W9-CDE-039

THE OFFICIAL®
PRICE GUIDE TO

Records

NINTH EDITION

THE OFFICIAL®
PRICE GUIDE TO

Records

NINTH EDITION

JERRY OSBORNE

HOUSE OF COLLECTIBLES • NEW YORK

© 1990 by Jerry Osborne

Cover photo by George Kerrigan

This is a registered trademark of Random House, Inc.

All rights reserved under International and Pan-American Copyright Conventions.

Published by: The House of Collectibles
201 East 50th Street
New York, New York 10022

Distributed by Ballantine Books, a division of Random House, Inc., New York, and simultaneously in Canada by Random House of Canada Limited, Toronto.

Manufactured in the United States of America

Library of Congress Catalog Card Number: 84-644340

ISBN: 0-876-37819-X

Ninth Edition: May 1990

10 9 8 7 6 5 4

CONTENTS

ACKNOWLEDGMENTS

The single most important element in the updating and revision of a price and reference guide is reader input.

From dealers and collectors, based in every state and in nearly every country around the globe, we receive suggestions, additions and corrections. Every single piece of data we acquire from readers is carefully reviewed, with all appropriate and usable information utilized in the next edition of this guide.

As enthusiastically as we encourage your contribution, let us equally encourage that when you write, you'll either type or print your name clearly on both the envelope and contents. It's as frustrating for us to receive a mailing of useful information, and not be able to credit the sender, as it probably is for the sender to not see his or her name in the Acknowledgments section.

In compiling this edition, information supplied by the people whose names appear below was of great importance. To these good folks, our deepest gratitude is extended. The amount of data and investment of time, of course, varied, but without each and every one of them this book would have been something less than it is.

Here then, alphabetically listed, is the board of advisors and contributors to this edition:

Jeff Aaron	Cindy Berman	Pat Carr	Kevin Crey
Marilee Albertsen	Lynn Best	Frank Castillo	Ross Crump
Davie Allan	Edward R. Blair	Jerry Chamberlain	Bill Cullvane
Ed Allan	John Blair	Jeff Chandler	Linda Curie-Cohen
Russ Allie	Harry Blaisure	Rich Cherry	Jeff Custer
Joseph Alterio	Peter Blecha	Presley M. Cheshire	David Cutler
Dan Alvino	Dee Bolt, III	Pete Chilkewitz	William D.
Amber's Records	Jim Borders	Erik Christensen	Robert J. Dalley
Michael H. Andrews	Boxcar Bill	Cory Church	Nicky D'Andrea
Jose C. Arocas	Bill Bram	Stephen M. Clark	Sherman Daniel
Jim Arslanian	Mike Bricker	Thomas Clark	Sherry Daniel
Loren Ayresman	Ed Broderick	Ron Clemmens	Neil T. Daniels
Saul Barbosa	John Brooks	Robert B. Clere	Frank Davella
Brent Barker Jr.	Richard Brooks	Al Cocorochio Jr.	James Calvin
John Barley	Fred Broughton	Howard R. Cohen	Davidson
Stanley Barron	Davis B. Brown	Jeff Collins	G. P. Davis
Jerry Barthelemy	Jean Brown	Bob Compeau	Gary Davis
Reginald Bartlette	Kip Brown	Loren Cone	Hank Davis
Chris Beachley	Pat Brown	Katherine Connella	Ken Davis
Rick Behrend	Kelly K. Bub	Wendy Cook	Lloyd Davis
Tim Behrens	Dave Budlong	Stan Cooper	Michael Dean
Richard J. Bell	Billy J. Burdette	Ronald L. Cornelius	Cathy Dee
Russ Bell	Robert Burroughs	Michael Corns	William Deibert
Randal Bender	Bud Buschardt	Lee Cotten	Les Derby
Maxine Bennett	Roger Bush	Perry Cox	Ted Despres
Jerry Bentsch	A. G. Bustos	Erik Cram	Michael Devich
Randy Berger	Dale Butler	Creative Radio	Jack Dey
Daniel S. Berkman	Terry Campbell	Service	Edward Dickhart

Acknowledgments

Bobby Diskin
Ronald R. Ditty Jr.
Frank Dix
Terry Dobrucki
Edward D. Donati
Larry Donn
Fred Dougherty
Steve Dougherty
Ralph Doyle
Alice L. Drake
Frances Easton
John Ebner
Judith M. Ebner
Chuck Edwards
Dave Eimer
Don Ell
P.W. Elliott
Bruce Elrod
John Evans
Larry Evans
Jerry Falk
Ron Feldhaus
Stan Feldman
Philip M. Finlay
Bill Finneran
John Fischer
Lindsey C. Flaherty
Eric Flaum
Ed Forcier
Sven Forsberg
Jeffery A. Frankel
Jonathan Frisch
Fred Frommholz
Maxim W. Furek
Jean-Marc Gargiulo
Tony Gargiulo
Brian Gari
Lee J. Garvin
Joseph Gavin
David Gayle
Guy H. Geest
Frank S. Gengar
Roger Gernert
Rich C. Gesner
Joel W. Getschman
Steve Goddard
Ed Godin
Marv Goldberg
Fernando Gonzalez
Fred Goss

Brian Granville
F. Gravereau
Charles T. Gray
Robert Green
James P. Greene
Hal Greimann
Paul Grenyo
Fred J. Griego
Gary Griffin
Will Griffith
Bill Griggs
John L. Grimes
Thomas Grosh
Jean-Philippe
  Guichard
James O. Guthrie
Buck Hafeman
Indra Haim
Bill Hall Jr.
Marshall S. Hall
Bruce Hamilton
Carolyn Hamilton
Brent Hample
Gary L. Hampton
John Hanager
Audrey Hansen
Lyle Hansen
Terry Hansen
Wes Harr
Dorothy Harris
Les Harris
Michael Harris
Steven Harris
Chris Hartlaub
Dennis Hartman
Peter Harvey
Robert Harvey
Walter F. Harwood
Marvin Hauschild
Randall Henderson
Jim Henkel
Walter Hering
Dennis V. Hickey
John Hillyard
Richard Hite
Chuck Hlava
Danny Holiday
Sid Holmes
Catherine Hopkins
Alexander Horvath

Bob Hover
Paul M. Hubbard
Bill Hughes
Elaine Hughes
Bill Humphreys
Tom Huxhold
Bob Hyde
Susan Jacob
Paul Jacobs Jr.
Alexander James
Ed Johnson
Jon E. Johnson
Linda Jones
Paula Jones
Miles Jordan
Steve Joyce
Ed Juska Jr.
George H. Kane
George Kapral
Norm Katuna
Artie Kauffman
J. Keener
Vaughn Keith
Jim Keller
Dave Kemp
Larry Ketchie
Fran Killian
Colin Kilts
Dave Kims
John P. King
Don R. Kirsch
Jeff Klein
Pete Kline
Don Kleiner
Ron Kowal
Frank Kramer
Walt Kubis
Kerry Kudlacek
Gladys Lambert
Darwin Lamm
George Langabeer
George J. Lapata
Rosalind Lardieri
Creig Lavine
Alan Leatherwood
Douglas C. Lembke
Scooter Lesley
Terry Lewis
Michael D. Linder
Joe Lindsey

David Link
Jerry D. Linn
Robert G. Livingston
Steve Loftness
Cyndee Long
Mark D. Long
Daniel Lorenzi
Dante Lorenzi
Frank Loux
Gary J. Lovell
Bob Lowenthal
Nancy Lucas
Peter Lucas
Curt Lundgren
Malcolm A.
  MacQuillan
Al Madden
Joseph Madrano
James M. Mains
Eric Maloney
Teri Marinko
Jay Marker
Mike Markesich
John Marlowe
Patricia Marsolais
Jim Martin
Larry L. Martin
Tom Martin
Tony Mastrianni
Harold D. Mathews
George Maupin
Ruth Maupin
Ernest Ray Maxwell
Ron McClure
Robbie McCurdy
Scott McGredy
Stephen J. McParland
Ken McPeck
Nick Mele
Jeff Melius
Richard S. Melrose
Robert Mercer
Sam Meroney
Joseph Merrell
Robert Michalski
Dale D. Mikolaczyk
Ian Miles
Paul Mochinal
Craig Moerer
Don Monfredi

Acknowledgments

George A.
Moonoogian
Les Moss
Gordon Mulholland
Steve Muller
George Mull
Brian Murphy
Keith Murphy
Mike Murray
Kim Murrie
Allen E. Mushin
Derek J. Myers
John Neilson
Gefforey Niswander
Joe Nix
Nedra Nelson
Bob Norberg
Carole Norris
Judy Norwood
Dave Nowlen
Jose Y. Nunez
Joseph Nunzio
Tom B. Ogilvy
Mike Ohr
Cathi Olsen
Tim O'Mara
Pete Oprisko
Johnny Otis
Ilse M. Ouellette
Jim Padrick
Frank B. Paino
Philip Palmer
Pam & Tony
David Paschen
Don Wayne
Patterson
Al Pavlow
Chris Peake
Victor Pearlin
Robert B. Perkins
Bob Phillips
Calman P. Phillips
Mark Phillips
Paul Phillips
Alex Pierce
Alex Pilepic
Steve Pimper
Walter Piotrowski
Steve C. Plucker

F. Darryl Porter
Alfred J. Powell
Tom Prestopnik
Danny Prisco
Chester Prudhomme
Robert Pruter
Frank J. Queen
Bill Quilty
Gilbert Quintero
Peter A. Rafter
Steven I. Ramm
Ray Randall
Jerry A. Rayburn
Walker Reddick
Steven S. Rickman
Mary A. Riggins
Don Riswick
Tom Robbins
Phil Roberts Jr.
David Robertson
Velpo F.
Robertson Jr.
Cliff Robnett
Norman Rodger
Alice Rogers
April Rogers
Jim Ronat
Arthur Root
Nicholas D. Rosati
Ric Ross
Gary Rowe
Ron Rowe
Wayne Russell
Marc Ryan
Richard T. Ryan
William Sabath
Sonia Sanchez
Ed Sanders
Greg Sanders
Ron Sataloff
Nina Schacherer
George F. Scheufel
Frederick Schmid
Bob Schmidt
Mario Schöppen
Joseph Scott
Rowland Scott
Bill Screws
Kevin Segura

Steve Seim
Rodney Selby
David Sellers Sr.
Laura Serra
Frank Sharpe
Greg Shaw
Dan Shellenbarger
Joe Shillair
Lee Shockley
Louis Silvani
Michael J. Silver
Mike Simko
Joseph F. Simon
David Slone
Jim Small
Al Smith
Ed Smith
John Smith
Kenneth Howard
Smith
Walter Smith
Robert Snyder
Mark G. Speck
Ulrich Springer
Danny Spurgeon
Jennifer Spurlock
John M. Squires
Denny Srnel
Tom Stein
Carlo Stevan
Michael Stevens
Jack Stevenson
Wayne Stierle
Doug Stitt
Bill Stone
Richard Strite
Howell Q. Strye
Paul Studstill
Tony Sturiale
Greg Surek
Scott Sutton
Robert L. Swan
Rod Sweetland
Ed Tataryn
Jeff Thames
Steve Thompson
Andy Thurston
Terry Titus
Joe Tomkus

P. M. Tortorice
Tom Tourville
Mike Townsend
Dan Trebik
Bill Trent
Lou Ukelson
Ronald Vaughan
Bernard Vasek
Tom Ventris Jr.
Very English &
Rolling Stone
Richard Vining
Ray Wade
Max Waller
Yvonne V. Walters
Mike Waston
Jim Weaver
Carrollyn Webster
Jeffrey Weinstein
Tom Wenzel
Don Weston
Danny A. White
Scott Wikle
Barbara Williams
Gary C. Williams
Robert B. Williams
Eric Wincentsen
Don Wiur
David R. Wolfe
Mike Wolstein
Rick Woodby
Barbara Wright
Richard Yeandle
Bill Yoder
Zee's Records
Pinhas Zilbergeld

Records

INTRODUCTION

In determining what should be included in *The Official Price Guide to Records,* we've considered many factors. Our goal is to make the guide helpful, convenient, and applicable; for avid record connoisseurs as well as for those who are simply curious about the value of their old records.

As an author-publisher team, we have put together nearly 40 record guides and reference books over the past 15 years. As a result of this considerable experience, we have developed some basic criteria that serve as the foundation for the guide.

First, we had to establish which records most people would own. The solution was to include those records made by *charted artists.* Thus, we began with the national pop and rock charts published by *Billboard, Cash Box,* and other trade publications. Then, because there has been so much chart crossover since the development of rock and roll, particularly between the black (rhythm and blues) music surveys and the top pop hits, we have included these charts as well.

Whether a song charted as a *single,* an *extended play (EP),* or a *long-playing (LP)* record, and regardless of whether it charted as "Race," "Rhythm and Blues," "Soul," "Disco," "Dance music," or "Sepia," you'll find that record priced here.

Performers who regularly appear on other charts — such as "Jazz," "Adult Contemporary," "Country," "Gospel," and "Classical" — do occasionally cross over to the pop/rock and black charts. All who have done so are included in this edition. However, these music forms are intrinsically diverse enough to require separate publications for truly comprehensive coverage.

It is important to recognize these guidelines from the start. The country music fan, for example, might find it hard to understand why Eddy Arnold is listed in this book while Ernest Tubb is not. Similarly, the jazz buff might be bewildered when finding Dave Brubeck here but not Art Farmer. While both Tubb and Farmer had numerous hits on their respective charts, they have never appeared on the pop (or black) charts. Eddy Arnold and Dave Brubeck, on the other hand, placed both singles and albums on the pop charts.

Just because we're listing all of the aforementioned charted artists, however, does not mean we are listing *only* charted records by those artists. Once an artist is included in the guide, we list and price *every known release* by that performer. Using country singer Hank Thompson as an example, let's show how comprehensive the coverage in this guide really is:

Despite his prominence in country and western music, Hank had only one song on the *Billboard* Hot 100; a single that remained on the chart for just one week and only managed to reach #99. Nevertheless, having qualified for this guide with one charted appearance, every known single, extended play, and long-playing album by Hank Thompson, from 1946 to present, is documented and priced in this edition. The reason behind the extensiveness of this coverage is if people like a performer well enough to put one of his/her records on the chart, they may own other records by that artist — without regard to chart success.

In summary, everyone who made the pop/rock (1950-1988) or black music charts (1942-1988) is included here, with not only their charted records, but their *entire* recorded output. This often includes 78rpm issues made twenty or thirty years before the '50s and should effectively cover most of the records to be found in the library of the average person.

Unlike previous editions of this guide, which did not include 78rpm singles, one can now price tens of thousands of 78s with this book; records originally issued as far back as the 1920s and as recently as 1962. Plus, for the first time in any record guide, this edition provides separate sections and pricing for simultaneously released 45s and 78s, a common practice for most labels in the '50s.

If you are seeking information on recordings not covered in this book, please write to the author (address on next page). We'll even provide you with information on upcoming titles now in various stages of production.

RECORD COLLECTING GUIDELINES: HOW THE RECORD PRICES ARE DETERMINED

Record values shown in this new *Official Price Guide to Records* are averaged using information derived from a number of traditional sources. Most influential in arriving at current values is our established "marked copy" review program. Dozens of the world's most active dealers and collectors receive a copy of the most recent edition in which, throughout the year, they mark changing prices. When it's time to prepare a revised edition, all marked copies are returned to us for analysis and processing.

Besides the annotated copies, we receive hundreds of letters each year, from folks like yourself, suggesting corrections and/or additions to the guide.

Another extremely important source of pricing information is *DISCoveries* magazine, the monthly publication where hobbyists buy, sell, and trade music collectibles. We painstakingly review each issue of *DISCoveries,* carefully comparing prices being asked to those shown in the most recent edition of the *Official Price Guide to Records.* If trading in *DISCoveries* indicates prices in the guide need to be increased or decreased, the changes are made. With our frequent publishing schedule, it is never long before the corrected prices appear in print.

What makes this step in the pricing process so vital is that nothing more verifiably illustrates the out-of-print record marketplace than everyday sales lists placed in *DISCoveries* by dealers from around the country and around the globe.

Record prices, as with most collectibles, can vary drastically from one area of the country to another. Having reviewers and annotators in every state, as well as in Europe, Asia, and beyond, enables us to present a realistic average of the highest and lowest current asking prices for an identically graded copy of each record.

Other sources of consequential information include: set sales and auction lists in other magazines as well as private sales list mailings, record convention trading, personal visits with collectors and to retail locations around the country, and hundreds of hours on the telephone with key advisors.

Although the record marketplace information in this edition was believed accurate at press time, it is ever subject to market changes. At any time, major bulk discoveries, quantity dumps, sudden increases wrought by an artist's death, overnight stardom that creates a greater demand for earlier material, and other such events and trends can easily affect scarcity and demand. Through diurnal research, keeping track of the day-to-day changes and discoveries taking place in the fascinating world of record collecting is a relatively simple and ongoing procedure.

To ensure the greatest possible accuracy, *Official Price Guide to Records* prices are averaged from data culled from all of the aforementioned sources.

HOW YOU CAN HELP

Obviously, we can never get too much input or too many reviewers. We wholeheartedly encourage you to submit whatever information you feel would be useful in building a better record guide. The quantity of data is not a factor. No amount is too little or too much.

When preparing additions for the *Official Price Guide to Records,* please try to list records in generally the same format as is used in the guide: artist's name, label, catalog number, title, year of release (if known), and price range. Since our data base is computer stored alphabetically by artist, there's no need to note the *Official Price Guide to Records* page number.

WAX FAX

One frequently used method of forwarding data to us is by FAX. For your convenience, we now have a full-time, dedicated FAX line (206 385-6572). Use this service to quickly and easily transmit additions, corrections, price updates, and suggestions. Be sure to include your name, address, and phone number so we can acknowledge your contribution and, if necessary, contact you.

Whether it's a marked copy of the guide, a letter, or a FAX, type or clearly print your name so we may accurately credit you in the next edition. Please submit all additions, corrections, and suggestions to:

Jerry Osborne
P.O. Box 255
Port Townsend, WA 98368

ABOUT THE FORMAT

Our arrangement of listings is the most logical way to present so much information in such a convenient, easy-to-carry package. It is clearly a format — the *only* format — with unlimited potential for expansion.

The structure of the *Official Price Guide to Records* allows us to include all of the following in one multi-purpose guidebook: 7-inch 45rpm singles, both 33rpm and 45rpm; 78rpm singles; 12-inch singles, both 33rpm and 45rpm; extended play 33rpm and 45rpm EPs; long play 10, and 12-inch LPs; picture sleeves; promotional issues, and more.

Once you locate an artist's section, his/her records are listed alphabetically by LABEL. Individual listings for each label appear in numerical order. In many instances, listings that are numerical by catalog number are also chronological in sequence of release, but there are also times where this is not the case. This format is especially helpful when using the guide along with an artist or label discography. Since the year of release is also provided for each listing, the reader knows immediately the pattern being followed by the label at the time.

Once familiar with the format, you'll find it easy and functional. However, do take time to familiarize yourself with the array. Reading all of the introductory pages should answer most reader questions. Having exhausted the supplied introductory material, please feel free to write or call if you have a question about the guide.

The documenting and pricing of so many recordings is made possible by selectively economizing on space; listing individual titles when necessary but not when it's possible to group a number of equally valuable releases together on one line. Again, *any time* it is necessary to have a separate listing on a record in order to clearly and accurately present the information, we will do it. Also, whenever a specific catalog number is noted, whether listed as an exception or not, the title will also be given for easy identification.

One facet of our approach of great concern is the artist who had one or more records of a value indicated for a particular label or series, but who also had one release (or more) that is a notable exception. Every effort has been made to separately document such exceptions; however, due to the sheer bulk of information herein, some may be missed. If you know of any, let us know about them.

You will find that the expansion of an artist's section, moving more toward individual rather than grouped listings, will be as commonplace in subsequent volumes of this series, as with this edition. There are hundreds of artists with revised sections in this volume, listing many more individual titles and catalog numbers than ever before. With some performers, it is, or perhaps soon will be, necessary to list every single record separately.

The decision to expand a section is partly based on reader input. Many examples of individual pricing in this edition can be directly attributed to a letter or call suggesting the need to do so. We're always listening and would love to hear from *you*.

RECORD GRADING AND THE PRICE RANGE

The pricing shown in this edition represents the PRICE RANGE for NEAR-MINT condition copies. The value range allows for the countless variables that affect record pricing. Often, the range will widen as the dollar amount increases, making a $750-$1000 range as logical as a $3-$5 range.

The standardized system of record grading, used and endorsed by Osborne Enterprises, the House of Collectibles, *DISCoveries* magazine, and buyers and sellers worldwide, is as follows:

MINT: A *mint* item must be absolutely perfect. Nothing less can be honestly described as mint. Even brand new purchases can easily be flawed in some manner and not qualify as mint. To allow for tiny blemishes, the highest grade used in our record guide series is *near-mint*. An absolutely pristine mint, or still sealed, item may carry a slight premium above the near-mint range shown in this guide.

VERY GOOD: Records in *very good* condition should have a minimum of visual or audible imperfections, which should not detract much from your enjoyment of owning them. This grade is halfway between good and near-mint.

GOOD: Practically speaking, the grade of *good* means that the item is good enough to fill a gap in your collection until a better copy becomes available. Good condition merchandise will show definite signs of wear and tear, probably evidencing that no protective care was given the item. Even so, records in good condition should play all the way through without skipping.

Most older records are going to be in something less than near-mint condition. It is very important to use the near-mint price range in this guide only as a starting point in record appraising. Be honest about actual condition. Apply the same standards to the records you trade or sell as you would want one from whom you were buying to observe. Visual grading may be unreliable. Accurate grading may require playing the record (play-grading).

Use the following formula to determine values on lesser condition copies:

For VERY GOOD condition, figure about 60% to 80% of the near-mint price range given in this guide.

Some dealers now report that a VG+ record priced at $4 or $40 will sell ahead of a mint item priced at $5 or $50. Also, with many of the older pieces that cannot be found in near-mint, VG or VG+ may be the highest grade available. This significantly narrows the gap between VG and the near-mint range.

For GOOD condition, figure about 20% to 40% of the near-mint price range given in this guide.

A plus sign or minus sign following the grade (G+, VG+, etc.) indicates an appreciation or depreciation of that grade, equivalent to about half the distance between grades. In other words, there's very little difference between G+ (good plus) and VG- (very good minus).

THE BOTTOM LINE

All the price guides and reporting of previous sales in the world won't change the rudimentary fact that true value is nothing more than what one person is willing to accept and what another is prepared to pay. Actual value is based on scarcity and demand. It's always been that way and always will.

A recording — or anything for that matter — can be 50 or 100 years old, but if no one wants it, the actual value will certainly be minimal. Just because something is old does not necessarily make it valuable. Someone has to want it!

On the other hand, a recent release, perhaps just weeks old, can have exceptionally high value if it has already become scarce and is by an artist whose following has created a demand. A record does not have to be old to be valuable.

RECORD TYPES DEFINED

With the inconsistent language used by the record companies in describing an EP or an LP, we've determined that a language guideline of some sort was needed in order to compile a useful record guide.

Some labels call a 10-inch LP an "EP" if it has something less than the prescribed number of tracks found on their LPs. Others call an EP a "Little LP." A few companies have even created special names, associated only with their own label, for the basic record formats.

Having carefully analyzed all of this, we have adopted the following classifications of record configurations, which consistently categorize all types, sizes, and speeds in one section or another:

Singles: 78rpm are those that play at 78rpm! Though 78s are almost always 10-inch discs, a few 7-inch 78rpm singles have been made.

Singles: 7-Inch can be either 45rpm or 33 1/3 (always referred to simply as "33") speed singles. If a 7-inch single has more than one track on either side, then it's an EP.

Singles are priced strictly as a disc, with a separate section devoted to picture sleeves (which are often traded separately). If we know that picture sleeves exist for a given artist, a separate grouping will appear for the label, price, and applicable year of release. Should you know of picture sleeves not documented in this edition, please advise us accordingly.

There have been a few 5-inch discs manufactured, but for the sake of keeping singles with singles (and since we don't want to establish a "Singles: 5-Inch" category), such curios will be included with the 7-inch singles.

EPs: 7-Inch 33/45rpm are 7-inch discs that have more than one track on one or both sides. Even if labeled an "EP" by the manufacturer, if it's pressed on a 10, or 12-inch disc it's an LP in our book. Unless so noted, all EPs are presumed to be accompanied by their original covers, in a condition about equal to the disc. An appropriate adjustment in value should be made to compensate for any differences in this area. Exceptions, such as EPs with paper sleeves or no sleeve at all, are designated as such when known.

LPs: 10/12-Inch 33rpm is self explanatory. The only possible confusion that might exist here is with 12-inch singles. If it's 10 or 12 inches in diameter, and labeled, priced, and marketed as a 12-inch single (Maxi-Single, etc.), then that's where you'll find it in this guide, regardless of its speed. Often, 12-inch singles will have a 12-inch die-cut cardboard sleeve or jacket; but many have covers that are exactly like LP jackets, with photos of the artist, etc. Unless so noted, all LPs are presumed to be accompanied by their original covers, in a condition about equal to the disc. An appropriate adjustment in value should be made to compensate for any differences in this area.

Other record type headings used in this edition, such as **Picture Sleeves, Promotional Singles,** etc., should be crystal-clear.

CROSS-REFERENCING AND MULTIPLE ARTISTS

The cross-referencing in this edition should provide the easiest possible method of discovering other sections of the book where a particular artist is featured or appears in any capacity.

We've tried to hold to a minimum unexplained cross-references, opting to concentrate more on those cross-references for which the reader can effortlessly understand the rationalization. Minimized is the unnecessary duplication of cross-references. For example, it is not necessary to list every group in which Eric Clapton played, under each and every one of those sections. What we've done is simply indicate "Also see Eric Clapton," where you *will* find a complete cross-referencing to all other sections where he appears.

Some artists have several sections, one right after the other, because they were involved in different duets and/or compilation releases. In such instances, the primary artist (whose section begins first) is not cross-referenced after each and every subsequent section, but only after the last section wherein that artist is involved. This, in effect, blocks the beginning and the end of releases pertaining to that performer. If you don't find the listing you're searching for right away, remember to check the sections that follow, as the artist may have been joined by someone else on that recording causing it to appear in a separate section.

Artist headings and resultant cross-referencing appear in two different formats in this guide. For example:

LEWIS, Jerry Lee, Carl Perkins & Johnny Cash

Listings under this type heading are those wherein the artists perform *together*. Often these releases will also include solo tracks by one or all of the performers in addition to those on which they collaborate.

LEWIS, Jerry Lee / Carl Perkins / Johnny Cash

This heading, with names separated by a slash, indicates there are selections, on separate tracks, by each of the named artists, but they do not perform together. The parameter set for these compilation releases is four different performers or less. Compilations containing five or more individual performers are, for purposes of compiling this edition, classified as **Various Artists** issues and will be documented in a separate future guide.

Whenever more than one act is featured on a record, cross-references appear under all of the other artists on the disc, who have a section of their own in this edition, directing the reader to the location of the listing in question. If you're looking up a record with a different artist on each side, and you don't find it under one artist, be sure to try looking for the flip-side artist.

Not all releases containing more than one artist are given separate sections. In some cases it makes more sense to include such records in the primary section for the most important artist. We will rarely create separate sections for multiple artist discs when the other performers on the issue do not have a section of their own in this edition.

To illustrate this point, Hank Williams, Jr. had several duet issues with Lois Johnson; Gene Ammons shared an LP with Sonny Stitt.

Even though Johnson and Stitt do not have individual sections in this book (they didn't make the *Billboard* pop singles or LPs charts), such recordings may be important to collectors of Williams and Ammons. For that reason, they are included in their respective artist's section. On the other hand, a duet by Brenda Lee and Willie Nelson requires a separate section, since either or both may be of interest to the researcher. Also, both are individually pop-charted artists. There are a few isolated exceptions to this policy, simply because every section in this edition was separately prepared and customized in whatever manner necessary to provide the user with the most usable information.

PROMOTIONAL ISSUES

The separate documenting and pricing of promotional issues is, in most cases, unnecessary. Because most of the records issued during the primary four decades covered in this guide were simultaneously pressed for promotional purposes, a separate listing of them would theoretically double the size of an already large book.

Rather, we've chosen to list promotional copies separately when we have the knowledge that a separate price (either higher or lower) consistently is asked for them. For the most part, promos of everyday releases will fall into the same range — usually toward the high end — given for store stock copies. Some may stretch the range slightly, but not enough to warrant separate pricing. Premiums may be paid for promos that have different (longer, shorter, differently mixed, etc.) versions of tunes, even though the artist may not be particularly hot in the collecting marketplace.

When identified as a "Promotional issue," we are usually describing a record with a special promotional ("Not For Sale," "Dee Jay Copy," etc.) label or sleeve, and not a *designate* promo. Designate promos are identical to commercial releases, except they have been rubber or mechanically stamped, stickered, written on by hand, or in some way altered to accommodate their use for promotional purposes. There are very few designate promos listed in this edition, and those that are (such as in the Elvis Presley section) are clearly identified as such.

COLORED VINYL PRESSINGS

Records known to exist on both black vinyl and colored vinyl (vinyl is the term used regardless of whether it's polystyrene or vinyl) are listed separately since there is usually a value difference. However, some colored vinyl releases were never pressed on black vinyl, and since there is no way to have the record other than on colored vinyl, it may or may not be specifically noted as being on colored vinyl.

Because the true color of some colored vinyl pressings may be a judgment call (is it red or is it dark pink . . . is it dark blue or is it purple?), we're using "colored vinyl" to indicate any pressings that are not standard black vinyl. This also applies to multi-color and clear vinyl issues.

FOREIGN RELEASES

This edition by design lists only U.S. releases. There is, however, an occasional exception. A handful of records that were widely distributed in the U.S. or sold via widespread U.S. advertising, even though manufactured outside the country, are included. Such anomalies would appear only in the more sophisticated sections of the guide. There is also a sprinkling of Canadian releases.

The collectors' market for out-of-print Canadian records is mostly a U.S. market. The trading of rare Canadian discs between Canadian collectors is not nearly as widespread as those instances that involve a U.S. buyer or seller.

The millions of overseas releases certainly have collector value to both fans in those countries as well as to many stateside collectors. Unfortunately, the tremendous volume of material and the variances in pricing make it impossible to comprehensively document and price imports.

BOOTLEGS AND COUNTERFEITS

Bootleg and counterfeit records are not listed in this guide. Should such a recording have slipped by, it was quite unintentional. For the record, a bootleg recording is one illegally manufactured, usually containing material not previously available in a legitimate form. Often, with the serious collector in mind, a boot will package previously issued tracks that have achieved some degree of value or scarcity. If the material is easily available, legally, then there would be no gain for the bootlegger.

The counterfeit record is one manufactured as close as possible in sound and appearance to the source disc from which it was inspired. Not all counterfeits were created to fool an unsuspecting buyer into thinking he or she was buying an authentic issue, but some were. Many were designated in some way, such as a slight marking or variance, so as not to allow them to be confused with originals. Such a fake record primarily exists to fill a gap in the collector's file until the real thing comes along.

With both bootleg and with counterfeit records, the appropriate and deserving recipients of royalties are, of course, denied remuneration for their works.

Since most of the world's valuable records have been counterfeited, it is always a good idea to consult with an expert when there is any doubt. The trained eye can usually spot a fake.

This is not to say *unauthorized* releases are excluded from the book. There are many legitimate releases that are unauthorized by one entity or another; records that are neither bootleg or counterfeit. Unauthorized does not necessarily mean illegal.

GROUP NAMES AND PERSONNEL

One chronic problem that we'll probably never cure completely is the many instances where groups using the exact same name are lumped together with other groups who are, in fact, completely different and contain none of the same personnel. Whenever known to be different, these groups are given separate sections; but there are times when we simply do not know. If you can shed any light in this area, we'd love to hear from you. Thanks to readers, many such groups have been sorted since our last edition.

The listing sequence for artists using the same name is chronological. Thus, the ABC group, Silk, who had a release in 1969, is listed ahead of the Philadelphia International group, Silk, that first recorded in 1979.

As often as not, there will have been group members that have come and gone over the years. Reflecting this turnover in our listing of members' names may cause some confusion, when the reader sees 12 different members shown for a group named the Five Satins. We've tried, whenever possible, to list the original line-up first, followed by later members. Also, the lead singer is usually listed first. We welcome additional information on group members from readers. One of the most reliable sources of this data is the LP covers, which often list members. If you can fill in the members' names on any groups where we don't list that information, we'll see that it gets into our next edition. Hundreds of group members have been added since the eighth edition of this guide.

When group members' names are given, there is a likelihood that not all of the members named appear on *all* of the releases documented. It is also possible that not all of the members named ever recorded with all of the other members shown at the same time.

When members' names are given for a solo performer, those named are noteworthy sidemen.

As more and more group members are named in future editions, there will be added cross-referencing to reflect the constant shuffle of performers from one group to another.

PARENTHETICAL NOTES

Some of the information that may be found in parentheses following the artist heading has already been covered. However, other uses of this space include:

• Complete artist and group or artist and band names. Some artists were shown as being with one group on a few releases and with another on other issues. We've tried to present the information the way, or many ways, that it was shown on the actual record label.

• Variations of spelling or names for the same artist. With some artists, it's convenient to have everything in one section; however, when it is illogical to combine listings, perhaps because the performer was popular under more than one name (such as Johnny Cymbal and Derek), you'll find individual sections for each name. As you would expect, cross-references will be used to help you locate things easily. When you see "Kenneth Rogers" in parentheses, we certainly are not trying to tell you that Kenneth is Kenny's real name. Rather, we're letting you know that on some releases he was shown as Kenneth Rogers instead of Kenny Rogers.

• Names of guest performers who may or may not be credited on the actual label, but who we feel you should know were involved in one or more of the records listed in that section.

• Real names of artists, but only when we feel they need to be given. We have no desire to give the real names of everyone who has recorded under a pseudonym, but there are times when you do need this information, particularly when they have also recorded under their real name or when more than one person has recorded under the same pseudonym. To help sort things out, we will, when known, give you the real name of someone who has recorded under a *nom de guerre,* such as Guitar Slim (Johnny Winter).

OLDIES LABELS AND REISSUES

An effort has been made to include many "oldies" or reissue records in the guide. Though many reissues of this type are of no value beyond their current retail cost, some are. Look at some of the early RCA Victor Gold Standard Series Elvis Presley releases, for example. Once in a blue moon a tune will turn up in true stereo on a reissue label that previously was hard to find in stereo (such as *I Ran All The Way Home,* on Collectables). Otherwise, it's just our desire to report comprehensively on all artists that prompted the listing of reissues.

The main reason we've included these reissues is to eliminate confusion, especially among younger collectors. Often, they'll discover a hit tune on a label, like Lana or Lost-Nite, and think it's an original release predating the label that had the hit single.

If there are reissues numbered as part of a label's standard release series, and not documented in this edition, please tell us about them.

USING THIS GUIDE:
ADDITIONAL POINTS

• Every "money record" — one hitting at least $100 on the high end of the range — is listed individually with label, catalog number, and title. Anything worth a hundred bucks deserves a separate listing.

- The alphabetization used makes finding any artist or label easy, but a few guidelines may speed the process along for you:

- Names that are simply letters (and are not intended to be pronounced as a word) are found at the beginning of the listings under each letter of the alphabet (i.e., ABC, AC-DC, GQ, SSQ, etc.). The same rule applies to acronyms and to initials (i.e., G.T.O, MFSB, etc.). When known, we'll parenthetically tell you what the abbreviation represents.

- Names are listed in the alphabetical order of the first word. This means you'll find **Rock Squad** before **Rocket.** Hyphenated words are looked upon as whole words (i.e., Mello-Kings is treated the same as Mellokings). Divided names (i.e., De Vorzon, El Dorados, etc.) are alphabetically listed as though they were a one-word name.

- Possessive names precede similarly spelled names that are not possessive. For example, KNIGHT'S would be found before KNIGHTS, regardless of what follows the comma.

- The articles "A" or "The" have been dropped from group names in this guide even though they may appear on the records as part of the name.

- With record labels, the listings appear in alphabetical/numeric/chronological order. Prefixes are generally not used (they make it more difficult to scan the numbers) unless they are necessary for identification. With some artists (Beatles, Elvis, etc.) it is essential at times because of constant reissues.

- Some sections make use of the label prefixes to sort things out, but most use a number series. If the numbers are duplicated by the label, or if any of a variety of confusing similarities exist, we may resort to the prefixes for clarity.

- Anytime we find that the monaural or the stereo issue of a particular record is in need of a separate listing (because there is a price difference for one that is outside the boundaries of the price range of the other), we will gladly provide same. If there is but one listing, this indicates that we have no reason to believe there is much difference in the two forms. A little application of the known variables will help in this area. For example, if the range is $20-$30 for a 1963 LP and you know that the stereo issue is in true stereo, it's safe to place the mono at the low end of the range ($20-$25) and the stereo at the high end ($25-$30). The calculation may be reversed for late sixties and for most electronically reprocessed issues.

- We believe the year or years of release given in the far-right column to be accurate. If we don't know the correct year, the column is left blank. In some cases the record may have been released in one year and debuted on the nation's music charts the following year. This is common for year-end issues and explains why you may remember a hit as being from 1966, although we list it as a 1965 release.

- When multiple years are indicated, such as "64-66," it means the records described on that line spanned the years 1964 through 1966. They may have had one issue in 1964 and another in 1966, or may have had eight releases during those years. It does *not* mean that we believe the release came out sometime between 1964 and 1966.

- Unusual though it may be, some records have been issued with no artist or label given. You will find this on both singles and albums. These items are filed by title in the *Official Price Guide to Records*.

• There are hundreds of double albums (two discs in one package) priced in the guide, but they are not necessarily identified as double LPs. They are, nevertheless, included in the price range.

GUIDELINES FOR PRICING RECORDS NOT FOUND IN THIS EDITION

Since it is impossible for us to include *every* record ever produced, a few guidelines may assist you in evaluating records not found in this edition:

Pop Singles on 45rpm: Most pop, non-rock vocal, and instrumental 45s from the '50s are available for under $10. From many rock-oriented dealers, pop singles can often be bought for less than $5. The few exceptions are likely to be folks with charted hits, and those will be found in the guide.

Pop music singles from the '60s to present are seldom going to sell for over $3 or $4; usually $1 or $2.

Pop Singles on 78rpm: Most pop 78s are available for under $5. Until the late '40s or early '50s, an *album* was a gatefold binder with a number of 78s, usually in individual paper sleeves. Prices on these pop albums will vary, but most will fall in the $20-50 range.

Pop Long Play Albums: From the '50s, 12-inch pop LPs generally are found for under $20-40. Ten-inch LPs may go for $25-50. Pop vocalists with jazz-related releases (such as Johnny Mathis' first LP) are a different story; some are now valued in the $50-150 range.

Most pop LPs from the '60s to present can be found for $5-15.

Pop Extended Play Albums: Pop EPs are scarce, as are all EPs, but many are still very reasonable. Most can be found for under $10-25.

Easy Listening Music: The average easy listening record will be worth about half of the price ranges shown for Pop Music.

Country Music on 45rpm: Most country music vocal and instrumental 45s from the '50s are available for under $15; many for less than $10. Obvious exceptions are any that border on rockabilly or country rock. Don't take any country record for granted! Play both sides of every disc, as it is always possible you'll discover a great country rocker.

Country music singles from the '60s to present are seldom going to sell for over $5; usually less.

Country Music on 78rpm: Most of the country 78s should fall into the $10 to $40 range. There are, however, many older 78s with prices well into three figures; some even higher.

Country Music Long Play Albums: From the '50s, 12-inch C&W LPs generally are found for under $30-60. Ten-inch LPs may go for $50-100. As already mentioned, the range will vary widely depending on the following and collectibility of the artist.

Country Music Extended Play Albums: Very, very few country music EPs were big sellers, which means nearly all are rare. You may find they are in the same price range as the '50s LPs above; some will bring even more than LPs from the same time period.

Most country LPs from the '60s to present can be found for $5-25. Again, there are exceptions.

Jazz Singles on 45rpm: Most jazz 45s from the '50s are available for under $10; perhaps even less than $5. The few exceptions are likely to be artists with charted hits, which will be found in the guide.

Jazz singles from the '60s to present are seldom going to sell for over $3 or $4; usually $1 or $2.

13

Jazz Singles on 78rpm: Most jazz 78s are available for under $20. Until the late '40s or early '50s, an *album* was a gatefold binder with a number of 78s, usually in individual paper sleeves. Prices on these jazz albums will vary, but most will fall in the $25-75 range.

Jazz Long Play Albums: From the '50s, 12-inch jazz LPs generally are found for under $50-100. Ten-inch LPs may go for $75-200.

Most jazz LPs from the '60s to present can be found for $10-30.

Jazz Extended Play Albums: As with country, very few jazz EPs were big sellers. All are rare. You may find they are in the same price range as the '50s jazz LPs above; some will bring even more than LPs from the same time period.

Comedy and Personality Long Play Albums: From the '50s and '60s, 12-inch comedy and personality (not soundtrack or original cast) LPs generally are found for under $15-40.

Most comedy and personality LPs from the '70s to present can be found for $5-15.

In summary, there is no way these few paragraphs can constitute a complete price guide for the millions of non-rock records that exist. If such generic generalizations were possible, while guaranteeing unerring accuracy, the entire price guide would be about ten pages. It is the exceptions that make record pricing so complicated and difficult to document.

Our goal here is simply to provide a rough idea of the value of recordings that are outside the parameters of the guide.

WHAT TO EXPECT WHEN SELLING YOUR RECORDS TO A DEALER

As nearly everyone in the hobby knows, there is a noteworthy difference between the prices reported in this guide and the prices that one can expect a dealer to pay when buying records for resale. Unless a dealer is buying for a personal collection and without thoughts of resale, he or she is simply not in a position to pay full price. Dealers work on a percentage basis, largely determined by the total dollar investment, quality, and quantity of material offered as well as the general financial condition and inventory of the dealer at the time.

Another very important consideration is the length of time it will take the dealer to recover at least the amount of the original investment. The greater the demand for the stock and the better the condition, the quicker the return and therefore the greater the percentage that can be paid. Our experience has shown that, day-in and day-out, most dealers will pay from 25% to 50% of *guide* prices. And that's assuming they are planning to resell at guide prices. If they traditionally sell below guide, that will be reflected in what they can pay for stock.

If you have records to sell, it would be wise to check with several shops. In doing so you'll begin to get a good idea of the value of your collection to a dealer.

Also, consult the Buyer-Seller Directory in this guide for the names of many dealers who not only might be interested in buying, but from whom many collectible records are available for purchase.

Whether you wish to sell the records you have, or add out-of-print discs to your collection, you'll want *DISCoveries* magazine. Each issue is jam-packed with ads, features, discographies, collecting tips and more. *DISCoveries* is prepared by collectors . . . for collectors. If getting into the record marketplace is important to you, *DISCoveries* is essential (*DISCoveries,* P.O. Box 255, Port Townsend, WA 98368; sample issue available upon request).

CONCLUDING THOUGHTS

The purpose of this guide is to report as accurately as possible the most recent prices asked and paid for records within the area of its coverage. There are two key words here that deserve emphasis: **Guide** and **Report.**

We cannot stress enough that this book is only a guide. There always have and always will be instances of records selling well above and below the prices shown within these pages. These extremes are recognized in the final averaging process; but it's still important to understand that just because we've reported a 30-year old record as having a $25-50 near-mint value, doesn't mean that a collector of that material should be hesitant to pay $75 for it. How badly he or she wants it and how often it's possible to purchase it *at any price* should be the prime factors considered, not the fact that we last reported it at a lower price. Of course, we'd like to know about sales of this sort so that the next edition can reflect the new pricing information.

Our objective is to report and reflect record marketplace activity; not to *establish* prices. For that reason, and if given the choice, we'd prefer to be a bit behind the times rather than ahead. With this guide being regularly revised, it will never be long before the necessary changes are reported within these pages.

We encourage record companies, artist management organizations, talent agencies, publicists, and performers to make certain that we are on the active mailing list for new release information, press releases, bios, publicity photos, and anything pertaining to recordings.

There is an avalanche of helpful information in this guide to aid the collector in determining what is valuable and what may not be worth fooling with, but the wise fan will also keep abreast of current trends and news through the pages of the fanzines and publications devoted to his/her favorite forms of music.

A

A FLOCK OF SEAGULLS:
see FLOCK OF SEAGULLS

A TASTE OF HONEY:
see TASTE OF HONEY

A's
Singles: 7-Inch
ARISTA: 79 .... $1-3
LPs: 10/12-Inch 33rpm
ARISTA: 79-81 5-8
Members: Richard Bush; Rick DiFonzo; Michael
Snyder; Terry Bortman; Rocco Nolte.

A.B. SKHY
Singles: 7-Inch
MGM: 69-70 2-4
LPs: 10/12-Inch 33rpm
MGM: 69-70 10-12

ABC
Singles: 12-Inch 33/45rpm
MERCURY: 83-87 4-6
Singles: 7-Inch
MERCURY: 82-87 1-3
Picture Sleeves
MERCURY: 82-87 1-3
LPs: 10/12-Inch 33rpm
MERCURY: 82-87 5-8

AC-DC
Singles: 12-Inch 33/45rpm
ATLANTIC: 79 4-8
(Promotional issues only.)
Singles: 7-Inch
ATCO: 77 2-4
ATLANTIC: 77-85 1-3
Picture Sleeves
ATLANTIC: 81 1-3
LPs: 10/12-Inch 33rpm
ATCO: 76-77 8-12
ATLANTIC: 77-88 5-10
Members: Bonn Scott; Angus Young; Malcomb
Young; Phil Rudd; Cliff Williams; Brian Johnson.

ADC BAND
Singles: 7-Inch
COTILLION: 78-82 1-3
LPs: 10/12-Inch 33rpm
COTILLION: 78-82 5-8
Members: Michael Judkins; Arwell Mathew Jr;
Audrey Mathew; Mark Patterson.

AM-FM
Singles: 7-Inch
DAKAR: 82 .... $1-3

APB
Singles: 12-Inch 33/45rpm
IMPORT: 83 4-6
SLEEPING BAG: 84 4-6
Singles: 7-Inch
IMPORT: 83 1-3
LPs: 10/12-Inch 33rpm
MCA: 83 5-8

AWB: see AVERAGE WHITE BAND

AALON
Singles: 7-Inch
ARISTA: 77 1-3
LPs: 10/12-Inch 33rpm
ARISTA: 77 5-8

ABACO DREAM
Singles: 7-Inch
A&M: 69-70 2-4

ABBA
Singles: 12-Inch 33/45rpm
ATLANTIC: 77-79 4-8
Singles: 7-Inch
ATLANTIC: 75-82 3-6
Picture Sleeves
ATLANTIC: 77-81 3-6
LPs: 10/12-Inch 33rpm
ATLANTIC (Except 300): 74-84 8-10
ATLANTIC (300; "Abba"): 78 10-20
(Promotional issue only.)
CBS INT'L: 80 8-12
K-TEL: 80 8-10
NAUTILUS: 82 10-15
(Half-speed mastered.)
SILVER EAGLE: 84 5-10
Members: Anni-frid Lyngstad; Bjorn Ulvaeus;
Benny Andersson; Agnetha Faltskog.
Also see FALTSKOG, Agnetha
Also see FRIDA

**ABBA / Spinners / Firefall / England
Dan & John Ford Coley**
EPs: 7-Inch 33/45rpm
WARNER SPECIAL
PRODUCTS: 78 5-10
(Coca-Cola/Burger King promotional issue. Issued
with paper sleeve.)
Also see ABBA
Also see ENGLAND DAN & JOHN
  FORD COLEY
Also see FIREFALL
Also see SPINNERS

ABBEY TAVERN SINGERS
Singles: 7-Inch
HBR: *66* $2-4

ABBOTT, Billy, & The Jewels
Singles: 7-Inch
PARKWAY: *63-64* 3-5

ABBOTT, Gregory
Singles: 12-Inch 33/45rpm
COLUMBIA: *87* 4-6
Singles: 7-Inch
COLUMBIA: *87-88* 1-3
Picture Sleeves
COLUMBIA: *87* 1-3
LPs: 10/12-Inch 33rpm
COLUMBIA: *87-88* 5-8

ABDUL, Paula
Singles: 7-Inch
VIRGIN: *88* 1-3
LPs: 10/12-Inch 33rpm
VIRGIN: *88* 5-8

ABRAMS, Colonel
Singles: 12-Inch 33/45rpm
MCA: *85-87* 4-6
STREETWISE: *84* 4-6
Singles: 7-Inch
MCA: *85-87* 1-3
STREETWISE: *84* 1-3

ABRAMS, Miss, & The Strawberry
Point School Third Grade Class
Singles: 7-Inch
REPRISE: *70* 1-3
Picture Sleeves
REPRISE: *70* 2-3

ACCENTS
Singles: 7-Inch
BRUNSWICK (55100; "Wiggle
Wiggle"): *58* 5-8
BRUNSWICK (55123; "Ching
A Ling"): *58-59* 8-10
CORAL: *59* 8-10
JUBILEE: *59* 4-6
Member: Robert Draper Jr.

ACCEPT
Singles: 7-Inch
PORTRAIT: *84-86* 1-3
Picture Sleeves
PORTRAIT: *84-86* 1-3
LPs: 10/12-Inch 33rpm
PVC: *83* 5-8
PASSPORT: *81* 6-10
PORTRAIT: *84-86* 5-8

ACCUSED
EPs: 7-Inch 33/45rpm
MARTHA
SPLATTERHEAD: *82* $8-12
LPs: 10/12-Inch 33rpm
COMBAT: *87* 5-8
Members: Blaine Cook; Tom Niemeyer; Dana Collins; Alex Sibbald.

ACE
Singles: 7-Inch
ABC: *76-78* 1-3
ANCHOR: *75-77* 2-4
LPs: 10/12-Inch 33rpm
ANCHOR: *75-77* 8-10
Members: Paul Carrack; Fran Byrne; Tex Comer; Phil Harris; Bam King; Jon Woodhead.
Also see CARRACK, Paul

ACE, Buddy
Singles: 7-Inch
DUKE: *60-69* 3-5
FIDELITY: *59* 4-6
PAULA: *70-72* 2-4
SPECIALTY: *59* 5-8
(Most Specialty singles are currently available, using original catalog numbers.)

ACE, Johnny
(Johnny Ace & The Beale Streeters)
Singles: 78rpm
DUKE: *52-55* 5-10
FLAIR: *53* 15-25
Singles: 7-Inch
ABC: *73* 1-3
DUKE: *52-55* 8-12
FLAIR: *53* 35-45
MCA: *84* 1-3
EPs: 7-Inch 33/45rpm
DUKE (71; "Memorial
Album"): *63* 12-20
(Jukebox issue only.)
DUKE (80; "Memorial
Album"): *55* 50-75
DUKE (81; "Tribute
Album"): *55* 50-75
LPs: 10/12-Inch 33rpm
DUKE (70; "Memorial
Album"): *55* 400-500
(10-Inch LP.)
DUKE (71; "Memorial
Album"): *56* 150-250
(No playing card shown on cover.)
DUKE (71; "Memorial
Album"): *61* 30-35
(Playing card shown on cover.)

DUKE

45 R.P.M.
VOCAL 3:02 B/\l
R-102-A

PEACOCK RECORDS
AFFILIATE
Houston, Texas

MY SONG
(James)
Johnny ACE
with
The Beale Streeters

DUKE (71; "Memorial Album"): 74 ..... $8-10
(With an "X" prefix.)
MCA: 83 4-6

ACE, Johnny / Earl Forrest
Singles: 78rpm
FLAIR (1015; "Midnight Hours
Journey"): 53 20-30
Singles: 7-Inch
FLAIR (1015; "Midnight Hours
Journey"): 53 40-60
Also see ACE, Johnny
Also see FORREST, Earl

ACE SPECTRUM
Singles: 7-Inch
ATLANTIC: 74-76 2-4
LPs: 10/12-Inch 33rpm
ATLANTIC: 74-76 8-10

ACKLES, David
Singles: 7-Inch
ELEKTRA: 68-72 2-4
LPs: 10/12-Inch 33rpm
COLUMBIA: 73 5-10
ELEKTRA: 69-72 8-12

ACKLIN, Barbara
Singles: 7-Inch
BRUNSWICK: 67-73 2-4
CAPITOL: 74-75 2-3
ERIC: 83 1-3
Picture Sleeves
BRUNSWICK: 68 3-5
LPs: 10/12-Inch 33rpm
BRUNSWICK: 68-71 8-12
CAPITOL: 75 5-8
Also see CHANDLER, Gene, &
Barbara Acklin

ACT I
Singles: 7-Inch
SPRING: 73-74 .... $2-4
LPs: 10/12-Inch 33rpm
SPRING: 74 5-8

AD LIBS
Singles: 7-Inch
A.G.P.: 66 3-5
BLUE CAT: 65 4-6
CAPITOL: 70 2-4
KAREN: 66 3-5
PHILIPS: 67 3-5
SHARE: 69 2-4

ADAM & THE ANTS
Singles: 12-Inch 33/45rpm
EPIC: 81 4-6
Singles: 7-Inch
EPIC: 81 1-3
LPs: 10/12-Inch 33rpm
EDITIONS EG: 82 5-8
EPIC: 81-82 8-10
Members: Adam Ant; Johnny Bivouac; Andy Wat-
son; Dave Barb.
Also see ANT, Adam
Also see BOW WOW WOW

ADAMS, Bobby
Singles: 7-Inch
BATTLE: 63 3-5
COLPIX: 61 4-8
HOMETOWN: 70 2-4
PET: 58 12-15
PURDY: 64 3-5

**ADAMS, Bobby, & Norma Jean
Carpenter**
Singles: 7-Inch
KINGSTAR: 71 2-4
Also see ADAMS, Bobby

ADAMS, Bryan
Singles: 12-Inch 33/45rpm
A&M: 82-87 4-6
Singles: 7-Inch
A&M (Black vinyl): 80-87 1-3
A&M (Colored vinyl) 2-4
Picture Sleeves
A&M: 80-87 1-3
LPs: 10/12-Inch 33rpm
A&M: 80-87 5-8

ADAMS, Bryan, & Tina Turner
Singles: 7-Inch
A&M: 85 1-3
Picture Sleeves
A&M: 85 1-3

Also see ADAMS, Bryan
Also see TURNER, Tina

ADAMS, Faye
Singles: 78rpm
ATLANTIC: *52-53* $5-10
HERALD: *53-57* 5-10
IMPERIAL: *55-57* 4-8
Singles: 7-Inch
ABC: *73* .... , 1-3
ATLANTIC: *52-53* 15-20
COLLECTABLES: *82* 1-3
HERALD (Black vinyl): *53-57* 8-12
HERALD (Colored vinyl): *53* 20-30
IMPERIAL: *55-57* 8-12
LIDO: *59-60* 4-8
SAVOY: *61* 3-5
WARWICK: *61* 3-5
LPs: 10/12-Inch 33rpm
COLLECTABLES: *88* 6-8
SAVOY: *76* 5-8
WARWICK: *61* 40-50
Also see MORRIS, Joe, & His
Orchestra

ADAMS, Gayle
Singles: 7-Inch
PRELUDE: *80-81* 1-3
LPs: 10/12-Inch 33rpm
PRELUDE: *82* 5-8

ADAMS, Johnny
Singles: 7-Inch
ARIOLA AMERICAN: *78* 1-3
ATLANTIC: *71-72* 2-4
HELP ME: *74-76* 2-4
J.B.: *76* 2-3
MODERN: *67* 3-5
PAID: *84* 1-3
RIC: *59-62* 5-8
RON: *64-65* 3-5
SSS INT'L: *68-74* 2-4
WATCH: *63* 3-5
LPs: 10/12-Inch 33rpm
ARIOLA AMERICAN: *78* 5-8
CHELSEA: *77* 10-20
HELP ME: *74-76* 8-10
SSS INT'L: *70* 10-15

ADAMS, Johnny, & The Gondoliers
Singles: 7-Inch
RIC: *59* 10-15
Also see ADAMS, Johnny

ADAMS, Marie
(Marie Adams With Three Tons Of Joy)
Singles: 78rpm
PEACOCK: *51-54* $4-8
Singles: 7-Inch
CAPITOL: *58* 4-8
PEACOCK: *51-54* 8-10
VANTAGE: *73* 2-4
Also see OTIS, Johnny

ADDEO, Leo
LPs: 10/12-Inch 33rpm
CAMDEN: *59-68* 4-8
RCA VICTOR: *61-64* 4-8

ADDERLEY, Julian "Cannonball"
Singles: 7-Inch
BLUE NOTE: *59* 2-4
CAPITOL: *61-73* 2-4
RIVERSIDE: *61-64* 2-4
EPs: 7-Inch 33/45rpm
EMARCY: *55* 10-15
LPs: 10/12-Inch 33rpm
BLUE NOTE: *58* 15-25
(Label reads "Blue Note Records Inc. - New York, U.S.A.")
BLUE NOTE: *66* 10-20
(Label reads "Blue Note Records - A Division Of Liberty Records Inc.")
CAPITOL (Except 2200 & 2300 series): *66-80* 6-15
CAPITOL (2200 & 2300 series): *64-65* 10-20
DOBRE: *77* 5-8
EMARCY (400 series): *76* 8-12
EMARCY (36000 series): *55-58* 20-25
EVEREST: *71* 5-10
FANTASY: *73-75* 6-10
LIMELIGHT: *66* 8-15
MERCURY (1000 series): *81* 5-8
MERCURY (20000 & 60000 series): *61-62* 12-18
MILESTONE: *73-82* 6-12
PACIFIC JAZZ: *62* 10-20
RIVERSIDE (032 through 142): *82-85* 5-8
RIVERSIDE (200 through 400 series): *58-63* 12-25
RIVERSIDE (1100 series): *59-60* 12-25
RIVERSIDE (3000 series): *68* 6-12
RIVERSIDE (9000 series): *60-63* 10-20
SAVOY (2200 series): *76* 8-12
SAVOY (12000 series): *55* 25-35

Aerosmith: (L-R) Tom Hamilton; Joe Perry; Steven Tyler; Joey Kramer; Brad Whitford (Photo: Norman Seeff)

TRIP: 75 .... $5-8

VSP: 65 10-15

WING: 68 6-12
   Also see WILSON, Nancy, & Cannonball Adderley

ADDERLEY, Julian
"Cannonball" & John Coltrane
     LPs: 10/12-Inch 33rpm

LIMELIGHT: 65 10-15

MERCURY: 61 12-18
   Also see COLTRANE, John

ADDERLEY, Julian
"Cannonball" & Sergio Mendes
     LPs: 10/12-Inch 33rpm

CAPITOL: 68-71 8-12

EVEREST: 73 5-8
   Also see ADDERLEY, Julian
   "Cannonball"
   Also see MENDES, Sergio

ADDRISI, Dick
     Singles: 7-Inch

VALIANT: 66 6-12
   Also see ADDRISI BROTHERS

ADDRISI BROTHERS
     Singles: 7-Inch

BELL: 74 2-4

BRAD: 58 5-8

BUDDAH: 77 2-3

COLUMBIA: 72-73 2-4

DEL-FI: 59 5-8

ELEKTRA: 81 1-3

IMPERIAL: 60 4-6

POM POM: 62 .... $4-6

PRIVATE STOCK: 75 2-3

SCOTTI BROTHERS: 79 2-3

VALIANT: 64-65 3-5

WARNER BROS.: 62-68 3-5
     Picture Sleeves

SCOTTI BROTHERS: 79 2-3
     LPs: 10/12-Inch 33rpm

BUDDAH: 77 5-10

COLUMBIA: 72 5-10
   Members: Dick Addrisi; Don Addrisi.
   Also see ADDRISI, Dick

ADE, King Sunny
(King Sunny Ade & His African Beats)
     Singles: 12-Inch 33/45rpm

MANGO: 83 4-6
     Singles: 7-Inch

MANGO: 83 1-3
     LPs: 10/12-Inch 33rpm

MANGO: 83 5-8

ADVANCE
     Singles: 12-Inch 33/45rpm

POLYDOR: 83 4-6
     Singles: 7-Inch

POLYDOR: 83 1-3

ADVENTURERS
     Singles: 12-Inch 33/45rpm

CHRYSALIS: 86 4-6
     Singles: 7-Inch

CHRYSALIS: 86 1-3

ELEKTRA: 88 1-3

Picture Sleeves
CHRYSALIS: *86* $1-3
LPs: 10/12-Inch 33rpm
CHRYSALIS: *86* 5-8
ELEKTRA: *88* 5-8

AEROSMITH
Singles: 7-Inch
COLUMBIA: *73-80* 2-4
GEFFEN: *85-88* 1-3
Picture Sleeves
GEFFEN: *85-87* 1-3
LPs: 10/12-Inch 33rpm
COLUMBIA (Except KC-32005 with
  orange cover): *73-88* 6-10
COLUMBIA (32005;
  "Aerosmith"): *73* 20-25
(Orange cover. Incorrectly shows *Walking the Dog*
as *Walking the Dig*. With "KC" prefix.)
GEFFEN: *85-88* 5-8
Promotional LPs
COLUMBIA (187; "Pure
  Gold"): *76* 50-55
(Boxed set of the group's first three LPs.)
Members: Steve Tyler; Tom Hamilton; Joey
Kramer; Joe Perry; Brad Whitford.
Also see PERRY, Joe, Project
Also see RUN-D.M.C.

AFRIKA BAMBAATAA:
see BAMBAATAA, Afrika

AFRIQUE
Singles: 7-Inch
MAINSTREAM: *73* 2-4
LPs: 10/12-Inch 33rpm
MAINSTREAM: *73* 8-12

AFRO CUBAN BAND
Singles: 7-Inch
ARISTA: *78* 1-3
LPs: 10/12-Inch 33rpm
ARISTA: *78* 5-8

AFTER THE FIRE
Singles: 12-Inch 33/45rpm
EPIC: *83* 4-6
Singles: 7-Inch
EPIC: *83-84* 1-3
LPs: 10/12-Inch 33rpm
EPIC: *82* 5-8
Members: Peter Banks; Iver Piercy; Tim Haywell;
Nick Battle.
Also see BANKS, Peter

AFTERBACH
Singles: 7-Inch
COLUMBIA/ARC: *81* 1-3

LPs: 10/12-Inch 33rpm
COLUMBIA/ARC: *81* $5-8

AFTERNOON DELIGHTS
Singles: 12-Inch 33/45rpm
MCA: *81* 4-6
Singles: 7-Inch
MCA: *81* 1-3
LPs: 10/12-Inch 33rpm
MCA: *81* 5-8

AGENT ORANGE
Singles: 7-Inch
ENIGMA: *86* 1-3
POSH BOY: *81* 2-4
LPs: 10/12-Inch 33rpm
ENIGMA: *86-87* 5-8

A-HA
Singles: 7-Inch
REPRISE: *85-86* 1-3
WARNER BROS.: *85-88* 1-3
Picture Sleeves
WARNER BROS.: *85-87* 1-3
LPs: 10/12-Inch 33rpm
REPRISE: *85-86* 5-8
WARNER BROS.: *85-88* 5-8
Member: Morten Harket.

AIDA
Singles: 12-Inch 33/45rpm
VANGUARD: *84* 4-6
Singles: 7-Inch
VANGUARD: *84* 1-3
LPs: 10/12-Inch 33rpm

AIR SUPPLY
Singles: 7-Inch
ARISTA: *80-86* 1-3
FLASHBACK: *82* 1-3
Picture Sleeves
ARISTA: *80-82* 1-3
LPs: 10/12-Inch 33rpm
ARISTA: *80-86* 5-8
COLUMBIA: *77* 10-15
MFSL: *84* 20-25
Members: Graham Russell; Russell Hitchcock;
David Moyse; Criston Barker; Ralph Cooper;
David Green; Frank Esler-Smith; Rex Goh.
Also see HITCHCOCK, Russell

AIRWAVES
Singles: 7-Inch
A&M: *78-79* 1-3
LPs: 10/12-Inch 33rpm
A&M: *78-79* 5-8
Members: John David; Dave Charles; Ray Mar-
tinez.

AKENS, Jewel
Singles: 7-Inch
AMERICAN INT'L ARTISTS: *75* $2-4
CAPEHART: *61* 3-5
COLGEMS: *67* 3-5
ERA: *65* 3-5
MINASA: *65* 3-5
RTV: *72* 2-4
LPs: 10/12-Inch 33rpm
ERA: *65* 15-25

AKKERMAN, Jan
(Jan Akkerman & Kaz Lux)
Singles: 7-Inch
ATLANTIC: *77-79* 1-3
LPs: 10/12-Inch 33rpm
ATCO: *73* 10-12
ATLANTIC: *76-79* 5-10
SIRE: *73* 10-15
Also see FOCUS

AL B. SURE!
Singles: 7-Inch
WARNER BROS.: *88* 1-3
LPs: 10/12-Inch 33rpm
WARNER BROS.: *88* 5-8

ALABAMA
(Alabama Band)
Singles: 7-Inch
GRT: *77* 3-6
MDJ: *79-80* 2-4
RCA VICTOR: *80-88* 1-3
SUN (Colored vinyl): *81* 4-8
Picture Sleeves
GRT: *77* 10-20
RCA VICTOR: *80-88* 1-3

LPs: 10/12-Inch 33rpm
ALABAMA RECORDS (78 9-01;
"The Alabama Band"): *78* $200-400
PLANTATION: *81* 40-60
RCA VICTOR: *80-88* 5-8
SONNY: *79* 30-50
Members: Randy Owen; Jeff Cook; Teddy Gentry;
R. Scott; Mark Herndon.
Also see RICHIE, Lionel, & Alabama

ALAIMO, Chuck
(Chuck Alaimo Quartet)
Singles: 78rpm
KEN: *57* 4-8
MGM: *57* 4-8
Singles: 7-Inch
KEN: *57* 8-12
MGM: *57* 8-10

ALAIMO, Steve
(Steve Alaimo & The Redcoats)
Singles: 7-Inch
ABC: *66-67* 2-4
ABC-PARAMOUNT: *64-66* 3-5
ATCO: *67-71* 3-5
CHECKER: *61-63* 6-12
DADE: *59* 4-6
DICKSON: *60* 6-10
ENTRANCE: *71-72* 2-4
ERIC: *83* 1-3
IMPERIAL: *60-63* 3-6
LIFETIME: *58* 15-20
MARLIN (Except 6064): *59* 8-10
MARLIN (6064, "I Want You To
Love Me"): *59* 10-15
EPs: 7-Inch 33/45rpm
ABC-PARAMOUNT (531; "Where
The Action Is"): *65* 8-15
(Jukebox issue only.)
LPs: 10/12-Inch 33rpm
ABC-PARAMOUNT: *65-66* 15-20
CHECKER: *61-63* 20-30
CROWN: *63* 10-12

ALAIMO, Steve, & Betty Wright
Singles: 7-Inch
ATCO: *69* 2-4
Also see ALAIMO, Steve
Also see WRIGHT, Betty

ALARM
Singles: 7-Inch
I.R.S.: *83-88* 1-3
Picture Sleeves
I.R.S.: *83-87* 1-3
LPs: 10/12-Inch 33rpm
I.R.S.: *83-88* 5-8

Members: Mike Peters; Nigel Twist; Dave Sharp; Eddie MacDonald.

ALBERT, Eddie
Singles: 78rpm
KAPP: *54-5 6* $2-4
Singles: 7-Inch
COLUMBIA: *68* 2-3
HICKORY: *64-65* 2-3
KAPP: *54-56* 3-5
LPs: 10/12-Inch 33rpm
COLUMBIA: *68* 8-12
HAMILTON: *59* 5-15

ALBERT, Eddie, & Sondra Lee
Singles: 7-Inch
KAPP: *56* 2-4
Also see ALBERT, Eddie

ALBERT, Morris
Singles: 7-Inch
RCA VICTOR: *75-76* 2-3
LPs: 10/12-Inch 33rpm
RCA VICTOR: *75-76* 5-8

ALBERTI, Willy
Singles: 7-Inch
EPIC: *59* 2-4
LONDON: *59* 2-4
LPs: 10/12-Inch 33rpm
LONDON: *59* 5-10

ALBRIGHT, Gerald
Singles: 7-Inch
ATLANTIC: *87-88* 1-3
LPs: 10/12-Inch 33rpm
ATLANTIC: *88* 5-8

ALCATRAZZ
Singles: 7-Inch
ROCSHIRE: *83* 1-3
Picture Sleeves
ROCSHIRE: *83* 1-3
LPs: 10/12-Inch 33rpm
CAPITOL: *85* 5-8
ROCSHIRE: *83-84* 5-8
Member: Graham Bonnet.
Also see RAINBOW
Also see SCHENKER, Michael

ALDO NOVA: see NOVA, Aldo

ALDRICH, Renee
Singles: 7-Inch
JAM PACKED: *87* 1-3

ALDRICH, Ronnie
Singles: 7-Inch
LONDON: *60-62* 1-3
LPs: 10/12-Inch 33rpm
LONDON: *61-76* 4-8

RICHMOND: *59* $5-10

ALEEM
Singles: 12-Inch 33/45rpm
ATLANTIC: *87* 4-6
Singles: 7-Inch
ATLANTIC: *86* 1-3
LPs: 10/12-Inch 33rpm
ATLANTIC: *87* 5-8
Member: Leroy Burgess.

ALEEMS
Singles: 12-Inch 33/45rpm
NIA: *85* 4-6
Singles: 7-Inch
ATLANTIC: *86-87* 1-3
NIA: *84-85* 1-3

ALEXANDER, Arthur
Singles: 7-Inch
BUDDAH: *75-76* 2-4
DOT: *62-64* 4-8
MONUMENT: *68* 3-6
MUSIC MILL: *77* 3-5
SOUND STAGE 7: *65-71* 3-5
WARNER BROS: *72-73* 2-4
EPs: 7-Inch 33/45rpm
DOT: *62* 25-35
LPs: 10/12-Inch 33rpm
DOT: *62* 20-30
WARNER BROS: *72* 5-8

ALEXANDER, David
Singles: 7-Inch
SOUNDTOWN: *87* 1-3

ALEXANDER, Goldie
Singles: 7-Inch
ARISTA: *82* 1-3

ALEXANDER, Margie
Singles: 12-Inch 33/45rpm
CHI-SOUND: *77* 4-6
Singles: 7-Inch
ATLANTIC: *71* 2-4
CHI-SOUND: *76-77* 2-3
FUTURE STARS: *74* 2-4

ALFIE: see SILAS, Alfie

ALFONZO
(Alfonzo Jones)
Singles: 12-Inch 33/45rpm
JOE-WES: *83* 4-6
Singles: 7-Inch
JOE-WES: *82* 1-3
LARC: *82* 1-3
LPs: 10/12-Inch 33rpm
LARC: *83* 5-8

ALI, Muhammad:
see CLAY, Cassius

ALICE COOPER:
see COOPER, Alice

ALICE WONDER LAND
Singles: 7-Inch
BARDELL: *63* $10-15
UNITED INTERNATIONAL: 10-15

ALISHA
Singles: 12-Inch 33/45rpm
VANGUARD: *84-86* 4-6
Singles: 7-Inch
RCA VICTOR: *87* 1-3
VANGUARD: *84-86* 1-3

ALIVE 'N KICKING
Singles: 7-Inch
ROULETTE: *70-71* 3-5
LPs: 10/12-Inch 33rpm
ROULETTE: *70* 20-30
ROULETTE: *70* 40-55
(Promotional issue.)

ALL POINTS BULLETIN BAND
Singles: 7-Inch
LITTLE CITY: *75-79* 2-3

ALL SPORTS BAND
Singles: 7-Inch
RADIO: *81-82* 1-3
LPs: 10/12-Inch 33rpm
RADIO: *81* 5-8

ALLAN, Davie
(Davie Allan & The Arrows)
Singles: 7-Inch
A.O.A.: *76* 2-4
CUDE: *63* 10-15
MARC: *63* 8-12
MGM: *71-73* 2-4
MRC: *84* 1-3
PRIVATE STOCK: *74* 2-4
SIDEWALK: *64* 5-10
TOWER: *65-68* 3-5
WHAT: *82* 1-3
LPs: 10/12-Inch 33rpm
ALKOR: *84* 5-8
ARROW DYNAMICS: *85* 8-12
TOWER: *65-68* 15-20
WHAT: *83* 5-8
  Also see ANNETTE
  Also see CURB, Mike
  Also see DALE, Dick
  Also see FROST, Max, & The Troopers
  Also see HONDELLS
  Also see NAYLOR, Jerry

  Also see PARIS SISTERS
  Also see RONSTADT, Linda
  Also see STAFFORD, Terry
  Also see STARLETS

ALLEN, Annisteen
(Annisteen Allen & Her Home Town Boys)

Singles: 78rpm
CAPITOL: *55* $5-10
DECCA: *56-57* 5-10
FEDERAL: *51-52* 5-8
KING: *46-54* 6-10
Singles: 7-Inch
CAPITOL: *55* 5-10
DECCA: *56-57* 5-10
KING: *53-54* 10-15
TRUE SOUND: 4-6
WIG: *59* 4-6

**ALLEN, Annisteen, & Melvin
Moore**
Singles: 7-Inch
TODD: *59* 4-6
  Also see ALLEN, Annisteen

ALLEN, Dayton
LPs: 10/12-Inch 33rpm
GRAND AWARD: *60* 6-12

ALLEN, Donna
Singles: 7-Inch
OCEANA: *88* 1-3
TWENTY-ONE: *86-87* 1-3
LPs: 10/12-Inch 33rpm
OCEANA: *88* 5-8
TWENTY-ONE: *86-87* 5-8

ALLEN, Jonelle
Singles: 7-Inch
ALEXANDER STREET: *78* 1-3

ALLEN, Lee
Singles: 78rpm
ALADDIN: *56* 5-8
Singles: 7-Inch
ALADDIN: *56* 8-12
COLLECTABLES: *82* 1-3
EMBER: *58-59* 3-5
EPs: 7-Inch 33/45rpm
EMBER: *58* 40-50
LPs: 10/12-Inch 33rpm
EMBER (200; "Walkin' With
Mr. Lee"): *58* 75-100
(Red label.)
EMBER ("Logs" label): *58* 60-75
(Ember logo is formed with logs.)

EMBER (Black label): *60* $25-30
Also see BLASTERS

ALLEN, Peter
Singles: 12-Inch 33/45rpm
A&M: *79* 4-6
Singles: 7-Inch
A&M: *74-82* 1-3
ARISTA: *83-84* 1-3
METROMEDIA: *71-73* 2-4
LPs: 10/12-Inch 33rpm
A&M: *74-82* 5-8
ARISTA: *83-84* 5-8
METROMEDIA: *71-72* 10-12

ALLEN, R. Justice
Singles: 7-Inch
CATAWBA: *86* 1-3

ALLEN, Rance, Group
Singles: 7-Inch
CAPITOL: *77-79* 1-3
GOSPEL TRUTH: *72-73* 2-4
STAX: *78-81* 1-3
TRUTH: *74-75* 2-3
LPs: 10/12-Inch 33rpm
CAPITOL: *77-79* 5-8
GOSPEL TRUTH: *72-74* 8-12
MYRRH: *84* 5-8
STAX: *78-81* 5-8
TRUTH: *75* 8-10
Members: Rance Allen; Thomas Allen; Steven
Allen.

ALLEN, Rex
Singles: 78rpm
DECCA (Except 30651): *56-57* 2-5
DECCA (30651; "Knock Knock,
Rattle"): *56* 8-12
MERCURY: *53-55* 2-4
Singles: 7-Inch
BUENA VISTA: *59* 2-4
DECCA (Except 28000 through
30000 series): *56-72* 2-5
DECCA (28000 & 29000 series): *52-56* 3-6
DECCA (30000 series,
except 30651): *56* 3-6
DECCA (30651; "Knock Knock,
Rattle"): *56* 10-15
JMI: *73* 1-3
MERCURY: *53-62* 2-5
WILDCAT: 3-5
Picture Sleeves
MERCURY: *63* 5-10
EPs: 7-Inch 33/45rpm
DECCA: *56* 8-15
MERCURY: *53-56* 8-15

LPs: 10/12-Inch 33rpm
BUENA VISTA: *61* $18-22
COLLECTOR'S CLASSICS: 5-8
CORAL: *73* 4-6
DECCA (5000 series): *68-70* 10-12
(Decca LP numbers in this series preceded by a "7"
or a "DL-7" are stereo issues.)
DECCA (8000 series): *56-58* 20-25
DESIGN: *62* 10-12
DISNEYLAND: *70* 6-10
HACIENDA: 20-22
JMI: 5-8
MCA: 4-6
MERCURY: *62* 12-15
PICKWICK/HILLTOP: *65* 10-12
VOCALION: *70* 6-10
WING: *64-66* 10-12

ALLEN, Richie
(Richie Allen & The Pacific Surfers)
Singles: 7-Inch
ERA: *61* 4-6
IMPERIAL: *60-63* 5-10
TOWER: *66* 3-6
LPs: 10/12-Inch 33rpm
IMPERIAL: *63* 35-70
Member: Richie Podolor.

ALLEN, Steve
Singles: 78rpm
BRUNSWICK: *53* 3-5
CORAL: *55-56* 3-5
Singles: 7-Inch
BRUNSWICK: *53* 3-6
CORAL: *55-56* 3-6
DOT: *59-66* 2-4
DUNHILL (Except 4097): *67-68* 1-3
DUNHILL (4097; "Here Comes Sgt.
Pepper"): *67* 3-6
SIGNATURE: *59-60* 2-4
Picture Sleeves
DOT: *65* 4-8
EPs: 7-Inch 33/45rpm
BRUNSWICK: *53* 10-15
CORAL: *55-56* 10-15
DECCA: *55* 15-20
LPs: 10/12-Inch 33rpm
COLUMBIA (2554; "Steve
Allen"): *56* 20-30
(10-Inch LP.)
CORAL (100; "Jazz Story"): *59* 25-35
(Narration by Steve Allen, music by various artists.)
CORAL (57000 series,
except 57099): *55-56* 15-20

CORAL (57099; "The James Dean
Story"): *56* $35-50
(With Bill Randle.)
CORAL (57400 series): *63* 10-15
(Coral LP numbers in this series preceded by a "7"
are stereo issues.)
DECCA: *55* 20-25
DOT (Except 3472 & 3517): *59-66* 8-12
DOT (3472; "Steve Allen's Funny Fone
Calls"): *63* 15-20
DOT (3517; "More Funny Fone
Calls"): *63* 15-20
DUNHILL: *67* 8-10
EMARCY: *58* 15-20
HAMILTON: *59-64* 10-15
MERCURY: *61* 10-15
PETE: *69* 5-10
ROULETTE: *59* 15-20
SIGNATURE (Except 1004): *59* 15-20
SIGNATURE (1004; "Man On The
Street"): *59* 30-40
(With Louis Nye, Tom Poston & Don Knotts.)

ALLEN, Steve, & Jayne Meadows
Singles: 78rpm
CORAL: *55* 3-5
Singles: 7-Inch
CORAL: *55* 3-6
Also see ALLEN, Steve

ALLEN, Vee
Singles: 7-Inch
LION: *73* 2-4
MCA: *83* 1-3
LPs: 10/12-Inch 33rpm
MCA: *83* 5-8

ALLEN, Woody
Singles: 7-Inch
UNITED ARTISTS: *72* 2-4
Picture Sleeves
UNITED ARTISTS: *72* 3-6
LPs: 10/12-Inch 33rpm
BELL: *67* 10-15
CAPITOL: *68* 8-12
CASABLANCA: *79* 5-10
COLPIX: *64-65* 15-20
UNITED ARTISTS (800 series): *77* 6-10
UNITED ARTISTS (9900 series): *72* 8-12

ALLEY CATS
Singles: 7-Inch
PHILLES: *62* 8-12

ALLISON, Gene
Singles: 78rpm
CALVERT: *56* 4-8
DECCA: *57* 4-8

VEE JAY: *57* $4-8
Singles: 7-Inch
CALVERT: *56* 8-10
CHAMPION: *59* 4-6
CHEROKEE: *59* 4-6
DECCA: *57* 5-8
MONUMENT: *65* 3-5
VALDOT: *62* 3-5
VEE JAY: *57-60* 5-8
LPs: 10/12-Inch 33rpm
VEE JAY (1009; "Gene
Allison"): *59* 100-125
(Maroon label.)
VEE JAY (1009; "Gene
Allison"): *59* 25-40
(Black label.)

ALLISONS
Singles: 7-Inch
TIP: *63* 5-8

ALLMAN, Duane
LPs: 10/12-Inch 33rpm
CAPRICORN: *72-74* 8-12
Also see DEREK & THE DOMINOS

ALLMAN, Duane & Gregg
Singles: 7-Inch
BOLD: *73* 5-8
LPs: 10/12-Inch 33rpm
BOLD (301; "Duane & Gregg
Allman"): *72* 20-25
(With gatefold cover.)
BOLD (301; "Duane & Gregg
Allman"): *73* 8-10
(With standard cover.)
SPRINGBOARD: *75* 8-10
Also see ALLMAN, Duane
Also see ALLMAN, Gregg
Also see ALLMAN BROTHERS BAND
Also see ALLMAN JOYS

ALLMAN, Gregg
(Gregg Allman Band)
Singles: 7-Inch
CAPRICORN: *73-77* 2-4
EPIC: *87-89* 1-3
LPs: 10/12-Inch 33rpm
CAPRICORN: *73-77* 8-12
EPIC: *87-89* 5-8
ROBERT KLEIN ("Interview"): *81* 40-60
(Promotional issue only.)
Also see ALLMAN, Duane & Gregg
Also see ALLMAN & WOMAN
Also see ALLMAN BROTHERS BAND
Also see ALLMAN JOYS

ALLMAN & WOMAN
Singles: 7-Inch
WARNER BROS: 77 .... $2-4
LPs: 10/12-Inch 33rpm
WARNER BROS: 77 8-10
Members: Gregg Allman; Cher.
Also see ALLMAN, Gregg
Also see CHER

ALLMAN BROTHERS BAND
Singles: 7-Inch
ARISTA: 80-81 1-3
CAPRICORN: 71-79 2-4
Picture Sleeves
ARISTA: 81 1-3
EPs: 7-Inch 33/45rpm
ATLANTIC: 73 10-20
(Jukebox issue only.)
CAPRICORN: 73 10-20
(Jukebox issue only.)
LPs: 10/12-Inch 33rpm
ARISTA: 80-81 5-8
ATCO: 69-73 15-20
CAPRICORN (Except 802): 72-79 8-12
CAPRICORN (802; "The Allman Brothers
Band At The Fillmore East"): 71 15-20
K-TEL: 5-8
MFSL: 85 15-25
POLYDOR (6339; "Best Of The
Allman Brothers Band"): 81 5-8
POLYDOR (839-417; "The Allman
Brothers Band"): 89 25-35
(6-LP boxed set, with booklet.)
Members: Duane Allman; Gregg Allman; Dicky
Betts; Les Dudek; David Goldflies; Paul Hornsby;
Berry Oakley; Dan Toler; Johnny Sandlin; Butch
Trucks; Johnny Johanson.
Also see ALLMAN, Duane & Gregg
Also see BETTS, Richard
Also see HOUR GLASS
Also see DUDEK, Les
Also see SEA LEVEL

ALLMAN JOYS
Singles: 7-Inch
DIAL: 66 20-25
LPs: 10/12-Inch 33rpm
DIAL: 73 10-15
Members: Duane Allman; Gregg Allman; Ralph
Balinger; Ronnie Wilkin; Tommy Amato; Jack
Jackson; Bobby Dennis.
Also see ALLMAN, Duane & Gregg

ALMEIDA, Laurindo
(Laurindo Almeida & The Modern Jazz Quartet)
Singles: 7-Inch
ATLANTIC: 64 2-3

CAPITOL: 55-65 .... $2-4
PACIFIC JAZZ: 55 3-5
EPs: 7-Inch 33/45rpm
CAPITOL: 56-59 5-10
CORAL: 54-56 2-4
PACIFIC JAZZ: 54 10-15
LPs: 10/12-Inch 33rpm
ATLANTIC: 64 10-15
CAPITOL(Except 8000
series): 59-65 10-15
CAPITOL(8000 series): 56-58 15-25
CORAL: 54-56 15-25
CRYSTAL CLEAR: 80 5-8
DAYBREAK: 73 5-8
DOBRE: 76-77 5-8
INNER CITY: 79 5-8
PACIFIC JAZZ: 54 25-35
(10-Inch LPs.)
SURREY: 65 8-12
WORLD PACIFIC: 56-62 10-20
Also see BYRD, Charlie
Also see DAVIS, Sammy, Jr., & Laurindo Almeida
Also see GETZ, Stan, & Laurindo Almeida
Also see SOMMERS, Joanie, & Laurindo Almeida

ALMEIDA, Laurindo / Chico Hamilton
LPs: 10/12-Inch 33rpm
JAZZTONE: 64 12-18
Also see ALMEIDA, Laurindo
Also see HAMILTON, Chico

ALMOND, Marc
LPs: 10/12-Inch 33rpm
CAPITOL: 88 5-8

ALPACA PHASE III
Singles: 7-Inch
ATLANTIC: 74 2-4

ALPERT, Herb
(Herb Alpert & The Tijuana Brass; Herbie Alpert)
Singles: 12-Inch 33/45rpm
A&M: 79-84 4-6
Singles: 7-Inch
A&M: 62-87 1-3
ANDEX: 59 2-4
CAROL: 59 2-4
ROWE/AMI: 66 4-8
("Play Me" Sales Stimulator promotional issue.)
Picture Sleeves
A&M: 65-81 1-3

EPs: 7-Inch 33/45rpm
A&M: *65-66* $3-6
(Jukebox issues only.)
LPs: 10/12-Inch 33rpm
A&M (Except 100 series): *66-87* 5-8
A&M (100 series): *62-66* 5-15
MFSL: *81* 25-50
Also see HALL, Lani, & Herb Alpert

ALPERT, Herb, & Hugh Masekela
Singles: 7-Inch
A&M/HORIZON: *78* 1-3
LPs: 10/12-Inch 33rpm
A&M/HORIZON: *78* 5-8
Also see ALPERT, Herb
Also see MASEKELA, Hugh

ALPHAVILLE
Singles: 12-Inch 33/45rpm
ATLANTIC: *84-86* 4-6
Singles: 7-Inch
ATLANTIC: *84-86* 1-3
Picture Sleeves
ATLANTIC: *84* 1-3
LPs: 10/12-Inch 33rpm
ATLANTIC: *84-86* 5-8

ALSTON, Gerald
Singles: 7-Inch
MOTOWN: *88* 1-3
LPs: 10/12-Inch 33rpm
MOTOWN: *88* 5-8

ALVIN, Dave
(Dave Alvin & The Red Devils)
Singles: 7-Inch
ENIGMA: *87* 5-8
LPs: 10/12-Inch 33rpm
EPIC: *87* 5-8
Also see BLASTERS
Also see X

ALVIN LEE: see LEE, Alvin

ALWAYS, Billy
Singles: 7-Inch
WAYLO: *82* 1-3

ALWAYS, Billy
Singles: 7-Inch
EPIC: *88* 1-3

AMAZING RHYTHM ACES
Singles: 7-Inch
ABC: *75-79* 2-3
COLUMBIA: *79* 2-3
WARNER BROS: *80* 1-3
LPs: 10/12-Inch 33rpm
ABC: *75-78* 8-10
COLUMBIA: *79* 5-8

WARNER BROS: *80* $5-8
Members: Russell Smith; James Brown, Jr; Byrd
Burton; Stick Davis; Billy Earhart III; James
Hooker; Butch McDade.

AMAZULU
Singles: 7-Inch
MANGO: *87* 1-3
Members: Ann Marie Ruddock; Sharon Bailey;
Lesley Beach.

AMBASSADORS
Singles: 7-Inch
ARCTIC: *68-69* 2-4
ATLANTIC: *67-68* 3-5
SOUND STAGE 7: *67-68* 3-5
TIME: 3-5
LPs: 10/12-Inch 33rpm
ARCTIC: *69* 10-12

AMBOY DUKES
Singles: 7-Inch
MAINSTREAM: *67-69* 5-10
LPs: 10/12-Inch 33rpm
MAINSTREAM (Except 801): *68-69* ... 20-25
MAINSTREAM (801; "Journeys &
Migrations"): *74* 10-12
POLYDOR: *70* 10-12
Members: Ted Nugent; Greg Arama; Rusty Day;
John Drake; Steve Farmer; Dave Palmer; Andy
Solomon; Rod Grange; K.J. Knight; John Angelos.
Also see NUGENT, Ted

AMBROSIA
Singles: 7-Inch
20TH CENTURY-FOX: *74-78* 2-3
WARNER BROS: *78-82* 1-3
LPs: 10/12-Inch 33rpm
NAUTILUS: *81* 10-15
(Half-speed mastered.)
20TH CENTURY-FOX: *74-78* 8-10
WARNER BROS: *78-82* 5-8
Members: David Pack; Burleigh Drummond; Joe
Puerta; Christopher North.
Also see PACK, David

**AMECHE, Don, & Frances
Langford**
EPs: 7-Inch 33/45rpm
COLUMBIA: *61* 5-15
(Promotional only.)
LPs: 10/12-Inch 33rpm
COLUMBIA (1000 & 8000
series): *61-62* 15-20
COLUMBIA (30000 series): *71* 8-12

AMERICA
Singles: 7-Inch
AMERICAN INT'L: *79* 3-6

CAPITOL: *80-85* $1-3
WARNER BROS: *72-77* 2-4
Picture Sleeves
AMERICAN INT'L: *79* 3-6
CAPITOL: *80-85* 1-3
WARNER BROS: *72-74* 2-5
LPs: 10/12-Inch 33rpm
CAPITOL: *80-85* 5-8
WARNER BROS (Except 2576): *72-77* . . 8-10
WARNER BROS (2576;
"America"): *71* 15-20
(For copies that do NOT include *A Horse With No Name*.)
WARNER BROS (2576;
"America"): *72* 8-10
(For copies that DO include *A Horse With No Name*.)
Members: Gerry Beckley; Dan Peek; Dewey Bunnell.
Also see PEEK, Dan

AMERICAN BREED
Singles: 7-Inch
ABC: *75* 1-3
ACTA: *67-69* 3-5
MCA: *84* 1-3
PARAMOUNT: *70* 2-4
Picture Sleeves
ACTA: *68* 5-10
LPs: 10/12-Inch 33rpm
ACTA: *67-68* 10-20
Members: Gary Loizzo; Al Ciner; Chuck Colbert; Lee Graziano; Kevin Murphy.
Also see RUFUS

AMERICAN COMEDY NETWORK
LPs: 10/12-Inch 33rpm
CRITIQUE: *84* 5-8

AMERICAN DREAM
Singles: 7-Inch
AMPEX: *70* 2-4
DEMIK: *68* 3-5
LPs: 10/12-Inch 33rpm
AMPEX: *70* 15-20
Members: Nick Jameson; Dooley Van Winkle; Nicky Indelicato; Don Ferris; Mickey Brook.

AMERICAN FLYER
Singles: 7-Inch
UNITED ARTISTS: *76-77* 2-4
Picture Sleeves
UNITED ARTISTS: *76-77* 2-5
LPs: 10/12-Inch 33rpm
UNITED ARTISTS: *76-77* 8-10
Members: Eric Kaz; Steve Katz; Craig Fuller; Doug Yule.
Also see PURE PRAIRIE LEAGUE

Also see VELVET UNDERGROUND

AMERICAN GIRLS
Singles: 7-Inch
I.R.S.: *86* $1-3
Picture Sleeves
I.R.S.: *86* 1-3
LPs: 10/12-Inch 33rpm
I.R.S.: *86* 5-8

AMES, Ed
Singles: 7-Inch
RCA VICTOR: *63-73* 2-3
Picture Sleeves
RCA VICTOR: *67* 2-4
LPs: 10/12-Inch 33rpm
CAMDEN: *72-73* 4-8
RCA VICTOR: *64-77* 5-15
Also see AMES BROTHERS

AMES, Nancy
Singles: 7-Inch
ABC: *68* 1-3
EPIC: *66-68* 2-3
LIBERTY: *61-65* 2-3
SC: *68* 1-3
Picture Sleeves
EPIC: *66* 2-4
LPs: 10/12-Inch 33rpm
EPIC: *66-68* 5-10
LIBERTY: *61-65* 5-12

AMES BROTHERS
Singles: 78rpm
CORAL: *50-53* 3-6
RCA VICTOR: *53-57* 2-5
Singles: 7-Inch
CORAL: *50-53* 5-10
EPIC: *62-63* 3-5
RCA VICTOR: *53-62* 5-15
Picture Sleeves
EPIC: *62* 3-5
RCA VICTOR: *60* 10-15
EPs: 7-Inch 33/45rpm
CORAL: *50-53* 10-20
RCA VICTOR: *53-61* 10-20
LPs: 10/12-Inch 33rpm
CORAL: *53-62* 15-30
EPIC: *63* 10-15
RCA VICTOR (1000 series): *75* 5-8
RCA VICTOR (1200 through 2200
series): *55-61* 15-30
RCA VICTOR (2800 series): *64* 8-15
RCA VICTOR (6000 series): *72* 5-10
VOCALION: *68* 5-10
Members: Ed Ames; Joe Ames; Gene Ames; Vic Ames.

Also see AMES, Ed
Also see COMO, Perry / Ames Brothers /
Harry Belafonte / Radio City Music Hall Orch.

AMESBURY, Bill
Singles: 7-Inch
CASABLANCA: *74-75* $2-4
LPs: 10/12-Inch 33rpm
CAPITOL: *76* 5-8
CASABLANCA: *74* 8-10

AMMONS, Gene
Singles: 78rpm
CHESS: *50* 4-8
DECCA: *54* 3-5
MERCURY: *47-53* 4-8
PRESTIGE: *51-57* 3-6
Singles: 7-Inch
ARGO: *62* 2-4
DECCA: *54* 3-5
MERCURY: *50-53* 3-6
PRESTIGE (100 through 400
    series): *60-68* 2-4
PRESTIGE (700 series): *69-73* 2-3
(This "700" series can easily be distinguished from
the early '50s "700" series that follows. The com-
pany address is shown as in New Jersey. In the '50s
the company was in New York.)
PRESTIGE (713 through 921): *51-57* 3-6
(Black vinyl.)
PRESTIGE (713 through 921): *51-57* 8-10
(Colored vinyl.)
SAVOY: *60* 2-4
UNITED: *53-54* 3-5
EPs: 7-Inch 33/45rpm
EMARCY: *54* 15-20
PRESTIGE: *51* 20-25
LPs: 10/12-Inch 33rpm
ARGO: *62* 15-20
CHESS: *59* 15-20
EMARCY (400 series): *76* 8-12
EMARCY (26000 series): *54* 40-50
    (10-Inch LPs.)
ENJA: *81* 5-8
MERCURY: *60-63* 15-20
OLYMPIC: *74* 5-8
PRESTIGE (014 through 192): *82-85* 5-8
PRESTIGE (7010 through 7132): *55-58* .. 20-30
(Each of the following LPs in this series was reis-
sued using the original catalog number but a dif-
ferent title: Prestige 7050, *All Star Jam Session*,
was reissued as *Woofin' & Tweetin*; Prestige 7039,
Hi-Fi Jam Session, was reissued as *Happy Blues*
and Prestige 7060, *Jammin' With Gene*, was reis-
sued as *Not Really The Blues*. These three 1960
reissues are valued in the $15-$20 range.)
PRESTIGE (7146 through 7287): *58-64* .. 15-20

PRESTIGE (7300 & 7400 series): *65-68* $10-15
PRESTIGE (7500 through 7800
    series): *68-70* 5-10
PRESTIGE (10000 series): *71-74* 5-10
PRESTIGE (24000 series): *73-81* 8-12
ROOTS: *76* 5-8
SAVOY: *61* 15-20
TRIP: *73-75* 5-8
VEE JAY: *60* 15-20
WING: *60-63* 12-15
    Also see MC DUFF, Brother Jack, & Gene
Ammons

AMMONS, Gene, & Richard "Groove" Holmes
LPs: 10/12-Inch 33rpm
PACIFIC JAZZ (32; "Groovin' With
    Jug"): *61* 15-20
    Also see HOLMES, Richard "Groove"

AMMONS, Gene, & Sonny Stitt
Singles: 78rpm
PRESTIGE: *50-51* 3-5
Singles: 7-Inch
PRESTIGE (700 series): *50-51* 3-5
(Black vinyl.)
PRESTIGE (700 series): *50-51* 8-10
(Colored vinyl.)
LPs: 10/12-Inch 33rpm
ARGO: *63* 12-15
CADET: *67* 10-15
CHESS: *60* 15-20
PRESTIGE (100 series): *51-54* 50-75
    (10-Inch LPs.)
PRESTIGE (7600 series): *69* 6-10
PRESTIGE (10000 series): *76* 5-8
VERVE (8400 series): *61-62* 15-20
(Reads"MGM Records - A Division Of Metro-
Goldwyn-Mayer, Inc." at bottom of label.)
VERVE (8800 series): *72* 8-12
(Reads"Manufactured By MGM Record Corp.," or
mentions either Polydor or Polygram at bottom of
label.)
Also see AMMONS, Gene
Also see STITT, Sonny

AMUZEMENT PARK
(Amusement Park Band)
Singles: 7-Inch
ATLANTIC: *84-85* 1-3
OUR GANG: *82-83* 1-3
LPs: 10/12-Inch 33rpm
ATLANTIC: *84* 5-8
    Member: Paul Richmond.

ANA
Singles: 7-Inch
PARC: *87* 1-3

ANACOSTIA
Singles: 7-Inch
COLUMBIA: 72-75 .... $2-4
MCA: 77 2-3
ROULETTE: 84 1-3
TABU: 78-79 1-3
LPs: 10/12-Inch 33rpm
MCA: 77 5-8
TABU: 78 5-8

ANDERSEN, Eric
Singles: 7-Inch
ARISTA: 75-77 1-3
COLUMBIA: 72 2-4
WARNER BROS: 68-71 2-4
LPs: 10/12-Inch 33rpm
ARISTA: 75-77 5-8
COLUMBIA: 72 8-10
VANGUARD: 65-70 15-20
WARNER BROS: 68-70 10-12

ANDERSON, Al
Singles: 7-Inch
VANGUARD: 73 2-4
LPs: 10/12-Inch 33rpm
TWIN/TONE: 88 5-8
VANGUARD: 73 10-12
Also see NRBQ

ANDERSON, Bill
(Bill Anderson & The Jordanaires)
Singles: 7-Inch
DECCA (30000 & 31000 series): 58-66 3-5
DECCA (32000 & 33000 series): 67-72 2-4
MCA: 73-81 1-3
SOUTHERN TRACKS: 82-87 1-3
SWANEE: 85 1-3
TNT: 59 4-6
Picture Sleeves
DECCA: 63-69 4-8
EPs: 7-Inch 33/45rpm
DECCA: 63-65 5-10
LPs: 10/12-Inch 33rpm
CORAL: 73 4-6
DECCA (4192 through 4686): 62-65 15-20
DECCA (4771 through 5344): 66-72 10-15
(Decca LP numbers in this series preceded by a "7"
or a "DL-7" are stereo issues.)
DECCA (7100 series): 69 15-20
DECCA (7200 series): 72 10-12
EPIC: 82-85 5-8
MCA: 73-80 5-10
SOUTHERN TRACKS: 84 5-8
VOCALION: 68-71 8-12
Also see COE, David Allan, & Bill Anderson

ANDERSON, Carl
Singles: 12-Inch 33/45rpm
EPIC: 82-86 .... $4-6
POLYDOR: 88 1-3
Singles: 7-Inch
EPIC: 82-86 1-3
LPs: 10/12-Inch 33rpm
EPIC: 82-86 5-8
Also see LORING, Gloria, & Carl Anderson

ANDERSON, Elton
Singles: 7-Inch
CAPITOL: 62 3-5
LANOR: 63 3-5
MERCURY: 59-61 8-10
VIN: 59 10-15

ANDERSON, Ernestine
Singles: 7-Inch
MERCURY: 60-62 2-4
SUE: 63-64 2-4
EPs: 7-Inch 33/45rpm
MERCURY: 59 5-10
LPs: 10/12-Inch 33rpm
MERCURY: 58-60 15-25
OMEGA DISK: 59 10-15
SUE: 63 10-15
WING: 64 10-15

ANDERSON, Jesse
Singles: 7-Inch
CADET: 67-68 3-5
JEWEL: 72 2-4
THOMAS: 70 2-4

ANDERSON, John
Singles: 7-Inch
WARNER BROS: 77-85 1-3
LPs: 10/12-Inch 33rpm
WARNER BROS: 80-85 5-8

ANDERSON, Jon
Singles: 12-Inch 33/45rpm
ATLANTIC: 82 4-6
Singles: 7-Inch
ATLANTIC: 76-82 1-3
COLUMBIA: 88 1-3
ELEKTRA: 84-85 1-3
LPs: 10/12-Inch 33rpm
ATLANTIC: 76-82 5-8
COLUMBIA: 88 5-8
ELEKTRA: 85 5-8
Promotional LPs
ATLANTIC ("An Evening With Jon
Anderson"): 76 20-30
(Interviews with Anderson and music from his
Olias Of Sunhillow LP, as well as selections by
Yes.)

Also see JON & VANGELIS
Also see TANGERINE DREAM / Jon Anderson / Bryan Ferry
Also see YES

ANDERSON, Lale
Singles: 7-Inch
KING: *61-62* $2-4
LPs: 10/12-Inch 33rpm
UNIVERSE: *61* 5-10

ANDERSON, Laurie
Singles: 12-Inch 33/45rpm
WARNER BROS: *81* 4-6
Singles: 7-Inch
WARNER BROS: *81* 1-3
EPs: 7-Inch 33/45rpm
WARNER BROS: *81* 3-5
LPs: 10/12-Inch 33rpm
WARNER BROS (Except 25192): *82-86* ... 5-8
WARNER BROS (25192; "United States Live"): *85* 30-40
(A 5-LP set.)

ANDERSON, Leroy
Singles: 78rpm
DECCA: *51-57* 2-4
Singles: 7-Inch
DECCA: *51-62* 2-4
EPs: 7-Inch 33/45rpm
DECCA: *51-58* 4-8
LPs: 10/12-Inch 33rpm
DECCA: *51-63* 5-15

ANDERSON, Liz & Lynn
Singles: 7-Inch
RCA VICTOR: *68* 3-5

ANDERSON, Lynn
Singles: 7-Inch
CHART: *66-71* 2-4
COLUMBIA: *70-80* 1-3
MERCURY: *86-88* 1-3
PERMIAN: *83* 1-3
RCA VICTOR: *68* 2-4
Picture Sleeves
COLUMBIA: *70-72* 3-6
LPs: 10/12-Inch 33rpm
ALBUM GLOBE: *76* 5-8
CHART (Except 1050): *67-71* 8-12
CHART (1050; "Lynn Anderson"): *72* ... 10-18
COLUMBIA: *70-80* 6-10
HARMONY: *71-73* 5-10
MOUNTAIN DEW: 5-10
PERMIAN: *83* 5-8
PICKWICK: 5-10
TIME-LIFE: *81* 5-8
Also see ANDERSON, Liz & Lynn

ANDERSON, Lynn, & Gary Morris
Singles: 7-Inch
PERMIAN: *83* $1-3
Also see ANDERSON, Lynn
Also see MORRIS, Gary

ANDERSON, Michael
Singles: 7-Inch
A&M: *88* 1-3
LPs: 10/12-Inch 33rpm
A&M: *88* 5-8

ANDERSON, Roshell
Singles: 7-Inch
EXCELLO: *71* 2-4
SUNBURST: *73-74* 2-4

ANDERSON, Vicki
(Vikki Anderson; Vickie Anderson)
Singles: 7-Inch
BROWNSTONE: *71-72* 2-4
DELUXE: *66* 3-5
FONTANA: *64* 3-5
KING: *66-70* 3-5
SMASH: *65* 3-5
TUFF: *67* 3-5
Also see BROWN, James, & Vickie Anderson

ANDREA TRUE CONNECTION:
see TRUE, Andrea

ANDREWS, Chris
Singles: 7-Inch
ATCO: *66* 3-5
RCA VICTOR: *69* 2-4

ANDREWS, Inez
(Inez Andrews & The Andrewettes)
Singles: 7-Inch
MCA: *84* 1-3
SONG BIRD: *64-73* 2-4
LPs: 10/12-Inch 33rpm
MCA: *84* 5-8
SAVOY: *80-81* 5-8

ANDREWS, Julie
Singles: 7-Inch
BUENA VISTA: *65* 2-3
COLUMBIA: *67* 2-3
DECCA: *67* 2-3
LONDON: *60* 2-4
RCA VICTOR: *70* 2-3
EPs: 7-Inch 33/45rpm
RCA VICTOR: *56* 10-15
LPs: 10/12-Inch 33rpm
ANGEL: *58* 15-20
COLUMBIA (1700 & 8500 series): *62* .. 15-20
COLUMBIA (31000 series): *72* 8-12
HARMONY: *70-72* 8-10

RCA VICTOR (1000 series): *70* **$8-12**
RCA VICTOR (1400 through 1600
   series): *56-58* **20-25**
RCA VICTOR (3800 series): *67* **8-12**
20TH CENTURY-FOX: *68* **8-12**

ANDREWS, Julie, & Carol Burnett
LPs: 10/12-Inch 33rpm
COLUMBIA (2200 & 5800
   series): *62* **15-20**
COLUMBIA (31000 series): *72* **8-12**
   Also see ANDREWS, Julie
   Also see BURNETT, Carol

**ANDREWS, Julie, & Andre Previn /
Vic Damone / Jack Jones / Marian
Anderson**
EPs: 7-Inch 33/45rpm
RCA VICTOR (277; "We Wish You
   A Merry Christmas"): *69* **2-4**
   (Radio Shack Special Collector's Edition.)
   Also see ANDREWS, Julie
   Also see DAMONE, Vic
   Also see JONES, Jack
   Also see PREVIN, Andre

ANDREWS, Lee
(Lee Andrews & The Hearts)
Singles: 78rpm
ARGO: *57* **10-20**
GOTHAM: *56* **25-50**
MAIN LINE: *57* **30-60**
RAINBOW: *54* **100-200**
Singles: 7-Inch
ARGO: *57* **15-25**
CASINO (110; "Baby, Come
   Back"): *58* **15-20**
CASINO (452; "Try The
   Impossible"): *58* **40-60**
CHESS: *57-58* **4-6**
COLLECTABLES: *82* **1-3**
CRIMSON: *67-68* **3-5**
GOTHAM (318; "Bluebird Of
   Happiness"): *56* **40-50**
GOTHAM (320; "Lonely Room"): *56* . . . **50-75**
GOTHAM (321; "Just Suppose"): *56* **50-75**
GOWEN: *61* **4-6**
GRAND: *62* **3-5**
JORDAN: *60* **10-15**
LOST NITE: *65* **3-5**
MAIN LINE (102; "Long Lonely
   Nights"): *57* **80-100**
   (Green label.)
MAIN LINE (Black label): *62* **5-8**
PARKWAY: *62-63* **3-5**

RAINBOW (252; "Maybe You'll Be
   There"): *54* **$200-250**
   (Black vinyl.)
RAINBOW (252; "Maybe You'll Be
   There"): *54* **400-500**
   (Colored vinyl. Small print.)
RAINBOW (252; "Maybe You'll Be
   There"): *62* **4-6**
   (Colored vinyl. Very large print.)
RAINBOW (256; "White Cliffs Of
   Dover"): *54* **250-300**
   (Yellow label.)
RAINBOW (256; "White Cliffs Of
   Dover"): *62* **4-6**
   (Blue label.)
RAINBOW (259; "The Bells Of St.
   Mary's"): *54* **200-250**
   (Yellow label.)
RAINBOW (259; "The Bells Of St.
   Mary's"): *62* **4-6**
   (Blue label.)
RCA VICTOR: *66* **3-5**
SWAN: *61* **3-5**
UNITED ARTISTS (100 series): *58-59* . . . **5-10**
UNITED ARTISTS (500 series): *63* **3-5**
LPs: 10/12-Inch 33rpm
COLLECTABLES: *82-85* **6-8**
LOST-NITE (1; "Lee Andrews & The
   Hearts"): *81* **8-10**
   (Colored vinyl 10-Inch LP.)
LOST-NITE (2; "Lee Andrews & The
   Hearts"): *81* **8-10**
   (Colored vinyl 10-Inch LP.)
LOST-NITE (100 series): *63* **10-15**
POST: **10-12**
   Members: Lee Andrews & The Hearts; Arthur
   Thompson; Roy Calhoun; Wendell Calhoun; Butch
   Curry; Ted Weems.

ANDREWS, Patty
Singles: 78rpm
CAPITOL: *55-56* **2-4**
DECCA: *50-54* **3-5**
Singles: 7-Inch
CAPITOL: *55-56* **2-4**
DECCA: *50-54* **3-5**
   Also see ANDREWS SISTERS

ANDREWS, Ruby
Singles: 7-Inch
ABC: *76-77* **2-3**
ZODIAC: *67-71* **2-4**
LPs: 10/12-Inch 33rpm
ABC: *77* **8-10**
ZODIAC: *72* **10-12**
   Also see STACKHOUSE, Ruby

ANDREWS SISTERS
Singles: 78rpm
CAPITOL: *56* $3-5
DECCA: *38-57* 3-8
Singles: 7-Inch
ABC: *74* 1-3
CAPITOL: *56* 3-6
DECCA: *50-57* 3-5
DOT: *64* 2-3
KAPP: *59* 2-4
PARAMOUNT: *73* 1-3
Picture Sleeves
DECCA: *57* 5-10
EPs: 7-Inch 33/45rpm
DECCA: *51-58* 5-15
LPs: 10/12 Inch 33rpm
ABC: *74* 5-8
CAPITOL: *64* 5-10
DECCA (4000 series): *67* 8-12
(Decca LP numbers in this series preceded by a "7"
or a "DL-7" are stereo issues.)
DECCA (5000 series): *51-54* 15-25
(10-Inch LPs.)
DECCA (8000 series): *55-58* 10-20
DOT: *61-67* 5-10
HAMILTON: *64-65* 4-6
MCA: *73* 8-12
PARAMOUNT: *73* 6-10
Members: Patty Andrews; Maxene Andrews;
Laverne Andrews.
Also see ANDREWS, Patty
Also see CROSBY, Bing

ANGEL
Singles: 7-Inch
CASABLANCA: *75-80* 1-3
LPs: 10/12-Inch 33rpm
CASABLANCA: *75-80* 5-10
Members: Barry Brandt; Frank Dimino; Greg Giuf-
fria; Mickey Jones; Punky Meadows; Felix Robin-
son.
Also see GIUFFRIA, Greg
Also see WILSON, Carl

ANGEL, Johnny T.:
see JOHNNY T. ANGEL

ANGEL CITY
Singles: 7-Inch
EPIC: *80-82* 1-3
LPs: 10/12-Inch 33rpm
EPIC: *80-82* 5-8
MCA: *85* 5-8
Members: Doc Neeson; Rick Brewster; John
Brewster.

ANGELS
Singles: 7-Inch
ASCOT: *63* $3-5
CAPRICE: *61-62* 4-6
COLLECTABLES: *82* 1-3
ERIC: *74* 1-3
POLYDOR: *74* 2-4
RCA VICTOR: *67-68* 4-6
SMASH: *63-64* 3-5
Picture Sleeves
SMASH: *63* 8-15
LPs: 10/12-Inch 33rpm
ASCOT: *64* 15-20
CAPRICE: *62* 40-45
SMASH: *63-64* 20-25
Members: Linda Jansen; Barbara Allbut; Phyllis
"Jiggs" Allbut; Peggy Santaglia.

ANIMALS
(Eric Burdon & The Animals; Original Animals)
Singles: 7-Inch
ABKCO: *75* 2-3
COLLECTABLES: *82* 1-3
I.R.S.: *83* 1-3
JET: *77* 2-3
MGM: *64-71* 4-6
MGM CELEBRITY SCENE ("The
Animals"): *66* 40-50
(Boxed set of five singles, bio insert & title strips.
Jukebox issue only.)
Picture Sleeves
MGM (Except 13264): *64-67* 5-10
MGM (13264; "House Of The Rising
Sun"): *64* 10-20
LPs: 10/12-Inch 33rpm
ABKCO: *73-76* 8-12
ACCORD: *82* 5-8
I.R.S.: *83-85* 5-8
MGM (Except 4264): *65-69* 12-20
MGM (4264; "The Animals"): *64* 15-20
PICKWICK: *71* 5-8
SCEPTER/CITATION: *76* 5-8
SPRINGBOARD: *72* 5-8
UNITED ARTISTS: *77* 5-8
WAND: *70* 8-12
Members: Eric Burdon; Alan Price; Hilton Valen-
tine; Chas Chandler; John Steel; John Weider.
Also see BURDON, Eric
Also see PRICE, Alan
Also see WEIDER, John

ANIMOTION
Singles: 12-Inch 33/45rpm
MERCURY: *85* 4-6
Singles: 7-Inch
CASABLANCA: *86* 1-3

MERCURY: *84-85* $1-3
Picture Sleeves
CASABLANCA: *86* 1-3
MERCURY: *84-85* 1-3
LPs: 10/12-Inch 33rpm
CASABLANCA: *86* 5-8
MERCURY: *84-85* 5-8

ANITA & THE SO-AND-SOs
(Anita Kerr Singers)
Singles: 7-Inch
RCA VICTOR: *62* 4-6
Also see KERR, Anita

ANKA, Paul
Singles: 78rpm
ABC-PARAMOUNT: *57* 5-15
RPM: *56* 10-20
Singles: 12-Inch 33/45rpm
COLUMBIA: *83* 4-6
Singles: 7-Inch
ABC-PARAMOUNT (Monaural): *57-62* .. 5-10
ABC-PARAMOUNT (Stereo): *58-60* ... 15-25
(With an "S" prefix. Add $5-$10 if
with picture insert.)
BARNABY: *71* 1-3
BUDDAH: *72-78* 2-3
COLUMBIA: *83-85* 1-3
ERIC: *74* 1-3
FAME: *73* 2-4
RCA VICTOR (Except 2000, 8000, &
10000 series): *67-79* 2-4
RCA VICTOR (2000 series): *62* 8-15
(With a "VLP" or "VP" prefix. Compact 33 stereo
single.)
RCA VICTOR (8000 series): *62-66* 3-6
RCA VICTOR (10000 series): *78-81* 1-3
RPM (472; "I Confess"): *56* 25-30
RPM (499; "I Confess"): *56* 20-30
UNITED ARTISTS: *75-77* 2-3
Promotional Singles
ABC-PARAMOUNT (104; "Share Your
Love"): 15-20
(Special fan club issue.)
Picture Sleeves
ABC-PARAMOUNT: *56-61* 10-15
COLUMBIA: *83* 1-3
ERIC: *74* 2-3
RCA VICTOR (Except 11000
series): *62-65* 5-10
RCA VICTOR (11000 series): *78* 2-3
UNITED ARTISTS: *75* 3-5
EPs: 7-Inch 33/45rpm
ABC: 12-15
(Jukebox issue only.)
ABC-PARAMOUNT: *59* 25-35

SIRE: *74* $10-12
(Jukebox issue only.)
LPs: 10/12-Inch 33rpm
ABC-PARAMOUNT (200 series): *58-59* .25-35
(With an "ABC" prefix. Monaural.)
ABC-PARAMOUNT (200 series): *58-59* .40-50
(With an "ABCS" prefix. Stereo.)
ABC-PARAMOUNT (300 & 400 series,
except ABCS-323): *60-61* 20-30
ABC-PARAMOUNT (ABCS-323; "Paul
Anka Sings His Big 15"): *60* 35-45
(Stereo.)
ACCORD: *81* 5-8
BUDDAH: *71-76* 6-10
CAMDEN: *74* 6-10
COLUMBIA: *83-85* 5-8
LIBERTY: *81-83* 5-8
PICKWICK: *75* 5-8
RCA VICTOR (Except "LPM" & "LSP"
series): *75-80* 5-8
RCA VICTOR ("LPM" or "LSP"
series): *62-70* 10-15
RANWOOD: *81* 5-8
RIVERA (0047; "Paul Anka &
Others"): *63* 25-40
(Contains two tracks by Paul Anka, remaining
songs by other artists.)
RHINO: *86* 5-8
SIRE: *74-78* 10-12
UNITED ARTISTS: *74-78* 5-8
Also see MARLO, Micki

ANKA, Paul, & Odia Coates
Singles: 12-Inch 33/45rpm
EPIC: *77* 4-6
Singles: 7-Inch
EPIC: *76* 2-3
UNITED ARTISTS: *74-75* 2-3
Also see COATES, Odia

ANKA, Paul / Sam Cooke / Neil
Sedaka
LPs: 10/12-Inch 33rpm
RCA VICTOR: *64* 15-20
Also see COOKE, Sam
Also see SEDAKA, Neil

ANKA, Paul, George Hamilton IV
& Johnny Nash
Singles: 7-Inch
ABC-PARAMOUNT: *58* 5-10
Also see ANKA, Paul
Also see HAMILTON, George
Also see NASH, Johnny

ANNETTE
(Annette Funicello; Annette & The Afterbeats;
Annette & The Upbeats)
Singles: 78rpm
DISNEYLAND (102; "How Will
I Know"): *58* $15-25
Singles: 7-Inch
BUENA VISTA (336, "Jo-Jo The Dog Faced
Boy"/"Lonely Guitar"). *59* 10-15
BUENA VISTA (336, "Jo-Jo The Dog Faced
Boy"/"Love Me Forever"): *59* 8-15
(Note different flip side.)
BUENA VISTA (339 through
354): *59-60* 8-15
BUENA VISTA (359 through
407): *60-62* 15-25
BUENA VISTA (414; "Teenage
Wedding"): *63* 20-30
BUENA VISTA (427 through
436): *63-64* 15-25
BUENA VISTA (337; "The Wah
Watusi"): *64* 10-15
BUENA VISTA (438; "Something
Borrowed"): *65* 15-25
BUENA VISTA (440; "The Monkey's
Uncle"): *65* 10-20
(With The Beach Boys.)
BUENA VISTA (442 through
475): *65-66* 10-15
BUENA VISTA (802; "The Parent
Trap"): *61* 25-25
BUENA VISTA (803; "The Parent
Trap"): *61* 25-40
(Compact 33 Single.)
DISNEYLAND: *57-58* 8-10
EPIC: *65* 4-6
STARVIEW: *83* 5-10

TOWER (326; "What's A Girl
To Do"): *67* $20-25
(Name misspelled, shown as by Annettte.)
Picture Sleeves
BUENA VISTA (339 through
354): *59-60* 10-20
BUENA VISTA (359 through
407): *60-62* 20-30
BUENA VISTA (414; "Teenage
Wedding"): *63* 25-40
BUENA VISTA (427 through
436): *63-64* 15-30
BUENA VISTA (337; "The Wah
Watusi"): *64* 10-15
BUENA VISTA (438; "Something
Borrowed"): *65* 20-30
BUENA VISTA (440; "The Monkey's
Uncle"): *65* 15-25
BUENA VISTA (442 through
475): *65-66* 10-15
BUENA VISTA (802; "The Parent
Trap"): *61* 20-30
DISNEYLAND: *58* 25-35
EPs: 7-Inch 33/45rpm
BUENA VISTA (3301;
"Annette"): *59* 40-60
DISNEYLAND (04; "Tall
Paul"): *58* 30-40
DISNEYLAND (69; "Mickey Mouse Club
Featuring Annette"): *58* 35-45
LPs: 10/12-Inch 33rpm
BUENA VISTA (3301;
"Annette"): *59* 35-50
BUENA VISTA (3302; "Annette Sings
Anka"): *60* 35-50
(With bonus color photo.)
BUENA VISTA (3302; "Annette Sings
Anka"): *60* 30-35
(Without bonus photo.)
BUENA VISTA (3303 through
3508): *60-64* 25-40
BUENA VISTA (4037; "Annette
Funicello"): *72* 15-25
DISNEYLAND (Except 3906): *62-75* ... 15-30
(Includes various Mouseketeer cast albums that in-
clude or feature Annette.)
DISNEYLAND (3906; "*Snow White* As Told
By Annette") 20-40
MICKEY MOUSE (12 through
24): *57-58* 35-50
(Includes various Mouseketeer cast albums that in-
clude or feature Annette.)
RHINO (Except 702): *84* 8-10
RHINO (702; "Best Of Annette"): *84* ... 12-15
(Picture disc.)

SILHOUETTE: *81* $10-15
STARVIEW (4001; "Country
Album"): *84* 8-12
(Standard issue.)
STARVIEW (4001; "Country
Album"): *84* 15-20
(Limited edition series.)
Also see ALLAN, Davie
Also see AVALON, Frankie, & Annette
Also see BEACH BOYS

ANNETTE / Jimmy Dodd
Singles: 78rpm
DISNEYLAND (758; "How Will I
Know"/"Annette"): *58* 15-25
(10-inch single.)
DISNEYLAND (758; "How Will I
Know"/"Annette"): *58* 20-30
(5-inch single.)
Picture Sleeves
DISNEYLAND (758; "How Will I
Know"/"Annette"): *58* 20-40

ANNETTE & HAYLEY MILLS
LPs: 10/12-Inch 33rpm
BUENA VISTA (3508; "Annette &
Hayley Mills"): *62* 50-100
(Issued with paper cover. Special products release.)
Also see MILLS, Hayley

ANNETTE & TOMMY SANDS
Singles: 7-Inch
BUENA VISTA: *61* 10-15
(45 single.)
BUENA VISTA: *61* 10-20
(Compact 33 Single.)
Picture Sleeves
BUENA VISTA: *61* 10-20
Also see ANNETTE
Also see SANDS, Tommy

ANNIE G.
Singles: 12-Inch 33/45rpm
MCA: *84* 4-6
Singles: 7-Inch
MCA: *84* 1-3

ANN-MARGRET
Singles: 12-Inch 33/45rpm
AVCO: *70* 8-10
FIRST AMERICAN: *81* 5-10
MCA: *80* 5-10
OCEAN/ARIOLA AMERICA: *79-80* 4-8
RAM: *81* 4-8
Singles: 7-Inch
FIRST AMERICAN: *81* 2-3
MCA: *79-80* 2-3
OCEAN/ARIOLA AMERICA: *79-80* 2-3

RCA VICTOR: *61-62* $10-20
(With a "37" prefix. Compact 33 Singles.)
RCA VICTOR: *61-66* 5-10
(With a "47" prefix.)
WARNER BROS: *59* 10-20
(With The Ja-Da Quartet.)
Picture Sleeves
RCA VICTOR: *61-64* 10-20
EPs: 7-Inch 33/45rpm
RCA VICTOR: *62-64* 15-30
LPs: 10/12-Inch 33rpm
LHI: *68-69* 12-15
LAGNIAPPE 1959 ("Be My
Guest"): *59* 100-200
(Cast LP produced by the Boys Tri-Ship Club of
New Trier High School. Includes *Tropical Heat
Wave* by Ann-Margret Olson.)
MCA: *80* 5-8
NORTHWESTERN UNIVERSITY/RCA
VICTOR (5760; "Among Friends"): *60* .50-100
(Cast LP for the *Waa-Mu Show of 1960* from
Northwestern University. Lists Ann-Margret Olson
as a dancer.)
RCA VICTOR (2399 through
2659): *61-66* 15-30
WARNER BROS: (1285; "It's The
Most Happy Sound"): *59* 50-100
(With The Ja-Da Quartet.)

ANN-MARGRET & JOHN GARY
LPs: 10/12-Inch 33rpm
RCA VICTOR: *64* 10-20
Also see GARY, John

ANN-MARGRET & LEE HAZLEWOOD
Singles: 7-Inch
LHI: *68-69* 3-5

LPs: 10/12-Inch 33rpm
LHI: *69* $12-15
Also see HAZLEWOOD, Lee

ANN-MARGRET & AL HIRT
Singles: 7-Inch
RCA VICTOR: *68* 3-6
LPs: 10/12-Inch 33rpm
RCA VICTOR: *64* 10-20
Also see HIRT, Al

**ANN-MARGRET / Kitty Kallen /
Della Reese**
LPs: 10/12-Inch 33rpm
RCA VICTOR: *63* 15-20
Also see ANN-MARGRET
Also see KALLEN, Kitty
Also see REESE, Della

ANQUETTE
LPs: 10/12-Inch 33rpm
LUKE SKYWALKER: *88* 5-8

ANT, Adam
Singles: 12-Inch 33/45rpm
EPIC: *82-85* 4-6
Singles: 7-Inch
EPIC: *82-85* 1-3
LPs: 10/12-Inch 33rpm
EPIC: *82-85* 5-8
Also see ADAM & THE ANTS

ANTELL, Peter
Singles: 7-Inch
BOUNTY: *65* 5-10
CAMEO: *62-63* 3-6
Also see WILD ONES

ANTHONY, Alan
Singles: 7-Inch
CHALET: *82* 1-3

ANTHONY, Mark
Singles: 7-Inch
TABU: *88* 1-3

ANTHONY, Markus
Singles: 7-Inch
ROCK 'N' ROLL: *86* 1-3

ANTHONY, Ray, & His Orchestra
Singles: 78rpm
CAPITOL: *49-62* 2-4
Singles: 7-Inch
CAPITOL: *50-62* 2-4
EPs: 7-Inch 33/45rpm
CAPITOL: *52-59* 4-8
LPs: 10/12-Inch 33rpm
CAPITOL: *52-62* 5-15
Also see BEACH BOYS

Also see SINATRA, Frank

ANTHONY & THE CAMP
Singles: 12-Inch 33/45rpm
WARNER BROS: *86* $4-6
Singles: 7-Inch
WARNER BROS: *86* 1-3
Picture Sleeves
WARNER BROS: *86* 1-3
LPs: 10/12-Inch 33rpm
WARNER BROS: *86* 5-8

ANTHONY & THE CAMP
Singles: 7-Inch
WARNER BROS: *86* 1-3

ANTHONY & THE IMPERIALS:
see LITTLE ANTHONY & THE IMPERIALS

ANTHRAX
LPs: 10/12-Inch 33rpm
ISLAND: *85-88* 5-8
MEGAFORCE: *87* 5-8

ANTON, Susan
Singles: 7-Inch
COLUMBIA: *78* 1-3
Picture Sleeves
COLUMBIA: *78* 2-3
Also see KNOBLOCK, Fred, & Susan Anton

AORTA
Singles: 7-Inch
ATLANTIC: *68* 5-10
COLUMBIA: *69* 4-6
LPs: 10/12-Inch 33rpm
COLUMBIA (9000 series): *69* 15-20
(With a "CS" prefix.)
COLUMBIA (38000 series): 5-8
HAPPY TIGER: *70* 12-20

APOLLO 100
Singles: 7-Inch
MEGA: *71-72* 1-3
LPs: 10/12-Inch 33rpm
MEGA: *72* 5-10

APOLLONIA 6
Singles: 12-Inch 33/45rpm
WARNER BROS: *84-85* 4-6
Singles: 7-Inch
WARNER BROS: *84-85* 1-3
Picture Sleeves
WARNER BROS: *84-85* 1-3
LPs: 10/12-Inch 33rpm
WARNER BROS: *84-85* 5-8
Also see VANITY 6

APOLLOS
LPs: 10/12-Inch 33rpm
CICADELIC: *86* $5-8

APPALACHIANS
Singles: 7-Inch
ABC-PARAMOUNT: *62-63* 3-5
GOLDIE: 6-10

APPALOOSA
(Robin Batteaux)
LPs: 10/12-Inch 33rpm
COLUMBIA: *69* 10-15
WHITE GOLD: *82* 5-8

APPLEJACKS
Singles: 78rpm
CAMEO: *57* 4-6
DECCA: *54* 5-8
PRESIDENT: *56* 4-6
TONE-CRAFT: *55* 4-6
Singles: 7-Inch
CAMEO (100 series): *57-60* 4-6
CAMEO (200 & 300 series): *61-64* 3-5
DECCA: *54* 5-8
PRESIDENT: *56* 4-6
TONE-CRAFT: *55* 4-8
Member: Dave Appell.

APRIL & NINO:
see TEMPO, Nino, & April Stevens

APRIL WINE
Singles: 7-Inch
BIG TREE: *72-75* 2-4
CAPITOL: *78-84* 1-3
LONDON: *76-78* 2-3
Picture Sleeves
CAPITOL (Except 4975): *81* 1-3
CAPITOL (4975; "Just Between You
& Me"): *81* 2-4
(Sleeve opens to a 22x15 poster.)
CAPITOL (4975; "Just Between You
& Me"): *81* 1-3
(Standard sleeve. Not a poster.)
LPs: 10/12-Inch 33rpm
AQUARIUS: 5-8
ATLANTIC: *81* 5-8
BIG TREE: *72-75* 10-15
CAPITOL: *78-84* 5-8
LONDON: *76-77* 10-12
Members: Steve Lang; Jerry Mercer; Myles Good-
wyn; Brian Greenway; Gary Moffet.

AQUARIAN DREAM
Singles: 7-Inch
BUDDAH: *76-77* 2-4
ELEKTRA: *78* 1-3

LPs: 10/12-Inch 33rpm
BUDDAH: *76* $8-10
ELEKTRA: *78-79* 5-8
Members: Claude Bartee; Pete Bartee; Jacques Bur-
vick; Mike Fowler; Valerie Horn; Gloria Jones; Pat
Shannon.
Also see CONNORS, Norman

AQUARIANS
Singles: 7-Inch
UNI: *69* 2-4
LPs: 10/12-Inch 33rpm
UNI: *69* 12-15

AQUATONES
Singles: 7-Inch
FARGO: *58-61* 4-6
LPs: 10/12-Inch 33rpm
FARGO (3001; "The Aquatones
Sing"): *64* 100-150
Member: Barbara Lee.

ARBORS
Singles: 7-Inch
COLUMBIA: *73* 2-5
(Black vinyl.)
COLUMBIA: *73* 5-8
(Colored vinyl. Promotional issue only.)
DATE: *66-70* 2-5
(Black vinyl.)
DATE: *66-70* 5-8
(Colored vinyl. Promotional issue only.)
MERCURY: *65* 3-5
LPs: 10/12-Inch 33rpm
DATE: *68* 12-15
VANGUARD: *62* 15-18

ARCADIA
Singles: 12-Inch 33/45rpm
CAPITOL: *85-86* 4-6
Singles: 7-Inch
CAPITOL: *85-86* 1-3
Picture Sleeves
CAPITOL: *85-86* 1-3
LPs: 10/12-Inch 33rpm
CAPITOL: *85-86* 5-8
Members: Roger Taylor; Simon LeBon.
Also see DURAN DURAN
Also see TAYLOR, Roger

ARCHIBALD
(Archibald With Dave Bartholomew's Band)
Singles: 78rpm
COLONY: *51* 20-30
IMPERIAL: *50-57* 15-30
Singles: 7-Inch
IMPERIAL (Except 5212): *52-57* 10-20

IMPERIAL (5212; "Early Morning
Blues"): 52 .... $45-55

ARCHIES
Singles: 7-Inch
CALENDAR: 68-69 3-6
ERIC: 81 1-3
KIRSHNER: 69-72 3-6
(Includes 5 1/2-inch flexi-discs.)
RCA VICTOR: 72 1-3
Picture Sleeves
CALENDAR: 68 5-10
KIRSHNER: 69-71 3-6
LPs: 10/12-Inch 33rpm
ACCORD: 81 5-8
BACK-TRAC: 85 5-8
CALENDAR: 68-70 10-15
51 WEST: 79 5-8
KIRSHNER: 69-71 8-10
RCA VICTOR (0221; "The
Archies"): 70 15-20
(Promotional issue only.)
Members: Ron Dante, Jeff Barry; Toni Wine, plus
assorted guests.
Also see BLOOM, Bobby
Also see GREENWICH, Ellie
Also see KIM, Andy
Also see STEVENS, Ray
Also see TEMPO, Nino

ARDEN, Toni
Singles: 78rpm
COLUMBIA: 49-54 2-5
DECCA: 57-57 2-4
RCA VICTOR: 55-56 2-4
Singles: 7-Inch
COLUMBIA: 50-54 2-5
DECCA: 57-59 2-4
MISHAWAKA: 2-4
RCA VICTOR: 55-56 2-4
EPs: 7-Inch 33/45rpm
DECCA: 58 4-6
COLUMBIA: 56 4-6
LPs: 10/12-Inch 33rpm
DECCA: 57-59 5-10

AREA CODE 615
Singles: 7-Inch
POLYDOR: 69-70 2-4
LPs: 10/12-Inch 33rpm
POLYDOR: 69-70 8-10

ARENA BRASS
LPs: 10/12-Inch 33rpm
EPIC: 62 4-6

ARGENT
Singles: 7-Inch
DATE: 70 .... $3-5
EPIC: 69-74 2-4
LPs: 10/12-Inch 33rpm
EPIC: 69-75 10-15
UNITED ARTISTS: 76 5-8
Members: Rod Argent, Russ Ballard; Robert Hen-
rit; Jim Rodford; John Verity.
Also see BALLARD, Russ
Also see ZOMBIES

ARKADE
Singles: 7-Inch
DUNHILL: 70-71 4-6

ARLEN, Harold, With "Friend"
LPs: 10/12-Inch 33rpm
COLUMBIA (2920; "Harold Sings
Arlen") 5-8
(With a "CSP" prefix.)
COLUMBIA (2920; "Harold Sings
Arlen"): 66 20-30
(With an "OS" prefix. Stereo issue.)
COLUMBIA (6520; "Harold Sings
Arlen"): 66 20-30
(With an "OL" prefix. Monaural issue.)
Members: Harold Arlen; Barbra Streisand.
Also see STREISAND, Barbra

ARMADA ORCHESTRA
LPs: 10/12-Inch 33rpm
SCEPTER: 75 4-6

ARMAGEDDON
Singles: 7-Inch
CAPITOL: 71-72 3-5
CREATIVE SOUND: 71 3-5
LPs: 10/12-Inch 33rpm
A&M: 75 8-10
AMOS: 70 15-18
Members: Keith Relf; Louis Cennamo; Martin
Pugh.
Also see RENAISSANCE
Also see YARDBIRDS

ARMATRADING, Joan
Singles: 12-Inch 33/45rpm
A&M: 83 4-6
Singles: 7-Inch
A&M: 74-88 1-3
Picture Sleeves
A&M: 83 1-3
LPs: 10/12-Inch 33rpm
A&M: 73-88 8-12

ARMEN, Kay
Singles: 78rpm
DECCA: 42-58 4-8

Singles: 7-Inch
DECCA: *55-59* $5-12
EPs: 7-Inch 33/45rpm
MGM: *54-55* 10-20
LPs: 10/12-Inch 33rpm
DECCA (5000 series): *54* 20-40
(10-Inch LP.)
DECCA (8000 series): *59* 10-20
MGM (200 series): *54* 20-40
MGM (3000 series): *55* 15-30

ARMORED SAINT
Singles: 12-Inch 33/45rpm
CHRYSALIS: *86* 4-6
Singles: 7-Inch
CHRYSALIS: *84-86* 1-3
LPs: 10/12-Inch 33rpm
CHRYSALIS: *84-87* 5-8

ARMS, Russell
Singles: 78rpm
EPIC: *54-56* 2-4
ERA: *56-57* 2-4
Singles: 7-Inch
EPIC: *54-56* 2-4
ERA: *56-57* 2-4
LPs: 10/12-Inch 33rpm
ERA: *57* 8-12

ARMSTEAD, Joshie "Jo"
Singles: 7-Inch
DE LEX: *62* 4-6
GIANT: *67-69* 2-4
TRUTH: *74* 2-3

ARMSTRONG, Chuck
Singles: 7-Inch
R&R: *76* 2-3

ARMSTRONG, Louis
(Louis Armstrong & The All Stars)
Singles: 78rpm
CAPITOL: *56* 3-6
COLUMBIA (2500 through 2700
series): *32* 15-25
COLUMBIA (40000 series): *56-66* 3-6
DECCA: *35-58* 5-15
OKEH: *26-31* 20-30
RCA VICTOR: *56* 3-6
VICTOR: *33* 10-20
VOCALION: *36* 10-15
Singles: 7-Inch
A&M: *88* 1-3
ABC: *67-73* 1-3
AMSTERDAM: *71* 1-3
AUDIO FIDELITY: *71* 1-3
AVCO EMBASSY: *71* 1-3
BRUNSWICK: *67-68* 3-6

BUENA VISTA: *68* $2-4
CAPITOL: *56* 3-6
COLUMBIA: *56-66* 3-6
CONTINENTAL: *71* 2-4
DECCA (25000 series): *61-64* 2-4
DECCA (27000 through 29000
series): *50-56* 4-8
DECCA (30000 through 31000
series): *56-59* 3-6
DOT: *59* 3-5
EPIC: *69* 2-4
KAPP: *64-69* 2-5
MGM: *59-60* 2-5
MERCURY: *64-66* 2-5
RCA VICTOR: *56* 3-6
UNITED ARTISTS: *68-69* 2-4
VERVE: *59-60* 2-5
Picture Sleeves
BUENA VISTA: *68* 3-5
CONTINENTAL: *71* 2-4
KAPP: *64* 4-6
MGM: *59* 6-12
MERCURY: *64* 5-8
EPs: 7-Inch 33/45rpm
COLUMBIA: *55-59* 5-15
DECCA: *55-57* 5-15
RCA VICTOR: *53-59* 10-20
LPs: 10/12-Inch 33rpm
ABC: *68-76* 5-10
AMSTERDAM: *70* 5-8
AUDIO FIDELITY: *60-64* 15-20
BIOGRAPH: *73* 5-8
BRUNSWICK: *68-71* 8-15
BUENA VISTA: *68* 8-12
CHIAROSCURO: *77* 5-8
COLUMBIA (500 through 900
series): *54-57* 20-35
COLUMBIA (2600 series): *67* 8-12
COLUMBIA (9400 series): *67* 8-12
COLUMBIA (30000 series): *71-80* 8-12
CORAL: *73* 5-8
DECCA (100 series): *65-66* 15-20
DECCA (4000 series): *61-63* 10-15
DECCA (5000 series): *51-54* 25-45
(10-Inch LPs.)
DECCA (8000 series): *55-59* 15-25
DECCA (9000 series): *67* 8-12
(Decca LP numbers in this series preceded by a "7"
or a "DL-7" are stereo issues.)
EVEREST: *71-76* 5-8
GNP/CRESCENDO: *77* 8-12
GUEST STAR: *64* 5-10
HARMONY: *69* 5-10
JAZZ HERITAGE: *80* 5-8

MCA: *73-82* $6-10
MERCURY: *66* 10-12
METRO: *65* 10-12
MILESTONE: *74-75* 5-8
OLYMPIC: *74* 5-8
PAUSA: *83* 5-8
RCA VICTOR (1300 & 1400
  series): *53-56* 20-40
RCA VICTOR (2300 through 2900
  series): *61-64* 10-15
  (With an "LPM" or "LSP" prefix.)
RCA VICTOR (2600 series): *77* 5-8
  (With a "CPL1" prefix.)
RCA VICTOR (5500 series): *77* 8-12
RCA VICTOR (6000 series): *71* 8-12
SAGA: *72* 5-8
STORYVILLE: *80* 5-8
TRIP: *72* 5-8
UNITED ARTISTS: *68-69* 2-3
VANGUARD: *76* 8-12
VERVE: *60-64* 15-20
VOCALION: *68-69* 5-10
  Also see BARRY, John
  Also see BRUBECK, Dave
  Also see CROSBY, Bing, & Louis Armstrong
  Also see CROSBY, Bing, Louis Armstrong,
Rosemary Clooney & The Hi-Los
  Also see FITZGERALD, Ella, & Louis
Armstrong
  Also see KAYE, Danny, & Louis Armstrong
  Also see JENKINS, Gordon
  Also see MILLS BROTHERS, & Louis
Armstrong

ARMSTRONG, Louis, & Duke Ellington
Singles: 7-Inch
ROULETTE: *63* 2-4
LPs: 10/12-Inch 33rpm
ROULETTE (100 series): *71* 8-12
ROULETTE (52000 series): *63* 15-20
  Also see ELLINGTON, Duke

ARMSTRONG, Louis, & Guy Lombardo
Singles: 7-Inch
CAPITOL: *66* 2-3
  Also see LOMBARDO, Guy

ARMSTRONG, Louis, & Oscar Peterson
Singles: 7-Inch
VERVE: *59* 2-4
LPs: 10/12-Inch 33rpm
VERVE: *59* 15-20
  Also see ARMSTRONG, Louis

  Also see PETERSON, Oscar

ARNELL, Ginny
Singles: 7-Inch
DECCA: *60* $4-8
MGM: *63-65* 4-8
WARWICK: *61* 5-10
LPs: 10/12-Inch 33rpm
MGM: *64* 15-25
  Also see JAMIE & JANE

ARNIE'S LOVE
Singles: 12-Inch 33/45rpm
PROFILE: *85-86* 4-6

ARNO, Audrey
Singles: 7-Inch
DECCA: *61* 3-5

ARNOLD, Calvin
Singles: 7-Inch
IX CHAINS: *75* 2-4
VENTURE: *67-69* 3-5

ARNOLD, Eddy
Singles: 78rpm
BLUEBIRD: *45* 25-50
RCA VICTOR (Except 1800 through 3100
  series): *46-49* 10-20
RCA VICTOR (1800 through 3100
  series): *46-49* 15-30
Singles: 7-Inch
DIAMOND P (1009; "If The Whole World
  Stopped Lovin"): *73* 2-5
  (Promotional issue only.)
MGM: *73-76* 1-3
RCA VICTOR (0100 through 0400
  series): *50-51* 4-6
  (Black or turquoise labels.)
RCA VICTOR (0500 through 0700
  series): *71-72* 1-3
  (Orange labels.)
RCA VICTOR (2000 series): *62* 4-8
  (Compact 33 stereo single.)
RCA VICTOR (4000 through 6000
  series): *51-57* 3-5
RCA VICTOR (7000 through 9000
  series): *57-71* 2-4
RCA VICTOR (10000 through 13000
  series): *76-83* 1-3
Picture Sleeves
RCA VICTOR: *56-66* 5-10
EPs: 7-Inch 33/45rpm
RCA VICTOR (100 series): *61* 10-12
  (With an "LPC" prefix. Compact 33 Double.)
RCA VICTOR (280; "Best
  Wishes"): 10-20
  (Promotional issue only.)

RCA VICTOR (200 through 900
   series): *52-56* $10-15
   (With an "EPA" prefix.)
RCA VICTOR (1100 & 1200
   series): *55-56* 15-20
   (With an "EPB" prefix.)
RCA VICTOR (1400 & 1500
   series): *57* 8-12
   (With an "EPA" prefix.)
RCA VICTOR (3000 series): *52-54* 20-25
   (With an "EPB" prefix.)
RCA VICTOR (4000 & 5000
   series): *57-59* 6-12
   (With an "EPA" prefix.)
         LPs: 10/12-Inch 33rpm
CAMDEN: *72-74* 5-10
   (With an "ACL1" prefix.)
CAMDEN (CAL & CAS series): *60-72* ... 8-15
   (With a "CAL," "CAS," or "CXS" prefix.)
GREEN VALLEY: *76* 8-10
K-TEL: *74* 8-10
MGM: *74-76* 8-12
RCA VICTOR (AHL1, ANL1, APL1,
   & AYL1 series): *73-81* 5-10
RCA VICTOR (CPL1 series): *83* 8-12
RCA VICTOR (209; "Eddy
   Arnold"): *66* 15-20
   (Promotional issue only.)
RCA VICTOR (1100 through 2200
   series): *55-60* 20-30
   (Monaural. With an "LPM" prefix.)
RCA VICTOR (2300 through 2900
   series): *60-64* 12-20
   (Monaural. With an "LPM" prefix.)
RCA VICTOR (3000 series): *52-54* 45-55
   (10-Inch LPs. With an "LPM" prefix.)
RCA VICTOR (3000 series): *64-68* 8-12
   (12-Inch LPs. With an "LPM" prefix.)
RCA VICTOR (1900 through 3400
   series): *60-65* 15-25
   (Stereo issues. With an "LSP" prefix. "LSP" num-
   bers below 1900 were reprocessed stereo issues of
   '50s LPs. They were issued in the '60s and are in
   the $10-$15 range.)
RCA VICTOR (3500 through 4800
   series): *66-73* 10-20
RCA VICTOR (6000 series): *70* 8-12
SUNRISE: *79* 5-8
TIME-LIFE: *81* 5-8
   Also see PRESLEY, Elvis / Hank Snow /
   Eddy Arnold / Jim Reeves

ARRINGTON, Steve
   (Steve Arrington's Hall Of Fame)
       Singles: 12-Inch 33/45rpm
ATLANTIC: *83-86* 4-6

Eddy Arnold
       Singles: 7-Inch
ATLANTIC: *83-86* $1-3
KONGLATHER: *82* 1-3
MANHATTAN: *87* 1-3
       LPs: 10/12-Inch 33rpm
ATLANTIC: *83-86* 5-8
   Also see SLAVE

ART ATTACK
       Singles: 12-Inch 33/45rpm
B.M.O.: *83* 4-6
       Singles: 7-Inch
B.M.O.: *83* 1-3
       LPs: 10/12-Inch 33rpm
B.M.O.: *83* 5-8

ART IN AMERICA
       Singles: 7-Inch
PAVILLION: *83* 1-3
       LPs: 10/12-Inch 33rpm
PAVILLION: *83* 5-8

ART OF NOISE
       Singles: 12-Inch 33/45rpm
CHINA: *86* 4-6
ISLAND: *83-84* 4-6
       Singles: 7-Inch
CHINA: *86* 1-3
ISLAND: *83-84* 1-3
       Picture Sleeves
CHINA: *86* 1-3
       LPs: 10/12-Inch 33rpm
CHINA: *86* 5-8
CHRYSALIS: *87* 5-8
ISLAND: *84-85* 5-8
   Also see HORN, Trevor, Paul Morley & The
   Art Of Noise

ART OF NOISE, & Duane Eddy
       Singles: 7-Inch
CHINA: *86* 1-3

Picture Sleeves
CHINA: *86* **$1-3**
Also see EDDY, Duane

ART OF NOISE, & Tom Jones
Singles: 7-Inch
CHINA: *88* 1-3
Also see ART OF NOISE
Also see JONES, Tom

ARTISTICS
Singles: 7-Inch
S&G: **10-12**

ARTISTICS
Singles: 7-Inch
BRUNSWICK: *66-73* **2-5**
OKEH: *63-66* **3-6**
LPs: 10/12-Inch 33rpm
BRUNSWICK: *67-73* **10-15**
OKEH: *67* **12-20**
Members: Jesse Bolian; Bernard Reed; Larry
Johnson; Tommy Green; Aaron Floyd; Marvin
Smith; Morris Williams.
Also see DUKAYS

ARTISTS UNITED AGAINST APARTHEID
Singles: 12-Inch 33/45rpm
MANHATTAN: *85* **4-6**
Singles: 7-Inch
MANHATTAN: *85* **1-3**
LPs: 10/12-Inch 33rpm
MANHATTAN: *85* **5-8**

ARVON, Bobby
Singles: 7-Inch
ARIOLA AMERICAN: *76* **2-3**
FIRST ARTISTS: *77-78* **1-3**
LPs: 10/12-Inch 33rpm
FIRST ARTISTS: *78* **5-8**

ASHE, Clarence
Singles: 7-Inch
ABC-PARAMOUNT: *65* **3-5**
CHESS: *64* **3-5**
J&S: *64* **3-5**

ASHE, Clarence, & Hartsy Maye
Singles: 7-Inch
J&S: *65* **3-5**
Also see ASHE, Clarence

ASHFORD, Nick
Singles: 7-Inch
ABC: *70* **2-4**
VERVE: *66-68* **3-5**
Also see ASHFORD & SIMPSON

ASHFORD & SIMPSON
Singles: 12-Inch 33/45rpm
CAPITOL: *82-86* **$4-6**
WARNER BROS: *79* **4-6**
Singles: 7-Inch
CAPITOL: *82-86* **1-3**
EMI AMERICA: *84-85* **1-3**
WARNER BROS: *73-81* **1-3**
Picture Sleeves
CAPITOL: *80-82* **1-3**
LPs: 10/12-Inch 33rpm
CAPITOL: *82-86* **5-8**
WARNER BROS (Except HS
series): *73-81* **5-10**
WARNER BROS (HS series): *79-80* **12-18**
(Half-speed mastered.)
Members: Nick Ashford; Valerie Simpson.
Also see ASHFORD, Nick
Also see JONES, Quincy
Also see SIMPSON, Valerie
Also see VALERIE & NICK

ASHLEY, Del
(David Gates)
Singles: 7-Inch
PLANETARY: *65* **8-15**
Also see GATES, David

ASHLEY, Tyrone
(Tyrone Ashley & The Funky Music Machine)
Singles: 7-Inch
PHIL-L.A. OF SOUL: *70-71* **2-4**
UNITED ARTISTS: *78* **1-3**
LPs: 10/12-Inch 33rpm
UNITED ARTISTS: *78* **5-8**

ASHTON, GARDNER & DYKE
Singles: 7-Inch
CAPITOL: *70-72* **2-4**

LPs: 10/12-Inch 33rpm
CAPITOL: *70-72* $8-10
Members: Tony Ashton; Kim Gardner; Roy Dyke.
Also see BADGER

ASIA
Singles: 12-Inch 33/45rpm
GEFFEN: *85* 4-6
Singles: 7-Inch
GEFFEN: *82-86* 1-3
Picture Sleeves
GEFFEN: *81* 1-3
LPs: 10/12-Inch 33rpm
GEFFEN: *82-86* 5-8
Members: Steve Howe; Carl Palmer; John Wetton;
Geoff Downes; Mandy Mayer.
Also see EMERSON, LAKE & PALMER
Also see HOWE, Steve, Band

ASLEEP AT THE WHEEL
Singles: 7-Inch
CAPITOL: *75-79* 2-4
EPIC: *74-88* 1-3
LPs: 10/12-Inch 33rpm
CAPITOL: *75-79* 5-8
EPIC (33000 series): *75* 12-15
(With a "BG" prefix.)
EPIC (33000 series): 10-12
(With an "EG" prefix.)
EPIC (33000 series): *74* 8-10
(With a "KE" prefix.)
EPIC (33000 series): 5-8
(With a "PE" prefix.)
EPIC (44000 series): *88* 5-8
MCA: *80-84* 5-8
UNITED ARTISTS: *73* 8-12
Member: Ray Benson.

ASPHALT JUNGLE
Singles: 7-Inch
TEC: *80* 1-3

ASSEMBLED MULTITUDE
Singles: 7-Inch
ATLANTIC: *70-72* 2-4
ERIC: *81* 1-3
LPs: 10/12-Inch 33rpm
ATLANTIC: *70* 8-10

ASSOCIATION
Singles: 7-Inch
COLUMBIA: *72* 2-4
ELEKTRA: *81* 2-3
JUBILEE: *65* 4-6
MUMS: *73* 2-4
RCA VICTOR: *75* 2-4
VALIANT: *66* 4-6
WARNER BROS: *67-71* 2-4

Picture Sleeves
VALIANT: *66* $5-10
LPs: 10/12-Inch 33rpm
COLUMBIA: *72* .8-10
VALIANT: *66* 12-20
WARNER BROS: *67-70* 8-12
Members: Gary Alexander; Ted Bluechel, Jr; Brian
Cole; Russ Giguere; Terry Kirkman; Cliff Nivison;
Larry Ramos; Richard Thompson; Jim Yester.
Also see MAMAS & THE PAPAS / Associa-
tion / Fifth Dimension

ASTLEY, Jon
Singles: 7-Inch
ATLANTIC: *88* 1-3
LPs: 10/12-Inch 33rpm
ATLANTIC: *88* 5-8

ASTLEY, Rick
Singles: 7-Inch
RCA VICTOR: *88* 1-3
LPs: 10/12-Inch 33rpm
RCA VICTOR: *88* 5-8

ASTORS
Singles: 7-Inch
STAX: *65-67* 3-5

ASTRONAUTS
Singles: 7-Inch
PALLADIUM (610; "Come Along
Baby"): *61* .75-125
RCA VICTOR: *63-65* 4-8
Picture Sleeves
RCA VICTOR: *63* 20-30
EPs: 7-Inch 33/45rpm
RCA VICTOR: *63* 25-40
RCA VICTOR WURLITZER
DISCOTHEQUE: *64* 30-40
(Promotional issue only.)
LPs: 10/12-Inch 33rpm
RCA VICTOR: *64-67* 20-30
Members: Stormy Patterson; Robert Demmon; Den-
nis Lindsey; James Gallagher; Richard Fifield.

ASYLUM CHOIR
Singles: 7-Inch
SHELTER: *71* 3-5
SMASH: *69* 4-6
LPs: 10/12-Inch 33rpm
SHELTER (2000 series): *74* 8-10
SHELTER (8000 series): *71* 12-15
SHELTER (52000 series): *75* 5-8
SMASH (67107; "Look Inside"): *68* 25-30
(With toilet tissue cover.)
SMASH (67107; "Look Inside"): *68* 10-15
(With photo cover.)
Members: Leon Russell; Marc Benno.

Also see BENNO, Marc
Also see RUSSELL, Leon

ASWAD
Singles: 7-Inch
MANGO: *88* $1-3
LPs: 10/12-Inch 33rpm
MANGO: *88* 5-8

ATILLA
LPs: 10/12-Inch 33rpm
BACK TRAC: *85* ....,5-8
EPIC: *70* 40-45
Member: Billy Joel.
Also see JOEL, Billy

ATKINS
Singles: 7-Inch
WARNER BROS: *82* 1-3
LPs: 10/12-Inch 33rpm
WARNER BROS: *82* 5-8

ATKINS, Chet
Singles: 78rpm
BLUEBIRD: *50* 10-20
RCA VICTOR: *50-57* 4-8
Singles: 7-Inch
RCA VICTOR (0100 through 0400
series): *50-51* 5-10
(Black or turquoise labels.)
RCA VICTOR (0100 through 0700
series): *71-74* 2-3
(Orange labels.)
RCA VICTOR (4000 through 6000
series): *51-57* 4-8
RCA VICTOR (7000 through 9000
series): *57-71* 2-5
RCA VICTOR (10000 through 13000
series): *75-83* 1-3
Picture Sleeves
RCA VICTOR: *61-67* 3-6
EPs: 7-Inch 33/45rpm
RCA VICTOR (100 series): *61* 8-12
(With an "LPC" prefix. Compact 33 Double.)
RCA VICTOR (500 through 900
series): *55-56* 8-12
(With an "EPA" prefix.)
RCA VICTOR (1100 & 1200
series): *55-56* 8-12
(With an "EPB" prefix.)
RCA VICTOR (1300 through 1500
series): *56-57* 8-12
(With an "EPA" prefix.)
RCA VICTOR (3000 series): *52-54* 15-20
(With an "EPB" prefix.)
RCA VICTOR (4000 & 5000
series): *58-60* 5-10

SESAC (13; "Mr. Atkins If You
Please"): *59* $20-30
(Promotional issue only.)
LPs: 10/12-Inch 33rpm
CAMDEN: *61-72* 8-12
CANDLELITE: 10-15
COLUMBIA: *83-85* 5-8
DOLTON: *67* 15-20
PICKWICK/CAMDEN: *75* 8-10
RCA VICTOR (AHL1, ANL1, APL1,
& AYL1 series): *73-83* 5-10
RCA VICTOR (CPL1 series): *77* 8-12
RCA VICTOR (1000 series): *54* 25-35
(With an "LPM" prefix.)
RCA VICTOR (1100 through 2200
series, except 1236): *55-60* 15-25
(With an "LPM" prefix.)
RCA VICTOR (1236: "Stringin' Along
With Chet Atkins"): *55* 30-40
(With an "LPM" prefix.)
RCA VICTOR (2300 through 2900
series): *60-64* 10-15
(With an "LPM" prefix.)
RCA VICTOR (3000 series): *53* 45-55
(10-Inch LPs. With an "LPM" prefix.)
RCA VICTOR (3000 series): *64-68* 8-12
(12-Inch LPs. With an "LPM" prefix.)
RCA VICTOR (2000 & 3000
series): *66-69* 10-15
(With an "LSC" prefix.)
RCA VICTOR (1900 through 3500
series): *60-66* 10-20
(With an "LSP" prefix, stereo issues. LSP numbers
below 1900 were reprocessed stereo issues of fif-
ties LPs. They were issued in the sixties are in the
$10-$15 range.)
RCA VICTOR (3500 through 4800
series): *68-73* 8-15
RCA VICTOR (6000 series): *70-72* 8-12
TIME-LIFE: *81* 5-8
Also see ATKINS STRING COMPANY
Also see CHARLES, Ray, George Jones &
Chet Atkins
Also see COUNTRY HAMS
Also see KERR, Anita
Also see REED, Jerry, & Chet Atkins
Also see SNOW, Hank, & Chet Atkins

ATKINS, Chet, & Les Paul
Singles: 7-Inch
RCA VICTOR: *78* 1-3
LPs: 10/12-Inch 33rpm
RCA VICTOR: *78* 5-8
Also see PAUL, Les

ATKINS, Chet / Faron Young
EPs: 7-Inch 33/45rpm
SESAC (48; "No Greater Love"): *59* ... **$20-30**
(Promotional issue only.)
Also see ATKINS, Chet
Also see YOUNG, Faron

ATKINS, Christopher
Singles: 7-Inch
POLYDOR: *82* **1-3**

ATKINS STRING COMPANY
Singles: 7-Inch
RCA VICTOR: *75* **1-3**
Also see ATKINS, Chet

ATLANTA
Singles: 7-Inch
MCA: *84-85* **1-3**
MDJ: *83* **1-3**
SO. TRACKS: *87-88* **1-3**
Picture Sleeves
MDJ: *83* **1-3**
LPs: 10/12-Inch 33rpm
MCA: *84* **5-8**

ATLANTA DISCO BAND
Singles: 7-Inch
ARIOLA AMERICA: *76* **1-3**
LPs: 10/12-Inch 33rpm
ARIOLA AMERICA: *76* **5-8**

ATLANTA RHYTHM SECTION
Singles: 7-Inch
COLUMBIA: *81* **1-3**
DECCA: *72* **2-4**
MCA: *73* **1-3**
POLYDOR: *74-80* **1-3**
LPs: 10/12-Inch 33rpm
COLUMBIA: *81* **5-8**
DECCA: *72* **12-15**
MCA: *77* **5-10**
MFSL: *79* **25-50**
POLYDOR: *74-80* **5-8**
Members: Ronnie Hammond; Rodney Justo;
Robert Nix; Barry Bailey; J.R. Cobb; Dean
Daughtry; Paul Goddard.
Also see CANDYMEN
Also see CLASSICS IV
Also see MANILOW, Barry / Atlanta Rhythm
Section

ATLANTIC STARR
Singles: 12-Inch 33/45rpm
A&M: *79-85* **4-6**
Singles: 7-Inch
A&M: *78-86* **1-3**
MANHATTAN: *86* **1-3**
WARNER BROS: *87-88* **1-3**

Picture Sleeves
A&M: *78-86* **$1-3**
LPs: 10/12-Inch 33rpm
A&M: *78-84* **5-8**
WARNER BROS: *87-88* **5-8**
Member: Sharon Bryant.

ATOMIC ROOSTER
Singles: 7-Inch
ELEKTRA: *71-72* **2-4**
LPs: 10/12-Inch 33rpm
ELEKTRA: *71-73* **12-15**
PVC: *83* **5-8**
Members: Chris Farlowe; Pete French; Steve Bol-
ton; John Cann; Vincent Crane; Paul Hammond;
Carl Palmer; Johnny Mandala; Rick Parnell.
Also see BROWN, Arthur

ATTACK, Art: see ART ATTACK

ATTITUDE
Singles: 12-Inch 33/45rpm
ATLANTIC: *83* **4-6**
Singles: 7-Inch
ATLANTIC: *83* **1-3**
LPs: 10/12-Inch 33rpm
ATLANTIC: *83* **5-8**

ATTITUDES
Singles: 7-Inch
DARK HORSE: *75-76* **2-4**
Picture Sleeves
DARK HORSE: *75* **3-5**
LPs: 10/12-Inch 33rpm
DARK HORSE: *76-77* **5-8**
Members: Danny Kortchmar; David Foster; Jim
Keltner; Paul Stallworth.

AUDIENCE
Singles: 7-Inch
ELEKTRA: *71-72* **2-4**
LPs: 10/12-Inch 33rpm
AUDIENCE: *71-72* **10-15**
Members: Trevor Williams; Howard Werth; Pat
Neubergh; Nick Judd; Tony Connor; Keith Gem-
mell.

AUDIO TWO
LPs: 10/12-Inch 33rpm
FIRST PRIORITY: *88* **5-8**

AUDREY
Singles: 78rpm
PLUS (104; "Dear Elvis"): *56* **10-20**
Singles: 7-Inch
PLUS (104; "Dear Elvis"): *56* **20-25**
(Break-in novelty. Contains excerpts of Elvis'
recordings.)
Also see PRESLEY, Elvis

AUGER, Brian
(Brian Auger & The Trinity; Brian Auger's
Oblivion Express)
Singles: 7-Inch
ATCO: 68-69 .... $3-5
RCA VICTOR: 70-74 2-4
LPs: 10/12-Inch 33rpm
ATCO: 69 12-15
CAPITOL: 69 10-12
POLYDOR: 74 5-8
RCA VICTOR: 70-77 6-10
WARNER BROS: 77 5-8

AUGIE: see MEYERS, Augie

AUGUST, Jan
Singles: 7-Inch
MERCURY: 50-62 2-4
EPs: 7-Inch 33/45rpm
MERCURY: 50-56 3-6
LPs: 10/12-Inch 33rpm
MERCURY: 50-62 5-10
WING: 59 4-8
Also see HAYMAN, Richard, Orchestra

AURRA
Singles: 12-Inch 33/45rpm
SALSOUL: 82 4-6
Singles: 7-Inch
DREAM: 80 1-3
SALSOUL: 81-83 1-3
LPs: 10/12-Inch 33rpm
DREAM: 80 5-8
SALSOUL: 81-83 5-8
Members: Curt Jones; Starleana Young.

AUSTIN, Gene
Singles: 78rpm
COLUMBIA: 54-56 2-4
DECCA: 56 2-4
VICTOR: 25-35 4-8
Singles: 7-Inch
COLUMBIA: 54-56 3-5
DECCA: 56 3-5
EPs: 7-Inch 33/45rpm
RCA VICTOR: 53 5-10
LPs: 10/12-Inch 33rpm
DOT: 8-15
RCA VICTOR: 53-57 10-20
X: 54 10-20

AUSTIN, Patti
Singles: 12-Inch 33/45rpm
QWEST: 84-86 4-6
Singles: 7-Inch
ABC: 68 2-4
CTI: 76-80 1-3
COLUMBIA: 71-73 2-3

CORAL: 65-68 .... $3-5
QWEST: 81-88 1-3
UNITED ARTISTS: 69-70 2-4
LPs: 10/12-Inch 33rpm
CTI: 77-80 5-8
QWEST: 81-88 5-8
Also see JONES, Quincy
Also see WALDEN, Narada Michael, & Patti
Austin
Also see YUTAKA

AUSTIN, Patti, & Jerry Butler
Singles: 7-Inch
CTI: 83 1-3
Also see BUTLER, Jerry

AUSTIN, Patti, & James Ingram
Singles: 7-Inch
QWEST: 82-84 1-3
Also see AUSTIN, Patti
Also see INGRAM, James

AUSTIN, Sil
Singles: 78rpm
JUBILEE: 54-55 4-6
MERCURY: 56-65 3-5
Singles: 7-Inch
JUBILEE: 54-55 5-8
MERCURY: 56-65 3-8
SSS INT'L: 70 1-3
SEW CITY: 66 2-4
EPs: 7-Inch 33/45rpm
MERCURY: 56-57 10-15
LPs: 10/12-Inch 33rpm
MERCURY: 59-67 10-20
SSS INT'L: 70-82 8-10
WING: 63-68 10-12

AUSTIN, Sil, & Red Prysock
Singles: 7-Inch
MERCURY: 61 3-5
LPs: 10/12-Inch 33rpm
MERCURY: 61 15-20
SSS INT'L: 69 8-10
WING: 63-68 10-12
Also see AUSTIN, Sil

AUTOGRAPH
Singles: 7-Inch
RCA VICTOR: 84-85 1-3
Picture Sleeves
RCA VICTOR: 84-85 1-3
LPs: 10/12-Inch 33rpm
RCA VICTOR: 84-87 5-8
Member: Steve Plunkett.

AUTOMATIC MAN
Singles: 7-Inch
ISLAND: *76-77* $2-4
LPs: 10/12-Inch 33rpm
ISLAND: *76-77* 5-8
Members: Michael Schrieve; Todd Cochran; Doni
Harvey; Pat Thrall.

AUTRY, Gene
Singles: 78rpm
QRS (1044; "Living In
The Mountains"):*29* 3500-4500
Singles: 7-Inch
COLUMBIA (20700 through
21500 series): *50-56* 3-5
COLUMBIA (38700 through
40500 series): *50-55* 3-5
COLUMBIA (44000 series): *68* 1-3
MISTLETOE: *74* 1-3

REPUBLIC: *69-76* 1-3
EPs: 7-Inch 33/45rpm
COLUMBIA: *51-56* 40-50
LPs: 10/12-Inch 33rpm
BIRCHMONT: 8-12
CHALLENGE: *58* 25-30
COLUMBIA (55 through
154): *51-55* 80-100
(10-Inch LPs.)
COLUMBIA (600 series): *55* 80-100
COLUMBIA (1000 series): *70-82* 8-10
COLUMBIA (1500 series): *61* 20-25
COLUMBIA (2500 series): *55* 80-100
(10-Inch LPs.)
COLUMBIA (6000 series): *51* 40-60
(10-Inch LPs.)
COLUMBIA (8000 series): 80-100
COLUMBIA (9000 series): 40-60
(10-Inch LPs.)
COLUMBIA (15000 series): *81* 8-10
COLUMBIA (37000 series): *82* 5-8
DESIGN 8-10
ENCORE: *80* 6-10
GRT: *77* 10-15
GRAND PRIX: 8-10
HALLMARK: 8-12
HARMONY (7100 through
7300 series): *56-65* 20-30
HARMONY (9000 series): *59-64* 20-25
HARMONY (11000 series): *64-66* 10-15
HURRAH: 5-8
MELODY RANCH: *65* 20-25
MISTLETOE: *74* 8-12

MURRAY HILL (897296;"Melody
Ranch Radio Show") $45-55
(4-LP set.)
RCA VICTOR (2600 series): *62* 25-30
RADIOLA: *75* 5-8
REPUBLIC (1900 series): 5-15
(2-LP sets.)
REPUBLIC (6000 series): *76-78* 5-15
STARDAY: *78* 6-10

AVALANCHE '77
Singles: 7-Inch
ABC: *77* 1-3
BOBLO: *77* 2-3
LPs: 10/12-Inch 33rpm
ABC: *77* 5-8

AVALON, Frankie
Singles: 78rpm
CHANCELLOR: *57-58* 5-10
X: *54* 5-10
Singles: 7-Inch
ABC: *74* 2-3
AMOS: *69* 3-5
BOBCAT: *83* 1-3
CHANCELLOR (1; "Shy Guy"): 8-10
(Acnecare promotional special products issue.)
CHANCELLOR (1004; "Cupid"): *57* 8-12
CHANCELLOR (1011 through
1139): *57-63* 5-10
(Monaural.)
CHANCELLOR (Stereo): *59-60* 10-20
COLLECTABLES: *81* 1-3
DE LITE: *76-78* 2-4
ERIC: *73* 1-3
LIBERTY: *82* 5-8
MCA: *84* 1-3
METROMEDIA: *70* 3-5
REGALIA: *72* 2-4
REPRISE: *68-69* 3-6
UNITED ARTISTS: *64-65* 3-5
X: *54* 10-20
Picture Sleeves
CHANCELLOR (1026 through
1045): *58-59* 10-20
CHANCELLOR (1048 through
1125): *60-63* 8-15
DE LITE: *78* 3-5
UNITED ARTISTS: *64* 4-8
EPs: 7-Inch 33/45rpm
CHANCELLOR: *58-60* 20-30
X: *55* 20-30
Promotional EPs
CHANCELLOR (303; "Ballad Of The
Alamo"): *60* 40-50
(With complete publicity kit.)

CHANCELLOR (303; "Ballad Of The
Alamo"): *60* $20-30
(Without publicity kit.)
CHANCELLOR (5004; "Swingin' On
A Rainbow"): *59* 20-30
(White label. Includes paper sleeve with note from
Frankie, thanking dee jays for their support.)
LPs: 10/12-Inch 33rpm
ABC: *73* 5-8
CHANCELLOR: *58-63* 25-35
DE-LITE: *76-78* 5-8
EVEREST: *82* 5-8
51 WEST: 5-8
MCA: *85* 5-8
METROMEDIA: *70* 5-8
SUNSET: *69* 8-10
TRIP: *77* 5-8
UNITED ARTISTS: *64* 12-15
(With a "UAL" or "UAS" prefix.)
UNITED ARTISTS: *75* 5-8
(With a "UA-LA" prefix.)
Also see FABIAN / Frankie Avalon

AVALON, Frankie, & Annette
Singles: 12-Inch 33/45rpm
PACIFIC STAR (5698; "Merry
Christmas"): *81* 15-25
(Picture disc.)
Singles: 7-Inch
PACIFIC STAR (569; "Merry
Christmas"): *81* 3-6
(Black vinyl.)
PACIFIC STAR (569; "Merry
Christmas"): *81* 15-20
(Colored vinyl.)
Picture Sleeves
PACIFIC STAR (569; "Merry
Christmas"): *81* 4-8
Also see ANNETTE
Also see AVALON, Frankie

AVANT-GARDE
Singles: 7-Inch
COLUMBIA: *67-68* 3-5

AVERAGE, Johnny, Band:
see JOHNNY AVERAGE BAND

AVERAGE WHITE BAND
(AWB)
Singles: 7-Inch
ARISTA: *80* 1-3
ATLANTIC: *74-80* 2-4
MCA: *73-74* 2-4
TRACK: *88* 1-3
LPs: 10/12-Inch 33rpm
ATLANTIC (Except 19000 series): *74-76* .8-12
ATLANTIC (19000 series): *77-80* 5-8

MCA (Except 345): *73-75* $8-10
MCA (345; "Show Your Hand"): *73* 15-20
(With "Jack-in-the-box" cover.)
MCA (345; "Show Your Hand"): *73* 8-10
(With standard cover.)
Members: Roger Ball; Malcolm Duncan; Steve Fer-
rone; Alan Garrie; Robbie McIntosh; Owen Mc-
Intyre.
Also see FOREVER MORE
Also see KARP, Charlie
Also see KING, Ben E., & The Average White
Band

AXE
Singles: 7-Inch
ATCO: *82-84* 1-3
MCA: *79-80* 2-4
LPs: 10/12-Inch 33rpm
ATCO: *82-84* 5-8
MCA: *79-80* 5-8
Members: Bobby Barth; Ted Mueller.

AXTON, Hoyt
(Hoyt Axton & The Sherwood Singers)
Singles: 7-Inch
A&M: *73-76* 2-4
BRIAR: *61* 4-6
CAPITOL: *71-72* 2-4
COLGEMS: *67* 3-6
COLUMBIA: *69* 3-5
ELEKTRA: *81* 1-3
HORIZON: *62-63* 4-8
JEREMIAH: *79-83* 2-4
MCA: *77-78* 1-3
20TH CENTURY-FOX: *66* 3-6
VEE JAY: *64-65* 3-6
Picture Sleeves
A&M: *73* 3-5
LPs: 10/12-Inch 33rpm
A&M: *73-77* 5-8
ACCORD: *82* 5-8
ALLEGIANCE: *84* 5-8
BRYLEN: *82* 5-8
CAPITOL: *71* 8-10
COLUMBIA: *69* 8-10
EXODUS: *66* 10-15
HORIZON: *62-63* 15-20
JEREMIAH: *79-82* 8-10
LAKE SHORE: *81* 5-8
MCA: *77-78* 5-8
SURREY: *65* 15-18
VEE JAY: *64-65* 10-15
VEE JAY INTERNATIONAL (Except 1000
series): *74-77* 5-8
VEE JAY INTERNATIONAL (1000
series): *74* 10-12

AXTON, Hoyt, & The Chambers Brothers
Singles: 7-Inch
HORIZON: *62* $3-5
LPs: 10/12-Inch 33rpm
HORIZON: *63* 15-20
Also see AXTON, Hoyt
Also see CHAMBERS BROTHERS

AYERS, Roy
(Roy Ayers' Ubiquity)
Singles: 12-Inch 33/45rpm
COLUMBIA: *84-85* 4-6
POLYDOR: *79* 4-6
Singles: 7-Inch
COLUMBIA: *84-86* 1-3
POLYDOR: *77* 2-3
LPs: 10/12-Inch 33rpm
ATLANTIC: *68-76* 8-12
COLUMBIA: *84-86* 5-8
ELEKTRA: *78* 5-8
ICHIBAN: *88* 5-8
POLYDOR: *70-81* 6-10
Also see DUNLAP, Gene
Also see UBIQUITY

AYERS, Roy, & Wayne Henderson
Singles: 7-Inch
POLYDOR: *79-80* 1-3
LPs: 10/12-Inch 33rpm
POLYDOR: *80* 5-8
Also see AYERS, Roy
Also see HENDERSON, Wayne

AZTEC CAMERA
Singles: 12-Inch 33/45rpm
SIRE: *84* 4-6
Singles: 7-Inch
SIRE: *83-85* 1-3
LPs: 10/12-Inch 33rpm
SIRE: *83-87* 5-8

AZTEC TWO STEP
Singles: 7-Inch
ELEKTRA: *72-73* 2-4
RCA VICTOR: *76-78* 2-3
LPs: 10/12-Inch 33rpm
ELEKTRA: *72* 10-12
RCA VICTOR: *76-80* 5-8
WATERHOUSE: *80* 5-8
Members: Rex Fowler; Alan Schwartzberg; Neal Schulman.

AZTECA
Singles: 7-Inch
COLUMBIA: *72-73* 2-4
LPs: 10/12-Inch 33rpm
COLUMBIA: *72-73* 10-12

Members: Coke Escovedo; Tony Smith.
Also see ESCOVEDO, Coke
Also see MALO
Also see SANTANA

B

B.B.C.S.& A.
Singles: 7-Inch
SAM: *82* $1-3

B.B.& Q. BAND
(Brooklyn, Bronx & Queens Band)
Singles: 12-Inch 33/45rpm
CAPITOL: *81-83* 4-6
Singles: 7-Inch
CAPITOL: *81-83* 1-3
IN YOUR FACE: *86* 1-3
LPs: 10/12-Inch 33rpm
CAPITOL: *81-83* 5-8

B. BEAT GIRLS
Singles: 12-Inch 33/45rpm
25 WEST: *83* 4-6
Singles: 7-Inch
25 WEST: *83* 1-3

B. BUMBLE & THE STINGERS
Singles: 7-Inch
MERCURY: *66* 3-5
RENDEZVOUS: *61-63* 4-6
Members: Billy Brumble; Ron Brady; Fred Richard.

B-52s
Singles: 12-Inch 33/45rpm
WARNER BROS: *86* 4-6
Singles: 7-Inch
DB-52: *78* 15-20
WARNER BROS (Except 927): *79-86* 1-3
WARNER BROS (927; "Give Me Back My Man"): *81* 2-4
(Promotional issue only.)
Picture Sleeves
WARNER BROS: *80-82* 1-3
LPs: 10/12-Inch 33rpm
WARNER BROS: *79-86* 5-8

B-H-Y
Singles: 7-Inch
SALSOUL: *79* 1-3
LPs: 10/12-Inch 33rpm
SALSOUL: *79* 5-8

B.T. EXPRESS
Singles: 12-Inch 33/45rpm
COAST TO COAST: *81* 4-6

COLUMBIA: *81* $4-6
Singles: 7-Inch
COAST TO COAST: *82* 1-3
COLUMBIA: *76-80* 1-3
EARTHTONE: *84* 1-3
ROADSHOW: *75* 2-4
SCEPTER: *74* 2-4
LPs: 10/12-Inch 33rpm
COAST TO COAST: *82* 5-8
COLUMBIA: *76-80* 5-8
ROADSHOW: *75 76* 10-12
SCEPTER: *74* 8-10

BTO:
see BACHMAN-TURNER OVERDRIVE

BABE RUTH
Singles: 7-Inch
CAPITOL: *76* 1-3
HARVEST: *73-76* 2-4
LPs: 10/12-Inch 33rpm
HARVEST: *73-76* 5-8
Members: Ellie Hope; Steve Gurl; Jenny Haan;
Dave Hewitt; Ray Knott; Bernie Marsden; Alan
Shacklock; Ed Spevock.

BABY JANE & THE ROCK-A-BYES
Singles: 7-Inch
SPOKANE: *63* 6-10
UNITED ARTISTS: *62* 5-8

BABY RAY
(Ray Eddlemon)
Singles: 7-Inch
IMPERIAL: *66-67* 4-8
LPs: 10/12-Inch 33rpm
IMPERIAL: *67* 12-20

BABY RAY & THE FERNS
Singles: 7-Inch
DONNA: *63* 20-25
Member: Frank Zappa.
Also see ZAPPA, Frank

BABYFACE
Singles: 7-Inch
SOLAR: *87-88* 1-3

BABYS
Singles: 7-Inch
CHRYSALIS: *77-81* 1-3
Picture Sleeves
CHRYSALIS: *79* 1-3
LPs: 10/12-Inch 33rpm
CHRYSALIS: *77-81* 5-8
Members: Mike Corby; John Waite; Tony Brock;
Wally Stocker.
Also see WAITE, John

BACHARACH, Burt
Singles: 7-Inch
A&M: *69-74* $1-3
CABOT: 2-4
KAPP: *63-65* 2-4
LIBERTY: *66* 1-3
UNITED ARTISTS: *67* 1-3
Picture Sleeves
A&M: *71* 1-3
LPs: 10/12-Inch 33rpm
A&M (Except 1): *67-74* 5-10
A&M (1; "Radio Interview"): *74* 8-15
(Promotional issue only.)
KAPP: *65* 8-15
MCA: *73* 5-8

BACHELORS
Singles: 7-Inch
LONDON: *63-72* 3-5
Picture Sleeves
LONDON: *64-65* 5-10
LPs: 10/12-Inch 33rpm
LONDON: *64-72* 10-15
Members: Con Cluskey; Declan Stokes; John
Stokes.

BACHMAN, Randy
Singles: 7-Inch
POLYDOR: *78* 1-3
LPs: 10/12-Inch 33rpm
POLYDOR: *78* 5-8
RCA VICTOR (1100 series): *75* 5-8
RCA VICTOR (4300 series): *70* 10-12
Also see BACHMAN-TURNER-BACHMAN
Also see BACHMAN-TURNER OVER-
DRIVE
Also see GUESS WHO
Also see IRONHORSE

BACHMAN-TURNER-BACHMAN
LPs: 10/12-Inch 33rpm
REPRISE: *75* 8-10
Members: Randy Bachman; C.F. Turner; Robin
Bachman.
Also see BACHMAN, Randy
Also see BACHMAN-TURNER OVER-
DRIVE
Also see BRAVE BELT

BACHMAN-TURNER OVERDRIVE
Singles: 7-Inch
COMPLEAT: *84-85* 1-3
MERCURY: *73-79* 2-4
Picture Sleeves
MERCURY: *74-75* 2-5
LPs: 10/12-Inch 33rpm
COMPLEAT: *84-85* 5-8

MERCURY: 73-78 . . . . $6-12
Members: Randy Bachman; C.F. Turner; Robin
Bachman; Tim Bachman; Jim Clench; Norman
Durkee; Blair Thornton.
Also see BACHMAN, Randy
Also see BACHMAN-TURNER-BACHMAN

BACK STREET CRAWLER
(Crawler)
Singles: 7-Inch
EPIC: 77-78 2-3
LPs: 10/12-Inch 33rpm
ATCO: 75-76 10-12
EPIC (Except "Crawler" picture
disc): 77-78 5-8
EPIC ("Crawler" picture
disc): 78 25-30
Members: Tony Braunagel; John Bundrick; Paul
Kossoff; Mike Montgomery; Geoff Whitehorn;
Terry Wilson Slesser.
Also see FREE
Also see KOSSOFF, Paul

BACKTRACK
Singles: 7-Inch
GOLDMINE: 85 1-3
Member: John Hunt.

BACKUS, Jim
(Jim Backus & Friend; Jim Bakus)
Singles: 7-Inch
JUBILEE: 58-59 4-8
LPs: 10/12-Inch 33rpm
DORE: 74 6-10

BAD BOYS FEATURING K LOVE
Singles: 12-Inch 33/45rpm
STARLITE: 85 4-6

BAD COMPANY
Singles: 7-Inch
ATLANTIC: 86 1-3
SWAN SONG: 74-84 2-4
Picture Sleeves
SWAN SONG: 79 1-3
LPs: 10/12-Inch 33rpm
ATLANTIC: 86-88 5-8
SWAN SONG: 74-84 5-10
Members: Paul Rodgers; Brian Howe; Boz Burrell;
Simon Kirke; Mick Ralphs; Mick Jones.
Also see FIRM
Also see FOREIGNER
Also see FREE
Also see KING CRIMSON
Also see NUGENT, Ted
Also see RODGERS, Paul

BAD GIRLS
Singles: 7-Inch
BC: 81 . . . . $1-3

BAD HABITS
Singles: 7-Inch
PAULA: 70-72 3-5
Members: Delaney Bramlett; Bonnie Bramlett.
Also see DELANEY & BONNIE

BADAROU, Wally
Singles: 7-Inch
ISLAND: 86 1-3
LPs: 10/12-Inch 33rpm
ISLAND: 86 5-8

BADFINGER
Singles: 7-Inch
APPLE: 70-73 4-6
ATLANTIC: 81 1-3
ELEKTRA: 79 2-3
RADIO: 81 1-3
WARNER BROS: 74 2-4
Promotional Singles
APPLE: 70-73 10-20
Picture Sleeves
APPLE: 72 8-15
LPs: 10/12-Inch 33rpm
APPLE (3364; "Magic Christian
Music"): 70 12-20
APPLE (3367; "No Dice"): 70 25-35
APPLE (3387; "Straight Up"): 71 75-100
APPLE (3411; "Ass"): 73 12-20
ELEKTRA: 79 5-8
RADIO: 81 5-8
WARNER BROS: 74 8-10
Members: Tom Evans; Mike Gibbons; Pete Ham;
Joey Molland; Peter Clarke; Tony Kaye.
Also see IVEYS

BADGER
LPs: 10/12-Inch 33rpm
ATCO: 73 10-12
EPIC: 74 8-10
Members: Roy Dyke; Kim Gardner; Dave Foster;
Tony Kaye; Jackie Lomax; Brian Parrish; Paul Pil-
nick.
Also see ASHTON, GARDNER & DYKE
Also see LOMAX, Jackie

BAEZ, Joan
Singles: 7-Inch
A&M: 72-77 2-4
DECCA: 72 2-4
PORTRAIT: 77-79 2-3
RCA VICTOR: 72 2-4
VANGUARD (35000 series): 63-69 3-5
VANGUARD (35100 series): 70-71 2-4

Picture Sleeves

A&M: *72* $3-5
PORTRAIT: *79* 1-3
RCA VICTOR: *72* 3-5
VANGUARD: *65-67* 4-8

LPs: 10/12-Inch 33rpm

A&M (Except 8375): *72-77* 6-10
A&M (8375; "Joan Baez - Radio
Airplay Album"): *76* 10-15
(Promotional issue only.)
EMUS: 8-12
FANTASY 10-15
NAUTILUS: *81* 25-35
(Half-speed mastered.)
PORTRAIT: *77-79* 5-8
SQUIRE: *63* 10-20
VANGUARD (41/42; "Ballad
Book"): *72* 10-12
VANGUARD (077 through 123): *60-63* . 20-30
VANGUARD (160 through 306): *64-69* . 12-25
VANGUARD (308 through 332): *69-73* .. 6-10
VANGUARD (400 series): 5-8
VANGUARD (6500 series): *71* 8-12
(Vanguard numbers 077 through 446 may be
preceded by a "2," indicating stereo or a "9" or
"79" for mono issues.)
VANGUARD (6500 series): *70-71* 10-12

BAGBY, Doc
Singles: 78rpm

OKEH: *57* 3-6

Singles: 7-Inch

END: *60* 3-5
KAISER: *59* 3-5
OKEH: *57* 4-6
RED TOP: *59* 10-15
TALLY HO: *61* 3-5
VIM: *57* 4-6

LPs: 10/12-Inch 33rpm

KING: *59* 20-25
Also see TERRY, Sonny

BAGBY, Doc / Luis Rivera
LPs: 10/12-Inch 33rpm

KING: *59* 20-25
Also see BAGBY, Doc

BAILEY, Arthur
Singles: 12-Inch 33/45rpm

ATLANTIC: *84* 4-6
Singles: 7-Inch
ATLANTIC: *84* 1-3

BAILEY, J.R.
Singles: 7-Inch

CALLA: *68* 3-5
MAM: *74* 2-4

MIDLAND INT'L: *75* $2-4
RCA VICTOR: *76* 2-4
SPRING: *84* 1-3
TOY: *72-73* 2-4
UNITED ARTISTS: *78* 1-3

LPs: 10/12-Inch 33rpm

MAM: *74* 8-10
UNITED ARTISTS: *78* 5-8

BAILEY, Pearl
Singles: 78rpm

COLUMBIA: *46-50* 3-6
CORAL: *52-55* 3-5
MERCURY: *56* 3-5
ROULETTE: *57* 3-5
SUNSET: *56* 3-5
VERVE: *56* 3-5

Singles: 7-Inch

COLUMBIA (38000 series): *50* 4-8
COLUMBIA (43000 series): *66* 2-4
CORAL: *52-55* 3-5
DECCA: *64* 2-4
MERCURY: *56* 3-5
PROJECT 3: *68-70* 1-3
RCA VICTOR (500 series): *71* 1-3
RCA VICTOR (9400 series): *67* 1-3
ROULETTE: *59-68* 1-3
SUNSET: *56* 3-5
VERVE: *56* 3-5

EPs: 7-Inch 33/45rpm

COLUMBIA: *52-56* 10-20
CORAL: *54* 10-20
ROULETTE: *57* 10-15

LPs: 10/12-Inch 33rpm

ACCORD: *83* 5-8
COLUMBIA (900 series): *57* 20-35
COLUMBIA (2600 series): *56* 25-40
(10-Inch LPs.)
COLUMBIA (6000 series): *50* 25-40
(10-Inch LPs.)
CORAL (56000 series): *54* 25-40
(10-Inch LPs.)
CORAL (57000 series): *57* 20-30
CO-STAR: *58* 15-20
MERCURY (Except 100 series): *56-58* .. 20-30
MERCURY (100 series): *69* 8-12
PROJECT 3: *70* 5-10
RCA VICTOR (4500 series): *71* 5-10
ROULETTE (100 series): *71* 8-12
ROULETTE (25000 & 25100
series): *57-63* 15-25
ROULETTE (25200 & 25300
series): *64-65* 10-15
VOCALION: *58* 15-25
WING: *59-63* 15-25

BAILEY, Pearl, & Mike Douglas
Singles: 7-Inch
PROJECT 3: 68 . . . . $1-3
Also see BAILEY, Pearl
Also see DOUGLAS, Mike

BAILEY, Philip
Singles: 12-Inch 33/45rpm
COLUMBIA: 83-86 4-6
Singles: 7-Inch
COLUMBIA: 83-86 1-3
LPs: 10/12-Inch 33rpm
COLUMBIA: 84-86 5-8
Also see EARTH, WIND & FIRE

BAILEY, Philip, & Phil Collins
Singles: 12-Inch 33/45rpm
COLUMBIA: 84 4-6
Singles: 7-Inch
COLUMBIA: 84 1-3
Also see BAILEY, Philip
Also see COLLINS, Phil

BAILEY, Razzy
(Razzie Bailey)
Singles: 7-Inch
ABC-PARAMOUNT: 67 4-6
B&K: 59 6-10
CAPRICORN: 75 2-4
ERASTUS: 76 2-4
MCA: 85-86 1-3
1-2-3: 69 2-4
PEACH: 66 3-5
RCA VICTOR: 77-84 1-3
SOA: 87-88 1-3
Picture Sleeves
RCA VICTOR: 80-81 1-3
LPs: 10/12-Inch 33rpm
MCA: 85-86 5-8
RCA VICTOR: 79-84 5-8

BAIO, Scott
Singles: 7-Inch
RCA VICTOR: 82-83 1-3
LPs: 10/12-Inch 33rpm
RCA VICTOR: 82-83 5-8

BAJA MARIMBA BAND
Singles: 7-Inch
A&M: 66-67 2-3
ALMO: 63-66 2-4
BELL: 73 1-3
SHOUT: 81 1-3
Picture Sleeves
A&M: 66-68 2-4
LPs: 10/12-Inch 33rpm
A&M: 64-70 5-10
BELL: 73 5-8

Member: Julius Wechter.
Also see DENNY, Martin

BAKER, Anita
Singles: 7-Inch
BEVERLY GLEN: 83-84 . . . . $1-3
ELEKTRA: 87-88 1-3
LPs: 10/12-Inch 33rpm
BEVERLY GLEN: 83 5-8
ELEKTRA: 87-88 5-8
Also see CHAPTER 8

BAKER, Bill
(Bill Baker & The Chestnuts; Bill Baker's Five Satins)
Singles: 7-Inch
AUDICON: 62 4-6
CORAL: 60 4-6
ETC: 63 3-5
ELGIN: 59 25-30
MUSIC TONE: 61-62 3-5
VIM: 60 25-30
LPs: 10/12-Inch 33rpm
DEL CAM (1000; "I'll Be Seeing
  You"): 87 8-10
Also see FIVE SATINS

BAKER, George
(George Baker Selection)
Singles: 7-Inch
COLOSSUS: 70 2-4
WARNER BROS: 75-76 2-4
Picture Sleeves
COLOSSUS: 70 3-6
LPs: 10/12-Inch 33rpm
COLOSSUS: 70 15-20
WARNER BROS: 76 10-12

BAKER, Ginger
(Ginger Baker's Air Force)
Singles: 7-Inch
ATCO: 70 2-4
LPs: 10/12-Inch 33rpm
ATCO: 70-72 12-15
SIRE: 77 5-8
POLYDOR: 72-79 8-10
Also see BAKER-GURVITZ ARMY
Also see BLIND FAITH
Also see CREAM
Also see WINWOOD, Steve

BAKER, Lavern
(Lavern Baker & The Gliders)
Singles: 78rpm
ATLANTIC: 59-65 3-6
KING: 55 5-10

Singles: 7-Inch
ATLANTIC (1000 series, except
1004): *55-58* $5-10
ATLANTIC (1004; "Soul On
Fire"): *53-54* 10-20
ATLANTIC (2000 series): *59-65* 4-8
BRUNSWICK: *66* 3-5
KING: *55* 10-20
EPs: 7-Inch 33/45rpm
ATLANTIC: *56-58* 40-60
LPs: 10/12-Inch 33rpm
ATCO: *71* 8-10
ATLANTIC (Except 8002, 8007, &
8030): *59-63* 15-20
ATLANTIC (8002; "Lavern"): *56* 40-50
(Black label.)
ATLANTIC (8002; "Lavern"): *59* 15-20
(Red label.)
ATLANTIC (8007; "Lavern
Baker"): *57* 35-45
ATLANTIC (8030; "Blues
Ballads"): *59* 35-45
(Black label.)
ATLANTIC (8030; "Blues
Ballads"): *59* 15-20
(Red label.)
BRUNSWICK: *70* 10-15
Also see KING, Ben E., & Lavern Baker
Also see KING CURTIS
Also see RHODES, Todd
Also see WILSON, Jackie, & Lavern Baker

BAKER, Lavern, & Jimmy Ricks
Singles: 7-Inch
ATLANTIC: *61* 3-5
Also see BAKER, Lavern

BAKER, Tammy Faye
Singles: 7-Inch
SUTRA: *88* 1-3
Picture Sleeves
SUTRA: *88* 1-3

BAKER, Teddy
Singles: 7-Inch
CASABLANCA: *81* 1-3

BAKER-GURVITZ ARMY
Singles: 7-Inch
ATCO: *74-76* 2-4
JANUS: *75* 2-4
LPs: 10/12-Inch 33rpm
ATCO: *75-76* 8-10
JANUS: *75* 10-12
Members: Ginger Baker; Adrian Gurvitz; Paul Gur-
vitz; Peter Lemer; John Norman; Snips.
Also see BAKER, Ginger

Also see GURVITZ, Adrian

BALAAM & THE ANGEL
LPs: 10/12-Inch 33rpm
VIRGIN: *88* $5-8

BALANCE
Singles: 7-Inch
PORTRAIT: *81-82* 1-3
LPs: 10/12-Inch 33rpm
PORTRAIT: *81-82* 5-8
Also see BLUES MAGOOS

BALDRY, Long John
(Long John Baldry & The Hootchie Cootchie
Men)
Singles: 7-Inch
A&M: *68* 3-5
ASCOT: *66-67* 4-6
EMI AMERICA: *79* 1-3
WARNER BROS: *68-72* 2-4
LPs: 10/12-Inch 33rpm
ASCOT: *65* 15-25
CASABLANCA: *75-76* 5-8
EMI AMERICA: *79-80* 5-8
UNITED ARTISTS: *71* 8-10
WARNER BROS: *71-72* 8-10

**BALDRY, Long John, & Kathi
McDonald**
Singles: 7-Inch
EMI AMERICA: *79* 1-3
Also see BALDRY, Long John
Also see MC DONALD, Kathi

BALIN, Marty
Singles: 7-Inch
CHALLENGE: *62* 15-20
EMI AMERICA: *81-84* 1-3
Picture Sleeves
EMI AMERICA: *81* 1-3
LPs: 10/12-Inch 33rpm
EMI AMERICA: *81-82* 8-10
Also see JEFFERSON AIRPLANE
Also see JEFFERSON STARSHIP

BALL, Kenny
(Kenny Ball & His Jazzmen)
Singles: 7-Inch
DECCA: *67* 1-3
GUYDEN: *61* 2-4
KAPP: *62-64* 2-4
Picture Sleeves
KAPP: *62* 4-8
LPs: 10/12-Inch 33rpm
JAZZOLOGY: *79* 5-8
KAPP: *62-64* 10-20

BALLADS
Singles: 7-Inch
VENTURE: *68* $3-5

BALLARD, Hank
**(Hank Ballard & The Midnight Lighters; Hank
Ballard & The Dapps)**
Singles: 7-Inch
KING: *68* 2-4
PEOPLE: *72* 2-4
POLYDOR: *72* 2-4
SILVER FOX: *70* 2-4
LPs: 10/12-Inch 33rpm
KING (1000 series): *69* 10-12

BALLARD, Hank & The Midnighters
Singles: 7-Inch
GUSTO: *78* 1-3
KING (5100 through 5500
   series): *59-62* 3-5
LE JOINT: *79* 1-3
Picture Sleeves
KING: *61* 5-10
EPs: 7-Inch 33/45rpm
KING: *58-63* 20-35
LPs: 10/12-Inch 33rpm
FEDERAL (90; "Their Greatest
   Hits"): *54* 800-1200
   (10-Inch LP.)
FEDERAL (541; "Their Greatest
   Hits"): *56* 400-450
   (White cover.)
FEDERAL (541; "Their Greatest
   Hits"): *56* 350-400
   (Tan or red cover.)
FEDERAL (581; "Midnighters,
   Vol. 2"): *57* 75-100
KING (500 through 800 series,
   except KS-740): *58-64* 25-35
KING (KS-740; "Spotlight On
   Hank Ballard"): *61* 75-100
   (Stereo.)
KING (900 series): *65-68* 15-20
KING (5000 series): *77* 8-10
   Also see BALLARD, Hank
   Also see MIDNIGHTERS
   Also see ROYALS

BALLARD, Russ
Singles: 7-Inch
EMI AMERICA: *84* 1-3
EPIC: *74-80* 1-3
LPs: 10/12-Inch 33rpm
EPIC: *74-80* 8-10
   Also see ARGENT
   Also see UNIT 4+2

BALLIN' JACK
Singles: 7-Inch
COLUMBIA: *71* $2-4
MERCURY: *73* 2-4
LPs: 10/12-Inch 33rpm
COLUMBIA: *70-72* 10-12
MERCURY: *73-74* 8-10

BALLOON FARM
Singles: 7-Inch
LAURIE: *68* 3-5

BALTIMORE & OHIO MARCHING
   BAND
Singles: 7-Inch
JUBILEE: *67* 2-4

BALUM & THE ANGELS
LPs: 10/12-Inch 33rpm
VIRGIN: *87* 5-8

BAMA
Singles: 7-Inch
FREE FLIGHT (Black vinyl): *79* 1-3
FREE FLIGHT (Colored vinyl): *79* 3-5
   (Promotional issues only.)
LPs: 10/12-Inch 33rpm
FREE FLIGHT: *79* 5-8

BAMBAATAA, Afrika
**(Afrika Bambaataa & James Brown; Afrika
Bambaataa & The Soul Sonic Force; Afrika
Bambaataa & Family)**
Singles: 12-Inch 33/45rpm
TOMMY BOY: *83-86* 4-6
Singles: 7-Inch
TOMMY BOY: *82-86* 1-3
LPs: 10/12-Inch 33rpm
TOMMY BOY: *83-86* 5-8
   Also see BROWN, James
   Also see SHANGO

BANANA SPLITS
Singles: 7-Inch
DECCA: *68-69* 4-8
Picture Sleeves
DECCA: *69-70* 8-10
EPs: 7-Inch 33/45rpm
KELLOGG: *69* 8-12
LPs: 10/12-Inch 33rpm
DECCA: *69* 10-15

BANANARAMA
Singles: 12-Inch 33/45rpm
LONDON: *83-88* 4-6
Singles: 7-Inch
LONDON: *82-88* 1-3
Picture Sleeves
LONDON: *82-88* 1-3

The Band: (L-R) Richard Manuel; Levon Helm; Rick Danko; Garth Hudson; Robbie Robertson (Photo: Elliott Landy)

LPs: 10/12-Inch 33rpm
LONDON: *83 88* **$5-8**
  Members: Satch Dallin; Kevin Woodward; S.
  Fahey.
  Also see BAND AID

BAND

Singles: 7-Inch
CAPITOL (Except 2000 series): *71-77* **3-5**
CAPITOL (2000 series): *67-70* **4-6**
WARNER BROS: *78* **2-4**
Picture Sleeves
CAPITOL: *70* **3-6**
LPs: 10/12-Inch 33rpm
CAPITOL (Except 2955): *69-85* **8-15**
CAPITOL (2955; "Music From
  Big Pink"): *68* **12-15**
MFSL: *80* **25-50**
WARNER BROS (737; "The Last
  Waltz"): *78* **15-20**
  (Promotional issue only.)
WARNER BROS (3146; "The Last
  Waltz"): *78* **15-20**
  (A 3-LP set.)
  Members: Levon Helm; Rick Danko; Garth Hud-
  son; Richard Manuel; Robbie Robertson; Jimmy
  Wieder.
  Also see DANKO, Rick
  Also see DYLAN, Bob
  Also see HAWKINS, Ronnie
  Also see HELM, Levon
  Also see LEVON & THE HAWKS
  Also see MILLER, Steve / Band / Quicksilver
Messinger Service

BAND AID

Singles: 7-Inch
COLUMBIA (04749; "Do They Know It's
  Christmas"): *84* **$1-3**
  Members: Bananarama; Boomtown Rats; Boy
  George, Phil Collins; Duran Duran; Bob Geldof;
  Heaven 17; Kool & The Gang; George Michael;
  John Moss; Spandau Ballet; Status Quo; Sting; U2;
  Ultravox; Paul Weller; Paul Young.
  Also see BANANARAMA
  Also see BOOMTOWN RATS
  Also see COLLINS, Phil
  Also see CULTURE CLUB
  Also see DURAN DURAN
  Also see GELDORF, Bob
  Also see HEAVEN 17
  Also see KOOL & THE GANG
  Also see SPANDAU BALLET
  Also see STATUS QUO
  Also see STING
  Also see STYLE COUNCIL
  Also see U2
  Also see ULTRAVOX
  Also see WHAM!
  Also see YOUNG, Paul

BAND OF GOLD

Singles: 7-Inch
RCA VICTOR: *85* **1-3**

BAND OF THE BLACK WATCH
Singles: 7-Inch
PRIVATE STOCK: 75-76 .... $2-4
LPs: 10/12-Inch 33rpm
PRIVATE STOCK: 76 5-8

BANDANA
(BANDANNA)
Singles: 7-Inch
HAVEN: 76 2-4
PARAMOUNT: 73 3-5
WARNER BROS: 81-86 1-3
LPs: 10/12-Inch 33rpm
WARNER BROS: 86 5-8
Also see PLAYER

BANDIT
Singles: 7-Inch
ABC: 75 2-3
ARISTA: 77 1-3
LPs: 10/12-Inch 33rpm
ABC: 75 8-10
ARISTA: 77 6-10
Members: Jim Diamond; Danny McIntosh; James
Litherland; Cliff Williams; Graham Broad.

BANDOLERO
Singles: 12-Inch 33/45rpm
SIRE: 84 4-6
Singles: 7-Inch
SIRE:84 1-3
LPs: 10/12-Inch 33rpm
ECLIPSE:75 8-10

BANDWAGON
Singles: 7-Inch
EPIC: 68 3-5

BANG
Singles: 7-Inch
CAPITOL: 72-74 2-4
LPs: 10/12-Inch 33rpm
CAPITOL: 72-73 8-12

BANGLES
Singles: 12-Inch 33/45rpm
COLUMBIA: 85-88 4-6
Singles: 7-Inch
COLUMBIA: 84-87 1-3
DEF JAM: 87 1-3
DOWNKIDDIE (001; "Getting Out
Of Hand"): 81 5-10
Picture Sleeves
COLUMBIA: 84-88 2-4
DOWNKIDDIE (001; "Getting Out
Of Hand"): 81 10-20
(Back of sleeve shows Downkiddie Records as
being in Los Angeles, California.)

DOWNKIDDIE (001; "Getting Out
Of Hand"): 81 ....$8-15
(Back of sleeve shows Downkiddie Records as
being in Torrance, California.)
LPs: 10/12-Inch 33rpm
COLUMBIA: 84-88 5-8
I.R.S.: 83 6-10
Members: Vicki Peterson; Debbi Peterson; Susanna
Hoffs; Annette Zilinskas; Michael Steele.
Also see BANGS

BANGOR FLYING CIRCUS
Singles: 7-Inch
DUNHILL: 70 2-4
LPs: 10/12-Inch 33rpm
DUNHILL: 69 12-15
Members: Michael Tegza; David Wolinski; Alan
DeCarlo.

BANGS
Singles: 7-Inch
DOWNKIDDIE (001; "Getting Out
Of Hand"): 81 20-30
Picture Sleeves
DOWNKIDDIE (001; "Getting Out
Of Hand"): 81 30-50
Members: Vicki Peterson; Debbi Peterson; Susanna
Hoffs.
Also see BANGLES

BANKS, Darrell
Singles: 7-Inch
ATCO: 67 3-6
COTILLION: 68 3-5
REVILOT: 66 4-8
SOULTOWN: 66 4-8
LPs: 10/12-Inch 33rpm
ATCO: 67 15-18
VOLT: 69 10-12

BANKS, Peter
Singles: 7-Inch
CAPITOL: 73 2-4
LPs: 10/12-Inch 33rpm
CAPITOL: 73 10-12
Also see AFTER THE FIRE
Also see BLODWYN PIG
Also see FLASH
Also see YES

BANKS, Ron
Singles: 12-Inch 33/45rpm
CBS ASSOCIATED: 83 4-6
Singles: 7-Inch
ABC: 75 2-3
CBS ASSOCIATED: 83 1-3
LPs: 10/12-Inch 33rpm
CBS ASSOCIATED: 83 5-8

Also see DRAMATICS

BANKS, Rose
Singles: 7-Inch
MOTOWN: 76 . . . .$2-3
SOURCE: 80 1-3
LPs: 10/12-Inch 33rpm
MOTOWN: 76 8-10
Also see SLY & THE FAMILY STONE

BANKS, Tony
Singles: 7-Inch
ATLANTIC: 83 1-3
CHARISMA: 79 2-3
LPs: 10/12-Inch 33rpm
ATLANTIC: 83 5-8
CHARISMA: 79 .5-10
Also see GENESIS

BANKS & HAMPTON
Singles: 7-Inch
WARNER BROS: 76-77 2-4
LPs: 10/12-Inch 33rpm
WARNER BROS: 77 5-8

BANZAII
Singles: 7-Inch
SCEPTER: 75 2-4

BARBARA & THE BROWNS
Singles: 7-Inch
SOUND OF MEMPHIS: 72 2-4
STAX: 64 3-5
Member: Barbara Brown.

BARBARA & THE UNIQUES
Singles: 7-Inch
ABBOTT: 72 2-4
ARDEN: 70 2-4
NEW CHICAGO SOUND: 70 2-4
20TH CENTURY-FOX: 74 2-4
Member: Barbara Blake.

BARBARA LYNN: see LYNN, Barbara

BARBARIANS
Singles: 7-Inch
JOY: 64 15-20
LAURIE: 65-66 10-12
LPs: 10/12-Inch 33rpm
LAURIE (2033; "The
Barbarians"): 66 50-60
RHINO: 79 5-8
Also see ELEGANTS

BARBER, Chris
(Chris Barber's Jazz Band)
Singles: 7-Inch
ATLANTIC: 59 2-4
LAURIE: 58-63 2-4

LONDON: 62 . . . .$2-4
Picture Sleeves
LAURIE: 59 3-6
LPs: 10/12-Inch 33rpm
ARCHIVE OF FOLK MUSIC: 68 8-12
ATLANTIC: 59 10-15
COLPIX: 59 10-15
LAURIE: 59-62 10-15

BARBER, Frank
Singles: 7 Inch
VICTORY: 82 1-3
LPs: 10/12-Inch 33rpm
VICTORY: 82 5-8

BARBIERI, Gato
Singles: 7-Inch
A&M: 76-79 1-3
UNITED ARTISTS: 73 1-3
LPs: 10/12-Inch 33rpm
A&M: 76-79 5-10
ARISTA: 75 8-10
FLYING DUTCHMAN: 70-80 5-10
IMPULSE: 73-75 8-10
UNITED ARTISTS: 73 5-10

BARBOUR, Dave
Singles: 78rpm
CAPITOL: 50-51 3-5
Singles: 7-Inch
ARWIN: 59 2-4
CAPITOL: 50-51 3-5
EPs: 7-Inch 33/45rpm
CAPITOL: 54 5-8
DECCA: 53 5-8
LPs: 10/12-Inch 33rpm
DECCA: 53 10-20

BARBOUR, Keith
Singles: 7-Inch
BARNABY: 71 2-4
EPIC: 69-70 3-5
LPs: 10/12-Inch 33rpm
EPIC: 69 12-18

BARBUSTERS
Singles: 7-Inch
CBS ASSOCIATED: 87 1-3
Also see JETT, Joan, & The Blackhearts

BARCLAY, Eddie
Singles: 7-Inch
RAMA: 55 4-6
TICO: 55 3-5

BARCLAY JAMES HARVEST
Singles: 7-Inch
HARVEST: 73 3-5
MCA: 76-77 2-4

POLYDOR: *75-79* $1-3
LPs: 10/12-Inch 33rpm
HARVEST: *73* 8-10
MCA: *77* 5-8
POLYDOR: *74-80* 8-10
SIRE: *70-71* 12-15
Members: Les Holroyd; John Lees; John Pritchard; Stewart "Wolly" Wolstenholme.

BARDENS, Pete
LPs: 10/12-Inch 33rpm
CAPITOL: *88* 5-8

BARDEUX
Singles: 7-Inch
SYNTHICIDE: *88* 1-3
LPs: 10/12-Inch 33rpm
SYNTHICIDE: *88* 5-8

BARE, Bobby
(Bobby Bare & The All American Boys; Bobby Bare & The Hillsiders; Bobby Bare & Bobby Bare, Jr.; Bobby Bare & The Family; Bobby & Jeannie Bare)
Singles: 78rpm
CAPITOL: *57* 4-8
Singles: 7-Inch
CAPITOL: *57* 5-8
COLUMBIA: *78-85* 1-3
EMI AMERICA: *85-86* 1-3
FRATERNITY (835 through
878): *58-61* 5-12
FRATERNITY (885 through
892): *61* 3-5
MERCURY: *70-72* 1-3
RCA VICTOR (Except 8000 & 9000
series): *69-77* 1-3
RCA VICTOR (8000 & 9000
series): *62-68* 2-4
RICE: *73-74* 1-3
Picture Sleeves
RCA VICTOR: *62-65* 4-8
LPs: 10/12-Inch 33rpm
CAMDEN: *68-73* 8-12
COLUMBIA: *78-85* 5-10
MERCURY: *70-72* 10-15
PICKWICK: *75-80* 5-10
PICKWICK/HILLTOP: *65* 10-15
RCA VICTOR (ANL1 & APL1
series): *73-77* 8-12
RCA VICTOR (AYL1 series): *81* 5-8
RCA VICTOR (2776 through
3994): *63-69* 15-20
(With an "LPM" or "LSP" prefix.)
RCA VICTOR (4000 series): *69-71* 10-15
(With an "LSP" prefix.)
RCA VICTOR (6000 series): *73* 10-15

SUN (136; "Bobby Bare's Greatest
Hits"): *74* $15-25
UNITED ARTISTS: *75-76* 8-12
Also see ORBISON, Roy / Bobby Bare / Joey Powers
Also see PARSONS, Bill

BARE, Bobby, Liz Anderson &
Norma Jean
Singles: 7-Inch
RCA VICTOR: *67* 3-5
LPs: 10/12-Inch 33rpm
RCA VICTOR: *67* 12-20

BARE, Bobby, & Rosanne Cash
Singles: 7-Inch
COLUMBIA: *79* 1-3
Also see CASH, Rosanne

BARE, Bobby, & Skeeter Davis
Singles: 7-Inch
RCA VICTOR (8000 & 9000
series): *65-70* 2-4
LPs: 10/12-Inch 33rpm
RCA VICTOR: *65-70* 10-15
Also see DAVIS, Skeeter

BARE, Bobby, / Donna Fargo /
Jerry Wallace
LPs: 10/12-Inch 33rpm
OUT OF TOWN DIST: *82* 5-8
Also see BARE, Bobby
Also see FARGO, Donna
Also see WALLACE, Jerry

BAR-KAYS
Singles: 12-Inch 33/45rpm
MERCURY: *79-85* 4-6
Singles: 7-Inch
MERCURY: *76-84* 1-3
STAX: *78-81* 1-3
VOLT: *67-74* 2-4
LPs: 10/12-Inch 33rpm
MERCURY: *76-87* 5-8
STAX: *78-81* 5-8
VOLT: *67-74* 10-12
Members: Jimmy King; Phalon Jones; Carl Cunningham; Ron Caldwell; Larry Dodson; James Alexander; Charles Allen; Vernon Burch; Ben Cauley; Donnelle Hagan; Harvey Henderson; Winston Stewart.
Also see REDDING, Otis

BARKLEY, Tyrone
Singles: 7-Inch
MIDSONG INT'L: *79* 1-3

BARNES, Cheryl
Singles: 7-Inch
MILLENNIUM: 77 .... $2-3
POLYDOR: 80 1-3
RCA VICTOR: 79 1-3

BARNES, J.J.
Singles: 7-Inch
BUDDAH: 69 3-5
GROOVESVILLE: 67 3-5
INVASION: 70 2-4
KABLE: 60 4-8
MAGIC TOUCH: 70 2-4
MICKAYS: 62-63 3-6
PERCEPTION: 74 2-4
REVILOT: 68 3-5
RICH: 3-5
RIC-TIC: 65-66 3-5
RING: 64 3-5
VOLT: 69 3-5

BARNES, J.J., & Steve Mancha
LPs: 10/12-Inch 33rpm
VOLT: 69 10-12
Also see BARNES, J.J.
Also see HOLIDAYS
Also see MANCHA, Steve

BARNES, Jimmy
(Jimmy Barnes & The Gibralters)
Singles: 7-Inch
GIBRALTAR: 59 4-6
SAVOY: 59-60 4-6
Also see BROWN, Nappy

BARNES, Jimmy
Singles: 7-Inch
GEFFEN: 86-88 1-3
LPs: 10/12-Inch 33rpm
GEFFEN: 86-88 5-8
Also see COLD CHISEL

BARNUM, H.B.
Singles: 7-Inch
CAPITOL: 65-68 3-5
DECCA: 71 2-4
ELDO: 60-61 4-8
IMPERIAL: 64 5-10
MUN RAB: 59 4-8
RCA VICTOR: 61-63 5-10
ULTRA SONIC: 60 3-5
UNITED ARTISTS: 73 1-3
Picture Sleeves
RCA VICTOR: 62 4-8
LPs: 10/12-Inch 33rpm
CAPITOL: 65 12-15
RCA VICTOR: 62 15-20
TROPIC ISLE: 59 15-25

Also see ROBINS

BARRABAS
Singles: 7-Inch
ATCO: 75-76 .... $2-4
LPs: 10/12-Inch 33rpm
ATCO: 75-76 5-8
RCA VICTOR: 72-73 8-10
Members: Jo Tejada; Ricky Morales; Miquel
Morales; Juan Videl; Daniel Louis; Ernest Duarte.

BARRACUDA
Singles: 7-Inch
RCA VICTOR: 68 4-8
Picture Sleeves
RCA VICTOR: 68 5-10

BARRACUDA
Singles: 7-Inch
20TH CENTURY-FOX: 73 2-4

BARRACUDA
Singles: 12-Inch 33/45rpm
EPIC: 83 4-6
Singles: 7-Inch
EPIC: 83 1-3

BARRETT, Richard
(Richie Barrett; Richard Barrett & The Chan-
tels; Richard Barrett & The Sevilles)
Singles: 7-Inch
ATLANTIC: 62 4-6
GONE: 59 10-15
MGM: 58 10-20
METRO: 58 5-10
SEVILLE: 60 5-10
20TH CENTURY-FOX: 59 5-10
Also see CHANTELS

BARRETT, Syd
LPs: 10/12-Inch 33rpm
HARVEST: 74 10-12
Also see PINK FLOYD

BARRETTO, Ray
Singles: 7-Inch
ASCOT: 66 1-3
ATLANTIC: 77-78 1-3
FANIA: 68-72 2-4
RIVERSIDE: 61 2-4
ROULETTE: 1-3
TICO: 63 3-5
UNITED ARTISTS: 65-67 2-4
LPs: 10/12-Inch 33rpm
ATLANTIC: 76-78 5-10
CTI: 81 5-8
FANIA: 68-73 5-10
FANTASY: 73 8-10
RIVERSIDE: 61-66 10-15

TICO: *62-63* $10-15
UNITED ARTISTS: *65-67* 8-15
  Also see LYTLE, Johnny, & Ray Barretto

BARRON, Blue
Singles: 7-Inch
MGM: *50-55* 2-4
EPs: 7-Inch 33/45rpm
MGM: *54-55* 3-6
LPs: 10/12-Inch 33rpm
MGM: *54* 8-12

BARRON KNIGHTS
Singles: 7-Inch
DECCA: *67* 5-8
EPIC (Except 9835): *79* 2-4
EPIC (9835; "Pop Go The
  Workers"): *65* 5-8
MERCURY: *72* 2-4
  Members: Barron Anthony; Peanut Langford;
  Butch Baker; Dave Ballinger; Duke D'mond.

BARROW, Keith
Singles: 12-Inch 33/45rpm
COLUMBIA: *79* 4-6
Singles: 7-Inch
CAPITOL: *80* 1-3
COLUMBIA: *76-79* 2-3
JEWEL: *73* 2-4
LPs: 10/12-Inch 33rpm
CAPITOL: *80* 5-8
UMBIA: *77* 5-8
JEWEL: *73* 8-10

BARRY, Claudja
Singles: 12-Inch 33/45rpm
CHRYSALIS: *79* 4-6
EPIC: *86-87* 4-6
PERSONAL: *83* 4-6
TSR: *85* 4-6
Singles: 7-Inch
CHRYSALIS: *79-84* 1-3
EPIC: *86-87* 1-3
MIRAGE: *82* 1-3
PERSONAL: *83* 1-3
SALSOUL: *77-78* 2-3
LPs: 10/12-Inch 33rpm
CHRYSALIS: *79-84* 5-8
HANDSHAKE: *82* 5-8
SALSOUL: *77* 5-8

BARRY, Claudja, & Ronnie Jones
LPs: 10/12-Inch 33rpm
HANDSHAKE: *82* 5-8
  Also see BARRY, Claudja

BARRY, Jan: see BERRY, Jan

BARRY, Joe
Singles: 7-Inch
ABC/DOT: *77* $1-3
JIN: *60-62* 5-10
NUGGET: 3-6
SMASH: *61-62* 4-8
Picture Sleeves
SMASH: *61* 8-15
LPs: 10/12-Inch 33rpm
ABC/DOT: *77* 5-10

BARRY, John, Orchestra
Singles: 7-Inch
A&M: *83* 1-3
CAPITOL (4200 series): *59* 2-4
CAPITOL (5400 series): *86* 1-3
COLUMBIA: *65-70* 2-3
EPIC: *72* 1-3
KING: *61* 2-4
MCA: *85* 1-3
MGM: *66* 2-3
MERCURY: *64* 2-4
20TH CENTURY-FOX: *64* 2-4
UNITED ARTISTS: *63-65* 2-3
WARNER BROS: *68* 2-3
Picture Sleeves
UNITED ARTISTS: *65* 4-8
LPs: 10/12-Inch 33rpm
ABC (852; "The Dove"): *74* 15-20
  (Soundtrack.)
BUENA VISTA (5008; "The Black
  Hole"): *80* 5-10
  (Soundtrack.)
CAPITOL (2500 series): *66* 10-15
CAPITOL (12413; "A View To
  Kill"): *86* 5-8
  (Soundtrack.)
COLUMBIA (1003; "Ready When You
  Are Mr. J.B."): *70* 8-12
COLUMBIA (2493; "Great Movie
  Themes"): *66* 10-15
COLUMBIA (2708; "You Only Live
  Twice"): *67* 8-12
  (Soundtrack.)
COLUMBIA (2710; "Sophia Loren In
  Rome"): *64* 20-30
  (Soundtrack.)
COLUMBIA (2960; "The Chase"): *66* . . .35-40
  (Soundtrack.)
COLUMBIA (3250; "The Lion In
  Winter"): *68* 12-15
  (Soundtrack.)
COLUMBIA (6310; "Sophia Loren In
  Rome"): *64* 50-60
  (Soundtrack.)

COLUMBIA (6560; "The
Chase"): 66 . . . . $40-45
(Soundtrack.)
COLUMBIA (9293; "Great Movie
Themes"): 66 10-15
COLUMBIA (9508; "You Only Live
Twice"): 67 10-12
(Soundtrack.)
DECCA (9124; "The Ipcress
File"): 65 15-20
(Soundtrack.)
DUNHILL (50102; "The Last
Valley"): 71 20-25
(Soundtrack.)
GEFFEN (24062; "The Cotton
Club"): 85 5-8
(Soundtrack.)
LIBERTY: 85 4-6
LONDON (912; "The Day Of The
Locust"): 75 10-15
(Soundtrack.)
MCA (5154; "Somewhere In
Time"): 80 5-8
(Soundtrack.)
MGM (4368; "Born Free"): 66 10-12
(Soundtrack.)
MAINSTREAM (6061; "King
Rat"): 65 25-30
(Soundtrack.)
MAINSTREAM (56061; "King
Rat"): 65 20-25
(Soundtrack.)
MAINSTREAM (6088; "The Wrong
Box"): 66 35-40
(Soundtrack.)
MAINSTREAM (56088; "The Wrong
Box"): 66 30-35
(Soundtrack.)
REPRISE (2260; "King Kong"): 76 8-12
(Soundtrack.)
ROULETTE (805; "Four In The
Morning"): 66 25-35
(Soundtrack.)
20TH CENTURY-FOX (3128; "Man
In The Middle"): 64 20-25
(Soundtrack.)
20TH CENTURY-FOX (4128; "Man
In The Middle"): 64 25-30
(Soundtrack.)
UNITED ARTISTS (91; "James Bond
Tenth Anniversary"): 72 8-12
UNITED ARTISTS (270; "The
Knack"): 74 8-12
(Soundtrack.)

UNITED ARTISTS (289; "You Only Live
Twice"): 74 . . . . $8-10
(Soundtrack.)
UNITED ARTISTS (299; "On Her Majesty's
Secret Service"): 74 8-12
(Soundtrack.)
UNITED ARTISTS (301; "Diamonds Are
Forever"): 74 8-10
(Soundtrack.)
UNITED ARTISTS (3424; "Goldfinger
& Other Favorites"): 65 8-12
UNITED ARTISTS (4114; "From Russia
With Love"): 64 10-15
(Soundtrack.)
UNITED ARTISTS (4117;
"Goldfinger"): 64 10-15
(Soundtrack.)
UNITED ARTISTS (4129; "The
Knack"): 65 20-25
(Soundtrack.)
UNITED ARTISTS (4132;
"Thunderball"): 65 15-20
(Soundtrack.)
UNITED ARTISTS (4155; "You Only
Live Twice"): 67 10-15
(Soundtrack.)
UNITED ARTISTS (4161; "The
Whisperers"): 67 15-18
(Soundtrack.)
UNITED ARTISTS (5114; "From Russia
With Love"): 64 15-20
(Soundtrack.)
UNITED ARTISTS (5117;
"Goldfinger"): 64 15-20
(Soundtrack.)
UNITED ARTISTS (5129; "The
Knack"): 65 25-30
(Soundtrack.)
UNITED ARTISTS (5132;
"Thunderball"): 65 20-25
(Soundtrack.)
UNITED ARTISTS (5155; "You Only
Live Twice"): 67 15-20
(Soundtrack.)
UNITED ARTISTS (5161; "The
Whisperers"): 67 18-20
(Soundtrack.)
UNITED ARTISTS (5204; "On Her Majesty's
Secret Service"): 69 12-18
(Soundtrack.)
UNITED ARTISTS (5220; "Diamonds
Are Forever"): 71 10-15
(Soundtrack.)
UNITED ARTISTS (6424; "Goldfinger
& Other Favorites"): 65 10-12

WARNER BROS (1755;
"Petulia"): *68* $15-20
(Soundtrack.)
WARNER BROS (2671; "Alice's Adventures
In Wonderland"): *72* 15-20
(Soundtrack.)
Also see ARMSTRONG, Louis
Also see BASIE, Count
Also see BASSEY, Shirley
Also see JONES, Tom
Also see MONRO, Matt
Also see SINATRA, Nancy

BARRY, Len
Singles: 7-Inch
AMY: *68-69* 3-5
BUDDAH: *72* 2-4
CAMEO: *64* 3-5
DECCA: *65-66* 3-5
MCA: *83* 1-3
MERCURY: *64* 3-5
PARAMOUNT: *73* 2-4
PARKWAY: *65* 3-5
RCA VICTOR: *67-68* 3-5
SCEPTER: *69-70* 2-4
EPs: 7-Inch 33/45rpm
DECCA (74720; "1-2-3"): *65* 8-15
(Jukebox issue only.)
LPs: 10/12-Inch 33rpm
BUDDAH: *72* 10-12
CAMEO: *64* 20-25
DECCA: *65* 20-25
RCA VICTOR: *67* 15-18
Also see DOVELLS

BARRY & THE TAMERLANES
Singles: 7-Inch
VALIANT: *63-65* 4-6
LPs: 10/12-Inch 33rpm
VALIANT: *63* 35-45
Members: Barry DeVorzon; Terry Smith; Bodie
Chandler.
Also see DE VORZON, Barry

BARTLEY, Chris
Singles: 7-Inch
BUDDAH: *71* 3-5
MUSICOR: *72* 2-4
VANDO: *67-68* 4-6
LPs: 10/12-Inch 33rpm
VANDO: *67* 15-20

BARTON, Eileen
Singles: 78rpm
CORAL: *51-56* 3-5
MERCURY: *53* 3-5
NATIONAL: *50* 4-8

Singles: 7-Inch
CORAL: *51-56* $3-5
CREST: *62* 2-4
MGM: *59* 2-4
MERCURY: *53* 3-5
20TH CENTURY-FOX: *63* 2-3
UNITED ARTISTS: *59* 2-4
EPs: 7-Inch 33/45rpm
CORAL: *54* 5-10
LPs: 10/12-Inch 33rpm
CORAL: *54* 15-20

BARTON, Lou Ann
Singles: 7-Inch
ASYLUM: *82* 1-3
LPs: 10/12-Inch 33rpm
ASYLUM: *82* 5-8

BARTZ, Gary
(Gary Bartz Nu Troop)
Singles: 7-Inch
ARISTA: *80* 1-3
CAPITOL: *77-78* 2-3
LPs: 10/12-Inch 33rpm
ARISTA: *80* 5-8
CAPITOL: *77-78* 5-10
CATALYST: *76* 5-10
MILESTONE: *68-69* 8-12
PRESTIGE: *73-75* 6-10
VEE JAY: *78* 5-8

BASIA
(Basia Trzetrzelewska)
Singles: 7-Inch
EPIC: *88* 1-3
LPs: 10/12-Inch 33rpm
EPIC: *88* 5-8

BASIE, Count
Singles: 78rpm
COLUMBIA: *43-51* 3-8
CLEF: *52-56* 3-5
DECCA (Except 1300 through
3000 series): *41-53* 3-8
DECCA (1300 through 3000
series): *37-40* 5-15
MERCURY: *52-53* 3-5
OKEH: *52* 3-5
Singles: 7-Inch
ABC-PARAMOUNT: *66* 2-3
BRUNSWICK: *67* 2-3
CLEF: *52-56* 3-5
COLUMBIA (33000 series): *76* 1-3
COLUMBIA (38000 & 39000
series): *50-51* 3-5
COMMAND: *67* 2-3
DECCA: *53* 3-5

HAPPY TIGER: *70*	$1-3
MERCURY: *52-53*	3-5
OKEH: *52*	3-5
REPRISE: *63*	2-3
ROULETTE: *58-63*	2-4
UNITED ARTISTS: *66*	2-3
VERVE: *60-67*	2-4

EPs: 7-Inch 33/45rpm

BRUNSWICK: *54*	10-15
CAMDEN: *58*	8-12
CLEF: *52-55*	10-15
COLUMBIA: *50*	10-15
CORAL:	10-15
DECCA: *53*	10-15
EPIC: *55*	10-15
RCA VICTOR (Except 5000 series): *54*	10-15
RCA VICTOR (5000 series): *59*	6-10
ROULETTE: *58-60*	8-12
VERVE: *56*	8-12

LPs: 10/12-Inch 33rpm

ABC: *76*	5-8
ABC-PARAMOUNT: *66*	10-15
ACCORD: *82-83*	5-8
AMERICAN: *57*	15-25
BRIGHT ORANGE: *73*	5-8
BRUNSWICK (54000 series): *63-67*	10-20
BRUNSWICK (58000 series): *54*	25-35
(10-Inch LPs.)	
CAMDEN: *58-60*	10-20
CIRCLE: *54*	40-50
CLEF (120; "Count Basie & His Orchestra"): *52*	100-200
(10-Inch LP.)	
CLEF (148; "The Count Basie Big Band"): *52*	100-200
(10-Inch LP.)	
CLEF (164; "The Count Basie Sextet"): *52*	100-200
(10-Inch LP.)	
CLEF (626; "Dance Session"): *53*	50-100
CLEF (647; "Dance Session, Volume 2"): *53*	50-100
CLEF (633; "Basieana"): *53*	50-100
CLEF (666; "Basie"): *54*	50-100
CLEF (678; "Basie Swings/Joe Williams Sings"): *55*	50-100
CLEF (685; "Count Basie"): *56*	50-80
CLEF (700 series): *56*	20-30
COLISEUM: *67*	8-12
COLUMBIA (700 & 900 series): *56-57*	20-30
COLUMBIA (6000 series): *50*	25-35
(10-Inch LPs.)	
COLUMBIA (31000 series): *72*	10-12

COMMAND: *66-71*	$10-15
DAYBREAK: *71*	6-10
DECCA (100 series): *64*	15-25
DECCA (5000 series): *50-53*	25-35
(10-Inch LPs.)	
DECCA (8000 series): *65*	10-15
DOCTOR JAZZ: *85-86*	5-8
DOT: *68*	8-12
EMARCY (26000 series): *54*	30-45
(10-Inch LPs.)	
EPIC (1000 & 1100 series): *54*	25-35
(10-Inch LPs.)	
EPIC: *55*	25-35
FLYING DUTCHMAN: *71*	6-10
HAPPY TIGER: *70*	8-12
HARMONY (7000 series): *60*	10-20
HARMONY (11000 series): *67-69*	5-10
IMPULSE: *62*	10-20
JAZZ PANORAMA: *52*	50-75
MCA: *77-82*	8-12
MGM: *70*	6-10
MFSL: *85*	15-25
MPS: *72*	10-12
MERCURY (25000 series): *50-51*	25-35
(10-Inch LPs.)	
METRO: *65-66*	6-10
OLYMPIC: *74*	5-10
PABLO: *74-83*	5-10
PAUSA: *83*	5-8
PRESTIGE: *82*	5-8
RCA VICTOR (500 series): *65*	10-15
RCA VICTOR (1100 series): *54*	25-35
REPRISE: *63-65*	10-15
ROULETTE (100 series): *71*	12-18
ROULETTE (52003 through 52106): *58-64*	15-20
ROULETTE (52111/12/13; "The World Of Count Basie"): *64*	30-40
(A 3-LP set.)	
SCEPTER: *74*	5-10
SOLID STATE: *68*	8-12
TRIP: *75*	5-10
UNITED ARTISTS: *66*	10-15
VSP: *66*	10-15
VANGUARD: *57*	15-25
VERVE: *73-84*	5-10
(Reads "Manufactured By MGM Record Corp.," or mentions either Polydor or Polygram at bottom of label.)	
VERVE (2000 series): *56*	20-30
(Reads "Verve Records, Inc." at bottom of label.)	
VERVE (2500 series): *77-82*	8-12
VERVE (2600 series): *82*	5-8
VERVE (6000 series): *56*	20-30
(Reads "Verve Records, Inc." at bottom of label.)	

VERVE (8000 & 8100 series): *56-57* ... **$15-25**
(Reads "Verve Records, Inc." at bottom of label.)
VERVE (8200 through 8400): *58-61* **15-20**
(Reads "Verve Records, Inc." at bottom of label.)
VERVE (8500 through 8600
series): *62-67* **10-15**
(Reads "MGM Records - A Division Of Metro-
Goldwyn-Mayer, Inc." at bottom of label.)
VERVE (8700 series): *69* **6-10**
(Reads "MGM Records - A Division Of Metro-
Goldwyn-Mayer, Inc." at bottom of label.)
VERVE (68000 series): *63-65* **10-20**
(Reads "MGM Records - A Division Of Metro-
Goldwyn-Mayer, Inc." at bottom of label.)
Also see BARRY, John
Also see BREWER, Teresa, & Count Basie
Also see CROSBY, Bing, & Count Basie
Also see DAVIS, Sammy, Jr., & Count Basie
Also see FITZGERALD, Ella, & Count Basie
Also see MILLS BROTHERS, & Count Basie
Also see PRYSOCK, Arthur, & Count Basie
Also see SINATRA, Frank, & Count Basie
Also see STARR, Kay, & Count Basie
Also see WILSON, Jackie, & Count Basie

BASIE, Count, & Tony Bennett
EPs: 7-Inch 33/45rpm
ROULETTE: *59* **6-10**
LPs: 10/12-Inch 33rpm
ROULETTE: *59-63* **10-20**
Also see BENNETT, Tony

BASIE, Count, & Billy Eckstine
LPs: 10/12-Inch 33rpm
ROULETTE: *59* **15-20**
Also see ECKSTINE, Billy

BASIE, Count, & Duke Ellington
Singles: 7-Inch
COLUMBIA: *62* **2-4**
LPs: 10/12-Inch 33rpm
ACCORD: *82* **5-8**
COLUMBIA: *62* **15-20**
Also see ELLINGTON, Duke

BASIE, Count, & Maynard Ferguson
LPs: 10/12-Inch 33rpm
ROULETTE: *65* **10-15**
Also see FERGUSON, Maynard

BASIE, Count, & Benny Goodman
LPs: 10/12-Inch 33rpm
ABC: *73* **10-12**
VANGUARD: *59* **15-20**
Also see GOODMAN, Benny

BASIE, Count, & Oscar Peterson
LPs: 10/12-Inch 33rpm
PABLO: *75-83* **5-10**

VERVE: *59* **$15-20**
Also see PETERSON, Oscar

BASIE, Count, & Sarah Vaughan
LPs: 10/12-Inch 33rpm
ROULETTE: *61* **15-20**
Also see VAUGHAN, Sarah

**BASIE, Count, Sarah Vaughan &
Joe Williams**
Singles: 7-Inch
ROULETTE: *60* **2-4**
LPs: 10/12-Inch 33rpm
ROULETTE: *60* **15-20**
Note: Joe Williams is a featured vocalist on many
of the recordings included in the section of listings
for Count Basie.
Also see BASIE, Count
Also see VAUGHAN, Sarah

BASIL, Toni
Singles: 12-Inch 33/45rpm
CHRYSALIS: *82-85* **4-6**
Singles: 7-Inch
A&M: *66* **5-10**
CHRYSALIS: *82-85* **1-3**
Picture Sleeves
CHRYSALIS: *82* **1-3**
LPs: 10/12-Inch 33rpm
CHRYSALIS: *82-84* **5-8**

BASKERVILLE HOUNDS
Singles: 7-Inch
AVCO EMBASSY: *69* **3-5**
BUDDAH: *67* **5-10**
DOT: *67* **5-10**
TEMA: *67* **10-15**
LPs: 10/12-Inch 33rpm
DOT: *67* **15-20**

BASS, Fontella
Singles: 7-Inch
ABC: *74* **1-3**
BOBBIN: *61* **4-6**
CHECKER: *65-66* **3-5**
CHESS: *75-85* **1-3**
ERIC: *73* **1-3**
MCA: *83* **1-3**
PAULA: *74* **2-4**
SONJA: *62* **4-6**
LPs: 10/12-Inch 33rpm
CHECKER: *66* **15-20**
PAULA: *71* **5-8**

BASS, Fontella, & Bobby McClure
Singles: 7-Inch
CHECKER: *65-66* **3-5**
Also see BASS, Fontella

Also see MC CLURE, Bobby

BASSEY, Shirley
Singles: 12-Inch 33/45rpm
UNITED ARTISTS: 79 . . . . $4-6
Singles: 7-Inch
EPIC: 59 2-5
MGM: 60 2-4
UNITED ARTISTS: 61-79 1-3
LPs: 10/12-Inch 33rpm
EPIC: 62 10-20
LIBERTY: 81-82 4-6
MGM: 60 12-20
PHILIPS: 65 10-15
SPRINGBOARD: 75 5-10
UNITED ARTISTS: 80 4-6
(With an "LM" prefix.)
UNITED ARTISTS: 62-72 10-15
(With a "UAL" or "UAS" prefix.)
UNITED ARTISTS: 73-79 5-10
(With a "UA-LA" prefix.)
Also see BARRY, John

BATAAN, Joe
(Joe Bataan & The Mestizo Band)
Singles: 7-Inch
SALSOUL: 80 1-3
UPTITE: 69 2-5
LPs: 10/12-Inch 33rpm
SALSOUL: 80-81 5-8

BATDORF, John
LPs: 10/12-Inch 33rpm
20TH CENTURY-FOX: 81 5-8
Also see BATDORF & RODNEY
Also see SILVER

BATDORF & RODNEY
Singles: 7-Inch
ARISTA: 75 1-3
ASYLUM: 72 2-4
ATLANTIC: 71-72 2-4
LPs: 10/12-Inch 33rpm
ATLANTIC: 71 8-12
ARISTA: 75 6-10
ASYLUM: 72 8-10
Members: John Batdorf: Mark Rodney.
Also see BATDORF, John
Also see SILVER

BAUMANN, Peter
Singles: 12-Inch 33/45rpm
PORTRAIT: 82-83 4-6
Singles: 7-Inch
PORTRAIT: 83 1-3
LPs: 10/12-Inch 33rpm
PORTRAIT: 82-83 5-8
VIRGIN: 77 8-10

Also see TANGERINE DREAM

BAXTER, Duke
Singles: 7-Inch
MERCURY: 70 . . . . $2-4
VMC: 69 3-5
LPs: 10/12-Inch 33rpm
VMC: 69 12-20

BAXTER, Les
(Les Baxter & His Orchestra & Chorus; Les Baxter Balladeers)
Singles: 78rpm
CAPITOL: 50-57 2-4
Singles: 7-Inch
A/S: 70 1-3
CAPITOL: 50-61 2-5
GNP/CRESCENDO: 64-69 2-3
LINK: 64 2-4
REPRISE: 62-63 2-3
EPs: 7-Inch 33/45rpm
CAPITOL: 51-56 4-8
GNP/CRESCENDO: 67-69 5-10
RCA VICTOR: 52 5-10
LPs: 10/12-Inch 33rpm
ALSHIRE: 70-85 5-8
AMERICAN INTERNATIONAL (1028;
"Dunwich Horror"): 70 15-20
(Soundtrack.)
CAPITOL (200 through 900
series): 51-58 8-18
CAPITOL (1000 through 1800
series): 58-63 4-10
CAPITOL (11000 series): 77-79 4-6
GNP/CRESCENDO: 69 5-10
RCA VICTOR: 52 15-20
REPRISE: 62-63 10-15

BAY CITY ROLLERS
Singles: 7-Inch
ARISTA: 75-78 2-3
BELL: 72-76 2-4
FLASHBACK: 80 1-3
Picture Sleeves
ARISTA: 75-78 1-3
LPs: 10/12-Inch 33rpm
ARISTA: 75-79 5-8
Members: Les McKeowen; Eric Faulkner; Stuart
Wood; Alan Longmuir; Derek Longmuir; Billy
Lyall; Pat McGlynn; Ian Mitchell.
Also see ROLLERS

BAYER, Carole:
see SAGER, Carole Bayer

The Beach Boys: (L-R) Mike Love; Carl Wilson; Brian Wilson; Bruce Johnston; Al Jardine (Photo: Harry Langdon)

BAZUKA
(Tony Camillo's Bazuka)
Singles: 7-Inch
A&M: 75 .... $2-4
VENTURE: 79 1-3
LPs: 10/12-Inch 33rpm
A&M: 75 5-8

BEACH BOYS
Singles: 12-Inch 33/45rpm
CARIBOU (9028; "Here Comes
  The Night"): 79 4-6
CARIBOU (9028; "Here Comes
  The Night"): 79 20-25
  (Promotional issue only.)
Singles: 7-Inch
BROTHER: 67 5-8
CANDIX (301; "Surfin"): 61 50-60
  (Label reads "Distributed by Era Record Sales
  Inc.")
CANDIX (301; "Surfin"): 61 75-100
  (Label does NOT say "Distributed by Era Record
  Sales Inc.")
CANDIX (331; "Surfin"): 62 60-75
CAPITOL (2000 series
  except 2765): 67-69 5-8
CAPITOL (2765;
  "Cottonfields"): 70 12-15
CAPITOL (4000 series,
  except 4880): 62-63 8-10

CAPITOL (4880; "Ten Little
  Indians"): 62 .... $15-20
CAPITOL (5000 series, except
  5096 & 5312): 63-66 5-8
  (Orange/yellow labels.)
CAPITOL (5096; "Little Saint
  Nick"): 63 12-15
CAPITOL (5312; "The Man With
  All The Toys"): 63 12-15
CAPITOL (5000 series): 81-86 2-4
  (Purple labels.)
CAPITOL (6000 series): 67-68 5-8
CARIBOU: 79-85 3-5
ELEKTRA: 88 1-3
ODE '70: 71 12-15
REPRISE (0894; "Add Some Music
  To Your Day"): 70 5-10
REPRISE (0929; "Slip On
  Through"): 70 5-10
REPRISE (0957; "Tears In
  The Morning"): 70 12-15
REPRISE (0998; "Cool, Cool
  Water"): 71 60-75
REPRISE (1015; "Long Promised
  Road"): 71 20-25
REPRISE (1047; "Long Promised
  Road"): 71 20-25
REPRISE (1058; "Surf's Up"): 71 45-50
REPRISE (1091; "Cuddle Up"): 72 25-30
REPRISE (1101; "Marcella"): 72 25-30

REPRISE (1138; "Sail On
Sailor"): 73 ....$10-12
REPRISE (1156; "California
Saga"): 73 5-10
REPRISE (1310; "I Can Hear
Music"): 74 3-5
REPRISE (1321; "Child Of
Winter"): 74 20-30
REPRISE (1325; "Sail On
Sailor"): 75 5-8
REPRISE (1336; "Wouldn't It
Be Nice"): 75 5-8
REPRISE (1354 through 1394): 76-78 3-5
X (301; "Surfin"): 61 125-150
Promotional Singles
CAPITOL (2360; "Bluebirds Over
The Mountain"): 69 15-20
CAPITOL (2936/7; "Salt Lake
City"): 65 175-200
CAPITOL CUSTOM ("Spirit Of
America"): 63 125-150
CARIBOU (557; "Here Comes The
Night"): 79 10-12
(Blue vinyl.)
CARIBOU (557; "Here Comes The
Night"): 79 50-60
(Special Edition autographed copies. Blue vinyl.)
CARIBOU (9026; "Here Comes The
Night"): 79 10-15
EVA-TONE (0300; "Living Doll"): 87 1-3
(Barbie Doll promotional issue.)
ODE '70 (66016; "Wouldn't It Be
Nice-Live Version"): 71 35-40
REPRISE (557-2; "Sail On
Sailor"): 73 75-100
REPRISE (0998; "Cool, Cool
Water"): 71 45-50
REPRISE (1310; "I Can Hear
Music"): 74 30-50
WHAT'S IT ALL ABOUT (449/450 &
507/508): 20-22
(Public service radio station issues. Program disc
449/450 has The Beach Boys on one side and Dr.
Hook on the flip. 507/508 features The Beach Boys
on one side and The Rolling Stones on the other.)
Picture Sleeves
BROTHER (1001; "Heroes &
Villains"): 67 50-100
CAPITOL (4777; "Surfin'
Safari"): 62 20-30
CAPITOL (4880; "Ten Little
Indians"): 62 75-100
CAPITOL (5000 series,
except 5561): 63-66 10-20

CAPITOL (5561; "Barbara
Ann"): 65 ....$90-125
CARIBOU: 79-85 3-5
EPs: 7-Inch 33/45rpm
BROTHER (1; "Radio Spot Backing
Tracks"): 73 225-250
(Promotional issue only.)
CAPITOL (189; "Best Of The Beach
Boys"): 66 15-20
(With an "LLP" prefix. Jukebox issue only.)
CAPITOL (1981; "Surfer Girl"): 63 45-55
CAPITOL (2186; "10 Little
Indians"): 64 300-325
(One side of this EP contains selections by Ray An-
thony.)
CAPITOL (2027; "Shut Down,
Vol. 2"): 64 45-55
CAPITOL (2269; "The Beach Boys
Today"): 65 50-75
(Jukebox issue only.)
CAPITOL (2293/94; "Beach Boys'
Party"): 65 125-150
(Jukebox issue only.)
CAPITOL (2545; "Best Of The Beach
Boys"): 66 50-75
(With a "DU" prefix. Jukebox issue only.)
CAPITOL (2545; "Best Of The Beach
Boys"): 66 15-20
CAPITOL (2754/55; "Brian Wilson Introduces
Selections"): 64 350-375
(Promotional issue only. Includes selections from
"Beach Boys Concert" & "Beach Boys Songbook.")
CAPITOL (5267; "4 By The Beach
Boys"): 66 35-45
REPRISE (2118; "Mount Vernon &
Fairway"): 73 8-10
(Originally packaged with Reprise LP 2118, "Hol-
land.")
ROCK SHOPPE ("The Beach
Years"): 75 75-100
(Demo disc for "A Six Hour Radio Special." Also
contains excerpts by Jan & Dean, Dick Dale & The
Surfaris, narrated by Roger Christian. Promotional
issue, pressed in a quantity of 200 copies.)
WARNER BROS (422; "Sunflower Promo
Spots"): 70 100-125
WARNER BROS (534; "Vote
'72"): 72 35-45
(Promotional issue only.)
WHAT'S IT ALL ABOUT: 20-25
(Promotional issue only.)
LPs: 10/12-Inch 33rpm
ACCORD: 83 5-8
BROTHER (9001; "Smiley
Smile"): 67 15-20
CAPITOL (133; "20/20"): 69 10-20

CAPITOL (133; "20/20"): *69* $30-35
(With an "SKAO-8" prefix. Capitol Record Club
issue.)

CAPITOL (253; "Close Up"): *69* 35-40

CAPITOL (442; "Good
Vibrations"): *70* 20-25

CAPITOL (500; "All Summer Long/
California Girls"): *70* 8-10

CAPITOL (701; "Dance, Dance, Dance/
Fun, Fun, Fun"): *71* 8-10

CAPITOL (1808 through 1998): *63-67* . . 10-15
(With a "DT" prefix.)

CAPITOL (1808 through 1998): *75-78* 5-8
(With an "SM" prefix.)

CAPITOL (1808 through 1998): *62-63* . . 20-35
(With a "T" or "ST" prefix.)

CAPITOL (2027; "Shut Down,
Volume 2"): *63* 8-15
(With a "DT" prefix.)

CAPITOL (2027; "Shut Down,
Volume 2"): *75* 5-8
(With an "SM" prefix.)

CAPITOL (2027; "Shut Down,
Volume 2"): *63* 15-20
(With a "T" or "ST" prefix.)

CAPITOL (2110; "All Summer
Long"): *64* 25-30
(With *Don't Break Down*. On this pressing, *Don't
Back Down* was incorrectly shown as *Don't Break
Down*.)

CAPITOL (2110; "All Summer
Long"): *64* 15-20
(With "Don't Back Down" shown correctly.)

CAPITOL (2164; "Beach Boys' Christmas
Album"): *75* 5-8
(With an "SM" prefix.)

CAPITOL (2164; "Beach Boys' Christmas
Album"): *64* 20-35
(With a "T" or "ST" prefix.)

CAPITOL (2198; "Beach Boys
Concert"): *64* 10-15

CAPITOL (2269; "The Beach Boys
Today"): *65* 15-20
(With a "T" or "DT" prefix.)

CAPITOL (2354; "Summer Days &
Summer Nights"): *65* 20-35
(With a "T" or "DT" prefix.)

CAPITOL (2398; "Beach Boys
Party"): *65* 30-35
(With a "SMAS" prefix. Price includes 15 bonus
photos. Deduct $8-12 if these photos are missing.)

CAPITOL (2398; "Beach Boys
Party"): *65* 20-30
(With a "DMAS" prefix. Price includes 15 bonus
photos. Deduct $8-12 if these photos are missing.)

CAPITOL (2458; "Pet Sounds"): *66* $15-20
(With a "T" or "DT" prefix.)

CAPITOL (2545; "Best Of The Beach
Boys"): *66* 10-15
(With a "T" or "DT" prefix.)

CAPITOL (2706; "Best Of The Beach
Boys, Volume 2"): *67* 10-15
(With a "T" or "DT" prefix.)

CAPITOL (2813; "Beach Boys Deluxe
Set"): *67* 100-125
(With a "TCL" prefix.)

CAPITOL (2813; "Beach Boys Deluxe
Set"): *67* 35-40
(With a "DTCL" prefix.)

CAPITOL (2859; "Wild Honey"): *67* 10-15
(With a "T" or "DT" prefix.)

CAPITOL (ST-8-2891; "Smiley
Smile"): *69* 60-75
(With an "ST-8" prefix. Capitol Record Club issue.)

CAPITOL (2893; "Stack-o-
Tracks"): *68* 100-150
(With music-lyrics booklet.)

CAPITOL (2893; "Stack-o-
Tracks"): *68* 50-75
(Without music-lyrics booklet.)

CAPITOL (2893; "Stack-o-
Tracks"): *69* 100-125
(With an "ST-8" prefix. Capitol Record Club issue.)

CAPITOL (2895; "Friends"): *68* 10-15

CAPITOL (2945; "Best Of The Beach
Boys, Volume, 3"): *68* 35-40

CAPITOL (3352; "Sunflower"): *70* 30-35
(With an "SKAO-9" prefix. Capitol Record Club
issue.)

CAPITOL (6994; "Golden Years Of
The Beach Boys"): *75* 25-30
(TV mail-order offer.)

CAPITOL (92639; "Still
Cruisn"): *89* 5-8

CAPITOL (10000 through 12000
series): *78-86* 5-10

CAPITOL (153477; "Rarities"): *75* 20-25
(RCA Record Club issue.)

CAPITOL (233559; "Endless
Summer"): *74* 20-25
(RCA Record Club issue.)

CAPITOL (233593; "American
Summer"): *75* 20-25
(RCA Record Club issue.)

CAPITOL (511384; Spirit Of
America"): *75* 15-20

CARIBOU: *78-85* 5-10

ERA: *69* 12-18

EVEREST: *81* 5-8

MFSL: *84* 15-25

PICKWICK: *72-75* 8-12

REPRISE (2083; "Carl & The Passions - So
Tough/Pet Sounds") : *72* $10-12
REPRISE (2118; "Holland"): *73* 15-20
(With *Mount Vernon & Fairway* EP.)
REPRISE (2118; "Holland"): *73* 8-12
(Without *Mount Vernon & Fairway* EP.)
REPRISE (2166; "Wild Honey/
20-20"): *74* 8-10
REPRISE (2166; "Friends/
Smiley Smile"): *74* 8-10
REPRISE (2223; "Good Vibrations/Best
Of The Beach Boys"): *75* 8-10
REPRISE (2251; "15 Big
Ones"): *76* 8-10
REPRISE (2258; "Love You"): *77* 8-10
REPRISE (2268; "M.I.U. Album"): *78* 8-10
REPRISE (6382;
"Sunflower"): *70* 8-12
REPRISE (6453; "Surf's Up"): *71* 20-25
(Capitol Record Club issue.)
REPRISE (6484; "The Beach Boys
In Concert"): *73* 8-10
RONCO: *78* 8-10
SEARS (608; "Summertime
Blues"): *70* 100-125
(Sold only at Sears retail stores.)
SESSIONS: *80* 15-20
SPRINGBOARD: *72* 5-8
WAND (688, "Greatest
Hits"): *72* 10-15

Promotional LPs

BROTHER (9431; "Good Vibrations From
The Beach Boys"): *86* 10-15
(Sunkist promotional issue.)
CAPITOL (1; "Open House"): *78* 175-200
CAPITOL (2754/5; "Beach Boys'
Concert"): *64* 300-350
CAPITOL (3123; "Silver Platter
Service"): *64* 75-100
(With selections by The Hollyridge Strings.)
CAPITOL (3133; "Silver Platter
Service"): *64* 125-150
("Beach Boys Christmas Special.")
CAPITOL (3266; "Silver Platter
Service"): *67* 75-100
CARIBOU (1024; "Keepin' The Summer
Alive"): *80* 45-50
CRAWDADDY ("Brian Wilson
Interview"): *77* 90-100
MORE MUSIC (03-179-72; "Good
Vibrations From London"): 50-60
MUTUAL RADIO ("Dick Clark Presents
The Beach Boys"): *81* 150-175
(A 3-LP boxed set.)

REPRISE ("Radio Spot Backing Tracks For
Beach Boys In Concert"): *73* $225-250
Members: Brian Wilson; Carl Wilson; Dennis Wilson; Mike Love; Al Jardine.
Note: Promos NOT listed separately are priced in the same range as commercial issues.
Also see ANNETTE
Also see ANTHONY, Ray
Also see BEATLES / Beach Boys / Buddy Holly
Also see BEATLES / Beach Boys / Kingston Trio
Also see CAMPBELL, Glen
Also see CHICAGO
Also see CLAYTON, Merry
Also see DR. HOOK
Also see FLAME
Also see JAN & DEAN / Beach Boys
Also see JETT, Joan, & The Blackhearts
Also see KENNY & THE CADETS
Also see PETERSEN, Paul
Also see ROLLING STONES
Also see ROTH, David Lee
Also see SURVIVORS
Also see WILSON, Brian
Also see WILSON, Carl
Also see WILSON, Dennis

**BEACH BOYS / Dick Dale /
Surfaris / Surf Kings**
LPs: 10/12-Inch 33rpm
GUEST STAR (1433; "The Beach
Boys"): *63* 15-25
Also see DALE, Dick
Also see SURFARIS

**BEACH BOYS & FRANKIE VALLI
& 4 SEASONS**
Singles: 7-Inch
FBI: *84* 3-5
Also see 4 SEASONS

BEACH BOYS & LITTLE RICHARD
Singles: 7-Inch
CRITIQUE: *87* 2-5
Also see LITTLE RICHARD

BEACH BOYS / Carl Wilson
LPs: 10/12-Inch 33rpm
BROTHER (2083; "Pet Sounds/
So Tough"): *72* 10-20
Also see WILSON, Carl

BEACH BOYS / Tony & Joe
Singles: 7-Inch
ERA: *70* 2-4
Also see BEACH BOYS
Also see TONY & JOE

BEACH BUMS
Singles: 7-Inch
ARE YOU KIDDING ME?: *66* $20-30
Member: Bob Seger.
Also see SEGER, Bob

BEACON STREET UNION
Singles: 7-Inch
MGM: *67-69* 4-6
RTP: *69* 3-5
LPs: 10/12-Inch 33rpm
MGM: *68* 15-25
Members: John Lincoln Wright; Robert Rhodes;
Paul Tartachny; Wayne Ulaky; Richard Weisberg.

BEAR, Edward: see EDWARD BEAR

BEAR ESSENCE STARRING
MARIANNA
Singles: 12-Inch 33/45rpm
MOBY DICK: *84* 4-6

BEARS
LPs: 10/12-Inch 33rpm
I.R.S.: *88* 5-8

BEASLEY, Walter
Singles: 7-Inch
POLYDOR: *88* 1-3
LPs: 10/12-Inch 33rpm
POLYDOR: *88* 5-8

BEAST
LPs: 10/12-Inch 33rpm
COTILLION: *69* 10-12
EVOLUTION: *70* 8-10

BEAT, B: see B. BEAT GIRLS

BEAT FARMERS
LPs: 10/12-Inch 33rpm
MCA/CURB: *87* 5-8
RHINO: *85* 5-8

BEATLES
Singles: 12-Inch 33/45rpm
ULTIMIX (120: "Twist And Shout"): *88* . 40-60
(Promotional issue only.)
Singles: 7-Inch
APPLE: *71-75* 3-5
ATCO (6302; "Sweet Georgia
Brown"): *64* 25-35
(Shown as by "The Beatles With Tony Sheridan.")
ATCO (6308; "Ain't She Sweet"): *64* 8-12
(Shown as by "The Beatles - Vocal By John
Lennon.")
ATLANTIC: *83-86* 1-3
CAPITOL (Orange, black or
purple label): *75-86* 2-3
(Includes reissues of 1964-1975 material and
original pressings of 1975-1986 releases.)

CAPITOL (2056; "Hello Goodbye"): *67* ...$4-6
(Orange/yellow "swirl" label.)
CAPITOL (2056; "Hello Goodbye"): *68* ...8-10
(Red/orange "target" label.)
CAPITOL (2138; "Lady Madonna"): *68* 4-6
(Orange/yellow "swirl" label.)
CAPITOL (2138; "Lady Madonna"): *68* ...8-10
(Red/orange "target" label.)
CAPITOL (5100; "Movie Medley"/"Fab
Four On Film"): *81* 60-70
(First issued with *Movie Medley* backed with *Fab
Four On Film*, which was the Beatles talking about
the film *A Hard Day's Night*. With a "B" prefix.)
CAPITOL (5100; "Movie Medley"/"I'm Happy
Just To Dance With You"): *81* 2-3
(With a "B" prefix.)
CAPITOL (5107; "Movie Medley"): *82* 2-3
(With a "B" prefix.)
CAPITOL (5189; "Love Me Do"): *82* 2-3
(With a "B" prefix. This recent Capitol 5000 series
differs from the 5000 series of 1964 by its use of
the "B" prefix.)
CAPITOL (5112 through 5964): *64-67* 8-12
(Price here is for orange/yellow swirl label issues.)
CAPITOL (5112; "I Want To Hold
Your Hand"): *84* 2-3
(*I Want To Hold Your Hand* was reissued as a
STEREO single in 1984. Even though the reissue is
on the orange/yellow label, it has black print
around the border of the label. 1964 issues have
this print in white letters.)
CAPITOL (5112 through 5964): *68* 12-15
(Red/orange target label issues.)
CAPITOL (5555; "We Can Work It
Out"): *68* 450-500
(Red and white "Starline" label. Issued in error.)
CAPITOL (6061 through 6066): *65* 25-35
(Green label "Starline" series.)
CAPITOL (6278 through 6300): *81* 2-3
(Blue label "Starline" series.)
CAPITOL (72144; "All My
Loving"): *72* 80-100
(An error in production created a U.S. pressing of
the Canadian release, *All My Loving/This Boy*.)
COLLECTABLES: *82* 2-3
DECCA (31382; "My
Bonnie"): *62* 2000-3000
(Shown as by Tony Sheridan and the Beat
Brothers. Note: Price is for a *COMMERCIAL*, not
promotional, issue. Commercial copies are on
Decca's black label with silver print and a multi-
color stripe across the center of the label. Black and
silver Decca labels without the other colors are
bootlegs.)

IBC (0082; "Murray The 'K' & The
Beatles As It Happened"): *76* $4-6
MGM (13213; "My Bonnie"): *64* 10-15
(Shown as by The Beatles With Tony Sheridan.)
MGM (13227; "Why"): *64* 15-20
(Shown as by The Beatles With Tony Sheridan.)
MURRAY THE "K" & THE BEATLES
(33 Single): *64* 20-25
(Reissued in 1976 as IBC 0082.)
OLDIES 45: *64* 5-8
SWAN (4152; "She Loves You"): *63* .. 150-200
(White label, with red print. Titles are in quotes.
Does NOT have "Don't Drop Out" on label.)
SWAN (4152; "She Loves You"): *63* .. 125-175
(White label, with red print. No quotes on titles.
Does NOT have "Don't Drop Out" on label.)
SWAN (4152; "She Loves You"): *63* .. 100-150
(White label, with red print. No quotes on titles.
Says "Don't Drop Out" on label.)
SWAN (4152; "She Loves You"): *63* .. 100-150
(White label, with blue print. No quotes on titles.
Says "Don't Drop Out" on label.)
SWAN (4152; "She Loves You"): *64* 10-20
(Black label.)
SWAN (4182; "Sie Liebt Dich"): *64* 35-45
(With "She Loves You" following "Sie Liebt Dich"
on the same line. White label with red print.)
SWAN (4182; "Sie Liebt Dich"): *64* 30-60
(With "She Loves You" under "Sie Liebt Dich" on
a separate line. White label with orange print.)
SWAN (4182; "Sie Liebt Dich"): *64* 25-35
(With "She Loves You" under "Sie Liebt Dich" on
a separate line. White label with red print.)
TOLLIE: *64* 15-25
(Black label.)
TOLLIE: *64* 25-30
(Yellow label with blue print.)
TOLLIE: *64* 30-40
(Yellow label, black print. Label name in brackets.)

TOLLIE: *64* $12-18
(Yellow label with black print. Label name is either
in a box or is by itself, with no lines, box or brack-
ets.)
TOLLIE: *64* 20-25
(Yellow label with green print. Label name is all
uppercase.)
TOLLIE: *64* 15-18
(Yellow label with green print. Label name is all
lowercase.)
VEE JAY (498; "Please Please
Me"): *63* 500-600
(Showing group as The "BEATTLES." With thin
lettering and oval label logo.)
VEE JAY (498; "Please Please
Me"): *63* 350-400
(Showing group as The "BEATTLES." With bold
lettering and oval label logo.)
VEE JAY (498; "Please Please
Me"): *63* 500-600
(Showing group as The "BEATTLES." With
'brackets' label logo.)
VEE JAY (498; "Please Please
Me"): *63* 350-400
(Showing group as The "BEATLES." With thin let-
tering and oval label logo.)
VEE JAY (498; "Please Please
Me"): *63* 400-500
(Showing group as The "BEATLES." With
'brackets' label logo.)
VEE JAY (498; "Please Please
Me"): *63* 600-700
(Showing group as The "BEATLES." With thin let-
tering and oval label logo. Catalog number, at bot-
tom of label, is preceded by the number symbol:
"#498.")
VEE JAY (522; "From Me To
You"): *63* 125-150
(Black label with horizontal silver lines.)
VEE JAY (522; "From Me To
You"): *63* 75-100
(Black label. With rainbow circle.)
VEE JAY (581; "Please Please
Me"): *64* 100-125
(Purple label.)
VEE JAY (581; "Please Please Me"): *64* . 50-75
(White label.)
VEE JAY (581; "Please Please Me"): *64* . 30-40
(Yellow label.)
VEE JAY (581; "Please Please Me"): *64* . 15-20
(Black label with horizontal silver lines.)
VEE JAY (581; "Please Please Me"): *64* . 12-15
(Black label. No rainbow circle.)
VEE JAY (581; "Please Please Me"): *64* . 20-25
(Black label with rainbow circle.)

VEE JAY (587; "Do You Want To Know
A Secret"): *64* **$30-40**
(Yellow label.)
VEE JAY (587; "Do You Want To Know
A Secret"): *64* **15-20**
(Black label with horizontal silver lines.)
VEE JAY (587; "Do You Want To Know
A Secret"): *64* **10-15**
(Black label. No horizontal lines. With either "Vee
Jay" or "VJ" logo.)
VEE JAY (587; "Do You Want To Know
A Secret"): *64* **25-30**
(Black label. No rainbow circle. Brackets Vee Jay
logo.)
VEE JAY (587; "Do You Want To Know
A Secret"): *64* **15-20**
(Black label. No rainbow circle. Oval Vee Jay
logo.)
VEE JAY (587; "Do You Want To Know
A Secret"): *64* **12-16**
(Black label with rainbow circle.)

Picture Sleeves

APPLE (Except 2531): *68-70* **12-18**
APPLE (2531; "Ballad Of John &
Yoko"): *69* **15-20**
ATCO (6308; "Ain't She Sweet"): *64* . **100-125**
CAPITOL/HOLIDAY INN
SLEEVE: *64* **250-300**
(Promotional sleeve, pictures the four Beatles on
front and their first three Capitol LPs on the back.
Not known to have been issued containing any par-
ticular single.)
CAPITOL (2056; "Hello Goodbye"): *67* . **18-20**
CAPITOL (2138; "Lady Madonna"): *68* . **12-18**
CAPITOL (4000 series, except 4506): *76* . . **4-6**
CAPITOL (4506; "Girl"): *78* **10-15**
CAPITOL (5100; "Movie Medley"/
"Fab Four On Film"): *81* **10-15**
(With a "B" prefix.)
CAPITOL (5107; "Movie Medley"/"I'm Happy
Just To Dance With You"): *81* **2-3**
(With a "B" prefix.)
CAPITOL (B-5189; "Love Me Do"): *82* . . . **2-3**
(With a "B" prefix. This recent Capitol 5000 series
differs from the 5000 series of 1964 by its use of
the "B" prefix.)
CAPITOL (5112; "I Want To Hold
Your Hand"): *64* **20-30**
CAPITOL (5112; WMCA Radio Promotional
Sleeve): *64* **650-750**
(Back of sleeve pictures WMCA dee jays. Front
side is identical to standard commercial issue.)
CAPITOL (5112; "I Want To Hold
Your Hand"): *84* **2-3**
(This reissue sleeve is clearly dated "1984" in
lower left corner.)

CAPITOL (5150; "Can't Buy Me
Love"): *64* **$250-300**
CAPITOL CUSTOM ("Music City
KFWBeatles"): *64* **550-600**
(Promotional sleeve for the "Souvenir Record"
from KFWB and Wallichs Music City.)
CAPITOL (5222; "A Hard Day's
Night"): *64* **20-25**
CAPITOL (5234; "I'll Cry Instead"): *64* . . **35-45**
CAPITOL (5235; "And I Love
Her"): *64* **30-35**
CAPITOL (5255; "Slow Down"): *64* **35-40**
CAPITOL (5327; "I Feel Fine"): *64* **12-15**
CAPITOL (5371; "Eight Days A
Week"): *65* **10-12**
CAPITOL (5407; "Ticket To Ride"): *65* . . **35-50**
CAPITOL (5439; "Leave My Kitten
Alone"): *85* **450-500**
CAPITOL (5476; "Help"): *65* **15-20**
CAPITOL (5498; "Yesterday"): *65* **12-18**
CAPITOL (5555; "We Can Work It
Out"): *65* **15-20**
CAPITOL (5587; "Nowhere Man"): *66* . . **12-18**
CAPITOL (5651; "Paperback
Writer"): *66* **12-18**
CAPITOL (5715; "Yellow
Submarine"): *66* **12-18**
CAPITOL (5810; "Penny Lane"): *67* **25-30**
CAPITOL (5964; "All You Need Is
Love"): *67* **8-12**
COLLECTABLES: *82* **2-3**
IBC (0082; "Murray The 'K' & The
Beatles As It Happened"): *76* **4-6**
MGM (13213; "My Bonnie"): *64* **35-40**
MGM (13227; "Why"): *64* **75-100**
MURRAY THE "K" & THE
BEATLES: *64* **60-75**
(Reissued in 1976 as IBC 0082.)
SWAN: *63* **30-35**
TOLLIE: *64* **35-40**

VEE JAY SPECIAL CHRISTMAS
SLEEVE: *64* $30-40
(Standard center-cut paper sleeve printed with the
Beatles' faces and "We Wish You A Merry
Christmas And A Happy New Year." Issued with
assorted Vee Jay singles during the holiday season.)
VEE JAY (581; "Please Please Me"
Commercial Issue): *64* 100-125
(Pictures the four Beatles.)
VEE JAY (581; "Please Please Me"
Promotional Issue): *64* 500-600
(Reads "The Record That Started Beatlemania"
across the top. Does not picture the group.)
VEE JAY (587; "Do You Want To Know
A Secret"): *64* 35-40

Promotional Singles

APPLE ("Let It Be"): *70* 20-25
(Identified as "Beatles Promo 1970." A one-sided
promo issue.)
ATCO (6302; "Sweet Georgia
Brown": *64* 75-125
ATCO (6308; "Ain't She
Sweet"): *64* 90-100
BACKSTAGE (1100 series,
except 1112 and 1122): *82-83* 8-10
(Picture discs.)
BACKSTAGE (1112; "*Oui* Presents
The Silver Beatles"): *82* 5-8
(*Oui* magazine promotional giveaway. Features a
Like Dreamers Do/Love Of The Loved montage.
Mailing also included *Oui* News Release and sub-
scription form. This is not a picture disc single, as
the other Backstage 1100 singles are.)
BACKSTAGE (1122; "Like
Dreamers Do"): *82* 25-35
(Picture disc, with photo of Penthouse "Pet.")
CAPITOL (2056; "Hello
Goodbye"): *67* 60-80
CAPITOL (2138; "Lady
Madonna"): *68* 50-75
CAPITOL (4274; "Got To Get You
Into My Life"): *76* 20-25
CAPITOL (4347; "Helter
Skelter"): *76* 20-25
CAPITOL (4347; "Ob-La-Di,
Ob-La-Da"): *76* 20-25
CAPITOL (4506; "Girl"): *78* 75-90
CAPITOL (4612; "Sgt. Pepper's Lonely
Hearts Club Band"-"With A Little
Help From My Friends"): *78* 12-15

CAPITOL (5100; "Movie Medley"/
"Fab Four On Film"): *81* $15-20
(First issued with *Movie Medley* backed with *Fab
Four On Film*, which was The Beatles talking
about the film *A Hard Day's Night*. Later issues
had *I'm Happy Just To Dance With You* on the flip
side.)
CAPITOL (5112; "I Want To Hold
Your Hand"): *84* 8-10
(Though the promo of this single is actually num-
bered 9076, we have it listed both ways for your
convenience.)
CAPITOL (PB-5189; "Love Me
Do"): *82* 10-12
(With a "PB" prefix. Promo copies of this issue
were on commercial stock labels, but are quickly
identified by the printing of an "Intro" time of :13
on the right side of the label. Also, store stock
copies were B-5189, not PB-5189.)
CAPITOL (5624; "Twist &
Shout"): *86* 8-10
CAPITOL (5810; "Penny Lane"): *67* ...90-100
CAPITOL (5964; "All You Need
Is Love"): *67* 70-85
(This promo, as well as many Capitol issues by
other artists, was shipped in a "Rush" paper sleeve.
It's possible a slight premium may be placed on
these sleeves, although they were NOT identified
in any way as a Beatles item.)
CAPITOL (9076; "I Want To Hold
Your Hand"): *84* 8-10
CAPITOL (9758; "Movie
Medley"): *81* 30-35
(With an "SPRO" prefix.)
CAPITOL CUSTOM (2637; "Music City
KFWBeatles"): *64* 200-250
(Radio KFWB & Wallichs Music City promo disc,
The Beatles Talking/You Can't Do That.)
CREATIVE RADIO (B-1; "The Beatle
Invasion"): 10-20
(Radio show demo. Flip side is *Inside Paul Mc-
Cartney*.)
DECCA (31382; "My Bonnie"): *62* ...500-600
(Shown as by Tony Sheridan And The Beat
Brothers. Pink label with black lettering.)
MBRF (55551; "Decade"): *72* 100-150
(Contains repeat spots for the *Beatles 1962-1966*
and *Beatles 1967-1970*.)
MGM (13213; "My Bonnie"): *64* 90-100
(Shown as by The Beatles With Tony Sheridan.)
MGM (13227; "Why"): *64* 75-125
(Shown as by The Beatles With Tony Sheridan.)
SWAN (4152; "She Loves
You"): *63* 150-200
SWAN (4152; "I'll Get You"): *64* 175-225
(One-sided pressing. Flip side has blank grooves.)

SWAN (4182; "Sie Liebt Dich"): *64* . $125-150
TOLLIE:(9001; "Twist & Shout") *64* . . 100-125
TOLLIE (9008; "Love Me Do"):*64* . . . 100-125
UNITED ARTISTS (2357; "A Hard Day's
Night"): *64* **800-1100**
UNITED ARTISTS (42370; "Let It
Be"): *70* **400-700**
(Contains three radio advertisements for the film.)
VEE JAY (8; "Anna"/"Ask Me
Why"): *64* **2500-3000**
VEE JAY (498; "Please Please
Me"): *63* **350-450**
VEE JAY (522; "From Me To
You"): *63* **100-150**
VEE JAY (581; "Please Please Me,"
Purple label): *64* **100-150**
VEE JAY (581; "Please Please Me,"
White label): *64* **100-125**
VEE JAY (587; "Do You Want To Know
A Secret"): *64* **100-125**
WHAT'S IT ALL ABOUT: **15-20**
Plastic Soundsheets/Flexi-Discs
AMERICOM: *69* **350-450**
(4-inch "Pocket Discs.")
EVA-TONE (8464; "All My Loving"): *82* . . **5-8**
(Back side reads either "Compliments Of
Musicland" or "Compliments Of Discount.")
EVA-TONE (8464; "All My
Loving"): *82* **15-20**
(Back side reads "Compliments Of Sam Goody.")
EVA-TONE (830771; "Till There
Was You"): *83* **3-5**
EVA-TONE (420826; "All My
Loving"): *82* **5-8**
(Back side reads either "Compliments Of
Musicland" or "Compliments Of Discount.")
EVA-TONE (420826; "All My
Loving"): *82* **15-20**
(Back side reads "Compliments Of Sam Goody.")
EVA-TONE (420827; "Magical Mystery
Tour"): *82* **5-8**
(Back side reads either "Compliments Of
Musicland" or "Compliments Of Discount.")
EVA-TONE (420827; "Magical Mystery
Tour"): *82* **15-20**
(Back side reads "Compliments Of Sam Goody.")
EVA-TONE (420828; "Rocky
Raccoon"): *82* **5-8**
(Back side reads either "Compliments Of
Musicland" or "Compliments Of Discount.")
EVA-TONE (420828; "Rocky
Raccoon"): *82* **15-20**
(Back side reads "Compliments Of Sam Goody.")
EVA-TONE (1214825; "The Beatles
German Medley): *83* **30-40**

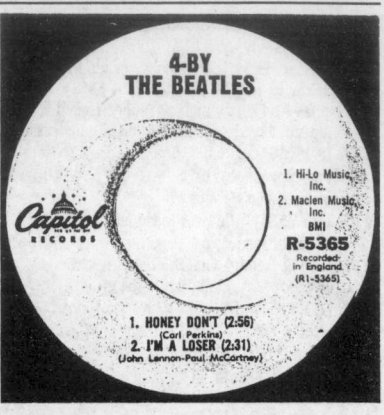

OFFICIAL BEATLES FAN CLUB ("1964
Season's Greetings From The
Beatles"): *64* $175-200
OFFICIAL BEATLES FAN CLUB ("1965
Beatles Christmas Record"): *65* 100-125
OFFICIAL BEATLES FAN CLUB ("1966
Season's Greetings From The
Beatles"): *66* .100-125
OFFICIAL BEATLES FAN CLUB ("1967
Christmas Time Is Here
Again"): *67* 100-125
OFFICIAL BEATLES FAN CLUB ("1968
Beatles Christmas Record"): *68* 50-75
OFFICIAL BEATLES FAN CLUB ("1969
Happy Christmas"): *69* 40-50
SILHOUETTE: *86* .6-10
EPs: 7-Inch 33/45rpm
CAPITOL (EAP 1-2121; "Four By The
Beatles"): *64* .100-150
CAPITOL (R-5365; "4-By The
Beatles"): *65* .100-125
VEE JAY (VJEP 1-903; "Souvenir Of
Their Visit To America"): *64* 65-80
(Solid black label with either oval or block style
Vee Jay logo.)
VEE JAY (VJEP 1-903; "Souvenir Of
Their Visit To America"): *64* 80-100
(Solid black label with brackets Vee Jay logo.)
VEE JAY (VJEP 1-903; "Souvenir Of
Their Visit To America"): *64* 45-50
(Black label with rainbow color-band. All four
song titles in same size type.)
VEE JAY (VJEP 1-903; "Souvenir Of
Their Visit To America"): *64* 60-75
(Black label with rainbow color-band. Has "Ask
Me Why" in much larger type size than other titles.)

Promotional EPs

CAPITOL 33 COMPACT (2047; "Meet
The Beatles"): *64* **$175-225**
(Jukebox issue only.)

CAPITOL 33 COMPACT (2080; "Beatles
Second Album"): *64* **175-225**
(Jukebox issue only.)

CAPITOL 33 COMPACT (2108; "Something
New"): *64* **250-300**
(Jukebox issue only.)

CAPITOL 33 COMPACT (2548/49;
"Open-End Interview"): *64* **550-600**
(Issued with a paper sleeve and script, which repre-
sents about $300-$400 of the value.)

CAPITOL 33 COMPACT (2598/99 "Second
Open-End Interview"): *64* **500-600**
(Issued with a paper sleeve and script, which repre-
sents about $300-$400 of the value.)

CAPITOL (2720/21; "The Beatles
Introduce New Songs"): *64* **500-600**
(A 45 rpm EP with John Lennon about Cilla
Black's *It's For You*, and Paul talking about Peter
and Gordon's *I Don't Want To See You Again*.)

CAPITOL 33 COMPACT (2905/06; "The
Capitol Souvenir Record"): *64* **250-300**
(Issued with a paper sleeve and script, which represents about $100-$125 of the value. Contains excerpts of 15 different songs by 15 artists, including
the Beatles.)

VEE JAY (903; "Souvenir Of
Their Visit To America"): *64* **100-150**
(White label with blue print. Price is for disc only.)

VEE JAY (903; "Souvenir Of
Their Visit To America"): *64* **1500-2000**
(Special sleeve in which some copies of the EP
were supplied to radio stations.)

LPs: 10/12-Inch 33rpm

ALBUM GLOBE (8146; "Happy
Michaelmas"): *81* **8-12**

APPLE (101; "The Beatles"): *68* **25-30**
(With Capitol logo at bottom of label.)

APPLE (101; "The Beatles"): *71* **20-25**
(Without Capitol logo at bottom of label.)

APPLE (153; "Yellow Submarine"): *69* .. **12-18**
(With Capitol logo at bottom of label.)

APPLE (153; "Yellow Submarine"): *71* .. **10-12**
(Without Capitol logo at bottom of label.)

APPLE (383; "Abbey Road"): *69* **12-18**
(With Capitol logo at bottom of label.)

APPLE (383; "Abbey Road"): *71* **10-12**
(Without Capitol logo at bottom of label.)

APPLE (385; "Hey Jude"): *70* **15-25**
(With Capitol logo at bottom of label.)

APPLE (385; "Hey Jude"): *71* **10-12**
(Without Capitol logo at bottom of label.)

APPLE (ST-2047; "Meet The
Beatles"): *71* **$12-18**
(With Capitol logo at bottom of label.)

APPLE (ST-2047; "Meet The
Beatles"): *71* **10-12**
(Without Capitol logo at bottom of label.)

APPLE (ST-2080; "The Beatles'
Second Album"): *71* **12-18**
(With Capitol logo at bottom of label.)

APPLE (ST-2080; "The Beatles'
Second Album"): *71* **10-12**
(Without Capitol logo at bottom of label.)

APPLE (ST-2108; "Something
New"): *71* **12-18**
(With Capitol logo at bottom of label.)

APPLE (ST-2108; "Something
New"): *71* **10-12**
(Without Capitol logo at bottom of label.)

APPLE (ST-2222; "The Beatles'
Story"): *71* **12-18**
(With Capitol logo at bottom of label.)

APPLE (ST-2228; "The Beatles'
Story"): *71* **10-12**
(Without Capitol logo at bottom of label.)

APPLE (ST-2228; "Beatles '65"): *71* ... **12-18**
(With Capitol logo at bottom of label.)

APPLE (ST-2228; "Beatles '65): *71* ... **10-12**
(Without Capitol logo at bottom of label.)

APPLE (ST-2309; "The Early
Beatles"): *71* **12-18**
(With Capitol logo at bottom of label.)

APPLE (ST-2309; "The Early
Beatles"): *71* **10-12**
(Without Capitol logo at bottom of label.)

APPLE (ST-2358; "Beatles VI"): *71* **12-18**
(With Capitol logo at bottom of label.)

APPLE (ST-2358; "Beatles VI"): *71* **10-12**
(Without Capitol logo at bottom of label.)

APPLE (ST-2386; "Help"): *71* **12-18**
(With Capitol logo at bottom of label.)

APPLE (ST-2386; "Help"): *71* **10-12**
(Without Capitol logo at bottom of label.)

APPLE (ST-2442; "Rubber Soul"): *71* .. **12-18**
(With Capitol logo at bottom of label.)

APPLE (ST-2442; "Rubber Soul"): *71* .. **10-12**
(Without Capitol logo at bottom of label.)

APPLE (ST-2576; "Revolver"): *71* **12-18**
(With Capitol logo at bottom of label.)

APPLE (ST-2576; "Revolver"): *71* **10-12**
(Without Capitol logo at bottom of label.)

APPLE (SMAS-2653; "Sgt. Pepper's
Lonely Hearts Club Band"): *71* **12-18**
(With Capitol logo at bottom of label.)

APPLE (SMAS-2653; "Sgt. Pepper's
Lonely Hearts Club Band"): *71* **10-12**
(Without Capitol logo at bottom of label.)

APPLE (SMAL-2835; "Magical Mystery
Tour"): *71* $12-18
(With Capitol logo at bottom of label.)
APPLE (SMAL-2835; "Magical Mystery
Tour"): *71* **10-12**
(Without Capitol logo at bottom of label.)
APPLE (3403; "The Beatles/
1962-1966"): *73* **15-20**
APPLE (3404; "The Beatles/
1967-1970"): *73* **15-20**
APPLE (34001; "Let It Be"): *70* **10-15**
ATCO (169; "Ain't She Sweet"): *64* ... **75-100**
(Monaural. Also contains selections by the Swal-
lows.)
ATCO (169; "Ain't She Sweet"): *64-69* **100-150**
(Stereo. Also contains selections by the Swallows.)
AUDIO FIDELITY (339; "First Movement,"
Picture disc): *82* **8-12**
AUDIO RARITIES (2452; "The Complete
Silver Beatles"): *82* **6-10**
AUDIO RARITIES (30003; "The Silver
Beatles"): *82* **15-20**
(Picture disc.)
BACKSTAGE (Except 1111): *82-83* **10-15**
BACKSTAGE (1111; "Like Dreamers
Do"): *82* **20-25**
(3-LP set. Contains two picture discs and a white
vinyl LP.)
BACKSTAGE (1111; "Like Dreamers
Do"): *82* **30-45**
(3-LP set. Contains two picture discs and a gray
vinyl LP.)
BACKSTAGE (1111; "Like Dreamers
Do"): *82* **30-40**
(3-LP set. Includes any of the custom issues,
which had various logos printed on the reverse side
of the picture discs.)
BACKSTAGE (1111; "Like Dreamers
Do"): *82* **15-20**
(3-LP set. No custom artwork on picture disc.
With gatefold cover.)
BACKSTAGE (1111; "Like Dreamers
Do"): *82* **12-15**
(A 2-LP set. With standard cover.)
BACKSTAGE (1111; "Like Dreamers
Do"): *82* **20-25**
CAPITOL (101; "The Beatles"): *76* **10-12**
(Orange label.)
CAPITOL (101; "The Beatles"): *78* **8-12**
(Purple label.)
CAPITOL (101; "The Beatles"): *84* **6-10**
(Black label.)
CAPITOL (153; "Yellow
Submarine"): *76* **8-10**
(Orange label.)

CAPITOL (153; "Yellow
Submarine"): *78* $6-10
(Purple label.)
CAPITOL (153; "Yellow
Submarine"): *84* 5-8
(Black label.)
CAPITOL (383; "Abbey Road"): *76* 8-10
(Orange label.)
CAPITOL (383; "Abbey Road"): *78* 6-10
(Purple label.)
CAPITOL (383; "Abbey Road"): *84* 5-8
(Black label.)
CAPITOL (385; "Hey Jude"): *76* 8-10
(Orange label.)
CAPITOL (385; "Hey Jude"): *78* 6-10
(Purple label.)
CAPITOL (385; "Hey Jude"): *84* 5-8
(Black label.)
CAPITOL (T-2047; "Meet The
Beatles"): *64* 30-45
(Monaural.)
CAPITOL (ST-2047; "Meet The
Beatles"): *64* 20-25
(Stereo. Black label, white print around border.)
CAPITOL (ST-2047; "Meet The
Beatles"): *69* 20-30
(Green label.)
CAPITOL (ST-2047; "Meet The
Beatles"): *76* 8-12
(Orange label.)
CAPITOL (ST-2047; "Meet The
Beatles"): *78* 6-10
(Purple label.)
CAPITOL (ST-2047; "Meet The
Beatles"): *84* 5-8
(Black label, black print around border.)
CAPITOL (ST-8-2047; "Meet The
Beatles"): *64-69* 25-30
(Capitol Record Club issue.)
CAPITOL (T-2080; "The Beatles'
Second Album"): *64* 30-40
(Monaural.)
CAPITOL (ST-2080; "The Beatles'
Second Album"): *64* 20-25
(Stereo. Black label, white print around border.)
CAPITOL (ST-2080; "The Beatles'
Second Album"):·*69* 20-30
(Green label.)
CAPITOL (ST-2080; "The Beatles'
Second Album"): *76* 8-12
(Orange label.)
CAPITOL (ST-2080; "The Beatles'
Second Album"): *78* 6-10
(Purple label.)

CAPITOL (ST-2442; "Rubber
Soul"): 69 . . . . $20-25
(Green label.)

CAPITOL (ST-2442; "Rubber
Soul"): 76 8-12
(Orange label.)

CAPITOL (ST-2442; "Rubber
Soul"): 78 6-10
(Purple label.)

CAPITOL (ST-2442; "Rubber Soul"): 84 . . 5-8
(Black label, black print around border.)

CAPITOL (ST-8-2442; "Rubber
Soul"): 65-69 25-35
(Capitol Record Club issue.)

CAPITOL (T-2553; "Yesterday And
Today"): 66 1500-2000
(Monaural. FIRST STATE "Butcher cover" issues.)

CAPITOL (ST-2553; "Yesterday And
Today"): 66 3500-4500
(Stereo. FIRST STATE "Butcher cover" issues.)

CAPITOL (T-2553; "Yesterday And
Today"): 66 300-600
(Monaural. PASTE OVER or PEELED "Butcher
cover" copies.)

CAPITOL (ST-2553; "Yesterday And
Today"): 66 750-1000
(Stereo. PASTE OVER or PEELED "Butcher
cover" copies.)

Note: The wide range of values exists here due to
varied opinions on the practice of peeling the
"Trunk cover" from the "Butcher cover." The exper-
tise used in the peeling is also a major factor affect-
ing the value of these LPs.

CAPITOL (T-2553; "Yesterday And
Today"): 66 25-40
(Monaural. "Trunk cover.")

CAPITOL (ST-2553; "Yesterday And
Today"): 66 20-25
(Stereo. Black label, white print around border.
"Trunk cover.")

CAPITOL (ST-2553; "Yesterday And
Today"): 69 20-25
(Green label.)

CAPITOL (ST-2553; "Yesterday And
Today"): 76 8-12
(Orange label.)

CAPITOL (ST-2553; "Yesterday And
Today"): 78 6-10
(Purple label.)

CAPITOL (ST-2553; "Yesterday And
Today"): 84 5-8
(Black label, black print around border.)

CAPITOL (ST-8-2553; "Yesterday And
Today"): 66-69 25-35
(Capitol Record Club issue.)

CAPITOL (T-2576; "Revolver"): 66 . . . . $30-40
(Monaural.)

CAPITOL (ST-2576; "Revolver"): 66 20-25
(Stereo. Black label, white print around border.)

CAPITOL (ST-2576; "Revolver"): 69 20-25
(Green label.)

CAPITOL (ST-2576; "Revolver"): 76 8-12
(Orange label.)

CAPITOL (ST-2576; "Revolver"): 78 6-10
(Purple label.)

CAPITOL (ST-2576; "Revolver"): 84 5-8
(Black label, black print around border.)

CAPITOL (ST-8-2576;
"Revolver"): 66-69 25-35
(Capitol Record Club issue.)

CAPITOL (MAS-2653; "Sgt. Pepper's Lonely
Hearts Club Band"): 67 50-100
(Monaural.)

CAPITOL (SMAS-2653; "Sgt. Pepper's Lonely
Hearts Club Band"): 67 30-40
(Stereo. Black label, white print around border.)

CAPITOL (SMAS-2653; "Sgt. Pepper's Lonely
Hearts Club Band"): 69 18-22
(Green label.)

CAPITOL (SMAS-2653; "Sgt. Pepper's Lonely
Hearts Club Band"): 76 8-12
(Orange label.)

CAPITOL (SMAS-2653; "Sgt. Pepper's Lonely
Hearts Club Band"): 78 6-10
(Purple label.)

CAPITOL (SMAS-2653; "Sgt. Pepper's Lonely
Hearts Club Band"): 84 5-8
(Black label, black print around border.)

CAPITOL (MAL-2835; "Magical Mystery
Tour"): 67 75-150
(Monaural.)

CAPITOL (SMAL-2835; "Magical Mystery
Tour"): 67 30-40
(Stereo. Black label, white print around border.)

CAPITOL (SMAL-2835; "Magical Mystery
Tour"): 69 18-22
(Green label.)

CAPITOL (SMAL-2835; "Magical Mystery
Tour"): 76 8-12
(Orange label.)

CAPITOL (SMAL-2835; "Magical Mystery
Tour"): 78 6-10
(Purple label.)

CAPITOL (SMAL-2835; "Magical Mystery
Tour"): 84 5-8
(Black label, black print around border.)

CAPITOL (3403; "The Beatles/
1962-1966"): 78 8-12

CAPITOL (3404; "The Beatles/
1967-1970"): 78 8-12

CAPITOL (11537; "Rock 'N' Roll
  Music"): 76 .... $12-18
CAPITOL (11638; "Beatles At The
  Hollywood Bowl"): 77 8-10
CAPITOL (11711; "Love Songs"): 77 6-10
CAPITOL (11840; "Sgt. Pepper's Lonely
  Hearts Club Band"): 78 15-20
  (Picture disc.)
CAPITOL (11841; "Abbey
  Road"): 78 20-30
  (Colored vinyl.)
CAPITOL (11842; "The Beatles/
  1962-1966"): 78 20-25
CAPITOL (11843; "The Beatles/
  1967-1970"): 78 20-25
CAPITOL (11900; "Abbey Road,"
  Picture disc): 78 20-30
CAPITOL (11921; "A Hard Day's
  Night"): 79 8-10
  (Purple label.)
CAPITOL (11921; "A Hard Day's
  Night"): 84 5-8
  (Black label, black print around border.)
CAPITOL (11922; "Let It Be"): 79 8-10
  (Purple label.)
CAPITOL (11922; "Let It Be"): 84 5-8
  (Black label, black print around border.)
CAPITOL (12009; "Rarities"): 78 40-60
CAPITOL (12060; "The Beatles
  Rarities"): 80 6-10
CAPITOL (12199; "Reel Music"): 82 6-10
CAPITOL (12245; "The Beatles 20
  Greatest Hits"): 82 8-12
  (Purple label.)
CAPITOL (12245; "The Beatles 20
  Greatest Hits"): 84 5-8
  (Black label.)
CAPITOL (16020; "Rock 'N' Roll
  Music, Volume I"): 80 5-8
CAPITOL (16021; "Rock 'N' Roll
  Music, Volume II"): 80 5-8
CAPITOL (91135;
  "Past Masters"): 88 10-12
CAPITOL/APPLE: 68-75 10-12
  (A "Capitol/Apple" label is simply the Apple label
  with the Capitol logo near the bottom of the label.)
CAPITOL RECORD CLUB ISSUES
  (Except ST-8-2553): 25-35
  (Includes Record Club issues on the Capitol label
  only. Releases on other labels, available through
  the club, are listed by their label name.)
CAPITOL RECORD CLUB (ST-8-2553;
  "Yesterday And Today"): 66 40-45
CICADELIC: 85-87 5-10

CLARION (601; "The Amazing Beatles
  & Other Great English Sounds"): 66 .. $60-75
  (Stereo. Back cover lists song titles. Also contains
  selections by the Swallows.)
CLARION (601; "The Amazing Beatles
  & Other Great English
  Sounds"): 66 75-100
  (Stereo. Back cover does NOT list song titles. Also
  contains selec tions by the Swallows.)
CLARION (601; "The Amazing Beatles
  & Other Great English Sounds"): 66 ... 50-75
  (Monaural. Also contains selections by the Swal-
  lows.)
CREATIVE RADIO ("The Beatle
  Invasion"): 5 35-4
  (3-LP set, includes 12 x 19 poster.)
GREAT NORTHWEST MUSIC CO: 78 .. 5-8
H.S.R.D.: 82 8-12
HALL OF MUSIC: 81 12-18
HERITAGE SOUND: 82 8-10
I-N-S RADIO NEWS ("American Tour
  With Ed Rudy #2"): 80 12-18
LINGASONG: 77 10-12
LLOYDS ("The Great American Tour-1965
  Live Beatlemania Concert"): 65 125-175
  (With selections by The Liverpool Lads.)
MFSL (1; "The Beatles, The
  Collection"): 82 375-425
  (13-LP boxed set. Includes booklet and alignment
  tool.)
MFSL (023; "Abbey Road"): 79 25-50
MFSL (047; "Magical Mystery
  Tour"): 81 20-40
MFSL (072; "The Beatles"): 82 20-30
MFSL/UHQR (100; "Sgt. Pepper's Lonely
  Hearts Club Band"): 82 200-400
  (Silver label. Boxed set. Reads "UHQR" near top.)
MFSL (100; "Sgt. Pepper's Lonely
  Hearts Club Band"): 84 15-25
  (White label. No "UHQR" on label.)
MFSL (101; "Please Please Me"): 84 15-25
MFSL (102; "With The Beatles"): 84 ... 15-25
MFSL (103; "A Hard Day's
  Night"): 84 15-25
MFSL (104; "Beatles For Sale"): 84 15-25
MFSL (105; "Help"): 84 15-25
MFSL (106; "Rubber Soul"): 84 15-25
MFSL (107; "Revolver): 84 15-25
MFSL (108; "Yellow Submarine"): 84 .. 15-25
MFSL (109; "Let It Be"): 84 15-25
MGM (E-4215; "The Beatles With
  Tony Sheridan & Guests"): 64 45-55
  (Monaural. With selections by Tony Sheridan and
  by the Titans.)

MGM (SE-4215; "The Beatles With
Tony Sheridan & Guests"): *64* **$75-100**
(Stereo. With selections by Tony Sheridan and by
the Titans.)

METRO (M-563; "This Is Where It
Started"): *66* **40-50**
(Also contains selections by Tony Sheridan and by
the Titans.)

METRO (MS-563; "This Is Where It
Started"): *66* **50-75**
(Also contains selections by Tony Sheridan and by
the Titans.)

MUSIC INTERNATIONAL: *85* **5-8**

PAC: *81* **15-20**

PBR INT'L: *78* **20-30**

PHOENIX 10: *82* **5-8**

PHOENIX 20: *83* **5-8**

PICKWICK (Except 90071: *78-79* **8-12**

PICKWICK (90071; "Recorded Live In
Hamburg, 1962, Volume 3"): *78* **15-20**

POLYDOR (4504; "In The Beginning,
Circa 1960"): *70* **12-15**
(With gatefold cover.)

POLYDOR (4504; "In The Beginning,
Circa 1960"): *81-84* **5-8**
(With standard cover.)

POLYDOR (93199; "In The Beginning,
Circa 1960"): *70* **15-18**
(Capitol Record Club issue.)

RPN (RADIO PULSEBEAT NEWS)
"American Tour
With Ed Rudy #2"): *64* **40-50**
(This LP was occasionally issued with a "Teen
Talk" booklet. The value of the booklet is ap-
proximately the same as for the LP. This edition
has NO pictures of The Beatles on the LP cover.)

RPN (RADIO PULSEBEAT NEWS) ("1965
Talk Album, Ed Rudy With New
U.S. Tour"): *65* **50-75**

RAVEN: *81* **5-8**

SAVAGE (69; "The Savage Young
Beatles"): *68* **75-100**
(Label is yellow. Cover is orange.)

SAVAGE (69; "The Savage Young
Beatles"): *68* **40-50**
(Label is orange. Cover is yellow.)

SILHOUETTE: *81-84* **8-12**

STERLING PRODUCTIONS (6481;
"I Apologize"): *66* **70-80**
(Price includes bonus 8x10 photo, which represents
$5-$15 of the value.)

UNITED ARTISTS (UAL-3366; "A Hard
Day's Night"): *64* **30-50**
(Monaural.)

UNITED ARTISTS (UAS-6366; "A Hard
Day's Night"): *64* **$30-50**
(Stereo. Black label.)

UNITED ARTISTS (UAS-6366; "A Hard
Day's Night"): *68-70* **20-25**
(Stereo. Pink and orange or black and orange label.)

UNITED ARTISTS (UAS-6366; "A Hard
Day's Night"): *71* **10-15**
(Stereo. Tan label.)

UNITED ARTISTS (UAS-6366; "A Hard
Day's Night"): *77* **8-12**
(Stereo. Orange and yellow label.)

UNITED ARTISTS (90828; "A Hard
Day's Night"): *65* **75-100**
(Capitol Record Club issue.)

VEE JAY (202; "Hear The Beatles
Tell All"): *64* **50-60**
(Monaural. Black label with rainbow color-band.)

VEE JAY (202; "Hear The Beatles
Tell All"): *79* **5-8**
(Stereo.)

VEE JAY (202; "Hear The Beatles
Tell All"): *87* **5-10**
(Picture disc.)

VEE JAY (1062; "Introducing The
Beatles"): *63* **500-750**
(Monaural. With *Love Me Do* and *P.S. I Love You.*
Back cover pictures 25 other Vee Jay albums.)

VEE JAY (1062; "Introducing The
Beatles"): *63* **800-1200**
(Stereo. With *Love Me Do* and *P.S. I Love You.*
Back cover pictures 25 other Vee Jay albums.)

VEE JAY (1062; "Introducing The
Beatles"): *63-64* **250-400**
(Monaural. With *Love Me Do* and *P.S. I Love You.*
Back cover is blank. May be regarded as a promo-
tional issue; however, nothing on the LP supports
that theory.)

VEE JAY (1062; "Introducing The
Beatles"): *63-64* **600-800**
(Stereo. With *Love Me Do* and *P.S. I Love You.*
Back cover is blank. May be regarded as a promo-
tional issue; however, nothing on the LP supports
that theory.)

VEE JAY (1062; "Introducing The
Beatles"): *64* **75-100**
(Monaural. With *Love Me Do* and *P.S. I Love You.*
Back cover lists contents. Has brackets style label
logo.)

VEE JAY (1062; "Introducing The
Beatles"): *64* **60-75**
(Monaural With *Love Me Do* and *P.S. I Love You.*
Back cover lists contents. Oval style label logo.)

VEE JAY (1062; "Introducing The
Beatles"): *64* **150-200**
(Stereo. With *Ask Me Why* and *Please Please Me.*
Covers either label style or design.)

VEE JAY (1062; "Introducing The
Beatles"): *64* $40-60
(Monaural, rainbow color-band label. With *Ask Me
Why* and *Please Please Me*.)

VEE JAY (1062; "Introducing The
Beatles"): *64* 65-80
(Monaural, black label, no color-band. With *Ask
Me Why* and *Please Please Me*. Has brackets style
label logo.)

VEE JAY (1062; "Introducing The
Beatles"): *64* 35-45
(Monaural, black label, no color-band. With *Ask
Me Why* and *Please Please Me*. Label logo has
neither oval nor brackets.)

VEE JAY (1092; "Songs, Pictures
And Stories"): *64* 50-75
(Monaural.)

VEE JAY (1092; "Songs, Pictures
And Stories"): *64* 150-200
(Stereo.)

Promotional LPs

ABC/WATERMARK ("Ringo's Yellow
Submarine"): *84* 700-800
(A set of 24 LPs in eight boxed sets, featuring
Ringo Starr telling the story of The Beatles. Issued
to radio stations only.)

APPLE (SBC-100; "The Beatles'
Christmas Album"): *70* 90-100
(Special issue for Beatles' fan club members.)

APPLE FILMS (004; The Yellow
Submarine"): *69* 400-450
(Contains the advertisements used on radio stations
to promote the film.)

ATCO (33-169; "Ain't She
Sweet"): *64* 300-350
(Also contains selections by the Swallows.)

BACKSTAGE (Colored vinyl): *82* 20-30

CAPITOL ("Help, Open-End
Interview"): *65* 550-650
(Issued with programmer's script.)

CAPITOL ("The Platinum Beatles
Collection"): *84* 475-500
(18-LP boxed set.)

CAPITOL (SPRO-8969;
"Rarities"): *78* .35-40

CAPITOL (SMAS-11638; "Beatles At The
Hollywood Bowl"): *77* 90-100

CAPITOL (12199; "Reel Music"): *82* 45-55
(Colored vinyl.)

CAPITOL/EMI (BC-13; "The Beatles
Collection"): *78* 250-300
(14-LP boxed set.)

I-N-S RADIO NEWS (1; "Beatlemania
Tour Coverage"): *64* 150-200
(An open-end interview. Includes a script.)

LINGASONG (7001; "Live! At The
Star-Club"): *77* $90-100
(Blue vinyl.)

LINGASONG (7001; "Live! At The
Star-Club"): *77* 75-90
(Red vinyl.)

LINGASONG (7001; "Live! At The
Star-Club"): *77* 30-40
(Black vinyl.)

ORANGE (12880; "The Silver
Beatles"): *85* 35-45

RAVEN: *81* 15-20

UNITED ARTISTS (UA-HELP; "United
Artists Presents 'Help!'"): *65* 400-450
(Contains the advertisements used on radio stations
to promote the film.)

UNITED ARTISTS (UA-HELP INT; "Special
Open-End Interview"): *65* 500-550
(Price includes script and programming informa-
tion, which represents about $50-$75 of the value.)

UNITED ARTISTS (2359/60; "Special Beatles
Half Hour Open End Interview"): *64* . 500-550
(Price includes 12-pages of script and programming information, which represents about $50-$75
of the value.)

UNITED ARTISTS (2362/63; "United Artists
Presents *A Hard Day's Night*): *64* . . . 400-450
(Contains the advertisements used on radio stations
to promote the film.)

UNITED ARTISTS (UAL 6366; "A Hard
Day's Night"): *64* 300-350
(White label.)

Members: John Lennon; Paul McCartney; George
Harrison; Pete Best; Ringo Starr.

Also see BEST, Pete

Also see HARRISON, George

Also see LENNON, John

Also see MARTIN, George

Also see McCARTNEY, Paul

Also see PRESLEY, Elvis / Beatles

Also see PRESTON, Billy

Also see SHANKAR, Ravi

Also see STARR, Ringo

BEATLES / Beach Boys / Buddy Holly
LPs: 10/12-Inch 33rpm

CREATIVE RADIO SHOWS (Demo of
"Specials"): *79* 75-100
(Promotional issue only.)

Also see BEACH BOYS

Also see HOLLY, Buddy

BEATLES / Beach Boys / Kingston Trio
Plastic Soundsheets/Flexi-Discs:
EVA-TONE (8464; "A Surprise Gift From
The Beatles, Beach Boys, And The
Kingston Trio"): *64* $300-350
(Plastic soundsheet.)
EVA-TONE (8464; "A Surprise Gift From
The Beatles, Beach Boys, And The
Kingston Trio"): *64* 200-250
(5-inch edition of the above plastic soundsheet.)
Also see BEACH BOYS
Also see KINGSTON TRIO

BEATLES / 4 Seasons
LPs: 10/12-Inch 33rpm
VEE JAY (DX-30; "Beatles Vs.
The Four Seasons"): *64* 250-400
(Monaural.)
VEE JAY (DXS-30; "Beatles Vs.
The Four Seasons"): *64* 500-750
(Stereo.)
Note: Price ranges include a bonus Beatles poster,
which represents $80-$100 of the value.
Also see 4 SEASONS

BEATLES / Frank Ifield
LPs: 10/12-Inch 33rpm
VEE JAY (1085; "The Beatles &
Frank Ifield"): *64* 750-1000
(Monaural. Pictures the Beatles on cover.)
VEE JAY (1085; "The Beatles &
Frank Ifield"): *64* 2000-3000
(Stereo. Pictures the Beatles on cover.)
VEE JAY (1085; "Jolly What!
The Beatles & Frank Ifield"): *64* 75-90
(Monaural. Pictures an Englishman on cover.)
VEE JAY (1085; "Jolly What!
The Beatles & Frank Ifield"): *64* 150-200
(Stereo. Pictures an Englishman on cover.)
Also see IFIELD, Frank

BEATLES / Jerry Blabber
Singles: 7-Inch
QUEST: *65* 5-10

BEATMASTER
Singles: 7-Inch
TOMMY BOY: *84* 1-3

BEATTY, E.C
Singles: 7-Inch
CAMPBELL: *64* 3-5
COLONIAL: *59-61* 8-10

BEAU, Toby: see TOBY BEAU

BEAU BRUMMELS
Singles: 7-Inch
AUTUMN: *64-65* 5-10
PEP: 1-3

RHINO: *82* $1-3
WARNER BROS: *66-75* 4-8
Picture Sleeves
PEP: 1-3
RHINO: *82* 2-4
LPs: 10/12-Inch 33rpm
ACCORD: *82* 5-8
AUTUMN: *65* 35-40
JAS: 8-10
POST: 8-10
RHINO: *81-82* 5-8
VAULT (114; "Best Of The Beau
Brummels"): *67* 25-30
VAULT (121; "Beau Brummels,
Vol. 44"): *68* 15-20
WARNER BROS (Except 1644): *67-75* ..20-25
WARNER BROS (1644; "Beau
Brummels '66"): *66* 30-35
Members: Sal Valentino; Ron Elliott; Ron
Meagher; Dee Mulligan; John Petersen.

BEAU COUP
Singles: 7-Inch
AMHERST: *87* 1-3
ROCK 'N' ROLL: *84-85* 1-3

BEAU-MARKS
Singles: 7-Inch
MAINSTREAM: *68* 3-5
PORT: *62* 4-6
RUST: *61* 4-6
SHAD: *60* 8-10
TIME: *59* 30-40

BEAUMONT, Jimmy
(Jimmy Beaumont & The Skyliners)
Singles: 7-Inch
BANG: *66* 4-6
CAPITOL: *74* 2-4
COLPIX: *61* 4-6
DRIVE: *76* 2-4
GALLANT: 4-6
MAY: *61-63* 4-6
Also see SKYLINERS

BEAUVOIR, Jean
Singles: 12-Inch 33/45rpm
COLUMBIA: *86* 4-6
Singles: 7-Inch
COLUMBIA: *86* 1-3
LPs: 10/12-Inch 33rpm
COLUMBIA: *86* 5-8
Also see LITTLE STEVEN & THE
DISCIPLES OF SOUL
Also see PLASMATICS

BE-BOP DELUXE
Singles: 7-Inch
HARVEST: 75-78 .... $1-3
LPs: 10/12-Inch 33rpm
HARVEST (Black vinyl): 76-78 5-8
HARVEST (Colored vinyl): 77-78 15-20
Promotional LPs
HARVEST (8531; "Be Bop's
Biggest"): 75 25-30
Members: Richard Brown; Robert Bryan; Nicholas Chatterton-Dew; Andrew Clarke; Simon Fox; Paul Jeffreys; Milton R. James; Bill Nelson; Ian Parkin; Charles Tumahai.

BECK, Jeff
(Jeff Beck Group)
Singles: 7-Inch
EPIC (10000 series): 67-69 4-6
EPIC (50000 series): 75-76 3-5
LPs: 10/12-Inch 33rpm
ACCORD: 81 5-8
EPIC (Except 43000
series): 69-85 5-12
EPIC (43000 series): 80-82 12-15
(Half-speed mastered LPs.)
MFP: 8-10
SPRINGBOARD: 75 5-8
Promotional LPs
EPIC (151; "Everything You Always
Wanted To Hear"): 76 15-20
Also see BECK, BOGERT & APPICE
Also see DONOVAN
Also see HARRISON, George / Dave Edmunds / Jeff Beck
Also see HONEYDRIPPERS
Also see LORD SUTCH
Also see POWELL, Cozy
Also see WOOD, Ron
Also see YARDBIRDS

BECK, Jeff, & Rod Stewart
Singles: 7-Inch
EPIC: 85 1-3
Also see BECK, Jeff
Also see STEWART, Rod

BECK, Jimmy
Singles: 7-Inch
ASTRA: 4-6
CHAMPION: 59 10-20

BECK, Joe
Singles: 7-Inch
POLYDOR: 77 1-3
LPs: 10/12-Inch 33rpm
KUDU: 75 8-10
POLYDOR: 77 5-8

VERVE/FORECAST: 69 .... $10-12
Also see PHILLIPS, Esther, & Joe Beck

BECK, BOGERT & APPICE
Singles: 7-Inch
EPIC: 73 2-4
LPs: 10/12-Inch 33rpm
EPIC: 73 10-12
Members: Jeff Beck; Tim Bogert; Carmine Appice.
Also see BECK, Jeff
Also see CACTUS
Also see VANILLA FUDGE

BECK FAMILY
Singles: 7-Inch
LE JOINT: 79 1-3

BECKHAM, Bob
Singles: 7-Inch
DECCA: 59-63 2-4
MONUMENT: 67 1-3
SMASH: 65 1-3
Picture Sleeves
DECCA: 59-60 4-8
LPs: 10/12-Inch 33rpm
DECCA: 59 12-15
Singles: 7-Inch
CASABLANCA: 80 1-3
LPs: 10/12-Inch 33rpm
CASABLANCA: 80 5-8

BECKMEIER BROTHERS
Singles: 7-Inch
CASABLANCA: 79 1-3
LPs: 10/12-Inch 33rpm
CASABLANCA: 79 5-8
Members: Fred Beckmeier; Steve Beckmeier.

BEE, Jimmy
(Jimmy Bee With Ernie Fields Jr.'s Orchestra)
Singles: 7-Inch
ALA: 73 2-4
CALLA: 76 1-3
KENT: 70 2-4
20TH CENTURY-FOX: 66-67 3-5
UNITED ARTISTS: 71 2-4

BEE GEES
Singles: 7-Inch
ATCO: 67-72 3-5
RSO: 73-84 1-3
WARNER BROS: 87 1-3
EPs: 7-Inch 33/45rpm
ATCO (4535; "Odessa"): 69 8-15
(Promotional issue only.)
ATCO (37264; "Rare, Precious &
Beautiful"): 69 8-15
(Promotional issue only.)

RSO (200; "Greatest Hits"): *79* **$5-10**
(Promotional issue only.)
LPs: 10/12-Inch 33rpm
ATCO (Except TL-ST-142): *67-72* **12-25**
ATCO (TL-ST-142; "Odessa"): *69* **30-50**
(Promotional issue only.)
RSO (Except 1): *73-84* **5-8**
RSO (1; "Words & Music"): **40-60**
(Promotional issue only.)
WARNER BROS: *87* **5-8**
Members: Barry Gibb; Maurice Gibb; Robin Gibb;
Vince Melouney; Colin Petersen.
Also see GIBB, Andy
Also see GIBB, Barry
Also see GIBB, Maurice
Also see GIBB, Robin
Also see SANG, Samantha

BEECHER, Johnny, & His
Buckingham Road Quintet
Singles: 7-Inch
CHARTER: *63* **3-5**
WARNER BROS: *63* **2-4**
LPs: 10/12-Inch 33rpm
CHARTER: *63* **10-20**

BEEFEATERS
Singles: 7-Inch
ELEKTRA: *64* **35-45**
Members: David Crosby; Gene Clark; Jim Mc-
Guinn.
Also see BYRDS

BEGINNING OF THE END
Singles: 7-Inch
ALSTON: *71-72* **2-4**
LPs: 10/12-Inch 33rpm
ALSTON: *71-76* **10-12**

BELAFONTE, Harry
Singles: 78rpm
JUBILEE: *54* **6-12**
RCA VICTOR: *52-57* **3-6**
ROOST (501; "Lean On Me"): *49* **8-15**
Singles: 7-Inch
COLUMBIA: *81* **1-3**
JUBILEE: *54* **10-20**
RCA VICTOR (0300 series): *57* **3-6**
RCA VICTOR (0400 through
0600 series): *71-72* **1-3**
RCA VICTOR (4000 & 5000
series): *52-55* **4-8**
RCA VICTOR (6000 & 7000
series): *55-62* **3-6**
RCA VICTOR (8000 & 9000
series): *62-67* **2-4**

Picture Sleeves
RCA VICTOR (Except 9200
series): *55-59* **$5-10**
RCA VICTOR (9200 series): *69* **3-5**
EPs: 7-Inch 33/45rpm
CAPITOL: *55* **15-20**
JUBILEE: *54* **20-25**
RCA VICTOR: *54-61* **10-20**
LPs: 10/12-Inch 33rpm
BOOK OF THE MONTH
RECORDS: *83* **15-20**
CAMDEN: *73-74* **5-10**
COLUMBIA: *81* **5-8**
CORONET: **8-15**
RCA VICTOR (0000 through 0900
series): *73* **5-10**
RCA VICTOR (1000 through 1900
series): *54-59* **15-25**
(With an "LPM" or "LSP" prefix.)
RCA VICTOR (2400 series): *78-81* **5-8**
(With an "AYL1" or "CPL1" prefix.)
RCA VICTOR (2000 & 3000 series,
except 2449): *60-67* **10-20**
(With an "LPM" or "LSP" prefix.)
RCA VICTOR (2449; "The Midnight
Special"): *62* **20-40**
(With Bob Dylan playing harmonica on the title
track, his first appearance on record.)
RCA VICTOR (4000 series): *68-71* **10-15**
RCA VICTOR (6000 series): *59-72* **15-25**
Also see COMO, Perry / Ames Brothers /
Harry Belafonte / Radio City Music Hall Orch.
Also see DYLAN, Bob

BELAFONTE, Harry, & Miriam
Makeba
LPs: 10/12-Inch 33rpm
RCA VICTOR: *65* **10-15**
Also see BELAFONTE, Harry
Also see MAKEBA, Miriam

BELEW, Adrian
LPs: 10/12-Inch 33rpm
ISLAND: *82-83* **5-8**

BELL, Archie
(Archie Bell & The Drells)
Singles: 12-Inch 33/45rpm
PHILADELPHIA INT'L: *79* **4-6**
PLAYHOUSE: *84* **4-6**
Singles: 7-Inch
ATLANTIC: *68-72* **2-4**
BECKETT: *81-84* **1-3**
EAST-WEST: **2-3**
GLADES: *73* **2-4**
OVIDE: *67* **3-8**

PHILADELPHIA INT'L: 76-79 . . . . $1-3
TSOP: 75-76 2-3
 LPs: 10/12-Inch 33rpm
ATLANTIC: 68-69 10-12
BECKETT: 81-84 5-8
PHILADELPHIA INT'L: 75-79 8-10
 Also see PHILADELPHIA INTERNATION-
AL ALL STARS

BELL, Benny
 Singles: 7-Inch
ENTERPRISE: 62 3-5
VANGUARD: 75 2-4

BELL, Jerry
 Singles: 7-Inch
MCA: 80-81 1-3

BELL, Madeline
 Singles: 7-Inch
ASCOT: 64-65 3-5
BRUT: 73 2-4
MOD: 67 3-5
PHILIPS: 67-68 2-4
PYE: 76 2-3
 LPs: 10/12-Inch 33rpm
PHILIPS: 68 15-18
PYE: 76 8-10
 Also see BLUE MINK
 Also see WATERS, Roger

BELL, Maggie
 Singles: 7-Inch
ATLANTIC: 73-74 2-4
SWAN SONG: 76 2-3
 LPs: 10/12-Inch 33rpm
ATLANTIC: 74 10-12
SWAN SONG: 75 8-10

BELL, Maggie, & Bobby Whitlock
 Singles: 7-Inch
SWAN SONG: 83-84 1-3
 Also see BELL, Maggie
 Also see WHITLOCK, Bobby

BELL, Randy
 Singles: 7-Inch
EPIC: 84 1-3

BELL, Rueben
 Singles: 7-Inch
ALARM: 75-77 2-3
DELUXE: 72-73 2-4
MURCO: 68 3-5
SILVER FOX: 69 2-4

BELL, Trudy
 Singles: 7-Inch
PHILIPS: 62-63 3-5

BELL, Vincent
 (Vinnie Bell & The Bell Men)
 Singles: 7-Inch
DECCA: 67-70 . . . . $2-5
INDEPENDENT: 60 5-10
MUSICOR: 64 2-4
VERVE: 63 3-5
 LPs: 10/12-Inch 33rpm
DECCA: 67-70 8-12
INDEPENDENT: 60 20-30
MUSICOR: 64 10-12
VERVE: 64 10-12

BELL, William
 Singles: 7-Inch
KAT FAMILY: 83-84 1-3
MERCURY: 76-77 2-3
STAX (Except 100 series): 67-74 2-4
STAX (100 series): 61-67 3-8
WILBE: 86 1-3
 LPs: 10/12-Inch 33rpm
KAT FAMILY: 83-84 5-8
MERCURY: 77 8-10
STAX: 67-74 10-12

BELL, William, & Janice Bullock
 Singles: 7-Inch
WILBE: 86 1-3
 Also see BULLOCK, Janice

BELL, William, & Judy Clay
 Singles: 7-Inch
STAX: 68 2-4
 Also see CLAY, Judy

BELL, William, & Mavis Staples
 Singles: 7-Inch
STAX: 69 2-4
 Also see STAPLES, Mavis

BELL, William, & Carla Thomas
 Singles: 7-Inch
STAX: 69-70 2-4
 Also see BELL, William
 Also see THOMAS, Carla

BELL & JAMES
 Singles: 12-Inch 33/45rpm
A&M: 79 4-6
LORIMAR: 80 4-6
 Singles: 7-Inch
A&M: 78-84 1-3
LORIMAR: 80 1-3
 LPs: 10/12-Inch 33rpm
A&M: 79-84 5-8
Members: Leroy Bell; Casey James.

Bellamy Brothers: (L-R) David Bellamy; Howard Bellamy

BELL NOTES
Singles: 7-Inch
AUTOGRAPH: *60* $4-6
ERIC: *73* 1-3
MADISON: *60* 4-6
TIME (Blue label): *59* 10-12
TIME (Red label): *59-60* 3-5
EPs: 7-Inch 33/45rpm
TIME (100; "I've Had It"): *59* 60-100
Members: Carl Bonura; Ray Ceroni; Lenny Giambalvo; Pete Kane; John Casey.

BELL SISTERS
Singles: 78rpm
BERMUDA: 4-6
RCA VICTOR: *50-53* 3-5
Singles: 7-Inch
BERMUDA: 4-6
RCA VICTOR: *50-53* 3-5
Also see RENE, Henri, & His Orchestra

BELLAMY, David
Singles: 7-Inch
WARNER BROS: *75* 2-3
Also see BELLAMY BROTHERS

BELLAMY BROTHERS
Singles: 7-Inch
CURB: *84* 1-3
ELEKTRA: *83* 1-3
MCA/CURB: *85-88* 1-3
WARNER BROS: *76-83* 1-3
LPs: 10/12-Inch 33rpm
ELEKTRA: *83* 5-8
MCA/CURB: *84-88* 5-8
WARNER BROS: *76-83* 8-10
Members: David Bellamy; Howard Bellamy.
Also see BELLAMY, David

BELLE, Regina
Singles: 7-Inch
COLUMBIA: *87-88* $1-3
ELEKTRA: *87* 1-3
LPs: 10/12-Inch 33rpm
COLUMBIA: *87-88* 5-8
Also see BRYSON, Peabo, & Regina Belle

BELLE EPOQUE
Singles: 7-Inch
BIG TREE: *78* 2-3

BELLE STARS
Singles: 12-Inch 33/45rpm
WARNER BROS: *83-84* 4-6
Singles: 7-Inch
WARNER BROS: *83-84* 1-3
LPs: 10/12-Inch 33rpm
WARNER BROS: *83-84* 5-8

BELLS
Singles: 7-Inch
MGM: *73* 2-4
POLYDOR: *70-73* 2-4
LPs: 10/12-Inch 33rpm
POLYDOR: *71-72* 10-12
Members: Jacki Ralph; Cliff Edwards; Frank Mills.
Also see MILLS, Frank

BELLUS, Tony
Singles: 7-Inch
ABC: *73* 1-3
COLLECTABLES: *81* 1-3
KING: *65* 3-5
NRC: *59-60* 5-8
Picture Sleeves
NRC (035; "Hey Little
Darlin"): *59* 20-30
NRC (051; "The Echo Of
An Old Song"): *60* 15-20
LPs: 10/12-Inch 33rpm
NRC: *60* 35-45

BELLY, P.J.
(Rob Gamble)
Singles: 7-Inch
NOR VA JAK: *87* 2-3

BELMONTS
(Belmonts With Dion)
Singles: 7-Inch
COLLECTABLES: *81* 1-3
CRYSTAL BALL: *79* 4-6
DOT: *68* 8-10
LAURIE: *75* 2-4
MOHAWK: *57* 20-25
ROULETTE: 1-3
SABINA (Except 521): *61-64* 8-12

SABINA (521 "Nothing In Return"): *64* . **$15-20**
SABINA: *61* **10-15**
(Sabrina changed its name to Sabina in 1961.)
STRAWBERRY: *76* **2-4**
SURPRISE: *61* **25-30**
UNITED ARTISTS (800 & 900
  series): *65* **5-8**
UNITED ARTISTS (50000
  series): *66* **10-12**
LPs: 10/12-Inch 33rpm
BUDDAH: *72* **25-50**
DOT: *69* **20-25**
SABINA: *62* **40-60**
STRAWBERRY: *78* **8-10**
  Also see DION & THE BELMONTS
  Also see SOUL, Jimmy / Belmonts

**BELMONTS, Freddy Cannon &
Bo Diddley**
Singles: 12-Inch 33/45rpm
ROCK & ROLL TRAVELLING
  SHOW: **2-4**
  Also see BELMONTS
  Also see CANNON, Freddy
  Also see DIDDLEY, Bo

BELOUIS SOME
Singles: 12-Inch 33/45rpm
CAPITOL: *85* **4-6**
Singles: 7-Inch
CAPITOL: *85* **1-3**
LPs: 10/12-Inch 33rpm
CAPITOL: *85* **5-8**

BELOYD
Singles: 7-Inch
20TH CENTURY-FOX: *77* **2-3**

BELTONES
Singles: 7-Inch
COLLECTABLES: *81* **1-3**
HULL (Black label): *57* **30-35**
HULL (Red label): *58* **15-20**
ROULETTE: *73* **1-3**

BELUSHI, John
Singles: 7-Inch
MCA: *78* **2-3**
  Also see BLUES BROTHERS
  Also see NATIONAL LAMPOON

BELVIN, Jesse
(Jesse Belvin & The Sharptones)
Singles: 78rpm
CASH: *56* **10-15**
HOLLYWOOD: *56* **15-25**
MODERN: *56* **5-8**
SPECIALTY: *52-53* **20-30**

Singles: 7-Inch
ALADDIN: *58* **$10-12**
CASH: *56* **25-35**
CLASS: *60* **3-5**
COLLECTABLES: *81* **1-3**
CUSTOM: **3-5**
ERIC: *73* **1-3**
HOLLYWOOD: *56* **35-45**
IMPACT: *62* **4-6**
JAMIE: *59* **4-8**
KENT: *59* **4-8**
KNIGHT: *59* **5-8**
MODERN: *56* **5-10**
RCA VICTOR (7000 series): *58-60* **5-10**
(With a "47" prefix.)
RCA VICTOR (7000 series): *59 60* **15 25**
(With a "61" prefix. Stereo.)
SPECIALTY (400 series): *52-53* **40-50**
SPECIALTY (500 series): *54-55* **12-15**
(Most Specialty singles are currently available,
using original catalog numbers.)
TENDER: *59* **15-20**
EPs: 7-Inch 33/45rpm
RCA VICTOR: *59-60* **20-35**
LPs: 10/12-Inch 33rpm
CAMDEN: *66* **12-15**
CORONET: **8-10**
CROWN: *60-63* **15-20**
RCA VICTOR (0900 series): *75* **8-10**
RCA VICTOR (2000 & 2100
  series): *59-60* **25-30**
UNITED: **10-12**
  Also see BENTON, Brook / Jesse Belvin
  Also see CHARGERS
  Also see CLIQUES
  Also see JESSE & MARVIN

BELVIN, Jesse, & Three Dots & A Dash
Singles: 78rpm
IMPERIAL (5164; "I'll Never Love
  Again"): *51* **25-50**

Singles: 7-Inch
IMPERIAL (5164; "I'll Never Love
  Again"): *51* **75-100**
  Also see BELVIN, Jesse

BENATAR, Pat
Singles: 12-Inch 33/45rpm
CHRYSALIS: *79-88* **4-6**
Singles: 7-Inch
CHRYSALIS: *79-88* **1-3**
SUNSHINE: *78* **4-8**
Picture Sleeves
CHRYSALIS: *79-88* **1-3**

LPs: 10/12-Inch 33rpm
CHRYSALIS: *79-88* $5-8
MFSL: *81* 20-40

BENNETT, Boyd
(Boyd Bennett & The Rockets; Boyd Bennett &
The Southlanders)
Singles: 78rpm
KING: *54-57* 5-10
Singles: 7-Inch
KING (1400 series): *54-55* 20-30
(Maroon labels.)
KING (1400 series): *56* 10-20
(Blue labels.)
KING (4000 series): *56-58* 10-15
KING (5000 series): *58-63* 5-10
MERCURY: *59-61* 5-10
EPs: 7-Inch 33/45rpm
KING (377; "Rock & Roll"): *57* 100-200
KING (383; "Rock & Roll"): *57* 100-200
LPs: 10/12-Inch 33rpm
KING (594; "Boyd Bennett"): *57* 800-1200

BENNETT, Joe, & The Sparkletones
Singles: 78rpm
ABC-PARAMOUNT: *57-58* 5-10
Singles: 7-Inch
ABC: *73* 2-4
ABC-PARAMOUNT: *57-58* 15-20
PARIS: *59-60* 10-15
LPs: 10/12-Inch 33rpm
MCA: *83* 5-8

BENNETT, Tony
Singles: 78rpm
COLUMBIA: *50-57* 3-6
Singles: 7-Inch
COLUMBIA (1600 series): 4-8
(Colored vinyl. Promotional issue only.)
COLUMBIA (06000 series): *86* 1-3
COLUMBIA (38000 through
41000 series): *50-61* 3-6
COLUMBIA (42000 through
45000 series): *61-70* 2-4
IMPROV: *75-77* 1-3
MGM: *73* 1-3
VERVE: *72-73* 1-3
Picture Sleeves
COLUMBIA (1600 series): 3-5
(Promotional issue only.)
COLUMBIA (40000 & 41000
series): *53-61* 5-10
COLUMBIA (42000 through 44000
series): *61-67* 3-6
IMPROV: *75* 1-3
LPs: 10/12-Inch 33rpm
COLUMBIA (Except 600 through

George Benson (Photo: Harris Savides)

1200 series): *59-86* $6-12
COLUMBIA (600 through
1200 series): *55-59* 10-20
FANTASY: 8-12
HARMONY: *69-73* 5-8
IMPROV: *75-78* 5-8
MGM: *73* 6-10
MGM/VERVE: *72* 6-10
MFSL: *84* 20-30
Also see GETZ, Stan

BENNETT, Tony, & Count Basie
EPs: 7-Inch 33/45rpm
COLUMBIA: *59* 6-10
LPs: 10/12-Inch 33rpm
COLUMBIA: *59* 10-20
Also see BENNETT, Tony

BENNETT, Tony / Al Tornello
LPs: 10/12-Inch 33rpm
GUEST STAR: *64* 5-10
Also see BENNETT, Tony

BENNO, Marc
Singles: 7-Inch
A&M: *71-79* 2-4
LPs: 10/12-Inch 33rpm
A&M: *70-79* 8-10
MCA: 5-8
Also see ASYLUM CHOIR

BENSON, George
Singles: 12-Inch 33/45rpm
WARNER BROS: *80-83* $4-6
Singles: 7-Inch
A&M: *68-70* 2-4
ARISTA: *77* 2-3
CTI: *75-78* 2-3
COLUMBIA: *66-67* 3-5
GROOVE: *54* 15-25
PRESTIGE: *64* 3-5
WARNER BROS: *76-88* 1-3
Picture Sleeves
WARNER BROS: *78-86* 1-3
LPs: 10/12-Inch 33rpm
A&M: *68-70* 8-12
CTI: *71-78* 8-10
COLUMBIA: *66-67* 8-10
(With a "CL" or "CS" prefix.)
COLUMBIA: *76* 5-8
(With a "CG" or "PC" prefix.)
MFSL: *78* 25-50
POLYDOR: *76* 5-8
VERVE: *69* 10-12
WARNER BROS: *75-88* 5-8
Also see FRANKLIN, Aretha, & George Benson
Also see MC DUFF, Brother Jack

BENT FABRIC: see FABRIC, Bent

BENTLEY, Erlene
Singles: 12-Inch 33/45rpm
MEGATONE: *83* 4-6
TVI: *84* 4-6
Singles: 7-Inch
MEGATONE: *83* 1-3

BENTON, Brook
Singles: 78rpm
EPIC: *56* 5-10
OKEH: *55* 5-10
Singles: 7-Inch
ALL PLATINUM: *76* 2-5
BRUT: *73* 3-5
COTILLION: *68-72* 3-6
EPIC: *56* 10-20
MGM: *72* 3-5
MERCURY (Monaural): *59-65* 5-10
MERCURY (Stereo): *60-61* 10-20
MUSICOR: *77* 2-5
OKEH: *55* 10-20
OLDE WORLD: *77-78* 2-4
RCA VICTOR: *65-67* 4-8
REPRISE: *67-68* 4-6
STAX: *74* 3-5

VIK: *57-58* $8-15
Picture Sleeves
MERCURY: *60-62* 5-10
RCA VICTOR: *65* 4-8
EPs: 7-Inch 33/45rpm
MERCURY: *59-61* 10-20
LPs: 10/12-Inch 33rpm
ALL PLATINUM: *76* 8-10
CAMDEN (Except 564): *70* 8-10
CAMDEN (564; "Brook Benton"): *60* ... 15-20
(With a "CAL" prefix.)
COTILLION: *70-72* 8-10
EPIC: *59* 15-20
HARMONY: *65* 8-12
MGM: *73* 8-10
MERCURY (MG & SR series): *59-65* .. 12-20
(With an "MG" or "SR" prefix.)
MERCURY: *84* 5-8
(With an "822" prefix.)
MUSICOR: *77* 8-10
OLDE WORLD: *77* 5-8
RCA VICTOR (APL1 series): *75* 8-10
(With an "APL1" prefix.)
RCA VICTOR (LPM/LSP series): *66* ... 10-12
(With an "LPM" or "LSP" prefix.)
REPRISE: *67-68* 8-12
WING: *66* 8-10
Also see KING CURTIS

BENTON, Brook / Jesse Belvin
LPs: 10/12-Inch 33rpm
CROWN: *63* 12-15
Also see BELVIN, Jesse

BENTON, Brook, & Damita Jo
Singles: 7-Inch
MERCURY: *63* 3-5
Also see DAMITA JO

BENTON, Brook, & Dinah Washington
Singles: 7-Inch
MERCURY: *60* 3-5
Picture Sleeves
MERCURY: *60* 4-8
EPs: 7-Inch 33/45rpm
MERCURY: *60* 10-15
LPs: 10/12-Inch 33rpm
MERCURY: *60* 15-25
Also see BENTON, Brook
Also see WASHINGTON, Dinah

BERG, Gertrude
LPs: 10/12-Inch 33rpm
AMY: *65* 6-12

BERGEN, Polly
Singles: 78rpm
COLUMBIA: *57* 2-4

RCA VICTOR: 50-51 .... $2-5
Singles: 7-Inch
COLUMBIA: 57-61 2-4
RCA VICTOR: 50-51 2-5
EPs: 7-Inch 33/45rpm
JUBILEE: 56 6-10
LPs: 10/12-Inch 33rpm
CAMDEN: 56 10-15
COLUMBIA: 57-61 10-15
HARMONY: 60 8-12
JUBILEE: 56 10-20
PHILIPS: 63 8-12
LPs: 10/12-Inch 33rpm
RKO: 59 8-15

BERLIN
Singles: 12-Inch 33/45rpm
GEFFEN: 83-84 4-6
Singles: 7-Inch
COLUMBIA: 86 1-3
GEFFEN: 82-86 1-3
I.R.S.: 80 1-3
LPs: 10/12-Inch 33rpm
ENIGMA ("Pleasure Victim"): 82 50-100
GEFFEN: 82-86 5-8

BERLIN PHILHARMONIC
Singles: 7-Inch
POLYDOR: 69 2-3
Member: Karl Boehm.

BERMAN, Shelley
LPs: 10/12-Inch 33rpm
METRO: 65 8-12
VERVE (15000 series): 59-64 10-20

BERMUDAS
Singles: 7-Inch
ERA: 64 4-6
Member: Rickie Page.

BERNARD, Chuck
Singles: 7-Inch
LAWRENCE: 67 3-5
SATELLITE: 65-66 3-5
ZODIAC: 70-71 2-4

BERNARD, Rod
(Rod Bernard & The Twisters)
Singles: 7-Inch
ABC: 74 1-3
ARBEE: 65-66 3-6
ARGO: 59 4-6
COLLECTABLES: 81 1-3
COPYRIGHT: 68 2-4
CRAZY CAJUN: 78 2-3
HALL: 61-64 3-5
HALLWAY: 61-64 3-5
JIN (105; "This Should Go On

Forever"): 59 .... $25-30
JIN (200 series): 74-76 2-3
MERCURY: 59-61 3-5
TEARDROP: 64-65 3-5
LPs: 10/12-Inch 33rpm
JIN: 50-60
Also see SHONDELLS / Rod Bernard / War-
ren Storm / Skip Stewart

BERNSTEIN, Elmer, Orchestra
Singles: 78rpm
DECCA: 56 2-5
Singles: 7-Inch
AVA: 62-65 2-3
CAPITOL: 59-60 2-3
CHOREO: 62 2-3
COLUMBIA: 65 2-3
DECCA: 56 3-6
DOT: 66 2-4
UNITED ARTISTS: 65-68 2-3
EPs: 7-Inch 33/45rpm
CAPITOL: 59-60 3-6
LPs: 10/12-Inch 33rpm
AVA (4; "Walk On The Wild Side"): 62 .. 25-35
(Soundtrack.)
AVA (20; "To Kill A Mockingbird"): 63 .25-40
(Soundtrack.)
AVA (31; "The Caretakers"): 63 25-35
(Soundtrack.)
AVA (45; "The Carpetbaggers"): 64 25-35
(Soundtrack.)
AVA (53; "Baby The Rain
   Must Fall"): 65 30-35
(Soundtrack.)
CAPITOL : 59-60 4-8
CHOREO (4; "Walk On The Wild
   Side"): 62 25-35
(Soundtrack.)
CHOREO (11; "Movie & TV
   Themes"): 62 10-15
(Soundtrack.)
COLUMBIA: 60 5-15
DOT: 59 5-10
HAMILTON: 59 4-8
MAINSTREAM (6056; "Baby The Rain
   Must Fall"): 65 30-35
(Soundtrack.)
MAINSTREAM (6083; "Walk On The
   Wild Side"): 67 20-30
(Soundtrack.)
MAINSTREAM (6094; "A Man & His
   Movies"): 67 8-15
RCA VICTOR (1120; "The
   Silencers"): 66 15-25
(Soundtrack.)

UNITED ARTISTS (304; "The Ten
Commandments"): 74 .... $5-10
(Soundtrack.)
UNITED ARTISTS (3495; "The Ten
Commandments"): 66 15-25
(Soundtrack. Monaural.)
UNITED ARTISTS (4127; "The
Hallelujah Trail"): 65 25-30
(Soundtrack. Monaural.)
UNITED ARTISTS (4138; "Cast A
Giant Shadow"): 66 20-25
(Soundtrack. Monaural.)
UNITED ARTISTS (4143;
"Hawaii"): 66 15-20
(Soundtrack. Monaural.)
UNITED ARTISTS (4146; "Return Of The
Seven"): 66 10-20
(Soundtrack. Monaural.)
UNITED ARTISTS (4176; "The
Scalphunters"): 68 15-20
(Soundtrack. Monaural.)
UNITED ARTISTS (5127; "The
Hallelujah Trail"): 65 30-35
(Soundtrack. Stereo.)
UNITED ARTISTS (5138, "Cast A
Giant Shadow"): 66 25-30
(Soundtrack. Stereo.)
UNITED ARTISTS (5143;
"Hawaii"): 66 15-25
(Soundtrack. Stereo.)
UNITED ARTISTS (5146; "Return
Of The Seven"): 66 10-20
(Soundtrack. Stereo.)
UNITED ARTISTS (5176; "The
Scalphunters"): 68 20-30
(Soundtrack. Stereo.)
UNITED ARTISTS (6495; "The Ten
Commandments"): 66 15-25
(Soundtrack. Stereo.)

BERNSTEIN, Leonard, Orchestra
LPs: 10/12-Inch 33rpm
CAMDEN: 55-56 8-15
COLUMBIA ("What Is Jazz"): 56 20-40

BERRY, Chuck
Singles: 78rpm
CHESS (1600 series): 55-58 10-20
CHESS (1700 through 1729): 58-59 15-25
CHESS (1737; "My Childhood
Sweetheart"): 59 20-30
CHESS (1747; "Too Pooped
To Pop"): 60 40-60
Singles: 7-Inch
ATCO: 79 1-3
CHESS (1604 through 1615): 55-56 10-20
CHESS (1626 through 1645): 56 8-15

CHESS (1653 through 1729): 57-59 5-10
CHESS (1737 through 1963): 59-69 4-8
CHESS (2000 & 9000 series): 70-73 2-4
ERIC: 73 1-3
MERCURY: 66-72 3-5
PHILO: 66 8-15
("Hip Pocket" Record.)
Picture Sleeves
CHESS: 64-65 10-20
EPs: 7-Inch 33/45rpm
CHESS: 57-59 40-60
LPs: 10/12-Inch 33rpm
ACCORD: 82 5-8
ATCO: 79 5-8
BROOKVILLE: 73 12-15
CHESS (Except 1400 &
9000 series): 66-76 10-20
CHESS (1426; "After School
Session"): 57 50-75
CHESS (1432; "One Dozen
Berrys"): 58 50-75
CHESS (1435; "Chuck Berry's
On Top"): 59 50-75
CHESS (1440, "Rockin' At The
Hops"): 59 50-75
CHESS (1456; "Chuck Berry's New
Jukebox Hits"): 61 25-40
CHESS (1465; "More Chuck Berry"): 63   25-40
CHESS (1466; "Chuck Berry
Twist"): 62 20-25
CHESS (1480; "Chuck Berry On
Stage"): 63 20-25
CHESS (1485; "Chuck Berry's
Greatest Hits"): 64 25-30
CHESS (1488; "St. Louis To
Liverpool"): 64 20-25
CHESS (1495; "Chuck Berry In
London"): 65 25-30
CHESS (1498; "Fresh Berrys"): 65 20-25
CHESS (9000 series): 85 5-8
EVEREST: 76 8-10
GUSTO: 78 5-8
MCA: 86 8-12
MAGNUM: 69 10-12
MERCURY: 67-72 10-15
PICKWICK: 72 8-10
TRIP: 78 8-10
UPFRONT: 79 5-8

BERRY, Chuck, & Bo Diddley
Singles: 7-Inch
CHECKER: 64 3-5
LPs: 10/12-Inch 33rpm
CHECKER: 64 20-25
Also see DIDDLEY, Bo

BERRY, Chuck, & Howlin' Wolf
LPs: 10/12-Inch 33rpm
CHESS: 69 .... $15-20
Also see BERRY, Chuck
Also see HOWLIN' WOLF

BERRY, Jan
(Jan; Jan Barry)
Singles: 7-Inch
A&M: 77-78 3-5
LIBERTY (55845; "The Universal
Coward"): 66 4-6
ODE '70 (Except 66023 &
66034): 72-77 12-20
ODE '70 (66023 "Mother Earth"): 72 ... 20-30
(With insert note from Jan. Promotional issue only.)
ODE '70 (66023 "Mother Earth"): 72 ... 15-20
(Without insert note from Jan.)
ODE '70 (66034 "Don't You Just
Know It"): 73 30-35
(With Brian Wilson.)
RIPPLE: 61 25-30
Picture Sleeves
LIBERTY (55845; "The Universal
Coward"): 66 75-100
Also see JAN & ARNIE
Also see JAN & DEAN
Also see WILSON, Brian

BERTEI, Adele
Singles: 12-Inch 33/45rpm
GEFFEN: 83 4-6
Singles: 7-Inch
GEFFEN: 83 1-3

BEST, Peter
Singles: 7-Inch
CAMEO: 66 15-20
CAPITOL: 67 15-20
COLLECTABLES: 87 2-3
(Shown as by the Beatles, but actually Pete Best
tracks.)
HAPPENING: 66 30-40
MR. MAESTRO: 65 30-40
ORIGINAL BEATLES
DRUMMER: 64 30-40
Picture Sleeves
CAMEO: 66 40-50
LPs: 10/12-Inch 33rpm
BEST FAN CLUB: 66 25-30
PHOENIX 10: 82 8-10
SAVAGE (71; "Best Of The
Beatles"): 65 75-100
Also see BEATLES

BETH, Karen
Singles: 7-Inch
BUDDAH: 75 .... $2-4
LPs: 10/12-Inch 33rpm
BUDDAH: 75 8-10

BETHEA, Harmon
(Bethea; Bethea With The Maskman & The
Agents)
Singles: 7-Inch
DYNAMO: 69-71 2-4
MUSICOR: 70-74 1-3

BETTERS, Harold
Singles: 7-Inch
GATEWAY: 63-65 3-5
REPRISE: 66-67 3-5
LPs: 10/12-Inch 33rpm
GATEWAY: 64-66 12-15
REPRISE: 65-67 12-15

BETTS, Richard
(Dickey Betts & Great Southern; Dickey Betts
Band)
Singles: 7-Inch
ARISTA: 77-78 2-3
CAPRICORN: 74-76 2-4
LPs: 10/12-Inch 33rpm
ARISTA: 78 5-8
CAPRICORN: 74 8-10
EPIC: 88 5-8
Also see ALLMAN BROTHERS BAND

BEVEL, Charles "Mississippi"
Singles: 7-Inch
A&M: 73-74 2-4

BEVERLY & DUANE
Singles: 7-Inch
ARIOLA AMERICA: 78-79 2-3
Members: Beverly Wheeler; Duane Williams.

BEVERLY SISTERS
Singles: 7-Inch
MERCURY: 60 3-5
LPs: 10/12-Inch 33rpm
CAPITOL: 61 10-12

BEY, Salome, & Brotherhood
Singles: 7-Inch
BUDDAH: 76 2-3

BIBLE
LPs: 10/12-Inch 33rpm
CHRYSALIS: 88 5-8

BICKERSONS:
see AMECHE, Don, & Frances Langford

BIDDU
(Biddu & Orchestra)
Singles: 7-Inch
COLOSSUS: *70* **$2-4**
EPIC: *75-77* **2-3**
LPs: 10/12-Inch 33rpm
EPIC: *76-77* **5-8**

BIG AUDIO DYNAMITE
Singles: 12-Inch 33/45rpm
COLUMBIA: *85-88* **4-6**
Singles: 7-Inch
COLUMBIA: *85-88* **1-3**
LPs: 10/12-Inch 33rpm
COLUMBIA: *85-88* **5-8**
Member: Mick Jones.
Also see CLASH

BIG BOPPER
(Jape Richardson; Jiles Perry Richardson, Jr.)
Singles: 7-Inch
D (1008; "Chantilly
Lace"): *58* **50-75**
MERCURY (71300 series): *58* **4-6**
(Black vinyl.)
MERCURY (71400 series): *59* **8-10**
LPs: 10/12-Inch 33rpm
MERCURY (20402; "Chantilly
Lace"): *59* **100-200**
(Black label.)
MERCURY (20402; "Chantilly
Lace"): *64* **75-100**
(Red label.)
MERCURY (20402; "Chantilly
Lace"): *81* **10-15**
(Chicago "skyline" label.)
PICKWICK: *73* **20-30**
Also see RICHARDSON, Jape

BIG BROTHER & THE HOLDING COMPANY
(Big Brother)
Singles: 7-Inch
COLUMBIA: *68-71* **5-8**
MAINSTREAM: *67-68* **5-8**
Picture Sleeves
COLUMBIA: *68* **5-10**

LPs: 10/12-Inch 33rpm
COLUMBIA: *68-71* **15-25**
MADE TO LAST: *84* **5-8**
MAINSTREAM: *67* **20-35**
Members: Janis Joplin; David Getz; Sam Andrew;
Peter Albin; Jim Gurley; David Schallock; Nick
Gravenites; Sam Andres.
Also see JOPLIN, Janis

BIG COUNTRY
Singles: 12-Inch 33/45rpm
MERCURY: *83-86* **$4-6**
Singles: 7-Inch
MERCURY: *83-86* **1-3**
REPRISE: *88* **1-3**
LPs: 10/12-Inch 33rpm
MERCURY: *83-86* **5-8**
REPRISE: *88* **5-8**

BIG MAYBELLE
(Mable Smith)
Singles: 78rpm
KING: *48-49* **4-8**
OKEH: *53-56* **5-15**
SAVOY: *56-58* **5-10**
Singles: 7-Inch
BRUNSWICK: *63* **3-5**
CHESS: *66* **3-5**
OKEH: *53-56* **10-20**
PARAMOUNT: *73* **2-4**
PORT: *65* **3-5**
ROJAC: *64-69* **3-5**
SAVOY: *56-61* **5-10**
EPs: 7-Inch 33/45rpm
EPIC: *57* **20-40**
LPs: 10/12-Inch 33rpm
BRUNSWICK: *62-68* **12-15**
ENCORE: *67* **10-12**
EPIC: *83* **8-10**
PARAMOUNT: *73* **8-10**
ROJAC: *67-69* **10-12**
SAVOY (14000 series): *58-61* **25-35**
SCEPTER: *64* **12-15**
UPFRONT: *73* **8-10**

BIG PIG
Singles: 7-Inch
A&M: *88* **1-3**
LPs: 10/12-Inch 33rpm
A&M: *88* **5-8**

BIG RIC
Singles: 7-Inch
ROCK 'N' ROLL: *83* **1-3**
SCOTTI BROTHERS: *83* **1-3**
LPs: 10/12-Inch 33rpm
SCOTTI BROTHERS: *83-84* **5-8**

BIG SAMBO
(Big Sambo & The House Wreckers; Big Sam &
The House Wreckers)
Singles: 7-Inch
ERIC: *62* **3-5**

BIG THREE
Singles: 7-Inch
FM: *63* **4-8**

ROULETTE: *66* $3-5
TOLLIE: *64* 4-6
      LPs: 10/12-Inch 33rpm
ACCORD: *82* 5-8
FM: *63-64* 15-25
ROULETTE: *68* 15-20
Members: Cass Elliott; Tim Rose; Denny Dougherty.
Also see ELLIOTT, Cass
Also see MAMAS & THE PAPAS

BILK, Mr. Acker
(With The Leon Young String Chorale)
      Singles: 7-Inch
ATCO: *61-66* 2-4
REPRISE: *62* 2-4
      LPs: 10/12-Inch 33rpm
ASCOT: *62* 8-12
ATCO: *62-66* 8-12

BILK, Mr. Acker, & Bent Fabric
      LPs: 10/12-Inch 33rpm
ATCO: *65* 8-12
Also see BILK, Mr. Acker
Also see FABRIC, Bent

BILL & TAFFY
      Singles: 7-Inch
RCA VICTOR: *74* 3-5
      LPs: 10/12-Inch 33rpm
RCA VICTOR: *73-74* 10-12
Members: Bill Danoff; Taffy Danoff.
Also see STARLAND VOCAL BAND

BILL BLACK'S COMBO:
  see BLACK, Bill

BILLION DOLLAR BABIES
      Singles: 7-Inch
POLYDOR (Except 14406): *77* 3-5
POLYDOR (14406; "Too Young"): *77* ... 8-10
(Promotional issue only.)
      LPs: 10/12-Inch 33rpm
POLYDOR (Except 022): *77* 12-15
POLYDOR (022; "Battle Axe"): *77* 20-25
(Promotional issue only.)
Also see COOPER, Alice

BILLY ALWAYS: see ALWAYS, Billy

BILLY & BABY GAP
      Singles: 7-Inch
TOTAL EXPERIENCE: *85* 1-3

BILLY & LILLIE
(Billy & Lillie & The Thunderbirds)
      Singles: 78rpm
SWAN: *57* 4-6
      Singles: 7-Inch
ABC: *73* 1-3

ABC-PARAMOUNT: *63* $4-6
CAMEO: *66* 3-5
COLLECTABLES: *81* 1-3
SWAN: *57-61* 5-10
Members: Billy Ford; Lillie Bryant.
Also see BRYANT, Lillie

BILLY & SUE
      Singles: 7-Inch
CREW: *70* 3-5
Members: William Oliver Swofford; Lesley Gore.
Also see GORE, Lesley
Also see OLIVER

BILLY & THE BEATERS
      Singles: 7-Inch
ALFA: *81* 1-3
      LPs: 10/12-Inch 33rpm
ALFA: *81* 5-8
Member: Billy Vera.
Also see VERA, Bill

BILLY JOE & THE CHECKMATES
(Billy Joe Hunter)
      Singles: 7-Inch
DORE: *61-66* 4-8

BILLY SATELLITE
      Singles: 7-Inch
CAPITOL: *84* 1-3
      LPs: 10/12-Inch 33rpm
CAPITOL: *84* 5-8

BIMBO JET
      Singles: 7-Inch
SCEPTER: *75* 2-3

BIONIC BOOGIE
      Singles: 7-Inch
POLYDOR: *77-78* 1-3
      LPs: 10/12-Inch 33rpm
POLYDOR: *78* 5-8
Member: Gregg Diamond.

BIRD, J.
      Singles: 12-Inch 33/45rpm
WARRIOR: *84* 4-6

BIRDLEGS & PAULINE
      Singles: 7-Inch
VEE JAY: *63* 4-8

BIRDSONG, Edwin
      Singles: 12-Inch 33/45rpm
PHILADELPHIA INT'L: *78-79* 4-6
SALSOUL: *81-84* 4-6
      Singles: 7-Inch
PHILADELPHIA INT'L: *78* 1-3
POLYDOR: *71-72* 2-4

SALSOUL: *81-84* $1-3
LPs: 10/12-Inch 33rpm
PHILADELPHIA INT'L: *78* 5-8
POLYDOR: *71-73* 8-10

BIRKIN, Jane, & Serge Gainsbourg
Singles: 7-Inch
FONTANA: *69* 2-3
LPs: 10/12-Inch 33rpm
FONTANA: *70* 5-10

BISHOP, Elvin
(Elvin Bishop Group; Elvin Bishop & Crabshaw Rising)
Singles: 7-Inch
CAPRICORN: *74-79* 2-3
EPIC: *72-75* 2-4
FILLMORE: *70-71* 2-4
WARNER BROS: *72* 2-4
LPs: 10/12-Inch 33rpm
CAPRICORN: *74-78* 5-8
EPIC: *72-75* 8-10
FILLMORE: *69-72* 10-12
Also see BUTTERFIELD, Paul
Also see GRATEFUL DEAD / Elvin Bishop Group

BISHOP, Stephen
Singles: 7-Inch
ABC: *76-78* 2-3
WARNER BROS: *80-83* 1-3
Picture Sleeves
ABC: *78* 2-3
LPs: 10/12-Inch 33rpm
ABC: *76-78* 5-8
MCA: *80* 5-8
WARNER BROS: *80* 5-8
Also see GRUSIN, Dave
Also see NEWMAN, Randy

BISHOP, Stephen, & Yvonne Elliman
Singles: 7-Inch
WARNER BROS: *80* 1-3
Also see BISHOP, Stephen
Also see ELLIMAN, Yvonne

BITS & PIECES
Singles: 7-Inch
MANGO: *81* 1-3
NASCO: *73-74* 2-4
PARAMOUNT: *74* 2-4

BIZ MARKIE
Singles: 7-Inch
COLD CHILL: *88* 1-3
PRISM: *86* 1-3

BLACK, Bill
(Bill Black's Combo)
Singles: 7-Inch
COLUMBIA: *70* $2-4
ECHO: *72* 2-4
GUSTO: *83* 1-3
HI (Except 2000 series): *67-76* 2-4
HI (2000 series): *59-66* 3-5
LONDON: *84* 1-3
MEGA: *71-74* 2-4
MOTOWN: *83* 1-3
Picture Sleeves
HI: *60-62* 4-8
LPs: 10/12-Inch 33rpm
COLUMBIA: *69-70* 8-10
51 WEST: *84* 5-8
HI (6000 & 8000 series): *77-78* 5-8
HI (12001 through
12005): *60-62* 15-30
HI (12006 through
12041): *62-68* 8-18
HI (32000 through
32010): *61-63* 15-30
HI (32011 through
32110): *63-77* 8-18
MEGA: *71-74* 5-8
ZODIAC: *77* 5-8
Also see PRESLEY, Elvis

BLACK, Cilla
Singles: 7-Inch
BELL: *68* 3-4
CAPITOL: *64-66* 3-5
DJM: *68-70* 2-4
EMI AMERICA: *74* 2-4
PRIVATE STOCK: *75-76* 2-3
LPs: 10/12-Inch 33rpm
CAPITOL: *65* 20-25

BLACK, Jay
Singles: 7-Inch
ATLANTIC: *75* 2-4
MIDSONG: *80* 1-3
MIGRATION: *75* 2-4
MILLENNIUM: *78* 1-3
PRIVATE STOCK: *76* 2-3
ROULETTE: *76* 2-4
UNITED ARTISTS: *67* 3-5
Picture Sleeves
UNITED ARTISTS: *67* 5-10
Also see JAY & THE AMERICANS

BLACK, Jeanne
Singles: 7-Inch
CAPITOL: *60-62* 2-5

LPs: 10/12-Inch 33rpm
CAPITOL: *60* $15-20

BLACK, Marion
Singles: 7-Inch
AVCO EMBASSY: *71* 2-4
SHAKAT: *74* 2-3

BLACK, Oscar
Singles: 78rpm
ATLANTIC: *51* 10-20
GROOVE: *54-55* 5-10
Singles: 7-Inch
ATLANTIC: *51* 25-40
GROOVE: *54-55* 10-20
SAVOY: *61* 3-6

BLACK, Oscar, & Sue Allen
Singles: 78rpm
GROOVE: *54-55* 5-10
Singles: 7-Inch
GROOVE: *54-55* 10-20
Also see BLACK, Oscar

BLACK, Shelly
Singles: 7-Inch
VIGOR: *76-77* 1-3

BLACK, Stanley
Singles: 7-Inch
LONDON: *50-55* 2-4
EPs: 7-Inch 33/45rpm
LONDON: *55* 3-6
LPs: 10/12-Inch 33rpm
LONDON: *51-65* 4-8

BLACK, Terry
Singles: 7-Inch
DUNHILL: *65-66* 3-5
TOLLIE: *64-65* 3-6
Picture Sleeves
TOLLIE: *65* 4-8

BLACK, Terry, & Laurel Ward
Singles: 7-Inch
KAMA SUTRA: *72* 2-4
Also see BLACK, Terry

BLACK 'N BLUE
Singles: 7-Inch
GEFFEN: *84* 1-3
MERCURY: *70* 2-4
LPs: 10/12-Inch 33rpm
GEFFEN: *84-88* 5-8

BLACK BLOOD
Singles: 7-Inch
CHRYSALIS: *77* 2-3
MAINSTREAM: *75* 2-4

LPs: 10/12-Inch 33rpm
CHRYSALIS: *77* $5-8
MAINSTREAM: *75* 8-10

BLACK FLAMES
Singles: 7-Inch
DEF JAM: *87* 1-3

BLACK HEAT
Singles: 7-Inch
ATLANTIC: *72-74* 2-4
LPs: 10/12-Inch 33rpm
ATLANTIC: *72-75* 8-10

BLACK ICE
Singles: 7-Inch
AMHERST: *76* 2-4
HDM: *77* 2-3
MONTAGE: *81-84* 1-3
LPs: 10/12-Inch 33rpm
AMHERST: *76* 8-10
MONTAGE: *82* 5-8

BLACK IVORY
Singles: 7-Inch
BUDDAH: *75-84* 1-3
KWANZA: *74* 2-4
PANORAMIC: *85* 1-3
PERCEPTION: *72* 2-4
TODAY: *71-73* 2-4
LPs: 10/12-Inch 33rpm
BUDDAH: *75-84* 5-8
TODAY: *72* 10-12

BLACK MAMBA
Singles: 12-Inch 33/45rpm
GARAGE: *84* 4-6

BLACK OAK ARKANSAS
(Black Oak)
Singles: 7-Inch
ATCO: *71-75* 2-4
CAPRICORN: *77-78* 2-3
ENTERPRISE: *70* 2-4
MCA: *75-77* 1-3
LPs: 10/12-Inch 33rpm
ATCO: *71-84* 10-12
CAPRICORN: *77-78* 5-8
MCA: *75-77* 8-10
STAX: *74* 10-12
Members: Jim Mangrum; Ruby Starr; Rickie
Reynolds; Stanley Knight; Harvey Jett; Jimmy
Henderson; Pat Daugherty; Tom Aldridge.

**BLACK OAK ARKANSAS /
COOPER BROTHERS**
LPs: 10/12-Inch 33rpm
CAPRICORN (0005; "I'd Rather Be
Sailing"): 78 .... $10-15
(Promotional issue only.)
Also see BLACK OAK ARKANSAS
Also see COOPER BROTHERS

BLACK PEARL
Singles: 7-Inch
ATLANTIC: 69 2-4
PROPHESY: 70 2-4
LPs: 10/12-Inch 33rpm
ATLANTIC: 69 12-15
PROPHESY: 70 15-20

BLACK SABBATH
Singles: 7-Inch
WARNER BROS: 70-76 2-3
LPs: 10/12-Inch 33rpm
WARNER BROS (Except 1000 &
2000 series): 76-84 5-10
WARNER BROS (1000 & 2000
series): 70-76 8-12
WARNER BROS: 87 5-8
Members: Ozzy Osbourne; Tony Iommi; Kip
Treavor; Bill Ward; Ronnie Dio; Terry "Geezer"
Butler.
Also see OSBOURNE, Ozzy

BLACK SATIN
Singles: 7-Inch
BUDDAH: 75 2-4
LPs: 10/12-Inch 33rpm
BUDDAH: 76 8-10
BUDDAH: 76 20-35
(Promotional issue.)
Member: Fred Parris.
Also see FIVE SATINS

BLACK UHURU
LPs: 10/12-Inch 33rpm
ISLAND: 84 5-8
MANGO: 80-85 5-8

BLACKBYRDS
Singles: 7-Inch
FANTASY: 74-84 1-3
LPs: 10/12-Inch 33rpm
FPM: 75 10-12
FANTASY: 74-84 10-12
Members: Gary Hart; Joe Hall III; Stephe Johnson;
Keith Killgo; Orville Saunders; Kevin Toney.
Also see BYRD, Donald

BLACKFOOT
Singles: 7-Inch
ATCO: 79-84 1-3

LPs: 10/12-Inch 33rpm
ANTILLES: 78 .... $5-8
ATCO: 79-84 5-8
EPIC: 76 8-10
ISLAND: 75 10-12
Members: Rick Medlocke; Jackson Spires; Charlie
Hargrett; Greg Walker.

BLACKFOOT, J.
Singles: 7-Inch
EDGE: 86-87 1-3
SOUND TOWN: 83-86 1-3
LPs: 10/12-Inch 33rpm
SOUND TOWN: 84-85 5-8

BLACKJACK
Singles: 7-Inch
POLYDOR: 79-84 1-3
20TH CENTURY-FOX: 76 2-4
LPs: 10/12-Inch 33rpm
POLYDOR: 79-80 5-8
Also see BOLTON, Michael

BLACKMORE, Ritchie
Singles: 7-Inch
POLYDOR: 75 2-4
LPs: 10/12-Inch 33rpm
POLYDOR: 75 8-10
Also see BLACKMORE'S RAINBOW
Also see LORD SUTCH

BLACKMORE'S RAINBOW
Singles: 7-Inch
OYSTER: 76 2-4
POLYDOR: 75-79 2-3
LPs: 10/12-Inch 33rpm
OYSTER: 75 8-10
Members: Ritchie Blackmore; Roger Glover; Ron-
nie Dio.
Also see BLACKMORE, Ritchie
Also see DEEP PURPLE
Also see RAINBOW

BLACKSMOKE
Singles: 7-Inch
CHOCOLATE CITY: 76 2-3

BLACKWELL
Singles: 7-Inch
ASTRO: 69-70 2-4
BUTTERFLY: 78 2-3
LPs: 10/12-Inch 33rpm
ASTRO: 69 8-10
BUTTERFLY: 78 5-8

BLACKWELL, Charlie
Singles: 7-Inch
WARNER BROS: 59 3-5

BLADES OF GRASS
Singles: 7-Inch
FINE: *67* $6-12
JUBILEE: *67-68* 3-5
LPs: 10/12-Inch 33rpm
JUBILEE: *67* 12-15
Members: Bruce Ames; Marc Black; Frank Di-
Chiara; Dave Gordon.

BLAKE & HINES
Singles: 7-Inch
MOTOWN:*87* 1-3

BLANC, Mel
Singles: 78rpm
CAPITOL (5221; "Seasons Greetings
From Capitol"): *49* 10-15
(Promotional issue only. Also contains greetings
from other Capitol artists.)
CAPITOL: *48-54* 5-10
Singles: 7-Inch
CAPITOL (Except PRO-15): *50-54* 5-10
CAPITOL (PRO-15; "I Taut I Taw A
Record Dealer"): *51* 10-20
(With Mel Blanc as assorted cartoon characters, but
not credited on label to Blanc. Promotional issue
only.)
WARNER BROS: *60* 2-5
EPs: 7-Inch 33/45rpm
CAPITOL: *51-53* 15-20
LPs: 10/12-Inch 33rpm
CAPITOL (400 series): *53* 20-30
(10-Inch LPs.)
CAPITOL (3200 series): *61-63* 10-20
GOLDEN: *61* 10-15
Also see HUNT, Pee Wee

Bobby Bland

BLANCHARD, Jack, & Misty Morgan
Singles: 7-Inch
EPIC: *73-75* $1-3
MEGA: *71-73* 2-3
WAYSIDE: *69-70* 2-4
LPs: 10/12-Inch 33rpm
MEGA: *72* 8-12
WAYSIDE: *70* 10-15

BLANCMANGE
Singles: 12-Inch 33/45rpm
ISLAND: *83-84* 4-6
SIRE: *84-85* 4-6
Singles: 7-Inch
ISLAND: *83-84* 1-3
SIRE: *84-85* 1-3
LPs: 10/12-Inch 33rpm
ISLAND: *82-84* 5-8
SIRE: *84-85* 5-8

BLAND, Billy
Singles: 78rpm
OLD TOWN: *55-57* 4-8
Singles: 7-Inch
ATLANTIC: *84* 1-3
COLLECTABLES: *81* 1-3
TIP TOP: *58* 4-6
OLD TOWN (1016 through
1035): *55-57* 8-15
OLD TOWN (1076 through
1143): *60-63* 5-10

BLAND, Bobby
(Bobby "Blue" Bland)
Singles: 78rpm
CHESS: *54* 10-12
MODERN: *52* 12-15
Singles: 7-Inch
ABC: *73-78* 1-3
DUKE (105; "I.O.U. Blues"): *54* 40-60
DUKE (115; "No Blow No
Show"): *54* 30-40
DUKE (141; "It's My Life,
Baby"): *56* 20-25
DUKE (146 through 196): *57-58* 5-10
DUKE (300 series): *60-66* 4-8
DUKE (400 series): *66-72* 3-5
DUNHILL: *74* 2-3
MCA: *79-84* 1-3
LPs: 10/12-Inch 33rpm
ABC: *75-78* 5-8
ABC/DUKE: *73* 5-8
BLUESWAY: *73* 5-8
DUKE (74 through 78): *62-64* 20-25
DUKE (79 through 89): *66-69* 15-20
DUKE (90 through 92): *70-74* 10-15

DUNHILL: 73-74 .... $8-10
MALACO: 88 5-8
MCA: 79-84 5-8

BLAND, Bobby, & B. B. King
Singles: 7-Inch
ABC: 78 1-3
IMPULSE: 76 2-3
LPs: 10/12-Inch 33rpm
DUNHILL: 74 10-12
IMPULSE: 76 8-10
MCA: 82 5-8
  Also see KING, B. B.

BLAND, Bobby / Little Junior Parker
LPs: 10/12-Inch 33rpm
DUKE: 74 8-10
  Also see PARKER, Little Junior

BLAND, Bobby, & Ike Turner
Singles: 7-Inch
KENT: 62 3-5
  Also see TURNER, Ike

BLAND, Bobby / Johnny Guitar Watson
LPs: 10/12-Inch 33rpm
CROWN: 63 15-20
  Also see BLAND, Bobby
  Also see WATSON, Johnny

BLANE, Marcie
Singles: 7-Inch
LONDON: 84 1-3
SEVILLE: 62-65 3-5

BLAST, C.L.
Singles: 7-Inch
ATLANTIC: 69 2-4
COTILLION: 80 1-3
PARK PLACE: 85 1-3
STAX: 67 3-5
UNITED: 70-71 2-4
LPs: 10/12-Inch 33rpm
COTILLION: 80 5-8

BLASTERS
Singles: 7-Inch
MCA: 84 1-3
SLASH: 82-85 3-5
LPs: 10/12-Inch 33rpm
ROLLIN' ROCK: 80 30-50
SLASH: 81-85 8-12
WARNER BROS: 5-8
  Members: David Alvin; Phil Alvin; John Bazz;
  Gene Taylor; Bill Bateman; Steve Berlin.
  Also see ALLEN, Lee
  Also see ALVIN, David
  Also see X

BLAZE
Singles: 7-Inch
EPIC: 76-77 .... $2-3
FRATERNITY: 76 2-4

BLEND
Singles: 7-Inch
MCA: 78-79 1-3
LPs: 10/12-Inch 33rpm
MCA: 78-79 5-8

BLENDELLS
Singles: 7-Inch
COLLECTABLES: 81 1-3
COTILLION: 68 3-5
ERA: 73 2-4
RAMPART: 64 5-8
REPRISE: 64-65 3-5

BLENDERS
Singles: 7-Inch
CORTLAND: 62 4-6
MAR-V-LOUS: 66 3-5
VISION: 62 4-6
WITCH: 63 8-10

BLESSING, Michael
(Michael Nesmith)
Singles: 7-Inch
COLPIX: 65 10-20
  Also see NESMITH, Michael

BLEYER, Archie
(Archie Blyer & Maria Alba)
Singles: 78rpm
ARC: 35 8-15
VOCALION: 34 8-15
Singles: 7-Inch
CADENCE: 54-57 5-10
LPs: 10/12-Inch 33rpm
CADENCE: 62 10-20
  Also see CHORDETTES
  Also see HAYES, Bill

BLIND FAITH
Singles: 7-Inch
RSO: 77 3-6
LPs: 10/12-Inch 33rpm
ATCO (304A; "Blind Faith"): 69 20-30
  (Front cover pictures a nude girl.)
ATCO (304B; "Blind Faith"): 69 10-12
  (Front cover pictures the group.)
RSO: 76 5-8
  (Reissue. Pictures the nude girl.)
  Members: Eric Clapton; Ginger Baker; Steve Win-
  wood; Rick Gretch.
  Also see BAKER, Ginger
  Also see CLAPTON, Eric
  Also see FAMILY

Also see WINWOOD, Steve

BLODWYN PIG
Singles: 7-Inch
A&M: *69-70* $2-4
LPs: 10/12-Inch 33rpm
A&M (3000 series): *82* 5-8
A&M (4000 series): *69-70* 10-15
Members: Blodwyn; Mick Abrahams; Peter Banks; Ron Berg; Clive Bunker; Jack Lancaster; Andy Pyle.
Also see BANKS, Peter

BLONDIE
Singles: 12-Inch 33/45rpm
CHRYSALIS: *78-84* 5-8
Singles: 7-Inch
CHRYSALIS: *77-84* 1-3
PRIVATE STOCK: *76-77* 6-10
Picture Sleeves
CHRYSALIS: *79-81* 2-4
LPs: 10/12-Inch 33rpm
CHRYSALIS (Except 5001): *76-84* 5-10
CHRYSALIS (5001; "Parallel
Lines"): *78* 15-25
(Picture disc.)
MFSL: *81* 20-40
PRIVATE STOCK: *75* 15-20
Members: Deborah Harry; Clem Burke; Jimmy Destri; Chris Stein; Gary Valentine; Fred Smith; Clem Burke; Nigel Harrison.
Also see HARRY, Debbie

BLOOD, SWEAT & TEARS
Singles: 7-Inch
ABC: *78* 1-3
COLUMBIA: *69-77* 2-4
Picture Sleeves
COLUMBIA: *70-72* 2-5
LPs: 10/12-Inch 33rpm
ABC: *77* 5-8
COLUMBIA (Except 9619 &
49000 series): *69-76* 10-12
COLUMBIA (9619; "Child Is Father
To The Man"): *68* 15-20
COLUMBIA (49000 series): *81* 12-15
(Half-speed mastered.)
LAX (1865; "Nuclear Blues"): *80* 5-8
(Black vinyl.)
LAX (1865; "Nuclear Blues"): *80* 10-12
(Colored vinyl. Promotional issue only.)
Members: David Clayton-Thomas; Jerry Hyman; Fred Lipsius; Dick Halligan; Bobby Colomby; Lew Soloff; Chuck Winfield; Steve Katz; James Thomas Fielder.
Also see CLAYTON-THOMAS, David
Also see KOOPER, Al

BLOODROCK
Singles: 7-Inch
CAPITOL: *69-75* $2-4
LPs: 10/12-Inch 33rpm
CAPITOL: *69-75* 10-15
Members: Rick Cobb; Eddie Grundy; Steve Hill; Lee Pickens; Nick Taylor; Warren Ham.

BLOODSTONE
Singles: 12-Inch 33/45rpm
MOTOWN: *79* 4-6
T-NECK: *82-85* 4-6
Singles: 7-Inch
EPIC: *82* 1-3
LONDON: *73-76* 2-3
MOTOWN: *79* 1-3
T-NECK: *82-85* 1-3
Picture Sleeves
LONDON: *74-76* 2-4
LPs: 10/12-Inch 33rpm
LONDON: *73-74* 8-10
MOTOWN: *78* 5-8
T-NECK: *82* 5-8
Members: Harry Williams; Charles McCormick; Charles Love; Steve Ferrone; Roger Lee Durham; Willis Draffen.

BLOOM, Bobby
Singles: 7-Inch
EARTH: *69* 2-4
KAMA SUTRA: *67* 3-5
L&R: *70* 2-4
MGM: *70-73* 2-4
ROULETTE: *70* 2-4
WHITE WHALE: *69* 2-4
LPs: 10/12-Inch 33rpm
BUDDAH: *71* 8-10
L&R: *70* 10-12
Also see ARCHIES
Also see MANN, Bobby
Also see MUSIC EXPLOSION

BLOOMFIELD, Mike
LPs: 10/12-Inch 33rpm
CLOUDS: *78* 5-8
COLUMBIA (9000 series): *69* 12-15
COLUMBIA (37000 series): *81-83* 6-10
GUITAR PLAYER: *77* 8-10
HARMONY: *71* 8-10
TAKOMA: *77-81* 5-8
WATERHOUSE: *81* 5-8
Also see KGB

BLOOMFIELD, Mike, Dr. John &
John Paul Hammond
LPs: 10/12-Inch 33rpm
COLUMBIA: *73* 8-10

The Blossoms featuring Darlene Love

Also see DR. JOHN

BLOOMFIELD, Mike, & Nick Graventes
LPs: 10/12-Inch 33rpm
COLUMBIA: *69* $10-12
Also see ELECTRIC FLAG

BLOOMFIELD, Mike, & Al Kooper
LPs: 10/12-Inch 33rpm
COLUMBIA: *68* 12-15
Also see BLOOMFIELD, Mike
Also see KOOPER, Al
Also see MOBY GRAPE

BLOOMFIELD, Mike, Al Kooper & Steve Stills
Singles: 7-Inch
COLUMBIA: *68* 2-4
LPs: 10/12-Inch 33rpm
COLUMBIA: *68* 10-12
MFSL: *85* 15-20
Also see BLOOMFIELD, Mike
Also see KOOPER, Al
Also see STILLS, Stephen

BLOSSOMS
Singles: 7-Inch
BELL: *69-70* 4-6
CAPITOL: *57-58* 4-8
CHALLENGE: *61-62* 10-12
CLASSIC ARTISTS: *89* 2-3

EEOC (8472; "Things Are
   Changing"): *65* $75-100
(Promotional issue for the Equal Employment Op-
portunity Center. With Brian Wilson on piano.)
EPIC: *77* 2-3
LION: *72* 2-4
MGM: *68* 6-12
ODE: *67-69* 3-5
OKEH: *62-63* 4-6
REPRISE: *65-67* 3-5
Picture Sleeves
EEOC: "Things Are
   Changing"): *65* 75-100
(Promotional issue only.)
LPs: 10/12-Inch 33rpm
LION: *72* 8-10
Members: Darlene Love; Gloria Jones; Fanita Bar-
rett; Annette Williams; Nanette Jackson.
Also see BOB B. SOXX & THE BLUE
JEANS
Also see EDDY, Duane
Also see LOVE, Darlene
Also see PRESLEY, Elvis

BLOW, Kurtis
Singles: 12-Inch 33/45rpm
MERCURY: *80-88* 4-6
Singles: 7-Inch
MERCURY: *80-86* 1-3
POLYDOR: *85* 1-3
LPs: 10/12-Inch 33rpm
MERCURY: *80-86* 5-8
Also see KING DREAM CHORUS &
HOLIDAY CREW
Also see KRUSH GROVE ALL STARS

BLOWFLY
Singles: 7-Inch
WEIRD WORLD: *80* 1-3

BLUE
Singles: 7-Inch
IRIS: 1-3
MCA/PIG (Colored vinyl): *77* 3-5
(Promotional issue only.)
RSO: *73-75* 2-4
ROCKET: *77* 1-3
LPs: 10/12-Inch 33rpm
RSO: *73* 8-10
ROCKET: *77* 5-8
Members: Tim Donald; Ian MacMillan; Jimmy Mc-
Cullough; Hugh Nicholson.
Also see MARMALADE

BLUE, David
(David Cohen)
Singles: 7-Inch
ASYLUM: *73* 2-3

REPRISE: *69* $2-4
LPs: 10/12-Inch 33rpm
ASYLUM: *73-76* 8-10
ELEKTRA: *66* 12-15
REPRISE: *68* 12-15

BLUE BARRON: see BARRON, Blue

BLUE BELLES
Singles: 7-Inch
NEWTOWN: *62* 4-6
PEAK: *62* 4-6
Picture Sleeves
PEAK: *62* 15-25
Member: Patti Labelle
Also see LABELLE, Patti

BLUE CHEER
Singles: 7-Inch
MERCURY: *76* 2-4
PHILIPS: *68-70* 3-5
Picture Sleeves
PHILIPS: *68* 8-15
LPs: 10/12-Inch 33rpm
PHILIPS (9000 series): *80* 5-8
PHILIPS (600000 series): *68-71* 20-40
Members: Leigh Stephens; Paul Whaley; Dick Peterson; Randy Holden; Tony Rainer; Bruce Stephens; Ralph Kellogg; Gary Yoder.

BLUE DIAMONDS
Singles: 78rpm
SAVOY: *54* 5-10
Singles: 7-Inch
SAVOY: *54* 15-25
Member: Ernie Kador.
Also see K-DOE, Ernie

BLUE HAZE
Singles: 7-Inch
A&M: *72-74* 2-4

BLUE JAYS
Singles: 7-Inch
COLLECTABLES: *81* 1-3
ERA: *72* 1-3
MILESTONE: *61-62* 5-10
Member: Leon Peels.

BLUE JAYS / Little Caesar & The Romans
LPs: 10/12-Inch 33rpm
MILESTONE: *62* 40-50
Also see BLUE JAYS
Also see LITTLE CAESAR & THE ROMANS

BLUE MAGIC
Singles: 12-Inch 33/45rpm
MIRAGE: *83* 4-6

Singles: 7-Inch
ATCO: *73-76* $2-4
CAPITOL: *81* 1-3
LIBERTY: *69* 2-4
MIRAGE: *83* 1-3
LPs: 10/12-Inch 33rpm
ATCO: *74-77* 8-10
ATLANTIC: *83* 5-8
CAPITOL: *81* 5-8
COLLECTABLES: *86* 6-8
MIRAGE: *83* 5-8
Members: Ted Mills; Margie Joseph; Vernon Sawyer; Wendell Sawyer; Richard Pratt; Keath Beaton.
Also see JOSEPH, Margie

BLUE MINK
Singles: 7-Inch
BELL: *71-72* 2-4
MCA: *73-74* 1-3
PHILIPS: *69-70* 3-5
Picture Sleeves
PHILIPS: *70* 3-6
LPs: 10/12-Inch 33rpm
MCA: *73* 8-10
PHILIPS: *69-70* 12-15
Members: Madeline Bell; Roger Cook; Barry Morgan; Herbie Flowers; Alan Parker; Ann Odell; Roger Coulan; Ray Cooper.
Also see BELL, Madeline

BLUE NOTES
Singles: 7-Inch
COLLECTABLES: *81* 1-3
JOSIE (800; "If You Love
Me"): *56-57* 50-75
PORT: *58* 10-20
RAMA (25; "If You'll Be Mine"): *53* . .100-200
3 SONS: *62* 8-12
TICO: *51* 15-25
UNI: *69* 3-6
VAL-UE: *60* 10-20
COLLECTABLES: *82* 6-8
Member: Harold Melvin.
Also see MELVIN, Harold, & The Blue Notes

BLUE OYSTER CULT
Singles: 12-Inch 33/45rpm
COLUMBIA: *80* 4-6
Singles: 7-Inch
COLUMBIA: *72-84* 1-3
WHAT'S IT ALL ABOUT: 8-12
(Promotional issue only.)
Picture Sleeves
COLUMBIA (45000 series): *72* 4-8
EPs: 7-Inch 33/45rpm
COLUMBIA (40; "Bootleg EP"): *72* 20-25

LPs: 10/12-Inch 33rpm
ABC RADIO ("A Night On The
Road"): *81* **$35-50**
(Promotional issue only.)
COLUMBIA (Except 31000 through
33000 series): *76-84* **5-8**
COLUMBIA (31000 through 33000
series): *72-75* **6-12**
COLUMBIA: *88* **5-8**
Members: Al Bouchard; Joe Bouchard; Eric
Bloom; Alan Lanier; Donald "Buck Dharma"
Roeser.

BLUE PRINT
Singles: 12-Inch 33/45rpm
FANTASY: *83* **4-6**
Singles: 7-Inch
FANTASY: *83* **1-3**

BLUE RIDGE RANGERS
(John Fogerty)
Singles: 7-Inch
FANTASY: *72-73* **2-4**
LPs: 10/12-Inch 33rpm
FANTASY: *73* **10-12**
Also see FOGERTY, John

BLUE STARS
Singles: 78rpm
MERCURY: *55-56* **3-5**
Singles: 7-Inch
MERCURY: *55-56* **3-5**

BLUE SWEDE
Singles: 7-Inch
EMI AMERICA: *73-75* **2-4**
Picture Sleeves
EMI AMERICA: *73-74* **2-4**
LPs: 10/12-Inch 33rpm
EMI AMERICA: *74-75* **8-10**
Members: Bjorn Skifs; Jan Guldback; Bosse Lil-
jedahl; Michael Areklew; Ladislau Balaz; Tommy
Berglund; Hinke Ekestubble.

BLUENOTES
Singles: 7-Inch
BROOKE: *59-60* **6-10**
Picture Sleeves
BROOKE: *60* **15-25**

BLUES BROTHERS
Singles: 7-Inch
ATLANTIC: *78-81* **1-3**
Picture Sleeves
ATLANTIC: *80* **2-5**
LPs: 10/12-Inch 33rpm
ATLANTIC: *78-81* **6-10**
Members: Dan Aykroyd; John Belushi.
Also see BELUSHI, John

John Fogerty, the voice of the Blue Ridge Rangers

BLUES IMAGE
Singles: 7-Inch
ATCO: *69-71* **$3-5**
LPs: 10/12-Inch 33rpm
ATCO: *69-70* **10-12**
Members: Mike Pinera; Joe Lala; Frank Konte;
Malcolm Jones; Manuel Bertematti.
Also see PINERA, Mike

BLUES MAGOOS
Singles: 7-Inch
ABC: *68-70* **3-5**
GANIM: *69* **15-20**
MERCURY (30000 series): *76* **2-4**
MERCURY (70000 series): *66-68* **5-8**
VERVE/FOLKWAYS (5006; "So I'm
Wrong"): *66* **15-20**
VERVE/FOLKWAYS (5044; "So I'm
Wrong"): *67* **10-15**
Picture Sleeves
MERCURY: *67* **10-15**
LPs: 10/12-Inch 33rpm
ABC: *69-70* **8-10**
MERCURY: *66-68* **30-40**
(Red label.)
MERCURY: *81* **5-8**
(Chicago "skyline" label.)
Members: Geoff Daking; Mike Esposito; Ron Gil-
bert; Ralph Scala; Emil Thielhelm.
Also see BALANCE

BLUES PROJECT
Singles: 7-Inch
CAPITOL: *72* **4-6**

MCA: *73* $1-3
VERVE/FOLKWAYS: *66-67* 8-10
LPs: 10/12-Inch 33rpm
CAPITOL: *72* 10-12
ELEKTRA: *80* 5-8
MCA: *73* 8-10
MGM: *70-74* 8-12
VERVE/FOLKWAYS: *66* 15-18
VERVE/FORECAST: *67-70* 12-15
Members: Al Kooper; Roy Blumenfeld; David
Cohen; Tommy Flanders; Richard Green; John
Gregory; Don Gretmar; Danny Kalb; Steve Katz;
Andy Kulbert; Bill Lussenden; Chicken Hirsch.
Also see KOOPER, Al
Also see SEATRAIN

BO, Eddie
Singles: 78rpm
ACE: *57* 4-8
APOLLO: *55-56* 5-10
Singles: 7-Inch
ACE: *57-59* 5-10
APOLLO: *55-56* 10-20
AT LAST: *63* 3-5
BLUE JAY: *64* 3-5
BO-SOUND: *71* 2-4
CAPITOL: *61* 3-5
CHECKER: *58* 5-10
CHESS (Except 1600 series): *62* 3-5
CHESS (1600 series): *58* 5-8
CINDERELLA: *63* 3-5
RIC: *59-62* 4-8
SEVEN B: *66-68* 3-5
SCRAM: *69* 2-4
SWAN: *62* 3-5
Also see PARKER, Robert

BO, Eddie, & Inez Cheatham
Singles: 7-Inch
SEVEN B: *68* 2-4
Also see BO, Eddie

BO DIDDLEY: see DIDDLEY, Bo

BOB & EARL
Singles: 7-Inch
CLASS: *59* 4-8
Members: Earl Nelson; Bobby Byrd.
Also see BYRD, Bobby
Also see LEE, Jackie

BOB & EARL
Singles: 7-Inch
ABC: *73* 1-3
CHENE: *64* 3-5
COLLECTABLES: *81* 1-3
CRESTVIEW: *69* 2-4
MARC: *63-64* 3-5

MIRWOOD: *66* $3-5
TEMPE: *62* 3-5
UNI: *70* 2-4
WHITE WHALE: *69* 2-4
LPs: 10/12-Inch 33rpm
CRESTVIEW: *69* 15-20
TIP: *64* 20-25
UPFRONT: 10-15
Members: Earl Nelson; Bobby Relf.
Also see WHITE, Barry

BOB B. SOXX & THE BLUE JEANS
Singles: 7-Inch
PHILLES: *62-63* 5-8
LPs: 10/12-Inch 33rpm
PHILLES: *63* 50-60
Members: Bobby Sheen; Darlene Love; Fanita Bar-
rett-James.
Also see BLOSSOMS
Also see LOVE, Darlene
Also see RONETTES / Crystals / Darlene
Love / Bob B. Soxx & The Blue Jeans
Also see SHEEN, Bobby

BOBBETTES
Singles: 78rpm
ATLANTIC: *57* 5-10
Singles: 7-Inch
ATLANTIC: *57-60* 10-15
DIAMOND: *62-65* 3-5
END: *61* 3-5
GALLIANT: *60* 5-8
GONE: *61* 5-8
JUBILEE: *62* 3-5
KING: *61-62* 3-5
MAYHEW: *72-74* 2-4
RCA VICTOR: *66* 3-5
TRIPLE-X: *60* 8-10
Members: Emma Pought; Jannie Pought; Heather
Dixon; Laura Webb; Helen Gathers.

BOBBY & THE MIDNITES
Singles: 7-Inch
ARISTA: *81* 1-3
COLUMBIA: *84* 1-3
LPs: 10/12-Inch 33rpm
ARISTA: *81* 5-8
COLUMBIA: *84* 5-8
Member: Bob Weir.
Also see WEIR, Bob

BOBBY LEE: see LEE, Bobby

BOBO, Willie
Singles: 7-Inch
BLUE NOTE : *77* 1-3
CAPITOL: *76* 2-3
JUPITER JAZZ: *75* 2-3

TICO: 59 .... $5-10
VERVE: 65-69 2-4
LPs: 10/12-Inch 33rpm
BLUE NOTE: 77 5-8
ROULETTE: 63-64 10-15
VERVE: 65-69 8-12
Also see HANCOCK, Herbie, & Willie Bobo

BOFILL, Angela
Singles: 12-Inch 33/45rpm
ARISTA: 81-85 4-6
Singles: 7-Inch
ARISTA: 81-85 1-3
GRP: 79 2-3
LPs: 10/12-Inch 33rpm
ARISTA: 81-85 5-8
CAPITOL: 88 5-8
GRP: 78 5-10

BOHANNON
(Hamilton Bohannon)
Singles: 12-Inch 33/45rpm
COMPLEAT: 84-85 4-6
MERCURY: 77-80 4-6
MCA: 84 4-6
PHASE II: 80-83 4-6
Singles: 7-Inch
DAKAR: 73-75 2-4
MERCURY: 77-80 1-3
PHASE 2: 80-83 1-3
LPs: 10/12-Inch 33rpm
DAKAR: 73-75 10-12
MERCURY: 77-80 8-10
PHASE 2: 80-83 5-8

BOHANNON, Hamilton, & Dr.
Perri Johnson
Singles: 12-Inch 33/45rpm
PHASE 2: 81 4-6
Singles: 7-Inch
PHASE 2: 81 1-3
Also see BOHANNON

BOHN, Rudi, & His Band
EPs: 7-Inch 33/45rpm
LONDON: 59 3-6
LPs: 10/12-Inch 33rpm
LONDON: 59-61 5-10

BOILING POINT
Singles: 7-Inch
BULLET: 78 1-3

BOLGER, Ray
Singles: 78rpm
DECCA: 49-51 3-5
Singles: 7-Inch
ARMOUR: 63 2-4

DECCA: 50-51 .... $3-6
LPs: 10/12-Inch 33rpm
DISNEYLAND: 65 6-10

BOLIN, Tommy
Singles: 7-Inch
NEMPEROR: 76 2-4
LPs: 10/12-Inch 33rpm
COLUMBIA: 76 8-10
NEMPEROR (400 series): 75 10-12
NEMPEROR (37000 series): 81 5-8
Also see JAMES GANG
Also see ZEPHYR

BOLTON, Michael
Singles: 7-Inch
COLUMBIA: 83-88 1-3
RCA VICTOR: 75-76 2-4
LPs: 10/12-Inch 33rpm
COLUMBIA: 83-88 5-8
RCA VICTOR: 75-76 8-10
Also see BLACKJACK

BOMBERS
Singles: 7-Inch
WEST END: 79 1-3
LPs: 10/12-Inch 33rpm
WEST END: 79 10-12

BON JOVI
Singles: 7-Inch
MERCURY: 84-88 1-3
LPs: 10/12-Inch 33rpm
MERCURY: 85-88 5-8
Members: Jon Bon Jovi; Richie Sambora; David
Bryan; Alec John Such; Tico Torres.

BON ROCK
Singles: 12-Inch 33/45rpm
EARTHTONE: 84 4-6
LPs: 10/12-Inch 33rpm
EARTHTONE: 84 5-8
Member: Keith Rogers.

BOND, Angelo
Singles: 7-Inch
ABC: 75-76 2-3
LPs: 10/12-Inch 33rpm
ABC: 75-77 8-10

BOND, Johnny
Singles: 78rpm
COLUMBIA (Except 21521): 50-56 3-6
COLUMBIA (21521; "The Little Rock
Roll"): 56 5-10
Singles: 7-Inch
COLUMBIA (Except 21521): 50-56 4-8
COLUMBIA (21521; "The Little Rock
Roll"): 56 10-20

DITTO: *59* $3-5
LAMB & LION: *74* 1-3
MGM: *73* 1-3
ORCHID: *89* 1-3
REPUBLIC: *60* 3-5
SMASH: *62* 2-4
STARDAY (600 through 900
series): *63-72* 2-4
STARDAY (8000 series): *72* 1-3
EPs: 7-Inch 33/45rpm
COLUMBIA: *58* **10-15**
REPUBLIC: *60* **10-15**
LPs: 10/12-Inch 33rpm
CMH: *77* 5-8
HARMONY: *64-65* 10-20
LAMB & LION: *74* 5-8
NASHVILLE: *71* 5-8
SHASTA: 10-15
STARDAY (100 & 200 series): *61-64* ... 20-25
STARDAY (300 series,
except 354): *65-66* **15-20**
STARDAY (354; "Famous Hot
Rodders I Have Known"): *65* 25-30
STARDAY (400 series): *67-71* 10-15
STARDAY (900 series): *74* 6-10

BONDS, Gary "U.S."
(U.S. Bonds)
Singles: 7-Inch
ABC: *73* 1-3
ATCO: *69* 2-4
BLUFF CITY: *74* 2-4
BOTANIC: *68* 3-5
COLLECTABLES: *81* 1-3
EMI AMERICA: *81-82* 1-3
LEGRAND (1003 through 1020): *60-62* ... 4-8
LEGRAND (1022 through 1041): *62-66* . 10-20
LEGRAND (1043 through 1046): *66-67* .. 5-15
MCA: *84* 1-3
PRODIGAL: *75* 2-3
SUE: *70* 2-4
Picture Sleeves
EMI AMERICA: *81-82* 1-3
LEGRAND: *61* 8-15
LPs: 10/12-Inch 33rpm
EMI AMERICA: *81-82* 5-8
LEGRAND (1000 series): *86* 5-8
LEGRAND (3000 series): *61-62* 25-30
MCA: *84* 5-8
PHOENIX: *84* 5-8
RHINO: *84* 5-8
Also see CHECKER, Chubby / Gary U.S.
Bonds
Also see GREENWICH, Ellie
Also see JACKSON, Chuck

Also see KING, Ben E.
Also see SPRINGSTEEN, Bruce

BONDS, U.S.: see BONDS, Gary "U.S."
BONE SYMPHONY
Singles: 12-Inch 33/45rpm
CAPITOL: *83* $4-6
Singles: 7-Inch
CAPITOL: *83* 1-3
LPs: 10/12-Inch 33rpm
CAPITOL: *83* 5-8
BONES
Singles: 7-Inch
MCA: *73* 2-4
SIGNPOST: *72* 3-5
LPs: 10/12-Inch 33rpm
MCA: *73* 8-10
SIGNPOST: *72* 10-12

BONES, Elbow: see ELBOW BONES
BONEY M
Singles: 12-Inch 33/45rpm
CARRERE: *85* 4-6
SIRE: *79* 4-6
Singles: 7-Inch
ATCO: *76-77* 2-4
ATLANTIC: *77* 2-3
SIRE: *78-79* 1-3
Picture Sleeves
SIRE: *79* 1-3
LPs: 10/12-Inch 33rpm
ATCO: *76* 10-12
ATLANTIC: *77* 8-10
SIRE: *77-79* 5-8
Members: Marcia Barrett; Bobby Farrell; Liz
Mitchell; Maizie Williams.

BONNIE & THE TREASURES
(Featuring Charlott O'Hara)
Singles: 7-Inch
PHI DAN (5505; "Home Of The
Brave"): *65* 25-30
BONNIE SISTERS
(With Mickey "Guitar" Baker)
Singles: 78rpm
RAINBOW: *56* 5-10
Singles: 7-Inch
RAINBOW: *56* 10-15

BONO, Sonny: see SONNY
BONOFF, Karla
Singles: 7-Inch
COLUMBIA: *77-84* 1-3
Picture Sleeves
COLUMBIA: *77-84* 1-3

LPs: 10/12-Inch 33rpm
COLUMBIA: 77-82 .... $5-8

BONZO DOG BAND
(Bonzo Dog Doo-Dah Band)
Singles: 7-Inch
IMPERIAL: 69 2-4
LIBERTY: 68 3-5
UNITED ARTISTS: 71-72 2-4
LPs: 10/12-Inch 33rpm
IMPERIAL: 68-70 15-18
LIBERTY: 83 5-8
UNITED ARTISTS: 71-74 10-12
Members: Vivian Stanshall; Neil Innes; Roger Ruskin Spear; Hughie Flint; Tony Kaye; Dave Richards; Andy Roberts.
Also see RUTLES

BONZO GOES TO WASHINGTON
Singles: 12-Inch 33/45rpm
SLEEPING BAG: 84 4-6

BOOGIE BOYS
Singles: 12-Inch 33/45rpm
CAPITOL: 84-87 4-6
Singles: 7-Inch
CAPITOL: 84-88 1-3
LPs: 10/12-Inch 33rpm
CAPITOL: 85-88 5-8
Member: William Stroman.

BOOGIE MAN ORCHESTRA
Singles: 7-Inch
BOOGIE MAN : 75 2-3

BOOK OF LOVE
Singles: 12-Inch 33/45rpm
SIRE: 84-88 4-6
LPs: 10/12-Inch 33rpm
SIRE: 86-88 5-8

BOOKER, James
Singles: 7-Inch
PEACOCK: 60-64 3-5
LPs: 10/12-Inch 33rpm
ROUNDER: 84 5-8
Also see LITTLE BOOKER

BOOKER T. & PRISCILLA
Singles: 7-Inch
A&M: 71-73 2-4
LPs: 10/12-Inch 33rpm
A&M: 71-73 8-10
Members: Booker T. Jones; Priscilla Coolidge-Jones.

BOOKER T. & THE MGs
(Booker T. Jones)
Singles: 12-Inch 33/45rpm
A&M: 82-84 .... $4-6
Singles: 7-Inch
A&M: 81-82 1-3
ASYLUM: 77 2-3
EPIC: 75 2-3
STAX (Except 100 series): 67-71 3-6
STAX (100 series): 62-66 4-8
LPs: 10/12-Inch 33rpm
A&M: 72-81 8-10
ASYLUM: 77 5-8
ATLANTIC: 68 10-12
EPIC: 74 8-10
PICKWICK: 5-10
STAX (700 series,
except 701): 65-68 20-30
STAX (701; "Green Onions"): 62 25-40
STAX (2000 series): 68-71 15-20
STAX (8000 series): 81-84 5-8
Also see MGs
Also see MAR-KEYS / Booker T. & The MGs
Also see SANTANA
Also see SIMON, PAUL

BOOM, Taka
Singles: 7-Inch
ARIOLA: 79 1-3
MIRAGE: 85 1-3
LPs: 10/12-Inch 33rpm
ARIOLA: 79 5-8

BOOMTOWN RATS
Singles: 7-Inch
COLUMBIA: 79-80 1-3
LPs: 10/12-Inch 33rpm
COLUMBIA: 79-85 5-8
MERCURY: 77 8-12
Members: Bob Geldof; Pete Briquette; Gerry Cott; Simon Crowe; Johnny Fingers; Garry Roberts.
Also see BAND AID
Also see GELDOF, Bob

BOONE, Daniel
Singles: 7-Inch
EPIC: 72 2-4
MERCURY: 72-74 2-4
PYE: 75 2-3
LPs: 10/12-Inch 33rpm
MERCURY: 72 10-12

BOONE, Debbie
Singles: 7-Inch
LAMB & LION: 80-84 1-3
WARNER BROS: 77-80 1-3

Picture Sleeves
WARNER BROS: *78* $1-3
LPs: 10/12-Inch 33rpm
LAMB & LION: *80-84* 5-8
WARNER BROS: *77-80* 5-8
Also see BOONE, Pat, & The Boone Girls
Also see BOONE GIRLS

BOONE, Pat
Singles: 78rpm
DOT: *55-58* 3-6
REPUBLIC: *54* 4-8
Singles: 7-Inch
ABC: *74-75* 1-3
BUENA VISTA: *73* 2-3
CAPITOL: *70* 2-4
CHEVROLET/RCA Victor (4988; "June
   Is Bustin' Out All Over"): *58* 5-8
(Promotional issue for Chevrolet dealers. Narration
by Bob Lund.)
DOT (15000 series): *55-57* 4-8
   (Maroon label.)
DOT (15000 & 16000 series,
   except 16658): *57-66* 3-6
   (Black label.)
DOT (16658; "Beach Girl"): *64* 4-8
   (With Bruce Johnston and Terry Melcher.)
DOT (200 series): *59-60* 5-10
   (Stereo.)
DOT (17000 series): *66-75* 2-4
HITSVILLE: *76-77* 2-3
LION: *72* 2-3
MC: *77* 2-3
MCA: *84* 1-3
MGM: *71-73* 2-3
MELODYLAND: *74-76* 2-3
REPUBLIC: *54* 6-10
SRG: *88* 1-3
TETRAGRAMMATON: *69* 2-4
WARNER BROS: *80-81* 1-3
Picture Sleeves
DOT: *57-62* 5-10
EPs: 7-Inch 33/45rpm
DOT: *57-60* 8-12
LPs: 10/12-Inch 33rpm
ABC: *74* 5-8
BIBLE VOICE: *70* 5-8
CANDLELITE: 6-10
   (A mail-order LP offer.)
DOT (Maroon label): *55-56* 10-25
DOT (Black label, black
   vinyl): *57-68* 10-20
DOT (25270; "Moonglow"): *60* 30-50
   (Colored vinyl.)
HAMILTON: *65* 10-12
HITSVILLE: *76* 8-10

LAMB & LION: *73-81* $5-8
MC: *77* 5-8
MCA: *82* 5-8
MGM: *73* 5-8
PARAMOUNT: *74* 5-8
PICKWICK: , ... 5-8
SUPREME: *70* 6-10
TETRAGRAMMATON: *69* 10-12
WORD: *75-84* 5-8
Also see BRUCE & TERRY
Also see JENKINS, Gordon, & His Orchestra

BOONE, Pat & Shirley
(Pat Boone Family)
Singles: 7-Inch
DOT: *62-64* 2-4
MGM: *72* 2-3
MELODYLAND: *75* 2-3
MOTOWN: *74* 2-3
WARNER BROS: *79* 1-3
EPs: 7-Inch 33/45rpm
DOT: *59* 5-8
LPs: 10/12-Inch 33rpm
LION: *72* 5-8
WORD: *71* 5-8

BOONE, Pat, & The Boone Girls
Singles: 7-Inch
LION: *72* 2-3
Also see BOONE, Debbie
Also see BOONE, Pat & Shirley
Also see BOONE GIRLS

BOONE FAMILY:
see BOONE, Pat & Shirley

BOONE GIRLS
(Boones)
Singles: 7-Inch
LAMB & LION: *77* 1-3
LION: *72* 2-3
MGM: *71-73* 2-4
MOTOWN: *75* 2-3
WARNER BROS: *77* 1-3
LPs: 10/12-Inch 33rpm
LAMB & LION: *77-83* 5-8
Also see BOONE, Debbie
Also see BOONE, Pat, & The Boone Girls

BOOTEE, Duke
Singles: 7-Inch
MERCURY: *84* 1-3

BOOTSY'S RUBBER BAND
(William "Bootsy" Collins)
Singles: 12-Inch 33/45rpm
WARNER BROS : *79-82* 4-6
Singles: 7-Inch
WARNER BROS: *75-82* 1-3

LPs: 10/12-Inch 33rpm
WARNER BROS: 76-82 . . . . $5-8
Also see PARLIAMENT
Also see SWEAT BAND
Also see ZAPP

BOOTY PEOPLE
Singles: 7-Inch
CALLA: 76 2-3
LPs: 10/12-Inch 33rpm
ABC: 77 5-8

BOSTIC, Earl
Singles: 78rpm
GOTHAM: 46-48 4-8
KING: 47-58 3-6
MAJESTIC: 46 5-10
Singles: 7-Inch
KING (4000 series): 52-56 8-12
(Colored vinyl.)
KING (4000 series,
except 4491): 50-57 4-6
(Black vinyl.)
KING (4491; "I Got Loaded"): 52 10-20
KING (5000 series): 57-65 3-8
KING (6000 series): 65-69 2-4
KING (15000 series): 72 1-3
EPs: 7-Inch 33/45rpm
KING: 52-62 8-15
LPs: 10/12-Inch 33rpm
KING (72; "Earl Bostic"): 52 50-100
KING (76; "Earl Bostic"): 52 50-100
KING (77; "Earl Bostic"): 52 50-100
KING (78; "Earl Bostic"): 52 50-100
KING (79; "Earl Bostic"): 52 50-100
KING (95; "Earl Bostic Plays Old
Standards"): 52 50-100
KING (103; "Earl Bostic"): 52 50-100
KING (119; "Earl Bostic"): 52 50-100
Note: King 72 through 119 are 10-inch LPs. More
precise titles would be appreciated, since our King
catalog simply titles them all as "Bill Bostic."
KING (500 series): 54-58 10-20
KING (600 through 1000
series): 59-70 8-15
PHILLIPS: 68 8-12

BOSTIC, Earl, & Bill Doggett
Singles: 78rpm
KING: 56 2-4
Singles: 7-Inch
KING: 56 3-5
Also see BOSTIC, Earl
Also see DOGGETT, Bill

BOSTIC, Sam
Singles: 7-Inch
ATLANTIC: 85 . . . . $1-3

BOSTON
Singles: 7-Inch
EPIC: 76-79 2-3
MCA: 85-87 1-3
Picture Sleeves
MCA: 85-87 1-3
LPs: 10/12-Inch 33rpm
EPIC (34188 "Boston"): 78 15-25
(With an "E99" prefix. Picture disc.)
EPIC (34188; "Boston"): 80 12-15
(With an "HE" prefix. Half-speed mastered.)
EPIC (34188; "Boston"): 76 15-25
(With a "PE" prefix.)
EPIC (35000 series): 78 10-12
EPIC (45000 series): 81 12-15
(With an "HE" prefix. Half-speed mastered.)
MCA: 85-87 5-8
Members: Brad Delp; Tom Scholz; Barry
Goudreau; Sib Hashian; Fran Sheehan.
Also see GOUDREAU, Barry
Also see ORION THE HUNTER

BOSTON POPS ORCHESTRA
(Conducted by Arthur Fiedler)
Singles: 78rpm
RCA VICTOR: 50-57 2-4
Singles: 7-Inch
RCA VICTOR: 50 65 2-5
EPs: 7-Inch 33/45rpm
RCA VICTOR: 50-61 4-8
LPs: 10/12-Inch 33rpm
DEUTSCHE GRAMMOPHON: 78 4-8
MIDSONG INT'L: 79 4-8
POLYDOR: 71-72 5-10
RCA VICTOR: 50-69 8-18

BOSTON POPS ORCHESTRA
(Conducted by John Williams)
LPs: 10/12-Inch 33rpm
PHILIPS: 80 5-8
Also see WILLIAMS, John

BOSWELL, Connie
Singles: 78rpm
BRUNSWICK: 32-34 4-8
DECCA: 35-56 2-5
Singles: 7-Inch
CHARLES: 62 2-4
DECCA: 50-56 3-5
Also see CROSBY, Bing, & Connie Boswell

BOTTOM & COMPANY
Singles: 7-Inch
MOTOWN: 74-75 2-4

LPs: 10/12-Inch 33rpm
GORDY: 76 . . . . $8-10

BOTTOM LINE
Singles: 7-Inch
GREEDY: 76 2-3
LPs: 10/12-Inch 33rpm
GREEDY: 76 8-10

BOUNTY, Rick, & The Rockits
Singles: 7-Inch
BOW (6144; "It'll Be Me"): 58 50-75
MASSABESIC: 86 3-5
Picture Sleeves
MASSABESIC: 86 3-5

BOURGEOIS-TAGG
Singles: 7-Inch
ISLAND: 86-87 1-3
LPs: 10/12-Inch 33rpm
ISLAND: 86-87 5-8
Members: Brent Bourgeois; Larry Tagg.

BOW WOW WOW
Singles: 12-Inch 33/45rpm
RCA VICTOR: 83 4-6
Singles: 7-Inch
RCA VICTOR: 81-84 1-3
Picture Sleeves
RCA VICTOR: 82 1-3
LPs: 10/12-Inch 33rpm
HARVEST: 82 5-8
RCA VICTOR: 81-84 5-8
Promotional LPs
RCA VICTOR "Special Radio
Series"): 81 10-15
Also see ADAM & THE ANTS

BOWEN, Jimmy
Singles: 78rpm
ROULETTE: 57 4-8
Singles: 7-Inch
CAPEHART: 61-62 3-5
CREST: 61 3-5
REPRISE: 64-66 3-5
ROULETTE: 57-60 4-8
Picture Sleeves
CAPEHART: 61 25-35
EPs: 7-Inch 33/45rpm
ROULETTE: 57 30-40
LPs: 10/12-Inch 33rpm
REPRISE: 66 15-20
ROULETTE (25004; "Jimmy
Bowen"): 57 75-100
Also see KNOX, Buddy / Jimmy Bowen

BOWIE, David
Singles: 12-Inch 33/45rpm
EMI AMERICA: 82-87 . . . . $4-8
RCA VICTOR: 79-80 8-15
Promotional 12-Inch Singles
EMI AMERICA: 82-87 6-15
RCA VICTOR: 79-80 10-20
Singles: 7-Inch
BACKSTREET: 82 1-3
DERAM: 67 15-20
EMI AMERICA: 83-87 1-3
LONDON: 74 5-8
MERCURY: 69-71 20-25
RCA VICTOR: 71-84 2-5
WARNER BROS: 66 40-50
Picture Sleeves
EMI AMERICA: 83-87 2-4
RCA VICTOR: 72-85 5-10
Promotional Singles
BACKSTREET: 82 5-8
DERAM: 67 20-30
EMI AMERICA (Except boxed
8380): 83-87 4-8
EMI AMERICA (8380; "Day In Day Out"
boxed edition): 87 15-20
(Colored vinyl.)
LONDON: 74 8-15
MERCURY: 69-71 20-35
RCA VICTOR: 71-84 5-12
WARNER BROS: 66 40-60
WHAT'S IT ALL ABOUT : 10-20
EPs: 7-Inch 33/45rpm
RCA VICTOR: 20-25
(Promotional issues only.)
LPs: 10/12-Inch 33rpm
DERAM (18003; "David
Bowie"): 67 100-125
EMI AMERICA: 83-86 5-8
LONDON: 73-85 8-12

MFSL (064; "Rise & Fall Of
Ziggy Stardust"): 82 . . . . $20-40
MFSL ("Let's Dance"): 82 15-25
MERCURY (61246; "Man Of Words/
Man Of Music"): 69 60-80
MERCURY (61246; "Space
Oddity"): 72 10-12
MERCURY (61325; "The Man Who Sold
The World"): 71 20-25
RCA VICTOR (0291; "Bowie Pin
Ups"): 73 8-12
RCA VICTOR (0576; "Diamond
Dogs"): 74 500-1000
(With "Dog Genitals" cover.)
RCA VICTOR (0576; "Diamond
Dogs"): 74 6-10
(With dog's genitals covered.)
RCA VICTOR (0700 through 1300
series): 74-76 8-15
RCA VICTOR (1732; "Changesone
Bowie"): 76 60-80
(With the alternate take of "John, I'm Only Danc-
ing.")
RCA VICTOR (1732; "Changesone
Bowie"): 76 6-10
(With the commonly issued take of "John, I'm
Only Dancing.")
RCA VICTOR (2000 through
2500): 77 6-10
RCA VICTOR (2743; "Peter & The
Wolf"): 78 6-10
(Black vinyl.)
RCA VICTOR (2743; "Peter & The
Wolf"): 78 15-25
(Colored vinyl.)
RCA VICTOR (2900 through 4200
series): 79-82 5-10
RCA VICTOR (4600 through 4800
series): 71-73 8-15
(With an "LSP" prefix.)
RCA VICTOR (4700 through 4900
series, except 4862): 83-84 5-10
(With an "AFL" or "CPL" prefix.)
RCA VICTOR 4862; "Ziggy
Stardust"): 83 5-10
(Black vinyl.)
RCA VICTOR 4862; "Ziggy
Stardust"): 83 10-20
(Clear vinyl.)

Promotional LPs

DERAM (18003; "David
Bowie"): 67 100-200
EMI AMERICA (9960; "Let's
Talk"): 83 30-40

MERCURY (61246; "Man Of Words/
Man Of Music"): 69 . . . . $70-80
RCA VICTOR (0200 through 4800
series): 71-73 15-20
(With programmer's strip on front cover.)
RCA VICTOR (2697; "Bowie Now"): 78 25-30
RCA VICTOR (3016; "An Evening With
David Bowie"): 78 75-100
RCA VICTOR (3545; "Bowie 1980"): 80 30-40
RCA VICTOR (3829; "RCA Special
Radio Series"): 80 25-40
RCA VICTOR (3840; "David Bowie
Interview"): 80 35-40
RCA VICTOR (11306; "Peter & The
Wolf"): 78 25-30
Also see HOUSTON, Cissy
Also see KHAN, Chaka
Also see QUEEN & DAVID BOWIE
Also see SPIDERS FROM MARS
Also see TURNER, Tina
Also see VANDROSS, Luther

BOWIE, David / Joe Cocker /
Youngbloods
LPs: 10/12-Inch 33rpm
MERCURY (SRD-2-29; "Zig Zag
Festival"): 70 35-40
(Promotional issue only.)
Also see COCKER, Joe
Also see YOUNGBLOODS

BOWIE, David, & Mick Jagger
Singles: 12-Inch 33/45rpm
EMI AMERICA (19200; "Dancing In The
Streets"): 85 5-8
Singles: 7-Inch
EMI AMERICA (8288; "Dancing In The
Streets"): 85 2-3
Also see JAGGER, Mick

BOWIE, David, & The Pat
Metheny Group
Singles: 12-Inch 33/45rpm
EMI AMERICA: 85 4-6
Singles: 7-Inch
EMI AMERICA: 85 2-3
LPs: 10/12-Inch 33rpm
EMI AMERICA: 85 5-8
Also see METHENY, Pat

BOWIE, David / Iggy Pop
Singles: 12-Inch 33/45rpm
RCA VICTOR: 77 25-35
(Promotional issue only.)
Also see BOWIE, David
Also see POP, Iggy

BOWIE, Roz
Singles: 7-Inch
BLUESTEM (Black vinyl): 87 .... $1-3
BLUESTEM (Colored vinyl): 87 2-4
Picture Sleeves
BLUESTEM: 87 1-3
LPs: 10/12-Inch 33rpm
BLUESTEM: 87 5-8

BOWLES, Rick
Singles: 7-Inch
POLYDOR: 82 1-3
LPs: 10/12-Inch 33rpm
POLYDOR: 82 5-8

BOX OF FROGS
Singles: 7-Inch
EPIC: 84-86 1-3
LPs: 10/12-Inch 33rpm
EPIC: 84-86 5-8
Members: Chris Dreja; Jim McCarty; Jeff Beck.
Also see YARDBIRDS

BOX TOPS
Singles: 7-Inch
BELL: 70-71 2-4
GUSTO: 84 1-3
HI: 71 2-4
MALA: 67-69 3-5
SPEHRE SOUND : 67 3-5
STAX: 74 2-4
LPs: 10/12-Inch 33rpm
BELL: 67-69 10-15
COTILLION: 71 10-12
KORY: 77 5-8
RHINO: 82 5-8
Members: Alex Chilton; Rick Allen; Tom Boggs;
Harold Cloud; Bill Cunningham; John Evans;
Swain Scharfar; Gary Talley; Danny Smythe.

BOY GEORGE
Singles: 7-Inch
VIRGIN: 87-88 1-3
LPs: 10/12-Inch 33rpm
VIRGIN: 87-88 5-8
Also see CULTURE CLUB

BOY MEETS GIRL
Singles: 7-Inch
A&M: 85-88 1-3
LPs: 10/12-Inch 33rpm
A&M: 85-88 5-8
Members: George Merrill; Shannon Rubicam.

BOYCE, Tommy
Singles: 7-Inch
A&M (Except 826): 66 2-4
A&M (826; "In Case The Wind
Should Blow"): 66 8-12

CAPITOL: 71 .... $2-4
COLPIX: 66 5-8
DOT: 60 8-12
MGM: 65 5-8
RCA VICTOR (7000 series): 61 8-10
RCA VICTOR (8000 series): 62-63 5-8
R-DELL: 58 10-15
WOW: 61 5-8
LPs: 10/12-Inch 33rpm
CAMDEN: 68 10-15
Also see CLOUD, Christopher

BOYCE, Tommy, & Bobby Hart
(Boyce & Hart)
Singles: 7-Inch
A&M: 67-69 3-5
AQUARIAN: 68 3-5
Picture Sleeves
A&M: 67-69 3-6
AQUARIAN: 68 4-8
LPs: 10/12-Inch 33rpm
A&M: 67-69 10-12
Also see BOYCE, Tommy
Also see DOLENZ, JONES, BOYCE &
HART

BOYD, Eddie
(Eddie Boyd & His Chess Men; Eddie Boyd
Blues Combo; Little Eddie Boyd & His Boogie
Band)
Singles: 78rpm
CHESS: 50-56 10-20
HERALD: 52 40-60
J.O.B.: 52-58 20-25
RCA VICTOR: 47-50 5-15
Singles: 7-Inch
ART TONE: 62 3-5
BEA & BABY: 59 4-6
CHESS (1500 & 1600 series): 54 50-75
(Colored vinyl.)
CHESS (1500 & 1600 series,
except 1523): 52-56 20-40
(Black vinyl.)
CHESS (1523; "Cool Kind
Treatment"): 52 30-40
HERALD (406; "I'm Goin'
Downtown"): 52 75-125
J.O.B.: 52-58 35-50
LA SALLE: 61 3-5
MOJO: 3-5
ORIOLE: 58 15-20
PALOS: 63-64 3-5
PUSH: 62 3-5
RCA VICTOR (50-0000 series): 50 35-50
EPs: 7-Inch 33/45rpm
ESQUIRE: 60 12-15

LPs: 10/12-Inch 33rpm	
EPIC: *69* $18-20	
LONDON: *69* 15-20	
Also see GREEN, Peter	

BOYD, Jimmy
(Little Jimmy Boyd)
Singles: 78rpm
COLUMBIA (Except 21571): *52-56* 3-6
COLUMBIA (21571; "Rockin' Down
The Mississippi"): *56* 10-15
Singles: 7-Inch
CAPITOL: *63* 2-4
COLUMBIA (MJV-100
series): *52* 6-12
COLUMBIA (21571; "Rockin' Down
The Mississippi"): *56* 20-30
COLUMBIA (39000 & 40000
series): *52-56* 5-10
IMPERIAL: *66-67* 3-5
MGM (12788; "Cream Puff"): *59* 30-40
TAKE TEN: *63* 3-5
VEE JAY: *65* 2-4
Picture Sleeves
COLUMBIA (MJV-100
series): *52* 15-25
Also see LAINE, Frankie, & Jimmy Boyd

BOYD, Jimmy, & Rosemary Clooney
Singles: 78rpm
COLUMBIA: *53* 3-5
Singles: 7-Inch
COLUMBIA (39000 series): *53* 5-8
COLUMBIA (41000 series): *60* 3-5
Also see BOYD, Jimmy
Also see CLOONEY, Rosemary

BOYD, Little Eddie:
see BOYD, Eddie

BOYER, Bonnie
Singles: 12-Inch 33/45rpm
COLUMBIA: *79* 4-6
Singles: 7-Inch
COLUMBIA: *79* 1-3
LPs: 10/12-Inch 33rpm
COLUMBIA: *79* 5-8

BOYER, Charles
Singles: 7-Inch
VALIANT: *65* 2-4
LPs: 10/12-Inch 33rpm
VALIANT: *65* 10-15

BOYLAN, Terence
Singles: 7-Inch
ASYLUM: *77-80* 1-3

LPs: 10/12-Inch 33rpm
ASYLUM: *77-80* $5-8
VERVE/FORECAST: *69* 12-15

BOYS BAND
Singles: 7-Inch
ELEKTRA: *82* 1-3
LPs: 10/12-Inch 33rpm
ASYLUM: *82* 5-8

BOYS DON'T CRY
Singles: 12-Inch 33/45rpm
PROFILE: *86* 4-6
Singles: 7-Inch
PROFILE: *86* 1-3
LPs: 10/12-Inch 33rpm
PROFILE: *86* 5-8
Member: Nick Richards.

BOYS IN THE BAND
Singles: 7-Inch
SPRING: *70* 2-4

BOYS ON THE BLOCK
Singles: 7-Inch
FANTASY: *87* 1-3

BOZE, Calvin
Singles: 78rpm
ALADDIN: *50-51* 10-15
SCORE: *48* 8-12
Singles: 7-Inch
ALADDIN (Except 3055 & 3065): *51-52* 20-35
ALADDIN (3055; "Safronia B."): *50* ... 40-50
ALADDIN (3065; "Lizzie Lou"): *51* 35-40
ASTRA: 4-8
G&G: 25-35
IMPERIAL: *62* 3-5

BRADLEY, James
(James Bradley & The Bill Smith Combo)
Singles: 7-Inch
CHESS: *60* 4-6
MALACO: *79-84* 1-3
MANCO: *61* 3-5
LPs: 10/12-Inch 33rpm
MALACO: *84* 5-8

BRADLEY, Jan
Singles: 7-Inch
CHESS: *62-68* 4-8
ERIC: *73* 1-3
FORMAL: *62* 10-15
HOOTENANNY: *63* 3-5
NIGHT OWL: *63* 3-5
SOUND SPECTRUM: 3-5

BRADLEY, Owen
(Owen Bradley Quintet)
Singles: 78rpm
CORAL : *49-50* $3-6
DECCA: *54-57* 3-6
Singles: 7-Inch
CORAL : *50* 4-8
DECCA: *54-61* 5-10
EPs: 7-Inch 33/45rpm
CORAL: *54* 10-20
DECCA: *58* 10-20
LPs: 10/12-Inch 33rpm
CORAL: *53-55* 15-25
DECCA: *58-60* 15-25

BRADSHAW, Terry
Singles: 7-Inch
BENSON: *80* 1-3
MERCURY: *76* 2-4
Picture Sleeves
BENSON: *80* 2-3
LPs: 10/12-Inch 33rpm
BENSON: *80* 5-8
HEARTWARMING: *82* 5-8
MERCURY: *76* 6-12

BRADSHAW, Tiny
Singles: 78rpm
KING: *50-55* 5-10
Singles: 7-Inch
GUSTO: *80-83* 1-3
KING (4300 through 4500
series): *50-53* 10-20
(Black vinyl.)
KING (4300 through 4500
series): *50-53* 25-40
(Colored vinyl.)
KING (4600 through 4800
series): *54-55* 5-10
EPs: 7-Inch 33/45rpm
KING: *50-57* 20-35
LPs: 10/12-Inch 33rpm
KING: *55-57* 20-40

BRAINSTORM
Singles: 12-Inch 33/45rpm
TABU: *77-79* 4-6
Singles: 7-Inch
RCA VICTOR: *82* 1-3
TABU: *76-79* 1-3
LPs: 10/12-Inch 33rpm
RCA VICTOR: *82* 5-8
TABU: *77-79* 5-8

BRAM TCHAIKOVSKY:
see TCHAIKOVSKY, Bram

BRAMLETT, Bonnie
Singles: 7-Inch
CAPRICORN: *75-78* $2-3
COLUMBIA: *72-73* 2-4
REFUGE: *81* 1-3
LPs: 10/12-Inch 33rpm
CAPRICORN: *75-78* 8-10
COLUMBIA: *72-73* 10-12
Also see DELANEY & BONNIE
Also see LITTLE FEAT

BRAMLETT, Delaney
(Delaney & Bekka Bramlett; Delaney Bramlett
& Blue Diamond)
Singles: 7-Inch
COLUMBIA (45950; "Are You A Beatle
Or A Rolling Stone"): *73* 5-10
CREAM: *81* 1-3
GNP/CRESCENDO: *64-66* 3-5
INDEPENDENCE: *67* 3-5
LPs: 10/12-Inch 33rpm
COLUMBIA: *72-73* 8-10
MGM: *75* 8-10
PRODIGAL: *77* 8-10
Also see DELANEY & BONNIE

BRAND X
Singles: 7-Inch
PASSPORT: *78* 1-3
LPs: 10/12-Inch 33rpm
PASSPORT: *76-84* 5-8
Members: Phil Collins; John Goodsall; Percy
Jones; Robin Lumley; Morris Pert.
Also see COLLINS, Phil

BRANDON, Bill
Singles: 7-Inch
MOONSONG: *72-73* 2-4
PIEDMONT: *76* 2-3
PRELUDE: *77-78* 1-3
SOUTH CAMP: *67* 3-5
TOWER: *68* 2-4

BRANIGAN, Laura
Singles: 12-Inch 33/45rpm
ATLANTIC: *82-87* 4-6
Singles: 7-Inch
ATLANTIC: *80-87* 1-3
EMI AMERICA: *84* 1-3
LPs: 10/12-Inch 33rpm
ATLANTIC: *82-87* 5-8
EMI AMERICA: *84* 5-8

BRASS CONSTRUCTION
Singles: 12-Inch 33/45rpm
CAPITOL: *83* 4-6
LIBERTY: *82* 4-6

LPs: 10/12-Inch 33rpm
ARISTA: *75-81* $5-8
Members: Mike Brecker; Randy Brecker; Dave Sanborn.
Also see DREAMS

BREMERS, Beverly
Singles: 7-Inch
COLUMBIA: *75-77* 2-3
ERIC: *83* 1-3
SCEPTER: *71-75* 2-4
Picture Sleeves
SCEPTER: *72* 2-5
LPs: 10/12-Inch 33rpm
SCEPTER: *72* 8-10

BRENDA & HERB
Singles: 7-Inch
H&L: *78* 2-3
Members: Brenda Reid; Herb Rooney.
Also see EXCITERS

BRENDA & THE TABULATIONS
Singles: 12-Inch 33/45rpm
CHOCOLATE CITY: *77* 4-6
Singles: 7-Inch
CHOCOLATE CITY: *76-77* 2-3
DIONN: *67-69* 5-8
EPIC: *72-75* 2-4
TOP & BOTTOM: *69-71* 4-6
LPs: 10/12-Inch 33rpm
CHOCOLATE CITY: *77* 5-8
DIONN: *67* 20-25
TOP & BOTTOM: *70* 12-15

BRENDA LEE: see LEE, Brenda

BRENNAN, Walter
Singles: 7-Inch
DOT: *60* 2-4
KAPP: *71* 1-3
LIBERTY: *62-64* 2-4
RPC: *61* 2-4
Picture Sleeves
DOT: *60* 4-8
LIBERTY: *62-63* 3-6
LPs: 10/12-Inch 33rpm
DOT: *60* 10-15
EVEREST: *60* 10-15
HAMILTON: *65* 8-10
LIBERTY: *62* 10-15
LONDON: *70* 6-10
RPC: *62* 10-15
SUNSET: *66* 8-10
UNITED ARTISTS: *75* 5-8

BRENSTON, Jackie
Singles: 78rpm
CHESS (Except 1458): *51-52* 10-20

CHESS (1458; "Rocket 88"): *51* $20-30
FEDERAL: *56-57* 5-10
Singles: 7-Inch
CHESS: *51-52* 40-60
FEDERAL: *56-57* 10-20
SUE: *61* 3-6

BREWER, Teresa
(Teresa Brewer & The Lancers)
Singles: 78rpm
CORAL: *52-57* 3-5
LONDON: *50-52* 3-6
Singles: 7-Inch
ABC: *67* 2-3
AMSTERDAM: *72-73* 2-3
CORAL (60000 &
  61000 series): *52-58* 4-6
CORAL (62000 & 65000
  series): *58-64* 3-5
DOCTOR JAZZ: *83* 1-3
FLYING DUTCHMAN: *72* 1-3
LONDON: *50-52* 4-6
PHILIPS: *63-67* 2-4
PROJECT 3: *82* 1-3
SSS INT'L: *68* 2-3
SIGNATURE: *74-83* 1-3
Picture Sleeves
CORAL: *58-60* 4-8
SIGNATURE: *80* 1-3
EPs: 7-Inch 33/45rpm
CORAL: *55-60* 8-12
LONDON: *52* 10-15
LPs: 10/12-Inch 33rpm
AMSTERDAM: *73-74* 6-10
COLUMBIA: *81* 5-8
CORAL (7; "Best Of Teresa
  Brewer"): *65* 12-18
CORAL (56072 through 57297): *56-59* . 15-20
CORAL (57315 through 57351): *60-65* . 10-15
DOCTOR JAZZ: *79-83* 5-8
FLYING DUTCHMAN: *74* 6-10
IMAGE: *78* 5-8
LONDON: *52* 20-30
MCA: *83* 5-8
PHILIPS: *63-67* 10-15
PROJECT 3: *82* 5-8
RCA VICTOR: *75* 5-8
SIGNATURE: *74-75* 5-8
VOCALION: *69* 8-12
WING: *66* 8-10

BREWER, Teresa, & Count Basie
LPs: 10/12-Inch 33rpm
DOCTOR JAZZ: *84* 5-8
Also see BASIE, Count
Also see BREWER, Teresa

BREWER, Teresa, & Duke Ellington
LPs: 10/12-Inch 33rpm
COLUMBIA: 81 .... $5-8
FLYING DUTCHMAN: 74 6-10
 Also see BREWER, Teresa
 Also see ELLINGTON, Duke

BREWER & SHIPLEY
Singles: 7-Inch
A&M: 68-69 3-5
BUDDAH: 70 2-4
CAPITOL: 74-75 2-3
KAMA SUTRA: 70-73 2-4
Picture Sleeves
KAMA SUTRA: 72 2-5
LPs: 10/12-Inch 33rpm
A&M: 68 12-15
ACCORD: 83 5-8
CAPITOL: 75 8-10
KAMA SUTRA: 70-76 10-12
 Members: Mike Brewer; Tom Shipley.

BRIAN & BRENDA
Singles: 7-Inch
ROCKET: 76-78 2-3
 Members: Brian Russell; Brenda Russell.

BRICK
Singles: 12-Inch 33/45rpm
BANG: 79-82 4-6
Singles: 7-Inch
BANG: 76-82 1-3
MAINSTREET: 76 2-3
STREET: 76 2-3
LPs: 10/12-Inch 33rpm
BANG: 76-82 5-8
 Members: Jimmy Brown; Regi Harris; Eddie Irons; Ray Ransom; Don Nevins.

BRIDES OF FUNKENSTEIN
Singles: 7-Inch
ATLANTIC: 78-80 1-3
LPs: 10/12-Inch 33rpm
ATLANTIC: 78-80 5-8
 Members: Lynn Mabry; Dawn Silva.
 Also see PARLIAMENT

BRIDGES, Alicia
Singles: 12-Inch 33/45rpm
SECOND WAVE: 84 4-6
POLYDOR: 78-79 4-6
Singles: 7-Inch
A.V.I.: 82 1-3
MEGA: 72 2-3
POLYDOR: 78-79 1-3
SECOND WAVE: 84 1-3
ZODIAC: 73 2-4

LPs: 10/12-Inch 33rpm
POLYDOR: 78-79 .... $5-8

BRIDGEWATER, Dee Dee
Singles: 12-Inch 33/45rpm
ELEKTRA: 79-80 4-6
Singles: 7-Inch
ELEKTRA: 78-79 1-3
LPs: 10/12-Inch 33rpm
ATLANTIC: 76 8-10
ELEKTRA: 78-80 5-8

BRIEF ENCOUNTER
Singles: 7-Inch
CAPITOL: 76-77 1-3
SEVENTY SEVEN: 72-73 2-4

BRIGGS, Lillian
Singles: 78rpm
EPIC: 56 3-5
Singles: 7-Inch
ABC-PARAMOUNT: 61 3-5
CORAL: 59-60 5-8
EPIC: 56 4-6

BRIGHT, Larry
Singles: 7-Inch
BRIGHT: 65 3-5
DEL FI: 63 4-8
DOT: 66 3-5
EDIT: 62 3-5
HIGHLAND: 61 4-6
ORIGINAL SOUND: 3 2-
RENDEZVOUS: 60 4-6
TIDE: 60-67 5-10

BRIGHTER SIDE OF DARKNESS
Singles: 7-Inch
20TH CENTURY-FOX: 72-75 2-4
LPs: 10/12-Inch 33rpm
20TH CENTURY-FOX: 73 8-10

BRILEY, Martin
Singles: 7-Inch
EMI AMERICA: 84 1-3
MERCURY: 81-84 1-3
LPs: 10/12-Inch 33rpm
MERCURY: 81-85 5-8

BRILL, Marty, & Larry Foster
LPs: 10/12-Inch 33rpm
COLPIX: 65 10-15
LAURIE: 62 15-20

BRIMMER, Charles
Singles: 7-Inch
CHELSEA: 75-76 2-3
LPs: 10/12-Inch 33rpm
CHELSEA: 76-77 8-10

BRINKLEY, Charles
Singles: 7-Inch
MUSIC MACHINE: 75 .... $2-3

BRINKLEY & PARKER
Singles: 7-Inch
DARNEL: 74 2-4

BRISCOE, Jimmy, & The Little Beavers
Singles: 7-Inch
ATLANTIC: 71 2-4
J-CITY: 72 2-4
PHI-KAPPA: 73-75 2-4
SALSOUL: 79 1-3
WANDERICK: 77 2-3
LPs: 10/12-Inch 33rpm
PHI-KAPPA: 74 10-12
WANDERICK: 77 8-10

BRISTOL, Johnny
Singles: 7-Inch
ATLANTIC: 76-78 2-3
HANDSHAKE: 80-81 1-3
MGM: 74-75 2-4
LPs: 10/12-Inch 33rpm
ATLANTIC: 76-78 5-8
HANDSHAKE: 81 5-8
MGM: 74-75 8-10
  Also see STEWART, Amii, & Johnny Bristol

BRISTOL, Johnny, & Alton McClain
Singles: 7-Inch
POLYDOR: 80 1-3
  Also see MC CLAIN, Alton, & Destiny

BRISTOL, Johnny, & Spyder Turner
Singles: 7-Inch
POLYDOR: 83 1-3
  Also see BRISTOL, Johnny
  Also see TURNER, Spyder

BRISTOL, Marc
LPs: 10/12-Inch 33rpm
KING NOODLE: 87 5-8

BRITISH LIONS
Singles: 7-Inch
RSO: 78 2-3
LPs: 10/12-Inch 33rpm
RSO: 78 5-8
  Members: John Fiddler; Dale Griffin; Overend
  Watts; Ray Major; Morgan Fisher.
  Also see MOTT THE HOOPLE

BRITT, Tina
Singles: 7-Inch
EASTERN: 65 3-5
MINIT: 69 2-4
VEEP: 68-69 2-4

LPs: 10/12-Inch 33rpm
MINIT: 69 .... $12-15

BROADWAY
Singles: 7-Inch
GRANITE: 76 2-3
HILLTAK: 78 1-3
LPs: 10/12-Inch 33rpm
HILLTAK: 79 8-10

BROMBERG, David
Singles: 7-Inch
COLUMBIA: 72-73 2-4
FANTASY: 77-79 2-3
LPs: 10/12-Inch 33rpm
ATLANTIC: 80 5-8
COLUMBIA: 72-77 8-10
FANTASY: 76-80 8-12
  Also see GRATEFUL DEAD
  Also see HARRISON, George
  Also see LOGGINS & MESSINA / David
  Bromberg
  Also see SAHM, Doug

BRONNER BROTHERS
Singles: 7-Inch
NEIGHBOR: 84 1-3

BRONSKI BEAT
Singles: 12-Inch 33/45rpm
MCA: 84-85 4-6
Singles: 7-Inch
MCA: 84-85 1-3
LPs: 10/12-Inch 33rpm
MCA: 85 5-8
  Member: Steve Bronski.
  Also see COMMUNARDS

BROOD, Herman
(Herman Brood & Wild Romance)
Singles: 7-Inch
ARIOLA AMERICA: 79 1-3
LPs: 10/12-Inch 33rpm
ARIOLA AMERICA: 79-80 8-10
TOWNHOUSE: 82 5-8

BROOKINS, Robert
Singles: 12-Inch 33/45rpm
MCA: 86-88 4-6
Singles: 7-Inch
MCA: 86 1-3

BROOKLYN BRIDGE
(Johnny Maestro & The Brooklyn Bridge)
Singles: 7-Inch
BUDDAH: 68-72 3-5
ERIC: 78 1-3
LPs: 10/12-Inch 33rpm
BUDDAH: 69-72 20-25

COLLECTABLES: **$5-8**
Members: Johnny Maestro; Fred Ferrara; Les
Cauchi; Mike Gregorio; Tom Sullivan; Carolyn
Wood; Jimmy Rosica; Richie Macioce; Artie Can-
tanzarita; Shelly Davis; Joe Ruvio.
Also see MAESTRO, Johnny

BROOKLYN DREAMS
Singles: 12-Inch 33/45rpm
CASABLANCA: 79 4-6
MILLENNIUM: 78 4-6
Singles: 7-Inch
CASABLANCA: 79-80 1-3
MILLENNIUM: 77-78 2-3
LPs: 10/12-Inch 33rpm
CASABLANCA: 79-80 5-8
MILLENNIUM: 77 8-10
Members: Joe Esposito; Eddie Hokenson; Bruce
Sudano.
Also see ESPOSITO, Joe "Bean"
Also see SUMMER, Donna

BROOKS, Donnie
Singles: 7-Inch
CHALLENGE: 66 3-5
COLLECTABLES: 81 1-3
DJ: 65 3-5
ERA: 59-68 3-6
HAPPY TIGER: 70-71 2-4
REPRISE: 64-65 3-5
YARDBIRD: 68-69 2-5
Picture Sleeves
ERA: 60-61 5-10
Promotional Singles
ERA ("Mission Bell"/
"Doll House"): 60 15-25
(Distributed during a personal appearance.)
LPs: 10/12-Inch 33rpm
ERA: 61 25-30
OAK: 71 8-10
WISHBONE: 75 5-10

BROOKS, Louis
(Louis Brooks & His Hi-Toppers)
Singles: 78rpm
EXCELLO: 52-57 8-15
Singles: 7-Inch
EXCELLO (2000 series): 52-53 15-25
EXCELLO (2100 series): 57-59 5-10

BROOKS, Nancy
Singles: 7-Inch
ARISTA: 79 1-3

BROOKS, Nancy / Bud Roman
Singles: 7-Inch
TOPS: 20-35

BROOKS, Ramona

Singles: 7-Inch
MANHATTAN: 77 .... $2-3
UNITED ARTISTS: 77 2-3
LPs: 10/12-Inch 33rpm
MANHATTAN: 78 8-10

BROOM, Bobby
Singles: 7-Inch
ARISTA: 81-84 1-3
GRP: 81 1-3
LPs: 10/12 Inch 33rpm
GRP: 81 5-8

BROTHER TO BROTHER
Singles: 7-Inch
SUGAR HILL: 81 1-3
TURBO: 74-77 2-3
LPs: 10/12-Inch 33rpm
SUGAR HILL: 81 5-8
TURBO: 74-77 10-12

BROTHERHOOD
Singles: 7-Inch
COLUMBIA: 70 2-4
DIAL: 69 2-5
MCA: 78 2-3
RCA VICTOR: 69 2-3
Picture Sleeves
RCA VICTOR: 69 3-5
LPs: 10/12-Inch 33rpm
MCA: 78 5-8
RCA VICTOR: 69 12-15
Members: Drake Levin; Michael Smith; Phil Volk;
Ron Collins.
Also see REVERE, Paul, & The Raiders
Also see WOMACK, Bobby

BROTHERHOOD OF MAN
Singles: 7-Inch
BELL: 74 2-3
DERAM: 70-72 2-4
PRIVATE STOCK: 77 2-3
PYE: 75-76 2-3
LPs: 10/12-Inch 33rpm
DERAM: 70 10-12
PYE: 76 8-10

BROTHERLY LOVE
Singles: 7-Inch
MUSIC MERCHANT: 72 2-4

BROTHERS BY CHOICE
Singles: 7-Inch
ALA: 78-80 1-3
FRETONE: 75 2-3

BROTHERS FOUR
Singles: 7-Inch
COLUMBIA (Except 43547): 59-69 3-6

COLUMBIA (43547; "Ratman & Bobbin
In The Clipper Caper"): *69* $5-8
FANTASY: *70* 1-3
Picture Sleeves
COLUMBIA: *60-63* 4-8
LPs: 10/12-Inch 33rpm
COLUMBIA: *59-69* 10-20
FANTASY: *70* 8-12
FIRST AMERICAN: *81* 5-8
HARMONY: *69-72* 6-10
Members: Bob Flick; Dick Foley; John Paine;
Mike Kirkland.

BROTHERS GUIDING LIGHT
(Brothers Guiding Light Featuring David)
Singles: 7-Inch
MERCURY: *73* 2-4

BROTHERS JOHNSON
Singles: 12-Inch 33/45rpm
A&M (Black vinyl): *78-85* 4-6
A&M (Colored vinyl): *78-85* 5-8
Singles: 7-Inch
A&M: *76-88* 1-3
Picture Sleeves
A&M: *76-85* 1-3
LPs: 10/12-Inch 33rpm
A&M (Except PR-4714): *76-85* 5-8
A&M (PR-4714; "Blam"): *79* 15-25
(Picture disc.)
Members: Louis Johnson; George Johnson.
Also see JONES, Quincy

BROTHERS OF SOUL
Singles: 7-Inch
BOO: *68-70* 2-4

BROWN, Al, & His Tunetoppers
(Al Brown's Tunetoppers)
Singles: 7-Inch
AMY: *60-61* 3-6
LPs: 10/12-Inch 33rpm
AMY: *60* 45-50

BROWN, Alex
Singles: 12-Inch 33/45rpm
MERCURY: *85* 4-6
Singles: 7-Inch
MERCURY: *85* 1-3
ROXBURY: *76* 2-3

BROWN, Arthur
(Crazy World Of Arthur Brown; Arthur
Brown's Kingdom Come)
Singles: 7-Inch
ATLANTIC: *68* 2-4
TRACK: *68-69* 2-4
LPs: 10/12-Inch 33rpm
ATLANTIC: *68* 12-15

GULL: *75* $8-10
PASSPORT: *74* 10-12
RECKLESS: *88* 6-8
Also see ATOMIC ROOSTER

BROWN, Boots
(Boots Brown & His Blockbusters; Boots Brown
& The Pelugelpipers; Boots Brown & Dan Drew)
Singles: 78rpm
RCA VICTOR: *53-57* 3-5
Singles: 7-Inch
DOT: *68* 2-4
RCA VICTOR: *53-60* 4-8
EPs: 7-Inch 33/45rpm
RCA VICTOR: *58* 15-20
LPs: 10/12-Inch 33rpm
GROOVE: 50-60
RCA VICTOR: *58* 25-30

BROWN, Buster
Singles: 78rpm
FIRE (Except 1008): *59-60* 35-45
FIRE (1008; "Fannie Mae"): *59* 125-175
Singles: 7-Inch
ABC: *73* 1-3
CHECKER: *63* 4-6
FIRE: *59-62* 4-8
GWENN: *62* 3-5
RCA VICTOR: *74* 2-4
ROULETTE: *72* 1-3
SEROCK: *63* 3-5
LPs: 10/12-Inch 33rpm
COLLECTABLES: *88* 6-8
FIRE: *60* 60-70
SOUFFLE: *73* 10-12

BROWN, Charles
(Charles Brown With Johnny Moore's Three
Blazers)
Singles: 78rpm
ALADDIN: *49-57* 5-15
CASH: *57* 4-8
HOLLYWOOD: *54* 6-12
SWING TIME: *52* 15-25
Singles: 7-Inch
ACE: *59* 4-8
ALADDIN (3076; "Black Night"): *51* 30-40
ALADDIN (3091 through 3138): *51-52* .. 15-25
ALADDIN (3157; "Rollin' Like A Pebble
In The Sand"): *52* 25-35
ALADDIN (3163 "Hard Times"): *52* 15-20
ALADDIN (3176 through 3191): *53* 25-35
ALADDIN (3200 & 3300 series): *53-58* .. 10-20
CASH: *57* 8-12
EAST-WEST: *58* 5-10
GALAXY: *66* 3-5
HOLLYWOOD: *54* 15-25

IMPERIAL: 62-63	$3-5
JEWEL: 71-74	2-4
KING: 60-64	3-5
LIBERTY: 84	1-3
LILLY: 62	3-5
MAINSTREAM: 65	3-5
NOLA: 63	3-5
STARDAY: 69	2-4
SWING TIME: 52	40-55

LPs: 10/12-Inch 33rpm

ALADDIN (702; "Mood Music"): 54	200-250
(10-Inch LP. Black vinyl.)	
ALADDIN (702; "Mood Music"): 54	300-450
(10-Inch LP. Colored vinyl.)	
ALADDIN (809; "Mood Music"): 56	75-125
BIG TOWN: 77-78	8-10
BLUESWAY: 70	8-10
IMPERIAL: 61	35-45
JEWEL: 72	8-10
KING (700 & 800 series): 61-63	20-30
KING (5000 series):	5-8
MAINSTREAM (300 series): 72	8-10
MAINSTREAM (6000/56000 series): 65	10-12
SCORE: 57	50-75

Also see MOORE, Johnny

BROWN, Charles / Basin Street Boys
Singles: 7-Inch

CASH (1052; "Lost In The Night"): 57	8-12

BROWN, Charles, & Jimmy McCracklin
LPs: 10/12-Inch 33rpm

IMPERIAL: 64	15-25

Also see MC CRACKLIN, Jimmy

BROWN, Charles, & Amos Milburn
Singles: 7-Inch

ACE: 59	4-6
KING: 61	3-5

LPs: 10/12-Inch 33rpm

GRAND PRIX:	10-12

Also see BROWN, Charles
Also see MILBURN, Amos

BROWN, Chuck
Singles: 7-Inch

EXCELLO: 62	3-5

BROWN, Chuck, & The Soul Searchers
Singles: 12-Inch 33/45rpm

SOURCE: 78-79	4-6

Singles: 7-Inch

SOUL SEARCHERS: 84	1-3
SOURCE: 78-80	1-3

T.T.E.D.: 84	$1-3

LPs: 10/12-Inch 33rpm

SOURCE: 79	5-8

BROWN, Clyde
Singles: 7-Inch

ATLANTIC: 73-74	2-4

**BROWN, Danny Joe
& The Danny Joe Brown Band**
Singles: 7-Inch

EPIC: 81	1-3

LPs: 10/12-Inch 33rpm

EPIC: 81	5-8

Also see MOLLY HATCHET

BROWN, Dee, & Lola Grant
Singles: 7-Inch

SHURFINE: 66	3-5

BROWN, Dennis
Singles: 12-Inch 33/45rpm

A&M: 82	4-6

Singles: 7-Inch

A&M: 81-82	1-3

LPs: 10/12-Inch 33rpm

A&M: 81-82	5-8

BROWN, Don
Singles: 7-Inch

FIRST AMERICAN: 77-78	2-3

BROWN, James
(James Brown & His Famous Flames; James
Brown & The J.B.s)
Singles: 78rpm

FEDERAL: 56-60	5-8

Singles: 12-Inch 33/45rpm

CHURCHILL: 83	4-6
POLYDOR: 78	4-6

Singles: 7-Inch

AUGUSTA: 83	1-3
BACKSTREET: 83	1-3
BETHLEHEM: 69	5-10
CHURCHILL: 83	1-3
FEDERAL (Monaural): 56-60	5-8
FEDERAL (Stereo): 59	8-15
KING (5000 series): 60-65	3-5
KING (6000 series): 65-71	2-4
PEOPLE: 71-76	2-4
POLYDOR: 71-84	1-3
SCOTTI BROTHERS: 86-88	1-3
SMASH: 64-66	3-5
T.K.: 80-81	1-3

Picture Sleeves

KING (5000 series): 60-65	4-8
KING (6000 series): 65-71	3-6
POLYDOR: 71-84	1-3

SCOTTI BROTHERS: *86* $1-3
SMASH: *64* 4-8
    EPs: 7-Inch 33/45rpm
KING: *59-63* 15-30
SMASH: *65-66* 10-20
(Jukebox issues only.)
    LPs: 10/12-Inch 33rpm
CHURCHILL: *83* 5-8
HRB: *73* 8-10
KING (683; "James Brown & His
  Famous Flames *Think*"): *60* 75-125
KING (743; "The Always Amazing James
  Brown & The Famous Flames"): *61* 50-75
KING (780; "The Exciting
  James Brown"): *62* 50-75
KING (804; "James Brown & The Famous
  Flames Tour The U.S.A."): *62* 50-75
KING (826; "The Apollo Theatre Presents, In
  Person, The James Brown Show"): *63* .. 40-60
KING (883; "Pure
  Dynamite"): *64* 25-50
KING (900 series): *65-66* 15-25
KING (1000 & 1100 series,
  except 1038): *67-71* 10-15
KING (1038; "Thinking About Little
  Willie John"): *68* 30-35
POLYDOR: *71-84* 5-8
SCOTTI BROTHERS: *88* 5-8
SMASH: *64-68* 10-20
SOLID SMOKE: *80-81* 5-8
T.K.: *80* 5-8
Also see BAMBAATAA, Afrika
Also see BYRD, Bobby, & James Brown
Also see J.B.s

BROWN, James, & Vicki Anderson
    Singles: 7-Inch
KING: *67-70* 2-4
Also see ANDERSON, Vicki

BROWN, James, Band
    Singles: 7-Inch
KING: *61* 3-5
Also see WESLEY, Fred, & The Horny Horns

BROWN, James, & Lyn Collins
    Singles: 7-Inch
POLYDOR: *72* 2-4
Also see COLLINS, Lyn

BROWN, James, & Marva Whitney
    Singles: 7-Inch
KING: *69* 2-4
Also see BROWN, James
Also see WHITNEY, Marva

BROWN, Jim Edward
(Jim Edward Brown & Helen Cornelius)
    Singles: 7-Inch
RCA VICTOR (Except 8000 &
  9000 series): *69-81* $1-3
RCA VICTOR (8000 & 9000
  series): *65-68* 2-4
    LPs: 10/12-Inch 33rpm
RCA VICTOR (Except 3000 &
  4000 series): *73-81* 5-10
RCA VICTOR (3000 & 4000
  series): *66-72* 8-12
(With an "LPM" or "LSP" prefix.)
Also see BROWNS

BROWN, Jocelyn
    Singles: 12-Inch 33/45rpm
JELLYBEAN: *86* 4-6
VINYL DREAMS: *84* 4-6
    Singles: 7-Inch
JELLYBEAN: *86* 1-3
TRI-WORLD: *88* 1-3
WARNER BROS: *86-87* 1-3
    LPs: 10/12-Inch 33rpm
JELLYBEAN: *86* 5-8
VINYL DREAMS: *84* 5-8

BROWN, Julie
    Singles: 7-Inch
RHINO: *84* 1-3
    LPs: 10/12-Inch 33rpm
RHINO: *85* 5-8

BROWN, Les, & His Band Of Renown
    Singles: 7-Inch
CAPITOL: *56-59* 2-4
COLUMBIA: *50-60* 2-5
CORAL: *59* 2-3
SIGNATURE: *60* 2-3
    EPs: 7-Inch 33/45rpm
CAPITOL: *56-58* 4-8
COLUMBIA: *54-56* 5-10
CORAL: *53-56* 5-10
    LPs: 10/12-Inch 33rpm
CAPITOL: *56-59* 5-15
COLUMBIA: *50-61* 5-15
CORAL: *59-60* 5-12
HARMONY: *59* 5-10
KAPP: *59* 4-8
MEDALLION: *61* 4-8

BROWN, Louise
    Singles: 7-Inch
WITCH: *61* 3-5

BROWN, Maxine
    Singles: 7-Inch
ABC: *75* 1-3

ABC-PARAMOUNT: *61-62* **$3-6**
AVCO EMBASSY: *71* **2-4**
COLLECTABLES: *81* **1-3**
COMMONWEALTH UNITED: *69-70* **2-4**
ERIC: *83* **1-3**
NOMAR: *61* **5-10**
WAND: *63-67* **3-8**
WHAM: **3-5**
　　　　　　Picture Sleeves
WAND: *63* **5-10**
WHAM: **8-12**
　　　　LPs: 10/12-Inch 33rpm
COLLECTABLES: *88* **6-8**
COMMONWEALTH UNITED: *69* **10-12**
GUEST STAR: *64* **10-12**
WAND: *63-67* **15-25**
　　Also see JACKSON, Chuck, & Maxine Brown

BROWN, Maxine / Irma Thomas
　　　　LPs: 10/12-Inch 33rpm
GRAND PRIX: *64* **12-15**
　　Also see BROWN, Maxine
　　Also see THOMAS, Irma

BROWN, Miquel
　　　　Singles: 12-Inch 33/45rpm
TSR: *83* **4-6**
　　　　　　Singles: 7-Inch
POLYDOR: *79* **1-3**
TSR: *83* **1-3**
　　　　LPs: 10/12-Inch 33rpm
POLYDOR: *78* **5-8**
TSR: *85* **5-8**

BROWN, Nappy
(Nappy Brown & The Gibralters; Nappy Brown & The Southern Sisters)
　　　　　　Singles: 7-Inch
SAVOY (1100 series): *55* **5-10**
SAVOY (1500 series): *57-60* **5-12**
SAVOY (1600 series): *61-63* **3-6**
　　　　LPs: 10/12-Inch 33rpm
SAVOY (14000 series): *58-60* **35-45**
SAVOY (14400 series): *77* **8-10**
　　Also see BARNES, Jimmy

BROWN, Odell
(Odell Brown & The Organ-Izers)
　　　　　　Singles: 7-Inch
CADET: *67-68* **2-4**
　　　　LPs: 10/12-Inch 33rpm
CADET: *67-69* **12-15**
PAULA: *74* **8-10**

BROWN, Oscar, Jr.
　　　　　　Singles: 7-Inch
ATLANTIC: *74* **2-3**
COLUMBIA: *60-62* **3-5**

FONTANA: *65-66* **$3-5**
MAD: *59* **5-8**
　　　　LPs: 10/12-Inch 33rpm
ATLANTIC: **5-8**
COLUMBIA: *61-63* **15-20**
FONTANA: *66* **10-12**

BROWN, Peter
　　　　Singles: 12-Inch 33/45rpm
COLUMBIA: *84* **4-6**
RCA VICTOR: *83* **4-6**
　　　　　　Singles: 7-Inch
COLUMBIA: *84* **1-3**
DRIVE: *77-80* **1-3**
RCA VICTOR: *83* **1-3**
　　　　LPs: 10/12-Inch 33rpm
COLUMBIA: *84* **5-8**
DRIVE: *78* **5-8**
RCA VICTOR: *82-83* **5-8**

BROWN, Peter, & Betty Wright
　　　　　　Singles: 7-Inch
DRIVE: *78* **2-3**
　　Also see BROWN, Peter
　　Also see WRIGHT, Betty

BROWN, Polly
　　　　　　Singles: 7-Inch
ARIOLA AMERICA: *75-76* **2-3**
BEL: *73* **2-4**
GTO: *74* **2-4**
　　Also see PICKETTYWITCH

BROWN, Randy
(Randy Brown & Company)
　　　　Singles: 12-Inch 33/45rpm
MILLENNIUM: *78* **4-6**
　　　　　　Singles: 7-Inch
CHOCOLATE CITY: *80-81* **1-3**
IX CHAINS: *75* **2-3**
PARACHUTE: *78-79* **1-3**
STAX: *80* **1-3**
TRUTH: *74-75* **2-4**
　　　　LPs: 10/12-Inch 33rpm
CHOCOLATE CITY: *80-81* **5-8**
PARACHUTE: *78-79* **5-8**
STAX: *80-81* **5-8**

BROWN, Ray, & The Whispers
　　　　　　Singles: 7-Inch
GNP/CRESCENDO: *65* **4-8**
PARKWAY: *66* **4-8**

BROWN, Roy
(Roy Brown & His Mighty, Mighty Men)
　　　　　　Singles: 78rpm
DELUXE (1000 series): *47-48* **10-15**
DELUXE (3300 through 3318): *49-51* . . **10-15**

GOLD STAR: *48* $10-15
IMPERIAL: *57* 4-8
KING: *52-57* 5-10
Singles: 7-Inch
BLUESWAY: *67* 3-5
DELUXE (3319; "Bar Room
  Blues"): *51* 75-100
  (Black vinyl.)
DELUXE (3319; "Bar Room
  Blues"): *51* 100-200
  (Colored vinyl.)
DELUXE (3323; "I've Got The Last
  Laugh Now"): *51* 40-60
  (Black vinyl.)
DELUXE (3323; "I've Got The Last
  Laugh Now"): *51* 75-125
  (Colored vinyl.)
FRIENDSHIP: 4-6
GUSTO: *83* 1-3
HOME OF THE BLUES: *60-61* 10-20
IMPERIAL: *57* 8-12
KING (4000 series): *52-56* 15-25
KING (5247 through 5333): *59-60* 4-6
MERCURY: *71* 2-3
TRU-LOVE: 4-6
EPs: 7-Inch 33/45rpm
KING: 40-60
LPs: 10/12-Inch 33rpm
BLUESWAY: *68-73* 10-20
EPIC: *71* 10-12
INTERMEDIA: *84* 5-8
KING (900 series): *66* 30-35
KING (1100 series): *71* 10-12
KING (5000 series): *79* 8-10
  Also see HARRIS, Wynonie / Roy Brown
  Also see HARRIS, Wynonie / Roy Brown /
Eddie Vinson

BROWN, Ruth
(Ruth Brown & The Rhythmakers)
Singles: 78rpm
ATLANTIC (Except 800 series): *51-57* ... 5-10
ATLANTIC (800 series): *49-50* 6-12
Singles: 7-Inch
ATLANTIC (919; "Teardrops From
  My Eyes"): *50* 200-250
ATLANTIC (948; "Shine On"): *51* 20-40
ATLANTIC (962 through 993): *52-53* ... 10-25
ATLANTIC (1005 through 1091): *53-56* .. 8-15
ATLANTIC (1100 series): *57-58* 4-8
ATLANTIC (2000 series): *59-60* 3-6
DECCA: *64* 3-5
NOSLEN: *64* 3-5
PHILIPS: *62* 3-5
SYKE: *69* 3-5

EPs: 7-Inch 33/45rpm
ATLANTIC: *54-57* $30-50
PHILIPS: *62* 12-20
LPs: 10/12-Inch 33rpm
ATLANTIC (1308; "Last Date With
  Ruth Brown"): *59* 25-35
ATLANTIC (8004; "Ruth Brown"): *57* ..50-75
  (Black label.)
ATLANTIC (8004; "Ruth Brown"): *57* ..25-35
  (Red label.)
ATLANTIC (8026; "Miss
  Rhythm"): *59* 35-50
  (Black label.)
ATLANTIC (8026; "Miss
  Rhythm"): *59* 15-25
  (Red label.)
ATLANTIC (8080; "Best Of Ruth
  Brown"): *63* 15-20
COBBLESTONE: *72* 8-10
DOBRE: *78* 5-8
MAINSTREAM (300 series): *72* 8-10
MAINSTREAM (6000 series): *65* 12-15
PHILIPS: *62* 12-15
SKYE: *70* 10-12
  Also see JOHNSON, Buddy

BROWN, Savoy:
see SAVOY BROWN

BROWN, Sawyer:
see SAWYER BROWN

BROWN, Sharon
Singles: 12-Inch 33/45rpm
PROFILE: *83* 4-6
Singles: 7-Inch
PROFILE: *82-83* 1-3

BROWN, Shawn
Singles: 12-Inch 33/45rpm
JWP: *85* 4-6

BROWN, Sheree
Singles: 12-Inch 33/45rpm
CAPITOL: *81* 4-6
Singles: 7-Inch
CAPITOL: *81-82* 1-3
LPs: 10/12-Inch 33rpm
CAPITOL: *81-82* 5-8

BROWN, Shirley
Singles: 12-Inch 33/45rpm
MERCURY: *83* 4-6
Singles: 7-Inch
ABET: *71* 2-4
ARISTA: *77-78* 2-3
SOUND TOWN: *84-85* 1-3
STAX: *79* 1-3
TRUTH: *74-76* 2-3

20TH CENTURY-FOX: *80* $1-3
    LPs: 10/12-Inch 33rpm
ARISTA: *77* 5-8
COLUMBIA: *68-72* 10-12
SOUND TRACK: *85* 5-8
STAX: *77-79* 5-8
TRUTH: *75* 8-10

BROWN, Veda
    Singles: 7-Inch
RAKEN: *75* 2-3
STAX: *73-74* 2-4

BROWN, Wini
(Wini Brown & The Boyfriends)
    Singles: 7-Inch
JARO: *60* 5-10
MERCURY: *52* 50-75
    LPs: 10/12-Inch 33rpm
JARO: *60* 20-30
   Members: Wini Brown; Joe Van Loan; Percy
   Green; Fred Francis; Warren Suttles.

BROWN, Wini, & Cootie Williams
    LPs: 10/12-Inch 33rpm
JARO: *60* 20-30
   Also see BROWN, Wini

BROWN SUGAR
    Singles: 7-Inch
ABKCO: *72* 2-4
CAPITOL: *76* 1-3
CHELSEA: *73-74* 2-4
   Member: Clydie King.

BROWNE, Duncan
    Singles: 7-Inch
IMMEDIATE: *69* 2-4
RAK: *72* 2-4
SIRE: *79* 1-3
    LPs: 10/12-Inch 33rpm
IMMEDIATE: *68* 10-12
SIRE: *79* 5-8

BROWNE, Jackson
    Singles: 12-Inch 33/45rpm
ASYLUM: *81-82* 4-6
    Singles: 7-Inch
ASYLUM: *72-86* 1-3
COLUMBIA: *86* 1-3
ELEKTRA: *80* 1-3
    Picture Sleeves
ASYLUM: *82-84* 1-3
ELEKTRA: *80* 1-3
    LPs: 10/12-Inch 33rpm
ASYLUM (Except 5051): *72-86* 6-10
ASYLUM (5051; "Jackson
  Browne"): *72* 10-15
  (With burlap cover.)

ASYLUM (5051; "Jackson
  Browne"): *72* $6-10
  (Without burlap.)
ELEKTRA ("Jackson Browne's First
  Album"): *67* 20-30
  (Promotional issue only.)
MFSL: *81* 20-40
   Also see CLEMONS, Clarence
   Also see LINDLEY, David

BROWNE, Tom
    Singles: 12-Inch 33/45rpm
ARISTA: *83* 4-6
    Singles: 7-Inch
ARISTA: *83-84* 1-3
GRP: *79-82* 1-3
    LPs: 10/12-Inch 33rpm
ARISTA: *83-84* 5-8
GRP: *79-82* 5-8

BROWNS
**(Jim Edward Brown & Maxine Brown With The
Louisiana Hayride Band)**
    Singles: 78rpm
FABOR: *54-55* 4-8
RCA VICTOR: *56-57* 3-5
    Singles: 7-Inch
COLUMBIA: *62* 2-4
FABOR: *54-55* 5-10
RCA VICTOR: *56-61* 3-6
    Picture Sleeves
RCA VICTOR: *60* 5-10
    EPs: 7-Inch 33/45rpm
RCA VICTOR: *57-60* 5-10
    LPs: 10/12-Inch 33rpm
CAMDEN: *65-68* 8-12
RCA VICTOR (1000 through 3000
  series): *75-81* 5-8
  (With an "ANL1" or "AYL1" prefix.)
RCA VICTOR (1400 series): *57* 30-40
  (With an "LPM" prefix.)
RCA VICTOR (2000 series): *59-65* 15-25
  (With an "LPM" or "LSP" prefix.)
RCA VICTOR (3000 series): *65-67* 12-15
  (With an "LPM" or "LSP" prefix.)
   Members: Jim Edward Brown; Maxine Brown;
  Bonnie Brown.
   Also see BROWN, Jim Edward
   Also see COOKE, Sam / Rod Lauren / Neil
Sedaka / Browns

BROWNSVILLE STATION
    Singles: 7-Inch
BIG TREE: *72-74* 2-4
EPIC: *79* 2-3
HIDEOUT: *69* 5-8
PALLADIUM: *70* 2-4

POLYDOR: *70* $2-4
PRIVATE STOCK: *77* 2-3
WARNER BROS: *71* 2-4
LPs: 10/12-Inch 33rpm
BIG TREE: *72-75* 10-12
EPIC (Black vinyl): *78* 8-10
EPIC (Colored vinyl): *78* 10-20
(Promotional issue only.)
PALLADIUM: *70* 12-15
PRIVATE STOCK: *77* 8-10
WARNER BROS: *70* 12-15
Members: Tony Driggins; Cub Koda; Michael
Lutz; Henry Weck; Bruce Nazarian.

BRUBECK, Dave, Quartet
Singles: 78rpm
COLUMBIA: *55-57* 2-5
FANTASY: *52-55* 3-6
Singles: 7-Inch
COLUMBIA (Except 40000 &
41000 series): *62-65* 1-3
COLUMBIA (40000 & 41000
series): *55-61* 3-5
FANTASY (500 series): *52-55* 4-8
FANTASY (4000 series): *56* 4-6
Picture Sleeves
COLUMBIA: *61-63* 3-6
EPs: 7-Inch 33/45rpm
COLUMBIA: *55-59* 10-15
FANTASY: *51-57* 10-20
LPs: 10/12-Inch 33rpm
COLUMBIA (500 through 900
series): *54-57* 35-50
COLUMBIA (1000 through 1200
series): *57-59* 15-25
COLUMBIA (1300 through 2300
series): *59-65* 10-20
COLUMBIA (6000 series): *54* 35-45
COLUMBIA (8000 series): *57-59* 20-30
COLUMBIA (8100 through 9300
series): *59-66* 10-20
CROWN: *62-64* 10-15
FANTASY (1 through 16): *51-54* 40-50
(10-Inch LPs.)
FANTASY (200 series): *56-57* 20-30
(Numbers in the 200 series may be preceded by a
"3.")
FANTASY (3300 series): 15-25
JAZZTONE: *57* 20-30
Also see ARMSTRONG, Louis
Also see TJADER, Cal

BRUBECK, Dave, & Paul Desmond
Singles: 7-Inch
A&M: *76* 1-3

LPs: 10/12-Inch 33rpm
HORIZON: *75* $6-10
Also see DESMOND, Paul

BRUBECK, Dave & Gerry Mulligan
Singles: 7-Inch
COLUMBIA: *68* 2-3
LPs: 10/12-Inch 33rpm
COLUMBIA: *68-73* 8-15
VERVE: *73* 8-12
Also see BRUBECK, Dave, Quartet
Also see MULLIGAN, Gerry

BRUCE, Jack
(Jack Bruce Band; Jack Bruce & Friends)
Singles: 7-Inch
RSO: *75* 2-3
LPs: 10/12-Inch 33rpm
ATCO: *69-71* 10-12
EPIC: *80* 5-8
POLYDOR: *72* 8-10
RSO: *77* 5-8
Also see CREAM
Also see MAYALL, John
Also see WEST, BRUCE & LAING

BRUCE, Jack, & Robin Trower
LPs: 10/12-Inch 33rpm
CHRYSALIS: *82* 5-8
Also see BRUCE, Jack
Also see TROWER, Robin

BRUCE, Lenny
Singles: 7-Inch
FANTASY (Black vinyl): 5-10
FANTASY (Colored vinyl): 5-10
LPs: 10/12-Inch 33rpm
CAPITOL (2630; "Why Did Lenny
Bruce Die"): *66* 15-20
DOUGLAS: *68-71* 12-18
FANTASY (1; "Lenny Bruce"): 30-40
FANTASY (7001; "Lenny Bruce's
Interviews Of Our Times"): *59* 25-30
(THICK red vinyl.)
FANTASY (7001; "Lenny Bruce's
Interviews Of Our Times"): 12-18
(Black vinyl.)
FANTASY (7001; "Lenny Bruce's
Interviews Of Our Times"): 6-10
(THIN red vinyl.)
FANTASY (7003; "The Sick Humor
Of Lenny Bruce"): *59* 25-30
(THICK red vinyl.)
FANTASY (7003; "The Sick Humor
Of Lenny Bruce"): 12-18
(Black vinyl.)

FANTASY (7003; "The Sick Humor
Of Lenny Bruce"): $6-10
(THIN red vinyl.)
FANTASY (7007; "I Am Not A Nut,
Elect Me"): *60* 25-30
(THICK red vinyl.)
FANTASY (7007; "I Am Not A Nut,
Elect Me"): 12-18
(Black vinyl.)
FANTASY (7007; "I Am Not A Nut,
Elect Me"): 6-10
(THIN red vinyl.)
FANTASY (7011; "Lenny Bruce,
American"): *62* 25-30
(THICK red vinyl.)
FANTASY (7011; "Lenny Bruce,
American"): 12-18
(Black vinyl.)
FANTASY (7011; "Lenny Bruce,
American"): 6-10
(THIN red vinyl.)
FANTASY (7012; "The Best Of
Lenny Bruce"): *63* 25-30
(THICK red vinyl.)
FANTASY (7012; "The Best Of
Lenny Bruce"): 12-18
(Black vinyl.)
FANTASY (7012; "The Best Of
Lenny Bruce"): 6-10
(THIN red vinyl.)
FANTASY (7017; "Thank You
Masked Man"): *72* 10-15
FANTASY (34201; "Lenny Bruce Live
At The Curran Theatre"): *72* 10-15
FANTASY (79003; "The Real Lenny
Bruce"): *75* 6-10
LENNY BRUCE RECORDS ("Recordings
Submitted As Evidence In The San Francisco
Obscenity Trial In March 1962"): *62* ...50-75
PHILLES (4010; "Lenny Bruce Is Out
Again"): *66* 20-40
REPRISE (6329; "The Berkeley
Concert"): *69* 10-12
UNITED ARTISTS (3580; "Midnight
Concert"): *67* 12-18
UNITED ARTISTS (9800; "Lenny Bruce
At Carnegie Hall"): *71* 12-18
WARNER BROS. (9101; "The Law, Language
& Lenny Bruce"): 10-15
(Promotional issue only.)

BRUCE & TERRY
Singles: 7-Inch
COLUMBIA: *64-66* 4-8
Members: Bruce Johnston; Terry Melcher.
Also see CALIFORNIA MUSIC

Also see BOONE, Pat
Also see NEWTON, Wayne
Also see RIP CHORDS
Also see SAGITTARIUS

BRUNSON, Tyrone "Tystick"
Singles: 12-Inch 33/45rpm
BELIEVE IN A DREAM: *82-84* $4-6
Singles: 7-Inch
BELIEVE IN A DREAM: *82-84* 1-3
LPs: 10/12-Inch 33rpm
BELIEVE IN A DREAM: *82-84* 5-8

BRYAN, Billy
(Gene Pitney)
Singles: 7-Inch
BLAZE: *59* 10-20
Also see PITNEY, Gene

BRYANT, Anita
Singles: 7-Inch
CARLTON: *58-61* 2-4
COLUMBIA: *61-67* 2-3
DISNEYLAND: 2-3
Picture Sleeves
COLUMBIA: *61-67* 3-6
DISNEYLAND: 2-4
LPs: 10/12-Inch 33rpm
CARLTON: *59-61* 10-15
COLUMBIA: *62-64* 5-10

BRYANT, Lillie
Singles: 7-Inch
CAMEO: *58* 3-5
SWAN: *59* 3-5
Also see BILLY & LILLIE

BRYANT, Ray, Combo
Singles: 7-Inch
COLUMBIA: *60-64* 2-4
Picture Sleeves
COLUMBIA: *60* 3-6
LPs: 10/12-Inch 33rpm
COLUMBIA: *60-62* 15-20
EPIC: *56* 30-40
PRESTIGE/NEWJAZZ: *62* 15-20
SIGNATURE: *60* 15-20
SUE: *63-64* 10-15

BRYSON, Peabo
Singles: 7-Inch
BULLET: *76-77* 2-3
CAPITOL: *77-82* 1-3
ELEKTRA: *84-88* 1-3
MCA: *84* 1-3
SHOUT: *75* 2-4
Picture Sleeves
CAPITOL: *81* 1-3

LPs: 10/12-Inch 33rpm
BULLET: 76 . . . . **$8-10**
CAPITOL: *78-84* **5-8**
ELEKTRA: *84-88* **5-8**
   Also see MANCHESTER, Melissa, & Peabo
Bryson
   Also see ZAGER, Michael, Moon Band, &
Peabo Bryson

BRYSON, Peabo, & Regina Belle
Singles: 7-Inch
ELEKTRA: *88* **1-3**
   Also see BELLE, Regina

BRYSON, Peabo, & Natalie Cole
Singles: 7-Inch
CAPITOL: *79* **1-3**
LPs: 10/12-Inch 33rpm
CAPITOL: *79* **5-8**
   Also see COLE, Natalie

BRYSON, Peabo, & Roberta Flack
Singles: 7-Inch
ATLANTIC: *80* **1-3**
CAPITOL: *83* **1-3**
LPs: 10/12-Inch 33rpm
ATLANTIC: *80* **5-8**
CAPITOL: *83* **5-8**
   Also see BRYSON, Peabo
   Also see FLACK, Roberta

BUBBLE PUPPY
Singles: 7-Inch
INTERNATIONAL ARTISTS: *69-70* **8-15**
Promotional Singles
INTERNATIONAL ARTISTS
   (Black vinyl): *69-70* **10-20**
INTERNATIONAL ARTISTS
   (Colored vinyl): *70* **20-30**
LPs: 10/12-Inch 33rpm
INTERNATIONAL ARTISTS (10; "A
   Gathering Of Promises")
   (Green label): *69* **100-125**
INTERNATIONAL ARTISTS (10; "A
   Gathering Of Promises")
   (White label): *69* **150-200**
   (Promotional issue only.)
   Members: Red Prince; Todd Potter; Rory Cox; M.
   Taylor; Dave Fore.

BUCHANAN, Bill
Singles: 7-Inch
GONE: *58* **10-15**
UNITED ARTISTS: *62* **4-6**
   Also see BUCHANAN & ANCELL
   Also see BUCHANAN & CELLA
   Also see BUCHANAN & GOODMAN
   Also see BUCHANAN & GREENFIELD

BUCHANAN, Roy
Singles: 7-Inch
ALLIGATOR: *85-86* **$1-3**
ATLANTIC: *76-78* **2-3**
BOMARC: *61* **5-8**
POLYDOR: *72-75* **2-4**
SWAN: *61* **3-6**
LPs: 10/12-Inch 33rpm
ALLIGATOR: *85* **5-8**
ATLANTIC: *76-77* **5-8**
BIOYA: *71* **15-20**
POLYDOR: *72-75* **8-10**
WAREHOUSE: *81* **5-8**
   Also see CANNON, Freddy
   Also see HAWKINS, Dale

BUCHANAN & ANCELL
Singles: 78rpm
FLYING SAUCER: *57* **5-10**
Singles: 7-Inch
FLYING SAUCER: *57* **10-15**
   Members: Bill Buchanan; Bob Ancell.
   Also see BUCHANAN, Bill

BUCHANAN & CELLA
Singles: 7-Inch
ABC-PARAMOUNT: *59* **8-10**
   Member: Bill Buchanan.
   Also see BUCHANAN, Bill

BUCHANAN & GOODMAN
Singles: 78rpm
LUNIVERSE (Except 101X): *56-58* **5-10**
LUNIVERSE (101X; "Back To
   Earth"): *56* **20-40**
Singles: 7-Inch
COMIC: *59* **8-10**
LUNIVERSE (Except 101X): *56-58* **10-20**
LUNIVERSE (101X; "Back To
   Earth"): *56* **50-75**
NOVELTY: *59* **8-10**
RADIOACTIVE: **12-20**
   Members: Bill Buchanan; Dickie Goodman.
   Also see BUCHANAN, Bill
   Also see GOODMAN, Dickie

BUCHANAN & GREENFIELD
Singles: 7-Inch
NOVEL (Red label): *64* **8-10**
NOVEL (Red & white label): *72* **2-4**
   Members: Bill Buchanan; Howard Greenfield.
   Also see BUCHANAN, Bill

BUCHANAN BROTHERS
Singles: 7-Inch
EVENT: *69-71* **2-4**
LPs: 10/12-Inch 33rpm
EVENT: *69* **15-20**

Members: Terry Cashman; Gene Pistilli; Tommy West.
Also see CASHMAN, PISTILLI & WEST

BUCK
Singles: 7-Inch
PLAYBOY: 75 ....$2-3

BUCKEYE
Singles: 7-Inch
POLYDOR: 79 1-3
LPs: 10/12-Inch 33rpm
POLYDOR: 79 5-8

BUCKINGHAM, Lindsey
Singles: 7-Inch
ASYLUM: 81 1-3
ELEKTRA: 84 1-3
WARNER BROS: 83 1-3
Picture Sleeves
ASYLUM: 81 1-3
LPs: 10/12-Inch 33rpm
ASYLUM: 81 5-8
ELEKTRA: 84 5-8
Also see BUCKINGHAM NICKS
Also see EGAN, Walter
Also see FLEETWOOD MAC
Also see STEWART, John

BUCKINGHAM NICKS
Singles: 7-Inch
POLYDOR: 73-79 2-4
Picture Sleeves
POLYDOR: 73 2-4
LPs: 10/12-Inch 33rpm
POLYDOR: 73 20-30
Members: Lindsey Buckingham; Stevie Nicks.
Also see BUCKINGHAM, Lindsey
Also see NICKS, Stevie

BUCKINGHAMS
Singles: 7-Inch
COLUMBIA: 67-70 3-5
RED LABEL: 85 1-3
ROWE/AMI: 66 5-10
("Play Me" Sales Stimulator promotional issue.)
SPECTRA-SOUND: 67 10-15
U.S.A.: 66-67 5-8
Picture Sleeves
COLUMBIA: 67-68 5-10
LPs: 10/12-Inch 33rpm
COLUMBIA: 67-75 15-20
RED LABEL: 85 5-8
U.S.A. (107; "Kind Of A Drag"): 67 30-40
(With 13 tracks.)
U.S.A. (107; "Kind Of A Drag"): 67 15-25
(With 12 tracks.)

Members: Dennis Tufano; Carl Giammerse; Nick Fortune; Marty Grebb; Dennis Miccoli; Jon-Jon Poulos.
Also see CENTURIES
Also see FALLING PEBBLES
Also see TUFANO & GIAMMERSE

BUCKLEY, Tim
Singles: 7-Inch
DISC REET: 73-74 ....$2-4
ELEKTRA: 66-67 3-5
LPs: 10/12-Inch 33rpm
DISC REET: 73-74 8-10
ELEKTRA: 66-70 12-15
RHINO: 83 5-8
STRAIGHT: 66-69 15-18
WARNER BROS: 70-72 10-12

BUCKNER & GARCIA
Singles: 12-Inch 33/45rpm
COLUMBIA: 82 4-6
Singles: 7-Inch
BGO: 81 3-5
COLUMBIA: 81 1-3
Picture Sleeves
COLUMBIA: 81 2-3
LPs: 10/12-Inch 33rpm
COLUMBIA: 82 5-8
Members: Jerry Buckner; Gary Garcia.
Also see WILLIS "THE GUARD" & VIGORISH

BUCKWHEAT
Singles: 7-Inch
LONDON: 71-73 2-4
LPs: 10/12-Inch 33rpm
LONDON: 71-73 10-12

BUCKWHEAT ZYDECO
LPs: 10/12-Inch 33rpm
ISLAND: 87-88 5-8

BUD & TRAVIS
Singles: 7-Inch
LIBERTY: 59-65 3-5
WORLD PACIFIC: 59 3-5
LPs: 10/12-Inch 33rpm
LIBERTY: 59-65 10-20
SUNSET: 67 8-12
Members: Bud Dashiel; Travis Edmonson.

BUENA VISTAS
Singles: 7-Inch
MARQUEE: 68 3-5
SWAN: 66 6-12

BUFFALO REBELS
Singles: 7-Inch
MAR-LEE: 60-61 10-15

Also see REBELS
Also see ROCKIN' REBELS

BUFFALO SPRINGFIELD
Singles: 7-Inch
ATCO: *67-68* $4-6
LPs: 10/12-Inch 33rpm
ATCO (105; "Retrospective"): *75* 5-8
ATCO (200; "Buffalo
Springfield"): *66* 35-40
(With *Baby Don't Scold Me.*)
ATCO (200; "Buffalo
Springfield"): *67* 15-20
(With *Baby Don't Scold Me* replaced by *For What
It's Worth.*)
ATCO (226 through 283): *67-69* 15-25
ATCO (806; "Buffalo
Springfield"): *73* 15-20
Members: Stephen Stills; Neil Young; Jim Mes-
sina; Richie Furay; Jim Fielder; Doug Hastings;
Dewey Martin.
Also see FURAY, Richie
Also see MESSINA, Jim
Also see POCO
Also see STILLS, Stephen
Also see YOUNG, Neil

BUFFETT, Jimmy
Singles: 7-Inch
ABC: *75-78* 2-3
ASYLUM: *80* 1-3
BARNABY: *70-72* 2-4
DUNHILL: *73-75* 2-4
FULL MOON: *80* 1-3
MCA (Black vinyl): *79-88* 1-3
MCA (Colored vinyl): *85* 3-6
LPs: 10/12-Inch 33rpm
ABC: *76-78* 8-10
BARNABY: *70-77* 10-12
DUNHILL: *73-74* 10-12
MCA: *79-88* 5-8
UNITED ARTISTS: *75* 8-10

BUFFETT, Mary
Singles: 12-Inch 33/45rpm
MOBY DICK: *84* 4-6
Singles: 7-Inch
MOBY DICK: *84* 1-3

BUGGLES
Singles: 7-Inch
CARRERE: *82* 1-3
ISLAND: *79-83* 1-3
Promotional Singles
CARRERE ("Fade Away"): *82* 2-3
(Soundsheet. Originally included in a magazine.)
LPs: 10/12-Inch 33rpm
CARRERE: *82* 5-8

ISLAND: *80* $5-8
Members: Trevor Horn; Geoff Downes.
Also see YES

BULAWAYO SWEET RHYTHM BOYS
Singles: 78rpm
LONDON: *54* 2-4
Singles: 7-Inch
LONDON: *54* 3-5

BULL & THE MATADORS
Singles: 7-Inch
TODDLIN' TOWN: *68-69* 4-6

BULLDOG
Singles: 7-Inch
BUDDAH: *72-74* 2-4
DECCA: *72* 2-4
GUYDEN: *71* 2-4
MCA: *73* 2-3
LPs: 10/12-Inch 33rpm
BUDDAH: *74* 8-10
DECCA: *72* 12-15
Members: Gene Cornish; Dino Danelli; Billy
Hocher; Eric Thorngren; John Turi.
Also see RASCALS

BULLENS, Cindy
Singles: 7-Inch
CASABLANCA: *79-80* 1-3
UNITED ARTISTS: *78-79* 2-3
LPs: 10/12-Inch 33rpm
CASABLANCA: *79* 5-8
UNITED ARTISTS: *78* 5-8

BULLOCK, Janice
Singles: 7-Inch
WRC: *87* 1-3
Also see BELL, William, & Janice Bullock

BUMBLE, B:
see B. BUMBLE & THE STINGERS

BUMBLE BEE UNLIMITED
Singles: 7-Inch
MERCURY: *76-77* 2-3
RCA VICTOR: *79* 1-3
LPs: 10/12-Inch 33rpm
RCA VICTOR: *79* 5-8

BUNN, Allen
(Alden Bunn)
Singles: 78rpm
APOLLO: *52* 25-50
Singles: 7-Inch
APOLLO (436; "She'll Be Sorry"): *52* . . 75-100
APOLLO (439; "Discouraged"): *52* 75-100
Also see LARKS
Also see TARHEEL SLIM

Jimmy Witherspoon (left) joins Eric Burdon in a 1971 recording session

LPs: 10/12-Inch 33rpm
MGM: 71 . . . . $10-12
  Also see BURDON, Eric
  Also see WITHERSPOON, Jimmy

BURGESS, Richard James
Singles: 12-Inch 33/45rpm
CAPITOL: 84 4-6
Singles: 7-Inch
CAPITOL: 84 1-3
LPs: 10/12-Inch 33rpm
CAPITOL: 84 5-8

BURKE, Keni
Singles: 7-Inch
DARK HORSE: 77-78 2-3
RCA VICTOR: 81-82 1-3
LPs: 10/12-Inch 33rpm
DARK HORSE: 77 8-10
RCA VICTOR: 81-82 5-8

BURKE, Solomon
Singles: 12-Inch 33/45rpm
SAVOY: 84 4-6
Singles: 7-Inch
ABC/DUNHILL: 74 2-3
AMHERST: 78 2-3
APOLLO: 56-58 10-15
ATLANTIC: 61-68 3-5
BELL: 69-70 2-4
CHESS: 75-77 2-3
DUNHILL: 74 2-4
INFINITY: 79 2-3
MGM: 70-73 2-4
PRIDE: 72-73 2-4
SINGULAR: 60 4-6
LPs: 10/12-Inch 33rpm
ABC/DUNHILL: 74 10-12
APOLLO: 62 50-75
ATLANTIC (8000 series): 62-64 15-20
ATLANTIC (8100 series): 65-68 12-15
BELL: 69 12-15
CHESS: 75-76 8-10
CLARION: 64 12-15
INFINITY: 79 5-8
KENWOOD: 64 12-15
MGM: 71-72 10-12
PRIDE: 73 8-10
ROUNDER: 84 5-8
SAVOY: 81-83 5-8
  Also see SOUL CLAN

BURKE, Solomon, & Lady Lee
Singles: 7-Inch
PRIDE: 73 2-4
  Also see BURKE, Solomon

BURNETT, Carol
LPs: 10/12-Inch 33rpm
DECCA: 61-64 . . . . $15-20
COLUMBIA: 71 8-12
RCA VICTOR: 67 10-15
TETRAGRAMMATON: 69 8-12
VOCALION: 68 8-12
  Also see ANDREWS, Julie, & Carol Burnett

BURNETT, T-Bone
Singles: 7-Inch
WARNER BROS: 83 1-3
LPs: 10/12-Inch 33rpm
TAKOMA: 80 5-8
WARNER BROS: 82-83 5-8

BURNETTE, Billy
(Billy Burnette & Jawbone)
Singles: 7-Inch
A&M: 76 2-3
COLUMBIA: 80-81 1-3
MCA/CURB: 86 1-3
POLYDOR: 79 1-3
WARNER BROS: 69 2-4
LPs: 10/12-Inch 33rpm
COLUMBIA: 80-81 5-8
ENTRANCE: 72 10-12
MCA/CURB: 86 5-8
POLYDOR: 79 5-8
  Also see FLEETWOOD MAC

BURNETTE, Dorsey
Singles: 78rpm
ABBOTT: 55 5-10
Singles: 7-Inch
ABBOTT: 55 10-20
CALLIOPE: 77 2-3
CAPITOL: 71-74 2-4
CEE-JAM: 57 10-15
COLLECTABLES: 81 1-3
CONDOR: 70 2-4
DOT: 61 4-6
ELEKTRA: 79-80 2-3
ERA: 60-69 3-5
HAPPY TIGER: 70 2-4
HICKORY: 67 3-5
IMPERIAL: 59-63 10-15
LIBERTY: 69 2-4
MC: 77 2-3
MEL-O-DY: 64 3-6
MELODYLAND: 75-76 2-4
MERRI: 60 4-6
MOVIE STAR: 3-5
MUSIC FACTORY: 68 2-4
REPRISE: 62-63 3-5
SMASH: 66 3-5

U.S. NAVY ("Be A Navy Man"): $8-10
(U.S. Navy recruiting promotional issue.)
Picture Sleeves
ERA: *61* 10-20
REPRISE: *63* 5-10
U.S. NAVY ("Be A Navy Man"): 15-25
(U.S. Navy recruiting promotional issue.)
LPs: 10/12-Inch 33rpm
CALLIOPE: *77* 8-10
CAPITOL: *72-73* 10-12
DOT: *63* 15-20
ERA (100 series): *60* 25-30
ERA (800 series): *69* 15-20
GUSTO: 5-8
TRIP: *74* 8-10
 Also see BURNETTE, Johnny & Dorsey
 Also see BURNETTE, Johnny, & The Rock'n
Roll Trio

BURNETTE, Johnny
Singles: 78rpm
CORAL: *56* 15-25
Singles: 7-Inch
CAPITOL: *63-64* 4-6
CHANCELLOR: *62* 8-10
CORAL: *57* 40-50
FREEDOM: *59* 15-30
LIBERTY: *60-62* 4-6
MAGIC LAMP (515; "Bigger
Man"): *64* 15-20
SAHARA: *64* 4-6
UNITED ARTISTS: *84* 1-3
VON (106; "Go Mule Go"): *54* 150-175
Picture Sleeves
LIBERTY: *60-61* 8-15
MAGIC LAMP (515; "Bigger
Man"): *64* 75-100
EPs: 7-Inch 33/45rpm
LIBERTY (1004; "Dreamin"): *60* 30-60
LIBERTY (1011; "Johnny Burnette's
Hits"): *61* 40-60
LPs: 10/12-Inch 33rpm
LIBERTY (7100 & 7200 series): *60-62* ..35-40
LIBERTY (7300 series): *63* 25-30
LIBERTY (10000 series): *81* 5-8
SUNSET: *67* 15-20
UNITED ARTISTS: *75* 8-10
 Also see BURNETTE, Johnny & Dorsey
 Also see BURNETTE, Johnny, & The Rock'n
Roll Trio
 Also see VEE, Bobby / Johnny Burnette / Ventures / Fleetwoods

BURNETTE, Johnny & Dorsey
(Burnette Brothers)
Singles: 7-Inch
CORAL: *60* $20-25
IMPERIAL: *58* 15-20
REPRISE: *63* 4-6
 Also see BURNETTE, Johnny, & The Rock'n
Roll Trio
 Also see TEXANS

**BURNETTE, Johnny, & The
Rock'n Roll Trio**
Singles: 78rpm
CORAL: *56* 15-30
Singles: 7-Inch
CORAL (61000 series): *56* 30-50
CORAL (62000 series): *60* 20-25
LPs: 10/12-Inch 33rpm
CORAL (57080; "Johnny Burnette
And The Rock'n Roll Trio"): *56* .. 1000-1200
(A Canadian issue of this LP exists and is worth as
much or more as the U.S. edition.)
MCA: *82* 5-8
SOLID SMOKE (Black vinyl): *78-80* 5-8
SOLID SMOKE (Colored vinyl): *78* 8-12
Members: Johnny Burnette; Dorsey Burnette; Paul
Burlison.
 Also see BURNETTE, Johnny & Dorsey
 Also see BURNETTE, Dorsey
 Also see BURNETTE, Johnny

BURNETTE, Rocky
(Rocky Burnette & The Rock 'N Roll Trio)
Singles: 7-Inch
EMI AMERICA: *80* 1-3
LPs: 10/12-Inch 33rpm
EMI AMERICA: *80-82* 5-8
GOODS: *82* 5-8
KYD: *83* 5-8

BURNING SENSATIONS
Singles: 7-Inch
CAPITOL: *83* 1-3
LPs: 10/12-Inch 33rpm
CAPITOL: *83* 5-8

BURNS, George
Singles: 7-Inch
MERCURY: *80-81* 1-3
Picture Sleeves
MERCURY: *80* 1-3
LPs: 10/12-Inch 33rpm
BUDDAH: *72* 6-10
MERCURY: *80* 5-8
PRIDE: 5-8
 Also see MARTIN, Dean

BURRAGE, Harold
(Harold Barrage)
Singles: 7-Inch
ALADDIN: 50 .... $20-30
COBRA: 56 10-20
DECCA: 50 20-30
M-PAC!: 62-65 3-6
PASO: 61 3-6
STATES (144; "Feel So Fine"): 50 25-40
(Black vinyl.)
STATES (144; "Feel So Fine"): 50 50-80
(Colored vinyl.)
VEE JAY: 60 4-8
VIVID: 64 3-5

BURRELL, Kenny
Singles: 7-Inch
BLUE NOTE: 62 2-4
LPs: 10/12-Inch 33rpm
ARGO: 60 15-25
BLUE NOTE: 56-57 20-40
(Label gives New York street address for Blue
Note Records.)
BLUE NOTE: 58-63 15-25
(Label reads "Blue Note Records Inc. - New York,
U.S.A.")
BLUE NOTE: 66 10-20
(Label shows Blue Note Records as a division of
either Liberty or United Artists.)
COLUMBIA: 61 15-20
KAPP: 62 12-18
MOODSVILLE: 63 15-20
NEW JAZZ: 58 20-25
PRESTIGE (Except 7308): 57-58 20-30
(Yellow label.)
PRESTIGE (7308; "Blue Moods"): 64 ... 10-15
VERVE: 63-65 12-20

BURRELL, Kenny, & Brother
Jack McDuff
LPs: 10/12-Inch 33rpm
PRESTIGE: 64 10-15
Also see BURRELL, Kenny
Also see McDUFF, Brother Jack

BURRITO BROTHERS
Singles: 7-Inch
CURB: 81-84 1-3
EPIC: 81 1-3
LPs: 10/12-Inch 33rpm
A&M: 80 6-10
CURB: 81-82 5-8
Also see FLYING BURRITO BROTHERS

BURROWS, Tony
Singles: 7-Inch
BELL: 70-72 2-4

BURTON, Jenny
Singles: 12-Inch 33/45rpm
ATLANTIC: 83-85 .... $4-6
Singles: 7-Inch
ATLANTIC: 83-86 1-3
LPs: 10/12-Inch 33rpm
ATLANTIC: 83-85 5-8

BURTON, Jenny, & Patrick Jude
Singles: 7-Inch
ATLANTIC: 84 1-3
Also see BURTON, Jenny

BURTON, Richard
Singles: 7-Inch
MGM: 65 3-5

BUS BOYS
Singles: 7-Inch
ARISTA: 80-84 2-3
VOSS: 88 1-3
LPs: 10/12-Inch 33rpm
ARISTA: 80-82 5-8
Members: Gus Loundermon; Brian O'Neal; Kevin
O'Neal; Michael Jones; Victor Johnson; Steve
Felix.

BUSCH, Lou, Orchestra
Singles: 78rpm
CAPITOL: 55-56 2-4
Singles: 7-Inch
CAPITOL: 55-56 3-5
Also see CARR, Joe "Fingers"

BUSH, Kate
Singles: 12-Inch 33/45rpm
EMI AMERICA: 85-86 5-10
Singles: 7-Inch
EMI AMERICA: 78-86 2-5
GEFFEN: 87 2-4
LPs: 10/12-Inch 33rpm
CBS: 89 5-8
EMI AMERICA: 78-86 5-10
HARVEST: 78 5-10
Also see GABRIEL, Peter

BUSHKIN, Joe
EPs: 7-Inch 33/45rpm
CAPITOL: 56 3-6
COLUMBIA: 51 4-8
SAVOY: 55 4-8
LPs: 10/12-Inch 33rpm
CAPITOL: 56-59 5-15
COLUMBIA: 51-52 8-18
EPIC: 56 5-15
MGM: 50-55 8-18
RONDO: 59 4-8

BUSTERS
Singles: 7-Inch
ARLEN: 63-64 .... $10-15

BUTANES
Singles: 7-Inch
ENRICA: 61 10-15

BUTCHER, John, Axis
Singles: 7-Inch
POLYDOR: 83 1-3
LPs: 10/12-Inch 33rpm
CAPITOL: 85 5-8
POLYDOR: 83 5-8

BUTLER, Billy
(Billy Butler & Infinity; Billy Butler & The Chanters; Billy Butler & The Enchanters)
Singles: 7-Inch
BRUNSWICK: 66-68 3-5
CURTOM: 76 2-3
OKEH: 63-66 3-5
MEMPHIS: 71 2-4
PRIDE: 72-73 2-4
LPs: 10/12-Inch 33rpm
EDSEL: 86 5-8
OKEH: 66 15-18
PRESTIGE: 69-70 10-12
PRIDE: 73 10-12
Also see INFINITY

BUTLER, Carl
Singles: 7-Inch
COLUMBIA: 61-63 2-4
LPs: 10/12-Inch 33rpm
COLUMBIA: 63 12-15
HARMONY: 66-71 8-12

BUTLER, Carl & Pearl
Singles: 7-Inch
COLUMBIA: 63-69 2-4
LPs: 10/12-Inch 33rpm
CMH: 80 5-8
COLUMBIA: 64-70 10-15
HARMONY: 72 8-12
PEDACA: 5-8
Also see BUTLER, Carl

BUTLER, Champ
Singles: 78rpm
COLUMBIA: 50-54 2-5
CORAL: 55-56 2-4
Singles: 7-Inch
COLUMBIA: 50-54 3-5
CORAL: 55-56 2-4
GILLETTE: 62 1-3
EPs: 7-Inch 33/45rpm
COLUMBIA: 53 5-8

LPs: 10/12-Inch 33rpm
GILLETTE: 62 .... $5-10

BUTLER, Jerry
(Jerry Butler & The Impressions)
Singles: 78rpm
ABNER (1013; "For Your Precious
Love"): 58 10-15
(Issued on 45, as FALCON 1013. This Abner 78
uses the Falcon number.)
Singles: 7-Inch
ABNER: 58-60 5-10
COLLECTABLES: 81 1-3
ERIC: 73 1-3
FALCON: 58 15-20
FOUNTAIN: 82 2-3
MCA: 83 1-3
MERCURY: 67-74 3-5
MISTLETOE: 75 2-4
MOTOWN: 76-77 2-3
PHILADELPHIA INT'L: 78-81 1-3
VEE JAY (280; "For Your Precious
Love"): 58 450-600
VEE JAY (300 through 700 series): 60-66 . 3-5
VEE JAY (1971; "Aware Of Love"): 63 . 10-15
(Stereo compact 33 single.)
Picture Sleeves
VEE JAY: 61-64 4-8
LPs: 10/12-Inch 33rpm
ABNER (2001; "Jerry Butler
Esquire"): 59 75-100
BUDDAH: 69 12-15
EXODUS: 5-8
FOUNTAIN: 82 5-8
DYNASTY: 12-15
KENT: 68 10-12
LOST-NITE: 81 8-10
MERCURY: 67-84 10-12
MOTOWN: 76-77 5-8
PHILADELPHIA INT'L: 78-81 5-8
POST: 5-8
PRIDE: 72 8-10
UPFRONT: 8-10
SCEPTER: 8-10
SUNSET: 68 10-12
TRIP: 71-78 10-12
UNITED ARTISTS: 75 8-10
VEE JAY (1000 series): 60-64 20-25
VEE JAY (1100 series): 64-65 15-20
Members (Impressions): Jerry Butler; Sam
Gooden; Richard Brooks; Arthur Brooks; Curtis
Mayfield.
Also see AUSTIN, Patti, & Jerry Butler
Also see CHANDLER, Gene, & Jerry Butler
Also see IMPRESSIONS

BUTLER, Jerry, & Brenda Lee Eager
Singles: 7-Inch
MERCURY: 71-73 .... $2-4
LPs: 10/12-Inch 33rpm
MERCURY: 73 8-10
Also see EAGER, Brenda Lee

BUTLER, Jerry, & Betty Everett
Singles: 7-Inch
ABC: 73 1-3
VEE JAY: 64 3-5
LPs: 10/12-Inch 33rpm
BUDDAH: 69 10-12
TRADITION: 82 5-8
VEE JAY: 64 15-20
Also see DELLS
Also see EVERETT, Betty

BUTLER, Jerry, & Debra Henry
Singles: 7-Inch
PHILADELPHIA INT'L: 80 1-3
Also see SILK

BUTLER, Jerry, & Stix Hooper
Singles: 7-Inch
MCA: 83 1-3
Also see HOOPER, Stix

BUTLER, Jerry, & Thelma Houston
Singles: 7-Inch
MOTOWN: 77 2-3
LPs: 10/12-Inch 33rpm
MOTOWN: 77 5-8
Also see BUTLER, Jerry
Also see HOUSTON, Thelma

BUTLER, Jonathan
Singles: 7-Inch
JIVE: 86-88 1-3
LPs: 10/12-Inch 33rpm
JIVE: 86-88 5-8
Also see TURNER, Ruby

BUTTERFIELD, Paul
(Butterfield Blues Band)
Singles: 7-Inch
BEARSVILLE: 73-81 2-4
ELEKTRA: 67-69 4-6
Picture Sleeves
ELEKTRA: 67 4-8
LPs: 10/12-Inch 33rpm
BEARSVILLE: 73-81 8-10
ELEKTRA: 65-76 10-20
RED LIGHTNIN': 72 25-30
Also see BISHOP, Elvin

BUTTERFLYS
Singles: 7-Inch
RED BIRD: 64 5-8

BUTTONS, Red
Singles: 7-Inch
COLUMBIA: 53 .... $3-5

BUZZARD, Dr.: see DR. BUZZARD

BUZZCOCKS
Singles: 7-Inch
I.R.S.: 79-80 1-3
LPs: 10/12-Inch 33rpm
I.R.S.: 79 5-8
Members: Pete Shelley; Steve Diggle; Howard
Devoto; Steve Garvey; John Maher.
Also see SHELLEY, Pete

BYRD, Bobby
(Robert Byrd & His Birdies; Bobby Day)
Singles: 78rpm
CASH: 56 15-20
JAMIE: 57 5-10
SAGE & SAND: 55 5-10
SPARK: 8-15
Singles: 7-Inch
CASH: 56 30-40
JAMIE: 57 8-12
SAGE & SAND: 55 10-20
SPARK: 15-25
Also see BOB & EARL
Also see DAY, Bobby
Also see HOLLYWOOD FLAMES
Also see NUNN, Bobby

BYRD, Bobby
(Bobby Byrd & The Byrds)
Singles: 7-Inch
BROWNSTONE: 71-72 2-4
FEDERAL: 63 3-5
INTERNATIONAL BROTHERS: 75 2-3
KING: 67-71 2-4
KWANZA: 73 2-3
SMASH: 64-65 3-5
LPs: 10/12-Inch 33rpm
KING: 70 10-12
Also see KING, Anna, & Bobby Byrd

BYRD, Bobby, & James Brown
Singles: 7-Inch
KING: 68 2-4
Also see BROWN, James
Also see BYRD, Bobby

BYRD, Charlie
Singles: 7-Inch
RIVERSIDE: 62-63 2-3
LPs: 10/12-Inch 33rpm
OFFBEAT: 59-60 20-30
RIVERSIDE: 62-82 15-25
SAVOY: 58 25-35

Also see ALMEIDA, Laurindo
Also see GETZ, Stan, & Charlie Byrd

BYRD, Charlie, & Woody Herman
LPs: 10/12-Inch 33rpm
EVEREST: *63* $10-15
PICKWICK: *66* 6-12
Also see BYRD, Charlie
Also see HERMAN, Woody

BYRD, Donald
(Donald Byrd & 125th Street, N.Y.C.)
Singles: 7-Inch
BLUE NOTE: *75-77* 1-3
ELEKTRA: *78-82* 1-3
LPs: 10/12-Inch 33rpm
BETHLEHEM: *60* 15-25
BLUE NOTE: *59-65* 15-25
(Label reads "Blue Note Records Inc. - New York, U.S.A.")
BLUE NOTE: *66* 10-20
(Label reads "Blue Note Records - A Division Of Liberty Records Inc.")
COLUMBIA: *57-58* 20-30
ELEKTRA: *78-82* 5-8
JUBILEE: *57* 20-30
PRESTIGE: *56* 40-55
(Yellow label.)
REGENT: *57* 20-30
SAVOY: *55* 20-30
TRANSITION: *56* 35-50
VERVE: *58* 15-20
Also see BLACKBYRDS

BYRD, Donald, & Stanley Turrentine
LPs: 10/12-Inch 33rpm
VERVE: *64* 15-20
Also see BYRD, Donald
Also see TURRENTINE, Stanley

BYRD, Gary
(Gary Byrd & The G.B. Experience)
Singles: 12-Inch 33/45rpm
WONDIRECTION: *83* 4-6
Singles: 7-Inch
RCA VICTOR: *73* 2-3

BYRD, Jerry
Singles: 7-Inch
MONUMENT: *60-62* 3-6
EPs: 7-Inch 33/45rpm
DECCA: *58* 6-10
MERCURY: *53-55* 10-15
LPs: 10/12-Inch 33rpm
DECCA: *58* 15-20
LEHUA: 8-10
MERCURY (Except 25000 series): *58-64* 10-20

MERCURY (25000 series): *53-54* $15-25
(10-Inch LPs.)
MONUMENT: *61-63* 10-20
WING: *60-66* 10-15

BYRD, Russell
Singles: 7-Inch
SYMBOL: *62* 3-5
WAND: *61* 3-5

BYRDS
Singles: 7-Inch
ASYLUM: *73* 3-5
COLUMBIA: *65-71* 5-10
(Black vinyl.)
COLUMBIA: *65* 25-40
(Colored vinyl. Promotional issues only.)
SCHOLASTIC: *66* 5-8
Picture Sleeves
COLUMBIA (Except 43271): *65-71* 12-25
COLUMBIA (43271; "Mr. Tambourine Man"): *65* 60-80
(Promotional issue only.)
EPs: 7-Inch 33/45rpm
COLUMBIA (10287; "The Byrds"): *66* 25-35
(Columbia Special Products issue for the Scholastic Book Services.)
COLUMBIA (116003/4; "Fifth Dimension Open-End Interview"): *66* 40-55
(Promotional issue only.)
LPs: 10/12-Inch 33rpm
ASYLUM: *73* 8-10
COLUMBIA (2000 series): *65-67* 20-25
COLUMBIA (9000 series): *65-69* 15-25
COLUMBIA (30000 through 33000 series): *70-75* 8-12
COLUMBIA (34000 through 37000 series): *75-84* 5-8
TOGETHER: *69* 15-20
Promotional LPs
BROADCAST ("Byrds Live"): *81* 35-40
COLUMBIA (2000 series): *65-67* 40-50
(White label.)
COLUMBIA (9000 series): *65-69* 35-45
(White label.)
COLUMBIA (116003/4; "Fifth Dimension" Interview Album): *66* 75-125
Members: David Crosby; Gene Clark; Chris Hillman; Roger McGuinn; Mike Clark; Skip Battin; John Guerin; Kevin Kelley.
Also see BEEFEATERS
Also see CLARK, Gene
Also see CROSBY, David
Also see HILLMAN, Chris
Also see MC GUINN, CLARK & HILLMAN
Also see PARSONS, Gram

BYRNE, David
Singles: 12-Inch 33/45rpm
SIRE: *82* $4-6
LPs: 10/12-Inch 33rpm
SIRE: *81* 5-8
Also see ENO, Brian
Also see TALKING HEADS

BYRNES, Edd "Kookie," With Joanie Sommers & The Mary Kaye Trio
Singles: 7-Inch
WARNER BROS: *59* 3-5
Picture Sleeves
WARNER BROS: *59* 5-10
Also see BYRNES, Edward
Also see KAYE, Mary
Also see SOMMERS, Joanie

BYRNES, Edward
(Edd "Kookie" Byrnes; Edd Byrnes With Connie Stevens; Edd Byrnes With Friend; Edd Byrnes & The Mary Kaye Trio.)
Singles: 7-Inch
WARNER BROS (Monaural): *59* 4-6
WARNER BROS (Stereo): *59* 10-15
Picture Sleeves
WARNER BROS: *59* 10-20
LPs: 10/12-Inch 33rpm
WARNER BROS: *59* 20-30
Also see BYRNES, Edd "Kookie," With Joanie Sommers & The Mary Kaye Trio
Also see STEVENS, Connie

BYRON, D.L.
Singles: 7-Inch
ARISTA: *80* 1-3
LPs: 10/12-Inch 33rpm
ARISTA: *80* 5-8

C

C., Fantastic Johnny:
see FANTASTIC JOHNNY C.

C & THE SHELLS
Singles: 7-Inch
COTILLION: *69-70* 2-4
ZANZEE: *72* 2-4
Also see SANDPEBBLES

C.C. & COMPANY
Singles: 7-Inch
SUSSEX: *75* 2-3
20TH CENTURY/WESTBOUND: *75* 2-3

C.C.S.
Singles: 7-Inch
BELL: *73* $2-4
RAK: *71* 2-4
LPs: 10/12-Inch 33rpm
RAK: *71-72* 8-10

C.J. & CO.
Singles: 7-Inch
WESTBOUND: *77-78* 2-3
LPs: 10/12-Inch 33rpm
WESTBOUND: *77-78* 2-3

C.L. BLAST: see BLAST, C.L.

C.O.D.s
Singles: 7-Inch
ERIC: *74* 1-3
KELLMAC: *65-66* 3-6

C.Q.D.
Singles: 12-Inch 33/45rpm
EMERGENCY: *83* 4-6

CABOOSE
Singles: 7-Inch
ENTERPRISE: *70* 2-4
LPs: 10/12-Inch 33rpm
ENTERPRISE: *71* 10-12

CACTUS
Singles: 7-Inch
ATCO: *70-72* 3-5
LPs: 10/12-Inch 33rpm
ATCO: *70-72* 15-20
Members: Carmine Appice; Tim Bogert; Pete French; Werner Fritzschings; Duane Hitchings; Jerry Norris; Mike Pinera; Roland Robinson; Rusty Day; Jim McCarty.
Also see BECK, BOGERT & APPICE
Also see NEW CACTUS BAND
Also see PINERA, Mike
Also see YARDBIRDS

CACTUS WORLD NEWS
Singles: 7-Inch
MCA: *86* 1-3
LPs: 10/12-Inch 33rpm
MCA: *86* 5-8

CADETS
Singles: 78rpm
MODERN: 55-57 5-10
Singles: 7-Inch
COLLECTABLES: *81* 1-3
MODERN (Except 971): *55-57* 10-20
MODERN (971: "If It Is Wrong"): *55* 50-75
SHERWOOD: *60* 3-5

LPs: 10/12-Inch 33rpm
CROWN (370; "The Cadets"): *63* $15-25
CROWN (5015; "Rockin' 'N
  Reelin"): *57* 50-75
RELIC: 10-12
  Members: Ted Taylor; Aaron Collins; Will "Dub"
  Jones; Willie Davis; Lloyd McGraw; Prentice
  Moreland; Tom Fox; Randolph Jones.
  Also see FLARES
  Also see JACKS
  Also see TAYLOR, Ted

CADILLAC, Flash:
see FLASH CADILLAC & THE CONTINEN-TAL KIDS

CADILLACS
Singles: 78rpm
JOSIE (765; "Gloria"): *54* 50-100
JOSIE (769; "Wishing Well"): *54* 50-100
JOSIE (773; "No Chance"): *55* 15-25
JOSIE (778; "Down The Road"): *55* 15-25
JOSIE (785 through 798): *56* 6-12
JOSIE (800 series except 820): *56* 5-10
JOSIE (820; "My Girl Friend"): *57* 10-20
Singles: 7-Inch
ABC: *73* 1-3
CAPITOL: *62* 3-5
JOSIE (765; "Gloria"): *54* 150-200
JOSIE (769; "Wishing Well"): *54* 150-200
JOSIE (773; "No Chance"): *55* 30-40
JOSIE (778; "Down The Road"): *55* 30-40
JOSIE (785 through 798): *56* 10-20
JOSIE (800 series except 820): *56-60* 5-10
JOSIE (820; "My Girl Friend"): *57* 25-30
JOSIE (900 series): *63* 3-5
MERCURY: *61* 3-5
SMASH: *61* 3-5
VIRGO: *72-73* 1-3
LPs: 10/12-Inch 33rpm
CADAVER: 5-8
HARLEM HITPARADE: 10-12
JUBILEE (1045; "The Fabulous
  Cadillacs"): *57* 300-400
  (Blue label.)
JUBILEE (1045; "The Fabulous
  Cadillacs"): *59* 100-150
  (Flat black label.)
JUBILEE (1045; "The Fabulous
  Cadillacs"): *60* 50-100
  (Glossy black label.)
JUBILEE (1089; "The Crazy
  Cadillacs"): *59* 150-250
  (Flat black label.)

JUBILEE (1089; "The Crazy
  Cadillacs"): *60* $75-125
  (Glossy black label.)
JUBILEE (5009; "Twistin' With
  The Cadillacs"): *62* 25-30
MURRAY HILL (5-LP boxed set): 30-35
  Members: Earl "Speedo" Carroll; Jim "Papa"
  Clark; Gus Willingham; Bobby Phillips; Laverne
  Drake; Charles Brooks; James Bailey; Earl Wade.
  Also see NEW YORK CITY
  Also see ORIGINAL CADILLACS
  Also see SCHOOLBOYS
  Also see SPEEDO & THE CADILLACS

CADILLACS / Orioles
LPs: 10/12-Inch 33rpm
JUBILEE (1117; "The Cadillacs Meet
  The Orioles"): *61* 40-50
  Also see CADILLACS
  Also see ORIOLES

CAESAR, Shirley
(Shirley Caesar & The Caesar Singers)
Singles: 7-Inch
HOB/SCEPTER: *73-75* 1-3
ROADSHOW: *77-78* 1-3
LPs: 10/12-Inch 33rpm
HOB: *70-75* 6-10
ROADSHOW: *77* 5-8
TRIP: *77* 5-8

CAESAR & CLEO
Singles: 7-Inch
REPRISE: *64-65* 8-15
VAULT: *63* 15-25
Picture Sleeves
REPRISE (0419; "Let The Good
  Times Roll"): *65* 25-50
  Members: Salvatore "Sonny" Bono; Cher LaPiere.
  Also see SONNY & CHER

CAESAR & THE ROMANS:
see LITTLE CAESAR & THE ROMANS

CAESARS
Singles: 7-Inch
LANIE: *67* 3-5

CAFE
(With The Hearns Sisters)
Singles: 12-Inch 33/45rpm
MONTAGE: *84* 4-6

CAFFERTY, John
(John Cafferty & The Beaver Brown Band)
Singles: 7-Inch
SCOTTI BROTHERS: *83-88* 1-3
LPs: 10/12-Inch 33rpm
SCOTTI BROTHERS: *84-88* 5-8

CAIN, Joe, & The Red Parrot Orchestra
Singles: 7-Inch
ZOO YORK: *83* $1-3

CAIN, Jonathan
(Jonathan Cain Band)
Singles: 7-Inch
BEARSVILLE: *76* 1-3
OCTOBER: *75-76* 2-4
LPs: 10/12-Inch 33rpm
BEARSVILLE: *77* 5-8
Also see CAIN, Tane
Also see JOURNEY

CAIN, Tane
Singles: 7-Inch
RCA VICTOR: *82-83* 1-3
LPs: 10/12-Inch 33rpm
RCA VICTOR: *82* 5-8
Also see CAIN, Jonathan

CAINE, General
Singles: 12-Inch 33/45rpm
CAPITOL: *84* 4-6
TABU: *82-84* 4-6
Singles: 7-Inch
CAPITOL: *84* 1-3
TABU: *82-84* 1-3
LPs: 10/12-Inch 33rpm
TABU: *82-84* 5-8

CAIOLA, Al
Singles: 78rpm
REGENCY: *56* 2-5
Singles: 7-Inch
AVLANCHE: *73* 1-3
PREFERRED: *59-60* 2-4
RCA VICTOR: *53-55* 3-5
REGENCY: *56* 3-5
UNITED ARTISTS: *60-68* 2-4
EPs: 7-Inch 33/45rpm
RCA VICTOR: *53* 5-10
LPs: 10/12-Inch 33rpm
ATCO: *60* 10-15
CAMDEN: *62* 8-12
CHANCELLOR: *60* 10-15
RCA VICTOR: *59* 10-15
ROULETTE: *60* 10-15
SAVOY: *56* 15-25
TIME: *60-61* 10-15
TWO WORLDS: *72* 8-10
UNART: *67* 8-12
UNITED ARTISTS: *60-69* 10-15

CALDERA
Singles: 7-Inch
CAPITOL: *76* 2-3

LPs: 10/12-Inch 33rpm
CAPITOL: *76-79* $8-10

CALDWELL, Bobby
Singles: 12-Inch 33/45rpm
MCA: *84-85* 4-6
Singles: 7-Inch
CLOUDS: *78-80* 1-3
PBR INT'L: *76* 1-3
POLYDOR: *82-83* 1-3
MCA: *84-85* 1-3
LPs: 10/12-Inch 33rpm
CLOUDS: *78-80* 5-8
MCA: *84* 5-8
POLYDOR: *82* 5-8
Also see CAPTAIN BEYOND

CALDWELL, Rue
Singles: 12-Inch 33/45rpm
CRITIQUE: *83* 4-6
Singles: 7-Inch
CRITIQUE: *83* 1-3

CALE, J.J.
Singles: 7-Inch
LIBERTY: *66* 5-10
MERCURY: *83-84* 1-3
SHELTER: *71-81* 2-5
LPs: 10/12-Inch 33rpm
MCA: *81* 5-8
MERCURY: *82-85* 5-8
SHELTER: *71-79* 10-15

CALE, John
Singles: 7-Inch
A&M: *81* 1-3
COLUMBIA: *70* 2-4
I.R.S.: *79-80* 1-3
REPRISE: *72* 2-4
Picture Sleeves
I.R.S.: *79-80* 1-3
LPs: 10/12-Inch 33rpm
A&M: *81* 5-8
COLUMBIA: *70-71* 12-15
I.R.S.: *79* 5-8
ISLAND: *75-77* 8-10
PASSPORT: *84* 5-8
REPRISE: *72-73* 10-12
ZE: *83* 5-8
Also see VELVET UNDERGROUND

CALEN, Frankie
Singles: 7-Inch
BEAR: *62* 3-5
EPIC: *63-64* 3-5
NRC: *59* 3-5
SPARK: *61* 3-5
UNITED ARTISTS: *62* 3-5

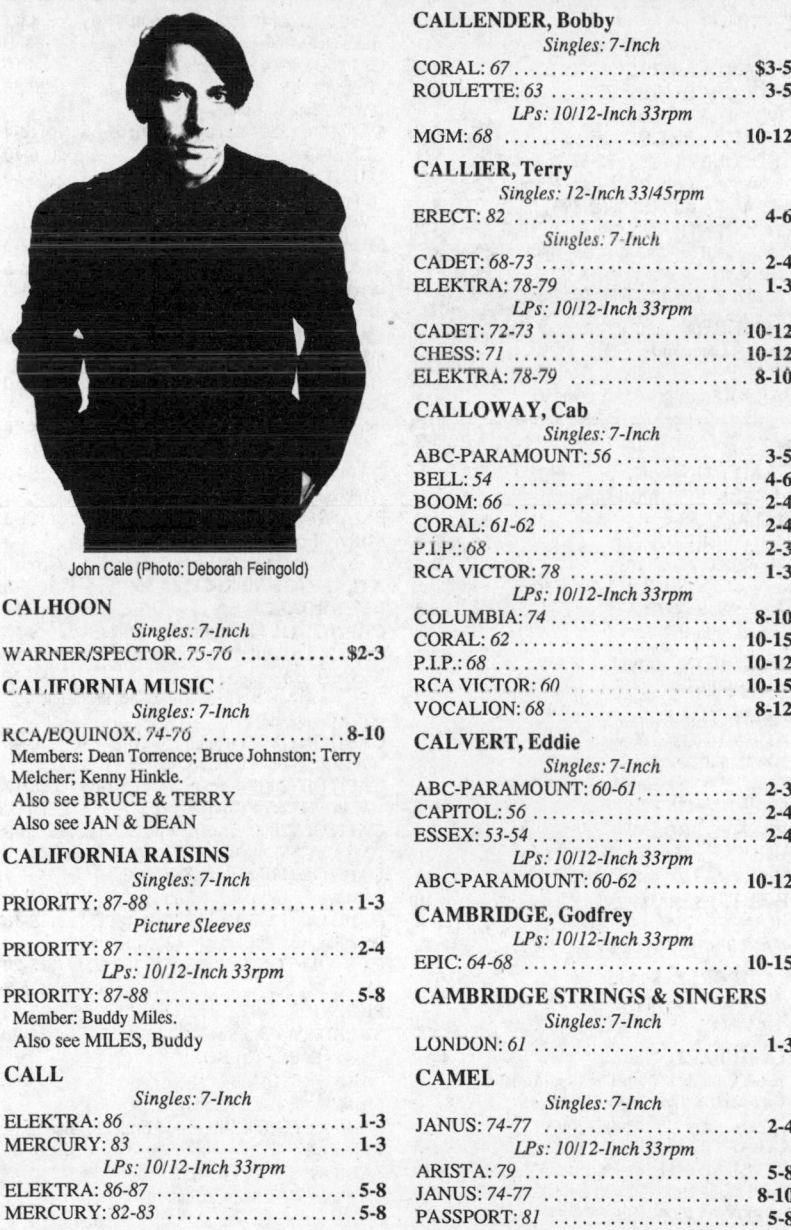

John Cale (Photo: Deborah Feingold)

CALHOON
Singles: 7-Inch
WARNER/SPECTOR. *75-76* $2-3

CALIFORNIA MUSIC
Singles: 7-Inch
RCA/EQUINOX. *74-76* 8-10
  Members: Dean Torrence; Bruce Johnston; Terry
  Melcher; Kenny Hinkle.
  Also see BRUCE & TERRY
  Also see JAN & DEAN

CALIFORNIA RAISINS
Singles: 7-Inch
PRIORITY: *87-88* 1-3
Picture Sleeves
PRIORITY: *87* 2-4
LPs: 10/12-Inch 33rpm
PRIORITY: *87-88* 5-8
  Member: Buddy Miles.
  Also see MILES, Buddy

CALL
Singles: 7-Inch
ELEKTRA: *86* 1-3
MERCURY: *83* 1-3
LPs: 10/12-Inch 33rpm
ELEKTRA: *86-87* 5-8
MERCURY: *82-83* 5-8

CALLENDER, Bobby
Singles: 7-Inch
CORAL: *67* $3-5
ROULETTE: *63* 3-5
LPs: 10/12-Inch 33rpm
MGM: *68* 10-12

CALLIER, Terry
Singles: 12-Inch 33/45rpm
ERECT: *82* 4-6
Singles: 7-Inch
CADET: *68-73* 2-4
ELEKTRA: *78-79* 1-3
LPs: 10/12-Inch 33rpm
CADET: *72-73* 10-12
CHESS: *71* 10-12
ELEKTRA: *78-79* 8-10

CALLOWAY, Cab
Singles: 7-Inch
ABC-PARAMOUNT: *56* 3-5
BELL: *54* 4-6
BOOM: *66* 2-4
CORAL: *61-62* 2-4
P.I.P.: *68* 2-3
RCA VICTOR: *78* 1-3
LPs: 10/12-Inch 33rpm
COLUMBIA: *74* 8-10
CORAL: *62* 10-15
P.I.P.: *68* 10-12
RCA VICTOR: *60* 10-15
VOCALION: *68* 8-12

CALVERT, Eddie
Singles: 7-Inch
ABC-PARAMOUNT: *60-61* 2-3
CAPITOL: *56* 2-4
ESSEX: *53-54* 2-4
LPs: 10/12-Inch 33rpm
ABC-PARAMOUNT: *60-62* 10-12

CAMBRIDGE, Godfrey
LPs: 10/12-Inch 33rpm
EPIC: *64-68* 10-15

CAMBRIDGE STRINGS & SINGERS
Singles: 7-Inch
LONDON: *61* 1-3

CAMEL
Singles: 7-Inch
JANUS: *74-77* 2-4
LPs: 10/12-Inch 33rpm
ARISTA: *79* 5-8
JANUS: *74-77* 8-10
PASSPORT: *81* 5-8
  Members: Peter Bardens; Doug Ferguson; Andy
  Latimer; Andy Ward.

CAMEO
Singles: 12-Inch 33/45rpm
ATLANTA ARTISTS: *83-86* $4-6
CHOCOLATE CITY: *78-80* 4-6
Singles: 7-Inch
ATLANTA ARTISTS: *83-88* 1-3
CHOCOLATE CITY: *75-82* 1-3
LPs: 10/12-Inch 33rpm
ATLANTA ARTISTS: *83-88* 5-8
CHOCOLATE CITY: *77-82* 5-8
Members: Tomi Jenkins; Larry Blackmon; Nathan Leftenant.
Also see SINGLETON, Charlie

CAMERON
(Rafael Cameron)
Singles: 7-Inch
SALSOUL: *80-82* 1-3
LPs: 10/12-Inch 33rpm
SALSOUL: *80-82* 5-8

CAMERON, G.C.
Singles: 7-Inch
MALACO: *83* 1-3
MOTOWN: *73-77* 1-3
MOWEST: *71-73* 2-4
LPs: 10/12-Inch 33rpm
MOTOWN: *74-77* 5-8
Also see SPINNERS

CAMERON, Rafael:
see CAMERON

CAMP, Hamilton
(Hamid Hamilton Camp & The Skymonters; Bob Camp)
Singles: 7-Inch
AMERICAN INT'L: *71* 1-3
WARNER BROS: *68* 2-4
LPs: 10/12-Inch 33rpm
ELEKTRA (200 series): *64* 12-15
ELEKTRA (75000 series): *73* 8-10
MOUNTAIN RAILROAD: 5-8
WARNER BROS: *67-69* 10-12

CAMPBELL, Debbie
Singles: 7-Inch
PLAYBOY: *75* 2-4

CAMPBELL, Glen
(Glen Campbell With The Glen-Aires; Glen Campbell & The Green River Boys)
Singles: 7-Inch
ATLANTIC AMERICA: *82-86* 1-3
CAPEHART: *61* 8-10
CAPITOL (2000 & 3000 series): *68-74* 1-3
CAPITOL (4000 series): *75-81* 1-3
(Orange or purple labels.)

CAPITOL (4783 through 5360): *61-65* $3-5
(Orange/yellow swirl labels.)
CAPITOL (5441; "Guess I'm Dumb"): *65* 20-25
(With Brian Wilson.)
CAPITOL (5504 through 5939): *65-67* 2-4
CENECO: 6-10
CREST: *61-62* 6-10
(Shown as Glen Cambpell on some Crest labels.)
EVEREST: *69* 1-3
MCA: *87-88* 1-3
STARDAY: *68* 3-5
WARNER BROS: *80* 1-3
Picture Sleeves
CAPITOL (Except 4856 & 5279): *68-74* ...1-3
CAPITOL (4856; "Long Black Limousine"): *62* 5-10
CAPITOL (5279; "Summer, Winter, Spring & Fall"): *64* 5-10
EPs: 7-Inch 33/45rpm
CAPITOL: *68-69* 5-10
(Jukebox issues only.)
MCA: *84* 1-3
MIRAGE: *81* 1-3
LPs: 10/12-Inch 33rpm
ATLANTIC AMERICA: *82-86* 5-8
BUCKBOARD: 8-10
CAPITOL (103 through 733): *68-71* 8-12
CAPITOL (1810; "Big Bluegrass Special"): *62* 60-75
(Shown as by The Green River Boys Featuring Glen Campbell.)
CAPITOL (1881 through 2392): *63-65* ...20-40
(With a "T" or "ST" prefix.)
CAPITOL (2809 through 2928): *67-68* 8-12
(With a "T" or "ST" prefix.)
CAPITOL (2000 series): *78* 5-8
(With an "SM" prefix.)
CAPITOL (11000 through 16000 series): *72-82* 5-8
CAPITOL (120000 series): 5-10
(Capitol Record Club issues.)
CUSTOM TONE: 15-20
MCA: *88* 5-8
PICKWICK: *64-73* 8-10
STARDAY: *68-69* 15-20
Also see BEACH BOYS
Also see CHAMPS
Also see FOLKSWINGERS
Also see FORD, Tennessee Ernie, & Glen Campbell
Also see SAGITTARIUS
Also see WILSON, Brian

CAMPBELL, Glen, & Rita Coolidge
Singles: 7-Inch
CAPITOL: *80* $2-3
Also see COOLIDGE, Rita

CAMPBELL, Glen, & Bobbie Gentry
Singles: 7-Inch
CAPITOL: *68-70* 2-5
EPs: 7-Inch 33/45rpm
CAPITOL: *68* 8-10
(Jukebox issue only.)
LPs: 10/12-Inch 33rpm
CAPITOL: *68* 8-10
Also see GENTRY, Bobbie

CAMPBELL, Glen, & Anne Murray
Singles: 7-Inch
CAPITOL: *71-72* 2-4
LPs: 10/12-Inch 33rpm
CAPITOL: *71-80* 5-10
Also see MURRAY, Anne

CAMPBELL, Glen, & Billy Strange
LPs: 10/12-Inch 33rpm
SURREY: *65* 12-15
Also see STRANGE, Billy

CAMPBELL, Glen, & Tanya Tucker
Singles: 7-Inch
CAPITOL: *81* 2-3
Also see CAMPBELL, Glen
Also see TUCKER, Tanya

CAMPBELL, Jim
Singles: 7-Inch
LAURIE: *69-70* 3-5

CAMPBELL, Jo Ann
Singles: 78rpm
ELDORADO: *57* 5-10
POINT: *56* 6-12
Singles: 7-Inch
ABC-PARAMOUNT (Monaural): *60-62* .. 5-10
ABC-PARAMOUNT (Stereo): *60* 20-30
CAMEO: *62-63* 5-10
ELDORADO: *57* 15-20
GONE: *59* 10-20
POINT: *56* 15-25
RORI: 5-10
LPs: 10/12-Inch 33rpm
ABC-PARAMOUNT: *62* 50-60
CAMEO: *62* 25-30
CORONET: 25-30
END: *59* 40-45
Also see JO ANN & TROY

CANDELA
Singles: 12-Inch 33/45rpm
ARISTA: *83* 4-6

Singles: 7-Inch
ARISTA: *82-83* $1-3

CANDY & THE KISSES
Singles: 7-Inch
CAMEO: *64* 8-10
COLLECTABLES: *81* 1-3
DECCA: *68* 3-5
R&L: *63* 8-10
SCEPTER: *65-66* 5-10

CANDYMEN
Singles: 7-Inch
ABC: *67-69* 3-5
LIBERTY: *70* 2-4
LPs: 10/12-Inch 33rpm
ABC: *67-68* 15-20
Members: Rodney Justo; Barry Bailey; Dean Daughtry; Billy Gilmore; Paul Goddard; John Adkins; Bob Nix.
Also see ATLANTA RHYTHM SECTION
Also see CLASSICS IV
Also see ORBISON, Roy

CANE, Gary
(Gary Cane & His Friends)
Singles: 7-Inch
SHELL: *60-61* 3-5

CANNED HEAT
(Heat Brothers)
Singles: 7-Inch
ALA: *84* 2-4
ATLANTIC: *74* 2-3
LIBERTY: *68-71* 4-6
UNITED ARTISTS: *71-73* 3-5
Picture Sleeves
LIBERTY: *67-69* 3-6
LPs: 10/12-Inch 33rpm
ACCORD: *81* 5-8
ALA: *84* 8-10
ATLANTIC: *73-74* 10-12
JANUS: *69* 12-15
LIBERTY (1000 series): *80* 5-8
LIBERTY (7000 series): *67-69* 12-20
LIBERTY (10000 series): *81* 5-8
LIBERTY (11000 series): *69-70* 10-15
SCEPTER: 10-12
SUNSET: *71* 10-12
UNITED ARTISTS: *71-75* 10-12
WAND: *70* 15-20
Members: Bob Hite; Joel Scott Hill; Harvey Mandel; Mark Andex; Ed Bayer; Frank Cook; Richard Hite; Chris Morgan; James Shane; Gene Taylor; Larry Taylor; Henry Vestine; Alan Wilson; Nolfo De LaParra.
Also see HOOKER, John Lee, & Canned Heat
Also see LITTLE RICHARD

Also see MANDEL, Harvey

CANNED HEAT & THE CHIPMUNKS
Singles: 7-Inch
LIBERTY: *68-70* $15-20
Also see CANNED HEAT
Also see CHIPMUNKS

CANNIBAL & THE HEADHUNTERS
Singles: 7-Inch
AIRES: *68* 3-5
CAPITOL: *69* 3-5
COLLECTABLES: *81* 1-3
DATE: *66* 3-5
ERA: *73* 2-4
RAMPART: *65-66* 4-6
LPs: 10/12-Inch 33rpm
DATE: *66* 20-25
RAMPART (3302; "Land Of 1000
Dances"): *65* 40-50
Members: Frankie "Cannibal" Garcia; Robert
Jaramillo; Joe Jaramillo; Richard Lopez.

CANNON, Ace
(Johnny "Ace" Cannon)
Singles: 7-Inch
FERNWOOD: *63-64* 3-5
HI (2000 series): *61-66* 3-5
HI (2100 through 2300 series): *66-76* 2-4
MOTOWN: *82* 1-3
SANTO: *62* 3-5
Picture Sleeves
HI: *62-63* 4-8
LPs: 10/12-Inch 33rpm
ALLEGIANCE: *84* 5-8
GUSTO: *80* 5-8
HI (007 through 040): *62-67* 10-15
(Hi numbers in this series were preceded by a "12"
for mono or a "32" for stereo issues.)
HI (043 through 090): *68-75* 6-10
(All numbers in this series were preceded by a
"32," indicating stereo.)
HI (6000 & 8000 series): *77-79* 8-10
MOTOWN: *83* 5-8

CANNON, Dean
Singles: 7-Inch
VALIANT: *63* 3-5

CANNON, Freddy
(Freddie Cannon)
Singles: 7-Inch
BUDDAH: *71* 2-4
CLARIDGE: *74-76* 2-3
ERIC: *78* 1-3
MCA: *74* 2-3
METROMEDIA: *72* 2-4
ROYAL AMERICAN: *69-70* 2-4

SIRE: *69* $2-4
SWAN: *59-64* 4-8
WARNER BROS: *64-67* 3-5
WE MAKE ROCK & ROLL
RECORDS: *68* 2-4
Picture Sleeves
SWAN: *59-62* 12-25
WARNER BROS: *64-65* 10-20
LPs: 10/12-Inch 33rpm
RHINO: *82* 5-8
SWAN: *60-63* 40-70
WARNER BROS: *64-66* 30-35
Also see BUCHANAN, Roy
Also see DANNY & THE JUNIORS
Also see G-CLEFS
Also see SLAY, Frank, & His Orchestra

CANNON, Freddy, & The Belmonts
Singles: 7-Inch
MIA SOUND: *81* 3-6
Also see BELMONTS, Freddy Cannon & Bo
Diddley
Also see CANNON, Freddy

CANO, Eddie
Singles: 7-Inch
DUNHILL: *66-67* 2-3
GNP/CRESCENDO: *62* 2-4
REPRISE: *62-65* 2-3
LPs: 10/12-Inch 33rpm
GNP/CRESCENDO: *61-62* 8-15
RCA VICTOR: *62* 8-15
REPRISE: *62-65* 8-15

CANTINA BAND
Singles: 7-Inch
MILLENNIUM: *81* 1-3
Member: Lou Christie.
Also see CHRISTIE, Lou

CANTRELL, Lana
Singles: 7-Inch
EAST COAST: *74* 2-4
POLYDOR: *74-75* 2-4
RCA VICTOR: *66-69* 3-5
LPs: 10/12-Inch 33rpm
RCA VICTOR: *67-69* 6-15

CANYON
Singles: 7-Inch
MAGNA-GLIDE: *75* 2-4

CAPALDI, Jim
Singles: 12-Inch 33/45rpm
RSO: *79* 4-6
Singles: 7-Inch
ATLANTIC: *83* 1-3
ISLAND: *72-76* 2-4

ISLAND: *88* $1-3
RSO: *78* 2-3
LPs: 10/12-Inch 33rpm
ATLANTIC: *83* 5-8
CAPITOL: *72* 8-10
ISLAND: *74-75* 10-12
ISLAND: *88* 5-8
RSO: *78-79* 5-8
  Also see TRAFFIC

CAPITOLS
Singles: 7-Inch
COLLECTABLES: *81* 1-3
KAREN: *66-68* 4-6
LPs: 10/12-Inch 33rpm
ATCO: *66* 15-20
COLLECTABLES: *88* 6-8
SOLID SMOKE: *85* 5-8

CAPRELLS
Singles: 7-Inch
ARIOLA AMERICA: *76* 2-3

CAPRIS
Singles: 7-Inch
AMBIENT SOUND: *82* 3-6
COLLECTABLES: *81* 2-4
LOST NITE (Pink label): *60* 15-20
MR. PEEKE: *63* 5-10
OLD TOWN: *60-61* 8-12
PLANET (1010; "There's A Moon
  Out Tonight"): *60* 75-100
TROMMERS: *60* 25-30
LPs: 10/12-Inch 33rpm
AMBIENT SOUND: *82* 5-8
COLLECTABLES: *84* 6-8
  Members: Nick "Santos" Santamaria; Mike
  Mitchell; Vince Narcardo; John Apostol; Frank
  Reina.

CAPTAIN & TENNILLE
Singles: 7-Inch
A&M: *75-78* 2-4
BUTTERSCOTCH CASTLE: *73* 40-50
JOYCE: *74* 15-20
CASABLANCA: *79-80* 2-3
Picture Sleeves
A&M: *75-78* 2-4
LPs: 10/12-Inch 33rpm
A&M: *75-79* 8-10
CAASABLANCA: *79* 5-8
  Members: Daryl Dragon; Toni Tennille.
  Also see TENNILLE, Toni
  Also see YELLOW BALLOON

CAPTAIN BEEFHEART
(Captain Beefheart & His Magic Band)
Singles: 7-Inch
A&M (818; "Frying Pan"):*66* $30-50
BUDDAH: *67-69* 4-8
MERCURY: *74* 3-5
REPRISE: *72* 3-6
VIRGIN: *82* 2-4
Promotional Singles
REPRISE (434; "Lick My Decals
  Off, Baby"): *70* 40-50
REPRISE (447; "Talking About"): *71* . . . 40-50
REPRISE (514; "Click Clack"): *71* 25-40
REPRISE (547; "Love Yo Yo
  Stuff"): *72* 40-50
  (Issued with gatefold, EP-like, cover.)
LPs: 10/12-Inch 33rpm
A&M: *84* 5-8
ACCORD: *83* 5-8
BIZARRE: *72* 10-12
BLUE THUMB (1; "Strictly
  Personal"): *68* 15-20
  (Black label.)
BLUE THUMB (1; "Strictly
  Personal"): *69* 8-12
  (Tan label.)
BLUE THUMB (Tan label): *69* 8-12
BUDDAH (1001; "Safe As Milk"): *67* . . 25-35
  (Monaural. With 4"x15" "Safe As Milk" bumper
  sticker. Without sticker, deduct $10-$15.)
BUDDAH (5001; "Safe As Milk"): *67* . . 25-30
  (Stereo. With bumper sticker. Without sticker,
  deduct $10 $15.)
BUDDAH (5077; "Mirror Man"): *71* 10-15
BUDDAH (5063; "Safe As Milk"): *70* . . . 8-10
D.I.R. (57; "Direct News, Week
  Of 12-18-78"): *78* 25-40
  (Contains five 5-minute radio programs, one of
  which has an interview with Don Van Vliet. Promo-
  tional issue only.)
EPIC: *82* 5-8
MERCURY (709; "Unconditionally
  Guaranteed"): *74* 8-12
MERCURY (1018; "Bluejeans &
  Moonbeams"): *74* 8-12
REPRISE (2050; "Spotlight
  Kid"): *72* 10-15
REPRISE (2115; "Clear Spot"): *72* 10-18
  (With embossed "Clear Spot" plastic bag.)
REPRISE (2115; "Clear Spot"): *72* 15-20
  (White label. With printed inserts instead of stand-
  ard cover. Promotional issue only.)
STRAIGHT (1053; "Trout Mask
  Replica"): *68* 30-40
  (With lyrics sleeve.)

FRYING PAN
(Don Vliet)
PROMOTIONAL
COPY   NOT FOR SALE
A&M   Stelen Music
RECORDS   (BMI)
                       Time 2:02
                       (1229)
                       Prod. by Dave Gates

CAPTAIN BEEFHEART
and HIS MAGIC BAND
Supervised by Leonard Grant
A Product of Quintus Productions, Inc.
818

STRAIGHT (1053; "Trout Mask
  Replica"): 68 .... $20-25
  (Without lyrics sleeve.)
STRAIGHT (6420; "Lick My Decals
  Off, Baby"): 70 10-15
VIRGIN: 80-82 5-8
WARNER BROS: 78 5-8
  Members: Don "Captain Beefheart" Van Vliet;
  Doug Moon; Paul Blakely; Alex St. Claire; Jerry
  Handley; Ry Cooder; Jeff Cotton; John French; Bill
  "Zoot Horn Rollo" Harkleroad; Rockette Morton;
  Jimmy Semens; Jerry Handsley.
  Also see COODER, Ry
  Also see MOTHERS OF INVENTION

CAPTAIN BEYOND
            Singles: 7-Inch
CAPRICORN: 73 2-4
        LPs: 10/12-Inch 33rpm
CAPRICORN (Except 0105): 72-73 8-12
CAPRICORN (0105; "Captain
  Beyond"): 72 30-40
  (With 3-D cover.)
CAPRICORN (0105; "Captain
  Beyond"): 72 8-12
  (With standard cover.)
WARNER BROS: 77 8-10
  Members: Bobby Caldwell; Rod Evans; Willie Daf-
  fern; Lee Dorman; Larry Reinhardt.
  Also see CALDWELL, Bobby
  Also see DEEP PURPLE

CAPTAIN RAPP
        Singles: 12-Inch 33/45rpm
BECKET: 83 4-6
            Singles: 7-Inch
BECKET: 83 1-3

CAPTAIN SKY
(Daryl Cameron)
        Singles: 12-Inch 33/45rpm
WMOT: 81 .... $4-6
            Singles: 7-Inch
A.V.I.: 79-82 1-3
TEC: 80 1-3
TRIPLE: 86 1-3
WMOT: 81 1-3
        LPs: 10/12-Inch 33rpm
A.V.I.: 78-82 5-8
TEC: 80 5-8

CARA, Irene
        Singles: 12-Inch 33/45rpm
CASABLANCA: 83 4-6
GEFFEN: 83 4-6
            Singles: 7-Inch
CASABLANCA: 83 1-3
GEFFEN: 83-85 1-3
RSO: 80 1-3
NETWORK: 81 1-3
        LPs: 10/12-Inch 33rpm
GEFFEN: 83-85 5-8
NETWORK: 82 5-8
RSO: 80 5-8

CARAVAN
            Singles: 7-Inch
BTM: 75 2-3
DK: 83 1-3
LONDON: 71 2-4
        LPs: 10/12-Inch 33rpm
ARISTA: 76 5-8
BTM: 75 5-8
LONDON: 71-75 12-15
VERVE/FORECAST: 69 15-20
  Members: Steve Miller; Richard Coughlan; Pye
  Hastings; John Perry; Geoff Richards; Jan Schel-
  haas; Dave Sinclair; Richard Sinclair; Mike
  Wedgewood.

CARAVELLES
            Singles: 7-Inch
SMASH: 63-65 3-6
        LPs: 10/12-Inch 33rpm
SMASH: 63 20-25
  Members: Lois Wilkinson; Andrea Simpson.

CARDINALS
            Singles: 78rpm
ATLANTIC: 51 12-25
            Singles: 7-Inch
ATLANTIC (952 through 995): 51-53 ... 50-75
ATLANTIC (1000 series,
  except 1025): 54-56 20-40

ATLANTIC (1025; "Under A Blanket
Of Blue"): *54* $40-60
ATLANTIC (1100 series): *57* 5-10
Members: Ernie Warren; Meredith Brothers; Leon
Tree; Don Johnson; Sam Aydelotte; Luther Mac-
Arthur; James Brown; Lee Tarver.

CAREFREES
Singles: 7-Inch
LONDON INT'L (Except 10614): *64* 4-6
LONDON INT'L (10614; "We Love
You Beatles"): *64* 5-10

Picture Sleeves
LONDON INT'L (10614; "We Love
You Beatles"): *64* 10-20

LPs: 10/12-Inch 33rpm
LONDON: *64* 35-40
Members: Lyn Cornell; Betty Prescott; Barbara
Kay.

CAREY, Tony
Singles: 7-Inch
MCA: *84* 1-3
ROCSHIRE: *83* 1-3

LPs: 10/12-Inch 33rpm
MCA: *84* 5-8
ROCSHIRE: *83* 5-8
Also see PLANET P PROJECT
Also see RAINBOW

CARGILL, Henson
Singles: 7-Inch
ARCO: *67* 2-4
ATLANTIC: *73-74* 1-3
COPPER MOUNTAIN: *79-80* 1-3
ELEKTRA: *75* 1-3
MEGA: *71-73* 2-3
MONUMENT: *67-70* 2-3
TOWER: *68* 2-4

LPs: 10/12-Inch 33rpm
ATLANTIC: *73* 6-10
HARMONY: *72* 6-10
MEGA: *72* 6-10
MONUMENT: *68-70* 8-12

CARLA & RUFUS:
see RUFUS & CARLA

CARLIN, George
Singles: 7-Inch
LITTLE DAVID: *72-75* 2-3
RCA VICTOR: *67* 3-5

Belinda Carlisle (Photo: Herb Ritts)

Picture Sleeves
LITTLE DAVID: *72* 5-8
LPs: 10/12-Inch 33rpm
ATLANTIC: *81* 5-8
CAMDEN: *72* 8-10
EARDRUM: *84* 5-8
ERA: *72* $8-12
LITTLE DAVID: *72-85* 5-10
RCA VICTOR: *67* 10-15

CARLISLE, Belinda
Singles: 12-Inch 33/45rpm
I.R.S.: *86* 4-6
Singles: 7-Inch
I.R.S.: *86-87* 1-3
MCA: *88* 1-3
LPs: 10/12-Inch 33rpm
I.R.S.: *86-87* 5-8
MCA: *88* 5-8
Also see GO-GOs

CARLISLE, Steve
Singles: 7-Inch
MCA: *81-82* 1-3
LPs: 10/12-Inch 33rpm
MCA: *82* 5-8

CARLOS, Walter
LPs: 10/12-Inch 33rpm
COLUMBIA: 69-72 .... $5-10

CARLTON, Carl
(Little Carl Carlton)
Singles: 12-Inch 33/45rpm
20TH CENTURY-FOX: 80 4-6
Singles: 7-Inch
ABC: 73-76 2-3
BACK BEAT: 68-75 2-4
CASABLANCA: 86 1-3
GOLDEN WORLD: 65 3-5
LANDO: 65 3-5
MCA: 84 1-3
MERCURY: 77 2-3
RCA VICTOR: 82 1-3
20TH CENTURY-FOX: 81-82 1-3
LPs: 10/12-Inch 33rpm
ABC: 10-12
BACK BEAT: 73 12-15
CASABLANCA: 86 5-8
RCA VICTOR: 82 5-8
20TH CENTURY-FOX: 81 5-8

CARLTON, Larry
Singles: 7-Inch
MCA: 85-86 1-3
UNI: 68-69 2-4
WARNER BROS: 78-83 1-3
LPs: 10/12-Inch 33rpm
ATLANTIC: 84 5-8
BLUE THUMB: 73 10-12
MCA: 85-87 5-8
UNI: 68 12-15
WARNER BROS: 78-83 5-8

CARMAN, Pauli
Singles: 12-Inch 33/45rpm
COLUMBIA: 86 4-6
Singles: 7-Inch
COLUMBIA: 86-87 1-3
LPs: 10/12-Inch 33rpm
COLUMBIA: 86 5-8

CARMEN, Eric
Singles: 12-Inch 33/45rpm
GEFFEN: 85 4-6
Singles: 7-Inch
ARISTA: 75-88 1-3
COOL: 86 2-4
EPIC: 70 3-5
GEFFEN: 85 1-3
RCA VICTOR: 87 1-3
Picture Sleeves
ARISTA: 77 1-3

LPs: 10/12-Inch 33rpm
ARISTA: 75-88 .... $5-10
GEFFEN: 85 5-8
Also see CHOIR
Also see QUICK
Also see RASPBERRIES

CARNE, Jean
(Jean Carn)
Singles: 7-Inch
ATLANTIC: 88 1-3
MOTOWN: 82 1-3
OMNI: 86 1-3
PHILADELPHIA INT'L: 77-80 1-3
TSOP: 81 1-3
LPs: 10/12-Inch 33rpm
ATLANTIC: 88 5-8
OMNI: 86 5-8
PHILADELPHIA INT'L: 76-80 5-8
MOTOWN: 82 5-8
TSOP: 81 5-8
Also see JOHNSON, Al, & Jean Carne
Also see MILITELLO, Bobby

CARNES, Kim
Singles: 12-Inch 33/45rpm
EMI AMERICA: 80-85 4-6
Singles: 7-Inch
A&M: 75-82 1-3
AMOS: 71-72 2-4
EMI AMERICA: 79-86 1-3
ELEKTRA: 84 1-3
MCA: 88 1-3
Picture Sleeves
EMI AMERICA: 80-85 1-3
LPs: 10/12-Inch 33rpm
A&M (3000 series): 82 5-8
A&M (4000 series): 75-77 8-10
AMOS: 71 12-15
EMI AMERICA: 79-86 5-8
MCA: 84-88 5-8
MFSL: 82 20-30
Also see COTTON, Gene, & Kim Carnes
Also see ROGERS, Kenny, & Kim Carnes
Also see ROGERS, Kenny, Kim Carnes &
James Ingram
Also see STREISAND, Barbra, & Kim Carnes
Also see U.S.A. FOR AFRICA

CARNES, Kim, & Dave Ellington
Singles: 7-Inch
AMOS: 72 2-4
Also see CARNES, Kim

CARNIVAL
Singles: 7-Inch
UNITED ARTISTS: 71 2-4

WORLD PACIFIC: *69* $3-5
    LPs: 10/12-Inch 33rpm
WORLD PACIFIC: *69* 10-12
  Member: Terry Fisher.

CAROSONE, Renato
    Singles: 7-Inch
CAPITOL: *58* 2-4

CARPENTER, Carleton, & Debbie Reynolds
    Singles: 78rpm
MGM: *51* 2-5
    Singles: 7-Inch
MGM: *51* 3-5
    EPs: 7-Inch 33/45rpm
MGM: *51* 5-10
  Also see REYNOLDS, Debbie

CARPENTER, Thelma
    Singles: 78rpm
COLUMBIA (30100 series): *50* 3-6
MAJESTIC: *45-46* 3-6
    Singles: 7-Inch
COLUMBIA (30200 series): *50* 3-5
CORAL: *60-62* 3-5
    LPs: 10/12-Inch 33rpm
CORAL: *63* 10-15

CARPENTERS
    Singles: 7-Inch
A&M: *69-82* 1-3
    Picture Sleeves
A&M: *70-81* 3-6
    EPs: 7-Inch 33/45rpm
A&M: *72-80* 10-15
  (Jukebox issues only.)
    LPs: 10/12-Inch 33rpm
A&M: *70-85* 5-12
  Members: Karen Carpenter; Richard Carpenter; Tony Peluso.

CARR, Cathy
    Singles: 78rpm
CORAL: *53-56* 3-5
FRATERNITY: *55-56* 3-5
    Singles: 7-Inch
ABC: *73* 1-3
COLLECTABLES: *81* 1-3
CORAL: *53-56* 4-6
FRATERNITY: *55-56* 4-6
LAURIE: *62-63* 3-5
ROULETTE: *59-61* 3-5
SMASH: *61* 3-5
    LPs: 10/12-Inch 33rpm
DOT: *66* 15-18
FRATERNITY: *56* 25-40
ROULETTE: *59* 25-30

CARR, James
    Singles: 7-Inch
ATLANTIC: *71* $2-4
GOLDWAX: *65-69* 3-5
    LPs: 10/12-Inch 33rpm
GOLDWAX: *67-68* 12-15

CARR, Jerry
    Singles: 7-Inch
CHERIE: *81* 1-3

CARR, Joe "Fingers"
(Lou Busch)
    Singles: 78rpm
CAPITOL: *50-57* 2-4
    Singles: 7-Inch
CAPITOL: *50-59* 2-5
CORAL: *63* 2-3
DOT : *66* 1-3
WARNER BROS: *60-62* 2-3
    EPs: 7-Inch 33/45rpm
CAPITOL: *51-57* 5-10
    LPs: 10/12-Inch 33rpm
CAPITOL (Except 2000 series): *51-61* .. 10-20
CAPITOL (2000 series): *64* 8-12
CORAL: *63* 8-12
DOT: *66* 8-12
WARNER BROS: *60-62* 8-12
  Also see BUSCH, Lou
  Also see FRAZIER, Dallas, & Joe "Fingers" Carr
  Also see PROVINE, Dorothy, & Joe "Fingers" Carr

CARR, Valerie
    Singles: 7-Inch
ATLAS: *64* 4-6
ROULETTE: *58-61* 3-5
    LPs: 10/12-Inch 33rpm
ROULETTE: *59* 25-30

CARR, Vikki
    Singles: 7-Inch
COLUMBIA: *71-75* 1-3
LIBERTY: *62-69* 2-4
    Picture Sleeves
COLUMBIA: *74* 1-3
LIBERTY: *67* 2-5
    LPs: 10/12-Inch 33rpm
COLUMBIA: *71-75* 6-10
LIBERTY (Except 10000 series): *63-70* . 10-15
LIBERTY (10000 series): *81* 5-8
UNITED ARTISTS: *71-80* 5-10

CARR, Wynona
    Singles: 7-Inch
REPRISE: *61-63* 3-5
SPECIALTY: *59-60* 3-6

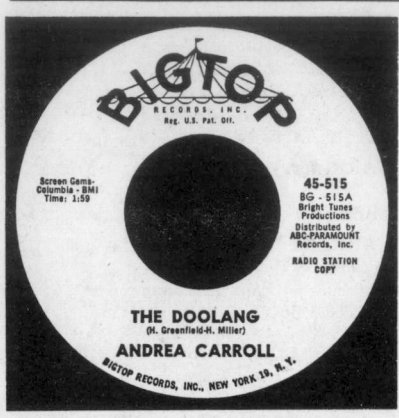

(Most Specialty singles are currently available, using original catalog numbers.)
LPs: 10/12-Inch 33rpm
REPRISE: *62* $12-15
SPECIALTY: *88* 6-10

CARRACK, Paul
Singles: 7-Inch
CHRYSALIS: *87-88* 1-3
EPIC: *82* 1-3
LPs: 10/12-Inch 33rpm
CHRYSALIS: *87-88* 5-8
EPIC: *81* 5-8
Also see ACE
Also see MIKE + THE MECHANICS
Also see SQUEEZE

CARRADINE, Keith
Singles: 7-Inch
ABC: *75* 2-3
ASYLUM: *78* 1-3
VALA: *83* 1-3
LPs: 10/12-Inch 33rpm
ASYLUM: *77* 8-10

CARROLL, Andrea
Singles: 7-Inch
BIG TOP (515; "The Doolang"): *64* 25-40
BIG TOP (3156; "It Hurts To
   Be Sixteen"): *63* 4-8
EPIC (Except 9438): *61-62* 5-10
EPIC (9438; "Young And
   Lonely"): *61* 50-100
   (Yellow label.)
EPIC (9438; "Young And
   Lonely"): *61* 40-75
   (White label. Promotional issue.)
RCA VICTOR: *65* 5-10
UNITED ARTISTS: *66* 8-15

CARROLL, Bernadette
Singles: 7-Inch
COLLECTABLES: *81* $1-3
JULIA: *62* 3-5
LAURIE: *63-64* 5-8

CARROLL, Bob
Singles: 78rpm
BALLY: *56-57* 2-5
DERBY: *53* 3-5
MGM: *55* 2-5
Singles: 7-Inch
BALLY: *56-57* 3-5
DERBY: *53* 3-5
DOT: *66* 2-4
MGM: *55* 3-5
MURBO: *67* 2-4
UNART: *59* 3-5
UNITED ARTISTS: *59-59* 2-4
Picture Sleeves
UNITED ARTISTS: *58* 4-8

CARROLL, Cathy
Singles: 7-Inch
CHEER: *63-64* 5-8
DOT: *66* 3-5
MUSICOR: *65* 3-5
PHILIPS: *63* 3-5
TRIODEX: *61* 5-8
WARNER BROS: *62-63* 3-6

CARROLL, David, Orchestra
Singles: 78rpm
MERCURY: *53-57* 2-4
Singles: 7-Inch
MERCURY: *53-62* 2-4
EPs: 7-Inch 33/45rpm
MERCURY: *54-59* 3-6
LPs: 10/12-Inch 33rpm
MERCURY: *53-62* 5-12
WING: *59* 4-8

CARROLL, Jim
(Jim Carroll Band)
Singles: 7-Inch
A&M: *72* 2-4
ATCO: *80-81* 1-3
ATLANTIC: *83* 1-3
LPs: 10/12-Inch 33rpm
A&M: *71* 10-12
ATCO: *80-82* 5-8
ATLANTIC: *83* 5-8

CARROLL, Ronnie
Singles: 7-Inch
PHILIPS: *63-66* 3-6

CARROLL BROTHERS
Singles: 7-Inch
CAMEO (100 series): *58* **$20-25**
CAMEO (200 series): *62* **3-5**
FELSTED: *59* **4-6**
LPs: 10/12-Inch 33rpm
CAMEO: *62* **20-25**
Member: Pete Carroll.

CARS
Singles: 12-Inch 33/45rpm
ELEKTRA: *86* **4-6**
(Promotional issues only.)
Singles: 7-Inch
ELEKTRA (Except picture
discs): *78-88* **1-3**
ELEKTRA (Picture discs): *78-86* **4-8**
Picture Sleeves
ELEKTRA: *78-86* **1-3**
LPs: 10/12-Inch 33rpm
ELEKTRA (Except picture discs): *78-87* . . . **5-8**
ELEKTRA ("Shake It Up"): *81* **12-15**
(Picture disc. Promotional issue only.)
ELEKTRA ("Since You're Gone"): *82* . . . **10-15**
(Picture disc. Promotional issue only.)
NAUTILUS: *82* **15-20**
(Half-speed mastered.)
Members: Ric Ocasek; Elliot Easton; Benjamin
Orr; Greg Hawkes; Dave Robinson.
Also see EASTON, Elliot
Also see OCASEK, Ric

CARSON, Kit
Singles: 78rpm
CAPITOL: *55* **2-5**
Singles: 7-Inch
CAPITOL: *55* **3-5**

CARSON, Mindy
Singles: 78rpm
COLUMBIA: *52-56* **3-5**
SIGNATURE: *48* **3-6**
RCA VICTOR: *50-51* **3-5**
Singles: 7-Inch
COLUMBIA: *52-56* **5-10**
JOY: *60* **3-5**
RCA VICTOR: *50-52* **4-8**
Also see MITCHELL, Guy, & Mindy Carson

CARTEE, Wayne
Singles: 7-Inch
GROOVY: *77* **2-3**

CARTER, Carlene
(Carlene Carter & Rockpile)
Singles: 7-Inch
EPIC: *83* **1-3**
WARNER BROS: *78-82* **1-3**

LPs: 10/12-Inch 33rpm
EPIC: *83* **$5-8**
WARNER BROS: *78-82* **5-8**
Also see EDMUNDS, Dave, & Carlene Carter
Also see ORRALL, Robert Ellis
Also see ROCKPILE

CARTER, Clarence
Singles: 7-Inch
ABC: *75-76* **1-3**
ATLANTIC: *68-72* **2-4**
FAME (Except 1000 series): *72-73* **2-4**
FAME (1000 series): *67* **3-5**
ICHIBAN **2-3**
RONN: *77* **1-3**
VENTURE: *80-81* **1-3**
LPs: 10/12-Inch 33rpm
ABC: *74-76* **8-10**
ATLANTIC: *68-71* **10-15**
BIG C: *83* **5-8**
BRYLEN: *84* **5-8**
FAME: *73* **10-12**
VENTURE: *80-81* **5-8**

CARTER, Clarence & Candi
Singles: 7-Inch
ATLANTIC: *72* **2-4**
Also see CARTER, Clarence

CARTER, Mel
Singles: 7-Inch
ABKCO: *84* **1-3**
AMOS: *69-70* **2-4**
ARWIN: *60* **4-6**
BELL: *68-69* **2-4**
CREAM: *81* **1-3**
DERBY: *63* **4-6**
IMPERIAL: *64-66* **3-5**
LIBERTY: *67-68* **2-4**
MERCURY: *62* **3-5**
PHILLIPS: *62* **3-5**
ROMAR: *73-74* **2-4**
LPs: 10/12-Inch 33rpm
AMOS: *70* **10-12**
DERBY: *63* **30-40**
IMPERIAL: *65-66* **15-20**
LIBERTY: *67* **12-15**
SUNSET: *68-70* **10-12**

CARTER, Mel, & Clydie King
Singles: 7-Inch
PHILIPS: *62* **3-5**
Also see CARTER, Mel

CARTER, Ralph
Singles: 7-Inch
MERCURY: *75-76* **2-3**

CARTER, Ron
LPs: 10/12-Inch 33rpm
MILESTONE: *77-78* $5-8
NEW JAZZ: *61* 15-20

CARTER, Valerie
Singles: 7-Inch
COLUMBIA: *77-79* 1-3
LPs: 10/12-Inch 33rpm
COLUMBIA: *77-78* 8-10
Also see LITTLE FEAT
Also see MONEY, Eddie, & Valerie Carter

CARTER, Valerie, & Henry Paul
Singles: 7-Inch
ATLANTIC: *82* 1-3
Also see CARTER, Valerie

CARTER BROTHERS
Singles: 7-Inch
COLEMAN: *64* 5-8
JEWEL: *65-67* 3-5
Members: Jerry Carter; Al Carter; Roman Carter.

CARTRELL, Delia
Singles: 7-Inch
RIGHT ON: *71-72* 2-4

CARTRIDGE, Flip
Singles: 7-Inch
PARROT: *66-67* 3-5

CARUSO, Marian
Singles: 78rpm
DECCA: *54-55* 2-5
DEVON: *52* 3-6
Singles: 7-Inch
DECCA: *54-55* 2-5
DEVON: *52* 3-6

CASCADES
Singles: 7-Inch
ABC: *73* 1-3
ARWIN: *66* 3-5
CANBASE: *72* 2-4
CHARTER: *64* 3-5
COLLECTABLES: *81* 1-3
LIBERTY: *65* 3-5
MRC: 4-8
PROBE: *68* 2-4
RCA VICTOR: *63-64* 3-5
SMASH: *67* 3-5
UNI: *69-70* 2-4
VALIANT: *62-63* 3-5
Picture Sleeves
PROBE: *68* 3-6
RCA VICTOR: *63* 5-10
LPs: 10/12-Inch 33rpm
BLOSSOM: 10-15

CASCADES: $10-12
UNI: *69* 15-20
VALIANT: *63* 35-40
Also see LIND, Bob
Also see YOUNG, Neil

CASCADES / Sir Douglas Quintet
Singles: 7-Inch
TRIP: 2-3
Also see CASCADES
Also see SIR DOUGLAS QUINTET

CASEY, Al
(Al Casey Combo; Al Casey & The K-C Ettes)
Singles: 7-Inch
CHALLENGE: *60* 3-5
GREGMARK (5; "Caravan"): *61* 4-6
(This release was shown as by Al Casey, but was
actually Duane Eddy.)
HIGHLAND (Except 1002): *60* 10-15
HIGHLAND (1002; "Got The Teenage
Blues"): *60* 20-25
LIBERTY: *58* 8-10
MCI: *55* 8-10
STACY: *62-64* 4-6
UNITED ARTISTS: *59* 4-6
LPs: 10/12-Inch 33rpm
PRESTIGE: *60-61* 15-20
STACY (100; "Surfin'
Hootenany"): *63* 25-40
(Black vinyl.)
STACY (100; "Surfin'
Hootenany"): *63* 100-125
(Colored vinyl.)
Also see CLARK, Sanford
Also see EDDY, Duane
Also see EXOTIC GUITARS
Also see REYNOLDS, Jody

CASH, Alvin
(Alvin Cash & The Crawlers; Alvin Cash & The
Registers)
Singles: 7-Inch
CHESS: *70* 2-4
COLLECTABLES: *81* 1-3
DAKAR: *76* 2-3
ERIC: *73* 1-3
MAR-V-LUS: *65-67* 3-5
SEVENTY SEVEN: *72* 2-4
TODDLIN' TOWN: *68-69* 2-4
LPs: 10/12-Inch 33rpm
MAR-V-LUS: *65* 15-20
SOUND STAGE "7": *73* 10-12

CASH, Johnny
(Johnny Cash & The Tennessee Two; Johnny
Cash & The Tennessee Three)
Singles: 78rpm
SUN: *55-57* $4-8
Singles: 7-Inch
CACHET: *80* 1-3
COLUMBIA (Except 41000 through
43000 series): *67-85* 1-3
COLUMBIA (41000 & 42000
series): *60-62* 6-10
(With a "3" prefix. Compact 33 singles.)
COLUMBIA (41000 & 42000
series): *58-64* 3-5
(With a "4" prefix.)
COLUMBIA (43000 series): *64-66* 2-4
MERCURY: *88* 1-3
SSS/SUN (Black vinyl): *69-70* 1-3
SSS/SUN (Colored vinyl): *69-70* 2-4
(Promotional issues only.)
SCOTTI BROS: *82* 1-3
SUN (200 series): *55-58* 5-8
SUN (300 series): *58-62* 3-5
EPs: 7-Inch 33/45rpm
COLUMBIA (Except jukebox
EPs): *58-60* 10-20
COLUMBIA (Stereo jukebox
EPs): *69* 25-30
SUN: *58* 10-20
Picture Sleeves
COLUMBIA (Except 41000 & 42000
series): *67-85* 1-3
COLUMBIA (41000 series): *58-61* 5-10
COLUMBIA (42000 series): *61-64* 3-6
SUN: *58* 8-15
LPs: 10/12-Inch 33rpm
COLUMBIA (29; "The World Of
Johnny Cash"): *70* 8-10
COLUMBIA (1200 through 1799): *58-61* 15-25
(With a "CL" prefix. Monaural.)
COLUMBIA (8100 through 8599): *58-61* 20-30
(With a "CS" prefix. Stereo.)
COLUMBIA (1800 through 2650): *62-68* 10-15
(With a "CL" prefix. Monaural.)
COLUMBIA (8600 through 9450): *62-68* 10-15
(With a "CS" prefix. Stereo.)
COLUMBIA (9700 through 9943): *69-70* . 8-10
(With a "CS" prefix.)
COLUMBIA (10000 series): *73* 5-10
COLUMBIA (30000 through 38000
series): *70-82* 5-15
COLUMBIA/SUFFOLK
MARKETING: *79* 6-10

DORAL: $20-40
(Promotional mail-order LP, from Doral cigarettes.)
OUT OF TOWN DIST: *82* 5-8
PRIORITY: *81-82* 5-8
SSS/SUN: *69-84* 5-8
SHARE: 5-10
SUN (100 series): *56-64* 20-30
TRIP: *74* 8-10
UNITED ARTISTS: *68* 10-12
Also see LEWIS, Jerry Lee / Johnny Cash
Also see RICH, Charlie
Also see ROBBINS, Marty / Johnny Cash /
Ray Price
Also see STATLER BROTHERS

CASH, Johnny, & June Carter
(Johnny Cash & June Carter Cash)
Singles: 7-Inch
COLUMBIA: *67-83* 1-3
LPs: 10/12-Inch 33rpm
COLUMBIA (9500 series): *64-67* 10-12
COLUMBIA (32000 series): *73* 5-10
HARMONY: *72* 6-10

CASH, Johnny / Billy Grammer /
Wilburn Brothers
LPs: 10/12-Inch 33rpm
PICKWICK/HILLTOP: *65* 10-15
Also see GRAMMER, Billy

CASH, Johnny, & Levon Helm
Singles: 7-Inch
A&M: *80* 1-3
Also see HELM, Levon

CASH, Johnny, & Waylon Jennings
Singles: 7-Inch
COLUMBIA: *78-86* 1-3
EPIC: *80* 1-3
Also see JENNINGS, Waylon

CASH, Johnny, Carl Perkins &
Jerry Lee Lewis
LPs: 10/12-Inch 33rpm
COLUMBIA: *82* 5-8
Also see PERKINS, Carl, Jerry Lee Lewis,
Roy Orbison & Johnny Cash

CASH, Johnny / Tammy Wynette
LPs: 10/12-Inch 33rpm
COLUMBIA (5418; "The King &
Queen"): 10-15
(Columbia Musical Treasury issue.)
Also see CASH, Johnny
Also see WYNETTE, Tammy

CASH, Rosanne
Singles: 7-Inch
COLUMBIA: *80-88* 1-3

LPs: 10/12-Inch 33rpm
COLUMBIA: *79-88* $6-10
Also see BARE, Bobby, & Rosanne Cash

CASH, Tommy
Singles: 7-Inch
AUDIOGRAPH: *83* 1-3
ELEKTRA: *75* 2-3
EPIC: *68-73* 2-3
MONUMENT: *77-79* 1-3
MUSICOR: *65* 2-4
20TH CENTURY-FOX: *76* 2-3
UNITED ARTISTS: *66-68* 2-4
LPs: 10/12-Inch 33rpm
EPIC: *69-72* 8-12
MONUMENT: *78* 5-8
UNITED ARTISTS: *68* 10-12

CA$HFLOW
Singles: 12-Inch 33/45rpm
ATLANTA ARTISTS: *86* 4-6
Singles: 7-Inch
ATLANTA ARTISTS: *86-88* 1-3
MERCURY: *86-88* 1-3
LPs: 10/12-Inch 33rpm
ATLANTA ARTISTS: *86-88* 5-8

CASHMAN, Terry
Singles: 7-Inch
BOOM: *66* 3-5
LIFESONG: *76-82* 1-3
LPs: 10/12-Inch 33rpm
LIFESONG: *76-77* 5-8
Also see CASHMAN, PISTILLI & WEST

CASHMAN & WEST
Singles: 7-Inch
ABC: *74* 2-3
DUNHILL: *72-74* 2-4
LIFESONG: *75* 2-3
LPs: 10/12-Inch 33rpm
ABC: *74* 8-10
DUNHILL: *72-74* 8-10
Members: Terry Cashman; Tommy West.
Also see GENE & TOMMY
Also see MORNING MIST

CASHMAN, PISTILLI & WEST
Singles: 7-Inch
ABC: *68* 2-4
CAPITOL: *69-71* 2-4
LPs: 10/12-Inch 33rpm
ABC: *68* 12-15
CAPITOL: *69-71* 12-15
Members: Terry Cashman; Gene Pistilli; Tommy West.
Also see BUCHANAN BROTHERS
Also see CASHMAN, Terry

CASHMERE
Singles: 12-Inch 33/45rpm
PHILLY WORLD: *83* $4-6
TNT: *84* 4-6
Singles: 7-Inch
PHILLY WORLD: *83-85* 1-3
LPs: 10/12-Inch 33rpm
PHILLY WORLD: *83-85* 5-8

CASINOS
(Gene Hughes & The Casinos)
Singles: 7-Inch
ABC: *73* 1-3
AIRTOWN: *67* 3-5
CERTRON: *70* 2-4
COLLECTABLES: *81* 1-3
FRATERNITY: *65-71* 3-5
MILLION: *72* 2-4
UNITED ARTISTS: *68* 2-4
LPs: 10/12-Inch 33rpm
FRATERNITY: *67* 15-25
Member: Gene Hughes.

CASLONS
Singles: 7-Inch
AMY: *61-62* 10-15
SEECO: *61* 10-15

CASON, Rich, & The Galactic Orchestra
Singles: 12-Inch 33/45rpm
PRIVATE I: *84* 4-6
Singles: 7-Inch
LARC: *83* 1-3
PRIVATE I: *84* 1-3

CASPER
Singles: 7-Inch
SUNFLOWER: *71* 2-4

CASPER
Singles: 7-Inch
A.V.I.: *84* 1-3
ATLANTIC: *83* 1-3
LPs: 10/12-Inch 33rpm
A.V.I.: *84* 5-8
ATLANTIC: *83* 5-8

CASSIDY, David
Singles: 7-Inch
BELL: *71-73* 2-4
FLASHBACK: *73* 1-3
MCA: *79* 1-3
RCA VICTOR: *75-77* 2-3
Picture Sleeves
BELL: *71-73* 2-5
LPs: 10/12-Inch 33rpm
BELL: *72-74* 10-12

RCA VICTOR: 74-76 .... $8-10
   Also see PARTRIDGE FAMILY

CASSIDY, Shaun
            Singles: 7-Inch
WARNER BROS: 77-80 2-3
            Picture Sleeves
WARNER BROS: 77-80 2-3
            LPs: 10/12-Inch 33rpm
WARNER BROS: 77-80 8-10

CASSIDY, Shaun, & Todd
Rundgren's Utopia
            Singles: 7-Inch
WARNER BROS: 80 1-3
   Also see CASSIDY, Shaun
   Also see UTOPIA

CASTAWAYS
            Singles: 7-Inch
COLLECTABLES: 81 1-3
ERA: 72 2-3
ERIC: 78 1-3
FONTANA: 68 4-6
LANA: 2-4
SOMA: 65 5-10
   Members: Richard Robey; Robert Folschon; Ron
   Hensley; James Donna; Dennis Caswell.

CASTELLS
            Singles: 7-Inch
COLLECTABLES: 80 1-3
DECCA: 65-66 3-5
ERA: 61-63 4-8
LAURIE: 68 3-5
UNITED ARTISTS: 68 3-5
WARNER BROS. (Except 5421): 64 3-5
WARNER BROS. (5421; "I Do"): 64 50-60
            LPs: 10/12-Inch 33rpm
ERA: 62 30-40

CASTER, Jimmy: see CASTOR, Jimmy

CASTLE, David
            Singles: 7-Inch
PARACHUTE: 77-79 1-3
            LPs: 10/12-Inch 33rpm
PARACHUTE: 77-79 8-10

CASTLE SISTERS
            Singles: 7-Inch
ROULETTE: 59-60 5-10
TERRACE: 62-63 4-8
TRIODEX: 61 4-8
            Picture Sleeves
TERRACE: 62 8-15

CASTLEMAN, Boomer
            Singles: 7-Inch
MUMS: 75 2-4

CASTOR, Jimmy
(Jimmy Castor Bunch; Jimmy Caster Quintet)
            Singles: 12-Inch 33/45rpm
SALSOUL: 83 .... $4-6
            Singles: 7-Inch
ATLANTIC: 74-77 2-4
CAPITOL: 68-69 3-6
CLOWN: 62 5-10
COMPASS: 68 3-6
COTILLION: 79 2-3
DECCA: 66 4-6
DREAM: 84-85 1-3
DRIVE: 78 2-3
JET SET: 65 4-8
KINETIC: 70 3-5
LONG DISTANCE: 81 1-3
RCA VICTOR: 71-73 3-5
SALSOUL: 82 1-3
SLEEPING BAG: 88 1-3
SMASH: 66-67 4-8
            LPs: 10/12-Inch 33rpm
ATLANTIC: 74-77 8-10
COTILLION: 79 5-8
DREAM: 83 5-8
DRIVE: 78 5-8
LONG DISTANCE: 80 5-8
PAUL WINLEY: 5-15
RCA VICTOR: 72-75 10-12
SMASH: 67 15-18

CASTOR, Jimmy, & The Juniors
            Singles: 78rpm
WING: 56 15-25
            Singles: 7-Inch
ATOMIC (100; "This Girl Of
   Mine"): 57 60-100
WING: 56 30-40
   Also see CASTOR, Jimmy

CASWELL, Johnny
            Singles: 7-Inch
DECCA: 66 4-8
LUV: 67 3-5
SMASH: 63-64 4-8
   Also see CRYSTAL MANSION

CAT MOTHER
(Cat Mother & The All Night News Boys)
            Singles: 7-Inch
POLYDOR: 69-72 3-5
            LPs: 10/12-Inch 33rpm
POLYDOR: 69-73 20-30

CATCH
            Singles: 12-Inch 33/45rpm
COLUMBIA: 84-85 4-6

Singles: 7-Inch
COLUMBIA: *84-85* $1-3

CATE BROTHERS
(Cates Gang)
Singles: 7-Inch
ASYLUM: *76-78* 2-3
ELEKTRA: *77* 2-3
METROMEDIA: *70* 2-4
LPs: 10/12-Inch 33rpm
ASYLUM: *75-77* 5-8
ATLANTIC: *79* 5-8
METROMEDIA: *70-73* 10-12
Members: Earl Cate; Ernie Cate.

CATES, George
Singles: 78rpm
CORAL: *51-57* 2-4
Singles: 7-Inch
CORAL: *51-57* 2-5
DOT: *62* 2-3
SIGNATURE: *59-60* 2-3
EPs: 7-Inch 33/45rpm
CORAL: *54-57* 3-6
LPs: 10/12-Inch 33rpm
CORAL: *54-57* 5-12

CATHY & JOE
Singles: 7-Inch
SMASH: *64-65* 3-5

CATHY JEAN
(Cathy Jean & The Roomates)
Singles: 7-Inch
ERIC: *73* 1-3
PHILIPS (Except 40014): *63* 5-10
PHILIPS (40014; "Believe Me"): *62* 10-15
VALMOR: *61-62* 8-10
LPs: 10/12-Inch 33rpm
VALMOR (78; "At The Hop"): *61* 500-750
VALMOR (789; "At The Hop"): *61* ... 350-450
(Note slightly different catalog numbers. These two
LPs also have completely different covers. Valmor
789 pictures the group, whereas # 78, the first
issue, does not.)
Also see ROOMATES

CAVALIERE, Felix
Singles: 7-Inch
BEARSVILLE: *74-75* 2-4
EPIC: *80* 1-3
LPs: 10/12-Inch 33rpm
BEARSVILLE: *74-75* 10-12
EPIC: *80* 5-8
Also see KARP, Charlie
Also see RASCALS

CAVALLARO, Carmen
Singles: 7-Inch
DECCA: *50-61* $2-4
EPs: 7-Inch 33/45rpm
DECCA: *50-59* 4-8
LPs: 10/12-Inch 33rpm
DECCA (Except "The Eddy
Duchin Story"): *50-61* 5-15
DECCA (8289; "The Eddy
Duchin Story"): *54* 30-40
DECCA (8289; "The Eddy
Duchin Story"): *59* 20-30
(With a "DL-7" prefix. Soundtrack.)
DECCA (8396; "The Eddy
Duchin Story"): *56* 55-65
(Soundtrack.)
DECCA (9121; "The Eddy
Duchin Story"): *65* 12-18
VOCALION: *59* 4-8

CAZZ
(Robert Lewis)
Singles: 7-Inch
NUMBER: *78* 2-3

CELEBRATION
(Celebration Featuring Mike Love)
Singles: 7-Inch
MCA: *78* 2-3
PACIFIC ARTS: *79* 5-8
Promotional Singles
MCA (1982; "Almost Summer,
KRTH 101 Version"): *78* 10-12
LPs: 10/12-Inch 33rpm
MCA (3037; "Almost Summer"): *78* 8-10
(Soundtrack.)
PACIFIC ARTS: *79* 8-10
Members: Mike Love; Charles Lloyd.

CELI BEE & THE BUZZY BUNCH
Singles: 7-Inch
APA: *77-78* 1-3
LPs: 10/12-Inch 33rpm
APA: *77-79* 5-8

CELLOS
Singles: 7-Inch
APOLLO: *57-58* 15-25
Members: Cliff Williams; Ken Levinson; Alvin
Campbell; Bill Montgomery; Alton Thomas.

CENTRAL LINE
Singles: 12-Inch 33/45rpm
MERCURY: *84-85* 4-6
Singles: 7-Inch
MERCURY: *81-85* 1-3
LPs: 10/12-Inch 33rpm
MERCURY: *82-85* 5-8

CENTURIES
Singles: 7-Inch
SPECTRA-SOUND: $10-15
Also see BUCKINGHAMS

CERRONE
Singles: 12-Inch 33/45rpm
PAVILLION: *82* 4-6
Singles: 7-Inch
ATLANTIC: *79* 1-3
COTILLION: *77-78* 2-3
PAVILLION: *82* 1-3
LPs: 10/12-Inch 33rpm
ATLANTIC: *79* 5-8
COTILLION: *77-79* 5-8
PAVILLION: *82* 5-8

CETERA, Peter
Singles: 7-Inch
FULL MOON: *82-88*...................1-3
Picture Sleeves
FULL MOON: *82-86*...................1-3
LPs: 10/12-Inch 33rpm
FULL MOON: *81-88*...................5-8
Also see CHICAGO

CETERA, Peter, & Amy Grant
Singles: 7-Inch
FULL MOON: *86* 1-3
Also see CETERA, Peter
Also see GRANT, Amy

CHABUKOS
Singles: 7-Inch
MAINSTREAM: *73* 2-3

CHACKSFIELD, Frank, Orchestra
Singles: 7-Inch
LONDON: *53-61* 2-3
EPs: 7-Inch 33/45rpm
LONDON: *53-61* 3-6
LPs: 10/12-Inch 33rpm
LONDON: *53-61* 5-10
RICHMOND: *59-62* 4-8

CHAD & JEREMY
Singles: 7-Inch
COLLECTABLES: *81* 1-3
COLUMBIA (Black vinyl): *65-68* 3-5
COLUMBIA (Colored vinyl): *65* 5-10
(Promotional issues only.)
ERIC: *73* 1-3
ROCSHIRE: *84* 1-3
WORLD ARTISTS: *64-65* 3-5
Picture Sleeves
COLUMBIA: *65-66* 5-10
WORLD ARTISTS: *64-65* 5-10

LPs: 10/12-Inch 33rpm
CAPITOL (2000 series): *66* $15-20
CAPITOL (12000 & 16000
series): *80* 5-8
COLUMBIA: *65-68* 20-25
FIDU: 10-12
HARMONY: *69* 12-15
ROCSHIRE: *84* 5-8
SIDEWALK: *69* 12-15
TRADITION REST: 10-12
WORLD ARTISTS (2000 series): *64-65* . 40-60
(Monaural.)
WORLD ARTISTS (3002; "Yesterday's
Gone"): *64* 75-150
(Stereo.)
WORLD ARTISTS (3005; "Chad & Jeremy
Sing For You"): *64* 75-150
(Stereo.)
Members: Chad Stuart; Jeremy Clyde.

CHAIN REACTION
Singles: 7-Inch
ARIOLA AMERICA: *76* 2-4
DATE: *66* 5-10
DELICKS: *69* 5-10
DIAL: *68* 5-10
VERVE: *68* 8-12

CHAIRMEN OF THE BOARD
Singles: 7-Inch
INVICTUS: *70-76* 2-4
Picture Sleeves
INVICTUS: *70-72* 2-5
LPs: 10/12-Inch 33rpm
INVICTUS: *70-74* 12-20
Members: General Johnson; Eddie Curtis; Harrison
Kennedy; Danny Woods.
Also see JOHNSON, General

CHAKA KHAN: see KHAN, Chaka

CHAKACHAS
Singles: 7-Inch
AVCO EMBASSY: *72* 2-3
JANUS: *74* 2-3
POLYDOR: *71-75* 2-3
LPs: 10/12-Inch 33rpm
AVCO EMBASSY: *72* 8-10
POLYDOR: *72* 8-10

CHAKIRIS, George
Singles: 7-Inch
CAPITOL: *62-65* 2-4
HORIZON: *62* 2-4
Picture Sleeves
CAPITOL: *63* 5-10
LPs: 10/12-Inch 33rpm
CAPITOL: *62-65* 10-20

HORIZON: 62 .... $15-20

CHAMBERLAIN, Richard
Singles: 7-Inch
MCA: 77 1-3
MGM: 62-65 2-4
Picture Sleeves
MGM: 62-65 5-10
LPs: 10/12-Inch 33rpm
MGM: 63-65 15-20
METRO: 66 8-12

CHAMBERS BROTHERS
Singles: 7-Inch
AVCO: 74-75 2-4
COLUMBIA: 67-73 3-6
TEAR DROP: 74 2-4
VAULT: 65-69 5-10
Picture Sleeves
COLUMBIA: 68-69 3-6
LPs: 10/12-Inch 33rpm
AVCO: 74-75 8-10
COLUMBIA (2000 & 9000
series): 67-68 15-20
COLUMBIA (30000 series,
except 31158): 71-75 10-12
COLUMBIA (31158; "Oh My
God"): 72 40-50
FOLKWAYS: 8-10
ROXBURY: 76 8-10
VAULT (100 series): 67-70 15-20
VAULT (9000 series): 66 20-25
  Members: Joe Chambers; Willie Chambers; Lester
  Chambers; George Chambers.
  Also see AXTON, Hoyt, & The Chambers
Brothers

CHAMPAGNE
Singles: 7-Inch
ARIOLA AMERICA: 77-78 2-3

CHAMPAIGN
Singles: 12-Inch 33/45rpm
COLUMBIA: 83 4-6
Singles: 7-Inch
COLUMBIA: 81-85 1-3
LPs: 10/12-Inch 33rpm
COLUMBIA: 81-85 5-8

CHAMPLIN, Bill
Singles: 7-Inch
ELEKTRA: 81-82 2-4
EPIC: 78 2-4
LPs: 10/12-Inch 33rpm
ELEKTRA: 82 5-8
EPIC: 78 5-8
  Also see SONS OF CHAMPLIN

CHAMPS
Singles: 7-Inch
CHALLENGE: 58 .... $5-10
Singles: 7-Inch
CHALLENGE: 58-65 4-8
ERIC: 78 1-3
LANA: 2-4
REPUBLIC: 76 2-3
EPs: 7-Inch 33/45rpm
CHALLENGE: 58 20-30
LPs: 10/12-Inch 33rpm
CHALLENGE (Except 601): 59-62 25-35
CHALLENGE (601; "Go Champs
Go!"): 58 30-40
(Black vinyl.)
CHALLENGE (601; "Go Champs
Go!"): 58 200-300
(Colored vinyl.)
DESIGN SPOTLIGHT SERIES: 10-15
INTERNATIONAL AWARD: 10-15
POINT: 10-15
SPECTRUM: 10-15
  Members: Dave Burgess; Danny "Chuck Rio"
  Flores; Gene Alden; Dale Norris; Joe Burness; Van
  Norman; Jim Seals; Dash Crofts; Dean Beard;
  Bobby Morris; Glen Campbell; Jerry Cole.
  Also see CAMPBELL, Glen
  Also see SEALS & CROFTS

CHAMPS / Cyclones
LPs: 10/12-Inch 33rpm
DESIGN SPOTLIGHT SERIES: 10-12
  Also see CHAMPS

CHAMPS' BOYS ORCHESTRA
Singles: 7-Inch
JANUS: 76 2-3

CHANDLER, Gene
(Eugene Dixon)
Singles: 12-Inch 33/45rpm
20TH CENTURY-FOX: 79 4-6
Singles: 7-Inch
BRUNSWICK: 67-68 3-5
CHECKER: 66-69 3-5
CHI-SOUND: 79-82 1-3
COLLECTABLES: 81 1-3
CONSTELLATION: 63-66 3-5
CURTOM: 72-73 2-3
ERIC: 73 1-3
FASTFIRE: 86 1-3
MCA: 84 1-3
MARSEL: 76 2-3
MERCURY: 70 2-3
SOLID SMOKE: 84 1-3
20TH CENTURY-FOX: 78-79 2-3
VEE JAY: 61-63 3-6

LPs: 10/12-Inch 33rpm
BRUNSWICK: 67-69 . . . . $12-15
CHECKER: 67 12-15
CHI-SOUND/20TH
  CENTURY-FOX: 78-79 5-8
CONSTELLATION: 64-66 15-20
KENT: 86 5-8
MERCURY: 70 10-12
SOLID SMOKE: 84 5-8
20TH CENTURY-FOX: 78-81 5-8
UPFRONT: 8-10
VEE JAY (1040; "The Duke
  Of Earl"): 62 50-100
  (Monaural.)
VEE JAY (1040; "The Duke
  Of Earl"): 62 100-150
  (Stereo.)
  At least six early Vee Jay tracks, including "Duke
  Of Earl," were actually by The Dukays and not just
  Gene Chandler.
  Also see DUKAYS
  Also see DUKE OF EARL

CHANDLER, Gene, & Barbara Acklin
Singles: 7-Inch
BRUNSWICK: 68-69 3-5
  Also see ACKLIN, Barbara

CHANDLER, Gene, & Jerry Butler
(Gene & Jerry)
Singles: 7-Inch
MERCURY: 70 2-4
  Also see BUTLER, Jerry

CHANDLER, Gene, & Jamie Lynn
Singles: 7-Inch
SALSOUL: 83 1-3
  Also see CHANDLER, Gene

CHANDLER, Karen
Singles: 78rpm
CORAL: 52-55 2-5
DECCA: 56 2-5
Singles: 7-Inch
CARLTON: 60 2-3
CORAL: 52-55 3-5
DECCA: 56 3-5
DOT: 67-68 2-3
MOHAWK: 62 2-3
STRAND: 61 2-3
SUNBEAM: 59 2-4
TIVOLI: 65 2-3
EPs: 7-Inch 33/45rpm
CORAL: 52 5-10
LPs: 10/12-Inch 33rpm
STRAND: 61 10-15

CHANDLER, Karen, & Jimmy Wakely
Singles: 78rpm
DECCA: 56 . . . . $2-5
Singles: 7-Inch
DECCA: 56 3-5
  Also see CHANDLER, Karen
  Also see WAKELY, Jimmy

CHANDLER, Kenny
Singles: 7-Inch
AMY: 63 3-5
COLLECTABLES: 81 1-3
CORAL: 62 3-5
EPIC: 65-66 3-5
LAURIE: 62-63 3-5
TOWER: 67-68 3-5
UNITED ARTISTS: 61 3-5

CHANGE
Singles: 12-Inch 33/45rpm
ATLANTIC: 84 4-6
RFC: 83 4-6
Singles: 7-Inch
ATLANTIC: 81-85 1-3
RFC: 80 1-3
WARNER BROS: 80 1-3
LPs: 10/12-Inch 33rpm
ATLANTIC: 81-85 5-8
RFC: 80 5-8
WARNER BROS: 80 5-8
  Also see VANDROSS, Luther

CHANGIN' TIMES
Singles: 7-Inch
BELL: 67 5-10
PHILIPS: 65-66 4-8

CHANNEL, Bruce
Singles: 7-Inch
CHARAY: 68 2-4
COLLECTABLES: 81 1-3
ELEKTRA: 80 1-3
KING: 59-60 3-5
LE CAM (100 series): 64 3-5
LE CAM (953; "Hey Baby"): 62 8-15
LE CAM (1100 & 7200 series): 77 2-3
MALA: 67-68 2-4
MANCO: 62 3-5
MEL-O-DY: 64 3-5
NAP: 2-4
SHAH: 64 3-5
SMASH: 62-63 3-5
SOFT: 3-5
TEEN AGER: 59 10-20
ZUMA: 77 2-4
Picture Sleeves
SMASH: 62-63 5-10

LPs: 10/12-Inch 33rpm
SMASH: *62* $20-25

CHANNEL, Bruce / Paul & Paula
Singles: 7-Inch
ERA: 1-3
  Also see CHANNEL, Bruce
  Also see PAUL & PAULA

CHANSON
Singles: 7-Inch
ARIOLA AMERICA: *78-79* 2-3
LPs: 10/12-Inch 33rpm
ARIOLA AMERICA: *78* 5-8

CHANTAYS
Singles: 7-Inch
ABC: *74* 1-3
COLLECTABLES: *81* 1-3
DOT: *63* 3-5
DOWNEY (104; "Pipeline"): *63* 12-15
DOWNEY (108; "Monsoon"): *63* 12-15
DOWNEY (116 through 130): *63-65* 8-10
MCA: *84* 1-3
LPs: 10/12-Inch 33rpm
DOT: *63-66* 25-30
DOWNEY: *63* 50-60
  Members: Bob Marshall; Bob Welch; Bob Spick-
  ard; Brian Carmen; Steve Cahn; Warren Waters

CHANTELS
Singles: 78rpm
END: *57* 15-25
Singles: 7-Inch
ABC: *73* 1-3
CARLTON: *61* 3-6
END (Black label): *57* 25-40
END (White or gray label): *58-59* 8-10
END (Multi-color label): *58-61* 4-8
ERIC: *73* 1-3
LANA: *63* 2-4
LUDIX: *63* 3-5
RCA VICTOR: *70* 2-4
ROULETTE: *69-71* 2-4
TCF: *65* 3-5
VERVE: *66* 3-5
EPs: 7-Inch 33/45rpm
END (201; "I Love You So"): *58* 100-125
END (202; "I Love You So"): *58* 75-100
LPs: 10/12-Inch 33rpm
CARLTON: *62* 35-45
END (301; "We're The
  Chantels"): *58* 500-600
  (Pictures the group on front cover.)
END (301; "The Chantels"): *61* 40-50
  (Pictures a juke box on front cover.)

END (312; "There's Our Song
  Again"): *62* $25-35
FORUM: 20-25
ROULETTE: 5-8
  Members: Arlene Smith; Lois Harris; Renee
  Minus; Sonia Gorring; Jackie Landry.
  Also see BARRETT, Richard

CHANTERS
Singles: 7-Inch
DE LUXE (6100 series): *58-61* 20-25
DE LUXE (6200 series): *63* 3-5
GUSTO: *77* 1-3
  Members: Bud Johnson, Jr; Larry Pendegrass; Fred
  Paige; Bobby Thompson; Elliot Green.

CHAPIN, Harry
Singles: 7-Inch
BOARDWALK: *80-81* 1-3
DUNHILL: *88* 1-3
ELEKTRA: *72-79* 2-3
LPs: 10/12-Inch 33rpm
BOARDWALK: *80* 5-8
DUNHILL: *88* 5-8
ELEKTRA: *72-79* 8-10

CHAPLAIN, Paul
(Paul Chaplain & His Emeralds)
Singles: 7-Inch
HARPER: *60-61* 8-12

CHAPTER 8
Singles: 12-Inch 33/45rpm
ARIOLA AMERICA: *79* 4-6
Singles: 7-Inch
ARIOLA AMERICA: *79-80* 1-3
BEVERLY GLEN: *85* 1-3
CAPITOL: *88* 1-3
LPs: 10/12-Inch 33rpm
ARIOLA AMERICA: *79* 5-8
CAPITOL: *88* 5-8
  Also see BAKER, Anita

CHARADE
(Featuring Jessica)
Singles: 12-Inch 33/45rpm
PROFILE: *83* 4-6

CHARGERS
Singles: 7-Inch
RCA VICTOR: *58* 10-20
  Members: Jesse Belvin; Jimmy Norman.
  Also see BELVIN, Jesse

CHARLENE
(Charlene Duncan)
Singles: 7-Inch
MOTOWN: *80-85* 1-3
PRODIGAL: *76* 1-3
LPs: 10/12-Inch 33rpm

MOTOWN: *82-85* $5-8
PRODIGAL: *76* 8-10

CHARLENE & STEVIE WONDER
Singles: 7-Inch
MOTOWN: *82* 1-3
Also see CHARLENE
Also see WONDER, Stevie

CHARLES, Jimmy
(Jimmy Charles & The Revelletts)
Singles: 7-Inch
ABC: *73* 1-3
COLLECTABLES: *81* 1-3
ERIC: *79* 1-3
MCA: *84* 1-3
PROMO: *60* 5-8
ROULETTE: *71* 1-3
Picture Sleeves
PROMO: *60-61* 15-25

CHARLES, Lee
Singles: 7-Inch
BAMBOO: *70-71* 2-3
BRUNSWICK: *69* 2-4
HOT WAX: *73* 2-3
INVICTUS: *74* 2-3
REVUE: *68* 2-4

CHARLES, Ray
(Ray Charles & The Raelettes)
Singles: 78rpm
ATLANTIC: *52-58* 4-8
JAX: *52* 10-20
ROCKIN': *53* 5-10
SWING TIME: *50-53* 40-50
SWING BEAT: *49* 8-12
SWING TIME: *50-53* 5-10
ATLANTIC: *52-58* 5-10
Singles: 7-Inch
ABC: *66-73* 2-4
ABC-PARAMOUNT (Monaural): *60-66* ...3-6
ABC-PARAMOUNT (Stereo): *61-62* 6-12
ATLANTIC (900 series): *62* 25-35
ATLANTIC (1008 through 1076): *53-55* .. 8-15
ATLANTIC (1085 through 1199): *56-57* .. 5-10
ATLANTIC (2000 through 2470): *58-68* ... 3-5
ATLANTIC (3000 series): *77-79* 2-3
BARONET: *62* 3-5
COLUMBIA: *82-87* 1-3
CROSSOVER: *73-78* 2-3
IMPULSE: *61* 3-5
RCA VICTOR: *76* 2-3
ROCKIN': *53* 30-45
SITTIN IN WITH (641; "Baby
Let me Hear You Call My Name"): *52* .50-100
SWING TIME: *50-53* 40-50

TANGERINE: *71* $2-3
TIME: *62* 3-5
Picture Sleeves
ABC: *68-70* 3-6
EPs: 7-Inch 33/45rpm
ABC-PARAMOUNT: *60-62* 10-20
ATLANTIC: *56-59* 20-25
LPs: 10/12-Inch 33rpm
ABC (Except 590): *66-73* 10-12
ABC (590; "A Man And His
Soul"): *67* 20-25
ABC-PARAMOUNT (300 & 400
series): *60-64* 15-25
ABC-PARAMOUNT (400 & 500
series): *65-66* 12-15
ATLANTIC (500 series): *73* 10-12
ATLANTIC (900 series): *62* 25-30
ATLANTIC (1200 series): *57-58* 25-35
ATLANTIC (1300 series): *59-62* 15-20
ATLANTIC (1500 series): *70* 8-10
ATLANTIC (3700 series): *82* 20-22
ATLANTIC (7000 series): *64* 12-15
ATLANTIC (8006 through 8039): *57-61* 25-35
(Black label.)
ATLANTIC (8006 through 8039): *59-61* 12-15
(Red label.)
ATLANTIC (8063 through 8094): *62-64* 20-25
ATLANTIC (19000 series): *77-80* 5-8
BARONET: *62* 15-20
BLUESWAY: *73* 8-10
BULLDOG: *84* 5-8
COLUMBIA: *83-86* 5-8
CORONET: 8-10
CROSSOVER: *73-76* 8-10
DESIGN: 8-10
EVEREST: *70-82* 8-10
GUEST STAR: *64* 10-15

HOLLYWOOD (505; "The Fabulous
Ray Charles"): 59 .... $75-100
HURRAH: 5-10
IMPULSE: 61 15-20
INTERMEDIA: 84 5-8
KING: 77 8-10
PALACE: 5-10
PREMIER: 8-10
STRAND: 10-12
TANGERINE: 70-73 10-12
UPFRONT: 8-10
  Also see JOEL, Billy, & Ray Charles
  Also see RAELETTES
  Also see THOMAS, B.J., & Ray Charles
  Also see U.S.A. FOR AFRICA

CHARLES, Ray, & Betty Carter
Singles: 7-Inch
ABC-PARAMOUNT: 61-62 3-5
LPs: 10/12-Inch 33rpm
ABC-PARAMOUNT: 61 20-25

CHARLES, Ray, & Clint Eastwood
Singles: 7-Inch
WARNER BROS: 80 1-3
  Also see EASTWOOD, Clint

CHARLES, Ray, & Mickey Gilley
Singles: 7-Inch
COLUMBIA: 85 1-3
  Also see GILLEY, Mickey

CHARLES, Ray / Ivory Joe
Hunter / Jimmy Rushing
LPs: 10/12-Inch 33rpm
DESIGN: 8-10
  Also see HUNTER, Ivory Joe

CHARLES, Ray, George Jones &
Chet Atkins
Singles: 7-Inch
COLUMBIA: 83 1-3
  Also see ATKINS, Chet
  Also see JONES, George

CHARLES, Ray, & Cleo Laine
LPs: 10/12-Inch 33rpm
RCA VICTOR: 76 10-12
  Also see LAINE, Cleo

CHARLES, Ray & Jimmy Lewis
Singles: 7-Inch
ABC: 69 2-3
TANGERINE: 68 2-4

CHARLES, Ray, & Willie Nelson
Singles: 7-Inch
COLUMBIA: 84 1-3
  Also see NELSON, Willie

CHARLES, Ray, & Hank Williams Jr.
Singles: 7-Inch
COLUMBIA: 85 .... $1-3
  Also see CHARLES, Ray
  Also see WILLIAMS, Hank, Jr.

CHARLES, Ray, Singers
Singles: 7-Inch
COMMAND: 64-70 2-4
DECCA: 58-59 2-3
JUBILEE: 54 2-4
MGM: 51-56 2-4
EPs: 7-Inch 33/45rpm
DECCA: 59 4-6
JAMESTOWN: 57 8-15
MGM: 55-57 5-8
LPs: 10/12-Inch 33rpm
ABC: 73 5-8
ALSHIRE: 70 5-8
ATCO: 68 8-12
CAMDEN: 67 6-10
COMMAND: 62-71 8-12
DECCA: 58-60 8-12
MCA: 82 4-6
MGM (100 series): 71 5-10
MGM (3000 series): 55-60 10-12
MGM (4000 series): 63-66 8-12
METRO: 65 6-10
VOCALION: 66 6-10

CHARLES, Ronnie
LPs: 10/12-Inch 33rpm
20TH CENTURY-FOX: 75 5-8

CHARLES, Rosevelt
LPs: 10/12-Inch 33rpm
VANGUARD: 64 10-15

CHARLES, Sonny
(Sonny Charles & Checkmates Ltd.)
Singles: 7-Inch
A&M: 68-73 3-5
CAPITOL: 66-67 3-5
FRATERNITY: 64 4-6
HIGHRISE: 82 1-3
RCA VICTOR: 72 2-3
LPs: 10/12-Inch 33rpm
HIGHRISE: 82 5-8
A&M: 69 15-20
  Also see CHECKMATES LTD.

CHARLES, Tommy
Singles: 7-Inch
DECCA: 56 5-8
WILLETT: 57 25-35

CHARLESTON CITY ALL-STARS
LPs: 10/12-Inch 33rpm
GRAND AWARD: 57-59 .... $5-12

CHARLIE
Singles: 7-Inch
ARISTA: 79 1-3
JANUS: 77-78 2-3
MIRAGE: 83 1-3
RCA VICTOR: 81 1-3
LPs: 10/12-Inch 33rpm
ARISTA: 79 5-8
COLUMBIA: 76 8-10
JANUS: 77-78 8-10
MIRAGE: 83 5-8
RCA VICTOR: 81 5-8

CHARME
Singles: 7-Inch
ATLANTIC: 84 1-3
RCA VICTOR: 79-85 1-3
LPs: 10/12-Inch 33rpm
RCA VICTOR: 79-85 5-8

CHARMETTES
Singles: 7-Inch
FEDERAL: 59 4-6
HI: 59 4-6
KAPP: 63-64 5-10
MALA: 64 5-10
MARLIN: 62 3-5
MELOMEGA: 62 3-5
MONA: 60 3-5
WORLD ARTISTS: 65 3-5

CHARMS
(Otis Williams & The Charms)
Singles: 78rpm
DELUXE (Except 600 through
6056): 54-57 5-10
DELUXE (6000 through 6056): 53-54 ... 20-40
Singles: 7-Inch
CHART: 55-56 10-15
DELUXE (6000 through 6034): 53-54 ... 60-80
DELUXE (6050; "Quiet Please"): 54 30-40
DELUXE (6056; "My Baby Dearest
Darling"): 54 30-40
DELUXE (6062 through 6098): 54-56 ... 10-15
DELUXE (6100 series): 57-59 4-6
(Monaural.)
DELUXE (6100 series): 59 10-20
(Stereo.)
GUSTO: 77 1-3
KING: 60-63 3-5
OKEH: 65-66 2-4
ROCKIN' (516; "Heaven Only
Knows"): 53 100-150

EPs: 7-Inch 33/45rpm
DELUXE (357; "Hits By The
Charms"): 55 .... $150-200
DELUXE (385; "Otis Williams &
The Charms"): 56 100-200
KING (357; "Hits By The
Charms"): 57 50-75
KING (364; "Hits By The Charms,
Vol. 2"): 57 50-75
KING (385; "Otis Williams & His
Charms"): 57 50-75
LPs: 10/12-Inch 33rpm
DELUXE (570; "All Their Hits"): 57 . 200-300
KING (614; "This Is Otis Williams &
The Charms"): 59 75-100
Members: Otis Williams & The Charms; Otis Wil-
liams; Ron Bradley; Don Peark; Joe Renn; Richard
Parker.
Also see WILLIAMS, Otis

CHARO
(Charo With The Salsoul Orchestra)
Singles: 7-Inch
CAPITOL: 76 1-3
SALSOUL: 77-78 1-3
LPs: 10/12-Inch 33rpm
SALSOUL: 77-78 5-8
Also see SALSOUL ORCHESTRA

CHARTBUSTERS
Singles: 7-Inch
BELL: 67 3-5
CRUSADER: 65 4-6
MUTUAL: 64-65 3-5

CHARTS
Singles: 78rpm
EVERLAST: 57 5-10
Singles: 7-Inch
ABC: 73 1-3
COLLECTABLES: 1-3
EVERLAST (5001; "Desiree"): 57 10-20
EVERLAST (5002 through 5010): 57 ... 15-20
EVERLAST (5026; "Desiree"): 63 5-8
GUYDEN: 59 4-6
VELVTONE: 5-10
WAND (1112; "Desiree"): 66 4-6
WAND (1124; "Livin' The
Nightlife"): 66 3-5
LPs: 10/12-Inch 33rpm
COLLECTABLES: 86 6-8
LOST-NITE: 81 8-10
Members: Joe Grier; Steve Brown; Ross Buford;
Glen Jackson; Leroy Binns.

CHASE
Singles: 7-Inch
EPIC: *71-76* $2-4
LPs: 10/12-Inch 33rpm
EPIC: *71-76* 10-12
Members: Bill Chase; Jerry Van Blair; Jay Burrid; Dennis Johnson; Ted Piercefield: Phil Porter; Terry Richards; Angel South; Alan Ware.

CHASE, Ellison
Singles: 7-Inch
BIG TREE: *76-77* 2-4
COLUMBIA: *82* 1-3
MAGNA-GLIDE: *75* 2-3
LPs: 10/12-Inch 33rpm
COLUMBIA/ARC: *82* 5-8

CHATER, Kerry
Singles: 7-Inch
WARNER BROS: *76-78* 2-4
LPs: 10/12-Inch 33rpm
WARNER BROS: *77* 5-8

CHAZ
Singles: 7-Inch
PROMISE: *82* 1-3

CHEAP TRICK
Singles: 12-Inch 33/45rpm
EPIC: *83* 4-6
Singles: 7-Inch
ASYLUM: *81* 2-4
EPIC: *77-88* 2-4
PASHA: *84* 2-3
EPs: 7-Inch 33/45rpm
CSP: *81* 3-6
(Nestles candy promotional issue.)
LPs: 10/12-Inch 33rpm
EPIC: *76-88* 5-8
EPIC/NU-DISC: *80* 10-15
(Includes bonus single.)
PASHA: *84* 5-8
Members: Robert Zander; Tom Petersson; Rick Nielson; Bun E. Carlos.

CHEATHAM, Oliver
Singles: 7-Inch
CRITIQUE: *86-87* 1-3
MCA: *83* 1-3
LPs: 10/12-Inch 33rpm
MCA: *83* 5-8

CHECKER, Chubby
Singles: 7-Inch
ABKCO: *72* 1-3
AMHERST: *76* 2-3
BUDDAH: *69* 3-6
MCA: *82* 2-4
PARKWAY (006; "The Jet"): *62* 3-6

PARKWAY (804 through 810): *59-60* ... $8-10
PARKWAY (811; "The Twist"/
"Toot"): *60* 10-15
(White label.)
PARKWAY (811; "The Twist"/
"Twistin' U.S.A."): *61* 10-15
(Yellow/orange or orange label.)
PARKWAY (811; "The Twist"): *61* 15-20
(Colored vinyl.)
PARKWAY (813 through 989): *60-66* 4-8
20TH CENTURY-FOX: *73-74* 2-3
Picture Sleeves
PARKWAY: *61-65* 4-8
EPs: 7-Inch 33/45rpm
PARKWAY: *61* 15-20
(Includes Compact 33 Doubles.)
LPs: 10/12-Inch 33rpm
ABKCO: *72* 8-10
D.C.M.: 4-6
EVEREST: *81* 5-8
51 WEST: *84* 5-8
MCA: *82* 8-10
PARKWAY: *60-66* 15-20
Also see DREAMLOVERS
Also see FAT BOYS

CHECKER, Chubby / Gary U.S. Bonds
LPs: 10/12-Inch 33rpm
EXACT: *80* 5-8
Also see BONDS, Gary "U.S."

CHECKER, Chubby, & Bobby Rydell
Singles: 7-Inch
CAMEO (12; "Your Hits And
Mine"): *61* 8-10
(Promotional issue only.)
CAMEO (200 series): *61-62* 4-8
Picture Sleeves
CAMEO: *61* 4-8
LPs: 10/12-Inch 33rpm
CAMEO: *61-63* 15-20
Also see RYDELL, Bobby

CHECKER, Chubby, & Dee Dee Sharp
LPs: 10/12-Inch 33rpm
CAMEO: *62* 20-30
Also see CHECKER, Chubby
Also see SHARP, Dee Dee

CHECKMATES LTD.
Singles: 7-Inch
A&M: *69* 4-8
CAPITOL: *66-67* 4-8
FANTASY: *77-78* 2-3
GREEDY: *77* 2-3
RUSTIC: *74* 2-4

LPs: 10/12-Inch 33rpm
A&M: *69* $15-20
CAPITOL: *67* 15-20
FANTASY: *77* 8-10
IKON: 5-8
POLYDOR: *76* 8-10
RUSTIC: *74* 8-10
Members: Sonny Charles; Bill Van Buskirk; Marvin Smith; Bobby Stevens; Harvey Trees.
Also see CHARLES, Sonny

CHEE-CHEE & PEPPY
Singles: 7-Inch
BUDDAH: *71* 2-4
LPs: 10/12-Inch 33rpm
BUDDAH: *72* 10-12

CHEECH & CHONG
Singles: 7-Inch
A&M: 1-3
EPIC/ODE: *77* 2-4
MCA: *85* 1-3
ODE: *71-77* 2-5
WARNER BROS: *78* 1-3
Picture Sleeves
A&M: 1-3
MCA: *85* 1-3
ODE: *73-77* 6-12
WARNER BROS: *78* 1-3
LPs: 10/12-Inch 33rpm
EPIC/ODE: *77* 5-8
ODE: *71-76* 8-12
WARNER BROS: *78-80* 6-10
Members: Richard Marin; Thomas Chong.
Also see TAYLOR, Bobby

CHEEKS, Judy
Singles: 7-Inch
DREAM: *80* 1-3
SALSOUL: *78* 1-3
UNITED ARTISTS: *73* 2-3
LPs: 10/12-Inch 33rpm
SALSOUL: *78* 5-8
UNITED ARTISTS: *73* 8-10

CHEERS
Singles: 78rpm
CAPITOL: *54-56* 4-8
MERCURY: *57* 3-6
Singles: 7-Inch
CAPITOL: *54-56* 5-10
MERCURY: *57* 4-6
EPs: 7-Inch 33/45rpm
CAPITOL: *55* 40-50
Members: Bert Convy; Gil Garfield; Susan Allen.

CHEMAY, Joe
(Joe Chemay Band)
Singles: 7-Inch
UNICORN: *81* $1-3
LPs: 10/12-Inch 33rpm
UNICORN: *81* 5-8

CHEQUERED PAST
Singles: 7-Inch
EMI AMERICA: *84* 1-3
LPs: 10/12-Inch 33rpm
EMI AMERICA: *84* 5-8
Members: Clem Burke; Nigel Harrison.

CHER
(Cher Bono; Cher Allman)
Singles: 12-Inch 33/45rpm
CASABLANCA: *79-82* 8-10
Singles: 7-Inch
ATCO: *69-72* 2-4
ATLANTIC: *69* 2-4
CASABLANCA: *79* 2-3
COLUMBIA: *82* 1-3
GEFFEN: *87-88* 1-3
IMPERIAL: *64-68* 3-5
KAPP: *71-72* 2-3
LIBERTY: *82* 1-3
MCA: *73-75* 2-3
UNITED ARTISTS: *71-72* 2-3
WARNER BROS: *75-77* 2-3
WARNER BROS/SPECTOR: *74* 2-4
Picture Sleeves
COLUMBIA: *82* 2-4
LPs: 10/12-Inch 33rpm
ATCO: *69* 15-20
CASABLANCA (Except "Take Me Home" picture disc): *79* 8-12
CASABLANCA ("Take Me Home" picture disc): *79* 25-30
COLUMBIA: *82* 5-8
GEFFEN: *87* 5-8
IMPERIAL: *65-68* 15-25
KAPP: *71-72* 12-15
LIBERTY: *81* 5-8
MCA: *73-74* 10-15
SPRINGBOARD: *72* 8-10
SUNSET: *70* 8-10
UNITED ARTISTS: *71-75* 8-10
WARNER BROS: *75-77* 8-15
Also see ALLMAN & WOMAN
Also see CHERILYN
Also see MASON, Bonnie Jo
Also see SONNY & CHER

CHER & NILSSON
Singles: 7-Inch
SPECTOR: 75 .... $2-4
Members: Cher; Harry Nilsson.
Also see CHER
Also see NILSSON

CHERI
Singles: 12-Inch 33/45rpm
21: *83* 4-6
Singles: 7-Inch
21: *83* 1-3
VENTURE: *82* 1-3

CHERILYN
(Cher Bono) / Cherilyn's Group
Singles: 7-Inch
IMPERIAL: *64* 15-20
Also see CHER

CHERRELLE
(Cherrelle & Alexander O'Neal)
Singles: 12-Inch 33/45rpm
TABU: *84-86* 4-6
Singles: 7-Inch
TABU: *84-88* 1-3
LPs: 10/12-Inch 33rpm
TABU: *84-88* 5-8
Also see O'NEAL, Alexander

CHERRY, Ava
Singles: 12-Inch 33/45rpm
CAPITOL: *82* 4-6
Singles: 7-Inch
CAPITOL: *82* 1-3
CURTOM: *80* 1-3
RSO: *80* 1-3
LPs: 10/12-Inch 33rpm
RSO: *80* 5-8

CHERRY, Don
Singles: 7-Inch
COLUMBIA: *55-59* 3-5
DECCA: *50-56* 3-5
MONUMENT: *65-78* 1-3
STRAND: *59* 2-3
VERVE: *62* 2-3
WARWICK: *60* 2-3
EPs: 7-Inch 33/45rpm
COLUMBIA: *56* 6-10
LPs: 10/12-Inch 33rpm
COLUMBIA: *56* 15-20
HARMONY: *59* 10-12
MONUMENT: *66-73* 8-10
Also see DAY, Doris, & Don Cherry

CHERRY PEOPLE
Singles: 7-Inch
HERITAGE: *68-69* $3-5
Picture Sleeves
HERITAGE: *68* 5-10
LPs: 10/12-Inch 33rpm
HERITAGE: *68* 15-20

CHERYL LYNN: see LYNN, Cheryl

CHEYNE
Singles: 12-Inch 33/45rpm
MCA: *85* 4-6

CHIC
Singles: 12-Inch 33/45
ATLANTIC: *78-83* 4-6
Singles: 7-Inch
ATLANTIC: *77-83* 1-3
MIRAGE: *82* 1-3
Picture Sleeves
ATLANTIC: *78-80* 1-3
LPs: 10/12-Inch 33rpm
ATLANTIC: *77-82* 5-8
Also see HONEYDRIPPERS
Also see NORMA JEAN
Also see RODGERS, Nile

CHIC / Leif Garrett / Roberta Flack / Genesis
EPs: 7-Inch 33/45rpm
WARNER SPECIAL PRODUCTS: *78* 5-10
(Coca-Cola/Burger King promotional issue. Issued with paper sleeve.)
Also see CHIC
Also see FLACK, Roberta
Also see GARRETT, Leif
Also see GENESIS

CHICAGO
Singles: 12-Inch 33/45rpm
COLUMBIA: *80* 4-6
Singles: 7-Inch
COLUMBIA: *69-80* 1-3
FULL MOON: *82-86* 1-3
REPRISE: *88* 1-3
WARNER BROS: *87* 1-3
Picture Sleeves
COLUMBIA: *70-80* 1-3
EPs: 7-Inch 33/45rpm
COLUMBIA: *70-73* 10-15
(Jukebox issues only.)
LPs: 10/12-Inch 33rpm
ACCORD: *81* 5-8
COLUMBIA: *69-82* 8-12
FULL MOON: *82-86* 5-8
MFSL: *85* 15-25
MAGNUM: *78* 10-12

REPRISE: *88* **$5-8**
Members: Peter Cetera; Terry Kath; Robert Lamm;
James Pankow; Lee Loughnane; Daniel Seraphine;
Walter Parazaider.
Also see BEACH BOYS
Also see CETERA, Peter

CHICAGO GANGSTERS
Singles: 7-Inch
GOLD PLATE: *75-76* 2-3
RCA VICTOR: *78* 1-3
RED COACH: *74-75* 2-3
LPs: 10/12-Inch 33rpm
GOLD PLATE: *75-76* 10-12

CHICAGO LOOP
Singles: 7-Inch
DYNO VOICE: *66-67* 3-5
MERCURY: *67-68* 3-5

CHICANO, El: see EL CHICANO

CHICORY
(Chicory Tip)
Singles: 7-Inch
EPIC: *72-73* 2-4
LPs: 10/12-Inch 33rpm
EPIC: *72* 10-12

CHIEFTAINS
Singles: 7-Inch
ISLAND: *76* 2-3
LPs: 10/12-Inch 33rpm
COLUMBIA: *78-80* 5-8
ISLAND: *75-78* 5-10

CHIFFONS
Singles: 7-Inch
B.T. PUPPY: *70* 2-4
BIG DEAL: *60* 30-35
BUDDAH: *71* 2-4
LAURIE: *63-76* 4-8
REPRISE: *62* 4-8
WILDCAT: 10-15
LPs: 10/12-Inch 33rpm
B.T. PUPPY: *70* 20-30
COLLECTABLES: *87* 6-8
LAURIE (2000 series): *63-66* 25-35
LAURIE (4000 series): *75* 10-15
Members: Judy Craig; Barbara Lee; Patricia Ben-
nett; Sylvia Peterson.
Also see COASTERS / Crew-Cuts / Chiffons
Also see FOUR PENNIES
Also see ISLEY BROTHERS / Chiffons

CHILD, Desmond, & Rouge
Singles: 12-Inch 33/45rpm
CAPITOL: *79* 4-6

Singles: 7-Inch
CAPITOL (Black vinyl): *79-82* **$1-3**
CAPITOL (Colored vinyl): *79* 3-5
LPs: 10/12-Inch 33rpm
CAPITOL (Black vinyl): *79* 5-8
CAPITOL (Colored vinyl): *79* 15-20
Also see VIDAL, Maria

CHI-LITES
Singles: 12-Inch 33/45rpm
LARC: *83* 4-6
PRIVATE I: *84* 4-6
Singles: 7-Inch
BLUE ROCK: *65* 3-5
BRUNSWICK: *69-78* 2-3
ERIC: *83* 1-3
INPHASION: *79* 1-3
LARC: *83* 1-3
MERCURY: *76-77* 2-3
O'RETTA: *70* 2-4
PRIVATE I: *84* 1-3
REVUE: *67-68* 3-5
20TH CENTURY-FOX: *81* 1-3
LPs: 10/12-Inch 33rpm
BRUNSWICK: *69-74* 10-12
EPIC: *83-84* 5-8
LARC: *83* 5-8
MERCURY: *77* 5-8
20TH CENTURY-FOX: *80-81* 5-8
Members: Eugene Record; Creadel Jones; Robert
Lester; Marshall Thompson.
Also see RECORD, Eugene
Also see WILSON, Jackie, & The Chi-Lites

CHILLIWACK
Singles: 7-Inch
A&M: *72* 2-4
MILLENNIUM: *81-83* 1-3
MUSHROOM: *76-80* 1-3
PARROT: *71* 2-4
SIRE: *74-76* 2-3
LPs: 10/12-Inch 33rpm
A&M: *71-73* 12-15
MILLENNIUM: *81-82* 5-8
MUSHROOM: *77-80* 8-10
PARROT: *70* 15-18
SIRE: *75* 10-12
Members: Bill Henderson; Howard Froese; Claire
Lawrence; Glen Miller; Ross Turney.

CHILLTOWN
Singles: 12-Inch 33/45rpm
A&M: *83* 4-6

CHIMES
Singles: 7-Inch
ABC: *75* 1-3

COLLECTABLES: *81* $1-3
LAURIE: *60* 5-10
LIMELIGHT: *57* 8-10
METRO INT'L: *63* 5-10
MUSIC NOTE: *60* 10-15
RESERVE: *57* 5-8
TAG (444; "Once in Awhile"/"Summer
Night"): *60* 4-8
TAG (444; "Once in Awhile"/"Oh How
I Love You So"): *60* 10-20
(Note different flip side.)
TAG (445; "I'm In The Mood
For Love"): *61* 5-10
TAG (447; "Let's Fall In
Love"): *61* 8-12

CHINA CRISIS
Singles: 12-Inch 33/45rpm
VIRGIN: *82* 4-6
WARNER BROS: *83* 4-6
Singles: 7-Inch
VIRGIN: *82* 1-3
WARNER BROS: *84* 1-3
LPs: 10/12-Inch 33rpm
A&M: *87* 5-8
WARNER BROS: *84* 5-8

CHIP E. INC. FEATURING K. JOY
Singles: 12-Inch 33/45rpm
D.J. INT'L: *85* 4-6

CHIPMUNKS
**(Starring Alvin, Theodore, & Simon; Featuring
David Seville)**
Singles: 7-Inch
LIBERTY (Except 77000 series): *58-74* ... 4-8
LIBERTY (77000 series): *59* 8-10
(Stereo singles.)
MISTLETOE: *75* 2-3
SUNSET: *68* 2-3
UNITED ARTISTS: *74* 1-3
Picture Sleeves
LIBERTY: *59-65* 5-10
EPs: 7-Inch 33/45rpm
LIBERTY: *59-64* 10-20
LPs: 10/12-Inch 33rpm
LIBERTY (Except 100 series &
LN series): *61-65* 10-15
LIBERTY (100 & 10000 series): *59-60* .. 20-25
(Black vinyl. With covers picturing the Chipmunks
as animals.)
LIBERTY (100 series) 12-15
(Black vinyl. With covers picturing the Chipmunks
as cartoon characters.)
LIBERTY (100 series): *59* 35-45
(Colored vinyl.)

Note: Liberty 100 series numbers were preceded by
a "3" for mono or a "7" for stereo issues.
LIBERTY (10000 series): *82* $5-8
PICKWICK: *80* 5-8
SUNSET: *68-69* 10-12
UNITED ARTISTS: *74-76* 6-10
Also see CANNED HEAT & THE CHIP-
MUNKS
Also see SEVILLE, David

CHIPMUNKS
**(Starring Alvin, Theodore, & Simon; Featuring
David Seville, Jr.)**
Singles: 7-Inch
EXCELSIOR: *80* 1-3
RCA VICTOR: *81-82* 1-3
Picture Sleeves
EXCELSIOR: *80* 1-3
RCA VICTOR: *81* 1-3
LPs: 10/12-Inch 33rpm
EXCELSIOR: *80* 5-8
PICKWICK INT'L: *80* 5-8
RCA VICTOR: *81-82* 5-8

CHIYO & THE CRESCENTS
Singles: 7-Inch
BREAK OUT: *63* 5-8
Also see CRESCENTS

CHOCOLATE MILK
Singles: 12-Inch 33/45rpm
RCA VICTOR: *83* 4-6
Singles: 7-Inch
RCA VICTOR: *75-83* 2-4
LPs: 10/12-Inch 33rpm
RCA VICTOR: *77-82* 5-8

CHOCOLETE
Singles: 12-Inch 33/45rpm
SUPERTRONICS: *85* 4-6

CHOICE FOUR
Singles: 7-Inch
RCA VICTOR: *74-76* 2-4
LPs: 10/12-Inch 33rpm
RCA VICTOR: *74-75* 8-10

CHOICE MCs FEATURING
FRESH GORDON
Singles: 12-Inch 33/45rpm
TOMMY BOY: *85* 4-6

CHOIR
Singles: 7-Inch
CANADIAN AMERICAN: *67* 20-25
INTREPID: *70* 4-6
ROULETTE: *67-68* 8-10
EPs: 7-Inch 33/45rpm
BOMP: *76* 8-10

Member: Eric Carmen.
Also see CARMEN, Eric

CHOPS
Singles: 12-Inch 33/45rpm
ATLANTIC: *84* $4-6
Singles: 7-Inch
ATLANTIC: *84* 1-3
LPs: 10/12-Inch 33rpm
ATLANTIC: *84* 5-8

CHORDCATS
Singles: 78rpm
CAT: *54* 8-12
Singles: 7-Inch
CAT: *54* 15-25
Members: Carl Feaster; Claude Feaster; Jimmy
Keys; Floyd McRae; William Edwards.
Also see CHORDS

CHORDETTES
(Chordettes With Archie Bleyer)
Singles: 78rpm
CADENCE: *54-57* 5-10
COLUMBIA: *50-54* 5-10
Singles: 7-Inch
BARNABY: *70-76* 2-3
CADENCE: *54-63* 5-12
COLUMBIA: *50-54* 5-12
ERIC: *78* 1-3
Picture Sleeves
CADENCE: *58-61* 5-10
EPs: 7-Inch 33/45rpm
CADENCE: *57-59* 10-15
COLUMBIA: *50-54* 15-20
LPs: 10/12-Inch 33rpm
BACK-TRAC: 5-8
BARNABY: *76* 8-10
CADENCE (1000 series): *57* 20-25
CADENCE (3000 & 25000
series): *58-61* 15-20
COLUMBIA (900 series): *57* 20-25
COLUMBIA (2000 & 6000
series): *50-54* 25-35
EVEREST: *82* 5-8
HARMONY: *59* 12-15
Members: Margie Needham; Janet Ertel; Carol
Bushman; Lynn Evans.
Also see BLEYER, Archie

CHORDS
Singles: 78rpm
CAT (104; "Sh-Boom"/"Cross Over
The Bridge"): *54* 20-25
CAT (104; "Sh-Boom"/"Little
Maiden"): *54* 10-20
CAT (109; "Zippety Zum"): *54* 8-12

Singles: 7-Inch
CAT (104; "Sh-Boom"/"Cross Over
The Bridge"): *54* $30-50
CAT (104; "Sh-Boom"/"Little
Maiden"): *54* 15-30
CAT (109; "Zippety Zum"): *54* 10-15
Members: Carl Feaster; Claude Feaster; Jimmy
Keys; Floyd McRae; William Edwards.
Also see CHORDCATS
Also see SH-BOOMS

CHRIS & KATHY
Singles: 7-Inch
MONOGRAM: *64* 8-10
Members: Chris Montez; Kathy Young.
Also see MONTEZ, Chris
Also see YOUNG, Kathy

CHRISTIAN, Chris
Singles: 7-Inch
BOARDWALK: *81-82* 1-3
LPs: 10/12-Inch 33rpm
BORADWALK: *81* 5-8
HOME SWEET HOME: *81* 5-8
MYRRH: *83-84* 5-8

CHRISTIE
Singles: 7-Inch
EPIC: *70-71* 2-3
LPs: 10/12-Inch 33rpm
EPIC: *70* 12-15
Members: Jeff Christie; Mike Blakely; Vic Elmes.

CHRISTIE, Dean
Singles: 7-Inch
MERCURY: *63-64* 3-5
SWL: *62* 3-5
SELECT: *62* 15-20
TOP FLIGHT: 20-25

CHRISTIE, Janice
Singles: 12-Inch
SUPERTRONICS: *85-86* 4-6

CHRISTIE, Lou
(Lou Christie & The Classics)
Singles: 12-Inch 33/45rpm
PLATEAU: *81* 6-10
Singles: 7-Inch
ABC: *73* 2-3
ALCAR: *63* 15-20
AMERICAN MUSIC MAKERS: 4-6
BUDDAH (Except 116): *68-72* 5-8
BUDDAH (116; "I'm Gonna Make
You Mine"): *69* 3-5
C AND C (102; "The Gypsy
Cried"): *62* 75-100
CO & CE: *66* 10-15
COLPIX: *64-66* 5-10

COLUMBIA: *67* $5-8
EPIC: *76* 2-4
MGM: *65-66* 4-8
MIDLAND INT'L: *76-77* 2-4
MIDSONG: *77* 2-4
PLATEAU: *81* 2-4
ROULETTE: *62-64* 4-6
SLIPPED DISC: *76* 6-10
THREE BROTHERS: *73-75* 3-6
WORLD: 5-8

Picture Sleeves

COLPIX: *64* 10-20
MGM (Except 13576): *65-66* 8-15
MGM (13576; "If My Car Could Only
Talk"): *66* 10-20

LPs: 10/12-Inch 33rpm

BUDDAH: *69-71* 15-20
CO & CE (1231; "Lou Christie Strikes
Back"): *66* 60-100
COLPIX: *66* 20-25
51 WEST: *83* 5-8
MGM: *66* 20-25
ROULETTE: *63* 20-30
SPIN-O-RAMA: *66* 15-20
THREE BROTHERS: *74* 15-20
   Also see CANTINA BAND
   Also see CHRISTY, Chic
   Also see CLASSICS
   Also see LA RUE, D.C.
   Also see LUGEE & THE LIONS
   Also see MARCY JOE
   Also see SACCO

CHRISTIE, Lou, & Leslie Gore
Singles: 7-Inch
EMI AMERICA: *86* 2-3
   Also see CHRISTIE, Lou
   Also see GORE, Leslie

CHRISTIE, Susan
Singles: 7-Inch
COLUMBIA: *66-67* 3-5

CHRISTMAS SPIRIT
Singles: 7-Inch
WHITE WHALE (290; "Christmas Is My
Time Of Year"): *69* 45-55
   Members: Mark Volman; Howard Kaylan; Linda
   Ronstadt.
   Also see RONSTADT, Linda
   Also see TURTLES

CHRISTOPHER, Gavin
Singles: 7-Inch
ISLAND: *76* 2-3
E.M.I./MANHATTAN: *86-88* 1-3
RSO: *79* 1-3

LPs: 10/12-Inch 33rpm
ISLAND: *76* $8-10
E.M.I./MANHATTAN: *86-88* 5-8
RSO: *79* 5-8

CHRISTOPHER, Paul & Shawn
Singles: 7-Inch
CASABLANCA: *75* 2-3

CHRISTY, Chic
Singles: 7-Inch
HAC: *62* 10-20
   Members: Lou Christie; Kay Chick; Susan Christie.
   Also see CHRISTIE, Lou

CHRISTY, Don
(Sonny Bono)
Singles: 7-Inch
FIDELITY: *60* 5-10
GO: *60* 5-10
NAME: *60* 5-10
SPECIALTY: *59* 5-10
   Also see SONNY

CHRISTY, June
Singles: 78rpm
CAPITOL: *51-57* 3-5
Singles: 7-Inch
CAPITOL (1800 through 3900
series): *51-58* 3-5
CAPITOL (4000 through 4800
series): *59-62* 2-4
EPs: 7-Inch 33/4rpm
CAPITOL: *53-55* 5-10
LPs: 10/12-Inch 33rpm
CAPITOL (516; "Something Cool"): *54* . . 20-30
(With an "H" prefix. 10-Inch LP.)
CAPITOL (516; "Something Cool"): *55* . . 15-20
(Green label. With a "T" prefix.)
CAPITOL (516; "Something Cool"): *60* . . 10-12
(Black label. With a "T" or "ST" prefix.)
CAPITOL (516; "Something Cool"): *75* 5-8
(With an "SM" prefix.)
CAPITOL (600 through 900
series): *55-57* 12-18
(Green label.)
CAPITOL (600 through 900
series): *60* 10-12
(Black label.)
CAPITOL (1000 through 2400
series): *60-65* 10-15
CAPITOL (11000 series): *79* 5-8
DISCOVERY: *82* 5-8
SEABREEZE: *80* 5-8
   Also see JONES, Jonah
   Also see KENTON, Stan, & His Orchestra

CHUCKLES
(Featuring Teddy Randazzo)
Singles: 7-Inch
ABC-PARAMOUNT: *61* $3-6
Also see RANDAZZO, Teddy
Also see THREE CHUCKLES

CHUNG, Wang:
see WANG CHUNG

CHURCH, Eugene
(Eugene Church & The Fellows)
Singles: 7-Inch
CLASS: *58-60* 4-6
COLLECTABLES: *81* 1-3
KING: *61-63* 3-5
RENDEZVOUS: *60* 3-5
SPECIALTY: *57* 5-10
(Most Specialty singles are currently available, using original catalog numbers.)
WORLD PACIFIC: *67* 3-5
Also see CLIQUES

CHURCHILL, Savannah
(Savannah Churchill & The Five Kings; Savannah Churchill & The Striders; Savannah Churchill & The Four Tunes)
Singles: 78rpm
ARGO: *56* 3-6
DECCA: *53-55* 3-6
KAY-RON: *56* 5-10
MANOR: *45-48* 5-10
RCA VICTOR: *51-52* 4-6
REGAL (3309; "Once There Lived
A Fool"): *50* 25-50
REGAL (3313; "Wedding Bells"): *50* 5-10
Singles: 7-Inch
ARGO: *56* 4-6
DECCA: *53-55* 4-6
JAMIE: *60* 3-6
KAY-RON: *56* 5-10
RCA VICTOR: *51-52* 4-8
REGAL (3309; "Once There Lived
A Fool"): *50* 75-125
EPs: 7-Inch 33/45rpm
CAMDEN: *54* 25-50
Also see FOUR TUNES

CINDERELLA
Singles: 7-Inch
MERCURY: *86-88* 1-4
LPs: 10/12-Inch 33rpm
MERCURY: *86-88* 5-8

CINDY & ROY
Singles: 12-Inch 33/45rpm
CASABLANCA: *79* 4-6

Singles: 7-Inch
CASABLANCA: *79* $1-3
LPs: 10/12-Inch 33rpm
CASABLANCA: *79* 5-8

CIRCUS
Singles: 7-Inch
METROMEDIA: *72-73* 2-3
LPs: 10/12-Inch 33rpm
HEMISPHERE: *74* 10-12
METROMEDIA: *73* 10-12

CIRCUT
Singles: 12-Inch 33/45rpm
4TH & BROADWAY: *84-85* 4-6

CISSEL, Chuck
Singles: 7-Inch
ARISTA: *79-80* 1-3
LPs: 10/12-Inch 33rpm
ARISTA: *80* 5-8

CISSEL, Chuck, & Marva King
Singles: 7-Inch
ARISTA: *82* 1-3
Also see CISSEL, Chuck

CITY
LPs: 10/12-Inch 33rpm
CHRYSALIS: *86* 5-8

CITY BOY
Singles: 7-Inch
AIRBOY: *77* 2-3
ATLANTIC: *79-81* 1-3
MERCURY: *76-78* 2-3
LPs: 10/12-Inch 33rpm
ATLANTIC: *80* 5-8
MERCURY: *76-78* 8-10
Members: Steve Broughton; Lol Mason; Mike Slamer; Max Thomas; Roy Ward; Chris Dunn; Roger Kent.

CLANCY BROTHERS
(Clancy Brothers & Lou Killen; Clancy Brothers & Robbie O'Connell)
LPs: 10/12-Inch 33rpm
AUDIO FIDELITY: *71-73* 8-12
COLUMBIA: *70* 8-12
VANGUARD: *74-83* 5-12

CLANCY BROTHERS & TOMMY MAKEM
Singles: 7-Inch
COLUMBIA: *62-69* 2-4
LPs: 10/12-Inch 33rpm
COLUMBIA: *62-69* 10-15
HARMONY: *71-72* 6-10
SHANACHIE: 5-10

TRADITION: *67-69* $10-12
  Also see CLANCY BROTHERS

CLANNAD
  LPs: 10/12-Inch 33rpm
RCA VICTOR: *84-88* 5-8

CLANTON, Ike
  Singles: 7-Inch
ACE: *59-60* 3-5
MERCURY: *62-63* 3-5

CLANTON, Jimmy
(Jimmie Clanton)
  Singles: 78rpm
ACE: *57* 5-10
  Singles: 7-Inch
ABC: *73* 1-3
ACE (Monaural): *57-63* 4-8
ACE (Stereo): *59* 10-15
COLLECTABLES: *81* 1-3
ERIC: *73* 1-3
IMPERIAL: *67-68* 3-5
LAURIE: *69* 2-4
MALA: *65* 3-5
PHILIPS: *63-64* 3-5
SPIRAL: *71* 2-4
STARCREST: *76* 2-3
STARFIRE: *78* 2-4
VIN: *62* 3-5
  Picture Sleeves
ACE (Except 51860): *59-63* 8-15
ACE (51860; "The Slave"): *60* 12-25
  (Promotionally issued, mail-order bonus offer to
  buyers of the *Jimmy's Happy/Jimmy's Blue* LP. All
  copies of this sleeve were autographed by Clanton.)
PHILIPS: *64* 5-10
STARCREST: *76* 3-5
  Promotional Singles
ACE (644; "Venus In Blue
  Jeans"): *62* 10-15
ACE (51860; "The Slave"): *60* 5-10
  (Promotional issue only. A bonus disc with the
  Jimmy's Happy/Jimmy's Blue LP.)
UNITED ARTISTS ("Teenage
  Millionaire"): *62* 5-8
  (5-inch cardboard flexi-disc.)
  EPs: 7-Inch 33/45rpm
ACE (Black vinyl): *59-61* 20-30
ACE (Colored vinyl): *60* 30-50
  LPs: 10/12-Inch 33rpm
ACE: *59-62* 40-80
PHILLIPS: *64* 15-20
  Also see DALE, Jimmy

CLANTON, Jimmy /Bristow Hopper
  LPs: 10/12-Inch 33rpm
DESIGN: $10-15

CLANTON, Jimmy, & MaryAnn Mobley
  Singles: 7-Inch
ACE: *61* 3-5
  Picture Sleeves
ACE: *61* 10-15
  Also see CLANTON, Jimmy

CLAPTON, Eric
  Singles: 12-Inch 33/45rpm
WARNER BROS (2248; "Forever Man"): 5-10
  (Promotional issue only.)
  Singles: 7-Inch
ATCO: *70-71* 2-4
DUCK: *83-86* 1-3
POLYDOR: *72-73* 2-3
POLYDOR: *88* 1-3
RSO: *74-82* 1-3
  Picture Sleeves
RSO: *80-81* 1-3
  LPs: 10/12-Inch 33rpm
ATCO (329; "Eric Clapton"): *70* 30-40
  (With studio chatter between takes, and reverb.)
ATCO (329; "Eric Clapton"): *70* 15-25
  (Omits chatter and reverb.)
ATCO (803; "History Of
  Eric Clapton "): *72* 15-25
DUCK: *83-86* 5-8
MFSL (030; "Slowhand"): *79* 25-50
MFSL (183; "Bluesbreakers"): *87* 15-20
POLYDOR: *72-73* 8-12
POLYDOR: *88* 5-8
RSO: *73-82* 6-10
  Also see BLIND FAITH
  Also see COOLIDGE, Rita
  Also see CREAM
  Also see DELANEY & BONNIE & FRIENDS
  Also see DEREK & THE DOMINOES
  Also see HARRISON, George
  Also see LEVY, Marcy
  Also see LOMAX, Jackie
  Also see MAYALL, John
  Also see RUSSELL, Leon
  Also see STARR, Ringo
  Also see WATERS, Roger
  Also see YARDBIRDS

CLARK, Chris
  Singles: 7-Inch
MOTOWN: *67-68* 3-5
V.I.P.: *65-67* 3-5

LPs: 10/12-Inch 33rpm
MOTOWN: *67* $12-15
WEED: 10-12

CLARK, Claudine
(Claudine Clark & The Spinners)
Singles: 7-Inch
CHANCELLOR: *62-63* 3-5
COLLECTABLES: *81* 1-3
ERIC: *73* 1-3
HERALD: *58* 10-20
JAMIE: *64* 3-5
LPs: 10/12-Inch 33rpm
CHANCELLOR: *62* 30-40

CLARK, Dave, Five
(Dave Clark & Friends)
Singles: 7-Inch
CONGRESS: *64* 4-6
EPIC (9656 through 10265): *64-67* 3-5
(Black vinyl.)
EPIC (9700 & 9800 series): *65* 8-10
(Colored vinyl. Promotional issues only.)
EPIC (10325 through 10894): *68-72* 6-10
JUBILEE: *64* 10-12
LAURIE: *63* 15-25
RUST: *64* 20-30
Picture Sleeves
CONGRESS (212; "I Knew It All
  The Time"): *64* 15-25
EPIC: *64-70* 8-15
EPs: 7-Inch 33/45rpm
COLUMBIA: *64-65* 20-40
EPIC: *66* 15-25
(Jukebox issues only.)
LPs: 10/12-Inch 33rpm
CORTLEIGH: 15-20
CROWN: *65* 20-25
CUSTOM: 15-20
EPIC (Except 24093): *64-75* 15-30
Note: Monaural Epic LPs are near the higher end of
the price range, whereas reprocessed stereo issues
are valued toward the lower end.
EPIC (24093; "Glad All
  Over"): *64* 75-120
(Instruments are not pictured on cover.)
EPIC (24093; "Glad All
  Over"): *64* 20-30
(Instruments are pictured on cover.)
Promotional LPs
EPIC (77238; "The Dave Clark
  Interviews"): *65* 40-45
I-N-S RADIO NEWS: *64* 60-80
Members: Dave Clark; Mike Smith; Lenny David-
son; Denny Payton; Rick Huxley.

CLARK, Dave, Five / Lulu
Singles: 7-Inch
EPIC (10260/65; "Everybody Knows"/
  "Best Of Both Worlds"): *67* $10-15
(Promotional issue only.)
Also see CLARK, Dave, Five
Also see LULU

CLARK, Dee
Singles: 7-Inch
ABC: *73* 1-3
ABNER (Monaural): *58-60* 4-6
ABNER (Stereo): *59-60* 10-15
CHELSEA: *75* 2-3
COLLECTABLES: *83* 1-3
ERIC: *73* 1-3
COLUMBIA: *67* 3-5
CONSTELLATION: *63-65* 3-5
FALCON: *58* 10-20
LIBERTY: *70* 2-3
MCA: *84* 1-3
VEE JAY (Monaural): *60-63* 4-6
VEE JAY (Stereo): *60-63* 10-15
UNITED ARTISTS: *71* 2-3
WAND: *68* 3-5
WARNER BROS: *73* 2-3
Picture Sleeves
ABNER: *59* 10-20
EPs: 7-Inch 33/45rpm
ABNER: *61* 35-45
VEE JAY: *61* 25-35
LPs: 10/12-Inch 33rpm
ABNER: *59-60* 30-40
SOLID SMOKE: *84* 5-8
SUNSET: *68* 10-12
VEE JAY: *60-64* 20-30

CLARK, Gene
(Gene Clark & The Gosdin Brothers)
Singles: 7-Inch
ASYLUM: *74* 2-3
COLUMBIA: *66* 3-5
RSO: *77* 1-3
Picture Sleeves
COLUMBIA: *80-81* 1-3
LPs: 10/12-Inch 33rpm
A&M: *71* 10-15
ASYLUM: *74* 8-10
COLUMBIA (2618; "Gene
  Clark"): *67* 20-30
(Monaural.)
COLUMBIA (9418; "Gene
  Clark"): *67* 20-30
(Stereo.)

Roy Clark in a 1963 photo

COLUMBIA (31123; "Early L.A.
  Sessions"): 72 .... $10-12
RSO: 77 5-8
TAKOMA: 84 5-8
  Also see BYRDS

CLARK, Petula
(Pet Clark)
Singles: 78rpm
CORAL: 53-54 4-8
Singles: 7-Inch
CORAL: 53-54 8-10
DUNHILL: 74 2-3
ERIC: 83 1-3
IMPERIAL: 59-60 4-6
JANUS: 76 2-3
KING: 54 8-10
LAURIE: 62-63 3-5
LONDON: 62 3-5
MGM (12000 series): 55 5-8
MGM (14000 series): 72-74 2-3
ROWE/AMI: 66 4-8
  ("Play Me" Sales Stimulator promotional issue.)
SCOTTI BROTHERS: 82 1-3
WARNER BROS: 64-69 2-4
WARWICK: 61 3-5
EPs: 7-Inch 33/45rpm
WARNER BROS: 65-66 4-8
  (Jukebox issues only.)
LPs: 10/12-Inch 33rpm
GNP/CRESCENDO: 73 8-10
IMPERIAL: 65 15-20
LAURIE: 65 15-20
MGM: 72 8-10
PREMIER: 64 15-20

SUNSET: 66 .... $10-12
WARNER BROS: 65-71 10-20

CLARK, Roy
Singles: 7-Inch
ABC: 74-79 1-3
ABC/DOT: 75-77 2-3
CAPITOL: 61-66 3-5
CHURCHILL: 82-84 1-3
DOT: 68-74 2-4
MCA: 79-84 1-3
SILVER DOLLAR: 86 1-3
SONGBIRD: 81 1-3
TOWER: 67 2-4
LPs: 10/12-Inch 33rpm
ABC: 77-79 5-10
ABC/DOT: 74-77 6-10
CAPITOL (300 series): 69 10-12
CAPITOL (1700 through 2500
  series): 62-66 12-18
  (With a "T" or "ST" prefix.)
CAPITOL (2400 series): 81 5-8
  (With an "SM" prefix.)
CAPITOL (11000 series): 74-75 8-12
CAPITOL (12000 through 16000
  series): 80-81 5-8
CHURCHILL: 82 5-8
DOT: 68-74 8-12
MCA: 79-84 4-8
PICKWICK/HILLTOP: 66 10-15
SONGBIRD: 81 5-8
TOWER: 67-68 10-15
WORD: 75 5-8

CLARK, Sanford
Singles: 78rpm
DOT: 56 5-10
MCI (1003; "The Fool"): 55 20-30
Singles: 7-Inch
ABC: 74 1-3
DOT (15000 series): 56 10-20
  (Maroon label.)
DOT (15000 series,
  except 15738): 56-58 8-15
  (Black label.)
DOT (15738; "Modern
  Romance"): 58 40-50
JAMIE: 58-60 5-8
LHI: 67-68 3-5
MCI (1003; "The Fool"): 55 40-50
RAMCO: 66 4-6
TREY: 61 3-5
WARNER BROS: 64-65 3-5
  Also see CASEY, Al

CLARK, Sanford, & Duane Eddy
Singles: 7-Inch
JAMIE (1107; "Sing 'Em Some
Blues"): 58 ....$10-15
  Also see CLARK, Sanford
  Also see EDDY, Duane

CLARK SISTERS
Singles: 12-Inch 33/45rpm
ELEKTRA: 83 4-6
Singles: 7-Inch
ELEKTRA: 83 1-3

CLARKE, Allan
Singles: 7-Inch
ASYLUM: 76 2-3
ATLANTIC: 78 2-3
ELEKTRA: 80 1-3
EPIC: 72 2-4
LPs: 10/12-Inch 33rpm
ASYLUM: 76 8-10
ATLANTIC: 78 5-8
ELEKTRA: 80 5-8
EPIC: 72 10-12
  Also see HOLLIES

CLARKE, Stanley
(Stan Clarke)
Singles: 12-Inch 33/45rpm
EPIC: 83-85 4-6
NEMPEROR: 79 4-6
Singles: 7-Inch
EPIC: 80-85 1-3
NEMPEROR: 75-79 2-3
LPs: 10/12-Inch 33rpm
EPIC: 80-85 5-8
NEMPEROR: 74-78 8-10
POLYDOR: 73 10-12
  Also see RETURN TO FOREVER

CLARKE, Stanley, & George
Duke
Singles: 12-Inch 33/45rpm
EPIC: 83 4-6
Singles: 7-Inch
EPIC: 81-84 1-3
LPs: 10/12-Inch 33rpm
EPIC: 81-83 5-8
  Also see CLARKE, Stanley
  Also see DUKE, George

CLARKE, Tony
Singles: 7-Inch
CHESS: 64-65 3-5
CHICKORY: 70 2-4

ERIC: 78 ....$1-3
M-S: 68 3-5

CLASH
Singles: 12-Inch 33/45rpm
EPIC: 81-82 5-10
Singles: 7-Inch
EPIC (1178; "Gates Of The
West"): 79 4-6
(Promotional issue only.)
EPIC (50000 series, except
50738): 79-85 1-3
EPIC (50738; "White Man In
Hammersmith Palais"): 79 5-8
LPs: 10/12-Inch 33rpm
EPIC (952; "If Music Could Talk"): 81 .. 15-20
(Promotional issue only.)
EPIC (30000 series, except
37037): 78-85 5-8
EPIC (37037; "Sandinista"): 82 10-12
EPIC/NU-DISC: 80 10-15
  Members: Mick Jones; Joe Strummer; Nick Shep-
  pard; Pete Howard; Vince White.
  Also see BIG AUDIO DYNAMITE

CLASSIC SULLIVANS
Singles: 7-Inch
KWANZA: 73 2-3

CLASSICS
Singles: 7-Inch
ALCAR: 63 15-25
STARR (508; "Close Your Eyes"): 60 .. 75-100
  Members: Lou Christie; Kay Chick; Shirley Her-
  bert; Ken Krease.
  Also see CHRISTIE, Lou
  Also see LUGEE & THE LIONS

CLASSICS

Singles: 7-Inch

COLLECTABLES: *83* $1-3
DART: *60-61* 10-15
ERIC: *82* 1-3
MERCURY: *61* 10-15
MUSIC NOTE: *63* 4-6
MUSICTONE: 4-6
PICCOLO: *65* 3-5
STORK: *64* 3-6
STREAM LINE: *61* 3-5
Members: Emil Stuccio; Tony Victor; John Gamble; Jamie Troy.

CLASSICS IV
(Dennis Yost & The Classics IV; Classics)

Singles: 7-Inch

ARLEN: *64* 10-15
CAPITOL: *66-67* 8-10
IMPERIAL: *67-70* 3-5
LIBERTY: *70* 2-4
MGM: *75* 2-3
MGM/SOUTH: *72-73* 2-3
UNITED ARTISTS: *71* 2-3

LPs: 10/12-Inch 33rpm

ACCORD: *81* ....,..... 5-8
IMPERIAL: *68-69* 12-15
LIBERTY (10000 series): *82-83* 5-8
LIBERTY (11000 series): *70* 10-12
MGM/SOUNDS OF THE SOUTH: *73* ... 8-10
SUNSET: *70* 10-12
UNITED ARTISTS: *75* 8-10
Members: Dennis Yost; James Cobb; Dean Daughtry; Wally Eaton; Auburn Burrell; Kim Venable; Joe Wilson.
Also see ATLANTA RHYTHM SECTION
Also see CANDYMEN
Also see YOST, Dennis

CLAY, Cassius
(Cassius Marcellus Clay Jr.; Muhammed Ali)

Singles: 7-Inch

COLUMBIA (43007; "Stand By Me"): *64* 10-15
COLUMBIA (75717; "Will The Real Sonny Liston Please Fall Down"): *64* 25-35
(Promotional issue only.)

Picture Sleeves

COLUMBIA (43007; "Stand By Me"): *64* 20-30

LPs: 10/12-Inch 33rpm

COLUMBIA: *63* 30-45

CLAY, Judy

Singles: 7-Inch

ATLANTIC: *69-70* $2-3
EMBER: *61-62* 3-5
SCEPTER: *64-66* 3-5
STAX: *68-69* 2-4
Also see BELL, William, & Judy Clay
Also see VERA, Billy, & Judy Clay

CLAY, Otis

Singles: 7-Inch

COTILLION: *68-71* 2-4
DAKAR: *69* 2-4
ELKA: *75* 2-3
HI: *72-73* 2-3
KAYVETTE: *77* 2-3
ONE-DERFUL: *65-67* 3-5

LPs: 10/12-Inch 33rpm

HI: *73-77* 8-10

CLAY, Tom
(Tom Clay & The Blackberries)

Singles: 7-Inch

BIG TOP: *60* 4-6
CHANT: 5-8
MOTOWN: *81* 1-3
MOWEST: *71* 2-4

LPs: 10/12-Inch 33rpm

MOWEST: *71* 10-12

CLAYDERMAN, Richard

LPs: 10/12-Inch 33rpm

COLUMBIA: *84* 4-8

CLAYTON, Merry

Singles: 7-Inch

CAPITOL: *63-65* 3-5
MCA: *80* 1-3
ODE '70: *70-76* 2-3

LPs: 10/12-Inch 33rpm

MCA: *80* 5-8
ODE (34000 series): *77* 5-8
ODE (77000 series): *71-75* 10-12
RCA: *88* 5-8
Also see BEACH BOYS
Also see SCOTT, Tom
Also see SMITH, Leslie, & Merry Clayton
Also see WYCOFF, Michael

CLAYTON, Willie

Singles: 7-Inch

COMPLEAT: *85* 1-3

CLAYTON-THOMAS, David

Singles: 7-Inch

COLUMBIA: *72* 2-4

DECCA: 69 .... $2-5
RCA VICTOR: 73 2-4
     LPs: 10/12-Inch 33rpm
ABC: 78 5-8
COLUMBIA: 72 10-12
DECCA: 69 15-18
RCA VICTOR: 73-74 8-10
  Also see BLOOD, SWEAT & TEARS

CLEAN LIVING
     Singles: 7-Inch
VANGUARD: 72 2-4
     LPs: 10/12-Inch 33rpm
VANGUARD: 72-73 8-10

CLEAR LIGHT
     Singles: 7-Inch
ELEKTRA: 67 3-5
     LPs: 10/12-Inch 33rpm
ELEKTRA: 67 12-15
  Members: Cliff DeYoung; Douglas Lubahn;
  Michael Ney; Ralph Schuckett; Bob Seal; Dallas
  Taylor.

CLEFS OF LAVENDER HILL
     Singles: 7-Inch
DATE: 66-67 8-12
THAMES: 66 8-12

CLEFTONES
     Singles: 78rpm
GEE: 56-57 5-10
     Singles: 7-Inch
ABC: 73 1-3
GEE (Red label): 56-58 10-12
GEE (Gray label): 61-63 3-6
ROULETTE: 58-60 4-8
WARE: 64 3-6
     LPs: 10/12-Inch 33rpm
GEE (705; "Heart & Soul"): 61 100-200
GEE (707; "For Sentimental
  Reasons"): 62 100-200
  (Monaural.)
GEE (707; "For Sentimental
  Reasons"): 62 150-250
  (Stereo.)
  Members: Herbie Cox; Berman Patterson; Bill Mc-
  Clain; Charles James; Warren Corbin; Pat Span;
  Eugene Pearson.
  Also see HARPTONES / Cleftones

CLEMMONS, Angela
     Singles: 12-Inch 33/45rpm
PORTRAIT: 82 4-6
     Singles: 7-Inch
EPIC: 80 2-4

PORTRAIT: 82-87 .... $1-3
     LPs: 10/12-Inch 33rpm
PORTRAIT: 82 5-8

CLEMONS, Clarence
(Clarence Clemons & The Red Bank Rockers)
     Singles: 7-Inch
COLUMBIA: 83-85 1-3
     LPs: 10/12-Inch 33rpm
COLUMBIA: 83-85 5-8
  Also see BROWNE, Jackson
  Also see FRANKLIN, Aretha
  Also see SPRINGSTEEN, Bruce

CLIFF, Jimmy
     Singles: 12-Inch 33/45rpm
COLUMBIA: 83-84 4-6
     Singles: 7-Inch
A&M: 69-70 2-4
COLUMBIA: 82-84 1-3
MANGO: 73 2-3
MCA: 81 1-3
REPRISE: 74-77 2-3
VEEP: 67-68 3-5
     LPs: 10/12-Inch 33rpm
A&M: 70 12-15
COLUMBIA: 82 5-8
ISLAND: 74 8-10
MCA: 80-81 5-8
REPRISE: 73 76 8-10
VEEP: 69 15-20
WARNER BROS: 78 5-8

CLIFFORD, Buzz
     Singles: 7-Inch
BOW: 4-6
CAPITOL: 67 2-4
COLUMBIA (41876; "Baby Sittin'
  Boogie"): 60 10-15
  (With a "3" prefix. Compact 33 Single.)
COLUMBIA (41979; "Simply
  Because"): 61 25-30
  (With a "3" prefix. Compact 33 Single.)
COLUMBIA (42019; "I'll Never
  Forget"): 61 25-30
  (With a "3" prefix. Compact 33 Single.)
COLUMBIA (42290; "Forever"): 62 25-30
  (With a "3" prefix. Compact 33 Single.)
COLUMBIA (41774; "Hello Mr.
  Moonlight"): 60 8-10
  (With a "4" prefix.)
COLUMBIA (41876; "Baby Sitter
  Boogie"): 60 15-20
  (Note slightly different title. With a "4" prefix.)

COLUMBIA (41876; "Baby Sittin'
  Boogie"): *61* $3-5
(With a "4" prefix.)
COLUMBIA (41979; "Simply
  Because"): *61* 15-20
(With a "4" prefix.)
COLUMBIA (42019; "I'll Never
  Forget"): *61* 15-20
(With a "4" prefix.)
COLUMBIA (42177; "Moving
  Day"): *61* 3-5
(With a "4" prefix.)
COLUMBIA (42290; "Forever"): *62* 15-20
(With a "4" prefix.)
DOT: *69-70* 2-3
ERIC: *83* 1-3
RCA VICTOR: *66* 2-4
ROULETTE: *62-63* 4-6
Picture Sleeves
COLUMBIA: *61-62* 15-20
LPs: 10/12-Inch 33rpm
COLUMBIA (1616; "Baby Sittin'
  Boogie"): *61* 40-50
(Monaural.)
COLUMBIA (8416; "Baby Sittin'
  Boogie"): *61* 50-60
(Monaural.)
DOT: *69* 12-15

CLIFFORD, Linda
Singles: 12-Inch 33/45rpm
CAPITOL: *82* 4-6
RSO: *79* 4-6
RED LABEL: *85* 4-6
Singles: 7-Inch
CAPITOL: *80-82* 1-3
CURTOM: *77-78* 2-3
GEMIGO: *75* 2-3
PARAMOUNT: *74* 2-3
POLYDOR: *73* 2-3
RSO: *79-80* 1-3
RED LABEL: *84-85* 1-3
LPs: 10/12-Inch 33rpm
CAPITOL: *80-82* 5-8
CURTOM: *77-80* 8-10
RSO: *79-80* 5-8
Also see MAYFIELD, Curtis, & Linda Clifford

CLIFFORD, Mike
Singles: 7-Inch
AIR: *71* 2-4
AMERICAN INT'L: *70* 2-4
CAMEO: *65-66* 3-5

COLUMBIA: *61-62* $3-5
LIBERTY: *59* 3-5
SIDEWALK: *67-68* 2-5
UNITED ARTISTS: *62-65* 3-5
Picture Sleeves
COLUMBIA: *61* 4-8
LPs: 10/12-Inch 33rpm
UNITED ARTISTS: *65* 15-20

CLIFFORD, Mike, & Patience & Prudence
Singles: 7-Inch
LIBERTY: *59* 3-5
Also see CLIFFORD, Mike
Also see PATIENCE & PRUDENCE

CLIMAX
Singles: 7-Inch
ARISTA: *81* 1-3
BELL: *71* 2-3
CAROUSEL: *70-71* 2-3
FLASHBACK: *73* 1-3
PARAMOUNT: *70* 2-4
PATTI PLATTERS: *67* 3-5
ROCKY ROAD: *72* 2-3
LPs: 10/12-Inch 33rpm
ROCKY ROAD: *72* 12-15
Members: Sonny Geraci; John Bahler; Tom Bahler;
Jon Jon Gultman; Walt Nims.
Also see LOVE GENERATION
Also see OUTSIDERS

CLIMAX BLUES BAND
Singles: 7-Inch
SIRE: *71-79* 2-3
WARNER BROS: *79-82* 1-3
LPs: 10/12-Inch 33rpm
SIRE (Except 6000 series): *69-76* 10-15
SIRE (6000 series): *77-78* 8-10
VIRGIN: *83* 5-8
WARNER BROS: *79-81* 5-8
Members: The Climax Chicago Blues Band; Colin
Cooper; John Cuffley; Peter Haycock; Derek Holt;
Richard Jones; Arthur Wood.

CLINE, Patsy
Singles: 78rpm
CORAL: *55-56* 5-10
DECCA: *57* 5-10
Singles: 7-Inch
CORAL: *55-56* 5-10
DECCA (25000 series): *65-69* 3-5
DECCA (29963 through 30846): *57-59* 4-8
DECCA (30929; "Gotta Lot Of
  Rhythm In My Soul"): *59* 8-12

DECCA (31000 series): 59-64 .... $3-6
EVEREST (2000 series): 62-64 3-5
EVEREST (20005; "I Don't
Wanta"): 62 8-12
FOUR STAR (Except 1000 series): 56 5-10
FOUR STAR (1000 series): 78 1-3
KAPP: 65 4-8
MCA: 73-80 1-3
STARDAY (7000 series): 65 3-5
STARDAY (8000 series): 71 1-3
Picture Sleeves
DECCA: 57-63 8-15
EPs: 7-Inch 33/45rpm
CORAL: 58 15-30
DECCA: 57-65 10-20
FOUR STAR: 57 20-35
(Promotional issue only.)
PATSY CLINE: 57 20-30
LPs: 10/12-Inch 33rpm
ACCORD: 81 5-8
ALBUM GLOBE: 5-8
ALLEGIANCE: 84 5-8
COLUMBIA: 69 12-15
(Columbia Musical Treasury issue.)
COUNTRY FIDELITY: 82 5-8
DECCA (4200 series): 61-62 20-25
DECCA (4500 series): 64 15-20
DECCA (4800 series): 67 10-15
DECCA (8600 series): 57 25-35
EVEREST (300 series): 75 5-8
EVEREST (1200 series): 62-64 15-20
51 WEST: 82 5-8
H.S.R.D.: 84 8-10
LONGINES: 8-12
MCA: 80-85 5-10
METRO: 65 12-18
PICKWICK/HILLTOP: 65-68 10-12
SEARS: 10-15

VOCALION: 65-69 .... $10-15
Also see HAGGARD, Merle / Patsy Cline
Also see REEVES, Jim, & Patsy Cline

CLINE, Patsy / Cowboy Copas / Hawkshaw Hawkins
LPs: 10/12-Inch 33rpm
STARDAY: 65 12-18
Also see COPAS, Cowboy
Also see HAWKINS, Hawkshaw

CLINE, Patsy / Pete Pike / Jack Bradshaw / Miller Brothers
EPs: 45rpm
FOUR STAR (137; "Come On
In"): 56 10-20
(10-Inch EP.)
Also see CLINE, Patsy

CLINTON, George
(George Clinton Band)
Singles: 12-Inch 33/45rpm
CAPITOL: 82-86 4-6
Singles: 7-Inch
ABC: 74 2-3
CAPITOL: 83-86 1-3
LPs: 10/12-Inch 33rpm
ABC: 74 8-10
CAPITOL: 82-86 5-8
INVICTUS: 73 10-12
Also see PARLIAMENTS

CLIQUE
Singles: 7-Inch
ABC: 73 1-3
CINEMA: 67 5-10
SCEPTER: 67 5-10
WHITE WHALE: 69-71 4-8
LPs: 10/12-Inch 33rpm
WHITE WHALE: 69 20-25

CLIQUES
Singles: 78rpm
MODERN: 56 8-12
Singles: 7-Inch
MODERN: 56 15-20
Members: Jesse Belvin; Eugene Church.
Also see BELVIN, Jesse
Also see CHURCH, Eugene

CLOCKS
Singles: 7-Inch
BOULEVARD: 82 1-3
LPs: 10/12-Inch 33rpm
BOULEVARD: 82 5-8

CLOCKWORK
Singles: 12-Inch 33/45rpm
PRIVATE 1: *84* $4-6
Singles: 7-Inch
PRIVATE 1: *84* 1-3

CLOONEY, Rosemary
Singles: 78rpm
COLUMBIA: *50-57* 3-5
Singles: 7-Inch
APCO: *75* 1-3
COLUMBIA (38000 through 40000
  series): *50-57* 5-10
CORAL: *59* 2-4
DOT: *68* 2-3
GIBSON/COLUMBIA: *55* 8-15
(A "Musicard," with fold-out cover.)
MGM: *59-65* 2-4
RCA VICTOR: *60-61* 2-4
REPRISE: *63-64* 2-4
SATURDAY EVENING POST (1055;
  "Hollywood's Favorite
  Songbird"): *54* 10-20
(Promotional issue only. Includes interview script.)
Picture Sleeves
RCA VICTOR: *60* 3-6
EPs: 7-Inch 33/45rpm
COLUMBIA: *51-56* 10-20
MGM: *58-60* 5-10
LPs: 10/12-Inch 33rpm
COLUMBIA (500 through 1200
  series): *54-58* 15-25
CONCORD JAZZ: *78-83* 5-8
CORAL: *59* 10-15
HARMONY: *59-68* 8-12
MGM (Except 1000 series): *59-62* 10-15
MGM (1000 series): *67* 8-12
RCA VICTOR: *60-63* 10-12

REPRISE: *63-64* $8-12
Also see BOYD, Jimmy, & Rosemary Clooney
Also see CROSBY, Bing, Louis Armstrong,
Rosemary Clooney & The Hi-Los
Also see CROSBY, Bing, & Rosemary
Clooney
Also see GOODMAN, Benny, Trio, With
Rosemary Clooney
Also see HERMAN, Woody

CLOONEY, Rosemary, & Bing Crosby
Singles: 7-Inch
RCA VICTOR: *59* 3-5
LPs: 10/12-Inch 33rpm
CAMDEN: *69* 5-10
CAPITOL (2300 series): *65* 8-12
CAPITOL (11000 series): *77* 5-8
RCA VICTOR: *58* 10-15
Also see CROSBY, Bing
Also see CROSBY, Bing, Louis Armstrong,
Rosemary Clooney & The Hi-Los

CLOONEY, Rosemary, & Jose Ferrer
EPs: 7-Inch 33/45rpm
MGM: *58* 10-18
Also see FERRER, Jose

CLOONEY, Rosemary, & Dick Haymes
LPs: 10/12-Inch 33rpm
EXACT: *80* 5-8
Also see HAYMES, Dick

CLOONEY, Rosemary, & Guy Mitchell
(With Joanne Gilbert)
EPs: 7-Inch 33/45rpm
COLUMBIA (377; "Red Garters"): *54* . . . 10-18
(Soundtrack.)
LPs: 10/12-Inch 33rpm
COLUMBIA (6282; "Red
  Garters"): *54* 40-50
(10-Inch LP. Soundtrack.)
Also see MITCHELL, Guy

CLOONEY, Rosemary, & Perez Prado
Singles: 7-Inch
RCA VICTOR: *60* 2-4
LPs: 10/12-Inch 33rpm
RCA VICTOR: *60* 10-12
Also see CLOONEY, Rosemary
Also see PRADO, Perez

CLOUD, Christopher
(Tommy Boyce)
Singles: 7-Inch
CHELSEA: *72-73* 2-4
LPs: 10/12-Inch 33rpm
CHELSEA: *73* 10-15

Also see BOYCE, Tommy

CLOUT
Singles: 7-Inch
EPIC: 78-79 .... $2-3
LPs: 10/12-Inch 33rpm
EPIC: 79-80 5-8

CLOVERS
Singles: 78rpm
ATLANTIC (900 series): 51-53 20-40
ATLANTIC (1000 series): 53-56 5-15
RAINBOW: 51 100-150
Singles: 7-Inch
ATLANTIC (900 series,
except 934 & 944): 52-53 25-50
ATLANTIC (934; "Don't You Know
I Love You"): 51 75-100
ATLANTIC (944; "Fool, Fool,
Fool"): 51 50-75
ATLANTIC (1000 series,
except 1000): 53-56 10-20
ATLANTIC (1000; "Good Lovin"): 53 .. 30-40
ATLANTIC (1100 series): 56-58 5-10
ATLANTIC (2000 series): 61 3-6
BRUNSWICK: 63 3-5
JOSIE: 68 3-5
POPLAR: 58 8-15
PORT: 65 3-5
PORWIN: 63 3-5
RIPETE: 88 2-3
UNITED ARTISTS: 59-61 4-8
WINLEY: 61-62 3-5
EPs: 7-Inch 33/45rpm
ATLANTIC (504; "The Clovers
Sing"): 56 60-100
ATLANTIC (537; "The Clovers
Sing"): 56 60-100
ATLANTIC (590; "The Clovers
Sing"): 57 50-75
LPs: 10/12-Inch 33rpm
ATCO: 71 10-12
ATLANTIC (1248; "The
Clovers"): 56 100-200
ATLANTIC (8009; "The
Clovers"): 57 75-100
(Black label.)
ATLANTIC (8009; "The
Clovers"): 59 25-40
(Red label.)
ATLANTIC (8034; "The Clovers'
Dance Party"): 59 25-50
GRAND PRIX: 64 10-12
POPLAR (1001; "The Clovers In

Clover"): 58 .... $50-80
TRIP: 72 8-10
UNITED ARTISTS: 59-60 35-45
Members: John "Buddy" Bailey; Harold Winley;
Hal Lucas; Bill Harris; Matthew McQuater; Charlie
White; Billy Mitchell.
Also see JACKSON, Willis
Also see KING CURTIS
Also see MITCHELL, Billy

CLUB HOUSE
Singles: 12-Inch 33/45rpm
ATLANTIC: 83 4-6
Singles: 7-Inch
ATLANTIC: 83 1-3

CLUB NOUVEAU
Singles: 12-Inch 33/45rpm
WARNER BROS: 86 4-6
Singles: 7-Inch
TOMMY BOY: 88 1-3
WARNER BROS: 86-88 1-3
LPs: 10/12-Inch 33rpm
WARNER BROS: 86-88 5-8

COASTERS
Singles: 78rpm
ATCO: 56-57 5-10
Singles: 7-Inch
ATCO (6000 series): 56 15-20
(Maroon label.)
ATCO (6000 series): 56-57 5-10
(Yellow & white label.)
ATCO (6100 series): 57-61 4-8
ATCO (6200 through 6400
series): 61-66 3-5
DATE: 67-68 3-5
KING: 71-73 2-4
TURNTABLE: 69 3-5
EPs: 7-Inch 33/45rpm
ATCO: 58-59 25-45
LPs: 10/12-Inch 33rpm
ATCO (100 series, except 101): 59-71 .. 20-30
ATCO (101; "The Coasters"): 58 35-50
(Yellow label.)
ATCO (101; "The Coasters"): 59 20-30
(Yellow & white label.)
ATCO (300 series): 71 10-12
ATLANTIC: 82 10-12
CLARION: 64 12-15
KING: 71 10-12
POWER PAK: 83 5-8
TRIP: 72-76 8-10
Members: Bobby Nunn; Leon Hughes; Carl
Gardner; Billy Guy; Adolph Jacobs; Cornel

Gunter; Will Jones; Earl Carroll; Ronnie Bright; Jimmy Norman.
Also see HENDRICKS, Bobby
Also see KING CURTIS
Also see NORMAN, Jimmy
Also see NUNN, Bobby
Also see ROBINS

COASTERS / Crew-Cuts / Chiffons
LPs: 10/12-Inch 33rpm
EXACT: *80* $5-8
Also see CHIFFONS
Also see CREW-CUTS

COASTERS / Drifters
LPs: 10/12-Inch 33rpm
TVP: 10-12
(A TV mail-order LP offer.)
Also see DRIFTERS

COATES, Odia
Singles: 12-Inch 33/45rpm
EPIC: *77* 4-6
Singles: 7-Inch
BUDDAH: *73* 2-3
EPIC: *78* 2-3
UNITED ARTISTS: *74-75* 2-3
LPs: 10/12-Inch 33rpm
UNITED ARTISTS: *75* 8-10
Also see ANKA, Paul, & Odia Coates

COBB, Joyce
Singles: 7-Inch
CREAM: *79-80* 1-3
TRUTH: *75* 2-3

COBHAM, Billy
(Billy Cobham's Glass Menagerie; Billy Cobham With The George Duke Band)
Singles: 12-Inch 33/45rpm
COLUMBIA: *80* 4-6
Singles: 7-Inch
ATLANTIC: *75-77* 2-3
COLUMBIA: *78-80* 1-3
LPs: 10/12-Inch 33rpm
ATLANTIC: *73-79* 5-8
COLUMBIA: *77-80* 5-8
ELEKTRA: *82-83* 5-8
Also see DUKE, George
Also see SINGLETON, Charlie

COCA-NUTS
Singles: 7-Inch
"BRING IT BACK!": *86* 3-5
(No label name is given on this release.)

COCCIANTE, Richard
Singles: 7-Inch
20TH CENTURY-FOX: *76* $1-3
LPs: 10/12-Inch 33rpm
20TH CENTURY-FOX: *76* 5-8

COCHISE
Singles: 7-Inch
UNITED ARTISTS: *71* 2-4
EPs: 7-Inch 33/45rpm
UNITED ARTISTS: *71* 10-12
LPs: 10/12-Inch 33rpm
UNITED ARTISTS: *71* 10-12
Member: Mick Grabham.

COCHRAN, Eddie
Singles: 78rpm
CREST (1026; "Skinny Jim"): *56* 50-100
LIBERTY: *57* 10-15
Singles: 7-Inch
CAPEHART: *60* 10-20
CREST (1026; "Skinny Jim"): *56* 100-150
LIBERTY (54000 series): *62* 5-10
LIBERTY (55056; "Sittin' In The Balcony"): *57* 10-20
LIBERTY (55070; "Mean When I'm Mad"): *58* 10-20
LIBERTY (55087; "Drive In Show"): *57* 10-20
LIBERTY (55112; "Twenty Flight Rock"): *58* 15-25
LIBERTY (55123; "Jeannie Jeannie Jeannie"): *58* 15-25
LIBERTY (55138; "Pretty Girl"): *58* 10-20
LIBERTY (55144; "Summertime Blues"): *58* 10-20
LIBERTY (55166; "C'mon Everybody"): *58* 10-20
LIBERTY (55177; "Teenage Heaven"): *59* 10-20
LIBERTY (55203; "Somethin' Else"): *59* 10-20
(With horizontal silver lines.)
LIBERTY (55203; "Somethin' Else"): *59* 5-10
(Without horizontal silver lines.)
LIBERTY (55217; "Hallelujah, I Love Her So"): *59* 5-10
LIBERTY (55242; "Cut Across Shorty"): *60* 10-20
(Green label.)
LIBERTY (55242; "Cut Across Shorty"): *61* 5-10
(Black label.)

LIBERTY (55278; "Sweetie Pie"): *60* . . . **$8-12**
LIBERTY (55389; "Weekend"): *61* **15-25**
Picture Sleeves
CAPEHART: *60* **25-35**
LIBERTY (55070; "Mean When
I'm Mad"): *58* **75-100**
EPs: 7-Inch 33/45rpm
LIBERTY (3061; "Singin' To
My Baby"): *58* **75-100**
(Price is for any of three volumes with this title.)
LPs: 10/12-Inch 33rpm
LIBERTY (3000 series,
except 3061): *60-62* **40-50**
LIBERTY (3061; "Singin' To
My Baby"): *58* **100-200**
(Green label.)
LIBERTY (3061; "Singin' To
My Baby"): *60* **25-30**
(Black label.)
LIBERTY (10000 series): *81-83* **5-8**
SUNSET: *66* **12-15**
UNITED ARTISTS: *71-75* **10-12**
Also see COCHRAN BROTHERS

COCHRAN, Hank
Singles: 7-Inch
CAPITOL: *78* **1-3**
DOT: *70* **2-3**
ELEKTRA: *80* **1-3**
GAYLORD: *62-63* **3-5**
LIBERTY: *62-63* **3-6**
MONUMENT: *67-68* **2-3**
RCA VICTOR: *64-66* **2-4**
LPs: 10/12-Inch 33rpm
CAPITOL: *78* **5-8**
ELEKTRA: *80* **5-8**
MONUMENT: *68* **10-12**
RCA VICTOR: *65* **12-18**
Also see COCHRAN BROTHERS

COCHRAN, Hank, & Willie Nelson
Singles: 7-Inch
CAPITOL: *78* **1-3**
Also see COCHRAN, Hank
Also see NELSON, Willie

COCHRAN, Wayne
(Wayne Cochran & The C.C. Riders)
Singles: 7-Inch
BETHLEHEM: *70* **2-4**
CHESS: *67-68* **3-5**
DECK: **2-4**
EPIC: *72* **2-4**
KING (5000 series): *63-65* **4-8**
KING (6000 series): *65-71* **3-6**

MERCURY: *65-67* **$3-5**
SCOTTIE: *59* **8-12**
SOFT: *65* **3-5**
Picture Sleeves
CHESS: *67* **3-6**
MERCURY: *65* **4-8**
LPs: 10/12-Inch 33rpm
BETHLEHEM: *70* **12-15**
CHESS: *68* **20-30**
EPIC: *72* **8-10**
KING: *70* **15-25**

COCHRAN BROTHERS
Singles: 78rpm
EKKO (1000 series): *56* **30-45**
EKKO (3001; "Tired &
Sleepy"): *56* **50-100**
Singles: 7-Inch
EKKO (1000 series): *56* **60-85**
EKKO (3001; "Tired &
Sleepy"): *56* **100-150**
Members: Eddie Cochran; Hank Cochran (not really brothers).
Also see COCHRAN, Eddie
Also see COCHRAN, Hank

COCHRANE, Tom, & Red Rider
Singles: 7-Inch
CAPITOL: *86* **1-3**
RCA: *88* **1-3**
LPs: 10/12-Inch 33rpm
CAPITOL: *86* **5-8**
RCA: *88* **5-8**
Also see RED RIDER

COCK ROBIN
Singles: 12-Inch 33/45rpm
COLUMBIA: *85* **4-6**
Singles: 7-Inch
COLUMBIA: *85* **1-3**
LPs: 10/12-Inch 33rpm
COLUMBIA: *85-87* **5-8**

COCKBURN, Bruce
Singles: 7-Inch
GOLD MOUNTAIN: *84* **1-3**
MCA: *86* **1-3**
MILLENNIUM: *80* **1-3**
LPs: 10/12-Inch 33rpm
EPIC: *71-72* **10-12**
GOLD MOUNTAIN: *84* **5-8**
ISLAND: *77-78* **8-10**
MCA: *86* **5-8**
MILLENNIUM: *80-81* **5-8**
TRUE NORTH: *77-78* **8-10**

Joe Cocker (Photo: Timothy White)

COCKER, Joe
Singles: 7-Inch
A&M: *68-78* $2-4
ASYLUM: *78-79* 2-3
CAPITOL: *84-88* 1-3
ISLAND: *83* 1-3
PHILIPS: *65* 6-10
Picture Sleeves
A&M: *69-74* 2-5
LPs: 10/12-Inch 33rpm
A&M (Except 3100 series): *69-77* 8-12
A&M (3100 series): *82* 5-8
ASYLUM (Except "Luxury You Can
  Afford" picture disc): *78-79* 5-8
ASYLUM ("Luxury You Can Afford"
  picture disc): *79* 20-30
  (Promotional issues only.)
CAPITOL: *84-87* 5-8
  Also see BOWIE, David / Joe Cocker /
Youngbloods
  Also see CRUSADERS
  Also see RUSSELL, Leon

COCKER, Joe, & Jennifer Warnes
Singles: 7-Inch
ISLAND: *82* 1-3
Picture Sleeves
ISLAND: *82* 1-3
  Also see COCKER, Joe
  Also see WARNES, Jennifer

COCO, El: see EL COCO

CODAY, Bill
Singles: 7-Inch
CRAYON: *71* 2-4
EPIC: *73-75* 2-3
GALAXY: *71* 2-4

CODY, Commander:
  see COMMANDER CODY

COE, David Allan
Singles: 7-Inch
COLUMBIA: *74-87* $1-3
SSS INT'L (Black vinyl): *71-72* 2-4
SSS INT'L (Colored vinyl): *71-72* 4-8
  (Promotional issues only.)
LPs: 10/12-Inch 33rpm
COLUMBIA: *72-86* 5-10
SSS INT'L (9; "Penitentiary
  Blues"): *70* 20-30
  Also see JONES, George, & David Allan Coe

COE, David Allan, & Bill Anderson
Singles: 7-Inch
COLUMBIA: *80* 1-3
  Also see ANDERSON, Bill

COE, David Allan, & Willie Nelson
Singles: 7-Inch
COLUMBIA: *86* 1-3
  Also see COE, David Allan
  Also see NELSON, Willie
  Also see NELSON, Willie / Jerry Lee Lewis /
Carl Perkins / David Allan Coe

COFFEE
Singles: 7-Inch
DELITE: *80-82* 1-3

COFFEY, Dennis
(Dennis Coffey & The Detroit Guitar Band; Dennis Coffey & Lyman Woodward Trio)
Singles: 7-Inch
MAVERICK: *69* 2-4
SUSSEX: *70-74* 2-3
WARNER BROS: *74* 2-3
20TH CENTURY/WESTBOUND: *75-76* ..2-3
WESTBOUND: *77-78* 1-3
LPs: 10/12-Inch 33rpm
SUSSEX: *70-75* 10-12
20TH CENTURY/WESTBOUND: *75-76* .8-10
WESTBOUND: *77* 5-8

COHEN, Leonard
Singles: 7-Inch
COLUMBIA: *68-73* 2-4
LPs: 10/12-Inch 33rpm
COLUMBIA: *68-85* 10-12
WARNER BROS: *77* 8-12

COHEN, Myron
LPs: 10/12-Inch 33rpm
RCA VICTOR: *66* 10-12

COLD BLOOD
Singles: 7-Inch
ABC: *75* 2-3

REPRISE: *72-73* $2-4
SAN FRANCISCO: *70* 3-5
LPs: 10/12-Inch 33rpm
ABC: *76* 8-10
REPRISE: *72-73* 10-12
SAN FRANCISCO: *69-70* 12-15
WARNER BROS: *74* 8-10
Members: Lydia Pense; Michael Andreas; Rod Ellicott; Frank Davis; Jerry Jonutz; Danny Hull; Larry Field.

COLD CHISEL
Singles: 7-Inch
ELEKTRA: *81* 1-3
LPs: 10/12-Inch 33rpm
ELEKTRA: *80-82* 5-8
Members: Jimmy Barnes; Don Walker; Steve Prestwich; Phil Small; Ian Moss.
Also see BARNES, Jimmy

COLDER, Ben
(Sheb Wooley)
Singles: 7-Inch
MGM: *62-73* 2-4
SUNBIRD: *80* 1-3
LPs: 10/12-Inch 33rpm
MGM (Except 4100 series): *66-73* 10-15
MGM (4100 series): *61-63* 15-20
Also see WOOLEY, Sheb

COLE, Ann
(Ann Cole & The Suburbans)
Singles: 78rpm
BATON: *56-57* 4-8
TIMELY: *54* 4-8
Singles: 7-Inch
BATON: *56-57* 5-8
MGM: *60* 3-5
ROULETTE: *62* 10-15
SIR: *59-60* 4-6
TIMELY: *54* 5-8

COLE, Bobby
Singles: 7-Inch
DATE: *68-69* 2-4

COLE, Cozy
(Cozy Cole & His All Stars; Cozy Cole & Gary Chester; Cozy Cole & Pete Johnson; Cozy Cole & Red Norvo)
Singles: 78rpm
MGM: *54* 3-6
Singles: 7-Inch
ARTISTIQUE: *61* 2-4
BETHLEHEM: *63* 2-4
CHARLIE PARKER: *62* 2-4

CORAL: *62-67* $3-6
KING: *59-60* 2-4
LOVE: *58-59* 4-8
MGM: *54* 4-6
RANDOM: *60* 2-4
Picture Sleeves
RANDOM: *60* 3-6
EPs: 7-Inch 33/45rpm
AFTER HOURS: *55* 15-20
MGM: *54* 15-20
LPs: 10/12-Inch 33rpm
AFTER HOURS: *55* 25-30
CHARLIE PARKER: *62* 15-20
COLUMBIA: *66* 10-15
CORAL: *62-64* 15-20
EVEREST: *74* 8-10
FELSTED: *59* 15-20
KING: *59-60* 20-25
LOVE: *59* 20-25
PARIS: *58* 20-25
SAVOY: *72-77* 8-12
TRIP: *74* 8-10

COLE, Cozy, & Illinois Jacquet
LPs: 10/12-Inch 33rpm
AUDITION: *55* 25-35
Also see COLE, Cozy
Also see JACQUET, Illinois

COLE, Nat "King"
(King Cole Trio)
Singles: 78rpm
CAPITOL (100 through 700
  series): *43-49* 5-10
CAPITOL (800 through 4600
  seriesl): *50-58* 3-5
CAPITOL (15000 series): *47-49* 3-8
DECCA (8000 series): *42* 10-20
EXCELSIOR: *45* 10-20
Singles: 7-Inch
CAPITOL (Except 800 through
  4600 series): *61-69* 3-5
CAPITOL (800 through 4600 series): *50-61*   4-8
(Purple labels.)
Picture Sleeves
CAPITOL: *59-66* 3-6
EPs: 7-Inch 33/45rpm
CAPITOL: *50-60* 5-10
LPs: 10/12-Inch 33rpm
CAPITOL (Except 100 through
  2900 series): *61-82* 5-10
CAPITOL (100 through 300
  series): *50-52* 20-35
(With an "H" prefix. 10-Inch LPs.)

MOODS IN SONG

Nat 'King' Cole

A BLOSSOM FELL

DARLING, JE VOUS
AIME BEAUCOUP

IF I MAY

THE SAND
AND THE SEA

CAPITOL (100 through 300
series): *52-53* $15-30
(With a "T" prefix.)
CAPITOL (400 through 2900
series): *52-68* 10-25
CROWN: *64* 8-12
DYNAMIC HOUSE: *72* 5-8
MCA: *73* 5-8
MARK '56: *76* 5-8
MONARCH ("Nat 'King' Cole"): *53* . . . 75-100
(Colored vinyl.)
PICKWICK: 4-8
SCORE: *57* 15-20
VSP: *66* 10-15
  Also see FOUR KNIGHTS
  Also see KENTON, Stan
  Also see MARTIN, Dean, & Nat "King" Cole
  Also see PRESLEY, Elvis / Frank Sinatra /
Nat King Cole

COLE, Nat "King," & Stubby Kaye
Singles: 7-Inch
CAPITOL: *65* 2-3
Picture Sleeves
CAPITOL: *65* 3-6

COLE, Nat "King," & George Shearing
LPs: 10/12-Inch 33rpm
CAPITOL: *61* 15-25
  Also see COLE, Nat "King"
  Also see SHEARING, George

COLE, Natalie
(Natalie Cole & George Shearing)
Singles: 12-Inch 33/45rpm
EPIC: *83* 4-6
MODERN: *85* 4-6
Singles: 7-Inch
CAPITOL: *75-80* 2-3
EPIC: *83* 1-3

E.M.I./MANHATTAN: *87-88* $1-3
MODERN: *85* 1-3
LPs: 10/12-Inch 33rpm
CAPITOL: *75-82* 8-12
EPIC: *83* 5-8
MANHATTAN: *87* 5-8
MFSL: *79-82* 25-50
MODERN: *85* 5-8
  Also see BRYSON, Peabo, & Natalie Cole

COLE, Sami Jo
Singles: 7-Inch
ELEKTRA: *81* 1-3

COLE, Tony
Singles: 7-Inch
20TH CENTURY-FOX: *73-74* 2-3
LPs: 10/12-Inch 33rpm
20TH CENTURY-FOX: *73* 8-10

COLEMAN, Albert
(Albert Coleman's Atlanta Pops)
Singles: 7-Inch
EPIC: *82* 1-3

COLEMAN, Durell
Singles: 7-Inch
ISLAND: *85* 1-3
LPs: 10/12-Inch 33rpm
ISLAND: *85* 5-8

COLICCHIO, Victor
Singles: 12-Inch 33/45rpm
3C: *88* 5-10
(With cover.)

COLLAGE
Singles: 12-Inch 33/45rpm
CONSTELLATION: *86* 4-6
MCA: *85* 4-6
SOLAR: *83* 4-6
Singles: 7-Inch
CONSTELLATION: *86* 1-3
MCA: *85* 1-3
SOLAR: *82-83* 1-3
LPs: 10/12-Inch 33rpm
CONSTELLATION: *86* 5-8
SOLAR: *81-83* 5-8

COLLAY & THE SATELLITES
Singles: 7-Inch
SHO-BIZ: *60* 10-12

COLLEY, Keith
Singles: 7-Inch
CHALLENGE: *66-70* 3-5
COLUMBIA: *68* 2-4
ERA: *61-62* 3-5

UNICAL: *63-64* $3-5
VEE JAY: *65* 3-5

COLLIER, Mitty
Singles: 7-Inch
CHESS: *61-68* 3-5
ENTRANCE: *72* 2-4
ERIC: *78* 1-3
PEACHTREE: *69-70* 2-4
LPs: 10/12-Inch 33rpm
CHESS: *65-66* 15-20
GOSPEL ROOTS: *79* 5-8

COLLINS, Albert
(Albert Collins & The Ice Breakers)
Singles: 7-Inch
GREAT SCOTT: 10-15
HALL: *64* 4-6
HALL WAY: *63* 5-8
IMPERIAL: *69* 2-4
KANGAROO: *58* 12-20
LIBERTY: *70* 2-4
TCF HALL: *65-66* 3-5
TUMBLEWEED: *72-73* 2-3
20TH CENTURY-FOX: *68* 2-4
LPs: 10/12-Inch 33rpm
ALLIGATOR: *79-84* 5-8
BLUE THUMB: *69* 10-12
BRYLEN: *84* 5-8
IMPERIAL: *69-70* 10-12
TCF HALL: *65* 30-35
TUMBLEWEED: *71* 10-12

COLLINS, Albert, Robert Cray &
Johnny Copeland
LPs: 10/12-Inch 33rpm
ALLIGATOR: *86* 5-8
 Also see COLLINS, Albert
 Also see CRAY, Robert

COLLINS, Big Tom
(Brownie McGhee)
Singles: 78rpm
KING: *51-52* 15-25
Singles: 7-Inch
KING: *51-52* 40-50

COLLINS, Bill
Singles: 7-Inch
BRENT: *59* 4-6

COLLINS, Bob
Singles: 7-Inch
MARK IV: 3-5

COLLINS, Bob, & The Fabulous Five
Singles: 7-Inch
MAINLINE: $10-15

COLLINS, Bonnie
Singles: 7-Inch
RINGO: *65* 3-5

COLLINS, Boots
Singles: 7-Inch
UPLAND: *64* 3-5

COLLINS, Carol
Singles: 7-Inch
DUNES: *61* 10-15

COLLINS, Cecil
Singles: 7-Inch
BLUE MOON: *59* 25-35

COLLINS, Dave
Singles: 7-Inch
CAPITOL: *73* 2-3

COLLINS, Dave & Ansell
Singles: 7-Inch
BIG TREE: *71-72* 2-4
LPs: 10/12-Inch 33rpm
BIG TREE: *71* 10-12
 Also see COLLINS, Dave

COLLINS, Dorothy
Singles: 78rpm
AUDIOVOX: *54-55* 3-5
CORAL: *55-56* 2-5
DECCA: *52* 3-5
MGM: *50-51* 3-5
Singles: 7-Inch
AUDIOVOX: *54-55* 3-6
CORAL: *55-56* 3-5
DECCA: *52* 3-6
GOLD EAGLE: *61* 2-3
MGM: *50-51* 4-6
ROULETTE: *63* 2-3
TOP RANK: *59-60* 2-4
EPs: 7-Inch 33/45rpm
CORAL: *55-56* 5-8
MGM: *55* 5-8
LPs: 10/12-Inch 33rpm
CORAL: *55-57* 10-15
MOTIVATION: *62* 8-12
TOP RANK: *60* 10-12
VOCALION: *65* 5-10

COLLINS, Judy
Singles: 7-Inch
ELEKTRA (Except 45008
through 45601): *66-84* $1-3
ELEKTRA (45008 through
45601): *64-66* 2-5
Picture Sleeves
ELEKTRA (Except
"The Hostage"): *69-84* 1-3
ELEKTRA ("The Hostage"): *73* 3-6
(Promotional issue only.)
LPs: 10/12-Inch 33rpm
ELEKTRA (Except 200 & 300
series): *67-84* 10-12
ELEKTRA (200 series): *61-64* 25-40
ELEKTRA (300 series): *65-72* 15-20

COLLINS, Judy, & T.G. Sheppard
Singles: 7-Inch
ELEKTRA: *84* 1-3
Also see COLLINS, Judy
Also see SHEPPARD, T.G.

COLLINS, Keanya
Singles: 7-Inch
BLUE ROCK: *69* 2-4
ITCO: *69* 2-4

COLLINS, Lyn
(Lyn Collins & The Famous Flames)
Singles: 7-Inch
PEOPLE: *72-76* 2-3
LPs: 10/12-Inch 33rpm
PEOPLE: *72-75* 10-12
Also see BROWN, James & Lyn Collins

COLLINS, Phil
Singles: 12-Inch 33/45rpm
ATLANTIC: *84-86* 4-6
Singles: 7-Inch
ATLANTIC: *81-88* 1-3
Picture Sleeves
ATLANTIC: *81-86* 1-3
LPs: 10/12-Inch 33rpm
ATLANTIC: *81-86* 5-8
Also see BAILEY, Philip, & Phil Collins
Also see BAND AID
Also see BRAND X
Also see GENESIS

COLLINS, Phil, & Marilyn Martin
Singles: 7-Inch
ATLANTIC: *85* 1-3
Picture Sleeves
ATLANTIC: *85* 1-3
Also see COLLINS, Phil

Also see MARTIN, Marilyn

COLLINS, Rodger
(Roger Collins)
Singles: 7-Inch
FANTASY: *73* $2-3
GALAXY: *66-73* 3-6
POMPEII: *69* 2-4

COLLINS, William:
see BOOTSY'S RUBBER BAND

COLLINS, Willie
Singles: 7-Inch
CAPITOL: *86* 1-3

COLLINS & COLLINS
Singles: 7-Inch
A&M: *80* 1-3
LPs: 10/12-Inch 33rpm
A&M: *80* 5-8

COLLINS KIDS
Singles: 78rpm
COLUMBIA: *55-57* 5-15
Singles: 7-Inch
COLUMBIA (21000 series): *55-56* 10-20
COLUMBIA (40824 through
41225): *57-58* 20-30
COLUMBIA (41329 through
41541): *59-60* 5-10
LPs: 10/12-Inch 33rpm
COLUMBIA: *83* 5-8
Members: Larry Collins; Lawrencine "Lorrie" Collins.

COLOMBO, Chris:
see COLUMBO, Chris

COLONEL ABRAMS:
see ABRAMS, Colonel

COLORS
Singles: 12-Inch 33/45rpm
FIRST TAKE: *83* 4-6
Singles: 7-Inch
BECKET: *82* 1-3

COLTER, Jessi
Singles: 7-Inch
CAPITOL: *75-82* 1-3
RCA VICTOR: *69-72* 2-4
LPs: 10/12-Inch 33rpm
CAPITOL: *75-81* 6-10
RCA VICTOR: *70* 8-12
Also see JENNINGS, Waylon, & Jessi Colter

COLTRANE, Alice
LPs: 10/12-Inch 33rpm
IMPULSE: *71-74* **$8-10**
WARNER BROS: *77-78* **5-10**

COLTRANE, Alice, & Carlos Santana
LPs: 10/12-Inch 33rpm
COLUMBIA: *74* **6-10**
Also see COLTRANE, Alice
Also see SANTANA

COLTRANE, Chi
Singles: 7-Inch
CLOUDS: *78* **1-3**
COLUMBIA: *72-73* **2-4**
LPs: 10/12-Inch 33rpm
CLOUDS: *77* **5-8**
COLUMBIA: *72-73* **8-10**

COLTRANE, John
(John Coltrane Trio; John Coltrane Quartet)
Singles: 7-Inch
ATLANTIC: *60-61* **2-4**
IMPULSE: *62* **2-3**
PRESTIGE: *57-63* **2-4**
LPs: 10/12-Inch 33rpm
ATLANTIC (300 series): *73* **8-12**
ATLANTIC (1300 & 1400
 series): *59-66* **15-20**
ATLANTIC (1500 series): *69-70* **8-12**
ATLANTIC (1600 series): *75* **5-10**
ATLANTIC (90000 series): *82* **5-8**
BETHLEHEM (6000 series): *63* **12-18**
 (Maroon label.)
BETHLEHEM (6000 series): *76* **10-12**
 (Gray label.)
BLUE NOTE (400 series): *75* **8-10**
BLUE NOTE (1500 series): *60* **15-25**
 (Label reads "Blue Note Records Inc.- New York,
 U.S.A.")
BLUE NOTE (1500 series): *66* **10-15**
 (Label shows Blue Note Records as a division of
 either Liberty or United Artists.)
COLTRANE: *66* **50-75**
IMPULSE (6 through 95): *61-65* **12-20**
IMPULSE (9000 & 9100
 series): *66-72* **10-15**
IMPULSE (9200 & 9300
 series): *73-79* **8-12**
NEW JAZZ: *63* **10-15**
PABLO: *77-83* **6-10**
PRESTIGE (020 through 2507): *81-83* **6-10**
PRESTIGE (7000 & 7100
 series): *56-60* **20-30**
 (Yellow label.)

PRESTIGE (7200 series): *61-64* **$15-20**
 (Yellow label.)
PRESTIGE (7000 through
 7400 series): *64-66* **10-15**
 (Blue label.)
PRESTIGE (7500 through
 7800 series): *68-70* **8-12**
PRESTIGE (24000 series): *72-83* **8-12**
RIVERSIDE: *82* **5-8**
ROULETTE: *63* **10-20**
SAVOY: *76-77* **8-12**
SOLID STATE: *68* **8-12**
TRIP: *73* **5-10**
UNITED ARTISTS (5600 series): *72* **8-12**
UNITED ARTISTS (14000 &
 15000 series): *63* **10-15**
Also see ADDERLEY, Julian "Cannonball,"
& John Coltrane
Also see ELLINGTON, Duke, & John
Coltrane

COLTRANE, John, & Miles Davis
LPs: 10/12-Inch 33rpm
PRESTIGE: *64* **10-15**
Also see DAVIS, Miles

COLTRANE, John & Thelonious Monk
LPs: 10/12-Inch 33rpm
JAZZLAND: *61* **15-25**
MILESTONE: *73* **8-12**
RIVERSIDE (Except 039): *65-68* **10-15**
RIVERSIDE (039; "Thelonious
 Monk & John Coltrane"): *82* **5-8**
Also see COLTRANE, John
Also see MONK, Thelonious

COLTS
Singles: 78rpm
MAMBO (112; "Adorable"): *55* **35-50**
VITA: *55-56* **10-20**
Singles: 7-Inch
ANTLER: *59* **10-20**
MAMBO (112; "Adorable"): *55* **75-100**
PLAZA: *62* **4-8**
VITA: *55-56* **25-40**
 Members: Joe Crunby; Rubin Crunby; Leroy
 Smith; Carl Moland.

COLTS / Red Coats
Singles: 7-Inch
DEL-CO: *59* **10-15**
Also see COLTS

COLUMBO, Chris
(Chris Colombo Quintet)
Singles: 7-Inch
BATTLE: 62 .... $2-4
MAXX: 64 2-3
STRAND: 63 2-4
LPs: 10/12-Inch 33rpm
MERCURY: 75 5-8
STRAND: 63 10-15

COMATEENS
Singles: 12-Inch 33/45rpm
MERCURY: 83-84 4-6
Singles: 7-Inch
MERCURY: 83-84 1-3
LPs: 10/12-Inch 33rpm
CACHALOT: 81 5-8
MERCURY: 83 5-8

COMER, Tony & Crosswinds
Singles: 7-Inch
VIDCOM: 84 1-3

COMMANDER CODY
(Commander Cody & His Lost Planet Airmen)
Singles: 7-Inch
ABC: 75 2-3
ARISTA: 77 2-3
DOT: 73-74 2-3
MCA: 83 1-3
PARAMOUNT: 71-74 2-4
WARNER BROS: 75 2-3
LPs: 10/12-Inch 33rpm
ARISTA: 78 5-8
PARAMOUNT: 71-74 10-12
WARNER BROS: 75 8-10

COMMODORES
Singles: 12-Inch 33/45rpm
MOTOWN: 79-85 4-6
POLYDOR: 86 4-6
Singles: 7-Inch
MOTOWN: 74-85 1-3
MOWEST: 72 2-4
POLYDOR: 86-88 1-3
LPs: 10/12-Inch 33rpm
MOTOWN (Except 39): 75-87 8-10
MOTOWN (39; "1978 Platinum
  Tour"): 78 15-20
(Promotional issue only.)
POLYDOR: 86 5-8
Members: Lionel Ritchie; William King; Ronald
LaPread; Tommy McClary; Walter Orange; Milan
Williams.
Also see MC CLARY, Thomas

Also see RICHIE, Lionel

COMMON BOND
LPs: 10/12-Inch 33rpm
FRONTLINE: 86-87 .... $5-8

COMMON SENSE
Singles: 7-Inch
BC: 81 1-3

COMMUNARDS
Singles: 12-Inch 33/45rpm
MCA: 86 4-6
Singles: 7-Inch
MCA: 86-88 1-3
LPs: 10/12-Inch 33rpm
MCA: 86-88 5-8
Members: Jimmy Sommerville; Sara Jane Morris;
Richard Coles.
Also see BRONSKI BEAT

COMO, Perry
Singles: 78rpm
RCA VICTOR: 43-58 3-8
Singles: 7-Inch
RCA VICTOR (0100 through
  0900 series): 69-73 1-3
RCA VICTOR (2000 series): 59 5-10
(Stereo. With a "VP" prefix.)
RCA VICTOR (3800 through
  7100 series): 50-58 5-10
RCA VICTOR (7200 through
  9700 series): 58-69 3-6
RCA VICTOR (10000 through
  13000 series): 74-83 1-3
Picture Sleeves
RCA VICTOR (3800 through
  7100 series): 53-58 8-15
RCA VICTOR (7200 through
  9700 series): 58-69 5-10
EPs: 7-Inch 33/45rpm
RCA VICTOR (Except SPD
  series): 52-70 10-20
RCA VICTOR (SPD-27; "Perry
  Como"): 56 30-60
(10-EP boxed set. Includes inserts and biography
booklet.)
RCA VICTOR (SPD-28; "Perry Como
  Highlighter"): 56 15-30
(Special sampler from Kleenex Tissue.)
LPs: 10/12-Inch 33rpm
CAMDEN: 60-74 5-10
RCA VICTOR (0100 through 4000
  series): 73-83 5-10
(With an "AFL1," "ANL1," "APL1," "AQL1,"
"AYL1," or "CPL1" prefix.)

RCA VICTOR (400 through 1900
series): *52-58* $12-20
(With an "LPM" prefix.)
RCA VICTOR (400 through 1900
series): *62-68* 5-10
(With an "LSP" prefix. Electronic stereo reissues.)
RCA VICTOR (2000 through 2900
series): *59-63* 10-15
(With an "LPM" or "LSP" prefix.)
RCA VICTOR (LPM-3100 series): *53-54* 15-25
(10-Inch LPs. With an LPM prefix.)
RCA VICTOR (3300 through 4500
series): *64-71* 8-12
(With an "LPM" or "LSP" prefix.)
READER'S DIGEST: *75* 8-15

**COMO, Perry / Ames Brothers / Harry
Belafonte / Radio City Music Hall Orch.**
EPs: 7-Inch 33/45rpm
RCA VICTOR (SP-35; "Merry
Christmas"): *56* 5-10
(Record dealer giveaway. Issued with paper sleeve.)
Also see AMES BROTHERS
Also see BELAFONTE, Harry

COMO, Perry, & Eddie Fisher
Singles: 78rpm
RCA VICTOR: *52* 3-5
Singles: 7-Inch
RCA VICTOR: *52* 3-5
Also see FISHER, Eddie

COMO, Perry, & The Fontane Sisters
Singles: 78rpm
RCA VICTOR: *50-51* 3-5
Singles: 7-Inch
RCA VICTOR: *50-51* 3-6
Also see FONTANE SISTERS

COMO, Perry, & Jaye P. Morgan
Singles: 7-Inch
RCA VICTOR: *55* 3-5
Also see COMO, Perry
Also see MORGAN, Jaye P.

COMPAGNONS DE LA CHANSON:
see LES COMPAGNONS DE LA CHANSON

COMSTOCK, Bobby
(Bobby Comstock & The Counts)
Singles: 7-Inch
ASCOT: *64-66* 4-6
ATLANTIC: *60* 4-8
BLAZE: *59* 10-15
ERIC: *73* 1-3
FESTIVAL: *61* 3-6
JUBILEE: *60-63* 4-6

LAWN: *62-64* $4-8
MARLEE: *58* 15-25
MOHAWK: *61* 3-6
TRIUMPH: *59* 4-8
LPs: 10/12-Inch 33rpm
ASCOT: *66* 30-35
BLAZE: 50-75
Also see KING CURTIS

CON FUNK SHUN
Singles: 12-Inch 33/45rpm
MERCURY: *83-86* 4-6
Singles: 7-Inch
FRETONE: *74* 2-4
MERCURY: *77-86* 1-3
LPs: 10/12-Inch 33rpm
51 WEST: *83* 5-8
MERCURY: *76-86* 5-8

CONCEPT
Singles: 7-Inch
TUCKWOOD: *85* 1-3

CONDUCTOR
Singles: 7-Inch
JAMIE: *61* 4-8
MONTAGE: *82* 1-3
LPs: 10/12-Inch 33rpm
MONTAGE: *82* 5-8

CONEY HATCH
LPs: 10/12-Inch 33rpm
MERCURY: *83-85* 5-8

CONLEE, John
Singles: 7-Inch
ABC: *78* 1-3
ABC/DOT: *76-77* 2-3
COLUMBIA: *87* 1-3
MCA: *79-86* 1-3
LPs: 10/12-Inch 33rpm
ABC: *78* 8-10
COLUMBIA: *86* 5-8
MCA: *79-86* 5-8

CONLEY, Arthur
Singles: 7-Inch
ATCO: *67-70* 3-5
CAPRICORN: *71-74* 2-4
FAME: *66* 3-5
JOTIS: *66* 3-5
LPs: 10/12-Inch 33rpm
ATCO: *67-69* 12-20
Also see SOUL CLAN

CONNIE
Singles: 12-Inch 33/45rpm
SUNNYVIEW: *85-86* $4-6
Singles: 7-Inch
SUNNYVIEW: *85-86* 1-3

CONNIFF, Ray, Orchestra & Chorus
Singles: 78rpm
COLUMBIA: *56-57* 2-3
Singles: 7-Inch
COLUMBIA: *56-82* 2-5
Picture Sleeves
COLUMBIA: *60-64* 2-4
EPs: 7-Inch 33/45rpm
COLUMBIA: *56-59* 4-6
LPs: 10/12-Inch 33rpm
COLUMBIA: *57-82* 5-15
HARMONY: *69* 4-8

CONNOR, Chris
Singles: 78rpm
ATLANTIC: *56-57* 3-5
BETHLEHEM: *54-55* 3-5
Singles: 7-Inch
ATLANTIC: *56-62* 3-5
BETHLEHEM (1200 & 1300
series): *54-55* 3-6
BETHLEHEM (3000 series): *64* 2-4
FM: *63* 2-4
EPs: 7-Inch 33/45rpm
ATLANTIC: *56-57* 5-10
BETHLEHEM: *54-56* 8-12
LPs: 10/12-Inch 33rpm
ABC-PARAMOUNT: *65-66* 8-12
ATLANTIC (1200 & 1300
series): *56-59* 15-25
ATLANTIC (8000 series): *56-62* 15-25
BETHLEHEM (Except 1000
series): *55-60* 15-25
(Maroon label.)
BETHLEHEM (1000 series): *54* 40-60
(10-Inch LPs.)
BETHLEHEM (6000 series): *78* 10-12
(Gray label.)
FM: *63* 10-15

CONNOR, Chris, & Maynard Ferguson
Singles: 7-Inch
ATLANTIC: *61* 2-4
LPs: 10/12-Inch 33rpm
ATLANTIC: *61* 12-20
ROULETTE: *58* 20-30
Also see CONNOR, Chris
Also see FERGUSON, Maynard

Also see SIMONE, Nina, Chris Connor & Carmen McRae

CONNORS, Norman
Singles: 7-Inch
ARISTA: *78-80* $1-3
BUDDAH: *74-77* 2-3
CAPITOL: *88* 1-3
LPs: 10/12-Inch 33rpm
ARISTA: *78-80* 5-8
BUDDAH: *75-78* 10-12
NOVUS: *81* 5-8
Members: Michael Henderson; Pharoah Sanders;
Jean Cain; Phyllis Hyman.
Also see AQUARIAN DREAM
Also see HENDERSON, Michael
Also see HYMAN, Phyllis

CONTI, Bill
Singles: 7-Inch
ARISTA: *82* 1-3
UNITED ARTISTS: *77-78* 1-3
LPs: 10/12-Inch 33rpm
MCA: *79* 5-10
UNITED ARTISTS: *78-79* 8-12

CONTINENTAL 4
(Continental Four)
Singles: 7-Inch
JAY WALKING: *71-72* 2-4
LPs: 10/12-Inch 33rpm
JAY WALKING: *71* 10-15

CONTINO, Dick
Singles: 78rpm
MERCURY: *54-57* 2-4
Singles: 7-Inch
DOT: *66-67* 2-3
MERCURY: *54-64* 2-4
EPs: 7-Inch 33/45rpm
MERCURY: *55-59* 5-8
LPs: 10/12-Inch 33rpm
DOT: *64-66* 5-10
HAMILTON: *64-66* 5-10
MERCURY: *56-63* 8-12
WING: *63* 6-10

CONTOURS
Singles: 7-Inch
GORDY: *62-67* 5-10
MOTOWN (400 series): *82* 1-3
MOTOWN (1008; "Whole Lotta
Woman"): *61* 100-125
MOTOWN (1012; "Funny"): *61* 150-175
ROCKET: *80* 1-3

LPs: 10/12-Inch 33rpm
GORDY: 62 .... $35-40
MOTOWN: 82 5-8
  Members: Bill Gordon; Sylvester Potts; Billy
  Hoggs; Joe Billingslea; Hubert Johnson.

CONTROLLERS
(Controllers With Valerie DeMece)
Singles: 12-Inch 33/45rpm
MCA: 85-86 4-6
Singles: 7-Inch
JUANA: 76-82 1-3
MCA: 85-88 1-3
LPs: 10/12-Inch 33rpm
JUANA: 77-79 8-10
MCA: 86 5-8
WINDHAM HILL: 85 5-8

CONVERTION
Singles: 7-Inch
SAM: 81 1-3
VANGUARD: 83 1-3
LPs: 10/12-Inch 33rpm
VANGUARD: 83 5-8

CONWAY BROTHERS
Singles: 7-Inch
ICHIBAN: 87 1-3
PBT: 86 1-3
PAULA: 85 1-3

COODER, Ry
Singles: 7-Inch
MUSICOR: 66 3-5
REPRISE: 69-72 2-4
WARNER BROS: 77-82 1-3
LPs: 10/12-Inch 33rpm
MFSL: 82 25-50
REPRISE: 72-76 8-10
WARNER BROS: 77-82 5-8
  Also see CAPTAIN BEEFHEART
  Also see LENNEAR, Claudia
  Also see LITTLE FEAT
  Also see LONGBRANCH PENNYWHISTLE

COOK, Tony
Singles: 12-Inch 33/45rpm
HALFMOON: 84 4-6

COOKE, SAM
(Sam Cooke & The Soul Stirrers)
Singles: 78rpm
KEEN: 57 4-8
SPECIALTY: 57 4-8
Singles: 7-Inch
CHERIE: 71 2-4
COLLECTABLES: 81 1-3

KEEN (2000 series): 58-60 .... $8-15
  (Stereo. With a "5" prefix.)
KEEN (2000 & 4000 series): 57-61 4-6
  (With a "3" prefix.)
RCA VICTOR (7000 series): 60-61 10-15
  (Stereo. With a "61" prefix.)
RCA VICTOR (7000 & 8000 series): 60-66 3-6
  (With a "47" prefix.)
SPECIALTY (SPBX series): 87 12-15
  (Boxed sets of six colored vinyl 45s.)
SPECIALTY (500 & 600 series): 57-59 ... 4-6
SPECIALTY (900 series): 70-72 2-3
  (Most Specialty singles are currently available,
  using original catalog numbers.)
Picture Sleeves
RCA VICTOR: 60-65 8-15
EPs: 7-Inch 33/45rpm
KEEN: 57-59 20-30
RCA VICTOR: 61-63 15-20
LPs: 10/12-Inch 33rpm
CAMDEN: 68-74 8-10
CANDLELITE: 15-20
  (A mail-order offer.)
CHERIE: 71 8-10
FAMOUS: 69 12-15
KEEN: 58-60 20-30
PHOENIX 10: 81 5-8
PICKWICK: 76 5-8
RCA VICTOR (2000 & 3000
  series): 60-68 15-30
  (With an "LPM" or "LSP" prefix.)
RCA VICTOR (2000 through
  5000 series): 78-85 5-8
  (With an "AFL1," "ANL1," or "AYL1" prefix.)
RCA VICTOR (7000 series): 86 8-12
SAR: 61 3-5
SPECIALTY: 69-85 5-12
TRIP: 72-76 8-10
UPFRONT: 73 8-10
  Also see ANKA, Paul / Sam Cooke / Neil
Sedaka
  Also see COOKE, Dale
  Also see RAWLS, Lou
  Also see SOUL STIRRERS

COOKE, Sam / Rod Lauren / Neil
Sedaka / Browns
EPs: 7-Inch 33/45rpm
RCA VICTOR (33-99; "Compact 33
  Double"): 60 15-20
  (Has the same four songs on each side, but is mono
  on one side and stereo on the reverse.)
  Also see BROWNS
  Also see LAUREN, Rod

Also see SEDAKA, Neil

COOKE, Sam / Lloyd Price / Larry Williams
LPs: 10/12-Inch 33rpm
SPECIALTY: 60 . . . . $20-25
  Also see COOKE, Sam
  Also see PRICE, Lloyd
  Also see WILLIAMS, Larry

COOKE, Samona
Singles: 7-Inch
EPIC: 76-77 2-3
MERCURY: 78 2-3

COOKER
(Norman Des Rosiers)
Singles: 7-Inch
SCEPTER: 73-74 2-3
LPs: 10/12-Inch 33rpm
SCEPTER: 74 8-10

COOKIE & HIS CUPCAKES
(Terry "Cookie" Clinton)
Singles: 7-Inch
CHESS: 63 3-5
JUDD: 59 10-15
KHOURY'S: 59 15-20
LYRIC: 63-64 8-10
MERCURY: 61 3-5
PAULA: 65-68 3-5
  Also see BOOGIE RAMBLERS
  Also see CLINTON, Terry, & The Berry Cups

COOKIES
Singles: 7-Inch
ABC: 74 1-3
DIMENSION: 62-64 5-8
ERIC: 73 1-3
MCA: 83 1-3
  Member: Earl-Jean McCree.
  Also see EARL-JEAN

COOKIES / Little Eva / Carole King
LPs: 10/12-Inch 33rpm
DIMENSION: 63 40-50
  Also see COOKIES
  Also see KING, Carole
  Also see LITTLE EVA

COOL HEAT
Singles: 7-Inch
FORWARD: 70 2-4
  Also see WIND

COOLEY, Eddie
(Eddie Cooley & The Dimples)
Singles: 78rpm
ROYAL ROOST: 56-57 . . . . $5-10
Singles: 7-Inch
ABC: 73 1-3
ROULETTE: 60 3-5
ROYAL ROOST: 56-57 8-10
TRIUMPH: 59 5-10

COOLIDGE, Rita
Singles: 7-Inch
A&M: 71-80 1-3
PEPPER: 68-69 3-5
Picture Sleeves
A&M: 72-80 1-3
LPs: 10/12-Inch 33rpm
A&M: 71-83 6-10
Promotional LPs
A&M ("In-Store Sampler-Rita
  Coolidge"): 8-12
  Also see CAMPBELL, Glen, & Rita Coolidge
  Also see CLAPTON, Eric

COOLIDGE, Rita, & Kris Kristofferson
Singles: 7-Inch
A&M: 73-74 2-3
MONUMENT: 74-75 2-3
Picture Sleeves
A&M: 73 2-3
LPs: 10/12-Inch 33rpm
A&M: 73-79 8-10
MONUMENT: 74 8-10
  Also see COOLIDGE, Rita
  Also see KRISTOFFERSON, Kris

COOPER, Alice
(Alice Cooper Group)
Singles: 12-Inch 33/45rpm
WARNER BROS: 80 10-15
(Promotional issue only.)
Singles: 7-Inch
ATLANTIC: 75 2-4
MCA: 86 1-3
STRAIGHT: 69-70 12-15
WARNER BROS: 70-80 2-4
Promotional Singles
ATLANTIC: 75 4-6
MCA: 86 3-5
WARNER BROS: 70-80 5-8
Picture Sleeves
WARNER BROS: 72-80 3-6

Alice Cooper (center) and his band

EPs: 7-Inch 33/45rpm

WARNER BROS: *73* $15-20
(Jukebox issues only.)

LPs: 10/12-Inch 33rpm

ATLANTIC: *75-78* 5-8
MFSL: *82* 25-50
MCA: *86-87* 5-8
STRAIGHT (1051; "Pretties For
  You"): *69* 30-40
  (Cover pictures drawing of a woman raising her
  dress, with a yellow sticker covering her crotch
  area. Price is for cover with sticker still intact.)
STRAIGHT (1051; "Pretties For
  You"): *69* 20-30
  (Cover shows the woman with the sticker removed
  and panties showing.)
WARNER BROS (Except 1883, 2567
  & 2623): *73-84* 8-12
WARNER BROS (1883; "Love It To
  Death"): *71* 25-30
  (Black cover has Cooper's right thumb showing
  through his wrap. Does NOT have white block
  reading "Including Their Hit I'm Eighteen.")
WARNER BROS (1883; "Love It To
  Death"): *71* 15-20
  (Black cover has Cooper's right thumb showing
  through his wrap. Has white block reading "Includ-
  ing Their Hit I'm Eighteen." Also includes issue
  with huge white stripes at top and bottom of cover.)
WARNER BROS (1883; "Love It To
  Death"): *71* 5-8
  (Black cover does NOT have Cooper's right thumb
  showing through his wrap. Has the white block
  reading "Including Their Hit I'm Eighteen.")
WARNER BROS (2567; "Killer"): *71* ... 15-18
  (With poster & 1972 calendar.)
WARNER BROS (2567; "Killer"): *72* 5-8
  (Without poster & calendar.)

WARNER BROS (2623; "School's
  Out"): *72* $30-40
  (With panties attached. Panties came in four dif-
  ferent colors; pink, white, yellow, and blue. Back
  cover does not list titles.)
WARNER BROS (2623; "School's
  Out"): *72* 15-18
  (With panties attached. Back cover lists titles.)
WARNER BROS (2623; "School's
  Out"): *72* 5-8
  (With no paper panties. Back cover lists titles.)
WARNER BROS/STRAIGHT (1051; "Pretties
  For You"): *69* 15-18
WARNER BROS/STRAIGHT (1845;
  "Easy Action"): *70* 30-35
  (With the name "Alice Cooper" in black letters on
  front cover.)
WARNER BROS/STRAIGHT (1845; "Easy
  Action"): *70* 5-8
  (With the name "Alice Cooper" in white letters on
  front cover.)

Promotional LPs

CHELSEA PROD ("Allison's Tea
  House"): *74* 25-30
STRAIGHT (1051;
  "Pretties For You"): *69* 40-55
  (Cover pictures drawing of a woman raising her
  dress, with a yellow sticker covering her crotch
  area. Price is for cover with sticker still intact.)
STRAIGHT (1051; "Pretties For
  You"): *69* 30-40
  (Cover shows the woman with the sticker removed
  and panties showing.)
STRAIGHT (1845; "Easy
  Action"): *70* 25-30
STRAIGHT (1883; "Love It To
  Death"): *71* 20-25

WARNER BROS (White label
promos): *71-78* $20-40
WARNER BROS/STRAIGHT ("Pretties
For You"): *69* 25-30
Members: Kane Roberts; Ken K. Mary.
Also see BILLION DOLLAR BABIES
Also see BRUCE, Michael
Also see FROST
Also see NAZZ
Also see SPIDERS

COOPER, Les, & The Soul Rockers
Singles: 7-Inch
ABC: *73* 1-3
ARRAWAK: *65* 3-5
ATCO: *69* 2-4
ENJOY: *65* 3-5
EVERLAST: *62* 3-5
SAMAR: *66* 3-5
LPs: 10/12-Inch 33rpm
EVERLAST: *63* 40-50
Also see EMPIRES
Also see WHIRLERS

COOPER, Pat
LPs: 10/12-Inch 33rpm
UNITED ARTISTS: *66-69* 8-15

COOPER BROTHERS
Singles: 7-Inch
CAPRICORN: *78-79* 1-3
LPs: 10/12-Inch 33rpm
CAPRICORN: *78-79* 5-8
Also see BLACK OAK ARKANSAS /
Cooper Brothers

COPAS, Cowboy
(Lloyd Copas)
Singles: 78rpm
KING: *46-57* 3-8
Singles: 7-Inch
KING (900 through 1500
series): *50-55* 4-6
KING (4800 through 5200
series): *55-59* 3-5
KING (5300 through 5700
series): *60-63* 2-4
STARDAY (400 through 700
series): *60-66* 2-4
STARDAY (7000 series): *64* 2-3
STARDAY (8000 series): *71* 1-3
EPs: 7-Inch 33/45rpm
KING: *57* 15-20
STARDAY: *60* 10-12

LPs: 10/12-Inch 33rpm
GUEST STAR: $10-15
KING (500 series): *57* 30-40
KING (600 through 800
series): *59-64* 25-35
KING (1000 series): *69* 8-12
NASHVILLE: *68-70* 8-12
PICKWICK/HILLTOP: *66* 10-12
STARDAY (100 & 200
series): *60-64* 20-25
STARDAY (300 series): *65-67* 12-20
STARDAY (400 series): *68-70* 8-12

COPAS, Cowboy / Hawkshaw Hawkins
LPs: 10/12-Inch 33rpm
KING: *63-66* 10-15
Also see CLINE, Patsy / Cowboy Copas /
Hawkshaw Hawkins
Also see COPAS, Cowboy
Also see HAWKINS, Hawkshaw

COPAS, Lloyd
Singles: 7-Inch
DOT (15735; "Circle Rock"): *58* 40-60
Also see COPAS, Cowboy

COPELAND, Ken
Singles: 78rpm
IMPERIAL: *57* 3-6
LIN (5007; "Fanny Brown"): *58* 10-15
Singles: 7-Inch
DOT: *58* 4-6
IMPERIAL: *57* 4-8
LIN (5007; "Fanny Brown"): *58* 15-25

COPELAND, Ken / Mints
Singles: 78rpm
LIN (5007; "Pledge Of
Love"): *57* 5-10
Singles: 7-Inch
IMPERIAL: *57* 4-6
LIN (5007; "Pledge Of
Love"): *57* 10-15
Also see COPELAND, Ken
Also see MINTS

COPELAND, Stewart
LPs: 10/12-Inch 33rpm
A&M: *83* 5-8
Also see POLICE

COPELAND, Stewart, & Stan Ridgway
Singles: 7-Inch
A&M: *83* 1-3
Also see COPELAND, Stewart
Also see WALL OF VOODOO

COPELAND, Vivian
Singles: 7-Inch
D'ORO: *69* $2-3
MALA: *67* 3-5

COREA, Chick
Singles: 7-Inch
POLYDOR: *79* 1-3
LPs: 10/12-Inch 33rpm
BLUE NOTE: *75-78* 8-12
ECM: *75-80* 6-10
ELEKTRA: *83* 5-8
PACIFIC JAZZ: *81* 5-8
POLYDOR: *76-78* 6-10
VERVE: *76* 5-8
WARNER BROS: *80-81* 5-8
Also see HANCOCK, Herbie, & Chick Corea

COREY, Jill
Singles: 7-Inch
COLUMBIA: *54-60* 2-5
MERCURY: *62* 2-4
EPs: 7-Inch 33/45rpm
COLUMBIA: *55-57* 6-10
LPs: 10/12-Inch 33rpm
COLUMBIA: *56-57* 10-15

CORLEY, Al
Singles: 7-Inch
MERCURY: *85* 1-3

CORLEY, Bob
Singles: 78rpm
RCA VICTOR: *56* 3-5
STARS: *55* 4-6
Singles: 7-Inch
RCA VICTOR: *56* 3-5
STARS: *55* 4-6

CORNBREAD & BISCUITS
Singles: 7-Inch
MASKE: *60* 3-5

**CORNELIUS BROTHERS &
SISTER ROSE**
Singles: 7-Inch
PLATINUM: *70* 5-10
UNITED ARTISTS: *70-74* 2-5
LPs: 10/12-Inch 33rpm
PICKWICK: *76* 5-8
UNITED ARTISTS: *72-76* 10-12
Members: Ed Cornelius; Carter Cornelius; Rose Cornelius.

CORNELL, Don
Singles: 78rpm
CORAL: *52-57* 3-5

Singles: 7-Inch
ABC-PARAMOUNT: *65* $2-3
CORAL: *52-57* 4-8
DOT: *59-60* 2-4
JAYBEE: *69* 1-3
JUBILEE: *62* 2-3
SIGNATURE: *59-60* 2-4
20TH CENTURY-FOX: *64* 2-3
EPs: 7-Inch 33/45rpm
CORAL: *54-56* 5-10
LPs: 10/12-Inch 33rpm
ABC-PARAMOUNT: *66* 5-10
CORAL: *54-57* 10-15
DOT: *59* 8-12
MOVIETONE: *66* 5-10
SIGNATURE: *59* 6-10
VOCALION: *59* 8-12

CORNELL, Don
Johnny Desmond & Alan Dale
Singles: 78rpm
CORAL: *53* 3-5
Singles: 7-Inch
CORAL: *53* 3-5
EPs: 7-Inch 33/45rpm
CORAL: *54* 5-10
Also see CORNELL, Don
Also see DALE, Alan
Also see DESMOND, Johnny

CORNER BOYS
Singles: 7-Inch
NEPTUNE: *69* 2-4

CORPORATION
Singles: 7-Inch
CAPITOL: *69* 4-8
MUSICOR: *70* 3-6
LPs: 10/12-Inch 33rpm
AGE OF AQUARIUS: *69* 15-20
CAPITOL: *69* 15-20
Also see SKUNKS

CORSAIRS
(Featuring Jay "Bird" Uzzell)
Singles: 7-Inch
CHESS: *62* 3-5
ERIC: *78* 1-3
SMASH: *61* 3-5
TUFF: *61-64* 4-8

CORTEZ, Dave "Baby"
(Baby Cortez)
Singles: 7-Inch
ABC: *74* 1-3
ALL PLATINUM: *72* 2-4

ARGO: *64* $3-5
CHESS: *63* 3-5
CLOCK: *59-62* 4-6
COLLECTABLES: *81* 1-3
EMIT: *62* 3-5
ERIC: *73* 1-3
FIRE: *60* 4-6
JULIA: *62* 15-20
OKEH (7100 series): *58* 10-15
OKEH (7200 series): *64* 3-5
ROULETTE: *65-68* 3-5
SOUND: *71* 2-4
T-NECK: *69* 2-4
WINLEY: *62* 3-5
EPs: 7-Inch 33/45rpm
CLOCK: *59-61* 15-20
RCA VICTOR (4300 series): *59* 15-25
(With an "EPA" prefix. Monaural.)
RCA VICTOR (4300 series): *59* 25-50
(With an "ESP" prefix. Stereo.)
LPs: 10/12-Inch 33rpm
CHESS: *62* 25-30
CLOCK: *60-63* 25-30
CORONET: 10-12
CROWN: *63* 12-15
DESIGN: 10-12
METRO: *65* 12-15
RCA VICTOR: *59* 25-30
ROULETTE: *65-66* 15-20
Also see BLAZERS
Also see ISLEY BROTHERS & Dave "Baby"
Cortez
Also see PEARLS
Also see VALENTINES

CORTEZ, Dave "Baby" / Jerry's House Rockers
LPs: 10/12-Inch 33rpm
CROWN: *63* 12-15
Also see CORTEZ, Dave "Baby"

CORY
Singles: 7-Inch
PHANTOM: *77* 2-3

CORYELL, Larry
LPs: 10/12-Inch 33rpm
VANGUARD: *69* 8-12
Also see ELEVENTH HOUSE
Also see MOUZON, Alphonse, & Larry
Coryell

COSBY, Bill
Singles: 12-Inch 33/45rpm
MOTOWN (110; "Super Special
For Radio"): *82* $5-10
(Promotional issue only.)
Singles: 7-Inch
CAPITOL: *76-78* 1-3
UNI: *69-70* 2-4
WARNER BROS: *65-67* 3-5
LPs: 10/12-Inch 33rpm
CAPITOL: *76-78* 5-8
COLUMBIA (40270; "Music From
The Bill Cosby Show"): *86* 5-8
(Featuring Grover Washington, Jr.)
GEFFEN: *86* 5-8
MCA: 5-8
MOTOWN: *82* 5-8
PARTEE: 6-10
TETRAGRAMMATON: *69* 6-10
UNI: *69-72* 6-10
WARNER BROS (Except 249): *64-70* 8-15
WARNER BROS (249; "Best Of
Bill Cosby"): *69* 15-20
(Promotional issue only.)
Also see ROSS, Diana, & Bill Cosby / Diana
Ross With The Jackson Five
Also see WASHINGTON, Grover, Jr.

COSBY, Bill, & Ozzie Davis
LPs: 10/12-Inch 33rpm
BLACK FORUM: *72* 8-12
Also see COSBY, Bill

COSTA, Don, Orchestra
ABC-PARAMOUNT: *56-57* 2-4
COLUMBIA: *62-63* 2-3
DCP: *64-65* 1-3
ESSEX: *55* 2-4
Singles: 7-Inch
ABC-PARAMOUNT: *56-57* 2-4
COLUMBIA: *62-63* 2-3
DCP: *64-65* 1-3
ESSEX: *55* 2-4
JAMIE: *59* 2-4
MGM: *66-72* 1-3
MERCURY: *68* 1-3
UNITED ARTISTS: *59-62* 2-4
VERVE: *67* 1-3
Picture Sleeves
UNITED ARTISTS: *60* 5-10
VERVE: *67* 4-8
LPs: 10/12-Inch 33rpm
ABC-PARAMOUNT: *56-61* 10-15
COLUMBIA: *62-63* 8-10

DCP: *64-65* $5-10
HARMONY: *65* 5-10
MERCURY: *68-69* 5-10
UNITED ARTISTS: *59-62* 8-12
VERVE: *67* 5-10

COSTANDINOS, Alec R.
(With The Syncophonic Orchestra)
Singles: 7-Inch
CASABLANCA: *79* 1-3
LPs: 10/12-Inch 33rpm
CASABLANCA: *78-79* 5-8

COSTELLO, Elvis
(Elvis Costello & The Attractions; Costello Show)
Singles: 12-Inch 33/45rpm
COLUMBIA: *83-85* 5-8
Singles: 7-Inch
CBS (Black vinyl): *79* 2-3
CBS (Colored vinyl): *79* 10-15
COLUMBIA: *77-86* 2-4
WARNER BROS: *89* 1-3
Promotional Singles
COLUMBIA: *77-86* 4-8
Picture Sleeves
COLUMBIA (Except 1171): *81-85* 2-5
COLUMBIA (1171; "Accidents Will
Happen"): *78* 10-20
(Promotional issue only.)
EPs: 7-Inch 33/45rpm
COLUMBIA: *80* 10-15
LPs: 10/12-Inch 33rpm
COLUMBIA (Black vinyl): *77-86* 6-12
COLUMBIA (Colored vinyl): *79* 20-30
COLUMBIA/COSTELLO: *78* 20-25
WARNER BROS: *89* 5-8
Promotional EPs
COLUMBIA: *78-80* 10-15
Promotional LPs
COLUMBIA (Picture Disc; "My Aim Is
True"/"This Year's Model"): *79* 125-150
COLUMBIA (529; "Live At Hollywood
High"): *79* 20-30
COLUMBIA (958; "Tom Snyder
Interview"): *81* 20-30
COLUMBIA (1318; "Almost
Blue"): *81* 25-30
COLUMBIA/COSTELLO ("Taking
Liberties"): *80* 30-35
Also see NICK & ELVIS

COTTON, Gene
Singles: 7-Inch
ABC: *75-77* 2-3

ARIOLA AMERICA: *77-79* $1-3
KNOLL: *81-82* 1-3
MYRRH: *74* 1-3
LPs: 10/12-Inch 33rpm
ABC: *76-77* 8-10
ACCORD: *83* 5-8
ARIOLA AMERICA: *78-79* 5-8
BUDDAH: *74-75* 8-10
CAPITOL: *71* 8-10
IMPACT: 15-20
KNOLL: *81-82* 5-8
MYRRH: *73* 8-10

COTTON, Gene, & Kim Carnes
Singles: 7-Inch
ARIOLA AMERICA: *78* 2-3
Also see CARNES, Kim
Also see COTTON, Gene

COTTON, James
(James Cotton Blues Band; With Matt "Guitar"
Murphy & Luther Tucker)
Singles: 12-Inch 33/45rpm
ERECT: *82* 4-6
Singles: 7-Inch
BUDDAH: *75* 2-3
LOMA: *66* 8-12
SUN (199; "My Baby"): *54* 200-300
SUN (206; "Cotton Crop Blues"): *54* .200-250
VERVE/FOLKWAYS: *67* 2-4
VERVE/FORECAST: *67-69* 2-4
LPs: 10/12-Inch 33rpm
ACCORD: *83* 5-8
ALLIGATOR: *84* 5-8
ANTONE'S: *88* 5-8
BUDDAH: *74-76* 10-12
CAPITOL: *71* 10-12
ERECT: *82* 5-8
INTERMEDIA: *84* 5-8
VANGUARD: *68* 10-15
VERVE/FOLKWAYS: *67* 10-15
VERVE/FORECAST: *68-69* 10-15
Also see WATERS, Muddy

COTTON, Josie
Singles: 12-Inch 33/45rpm
BOMP: *80* 5-10
Singles: 7-Inch
ELEKTRA (Black vinyl): *82* 1-3
ELEKTRA (Colored vinyl): *82* 5-10
LPs: 10/12-Inch 33rpm
ELEKTRA: *82* 5-8

DOUBLE-
SHOT
every shot counts

1608 Argyle Ave.   Hollywood, Calif.

HOT SHOT
MUSIC, INC.   104
(B.M.I.)   (DS-107)
2:56   VOCAL

"PSYCHOTIC REACTION"
(Ellner-Chaney-Atkinson-Byrne-Michalski)
COUNT FIVE

COTTON, LLOYD & CHRISTIAN
Singles: 7-Inch
20TH CENTURY-FOX: 75-76 .... $2-4
LPs: 10/12-Inch 33rpm
20TH CENTURY-FOX: 75-76 8-10
Members: Darryl Cotton; Michael Lloyd; Chris
Christian.
Also see LLOYD, Michael

COUCHOIS
Singles: 7-Inch
WARNER BROS: 79-80 1-3
LPs: 10/12-Inch 33rpm
WARNER BROS: 79-80 5-8

COUGAR, John:
see MELLENCAMP, John Cougar

COULTER, Clifford
Singles: 7-Inch
COLUMBIA: 80 1-3
LPs: 10/12-Inch 33rpm
COLUMBIA: 80 5-8

COUNT BASIE:
see BASIE, Count

COUNT FIVE
Singles: 7-Inch
DOUBLE SHOT: 66-69 5-8
LPs: 10/12-Inch 33rpm
DOUBLE SHOT: 66 30-40

COUNT 5
Singles: 7-Inch
LES COUNTS: 10-15

COUNTRY BOYS & CITY GIRLS
Singles: 7-Inch
HAPPY FOX: 76 2-4
Member: Lee Maye.
Also see MAYE, Arthur Lee

COUNTRY COALITION
Singles: 7-Inch
ABC: 70-73 .... $2-4
ABC/BLUESWAY: 70 2-4

COUNTRY HAMS
Singles: 7-Inch
EMI: 74 10-15
Picture Sleeves
EMI: 74 35-45
Promotional Singles
EMI: 74 15-25
Members: Paul McCartney & Wings; Chet Atkins;
Floyd Cramer.
Also see ATKINS, Chet
Also see CRAMER, Floyd
Also see McCARTNEY, Paul

COUNTRY JOE & THE FISH
Singles: 7-Inch
VANGUARD: 67-69 4-6
Picture Sleeves
VANGUARD: 68 5-10
EPs: 7-Inch 33/45rpm
RAG BABY: 25-30
LPs: 10/12-Inch 33rpm
FANTASY: 77 8-10
VANGUARD (Except 9266): 67-71 10-20
VANGUARD (9266; "I Feel Like
   I'm Fixin' To Die"): 67 20-30
(With cut-out pictures and poster game.)
VANGUARD (9266; "I Feel Like
   I'm Fixin' To Die"): 67 12-15
(Without pictures and poster.)
Also see McDONALD, Country Joe

COUNTS
Singles: 78rpm
DOT: 53-56 5-15
Singles: 7-Inch
DOT (1199; "Hot Tamales"): 54 15-25
DOT (1188; "Darling Dear"): 53 30-40
DOT (1210; "My Dear, My
   Darling"): 54 30-40
DOT (1226; "Baby, I Want
   You"): 54 30-40
DOT (1235; "Let Me Go
   Lover"): 54 15-25
DOT (1243; "From This
   Day On"): 55 15-20
DOT (1265; "Sally Walker"): 55 15-20
DOT (1275; "Heartbreaker"): 56 15-20
DOT (16000 series): 60 3-5

COUNTS
Singles: 7-Inch
AWARE: 74 ....$2-3
WESTBOUND: 72 2-4
LPs: 10/12-Inch 33rpm
AWARE: 75.........................8-10
AWARE/GRC: 73 8-10
GRC: 73 8-10
WESTBOUND: 72 8-10

COURTNEY, David
LPs: 10/12-Inch 33rpm
UNITED ARTISTS: 75 8-10

COURTNEY, Lou
(Lew Courtney)
Singlas: 7-Inch
BUDDAH: 69 2-5
EPIC: 73-75 2-3
IMPERIAL: 63-64 3-5
PHILIPS: 65 3-5
POP SIDE: 67 3-5
RAGS: 73 4-6
RIVERSIDE: 66-67 3-5
VERVE: 68 2-5
LPs: 10/12-Inch 33rpm
EPIC: 74 8-10
RCA VICTOR: 76 8-10
RIVERSIDE: 67 15-20

COURTSHIP
Singles: 7-Inch
CAPITOL: 70 2-4
GLADES: 72 2-4
TAMLA: 72 2-4

COUSIN ICE
Singles: 7-Inch
URBAN ROCK: 85 4-6

COVAY, Don
(Don Covay & The Goodtimers; Don Covay &
The Jefferson Lemon Blues Band)
Singles: 7-Inch
ATLANTIC: 65-70 3-5
BIG TOP: 60 4-6
CAMEO: 62-63 3-5
COLUMBIA: 61 3-5
LANDA: 64 3-5
MERCURY: 72-75 2-3
NEWMAN: 80 1-3
PARKWAY: 63-64 3-5
PHILADELPHIA INT'L: 76.............2-3
ROSEMART: 64 3-5
LPs: 10/12-Inch 33rpm
ATLANTIC: 65-69 15-20

JANUS: 72 ....$8-10
MERCURY: 74 8-10
PHILADELPHIA INT'L: 76 8-10
VERSATILE: 78 8-10
Also see GOODTIMERS
Also see PRETTY BOY
Also see RAINBOWS
Also see SOUL CLAN

COVEN
Singles: 7 Inch
BUDDAH: 74 2-3
MGM: 71-73 2-4
MERCURY: 69 2-4
SGC: 68 4-8
WARNER BROS: 71-73 2-4
LPs: 10/12-Inch 33rpm
BUDDAH: 74 8-10
MGM: 71-72 10-12
MERCURY: 69 12-15
Member: Teresa Kelly.

COVER GIRLS
Singles: 7-Inch
FEVER: 87 1-3
LPs: 10/12-Inch 33rpm
FEVER: 87 5-8

COWBOY COPAS:
see COPAS, Cowboy

COWBOY CHURCH SUNDAY SCHOOL
Singles: 78rpm
DECCA: 54-55 2-4
VOSS: 54 3-5
Singles: 7-Inch
DECCA: 54-55 2-4
VOSS: 54 3-5
EPs: 7-Inch 33/45rpm
DECCA: 55......................... 5-8

COWSILLS
Singles: 7-Inch
JODA: 65 10-15
LONDON: 71-72 2-3
MGM: 67-71 2-4
PHILIPS: 66-67 3-5
Picture Sleeves
MGM: 67-69 3-6
PHILIPS: 66 5-10
LPs: 10/12-Inch 33rpm
LONDON: 71 8-10
MGM: 67-71 10-12
WING: 68 10-12
Also see COWSILL, Bill

Also see COWSILL, John
Also see COWSILL, Susan

COX, Wally
Singles: 78rpm
RCA VICTOR: *53* $3-5
Singles: 7-Inch
ARVEE: *60* 2-4
GEORGE: *61* 2-4
RCA VICTOR (5278; "What A Crazy
Guy"): *53* 3-5
WAND: *70* 1-3
Picture Sleeves
RCA VICTOR (5278; "What A Crazy
Guy"): *53* 10-20

COYOTE SISTERS
Singles: 7-Inch
MOROCCO: *84* 1-3
Picture Sleeves
MOROCCO: *84* 1-3
LPs: 10/12-Inch 33rpm
MOROCCO: *84* 5-8
Members: Leah Kunkel; Marty Gwinn; Renee Armand.

CRABBY APPLETON
Singles: 7-Inch
ELEKTRA: *70-72* 2-4
LPs: 10/12-Inch 33rpm
ELEKTRA: *70-71* 8-10

CRACK THE SKY
Singles: 7-Inch
LIFESONG: *76-79* 2-3
LPs: 10/12-Inch 33rpm
LIFESONG (Except 8000
series): *75-78* 10-15
LIFESONG (8000 series): *81* 5-8

CRADDOCK, Billy "Crash"
(Billy Craddock; "Crash" Craddock)
Singles: 7-Inch
ABC: *72-78* 1-3
ABC/DOT: *75-77* 2-3
CAPITOL: *78-82* 1-3
CARTWHEEL: *71-72* 2-3
CEE CEE: *83* 1-3
CHART: *67-73* 2-3
COLONIAL: *58* 8-10
COLUMBIA: *59-60* 4-6
DATE: *58* 5-8
KING (Except 5912): *64-65* 3-5
KING (5912; "Betty Betty"): *64* 10-12
MERCURY: *61-62* 3-5

Picture Sleeves
COLUMBIA: *59* $12-25
EPs: 7-Inch 33/45rpm
ABC: *74* 4-8
(Jukebox issue only.)
LPs: 10/12-Inch 33rpm
ABC: *72-78* 6-10
ABC/AT EASE: *78* 10-12
(Special issue for the Armed Forces.)
ABC/DOT: *76-77* 6-10
CAPITOL: *78-83* .5-8
CARTWHEEL: *71-72* 10-12
CHART: *73* 8-12
HARMONY: *73* .10-12
KING: *64* 40-50
STARDAY: 8-10
MCA: *82* 5-10

CRAMER, Floyd
Singles: 78rpm
ABBOTT: *53-54* .3-5
MGM: *55-57* 2-4
Singles: 7-Inch
ABBOTT: *53-54* .3-6
MGM: *55-57* 2-4
RCA VICTOR: *60-81* 1-3
Picture Sleeves
RCA VICTOR: *60-79* 5-12
EPs: 7-Inch 33/45rpm
MGM: *57* 5-10
RCA VICTOR: *61-63* 5-10
LPs: 10/12-Inch 33rpm
ALSHIRE: *68* 8-12
CAMDEN: *65-74* 6-12
MGM (3500 series): *57* 15-20
MGM (4200 series): *64* 10-15
MGM (4600 series): *70* 8-12
RCA VICTOR (0100 through 4000
series): *73-81* 5-10
(With an "AHL1," ANL1," "APD1," "APL1," or
"AYL1" prefix.)
RCA VICTOR (2000 through 4000
series): *60-73* 10-20
(With an "LPM" or "LSP" prefix.)
Also see COUNTRY HAMS
Also see PRESLEY, Elvis
Also see REEVES, Jim

CRAMPS
Singles: 12-Inch 33/45rpm
I.R.S.: *82* 10-15
Singles: 7-Inch
I.R.S. (Black vinyl): *81* 4-6
I.R.S. (Colored vinyl)*81* 30-40

ILLEGAL/I.R.S.: *80* $10-15
NEW ROSE (Picture discs): *84* 10-15
VENGEANCE: *78* 50-60
Picture Sleeves
VENGEANCE: *78* 50-75
EPs: 7-Inch 33/45rpm
BIG BEAT: *83* 8-12
ILLEGAL/I.R.S: *79* 8-10
LPs: 10/12-Inch 33rpm
ENIGMA: 5-8
I.R.S.: *79-84* 8-10
ILLEGAL/I.R.S. (Except 012): *79-80* 8-10
ILLEGAL/I.R.S. (012; "Off The
  Bone"): *83* 15-20
  (With 3-D cover AND glasses.)
ILLEGAL/I.R.S. (012; "Off The
  Bone"): *83* 5-8
  (With standard cover.)
LAST RECORD: *78* 15-20
NST: *85* 5-8
NEW ROSE: *86* 5-8
MIDNIGHT: *78* 15-20
  Members: Lux Interior; Poison Ivy; Congo Powers;
  Bryan Gregory; Nick Knox; Ivy Rorschach.

CRAMPTON SISTERS
Singles: 7-Inch
ABC: *66* 3-5
DCP: *64* 4-6

CRANE, Les
Singles: 7-Inch
WARNER BROS: *71* 2-3
LPs: 10/12-Inch 33rpm
WARNER BROS: *71* 6-10

CRAWFORD, Caroline
Singles: 7-Inch
MERCURY: *78-79* 1-3
LPs: 10/12-Inch 33rpm
MERCURY: *78-79* 5-8

CRAWFORD, Carolyn
Singles: 7-Inch
MERCURY: *79* 2-3
MOTOWN: *63-64* 8-10
PHILADELPHIA INT'L: *74-75* 2-3

CRAWFORD, Hank
Singles: 7-Inch
ATLANTIC: *61-70* 2-4
KUDU: *72* 2-3
LPs: 10/12-Inch 33rpms
ATLANTIC: *61-73* 10-20
KUDU: *72-76* 10-12

CRAWFORD, Johnny
Singles: 7-Inch
ABC: *73* $1-3
CINDY: 3-6
COLLECTABLES: *81* 1-3
DEL-FI: *61-64* 4-8
SIDEWALK: *67-68* 3-5
WYNNE: *60* 5-8
Picture Sleeves
DEL-FI: *61-63* 8-15
SIDEWALK: *68* 4-6
LPs: 10/12-Inch 33rpm
DEL-FI: *62-63* 20-30
GUEST STAR: *63* 15-20
RHINO: *82* 5-8
SUPREME: *66* 15-20
  Also see CRAWFORD BROTHERS
  Also see MOUSEKETEERS

CRAWFORD, Randy
Singles: 12-Inch 33/45rpm
WARNER BROS: *83* 4-6
Singles: 7-Inch
COLUMBIA: *72-73* 2-3
MCA: *81* 1-3
WARNER BROS: *77-86* 1-3
LPs: 10/12-Inch 33rpm
RCA VICTOR: *84* 5-8
WARNER BROS: *76-86* 6-10
  Also see CRUSADERS
  Also see JARREAU, Al, & Randy Crawford
  Also see SPRINGFIELD, Rick, & Randy
Crawford

CRAWLER:
see BACK STREET CRAWLER

CRAYTON, Pee Wee
Singles: 78rpm
ALADDIN: *51* $10-20
FLAIR: *55* 6-12
FOUR STAR: *47* 10-20
IMPERIAL: *54-55* 15-30
MODERN: *49-51* 8-12
POST: *55* 6-12
RECORDED IN HOLLYWOOD: *54* ... 10-20
VEE JAY: *56-57* 6-12
Singles: 7-Inch
ALADDIN: *51* 25-40
EDCO: 10-20
FLAIR: *55* 10-20
FOX: 10-15
GUYDEN: *61* 3-5
IMPERIAL: *54-55* 15-30
JAMIE: *61* 3-5
MODERN: *51* 20-30
POST: *55* 10-20
RECORDED IN HOLLYWOOD: *54* ... 25-40
SMASH: *62* 3-5
VEE JAY: *56-57* 15-25
LPs: 10/12-Inch 33rpm
CROWN: *59* 35-40
MURRAY BROTHERS: *83* 5-8
VANGUARD: *71* 8-10
Also see CARROLL COUNTRY BOYS
Also see HOMER THE GREAT

CRAZY ELEPHANT
Singles: 7-Inch
BELL: *69-70* 3-5
SPHERE SOUND: *69* 2-4
LPs: 10/12-Inch 33rpm
BELL: *69* 12-15

CRAZY HORSE
Singles: 7-Inch
EPIC: *72* 2-4
M.O.C.: 3-5
REPRISE: *71-72* 2-4
LPs: 10/12-Inch 33rpm
EPIC: *72-76* 8-10
RCA VICTOR: *78* 5-8
REPRISE: *71-72* 10-12
Also see YOUNG, Neil

CRAZY OTTO
Singles: 78rpm
DECCA: *55-57* 2-4
Singles: 7-Inch
DECCA: *55-61* 2-4
MGM: *62* 2-3

EPs: 7-Inch 33/45rpm
DECCA: *55-58* $5-8

LPs: 10/12-Inch 33rpm
DECCA: *55-61* 8-12
MGM: *63* 6-10
VOCALION: *59* 8-10

CRAZY WORLD OF ARTHUR BROWN:
see BROWN, Arthur

CREACH, Papa John
Singles: 7-Inch
BUDDAH: *76* 2-3
DJM: *79* 1-3
GRUNT: *71-72* 2-4
LPs: 10/12-Inch 33rpm
BUDDAH: *75-77* 10-12
DJM: *77-78* 8-10
GRUNT: *71-74* 12-15
Also see JEFFERSON STARSHIP
Also see SUNRISE

CREAM
Singles: 7-Inch
ATCO: *67-70* 4-6
EPs: 7-Inch 33/45rpm
ATCO ("Goodbye Cream"): *69* 8-12
(Promotional issue only.)
LPs: 10/12-Inch 33rpm
ATCO: *67-72* 15-20
MFSL: *82* 15-20
POLYDOR: *72-73* 10-12
RSO (Except 015): *72-83* 5-8
RSO (015; "Classic Cuts"): *75* 35-40
(Promotional issue only.)
SPRINGBOARD: 10-12
Members: Eric Clapton; Jack Bruce; Ginger Baker.
Also see BAKER, Ginger
Also see BRUCE, Jack
Also see CLAPTON, Eric

CREATIVE SOURCE
Singles: 7-Inch
POLYDOR: *75* 2-3
SUSSEX: *73-74* 2-3
LPs: 10/12-Inch 33rpm
POLYDOR: *75-76* 8-10
SUSSEX: *74* 10-12

CREEDENCE CLEARWATER REVIVAL
Singles: 12-Inch 33/45rpm
FANTASY (238; "Creedence
Medley"): *85* 10-15

FANTASY ('/59; "I Heard It Through
The Grapevine"): *76* $15-20
(Promotional issue only.)
Singles: 7-Inch
FANTASY (Except 2832): *69-85* 2-4
SCORPIO (412; "Porterville"): *68* 15-25
Promotional Singles
FANTASY (2832; "45 Revolutions
Per Minute"): *70* 40-60
Picture Sleeves
FANTASY (Except 2832): *69-76* 3-6
FANTASY (2832; "45 Revolutions
Per Minute"): *70* 20-25
LPs: 10/12-Inch 33rpm
FANTASY (1 through 70): *73-78* 8-12
FANTASY (4500 series): *80-85* 5-8
(Includes reissues of 8382 through 9404.)
FANTASY (8382 through
9404): *68-72* 8-15
FANTASY (9418 through 9621): *72-82* 5-8
K-TEL: *78* 8-12
MFSL: *79* 25-50
SWEET THUNDER: *75* 40-80
(Half-speed mastered.)
WARNER SPECIAL PRODUCTS
(3514; "Greatest Hits"): *85* 10-15
(A TV mail-order offer.)
Members: John Fogerty; Tom Fogerty; Doug Clif-
ford; Stuart Cook.
Also see CLIFFORD, Doug "Cosmo"
Also see DA SHIELL, Russell
Also see FOGERTY, John
Also see FOGERTY, Tom
Also see GOLLIWOGS
Also see HARRISON, Don

CREME, Lol, & Kevin Godley:
see GODLEY, Kevin, & Lol Creme

CREME D'COCOA
Singles: 7-Inch
VENTURE: *78-80* 1-3
LPs: 10/12-Inch 33rpm
VENTURE: *79* 8-10

CRENSHAW, Marshall
Singles: 12-Inch 33/45rpm
SHAKE: *81* 20-25
WARNER BROS: *82* 5-8
Singles: 7-Inch
WARNER BROS: *82-85* 1-3
LPs: 10/12-Inch 33rpm
WARNER BROS: *82-85* 5-8

CREOLE, Kid: see KID CREOLE

CRESCENDOS
Singles: 78rpm
NASCO: *57* $5-10
Singles: 7-Inch
ABC: *73* 1-3
MCA: *84* 1-3
NASCO: *57-58* 10-15
SCARLET: *60-61* 10-15
TAP: 8-10
Picture Sleeves
NASCO: *58* 15-25
TAP: 10-20
LPs: 10/12-Inch 33rpm
GUEST STAR: 20-25
Member: Dale Ward.
Also see BURT, Wanda
Also see GREEN, Janice
Also see WARD, Dale

CRESCENTS
Singles: 7-Inch
ERA: *63* 3-6
Also see CHIYO & THE CRESCENTS

CRESTS
Singles: 78rpm
JOYCE: *57* 20-40
Singles: 7-Inch
ABC: *73* 1-3
APT: *65* 5-10
CAMEO: *63-64* 5-10
COED (Except 501): *58-62* 8-15
COED (501; "Pretty Little
Angel"): *58* 25-35
COLLECTABLES: *81-83* 1-3
CORAL: *64* 15-20
ERIC: *73* 1-3
JOYCE 103; ("Sweetest One"): *57* 40-60
(With the oversize letter "Y" in the Joyce logo.)
JOYCE 103; ("Sweetest One"): 10-15
(With all of the letters the same size in the Joyce
logo.)
JOYCE 105; ("No One To Love"): *57* ... 50-75
KING TUT: 3-5
LANA: 2-4
MUSICTONE: *62* 5-10
SELMA: *62-63* 10-15
TIMES SQUARE: *62-64* 4-6
TRANS ATLAS: *62* 10-15
TRIP: 2-3
UNITED ARTISTS: *62* 15-20
EPs: 7-Inch 33/45rpm
COED (101; "The Angels Listened
In"): *59* 150-250

LPs: 10/12-Inch 33rpm

COED (901; "The Crests Sing
All Biggies"): 60 .... $125-175
COED (904; "The Best Of The
Crests"): 60 100-150
COLLECTABLES: 83 6-8
POST: 8-10
　Members: Johnny Maestro; Tom Gough; Harold
　Torres; Jay Carter.
　Also see CARTER, J.T.
　Also see MAESTRO, Johnny

CRETONES
Singles: 7-Inch
PLANET: 80 1-3
LPs: 10/12-Inch 33rpm
PLANET: 81 5-8

CREW-CUTS
Singles: 78rpm
MERCURY: 54-57 4-6
Singles: 7-Inch
ABC-PARAMOUNT: 63 3-5
CHESS: 64 3-5
FIREBIRD: 70 2-4
MERCURY: 54-57 4-6
RCA VICTOR: 58-60 3-5
VEE JAY: 63 3-5
WARWICK: 60-61 3-5
WHALE: 62 3-5
EPs: 7-Inch 33/45rpm
MERCURY: 54-57 10-20
LPs: 10/12-Inch 33rpm
MERCURY: 55-56 20-25
RCA VICTOR: 59-60 15-20
WING: 59-60 15-20
　Members: Ray Perkins; John Perkins; Rudi
　Maugeri; Pat Barrett.
　Also see COASTERS / Crew-Cuts / Chiffons

CREWE, Bob
(Bob Crewe Generation; Bob Crew & The Rays)
Singles: 78rpm
CORAL: 56 .... $3-6
Singles: 7-Inch
ABC-PARAMOUNT: 61 3-5
DYNO VOICE: 66-68 1-3
CORAL: 56 4-6
CREWE: 71 2-3
ELEKTRA: 76-77 1-3
ERIC: 73 1-3
JUBILEE: 54 5-8
MELBA: 57 4-6
METROMEDIA: 72 2-3
SPOTLIGHT: 56 15-25
20TH CENTURY-FOX: 76 1-3
U.T.: 59 8-10
VIK: 57 4-6
WARWICK: 59-61 3-5
Picture Sleeves
DYNO VOICE: 67 2-4
LPs: 10/12-Inch 33rpm
CGC: 70 10-12
DYNO VOICE: 67-68 10-12
ELEKTRA: 76-77 8-10
GAMBLE: 69 2-3
PHILIPS: 67 10-15
WARWICK: 60-61 15-20
　Also see LA ROSA, Julius, & The Bob Crew
Generation

CRICKETS
Singles: 7-Inch
BARNABY: 72 15-20
BRUNSWICK (55124; "Love's Made
A Fool Of You"): 59 12-20
BRUNSWICK (55153; "When You
Ask About Love"): 59 12-20
CORAL: 60 15-20
(Records by Buddy Holly & The Crickets, even if
shown only as by "The Crickets," are listed in the
BUDDY HOLLY section of this guide.)
LIBERTY: 61-65 8-12
MGM: 73 10-12
MUSIC FACTORY: 68 12-15
Promotional Singles
BRUNSWICK (55124; "Love's Made
A Fool Of You"): 59 15-25
BRUNSWICK (55153; "When You
Ask About Love"): 59 15-25
CORAL: 60 20-30
EPs: 7-Inch 33/45rpm
B.H.M.S.: 78 3-5

CORAL (81192; "The Crickets"): *63* ... **$50-75**
(With Buddy Holly on one track, *It's Too Late*")
LPs: 10/12-Inch 33rpm
BARNABY: *70* **10-20**
CORAL: *60* **40-60**
(Records by Buddy Holly & The Crickets, even if
shown only as by "The Crickets," are listed in the
BUDDY HOLLY section of this guide.)
KOALA: **8-10**
LIBERTY: *62-64* **25-30**
VERTIGO: *73* **12-15**
Members: Sonny Curtis; Jerry Naylor; Glen D. Hardin; Jerry Allison; Joe Mauldin; Earl Sinks; David Box.
Also see ALLISON, Jerry, & The Crickets
Also see BOX, David
Also see CAMPERS
Also see CURTIS, Sonny
Also see HOLLY, Buddy
Also see IVAN
Also see JENNINGS, Waylon
Also see NAYLOR, Jerry
Also see PRESLEY, Elvis
Also see SULLIVAN, Niki
Also see VEE, Bobby, & The Crickets

CRISS, Peter
Singles: 7-Inch
CASABLANCA: *79-80* **1-3**
LPs: 10/12-Inch 33rpm
CASABLANCA (Except picture
discs): *78 80* **20-30**
CASABLANCA (Picture discs): *79* **40-50**
Also see KISS

CRISS, Sonny

CRITTERS
Singles: 7-Inch
KAPP: *65-69* **4-6**
MCA: *84* **1-3**
MUSICOR: *65* **4-6**
PRANCER: *68* **3-5**
PROJECT 3: *67-69* **3-5**
Picture Sleeves
KAPP: *66* **5-10**
PROJECT 3: *67-69* **4-8**
LPs: 10/12-Inch 33rpm
BACK-TRAC: *85* **5-8**
KAPP: *66* **25-30**
PROJECT 3: *68* **15-20**
Also see CICCONE, Don

**CRITTERS / Young Rascals / Lou
Christie**
LPs: 10/12-Inch 33rpm
BOTIQUE: *66* **$10-20**
(Tracks shown as by the "Young Rascals" are actually by Felix & The Escorts.)
Also see CHRISTIE, Lou
Also see CRITTERS
Also see FELIX & THE ESCORTS
Also see RASCALS

CROCE, Jim
Singles: 7-Inch
ABC: *72-74* **2-4**
LIFESONG: *75-76* **2-3**
Picture Sleeves
ABC: *73* **2-5**
EPs: 7-Inch 33/45rpm
ABC: *73* **10-12**
(Jukebox issue only.)
LPs: 10/12-Inch 33rpm
ABC: *72-74* **10-12**
BURNS MEDIA (1-2 "The Faces
I've Been"): *75* **40-60**
(2-LP set. Promotional issue only.)
CASHWEST: *77* **8-10**
COMMAND: *74-75* **12-15**
LIFESONG: *75-78* **8-10**
MFSL: *82* **25-50**

CROCE, Jim & Ingrid
(Jim & Ingrid)
Singles: 7-Inch
CAPITOL: *69* **10-15**
LPs: 10/12-Inch 33rpm
CAPITOL: *69* **30-35**
Also see CROCE, Jim

CROCHET, Cleveland
(Cleveland Crochet & The Sugar Bees;
Cleveland Crochet & His Hillbilly Ramblers)
Singles: 7-Inch
GOLDBAND: *60-61* **3-6**
LYRIC: **4-8**
LPs: 10/12-Inch 33rpm
GOLDBAND: *61* **30-35**

CROCKETT, G. L.
(G. Davy Crockett)
Singles: 78rpm
CHIEF: *57* **10-20**
Singles: 7-Inch
CHECKER: *65* **15-20**
CHIEF: *57* **30-40**
4 BROTHERS: *65* **3-5**

CROCKETT, Howard
Singles: 7-Inch

DOT (15593; "If You'll Let
  Me"): *57* $25-30
DOT (17000 series): *73* 2-3
MANCO: *60* 4-6
MEL-O-DY: *64* 8-15

CROOK, General
Singles: 7-Inch

CAPITOL: *69* 2-4
DOWN TO EARTH: *70-71* 3-5
WAND: *74* 2-3
LPs: 10/12-Inch 33rpm
CAPITOL: *70* 10-15
WAND: *74* 10-12

CROSBY, Beverly
Singles: 7-Inch

BAREBACK: *77* 2-3

CROSBY, Bing
**(Bing Crosby & The Andrews Sisters; Bing &
Gary Crosby)**
Singles: 78rpm

BRUNSWICK: *31-34* 5-15
DECCA: *34-57* 5-10
KAPP: *57* 2-4
VICTOR: *31* 8-15
Singles: 7-Inch
AMOS: *69* 2-3
CAPITOL: *63* 2-3
COLUMBIA: *59* 2-4
DAYBREAK: *71* 2-3
DECCA (23700 through 25600
  series): *51-65* 2-4
  (Includes 45rpm reissues of material originally is-
  sued on 78rpm.)
DECCA (27000 through 30000
  series): *50-59* 3-5

KAPP: *57* $3-5
LONDON: *77* 2-3
MGM: *60* 2-4
POLYDOR: *78* 2-3
RCA VICTOR: *60* 2-4
REPRISE: *64-67* 2-3
UNITED ARTISTS: *75* 2-3
VERVE: 2-4
Picture Sleeves
DECCA: *53-63* 5-10
KAPP: *57* 4-8
EPs: 7-Inch 33/45rpm
BRUNSWICK: *55* 5-10
COLUMBIA: *50-52* 8-12
DECCA (Except 1700): *50-59* 6-15
DECCA (1700; "Deluxe
  Box Set"): 75-100
  (15-EP set.)
RCA VICTOR: *57* 5-8
LPs: 10/12-Inch 33rpm
AMOS: *69* 8-10
ARGO: *76* 10-15
BIOGRAPH: *73* 5-10
BRUNSWICK: *55* 15-20
CAPITOL (2300 series): *65* 8-12
CAPITOL (11000 series): *77-78* 5-8
CITADEL: *78* 5-8
COLUMBIA (43; "Bing In
  Hollywood"): *67* 10-15
COLUMBIA (6000 series): *50* 15-25
COLUMBIA (35000 series): *78-79* 5-10
DECCA (100 series): *54-65* 10-25
DECCA (4000 series): *61-64* 8-12
DECCA (5000 series): *50-55* 15-25
  (10-Inch LPs.)
DECCA (8000 series): *54-59* 10-20
  (Black label with silver print.)
DECCA (8000 series): *60-72* 8-12
  (Black label with horizontal rainbow stripe.)
DECCA (8700 series): *64* 6-10
DECCA (9000 series): *61-62* 10-15
  (Decca LP numbers in this series preceded by a "7"
  or a "DL-7" are stereo issues.)
ENCORE: *68* 8-10
GOLDEN: *57* 10-15
HARMONY (7000 series): *57* 10-15
HARMONY (11000 series): *69* 5-10
LONDON: *77* 5-8
MCA: *77-82* 5-10
MGM: *61-64* 10-12
METRO: *65* 5-10
P.I.P.: *71* 5-10
POLYDOR: *77* 5-8

RCA VICTOR (500 series): 72 ....$6-10
RCA VICTOR (1400 through 2000
  series): 57-59 10-15
  (With an "LPM" or "LSP" prefix.)
RCA VICTOR (2000 series): 77 5-8
  (With a "CPL1" prefix.)
REPRISE: 64 8-12
20TH CENTURY-FOX: 79 5-8
UNITED ARTISTS: 76 5-8
VOCALION (3600 series): 57 10-15
VOCALION (3700 series): 66 5-10
WARNER BROS: 60-62 10-15
  Also see ANDREWS SISTERS
  Also see CROSBY, Gary, Phillip, Dennis,
  Lindsay & Bing
  Also see DORSEY, Jimmy
  Also see YOUNG, Victor

CROSBY, Bing & Gary
  Singles: 7-Inch
DECCA: 50-51 3-6

CROSBY, Bing, & Louis Armstrong
  Singles: 78rpm
CAPITOL: 56 2-5
  Singles: 7-Inch
CAPITOL: 56 3-5
DECCA: 51 4-8
MGM: 60 2-4
  LPs: 10/12-Inch 33rpm
MGM (100 series): 70 5-10
MGM (3800 series): 60 10-20
SOUNDS RARE: 83 5-8

**CROSBY, Bing, Louis Armstrong,
  Rosemary Clooney, & The Hi-Los**
  Singles: 7-Inch
COLUMBIA (6277; "Music To
  Shave By"): 5-10
  (Special products flexi-disc from Remington.)
  Also see ARMSTRONG, Louis
  Also see CLOONEY, Rosemary

CROSBY, Bing, & Count Basie
  LPs: 10/12-Inch 33rpm
DAYBREAK: 72 8-12
  Also see BASIE, Count

CROSBY, Bing, & Connee Boswell
  Singles: 78rpm
DECCA: 38-40 4-8
  Also see BOSWELL, Connee

CROSBY, Bing, & Judy Garland
  Singles: 78rpm
DECCA: 45 5-10

Also see GARLAND, Judy

CROSBY, Bing, & Bob Hope
  Singles: 78rpm
DECCA: 45 ....$4-8
  Also see HOPE, Bob

CROSBY, Bing, & Louis Jordan
  Singles: 78rpm
DECCA: 45 4-8
  Also see JORDAN, Louis

CROSBY, Bing, & Grace Kelly
  Singles: 78rpm
CAPITOL: 56 2-5
  Singles: 7-Inch
CAPITOL: 56 3-5

CROSBY, Bing, & Peggy Lee
  Singles: 78rpm
DECCA: 52 3-5
  Singles: 7-Inch
DECCA: 52 4-6
  Also see LEE, Peggy

CROSBY, Bing, & The Mills Brothers
  Singles: 78rpm
BRUNSWICK: 32 5-10
  Also see MILLS BROTHERS

CROSBY, Bing, & Frank Sinatra
  Singles: 78rpm
CAPITOL: 56 2-5
  Singles: 7-Inch
CAPITOL: 56 3-5
  Also see SINATRA, Frank

CROSBY, Bing, & Mel Torme
(With The Mel-Tones)
  Singles: 78rpm
DECCA: 46 4-8
  Also see TORME, Mel

CROSBY, Bing, & Orson Welles
  LPs: 10/12-Inch 33rpm
DECCA (6000; "The Small One, The
  Happy Prince"): 50 10-25
  Also see CROSBY, Bing
  Also see WELLES, Orson

CROSBY, Chris
  Singles: 7-Inch
ATLANTIC: 67 3-5
CHALLENGE: 64-65 3-5
COLUMBIA: 69 2-4
DORE: 61 3-5
MGM: 64 3-5
WARNER BROS: 63 3-5

Picture Sleeves
MGM: *64* $4-8
LPs: 10/12-Inch 33rpm
MGM: *64* 15-20

CROSBY, David
Singles: 7-Inch
ATLANTIC: *71* 2-4
LPs: 10/12-Inch 33rpm
ATLANTIC: *71* 10-12
Also see BYRDS
Also see GRATEFUL DEAD
Also see SLICK, Grace

CROSBY, David, & Graham Nash
Singles: 7-Inch
ABC: *75-77* 2-3
ATLANTIC: *72* 2-4
LPs: 10/12-Inch 33rpm
ABC: *75-78* 8-10
ATLANTIC: *72* 10-12
Also see CROSBY, David
Also see NASH, Graham

CROSBY, STILLS & NASH
Singles: 7-Inch
ATLANTIC: *69-82* 2-4
Picture Sleeves
ATLANTIC: *70-82* 2-4
LPs: 10/12-Inch 33rpm
ATLANTIC (Except 8000 series): *77-83* .. 8-10
ATLANTIC (8000 series): *69* 12-18
Members: David Crosby; Stephen Stills; Graham Nash.
Also see CROSBY, David
Also see NASH, Graham
Also see STILLS, Stephen

CROSBY, STILLS, NASH & YOUNG
Singles: 7-Inch
ATLANTIC: *70* 2-4
ATLANTIC: *88* 1-3
Picture Sleeves
ATLANTIC: *70* 2-4
EPs: 7-Inch 33/45rpm
ATLANTIC: *70* 10-12
(Jukebox issue only.)
LPs: 10/12-Inch 33rpm
ATLANTIC (Except 19000 series): *70-74* 10-20
ATLANTIC (19000 series): *81* 5-8
ATLANTIC: *88* 5-8
MFSL: *82* 25-50

Promotional LPs
ATLANTIC (165; "Celebration Copy"): $25-30
Members: David Crosby; Stephen Stills; Graham Nash; Neil Young.
Also see CROSBY, David
Also see NASH, Graham
Also see STILLS, Stephen
Also see YOUNG, Neil

CROSS, Christopher
Singles: 7-Inch
COLUMBIA: *85* 1-3
WARNER BROS: *80-88* 1-3
Picture Sleeves
WARNER BROS: *80-81* 1-3
LPs: 10/12-Inch 33rpm
COLUMBIA: *85* 5-8
WARNER BROS: *80-88* 5-8

CROSS, Jimmy
Singles: 7-Inch
CHICKEN: *65* 3-5
RECORDO: *61* 4-6
RED BIRD: *65* 3-5
TOLLIE: *64* 4-6

CROSS COUNTRY
(Tokens)
Singles: 7-Inch
ATCO: *73-74* 2-4
LPs: 10/12-Inch 33rpm
ATCO: *73* 10-12
Also see TOKENS

CROUCH, Andrae
(Andrae Crouch & The Disciples)
Singles: 7-Inch
LIGHT: *76-80* 1-3
WARNER BROS: *81* 1-3
LPs: 10/12-Inch 33rpm
ACCORD: *82* 5-8
LIGHT: *68-82* 5-10
WARNER BROS: *81* 5-8

CROW
(David Wagner)
Singles: 7-Inch
AMARET: *69-72* 2-4

LPs: 10/12-Inch 33rpm
AMARET: *69-73* 10-15

CROWD PLEASERS
Singles: 7-Inch
WESTBOUND: *79* 2-3

LPs: 10/12-Inch 33rpm
WESTBOUND: *79* $5-8

CROWDED HOUSE
Singles: 12-Inch 33/45rpm
CAPITOL: *86* 4-6
Singles: 7-Inch
CAPITOL: *86-88* 1-3
LPs: 10/12-Inch 33rpm
CAPITOL: *86-88* 5-8
Member: Neil Finn.
Also see SPLIT ENZ

CROWELL, Rodney
Singles: 7-Inch
COLUMBIA: *86-88* 1-3
WARNER BROS: *78-82* 1-3
LPs: 10/12-Inch 33rpm
WARNER BROS: *78-81* 5-8

CROWN HEIGHTS AFFAIR
Singles: 7-Inch
DELITE: *75-82* 1-3
RCA VICTOR: *73-74* 2-3
LPs: 10/12-Inch 33rpm
DELITE: *75-82* 5-8
RCA VICTOR: *74-78* 10-12

CROWS
Singles: 78rpm
RAMA (3; "Seven Lonely
Days"): *53* 20-40
RAMA (5; "Gee"): *53* 20-40
RAMA (10; "Heartbreaker"): *53* 50-100
RAMA (29; "Baby"): *54* 40-60
RAMA (30; "Miss You"): *54* 50-100
RAMA (50; "Baby Doll"): *54* 40-60
TICO (1082; "Mambo Shevitz"): *51* 30-60
Singles: 7-Inch
RAMA (3; "Seven Lonely
Days"): *53* 100-150
RAMA (5; "Gee"): *53* 40-60
(Black vinyl.)
RAMA (5; "Gee"): *53* 150-200
(Colored vinyl.)
RAMA (10; "Heartbreaker"): *53* 200-250
(Black vinyl.)
RAMA (10; "Heartbreaker"): *53* 400-450
(Colored vinyl.)
RAMA (29; "Baby"): *54* 100-125
RAMA (30; "Miss You"): *54* 200-250
(Black vinyl.)
RAMA (30; "Miss You"): *54* 400-450
(Colored vinyl.)
RAMA (50; "Baby Doll"): *54* 100-125

TICO (1082; "Mambo Shevitz"): *51* .. $75-100
(Black vinyl.)
TICO (1082; "Mambo Shevitz"): *51* .. 150-200
(Colored vinyl.)
Members: Sonny Norton; Harold Major; Jerry
Hamilton; Mark Jackson; Bill Davis.
Also see HARPTONES / Crows
Also see JEWELS

CRUDUP, Big Boy
(Arthur "Big Boy" Crudup)
Singles: 78rpm
ACE (503; "I Wonder"): *53* 175-225
BLUEBIRD: *41-46* 5-10
GROOVE: *53-54* 8-15
RCA VICTOR: *47-53* 4-8
Singles: 7-Inch
FIRE: *62* 5-10
GROOVE: *53-54* 20-30
RCA VICTOR (4000 & 5000
series): *52-53* 20-35
(With a "47" prefix.)
RCA VICTOR (50-0000; "That's All
Right"): *50* 40-60
RCA VICTOR (50-0001 through
50-0141): *50-51* 25-50
EPs: 7-Inch 33/45rpm
CAMDEN: 50-75
LPs: 10/12-Inch 33rpm
COLLECTABLES: *88* 6-8
DELMARK: *69* 10-12
FIRE (103; "Mean Ol' Frisco"): *62* ... 125-175
RCA VICTOR: *71* 10-12
TRIP: *75* 8-10
Also see CRUDUP, Percy Lee
Also see JAMES, Elmore

CRUDUP, Percy Lee
(Arthur Crudup)
Singles: 78rpm
CHECKER: *52* 15-20
Also see CRUDUP, Big Boy

CRUISE, Pablo:
see PABLO CRUISE

CRUM, Simon
(Ferlin Husky)
Singles: 78rpm
CAPITOL: *55-57* 4-8

Singles: 7-Inch
ABC: *74* 2-3
CAPITOL: *55-63* 6-12
LPs: 10/12-Inch 33rpm
CAPITOL: *63* 50-75

Also see HUSKY, Ferlin

CRUSADERS
Singles: 7-Inch
ABC: 78 . . . . $1-3
BLUE THUMB: 72-77 2-3
CHISA: 71 2-4
MCA: 79-86 1-3
LPs: 10/12-Inch 33rpm
BLUE THUMB: 73-77 10-12
MCA: 79-86 8-10
MFSL: 78 25-50
MOTOWN: 73 10-12
MOWEST: 72 10-12
Also see COCKER, Joe
Also see CRAWFORD, Randy
Also see HOOPER, Stix
Also see JAZZ CRUSADERS
Also see SAMPLE, Joe

CRUSADERS & B. B. King
Singles: 7-Inch
MCA: 82 1-3
LPs: 10/12-Inch 33rpm
MCA: 82 8-10
Also see CRUSADERS
Also see KING, B. B.

CRYAN' SHAMES
Singles: 7-Inch
COLUMBIA: 66-70 3-6
DESTINATION: 66 4-8
Picture Sleeves
COLUMBIA: 67 5-10
LPs: 10/12-Inch 33rpm
BACK-TRAC: 85 5-8
COLUMBIA (Except 2589 &
  9389): 67-69 15-20
COLUMBIA (2589; "Sugar &
  Spice"): 66 20-25
  (Monaural.)
COLUMBIA (9389; "Sugar &
  Spice"): 66 20-30
  (Stereo.)

CRYSTAL, Billy
Singles: 12-Inch 33/45rpm
A&M: 85 4-6
Singles: 7-Inch
A&M: 85 1-3
Picture Sleeves
A&M: 85 3-5

CRYSTAL GAYLE:
see GAYLE, Crystal

CRYSTAL GRASS
Singles: 7-Inch
POLYDOR: 75 . . . . $2-3
PRIVATE STOCK: 76 2-3
LPs: 10/12-Inch 33rpm
MERCURY: 78 5-8
POLYDOR: 75 8-10

CRYSTAL MANSION
Singles: 7-Inch
CAPITOL: 68-70 2-4
COLOSSUS: 70-71 2-4
RARE EARTH: 72 2-3
20TH CENTURY-FOX: 79 1-3
LPs: 10/12-Inch 33rpm
CAPITOL: 69 12-15
RARE EARTH: 72 10-12
20TH CENTURY-FOX: 79 5-8
Also see CASWELL, Johnny

CRYSTALS
Singles: 7-Inch
INDIGO: 61 10-20
MICHELLE: 67 3-5
PAVILLION: 82 2-3
PHILLES (Except 105 & 111): 61-64 8-10
PHILLES (105; "He Hit Me"): 62 15-20
PHILLES (111; "Let's Dance The
  Screw"): 63 350-400
  (White label promotional issue only. Light blue
  labels are counterfeit copies.)
UNITED ARTISTS: 65-66 4-6
LPs: 10/12-Inch 33rpm
PHILLES (4000; "The Crystals Twist
  Uptown"): 62 75-100
  (Monaural.)
PHILLES (4000; "The Crystals Twist
  Uptown"): 62 400-500
  (Stereo.)
PHILLES (4001; "He's A Rebel"): 63 . . . 60-75
PHILLES (4003; "The Crystals"): 63 60-75
Also see LOVE, Darlene
Also see RONETTES / Crystals / Darlene
Love / Bob B. Soxx & The Blue Jeans

CUBA, Joe
(Joe Cuba Sextet)
Singles: 7-Inch
ROULETTE: 71 2-3
TICO: 66 2-5

CUES
Singles: 78rpm
CAPITOL: 55-56 5-10
JUBILEE: 55 4-8

LAMP: *54* $5-10
PREP: *57* 4-8
Singles: 7-Inch
CAPITOL: *55-56* 10-20
JUBILEE: *55* 8-12
LAMP: *54* 10-20
PREP: *57* 5-10
Members: Ollie Jones; Jimmy Breedlove; Abe De
Costa; Robey Kirk; Eddie Barnes.
Also see RAVENS

CUFF LINKS
Singles: 7-Inch
ATCO: *72* 2-3
DECCA: *69-71* 2-4
MCA: *84* 1-3
LPs: 10/12-Inch 33rpm
DECCA: *69-70* 15-25
Members: Ron Dante; Rupert Holmes.

CUGINI
Singles: 7-Inch
SCOTTI BROTHERS: *79* 2-3

CULT
(Southern Death Cult; Death Cult)
Singles: 12-Inch 33/45rpm
SIRE: *85-86* 4-6
Singles: 7-Inch
SIRE: *85-86* 1-3
LPs: 10/12-Inch 33rpm
SIRE: *85-87* 5-8
Members: Ian Astbury; Billy Duffy; Jamie Stewart;
Les Warner.

CULTURE CLUB
(Featuring Boy George)
Singles: 12-Inch 33/45rpm
EPIC/VIRGIN: *82-86* 4-6
Singles: 7-Inch
EPIC/VIRGIN: *82-86* 1-3
Picture Sleeves
EPIC/VIRGIN: *82-86* 1-3
LPs: 10/12-Inch 33rpm
EPIC/VIRGIN (Except picture
discs): *82-86* 5-8
EPIC/VIRGIN (Picture discs): *83* 8-10
Also see BAND AID
Also see BOY GEORGE

CUMMINGS, Burton
Singles: 7-Inch
ALFA: *81* 1-3
PORTRAIT: *76-78* 2-3
Picture Sleeves
ALFA: *81* 1-3

EPs: 7-Inch 33/45rpm
PORTRAIT: *77* $3-5
(Issued with a paper sleeve.)
LPs: 10/12-Inch 33rpm
ALFA: *81* 5-8
PORTRAIT: *76-78* 8-10
Also see GUESS WHO

CUNHA, Rick
Singles: 7-Inch
COLUMBIA: *75* 2-3
GRC: *74* 2-3
LPs: 10/12-Inch 33rpm
COLUMBIA: *75* 8-10
GRC: *74* 10-12
Also see JENNINGS, Waylon

CUPIDS
Singles: 7-Inch
AANKO: *63* 30-35
KC: *63* 10-15

CURB, Mike
(Mike Curb & The Sidewalk Sounds; Mike Curb
& The Curbstones; Mike Curb & The Rebalairs;
The Mike Curb Congregation)
Singles: 7-Inch
BUENA VISTA: *75* 2-4
MGM: *70* 2-3
REPRISE: *64* 5-8
SMASH: *64* 3-6
TOWER: *66* 4-6
Picture Sleeves
BUENA VISTA: *75* 5-10
LPs: 10/12-Inch 33rpm
BUENA VISTA: 8-12
FORWARD: 5-8
MGM: *71* 5-8
Also see ALLAN, Davie
Also see DAVIS, Sammy, Jr.
Also see LEGRAND, Michel, & The Mike
Curb Congregation

CURE
Singles: 12-Inch 33/45rpm
ELEKTRA: *85-86* 4-6
SIRE: *83-85* 4-6
Singles: 7-Inch
ELEKTRA: *85-88* 1-3
SIRE: *83-85* 1-3
LPs: 10/12-Inch 33rpm
A&M: *81* 8-10
ELEKTRA: *85-87* 5-8
PVC: *80* 8-10
SIRE: *83-85* 5-8

Members: Robert Smith; Laurence Tolhurst.

CURIOSITY KILLED THE CAT
Singles: 7-Inch
MERCURY: 87 .... $1-3
LPs: 10/12-Inch 33rpm
MERCURY: 87 1-3

CURTIS, Sonny
Singles: 78rpm
CORAL: 53 5-10
Singles: 7-Inch
A&M: 72 10-15
CAPITOL: 75-76 8-12
CORAL (61023; "The Best Way To
Hold A Girl"): 53 10-20
CORAL (62207; "Red Headed
Stranger"): 60 15-20
DIMENSION: 63-64 5-8
DOT: 58 10-15
ELEKTRA: 79-81 1-3
LIBERTY: 64 10-15
MERCURY: 73 8-10
OVATION: 70 10-15
STEEM: 85 1-3
VIVA: 66-69 8-10
LPs: 10/12-Inch 33rpm
ELEKTRA: 79-81 8-15
IMPERIAL: 64 25-40
VIVA: 68-69 20-30
Also see CLAPTON, Eric
Also see CRICKETS

CURTIS, T.C.
Singles: 12-Inch 33/45rpm
SIRE: 85 4-6

CURTIS LEE: see LEE, Curtis

CURTOLA, Bobby
Singles: 7-Inch
DEL-FI: 61-63 3-5
KING: 67 3-5
TARTAN AMERICAN: 66 3-5
Picture Sleeves
DEL-FI: 61-62 8-15

CUT
Singles: 7-Inch
SUPERTRONICS: 86 1-3

CUTTING CREW
Singles: 7-Inch
VIRGIN: 87 1-3
LPs: 10/12-Inch 33rpm
VIRGIN: 87 5-8

CYCLONES

Singles: 7-Inch
TROPHY: 58 .... $10-20
Member: Bill Taylor.

CYMANDE
Singles: 7-Inch
JANUS: 72-73 2-4
LPs: 10/12-Inch 33rpm
JANUS: 72-74 10-12

CYMARRON
Singles: 7-Inch
ENTRANCE: 71-72 2-4
LPs: 10/12-Inch 33rpm
ENTRANCE: 71 10-12

CYMBAL, Johnny
Singles: 7-Inch
AMARET: 69 2-4
COLUMBIA: 66 3-5
DCP: 65 3-5
KAPP: 63-64 4-6
KEDLEN: 63 8-10
MCA: 84 1-3
MGM: 60-61 4-6
MUSICOR: 67 3-5
VEE JAY: 63 4-6
LPs: 10/12-Inch 33rpm
KAPP: 63 30-35
Also see DEREK

CYMONE, Andre
Singles: 12-Inch 33/45rpm
COLUMBIA: 82-86 4-6
Singles: 7-Inch
COLUMBIA: 82-86 1-3
LPs: 10/12-Inch 33rpm
COLUMBIA: 82-86 5-8

CYRÉ
Singles: 7-Inch
FRESH: 87 1-3

CYRKLE
Singles: 7-Inch
COLUMBIA (Black vinyl): 65-68 3-5
COLUMBIA (Colored vinyl): 66 5-10
(Promotional issues only.)
Picture Sleeves
COLUMBIA: 66-68 20-30
LPs: 10/12-Inch 33rpm
COLUMBIA: 66-67 20-25
FLYING DUTCHMAN/AMSTERDAM
(12007; "The Minx"): 70 20-25
(Soundtrack.)

Also see REVERE, Paul, & The Raiders /
Cyrkle
Also see SIMON, Paul

D

D., Eddie: see EDDIE D.

DA
LPs: 10/12-Inch 33rpm
FRONTLINE: 85-86 . . . .$5-8

DB's
LPs: 10/12-Inch 33rpm
I.R.S.: 87 5-8

D.J. DOC & SPYDER D.
Singles: 7-Inch
PROFILE: 86 4-6

**D.J. JAZZY JEFF & THE FRESH
   PRINCE**
Singles: 7-Inch
WORD-UP: 86 1-3
LPs: 10/12-Inch 33rpm
JIVE: 87 5-8

"D" TRAIN
Singles: 12-Inch 33/45rpm
PRELUDE: 81-85 .4-6
Singles: 7-Inch
PRELUDE: 81-85 .1-3
LPs: 10/12-Inch 33rpm
PRELUDE: 82-85 .5-8

DFX2
Singles: 7-Inch
MCA: 83 1-3
LPs: 10/12-Inch 33rpm
MCA: 83 5-8

DMX, Davy: see DAVY DMX

D.O.X.
(Defenders Of the Cross)
LPs: 10/12-Inch 33rpm
FRONTLINE: 86 5-8

DADDY DEWDROP
Singles: 7-Inch
CAPITOL: 75 2-3
INPHASION: 78-79 2-3
SUNFLOWER: 70-72 2-4
SUNFLOWER/MGM: 73 2-3
LPs: 10/12-Inch 33rpm
SUNFLOWER: 71 12-15

DADDY O's
Singles: 7-Inch
CABOT: 58 . . . .$4-6

DAHL, Steve, & The Teenage Radiation
Singles: 7-Inch
COHO: 79 2-3
OVATION: 79 2-3
Picture Sleeves
OVATION: 79 2-3

DAILY, E.G.
(Elizabeth G. Daily)
Singles: 12-Inch 33/45rpm
A&M: 86 4-6
Singles: 7-Inch
A&M: 86 1-3
LPs: 10/12-Inch 33rpm
A&M: 86 5-8

**DAISY DILLMAN BAND:
  see DILLMAN BAND**

DA'KRASH
Singles: 7-Inch
CAPITOL: 88 1-3
LPs: 10/12-Inch 33rpm
CAPITOL: 88 5-8

DALBELLO
Singles: 12-Inch 33/45rpm
CAPITOL: 84 4-6
Singles: 7-Inch
CAPITOL: 84 1-3

DALE, Alan
Singles: 78rpm
COLUMBIA: 50-51 3-5
CORAL: 52-56 2-5
Singles: 7-Inch
ABC-PARAMOUNT: 64 1-3
ADVANCE: 2-4
COLUMBIA: 50-51 3-5
CORAL (60000 & 61000 series): 52-56 . . .2-5
CORAL (62000 series): 63 2-3
DECCA: 52 3-5
EMKAY: 62 2-3
FTP: 61 2-3
MGM: 59 2-3
SINCLAIR: 61 2-3
EPs: 7-Inch 33/45rpm
CORAL: 52-56 6-10
LPs: 10/12-Inch 33rpm
CORAL: 55-56 .12-20
FORD: 63 6-10
UNITED ARTISTS: 60 8-12

Also see CORNELL, Don, Johnny Desmond, & Alan Dale

DALE, Dick
(Dick Dale & His Del-tones)
Singles: 7-Inch
ACCENT: 68 .... $4-6
CAPITOL: 63-64 5-8
COLUMBIA: 87 3-5
CONCERT ROOM: 63 4-6
COUGAR: 67 3-5
CUPID: 60 10-12
DEL-TONE (5012 through 5014): 59-60 . 25-35
DEL-TONE (5017 through 5028): 61-63 .. 8-12
GNP/CRESCENDO: 75 2-4
SATURN: 63 8-10
YES: 3-5
Promotional Singles
CAPITOL ("Thunder Wave"/
"Spanish Kiss"): 64 5-8
(Bonus single, packaged with an LP by Jerry Cole & His Spacemen.)
CAPITOL (2320; "Peppermint
Man"): 63 25-35
(Compact 33 Single)
Picture Sleeves
CAPITOL (Except 2320): 63 12-25
CAPITOL (2320; "Peppermint
Man"): 63 35-45
(Promotional Compact 33 Single sleeve.)
COLUMBIA: 87 4-6
YES: 4-8
LPs: 10/12-Inch 33rpm
ACCENT: 67 15-20
BALBOA: 83 5-8
CAPITOL (1886; "Surfer's Choice"): 63 . 15-25
CAPITOL (1930; "King Of The Surf
Guitar"): 63 30-35
CAPITOL (2002; "Checkered
Flag"): 63 25-35
CAPITOL (2053; "Mr.
Eliminator"): 64 30-35
CAPITOL (2111; "Summer Surf"): 64 ... 30-35
(Includes the bonus single by Jerry Cole & His Spacemen.)
CAPITOL (2111; "Summer Surf"): 64 ... 20-30
(Without the bonus single by Jerry Cole & His Spacemen.)
CAPITOL (2293; "Rock Out With Dick
Dale Live At Ciro's"): 65 30-35
DEL-TONE (1001; "Surfer's
Choice"): 61 30-40
DEL-TONE (1886; "Surfer's
Choice"): 63 20-25

DUBTONE: 63 .... $15-20
GNP/CRESCENDO: 75 8-12
Also see ALLAN, Davie
Also see BEACH BOYS / Dick Dale / Surfaris / Surf Kings

DALE, Jimmy
(Jimmy Clanton)
Singles: 7-Inch
DREW-BLAN: 61 15-20
Also see CLANTON, Jimmy

DALE & GRACE
Singles: 7-Inch
COLLECTABLES: 1-3
ERIC: 1-3
HBR: 66 3-5
MICHELLE: 63-64 5-10
MONTEL: 63-67 3-5
MONTEL MICHELLE (942; "What Am
I Living For"): 64 4-6
(Uses both label names.)
TRIP: 2-3
LPs: 10/12-Inch 33rpm
MONTEL: 64 30-35
Members: Dale Houston; Grace Broussard.

DALLARA, Tony
Singles: 7-Inch
MERCURY: 58-60 2-4
VESUVIUS: 61-62 2-3
LPs: 10/12-Inch 33rpm
VESUVIUS: 62 6-10

DALTON, Kathy
Singles: 7-Inch
DISC REET: 74 2-3
LPs: 10/12-Inch 33rpm
DISC REET: 73-74 8-10

DALTON & DUBARRI
Singles: 7-Inch
ABC: 76 2-3
COLUMBIA: 73-74 2-3
HILLTAK: 79 1-3
LPs: 10/12-Inch 33rpm
ABC: 76 8-10
COLUMBIA: 73-74 10-12
HILLTAK: 79 5-8

DALTREY, Roger
Singles: 7-Inch
A&M: 75-76 2-3
ATLANTIC: 84-86 1-3
MCA: 73-82 1-3
MCA/GOLDHAWKE: 75-77 2-3

ODE: 72-73 ....$2-4
POLYDOR: 80-81 1-3
TRACK: 73 2-3
LPs: 10/12-Inch 33rpm
ATLANTIC: 84-86 5-8
MCA: 71-82 10-12
TRACK: 73 10-12
Also see WHO

DALTREY, Roger, & Steve Gibbons
Singles: 12-Inch 33/45rpm
MCA: 5-8
(Promotional issue only.)
Also see DALTREY, Roger
Also see GIBBONS, Steve, Band

DALTREY, Roger, & Rick Wakeman
Singles: 7-Inch
A&M: 75 2-3
LPs: 10/12-Inch 33rpm
A&M: 75 8-10
Also see DALTREY, Roger
Also see WAKEMAN, Rick

DAMIAN, Michael
Singles: 7-Inch
LEG: 81 1-3

DAMARIS
Singles: 7-Inch
COLUMBIA: 84 1-3

DAMIANO, Joe
(Josef Damiano)
Singles: 7-Inch
CHANCELLOR: 59-60 3-5

DAMION & DENITA
LPs: 10/12-Inch 33rpm
ROCKET: 80 5-8

DAMITA JO
(Damita Joe)
Singles: 7-Inch
EPIC (Black vinyl): 65-67 2-3
EPIC (Colored vinyl): 66 4-8
MELIC: 64 2-3
MERCURY: 60-64 2-4
RANWOOD: 68-71 1-3
VEE JAY: 65 2-3
Picture Sleeves
EPIC: 65 3-6
MERCURY: 61-63 4-8
EPs: 7-Inch 33/45rpm
MERCURY: 60-61 5-8
LPs: 10/12-Inch 33rpm
CAMDEN: 65 6-10

EPIC: 65-67 ....$8-12
MERCURY: 61-63 10-20
RANWOOD: 68 5-8
VEE JAY: 65 8-12
Also see BENTON, Brook, & Damita Jo

DAMITA JO & BILLY ECKSTINE
Singles: 7-Inch
MERCURY: 63 2-3
Also see ECKSTINE, Billy

DAMITA JO & STEVE GIBSON & THE RED CAPS
Singles: 7-Inch
ABC-PARAMOUNT: 61 4-6
LPs: 10/12-Inch 33rpm
ABC-PARAMOUNT: 61 30-40
Also see DAMITA JO
Also see GIBSON, Steve

DAMNATION
(Featuring Adam Blessing)
Singles: 7-Inch
UNITED ARTISTS: 71-72 2-4
LPs: 10/12-Inch 33rpm
UNITED ARTISTS: 69-71 10-15

DAMON, Liz
(Liz Damon's Orient Express)
Singles: 7-Inch
ABC: 73 1-3
ANTHEM: 71-72 2-4
MAKAHA: 70 3-5
WHITE WHALE: 70 2-3
LPs: 10/12-Inch 33rpm
WHITE WHALE: 71 8-12

DAMONE, Vic
Singles: 78rpm
COLUMBIA: 56-57 2-4
MERCURY: 50-55 2-4
Singles: 7-Inch
CAPITOL: 61-64 2-3
COLUMBIA: 56-61 2-4
DOLTON: 62 2-3
MGM: 72-73 2-3
MERCURY: 50-55 2-4
RCA VICTOR: 66-69 1-3
REBECCA: 77 1-3
UNITED TALENT: 70 1-3
WARNER BROS: 65-66 2-3
EPs: 7-Inch 33/45rpm
COLUMBIA: 56-58 5-8
MERCURY: 50-56 6-10
LPs: 10/12-Inch 33rpm
CAPITOL: 62-64 8-12

COLUMBIA (1000 through 1500
series): *58-61* $10-15
COLUMBIA (1900 series): *62* 8-12
COLUMBIA (8000 through 8300
series): *58-61* 10-15
COLUMBIA (8700 series): *62* 8-12
DOLTON: *64* 6-10
HARMONY: *66-67* 5-8
MERCURY (Except 25000
series): *69* 6-10
MERCURY (25000 series): *50-56* 12-20
RCA VICTOR: *66-68* 5-10
WARNER BROS: *65* 5-10
WING: *59-63* 6-10
   Also see ANDREWS, Julie & Andre Previn /
Vic Damone / Jack Jones / Marian Anderson

DANA, Bill
(Jose Jimenez)
Singles: 7-Inch
A&M: *65-66* 2-4
KAPP: *61-63* 2-5
SIGNATURE: *60* 3-5
Picture Sleeves
KAPP: *61-62* 4-8
LPs: 10/12-Inch 33rpm
A&M: *68* 8-12
CAPITOL: *70* 6-10
HBR: *66* 8-10
KAPP: *60-64* 10-15
ROULETTE: *61* 12-20
SIGNATURE: *60* 20-25

DANA, Vic
Singles: 7-Inch
CASINO: *76* 1-3
COLUMBIA: *71* 1-3
DOLTON: *61-65* 2-4
LIBERTY: *68-70* 2-3
MGM: *75* 1-3
Picture Sleeves
DOLTON: *62-66* 3-6
LPs: 10/12-Inch 33rpm
DOLTON: *61-65* 10-15
LIBERTY: *67-70* 8-12
SUNSET: *67* 6-10

DANCER, PRANCER & NERVOUS
Singles: 7-Inch
CAPITOL: *59* 3-5
Picture Sleeves
CAPITOL: *59* 5-10
Member: Russ Regan.

DANDERLIERS
Singles: 78rpm
STATES (147; "Chop Chop
Boom"): *55* $40-60
STATES (150; "Shu-Wop"): *55* 20-40
STATES (152; "May God Be
With You"): *55* 20-40
STATES (160; "My Love"): *56* 35-50
Singles: 7-Inch
B&F: *61* 4-6
STATES (147; "Chop Chop
Boom"): *55* 75-125
(Black vinyl.)
STATES (147; "Chop Chop
Boom"): *55* 200-300
(Colored vinyl.)
STATES (150; "Shu-Wop"): *55* 40-60
STATES (152; "May God Be
With You"): *56* 50-75
STATES (160; "My Love"): *56* 75-100
Members: Dallas Taylor; James Campbell; Richard
Thomas; Walter Stephenson; Bernard Dixon; Louis
Johnson.

DANDLEERS: see DANLEERS

DANGERFIELD, Rodney
Singles: 12-Inch 33/45rpm
RCA VICTOR: *83* 4-6
Singles: 7-Inch
RCA VICTOR: *83* 1-3
LPs: 10/12-Inch 33rpm
DECCA: *66* 15-20
CASABLANCA: *80* 5-8
RCA VICTOR: *83* 5-8
RHINO: *80* 5-8

DANIELS, Charlie, Band
(Charley Daniels & The Jaguars)
Singles: 7-Inch
EPIC: *76-88* 1-3
HANOVER: *59* .8-10
KAMA SUTRA: *73-76* 2-3
PAULA (200 series): *66* 3-5
PAULA (400 series): *76* 2-3
LPs: 10/12-Inch 33rpm
CAPITOL (11000 series): *75* 8-10
CAPITOL (16000 series): *80* 5-8
EPIC (Except 273): *76-88* 5-8
EPIC (273; "Everything You Always
Wanted To Hear"): *77* 8-12
(Promotional issue only.)
KAMA SUTRA: *73-76* 10-12
MFSL: *85* 15-20

DANKO, Rick
Singles: 7-Inch
ARISTA: 78 . . . . $2-3
LPs: 10/12-Inch 33rpm
ARISTA: 77 8-10
Also see BAND

DANKWORTH, Johnny
(Johnnie Dankworth)
Singles: 78rpm
CAPITOL: 55-56 2-4
Singles: 7-Inch
CAPITOL: 55-56 2-4
FONTANA: 63-66 2-3
20TH CENTURY-FOX: 66 2-3
LPs: 10/12-Inch 33rpm
FONTANA (Except 7559): 64-69 6-10
FONTANA (7559; "The Idol"): 66 15-20
(Soundtrack.)
ROULETTE: 60-61 10-15
TOP RANK: 60 10-15

DANLEERS
(Dandleers)
Singles: 7-Inch
ABC: 75 1-3
AMP 3: 58 20-25
EPIC: 60 4-6
EVEREST: 61 4-6
LE MANS: 64 3-5
MERCURY: 58-59 8-10
SMASH: 64 3-5
Members: Jimmy Weston; Johnny Lee; Nat Mc-
Cune; Willie Ephraim; Roosevelt Mays; Doug
Ebron; Louis Williams; Terry Wilson; Frank
Clemens; Bill Carey.

DANNY & THE JUNIORS
Singles: 78rpm
ABC-PARAMOUNT: 57-58 10-15
Singles: 7-Inch
ABC: 73 1-3
ABC-PARAMOUNT: 57-59 5-8
CRUNCH: 73 2-4
GUYDEN: 62 4-6
LUB: 68 2-4
MCA: 1-3
MERCURY: 64 3-5
RONN: 68 3-5
ROULETTE: 1-3
SINGULAR (711; "At The Hop"): 57 . . . 50-75
SINGULAR (Black label): 2-3
SWAN: 60-62 5-8

DANNY and the JUNIORS
AT THE HOP

EPs: 7-Inch 33/45rpm
ABC-PARAMOUNT (11; "At The
Hop"): 57 . . . . $150-200
Picture Sleeves
SWAN: 60 20-30
LPs: 10/12-Inch 33rpm
MCA: 5-8
Members: Danny Rapp; Frank Maffei; Joe Terry;
Dave White.
Also see CANNON, Freddy

DANNY WILSON
Singles: 7-Inch
VIRGIN: 87 1-3
LPs: 10/12-Inch 33rpm
VIRGIN: 87 5-8

DANSE SOCIETY
Singles: 12-Inch 33/45rpm
ARISTA: 84 4-6
Singles: 7-Inch
ARISTA: 84 1-3

DANTE
(Dante & The Evergreens; Dante & His Friends)
Singles: 7-Inch
A&M: 66 3-5
DECCA: 60-61 4-6
IMPERIAL: 61-62 4-6
MADISON: 60-61 4-6
MERCURY: 60 4-6
TIDE: 60 4-6
LPs: 10/12-Inch 33rpm
MADISON (1002; "Dante & The
Evergreens"): 61 60-100

D'ARBY, Terence Trent
Singles: 7-Inch
COLUMBIA: 87-89 1-3
LPs: 10/12-Inch 33rpm
COLUMBIA: 87-89 5-8

DARENSBOURG, Joe, & His
Dixie Flyers
Singles: 7-Inch
LARK: *58-59* $2-5
LPs: 10/12-Inch 33rpm
DIXIELAND JUBILEE: *75* 5-8
GHB: *77* 5-8

DARIAN, Fred
(Freddy Darian)
Singles: 7-Inch
DEL-FI: *60* 3-5
GARDENA: *61* 3-5
JAF: *61-63* 3-5
MAHALO: *63* 3-5
OKEH: *59* 4-6
RCA VICTOR: *59* 4-6
UNITED ARTISTS: *63* 3-5

DARIN, Bobby
(Bobby Darin & The Jaybirds; Bobby Darin &
The Rinky Dinks; Bob Darin)
Singles: 78rpm
ATCO: *57-58* 5-10
DECCA: *56-57* 5-10
Singles: 7-Inch
ATCO (Monaural): *57-65* 5-10
ATCO (Stereo): *59* 15-20
(With an "SD" prefix.)
ATLANTIC: *65-67* 3-5
CAPITOL: *62-65* 4-6
DECCA (Except 29922 &
30737): *56-57* 15-20
DECCA (29922; "Blue Eyed
Mermaid"): *56* 25-50
DECCA (30737; "Dealer In
Dreams"): *59* 8-10
DIMENSION: *70* 3-5
DIRECTION: *68-70* 3-5
MOTOWN: *71-72* 2-4
Picture Sleeves
ATCO (Except 6211): *59-62* 6-10
ATCO (6211; "Ave Maria"): *61* 75-100
CAPITOL: *62-65* 4-8
EPs: 7-Inch 33/45rpm
ATCO: *58-60* 20-30
CAPITOL CUSTOM/ARTISTIC: *63* 15-25
(Issued with paper sleeve.)
CAPITOL CUSTOM/SCRIPTO: *63* 15-25
(Issued with printed, 45 rpm-type paper sleeve.)
DECCA (2676; "Bobby Darin"): *60* 40-60
LPs: 10/12-Inch 33rpm
ATCO (Except 102 & 131): *59-67* 20-30
ATCO (102; "Bobby Darin"): *58* 35-45

ATCO (131; "The Bobby Darin
Story"): *61* $35-40
(White cover.)
ATCO (131; "The Bobby Darin
Story"): *72* 8-12
(Black cover.)
ATLANTIC: *66-67* 15-25
BAINBRIDGE: *81* 5-8
CANDLELITE: *76* 12-15
CAPITOL: *62-66* 15-25
CLARION: *64* 15-20
DIRECTION: *68-70* 12-15
IMPERIAL HOUSE: *76* 12-15
MOTOWN (100 series): *82* 5-8
MOTOWN (700 & 800 series): *72-74* 10-12
WARNER BROS. (3501; "The Original
Bobby Darin"): *76* 20-30
(3-LP, mail-order offer.)
Also see DING DONGS
Also see RINKY DINKS

DARLIN, Florraine
Singles: 7-Inch
EPIC: *62-63* 5-8
RIC: *64* 3-5

DARNEL, Bill
(Bill Darnel & The Heathertones)
Singles: 78rpm
CORAL: *50-51* 2-5
DECCA: *52-53* 2-5
Singles: 7-Inch
CORAL: *50-51* 3-5
DECCA: *52-53* 3-5
JUBILEE: *59* 3-5
LONDON (Except 1665): *56* 3-5
LONDON (1665; "Rock-A-Boogie
Baby"): *56* 6-10
PARIS: *59* 10-15

X: *54-55* $4-8
    EPs: 7-Inch 33/45rpm
X: *55* 10-15
    LPs: 10/12-Inch 33rpm
X: *55* 20-30

DARNELL, Larry
Singles: 78rpm
DELUXE: *57* 4-8
OKEH: *51-53* 4-8
REGAL: *49-51* 5-10
Singles: 7-Inch
ANNA: *60* 10-15
ARGO: *60* 5-10
DELUXE: *57* 5-10
OKEH: *51-53* 10-15
REGAL: *51* 10-15
WARWICK: *59* 5-10
EPs: 7-Inch 33/45rpm
EPIC: *61* 20-30

DARRELL, Johnny
Singles: 7-Inch
CAPRICORN: *74-75* 1-3
CARTWHEEL: *71-72* 1-3
GUSTO: *78* 1-3
MONUMENT: *73* 1-3
UNITED ARTISTS: *65-70* 2-3
Picture Sleeves
UNITED ARTISTS: *67* 2-5
LPs: 10/12-Inch 33rpm
CAPRICORN: *75* 6-10
GUSTO: 5-8
SUNSET: *68-70* 6-10
UNITED ARTISTS: *66-70* 8-12

DARRELL, Johnny / George
Jones / Willie Nelson
LPs: 10/12-Inch 33rpm
SUNSET: *69* 8-10
    Also see DARRELL, Johnny
    Also see JONES, George
    Also see NELSON, Willie

DARREN, James
(Jimmy Darren)
Singles: 7-Inch
ABC: *74* 1-3
BUDDAH: *70* 3-5
COLPIX (Except 758 and "SCP"
    series): *58-64* 5-10
COLPIX (758; "Punch & Judy"): *64* 10-20
COLPIX ("SCP" series): *59* 8-15
    (Stereo.)
ERIC: 1-3

MIGHTY PRETTY TERRITORY

"THE NAKED CITY"

JIMMY DARREN

In the two years since he was discovered by a Columbia Pictures talent scout while riding in a Tin Pan Alley building elevator in New York, 22 year old Jimmy Darren has had a meteoric Hollywood success story. After playing a few top supporting roles, his fan mail grew to such huge proportions that Columbia awarded him the romantic lead opposite Sandra Dee in the Cinemascope and color production, "Gidget." He sings "There's No Such Thing" in the new film. Although stix maces his film singing status, Jimmy did some night club singing in his native Philadelphia before he ever thought of becoming an actor.

"THE NAKED CITY"

KIRSHNER: *71-72* $3-5
MCA: 1-3
MGM: *73* 2-5
PRIVATE STOCK: *75-77* 2-4
RCA VICTOR: *78* 2-3
WARNER BROS: *65-68* 4-6
Picture Sleeves
COLPIX: *58-61* 5-15
LPs: 10/12-Inch 33rpm
COLPIX: *60-62* 15-25
KIRSHNER: *71-72* 10-15
WARNER BROS: *67* 15-20

DARREN, James / Shelley
Fabares / Paul Petersen
LPs: 10/12-Inch 33rpm
COLPIX: *63-64* 20-30
    Also see DARREN, James
    Also see FABARES, Shelley
    Also see PETERSEN, Paul

DARTELLS
Singles: 7-Inch
ARLEN (Black vinyl): *63* 10-15
ARLEN (Colored vinyl): *63* 20-25
DOT: *63-64* 5-10
HBR: *66* 5-8
LPs: 10/12-Inch 33rpm
DOT: *63* 25-30
    Member: Doug Phillips.

DASH, Sarah
Singles: 7-Inch
KIRSHNER: *79* 1-3
LPs: 10/12-Inch 33rpm
KIRSHNER: *78* 5-8
    Also see LABELLE, Patti

DAVE & SUGAR
(Dave Rowland & Sugar)
Singles: 7-Inch
ELEKTRA: 81 .... $1-3
RCA VICTOR: 75-82 1-3
LPs: 10/12-Inch 33rpm
ELEKTRA: 81 5-8
RCA VICTOR: 76-82 5-10
Members: Dave Rowland; Vicki Hackeman-Baker;
Jackie Frantz; Sue Powell; Melissa Dean; Jamie
Kaye.
Also see PRIDE, Charley

DAVID, F.R.
Singles: 7-Inch
CARRERE AMERICA: 83 1-3
LPs: 10/12-Inch 33rpm
CARRERE AMERICA: 83 5-8

DAVID & JONATHAN
Singles: 7-Inch
AMY: 68 3-5
CAPITOL: 66-67 4-6
20TH CENTURY-FOX: 66 4-6
Picture Sleeves
CAPITOL: 66 4-8
LPs: 10/12-Inch 33rpm
CAPITOL: 66 20-25
Members: Roger Greenaway; Roger Cook.
Also see WHITE PLAINS

DAVID & LEE
Singles: 7-Inch
G.S.P.: 62 12-18
Members: David Gates; Leon Russell.
Also see GATES, David
Also see RUSSELL, Leon

DAVIDSON, John
Singles: 7-Inch
COLUMBIA: 66-71 2-3

MERCURY: 73 .... $1-3
20TH CENTURY-FOX: 73-77 1-3
Picture Sleeves
COLUMBIA: 66-69 2-4
LPs: 10/12-Inch 33rpm
COLPIX: 65 10-15
COLUMBIA: 66-80 5-10
HARMONY: 72 4-6
MERCURY: 73 5-8
20TH CENTURY-FOX: 74-76 5-8

DAVIE, Hutch
(Hutch Davie & His Honky-Tonkers)
Singles: 7-Inch
ATCO: 58-59 3-5
CLARIDGE: 66 2-4
DYNO VOICE: 68 2-3
LPs: 10/12-Inch 33rpm
ATCO: 59 20-25

DAVIES, Dave
Singles: 7-Inch
REPRISE: 67-68 15-20
WARNER BROS: 83 1-3
LPs: 10/12-Inch 33rpm
RCA VICTOR: 80-81 8-10
WARNER BROS: 83 5-8
Also see KINKS

DA VINCI, Paul
Singles: 7-Inch
MERCURY: 72-74 2-3

DAVIS, Betty
Singles: 7-Inch
ISLAND: 75-76 2-3
JUST SUNSHINE: 73-74 2-4
LPs: 10/12-Inch 33rpm
ISLAND: 75 5-8
JUST SUNSHINE: 73-74 6-10

DAVIS, Billy
Singles: 7-Inch
ABC: 75 2-3
COBBLESTONE: 69 2-4
HI: 68 3-5

DAVIS, Carl, & The Chi-Sound Orch.
Singles: 7-Inch
CHI-SOUND: 77 2-3

DAVIS, Danny
(Danny Davis & The Nashville Brass; Danny
Davis Orchestra; Danny Davis & The Titans;
Danny Davis & The Nashville Strings)
Singles: 78rpm
BLUE JAY: 54 2-4

COLUMBIA (820; "Friday & Saturday
Nights In Person"): *61* $25-35
(Stereo.)
COLUMBIA (900 through 1600
series): *57-61* 15-25
(With six black Columbia "eye" logos on red label.)
COLUMBIA (1800 through 2300
series): *61-65* 10-20
COLUMBIA (8000 through 8400
series): *58-61* 20-30
(With six black Columbia "eye" logos on red label.)
COLUMBIA (8600 through 9800
series): *61-69* 10-20
COLUMBIA (10000 series): *73* 6-10
COLUMBIA (30000 series,
except 36976): *70-85* 6-12
COLUMBIA (36976; "The Miles
Davis Collection"): *80* 30-40
(6-LP set.)
COLUMBIA (40000 series): *81* 8-12
DEBUT (043; "Blue Moods"): *83* 5-8
DEBUT (120; "Blue Moods"): *55* 40-50
FANTASY: *62* 15-20
FONTANA: *65* 10-15
MOODSVILLE: *63* 15-20
NEW JAZZ: *64* 10-15
PRESTIGE (004 through 093): *80-85* 5-8
PRESTIGE (100 series): *52-54* 50-75
(10-Inch LPs.)
PRESTIGE (7007 through 7166): *55-59* . 20-30
(Yellow label.)
PRESTIGE (7168 through 7281): *60-64* . 12-20
(Yellow label.)
PRESTIGE (7000 through 7600
series): *64-69* 6-12
(Blue label.)
PRESTIGE (7700 through 7800
series): *70-71* 6-12
PRESTIGE (24000 series): *72-78* 8-12
SAVOY: *61* 12-20
TRIP: *73* 5-10
UNITED ARTISTS: *71* 8-10
Also see COLTRANE, John, & Miles Davis
Also see FORREST, Jimmy

DAVIS, Miles, & Thelonious Monk
LPs: 10/12-Inch 33rpm
COLUMBIA: *64* 10-20
Also see DAVIS, Miles
Also see MONK, Thelonious

DAVIS, Miz
Singles: 7-Inch
NEW: *76* 2-3

DAVIS, Paul
Singles: 7-Inch
ARISTA: *81-82* $1-3
BANG (Except 500 series): *73-80* 1-3
BANG (500 series): *68-72* 2-4
FLASHBACK: *82* 1-3
SOLID GOLD : *73* 1-3
LPs: 10/12-Inch 33rpm
ARISTA: *81* 5-8
BANG: *72-82* 10-12
Also see OSMOND, Marie, & Paul Davis

DAVIS, Ruth
Singles: 7-Inch
CLARIDGE: *78* 2-3
Also see KIRKLAND, Bo, & Ruth Davis

DAVIS, Sammy, Jr.
(Sammy Davis)
Singles: 7-Inch
A.L.B.B. (38032; "The House I
Live In"): 3-5
(Promotional issue only.)
DECCA (25500 series): *62* 2-3
DECCA (29000 through 31000
series): *54-60* 2-5
DECCA (32000 series): *69* 2-3
ECOLOGY: *71* 1-3
MGM: *71-79* 1-3
VERVE: *60* 2-3
REPRISE: *61-71* 2-3
20TH CENTURY-FOX: *75-76* 1-3
WARNER BROS: *77* 1-3
Picture Sleeves
A.L.B.B. (38032; "The House I
Live In"): 5-10
(Promotional issue only.)
EPs: 7-Inch 33/45rpm
CAPITOL: *54* 4-6
DECCA: *54-55* 6-10
LPs: 10/12-Inch 33rpm
DECCA (100 series): *66* 8-12
DECCA (4000 series): *61-65* 8-12
DECCA (8100 through 8700
series): *54-58* 15-25
DECCA (8900 series): *59* 10-15
HARMONY: *69-71* 5-10
MCA: *77* 5-10
MGM: *72-73* 5-10
MOTOWN: *70* 6-10
RCA VICTOR (1086; "The Three Penny
Opera"): *64* 15-25
REPRISE: *61-69* 10-18

20TH CENTURY-FOX (Except
   5014): *76* $5-8
20TH CENTURY-FOX (5014; "Of Love &
   Desire"): *64* 25-35
   (Soundtrack.)
WARNER BROS: *77* 5-8
UNITED ARTISTS (5187; "Salt &
   Pepper"): *68* 10-15
   (Soundtrack.)
VOCALION: *68* 5-10
   Also see CURB, Mike
   Also see SINATRA, Frank, Sammy Davis, Jr.
   & Dean Martin

DAVIS, Sammy, Jr., & Laurindo Almeida
LPs: 10/12-Inch 33rpm
REPRISE: *67* 8-12
   Also see ALMEIDA, Laurindo

DAVIS, Sammy, Jr., & Count Basie
Singles: 7-Inch
VERVE: *65* 1-3
LPs: 10/12-Inch 33rpm
MGM: *73* 6-10
VERVE: *65* 10-15
   Also see BASIE, Count

DAVIS, Sammy, Jr., & Carmen McRae
Singles: 7-Inch
DECCA: *55* 2-4
EPs: 7-Inch 33/45rpm
DECCA: *59* 5-8
LPs: 10/12-Inch 33rpm
DECCA: *59* 10-20
   Also see MC RAE, Carmen

DAVIS, Sammy, Jr. / Joya Sherril
LPs: 10/12-Inch 33rpm
DESIGN: 5-8
   Also see DAVIS, Sammy, Jr.

DAVIS, Skeeter
Singles: 7-Inch
MERCURY: *76-77* 1-3
PART TWO: *80* 1-3
RCA VICTOR (Except 7400 through
   9600 series): *69-74* 1-3
RCA VICTOR (7400 through 8300
   series): *59-64* 3-5
RCA VICTOR (8400 through 9600
   series): *64-68* 1-3
Picture Sleeves
RCA VICTOR: *63* 4-8
EPs: 7-Inch 33/45rpm
RCA VICTOR: *63* 5-10

The Davis Sisters: Skeeter (left) and Betty.

LPs: 10/12-Inch 33rpm
CAMDEN: *65-74* $5-10
GUSTO: *78* 5-8
RCA VICTOR (2000 & 3000 series,
   except 3790): *60-68* 10-15
RCA VICTOR (3790; "Skeeter Davis
   Sings Buddy Holly"): *67* 20-30
TUDOR: *81* 5-8
   Also see BARE, Bobby, & Skeeter Davis
   Also see HAMILTON, George IV, & Skeeter
Davis
   Also see JENNINGS, Waylon
   Also see POSEY, Sandy / Skeeter Davis
   Also see WAGONER, Porter, & Skeeter Davis

DAVIS, Spencer
(Spencer Davis Group; Spencer Davis & Peter
Jameson)
Singles: 7-Inch
ALLEGIANCE: *84* 1-3
ATCO: *66* 4-6
FONTANA: *64* 5-10
UNITED ARTISTS: *66-72* 3-6
VERTIGO: *73-74* 1-3
Picture Sleeves
UNITED ARTISTS: *66-67* 5-10
LPs: 10/12-Inch 33rpm
ALLEGIANCE: *84* 5-8
DATE: *70* 10-12
FONTANA: *66* 20-30
ISLAND: *83* 5-8
MEDIARTS: *71* 10-12
RHINO: *84* 5-8
UNITED ARTISTS: *67-75* 20-30
VERTIGO: *73-74* 10-12

WING: $10-15
Members: Spencer Davis; Steve Winwood; Pete
York; Brian Dexter; Ray Fenwick; Ken Salmon.
Also see WINWOOD, Steve

DAVIS, Tim
Singles: 7-Inch
METROMEDIA: 72-73 2-3
LPs: 10/12-Inch 33rpm
METROMEDIA: 72-74 8-10

DAVIS, Tyrone
Singles: 7-Inch
ABC: 68 3-5
COLUMBIA: 76-81 1-3
DAKAR: 68-77 2-3
EPIC: 83 1-3
FUTURE: 87-88 1-3
HIGHRISE: 82-83 1-3
OCEAN FRONT: 83-84 1-3
LPs: 10/12-Inch 33rpm
COLUMBIA: 76-81 8-10
DAKAR: 69-76 10-15
EPIC: 83 5-8
FUTURE: 88 5-8
HIGHRISE: 82 5-8

DAVY DMX
(DAVY D)
Singles: 12-Inch 33/45rpm
CBS ASSOCIATED: 84 4-6
Singles: 7-Inch
CBS ASSOCIATED: 84 1-3
DEF JAM: 87 1-3

DAWN
Singles: 7-Inch
ARISTA: 75 2-3
ELEKTRA: 76-77 2-3
Members: Joyce Wilson; Telma Hopkins.
Also see DAWN (With Tony Orlando)

DAWN
(With Tony Orlando)
Singles: 7-Inch
BELL: 70-72 2-4
LPs: 10/12-Inch 33rpm
BELL: 70-71 10-12
Members: Tony Orlando; Joyce Wilson; Telma
Hopkins.
Also see DAWN
Also see ORLANDO, Tony, & Dawn

DAWSON, Cliff
Singles: 7-Inch
BOARDWALK: 82 1-3

DAWSON, Cliff, & Renee Diggs
Singles: 7-Inch
BOARDWALK: 83 .... $1-3
Also see DAWSON, Cliff
Also see STARPOINT

DAY, Arlan
Singles: 7-Inch
PASHA: 81 1-3

DAY, Bobby
(Bobby Day & The Satellites; Bobby Day & The Blossoms; Bobby Byrd)
Singles: 78rpm
CLASS: 57 5-8
Singles: 7-Inch
CLASS: 57-59 5-8
RCA VICTOR: 63-64 3-5
RENDEZVOUS: 60-62 4-6
SURE SHOT: 67 3-5
LPs: 10/12-Inch 33rpm
CLASS: 59 45-55
RHINO: 84 5-8
Also see BYRD, Bobby

DAY, Dennis
Singles: 78rpm
CAPITOL: 56 2-5
RCA VICTOR: 50-54 3-5
Singles: 7-Inch
CAPITOL: 56 3-5
RCA VICTOR: 50-54 3-5
SHAMROCK: 59 2-4
EPs: 7-Inch 33/45rpm
CAPITOL: 56 5-10
RCA VICTOR: 50-59 4-8
LPs: 10/12-Inch 33rpm
BLUEBIRD: 60 5-10
CAMDEN: 64-66 5-10
CAPITOL: 56 10-20
MASTERSEAL: 10-20
REPRISE: 63 5-10
ROULETTE: 63 8-12

DAY, Doris
(Doris Day & The Mellomen; Doris Day & The Norman Luboff Choir)
Singles: 78rpm
COLUMBIA: 47-57 4-8
Singles: 7-Inch
COLUMBIA (38000 & 39000
series): 50-53 5-10
COLUMBIA (40000 through 44000
series): 54-67 4-8

Picture Sleeves
COLUMBIA: *57-61* $10-20
EPs: 7-Inch 33/45rpm
COLUMBIA (Except 540): *50-59* 10-20
COLUMBIA (540; "Love Me Or
Leave Me"): *55* 15-25
LPs: 10/12-Inch 33rpm
COLUMBIA (1; "Listen To Day"): *60* ...20-30
COLUMBIA (600 through 1300
series): *55-59* 15-30
COLUMBIA (1400 through 2100
series): *60-64* 10-20
COLUMBIA (8000 through 8900
series): *58-64* 15-25
COLUMBIA (2200 through 2300
series): *64-65* 10-20
COLUMBIA (9000 through 9100
series): *64-65* 10-20
COLUMBIA (6000 series): *50-54* 25-50
(10-Inch LPs.)
HARMONY: *66-72* 8-12

DAY, Doris, & Don Cherry
EPs: 7-Inch 33/45rpm
COLUMBIA: *56* 10-20
Also see CHERRY, Don
Also see DAY, Doris

DAY, Doris, & Frankie Laine
Singles: 78rpm
COLUMBIA: *52* 3-5
Singles: 7-Inch
COLUMBIA: *52* 3-6
Also see LAINE, Frankie

DAY, Doris, & Andre Previn
LPs: 10/12-Inch 33rpm
COLUMBIA: *62* 10-20
Also see PREVIN, Andre

DAY, Doris, & Johnnie Ray
Singles: 78rpm
COLUMBIA: *52-53* 3-5
Singles: 7-Inch
COLUMBIA: *52-53* 3-6
Also see RAY, Johnnie

DAY, Doris / Frank Sinatra
LPs: 10/12-Inch 33rpm
COLUMBIA (6000 series): *55* 25-50
(10-Inch LPs.)
Also see DAY, Doris
Also see SINATRA, Frank, & Doris Day

DAY, Morris
Singles: 12-Inch 33/45rpm
WARNER BROS: *85-86* $4-6
Singles: 7-Inch
WARNER BROS: *85-88* 1-3
LPs: 10/12-Inch 33rpm
WARNER BROS: *85-88* 5-8
Also see TIME

DAYBREAK
Singles: 7-Inch
PRELUDE: *80* 1-3
UNI: *70* 2-4

DAYE, Cory
Singles: 7-Inch
N.Y.I.: *79* 1-3
LPs: 10/12-Inch 33rpm
N.Y.I.: *79* 5-8
Also see DR. BUZZARD'S ORIGINAL
SAVANNAH BAND

DAYE, Johnny
Singles: 7-Inch
JOMADA: *65-66* 3-5
PARKWAY: *66* 3-5
STAX: *68* 3-5

DAYNE, Taylor
Singles: 7-Inch
ARISTA: *87-88* 1-3
LPs: 10/12-Inch 33rpm
ARISTA: *88* 5-8

DAYTON
Singles: 7-Inch
CAPITOL: *82-85* 1-3
LIBERTY: *81-82* 1-3
UNITED ARTISTS: *80* 1-3
LPs: 10/12-Inch 33rpm
CAPITOL: *83* 5-8
LIBERTY: *81-82* 5-8
UNITED ARTISTS: *80* 5-8

DAZZ BAND
Singles: 12-Inch 33/45rpm
GEFFEN: *86* 4-6
MOTOWN: *80-85* 4-6
Singles: 7-Inch
GEFFEN: *86* 1-3
MOTOWN: *80-85* 1-3
RCA VICTOR: *88* 1-3
LPs: 10/12-Inch 33rpm
GEFFEN: *86* 5-8
MOTOWN: *80-85* 5-8
RCA: *88* 5-8

Also see KINSMAN DAZZ

D'COCOA, Creme:
see CREME D'COCOA

DEACONS
Singles: 7-Inch
SHAMA: 68 .... $8-12

DEAD BOYS
Singles: 7-Inch
SIRE (Commercial): 77-78 1-3
SIRE (Promotional): 77-78 5-8
LPs: 10/12-Inch 33rpm
BOMP: 80 8-10
SIRE: 77-78 8-10

DEAD KENNEDYS
Singles: 7-Inch
ALTERNATIVE TENTACLES: 83-86 3-8
LPs: 10/12-Inch 33rpm
ALTERNATIVE TENTACLES: 83-86 ... 5-10
I.R.S.: 81 5-8
Members: Jello Biafra; Ray Papperell; Paul
Roessler; Klaus Flouride.

DEAD MILKMEN
LPs: 10/12-Inch 33rpm
ENIGMA: 87-88 5-8

DEAD OR ALIVE
Singles: 12-Inch 33/45rpm
EPIC: 84-86 4-6
Singles: 7-Inch
EPIC: 84-87 1-3
LPs: 10/12-Inch 33rpm
EPIC: 84-88 5-8
Member: Pete Burns.

DEADLY NIGHTSHADE
Singles: 7-Inch
PHANTOM: 76 2-3
LPs: 10/12-Inch 33rpm
PHANTOM: 76 8-10

DEAL, Bill
(Bill Deal & The Rhondels)
Singles: 7-Inch
BUDDAH: 71-72 2-3
COLLECTABLES: 1-3
ERIC: 1-3
HERITAGE: 68-70 3-5
POLYDOR: 70-73 2-3
RED LION: 79 2-3
Picture Sleeves
HERITAGE: 69 4-6
LPs: 10/12-Inch 33rpm
HERITAGE: 69 12-15

RHINO: 86 .... $5-8

DEAN, Alan
Singles: 78rpm
LONDON: 51 2-5
MGM: 51-56 2-4
RAMA: 56-57 3-6
Singles: 7-Inch
LONDON: 51 3-5
MGM: 51-56 2-4
RAMA: 56-57 3-6

DEAN, Debbie
(Debbie Deane & The Petites; Debbie Dean &
The Paulette Singers)
Singles: 7-Inch
MOTOWN: 61-62 25-30
TREVA: 66 3-5
V.I.P: 66-68 3-5
Picture Sleeves
MOTOWN: 62 20-35

DEAN, Hazell
(Hazel Dean)
Singles: 12-Inch 33/45rpm
QUALITY: 84 4-6
Singles: 7-Inch
LONDON: 76 1-3

DEAN, Jimmy
(Jimmie Dean)
Singles: 78rpm
COLUMBIA: 57 3-6
FOUR STAR: 54 4-8
Singles: 7-Inch
CASINO: 76 1-3
COLUMBIA (40000 through 43000 series,
except 42175): 57-66 2-4
COLUMBIA (42175; "Big Bad John"): 61 .. 4-6
(With words: "At the bottom of this mine
lies one hell of a man.")
COLUMBIA (42175; "Big Bad John"): 61 .. 2-4
(With words: "At the bottom of this mine
lies a big, big man.")
COLUMBIA (45000 through 46000
series): 74 1-3
FOUR STAR (1600 series): 54 4-6
FOUR STAR (1700 series): 59 3-5
KING: 64 2-3
MERCURY: 56 3-5
RCA VICTOR: 66-71 2-3
Picture Sleeves
COLUMBIA (Except 41025): 59-66 4-8
COLUMBIA (41025; "Little Sandy
Sleighfoot"): 57 10-15

EPs: 7-Inch 33/45rpm
COLUMBIA: *57* $6-12
LPs: 10/12-Inch 33rpm
ACCORD: *82* 5-8
BRYLEN: 5-8
CASINO: *76* 5-8
COLUMBIA (1000 series): *57* 15-25
COLUMBIA (1500 through 2500
  series): *61-66* 10-20
  (Monaural.)
COLUMBIA (8000 & 9000
  series): *61-68* 10-20
  (Stereo. With a "CS" prefix.)
COLUMBIA (9200 series): 5-8
  (With a "PC" prefix.)
COLUMBIA (10000 series): *73* 6-10
GRT: *77* 5-8
GUEST STAR: 8-10
HARMONY: *60-69* 8-12
KING: *61* 12-18
MERCURY: *57* 15-20
PICKWICK/HILLTOP: *65* 10-12
RCA VICTOR: *67-71* 8-12
SPIN-O-RAMA: 8-10
WING: *64* 8-12
WYNCOTE: 8-10

DEAN, Jimmy / Johnny Horton
LPs: 10/12-Inch 33rpm
STARDAY: *65* 15-20
  Also see HORTON, Johnny

DEAN, Jimmy, & Dottie West
Singles: 7-Inch
RCA VICTOR: *71* 2-3
LPs: 10/12-Inch 33rpm
RCA VICTOR: *70* 8-10
  Also see DEAN, Jimmy
  Also see WEST, Dottie

DEAN & JEAN
Singles: 7-Inch
EMBER: *59-62* 4-6
RUST: *63-65* 3-5

DEAN & MARC
Singles: 7-Inch
BULLSEYE: *59* 4-6
HICKORY: *63-65* 3-5
MAY: *63* 3-5
  Members: Dean Mathis; Marc Mathis.
  Also see NEWBEATS

DEANE, Shelbra
Singles: 7-Inch
CASINO: *76-77* 1-3

DE BARGE
(DeBarges)
Singles: 12-Inch 33/45rpm
GORDY: *85-86* $4-6
Singles: 7-Inch
GORDY: *81-86* 1-3
STRIPED H.: *87* 1-3
LPs: 10/12-Inch 33rpm
GORDY: *81-86* 5-8
MOTOWN: 4-6
  Members: Eldra BeBarge; Marty DeBarge; James
  DeBarge; Bunny De Barge.
  Also see DE BARGE, Bunny
  Also see DE BARGE, EL
  Also see KING DREAM CHORUS &
HOLIDAY CREW

DE BARGE, Bunny
Singles: 12-Inch 33/45rpm
GORDY: *87* 4-6
Singles: 7-Inch
GORDY: *87* 1-3
LPs: 10/12-Inch 33rpm
MOTOWN: *87* 1-3
  Also see DE BARGE

DE BARGE, Chico
Singles: 12-Inch 33/45rpm
MOTOWN: *86-87* 4-6
Singles: 7-Inch
MOTOWN: *86-88* 1-3
LPs: 10/12-Inch 33rpm
MOTOWN: *86-87* 5-8

DE BARGE, El
(El DeBarge With DeBarge)
Singles: 12-Inch 33/45rpm
GORDY: *86-87* 4-6
Singles: 7-Inch
GORDY: *81-87* 1-3
LPs: 10/12-Inch 33rpm
GORDY: *81-87* 5-8
  Also see DE BARGE

DEBBIE DEB
Singles: 12-Inch 33/45rpm
JAMPACKED: *85* 4-6
SUNNYVIEW: *84* 4-6
Singles: 7-Inch
JAMPACKED: *87* 1-3

DE BLANC
Singles: 7-Inch
ARISTA: *75-76* 2-3

DE BURGH, Chris
Singles: 7-Inch
A&M: 75-88 .... $1-3
LPs: 10/12-Inch 33rpm
A&M: 76-86 8-10

DE CARO, Nick, Orchestra
Singles: 7-Inch
A&M: 67-69 2-3
LPs: 10/12-Inch 33rpm
A&M: 69 6-10
BLUE THUMB: 77 5-8

DE CASTRO, Peggy
Singles: 7-Inch
SPOTLITE: 62 5-15
Also see DE CASTRO SISTERS

DE CASTRO SISTERS
Singles: 7-Inch
ABC-PARAMOUNT: 58 2-4
ABBOTT: 54-56 2-4
CAPITOL: 60-61 2-3
RCA VICTOR: 56 2-4
TICO: 52 3-5
ZODIAC: 77 1-3
LPs: 10/12-Inch 33rpm
ABBOTT: 56 20-30
CAPITOL: 60-61 12-18
20TH CENTURY-FOX: 65 8-12
Members: Peggy DeCastro; Babette DeCastro;
Cherie DeCastro.
Also see DE CASTRO, Peggy

DECO
Singles: 12-Inch 33/45rpm
QWEST: 84-85 4-6
Singles: 7-Inch
QWEST: 84-85 1-3
LPs: 10/12-Inch 33rpm
QWEST: 84 5-8

DEE, Dave, Dozy, Beaky, Mick, & Tich
Singles: 7-Inch
ATLANTIC: 83 1-3
FONTANA: 66-67 4-8
IMPERIAL: 67-68 3-5
LPs: 10/12-Inch 33rpm
FONTANA: 67 20-30
IMPERIAL: 68 12-20

DEE, Jackie
(Jackie DeShannon)
Singles: 78rpm
GONE: 57 30-35

Singles: 7-Inch
GONE: 57 .... $30-35
LIBERTY: 58 25-30
Also see DE SHANNON, Jackie

DEE, Jimmy
(Jimmy Dee & The Offbeats)
Singles: 7-Inch
CUTIE: 63 3-5
DOT: 57-58 10-20
HEAR ME: 3-5
INNER-GLO: 50-60
SCOPE: 59 10-15
TNT: 57-59 20-30
TAPER: 59 25-35

DEE, Joey
(Joey Dee & The Starliters; Joey Dee & The New
Starliters; Joey Dee & Hawk)
Singles: 7-Inch
ABC: 73 1-3
CANEIL: 2-4
JUBILEE: 66-67 3-5
ROULETTE: 61-63 3-5
SCEPTER: 60 4-6
SUNBURST: 73 3-5
TONSIL RECORDS: 70 2-4
VASELINE HAIR TONIC: 62 10-15
(Special products issue from Chesebrough-Ponds.)
Picture Sleeves
ROULETTE: 62 4-8
EPs: 7-Inch 33/45rpm
DIPLOMAT: 62 10-12
LPs: 10/12-Inch 33rpm
ACCORD: 82 5-8
ROULETTE: 61-63 15-25
SCEPTER: 62 15-25

Chesebrough-Pond's
VASELINE HAIR TONIC
45 RPM   SIDE 1
Learn To Dance The Authentic Peppermint Twist
JOEY DEE

DEE, Joey, & The Starliters / Dion
Singles: 7-Inch
MONUMENT: *61* $4-6
Also see DION

DEE, Joey, & The Starliters /
Randy Andy & The Candymen
EPs: 7-Inch 33/45rpm
DIPLOMAT: *62* 15-20
Also see DEE, Joey

DEE, Johnny
(John D. Loudermilk)
Singles: 7-Inch
BULLET: *53* 5-10
COLONIAL: *57* 10-15
DOT: *58* 4-8
Also see LOUDERMILK, John D.

DEE, Kiki
Singles: 7-Inch
LIBERTY: *68* 3-5
MCA: *73-77* 2-3
POSSE: *81* 1-3
RCA VICTOR: *81* 1-3
RARE EARTH: *71* 2-3
ROCKET: *73-79* 1-3
TAMLA: *70* 2-4
WORLD PACIFIC: *66* 3-5
LPs: 10/12-Inch 33rpm
LIBERTY (7600 series): *69* 15-20
LIBERTY (10000 series): *81* 5-8
MCA/ROCKET: *73-74* 8-12
RCA VICTOR: *81* 5-8
ROCKET: *77-78* 8-10
TAMLA: *70* 15-20
Also see JOHN, Elton, & Kiki Dee

DEE, Lenny
Singles: 78rpm
DECCA: *56-61* 2-3
Singles: 7-Inch
DECCA: *56-61* 2-3
EPs: 7-Inch 33/45rpm
DECCA: *59* 3-6
LPs: 10/12-Inch 33rpm
DECCA: *55-70* 5-15

DEE, Lola
Singles: 78rpm
BALLY: *57* 3-6
MERCURY: *54-56* 3-5
WING: *55-56* 5-10
Singles: 7-Inch
BALLY: *57* 3-6

MERCURY: *54-56* $3-6
WING: *55-56* 10-20

DEE, Lola, & Rusty Draper
Singles: 78rpm
MERCURY: *56* 3-5
Singles: 7-Inch
MERCURY: *56* 4-8
Also see DEE, Lola
Also see DRAPER, Rusty

DEE, Neecy
Singles: 12-Inch 33/45rpm
TNT: *85* 4-6

DEE, Tommy,
(Tommy Dee With Carol Kay & The Teen-Aires)
Singles: 7-Inch
CHALLENGE: *60* 6-10
CREST (Monaural): *59* 4-6
CREST (Stereo): *59* 15-20
PIKE: *61* 3-5
SIMS: *66* 3-6

DEE JAY & THE RUNAWAYS
Singles: 7-Inch
COULEE: 20-35
IGL (100; "Jenny Jenny"): *64* 50-100
SMASH: *66* 3-5
SONIC: *68* 4-6
Members: Gary Lind; John Senn; Terry Klein;
Denny; Bob; Tom.

DEELE
Singles: 7-Inch
SOLAR: *83-88* 1-3
LPs: 10/12-Inch 33rpm
SOLAR: *85-88* 5-8

DEEP PURPLE
Singles: 7-Inch
GRP: *73* 2-4
MERCURY: *84-88* 1-3
TETRAGRAMMATON: *68-69* 5-10
WARNER BROS: *70-73* 3-5
WARNER BROS/PURPLE: *74-75* 2-4
Picture Sleeves
TETRAGRAMMATON: *68* 5-15
WARNER BROS/PURPLE : *74-75* 3-5
LPs: 10/12-Inch 33rpm
MERCURY: *84-88* 5-8
PASSPORT: *88* 5-8
PORTRAIT: *82* 5-8
SCEPTER/CITATION: *72* 8-10
TETRAGRAMMATON: *68-69* 20-30

WARNER BROS (Except 3000
series): *70-74* **$15-20**
WARNER BROS (3000 series): *77* **5-8**
WARNER BROS/PURPLE: *74-80* **10-12**
Members: Ritchie Blackmore; Jon Lord; Ian Paice;
Rod Evans; Nick Simper; Roger Glover; Ian Gil-
lan; David Coverdale.
Also see BLACKMORE'S RAINBOW
Also see CAPTAIN BEYOND
Also see GILLAN, Ian
Also see GLOVER, Roger
Also see TRAPEZE
Also see WHITESNAKE

DEEP VELVET
Singles: 7-Inch
AWARE: *73* **2-3**

DEES, Rick
(Rick Dees & His Cast Of Idiots)
Singles: 12-Inch 33/45rpm
RSO: *78* **4-6**
STAX: *78* **4-6**
Singles: 7-Inch
ATLANTIC: *86* **1-3**
FRETONE (040; "Disco Duck"): *76* **5-10**
RSO (Except 860): *76-77* **1-3**
RSO (860; "He Ate Too Many
Jelly Donuts"): *77* **5-8**
RSO/POLYDOR: *76-77* **1-3**
STAX: *78* **1-3**
Picture Sleeves
ATLANTIC: *86* **2-3**
STAX: *78* **1-3**
LPs: 10/12-Inch 33rpm
ATLANTIC: *85* **5-8**
RSO: *77* **8-10**

DEES, Sam
Singles: 7-Inch
ATLANTIC: *73-75* **2-3**
CHESS: *71* **2-3**
LOLO: *69* **2-4**
POLYDOR: *78* **1-3**
LPs: 10/12-Inch 33rpm
ATLANTIC: *75* **5-8**

DEES, Sam, & Bettye Swann
Singles: 7-Inch
BIG TREE: *76* **2-3**
Also see DEES, Sam
Also see SWANN, Bettye

DEF LEPPARD
Singles: 7-Inch
MERCURY: *80-88* **1-3**

EPs: 7-Inch 33/45rpm
BLUDGEON RIFFOLA: *78* **$10-15**
Picture Sleeves
MERCURY: *80-84* **1-3**
LPs: 10/12-Inch 33rpm
MERCURY: *80-87* ..,................... **5-8**
Members: Joe Elliott; Rick Allen; Steve Clark; Phil
Collen.

DE FRANCO FAMILY
Singles: 7-Inch
20TH CENTURY-FOX (Except
2214): *73-74* **2-3**
20TH CENTURY-FOX (2214; "We
Belong Together"): *75* **3-5**
Picture Sleeves
20TH CENTURY-FOX: *73-74* **2-3**
LPs: 10/12-Inch 33rpm
20TH CENTURY-FOX: *73-74* **8-10**
Member: Tony DeFranco.

DEJA
Singles: 7-Inch
VIRGIN: *87-88* **1-3**
LPs: 10/12-Inch 33rpm
VIRGIN: *87-88* **5-8**

DE JOHN SISTERS
Singles: 78rpm
COLUMBIA: *57* **3-6**
EPIC: *54-56* **3-6**
OKEH: *53* **3-5**
Singles: 7-Inch
COLUMBIA: *57* **5-15**
EPIC: *54-56* **5-10**
OKEH: *53* **4-8**
SUNBEAM: *59* **3-6**
UNITED ARTISTS: *60* **3-5**
LPs: 10/12-Inch 33rpm
UNITED ARTISTS: *60* **10-20**
Members: Julie DeGiovanni; Dux DeGiovanni.

DEJONAY, Zena
Singles: 12-Inch 33/45rpm
TVI: *84* **4-6**

DEKKER, Desmond, & The Aces
Singles: 7-Inch
UNI: *69-70* **2-4**
LPs: 10/12-Inch 33rpm
UNI: *69* **15-20**

DELACARDOS
Singles: 7-Inch
ELGEY: *59* **25-30**
IMPERIAL: *63* **4-6**
SHELL: *61-62* **4-6**

UNITED ARTISTS: *61* $10-15

DELANEY & BONNIE
(Delaney & Bonnie & Friends)
Singles: 7-Inch
ATCO: *70-72* 3-5
COLUMBIA: *72-73* 2-4
ELEKTRA: *69* 3-5
INDEPENDENCE: *67* 4-6
STAX: *68-69* 3-5
LPs: 10/12-Inch 33rpm
ATCO: *70-72* 15-25
COLUMBIA: *72* .15-25
ELEKTRA: *69* 15-25
GNP/CRESCENDO: *70* 15-25
STAX: *69* 15-25
Members: Delaney Bramlett; Bonnie Bramlett.
Also see BAD HABITS
Also see BRAMLETT, Bonnie
Also see BRAMLETT, Delaney
Also see CLAPTON, Eric
Also see LANI & BONI
Also see SHINDOGS
Also see WHITLOCK, Bobby

DELBERT & GLEN
Singles: 7-Inch
CLEAN: *72-73* 2-4
LPs: 10/12-Inch 33rpm
CLEAN: *72-73* 12-20
Members: Delbert McClinton; Glen Clark.
Also see MC CLINTON, Delbert
Also see PRINE, John / Daryl Hall & John
Oates / Barnaby Bye / Delbert & Glen

DELEGATES
Singles: 7-Inch
MAINSTREAM: *72* 5-8
LPs: 10/12-Inch 33rpm
MAINSTREAM: *73* 10-15

DELEGATION
Singles: 12-Inch 33/45rpm
SHADYBROOK: *77* 4-6
Singles: 7-Inch
MCA: *76* 2-3
MERCURY: *80-81* 1-3
SHADYBROOK: *77-79* 1-3
LPs: 10/12-Inch 33rpm
MERCURY: *80-81* 5-8
SHADYBROOK: *79* 5-8

DELFONICS
Singles: 7-Inch
CAMEO: *67* 3-5
COLLECTABLES: 1-3

MOON SHOT: *68* $3-5
PHILLY GROOVE: *68-73* 2-4
ROULETTE: *73* 1-3
LPs: 10/12-Inch 33rpm
KORY: *77* 8-10
PHILLY GROOVE: *68-74* 8-12
POOGIE: *81* 5-8
COLLECTABLES: *88* 6-8
Member: Major Harris.
Also see HARRIS, Major

DEL FUEGOS
LPs: 10/12-Inch 33rpm
SLASH: *85-87* 5-8

DELIVERANCE
Singles: 7-Inch
COLUMBIA: *80* 1-3

DELLS
Singles: 78rpm
VEE JAY (166; "Dreams Of
  Contentment"): *55* 50-75
VEE JAY (200 series): *56-57* 8-15
Singles: 12-Inch 33/45rpm
ABC: *79* 4-6
Singles: 7-Inch
A&M: *76* 2-3
ABC: *73-78* 1-3
ARGO: *62* 4-6
CADET: *67-75* 2-4
CHESS: *73* 2-4
COLLECTABLES: 1-3
MCA: *79* 1-3
MERCURY: *75-77* 2-3
PRIVATE I: *84* 1-3
20TH CENTURY-FOX: *80-82* 1-3
VEE JAY (166; "Dreams Of
  Contentment"): *55* 100-150
Note: Vee Jay 134, *Tell The World*, is listed in the
following section for DELLS / Count Morris.
VEE JAY (200 series): *56-58* 10-20
VEE JAY (300 series,
  except 300): *59-61* 5-12
VEE JAY (300; "Wedding Day"): *58* . . . 25-50
VEE JAY (500 through 700 series): *64-65* . 4-8
LPs: 10/12-Inch 33rpm
ABC: *78* 8-10
BUDDAH: *69* 10-15
CADET: *68-75* 10-20
LOST-NITE: *81* 6-10
MERCURY: *75-77* 10-12
PRIVATE I: *84* 5-8
TRIP: *73* 10-12

20TH CENTURY-FOX: *80-81* $5-8
UPFRONT: *68* 10-12
VEE JAY (1010; "Oh What
  A Night"): *59* 400-500
(With thin circular ring on label.)
VEE JAY (1010; "Oh What
  A Night"): *59* 300-400
(With thick circular ring on label.)
VEE JAY (1141; "It's Not
  Unusual"): *65* 100-200
Members: Johnny Funches; Mike McGill; Marvin
Junior; Vern Allison; Johnny Carter.
Also see BUTLER, Jerry, & Betty Everett
Also see SOUTH, Joe / Dells

DELLS / Count Morris
        Singles: 78rpm
VEE JAY (134; "Tell The World"): *55* . 75-150
        Singles: 7-Inch
VEE JAY (134; "Tell The World"): *55* 250-350
(Black vinyl.)
VEE JAY (134; "Tell The World"): *55* 500-600
(Colored vinyl.)

DELLS & The Dramatics
        Singles: 7-Inch
CADET: *75* 2-3
Also see DELLS
Also see DRAMATICS

DE LORY, Al
        Singles: 7-Inch
CAPITOL: *68-71* 2-5
EUREKA: *61* 3-5
PHI DAN: *65* 2-5
     LPs: 10/12-Inch 33rpm
CAPITOL: *69-70* 5-15

DELPHS, Jimmy
        Singles: 7-Inch
CARLA: *67* 3-5
KAREN: *68* 3-5

DEL-VIKINGS
(Dell-Vikings)
        Singles: 78rpm
DOT: *57* 6-12
FEE BEE: *56-57* 20-40
        Singles: 7-Inch
ABC: *75* 1-3
ABC-PARAMOUNT: *61-63* 5-10
ALPINE: *60* 10-20
BIM BAM BOOM: *72* 2-4
BLUE SKY: 2-4
BROADCAST: 2-4
COLLECTABLES: *80* 1-3

DOT: *57-60* $6-12
FEE BEE (205; "Come Go With
  Me"): *56* 40-80
FEE BEE (206; "Down In Bermuda"): *56* . 40-80
FEE BEE (210; "What Made
  Maggie Run"): *56* 40-80
FEE BEE (214; "Whispering Bells): *57* . . 40-80
FEE BEE (218; "I'm
  Spinning"): *57* 40-80
FEE BEE (221; "Willette"): *57* 40-80
FEE BEE (902; "True Love"): *61* 20-40
GATEWAY: *64* 4-8
LUNIVERSE: *57* 20-30
MERCURY: *57-63* 5-10
SCEPTER: *72* 2-4
    EPs: 7-Inch 33/45rpm
DOT (1058; "Come Go
  With Us"): *57* 100-200
MERCURY (3359/62/63; "They Sing,
  They Swing"): *57* 75-100
(Price is for any in the series of three EPs.)
    LPs: 10/12-Inch 33rpm
COLLECTABLES: *80-83* 6-8
DOT (3695; "Come Go With
  Me"): *66* 150-225
LUNIVERSE (1000; "Come Go
  With The Del Vikings"): *57* 250-400
MERCURY (20314; "They Sing,
  They Swing"): *57* 60-80
MERCURY (20353; "Del Vikings'
  Record Session"): *57* 60-80
Members: Kripp Johnson; Norman Wright;
Clarence Quick; Don Jackson; Gus Backus; Bill
Blakely; David Lerchey.

DEL-VIKINGS / Sonnets
    LPs: 10/12-Inch 33rpm
CROWN (5368; "The Del-Vikings &
  The Sonnets"): *63* 20-30
(Tracks shown by The Sonnets are actually by The
Meadowlarks and by The Sounds.)
Also see DEL-VIKINGS
Also see JULIAN, Don, & The Meadowlarks

DE MARCO, Ralph
        Singles: 7-Inch
GUARANTEED: *59* 2-4
SHELLEY: *60* 2-4
20TH CENTURY-FOX: *62* 2-3

DE MATTEO, Nicky
(Nicky DeMatteo & The Sorrows)
        Singles: 7-Inch
ABC-PARAMOUNT: *61* 3-5
CAMEO: *65-66* 5-8

DIAMOND: *63* $5-15
END: *58* 10-15
GUYDEN: *60* 3-5
PARIS: *59* 5-8
TORE: *59* 5-8

DEMENSIONS
(Dimensions)
Singles: 7-Inch
COLLECTABLES: 1-3
CORAL (Except 65600 series): *61-63* ... 10-15
CORAL (65600 series): *67* 3-5
MOHAWK: *60-61* 5-8
Picture Sleeves
CORAL: *63* 12-25
LPs: 10/12-Inch 33rpm
CORAL: *63* 60-75
Member: Lenny Dell.

DENNY, Martin
Singles: 7-Inch
LIBERTY (55000 series): *59-67* 2-4
LIBERTY (56000 series): *69* 1-3
LIBERTY (77000 series): *59-60* 4-6
(Stereo.)
Picture Sleeves
LIBERTY: *59-63* 3-6
LPs: 10/12-Inch 33rpm
FIRST AMERICAN: *81* 5-8
LIBERTY: *59-69* 8-12
SUNSET: *66-68* 5-10
UNITED ARTISTS: *74-80* 5-8
Also see BAJA MARIMBA BAND
Also see ZENTER, Si

DENNY, Sandy
Singles: 7-Inch
A&M: *72-73* 2-4
LPs: 10/12-Inch 33rpm
A&M: *71-72* 8-10
ISLAND: *74-76* 8-10
Also see FAIRPORT CONVENTION
Also see LED ZEPPELIN

DENVER, John
Singles: 12-Inch 33/45rpm
RCA VICTOR (11189; "Bet On The
   Blues"): *77* 5-10
(Promotional issue only.)
Singles: 7-Inch
RCA VICTOR (Except 0067 through
   0955): *74-86* 1-3
RCA VICTOR (0067 through 0955): *70-74* . 3-6
Promotional Singles
RCA VICTOR (Colored vinyl): 4-8

Picture Sleeves
RCA VICTOR: *74-86* $1-3
WINDSTAR: *88* 1-3
LPs: 10/12-Inch 33rpm
HJD: 40-50
RCA VICTOR: *70-86* 6-10
Also see DENVER, BOISE & JOHNSON
Also see MITCHELL, Chad, Trio

DENVER, John, & Placido Domingo
Singles: 7-Inch
COLUMBIA: *82* 1-3
Also see DOMINGO, Placido

**DENVER, John, & Emmylou
Harris**
Singles: 7-Inch
RCA VICTOR: *83* 1-3
Also see HARRIS, Emmylou

DENVER, John, & The Muppets
Singles: 7-Inch
RCA VICTOR: *79* 1-3
LPs: 10/12-Inch 33rpm
RCA VICTOR: *79-83* 5-8
Also see MUPPETS

DENVER, John & Olivia Newton-John
Singles: 7-Inch
RCA VICTOR: *75* 2-3
Also see DENVER, John
Also see NEWTON-JOHN, Olivia

DENVER, BOISE & JOHNSON
Singles: 7-Inch
REPRISE: *68* 5-10
Member: John Denver; Michael Johnson.
Also see DENVER, John

DEODATO
(Eumir Deodato)
Singles: 12-Inch 33/45rpm
WARNER BROS: *84* 4-6
Singles: 7-Inch
CTI: *73-77* 1-3
MCA: *74-76* 1-3
WARNER BROS: *78-84* 1-3
LPs: 10/12-Inch 33rpm
CTI: *73-74* 8-10
MCA: *76* 6-10
MUSE: *73* 8-10
WARNER BROS: *78-82* 5-8

DEPECHE MODE
Singles: 12-Inch 33/45rpm
SIRE: *81-86* 4-6

Singles: 7-Inch
SIRE: *81-88* $1-3
LPs: 10/12-Inch 33rpm
SIRE: *81-88* 5-8

DEREK
(Johnny Cymbal)
Singles: 7-Inch
BANG: *68-69* 3-5
SOLID GOLD: *73* 1-3
Also see CYMBAL, Johnny

DEREK & CYNDI
Singles: 7-Inch
THUNDER: *74* 2-3
Picture Sleeves
THUNDER: *74* 2-3

DEREK & THE DOMINOS
Singles: 7-Inch
ATCO: *70-72* 2-4
RSO: *73* 2-3
LPs: 10/12-Inch 33rpm
ATCO: *70-71* 20-30
POLYDOR: *74* 8-10
RSO: *77* 5-8
Members: Eric Clapton; Jim Gordon; Carl Radle;
Bobby Whitlock; Duane Allman.
Also see ALLMAN, Duane
Also see CLAPTON, Eric
Also see WHITLOCK, Bobby

DERRINGER, Rick
(Derringer; Rick Derringer & The McCoys)
Singles: 7-Inch
BLUE SKY: *74-80* 2-3
EPIC: *83* 1-3
LPs: 10/12-Inch 33rpm
BLUE SKY: *73-81* 8-12
MERCURY: *74* 10-12
PASSPORT: *83* 5-8
Also see MC COYS

DERRINGER, Rick, & The Edgar
Winter Group
LPs: 10/12-Inch 33rpm
BLUE SKY: *75* 8-10
Also see DERRINGER, Rick
Also see WINTER, Edgar

DE SANTO, Sugar Pie
Singles: 7-Inch
BRUNSWICK: *67-68* 3-5
CADET: *66* 3-5
CHECK: *60* 5-10
CHECKER: *63-66* 3-5

GEDINSON: *62* $3-5
SOUL CLOCK: *69* 2-4
VELTONE: *60* 8-15
WAX: *64* 3-5
EPs: 7-Inch 33/45rpm
CHECKER: *61* .20-40
LPs: 10/12-Inch 33rpm
CHECKER: *61* .30-50
Also see JAMES, Etta, & Sugar Pie DeSanto

DE SARIO, Teri
Singles: 7-Inch
CASABLANCA: *78* 1-3
LPs: 10/12-Inch 33rpm
CASABLANCA: *80* 5-8

DE SARIO, Teri, & K.C.
Singles: 7-Inch
CASABLANCA: *79-80* 1-3
Also see DE SARIO, Teri
Also see K.C. & THE SUNSHINE BAND

DE SHANNON, Jackie
Singles: 7-Inch
AMHERST: *78* 6-12
ATLANTIC: *72-74* 5-10
CAPITOL: *71* 5-10
COLUMBIA (Except 10221): *75* 5-10
COLUMBIA (10221; "Boat To
Sail"): *76* 10-15
(With Brian Wilson.)
EDISON INT'L (416; "I Wanna
Go Home"): *60* 50-100
EDISON INT'L (418; "Put My
Baby Down"): *60* 50-100
IMPERIAL: *65-70* 3-6
LIBERTY (55000 series): *60-64* 15-25
LIBERTY (56000 series): *70* 5-8
MGM: *65* 4-6
RCA VICTOR: *80* 2-3
Picture Sleeves
LIBERTY: *63* .50-100
LPs: 10/12-Inch 33rpm
AMHERST: *77* 15-25
ATLANTIC: *72-74* 10-12
CAPITOL: *71* .12-15
COLUMBIA: *75* 10-12
IMPERIAL: *65-70* 25-50
LIBERTY (3320; "Jackie
De Shannon"): *63* 50-100
(Monaural.)
LIBERTY (3390; "Breakin' It Up On
The Beatles Tour"): *64* 50-100
(Monaural.)

LIBERTY (7320; "Jackie
De Shannon"): *63* $75-100
(Stereo.)
LIBERTY (7390; "Breakin' It Up On
The Beatles Tour"): *64* 75-100
(Stereo.)
LIBERTY (10000 series): *82* 5-8
SUNSET: *68-71* 10-15
UNITED ARTISTS: *75* 8-10
Also see DEE, Jackie
Also see SHANNON, Jackie

DESMOND, Johnny
Singles: 78rpm
CORAL: *52-56* 2-5
MGM: *50-51* 3-6
Singles: 7-Inch
COLUMBIA: *59-60* 4-8
CORAL: *52-56* 4-8
DIAMOND: *62* 2-4
EDGEWOOD: *62* 2-4
MGM: *50-51* 4-8
MUSICANZA: 2-3
RCA VICTOR: *63* 2-4
20TH CENTURY-FOX: *64* 2-4
VIGOR: *73* 1-3
Picture Sleeves
CORAL: *55* 5-10
EPs: 7-Inch 33/45rpm
CORAL: *54-56* 8-15
MGM: *52* 10-20
LPs: 10/12-Inch 33rpm
CAMDEN: *53-54* 10-20
COLUMBIA: *59-60* 5-10
CORAL: *55-56* 15-25
LION: *56* 10-15
MGM: *55* 10-20
MAYFAIR: *58* 10-15
MOVIETONE: *66* 5-8
VOCALION: *66* 5-10
Also see CORNELL, Don, Johnny Desmond
& Alan Dale

DESMOND, Paul
(Paul Desmond Quartet)
Singles: 7-Inch
A&M: *69-70* 1-3
RCA VICTOR: *62-63* 2-3
LPs: 10/12-Inch 33rpm
A&M: *69-76* 6-12
CTI: *75* 6-10
CAMDEN: *73* 5-10
DISCOVERY: *81* 5-8

FANTASY (21; "Paul Desmond"): *54* .. $40-60
(10-Inch LP.)
FANTASY (220; "Paul Desmond"): *56* .. 20-25
RCA VICTOR (2400 & 2500
series): *62-63* 10-20
RCA VICTOR (2800 series): *78* 5-8
RCA VICTOR (3300 & 3400
series): *65-66* 10-15
WARNER BROS: *60* 15-25
Also see BRUBECK, Dave, & Paul Desmond
Also see MULLIGAN, Gerry, & Paul Desmond

DESTINATION
Singles: 7-Inch
A.V.I.: *77* 2-3
LPs: 10/12-Inch 33rpm
A.V.I.: *77* 8-10

DESTINATION
Singles: 12-Inch 33/45rpm
BUTTERFLY: *79* 4-6
Singles: 7-Inch
BUTTERFLY: *79* 1-3
LPs: 10/12-Inch 33rpm
BUTTERFLY: *79* 5-8

**DET REIRRUC & THE CLUB
RAPPERS**
Singles: 12-Inch 33/45rpm
CLUB: *85* 4-6

DETECTIVE
Singles: 7-Inch
SWAN SONG: *77-78* 1-3
LPs: 10/12-Inch 33rpm
SWAN SONG: *77* 10-12
Member: Michael Des Barres.

DETERGENTS
Singles: 7-Inch
KAPP: *66* 4-6
ROULETTE: *64-65* 4-6
Picture Sleeves
ROULETTE: *64-65* 15-25
LPs: 10/12-Inch 33rpm
ROULETTE: *65* 20-30
Members: Ron Dante; Tommy Wynn; Danny Jordan.

DETROIT
Singles: 7-Inch
PARAMOUNT: *70-71* 2-3
LPs: 10/12-Inch 33rpm
PARAMOUNT: *71-72* 10-12
Also see DETROIT WHEELS

Also see ROCKETS
Also see RYDER, Mitch, & The Detroit
Wheels

DETROIT EMERALDS
Singles: 7-Inch
RIC-TIC: *68* $3-5
WESTBOUND: *70-78* 2-4
LPs: 10/12-Inch 33rpm
WESTBOUND: *71-78* 10-12

DETROIT WHEELS
Singles: 7-Inch
INFERNO: *68* 3-5
Also see DETROIT
Also see RYDER, Mitch, & The Detroit
Wheels
Also see ROCKETS

DETROYT
Singles: 7-Inch
TABU: *84* 1-3

DE VAUGHN, William
Singles: 7-Inch
ROXBURY: *74* 2-3
TEC: *80* 1-3
LPs: 10/12-Inch 33rpm
ROXBURY: *74* 8-10
TEC: *80* 5-8

DEVICE
Singles: 7-Inch
CHRYSALIS: *86* 1-3

DEVO
Singles: 12-Inch 33/45rpm
ENIGMA: *88* 4-6
WARNER BROS: *80-85* 4-6
Singles: 7-Inch
ASYLUM: *81* 1-3
BOOJI BOY: *78* 2-4
ENIGMA: *88* 1-3
FULL MOON: *81* 1-3
WARNER BROS: *78-85* 1-3
Promotional Singles
WARNER BROS ("Beautiful
World"): *81* 8-12
(Space helmet shaped disc.)
Picture Sleeves
WARNER BROS: *79-85* 1-3
LPs: 10/12-Inch 33rpm
ENIGMA: *88* 5-8
WARNER BROS: *78-88* 5-10
Members: Mark Mothersbaugh; Bob
Mothersbaugh; David Kendrick; Bob Casale;
Gerald Casale.

DE VOL, Frank, Orchestra
(Frank De Vol & The Rainbow Strings)
Singles: 78rpm
CAPITOL: *50-56* $2-4
KEM: *55* 2-4
Singles: 7-Inch
ABC-PARAMOUNT: *64-65* 2-3
CAPITOL: *50-56* 2-4
COLGEMS: *68* 2-3
COLUMBIA: *59-62* 2-3
KEM: *55* 2-4
Picture Sleeves
COLGEMS: *68* 2-4
LPs: 10/12-Inch 33rpm
ABC-PARAMOUNT: *65-66* 5-10
COLGEMS (108; "Guess Who's
Coming To Dinner"): *68* 20-25
(Soundtrack.)
COLGEMS (5006; "The
Happening"): *67* 15-20
(Soundtrack.)
COLUMBIA: *59-63* 8-10
HARMONY: *65* 5-8

DEVONS
Singles: 7-Inch
KING: *69* 2-4

DE VORZON, Barry
Singles: 7-Inch
COLUMBIA: *59-61* 6-10
RCA VICTOR: *57-59* 5-15
WARNER BROS: *81* 1-3
LPs: 10/12-Inch 33rpm
ARISTA: *76* 5-8
Also see BARRY & THE TAMERLANES

DE VORZON, Barry, & Perry Botkin Jr.
Singles: 7-Inch
A&M: *76-77* 1-3
Picture Sleeves
A&M: *76* 1-3
Also see DE VORZON, Barry
Also see MC COY BOYS

DEVOTIONS
Singles: 7-Inch
DELTA (1001; "Rip Van
Winkle"): *61* 50-75
KAPE: 3-5
ROULETTE (Except 4406 &
4541): *64* 8-10
ROULETTE (4406; "Rip Van
Winkle"): *61* 25-30
(White label.)

ROULETTE (4541; "Rip Van
   Winkle"): *64* $6-10
   (Orange label.)
   Members: Joe Pardo; Frank Pardo; Bob Weisbrod;
   Ray Sanchez; Bob Havorka; Louis DeCarlo; Larry
   Frank

DEVOTO, Howard
   Singles: 12-Inch 33/45rpm
I.R.S.: *86* 4-6
   Singles: 7-Inch
I.R.S.: *86* 1-3
   LPs: 10/12-Inch 33rpm
I.R.S.: *86* 5-8

DEXY'S MIDNIGHT RUNNERS
   Singles: 7-Inch
EMI AMERICA: *81* 1-3
MERCURY: *82-83* 1-3
   LPs: 10/12-Inch 33rpm
EMI AMERICA: *81* 5-8
MERCURY: *82* 5-8

DEY, Tracey
   Singles: 7-Inch
AMY: *63-65* 5-10
COLUMBIA: *66* 3-6
LIBERTY: *63* 8-15
VEE JAY: *62* 5-10

DE YOUNG, Cliff
   Singles: 7-Inch
MCA: *73-75* 2-3
   LPs: 10/12-Inch 33rpm
MCA: *73-75* 10-12

DE YOUNG, Dennis
   Singles: 7-Inch
A&M: *83-86* 1-3
   LPs: 10/12-Inch 33rpm
A&M: *84-86* 5-8
   Also see STYX

DIAMOND, Gregg
   (Gregg Diamond's Starcruiser; Gregg
   Diamond's Bionic Boogie)
   Singles: 12-Inch 33/45rpm
POLYDOR: *79* 4-6
   Singles: 7-Inch
MARLIN: *78* 1-3
POLYDOR: *79-80* 1-3
   LPs: 10/12-Inch 33rpm
MARLIN: *78* 5-8
MERCURY: *79* 5-8
POLYDOR: *77-78* 5-8

DIAMOND, Joel
   (Joel Diamond Experience)
   Singles: 12-Inch 33/45rpm
CASABLANCA: *79* $4-6
   Singles: 7-Inch
ATLANTIC: *82* 1-3
CASABLANCA: *79-84* 1-3
MOTOWN: *81* 1-3
   LPs: 10/12-Inch 33rpm
CASABLANCA: *79* 8-10

DIAMOND, Leo
   Singles: 78rpm
RCA VICTOR: *55* 2-4
   Singles: 7-Inch
RCA VICTOR: *55* 2-4

DIAMOND, Neil
   Singles: 12-Inch 33/45rpm
COLUMBIA (1586;
   "Heartlight"): *82* 6-10
   Singles: 7-Inch
BANG (100 series): 2-3
   ("Best Hits" reissue series.)
BANG (500 & 700 series): *66-73* 3-6
CAPITOL: *90-91* 1-3
COLUMBIA (02600 through 06100
   series): *81-86* 1-3
COLUMBIA (10000 & 11000
   series): *74-80* 1-3
COLUMBIA (33000 series): 1-3
   ("Hall Of Fame" series.)
COLUMBIA (42809; "Clown
   Town"): *63* 150-200
COLUMBIA (45000 series): *73-74* 2-4
MCA (40000 series): *73* 2-4
MCA (60000 series): *73* 1-3
PHILCO: *66-67* 10-20
   ("Hip-Pocket" Record.)
SOLID ROCK: 2-3
UNI: *68-72* 3-5
   Promotional Singles
BANG (Except 55075): *66-73* 4-8
UNI (55075; "Two-Bit Manchild"): *68* .. 10-20
   (Colored vinyl.)
CAPITOL: *80-81* 2-4
COLUMBIA (1115; "Song Sung
   Blue"): *77* 3-5
COLUMBIA (1193; "September
   Morn"): *79* 3-5
   (Contains an alternate version of the song.)
COLUMBIA (02600 through 11000): *74-86* 2-5
COLUMBIA (42809; "Clown
   Town"): *63* 100-200

COLUMBIA (45000 series): *73-74* $3-6
MCA: *73* 2-4
UNI: *68-72* 5-10
WHAT'S IT ALL ABOUT: 8-15
Picture Sleeves
CAPITOL: *80-81* 1-3
COLUMBIA: *73-85* 2-3
UNI: *68-70* 3-6
EPs: 7-Inch 33/45rpm (Jukebox)
COLUMBIA (32919; "Serenade"): *74* ... 10-20
MCA (34989; "12 Greatest Hits"): *74* ... 10-20
UNI (34818; "Neil Diamond Gold"): *71* . 10-20
UNI (34871; "Stones"): *71* 10-20
LPs: 10/12-Inch 33rpm
BANG (214; "The Feel Of Neil
 Diamond"): *66* 50-100
BANG (217; "Just For You"): *67* 20-40
BANG (219; "Greatest Hits"): *68* 20-40
BANG (221; "Shilo"): *70* 20-30
BANG (224; "Do It"): *71* 20-30
BANG (227; "Double Gold"): *73* 20-35
CAPITOL: *80* 5-8
COLUMBIA (30000 series): *73-86* 6-12
COLUMBIA (40000 series): *78-82* 10-15
 (Half-speed mastered.)
DIRECT-TO-DISK: 10-20
FROG KING (1; "Early
 Classics"): *78* 25-50
 (Includes music & lyrics songbook. Columbia
 Record Club issue.)
HARMONY (30023;
 "Chartbusters"): *70* 15-25
 (A various artists LP, containing the 1963 Colum-
 bia track *Clown Town*, and the otherwise unavail-
 able *I've Never Been The Same*.)
MCA: *72-81* 6-15
MFSL: *79-82* 25-50
UNI (11; Neil Diamond D.J.
 Sampler"): *71* 25-50
 (Promotional souvenir issue only.)
UNI (1913; "Open-End Interview
 With Neil Diamond"): *72* 25-50
 (Promotional issue only.)
UNI (73030; "Velvet Gloves &
 Spit"): *68* 20-35
 (Does not contain *Shilo*.)
UNI (73030; "Velvet Gloves &
 Spit"): *70* 15-25
 (With *Shilo*.)
UNI (73047; "Brother Love's Traveling
 Salvation Show"): *69* 20-35
UNI (73047; "Sweet Caroline/Brother Love's
 Traveling Salvation Show"): *69* 15-25

UNI (73071; "Touching You,
 Touching Me"): *69* $15-25
UNI (73084; "Gold"): *70* 15-25
UNI (73092; "Tap Root Manuscript"): *70* . 15-25
 (Some 70000 series LPs were reissued in the 90000
 series, with the only change being the first digit.)
UNI (93106; "Stones"): *71* 15-25
UNI (93136; "Moods"): *72* 15-25
Also see NEIL & JACK
Also see STREISAND, Barbra, & Neil
Diamond

DIAMOND, Neil / Diana Ross & The Supremes
LPs: 10/12-Inch 33rpm
MCA (734727; "It's Happening"): *72* ... 20-40
 (One side of LP devoted to each artist.)
Also see DIAMOND, Neil
Also see SUPREMES

DIAMOND REO
Singles: 7-Inch
BIG TREE: *75* 2-3
BUDDAH: *77* 2-3
LPs: 10/12-Inch 33rpm
BIG TREE: *75* 8-10
KAMA SUTRA: *76* 8-10
PICCADILLY: *79* 5-8

DIAMONDS
Singles: 78rpm
CORAL: *55-56* 3-6
MERCURY: *56-57* 2-5
Singles: 7-Inch
CHURCHILL: *87* 1-3
CORAL: *55-56* 5-10
MERCURY: *56-62* 4-8
Picture Sleeves
MERCURY: *58* 10-20
EPs: 7-Inch 33/45rpm
BRUNSWICK: *57* 15-20
MERCURY: *56-61* 10-20
LPs: 10/12-Inch 33rpm
MERCURY: *56-60* 20-30
WING: *59* 15-20
 Members: David Somerville; Phil Leavitt; Bill
 Reed; Ted Kowalski

DIAMONDS & Pete Rugolo
LPs: 10/12-Inch 33rpm
MERCURY: *59* 45-55
Also see DIAMONDS

DIANE RAY: see RAY, Diane

DIBANGO, Manu
Singles: 7-Inch
ATLANTIC: 73 .... $2-3
LPs: 10/12-Inch 33rpm
ATLANTIC: 73 8-10

DICK & DEE DEE
Singles: 7-Inch
DOT: 68-69 3-5
LAMA: 61 10-15
LIBERTY: 61-62 5-8
UNITED ARTISTS: 2-3
WARNER BROS: 62-69 4-6
Picture Sleeves
WARNER BROS: 63-64 10-20
LPs: 10/12-Inch 33rpm
LIBERTY (3236/7236; "Tell Me / The
Mountain's High"): 62 40-50
WARNER BROS: 63-65 20-30
Members: Dick St. John; Dee Dee Sperling.

DICK & DON:
see ADDRISI BROTHERS

DICK LEE: see LEE, Dick

DICKENS, Jimmy
(Little Jimmy Dickens)
Singles: 78rpm
COLUMBIA: 50-57 4-8
Singles: 7-Inch
COLUMBIA (10000 series): 76 1-3
COLUMBIA (20000 & 21000
series): 50-56 5-10
COLUMBIA (40000 series): 56 4-6
COLUMBIA (41000 series,
except 41173): 57-60 4-6
COLUMBIA (41137; "I Got A Hole
In My Pocket"): 57 20-30
COLUMBIA (42000 through 44000
series): 60-67 3-5
DECCA: 67-69 2-4
LITTLE GEM: 75 1-3
PARTRIDGE: 80 1-3
STARDAY: 73 1-3
UNITED ARTISTS: 70-72 2-3
EPs: 7-Inch 33/45rpm
COLUMBIA (Except 2800
series): 52-57 15-20
COLUMBIA (2800 series): 57-58 10-15
LPs: 10/12-Inch 33rpm
COLUMBIA (1047; "Raisin' The
Dickens"): 57 40-50

COLUMBIA (1500 through 2500
series): 60-66 .... $10-20
(Monaural.)
COLUMBIA (8300 through 9600
series): 60-68 12-20
(Stereo.)
COLUMBIA (10000 & 11000
series): 70-73 6-10
COLUMBIA (38000 series): 84 5-8
DECCA: 68-69 10-12
GUSTO: 5-8
HARMONY (7000 series): 64-65 10-15
HARMONY (9000 series): 54 20-30
(10-Inch LPs.)
HARMONY (11000 series): 67 8-12
QCA: 75 6-10

DICKEY DOO & THE DONT'S
Singles: 7-Inch
ASCOT: 65 3-5
DANNA: 67 3-5
SWAN: 58-59 5-8
UNITED ARTISTS: 60-61 5-8
LPs: 10/12-Inch 33rpm
UNITED ARTISTS: 60 25-35
Member: Gerry Granahan
Also see GRANAHAN, Gerry

DICKIE LEE: see LEE, Dickie

DICTATORS
Singles: 7-Inch
ASYLUM: 77 2-3
LPs: 10/12-Inch 33rpm
ASYLUM: 77-78 8-10
EPIC: 75 10-12

DIDDLEY, Bo
Singles: 78rpm
CHECKER: 55-57 6-12
Singles: 7-Inch
ABC: 74 1-3
CHECKER (800 series): 55-58 8-10
CHECKER (900 series): 59-62 4-6
CHECKER (1000 through 1200
series): 62-69 3-5
CHESS: 71-72 2-4
RCA VICTOR: 76 2-3
EPs: 7-Inch 33/45rpm
CHESS (5125; "Bo Diddley"): 58 25-35
(This EP was issued with two different covers; one
of the conventional cardboard style, the other made
of paper.)
LPs: 10/12-Inch 33rpm
ACCORD: 82 5-8

CHECKER (Except 1436): *59-69* $25-50
CHECKER (1436; "Go Bo
   Diddley"): *57* 50-100
CHESS (Except 1431): *71-74* 10-15
CHESS (1431; "Bo Diddley"): *58* 50-100
RCA VICTOR: *76* 8-10
   Also see BELMONTS, Freddy Cannon & Bo
   Diddley
   Also see BERRY, Chuck, & Bo Diddley
   Also see MOONGLOWS

DIDDLEY, Bo, Howlin' Wolf &
Muddy Waters
         LPs: 10/12-Inch 33rpm
CHECKER: *68* 15-20
   Also see DIDDLEY, Bo
   Also see HOWLIN' WOLF
   Also see WATERS, Muddy

DIESEL
         Singles: 7-Inch
REGENCY: *81* 2-3
         LPs: 10/12-Inch 33rpm
REGENCY: *81* 8-10

DIFFORD & TILBROOK
         Singles: 7-Inch
A&M: *84* 1-3
         LPs: 10/12-Inch 33rpm
A&M: *84* 5-8
   Members: Chris Difford; Glenn Tilbrook.
   Also see SQUEEZE

DIFOSCO
         Singles: 7-Inch
EARTHQUAKE: *71* 2-4
ROXBURY: *76* 1-3
20TH CENTURY-FOX: *78* 1-3

DILLARD, Varetta
(Varetta Dillard & The Roamers)
         Singles: 78rpm
GROOVE: *55-56* 4-8
SAVOY: *53-55* 4-8
         Singles: 7-Inch
CUB: *60-61* 4-6
GROOVE: *55-56* 5-10
RCA VICTOR: *57* 8-12
SAVOY: *53-55* 5-10
TRIUMPH: *59* 5-10

DILLARD, Varetta
(Varetta Dillard & The Four Students)
         Singles: 78rpm
GROOVE: *55-56* 10-20

         Singles: 7-Inch
GROOVE: *55-56* $20-40
DILLARDS
         Singles: 7-Inch
ANTHEM: *71-72* 2-3
CAPITOL: *65* .2-4
ELEKTRA: *63-69* 2-4
POPPY: *74* 2-3
UNITED ARTISTS: *75* 2-3
WHITE WHALE: *70* 2-3
         LPs: 10/12-Inch 33rpm
ANTHEM: *72* .6-10
ELEKTRA (200 series): *63-65* 20-30
   (Gold label.)
ELEKTRA (7-200 series): *63-65* 20-30
   (Gold label.)
ELEKTRA (7-200 series): 10-15
   (Brown label.)
ELEKTRA (74000 series): *68* 8-12
FLYING FISH: *77-81* 5-8
POPPY: *73* 8-12
20TH CENTURY-FOX: *73* 8-12
   Members: Doug Dillard; Rodney Dillard; Dean
   Webb; Mitch Jayne.

DILLARDS & John Hartford
         LPs: 10/12-Inch 33rpm
FLYING FISH: .5-8
   Also see DILLARDS
   Also see HARTFORD, John

DILLMAN BAND
(Daisy Dillman Band)
         Singles: 7-Inch
RCA: *81* 1-3
UNITED ARTISTS: *77-78* 2-3
         LPs: 10/12-Inch 33rpm
RCA: *81* 5-8
UNITED ARTISTS: *78* 5-8

DI MEOLA, Al
(Al Di Meola Project)
         Singles: 7-Inch
COLUMBIA: *76-84* 1-3
         LPs: 10/12-Inch 33rpm
COLUMBIA: *76-83* 5-8
E.M.I./MANHATTAN: *88* 5-8
   Also see RETURN TO FOREVER
DING DONGS
(Bobby Darin)
         Singles: 7-Inch
BRUNSWICK (55073; "Early In The
   Morning"): *58* $50-75
   Also see DARIN, Bobby

DINNING, Mark
Singles: 78rpm
MGM: *57* $4-8
Singles: 7-Inch
CAMEO: *64* 3-5
HICKORY: *65-66* 3-5
MGM (Except 12775 & 12980): *57-63* 4-6
MGM (12775; "Cutie Cutie"): *59* 8-12
MGM (12980; "Top 40, News,
   Weather & Sports"): *61* 5-10
   (With mention of "Patrice Lumumba" in lyrics.)
MGM (12980; "Top 40, News, Weather
   & Sports"): *61* 4-6
   (With no mention of "Patrice Lumumba" in lyrics.)
UNITED ARTISTS: *67-68* 3-5
Picture Sleeves
MGM: *60* 8-15
LPs: 10/12-Inch 33rpm
MGM (3828; "Teen Angel"): *60* 40-80
MGM (3855; "Wanderin"): *60* 40-80

DINO, DESI & BILLY
Singles: 7-Inch
COLUMBIA: *69* 2-4
UNI: *69* 3-5
REPRISE (Except 0965): *64-69* 4-6
REPRISE (0965; "Lady Love"): *70* 10-15
Picture Sleeves
REPRISE: *65-68* 4-8
LPs: 10/12-Inch 33rpm
REPRISE: *65-66* 15-20
UNI: *69* 12-15
   Members: Dino Martin; Desi Arnaz Jr.; Billy
   Hinsche.

DINO, Kenny
Singles: 12-Inch 33/45rpm
KDK PRODUCTIONS ("Love Songs
   For Seka"): *80* 20-30
   (Picture disc with photo of adult-film star, Seka.)
Singles: 7-Inch
COLUMBIA: *64* 3-5
DOT: *61* 3-5
MUSICOR: *61-62* 4-6
SMASH: *63-64* 3-5

DINO, Paul
Singles: 7-Inch
ENTRE: *63* 3-5
PROMO: *60-61* 3-5

DIO
Singles: 7-Inch
WARNER BROS: *85-86* 1-3
LPs: 10/12-Inch 33rpm
WARNER BROS: *85-87* 5-8

Dion DiMucci

DION
(Dion DiMucci)
Singles: 7-Inch
BIG TREE/SPECTOR: *76* $2-3
COLUMBIA (40000 series): *62* 15-20
   (With a "3" prefix. Compact 33 Singles.)
COLUMBIA (40000 series): *62-65* 4-6
   (With a "4" prefix. Black vinyl.)
COLUMBIA (42852; "Donna The
   Prima Donna"): *63* 10-15
   (Colored vinyl. Promotional issue only.)
LAURIE: *60-69* 4-6
LIFESONG: *78-79* 2-3
SPECTOR: *75* 2-3
WARNER BROS (Except 814): *69-79* 2-4
WARNER BROS (814; "The
   Wanderer"): *79* 4-8
   (Promotional issue only.)
WARNER BROS/SPECTOR: *75* 2-3
Picture Sleeves
COLUMBIA (Except 42662): *64-66* 8-15
COLUMBIA (42662; "Ruby
   Baby"): *62* 25-40
   (Promotional issue sleeve sent with "Ruby Baby,"
   but does not list title or number. Simply reads,
   "Dion Is Now On Columbia Records.")
COLUMBIA (42662; "Ruby
   Baby"): *62* 5-10
   (Commercially issued sleeve.)
LAURIE: *60-62* 5-10
LPs: 10/12-Inch 33rpm
ABEL: 8-10
ARISTA: *77* 8-12
COLLECTABLES: *85-87* 6-8
COLUMBIA: *63-73* 15-20
DAYSPRING: *80* 5-8
LAURIE (2000 series,
   except 2009 & 2047): *61-63* 20-30

LAURIE (2009; "Runaround Sue"): *61* . $20-30
(Black vinyl.)
LAURIE (2009; "Runaround Sue"): *61* . . 30-60
(Colored vinyl.)
LAURIE (2047; "Dion"): *68* 10-15
LAURIE (4000 series): 8-15
LIFESONG: *78* 5-8
WARNER BROS: *69-76* 10-15
Also see DEE, Joey, & The Starliters / Dion

DION / Glen Stuart Chorus
LPs: 10/12-Inch 33rpm
ABEL: 8-10

DION & THE BELMONTS
(Featuring Dion DiMucci)
Singles: 7-Inch
ABC: *66-67* 3-5
COLLECTABLES: 1-3
LAURIE (Gray label): *58* 25-30
LAURIE (Blue label): *58* 15-20
LAURIE (Red & white label): *58-60* 4-8
(Monaural.)
LAURIE (Stereo): *59* 20-25
(With an "S" prefix.)
MOHAWK: *57* 25-30
Picture Sleeves
LAURIE: *59-60* 10-20
EPs: 7-Inch 33/45rpm
LAURIE: *59* 30-50
LPs: 10/12-Inch 33rpm
ABC: *67* 15-20
ARISTA: *84* 8-12
COLLECTABLES: *85* 6-8
GRT: *75* 8-10
LAURIE (1002; "Presenting Dion
& The Belmonts"): *59* 50-100
LAURIE (2002; "Presenting Dion
& The Belmonts"): *60* 40-80
LAURIE (2006; "Wish Upon
A Star"): *60* 30-35
LAURIE (2013; "Dion With
The Belmonts"): *62* 20-30
LAURIE (2016; "By Special
Request"): *62* 20-30
LAURIE (4001; "Everything You
Always Wanted To Hear"): *76* 8-12
LAURIE (6000; "60 Greatest"): 12-15
PICKWICK: *75* 8-10
WARNER BROS: *73* 8-10
Also see BELMONTS

DION & THE TIMBERLANES
(Featuring Dion DiMuci)
Singles: 7-Inch
JUBILEE: *57* 25-30
MOHAWK: *57* 30-35

VIRGO: *73* $1-3
Also see DION

DIONNE & FRIENDS
Singles: 7-Inch
ARISTA: *85* 1-3
Members: Dionne Warwick; Elton John; Stevie
Wonder; Gladys Knight.
Also see JOHN, Elton
Also see KNIGHT, Gladys
Also see WARWICK, Dionne
Also see WONDER, Stevie

DIPLOMATS
Singles: 7-Inch
AROCK: *64* 3-5
DYNAMO: *68-69* 3-5
MAY: *61* 4-6
MINIT: *66* 3-5
WAND: *65* 3-5

DIRECT CURRENT
Singles: 7-Inch
TEC: *79* 1-3

DIRE STRAITS
Singles: 12-Inch 33/45rpm
WARNER BROS: *83* 4-6
Singles: 7-Inch
WARNER BROS: *79-86* 1-3
Picture Sleeves
WARNER BROS: *80* 1-3
LPs: 10/12-Inch 33rpm
WARNER BROS: *78-88* 5-8
Member: Mark Knopfler.

DIRT BAND:
see NITTY GRITTY DIRT BAND

DIRKSEN, Senator Everett McKinley
Singles: 7-Inch
CAPITOL: *66* 2-4
Picture Sleeves
CAPITOL: *66* 2-4
LPs: 10/12-Inch 33rpm
BELL: *70* 5-10
CAPITOL: *66-67* 10-15

DISCO FOUR
Singles: 12-Inch 33/45rpm
PROFILE: *83* 4-6
Singles: 7-Inch
PROFILE: *82-83* 1-3

DISCO-TEX & HIS SEX-O-LETTES
Singles: 7-Inch
CHELSEA: *74-76* 2-3
LPs: 10/12-Inch 33rpm
CHELSEA: *75-76* 8-10
MUSICOR: *79* 5-8

DISCO 3
Singles: 12-Inch 33/45rpm
SUTRA: *83* $4-6
Singles: 7-Inch
SUTRA: *84* 1-3

DIVINYLS
Singles: 12-Inch 33/45rpm
CHRYSALIS: *85* 4-6
Singles: 7-Inch
CHRYSALIS: *83-86* 1-3
LPs: 10/12-Inch 33rpm
CHRYSALIS: *83-86* 5-8
Member: Christina Amphlett.

DIXIE CUPS
Singles: 7-Inch
ABC-PARAMOUNT: *65-66* 3-5
ANTILLES: *87* 1-3
RED BIRD: *64-65* 4-6
Picture Sleeves
ANTILLES: *87* 1-3
EPs: 7-Inch 33/45rpm
ABC-PARAMOUNT: *65* 15-25
LPs: 10/12-Inch 33rpm
ABC-PARAMOUNT: *65* 20-25
RED BIRD: *64-65* 25-35
Members: Barbara Hawkins; Rosa Hawkins; Joan
Johnson.

DIXIE DREGS
(Dregs)
Singles: 7-Inch
ARISTA: *80-82* 1-3
CAPRICORN: *77-79* 2-3
LPs: 10/12-Inch 33rpm
ARISTA: *80-82* 5-8
CAPRICORN: *78-79* 5-8
Member: Steve Morse.
Also see MORSE, Steve, Band

DIXIE DRIFTER
Singles: 7-Inch
AMY: *68* 2-4
IX CAHINS: *74* 2-4
ROULETTE: *65* 3-5

DIXIE HUMMINGBIRDS
Singles: 78rpm
OKEH: *53* 2-4
Singles: 7-Inch
ABC: *73-74* 1-3
OKEH: *53* 2-4
PEACOCK: *59-74* 1-3
LPs: 10/12-Inch 33rpm
CONSTELLATION: *64* 5-10
GOSPEL ROOTS: *80* 5-8
PEACOCK: *59-78* 5-10

DIXIEBELLES
Singles: 7-Inch
MONUMENT: *72* $1-3
SOUND STAGE 7: *63-64* 3-5
EPs: 7-Inch 33/45rpm
SOUND STAGE 7: *63* 12-15
LPs: 10/12-Inch 33rpm
SOUND STAGE 7: *63* 20-25
MONUMENT: *65* 12-15
Also see SMITH, Jerry

DIXON, Floyd
(Floyd Dixon & His Band)
Singles: 78rpm
ALADDIN: *50-52* 10-20
CASH: *54* 8-15
CAT: *54* 8-15
MODERN: *49-50* 5-10
PEACOCK: *50* 5-10
SUPREME: *47* 8-12
SWING TIME: *47* 8-12
Singles: 7-Inch
ALADDIN (Black vinyl): *50-52* 25-40
ALADDIN (Colored vinyl): *50-52* 40-60
CASH: *54* 10-20
CAT: *54* 10-20
CHATTAHOOCHEE: *64* 3-5
CHECKER: *58* 8-12
DODGE: *61* 3-6
EBB: *57* 10-15
JELLO: *60* 8-10
KENT: *58* 4-8
SPECIALTY (Black vinyl): *53* 10-20
SPECIALTY (Colored vinyl): *53* 20-40
(Most Specialty singles are currently available,
using original catalog numbers.)
SWINGIN': *60* 4-8

**DIXON, Floyd, & Johnny Moore's
Three Blazers**
Singles: 78rpm
ALADDIN: *50* 15-20
Singles: 7-Inch
ALADDIN: *50* 25-35
Also see MOORE, Johnny

DOBKINS, Carl, Jr.
Singles: 7-Inch
ATCO: *64* 3-5
CHALET: *69* 2-3
COLPIX: *65* 3-5
DECCA: *59-62* 4-6
FRATERNITY: *58* 4-6
MCA: 1-3
Picture Sleeves
DECCA: *59-60* 5-10

EPs: 7-Inch 33/45rpm

DECCA (2664; "My Heart Is An
Open Book"): *59* $50-75
LPs: 10/12-Inch 33rpm

DECCA (DL-8938; "Carl
Dobkins Jr."): *59* 30-40
(Monaural.)

DECCA (DL7-8938; "Carl
Dobkins, Jr."): *59* 40-50
(Stereo.)
Also see LEE, Brenda / Carl Dobkins, Jr.

DOCKETT, Jimmy
Singles: 7-Inch

FLO FEEL: *73* 2-4
HULL: *64-65* 3-5

**DR. BUZZARD'S ORIGINAL
SAVANNAH BAND**
Singles: 7-Inch

RCA VICTOR: *76-80* 1-3
LPs: 10/12-Inch 33rpm

ELEKTRA: *79* 5-8
PASSPORT: 5-8
RCA VICTOR: *76-80* 8-10
Also see DAYE, Cory
Also see KID CREOLE & THE COCONUTS

DOCTOR FEELGOOD
(Doctor Feelgood & The Interns)
Singles: 7-Inch

COLUMBIA: *65-66* 3-5
EPIC: 2-3
MASTER SOUND: *67* 3-5
OKEH: *62-63* 4-8
1-2-3: *68* 3-5
LPs: 10/12-Inch 33rpm

OKEH: *62* 20-25
NUMBER ONE: 15-20
Also see PIANO RED

DR. HOOK
(Doctor Hook & The Medicine Show)
Singles: 7-Inch

CAPITOL: *75-80* 1-3
CASABLANCA: *80-82* 1-3
COLUMBIA: *71-74* 2-3
Picture Sleeves

CAPITOL: *75-80* 1-3
COLUMBIA: *71-72* 2-4
LPs: 10/12-Inch 33rpm

CAPITOL: *75-81* 8-10
CASABLANCA: *80-82* 5-8
COLUMBIA (Except 34147): *72-74* 15-20
COLUMBIA (34147; "Best Of
Dr. Hook"): *76* 5-8
Also see BEACH BOYS

Also see SAWYER, Ray

**DR. J.R. KOOL & THE OTHER
ROXANNES**
Singles: 12-Inch 33/45rpm

COMPLEAT: *85* $4-6
Singles: 7-Inch

COMPLEAT: *85* 1-3
LPs: 10/12-Inch 33rpm

COMPLEAT: *85* 5-8

DR. JECKYLL & MR. HYDE
Singles: 12-Inch 33/45rpm

PROFILE: *83-86* 4-6
Singles: 7-Inch

PROFILE: *83-86* 1-3
LPs: 10/12-Inch 33rpm

PROFILE: *84-86* 5-8

DR. JOHN
(Mac Rebennack)
Singles: 7-Inch

ATCO: *72-74* 2-4
COLUMBIA: *82* 1-3
HORIZON: *79* 2-3
RCA VICTOR: *78* 2-3
STREETWISE: *84* 1-3
WARNER BROS: *81* 1-3
LPs: 10/12-Inch 33rpm

A&M: *79* 8-10
ACCORD: *81* . . . . :5-8
ACE: 10-12
ATCO (Except 200 & 300
series): *72-74* 8-10
ATCO (200 & 300 series): *68-71* 12-15
BAROMETER: *74* 10-12
CLEANCUTS: *82-84* 5-8
KARATE: *78* 8-10
SPRINGBOARD: *72* 10-12
TRIP: *75-76* 8-10
UNITED ARTISTS: *75* 8-10
Also see BLOOMFIELD, Mike, Dr. John &
John Paul Hammond
Also see SAHM, Doug

DR. JOHN & LIBBY TITUS
Singles: 7-Inch

WARNER BROS: *81* 1-3
Also see DR. JOHN

**DR. WEST'S MEDICINE SHOW &
JUNK BAND**
Singles: 7-Inch

GO GO: *66-67* 4-6
GREGAR: *68* 3-5
ROWE/AMI: *66* 4-8
("Play Me" Sales Stimulator promotional issue.)

LPs: 10/12-Inch 33rpm
GO GO: *67* $20-25
GREGAR: 12-15
  Also see GREENBAUM, Norman

DODDS, Nella
Singles: 7-Inch
WAND: *64-66* 3-6

DOGGETT, Bill
Singles: 78rpm
KING: *53-57* 3-6
Singles: 7-Inch
ABC-PARAMOUNT: *64* 2-4
CHUMLEY: *74* 1-3
COLUMBIA: *62-63* 3-6
GUSTO: 1-3
KING (4000 series): *53-56* 4-8
KING (5000 series): *56-65* 3-6
KING (6000 series): *66-71* 2-4
ROULETTE: *67* .2-5
SUE: *64* 2-5
WARNER BROS: *61* 2-5
Picture Sleeves
COLUMBIA: *62* .5-10
EPs: 7-Inch 33/45
KING: *54-59* 5-10
LPs: 10/12-Inch 33rpm
ABC-PARAMOUNT: *65* 10-15
COLUMBIA: *62-63* 12-15
HARMONY: *67* 10-15
KING: *54-66* 15-30
ROULETTE: *66* 10-15
STARDAY: 5-8
WARNER BROS: *61-62* 12-15
  Members: Bill Butler; Clifford Scott.
  Also see BOSTIC, Earl, & Bill Doggett
  Also see FITZGERALD, Ella, & Bill Doggett
  Also see JACQUET, Illinois

DOKKEN
(Don Dokken)
Singles: 7-Inch
ELEKTRA: *83-88* .1-3
LPs: 10/12-Inch 33rpm
ELEKTRA: *83-88* .5-8

DOLBY, Thomas
Singles: 12-Inch 33/45rpm
CAPITOL: *83-84* .4-6
Singles: 7-Inch
CAPITOL: *83* 1-3
HARVEST: *82* 1-3
LPs: 10/12-Inch 33rpm
CAPITOL: *83-84* .5-8
E.M.I./MANHATTAN: *88* 5-8
HARVEST: *83* 5-8

Also see DOLBY'S CUBE

DOLBY'S CUBE
(Thomas Dolby)
Singles: 12-Inch 33/45rpm
CAPITOL: *84* $4-6
Singles: 7-Inch
CAPITOL: *84* 1-3
Also see DOLBY, Thomas

DOLCE, Joe
Singles: 7-Inch
MCA: *81* 1-3
METROMEDIA: *81* 1-3

DOLENZ, Mickey
Singles: 7-Inch
CHALLENGE: *66-67* 10-15
MGM: *71-72* 5-10
ROMAR: *73-74* .5-10
Picture Sleeves
CHALLENGE: *66-67* 20-25
LPs: 10/12-Inch 33rpm
CHRYSALIS: *79* 8-10
Also see MONKEES

**DOLENZ, Mickey, Davy Jones &
Peter Tork**
Singles: 7-Inch
CHRISTMAS RECORDS: *76* 8-12
(Fan club, mail-order issue. Issued with special
poster.)
Members: Mickey Dolenz; David Jones; Peter Tork.
Also see MONKEES

DOLENZ, JONES, BOYCE & HART
Singles: 7-Inch
CAPITOL: *75-76* 10-15
LPs: 10/12-Inch 33rpm
CAPITOL: *76* 10-15
Members: Mickey Dolenz; David Jones; Tommy
Boyce; Bobby Hart.
Also see BOYCE, Tommy, & Bobby Hart
Also see DOLENZ, Mickey
Also see JONES, Davy, & Mickey Dolenz

DOLLAR
Singles: 7-Inch
CARRERE: *79* 1-3

DOLPHINS
Singles: 7-Inch
EMPRESS: *61* 4-6
FRATERNITY: *64-65* 3-5
GEMINI: *62* 4-6
LAURIE: *63* 4-6
SHAD: *60* 10-12
YORKSHIRE: *66* 5-10

DOMINATRIX
Singles: 12-Inch 33/45rpm
STREETWISE: $4-6

DOMINGO, Placido
Singles: 7-Inch
COLUMBIA: *81-84* 1-3
LPs: 10/12-Inch 33rpm
COLUMBIA: *81-84* 5-8
RCA VICTOR: *82* 5-8
Also see DENVER, John, & Placido Domingo

DOMINO, Fats
Singles: 78rpm
IMPERIAL: *50-57* 5-15
Singles: 7-Inch
ABC: *73* 1-3
ABC-PARAMOUNT: *63-64* 3-5
BROADMOOR: *67* 4-8
IMPERIAL (5099; "Korea Blues"): *52* . **150-200**
IMPERIAL (5167; "You Know I
Miss You"): *52* **125-150**
IMPERIAL (5180; "Goin' Home"): *52* .. **50-75**
IMPERIAL (5197 through 5251): *52-53* . **25-40**
(Black vinyl.)
IMPERIAL (5197 through 5251): *52-53* . **50-75**
(Colored vinyl.)
IMPERIAL (5262 through 5340): *53-55* . **15-25**
(Black vinyl.)
IMPERIAL (5262 through 5340): *53-55* . **35-50**
(Colored vinyl.)
IMPERIAL (5348 through 5454): *55-57* .. **5-10**
IMPERIAL (5467 through
5900 series): *57-63* 4-6
IMPERIAL (66000 series): *64* 3-5
MERCURY: *65* 3-5
REPRISE: *68-70* 3-5
UNITED ARTISTS: *74* 1-3
WARNER BROS: *80* 2-3
Picture Sleeves
IMPERIAL: *57-59* 10-20
MERCURY: *65* 8-15
EPs: 7-Inch 33/45rpm
ABC-PARAMOUNT: *64-65* 12-20
IMPERIAL (Red script label): *55-55* 30-50
IMPERIAL (Maroon label): *56-57* 20-30
MERCURY: *65* 15-20
(Jukebox issues only.)
LPs: 10/12-Inch 33rpm
ABC-PARAMOUNT: *63-65* 15-20
CANDLELITE: *76* 12-15
EVEREST: *74-77* 8-10
GRAND AWARD: 10-15
HARLEM HITPARADE: *75* 8-10
HARMONY: *69* 10-15

IMPERIAL (Except 9004 through
9103): *60-63* $20-30
IMPERIAL (9004 through 9103): *56-60* .. 40-80
LIBERTY: *80-81* 5-8
MERCURY (21039; "Fats
Domino '65"): *65* 15-20
(Monaural.)
MERCURY (61039; "Fats
Domino '65"): *65* 15-20
(Stereo.)
REPRISE (6304; "Fats Is Back"): *68* 20-30
REPRISE (6439; "Fats"): *71* 100-200
SUNSET: *66-71* 12-15
UNITED ARTISTS: *71-80* 8-10
Also see PRICE, Lloyd

DOMINOES
Singles: 78rpm
FEDERAL (12001; "Do Something
For Me"): *50* 75-150
FEDERAL (12022; "Sixty Minute
Man"): *51* 50-100
FEDERAL (12039; "I Am With
You"): *51* 75-125
FEDERAL (12059; "That's What
You're Doing To Me"): *52* 100-175
FEDERAL (12068; "Have Mercy
Baby"): *52* 50-100
FEDERAL (12072; "Love, Love,
Love"): *52* 40-80
Singles: 7-Inch
FEDERAL (12001; "Do Something
For Me"): *50* 200-250
FEDERAL (12022; "Sixty Minute
Man"): *51* 75-125
FEDERAL (12039; "I Am With
You"): *51* 150-200
FEDERAL (12059; "That's What
You're Doing To Me"): *52* 250-300
FEDERAL (12068; "Have Mercy
Baby"): *52* 75-125
FEDERAL (12072; "Love, Love,
Love"): *52* 75-100
Later Federal numbers, as well as EPs & LPs, are
listed under Billy Ward & The Dominoes.
GUSTO: 1-3
Members: Billy Ward; Clyde McPhatter; Charlie
White; William Lamont; Bill Brown.
Also see LITTLE ESTHER & THE
DOMINOES
Also see MC PHATTER, Clyde
Also see WARD, Billy, & The Dominoes

DON & DEWEY
(Don & Dewey With The Titans)
Singles: 78rpm
SHADE: *56* $5-10
Singles: 7-Inch
FIDELITY: 4-8
HIGHLAND: *62* 4-8
RUSH. *63*...........................3-5
SHADE: *56* 12-20
SPECIALTY (SPBX series): *86* 12-15
(Boxed sets of six colored vinyl 45s.)
SPECIALTY (599; "Jungle Hop"): *57* 8-12
SPECIALTY (Except 617): *59-64* 4-8
SPECIALTY (600 series,
cxccpt 617): *57-64* 4-8
SPECIALTY (617; "Just A Little
Lovin"): *57* 8-12
SPOT: *56* 5-10
LPs: 10/12-Inch 33rpm
SPECIALTY: *70* 8-10
Note: most Specialty singles and LPs are currently
available, using original catalog numbers.
Members: Don Harris (aka Don Bowman); Dewey
Terry.

DON & JUAN
Singles: 7-Inch
BIG TOP: *61-63* 4-6
ERIC: 1-3
MALA: *63-65* 3-5
TWIRL: *66* 3-5
Members: Roland Trone: Claude Johnson.
Also see GENIES

DON & THE GOODTIMES
(Don Gallucci)
Singles: 7-Inch
BURDETTE: *66* 5-10
DUNHILL: *65* 4-6
EPIC: *67-68* 4-6
JERDEN: *66* 5-8
WAND: *64* 4-8
Picture Sleeves
EPIC: *67* 8-15
LPs: 10/12-Inch 33rpm
BURDETTE: *66* 30-35
EPIC: *67* 15-20
PANORAMA: 20-25
WAND: *67* 20-25
Also see KINGSMEN
Also see TOUCH

DON, DICK, & JIMMY
Singles: 7-Inch
CROWN: *54-55* 4-6
DOT: *54* 4-6

LPs: 10/12-Inch 33rpm
CROWN: *57* $20-25
DOT: *59* 15-20
MODERN: 25-30
VERVE: *59* 15-20
Members: Don Sutton; Dick Rock; Jimmy Cook.

DONALDSON, Bo, & The Heywoods
Singles: 7-Inch
ABC: *73-75*........................ 2-3
CAPITOL: *76* 2-3
FAMILY: *72-74* 2-4
PLAYBOY: *77* 2-3
Picture Sleeves
ABC: *74* 1-3
LPs: 10/12-Inch 33rpm
ABC: *74* 6-10
FAMILY: *73* 8-12

DONALDSON, Lou
(Lou Donaldson Quintet)
Singles: 78rpm
BLUE NOTE: *52-57* 3-5
Singles: 7-Inch
ARGO: *63-65* 2-3
BLUE NOTE (100 through 300
series): *73-74* 1-3
BLUE NOTE (1500 & 1600
series): *52-58* 4-6
BLUE NOTE (1700 through 1900
scrics): *58-72* 2-5
LPs: 10/12-Inch 33rpm
ARGO: *63-65* 10-20
BLUE NOTE: *64-80* 8-15
(Label shows Blue Note Records as a division of
either Liberty or United Artists.)
BLUE NOTE (1500 series): *57-58* 25-50
(Label gives New York street address for Blue
Note Records.)
BLUE NOTE (1500 series): *58* 15-25
(Label reads "Blue Note Records Inc. - New York,
USA.")
BLUE NOTE (1500 series): *66* 10-20
(Label shows Blue Note Records as a division of
either Liberty or United Artists.)
BLUE NOTE (4000 & 84000
series): *58-63* 15-25
(Label reads "Blue Note Records Inc. - New York,
U.S.A.")
BLUE NOTE (5000 series): *52-54* 50-75
(10-Inch LPs.)
BLUE NOTE (5000 series): *52-54* 50-75
(10-Inch LPs.)
CADET: *65-71* 8-12
COTILLION: *76-77* 5-8
SUNSET: *69-71* 5-10
TRIP: *79* 5-8

DONEGAN, Lonnie
(Lonnie Donegan & His Skiffle Group)
Singles: 78rpm
LONDON: *56* $3-6
MERCURY: *56* 3-6
Singles: 7-Inch
ABC: *76* 1-3
APT: *62* 3-5
ATLANTIC: *60-61* 3-5
DOT: *61* 3-5
FELSTED: *61* 3-5
HICKORY: *64-65* 3-5
LONDON: *56* 5-8
MCA: 2-3
MERCURY: *56* 4-6
LPs: 10/12-Inch 33rpm
ABC-PARAMOUNT: *63* 15-20
ATLANTIC: *60* 20-25
DOT (3159; "Lonnie
Donegan"): *59* 20-30
DOT (3394; "Lonnie
Donegan"): *61* 15-25
UNITED ARTISTS: *77* 10-12
DONNA LYNN:
see LYNN, Donna

DONNER, Ral
(Ral Donner & The Starfires; Ral Donner With
Scotty Moore, D.J.Fontana, & The Jordanaires)
Singles: 7-Inch
ABC: *73* $1-3
CHICAGO FIRE: *74* 5-8
END: *63* 10-12
FONTANA: *64-65* 10-15
GONE (5102; "Girl Of My Best
Friend"): *60* 20-25
(Black label.)
GONE (5100 series, except
5108 & 5119): *61-62* 4-6
(Multi-color labels.)
GONE (5108; "To Love"/
"And Then"): *61* 15-20
(Shortly after this release, *You Don't Know What
You've Got* was issued using the same catalog num-
ber.)
GONE (5108; "You Don't Know What
You've Got"): *61* 4-6
GONE (5114; "Please Don't Go"): *61* 5-10
GONE (5119; "School Of
Heartbreakers"): *61* 15-25
GONE (5121; "She's Everything"/
"Because We're Young"): *61* 8-10
GONE (5121; "She's Everything"/
"Will You Love Me In Heaven"): *61* 8-10

(*Will You Love Me In Heaven* is by a girl group on this release though credited on the label to Ral. We don't yet know the name of the group.)
GONE (5125; "Will You Love Me
In Heaven"): *61* $8-10
(*Will You Love Me In Heaven* is by Ral on this release.)
GONE (5129; "Loveless Life"): *62* 4-8
GONE (5133; "To Love"): *61* 5-10
MJ: *70* 3-5
MID-EAGLE. *68-76* 3-5
RED BIRD (057; "Love Isn't
Like That"): *66* 75-100
REPRISE: *62-63* 15-20
RISING SONS: *68* 3-5
ROULETTE: *71* 1-3
SCOTTIE: *59* 40-50
SMASH: *65* 15-20
(Promotional issue only.)
STARFIRE (Colored vinyl): *78-79* 4-6
STARFIRE (Except "Rip It Up"
picture disc): *78-79* 2-3
(Black vinyl.)
STARFIRE (114; "Rip It Up"
picture disc): *79* 8-12
SUNLIGHT: *72* 5-8
TAU: *63* 15-20
THUNDER: *78* 2-3
Picture Sleeves
MJ: *70* 5-8
REPRISE: *63* 40-50
STARFIRE: *78-79* 1-3
LPs: 10/12-Inch 33rpm
AUDIO RESEARCH: *80* 12-15
GONE (5012; "Takin' Care Of
Business"): *61* 50-60
GONE (5033; "Elvis Scrapbook"): 10-15
GYPSY: *79* 8-12
MURRAY HILL: *88* 5-8
STARFIRE: *82* 8-10
Also see PRESLEY, Elvis

DONNER, Ral / Ray Smith / Bobby Dale
LPs: 10/12-Inch 33rpm
CROWN: *63* 15-20
Also see SMITH, Ray

DONNER, Ral / Zantees
Singles: 7-Inch
EVA-TONE/GOLDMINE: *79* 1-3
(Soundsheet.)
Also see DONNER, Ral

DONNIE & THE DREAMERS
Singles: 7-Inch
DECCA: *61* 15-20
WHALE: *61* 15-25

The Doobie Brothers: (L-R) Michael Hossack; John Hartman; Tiran Porter; Tom Johnston; Bobby LaKind; Patrick Simmons (Photo: Joyce Ravid)

DONOVAN
(Donovan P. Leitch)
Singles: 12-Inch 33/45rpm
ALLEGIANCE (1437; "Donovan"): *83* .. $5-10
Singles: 7-Inch
ALLEGIANCE: *83* 1-3
ARISTA: *77* 2-3
EPIC: *66-76* 3-5
HICKORY: *65-68* 5-15
Picture Sleeves
EPIC: *66-70* 5-10
LPs: 10/12-Inch 33rpm
ALLEGIANCE: *83* 5-8
ARISTA: *77* 8-10
BELL: *73* 10-12
COLUMBIA: *73* 5-10
EPIC (Except 26439): *67-76* 10-15
EPIC (26439; "Donovan's Greatest
Hits"): *69* 15-20
(With a "BXN" prefix. Gatefold cover. Includes booklet.)
EPIC (26439; "Donovan's Greatest
Hits"): *77* 5-8
(With a "PE" prefix.)
HICKORY: *65-69* 25-50
JANUS: *70-71* 10-12
KORY: *77* 5-8
PYE: *76* 8-10
Also see BECK, Jeff

DOO, Dickey:
see DICKEY DOO & THE DON'TS

DOOBIE BROTHERS
Singles: 12-Inch 33/45rpm
WARNER BROS: *79* 4-6

Jim Morrison, lead voice of the Doors
Singles: 7-Inch
ASYLUM: *80* **$1-3**
SESAME STREET: *81* **1-3**
WARNER BROS: *71-83* **1-3**
Picture Sleeves
WARNER BROS: *72-80* **1-3**
LPs: 10/12-Inch 33rpm
NAUTILUS (5; "Captain & Me"): *80* ... **25-35**
(Half-speed mastered.)
NAUTILUS (18; "Minute By
Minute"): *81* **15-20**
(Half-speed mastered.)
PICKWICK: *80* **6-10**
WARNER BROS: *71-83* **8-12**
Members: Michael McDonald; Tom Johnston;
Patrick Simmons.
Also see JOHNSTON, Tom
Also see MC DONALD, Michael
Also see SIMMONS, Patrick

DOOBIE BROTHERS, James Hall
& James Taylor
Singles: 7-Inch
ASYLUM: *80* **1-3**
Also see TAYLOR, James

DOOBIE BROTHERS, & Nicolette
Larson
Singles: 7-Inch
WARNER BROS: *79* **1-3**
Also see LARSON, Nicolette

DOOBIE BROTHERS / Kate Taylor &
The Simon-Taylor Family
Singles: 7-Inch
WARNER BROS: *80* **1-3**
Picture Sleeves
WARNER BROS: *80* **1-3**
Also see DOOBIE BROTHERS

Also see SIMON SISTERS
Also see TAYLOR, James
Also see TAYLOR, Kate
Also see TAYLOR, Livingston

DOOLITTLE BAND
(Dandy & The Doolittle Band)
Singles: 7-Inch
COLUMBIA: *80* **$1-3**

DOORS
Singles: 7-Inch
ELEKTRA (Except 45000 series): *79-83* ...**1-3**
ELEKTRA (45000 series): *67-72* **4-6**
Promotional Singles
ELEKTRA (45000 series): *67-72* **8-12**
Picture Sleeves
ELEKTRA: *67-78* **5-10**
LPs: 10/12-Inch 33rpm
ELEKTRA (500 series): *78-80* **5-8**
ELEKTRA (4007; "The Doors"): *67* **15-25**
ELEKTRA (4014; "Strange Days"): *67* ..**15-25**
(Elektra 4000 series numbers were mono issues.
Stereo numbers were preceeded by a "7.")
ELEKTRA (5035; "Best Of The
Doors"): *73* **15-20**
ELEKTRA (EKS-6001; "Weird Scenes
Inside The Gold Mine"): *72* **12-15**
ELEKTRA (8E-6001; "Weird Scenes
Inside The Gold Mine"): *73* **8-12**
ELEKTRA (9002; "Absolutely
Live"): *70* **15-20**
ELEKTRA (74024; "Waiting For
The Sun"): *68* **15-20**
ELEKTRA (75005; "The Soft
Parade"): *69* **12-15**
ELEKTRA (75007; "Morrison Hotel /
Hard Rock Cafe"): *70* **12-15**
ELEKTRA (74079; "Doors 13"): *70* **12-15**
ELEKTRA (75011; "L.A.
Woman"): *71* **15-20**
(With die-cut cover.)
ELEKTRA (75011; "L.A. Woman"): **5-8**
(With standard cover.)
ELEKTRA (75017; "Other Voices"): *71* ...**8-12**
ELEKTRA (75038; "Full Circle"): *72* **8-12**
ELEKTRA (60000 series): *84-87* **5-8**
MFSL: *76* **15-20**
Members: Jim Morrison; Robbie Krieger; Ray
Manzarek; John Densmore.
Also see MANZAREK, Ray

DORADOS, El:
see EL DORADOS

DORE, Charlie
Singles: 7-Inch
CHRYSALIS: *81* **1-3**

ISLAND: *80-81* $1-3
      LPs: 10/12-Inch 33rpm
ISLAND: *80-81* 5-8

DORMAN, Harold
      Singles: 7-Inch
ABC: *73* 1-3
COLLECTABLES: 1-3
RITA: *60* 4-6
SANTO: *62* 3-5
SUN: *61-62* 3-5
TINCE: *60* 4-6

DORSEY, Jimmy, Orchestra & Chorus
      Singles: 78rpm
BELL: *54* 2-5
COLUMBIA: *50-52* 3-5
DECCA: *35-57* 2-5
FRATERNITY: *57* 2-5
MGM: *54* 2-5
OKEH: *29* 10-15
      Singles: 7-Inch
ABC: *73* 1-3
BELL: *54* 3-5
COLUMBIA: *50-52* 3-5
DECCA: *51-67* 2-5
DOT: *63* 2-4
EPIC: *59* 2-4
FRATERNITY: *57-60* 2-5
MGM: *54* 2-4
      EPs: 7-Inch 33/45rpm
COLUMBIA: *52-56* 4-6
      LPs: 10/12-Inch 33rpm
COLUMBIA: *55-56* 10-20
CORAL: *54* 10-20
DECCA: *57-66* 10-20
EPIC: *59* 8-12
FRATERNITY: *57* 10-20
HINDSIGHT: *81* 5-8
LION: *56* 10-20
MCA: *75* 5-8
  Also see CROSBY, Bing, & Jimmy Dorsey

DORSEY, Lee
      Singles: 7-Inch
ABC: *78* 1-3
ABC-PARAMOUNT: *60* 4-6
AMY: *65-69* 3-5
CONSTELLATION: *64* 3-5
FLASHBACK: *65* 1-3
FURY: *61-63* 4-6
GUSTO: 1-3
POLYDOR: *70-72* 2-3
REX: *57* 15-20
ROULETTE: 1-3
SANSU: *67* 3-5

SMASH: *63* $3-5
SPRING: *71* 2-3
VALIANT: *58* 10-15
      LPs: 10/12-Inch 33rpm
AMY: *66* 20-25
ARISTA: *85* 5-8
FURY: *62* 30-35
POLYDOR: *70* 10-12
SPHERE SOUND: *67* 15-20

DORSEY, Tommy, Orchestra
(Tommy Dorsey's Sentimentalists; Tommy Dorsey Orchestra Starring Warren Covington)
      Singles: 78rpm
BELL: *54* 4-8
  (7-Inch single.)
BLUEBIRD: *40* 3-6
DECCA: *52-64* 2-5
OKEH: *29* 10-15
RCA VICTOR: *49-57* 2-5
VICTOR: *35-48* 3-6
      Singles: 7-Inch
DECCA: *52-64* 2-5
MCA: *73* 1-3
RCA VICTOR: *50-57* 2-5
      EPs: 7-Inch 33/45rpm
COLUMBIA: *52-56* 4-6
DECCA: *52-63* 4-6
RCA VICTOR: *51-61* 4-6
      LPs: 10/12-Inch 33rpm
ACCORD: *82* 5-8
BRIGHT ORANGE: *73* 5-10
CAMDEN (Except 200 series): *61-73* 5-10
CAMDEN (200 series): *53-55* 10-20
COLPIX: *58-63* 10-20
CORAL: *73* 5-8
CORONET: 5-10
DECCA: *52-60* 10-20
GOLDEN MUSIC SOCIETY: *56* 15-20
HARMONY: *65-72* 5-10
MCA: *75-81* 5-8
MOVIETOWN: *67* 8-10
RCA VICTOR: *51-82* 10-20
SPRINGBORAD: *77* 6-10
20TH CENTURY-FOX: *59-73* 10-15
  Also see GARLAND, Judy / Tommy Dorsey
  Also see SINATRA, Frank

DOSS, Kenny
      Singles: 7-Inch
BEARSVILLE: *80* 1-3
      LPs: 10/12-Inch 33rpm
BEARSVILLE: *80* 5-8

DOTTIE & RAY
Singles: 7-Inch
LE SAGE: *65* $3-5

DOUBLE
Singles: 7-Inch
A&M: *86* 1-3
LPs: 10/12-Inch 33rpm
A&M: *86* 5-8
Members: Kurt Maloo; Felix Haug.

DOUBLE ENTENTE
Singles: 12-Inch 33/45rpm
COLUMBIA: *84* 4-6
Singles: 7-Inch
COLUMBIA: *84* 1-3

DOUBLE EXPOSURE
Singles: 12-Inch 33/45rpm
GOLD COAST: *81* 4-6
Singles: 7-Inch
SALSOUL: *76-79* 1-3
LPs: 10/12-Inch 33rpm
SALSOUL: *78-79* 8-10

DOUBLE IMAGE
Singles: 7-Inch
CBS ASSOCIATED: *83* 1-3
CURB: *83* 1-3
LPs: 10/12-Inch 33rpm
ECM: *79* 5-8

DOUBLE VISION
Singles: 12-Inch 33/45rpm
PROFILE: *84* 4-6

DOUCETTE
(Jerry Doucette)
Singles: 7-Inch
MUSHROOM: *77-79* 1-3
LPs: 10/12-Inch 33rpm
MUSHROOM: *78-79* 5-8

DOUGLAS, Carl
(Carl Douglas & The Big Stampede)
Singles: 7-Inch
ERIC: 1-3
OKEH: *66-67* 3-5
20TH CENTURY-FOX: *74-75* 2-3
LPs: 10/12-Inch 33rpm
20TH CENTURY-FOX: *74* 10-15

DOUGLAS, Carol
Singles: 12-Inch 33/45rpm
MIDSONG INT'L: *78* 4-6
Singles: 7-Inch
MIDLAND INT'L: *74-79* 2-3
RCA VICTOR: *76* 2-3
20TH CENTURY-FOX: *81* 1-3

Picture Sleeves
MIDLAND INT'L: *77-88* $1-3
LPs: 10/12-Inch 33rpm
MIDLAND INT'L: *76-80* 8-10

DOUGLAS, Mike
Singles: 7-Inch
BANANA: 4-8
BLUE RIVER: *66* 2-4
DECCA: *69* 1-3
EPIC: *65-67* 2-4
IMAGE: *77* 1-3
MGM: *71-73* 1-3
PROJECT 3: *68* 2-3
STAX: *74* 1-3
Picture Sleeves
EPIC: *65-66* 3-6
LPs: 10/12-Inch 33rpm
ATLANTIC: *76* 5-8
EPIC: *65-67* 10-15
HARMONY: *68* 8-12
Also see BAILEY, Pearl, & Mike Douglas

DOUGLAS, Ronny, & Bobby Lonero
Singles: 7-Inch
COLUMBIA: *71-72* 2-3

DOVALE, Debbie
Singles: 7-Inch
ROULETTE: *63-64* 5-15

DOVE, Ronnie
(Ronnie Dove & The Beltones)
Singles: 7-Inch
ABC: *74* 1-3
DECCA (31000 series): *61* 6-10
DECCA (32000 & 33000 series): *71-73* 2-3
DIAMOND: *64-70* 3-5
DIAMOND: *87* 1-3
ERIC: 1-3
HITSVILLE: *76* 2-3
JALO: *62* 6-10
MC: *78* 2-3
MCA: *73* 1-3
MELODYLAND: *75-76* 2-3
MOTION: *81* 2-3
MOON SHINE: *83* 1-3
SWAN: *63* 3-5
WRAYCO: *71* 2-3
Picture Sleeves
DIAMOND: *65-66* 3-6
LPs: 10/12-Inch 33rpm
CERTRON: *70* 10-12
DIAMOND: *65-70* 15-25
MCA: *73* 8-10

DOVELLS
Singles: 7-Inch
ABKCO: *83* $1-3
COLLECTABLES: 1-3
DECCA: *70* 3-5
EVENT: *70-74* 3-5
MGM: *66-73* 3-5
PARKWAY (Except 819 & 827): *62-63* ...3-5
PARKWAY (819; "No No No"): *61* 8-10
PARKWAY (827; "Bristol Stomp"/
"Out In The Cold"): *61* 8-10
PARKWAY (827; "Bristol Stomp"/
"Letters Of Love"): *61* 3-5
VERVE: *73* 2-3
Picture Sleeves
PARKWAY: *62-63* 4-8
LPs: 10/12-Inch 33rpm
DOVCO: *76* 5-8
PARKWAY: *61-63* 25-50
WYNCOTE: *65* 10-15
Members: Len Barry; Arnie Satin; Jerry Summers;
Danny Brooks; Mike Dennis.
Also see BARRY, Len
Also see MAGISTRATES
Also see ORLONS / Dovells

DOWELL, Joe
Singles: 7-Inch
JOURNEY: *73* 2-3
MONUMENT: *66* 3-5
SMASH: *61-63* 4-6
Picture Sleeves
JOURNEY: *73* 2-3
SMASH: *61-62* 4-8
LPs: 10/12-Inch 33rpm
SMASH: *61-62* 15-20
WING: *66* 10-12

DOWNING, Al
(Big Al Downing)
Singles: 7-Inch
CARLTON: *58-59* 10-20
CHALLENGE: *58* 15-20
CHESS (1000 series): *62* 3-5
CHESS (2000 series): *75* 2-3
COLUMBIA: *64* 3-5
HOUSE OF THE FOX: *71* 2-4
JANUS: *74* 2-3
KANSOMA: *62* 3-5
LENOX: *63* 3-5
POLYDOR: *76* 2-3
SILVER FOX: 2-4
TEAM: *82-84* 1-3
VINE ST: *87* 1-3
V-TONE: *61* 3-5
WARNER BROS: *78-80* 1-3

WHITE ROCK: *58* $40-50
LPs: 10/12-Inch 33rpm
TEAM: *83-85* 5-8
Also see PHILLIPS, Little Esther, & Big Al
Downing

DOWNING, Don
Singles: 7-Inch
ABNER: *62* 3-5
CHAN: 3-5
ROADSHOW: *73* 2-3
SCEPTER: *74* 2-3
LPs: 10/12-Inch 33rpm
ROADSHOW: *79* 5-8

DOZIER, Gene, & The Brotherhood
Singles: 7-Inch
MINIT: *67-68* 3-5
LPs: 10/12-Inch 33rpm
MINIT: *67* 10-15

DOZIER, Lamont
Singles: 12-Inch 33/45rpm
WARNER BROS: *79* 4-6
Singles: 7-Inch
ABC: *73-76* 2-3
COLUMBIA: *81* 1-3
INVICTUS: *72* 2-4
MEL-O-DY (102; "Dearest One"): *62* ... 20-40
LPs: 10/12-Inch 33rpm
ABC: *73-74* 8-10
COLUMBIA: *81* 5-8
INVICTUS: *74* 8-10
M&M: *82* 5-8
WARNER BROS: *76-79* 8-10
Also see HOLLAND, Eddie, & Lamont Dozier
Also see VOICE MASTERS

DRAFI
Singles: 7-Inch
LONDON: *66-67* 4-6

DRAGON
Singles: 12-Inch 33/45rpm
POLYDOR: *84* 4-6
Singles: 7-Inch
POLYDOR: *83-84* 1-3
PORTRAIT: *78-79* 1-3
LPs: 10/12-Inch 33rpm
POLYDOR: *83* 5-8
PORTRAIT: *78* 5-8

DRAKE, Charlie
Singles: 7-Inch
UNITED ARTISTS (Except 398): *61-62* .. 3-5

UNITED ARTISTS (398; "My Boomerang
 Won't Come Back"): *61* **$10-20**
 (Sings "Practiced Till I Was BLACK in the Face.")
UNITED ARTISTS (398; "My Boomerang
 Won't Come Back"): *61* **3-5**
 (Sings "Practiced Till I Was BLUE in the Face.")

DRAKE, Guy
Singles: 7-Inch
MALLARD: *71* **2-3**
ROYAL AMERICAN: *70* **2-4**
LPs: 10/12-Inch 33rpm
OVATION: *74* **5-8**
ROYAL AMERICAN: *70* **15-20**

DRAKE, Pete
Singles: 7-Inch
SMASH: *64-65* **2-4**
STARDAY: *66* **2-3**
STOP: *68-70* **1-3**
LPs: 10/12-Inch 33rpm
CANAAN: *68* **8-12**
CUMBERLAND: *63* **12-18**
PICKWICK/HILLTOP: *67* **8-12**
MOUNTAIN DEW: **8-10**
SMASH: *64-65* **10-15**
STARDAY: *62-65* **15-25**
STOP: *70* **6-10**

DRAMATICS
Singles: 7-Inch
ABC: *75-77* **2-3**
CADET: *74* **2-3**
CAPITOL: *82* **1-3**
CRACKERJACK: **15-30**
FANTASY: *86* **1-3**
MAINSTREAM: *75* **2-3**
MCA: *79-80* **1-3**
SPORT: *67* **3-5**
VOLT: *71-73* **2-3**
WINGATE: **4-8**
LPs: 10/12-Inch 33rpm
ABC: *75-78* **8-10**
CADET: *74* **8-10**
CAPITOL: *82* **5-8**
FANTASY: *86* **5-8**
MCA: *80* **5-8**
STAX: *77-78* **8-10**
VOLT: *72-74* **10-12**
 Members: Ron Banks; Elbert Wilkins; L.J.
 Reynolds; William Howard; Larry Demps; Lenny
 Mayes; Carl Smalls; Willie Ford.
 Also see BANKS, Ron
 Also see DELLS / Dramatics
 Also see REYNOLDS, L.J.
 Also see UNDISPUTED TRUTH

DRAPER, Rusty
Singles: 78rpm
MERCURY: *52-57* **$3-6**
Singles: 7-Inch
MERCURY: *52-62* **4-8**
MONUMENT: *63-70* **2-5**
EPs: 7-Inch 33/45rpm
MERCURY: *54-56* **10-15**
LPs: 10/12-Inch 33rpm
GOLDEN CREST: *73* **5-10**
HARMONY: *72* **5-10**
MERCURY: *54-62* **10-20**
MONUMENT: *65-75* **8-12**
WING: *63-64* **8-12**
 Also see DEE, Lola, & Rusty Draper

DREAM ACADEMY
Singles: 7-Inch
MCA: *79* **2-3**
WARNER BROS: *85-86* **1-3**
LPs: 10/12-Inch 33rpm
REPRISE: *87* **5-8**
WARNER BROS: *85-86* **5-8**

DREAM SYNDICATE
LPs: 10/12-Inch 33rpm
A&M: *84* **5-8**
SLASH: **5-8**
 Also see TEXTONES

DREAM WEAVERS
Singles: 78rpm
DECCA: *55-56* **3-5**
Singles: 7-Inch
DECCA: *55-56* **3-6**
EPs: 7-Inch 33/45rpm
DECCA: *56* **10-15**
 Member: Wade Buff.

DREAMBOY
Singles: 7-Inch
QWEST: *83-84* **1-3**
LPs: 10/12-Inch 33rpm
QWEST: *83-84* **5-8**

DREAMLOVERS
Singles: 7-Inch
CAMEO: *64* **4-6**
CASINO: **10-15**
COLLECTABLES: *82* **1-3**
COLUMBIA: *63* **30-40**
END: *62* **8-12**
HERITAGE: *61-62* **5-10**
MERCURY: *66-67* **5-8**
SWAN: *63* **3-5**
V-TONE: *60-61* **10-15**
WARNER BROS: *65* **3-5**

LPs: 10/12-Inch 33rpm
COLLECTABLES: 82 .... $6-8
COLUMBIA: 63 30-45
HERITAGE: 79 8-12
Also see CHECKER, Chubby

DREAMS
Singles: 7-Inch
COLUMBIA: 71-72 3-5
D.C: 69 4-6
LPs: 10/12-Inch 33rpm
COLUMBIA: 70-71 10-15
Also see BRECKER BROTHERS

DREAMS SO REAL
Singles: 7-Inch
ARISTA. 88 1-3
LPs: 10/12-Inch 33rpm
ARISTA: 88 5-8
FATHER'S HOUSE: 86 8-10
I.R.S.: 87 5-8
Members: Barry Marler; Drew Worsham; Trent
Allen.

DREGS: see DIXIE DREGS

DRENNON, Eddie, & B.B.S. Unlimited
Singles: 7-Inch
FRIENDS & CO: 75 2-3

DRESSLER, Len
Singles: 78rpm
MERCURY. 56 5-10
Singles: 7-Inch
CAPITOL: 63 4-6
MERCURY: 56 8-15

DREW, Patti
(Patti Drew & The Drew-Vels)
Singles: 7-Inch
CAPITOL: 67-69 4-6
INNOVATION: 75 3-5
QUILL: 65 4-8
LPs: 10/12-Inch 33rpm
CAPITOL: 69-70 12-15
Also see DREW-VELS

DREW-VELS
(Featuring Patti Drew)
Singles: 7-Inch
CAPITOL: 63-64 5-10
LPs: 10/12-Inch 33rpm
CAPITOL (2804; "Tell
  Him"): 67 20-30
Members: Patti Drew; Erma Drew; Lorraine Drew;
Carlton Black.
Also see DREW, Patti

DREWS, J.D.
Singles: 7-Inch
UNICORN: 80 .... $1-3

DRIFTER, Dixie: see DIXIE DRIFTER

DRIFTERS
(Clyde McPhatter & The Drifters)
Singles: 78rpm
ATLANTIC: 53-57 8-15
Singles: 7-Inch
ATLANTIC (1006 through
  1029): 53-54 25-50
ATLANTIC (1043 through
  1078): 54-55 15-30
ATLANTIC (1089 through
  2127): 56-62 5-10
ATLANTIC (2134 through
  2786): 62-71 4-6
BELL: 73-74 3-5
CROWN (108; "The World Is
  Changing"): 54 100-150
Picture Sleeves
ATLANTIC: 64 8-15
EPs: 7-Inch 33/45rpm
ATLANTIC: 55-58 30-40
LPs: 10/12-Inch 33rpm
ATCO: 71 10-12
ATLANTIC (Except 8003 &
  8022): 59-68 25-35
ATLANTIC (8003; "Clyde McPhatter
  & The Drifters"): 56 100-200
(Black label.)
ATLANTIC (8003; "Clyde McPhatter
  & The Drifters"): 59 30-40
(Red label.)
ATLANTIC (8022; "Rockin' &
  Driftin'"): 58 75-150
(Black label.)
ATLANTIC (8022; "Rockin' &
  Driftin'"): 59 25-35
(Red label.)
CANDLELITE: 10-15
CLARION: 64 15-20
GUSTO: 80 5-8
TRIP: 76 5-8
Members: Clyde McPhatter; Bill Pinckney; Johnny
Moore; Ben E. King; Rudy Lewis; Elsbeary Hobbs;
Charlie Hughes; Jim Millender; Charlie Thomas;
Andrew Thrasher; Gerhart Thrasher; Willie Ferbie;
Jimmy Oliver; David Baughan; Bobby Lee Hollis;
Bobby Hendricks; Tommy Evans; Johnny Wil-
liams; Gene Pearson; Abdul Samad; Tommy
Evans; Dock Green; Freddie Houston.
Also see COASTERS / Drifters
Also see DUVALS

Also see HENDRICKS, Bobby
Also see KING, Ben E.
Also see MC PHATTER, Clyde
Also see MOONGLOWS

DRIFTERS / Lesley Gore / Roy Orbison / Los Bravos
EPs: 7-Inch 33/45rpm
SWINGERS FOR COKE: 66 .... $10-20
(Promotional issue only. Each artist sings a song about Coca Cola.)
Also see DRIFTERS
Also see GORE, Lesley
Also see LOS BRAVOS
Also see ORBISON, Roy

DRUPI
Singles: 7-Inch
A&M: 73 1-3

DRUSKY, Roy
Singles: 7-Inch
CAPITOL: 76 1-3
DECCA: 60-62 2-5
MERCURY: 63-72 2-4
PLANTATION: 79-80 1-3
EPs: 7-Inch 33/45rpm
DECCA: 61-63 4-8
LPs: 10/12-Inch 33rpm
CAPITOL: 76 5-10
DECCA: 61-62 12-20
HARMONY: 65 10-12
MCA: 4-8
MERCURY: 64-72 8-15
PICKWICK/HILLTOP: 8-12
PLANTATION: 79-80 5-8
SCORPION: 76 5-10
VOCALION: 70 8-12
WING: 64-66 10-15
Also see WELLS, Kitty, & Roy Drusky

DUALS
Singles: 7-Inch
ARC: 59 8-12
COLLECTABLES: 1-3
STAR REVUE: 61 15-25
SUE: 61 4-6
LPs: 10/12-Inch 33rpm
SUE: 61 40-50

DUBS
Singles: 7-Inch
ABC-PARAMOUNT: 59-61 8-15
CLIFTON: 73 2-4
END: 62 5-10
GONE (Except 5002): 58-62 10-20
GONE (5002; "Don't Ask Me To Be Lonely"): 57 15-25

JOHNSON (Except 1021): 73 .... $2-4
JOHNSON (102; "Don't Ask Me To Be Lonely"): 57 200-250
JOSIE: 63 3-5
MARK-X: 60 5-8
ROULETTE: 1-3
WILSHIRE: 63 5-10
LPs: 10/12-Inch 33rpm
CANDLELITE: 73 10-15
MURRAY HILL: 88 5-8
Members: Richard Blandon; Billy Carlisle; Cleveland Still; James Miller; Tom Gardner; Tom Grate; Cordell Brown; Dave Shelley.

DUBS / Actuals
Singles: 78rpm
CANDLELITE (438; "We Three"): 72 5-10

DUBS / Shells
LPs: 10/12-Inch 33rpm
CANDLELITE: 8-10
JOSIE (4001; "The Dubs Meet The Shells"): 62 75-150
Also see DUBS
Also see SHELLS

DUBSET
Singles: 12-Inch 33/45rpm
ELEKTRA: 84 4-6

DUCES OF RHYTHM & TEMPO TOPPERS
(Featuring Little Richard)
Singles: 78rpm
PEACOCK: 53-54 20-30
Singles: 7-Inch
PEACOCK: 53-54 40-60
Also see LITTLE RICHARD
Also see TEMPO TOPPERS

DUCHIEN, Armand
Singles: 12-Inch 33/45rpm
A&M: 84 4-6

DUDEK, Les
Singles: 7-Inch
COLUMBIA: 77-78 1-3
LPs: 10/12-Inch 33rpm
COLUMBIA: 75-81 8-10
Also see ALLMAN BROTHERS BAND

DUDLEY, Dave
Singles: 78rpm
KING: 55-56 4-8
Singles: 7-Inch
COLUMBIA: 78 1-3
GOLDEN WING: 63 3-5
JUBILEE: 62 3-5
KING (4000 series): 55-56 6-12

KING (5000 series): *63* $2-4
MERCURY: *63-73* 2-3
NRC: *59* 4-6
NEW STAR: *62* 4-6
RICE: *73-78* 1-3
STARDAY: *60* 3-5
SUN (Black vinyl): *79-80* 1-3
SUN (Colored vinyl): *79-80* 3-5
UNITED ARTISTS: *75-76* 1-3
VEE: *61* 4-8

LPs: 10/12-Inch 33rpm
GOLDEN WING: *63* 25-30
MERCURY: *64-73* 10-15
MOUNTAIN DEW: *69* 8-12
NASHVILLE: *68* 8-12
PLANTATION: *81* 5-8
RICE: *78* 1-3
SUN: *80* 5-8
UNITED ARTISTS: *75-76* 8-12
WING: *68* 8-12

DUDLEY, Dave, & Tom T. Hall
Singles: 7-Inch
MERCURY: *70* 2-3
Also see HALL, Tom T.

DUDLEY, Dave / Link Wray
LPs: 10/12-Inch 33rpm
GUEST STAR: *63* 10-20
Also see DUDLEY, Dave
Also see WRAY, Link

DUDLEY, Kay
Singles: 7-Inch
TEEN ED: *61* 3-5

DU DROPPERS
Singles: 78rpm
GROOVE: *53-55* 15-30
RCA VICTOR: *53* 10-20
RED ROBIN (108; "Can't Do
 Sixty No More"): *52* 35-50
RED ROBIN (116; "Come On &
 Love Me Baby"): *53* 20-40
Singles: 7-Inch
GROOVE (Except 0013): *54-55* 20-40
GROOVE (0013; "Just Whisper"): *54* ... 40-60
RCA VICTOR: *53* 20-30
RED ROBIN (108; "Can't Do
 Sixty No More"): *52* 75-100
 (Black vinyl.)
RED ROBIN (108; "Can't Do
 Sixty No More"): *52* 200-300
 (Colored vinyl.)
RED ROBIN (116; "Come On &
 Love Me Baby"): *53* 50-75

EPs: 7-Inch 33/45rpm
GROOVE (2; "Talk That Talk"): *55* .. $75-100
GROOVE (5; "Tops In Rhythm
 & Blues"): *55* 75-100
Members: Julius Ginyard; Willie Ray; Eddie
Hashaw; Harvey Ray; Bob Kornegay; Prentice
Moreland; Joe Van Loan; Charlie Hughes.
Also see GALE, Sunny, & The Du Droppers

DUKAYS
Singles: 7-Inch
JERRY-O: *64* 3-5
NAT: *61-62* 5-10
VEE JAY: *62* 4-8
Members: Eugene "Gene Chandler" Dixon; James
Lowe; Earl Edwards; Ben Broyles; Shirley Jones;
Charles Davis Claude McRae.
Also see ARTISTICS
Also see CHANDLER, Gene

DUKE, Doris
Singles: 7-Inch
CANYON: *70* 2-3

DUKE, George
Singles: 12-Inch 33/45rpm
ELEKTRA: *85-86* 4-6
EPIC: *83* 4-6
Singles: 7-Inch
ELEKTRA: *85-86* 1-3
EPIC: *77-83* 1-3
LPs: 10/12-Inch 33rpm
ELEKTRA: *85-86* 5-8
EPIC: *77-83* 5-8
MPS/BASF: *74-76* 8-10
Also see CLARKE, Stanley, & George Duke
Also see COBHAM, Billy
Also see MOTHERS OF INVENTION

DUKE, Patty
Singles: 7-Inch
UNITED ARTISTS: *65-68* 3-5
Picture Sleeves
UNITED ARTISTS: *65* 5-10
LPs: 10/12-Inch 33rpm
UNITED ARTISTS: *65-68* 15-20

DUKE & THE DRIVERS
Singles: 7-Inch
ABC: *75* 2-3
LPs: 10/12-Inch 33rpm
ABC: *76* 8-10

DUKE JUPITER
Singles: 7-Inch
COAST TO COAST: *82* 1-3
MOROCCO: *84-85* 1-3
LPs: 10/12-Inch 33rpm
COAST TO COAST: *82-83* 5-8

MERCURY: *80* $5-8
MOROCCO: *84* 5-8

DUKE OF EARL
(Gene Chandler)
Singles: 7-Inch
VEE JAY: *62* 3-6
Also see CHANDLER, Gene

DUKES OF DIXIELAND
LPs: 10/12-Inch 33rpm
AUDIO FIDELITY: *55-61* 5-15
COLUMBIA: *62* 4-8
EPIC: *56* 5-12
RCA VICTOR: *59* 5-10

DUKES OF STRATOSPHERE
Singles: 12-Inch 33/45rpm
GEFFEN (2840; "Vanishing
Girl"): *87* 5-10
(Promotional issue only.)
LPs: 10/12-Inch 33rpm
GEFFEN: *87* 5-8
Also see XTC

DUNCAN, Jamie
Singles: 7-Inch
SOUTHERN GOLD: *86* 2-3

DUNCAN SISTERS
Singles: 12-Inch 33/45rpm
EAR MARC: *79* 4-6
Singles: 7-Inch
EAR MARC: *79-80* 1-3

DUNDAS, David
Singles: 7-Inch
CHRYSALIS: *76-77* 2-3
LPs: 10/12-Inch 33rpm
CHRYSALIS: *77* 8-10

DUNLAP, Gene
(Gene Dunlap & The Ridgeways)
Singles: 12-Inch 33/45rpm
CAPITOL: *82* 4-6
Singles: 7-Inch
CAPITOL: *81-83* 1-3
LPs: 10/12-Inch 33rpm
CAPITOL: *81-83* 5-8
Also see AYERS, Roy
Also see WYNNE, Philippe

DUNN & BRUCE STREET
Singles: 7-Inch
DEVAKI: *81-82* 1-3
Members: Dunn Pearson; Bruce Gray

DUNN & MC CASHEN
Singles: 7-Inch
CAPITOL: *69-70* 2-3
LPs: 10/12-Inch 33rpm

CAPITOL: *69-70* $10-12
COLUMBIA: *71* .12-15

DUPREE, Champion Jack
(Jack Dupree & His Band)
Singles: 78rpm
ALERT: *46* 8-12
APOLLO: *49-50* .8-12
CELEBRITY: *46* .8-12
CONTINENTAL: *45* 10-15
JOE DAVIS: *46* 8-12
KING: *53-55* 5-10
RED ROBIN: *53-54* 30-50
VIK: *57* 5-10
Singles: 7-Inch
ATLANTIC: *61* 3-5
EVERLAST: *64* 3-5
FEDERAL: *61* 3-5
GUSTO: 1-3
KING: *53-55* 10-20
RED ROBIN (109; "Stumblin' Block
Blues"): *53* 75-100
RED ROBIN (112; "Highway
Blues"): *53* 75-100
RED ROBIN (130; "Drunk Again"): *54* .75-100
VIK: *57* 10-20
LPs: 10-Inch 33rpm
ARCHIVE OF FOLK MUSIC: *68* 10-12
ATLANTIC (Except 8019 & 8255): *61* . .25-30
ATLANTIC (8019; "Blues From
The Gutter"): *59* 50-75
(Green label.)
ATLANTIC (8019; "Blues From
The Gutter"): *59* 25-40
(Black label.)
ATLANTIC (8019; "Blues From
The Gutter"): *59* 15-25
(Red label.)
ATLANTIC (8255; "Blues From
The Gutter"): *70* 8-10
BLUE HORIZON: *69* 10-12
EVEREST: 8-12
FOLKWAYS: *61* 20-25
GNP/CRESCENDO: *74* 8-10
JAZZMAN: *82* 5-8
KING (700 series): *61* 45-60
KING (1000 series): *70* 10-12
LONDON: *69* 10-12
OKEH: *63* 25-30
STORYVILLE: *82* 5-8

DUPREE, Champion Jack, &
Mickey Baker
LPs: 10/12-Inch 33rpm
SIRE: *69* 10-12
Also see DUPREE, Champion Jack

DUPREE, Robbie
Singles: 7-Inch
ELEKTRA: *80-81* $1-3
Picture Sleeves
ELEKTRA: *80* 1-3
LPs: 10/12-Inch 33rpm
ELEKTRA: *80-81* 5-8

DUPREES
Singles: 7-Inch
COED: *62-65* 4-6
COLLECTABLES: *80* 1-3
COLUMBIA: *65-67* 5-8
ERIC: 1-3
HERITAGE: *68-70* 3-5
RCA VICTOR: *75* 3-5
Picture Sleeves
COLUMBIA: *66* 10-20
HERITAGE: *68* 4-8
LPs: 10/12-Inch 33rpm
COED (905; "You Belong To Me"): *63* .50-100
COED (906; "Have You Heard"): *63* ...50-100
COLLECTABLES: *80* 6-8
HERITAGE: *68* 15-30
POST: 15-25
Members: Joey "Vann" Canzano; Mike Arnone;
Tom Bialaglow; John Salvato; Joe Santollo.
Also see ITALIAN ASPHALT & PAVE-
MENT COMPANY
Also see VANN, Joey

DURAN DURAN
Singles: 12-Inch 33/45rpm
CAPITOL: *83-87* 4-6
Singles: 7-Inch
CAPITOL (Black vinyl): *83-88* 1-3
CAPITOL (Colored vinyl): *86-87* 4-8
(Promotional issues only.)
HARVEST: *81-82* 1-3
Picture Sleeves
CAPITOL: *83-86* 1-3
EPs: 7-Inch 33/45rpm
HARVEST: *82* 12-20
LPs: 10/12-Inch 33rpm
CAPITOL: *83-88* 5-8
HARVEST: *82* 5-8
Members: John Taylor, Andy Taylor; Simon
LeBon.
Also see ARCADIA
Also see BAND AID
Also see POWER STATION
Also see TAYLOR, Andy
Also see TAYLOR, John

DURANTE, Jimmy
Singles: 78rpm
BRUNSWICK: *34* 5-10

DECCA: *44-57* $4-8
Singles: 7-Inch
DECCA: *51-59* 2-5
WARNER BROS: *63-70* 2-3
EPs: 7-Inch 33/45rpm
DECCA: *54-56* 5-10
MGM: *53-55* 5-10
VARSITY: *55* 5-10
LPs: 10/12-Inch 33rpm
DECCA (9000 series): *54-56* 15-25
DECCA (78000 series): *70* 8-12
HARMONY: *68* 8-12
LIGHT: *71* 5-10
LION: *56* 15-20
MGM (3200 series): *55* 15-25
MGM (4200 series): *64* 10-15
ROULETTE: *61* 15-20
WARNER BROS: *63-67* 10-15
Also see MARTIN, Dean

DURY, Ian, & The Blockheads
Singles: 7-Inch
STIFF (Except 1179): *79-81* 1-3
STIFF (1179; "Hit Me With Your
Rhythm Stick"): *80* 2-4
(Promotional issue only.)
Picture Sleeves
STIFF (Except 1179): *79-81* 1-3
STIFF (1179; "Hit Me With Your
Rhythm Stick"): *80* 2-4
(Promotional issue only.)
LPs: 10/12-Inch 33rpm
POLYDOR: *81* 5-8
STIFF: *78-82* 5-8
Also see JANKEL, Chas

DUSK
Singles: 7-Inch
BELL: *71-72* 2-3

DUVALL, Huelyn
Singles: 7-Inch
CHALLENGE (Except 1012): *58-60* ... 15-20
CHALLENGE (1012; "Comin' Or
Goin'"): *58* 25-35
(Blue label.)
CHALLENGE (1012; "Comin' Or
Goin'"): *58* 10-20
(Maroon label.)
STARFIRE: *59* 30-35

DUVALS
(Five Crowns)
Singles: 7-Inch
RAINBOW (335; "You Came
To Me"): *57* 50-75
(Yellow label.)

RAINBOW (335; "You Came
To Me"): *61* $4-6
(Yellow label.)
Members: Wilbur Paul; Jesse Facing; Richard
Lewis; Dock Green; William Bailey.
Also see DRIFTERS

DYER, Ada
Singles: 7-Inch
MOTOWN: *88* 1-3

DYKE & THE BLAZERS
Singles: 7-Inch
ARTCO: *67* 8-10
ORIGINAL SOUND: *67-70* 3-6
LPs: 10/12-Inch 33rpm
ORIGINAL SOUND: *67-69* 30-35
Member: Arlester "Dyke" Christian.

DYLAN, Bob
(Bob Dylan With The Band)
Singles: 7-Inch
ASYLUM: *74* 3-5
COLUMBIA (10106; "Tangled Up In
Blue"): *75* 8-10
COLUMBIA (10217; "Million Dollar
Bash"): *75* 8-10
COLUMBIA (10245; "Hurricane"): *75* 2-4
COLUMBIA (10298; "Mozambique"): *75* .. 2-4
COLUMBIA (10454; "Rita Mae"): *77* 8-10
COLUMBIA (10805; "Baby Stop
Crying"): *78* 4-6
COLUMBIA (10851; "Changing Of
The Guards"): *78* 5-8
COLUMBIA (11000 series): *79-80* 2-4
COLUMBIA (18-0000 series): *81* 2-3
COLUMBIA (38-0000 through
0400): *84-86* 1-3
COLUMBIA (42656; "Mixed Up
Confusion"): *63* 250-300
COLUMBIA (42856; "Blowin' In
The Wind"): *63* 125-175
COLUMBIA (43242; "Subterranean
Homesick Blues"): *65* 10-15
(Gray label.)
COLUMBIA (43242; "Subterranean
Homesick Blues"): *65* 4-6
(Red label.)
COLUMBIA (43346; "Like A Rolling
Stone"): *65* 4-6
COLUMBIA (43389; "Positively
4th Street"): *65* 10-15
(Gray label.)
COLUMBIA (43389; "Positively
4th Street"): *65* 4-6
(Red label.)

COLUMBIA (43477; "Can You Please
Crawl Out Your Window"): *65* $10-15
COLUMBIA (43683; "I Want You"): *66* ..4-6
COLUMBIA (43541; "One Of Us
Must Know"): *66* 8-10
COLUMBIA (43592; "Rainy Day
Women #12 & 35"): *66* 4-6
COLUMBIA (43792; "Just Like
A Woman"): *66* 4-6
COLUMBIA (44069; "Leopard-Skin
Pill-Box Hat"): *67* 8-10
COLUMBIA (44826; "I Threw It
All Away"): *69* 5-8
COLUMBIA (44926; "Lay Lady,
Lay"): *69* 4-6
COLUMBIA (45004; "Tonight I'll Be
Staying Here With You"): *69* 5-8
COLUMBIA (45199; "Wigwam"): *69* 5-10
COLUMBIA (45409; "Watching The
River Flow"): *71* 5-10
COLUMBIA (45516; "George
Jackson"): *71* 8-10
COLUMBIA (45913; "Knockin' On
Heaven's Door"): *73* 2-4
COLUMBIA (45982; "A Fool Such
As I"): *73* 3-5
Picture Sleeves
COLUMBIA (10245; "Hurricane"): *75* .200-300
(Promotional issue only.)
COLUMBIA (11235; "Slow Train"): *80* 5-8
COLUMBIA (43242; "Subterranean
Homesick Blues"): *65* 200-250
(Promotional issue only.)
COLUMBIA (43242; "Subterranean
Homesick Blues"): *65* 30-50
(Columbia "Hit Pack" picture sleeve.)
COLUMBIA (43389; "Positively
4th Street"): *65* 15-20
COLUMBIA (43683; "I Want
You"): *66* 15-20
COLUMBIA (18-0000 series): *81* 4-6
Promotional Singles
ASYLUM: *74* 5-8
COLUMBIA (25; "All The
Tired Horses"): *70* 25-35
COLUMBIA (1039; "If Not
For You"): *71* 25-35
COLUMBIA (10106; "Tangled Up
In Blue"): *75* 10-15
COLUMBIA (10245; "Hurricane"): *75* ...10-15
COLUMBIA (10245; "Hurricane"): *75* ...20-25
(Compact 33 Single.)
COLUMBIA (10298; "Mozambique"): *75* ..5-8
COLUMBIA (10454; "Rita Mae"): *77* ...10-15

COLUMBIA (10805; "Baby Stop
  Crying"): *78* $10-15
COLUMBIA (11000 series): *79-80* 4-6
COLUMBIA (18-0000 series): *81* 3-5
COLUMBIA (38-0000 through
  0400): *84-86* 2-4
COLUMBIA (42856; "Blowin' In
  The Wind"): *63* 200-275
  (Price includes "Rebel With A Cause," a letter-in-
  sert introducing Dylan, which represents $75-$100
  of the value.)
COLUMBIA (43242; "Subterranean
  Homesick Blues"): *65* 30-40
  (Black vinyl.)
COLUMBIA (43242; "Subterranean
  Homesick Blues"): *65* 35-50
  (Colored vinyl.)
COLUMBIA (43346; "Like A Rolling
  Stone"): *65* 30-40
  (Black vinyl.)
COLUMBIA (43346; "Like A Rolling
  Stone"): *65* 35-50
  (Colored vinyl.)
COLUMBIA (43389; "Positively
  4th Street"): *65* 25-40
  (Black vinyl.)
COLUMBIA (43389; "Positively
  4th Street"): *65* 35-50
  (Colored vinyl.)
COLUMBIA (43389; "Positively
  4th Street"): *65* 75-100
  (Outtake promo. Actually contains an alternate take
  of *Can You Please Crawl Out Your Window*.)
COLUMBIA (43477; "Can You Please
  Crawl Out Your Window"): *65* 30-45
COLUMBIA (43683; "I Want You"): *66* . 25-35
  (Black vinyl.)
COLUMBIA (43683; "I Want You"): *66* . 35-50
  (Colored vinyl.)
COLUMBIA (43541; "One Of Us
  Must Know"): *66* 30-45
COLUMBIA (43592; "Rainy Day
  Women #12 & 35"): *66* 25-35
COLUMBIA (43792; "Just Like A
  Woman"): *66* 25-35
  (Black vinyl.)
COLUMBIA (43792; "Just Like A
  Woman"): *66* 35-50
  (Colored vinyl.)
COLUMBIA (44069; "Leopard-Skin
  Pill-Box Hat"): *67* 20-30
COLUMBIA (44826; "I Threw It
  All Away"): *69* 15-20
COLUMBIA (44926; "Lay Lady,
  Lay"): *69* 15-20

COLUMBIA (45004; "Tonight I'll Be
  Staying Here With You"): *69* $15-20
COLUMBIA (45199; "Wigwam"): *69* . . . 15-20
COLUMBIA (45409; "Watching The
  River Flow"): *71* 15-20
COLUMBIA (45516; "George
  Jackson"): *71* 15-20
COLUMBIA (45913; "Knockin' On
  Heaven's Door"): *73* 10-15
COLUMBIA (45982; "A Fool Such
  As I"): *73* 10-15
          EPs: 7-Inch 33/45rpm
COLUMBIA (319; "Step Lively"): *65* . . 75-100
COLUMBIA (9128; "Bringing It All
  Back Home"): *65* 100-125
  (Jukebox issue only.)
COLUMBIA/PLAYBACK: *73* 60-85
  (Promotional issue only. Contains four tracks by
  four different artists.)
          LPs: 10/12-Inch 33rpm
ASYLUM (201; "Before The Flood"): *74* 10-15
ASYLUM (1003; "Planet Waves"): *74* . . 15-20
  (Without cut corner.)
ASYLUM (1003; "Planet Waves"): *74* . . . 8-10
  (With cut corner.)
ASYLUM (1003; "Planet Waves"): *74* . . 15-20
  (With an "EQ" prefix. Quad LP.)
COLUMBIA (C2L-41/C2S-841;
  "Blonde On Blonde"): *66* 40-80
  (With "female photos.")
COLUMBIA (C2L-41/C2S-841;
  "Blonde On Blonde"): *66* . . . : 10-12
  (With Dylan photo replacing female photos.)
COLUMBIA (CL-1779/CS-8579;
  "Bob Dylan"): *62* 100-150
  (Red & black label with six Columbia "eye" boxes.)
COLUMBIA (CL-1779/CS-8579;
  "Bob Dylan"): *62* 20-30
  (Red label, without six Columbia "eye" boxes.)

COLUMBIA (CL-1986/CS-8786; "The
Freewheelin' Bob Dylan"): *63* ... **$1000-2000**
(With the tracks: *Let Me Die In My Footsteps,
Talkin' John Birch Society Blues, Gamblin'
Willie's Dead Man's Hand*, and *Rocks & Gravel*,
which may also be shown as *Solid Gravel*. We suggest verification of the above tracks by listening to
the LP, rather than accepting the information
printed on the label.)

COLUMBIA (CL-1986/CS-8786; "The
Freewheelin' Bob Dylan"): *63* **25-35**
(Reissued with the above tracks replaced by four
others.)

COLUMBIA (CL-2105/CS-8905; "The
Times They Are A-Changin'"): *64* **20-30**

COLUMBIA (CL-2193/CS-8993; "Another
Side Of Bob Dylan"): *64* **15-20**

COLUMBIA (CL-2328/CS-9128; "Bringin'
It All Back Home"): *65* **15-25**

COLUMBIA (CL-2389/CS-9189; "Highway
61 Revisited"): *65* **75-100**
(With an alternate take of *From A Buick 6*. The alternate take begins with a harmonica riff and that
pressing has a "-1" at the end of the matrix number,
stamped in the vinyl trailoff.)

COLUMBIA (CL-2389/CS-9189; "Highway
61 Revisited"): *65* **10-15**

COLUMBIA (KCL-2663/KCS-9463; "Bob
Dylan's Greatest Hits"): *67* **15-25**

COLUMBIA (CL-2804; "John Wesley
Harding"): *68* **60-100**
(Monaural issue.)

COLUMBIA (CS-9604; "John Wesley
Harding"): *68* **10-15**
(Stereo issue.)

COLUMBIA (KCS-9825; "Nashville
Skyline"): *68* **8-12**

COLUMBIA (Q-30000 series): *74-75* ... **20-30**
(Quadrophonic issues.)

COLUMBIA (30050; "Self Portrait"): *70* . **50-60**
(With "360-Degree Stereo" at bottom of label.)

COLUMBIA (30050; "Self
Portrait"): *70* **10-15**
(Without "360-Degree Stereo" at bottom of label.)

COLUMBIA (30290 through
32747): *70-73* **6-10**

COLUMBIA (33235; "Blood On
The Tracks"): *75* **25-35**
(With a mural pictured on the back cover.)

COLUMBIA (33235; "Blood On
The Tracks"): *75* **8-12**
(With liner notes on the back cover.)

COLUMBIA (33893 through
38819): *76-83* **6-10**

COLUMBIA (38830; "Biography"): *85* .. **10-15**
(Boxed set, includes 36-page booklet.)

COLUMBIA (39944; "Real Live"): *84* **$5-8**

COLUMBIA (40110; "Empire
Burlesque"): *85* **5-8**

COLUMBIA (40439; "Knocked Out
Loaded"): *86* **5-8**

COLUMBIA (HC-40000 series): *81-82* ..**15-20**
(Half-speed mastered.)

FOLKWAYS (5322; "Bob Dylan
Vs. A.J. Weberman"): **100-150**

ISLAND: *74* **20-30**

Promotional LPs

ASYLUM (201; "Before The Flood"): *74* .**20-30**
(White label.)

ASYLUM (1003; "Planet Waves"): *74* ...**20-30**
(White label.)

COLUMBIA (422; "Renaldo &
Clara"): *76* **20-25**

COLUMBIA (798; "Saved"): *80* **25-30**

COLUMBIA (1259; "Dylan London
Interview"): *80* **20-30**

COLUMBIA (1263; "Shot Of Love"): *81* .**25-30**

COLUMBIA (1471; "Electric
Lunch"): *83* **10-15**

COLUMBIA (1770; "Infidels"): *83* **10-15**

COLUMBIA (C2L-41/C2S-841;
"Blonde On Blonde"): *66* **60-75**
(White label.)

COLUMBIA (CL-1779/CS-8579;
"Bob Dylan"): *62* **200-300**
(White label.)

COLUMBIA (CL-1986/CS-8786; "The
Freewheelin' Bob Dylan"): *63* **2000-3000**
(White label. With the tracks: *Let Me Die In My
Footsteps, Talkin' John Birch Society Blues,
Gamblin' Willie's Dead Man's Hand*, and *Rocks &
Gravel*, which may also be shown as *Solid Gravel*.
We suggest verification of the above tracks by lis-
tening to the LP, rather than accepting the informa-
tion printed on the label.)

COLUMBIA (CL-1986/CS-8786; "The
Freewheelin' Bob Dylan"): *63* **75-100**
(White label reissue, with the above tracks replaced
by four others.)

COLUMBIA (CL-2105/CS-8905; "The
Times They Are A-Changin'"): *64* **75-100**
(White label.)

COLUMBIA (CL-2193/CS-8993; "Another
Side Of Bob Dylan"): *64* **60-75**
(White label.)

COLUMBIA (CL-2328/CS-9128; "Bringin'
It All Back Home"): *65* **60-75**
(White label.)

COLUMBIA (CL-2389/CS-9189; "Highway
61 Revisited"): *65* **60-75**
(White label.)

COLUMBIA (KCL-2663/KCS-9463; "Bob
Dylan's Greatest Hits"): *67* **$60-75**
(White label.)
COLUMBIA (CL-2804; "John Wesley
Harding"): *68* **50-60**
(White label.)
COLUMBIA (KCS-9825; "Nashville
Skyline"): *68* **50-60**
(White label.)
COLUMBIA (30050; "Self Portrait"): *70* . **50-60**
(White label.)
COLUMBIA (30290 through
32747): *70-73* **15-20**
(White labels.)
COLUMBIA (33235; "Blood On
The Tracks"): *75* **20-25**
(White label.)
COLUMBIA (33893 through
38819): *76-83* **10-15**
(White labels.)
COLUMBIA (39944; "Real Live"): *84* ... **10-15**
(White label.)
COLUMBIA (40000 series): *85-86* **5-8**
(With an "FC" or "OC" prefix.)
COLUMBIA (40000 series): *81-82* **15-20**
(With an "HC" prefix. Half-speed mastered.)
FOLKWAYS (5322; "Bob Dylan Vs.
A.J. Weberman"): **75-100**
ISLAND: *74* **20-30**
WESTWOOD ONE ("Dylan On
Dylan"): *84* **150-175**
(5-LP set. Issued for radio broadcast only.)
WESTWOOD ONE ("Dylan On
Dylan"): *84* **100-125**
(3-LP set. Shorter version of the show listed above.)
Also see BAND
Also see BELAFONTE, Harry
Also see HARRISON, George
Also see SAHM, Doug
Also see U.S.A. FOR AFRICA

DYLAN, Bob, & The Heartbreakers / Michael Rubini
Singles: 7-Inch
MCA: *86* **1-3**
Also see DYLAN, Bob
Also see PETTY, Tom, & The Heartbreakers

DYNAMIC BREAKERS
Singles: 12-Inch 33/45rpm
SUNNYVIEW: *85* **4-6**
Singles: 7-Inch
SUNNYVIEW: *85* **1-3**

DYNAMIC CORVETTES
Singles: 7-Inch
ABET: *75* **2-3**

DYNAMIC SUPERIORS
Singles: 12-Inch 33/45rpm
MOTOWN: *77* **$4-6**
Singles: 7-Inch
MOTOWN: *74-77* **2-3**
LPs: 10/12-Inch 33rpm
MOTOWN: *74-77* **8-10**
Members: Tony Washington; Maurice Washington;
Michael McCalpin; George Spann; George Peter-
back.

DYNAMICS
Singles: 7-Inch
ARC: *59* **4-6**
CAPRI: *59* **4-6**
DELTA: *59* **4-6**
DYNAMIC: *59-62* **8-12**
GUARANTEED: *59* **4-6**
IMPALA: *59* **12-15**
LAVERE: *61* **3-5**
LI BAN: *62* **3-5**
LIBERTY: *63* **3-5**
REPRISE: *63* **8-10**
SEECO: *59* **5-8**
U.S.A: *64* **3-5**

DYNA-SORES
Singles: 7-Inch
RENDEZVOUS: *60* **5-8**
Member: Jimmy Norman.
Also see NORMAN, Jimmy

DYNASTY
Singles: 7-Inch
SOLAR: *79-88* **1-3**
LPs: 10/12-Inch 33rpm
SOLAR: *79-88* **5-8**

DYNATONES
Singles: 7-Inch
HBR: *66* **3-5**
ST. CLAIR: *66* **5-8**
LPs: 10/12-Inch 33rpm
HBR: *66* **20-25**

DYNELL, Johnny, & The New York 88
Singles: 12-Inch 33/45rpm
ACME: *83-84* **4-6**

DYSON, Clifton
Singles: 12-Inch 33/45rpm
MOTOWN: *79* **4-6**
Singles: 7-Inch
MOTOWN: *79* **2-3**
NETWORK: *82* **1-3**
LPs: 10/12-Inch 33rpm
AFTER HOURS: *82* **5-8**
NETWORK: *82* **5-8**

DYSON, Ronnie
Singles: 12-Inch 33/45rpm
COTILLION: *83* **4-6**
Singles: 7-Inch
COLUMBIA: *69-78* **2-3**
COTILLION: *82-83* **1-3**
Picture Sleeves
COLUMBIA: *73-75* **2-4**
LPs: 10/12-Inch 33rpm
COLUMBIA: *70-79* **8-10**
COTILLION: *82-83* **5-8**

E

E., Sheila
(Sheila Escovedo)
Singles: 12-Inch 33/45rpm
WARNER BROS: *84-85* **$4-6**
Singles: 7-Inch
PAISLEY PARK: *85-87* **1-3**
WARNER BROS: *84-85* **1-3**
LPs: 10/12-Inch 33rpm
PAISLEY PARK: *85-87* **5-8**
WARNER BROS: *84* **5-8**
Also see KRUSH GROOVE ALL-STARS
Also see PRINCE

EQ
Singles: 12-Inch 33/45rpm
ATLANTIC: *86* **4-6**

E.U.
(Experience Unlimited)
Singles: 7-Inch
ISLAND: *86* **1-3**
MANHATTAN: *88* **1-3**
LPs: 10/12-Inch 33rpm
ISLAND: *86* **5-8**

EAGER, Brenda Lee
(Brenda Lee Eager & Peaches)
Singles: 12-Inch 33/45rpm
PRIVATE I: *84* **4-6**
Singles: 7-Inch
MERCURY: *72-74* **2-4**
PLAYBOY: *75* **2-3**
PRIVATE I: *84* **1-3**
Also see BUTLER, Jerry, & Brenda Lee Eager

EAGLES
Singles: 7-Inch
ASYLUM: *72-80* **2-4**
FULL MOON: *81* **1-3**
Picture Sleeves
ASYLUM: *72-80* **2-4**

LPs: 10/12-Inch 33rpm
ASYLUM: *72-82* **$8-12**
Members: Don Felder; Glenn Frey; Don Henley;
Randy Meisner; Timothy B. Schmit; Joe Walsh.
Also see FELDER, Don
Also see FREY, Glenn
Also see HENLEY, Don
Also see LEADON, Bernie
Also see LEE, Johnny / Eagles
Also see MEISNER, Randy
Also see NEWMAN, Randy
Also see POCO
Also see RONSTADT, Linda
Also see SCHMIT, Timothy B.
Also see SIMMONS, Patrick
Also see VITALE, Joe
Also see WALSH, Joe

EARLAND, Charles
(Charles Earland's Odyssey; Charlie Earland Jr.)
Singles: 7-Inch
COLUMBIA: *81-82* **1-3**
MERCURY: *76* **1-3**
PRESTIGE: *70-74* **2-3**
QUAKER TOWN: *64* **2-4**
LPs: 10/12-Inch 33rpm
COLUMBIA: *80* **5-8**
MERCURY: *76-78* **5-8**
MUSE: *80* **5-8**
PRESTIGE: *70-75* **5-10**
RARE BIRD: *71* **5-10**
TRIP: *73* **5-10**

EARLE, Steve
(Steve Earle & The Dukes)
Singles: 12-Inch 33/45rpm
MCA: *86* **4-6**
Singles: 7-Inch
EPIC: *84-85* **1-3**
HUGHES: *88* **1-3**
MCA: *86-87* **1-3**
Picture Sleeves
EPIC: *84* **1-3**
EPs: 7-Inch 33/45rpm
LSI: *82* **4-8**
LPs: 10/12-Inch 33rpm
MCA: *86-87* **5-8**
UNI 7: *88* **5-8**

EARL-JEAN
(Earl Jean McCree)
Singles: 7-Inch
COLPIX: *64* **3-5**
Also see COOKIES

EARLS
Singles: 12-Inch 33/45rpm
WOODBURY: *76-77* **$6-10**
Singles: 7-Inch
ABC: *68* **5-8**
ATLANTIC: **1-3**
BARRY: *63* **3-5**
CLIFTON: *74* **2-4**
COLLECTABLES: **1-3**
COLUMBIA: *76* **2-4**
MR. "G": *67* **5-8**
OLD TOWN (Light-blue label): *63* **20-25**
OLD TOWN (Multi-color label,
except 1130): *63-65* **8-12**
OLD TOWN (1130; "Remember
Then"): *62* **5-8**
ROME (101; "Life Is But a Dream"/
"It's You"): *61* **20-25**
ROME (101; "Life Is But a Dream"/
"Without You"): *61* **15-20**
ROME (102; "Lookin' For
My Baby"): *61* **15-20**
ROME (112; "Little Boy &
Girl"): *76* **2-4**
ROME (114; "All Through Our
Teens"): *76* **6-8**
(Black vinyl.)
ROME (114; "All Through Our
Teens"): *76* **6-8**
(Colored vinyl.)
ROME (5117; "My Heart's
Desire"): *62* **20-25**
(Colored vinyl.)
WOODBURY: *76* **2-3**
EPs: 7-Inch 33/45rpm
CRYSTAL BALL: **5-8**
LPs: 10/12-Inch 33rpm
CRYSTAL BALL: **8-10**
OLD TOWN (104; "Remember Me
Baby"): *63* **100-200**
(Counterfeits exist but can be identified by their
1/2-inch vinyl trail-off and poor fidelity. Originals
have a 3/4-inch trail-off and excellent fidelity.)
Members: Larry Chance; Robert Del Din; Jack
Wray; Ed Harder.

EARONS
Singles: 12-Inch 33/45rpm
ISLAND: *84* **4-6**
Singles: 7-Inch
BOARDWALK: *83* **1-3**
ISLAND: *84* **1-3**

EARTH OPERA
Singles: 7-Inch
ELEKTRA: *67-69* **3-5**

LPs: 10/12-Inch 33rpm
ELEKTRA: *68-69* **$10-12**

EARTH QUAKE:
see EARTHQUAKE

EARTH, WIND & FIRE
Singles: 12-Inch 33/45rpm
COLUMBIA: *75-83* **4-6**
Singles: 7-Inch
ARC: *78-82* **1-3**
COLUMBIA: *73-88* **1-3**
WARNER BROS: *71* **2-3**
Picture Sleeves
COLUMBIA: *74-80* **1-3**
LPs: 10/12-Inch 33rpm
COLUMBIA (Except 47000
series): *72-88* **8-12**
COLUMBIA (47000 series): *81-82* **15-20**
(Half-speed mastered.)
COLUMBIA/ARC (Except picture
discs): *75-81* **8-10**
COLUMBIA/ARC (Picture discs): *79* ...**10-15**
WARNER BROS: *71-74* **12-15**
Member: Philip Bailey.
Also see BAILEY, Philip

EARTH, WIND & FIRE & THE EMOTIONS
Singles: 12-Inch 33/45rpm
ARC: *79* **4-6**
Singles: 7 Inch
ARC: *79-80* **1-3**
LPs: 10/12-Inch 33rpm
ARC: *79* **5-8**
Also see EMOTIONS

EARTH, WIND & FIRE & RAMSEY LEWIS
Singles: 7-Inch
COLUMBIA: *74-75* **2-3**
Also see EARTH, WIND & FIRE
Also see LEWIS, Ramsey

EARTHQUAKE
(Earth Quake)
Singles: 7-Inch
A&M: *72* **2-4**
BESERKLEY: *76-77* **2-3**
LPs: 10/12-Inch 33rpm
A&M: *71-78* **10-12**
BESERKLEY: *76-80* **8-10**

EAST, Thomas
(Thomas East & The Fabulous Playboys)
Singles: 7-Inch
LION: *73* **2-3**
MGM: *73* **2-3**

TODDLIN' TOWN: *68-69* $3-6

EAST COAST
Singles: 7-Inch
RSO: *79* 1-3

EAST L.A. CAR POOL
Singles: 7-Inch
GRC: *75* 2-3

EASTBOUND EXPRESSWAY
Singles: 7-Inch
AVI: *78-79* 2-3

EASTON, Elliot
Singles: 7-Inch
ELEKTRA: *85* 1-3
LPs: 10/12-Inch 33rpm
ELEKTRA: *85* 5-8
Also see CARS

EASTON, Sheena
Singles: 12-Inch 33/45rpm
EMI AMERICA: *81-86* 4-6
Singles: 7-Inch
EMI AMERICA: *81-86* 1-3
LIBERTY: *81* 1-3
Picture Sleeves
EMI AMERICA: *81-86* 1-3
LPs: 10/12-Inch 33rpm
EMI AMERICA: *81-86* 5-8
MCA: *88* 5-8

EASTON, Sheena, & Kenny Rogers
Singles: 7-Inch
LIBERTY: *83* 1-3
LPs: 10/12-Inch 33rpm
LIBERTY: *84* 5-8
Also see EASTON, Sheena
Also see ROGERS, Kenny

EASTWOOD, Clint
Singles: 7-Inch
CAMEO: *63* 10-15
CERTRON: *70* 2-4
GOTHIC: *61* 8-12
PARAMOUNT: *69* 2-5
WARNER BROS: *81* 1-3
Picture Sleeves
CAMEO: *63* 25-40
CERTRON: *70* 2-4
LPs: 10/12-Inch 33rpm
CAMEO (1056; "Cowboy
Favorites"): *63* 50-100
Also see CHARLES, Ray, & Clint Eastwood
Also see HAGGARD, Merle, & Clint
Eastwood

EASTWOOD, Clint, & T.G. Sheppard
Singles: 7-Inch
WARNER BROS: *84* $1-3
Also see EASTWOOD, Clint
Also see SHEPPARD, T.G.

EASY STREET
Singles: 7-Inch
CAPRICORN: *76* 2-3
LPs: 10/12-Inch 33rpm
CAPRICORN: *76-77* 8-10

EASYBEATS
Singles: 7-Inch
ASCOT: *66* 8-10
RARE EARTH: *69* 3-5
UNITED ARTISTS: *67-69* 4-6
Picture Sleeves
ASCOT: *66* 10-15
LPs: 10/12-Inch 33rpm
RARE EARTH: *70* 10-15
UNITED ARTISTS: *67-68* 30-40
Also see FLASH & THE PAN

EBB TIDE
(Ebb K. Harrison, Sr.)
Singles: 7-Inch
SOUND GEMS: *75-76* 2-3

EBN/OZN
Singles: 12-Inch 33/45rpm
ELEKTRA: *84* 4-6
Singles: 7-Inch
ELEKTRA: *84* 1-3
LPs: 10/12-Inch 33rpm
ELEKTRA: *84* 5-8
Members: Ebn; Ozn.

EBONEE WEBB
(Ebony Web)
Singles: 7-Inch
CAPITOL: *81-84* 1-3
HI: *70-72* 2-4
LPs: 10/12-Inch 33rpm
CAPITOL: *81-84* 5-8

EBONY
Singles: 12-Inch 33/45rpm
QUALITY/RFC: *84* 4-6

EBONY, IVORY & JADE
Singles: 7-Inch
COLUMBIA: *75* 2-3

EBONY RHYTHM FUNK CAMPAIGN
Singles: 7-Inch
INNOVATION: *75* 2-4
MCA: *72* 2-4
LPs: 10/12-Inch 33rpm
UNI: *72* 6-10

EBONY WEB:
see EBONEE WEBB

EBONYS
Singles: 7-Inch
BUDDAH: 76 . . . . $2-3
PHILADELPHIA INT'L: 71-74 2-3
LPs: 10/12-Inch 33rpm
PHILADELPHIA INT'L: 73 8-10

ECHO & THE BUNNYMEN
Singles: 12-Inch 33/45rpm
SIRE: 81-86 5-8
Singles: 7-Inch
SIRE: 81-86 1-3
LPs: 10/12-Inch 33rpm
SIRE: 81-87 5-8

ECHOES
Singles: 7-Inch
ASCOT: 65 6-10
COLUMBIA: 60 4-6
FELSTED: 61 5-8
SRG: 61 15-20
SEG-WAY: 60-61 8-12
EPs: 7-Inch 33/45rpm
CRYSTAL BALL: 4-6
Members: Harry Doyle; Tom Morrissey; Tom
Duffy.

ECKSTINE, Billy
Singles: 78rpm
DELUXE: 45 10-15
MGM (10000 through 10500
series): 47-56 3-5
NATIONAL: 45-48 4-8
RCA VICTOR: 56 3-6
Singles: 7-Inch
A&M: 76 1-3
ENTERPRISE: 70-74 1-3
MGM (8000 series): 3-5
MGM (10600 through 12000
series): 50-56 3-6
MERCURY: 59-64 2-4
MOTOWN: 65-68 2-4
RCA VICTOR: 56 3-6
ROULETTE: 59-60 2-4
Picture Sleeves
MERCURY: 62 5-10
EPs: 7-Inch 33/45rpm
EMARCY: 54-55 10-20
KING: 54 10-20
MGM: 50-56 10-20
MOTOWN: 65 5-10
RENDITION: 50 15-25
LPs: 10/12-Inch 33rpm
AUDIO LAB: 60 10-20

EMARCY (26000 series): 54-55 . . . . . . $25-50
(10-Inch LPs.)
EMARCY (36000 series): 54-56 15-25
ENTERPRISE: 71-74 5-10
FELSTED: 50-75
KING (265 series): 54 40-60
(10 Inch LP.)
MGM (100 & 200 series): 52-53 25-50
(10-Inch LPs.)
MGM (3100 & 3200 series): 54-55 15-25
MERCURY: 57-64 10-20
METRO: 65 8-12
MOTOWN: 65-69 10-15
NATIONAL (2000 series): 50 30-60
(10-Inch LP.)
REGENT: 56-57 15-25
ROULETTE: 60 10-20
SAVOY: 76-79 8-10
TRIP: 75 5-8
WING: 67 6-10
Also see BASIE, Count, & Billy Eckstine
Also see DAMITA JO & BILLY ECKSTINE

ECKSTINE, Billy, & Quincy Jones
Singles: 7-Inch
MERCURY: 62 2-4
LPs: 10/12-Inch 33rpm
MERCURY: 62 12-20
Also see JONES, Quincy

ECKSTINE, Billy /Arthur Prysock
LPs: 10/12-Inch 33rpm
GUEST STAR: 64 5-10
Also see PRYSOCK, Arthur

ECKSTINE, Billy, & Sarah Vaughan
Singles: 7-Inch
MERCURY: 57-59 2-4
LPs: 10/12-Inch 33rpm
GUEST STAR: 64 5-10

LION: 59 .... $12-15
MERCURY: 57 15-20
Also see ECKSTINE, Billy
Also see VAUGHAN, Sarah

ECSTASY, PASSION & PAIN
Singles: 12-Inch
ROULETTE: 84 4-6
Singles: 7-Inch
ROULETTE: 74-76 2-3
LPs: 10/12-Inch 33rpm
· ROULETTE: 74 8-10
Member: Barbara Roy.
Also see ROY, Barbara

EDDIE, John
Singles: 7-Inch
COLUMBIA: 86 1-3
LPs: 10/12-Inch 33rpm
COLUMBIA: 86 5-8

EDDIE & BETTY
Singles: 7-Inch
LARK: 59 4-6
SIX THOUSAND: 57 5-8
WARNER BROS: 59 4-6
LPs: 10/12-Inch 33rpm
WARNER BROS: 59 15-20
Members: Eddie Cole; Betty Cole.

EDDIE & DUTCH
Singles: 7-Inch
IVANHOE: 70 2-3

EDDIE & ERNIE
Singles: 7-Inch
CHESS: 66 3-5
EASTERN: 65-66 3-5
REVUE: 69 2-4

EDDIE & FREDDIE
Singles: 7-Inch
OCTOBER: 77 2-3

EDDIE & THE TIDE
(Eddie Rice)
Singles: 7-Inch
ATCO: 85 1-3

EDDIE D.
Singles: 12-Inch 33/45rpm
PHILLY WORLD: 85 4-6
Singles: 7-Inch
PHILLY WORLD: 85 1-3

EDDY, Duane
(Duane Eddy & The Rebels; Duane Eddy & The
Rebelettes; Duane Eddy & His Rock-a-billies;
Duane Eddy & His Twangy Guitar)
Singles: 78rpm
FORD: 57 15-25

DUANE EDDY | YOUR BABY'S GONE SURFIN' | 45 RPM RCA VICTOR 47-8214 SHUCKIN'

JAMIE: 58 .... $5-10
Singles: 7-Inch
BIG TREE: 72 2-4
COLPIX: 65-66 4-6
CONGRESS: 70 2-4
ELEKTRA: 77 2-3
FORD: 57 25-30
GREGMARK (5; "Caravan"): 61 5-8
(Shown as by Duane Eddy, but was actually Al
Casey.)
JAMIE (Monaural): 58-62 5-10
JAMIE (Stereo): 59-60 15-25
RCA VICTOR: 61-65 4-8
REPRISE: 66-68 3-6
UNI: 70 2-4
Picture Sleeves
COLPIX: 66 15-25
JAMIE: 59-61 12-25
RCA VICTOR: 62-63 8-15
EPs: 7-Inch 33/45rpm
JAMIE: 59-60 20-30
RCA VICTOR/WURLITZER
DISCOTHEQUE MUSIC: 64 15-25
LPs: 10/12-Inch 33rpm
CAMDEN: 8-15
CAPITOL: 87 6-10
COLPIX: 65 25-30
JAMIE (Except 3000, 3011, &
3026): 59-63 15-30
JAMIE (3000; "Have Twangy Guitar,
Will Travel"): 58 20-40
(White cover.)
JAMIE (3000; "Have Twangy Guitar,
Will Travel"): 58 15-30
(Red cover.)
JAMIE (3011; "Songs Of Our
Heritage"): 60 40-60
(Colored vinyl.)

JAMIE (3011; "Songs Of Our
Heritage"): *60* **$20-30**
(With gatefold cover. Black vinyl.)
JAMIE (3011; "Songs Of Our
Heritage"): *61* **15-20**
(Standard cover. Black vinyl.)
JAMIE (3026; "16 Greatest Hits"): *64* . . . **12-20**
RCA VICTOR (LPM/LSP series): *62-66* . **25-30**
RCA VICTOR (ANL series): *78* **5-8**
REPRISE: *66-67* **15-20**
SIRE: *75* **10-12**
Members: Duane Eddy; Steve Douglas.
Also see ART OF NOISE
Also see BLOSSOMS
Also see CASEY, Al
Also see CLARK, Sanford, & Duane Eddy
Also see FOGERTY, John
Also see JIMMY & DUANE
Also see THOMAS, B.J.

EDELMAN, Randy
Singles: 7-Inch
ARISTA: *77-79* **1-3**
LION: *73* **2-3**
MGM: *73* **2-3**
SUNFLOWER: *71-72* **2-4**
20TH CENTURY-FOX: *74-76* **2-3**
LPs: 10/12-Inch 33rpm
ARISTA: *77-79* **5-8**
LION: *73* **8-10**
MGM: *72* **8-10**
SUNFLOWER: *71* **8-10**
20TH CENTURY-FOX: *74-78* **8-10**

EDEN'S CHILDREN
Singles: 7-Inch
ABC: *68* **2-4**
LPs: 10/12-Inch 33rpm
ABC: *68* **10-15**

EDGE, Graeme
(Graeme Edge Band)
Singles: 7-Inch
LONDON: *77* **1-3**
THRESHOLD: *74* **2-3**
LPs: 10/12-Inch 33rpm
LONDON: *77* **8-10**
THRESHOLD: *75* **8-10**
Also see GURVITZ, Adrian
Also see MOODY BLUES

EDISON LIGHTHOUSE
Singles: 7-Inch
BELL: *70-71* **2-4**

EDMUNDS, Dave
(Dave Edmunds Band)
Singles: 7-Inch
COLUMBIA: *80-85* **$1-3**
MAM: *70-71* **3-5**
RCA VICTOR: *73-74* **3-5**
SWAN SONG: *77-81* **2-3**
Promotional Singles
COLUMBIA (1576; "Run Rudolph
Run"): *82* **3-5**
(Compact 33 Single.)
COLUMBIA (03428; "Run
Rudolph Run"): *82* **2-4**
Picture Sleeves
SWAN SONG: *81* **2-3**
LPs: 10/12-Inch 33rpm
ATLANTIC (320; "College Network"): . **35-40**
(Promotional issue only.)
COLUMBIA (Except 1725): *80-87* **5-8**
COLUMBIA (1725; "Information"): *83* . **15-25**
(Picture disc. Promotional issue only.)
MAM: *72* **30-40**
RCA VICTOR (4000 series): *82* **5-8**
RCA VICTOR (5000 series): **10-12**
SWAN SONG: *77-81* **8-10**
Also see HARRISON, George / Dave Ed-
munds
Also see HARRISON, George / Dave Ed-
munds / Jeff Beck
Also see LEWIS, Huey, & The News
Also see LOWE, Nick, & Dave Edmunds

EDMUNDS, Dave, & Carlene Carter
Singles: 7-Inch
WARNER BROS: *80* **1-3**
Also see CARTER, Carlene
Also see EDMUNDS, Dave

EDSELS
Singles: 7-Inch
ABC: *75* **1-3**

CAPITOL: *61-62* $3-5
DOT: *62* 5-8
DUB (2843; "Lama Rama
  Ding Dong"): *58* 30-50
DUB (2843; "Rama Lama
  Ding Dong"): *58* 12-20
(Note slight variation in above titles.)
EMBER: *61* 5-8
MUSICTONE: *61* 5-8
ROULETTE (4000 series): *59* 15-20
TAMMY: *60-61* 15-20
TWIN: *61* 5-8
  Members: George Jones Jr.; Larry Green; James
  Reynolds; Marshall Sewell; Harry Green.

EDWARD BEAR
Singles: 7-Inch
CAPITOL: *70-74* 2-3
Picture Sleeves
CAPITOL: *72-73* 2-4
LPs: 10/12-Inch 33rpm
CAPITOL: *70-73* 8-10

EDWARDS, Alton
Singles: 12-Inch 33/45rpm
COLUMBIA: *82* 4-6
Singles: 7-Inch
COLUMBIA: *82* 1-3

EDWARDS, Bobby
Singles: 7-Inch
BLUEBONNET: *59* 3-5
CAPITOL: *61-63* 2-4
CHART: *68* 1-3
CREST: *61* 4-6
MANCO: *62* 3-5
MUSICOR: *65* 2-3
POLARIS: 2-4

EDWARDS, Dee
Singles: 12-Inch 33/45rpm
COTILLION: *79* 4-6
Singles: 7-Inch
COTILLION: *78-80* 1-3
D TOWN: *65* 4-6
RCA VICTOR: *72* 2-4
LPs: 10/12-Inch 33rpm
COTILLION: *80* 5-8

EDWARDS, Dennis
Singles: 12-Inch 33/45rpm
GORDY: *84* 4-6
Singles: 7-Inch
GORDY: *84-85* 1-3
MOTOWN: 1-3
LPs: 10/12-Inch 33rpm
GORDY: *84-85* 5-8
Also see TEMPTATIONS

EDWARDS, Jayne
Singles: 12-Inch 33/45rpm
PROFILE: *83-84* $4-6
Singles: 7-Inch
PROFILE: *83-84* 1-3
LPs: 10/12-Inch 33rpm
PROFILE: *84* 5-8

EDWARDS, Jimmy
(Jimmie Edwards)
Singles: 7-Inch
MERCURY: *57-58* 5-8
RCA VICTOR: *59-60* 4-6

EDWARDS, John
Singles: 7-Inch
AWARE: *73-74* 2-3
BELL: *72* 2-4
COTILLION: *76-77* 2-3
LPs: 10/12-Inch 33rpm
AWARE: *74* 5-10
CREED: *75* 5-10
GENERAL/GRC: *74* 5-10

EDWARDS, Jonathan
Singles: 7-Inch
ATCO: *72-73* 2-3
CAPRICORN: *71* 2-3
WARNER BROS: *77* 2-3
LPs: 10/12-Inch 33rpm
ATCO: *72-74* 8-10
CAPRICORN: *71* 10-12
REPRISE: *74* 8-10
WARNER BROS: *77* 8-10

EDWARDS, Tom
Singles: 7-Inch
CORAL: *57* 3-5

EDWARDS, Tommy
Singles: 78rpm
MGM: *51-58* 2-5
Singles: 7-Inch
MGM (10000 & 11000 series): *51-55* 3-6
MGM (12000 & 13000 series): *55-65* 2-5
MGM (50000 series): *59* 5-8
(Stereo.)
Picture Sleeves
MGM: *60* 4-8
EPs: 7-Inch 33/45rpm
MGM (Except 1001): *59* 8-12
MGM (1001; "It's All In
  The Game"): *52* 10-15
LPs: 10/12-Inch 33rpm
LION: *59* 10-15
MGM: *59-63* 10-20
METRO: *65* 8-12
REGENT: 10-15

EDWARDS, Vincent
Singles: 7-Inch
CAPITOL: 62 .... $2-4
COLPIX: 65 2-4
DECCA (Monaural): 62-63 2-4
DECCA (Stereo 33 series): 62 4-6
KAMA SUTRA: 67 3-6
RUSS-FI (1 "Oh Babe"): 59 4-6
RUSS-FI (7001; "Why Did You
    Leave Me"): 62 3-5
Picture Sleeves
COLPIX: 65 3-6
DECCA: 62 4-8
KAMA SUTRA: 67 3-6
EPs: 7-Inch 33/45rpm
DECCA: 62 8-10
LPs: 10/12-Inch 33rpm
DECCA: 62-63 10-15

EGAN, Walter
Singles: 7-Inch
COLUMBIA: 77-79 1-3
LPs: 10/12-Inch 33rpm
COLUMBIA: 77-80 5-8
Also see BUCKINGHAM, Lindsey
Also see NICKS, Stevie

EGG CREAM
Singles: 7-Inch
PYRAMID: 77 1-3
LPs: 10/12-Inch 33rpm
PYRAMID: 77 5-8
Member: Andy Adams.

EGYPTIAN LOVER
Singles: 12-Inch 33/45rpm
EGYPTIAN: 84-86 4-6
Singles: 7-Inch
EGYPTIAN: 84-86 1-3
FREAK BEAT: 84 1-3

LPs: 10/12-Inch 33rpm
EGYPTIAN: 85 .... $5-8
PRIORITY: 88 5-8

801
LPs: 10/12-Inch 33rpm
EDITIONS E.G.: 86 5-8
Members: Phil Manzanera; Brian Eno.
Also see ENO, Brian
Also see MANZANERA, Phil

8TH DAY
(Eighth Day)
Singles: 7-Inch
A&M: 83 1-3
INVICTUS: 71-72 2-4
KAPP: 67-69 3-5
Picture Sleeves
KAPP: 68 4-8
LPs: 10/12-Inch 33rpm
A&M: 83 5-8
INVICTUS: 71-73 8-10
KAPP: 68 10-15

EL CHICANO
Singles: 7-Inch
GORDO: 70 3-5
KAPP/GORDO: 70-72 2-4
MCA: 73-75 2-3
RFR: 82 1-3
SHADYBROOK: 77-78 1-3
LPs: 10/12-Inch 33rpm
KAPP: 70-72 10-12
MCA: 73-74 8-10
Also see TIERRA

EL COCO
(Coco)
Singles: 12-Inch 33/45rpm
A.V.I.: 78-85 4-6
Singles: 7-Inch
A.V.I.: 75-85 1-3
LPs: 10/12-Inch 33rpm
A.V.I.: 75-85 5-8

EL DEBARGE:
see DE BARGE, El

EL DORADOS
Singles: 78rpm
VEE JAY (115; "Baby I Need You"): 54   10-20
VEE JAY (118; "Annie's Answer"): 54   20-40
    (With Hazel McCollum.)
VEE JAY (127: "One More Chance"): 54   35-60
VEE JAY (147; "At My Front Door"): 55   10-20
VEE JAY (165; "I'll Be Forever
    Lovin' You"): 55 10-20
VEE JAY (180 through 263): 56-57 10-20

Singles: 7-Inch
COLLECTABLES: $1-3
VEE JAY (115; "Baby I Need You"): *54* . 15-20
(Black vinyl.)
VEE JAY (115; "Baby I Need You"): *54* . 60-75
(Colored vinyl.)
VEE JAY (118; "Annie's Answer"): *54* .. 50-75
(Black vinyl. With Hazel McCollum.)
VEE JAY (118; "Annie's
Answer"): *54* 150-200
(Colored vinyl.)
VEE JAY (127; "One More
Chance"): *54* 75-125
VEE JAY (147; "At My Front
Door"): *55* 15-25
VEE JAY (165; "I'll Be Forever
Lovin' You"): *55* 20-30
VEE JAY (180; "Now That You've
Gone"): *56* 20-30
VEE JAY (197; "A Fallen Tear"): *56* 20-30
VEE JAY (211; "Bim Bam Boom"): *56* .. 20-30
VEE JAY (250; "Tears On My
Pillow"): *57* 15-25
VEE JAY (263; "3 Reasons Why"): *58* .. 25-50
VEE JAY (302; "Lights Are Low"): *58* .. 30-50
LPs: 10/12-Inch 33rpm
LOST-NITE: *81* 5-8
VEE JAY (1001; "Crazy Little
Mama"): *58* 300-400
(This LP contains two tracks by The Magnificents.)
Members: Pirkle Lee Moses Jr.; Arthur Bassett;
Louis Bradley; James Maddox; Jewel Jones;
Richard Nickens; Johnny Carter; Ted Long; John
McCall; Douglas Brown.
Also see MAGNIFICENTS

ELAINE & ELLEN
Singles: 7-Inch
OVATION: *80* 1-3

ELBERT, Donnie
Singles: 78rpm
DELUXE: *57* 5-10
Singles: 7-Inch
ALL PLATINUM: *72* ...`.............. 2-3
AVCO: *72* 2-3
CUB: *63* 3-5
DELUXE: *57* 10-20
GATEWAY: *64-65* 3-5
GUSTO: 1-3
JALYNNE: *61-62* 3-5
RARE BULLET: *70* 2-4
VEE JAY: *60* 5-15
LPs: 10/12-Inch 33rpm
ALL PLATINUM: *71* 10-12
DELUXE: *71* 10-15

KING: *59* $30-40
SUGARHILL: *81* 5-8
TRIP: *72* 8-10

ELBOW BONES & THE RACKETEERS
Singles: 12-Inch 33/45rpm
EMI AMERICA: *83* 4-6
Singles: 7-Inch
EMI AMERICA: *84* 1-3
Members: Ginchy Dan; Stephanie Fuller.

ELECTRIC EXPRESS
Singles: 7-Inch
LINCO: *71* 2-3

ELECTRIC FLAG
(Electric Flag Music Band)
Singles: 7-Inch
ATLANTIC: *74-75* 2-3
COLUMBIA: *67* 3-5
SIDEWALK: *67* 8-10
Picture Sleeves
COLUMBIA: *67* 4-8
LPs: 10/12-Inch 33rpm
ATLANTIC: *74* 8-10
COLUMBIA: *68-71* 10-12
Also see BLOOMFIELD, Mike, & Nick
Graventes
Also see MILES, Buddy

ELECTRIC INDIAN
Singles: 7-Inch
MARMADUKE: *69* 5-8
UNITED ARTISTS: *69* 2-4
LPs: 10/12-Inch 33rpm
UNITED ARTISTS: *69* 10-12

ELECTRIC LIGHT ORCHESTRA
(ELO)
Singles: 12-Inch 33/45rpm
JET: *78* 8-12
Singles: 7-Inch
JET/CBS: *77-86* 1-3
JET/UNITED ARTISTS: *77* 2-3
MCA: *80* 1-3
UNITED ARTISTS: *72-77* 2-4
Picture Sleeves
JET: *78-79* 2-3
JET/UNITED ARTISTS: *77* 2-3
MCA: *80* 1-3
UNITED ARTISTS: *72-77* 2-5
LPs: 10/12-Inch 33rpm
JET/CBS (Except 40000
series): *78-81* 5-8
JET/CBS (40000 series): *80-81* 15-20
(Half-speed mastered.)
UNITED ARTISTS: *72-75* 10-12

UNITED ARTISTS/JET: *76-77* $8-10
(Black vinyl.)
UNITED ARTISTS/JET: *76-77* 25-30
(Colored vinyl. Promotional issues only.)
  Also see LYNNE, Jeff
  Also see NEWTON-JOHN, Olivia, & The
Electric Light Orchestra
  Also see WOOD, Roy

ELECTRIC MIND
Singles: 12-Inch 33/45rpm
EMERGENCY: *83* 4-6

ELECTRIC PRUNES
Singles: 7-Inch
REPRISE (Except 0300 &
0400 series): *67-69* 8-15
REPRISE (0300 & 0400
series): *65-66* 15-25
Promotional Singles
REPRISE (277; "Sanctus"): *67* 25-40
REPRISE (305; "Help Us"): *68* 25-40
LPs: 10/12-Inch 33rpm
REPRISE: *67-69* 20-30

ELECTRONIC CONCEPT
ORCHESTRA
LPs: 10/12-Inch 33rpm
LIMELIGHT: *69* 5-10
MERCURY: *70* 5-10
Member: Eddie Higgins.

ELEGANTS
(Vito & The Elegants)
Singles: 7 Inch
ABC: *73* 1-3
ABC-PARAMOUNT: *61* 10-12
APT (Except 25005): *59* 25-50
APT (25005; "Little Star"): *58* 25-30
(With silver letters on black label.)
APT (25005; "Little Star"): *58* 8-10
(With multi-color label.)
BIM BAM BOOM: *74* 5-8
(Black vinyl.)
BIM BAM BOOM: *74* 2-4
(Colored vinyl.)
CRYSTAL BALL: 3-5
HULL: *60* 35-40
LAURIE: *65* 8-12
MCA: 1-3
PHOTO: *63* 8-10
ROULETTE: *71* 1-3
UNITED ARTISTS: *60-61* 10-15
Picture Sleeves
CRYSTAL BALL: 3-5
PHOTO: *63* 30-40
(Price includes special insert, which represents $10-
$15 of the value.)

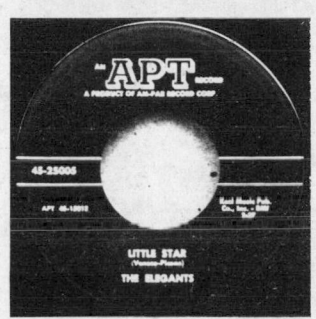

Members: Vito Picone; Frank Tardagno; Carman
Romano; Jimmy Moschella; Artie Venosa.
  Also see BARBARIANS

ELEKTRIK DRED
Singles: 7-Inch
SOUNDS OF FLORIDA: *83* $1-3

ELEKTRO, Eve
Singles: 12-Inch 33/45rpm
BLACK SUIT: *84* 4-6

ELEPHANT'S MEMORY
Singles: 7-Inch
APPLE: *72* 3-5
BUDDAH: *69* 3-5
METROMEDIA: *70-71* 2-4
RCA VICTOR: *74* 2-3
Picture Sleeves
METROMEDIA: *70* 3-5
LPs: 10/12-Inch 33rpm
APPLE: *72* 10-15
BUDDAH: *69-74* 10-15
METROMEDIA: *70* 10-12
MUSE: 8-10
RCA VICTOR: *74* 8-10
  Also see LENNON, John

ELEVENTH HOUSE
Singles: 7-Inch
20TH CENTURY-FOX: *74-75* 2-3
LPs: 10/12-Inch 33rpm
ARISTA: *75* 6-10
20TH CENTURY-FOX: *74* 8-10
  Member: Larry Coryell.
  Also see CORYELL, Larry
  Also see MOUZON, Alphonse, & Larry
Coryell

ELGART, Larry
(Larry Elgart & His Manhattan Swing Orchestra)
Singles: 78rpm
DECCA: *54-55* $2-4
Singles: 7-Inch
DECCA: *54-55* 2-4
MGM: *61-62* 2-3
RCA VICTOR: *59-83* 1-3
EPs: 7-Inch 33/45rpm
BRUNSWICK: *54* 5-10
DECCA: *54-55* 5-10
LPs: 10/12-Inch 33rpm
BRUNSWICK: *54* 15-25
(10-Inch LPs.)
CAMDEN: *60-73* 5-10
DECCA: *54-55* 10-20
MGM: *60-62* 8-12
RCA VICTOR: *59-83* 5-10

ELGART, Les
(Les Elgart & His Orchestra)
Singles: 78rpm
COLUMBIA: *53-57* 2-4
Singles: 7-Inch
COLUMBIA (40000 series,
 except 40180): *53-62* 2-4
COLUMBIA (40180; "Bandstand
 Boogie"): *54* 15-20
("Bandstand Boogie" was the American Bandstand
TV show theme.)
COLUMBIA (56767; "Bandstand
 Twist"): *62* 5-8
(Promotional issue only.)
GOLD-MOR: *73* 1-3
EPs: 7-Inch 33/45rpm
COLUMBIA: *53-59* 5-10
LPs: 10/12-Inch 33rpm
COLUMBIA: *53-62* 10-20
HARMONY: *66* 5-10

ELGART, Les & Larry
Singles: 7-Inch
COLUMBIA: *64-68* 2-3
SWAMPFIRE: *69* 1-3
LPs: 10/12-Inch 33rpm
COLUMBIA (Except 38000
 series): *57-68* 8-15
COLUMBIA (38000 series): *82* 5-8
HARMONY: *68-73* 5-10
SWAMPFIRE: *70* 5-8
Also see ELGART, Larry
Also see ELGART, Les

ELGINS
Singles: 7-Inch
V.I.P.: *66-71* 3-5

LPs: 10/12-Inch 33rpm
V.I.P.: *66* $15-20
Member: Saundra Mallet.

ELI'S SECOND COMING
Singles: 7-Inch
SILVER BLUE: *76-78* 2-3

ELLEDGE, Jimmy
Singles: 7-Inch
FOUR STAR: *75* 1-3
HICKORY: *65-67* 2-3
LITTLE DARLIN': *68* 1-3
RCA VICTOR (Except 8012): *61-64* 3-8
RCA VICTOR (8012; "Can't You
 See It In My Eyes"): *62* 10-20
SIMS: *64* 2-4
Picture Sleeves
RCA VICTOR: *62-63* 4-8

ELLIMAN, Yvonne
Singles: 7-Inch
DECCA: *71-72* 2-3
MCA: 1-3
RSO: *74-79* 1-3
LPs: 10/12-Inch 33rpm
DECCA: *72* 12-15
MCA: *73* 8-10
RSO: *77-79* 5-8
Also see BISHOP, Stephen, & Yvonne Elliman

ELLINGTON, Duke
Singles: 7-Inch
BELL: *73* 1-3
BETHLEHEM: *58-60* 3-5
CAPITOL (2000 series): *53-56* 3-5
COLUMBIA (33000 series): *76* 1-3
COLUMBIA (39000 series): *50-53* 3-5
COLUMBIA (40000 through
 42000 series): *58-61* 3-5
RCA VICTOR (0300 series): *74* 1-3
RCA VICTOR (4000 through
 6000 series): *51-55* 4-6
REPRISE: *67* 2-4
EPs: 7-Inch 33/45rpm
BRUNSWICK: *54* 10-20
CAPITOL: *53-56* 10-20
COLUMBIA: *50-56* 10-20
RCA VICTOR: *52-60* 10-20
ROYALE: 10-20
LPs: 10/12-Inch 33rpm
ALLEGIANCE: *84* 5-8
ALLEGRO: *54* 25-50
(10-Inch LPs.)
ATLANTIC: *71-82* 5-10
BASF: *73* 5-10
BETHLEHEM: *56-57* 15-30

BRIGHT ORANGE: *73* $5-10
BRUNSWICK (54000 series): *56* 15-30
BRUNSWICK (58000 series): *54* 30-50
  (10-Inch LPs.)
CAMDEN (400 series): *58* 15-25
CAPITOL (400 series): *53* 25-50
  (With an "H" prefix. 10-Inch LPs.)
CAPITOL (400 through
  600 series): *55-57* 25-40
CAPITOL (1600 series): *61* 10-20
  (With a "T" prefix.)
CAPITOL (11000 series): *72-77* 5-10
CAPITOL (16000 series): *81* 4-6
COLUMBIA (27; "The Ellington
  Era, Volume 1"): *63* 25-40
COLUMBIA (39; "The Ellington
  Era, Volume 2, 1927-1940"): *66* 25-40
COLUMBIA (500 through 900
  series): *54-57* 20-30
COLUMBIA (1085 through 2029
  except 1360): *57-63* 15-30
  (Monaural.)
COLUMBIA (1360; "Anatomy of a
  Murder"): *59* 35-50
  (Soundtrack. Monaural.)
COLUMBIA (4000 series): *55* 25-50
COLUMBIA (6000 series): *50* 30-60
  (10-Inch LPs.)
COLUMBIA (8053 through 9600,
  except 8166): *57-68* 10-20
  (Stereo.)
COLUMBIA (8166; "Anatomy of a
  Murder"): *59* 45-60
  (Soundtrack. Stereo.)
COLUMBIA (14000 series): *79* 5-10
  (Columbia Special Products series.)
COLUMBIA (32000 through
  38000 series): *73-82* 5-10
DECCA: *67-70* 8-15
DOCTOR JAZZ: *84* 5-8
EVEREST: *70-73* 5-10
FANTASY: *71-75* 6-12
FLYING DUTCHMAN: *69* 5-10
HARMONY: *67-71* 5-10
IMPULSE (Except 9200 series): *62* 15-20
IMPULSE (9200 series): *73* 8-12
ODYSSEY: *68* 8-12
PABLO: *76-80* 5-10
PRESTIGE: *73-77* 6-12
RCA VICTOR (500 series): *64-69* 10-20
RCA VICTOR (0700 through
  2000 series): *75-78* 5-8
  (With an "ANL1" or "APL1" prefix.)
RCA VICTOR (1000 series): *54* 25-40
  (With an "LJM" or "LPT" prefix.)

RCA VICTOR (1300 through
  2800 series): *57-66* $12-30
  (With an "LPM" or "LSP" prefix.)
RCA VICTOR (3000 series): *52-53* 25-50
  (10-Inch LPs.)
RCA VICTOR (3500 through
  3900 series): *66-68* 8-15
RCA VICTOR (4000 series): *81* 8-10
RCA VICTOR (6009; "The Indispensible
  Duke Ellington"): *61* 20-30
RCA VICTOR (6042; "This Is Duke
  Ellington"): *71* 10-15
REPRISE: *63-68* 10-20
RIVERSIDE (Except 100
  series): *62-64* 10-20
RIVERSIDE (100 series): *56-59* 15-30
RON-LETTE: *58* 15-30
SOLID STATE: *70* 5-10
SUNSET: *69* 5-10
TRIP: *75-76* 5-10
UNITED ARTISTS (Except 14000 &
  15000 series): *72* 5-10
UNITED ARTISTS (14000 & 15000
  series): *62* 15-25
VERVE: *67* 10-12
X: *54* 25-50
  (10-Inch LPs.)
Also see ARMSTRONG, Louis, & Duke El-
lington
Also see BASIE, Count, & Duke Ellington
Also see BREWER, Teresa, & Duke Ellington
Also see FITZGERALD, Ella, & Duke El-
lington
Also see HIBBLER, Al, & Duke Ellington
Also see SINATRA, Frank, & Duke Ellington

ELLINGTON, Duke, & John Coltrane
    LPs: 10/12-Inch 33rpm
IMPULSE: *63* 15-25
Also see COLTRANE, John

ELLINGTON, Duke, & Johnny Hodges
    LPs: 10/12-Inch 33rpm
PRESTIGE: *81* 8-10
VERVE (Except 8800
  series): *59-60* 15-30
VERVE (8800 series): *73* 8-12
Also see ELLINGTON, Duke
Also see HODGES, Johnny

ELLIOT, Cass
  (Mama Cass)
    Singles: 7-Inch
DUNHILL: *68-70* 2-5
RCA VICTOR: *71-73* 2-3
    LPs: 10/12-Inch 33rpm
DUNHILL: *68-72* 10-20

RCA VICTOR: 72-73 . . . . $10-15
Also see BIG THREE
Also see MAMAS & THE PAPAS
Also see MASON, Dave, & Mama Cass

ELLIOT, Mike, & Bud Latour
Singles: 7-Inch
MCA: 86 2-4
(Promotional issues only.)
TRI-FIVE: 86 2-4

ELLIS, Jimmy
Singles: 7-Inch
BOBLO: 77-78 5-10
CHALLENGER: 73 4-6
DRADCO: 64 8-10
KRISTAL: 85 1-3
MCA: 73 2-4
SOUTHERN TRACKS: 86-87 1-3
SUN: 72-77 3-6
TONY LAWRENCE: 83-84 1-3
EPs: 7-Inch 33/45rpm
JIMMY ELLIS FAN CLUB ("Merry
Christmas"): 81 4-6
LPs: 10/12-Inch 33rpm
BOBLO (829; "By Request, Ellis
Sings Elvis"): 77 50-100
ROLLER SKATE: 82 8-10
Also see LEWIS, Jerry Lee, Carl Perkins, &
Charlie Rich

ELLIS, Ray, Orchestra
Singles: 7-Inch
MGM: 59-60 2-3
RCA VICTOR: 61 2-3
LPs: 10/12-Inch 33rpm
HARMONY: 59 4-8
MGM: 59-60 5-10
RCA VICTOR: 61 4-8

ELLIS, Shirley
Singles: 7-Inch
COLUMBIA: 67 2-4
CONGRESS: 63-65 3-5
Picture Sleeves
CONGRESS: 64-65 5-10
LPs: 10/12-Inch 33rpm
COLUMBIA: 67 15-20
CONGRESS: 64-65 20-25

ELLISON, Lorraine
Singles: 7-Inch
LOMA: 67-68 2-4
MERCURY: 65-66 3-5
SHARP: 63 3-5
WARNER BROS: 66-69 2-4
LPs: 10/12-Inch 33rpm
WARNER BROS (1000 series): 67-69 . . 15-20

WARNER BROS (2000 series): 74 . . . . . . $8-10

ELMO & ALMO
Singles: 7-Inch
DADDY BEST: 67 2-4

ELUSION
Singles: 7-Inch
COTILLION: 81 1-3
LPs: 10/12-Inch 33rpm
COTILLION: 81 5-8

ELY, Joe
Singles: 7-Inch
MCA: 77-81 1-3
SOUTHCOAST: 81 1-3
LPs: 10/12-Inch 33rpm
MCA: 77-81 1-3
SOUTHCOAST: 81 5-8

EMERSON, Keith
LPs: 10/12-Inch 33rpm
BACKSTREET: 81 5-10
Also see EMERSON, Keith, & The Nice
Also see EMERSON, LAKE & PALMER
Also see EMERSON, LAKE & POWELL

EMERSON, Keith, & The Nice
Singles: 7-Inch
MERCURY: 72 2-4
LPs: 10/12-Inch 33rpm
MERCURY: 72 12-15
Also see EMERSON, Keith
Also see EMERSON, LAKE & PALMER
Also see NICE

EMERSON, LAKE & PALMER
Singles: 7-Inch
ATLANTIC: 77-80 1-3
COTILLION: 71-72 2-3
MANTICORE: 74 2-3
Promotional Singles
ATLANTIC ("Brain Salad
Surgery"): 78 2-4
LPs: 10/12-Inch 33rpm
ATLANTIC (Except 281): 77-80 8-10
ATLANTIC (281; "Emerson, Lake
& Palmer"): 77 12-15
(With The London Philharmonic Orchestra. Also
contains interviews with the three members. Promo-
tional issue only.)
COTILLION: 71-72 12-15
MANTICORE: 73-74 10-12
Members: Keith Emerson; Greg Lake; Carl Palmer.
Also see ASIA
Also see EMERSON, Keith, & The Nice
Also see EMERSON, LAKE & POWELL
Also see 3

EMERSON, LAKE & POWELL
Singles: 7-Inch
POLYDOR: 86 ....$1-3
LPs: 10/12-Inch 33rpm
POLYDOR: 86 5-8
Members: Keith Emerson; Greg Lake; Cozy
Powell.
Also see EMERSON, Keith
Also see EMERSON, LAKE & PALMER
Also see LAKE, Greg
Also see POWELL, Cozy

EMMERSON, Les
Singles: 7-Inch
LION: 73 2-3

EMOTIONS
Singles: 7-Inch
BRAINSTORM: 68 3-5
CALLA: 65 4-6
JASON SCOTT: 4-8
KAPP: 62-63 4-6
KARATE: 64 4-6
LAURIE (3167; "Starlit
Night"): 63 4-6
PIO: 61 8-10
20TH CENTURY-FOX: 63-64 10-15
VARDAN: 65 3-5
LPs: 10/12-Inch 33rpm
MAGIC CARPET: 8-10
Members: Joe Favale; Tony Maltese; Don Colluri;
Larry Cusamanno; Joe Nigro; Sal Covais.

EMOTIONS
Singles: 12-Inch 33/45rpm
RED LABEL: 84 4-6
Singles: 7-Inch
ARC: 80-81 1-3
COLUMBIA: 76-81 1-3
STAX: 77-79 1-3
MOTOWN: 85 1-3
RED LABEL: 84 1-3
TWIN STACKS: 68 3-5
VOLT: 69-74 2-3
LPs: 10/12-Inch 33rpm
COLUMBIA: 76-81 5-8
MOTOWN: 85 5-8
RED LABEL: 84 5-8
STAX: 77-79 5-8
VOLT: 69-74 10-20
Members: Sheila Hutchinson; Wanda Hutchinson;
Jeanette Hutchinson.
Also see EARTH, WIND & FIRE & THE
EMOTIONS

EMPERORS
Singles: 7-Inch
BRUNSWICK: 67 ....$3-6
MALA: 66-67 4-8
TWO PLUS TWO: 66 4-8

ENCHANTERS
Singles: 7-Inch
BALD EAGLE: 58 4-6
BAMBOO: 61 4-6
EPSOM: 62 3-5
J.J. & M: 62 8-10
LOMA: 65-66 3-5
MERCER: 4-6
MUSITRON: 61 3-5
ORBIT: 59 10-15
SHARP: 60 12-20
STARDUST: 10-15
TOM TOM: 63 5-10
WARNER BROS: 64 3-5

ENCHANTMENT
Singles: 7-Inch
COLUMBIA: 82-84 1-3
DESERT MOON: 76 2-3
RCA VICTOR: 80 1-3
ROADSHOW: 77-78 1-3
UNITED ARTISTS: 76-77 1-3
LPs: 10/12-Inch 33rpm
COLUMBIA: 82 5-8
RCA VICTOR: 80 5-8
ROADSHOW: 77-78 8-10
UNITED ARTISTS: 77 8-10

ENDGAMES
Singles: 12-Inch 33/45rpm
FLIP: 83 4-6
MCA: 83 4-6
Singles: 7-Inch
MCA: 84 1-3
LPs: 10/12-Inch 33rpm
MCA: 84 5-8

ENERGETICS
Singles: 7-Inch
ATLANTIC: 79 1-3
LPs: 10/12-Inch 33rpm
ATLANTIC: 79 5-8

ENERGY
Singles: 7-Inch
SHOUT: 74 2-3

ENGLAND DAN & JOHN FORD COLEY
Singles: 7-Inch
A&M: 71-77 2-4
BIG TREE: 76-80 1-3

MCA: *80* $1-3
LPs: 10/12-Inch 33rpm
A&M: *71-73* 10-12
BIG TREE: *76-79* 8-10
MCA: *80* 5-8
Members: Dan Seals; John Ford Coley.
Also see ABBA / Spinners / Firefall / England
Dan & John Ford Coley
Also see SEALS, Dan
Also see SOUTHWEST F.O.B.

ENGLE, Priscilla
LPs: 10/12-Inch 33rpm
FRONTLINE: *86* 5-8

ENGLISH, Barbara Jean
Singles: 7-Inch
ALITHIA: *73-74* 2-3
LPs: 10/12-Inch 33rpm
ALITHIA: *73* 8-10

ENGLISH, Jackie
Singles: 7-Inch
VENTURE: *80* 1-3

ENGLISH, Scott
(Scott English & The Accents; Scott English &
The Dedications)
Singles: 7-Inch
DOT: *60* 8-10
JANUS (Except 171): *72* 2-3
JANUS (171; "Brandy"): *71* 8-10
JOKER: *62* 4-6
SPOKANE: *64* 10-15
SULTAN: *63* 10-15

ENGLISH BEAT
Singles: 12-Inch 33/45rpm
I.R.S.: *83-85* 4-6
Singles: 7-Inch
I.R.S.: *83-85* 1-3
LPs: 10/12-Inch 33rpm
I.R.S.: *82-85* 5-8
SIRE: *80-81* 5-8
Members: Andy Cox; David Steele.
Also see FINE YOUNG CANNIBALS

ENGLISH CONGREGATION
Singles: 7-Inch
ATCO: *72* 2-3
SIGNPOST: *73* 2-3
LPs: 10/12-Inch 33rpm
SIGNPOST: *73* 8-10

ENNIS, Ethel
Singles: 7-Inch
BASF: *73* 1-3
RCA VICTOR: *64-66* 2-3
SPIRAL: *71-72* 1-3

LPs: 10/12-Inch 33rpm
BASF: *73* $5-10
CAMDEN: *73* 5-8
RCA VICTOR: *64-65* 10-15

ENO, Brian
(Eno)
Singles: 7-Inch
ISLAND: *72* 2-3
LPs: 10/12-Inch 33rpm
ANTILLES: *73-78* 8-10
EDITIONS E.G.: *81-82* 5-8
ISLAND: *73-78* 8-10
PVC: *79* 5-8
SIRE: *81* 5-8
Also see BYRNE, David
Also see 801
Also see FRIPP & ENO
Also see ROXY MUSIC

ENTERTAINERS IV
Singles: 7-Inch
DORE: *66* 3-5

ENTWISTLE, John
(John Entwistle's Rigor Mortis; John Entwistle's
Ox)
Singles: 7-Inch
DECCA: *72* 2-4
TRACK: *73* 2-3
LPs: 10/12-Inch 33rpm
ATCO: *81* 5-8
DECCA: *71-72* 10-15
MCA/TRACK: *73-75* 8-10
Also see TOWNSHEND, Pete, & Ronnie Lane
Also see WHO

EON
Singles: 7-Inch
ARIOLA AMERICA: *78* 1-3
LPs: 10/12-Inch 33rpm
ARIOLA AMERICA: *78* 5-8
SCEPTER: *73* 8-10

EPIC SPLENDOR
Singles: 7-Inch
HOT BISCUIT: *67-68* 3-5
Picture Sleeves
HOT BISCUIT: *67* 5-10

EPOQUE, Belle:
see BELLE EPOQUE

EPPS, Preston
Singles: 7-Inch
ADMIRAL: *65* 3-5
EMBASSY: *62* 3-5
JO JO: *69* 2-4
MAJESTY: 3-5

ORIGINAL SOUND (Monaural): *59-61* . . **$4-6**
ORIGINAL SOUND (Stereo): *59* **8-10**
EPs: 7-Inch 33/45rpm
ORIGINAL SOUND: *60* **10-20**
LPs: 10/12-Inch 33rpm
ORIGINAL SOUND: *60-63* **25-50**
TOP RANK: *61* **25-50**

EQUALS
Singles: 7-Inch
PRESIDENT: *67-68* **4-8**
RCA VICTOR: *68* **3-6**
LPs: 10/12-Inch 33rpm
LAURIE: *67* **20-25**
PRESIDENT: *68-69* **15-20**
RCA VICTOR: *68* **10-12**
Member: Eddy Grant.
Also see GRANT, Eddy

ERAMUS HALL
Singles: 12-Inch 33/45rpm
CAPITOL: *84* **4-6**
Singles: 7-Inch
CAPITOL: *84* **1-3**
LPs: 10/12-Inch 33rpm
CAPITOL: *84* **5-8**

ERIC
Singles: 12-Inch 33/45rpm
MEMO: *84* **4-6**

ERIC B. & RAKIM
Singles: 7-Inch
4TH & B'WAY: *87-88* **1-3**
ZAKIA: *86* **1-3**
LPs: 10/12-Inch 33rpm
4TH & B'WAY: *87* **5-8**

ERNIE
(Jim Henson) / Sesame Street Kids
Singles: 7-Inch
COLUMBIA: *70* **1-3**
Also see HENSON, Jim

ERUPTION
Singles: 12-Inch 33/45rpm
ARIOLA AMERICA: *78* **4-6**
Singles: 7-Inch
ARIOLA AMERICA: *78* **1-3**
LPs: 10/12-Inch 33rpm
ARIOLA AMERICA: *78* **5-8**

ERWIN, Dee
(Big Dee Erwin)
Singles: 7-Inch
CUB: *68* **3-5**
ROULETTE: *65* **3-5**
Also see IRWIN, Big Dee

ESCORTS
Singles: 7-Inch
ALITHIA: *73-74* **$2-4**
LPs: 10/12-Inch 33rpm
ALITHIA: *73-74* **8-10**

ESCOVEDO, Coke
Singles: 7-Inch
MERCURY: *76-77* **1-3**
LPs: 10/12-Inch 33rpm
MERCURY: *76-77* **5-8**
Also see AZTECA
Also see SANTANA

ESMERALDA, Santa
Singles: 12-Inch 33/45rpm
CASABLANCA: *77-78* **4-6**
Singles: 7-Inch
CASABLANCA: *77-78* **2-3**
LPs: 10/12-Inch 33rpm
CASABLANCA: *77-80* **5-8**
Member: Leroy Gomez.

ESPOSITO, Joe "Bean"
Singles: 7-Inch
CASABLANCA: *83* **1-3**
Also see BROOKLYN DREAMS

ESQUIRE
LPs: 10/12-Inch 33rpm
GEFFEN: *87* **5-8**

ESQUIRES
Singles: 7-Inch
B&G: **3-6**
BUNKY: *67-68* **4-6**
CAPITOL: *69* **3-5**
JU-PAR: *76* **2-4**
LAMARR: *71* **2-4**
SALEM: *65* **4-8**
TOWER: *65* **4-8**
WAND: *68-69* **4-6**
LPs: 10/12-Inch 33rpm
BUNKY: *68* **12-15**
Member: Mill Edwards.

ESSENCE
Singles: 7-Inch
EPIC: *75-77* **2-3**
LPs: 10/12-Inch 33rpm
SAVOY: *78* **5-8**

ESSEX
Singles: 7-Inch
BANG: *66* **3-5**
ROULETTE: *63-64* **4-6**
LPs: 10/12-Inch 33rpm
ROULETTE: *63-64* **15-20**

Members: Anita Humes; Walter Vickers; Rodney
Taylor; Billie Hill; Rudolph Johnson.

ESSEX, David
Singles: 7-Inch
COLUMBIA: 73-76 .... $2-3
RSO: 79 1-3
UNI: 67 4-6
Picture Sleeves
UNI: 67 5-10
LPs: 10/12-Inch 33rpm
COLUMBIA: 73-75 8-10
MERCURY: 83 5-8

ETERNALS
Singles: 7-Inch
COLLECTABLES: 1-3
HOLLYWOOD: 59 10-15
WARWICK: 60 5-8
Members: Charles Girona; Alex Miranda; Fred
Hodge; Ernie Sierra; Arnold Torres; George Vil-
lanueva.

ETERNITY'S CHILDREN
Singles: 7-Inch
A&M: 67 3-5
TOWER: 68-69 3-5
Picture Sleeves
TOWER: 68 5-10
LPs: 10/12-Inch 33rpm
TOWER: 68 15-20

ETTA & HARVEY
Singles: 7-Inch
CHESS: 60 3-5
Members: Etta James; Harvey Fuqua.
Also see HARVEY & THE MOONGLOWS
Also see JAMES, Etta

ETZEL, Roy
Singles: 7-Inch
HICKORY: 63 2-3
MGM: 65-67 2-3
PRESIDENT: 61 2-4
TIME: 61 2-4
LPs: 10/12-Inch 33rpm
MGM: 65 8-12

EUBANKS, Jack
Singles: 7-Inch
MONUMENT: 61-64 3-8
LPs: 10/12-Inch 33rpm
MONUMENT: 66 10-20

EUCLID BEACH BAND
Singles: 7-Inch
EPIC/CLEVELAND INT'L: 78-79 1-3
SCENE: 78 2-3

LPs: 10/12-Inch 33rpm
EPIC: 79 .... $5-8

EUNICE
(With The Earl Palmer Combo; Eunice Russ
Frost)
Singles: 7-Inch
CLASSIC ARTISTS: 89 2-3
Also see GENE & EUNICE

EUROGLIDERS
Singles: 7-Inch
COLUMBIA: 84 1-3
LPs: 10/12-Inch 33rpm
COLUMBIA: 84 5-8
Member: Grace Knight.

EUROPE
Singles: 7-Inch
EPIC: 86-87 1-3
LPs: 10/12-Inch 33rpm
EPIC: 86-88 5-8
Members: Joey Tempest; John Leven; Mic
Michaeli; Kee Marcello; Ian Haughland.

EURYTHMICS
Singles: 12-Inch 33/45rpm
RCA VICTOR: 83-86 4-6
Singles: 7-Inch
RCA VICTOR: 83-87 1-3
LPs: 10/12-Inch 33rpm
RCA VICTOR: 83-88 5-8
Members: Annie Lennox; Dave Stewart.
Also see TOURISTS

EURYTHMICS, & Aretha Franklin
Singles: 12-Inch 33/45rpm
RCA VICTOR: 85 4-6
Singles: 7-Inch
RCA VICTOR: 85 1-3
Also see EURYTHMICS
Also see FRANKLIN, Aretha

EVANS, Linda
Singles: 7-Inch
ARIOLA: 79 1-3

EVANS, Margie
Singles: 7-Inch
ICA: 77 2-3
UNITED ARTISTS: 73 2-3

EVANS, Paul
(Paul Evans & The Curls)
Singles: 7-Inch
ATCO: 59-60 3-5
CARLTON: 61-62 3-5
CINNAMON INT'L: 80 1-3
COLLECTABLES: 1-3
COLUMBIA: 68 2-4

DECCA: *58* $4-6
DOT: *73* 2-3
EPIC: *64-65* 3-5
GUARANTEED: *59-60* 4-6
KAPP: *62-63* 3-5
LAURIE: *71* 2-3
MERCURY: *74-75* 2-3
MUSICOR: *77* 2-3
RCA VICTOR: *57* 4-6
RANWOOD: *72* 2-3
SPRING: *78-79* 1-3
LPs: 10/12-Inch 33rpm
CARLTON: *61* 25-50
GUARANTEED: *60* 30-50
KAPP: *64-66* 20-45

EVANS, Paul & Mimi
Singles: 7-Inch
EPIC: *64* 3-5
Also see EVANS, Paul

EVASIONS
Singles: 7-Inch
SAM: *81* 1-3

EVE
LPs: 10/12-Inch 33rpm
LHI: *70* 10-12

EVE ELEKTRO:
see ELEKTRO, Eve

EVERETT, Betty
(Betty Everett & The Daylighters)
Singles: 7-Inch
ABC: *66-67* 3-5
C.J.: *61-64* 4-6
CODRA: *57-58* 10-20
COLLECTABLES: 1-3
ERIC: 1-3
FANTASY: *70-74* 2-3
ONE-DERFUL: *62* 3-5
UNI: *68-69* 2-4
VEE JAY: *63-65* 3-5
LPs: 10/12-Inch 33rpm
FANTASY: *75* 8-10
SUNSET: *68* 10-12
UNI: *69* 10-12
VEE JAY: *64* 25-50
Also see BUTLER, Jerry, & Betty Everett

EVERETT, Betty / Ketty Lester
LPs: 10/12-Inch 33rpm
GRAND PRIX: 10-12
Also see LESTER, Ketty

EVERETT, Betty / Impressions
LPs: 10/12-Inch 33rpm
CUSTOM: 10-12

Also see EVERETT, Betty
Also see IMPRESSIONS

EVERETT, Leon
Singles: 7-Inch
ORLANDO: *80-86* $1-3
RCA VICTOR: *81-84* 1-3
TRUE: *77* 3-6
LPs: 10/12-Inch 33rpm
ORLANDO 1: *86* 5-8
RCA VICTOR: *81-84* 5-8
TRUE (1002; "Goodbye King Of
Rock & Roll"): *77* 10-20
(Price includes 18x23 bonus poster of Elvis Presley. Deduct $4-$8 if this poster is missing.)

EVERLY, Don
Singles: 7-Inch
ABC/HICKORY: *75-77* 2-3
ODE: *70-74* 2-4
LPs: 10/12-Inch 33rpm
ABC/HICKORY: *76-77* 8-10
ODE: *70-74* 8-10
Also see HARRIS, Emmylou

EVERLY, Phil
Singles: 7-Inch
CAPITOL: *83* 1-3
CURB: *80-81* 1-3
ELEKTRA: *79* 2-3
PYE: *73-76* 2-3
RCA VICTOR: *73* 2-4
LPs: 10/12-Inch 33rpm
ELECTRA: *79* 5-8
PYE: *75-76* 8-10
RCA VICTOR: *73* 8-10

EVERLY BROTHERS
Singles: 78rpm
CADENCE: *57-58* 10-20
COLUMBIA: *56* 15-25
Singles: 7-Inch
BARNABY: *70-76* 2-3
CADENCE (Silver & maroon
label): *57-61* 5-10
CADENCE (Red label): *61-62* 3-5
COLUMBIA: *56* 30-40
ERIC: 1-3
MERCURY: *84-86* 1-3
RCA VICTOR: *72-73* 2-3
WARNER BROS (Colored vinyl): 25-45
(Promotional issues only.)
WARNER BROS (Monaural): *60-74* 3-6
(Black vinyl.)
WARNER BROS (Stereo): *60* 15-25
(With an "S" prefix.)

Picture Sleeves

CADENCE: *57-60* $15-30
WARNER BROS: *60-66* 10-25

EPs: 7-Inch 33/45rpm

CADENCE: *57-61* 25-40
WARNER BROS: *60* 15-25

LPs: 10/12-Inch 33rpm

ARISTA: *84* 8-12
BARNABY (Except 4000 series): *70-74* .. 8-12
BARNABY (4000 series): *77* 6-10
CADENCE (3003; "The Everly
  Brothers"): *58* 75-125
CADENCE (3016; "Songs Our Daddy
  Taught Us"): *58* 45-60
CADENCE (3025; "The Everly
  Brothers Best"): *59* 75-100
  (With blue cover.)
CADENCE (3040; "The Fabulous Style
  Of The Everly Brothers"): *60* 50-75
CADENCE (3059; "Folk Songs"): *63* ... 35-40
CADENCE (3062; "15 Everly
  Hits"): *63* 45-65
CADENCE (25040; "The Fabulous Style
  Of The Everly Brothers"): *60* 55-65
CANDLELITE: *76* 10-15
HARMONY: *68-70* 10-12
MERCURY: *84-86* 5-8
PAIR: *84* 8-12
PASSPORT: *84-86* 5-8
RCA VICTOR: *72* 8-12
RHINO (Except picture discs): *85* 5-8
RHINO (Picture discs): *85* 8-10
RONCO: 8-10
WARNER BROS (135; "Souvenir
  Sampler, 10 Songs"): *61* 50-80
  (Promotional issue only.)
WARNER BROS (1381; "It's Everly
  Time"): *60* 25-40
WARNER BROS (1395; "A Date With
  The Everly Brothers"): *60* 30-40
  (With gatefold cover and wallet photos.)
WARNER BROS (1395; "A Date With
  The Everly Brothers"): *61* 15-20
  (With standard cover.)
WARNER BROS (1418; "Both Sides Of
  An Evening"): *61* 25-30
WARNER BROS (1430; "Instant
  Party"): *62* 20-30
WARNER BROS (1471; "Golden
  Hits"): *62* 20-30
WARNER BROS (1483; "Christmas With
  The Everly Brothers"): *61* 20-25
WARNER BROS (1513; "Great Country
  Hits"): *63* 20-25
WARNER BROS (1554; "Very Best Of

The Everly Brothers"): *64* $15-20
  (Yellow cover.)
WARNER BROS (1554; "Very Best Of
  The Everly Brothers"): *64* 10-15
  (Blue cover.)
WARNER BROS (1578; "Rock 'N'
  Soul"): *65* 20-25
WARNER BROS (1585; "Gone Gone
  Gone"): *65* 20-25
WARNER BROS (1605; "Beat &
  Soul"): *65* 15-25
WARNER BROS (1620; "In Our
  Image"): *66* 15-25
WARNER BROS (1646; "Two Yanks
  In London"): *66* 15-25
WARNER BROS (1676; "The Hit Sound
  Of The Everly Brothers"): *67* 15-20
WARNER BROS (1708; "The Everly
  Brothers Sing"): *67* 15-25
WARNER BROS (1752; "Roots"): *68* ...15-25
WARNER BROS (1858; "The Everly
  Brothers Show"): *70* 12-15
Members: Don Everly; Phil Everly.
Also see EVERLY, Don
Also see EVERLY, Phil

EVERY FATHER'S TEENAGE SON
Singles: 7-Inch

BUDDAH: *67* 3-5

EVERY MOTHER'S SON
Singles: 7-Inch

MGM: *67-68* 3-5
POLYDOR: 1-3

Picture Sleeves

MGM: *67* 3-6

LPs: 10/12-Inch 33rpm

MGM: *67* 10-20

EVERYTHING IS EVERYTHING
Singles: 7-Inch

VANGUARD APOSTOLIC: *69* 3-5

LPs: 10/12-Inch 33rpm

VANGUARD: *69* 15-20

EXCELLENTS
Singles: 7-Inch

BLAST (Red label): *62* 25-30
BLAST (Red & white label): *62-63* 8-15
BLAST (White label): *62* 40-60
  (Promotional issue only.)
COLLECTABLES: 1-3
MERMAID (106; "Love No One
  But You"): 60-75
  (Label pictures a mermaid.)

MERMAID (106; "Love No One
  But You"): $20-25
  (Label does not picture mermaid.)
OLD TIMER: *64* 4-6
  Also see EXCELLONS

EXCELLONS
(Excellents)
        Singles: 7-Inch
BOBBY: *64* 15-20
  Also see EXCELLENTS

EXCELS
        Singles: 7-Inch
GONE: *60* 10-15
R.S.V.P.: *61* 10-15

EXCITERS
        Singles: 7-Inch
BANG: *66* 3-5
LIBERTY: 2-3
ROULETTE: *64* 4-8
RCA VICTOR: *68-69* 3-6
SHOUT: *66-67* 3-6
TODAY: *70* 3-5
UNITED ARTISTS: *62-63* 5-10
        Picture Sleeves
ROULETTE: *64* 8-15
        LPs: 10/12-Inch 33rpm
RCA VICTOR: *69* 10-12
ROULETTE: *66* 15-20
SUNSET: *70* 10-12
TODAY: *71* 8-10
UNITED ARTISTS: *63* 25-50
  Members: Brenda Reid; Herb Rooney.
  Also see BRENDA & HERB

EXECUTIVE
        Singles: 7-Inch
20TH CENTURY-FOX: *81* 1-3

EXECUTIVE SUITE
        Singles: 7-Inch
BABYLON: *73-74* 2-3
UNITED ARTISTS: *75* 2-3

EXILE
        Singles: 7-Inch
ATCO: *77* 2-4
COLUMBIA: *69-70* 3-5
EPIC: *83-88* 1-3
WARNER BROS/CURB: *78-81* 1-3
WOODEN NICKEL: *72-73* 2-3
        LPs: 10/12-Inch 33rpm
EPIC: *83-86* 5-8
RCA VICTOR: *78* .5-8
WARNER BROS: *78-81* 5-8
WOODEN NICKEL: *73* 8-10

Members: J.P. Pennington; Les Taylor; Sonny Le-
Maire; Marlon Hargis; Steve Goetzman.

EXITS
        Singles: 7-Inch
GEMINI: *67* $3-5

EXODUS
        LPs: 10/12-Inch 33rpm
ARISTA: *87* 5-8

EXOTIC GUITARS
        Singles: 7-Inch
RANWOOD: *68-70* 2-4
        LPs: 10/12-Inch 33rpm
RANWOOD: *68-70* 5-8
  Member: Al Casey.
  Also see CASEY, Al

EXPOSE
        Singles: 12-Inch 33/45rpm
ARISTA: *85-87* 4-6
        Singles: 7-Inch
ARISTA: *85-88* 1-3
        LPs: 10/12-Inch 33rpm
ARISTA: *86-88* 5-8
  Members: Jeanette Jurado; Gioia Bruno; Ann Cur-
less.

EXPRESS, B.T: see B.T. EXPRESS

EXTRA Ts
        Singles: 7-Inch
SUNNYVIEW: *82* 1-3

EYE TO EYE
        Singles: 7-Inch
WARNER BROS: *82-83* 1-3
        LPs: 10/12-Inch 33rpm
WARNER BROS: *82* 5-8
  Also see MARSHALL-HAIN

EZO
        LPs: 10/12-Inch 33rpm
GEFFEN: *87* 5-8

F

F., Simon
(Simon Fellowes)
        Singles: 7-Inch
REPRISE: *87* 1-3

FCC
(Funky Communication Committee)
        Singles: 7-Inch
FREE FLIGHT (Black vinyl): *79* 2-3

FREE FLIGHT (Colored vinyl): *79* $3-5
(Promotional issue only.)
LPs: 10/12-Inch 33rpm
RCA VICTOR: *80* 5-8
FLB
Singles: 12-Inch 33/45rpm
WMOT: *78* 4-6
Singles: 7-Inch
WMOT: *78* 1-3
LPs: 10/12-Inch 33rpm
WMOT: *78* 5-8
F.R. DAVID: see DAVID, F.R.

FABARES, Shelley
Singles: 7-Inch
COLPIX (Except 721): *62-64* 4-8
COLPIX (721; "Football Season's
Over"): *64* 15-25
DUNHILL: *65-66* 10-20
ERIC: 1-3
VEE JAY: *64* 10-15
Picture Sleeves
COLPIX: *62* 15-25
LPs: 10/12-Inch 33rpm
COLPIX: *62* 30-35
Also see DARREN, James / Shelley Fabares /
Paul Petersen
Also see PETERSEN, Paul, & Shelley Fabares

FABIAN
(Fabian & The Fabulous Four)
Singles: 7-Inch
ABC: *74* 1-3
CHANCELLOR (Monaural): *58-61* 5-8
CHANCELLOR (Stereo): *58-60* 15-20
(With an "SC" prefix.)
COLLECTABLES: 1-3
CREAM: *77* 2-4
DOT: *62* 4-6
ERIC: 1-3
Picture Sleeves
CHANCELLOR: *59-61* 10-20
CREAM: *77* 2-4
EPs: 7-Inch 33/45rpm
CHANCELLOR: *59-60* 15-25
Promotional EPs
CHANCELLOR (5003; "Hold That
Tiger!"): *60* 20-30
(Promotional issue only.)
CHANCELLOR (5005; "The Fabulous
Fabian"): *60* 20-30
(Promotional issue only.)
CHANCELLOR (9802; "Young &
Wonderful"): *60* 20-30

4 SONGS FROM FABE'S NEWEST L. P.

THE

FABIAN "FACADE"

"YOUNG AND WONDERFUL"

Chancellor
RECORDS

LPs: 10/12-Inch 33rpm
ABC: *73* $10-12
CHANCELLOR: *59-62* 20-30
EVEREST: *83* 5-8
MCA: *85* 5-8
TRIP: *77* 8-10
UNITED ARTISTS: *75* 10-12
Also see FOUR DATES

FABIAN / Frankie Avalon
LPs: 10/12-Inch 33rpm
CHANCELLOR: *60* 30-35
MCA: *85* 5-8
Also see AVALON, Frankie
Also see FABIAN

FABRIC, Bent
Singles: 7-Inch
ATCO: *62-65* 2-3
Picture Sleeves
ATCO: *62* 3-6
LPs: 10/12-Inch 33rpm
ATCO: *62-63* 6-10
Also see BILK, Mr. Acker, & Bent Fabric

FABRIQUE, Tina
Singles: 12-Inch 33/45rpm
PRISM: *84* 4-6

FABULOUS COUNTS
Singles: 7-Inch
MOIRA: *68-70* 2-4
LPs: 10/12-Inch 33rpm
COTILLION: *69* 10-12

FABULOUS FARQUAHR
(Farquhr)
Singles: 7-Inch
ELEKTRA: *71* 2-3
VERVE/FORECAST: *68-69* 3-5
WARNER BROS: *70* 2-4

LPs: 10/12-Inch 33rpm
ELEKTRA: 70 . . . .$8-10
VERVE/FORECAST: 69 10-12

FABULOUS POODLES
Singles: 7-Inch
EPIC: 79 1-3
LPs: 10/12-Inch 33rpm
EPIC: 76-79 5-8

FABULOUS RHINESTONES
Singles: 7-Inch
JUST SUNSHINE: 72 2-4
LPs: 10/12-Inch 33rpm
JUST SUNSHINE: 72-73 8-10

FABULOUS THUNDERBIRDS
Singles: 7-Inch
CBS ASSOCIATED: 86-87 1-3
CHRYSALIS: 79-81 1-3
ELEKTRA: 88 1-3
LPs: 10/12-Inch 33rpm
CBS ASSOCIATED: 86-87 5-8
CHRYSALIS: 79-81 5-8
TAKOMA: 79 10-15
Members:Kim Wilson; Jimmie Vaughan; Preston
Hubbard; Fran Christina.
Also see SANTANA

FACE TO FACE
Singles: 12-Inch 33/45rpm
EPIC: 84 4-6
PORTRAIT: 84 4-6
Singles: 7-Inch
EPIC: 84 1-3
PORTRAIT: 84 1-3
LPs: 10/12-Inch 33rpm
EPIC: 84 5-8
MERCURY: 88 5-8

FACENDA, Tommy
Singles: 7-Inch
ATLANTIC: 59 8-15
LEGRANDE: 59 5-10
NASCO: 58 4-8
Also see KING CURTIS

FACES
Singles: 7-Inch
WARNER BROS: 71-75 3-5
LPs: 10/12-Inch 33rpm
MERCURY: 73 8-10
WARNER BROS: 71-76 10-20
Members: Rod Stewart; Ron Wood; Ronnie Lane.
Also see MC LAGAN, Ian
Also see SMALL FACES
Also see STEWART, Rod
Also see WOOD, Ron

FACHIN, Eria
Singles: 7-Inch
CRITIQUE: 88 . . . .$1-3

FACTS OF LIFE
Singles: 7-Inch
KAYVETTE: 76-77 2-3
LPs: 10/12-Inch 33rpm
KAYVETTE: 77 8-10

FAGEN, Donald
Singles: 7-Inch
WARNER BROS: 82-88 1-3
LPs: 10/12-Inch 33rpm
WARNER BROS: 82 5-8
Also see STEELY DAN

FAGEN, Donald, & Walter Becker
LPs: 10/12-Inch 33rpm
PVC: 85 5-8
Also see FAGEN, Donald

FAGIN, Joe
Singles: 7-Inch
MILLENNIUM: 82 1-3

FAIR, Yvonne
Singles: 7-Inch
DADE: 63 3-5
KING: 62 3-5
MOTOWN: 74-76 2-3
SMASH: 66 3-5
SOUL: 70 2-4
LPs: 10/12-Inch 33rpm
MOTOWN: 76 5-8

FAIRCHILD, Barbara
Singles: 7-Inch
CAPITOL: 86 1-3
COLUMBIA: 69-78 1-3
DOWN HOME: 80 1-3
KAPP: 68 2-4
LPs: 10/12-Inch 33rpm
AUDIOGRAPH: 82 5-8
COLUMBIA: 70-78 8-12
PAID: 81 5-8
Also see WALKER, Billy, & Barbara Fairchild

FAIRGROUND ATTRACTION
Singles: 7-Inch
RCA VICTOR: 88 1-3

FAIRPORT CONVENTION
Singles: 7-Inch
A&M: 71-72 2-4
LPs: 10/12-Inch 33rpm
A&M: 69-74 10-12
COTILLION: 70 10-15
ISLAND: 74-75 8-10

Also see DENNY, Sandy
Also see MATTHEWS, Ian
Also see THOMPSON, Richard

FAIRWEATHER
(Andy Fairweather-Low)
LPs: 10/12-Inch 33rpm
NEON: *71* $8-10
Also see FAIRWEATHER-LOW, Andy

FAIRWEATHER-LOW, Andy
Singles: 7-Inch
A&M: *75-77* 2-3
LPs: 10/12-Inch 33rpm
A&M: *74-76* 8-10
WARNER BROS: *80* 5-8
Also see WILLIE & THE POOR BOYS

FAITH, Adam
Singles: 7-Inch
AMY: *64-65* 3-5
CAPITOL: *65-66* 3-5
CUB: *59* 4-6
DOT: *62* 3-5
LPs: 10/12-Inch 33rpm
AMY: *65* 25-30
MGM: *61* 25-30
WARNER BROS: *74* 8-10

FAITH, Gene
Singles: 7-Inch
VIRTUE: *69-70* 2-4

FAITH, Percy, Orchestra
Singles: 78rpm
COLUMBIA: *50-57* 2-4
Singles: 7-Inch
COLUMBIA: *50-76* 2-5
Picture Sleeves
COLUMBIA: *60* 3-6
EPs: 7-Inch 33/45rpm
COLUMBIA: *50-59* 4-6
ROYALE: 4-8
LPs: 10/12-Inch 33rpm
COLUMBIA: *51-82* 5-15
HARMONY: *68-72* 5-10
Also see SANDERS, Felicia

FAITH BAND
Singles: 7-Inch
MERCURY/VILLAGE: *78-79* 1-3
VILLAGE: *78* 2-3
LPs: 10/12-Inch 33rpm
BROWN BAG: *73* 10-12
MERCURY: *78-79* 5-8
VILLAGE: *77* 8-10

FAITH, HOPE & CHARITY
Singles: 7-Inch
MAXWELL: *70* $2-4
RCA VICTOR: *75-77* 2-3
SUSSEX: *72* 2-4
20TH CENTURY-FOX: *78-80* 1-3
LPs: 10/12-Inch 33rpm
RCA VICTOR: *75* 8-10
SUSSEX: *72* 8-10
20TH CENTURY-FOX: *80* 5-8

FAITHFULL, Marianne
Singles: 12-Inch 33/45rpm
ISLAND: *83* 4-6
Singles: 7-Inch
ISLAND: *79* 1-3
LONDON (Except 1022): *64-72* 3-6
LONDON (1022; "Sister Morphine"): *69* .50-75
(With The Rolling Stones.)
Picture Sleeves
LONDON: *65* 4-8
LPs: 10/12-Inch 33rpm
ISLAND: *79-83* 5-8
LONDON: *65-69* 15-25
Also see ROLLING STONES

FALANA, Lola
Singles: 7-Inch
RCA VICTOR: *75* 2-3
REPRISE: *67* 5-10

FALCO
Singles: 12-Inch 33/45rpm
A&M: *83-86* 4-6
Singles: 7-Inch
A&M: *83-86* 1-3
LPs: 10/12-Inch 33rpm
A&M: *83-86* 5-8

FALCONS
Singles: 7-Inch
ANNA: *60* $30-40
ATLANTIC: *62-63* 3-5
BIG WHEEL: *66* 3-5
CHESS: *59* 4-6
FALCON: *57* 25-35
FLICK (Except 001): *59* 10-20
FLICK (001; "You're So Fine"): *59* ... 40-60
KUDO: *58* 10-20
LIBERTY: 1-3
LU PINE: *62-64* 3-5
MERCURY: *56* 15-20
SILHOUETTE: *57* 20-25
UNART: *59* 4-6
UNITED ARTISTS: *59-60* 4-6
Members: Wilson Pickett; Eddie Floyd; Arnet
Robinson; Joe Stubbs; Ben Rice; Lance Finnie.
Also see FLOYD, Eddie
Also see PICKETT, Wilson

FALLING PEBBLES
(Buckinghams)
Singles: 7-Inch
ALLEY CAT: 12-15
Also see BUCKINGHAMS

FALTERMEYER, Harold
Singles: 7-Inch
MCA: *85* 1-3
Also see LABELLE, Patti, & Harold Falter-
meyer

FALTSKOG, Agnetha
Singles: 7-Inch
POLYDOR: *83* 1-3
LPs: 10/12-Inch 33rpm
POLYDOR: *83* 5-8
Also see ABBA

FALTSKOG, Agnetha, & Peter Cetera
Singles: 7-Inch
ATLANTIC: *88* 1-3

FAME: see KIDS FROM "FAME"

FAME, Georgie
(Georgie Fame & The Blue Flames)
Singles: 7-Inch
EPIC: *68-70* 3-5
IMPERIAL: *65-67* 3-5
ISLAND: *75* 2-3
EPs: 7-Inch 33/45rpm
EPIC: *68* 4-8
(Jukebox issues only.)
LPs: 10/12-Inch 33rpm
EPIC: *68-70* 10-15
IMPERIAL: *65-66* 15-20
ISLAND: *75* 8-10

FAMILY
Singles: 7-Inch
LITTLE CITY: *77* $2-3
UNITED ARTISTS: *71-73* 2-4
LPs: 10/12-Inch 33rpm
REPRISE: *68-70* 15-20
UNITED ARTISTS: *71-73* 10-12
Members; Rick Gretch; John Weider.
Also see BLIND FAITH
Also see WEIDER, John

FAMILY
Singles: 12-Inch 33/45rpm
PAISLEY PARK: *85* 4-6
Singles: 7-Inch
PAISLEY PARK: *85* 1-3
LPs: 10/12-Inch 33rpm
PAISLEY PARK: *85* 5-8

FAMILY PLANN
Singles: 7-Inch
DRIVE: *75* 2-3

FANCY
Singles: 7-Inch
BIG TREE: *74* 2-3
POISON RING: *71* 3-5
LPs: 10/12-Inch 33rpm
BIG TREE: *74* 8-10
POISON RING: *71* 12-20
RCA VICTOR: *79* 5-8
Members: Al Ranaudo; Billy Durso.

FANNY
Singles: 7-Inch
CASABLANCA: *74-75* 2-3
REPRISE: *70-73* 2-5
LPs: 10/12-Inch 33rpm
CASABLANCA: *74* 8-10
REPRISE: *70-73* 10-12
Members: Jean Millington; June Millington; Alice
de Buhr; Nickey Barclay; Patti Quatro; Wendy
Haas; Brie Howard.

FANTASTIC FIVE KEYS
Singles: 7-Inch
CAPITOL: *62* 3-6
Also see FIVE KEYS

FANTASTIC FOUR
Singles: 7-Inch
EASTBOUND: *73-74* 2-3
RIC-TIC: *66-68* 3-5
SOUL: *68-70* 2-4
EASTBOUND: *74* 2-3
WESTBOUND: *75-79* 1-3
LPs: 10/12-Inch 33rpm
SOUL: *69* 10-12

20TH CENTURY-FOX/
  WESTBOUND: 76 .... $8-10
  WESTBOUND: 75-78 8-10

FANTASTIC JOHNNY C.
(Johnny Corley)
Singles: 7-Inch
KAMA SUTRA: 70 2-4
PHIL L.A. OF SOUL: 67-73 3-5
LPs: 10/12-Inch 33rpm
PHIL L.A. OF SOUL: 68 15-20

FANTASTICS
Singles: 7-Inch
BELL: 71-72 2-3
DERAM: 69 2-4

FANTASY
Singles: 7-Inch
IMPERIAL: 69 2-4
LIBERTY: 70 2-3
LPs: 10/12-Inch 33rpm
LIBERTY: 70 10-12

FANTASY
Singles: 12-Inch 33/45rpm
QUALITY: 83 4-6
Singles: 7-Inch
PAVILLION: 81 1-3
LPs: 10/12-Inch 33rpm
PAVILLION: 81-82 5-8

FANTAYZEE, Haysi:
see HAYSI FANTAYZEE

FARAGHER BROTHERS
Singles: 7-Inch
ABC: 76-77 2-3
POLYDOR: 79 1-3
LPs: 10/12-Inch 33rpm
ABC: 79 5-8
POLYDOR: 78-79 5-8

FARDON, Don
Singles: 7-Inch
CHELSEA: 73 2-3
GNP/CRESCENDO: 68 3-5
LPs: 10/12-Inch 33rpm
DECCA: 70 10-12
GNP/CRESCENDO: 68 15-20

FARGO, Donna
Singles: 7-Inch
ABC: 78 1-3
ABC/DOT: 74-77 1-3
CHALLENGE: 68 2-4
CLEVELAND INT'L: 84 1-3
COLUMBIA: 83 1-3
DECCA: 72 2-3
DOT: 72-74 2-3

MCA: 81 .... $1-3
MERCURY: 86-87 1-3
RCA VICTOR: 82 1-3
RAMCO: 67 3-5
SONGBIRD: 81 1-3
WARNER BROS: 76-81 1-3
Picture Sleeves
DOT: 72-74 2-4
WARNER BROS: 76-80 1-3
LPs: 10/12-Inch 33rpm
ABC/DOT: 74-77 5-10
DOT: 72-73 8-12
MCA: 4-6
MERCURY: 86 5-8
PICKWICK/HILLTOP: 6-10
RCA VICTOR: 83 5-8
SONGBIRD: 81 4-8
WARNER BROS: 76-80 5-10
  Also see BARE, Bobby / Donna Fargo / Jerry
Wallace

FARQUAHR:
see FABULOUS FARQUAHR

FARRELL, Eileen
Singles: 7-Inch
LONDON: 65 2-3
LPs: 10/12-Inch 33rpm
COLUMBIA: 60-63 10-20
HARMONY: 68 5-10

FARRENHEIT
LPs: 10/12-Inch 33rpm
WARNER BROS: 87 5-8

FARROW, Cee
Singles: 7-Inch
ROCSHIRE: 83 1-3

FASCINATIONS
Singles: 7-Inch
MAYFIELD: 66-67 3-5

FAST RADIO
Singles: 12-Inch 33/45rpm
RADAR: 83 4-6

FASTER PUSSYCAT
LPs: 10/12-Inch 33rpm
ELEKTRA: 87 5-8

FASTWAY
Singles: 7-Inch
COLUMBIA: 83-86 1-3
LPs: 10/12-Inch 33rpm
COLUMBIA: 83-86 5-8

FAT BOYS
Singles: 12-Inch 33/45rpm
SUTRA: 84-86 4-6

Also see JAZZ CRUSADERS
Also see TASTE OF HONEY

FELDER, Wilton, & Bobby Womack
Singles: 7-Inch
MCA: *80* $1-3
Also see FELDER, Wilton
Also see WOMACK, Bobby

FELDMAN, Victor
(Victor Feldman All Stars; Victor Feldman
Quartet; Victor Feldman Trio; Vic Feldman)
Singles: 7-Inch
AVA: *63* 2-3
INFINITY: *62* 2-3
PACIFIC JAZZ: *66* 2-3
VEE JAY: *64* 2-3
LPs: 10/12-Inch 33rpm
AVA: *63* 12-20
CONTEMPORARY: *58-60* 15-25
INTERLUDE: *59* 15-20
MODE: *58* 20-30
NAUTILUS: *82* 10-20
(Half-speed mastered.)
PACIFIC JAZZ: *67-68* 10-15
PALTO ALTO: *83-84* 5-8
RIVERSIDE: *61* 15-20
VEE JAY: *59-65* 15-25
WORLD PACIFIC: *62* 15-25

FELICIANO, Jose
Singles: 7-Inch
ALA: *80* 1-3
MOTOWN: *81-83* 1-3
PRIVATE STOCK: *76-77* 1-3
RCA VICTOR: *64-75* 2-4
LPs: 10/12-Inch 33rpm
CAMDEN: *72* 8-10
MOTOWN: *81* 5-8
PRIVATE STOCK: *76-77* 6-10
RCA VICTOR: *65-76* 8-15

FELICIANO, Jose
& Quincy Jones
LPs: 10/12-Inch 33rpm
RCA VICTOR(4096;"Mac Kenna's
Gold") : *69* 20-25
(Soundtrack.)
Also see FELICIANO, Jose
Also see JONES, Quincy

FELIX & JARVIS
Singles: 7-Inch
RFC/QUALITY: *82-83* 1-3

FELLER, Dick
Singles: 7-Inch
ASYLUM: *74-75* 1-3

UNITED ARTISTS: *72-80* $1-3
LPs: 10/12-Inch 33rpm
ASYLUM: *75* 6-10
AUDIOGRAPH ALIVE: *84* 5-8
UNITED ARTISTS: *73* 8-12

FELLINI, Suzanne
Singles: 7-Inch
CASABLANCA: *80* 1-3
LPs: 10/12-Inch 33rpm
CASABLANCA: *80* 5-8

FELONY
Singles: 7-Inch
ROCK 'N' ROLL: *83-84* 1-3
LPs: 10/12-Inch 33rpm
ROCK 'N' ROLL: *83* 5-8

FELTS, Narvel
Singles: 78rpm
MERCURY: *57* 5-10
Singles: 7-Inch
ABC: *76* 2-3
ABC/DOT: *75-77* 2-3
CINNAMON: *73-74* 2-3
COLLAGE: *79* 2-3
COMPLEAT: *82-83* 1-3
EVERGREEN: *82-87* 1-3
GMC: *81* 1-3
GROOVE: *63* 3-5
HI (2100 series): *67* 3-5
HI (2300 series): *76* 2-3
KARI: *80* 1-3
LOBO: *82* 1-3
MCA: *79* 1-3
MERCURY: *57* 5-10
PINK: *59-60* 8-15
LPs: 10/12-Inch 33rpm
ABC: *78* 5-8
ABC/DOT: *75-77* 8-10
CINNAMON: *73-74* 8-10
HI: *76* 8-10

FELTS, Narvel / Red Sovine / Mel Tillis
LPs: 10/12-Inch 33rpm
POWER PAK: 5-8
Also see FELTS, Narvel
Also see SOVINE, Red

FEMALE BODY INSPECTORS
Singles: 12-Inch 33/45rpm
WARNER BROS: *86* 4-6
Singles: 7-Inch
WARNER BROS: *86* 1-3

FENDER, Freddy
(Baldemar Huerta)
Singles: 7-Inch
ABC: 76-79 ....$2-3
ABC/DOT: 75-77 2-3
ARV INT'L: 75 2-3
ARGO: 60 8-10
DUNCAN: 59 10-15
GRT: 75-76 2-3
GOLDBAND: 4-6
IMPERIAL: 60 8-12
MCA: 82 1-3
NORCO: 63-65 4-6
STARFLITE: 79-80 2-3
WARNER BROS: 83 1-3
LPs: 10/12-Inch 33rpm
ABC: 78-79 5-8
ABC/DOT: 75-77 8-10
ACCORD: 81 5-8
GRT: 75 8-10
STARFLITE: 80 5-8

FENDERMEN
Singles: 7-Inch
COLLECTABLES: 1-3
CUCA: 60 30-40
DAB: 3-5
ERA: 72 1-3
ERIC: 1-3
SOMA: 60-61 4-8
LPs: 10/12-Inch 33rpm
SOMA (1240; "Mule Skinner
Blues"): 60 800-1200
Members: Phil Humphrey; Jim Sundquist.

FERGUSON, Helena
Singles: 7-Inch
COMPASS: 67-68 3-5

FERGUSON, Jay
Singles: 7-Inch
ASYLUM: 77-79 2-3
CAPITOL: 82 1-3
LPs: 10/12-Inch 33rpm
ASYLUM: 76-79 8-10
CAPITOL: 80-82 5-8
Also see SPIRIT

FERGUSON, Johnny
Singles: 7-Inch
MGM: 59-60 3-5

FERGUSON, Maynard
(Maynard Ferguson Sextet)
Singles: 78rpm
CAPITOL: 50-51 3-5
EMARCY: 54 3-5
MERCURY: 55 2-4

Singles: 12-Inch 33/45rpm
COLUMBIA: 79 ....$4-6
Singles: 7-Inch
CAMEO: 63 2-3
CAPITOL: 50-51 3-5
COLUMBIA: 71-82 1-3
EMARCY: 54 3-5
MERCURY: 55 2-4
ROULETTE: 59-62 2-4
EPs: 7-Inch 33/45rpm
EMARCY: 54-57 5-15
LPs: 10/12-Inch 33rpm
BETHLEHEM: 78 5-8
CAMEO: 63 12-20
COLUMBIA: 71-82 5-10
EMARCY (400 series): 76 5-10
EMARCY (1000 series): 81 5-8
EMARCY (26017; "Hollywood
Party"): 54 50-100
(10-Inch LP.)
EMARCY (26024;
"Dimensions"): 54 50-100
(10-Inch LP.)
EMARCY (36000 series): 55-57 20-40
ENTERPRISE: 68 8-12
MAINSTREAM (300 series): 71-72 ...6-10
MAINSTREAM (6000 series): 64 15-20
(Stereo.)
MAINSTREAM (56000 series): 64 12-20
(Monaural.)
MERCURY: 60 12-20
PALTO ALTO: 83 5-8
PRESTIGE: 69 8-12
ROULETTE: 58-72 12-25
SKYLARK: 53 20-40
TRIP: 74 5-8
Also see BASIE, Count, & Maynard Ferguson
Also see CONNOR, Chris, & Maynard Ferguson
Also see KENTON, Stan
Also see MANN, Herbie / Maynard Ferguson

FERKO STRING BAND
Singles: 78rpm
MEDIA: 55 2-4
SAVOY: 55 2-4
Singles: 7-Inch
ARGO: 63 2-3
MEDIA: 55 2-4
SAVOY: 55 2-4
LPs: 10/12-Inch 33rpm
ABC-PARAMOUNT: 63 10-15
ALSHIRE: 76 4-6
REGENT: 56-59 12-20
SURE: 65-73 6-12

FERRANTE & TEICHER
Singles: 78rpm
COLUMBIA: *53* $2-5
ENTRE: *53* 3-6
Singles: 7-Inch
ABC-PARAMOUNT: *58-62* 2-4
COLUMBIA: *53* 2-5
ENTRE: *53* 3-6
UNITED ARTISTS: *59-79* 1-3
Picture Sleeves
UNITED ARTISTS: *60-69* 2-4
EPs: 7-Inch 33/45rpm
ABC-PARAMOUNT: 4-8
MGM: *54* 10-20
UNITED ARTISTS: *69* 4-8
LPs: 10/12-Inch 33rpm
ABC: *73-76* 5-10
ABC-PARAMOUNT: *58-66* 8-15
COLUMBIA: *55-73* 8-15
DORAL: 10-20
(Promotional mail-order issue, from Doral cigarettes.)
GUEST STAR: *64* 4-8
HARMONY: *64-70* 5-10
LIBERTY: *81-84* 5-8
MGM: *54* 20-40
METRO: *66* 5-10
MISTLETOE: *75* 4-6
SUNSET: *70-71* 5-10
WESTMINSTER: *55-58* 12-20
UNART: *67* 5-10
UNITED ARTISTS: *60-80* 5-15
URANIA: 4-8
Members: Arthur Ferrante; Louis Teicher.

FERRARI
Singles: 12-Inch 33/45rpm
SUGAR HILL: *82* 4-6

FERRER, Jose
(Jose Ferrer & The Ferrers)
Singles: 78rpm
COLUMBIA: *54-55* $2-4
Singles: 7-Inch
COLUMBIA: *54-55* 2-4
EPIC: *68* 1-3
RCA VICTOR: *60* 2-3
Picture Sleeves
RCA VICTOR: *60* 3-6
LPs: 10/12-Inch 33rpm
MGM: *62-65* 6-12
Also see CLOONEY, Rosemary, & Jose Ferrer

FERRY, Bryan
Singles: 12-Inch 33/45rpm
WARNER BROS: *85* 4-6
Singles: 7-Inch
ATLANTIC: *74-79* 2-3
WARNER BROS: *85* 1-3
LPs: 10/12-Inch 33rpm
ATLANTIC: *72-78* 10-12
REPRISE: *87-88* 5-8
WARNER BROS: *85* 5-8
Also see ROXY MUSIC
Also see TANGERINE DREAM / Jon Anderson / Bryan Ferry

FESTIVAL
Singles: 7-Inch
RSO: *80* 1-3
LPs: 10/12-Inch
RSO: *80* 5-8

FEVA, Sandra
Singles: 7-Inch
CATAWBA: *87* 1-3
KRISMA: *86* 1-3
VENTURE: *79-81* 1-3
LPs: 10/12-Inch 33rpm
VENTURE: *81* 5-8

FEVER
Singles: 12-Inch 33/45rpm
FANTASY: *79-82* 4-6
JDC: *85* 4-6
Singles: 7-Inch
FANTASY: *79-82* 1-3
LPs: 10/12-Inch 33rpm
FANTASY: *79-80* 5-8

FEVER TREE
Singles: 7-Inch
AMPEX: *70* 4-8
MAINSTREAM: *67* 5-10
UNI: *68-69* 5-10
LPs: 10/12-Inch 33rpm
AMPEX: *70* 12-20

MCA: 76 .... $8-10
UNI: 68-70 15-30

FIDELITYS
Singles: 7-Inch
BATON: 58 10-15
SIR: 59-60 8-10

FIEDLER, Arthur:
see BOSTON POPS ORCHESTRA

FIELD, Sally
Singles: 7-Inch
COLGEMS: 67-68 2-4
Picture Sleeves
COLGEMS: 67 3-6
LPs: 10/12-Inch 33rpm
COLGEMS: 67 10-20

FIELDS, Ernie
Singles: 7-Inch
CAPITOL: 64 2-4
RENDEZVOUS: 59-62 3-5
LPs: 10/12-Inch 33rpm
RENDEZVOUS: 60 30-40

FIELDS, Kim
Singles: 7-Inch
CRITIQUE: 84 1-3

FIELDS, Richard "Dimples"
Singles: 12-Inch 33/45rpm
RCA VICTOR: 84-85 4-6
Singles: 7-Inch
BOARDWALK: 81-83 1-3
COLUMBIA: 87 1-3
RCA VICTOR: 84-85 1-3
LPs: 10/12-Inch 33rpm
BOARDWALK: 81-82 5-8
RCA VICTOR: 84 5-8

FIELDS, W. C.
LPs: 10/12-Inch 33rpm
AMERICAN: 75 .... $5-8
COLUMBIA: 69-77 6-10
DECCA: 68 8-12
HARMONY: 70 6-10
HUDSON: 60 15-20
MARK '56 ("Original Radio Broadcast") 10-15
(Coca-Cola special products issue.)

FIELDS, W. C., & Mae West
LPs: 10/12-Inch 33rpm
HARMONY: 70 6-10
PROSCENIUM: 60 15-20
  Also see FIELDS, W. C.
  Also see WEST, Mae

FIESTA
Singles: 7-Inch
ARISTA: 78 1-3

FIESTAS
Singles: 7-Inch
ATLANTIC: 1-3
COLLECTABLES: 1-3
OLD TOWN (1000 series): 59-60 5-10
OLD TOWN (1100 series): 61-65 4-8
RESPECT: 75 2-3
STRAND: 61 10-15
VIGOR: 74 1-3
  Members: Tom Bullock; Eddie Morris; Sam In-
  galls; Preston Love.
  Also see ROBERT & JOHNNY / Fiestas

FIFTH ANGEL
LPs: 10/12-Inch 33rpm
EPIC: 88 5-8

FIFTH DIMENSION
Singles: 7-Inch
ABC: 75-76 1-3
ARISTA: 75 2-3
BELL: 70-74 2-4
MOTOWN: 78-79 1-3
SOUL CITY: 66-70 2-4
SUTRA: 83 1-3
Picture Sleeves
SOUL CITY: 67-69 3-6
LPs: 10/12-Inch 33rpm
ARISTA: 75 8-10
BELL: 70-74 8-10
KORY: 77 8-10
MOTOWN: 78-79 5-8
RHINO: 86 5-8
SOUL CITY: 67-70 10-15
  Members: Marilyn McCoo; Billy Davis, Jr;
  Lamonte McLemore; Florence LaRue; Ron
  Townson.

Also see MAMAS & THE PAPAS / Association / Fifth Dimension
Also see MC COO, Marilyn, & Billy Davis Jr.

FIFTH ESTATE
Singles: 7-Inch
JUBILEE: 67-69 .... $3-5
RED BIRD: 66 3-5
LPs: 10/12-Inch 33rpm
JUBILEE: 67 20-25

50 GUITARS OF TOMMY GARRETT
Singles: 7-Inch
LIBERTY: 66-68 1-3
LPs: 10/12-Inch 33rpm
LIBERTY: 61-71 5-10
MUSICOR: 76-78 4-6
UNITED ARTISTS: 73 5-8
Also see GARRETT, Tommy

52ND STREET
Singles: 12-Inch 33/45rpm
A&M: 83 4-6
MCA: 85-87 4-6
PROFILE: 84 4-6
Singles: 7-Inch
MCA: 85-86 1-3
LPs: 10/12-Inch 33rpm
MCA: 86 5-8

FIGURES ON THE BEACH
Singles: 12-Inch 33/45rpm
METRO AMERICAN: 84 4-6

FILE 13
Singles: 12-Inch 33/45rpm
PROFILE: 84 4-6

FINE YOUNG CANNIBALS
Singles: 12-Inch 33/45rpm
I.R.S.: 86 4-6
Singles: 7-Inch
I.R.S.: 86 1-3
LPs: 10/12-Inch 33rpm
I.R.S.: 86 5-8
Members: Roland Gift; Danny Cox; David Steele.
Also see ENGLISH BEAT

FINESSE & SYNQUIS
LPs: 10/12-Inch 33rpm
MCA: 88 5-8

FINISHED TOUCH
Singles: 7-Inch
MOTOWN: 78 1-3
LPs: 10/12-Inch 33rpm
MOTOWN: 78 5-8

FINN, Tim
Singles: 7-Inch
A&M: 83 .... $1-3
LPs: 10/12-Inch 33rpm
A&M: 83 5-8
Also see SPLIT ENZ

FINNEGAN, Larry
Singles: 7-Inch
CORAL: 62 3-5
OLD TOWN: 62-63 5-8
RIC: 64 8-10

FINNEY, Albert
Singles: 7-Inch
MOTOWN: 77 1-3
LPs: 10/12-Inch 33rpm
MOTOWN: 77 5-8

FIONA
(Fiona Flanagan)
Singles: 7-Inch
ATLANTIC: 84-85 1-3
LPs: 10/12-Inch 33rpm
ATLANTIC: 84-85 5-8

FIORILLO, Elisa
Singles: 7-Inch
CHRYSALIS: 88 1-3
LPs: 10/12-Inch 33rpm
CHRYSALIS: 88 5-8

FIRE & RAIN
Singles: 7-Inch
MERCURY: 73 2-4
LPs: 10/12-Inch 33rpm
MERCURY: 73 8-10

FIRE INC.
Singles: 7-Inch
MCA: 84 1-3

FIREBALLET
Singles: 7-Inch
PASSPORT: 75-76 1-3
LPs: 10/12-Inch 33rpm
PASSPORT: 75-76 8-10

FIREBALLS
Singles: 7-Inch
ATCO: 67-70 3-5
DOT: 63-67 4-6
KAPP (248; "Fireball"): 59 35-50
TOP RANK (Monaural): 59-61 5-10
TOP RANK (Stereo): 59-60 15-20
(With an "ST" following the number.)
WARWICK: 61 4-6
EPs: 7-Inch 33/45rpm
TOP RANK (1000; "The Fireballs"): 60 . . 40-60

LPs: 10/12-Inch 33rpm
ATCO: *68* $10-14
TOP RANK: *60* 35-45
WARWICK (2042; "Here Are The
  Fireballs"): *61* 45-55
  Members: Chuck Tharp; George Tomsco; Dan
  Trammell; Eric Budd; Stan Lark; Doug Roberts;
  Jimmy Gilmer; Keith McCormick.
  Also see GILMER, Jimmy
  Also see STRING-A-LONGS

FIREFALL
Singles: 7-Inch
ATLANTIC: *76-81* 1-3
Picture Sleeves
ATLANTIC: *78* 1-3
LPs: 10/12-Inch 33rpm
ATLANTIC: *76-82* 5-8
  Members: Rick Roberts; Jock Bartley; Larry Bur-
  nette; Mike Clark; Scott Kirkpatrick; Dave Muse;
  Mark Andes; Peter Graves.
  Also see ABBA / Spinners / Firefall / England
Dan & John Ford Coley
  Also see MANILOW, Barry / Firefall

FIREFLIES
Singles: 7-Inch
CANADIAN AMERICAN: *60* 4-6
ERIC: 1-3
HAMILTON: *63* 3-5
RIBBON: *59-60* 5-8
TAURUS: *62-64* 8-12
LPs: 10/12-Inch 33rpm
TAURUS (1002; "You Were
  Mine"): *61* 75-100
  (Monaural.)
TAURUS (1002; "You Were
  Mine"): *61* 250-350
  (Stereo.)
  Member: Ritchie Adams.

FIREFLY
Singles: 7-Inch
A&M: *75* 2-3
EMERGENCY: *81* 1-3

FIRESIGN THEATRE
Singles: 7-Inch
COLUMBIA (Except 34): *69* 2-4
COLUMBIA (34; "This Side"): *70* 3-5
  (One-sided promotional issue.)
Picture Sleeves
COLUMBIA (34; "This Side"): *70* 4-6
LPs: 10/12-Inch 33rpm
BUTTERFLY: *77* 5-8
COLUMBIA: *69-74* 8-12
EPIC: *74* 5-10
RHINO: *79-82* 5-8

FIRM
Singles: 7-Inch
ATLANTIC: *85-86* $1-3
LPs: 10/12-Inch 33rpm
ATLANTIC: *85-86* 5-8
  Members: Jimmy Page; Paul Rodgers; Tony
  Franklin; Chris Slade.
  Also see BAD COMPANY
  Also see MANN, Manfred
  Also see PAGE, Jimmy
  Also see RODGERS, Paul

FIRST CHOICE
Singles: 12-Inch 33/45rpm
FIRST CHOICE: *83* 4-6
SALSOUL: *84* 4-6
Singles: 7-Inch
GOLD MINE: *77-79* 2-3
PHILLY GROOVE: *73-74* 2-4
WARNER BROS: *76* 2-3
LPs: 10/12-Inch 33rpm
GOLD MINE: *77-80* 5-8
KORY: *77* 8-10
PHILLY GROOVE: *73-74* 8-10

FIRST CIRCLE
Singles: 7-Inch
EMI AMERICA: *87* 1-3

FIRST CLASS
Singles: 7-Inch
ALL PLATINUM: *76-77* 2-3
EBONY SOUNDS: *75* 2-3
PRIVATE STOCK/UK: *76* 1-3
TODAY: *74* 2-4
UK: *74-75* 2-3
LPs: 10/12-Inch 33rpm
ALL PLATINUM: *76* 5-8
PARK-WAY: *80* 5-8
SUGARHILL: *81* 5-8
UK: *74* 8-10
  Members: John Carter; Charles Mills; Tony Bur-
  rows; Del John; Spencer James; Eddie Richards;
  Robin Shaw; Clive Barrett.

FIRST EDITION
Singles: 7-Inch
REPRISE: *67-68* 3-6
LPs: 10/12-Inch 33rpm
REPRISE: *67-68* 12-20
  Members: Kenny Rogers; Mike Settle; Thelma Lou
  Camacho; Terry Williams; Mickey Jones.
  Also see NEW CHRISTY MINSTRELS
  Also see ROGERS, Kenny, & The First Edi-
tion

FIRST FAMILY
Singles: 7-Inch
POLYDOR: 74 .... $2-4

FIRST FIRE
LPs: 10/12-Inch 33rpm
TORTOISE INT'L: 78 5-8

FIRST FOUR
Singles: 7-Inch
STRATA: 65 3-5

FIRST GEAR
LPs: 10/12-Inch 33rpm
MYRRH: 72 8-10

FIRST LOVE
Singles: 12-Inch 33/45rpm
CHYCAGO INT'L: 82 4-6
Singles: 7-Inch
CHYCAGO INT'L: 82 1-3
CIM: 83 1-3
DAKAR: 80 1-3
LPs: 10/12-Inch 33rpm
CHYCAGO INT'L: 82 5-8

FISCHOFF, George
(George Fischoff Keyboard Komplex; George
Fischoff & The Peppers; George Fischoff & The
Luv Ens)
Singles: 7-Inch
COLUMBIA: 77 1-3
DRIVE: 79 1-3
HERITAGE: 81 1-3
P.I.P.: 75 1-3
RANWOOD: 76 1-3
REWARD: 84 1-3
UNITED ARTISTS: 72-74 2-3

FISHBONE
LPs: 10/12-Inch 33rpm
COLUMBIA: 88 5-8

FISCHOFF, George
(George Fischoff Keyboard Komplex; George
Fischoff & The Peppers; George Fischoff & The
Luv Ens)
Singles: 7-Inch
COLUMBIA: 77 1-3
DRIVE: 79 1-3
HERITAGE: 81 1-3
P.I.P: 75 1-3
RANWOOD: 76 1-3
REWARD: 84 1-3
UNITED ARTISTS: 72-74 2-3

FISHER, Eddie
Singles: 78rpm
RCA VICTOR: 50-57 2-5

Singles: 7-Inch
ABC-PARAMOUNT: 61 .... $2-4
DOT: 65-66 2-5
MUSICOR: 69 2-4
RCA VICTOR (3000 through 6000
   series): 50-57 4-8
RCA VICTOR (7000 through 9000
   series): 7-68 3-6
RAMROD: 60-63 2-3
7 ARTS: 61 2-3
TRANS ATLAS: 62 2-3
Picture Sleeves
RCA VICTOR (5000 series): 53-55 10-20
RCA VICTOR (6000 series): 55-57 8-15
EPs: 7-Inch 33/45rpm
RCA VICTOR: 51-58 10-20
LPs: 10/12-Inch 33rpm
CAMDEN: 63 6-10
DOT: 65-67 8-15
HAMILTON: 66 6-10
RCA VICTOR (Except ANL1
   series): 51-72 10-20
RCA VICTOR (ANL1 series): 75 5-8
RAMROD: 60-63 10-15
Also see COMO, Perry, & Eddie Fisher

FISHER, Mary Ann
Singles: 7-Inch
FIRE: 59-60 3-5
IMPERIAL: 62 3-6
SEG-WAY: 61 5-10

FISHER, Toni
(Miss Toni Fisher)
Singles: 7-Inch
BIG TOP: 62 3-6
CAPITOL: 67 2-4
COLLECTABLES: 1-3
COLUMBIA: 61 3-6
ERA: 72 1-3
SIGNET: 59-64 4-8
SMASH: 63 4-8

FISHER, Willie
Singles: 7-Inch
TIGRESS: 77 1-3

FIT
Singles: 7-Inch
A&M: 88 1-3

FITZGERALD, Ella
Singles: 78rpm
DECCA (800 through 3000 series): 36-41 .5-10
DECCA (18000 through 26000
   series): 42-49 4-8
VERVE: 54-57 2-5

Singles: 7-Inch
CAPITOL: *67-68* $1-3
DECCA (27000 through 29000
   series): *50-56* 3-5
DECCA (30000 series): *56-67* 2-3
PABLO: *75* 1-3
PRESTIGE: *69* 2-4
REPRISE: *69-71* 1-3
VERVE: *54* 3-5
VERVE (10000 series): *56-59* 2-4
VERVE (10100 through 10300 series,
   except 10340): *60-65* 2-3
VERVE (10340; "Ringo Beat"): *64* 6-12
Picture Sleeves
VERVE: *59-60* 4-8
EPs: 7 Inch 33/45rpm
DECCA: *50-58* 15-30
VERVE: *56-61* 10-25
LPs: 10/12-Inch 33rpm
ATLANTIC: *72* 5-10
BAINBRIDGE: *81* 5-8
CAPITOL (2000 series): *67-68* 8-12
CAPITOL (11000 series): *78* 5-8
CAPITOL (16000 series): *80* 4-6
COLUMBIA: *73* 5-8
CORAL: *73* 4-6
DECCA (156; "The Best Of Ella
   Fitzgerald"): *58* 25-35
   (Black label with silver print.)
DECCA (156; "The Best Of Ella
   Fitzgerald"): *65* 15-20
   (Black label with horizontal rainbow band.)
DECCA (4000 series): *61-67* 10-20
DECCA (5084; "Souvenir Album"): *50* . 75-125
   (10-Inch LP.)
DECCA (5300; "Gershwin Songs"): *51* . 75-125
   (10-Inch LP.)
DECCA (8000 series): *55-59* 20-40
EVEREST: *73* 5-8
MCA: *76-82* 5-8
MGM: *70* 6-12
MPS: *72* 6-10
METRO: *65-66* 10-15
OLYMPIC: *74* 5-8
PABLO: *75-83* 5-8
REPRISE: *69-71* 8-12
VERVE (2500 & 2600 series): *76-82* 5-10
   (Reads "Manufactured By MGM Record Corp.," or
   mentions either Polydor or Polygram at bottom of
   label.)
VERVE (4001 through 4009): *56* 25-50
   (Reads "Verve Records, Inc." at bottom of label.)

VERVE (4010;"Ella Fitzgerald
   Sings The Duke Ellington Song
   Book"): *56* $75-125
   (4-LP set.)
VERVE (4013 through 4015): *57* 20-40
   (Reads "Verve Records, Inc." at bottom of label.)
VERVE (4019; "Ella Fitzgerald Sings
   The Irving Berlin Song Book"): *58* 20-40
VERVE (4020 through 4028): *58-59* 20-40
   (Reads "Verve Records, Inc." at bottom of label.)
VERVE (4029; "Ella Fitzgerald Sings The
   George & Ira Gershwin
   Songbook"): *59* 40-60
   (5-LP boxed set, containing individual LPs 4024
   through 4028.)
VERVE (4036 through 4071): *59-66* 10-20
VERVE (6000 series): *57-59* 20-35
   (Reads"Verve Records, Inc." at bottom of label.)
VERVE (6100 series): *60* 15-20
   (Reads"Verve Records, Inc." at bottom of label.)
VERVE (8200 series): *58* 20-30
   (Reads"Verve Records, Inc." at bottom of label.)
VERVE (64036 through 64071): *59-66* .. 10-20
VERVE (67000 & 68000 series): *67-73* .. 8-15
VERVE (2610000 series): *83* 20-30
VOCALION: *67* 6-10
   Also see RIDDLE, Nelson

FITZGERALD, Ella, & Louis Armstrong
EPs: 7-Inch 33/45rpm
VERVE: *56* 15-30
LPs: 10/12-Inch 33rpm
METRO: *67* 5-10
VERVE: *56* 30-45
   Also see ARMSTRONG, Louis

FITZGERALD, Ella, & Count Basie
LPs: 10/12-Inch 33rpm
PABLO: *79* 5-8
VERVE: *63* 15-20
   Also see BASIE, Count

FITZGERALD, Ella / Bill Doggett
Singles: 7-Inch
DECCA: *53* 2-5
LPs: 10/12-Inch 33rpm
VERVE: *62* 10-20
   Also see DOGGETT, Bill

FITZGERALD, Ella, & Duke Ellington
Singles: 7-Inch
VERVE: *66* 2-3
LPs: 10/12-Inch 33rpm
VERVE: *65-67* 10-20
   Also see ELLINGTON, Duke

FITZGERALD, Ella / Billie Holiday
LPs: 10/12-Inch 33rpm
MCA: 76 .... $5-8
VERVE: 58 25-40
Also see HOLIDAY, Billie

FITZGERALD, Ella / Billie Holiday / Lena Horne
LPs: 10/12-Inch 33rpm
COLUMBIA: 56 25-50
Also see HOLIDAY, Billie
Also see HORNE, Lena

FITZGERALD, Ella, & The Ink Spots
Singles: 78rpm
DECCA (18000 series): 44-45 3-6
EPs: 7-Inch 33/45rpm
DECCA: 53 5-10
Also see INK SPOTS

FITZGERALD, Ella, & Antonio Carlos Jobim
LPs: 10/12-Inch 33rpm
PABLO: 81 5-8
Also see JOBIM, Antonio Carlos

FITZGERALD, Ella, & Louis Jordan
Singles: 78rpm
DECCA (23000 series): 46 3-6
Also see JORDAN, Louis

FITZGERALD, Ella, & Peggy Lee
LPs: 10/12-Inch 33rpm
DECCA (8166; "Pete Kelly's
Blues"): 56 35-50
Also see LEE, Peggy

FITZGERALD, Ella, & Oscar Peterson
LPs: 10/12-Inch 33rpm
PABLO: 76 5-8
Also see FITZGERALD, Ella
Also see PETERSON, Oscar

FIVE AMERICANS
Singles: 7-Inch
ABC-PARAMOUNT: 65 4-6
ABNAK (Except 109): 67-69 5-10
ABNAK (109; "I See The Light"): 65 ... 15-20
Note: Most Abnak singles were colored vinyl.
HBR: 65-66 3-5
JETSTAR: 65 4-6
Picture Sleeves
ABNAK: 68 10-15
HBR: 66 10-20
LPs: 10/12-Inch 33rpm
ABNAK: 67-68 20-30
HBR: 66 20-30

FIVE BLOBS

Singles: 7-Inch
COLUMBIA: 58 .... $4-8
JOY: 59 8-15
Member: Bernie Nee.

FIVE BOROUGHS
Singles: 7-Inch
AVENUE D (Black vinyl): 88 2-3
AVENUE D (Colored vinyl): 88 3-5
Members: Frank Iovino; Dave Strum; Geno
Radicello; Charlie Notobartolo; Bruce Goldie.

FIVE BY FIVE
Singles: 7-Inch
PAULA: 67-70 3-6
LPs: 10/12-Inch 33rpm
PAULA: 69 15-20

5 CHANELS
(Chanels)
Singles: 7-Inch
DEB: 58 8-10

FIVE DU-TONES
Singles: 7-Inch
ONE-DERFUL: 63-65 4-6

FIVE EMPREES
Singles: 7-Inch
FREEPORT: 65-66 3-5
SMASH: 66 3-5
LPs: 10/12-Inch 33rpm
FREEPORT: 65-66 25-35
Also see FIVE EMPRESSIONS

FIVE EMPRESSIONS
Singles: 7-Inch
FREEPORT: 65 6-10
Also see FIVE EMPREES

FIVE FLIGHTS UP
Singles: 7-Inch
T.A.: 70-71 2-4

FIVE KEYS

Singles: 78rpm

ALADDIN (3085; "With A Broken
Heart"): *51* $50-100
ALADDIN (3099; "The Glory Of
Love"): *51* 50-100
ALADDIN (3113; "It's Christmas
Time"): *51* 50-100
ALADDIN (3127; "Red Sails In
The Sunset"): *52* 75-125
ALADDIN (3131; "Mistakes"): *52* 200-350
ALADDIN (3136; "I Hadn't Anyone
Til You"): *52* 50-100
ALADDIN (3158; "I Cried For
You"): *52* 150-300
ALADDIN (3167; "Can't Keep
From Crying"): *53* 150-250
ALADDIN (3175; "There Ought
To Be A Law"): *53* 50-100
ALADDIN (3190; "These Foolish
Things"): *53* 40-80
ALADDIN (3204; "Teardrops In
Your Eyes"): *53* 40-80
ALADDIN (3214; "My Saddest
Hour"): *53* 40-80
ALADDIN (3228; "Someday
Sweetheart"): *54* 40-60
ALADDIN (3245; "Deep In My
Heart"): *54* 40-60
ALADDIN (3263; "My Love"): *55* 75-125
ALADDIN (3312; "Story Of Love"): *56* .25-50
CAPITOL: *54-57* 8-15
GROOVE (0031; "I'll Follow
You"): *51* 400-600

Singles: 7-Inch

ALADDIN (3085; "With A Broken
Heart"): *51* 400-600
ALADDIN (3099; "The Glory Of
Love"): *51* 250-500
ALADDIN (3113; "It's Christmas
Time"): *51* 250-500
ALADDIN (3127; "Red Sails In
The Sunset"): *52* 500-750
ALADDIN (3131; "Mistakes"): *52* 500-750
ALADDIN (3136; "I Hadn't Anyone
Til You"): *52* 500-750
ALADDIN (3158; "I Cried For
You"): *52* 300-600
ALADDIN (3167; "Can't Keep
From Crying"): *53* 250-500
ALADDIN (3175; "There Ought
To Be A Law"): *53* 250-500
ALADDIN (3190; "These Foolish
Things"): *53* 600-900

ALADDIN (3204; "Teardrops In
Your Eyes"): *53* $250-500
ALADDIN (3214; "My Saddest
Hour"): *53* 250-500
ALADDIN (3228; "Someday
Sweetheart"): *54* 250-500
ALADDIN (3245; "Deep In My
Heart"). *54* 250-500
ALADDIN (3263; "My Love"): *55* ...200-250
ALADDIN (3312; "Story Of
Love"): *56* 200-250
CAPITOL: *54-57* 10-20
GROOVE (0031; "I'll Follow
You"): *51* 2000-2500
(Promotional issue only.)
GUSTO: 1-3
IMPERIAL: *62* 2-3
KING: *59-64* 8-15
LANDMARK: *73* 2-5
OWL: *73* 2-5

EPs: 7-Inch 33/45rpm

CAPITOL (572; "The Five Keys"): *55* . 75-100
CAPITOL (828; "The Five Keys
On Stage"): *57* 100-125
(Covers picture a group member's thumb in a phal-
lic-like position.)
CAPITOL (828; "The Five Keys
On Stage"): *57* 150-100
(Reworked cover, with member's thumb removed
from picture.)

LPs: 10/12-Inch 33rpm

ALADDIN (806; "The Best Of The
Five Keys"): *56* 400-500
CAPITOL (828; "The Five Keys
On Stage"): *57* 75-150
(Cover pictures a group member's thumb in a phal-
lic position.)
CAPITOL (828; "The Five Keys
On Stage"): *57* 40-80
(Reworked cover, with member's thumb removed
from picture.)
CAPITOL (1769; "The Fantastic
Five Keys"): *62* 30-60
(With a "T" prefix.)
CAPITOL (1769; "The Fantastic
Five Keys"): *77* 8-10
(With an "M" prefix.)
HARLEM HITPARADE: *72* 10-12
KING (688; "The Five Keys"): *60* 150-250
SCORE (4003; "On The
Town"): *57* 200-300
Members: Rudy West; Ripley Ingram; Maryland
Pierce; Dickie Smith; Ray Loper; Bernie West;
Ulysses Hicks; Thomas Threat.
Also see FANTASTIC FIVE KEYS

FIVE MAN ELECTRICAL BAND
Singles: 7-Inch
CAPITOL: 68-69 .... $3-5
LION: 72-73 2-3
LIONEL: 71 2-3
MGM: 70 4-6
POLYDOR: 74 2-3
LPs: 10/12-Inch 33rpm
CAPITOL: 69 15-20
LION: 73 10-12
LIONEL: 70-71 10-15
MGM: 70 10-15

FIVE ROYALES
(5 Royales)
Singles: 78rpm
APOLLO: 51-55 10-20
KING: 54-56 6-12
Singles: 7-Inch
ABC-PARAMOUNT: 62 4-6
APOLLO (Black vinyl): 51-55 15-25
APOLLO (Colored vinyl): 52 40-60
GUSTO: 1-3
HOME OF THE BLUES: 60-62 3-5
KING (4000 series): 54-56 10-20
KING (5000 series): 57-64 5-10
SMASH: 64-65 3-5
TODD: 63 4-6
VEE JAY: 61-62 3-5
LPs: 10/12-Inch 33rpm
APOLLO (488; "The Rockin'
5 Royales"): 55 500-1000
KING (580; "Dedicated To
You"): 57 200-300
KING (616; "The 5 Royales Sing
For You"): 59 100-150
KING (678; "The 5 Royales"): 60 150-250
KING (955; "24 All Time Hits"): 66 30-60
Members: Johnny Tanner; Eugene Tanner; Low-
man Pauling; Jim Moore; Otto Jeffries; Obadiah
"Scoop" Carter.

FIVE SATINS
Singles: 78rpm
EMBER: 56-57 8-15
STANDORD (100; "All Mine"): 56 50-100
STANDORD (200; "In The Still Of
The Nite"): 56 75-125
Singles: 7-Inch
ABC: 73 1-3
CANDLELITE: 2-4
CHANCELLOR: 62 4-6
COLLECTABLES: 1-3
CUB: 60-61 10-15
EMBER: 56-61 10-20
ELEKTRA: 82 2-3

FIRST: 59 .... $10-15
FLASHBACK: 65 2-4
KIRSHNER: 73-74 2-4
LANA: 1-3
NIGHTRAIN: 70 3-5
RCA VICTOR: 71 2-4
ROULETTE: 64 3-6
STANDORD (100; "All Mine"): 56 ...200-225
(Red label. Copies on a maroon-brown label are un-
authorized reissues.)
STANDORD (200; "In The Still Of
The Nite"): 56 200-250
TIME MACHINE: 62 4-6
TIMES SQUARE: 62-64 3-5
UNITED ARTISTS: 61 10-20
WARNER BROS: 63 3-6
EPs: 7-Inch 33/45rpm
EMBER (Red label): 60 50-75
EMBER (Black or "logs" label): 60-61 ...20-30
LPs: 10/12-Inch 33rpm
CELEBRITY SHOWCASE: 70 10-12
COLLECTABLES: 84 6-8
EMBER (100; "The Five Satins
Sing"): 57 200-300
(Red label. Cover pictures the group on the front.)
EMBER (100; "The Five Satins
Sing"): 58 50-100
(Black vinyl. "Logs" label.)
EMBER (100; "The Five Satins
Sing"): 58 500-700
(Colored vinyl. "Logs" label.)
EMBER (100; "The Five Satins
Sing"): 60 25-40
(Black label.)
EMBER (401; "The Five Satins
Encore"): 60 50-75
(Black label.)
EMBER (401; "The Five Satins
Encore"): 61 25-40
("Logs" label.)
LOST-NITE: 81 6-10
MT. VERNON: 20-25
RELIC: 8-10
Members: Fred Parris; Louis Peebles; Stan Dortch;
Jim Freeman; Nate Moseley; Bill Baker; Jimmy
Curtis; Nate Marshall; Ed Martin; Tom Killebrew;
Al Denby; Jess Murphy; Wes Forbes; Richard
Freeman.
Also see BAKER, Bill
Also see BLACK SATIN
Also see GRANAHAN, Gerry
Also see NEW YORK CITY
Also see NEW YORKERS
Also see PARRIS, Fred

Also see SOUTHSIDE JOHNNY & THE AS-
BURY DUKES

FIVE SPECIAL
Singles: 7-Inch
ELEKTRA: 79-80 .... $1-3
LPs: 10/12-Inch 33rpm
ELEKTRA: 79 5-8

FIVE STAIRSTEPS
(Stairsteps; Five Stairsteps & Cubie)
Singles: 7-Inch
BUDDAH: 67-68 2-4
COLLECTABLES: 1-3
CURTOM: 68-69 2-4
WINDY C: 66-67 3-5
Picture Sleeves
BUDDAH: 67-68 3-5
LPs: 10/12-Inch 33rpm
BUDDAH: 68-70 10-12
COLLECTABLES: 85 6-8
CURTOM: 69 8-10
WINDY C: 67 10-12
Also see INVISIBLE MAN'S BAND
Also see STAIRSTEPS

FIVE STAR
Singles: 12-Inch 33/45rpm
RCA VICTOR: 85-86 4-6
Singles: 7-Inch
RCA VICTOR: 85-88 1-3
LPs: 10/12-Inch 33rpm
RCA VICTOR: 85-88 5-8

5000 VOLTS
Singles: 7-Inch
PHILIPS: 75 2-3
PRIVATE STOCK: 76 1-3

FIXX
Singles: 12-Inch 33/45rpm
MCA: 82-86 4-6
Singles: 7-Inch
MCA: 82-86 1-3
LPs: 10/12-Inch 33rpm
MCA (Except 8642): 82-87 5-8
MCA (8642; "Talkabout"): 8-12
(Interviews with Fixx. Promotional issue only.)

FLACK, Roberta
Singles: 7-Inch
ATLANTIC: 69-88 1-3
MCA: 81 1-3
VIVA: 83 1-3
Picture Sleeves
ATLANTIC: 78-82 1-3
LPs: 10/12-Inch 33rpm
ATLANTIC: 69-88 5-10

VIVA: 83 .... $5-8
Also see BRYSON, Peabo, & Roberta Flack
Also see CHIC / Leif Garrett / Roberta Flack /
Genesis
Also see MC CANN, Les

FLACK, Roberta & Donny Hathaway
Singles: 7-Inch
ATLANTIC: 71-80 1-3
LPs: 10/12-Inch 33rpm
ATLANTIC: 72-80 5-10
Also see HATHAWAY, Donny

FLACK, Roberta, & Eric Mercury
Singles: 7-Inch
ATLANTIC: 83 1-3
Also see FLACK, Roberta
Also see MERCURY, Eric

FLAGG, Fannie
LPs: 10/12-Inch 33rpm
RCA VICTOR: 67-77 6-12
SUNFLOWER: 71 6-10

FLAME
Singles: 7-Inch
BROTHER: 70-71 10-12
LPs: 10/12-Inch 33rpm
BROTHER: 70 15-25
Also see BEACH BOYS

FLAMIN' GROOVIES
Singles: 7-Inch
BOMP: 74 3-5
EPIC: 69-70 3-5
KAMA SUTRA: 71 3-5
Picture Sleeves
BOMP: 4-8
LPs: 10/12-Inch 33rpm
BUDDAH: 77 10-12
EPIC: 69 35-45
KAMA SUTRA (2021;
"Flamingo"): 70 20-25
(Pink label.)
KAMA SUTRA (2021;
"Flamingo"): 10-12
(Blue label.)
KAMA SUTRA (2031; "Teenage
Head"): 71 15-20
(Pink label.)
KAMA SUTRA (2031; "Teenage
Head"): 10-12
(Blue label.)
SIRE: 76-79 10-12
VOXX: 5-8
Members: Roy Loney; Cyril Jordan; George
Alexander; Tim Lynch; Danny Mihm; Chris Wil-
son; James Farrell; David Wright.

FLAMING EMBER
Singles: 7-Inch
HOT WAX: 69-70 . . . . **$2-4**
LPs: 10/12-Inch 33rpm
HOT WAX: 70-71 . . . . **10-15**

FLAMINGOS
Singles: 78rpm
CHANCE (1133; "Someday,
Someway"): *53* **50-100**
CHANCE (1140; "That's My
Desire"): *53* **50-100**
CHANCE (1145; "Golden
Teardrops"): *53* **50-100**
CHANCE (1149; "Plan For Love"): *53* . **50-100**
CHANCE (1154; "Cross Over
The Bridge"): *54* **50-100**
CHANCE (1162; "Blues In The
Letter"): *54* **50-100**
CHECKER (815; "When"): *55* **15-25**
CHECKER (821; "Please Come
Back Home"): *55* **15-30**
CHECKER (830; "I'll Be Home"): *56* . . . **15-30**
CHECKER (837 through 915): *56-57* **8-15**
DECCA: *57* **5-10**
PARROT (808; "Dream Of A
Lifetime"): *54* **50-100**
PARROT (812; "I'm Yours"): *55* **75-150**
Singles: 7-Inch
ABC: *73* **1-3**
CHANCE (1133; "Someday,
Someway"): *53* **400-600**
(Colored vinyl.)
CHANCE (1133; "Someday,
Someway"): *53* **200-300**
(Black vinyl.)
CHANCE (1140; "That's My
Desire"): *53* **400-600**
(Colored vinyl.)
CHANCE (1140; "That's My
Desire"): *53* **200-300**
(Black vinyl.)
CHANCE (1145; "Golden
Teardrops"): *53* **500-750**
(Colored vinyl.)
CHANCE (1145; "Golden
Teardrops"): *53* **250-350**
(Black vinyl.)
CHANCE (1149; "Plan For
Love"): *53* **175-300**
CHANCE (1154; "Cross Over
The Bridge"): *54* **150-250**
CHANCE (1162; "Blues In The
Letter"): *54* **150-250**
CHECKER (815; "When"): *55* **25-50**

The Flamingos

CHECKER (821; "Please Come
Back Home"): *55* **$30-60**
CHECKER (830; "I'll Be Home"): *56* . . .**25-50**
CHECKER (837 through 915): *56-59* **15-25**
CHECKER (1000 series): *64* **6-10**
CHESS: *73* **1-3**
COLLECTABLES: **1-3**
DECCA: *57-59* **10-20**
END (Monaural): *58-62* **5-10**
END (Stereo): *59* **15-25**
JULMAR: *69* **3-5**
PARROT (808; "Dream Of A
Lifetime"): *54* **400-600**
(Colored vinyl.)
PARROT (808; "Dream Of A
Lifetime"): *54* **200-300**
(Black vinyl.)
PARROT (811; "I Really Don't
Want To Know"): *55* **500-750**
PARROT (812; "I'm Yours"): *55* **400-600**
(Colored vinyl.)
PARROT (812; "I'm Yours"): *55* **200-300**
(Black vinyl.)
PHILIPS: *66* **3-5**
POLYDOR: *70* **2-4**
RONZE: *71-76* **2-4**
ROULETTE: *63* **3-6**
TIMES SQUARE: *64* **3-5**
VEE JAY: *61* **3-5**
WORLDS: *75* **2-3**
EPs: 7-Inch 33/45rpm
END (205; "Goodnight Sweetheart"): *59* .**25-50**
(Monaural.)
END (205; "Goodnight Sweetheart"): *59* .**50-75**
(Stereo.)
LPs: 10/12-Inch 33rpm
CHECKER (1433; "The Flamingos"): *59* .**40-60**
(Monaural.)

CHECKER (3005; "The
Flamingos"): *59* $20-40
(Stereo.)
CHESS: *76* 8-10
CONSTELLATION: *64* 15-20
EMUS: 8-10
END (Except 304): *60-62* 25-30
END (304; "Flamingo Serenade"): *59* ... 25-40
(Monaural.)
END (304; "Flamingo Serenade"): *59* ... 50-75
(Stereo.)
LOST-NITE: *81* 5-8
MEKA: 10-12
PHILLIPS: *66* 15-20
RONZE: *72* 10-12
SOLID SMOKE: *82* 5-8
Members. Sollie McElroy, John Carter, Zeke
Carey; Jake Carey; Paul Wilson; Nate Nelson;
Tommy Hunt; Terry Johnson.
Also see HUNT, Tommy
Also see PLATTERS

FLAMINGOS / Moonglows
LPs: 10/12-Inch 33rpm
VEE JAY: *62* 30-40
Also see FLAMINGOS
Also see MOONGLOWS

FLANAGAN, Ralph
Singles: 7-Inch
CORAL: *61* 2-3
IMPERIAL: *59* 2-3
RCA VICTOR: *50-57* 2-4
EPs: 7-Inch 33/45rpm
CAMDEN: *54* 4-6
RCA VICTOR: *51-57* 4-6
LPs: 10/12-Inch 33rpm
CAMDEN: *54* 5-10
GOLDEN ERA: *76* 4-6
IMPERIAL: *58-59* 5-10
RCA VICTOR: *51-57* 5-10

FLARES
(Flairs)
Singles: 7-Inch
COLLECTABLES: 1-3
FELSTED: *60-61* 8-12
PRESS: *62-63* 5-10
Picture Sleeves
FELSTED: *60* 20-30
LPs: 10/12-Inch 33rpm
PRESS: *61* 25-40
Members: Aaron Collins; Willie Davis; Tom
Miller; Randy Jones.
Also see CADETS

FLASH
Singles: 7-Inch
CAPITOL: *72* $2-3
LPs: 10/12-Inch 33rpm
CAPITOL (11000 series): *77* 5-8
(With an "SM" prefix.)
CAPITOL (11000 series): *72-73* 8-10
(With an "SMAS" & "ST" prefix.)
Also see BANKS, Peter

FLASH & THE PAN
Singles: 12-Inch 33/45rpm
EPIC: *81-83* 4-6
Singles: 7-Inch
EPIC: *79-83* 1-3
LPs: 10/12-Inch 33rpm
EPIC: *79-82* 5-8
Members: Harry Vanda; George Young.
Also see EASYBEATS

**FLASH CADILLAC & THE
CONTINENTAL KIDS**
Singles: 7-Inch
EPIC: *72-74* 4-6
PRIVATE STOCK: *74-77* 4-6
LPs: 10/12-Inch 33rpm
EPIC: *72-74* 10-12
PRIVATE STOCK: *75* 8-10
Also see WOLFMAN JACK

FLASHCATS
Singles: 7-Inch
BOGUS: *86* 1-3
Also see JACKSON, Bull Moose

FLATT, Lester, & Earl Scruggs
Singles: 78rpm
COLUMBIA: *51-57* 3-6
MERCURY: *49-50* 4-8
Singles: 7-Inch
COLUMBIA (20000 & 21000
series): *51-56* 4-6
COLUMBIA (40000 through 42000
series): *56-63* 3-5
COLUMBIA (43000 through 45000
series): *64-67* 2-4
Picture Sleeves
COLUMBIA: *62-67* 4-8
MERCURY: *68* 3-5
EPs: 7-Inch 33/45rpm
COLUMBIA: *57-60* 8-12
LPs: 10/12-Inch 33rpm
COLUMBIA (30; "Flatt &
Scruggs"): *75* 8-12
COLUMBIA (400 series): *69* 12-15
COLUMBIA (1000 & 2000 series,
except 1019): *60-68* 10-20

Lester Flatt (with the Nashville Grass)

COLUMBIA (1019; "Foggy Mountain
Jamboree"): *57* **$25-35**
COLUMBIA (8000 & 9000
series): *60-70* **10-20**
(With a "CS" prefix.)
COLUMBIA (8000 & 9000 series): **5-8**
(With a "PC" prefix.)
COLUMBIA (10000 series): *73* **6-12**
COLUMBIA (30000 through 37000
series): *70-82* **5-12**
COUNTY: **5-10**
EVEREST: *71-82* **5-10**
51 WEST: **5-8**
HARMONY: *60-71* **8-15**
MERCURY (20000 series): *58-63* **20-30**
(Monaural.)
MERCURY (60000 series): *63* **20-30**
(Stereo.)
MERCURY (61000 series): *68* **10-15**
NASHVILLE: *70* **8-10**
PICKWICK/HILLTOP: *68* **8-12**
POWER PAK: **5-8**
ROUNDER: **5-8**
WING: *68* **8-12**
Also see HALL, Tom T., & Earl Scruggs
Also see SCRUGGS, Earl

FLATT, Lester, Earl Scruggs, & Doc Watson
LPs: 10/12-Inch 33rpm
COLUMBIA: *67* **10-15**
Also see FLATT, Lester, & Earl Scruggs
Also see WATSON, Doc

FLAVOR
Singles: 7-Inch
COLUMBIA: *68* **2-4**
Picture Sleeves
COLUMBIA: *68* **3-6**
LPs: 10/12-Inch 33rpm
JU-PAR: *77* **8-10**

FLAVOUR, La: see LA FLAVOUR

FLEETWOOD, Mick
LPs: 10/12-Inch 33rpm
RCA VICTOR: *81* **$5-8**
Also see FLEETWOOD MAC

FLEETWOOD MAC
Singles: 7-Inch
BLUE HORIZON: *70* **4-6**
DJM: *73* **4-6**
EPIC (Except 11029): *68-69* **5-8**
EPIC (11029; "Albatross"/
"Black Magic Woman"): *73* **2-3**
REPRISE: *69-76* **2-4**
WARNER BROS (Except 8304): *77-88* **1-3**
WARNER BROS (8304; "Silver
Spring"): *76* **6-12**
(The flip, *Go Your Own Way,* was the hit, but *Silver Spring* is the collectible side of this single.)
Picture Sleeves
WARNER BROS: *77-83* **1-3**
LPs: 10/12-Inch 33rpm
BLUE HORIZON: *69-71* **20-25**
EPIC (Except 33740): *68-69* **20-25**
EPIC (33740; "English Rose"): *73* **8-12**
(Price range also includes reissue 2-LP set, *Fleetwood Mac/English Rose*, which carries the same catalog number and was issued in 1974.)
MFSL (012; "Fleetwood Mac"): *78* **30-60**
MFSL (119; "Mirage"): *84* **20-30**
NAUTILUS: *80* **15-20**
(Half-speed mastered.)
REPRISE: *69-77* **8-15**
SIRE: *75-77* **8-10**
WARNER BROS: *77-88* **8-12**
Members: Mick Fleetwood; John McVie; Peter Green; Jeremy Spencer; Danny Kirwin; Christine McVie; Bob Welch; Bob Weston; Dave Walker; Lindsey Buckingham; Stevie Nicks; Rick Vito; Billy Burnette.
Also see BUCKINGHAM, Lindsey
Also see BURNETTE, Billy
Also see FLEETWOOD, Mick
Also see GREEN, Peter
Also see MAYALL, John
Also see MC VIE, Christine
Also see NICKS, Stevie
Also see WELCH, Bob

FLEETWOODS
Singles: 7-Inch
DOLPHIN: *59* **8-12**
DOLTON (1; "Come Softly To Me"): *59* .. **6-10**
DOLTON (3; "Graduation's Here"): *59* **4-8**
(Monaural.)
DOLTON (3; "Graduation's Here"): *59* .. **10-15**
(Stereo. With an "S" prefix.)

DOLTON (5 through 315): *59-66* $3-8
LIBERTY (55188; "Come Softly
  To Me"): *59* 4-8
  (Monaural.)
LIBERTY (77188; "Come Softly
  To Me"): *59* 10-15
  (Stereo.)
UNITED ARTISTS: *74* 1-3
Picture Sleeves
DOLTON: *60-62* 5-12
EPs: 7-Inch 33/45rpm
DOLTON: *60* 15-30
LPs: 10/12-Inch 33rpm
DOLTON: *59-65* 15-20
LIBERTY: *82-83* 5-8
SUNSET: *66* 10-15
UNITED ARTISTS: *75* 8-10
  Members: Gary Troxel; Barbara Ellis; Gretchen
  Christopher.
  Also see VEE, Bobby / Johnny Burnette / Ven-
  tures / Fleetwoods

FLEMONS, Wade
(Wade Flemons & The Newcomers)
Singles: 7-Inch
VEE JAY (Maroon label): *58-59* 5-10
VEE JAY (Black label): *61-63* 3-6
LPs: 10/12-Inch 33rpm
VEE JAY (Maroon label): *59* 40-50
VEE JAY (Black label): *61* 15-25

FLENOY, Julian
Singles: 7-Inch
KMA: *86* 1-3

FLESH FOR LULU
Singles: 12-Inch 33/45rpm
MCA: *85* 4-6
Singles: 7-Inch
MCA: *85* 1-3
LPs: 10/12-Inch 33rpm
CAPITOL: *87* 5-8
MCA: *85* 5-8
  Members: Nick Marsh; James Mitchell; Rocco
  Barker; Kevin Mills; Derek Grenning.

FLESHTONES
Singles: 7-Inch
I.R.S.: *81-82* 1-3
LPs: 10/12-Inch 33rpm
I.R.S.: *81-82* 5-8
  Member: Jonithan Weiss.
  Also see VIPERS

FLETCHER, Darrow
Singles: 7-Inch
CONGRESS: *70* 2-3
CROSSOVER: *75-79* 2-3

Flesh For Lulu: (L-R) Hans Perrson; Derek Greening; Nick
Marsh; Rocco Barker; Mike Steed (Photo: Simon Fowler)

GROOVY: *66* $3-5
REVUE: *68* 2-4
UNI: *70-71* 2-3

FLETCHER, Lois
Singles: 7-Inch
PLAYBOY: *74* 2-3

FLINT, Shelby
Singles: 7-Inch
CADENCE: *58* 5-8
VALIANT: *60-66* 3-6
LPs: 10/12-Inch 33rpm
VALIANT (400 series): *61-63* 20-25
VALIANT (25000 series): *66* 15-20

FLIP CARTRIDGE:
  see CARTRIDGE, Flip

FLIRTATIONS
Singles: 7-Inch
DERAM: *69* 3-5
PARROT: *68* 2-4
LPs: 10/12-Inch 33rpm
DERAM: *69* 12-20

FLIRTS
Singles: 12-Inch 33/45rpm
CBS ASSOCIATES: *86* 4-6
Singles: 7-Inch
CBS ASSOCIATES: *86* 1-3
O RECORDS: *82* 1-3
LPs: 10/12-Inch 33rpm
CBS ASSOCIATES: *86* 5-8
O RECORDS: *82* 5-8

FLOATERS
Singles: 7-Inch
ABC: *77-79* 1-3

Picture Sleeves
ABC: 77-78 .... $1-3
LPs: 10/12-Inch 33rpm
ABC: 77-79 5-8

FLOATING BRIDGE
Singles: 7-Inch
VAULT: 69 3-5
LPs: 10/12-Inch 33rpm
VAULT: 69 10-12

FLOCK
Singles: 7-Inch
COLUMBIA: 69-70 3-5
DESTINATION: 66-67 5-8
U.S.A.: 68 4-6
LPs: 10/12-Inch 33rpm
COLUMBIA: 69-71 10-15
MERCURY: 75 8-10

FLOCK OF SEAGULLS
Singles: 12-Inch 33/45rpm
JIVE: 82-83 4-6
Singles: 7-Inch
JIVE: 82-86 1-3
LPs: 10/12-Inch 33rpm
JIVE: 82-86 5-8

FLOOD, Dick
(Dick Flood & The Pathfinders)
Singles: 7-Inch
EPIC: 61-62 2-4
KAPP: 65 2-4
MONUMENT: 59-60 3-5
NASCO: 71-72 1-3
NUGGET: 68 2-3
TOTEM: 67 2-4

FLOS
Singles: 7-Inch
SUPERSTAR I: 87 1-3

FLOTSAM & JETSAM
LPs: 10/12-Inch 33rpm
ELEKTRA: 88 5-8

FLOYD, Eddie
Singles: 7-Inch
ATLANTIC: 65 3-5
LUPINE: 63 4-6
MALACO: 77 2-3
MERCURY: 78 1-3
SAFICE: 64 4-6
STAX: 66-75 3-5
LPs: 10/12-Inch 33rpm
ATCO: 74 8-10
MALACO: 77 5-8
STAX: 67-79 10-15
Also see FALCONS

Also see MOORE, Dorothy, & Eddie Floyd

FLOYD, Eddie, & Mavis Staples
Singles: 7-Inch
STAX: 69 .... $2-3
Also see FLOYD, Eddie
Also see STAPLES, Mavis

FLOYD, King:
see KING FLOYD

FLYING BURRITO BROTHERS
Singles: 7-Inch
A&M: 69-70 2-4
COLUMBIA: 76 2-3
LPs: 10/12-Inch 33rpm
A&M: 69-76 10-15
COLUMBIA: 75-76 8-10
REGENCY: 80 5-8
Also see BURRITO BROTHERS
Also see HILLMAN, Chris
Also see PARSONS, Gram

FLYING LIZARDS
Singles: 7-Inch
VIRGIN: 79 1-3
Picture Sleeves
VIRGIN: 79 1-3
LPs: 10/12-Inch 33rpm
VIRGIN: 80 5-8

FLYING MACHINE
Singles: 7-Inch
CONGRESS: 69-70 3-5
RAINY DAY: 67 3-5
LPs: 10/12-Inch 33rpm
JANUS: 69 10-15
Also see TAYLOR, James

FOCUS
Singles: 7-Inch
ATCO: 75 2-3
SIRE: 73 2-3
LPs: 10/12-Inch 33rpm
ATCO: 74-75 8-10
SIRE: 72-77 8-10
Also see AKKERMAN, Jan

FOCUS
Singles: 7-Inch
EMI AMERICA: 87 1-3

FOCUS & P. J. PROBY
LPs: 10/12-Inch 33rpm
HARVEST: 78 5-10
Also see FOCUS
Also see PROBY, P. J.

FOGELBERG, Dan
Singles: 7-Inch
COLUMBIA: *73* $4-6
EPIC: *74-75* 2-3
FULL MOON/EPIC: *75-82* 1-3
FULL MOON: *82-87* 1-3
Picture Sleeves
FULL MOON/EPIC: *80* 1-3
LPs: 10/12-Inch 33rpm
COLUMBIA: *72* 10-15
EPIC: *74-78* 8-10
EPIC/FULL MOON: *75-82* 8-10
FULL MOON: *82-87* 5-8

FOGELBERG, Dan, & Tim Weisberg
Singles: 7-Inch
FULL MOON/EPIC: *78-80* 1-3
LPs: 10/12-Inch 33rpm
FULL MOON/EPIC: *78* 5-8
Also see FOGELBERG, Dan
Also see WEISBERG, Tim

FOGERTY, John
Promotional Singles: 12-Inch 33/45rpm
WARNER BROS (2234; "Old Man
Down The Road"): *84* 5-10
WARNER BROS (2267; "Rock & Roll
Girls"): *85* 5-10
WARNER BROS (2337; "I Can't Help
Myself"): *85* 5-10
WARNER BROS (2362; "Vanz Kant
Danz): *85* 5-10
WARNER BROS (2363; "Vanz Kant
Danz-Edit"): *85* 5-10
WARNER BROS (2514; "Eye Of The
Zombie"): *86* 5-10
Singles: 7-Inch
ASYLUM: *75-76* 2-3
FANTASY: *73* 3-5
WARNER BROS: *84-86* 1-3
Picture Sleeves
WARNER BROS: *84-87* 1-3
LPs: 10/12-Inch 33rpm
ASYLUM: *75* 5-8
WARNER BROS: *85-86* 5-8
Also see BLUE RIDGE RANGERS
Also see CREEDENCE CLEARWATER
REVIVAL
Also see EDDY, Duane

FOGERTY, Tom
(Tommy Fogerty & The Blue Velvets)
Singles: 7-Inch
FANTASY: *71-82* 2-4
ORCHESTRA: *61-62* 25-50

Picture Sleeves
FANTASY: *71* $3-5
LPs: 10/12-Inch 33rpm
FANTASY: *72-81* 8-10
Members: Tom Fogerty; John Fogerty; Doug Clifford; Stuart Cook.
Also see CREEDENCE CLEARWATER
REVIVAL
Also see SAUNDERS, Merl

FOGHAT
Singles: 7 Inch
BEARSVILLE: *72-80* 1-3
Picture Sleeves
BEARSVILLE: *79* 1-3
LPs: 10/12-Inch 33rpm
BEARSVILLE: *72-82* 5-10
Also see SAVOY BROWN
Also see WISHBONE ASH

FOLEY, Ellen
Singles: 7-Inch
EPIC/CLEVELAND INT'L: *79-83* 1-3
LPs: 10/12-Inch 33rpm
EPIC/CLEVELAND INT'L: *79-83* 5-8
Also see MEAT LOAF

FOLEY, Red
Singles: 78rpm
DECCA (Except 30067 & 30674): *42-57* . . 3-6
DECCA (30067; "Rock 'N
Reelin'"): *56* 5-10
DECCA (30674; "Crazy Little
Guitar Man"): *58* 5-10
Singles: 7-Inch
DECCA (25000 series): *61-67* 2-3
DECCA (27000 through 29000
series): *50-56* 3-6
DECCA (30000 series,
except 30067 & 30674): *56-59* 3-6

Also see COMO, Perry, & The Fontane Sisters

FOOLS
Singles: 12-Inch 33/45rpm
PVC: $4-6
Singles: 7-Inch
EMI AMERICA: *80-81* 1-3
Picture Sleeves
EMI AMERICA: *80* 1-3
LPs: 10/12-Inch 33rpm
EMI AMERICA (Except 9393): *80-81* 5-8
EMI AMERICA (9393; "April Fools
Day"): *80* 10-15
(Promotional issue only.)

FOOLS GOLD
Singles: 7-Inch
COLUMBIA: *77* 2-3
MORNING SKY: *76* 2-3
LPs: 10/12-Inch 33rpm
COLUMBIA: *77* 8-10
MORNING SKY: *76* 8-10

FORBERT, Steve
Singles: 7-Inch
NEMPEROR: *79-82* 1-3
LPs: 10/12-Inch 33rpm
NEMPEROR: *79-82* 5-8

FORCE MDs
Singles: 12-Inch 33/45rpm
TOMMY BOY: *84-86* 4-6
Singles: 7-Inch
TOMMY BOY: *84-88* 1-3
LPs: 10/12-Inch 33rpm
TOMMY BOY: *84-88* 5-8

FORD, Dee Dee: see GARDNER,
Don, & Dee Dee Ford

FORD, Frankie
Singles: 7-Inch
ABC: *73-74* 1-3
ACE: *58-60* 5-8
COLLECTABLES: *81* 1-3
CONSTELLATION: *63* 3-5
DOUBLOON: *67* 3-5
IMPERIAL: *60-62* 4-6
PAULA: *71* 2-4
SYC: *82* 1-3
Picture Sleeves
ACE: *60* 15-25
EPs: 7-Inch 33/45rpm
ACE: *59* 25-50
LPs: 10/12-Inch 33rpm
ACE: *59* 40-60
BRIARMEADE: *76* 8-10
Also see SMITH, Huey

FORD, Lita
Singles: 7-Inch
MERCURY: *84* $1-3
RCA VICTOR: *88* 1-3
LPs: 10/12-Inch 33rpm
MERCURY: *84* 5-8
RCA VICTOR: *88* 5-8
Also see RUNAWAYS

FORD, Mary:
see PAUL, Les, & Mary Ford

FORD, Pennye
Singles: 12-Inch 33/45rpm
TOTAL EXPERIENCE: *84-85* 4-6
Singles: 7-Inch
TOTAL EXPERIENCE: *84-85* 1-3
LPs: 10/12-Inch 33rpm
TOTAL EXPERIENCE: *85* 5-8

FORD, Robben
LPs: 10/12-Inch 33rpm
WARNER BROS: *88* 5-8

FORD, Tennessee Ernie
Singles: 78rpm
CAPITOL (1; "Sixteen Tons"): *69* 3-6
(Promotional "Special Commemorative Pressing"
for Ford's 20th year on Capitol.)
CAPITOL (1200 through 2900
series): *50-57* 3-6
CAPITOL (40000 series): *49-50* 3-6
Singles: 7-Inch
CAPITOL (1275 through 2900
series): *50-54* 4-8
(Purple labels. Ford's many "Boogie" titles repre-
sent the higher end of this price range.)
CAPITOL (2000 through 4100
series): *70-75* 1-3
(Orange labels.)
CAPITOL (3000 through 4400
series): *54-60* 2-4
CAPITOL (4500 through 5700
series): *61-67* 1-3
Picture Sleeves
CAPITOL: *55-60* 4-8
EPs: 7-Inch 33/45rpm
CAPITOL (Except 413): *55-61* 5-10
CAPITOL (413; "Backwoods Boogie
& Blues"): *53* 15-25
LPs: 10/12-Inch 33rpm
CAPITOL (Except 888): *56-80* 5-15
CAPITOL (888; "Ol' Rockin'
Ern"): *57* 30-40
Also see LAWRENCE, Steve / Tennessee
Ernie Ford
Also see LEE, Brenda / Tennessee Ernie Ford

Foreigner: (top) Lou Gramm; Mick Jones
(bottom) Rick Wills; Dennis Elliott

Also see STARR, Kay, & Tennessee Ernie
Ford

**FORD, Tennessee Ernie, & Glen
Campbell**
LPs: 10/12-Inch 33rpm
CAPITOL: *75* $10-12
Also see CAMPBELL, Glen

FORDHAM, Julia
LPs: 10/12-Inch 33rpm
VIRGIN: *88* 5-8

FORECAST
Singles: 12-Inch 33/45rpm
RCA VICTOR: *83* 4-6
Singles: 7-Inch
ARIOLA: *80* 1-3
RCA VICTOR: *83* 1-3
LPs: 10/12-Inch 33rpm
RCA VICTOR: *83* 5-8

FOREIGNER
Singles: 7-Inch
ATLANTIC: *77-88* 1-3
ATLANTIC/WARNER: *79* 1-3
Picture Sleeves
ATLANTIC: *78-88* 1-3
LPs: 10/12-Inch 33rpm
ATLANTIC (Except "Foreigner"
picture disc): *77-88* 5-8
ATLANTIC ("Foreigner" picture
disc): *79* 20-25
GEFFEN: *85* 5-8

MFSL: *81* $25-50
Members: Lou Gramm; Rick Wills; Mick Jones;
Dennis Elliott; Ian McDonald; Al Greenwood.
Also see BAD COMPANY
Also see NEW JERSEY MASS CHOIR
Also see SPYS

FOREVER MORE
Singles: 7-Inch
RCA VICTOR: *69-70* 2-5
LPs: 10/12-Inch 33rpm
RCA VICTOR: *69-70* 10-15
Also see AVERAGE WHITE BAND

FORMATIONS
Singles: 7-Inch
BANK: *68* 5-8
MGM: *68-69* 3-5

FORREST
Singles: 12-Inch 33/45rpm
PROFILE: *83* 4-6

FORREST, Earl
Singles: 78rpm
DUKE(103; "Rock The Bottle"): *52* 10-15
Singles: 7-Inch
DUKE(108 through 130): *52-54* 15-25
DUKE(300 series): *62-63* 3-5
METEOR: *53* 30-45
Also see ACE, Johnny / Earl Forrest

FORREST, Jimmy
Singles: 78rpm
UNITED: *52-55* 5-10
Singles: 7-Inch
PRESTIGE: *61-62* 2-4
TRIUMPH: *59* 3-5
UNITED (Black vinyl): *52-55* 5-10
UNITED (Colored vinyl): *52* 10-20
LPs: 10/12-Inch 33rpm
NEW JAZZ: *60-64* 15-25
PRESTIGE: *61-62* 15-25
(Yellow label.)
PRESTIGE: *64* 10-15
(Blue label.)
UNITED: *57* 60-75
Also see DAVIS, Miles

FORTUNES
Singles: 7-Inch
CAPITOL: *71-74* 2-3
LONDON: 1-3
PRESS: *65-66* 4-6
UNITED ARTISTS: *67-68* 3-5
WORLD PACIFIC: *70* 2-3
LPs: 10/12-Inch 33rpm
CAPITOL: *71-73* 8-10
COCA-COLA: 25-35

PRESS: 65 . . . . $25-30
WORLD PACIFIC: 70 8-10

FORUM
Singles: 7-Inch
MIRA: 67 8-12
PENTHOUSE: 66 8-12
LPs: 10/12-Inch 33rpm
MIRA: 67 15-20
Members: Phil Campos; Rene Nole; Riselle Vaine.

FOSTER, Bruce
Singles: 7-Inch
MILLENIUM: 77 3-5
Picture Sleeves
MILLENIUM: 77 5-10
LPs: 10/12-Inch 33rpm
MILLENIUM: 77 8-15

FOSTER, David
Singles: 7-Inch
ATLANTIC: 85-88 1-3
LPs: 10/12-Inch 33rpm
ATLANTIC: 86-88 5-8

FOSTER, David, & Olivia Newton-John
Singles: 7-Inch
ATLANTIC: 86 1-3
Also see FOSTER, David
Also see NEWTON-JOHN, Olivia

FOSTER, Ian
Singles: 7-Inch
MCA: 87 1-3

FOSTER & LLOYD
LPs: 10/12-Inch 33rpm
RCA VICTOR: 86 5-8

FOTOMAKER
Singles: 7-Inch
ATLANTIC: 78-79 2-3
LPs: 10/12-Inch 33rpm
ATLANTIC: 78-79 5-8
Members: Gene Cornish; Dino Dannelli; Wally Bryson.
Also see RASCALS
Also see RASPBERRIES

FOUNDATIONS
Singles: 7-Inch
UNI: 67-71 3-5
LPs: 10/12-Inch 33rpm
UNI: 68-69 15-20

FOUNTAIN, Pete
Singles: 7-Inch
CORAL: 58-62 2-3
LPs: 10/12-Inch 33rpm
CORAL: 59-69 5-15
FIRST AMERICAN: 78 4-6

GUEST STAR: 64 . . . . $4-8
Also see HIRT, Al, & Pete Fountain
Also see LEE, Brenda, & Pete Fountain

FOUNTAIN, Roosevelt, & The Pens of Rhythm
Singles: 7-Inch
PRINCE-ADAMS: 62-63 3-5

FOUR ACES
Singles: 78rpm
DECCA: 51-57 2-5
FLASH: 50 5-10
MERION: 52 5-10
VICTORIA : 51 5-10
Singles: 7-Inch
ABC PARAMOUNT: 60 2-4
DECCA (25000 series): 61-64 2-3
DECCA (27000 & 28000 series): 51-53 . . . 5-8
DECCA (29000 through 31000
series): 54-60 4-6
FLASH: 50 10-15
MERION: 52 10-15
RADNOR: 69 1-3
VICTORIA (Black vinyl): 51 10-20
VICTORIA (Colored vinyl): 51 25-40
Picture Sleeves
ABC-PARAMOUNT: 60 3-6
EPs: 7-Inch 33/45rpm
DECCA: 52-59 10-20
LPs: 10/12-Inch 33rpm
ACCORD: 81-82 5-8
DECCA (8100 through 8500
series): 55-56 15-25
DECCA (8600 through 8900
series): 57-59 10-20
MCA: 74 5-10
RADNOR: 5-8
UNITED ARTISTS: 61 10-15
VOCALION: 69 5-10
WESTOWN: 5-8
Members: Al Alberts; Louis Silvestri; Dave
Mahoney; Sol Vocarro.

FOUR ACES / Four Lads / Four Preps
LPs: 10/12-Inch 33rpm
EXACT: 80 5-8
Also see FOUR ACES
Also see FOUR LADS
Also see FOUR PREPS

FOUR BLAZES
Singles: 7-Inch
UNITED (114; "Mary Jo"): 52 30-50
(Black vinyl.)
UNITED (114; "Mary Jo"): 52 75-100
(Colored vinyl.)

UNITED (125 through 177): *52-54* $15-25
(Black vinyl.)
UNITED (125 through 177): *52-54* 30-50
(Colored vinyl.)
Member: Tommy Braden.

FOUR BUDDIES
Singles: 78rpm
SAVOY: *51-53* 20-45
Singles: 7-Inch
SAVOY (769; "I Will Wait"): *51* 75-100
SAVOY (779; "Don't Leave Me
Now"): *51* 75-100
SAVOY (789; "My Summer's
Gone"): *51* 75-100
SAVOY (817; "Heart & Soul"): *51* 75-100
SAVOY (845; "You're Part
Of Me"): *52* 50-75
SAVOY (866; "What's The Matter
With Me"): *52* 50-75
SAVOY (888; "My Mother's
Eyes"): *53* 40-60
Members: Leon Harrison; Greg Carroll; Bert Palmer; Tommy Smith.

FOUR COINS
Singles: 78rpm
EPIC: *54-59* 2-5
Singles: 7-Inch
COLUMBIA: *67* 2-3
EPIC: *54-59* 2-5
JOY: *64* 1-3
JUBILEE: *61-62* 2-3
MGM: *60-61* 2-3
VEE JAY: *62-63* 2-3
Picture Sleeves
EPIC: *57* 4-8
EPs: 7-Inch 33/45rpm
EPIC: *55-58* 5-10
LPs: 10/12-Inch 33rpm
EPIC: *55-58* 10-15
MGM: *61* 8-12
ROULETTE: *65* 6-10

FOUR DATES
Singles: 7-Inch
CHANCELLOR: *58* 5-8
Also see FABIAN

FOUR ESQUIRES
Singles: 78rpm
CADENCE: *55* 4-8
PARIS: *57* 4-8
PILGRIM: *56* 4-8
Singles: 7-Inch
CADENCE: *55* 5-10
PARIS: *57* 8-15

PILGRIM: *56* $5-10
ROULETTE: 1-3
TERRACE: *63* 3-6

FOUR FELLOWS
Singles: 78rpm
DERBY (862; "I Tried"): *54* 15-25
GLORY (Except 242): *55-57* 8-15
GLORY (242; "Darling You"): *56* 20-30
Singles: 7-Inch
DERBY (862; "I Tried"): *54* 25-50
GLORY (Except 242): *55-57* 15-25
GLORY (242; "Darling You"): *56* 50-75
Members: David Jones; Ted Williams; Larry Banks; Jim McGowan.
Also see MC LAURIN, Bette

450 SL
Singles: 7-Inch
GOLDEN BOY: *85* 1-3

FOUR FRESHMEN
Singles: 78rpm
CAPITOL: *50-57* 2-4
Singles: 7-Inch
CAPITOL: *50-65* 2-4
DECCA: *67* 2-3
LIBERTY: *68* 1-3
Picture Sleeves
CAPITOL: *63* 3-6
EPs: 7-Inch 33/45rpm
CAPITOL: *54-59* 5-10
LPs: 10/12-Inch 33rpm
CAPITOL ("SM" prefix): *75-79* 5-8
CAPITOL ("T" or "ST" prefix): *54-64* ... 10-15
LIBERTY: *68-82* 5-10
SUNSET: *70* 5-8
Members: Don Barbour; Ross Barbour; Ken Errair; Bob Flanagan.

FOUR JACKS & A JILL
Singles: 7-Inch
RCA: *68* 3-5
LPs: 10/12-Inch 33rpm
RCA VICTOR: *68* 10-15

FOUR KNIGHTS
Singles: 78rpm
CAPITOL: *51-57* 5-8
CORAL (60046; "Wrapped Up In
A Dream"): *49* 8-15
CORAL (60072; "The Crystal
Gazer"): *49* 8-15
DECCA: *46-47* 8-15
Singles: 7-Inch
CAPITOL (346; "Spotlight
Songs"): *52* 30-50
(Boxed set of three 45rpm singles.)

CAPITOL (1000 & 2000 series): *51-54* . . **$8-15**
CAPITOL (3000 series): *55-57* **5-10**
CORAL (61000 & 62000 series): *58-59* . . . **5-10**
DECCA (48018; "He'll Understand And
Say Well Done"): *52* **20-25**
(Reissue of a 1947 78rpm.)
SOUVENIR: *62* **3-5**
EPs: 7-Inch 33/45rpm
CAPITOL: *52-54* **40-60**
LPs: 10/12-Inch 33rpm
CAPITOL (346; "Spotlight
Songs"): *52* **75-100**
(10-Inch LP.)
Members: Gene Alford; John Wallace; Clarence
Dixon; Oscar Broadway.
Also see COLE, Nat "King"
Also see HUNT, Pee Wee

FOUR LADS
Singles: 78rpm
COLUMBIA: *52-58* **3-5**
OKEH: *52* **3-5**
Singles: 7-Inch
COLUMBIA: *52-60* **4-8**
DOT: *62* **3-5**
FONA: *77-78* **2-3**
KAPP: *60-61* **3-5**
OKEH: *52* **5-10**
UNITED ARTISTS: *63-69* **3-5**
Picture Sleeves
COLUMBIA: *57-59* **5-10**
KAPP: *60* **4-8**
EPs: 7-Inch 33/45rpm
COLUMBIA: *55-59* **5-10**
LPs: 10/12-Inch 33rpm
COLUMBIA: *54-60* **10-15**
DOT: *62-63* **8-12**
KAPP: *61* **8-12**
HARMONY: *69* **5-10**
UNITED ARTISTS: *64* **6-10**
Members: Frankie Busseri; Jimmy Arnold; Connie
Coderini; Bernie Toorish.
Also see FOUR ACES / Four Lads / Four
Preps
Also see LAINE, Frankie, & The Four Lads
Also see RAY, Johnnie

FOUR LOVERS
Singles: 78rpm
EPIC (9255; "My Life For
Your Love"): *57* **50-100**
RCA VICTOR: *56-57* **5-10**
Singles: 7-Inch
EPIC (9255; "My Life For
Your Love"): *57* **150-200**
MAGIC CARPET: **3-5**

RCA VICTOR: *56-57* **$20-25**
EPs: 7-Inch 33/45rpm
RCA VICTOR (47; "The Four Lovers/
Homer & Jethro"): *56* **25-35**
(Promotional issue only. Not issued with cover.)
RCA VICTOR (64; "The Four Lovers/
Teddi King"): *56* **25-35**
(Promotional issue only. Not issued with cover.)
RCA VICTOR (869; "The Four
Lovers"): *56* **175-250**
RCA VICTOR (871, "Joyride"): *56* . . . **100-150**
LPs: 10/12-Inch 33rpm
RCA VICTOR (1317; "Joyride"): *56* . . **350-400**
Members: Frankie Valli; Tom Devito; Nick Devito;
Hank Majewski.
Also see HOMER & JETHRO
Also see 4 SEASONS
Also see VALLI, Frankie

FOUR PENNIES
Singles: 7-Inch
LAURIE: **5-10**
RUST: *63* **15-25**
Members: Judy Craig; Barbara Lee; Patricia Ben-
nett; Sylvia Peterson.
Also see CHIFFONS

FOUR PREPS
Singles: 78rpm
CAPITOL: *56-57* **3-6**
Singles: 7-Inch
CAPITOL (Purple label): *56-61* **4-8**
CAPITOL (Orange & yellow label): *62-67* . **3-5**
Picture Sleeves
CAPITOL: *61* **5-10**
EPs: 7-Inch 33/45rpm
CAPITOL: *56-58* **8-15**
LPs: 10/12-Inch 33rpm
CAPITOL: *58-67* **10-20**

more money for you and me
(MEDLEY)

The Four Preps

Members: Bruce Belland; Glen Larson; Marv Ingraham; Ed Cobb.
Also see FOUR ACES / Four Lads / Four Preps

4 SEASONS
(The Four Seasons; Frankie Valli & The 4 Seasons)

Singles: 7-Inch
BOB CREWE PRESENTS: 70 . . . . $10-12
(Promotional issue only.)
COLLECTABLES: 81 1-3
COLUMBIA (6675; "Big Man's
World"): 64 25-30
(Promotional soundsheet.)
CREWE: 69 3-5
GONE: 61 20-40
GORDA: 65 4-6
MOTOWN: 73 5-8
MOWEST: 72 5-8
OLDIES 45: 62-63 3-5
PHILIPS (40166 through 40662): 64-69 . . . 3-5
PHILIPS (40688; "Lay Me
Down"): 70 15-20
PHILIPS (40694; "Where Are
My Dreams"): 70 20-25
RAINBOW: 62 3-5
SEASONS 4-EVER (Black vinyl): 71 4-6
SEASONS 4-EVER (Colored
vinyl): 71 10-12
VEE JAY (456 through 562): 62-63 4-6
VEE JAY (576; "Stay"/
"Peanuts"): 63 40-50
VEE JAY (582; "Stay"/
"Goodnight My Love"): 64 3-5
VEE JAY (597; "Alone"): 64 10-12
(Yellow label.)
VEE JAY (597; "Alone"): 64 4-6
(Black label.)

VEE JAY (608 through 719): 64-66 . . . . . . $5-8
WABC RADIO: 64 50-75
(Special products custom pressing.)
WXYZ-DETROIT: 65 25-40
(Special products custom pressing.)
WARNER BROS: 75-80 2-3
WIBBAGE: 65 25-35
(Special products custom pressing.)

Picture Sleeves
PHILIPS (Except 40524): 64-68 10-20
PHILIPS (40524; "Saturday's
Father"): 68 20-30
(Fold-out sleeve.)
PHILIPS (40524; "Saturday's Father"): 68 .5-10
(Standard sleeve.)
VEE JAY: 64 12-25

EPs: 7-Inch 33/45rpm
MAGIC CARPET: 4-8
PHILIPS: 68 15-20
VEE JAY: 64 15-20

LPs: 10/12-Inch 33rpm
ARISTA: 84 8-12
GUEST STAR: 64 10-15
K-TEL: 77 15-20
LONGINES: 20-25
(TV mail-order offer.)
MCA: 85 5-8
MOTOWN: 80 5-8
MOWEST: 10-12
PHILLIPS (124; "Dawn & 11 Other
Great Hits"): 64 15-20
PHILLIPS (129; "Born To Wander"): 64 .15-20
PHILLIPS (146; "Rag Doll"): 64 15-20
PHILLIPS (150; "All The Song
Hits"): 64 15-20
PHILLIPS (164; "The 4 Seasons
Entertain You"): 65 15-20
PHILLIPS (193; "The 4 Seasons Sing Big
Hits By Burt Bacharach, Hal David, &
Bob Dylan"): 65 50-65
(With photos of the group on the front and back
cover.)
PHILLIPS (193; "The 4 Seasons Sing Big
Hits By Burt Bacharach, Hal David, &
Bob Dylan"): 65 15-20
(Does not have group photos on front and back
cover.)
PHILLIPS (196; "Gold Vault Of
Hits"): 65 15-20
PHILLIPS (201; "Working My Way
Back To You"): 66 15-20
PHILLIPS (221; "2nd Gold Vault
Of Hits"): 66 .15-20
PHILLIPS (222; "Lookin' Back"): 66 15-20

THE FOUR SEASONS

PHILLIPS (223; "Christmas
  Album"): *66* $12-15
PHILLIPS (243; "New Gold Hits"): *67* ..15-20
PHILLIPS (290; "Genuine Imitation
  Life Gazette"): *69* 35-45
  (With yellow cover.)
PHILLIPS (290; "Genuine Imitation
  Life Gazette"): *69* 10-12
  (With white cover.)
PHILLIPS (341; "Half & Half"): *70* 10-12
PHILLIPS (2-6501; "Edizone
  D'Oro"): *68* 20-25
PICKWICK: *70* 8-10
PRIVATE STOCK: *75* 10-12
SEARS: *70* 20-25
VEE JAY (1000 series
  except 1082 & 1088): *62-63* 30-35
VEE JAY (1082; "Folk-Nanny"): *64* 30-40
VEE JAY (1082; "Stay & Other
  Great Hits"): *64* 15-20
  (Repackage of "Folk-Nanny.")
VEE JAY (1088; "More Golden
  Hits"): *64* 15-20
VEE JAY (1100 series): *64-65* 15-20
WARNER BROS: *75-81* 8-10
  Members: Frankie Valli; Tom Devito; Nick Devito;
  Hank Majewski; Bob Gaudio; Charlie Calello;
  Nick Massi; Joe Long; Don Ciccione; Bill
  Deloach; Paul Wilson.
  Also see BEACH BOYS & FRANKIE
VALLI & THE FOUR SEASONS
  Also see BEATLES / 4 Seasons
  Also see FOUR LOVERS
  Also see JAN & DEAN / Roy Orbison / 4
Seasons / Shirelles
  Also see SANTOS, Larry
  Also see SIMON, Paul
  Also see VALLI, Frankie

Also see WONDER WHO?

4 SEASONS / Scarlets
    Singles: 7-Inch
OLDIES 45: *63* $5-8

4 SEASONS / Shirelles
    Singles: 7-Inch
COKE: *65* 20-30
  (Coca-Cola radio spots. Issued to radio stations
  only.)

4 SEASONS / Ray Stevens
    Singles: 7-Inch
OLDIES 45: *63* 5-8
  Also see 4 SEASONS
  Also see STEVENS, Ray

FOUR SONICS
    Singles: 7-Inch
SPORT: *68* 3-5

FOUR SPORTSMEN
    Singles: 7-Inch
SUNNYBROOK: *60-62* 4-6

FOUR TOPS
    Singles: 12-Inch 33/45rpm
ABC: *77-78* 4-6
MOTOWN: *80* 4-8
    Singles: 7-Inch
ABC: *75-79* 2-3
ARISTA : *88* 1-3
CASABLANCA: *81-82* 2-3
CHESS (1623; "Could It
  Be You"): *56* 50-75
COLUMBIA (41755; "Ain't That
  Love"): *60* 20-35
COLUMBIA (43356; "Ain't That
  Love"): *65* 4-8
DUNHILL: *72-74* 2-3
MOTOWN (400 series): 1-3

MOTOWN (1000 through 1200
series): *64-72* $3-5
MOTOWN (1700 series): *83-85* 1-3
MOTOWN/TOPPS ("I Can't Help
Myself"): *67* 50-75
(Topps Chewing Gum promotional item.
Cardboard flexi, picture disc. Issued with generic
paper sleeve.)
RSO: *82* 2-3
RIVERSIDE (4534; "Pennies From
Heaven"): *62* 20-35
Picture Sleeves
MOTOWN: *66-70* 4-8
LPs: 10/12-Inch 33rpm
ABC: *75-78* 8-10
ARISTA: *88* 5-8
CASABLANCA: *81-82* 5-8
COMMAND: *74* 10-12
DUNHILL: *72-74* 8-10
MOTOWN (Except 100 & 200
series): *64-72* 10-20
MOTOWN (100 & 200 series): *82-84* 5-8
NATURAL RESOURCES: *78* 8-10
WORKSHOP (217; "Jazz
Impressions"): *62* 250-350
Members: Levi Stubbs; Lawrence Payton; Abdul
"Duke" Fakir; Obie Benson.
Also see HOLLAND, Eddie, & Lamont Dozier
Also see PAYTON, Lawrence
Also see SUPREMES & Four Tops

FOUR TOPS / Temptations
LPs: 10/12-Inch 33rpm
SILVER EAGLE: *87* 6-10
Also see FOUR TOPS
Also see TEMPTATIONS

FOUR TUNES
Singles: 78rpm
ARCO: *50* 4-6
COLUMBIA: *48* 4-6
JUBILEE: *53-57* 4-8
MANOR: *46-49* 5-10
RCA VICTOR: *49-53* 5-15
Singles: 7-Inch
JUBILEE: *53-57* 4-8
KAY-RON: 5-8
RCA VICTOR (3881 through
4102): *50-51* 20-30
RCA VICTOR (4241 through
4305): *51* 15-20
RCA VICTOR (4427; "I'll See You
In My Dreams"): *51* 20-25
RCA VICTOR (4489 through
5532): *52-53* 5-10
RCA VICTOR (50-0000 series): *49-51* .. 25-40

VIRGO: *72* $1-3
EPs: 7-Inch 33/45rpm
RCA VICTOR: *54* 30-50
LPs: 10/12-Inch 33rpm
JUBILEE (1039; "12 x 4"): *57* 40-60
Members: Jim Nabbie; Danny Owens; William
"Pat" Best; Jimmy Gordon; Deek Watson.
Also see CHURCHILL, Savannah

FOUR TUNES /Shadows
LPs: 10/12-Inch 33rpm
CHICAGO: *88* 8-10
Also see FOUR TUNES

FOUR VOICES
Singles: 78rpm
COLUMBIA: *55-57* 3-5
Singles: 7-Inch
COLUMBIA: *55-60* 3-5
PEACOCK: *62* 2-3

FOUR-EVERS
Singles: 7-Inch
CHATTAHOOCHEE: *64* 3-5
COLUMBIA (Except 42303): *66* 3-5
COLUMBIA (42303; "You Belong
To Me"): *62* 20-25
CONSTELLATION: *65* 10-12
CRYSTAL BALL: 3-6
JAMIE: *63* 5-10
JASON SCOTT: 3-5
RED BIRD: *66* 10-15
SMASH (1887; "Please Be Mine"): *63* 5-8
SMASH (1887; "Be My Girl"): *64* 3-5

FOWLEY, Kim
Singles: 7-Inch
CAPITOL: *72-73* 2-4
CORBY: *65* 8-10
CREATIVE FAMILY: 15-25
IMPERIAL: *68-69* 3-5
LIVING LEGEND: *65-66* 8-10
LOMA: *66* 4-6
REPRISE: *67* 3-5
TOWER: *67* 3-5
LPs: 10/12-Inch 33rpm
CAPITOL: *72-74* 10-12
IMPERIAL: *68-69* 15-20
PVC: *79* 5-8
TOWER: *67* 15-20
Also see KING LIZARD

FOX
Singles: 7-Inch
ARIOLA/GTO: *75* 2-3
GTO: *74* 2-4
LPs: 10/12-Inch 33rpm
ARIOLA AMERICA: *75* 8-10

FOX, Charles
Singles: 7-Inch
HANDSHAKE: *81* $1-3

FOX, Samantha
Singles: 12-Inch 33/45rpm
JIVE: *86* 4-6
Singles: 7-Inch
JIVE: *86-88* 1-3
LPs: 10/12-Inch 33rpm
JIVE: *86-88* 5-8

FOX, Virgil
LPs: 10/12-Inch 33rpm
DECCA : *71* 5-10

FOXX, Inez
(Inez & Charlie Foxx)
Singles: 7-Inch
DYNAMO: *67-70* 3-5
LANA: 2-4
MUSICOR: *66-68* 3-5
SUE: *65* 3-6
SYMBOL: *63-64* 5-8
VOLT: *72-73* 2-4
UNITED ARTISTS: *74* 2-3
LPs: 10/12-Inch 33rpm
DYNAMO: *67* 10-15
SUE: *65* 20-25
SYMBOL : *63* 25-30
VOLT: *73* 8-10
    Also see PLATTERS / Inez & Charlie Foxx /
Jive Five / Tommy Hunt

FOXX, Redd
(Redd Foxx & Hattie Noel)
Singles: 78rpm
DOOTO (Except 416): *57-61* 2-5
DOOTO (416; "Real Pretty
    Mama"): *57* 5-10
DOOTONE: *56-57* 3-6
SAVOY: *46* 5-10
Singles: 7-Inch
DOOTO (Except 416): *57-61* 2-5
DOOTO (416; "Real Pretty Mama"): *57* . . 10-20
DOOTONE: *56-57* 3-6
EPs: 7-Inch 33/45rpm
DOOTO: *57-61* 5-8
DOOTONE: *56-57* 5-10
LPs: 10/12-Inch 33rpm
ATLANTIC: *75* 5-8
AUTHENTIC: *55-56* 15-25
DOOTO: *60-74* 5-15
DOOTONE: *57* 10-20
KING: *69-71* 5-10
LAFF: *79* 5-8
LOMA: *66-68* 8-12

RCA VICTOR: *72* $5-10
WARNER BROS: *69* 8-10

FOXY
Singles: 7-Inch
DASH: *76-80* 1-3
LPs: 10/12-Inch 33rpm
DASH: *78-80* 5-8
Also see OXO

FOZZIE BEAR:
see KERMIT / Fozzie Bear

FRAMPTON, Peter
Singles: 7-Inch
A&M (Except 1988): *74-81* 2-5
A&M (1988; "Tried To Love"): *77* 3-5
    (Commerical issue. With Mick Jagger.)
A&M (1988; "Tried To Love"): *77* 10-15
    (White label, promotional issue.)
ATLANTIC: *86* 1-3
Picture Sleeves
A&M (Except 1988): *74-81* 2-5
A&M (1988; "Tried To Love"): *77* 4-6
LPs: 10/12-Inch 33rpm
A&M (Except picture discs): *73-82* 6-12
A&M ("I'm In You"): *77* 50-60
    (Picture disc.)
A&M ("Frampton Comes Alive"): *79* ... 15-20
    (Picture disc. Promotional issue only.)
ATLANTIC: *86* 5-8
    Also see FRAMPTON'S CAMEL
    Also see JAGGER, Mick
    Also see STARR, Ringo

FRAMPTON'S CAMEL
(Peter Frampton)
Singles: 7-Inch
A&M: *72-73* 5-8
    Also see FRAMPTON, Peter
    Also see HUMBLE PIE

FRANCE JOLI:
see JOLI, France

FRANCHI, Sergio
Singles: 7-Inch
LAX: *79* 1-3
METROMEDIA: *71-72* 1-3
RCA VICTOR: *62-67* 2-3
UNITED ARTISTS: *69-70* 1-3
LPs: 10/12-Inch 33rpm
FOUR CORNERS: *66* 6-10
RCA VICTOR: *62-77* 5-15
UNITED ARTISTS: *70* 5-10

FRANCIS, Connie
Singles: 78rpm
MGM: *55-58* 4-8

FRANCIS, Connie, & Hank Williams Jr.
LPs: 10/12-Inch 33rpm

FRANKE & THE KNOCKOUTS

FRANKIE & THE SPINDELS

FRANKIE GOES TO HOLLYWOOD

FRANKLIN, Aretha

CANDLELITE: 77 .... $8-10
CHECKER: 65 12-15
COLUMBIA (12; "Aretha
  Franklin"): 68 10-15
COLUMBIA (1612 through 2281): 61-64 12-20
COLUMBIA (2300 through 2700
  series): 65-67 10-15
COLUMBIA (8402 through 9081): 61-64 12-25
  (With a "CS" prefix.)
COLUMBIA (9100 through 9700
  series): 65-69 10-15
  (With a "CS" prefix.)
COLUMBIA (10000 series): 73 5-10
COLUMBIA (30000 series): 72-82 5-10
HARMONY: 68-71 10-12
UPFRONT: 79 5-8
  Also see CLEMONS, Clarence
  Also see EURYTHMICS & Aretha Franklin
  Also see GRAHAM, Larry
  Also see MICHAEL, George
  Also see SANTANA
  Also see SIMON, Paul
  Also see SWEET INSPIRATIONS
  Also see WOLF, Peter

FRANKLIN, Aretha, & George Benson
Singles: 7-Inch
ARISTA: 81 1-3
  Also see BENSON, George

**FRANKLIN, Aretha, With James
Cleveland & The Southern California
Community Choir**
EPs: 7-Inch 33/45rpm
ATLANTIC (1025; "Amazing Grace"): 72 . 4-6
  (Promotional issue only.)
LPs: 10/12-Inch 33rpm
ATLANTIC: 72 6-10
  Also see FRANKLIN, Aretha

FRANKLIN, Bobby
(Bobby Franklin & Insanity; Boby Franklin)
Singles: 7-Inch
BABY: 75 2-3
COLUMBIA: 76 2-3
THOMAS: 69 2-4

FRANKLIN, Carolyn
Singles: 7-Inch
RCA VICTOR: 69-73 2-3
LPs: 10/12-Inch 33rpm
RCA VICTOR: 69-73 10-12

FRANKLIN, Doug
(Doug Franklin & The Bluenotes)
Singles: 7-Inch
COLONIAL: 58-59 4-8

FRANKLIN, Erma
Singles: 7-Inch
BRUNSWICK: 69 .... $2-3
EPIC: 61-63 3-5
SHOUT: 67-68 2-4
LPs: 10/12-Inch 33rpm
BRUNSWICK: 69 10-15
EPIC: 62 15-20

FRANKLIN, Rodney
Singles: 7-Inch
COLUMBIA: 80-86 1-3
LPs: 10/12-Inch 33rpm
COLUMBIA: 80-86 5-8

FRANKS, Michael
Singles: 7-Inch
REPRISE: 76 2-3
WARNER BROS: 77-83 1-3
LPs: 10/12-Inch 33rpm
JOHN HAMMOND: 5-8
REPRISE: 76 5-8
WARNER BROS: 77-87 5-8

FRANTICS
Singles: 7-Inch
BOLO: 62 4-6
DOLTON: 59-61 4-8
SEAFAIR: 64 4-6

FRASER, Andy
Singles: 7-Inch
ISLAND: 84 1-3

FRAZIER, Dallas
Singles: 78rpm
CAPITOL: 54 3-5
Singles: 7-Inch
CAPITOL (2000 through 2400
  series): 67-69 2-4
CAPITOL (2800 & 2900 series): 54 3-5
CAPITOL (5500 series): 65 2-5
JAMIE: 59 3-5
MERCURY: 64 2-4
MUSIKRON: 61 3-5
RCA VICTOR: 71-73 1-3
20TH CENTURY-FOX: 75 2-4
LPs: 10/12-Inch 33rpm
CAPITOL: 66-67 10-15
RCA VICTOR: 70-71 8-12

FRAZIER, Dallas, & Joe "Fingers" Carr
Singles: 78rpm
CAPITOL: 54 3-5
Singles: 7-Inch
CAPITOL: 54 3-5
EPs: 7-Inch 33/45rpm
CAPITOL: 54 5-10

Also see CARR, Joe "Fingers"
Also see FRAZIER, Dallas

FREBERG, Stan
(The Stan Freberg Show)
Singles: 78rpm
CAPITOL: *50-57* $5-15
Singles: 7-Inch
BELFAST SPARKLING WATER (1515;
"Invisible Bubbles"): 50-75
(Product commercials for radio use.)
BIG SOUND (2; "Jockey's Little
Helper"): 35-50
(Product commercials for radio use.)
BUBBLE UP (2227; "Music To
Bubble Up By"): 20-30
(Product commercials for radio use.)
BUTTERNUT COFFEE (2000; "Instant
Sales For Instant Butternut
By Instant Freberg"): 40-50
(Product commercials for radio use.)
BUTTERNUT COFFEE (2237; "Amazing
Butternut Coffee"): 25-35
(Product commercials for radio use.)
CAPITOL (415; "Wun'erful
Wun'erful"): *57* 10-15
(One-sided disc. Promotional issue only.)
CAPITOL (1200 through 3100
series, except 2125): *50-54* 10-20
CAPITOL (2125; "Abe Snake For
President"): *52* 30-40
CAPITOL (3200 through 5700
series): *54-66* 5-10
COCA COLA BOTTLING CO. (2227;
"Music To Bubble-Up By"): 30-50
(Product commercials for radio use.)
CONTADINA (4476; "The Whole
Peeled Bounce"): 35-50
(Product commercials for radio. With The Hi Lo's.)
MILKY WAY (23300; "Tom Sweet &
His Milky Way Machine"): 35-50
PITTSBURGH PAINT (1/2; "Four
Pittsburgh Paint commercials"): 20-30
(Product commercials for radio use.)
RADIO (2225; "Who Listens To
Radio"): 25-40
(Promotional spots for advertising with radio.)
SOUTHERN BAPTIST CHURCH (101578;
"Southern Baptist Radio &
TV Commission"): 15-20
(Product commercials for radio use.)
STAINLESS STEEL (1369; "Stainless
Steel"): 35-50
(Product commercials for radio use.)

STAN FREBERG ON COMMERCIALS
("Rubblemeyer Farms"): $40-60
(Promotional issue only. Commercial parodies,
comparing the right and wrong approach to produc-
ing radio spots.)
TERMINIX (3540; "Floor Show, Now
Going On At Your House"): 30-40
(Product commercials for radio use.)
UNITED PRESBYTERIAN CHURCH
(101578; "The Presbyterian Church"): ...15-20
(Product commercials for radio use.)
ZEE (2020; "Zee With Freberg - Hey
You Up There"): 35-50
(Product commercials for radio use.)
ZEE (24005; "Zee Spot Commercials"): .35-50
(Product commercials for radio use.)
Picture Sleeves
BUBBLE UP (2227; "Music To
Bubble Up By"): 85-100
(Gatefold sleeve.)
CAPITOL (415; "Wun'erful
Wun'erful"): *57* 15-20
(Promotional issue only.)
CAPITOL (4097; "Green
Christmas"): *58* 6-12
CAPITOL (4329; "The Old Payola
Roll Blues"): *60* 15-20
CAPITOL (5726; "Flackman &
Reagan"): *66* 10-15
PITTSBURGH PAINT (1/2; "Four
Pittsburgh Paint commercials"): 20-30
(Reads: "The Stations Representatives Assn.
presents: Some Exciting new commercials for
Radio!")
RADIO (2225; "Who Listens To Radio"): 25-40
SOUTHERN BAPTIST CHURCH
(101578;"Southern Baptist
Radio & TV Commission"): 15-20
TERMINIX (3540; "Floor Show"): 10-20
ZEE (2020; "Zee Here, Mr. Freberg"): ...35-50
EPs: 7-Inch 33/45rpm
CAPITOL (496; "Any Requests"): *54* 20-30
CAPITOL (628; "Real St. George"): *55* ..15-25
CAPITOL (731; "Elderly Man
River"): *58* 35-50
CAPITOL (732; "The Best Of The
Stan Freberg Show"): *58* 40-50
(Promotional issue only.)
CAPITOL (1101; "Omaha"): *59* 15-25
CAPITOL (1589; "Stan
Freberg"): *61* 25-40
(Compact 33 issue.)
CAPITOL (3192; "Ugly
Duckling"): 15-25

SWIMSUITSMANSHIP (2080;
"Swimsuitsmanship"): $100-125
(Promotional issue only. Cover reads: "Fit Facts &
Figures You & Rose Marie Reid.")
UNITED PRESBYTERIAN CHURCH
(1400; "Is God Dead?"): 30-45
(Product commercials for radio use.)
LPs: 10/12-Inch 33rpm
BEKINS (27713; "Bekins Presents
The Sound Of Moving"): 35-50
(Product commercials for radio use.)
BUTTERNUT COFFEE (2000;
"Instant Butternut Coffee"): 40-60
(Product commercials for radio use.)
CAPITOL (777; "A Child's Garden
Of Freberg"): *57* 20-40
CAPITOL (1035; "The Best Of The
Stan Freberg Shows"): *58* 40-60
CAPITOL (1242; "Stan Freberg
With The Original Cast"): *59* 20-35
(With a "T" prefix.)
CAPITOL (1242; "Stan Freberg
With The Original Cast"): *69* 12-20
(With a "DT" prefix.)
CAPITOL (1242; "Stan Freberg
With The Original Cast"): *75* 5-8
(With an "SM" prefix.)
CAPITOL (1573; "Stan Freberg Presents The
United States Of America, Volume 1 - The
Early Years"): *61* 25-25
(With a "W" or "SW" prefix.)
CAPITOL (1694; "Face The
Funnies"): *62* .25-35
CAPITOL (1816; "Madison Avenue
Werewolf"): *62* 25-35
CAPITOL (2020; "Best Of Stan
Freberg"): *64* .15-25
CAPITOL (2551; "Freberg
Underground"): *66* 15-25
(With a "T" or "ST" prefix.)
CAPITOL (2551; "Freberg
Underground"): *75* 5-8
(With an "SM" prefix.)
CAPITOL (3264; "Mickey Mouse's
Birthday Party"): *63* 15-25
CAPITOL (11000 series): *78* 5-8
CAPITOL (80700; "Uncle Stan
Wants You"): *61* 60-80
(Promotional issue for the LP series, "Stan Freberg
Presents The United States Of America.")
COCA COLA (2468; "The Freedle Family
Singers"): 175-200
COLUMBIA (105948; "Hey, Look
Us Over"): 60-75
(Promotional issue only. With booklet.)

KAISER FOIL (22077; "A Kaiser Foil
Salesman Faces Life"): $125-175
(A 10-Inch LP. Product commercials for radio use.
MEADOWGOLD (2152; "Meadowgold
Dairies"): 85-100
(Product commercials for radio use.)
OREGON (2039; "Oregon
Soundtrack"): 125-150
(Product commercials for radio use. Includes press
kit.)
RADIO (3; "Radio Briefings"): 35-50
(Promotional spots for using radio advertising.)
RADIO (1499; "More Here Than
Meets The Ear"): 30-45
(Promotional spots for using radio advertising.)
RADIO (2226; "Who Listens
To Radio"): 35-50
(Promotional spots for using radio advertising.)
TV GUIDE (2889; "TV Guide
Spots"): 60-75
(Product commercials for radio use.)
Note: Advertising agency discs, containing com-
mercials for radio station use, are listed by product
name since there are no label names used.
Members: Stan Freberg; Daws Butler; June Foray;
George Burns; Jesse White; Peter Leeds; Paul
Frees; Billy May.

FRED, John
(John Fred & His Playboy Band)
Singles: 7-Inch
JEWEL: *64-65* 5-8
MONTEL: *59-62* 10-12
N-JOY: 8-10
PAULA: *65-69* 3-5
UNI: *69-70* 2-4
LPs: 10/12-Inch 33rpm
PAULA: *66-68* 20-25
UNI: *70* 10-15

FRED & THE NEW J. B.s
Singles: 7-Inch
PEOPLE: 75 .... $2-3

FREDDIE & THE DREAMERS
Singles: 7-Inch
CAPITOL: 63-64 15-20
ERIC: 1-3
MERCURY: 64-65 3-6
SUPER K: 70 2-4
Picture Sleeves
MERCURY: 65 5-10
EPs: 7-Inch 33/45rpm
MERCURY (74; "Interview With The
Dreamers"): 65 20-25
(Promotional issue only.)
LPs: 10/12-Inch 33rpm
CAPITOL: 76-79 8-10
MERCURY: 65-66 20-25
TOWER: 65 20-25
Also see JONES, Tom / Freddie & The
Dreamers / Johnny Rivers

FREDERICK
Singles: 12-Inch 33/45rpm
HEAT: 85 4-6

FREDERICK II
Singles: 7-Inch
VULTURE: 71 2-4

FREE
Singles: 7-Inch
A&M: 70-71 3-5
ISLAND: 72 3-5
LPs: 10/12-Inch 33rpm
A&M: 69-75 8-15
ISLAND: 73 8-10
Members: Andy Fraser; Paul Rodgers; Simon
Kirke; Paul Kossoff.
Also see BACK STREET CRAWLER
Also see BAD COMPANY
Also see KOSSOFF, Paul

FREE EXPRESSION
Singles: 7-Inch
VANGUARD: 81 2-3

FREE MOVEMENT
Singles: 7-Inch
COLUMBIA: 71 2-4
DECCA: 71 2-4
LPs: 10/12-Inch 33rpm
COLUMBIA: 72 8-10

FREEMAN, Bobby
Singles: 7-Inch
ABC: 73 1-3
AUTUMN: 63-64 3-6

DOUBLE SHOT: 69-70 .... $3-5
GUSTO: 1-3
JOSIE: 58-62 8-15
KING: 60-65 4-8
LOMA: 67 3-5
RNOR: 2-4
VIRGO: 72 1-3
Picture Sleeves
RNOR: 4-8
LPs: 10/12-Inch 33rpm
AUTUMN: 64 20-25
JOSIE: 65 15-20
JUBILEE (1000 series): 59 35-45
JUBILEE (5000 series): 62 20-25
KING: 65 30-35

FREEMAN, Ernie
Singles: 78rpm
CASH: 56 3-6
Singles: 7-Inch
AVA: 64 3-5
CASH: 56 6-10
IMPERIAL (Except 5752): 57-62 4-8
IMPERIAL (5752; "Theme From
Igor"): 61 6-12
KING: 60 3-5
LIBERTY: 62 3-5
LPs: 10/12-Inch 33rpm
DUNHILL: 67 10-12
IMPERIAL: 57-62 15-25
LIBERTY: 62-63 12-15
Also see OTIS, Johnny
Also see SIR CHAUNCEY
Also see WITHERSPOON, Jimmy

FREEMAN, John
Singles: 7-Inch
DAKAR: 77 1-3

FREESTYLE
(Freestyle Express)
Singles: 7-Inch
MUSIC SPECIALISTS: 84-86 1-3

FREEZ
Singles: 12-Inch 33/45rpm
STREETWISE: 83 4-6
Singles: 7-Inch
STREETWISE: 83 1-3
LPs: 10/12-Inch 33rpm
STREETWISE: 83 5-8
Also see ROCCA, John

FREHLEY, Ace
Singles: 7-Inch
CASABLANCA: 78 2-4

LPs: 10/12-Inch 33rpm
CASABLANCA (Except picture
discs): *78-80* **$20-30**
CASABLANCA (Picture discs): *79* **40-50**
MEGAFORCE: *87* **5-8**
  Also see KISS

FREHLEY'S COMET
LPs: 10/12-Inch 33rpm
MEGAFORCE: *88* **5-8**

FRENCH, Don
Singles: 7-Inch
LANCER: *59* **5-10**

FRESH, Doug E., & The Get
Fresh Band
Singles: 12-Inch 33/45rpm
REALITY: *85* **4-6**
Singles: 7-Inch
REALITY: *85-88* **1-3**

FRESH BAND
Singles: 12-Inch 33/45rpm
ARE 'N BE: *84* **4-6**

FRESH 3 MCu
Singles: 12-Inch 33/45rpm
PROFILE: *84* **4-6**
Singles: 7-Inch
PROFILE: *84* **1-3**
LPs: 10/12-Inch 33rpm
PROFILE: *84* **5-8**

FREY, Glenn
Singles: 12-Inch 33/45rpm
MCA: *84-85* **4-6**
Singles: 7-Inch
ASYLUM: *82* **1-3**
MCA: *84-88* **1-3**
Picture Sleeves
MCA: *85* **1-3**
LPs: 10/12-Inch 33rpm
ASYLUM: *82* **5-8**
MCA: *84-88* **5-8**
  Also see EAGLES

FRIDA
Singles: 7-Inch
ATLANTIC: *82* **1-3**
LPs: 10/12-Inch 33rpm
ATLANTIC: *82* **5-8**
  Also see ABBA

FRIEDMAN, Dean
Singles: 7-Inch
LIFESONG: *77-78* **1-3**
LPs: 10/12-Inch 33rpm
LIFESONG: *77-78* **5-8**

RECORD CO-OP: *82* **$5-8**

FRIEDMAN, Kinky
Singles: 7-Inch
ABC: *75* **1-3**
EPIC: *76* **1-3**
SUNRISE: *83* **1-3**
LPs: 10/12-Inch 33rpm
ABC: *74* **5-10**
EPIC: *76* **5-8**
VANGUARD: *73* **6-10**

FRIEND & LOVER
Singles: 7-Inch
ABC: *67* **3-5**
CADET CONCEPT: **2-4**
VERVE/FORECAST: *68* **3-5**
LPs: 10/12-Inch 33rpm
VERVE/FORECAST: *68* **12-15**
  Members: James Post; Cathy Post.

FRIENDS OF DISTINCTION
Singles: 7-Inch
RCA VICTOR: *69-73* **2-4**
LPs: 10/12-Inch 33rpm
COLLECTABLES: *88* **6-8**
RCA VICTOR: *69-73* **10-12**

FRIJID PINK
Singles: 7-Inch
LION: *72* **3-5**
LONDON: **1-3**
PARROT: *69-71* **4-6**
LPs: 10/12-Inch 33rpm
FANTASY: *74* **8-10**
LION: *72* **8-10**
PARROT: *70* **12-15**

FRIPP, Robert
LPs: 10/12-Inch 33rpm
EDITIONS E.G: *79-81* **5-8**
POLYDOR: *79-81* **5-8**
  Also see KING CRIMSON

FRIPP, Robert, & Andy Summers
LPs: 10/12-Inch 33rpm
A&M: *83-84* **5-8**
  Also see FRIPP, Robert
  Also see POLICE

FRIPP & ENO
LPs: 10/12-Inch 33rpm
ANTILLES: *73* **8-10**
  Members: Robert Fripp; Brian Eno.
  Also see ENO, Brian
  Also see FRIPP, Robert

FRIZZELL, Lefty
Singles: 78rpm
COLUMBIA: *50-57* **4-8**

Singles: 7-Inch
ABC: *73-75* $1-3
COLUMBIA (20000 & 21000
  series): *50-56* 5-10
COLUMBIA (40000 & 41000
  series): *56-61* 3-6
COLUMBIA (42000 through 45000
  series): *61-72* 2-4
EPs: 7-Inch 33/45rpm
COLUMBIA: *51-59* 10-20
LPs: 10/12-Inch 33rpm
ABC: *73-77* 8-12
COLUMBIA (CG series): *75* 10-12
COLUMBIA (1000 & 2000 series,
  except 1342): *64-67* 10-20
COLUMBIA (1342; "The One &
  Only Lefty Frizzell"): *59* 20-30
COLUMBIA (8000 & 9000
  series): *64-67* 10-20
  (With a "CS" prefix.)
COLUMBIA (8000 & 9000 series): 5-8
  (With a "PC" prefix.)
COLUMBIA (9000 series): *51-52* 35-50
  (10-Inch LPs. With an "HL" prefix.)
COLUMBIA (10000 series): *73-83* 5-12
COLUMBIA (30000 series): *75-82* 5-12
HARMONY (7200 series): *60* 15-20
HARMONY (11000 series): *66-68* 8-15
MCA: *82* 5-8
ROUNDER: *80-83* 5-8
  Also see PRICE, Ray / Lefty Frizzell / Carl
Smith
  Also see SMITH, Carl / Lefty Frizzell / Marty
Robbins

FROGMEN
Singles: 7-Inch
ASTRA: *61* 10-15
CANDIX: *61* 5-10
SCOTT: *64* 4-8
TEE JAY (Black vinyl): *64* 5-10
TEE JAY (Colored vinyl): *64* 10-20

FROMAN, Jane
Singles: 78rpm
CAPITOL: *52-56* 2-5
Singles: 7-Inch
CAPITOL: *52-56* 2-5
EPs: 7-Inch 33/45rpm
CAPITOL: *52-56* 5-15
LPs: 10/12-Inch 33rpm
CAPITOL: *52-56* 15-25
  Also see MARTIN, Dean / Jane Froman

FROST
(Dick Wagner & Frost)
Singles: 7-Inch
DATE: *68* $4-8
VANGUARD: *69-70* 3-6
LPs: 10/12-Inch 33rpm
VANGUARD: *69-70* 12-15
  Also see COOPER, Alice

FROST, Frank, With The Night Hawks
Singles: 7-Inch
JEWEL: *66-67* 3-5
PHILLIPS INT'L: *61* 5-12
LPs: 10/12-Inch 33rpm
JEWEL: *74* 8-10
PHILLIPS INT'L. (1975; "Hey
  Boss Man!"): *61* 400-700

FROST, Max, & The Troopers
Singles: 7-Inch
SIDEWALK: *68* 6-12
TOWER: *68-69* 5-10
LPs: 10/12-Inch 33rpm
TOWER: *68* 20-30
  Also see ALLAN, Davie

FROST, Thomas & Richard
Singles: 7-Inch
IMPERIAL: *69* 2-3
LPs: 10/12-Inch 33rpm
UNI: *72* 8-10

FROZEN GHOST
Singles: 7-Inch
ATLANTIC: *87* 1-3
LPs: 10/12-Inch 33rpm
ATLANTIC: *87* 5-8

FUGS
Singles: 7-Inch
ESP: *66* 4-6
LPs: 10/12-Inch 33rpm
BROADSIDE: *66* 30-35
ESP: *66-67* 20-25
PVC: *82* 5-8
REPRISE: *67-70* 10-15
  Members: Ed Saunders; John Anderson; Lee
Crabtree; Pete Kearney; Tuli Kupferberg; Vinny
Leary; Ken Weaver; Pete Stampfel; Steve Weber.

FULL FORCE
Singles: 12-Inch 33/45rpm
COLUMBIA: *85-86* 4-6
Singles: 7-Inch
COLUMBIA: *85-88* 1-3
LPs: 10/12-Inch 33rpm
COLUMBIA: *85-88* 5-8
  Also see LISA LISA

FULLER, Bobby
(Bobby Fuller Four; Bobby Fuller With Jim Reese & The Embers; Bobby Fuller & The Fanatics)

Singles: 7-Inch

ABC: 73	$1-3
HI-TONE:	3-5
DONNA: 65	25-35
EASTWOOD: 62	15-20
ERIC:	1-3
EXETER (Except 124): 64	15-20
EXETER (124; "I Fought The Law"): 64	30-40
LIBERTY: 65	8-10
MUSTANG: 65-66	4-6
TODD:	15-18
YUCCA: 62	20-30

LPs: 10/12-Inch 33rpm

MUSTANG (900; "KRLA King Of The Wheels"): 66	50-60
MUSTANG (901; "I Fought The Law"): 66	30-40
RHINO: 81	5-8
VOXX: 84	5-8

Members: Bobby Fuller; Randy Fuller; Duane Quirico; Jim Reese; Dalton Powell; Johnny Barbata.

FULLER, Jerry
Singles: 7-Inch

CHALLENGE (Except 59052): 60-66	4-6
CHALLENGE (59052; "Betty My Angel"): 59	10-12
COLUMBIA: 70	2-4
LIN: 58-59	10-12

LPs: 10/12-Inch 33rpm

LIN: 60	25-35
MCA: 79	5-8

FULLER, Jerry, & Diane Maxwell
Singles: 7-Inch

CHALLENGE: 60	3-5

Also see FULLER, Jerry
Also see MAXWELL, Diane

FULSON, Lowell
(Lowell Folsom; Lowel Fulsom)

Singles: 78rpm

ALADDIN: 51	15-25
BIG TOWN: 46-47	5-10
CASH: 57	4-8
CHECKER: 54-57	5-10
DOWN TOWN: 49	5-10
GILT EDGE: 51	5-10
HOLLYWOOD: 55	5-10
PARROT: 53	15-25
RPM: 50	5-10
SCOTTY'S RADIO: 46	5-10

SWING TIME: 46-53	$5-10
TRILON: 47-48	5-10

Singles: 7-Inch

ALADDIN (3088 through 3104): 51 (Black vinyl.)	30-60
ALADDIN (3104; "Stormin' & Rainin'"): 53 (Colored vinyl.)	50-100
ALADDIN (3200 series): 53-54	15-20
CASH: 57	8-12
CHECKER (Except 800 series): 59-62	4-8
CHECKER (800 series): 54-58	10-20
GRANITE: 76	2-3
HOLLYWOOD: 55	10-15
JEWEL: 69	2-4
KENT: 64-67	3-5
MOVIN': 64	3-5
PARROT (Black vinyl): 53	25-50
PARROT (Colored vinyl): 53	50-75
SWING TIME: 51-53	15-20

Picture Sleeves

KENT: 67	3-6

LPs: 10/12-Inch 33rpm

ARHOOLIE: 62	10-12
BIG TOWN: 78	5-8
CHESS:	15-18
JEWEL: 70-73	8-10
KENT: 65-71	10-15

Also see GLENN, Lloyd

FUN & GAMES
Singles: 7-Inch

UNI: 68	3-5

LPs: 10/12-Inch 33rpm

UNI: 68	12-15

FUN BOY THREE
Singles: 7-Inch

CHRYSALIS: 82-83	1-3

LPs: 10/12-Inch 33rpm
CHRYSALIS: 82-83 .... $5-8
Also see SPECIALS

FUN FUN
Singles: 12-Inch 33/45rpm
TSR: 84-85 4-6

FUNICELLO, Annette:
see ANNETTE

FUNK, Professor:
see PROFESSOR FUNK

FUNK DELUXE
Singles: 7-Inch
PLAZA: 88 1-3
SALSOUL: 83-84 1-3
LPs: 10/12-Inch 33rpm
SALSOUL: 83 5-8

FUNKADELIC
(Featuring George Clinton)
Singles: 7-Inch
WARNER BROS: 78-79 1-3
WESTBOUND: 69-76 2-3
Picture Sleeves
WARNER BROS: 78-81 1-3
LPs: 10/12-Inch 33rpm
20TH CENTURY/WESTBOUND: 75 5-8
WARNER BROS: 76-81 5-8
WESTBOUND: 70-79 8-10
Also see PARLIAMENTS

FUNKADELIC
Singles: 7-Inch
LAX: 81 1-3
LPs: 10/12-Inch 33rpm
LAX: 81 5-8
Note: This group was formed by three former members of the preceding Westbound/Warner Bros. band.
Also see FUNKADELIC (Featuring George Clinton)
Also see JUNIE

FUNKY COMMUNICATION COMMITTEE: see FCC

FUNKY KINGS
Singles: 7-Inch
ARISTA: 76 1-3
LPs: 10/12-Inch 33rpm
ARISTA: 76 5-8

FUNN
Singles: 7-Inch
MAGIC: 81 1-3

FURAY, Richie
Singles: 7-Inch
ASYLUM: 77-79 ....$1-3
LPs: 10/12-Inch 33rpm
ASYLUM: 76-82 5-8
Also see POCO
Also see SOUTHER-HILLMAN-FURAY

FURIOUS FIVE
Singles: 12-Inch 33/45rpm
SUGAR HILL: 84-85 4-6

FURIOUS FIVE & THE SUGARHILL GANG
Singles: 12-Inch 33/45rpm
SUGAR HILL: 81 4-6
Also see FURIOUS FIVE
Also see SUGARHILL GANG

FURYS
Singles: 7-Inch
MACK IV: 63 4-8

FUSE ONE
LPs: 10/12-Inch 33rpm
CTI: 82 5-8

FUTURE
Singles: 7-Inch
HOUSTON INT.: 87-88 1-3

FUTURES
Singles: 7-Inch
AVALANCHE: 1-3
GAMBLE: 73 2-4
PHILADELPHIA INT'L: 81 1-3
LPs: 10/12-Inch 33rpm
PHILADELPHIA INT'L: 81 5-8
Also see MASON, Barbara

FUZZ
Singles: 7-Inch
CALLA: 71 2-3
ROULETTE: 1-3
LPs: 10/12-Inch 33rpm
CALLA: 71 10-12

G

G., Kenny
(Kenny Gorelick)
Singles: 7-Inch
ARISTA: 83-87 1-3
LPs: 10/12-Inch 33rpm
ARISTA: 83-86 5-8
Also see LORBER, Jeff

G., Kenny, & Lenny Williams
Singles: 7-Inch
ARISTA: 83-86 . . . .$1-3
  Also see G., Kenny
  Also see WILLIAMS, Lenny

G.L.O.B.E. & WHIZ KID
Singles: 12-Inch 33/45rpm
TOMMY BOY: 83 4-6
Singles: 7-Inch
TOMMY BOY: 83 1-3

GQ
Singles: 7-Inch
ARISTA: 79-82 1-3
LPs: 10/12-Inch 33rpm
ARISTA: 79-81 5-8

G.T.
Singles: 7-Inch
A&M: 83 1-3

GTR
Singles: 78rpm
ARISTA: 86 4-6
Singles: 7-Inch
ARISTA: 86 1-3
LPs: 10/12-Inch 33rpm
ARISTA: 86 5-8
  Members: Max Bacon; Steve Howe; Steve Hackett;
  Phil Spalding; Jonathan Mover.
  Also see HACKETT, Steve
  Also see HOWE, Steve
  Also see MARILLION

GABOR SZABO:
see SZABO, Gabor

GABRIEL
Singles: 7-Inch
ABC: 76-77 2-4
EPIC: 78-79 1-3
LPs: 10/12-Inch 33rpm
ABC: 75-76 8-10
EPIC: 78 5-8

GABRIEL, Peter
Singles: 12-Inch 33/45rpm
GEFFEN: 82-86 4-6
Singles: 7-Inch
ATCO: 77 2-3
ATLANTIC: 78 2-3
GEFFEN: 82-87 1-3
MERCURY: 80 1-3
WARNER BROS: 86 1-3
Picture Sleeves
GEFFEN: 82-86 1-3
LPs: 10/12-Inch 33rpm
ATCO: 77 10-12

Peter Gabriel (Photo: Annie Leibovitz)

ATLANTIC: 78 . . . .$8-10
GEFFEN: 82-86 5-8
MERCURY: 80 5-8
  Also see BUSH, Kate
  Also see GENESIS

GABRIEL & THE ANGELS
Singles: 7-Inch
AMY: 61 30-35
NORMAN: 61-62 8-10
SWAN: 62-63 5-10

GADABOUTS
Singles: 7-Inch
JARO: 60 4-8
MERCURY: 54-56 5-10
WING: 55 5-10

GADSON, James
Singles: 7-Inch
CREAM.: 72 2-4

GADSON, Mel
Singles: 7-Inch
BIG TOP: 60 5-10

GAGE, Yvonne
Singles: 7-Inch
CIM: 84 1-3

GAGNON, Andre
Singles: 7-Inch
LONDON: 76 2-4

GAIL, Sunny:
see GALE, Sunny

GAINES, Earl
(Earl Gains)
Singles: 7-Inch
CHAMPION: *58-60* $4-6
DELUXE: *68-69* 2-4
HBR: *66* 3-5
HOLLYWOOD: *67* 3-5
SEVENTY SEVEN: *73* 2-3
LPs: 10/12-Inch 33rpm
DELUXE: *69* 10-15
EXCELLO: *62* 3-5

GAINES, Rosie
Singles: 7-Inch
EPIC: *85* 1-3

GALE, Eric
Singles: 7-Inch
COLUMBIA: *78-80* 1-3
LPs: 10/12-Inch 33rpm
COLUMBIA: *77-80* 5-8
ELEKTRA: *83* 5-8
KUDU: *73* 8-10
Also see GRUSIN, Dave

GALE, Sunny
(Sunny Gale & The Saints & Sinners Dixieland Band; Sunny Gail)
Singles: 78rpm
DECCA: *56-57* 3-5
RCA VICTOR: *52-56* 3-5
Singles: 7-Inch
BLAINE: *65* 3-5
CANADIAN AMERICAN: *63-64* 3-5
DECCA: *56-59* 5-10
RCA VICTOR (4000 through 6000 series): *52-56* 6-12
RCA VICTOR (9000 series): *68* 2-4
RIVERSIDE: *63* 3-5
TERRACE: *62* 3-5
THIMBLE: *74* 1-3
WARWICK: *60-61* 3-5
LPs: 10/12-Inch 33rpm
CANADIAN AMERICAN: *64* 10-20
Also see WILCOX, Eddie

GALE, Sunny, & The Du Droppers
Singles: 7-Inch
RCA VICTOR: *53* 10-20
Also see DU DROPPERS
Also see GALE, Sunny

GALENS
Singles: 7-Inch
CHALLENGE: *63-65* 3-6

GALLAGHER, Rory
LPs: 10/12-Inch 33rpm
ATCO: *71-72* $10-12
CHRYSALIS: *75-80* 5-8
MERCURY: *82* 5-8
POLYDOR: *72-75* 8-10
Also see TASTE

GALLAGHER & LYLE
Singles: 7-Inch
A&M: *73-78* 2-3
LPs: 10/12-Inch 33rpm
A&M: *73-78* 8-10
CAPITOL (10000 series): *77* 5-8
(With an "SM" prefix.)
CAPITOL (11000 series): *72* 8-12
(With an "ST" prefix.)
Members: Ben Gallagher; Graham Lyle.
Also see MC GUINNESS-FLINT

GALLAHADS
Singles: 78rpm
CAPITOL: *55* 3-5
JUBILEE: *56* 3-5
VIK: *57* 3-5
Singles: 7-Inch
CAPITOL: *55* 5-10
JUBILEE: *56* 5-8
VIK: *57* 4-8

GALLERY
Singles: 7-Inch
SUSSEX: *72* 2-3
Picture Sleeves
SUSSEX: *72* 2-4
LPs: 10/12-Inch 33rpm
SUSSEX: *72-73* 10-12
Member: Jim Gold.

GALLOP, Frank
Singles: 7-Inch
ABC-PARAMOUNT: *58* 3-5
KAPP: *66* 2-4
MUSICOR: *66* 2-3
Picture Sleeves
MUSICOR: *66* 3-6
LPs: 10/12-Inch 33rpm
MUSICOR: *66* 8-12

GALLOWAY, Leata
Singles: 7-Inch
COLUMBIA: *88* 1-3

GAMBLE, Dee Dee Sharp:
see SHARP, Dee Dee

GAME THEORY
EPs: 7-Inch 33/45rpm
ENIGMA: *82-86* 4-6

LPs: 10/12-Inch 33rpm
ENIGMA: 82-86 ....$5-8
Members: Scott Miller; Gil Ray; Shelley La-
Freniere; Guillaume Gassuan; Donteet Thayer.

GAMMA
Singles: 7-Inch
ELEKTRA: 79-82 1-3
LPs: 10/12-Inch 33rpm
ELEKTRA: 79-82 5-8
Also see MONTROSE

GANG OF FOUR
Singles: 12-Inch 33/45rpm
WARNER BROS: 80-84 4-6
Singles: 7-Inch
WARNER BROS: 80-84 1-3
LPs: 10/12-Inch 33rpm
WARNER BROS: 80-83 5-8
Also see SHRIEKBACK

GANG'S BACK
Singles: 7-Inch
HANDSHAKE: 82 1-3

GANGSTERS
Singles: 7-Inch
HEAT: 79-81 2-3
MONTAGE: 82 1-3
LPs: 10/12-Inch 33rpm
MONTAGE: 82 5-8

GANTS
Singles: 7-Inch
LIBERTY: 65-67 4-8
LPs: 10/12-Inch 33rpm
LIBERTY: 65-66 15-25

GAP, Billy & Baby:
see BILLY & BABY GAP

GAP BAND
Singles: 12-Inch 33/45rpm
PASSPORT: 83 4-6
TOTAL EXPERIENCE: 82-86 4-6
Singles: 7-Inch
A&M: 75 2-3
MEGA: 84 1-3
MERCURY: 1-3 79-84
PASSPORT: 83 1-3
RCA VICTOR: 87 1-3
SHELTER: 74 2-3
TATTOO: 77 1-3
TOTAL EXPERIENCE: 82-87 1-3
LPs: 10/12-Inch 33rpm
MERCURY: 79-80 5-8
PASSPORT: 83 5-8
SHELTER: 74 8-10
TATTOO: 77 8-10

TOTAL EXPERIENCE: 82-86 ....$5-8

GARCIA, Jerry
(The Jerry Garcia Band)
Singles: 7-Inch
DOUGLAS: 73 3-5
ROUND: 72-74 3-5
WARNER BROS: 72 3-5
LPs: 10/12-Inch 33rpm
ARISTA: 78-82 5-8
ROUND: 74-75 8-10
UNITED ARTISTS: 76 8-10
WARNER BROS (2582;
"Garcia"): 72 20-35
Also see GRATEFUL DEAD
Also see IT'S A BEAUTIFUL DAY
Also see JEFFERSON AIRPLANE
Also see JEFFERSON STARSHIP
Also see OLD & IN THE WAY
Also see ROWANS
Also see SAUNDERS, Merl

GARCIA, Jerry, & Robert Hunter
Singles: 7-Inch
ROUND (102; "Sampler For Dead
Heads"): 74 20-30
(Price includes a letter about the Grateful Dead LP,
The Mars Hotel, and a few miniature LP covers.
Promotional fan club issue.)
ROUND (102; "Sampler For Dead
Heads"): 74 15-20
(Price for disc by itself, without inserts.)
Also see GARCIA, Jerry

GARDNER, Dave
(Brother Dave Gardner)
Singles: 7-Inch
OJ: 57 4-8
RCA VICTOR: 59-61 3-6
LPs: 10/12-Inch 33rpm
CAMDEN: 73 5-10
CAPITOL: 63 15-20
RCA VICTOR: 60-64 15-25
TOWER: 67 8-15

GARDNER, Don, & Dee Dee Ford
Singles: 7-Inch
FIRE: 62 4-6
FLASHBACK: 65 1-3
KC: 62 3-5
LUDIX: 63 3-5
RED TOP: 63 3-5
TRU-GLO-TOWN: 66 3-5
LPs: 10/12-Inch 33rpm
FIRE: 62 35-45
SUE: 66 15-20

(L-R) Art Garfunkel co-starred with Candice Bergen, Jack Nicholson and Ann-Margret in *Carnal Knowledge*

Also see WASHINGTON, Baby, & Don Gardner

GARDNER, Joanna
Singles: 7-Inch
PHILLY WORLD: *85* $1-3

GARDNER, Reggie
Singles: 7-Inch
CAPITOL: *71* 2-3

GARDNER, Taana
Singles: 7-Inch
WEST END: *81* 1-3

GARFUNKEL, Art
Singles: 7-Inch
COLUMBIA: *73-88* 1-3
Picture Sleeves
COLUMBIA: *81* 1-3
LPs: 10/12-Inch 33rpm
COLUMBIA (30000 series): *73-81* 8-12
(With an "FC," "JC," "KC," or "PC" prefix.)
COLUMBIA (30000 series): *73-75* 10-15
(With a "CQ" or "PCQ" prefix. Quad issues.)
COLUMBIA (47000 series): *78* 12-15
(Half-speed mastered.)
COLUMBIA: *88* 5-8
Also see GARR, Artie
Also see SIMON & GARFUNKEL
Also see TAYLOR, James

GARI, Frank
Singles: 7-Inch
ATLANTIC: *62* 3-5
CAPITOL: *68* 2-4
CRUSADE: *60-62* 3-5
RIBBON: *59* 4-6

Picture Sleeves
CRUSADE: *61-62* $8-15

GARLAND, Judy
Singles: 78rpm
CAPITOL: *56-57* 3-5
COLUMBIA: *53-54* 3-5
DECCA (Except 2000 through
  4000 series): *42-55* 4-8
DECCA (2000 through 4000
  series): *39-42* 8-15
Singles: 7-Inch
ABC: *67* 2-4
CAPITOL: *56-63* 4-8
COLUMBIA (40000 series): *53-54* 5-10
DECCA (25000 series): *65* 4-8
DECCA (29000 series): *55* 5-10
WARNER BROS: *63* 3-5
Promotional Singles
CAPITOL ("After You've Gone"/
  "When You're Smiling"): *59* 10-20
Picture Sleeves
CAPITOL ("After You've Gone"/
  "When You're Smiling"): *59* 15-25
(Sleeve reads "Two Of The Top Tunes From Garland At The Grove.")
EPs: 7-Inch 33/45rpm
CAPITOL (676; "Miss Show
  Business"): *55* 10-20
CAPITOL (734; "Judy"): *56* 10-20
CAPITOL (835; "Alone"): *57* 10-20
CAPITOL (1569; "Judy At Carnegie
  Hall"): *62* 10-15
COLUMBIA (1201; "A Star Is
  Born"): *54* 15-20
(Soundtrack.)

COLUMBIA (2598; "Judy
Garland"): *57* $20-30
COLUMBIA (7621; "Born In A
Trunk"): *56* 25-50
DECCA (620; "Judy Garland At The Palace/
Greatest Performances"): *55* 10-20
DECCA (661; "The Wizard Of Oz"): *51* . 15-25
DECCA (2050; "Judy Garland,
Volume 2"): *53* 12-20
MGM (268; "If You Feel Like Singing,
Sing"): *54* 10-20
MGM (1038; "Get Happy"): *55* 10-20
MGM (1116; "Look For The Silver
Lining"): *55* 10-20
MGM (1122; "Judy Garland"): *55* 10-20

LPs: 10/12-Inch 33rpm

ABC (620; Judy Garland At Home At
The Palace"): *67* 10-15
ABC (30007; "Judy Garland - The
ABC Collection"): *76* 5-10
AEI: 8-12
ACCESSOR: 8-15
C.I.T.: 8-12
CAPITOL (676; "Miss Show
Business"): *55* 25-40
(With a "W" prefix.)
CAPITOL (676; "Miss Show
Business"): *63* 10-20
(With an "SW" prefix.)
CAPITOL (734; "Judy"): *56* 25-35
(With a "T" prefix.)
CAPITOL (734; "Judy"): *63* 10-20
(With a "DT" prefix.)
CAPITOL (835; "Alone"): *57* 25-35
(With a "T" prefix.)
CAPITOL (835; "Alone"): *63* 10-20
(With a "DT" prefix.)
CAPITOL (1036; "Judy In Love"): *58* ... 20-35
CAPITOL (1118; "Garland At The
Grove"): *59* 40-60
CAPITOL (1188; "The Letter"): *59* 20-30
(With John Ireland.)
CAPITOL (1467; "Judy - That's
Entertainment"): *60* 20-35
CAPITOL (1569; "Judy At Carnegie
Hall"): *61* 20-35
CAPITOL (1710; "The Garland
Touch"): *62* 20-30
CAPITOL (1861; "I Could Go On
Singing"): *63* 25-35
(Soundtrack.)
CAPITOL (1941; "Our Love Letter"): *63* . 15-20
(With John Ireland.)

Judy Garland

CAPITOL (1999; "The Hits Of
Judy Garland"): *64* $20-30
(With a "T" or "ST" prefix.)
CAPITOL (1999; "The Hits Of
Judy Garland"): *75* 5-8
(With an "SM" prefix.)
CAPITOL (2062; "Just For Openers"): *64* 15-25
CAPITOL (2988; "Judy Garland -
Deluxe Set"): *68* 20-35
CAPITOL (11763; "Alone"): *78* 5-8
CAPITOL (11876; "Judy - That's
Entertainment"): *79* 5-8
CAPITOL (12034; "Just For Openers"): *80* . 5-8
CAPITOL (16175; "The Hits Of
Judy Garland"): *81* 4-6
COLUMBIA (762; "Born In A
Trunk"): *56* 50-100
(10-inch LP.)
COLUMBIA (1101; "A Star Is
Born"): *58* 20-30
(Soundtrack.)
COLUMBIA (1201; "A Star Is
Born"): *54* 40-55
(Soundtrack. Deluxe boxed edition.)
COLUMBIA (8740; "A Star Is
Born"): *63* 20-30
(Soundtrack. Reprocessed stereo.)
COLUMBIA (10011; "A Star Is
Born"): *73* 5-12
(Soundtrack.)
COLUMBIA/CSP (8740; "A Star Is
Born"): 5-10
(Soundtrack. Reprocessed stereo.)

COMPUNSONIC: $8-12
DRG: 10-20
DECCA (5; "Collector's Items:
1936-1945"): *70* 15-25
DECCA (172; "The Best Of Judy
Garland"): *63* 15-20
DECCA (4199; "The Magic Of Judy
Garland"): *61* 15-20
DECCA (5152; "The Wizard Of
Oz"): *51* 50-100
(10-Inch LP.)
DECCA (6020; "Judy Garland At
The Palace"): *55* 35-45
DECCA (8190; "Judy Garland - Greatest
Performances"): *55* 35-45
DECCA (8387; "The Wizard Of
Oz"): *56* 30-40
(One side of this LP, *The Song Hits From Pinoc-
chio*, does not feature Judy.)
DECCA (75150; "Judy Garland's
Greatest Hits"): *69* 8-12
DECCA (78387; "The Wizard Of
Oz"): *67* 10-15
51 WEST: 5-8
HARMONY (11366; "A Star Is
Born"): *69* 10-15
JUNO (1000; "Judy - London
1969"): *69* 6-12
MCA (4003; "The Best Of
Judy Garland"): *73* 10-15
MGM (1; "Golden Years
At MGM"): *69* 15-25
MGM (21; "The Pirate"): *51* 75-150
(Soundtrack, with Gene Kelly. 10-Inch LP.)
MGM (82; "Judy Garland Sings"): *51* .. 50-100
MGM (113; "Judy Garland"): *70* 8-12
MGM (3149; "Judy Garland"): *54* 35-45
MGM (3234; "The Pirate"): *55* 20-35
(Soundtrack, with Gene Kelly.)
MGM (3771; "Words & Music"): *60* 15-25
MGM (3989; "The Judy Garland
Story, Volume 1"): *61* 15-20
MGM (3996; "The Wizard Of Oz"): *61* .. 15-20
MGM (4005; "The Judy Garland
Story, Volume 2"): *61* 15-20
MGM (4204; "The Very Best Of
Judy Garland"): *64* 12-20
MARK '56: 8-15
METRO (505; "Judy Garland"): *65* 10-15
METRO (581; "Judy Garland
In Song"): *66* 10-15
PARAGON: 5-10
PHOENIX 10: 8-12
PICKWICK: 5-10
RADIANT: 6-12

RADIOLA: $5-10
SPRINGBOARD: 5-10
TRIP (9; "16 Greatest Hits - Judy
Garland"): *76* 5-8
TROPHY: 5-10
Also see CROSBY, Bing, & Judy Garland
Also see MARTIN, Dean
Also see YOUNG, Victor

GARLAND, Judy / Tommy Dorsey
Singles: 78rpm
VOGUE ("The Trolley Song"): *47* 200-300
(Picture disc.)
Also see DORSEY, Tommy

GARLAND, Judy, & Liza Minnelli
Singles: 7-Inch
CAPITOL: *65* 2-4
LPs: 10/12-Inch 33rpm
CAPITOL (2295; "Live At The London
Palladium"): *65* 15-20
CAPITOL (11191; "Live At The London
Palladium"): *73* 5-8
MFSL: *81* 20-35
TROLLEY CAR: 5-10
Also see GARLAND, Judy
Also see MINNELLI, Liza

GARLOW, Clarence
Singles: 78rpm
ALADDIN: *52* 8-15
FEATURE: *51-54* 8-15
FOLK STAR: *54* 5-10
FLAIR: *54* 10-20
GOLDBAND: *56-57* 5-10
LYRIC: *51* 10-15
MACY'S: *49* 5-10
Singles: 7-Inch
ALADDIN: *52* 25-50
FEATURE: *54* 20-40
FLAIR: *54* 25-50
FOLK STAR: *54* 15-20
GOLDBAND: *56-57* 8-15

GARNER, Erroll
(Erroll Garner Trio)
Singles: 7-Inch
ABC-PARAMOUNT: *61-62* 2-3
COLUMBIA: *50-70* 2-4
MGM: *66-69* 2-3
MERCURY (70000 series): *54* 2-4
MERCURY (72000 & 73000
series): *63-71* 2-3
REPRISE: *63* 2-3
EPs: 7-Inch 33/45rpm
ATLANTIC: *52-56* 5-10
BRUNSWICK: *53* 5-10

COLUMBIA: *50-75*	$5-15
EMARCY: *56*	5-10
KING: *54*	5-10
MERCURY: *54-56*	5-10
SAVOY: *51-55*	5-10

LPs: 10/12-Inch 33rpm

ABC-PARAMOUNT: *61*	10-20
ATLANTIC (100 series): *50-52*	20-40
(10-Inch LPs.)	
ATLANTIC (1200 series): *56*	10-20
BARONET: *61*	10-20
BLUE NOTE (5000 series): *52-53*	20-40
10-Inch LPs.)	
COLUMBIA (500 through 1500 series): *54-61*	10-20
COLUMBIA (2500 series): *56*	15-25
(10-Inch LPs.)	
COLUMBIA (6000 series): *50-51*	20-40
(10-Inch LPs.)	
COLUMBIA (8000 series): *60*	10-20
COLUMBIA (9000 series): *70*	5-10
COLUMBIA SPECIAL PRODUCTS: *79*	5-8
DIAL: *50*	25-50
(10-Inch LPs.)	
EMARCY (26000 series): *54*	20-35
(10-Inch LPs.)	
EMARCY (36000 series): *55-56*	15-25
ENRICA: *59*	15-20
EVEREST: *70*	5-10
GRAND AWARD: *56*	15-25
HARMONY: *68*	5-10
JAZZTONE: *57*	15-20
KING (200 series): *54*	20-35
(10-Inch LPs.)	
KING (500 series): *58*	12-20
LONDON: *72-73*	5-10
MGM: *65-68*	8-15
MERCURY (20000 series): *54-63*	10-25
(Monaural.)	
MERCURY (25000 series): *51*	20-40
(10-Inch LPs.)	
MERCURY (60000 series): *62-63*	10-20
(Stereo.)	
MERCURY (61000 series): *70*	5-10
REPRISE: *63*	10-20
RONDO-LETTE: *58*	15-20
ROOST: *52*	20-40
(10-Inch LPs.)	
ROOST (2000 series): *56*	15-25
SAVOY (1100 series): *78*	5-8
SAVOY (2000 series): *76*	5-10
SAVOY (12000 series): *55*	15-25
SAVOY (15000 series): *50-51*	20-40
(10-Inch LPs.)	
TRIP: *74*	5-8

WING: *62*	$10-15

Also see STARR, Kay / Erroll Garner

GARNETT, Gale
(Gale Garnett & The Gentle Reign)
Singles: 7-Inch

COLUMBIA: *68*	2-3
RCA VICTOR: *64-67*	2-4

Picture Sleeves

RCA VICTOR: *64*	3-6

LPs: 10/12-Inch 33rpm

COLUMBIA: *68-69*	8-12
RCA VICTOR: *64-66*	8-12

GARR, Artie
(Art Garfunkel)
Singles: 7-Inch

OCTAVIA: *61*	15-20
WARWICK: *59*	20-25

Also see GARFUNKEL, Art

GARRAFFA, Donna
Singles: 12-Inch 33/45rpm

ARTIST INT'L: *85*	4-6

GARRETT, Lee
Singles: 7-Inch

CHRYSALIS: *76*	2-3

GARRETT, Leif
Singles: 7-Inch

ATLANTIC: *77-78*	1-3
SCOTTI BROS: *78-81*	1-3

Picture Sleeves

ATLANTIC: *77-78*	1-3
SCOTTI BROS: *78-81*	1-3

LPs: 10/12-Inch 33rpm

ATLANTIC: *77*	5-8
SCOTTI BROS: *78-80*	5-8

Also see CHIC / Roberta Flack / Leif Garrett / Genesis

GARRETT, Scott
(Scott Garret)
Singles: 7-Inch

LAURIE (Except 3029): *59*	4-6
LAURIE (3029; "Love Story"): *59*	15-20
(With The Mystics.)	
OKEH: *60*	5-10

Also see MYSTICS

GARRETT, Siedah
Singles: 12-Inch 33/45rpm

QWEST: *85*	4-6

Singles: 7-Inch

QWEST: *85-88*	1-3

LPs: 10/12-Inch 33rpm

QWEST: *88*	5-8

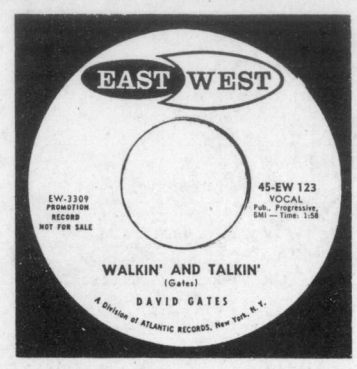

GARRETT, Tommy
(Tommy Garrett & 25 Pianos)
LPs: 10/12-Inch 33rpm
LIBERTY: *62* **$8-12**
Also see 50 GUITARS OF TOMMY GARRETT

GARRETT, Vernon, & Marie Franklin
Singles: 7-Inch
VENTURE: *76* 2-4

GARRETT'S CREW
Singles: 7-Inch
CLOCKWORK: *83* 1-3

GARY, John
Singles: 7-Inch
ACE: *62* 2-4
BIG B: *64* 2-4
FRATERNITY: *59-66* 2-4
RCA VICTOR: *63-71* 2-3
ST. JAMES: *63* 2-4
LPs: 10/12-Inch 33rpm
CAMDEN: *68* 5-10
CHURCHILL: *77* 4-8
METRO: *65* 5-10
RCA VICTOR: *63-78* 5-15
Also see ANN-MARGRET & JOHN GARY

GARY & DAVE
Singles: 7-Inch
LONDON: *73* 2-3

GARY & THE HORNETS
Singles: 7-Inch
SMASH: *66-68* 3-5
Picture Sleeves
SMASH: *66-67* 5-10

GARY O'
LPs: 10/12-Inch 33rpm
CAPITOL: *81* 5-8

GARY'S GANG
Singles: 12-Inch 33/45rpm
COLUMBIA: *79* $4-6
RADAR: *83* 4-6
Singles: 7-Inch
COLUMBIA: *79* 1-3
RADAR: *83* 1-3
LPs: 10/12-Inch 33rpm
COLUMBIA: *79* 5-8
Members: Gary Turnier; Eric Matthew.

GASCA, Luis
LPs: 10/12-Inch 33rpm
BLUE THUMB: *72* 8-10

GATES, David
(David Gates & The Accents)
Singles: 7-Inch
ARISTA: *81* 2-3
DEL-FI: *63* 10-15
EAST WEST (123; "Walkin' & Talkin"): *59* 75-100
ELEKTRA: *73-80* 2-4
MALA: *60-61* 40-50
PLANETARY: *65* 8-10
ROBBINS: *61* 35-45
Picture Sleeves
ELEKTRA: *77* 1-3
LPs: 10/12-Inch 33rpm
ARISTA: *81* 5-8
ELEKTRA: *73-80* 8-15
Also see ASHLEY, Del
Also see BREAD
Also see DAVID & LEE

GATLIN, Larry
**(Larry Gatlin & The Gatlin Brothers Band;
Larry Gatlin With Family & Friends)**
Singles: 7-Inch
COLUMBIA: *79-88* 1-3
MONUMENT: *73-78* 2-3

Larry Gatlin (center) and the Gatlin Brothers Band

LPs: 10/12-Inch 33rpm
COLUMBIA: *79-86* **$5-8**
MONUMENT: *74-78* **5-10**
Members: Larry Gatlin; Steve Gatlin; Rudy Gatlin.

GAYE, Marvin
Singles: 12-Inch 33/45rpm
COLUMBIA: *83-85* **4-6**
Singles: 7-Inch
COLUMBIA: *82-85* **1-3**
DETROIT FREE PRESS ("The Teen
Beat Song"): *66* **20-30**
(Promotional issue only.)
MOTOWN: **1-3**
MOTOWN/TOPPS ("How Sweet It Is
To Be Loved By You"): *67* **50-75**
(Topps Chewing Gum promotional item.
Cardboard flexi, picture disc. Issued with generic
paper sleeve.)
TAMLA (1800 series): *86* **1-3**
TAMLA (54041; "Let Your Conscience
Be Your Guide"): *61* **20-25**
TAMLA (54055; "Sandman"): *62* **45-55**
TAMLA (54063; "Taking My Time"): *62* **10-15**
TAMLA (54068 through 54170): *62-68* **4-8**
TAMLA (54176 through 54280): *68-77* **2-5**
Picture Sleeves
TAMLA (1800 series): *86* **1-3**
TAMLA (54000 series): *64-77* **3-6**
LPs: 10/12-Inch 33rpm
COLUMBIA: *82-85* **5-8**
KORY: *76-77* **8-10**
MOTOWN: *64-88* **8-15**
NATURAL RESOURCES: *78* **5-8**
TAMLA (221 through 251): *61-64* **25-35**
TAMLA (252 through 299): *64-69* **15-20**
TAMLA (300 series): *70-81* **8-12**
TAMLA (6100 series): *86* **5-8**
Also see MARTHA & THE VANDELLAS
Also see MOONGLOWS

GAYE, Marvin / Gladys Knight & The Pips
Singles: 7-Inch
MOTOWN: *68* **3-5**
Also see KNIGHT, Gladys

GAYE, Marvin, & Diana Ross
Singles: 7-Inch
MOTOWN: *73-74* **2-3**
Also see ROSS, Diana

GAYE, Marvin, & Tammi Terrell
Singles: 7-Inch
TAMLA: *67-70* **3-5**
LPs: 10/12-Inch 33rpm
MOTOWN: *80-82* **5-8**

TAMLA: *67-70* **$10-15**
Also see TERRELL, Tammi

GAYE, Marvin, & Mary Wells
Singles: 7-Inch
MOTOWN: *64* **3-5**
Picture Sleeves
MOTOWN: *64* **4-6**
LPs: 10/12-Inch 33rpm
MOTOWN: *64* **20-25**
Also see WELLS, Mary

GAYE, Marvin, & Kim Weston
Singles: 7-Inch
TAMLA: *64-67* **3-5**
LPs: 10/12-Inch 33rpm
TAMLA: *66* **20-25**
Also see GAYE, Marvin
Also see WESTON, Kim

GAYLE, Crystal
Singles: 7-Inch
COLUMBIA: *79-82* **1-3**
DECCA: *70-72* **2-4**
ELEKTRA: *82* **1-3**
MCA: *77* **1-3**
UNITED ARTISTS: *74-80* **1-3**
WARNER BROS: *83-88* **1-3**
Picture Sleeves
COLUMBIA: *79-82* **1-3**
UNITED ARTISTS: *77-79* **1-3**
LPs: 10/12-Inch 33rpm
COLUMBIA: *79-83* **5-8**
ELEKTRA: *82* **5-8**
LIBERTY: *80-82* **5-8**
MCA: *78* **5-8**
MFSL: *80* **20-40**
UNITED ARTISTS: *75-80* **5-10**
WARNER BROS: *83-88* **5-8**
Also see RABBITT, Eddie, & Crystal Gayle

GAYLE, Crystal, & Gary Morris
Singles: 7-Inch
WARNER BROS: *85-88* **1-3**
Also see MORRIS, Gary

GAYLE, Crystal, & Tom Waits
LPs: 10/12-Inch 33rpm
COLUMBIA: *82* **5-8**
Also see GAYLE, Crystal
Also see WAITS, Tom

GAYLORD, Ronnie
Singles: 78rpm
MERCURY: *54-55* **3-5**
WING: *55-56* **3-5**
Singles: 7-Inch
MERCURY: *54-55* **3-5**

WING: *55-56* $3-5
EPs: 7-Inch 33/45rpm
MERCURY: *55* 5-10
Also see GAYLORD & HOLIDAY

GAYLORD & HOLIDAY
Singles: 7-Inch
NATURAL RESOURCES: *77* 1-3
PALMER: *67* 2-3
PRODIGAL: *76* 1-3
VERVE: *66* 2-3
LPs: 10/12-Inch 33rpm
NATURAL RESOURCES: *76* 5-8
PRODIGAL: *75* 5-8
VMI: *72* 5-10
Members: Ronnie Gaylord; Burt Holiday.
Also see GAYLORD, Ronnie
Also see GAYLORDS

GAYLORDS
Singles: 78rpm
MERCURY: *52-62* 4-6
Singles: 7-Inch
MERCURY: *52-62* 4-8
TIME: *64* 2-4
EPs: 7-Inch 33/45rpm
MERCURY: *54-56* 5-12
LPs: 10/12-Inch 33rpm
MERCURY: *54-63* 10-20
TIME: *64* 8-15
WING: *59-64* 8-15
Members: Don Rea; Burt "Holiday" Bonaldi; Billy
Christ.
Also see GAYLORD & HOLIDAY

GAYNOR, Gloria
Singles: 12-Inch 33/45rpm
POLYDOR: *78* 4-6
SILVER BLUE: *83* 4-6
Singles: 7-Inch
COLUMBIA: *73* 2-3
JOCIDA: *65* 3-5
MGM: *74-75* 2-3
POLYDOR: *76-81* 1-3
SILVER BLUE: *83* 1-3
LPs: 10/12-Inch 33rpm
ATLANTIC: *82* 5-8
MGM: *75* 8-10
POLYDOR: *77-80* 5-8

GAYTEN, Paul
Singles: 78rpm
ARGO: *57* 5-10
CHECKER: *55-56* 5-10
DELUXE: *47-49* 5-10
OKEH: *52-55* 5-10
REGAL: *49-51* 5-10

Singles: 7-Inch
ANNA: *59-60* $5-8
ARGO: *57-58* 10-15
CHECKER (801 through 836): *55-56* 10-20
CHECKER (872 through 880): *57-58* 5-10
OKEH: *52-55* 10-15

G-CLEFS
Singles: 78rpm
PARIS: *57* 3-6
PILGRIM: *56* 3-6
Singles: 7-Inch
LOMA: *66* 3-5
PARIS: *57* 5-8
PILGRIM: *56* 5-10
REGINA: *64* 3-5
ROULETTE: 1-3
TERRACE: *61-63* 4-8
VEEP: *65-66* 3-5
Also see CANNON, Freddy

GEDDES, David
Singles: 7-Inch
ATCO: *75* 2-3
BIG TREE: *75* 2-3
H&L: *77* 2-3
ZODIAC: *77* 2-3
LPs: 10/12-Inch 33rpm
BIG TREE: *75* 8-10

GEE, Spoonie:
see SPOONIE GEE

GEILS, J., Band,
(Geils)
Singles: 12-Inch 33/45rpm
EMI AMERICA: *82-84* 4-6
Singles: 7-Inch
ATLANTIC: *71-78* 2-3
EMI AMERICA: *78-84* 1-3
PRIVATE I: *85* 1-3
Picture Sleeves
ATLANTIC: *73-78* 2-3
EMI AMERICA: *78-84* 1-3
PRIVATE I: *85* 2-3
LPs: 10/12-Inch 33rpm
ATLANTIC (Black vinyl): *70-80* 8-12
ATLANTIC (Colored vinyl): *73* 15-20
EMI AMERICA: *78-84* 5-8
NAUTILUS: 15-20
Also see WOLF, Peter

GELDOF, Bob
Singles: 7-Inch
ATLANTIC: *86* 1-3
LPs: 10/12-Inch 33rpm
ATLANTIC: *86* 5-8
Also see BAND AID

Also see BOOMTOWN RATS

GEM
Singles: 7-Inch
STREETKING: *84* $1-3

GENE & DEBBE
Singles: 7-Inch
HICKORY: *70* 2-4
TRX: *67-69* 3-5
LPs: 10/12-Inch 33rpm
TRX: *68* 15-20
Members: Gene Thomas; Debbe Nevills.
Also see THOMAS, Gene

GENE & EUNICE
Singles: 78rpm
ALADDIN: *55* 4-8
COMBO: *55* 4-8
Singles: 7-Inch
ALADDIN: *55* 8-12
CASE: *59* 4-6
COLLECTABLES: 1-3
COMBO: *55* 8-12
ERA: *72* 1-3
LILLY: *62* 3-5
EPs: 7-Inch 33/45rpm
CASE: *59* 20-30
(Issued with a paper sleeve.)
Members: Gene Forrest; Eunice Levy.
Also see EUNICE

GENE & JERRY (Chandler & Butler):
see CHANDLER, Gene, & Jerry Butler

GENE & TOMMY
Singles: 7-Inch
ABC: *67* 3-5
Members: Terry Cashman; Tommy West.
Also see CASHMAN & WEST

GENE & WENDELL
Singles: 7-Inch
PHILIPS: *62-63* 3-5
RAY STARR: *61-62* 3-5

GENE LOVES JEZEBEL
Singles: 12-Inch 33/45rpm
GEFFEN: *86* 4-6
Singles: 7-Inch
GEFFEN: *86-88* 1-3
LPs: 10/12-Inch 33rpm
GEFFEN: *86-87* 5-8
Members: Michael Aston; Jay Aston; James Stevenson; Chris Bell; Peter Rizzo.
Also see THOMPSON TWINS

GENE THE HAT
Singles: 7-Inch
CHECKER: *61* 3-5

DEAUVILLE: *62* $3-5
GEE: *62* 3-5

GENELLS
Singles: 7-Inch
DEWEY: *63* 5-8

GENERAL CAINE:
see CAINE, General

GENERAL KANE
Singles: 12-Inch 33/45rpm
MOTOWN: *86* 5-8
Singles: 7-Inch
MOTOWN: *86-87* 1-3
LPs: 10/12-Inch 33rpm
MOTOWN: *86* 5-8

GENERAL PUBLIC
Singles: 12-Inch 33/45rpm
I.R.S.: *84-86* 4-6
Singles: 7-Inch
I.R.S.: *84-86* 1-3
LPs: 10/12-Inch 33rpm
I.R.S.: *84-86* 5-8

GENESIS
Singles: 12-Inch 33/45rpm
ATLANTIC: *86* 4-6
Singles: 7-Inch
ATCO: *76-77* 2-3
ATLANTIC: *78-87* 1-3
CHARISMA: *73* 4-6
PARROT: *68* 10-15
Picture Sleeves
ATLANTIC: *78-86* 1-3
Promotional Singles
ATCO: *76-77* 3-5
ATLANTIC: *78-86* 2-4
CHARISMA: *73* 4-8
PARROT: *68* 10-15
LPs: 10/12-Inch 33rpm
ABC: *74* 8-10
BUDDAH (5659; "The Best Of
Genesis"): *76* 10-12
CHARISMA: *72-79* 8-12
IMPULSE: *70* 15-25
LONDON (600 series): *74* 10-15
LONDON (50000 series): *77* 5-8
MCA: *78* 5-8
MFSL: *82* 25-50
Members: Phil Collins; Peter Gabriel; Tony Banks; Steve Hackett; Anthony Phillips; Mike Rutherford.
Also see BANKS, Tony
Also see CHIC / Roberta Flack / Leif Garrett / Genesis
Also see COLLINS, Phil
Also see GABRIEL, Peter

Also see HACKETT, Steve
Also see PHILLIPS, Anthony
Also see RUTHERFORD, Mike

GENIES
Singles: 7-Inch
ERIC: $1-3
HOLLYWOOD: 59 5-10
SHAD: 59 5-10
WARWICK: 60-61 8-12
Members: Eugene Pitt; Roy Charles Hammond;
Claude Johnson; Roland Trone; Jay Washington.
Also see DON & JUAN
Also see JIVE FIVE
Also see ROY C.

GENTLE GIANT
Singles: 7-Inch
CAPITOL: 74-78 2-3
COLUMBIA: 72-73 2-4
LPs: 10/12-Inch 33rpm
CAPITOL: 74-80 5-8
COLUMBIA: 72-73 8-10
VERTIGO: 71 10-12

GENTLE PERSUASION
Singles: 7-Inch
CAPITOL: 83 1-3
WARNER BROS: 78 5-8

GENTRY, Bobbie
Singles: 7-Inch
BRUNSWICK: 75 2-3
CAPITOL: 67-76 2-4
WARNER BROS: 76-78 1-3
Picture Sleeves
CAPITOL: 67-72 2-5
LPs: 10/12-Inch 33rpm
CAPITOL (Except "SM" series): 67-71 ... 8-15
CAPITOL ("SM" series): 81 5-8
WARNER BROS. ("Ode To Billie Joe: Special
Radio Salute To Bobbie Gentry"): 76 ... 15-20
(Promotional issue only.)
Also see CAMPBELL, Glen, & Bobbie Gentry
Also see REYNOLDS, Jody, & Bobbie Gentry

GENTRYS
Singles: 7-Inch
BELL: 68 3-5
CAPITOL: 72 2-4
MGM (Except 13690): 65-67 4-8
MGM (13690; "There's A
Love"): 67 6-10
STAX: 74 2-3
SUN (Except 1126): 70-71 2-4
SUN (1126; "God Save Our
Country"): 71 10-20
YOUNGSTOWN: 65 15-25

Picture Sleeves
MGM: 66 .... $5-10
Promotional Singles
SUN (Colored vinyl): 71 8-15
LPs: 10/12-Inch 33rpm
MGM: 65-70 15-20
SUN: 70 10-15
Members: Larry Raspberry; Jimmy Johnson; Bruce
Bowles; Pat Neal.

GENTY
Singles: 7-Inch
VENTURE: 80 1-3

GEORGE, Barbara
Singles: 7-Inch
AFO: 61-62 3-5
SUE: 62-63 3-5
UNITED ARTISTS: 74 1-3
LPs: 10/12-Inch 33rpm
AFO: 62 30-40

GEORGE, Lowell
Singles: 7-Inch
WARNER BROS: 78-79 2-3
LPs: 10/12-Inch 33rpm
WARNER BROS: 78-79 5-8
Also see LITTLE FEAT

GEORGE & GENE (Jones & Pitney):
see JONES, George, & Gene Pitney

GEORGIA SATELLITES
Singles: 7-Inch
ELEKTRA: 86-88 1-3
LPs: 10/12-Inch 33rpm
ELEKTRA: 86-88 5-8
Member: Dan Baird.

GEORGIO
Singles: 7-Inch
MACOLO: 87 1-3
MOTOWN: 87-88 1-3
LPs: 10/12-Inch 33rpm
MOTOWN: 87-88 5-8

GERARD, Danyel
Singles: 7-Inch
COLUMBIA: 72 3-5
MGM/VERVE: 72 2-4
LPs: 10/12-Inch 33rpm
VERVE: 71 8-10

GERRARD, Donny
Singles: 7-Inch
GREEDY: 76-77 2-3
ROCKET: 76 2-3
LPs: 10/12-Inch 33rpm
GREEDY: 8-10
Also see SKYLARK

GERRY & THE PACEMAKERS
Singles: 7-Inch
ERIC: $1-3
LAURIE (Except 3100 series): *64-67* 5-10
LAURIE (3100 series): *63* 10-15
LPs: 10/12-Inch 33rpm
ACCORD: *81* 5-8
CAPITOL: *79* 5-8
LAURIE: *64-66* 15-20
Member: Gerry Marsden.
Also see MARTIN, George, & His Orchestra

GESTURES
Singles: 7-Inch
SOMA: *64-65* 5-8

GET WET
Singles: 7-Inch
BOARDWALK: *81* 1-3
LPs: 10/12-Inch 33rpm
BOARDWALK: *81* 5-8

GETZ, Stan
(Stan Getz Quintet)
Singles: 7-Inch
CLEF: *53-54* 3-5
COLUMBIA: *75-80* 1-3
DAWN: *54* 3-5
MGM: *65* 2-3
MERCURY: *53* 3-5
NORGRAN: *54-55* 3-5
PRESTIGE: *50-53* 3-5
ROOST: *50-53* 3-5
VERVE: *60-72* 1-3
EPs: 7-Inch 33/45rpm
CLEF: *53* 10-20
DALE: *51* 15-25
NORGRAN (100 series): *55* 10-15
NORGRAN (2000 series): *54* 20-40
(Boxed set series.)
PRESTIGE: *50* 15-25
ROOST: *51-52* 15-25
LPs: 10/12-Inch 33rpm
AMERICAN RECORDING
  SOCIETY: *57* 20-30
BARONET: *62* 10-20
BLUE RIBBON: *61* 10-20
CLEF (100 series): *53* 60-80
(10-Inch LPs.)
COLUMBIA: *74-82* 5-10
CONCORD JAZZ: *81* 5-8
DALE (21; "Retrospect"): *51* 75-100
(10-Inch LPs.)
INNER CITY: *78* 5-8
JAZZ MAN: *82* 5-8
JAZZTONE: *57* 15-25
MGM (Except 4312): *70* 5-10

MGM (4312; "Mickey One"): *65* $15-20
(Soundtrack.)
METRO: *65* 10-15
MODERN: *56* 20-30
NEW JAZZ: *59* 15-25
NORGRAN (4; "Stan Getz"): *53* 75-100
(10-Inch LP.)
NORGRAN (1000 series): *54-56* 30-50
NORGRAN (2000 series): *54* 100-125
(Boxed set series.)
PRESTIGE (100 series): *52* 75-100
(10-Inch LPs.)
PRESTIGE (7002 through 7022): *56* 25-50
(Yellow label.)
PRESTIGE (7252 through 7256): *56* 25-50
(Yellow label.)
PRESTIGE (7000 series): *64-68* 8-18
(Blue label.)
PRESTIGE (24000 series): *72-79* 8-12
ROOST (400 series): *51-52* 60-90
(10-Inch LPs.)
ROOST (2000 series): *58-64* 12-25
ROULETTE: *71-72* 8-12
SAVOY (1100 series): *77* 5-8
SAVOY (9000 series): *53* 60-80
(10-Inch LPs.)
SEECO: *54* 50-75
(10-Inch LPs.)
VSP: *66-67* 8-12
VERVE: *58-60* 15-30
(Reads "Verve Records, Inc." at bottom of label.)
VERVE: *61-72* 10-20
(Reads "MGM Records — A Division Of Metro-
Goldwyn-Mayer, Inc." at bottom of label.)
VERVE: *73-84* 5-10
(Reads "Manufactured By MGM Record Corp.," or
mentions either Polydor or Polygram at bottom of
label.)
Also see BENNETT, Tony
Also see HOLIDAY, Billie, & Stan Getz
Also see TJADER, Cal, & Stan Getz

GETZ, Stan, & Laurindo Almeida
Singles: 7-Inch
VERVE: 66 . . . . $2-3
LPs: 10/12-Inch 33rpm
VERVE: 66 8-15
Also see ALMEIDA, Laurindo

GETZ, Stan, & Charlie Byrd
Singles: 7-Inch
MGM: 78 1-3
VERVE: 62 2-5
LPs: 10/12-Inch 33rpm
VERVE: 62 10-20
Also see BYRD, Charlie

GETZ, Stan, & Astrud Gilberto
Singles: 7-Inch
MGM: 78 1-3
VERVE: 64-65 2-3
LPs: 10/12-Inch 33rpm
VERVE: 64 10-20
Also see GILBERTO, Astrud

GETZ, Stan, & Gerry Mulligan
LPs: 10/12-Inch 33rpm
VERVE: 58-60 20-30
(Reads "Verve Records, Inc." at bottom of label.)
VERVE: 61-63 10-20
(Reads "MGM Records - A Division Of Metro-Goldwyn-Mayer, Inc." at bottom of label.)
Also see MULLIGAN, Gerry

GETZ, Stan, & Oscar Peterson
LPs: 10/12-Inch 33rpm
VERVE: 60 15-25
(Reads "Verve Records, Inc." at bottom of label.)
VERVE: 61-81 8-18
(Reads "MGM Records - A Division Of Metro-Goldwyn-Mayer, Inc." at bottom of label.)
Also see GETZ, Stan
Also see PETERSON, Oscar

GIANT STEPS
Singles: 7-Inch
A&M: 88 1-3
LPs: 10/12-Inch 33rpm
A&M: 88 5-8

GIBB, Andy
Singles: 7-Inch
RSO: 77-81 1-3
Picture Sleeves
RSO: 77-78 1-3
LPs: 10/12-Inch 33rpm
RSO: 77-80 5-8
Also see BEE GEES
Also see NEWTON-JOHN, Olivia, & Andy Gibb

GIBB, Andy, & Victoria Principal
Singles: 7-Inch
RSO: 81 . . . . $1-3
Picture Sleeves
RSO: 81 1-3
Also see GIBB, Andy

GIBB, Barry
Singles: 7-Inch
ATCO: 77 2-3
MCA: 84 1-3
Picture Sleeves
MCA: 84 1-3
LPs: 10/12-Inch 33rpm
MCA: 84 5-8
Also see BEE GEES
Also see STREISAND, Barbra, & Barry Gibb
Also see WARWICK, Dionne

GIBB, Maurice
Singles: 7-Inch
ATCO: 70 2-3
Also see BEE GEES

GIBB, Robin
Singles: 7-Inch
ATCO: 69-71 2-3
EMI AMERICA: 85 1-3
MIRAGE: 84 1-3
POLYDOR: 83 1-3
RSO: 78 1-3
SESAME STREET: 78 1-3
Picture Sleeves
EMI AMERICA: 85 1-3
MIRAGE: 84 1-3
POLYDOR: 83 1-3
SESAME STREET: 78 1-3
LPs: 10/12-Inch 33rpm
ATCO: 70 8-10
MIRAGE: 84 5-8
POLYDOR: 83 5-8
Also see BEE GEES
Also see LEVY, Marcy, & Robin Gibb

GIBBONS, Steve, Band
Singles: 7-Inch
MCA/GOLD HAWKE: 76-78 1-3
POLYDOR: 78 1-3
LPs: 10/12-Inch 33rpm
MCA: 76-77 8-10
POLYDOR: 78-80 5-8
Also see DALTREY, Roger, & Steve Gibbons

GIBBS, Doug
Singles: 7-Inch
OAK: 72 2-3

GIBBS, Georgia
Singles: 78rpm
CORAL: *50-51* $3-5
Singles: 7-Inch
BELL: *64-66* 2-5
CORAL: *50-51* 5-10
EPIC (Except 9606): *63-64* 3-6
EPIC (9606; "Tater Poon"): *63* 5-15
IMPERIAL: *60* 2-4
KAPP: *59* 3-5
MERCURY: *51-57* 4-8
RCA VICTOR: *57-67* 3-6
ROULETTE: *58-59* 3-5
EPs: 7-Inch 33/45rpm
MERCURY: *54-56* 10-20
ROYALE 10-20
LPs: 10/12-Inch 33rpm
BELL: *66* 8-12
CORAL: *54* 15-25
EPIC: *63* 10-20
IMPERIAL: *60* 10-20
MERCURY: *54-56* 15-25
SUNSET: *66* 8-12

GIBBS, Terri
Singles: 7-Inch
HORIZON: *87* 1-3
MCA: *81-83* 1-3
TEM: *82* 1-3
WARNER BROS: *85* 1-3
LPs: 10/12-Inch 33rpm
MCA: *81-83* 5-8
PHONORAMA: *84* 5-8

GIBSON, Beverly Ann
Singles: 7-Inch
DEB: *59* 4-6
JUBILEE: *63* 3-5
LANDA: *61* 3-5

GIBSON, Debbie
Singles: 7-Inch
ATLANTIC: *87-88* 1-3
LPs: 10/12-Inch 33rpm
ATLANTIC: *87-88* 5-8

GIBSON, Don
Singles: 78rpm
COLUMBIA: *52-54* 4-8
MGM: *55-56* 3-6
RCA VICTOR: *51* 4-8
Singles: 7-Inch
ABC/HICKORY: *75-78* 1-3
COLUMBIA (20000 series): *52-54* 4-8
HICKORY: *70-72* 2-3
MCA: *79* 1-3
MGM (12000 series): *55-56* 10-20

Don Gibson

RCA VICTOR (0400 series): *51* $5-10
RCA VICTOR (4300 & 4400
 series): *51-52* 5-10
RCA VICTOR (7000 series): *58-61* 3-6
RCA VICTOR (8000 & 9000
 series): *62-70* 2-5
WARNER BROS: *80* 1-3
Picture Sleeves
RCA VICTOR: *63* 3-6
EPs: 7-Inch 33/45rpm
COLUMBIA: *57* 12-20
RCA VICTOR: *58-59* 8-15
LPs: 10/12-Inch 33rpm
ABC/HICKORY: *75-78* 6-10
CAMDEN: *65-74* 10-15
HARMONY (7300 series): *65* 12-20
HARMONY (31000 series): *72* 5-10
HICKORY: *70-72* 8-12
HICKORY/MGM: *73-75* 6-10
LION: *58* 25-35
MGM: *70* 8-12
METRO: *65* 12-18
RCA VICTOR (Except 1700 through
 2000 series): *60-70* 10-20
RCA VICTOR (1700 through
 2000 series): *58-59* 20-30

GIBSON, Don, & Sue Thompson
Singles: 7-Inch
HICKORY: *71-75* 2-3
LPs: 10/12-Inch 33rpm
HICKORY: *73* 8-12
HICKORY/MGM: *75* 5-10
Also see THOMPSON, Sue

GIBSON, Don, & Dottie West
Singles: 7-Inch
RCA VICTOR: *69-70* **$2-4**
LPs: 10/12-Inch 33rpm
RCA VICTOR: *69* **8-12**
Also see GIBSON, Don
Also see WEST, Dottie

GIBSON, Ginny
Singles: 78rpm
ABC-PARAMOUNT: *56* **3-5**
DERBY: *52* **3-5**
MGM: *51-55* **3-5**
Singles: 7-Inch
ABC-PARAMOUNT: *56* **3-5**
DERBY: *52* **3-5**
MGM: *51-55* **3-5**
EPs: 7-Inch 33/45rpm
JD: **5-8**

GIBSON, Jon
LPs: 10/12-Inch 33rpm
FRONTLINE: *86* **5-8**

GIBSON, Johnny
(Johnny Gibson Trio)
Singles: 7-Inch
BIG TOP: *61-63* **3-5**
TWIRL: **3-5**
Also see JOHNNY & THE HURRICANES

GIBSON, Steve
(Steve Gibson & The Red Caps; Steve Gibson &
The Original Red Caps)
Singles: 78rpm
ABC-PARAMOUNT: *56-57* **4-8**
BEACON: *44* **10-20**
MERCURY: *47-54* **6-12**
RCA VICTOR: *51-55* **5-10**
Singles: 7-Inch
ABC-PARAMOUNT: *56-60* **5-10**
BANDBOX: *62* **3-5**
HI LO: *58* **5-10**
HUNT: *59* **4-6**
JAY DEE: *54* **6-10**
MERCURY (8069 through 8093): *49* . . . **25-40**
MERCURY (8100 series): *49-50* **20-30**
MERCURY (70000 series): *54* **20-30**
RCA VICTOR (3986; "The
   Thing"): *50* **30-40**
RCA VICTOR (4294; "Shame"): *51* **30-40**
RCA VICTOR (4670 through
   5130): *52-53* **15-25**
RCA VICTOR (5900 & 6000 series): *55* . . **5-10**
RCA VICTOR (50-0000 series): *51* **20-30**
ROSE: *59* **5-10**
STAGE: **8-12**

EPs: 7-Inch 33/45rpm
MERCURY (3215; "Blueberry
   Hill"): *53* **$60-100**
LPs: 10/12-Inch 33rpm
MERCURY (25115; "You're Driving
   Me Crazy"): *53* **100-150**
   (10-Inch LP.)
MERCURY (25116; "Blueberry
   Hill"): *53* **100-150**
   (10-Inch LP.)
Also see DAMITA JO & STEVE GIBSON &
THE RED CAPS
Also see GREGG, Bobby

GIBSON BROTHERS
Singles: 12-Inch 33/45rpm
ISLAND: *79* **4-6**
Singles: 7-Inch
ISLAND: *79* **1-3**

GIDEA PARK
Singles: 7-Inch
PROFILE: *82* **1-3**
Member: Adrian Baker.

GILBERT, Regina, & Jan Midkiff
Singles: 7-Inch
FOUNTAIN: *86* **2-3**

GILBERTO, Astrud
Singles: 7-Inch
CTI: *71* **1-3**
VERVE: *67-70* **2-3**
LPs: 10/12-Inch 33rpm
IMAGE: *78* **5-8**
PERCEPTION: *72* **5-10**
VERVE: *65-70* **8-15**
Also see GETZ, Stan, & Astrud Gilberto
Also see JOBIM, Antonio Carlos
Also see JONES, Quincy
Also see WANDERLEY, Walter

GILBERTO, Astrud, & Stanley
Turrentine
LPs: 10/12-Inch 33rpm
CTI: *71* **8-12**
Also see GILBERTO, Astrud
Also see TURRENTINE, Stanley

GILDER, Nick
Singles: 7-Inch
CHRYSALIS: *76-79* **1-3**
Picture Sleeves
CHRYSALIS: *78* **1-3**
LPs: 10/12-Inch 33rpm
CASABLANCA: *80* **5-8**
CHRYSALIS: *77-79* **5-8**
Also see SWEENY TODD

GILKYSON, Terry
(Terry Gilkyson & The Easy Riders; Terry Gilkyson & The South Coasters)
Singles: 78rpm
COLUMBIA: *54-57* $3-5
DECCA: *51-52* 3-6
Singles: 7-Inch
COLUMBIA: *54-57* 3-5
DECCA: *51-52* 4-6
Picture Sleeves
COLUMBIA: *57* 5-10
EPs: 7-Inch 33/45rpm
COLUMBIA: *57* 5-10
DECCA: *51-53* 5-15
LPs: 10/12-Inch 33rpm
DECCA (5000 series): *51-53* 15-25
(10-Inch LPs.)
KAPP: *60-63* 10-20
Also see MARTIN, Dean

GILL, Johnny
Singles: 7-Inch
COTILLION: *83-85* 1-3
LPs: 10/12-Inch 33rpm
COTILLION: *83-85* 5-8
Also see LATTISAW, Stacy, & Johnny Gill
Also see NEW EDITION

GILLAN, Ian
(Gillan)
Singles: 7-Inch
OYSTER: *76* 1-3
LPs: 10/12-Inch 33rpm
ISLAND: *77-78* 5-8
OYSTER: *76* 8-10
VIRGIN: *80* 5-8
Also see DEEP PURPLE

GILLEY, Mickey
(Mickey Gilley & The Urban Cowboy Band)
Singles: 7-Inch
ACT 1: *66* 4-6
AIRBORNE: *88* 1-3
ASTRO (Except 100 series): *71-73* 2-4
ASTRO (100 series): *63-65* 10-12
DARYL: *63* 4-6
DOT: *58* 40-50
EPIC: *78-87* 1-3
ERIC: *64* 4-6
GOLDBAND: *64* 3-5
GRT: *70* 2-4
KHOURY'S: *59* 15-20
LYNN: *60-61* 10-15
MINOR: *57* 50-60
PAULA (Except 400 series): *66-68* 3-5
PAULA (400 series): *74-84* 1-3
PLAYBOY: *74-77* 2-3

POTOMAC: *60* $10-15
PRINCESS: *62* 5-8
RESCO: *74* 2-4
REX: *58* 15-20
SABRA: *61* 8-10
SAN: *63* 8-12
SUPREME: *62* 5-8
TCF HALL: *65* 3-5
LPs: 10/12-Inch 33rpm
ASTRO (Except 101): *73-78* 8-10
ASTRO (101; "Lonely Wine"): *64* 50-100
EPIC: *79-86* 5-8
PAULA (Except 2000 series): *81* 5-8
PAULA (2195; "Down The Line"): *67* ..20-25
PAULA (2224; "Mickey Gilley At
His Best"): *74* 10-12
PAULA (2234; "Mickey Gilley"): *78* 8-10
PLAYBOY: *74-78* 8-12
Also see CHARLES, Ray, & Mickey Gilley
Also see HAGGARD, Merle / Mickey Gilley /
Willie Knight

GILLEY, Mickey, & Barbi Benton
Singles: 7-Inch
PLAYBOY: *75* 2-3
Picture Sleeves
PLAYBOY: *75* 2-5

GILLEY, Mickey, & Johnny Lee
Singles: 7-Inch
EPIC: *81* 1-3
Also see LEE, Johnny
Also see NELSON, Willie / Johnny Lee /
Mickey Gilley

GILLEY, Mickey, & Charly McClain
Singles: 7-Inch
EPIC: *83-84* 1-3
Also see GILLEY, Mickey

GILMER, Jimmy
(Jimmy Gilmer & The Fireballs)
Singles: 7-Inch
ABC: *74* 1-3
ATCO: *68* 3-5
DECCA: *59* 8-10
DOT: *63-66* 3-5
HAMILTON: *63* 4-6
WARWICK: *60* 8-10
LPs: 10/12-Inch 33rpm
ATCO: *68-69* 10-12
CROWN: *63* 15-18
DOT (Except 3577 & 25577): *63-68* 20-25
DOT (3577; "Buddy's Buddy"): *64* 40-50
(Monaural.)
DOT (25577; "Buddy's Buddy"): *64* ...75-100
(Stereo.)

Also see FIREBALLS
Also see JIM & MONICA

GILMOUR, David
Singles: 12-Inch 33/45rpm
COLUMBIA: 84-86 .... $4-6
Singles: 7-Inch
COLUMBIA: 84-86 1-3
LPs: 10/12-Inch 33rpm
COLUMBIA: 78-85 5-8
Also see PINK FLOYD

GILREATH, James
Singles: 7-Inch
JOY: 63-64 3-5

GILSTRAP, Jim
Singles: 7-Inch
BELL: 74 2-3
ROXBURY: 75-76 2-3
LPs: 10/12-Inch 33rpm
ROXBURY: 75-76 5-8

GINIE LYNN: see LYNN, Ginie

GINO & GINA
Singles: 7-Inch
BRUNSWICK: 61 3-5
MERCURY: 58 8-10

**GIOVANNI, Nikki, & The New
York Community Choir**
LPs: 10/12-Inch 33rpm
RIGHT-ON: 71 4-8

GIPSY KINGS
LPs: 10/12-Inch 33rpm
MUSICIAN: 88 5-8

GIRLFRIENDS
Singles: 7-Inch
COLPIX: 63-64 10-15
MELIC: 63 5-10
PIONEER: 60 10-15

GIRLS CAN'T HELP IT
LPs: 10/12-Inch 33rpm
SIRE: 84 5-8

GIRLSCHOOL
Singles: 7-Inch
MERCURY: 82 1-3
LPs: 10/12-Inch 33rpm
MERCURY: 82 5-8
STIFF AMERICA: 82 5-8

GIRLTALK
Singles: 7-Inch
GEFFEN: 84 1-3

GIUFFRIA
(Gregg Giuffria)
Singles: 7-Inch
MCA/CAMEL: 84-86 .... $1-3
LPs: 10/12-Inch 33rpm
MCA/CAMEL: 84-86 5-8
Also see ANGEL

GIVENS FAMILY
Singles: 7-Inch
PJ: 86 1-3
SUGAR HILL: 85 1-3

GLADIOLAS
Singles: 78rpm
EXCELLO: 57 5-10
Singles: 7-Inch
EXCELLO: 57-58 15-25
Members: Maurice Williams; Norman Wade; Bill
Massey; Willie Jones; Earl Gainey; Bobby
Robinson.
Also see WILLIAMS, Maurice, & The Zodiacs

GLADSTONE
Singles: 7-Inch
ABC: 72 2-3
LPs: 10/12-Inch 33rpm
ABC: 72-73 8-10

GLAHE, Will, & His Orchestra
Singles: 78rpm
LONDON: 55-57 2-4
Singles: 7-Inch
LONDON: 55-60 2-4
LPs: 10/12-Inch 33rpm
LONDON: 55-60 5-15

GLASS, Philip
LPs: 10/12-Inch 33rpm
COLUMBIA: 85-86 5-10
Also see RONSTADT, Linda

GLASS BOTTLE
Singles: 7-Inch
AVCO: 71 2-3
AVCO EMBASSY: 70 2-4
Member: Gary Criss.

GLASS FAMILY
Singles: 7-Inch
JDC: 78 2-3

GLASS HARP
LPs: 10/12-Inch 33rpm
DECCA: 71-72 8-10
MCA: 5-8
Member: Phil Keaggy.

GLASS HOUSE
Singles: 7-Inch
INVICTUS: 69-72 2-4

LPs: 10/12-Inch 33rpm
INVICTUS: *71-72* $8-10
KIRSHNER: *71* 8-10
Members: Scherrie Payne; Ty Hunter.
Also see HUNTER, Ty
Also see PAYNE, Scherrie

GLASS MOON
Singles: 7-Inch
RADIO: *82* 1-3
LPs: 10/12-Inch 33rpm
RADIO: *80-82* 5-8

GLASS TIGER
Singles: 12-Inch 33/45rpm
EMI-MANHATTAN: *86* 4-6
Singles: 7-Inch
EMI-MANHATTAN: *86-88* 1-3
LPs: 10/12-Inch 33rpm
EMI-MANHATTAN: *86-88* 5-8

GLAZER, Tom
(Tom Glazer & The Children's Do-Re-Mi
Chorus; Tom Glazer With Dotty Evans & Robin
Morgan)
Singles: 78rpm
COLUMBIA: *53-55* 3-5
CORAL: *56* 2-5
Singles: 7-Inch
COLUMBIA: *53-55* 3-6
CORAL: *56* 3-6
KAPP: *63-64* 2-4
UNITED ARTISTS: *66-67* 2-4
Picture Sleeves
KAPP: *63* 3-8
LPs: 10/12-Inch 33rpm
CAMDEN: *64-65* 5-10
KAPP: *63-64* 8-12
COLUMBIA: *55* 15-30
HARMONY: *59* 8-15
MERCURY: *55* 15-25
MOTIVATION: *62* 5-10
RIVERSIDE: *61* 8-12
UNITED ARTISTS: *66* 8-12
WASHINGTON: *59* 8-15
WONDERLAND: *63* 6-12

GLEASON, Jackie
(Jackie Gleason's Orchestra)
Singles: 78rpm
CAPITOL: *52-57* 2-4
DECCA (27000 series): *51* 3-5
Singles: 7-Inch
CAPITOL: *52-62* 2-4
DECCA (27000 series): *51* 3-5
EPs: 7-Inch 33/45rpm
CAPITOL (Except 511): *53-60* 3-6

CAPITOL (511; "And Awa-a-ay
We Go"): *54* $25-50
(Double EP set, with contents same as LP listed
below.)
LPs: 10/12-Inch 33rpm
CAPITOL (Except 511): *53-69* 5-15
CAPITOL (511; "And Awa-a-y
We Go"): *54* 40-60
(10-Inch LP. Unlike Gleason's mood music
releases, this was a collection of songs by Jackie,
sung in character by: Joe The Bartender, The Loud
Mouth, Ralph Kramden, Fenwick Babbitt, Reggie
Van Gleason III, and The Poor Soul.)
Also see MARTIN, Dean / Jackie Gleason

GLENCOVES
Singles: 7-Inch
SELECT: *63-64* 3-5

GLENN, Darrell
Singles: 78rpm
DOT: *56* 3-6
RCA VICTOR: *54* 2-5
Singles: 7-Inch
COLUMBIA: *66-67* 2-3
DOT: *56* 4-8
FASHION: *60* 2-4
LONGHORN: *65* 2-4
NRC: *58* 4-6
POMPEII: *68 69* 2-3
RCA VICTOR: *54* 3-5
ROBBIE: *64* 2-4
TWINKLE: 25-30
VALLEY: *53* 3-5
LPs: 10/12-Inch 33rpm
NRC: *59* 12-20

GLENN, Garry
Singles: 7-Inch
MOTOWN: *87* 1-3

GLENN, Lloyd
Singles: 78rpm
ALADDIN: *56-57* 3-6
HOLLYWOOD: *54* 4-8
SWING TIME: *52-54* 5-10
Singles: 7-Inch
ALADDIN: *56-59* 5-8
HOLLYWOOD: *54* 5-8
IMPERIAL: *62* 3-5
SWING TIME: *52-54* 15-25
LPs: 10/12-Inch 33rpm
ALADDIN (808; "Chica-Boo"): *56* 40-50
(Black vinyl.)
ALADDIN (808; "Chica-Boo"): *56* 75-125
(Colored vinyl.)
BLACK & BLUE: *77* 8-10
IMPERIAL: *62* 20-30

SCORE: 57 .... $40-50
SWING TIME (1901; "Lloyd
  Glenn"): 54 100-125
  (10-Inch LP.)
Also see FULSON, Lowell

GLITTER, Gary
(Gary Glitter & The Glitter Band)
Singles: 7-Inch
ARISTA: 75 2-3
BELL: 72-74 2-3
LPs: 10/12-Inch 33rpm
BELL: 72 8-10
EPIC: 81 6-10
Also see GLITTER BAND

GLITTER BAND
Singles: 7-Inch
ARISTA: 75-76 2-3
LPs: 10/12-Inch 33rpm
ARISTA: 76 8-10
Member: Pete Gill.
Also see GLITTER, Gary
Also see MOTORHEAD

GLORIES
Singles: 7-Inch
DATE: 67-68 4-8

GLOVER, Roger
Singles: 7-Inch
21: 84 1-3
UK: 75 8-10
LPs: 10/12-Inch 33rpm
POLYDOR: 78 5-8
21: 84 5-8
UK: 75 8-10
Also see DEEP PURPLE
Also see RAINBOW

GO WEST
Singles: 7-Inch
CHRYSALIS: 85-87 1-3
LPs: 10/12-Inch 33rpm
CHRYSALIS: 85-87 5-8

GOANNA
Singles: 7-Inch
ATCO: 83 1-3
LPs: 10/12-Inch 33rpm
ATCO: 83 5-8

GODFATHERS
Singles: 7-Inch
EPIC : 88 1-3
LPs: 10/12-Inch 33rpm
EPIC: 88 5-8

GODFREY, Arthur
Singles: 78rpm
COLUMBIA: 50-56 .... $2-5
DECCA (29000 series): 55 2-4
Singles: 7-Inch
COLUMBIA: 50-56 3-5
CONTEMPO: 63-64 2-3
DECCA (29000 series): 55 3-5
MGM: 66 2-3
MTA: 69 1-3
SIGNATURE: 60 2-4
VEE JAY: 65 2-3
Picture Sleeves
MGM: 66 4-8
EPs: 7-Inch 33/45rpm
COLUMBIA: 52-56 5-8
LPs: 10/12-Inch 33rpm
ADMIRAL: 67 8-12
CAMDEN: 66-67 8-12
CAPITOL: 62 8-15
COLUMBIA: 53-61 10-20
CONTEMPO: 8-15
HARMONY: 59 10-15
RCA VICTOR: 73 5-8
SIGNATURE: 60 8-15
Also see MARINERS

GODFREY, Ray
Singles: 7-Inch
ABC: 67 3-5
COLUMBIA: 67 3-5
J&J: 60 4-6
PEACH: 62 10-12
SIMS: 63 3-5
SPRING: 70 2-4
TOLLIE: 65 4-8
YONAH: 61 4-6

GODLEY, Kevin, & Lol Creme
(Godley & Creme)
Singles: 12-Inch 33/45rpm
POLYDOR: 85 4-6
Singles: 7-Inch
MERCURY: 77 2-3
MIRAGE: 82 2-3
POLYDOR: 85 1-3
LPs: 10/12-Inch 33rpm
MERCURY: 77 10-15
MIRAGE: 82 5-8
POLYDOR: 85 5-10
Also see 10CC

GODSPELL
(Robin Lamont & Original "Godspell" Cast)
Singles: 7-Inch
BELL: 72 2-3

GODWIN, Peter
Singles: 12-Inch 33/45rpm
POLYDOR: 83 .... $4-6

GODZ
Singles: 7-Inch
MILLENIUM: 78 2-3
LPs: 10/12-Inch 33rpm
CASABLANCA: 78 5-8
MILLENIUM/CASABLANCA: 78 5-8

GOFFIN, Louise
Singles: 7-Inch
ASYLUM: 79 1-3
ELEKTRA: 79 1-3
WARNER BROS: 88 1-3
LPs: 10/12-Inch 33rpm
ASYLUM: 79-81 5-8

GO-GOs
Singles: 12-Inch 33/45
I.R.S.: 82 4-6
Singles: 7-Inch
I.R.S.. (Except 8001): 81-85 1-3
I.R.S.. (8001; "We Got The Beat"): 82 4-8
Picture Sleeves
I.R.S.: 81-85 1-3
LPs: 10/12-Inch 33rpm
I.R.S.: 81-85 5-8
Members: Belinda Carlisle; Charlotte Caffey; Jane
Wiedlin; Margot Olaverria; Elissa Bello; Gina
Schook; Kathy Valentine.
Also see CARLISLE, Belinda
Also see TEXTONES
Also see VENTURES
Also see WIEDLIN, Jane

GOLD, Andrew
Singles: 7-Inch
ASYLUM: 76-78 1-3
Picture Sleeves
ASYLUM: 77-78 1-3
LPs: 10/12-Inch 33rpm
ASYLUM: 75-80 5-8
Also see WAX

GOLD, Marty, & His Orchestra
Singles: 7-Inch
KAPP: 58-59 2-3
RCA VICTOR: 60-61 2-3
EPs: 7-Inch 33/45rpm
KAPP: 59 3-6
VIK: 56-57 4-8
LPs: 10/12-Inch 33rpm
KAPP: 59 4-8
RCA VICTOR: 59-63 4-8
VIK: 56-57 5-10

GOLDDIGGERS
Singles: 7-Inch
METROMEDIA: 69 .... $1-3
RCA VICTOR: 72 1-3
LPs: 10/12-Inch 33rpm
METROMEDIA: 69 6-10
RCA VICTOR: 71 5-10
Also see MARTIN, Dean

GOLDE, Frannie
Singles: 7-Inch
ATLANTIC: 77 1-3
BIG TREE: 76 2-3
PORTRAIT: 79 1-3

GOLDEN EARRING
Singles: 7-Inch
ATLANTIC: 70 2-4
MCA: 76-78 2-3
POLYDOR (2000 series): 79 1-3
POLYDOR (14000 series): 69 3-5
TRACK: 74-75 2-3
21: 82-86 1-3
LPs: 10/12-Inch 33rpm
ATLANTIC: 69 15-20
CAPITOL (Except 11315): 67-74 30-35
CAPITOL (11315; "Golden Earring"): 74 10-12
DWARF; 10-20
MCA: 75-81 6-10
POLYDOR: 79-80 5-8
TRACK (396; "Moontan"): 73 20-25
(With nude showgirl on cover.)
TRACK (396; "Moontan"): 73 10-12
(Showgirl not nude on cover.)
21: 82-86 5-8

GOLDEN GATE STRINGS
(With Stu Phillips)
LPs: 10/12-Inch 33rpm
EPIC: 67 5-10
Also see HOLLYRIDGE STRINGS

GOLDSBORO, Bobby
Singles: 7-Inch
CURB: 80-82 1-3
EPIC: 77 1-3
LAURIE: 62-63 3-5
UNITED ARTISTS (Except 600
through 900 series): 63-66 2-4
UNITED ARTISTS (600 through 900
series): 63-64 3-5
VISTA: 74 2-3
Picture Sleeves
UNITED ARTISTS (Except 700
series): 66-74 2-5
UNITED ARTISTS (700 series): 64 4-8

LPs: 10/12-Inch 33rpm
CURB: 80-82 .... $5-8
DORAL: 15-25
(Promotional mail-order issue, from Doral cigarettes.)
EPIC: 77 8-10
K-TEL: 5-8
LIBERTY: 81 5-8
SUNSET: 5-10
UNITED ARTISTS: 64-76 10-20
  Also see ORBISON, Roy
  Also see REEVES, Del, & Bobby Goldsboro

GOLLIWOGS
Singles: 7-Inch
FANTASY: 65 15-25
SCORPIO: 64-68 15-25
LPs: 10/12-Inch 33rpm
FANTASY: 75 8-10
  Also see CREEDENCE CLEARWATER
REVIVAL

GOMM, Ian
Singles: 7-Inch
STIFF: 79 1-3
LPs: 10/12-Inch 33rpm
STIFF: 79-80 5-8

GONE ALL STARS
Singles: 7-Inch
GONE: 58 8-10
ROULETTE: 71 1-3
EPs: 7-Inch 33/45rpm
GONE: 58 25-40

GONZALES, Terri
Singles: 7-Inch
BECKET: 82 1-3

GONZALEZ
Singles: 12-Inch 33/45rpm
CAPITOL: 79 .... $4-6
Singles: 7-Inch
CAPITOL: 78-79 1-3
LPs: 10/12-Inch 33rpm
CAPITOL: 78-80 5-8

GOOD QUESTION
Singles: 7-Inch
PAISLEY PARK: 88 1-3

GOODEES
Singles: 7-Inch
HIP: 68-69 4-6
LPs: 10/12-Inch 33rpm
HIP: 69 10-12

GOODIE
Singles: 12-Inch 33/45rpm
TOTAL EXPERIENCE: 82-84 4-6
Singles: 7-Inch
TOTAL EXPERIENCE: 82-84 1-3
LPs: 10/12-Inch 33rpm
TOTAL EXPERIENCE: 83 5-8

GOODIES
Singles: 7-Inch
20TH CENTURY-FOX: 75 2-3

GOODING, Cuba
Singles: 12-Inch 33/45rpm
STREETWISE: 83 4-6
Singles: 7-Inch
MOTOWN: 78-79 1-3
STREETWISE: 83 1-3
LPs: 10/12-Inch 33rpm
MOTOWN: 78-79 5-8
  Also see MAIN INGREDIENT

GOODMAN, Benny, Orchestra
Singles: 78rpm
COLUMBIA: 50-56 2-4
Singles: 7-Inch
CHESS: 59 2-3
COLUMBIA (Except 250): 50-56 2-5
COLUMBIA (250; "1938 Carnegie
  Hall Concert"): 25-35
(Boxed set.)
COMMAND: 67 1-3
DECCA: 62 1-3
RCA VICTOR: 50-59 2-4
EPs: 7-Inch 33/45rpm
BRUNSWICK: 54 4-8
CAPITOL: 55-56 4-8
COLUMBIA: 50-58 4-8
DECCA (798; "The Benny Goodman
  Story"): 56 10-15

The Many Heads Of DICKIE GOODMAN

RED PAJAMAS: *83* $5-8

GOODMAN, Steve, & Phoebe Snow
Singles: 7-Inch
ASYLUM: *80* 1-3
Also see GOODMAN, Steve
Also see SNOW, Phoebe

GOODTIMERS
Singles: 7-Inch
ARNOLD: *61* 4-6
EPIC: *61* 3-5
Member: Don Covay.
Also see COVAY, Don

GOODWIN, Don
Singles: 7-Inch
SILVER BLUE: *73* 2-3

GOODWIN, Ron, Orchestra
Singles: 78rpm
CAPITOL: *56-57* 2-4
Singles: 7-Inch
CAPITOL: *56-59* 2-4
KING: *61* 2-3
LPs: 10/12-Inch 33rpm
CAPITOL: *57-60* 5-15

GOODY GOODY
Singles: 7-Inch
ATLANTIC: *78* 1-3
LPs: 10/12-Inch 33rpm
ATLANTIC: *78* 5-8

GOON SQUAD
Singles: 12-Inch 33/45rpm
EPIC: *85* 4-6
Singles: 7-Inch
EPIC: *85* 1-3

GOOSE CREEK SYMPHONY
(Goose Creek)
Singles: 7-Inch
CAPITOL: *70-72* 2-4
LPs: 10/12-Inch 33rpm
CAPITOL: *70-72* 10-12
COLUMBIA: *74* 8-10
RLO: 8-10

GORDON, Barry
Singles: 78rpm
MGM: *55-56* 2-5
Singles: 7-Inch
ABC: *68* 2-3
CAPITOL: *71* 1-3
CADENCE: *62* 2-4
DUNHILL: *68* 2-3
ERA: *59* 2-4
MGM: *55-56* 3-5
MERCURY: *61* 2-4

UNITED ARTISTS: *64-66* $2-4
Picture Sleeves
MGM: *56* 4-8
LPs: 10/12-Inch 33rpm
UNITED ARTISTS: *66* 8-15

GORDON, Robert
(Robert Gordon & Link Wray)
Singles: 12-Inch 33/45rpm
PRIVATE STOCK: *78* 8-10
RCA VICTOR: *81* 8-10
(Promotional issue only.)
Singles: 7-Inch
PRIVATE STOCK: *77-78* 3-5
RCA VICTOR (Black vinyl): *79-81* 2-4
RCA VICTOR (Colored vinyl): *79-81* 5-10
(Promotional issue only.)
Picture Sleeves
PRIVATE STOCK: *79* 2-3
RCA VICTOR: *79* 3-6
LPs: 10/12-Inch 33rpm
PRIVATE STOCK: *77-78* 8-10
RCA VICTOR (Black vinyl): *79-82* 5-10
RCA VICTOR (Colored vinyl): *79* 20-25
Promotional LPs
RCA VICTOR (3411; "Robert Gordon"/"Live
From Paradise In Boston"): *79* 35-40
Also see WRAY, Link

GORDON, Roscoe
Singles: 78rpm
CHESS (1487; "Booted"): *52* 20-40
DUKE (101; "Tell Daddy"): *52* 25-30
DUKE (106; "T-Model Boogie"): *53* 25-30
DUKE (109 through 129): *53-54* 8-15
FLIP (227; "Just Love Me Baby"): *55* ... 50-100
FLIP (237; "The Chicken"): *56* 10-20
RPM (322; "Roscoe's Boogie"): *50* 20-25
RPM (324; "Saddle The Cow"): *50* 25-50
RPM (336; "A Dime A Dozen"): *50* 20-25
RPM (344 through 384): *51-53* 12-25
SUN (Except 227 & 237): *56-58* 8-15
SUN (227; "Just Love Me Baby"): *55* ... 50-100
SUN (237; "The Chicken"): *56* 30-60
Singles: 7-Inch
ABC-PARAMOUNT: *62-63* 3-5
CHESS (1487; "Booted"): *52* 75-100
COLLECTABLES: *81* 1-3
DUKE (109 through 129): *53-54* 25-35
DUKE (300 series): *60* 4-8
FLIP (227; "Just Love Me Baby"): *55* .. 200-300
FLIP (237; "The Chicken"): *56* 20-30
OLD TOWN: *64* 4-6
RPM (324; "Saddle The Cow"): *50* 75-100
RPM (344 through 384): *51-53* 25-45
SUN (Except 227 & 237): *56-58* 10-15

SUN (227; "Just Love Me Baby"): 55 . $400-500
SUN (237; "The Chicken"): 56 100-150
VEE JAY: 59-61 4-6

GORE, Lesley
Singles: 7-Inch
A&M: 75-76 2-4
CREWE: 70-71 2-4
MERCURY: 63-69 5-10
MOWEST: 72 2-4
Picture Sleeves
A&M: 75-76 4-6
MERCURY: 63-67 8-15
LPs: 10/12-Inch 33rpm
A&M: 75 8-10
MERCURY (8000 series): 80 5-8
MERCURY (20000 & 60000
series): 63-68 20-30
MOWEST: 72 8-10
POLYDOR: 85 5-8
WING: 67-69 10-20
Also see BILLY & SUE
Also see CHRISTIE, Lou, & Leslie Gore
Also see DRIFTERS / Leslie Gore / Roy Orbison / Los Bravos

GORE, Michael
Singles: 7-Inch
CAPITOL: 84 1-3

GORL, Robert
Singles: 7-Inch
ELEKTRA: 84 1-3

GORME, Eydie
Singles: 78rpm
ABC-PARAMOUNT: 55-62 2-4
Singles: 7-Inch
ABC-PARAMOUNT: 55-62 2-5
CALENDAR: 67 1-3
COLUMBIA: 62-68 2-4
CORAL: 53-55 5-10
MGM: 71-73 1-3
RCA VICTOR: 69-70 1-3
UNITED ARTISTS: 60-76 1-3
Picture Sleeves
COLUMBIA: 62-63 3-6
LPs: 10/12-Inch 33rpm
ABC-PARAMOUNT: 57-65 8-15
APPLAUSE: 81 4-6
COLUMBIA: 63-73 8-15
HARMONY: 68-71 5-10
MGM: 71 5-10
RCA VICTOR: 68-70 5-10
UNITED ARTISTS: 61-62 8-15
VOCALION: 63 6-10
Also see LAWRENCE, Steve, & Eydie Gorme

GOUDREAU, Barry
Singles: 7-Inch
PORTRAIT: 79 .... $1-3
LPs: 10/12-Inch 33rpm
PORTRAIT: 79 5-8
Also see BOSTON

GOULET, Robert
Singles: 7-Inch
ABC: 74 1-3
ARTISTS OF AMERICA: 75 1-3
COLUMBIA (Black vinyl): 61-70 2-4
COLUMBIA (Colored vinyl): 63 4-8
MGM: 73 1-3
MERLIN: 71 1-3
PARAMOUNT: 74 1-3
Picture Sleeves
ABC: 74 3-5
COLUMBIA (Except 59227): 62-65 3-5
COLUMBIA (59227; "The Moon
Was Yellow"): 63 5-10
(Promotional issue only.)
LPs: 10/12-Inch 33rpm
ARTISTS OF AMERICA: 76 5-8
COLUMBIA: 61-73 5-15
HARMONY: 71-72 5-10
MERLIN: 71 5-10
ORINDA: 78 5-8

GRACE, Fredi, & Rhinestone
Singles: 7-Inch
RCA VICTOR: 82 1-3

GRACE, Leda
Singles: 7-Inch
POLYDOR: 81 1-3

GRACIE, Charlie
Singles: 78rpm
CADILLAC: 54 10-20
CAMEO: 57 4-6
20TH CENTURY: 56 20-30
Singles: 7-Inch
ABKCO: 75 1-3
CADILLAC: 54 45-55
CAMEO: 57-59 4-6
CORAL: 59 4-6
DIAMOND: 65 3-5
FELSTED: 61 3-5
PRESIDENT: 62 3-5
ROULETTE: 59-61 3-5
20TH CENTURY: 56 20-30

GRADUATES
Singles: 7-Inch
CORSICAN: 59 10-15
SHAN-TODD: 59 10-15

Picture Sleeves
CORSICAN: *59* $20-30

GRAHAM, Jaki
Singles: 12-Inch 33/45rpm
CAPITOL: *86* 4-6
Singles: 7-Inch
CAPITOL: *86* 1-3
LPs: 10/12-Inch 33rpm
CAPITOL: *86* 5-8

GRAHAM, Jaki, & David Grant
Singles: 12-Inch 33/45rpm
CAPITOL: *86* 4-6
Singles: 7-Inch
CAPITOL: *86* 1-3
Also see GRAHAM, Jaki
Also see GRANT, David

GRAHAM, Larry
(Larry Graham & Graham Central Station;
Graham Central Station)
Singles: 7-Inch
ARISTA: *87* 1-3
WARNER BROS: *74-83* 1-3
Picture Sleeves
WARNER BROS: *80* 1-3
LPs: 10/12-Inch 33rpm
WARNER BROS: *73-83* 5-10
Also see FRANKLIN, Aretha
Also see SLY & THE FAMILY STONE

GRAINGERS
Singles: 7-Inch
BC: *81* 1-3

GRAMM, Lou
Singles: 7-Inch
ATLANTIC: *87* 1-3
LPs: 10/12-Inch 33rpm
ATLANTIC: *87* 5-8

GRAMMER, Billy
Singles: 7-Inch
DECCA: *61-66* 2-4
EPIC: *66-67* 2-3
EVEREST: *60* 2-4
MERCURY: *68-69* 2-3
MONUMENT (Except 400 series): *75-76* .. 1-3
MONUMENT (400 series): *59-63* 2-4
RICE: *67* 2-3
STOP: *69* 2-3
EPs: 7-Inch 33/45rpm
DECCA: *64* 4-6
LPs: 10/12-Inch 33rpm
CLASSIC CHRISTMAS: *77* 5-8
DECCA: *62-64* 10-15
EPIC: *67* 8-12

MONUMENT (4000; "Travelin'
On"): *59* $15-20
MONUMENT (8039; "Travelin'
On"): *66* 8-12
(Reissued with *Lost In A Small Cafe* replaced with
Gotta Travel On.)
STONEWAY: *75* 5-10
VOCALION: *68* 6-12
Also see CASH, Johnny / Billy Grammer /
Wilburn Brothers

GRANAHAN, Gerry
Singles: 7-Inch
CANADIAN AMERICAN: *60* 3-5
CAPRICE (Except 108): *61* 3-5
CAPRICE (108; "Dance Girl,
Dance"): *61* 25-35
(With The Wildwoods, aka The Five Satins.)
GONE: *59-60* 4-6
SUNBEAM: *58-59* 4-6
Picture Sleeves
GONE: *60* 15-25
Also see DICKY DOO & THE DON'TS
Also see FIVE SATINS

GRANATA, Rocca, & The
International Quintet
Singles: 7-Inch
LAURIE: *59* 2-4
Picture Sleeves
LAURIE: *59* 3-5

GRAND CANYON
Singles: 7-Inch
BANG: *74* 3-6
FAITHFUL VIRTUE: *70* 2-3

GRAND FUNK RAILROAD
(Grand Funk)
Singles: 7-Inch
CAPITOL (Black vinyl): *69-76* 2-4

CAPITOL (Colored vinyl): *73* $3-6
(Promotional issue only.)
FULL MOON: *81* 1-3
MCA: *76-77* 1-3
Picture Sleeves
CAPITOL: *72-76* 2-5
FULL MOON: *81* 1-3
MCA: *76* 2-3
LPs: 10/12-Inch 33rpm
CAPITOL (Except 12000 & 16000
series): *69-76* 8-10
CAPITOL (12000 & 16000 series): *80-81* . . 5-8
FULL MOON: *81-83* 5-8
MCA: *76* 8-10
Members: Mark Farner; Don Brewer; Mel
Schacher; Craig Frost.
Also see KNIGHT, Terry

GRANDMASTER FLASH & THE FURIOUS FIVE
**(Grandmaster Melle Mel & The Furious Five;
Grandmaster & Melle Mel; Grandmaster Flash)**
Singles: 12-Inch 33/45
ATLANTIC: *84* 4-6
ELEKTRA: *85-86* 4-6
SUGAR HILL: *80-85* 4-6
Singles: 7-Inch
ATLANTIC: *84* 1-3
ELEKTRA: *85-87* 1-3
MCA: *85* 1-3
SUGAR HILL: *80-85* 1-3
LPs: 10/12-Inch 33rpm
ELEKTRA: *86-88* 5-8
SUGAR HILL: *82-85* 5-8
Also see KING DREAM CHORUS &
HOLIDAY CREW
Also see MELLE MEL & DUKE BOOTEE

GRANDMIXER D. ST.
Singles: 12-Inch 33/45rpm
ISLAND: *83* 4-6
Singles: 7-Inch
ISLAND: *83* 1-3

GRANT, Amy
Singles: 7-Inch
A&M: *85-88* 1-3
Picture Sleeves
A&M: *85-86* 1-3
LPs: 10/12-Inch 33rpm
A&M: *85-88* 5-8
MYRRH: *80-85* 5-8
Also see CETERA, Peter, & Amy Grant

GRANT, David
Singles: 12-Inch 33/45rpm
CHRYSALIS: *83* 4-6

Singles: 7-Inch
CAPITOL: *86* $1-3
CHRYSALIS: *83* 1-3
Also see GRAHAM, Jaki, & David Grant
Also see LINX

GRANT, Earl
Singles: 7-Inch
DECCA: *58-70* 2-4
PRINCE: *56* 3-5
EPs: 7-Inch 33/45rpm
DECCA: *59-62* 4-8
LPs: 10/12-Inch 33rpm
DECCA: *59-70* 5-15
MCA: *76* 5-8
VOCALION: *69-70* 5-10

GRANT, Eddy
Singles: 12-Inch 33/45rpm
EPIC: *80-82* 4-6
PORTRAIT: *83-85* 4-6
Singles: 7-Inch
EPIC: *79-80* 1-3
PORTRAIT: *83-85* 1-3
LPs: 10/12-Inch 33rpm
EPIC: *79-80* 5-8
PORTRAIT: *83-85* 5-8
Also see EQUALS

GRANT, Eleanor
Singles: 7-Inch
CBS ASSOCIATED: *84-85* 1-3
CATAWBA: *83* 1-3
COLUMBIA: *76* 2-3

GRANT, Gogi
Singles: 78rpm
ERA: *55-56* 2-5
RCA VICTOR: *52-57* 2-5
Singles: 7-Inch
CHARTER: *63* 2-4
ERA: *55-56* 3-5
LIBERTY: *60-61* 3-5
MONUMENT: *66-67* 2-3
PETE: *68-69* 2-3
RCA VICTOR: *52-58* 3-5
20TH FOX: *61-62* 2-4
Picture Sleeves
20TH FOX: *61* 4-8
EPs: 7-Inch 33/45rpm
RCA VICTOR (Except 1030): *57-58* 5-10
RCA VICTOR (1030; "The Helen
Morgan Story"): *57* 20-30
(Soundtrack.)
LPs: 10/12-Inch 33rpm
CHARTER: *64* 8-12
ERA (Black vinyl): *56-61* 15-25

ERA (Colored vinyl): *56*	$25-50
LIBERTY: *60*	8-15
PETE: *68-70*	6-10
RCA VICTOR (Except 1030): *57-59*	10-20
RCA VICTOR (1030; "The Helen	
Morgan Story"): *57*	50-75
(Soundtrack.)	

GRANT, Janie
Singles: 7-Inch

CAPRICE: *61-62*	4-6
PARKWAY: *66*	3-5
UNITED ARTISTS: *63-65*	3-5
Also see RAY, James	

GRANT, Tom
Singles: 7-Inch

WMOT: *81*	1-3

GRAPEFRUIT
Singles: 7-Inch

EQUINOX: *68*	3-5

LPs: 10/12-Inch 33rpm

DUNHILL: *68*	10-12
RCA VICTOR: *69*	10-12

GRAPES OF WRATH
LPs: 10/12-Inch 33rpm

CAPITOL: *86-88*	5-8

Members: Kevin Kane; Tom Kane; Hooper Kane.

GRAPPELLI, Stephane, & David Grisman
LPs: 10/12-Inch 33rpm

WARNER BROS: *81*	5-8
Also see GRISMAN, David	

GRAPPELLI, Stephane, & Barney Kessel
LPs: 10/12-Inch 33rpm

MFSL: *84*	20-40

Also see GRAPPELLI, Stephane, & David Grisman

GRASS ROOTS
(Featuring Rob Grill)
Singles: 7-Inch

ABC: *70*	1-3
DUNHILL: *65-74*	3-5
HAVEN: *75-76*	2-3
MCA: *82*	1-3

Picture Sleeves

DUNHILL: *67-70*	3-6

EPs: 7-Inch 33/45rpm

DUNHILL (165; "The Grass	
Roots"): *71*	5-8
(Promotional issue only.)	

LPs: 10/12-Inch 33rpm

ABC: *76*	8-10

COMMAND: *74*	$8-10
DUNHILL: *66-73*	10-15
HAVEN: *75*	8-10
MCA: *82*	5-8

Members: Rob Grill; Warren Entner; Creed Bratton; Erik Coonce.

GRATEFUL DEAD
Singles: 7-Inch

ARISTA (Black vinyl): *77-87*	1-3
ARISTA (Colored vinyl): *87*	2-3
FLASHBACK: *80*	2-3
GRATEFUL DEAD: *73-76*	5-10
SCORPIO (201; "Don't Ease Me In"): *66*	50-75
WARNER BROS: *67-73*	5-10

Promotional Singles

ARISTA: *77-87*	2-5
GRATEFUL DEAD: *73-76*	8-15
WARNER BROS: *67-73*	8-15

Picture Sleeves

ARISTA: *80*	1-3
GRATEFUL DEAD: *74*	10-15

EPs: 7-Inch 33/45rpm

WARNER BROS (226; "American	
Beauty"): *70*	15-30
(Jukebox issue only.)	

LPs: 10/12-Inch 33rpm

ARISTA: *77-87*	5-10
DIRECT-DISK: *79*	10-15
GRATEFUL DEAD: *73-74*	12-20
(Without any mention on cover about "Distribution by United Artists.")	
GRATEFUL DEAD: *75-76*	8-15
(With "Distribution by United Artists" on cover.)	
MFSL (014; "American Beauty"): *78*	40-80
MFSL (172; "From The Mars Hotel"): *85*	15-25
PAIR: *84*	6-12
PRIDE: *73*	12-20
SUNFLOWER: *70-71*	25-35
WARNER BROS (1689; "The	
Grateful Dead"): *67*	40-60
(Monaural, with a "W" prefix. Gold label.)	
WARNER BROS (1689; "The	
Grateful Dead"): *67*	25-35
(Stereo, with a "WS" prefix. Gold label.)	
WARNER BROS (1689; "The	
Grateful Dead"): *67*	20-30
(With Warner Bros. - Seven Arts "W7" label.)	
WARNER BROS (1689; "The	
Grateful Dead"): *71*	10-20
(With Warner Bros. "Arrowhead" label. Cover has copyright date on back.)	
WARNER BROS (1749; "Anthem	
Of The Sun"): *68*	20-30
(Background cover color is purple. With Warner Bros. - Seven Arts "W7" label.)	

WARNER BROS (1749; "Anthem
  Of The Sun"): *71* $10-20
  (Background cover color is white. With Warner
  Bros. "Arrowhead" logo on label.)
WARNER BROS (1790;
  "Aoxomoxoa"): *68* 20-30
  (With Warner Bros. - Seven Arts "W7" label.)
WARNER BROS (1790;
  "Aoxomoxoa"): *71* 10-20
  (With Warner Bros. "Arrowhead" label. Cover has
  copyright date on back.)
WARNER BROS (1830; "Live
  Dead"): *69* 25-35
  (With Warner Bros. - Seven Arts "W7" label. Is-
  sued with bonus pamphlet.)
WARNER BROS (1830; "Live
  Dead"): *71* 15-20
  (With Warner Bros. "Arrowhead" label. Cover has
  copyright date on back.)
WARNER BROS (1869; "Workingman's
  Dead"): *70* 20-30
  (With Warner Bros. - Seven Arts "W7" label.)
WARNER BROS (1869; "Workingman's
  Dead"): *71* 10-15
  (With Warner Bros. "Arrowhead" label. Cover has
  copyright date on back.)
WARNER BROS (1893; "American
  Beauty"): *70* 15-25
  (With Warner Bros. - Seven Arts "W7" label.)
WARNER BROS (1893; "American
  Beauty"): *71* 10-15
  (With Warner Bros. "Arrowhead" label. Cover has
  copyright date on back.)
WARNER BROS (1935; "Skull &
  Roses"): *71* 15-25
  (Title shown is commonly used to describe what is
  actually an untitled LP. Includes bonus sticker pic-
  turing cover art.)
WARNER BROS (2668; "Europe
  '72"): *72* 15-25
WARNER BROS (2721; "History Of The
  Grateful Dead, Vol. 1"): *73* 10-15
WARNER BROS (2764; "Skeletons From
  The Closet"): *74* 8-12
WARNER BROS (3091; "What A Strange
  Trip It's Been"): *77* 8-10
    Promotional LPs
ARISTA (35; "Grateful Dead
  Sampler"): *78* 40-50
ARISTA (7001; "Terrapin Station"): *77* .. 20-25
  (The lengthy *Terrapin Station* track is banded for
  radio station airplay.)
  Members: Jerry Garcia; Ron McKernan; Bob Weir;
  Bill Kreutzman; Phil Lesh; Mickey Hart; Tom Con-
  stanten; Ned Lagin; Robert Hunter; Keith God-
  chaux; Donna Godchaux; Brent Mydland.

Also see BROMBERG, David
Also see CROSBY, David
Also see GARCIA, Jerry
Also see HART, Mickey
Also see KANTER, Paul, & Grace Slick
Also see KELLY, Mike
Also see NEW RIDERS OF THE PURPLE
SAGE
Also see SILVER
Also see WEIR, Bob

**GRATEFUL DEAD / Elvin Bishop
Group**
       Singles: 7-Inch
WARNER BROS (7627; "Johnny B.
  Goode"): *72* $6-10
Also see BISHOP, Elvin
Also see GRATEFUL DEAD

GRAVES, Billy
       Singles: 7-Inch
MONUMENT (Except 401): *59-66* 3-5
MONUMENT (401; "The Shag"): *59* 5-8

GRAVES, Carl
       Singles: 7-Inch
A&M: *74* 2-3
ARIOLA AMERICA: *75-77* 2-3

GRAY, Claude
       Singles: 7-Inch
COLUMBIA: *64-66* 2-3
COUNTRY INT'L: *81-86* 1-3
D: *59-60* 3-5
DECCA: *66-71* 2-3
GRANNY WHITE: *76-82* 1-3
MERCURY: *60-64* 2-4
MILLION: *72-73* 1-3
       LPs: 10/12-Inch 33rpm
DECCA: *67-68* 8-12
MERCURY: *62* 12-18
MILLION: *72* 5-10
PICKWICK/HILLTOP: *67* 8-12

GRAY, Diva & Oyster
       Singles: 7-Inch
COLUMBIA: *79-80* 1-3
       LPs: 10/12-Inch 33rpm
COLUMBIA: *79* 5-8

GRAY, Dobie
       Singles: 12-Inch 33/45rpm
INFINITY: *79* 4-6
       Singles: 7-Inch
ARISTA: *83* 1-3
CAPITOL (Except 5853): *86-87* 1-3
CAPITOL (5853; "River Deep,
  Mountain High"): *67* 3-5

CAPRICORN: *76-77* $2-3
CHARGER: *64-66* 3-5
COLLECTABLES: *81* 1-3
CORDAK: *62-64* 3-5
DECCA: *73* 2-3
ERIC: 1-3
GUSTO: *85* 1-3
INFINITY: *78-79* 2-3
JAF: *63* 4-6
MCA: *73-75* 2-3
REAL FINE: *62* 4-6
ROBOX: *81* 1-3
STRIPE: *60-61* 8-10
WHITE WHALE: *69* 3-5
LPs: 10/12-Inch 33rpm
CAPITOL: *86* 5-8
CAPRICORN: *76* 8-10
CHARGER: *65* 15-20
DECCA: *73* 8-10
INFINITY: *79* 6-10
MCA: *73-74* 8-10
ROBOX: *81* 5-8
STRIPE: 10-12

GRAY, Dolores
Singles: 7-Inch
DECCA: *51-55* 3-5

GRAY, Glen, & The Casa Loma Orchestra
Singles: 78rpm
CAPITOL: *56-57* 2-4
DECCA: *55* 2-4
Singles: 7-Inch
CAPITOL: *56-58* 2-4
DECCA: *55* 2-4
EPs: 7-Inch 33/45rpm
CAPITOL: *56-58* 3-6
LPs: 10/12-Inch 33rpm
CAPITOL: *56-61* 5-15

GRAY, Maureen
Singles: 7-Inch
CHANCELLOR: *61-62* 3-5
LANDA: *62* 8-10
MERCURY: *63-64* 3-5

GRAYSON, Kim
Singles: 7-Inch
SOUNDWAVES: *87* 1-3
Picture Sleeves
SOUNDWAVES: *87* 2-4

GREAN, Charles
(Charles Randolph Grean Sounde)
Singles: 7-Inch
DOT: *67* 2-3
RANWOOD: *69-79* 1-3

LPs: 10/12-Inch 33rpm
RANWOOD: *69-70* $6-12

GREASE BAND
Singles: 7-Inch
SHELTER: *71* 2-4
LPs: 10/12-Inch 33rpm
SHELTER: *71* 8-10
Member: Henry McCullough.
Also see MC CARTNEY, Paul

GREAT BELIEVERS
Singles: 7-Inch
CASCADE: *64* 30-40
Member: Johnny Winter.
Also see WINTER, Johnny

GREAT!! SOCIETY!!
Singles: 7-Inch
COLUMBIA: *68* 8-10
NORTHBEACH (1001; "Someone To
Love"): *66* 75-150
Member: Grace Slick.
Also see JEFFERSON AIRPLANE
Also see SLICK, Grace

GREAT WHITE
Singles: 7-Inch
CAPITOL: *86-88* 1-3
EMI AMERICA: *84* 1-3
LPs: 10/12-Inch 33rpm
CAPITOL: *86-87* 5-8
EMI AMERICA: *84* 5-8
ENIGMA: *88* 5-8
GREENWORLD: *85* 5-8

GREAVES, R.B.
Singles: 7-Inch
ATCO: *69-70* 2-4
BAREBACK: *77* 2-3
MGM: *73* 2-3
MIDSONG: *80* 1-3
SUNFLOWER: *72* 2-3
20TH CENTURY-FOX: *74* 2-3
LPs: 10/12-Inch 33rpm
ATCO: *69* 12-15

GRECCO, Cyndi
Singles: 7-Inch
PRIVATE STOCK: *76-77* 1-3

GRECH, Rick
Singles: 7-Inch
RSO: *73* 2-3
LPs: 10/12-Inch 33rpm
RSO: *73* 5-8

GRECO, Buddy
(Buddy Greco Trio)
Singles: 78rpm
CORAL: *51-55* $3-6
KAPP: *56* 2-5
Singles: 7-Inch
CORAL: *51-55* 5-10
EPIC: *58-67* 3-6
HERALD: *59* 3-5
KAPP: *56* 2-4
MGM: *71-72* 2-3
REPRISE: *66-68* 2-3
SCEPTER: *69* 2-3
Picture Sleeves
EPIC: *64-65* 3-6
EPs: 7-Inch 33/45rpm
CORAL: *55* 5-8
LPs: 10/12-Inch 33rpm
CORAL: *55* 10-20
EPIC: *60-66* 8-15
HARMONY: *68* 8-12
KAPP: *61* 8-15
REPRISE: *67* 8-12
SCEPTER: *69-73* 5-10
VOCALION: *64* 8-12

GREELEY, George
Singles: 7-Inch
WARNER BROS: *59-62* 2-3
Picture Sleeves
WARNER BROS: *62* 2-5
EPs: 7-Inch 33/45rpm
CAPITOL: *56* 4-8
LPs: 10/12-Inch 33rpm
CAPITOL: *56* 5-15
RAVE: *56* 8-18
WARNER BROS: *59-61* 5-10

GREEN, Al
(Al Greene & The Soul Mates)
Singles: 7-Inch
A&M: *87* 1-3
BELL: *72-73* 2-3
FLASHBACK: 1-3
HI: *70-78* 2-3
HOT LINE: *67* 5-10
MOTOWN: *82-85* 1-3
LPs: 10/12-Inch 33rpm
A&M: *87* 5-8
BELL: *71* 8-10
HI: *69-78* 10-12
HOT LINE: *67* 20-25
KORY: *77* 8-10
MOTOWN: *82-85* 5-8
MYRRH: *80-83* 5-8

GREEN, Darren
Singles: 7-Inch
RCA VICTOR: *73-74* $2-3

GREEN, Garland
Singles: 7-Inch
CASINO: *76* 2-4
COTILLION: *71* 3-5
GAMMA: *67* 3-5
OCEAN FRONT: *83* 1-3
RCA VICTOR: *77* 2-3
REVUE: *68* 3-6
SPRING: *74-75* 2-3
UNI: *69* 3-5
LPs: 10/12-Inch 33rpm
OCEAN FRONT: *83* 5-8
RCA VICTOR: *74-78* 8-10
UNI: *70* 10-12

GREEN, Grant
LPs: 10/12-Inch 33rpm
BLUE NOTE: *61-65* 10-20
(Label reads "Blue Note Records Inc. - New York, U.S.A.")
BLUE NOTE: *66* 8-12
(Label reads "Blue Note Records - A Division Of Liberty Records Inc.")
BLUE THUMB: *71* 5-10
VERVE: *65* 10-18
VERSATILE: *78* 5-8

GREEN, Jack
Singles: 7-Inch
RCA VICTOR: *80* 1-3
LPs: 10/12-Inch 33rpm
RCA VICTOR: *80* 5-8
Also see PRETTY THINGS
Also see T-REX

GREEN, Peter
LPs: 10/12-Inch 33rpm
REPRISE: *71* 8-10
SAIL: *79-80* 5-8
Also see BOYD, Eddie
Also see FLEETWOOD MAC

GREEN, Sonny
Singles: 7-Inch
HILL: *73* 2-3

GREEN BERETS
Singles: 7-Inch
UNI: *70* 2-4

GREEN RIVER BOYS:
see CAMPBELL, Glen

GREENBAUM, Norman
Singles: 7-Inch
GREGAR: *69-70* 4-6

REPRISE: *70-71* $3-5
Picture Sleeves
REPRISE: *69* 4-8
LPs: 10/12-Inch 33rpm
GREGAR: *70* 15-20
REPRISE: *69-72* 12-15
Also see DR. WEST'S MEDICINE SHOW & JUNK BAND

GREENBERG, Steve
Singles: 7-Inch
TRIP: *69* 3-5

GREENE, Al: see GREEN, Al

GREENE, Barbara
Singles: 7-Inch
ATCO: *63* 25-30
RENEE: *68* 8-10
VIVID: *64* 3-5

GREENE, Jack
(Jack Greene & The Jolly Green Giants)
Singles: 7-Inch
DECCA: *65-72* 2-3
EMH: *83-84* 1-3
FRONTLINE: *80* 1-3
MCA: *73-74* 1-3
LPs: 10/12-Inch 33rpm
CORAL: *73* 4-6
DECCA: *66-71* 8-12
51 WEST: *84* 5-8
FRONTLINE: *80* 5-8
MCA: *73* 5-10

GREENE, Jack, & Jeannie Seely
Singles: 7-Inch
DECCA: *69-72* 2-3
LPs: 10/12-Inch 33rpm
DECCA: *70-72* 8-10
MCA: *73* 4-6
PINNACLE: *78* 5-8
RDS: *79* 5-8
Also see GREENE, Jack
Also see SEELY, Jeannie

GREENE, Laura
Singles: 7-Inch
SOUND TREK: *80* 1-3

GREENE, Lorne
Singles: 7-Inch
COLUMBIA: *69* 2-3
GRT: *70-71* 1-3
RCA VICTOR: *62-66* 3-6
Picture Sleeves
RCA VICTOR: *63-65* 5-10
LPs: 10/12-Inch 33rpm
CAMDEN: *70* 5-10

MGM: *71* $5-10
RCA VICTOR: *63-66* 10-20

GREENWICH, Ellie
(Ellie Gaye)
Singles: 7-Inch
BELL: *69* 3-5
RED BIRD: *65* 4-6
RCA VICTOR: 8-15
UNITED ARTISTS: *67* 3-5
VERVE: *70-73* 2-4
LPs: 10/12-Inch 33rpm
UNITED ARTISTS: *68* 30-40
VERVE: *73* 10-12
Also see ARCHIES
Also see BONDS, Gary "U.S."
Also see RAINDROPS

GREENWOOD, Lee
(Lee Greenwood Affair)
Singles: 7-Inch
DOT: *69* 2-4
MCA: *81-88* 1-3
PARAMOUNT: *71* 2-3
LPs: 10/12-Inch 33rpm
MCA: *82-86* 5-8
Also see MANDRELL, Barbara, & Lee Greenwood

GREENWOOD COUNTY SINGERS
(Greenwoods)
Singles: 7-Inch
DECCA: *64-66* 2-4
KAPP: *64-66* 2-4
LPs: 10/12-Inch 33rpm
DECCA: *64* 10-15
KAPP: *64-66* 10-15
RCA VICTOR: *70* 8-12

GREER, John
(Big John Greer)
Singles: 78rpm
RCA VICTOR: *49-53* 5-10
Singles: 7-Inch
RCA VICTOR (Black vinyl): *50-53* 12-25
RCA VICTOR (Colored vinyl): *49-50* ... 25-50

GREER, Big John, & The Four Students
Singles: 78rpm
GROOVE: *55* 5-10
Singles: 7-Inch
GROOVE: *55* 10-20
Also see GREER, John

GREGG, Bobby
(Bobby Gregg & His Friends; Bobby Grego)
Singles: 7-Inch
COTTON: *62* 5-8
EPIC: *62-66* 4-6

LPs: 10/12-Inch 33rpm
EPIC: 63 .... $25-30
Also see GIBSON, Steve

GREGORY, Dick
Singles: 7-Inch
VEE JAY: 62 2-4
LPs: 10/12-Inch 33rpm
COLPIX: 61-64 10-20
POPPY: 69-73 8-15
VEE JAY: 62-64 10-20

GREY & HANKS
Singles: 7-Inch
RCA VICTOR: 78-80 1-3
LPs: 10/12-Inch 33rpm
RCA VICTOR: 79-80 5-8
Members: Zane Grey; Len Hanks

GRIFFIN
Singles: 7-Inch
QWEST: 84 1-3

GRIFFIN, Billy
Singles: 7-Inch
ATLANTIC: 86 1-3
COLUMBIA: 83-86 1-3
LPs: 10/12-Inch 33rpm
COLUMBIA: 84-86 5-8

GRIFFIN, Merv
(Merv Griffin & The Griffin Family Singers)
Singles: 78rpm
COLUMBIA: 53 3-5
RCA VICTOR: 51-52 3-5
Singles: 7-Inch
CAMEO: 63-64 2-4
CARLTON: 61 2-4
COLUMBIA: 53 3-5
CORAL: 66 2-3
DOT: 68 2-3
GRIFFIN: 73 1-3
MGM: 65-67 2-3
MERCURY: 62 2-4
METROMEDIA: 70 1-3
RCA VICTOR: 51-52 3-5
EPs: 7-Inch 33/45rpm
RCA VICTOR (3000 series): 52 5-10
LPs: 10/12-Inch 33rpm
CAMEO: 64 8-15
CARLTON: 61 10-20
MGM: 65-66 8-15
METROMEDIA: 69 5-10
RCA VICTOR (3000 series): 52 15-25
(10-Inch LPs.)
Also see MARTIN, Freddy, & His Orchestra

GRIFFIN, Reggie, & Technofunk
Singles: 7-Inch
SWEET MOUNTAIN: 82 .... $1-3

GRIFFIN BROTHERS
(Griffin Brothers Featuring Tommy Brown;
Griffin Brothers Featuring Margie Day)
Singles: 78rpm
DOT: 50-52 4-8
Singles: 7-Inch
DOT (1100 series,
except 1108): 51-53 10-20
DOT (1108; "Ace In The
Hole"): 52 20-30
DOT (16000 series): 60 4-6
Members: Jimmy Griffin; Edward "Buddy" Griffin.

GRIFFITH, Andy
(Deacon Andy Griffith)
Singles: 78rpm
CAPITOL: 53-57 3-6
Singles: 7-Inch
CAPITOL (2500 series): 69 1-3
CAPITOL (2600 through 3600
series): 53-57 5-15
CAPITOL (4000 & 5000 series): 59-63 4-6
(Purple or orange/yellow swirl label.)
CAPITOL (4000 series): 76 2-3
(Orange label.)
COLONIAL: 53 15-20
COLUMBIA: 72 5-10
EPs: 7-Inch 33/45rpm
CAPITOL: 54-61 15-30
LPs: 10/12-Inch 33rpm
CAPITOL (1100 through 1600
series): 59-61 15-25
CAPITOL (2000 series): 64-67 10-20
COLUMBIA: 72 5-10

GRIFFITH, Johnny, Inc.
Singles: 7-Inch
RCA VICTOR: 73 2-3

GRIM REAPER
Singles: 7-Inch
RCA VICTOR: 85-87 1-3
LPs: 10/12-Inch 33rpm
RCA VICTOR: 85-87 5-8

GRIN
Singles: 7-Inch
A&M: 74 2-3
SPINDIZZY: 71-72 2-3
LPs: 10/12-Inch 33rpm
A&M: 73 8-10
COLUMBIA: 5-8
SPINDIZZY: 71-72 8-10
Member: Nils Lofgren.

Also see LOFGREN, Nils

GRINDERSWITCH
Singles: 7-Inch
ATCO: 77-78 . . . . $2-3
LPs: 10/12-Inch 33rpm
ATCO: 77 8-10
CAPRICORN: 74-76 8-10

GRISMAN, David
LPs: 10/12-Inch 33rpm
WARNER BROS: 81 5-8
Also see GRAPPELLI, Stephane, & David
Grisman

GROCE, Larry
Singles: 7-Inch
PEACEABLE: 75 2-3
WARNER BROS: 75 2-3
LPs: 10/12-Inch 33rpm
DAYBREAK: 71-72 8-10
WARNER BROS: 76 8-10

GROSS, Henry
Singles: 7-Inch
A&M: 74-75 2-3
LIFESONG: 76-78 2-3
LPs: 10/12-Inch 33rpm
ABC-PARAMOUNT: 71 8-10
A&M: 73-75 8-10
CAPITOL: 81 5-8
LIFESONG: 76-78 8-10
Also see SHA NA NA

GROUND HOG
Singles: 7-Inch
GEMIGO: 74 2-3

GROVE, Harry, Trio
Singles: 78rpm
LONDON: 52 2-4
Singles: 7-Inch
LONDON: 52 2-4
LPs: 10/12-Inch 33rpm
LONDON: 52 10-15

GRUSIN, Dave
(Dave Grusin Quintet; Dave Grusin & The
NY/LA Dream Band)
Singles: 7-Inch
DECCA: 68-69 2-3
EPIC: 63 2-4
WARNER BROS: 83 1-3
LPs: 10/12-Inch 33rpm
COLUMBIA: 65 10-20
EPIC: 62 15-25
GRP: 80-83 5-8
POLYDOR: 77 5-8
SHEFFIELD LAB: 77-82 8-15

VERSATILE: 78 . . . . $5-8
Also see BISHOP, Stephen
Also see GALE, Eric
Also see RITENOUR, Lee

GUADALCANAL DIARY
LPs: 10/12-Inch 33rpm
ELEKTRA: 86-88 5-8
Members: Rhett Crowe; Murray Attaway; John
Poe; Jeff Walls.

GUARALDI, Vince
(Vince Guaraldi Trio)
Singles: 7-Inch
FANTASY: 62-66 2-4
LPs: 10/12-Inch 33rpm
FANTASY (3200 series): 56-58 15-25
FANTASY (3300 series): 62-66 10-20
FANTASY (8000 series): 62 15-25
FANTASY (8300 series): 63-66 10-20
MFSL: 84 20-40
WARNER BROS: 68-69 8-12

GUARD, Dave, & The Whiskeyhill
Singers
Singles: 7-Inch
CAPITOL: 62 3-5
LPs: 10/12-Inch 33rpm
CAPITOL: 62 15-20
Also see KINGSTON TRIO

GUCCI CREW II
LPs: 10/12-Inch 33rpm
GUCCI: 88 5-8

GUESS WHO
Singles: 7-Inch
AMY: 67 8-15
FONTANA: 69 5-8
HILLTAK: 78-79 2-3
RCA VICTOR: 69-76 3-5
SCEPTER: 65-73 4-8
Picture Sleeves
RCA VICTOR: 70 3-6
LPs: 10/12-Inch 33rpm
HILLTAK: 79 5-8
MGM: 69 12-15
PICKWICK: 72 8-10
PIP: 71 8-10
PRIDE: 73 8-10
RCA VICTOR (Except AYL1 & LSP
series): 73-80 8-12
RCA VICTOR (AYL1 series): 80 5-8
RCA VICTOR (LSP series): 69-72 15-25
SCEPTER: 73 8-10
SPRINGBOARD: 72 8-10
WAND: 69 12-15

Members: Chad Allen; Burton Cummings; Randy
Bachman; Domenic Troiano.
Also see BACHMAN, Randy
Also see CUMMINGS, Burton
Also see WOLFMAN JACK

GUIDRY, Greg
Singles: 7-Inch
COLUMBIA: 82 . . . . $1-3
LPs: 10/12-Inch 33rpm
COLUMBIA: 82 5-8

GUITAR, Bonnie
Singles: 78rpm
DOT: 57 3-5
Singles: 7-Inch
ABC: 74 1-3
COLUMBIA: 72 1-3
DOLTON: 59 3-5
DOT (15000 series): 57-59 5-10
DOT (16000 series): 66-67 3-5
FABOR: 64 2-3
FOUR STAR: 75 1-3
JERDEN: 63 4-8
MCA: 74 1-3
PARAMOUNT: 70 1-3
RCA VICTOR: 61-62 10-20
RADIO: 58 5-10
LPs: 10/12-Inch 33rpm
CAMDEN: 69 6-12
DOT (Except 3069): 59-68 10-15
DOT (3069; "Moonlight &
Shadows"): 57 15-20
HAMILTON: 65 8-12
PARAMOUNT: 70 8-12
PICKWICK: 70 6-12

GUITAR SLIM
(Johnny Winter)
Singles: 7-Inch
DIAMOND: 62 50-75
Also see WINTER, Johnny

GUNHILL ROAD
Singles: 7-Inch
KAMA SUTRA: 73 2-3
MERCURY: 72 2-3
LPs: 10/12-Inch 33rpm
KAMA SUTRA: 72 8-10
MERCURY: 71 8-10

GUNS N'ROSES
Singles: 7-Inch
GEFFEN: 88 1-3
LPs: 10/12-Inch 33rpm
GEFFEN: 88 5-8

GUNTER, Shirley
(Shirley Gunter & The Flairs; Shirley Gunter &
The Queens)
Singles: 78rpm
FLAIR: 55 . . . . $5-10
MODERN: 56 5-10
Singles: 7-Inch
FLAIR: 55 10-20
MODERN: 56 8-15
TANGERINE: 65 3-6
Member (Queens): Zola Taylor.

GURVITZ, Adrian
Singles: 7-Inch
JET: 79 2-3
Also see BAKER-GURVITZ ARMY
Also see EDGE, Graeme

GUTHRIE, Arlo
Singles: 7-Inch
REPRISE: 69-77 2-3
LPs: 10/12-Inch 33rpm
REPRISE: 70-76 8-10
WARNER BROS: 77-78 5-8
Also see SEEGER, Pete, & Arlo Guthrie

GUTHRIE, Gwen
Singles: 12-Inch 33/45rpm
GARAGE: 85 4-6
ISLAND: 83-85 4-6
Singles: 7-Inch
GARAGE: 85 1-3
ISLAND: 82-85 1-3
POLYDOR: 86-87 1-3
WARNER BROS: 88 1-3
LPs: 10/12-Inch 33rpm
GARAGE: 85 5-8
ISLAND: 85 5-8
Also see HOWARD, George

GUY
Singles: 7-Inch
UPTOWN: 88 1-3
LPs: 10/12-Inch 33rpm
UPTOWN : 88 5-8

GUY, Bob
(Frank Zappa)
Singles: 7-Inch
DONNA (1380; "Letter From
Jeepers"): 61 40-60
Also see ZAPPA, Frank

GUY, Buddy
(Buddy Guy & His Band)
Singles: 7-Inch
ARTISTIC: 58-59 5-10
CHESS: 60-65 4-8

LPs: 10/12-Inch 33rpm
BLUE THUMB: 70 .... $8-10
CHESS: 69 10-12
VANGUARD: 68 12-15
Also see WELLS, Junior, & Buddy Guy

GYPSIES
Singles: 7-Inch
CAPRICE: 66 3-5
OLD TOWN: 64-66 3-6

GYPSY
Singles: 7-Inch
METROMEDIA: 70 2-4
RCA VICTOR: 72 2-3
LPs: 10/12-Inch 33rpm
METROMEDIA: 70-71 8-10
RCA VICTOR: 72-73 8-10
Also see WALSH, James, Gypsy Band

H

HACKETT, Buddy
Singles: 78rpm
CORAL: 53-56 2-5
Singles: 7-Inch
CORAL: 53-56 3-5
LAUREL: 60 2-4
LPs: 10/12-Inch 33rpm
CORAL: 65 8-15
DOT: 59 10-15

HACKETT, Steve
Singles: 7-Inch
CHARISMA: 80 1-3
CHRYSALIS: 76-79 2-3
EPIC: 81 1-3
LPs: 10/12-Inch 33rpm
CHARISMA: 80 5-8
CHRYSALIS: 76-79 5-8
EPIC: 81 5-8
Also see GTR
Also see GENESIS

HAGAR, Sammy
Singles: 7-Inch
CAPITOL: 76-79 2-3
COLUMBIA: 87 1-3
GEFFEN: 82-87 1-3
LPs: 10/12-Inch 33rpm
CAPITOL: 77-82 5-8
GEFFEN: 82-87 5-8
Also see MONTROSE
Also see VAN HALEN

HAGAR, SCHON, AARONSON, SHRIEVE
Singles: 7-Inch
GEFFEN: 85 .... $1-3
LPs: 10/12-Inch 33rpm
GEFFEN: 85 5-8
Members: Sammy Hagar; Neal Schon; Ken Aaronson; Michael Shrieve.
Also see HAGAR, Sammy
Also see SCHON, Neal, & Jan Hammer
Also see SANTANA

HAGEN, Nina
(The Nina Hagen Band)
Singles: 12-Inch 33/45rpm
COLUMBIA: 84-85 4-6
Singles: 7-Inch
COLUMBIA: 80-85 1-3
LPs: 10/12-Inch 33rpm
COLUMBIA: 80-83 5-10

HAGGARD, Merle
(Merle Haggard & The Strangers)
Singles: 7-Inch
CAPITOL: 65-77 2-4
COLUMBIA: 83 1-3
EPIC: 81-88 1-3
MCA: 77-85 1-3
MERCURY: 83 1-3
TALLY: 63-65 5-10
Picture Sleeves
CAPITOL: 67-71 2-5
MCA: 77-80 1-3
EPs: 7-Inch 33/45rpm
CAPITOL: 71 5-8
(Jukebox issues only.)
LPs: 10/12-Inch 33rpm
ALBUM GLOBE: 5-8
CAPITOL (168 through 735): 69-71 8-15
(With a "T," "ST," "STBB," or "SWBB" prefix.)
CAPITOL (168 through 735): 69-71 4-8
(With an "SM" prefix.)
CAPITOL (796; "Merle Haggard's Strangers
& Friends Honky Tonkin'"): 71 20-30
CAPITOL (803; "Land Of Many
Churches"): 71 50-65
CAPITOL (823; "Truly The Best Of
Merle Haggard"): 71 40-60
CAPITOL (882; "Let Me Tell You
About A Song"): 72 10-12
CAPITOL (2300 through 2900
series): 65-68 15-25
(With a "T," "ST," or "SKAO" prefix.)
CAPITOL (2700 through 2900 series): 4-8
(With an "SM" prefix.)

CAPITOL (11000 through 16000
series): 72-82 ....$4-8
EPIC: 81-86 5-8
MCA: 77-84 4-8
MERCURY: 83 5-8
PICKWICK/HILLTOP: 8-12
SONGBIRD: 81 5-8

HAGGARD, Merle / Patsy Cline
LPs: 10-Inch 33rpm
OUT OF TOWN DIST: 82 5-8
Also see CLINE, Patsy

HAGGARD, Merle, & Clint Eastwood
Singles: 7-Inch
ELEKTRA: 80 1-3
Picture Sleeves
ELEKTRA: 80 2-3
Also see EASTWOOD, Clint

**HAGGARD, Merle / Mickey
Gilley / Willie Knight**
LPs: 10/12-Inch 33rpm
OUT OF TOWN DIST: 82 5-8
Also see GILLEY, Mickey

HAGGARD, Merle / Sonny James
LPs: 10/12-Inch 33rpm
CAPITOL: 12-15
Also see JAMES, Sonny

HAGGARD, Merle, & George Jones
Singles: 7-Inch
EPIC (03405; "C.C.
Waterback"): 82 1-3
EPIC (03405; "C.C.
Waterback"): 82 4-8
(Picture disc.)
LPs: 10/12-Inch 33rpm
EPIC: 82 5-8
Also see JONES, George

HAGGARD, Merle, & Willie Nelson
Singles: 7-Inch
EPIC: 83 1-3
LPs: 10/12-Inch 33rpm
EPIC: 83 5-8
Also see NELSON, Willie

HAGGARD, Merle, & Johnny Paycheck
Singles: 7-Inch
EPIC: 81 1-3
Also see HAGGARD, Merle
Also see PAYCHECK, Johnny

HAHN, Carol
Singles: 12-Inch 33/45rpm
NICKLE: 83 4-6

Merle Haggard

HAHN, Joyce
Singles: 7-Inch
CADENCE: 57 ....$2-4

HAIRCUT ONE HUNDRED
Singles: 7-Inch
ARISTA: 82 1-3
LPs: 10/12-Inch 33rpm
ARISTA: 82 5-8
Member: Nick Heyward.
Also see HEYWARD, Nick

HAIRSTON, Curtis
Singles: 12-Inch 33/45rpm
PRETTY PEARL: 83 4-6
Singles: 7-Inch
ATLANTIC: 87 1-3
PRETTY PEARL: 84-85 1-3

HALEY, Bill
(Bill Haley & The Comets; Bill Haley & The Sad-
dlemen; Bill Haley & His Saddle Men Featuring
Billy Williamson)
Singles: 78rpm
ATLANTIC (727; "I'm Gonna Dry
Ev'ry Tear With A Kiss"): 50 150-200
DECCA: 54-55 15-20
(Black label with gold print.)
DECCA: 54-57 10-15
(Black label with silver print.)
ESSEX: 52-55 10-20
KEYSTONE (5101; "Deal Me
A Hand"): 50 250-300
Singles: 7-Inch
APT: 65 10-15
ARZEE: 77 4-6

DECCA (29000 series): *54-56* **$10-15**
(With silver lines on both sides of the name Decca.)
DECCA (29000 series): *54-56* **6-10**
(With a star and silver lines under the name Decca.)
DECCA (30000 & 31000 series): *56-64* **4-6**
DECCA (72000 series): *69* **3-5**
ESSEX (303; "Rock The Joint"): *52* ... **150-200**
(Colored vinyl.)
ESSEX (303; "Rock The Joint"): *52* **50-60**
(Black vinyl.)
ESSEX (305; "Rocking Chair On
The Moon"): *52* **50-60**
ESSEX (310; "Real Rock Drive"): *52* ... **30-35**
ESSEX (321; "Crazy Man Crazy"): *53* ... **30-35**
ESSEX (327; "Fractured"): *53* **30-35**
ESSEX (332; "Live It Up"): *53* **25-30**
ESSEX (340; "Ten Little Indians"): *53* .. **25-30**
ESSEX (348; "Chattanooga
Choo-Choo"): *54* **25-30**
ESSEX (374; "Jukebox
Cannonball"): *54* **20-30**
ESSEX (381; "Rocket 88"): *54* **100-125**
ESSEX (399; "Rock The Joint"): *55* **20-25**
Note: Essex 102, *Rock Around the Clock*, is a '70s
bootleg.
GONE: *61* **10-12**
HOLIDAY (108; "Green Tree
Boogie"): *51* **150-200**
HOLIDAY (111; "A Year Ago This
Christmas"): *51* **150-200**
HOLIDAY (113; "Jukebox
Cannonball"): *51* **150-200**
JANUS: *71* **2-3**
KAMA SUTRA: *70* **3-5**
KASEY: *61* **5-8**
LOGO: *61* **5-8**
MCA: *74* **1-3**
NEWTOWN: *63-64* **5-8**

TRANSWORLD (200 & 300
series): *54* **$60-75**
TRANSWORLD (700 series): *53* **35-45**
UNITED ARTISTS: *69* **3-5**
WARNER BROS: *60* **10-20**
Picture Sleeves
DECCA: *57-58* **12-25**
EPs: 7-Inch 33/45rpm
DECCA: *55-59* **30-60**
ESSEX (102; "Dance Party"): *54* **50-75**
SOMERSET: *55* **40-60**
TRANSWORLD: *55* **30-50**
LPs: 10/12-Inch 33rpm
ACCORD: *81-82* **5-8**
ALSHIRE: *70-79* **8-10**
AMBASSADOR: **10-12**
CORAL: *73* **8-10**
DECCA (5560; "Shake, Rattle
& Roll"): *54* **150-250**
DECCA (7211; "Golden Hits"): *72* **12-15**
DECCA (8000 series): *55-59* **30-60**
DECCA (75027; "Greatest Hits"): *68* ... **12-15**
ESSEX ("Rock With Bill Haley & The
Comets"): *54* **200-275**
EXACT: *80* **5-8**
51 WEST: *83* **5-8**
GNP/CRESCENDO: *74-76* **8-10**
GUEST STAR: *65* **12-15**
JANUS: *72* **8-10**
KAMA SUTRA: *70* **10-12**
MCA: *73* **8-10**
PICKWICK: *71* **8-10**
ROULETTE: *62* **15-20**
SOMERSET ("Rock & Roll
Dance Party"): *55* **50-80**
(Also contains tracks by Bunny Paul & the
Harptones, Ken Carsonn, The Dinning Sisters, The
Swingers, and The House Rockers.)
SOMERSET (4600; "Rock With
Bill Haley"): *55* **50-80**
SPRINGBOARD: *77* **8-10**
SUN: *80* **5-8**
TRANSWORLD (202; "Rock With Bill
Haley & The Comets"): *55* **150-250**
VOCALION: *63* **12-15**
WARNER BROS: *60-70* **25-30**
Also see KINGSMEN

HALL, Daryl
(Daryl Hall With Gulliver)
Singles: 7-Inch
AMY: *69* **$3-5**
CHELSEA: *76* **2-4**
RCA VICTOR: *80-87* **1-3**

Picture Sleeves
RCA VICTOR: *80-86* $1-3
LPs: 10/12-Inch 33rpm
RCA VICTOR: *80-86* 5-8
Also see U.S.A. FOR AFRICA

HALL, Daryl, & John Oates
(Hall & Oates)
Singles: 12-Inch 33/45rpm
CHELSEA: *76* 2-4
RCA VICTOR: *81-85* 4-6
Singles: 7-Inch
ARISTA: *88* 1-3
ATLANTIC: *72-77* 2-3
RCA VICTOR: *76-84* 1-3
Picture Sleeves
RCA VICTOR: *77-84* 1-3
Promotional Singles
RCA VICTOR (Colored vinyl): *85* 3-5
(With one side by Daryl Hall and one side by John Oates.)
LPs: 10/12-Inch 33rpm
ARISTA: *88* 5-8
ATLANTIC: *72-77* 8-12
CHELSEA: *76* 10-12
MFSL: *82* 20-30
RCA VICTOR (Black vinyl): *75-84* 5-8
RCA VICTOR (Colored vinyl): *78* 10-12
Promotional LPs
RCA VICTOR ("Special Radio
Series"): *81* 15-25
Also see KENDRICKS, Eddie
Also see PRINE, John / Daryl Hall & John
Oates / Barnaby Bye / Delbert & Glen
Also see RUFFIN, David
Also see WHOLE OATS

HALL, Daryl, & Ruth Copeland
Singles: 7-Inch
RCA VICTOR: *76* 2-3
Also see HALL, Daryl

HALL, Ellis, Jr.
Singles: 7-Inch
H.C.R.C.: *83* 1-3

HALL, Jimmy
Singles: 7-Inch
EPIC: *80-82* 1-3
LPs: 10/12-Inch 33rpm
EPIC: *80* 5-8
Also see WET WILLIE

HALL, John, Band
Singles: 7-Inch
ASYLUM: *78* 2-3
COLUMBIA: *79* 1-3
EMI AMERICA: *81-83* 1-3

LPs: 10/12-Inch 33rpm
ASYLUM: *78* $5-8
COLUMBIA: *70* 8-10
EMI AMERICA: *81-82* 5-8
Also see ORLEANS

HALL, Lani
Singles: 7-Inch
A&M: *71-85* 1-3
Picture Sleeves
A&M: *80* 1-3
LPs: 10/12-Inch 33rpm
A&M: *72-85* 5-8
Also see MENDES, Sergio

HALL, Lani, & Herb Alpert
Singles: 7-Inch
A&M: *81* 1-3
Also see ALPERT, Herb
Also see HALL, Lani

HALL, Larry
Singles: 7-Inch
GOLD LEAF: *62* 3-5
HOT: *59* 8-10
STRAND: *59-62* 4-6
LPs: 10/12-Inch 33rpm
STRAND: *60* 35-45

HALL, Randy
Singles: 7-Inch
MCA: *84-88* 1-3
LPs: 10/12-Inch 33rpm
MCA: *84* 5-8

HALL, Tom T.
(Tom T. Hall & The Storytellers)
Singles: 7-Inch
MERCURY: *67-86* 1-3
RCA VICTOR: *77-81* 1-3
LPs: 10/12-Inch 33rpm
MERCURY (500 through 1100
series): *73-77* 5-10
MERCURY (5000 through 8000
series): *78-84* 5-8
MERCURY (61000 series): *69-71* 8-15
MERCURY (80000 series): *83-86* 5-8
OUT OF TOWN DIST: *82* 5-8
RCA VICTOR: *78-81* 4-8
Also see DUDLEY, Dave, & Tom T. Hall
Also see PAGE, Patti, & Tom T. Hall

HALL, Tom T., & Earl Scruggs
Singles: 7-Inch
COLUMBIA: *82* 1-3
LPs: 10/12-Inch 33rpm
COLUMBIA: *82* 5-8
Also see HALL, Tom T.

Also see FLATT, Lester, & Earl Scruggs

HALL & OATES:
see HALL, Daryl, & John Oates

HALLORAN, Jack, Singers
Singles: 7-Inch
DOT: 63 . . . . $2-3

HALOS
Singles: 7-Inch
7 ARTS: 61 8-10
TRANS ATLAS: 62 3-5
LPs: 10/12-Inch 33rpm
WARWICK: 62 35-45

HAMBLIN, Stuart
Singles: 7-Inch
BLUEBIRD: 59 2-5
COLUMBIA: 50-62 2-5
CORAL: 59 2-4
KAPP: 66 2-3
LAMB & LION: 74 1-3
RCA VICTOR (0500 series): 71 1-3
RCA VICTOR (5000 & 6000
series): 54-56 2-4
EPs: 7-Inch 33/45rpm
COLUMBIA: 58-59 5-8
RCA VICTOR: 54-60 5-12
LPs: 10/12-Inch 33rpm
CAMDEN: 59-66 6-12
COLUMBIA: 61-62 8-15
CORAL: 60 12-15
KAPP: 66 8-12
LAMB & LION: 74 4-6
RCA VICTOR: 54-57 10-20
SACRED: 4-8
WORD: 4-8

HAMILTON, Bobby
Singles: 7-Inch
APT: 58-59 5-10
DECCA: 59 4-6
DIANA: 59 4-6

HAMILTON, Chico
(Chico Hamilton Trio; Chico Hamilton Quartet;
Chico Hamilton Quintet; Chico Hamilton & The
Players)
Singles: 7-Inch
COLUMBIA: 61 2-3
CORAL: 62 2-3
ENTERPRISE: 74 1-3
IMPULSE: 64-67 1-3
PACIFIC JAZZ (600 series): 54-55 3-5
PACIFIC JAZZ (88000 series): 66 1-3
EPs: 7-Inch 33/45rpm
DECCA: 57 5-15
PACIFIC JAZZ: 55-56 10-20

LPs: 10/12-Inch 33rpm
BLUE NOTE: 75 . . . . $5-8
COLUMBIA: 60-62 15-25
CROWN: 63 10-15
DECCA: 57 25-35
DISCOVERY: 81 5-8
ELEKTRA: 80 5-8
EVEREST: 79 5-8
FLYING DUTCHMAN: 71 5-10
IMPULSE: 63-71 10-20
INSTANT: 64 10-15
MERCURY: 77 5-8
ODYSSEY: 68 8-12
PACIFIC JAZZ (17; "The Chico
Hamilton Trio"): 55 40-60
(10-Inch LP.)
PACIFIC JAZZ (39; "Spectacular
Chico Hamilton"): 62 10-15
PACIFIC JAZZ (1200 series): 55-57 20-40
PACIFIC JAZZ (20000 series): 68 8-12
REPRISE: 63 10-20
SESAC: 59 30-40
(Promotional issue only.)
SOLID STATE: 68-69 8-12
SUNSET: 68 5-10
WARNER BROS (1200 & 1300
series): 58-59 20-30
WORLD PACIFIC (1000 & 1200
series): 58-60 20-30
Also see ALMEIDA, Laurindo / Chico Hamil-
ton

HAMILTON, Chico, & Charles Lloyd
LPs: 10/12-Inch 33rpm
COLUMBIA: 68 8-10
Also see HAMILTON, Chico
Also see LLOYD, Charles, Quartet

HAMILTON, George, IV
(George Hamilton IV & The Country
Gentlemen)
Singles: 78rpm
ABC-PARAMOUNT: 56-65 3-6
COLONIAL: 56 6-12
Singles: 7-Inch
ABC: 78 1-3
ABC/DOT: 77 1-3
ABC-PARAMOUNT: 56-65 5-10
COLONIAL: 56 20-30
GRT: 76 2-3
MCA: 79-80 1-3
RCA VICTOR: 61-74 2-4
Picture Sleeves
ABC-PARAMOUNT: 65 10-15
EPs: 7-Inch 33/45rpm
ABC-PARAMOUNT: 58 8-12

LPs: 10/12-Inch 33rpm
ABC: 72-77 .... $8-10
ABC-PARAMOUNT: 58-63 25-35
CAMDEN: 68-73 8-10
HARMONY: 70 8-10
LAMB & LION: 74 8-10
MCA: 80 5-8
RCA VICTOR (APLI series): 74-76 8-10
RCA VICTOR (LPM & LSP
series): 61-73 10-15
   Also see ANKA, Paul, George Hamilton IV &
Johnny Nash

HAMILTON, George, IV, &
Skeeter Davis
LPs: 10/12-Inch 33rpm
RCA VICTOR: 70 10-12
   Also see DAVIS, Skeeter
   Also see HAMILTON, George, IV

HAMILTON, Roy
Singles: 78rpm
EPIC: 54-57 2-5
Singles: 7-Inch
AGP: 69 1-3
CAPITOL: 67 2-3
EPIC: 54-62 5-12
MGM: 63-65 3-5
RCA VICTOR: 65-67 2-4
Picture Sleeves
EPIC: 60-62 5-10
EPs: 7-Inch 33/45rpm
EPIC: 55-59 10-12
LPs: 10/12-Inch 33rpm
EPIC: 55-67 10-20
MGM: 63-64 10-15
RCA VICTOR: 66 8-12

HAMILTON, Russ
Singles: 78rpm
KAPP: 57 4-6
Singles: 7-Inch
KAPP: 57-64 4-6
MGM: 60 3-5
LPs: 10/12-Inch 33rpm
KAPP: 57 30-35

HAMILTON, JOE FRANK &
DENNISON
Singles: 7-Inch
PLAYBOY: 76-77 2-3
Picture Sleeves
PLAYBOY: 76 2-4
LPs: 10/12-Inch 33rpm
PLAYBOY: 76-77 8-10
   Members: Dan Hamilton; Joe Frank Carollo; Alan
Dennison.

   Also see HAMILTON, JOE FRANK &
REYNOLDS

HAMILTON, JOE FRANK &
REYNOLDS
Singles: 7-Inch
ABC: 72 .... $2-3
DUNHILL: 71 2-3
PLAYBOY: 75-76 2-3
Picture Sleeves
PLAYBOY: 76 2-4
LPs: 10/12-Inch 33rpm
DUNHILL: 71-72 8-10
PLAYBOY: 75-77 8-10
   Members: Dan Hamilton; Joe Frank Carollo; Tom
Reynolds.
   Also see HAMILTON, JOE FRANK & DEN-
NISON
   Also see T-BONES

HAMLISCH, Marvin
Singles: 12-Inch 33/45rpm
UNITED ARTISTS: 77 4-6
Singles: 7-Inch
A&M: 74-76 1-3
ARISTA: 79 1-3
MCA: 74-83 1-3
PLANET: 80 1-3
UNITED ARTISTS: 71-77 1-3
LPs: 10/12-Inch 33rpm
MCA: 74 5-10
SOUTHERN CROSS: 83 5-8

HAMMEL, Karl, Jr.
Singles: 7-Inch
ARLISS (1007; "Summer
Souvenirs"): 61 3-5
ARLISS (1011; "Sittin'
Alphabetically"): 61 12-15
LAURIE: 63 3-5
20TH CENTURY-FOX: 66 3-5

HAMMER, Jan
(Jan Hammer Group)
Singles: 12-Inch 33/45rpm
MCA: 85 4-6
Singles: 7-Inch
ASYLUM: 79 1-3
MCA: 85-88 1-3
NEMPEROR: 76-78 1-3
LPs: 10/12-Inch 33rpm
ECM: 5-8
MPS: 76 5-8
NEMPEROR: 74-76 5-10
VANGAURD: 77 5-8
   Also see BECK, Jeff
   Also see GOODMAN, Jerry, & Jan Hammer

Also see SCHON, Neal, & Jan Hammer

HAMMOND, Albert
Singles: 7-Inch
EPIC: 76 .... $2-3
MUMS: 72-75 2-3
LPs: 10/12-Inch 33rpm
COLUMBIA: 81-82 5-8
EPIC: 77 8-10
MUMS: 72-74 8-10
Also see MAGIC LANTERNS
Also see SPRINGSTEEN, Bruce / Albert
Hammond / Loudon Wainwright, III / Taj Mahal

HAMPSHIRE, Keith
Singles: 7-Inch
A&M: 72-74 2-3
RCA VICTOR: 71 2-3

HAMPTON, Lionel
(Lionel Hampton & His Orchestra; Lionel
Hampton Quartet; Lionel Hampton All Star
Alumni Big Band)
Singles: 7-Inch
CLEF: 55 2-4
BRUNSWICK: 74 1-3
COLUMBIA: 76 1-3
DECCA: 50-53 2-4
GLAD HAMP: 60-67 2-3
IMPULSE: 65 2-3
MGM: 51-61 2-4
NORGREN: 56 2-4
EPs: 7-Inch 33/45rpm
CLEF: 53-56 10-20
COLUMBIA: 56 5-15
DECCA: 51-53 5-15
EMARCY: 56 5-15
EPIC: 56 5-10
GLAD HAMP: 62 5-8

MGM: 56 .... $5-15
MERCURY: 55 5-15
NORGREN: 55 10-20
RCA VICTOR: 54-57 5-15
LPs: 10/12-Inch 33rpm
AMERICAN RECORDING
  SOCIETY: 56 40-60
AUDIO FIDELITY: 57-59 15-20
BLUE NOTE (5000 series): 53 40-60
  (10-Inch LPs.)
BRUNSWICK: 74 5-8
CAMDEN (400 & 500 series): 58-59 10-20
CLEF (100 series): 53 30-50
  (10-Inch LPs.)
CLEF (600 & 700 series): 53-56 20-35
COLUMBIA (1300 through
  1600 series): 59-61 10-20
  (Monaural.)
COLUMBIA (8100 through
  8400 series): 59-61 15-25
  (Stereo.)
CONTEMPORARY: 55 20-35
CORAL: 63 15-20
DECCA (4000 series): 61-63 15-20
DECCA (5000 & 7000
  series): 51-53 20-30
  (10-Inch LPs.)
DECCA (8200 series): 56 20-30
DECCA (9000 series): 58 15-25
DECCA (79000 series): 69 8-12
EMARCY (26000 series): 53 30-40
  (10-Inch LPs.)
EMARCY (36000 series): 56 15-25
EPIC (300 series): 56 15-25
EPIC (16000 & 17000
  series): 62 15-20
GENE NORMAN PRESENTS: 57 20-30
GLAD HAMP (1001 through
  1009): 61-65 10-15
GLAD HAMP (1020 & 1021): 80 5-8
GLAD HAMP (3000 series): 62 10-15
HARMONY (7000 series): 58-61 10-20
HARMONY (32000 series): 73 5-8
IMPULSE: 65 10-20
LAURIE: 78 5-8
MCA: 75-82 5-8
MGM (200 series): 51 20-30
  (10-Inch LPs.)
MGM (3300 series): 56 15-25
MUSE: 79 5-8
NORGREN (1000 series): 55 30-50
PERFECT: 59 20-30
RCA VICTOR (1000 series): 54 20-30
RCA VICTOR (1400 through
  2300 series): 57-61 15-25

RCA VICTOR (3900 series): *68* **$8-15**
RCA VICTOR (5536; "The Complete
Lionel Hampton"): *76* **45-60**
(6-LP boxed set.)
SUTRA: *81* **5-8**
VERVE (2500 series): *82* **5-10**
VERVE (8100 & 8200
series): *56-58* **20-30**
(Reads "Verve Records, Inc." at bottom of label.)
WHO'S WHO IN JAZZ: *78-81* **5-8**
Also see COREA, Chick, & Lionel Hampton

**HAMPTON, Lionel, & Dinah
Washington**
LPs: 10/12-Inch 33rpm
DECCA (8000 series): *54* **20-30**
Also see HAMPTON, Lionel
Also see WASHINGTON, Dinah

HANCOCK, Herbie
Singles: 12-Inch 33/45rpm
COLUMBIA: *79-85* **4-6**
Singles: 7-Inch
BLUE NOTE: *62-65* **2-3**
COLUMBIA: *74-88* **1-3**
WARNER BROS: *69-72* **2-3**
LPs: 10/12-Inch 33rpm
BLUE NOTE: *62-65* **15-25**
(Label reads "Blue Note Records Inc. - New York,
U.S.A.")
BLUE NOTE: *66-71* **8-15**
(Label shows Blue Note Records as a division of
either Liberty or United Artists.)
COLUMBIA: *73-88* **5-10**
WARNER BROS: *70-74* **8-15**
Also see SANTANA
Also see SUMMERS, Bill

HANCOCK, Herbie, & Chick Corea
LPs: 10/12-Inch 33rpm
COLUMBIA: *79* **5-10**
POLYDOR: *79* **8-10**
Also see COREA, Chick
Also see RETURN TO FOREVER

HANCOCK, Herbie, & Willie Bobo
LPs: 10/12-Inch 33rpm
BLUE NOTE: *73* **5-10**
Also see HANCOCK, Herbie
Also see BOBO, Willie

HANDY, John
(John Handy Quartet; John Handy Quintet)
Singles: 7-Inch
IMPULSE: *76-77* **1-3**
COLUMBIA: *66-69* **2-4**
LPs: 10/12-Inch 33rpm
IMPULSE: *76-77* **5-10**

COLUMBIA: *66-68* **$10-15**
RCA VICTOR: *67* **10-15**
ROULETTE (52000 series): *60* **15-25**
ROULETTE (52100 series): *66-67* **10-15**
WARNER BROS: *78* **5-8**

HANDY, John, III
LPs: 10/12-Inch 33rpm
ROULETTE (100 series): *76* **5-8**
ROULETTE (52000 series): *60* **15-25**
ROULETTE (52100 series): *66-67* **10-15**

HANNIBAL, King:
see KING HANNIBAL

HANSON & DAVIS
Singles: 12-Inch 33/45rpm
FRESH: *85-86* **4-6**

HANSSON, Bo
Singles: 7-Inch
CHARISMA: *73* **2-3**
SIRE: *76-77* **2-3**
LPs: 10/12-Inch 33rpm
FAMOUS CHARISMA: *72-73* **8-10**
PVC: *79* **5-8**
SIRE: *76-77* **8-10**

HAPPENINGS
Singles: 7-Inch
ABC: *73* **1-3**
B.T. PUPPY: *66-69* **3-5**
BIG TREE: *72* **2-3**
JUBILEE: *69-71* **3-5**
MIDLAND INT'L: *77* **2-3**
MUSICORE: *72* **2-3**
VIRGO: *72* **1-3**
Picture Sleeves
B.T. PUPPY: *67* **5-10**
LPs: 10/12-Inch 33rpm
B.T. PUPPY: *66-68* **12-15**
JUBILEE: *69* **10-12**
Member: Bob Miranda; Tom Guliano; Ralph De-
Vito; Dave Libert; Bernie Laporte; Mike LaNeue.
Also see TOKENS / Happenings

HARBOR, Pearl:
see PEARL HARBOR

HARD TIMES
Singles: 7-Inch
WORLD PACIFIC: *66-68* **5-10**
LPs: 10/12-Inch 33rpm
WORLD PACIFIC: *66-68* **15-25**
Also see STEPPENWOLF

HARDCASTLE, Paul
Singles: 12-Inch 33/45rpm
CHRYSALIS: *85-86* **4-6**
PROFILE: *84* **4-6**

Paul Hardcastle

Singles: 7-Inch
CHRYSALIS: *85-86* $1-3
PROFILE: *84-85* 1-3
LPs: 10/12-Inch 33rpm
CHRYSALIS: *86* 5-8
PROFILE: *85* 5-8

HARDEN TRIO
Singles: 7-Inch
COLUMBIA: *65-68* 2-4
PAPA JOE: *72* 2-3
LPs: 10/12-Inch 33rpm
COLUMBIA: *66-68* 10-15
HARMONY: *70* 8-12
Members: Arlene Harden; Bobby Harden; Robbie Harden.

HARDIN, Tim
Singles: 7-Inch
COLUMBIA: *69-72* 2-4
VERVE/FOLKWAYS: *66-70* 2-4
VERVE/FORECAST: *67-71* 2-4
LPs: 10/12-Inch 33rpm
ATCO: *67* 8-15
COLUMBIA: *69-81* 6-12
MGM: *70-74* 6-10
POLYDOR: *81* 5-8
VERVE/FOLKWAYS: *66-69* 10-15

HARDLY-WORTHIT PLAYERS
(Featuring Senator Bobby & Senator McKinley)
Singles: 7-Inch
PARKWAY: *67* 4-8
LPs: 10/12-Inch 33rpm
PARKWAY: *66-67* 10-20
Also see SENATOR BOBBY

HARDY, Hagood
Singles: 7-Inch
CAPITOL: *75-78* $1-3
HERITAGE: *71* 2-3
LPs: 10/12-Inch 33rpm
CAPITOL: *75-76* 4-8

HARDY BOYS
Singles: 7-Inch
RCA VICTOR: *69-70* 2-4
LPs: 10/12-Inch 33rpm
RCA VICTOR: *69-70* 8-10

HAREWOOD, Dorian
Singles: 7-Inch
EMERIC: *88* 1-3
LPs: 10/12-Inch 33rpm
EMERIC: *88* 5-8

HARLEM RIVER DRIVE
(Harlem River Drive Featuring Eddie Palmieri)
Singles: 7-Inch
ARISTA: *75* 2-3
ROULETTE: *70-72* 2-5
LPs: 10/12-Inch 33rpm
ROULETTE: *71* 8-10
TICO: *72* 5-10
Members: Eddie Palmieri; Jimmy Norman.
Also see NORMAN, Jimmy

HARLEY, Steve
(Steve Harley & Cockney Rebel)
Singles: 7-Inch
CAPITOL: *78* 1-3
EMI: *75-77* 2-3
LPs: 10/12-Inch 33rpm
CAPITOL: *78* 5-8
EMI: *75-77* 5-8

HARMONICATS
(Jerry Murad's Harmonicats)
Singles: 7-Inch
COLUMBIA: *61-67* 2-3
MERCURY: *50-60* 2-5
EPs: 7-Inch 33/45rpm
MERCURY: *50-61* 4-8
LPs: 10/12-Inch 33rpm
COLUMBIA: *61-67* 5-10
HARMONY: *66* 5-10
MERCURY: *50-69* 8-15
WING: *59-64* 8-12
Members: Jerry Murad; Al Fiore; Don Les.

HARNELL, Joe
(Joe Harnell & His Orchestra; Joe Harnell & His Trio)
Singles: 7-Inch
COLUMBIA: *66-68* 2-3
EPIC: *59-60* 2-3

KAPP: *61-65*	$2-3
MCA: *78*	1-3
MEDALLION: *61-62*	2-3
MOTOWN: *69-70*	1-3

Picture Sleeves

KAPP: *63*	4-6

LPs: 10/12-Inch 33rpm

CAPITOL: *77*	4-8
COLUMBIA: *66*	5-10
EPIC: *59-63*	8-12
KAPP: *63-66*	8-12
MEDALLION: *61*	6-10
MOTOWN: *70*	5-10

HARNEY, Ben, & Sheryl Lee Ralph
Singles: 7-Inch

GEFFEN: *83*	1-3

HAROLD, Prince:
see PRINCE HAROLD

HARPER, Janice
Singles: 7-Inch

CAPITOL: *58-60*	2-5
PREP: *57*	3-5
RCA VICTOR: *66*	2-4

HARPERS BIZARRE
Singles: 7-Inch

FOREST BAY CO: *76*	2-3
WARNER BROS: *67-72*	2-4

EPs: 7-Inch 33/45rpm

WARNER BROS: *68*	4-8

(Jukebox issues only.)

LPs: 10/12-Inch 33rpm

FOREST BAY CO: *76*	8-10
WARNER BROS: *67-68*	10-20

Members: Ted Templeman; John Petersen; Dick
Yount; Dick Scoppettone.

HARPO, Slim
Singles: 78rpm

EXCELLO: *57*	4-8

Singles: 7-Inch

ABC: *73*	1-3
EXCELLO (2100 series, except 2113): *59-61*	4-6
EXCELLO (2113; "I'm A King Bee"): *57*	8-10
EXCELLO (2200 series): *62-68*	3-5
EXCELLO (2300 series): *69-71*	2-4

LPs: 10/12-Inch 33rpm

EXCELLO (Except 8003 & 8005): *68-70*	10-12
EXCELLO (8003; "Raining In My Heart"): *61*	25-30
EXCELLO (8005; "Baby, Scratch My Back"): *66*	15-20

HARPTONES
(Harp-Tones)
Singles: 78rpm

ANDREA: *56*	$5-10
BRUCE: *53-55*	10-20
GEE: *57*	5-10
PARADISE: *56*	20-30
RAMA: *56-57*	5-10
TIP TOP: *56*	4-8

Singles: 7-Inch

AMBIENT SOUND: *82*	4-6
ANDREA: *56*	12-15
BRUCE (Except 101): *54-55*	25-50
BRUCE (101; "A Sunday Kind Of Love"): *53*	175-250
("Bruce" in script lettering.)	
BRUCE (101; "A Sunday Kind Of Love"): *53*	20-50
("Bruce" in block lettering.)	
COED: *60*	3-5
COMPANION: *61-62*	10-15
CUB: *61*	3-5
GEE: *57*	10-20
KT: *63*	10-12
PARADISE: *56*	50-75
RAMA: *56-57*	10-20
RAVEN: *62*	10-12
ROULETTE: *71*	1-3
TIP TOP: *56*	5-8
WARWICK: *59-60*	5-8

EPs: 7-Inch 33/45rpm

BRUCE (201; "The Sensational Harptones"): *54*	1000-2000

LPs: 10/12-Inch 33rpm

AMBIENT SOUND: *82*	5-8
HARLEM HITPARADE:	8-10
RARE BIRD:	6-10
RELIC:	5-8

Members: Willie Winfield; Nicky Clark; Bill Brown; Bill Dempsey; Bill Galloway; Raoul Cita; Jimmy Beckum; Lynn Daniels; Vicki Burgess; Margaret Moore; Fred Taylor.

HARPTONES / Cleftones
Singles: 7-Inch
ROULETTE: $1-3
Also see CLEFTONES

HARPTONES / Crows
LPs: 10/12-Inch 33rpm
ROULETTE: 72 12-20
Also see CROWS

HARPTONES / Paragons
LPs: 10/12-Inch 33rpm
MUSICNOTE: 64 20-25
Also see HARPTONES
Also see PARAGONS

HARRELL, Grady
Singles: 7-Inch
MCA: 85 1-3

HARRIS, Betty
Singles: 7-Inch
JUBILEE: 63-69 8-10
PROM: 2-4
SSS INT'L: 69 2-3
SANSU: 66-68 2-4

HARRIS, Bobby
Singles: 7-Inch
ATLANTIC: 65 3-5
Also see LUNDY, Pat, & Bobby Harris

HARRIS, Brenda Jo
Singles: 7-Inch
ROULETTE: 68 2-4

HARRIS, Damon
Singles: 12-Inch 33/45rpm
WMOT: 78-79 4-6
Singles: 7-Inch
WMOT: 78-79 1-3
LPs: 10/12-Inch 33rpm
WMOT: 78 5-8

HARRIS, David
Singles: 7-Inch
PLEASURE: 74 2-3

HARRIS, Eddie
Singles: 7-Inch
ABC: 73 1-3
ATLANTIC: 65-77 1-3
COLUMBIA: 64 2-3
VEE JAY: 61-63 2-4
WARNER BROS: 81 1-3

LPs: 10/12-Inch 33rpm
ANGELACO: 81 .... $5-8
ATLANTIC: 65-81 6-12
BUDDAH: 69 8-12
COLUMBIA: 64-68 10-20
CRUSADERS: 82 5-8
GNP/CRESCENDO: 73 5-8
HARMONY: 72 5-10
RCA VICTOR: 78 5-8
SUNSET: 69 5-10
TRIP: 73 5-8
VEE JAY (3016 through 3028): 61-62 ...20-35
VEE JAY (3031 through 3034): 63 15-25
Also see MC CANN, Les, & Eddie Harris

HARRIS, Eddie, & John Klemmer
LPs: 10/12-Inch 33rpm
CRUSADERS: 82 5-8
Also see KLEMMER, John

HARRIS, Emmylou
(Emmylou Harris & The Hot Band)
Singles: 7-Inch
HUGHES: 87 1-3
JUBILEE: 69-70 5-8
REPRISE (Except 1341): 75-77 2-3
REPRISE (1341; "Light Of The
    Stable"): 75 4-6
REPRISE: 88 1-3
WARNER BROS: 77-87 1-3
Picture Sleeves
REPRISE: 75-77 2-4
WARNER BROS: 80-86 1-3
LPs: 10/12-Inch 33rpm
EMUS: 79 10-15
JUBILEE: 69 25-30
MFSL: 78 30-50
REPRISE: 75 8-10
WARNER BROS: 77-87 5-8
Members: James Burton; Glen D. Hardin; Emory Gordy; Ronnie Tutt.
Also see DENVER, John
Also see EVERLY, Don
Also see LITTLE FEAT
Also see ORBISON, Roy, & Emmylou
Harris / Craig Hundley
Also see OWENS, Buck, & Emmylou Harris
Also see PARSONS, Gram
Also see PARTON, Dolly
Also see PRESLEY, Elvis
Also see RONSTADT, Linda, & Emmylou
Harris
Also see TUCKER, Tanya
Also see WINCHESTER, Jesse
Also see YOUNG, Neil

HARRIS, Gene
(Gene Harris & The Three Sounds)
Singles: 7-Inch
BLUE NOTE: *71-77* $1-3
LPs: 10/12-Inch 33rpm
BLUE NOTE: *71-77* 5-10

HARRIS, Huey "Baby"
Singles: 7-Inch
PROFILE: *85* 1-3

HARRIS, Major
Singles: 7-Inch
ATLANTIC: *75-76* 2-3
OKEH: *69* 2-4
POP ART: *83* 1-3
WMOT: *76-81* 1-3
LPs: 10/12-Inch 33rpm
ATLANTIC: *75* 8-10
RCA VICTOR: *78* 5-8
WMOT: *76* 8-10
Also see DELFONICS

HARRIS, Peppermint:
see PEPPERMINT HARRIS

HARRIS, Phil
Singles: 78rpm
ARA: *46* 4-8
RCA VICTOR: *50-54* 3-6
Singles: 7-Inch
COLISEUM: *68* 2-3
MEGA: *73* 1-3
MONTCLARE: *76* 1-3
RCA VICTOR: *50-54* 5-10
REPRISE: *62* 2-3
VISTA: *67-70* 2-3
EPs: 7-Inch 33/45rpm
RCA VICTOR: *53-60* 5-10
LPs: 10/12-Inch 33rpm
CAMDEN: *63* 8-12
MEGA: *72-74* 5-10
RCA VICTOR (1900 series): *59* 10-20
RCA VICTOR (3000 series): *53-54* 20-30
ZODIAC: *77* 5-8

HARRIS, Richard
Singles: 7-Inch
ATLANTIC: *74-75* 2-3
DUNHILL: *68-75* 2-4
Picture Sleeves
DUNHILL (Except 4134): *72* 4-6
DUNHILL (4134; "Mac Arthur Park"): *68* . 3-6
DUNHILL (4134; "Mac Arthur Park"): *68* . 5-10
(Specially printed promotional sleeve.)
EPs: 7-Inch 33/45rpm
DUNHILL: *68* 4-6
(Jukebox issues only.)

LPs: 10/12-Inch 33rpm
ATLANTIC: *74-75* $6-10
DUNHILL: *70-73* 8-12

HARRIS, Rolf
Singles: 7-Inch
EPIC (Except 9721): *63-66* 3-5
EPIC (9721; "Ringo For President"); *64* .. 5-10
MGM: *70* 2-4
20TH CENTURY-FOX: *60-61* 5-8
Picture Sleeves
EPIC: *63-64* 4-8
LPs: 10/12-Inch 33rpm
EPIC: *63-64* 15-20

HARRIS, Sam
Singles: 12-Inch 33/45rpm
MOTOWN: *84-86* 4-6
Singles: 7-Inch
MOTOWN: *84-86* 1-3
LPs: 10/12-Inch 33rpm
MOTOWN: *84-86* 5-8

HARRIS, Thurston
(Thurston Harris & The Sharps)
Singles: 78rpm
ALADDIN: *57* 3-6
Singles: 7-Inch
ALADDIN: *57-61* 4-8
CUB: *62* 3-5
DOT: *62-63* 3-5
IMPERIAL: *63* 3-5
REPRISE: *64* 3-5

HARRIS, Tony
Singles: 78rpm
EBB: *56-57* 5-10
Singles: 7-Inch
EBB: *56-57* 10-15

HARRIS, Wynonie
(Wynonie Harris & Lucky Millinder)
Singles: 78rpm
ALADDIN: *47* 5-10
APOLLO: *45-46* 5-10
BULLET: *46* 8-12
HAMP-TONE: *45* 5-10
KING: *47-57* 5-12
PHILO: *45* 8-12
Singles: 7-Inch
KING (4210 through 4724,
 except 4485): *51-54* 40-60
KING (4485; "Lovin' Machine"): *51* 40-60
 (Black vinyl.)
KING (4485; "Lovin' Machine"): *51* .. 125-200
 (Colored vinyl.)
KING (4763 through 4839): *54-55* 20-40
KING (4900 & 5000 series): *56-57* 10-20

KING (5100 through 5400 series): *58-60* . **$5-10**
ROULETTE: *60* **3-5**
      EPs: 7-Inch 33/45rpm
KING: **50-75**
      LPs: 10/12-Inch 33rpm
KING (1000 series): *72* **12-15**
  Also see MILLINDER, Lucky, & His
Orchestra
  Also see MILBURN, Amos / Wynonie
Harris / Crown Prince Waterford

HARRIS, Wynonie / Roy Brown
      LPs: 10/12-Inch 33rpm
KING (607; "Battle Of The
  Blues"): *58* **100-200**
KING (627; "Battle Of The
  Blues, Vol. 2"): *58* **100-200**

HARRIS, Wynonie / Roy Brown / Eddie Vinson
      LPs: 10/12-Inch 33rpm
KING (668; "Battle Of
  The Blues, Vol. 4"): *60* **200-300**
  Also see BROWN, Roy
  Also see HARRIS, Wynonie

HARRISON, Don, Band
      Singles: 7-Inch
ATLANTIC: *76* **2-3**
MERCURY: *77* **2-3**
      LPs: 10/12-Inch 33rpm
ATLANTIC: *76* **8-10**
MERCURY: *77* **8-10**
  Members: Don Harrison; Doug Clifford; Stu Cook.
  Also see CREEDENCE CLEARWATER
REVIVAL

HARRISON, George
      Singles: 12-Inch 33/45rpm
DARK HORSE (949; "All Those
  Years Ago"): *81* **25-30**
  (Promotional issue only.)
DARK HORSE (1075; "Wake Up My
  Love"): *82* **20-25**
  (Promotional issue only.)
DARK HORSE (2845; "Got My Mind
  Set On You"): *87* **15-20**
  (Promotional issue only.)
DARK HORSE (2885; "When We
  Was Fab"): *88* **10-15**
  (Promotional issue only.)
DARK HORSE (2889; "Devil's
  Radio"): *87* **15-20**
      Singles: 7-Inch
APPLE (1828; "What Is Life"): *71* **4-6**
APPLE (1836; "Bangladesh"): *71* **4-6**
APPLE (1862; "Give Me Love"): *73* **3-5**

APPLE (1877; "Dark Horse"): *74* **$3-5**
APPLE (1879; "Ding Dong;
  Ding Dong"): *74* **8-10**
  (Blue & white label.)
APPLE (1879; "Ding Dong;
  Ding Dong"): *74* **3-5**
  (Black & white label.)
APPLE (1884; "You"): *75* **4-6**
APPLE (1885; "This Guitar"): *75* **4-6**
APPLE (2995; "My Sweet Lord"): *70* **3-5**
CAPITOL (Orange label): *76* **4-6**
CAPITOL (Purple label): *78* **1-3**
CAPITOL (Black label): *83-86* **1-3**
CAPITOL STARLINE: *77-87* **1-3**
DARK HORSE (0410; "All Those
  Years Ago"): *81* **1-3**
DARK HORSE (8294; "This Song"): *76* ...**4-6**
DARK HORSE (8313; "Crackerbox
  Palace"): *77* **2-3**
DARK HORSE (8763; "Blow Away"): *79* ..**2-3**
DARK HORSE (8844; "Love Comes To
  Everyone"): *79* **2-3**
DARK HORSE (25643; "Cloud
  Nine"): *87* **2-3**
DARK HORSE (27913; "This Is Love"): *88* **2-3**
DARK HORSE (28131; "When We
  Was Fab"): *88* **2-3**
DARK HORSE (28178; "Got My Mind
  Set On You"): *87* **2-3**
DARK HORSE (29744; "I Really
  Love You"): *83* **4-6**
DARK HORSE (29864; "Wake Up
  My Love"): *82* **3-5**
DARK HORSE (49725; "All Those
  Years Ago"): *81* **2-3**
DARK HORSE (49785; "Teardrops"): *81* ..**3-5**
      Picture Sleeves
APPLE (1828; "What Is Life"): *71* **20-25**
APPLE (1836; "Bangladesh"): *71* **10-15**
APPLE (1877; "Dark Horse"): *74* **35-40**
APPLE (1879; "Ding Dong;
  Ding Dong"): *74* **10-15**
APPLE (1884; "You"): *75* **10-12**
APPLE (2995; "My Sweet Lord"): *70* **15-20**
DARK HORSE (8294; "This Song"): *76* .**15-20**
DARK HORSE (8294; "This Song"): *76* .**40-50**
  (Special promotional sleeve issued with promo
single. Price includes insert flyer with "The Story
Behind *This Song*, which represents about $15-$20
of the value.)
DARK HORSE (8763; "Blow Away"): *79* ..**4-6**
DARK HORSE (8844; "Love Comes
  To Everyone"): *79* **200-250**
DARK HORSE (28131; "When We Was
  Fab"): *88* **2-3**

DARK HORSE (28178; "Got My Mind
Set On You"): *87* $2-3
DARK HORSE (49725; "All Those
Years Ago"): *81* 2-3
Promotional Singles
APPLE (1879; "Ding Dong;
Ding Dong"): *74* 25-30
APPLE (1877; "Dark Horse"): *74* 20-25
APPLE (1879; "Ding Dong;
Ding Dong"): *74* 20-25
APPLE (1884; "You"): *75* 25-30
APPLE (1885; "This Guitar"): *75* 25-30
APPLE/20TH CENTURY-FOX (791;
"Concert For Bangla Desh"): *71* 300-350
(Contains radio spots. Issued only to radio stations.)
DARK HORSE (8294; "This Song"): *76* .10-15
DARK HORSE (8313; "Crackerbox
Palace"): *77* 10-12
DARK HORSE (8763; "Blow
Away"): *79* 10-12
DARK HORSE (8844; "Love Comes
To Everyone"): *79* 10-12
DARK HORSE (28131; "When We
Was Fab"): *88* 10-12
DARK HORSE (28178; "Got My Mind
Set On You"): *87* 10-15
DARK HORSE (29744; "I Really Love
You"): *83* 10-12
DARK HORSE (29864; "Wake Up
My Love"): *82* 10-12
DARK HORSE (49725; "All Those
Years Ago"): *81* 8-10
DARK HORSE (49725; "All Those
Years Ago"): *81* 10-12
LPs: 10/12-Inch 33rpm
APPLE (639; "All Things Must
Pass"): *70* 15-25
(Includes bonus poster.)
APPLE (3350; "Wonderwall Music"): *68* .15-20
APPLE (3385; "Concert For
Bangla Desh"): *71* 15-20
(Includes 64-page booklet. Also contains music by
Eric Clapton, Bob Dylan, Leon Russell, Ringo
Starr; Ravi Shankar, and others.)
APPLE (3410; "Living In The Material
World"): *73* 10-12
APPLE (3420; "Extra Texture"): *75* 10-12
CAPITOL (639; "All Things Must
Pass"): *76-78* 10-15
(Orange or purple labels.)
CAPITOL (639; "All Things Must
Pass"): *83* 10-12
(Black label.)
CAPITOL (3385; "Concert For Bangla
Desh"): *81* 10-12

CAPITOL (11578; "The Best Of George
Harrison"): *76* $6-10
(Custom label with six photos of Harrison. Also
contains tracks by the Beatles, featuring George.)
CAPITOL (11578; "The Best Of George
Harrison"): *78-83* 6-10
(Purple or black labels.)
CAPITOL (16000 series): *81* 5-8
DARK HORSE (3005; "Thirty-Three
& 1/3"): *76* 8-10
DARK HORSE (3255; "George
Harrison"): *79* 8-10
DARK HORSE (3418; "Dark
Horse"): *74* 10-12
DARK HORSE (3492; "Somewhere In
England"): *81* 5-10
DARK HORSE (23734; "Gone
Troppo"): *82* 8-12
DARK HORSE (25643; "Cloud
Nine"): *87* 5-8
ZAPPLE (3358; "Electronic
Music"): *69* 15-20
Promotional LPs
DARK HORSE ("Dark Horse Radio
Special"): *74* 100-125
DARK HORSE (649; "A Personal Music
Dialogue With George Harrison
At 33 1/3"): *76* 30-40
DARK HORSE (23734; "Gone
Troppo"): *82* 18-20
(An audiophile Quiex II vinyl pressing.)
Also see BEATLES
Also see BROMBERG, David
Also see CLAPTON, Eric
Also see DYLAN, Bob
Also see RUSSELL, Leon
Also see SCOTT, Tom
Also see SHANKAR, Ravi

HARRISON, George / Dave Edmunds
Singles: 12-Inch 33/45rpm
COLUMBIA (2085; "I Don't Want To
Do It"): *85* 10-15
(Promotional issue only.)
Singles: 7-Inch
COLUMBIA (04887; "I Don't Want To
Do It"): *85* 1-3
Promotional Singles
COLUMBIA (04887; "I Don't Want To
Do It"): *85* 6-10
Also see EDMUNDS, Dave

HARRISON, George / Dave Edmunds / Jeff Beck
Singles: 12-Inch 33/45rpm
COLUMBIA (2034; "I Don't Want To
Do It"): *85* $12-18
(Promotional issue only.)
Also see BECK, Jeff
Also see EDMUNDS, Dave
Also see HARRISON, George

HARRISON, Jerry, & The Casual Gods
LPs: 10/12-Inch 33rpm
SIRE: *88* 5-8

HARRISON, Noel
Singles: 7-Inch
LONDON: *65-67* 3-5
REPRISE: *67-70* 2-4
LPs: 10/12-Inch 33rpm
LONDON: *66-67* 15-20
REPRISE: *67-69* 10-15
RIVERSIDE: 10-12
Also see LEGRAND, Michel, & Noel Harrison

HARRISON, Reggie:
see HIPPIES / Reggie Harrison

HARRISON, Wes
LPs: 10/12-Inch 33rpm
PHILIPS: *63* 10-15

HARRISON, Wilbert
(Wilbert Harrison & The Roamers; Wilburt
Harrison)
Singles: 78rpm
DELUXE: *52-53* 10-20
Singles: 7-Inch
ABC: *73* 1-3
BRUNSWICK: *74* 2-3
CONSTELLATION: *64* 3-5
DELUXE: *52-53* 25-50
DOC: *62* 3-5
FURY: *59-62* 4-6
GLADES: *59* 5-8
HOUSE OF SOUND: 3-5
NEPTUNE: *61* 3-5
PORT: *65* 3-5
ROCKIN': *52* 50-75
ROULETTE: *67* 3-5
SSS INT'L: *71* 2-3
SAVOY (1100 series): *54* 8-10
SAVOY (1500 series): *59* 4-6
SEA HORN: *63* 3-5
SUE: *69* 2-4
LPs: 10/12-Inch 33rpm
BUDDAH: *71* 8-10
CHELSEA: *77* 8-10
JUGGERNAUT: *71* 8-10

SPHERE SOUND: *65* $25-30
SUE: *70* 12-15
WET SOUL: *70* 10-12

HARRY, Debbie
Singles: 12-Inch 33/45rpm
CHRYSALIS: *81-83* 4-6
GEFFEN: *85-86* 4-6
Singles: 7-Inch
CHRYSALIS: *81-83* 1-3
GEFFEN: *85-87* 1-3
Picture Sleeves
CHRYSALIS: *81* 1-3
LPs: 10/12-Inch 33rpm
CHRYSALIS: *81* 5-8
GEFFEN: *86* 5-8
Also see BLONDIE
Also see WIND IN THE WILLOWS

HART, Bonnie
Singles: 7-Inch
BADGER: *88* 3-5

HART, Corey
Singles: 7-Inch
EMI AMERICA: *84-88* 1-3
Picture Sleeves
EMI AMERICA: *84-88* 1-3
LPs: 10/12-Inch 33rpm
EMI AMERICA: *84-88* 5-8

HART, Freddie
(Freddie Hart & The Heartbeats)
Singles: 78rpm
CAPITOL: *53-55* 3-6
COLUMBIA (Except 21512): *56-63* 2-5
COLUMBIA (21512; "Dig Boy, Dig"): *56* . 5-10
Singles: 7-Inch
CAPITOL (2500 through 3000
series): *53-55* 4-8
(Purple labels.)
CAPITOL (2600 through 4600
series): *70-79* 1-3
(Orange labels.)
COLUMBIA (Except 21512): *56-63* 3-6
COLUMBIA (21512; "Dig Boy,
Dig"): *56* 15-25
EL DORADO: *85* 1-3
FIFTH ST: *87* 1-3
KAPP: *65-72* 2-4
MCA: *73* 1-3
MONUMENT: *63-64* 2-3
SUNBIRD: *80-81* 1-3
Picture Sleeves
KAPP: *68* 2-5
SUNBIRD: *80* 1-3

LPs: 10/12-Inch 33rpm
BRYLEN: *84* $5-8
CAPITOL: *70-79* 5-10
COLUMBIA (1700 series): *62* 20-25
COLUMBIA (13000 series): *72* 10-12
CORAL: *73* 4-8
HARMONY: *67-73* 8-12
KAPP: *65-69* 8-15
MCA: *75* 8-12
PICKWICK/HILLTOP: 8-12
SUNBIRD: *80* 5-8
VOCALION: *72* 8-10

HART, Freddie / Sammi Smith / Jerry Reed
LPs: 10/12-Inch 33rpm
HARMONY: *72* 6-10
Also see HART, Freddie
Also see REED, Jerry
Also see SMITH, Sammi

HART, Mickey
Singles: 7-Inch
WARNER BROS: *71-72* 3-5
LPs: 10/12-Inch 33rpm
RELIX: *85* 5-8
WARNER BROS: *72* 10-20
Also see GRATEFUL DEAD

HART, Mickey, Airto & Flora Purim
LPs: 10/12-Inch 33rpm
REFERENCE: *83* 6-10
Also see HART, Mickey
Also see PURIM, Flora

HART, Rita
Singles: 12-Inch 33/45rpm
ENVELOPE.: *84* 4-6

HART, Rod
Singles: 7-Inch
IBC: *80* 1-3
PHOENIX SUN: *68* 2-3
PLANTATION: *76-77* 2-3
LPs: 10/12-Inch 33rpm
PLANTATION: *76* 5-8

HARTFORD, John
Singles: 7-Inch
AMPEX: *71* 2-3
RCA VICTOR: *66-70* 2-4
LPs: 10/12-Inch 33rpm
FLYING FISH: *76-84* 5-8
RCA VICTOR: *67-70* 8-12
WARNER BROS: *71-72* 8-10
Also see DILLARDS & John Hartford

Debbie Harry (Photo: Brian Aris)

HARTLEY, Keef, Band
Singles: 7-Inch
DERAM: *70-73* $2-4
LPs: 10/12-Inch 33rpm
DERAM: *69-73* 10-12
Also see MAYALL, John

HARTMAN, Dan
Singles: 12-Inch 33/45rpm
BLUE SKY: *78-81* 4-6
MCA: *84-85* 4-6
Singles: 7-Inch
BLUE SKY: *76-81* 1-3
MCA: *84-85* 1-3
PORTRAIT: *81* 1-3
LPs: 10/12-Inch 33rpm
BLUE SKY (Except 246): *76-81* 5-8
BLUE SKY (246; "Who Is Dan
Hartman"): *75* 8-15
(Promotional issue only.)
MCA: *84-85* 5-8
Also see WINTER, Edgar

HARVEST, Barclay James:
see BARCLAY JAMES HARVEST

HARVEST, King:
see KING HARVEST

HARVEY
(Harvey Fuqua)
Singles: 7-Inch
CHESS: *59* 4-8
TRI-PHI: *62-63* 5-10
Also see HARVEY & THE MOONGLOWS
Also see NEW BIRTH

HARVEY, Alex
(Sensational Alex Harvey Band)
Singles: 7-Inch
ATLANTIC: 75 . . . . $2-3
CAPITOL: 72 2-4
VERTIGO: 73-75 2-3
LPs: 10/12-Inch 33rpm
CAPITOL: 72 8-12
ATLANTIC: 75 8-10
VERTIGO: 73-75 8-10

HARVEY, Steve
Singles: 12-Inch 33/45rpm
LONDON: 84 4-6
Singles: 7-Inch
LONDON: 84 1-3

HARVEY & THE MOONGLOWS
(Featuring Harvey Fuqua)
Singles: 7-Inch
CHESS: 58-59 4-8
Also see ETTA & HARVEY
Also see HARVEY
Also see MOONGLOWS

HARVEY BOYS
Singles: 78rpm
CADENCE: 57 2-5
Singles: 7-Inch
CADENCE: 57 3-5

HASHIM
Singles: 12-Inch 33/45rpm
CUTTING EDGE: 84 4-6

HASLAM, Annie
Singles: 7-Inch
SIRE: 78 2-4
LPs: 10/12-Inch 33rpm
SIRE: 77 8-12
Also see RENAISSANCE

HASSAN & 7-11
Singles: 7-Inch
EASY STREET: 84 1-3

HATCHER, Roger
Singles: 7-Inch
BROWN DOG: 76 2-3

HATFIELD, Bobby
Singles: 7-Inch
MOONGLOW: 63 3-5
VERVE: 68-69 2-4
WARNER BROS: 72 2-3
LPs: 10/12-Inch 33rpm
MGM: 71 10-12
Also see RIGHTEOUS BROTHERS

HATHAWAY, Donny
Singles: 7-Inch
ATCO: 69-78 . . . . $2-4
LPs: 10/12-Inch 33rpm
ATCO: 70-78 8-10
ATLANTIC: 80 5-8
Also see FLACK, Roberta, & Donny
Hathaway

HATHAWAY, Donny, & June Conquest
Singles: 7-Inch
CURTOM: 72 2-3

HATHAWAY, Donny, & Margie Joseph
Singles: 7-Inch
ATCO: 72 2-3
Also see HATHAWAY, Donny
Also see JOSEPH, Margie

HAVENS, Richie
Singles: 7-Inch
A&M: 77 2-3
DOUGLAS: 68 3-5
ELEKTRA: 80 1-3
MGM: 70 2-4
ODE '70: 72 2-3
STORMY FOREST: 70-74 2-3
VERVE/FOLKWAYS: 66-67 3-5
VERVE/FORECAST: 68 3-5
LPs: 10/12-Inch 33rpm
A&M: 77 8-10
DOUGLAS: 68 12-15
ELEKTRA: 80 5-8
MGM: 70 8-10
ODE '70: 73 8-10
RBI: 87 5-8
STORMY FOREST: 69-74 10-12
VERVE/FOLKWAYS: 67 12-15
VERVE/FORECAST: 67-68 12-15

HAWK
(Jerry Lee Lewis)
Singles: 7-Inch
PHILLIPS INT'L: 60 12-20
Also see LEWIS, Jerry Lee

HAWKINS, Dale
(Dale Hawkins With The Escapades)
Singles: 78rpm
CHECKER: 56-57 10-20
Singles: 7-Inch
ABC-PARAMOUNT: 65 3-5
ATLANTIC: 61-62 4-8
BELL: 69 3-5
CHECKER (800 series): 56-57 15-25
(Maroon label with "checkerboard" design at top.)
CHECKER (800 series): 57-58 5-8
(Maroon label with Checker name on side.)

CHECKER (900 series): *58-61* $4-8
CHESS: *76* 5-10
LINCOLN: 3-5
TILT: *61* 3-5
ZONK: *62* 5-8
Picture Sleeves
CHECKER: *60* 20-40
LPs: 10/12-Inch 33rpm
BELL: *69* 10-12
CHESS (1429; "Suzy-Q"): *58* 100-125
ROULETTE: *62* 30-35
Also see BUCHANAN, Roy

HAWKINS, Edwin, Singers
Singles: 7-Inch
BUDDAH: *71-72* 2-3
PAVILION: *69* 2-3
LPs: 10/12-Inch 33rpm
BUDDAH: *71-72* 8-12
PAVILION: *69* 10-12
Also see MELANIE
Also see MORRISON, Dorothy

HAWKINS, Erskine
Singles: 78rpm
BLUEBIRD: *39-44* 5-10
BRUNSWICK: *53* 4-8
DECCA: *56* 4-6
CORAL: *50-54* 4-8
KING: *51-52* 5-10
VICTOR/RCA VICTOR: *45-52* 5-10
VOCALION: *36-37* 5-10
Singles: 7-Inch
BRUNSWICK: *53* 5-10
DECCA: *56* 5-10
CORAL: *52-54* 5-10
KING (Black vinyl): *51-52* 10-20
KING (Colored vinyl): *51-52* 20-40
RCA VICTOR: *50-52* 10-15
EPs: 7-Inch 33/45rpm
RCA VICTOR: *59* 10-20
LPs: 10/12-Inch 33rpm
CORAL: *54* 20-30
DECCA: *61* 15-20
IMPERIAL: *62* 15-25
RCA VICTOR: *60* 20-30

HAWKINS, Erskine, & The Four Hawks
Singles: 78rpm
KING: *53* 10-20
Singles: 7-Inch
KING: *53* 25-50
Also see HAWKINS, Erskine

HAWKINS, Hawkshaw
Singles: 78rpm
KING: *46-53* 3-6

RCA VICTOR: *55-57* $2-5
Singles: 7-Inch
COLUMBIA: *59-62* 3-5
KING (900 through 1100
series): *50-53* 4-6
KING (5000 series): *60-64* 2-4
RCA VICTOR: *55-59* 3-5
STARDAY: *71* 1-3
EPs: 7-Inch 33/45rpm
KING: *53* 8-12
LPs: 10/12-Inch 33rpm
CAMDEN: *64-66* 10-15
GLADWYNNE: 40-60
HARMONY: *63* 10-15
KING (500 series): *58-59* 20-30
KING (800 series): *63-64* 15-25
KING (1000 series): *69* 8-12
LA BREA: 40-50
NASHVILLE: *69* 8-12
STARDAY: 5-8
Also see CLINE, Patsy / Cowboy Copas /
Hawkshaw Hawkins
Also see COPAS, Cowboy / Hawkshaw Haw-
kins

HAWKINS, Jennell
Singles: 7-Inch
AMAZON: *61-63* 3-5
DYNAMIC: *61* 3-5
DYNAMITE: *61* 3-5
LPs: 10/12-Inch 33rpm
AMAZON: *61-62* 25-35

HAWKINS, Ronnie
(Ronnie Hawkins & The Hawks)
Singles: 7-Inch
COTILLION: *70-71* 2-4
HAWK: 5-8
MONUMENT: *72-73* 2-4
ROULETTE (Monaural): *59-63* 5-8
ROULETTE (Stereo): *59* 20-25
(With an "SSR" prefix.)
LPs: 10/12-Inch 33rpm
ACCORD: *83* 5-8
COTILLION: *70-71* 10-15
MONUMENT: *72-75* 8-12
ROULETTE (25078; "Ronnie
Hawkins"): *59* 50-75
(Black vinyl.)
ROULETTE (25078; "Ronnie
Hawkins"): *59* 175-200
(Colored vinyl.)
ROULETTE (25102; "Mr.
Dynamo"): *60* 50-75
(Black vinyl.)

ROULETTE (25102; "Mr.
Dynamo"): 60 .... $175-200
(Colored vinyl.)
ROULETTE (25120; "Folk
Ballads"): 60 50-75
ROULETTE (25137; "Songs Of Hank
Williams"): 60 50-75
ROULETTE (42045; "Best Of Ronnie
Hawkins"): 70 25-35
UNITED ARTISTS: 79 5-8
Also see BAND
Also see LENNON, John
Also see LEVON & THE HAWKS

HAWKINS, Roy
Singles: 78rpm
DOWN TOWN: 48 10-20
MODERN: 48-54 8-15
RPM: 54 5-10
Singles: 7-Inch
KENT: 62 3-5
MODERN (Except 826): 51-54 15-25
MODERN (826; "The Thrill Is
Gone"): 51 25-40
RPM: 54 10-20
RHYTHM: 58 20-35

HAWKINS, Sam
(Sam Hawkins & The Crystals)
Singles: 7-Inch
ARNOLD: 63 3-5
BLUE CAT: 65 3-5
DECCA: 59-61 4-6
GONE: 59 4-6
SHELL: 3-5

HAWKS
Singles: 7-Inch
COLUMBIA: 81 1-3
LPs: 10/12-Inch 33rpm
COLUMBIA: 81 5-8

HAWKWIND
Singles: 7-Inch
ATCO: 75 2-3
UNITED ARTISTS: 71-73 2-3
LPs: 10/12-Inch 33rpm
ATCO: 75 8-10
SIRE: 78 5-8
UNITED ARTISTS: 71-74 10-15
Also see MOTORHEAD

HAWLEY, Deane
(Deane Hawley & The Crystals)
Singles: 7-Inch
DORE: 59-61 3-5
LIBERTY: 61-62 3-5
SUNDOWN: 3-5

VALOR: $5-8
WARNER BROS: 64 3-5

HAYES, Bill
(Bill Hayes With Archie Bleyer's Orchestra)
Singles: 78rpm
ABC-PARAMOUNT: 57 3-5
ABC-PARAMOUNT (9895; "Bop
Boy"): 58 8-15
CADENCE: 55-56 3-6
MGM: 55 2-5
Singles: 7-Inch
ABC-PARAMOUNT (Except 9895): 57 ...3-5
ABC-PARAMOUNT (9895; "Bop
Boy"): 58 20-30
ABLE: 3-6
BARNABY: 76 1-3
CADENCE: 55-56 4-6
DAYBREAK: 74 1-3
KAPP: 59 2-4
MGM: 55 4-6
SHAW: 65 2-3
Picture Sleeves
CADENCE: 55 10-15
EPs: 7-Inch 33/45rpm
MGM: 55 10-20
LPs: 10/12-Inch 33rpm
ABC-PARAMOUNT: 57 20-25
DAYBREAK: 74 5-10
KAPP: 60 8-15
Also see BLEYER, Archie

HAYES, Isaac
Singles: 12-Inch 33/45rpm
COLUMBIA: 85-86 4-6
Singles: 7-Inch
ABC: 77 1-3
BRUNSWICK: 64 3-5
COLUMBIA: 85-88 1-3
ENTERPRISE: 69-74 2-3
HBS/ABC: 75-76 2-3
POLYDOR: 78-80 1-3
SAN AMERICAN: 70 2-4
STAX: 78 1-3
LPs: 10/12-Inch 33rpm
ABC-PARAMOUNT: 75-77 8-10
ATLANTIC: 72 8-10
COLUMBIA: 86-88 5-8
ENTERPRISE: 68-75 10-12
POLYDOR: 77-81 5-8
STAX: 77-82 5-8

HAYES, Isaac, & Millie Jackson
Singles: 7-Inch
POLYDOR: 79-80 1-3

LPs: 10/12-Inch 33rpm
POLYDOR: 79 .... $5-8
Also see JACKSON, Millie

HAYES, Isaac, & David Porter
Singles: 7-Inch
ENTERPRISE: 72 2-3
Also see PORTER, David

HAYES, Isaac, & Dionne Warwick
Singles: 7-Inch
ABC: 77 1-3
Also see HAYES, Isaac
Also see WARWICK, Dionne

HAYES, Linda
(Linda Hayes With Tony Williams; Linda Hayes
& The Platters; Linda Hayes With The Flairs)
Singles: 78rpm
ANTLER: 56 5-10
DECCA: 55 5-10
HOLLYWOOD: 53-55 5-15
KING: 55 6-12
RECORDED IN HOLLYWOOD: 53 5-10
Singles: 7-Inch
ANTLER: 56 10-20
DECCA: 55 10-20
HOLLYWOOD (Except 1032): 53-55 ... 15-30
HOLLYWOOD (1032; "Our Love Is
Blessed"). 55 25-45
KING: 55 15-25
RECORDED IN HOLLYWOOD: 53 5-10
Also see PLATTERS

HAYES, Peter Lind, & Mary Healy
Singles: 7-Inch
COLUMBIA: 55 2-4
ESSEX: 53 2-4
KAPP: 56 2-4

HAYES, Richard
Singles: 7-Inch
ABC-PARAMOUNT: 56 5-15
COLUMBIA: 60-61 3-5
CONTEMPO: 64 2-4
DECCA: 61 3-5
MERCURY: 50-55 4-8
EPs: 7-Inch 33/45rpm
MERCURY: 54 8-15
LPs: 10/12-Inch 33rpm
MERCURY: 55 10-20

HAYES, Richard, & Kitty Kallen
Singles: 7-Inch
MERCURY: 50-51 2-4
Also see HAYES, Richard
Also see KALLEN, Kitty

HAYMAN, Richard, Orchestra
(Richard Hayman & Jan August)
Singles: 7-Inch
COMMAND: 69 .... $1-3
MGM: 65 1-3
MERCURY: 50-62 2-4
MUSICOR: 73 1-3
EPs: 7-Inch 33/45rpm
MERCURY: 51-59 3-6
LPs: 10/12-Inch 33rpm
ASCOT: 64 5-10
COMMAND: 69 5-10
MAINSTREAM: 67 5-10
MERCURY: 51-64 8-15
TIME: 63-64 5-10
WING: 62-64 5-10
Also see AUGUST, Jan

HAYMES, Dick
Singles: 78rpm
CAPITOL: 56 2-4
DECCA: 43-54 3-6
Singles: 7-Inch
CAPITOL: 56 3-5
GNP/CRESCENDO: 75 1-3
DECCA: 50-54 3-5
WARWICK: 60 2-4
EPs: 7-Inch 33/45rpm
CAPITOL: 56 5-10
DECCA: 50-54 5-10
LPs: 10/12-Inch 33rpm
AUDIOPHILE: 78 5-8
CAPITOL: 56 10-20
CORAL: 73 4-6
DAYBREAK: 74 5-10
DECCA: 50-54 10-20
GLENDALE: 84 5-8
MCA: 76-83 5-8
WARWICK: 60 8-15
Also see CLOONEY, Rosemary, & Dick
Haymes
Also see JAMES, Harry, & Dick Haymes
Also see MERMAN, Ethel, & Dick Haymes

HAYSI FANTAYZEE
Singles: 7-Inch
RCA VICTOR: 83 1-3
LPs: 10/12-Inch 33rpm
RCA VICTOR : 83 5-8
Members: Kate Garner; Jeremiah Healy.

HAYWARD, Justin
Singles: 7-Inch
COLUMBIA: 78 1-3
DERAM: 77 2-3

LPs: 10/12-Inch 33rpm
DERAM: *77-80* $5-8

HAYWARD, Justin, & John Lodge
Singles: 7-Inch
THRESHOLD: *75* 2-3
LPs: 10/12-Inch 33rpm
THRESHOLD: *75* 12-15
Also see HAYWARD, Justin
Also see LODGE, John
Also see MOODY BLUES

HAYWARD, Leon:
see HAYWOOD, Leon

HAYWOOD, Leon
(Leon Hayward)
Singles: 12-Inch 33/45rpm
CASABLANCA: *83* 4-6
MCA: *79* 4-6
20TH CENTURY-FOX: *80* 4-6
Singles: 7-Inch
ATLANTIC: *71-72* 2-3
CAPITOL: *69-70* 2-3
CASABLANCA: *83* 1-3
COLUMBIA: *76-77* 2-3
DECCA: *67-68* 2-4
EPIC: *80-81* 1-3
FAT FISH: *66* 3-5
GALAXY: *67* 2-4
IMPERIAL: *65-66* 3-5
MCA: *77-79* 1-3
MODERN: *84* 1-3
20TH CENTURY-FOX: *74-80* 1-3
LPs: 10/12-Inch 33rpm
CASABLANCA: *83* 5-8
DECCA: *67* 8-12
GALAXY: *67* 8-12
MCA: *78-79* 5-8
20TH CENTURY-FOX: *73* 5-10

HAZARD, Robert
Singles: 7-Inch
RCA VICTOR: *83* 1-3
LPs: 10/12-Inch 33rpm
RCA VICTOR: *83* 5-8

HAZE
Singles: 7-Inch
ASI: *75* 2-3
LPs: 10/12-Inch 33rpm
ASI: *74* 8-10

HAZLEWOOD, Lee
Singles: 7-Inch
CAPITOL: *72* 2-3
JAMIE: *60* 3-5
LHI: *68* 2-3

MCA: *79-80* $1-3
MGM: *66-67* 2-4
REPRISE: *65-68* 2-4
SMASH: *61* 3-5
LPs: 10/12-Inch 33rpm
CAPITOL: *72* 8-10
HARMONY: *67* 8-12
MGM: *66-67* 10-15
MERCURY: *63* 10-15
REPRISE: *64-65* 10-15
Also see ANN-MARGRET & LEE HAZ-
LEWOOD
Also see SHACKLEFORDS
Also see SINATRA, Nancy, & Lee Hazlewood

HEAD, Murray
(Murray Head With The Trinidad Singers;
Murry Head)
Singles: 12-Inch 33/45rpm
CHESS: *85* 4-6
Singles: 7-Inch
A&M: *76* 1-3
CAPITOL: *67* 2-4
CHESS: *85* 1-3
DECCA: *69-71* 2-3
Picture Sleeves
DECCA: *70-71* 2-5
LPs: 10/12-Inch 33rpm
A&M: *76* 8-10
COLUMBIA: *72* 5-10

HEAD, Roy
(Roy Head & The Traits)
Singles: 7-Inch
ABC: *73-79* 1-3
ABC/DOT: *76-77* 2-3
AVION: *83* 1-3
BACK BEAT: *65-67* 4-6
CHURCHILL: *81* 1-3
DUNHILL: *70* 2-3
ELEKTRA: *79-80* 1-3
MEGA: *74* 2-3
MERCURY: *68* 2-4
NSD: *82* 1-3
SCEPTER: *65-66* 3-5
SHANNON: *75* 2-3
TMI: *71-73* 2-3
LPs: 10/12-Inch 33rpm
ABC: *73-78* 8-10
DUNHILL: *70* 10-12
ELEKTRA: *79-80* 5-8
SCEPTER: *65* 15-20
TMI: *72* 8-10
TNT (101; "Roy Head & The
Traits"): *65* 100-150
Also see TRAITS

HEAD EAST
Singles: 7-Inch
A&M: 75-79 ....$1-3
LPs: 10/12-Inch 33rpm
A&M: 76-80 5-8
ALLEGIANCE: 83 5-8

HEADBOYS
Singles: 7-Inch
RSO: 79 1-3
LPs: 10/12-Inch 33rpm
RSO: 79 5-8

HEADHUNTERS
Singles: 7-Inch
FENTON: 3-5
LPs: 10/12-Inch 33rpm
ARISTA: 78 5-8

HEADPINS
Singles: 7-Inch
ATCO: 82 1-3
SGR: 83 1-3
LPs: 10/12-Inch 33rpm
ATCO: 83 5-8

HEALEY, Jeff, Band
LPs: 10/12-Inch 33rpm
ARISTA: 88 5-8

HEAP, Jimmy
(Jimmy Heap & The Melody Masters; Jimmy Heap & Perk Williams)
Singles: 7-Inch
CAPITOL: 53-55 5-10
D: 59 5-10
DART: 60 4-6
FAME (502; "Little Jewell"): 58 100-150
IMPERIAL: 60 4-8

HEART
Singles: 12-Inch 33/45rpm
CAPITOL: 85 4-6
MUSHROOM: 76 4-6
PORTRAIT: 77-79 4-6
Promotional 12-Inch Singles
MUSHROOM (7023, "Dreamboat
Annie): 76 8-10
PORTRAIT (16445, "Straight
On"): 78 8-10
Singles: 7-Inch
CAPITOL: 85-88 1-3
EPIC: 81-83 1-3
MUSHROOM: 76-79 2-3
NAUTILUS: 80 20-25
(Half-speed mastered.)
PORTRAIT: 77-79 2-3

Picture Sleeves
CAPITOL: 85-86 ....$1-3
LPs: 10/12-Inch 33rpm
CAPITOL: 85-87 5-8
EPIC: 80-82 5-8
MUSHROOM (MRS-5008
"Magazine"); 77 50-75
(First issue is easily identified: Last track on side
one is *Magazine*.)
MUSHROOM (MRS-5008
"Magazine"): 77 5-8
(Second issue. First track on side two is
Magazine."There are also other differences in song
order.)
MUSHROOM (MRS-1-SP;
"Magazine"): 78 8-12
(Picture Disc.)
MUSHROOM (MRS-2-SP; "Dreamboat
Annie"): 79 10-15
(Picture Disc.)
PORTRAIT (30000 series): 77-81 5-8
PORTRAIT (40000 series): 81 12-15
(Half-speed mastered.)
Members: Nancy Wilson; Ann Wilson; Howard
Leese; Steve Fossen; Roger Fisher; Mike Derosier;
Mark Andes; Denny Carmassi.
Also see SPIRIT
Also see WILSON, Ann & The Daybreaks

HEART BEATS QUINTET
(With Russell Jacquet & His Orchestra)
Singles: 10 Inch
CANDLELITE (437; "Tormented"): 72 . 10-20
(Colored vinyl. A 45rpm single.)
CANDLELITE (437; "Tormented"): 72 .. 8-15
(Black vinyl.)
Singles: 7-Inch
CANDLELITE (1135; "Tormented"): 76 .. 3-5
NETWORK (71200; "Tormented"): 55 . 50-75
Members: James Sheppard; Albert Crump; Vernon
Walker; Wally Roker; Rob Adams.
Also see HEARTBEATS
Also see JACQUET, Illnois

HEART OF GOLD BAND
LPs: 10/12-Inch 33rpm
RELIX: 86 5-8
Members: Keith Godchaux; Donna Godchaux.

HEARTBEATS
Singles: 7-Inch
GEE: 57-60 10-15
GUYDEN: 59 15-20
HULL (711; "Crazy For You"): 55 ... 100-150
(Pink label.)
HULL (713; "Darling How Long"): 56 .. 25-50
HULL (716; "People Are Talking"): 56 .. 25-50

HULL (720; "A Thousand Miles
Away"): *56* **$100-150**
(Black label.)
HULL (720; "A Thousand Miles
Away"): *56* **10-20**
(Red label.)
RAMA: *56-60* **5-10**
ROULETTE (4000 series): *58-59* **4-8**
LPs: 10/12-Inch 33rpm
EMUS: **8-10**
ROULETTE (25107; "A Thousand
Miles Away"): *60* **75-125**
(Roulette reissues have a "1981" copyright date at
the bottom of back cover and are currently avail-
able for $5-$8.)
Members: James Sheppard; Albert Crump; Vernon
Walker; Wally Roker; Rob Adams.
Also see HEART BEATS QUINTET
Also see SHEP & THE LIMELITES

**HEARTBEATS / Shep & The
Limelites**
LPs: 10/12-Inch 33rpm
ROULETTE (115; "Echoes Of A
Rock Era"): **25-35**
Also see HEARTBEATS
Also see SHEP & THE LIMELITES

HEARTS
Singles: 7-Inch
BATON: *55-56* **8-10**
J&S: *56-57* **8-10**
LAVENDER: *62* **4-6**
TUFF: *63* **3-5**
Members: Baby Washington; Rex Garvin; Pat Ford.
Also see WASHINGTON, Baby

HEARTSFIELD
Singles: 7-Inch
MERCURY: *74* **2-3**

LPs: 10/12-Inch 33rpm
COLUMBIA: *77* **$5-8**
MERCURY: *73-75* **8-10**

HEARTSMAN, Johnny
Singles: 7-Inch
MUSIC CITY: *57* **5-8**

HEAT
Singles: 7-Inch
MCA: *79-81* **1-3**
LPs: 10/12-Inch 33rpm
MCA: *79-81* **5-8**

HEATH, Ted
Singles: 7-Inch
LONDON: *50-61* **2-3**
EPs: 7-Inch 33/45rpm
LONDON: *51-56* **3-6**
LPs: 10/12-Inch 33rpm
LONDON: *50-62* **5-15**
RICHMOND: *62* **4-8**

HEATH, Walter
Singles: 7-Inch
BUDDAH: *74* **2-3**

HEATH BROTHERS
Singles: 7-Inch
COLUMBIA: *79-81* **1-3**
LPs: 10/12-Inch 33rpm
COLUMBIA: *79-81* **5-8**

HEATHERTON, Joey
Singles: 7-Inch
CORAL: *64-65* **2-4**
DECCA: *66* **2-4**
MGM: *72-73* **2-3**
Picture Sleeves
CORAL: *64* **4-8**
MGM: *72* **2-5**
LPs: 10/12-Inch 33rpm
MGM: *72* **8-12**

HEATWAVE
Singles: 12-Inch 33/45rpm
EPIC: *77-82* **4-6**
Singles: 7-Inch
EPIC: *77-82* **1-3**
LPs: 10/12-Inch 33rpm
EPIC: *77-82* **5-8**
Members: Keith Wilder; Rod Temperton; Ernie
Berger; John Wilder; Eric Johns.

HEAVEN & EARTH
Singles: 7-Inch
GEC: *76* **2-3**
MERCURY: *78-80* **1-3**
TEC: *80* **1-3**
WMOT: *81* **1-3**

LPs: 10/12-Inch 33rpm
MERCURY: 78-79 .... **$5-8**
WMOT: 81 .... **5-8**
Members: Dwight Dukes; Dean Williams; James
Dukes; Keith Steward.

HEAVEN BOUND
Singles: 7-Inch
MGM: 71 .... **2-3**
LPs: 10/12-Inch 33rpm
MGM: 72 .... **8-12**
Member: Tony Scotti.

HEAVEN 17
Singles: 12-Inch 33/45rpm
ARISTA: 83-84 .... **4-6**
Singles: 7-Inch
ARISTA: 83-84 .... **1-3**
LPs: 10/12-Inch 33rpm
ARISTA: 83 .... **8-10**
VIRGIN: 87 .... **5-8**
Also see BAND AID

HEAVY D. & THE BOYZ
Singles: 12-Inch 33/45rpm
MCA: 86 .... **4-6**
Singles: 7-Inch
MCA: 86-88 .... **1-3**
LPs: 10/12-Inch 33rpm
MCA: 86-87 .... **5-8**

HEBB, Bobby
Singles: 7-Inch
BOOM: 66 .... **3-5**
CADET: 72 .... **2-3**
FM: 61 .... **3-5**
LAURIE: 75 .... **2-3**
PHILIPS: 66 .... **3-5**
RICH: 60 .... **3-5**
SCEPTER: 66 .... **3-5**
Picture Sleeves
PHILIPS: 66 .... **3-6**
LPs: 10/12-Inch 33rpm
EPIC: 70 .... **10-12**
PHILLIPS: 66 .... **15-20**

HEDGEHOPPERS ANONYMOUS
Singles: 7-Inch
PARROT: 65-66 .... **4-6**
Also see KING, Jonathan

HEFTI, Neal
(Neal Hefti & His Orchestra; Neal Hefti Quintet;
Neal Hefti & The Mello-Larks)
Singles: 7-Inch
COLUMBIA: 65 .... **1-3**
CORAL: 51-59 .... **2-4**
DOT: 67-68 .... **1-3**
EPIC: 55-56 .... **2-4**

RCA VICTOR: 66 .... **$2-4**
REPRISE: 62 .... **2-3**
UNITED ARTISTS: 65-66 .... **1-3**
Picture Sleeves
RCA VICTOR: 66-67 .... **3-6**
EPs: 7-Inch 33/45rpm
CORAL: 52-56 .... **4-8**
X: 55 .... **4-8**
LPs: 10/12-Inch 33rpm
COLUMBIA: 60 .... **8-15**
CORAL: 52-60 .... **10-20**
DOT (803; "Barefoot In The Park"): 67 .. **20-25**
(Soundtrack.)
EPIC: 56 .... **10-15**
LIBERTY (413; "Synanon"): 65 .... **15-25**
(Soundtrack.)
RCA VICTOR (1121; "Boeing
Boeing"): 66 .... **20-25**
(Soundtrack.)
RCA VICTOR (3573; "Batman"): 66 ... **15-20**
(Soundtrack.)
RCA VICTOR (3621; "Hefti In
Gotham City"): 66 .... **10-20**
RCA VICTOR (3750; "Oh Dad, Poor Dad,
Mama's Hung You In The Closet & I'm
Feeling So Sad"): 67 .... **15-20**
(Soundtrack.)
REPRISE: 62 .... **8-15**
20TH CENTURY-FOX: 64 .... **8-12**
UNITED ARTISTS (119; "How To
Murder Your Wife"): 65 .... **10-15**
(Soundtrack.)
UNITED ARTISTS (139; "Duel At
Diablo"): 66 .... **15-20**
(Soundtrack.)
UNITED ARTISTS (573; "Definitely
Hefti"): 67 .... **8-15**
WARNER BROS (1572; "Sex & The
Single Girl"): 64 .... **20-25**
(Soundtrack.)
X: 55 .... **10-15**

HEIGHT, Donald
Singles: 7-Inch
JUBILEE: 63-69 .... **3-5**
KING: 60 .... **3-5**
OLD TOWN: 64 .... **3-5**
RCA VICTOR: 65 .... **3-5**
ROULETTE: 65 .... **3-5**
SHOUT: 66-68 .... **2-4**
SOOZEE: 62 .... **3-5**

HEIGHT, Ronnie
Singles: 7-Inch
BAMBOO: 61 .... **3-5**
DORE: 59 .... **4-6**

ERA: *59-61* $3-5

HEINTJE
Singles: 7-Inch
MGM: *70* 2-3
LPs: 10/12-Inch 33rpm
MGM: *70* 8-10

HELIX
LPs: 10/12-Inch 33rpm
CAPITOL: *83-87* 5-8

HELLO PEOPLE
Singles: 7-Inch
ABC/DUNHILL: *75-76* 2-3
PHILIPS: *68* 3-5
Picture Sleeves
PHILIPS: *68* 4-8
LPs: 10/12-Inch 33rpm
ABC/DUNHILL: *74* 8-10
ABC-PARAMOUNT: *75* 8-10
MEDIARTS: *70* 12-15
PHILLIPS: *68* 12-15

HELLOWEEN
LPs: 10/12-Inch 33rpm
RCA VICTOR: *88* 5-8

HELM, Levon
(Levon Helm & The RCO All-Stars)
Singles: 7-Inch
A&M: *80* 1-3
ABC: *78* 2-3
CAPITOL: *82* 1-3
MCA: *80* 1-3
LPs: 10/12-Inch 33rpm
ABC-PARAMOUNT: *77-78* 5-8
A&M: *80* 5-8
CAPITOL: *82* 5-8
MCA: *80* 5-8
Also see BAND
Also see CASH, Johnny, & Levon Helm
Also see LEVON & THE HAWKS

HELMS, Bobby
Singles: 7-Inch
BLACK ROSE: *83-84* 1-3
CAPITOL: *70* 2-3
CERTRON: *70* 2-4
COLUMBIA: *64* 2-4
DECCA (Except 29947): *57-62* 3-5
DECCA (29947; "Tennessee Rock &
Roll"): *56* 10-15
GUSTO: *74* 1-3
KAPP: *65-67* 2-3
LARRICK: *75* 2-3
LITTLE DARLIN': *67-79* 1-3
MCA: 1-3

MILLION: *72* $2-3
MISTLETOE: *74* 1-3
Picture Sleeves
CERTRON: *70* 3-6
DECCA: *57* 5-10
EPs: 7-Inch 33/45rpm
DECCA: *57-59* 10-20
LPs: 10/12-Inch 33rpm
CERTRON: *70* 8-10
COLUMBIA: *63* 12-15
DECCA: *57* 25-30
HARMONY: *67* 10-12
KAPP: *66* 10-12
LITTLE DARLIN': *68* 10-12
MCA: *83* 5-8
MISTLETOE: *74* 5-8
VOCALION: *65* 10-12
Also see KERR, Anita

HELMS, Jimmie
Singles: 7-Inch
EAST WEST: *58* 20-25
FOREST: *63* 3-5
SCOTTIE: *59* 5-10
SYMBOL: *63* 3-5

HENDERSON, Finis
Singles: 7-Inch
MOTOWN: *83* 1-3
LPs: 10/12-Inch 33rpm
MOTOWN: *83* 5-8

HENDERSON, Joe
Singles: 7-Inch
ABC: *73* 1-3
KAPP: *64* 3-5
RIC: *64* 3-5
TODD: *62-63* 3-5
VIRGO: *72* 1-3
LPs: 10/12-Inch 33rpm
TODD: *62* 20-25

HENDERSON, Michael
Singles: 12-Inch 33/45rpm
EMI AMERICA: *86* 4-6
Singles: 7-Inch
BUDDAH: *76-83* 1-3
EMI AMERICA: *86* 1-3
LPs: 10/12-Inch 33rpm
ACCORD: *8* 5-
BUDDAH: *76-83* 8-12
EMI AMERICA: *86* 5-8
Also see CONNORS, Norman
Also see HYMAN, Phyllis, & Michael
Henderson

HENDERSON, Ron, & Choice Of Colour
Singles: 7-Inch
CHELSEA: 77 .... $2-3

HENDERSON, Skitch, Orchestra
Singles: 7-Inch
CAPITOL: 50-51 2-4
COLUMBIA: 65-69 1-3
EPs: 7-Inch 33/45rpm
CAPITOL: 54 5-10
DECCA: 56 5-10
LPs: 10/12-Inch 33rpm
CAPITOL: 50-54 10-25
COLUMBIA: 62-69 8-12
DECCA: 56 10-20
HARMONY: 72 5-8
SEECO: 55 10-20
VOCALION: 66 5-10

HENDERSON, Wayne
(Wayne Henderson & The Freedom Sounds)
Singles: 7-Inch
POLYDOR: 78-79 1-3
LPs: 10/12-Inch 33rpm
ABC: 77 5-8
ATLANTIC: 67-68 8-12
POLYDOR: 78-79 5-8
Also see AYERS, Roy, & Wayne Henderson

HENDERSON, Willie
(Willie Henderson & The Soul Explosions)
Singles: 7-Inch
BRUNSWICK: 70 2-3
PLAYBOY: 74 2-3
LPs: 10/12-Inch 33rpm
BRUNSWICK: 69-74 10-12

HENDRICKS, Bobby
Singles: 7-Inch
MGM: 63 3-5
MERCURY: 61 3-5
SUE: 58-60 4-8
Also see COASTERS
Also see DRIFTERS

HENDRIX, Jimi
Singles: 7-Inch
AUDIO FIDELITY: 10-15
REPRISE (Except 0572 & 0665): 67-72 5-8
REPRISE (0572; "Hey Joe"): 67 20-30
REPRISE (0665; "Up From The
    Skies"): 68 10-15
TRIP: 72 2-4
Promotional Singles
REPRISE (Except 0572 & 0665): 67-72 ... 6-10
REPRISE (0572; "Hey Joe"): 67 25-30
REPRISE (0665; "Up From The
    Skies"): 68 10-20

Picture Sleeves
REPRISE (0572; "Hey Joe"): 67 ...... $60-80
EPs: 7-Inch 33/45rpm
REPRISE (595; "And A Happy
    New Year"): 74 100-150
(Promotional issue only.)
LPs: 10/12-Inch 33rpm
ABC (82-41; "Jimi Hendrix:
    A Tribute"): 82 150-200
(Five LPs plus cue sheets. Promotional issue only.)
ACCORD: 81 5-8
BBC ROCK HOUR/LONDON WAVE-
    LENGTH ("Jimi Hendrix Special"): 81 . 50-75
CAPITOL (12000 series): 86 5-8
CAPITOL (15000 series): 86 4-6
(Mini LP.)
CRAWDADDY: 75 200-250
PICKWICK: 75 5-8
NUTMEG: 75 15-20
REPRISE (840; "Jimi Hendrix - Christmas
    Medley"): 79 40-50
(Promotional issue only.)
REPRISE (2025; "Smash Hits"): 69 25-35
(Orange and brown label. Price includes bonus
poster, which represents about $15-$20 of the
value.)
REPRISE (2025; "Smash Hits"): 71 8-10
(Brown label.)
REPRISE (2029; "Historic
    Performances"): 70 8-10
REPRISE (2034; "The Cry Of Love"): 71 . 8-10
REPRISE (2040; "Rainbow Bridge"): 71 10-15
REPRISE (2049; "In The West"): 72 10-15
REPRISE (2103; "War Heroes"): 72 10-15
REPRISE (2204; "Crash Landing"): 75 .. 10-15
REPRISE (2229; "Midnight
    Lightning"): 75 10-15
REPRISE (2245; "Essential Jimi
    Hendrix"): 78 8-12
REPRISE (2276; "Smash Hits"): 77 5-8
REPRISE (2293; "Essential Jimi
    Hendrix, Vol. 2"): 79 10-20
(Includes the bonus single, "Gloria,"
extended version.)
REPRISE (2293; "Essential Jimi
    Hendrix, Vol. 2"): 79 5-10
(Without the bonus single.)
REPRISE (2299; "Nine To The
    Universe"): 80 5-8
REPRISE (R-6261; "Are You
    Experienced"): 67 35-65
(Monaural. Green, pink, and yellow label.)
REPRISE (6261; "Are You
    Experienced"): 68 12-20
(Orange and brown label.)

REPRISE (6261; "Are You
Experienced"): *71* **$5-8**
(Brown label.)
REPRISE (R-6281; "Axis: Bold
As Love"): *68* **150-200**
(Monaural. Orange and brown label.)
REPRISE (RS-6281; "Axis: Bold
As Love"): *68* **15-20**
(Stereo. Green, pink, and yellow label.)
REPRISE (RS-6281; "Axis: Bold
As Love"): *71* **5-8**
(Brown label.)
REPRISE (6307; "Electric
Ladyland"): *68* **12-15**
(Orange and brown label.)
REPRISE (6307; "Electric
Ladyland"): *71* **8-10**
(Brown label.)
REPRISE (22306; "Jimi Hendrix
Concerts"): *82* **8-10**
REPRISE (25358; "Jimi Plays
Monterey"): *86* **5-8**
RHINO: *82* **5-8**
ROLLING STONE PRODUCTIONS (82-24;
"The Jimi Hendrix Profile"): *82* **50-100**
(Two LPs plus cue sheets. Promotional issue only.)
RYKO: *87-88* **10-15**
SHOUT: *72* **10-15**
(White label with red and blue printing.)
SHOUT: **8-10**
(Yellow label.)
SPRINGBOARD: *72* **8-10**
TRIP: *72-74* **8-10**
UNITED ARTISTS: *75* **8-10**
WESTWOOD ONE ("Rock & Roll Never
Forgets Jimi Hendrix"): *83* **150-200**
(Five LPs plus cue sheets. Promotional issue only.)

WESTWOOD ONE ("Jimi Hendrix, Live
And Unreleased"): *88* **$400-500**
(Eight LPs plus cue sheets. Promotional issue only.)
Also see MILES, Buddy
Also see REDDING, Otis / Jimi Hendrix

HENDRIX, Jimi, & Buddy Miles
LPs: 10/12-Inch 33rpm
CAPITOL (472; "Band Of
Gypsies"): *70* **10-12**
Also see MILES, Buddy

HENDRIX, Jimi, & The Isley Bros.
LPs: 10/12-Inch 33rpm
T-NECK: *71* **10-15**
Also see ISLEY BROTHERS

HENDRIX, Jimi, & Curtis Knight
LPs: 10/12-Inch 33rpm
CAPITOL (659; "Flashing"): *70* **8-10**
CAPITOL (2856; "Get That
Feeling"): *67* **10-15**
CAPITOL (2894; "Flashing"): *68* **10-15**
51 WEST: *82* **5-8**

HENDRIX, Jimi, & Little Richard
Singles: 7-Inch
ALANNA: *72* **3-5**
LPs: 10/12-Inch 33rpm
ALANNA: *72* **10-12**
EVEREST: *74* **6-10**
PICKWICK: *73* **6-10**
Also see LITTLE RICHARD

HENDRIX, Jimi, & Lonnie Youngblood
LPs: 10/12-Inch 33rpm
MAPLE: *71* **20-25**
Also see HENDRIX, Jimi
Also see YOUNGBLOOD, Lonnie

HENDRIX, Patti
Singles: 7-Inch
HILLTAK: *78* **1-3**
20TH CENTURY-FOX: *74* **2-3**

HENDRYX, Nona
Singles: 12-Inch 33/45rpm
RCA VICTOR: *83-86* **4-6**
Singles: 7-Inch
EMI AMERICA: *87* **1-3**
EPIC: *77* **2-3**
RCA VICTOR: *83-87* **1-3**
LPs: 10/12-Inch 33rpm
EPIC: *77* **5-8**
RCA VICTOR: *83-87* **5-8**
Also see LABELLE, Patti

HENHOUSE FIVE PLUS TOO
Singles: 7-Inch
WARNER BROS/AHAB: *76-77* **2-3**

Member: Ray Stevens.
Also see STEVENS, Ray

HENLEY, Don
Singles: 12-Inch 33/45rpm
GEFFEN: *85* $4-6
Singles: 7-Inch
ASYLUM: *82-83* 1-3
GEFFEN: *84-85* 1-3
LPs: 10/12-Inch 33rpm
ASYLUM: *82-83* 5-8
GEFFEN: *84-85* 5-8
Also see EAGLES
Also see NICKS, Stevie, & Don Henley

HENRY, Clarence
(Clarence "Frogman" Henry)
Singles: 7-Inch
ARGO (5200 series): *56-58* 5-8
ARGO (5300 & 5400 series): *59-63* 4-6
DIAL: *67* 3-5
PARROT: *64-66* 3-5
CHESS: *73* 1-3
ERIC: *73* 1-3
LPs: 10/12-Inch 33rpm
ARGO: *61* 40-50
CADET: 20-30
(Some Cadet LPs were packaged in Argo covers,
using the same numbers.)
ROULETTE: *69* 15-20

HENSLEY, Ken
Singles: 7-Inch
MERCURY: *73* 2-3
LPs: 10/12-Inch 33rpm
MERCURY: *73* 8-10
WARNER BROS: *75* 8-10
Also see URIAH HEEP

HENSON, Jim
(Jim Henson's Muppets)
Singles: 7-Inch
COLUMBIA: *72* 1-3
SIGNATURE: *60* 3-5
Singles: 12-Inch 33/45rpm
COLUMBIA: *71* 5-8
Also see ERNIE
Also see KERMIT / Fozzie Bear
Also see MUPPETS

HERB THE "K"
Singles: 7-Inch
PRIVATE I: *85* 1-3

HERMAN, Keith
Singles: 7-Inch
RADIO: *79* 1-3

HERMAN, Woody, Orchestra
Singles: 7-Inch
CADET: *69* $1-3
CAPITOL: *54-56* 2-4
CENTURY: *79* 1-3
CHURCHILL: *79* 1-3
COLUMBIA: *65-76* 1-3
FANTASY: *73-74* 1-3
MCA: *73* 1-3
MARS: *52-53* 2-4
PHILIPS: *62* 1-3
EPs: 7-Inch 33/45rpm
CAPITOL: *55-56* 5-10
COLUMBIA: *52-54* 8-12
DECCA: *56* 5-10
MGM: *55* 5-10
LPs: 10/12-Inch 33rpm
ACCORD: *82* 5-8
ATLANTIC (1300 series): *60* 10-20
ATLANTIC (90000 series): *82* 5-8
BRIGHT ORANGE: *73* 5-8
CADET: *69-71* 8-12
CAPITOL: *72-75* 5-8
(With an "M" or "SM" prefix.)
CAPITOL: *55-62* 10-25
(With a "T" or "ST" prefix.)
CENTURY: *78* 5-8
CHESS: *76* 5-8
COLUMBIA (2300 & 2400 series): *65-66* 5-15
COLUMBIA (2500 series): *52-54* 15-25
(10-Inch LPs.)
COLUMBIA (6000 series): *52-55* 15-25
COLUMBIA (9000 series): *65-67* 5-15
COLUMBIA (32000 series): *74* 5-8
CONCORD JAZZ: *81-83* 5-8
CROWN: *59* 10-15
DECCA (4000 series): *64* 8-15
DECCA (8000 series): *56* 10-25
EVEREST (Except 200 & 300
series): *59-63* 10-20
EVEREST (200 & 300 series): *74-78* 5-8
FPM: *75* 5-8
FANTASY: *71-81* 5-10
HARMONY: *72* 5-8
JAZZLAND: *60* 10-20
MGM: *55* 10-25
METRO: *65* 5-12
PHILIPS: *62-65* 10-15
ROULETTE: *59* 10-20
SURREY: *66* 8-12
TREND: *81* 5-8
TRIP: *75* 5-8
VSP: *66-67* 8-12
VERVE: *63-68* 8-15

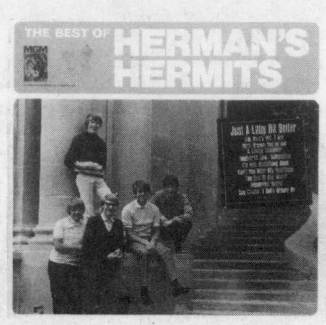

HIBBLER, Al
Singles: 78rpm
ALADDIN: 56 .... $3-5
ATLANTIC: 51 5-10
CLEF: 54 3-5
COLUMBIA: 50 3-5
DECCA: 55-57 3-5
MERCURY: 52-56 3-5
MIRACLE: 48 5-10
NORGRAN: 54-55 3-5
ORIGINAL: 55 4-8
Singles: 7-Inch
ALADDIN: 56 4-8
ATLANTIC (900 series): 51 20-30
ATLANTIC (1000 series): 55 10-20
CLEF: 54 3-6
COLUMBIA: 50 4-8
DECCA: 55-59 3-6
MCA: 74 1-3
MERCURY: 52-56 3-6
NORGRAN: 54-55 3-6
ORIGINAL: 55 5-8
REPRISE: 61-62 2-4
SATIN: 66 2-3
TOP RANK: 60 2-4
VEGAS: 67 2-3
EPs: 7-Inch 33/45rpm
CLEF: 51 10-15
DECCA: 55-57 5-10
NORGRAN: 53 10-15
RCA VICTOR: 55 5-10
LPs: 10/12-Inch 33rpm
ATLANTIC: 56 10-20
CLEF: 54 15-25
DECCA (8000 series): 56-59 10-20
DECCA (75000 series): 69 5-10
LMI: 65 8-12
MCA: 76 5-10
NORGRAN: 53 20-40
REPRISE: 61 8-15
TRIP: 77 4-8
VERVE: 55 10-20
Also see HOLIDAY, Billie, & Al Hibbler

HIBBLER, Al, & Duke Ellington
Singles: 7-Inch
COLUMBIA (33000 series): 76 1-3
LPs: 10/12-Inch 33rpm
COLUMBIA: 56 10-20
Also see ELLINGTON, Duke
Also see HIBBLER, Al

HICKEY, Ersel
Singles: 7-Inch
APOLLO: 62 3-5

BLACK CIRCLE: 72 .... $2-3
EPIC (Except 9278, 9298, & 9309): 58-60 . 5-8
EPIC (9278; "Goin' Down That
Road"): 58 8-10
EPIC (9298; "You Never Can Tell"): 58 .. 8-10
EPIC (9309; "You Threw A Dart"): 59 ... 8-10
JANUS: 71 2-3
KAPP: 61 4-6
LAURIE: 63 3-5
MAGNUM: 84 1-3
RAMESES: 76 2-3
TOOT: 8-10
UNIFAX: 74 2-3
EPs: 7-Inch 33/45rpm
EPIC (7206; "Ersel Hickey In
Lover's Land"): 58 75-100

HICKS, Clair
Singles: 12-Inch 33/45rpm
KN: 84 4-6

HICKS, Dan, & His Hot Licks
Singles: 7-Inch
BLUE THUMB: 73-74 2-4
LPs: 10/12-Inch 33rpm
BLUE THUMB: 71-72 8-10
EPIC: 69 10-12
WARNER BROS: 78 5-8

HIDDEN STRENGTH
Singles: 7-Inch
UNITED ARTISTS: 76 2-3

HI-FI FOUR
Singles: 78rpm
KING: 56 4-6
Singles: 7-Inch
KING: 56 4-6

HIGGINS, Bertie
Singles: 7-Inch
CBS ASSOCIATED: 85 1-3
KAT FAMILY: 81-82 1-3
SOUTHERN TRACKS: 87-88 1-3
LPs: 10/12-Inch 33rpm
KAT FAMILY: 82 5-8

HIGGINS, Monk
(Monk Higgins & The Specialties)
Singles: 7-Inch
BUDDAH: 74 2-3
CHESS: 67 2-4
SOLID STATE: 68 2-4
ST. LAWRENCE: 66 3-5
UNITED ARTISTS: 72-73 2-4
LPs: 10/12-Inch 33rpm
BUDDAH: 74 5-10
SOLID STATE: 69 8-12

UNITED ARTISTS: 72 .... $8-10
Also see MASON, Barbara

HIGH INERGY
Singles: 12-Inch 33/45rpm
GORDY: 83 4-6
Singles: 7-Inch
GORDY (Black vinyl): 77-83 1-3
GORDY (Colored vinyl): 3-5
(Promotional issue only.)
LPs: 10/12-Inch 33rpm
GORDY: 77-83 5-8
Also see ROBINSON, Smokey, & Barbara
Mitchell

HIGH KEYS
Singles: 7-Inch
ATCO: 63-64 8-10
VERVE: 66 3-5

HIGHLIGHTS
(Featuring Frank Pizani)
Singles: 78rpm
BALLY: 56-57 4-8
Singles: 7-Inch
BALLY: 56-58 5-10
Also see PIZANI, Frank

HIGHTOWER, Willie
Singles: 7-Inch
CAPITOL: 69 3-5
FAME: 70 2-4

HIGHWAYMEN
Singles: 7-Inch
ABC-PARAMOUNT: 65-66 2-4
LIBERTY: 81 1-3
UNITED ARTISTS: 61-64 3-5
LPs: 10/12-Inch 33rpm
ABC-PARAMOUNT: 66 8-15
LIBERTY: 82 4-8
UNITED ARTISTS: 61-65 10-20
Members: Steve Butts; Chan Daniels; Gil Robbins;
Dave Fisher.

HILL, Bunker
Singles: 7-Inch
MALA (Except 464): 62 3-5
MALA (464; "The Girl Can't
Dance"): 63 8-12

HILL, Dan
Singles: 7-Inch
COLUMBIA: 88 1-3
EPIC: 80-81 1-3
20TH CENTURY-FOX: 75-79 1-3
LPs: 10/12-Inch 33rpm
EPIC: 80-81 5-8
20TH CENTURY-FOX: 75-80 6-9

HILL, Dan, & Vonda Sheppard
Singles: 7-Inch
COLUMBIA: 87 .... $1-3
LPs: 10/12-Inch 33rpm
COLUMBIA: 87 5-8
Also see HILL, Dan

HILL, David
Singles: 78rpm
ALADDIN: 57 3-6
Singles: 7-Inch
ALADDIN: 57 5-8
KAPP: 59 4-6
RCA VICTOR: 57-58 4-6

HILL, Jessie
Singles: 7-Inch
DOWNEY: 64 3-5
MINIT: 60-62 8-10
LPs: 10/12-Inch 33rpm
BLUE THUMB: 72 8-10

HILL, Lonnie
Singles: 7-Inch
URBAN SOUND: 84-85 1-3
LPs: 10/12-Inch 33rpm
URBAN SOUND: 85 5-8

HILL, Z.Z.
Singles: 7-Inch
ATLANTIC: 69-70 3-5
AUDREY: 71-72 2-4
COLUMBIA: 77-78 1-3
HILL: 71-73 2-4
KENT: 64-71 3-5
M.H.: 63 3-5
M.H.R.: 75 2-3
MALACO: 82-84 1-3
MAILBU: 1-3
MESA: 64 3-5
MANKIND: 71-72 2-4
QUINCY: 70 2-4
RARE BULLET: 84 1-3
UNITED ARTISTS: 73-75 2-3
LPs: 10/12-Inch 33rpm
COLUMBIA: 78-79 5-8
KENT: 69-71 10-12
MALACO: 82-84 5-8
MANKIND: 71 8-10
UNITED ARTISTS: 72-75 8-10

HILLAGE, Steve
LPs: 10/12-Inch 33rpm
ATLANTIC: 76-77 8-10
VIRGIN: 75 8-10

HILLMAN, Chris
Singles: 7-Inch
ASYLUM: 76-77 .... $2-3
LPs: 10/12-Inch 33rpm
ASYLUM: 76-77 5-8
SUGAR HILL: 82-84 5-8
Also see BYRDS
Also see FLYING BURRITO BROTHERS
Also see MC GUINN & HILLMAN
Also see SOUTHER-HILLMAN-FURAY
BAND

HILLSIDE SINGERS
Singles: 7-Inch
METROMEDIA: 71-72 2-3
LPs: 10/12-Inch 33rpm
METROMEDIA: 71 8-12

HILLTOPPERS
(Hill Toppers)
Singles: 78rpm
DOT: 52-57 3-5
Singles: 7-Inch
ABC: 74 1-3
DOT (15000 series): 52-60 5-10
DOT (16000 series): 63 3-5
3-J: 66 2-3
EPs: 7-Inch 33/45rpm
DOT: 54-56 5-12
LPs: 10/12-Inch 33rpm
DOT: 54-56 10-25
SOUVENIR: 73 8-15
Members: Jimmy Sacca; Billy Vaughn; Don Mc-
Guire; Seymour Spiegelman.
Also see VAUGHN, Billy

HINDSIGHT
Singles: 7-Inch
VIRGIN: 88 1-3
LPs: 10/12-Inch 33rpm
VIRGIN: 88 5-8

HINE, Eric
Singles: 7-Inch
MONTAGE: 81 1-3

HINES, Gregory
Singles: 7-Inch
EPIC: 88 1-3
LPs: 10/12-Inch 33rpm
EPIC: 88 5-8

HINES, J., & The Fellows
Singles: 7-Inch
DELUXE: 73 2-4

HINTON, Joe
(Little Joe Hinton)
Singles: 7-Inch
ARVEE: 61 .... $4-6
BACKBEAT: 59-65 3-5
HOTLANTA: 74 8-10
Picture Sleeves
BACKBEAT: 59-65 8-15
LPs: 10/12-Inch 33rpm
BACKBEAT: 65 15-20
DUKE: 73 8-10

HIPPIES / Reggie Harrison
Singles: 7-Inch
PARKWAY (863; "Memory Lane"): 63 .. 6-10
Also see STEREOS
Also see TAMS

HIROSHIMA
Singles: 12-Inch 33/45rpm
EPIC: 85 4-6
Singles: 7-Inch
ARISTA: 80-84 1-3
EPIC: 85 1-3
LPs: 10/12-Inch 33rpm
ARISTA: 84 5-8
EPIC: 85-87 5-8

HIRT, Al
Singles: 7-Inch
CORAL: 65 2-3
GWP: 69-70 1-3
MONUMENT: 74 1-3
RCA VICTOR: 61-68 2-3
Picture Sleeves
RCA VICTOR: 61-66 2-5
EPs: 7-Inch 33/45rpm
RCA VICTOR: 62 4-6
LPs: 10/12-Inch 33rpm
ACCORD: 82 4-8
AUDIO FIDELITY: 59-61 10-15
CAMDEN: 67-71 5-10
GWP: 70-71 5-8
METRO: 65 5-10
MONUMENT: 74 4-8
RCA VICTOR: 61-78 5-15
VOCALION: 70 5-8
Also see ANN-MARGRET & AL HIRT

HIRT, Al, & Pete Fountain
Singles: 7-Inch
CORAL: 61 2-3
EPs: 7-Inch 33/45rpm
CORAL: 62 4-6
LPs: 10/12-Inch 33rpm
CORAL: 61-62 8-15
MGM: 64 8-15

Also see MULLIGAN, Gerry, & Johnny
Hodges

HODGES, Johnny, & Lawrence Welk
LPs: 10/12-Inch 33rpm
DOT: 66 . . . .$10-15
Also see WELK, Lawrence

HODGES, Johnny, & Wild Bill Davis
LPs: 10/12-Inch 33rpm
RCA VICTOR: 65-67 10-15
VERVE: 61-66 10-20
Also see HODGES, Johnny

HODGES, JAMES & SMITH
Singles: 12-Inch 33/45rpm
LONDON: 79 4-6
Singles: 7-Inch
LONDON: 76-79 2-3
20TH CENTURY-FOX: 75 2-3
LPs: 10/12-Inch 33rpm
LONDON: 78 5-8
Members: Pat Hodges; Denita James; Jessica Smith.

HODGSON, Roger
Singles: 7-Inch
A&M: 84 1-3
LPs: 10/12-Inch 33rpm
A&M: 84-87 5-8
Also see SUPERTRAMP

HOG HEAVEN
Singles: 7-Inch
ROULETTE: 71 .2-4
LPs: 10/12-Inch 33rpm
ROULETTE: 71 .10-12
Also see JAMES, Tommy, & The Shondells

HOGG, Smokey
(Andrew Hogg)
Singles: 78rpm
BULLET: 48 10-15
COLONY: 50 5-10
COMBO: 52 5-10
CROWN: 54 10-20
EXCLUSIVE: 47 10-15
FEDERAL: 53 10-20
FIDELITY: 52 5-10
IMPERIAL (5100 series): 50 4-8
IMPERIAL (5269; "When I've Been
  Drinkin'"): 53 .15-30
IMPERIAL (5290; "My Baby's
  Gone"): 53 10-20
INDEPENDENT: 49 10-15
MACY'S: 49 5-10
MERCURY: 51 .10-20
METEOR: 54 20-30
MODERN: 48-52 5-15

RAY'S RECORD: 52 . . . .$15-25
RECORDED IN HOLLYWOOD: 52 5-10
SHOW TIME: 54 10-20
SITTIN' IN WITH: 51-52 4-8
SPECIALTY (300 series): 49 5-10
TOP HAT: 52 10-15
Singles: 7-Inch
CROWN: 54 25-45
EBB: 58 10-15
FEDERAL: 53 25-50
IMPERIAL (5269; "When I've Been
  Drinkin'"): 53 50-75
IMPERIAL (5290; "My Baby's
  Gone"): 53 20-40
MERCURY: 51 25-50
METEOR: 54 30-60
MODERN (884 through 924): 51-52 25-50
RAY'S RECORD: 52 25-50
SHOW TIME: 54 25-45
LPs: 10/12-Inch 33rpm
CROWN: 62 15-20
KENT: 10-12
TIME: 62 30-40
UNITED: 5-8

HOLDEN, Ron
(Ron Holden & The Thunderbirds)
Singles: 7-Inch
ABC: 73 1-3
CHALLENGE: 67 3-5
DONNA: 60 61 8-10
ELDO: 61 4-6
NITE OWL: 60 20-25
NOW: 74 2-3
RAMPART: 65 3-5
LPs: 10/12-Inch 33rpm
DONNA: 60 45-55
Also see ROSIE & RON

HOLIDAY, Billie
Singles: 78rpm
CLEF: 53-55 4-6
COLUMBIA: 51-52 4-6
DECCA: 45-52 5-10
DECCA (27000 series): 50-52 4-6
DECCA (48000 series): 51-52 4-6
MERCURY: 52-53 4-6
Singles: 7-Inch
CLEF: 53-55 4-8
COLUMBIA (30000 series): 51-52 4-8
DECCA (250; "Lover Man"): 52 20-40
(Boxed set of four singles.)
DECCA (27000 series): 50-52 4-8
DECCA (48000 series): 51-52 4-8
KENT: 73 1-3
MGM: 59 3-5

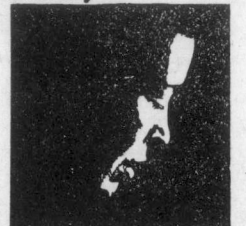

Hear her latest! MGM K12813

Billie Holiday SINGS DON'T WORRY 'BOUT ME AND JUST ONE MORE CHANCE

ORCHESTRA CONDUCTED BY RAY ELLIS

MERCURY (89000 series): *52-53* **$4-8**
UNITED ARTISTS: *72* **1-3**
VERVE: *59-62* **3-5**
Picture Sleeves
MGM: *59* **4-8**
EPs: 7-Inch 33/45rpm
CLEF: *53-54* **10-25**
COLUMBIA: *54-58* **10-25**
DECCA: *56* **5-15**
LPs: 10/12-Inch 33rpm
ALADDIN: *56* **40-60**
AMERICAN RECORDING
   SOCIETY: *56* **30-50**
ATLANTIC: *72* **5-10**
CLEF (118; "Favorites"): *53* **75-150**
   (10-Inch LPs.)
CLEF (144; "An Evening With
   Billie"): *53* **75-150**
   (10-Inch LP.)
CLEF (161; "Favorites"): *53* **75-150**
   (10-Inch LP.)
CLEF (600 & 700 series): *55-56* **30-50**
COLUMBIA (21; "The Golden
   Years"): *62* **20-40**
   (3-LP boxed set.)
COLUMBIA (40; "The Golden Years,
   Volume 2"): *66* **20-35**
   (3-LP boxed set.)
COLUMBIA (600 series): *54* **40-60**
   (Red label with gold colored printing.)
COLUMBIA (600 series): *56* **20-40**
   (Red label with black and white printing.)
COLUMBIA (2600 series): *67* **8-15**
COLUMBIA (6129; "Billie Holiday
   Sings"): *50* **100-150**
   (10-Inch LP.)
COLUMBIA (6163; "Billie Holiday
   Favorites"): *50* **100-150**
   (10-Inch LP.)

COLUMBIA (1100 series): *58* **$25-40**
COLUMBIA (30000 series): *72-73* . . . . . . **.8-15**
DECCA (100 series): *65* . . . . **.10-15**
DECCA (5345; "Lover Man"): *52* . . . . . . **.75-100**
   (10-Inch LP.)
DECCA (8000 series): *56-58* . . . . **.25-50**
DECCA (75000 series): *68* . . . . **.8-15**
ESP: *71-73* . . . . **.8-12**
EVEREST: *73-75* . . . . **.5-8**
HARMONY: *73* . . . . **.5-8**
JAZZTONE: *56* . . . . **.20-35**
JOLLY ROGER: *54* . . . . **.40-60**
KENT: *73* . . . . **.5-8**
MCA: *73* . . . . **.5-10**
MFSL: *87* . . . . **.15-20**
MGM (100 series): *70* . . . . **.6-10**
MGM (3700 series): *59* . . . . **.20-35**
MGM (4900 series): *74* . . . . **.5-8**
MAINSTREAM: *65* . . . . **.10-20**
METRO: *65* . . . . **.10-20**
MONMOUTH-EVERGREEN: *72* . . . . . . **.5-10**
PARAMOUNT: *73* . . . . **.5-8**
RIC: *64* . . . . **.10-20**
SCORE: *57* . . . . **.25-50**
SOLID STATE: *69* . . . . **.8-12**
TRIP: *73* . . . . **.5-8**
UNITED ARTISTS (5600 series): *72* . . . . **.5-10**
UNITED ARTISTS (14000 & 15000
   series): *62* . . . . **.20-30**
VSP: *66* . . . . **.8-15**
VERVE: *57-60* . . . . **.20-40**
   (Reads "Verve Records, Inc." at bottom of label.)
VERVE: *61-72* . . . . **.10-25**
   (Reads "MGM Records - A Division Of Metro-
   Goldwyn-Mayer, Inc." at bottom of label.)
VERVE: *73-84* . . . . **.5-10**
   (Reads "Manufactured By MGM Record Corp.," or
   mentions either Polydor or Polygram at bottom of
   label.)
   Also see FITZGERALD, Ella / Billie Holiday
   Also see FITZGERALD, Ella / Billie
Holiday / Lena Horne

HOLIDAY, Billie, & Stan Getz
LPs: 10/12-Inch 33rpm
DALE (25; "Billie & Stan"): *51* . . . . **.75-125**
   Also see GETZ, Stan

HOLIDAY, Billie, & Eddie Heywood
LPs: 10/12-Inch 33rpm
COMMODORE (20005; "Billie
   Holiday, Volume 1"): *50* . . . . **.75-100**
   (10-Inch LP.)
COMMODORE (20006; "Billie
   Holiday, Volume 2"): *50* . . . . **.75-100**
   (10-Inch LP.)

COMMODORE (30000 series): *59* $20-40
Also see HEYWOOD, Eddie

HOLIDAY, Billie, & Al Hibbler
LPs: 10/12-Inch 33rpm
IMPERIAL: *62* 15-25
SUNSET: *67* 8-15
Also see HIBBLER, Al
Also see HOLIDAY, Billie

HOLIDAY, Chico
Singles: 7-Inch
CORAL: *61-63* 2-4
KARATE: *65* 2-4
RCA VICTOR: *59* 3-5
SHAMLEY: *69* 2-4

HOLIDAY, Jimmy
Singles: 7-Inch
DIPLOMACY: *65* 3-5
EVEREST: *63-65* 3-5
KENT: *68* 3-5
MINIT: *66-68* 3-5
LPs: 10/12-Inch 33rpm
MINIT: *66* 15-20

HOLIDAY, Jimmy, & Clydie King
Singles: 7-Inch
MINIT: *67* 3-5
Also see HOLIDAY, Jimmy

HOLIDAYS
Singles: 7-Inch
GOLDEN WORLD: *66* 4-8
Members: Edwin Starr; Steve Mancha; J.J. Barnes.
Also see BARNES, J.J., & Steve Mancha
Also see STARR, Edwin

HOLIEN, Danny
Singles: 7-Inch
TUMBLEWEED: *72* 2-3

HOLLAND, Amy
Singles: 7-Inch
CAPITOL: *80-83* 1-3
Picture Sleeves
CAPITOL: *80* 1-3
LPs: 10/12-Inch 33rpm
CAPITOL: *80-83* 5-8
Also see McDONALD, Michael

HOLLAND, Brian
(Bryant Holland)
Singles: 7-Inch
INVICTUS: *73* 2-3
KUDO: *58* 8-12
Also see HOLLAND-DOZIER

HOLLAND, Eddie
Singles: 7-Inch
MERCURY: *58* $10-20
MOTOWN: *61-64* 5-8
TAMLA (102; "Merry-Go-
Round"): *59* 50-65
UNITED ARTISTS: *59-61* 5-10
Picture Sleeves
MOTOWN: *62* 10-20
LPs: 10/12-Inch 33rpm
MOTOWN: *63* 25-35

HOLLAND, Eddie, & Lamont Dozier
(Holland-Dozier With The Four Tops)
Singles: 7-Inch
MOTOWN: *63* 15-20
Also see DOZIER, Lamont
Also see FOUR TOPS
Also see HOLLAND, Eddie

HOLLAND-DOZIER
Singles: 7-Inch
INVICTUS: *72-73* 2-4
Members: Brian Holland; Lamont Dozier
Also see HOLLAND, Brian
Also see HOLLAND, Eddie, & Lamont Dozier

HOLLIDAY, Jennifer
Singles: 12-Inch 33/45rpm
GEFFEN: *83-86* 4-6
Singles: 7-Inch
GEFFEN: *82-87* 1-3
LPs: 10/12-Inch 33rpm
GEFFEN: *82-86* 5-8

HOLLIES
Singles: 7-Inch
ATLANTIC: *83* 1-3
EPIC (10000 series, except
10716): *67-74* 3-6
EPIC (10716; "Survival Of
The Fittest"): *71* 8-10
EPIC (50000 series): *75-78* 2-4
IMPERIAL (66026 through
66070): *64-65* 10-15
IMPERIAL (66099; "Yes I Will"): *65* ... 20-40
IMPERIAL (66119 through
66258): *66-68* 5-10
IMPERIAL (66271; "If I Needed
Someone"): *65* 20-40
LIBERTY: *64* 25-40
Picture Sleeves
EPIC: *67-68* 4-8
IMPERIAL: *67* 5-10
LPs: 10/12-Inch 33rpm
ATLANTIC: *83* 5-8
CAPITOL: *80* 5-8

The Hollies

EPIC (24315; "Evolution"): *67* **$15-25**
(Monaural.)
EPIC (26315; "Evolution"): *67* **15-20**
(Stereo.)
EPIC (26538; "He Ain't Heavy He's
My Brother"): *70* **10-15**
EPIC (30255; "Moving Finger"): *71* **10-15**
EPIC (30958; "Distant Light"): *72* **10-20**
(With a "KE" prefix. Gatefold cover.)
EPIC (30958; "Distant Light"): *77* **5-10**
(With an "AL" prefix. Standard cover.)
EPIC (31000 through 35000 series): *73-78* **6-12**
IMPERIAL: *64-67* **25-50**
LIBERTY: *84* **5-8**
 Also see CLARKE, Allan
 Also see NASH, Graham
 Also see SPRINGSTEEN, Bruce / Johnny
Winter / Hollies

HOLLIES / Peter Sellers
Singles: 7-Inch
UNITED ARTISTS (50079; "After
The Fox"): *66* **10-20**
LPs: 10/12-Inch 33rpm
UNITED ARTISTS (286; "After The
Fox"): *74* **8-10**
(Soundtrack.)
UNITED ARTISTS (4148; "After The
Fox"): *66* **20-35**
(Soundtrack. Monaural.)

UNITED ARTISTS (5148; "After The
Fox"): *66* **$25-40**
(Soundtrack. Stereo.)
Also see HOLLIES

HOLLOWAY, Brenda
(Brenda Holloway & The Carrolls)
Singles: 7-Inch
BREVIT: *63* **4-6**
CATCH: *64* **5-10**
DONNA: *62* **5-10**
TAMLA: *64-67* **3-5**
LPs: 10/12-Inch 33rpm
TAMLA: *65* **20-25**

HOLLOWAY, Brenda, & Jess Harris
Singles: 7-Inch
BREVIT: *63* **3-5**
 Also see HOLLOWAY, Brenda

HOLLOWAY, Loleatta
(Loleatta Holloway & The Salsoul Orchestra)
Singles: 12-Inch 33/45rpm
SALSOUL: *83* **4-6**
STREETWISE: *84* **4-6**
Singles: 7-Inch
AWARE: *73-75* **2-3**
GRC: *73* **2-3**
GALAXY: *71* **2-4**
GOLD MINE: *76-77* **1-3**
SALSOUL: *77-83* **1-3**

LPs: 10/12-Inch 33rpm
GOLD MINE: 77 .... $5-8
  Also see SALSOUL ORCHESTRA

HOLLOWAY, Loleatta, & Bunny Sigler
Singles: 7-Inch
GOLD MINE: 78 1-3
  Also see HOLLOWAY, Loleatta
  Also see SIGLER, Bunny

HOLLY, Buddy
(Buddy Holly & The Crickets; Buddy Holly &
The Three Tunes)
Singles: 12-Inch 33/45rpm
SOLID SMOKE: 79 5-8
Singles: 78rpm
BRUNSWICK (55009; "That'll Be
  The Day"): 57 40-50
BRUNSWICK (55035; "Oh Boy"): 58 ... 40-50
BRUNSWICK (55053; "Maybe
  Baby"): 58 40-50
BRUNSWICK (55072; "Think It
  Over"): 58 40-50
BRUNSWICK (55094; "It's So
  Easy"): 58 40-50
CORAL (61852; "Words Of Love"): 57 .. 60-80
CORAL (61885; "Peggy Sue"): 57 40-50
CORAL (61947; "Listen To Me"): 58 .. 40-50
CORAL (61985; "Rave On"): 58 40-50
CORAL (62006; "Early In The
  Morning"): 58 40-50
CORAL (62051; "Heartbeat"): 58 40-50
DECCA (29854; "Blue Days - Black
  Nights"): 56 50-75
DECCA (30166; "Modern Don
  Juan"): 56 50-75
DECCA (30434; "That'll Be
  The Day"): 57 50-75
DECCA (30543; "Love Me"): 58 50-75
DECCA (30650; "Ting-A-Ling"): 58 50-75
Note: All Buddy Holly 78rpms were simultaneously issued on 45rpm.
Singles: 7-Inch
BRUNSWICK (55009; "That'll Be
  The Day"): 57 10-15
BRUNSWICK (55035; "Oh Boy"): 58 ... 10-15
BRUNSWICK (55053; "Maybe
  Baby"): 58 10-15
BRUNSWICK (55072; "Think It
  Over"): 58 10-15
BRUNSWICK (55094; "It's So
  Easy"): 58 10-15
CORAL (61852; "Words Of
  Love"): 57 100-125
CORAL (61885; "Peggy Sue"): 57 10-15
CORAL (61947; "Listen To Me"): 58 ... 10-15

CORAL (61985; "Rave On"): 58 ...... $15-20
CORAL (62006; "Early In The
  Morning"): 58 10-15
CORAL (62051; "Heartbeat"): 58 10-15
CORAL (62074; "It Doesn't Matter
  Anymore"): 59 10-15
CORAL (62143; "Peggy Sue Got
  Married"): 59 15-20
CORAL (62210; "True Love Ways"): 60 20-25
CORAL (62329; "Reminiscing"): 62 15-20
CORAL (62352; "Bo Diddley"): 63 25-30
CORAL (62369; "Brown Eyed
  Handsome Man"): 63 20-25
CORAL (62390; "Rock Around
  With Ollie Vee"): 64 25-30
CORAL (62407; "Maybe Baby"): 64 20-25
CORAL (62448; "Slippin' &
  Slidin'"): 65 40-50
CORAL (62554; "Rave On"): 68 15-18
CORAL (62558; "Love Is Strange"): 69 .. 8-10
CORAL (65618; "That'll Be The Day"): 69 5-8
DECCA (29854; "Blue Days - Black
  Nights"): 56 60-70
DECCA (30166; "Modern Don
  Juan"): 56 40-50
DECCA (30434; "That'll Be
  The Day"): 57 75-100
DECCA (30543; "Love Me"): 58 35-45
DECCA (30650; "Ting-A-Ling"): 58 ... 40-50
MCA: 73-78 2-3
Promotional Singles
BRUNSWICK (55009; "That'll Be
  The Day"): 57 35-50
BRUNSWICK (55035; "Oh Boy"): 58 .. 35-50
BRUNSWICK (55053; "Maybe
  Baby"): 58 35-50
BRUNSWICK (55072; "Think It
  Over"): 58 35-50
BRUNSWICK (55094; "It's So
  Easy"): 58 35-50
CORAL (61852; "Words Of
  Love"): 57 80-100
CORAL (61885; "Peggy Sue"): 57 15-25
CORAL (61947; "Listen To Me"): 58 ... 15-25
CORAL (61985; "Rave On"): 58 15-25
CORAL (62006; "Early In
  The Morning"): 58 15-25
CORAL (62051; "Heartbeat"): 58 15-25
CORAL (62074; "It Doesn't Matter
  Anymore"): 59 15-25
CORAL (62134; "Peggy Sue Got
  Married"): 59 15-25
CORAL (62210; "True Love Ways"): 60 15-25
CORAL (62329; "Reminiscing"): 62 15-25

CORAL (62352; "Bo Diddley"): *63* **$15-25**
CORAL (62369; "Brown Eyed
Handsome Man"): *63* **15-25**
CORAL (62390; "Rock Around
With Ollie Vee"): *64* **20-25**
CORAL (62407; "Maybe Baby"): *64* **15-25**
CORAL (62448; "Slippin' &
Slidin'"): *65* **20-25**
CORAL (62554; "Rave On"): *68* **15-25**
CORAL (62558; "Love Is Strange"): *69* . **10-20**
CORAL (65618; "That'll Be
The Day"): *69* **10-20**
DECCA (29854; "Blue Days - Black
Nights"): *56* **50-60**
DECCA (30166; "Modern Don
Juan"): *56* **35-50**
DECCA (30434; "That'll Be
The Day"): *57* **50-75**
DECCA (30543; "Love Me"): *58* **35-50**
DECCA (30650; "Ting-A-Ling"): *58* ..:. **35-50**
Picture Sleeves
CORAL (62558; "Love Is Strange"): *69* . **10-15**
MCA: *78* **3-5**
EPs: 7-Inch 33/45rpm
BRUNSWICK (71036; "The Chirping
Crickets"): *57* **100-200**
BRUNSWICK (71038; "The Sound
Of The Crickets"): *58* **100-200**
CORAL (81169; "Listen To Me"): *58* . **200-300**
CORAL (81182; "The Buddy
Holly Story"): *59* **150-250**
CORAL (81191; "Buddy Holly"): *62* .. **150-250**
CORAL (81193; "Brown Eyed
Handsome Man"): *63* **100-200**
DECCA (2575; "That'll Be
The Day"): *58* **500-750**
(With liner notes on the back cover.)
DECCA (2575; "That'll Be
The Day"): *58* **400-600**
(With EP ads on the back cover.)
LPs: 10/12-Inch 33rpm
BRUNSWICK (54038; "The Chirping
Crickets"): *57* **200-300**
CORAL (8; "The Best Of
Buddy Holly"): *66* **75-125**
CORAL (57210; "Buddy Holly"): *58* ... **75-125**
(Maroon label.)
CORAL (57279; "The Buddy
Holly Story"): *59* **50-75**
(Maroon label. With red & black print on the back
cover.)
CORAL (57279; "The Buddy
Holly Story"): *59* **30-55**
(Maroon label. With black print on the back cover.)

CORAL (57279; "The Buddy
Holly Story"): *63* **$25-35**
(Black label. With pictures of other LPs on the
back cover.)
CORAL (57326; "The Buddy
Holly Story Vol. II"): *60* **100-125**
(Maroon label.)
CORAL (57326; "The Buddy
Holly Story Vol. II"): *63* **25-50**
(Black label.)
CORAL (57405; "Buddy Holly
And The Crickets"): *62* **50-75**
(Maroon label.)
CORAL (57405; "Buddy Holly
And The Crickets"): *63* **25-45**
(Black label.)
CORAL (57426; "Reminiscing"): *63* ... **50-75**
(Maroon label.)
CORAL (57426; "Reminiscing"): *63* ... **20-40**
(Black label.)
CORAL (57450; "Showcase"): *64* **40-50**
CORAL (57463; "Holly In
The Hills"): *65* **75-100**
CORAL (57492; "Buddy Holly's
Greatest Hits"): *67* **75-100**
CORAL (757279; "The Buddy
Holly Story"): *63* **25-35**
(Stereo.)
CORAL (757405; "Buddy Holly
And The Crickets"): *62* **50-75**
(Maroon label. Stereo.)
CORAL (757405; "Buddy Holly
And The Crickets"): *63* **25-45**
(Black label. Stereo.)
CORAL (757463; "Holly In
The Hills"): *65* **40-60**
(Stereo.)
CORAL (757504; "Giant"): *69* **40-80**
(Stereo.)
CREATIVE RADIO ("The Day The
Music Died"): **25-30**
(2-LP set, includes poster.)
DECCA (207; "A Rock & Roll
Collection"): *72* **15-20**
DECCA (8707; "That'll Be
The Day"): *58* **200-300**
(Black label.)
MCA (Except 6-80000): *75-85* **8-12**
MCA (6-80000; "The Complete
Buddy Holly"): *81* **30-40**
(6-LP boxed set.)
VOCALION (3811; "The Great
Buddy Holly"): *67* **90-110**
(Monaural.)

VOCALION (73811; "The Great
Buddy Holly"): 67 ....$20-30
(Reprocessed stereo.)
VOCALION (73923; "Good Rockin'
Buddy Holly"): 71 80-100
Promotional LPs
BRUNSWICK (54038; "The Chirping
Crickets"): 57 200-250
CORAL (Except 757504): 58-65 50-75
CORAL (757504; "Giant"): 69 35-45
DECCA (8707, "That'll Be
The Day"): 58 350-450
(Pink label.)
PICK (1111; "Buddy Holly & The
Picks"): 86 10-12
Also see BEATLES / Beach Boys / Buddy
Holly
Also see CRICKETS
Also see DAVIS, Sherry
Also see JENNINGS, Waylon
Also see PETTY, Norman, Trio
Also see PRESLEY, Elvis / Buddy Holly

HOLLY, Pete, & The Looks
Singles: 7 Inch
BOMP: 87 1-3
Picture Sleeves
BOMP: 87 1-3

HOLLY & THE ITALIANS
(Featuring Holly Beth Vincent)
Singles: 7-Inch
VIRGIN: 82 1-3
LPs: 10/12-Inch 33rpm
VIRGIN: 82 5-8

HOLLYRIDGE STRINGS
(Stu Phillips & The Hollyridge Strings)
Singles: 7-Inch
CAPITOL: 61-68 2-4
LPs: 10/12-Inch 33rpm
CAPITOL: 64-78 5-15
Also see GOLDEN GATE STRINGS
Also see PHILLIPS, Stu

HOLLYWOOD ARGYLES
Singles: 7-Inch
ABC: 74 1-3
CHATTAHOOCHEE: 65 3-5
ERA: 72 1-3
FELSTED: 63 3-5
FINER ARTS: 61 3-5
LUTE: 60 4-6
PAXLEY: 61 4-6
LPs: 10/12-Inch 33rpm
LUTE (9001; "Alley Oop"): 60 150-250
Member: Gary Paxton.

Buddy Holly

Also see NEW HOLLYWOOD ARGYLES

HOLLYWOOD FLAMES
Singles: 78rpm
DECCA: 54-55 ....$15-30
EBB: 57-59 5-10
LUCKY (001; "One Night With
A Fool"): 54 50-100
LUCKY (006; "Peggy"): 54 50-100
LUCKY (009; "Let's Talk It Over"): 54 . 40-60
SWING TIME (345; "Let's Talk
It Over"): 53 50-100
Singles: 7-Inch
ATCO: 59-60 4-8
CHESS: 61 3-5
DECCA: 54-55 40-60
EBB: 57-59 10-15
GOLDIE: 62 3-6
LUCKY (001; "One Night With
A Fool"): 54 150-250
LUCKY (006; "Peggy"): 54 125-200
LUCKY (009; "Let's Talk It
Over"): 54 100-175
SWING TIME (345; "Let's Talk
It Over"): 53 150-250
SYMBOL: 65-66 3-5
VEE JAY: 63 3-5
LPs: 10/12-Inch 33rpm
SPECIALTY: 88 6-10
Members: David Ford; Bobby Byrd; Gaynel
Hodge; Clyde Tillis; Earl Nelson; Curtis Williams;

Don Height; Ray Brewster; John Berry; George
Home.
Also see BYRD, Bobby

HOLLYWOOD STARS
Singles: 7-Inch
ARISTA: 77 .... $1-3
LPs: 10/12-Inch 33rpm
ARISTA: 77 8-10
Also see KINKS / Hollywood Stars

HOLLYWOOD STUDIO ORCHESTRA
Singles: 7-Inch
UNITED ARTISTS: 59 1-3
LPs: 10/12-Inch 33rpm
UNITED ARTISTS: 61 5-12

HOLM, Michael
Singles: 7-Inch
MERCURY: 74 2-3

HOLMAN, Eddie
Singles: 7-Inch
ABC: 69-71 2-4
AGAPE: 82 1-3
ASCOT: 63 3-5
BELL: 68 3-5
GSF: 73 2-4
PARKWAY: 65-67 3-5
SALSOUL: 77 1-3
SILVER BLUE: 74 2-3
LPs: 10/12-Inch 33rpm
ABC-PARAMOUNT: 70 10-12
SALSOUL: 77 5-8

HOLMES, Cecil
(Cecil Holmes' Soulful Sounds)
Singles: 7-Inch
BUDDAH: 73 2-3
LPs: 10/12-Inch 33rpm
BUDDAH: 73 6-12

HOLMES, Clint
Singles: 7-Inch
EPIC: 73 2-3
LPs: 10/12-Inch 33rpm
EPIC: 73 10-12

HOLMES, Jake
Singles: 7-Inch
COLUMBIA: 71-72 2-3
POLYDOR: 70 2-3
TOWER: 67 2-4
Picture Sleeves
TOWER: 67 3-5
LPs: 10/12-Inch 33rpm
POLYDOR: 70 8-12

HOLMES, Jan

Singles: 7-Inch
JAY JAY: 85 .... $1-3

HOLMES, Leroy, Orchestra
Singles: 78rpm
MGM: 51-57 2-4
Singles: 7-Inch
MGM: 51-61 2-4
METRO: 59 2-3
UNITED ARTISTS: 67-68 2-4
Picture Sleeves
UNITED ARTISTS: 67 4-8
EPs: 7-Inch 33/45rpm
MGM: 52-56 3-6
LPs: 10/12-Inch 33rpm
LION: 59-60 5-10
MGM: 52-62 5-15
UNITED ARTISTS: 67-68 4-8

HOLMES, Richard "Groove"
Singles: 7-Inch
BLUE NOTE: 71 2-3
FLYING DUTCHMAN: 76 1-3
PACIFIC JAZZ: 61-69 2-4
PRESTIGE: 66-69 2-4
LPs: 10/12-Inch 33rpm
BLUE NOTE: 71 5-10
FLYING DUTCHMAN: 75-76 5-8
GROOVE MERCHANT: 72-75 5-10
LOMA: 66 10-15
MUSE: 78-80 5-8
PACIFIC JAZZ (Except 20000
  series): 61-62 15-25
PACIFIC JAZZ (20000 series): 68-69 ... 8-15
PRESTIGE: 66-70 8-15
VERSATILE: 78 5-8
WARNER BROS: 64 10-20
WORLD PACIFIC JAZZ: 70 8-12
  Also see AMMONS, Gene, & Richard
"Groove" Holmes
  Also see JONES, Brenda, & "Groove" Holmes
  Also see MC GRIFF, Jimmy
  Also see WITHERSPOON, Jimmy

HOLMES, Richard "Groove," &
Les McCann
LPs: 10/12-Inch 33rpm
PACIFIC JAZZ: 62 15-25
  Also see HOLMES, Richard "Groove"
  Also see MC CANN, Les

HOLMES, Rupert
Singles: 7-Inch
EPIC: 74-76 3-6
INFINITY: 79 1-3
MCA: 80-81 1-3
PRIVATE STOCK: 78 1-3

Picture Sleeves
EPIC: 75 ....$2-3
LPs: 10/12-Inch 33rpm
ELEKTRA: 81 5-8
EPIC: 74-75 8-12
INFINITY: 79 5-8
MCA: 80 5-8
PRIVATE STOCK: 78 5-8
 Also see STREET PEOPLE

HOMBRES
Singles: 7-Inch
VERVE/FORECAST: 67-68 3-5
LPs: 10/12-Inch 33rpm
VERVE/FORECAST: 67 15-20

HOMER & JETHRO
Singles: 78rpm
KING: 46-53 5-15
FEDERAL: 51 8-15
RCA VICTOR: 50-58 5-10
Singles: 7-Inch
BLUEBIRD: 59 3-5
KING: 63 2-4
RCA VICTOR (0100 series): 50 10-20
(Colored vinyl.)
RCA VICTOR (0100 through 0400
 series): 50 5-10
(Black vinyl.)
RCA VICTOR (0500 series): 71 2-3
RCA VICTOR (4200 through 7500
 series): 51-59 5-15
RCA VICTOR (7600 through
 9900 series): 59-70 3-6
EPs: 7-Inch 33/45rpm
AUDIO LAB: 59 10-20
KING: 58 10-20
RCA VICTOR: 53-57 10-20
Picture Sleeves
RCA VICTOR (5000 series): 53 8-12
RCA VICTOR (8000 series): 64 3-6
LPs: 10/12-Inch 33rpm
AUDIO LAB: 58 20-30
CAMDEN: 62-71 10-18
DIPLOMAT: 8-12
GUEST STAR: 63 10-15
KING (600 series): 59 20-25
KING (800 series): 63 12-18
KING (1000 series): 67 8-12
NASHVILLE: 69 8-12
RCA VICTOR (1400 & 1500 series): 57 .25-40
RCA VICTOR (1400 through 1800
 series): 57-58 25-40
RCA VICTOR (2100 through 2900
 series): 60-64 12-20

RCA VICTOR (3100 series): 53 ......$40-50
(10-Inch LP.)
RCA VICTOR (3300 through 4600
 series): 65-72 8-15
Members: Henry "Homer" Haynes; Kenneth
"Jethro" Burns.
 Also see FOUR LOVERS

HONDELLS
Singles: 7-Inch
AMOS: 69-70 4-6
COLUMBIA: 67-68 4-6
MERCURY (Except 72563 &
 72605): 64-66 8-12
MERCURY (72563; "Younger Girl"): 67 ..5-8
MERCURY (72605; "Kissin' My
 Life Away"): 67 5-8
Promotional Singles
MERCURY (72324; "Hot Rod High"): 67 5-10
(White label. Shows *Hot Rod High* as the "A" side
instead of *Little Honda*.)
Picture Sleeves
MERCURY: 64-65 15-25
LPs: 10/12-Inch 33rpm
MERCURY: 64-65 25-35
Members: Gary Usher; Chuck Girard; Richie
Burns; Brian Wilson.
 Also see ALLEN, David
 Also see WILSON, Brian

HONDELLS / Del Shannon / Martha & The Vandellas
EPs: 7-Inch 33/45rpm
PEPSI-COLA (8256; "Pepsi-Cola Ad
 Radio Youth Market, 1966"): 66 10-20
(Promotional issue only.)
 Also see HONDELLS
 Also see MARTHA & THE VANDELLAS
 Also see SHANNON, Del

HONEY CONE
Singles: 7-Inch
HOT WAX: 69-76 2-4
LPs: 10/12-Inch 33rpm
HOT WAX: 70-72 8-10
Members: Edna Wright; Sharon Cash.

HONEYCOMBS
Singles: 7-Inch
INTERPHON: 64-65 5-8
WARNER BROS: 65-66 4-6
Picture Sleeves
INTERPHON: 64 10-15
LPs: 10/12-Inch 33rpm
INTERPHON: 64 20-25
VEE JAY: 64 35-45
Members: Honey; John; Martin; Denis; Alan.

HONEYCONES
Singles: 7-Inch
EMBER: *58-59* $8-10

HONEYCUTT, Miki
Singles: 7-Inch
PAULA: *77* 2-3

HONEYDRIPPERS
Singles: 7-Inch
ESPARANZA: *84-85* 1-3
Picture Sleeves
ESPARANZA: *84-85* 1-3
LPs: 10/12-Inch 33rpm
ESPARANZA: *84* 5-8
Members: Jeff Beck; Jimmy Page; Robert Plant;
Nile Rodgers.
Also see BECK, Jeff
Also see CHIC
Also see PAGE, Jimmy
Also see PLANT, Robert
Also see RODGERS, Nile

HONEYMOON SUITE
Singles: 7-Inch
WARNER BROS: *84-88* 1-3
LPs: 10/12-Inch 33rpm
WARNER BROS: *84-88* 5-8

HOOK, Dr.: see DR. HOOK

HOOKER, Frank
& The Positive People
Singles: 7-Inch
PANORAMA: *79-80* 1-3

HOOKER, John Lee
Singles: 78rpm
CHART: *53* 4-8
CHESS: *52-54* 15-30
JVB: *53* 15-30
MODERN: *48-56* 5-12
REGAL: *50-51* 5-10
SENSATION: *49-50* 5-10
SPECIALTY: *54* 5-10
Singles: 7-Inch
ABC: *71-73* 2-3
BATTLE: *62* 3-5
BLUESWAY: *67-69* 3-5
CHART: *53* 5-8
CHESS (1505; "High Priced
  Woman"): *52* 40-60
CHESS (1513; "Walkin' The
  Boogie"): *52* 30-50
CHESS (1562; "It's My Own Fault"): *54* . 20-30
CHESS (1900 series): *66* 3-5
FEDERAL: *60* 3-5
FORTUNE: *60* 3-5

GALAXY: *63* $3-5
HI-Q: *61* 3-5
JVB (30; "Boogie Rambler"): *53* 25-40
JEWEL: *70-77* 2-3
LAUREN: *61* 3-5
MODERN (800 series): *51-52* 25-50
MODERN (900 series): *53-56* 20-30
SPECIALTY: *54* 10-20
STARDAY: *70* 2-4
STAX: *69* 2-4
VEE JAY (Maroon label): *55-60* 10-20
VEE JAY (Black label): *60-65* 5-10
EPs: 7-Inch 33/45rpm
IMPULSE: *66* 8-10
(Jukebox issues only.)
LPs: 10/12-Inch 33rpm
ABC: *71-74* 8-12
ARCHIVE OF FOLK MUSIC: *68* 10-12
ATCO: *63* 25-30
ATLANTIC: *72* 8-10
BATTLE: 10-12
BLUESWAY: *66-73* 10-15
BRYLEN: *84* 5-8
BUDDAH: *69* 12-15
CHESS (1400 series): *61-63* 20-30
CHESS (1500 series): *66* 15-20
CROWN: *62-63* 10-15
CUSTOM: 12-15
EVEREST: *79-83* 5-8
EXODUS: 8-10
FANTASY: *72-77* 8-10
FORTUNE: *69* 8-12
GNP/CRESCENDO: *74* 8-10
GALAXY: *63* 20-25
GREEN BOTTLE: *72* 10-12
IMPULSE: *66* 12-15
JEWEL: *71* 10-12
KENT: *71* 10-12
KING (700 series): *61* 20-25
KING (1000 series): *70* 10-12
MCA: *83* 5-8
MUSE: *80* 5-8
SPECIALTY: *70* 10-12
(Specialty LP reissues, using original catalog num-
bers, are currently available.)
STAX (2000 series): *69* 10-12
STAX (4000 series): *77* 8-10
TOMATO: *78* 5-8
TRADITION: *69* 10-12
TRIP: *73-78* 8-10
UNITED: 10-12
UNITED ARTISTS: *71-73* 12-15
VEE JAY (1007; "I'm John Lee
  Hooker"): *59* 30-35
(Maroon label.)

VEE JAY (1007; "I'm John Lee
Hooker"): *61* **$15-20**
(Black label.)
VEE JAY (1023 through 1043): *60-62* . . . **25-30**
VEE JAY (1049 through 1078): *62-64* . . . **15-20**
VERVE/FOLKWAYS: *66* **10-15**
WAND: *70* **10-12**
Also see MC GHEE, Sticks / John Lee Hooker

HOOKER, John Lee & Canned Heat
Singles: 7-Inch
UNITED ARTISTS: *71* **2-3**
LPs: 10/12-Inch 33rpm
LIBERTY: *71* **10-12**
RHINO: *82* **5-8**
Also see CANNED HEAT

HOOKER, John Lee / Lightnin'
Hopkins / J. Carroll
LPs: 10/12-Inch 33rpm
GUEST STAR: *64* **15-20**
Also see HOPKINS, Lightnin'

HOOKER, John Lee, & Little
Eddie Kirkland
Singles: 7-Inch
MODERN: *52* **25-40**
Also see HOOKER, John Lee

HOOPER, Stix
Singles: 7-Inch
MCA: *79-82* **1-3**
LPs: 10/12-Inch 33rpm
MCA: *79-82* **5-8**
Also see BUTLER, Jerry, & Stix Hooper
Also see CRUSADERS

HOOTERS
Singles: 7-Inch
COLUMBIA: *85-87* **1-3**
MONTAGE: *83* **1-3**
LPs: 10/12-Inch 33rpm
COLUMBIA: *85-87* **5-8**
Also see LAUPER, Cyndi

HOPE, Ellie
Singles: 12-Inch 33/45rpm
QUALITY: *83* **4-6**

HOPE, Lynn
(Lynn Hope Quintet)
Singles: 78rpm
ALADDIN: *54-56* **4-6**
PREMIUM : *50* **3-6**
Singles: 7-Inch
ALADDIN: *54-56* **5-10**
KING: *60* **3-6**

LPs: 10/12-Inch 33rpm
ALADDIN (707; "Lynn Hope & His
Tenor Sax"): *55* **$75-100**
ALADDIN (850; "Lynn Hope"): *56* . . . **75-100**
IMPERIAL: *62* **15-20**
KING: *61* **15-20**
SCORE: *57* **20-25**

HOPKIN, Mary
(Mark Hopkins)
Singles: 7-Inch
APPLE: *68-72* **3-6**
ESKEE: *66* **3-6**
POCKET DISC: *69* **3-6**
RCA VICTOR: *76* **2-3**
Picture Sleeves
APPLE: *68-70* **3-6**
LPs: 10/12-Inch 33rpm
AIR: *72* **8-10**
APPLE: *69-72* **10-12**

HOPKINS, Lightnin'
Singles: 78rpm
ACE: *56* **5-10**
ALADDIN (100 & 200 series): *47-54* **5-10**
CHART: *55* **4-8**
DECCA: *53* **5-10**
GOLD STAR (Except 671): *47-50* **5-8**
GOLD STAR (671; "Henny Penny
Blues"): *49* **15-20**
MODERN: *47-49* . . . . : **5-10**
Singles: 7-Inch
ACE: *56* **10-20**
ALADDIN (3063; "Shotgun"): *50* **25-50**
ALADDIN (3077 through 3262): *51-54* . **15-25**
ARHOOLIE: *65* **3-5**
BLUESVILLE: *60-63* **3-5**
CANDID: *60-62* **3-5**
CHART: *55* **8-12**

DART: *60* $3-5
DECCA: *53* 10-20
FIRE: *61* 3-5
FLASHBACK: *65* 1-3
HARLEM (2321; "Contrary
  Mary"): *55* 75-100
HARLEM (2324; "Lightnin's
  Boogie"): *55* 75-100
HARLEM (2331; "Fast Life"): *55* 75-100
HARLEM (2336; "Old Woman
  Blues"): *55* 75-100
LIGHTNING (104; "Unsuccessful
  Blues"): *55* 200-300
HERALD (400 series): *54-58* 15-25
HERALD (500 series): *59-60* 8-15
IMPERIAL: *62* 5-15
IVORY: *61* 5-10
JAX (315; "No Good Woman"): *53* ... 100-150
  (Colored vinyl.)
JAX (318; "Automobile"): *53* 100-150
  (Colored vinyl.)
JAX (321; "Contrary Mary"): *53* 100-150
  (Colored vinyl.)
JAX (635; "Coffee Blues"): *53* 75-100
JEWEL: *68-72* 2-4
KENT: 2-4
KIMBERLEY: *60* 3-5
LIGHTNING (104; "Unsuccessful
  Blues"): *49* 200-300
MERCURY: *52* 20-40
PRESTIGE: *60-67* 3-5
RPM (337 through 351): *51-52* 25-40
RPM (359 through 398): *52-54* 20-30
SHAD: *59* 4-8
SITTIN' IN WITH (621; "New York
  Boogie"): *51* 100-200
  (Colored vinyl.)
SITTIN' IN WITH (642; "You Caused (My
  Heart To Weep"): *52* 100-200
  (Colored vinyl.)
SITTIN' IN WITH (644; "Jailhouse
  Blues"): *52* 100-200
  (Colored vinyl.)
SITTIN' IN WITH (647; "Dirty
  House"): *52* 100-200
  (Colored vinyl.)
SITTIN' IN WITH (652; "Papa Bones
  Boogie"): *52* 100-200
  (Colored vinyl.)
SITTIN' IN WITH (658; "Broken Hearted
  Blues"): *53* 100-200
  (Colored vinyl.)
SITTIN' IN WITH (660; "I've Been A
  Bad Man"): *53* 100-200
  (Colored vinyl.)

SITTIN' IN WITH (661; "Down To
  The River"): *53* $100-200
  (Colored vinyl.)
TNT (8010; "Moanin' Blues"): *53* 200-300
VAULT: *70* 2-4
Note: Even among blues experts there is confusion
over which of the Jax and Sittin' In With singles
were pressed on colored plastic, which were on
black, and which came both ways.

LPs: 10/12-Inch 33rpm

ARHOOLIE: *68* 10-15
BARNABY: *71* 8-10
BULLDOG: *65* 12-15
CANDID: *61* 20-25
COLLECTABLES: *88* 6-8
CROWN: *61* 20-25
DART: 10-15
EVEREST (241; "Lightnin'
  Hopkins"): *69* 10-12
EVEREST (342; "Autobiography In
  Blues"): *79* 5-8
FANTASY: *72-81* 8-10
FIRE (104; "Mojo Hand"): *62* 50-75
GUEST STAR: *64* 15-20
HARLEM HITPARADE: 5-10
HERALD (1012; "Lightnin' &
  The Blues"): *60* 75-100
IMPERIAL: *62* 20-25
INTERNATIONAL ARTISTS: *68* 20-25
JAZZ MAN: *82* 5-8
JEWEL: *67-70* 10-12
MAINSTREAM: *71-74* 8-10
MOUNT VERNON: 15-20
OLYMPIC: *73* 8-10
POPPY: *69* 12-15
PRESTIGE: *65-70* 10-15
PRESTIGE/BLUESVILLE: *61-64* 20-25
RHINO: *82* 5-8
SCORE: 40-60
TIME: *60-62* 25-30
TOMATO: *77* 5-8
TRADITION (1035 through
  1040): *60* 20-25
TRADITION (1056 through
  2000): *67-72* 10-12
TRIP: *71-78* 5-8
UNITED: 8-10
UPFRONT: 8-12
VAULT: *69* 10-12
VEE JAY: *62* 20-25
VERVE: *62* 15-20
VERVE/FOLKWAYS: *65-67* 12-15
  Also see HOOKER, John Lee / Lightnin' Hop-
kins / Johnny Carroll

HOPKINS, Lightnin', & Thunder Smith
Singles: 78rpm
ALADDIN: *46* $5-10

HOPKINS, Lightnin', & Sonny Terry
LPs: 10/12-Inch 33rpm
PRESTIGE BLUESVILLE: *61-63* 15-20
  Also see HOPKINS, Lightnin'
  Also see TERRY, Sonny

HOPKINS, Nicky
Singles: 7-Inch
COLUMBIA: *72* 2-4
LPs: 10/12-Inch 33rpm
COLUMBIA: *73* 8-10
ROLLING STONE: *72* 10-12
  Also see LORD SUTCH
  Also see QUICKSILVER
  Also see ROLLING STONES

HORAN, Eddie
Singles: 7-Inch
HDM: *78* 1-3

HORN, Trevor, Paul Morley & The Art Of Noise
Singles: 7-Inch
ISLAND: *86* 1-3
  Also see ART OF NOISE

HORNE, Jimmy "Bo"
Singles: 12-Inch 33/45rpm
SUNSHINE SOUND: *79* 4-6
Singles: 7-Inch
ALSTON: *75-77* 2-4
SUNSHINE SOUND: *77-80* 1-3
LPs: 10/12-Inch 33rpm
SUNSHINE SOUND: *78-80* 5-8

HORNE, Lena
Singles: 78rpm
RCA VICTOR: *52-57* 3-5
Singles: 7-Inch
BUDDAH: *71* 1-3
CHARTER: *63* 2-4
DRG: *86* 1-3
GRYPHON: *76* 1-3
MCA: *78* 1-3
RCA VICTOR (4000 through 7000
  series): *52-61* 3-5
20TH CENTURY-FOX: *63-64* 2-4
UNITED ARTISTS: *65-66* 2-3
Picture Sleeves
RCA VICTOR: *62* 3-6
EPs: 7-Inch 33/45rpm
MGM: *54-55* 5-10
RCA VICTOR: *56-59* 5-10

LPs: 10/12-Inch 33rpm
BUDDAH: *71* $5-10
CAMDEN: *56* 10-20
CHARTER: *63* 10-15
CORONET: 5-10
DRG: *86* 5-8
GRYPHON: *75-76* 5-8
LIBERTY: *81* 4-8
MFSL: *82* 20-40
MGM: *54-55* 10-20
POLYDOR: 4-8
QWEST: *81* 5-10
RCA VICTOR (Except 4300
  series): *52-63* 10-20
RCA VICTOR (4300 series): *81* 4-8
SPRINGBOARD: *77* 4-8
20TH CENTURY-FOX: *64* 8-15
UNITED ARTISTS: *65-66* 8-15
  Also see FITZGERALD, Ella / Billie
Holiday / Lena Horne

HORNE, Lena, & Michel Legrand
LPs: 10/12-Inch 33rpm
GRYPHON: *75* 5-8
  Also see LEGRAND, Michel, & His Orchestra

HORNE, Lena, & Gabor Szabo
Singles: 7-Inch
SKYE: *70* 1-3
LPs: 10/12-Inch 33rpm
BUDDAH: *70-76* 6-12
SKYE: *70* 6-12
  Also see HORNE, Lena
  Also see SZABO, Gabor

HORNSBY, Bruce, & The Range
Singles: 7-Inch
RCA VICTOR: *86-88* 1-3
LPs: 10/12-Inch 33rpm
RCA VICTOR: *86-88* 5-8

HORSLIPS
Singles: 7-Inch
DJM (Black vinyl): *77-79* 2-3
DJM (Colored vinyl): *77* 3-5
  (Promotional issues only.)
MERCURY: *79* 2-3
RCA VICTOR: *75* 2-3
LPs: 10/12-Inch 33rpm
ATCO: *73-74* 10-12
DJM: *77-79* 5-8
MERCURY: *79-80* 5-8
RCA VICTOR: *74* 8-10

HORTON, Jamie
Singles: 7-Inch
ERIC: *68* 1-3
JOY: *59-61* 8-10

HORTON, Johnny

Singles: 78rpm

ABBOTT: *53* $5-10
COLUMBIA: *56-57* 5-10
MERCURY: *54-55* 5-10

Singles: 7-Inch

ABBOTT: *53* 15-20
COLUMBIA (20000 series): *56* 5-8
COLUMBIA (40000 series,
except 40813): *57* 4-6
COLUMBIA (40813; "I'm Coming
Home"): *57* 10-20
COLUMBIA (41000 series, except
41043 & 41110): *57-61* 5-10
COLUMBIA (41043; "Lover's
Rock"): *57* 10-20
COLUMBIA (41110; "Honky Tonk
Hardwood Floor"): *58* 25-50
COLUMBIA (42000 through 44000
series): *61-67* 3-6
DOT: *59* 5-10
MERCURY: *54-55* 10-20

Picture Sleeves

COLUMBIA (Except 41308): *59-64* 8-10
COLUMBIA (41308; "When It's
Springtime In Alaska"): *59* 10-20
(Blue and white sleeve. Promotional issue only.)
DOT: *59* 5-8

EPs: 7-Inch 33/45rpm

COLUMBIA: *57-60* 10-20
MERCURY: *55* 15-25
SESAC: *59* 25-35
(Promotional issues only.)

LPs: 10/12-Inch 33rpm

BRIAR INT'L (104; "Done
Rovin"): 60-100
COLUMBIA (1300 through 1700
series): *60-62* 20-30
(With a "CL" prefix.)
COLUMBIA (8000 series): *60-63* 25-30
(With a "CS" prefix.)
COLUMBIA (8000 series): 5-8
(With a "PC" prefix.)
COLUMBIA (9000 series): *65-69* 15-20
(With a "CS" prefix.)
COLUMBIA (30000 series): *71* 10-15
CROWN: *63* 12-15
CUSTOM: 8-12
DOT: *59* 15-20
HARMONY: *70-71* 10-12
MERCURY: *59* 25-30
PICKWICK/HILLTOP: *65-68* 10-15
SEARS: 10-15
(Promotional issue only.)

SESAC (1201; "Free & Easy
Songs"): *59* $100-125
(Promotional issue only.)
Also see DEAN, Jimmy / Johnny Horton

HORTON, Johnny / Sonny James

LPs: 10/12-Inch 33rpm

CUSTOM: 8-12
Also see JAMES, Sonny
Also see HORTON, Johnny

HOSANNA

Singles: 7-Inch

CALLA: *76* 2-3

HOT

Singles: 7-Inch

BIG TREE: *77-79* 1-3

LPs: 10/12-Inch 33rpm

BIG TREE: *77-79* 5-8

HOT BUTTER

Singles: 7-Inch

MUSICOR: *72* 2-4

LPs: 10/12-Inch 33rpm

MUSICOR: *72-74* 8-10
Members: Steve Jerome; Bill Jerome; Johnny Abbott; Stan Free; Dave Mullaney.

HOT CHOCOLATE

Singles: 7-Inch

APPLE: *69* 3-5
BIG TREE: *75-77* 1-3
EMI AMERICA: *82* 1-3
INFINITY: *78-79* 1-3
RAK: *72-73* 2-3

LPs: 10/12-Inch 33rpm

BIG TREE: *74-77* 8-10
EMI AMERICA: *82* 5-8
INFINITY: *78-79* 5-8
Members: Errol Brown; Tony Wilson.

HOT CUISINE

Singles: 7-Inch

PRELUDE: *81* 1-3

HOT LINE

Singles: 12-Inch 33/45rpm

MEMO: *84* 4-6

Singles: 7-Inch

RED COACH: *74* 2-4

HOT SAUCE

Singles: 7-Inch

VOLT: *72-74* 2-3

HOT STREAK

Singles: 12-Inch 33/45rpm

EASY STREET: *83* 4-6

HOT TUNA
Singles: 7-Inch
GRUNT: 71-76 .... $2-4
Picture Sleeves
GRUNT: 72 3-6
LPs: 10/12-Inch 33rpm
GRUNT: 72-78 8-12
RCA VICTOR (3000 series): 81 5-8
RCA VICTOR (4000 series): 70-71 10-15
Members: Paul Cassady; Jorma Kaukonen.
Also see JOPLIN, Janis / Hot Tuna
Also see KAUKONEN, Jorma

HOTBOX
Singles: 12-Inch 33/45rpm
POLYDOR: 84 4-6
Singles: 7-Inch
POLYDOR: 84 1-3

HOTEL
Singles: 7-Inch
MCA: 79-80 1-3
MERCURY: 78 1-3
LPs: 10/12-Inch 33rpm
MCA: 79-80 5-8

HOTHOUSE FLOWERS
Singles: 7-Inch
LONDON: 88 1-3
LPs: 10/12-Inch 33rpm
LONDON: 88 5-8

HOTLEGS
Singles: 7-Inch
CAPITOL (Except 3043): 70-71 3-5
CAPITOL (3043; "Run Baby, Run"): 71 . 10-15
LPs: 10/12-Inch 33rpm
CAPITOL: 71 15-20
Members: Eric Stewart; Kevin Godley; Lol Cream.
Also see 10CC

HOT-TODDYS
Singles: 7-Inch
CORSICAN: 59 8-10
SHAN-TODD: 59 10-15
STRAND: 60 8-10
Also see ROCKIN' REBELS

HOUR GLASS
Singles: 7-Inch
LIBERTY: 68 8-10
Picture Sleeves
LIBERTY: 68 10-15
LPs: 10/12-Inch 33rpm
LIBERTY: 67-68 15-20
UNITED ARTISTS: 73 10-12
Members: Duane Allman; Gregg Allman.
Also see ALLMAN BROTHERS

HOUSE OF LORDS
LPs: 10/12-Inch 33rpm
RCA/SIMMONS: 88 .... $5-8

HOUSE OF LOVE
LPs: 10/12-Inch 33rpm
RELATIVITY: 88 5-8

HOUSEMARTINS
LPs: 10/12-Inch 33rpm
ELEKTRA: 88 5-8

HOUSTON, Cissy
(Sissie Houston)
Singles: 7-Inch
COLUMBIA: 79-80 1-3
COMMONWEALTH UNITED: 70 2-3
JANUS: 71 2-3
KAPP: 67 3-5
PRIVATE STOCK: 77-78 1-3
LPs: 10/12-Inch 33rpm
COLUMBIA: 79-80 5-8
JANUS: 70 8-10
PRIVATE STOCK: 77-78 5-8
Also see BOWIE, David
Also see MANN, Herbie, & Cissy Houston
Also see SWEET INSPIRATIONS

HOUSTON, David
Singles: 7-Inch
BLACK ROSE: 82 1-3
COLONIAL: 78 2-3
COUNTRY INT'L: 80 1-3
DERRICK: 79 1-3
ELEKTRA: 78-79 1-3
EXCELSIOR: 81 1-3
EPIC: 63-76 2-4
NRC: 59 3-5
PHILLIPS INTERNATIONAL: 61 4-6
RCA VICTOR (6611; "Sugar
Sweet"): 56 10-15
RCA VICTOR (6696; "Blue Prelude"): 56 . 5-8
RCA VICTOR (6927; "One & Only"): 57 20-25
RCA VICTOR (7001; "Teenage
Frankie & Johnny"): 57 8-10
SOUNDWAVES: 83 1-3
STARDAY: 77 1-3
SUN (400 series): 66 2-4
SUN (1100 series): 72 1-3
Picture Sleeves
EPIC: 66-69 2-5
LPs: 10/12-Inch 33rpm
CAMDEN: 66 8-12
COLUMBIA: 73 6-10
DELTA: 82 5-8
EPIC: 64-76 5-15
EXACT: 80 5-8

EXCELSIOR: *81* $5-8
51 WEST: *84* 5-8
GUEST STAR: *64* 6-12
GUSTO: *78* 5-8
HARMONY: *70-72* 8-12
STARDAY: *77* 6-10
 Also see JAMES, Sonny / David Houston

HOWARD, David, & Barbara Mandrell
Singles: 7-Inch
EPIC: *70-74* 2-4
LPs: 10/12-Inch 33rpm
EPIC: *72-75* 8-15
 Also see MANDRELL, Barbara

HOUSTON, David, & Tammy Wynette
Singles: 7-Inch
EPIC: *67* 2-4
LPs: 10/12-Inch 33rpm
EPIC: *67* 8-12
51 WEST: *82* 5-8
 Also see HOUSTON, David
 Also see WYNETTE, Tammy

HOUSTON, Don
Singles: 7-Inch
THUNDER: *59* 4-8

HOUSTON, Thelma
(Thelma Houston & Pressure Cooker)
Singles: 12-Inch 33/45rpm
MCA: *83* 4-6
Singles: 7-Inch
CAPITOL: *66* 3-5
DUNHILL (Except 11): *70* 2-4
DUNHILL (11; "Everybody Gets To
 Go To The Moon"): *69* 4-6
(Special Apollo 11 Mission promotional issue.
Price includes paper sleeve.)
MCA: *83* 1-3
MOTOWN: *74-78* 1-3
MOWEST: *71-73* 2-4
RCA VICTOR: *80-81* 1-3
TAMLA: *76-79* 2-3
LPs: 10/12-Inch 33rpm
DUNHILL: *69* 10-12
MCA: *83* 5-8
MOTOWN: *81-82* 5-8
MOWEST: *72* 8-10
RCA VICTOR: *80-81* 5-8
SHEFFIELD (2; "I've Got The
 Music In Me"): *74* 25-30
SHEFFIELD (200; "I've Got The
 Music In Me"): *82* 5-8
TAMLA: *76-79* 5-8
MYRRH: *74* 8-10
 Also see BUTLER, Jerry, & Thelma Houston

HOUSTON, Whitney
Singles: 12-Inch 33/45rpm
ARISTA: *85-88* $4-6
Singles: 7-Inch
ARISTA: *85-88* 1-3
LPs: 10/12-Inch 33rpm
ARISTA: *85-88* 5-8
 Also see KING DREAM CHORUS &
 HOLIDAY CREW
 Also see PENDERGRASS, Teddy

HOWARD, Camille, Trio
(Camille Howard)
Singles: 78rpm
FEDERAL: *53* 4-8
IMPERIAL: *53* 4-8
SPECIALTY: *51-53* 4-8
VEE JAY: *56* 3-6
Singles: 7-Inch
FEDERAL: *53* 10-20
IMPERIAL: *53* 10-15
SPECIALTY: *51-53* 10-20
(Most Specialty singles are currently available,
using original catalog numbers.)
VEE JAY: *56* 10-15
Members: Camille Howard; Roy Milton; Dallas
Bartley.
 Also see MILTON, Roy

HOWARD, Don
Singles: 78rpm
ESSEX: *52* 2-5
MERCURY: *56* 2-4
Singles: 7-Inch
ESSEX: *52* 3-5
MERCURY: *56* 2-4

HOWARD, Eddy
Singles: 78rpm
MERCURY: *50-57* 2-4
Singles: 7-Inch
MERCURY: *50-61* 2-5
MISHAWAKA: *72* 1-3
EPs: 7-Inch 33/45rpm
MERCURY: *50-59* 4-8
LPs: 10/12-Inch 33rpm
IMPERIAL: *61* 8-15
MERCURY: *50-65* 8-18
WING: *60-63* 5-10

HOWARD, George
(George Howard With Gwen Guthrie)
Singles: 12-Inch 33/45rpm
MCA: *86* 4-6
Singles: 7-Inch
MCA: *86* 1-3
PALO ALTO: *83* 1-3

TBA: *84-86* $1-3
    LPs: 10/12-Inch 33rpm
MCA: *86-88* 5-8
PALO ALTO: *83* 5-8
TBA: *84-86* 5-8
  Also see GUTHRIE, Gwen

HOWARD, Miki
    Singles: 7-Inch
ATLANTIC: *86-88* 1-3
    LPs: 10/12-Inch 33rpm
ATLANTIC: *86-88* 5-8
  Also see SIDE EFFECT

HOWARD, Miki, & Gerald Levert
    Singles: 7-Inch
ATLANTIC: *88* 1-3
  Also see HOWARD, Miki

HOWE, Steve, Band
    Singles: 7-Inch
ATLANTIC: *75-79* 1-3
    LPs: 10/12-Inch 33rpm
ATLANTIC: *75-79* 5-8
  Also see ASIA
  Also see GTR
  Also see YES

HOWLIN' WOLF
(Chester Burnett)
    Singles: 78rpm
CHESS (1400 series): *51-52* 8-15
CHESS (1500 & 1600 series): *52-57* 5-10
    Singles: 7-Inch
CHESS (1528; "My Last
  Affair"): *53* 50-75
CHESS (1557 through 1593): *53-55* 30-60
CHESS (1600 series): *55-57* 10-20
CHESS (1700 through 1900
  series): *58-66* 4-8
CHESS (2000 series): *67-71* 2-5
    LPs: 10/12-Inch 33rpm
CADET: *69* 10-12
CHESS (Except 1400 & 1500
  series): *71-77* 8-10
CHESS (1400 series): *58-62* 35-45
CHESS (1500 series,
  except 1502): *67-69* 15-20
CHESS (1502; "Real Folk
  Blues"): *66* 25-30
CROWN: *62* 15-20
CUSTOM: 10-12
KENT: *67* 10-15
UNITED: 8-10
  Also see BERRY, Chuck, & Howlin' Wolf
  Also see DIDDLEY, Bo, Howlin' Wolf &
Muddy Waters

  Also see ROBINSON, Freddy
  Also see WATERS, Muddy, & Howlin' Wolf

HUANG CHUNG:
see WANG CHUNG

HUBBARD, Freddie
    Singles: 12-Inch 33/45rpm
FANTASY: *81* $4-6
    Singles: 7-Inch
ATLANTIC: *69* 2-3
BLUE NOTE: *61-64* 2-4
COLUMBIA: *74-76* 1-3
    LPs: 10/12-Inch 33rpm
ATLANTIC: *67-76* 8-15
BLUE NOTE: *60-65* 15-25
(Label reads "Blue Note Records Inc. - New York,
U.S.A.")
BLUE NOTE: *66-76* 8-15
(Label shows Blue Note Records as a division of
either Liberty or United Artists.)
CTI: *70-75* 5-10
COLUMBIA: *74-83* 5-8
ELEKTRA: *82* 5-8
ENJA: *81* 5-8
FANTASY: *81-83* 5-8
IMPULSE: *63-73* 10-20
LIBERTY: *81* 5-8
PABLO: *82-83* 5-8
PAUSA: *82* 5-8

HUBBARD, Freddie, & Oscar Peterson
    LPs: 10/12-Inch 33rpm
PABLO: *80* 5-8
  Also see PETERSON, Oscar

HUBBARD, Freddie, & Stanley Turrentine
    LPs: 10/12-Inch 33rpm
CTI: *74* 5-8
  Also see HUBBARD, Freddie
  Also see TURRENTINE, Stanley

HUDMON, R.B., Jr.
    Singles: 7-Inch
ATLANTIC: *76-77* 2-3
CAPITOL: *71* 2-4
COTILLION: *78* 1-3
1-2-3: *68-70* 2-4
    LPs: 10/12-Inch 33rpm
COTILLION: *78* 5-8

HUDSON, Al
(Al Hudson & The Soul Partners)
    Singles: 12-Inch 33/45rpm
ABC: *77* 4-6
    Singles: 7-Inch
ABC: *76-79* 1-3
ATCO: *75-76* 2-3

LPs: 10/12-Inch 33rpm
ABC: 77 . . . . $8-10
Also see ONE WAY

HUDSON, David
Singles: 7-Inch
ALSTON: 80 1-3
LPs: 10/12-Inch 33rpm
ALSTON: 80 5-8

**HUDSON, "Emperor" Bob, &
Lawrence Welk**
Singles: 7-Inch
RANWOOD: 72 2-3
Also see HUDSON & LANDRY
Also see WELK, Lawrence

HUDSON, Lavine
Singles: 7-Inch
VIRGIN: 88 1-3

HUDSON, Pookie
(Pookie Hudson & The Spaniels)
Singles: 7-Inch
CHESS: 66 3-5
DOUBLE-L: 63 3-5
NEPTUNE: 61 3-5
PARKWAY: 62 3-5
Also see SPANIELS

HUDSON & LANDRY
Singles: 7-Inch
DORE: 71-74 2-3
LPs: 10/12-Inch 33rpm
DORE: 71-75 5-10
Members: Bob Hudson; Ron Landry.
Also see HUDSON, "Emperor" Bob, &
Lawrence Welk

HUDSON BROTHERS
Singles: 7-Inch
ARISTA: 76-78 1-3
CASABLANCA: 74 2-3
ROCKET: 74-76 2-3
Picture Sleeves
ROCKET: 75 1-3
LPs: 10/12-Inch 33rpm
CASABLANCA: 74 8-10
PLAYBOY: 72 8-10
ROCKET: 74-75 8-10
Members: Bill Hudson; Brett Hudson; Mark Hud-
son.

HUES CORPORATION
Singles: 7-Inch
RCA VICTOR: 73-75 2-3
WARNER BROS: 77 2-3
LPs: 10/12-Inch 33rpm
RCA VICTOR: 73-77 8-10

WARNER BROS: 77-78 . . . . $5-8
Members: St. Clair Lee; H. Ann Kelly; Tommy
Brown; Karl Russell.

HUFF, Terry
(Terry Huff & Special Delivery)
Singles: 7-Inch
MAINSTREAM: 76 2-3
PHILADELPHIA INT'L: 80 1-3
LPs: 10/12-Inch 33rpm
MAINSTREAM: 76 5-8

HUGH, Grayson
LPs: 10/12-Inch 33rpm
RCA VICTOR: 88 5-8

HUGHES, Freddie
(Fred Hughes)
Singles: 7-Inch
BRUNSWICK: 69-71 2-4
COLLECTABLES: 81 1-3
EXODUS: 66 3-5
MINASA: 65 3-5
VEE JAY: 65 5-10
WAND: 68-69 3-5
LPs: 10/12-Inch 33rpm
BRUNSWICK: 70 8-12
WAND: 68 10-15

HUGHES, Jimmy
Singles: 7-Inch
ATLANTIC: 68 2-3
COLLECTABLES: 81 1-3
FAME: 64-67 3-5
GUYDEN: 62 3-5
VOLT: 69 2-3
LPs: 10/12-Inch 33rpm
ATCO: 67 10-15
STAX: 85 5-8
VEE JAY: 64 15-20
VOLT: 69 10-12

HUGHES, Rhetta
Singles: 12-Inch 33/45rpm
ARIA: 83 4-6
Singles: 7-Inch
ARIA: 83 1-3
COLUMBIA: 67-68 3-5
SUTRA: 80 1-3
TETRAGRAMMATON: 68-69 2-3
LPs: 10/12-Inch 33rpm
SUTRA: 80 5-8
TETRAGRAMMATON: 69 10-12

HUGHES, Rhetta, & Tennyson Stephens
LPs: 10/12-Inch 33rpm
COLUMBIA: 65 12-18
Also see HUGHES, Rhetta
Also see STEPHENS, Tennyson

HUGHES-THRALL
Singles: 7-Inch
BOULEVARD: 82 .... $1-3
Members: Glenn Hughes; Pat Thrall.

HUGO & LUIGI
(Hugo & Luigi Chorus)
Singles: 78rpm
MERCURY: 55-56 2-4
Singles: 7-Inch
MERCURY: 55-56 2-4
RCA VICTOR: 59-60 2-3
ROULETTE: 58 2-5
Picture Sleeves
ROULETTE: 58 3-5
LPs: 10/12-Inch 33rpm
FORUM: 60 5-10
MERCURY: 56 5-15
RCA VICTOR: 60-63 5-10
ROULETTE: 59 5-12
WING: 60 5-10
Members: Hugo Peretti; Luigi Creatore.

HULIN, T.K.
Singles: 7-Inch
SMASH: 63 3-5
L.K. (Except 1001): 63 15-25
L.K. (1001; "Little Bitty
Boy"): 35-50
LPs: 10/12-Inch 33rpm
STARLITE: 10-12

HULLABALOOS
Singles: 7-Inch
ROULETTE: 64-65 4-6
Picture Sleeves
ROULETTE: 64-65 10-20
LPs: 10/12-Inch 33rpm
ROULETTE: 65 25-30

HUMAN BEINZ
(Human Beinz With The Mammals)
Singles: 7-Inch
CAPITOL: 67-69 4-6
GATEWAY: 66-67 5-10
Picture Sleeves
CAPITOL: 68 8-15
LPs: 10/12-Inch 33rpm
CAPITOL: 68 15-25
GATEWAY: 68 25-35

HUMAN BODY
Singles: 7-Inch
BEARSVILLE: 84 1-3

HUMAN LEAGUE
Singles: 12-Inch 33/45rpm
A&M: 82-86 4-6

Singles: 7-Inch
A&M: 82-86 .... $1-3
Picture Sleeves
A&M: 82-85 1-3
LPs: 10/12-Inch 33rpm
A&M: 82-86 5-8
Member: Phil Oakey.
Also see LEAGUE UNLIMITED OR-
CHESTRA
Also see MORODER, Giorgio, & Phil Oakey

HUMBLE PIE
Singles: 7-Inch
A&M: 71-75 2-4
ATCO: 80 1-3
IMMEDIATE: 69 4-6
LPs: 10/12-Inch 33rpm
A&M: 70-82 8-12
ACCORD: 82 5-8
ATCO: 80-81 5-8
IMMEDIATE: 68-72 12-15
Members: Steve Marriott; Peter Frampton.
Also see FRAMPTON'S CAMEL
Also see SMALL FACES

HUMPERDINCK, Engelbert
Singles: 7-Inch
EPIC: 76-83 1-3
PARROT: 67-73 2-3
Picture Sleeves
PARROT: 67-71 2-4
LPs: 10/12-Inch 33rpm
EPIC: 76-83 5-10
PARROT: 67-74 8-15

HUMPHREY, Bobbi
Singles: 12-Inch 33/45rpm
EPIC: 78-79 4-6
Singles: 7-Inch
BLUE NOTE: 72-76 2-3
EPIC: 77-79 1-3
LPs: 10/12-Inch 33rpm
BLUE NOTE: 71-76 5-10
EPIC: 78-79 5-8

HUMPHREY, Della
Singles: 7-Inch
ARCTIC: 68 3-5

HUMPHREY, Paul
& His Cool Aid Chemists
Singles: 7-Inch
LIZARD: 70-71 2-4
LPs: 10/12-Inch 33rpm
LIZARD: 71 8-12

HUMPHRIES, Teddy
Singles: 7-Inch
KING: *59* $3-5

HUNT, Geraldine
Singles: 7-Inch
ABC: *67* 2-4
BOMBAY: *64* 3-5
CHECKER: *62* 3-5
PRISM: *80* 1-3
ROULETTE: *70-73* 2-4

HUNT, Geraldine, & Charlie Hodges
Singles: 7-Inch
CALLA: *70* 2-4
  Also see HODGES, Charles
  Also see HUNT, Geraldine

HUNT, Pee Wee
Singles: 78rpm
CAPITOL: *50-57* 2-4
Singles: 7-Inch
CAPITOL: *50-62* 2-4
SAVOY: *51* 3-5
EPs: 7-Inch 33/45rpm
CAPITOL: *50-56* 4-8
SAVOY: *51* 5-10
LPs: 10/12-Inch 33rpm
CAPITOL: *78* 4-8
  (With an "SM" prefix.)
CAPITOL: *50-63* 10-20
  (With a "T" or "ST" prefix.)
GLENDALE: *78* 4-8
SAVOY: *51* 20-30
  Also see BLANC, Mel
  Also see FOUR KNIGHTS

HUNT, Tommy
Singles: 7-Inch
ATLANTIC: *65* 3-5
CAPITOL: *66* 3-5
DYNAMO: *67* 3-5
SCEPTER: *61-63* 4-6
LPs: 10/12-Inch 33rpm
DYNAMO: *67* 10-15
SCEPTER: *62* 20-25
  Also see FLAMINGOS
  Also see PLATTERS / Inez & Charlie Foxx /
  Jive Five / Tommy Hunt

HUNTER, Ian
Singles: 7-Inch
CHRYSALIS: *79* 1-3
COLUMBIA: *75* 2-3
LPs: 10/12-Inch 33rpm
CHRYSALIS: *79-81* 5-8
COLUMBIA: *75-79* 8-10
  Also see MOTT THE HOOPLE

HUNTER, Ivory Joe
(Ivory Joe Hunter & The Ivorytones)
Singles: 78rpm
ATLANTIC: *55-58* $5-8
EXCLUSIVE: *45* 6-12
FOUR STAR: *48* 5-10
KING: *47-50* 5-10
MGM: *49-54* 5-10
PACIFIC: *45-47* 8-12
Singles: 7-Inch
ATLANTIC: *55-58* 5-10
CAPITOL: *61-62* 3-5
DOT: *58-59* 4-6
GOLDISC: *60* 4-6
KING (4424 through 4455): *51* 20-30
KING (5200 series): *59* 5-8
MGM (500 series): *78* 1-3
MGM (8000 series): *49* 15-30
MGM (10000 & 11000 series): *49-54* 10-20
PARAMOUNT: *73* 2-3
SMASH: *63* 3-5
SOUND STAGE 7: *68* 3-5
VEE JAY: *62* 3-5
VEEP: *67* 3-5
EPs: 7-Inch 33/45rpm
ATLANTIC: *58* 20-40
KING: 25-50
MGM: *57* 20-40
LPs: 10/12-Inch 33rpm
ATLANTIC (Black label): *58* 30-50
ATLANTIC (Red label): *59* 15-25
DOT: *64* 15-20
EPIC: *71* 8-10
EVEREST: *74* 8-10
GOLDISC: *61* 20-30
GRAND PRIX: 10-15
KING: *58* 25-30
LION: 15-20
MGM: *57* 50-75
PARAMOUNT: *74* 8-10
SAGE: *59* 20-25
SMASH: *63* 15-20
SOUND: *57* 30-40
  Also see CHARLES, Ray / Ivory Joe Hunter /
  Jimmy Rushing

HUNTER, Ivory Joe / Memphis Slim
LPs: 10/12-Inch 33rpm
STRAND: 15-25
  Also see HUNTER, Ivory Joe

HUNTER, John
Singles: 7-Inch
PRIVATE I: *84-85* 1-3
LPs: 10/12-Inch 33rpm
PRIVATE I: *85* 5-8

HUNTER, Tab
Singles: 78rpm
DOT: *56-57* $3-5
Singles: 7-Inch
DOT: *56-62* 3-5
WARNER BROS (Monaural): *58-59* 3-5
WARNER BROS (Stereo): *59* 5-8
(With an "S" prefix.)
Picture Sleeves
WARNER BROS: *58-60* 5-10
EPs: 7-Inch 33/45rpm
WARNER BROS (1221; "Tab
Hunter"): *58* 15-25
(With an "EA" prefix. Monaural. Contains one
track not heard on stereo version.)
WARNER BROS (1221; "Tab
Hunter"): *58* 20-35
(With an "ESB" prefix. Stereo. Contains one track
not heard on mono version.)
LPs: 10/12-Inch 33rpm
DOT (3370; "Young Love"): *61* 25-30
(Monaural.)
DOT (25370; "Young Love"): *61* 20-25
(Stereo. Contains re-recorded tracks, for stereo, that
are the original recordings on the mono version.)
WARNER BROS: *58-60* 25-35

HUNTER, Ty
(Ty Hunter & The Voice Masters)
Singles: 7-Inch
ANNA: *60* 5-8
CHECK MATE: *61* 4-6
CHESS: *62-64* 3-5
  Also see GLASS HOUSE
  Also see ORIGINALS
  Also see VOICE MASTERS

HUNTLEY, Chet, & David Brinkley
LPs: 10/12-Inch 33rpm
RCA VICTOR: *64-66* 8-15

HUNTSBERRY, Howard
Singles: 7-Inch
MCA: *88* 1-3
LPs: 10/12-Inch 33rpm
MCA: *88* 5-8

HURBY'S MACHINE
LPs: 10/12-Inch 33rpm
SOUND CHECK: *88* 5-8

HURD, Debra
Singles: 7-Inch
GEFFEN: *83* 1-3

HURRICANE
LPs: 10/12-Inch 33rpm
ENIGMA: *88* 5-8

HURT, Jim
Singles: 7-Inch
SCOTTI BROTHERS: *80* $1-3

HURT 'EM BAD & THE S.C. BAND
Singles: 7-Inch
PROFILE: *82* 1-3

HUSKY, Ferlin
(Ferlin Husky & The Hush Puppies; Ferlin
Husky & The Coon Creek Girls; Ferlin & Bettie
Husky; Ferlin Huskey)
Singles: 78rpm
CAPITOL: *52-57* 3-5
Singles: 7-Inch
ABC: *73-75* 1-3
CAPITOL (2000 through 3400): *67-72* 2-3
(Orange labels.)
CAPITOL (2300 through 4300): *52-60* 3-5
(Purple labels.)
CAPITOL (4400 through 5900): *60-67* 2-4
CACHET: *80* 1-3
FIRST GENERATION: *78* 1-3
KING: *60-61* 2-4
EPs: 7-Inch 33/45rpm
CAPITOL: *57-60* 8-15
Picture Sleeves
CAPITOL: *62-68* 3-6
LPs: 10/12-Inch 33rpm
ABC: *73-75* 5-10
AUDIOGRAPH ALIVE: *82* 5-8
CAPITOL (700 & 800 series): *56-57* 25-40
CAPITOL (1200 through 2800
series): *60-68* 10-20
(With a "T" or "ST" prefix.)
CAPITOL (1200 through 2800
series): *68-75* 5-10
(With a "DT" or "SM" prefix.)
KING (600 & 700 series): *59-60* 25-35
PICKWICK: 6-12
PICKWICK/HILLTOP: *65* 8-12
  Also see CRUM, Simon
  Also see OWENS, Buck / Faron Young / Fer-
lin Husky
  Also see PRESTON, Terry
  Also see SHEPARD, Jean, & Ferlin Husky

HUTCH, Willie
Singles: 7-Inch
DUNHILL: *65* 3-5
MAVERICK: *68* 3-5
MOTOWN: *73-82* 1-3
RCA VICTOR: *69* 2-4
WHITFIELD: *78-79* 1-3
LPs: 10/12-Inch 33rpm
MOTOWN: *73-82* 5-10
RCA VICTOR: *69* 10-12

WHITFIELD: *78-79* $5-8

HUTSON, Leroy
(Leroy Hutson & The Free Spirit Symphony)
Singles: 7-Inch
CURTOM: *73-78* 2-3
RSO: *79* 1-3
LPs: 10/12-Inch 33rpm
CURTOM: *73-78* 8-10
Also see IMPRESSIONS

HUTTON, Danny
Singles: 7-Inch
HBR: *65* 3-5
MGM: *66* 3-5
Picture Sleeves
HBR: *65* 10-15
MGM: *66* 8-12
LPs: 10/12-Inch 33rpm
MGM: *70* 8-10
Also see THREE DOG NIGHT

HYDE, Paul, & The Payolas
Singles: 7-Inch
A&M: *85* 1-3
LPs: 10/12-Inch 33rpm
A&M: *85* 5-8

HYLAND, Brian
Singles: 7-Inch
ABC: *73* 1-3
ABC-PARAMOUNT: *61-64* 3-5
DOT: *67-69* 3-5
KAPP: *60-61* 4-6
LEADER: *60* 5-10
MCA: *73* 1-3
PHILIPS: *64-67* 3-5
ROWE/AMI: *66* 4-8
("Play Me" Sales Stimulator promotional issue.)
ROULETTE: 1-3
UNI: *70-72* 2-4
Picture Sleeves
ABC-PARAMOUNT: *61-63* 8-15
KAPP (Except 352): *60-61* 10-20
KAPP (352; "Four Little Heels"): *60* 20-30
(Black & white sleeve. Promotional issue only.)
KAPP (352; "Four Little
Heels"): *60* 10-20
(Color sleeve.)
PHILIPS: *64-67* 4-8
LPs: 10/12-Inch 33rpm
ABC-PARAMOUNT: *61-64* 20-25
DOT: *69* 10-12
KAPP: *60* 25-30
PHILIPS: *64-66* 15-20
PICKWICK: 5-8
PRIVATE STOCK: *77* 5-8

UNI: *71* $8-10
WING: *67* 10-12

HYMAN, Dick
(Dick Hyman Trio; Dick Hyman & His Electric
Eclectics)
Singles: 78rpm
MGM: *54-57* 2-4
Singles: 7-Inch
COLUMBIA: *74-75* 1-3
COMMAND: *61-70* 2-3
EVEREST: *60* 2-3
MGM: *54-62* 2-5
RCA VICTOR: *62* 2-3
LPs: 10/12-Inch 33rpm
ATLANTIC: *75* 5-8
COLUMBIA: *74* 5-8
COMMAND: *60-73* 5-15
EVEREST: *60* 5-10
FAMOUS DOOR: *73* 5-8
MCA: *77* 5-10
MGM: *54-63* 10-20
PROJECT 3: *71* 5-8
RCA VICTOR: *80-83* 4-8
SUNSET: *66* 5-10

HYMAN, Phyllis
Singles: 12-Inch 33/45rpm
ARISTA: *83* 4-6
Singles: 7-Inch
ARISTA: *78-83* 1-3
BUDDAH: *77* 1-3
DESERT MOON: *76* 2-3
PHILADELPHIA INT'L: *86* 1-3
LPs: 10/12-Inch 33rpm
ARISTA: *79-83* 5-8
BUDDAH: *77* 5-8
PHILADELPHIA INT'L: *86* 5-8

**HYMAN, Phyllis
& Michael Henderson**
Singles: 7-Inch
ARISTA: *81* 1-3
Also see CONNORS, Norman
Also see HENDERSON, Michael
Also see HYMAN, Phyllis

I

I LEVEL
Singles: 12-Inch 33/45rpm
VIRGIN: *82-84* 4-6
Singles: 7-Inch
VIRGIN: *82-84* 1-3

LPs: 10/12-Inch 33rpm
VIRGIN: *83* $5-8

I.R.T.
(Interboro Rhythm Team)
Singles: 12-Inch 33/45rpm
RCA VICTOR: *84* 4-6
Singles: 7-Inch
RCA VICTOR: *84* 1-3

IAN, Janis
Singles: 7-Inch
CAPITOL: *71* 2-3
CASABLANCA: *80* 1-3
COLUMBIA: *74-81* 1-3
POLYDOR: *78* 1-3
VERVE/FOLKWAYS: *66-67* 3-5
VERVE/FORECAST: *68-69* 2-4
Picture Sleeves
COLUMBIA: *75* 3-6
LPs: 10/12-Inch 33rpm
CAPITOL: *71-75* 8-12
COLUMBIA: *74-81* 8-10
MGM: *70* 8-10
POLYDOR: *75* 8-10
VERVE/FOLKWAYS: *67* 10-15
VERVE/FORECAST: *68-69* 10-15

ICEHOUSE
Singles: 12-Inch 33/45rpm
CHRYSALIS: *81-86* 4-6
Singles: 7-Inch
CHRYSALIS: *81-88* 1-3
LPs: 10/12-Inch 33rpm
CHRYSALIS: *81-87* 5-8

ICICLE WORKS
Singles: 7-Inch
ARISTA: *84* 1-3
LPs: 10/12-Inch 33rpm
ARISTA: *84* 5-8

ICE-T
Singles: 7-Inch
SIRE: *88* 1-3
LPs: 10/12-Inch 33rpm
SIRE: *88* 5-8

ICON
LPs: 10/12-Inch 33rpm
CAPITOL: *85* 5-8
Members: Steve Clifford; Dan Wexler; Pat Dixon; John Aquilino; Tracy Wallach; Jerry Harrison.

IDEALS
Singles: 7-Inch
SATELLITE: *66* 3-5

IDES OF MARCH
Singles: 7-Inch
KAPP: *69* $3-5
PARROT: *66-67* 5-8
RCA VICTOR: *72-73* 2-4
WARNER BROS: *69-71* 3-5
LPs: 10/12-Inch 33rpm
RCA VICTOR: *72-73* 8-12
WARNER BROS: *70-71* 10-15
Member: Jim Peterik.

IDLE RACE
Singles: 7-Inch
LIBERTY: *67* 10-15
LPs: 10/12-Inch 33rpm
LIBERTY: *69* 25-30
SUNSET: *72* 8-12
Members: Jeff Lynne; Greg Masters; Roger Spencer; Dave Pritchard.
Also see LYNNE, Jeff

IDOL, Billy
Singles: 12-Inch 33/45rpm
CHRYSALIS: *81-86* 4-6
Singles: 7-Inch
CHRYSALIS: *81-87* 1-3
LPs: 10/12-Inch 33rpm
CHRYSALIS: *82-87* 5-8

IF
Singles: 7-Inch
CAPITOL: *70-74* 2-4
METROMEDIA: *72* 2-3
LPs: 10/12-Inch 33rpm
CAPITOL: *69-74* 10-12
METROMEDIA: *72-73* 8-10

IFIELD, Frank
Singles: 7-Inch
CAPITOL: *63-65* 2-4
HICKORY: *66-71* 2-3
MAM: *71* 2-3
VEE JAY: *62-63* 3-5
WARNER BROS: *79* 1-3
LPs: 10/12-Inch 33rpm
CAPITOL: *63* 10-12
HICKORY: *66-68* 8-10
VEE JAY: *62* 10-15
Also see BEATLES / Frank Ifield

IGLESIAS, Julio
Singles: 7-Inch
COLUMBIA: *83-88* 1-3
LPs: 10/12-Inch 33rpm
COLUMBIA: *83-86* 5-8

IGLESIAS, Julio, & Willie Nelson
(Willie Nelson & Julio Iglesias)
Singles: 7-Inch
COLUMBIA (Except 04495): *84* $1-3
COLUMBIA (04495; "As Time
Goes By"): *84* 4-8
(Promotional issue only.)
Picture Sleeves
COLUMBIA (Except 04495): *84* 1-3
COLUMBIA (04495; "As Time
Goes By"): *84* 5-10
(Promotional issue only.)
Also see IGLESIAS, Julio
Also see NELSON, Willie

IGLESIAS, Julio, & Diana Ross
Singles: 7-Inch
COLUMBIA: *84* 1-3
Picture Sleeves
COLUMBIA: *84* 1-3
Also see IGLESIAS, Julio
Also see ROSS, Diana

IGGY & THE STOOGES:
see POP, Iggy

IKETTES
Singles: 7-Inch
ATCO: *61-62* 3-5
INNIS: *64* 3-5
MODERN: *64-66* 3-5
PHI-DAN: 3-5
POMPEII: *68* 3-5
TEENA: *63* 3-5
UNITED ARTISTS: *71-72* 2-4
LPs: 10/12-Inch 33rpm
MODERN: *65* 15-20
UNITED ARTISTS: *73-75* 8-10
Also see TURNER, Ike & Tina

ILLINOIS SPEED PRESS
Singles: 7-Inch
COLUMBIA: *68-70* 3-5
LPs: 10/12-Inch 33rpm
COLUMBIA: *69-70* 10-15
Member: Paul Cotton.
Also see POCO

ILLUSION
Singles: 7-Inch
DYNO VOICE: *68* 3-5
STEED: *69-71* 2-4
LPs: 10/12-Inch 33rpm
STEED: *69-70* 12-15

ILLUSION
Singles: 7-Inch
ISLAND: *77-78* 1-3

LPs: 10/12-Inch 33rpm
ISLAND: *77-78* $5-8

ILLUSION
Singles: 7-Inch
SUGAR HILL: *82* 1-3

ILLUSTRATED MAN
Singles: 7-Inch
CAPITOL: *84* 1-3

IMAGINATION
Singles: 12-Inch 33/45rpm
ELEKTRA: *84* 4-6
Singles: 7-Inch
ELEKTRA: *83* 1-3
MCA: *82-83* 1-3
RCA: *87* 1-3
LPs: 10/12-Inch 33rpm
MCA: *82* 5-8

IMPACT
Singles: 7-Inch
ATCO: *76* 2-3
FANTASY: *77-78* 2-3
LPs: 10/12-Inch 33rpm
ATCO: *75* 8-10
FANTASY: *77* 5-8

IMPALAS
(Featuring Joe "Speedo" Frazier)
Singles: 7-Inch
CUB (Except 9022): *59-60* 8-10
CUB (9022; "I Ran All The
Way Home"): *59* 20-25
CUB (9022; "Sorry, I Ran All
The Way Home"): *59* 8-10
(The difference between the two previous listings is
the use of the word "Sorry" in the title.)
HAMILTON: *59* 4-6
MGM: *64-78* 1-3
EPs: 7-Inch 33/45rpm
CUB (5000; "Sorry, I Ran All
The Way Home"): *59* 100-125
LPs: 10/12-Inch 33rpm
CUB (8003; "Sorry, I Ran All
The Way Home"): *59* 75-100
(Monaural.)
CUB (8003; "Sorry, I Ran All
The Way Home"): *59* 150-250
(Stereo.)

IMPALAS / Horst Jankowski & His Orchestra
Singles: 7-Inch
COLLECTABLES: *85* 1-3
(Contains a true stereo version of *I Ran All The
Way Home*.)
Also see IMPALAS

Also see JANKOWSKI, Horst, & His Orchestra

IMPELLITTERI
LPs: 10/12-Inch 33rpm
RELATIVITY: 88 . . . . $5-8

IMPERIALS
Singles: 7-Inch
CAPITOL: 63 3-5
CARLTON: 61 3-5
END (1027; "Tears On My Pillow"): 58 . . 15-20
(Reissues were shown as by "Little Anthony & The Imperials.")
LIBERTY: 58 4-6
Also see LITTLE ANTHONY & THE IMPERIALS

IMPERIALS
Singles: 7-Inch
OMNI: 78 2-3

IMPRESSIONS
Singles: 12-Inch 33/45rpm
20TH CENTURY-FOX: 79 4-6
Singles: 7-Inch
ABC: 66-68 3-5
ABC-PARAMOUNT: 61-66 4-6
ABNER: 59-60 5-8
BANDERA: 59 15-20
CHI-SOUND: 81 1-3
COTILLION: 76-77 2-3
CURTOM: 68-76 2-4
MCA: 87 1-3
SWIRL: 62 3-5
20TH CENTURY-FOX: 81 1-3
VEE JAY (400 series): 62 4-6
Picture Sleeves
CURTOM: 68 3-5
LPs: 10/12-Inch 33rpm
ABC: 66-76 10-15
ABC-PARAMOUNT: 63-66 15-20
COTILLION: 76 8-10
CURTOM: 68-76 8-10
MCA: 82 5-8
PICKWICK: 75 8-10
SCEPTER/CITATION: 8-10
SIRE: 76 8-10
20TH CENTURY-FOX: 79-81 5-8
UPFRONT: 8-10
Members: Curtis Mayfield; Sam Gooden; Richard Brooks; Fred Cash; Leroy Hutson; Reggie Torlan; Ralph Johnson; Nate Evans.
Also see EVERETT, Betty / Impressions
Also see HUTSON, Leroy
Also see MAYFIELD, Curtis
Also see MYSTIQUE

IMPRESSIONS / Jerry Butler
LPs: 10/12-Inch 33rpm
SIRE: 77 . . . . $5-8
Also see BUTLER, Jerry
Also see IMPRESSIONS

IN CROWD
Singles: 7-Inch
BRENT: 65 3-5
MUSICOR: 65 4-8
RONN: 5-10
SWAN: 65 3-5
TOWER: 65-66 3-5
VIVA: 66-67 3-5

INCREDIBLE BONGO BAND
Singles: 7-Inch
MGM: 73 2-3
PRIDE: 72-74 2-3
LPs: 10/12-Inch 33rpm
PRIDE: 73-74 8-10

INCREDIBLE STRING BAND
LPs: 10/12-Inch 33rpm
ELEKTRA: 67-72 8-12
REPRISE: 72-74 8-12

INCREDIBLES
Singles: 7-Inch
AUDIO ARTS: 66-68 3-5
CLASS: 66 3-5
TETRAGRAMMATON: 69 2-4
LPs: 10/12-Inch 33rpm
AUDIO ARTS: 70 10-12

INDEEP
Singles: 12-Inch 33/45rpm
SOUND OF NEW YORK: 83-85 4-6
Singles: 7-Inch
SOUND OF NEW YORK: 83-85 1-3
LPs: 10/12-Inch 33rpm
SOUND OF NEW YORK: 83 5-8

INDEPENDENTS
Singles: 7-Inch
WAND: 72-74 2-3
LPs: 10/12-Inch 33rpm
WAND: 72-74 8-10

INDIA
Singles: 12-Inch 33/45rpm
WEST END: 83 4-6

INDIOS TABAJARAS, Los:
see LOS INDIOS TABAJARAS

INDIVIDUALS
Singles: 7-Inch
P.I.P.: 75 2-3

INDUSTRY
Singles: 7-Inch
CAPITOL: *83* $1-3

INFINITY
(Infinity Featuring Billy Butler)
Singles: 7-Inch
FOUNTAIN: *69* 2-5
MERCURY: *70* 2-4
UNI: *72* 2-4
Also see BUTLER, Billy

INFORMATION SOCIETY
Singles: 7-Inch
TOMMY B: *88* 1-3
LPs: 10/12-Inch 33rpm
TOMMY B: *88* 5-8

INGMANN, Jorgen
Singles: 7-Inch
ATCO: *60-66* ....:................. 2-4
MERCURY: *56* 2-4
PARROT: *64* 2-3
UNITED ARTISTS INT'L: *68* 2-3
LPs: 10/12-Inch 33rpm
ATCO: *62* 20-30
MERCURY: *56* 15-25
UNITED ARTISTS INT'L: *68* 8-12

INGRAM
Singles: 7-Inch
H&L: *77* 1-3
LPs: 10/12-Inch 33rpm
H&L: *77* 8-10

INGRAM, James
Singles: 12-Inch 33/45rpm
QWEST: *83* 4-6
Singles: 7-Inch
MCA: *87* 1-3
QWEST: *83-86* 1-3
LPs: 10/12-Inch 33rpm
QWEST: *83* 5-8
Also see AUSTIN, Patti, & James Ingram
Also see JONES, Quincy, & James Ingram
Also see ROGERS, Kenny, Kim Carnes &
James Ingram
Also see RONSTADT, Linda, & James Ingram
Also see U.S.A. FOR AFRICA

INGRAM, James, & Michael McDonald
Singles: 7-Inch
QWEST: *83* 1-3
Also see INGRAM, James
Also see MC DONALD, Michael

INGRAM, Luther
(Luther Ingram & The G-Men)
Singles: 7-Inch
DECCA: *65* $3-5
ERIC: 1-3
HIB: *67* 3-5
KO KO: *67-78* 2-4
PROFILE: *86-87* 1-3
SMASH: *66* 3-5
LPs: 10/12-Inch 33rpm
KO KO: *71-76* 8-10
Note: The Ko Ko label name may be shown as one
word (Koko) on some issues.

INK SPOTS
Singles: 78rpm
BLUEBIRD: *36* 10-15
DECCA (800 series): *36* 8-12
DECCA (1000 through 4000
series): *36-42* 5-10
DECCA (18000 through 30000
series): *42-57* 3-6
Singles: 7-Inch
DECCA (25000 through 31000
series): *50-61* 2-5
GRAND AWARD: *56* 3-5
VERVE: *60* 2-3
X-TRA: *60* 2-4
EPs: 7-Inch 33/45rpm
DECCA: *54-56* 5-15
GRAND AWARD: *56* 5-15
WALDORF MUSIC HALL: *55* 5-15
LPs: 10/12-Inch 33rpm
AUDITION: *56* 10-20
CORAL: *73* 4-6
CROWN (144; "Greatest Hits"): *59* 10-15
(Black vinyl.)
CROWN (144; "Greatest Hits"): *59* 20-40
(Colored vinyl.)
DECCA (100 series): *65* 10-20
DECCA (4000 series): *63* 10-20
(Decca LP numbers in this series preceded by a "7"
or a "DL-7" are stereo issues.)
DECCA (5000 series): *51-53* 20-30
(10-Inch LPs.)
DECCA (7000 & 8000 series): *54-59* 15-25
DIPLOMAT: *64* 5-8
EVEREST: *82* 5-8
EXACT: *80* 5-8
GRAND AWARD: *56-59* 10-20
MCA: *73* 5-8
MAYFAIR: 8-15
PAULA: *72* 5-8
VERVE: *56-60* 15-25
VOCALION: *59-65* 8-15

WALDORF MUSIC HALL: *55* $20-30
  Members: Bill Kenny; Orville Jones; Herb Kenny;
  Charlie Fuqua; Ivory "Deek" Watson; Bernie Mackey; Cliff Givens; Billy Bowen.
  Also see FITZGERALD, Ella, & The Ink
Spots
  Also see KENNY, Bill

INK SPOTS
Singles: 78rpm
KING (1200 & 1300 series,
  except 1336): *53-54* 4-8
KING (1336; "Melody Of
  Love"): *54* 8-15
KING (1400 series): *54-55* 10-15
KING (1500 series): *55* 5-10
KING (4000 series,
  except 4670): *55* 5-10
KING (4670; "Here In My
  Lonely Room"): *54* 10-20
Singles: 7-Inch
KING (1200 & 1300 series,
  except 1336): *53-54* 12-15
KING (1336; "Melody Of
  Love"): *54* 25-30
KING (1400 series): *54-55* 20-25
KING (1500 series): *55* 12-15
KING (4000 series,
  except 4670): *55* 12-15
KING (4670; "Here In My
  Lonely Room"): *54* 40-50
EPs: 7-Inch 33/45rpm
KING: *57* 40-60
LPs: 10/12-Inch 33rpm
KING (535; "Something Old...Something
  New"): *57* 75-100
KING (642; "Something Old...Something
  New"): *59* 50-75
  Members: James Holmes; Charlie Fuqua; Harry
  Jackson; Isaac Royal; Leon Antoine.

INK SPOTS
Singles: 7-Inch
FORD: *62* 3-5
  Member: Joe Van Loan.

INMAN, Autry
Singles: 78rpm
DECCA (Except 28629 & 29936): *56* 3-6
DECCA (28629; "That's All
  Right"): *56* 4-8
DECCA (29936; "Be Bop Baby"): *56* 5-10
Singles: 7-Inch
DECCA (Except 28629 & 29936): *56* 4-8
DECCA (28629; "That's All
  Right"): *56* 8-12
DECCA (29936; "Be Bop Baby"): *56* 15-20

EPIC: *67-69* $2-3
GLAD: *60* 3-5
JUBILEE: *65-69* 2-4
MERCURY: *62* 2-4
MILLION: *72* 1-3
RCA VICTOR: *58* 4-6
SIMS: *63-64* 2-4
UNITED ARTISTS: *60* 2-4
LPs: 10/12-Inch 33rpm
ALSHIRE: *69* 8-12
EPIC: *68* 8-12
GUEST STAR: 8-12
JUBILEE: *64-69* 10-20
MOUNTAIN DEW: *63* 15-25
SIMS: *64* 15-20

INMATES
Singles: 7-Inch
POLYDOR/RADAR: *79* 1-3
LPs: 10/12-Inch 33rpm
POLYDOR: *79-80* 5-8

INNER CITY
Singles: 7-Inch
VIRGIN: *88* 1-3

INNER CITY JAM BAND
Singles: 7-Inch
BAREBACK: *77* 2-3

INNER LIFE
Singles: 12-Inch 33/45rpm
SALSOUL: *83* 4-6
Singles: 7-Inch
PERSONAL: *84* 1-3
PRELUDE: *79-80* 1-3
SALSOUL: *83* 1-3

INNERVISION
Singles: 7-Inch
ARIOLA AMERICA: *77* 2-3

ATLANTIC: *85-86* $4-6
Singles: 7-Inch
ATCO: *83-85* 1-3
ATLANTIC: *85-88* 1-3
LPs: 10/12-Inch 33rpm
ATCO: *83-85* 5-8
ATLANTIC: *85-87* 5-8
Members: Michael Hutchence; Tim Farriss;
Andrew Farriss; Jon Farriss; Gary Beers; Kirk Pen-
gilly.

IRIS, Donnie
Singles: 7-Inch
HME: *85* 1-3
MCA: *80-83* 1-3
LPs: 10/12-Inch 33rpm
HME: *85* 5-8
MCA: *80-83* 5-8
MIDWEST: *80* 5-8
Also see JAGGERZ

IRISH ROVERS
Singles: 7-Inch
DECCA: *68-70* 2-3
LPs: 10/12-Inch 33rpm
DECCA: *68-72* 8-15
MCA: *73-77* 5-8
SANDCASTLE: *76* 5-8
Also see ROVERS

IRON BUTTERFLY
Singles: 7-Inch
ATCO: *68-71* 3-5
MCA: *75* 2-3
LPs: 10/12-Inch 33rpm
ATCO (Except 227): *68-71* 10-15
ATCO (227; "Heavy"): *68* 15-20
MCA: *75* 8-10
Members: Doug Ingle; Mike Pinera; Larry Rein-
hardt; Ron Bushy; Lee Dorman; Erik Brann.
Also see PINERA, Mike

IRON MAIDEN
LPs: 10/12-Inch 33rpm
CAPITOL (Except picture discs): *82-88* 5-8
CAPITOL (Picture discs): *82* 8-10
HARVEST: *80-82* 5-8

IRONHORSE
Singles: 7-Inch
SCOTTI BROS: *79-80* 1-3
LPs: 10/12-Inch 33rpm
SCOTTI BROS: *79-80* 5-8
Member: Randy Bachman.
Also see BACHMAN, Randy

Ron Isley of the Isley Brothers (Photo: Jeff Katz)

IRWIN, Big Dee
(Dee Irwin; Big Dee Irwin With Little Eva)
Singles: 7-Inch
DIMENSION: *63-64* $4-6
FAIRMOUNT: *66* 3-5
IMPERIAL: *68* 3-5
ROTATE: *65* 3-5
Also see ERWIN, Dee
Also see LITTLE EVA
Also see PASTELLS

ISAAK, Chris
LPs: 10/12-Inch 33rpm
WARNER BROS: *87* 5-8

ISLANDERS
(Featuring Randy Starr)
Singles: 7-Inch
MAYFLOWER: *59-60* 3-6
LPs: 10/12-Inch 33rpm
MAYFLOWER: *60* 15-30
Also see STARR, Randy

ISLEY BROTHERS
Singles: 12-Inch 33/45rpm
T-NECK: *79-83* 4-6
Singles: 7-Inch
ATLANTIC: *61-65* 3-5
CINDY: *58* 15-25
GONE: *58* 10-20
MARK-X (7000 series): *57* 20-35
MARK-X (8000 series): *60* 5-10
RCA VICTOR (0500 series): *61* 2-3
(With a "447" prefix. Black label with dog on top.)
RCA VICTOR (7000 series): *59-60* 4-6
(With a "47" prefix.)
RCA VICTOR (7000 series): *59-60* 8-10
(With a "61" prefix. Stereo.)
T-NECK (Except 501): *69-84* 1-3

T-NECK (501; "Testify"): *64* $4-6
TAMLA: *66-69* 4-6
TEENAGE: *57* 50-60
UNITED ARTISTS: *63-64* 4-8
VEEP: *66* 4-8
WAND: *62-63* 5-10
WARNER BROS: *85-88* 1-3
LPs: 10/12-Inch 33rpm
BUDDAH: *76* 10-12
CAMDEN: *73-75* 8-10
COLLECTABLES: *88* 6-8
MOTOWN: *80-82* 5-8
PHILADELPHIA INT'L: *78* 5-8
PICKWICK: *77* 5-10
RCA VICTOR: *59* 30-35
SCEPTER: *66* 10-15
SUNSET: *69* 8-10
T-NECK: *69-84* 8-10
TAMLA: *66-69* 12-15
TRIP: *76* 8-10
UNITED ARTISTS (500 series): *75* 8-10
UNITED ARTISTS (6000 series): *63* ... 20-25
WAND: *62* 15-20
WARNER BROS: *85-87* 5-8
Members: Ron Isley; Rudy Isley; O'Kelly Isley;
Ernie Isley; Marvin Isley.
Also see HENDRIX, Jimi, & The Isley
Brothers
Also see ISLEY-JASPER-ISLEY

ISLEY BROTHERS / Chiffons
LPs: 10/12-Inch 33rpm
SPINORAMA: *63* 10-15
Also see CHIFFONS

ISLEY BROTHERS
& Dave "Baby" Cortez
LPs: 10/12-Inch 33rpm
T-NECK: *69* 8-10
Also see CORTEZ, Dave "Baby"

ISLEY BROTHERS / Go-Go's
EPs: 7-Inch 33/45rpm
RCA VICTOR/WURLITZER: *64* 8-15
(Promotional issue only.)

ISLEY BROTHERS / Marvin & Johnny
LPs: 10/12-Inch 33rpm
CROWN: *63* 10-20
Also see ISLEY BROTHERS
Also see MARVIN & JOHNNY

ISLEY-JASPER-ISLEY
Singles: 12-Inch 33/45rpm
CBS ASSOCIATED: *85-86* 4-6
Singles: 7-Inch
CBS ASSOCIATED: *85-87* 1-3

LPs: 10/12-Inch 33rpm
CBS ASSOCIATED: *85-86* $5-8
Members: Marvin Isley; Chris Isley; Ernie Isley.
Also see ISLEY BROTHERS

ITALIAN ASPHALT & PAVEMENT
COMPANY
(Duprees)
Singles: 7-Inch
COLOSSUS: *70* 2-4
Picture Sleeves
COLOSSUS: *70* 3-5
LPs: 10/12-Inch 33rpm
COLOSSUS: *70* 8-10
Also see DUPREES

IT'S A BEAUTIFUL DAY
(Featuring David LaFlamme)
Singles: 7-Inch
COLUMBIA: *69-73* 3-5
SAN FRANCISCO SOUND: 8-10
LPs: 10/12-Inch 33rpm
COLUMBIA (1000 series): *70* 15-20
COLUMBIA (9000 series): *69* 25-30
COLUMBIA (30000 series): *71-73* 10-12
SAN FRANCISCO SOUND: 15-25
Promotional LPs
COLUMBIA (32660; "A 1001
Nights"): *73* 30-40
Also see GARCIA, Jerry
Also see LA FLAMME, David
Also see PABLO CRUISE

IVAN
(Jerry Ivan Allison)
Singles: 7-Inch
CORAL (62017; "Real Wild
Child"): *59* 35-40
CORAL (62081; "Frankie
Frankenstein"): *59* 40-50
CORAL (65607; "Real Wild
Child"): *67* 15-20
Also see CRICKETS

IVAN / Johnny Tillotson
Singles: 7-Inch
OLDIES 45: *64* 3-5
Also see IVAN
Also see TILLOTSON, Johnny

IVES, Burl
(Burl Ives & The Trinidaddies)
Singles: 78rpm
COLUMBIA: *50-51* 3-6
DECCA: *48-57* 3-6
Singles: 7-Inch
BELL: *70* 1-3
BIG TREE: *71* 1-3

BUENA VISTA: *63* $2-4
COLUMBIA (39000 series): *50-51* 4-6
COLUMBIA (44000 series): *68-69* 2-3
COLUMBIA (70000 series): *69* 1-3
CYCLONE: *70* 1-3
DECCA (25000 series): *66-69* 2-3
DECCA (27000 through 31000
 series): *50-66* 3-6
DECCA (32000 & 33000 series): *67-73* 2-3
DISNEYLAND: *64* 2-3
MCA: *73-74* 1-3
MONKEY JOE: *78* 1-3
Picture Sleeves
BUENA VISTA: *63* 3-5
DECCA: *62* 3-6
UNITED ARTISTS: *62* 3-6
EPs: 7-Inch 33/45rpm
COLUMBIA: *51-55* 5-15
DECCA: *51-65* 5-15
LPs: 10/12-Inch 33rpm
BELL: *71* 5-8
CAEDMON: *72* 4-6
COLUMBIA (600 series): *55* 15-20
COLUMBIA (1400 series): *60* 10-20
COLUMBIA (2500 series): *55* 15-25
 (10-Inch LPs.)
COLUMBIA (6000 series): *50-51* 15-25
COLUMBIA (9000 series): *68-69* 8-12
CORAL: *73* 4-6
DECCA (100 series): *61* 10-20
DECCA (4000 series): *62-68* 8-15
 (Decca LP numbers in this series preceded by a "7"
 or a "DL-7" are stereo issues.)
DECCA (5000 series): *51-53* 15-25
 (10-Inch LPs.)
DECCA (5000 series): *68* 8-12
 (12-Inch LPs.)
DECCA (8000 series): *55-59* 10-20
DISNEYLAND: *63-64* 8-12
EVEREST: *78* 5-8
HARMONY: *59-70* 8-15
MCA: *73-75* 5-8
SUNSET: *70* 5-10
UNART: *67* 6-12
UNITED ARTISTS: *59-62* 10-20
WORD: *63-66* 5-10
 Also see MILLS, Hayley, & Burl Ives

IVEYS
Singles: 7-Inch
APPLE: *69* 5-8
 Also see BADFINGER

IVY LEAGUE
Singles: 7-Inch
CAMEO: *65-66* 5-8

LPs: 10/12-Inch 33rpm
CAMEO: *65* $20-30
 Member: John Carter.
 Also see OHIO EXPRESS

IVY THREE
Singles: 7-Inch
SHELL (Except 723): *60-61* 4-6
SHELL (723; "Hush Little
 Baby"): *60* 8-10

J

J. BIRD: see BIRD, J.

J.B.s
(J.B.'s Internationals)
Singles: 7-Inch
PEOPLE: *72-76* 2-3
POLYDOR: *77-78* 1-3
LPs: 10/12-Inch 33rpm
PEOPLE: *72-75* 5-8
 Also see BROWN, James

J.D. DREWS: see DREWS, J.D.

J.J. FAD
Singles: 7-Inch
RUTHLESS: *88* 1-3

JACK, Ballin': see BALLIN' JACK

JACKIE & THE STARLITES
Singles: 78rpm
FIRE/FURY (1000; "They Laughed
 At Me"): *57* 20-30
Singles: 7-Inch
FIRE/FURY (1000; "They Laughed
 At Me"): *57* 50-75
FURY: *62* 10-15
HULL: *64* 15-20
MASCOT: *62-63* 15-25
LPs: 10/12-Inch 33rpm
LOST-NITE: *81* 5-8
 Member: Jackie Rue

JACKIE LEE: see LEE, Jackie

JACKS
Singles: 78rpm
RPM (Except 428 & 433): *55-56* 5-10
RPM (428; "Why Don't You Write Me"/
 "Smack Dab In The Middle"): *55* 15-25
RPM (428; "Why Don't You Write Me"/
 "My Darling"): *55* 10-20
 (Note different flip side.)
RPM (433; "I'm Confessin'"): *55* 10-20

JACKS, Susan

JACKS, Terry

JACKSON, Bull Moose
(Bull Moose Jackson & His Buffalo Bearcats;
Bull Moose Jackson & The Flashcats; Moose
Jackson)

JACKSON, Chuck

JACKSON, Chuck, & Maxine Brown

JACKSON, Chuck / Percy Sledge

JACKSON, Chuck, & Tammi Terrell

JACKSON, Chuck / Young Jesse
LPs: 10/12-Inch 33rpm
GUEST STAR: *64* $8-12
Also see JACKSON, Chuck

JACKSON, Clarence
Singles: 7-Inch
R&R: *85* 1-3

JACKSON, Deon
Singles: 7-Inch
ABC: *75* 1-3
ATLANTIC: *63-64* 3-5
CARLA: *66-69* 3-5
LPs: 10/12-Inch 33rpm
ATCO: *66* 15-20
COLLECTABLES: *88* 6-8

JACKSON, Ernest
Singles: 7-Inch
STONE: *73* 2-3

JACKSON, Freddie
Singles: 12-Inch 33/45rpm
CAPITOL: *85-86* 4-6
Singles: 7-Inch
CAPITOL: *85-88* 1-3
LPs: 10/12-Inch 33rpm
CAPITOL: *85-88* 5-8
Also see MOORE, Melba, & Freddie Jackson

JACKSON, George
Singles: 78rpm
RPM: *55* 3-6
Singles: 7-Inch
ATLANTIC: *53* 15-25
CAMEO: *66* 3-5
DOT: *65* 3-5
MERCURY: *67-68* 3-5
RPM: *55* 8-10

JACKSON, J.J.
(J.J. Jackson & The Jackels; J.J. Jackson & The Jackals)
Singles: 7-Inch
ABC: *73* 1-3
CALLA: *66-67* 3-5
EVEREST: *62* 3-5
LOMA: *67-68* 3-5
MAGNA-GLIDE: *75* 2-3
PRELUDE: *59* 4-6
STORM: *59* 5-8
WARNER BROS: *69* 2-3
LPs: 10/12-Inch 33rpm
CALLA: *67* 15-25
CONGRESS: *68* 15-20
PERCEPTION: *69-70* 10-15
WARNER BROS: *69* 10-12

JACKSON, Janet
Singles: 12-Inch 33/45rpm
A&M: *82-86* $4-6
Singles: 7-Inch
A&M: *82-87* 1-3
Picture Sleeves
A&M: *82-86* 1-3
LPs: 10/12-Inch 33rpm
A&M: *82-86* 5-8

JACKSON, Jenny
Singles: 7-Inch
FARR: *76* 2-3

JACKSON, Jermaine
Singles: 12-Inch 33/45rpm
ARISTA: *84-86* 4-6
MOTOWN: *80-83* 4-6
Singles: 7-Inch
ARISTA: *84-87* 1-3
MOTOWN: *72-83* 1-3
Picture Sleeves
MOTOWN: *81* 1-3
LPs: 10/12-Inch 33rpm
ARISTA: *84-86* 5-8
MOTOWN: *72-82* 5-8
Also see JACKSONS

JACKSON, Jermaine, & Michael Jackson
Singles: 12-Inch 33/45rpm
ARISTA: *84* 4-6
Also see JACKSON, Jermaine
Also see JACKSON, Michael

JACKSON, Jermaine, & Pia Zadora
Singles: 7-Inch
CURB: *85* 1-3
Also see JACKSON, Jermaine
Also see ZADORA, Pia

JACKSON, Joe
Singles: 12-Inch 33/45rpm
A&M: *82-86* 4-6
Singles: 7-Inch
A&M (Except 18000): *79-86* 1-3
A&M (18000; "I'm The Man"): *79* 10-15
(Boxed set of five 45s with sleeves and poster. Labeled "The 7-Inch Album.")
Picture Sleeves
A&M: *80-86* 1-3
LPs: 10/12-Inch 33rpm
A&M: *79-88* 5-10
MFSL: *82* 20-30

JACKSON, LaToya
Singles: 12-Inch 33/45rpm
LARC: *83* 4-6

PRIVATE I: *84* $4-6
Singles: 7-Inch
LARC: *83* 1-3
POLYDOR: *80-81* 1-3
PRIVATE I: *84-86* 1-3
RCA VICTOR: *88* 1-3
LPs: 10/12-Inch 33rpm
POLYDOR: *80-81* 5-8
PRIVATE I: *84* 5-8

JACKSON, Mahalia
Singles: 78rpm
APOLLO: *50-57* 2-4
COLUMBIA: *55-57* 2-4
Singles: 7-Inch
APOLLO (200 through 500
series): *50-59* 2-5
APOLLO (600 through 700
series): *59-62* 2-3
COLUMBIA: *55-70* 2-4
GRAND AWARD: *58-59* 2-4
KENWOOD: *64-69* 1-3
EPs: 7-Inch 33/45rpm
APOLLO: *54-59* 5-10
COLUMBIA: *55-60* 5-10
LPs: 10/12-Inch 33rpm
APOLLO: *54-61* 10-20
CAEDMON: *73* 4-6
COLUMBIA (600 through 2100
series): *55-64* 10-20
COLUMBIA (2400 through 2600
series): *66-67* 5-15
COLUMBIA (8100 through 8900
series): *59-64* 10-20
COLUMBIA (9200 through 9900
series): *66-69* 5-15
COLUMBIA (10000 series): *73* 4-8
COLUMBIA (30000 series): *71-72* 5-10
GRAND AWARD: *56* 15-20
HARMONY: *68-72* 5-8
KENWOOD: *64-73* 5-10
PRIORITY: *82* 4-6

JACKSON, Marlon
LPs: 10/12-Inch 33rpm
CAPITOL: *87* 5-8

JACKSON, Michael
Singles: 12-Inch 33/45rpm
EPIC: *79-87* 4-6
Singles: 7-Inch
EPIC: *79-88* 1-3
MCA (1786; "Someone In
The Dark"): *83* 25-50
(Promotional issue only.)
MOTOWN: *71-88* 1-3

Picture Sleeves
EPIC: *82-87* $1-3
MCA (1786; "Someone In The Dark"): *83* 25-50
(Promotional issue only.)
MOTOWN: *72* 2-4
LPs: 10/12-Inch 33rpm
EPIC (35000 through
40000): *79-87* 5-8
EPIC (45000 series): *80* 10-15
(Half-speed mastered.)
MOTOWN: *72-85* .5-10
Also see JACKSON, Jermaine, & Michael
Jackson
Also see JACKSONS
Also see JONES, Quincy
Also see MC CARTNEY, Paul, & Michael
Jackson
Also see ROCKWELL
Also see ROSS, Diana, & Michael Jackson
Also see U.S.A. FOR AFRICA
Also see WONDER, Stevie, & Michael Jackson

JACKSON, Michael, & Mick Jagger / Jacksons
Singles: 12-Inch 33/45rpm
EPIC (5022; "State Of Shock"): *84* 8-10
(With special cover.)
EPIC (5022; "State Of Shock"): *84* 10-15
(Promotional issue with cover.)
Singles: 7-Inch
EPIC (4503; "State Of Shock"): *84* 1-3
Picture Sleeves
EPIC (4503; "State Of Shock"): *84* 2-5
Also see JACKSON, Michael
Also see JACKSONS
Also see JAGGER, Mick

JACKSON, Mick
Singles: 7-Inch
ATCO: *78* 2-3

JACKSON, Millie
Singles: 7-Inch
GEFFEN: *87* 1-3
JIVE: *86-88* 1-3
MGM: *69* 2-4
SPRING: *71-83* 1-3
LPs: 10/12-Inch 33rpm
SPRING: *73-83* 5-8
POLYDOR: *79* 5-8
Also see HAYES, Isaac, & Millie Jackson
Also see WHODINI

JACKSON, Paul, Jr.
Singles: 7-Inch
ATLANTIC: *88* 1-3

JACKSON, Python Lee:
see PYTHON LEE JACKSON

JACKSON, Randy
Singles: 7-Inch
EPIC: 78 . . . . $1-3

JACKSON, Rebbie
Singles: 12-Inch 33/45rpm
COLUMBIA: 84-86 4-6
Singles: 7-Inch
COLUMBIA: 84-88 1-3
LPs: 10/12-Inch 33rpm
COLUMBIA: 84-88 5-8

JACKSON, Rebbie, & Robin Zander
Singles: 7 Inch
COLUMBIA: 86 1-3
Also see JACKSON, Rebbie

JACKSON, Roddy
Singles: 7-Inch
SPECIALTY: 58-59 4-8
(Most Specialty singles are currently available,
using original catalog numbers.)

JACKSON, Shawn
Singles: 7-Inch
PLAYBOY: 74 2-3

JACKSON, Stonewall
Singles: 7-Inch
COLUMBIA (Except 41000
series): 61-73 2-3
COLUMBIA (41000 series): 58-61 3-5
FIRST GENERATION: 81 1-3
GRT: 74 1-3
LITTLE DARLIN': 78-79 1-3
MGM: 73 1-3
PHONORAMA: 83 1-3
EPs: 7-Inch 33/45rpm
COLUMBIA: 59 5-10
LPs: 10/12-Inch 33rpm
AUDIOGRAPH ALIVE: 82 5-8
COLUMBIA (1300 series): 59 15-20
COLUMBIA (1700 through 2700
series): 62-67 8-15
COLUMBIA (8100 series): 59 15-25
COLUMBIA (8500 through 9900
series): 62-70 8-15
COLUMBIA (10000 series): 73 5-8
COLUMBIA (30000 series): 70-72 5-10
GRT: 75-76 5-10
HARMONY: 66-74 6-12
LITTLE DARLIN': 79 5-8
MYRRH: 76 5-8
PHONORAMA: 5-8
RURAL RHYTHM: 5-10

Wanda Jackson

SUNBIRD: 80 . . . . $5-8

JACKSON, Walter
Singles: 7-Inch
BRUNSWICK: 73 2-3
CHI-SOUND: 76-78 2-3
COLUMBIA (02000 series): 81 1-3
COLUMBIA (42000 series): 62-63 3-5
COTILLION: 69 2-3
EPIC: 66-68 3-5
KELLI-ARTS: 83 1-3
OKEH: 64-67 3-5
20TH CENTURY-FOX: 79 1-3
Picture Sleeves
OKEH: 66-67 3-6
LPs: 10/12-Inch 33rpm
CHI-SOUND: 76-78 8-10
COLUMBIA: 81 5-8
EPIC: 77 8-10
OKEH: 65-69 10-20
20TH CENTURY-FOX: 79 5-8

JACKSON, Wanda
(Wanda Jackson & The Party Timers)
Singles: 78rpm
CAPITOL: 56-57 5-10
DECCA: 54-55 4-8
Singles: 7-Inch
ABC: 75 1-3
CAPITOL (2000 through 3000
series): 67-72 2-3
(Orange or orange/yellow labels.)
CAPITOL (3400 through 4500
series): 56-61 6-12
(Purple labels.)

CAPITOL (4600 through 5900
series): *61-67* $2-4
DECCA: *54-55* 8-15
MYRRH: *73-75* 1-3

Picture Sleeves
CAPITOL: *62-66* 4-8

EPs: 7-Inch 33/45rpm
CAPITOL: *58* 15-30

LPs: 10/12-Inch 33rpm
CAPITOL (100 through 600
series): *69-71* 8-12
CAPITOL (1041; "Wanda Jackson"): *58* . 40-50
CAPITOL (1384; "Rockin' With
Wanda"): *60* 50-60
CAPITOL (1511; "There's A Party
Goin' On"): *61* 60-75
CAPITOL (1596; "Right Or Wrong"): *61* 25-35
CAPITOL (1700 through 1900
series): *62-63* 10-20
CAPITOL (2030; "Two Sides Of
Wanda Jackson"): *64* 35-45
CAPITOL (2300 through 2900
series): *65-68* 8-15
CAPITOL (11000 series): *72-73* 5-8
DECCA: *62* 40-50
GUSTO: *80* 5-8
MYRRH: *73-76* 5-8
PICKWICK/HILLTOP: *65-68* 8-12
VARRICK/ROUNDER: *87* 5-8
VOCALION: *69* 8-12
WORD: *77* 4-6

JACKSON, Willis
(Willis "Gator Tail" Jackson & His Orchestra;
Vocal By The 4'Gaters)
Singles: 78rpm
APOLLO: *50* 4-8
ATLANTIC: *51-53* 5-10
DELUXE: *53* 3-6

Singles: 7-Inch
ATLANTIC (900 series): *51-53* 15-25
CADET: *66* 2-3
DELUXE: *53* 5-8
FIRE: *59* 4-6
PRESTIGE: *59-69* 2-4
VERVE: *64* 2-4

LPs: 10/12-Inch 33rpm
ATLANTIC: *75* 5-8
AUDIO-LAB: *59* 15-25
CADET: *66* 10-20
COTILLION: *76* 5-8
MGM: *64* 10-20
MOODSVILLE: *62* 15-20
MUSE: *76-81* 5-8
PRESTIGE (2500 series): *82* 5-8

PRESTIGE (7100 & 7200 series): *59-64* $15-25
(Yellow label.)
PRESTIGE (7100 & 7200 series): *65* 10-20
(Blue label.)
PRESTIGE (7300 through 7800
series): *65-71* 8-15
TRIP: *73* 5-10
VERVE: *64-69* 10-20
Also see CLOVERS
Also see MC DUFF, Brother Jack, & Willis
Jackson

JACKSON SISTERS
Singles: 7-Inch
PROPHESY: *73* 1-3

JACKSONS
(Jackson 5)
Singles: 12-Inch 33/45rpm
EPIC: *79-84* 4-6
MOTOWN: *83* 5-10

Singles: 7-Inch
DYNAMO (146; "You Don't Have
To Be Over 21"): *71* 5-15
EPIC: *76-81* 1-3
MCA: *87* 1-3
MOTOWN (Black vinyl): *69-75* 2-5
MOTOWN (Colored vinyl): *75* 8-12
(Promotional issue only.)
STEEL-TOWN (681; "Big Boy"): *68* 25-50
STEEL-TOWN (682; "We Don't Have To
Be Over 21"): *71* 20-40

Picture Sleeves
EPIC: *76-81* 1-3
MOTOWN: *71-75* 3-6

EPs: 7-Inch 33/45rpm
MOTOWN ("Jackson Five"): *70* 5-10
(Five track flexi-disc.)
MOTOWN (60718; "Jackson Five,
Third Album"): *70* 10-20

LPs: 10/12-Inch 33rpm
EPIC (30000 series, except
picture discs): *76-84* 5-8
EPIC (Picture discs): *79* 10-15
EPIC (46000 series): *81* 10-15
(Half-speed mastered.)
MCA: *87* 5-8
MOTOWN (100 series): *80* 5-10
MOTOWN (700 series,
except 713): *69-70* 8-15
MOTOWN (713; "The Jackson 5
Christmas Album"): *70* 10-20
MOTOWN (800 series): *75-76* 8-15
MOTOWN (5000 series): 5-8
NATURAL RESOURCES: *79* 8-12
(Promotional issues only.)

PICKWICK: $5-10
  Members: Michael Jackson; Jermaine Jackson;
  Jackie Jackson; Marlon Jackson; Tito Jackson;
  Randy Jackson.
  Also see JACKSON, Jermaine
  Also see JACKSON, Michael
  Also see JACKSON, Michael, & Mick Jagger
  / Jacksons
  Also see RIPPLES & WAVES PLUS
  MICHAEL
  Also see ROSS, Diana, & Bill Cosby / Diana
  Ross With The Jackson Five
  Also see WONDER, Stevie

JACOBI, Lou
  LPs: 10/12-Inch 33rpm
CAPITOL: 66 8-12
VERVE: 67 8-12

JACOBS, Debbie
  Singles: 12-Inch 33/45rpm
PERSONAL: 84 4-6
  Singles: 7-Inch
MCA: 79-80 1-3

JACOBS, Dick, & His Orchestra
  Singles: 78rpm
CORAL: 54-57 3-5
  Singles: 7-Inch
CORAL: 54-62 3-5
  EPs: 7-Inch 33/45rpm
CORAL: 56 5-15
  LPs: 10/12-Inch 33rpm
CORAL: 56-60 8-18
VOCALION: 60 4-8

JACOBS, Hank
  Singles: 7-Inch
IMPERIAL: 62 3-5
SUE: 63-64 3-5
  LPs: 10/12-Inch 33rpm
SUE: 64 15-20

JACQUET, Illinois
  (Illinois Jacquet & His All Stars; Jacque Rabbit;
  With Russell Jacquet)
  Singles: 78rpm
ARA: 46 5-10
ALADDIN: 45-54 4-8
APOLLO: 46-47 4-8
MERCURY: 52 4-8
PHILO: 45 5-10
RCA VICTOR: 48-51 4-8
SAVOY: 46 4-8
  Singles: 7-Inch
ALADDIN (3100 & 3200 series): 53-54 . 10-15
ARGO: 63-65 2-4
PRESTIGE: 68-69 2-3

RCA VICTOR (50-0000 series): 51 ... $15-20
VERVE: 62 2-4
  EPs: 7-Inch 33/45rpm
APOLLO: 50 45-55
CLEF: 51-54 20-30
RCA VICTOR: 53 20-30
SAVOY: 50-53 20-30
  LPs: 10/12-Inch 33rpm
ACCORD: 82 5-8
ALADDIN (700 series): 54 50-75
ALADDIN (800 series): 56 50-60
APOLLO (104; "Jam
  Session"): 50 125-150
ARGO: 63-65 10-20
CLEF (100 series): 51-52 40-60
  (10-Inch LPs.)
CLEF (600 & 700 series): 54-56 30-50
EPIC: 63 15-20
GRAND AWARD: 56 20-30
IMPERIAL: 62 15-20
JRC: 79 5-8
PRESTIGE: 69-75 8-12
RCA VICTOR (3200 series): 53 35-50
  (10-Inch LPs.)
ROULETTE: 60 15-25
SAVOY (500 series): 52 30-50
SAVOY (15000 series): 50 40-60
TRIP: 79 5-8
VERVE (2500 series): 82-87 5-10
VERVE (8000 series): 57-58 25-50
  (Reads "Verve Records, Inc." at bottom of label.)
VERVE (8000 series): 61-65 10-20
  (Reads "MGM Records - A Division Of Metro-
  Goldwyn-Mayer, Inc." at bottom of label.)
  Also see COLE, Cozy, & Illnois Jacquet
  Also see DOGGETT, Bill
  Also see HEART BEATS QUINTET

JACQUET, Illinois / Lester Young
  EPs: 7-Inch 33/45rpm
ALADDIN: 54 30-40
  LPs: 10/12-Inch 33rpm
ALADDIN (701; "Battle Of
  The Saxes"): 54 50-75
  (10-Inch LP. Black vinyl.)
ALADDIN (701; "Battle Of
  The Saxes"): 54 150-200
  (10-Inch LP. Colored vinyl.)
ALADDIN (800 series): 56 50-60
  Also see JACQUET, Illinois

JACQUET, Russell, & His Orch:
  see HEART BEATS QUINTET

JADE WARRIOR
  Singles: 7-Inch
VERTIGO: 71-72 2-4

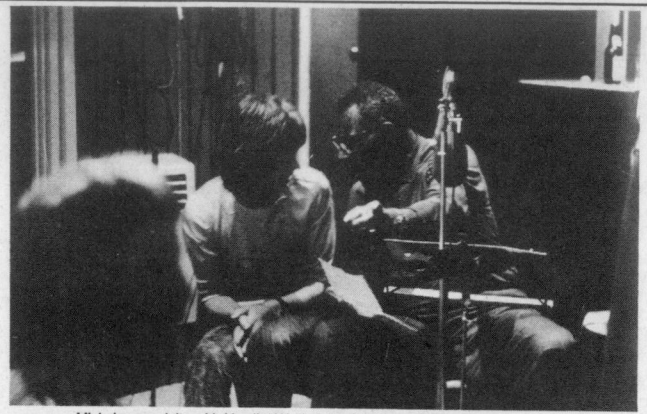

Mick Jagger visits with Howlin' Wolf at the Chess studios in Chicago

LPs: 10/12-Inch 33rpm
ANTILLES: *78* $5-8
ISLAND: *74-76* 8-10
VERTIGO: *71-72* 10-12

JAGGER, Chris
LPs: 10/12-Inch 33rpm
ASYLUM: *73-74* 8-10

JAGGER, Mick
Singles: 12-Inch 33/45rpm
COLUMBIA (2060; "Lucky In Love"): *85* . 4-6
(With special cover.)
COLUMBIA (2060; "Lucky In
Love"): *85* 12-15
(Promotional issue with special cover.)
COLUMBIA (5181; "Just Another
Night"): *85* 4-6
(With special cover.)
COLUMBIA (5181; "Just Another
Night"): *85* 10-15
(Promotional issue with special cover.)
COLUMBIA (6926; "Let's Work"): *87* 5-8
COLUMBIA (7492; "Throwaway"): *87* 5-8
EPIC (5931; "Ruthless People"): *86* 8-10
(With special cover.)
Singles: 7-Inch
COLUMBIA: *85-87* 1-3
EPIC: *86* 1-3
Promotional Singles
COLUMBIA: *85* 6-10
EPIC: *86* 5-10
LPs: 10/12-Inch 33rpm
COLUMBIA: *85-87* 6-10
EPIC: *86* 6-10
LONDON WAVELENGTH (006;
"The Mick Jagger Special"): *81* 50-75
(Promotional issue only.)

ROLLING STONES (164; "Interview
With Mick Jagger"): *71* $50-75
(Promotional issue only.)
UNITED ARTISTS (300; "Ned
Kelly"): *74* 8-10
(Soundtrack.)
UNITED ARTISTS (5213; "Ned
Kelly"): *70* 10-20
(Soundtrack.)
Also see BOWIE, David, & Mick Jagger
Also see FRAMPTON, Peter
Also see JACKSON, Michael, & Mick Jagger
/ Jacksons
Also see ROLLING STONES
Also see TOSH, Peter, & Mick Jagger
Also see WEST, Leslie

JAGGERZ
Singles: 7-Inch
KAMA SUTRA: *70* 2-4
WOODEN NICKEL: *75* 2-3
LPs: 10/12-Inch 33rpm
KAMA SUTRA: *70* 10-15
WOODEN NICKEL: *75* 8-10
Member: Donnie Iris.
Also see IRIS, Donnie
Also see Q

JAGS
Singles: 7-Inch
ISLAND: *80* 1-3
LPs: 10/12-Inch 33rpm
ISLAND: *80-81* 5-8

JAISUN
Singles: 7-Inch
JETT SETT: *78* 2-3

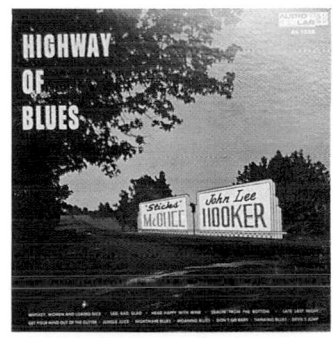

1.

2.

3.

4.

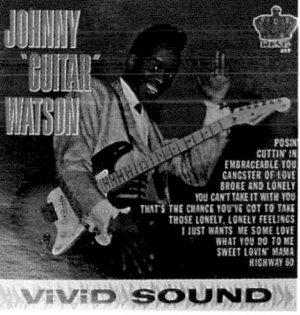

5.

6.

1. Tracks by Stick, or "Sticks," McGhee (younger brother of Brownie McGhee) make up one side of this 1959 LP. The other side is by the legendary John Lee Hooker. *2. Surfin' Bird,* by Minneapolis/St. Paul's Trashmen, has become a novelty classic. It reached the top-five in 1963.   *3.* The Sapphires hailed from Philadelphia. Their 1964 *Who Do You Love* was as smooth as their namesake jewel.   *4.* Issued in 1963, *Dynamite* was Ike and Tina Turner's second LP. The title says it all.   *5.* Mary Wells was Motown's first female star. *The One Who Really Loves You* appeared in 1962.   *6.* For nearly forty years Johnny "Guitar" Watson has been recording. His first R&B top-ten hit, *Cuttin' in,* is on this 1963 King LP.

1.

2.

3.

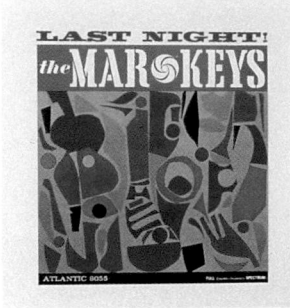

4.

5.

6.

1. Joanie Sommers had every tool necessary to be an immense star, but never quite lived up to expectations. Neither *Johnny Get Angry* (1963), nor any of her LPs, cracked the top-100.   *2.* Aaron Neville, one of the famous Neville Brothers, topped the charts in early 1967 with *Tell It Like It Is.*   *3.* Raphael ''Googie'' Rene was a classy keyboardist who also happened to record for the Class label. *Romesville* (1959) featured an all-star, thirty-member, modern jazz lineup.   *4.* Instrumentalists of a different genre, the Mar-Keys, from Memphis, turned *Last Night* into one of 1961's biggest hits.   *5. Double Dynamite* was the second hit album (1967) for Samuel Moore and David Prater.   *6.* The first LP for Missouri-born, Arizona/California-raised Jerry Wallace came in 1959 and featured his early rockers.

 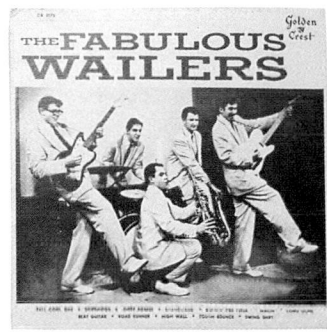

1.

2.

MOTHERMANIA

3.

4.

5.

6.

1. *Gone* topped both the pop and country music charts in 1957, although this LP wasn't released until 1960.   2. *Tall Cool One* was a top-forty hit twice for the Washington-based Wailers: in 1959 and again in '64.   3. *Mothermania*, a 1969 issue, is a "best of" collection of earlier tracks by the Frank Zappa-led Mothers of Invention.   4. The Jaynetts, a trio of teenage girls, had only one hit, *Sally Go 'Round the Roses*, which reached number two in 1963.   5. Denmark's Jorgen Ingmann rode to the top of the charts in early '61 with the ingratiating instrumental, *Apache*.   6. For years, England's premier instrumental group was the Shadows, who also backed Cliff Richard. This, their second U.S. LP, came in 1964.

 1.

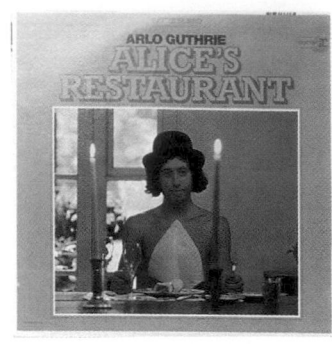 2.

 3.

 4.

 5.

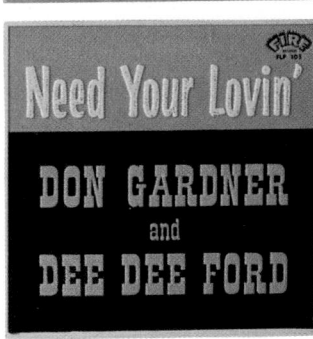 6.

1. After *Behind Closed Doors* (1973), eight Charlie Rich singles reached number one. This song turned his career around and fueled his selection as CMA Entertainer of the Year in 1974.   2. This 1967 LP, with an eighteen-minute version of *Alice's Restaurant (Massacree),* inspired the 1969 film of the same name.   3. Them, featuring Van Morrison, was a British Invasion group that hailed from Northern Ireland. This, their first LP, appeared in 1965.   4. A more attractive *Calendar Girl* than Julie London may not have existed in 1956, when this LP hit the top-twenty.   5. *Let's Try Again* was Clyde McPhatter's biggest MGM hit, but the label chose to title his 1960 LP *Let's Start Over Again.*   6. On Don Gardner and Dee Dee Ford's rare *Need Your Lovin'* LP (1962), cover art is reduced to its simplest form.

1.

2.

3.

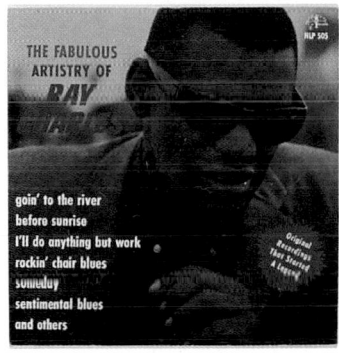

4.

5.

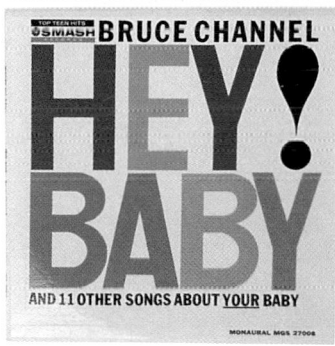

6.

1. Perky Claudine Clark, from Macon, Georgia, crafted one of 1962's liveliest tunes, *Party Lights*, which ignited interest in this LP.   *2.* The second of six different hits of *Land of 1000 Dances* was by Los Angeles' Cannibal and the Headhunters (1965). Theirs was also the second most popular—after Wilson Pickett's rendition.   *3.* Pictured for the first time in full color, this is the 1958 issue of *We Are the Chantels,* one of the most valuable albums in this guide.   *4. The Fabulous Artistry of Ray Charles* (1959) contains eight recordings made in the early '50s for Swingtime. To round out the LP, four tracks by Charles Brown are added.   *5.* A 1961 release, *Dance 'til Quarter to Three with U.S. Bonds* included his first three hits. The cover photo proved Bonds could have easily jumped his way into a Toyota commercial.   *6.* In 1958, Bruce Channel became a regular on the Louisiana Hayride. By early '62, he was holding down the number one spot on the pop charts with *Hey! Baby.*

1.

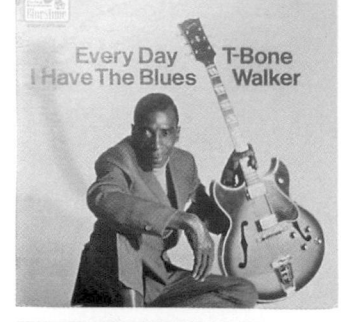

2.

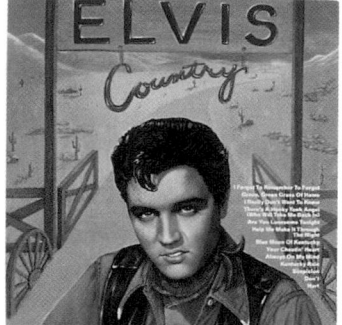

3.

4.

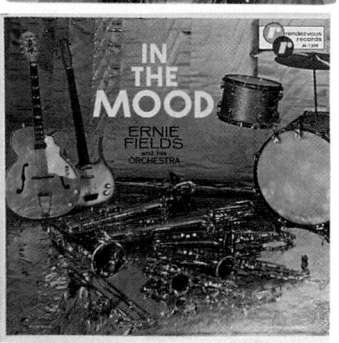

5.

6.

1. Peaches 'N Cream, the centerpiece of *Soul the Hits,* was a 1965 hit for the Ikettes, three girls from the Ike and Tina Turner Revue. *2.* Thibeaux "T-Bone" Walker had nine R&B top-twenty hits from 1947 to 1950. Unfortunately, none are included on this 1969 collection. *3. Elvis Country,* an already-scarce 1984 item, was a Special Products pressing for ERA, proving records do not have to be *old* to be valuable. *4. Pretty Mama Blues* became a number one blues tune in 1948, but didn't appear on an LP by Ivory Joe Hunter until this 1957 release. *5.* Ernie Fields played trombone while directing the orchestra on his 1959 hit remake of Glenn Miller's classic *In the Mood.* On this cover, the instruments are pictured but not the musicians. *6.* A string of four Standells' hits began in 1966, but two years earlier the boys were recorded live at P.J.'s club in Los Angeles for this LP.

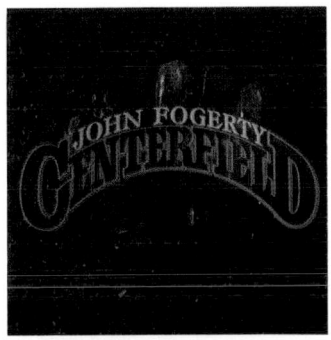

1.

2.

3.

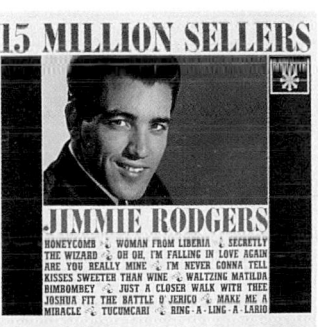

4.

5.

6.

1 In 1985, over a dozen years after the breakup of Creedence Clearwater Revival, John Fogerty returned to the top of the LP charts with *Centerfield*. *2. Duets* contained eleven old Jerry Lee Lewis tracks overdubbed in 1978 with the voice of Jimmy "Orion" Ellis. The duet effect was actually quite enjoyable, with Ellis singing in an Elvis Presley style. *3.* One of the great voices of the '60s belonged to Gene Pitney. *Only Love Can Break A Heart* (1962), Gene's first charted LP, featured seven of his best singles sides. *4.* In titling this 1962 gathering of Jimmie Rodgers hits, Roulette got a little carried away—15 fine tracks, yes, but not *15 Million Sellers*. *5.* From San Marcos, Texas, came Roy Head, who shot right up the charts in 1965 with *Treat Her Right*. This, his first LP, didn't contain *Treat Her Right* but offered an excellent assortment of rock and rhythm and blues. *6. Go Bo Diddley* (1957) was the second album for Bo—singer, songwriter, master of music's most distinctive guitar sound, and, more recently, star of a TV commercial with Bo Jackson.

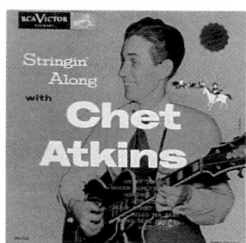  

1. Looking at *After School Session,* a 1957 Chuck Berry issue, it's easy to understand why EPs were so popular. Four great songs on one 45rpm disc, plus a cardboard jacket like those used on 12-inch albums. *2.* Most jukebox EPs used the same cover art as the LP. On this 1961 Little Willie John EP, twelve tracks are shown on the cover but only six are found on the disc. *3.* Homer and Jethro's hit parody of *Hernando's Hideaway* and three others made up this 1955 EP. *4.* The second EP (1957) for rock and roll's greatest duo, the Everly Brothers is, like all Cadence EPs, quite collectible. *5.* You don't have to know anything about opera or classical music to enjoy *Spike Jones Murders "Carmen"* (1955); you just have to know how to laugh. *6.* Issued in 1956, at the peak of his popularity, the *Little Richard* EP has four tracks recorded in '52, when he was unknown. *7. Hey Joe,* the first Jimi Hendrix single (1967), came with a now-quite-scarce picture sleeve. *8.* Jimi's . . . *and a Happy New Year* was a promotional, 1974 single that also came with a special sleeve. *9.* This eight-track, 10-inch LP by Chet Atkins (1953) demonstrated the five-fingered, folk/country style for which he is now famous. *10.* The 10-inch *Barrelhouse, Boogie and the Blues* (1954) spotlights Ella Mae Morse's cover versions of early '50s hits made popular by Ruth Brown and others. *11.* The *Don't Let Go* EP (1958) followed hot on the heels of the top-fifteen single of the same title. *12.* A real oddity, this 1960 EP has two songs by the Wailers backed with two by the Three Graces. The sleeve is actually a mailing envelope.

JAK
Singles: 7-Inch
EPIC: 84-86 ....$1-3
LPs: 10/12-Inch 33rpm
EPIC: 85 1-3

JAKKI
Singles: 7-Inch
PYRAMID: 76 1-3
WEST END: 1-3

JAM
Singles: 7-Inch
POLYDOR: 78-83 1-3
Picture Sleeves
POLYDOR: 80-83 1-3
LPs: 10/12-Inch 33rpm
POLYDOR: 77-83 5-8
Also see STYLE COUNCIL

JAMAICA BOYS
Singles: 7-Inch
WARNER BROS: 87-88 1-3

JAMAL, Ahmad
(Ahmad Jamal Trio; Ahmad Jamal Quintet)
Singles: 7-Inch
ARGO: 57-65 2-4
CADET: 66-68 2-3
CHESS: 73 1-3
PARROTT: 55 3-5
20TH CENTURY-FOX: 73-80 1-3
EPs: 7-Inch 33/45rpm
ARGO: 59-61 8-15
LPs: 10/12-Inch 33rpm
ABC: 68 8-12
ARGO (610 through 662): 56-60 20-40
ARGO (667 through 758): 61-65 10-20
CADET: 65-73 8-15
CATALYST: 76 5-8
EPIC (600 series): 63-65 10-20
EPIC (3200 series): 56 20-30
EPIC (3600 series): 59 15-25
IMPULSE: 69-73 8-15
MOTOWN: 80 5-8
PERSONAL CHOICE: 82 5-8
SHUBRA: 83 5-8
20TH CENTURY-FOX: 73-80 5-8
WHO'S WHO IN JAZZ: 81 5-8

JAMES, Bob
(Bob James Trio)
Singles: 7-Inch
CTI: 74-77 1-3
COLUMBIA: 79-83 1-3
TAPPAN ZEE/COLUMBIA: 77-85 1-3
Picture Sleeves
COLUMBIA: 79-80 1-3

LPs: 10/12-Inch 33rpm
CTI: 74-77 ....$5-10
COLUMBIA: 83 5-8
ESP: 65 10-15
MERCURY: 63 15-20
TAPPAN ZEE/COLUMBIA: 77-85 5-10
WARNER BROS: 88 5-8

JAMES, Bob, & Earl Klugh
Singles: 7-Inch
CAPITOL: 82 1-3
TAPPAN ZEE/COLUMBIA: 79 1-3
LPs: 10/12-Inch 33rpm
CAPITOL: 82 5-8
MFSL: 84 20-30
TAPPAN ZEE/COLUMBIA: 79 5-10

JAMES, Bob, & David Sanborn
LPs: 10/12-Inch 33rpm
WARNER BROS: 86 5-8
Also see JAMES, Bob
Also see SANBORN, David

JAMES, Elmore
(Elmore James & His Broomdusters; Elmo
James)
Singles: 78rpm
ACE (508; "My Time Ain't
Long"): 53 30-60
CHECKER (777; "Country
Boogie"): 53 30-60
CHIEF: 57 5-10
FLAIR (1011; "Early In The
Morning"): 54 20-40
FLAIR (1014; "Can't Stop Lovin'"): 54 . 20-40
FLAIR (1022 through 1079): 55-56 10-20
METEOR (5000; "I Believe"): 53 25-50
METEOR (5003; "Sinful
Woman"): 53 25-50
MODERN (983; "Wild About You"): 56 25-50
TRUMPET: 52 15-25
VEE JAY: 57 5-8
Singles: 7-Inch
ACE (508; "My Time Ain't
Long"): 53 75-125
CHECKER (777; "Country
Boogie"): 53 75-100
CHESS: 60 4-6
CHIEF: 57-60 10-20
ENJOY: 65 5-10
FIRE: 60-62 8-12
FLAIR (1011; "Early In The
Morning"): 54 50-100
FLAIR (1014; "Can't Stop Lovin'"): 54 50-100
FLAIR (1022 through 1079): 55-56 25-50
FLASHBACK: 65 1-3

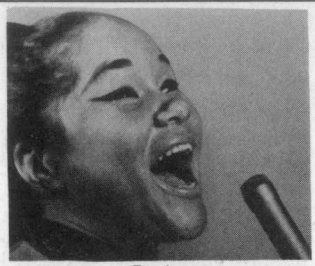

Etta James

JEWEL: *66-67* $3-5
(The reverse side of both Jewel 764 and 783 are actually by Big Boy Crudup, even though credited to Elmo James.)
KENT: *60-67* 3-5
METEOR (5000; "I Believe"): *53* 50-100
METEOR (5003; "Sinful
Woman"): *53* 50-100
MODERN (983; "Wild About
You"): *56* 50-100
M-PAC: 3-5
S&M: 4-6
SOUND: 3-5
SPHERE SOUND: *65* 3-5
VEE JAY: *57* 5-8
LPs: 10/12-Inch 33rpm
BELL: *68-69* 10-12
BLUE HORIZON: 10-12
CHESS: *69* 10-12
COLLECTABLES: *88* 6-8
CROWN: *61* 40-50
CUSTOM: 8-12
INTERMEDIA: *84* 5-8
KENT: *64-69* 10-15
KENT TREASURE SERIES: *86* 5-8
SPHERE SOUND: 20-25
TRIP: *71-78* 8-10
UNITED: 10-12
UPFRONT: 8-10
Also see CRUDUP, Big Boy

JAMES, Elmore, & John Brim
LPs: 10/12-Inch 33rpm
CHESS: *69* 10-12
Also see JAMES, Elmore

JAMES, Etta
(Etta "Miss Peaches" James)
Singles: 78rpm
MODERN: *55-56* 3-6
Singles: 7-Inch
ABC: *74* 1-3
ARGO: *60-64* 3-5
CADET: *67-72* 2-4

CHESS: *73-76* $2-3
KENT: *58-60* 3-5
MODERN (900 series): *55-56* 5-10
MODERN (1000 series): *57-58* 4-8
T-ELECTRIC: *80* 1-3
WARNER BROS: *78* 2-3
LPs: 10/12-Inch 33rpm
ARGO: *61-65* 20-25
CADET: *67-71* 10-15
CHESS: *71-76* 10-12
CROWN: *61-63* 20-30
INTERMEDIA: *84* 5-8
KENT (3002; "Miss Etta James"): *61* 15-20
(Black vinyl.)
KENT (3002; "Miss Etta James"): *61* 20-40
(Colored vinyl.)
T-ELECTRIC: *80* 5-8
UNITED: 10-12
WARNER BROS: *78* 5-8
WESTBOUND: 8-10
Also see ETTA & HARVEY

JAMES, Etta, & Sugar Pie DeSanto
Singles: 7-Inch
CADET: *65-66* 3-5
Also see DE SANTO, Sugar Pie
Also see JAMES, Etta

JAMES, Harry, & His Orchestra
Singles: 7-Inch
COLUMBIA (33000 series): *76* 1-3
COLUMBIA (38000 through
40000 series): *50-56* 2-4
DOT: *65-66* 1-3
GOLD-MOR: *73* 1-3
MGM: *59-63* 2-3
EPs: 7-Inch 33/45rpm
COLUMBIA: *50-56* 4-8
LPs: 10/12-Inch 33rpm
BAINBRIDGE: *83* 4-8
BRIGHT ORANGE: *73* 4-8
CAPITOL (600 through
1500 series): *55-61* 8-15
(With a "T" or "ST" prefix.)
CAPITOL (1500 series): *62* 8-10
(With a "DT" prefix.)
CAPITOL (1500 series): *77* 4-8
(With an "M" prefix.)
COLUMBIA: *50-67* 8-15
COLUMBIA SPECIAL PRODUCTS: *79* ...4-8
DOT: *66-67* 5-10
HARMONY: *59-72* 8-12
LONDON: *68* 5-10
MGM: *59-65* 8-15
METRO: *65-67* 5-10
SHEFFIELD LAB: *77-79* 5-10

Also see KALLEN, Kitty
Also see SINATRA, Frank

JAMES, Harry, & Dick Haymes
LPs: 10/12-Inch 33rpm
CIRCLE: *81* **$5-8**
Also see HAYMES, Dick
Also see JAMES, Harry, & His Orchestra

JAMES, Jesse
Singles: 7-Inch
T.T.E.D: *87* **1-3**
20TH CENTURY-FOX: *67-75* **2-4**
UNI: *69* **2-4**
ZEA (ZAY): *70-71* **2-4**
LPs: 10/12-Inch 33rpm
20TH CENTURY-FOX: *67* **8-10**

JAMES, Jimmy, & The Vagabonds
Singles: 7-Inch
ATCO: *67-68* **3-5**
PYE: *75-76* **2-3**
LPs: 10/12-Inch 33rpm
ATCO: *67* **10-15**
PYE: *76* **5-8**

JAMES, Joni
Singles: 78rpm
MGM: *52-57* **4-8**
SHARP ("You Belong To Me"): *52* **20-40**
Singles: 7-Inch
MGM: *52-64* **5-15**
MGM/GOLDEN CIRCLE: **2-4**
SHARP ("You Belong To Me"): *52* **50-100**
Picture Sleeves
MGM: *57-62* **5-10**
EPs: 7-Inch 33/45rpm
MGM: *53-59* **10-20**
LPs: 10/12-Inch 33rpm
MGM (200 series): *54* **25-50**
MGM (3200 through 4100
  series): *55-63* **20-35**
MGM (4200 series): *64-65* **10-20**

JAMES, Rick
(Rick James & The Stone City Band)
Singles: 12-Inch 33/45rpm
GORDY: *79-85* **4-6**
MOTOWN: *78-85* **4-6**
Singles: 7-Inch
GORDY: *78-85* **1-3**
MOTOWN: *86* **1-3**
REPRISE: *88* **1-3**
Picture Sleeves
GORDY: *79-85* **1-3**
LPs: 10/12-Inch 33rpm
GORDY: *78-86* **5-8**
REPRISE: *88* **5-8**

Also see STONE CITY BAND
Also see TEMPTATIONS, & Rick James

JAMES, Rick, & Friend
(Rick James & Smokey Robinson)
Singles: 7-Inch
GORDY: *83* **$2-5**
Also see ROBINSON, Smokey

JAMES, Rick, & Smokey Robinson
Singles: 7-Inch
GORDY: *83* **1-3**
Also see JAMES, Rick, & Friend
Also see ROBINSON, Smokey

JAMES, Rick, & Roxanne Shante
Singles: 7-Inch
REPRISE: *88* **1-3**
Also see JAMES, Rick
Also see SHANTE, Roxanne

JAMES, Sonny
(Sonny James & The Southern Gentlemen)
Singles: 78rpm
CAPITOL: *52-57* **3-5**
Singles: 7-Inch
CAPITOL (2000 through 3900): *67-74* **2-3**
(Orange labels.)
CAPITOL (2600 through 3800): *52-57* **3-6**
(Purple labels.)
CAPITOL (3900 through 5900): *57-67* **2-5**
COLUMBIA: *72-78* **1-3**
DIMENSION: *82* **1-3**
DOT: *62* **2-4**
GROOVE: *61* **3-5**
MONUMENT: *79* **1-3**
NRC: *60* **3-5**
RCA VICTOR: *61-62* **3-5**
Picture Sleeves
CAPITOL: *59-72* **3-6**
COLUMBIA: *72-75* **2-3**
DIMENSION: *76* **1-3**
NRC: *60* **5-8**
EPs: 7-Inch 33/45rpm
CAPITOL: *57-58* **8-15**
LPs: 10/12-Inch 33rpm
ABC: *77* **5-8**
BROOKVILLE: *75* **8-12**
CAMDEN: **8-12**
CAPITOL (100 through 800): *68-71* **8-12**
CAPITOL (700 through 900): *57-58* **20-30**
CAPITOL (1100 series): *59* **15-25**
CAPITOL (2000 through 2800): *64-68* ... **8-15**
CAPITOL (11000 series): *72-73* **5-8**
COLUMBIA: *72-78* **5-10**
CROWN: **8-12**
DIMENSION: *82* **5-8**

DOT: *62* $15-20
GUEST STAR: *64* 10-15
HAMILTON: *65* 8-12
MONUMENT: *79* 5-8
PICKWICK: *76* 5-8
PICKWICK/HILLTOP: *69* 8-12
TVP: *75* 8-12
  Also see HAGGARD, Merle / Sonny James
  Also see HORTON, Johnny / Sonny James

JAMES, Sonny / David Houston
LPs: 10/12-Inch 33rpm
PICKWICK/HILLTOP: *67* 8-12
  Also see HOUSTON, David

JAMES, Sonny / Seekers
Singles: 7-Inch
CAPITOL (5375; "I'll Keep Holding On"/
  "I'll Never Find Another You"): *65* 3-5
  (These two tracks were unintentionally pressed
  back-to-back.)
  Also see JAMES, Sonny
  Also see SEEKERS

JAMES, Tommy
(Tommy James & The Shondells)
Singles: 7-Inch
ABC: *73* 1-3
FANTASY: *75-80* 1-3
MCA: *74* 2-3
MILLENNIUM: *79-81* 1-3
ROULETTE: *66-73* 3-5
Picture Sleeves
ROULETTE: *66-67* 4-8
LPs: 10/12-Inch 33rpm
FANTASY: *76-80* 8-10
MILLENNIUM: *80* 5-8
ROULETTE: *66-72* 10-15
SCEPTER: *73* 8-10
SCEPTER/CITATION: *82* 5-8
TWENTY-ONE: *83* 5-8
  Members: Tommy James; Mike Vale; Ed Gray;
  Ron Rosman; Pete Lucia.
  Also see HOG HEAVEN
  Also see SHONDELLS

JAMES BOYS
Singles: 7-Inch
PHIL L.A. OF SOUL: *68* 2-4

JAMES GANG
Singles: 7-Inch
ABC: *70-72* 2-4
ATCO: *74-75* 2-3
BLUESWAY: *69* 3-5
LPs: 10/12-Inch 33rpm
ABC: *70-73* 10-12
ATCO: *74-76* 8-10

BLUESWAY: *69* $10-15
COMMAND: *74* 8-10
MCA: 5-8
  Members: Joe Walsh; Tommy Bolin; Dominic
  Troiano.
  Also see WALSH, Joe

JAMESON, Cody
Singles: 7-Inch
ATCO: *77* 2-3

JAMESON, Nick
Singles: 7-Inch
MOTOWN: *86* 1-3
LPs: 10/12-Inch 33rpm
MOTOWN: *86* 5-8

JAMESTOWN MASSACRE
Singles: 7-Inch
WARNER BROS: *72* 2-3

JAMIE & JANE
Singles: 7-Inch
DECCA: *59* 10-20
  Members: Gene Pitney; Ginny Arnell.
  Also see ARNELL, Ginny
  Also see PITNEY, Gene

JAMIES
Singles: 7-Inch
EPIC (9000 series): *58-63* 5-8
EPIC (11000 series): *74* 1-3
UNITED ARTISTS: *59* 4-6
Picture Sleeves
EPIC: *62* 10-20

JAMM
Singles: 7-Inch
EPIC: *88* 1-3

JAMMERS
Singles: 7-Inch
SALSOUL: *82-83* 1-3

JAMUL
Singles: 7-Inch
LIZARD: *70* 2-4
LPs: 10/12-Inch 33rpm
LIZARD: *70* 10-12

JAN & ARNIE
Singles: 7-Inch
ARWIN: *58* 10-20
DOT: *60* 8-10
DORE (522; "Baby Talk"): *59* 100-125
  (Actually by Jan & Dean but shown on first press-
  ings as by Jan & Arnie.)
EPs: 7-Inch 33/45rpm
DOT (1097; "Jan & Arnie"): *60* 200-300
  Members: Jan Berry; Arnie Ginsburg.
  Also see BERRY, Jan

Also see JAN & DEAN

JAN & DEAN
Singles: 7-Inch
CHALLENGE (Except 9111): *61* $5-12
CHALLENGE (9111; "Heart & Soul"/
"Those Words"): *61* 25-30
CHALLENGE (9111; "Heart & Soul"/
"Midsummer Night's Dream"): *61* 5-8
(Note different flip side.)
COLUMBIA: *67* .12-15
DORE: *59-61* 10-20
J&D: *66* 20-30
JAN & DEAN: *66* 45-50
LIBERTY (Except 55522): *61-66* 5-15
LIBERTY (55522; "She's Still Talkin'
Baby Talk"): *62* 20-25
MAGIC LAMP: *66* 15-20
ODE: *75* 20-25
UNITED ARTISTS: *72-76* 8-10
WARNER BROS: *67-68* 25-30
Picture Sleeves
DORE (555; "We Go
Together"): *60* .25-50
DORE (576; "Gee"): *60* 75-100
LIBERTY (Except 55766 &
55849): *63-65* .10-20
LIBERTY (55766; "From All Over
The World"): *65* 80-125
LIBERTY (55849; "Folk City"): *65* 20-25
UNITED ARTISTS: *71* 10-15
LPs: 10/12-Inch 33rpm
COLUMBIA (9461; "Save For A
Rainy Day"): *67* 400-700
(Promotional issue only.)
DEADMAN'S CURVE ("Live At The
Keystone Berkeley"): *79* 15-20
(With Papa Doo Ron Ron.)
DESIGN/STEREO SPECTRUM: *64* 10-15
DORE (101; "Jan & Dean"): *60* 100-150
(Price includes a 12x12 Jan & Dean color photo,
which represents about $25-$45 of the value.)
EXACT: *80* 5-8
IMPERIAL HOUSE: *80* 5-8
INTERNATIONAL AWARD
SERIES: 8-10
J&D (101; "Save For A
Rainy Day"): *67* 125-200
LIBERTY (LN series): *81-82* 5-8
LIBERTY (LRP & LST series,
except 414): *62-66* 20-30
LIBERTY (414; "Pop Symphony
Number 1"): *65* 40-50
(With an "LRP-3" prefix, for mono, or an
"LST-7" prefix for stereo issues.)

Jan and Dean

MAGIC CARPET: $10-12
RHINO: *82* 5-8
SUNSET: *67* 10-15
UNITED ARTISTS: *71-79* 10-12
Members: Jan Berry; Dean Torrence.
Also see BERRY, Jan
Also see CALIFORNIA MUSIC
Also see JAN & ARNIE

JAN & DEAN / Beach Boys
LPs: 10/12-Inch 33rpm
EXACT: *81* 5-8
Also see BEACH BOYS

JAN & DEAN / Roy Orbison / 4
Seasons / Shirelles
EPs: 7-Inch 33/45rpm
COKE: *65* 20-30
(Coca-Cola radio spots. Issued to radio
stations only.)
Also see 4 SEASONS
Also see ORBISON, Roy
Also see SHIRELLES

JAN & DEAN / Soul Surfers
LPs: 10/12-Inch 33rpm
L-J: *63* 35-45
Also see JAN & DEAN

JAN & KJELD
Singles: 7-Inch
ALONCA: *66* 2-4
IMPERIAL: *59* 3-5
JARO INT'L: *60* 3-5

KAPP: *60-61* $3-5
Picture Sleeves
JARO INT'L: *60* 4-8
KAPP: *60* 4-8
LPs: 10/12-Inch 33rpm
KAPP: *60* 15-20

JANE, Baby: see BABY JANE

JANE'S ADDICTION
LPs: 10/12-Inch 33rpm
WARNER BROS: *88* 5-8

JANIS, Johnny
Singles: 78rpm
ABC-PARAMOUNT: *57* 3-6
Singles: 7-Inch
ABC-PARAMOUNT: *57* 5-8
BOMARC: *59-60* 4-6
COLUMBIA: *60* 3-5
CORAL: *55* 5-8
MONUMENT: *66-68* 3-5
LPs: 10/12-Inch 33rpm
ABC-PARAMOUNT: *57* 20-25
COLUMBIA: *61* 15-18
MONUMENT: *65* 10-15

JANKEL, Chas
Singles: 12-Inch 33/45rpm
A&M: *83* 4-6
Singles: 7-Inch
A&M: *82* 1-3
LPs: 10/12-Inch 33rpm
A&M: *82* 5-8
Also see DURY, Ian, & The Blockheads

JANKOWSKI, Horst, & His Orchestra
Singles: 7-Inch
MERCURY: *65-68* 2-3
LPs: 10/12-Inch 33rpm
MERCURY: *65-69* 5-15
Also see IMPALAS / Horst Jankowski & His
Orchestra

JARMELS
Singles: 7-Inch
LAURIE: *61-63* 5-8
LPs: 10/12-Inch 33rpm
COLLECTABLES: *87* 6-8

JARRE, Jean-Michael
Singles: 12-Inch 33/45rpm
POLYDOR: *86* 4-6
Singles: 7-Inch
POLYDOR: *78-86* 1-3
LPs: 10/12-Inch 33rpm
DREYFUS: *85-86* 5-8
POLYDOR: *78-86* 5-8
Also see U.S.A. FOR AFRICA

JARREAU, Al
Singles: 7-Inch
MCA: *87* $1-3
REPRISE: *76* 2-3
REPRISE: *88* 1-3
WARNER BROS: *77-86* 1-3
LPs: 10/12-Inch 33rpm
MFSL: *78* 25-50
REPRISE: *76* 5-8
REPRISE: *88* 5-8
WARNER BROS: *77-86* 5-8
Also see U.S.A. FOR AFRICA

JARREAU, Al, & Randy Crawford
Singles: 7-Inch
WARNER BROS: *82* 1-3
Also see CRAWFORD, Randy
Also see JARREAU, Al

JARRETT, Keith
LPs: 10/12-Inch 33rpm
ATLANTIC: *75* 6-10
ECM: *76-80* 6-12
IMPULSE: *75-77* 6-10

JARVIS, Carol
Singles: 78rpm
DOT: *57* 3-5
Singles: 7-Inch
DOT: *57-59* 4-6
ERA: *60-61* 3-5

JARVIS, Marion
Singles: 7-Inch
ROXBURY: *74* 2-4

JASMIN
Singles: 12-Inch 33/45rpm
TVI: *84* 4-6

JASON & THE SCORCHERS
(Jason & The Nashville Scorchers)
Singles: 7-Inch
EMI AMERICA: *84-86* 1-3
PRAXIS: *83-84* 10-15
LPs: 10/12-Inch 33rpm
EMI AMERICA: *84-86* 5-8
Member: Jason Ringenberg.

JASPER, Chris
Singles: 7-Inch
CBS ASSOC: *87-88* 1-3
LPs: 10/12-Inch 33rpm
CBS ASSOC: *88* 5-8

JAY, Dee: see DEE JAY

JAY, Jazzy: see JAZZY JAY

JAY, Morty
(Morty Jay & The Surfin' Cats)
Singles: 7-Inch
LEGEND: *63* $5-8
20TH CENTURY-FOX: *63* 2-4

JAY & THE AMERICANS
(Featuring Jay Black)
Singles: 7-Inch
FUTURA: *72* 2-3
UNITED ARTISTS (Except 300
  through 600 series): *64-71* 3-5
UNITED ARTISTS (300 through
  600 series): *61-63* 4-6
Picture Sleeves
UNITED ARTISTS: *65-66* 3-6
LPs: 10/12-Inch 33rpm
SUNSET: *69-70* 10-12
UNART: *68* 8-12
UNITED ARTISTS (222; "She
  Cried"): *62* 20-25
  (With a "UAL" prefix, for mono, or "UAS" for
  stereo.)
UNITED ARTISTS (300; "At The
  Cafe Wha"): *63* 20-25
  (With a "UAL" prefix, for mono, or "UAS" for
  stereo.)
UNITED ARTISTS (300 series): *75* 5-8
  (With a "UA-LA" prefix.)
UNITED ARTISTS (400 through 700
  series): *65-70* 10-15
  (With a "UAL" prefix, for mono, or "UAS" for
  stereo.)
UNITED ARTISTS (1000 series): *80* 5-8
  (With an "LM" prefix.)
  Also see BLACK, Jay

JAY & THE TECHNIQUES
(Featuring Jay Proctor)
Singles: 7-Inch
EVENT: *76* 2-4
GORDY: *72* 2-3
SMASH: *67-69* 3-5
Picture Sleeves
SMASH: *67-68* 3-6
LPs: 10/12-Inch 33rpm
EVENT: *75* 8-10
SMASH: *67-68* 15-20

JAYE, Jerry
Singles: 7-Inch
COLUMBIA: *75* 2-3
HI (2100 series): *67-68* 3-5
HI (2300 series): *76-77* 2-3
LABEL: *59* 4-6
MEGA: *71-74* 2-3
RAINTREE: *72* 2-3

STEPHANY: *58* $8-15
LPs: 10/12-Inch 33rpm
HI (32000 series): *67* 15-20
HI (32100 series): *76* 5-8

JAYE, Miles
Singles: 7-Inch
ISLAND: *87-88* 1-3
LPs: 10/12-Inch 33rpm
MCA: *87* 5-8

JAYHAWKS
Singles: 78rpm
ALADDIN: *57* 6-12
FLASH (Except 105): *56* 5-10
FLASH (105; "Counting My
  Teardrops"): *56* 20-40
Singles: 7-Inch
ALADDIN: *57* 15-25
EASTMAN: *59* 10-20
FLASH (Except 105): *56* 10-20
FLASH (105; "Counting My
  Teardrops"): *56* 75-100
  Members: James Johnson; Carl Fisher; Dave
  Govan; Carver Bunkern; Richard Owens.
  Also see MARATHONS
  Also see VIBRATIONS

JAYNETTS
Singles: 7-Inch
J&S: *65* 3-6
TUFF: *63 64* 3-6
LPs: 10/12-Inch 33rpm
TUFF: *63* 30-35

JAZZ CRUSADERS
Singles: 7-Inch
CHISA: *70-71* 1-3
PACIFIC JAZZ: *62-68* 2-4
WORLD PACIFIC: *64-65* 2-3
LPs: 10/12-Inch 33rpm
BLUE NOTE: *75-80* 5-10
CHISA: *70* 8-12
LIBERTY: *70* 8-12
PACIFIC JAZZ (27 through 87): *61-64* .. 20-35
PACIFIC JAZZ (10000 & 20000
  series): *65-69* 10-20
PAUSA: *82* 5-8
WORLD PACIFIC: *65* 8-15
  Members: Wilton Felder; Nesbert Hooper; Wayne
  Henderson; Joe Sample.
  Also see CRUSADERS
  Also see FELDER, Wilton

JAZZY JAY
Singles: 7-Inch
ATLANTIC: *84* 1-3

JEAN, Cathy: see CATHY JEAN

JEAN, Earl: see EARL-JEAN

JEAN & THE DARLINGS
Singles: 7-Inch
VOLT: *67-69* $3-5

JECKYLL, Dr: see DR. JECKYLL

JEFF & ALETA
Singles: 7-Inch
SRI: *80* 1-3

JEFFERSON
Singles: 7-Inch
DECCA: *69* 2-4
JANUS: *69* 2-4
LPs: 10/12-Inch 33rpm
JANUS: *69* 10-12

JEFFERSON, Morris
Singles: 7-Inch
PARACHUTE: *78* 1-3
LPs: 10/12-Inch 33rpm
PARACHUTE: *78* 5-8

JEFFERSON AIRPLANE
Singles: 7-Inch
GRUNT: *71-73* 2-4
RCA VICTOR (Except 8700 & 8800
series): *67-70* 4-6
RCA VICTOR (8700 & 8800 series): *66* .. 8-10
Picture Sleeves
GRUNT (Except 0506): *71* 4-8
GRUNT (0506; "Long John Silver"): *72* . 10-20
RCA VICTOR: *68-69* 4-8
LPs: 10/12-Inch 33rpm
GRUNT (Except 1000 series): *73-82* 25-50
GRUNT (1001; "Bark"): *71* 30-60
GRUNT (1007; "Long John Silver"): *71* . 30-60
PAIR: *84* 8-10
RCA VICTOR (0320;
"Volunteers"): *73* 12-15
(With an "APD1" prefix. Quad issue.)
RCA VICTOR (1511; "After Bathing
At Baxters"): *67* 20-40
(Black label. With an "LOP" or "LSO" prefix.)
RCA VICTOR (1511; "After Bathing
At Baxters"): *71* 8-12
(Orange label. With an "AFL1" prefix.)
RCA VICTOR (3584; "Jefferson
Airplane Takes Off"): *66* 40-80
(Black label. Has 12 tracks. With an "LPM" or
"LSP" prefix.)
RCA VICTOR (3584; "Jefferson
Airplane Takes Off"): *66* 15-20
(Black label. Has 11 tracks. With an "LPM" or
"LSP" prefix.)

RCA VICTOR (3584; "Jefferson
Airplane Takes Off"): *66* $10-12
(Orange Label. With an "AYL1" prefix.)
RCA VICTOR (3661; "Worst Of
Jefferson Airplane"): *80* 5-8
(With an "AYL1" prefix.)
RCA VICTOR (3766; "Surrealistic
Pillow"): *67* 20-30
(Black label. With an "LPM" or "LSP" prefix.)
RCA VICTOR (3766; "Surrealistic
Pillow"): *69* 10-12
(Orange label. With an "AYL1" prefix.)
RCA VICTOR (3797; "Crown Of
Creation"): *80* 5-8
(With an "AYL1" prefix.)
RCA VICTOR (3798; "Bless Its
Pointed Little Head"): *80* 5-8
(With an "AYL1" prefix.)
RCA VICTOR (3867;
"Volunteers"): *81* 5-8
(With an "AYL1" prefix.)
RCA VICTOR (4058; "Crown Of
Creation"): *68* 10-15
(With an "LSP" prefix.)
RCA VICTOR (4238;
"Volunteers"): *69* 10-15
(With an "LSP" prefix.)
RCA VICTOR (4448; "Blows Against
The Empire"): *70* 10-15
(Price includes booklet insert, which represents
about $3-$5 of the value. With an "LSP" prefix.)
RCA VICTOR (4448; "Blows Against
The Empire"): *70* 50-100
(Clear vinyl. Promotional issue only.)
RCA VICTOR (4459; "Worst Of
Jefferson Airplane"): *70* 8-10
(With an "LSP" prefix.)
RCA VICTOR (4459; "Worst Of
Jefferson Airplane"): 5-8
(With an "AFL1" prefix.)
Members: Grace Slick; Marty Balin; Paul Kantner.
Also see BALIN, Marty
Also see GARCIA, Jerry
Also see GREAT!! SOCIETY!!
Also see JEFFERSON STARSHIP
Also see KBC BAND
Also see KAUKONEN, Jorma
Also see KANTNER, Paul, & Grace Slick
Also see QUICKSILVER
Also see SLICK, Grace

JEFFERSON STARSHIP
Singles: 7-Inch
GRUNT: *74-84* 1-3
Picture Sleeves
GRUNT: *77-83* 2-3

LPs: 10/12-Inch 33rpm
GRUNT (0717 through 1557): *74-76* **$8-12**
GRUNT (1255; "Flight Log,
  1966-1976"): *77* **12-15**
(With simulated leather cover. Also contains Jefferson Airplane, Hot Tuna, Grace Slick and Paul Kanter tracks.)
GRUNT (1255; "Flight Log
  1966-1976"): *81* **6-12**
(With standard cover.)
GRUNT (2515 through 3247): *78-79* **5-10**
GRUNT (3363; "Gold"): *79* **15-20**
(Picture disc.)
GRUNT (3452 through 4921): *79-84* **5-8**
RCA VICTOR: *81* **5-8**
Members: Grace Slick; Marty Balin; Paul Kantner; Aynsley Dunbar.
Also see BALIN, Marty
Also see CREACH, Papa John
Also see DUNBAR, Aynsley
Also see GARCIA, Jerry
Also see JEFFERSON AIRPLANE
Also see KANTNER, Paul, & Jefferson Starship
Also see STARSHIP

JEFFREE
Singles: 7-Inch
MCA: *78-79* **1-3**
LPs: 10/12-Inch 33rpm
MCA: *79* **5-8**

JEFFREY, Joe
(Joe Jeffrey Group)
Singles: 7-Inch
WAND: *69* **2-5**
LPs: 10/12-Inch 33rpm
WAND: *69* **10-15**

JEFFREYS, Garland
Singles: 7-Inch
A&M: *77-79* **1-3**
ARISTA: *75* **2-3**
ATLANTIC: *73* **2-4**
EPIC: *81-83* **1-3**
LPs: 10/12-Inch 33rpm
A&M: *77-79* **5-8**
ATLANTIC: *73* **8-10**
EPIC: *81-83* **5-8**

JELLY BEANS
Singles: 7-Inch
ESKEE: *65* **3-6**
RED BIRD: *64* **4-8**

JELLYBEAN
("Jellybean" Benitez)
Singles: 12-Inch 33/45rpm
EMI AMERICA: *84-86* **$4-6**
Singles: 7-Inch
CHRYSALIS: *87* **1-3**
EMI AMERICA: *84-86* **1-3**
LPs: 10/12-Inch 33rpm
CHRYSALIS: *87* **5-8**
EMI AMERICA: *84-86* **5-8**

JENKINS, Donald
(Donald Jenkins & The Delighters)
Singles: 7-Inch
CORTLAND: *63* **5-8**
DUCHESS: *65* **3-6**

JENKINS, Gordon, & His Orchestra
Singles: 78rpm
DECCA: *50-56* **2-4**
Singles: 7-Inch
COLUMBIA: *64* **1-3**
DECCA: *50-56* **2-5**
KAPP: *60-64* **2-3**
TIME: *62* **2-3**
X: *55* **2-4**
EPs: 7-Inch 33/45rpm
DECCA: *51-56* **5-10**
LPs: 10/12-Inch 33rpm
CAPITOL (700 series): *56* **12-20**
(With a "T" prefix.)
CAPITOL (700 series): *61* **8-15**
(With a "DT" prefix.)
CAPITOL (700 series): *75* **4-8**
(With an "SM" prefix.)
COLUMBIA: *62-63* **8-15**
CORAL: *73* **4-6**
DECCA: *51-63* **8-18**
(Decca LP numbers in this series preceded by a "7" or a "DL-7" are stereo issues.)
DOT: *66* **5-10**
GWP: *71* **5-10**
MCA: *73-75* **4-8**
SUNSET: *67* **5-10**
TIME: *62-64* **8-15**
Also see ARMSTRONG, Louis
Also see BOONE, Pat
Also see LEE, Peggy
Also see WEAVERS

JENKINS, Gus
(Gus Jinkins)
Singles: 78rpm
COMBO: *54* **6-12**
FLASH: *56-57* **4-6**
Singles: 7-Inch
CATALINA: *63* **3-5**

COMBO: *54* $25-30
FLASH: *56-57* 5-10
GENERAL ARTIST: *64-69* 3-5
PIONEER INT'L: *59-62* 3-5
SAR: *64* 3-5
TOWER: *64-65* 3-5

JENKINS, Kechia
Singles: 7-Inch
PROFILE: *88* 1-3

JENKINS, Norma
Singles: 7-Inch
DESERT MOON: *76* 2-3

JENNIFER
(Jennifer Warnes)
Singles: 7-Inch
PARROT: *67-70* 3-5
LPs: 10/12-Inch 33rpm
PARROT: *68-70* 12-18
Also see WARNES, Jennifer

JENNINGS, Waylon
(Waylon Jennings & The Waylors; Waylon Jennings & The Kimberlys; Waylon Jennings & The Crickets)
Singles: 7-Inch
A&M (Except 722): *64* 8-10
A&M (722; "Rave On"): *63* 10-15
BAT: *62* 10-15
BRUNSWICK (55130; "Jole
Blon"): *59* 80-100
(Maroon label. With Buddy Holly &
King Curtis.)
BRUNSWICK (55130; "Jole Blon"): *59* . 60-80
(Yellow label. Promotional issue only.)
MCA: *86-88* 1-3
RCA VICTOR (Except 8500 through
9600 series): *69-80* 1-3
RCA VICTOR (8500 through 9600 series): *65-68* 3-5
RAMCO: *67* 5-10
TREND '61: *61* 15-20
TREND '63: *63* 30-35
Picture Sleeves
RCA VICTOR: *80* 1-3
LPs: 10/12-Inch 33rpm
A&M: *69* 25-30
BAT (1001; "Waylon Jennings
At JD's"): *64* 150-200
CAMDEN: *67-76* 8-15
MCA: 4-6
PICKWICK: *75* 5-10
RCA VICTOR (0500 through
3300 series): *74-79* 5-10
RCA VICTOR (3400 series,
except 3406): *79* 5-8

RCA VICTOR (3406; "Greatest
Hits"): *79* $12-18
(Picture disc.)
RCA VICTOR (3500 through
3900 series): *66-68* 15-25
(With an "LPM" or "LSP" prefix.)
RCA VICTOR (3600 through
3900 series): *80-81* 4-8
(With an "AYL1" or "AHL1" prefix.)
RCA VICTOR (4000 through
4100 series): *68-69* 10-20
(With an "LPM" or "LSP" prefix.)
RCA VICTOR (4000 through
4300 series): *81-82* 4-8
(With an "AYL1" prefix.)
RCA VICTOR (4400 through
4800 series): *70-73* 8-15
(With an "LSP" prefix.)
RCA VICTOR (4400 through
4800 series): *83* 4-8
(With an "AHL1" prefix.)
SOUNDS (1001; "Waylon Jennings
At JD's"): *64* 125-150
TIME-LIFE: *81* 5-8
VOCALION: *69* 15-20
Also see CASH, Johnny, & Waylon Jennings
Also see CRICKETS
Also see CUNHA, Rick
Also see DAVIS, Skeeter
Also see HOLLY, Buddy
Also see KIMBERLYS
Also see KING CURTIS
Also see U.S.A. FOR AFRICA

JENNINGS, Waylon, & Jesse Colter
Singles: 7-Inch
RCA VICTOR: *69-71* 2-4
LPs: 10/12-Inch 33rpm
RCA VICTOR: *81* 5-8
Also see COLTER, Jesse

JENNINGS, Waylon / Johnny Paycheck
LPs: 10/12-Inch 33rpm
OUT OF TOWN DIST: *82* 5-8
Also see PAYCHECK, Johnny

JENNINGS, Waylon, & Jerry Reed
Singles: 7-Inch
RCA VICTOR: *83* 1-3
Also see REED, Jerry

JENNINGS, Waylon, & Willie Nelson
(Waylon & Willie)
Singles: 7-Inch
COLUMBIA: *83* 1-3
MCA: *86* 1-3
RCA VICTOR: *76-86* 1-3

LPs: 10/12-Inch 33rpm
AURA: *83* $5-8
RCA VICTOR (Black vinyl): *78-83* 5-8
RCA VICTOR (Colored vinyl): *78* 20-25
(Promotional issues only.)
Also see JENNINGS, Waylon
Also see NELSON, Willie

JENSEN, Kris
Singles: 7-Inch
A&M: *70* 2-4
COLPIX: *59* 4-6
HICKORY: *62-65* 3-5
KAPP: *61* 3-5
LEADER: *60-61* 3-5
Picture Sleeves
HICKORY: *62-64* 8-15
LPs: 10/12-Inch 33rpm
HICKORY: *62* 35-40

JEROME, Henry, & His Orchestra
Singles: 7-Inch
DECCA: *60-64* 2-4
LPs: 10/12-Inch 33rpm
DECCA: *60-64* 5-12
ROULETTE: *59* 5-15

JERRY, Mungo:
see MUNGO JERRY

JERRY O
Singles: 7-Inch
SHOUT: *67* 3-5
WHITE WHALE: *69* 2-4

JESSE & MARVIN
Singles: 78rpm
SPECIALTY: *52* 6-12
Singles: 7-Inch
SPECIALTY (447; "Dream Girl"): *52* ... 15-25
(Black vinyl.)
SPECIALTY (447; "Dream Girl"): *52* ... 30-50
(Colored vinyl.)
(Most Specialty singles are currently available,
using original catalog numbers.)
Members: Jesse Belvin; Marvin Phillips.
Also see BELVIN, Jesse
Also see MARVIN & JOHNNY

JESSE'S GANG
Singles: 7-Inch
GEFFEN: *87* 1-3
JES SAY: *85* 4-6

JESTERS
Singles: 78rpm
WINLEY (Except 218): *57* 5-8
WINLEY (218; "So Strange"): *57* 10-20
Singles: 7-Inch
ABC: *73* 1-3

AMY: *62* $3-5
COLLECTABLES: 1-3
CYCLONE: *58* 15-25
LOST-NITE: *63* 3-5
WINLEY (Except 218): *57-61* 8-15
WINLEY (218; "So Strange"): *57* 20-40
LPs: 10/12-Inch 33rpm
COLLECTABLES: *86* 6-8
LOST-NITE: *81* 5-8
Members: Len McKay; Adam Jackson; Jimmy
Smith; Noel Grant; Leo Vincent; Melvin Lewis;
Don Lewis.
Also see PARAGONS / Jesters

JESUS & MARY CHAIN
LPs: 10/12-Inch 33rpm
REPRISE: *86* 5-8
WARNER BROS: *87-88* 5-8

JETBOY
LPs: 10/12-Inch 33rpm
MCA: *88* 5-8

JETE, Le: see LE JETE

JETER, Genobia
Singles: 12-Inch 33/45rpm
RCA VICTOR: *86* 4-6
Singles: 7-Inch
RCA VICTOR: *86-87* 1-3
LPs: 10/12-Inch 33rpm
RCA VICTOR: *86* 5-8

JETER, Genobia, & Glenn Jones
Singles: 7-Inch
RCA VICTOR: *87* 1-3
Also see JETER, Genobia
Also see JONES, Glenn

JETHRO TULL
Singles: 7-Inch
CHRYSALIS: *72-84* 1-3

Jethro Tull: (L-R) Martin Barre; Ian Anderson;
Doan Perry; Martin Allock; Dave Pegg

CHRYSALIS/REPRISE: 69-72 .... $2-4
    LPs: 10/12-Inch 33rpm
CHRYSALIS (Except CH4 & V5X
  series): 73-87 6-12
CHRYSALIS (CH4 series): 73-74 10-12
  (Quadrophonic issues.)
CHRYSALIS (V5X-41653; "Twenty
  Years Of Jethro Tull"): 88 25-35
  (Five LP set.)
MFSL (061; "Aqualung"): 82 25-50
MFSL (092; "Broadsword &
  The Beast"): 82 20-30
REPRISE: 69-72 10-15
REPRISE/CHRYSALIS (2106; "Living
  In The Past"): 72 15-20
  (Price range includes bonus color booklet.)
  Members: Ian Anderson; Clive Bunker; Glen Cormick; John Evan; Barry Barlow; David Palmer; John Glascock; Jeff Hammond; Mick Abrahams; Martin Barre; Doane Perry; Martin Allock; Dave Pegg.
  Also see WILD TURKEY

JETS
    Singles: 12-Inch 33/45rpm
MCA: 85-88 4-6
    Singles: 7-Inch
MCA: 85-87 1-3

Joan Jett

    LPs: 10/12-Inch 33rpm
MCA: 85-87 .... $5-8
  Members: Elizabeth Wolfgram and the Wolfgram family.

JETT, Joan, & The Blackhearts
    Singles: 12-Inch 33/45rpm
MCA: 83 4-6
    Singles: 7-Inch
BLACKHEART/CBS: 83-88 1-3
BOARDWALK: 81-82 1-3
MCA: 83 1-3
    Picture Sleeves
BLACKHEART/CBS: 83-88 1-3
BOARDWALK: 81-82 1-3
    LPs: 10/12-Inch 33rpm
BLACKHEART/CBS: 80-88 5-8
BOARDWALK: 81-82 5-8
MCA: 83-84 5-8
  Also see BARBUSTERS
  Also see BEACH BOYS
  Also see RUNAWAYS

JEWELS
(Crows)
    Singles: 78rpm
RAMA (1010; "Heartbreaker"): 53 100-200
    Singles: 7-Inch
RAMA (1010; "Heartbreaker"): 53 300-500
  (Black vinyl. May show *Heartbreaker* as by the Crows and *Call A Doctor* by the Jewels.)
RAMA (1010; "Heartbreaker"): 53 500-750
  (Colored vinyl.)
  Also see CROWS

JEWELS
    Singles: 7-Inch
DIMENSION: 64-65 3-6

JIGSAW
    Singles: 7-Inch
CHELSEA: 75-76 2-3
20TH CENTURY-FOX: 77-78 1-3
    LPs: 10/12-Inch 33rpm
CHELSEA: 75 8-10
ELEKTRA: 82 5-8
20TH CENTURY-FOX: 77 5-8

JILL & RAY
    Singles: 7-Inch
LE CAM: 62 10-15
  Members: Jill Jackson; Ray Hildebrand.
  Also see PAUL & PAULA

JIM & JEAN
    Singles: 7-Inch
VERVE/FORECAST: 68 3-5
    LPs: 10/12-Inch 33rpm
VERVE/FOLKWAYS: 68 8-12

Members: Jim Glover; Jean Glover

JIM & MONICA
Singles: 7-Inch
BETTY: *64* $8-10
Member: Jimmy Gilmer.
Also see GILMER, Jimmy

JIMENEZ, Jose: see DANA, Bill

JIMMY, Bobby, & The Critters
Singles: 12-Inch 33/45rpm
MACOLA: *86* 4-6
LPs: 10/12-Inch 33rpm
MACOLA: *86* 5-8

JIMMY & DUANE
Singles: 7-Inch
EB X. PRESTON (212; "Soda
Fountain Girl"): 75-125
Members: Jimmy Delbridge; Duane Eddy.
Also see EDDY, Duane

JIMMY G. & THE TACKHEADS
Singles: 7-Inch
CAPITOL: *85-86* 1-3
LPs: 10/12-Inch 33rpm
CAPITOL: *86* 5-8

JIMMY LEE
(Jimmy Lee Robinson)
Singles: 7-Inch
BANDERA: *60* 10-15

JIMMY LEE & ARTIS:
see LEE, Jimmy, & Artis

JINKINS, Gus: see JENKINS, Gus

JIVE BOMBERS
(Featuring Clarence "Bad Boy" Palmer;
Clarence Palmer & The Jive Bombers)
Single: 78rpm
CITATION: *52* 15-25
SAVOY: *56-58* 5-10
Singles: 7-Inch
CITATION: *52* 25-50
COLLECTABLES: *85* 1-3
MIDDLE TONE: *64* 3-5
SAVOY: *56-59* 10-20
LPs: 10/12-Inch 33rpm
SAVOY: *86* 5-8
Members: Clarence Palmer; Earl Johnson; Allen
Tinney; William Tinny.

JIVE FIVE
Singles: 7-Inch
AMBIENT SOUND: *82* 3-5
BELTONE: *61-63* 4-6
DECCA: *70* 3-5
MUSICOR: *67-68* 3-5
SKETCH: *64* 10-15

UNITED ARTISTS: *64-66* $3-5
LPs: 10/12-Inch 33rpm
AMBIENT SOUND: *82* 5-8
COLLECTABLES: *85* 6-8
RELIC: 8-10
UNITED ARTISTS: *65* 25-35
Members: Eugene Pitt; Norm Johnson; Richard
Harris; Jerry Hannah; Billy Prophet; Johnny Wat-
son; Casey Spencer; Webster Harris.
Also see GENIES
Also see PLATTERS / Inez & Charlie Foxx /
Jive Five / Tommy Hunt

JIVIN' GENE
(Jivin' Gene & The Jokers)
Singles: 7-Inch
ABC: *73* 1-3
CHESS: *64* 3-5
HALL WAY: *64* 3-5
JIN: *59* 10-15
MERCURY: *59-62* 4-8
TFC/HALL: *65* 3-5
Member: Gene Bourgeois.

JO, Damita: see DAMITA JO

JO, Marcy: see MARCY JOE

JO, Sami: see SAMI JO

JO ANN & TROY
Singles: 7-Inch
ATLANTIC: *64* 8-10
Members: Jo Ann Campbell; Troy Seals.
Also see CAMPBELL, Jo Ann

JO JO GUNNE
Singles: 7-Inch
ASYLUM: *72* 2-3
LPs: 10/12-Inch 33rpm
ASYLUM (Except 5071): *72-74* 8-10
ASYLUM (5071; "Jumpin' The
Gunne"): *73* 10-12
(With gatefold cover.)
ASYLUM (5071; "Jumpin' The
Gunne"): *73* 6-10
(With standard cover.)
Member: Jay Ferguson.

JOBIM, Antonio Carlos
Singles: 7-Inch
A&M: *67* 2-3
CTI: *70* 1-3
MCA: *74* 1-3
VERVE: *63-64* 2-4
LPs: 10/12-Inch 33rpm
A&M: *67-70* 8-12
CTI: *70-71* 8-12
CAPITOL: *64* 10-20
DISCOVERY: *82* 5-8

MCA: *73* $5-8
VERSATILE: *78* 5-8
VERVE (Except 3000 series): *63* 10-20
VERVE (3000 series): *82* 5-8
WARNER BROS: *65-80* 8-15
   Also see FITZGERALD, Ella, & Antonio Carlos Jobim
   Also see GILBERTO, Astrud
   Also see SINATRA, Frank, & Antonio Carlos Jobim

JOBOXERS
Singles: 7-Inch
RCA VICTOR: *83* 1-3
LPs: 10/12-Inch 33rpm
RCA VICTOR: *83* 5-8

JOE, Billy: see BILLY JOE

JOE, Marcy: see MARCY JOE

JOE & ANN
Singles: 7-Inch
ACE: *60-62* 5-8

JOE & EDDIE
Singles: 7-Inch
CAPITOL: *59* 4-6
GNP/CRESCENDO: *62-65* 3-5
LPs: 10/12-Inch 33rpm
GNP/CRESCENDO: *63-66* 8-15
Members: Joe Gilbert; Eddie Brown.

JOEL, Billy
Singles: 12-Inch 33/45rpm
COLUMBIA: *83* 4-6
Singles: 7-Inch
COLUMBIA: *73-87* 1-3
EPIC: *86* 1-3
FAMILY: *71-73* 3-5
Picture Sleeves
COLUMBIA: *79-85* 1-3
LPs: 10/12-Inch 33rpm
COLUMBIA (30000 & 40000 series): *73-86* 5-8
  (With an "FC," "KC," "PC," or "TC" prefix.)
COLUMBIA (30000 series): *74-76* 10-15
  (With a "CQ" or "PCQ" prefix. Quad issues.)
COLUMBIA (40000 series): *80-87* 10-15
  (With an "HC" prefix. Half-speed mastered.)
FAMILY PRODUCTIONS: *71* 20-25
Promotional LPs
COLUMBIA (326; "Souvenir"): *75* 20-25
COLUMBIA (402; "Interchords"): *77* ... 20-25
   Also see ATTILA
   Also see KHAN, Steve
   Also see U.S.A. FOR AFRICA

JOEL, Billy, & Ray Charles
Singles: 7-Inch
COLUMBIA: *87* $1-3
   Also see CHARLES, Ray
   Also see JOEL, Billy

JOESKI LOVE
Singles: 7-Inch
VINTERTAINMENT: *86* 1-3

JOHANSEN, David
Singles: 7-Inch
BLUE SKY: *78-82* 1-3
LPs: 10/12-Inch 33rpm
BLUE SKY: *78-82* 5-8
   Also see NEW YORK DOLLS

JOHN, Dr.: see DR. JOHN

JOHN, Elton
Singles: 7-Inch
CONGRESS: *69-70* 15-30
DJM: *69* 15-18
EPIC: *87* 1-3
GEFFEN: *81-86* 1-3
MCA: *72-88* 1-3
MCA/ROCKET: *76-77* 2-3
ROCKET: *76* 2-3
UNI: *70-72* 2-3
VIKING: *69* 25-50
Picture Sleeves
GEFFEN: *81-86* 1-3
MCA: *74-88* 2-4
EPs: 7-Inch 33/45rpm
MCA: *73* 8-10
  (Jukebox issue only.)
UNI: *70* 10-12
  (Jukebox issue only.)
LPs: 10/12-Inch 33rpm
GEFFEN: *81-87* 5-8
MCA (1995; "A Single Man"): *79* 10-15
  (Picture disc.)
MCA (1995; "A Single Man"): *79* 35-45
  (Promotional issue picture disc. "B" side pictures Elton from the rear.)
MCA (2100 through 2130): *73-75* 6-10
MCA (2142; "Captain Fantastic & The Brown Dirt Cowboy"): *75* 10-12
  (Includes poster, lyrics booklet, bio scrapbook, and comic insert. Deduct $3-$5 if these items are missing.)
MCA ("Captain Fantastic"): *79* 35-45
  (Picture disc. Promotional issue only.)
MCA ("Captain Fantastic"): *79* 50-100
  (Colored vinyl. Promotional issue only.)
MCA (2163 through 5121): *75-80* 5-8
MCA (8000 series): *87* 10-12
MCA: *88* 5-8

MCA (10003; "Goodbye Yellow
   Brick Road"): 73 ....$10-12
MCA (37000 series): 79 4-6
MCA/ROCKET (Except 1953): 76-77 ...10-12
MCA/ROCKET (1953; "Get Up
   And Dance"): 77 20-25
   (Promotional issue only.)
NAUTILUS: 82 12-18
   (Half-speed mastered.)
UNI: 70-72 20-25
   Also see DIONNE & FRIENDS
   Also see OLSSON, Nigel
   Also see RUSH, Jennifer, & Elton John
   Also see SEDAKA, Neil
   Also see STARR, Ringo

JOHN, Elton, & Kiki Dee
Singles: 7-Inch
ROCKET: 76 2-3
Picture Sleeves
ROCKET: 76 2-3
   Also see DEE, Kiki

JOHN, Elton, & Lesley Duncan
Singles: 7-Inch
MCA (1938; "Love Song"): 76 10-15
   (Promotional issue only.)

JOHN, Elton / John Lennon
Singles: 7-Inch
MCA (40364; "Philadelphia Freedom"): 75 .3-5
Picture Sleeves
MCA (40364; "Philadelphia Freedom"): 75 .3-5
MCA (40364; WFIL radio "Philadelphia
   Freedom"): 75 25-30
   (Promotional issue only.)
   Also see LENNON, John

JOHN, Elton / Tina Turner
Singles: 7-Inch
POLYDOR (002; "Pinball
   Wizard"): 75 20-30
   (Promotional issue only.)
   Also see JOHN, Elton
   Also see TURNER, Tina

JOHN, Little Willie
Singles: 78rpm
KING: 56-57 3-6
Singles: 7-Inch
GUSTO: 1-3
KING (4818 through 5394): 56-60 4-8
KING (5428 through 5949): 61-64 3-6
EPs: 7-Inch 33/45rpm
KING: 58 20-30
LPs: 10/12-Inch 33rpm
BLUESWAY: 73 8-10

Elton John

KING (500 through 700 series,
   except 564): 58-61 ....$20-25
KING (564; "Fever"): 56 40-80
   (With brown cover.)
KING (564; "Fever"): 59 15-20
   (With blue cover.)
KING (800 through 1000 series): 62-70 .15-20
   Also see WILLIAMS, Paul

JOHN, Mable
Singles: 7-Inch
STAX: 66-68 3-5
TAMLA (54031; "Who Wouldn't Love
   A Man Like That"): 60 25-30
TAMLA (54040; "No Love"): 61 15-20
TAMLA (54050; "Take Me"): 61 15-20
TAMLA (54081; "Who Wouldn't Love
   A Man Like That"): 63 8-10

JOHN, Pope: see POPE JOHN

JOHN, Robert
(Bobby Pedrick, Jr.)
Singles: 12-Inch 33/45
CBS ASSOCIATED: 84 4-6
Singles: 7-Inch
A&M: 70-72 2-5
ARIOLA: 78 2-3
ATLANTIC: 72-73 2-4
COLUMBIA: 68-69 3-5
EMI AMERICA: 79-80 1-3
MOTOWN: 83 1-3
LPs: 10/12-Inch 33rpm
COLUMBIA: 68 10-20
EMI AMERICA: 79-82 5-8
HARMONY: 72 8-10
   Also see PEDRICK, Bobby

JOHN & ERNEST
Singles: 7-Inch
RAINY WEDNESDAY: *73* $4-8
Members: John Free; Ernest Smith.

JOHNNIE & JOE
Singles: 7-Inch
ABC-PARAMOUNT: *60* 5-8
AMBIENT SOUND: *82* 3-5
(Blue or multi-color labels.)
CHESS: *57* 10-15
(Silver and blue label.)
CHESS: *60* 8-10
J&S (Except 1664): *57-59* 10-15
J&S (1664; "Over The Mountain"): *57* ... 30-40
(First pressings had thick & thin horizontal lines
across the label.)
J&S (1664; "Over The Mountain"): *62* ... 10-15
(Without the horizontal lines across the label.)
LPs: 10/12-Inch 33rpm
AMBIENT SOUND: *82* 5-8
Members: Johnnie Richardson; Joe Rivers.

JOHNNY & THE DISTRACTIONS
Singles: 7-Inch
A&M: *82* 1-3
LPs: 10/12-Inch 33rpm
A&M: *82* 5-8

JOHNNY & THE EXPRESSIONS
Singles: 7-Inch
JOSIE: *65-66* 3-5

JOHNNY & THE HURRICANES
Singles: 7-Inch
ABC: *73* 1-3
ATILA: *64* 5-10
BIG TOP: *60-63* 4-6
JA-DA: 3-5
JEFF: *64* 4-6
MALA: *63* 3-5
TWIRL: *59* 10-15
WARWICK (Monaural): *59-60* 5-10
WARWICK (Stereo): *59* 15-25
(With an "S" prefix.)
Picture Sleeves
BIG TOP: *60-61* 10-15
WARWICK: *60* 10-20
EPs: 7-Inch 33/45rpm
WARWICK: *59* 30-40
LPs: 10/12-Inch 33rpm
ATILA: 30-35
BIG TOP: *60* 45-55
TWIRL: 50-75
WARWICK: *59-60* 50-60
Members: Johnny Paris; Paul Tesluk; Dave Yorko;
Lionel "Butch" Mattice; Bill Savitch.
Also see GIBSON, Johnny

JOHNNY & THE JAMMERS
Singles: 7-Inch
DART (131; "School Day Blues"): *59* .$75-100
Member: Johnny Winter.
Also see WINTER, Johnny

JOHNNY AVERAGE BAND
Singles: 7-Inch
BEARSVILLE: *81* 1-3
LPs: 10/12-Inch 33rpm
BEARSVILLE: *81* 5-8
Member: Nikki Wills.

JOHNNY HATES JAZZ
Singles: 7-Inch
VIRGIN: *88* 1-3
LPs: 10/12-Inch 33rpm
VIRGIN: *88* 5-8

JOHNNY LEE: see LEE, Johnny

JOHNNY O
Singles: 7-Inch
MICMAC: *88* 1-3

JOHNNY T. ANGEL
Singles: 7-Inch
BELL: *74* 2-3

JOHNS, Sammy
Singles: 7-Inch
GRC: *73-75* 2-3
REAL WORLD: *80* 1-3
WARNER/CURB: *76* 2-3
LPs: 10/12-Inch 33rpm
GRC: *75* 8-10

JOHNSON, Al
Singles: 7-Inch
COLUMBIA: *80* 1-3
LPs: 10/12-Inch 33rpm
COLUMBIA: *80* 5-8

JOHNSON, Al, & Jean Carn
Singles: 7-Inch
COLUMBIA: *80* 1-3
Also see CARN, Jean
Also see JOHNSON, Al

JOHNSON, Benny
Singles: 7-Inch
TODAY: *73* 2-3

JOHNSON, Betty
Singles: 78rpm
BALLY: *56-57* 4-6
Singles: 7-Inch
ATLANTIC: *58-60* 3-5
BALLY: *56-57* 4-6
BELL: *71* 2-4
COED: *60* 3-5

DOT: *60* $3-5
RCA VICTOR (6000 series): *55* 4-6
RCA VICTOR (8000 series): *63* 2-4
REPUBLIC: *60-61* 3-5
WORLD ARTISTS: *63* 2-4
EPs: 7-Inch 33/45rpm
RCA VICTOR: *57* 4-6
LPs: 10/12-Inch 33rpm
ATLANTIC: *58-59* 15-20
BALLY: *57* 20-25

JOHNSON, Bubber
(Bubber Johnson & The Dreamers)
Singles: 78rpm
KING: *55-56* 3-6
Singles: 7-Inch
KING (4000 series): *55-56* 5-10
KING (5000 series): *57-60* 4-8
MERCURY: *52* 20-25
LPs: 10/12-Inch 33rpm
KING (500 series): *57* 30-35
KING (600 series): *59* 20-25

JOHNSON, Buddy
(Buddy Johnson & His Orchestra)
Singles: 78rpm
ATLANTIC: *53* 3-5
DECCA: *42-54* 3-5
MERCURY: *53-56* 2-5
RCA VICTOR: *56* 2-5
Singles: 7-Inch
ATLANTIC: *53* 4-6
DECCA (24996 through 29058): *50-54* ..10-20
MERCURY: *53-56* 4-8
RCA VICTOR: *56* 4-8
ROULETTE: *59* 3-6
WING: *56* 4-8
LPs: 10/12-Inch 33rpm
FORUM: 10-15
MERCURY: *55-60* 25-30
WING (Except 12005): *63* 10-15
WING (12005; "Rock 'N Roll
Stage Show"): *56* 25-50
Also see BROWN, Ruth
Also see PRYSOCK, Arthur

JOHNSON, Buddy & Ella
Singles: 78rpm
MERCURY: *56-57* 2-5
Singles: 7-Inch
MERCURY: *56-61* 3-5
ROULETTE: *59* 3-5
LPs: 10/12-Inch 33rpm
MERCURY: *58* 20-25
ROULETTE: *59* 20-25
Also see JOHNSON, Buddy

JOHNSON, Danny
Singles: 7-Inch
FIRST AMERICAN: *79* $1-3
LPs: 10/12-Inch 33rpm
FIRST AMERICAN: *79* 5-8

JOHNSON, General
(General Johnson & The Chairmen; Norman
Johnson)
Singles: 12-Inch 33/45rpm
ARISTA: *78* 4-8
Singles: 7-Inch
ARISTA: *76-78* 2-4
INVICTUS: *71* 2-5
SURFSIDE: *80* 2-3
Also see CHAIRMEN OF THE BOARD
Also see SHOWMEN

JOHNSON, Howard
Singles: 12-Inch 33/45rpm
A&M: *82-85* 4-6
Singles: 7-Inch
A&M: *82-85* 1-3
LPs: 10/12-Inch 33rpm
A&M: *82-85* 5-8
Also see NITEFLYTE

JOHNSON, James Arthur
Singles: 7-Inch
TUXEDO MUSIC: *86* 1-3

JOHNSON, Janice Marie
Singles: 7-Inch
CAPITOL: *84* 1-3

JOHNSON, Jesse
(Jesse Johnson's Revue)
Singles: 12-Inch 33/45rpm
A&M: *85* 4-6
Singles: 7-Inch
A&M: *85-88* 1-3
OLD TOWN: *66* 3-5
LPs: 10/12-Inch 33rpm
A&M: *85-88* 5-8
Also see STONE, Sly
Also see TIME

JOHNSON, Jimmy
(Jimmy Johnson & His Band featuring Hank
Alexander)
Singles: 7-Inch
MAGNUM: *65* 3-5

JOHNSON, Kevin
Singles: 7-Inch
MAINSTREAM: *73* 2-3

JOHNSON, L.V.
Singles: 7-Inch
ICA: *80-81* 1-3

JOHNSON, Lonnie
(Lonnie Johnson & Victoria Spivey)
Singles: 78rpm

ALADDIN: 47 .... $4-8
ARCO: 3-5
BLUEBIRD: 44 4-8
DISC: 46-47 4-8
GROOVE: 55 4-8
HOLIDAY: 48 3-6
KING: 47-57 3-8
PARADISE: 52 3-6
RCA VICTOR: 46-50 4-8
RAMA: 56 4-8
SCORE: 49 3-6

Singles: 7-Inch

FEDERAL: 60 3-6
GROOVE: 55 10-15
KING (4201; "Tomorrow Night"): 51 ... 15-25
KING (4500 through 4600
series): 51-53 10-20
KING (4700 through 4900
series): 54-56 5-10
KING (5000 series): 57-65 3-6
KING (6000 series): 70 2-4
PRESTIGE: 60-64 3-5
RAMA (Black vinyl): 56 10-20
RAMA (Colored vinyl): 56 25-35

EPs: 7-Inch 33/45rpm

KING: 54 20-35

LPs: 10/12-Inch 33rpm

COLLECTOR'S CLASSICS: 10-15
KING (Except 520): 66-70 10-15
KING (520; "Lonesome
Road"): 54 60-75
PRESTIGE: 69 10-12
PRESTIGE BLUESVILLE: 60-63 15-20

JOHNSON, Lonnie, & Elmer Snowden
LPs: 10/12-Inch 33rpm

PRESTIGE BLUESVILLE: 61 15-20

JOHNSON, Lonnie / George Dawson's Chocolateers
Singles: 78rpm

PARADE: 52 3-6
Also see JOHNSON, Lonnie

JOHNSON, Lou
Singles: 7-Inch

BIG HILL: 64-66 3-5
BIG TOP: 62-67 3-5
COTILLION: 68-69 2-4
HILLTOP: 64 3-5

LPs: 10/12-Inch 33rpm

COTILLION: 69 10-12
VOLT: 71 8-10

JOHNSON, Marv
Singles: 7-Inch

GORDY: 65-68 .... $4-6
TAMLA (101; "Come To Me"): 59 125-150
UNITED ARTISTS: 59-64 3-5

EPs: 7-Inch 33/45rpm

UNITED ARTISTS: 60 25-35

LPs: 10/12-Inch 33rpm

UNITED ARTISTS: 60-62 25-40

JOHNSON, Michael
Singles: 7-Inch

ATCO: 73 2-4
EMI AMERICA: 78-80 1-3

Picture Sleeves

EMI AMERICA: 78 1-3

LPs: 10/12-Inch 33rpm

ATCO: 73 8-10
EMI AMERICA: 78-82 5-8

JOHNSON, Orlando, & Trance
Singles: 12-Inch 33/45rpm

EASYSTREET: 83 4-6

JOHNSON, Paul
Singles: 7-Inch

EPIC: 88 1-3

JOHNSON, Robert
Singles: 7-Inch

INFINITY: 78 2-3

LPs: 10/12-Inch 33rpm

INFINITY: 78 5-8

JOHNSON, Rozetta
Singles: 7-Inch

CLINTONE: 70 2-3

JOHNSON, Ruby
Singles: 7-Inch

NEBS: 65 3-5
VOLT: 66 3-5

JOHNSON, Syl
Singles: 12-Inch 33/45rpm

BOARDWALK: 82 4-6

Singles: 7-Inch

FEDERAL: 59-62 3-5
HI: 73-76 2-3
SHAMA: 77 2-3
TMP-TING: 65 3-5
TWILIGHT: 67-68 3-5
TWINIGHT: 69 2-4

LPs: 10/12-Inch 33rpm

HI: 73-75 8-10
TWINIGHT: 68 10-12

JOHNSON, Troy
Singles: 7-Inch
KALLISTA: *86* $1-3

JOHNSTON, Tom
Singles: 7-Inch
WARNER BROS: *79-81* 1-3
LPs: 10/12-Inch 33rpm
WARNER BROS: *81* 5-8
Also see DOOBIE BROTHERS

JOINER, ARKANSAS JUNIOR HIGH SCHOOL BAND
Singles: 7-Inch
LIBERTY: *60-61* 3-5

JOLI, France
Singles: 12-Inch 33/45rpm
EPIC: *83-85* 4-6
Singles: 7-Inch
EPIC: *83-85* 1-3
PRELUDE: *79-82* 1-3
LPs: 10/12-Inch 33rpm
EPIC: *83-85* 5-8
PRELUDE: *79-80* 5-8

JOLLY, Pete
(Pete Jolly Trio)
Singles: 7-Inch
A&M: *68-69* 1-3
AVA: *63-64* 2-4
COLUMBIA: *66* 1-3
MAINSTREAM: *69* 1-3
LPs: 10/12-Inch 33rpm
A&M: *68-71* 8-12
AVA: *63-64* 10-20
CHARLIE PARKER: *62* 15-20
COLUMBIA: *65* 10-20
MGM: *63* 8-15
METROJAZZ: *60* 15-25
RCA VICTOR (1100 through 1300 series): *55-57* 20-30
TRIP: *75* 5-8

JOLO
Singles: 12-Inch 33/45rpm
MEGATONE: *84* 4-6

JON & ROBIN
(Jon & Robin & The In Crowd)
Singles: 7-Inch
ABNAK: *67-68* 3-5
LPs: 10/12-Inch 33rpm
ABNAK: *67-68* 15-20
Members: Jon Abnor; Robin Abnor.

JON & VANGELIS
Singles: 7-Inch
POLYDOR: *77-83* 1-3

LPs: 10/12-Inch 33rpm
POLYDOR: *80-83* $5-8
Members: Jon Anderson; Vangelis.
Also see ANDERSON, Jon
Also see VANGELIS

JONAE, Gwen
Singles: 12-Inch 33/45rpm
ARIAL: *83* 4-6
C&M: *83* 4-6

JONES, Brenda
Singles: 7-Inch
FLYING DUTCHMAN: *76* 2-3
MERCURY: *74* 2-3
WAVE: *82* 1-3

JONES, Brenda, & "Groove" Holmes
Singles: 7-Inch
FLYING DUTCHMAN: *76* 2-3
Also see HOLMES, Richard "Groove"
Also see JONES, Brenda

JONES, Brian
LPs: 10/12-Inch 33rpm
ROLLING STONES (49100; "Pipes Of Pan"): *71* 10-15
Promotional LPs
ROLLING STONES (49100; "Pipes Of Pan"): *71* 30-35
(Price range includes poster and cue sheets.)
Also see ROLLING STONES

JONES, Corky
(Buck Owens)
Singles: 78rpm
DIXIE: *56* 10-15
PEP: *56* 20-35
Singles: 7-Inch
DIXIE: *56* 25-35
PEP: *56* 50-75
Also see OWENS, Buck

JONES, Davy
(David Jones)
Singles: 7-Inch
BELL: *71-72* 8-10
COLPIX: *65* 10-15
MGM: *72-73* 10-15
MY FAVORITE MONKEE-DAVY JONES SINGS ("A Little Bit Me, A Little Bit You"): *67* 25-50
(Promotional issue only.)
Picture Sleeves
COLPIX: *65* 15-20
LPs: 10/12-Inch 33rpm
BELL: *71* 15-20
COLPIX: *65* 20-25
Also see MONKEES

JONES, Davy, & Mickey Dolenz
Singles: 7-Inch
BELL: *71* $8-10
MCA: *78* 2-3
Picture Sleeves
MCA: *78* 2-4
Also see DOLENZ, Mickey
Also see JONES, Davy
Also see NILSSON, Harry

JONES, Etta
Singles: 7-Inch
KING: *61-62* 3-5
PRESTIGE: *60-65* 3-5
20TH CENTURY-FOX/
  WESTBOUND: *75* 1-3
LPs: 10/12-Inch 33rpm
GRAND PRIX: 8-12
KING (500 series): *58* 20-40
KING (700 series): *61* 15-25
MUSE: *77-81* 5-8
PRESTIGE (7100 & 7200 series): *60-63* . 20-30
  (Yellow labels.)
PRESTIGE (7100 & 7200 series): *65* 10-20
  (Blue labels.)
PRESTIGE (7400 through 7700
  series): *67-70* 8-15
ROULETTE: *66* 8-15
20TH CENTURY-FOX/WESTBOUND: *75* 5-8

JONES, George
(George Jones & The Jones Boys; George Jones
& Sonny Burns; George Jones & Jeanette Hicks)
Singles: 78rpm
DIXIE: *56* 15-25
MERCURY: *57* 2-5
STARDAY: *54-57* 4-8
Singles: 7-Inch
D: *65-66* 2-4
EPIC: *72-88* 1-3
MERCURY (71000 & 72000
  series): *57-64* 3-6
MUSICOR: *65-71* 2-4
PROMOTIONAL COPIES ("The
  Race Is On"): *64* 10-20
  (No label name, other than "Promotional Copies,"
  is shown on disc.)
RCA VICTOR: *72-74* 1-3
STARDAY (Except 100 & 200
  series): *64-71* 1-3
STARDAY (100 & 200
  series): *54-57* 5-15
UNITED ARTISTS: *62-67* 3-5
Picture Sleeves
MERCURY: *62-64* 5-10
MUSICOR: *65* 3-8

UNITED ARTISTS: *62-63* $3-8
EPs: 7-Inch 33/45rpm
DIXIE (501; "Why Baby Why"): *56* 25-50
  (Not issued with cover.)
DIXIE (505; "Heartbreak Hotel"): *56* 25-50
  (Not issued with cover.)
DIXIE (525; "Don't Do This
  To Me"): *59* 15-25
  (Contains one George Jones track. Not issued with
  cover.)
MERCURY: *61* 10-20
RECORD OF THE MONTH (280; "
  Heartbreak Hotel"): 20-40
  (Colored vinyl.)
STARDAY: *65* 8-15
  (Jukebox issues.)
LPs: 10/12-Inch 33rpm
ACCORD: *82* 4-6
ALBUM GLOBE: *81* 5-8
ALLEGIANCE: *84* 4-8
AMBASSADOR: 5-8
BUCKBOARD: *76* 5-8
BULLDOG: 8-10
CAMDEN: *72-74* 5-8
COLUMBIA: *80-83* 5-8
EPIC: *72-82* 5-10
EVEREST: *79* 5-8
51 WEST: *79-82* 5-8
GRASS COUNTRY: 8-10
GUEST STAR: *63* 20-30
GUSTO: *78-81* 5-8
I&M: *82* 5-8
KOALA: 5-8
K-TEL: 5-8
LIBERTY: *82* 5-8
MERCURY (8000 series): *72* 5-10
MERCURY (20306 through
  20477): *58-59* 30-40
MERCURY (20596 through
  20836): *60-63* 20-30
  (Monaural.)
MERCURY (20906 through
  21048): *64-65* 10-20
  (Monaural.)
MERCURY (60257 through
  60836): *60-63* 20-30
  (Stereo.)
MERCURY (60906 through
  61048): *64-65* 10-20
  (Stereo.)
MOUNTAIN DEW: 5-8
MUSIC DISC: *69* 6-10
MUSICOR: *65-77* 8-15
MUSICOR/RCA VICTOR: *74-75* 8-10
NASHVILLE: *70-71* 6-10

PHOENIX 10: *81* $5-8
PHOENIX 20: *81* 5-8
PICADILLY: *81* 5-8
PICKWICK: *80* 4-8
PICKWICK/HILLTOP: *69* 8-12
POWER PAK: *75* 5-8
RCA VICTOR: *72-75* 5-10
ROUNDER: *82* 5-8
RUBY: 5-8
SEARS: 8-12
STARDAY (100 series,
   except 101): *60-62* 25-35
STARDAY (101; "The Grand Ole
   Opry's New Star"): *58* 50-75
STARDAY (300 series): *65-66* 15-30
STARDAY (400 series,
   except 401): *69* 8-12
STARDAY (401; "George Jones Song
   Book & Picture Album"): *67* 30-35
   (With 32-page song booklet.)
STARDAY (401; "George Jones Song
   Book & Picture Album"): *68* 15-20
   (Without 32-page song booklet.)
STARDAY (3000 series): *77* 5-8
STARDAY (90000 series): 8-12
SUNRISE: 5-8
TIME-LIFE: *81-82* 5-8
TRIP: *76* 5-8
TROLLY CAR: 5-8
UNART: *67-68* 8-12
UNITED ARTISTS (85; "George
   Jones Superpak"): *71* 10-15
UNITED ARTISTS (100 series): *73* 5-8
UNITED ARTISTS (3000 series): *62-67* . 10-20
   (Monaural.)
UNITED ARTISTS (6000 series): *62-69* . 10-20
   (Stereo.)
WHITE LIGHTNING: 12-18
WING: *64-68* 8-12
WING/PICKWICK: 4-6
   Also see CHARLES, Ray, George Jones &
Chet Atkins
   Also see DARRELL, Johnny / George Jones /
Willie Nelson
   Also see HAGGARD, Merle, & George Jones
   Also see JONES, Thumper
   Also see PARTON, Dolly / George Jones

JONES, George, & David Allan Coe
     Singles: 7-Inch
COLUMBIA: *81* 1-3
   Also see COE, David Allan

JONES, George, & Melba Montgomery
     Singles: 7-Inch
MUSICOR: *66-67* 2-4

UNITED ARTISTS: *63-66* $2-4
     LPs: 10/12-Inch 33rpm
BUCKBOARD: *76* 5-8
GUEST STAR: 20-30
LIBERTY: *82* 4-6
MUSIC DISC: *69* 6-10
MUSICOR: *66-74* 8-12
MUSICOR/RCA VICTOR: *74* 8-10
UNITED ARTISTS (200 series): *73* 5-8
UNITED ARTISTS (3000 & 6000
   series): *63-66* 10-15
   Also see MONTGOMERY, Melba

JONES, George, & Johnny Paycheck
     Singles: 7-Inch
EPIC: *78-80* 1-3
     LPs: 10/12-Inch 33rpm
EPIC: *80* 5-8
   Also see PAYCHECK, Johnny

JONES, George, & Gene Pitney
(George & Gene, With The Jordanaires)
     Singles: 7-Inch
MUSICOR: *65-66* 3-5
     Picture Sleeves
MUSICOR: *65* 3-6
     LPs: 10/12-Inch 33rpm
DESIGN: 6-10
INTERNATIONAL AWARD: 8-10
MUSIC DISC: *69* 10-12
MUSICOR (3044; "George Jones &
   Gene Pitney"): *65* 15-20
   (Front cover shows title as "For The First Time!
   Two Great Stars, George Jones & Gene Pitney.")
MUSICOR (3044; "George Jones &
   Gene Pitney"): *65* 12-15
   (Front cover shows title as "Recorded In Nashville,
   Tennessee, George Jones & Gene Pitney.")
MUSICOR (3065; "It's Country
   Time Again"): *65* 12-15
   Also see PITNEY, Gene

JONES, George, Gene Pitney &
Melba Montgomery
     LPs: 10/12-Inch 33rpm
MUSICOR: *66* 12-15
   (Contains duets by these artists, but there are no
   tracks where all three perform together.)
   Also see MONTGOMERY, Melba
   Also see PITNEY, Gene

JONES, George, & Ernest Tubb
     Singles: 7-Inch
FIRST GENERATION: *81* 1-3

JONES, George, & Tammy Wynette
(George, Tammy, & Tina)
Singles: 7-Inch
EPIC: *71-80* $1-3
LPs: 10/12-Inch 33rpm
COLUMBIA: *81* 5-8
EPIC: *71-81* 8-12
TVP: 5-8
Also see JONES, George
Also see WYNETTE, Tammy

JONES, Glenn
Singles: 12-Inch 33/45rpm
RCA VICTOR: *83-85* 4-6
Singles: 7-Inch
JIVE: *87-88* 1-3
RCA VICTOR: *83-87* 1-3
LPs: 10/12-Inch 33rpm
JIVE: *87* 5-8
RCA VICTOR: *83-84* 5-8
Also see JETER, Genobia, & Glenn Jones
Also see WARWICK, Dionne, & Glenn Jones

JONES, Grace
Singles: 12-Inch 33/45rpm
ISLAND: *83* 4-6
MANHATTAN: *85* 4-6
Singles: 7-Inch
BEAM JUNCTION: *76-77* 2-3
ISLAND: *78-83* 1-3
MANHATTAN: *85-86* 1-3
LPs: 10/12-Inch 33rpm
ISLAND: *77-82* 5-8
MANHATTAN: *85* 5-8

JONES, Howard
Singles: 12-Inch 33/45rpm
ELEKTRA: *83-85* 4-6
Singles: 7-Inch
ELEKTRA: *83-87* 1-3
LPs: 10/12-Inch 33rpm
ELEKTRA: *83-85* 5-8

JONES, Ignatius
Singles: 12-Inch 33/45rpm
WARNER BROS: *83* 4-6
Singles: 7-Inch
WARNER BROS: *83* 1-3

JONES, Jack
Singles: 7-Inch
CAPITOL: *59-60* 2-4
KAPP: *60-67* 2-3
POLYDOR: *83* 1-3
RCA VICTOR: *67-77* 1-3
Picture Sleeves
CAPITOL: *59* 3-6
KAPP: *63-69* 2-5

LPs: 10/12-Inch 33rpm
CAMDEN: *73* $4-8
CAPITOL: *59-64* 10-15
KAPP: *61-69* 8-15
MCA: *77* 5-8
MGM: *79* 4-8
RCA VICTOR: *67-77* 5-10
Also see ANDREWS, Julie & Andre Previn /
Vic Damone / Jack Jones / Marian Anderson

JONES, Jimmy
(Jimmy Jones & The Jones Boys)
Singles: 7-Inch
ARROW: *57* 20-25
BELL: *67* 3-5
CUB: *59-62* 3-5
EPIC: *59* 3-5
MGM: *78* 1-3
PARKWAY: *66* 3-5
ROULETTE: *65* 3-5
SAVOY: *60* 4-6
VEE JAY: *63* 3-5
Picture Sleeves
CUB: *60* 10-20
LPs: 10/12-Inch 33rpm
JEN JILLUS: *77* 5-8
MGM: *60* 35-40

JONES, Joe
Singles: 7-Inch
ABC: *73* 1-3
RIC: *60* 4-6
ROULETTE: *60-61* 3-5
LPs: 10/12-Inch 33rpm
PRESTIGE: *69* 10-12
ROULETTE: *61* 25-30

JONES, Johnny
Singles: 7-Inch
FURY: *68* 3-5

JONES, Jonah
(Jonah Jones Quartet)
Singles: 7-Inch
BETHLEHEM: *59* 2-4
CAPITOL: *58-63* 2-4
DECCA: *65* 1-3
GROOVE: *56* 2-4
EPs: 7-Inch 33/45rpm
BETHLEHEM: *55* 8-12
CAMDEN: *69* 5-10
CAPITOL: *58-59* 5-10
GROOVE: *56* 5-10
RCA VICTOR: *59* 5-10
LPs: 10/12-Inch 33rpm
ANGEL: *56* 15-25
BETHLEHEM: *55-60* 15-30

CAPITOL (1000 through
2800 series): *58-67* $10-20
(With a "T" or "ST" prefix.)
CAPITOL (1600 series): *77* 4-8
(With an "SM" prefix.)
CAPITOL (11000 series): *75* 5-8
DECCA: *65-67* 8-15
GROOVE: *56* 15-25
INNER CITY: *81* 5-8
MOTOWN: *69* 8-12
RCA VICTOR: *59-63* 12-20
  Also see CHRISTY, June

JONES, Kay Cee
Singles: 7-Inch
AMERICAN: *56* 5-8
CHANCELLOR: *59* 4-6
DECCA: *57* 4-8

JONES, Klinte
Singles: 7-Inch
OH MY: *84* 4-6

JONES, Linda
(Linda Jones & The Whatnauts)
Singles: 7-Inch
ATCO: *65* 3-5
BLUE CAT: *65* 4-6
COTIQUE: *69* 3-5
LOMA: *67-68* 4-8
NEPTUNE: *69* 3-5
STANG: *72* 2-4
TURBO: *72* 2-4
WARNER BROS: *69* 3-5
LPs: 10/12-Inch 33rpm
LOMA: *67* 12-15
TURBO: *72* 8-10

JONES, Michael
LPs: 10/12-Inch 33rpm
NARADA LOTUS: *88* 5-8

JONES, Oran "Juice"
(Juice)
Singles: 7-Inch
DEF JAM: *86-87* 1-3

JONES, Quincy
Singles: 7-Inch
A&M: *69-81* 1-3
ABC: *68* 2-3
BELL: *69* 2-3
COLGEMS: *68* 2-3
IMPULSE: *62* 2-4
MERCURY: *59-66* 2-4
RCA VICTOR: *69* 2-3
REPRISE: *72* 1-3
UNI: *69* 2-3
UNITED ARTISTS: *70* 1-3

Rickie Lee Jones (Photo: Deborah Feingold)

Picture Sleeves
A&M: *77-81* $1-3
COLGEMS: *68* 2-5
LPs: 10/12-Inch 33rpm
A&M: *69* 5-10
ABC (7; "For Love Of Ivy"): *68* 12-15
(Soundtrack.)
ABC (700 series): *73* 8-12
ABC-PARAMOUNT: *56-57* 30-50
ALLEGIANCE: *84* 5-8
COLGEMS: *68* 20-25
EMARCY: *56* 25-50
IMPULSE (11; "The
Quintessence"): *62* 15-25
IMPULSE (9300 series): *78* 8-12
LIBERTY: *67* 12-15
MFSL: *82* 20-30
MERCURY (Black label): *59-63* 20-35
MERCURY (Red label): *64-72* 10-20
PRESTIGE (100 series): *53* 100-150
(10-Inch LPs.)
TRIP: *74-76* 5-8
UNITED ARTISTS: *70* 10-15
VERVE: *67* 15-20
WING: *69* 6-12
  Also see ASHFORD & SIMPSON
  Also see AUSTIN, Patti
  Also see BROTHERS JOHNSON
  Also see ECKSTINE, Billy, & Quincy Jones
  Also see FELICIANO, Jose, & Quincy Jones
  Also see GILBERTO, Astrud
  Also see JACKSON, Michael
  Also see KHAN, Chaka
  Also see RIPERTON, Minnie
  Also see U.S.A. FOR AFRICA

Also see VAUGHAN, Sarah, & Quincy Jones
Also see WASHINGTON, Dinah

JONES, Quincy, & James Ingram
Singles: 7-Inch
A&M: *81* $1-3
Also see INGRAM, James
Also see JONES, Quincy

JONES, Rickie Lee
Singles: 7-Inch
WARNER BROS: *79-84* 1-3
LPs: 10/12-Inch 33rpm
GEFFEN: *89* 5-8
MFSL: *82* 25-50
WARNER BROS: *79-84* 5-8

JONES, Shirley
Singles: 7-Inch
PHILADELPHIA INT'L: *86-87* 1-3
Also see JONES GIRLS

JONES, Spencer
Singles: 12-Inch 33/45rpm
NEXT PLATINUM: *83* 4-6
Singles: 7-Inch
PROFILE: *86* 1-3

JONES, Spike
(Spike Jones & The City Slickers)
Singles: 78rpm
BLUEBIRD: *42-43* 10-20
RCA VICTOR: *46-55* 5-10
VICTOR: *44-45* 8-12
Singles: 7-Inch
LIBERTY: *59-65* 3-5
RCA VICTOR (0500 series): *71* 2-4
RCA VICTOR (3287-89; "Spike
Jones Favorites"): *49* 25-50
(Three disc boxed set.)
RCA VICTOR (3600 through 6000
series): *50-55* 5-10
WARNER BROS: *59* 4-6
Picture Sleeves
RCA VICTOR: *53-54* 12-25
EPs: 7-Inch 33/45rpm
RCA VICTOR: *51-59* 15-30
VERVE: *56-57* 12-25
LPs: 10/12-Inch 33rpm
GLENDALE: *78* 5-8
LIBERTY: *60-65* 12-20
MGM: *70* 8-12
RCA VICTOR (18; "Spike Jones
Plays The Charleston"): *51* 50-75
RCA VICTOR (1000 series): *75* 5-8
RCA VICTOR (2200 series): *60* 15-25
RCA VICTOR (2300 series): *77* 5-8

RCA VICTOR (3000 & 3100
series): *52-53* $30-50
RCA VICTOR (3200 series): *71* 8-12
RCA VICTOR (3700 series): *80* 4-8
RCA VICTOR (3800 series): *67* 10-15
(With an "LPM" or "LSP" prefix.)
RCA VICTOR (3800 series): *81* 5-8
(With an "AYL1" prefix.)
UNITED ARTISTS: *75* 5-8
VERVE (Except 8500 series): *56-59* 20-30
VERVE (8500 series): *63* 12-20
WARNER BROS: *59-60* 15-25
Also see KATZ, Mickey, & His Orchestra

JONES, Tamiko
Singles: 7-Inch
A&M: *68-69* 2-4
ARISTA: *75* 2-3
ATLANTIC: *66* 3-5
ATLANTIS: *77* 2-3
CONTEMPO: *76* 2-3
DECEMBER: *67* 3-5
GOLDEN WORLD: *66* 3-5
POLYDOR: *79* 1-3
SUTRA: *86* 1-3
20TH CENTURY-FOX: *74* 2-3
LPs: 10/12-Inch 33rpm
A&M: *68* 10-12
DECEMBER: *68* 10-12

JONES, Tamiko, & Herbie Mann
Singles: 7-Inch
ATLANTIC: *66* 3-5
LPs: 10/12-Inch 33rpm
ATLANTIC: *67* 8-15
Also see JONES, Tamiko
Also see MANN, Herbie

JONES, Thelma
Singles: 7-Inch
BARRY: *66-68* 3-5
COLUMBIA: *78* 2-3

JONES, Thumper
(George Jones)
Singles: 78rpm
STARDAY (240; "Rock-It"): *56* 20-30
Singles: 7-Inch
STARDAY (240; "Rock-It"): *56* 50-60
EPs: 7-Inch 33/45rpm
DIXIE (502; "Thumper Jones"): *58* 15-25
(Contains three Jones tracks. Not issued with
cover.)
LPs: 10/12-Inch 33rpm
TEENAGE HEAVEN: 8-12
Also see JONES, George

CAPITOL (1851; "Mary Had A
 Little Lamb"): $2-3
CAPITOL (1857; "Hi Hi Hi"): 2-3
CAPITOL (1861; "My Love"): 2-3
CAPITOL (1863; "Live & Let Die"): 2-3
CAPITOL (1869; "Helen Wheels"): 2-3
CAPITOL (1871; "Jet"): 2-3
CAPITOL (1873; "Band On The Run"): ...2-3
CAPITOL (1875; "Junior's Farm"): 2-3
CAPITOL (4091; "Listen To What
 The Man Said"): 75 2-3
CAPITOL (4145; "Letting Go"): 75 2-3
CAPITOL (4175; "Venus & Mars
 Rock Show"): 75 2-3
CAPITOL (4256; "Silly Love Songs"): 76 ..3-5
 (Capitol custom label.)
CAPITOL (4256; "Silly Love Songs"): 2-3
 (Black label.)
CAPITOL (4293; "Let 'Em In"): 76 3-5
 (Capitol custom label.)
CAPITOL (4293; "Let 'Em In"): 2-3
 (Black label.)
CAPITOL (4385; "Maybe I'm
 Amazed"): 77 2-3
CAPITOL (4504; "Mull Of Kintyre"): 77 ...2-3
CAPITOL (4559; "With A
 Little Luck"): 78 2-3
CAPITOL (4594; "I've Had Enough"): 78 ..2-3
CAPITOL (4625; "London Town"): 78 2-3
CAPITOL (5537; "Spies Like Us"): 85 2-3
CAPITOL (5597; "Press"): 86 2-3
CAPITOL (5636;
 "Stranglehold"): 86 2-3
COLUMBIA (02171; "Silly Love
 Songs"): 81 2-3
COLUMBIA (03018; "Take It Away"): 82 .2-3
COLUMBIA (03235; "Tug Of War"): 82 ...2-3
COLUMBIA (04296; "So Bad"): 83 2-3
COLUMBIA (04581; "No More
 Lonely Nights"): 84 2-3
COLUMBIA (10939; "Goodnight
 Tonight"): 79 2-3
COLUMBIA (11020; "Getting Closer"): 79 .2-3
COLUMBIA (11070; "Arrow Through
 Me"): 79 2-3
COLUMBIA (11162; "Wonderful
 Christmastime"): 79 2-3
COLUMBIA (11263; "Coming Up"): 80 ...2-3
COLUMBIA (11335; "Waterfalls"): 80 2-3
COLUMBIA (33405; "Goodnight
 Tonight"): 80 2-3
COLUMBIA (33409; "My Love"): 80 2-3
COLUMBIA (33408; "Uncle Albert-
 Admiral Halsey"): 80 2-3

COLUMBIA (33409; "Band On
 The Run"): 80 .... $2-3
PROFILE (5147; "Let It Be"): 87 2-3
 Picture Sleeves
APPLE (1847; "Give Ireland Back
 To The Irish"): 72 10-15
APPLE (1851; "Mary Had A
 Little Lamb"): 72 20-25
 ("Little Woman Love" printed under photo, on
 reverse side of sleeve.)
APPLE (1851; "Mary Had A
 Little Lamb"): 72 10-12
 ("Little Woman Love" not printed under photo, on
 reverse side of sleeve.)
CAPITOL (4091; "Listen To What
 The Man Said"): 75 4-6
CAPITOL (4504; "Mull Of Kintyre"): 77 . 8-10
CAPITOL (5537; "Spies Like Us"): 85 ... 2-3
CAPITOL (5597; "Press"): 86 2-3
CAPITOL (5636; "Stranglehold"): 86 2-3
COLUMBIA (03018; "Take It Away"): 82 . 5-8
 (Reads "Not For Sale" on back side. Promotional
 issue only.)
COLUMBIA (03018; "Take It Away"): 82 . 2-4
COLUMBIA (04296; "So Bad"): 83 2-3
COLUMBIA (04296; "So Bad"): 83 5-8
 (Reads "Not For Sale" on back side. Promotional
 issue only.)
COLUMBIA (04581; "No More
 Lonely Nights"): 84 5-8
COLUMBIA (11020; "Getting
 Closer"): 79 20-25
COLUMBIA (11162; "Wonderful
 Christmastime"): 79 3-5
COLUMBIA (11263 "Coming Up"): 80 ... 3-5
COLUMBIA (11335; "Waterfalls"): 80 .. 12-15
PROFILE (5147; "Let It Be"): 87 2-3
 Promotional Singles
APPLE (1829; "Another Day"): 71 25-35
APPLE (1837; "Uncle Albert-
 Admiral Halsey"): 71 15-20
APPLE (1851; "Mary Had A
 Little Lamb"): 72 40-50
APPLE (1857; "Hi Hi Hi"): 72 10-15
APPLE (1861; "My Love"): 73 45-55
APPLE (1863; "Live & Let Die"): 73 ... 10-15
APPLE (1871; "Jet"): 74 20-30
APPLE (1873; "Band On The Run"): 74 . 20-30
APPLE (1875; "Junior's Farm"): 74 20-30
APPLE (1875; "Sally G"): 74 20-30
APPLE (6786; "Helen Wheels"): 73 25-35
APPLE (6787; "Country Dreamer"): 73 . 40-50
CAPITOL (4145; "Letting Go"): 75 12-15
CAPITOL (4175; "Venus & Mars
 Rock Show"): 75 12-15

JOPLIN, Janis / Hot Tuna
LPs: 10/12-Inch 33rpm
GRUNT ("The Last Interview"): 72 .... $25-35
(Promotional issue only. Includes bonus Joplin
home recording.)
Also see HOT TUNA
Also see JOPLIN, Janis

JORDAN, Frank
Singles: 7-Inch
A-STREET: 86 3-5

JORDAN, Jerry
(Jordans)
Singles: 7-Inch
MCA: 75-76 1-3
LPs: 10/12-Inch 33rpm
MCA: 75-76 5-8

JORDAN, Lonnie
Singles: 7-Inch
BOARDWALK: 82 1-3
MCA: 78 1-3
UNITED ARTISTS: 76-77 2-3
LPs: 10/12-Inch 33rpm
MCA: 78 5-8
Also see WAR

JORDAN, Louis
(Louis Jordan's Elk Rendezvous Band; Louis
Jordan & His Tympani 5)
Singles: 78rpm
DECCA (7500 through 8600
series): 38-43 5-8
DECCA (18000 through 30000
series): 44-50 3-6
VIK: 56 3-6
Singles: 7-Inch
ALADDIN: 54-56 12-25
DECCA (20000 through 30000
series): 50-54 8-15
LOU-WA: 60 3-6
MERCURY: 56-58 5-10
PZAZZ: 68 2-4
TANGERINE: 62-66 3-6
VIK: 56 4-8
WARWICK: 60-61 3-6
X: 55 5-8
EPs: 7-Inch 33/45rpm
DECCA: 56 15-20
MERCURY: 57 15-20
LPs: 10/12-Inch 33rpm
CLASSICAL JAZZ: 82 5-8
DECCA (5035; "Greatest Hits"): 68 10-15
DECCA (8500 series): 56 30-35
MCA: 75-80 5-8
MERCURY: 57-58 25-30

SCORE: $55-65
TANGERINE: 64 12-15
TRIP: 75 8-10
WING: 63 12-15
Also see CROSBY, Bing, & Louis Jordan
Also see FITZGERALD, Ella, & Louis Jordan

JORDAN, Stanley
LPs: 10/12-Inch 33rpm
BLUE NOTE: 87 5-8
EMI: 88 5-8

JORDAN, Tenita
Singles: 7-Inch
CBS ASSOCIATED: 85 1-3

JORDANS: see JORDAN, Jerry

JOSEPH, David
Singles: 12-Inch 33/45rpm
MANGO: 83 4-6
Singles: 7-Inch
MANGO: 83 1-3

JOSEPH, Margie
(Margie Joseph & Blue Magic)
Singles: 12-Inch 33/45rpm
H.C.R.C.: 83 4-6
Singles: 7-Inch
ATCO: 75 2-3
ATLANTIC: 72-78 2-3
COTILLION: 76-84 1-3
H.C.R.C.: 82-83 1-3
OKEH: 68 3-5
VOLT: 68-71 2-4
LPs: 10/12-Inch 33rpm
ATLANTIC: 73-74 8-10
H.C.R.C: 83 5-8
VOLT: 71 10-12
Also see BLUE MAGIC
Also see HATHAWAY, Donny, & Margie
Joseph

JOSIAS, Cory
Singles: 12-Inch 33/45rpm
SIRE: 83 4-6

JOURNEY
Singles: 7-Inch
COLUMBIA: 74-88 2-4
GEFFEN: 85 1-3
Picture Sleeves
COLUMBIA: 80-81 1-3
EPs: 7-Inch 33/45rpm
CSP: 81 3-6
(Nestle's candy promotional issue.)
LPs: 10/12-Inch 33rpm
COLUMBIA (662; "Live Sampler"): 75 ..12-15
(Promotional issue only.)

COLUMBIA (914; "Journey"): 75 ..... $12-15
(Promotional issue only.)
COLUMBIA (30000 series): 75-82 5-10
COLUMBIA (46000 & 47000
series): 81-82 12-15
(With an "HC" prefix. Half-speed mastered LPs.)
Members: Steve Perry; Neal Schon; Aynsley Dunbar.
Also see CAIN, Jonathan
Also see PERRY, Steve
Also see SCHON, Neal, & Jan Hammer

JOVI, Bon: see BON JOVI

JOY, Roddie
Singles: 7-Inch
PARKWAY: 66-67 3-5
RED BIRD: 65 3-6

JOY DIVISION
LPs: 10/12-Inch 33rpm
QWEST: 88 5-8

JOY OF COOKING
Singles: 7-Inch
BROWNSVILLE: 71 2-4
CAPITOL: 71-73 2-3
FANTASY: 77-78 1-3
LPs: 10/12-Inch 33rpm
CAPITOL: 71-72 8-10
Members: Terry Garthwaite; Toni Brown.

JUDAS PRIEST
Singles: 7-Inch
COLUMBIA: 79-84 1-3
Picture Sleeves
COLUMBIA: 81 1-3
LPs: 10/12-Inch 33rpm
COLUMBIA (Except "Screaming For
Vengeance" picture disc): 77-84 5-8
COLUMBIA ("Screaming For Vengeance"
picture disc): 84 8-15
COLUMBIA (40000 series): 87-88 10-12
(Some pressings of this disc may contain music by
Neil Diamond.)
JANUS: 76 6-10
OVATION: 80 5-8
RCA VICTOR: 83-84 5-8
VISA: 78-81 5-8
Members: Rob Halford; K.K. Downing; Glenn Tipton; Ian Hill; Dave Holland.

JUDDS
Singles: 7-Inch
RCA VICTOR: 84-88 1-3
LPs: 10/12-Inch 33rpm
RCA VICTOR: 83-88 5-8
Members: Naomi Judd; Wynonna Judd.

JUICY
Singles: 12-Inch 33/45rpm
ATLANTIC: 83-84 ....$4-6
PRIVATE I: 85 4-6
Singles: 7-Inch
ARISTA: 83 1-3
ATLANTIC: 83-84 1-3
CBS ASSOC: 86 1-3
PRIVATE I: 85-86 1-3
LPs: 10/12-Inch 33rpm
ARISTA: 83 5-8
ATLANTIC: 84 5-8
Members: Jerry Barnes; Katreese Barnes

JUKES:
see SOUTHSIDE JOHNNY & THE ASBURY
JUKES

JULIA LEE: see LEE, Julia

JULIAN, Don
(Don Julian & The Larks)
Singles: 7-Inch
DYNAMITE: 62 3-6
JERK: 65 3-5
ORIGINAL SOUND: 58-60 5-10
LPs: 10/12-Inch 33rpm
AMAZON: 63 30-40
Also see LARKS

JULIAN, Don & The Meadowlarks
Singles: 78rpm
DOOTO: 57 10-20
DOOTONE: 55-56 15-30
RPM (399; "Love Only You"): 54 25-50
RPM (406; "LSMFT Blues"): 54 50-100
Singles: 7-Inch
CLASSIC ARTISTS: 89 2-3
DOOTO: 57 20-40
DOOTONE: 55-56 30-60
ORIGINAL SOUND: 58-59 5-10
RPM (399; "Love Only You"): 54 75-125
RPM (406; "LSMFT Blues"): 54 100-200
EPs: 7-Inch 33/45rpm
DOOTO: 15-25
DOOTONE (203; "Don Julian & The
Meadowlarks"): 56 75-125
Members: Don Julian; Ronald Barrett; Earl Jonces;
Randy Jones; Glen Reagan; Freeman Bralton;
Benny Patricks.
Also see DEL-VIKINGS / Sonnets
Also see JULIAN, Don
Also see PENGUINS / Meadowlarks / Medallions / Dootones

JULIE
(Julie Budd)
Singles: 7-Inch
TOM CAT: 76 .... $2-3

JULUKA
Singles: 7-Inch
WARNER BROS: 83-84 1-3
LPs: 10/12-Inch 33rpm
WARNER BROS: 83-84 5-8

JUMBO
Singles: 7-Inch
PRELUDE: 77 2-3
LPs: 10/12-Inch 33rpm
PYE: 77 5-8

JUMP 'N THE SADDLE
Singles: 7-Inch
ATLANTIC: 83 1-3

JUNE & DONNIE
Singles: 7-Inch
CURTOM: 68 2-4

JUNGKLAS, Rob
Singles: 7-Inch
MANHATTAN: 87 1-3

JUNGLE BROTHERS
LPs: 10/12-Inch 33rpm
IDLERS: 88 5-8

JUNIE
(Walter Morrison; Junie Morrison)
Singles: 7-Inch
COLUMBIA: 81 1-3
EASTBOUND: 74 2-4
20TH CENTURY-FOX/
  WESTBOUND: 75-76 2-3
LPs: 10/12-Inch 33rpm
20TH CENTURY-FOX/
  WESTBOUND: 76 5-8
  Also see FUNKADELIC
  Also see MORRISON, Junie
  Also see OHIO PLAYERS

JUNIOR
(Junior Giscombe)
Singles: 12-Inch 33/45rpm
LONDON: 84 4-6
MERCURY: 83 4-6
Singles: 7-Inch
CASABLANCA: 83 1-3
LONDON: 84-88 1-3
MERCURY: 82-86 1-3
LPs: 10/12-Inch 33rpm
LONDON: 88 5-8
MERCURY: 82-83 5-8

JU-PAR UNIVERSAL ORCHESTRA
Singles: 7-Inch
JU-PAR: 77 .... $2-3

JUPITER, Duke: see DUKE JUPITER

JUST US
Singles: 7-Inch
ATLANTIC: 71 2-3
COLPIX: 66 2-4
KAPP: 66-67 2-4
MINUTEMAN: 66 3-5
Picture Sleeves
KAPP: 66 3-6
LPs: 10/12-Inch 33rpm
KAPP: 66 10-12

JUST-ICE
LPs: 10/12-Inch 33rpm
FRESH 5: 88 5-8

JUSTIS, Bill
(Bill Justis & The Jury; Bill Justis Orchestra)
Singles: 78rpm
PHILLIPS INT'L: 57 5-8
Singles: 7-Inch
BELL: 70 2-4
MONUMENT: 76 2-3
PHILLIPS INT'L: 57-59 5-10
PLAY ME: 59 4-8
MCA: 77 1-3
MONUMENT: 66 2-4
NRC: 60 4-8
SMASH: 63-65 3-6
Picture Sleeves
SMASH: 63 4-8
LPs: 10/12-Inch 33rpm
HARMONY: 72 8-10
PHILLIPS INT'L: 57 25-30
SMASH: 62-66 15-20
SUN: 69 8-10

JUVET, Patrick
Singles: 12-Inch 33/45rpm
CASABLANCA: 78-79 4-6
Singles: 7-Inch
CASABLANCA: 78-79 1-3
LPs: 10/12-Inch 33rpm
CASABLANCA: 78-79 5-8

KBC BAND
Singles: 7-Inch
ARISTA: 86 1-3
LPs: 10/12-Inch 33rpm
ARISTA: 86 5-8

Members: Paul Kantner; Marty Balin; Jack Casady.
Also see JEFFERSON AIRPLANE

KC & THE SUNSHINE BAND
(KC; Sunshine Band)
Singles: 12-Inch 33/45rpm
EPIC: 82 .... $4-6
MECA: 83-85 4-6
SUNSHINE SOUND: 81 4-6
Singles: 7-Inch
CASABLANCA: 80-83 1-3
EPIC: 81-83 1-3
MECA: 83-85 1-3
SUNSHINE SOUND: 81 1-3
TK: 73-81 1-3
Picture Sleeves
TK: 76-78 1-3
LPs: 10/12-Inch 33rpm
CASABLANCA: 81 5-8
EPIC: 81-82 5-8
MECA: 84 5-8
SUNSHINE SOUND: 81 5-8
TK: 74-80 8-10
Also see DE SARIO, Teri, & K.C.
Also see WRIGHT, Betty

KGB
Singles: 7-Inch
MCA: 76 2-3
LPs: 10/12-Inch 33rpm
MCA: 76 8-10
Members: Mike Bloomfield; Barry Goldberg; Rick
Gretch; Carmine Appice; Ray Kennedy.
Also see BLOOMFIELD, Mike
Also see KENNEDY, Ray

K.I.D.
Singles: 12-Inch 33/45rpm
SAM: 81 4-6
Singles: 7-Inch
SAM: 81 1-3

KTP
Singles: 7-Inch
MERCURY: 87 1-3

KADO, Ernie: see K-DOE, Ernie

KADOR, Ernest: see K-DOE, Ernie

KAEMPFERT, Bert, & His Orchestra
Singles: 7-Inch
DECCA: 60-71 2-3
EPs: 7-Inch 33/45rpm
DECCA: 61 3-6
LPs: 10/12-Inch 33rpm
CADENCE: 61 5-15

DECCA: 59-72 .... $5-15
MCA: 73-76 5-10

KAJAGOOGOO
(Kaja)
Singles: 12-Inch 33/45rpm
EMI AMERICA: 83-85 4-6
Singles: 7-Inch
EMI AMERICA: 83-85 1-3
LPs: 10/12-Inch 33rpm
EMI AMERICA: 83-85 5-8
Also see LIMAHL

KALEIDOSCOPE
Singles: 7-Inch
EPIC: 67-69 15-30
LPs: 10/12-Inch 33rpm
BACK-TRAC: 85 5-8
EPIC (24304; "Side Trips"): 67 50-100
(Monaural.)
EPIC (24333; "A Beacon From
Mars"): 67 50-100
(Monaural.)
EPIC (26304; "Side Trips"): 67 50-100
(Stereo.)
EPIC (26333; "A Beacon From
Mars"): 67 50-100
(Stereo.)
EPIC (26467; "Incredible
Kaleidoscope"). 69 20-40
EPIC (26508; "Bernice"): 70 15-20
PACIFIC ARTS: 78 5-10
Members: David Lindley; Solomon Feldthouse;
John Vidican; John Welsh; Rick O'Neil; Brian
Monsour; Chris Darrow.
Also see WILLIAMS, Larry, & Johnny Guitar
Watson

KALIN TWINS
Singles: 7-Inch
DECCA: 58-62 4-6
Picture Sleeves
DECCA: 59 5-10
EPs: 7-Inch 33/45rpm
DECCA: 59 10-20
LPs: 10/12-Inch 33rpm
DECCA: 58 20-25
VOCALION: 66 10-15
Members: Hal Kalin; Herb Kalin.

KALLEN, Kitty
Singles: 78rpm
DECCA: 54-57 2-5
COLUMBIA: 54 2-5
MERCURY: 51-54 3-5
Singles: 7-Inch
BELL: 67 2-3
DECCA: 54-59 2-5

COLUMBIA (40000 series): *54* **$3-5**
COLUMBIA (41000 series): *59-61* **2-4**
MGM: *65* **2-3**
MERCURY: *51-54* **3-5**
PHILIPS: *66* **2-3**
RCA VICTOR: *63* **2-4**
20TH CENTURY-FOX: *64* **2-3**
UNITED ARTISTS: *65* **2-3**
Promotional Singles
DECCA (78094; "Personal Introduction By
Kitty Kallen To The 1954 Christmas Seal
Song"): *54* **4-8**
(One-sided pressing. Promotional issue only.)
EPs: 7-Inch 33/45rpm
DECCA: *54-56* **5-10**
COLUMBIA: *54* **5-10**
MERCURY: *55* **5-10**
LPs: 10/12-Inch 33rpm
COLUMBIA: *60-61* **10-20**
DECCA: *56* **15-25**
MCA: *83* **4-8**
MOVIETONE: *67* **8-12**
RCA VICTOR: *63* **10-15**
20TH CENTURY-FOX: *64* **8-15**
VOCALION: *59* **10-15**
WING: *63* **8-15**
  Also see ANN-MARGRET / Kitty Kallen /
Della Reese
  Also see HAYES, Richard, & Kitty Kallen
  Also see JAMES, Harry, & His Orchestra

KALLEN, Kitty, & Georgie Shaw
Singles: 78rpm
DECCA: *55* **2-5**
Singles: 7-Inch
DECCA: *55* **3-5**
  Also see KALLEN, Kitty
  Also see SHAW, Georgie

KALLMANN, Gunter, Chorus
Singles: 7-Inch
4 CORNERS: *65-68* **2-4**
LPs: 10/12-Inch 33rpm
4 CORNERS: *65-68* **6-12**
POLYDOR: *70* **5-10**

KALYAN
Singles: 7-Inch
MCA: *77* **2-3**
LPs: 10/12-Inch 33rpm
MCA: *77* **8-10**

KAMIKAZE
Singles: 12-Inch 33/45rpm
A&M: *84* **4-6**
Singles: 7-Inch
A&M: *84* **1-3**

KAMON, Karen
Singles: 7-Inch
COLUMBIA: *84* **$1-3**

KANE, Big Daddy
Singles: 7-Inch
COLD CHILLIN': *88* **1-3**
LPs: 10/12-Inch 33rpm
COLD CHILLIN': *88* **5-8**

KANE, Madleen
Singles: 12-Inch 33/45rpm
CHALET: *82* **4-6**
TSR: *85* **4-6**
Singles: 7-Inch
CHALET: *82* **1-3**
WARNER BROS: *78-79* **1-3**
Picture Sleeves
WARNER BROS: *78-79* **1-3**
LPs: 10/12-Inch 33rpm
CHALET: *82* **5-8**
WARNER BROS: *78-79* **5-8**

KANE, Paul
(Paul Simon)
Singles: 7-Inch
TRIBUTE: *63* **25-30**
(Copies on Tribute showing "Paul Simon" as the
artist are bootleg issues.)
  Also see SIMON, Paul

KANE GANG
Singles: 12-Inch 33/45rpm
LONDON: *86* **4-6**
Singles: 7-Inch
CAPITOL: *87-88* **1-3**
LONDON: *86* **1-3**
LPs: 10/12-Inch 33rpm
CAPITOL: *87* **5-8**
LONDON: *86* **5-8**
POLYGRAM: *85* **5-8**

KANO
Singles: 7-Inch
EMERGENCY: *80* **1-3**
MIRAGE: *81* **1-3**
LPs: 10/12-Inch 33rpm
EMERGENCY: *81* **5-8**
MIRAGE: *81* **5-8**

KANSAS
Singles: 7-Inch
CBS ASSOCIATED: *83* **1-3**
KIRSHNER: *74-82* **1-3**
MCA: *86-87* **1-3**
LPs: 10/12-Inch 33rpm
BURNS MEDIA: *78* **15-20**
(Promotional issue only.)

KASENETZ-KATZ
SINGING ORCHESTRAL CIRCUS
(Kasenetz-Katz Super Cirkus; Kasenetz-Katz
Fighter Squadron)
Singles: 7-Inch
BELL (966; "When He Comes"): *71* $5-8
(With 10CC.)
BUDDAH: *68* 3-5
EPIC: *77* 2-3
MAGNA-GLIDE: *75* 2-3
SUPER K: *69-71* 2-4
LPs: 10/12-Inch 33rpm
BUDDAH: *68* 10-12
Also see MUSIC EXPLOSION
Also see 1910 FRUITGUM COMPANY
Also see OHIO EXPRESS
Also see 10CC

KASHIF
Singles: 12-Inch 33/45rpm
ARISTA: *83-86* 4-6
Singles: 7-Inch
ARISTA: *83-88* 1-3
LPs: 10/12-Inch 33rpm
ARISTA: *83-87* 5-8
Also see MOORE, Melba, & Kashif
Also see WARWICK, Dionne, & Kashif

KASHIF & Meli'sa Morgan
Singles: 7-Inch
ARISTA: *87* 1-3
Also see MORGAN, Meli'sa

KATFISH
Singles: 7-Inch
BIG TREE: *75* 2-3

KATRINA & THE WAVES
Singles: 7-Inch
CAPITOL: *85-86* 1-3
LPs: 10/12-Inch 33rpm
CAPITOL: *85-86* 5-8

KATZ, Mickey, & His Orchestra
Singles: 78rpm
CAPITOL: *51-57* 3-5
Singles: 7-Inch
CAPITOL: *51-62* 3-5
EPs: 7-Inch 33/45rpm
CAPITOL: *53-56* 5-10
LPs: 10/12-Inch 33rpm
CAPITOL (Except SM-298): *53-65* 10-20
CAPITOL (SM-298; "Mickey
Katz"): *78* 5-8
Also see JONES, Spike

KAUKONEN, Jorma
(Jorna Kaukonen & Vital Parts)
Singles: 7-Inch
GRUNT: *73* $2-3
LPs: 10/12-Inch 33rpm
GRUNT: *73* 8-10
RCA VICTOR: *79-81* 5-8
Also see HOT TUNA
Also see JEFFERSON AIRPLANE

KAY, John
(John Kay & Steppenwolf)
Singles: 7-Inch
DUNHILL: *72-73* 2-4
MERCURY: *78* 2-3
LPs: 10/12-Inch 33rpm
COLUMBIA: *69* 10-12
DUNHILL: *72-73* 8-10
MERCURY: *78* 5-8
QWIL: *87* 5-8
Also see STEPPENWOLF

KAY GEES: see KAY-GEES

KAYAK
Singles: 7-Inch
JANUS: *78* 2-3
MERCURY: *80* 1-3
LPs: 10/12-Inch 33rpm
HARVEST: *74* 8-10
JANUS (Except "Phantom Of The
Night," picture disc): *75-79* 8-10
JANUS ("Phantom Of The
Night"): *79* 25-30
(Picture disc. Promotional issue only.)
MERCURY: *80* 5-8
Also see WERNER, Max

KAYE, Danny
Singles: 78rpm
DECCA: *50-56* 2-5
Singles: 7-Inch
DECCA: *50-56* 3-5
REPRISE: *62* 2-4
Picture Sleeves
REPRISE: *62* 4-8
EPs: 7-Inch 33/45rpm
DECCA: *50-56* 8-15
LPs: 10/12-Inch 33rpm
DECCA: *50-67* 10-20
(Decca LP numbers in this series preceded by a "7"
or a "DL-7" are stereo issues.)
GOLDEN: *62* 5-10
HARMONY: *64* 5-10

KAYE, Danny, & Louis Armstrong
Singles: 7-Inch
DOT: *59-64* 2-4

Picture Sleeves

DOT: *59* $4-8
  Also see ARMSTRONG, Louis
  Also see KAYE, Danny

KAYE, Mary
(Mary Kaye Trio)
Singles: 78rpm

CAPITOL: *52* 2-5
DECCA: *55-56* 2-4
RCA VICTOR: *54* 2-4
Singles: 7-Inch
BLUE-J: 4-8
CAMELOT: *67* 2-3
CAPITOL: *52* 3-5
DECCA: *55-56* 2-4
LECTRON: *65* 2-3
RCA VICTOR: *54* 2-4
VERVE: *60* 2-4
WARNER BROS: *59* 2-4
EPs: 7-Inch 33/45rpm
DECCA: *56* 5-10
LPs: 10/12-Inch 33rpm
COLUMBIA: *62* 5-15
DECCA: *30* 10-20
MOVIETONE: *67* 8-12
20TH CENTURY-FOX: *64* 8-15
VERVE: *60-62* 10-15
WARNER BROS: *59* 10-20
  Also see BYRNES, Edd "Kookie," With
Joanie Sommers & The Mary Kaye Trio

KAYE, Sammy, & His Orchestra
Singles: 78rpm
COLUMBIA: *50-57* 2-4
Singles: 7-Inch
COLUMBIA: *50-60* 2-4
DECCA: *60-70* 1-3
PROJECT 3: *72* 1-3
EPs: 7-Inch 33/45rpm
COLUMBIA: *50-60* 5-10
DECCA: *64* 4-6
RCA VICTOR: *52-53* 5-10
LPs: 10/12-Inch 33rpm
CAMDEN: *53-56* 8-15
COLUMBIA: *50-62* 10-15
DECCA: *60-70* 8-15
  (Decca LP numbers in this series preceded by a "7"
or a "DL-7" are stereo issues.)
HARMONY: *59-68* 5-10
MCA: *74* 5-10
PROJECT 3: *72* 5-8
RCA VICTOR: *68-72* 5-10
VOCALION: *71* 5-10

KAY-GEES
Singles: 7-Inch
DE-LITE: *78-79* $2-3
GANG: *74-76* 2-3
LPs: 10/12-Inch 33rpm
DELITE: *78-79* 5-8
GANG: *75* 5-8

KAYLI, Bob
Singles: 7-Inch
ANNA: *59* 15-20
CARLTON: *58* 5-8
GORDY: *62* 20-25
TAMLA: *61* 15-20

K-DOE, Ernie
(Ernest Kador; Ernie Kado)
Singles: 78rpm
SPECIALTY: *55* 4-8
Singles: 7-Inch
DUKE: *64-69* 3-5
EMBER: *59-61* 4-8
INSTANT: *63-64* 3-6
MINIT: *59-63* 4-8
SPECIALTY: *55* 10-15
LPs: 10/12-Inch 33rpm
JANUS: *71* 8-10
MINIT (0002; "Mother In Law"): *61* 40-80
  Also see BLUE DIAMONDS
  Also see SPELLMAN, Benny

KEANE BROTHERS
Singles: 12-Inch 33/45rpm
ABC: *79* 4-6
Singles: 7-Inch
ABC: *79* 1-3
20TH CENTURY-FOX: *76* 2-3
LPs: 10/12-Inch 33rpm
ABC: *79* 5-8

KEEL
Singles: 7-Inch
GOLD MOUNTAIN: *84-85* 1-3
LPs: 10/12-Inch 33rpm
GOLD MOUNTAIN: *85* 5-8
MCA: *87* 5-8

KEENE, Tommy
Singles: 7-Inch
GEFFEN: *86* 1-3
LPs: 10/12-Inch 33rpm
GEFFEN: *86* 5-8

KEITH
Singles: 7-Inch
DISCREET: *71-74* 2-3
MERCURY: *66-68* 3-5
RCA VICTOR: *69* 2-4

Picture Sleeves
MERCURY: 66-68 .... $3-6
    LPs: 10/12-Inch 33rpm
MERCURY: 67 12-20
RCA VICTOR: 69 15-25

KEITH, David
Singles: 7-Inch
RCA VICTOR: 88 2-3
    Picture Sleeves
RCA VICTOR: 88 2-5
Also see PRESLEY, Elvis / David Keith

KELLEM, Manny, & His Orchestra
Singles: 7-Inch
EPIC: 68 1-3
METROMEDIA: 69 1-3
    LPs: 10/12-Inch 33rpm
EPIC: 68 5-10

KELLER, Jerry
Singles: 7-Inch
CAPITOL: 61 3-5
CORAL: 63-64 3-5
JUBILEE: 58 4-6
KAPP (Monaural): 59-60 4-6
KAPP (Stereo): 59 8-10
(With a "KS" prefix.)
RCA VICTOR: 67 3-5
REPRISE: 65 3-5
WEB: 58 4-6
    Picture Sleeves
KAPP: 59 8-10
    LPs: 10/12-Inch 33rpm
KAPP: 60 20-25

KELLUM, Murry
Singles: 7-Inch
CINNAMON: 74 2-3
EPIC: 71-72 2-4
MUSIC MILL: 76 2-3
PLANTATION: 78 1-3
RANWOOD: 76 2-3
    LPs: 10/12-Inch 33rpm
PLANTATION: 78 5-8

KELLUM, Murry, & Alton Lott
Singles: 7-Inch
K&M: 61 3-5
Also see KELLUM, Murry

KELLUM, Murry / Glenn Sutton
Singles: 7-Inch
ABC: 73 1-3
M.O.C. (Except 658): 63-64 3-5
M.O.C. (658; "I Dreamed I Was
    A Beatle"): 64 8-10
Also see KELLUM, Murry

Also see SUTTON, Glenn

KELLY, Casey
Singles: 7-Inch
ELEKTRA: 72-73 .... $2-3
PRIVATE STOCK: 77 2-3
    LPs: 10/12-Inch 33rpm
ELEKTRA: 72 8-10

KELLY, Grace:
see CROSBY, Bing, & Grace Kelly

KELLY, Herman, & Life
Singles: 7-Inch
ALSTON: 78 2-3

KELLY, J., & The Premiers
(J. Kely & The Premiers)
Singles: 7-Inch
ROADSHOW: 74 2-3

KELLY, Mike
LPs: 10/12-Inch 33rpm
RELIX: 86 5-8
Also see GRATEFUL DEAD
Also see KINGFISH

KELLY, Monty, & His Orchestra
Singles: 78rpm
ESSEX: 54 2-4
Singles: 7-Inch
CARLTON: 59-60 2-4
ESSEX: 54 2-5
    LPs: 10/12-Inch 33rpm
ALSHIRE: 72 4-8
CARLTON: 59 10-20

KELLY, Paul
Singles: 7-Inch
DIAL: 65-68 3-5
HAPPY TIGER: 70 2-4
PHILIPS: 66-68 3-5
WARNER BROS: 73-76 2-3
    Picture Sleeves
PHILIPS: 66 3-6
    LPs: 10/12-Inch 33rpm
HAPPY TIGER: 70 8-10
WARNER BROS: 72-76 8-10
Also see TEX, Joe

KELLY BROTHERS
Singles: 7-Inch
EXCELLO: 67-69 3-5
SIMS: 65-67 3-5
    LPs: 10/12-Inch 33rpm
EXCELLO: 68 12-15
Also see KING PINS

KELTON, Gene
Singles: 7-Inch
AVATAR: *87* $2-4

KEMP, Johnny
Singles: 7-Inch
COLUMBIA: *86-88* 1-3
LPs: 10/12 Inch 33rpm
COLUMBIA: *88* 5-8

KENDALL, Jeannie
(Jeanie Kendall)
Singles: 7-Inch
DOT: *72-73* 2-4
Also see KENDALLS

KENDALL SISTERS
Singles: 7-Inch
ARGO: *57-58* 3-5

KENDALLS
Singles: 7-Inch
DOT: *72-73* 2-4
MCA/CURB: *86* 1-3
MERCURY: *81-85* 1-3
OVATION: *77-80* 1-3
STEP ONE: *87-88* 1-3
STOP: *70* 2-4
UNITED ARTISTS: *75-76* 2-3
LPs: 10/12-Inch 33rpm
DOT: *72* 8-12
GUSTO: *78* 5-8
MCA/CURB: *86* 5-8
MERCURY: *81-85* 5-8
OVATION: *77-80* 5-10
STOP: *70* 10-15
POWER PAK: *74* 5-8
Members: Jeannie Kendall; Royce Kendall.
Also see KENDALL, Jeannie

KENDRICK, Nat, & The Swans
Singles: 7-Inch
DADE (1000 series): *59-60* 4-6
DADE (5000 series): *63* 3-5

KENDRICKS, Eddie
Singles: 7-Inch
ARISTA: *78-80* 1-3
ATLANTIC: *80-81* 1-3
CORNER STREET: *84* 1-3
RCA VICTOR: *85-88* 1-3
TAMLA: *71-77* 2-3
LPs: 10/12-Inch 33rpm
ARISTA: *78* 5-8
ATLANTIC: *81* 5-8
MOTOWN: *75-82* 5-8
MS. DIXIE: *83* 5-8
TAMLA: *71-78* 8-10

Also see HALL, Daryl, & John Oates
Also see RUFFIN, David, & Eddie Kendricks
Also see TEMPTATIONS

KENDRICKS, Linda
Singles: 12-Inch 33/45rpm
AIRWAVE: *84* $4-6
Singles: 7-Inch
AIRWAVE: *84* 1-3

KENNEDY, Edward M.
LPs: 10/12-Inch 33rpm
RCA VICTOR: *65* 8-15

KENNEDY, Jacqueline
LPs: 10/12-Inch 33rpm
AUDIO FIDELITY(703; "Jacqueline
Kennedy"): *66* 8-15
(LP contains Jackie's story as well as excerpts of
some of her speeches given as First Lady.)

KENNEDY, John Fitzgerald
LPs: 10/12-Inch 33rpm
CAEDMON: *64* 5-10
CHALLENGE: *64* 8-15
COLPIX: *64* 10-20
COLUMBIA: *65* 10-20
DECCA: *63* 10-20
DIPLOMAT: *63* 5-15
DOCUMENTARIES UNLIMITED: *63*   10-20
GATEWAY: *64* 8-15
HARMONIA: *64* 8-15
LEGACY: *65* 10-20
PALACE: *64* 8-15
PHILIPS: *64* 8-15
PICKWICK: *63* 8-12
PREMIER: *63* 10-20
RCA VICTOR: *64* 8-15
REGINA: *64* 5-15
SOMERSET: *63* 5-15
20TH CENTURY-FOX: *63* 10-20
Note: Most of the albums listed above were
released as a tribute of some type to President Ken-
nedy after his assassination on November 22, 1963.
Most contain excerpts of his speeches.

KENNEDY, John Fitzgerald /
Richard M. Nixon
LPs: 10/12-Inch 33rpm
COLUMBIA: *68* 10-15
Also see KENNEDY, John Fitzgerald

KENNEDY, Joyce
Singles: 7-Inch
A&M: *84-85* 1-3
LPs: 10/12-Inch 33rpm
A&M: *84* 5-8
Also see MOTHER'S FINEST

I LIKE IT LIKE THAT
(Chris Kenner)
CHRIS KENNER

KENNEDY, Joyce, & Jeffrey Osborne
Singles: 7-Inch
A&M: 84 . . . . $1-3
  Also see KENNEDY, Joyce
  Also see OSBORNE, Jeffrey

KENNEDY, Mike
Singles: 7-Inch
ABC: 72 2-3
LPs: 10/12-Inch 33rpm
ABC: 72 8-10
  Also see LOS BRAVOS

KENNEDY, Ray
Singles: 7-Inch
ARC: 80 1-3
LPs: 10/12-Inch 33rpm
CREAM: 72 10-12
  Also see KGB

KENNEDY, Robert Francis
LPs: 10/12-Inch 33rpm
COLUMBIA: 68 8-15

KENNER, Chris
Singles: 78rpm
BATON: 55 4-8
IMPERIAL: 57 3-6
Singles: 7-Inch
BATON: 55 10-15
IMPERIAL: 57-58 5-10
INSTANT: 61-64 4-8
PRIGAN: 61 4-8
RON: 61 4-6
UPTOWN: 65 3-5
VALIANT (3229; "I Like It Like
  That"): 61 15-25
LPs: 10/12-Inch 33rpm
ATLANTIC: 66 15-20

KENNY, Bill
(Bill Kenny & The Song Spinners)
Singles: 78rpm
DECCA: 50-53 . . . . $2-4
VIK: 56 2-4
X: 55 2-4
Singles: 7-Inch
DECCA: 50-53 3-5
MERCURY: 62 2-4
TEL: 59 2-4
VIK: 56 2-4
WARWICK: 60 2-4
X: 55 2-4
LPs: 10/12-Inch 33rpm
DECCA (5000 series): 51 10-20
  (10-Inch LPs.)
MERCURY: 62 10-15
  Also see INK SPOTS

KENNY & JOHNNY
Singles: 7-Inch
PHILADELPHIA INT'L: 86 1-3
  Members: Kenny Whitehead; Johnny Whitehead.
  Also see WHITEHEAD, Kenny & Johnny

KENNY & THE CADETS
Singles: 7-Inch
RANDY (422; "Barbie"): 62 250-300
  (Black vinyl.)
RANDY (422; "Barbie"): 62 350-400
  (Colored vinyl.)
  Members: Brian Wilson; Carl Wilson; Al Jardine;
  Audree Wilson.
  Also see BEACH BOYS

KENNY G.: see G., Kenny

KENT, Al
Singles: 7-Inch
BARITONE: 60 3-6
RIC-TIC: 67 3-5
WIZARD: 59 4-8

KENTON, Stan, & His Orchestra
Singles: 78rpm
CAPITOL: 50-57 2-4
Singles: 7-Inch
CAPITOL: 50-68 2-4
EPs: 7-Inch 33/45rpm
CAPITOL: 50-59 5-15
LPs: 10/12-Inch 33rpm
BRIGHT ORANGE: 73 5-8
CAPITOL (100 series): 75 4-8
  (With an "SM" prefix.)
CAPITOL (100 through 500
  series): 50-54 25-50
  (10-Inch LPs.)
CAPITOL (300 series): 69 5-10

CAPITOL (600 through 1200
  series): *56-59* $15-25
CAPITOL (1300 through 2900
  series): *60-68* 10-20
CAPITOL (11000 & 12000
  series): *72-80* 5-8
CAPITOL (16000 series): *81* 4-6
CREATIVE WORLD: *71-80* 5-8
HINDSIGHT: *84* 4-8
LONDON: *72-77* 5-8
MARK '56: *77* 5-8
MFSL: *82* 15-25
  Also see CHRISTY, June
  Also see COLE, Nat "King"
  Also see FERGUSON, Maynard
  Also see RITTER, Tex

KERMIT
(Jim Henson)
          Singles: 7-Inch
ATLANTIC: *79* 1-3
  Also see HENSON, Jim

KERMIT / Fozzie Bear
(Jim Henson)
          Singles: 7-Inch
ATLANTIC: *80* 1-3
  Also see KERMIT
  Also see HENSON, Jim
  Also see MUPPETS

KERR, Anita
(Anita Kerr Singers; Anita Kerr Quartette)
          Singles: 78rpm
DECCA: *51-57* 2-4
          Singles: 7-Inch
AMPEX: *71* 1-3
DECCA: *51-72* 2-4
DOT: *69-70* 1-3
RCA VICTOR: *63-75* 2-3
WARNER BROS: *66-68* 2-3
          LPs: 10/12-Inch 33rpm
AMPEX: *71* 5-8
BAINBRIDGE: *81* 4-6
CAMDEN: *68* 5-10
CENTURY: *79* 4-8
DECCA: *60-69* 8-15
DOT: *69-70* 5-10
RCA VICTOR: *62-77* 8-15
VOCALION: *70* 5-10
WARNER BROS: *66* 8-12
WORD: *75-77* 4-8
  Note: There are hundreds of artists whose record-
  ings contain the background vocals of The Anita
  Kerr Singers. Cross referenced here are those that
  would be of most interest to readers of this book.
  Also see ANITA & TH' SO-AND-SOs

Chaka Khan (Photo: Greg Gorman)

  Also see ATKINS, Chet
  Also see FOLEY, Red
  Also see HELMS, Bobby
  Also see LITTLE DIPPERS
  Also see PRESLEY, Elvis
  Also see REEVES, Jim

KERR, George
          Singles: 7-Inch
ALL PLATINUM: *70* $2-3

KERSHAW, Nik
          LPs: 10/12-Inch 33rpm
MCA: *84-85* 5-8

KEVIN & THE BLACKTEARS
          Singles: 7-Inch
KEVIN KAT: *87* 1-3
  Also see MEYERS, Augie

KEYES, Troy
          Singles: 7-Inch
ABC: *67-68* 3-5
CHUMLEY: *74* 2-3

KHAN, Chaka
          Singles: 12-Inch 33/45rpm
WARNER BROS: *79-86* 4-6
          Singles: 7-Inch
ATLANTIC: *86* 1-3
MCA: *80-86* 1-3
WARNER BROS: *78-88* 1-3
          Picture Sleeves
WARNER BROS: *78-88* 1-3
          LPs: 10/12-Inch 33rpm
WARNER BROS: *79-88* 5-8
  Also see BOWIE, David
  Also see JONES, Quincy

Also see RUFUS

KHAN, Steve
Singles: 7-Inch
TAPPAN ZEE: 78 .... $2-3
LPs: 10/12-Inch 33rpm
COLUMBIA: 79 5-8
NOVAS: 80 5-8
Also see JOEL, Billy

KHEMISTRY
Singles: 7-Inch
COLUMBIA: 82 1-3
LPs: 10/12-Inch 33rpm
COLUMBIA: 82 5-8

KIARA
Singles: 7-Inch
ARISTA: 88 1-3
LPs: 10/12-Inch 33rpm
ARISTA: 88 5-8
WARLOCK: 85 1-3

KICK AXE
LPs: 10/12-Inch 33rpm
PASHA: 84 5-8

KID CREOLE & THE COCONUTS
Singles: 12-Inch 33/45rpm
ATLANTIC: 84-85 4-6
Singles: 7-Inch
ANTILLES: 80 1-3
ATLANTIC: 84-85 1-3
SIRE: 81-82 1-3
ZE: 81 1-3
LPs: 10/12-Inch 33rpm
ANTILLES: 80 8-10
SIRE: 81-82 5-8
Also see DR. BUZZARD'S ORIGINAL
SAVANNAH BAND

KIDDO
Singles: 12-Inch 33/45rpm
A&M: 83 4-6
Singles: 7-Inch
A&M: 83-84 1-3
LPs: 10/12-Inch 33rpm
A&M: 83 5-8

KID 'N PLAY
Singles: 7-Inch
SELECT: 88 1-3
LPs: 10/12-Inch 33rpm
SELECT: 88 5-8

KIDS AT WORK
Singles: 7-Inch
CBS ASSOCIATED: 84 1-3

KIDS FROM "FAME"
LPs: 10/12-Inch 33rpm
RCA VICTOR: 82-83 .... $5-8

KIDS NEXT DOOR
Singles: 7-Inch
4 CORNERS OF THE WORLD: 65 3-5

KIHN, Greg, Band
Singles: 12-Inch 33/45rpm
BESERKLEY: 78-83 4-6
Singles: 7-Inch
BESERKLEY: 78-83 1-3
EMI AMERICA: 85-86 1-3
Picture Sleeves
BESERKLEY: 81 1-3
LPs: 10/12-Inch 33rpm
BESERKLEY: 76-83 8-10
EMI AMERICA: 85-86 5-8

KILGORE, Theola
Singles: 7-Inch
KT: 64 3-6
SEROCK: 63 3-6

KILLER DWARFS
LPs: 10/12-Inch 33rpm
EPIC: 88 5-8

KILLING JOKE
LPs: 10/12-Inch 33rpm
EDITIONS: 81-82 5-8
VIRGIN: 87 5-8

KILZER, John
LPs: 10/12-Inch 33rpm
GEFFEN: 88 5-8

KIM, Andy
Singles: 7-Inch
ABC: 74 1-3
CAPITOL: 74-76 2-3
RED BIRD: 65 4-6
STEED: 68-71 2-3
TCF: 64 3-5
20TH CENTURY-FOX: 68 2-3
UNI: 72-73 2-3
UNITED ARTISTS: 63 3-5
Picture Sleeves
CAPITOL: 74 2-3
STEED: 69 2-4
LPs: 10/12-Inch 33rpm
CAPITOL: 74-75 8-10
DUNHILL: 74 8-10
STEED: 68-71 10-12
UNI: 72-73 8-10
Also see ARCHIES

B.B. King (Photo: Brian Blauser)

KIMBERLY, Adrian
Singles: 7-Inch
CALLIOPE: *61* **$4-8**
Picture Sleeves
CALLIOPE: *61* **10-15**

KIMBERLYS
Singles: 7-Inch
CANADIAN AMERICAN: *62-63* **3-5**
COLUMBIA: *65-66* **2-4**
HAPPY TIGER: *70-71* **2-3**
RCA VICTOR: *69* **2-3**
LPs: 10/12-Inch 33rpm
HAPPY TIGER: *70* **8-12**
Also see JENNINGS, Waylon

KIMBLE, Neal
Singles: 7-Inch
VENTURE: *68* **3-5**

KIME, Warren, & His Brass
Impact Orchestra
LPs: 10/12-Inch 33rpm
COMMAND: *67* **5-10**

KIMMEL, Tom
Singles: 7-Inch
MERCURY: *87* **1-3**
LPs: 10/12-Inch 33rpm
MERCURY: *87* **5-8**

KINDLER, Steven
LPs: 10/12-Inch 33rpm
GLOBAL PACIFIC: *88* **5-8**

KINETICS
LPs: 10/12-Inch 33rpm
ETIQUETTE: *86* **$5-8**
Members: Roger Rogers; Daniel Davison; Roger
Baldwin; Denney Goodhew.

KING
(Paul King)
Singles: 12-Inch 33/45rpm
EPIC: *85* **4-6**
Singles: 7-Inch
EPIC: *85* **1-3**
LPs: 10/12-Inch 33rpm
ELEKTRA: *80-81* **5-8**
EPIC: *85* **5-8**

KING, Albert
Singles: 7-Inch
BOBBIN: *59-62* **4-6**
COUN-TREE: *65* **3-5**
KING: *61-63* **3-5**
PARROT (798; "Bad Luck
Blues"): *53* **60-100**
STAX: *66-74* **3-5**
TOMATO: *78-79* **2-3**
UTOPIA: *76-77* **2-3**
LPs: 10/12-Inch 33rpm
ATLANTIC: *69-82* **8-10**
KING (800 series): *63* **35-45**
KING (1000 series): *69* **10-12**
STAX (Except 700 & 2000
series): *72-81* **8-10**

STAX (700 series): *67* $12-15
STAX (2000 series): *68-71* 10-12
TOMATO: *77-79* 5-8
UTOPIA: *76-77* 8-10
  Also see LITTLE MILTON & ALBERT
KING

KING, Albert, & Otis Rush
LPs: 10/12-Inch 33rpm
CHESS: *69* 10-12
  Also see KING, Albert
  Also see RUSH, Otis

KING, Anna
Singles: 7-Inch
LUDIX: *63* 3-5
MALIBU: *61* 3-5
RUST: *64* 3-5
SMASH: *64-65* 3-5
LPs: 10/12-Inch 33rpm
SMASH: *64* 12-15

KING, Anna, & Bobby Byrd
Singles: 7-Inch
SMASH: *64* 3-5
  Also see BYRD, Bobby
  Also see KING, Anna

KING, B.B.
Singles: 78rpm
BULLET: *49-50* 20-30
RPM: *50-57* 4-8
Singles: 7-Inch
ABC: *66-78* 2-4
ABC-PARAMOUNT: *62-66* 3-5
BLUESWAY: *67-70* 2-4
KENT (300 series): *58-64* 3-5
KENT (400 series): *64-68* 2-4
KENT (4000 & 5000 series): 2-3
MCA: *80-85* 1-3
RPM (339 through 363): *51-52* 20-30
RPM (374 through 395): *52-54* 10-20
RPM (403 through 501): *54-57* 5-10
Picture Sleeves
BLUESWAY: *69* 3-5
EPs: 7-Inch 33/45rpm
ABC-PARAMOUNT: *63* 8-10
  (Jukebox issue only.)
LPs: 10/12-Inch 33rpm
ABC: *70-78* 8-10
ABC-PARAMOUNT: *63-65* 15-20
ACCORD: *82* 5-8
BLUESWAY: *67-73* 10-15
COMMAND: *74* 10-12
CROWN (Black vinyl): *59-63* 15-25

CROWN (147; "B.B. King
  Wails"): *60* .... ?.... $75-125
  (Colored vinyl.)
CRUSADERS: *82* 5-8
CUSTOM: 8-10
FANTASY: *81* 5-8
GALAXY: *63* 15-20
KENT : *64-73* 10-15
MCA: *80-85* 5-8
UNITED: 10-12
  Also see BLAND, Bobby, & B.B. King
  Also see CRUSADERS, & B.B. King

KING, B.B., Jr., & The Blues Messengers
Singles: 7-Inch
L. BROWN: *64* 3-5

KING, Ben E.
Singles: 7-Inch
ATLANTIC: *75-81* 1-3
ATCO (Except 6100 & 6200
  series): *64-69* 3-5
ATCO (6100 & 6200 series): *60-64* 4-6
ELEKTRA: *76* 2-3
MANDALA: *72-73* 2-3
MAXWELL: *69* 2-4
LPs: 10/12-Inch 33rpm
ATCO: *61-65* 20-25
ATLANTIC: *75-81* 8-10
KING: 10-12
MANDALA: *72* 8-10
MAXWELL: *70* 10-12
  Also see BONDS, Gary "U.S."
  Also see DRIFTERS
  Also see SOUL CLAN

KING, Ben E., & The Average White Band
Singles: 7-Inch
ATLANTIC: *77* 2-3
LPs: 10/12-Inch 33rpm
ATLANTIC: *77* 8-10
  Also see AVERAGE WHITE BAND

KING, Ben E., & Lavern Baker
Singles: 7-Inch
ATLANTIC: *60* 3-5
  Also see BAKER, Lavern

KING, Ben E., & Dee Dee Sharp
Singles: 7-Inch
ATCO: *68* 3-5
  Also see KING, Ben E.
  Also see SHARP, Dee Dee

KING, Bobby
(Featuring Alfie Silas)
Singles: 7-Inch
MOTOWN: 84 ....$1-3
  Also see SILAS, Alfie

KING, Carole
Singles: 7-Inch
ABC: 74 1-3
ABC-PARAMOUNT: 58-59 25-30
ALPINE: 60 35-40
ATLANTIC: 82-83 1-3
AVATAR: 77-78 2-3
CAPITOL: 77-80 1-3
COMPANION: 62 20-25
DIMENSION (Except 2000): 62-63 8-10
DIMENSION (2000; "It Might As Well
  Rain Until September"): 62 4-6
ODE: 71-76 2-3
RCA VICTOR (7560; "Short Mort"): 59 .25-35
TOMORROW: 66 8-10
Picture Sleeves
AVATAR: 77..........................2-3
CAPITOL: 80 1-3
ODE: 71-75 2-3
LPs: 10/12-Inch 33rpm
ATLANTIC: 82-83 5-8
CAPITOL (Except 11000 series): 80 5-8
CAPITOL (11000 series): 77-79 8-10
EMUS: 79 5-8
EPIC/ODE (30000 series): 78-80 5-8
EPIC/ODE (40000 series): 80 12-15
  (Half-speed mastered.)
ODE: 70-77 10-12
  Also see COOKIES / Little Eva / Carole King
  Also see SHIRELLES

KING, Claude
Singles: 7-Inch
CINNAMON: 74 .... $2-3
COLUMBIA: 61-71 2-4
DEE JAY: 57 25-30
TRUE: 77-80 1-3
Picture Sleeves
COLUMBIA: 61-69 3-6
LPs: 10/12-Inch 33rpm
COLUMBIA: 62-70 10-15
GUSTO: 80 5-8
HARMONY: 68 8-12
TRUE: 77 8-10
  Also see YOUNG, Faron / Carl Perkins /
Claude King

KING, Earl
Singles: 78rpm
KING: 55 3-6
Singles: 7-Inch
KING: 55 5-8

KING, Evelyn "Champagne"
Singles: 12-Inch 33/45rpm
PRIVATE I: 85 4-6
RCA VICTOR: 78-86 4-6
Singles: 7-Inch
EMI-MANHATTAN: 88 1-3
RCA VICTOR: 78-86 1-3
Picture Sleeves
RCA VICTOR: 78-85 1-3
LPs: 10/12-Inch 33rpm
EMI-MANHATTAN: 88 5-8
RCA VICTOR: 77-86 5-8

KING, Freddie
(Freddy King)
Singles: 78rpm
EL-BEE: 56 20-30
Singles: 7-Inch
COTILLION: 68-70 2-3
EL-BEE: 56 50-75
FEDERAL: 60-65 3-5
GUSTO: 78 1-3
KING: 69 2-3
LPs: 10/12-Inch 33rpm
COTILLION: 69-70 10-15
FEDERAL: 62 20-25
KING (700 series): 61 35-40
KING (800 series): 62-63 20-25
KING (900 series): 65-66 15-20
KING (1000 series): 69 12-15
MCA: 5-8
RSO: 74-77 8-10
SHELTER: 71-75 8-10
  Also see ROGERS, Jimmy, & Freddie King

KING, Freddie, & Lulu Reed
Singles: 7-Inch
FEDERAL: 62 . . . . $3-5
LPs: 10/12-Inch 33rpm
FEDERAL: 62 20-25

KING, Freddie / Lulu (Reed) /
Sonny Thompson
LPs: 10/12-Inch 33rpm
KING: 62 25-30
Also see KING, Freddie
Also see THOMPSON, Sonny

KING, Johnny
Singles: 7-Inch
DOT: 58 4-6
GUY: 61 3-5
MONTICELLO: 59 4-6
TIARA: 59 4-6

KING, Jonathan
Singles: 7-Inch
PARROT: 65-72 3-5
UK: 73-74 2-3
UK/BIG TREE: 75 2-3
LPs: 10/12-Inch 33rpm
PARROT: 67 25-30
UK: 72-73 10-12
Also see HEDGEHOPPERS ANONYMOUS

KING, Marcel
Singles: 12-Inch 33/45rpm
A&M: 84 4-6
Singles: 7-Inch
A&M: 84 1-3

KING, Marva
Singles: 7-Inch
TRI-WORLD: 88 1-3

KING, Morgana
Singles: 78rpm
MERCURY: 56 2-4
Singles: 7-Inch
MAINSTREAM: 64 2-4
MERCURY: 56 2-4
PARAMOUNT: 73-74 2-3
REPRISE: 66-67 2-3
20TH CENTURY-FOX: 59 2-4
VERVE: 68 2-3
WING: 56 2-4
Picture Sleeves
PARAMOUNT: 73 2-4
LPs: 10/12-Inch 33rpm
ASCOT: 65-66 10-20
CAMDEN: 60 10-20
EMARCY: 56 20-30
MAINSTREAM (300 series): 72 5-10

MAINSTREAM (6000 series): 64-65 . . . $10-20
MUSE: 79-82 5-8
PARAMOUNT: 73 5-10
REPRISE: 65-67 10-20
TRIP: 74 5-8
UNITED ARTISTS: 59 15-25
VERVE: 68 8-15
WING: 65 10-15

KING, Pee Wee
(Pee Wee King With Redd Stewart; Pee Wee
King & New Golden West Cowboys)
Singles: 78rpm
BLUEBIRD: 49 3-6
RCA VICTOR: 50-55 2-5
Singles: 7-Inch
BRIAR: 61 2-4
JARO: 60 2-4
CUCA: 64-66 2-4
LANDA: 61 2-4
RCA VICTOR: 50-55 3-6
STARDAY: 64-71 2-4
TODD: 59 2-4
LPs: 10/12-Inch 33rpm
BRIAR: 62 40-50
CAMDEN: 65-71 8-15
CAPITOL: 66 12-18
NASHVILLE: 8-12
RCA VICTOR: 77 5-8
STARDAY (200 series): 64 12-15
STARDAY (900 series): 75 8-10

KING, Peggy
Singles: 78rpm
COLUMBIA: 54-56 2-4
MGM: 52 2-4
Singles: 7-Inch
BUENA VISTA: 62 2-3
BULLET: 71 1-3
COLUMBIA: 54-56 2-4
MGM: 52 2-4
ROULETTE: 61 2-4
Picture Sleeves
BUENA VISTA: 62 3-5
EPs: 7-Inch 33/45rpm
COLUMBIA: 55 5-10
LPs: 10/12-Inch 33rpm
COLUMBIA: 55 10-20
IMPERIAL: 59 10-15
Also see VALE, Jerry, Peggy King & Felicia
Sanders

KING, Rev. Martin Luther, Jr.
Singles: 7-Inch
DOOTO: 68 2-3
GORDY: 68 2-3

MERCURY: *68* $2-3
LPs: 10/12-Inch 33rpm
BLACK FORUM: *70* 5-10
BUDDAH: *69* 8-15
CREED: *69-71* 8-12
DOTTO: *62-68* 8-15
EXCELLO: *68* 8-15
GORDY: *63-68* 8-15
MERCURY: *68* 8-15
MR. MAESTRO: *63* 10-15
NASHBORO: *72* 5-8
20TH CENTURY-FOX: *63-68* 8-15
UNART: *68* 8-12
Note: The above recordings contain speeches or
excerpts of speeches by King.
Also see LANDS, Liz / Martin Luther King

KING, Sleepy: see SLEEPY KING

KING, Willard
(Will King)
Singles: 7-Inch
CAPITOL: *73* 2-3
TOTAL EXPERIENCE: *85* 1-3

KING BISCUIT BOY
(King Biscuit Boy With Crowbar)
Singles: 7-Inch
EPIC: *75* 2-3
PARAMOUNT: *70-73* 2-4
LPs: 10/12-Inch 33rpm
EPIC: *74* 8-10
PARAMOUNT: *70-73* 10-15

KING COLE TRIO:
see COLE, Nat "King"

KING CRIMSON
Singles: 12-Inch 33/45rpm
WARNER BROS: *84* 4-6
Singles: 7-Inch
ATLANTIC: *70-74* 2-3
WARNER BROS: *81-84* 1-3
LPs: 10/12-Inch 33rpm
ATLANTIC (Except 18000 & 19000
series): *69-74* 10-15
ATLANTIC (18000 & 19000
series): *74-75* 8-10
MFSL: *82* 25-50
WARNER BROS: *81-82* 5-8
WIZARDO: 10-12
WORLD RECORD CLUB: 12-15
Members: Greg Lake; Robert Fripp; Boz Burrell.
Also see BAD COMPANY
Also see FRIPP, Robert
Also see LAKE, Greg

KING CURTIS
(King Curtis & The Kingpins; King Curtis &
The Nobel Knights)
Singles: 78rpm
GEM: *54* $10-15
MONARCH: *53* 15-20
Singles: 7-Inch
ABC-PARAMOUNT: *60* 3-5
ALCOR: *62* 3-5
ATCO: *59-71* 3-5
CAPITOL: *62-65* 3-6
ENJOY: *62* 3-5
EVEREST: *61* 3-5
GEM: *54* 25-35
KING: *62* 3-5
MONARCH: *53* 30-50
NEW JAZZ: *61* 3-5
TRU-SOUND: *61-63* 3-5
EPs: 7-Inch 33/45rpm
ATCO: *68* 3-5
(Jukebox issues only.)
CAPITOL: *63* 8-15
LPs: 10/12-Inch 33rpm
ATCO (110, "Have Tenor Sax,
Will Blow"): *59* 75-125
ATCO (189 through 385): *66-72* 10-15
CAMDEN: *68* 10-12
CAPITOL (2000 series): *64-68* 12-15
CAPITOL (11000 series): *78-79* 5-8
CLARION: 8-10
COLLECTABLES: *88* 6-8
ENJOY: *62* 25-30
EVEREST: *61* 20-25
HARLEM HIT PARADE: 8-10
MOUNT VERNON: 10-12
NEW JAZZ: *60* 20-25
PRESTIGE (7200 series): *62* 15-20
PRESTIGE (7700 series): *69-70* 8-12
TRU-SOUND: *62* 15-20
Note: The studio tenor saxophone work of King
Curtis is featured on the recordings of many artists,
a few of whom are referenced here.
Also see BAKER, Lavern
Also see CLOVERS
Also see COASTERS
Also see COMSTOCK, Bobby
Also see FACENDA, Tommy
Also see JENNINGS, Waylon
Also see KING PINS
Also see LED ZEPPELIN / King Curtis
Also see MITCHELL, Freddie
Also see PAT & THE SATELLITES
Also see PRETTY BOY
Also see RESTIVO, Johnny
Also see SEDAKA, Neil

Also see SHARPE, Ray
Also see SHIRELLES, & King Curtis
Also see TURNER, Joe
Also see TURNER, Sammy

KING DIAMOND
LPs: 10/12-Inch 33rpm
ROADACRE: 88 . . . . $5-8

KING DREAM CHORUS & HOLIDAY CREW
Singles: 12-Inch 33/45rpm
MERCURY: 86 4-6
Singles: 7-Inch
MERCURY: 86 1-3
Members: Kurtis Blow; El De Barge; Fat Boys;
Grandmaster Melle Mel; Whitney Houston; Stacy
Lattisaw; Lisa Lisa & Full Force; Teena Marie;
Menudo; Stephanie Mills; New Edition; Run-
DMC; James Taylor; Whodini.
Also see BLOW, Kurtis
Also see DE BARG
Also see FAT BOYS
Also see GRANDMASTER FLASH & THE
FURIOUS FIVE
Also see HOUSTON, Whitney
Also see LATTISAW, Stacy
Also see LISA LISA
Also see MARIE, Teena
Also see MENUDO
Also see MILLS, Stephanie
Also see NEW EDITION
Also see RUN-D.M.C.
Also see TAYLOR, James
Also see WHODINI

KING FAMILY
Singles: 7-Inch
WARNER BROS: 65 2-3
LPs: 10/12-Inch 33rpm
CAPITOL: 65 5-15
WARNER BROS: 65 5-15

KING FLOYD
Singles: 7-Inch
CHIMNEYVILLE: 70-76 2-4
ORIGINAL SOUND: 64 3-5
UPTOWN: 66 3-5
LPs: 10/12-Inch 33rpm
ATCO: 73 8-10
CHIMNEYVILLE: 72 8-10
PULSAR: 69 10-12

KING HANNIBAL
Singles: 7-Inch
AWARE: 73 2-3
LPs: 10/12-Inch 33rpm
AWARE: 73 8-10

KING HARVEST
Singles: 7-Inch
A&M: 75-76 . . . . $2-3
PERCEPTION: 72-73 2-3
LPs: 10/12-Inch 33rpm
A&M: 75 10-12
PERCEPTION: 73 8-10

KING KOBRA
Singles: 12-Inch 33/45rpm
CAPITOL: 86 4-6
Singles: 7-Inch
CAPITOL: 86 1-3
LPs: 10/12-Inch 33rpm
CAPITOL: 86 5-8
Members: Carmine Appice; Mark Free; David
Michael Phillips; Johnny Rod; Mick Sweda.

KING LIZARD
(Kim Fowley)
Singles: 7-Inch
ORIGINAL SOUND: 75 2-3
Also see FOWLEY, Kim

KING PINS
Singles: 7-Inch
ATCO: 67 3-5
FEDERAL: 63-64 3-5
LARSE: 66 8-12
MGM: 66 4-8
VEE JAY: 63 3-5
LPs: 10/12-Inch 33rpm
KING: 63 20-25
Also see KELLY BROTHERS
Also see KING CURTIS

KING PLEASURE:
see PLEASURE, King

KING RICHARD'S FLUEGEL KNIGHTS
Singles: 7-Inch
MTA: 66-68 1-3
LPs: 10/12-Inch 33rpm
MTA: 67-70 5-10

KING TEE
LPs: 10/12-Inch 33rpm
CAPITOL: 88 5-8

KINGBEES
(Nino Tempo & The Kingbees)
Singles: 7-Inch
RSO: 80-81 1-3
Picture Sleeves
RSO: 80-81 1-3
LPs: 10/12-Inch 33rpm
RSO: 80-81 5-8
Members: Jamie; Michael; Rex.

KINGDOM COME
Singles: 7-Inch
POLYDOR: *88* **$1-3**
LPs: 10/12-Inch 33rpm
POLYDOR: *88* **5-8**

KINGFISH
Singles: 7-Inch
JET: *78* **2-3**
ROUND: *76* **3-5**
LPs: 10/12-Inch 33rpm
ACCORD: *81* **5-8**
JET: *78* **8-10**
ROUND: *76* **10-20**
Members: Bob Weir; David Torbert; Matt Kelly.
Also see KELLY, Mike
Also see NEW RIDERS OF THE PURPLE
SAGE
Also see WEIR, Bob

KINGS
Singles: 7-Inch
ELEKTRA: *80* **1-3**
LPs: 10/12-Inch 33rpm
ELEKTRA: *80* **5-8**

KINGS OF THE SUN
Singles: 7-Inch
RCA VICTOR: *88* **1-3**
LPs: 10/12-Inch 33rpm
RCA VICTOR: *88* **5-8**

KING'S X
LPs: 10/12-Inch 33rpm
MEGAFORCE: *88* **5-8**

KINGSMEN
Singles: 7-Inch
EAST WEST: *58* **5-10**
Also see HALEY, Bill

KINGSMEN
Singles: 7-Inch
CAPITOL: *72* **2-4**
EARTH: *69* **3-5**
ERIC: **1-3**
JALYNNE: *61* **10-12**
JERDEN (712; "Louie Louie"): *63* **40-60**
WAND (Except 1107 & 1115): *63-68* **5-10**
WAND (1107; "It's Only
   The Dog"): *65* **8-12**
WAND (1115; "Killer Joe"): *65* **8-12**
LPs: 10/12-Inch 33rpm
ARISTA: *81* **8-10**
HEAVY WEIGHT: *67* **20-25**
RHINO: **5-8**
SCEPTER/CITATION: *72* **8-12**

WAND (657; "The Kingsmen
   In Person"): *64* **$30-35**
WAND (659; "The Kingsmen,
   Vol. 2"): *64* **50-100**
   (Without "Death Of An Angel.")
WAND (659; "The Kingsmen,
   Vol. 2"): *64* **25-35**
   (With "Death Of An Angel.")
WAND (662; "The Kingsmen,
   Vol. 3"): *65* **25-30**
WAND (670 through 681): *65-67* **20-25**
Members: Lynn Easton; Mike Mitchell; Don Gal-
lucci; Norm Sundholm; Gary Abbot; Jack Ely;
Barry Curtis; Dick Peterson.
Also see DON & THE GOODTIMES

KINGSTON TRIO
Singles: 7-Inch
CAPITOL: *58-64* **4-6**
DECCA: *64-66* **3-5**
Picture Sleeves
CAPITOL: *60-62* **10-20**
DECCA: *65-66* **10-25**
EPs: 7-Inch 33/45rpm
CAPITOL: *58-61* **10-20**
LPs: 10/12-Inch 33rpm
CANDLELITE: **10-15**
CAPITOL (500 series): *70* **8-15**
CAPITOL (900 through 1500
   series): *58-61* **25-40**
CAPITOL (1600 through 2600
   series, except 2180): *61-66* **15-25**
CAPITOL (2180; "The Folk Era"): *64* . . . **25-40**
   (3-LP set with bound-in booklet.)
CAPITOL (11000 series): *79* **5-8**
CAPITOL (16000 series): *81* **4-6**
DECCA: *64-65* **15-25**
INTERMEDIA: *85* **5-8**
NAUTILUS: *79* **5-8**
TETRAGRAMMATON: *69* **10-15**
XERES: *82* **5-8**
Members: John Stewart; Dave Guard; Nick
Reynolds; Bob Shane.
   Also see BEATLES / Beach Boys / Kingston
Trio
   Also see GUARD, Dave, & The Whiskeyhill
Singers
   Also see NEW KINGSTON TRIO
   Also see STEWART, John
   Also see STEWART, John, & Nick Reynolds

KINISON, Sam
LPs: 10/12-Inch 33rpm
WARNER BROS: *88* **5-8**

KINKS

Singles: 7-Inch
ARISTA: *77-85* **$1-3**
CAMEO (308; "Long Tall Sally"): *64* ... **50-75**
CAMEO (345; "Long Tall Sally"): *65* ... **35-45**
CAMEO (348; "You Still
 Want Me"): *65* **100-200**
ERIC: **1-3**
MCA: *86-88* **1-3**
RCA VICTOR: *72-76* **3-5**
REPRISE (0306 through 0647): *65-67* **5-8**
REPRISE (0691 through 0847): *68-69* ... **10-12**
REPRISE (0930 through 1017): *70-71* **3-5**
Promotional Singles
ARISTA (5; "Sleepwalker"): *77* **3-5**
REPRISE (0306 through 0647): *65-67* ... **10-12**
REPRISE (0691 through 0847): *68-69* ... **10-15**
REPRISE (0930 through 1094): *70-72* **5-10**
EPs: 7-Inch 33/45rpm
ARISTA (22; "The Kinks' Misfit
 Record"): *78* **20-25**
 (Promotional issue only.)
CAMEO: *78* **4-6**
Picture Sleeves
ARISTA (Except 5): *80* **2-4**
ARISTA (5; "Sleepwalker"): *77* **5-10**
LPs: 10/12-Inch 33rpm
ARISTA: *77-86* **6-12**
COMPLEAT: **5-8**
MCA: *86* **5-8**
MFSL: *82* **20-30**
PICKWICK: *72-79* **5-10**
PYE: *75-76* **8-10**
RCA VICTOR (Except AYL1
 series): *71-76* **10-15**
RCA VICTOR (AYL1 series): *80-82* **5-8**
REPRISE (2127; "The Great Lost
 Kinks' Album"): *73* **20-30**

REPRISE (R-6143; "You Really
 Got Me"): *64* **$50-100**
 (Monaural.)
REPRISE (RS-6143; "You Really
 Got Me"): *64* **20-30**
 (Stereo.)
REPRISE (R-6158; "Kinks Size"): *65* **50-75**
 (Monaural.)
REPRISE (RS-6158; "Kinks Size"): *65* ... **20-30**
 (Stereo.)
REPRISE (R-6173; "Kinda Kinks"): *65* .. **50-75**
 (Monaural.)
REPRISE (RS-6173; "Kinda Kinks"): *65* . **20-30**
 (Stereo.)
REPRISE (R-6184; "Kinks
 Kingdom"): *65* **50-75**
 (Monaural.)
REPRISE (RS-6184; "Kinks
 Kingdom"): *65* **20-30**
 (Stereo.)
REPRISE (R-6197; "The Kink
 Kontroversy"): *66* **50-75**
 (Monaural.)
REPRISE (RS-6197; "The Kink
 Kontroversy"): *66* **20-30**
 (Stereo.)
REPRISE (R-6217; "The Kinks'
 Greatest Hits"): *66* **50-75**
 (Monaural.)
REPRISE (RS-6217; "The Kinks'
 Greatest Hits"): *66* **20-30**
 (Stereo.)
REPRISE (6228; "Face To Face"): *66* **20-30**
REPRISE (6260; "The Live Kinks"): *67* . **20-30**
REPRISE (6279; "Something Else"): *67* . **20-30**
REPRISE (6327; "Village Green
 Preservation Society"): *69* **25-35**
REPRISE (6366; "Arthur"): *69* **15-20**
 (Price includes lyrics insert.)
REPRISE (6423; "Lola Vs.
 The Powerman"): *69* **12-15**
 (Blue & white cover.)
REPRISE (6423; "Lola Vs.
 The Powerman"): *69* **6-10**
 (Black, blue, and white cover.)
REPRISE (6454; "The Kink
 Kronikles"): *69* **8-12**
Note: Original Reprise Kinks LPs from the sixties
were on a multi-colored label. All 11 of these LPs
have been repressed on the brown Reprise label.
Promotional LPs
ARISTA (Except 69): *77-84* **10-15**
ARISTA (69; "Low Budget Radio
 Interview"): *79* **40-50**
REPRISE (2127; "The Great Lost
 Kinks Album"): *73* **50-75**

REPRISE (6143; "You Really
Got Me"): *64* $50-100
(White label, monaural.)
REPRISE (6158; "Kinks Size"): *65* ... 100-200
(White label, monaural.)
REPRISE (6173; "Kinda Kinks"): *65*   100-200
(White label, monaural.)
REPRISE (6184; "Kinks
Kingdom"): *65* 100-200
(White label, monaural.)
REPRISE (6197; "The Kink
Kontroversy"): *66* 100-200
(White label, monaural.)
REPRISE (6217; "The Kinks'
Greatest Hits"): *66* 100-200
(White label, monaural.)
REPRISE (6228; "Face To Face"): *66* .. 75-150
(White label, monaural.)
REPRISE (6260; "The Live Kinks"): *67* . 75-150
(White label, monaural.)
REPRISE (6279; "Something Else"): *67* . 75-150
REPRISE (6000 series): *64-72* 30-60
(White label, stereo.)
WARNER BROS (328; Complete "Kinks Kit"/
"Then, Now, And In-Between"): *69* ... 275-375
(Boxed set, includes *Then, Now, and In-Between*
LP, button, pin, postcard, letter, decal, and other
promotional materials.)
WARNER BROS (328; "Then, Now,
And In-Between"): *69* 75-100
(Price for LP only.)
Members: Ray Davies; Dave Davies.
Also see DAVIES, Dave

KINKS / Hollywood Stars
Singles: 7-Inch
ARISTA (5; "Sleepwalker"): *77* 8-10
Also see HOLLYWOOD STARS
Also see KINKS

KINNEY, Fern
Singles: 7-Inch
ATLANTIC: *68* $3-5
MALACO: *79-80* 1-3

KINSMAN DAZZ
Singles: 7-Inch
20TH CENTURY-FOX: *78-79* 2-3
LPs: 10/12-Inch 33rpm
20TH CENTURY-FOX: *79* 5-8
Also see DAZZ BAND

KIRBY, Kathy
Singles: 7-Inch
ASCOT: *67* 2-4
LONDON: *62-65* 3-5
PARROT: *65-66* 3-5

KIRK, Jim, & The TM Singers
Singles: 7-Inch
CAPITOL: *80* 1-3

KIRKLAND, Bo
Singles: 7-Inch
CLARIDGE: *75* 2-3

KIRKLAND, Bo, & Ruth Davis
Singles: 7-Inch
CLARIDGE: *75-78* 2-3
Also see DAVIS, Ruth
Also see KIRKLAND, Bo

KIRTON, Lew
Singles: 7-Inch
BELIEVE: *83* 1-3
MARLIN: *77* 2-3

KISS
Singles: 12-Inch 33/45rpm
MERCURY: *85* 5-10
Singles: 7-Inch
CASABLANCA: *74-82* 2-4
MERCURY: *83-88* 1-3
Picture Sleeves
CASABLANCA: *75-78* 5-10
LPs: 10/12-Inch 33rpm
CASABLANCA (7006; "Hotter Than
Hell"): *74* 15-25
CASABLANCA (7016; "Dressed To
Kill"): *75* 10-20
CASABLANCA (7020; "Alive"): *75* 10-20
CASABLANCA (7025; "Destroyer"): *75* 10-20
CASABLANCA (7032; "The
Originals"): *76* 30-55
CASABLANCA (7037; "Rock And
Roll Over"): *76* 15-20
(Price includes sticker, which represents about $4-
$6 of the value.)

CASABLANCA (7057; "Love
Gun"): 77 .... $25-50
(Price includes cardboard gun, which represents
about $15-$25 of the value.)

CASABLANCA (7057; "Love Gun"): 77   10-20
(Without cardboard gun.)

CASABLANCA (7076; "Alive II"): 77 .. 30-40
(Price includes tatoos booklet, which represents
about $15-$20 of the value.)

CASABLANCA (7100; "Double
Platinum"): 78 10-20
(Price includes platinum award, which represents
about $15-$25 of the value.)

CASABLANCA (7152; "Dynasty"): 79 .. 15-20
(Price includes poster, which represents about $4-
$6 of the value.)

CASABLANCA (7225; "Kiss
Unmasked"): 80 10-15
(Price includes poster, which represents about $4-
$6 of the value.)

CASABLANCA (7261; "Music From
The Elder"): 81 25-50

CASABLANCA (7270; "Creatures Of
The Night"): 82 15-20
(With makeup.)

CASABLANCA (9001; "Kiss"): 74 15-25

MERCURY (Except picture
discs): 83-88 5-8

MERCURY (Picture discs): 83-88 15-20

Promotional LPs

CASABLANCA (76; "Kiss Tour
Album"): 76 20-30

CASABLANCA (7001; "Kiss"): 74 40-60
(Without *Kissin' Time*.)

CASABLANCA (7032; "The
Originals"): 76 60-80
(With inserts.)

CASABLANCA (20137; "Criss, Frehley,
Simmons, Stanley"): 78 20-30
Members: Gene Simmons; Ace Frehley; Paul Stan-
ley; Peter Criss; Bruce Kulick; Eric Carr; Vinnie
Vincent.

Also see CRISS, Peter
Also see FREHLEY, Ace
Also see SIMMONS, Gene
Also see STANLEY, Paul
Also see VINCENT, Vinnie, Invasion

KISSING THE PINK
Singles: 7-Inch
ATLANTIC: 83 1-3
LPs: 10/12-Inch 33rpm
ATLANTIC: 83 5-8

KISSOON, Katie
Singles: 12-Inch 33/45rpm
JIVE: 84 4-6

KISSOON, Mac
LPs: 10/12-Inch 33rpm
DECCA: 70 .... $10-12

KISSOON, Mac & Katie
Singles: 7-Inch
ABC: 71 2-4
BELL: 72 2-3
MCA/STATE: 75-76 2-3
Also see KISSOON, Katie
Also see KISSOON, Mac
Also see WATERS, Roger

KITARO
(Mansanori Takahashi)
LPs: 10/12-Inch 33rpm
GEFFEN: 86-87 5-8
GRAMAVISION: 85-86 5-8

KITT, Eartha
Singles: 78rpm
RCA VICTOR: 53-57 3-5
Singles: 12-Inch 33/45rpm
STREETWISE: 83 4-6
Singles: 7-Inch
DECCA: 65 3-5
KAPP: 59-66 3-6
RCA VICTOR: 53-57 2-4
STREETWISE: 83 1-3
Picture Sleeves
RCA VICTOR: 54-55 8-15
EPs: 7-Inch 33/45rpm
RCA VICTOR: 53-57 10-20
LPs: 10/12-Inch 33rpm
CAEDMON: 69 5-10
DECCA: 65 10-15
GNP/CRESCENDO: 65 10-15
KAPP: 59-60 10-20
MGM: 62 10-20
PHILIPS: 68 8-15
RCA VICTOR: 53-57 15-30
STANYAN: 72 5-10

KITTY & THE HAYWOODS
Singles: 7-Inch
MERCURY: 77 2-3
LPs: 10/12-Inch 33rpm
MERCURY: 77 8-10

KIX
Singles: 7-Inch
ATLANTIC: 81-83 1-3
LPs: 10/12-Inch 33rpm
ATLANTIC: 81-88 5-8

KLAATU
Singles: 7-Inch
CAPITOL: 77-80 2-4

ISLAND: *75* $2-3
Picture Sleeves
CAPITOL: *77* 2-5
LPs: 10/12-Inch 33rpm
CAPITOL: *76-80* 6-10
Members: John Woloschuk; Cary Draper; David
Long; Dino Tome.

KLEEER
Singles: 7-Inch
ATLANTIC: *79-85* 1-3
LPs: 10/12-Inch 33rpm
ATLANTIC: *79-85* 5-8

KLEIN, Robert
Singles: 7-Inch
BRUT: *73* 3-5
CASABLANCA: *79* 2-3
LPs: 10/12-Inch 33rpm
BRUT: *73* 8-12

KLEIN & MBO
Singles: 12-Inch 33/45rpm
ATLANTIC: *83* 4-6
Singles: 7-Inch
ATLANTIC: *83* 1-3

KLEMMER, John
Singles: 7-Inch
ABC: *76* 1-3
LPs: 10/12-Inch 33rpm
ABC: *75-79* 5-10
CADET CONCEPT: *69* 8-12
CHESS: *76* 8-12
ELEKTRA: *80-83* 5-8
MCA: *79-82* 5-10
NAUTILUS: *80-81* 5-8
NOVUS: *79* 5-8
Also see HARRIS, Eddie, & John Klemmer

KLINE, Johnny
Singles: 7-Inch
JET: *88* 2-4
Members: Johnny Kline; Stan Butcler; Jim
Cochran.

KLINT, Pete, Quintet
Singles: 7-Inch
MERCURY: *67* 2-3

KLIQUE
Singles: 12-Inch 33/45rpm
MCA: *81-85* 4-6
Singles: 7-Inch
MCA: *81-85* 1-3
LPs: 10/12-Inch 33rpm
MCA: *81-85* 5-8

KLOCKWISE
Singles: 7-Inch
SINBAN: *84-85* $1-3

KLOWNS
Singles: 7-Inch
RCA VICTOR: *70* 2-3
LPs: 10/12-Inch 33rpm
RCA VICTOR: *70* 8-10

KLUGH, Earl
Singles: 7-Inch
BLUE NOTE: *77* 2-3
LIBERTY: *81* 1-3

KLYMAXX
Singles: 12-Inch 33/45rpm
CONSTELLATION: *84-86* 4-6
MCA: *84* 4-6
Singles: 7-Inch
CONSTELLATION: *84-87* 1-3
MCA: *84-86* 1-3
SOLAR: *81-83* 1-3
LPs: 10/12-Inch 33rpm
CONSTELLATION: *85* 5-8
SOLAR: *81-83* 5-8

KNACK
Singles: 7-Inch
CAPITOL (4000 series): *79-81* 2-4
Picture Sleeves
CAPITOL (Except 4731 & 4822): *79-81* . . 2-4
CAPITOL (4731; "My Sharona"): *79* 4-8
CAPITOL (4822; "Baby Talks Dirty"): *80* 8-10
LPs: 10/12-Inch 33rpm
CAPITOL: *79-81* 8-10
Member: Doug Fieger.
Also see SKY

KNICKERBOCKERS
Singles: 7-Inch
CHALLENGE: *65-67* $4-6
ERIC: 1-3
LPs: 10/12-Inch 33rpm
CHALLENGE (Except 622): *65* 25-30
CHALLENGE (622; "Lies"): *66* 30-40
Member: Buddy Randall.

KNIGHT, Frederick
Singles: 7-Inch
JUANA: *81* 1-3
MAXINE: *69* 2-4
STAX: *72* 2-3
TRUTH: *75* 2-3
LPs: 10/12-Inch 33rpm
STAX: *73* 8-10

KNIGHT, Gladys
(Gladys Knight & The Pips)
Singles: 12-Inch 33/45rpm
COLUMBIA: *79-85* 4-6
MCA: *86* 4-6
Singles: 7-Inch
ABC: *73* 1-3
BUDDAH: *73-79* 2-3
COLUMBIA: *79-85* 1-3
ENJOY: *64* 3-5
ERIC: *78* 1-3
FLASHBACK: *67* 1-3
FURY: *61-63* 4-8
MCA: *86-88* 1-3

Gladys Knight and the Pips

MAXX: *64-65* $3-5
SOUL (Except 35023 & 35033): *67-74* 2-3
SOUL (35023 & 35033): *66* 3-5
VEE JAY: *61-63* 4-6
Picture Sleeves
BUDDAH: *73-75* 2-3
COLUMBIA: *81* 1-3
LPs: 10/12-Inch 33rpm
ACCORD: *81-82* 5-8
ALLEGIANCE: *84* 5-8
BELL: *68-75* 10-12
BUDDAH: *73-78* 8-10
COLUMBIA: *79-85* 5-8
51 WEST: 5-8
FURY (1003; "Letter Full
Of Tears"): *62* 60-100
LOST-NITE: *81* 5-8
MCA: *87* 5-8
MCP: *76* 8-10
MAXX: 10-15
MOTOWN (Except 792): *80-82* 5-8
MOTOWN (792; "Anthology"): *74* 8-10
NATURAL RESOURCES: *78* 5-8
PICKWICK: *73* 8-10
SOUL: *67-75* 10-15
SPHERE SOUND: *65* 15-20
SPRINGBOARD: *75* 8-10
TRIP: *73* 8-10
UNITED ARTISTS: *75* 10-12
UPFRONT: 10-12
VEE JAY: *75* 10-12
Also see DIONNE & FRIENDS
Also see GAYE, Marvin / Gladys Knight &
The Pips
Also see PIPS

KNIGHT, Gladys, & Johnny Mathis
Singles: 7-Inch
COLUMBIA: *80* 1-3
Also see KNIGHT, Gladys
Also see MATHIS, Johnny

KNIGHT, Holly
Singles: 7-Inch
COLUMBIA: *88* 1-3

KNIGHT, Jean
(Jean Knight & Premium)
Singles: 7-Inch
CHELSEA: *75* 2-3
COTILLION: *81* 1-3
DIAL: *74* 2-4
MIRAGE: *85* 5-8
STAX: *71-73* 2-4
TRIBE: *65* 3-5

LPs: 10/12-Inch 33rpm
STAX: 71 ....$10-12

KNIGHT, Jerry
Singles: 7-Inch
A&M: 80-83 1-3
Picture Sleeves
A&M: 80 1-3
LPs: 10/12-Inch 33rpm
A&M: 80-81 5-8
Also see OLLIE & JERRY
Also see RAYDIO

KNIGHT, Marie
Singles: 7-Inch
DIAMOND: 63 3-5
MERCURY: 56 8-10
MUSICOR: 65-66 3-5
OKEH: 61-65 3-5
WING: 56 6-10
Picture Sleeves
OKEH: 61 4-8
LPs: 10/12-Inch 33rpm
CARLTON: 60 20-25
Also see MARIE & REX

KNIGHT, Robert
Singles: 7-Inch
DOT: 61 4-6
ELF: 68-69 3-5
MONUMENT: 74 2-4
RISING SONS: 67-68 3-5
LPs: 10/12-Inch 33rpm
MONUMENT: 67 12-15

KNIGHT, Sonny
Singles: 78rpm
ALADDIN: 53 6-12
DOT: 56 4-8
SPECIALTY: 57 3-6
Singles: 7-Inch
A&M: 63-64 3-5
ALADDIN: 53 15-25
AURA: 64-65 3-5
DOT (Maroon label): 56 8-12
DOT (Black label): 57 5-8
EASTMAN: 59 4-6
FIFO: 61 3-5
MERCURY: 62 3-5
SPECIALTY: 57 5-10
(Most Specialty singles are currently available, using original catalog numbers.)
STARLA (Except 1): 58-59 8-12
STARLA (1; "Dedicated To You"): 57 10-20
VITA: 56 15-20
WORLD PACIFIC (Except 403): 66 3-5

WORLD PACIFIC (403; "If You Want This Love"): 64 ....$4-6
(Reissued several months later on Aura 403.)
Picture Sleeves
AURA: 65 5-10
LPs: 10/12-Inch 33rpm
AURA: 64 15-20

KNIGHT, Terry
(Terry Knight & The Pack)
Singles: 7-Inch
ABKCO: 75 2-4
CAMEO: 67 4-8
CAPITOL: 69 5-10
FRATERNITY: 67 4-8
LUCKY ELEVEN: 66-67 5-10
LPs: 10/12-Inch 33rpm
ABKCO: 72 10-15
CAMEO: 67 25-30
LUCKY ELEVEN: 66 20-25
Also see GRAND FUNK RAILROAD

KNIGHT BROTHERS
Singles: 7-Inch
CHECKER: 63-66 3-5
MERCURY: 67-68 2-4
Member: Peter Knight.

KNIGHTSBRIDGE STRINGS
Singles: 7-Inch
MONUMENT: 66 1-3
TOP RANK: 59-60 2-3
LPs: 10/12-Inch 33rpm
MONUMENT: 66-69 5-10
PURIST: 61 5-10
RIVERSIDE: 62-64 5-12
TOP RANK: 59-60 5-15
Also see RANDOLPH, Boots

KNOBLOCK, Fred
Singles: 7-Inch
SCOTTI BROS: 80-82 1-3
LPs: 10/12-Inch 33rpm
SCOTTI BROS: 80-82 5-8

KNOBLOCK, Fred, & Susan Anton
Singles: 7-Inch
SCOTTI BROS: 80 1-3
Also see ANTON, Susan
Also see KNOBLOCK, Fred

KNOCKOUTS
Singles: 7-Inch
MGM: 61 3-5
SHAD: 59-60 15-20
TRIBUTE: 64-65 3-5
LPs: 10/12-Inch 33rpm
TRIBUTE: 64 45-50

KNOX, Buddy
(Buddy Knox & The Rhythm Orchids)
Singles: 78rpm
ROULETTE: 57 .... $5-10
Singles: 7-Inch
ABC: 73 1-3
LIBERTY: 60-64 4-6
REPRISE: 65-66 3-5
ROULETTE (4000 series): 57 10-15
(With the "roulette wheel" label.)
ROULETTE (4000 series): 57-58 5-10
(Orange label. No "roulette wheel.")
ROULETTE (4082 through 4262): 58-60 .. 4-6
RUFF: 65 3-5
UNITED ARTISTS: 68-71 3-5
Picture Sleeves
LIBERTY: 61 10-20
EPs: 7-Inch 33/45rpm
ROULETTE: 57 25-40
LPs: 10/12-Inch 33rpm
ACCORD: 82-83 5-8
LIBERTY: 62 20-25
ROULETTE (25003; "Buddy
Knox"): 57 50-100
UNITED ARTISTS: 69 10-12

KNOX, Buddy / Jimmy Bowen
(With The Rhythm Orchids)
Singles: 7-Inch
TRIPLE-D (797; "Party Doll"/"I'm
Stickin' With You"): 57 75-125
LPs: 10/12-Inch 33rpm
MURRAY HILL: 5-8
ROULETTE (25048; "Buddy Knox &
Jimmy Bowen"): 58 50-75
Also see BOWEN, Jimmy
Also see KNOX, Buddy

KOENEMANN, Randy, With
Midwests Best
Singles: 7-Inch
L. PARKS: 87 1-3

KOFFIE
Singles: 12-Inch 33/45rpm
PAN DISC: 83 4-6

KOFFMAN, Moe,
(Moe Koffman Quartette; Moe Koffman Quintet; Moe Koffman Septette)
Singles: 7-Inch
ABC: 73 1-3
ASCOT: 62 2-3
ATCO: 65 2-3
GOLD EAGLE: 61 2-3
JUBILEE: 58-68 2-4
PALETTE: 60-63 2-4

VIRGO: 72 .... $1-3
LPs: 10/12-Inch 33rpm
ASCOT: 62 10-15
JANUS: 78 5-8
JUBILEE: 68 8-12
UNITED ARTISTS: 62-63 10-20

KOKOMO
(James Wisner)
Singles: 7-Inch
FELSTED: 61-62 2-4
Picture Sleeves
FELSTED: 61 4-8
LPs: 10/12-Inch 33rpm
FELSTED: 61 15-20

KOKOMO
Singles: 7-Inch
COLUMBIA: 75-76 2-3
LPs: 10/12-Inch 33rpm
COLUMBIA: 75-76 8-10
Member: Tony Malley.
Also see 10CC

KOKO-POP
Singles: 7-Inch
MOTOWN: 84-85 1-3
LPs: 10/12-Inch 33rpm
MOTOWN: 84 5-8

KOLBY, Diane
Singles: 7-Inch
COLUMBIA: 70-71 2-4

KOMIKO
Singles: 7-Inch
SAM: 82 1-3

KON KAN
Singles: 7-Inch
ATLANTIC: 88 1-3

KONGAS
Singles: 7-Inch
POLYDOR: 78 2-3
LPs: 10/12-Inch 33rpm
POLYDOR: 78 5-8
SALSOUL: 78 5-8

KONGOS, John
(John T. Kongos; Johnny Kongos)
Singles: 7-Inch
ELEKTRA: 71-72 2-3
GROOVE: 61 3-5
KAPP: 67 3-5
RCA VICTOR: 63 3-5
Picture Sleeves
ELEKTRA: 71 2-3
LPs: 10/12-Inch 33rpm
ELEKTRA: 72 8-10

JANUS: *71* $8-10

KOOL, Dr. J.R.:
see DR. J.R. KOOL

KOOL & THE GANG
Singles: 12-Inch 33/45rpm
DE-LITE: *79-85* 4-6
MERCURY: *86* 4-6
Singles: 7-Inch
DE-LITE: *69-85* 1-3
MERCURY: *86-88* 1-3
LPs: 10/12-Inch 33rpm
DE-LITE: *69-83* 8-10
MERCURY: *86-88* 5-8
Also see BAND AID

KOOL KYLE & BILLY BILL
Singles: 12-Inch 33/45rpm
PROFILE: *86* 4-6
Singles: 7-Inch
PROFILE: *86* 1-3

KOOL MOE DEE
Singles: 7-Inch
JIVE: *87-88* 1-3
LPs: 10/12-Inch 33rpm
JIVE: *87* 5-8

KOOPER, Al
Singles: 7-Inch
AURORA: *67* 3-5
COLUMBIA: *69-71* 2-4
VERVE/FOLKWAYS: *66* 3-5
Picture Sleeves
COLUMBIA: *69* 3-5
LPs: 10/12-Inch 33rpm
COLUMBIA: *69-82* 10-12
UNITED ARTISTS: *76* 8-10
Also see BLOOD, SWEAT & TEARS
Also see BLOOMFIELD, Mike, & Al Kooper
Also see BLOOMFIELD, Mike, Al Kooper &
Steve Stills
Also see BLUES PROJECT
Also see ROYAL TEENS

KOOPER, Al, & Steve Mills
Singles: 7-Inch
COLUMBIA: *68* 3-5

KOOPER, Al, & Shuggie Otis
LPs: 10/12-Inch 33rpm
COLUMBIA: *69* 10-12
Also see KOOPER, Al
Also see OTIS, Shuggie

KOPPER
Singles: 7-Inch
KMA: *86-87* 1-3

KORGIS
Singles: 7-Inch
ASYLUM: *80* $1-3
LPs: 10/12-Inch 33rpm
ASYLUM: *80* 5-8

KORONA
Singles: 7-Inch
UNITED ARTISTS: *80* 1-3
LPs: 10/12-Inch 33rpm
UNITED ARTISTS: *80* 5-8

KOSSOFF, Paul
LPs: 10/12-Inch 33rpm
DJM: *77* 10-12
ISLAND: *73-75* 8-10
Also see BACK STREET CRAWLER
Also see FREE

KOSSOFF / Kirke / Tetsu / Rabbit
LPs: 10/12-Inch 33rpm
ISLAND: *72* 8-10
Members: Paul Kossoff; Simon Kirke.
Also see FREE
Also see KOSSOFF, Paul

**KOSTELANETZ, Andre, & His
Orchestra**
Singles: 78rpm
COLUMBIA: *50-57* 1-3
Singles: 7-Inch
COLUMBIA: *50-61* 1-3
EPs: 7-Inch 33/45rpm
COLUMBIA: *50-59* 3-6
LPs: 10/12-Inch 33rpm
COLUMBIA: *50-71* 5-15

KOTTKE, Leo
Singles: 7-Inch
CAPITOL: *75* 2-3
LPs: 10/12-Inch 33rpm
CAPITOL (Except 16000 series): *71-76* .. 8-10
CAPITOL (16000 series): *71-76* 5-8
CHRYSALIS: *76-81* 5-8
OBLIVION: 15-20
SYMPOSIUM: *70* 10-12
TAKOMA: *71-74* 8-12

**KOTTKE, Leo, John Fahey &
Peter Lang**
LPs: 10/12-Inch 33rpm
TAKOMA: *74* 8-10
Also see KOTTKE, Leo

KRAFTWERK
Singles: 12-Inch 33/45rpm
WARNER BROS: *83* 4-6
Singles: 7-Inch
CAPITOL: *76-78* 2-3

Note: Walter Scott vocal may be shown as by "Little Walter."

REPRISE: 70 .... $3-6
LPs: 10/12-Inch 33rpm
MUSICLAND U.S.A.: 66 20-25
Members: Walter Scott; Bob Kuban; John Krenski; Greg Hoeltzel.

KUF-LINX
Singles: 78rpm
CHALLENGE: 58 8-10
Singles: 7-Inch
CHALLENGE (White label): 58 8-10
CHALLENGE (Maroon label): 58 4-6
Member: Johnny Jennings.

KULIS, Charlie
Singles: 7-Inch
PLAYBOY: 75 2-3

KWICK
Singles: 12-Inch 33/45rpm
CAPITOL: 83 4-6
Singles: 7-Inch
CAPITOL: 83 1-3
EMI AMERICA: 80-82 1-3
LPs: 10/12-Inch 33rpm
CAPITOL: 83 5-8
EMI AMERICA: 80-81 5-8

KYM
Singles: 12-Inch 33/45rpm
AWARD: 84 4-6
Singles: 7-Inch
AWARD: 84 1-3

L

L.A. BOPPERS
Singles: 7-Inch
MCA: 82 1-3
MERCURY: 80-81 1-3
LPs: 10/12-Inch 33rpm
MCA: 82 5-8
MERCURY: 80-81 5-8

L.A. DREAM TEAM
Singles: 12-Inch 33/45rpm
MCA: 86 4-6
Singles: 7-Inch
MCA: 86 1-3
LPs: 10/12-Inch 33rpm
MCA: 86-87 5-8
Members: Rudy Pardee; Chris Wilson.

L.A. GUNS
LPs: 10/12-Inch 33rpm
VERTIGO: 88 .... $5-8

L.A. JETS
Singles: 7-Inch
RCA VICTOR: 76 2-3
LPs: 10/12-Inch 33rpm
RCA VICTOR: 76 8-10

L.L. COOL J
(Ladies Love Cool James; James Todd Smith)
Singles: 12-Inch 33/45rpm
COLUMBIA: 85-86 4-6
Singles: 7-Inch
COLUMBIA: 85-86 1-3
DEF JAM: 87-88 1-3
LPs: 10/12-Inch 33rpm
COLUMBIA: 85 5-8

L.T.D.
(Love, Togetherness & Devotion)
Singles: 7-Inch
A&M: 76-80 1-3
MONTAGE: 83 1-3
Picture Sleeves
A&M: 76-78 1-3
LPs: 10/12-Inch 33rpm
A&M: 74-81 8-10
MONTAGE: 83 5-8
SPRINGBOARD: 77 8-10
Member: Jeffrey Osborne.
Also see OSBORNE, Jeffrey

LTG EXCHANGE
Singles: 7-Inch
FANIA: 74 2-3
WAND: 74 2-3

LABAN
Singles: 7-Inch
CRITIQUE: 86 1-3

LABELLE, Patti
(Patti Labelle & The Blue Belles; Labelle)
Singles: 12-Inch 33/45rpm
EPIC: 78-79 4-6
MCA: 85 4-6
PHILADELPHIA INT'L: 83-85 4-6
Singles: 7-Inch
ATLANTIC: 65-70 2-4
EPIC: 74-80 1-3
KING: 63 4-6
MISTLETOE: 73 2-3
PHILADELPHIA INT'L: 81-85 1-3
MCA: 85-87 1-3
NEWTOWN: 62-63 4-6
NICETOWN: 64 4-6
PARKWAY: 64 3-5

RCA VICTOR: 73 .... $2-3
TRIP: 71 1-3
WARNER BROS: 71-72 2-3
LPs: 10/12-Inch 33rpm
ATLANTIC: 65-67 15-20
EPIC: 74-82 8-10
MCA: 85-86 5-8
MISTLETOE: 10-15
NEWTOWN (632; "Sleigh Bells, Jingle Bells,
 & Blue Bells"): 63 50-75
PARKWAY: 64 20-25
PHILADELPHIA INT'L: 81-85 5-8
RCA VICTOR (0200 series): 73 8-10
RCA VICTOR (4100 series): 82 5-8
TRIP: 71-75 8-10
UNITED ARTISTS: 74-75 8-10
UPFRONT: 10-12
WARNER BROS: 71-72 8-10
  Also see BLUE-BELLES
  Also see DASH, Sarah
  Also see HENDRIX, Nona
  Also see NYRO, Laura
  Also see WOMACK, Bobby, & Patti Labelle

LABELLE, Patti / Harold Faltermeyer
Singles: 7-Inch
MCA: 85 1-3
  Also see FALTERMEYER, Harold

LABELLE, Patti, & Michael McDonald
Singles: 7-Inch
MCA: 86 1-3
  Also see McDONALD, Michael

LABELLE, Patti, & Grover Washington Jr.
Singles: 7-Inch
ELEKTRA: 82 1-3
  Also see LABELLE, Patti
  Also see WASHINGTON, Grover, Jr.

LA BOUNTY, Bill
Singles: 7-Inch
20TH CENTURY-FOX: 75-76 2-3
WARNER BROS: 78 2-3

LABRADORS
Singles: 7-Inch
CHIEF: 58 35-50

LABYRINTH
Singles: 7-Inch
21: 85 1-3
  Member: Julie Loco.

LACE
LPs: 10/12-Inch 33rpm
WING: 88 5-8

LADD, Cheryl
Singles: 12-Inch 33/45rpm
CAPITOL (8894;
 "Skinnydippin'"): 78 .... $8-10
(Promotional issue only.)
Singles: 7-Inch
CAPITOL: 76-79 2-5
Picture Sleeves
CAPITOL: 78-79 2-5
WARNER BROS: 74 4-6
LPs: 10/12-Inch 33rpm
CAPITOL: 78-79 6-10
  Also see VALLI, Frankie, & Cheryl Ladd

LADIES CHOICE
Singles: 7-Inch
STREETWISE: 83 1-3

LADY
Singles: 7-Inch
MEGA: 82 1-3

LADY FLASH
Singles: 7-Inch
RSO: 76 2-3
LPs: 10/12-Inch 33rpm
RSO: 76 8-10
  Also see MANILOW, Barry

LAFAYETTES
Singles: 7-Inch
RCA VICTOR: 62 3-5

LA FLAMME, David
Singles: 7-Inch
AMHERST: 76-77 2-3
Picture Sleeves
AMHERST: 76 2-3
LPs: 10/12-Inch 33rpm
AMHERST: 76-78 8-10
  Also see IT'S A BEAUTIFUL DAY

LA FLAVOUR
Singles: 12-Inch 33/45rpm
SWEET CITY: 80 5-10
Singles: 7-Inch
MERCURY: 79 1-3
SWEET CITY: 80 1-3
LPs: 10/12-Inch 33rpm
SWEET CITY: 80 5-8

LA FORGE, Jack
(Jack LaForge & His Orchestra)
Singles: 7-Inch
LYRIC: 65-66 2-3
REGINA: 63-66 2-3
RIO: 62 2-4
LPs: 10/12-Inch 33rpm
AUDIO FIDELITY: 66 6-12

PURPLETONE: 62 .... $8-15
REGINA: 63-65 8-15

LA LA, Prince: see PRINCE LA LA

LAID BACK
Singles: 12-Inch 33/45rpm
SIRE: 84-85 4-6
WARNER BROS: 83 4-6
Singles: 7-Inch
SIRE: 84-85 1-3
WARNER BROS: 83-84 1-3
LPs: 10/12-Inch 33rpm
SIRE: 84 5-8
Members: Timothy Stahl; John Guldberg.

LAINE, Cleo
Singles: 7-Inch
RCA VICTOR: 74-80 1-3
LPs: 10/12-Inch 33rpm
BUDDAH: 74 8-10
FONTANA: 66 10-15
GNP/CRESCENDO: 74 5-10
QUINTESSENCE: 80 5-8
RCA VICTOR: 73-80 5-10
Also see CHARLES, Ray, & Cleo Laine

LAINE, Frankie
Singles: 78rpm
MERCURY: 47-51 3-6
COLUMBIA: 51-57 3-5
Singles: 7-Inch
ABC: 67-69 2-4
AMOS: 70-71 2-3
CAPITOL: 64-66 2-3
COLUMBIA (39000 through
40000): 51-57 3-6
COLUMBIA (41000 through
42000): 57-64 2-5
MAINSTREAM: 75 1-3
MERCURY (5000 series): 50-51 4-6
SUNFLOWER: 72 1-3
WARNER BROS: 74 1-3
Picture Sleeves
COLUMBIA: 56-57 8-15
EPs: 7-Inch 33/45rpm
COLUMBIA: 52-59 5-15
MERCURY: 51-54 8-15
LPs: 10/12-Inch 33rpm
ABC (600 series): 67-69 8-15
ABC (30000 series): 76 5-8
AMOS: 70-71 8-12
CAPITOL: 65 10-15
COLUMBIA (600 through 1200
series): 54-58 12-20
COLUMBIA (1300 through 1900
series): 59-63 10-20

COLUMBIA (6000 series): 53-54 ..... $15-30
(10-Inch LPs.)
COLUMBIA (8100 through 8700
series): 59-63 10-20
HARMONY: 65-71 8-15
HINDSIGHT: 84 4-8
MERCURY (20000 series): 54-61 10-20
MERCURY (25000 series): 51-52 20-30
(10-Inch LPs.)
MERCURY (60000 series): 61 10-20
TOWER: 67 8-15
TRIP: 75 5-8
WING: 60-67 8-15
Also see DAY, Doris, & Frankie Laine

LAINE, Frankie, & Jimmy Boyd
Singles: 78rpm
COLUMBIA: 53 3-5
Singles: 7-Inch
COLUMBIA: 53 3-5
Also see BOYD, Jimmy

LAINE, Frankie, & The Four Lads
Singles: 78rpm
COLUMBIA: 54 3-5
Singles: 7-Inch
COLUMBIA: 54 3-5
EPs: 7-Inch 33/45rpm
COLUMBIA: 56 5-15
LPs: 10/12-Inch 33rpm
COLUMBIA: 56 15-20
Also see FOUR LADS

LAINE, Frankie, & Jo Stafford
Singles: 78rpm
COLUMBIA: 51-53 3-5
Singles: 7-Inch
COLUMBIA: 51-53 3-5
EPs: 7-Inch 33/45rpm
COLUMBIA: 54 5-15
LPs: 10/12-Inch 33rpm
COLUMBIA: 54 15-20
Also see LAINE, Frankie
Also see STAFFORD, Jo

LAKE
Singles: 7-Inch
CARIBOU: 81 1-3
COLUMBIA: 77-79 1-3
LPs: 10/12-Inch 33rpm
CARIBOU: 81 5-8
COLUMBIA: 77-79 5-8

LAKE, Greg
Singles: 7-Inch
ATLANTIC: 75-77 2-3
CHRYSALIS: 81 1-3

LPs: 10/12-Inch 33rpm
CHRYSALIS: *81* $5-8
Also see EMERSON, LAKE & PALMER
Also see KING CRIMSON

LAKESIDE
Singles: 7-Inch
SOLAR: *78-87* 1-3
LPs: 10/12-Inch 33rpm
ABC-PARAMOUNT: *77* 8-10
SOLAR: *77-82* 5-8

LA LA
Singles: 7-Inch
ARISTA: *87* 1-3

LA LA, Prince:
see PRINCE LA LA

LAMAS, Lorenzo
Singles: 7-Inch
SCOTTI BROTHERS: *84-85* 1-3

LAMB, Kevin
Singles: 7-Inch
ARISTA: *78* 1-3

LAMONT, Lee
Singles: 7-Inch
BACK BEAT: *64-66* 3-5

L'AMOUR
Singles: 12-Inch 33/45rpm
BROCCOLLI: *84* 4-6

LAMP SISTERS
Singles: 7-Inch
DUKE: *68-69* 3-5

LANCE, Herb
(Herb Lance & The Classics)
Singles: 78rpm
SITTIN' IN WITH: *49* 5-10
Singles: 7-Inch
DELUXE: *57* 10-15
MALA: *59-60* 4-8
PROMO: *61* 4-6
LPs: 10/12-Inch 33rpm
CHESS: *66* 12-15

LANCE, Major
Singles: 12-Inch 33/45rpm
KAT FAMILY: *82* 4-6
Singles: 7-Inch
COLUMBIA: *77* 2-3
CURTOM: *70* 2-4
DAKAR: *69* 3-5
EPIC: *66* 1-3
KAT FAMILY: *82* 1-3
MERCURY: *60* 5-10
OKEH: *63-67* 3-5

OSIRIS: *75* $2-3
PLAYBOY: *74-75* 2-4
SOUL: *78* 2-3
VOLT: *72* 2-5
Picture Sleeves
OKEH: *63-64* 4-8
EPs: 7-Inch 33/45rpm
OKEH: *64* 10-15
(Jukebox issue only.)
LPs: 10/12-Inch 33rpm
BACK-TRAC: *85* 5-8
CONTEMPO: 10-12
KAT FAMILY: *83* 5-8
OKEH: *63-64* 15-20
SOUL: *78* 5-8

LANDIS, Jerry
(Paul Simon)
Singles: 7-Inch
AMY: *62* 20-25
CANADIAN AMERICAN: *61* 20-25
MGM: *59* 25-30
WARWICK: *60-61* 20-30
Also see SIMON, Paul

LANDS, Liz
Singles: 7-Inch
GORDY (7026; "What He
Lived For"): *63* 5-8
ONE-DERFUL: *67* 3-5

LANDS, Liz / Martin Luther King
Singles: 7-Inch
GORDY (7023; "We Shall
Overcome"): *63* 8-12
Also see KING, Rev. Martin Luther, Jr.
Also see LANDS, Liz

LANDS, Liz, & The Temptations
Singles: 7-Inch
GORDY (7030; "Keep Me"): *64* 8-12
Also see LANDS, Liz
Also see TEMPTATIONS

LANE, Mickey Lee
Singles: 7-Inch
MALA: *68* 5-8
SWAN: *64-66* 5-8

LANE, Robin, & The Chartbusters
Singles: 7-Inch
WARNER BROS: *80-81* 1-3
Picture Sleeves
WARNER BROS: *80* 1-3
LPs: 10/12-Inch 33rpm
WARNER BROS: *80-81* 5-8
Members: Robin Lane; Leroy Radcliffe; Asa Breb-
ner; Scott Baeren Wald; Tim Jackson.

LANE BROTHERS
Singles: 7-Inch
LEADER: 60 .... $3-5
RCA VICTOR: 57-58 3-6

LANE BROTHERS / Julius La Rosa
EPs: 7-Inch 33/45rpm
RCA VICTOR: 57 5-10
(Promotional issue only.)
Also see LANE BROTHERS
Also see LA ROSA, Julius

LANG, K. D.
Singles: 7-Inch
SIRE: 88-89 1-3
LPs: 10/12-Inch 33rpm
SIRE: 88-89 5-8

LANI & BONI
Singles: 7-Inch
GARPAX: 64 4-6
Members: Delaney Bramlett; Bonnie Bramlett.
Also see DELANEY & BONNIE

LANIER & CO.
Singles: 7-Inch
LARC: 82-83 1-3
LPs: 10/12-Inch 33rpm
LARC: 83 5-8

LANIN, Lester, & His Orchestra
Singles: 78rpm
EPIC: 56-57 2-3
Singles: 7-Inch
EPIC: 56-62 2-3
EPs: 7-Inch 33/45rpm
EPIC: 56-58 3-6
LPs: 10/12-Inch 33rpm
EPIC: 56-62 5-15

LANSON, Snooky
Singles: 78rpm
DECCA: 52 2-4
DOT: 55-56 2-4
LONDON: 50-51 2-5
REPUBLIC: 53 2-4
Singles: 7-Inch
DECCA: 52 2-4
DOT: 55-56 2-4
LONDON: 50-51 3-5
REPUBLIC: 53 2-4
STARDAY: 68 1-3
LPs: 10/12-Inch 33rpm
CAMDEN (200 series): 55 10-20
DOT: 60 10-15
STARDAY: 68 5-10

LANZ, David
LPs: 10/12-Inch 33rpm
NARADA EQUINOX: 88 .... $5-8
NARADA LOTUS: 88 5-8

LANZA, Mario
Singles: 78rpm
RCA VICTOR: 50-57 2-5
Singles: 7-Inch
RCA VICTOR (0400 series): 71 1-3
RCA VICTOR (3200 through
8500 series): 51-59 3-5
RCA VICTOR (1300 series): 50 4-6
Picture Sleeves
RCA VICTOR (3300; "The Lovliest Night
Of The Year"): 51 15-25
(Die-cut sleeve, with center hole.)
RCA VICTOR (4209; "Song Of
India"): 51 15-25
EPs: 7-Inch 33/45rpm
RCA VICTOR (Except 1837): 53-61 8-15
RCA VICTOR (1837; "The Student
Prince"): 54 15-25
(Soundtrack.)
LPs: 10/12-Inch 33rpm
CAMDEN (Except 400 series): 63 5-15
CAMDEN (400 series): 57 10-20
(With a "CAL" prefix.)
CAMDEN (400 series): 63 8-15
(With a "CAS" prefix.)
RCA VICTOR (75; "The Toast Of
New Orleans"): 51 45-60
(Soundtrack. A 10-Inch LP.)
RCA VICTOR (86 through 1181): 51-53 20-30
RCA VICTOR (1750; "A Legendary
Performer"): 76 5-8
RCA VICTOR (1837; "The Student
Prince"): 54 35-45
(Soundtrack.)
RCA VICTOR (1860 through
2090): 54-57 15-25
(Black labels.)
RCA VICTOR (1860 through 2090): 68 .. 6-12
(Orange labels.)
RCA VICTOR (2211; "Seven Hills
Of Rome"): 58 20-30
(Soundtrack songs on one side. Other Mario Lanza
songs on the second side.)
RCA VICTOR (2331 through 2333): 59 . 12-20
(Black labels.)
RCA VICTOR (2331 through 2333): 68 .. 6-12
(Orange labels.)
RCA VICTOR (2338; "For The First
Time"): 59 20-30
(Soundtrack.)

RCA VICTOR (2339 through
2790): *60-64* $10-20
(Black labels.)
RCA VICTOR (2339 through 2790): *68* . . **6-12**
(Orange labels.)
RCA VICTOR (2800 series): *78* **4-8**
RCA VICTOR (2900 through 3200): *68-71* **8-15**
RCA VICTOR (4158; "The Mario
Lanza Collection"): *81* **35-45**
(5-LP boxed set.)

LARKIN, Billy
(Billy Larkin & The Delegates)
Singles: 7-Inch
BRYAN: *75* **2-3**
CASINO: *76* **2-3**
MELODY: **25-30**
MERCURY: *78-79* **1-3**
SUNBIRD: *81* **1-3**
WORLD PACIFIC: *66* **3-5**
LPs: 10/12-Inch 33rpm
AURA: *65-66* **12-18**
BRYAN: *75* **5-10**
WORLD PACIFIC: *65-69* **10-15**

LARKS
Singles: 78rpm
APOLLO: *51-55* **25-60**
LLOYDS: *54* **25-50**
Singles: 7-Inch
APOLLO (435; "My Lost
Love"): *51* **400-500**
APOLLO (437; "Darlin'"): *52* **400-500**
APOLLO (475; "Honey From
The Bee"): *55* **75-100**
APOLLO (1180; "Hopefully
Yours"): *51* **400-500**
APOLLO (1184; "My
Reverie"): *51* **400-500**
(Black vinyl, if it exists. May have been on colored
vinyl only.)
APOLLO (1184; "My Reverie"): *51* . . **750-1000**
(Colored vinyl.)
APOLLO (1189; "Shadrack"): *52* **400-600**
APOLLO (1190; "Stolen
Love"): *52* **500-600**
APOLLO (1194; "Hold Me"): *52* **500-600**
LLOYDS (108; "Margie"): *54* **100-150**
LLOYDS (110; "If It's A
Crime"): *54* **250-300**
LLOYDS (112; "No Other Girl"): *54* . . **400-500**
LLOYDS (114; "Forget It"): *54* **100-150**
Members: Gene Mumford; Allen Bunn; Ray Bar-
nes; Thermon Ruth; Dave McNeil; Hadie Rowe;
Orville Brooks.
Also see BUNN, Allen

LARKS
(With Don Julian)
Singles: 7-Inch
JERK: *65* $3-5
MONEY: *64-71* 3-5
LPs: 10/12-Inch 33rpm
MONEY: *65-67* 15-20
Also see JULIAN, Don

LARKS
Singles: 7-Inch
CROSS FIRE: 10-15
GUYDEN: *63* 3-5
SHERYL: *61* 3-5
STACY: *63* 3-5
VIOLET: *63* 4-6

LA ROSA, Julius
Singles: 78rpm
CADENCE: *53-55* 2-5
Singles: 7-Inch
ABC: *67* 2-3
BARNABY: *70* 1-3
CADENCE (1200 series): *53-55* 3-5
CADENCE (1400 series): *63-64* 2-4
KAPP: *60-62* 2-4
MGM: *66* 2-3
METROMEDIA: *70* 1-3
RCA VICTOR (0900 series): *73* 1-3
RCA VICTOR (6000 & 7000
series): *56-58* 2-4
ROULETTE: *59* 2-4
EPs: 7-Inch 33/45rpm
CADENCE: *54-57* 5-10
RCA VICTOR: *56* 4-8
LPs: 10/12-Inch 33rpm
CADENCE: *56* 15-20
FORUM: *60* 8-15
KAPP: *61* 8-15
MGM: *66-67* 8-12
METROMEDIA: *71* 5-10
RCA VICTOR: *56* 12-20
ROULETTE: *59* 10-18
Also see LANE BROTHERS / Julius La Rosa

LA ROSA, Julius, & The Bob Crewe Generation
Singles: 7-Inch
CREWE: *69* 1-3
Also see CREWE, Bob
Also see LA ROSA, Julius

LARRICE
Singles: 12-Inch 33/45rpm
STREETWISE: *84* 4-6

LARRY LEE: see LEE, Larry

LARSEN, Neil
Singles: 7-Inch
A&M: *79* $1-3
WARNER BROS: *83* 1-3
LPs: 10/12-Inch 33rpm
A&M: *79* 5-8
HORIZON: *78-79* 8-10
WARNER BROS: *83* 5-8
Also see LARSEN-FEITEN BAND

LARSEN-FEITEN BAND
Singles: 7-Inch
WARNER BROS: *80* 1-3
LPs: 10/12-Inch 33rpm
WARNER BROS: *80* 5-8
Members: Neil Larsen; Buzz Feiten.
Also see LARSEN, Neil

LARSON, Nicolette
Singles: 7-Inch
MCA: *86* 1-3
WARNER BROS: *78-82* 1-3
LPs: 10/12-Inch 33rpm
MCA: *86* 5-8
WARNER BROS: *78-82* 5-8
Also see DOOBIE BROTHERS, & Nicolette
Larson
Also see WINCHESTER, Jesse
Also see YOUNG, Neil

LA RUE, D.C.
Singles: 12-Inch 33/45rpm
CASABLANCA: *79-80* 4-6
PYRAMID: *78-79* 4-6
Singles: 7-Inch
CASABLANCA: *79-80* 1-3
PYRAMID: *76-79* 1-3
LPs: 10/12-Inch 33rpm
CASABLANCA: *79-80* 5-8
PYRAMID: *76-79* 5-8
Also see CHRISTIE, Lou

LA SALLE, Denise
Singles: 7-Inch
ABC: *77-79* 1-3
CHESS: *68* 3-5
MCA: *79-80* 1-3
MALACO: *81-85* 1-3
WESTBOUND: *71-75* 2-4
LPs: 10/12-Inch 33rpm
ABC: *77-78* 8-10
MCA: *80* 5-8
MALACO: *81-85* 5-8
WESTBOUND: *72-75* 8-10

LASLEY, David
Singles: 7-Inch
EMI AMERICA: *82-84* 1-3

LASSER'S, Max, Ark
LPs: 10/12-Inch 33rpm
CBS: *88* $5-8

LASSIES
Singles: 7-Inch
DECCA: *56* 5-8

LAST, James
Singles: 7-Inch
POLYDOR: *71-82* 1-3
LPs: 10/12-Inch 33rpm
POLYDOR: *72-81* 5-10

LAST POETS
Singles: 7-Inch
DOUGLAS: *71* 2-3
LPs. 10/12-Inch 33rpm
BLUE THUMB: *72-73* 5-8
DOUGLAS: *70-71* 5-10
JUGGERNAUT: *71* 5-10

LAST WORD
Singles: 7-Inch
ATCO: *67-68* 3-5
BOOM: *66* 3-5
LPs: 10/12-Inch 33rpm
ATCO: *68* 10-15

LATEEF, Yusef
(Yusef Lateef Quintet)
Singles: 7-Inch
ATLANTIC: *68-70* 2-3
IMPULSE: *64* 2-4
NEW JAZZ: *60* 2-4
PRESTIGE: *63-69* 2-4
LPs: 10/12-Inch 33rpm
ATLANTIC: *68-76* 8-15
CTI: *77-79* 5-8
CADET: *69* 8-15
CHARLIE PARKER: *62* 15-25
EVEREST: *74* 5-8
IMPULSE (56 through
9125): *63-66* 10-20
IMPULSE (9200 & 9300
series): *73-78* 8-12
MILESTONE: *73* 8-12
MOODSVILLE: *61* 20-30
NEW JAZZ: *59-61* 20-35
PRESTIGE (7100 series): *57* 25-50
PRESTIGE (7400 through
7800 series): *66-71* 8-15
PRESTIGE (24000 series): *72-74* ...8-15
RIVERSIDE (300 series): *60* 20-30
(Riverside 300 series numbers may be preceded by
a "9" or a "12.")
RIVERSIDE (3000 series): *68* 10-15
SAVOY (2200 series): *76-79* 8-12

SAVOY (12000 & 13000 series): *56-59* $20-40
TRIP: *73* 5-8
VERVE: *57* 20-40

LATIMORE, Benny
(Latimore)
Singles: 7-Inch
ATLANTIC: *69* 2-4
DADE: *67-68* 3-5
GLADES: *73-79* 1-3
MALACO: *83-86* 1-3
LPs: 10/12-Inch 33rpm
GLADES: *73-78* 6-10
MALACO: *83-86* 5-8

LATTISAW, Stacy
Singles: 7-Inch
COTILLION: *79-84* 1-3
MOTOWN: *86-88* 1-3
LPs: 10/12-Inch 33rpm
COTILLION: *79-84* 5-8
MOTOWN: *86-88* 5-8
Also see KING DREAM CHORUS &
HOLIDAY CREW

LATTISAW, Stacy, & Johnny Gill
Singles: 7-Inch
COTILLION: *84-85* 1-3
LPs: 10/12-Inch 33rpm
COTILLION: *84* 5-8
Also see GILL, Johnny
Also see LATTISAW, Stacy

LAUGHING SOUP DISH
Singles: 7-Inch
VOXX: *87* 1-3
LPs: 10/12-Inch 33rpm
VOXX: *87* 5-8

LAUPER, Cyndi
Singles: 12-Inch 33/45rpm
PORTRAIT: *83-87* 4-6
Singles: 7-Inch
PORTRAIT: *83-88* 1-3
Picture Sleeves
PORTRAIT: *83-87* 1-3
LPs: 10/12-Inch 33rpm
PORTRAIT: *83-86* 5-8
Also see HOOTERS
Also see U.S.A. FOR AFRICA

LAURA & JOHNNY
Singles: 7-Inch
SILVER FOX: *69* 2-4

LAURA LEE: see LEE, Laura

LAURAN, Niki
Singles: 12-Inch 33/45rpm
WAVE: *83* 4-6

LAUREN, Rod
Singles: 7-Inch
CHANCELLOR: *62* $3-5
RCA VICTOR: *59-62* 4-6
Picture Sleeves
RCA VICTOR: *59-60* 4-8
LPs: 10/12-Inch 33rpm
RCA VICTOR: *61* 20-25
Also see COOKE, Sam / Rod Lauren / Neil
Sedaka / Browns

LAURENCE, Paul
Singles: 12-Inch 33/45rpm
CAPITOL: *86* 4-6
Singles: 7-Inch
CAPITOL: *85-86* 1-3
LPs: 10/12-Inch 33rpm
CAPITOL: *86* 5-8

LAURIE, Annie
Singles: 78rpm
DELUXE: *47-49* 4-8
REGAL: *49* 4-8
OKEH: *55* 3-6
SAVOY: *56* 3-5
Singles: 7-Inch
DELUXE: *57-60* 5-10
DOVE: *68* 2-4
GUSTO: *78* 1-3
OKEH: *55* 5-10
RITZ: *62* 3-5
SAVOY: *56* 5-8
LPs: 10/12-Inch 33rpm
AUDIO LAB (1510; "It Hurts To Be
In Love"): *58* 30-45

LAURIE, Linda
Singles: 7-Inch
ANDIE: *60* 3-5
GLORY: *59* 5-8
KEETCH: *64* 3-5
RECONA: *63* 3-5
RUST: *60-63* 4-6

LAURIE SISTERS
Singles: 78rpm
MERCURY: *54-55* 2-4
VIK: *56* 2-4
Singles: 7-Inch
MGM: *59-60* 3-5
MERCURY: *54-55* 4-6
PORT: *63* 3-5
VIK: *56* 4-6
LPs: 10/12-Inch 33rpm
CAMDEN: *60* 15-20

LAVERNE & SHIRLEY
Singles: 7-Inch
ATLANTIC: 76-77 .... $2-3
LPs: 10/12-Inch 33rpm
ATLANTIC: 76 8-10
· Members: Penny Marshall; Cindy Williams.

LAVETTE, Betty
(Betty Lavett; Bettye LaVette)
Singles: 7-Inch
ATCO: 72 2-3
ATLANTIC: 62-63 3-5
BIG WHEEL: 66 3-5
CALLA: 65 3-5
EPIC: 75 2-3
KAREN: 68-69 2-4
LUPINE: 64 4-6
MOTOWN: 81-82 1-3
SSS INT'L: 71 1-3
SILVER FOX: 69 2-3
TCA: 71 2-4
WEST END: 2-3
LPs: 10/12-Inch 33rpm
MOTOWN: 81 5-8

LAWRENCE, Eddie
Singles: 78rpm
CORAL: 56-57 2-4
Singles: 7-Inch
CORAL: 56-63 2-4
EPIC: 65 2-3
SHASTA: 60 2-4
SIGNATURE: 60 2-4
Picture Sleeves
CORAL: 56 5-10
EPIC: 65 3-5
LPs: 10/12-Inch 33rpm
CORAL: 55-62 10-25
EPIC: 65 8-15
SIGNATURE: 59 10-20

LAWRENCE, Steve
Singles: 78rpm
CORAL: 55-57 2-4
KING: 52-53 2-5
Singles: 7-Inch
ABC: 73 1-3
ABC-PARAMOUNT: 58-60 3-5
CALENDAR: 67-68 2-3
COLUMBIA: 62-68 2-4
CORAL: 55-59 3-5
KING (1200 series): 53 4-6
KING (5000 series): 60-64 2-4
KING (15000 series): 52-53 4-8
MGM: 71-73 1-3
RCA VICTOR: 69-70 1-3

ROULETTE: 73 .... $1-3
STAGE 2: 84 1-3
20TH CENTURY-FOX: 75-77 1-3
UNITED ARTISTS (200 & 300
series): 60-61 3-5
UNITED ARTISTS (900 through
1100 series): 76-78 1-3
WARNER BROS: 78 1-3
Picture Sleeves
COLUMBIA: 62-63 3-6
STAGE 2: 84 1-3
UNITED ARTISTS: 60-61 4-8
EPs: 7-Inch 33/45rpm
COLUMBIA: 64-69 5-10
(Jukebox issues only.)
CORAL: 60 5-10
(Jukebox issues only.)
KING: 55 10-15
RCA VICTOR: 70 4-8
LPs: 10/12-Inch 33rpm
ABC-PARAMOUNT: 57-60 20-30
APPLAUSE: 81 4-8
COLUMBIA: 63-68 10-20
COLUMBIA RECORD CLUB: 75 ... 8-15
CORAL: 56-63 15-35
GALA: 77 5-8
GUEST STAR: 64 5-10
HARMONY: 68-71 6-12
KING: 58 20-30
MGM: 71 5-10
RCA VICTOR: 69-70 6-12
SESAC: 59 10-20
(Promotional issues only.)
SPINORAMA: 8-15
UNITED ARTISTS: 61-64 10-20
VERSATILE: 77 5-8
VOCALION: 66-69 5-12

LAWRENCE, Steve / Tennessee Ernie Ford
LPs: 10/12-Inch 33rpm
CAMAY: 60 15-25
Also see FORD, Tennessee Ernie

LAWRENCE, Steve, & Eydie Gorme
(Steve & Eydie)
Singles: 78rpm
CORAL: 55 2-4
Singles: 7-Inch
CALENDAR: 68 2-3
COLUMBIA: 62-67 3-5
CORAL: 55 3-5
MGM: 72-73 1-3
RCA VICTOR: 68-69 1-3

EPs: 7-Inch 33/45rpm
ABC: *60* $5-10
(Jukebox issues only.)
ADVERTISING COUNCIL (5071;
"Celebrity Spots"): 15-30
(Promotional issue only. Includes other artists.)
COLUMBIA: *64-69* 5-10
(Jukebox issues only.)
CORAL: *56* 8-12
LPs: 10/12-Inch 33rpm
ABC: *73-76* 5-10
ABC/LONGINES ("Romantic
Treasury"): *67* 30-45
(6-LP boxed set.)
ABC-PARAMOUNT: *59-64* 15-25
CBS: *63* 10-15
CALENDAR: *68* 8-15
COLUMBIA: *63-67* 10-15
CORAL: *57-60* 10-15
ENCORE: *84* 5-8
HARMONY: *64-71* 5-10
MCA: 5-10
MGM: *72-73* 5-10
PICKWICK: 5-10
RCA VICTOR: *69-72* 6-12
STAGE 2: *78-84* 4-8
UNITED ARTISTS: *61-62* 10-20
VOCALION: *67* 5-12
Also see GORME, Eydie
Also see OSMONDS, Steve Lawrence &
Eydie Gorme

LAWRENCE, Steve / Trini Lopez
LPs: 10/12-Inch 33rpm
DIPLOMAT: *65* 8-12
Also see LAWRENCE, Steve
Also see LOPEZ, Trini

LAWRENCE, Vicki
Singles: 7-Inch
BELL: *73-74* 2-3
FLASHBACK: *74* 1-3
PRIVATE STOCK: *75-76* 2-3
UNITED ARTISTS: *71* 2-4
LPs: 10/12-Inch 33rpm
WINDMILL: *79* 5-8

LAWS, Debra
Singles: 7-Inch
ELEKTRA: *80-81* 1-3
LPs: 10/12-Inch 33rpm
ELEKTRA: *81* 5-8

LAWS, Eloise
Singles: 7-Inch
ABC: *77-78* 1-3
CAPITOL: *82* 1-3

COLUMBIA: *68-70* $2-3
INVICTUS: *75-77* 2-3
LIBERTY: *80-81* 1-3
MUSIC MERCHANT: *72-73* 2-3
Picture Sleeves
LIBERTY: *80* 1-3
LPs: 10/12-Inch 33rpm
ABC: *77-78* 8-10
CAPITOL: *82* 5-8
INVICTUS: *76* 5-8
LIBERTY: *80* 5-8

LAWS, Hubert
Singles: 7-Inch
ATLANTIC: *65* 2-4
CTI: *70-75* 2-3
COLUMBIA: *78* 1-3
LPs: 10/12-Inch 33rpm
ATLANTIC: *66-81* 8-15
CTI: *70-77* 8-15
COLUMBIA: *76-80* 5-10

LAWS, Ronnie
(Ronnie Laws & Pressure)
Singles: 7-Inch
BLUE NOTE: *75-77* 2-3
CAPITOL: *83-84* 1-3
LIBERTY: *80-81* 1-3
UNITED ARTISTS: *75-80* 1-3
LPs: 10/12-Inch 33rpm
BLUE NOTE: *75-77* 6-12
CAPITOL: *83* 5-8
LIBERTY: *81* 5-8
UNITED ARTISTS: *75-80* 5-10

LAYNA, Magda
Singles: 12-Inch 33/45rpm
MEGATONE: *83* 4-6

LAYNE, Joy
Singles: 78rpm
MERCURY: *57* 2-5
Singles: 7-Inch
LUCKY FOUR: *61* 3-5
MERCURY: *57* 4-6

LAZY COWGIRLS
Singles: 7-Inch
BOMP: *87* 1-3
Picture Sleeves
BOMP: *87* 1-3
LPs: 10/12-Inch 33rpm
BOMP: *87* 5-8

LAZY RACER
Singles: 7-Inch
A&M: *79-80* 1-3

ATLANTIC (2777; "The Immigrant
Song"): 70 . . . . $10-15
(With "Do What Thou Wilt Shall Be The Whole Of
The Law" etched in the vinyl trailoff, which indi-
cates a first pressing. Valued higher than other At-
lantic Led Zeppelin singles because the flip, *Hey
Hey, What Can I Do*, is not available otherwise.)
SWAN SONG: 74-79 2-3
Promotional Singles
ATLANTIC (157; "Gallows
Pole"): 71 25-35
ATLANTIC (175; "Stairway To
Heaven"): 72 35-45
(If accompanied by its special promotional sleeve,
the price range of this issue would be approximate-
ly double.)
ATLANTIC (269; "Stairway To
Heaven"): 72 30-35
ATLANTIC (1019; "Dazed &
Confused"): 10-15
ATLANTIC (2000 series): 69-73 5-10
(Includes Mono/Stereo and Long/Short version is-
sues.)
EPs: 7-Inch 33/45rpm
ATLANTIC (7-7208; "Led
Zeppelin"): 71 35-40
(May have been a promotional issue only. Has
Rock and Roll, and *Black Dog* backed with *Stair-
way to Heaven*.)
LPs: 10/12-Inch 33rpm
ATLANTIC (7000 series): 70-73 6-10
ATLANTIC (8000 series): 69 10-15
ATLANTIC (19000 series): 77 5-8
MFSL: 82 25-50
SWAN SONG: 75-79 8-12
Members: Robert Plant; Jimmy Page; John Paul
Jones; John Bonham.
Also see DENNY, Sandy
Also see PAGE, Jimmy

Also see PLANT, Robert

LED ZEPPELIN / King Curtis
Singles: 7-Inch
ATCO (6779; "Whole Lotta
Love"): 72 . . . . $25-40
Also see KING CURTIS
Also see LED ZEPPELIN

LEDERNACKEN
Singles: 12-Inch 33/45rpm
4TH & BROADWAY: 84 4-6

LEE, Alvin
(Alvin Lee & Company; Alvin Lee & Ten Years
Later)
Singles: 7-Inch
COLUMBIA: 74 2-3
RSO: 79 1-3
LPs: 10/12-Inch 33rpm
ATLANTIC: 80-81 5-8
COLUMBIA: 73-75 10-12
LONDON: 78 8-10
RSO: 77-79 10-12
Also see TEN YEARS AFTER

LEE, Alvin, & Mylon LeFevre
Singles: 7-Inch
COLUMBIA: 74 2-3
LPs: 10/12-Inch 33rpm
COLUMBIA: 73 10-12
Also see LEE, Alvin

LEE, Bobby
Singles: 7-Inch
A-B-S (106; "Miss Mary"): 100-200
CUCA: 62 3-5
DECCA: 60-61 3-5
FALEW: 64 3-5
PORT: 67 3-5
RAMCO: 67 3-5
SUE: 66 3-5

LEE, Brenda
(Brenda Lee & The Jordanaires)
Singles: 78rpm
DECCA: 56-58 5-15
Singles: 7-Inch
DECCA (30050; "Jambalaya"): 56 15-20
DECCA (30107 through 30885): 56-59 . .10-15
(Price range of 30050 through 30333 is for black,
pink, or green label originals. Pink and green were
promotional only. Decca multi-color labels in that
series are $2-$4 1960s reissues.)
DECCA (30967 through 31570): 59-63 4-6
DECCA (31599 through 32975): 64-72 2-5
DECCA (88215; "I'm Gonna Lasso
Santa Claus"): 56 20-25
(Decca "Children's Series" issue.)

ELEKTRA: *78* $2-3
MCA: *73-86* 1-3
Picture Sleeves
DECCA (30776; "Rockin' Around
The Christmas Tree"): *59* 12-25
DECCA (30967; "Sweet
Nothin's"): *59* 25-35
DECCA (31093 through 32428): *60-69* ... 5-15
DECCA (34000 series): *62* 5-10
(Compact 33 stereo.)
DECCA (88215; "I'm Gonna Lasso
Santa Claus"): *56* 25-40
(For either 45 or 78 rpm single sleeve.)
EPs: 7-Inch 33/45rpm
DECCA: *60-65* 10-20
LPs: 10/12-Inch 33rpm
CORAL: *73* 5-8
DECCA (4039 through 4104): *60-61* 20-25
DECCA (4176 through 4755): *61-66* 15-20
DECCA (4757; "10 Golden Years"): *66* .. 15-20
("Deluxe Limited Edition," with gatefold cover.)
DECCA (4757; "10 Golden Years"): 10-12
(With standard cover.)
DECCA (4825 through 75232): *66-70* ... 10-15
(Brenda's Decca LPs, 4039 through 4955, with a
"DL" prefix were mono. Decca stereo LPs were in-
dicated by a "DL7" prefix.)
MCA (Except 700 series): *73-86* 8-10
MCA (700 series): 5-8
VOCALION: *67-70* 10-12

LEE, Brenda / Carl Dobkins, Jr.
EPs: 7-Inch 33/45rpm
DECCA (38169; "Datesetters,
U.S.A."): *60* 15-25
(A Celanese Special Products issue.)
Also see DOBKINS, Carl, Jr.

LEE, Brenda / Tennessee Ernie Ford
LPs: 10/12-Inch 33rpm
DECCA (9226; "The Brenda Lee/
Tennessee Ernie Ford Show For
Christmas Seals"): 20-30
(Promotional issue only.)
Also see FORD, Tennessee Ernie

LEE, Brenda, & Pete Fountain
Singles: 7-Inch
DECCA: *68* 2-4
LPs: 10/12-Inch 33rpm
DECCA: *68* 8-15
Also see FOUNTAIN, Pete

LEE, Brenda, & The Oak Ridge Boys
Singles: 7-Inch
MCA: *82* 1-3
Also see OAK RIDGE BOYS

LEE, Brenda, & Willie Nelson
Singles: 7-Inch
MONUMENT: *83* $1-3
Also see LEE, Brenda
Also see NELSON, Willie

LEE, Curtis
Singles: 7-Inch
ABC: *74* 1-3
DUNES: *60-63* 5-8
HOT (7; "Gotta Have You"): *60* 20-30
MCA: 1-3
MIRA: *67* 3-5
ROJAC: *67* 3-5
SABRA: *61* 10-15
WARRIOR: *59* 10-15
Picture Sleeves
DUNES: *61* 10-20

LEE, Dick
Singles: 7-Inch
ABC: *67* 2-4
BLUE BELL: *61* 3-5
CAPITOL: *68* 2-3
CENTAUR: *59* 3-5
DOT: *66* 2-4
ESSEX: *54* 3-5
FELSTED: *60* 3-5
KAPP: *69* 2-3
MGM: *59* 3-5
METRO: *65* 3-5
ROULETTE: *62-63* 2-4
20TH CENTURY-FOX: *65* 2-4
VIK: *56* 3-5
X: *55* 3-5
Picture Sleeves
FELSTED: *60* 3-6

LEE, Dickey
(Dickey Lee With The Collegiates; Dickie Lee)
Singles: 78rpm
SUN (280; "Good Lovin'"): *57* 5-8
SUN (297; "Dreamy Nights"): *57* 8-15
TAMPA: *57* 6-12
Singles: 7-Inch
ABC: *73* 1-3
ATCO: *68* 3-5
DIAMOND: *69* 3-5
DICKIE LEE STORY: *77* 15-20
(Identified as "The Dickie Lee Story," since no
label name appears on this disc. Promotional issue
only.)
DOT: *60* 8-10
ERIC: 1-3
MERCURY: *79-82* 1-3
RCA VICTOR: *70-78* 1-3

RENDEZVOUS: *62* $5-8
SMASH: *62-64* 3-5
SUN (280; "Good Lovin"): *57* 10-15
SUN (297; "Dreamy Nights"): *57* 15-25
TCF: *65* 3-5
TCF HALL: *64-65* 3-5
TAMPA: *57* 12-15
TRACIE: *67* 3-5
LPs: 10/12-Inch 33rpm
RCA VICTOR: *71-76* 6-12
MERCURY: *79-80* 5-8
SMASH: *62* 20-25
TCF HALL: *65* 15-20

LEE, Jackie
(Jackie Lee & His Orchestra)
Singles: 78rpm
CORAL: *53* 2-4
Singles: 7-Inch
CORAL: *53* 2-4

LEE, Jackie
(Earl Nelson)
Singles: 7-Inch
FAYETTE: *64* 3-5
KEYMAN: *67-68* 3-5
MIRWOOD: *65-66* 3-5
SWAN: *59* 4-6
UNI: *70* 2-4
LPs: 10/12-Inch 33rpm
MIRWOOD: *66* 15-20
Also see BOB & EARL

LEE, Jimmy, & Artis
Singles: 78rpm
MODERN: *52* 10-15
Singles: 7-Inch
MODERN: *52* 25-30

LEE, Johnny
Singles: 7-Inch
ABC/DOT: *75* 2-3
ASTRO: *80* 1-3
ASYLUM: *80-82* 1-3
EPIC: *81* 1-3
FULL MOON/WARNER BROS: *80-86* ... 1-3
GRT: *76-78* 2-3
Picture Sleeves
ASYLUM: *80* 1-3
LPs: 10/12-Inch 33rpm
ACCORD: *83* 5-8
ASYLUM: *80-81* 5-8
FULL MOON/WARNER BROS: *80-86* ... 5-8
GRT: *77* 6-10
JMS: *83* 8-12
PLANTATION: *81* 4-8
Also see GILLEY, Mickey, & Johnny Lee

LEE, Johnny / Eagles
Singles: 7-Inch
ASYLUM: *80-81* $1-3
Picture Sleeves
ASYLUM: *80* 1-3
Also see EAGLES
Also see LEE, Johnny

LEE, Julia
(Julia Lee & Her Boyfriends)
Singles: 78rpm
CAPITOL: *46-52* 5-15
Singles: 7-Inch
CAPITOL: *52* 10-20

LEE, Larry
(Larry Lee & The Four Bel-Aires; Larry Lee & Frankie Valli)
Singles: 7-Inch
COLUMBIA: *82* 1-3
GENIUS: 4-6
M.Z.(006; "Stolen Love"): 100-125
Also see OZARK MOUNTAIN DAREDEVILS
Also see VALLI, Frankie

LEE, Laura
Singles: 7-Inch
ARIOLA AMERICA: *76* 2-3
CHESS: *67-69* 3-5
COTILLION: *69* 2-4
HOT WAX: *71-72* 2-3
INVICTUS: *74* 2-3
RIC TIC: *66* 3-5
LPs: 10/12-Inch 33rpm
CHESS: *72* 8-10
HOT WAX: *72-73* 8-10
INVICTUS: *74* 8-10

LEE, Leapy: see LEAPY LEE

LEE, Leon
Singles: 7-Inch
CROSSOVER: *74* 2-4

LEE, Michele
Singles: 7-Inch
ABC-PARAMOUNT: *62-63* 3-5
COLUMBIA: *65-69* 3-5
LPs: 10/12-Inch 33rpm
COLUMBIA: *66-68* 10-15

LEE, Nickie
Singles: 7-Inch
DADE: *67* 3-5
MALA: *68-69* 3-5

LEE, Peggy
(Peggy Lee With Benny Goodman's Orchestra)
Singles: 78rpm
CAPITOL: *47-58* $3-6
DECCA: *52-57* 3-5
OKEH (6000 series): *41-42* 4-8
Singles: 7-Inch
A&M: *75* 1-3
ATLANTIC: *74* 1-3
CAPITOL (801 through 2000 series): *49-51* 4-8
CAPITOL (2100 through 3400
    series): *68-72* 2-4
CAPITOL (3800 through 5900
    series): *58-67* 3-6
CAPITOL (90000 series): 3-5
COLUMBIA: *76* 1-3
DECCA (25000 series): *64* 2-4
DECCA (28000 & 29000 series): *52-58* 3-6
DECCA (30000 series): *58-59* 2-5
EPs: 7-Inch 33/45rpm
CAPITOL (Except 100 series): *57-59* 10-20
CAPITOL (100 series): *52* 20-40
COLUMBIA: *50-51* 20-40
DECCA: *52-55* 15-30
LPs: 10/12-Inch 33rpm
A&M: *75* 5-8
ATLANTIC: *74* 5-8
CAPITOL (100 & 200 series): *50* 40-60
    (With an "H" or "T" prefix. 10-Inch LPs.)
CAPITOL (100 through 810): *69-71* 5-12
CAPITOL (864 through 1100
    series): *56-59* 20-35
CAPITOL (1200 through 2800
    series): *60-68* 10-20
    (With a "T" or "ST" prefix.)
CAPITOL (1500 through 1800
    series): *75-77* 5-8
    (With an "SM" prefix.)
CAPITOL (11000 series): *72-79* 5-8
CAPITOL (16000 series): *80* 4-8
COLUMBIA (6033; "Benny Goodman
    & Peggy Lee"): *50* 30-60
    (10-Inch LP.)
DRG: *79* 5-8
DECCA (100 series): *60-66* 10-20
DECCA (4000 series): *64* 10-20
DECCA (5000 series): *52-53* 40-60
    (10-Inch LPs.)
DECCA (8000 series): *55-59* 15-30
EVEREST: *74* 5-8
GLENDALE: *82* 4-8
HARMONY (7000 series): *58* 10-15
HARMONY (30000 series): *70* 5-10
MERCURY: *77* 5-8
VOCALION: *66-70* 6-12

Also see CROSBY, Bing, & Peggy Lee
Also see FITZGERALD, Ella, & Peggy Lee
Also see GOODMAN, Benny, Orchestra
Also see JENKINS, Gordon, & His Orchestra

LEE, Peggy, & Dean Martin
Singles: 78rpm
CAPITOL: *49* $5-8
Also see MARTIN, Dean

LEE, Peggy, & George Shearing
Singles: 7-Inch
CAPITOL: *59* 2-4
LPs: 10/12-Inch 33rpm
CAPITOL (1219; "Beauty & The
    Beat"): *59* 20-30
    (With Capitol logo on left side of label.)
CAPITOL (1219; "Beauty & The
    Beat"): *62* 10-20
    (With Capitol logo at the top of label.)
Also see SHEARING, George, Quintet

LEE, Peggy, & Mel Torme
Singles: 78rpm
CAPITOL: *49* 3-5
Singles: 7-Inch
CAPITOL: *49* 4-6
Also see LEE, Peggy
Also see TORME, Mel

LEE, Roberta
Singles: 78rpm
DECCA: *51-54* 2-4
TEMPO: *50-51* 2-5
X: *54* 2-4
Singles: 7-Inch
DECCA: *51-54* 3-5
TEMPO: *50-51* 4-6
TOWER: *68* 1-3
X: *54* 3-5

LEE, Toney
Singles: 12-Inch 33/45rpm
RADAR: *83* 4-6
Singles: 7-Inch
CRITIQUE: *85* 1-3

LEE & PAUL
Singles: 7-Inch
COLUMBIA: *59-65* 3-5
Members: Lee Pockriss; Paul Vance.
Also see VANCE, Paul

LEFEVRE, Raymond, & His Orchestra
Singles: 7-Inch
ATLANTIC: *61* 2-3
4 CORNERS: *67-68* 2-3
JAMIE: *60* 2-3
KAPP: *58-66* 2-4

MERCURY: *60* $2-3
VERVE: *62* 2-3
LPs: 10/12-Inch 33rpm
ATLANTIC: *61* 8-15
BUDDAH: *71-72* 5-10
4 CORNERS: *67-68* 5-10
KAPP: *59-66* 8-15
MONUMENT: *67* 6-12

LEFT BANKE
Singles: 7-Inch
CON AMERICA: *78* 2-4
SMASH (Except 2243): *66-69* 3-5
SMASH (2243; "Myrah"): *69* 20-30
Picture Sleeves
SMASH: *67* 4-8
LPs: 10/12-Inch 33rpm
RHINO: *85* 5-8
SMASH: *67-69* 15-20
MERCURY: *81* 5-8
Members: Michael Brown; George Cameron; Tom
Finn; Steve Martin.

LEGACY
Singles: 7-Inch
BRUNSWICK: *82* 1-3
PRIVATE I: *85* 1-3

LEGRAND, Michel, & His Orchestra
Singles: 7-Inch
A&M: *83* 1-3
BELL: *71-72* 1-3
COLUMBIA: *55-59* 2-4
DECCA: *68* 1-3
FLASHBACK: *73* 1-3
MCA: *73-76* 1-3
MGM: *67-68* 1-3
PHILIPS: *63-66* 2-3
20TH CENTURY-FOX: *77* 1-3
UNITED ARTISTS: *70* 1-3
WARNER BROS: *68-76* 1-3
Picture Sleeves
MGM: *67* 8-15
EPs: 7-Inch 33/45rpm
COLUMBIA: *56-59* 5-10
LPs: 10/12-Inch 33rpm
BELL: *72-74* 5-10
COLUMBIA (Except 3140): *55-71* 10-20
COLUMBIA (3140; "How To Save A
Marriage & Ruin Your Life"): *68* 35-40
(Soundtrack.)
GRYPHON: *75-79* 5-8
HARMONY: *66-74* 5-10
KORY: *77* 4-8
MCA: *73-76* 8-15

MGM (14; "Ice Station Zebra"): *68* $40-50
(Soundtrack.)
MERCURY: *65* 8-15
PABLO: *83* 4-8
PHILIPS: *62-64* 8-15
SPRINGBOARD: *77* 4-8
20TH CENTURY-FOX: *77* 5-10
UNITED ARTISTS: *69* 6-12
VERVE: *68-72* 8-15
WARNER BROS: *71-76* 6-12
Also see HORNE, Lena, & Michel Legrand
Also see VAUGHAN, Sarah

**LEGRAND, Michel, & The Mike
Curb Congregation**
LPs: 10/12-Inch 33rpm
AMERICAN INT'L (1039; "Wuthering
Heights"): *71* 15-20
(Soundtrack.)
Also see CURB, Mike

LEGRAND, Michel, & Noel Harrison
LPs: 10/12-Inch 33rpm
UNITED ARTISTS (295; "The Thomas
Crown Affair"): *74* 5-10
(Soundtrack.)
UNITED ARTISTS (5182; "The Thomas
Crown Affair"): *68* 12-18
(Soundtrack.)
Also see HARRISON, Noel

LEGRAND, Michel, & Matt Monro
LPs: 10/12-Inch 33rpm
DECCA (9160; "A Matter Of
Innocence"): *68* 15-25
(Soundtrack.)
Also see LEGRAND, Michel
Also see MONRO, Matt

LEHRER, Tom
Singles: 7-Inch
REPRISE: *69* 2-4
LPs: 10/12-Inch 33rpm
LEHRER: *52-53* 20-40
REPRISE: *65-66* 10-20

LE JETE
Singles: 12-Inch 33/45rpm
MEGATONE: *83* 4-6

LEKAKIS, Paul
Singles: 7-Inch
ZYX: *87* 1-3

LEMMONS, Billy
Singles: 7-Inch
ARIOLA AMERICA: *77* 2-3

LEMON PIPERS
Singles: 7-Inch
BUDDAH: *67-69* $3-5
CAROL: 8-12
ERIC: *78* 1-3
Picture Sleeves
BUDDAH: *68* 4-8
LPs: 10/12-Inch 33rpm
BUDDAH: *68* 12-15
Member: Ivan Browne.
Also see 1910 FRUITGUM COMPANY /
Lemon Pipers
Also see RAM JAM

LENNON, John
(John & Yoko; Plastic Ono Band)
Singles: 12-Inch 33/45rpm
CAPITOL (9585/6; "Imagine"/
"Come Together"): *86* 25-30
CAPITOL (9894; "Happy Xmas"): *86* .150-200
(Promotional issue only.)
CAPITOL (9917; "Rock & Roll
People"): *86* 20-25
(Promotional issue only.)
CAPITOL (9929; "Happy Xmas"): *86* . . .30-40
(Promotional issue only.)
CAPITOL (79453; "Stand By Me"): *88* . .20-25
(Promotional issue only.)
GEFFEN (919; "Starting Over"): *80* 35-45
(Promotional issue only.)
GEFFEN (1079; "Happy Xmas"): *82* 25-30
(Price range includes special sleeve. Promotional
issue only.)
POLYDOR (250; "Nobody Told
Me"): *83* 25-30
Singles: 7-Inch
APPLE (1809; "Give Peace
A Chance"): *69* .3-5
APPLE (1813; "Cold Turkey"): *69* 4-8
APPLE (1818; "Instant
Karma"): *70* 3-5
APPLE (1827; "Mother"): *70* 5-10
APPLE (1830; "Power To The People"): *71* .3-5
APPLE (1840; "Imagine"): *71* 3-5
APPLE (1842; "Happy Xmas"): *71* 8-12
(Label pictures John and Yoko.)
APPLE (1842; "Happy Xmas"): *71* 5-8
(Standard Apple label.)
APPLE (1848; "Woman Is The
Nigger Of The World"): *72* 3-5
(With Elephant's Memory.)
APPLE (1868; "Mind Games"): *73* 3-5
APPLE (1874; "Whatever Gets You
Through The Night"): *74* 3-5
APPLE (1878; "#9 Dream"): *74* 3-5
APPLE (1881; "Stand By Me"): *75* 3-5

CAPITOL: *78* $4-8
(Orange labels.)
CAPITOL: *78-88* .2-3
(Purple or black labels.)
CAPITOL STAR LINE: *77-78* 2-4
GEFFEN (0408; "Starting Over"): *83* 2-3
GEFFEN (0415; "Watching The
Wheels"): *83* 2-3
GEFFEN (29855; "Happy Xmas"): *82* 2-3
GEFFEN (49604; "Starting Over"): *80* 2-3
GEFFEN (49644; "Woman"): *80* 2-3
GEFFEN (49695; "Watching The
Wheels"): *81* 2-3
ORANGE PEEL (70078; "Interview"): *81* 12-15
(John is interviewed by David Peel. Picture disc.)
POLYDOR: *84-86* 2-3
Promotional Singles
APPLE (1809; "Give Peace
A Chance"): *69* 8-10
APPLE (1813; "Cold Turkey"): *69* 20-25
APPLE (1818; "Instant Karma"): *70* 20-25
(With *Instant Karma* on both sides of disc.)
APPLE (1818; "Instant Karma"): *70* . . 125-175
(With *Instant Karma* on one side of disc. Flip side
is a blank pressing.)
APPLE (1827; "Mother"): *70* 25-35
APPLE (1830; "Power To The
People"): *71* 15-20
APPLE (1833; "Ain't That
A Shame"): *75* 80-100
APPLE (1840; "Imagine"): *71* 10-15
APPLE (1848; "Woman Is The
Nigger Of The World"): *72* 12-15
APPLE (1868; "Mind Games"): *73* 20-30
APPLE (1874; "Whatever Gets You
Through The Night"): *74* 20-25
APPLE (1878; "#9 Dream"): *74* 20-30
APPLE (1878; "What You Got"): *74* 40-50
(There were two separate promo singles using the
same 1878 catalog number. On commercial issues
these tracks were back to back.)
APPLE (1881; "Stand By Me"): *75* 20-30
APPLE (1883; "Ain't That
A Shame"): *75* 90-125
APPLE (1883; "Slipin' &
Slidin'"): *75* 90-125
(There were two separate promo singles using the
same 1883 catalog number.)
APPLE (47663/4; "Happy
Xmas"): *71* 175-200
(White label with black print.)
COTILLION (104/5; "John Lennon On
Ronnie Hawkins"): *70* 30-35
(John Lennon promotes a 1970 Ronnie Hawkins
Cotillion LP.)

EVA-TONE ("John Lennon
  Radio Play"): *69* **$150-200**
  (Soundsheet. Originally included with an issue of
  Aspen magazine.)
GEFFEN (29855; "Happy Xmas"): *82* **8-12**
GEFFEN (49604; "Starting Over"): *80* ... **10-15**
GEFFEN (49644; "Woman"): *80* **8-12**
GEFFEN (49695; "Watching The
  Wheels"): *81* **10-12**
KYA ("KYA 1969 Peace Talk"): *69* **50-60**
  (Radio KYA's Tom Campbell & Bill Holley's
  telephone interview with John Lennon.)
POLYDOR: *84-86* **5-12**
QUAKER: *86* **10-15**
  (Soundsheet, issued with Quaker Granola Dipps.)
QUAYE/TRIDENT (3419;
  "Rock 'N' Roll"): *75* **200-250**
  (Contains a one minute radio spot for the "Rock
  'N' Roll" LP. Issued to radio stations only.)
WHAT'S IT ALL ABOUT: **15-20**

Picture Sleeves

APPLE (1809; "Give Peace
  A Chance"): *69* **10-15**
APPLE (1813; "Cold Turkey"): *69* **50-75**
APPLE (1818; "Instant Karma"): *70* ... **10-15**
APPLE (1827; "Mother"): *70* **100-150**
APPLE (1830; "Power To
  The People"): *71* **15-20**
APPLE (1842; "Happy Xmas"): *71* **10-15**
APPLE (1848; "Woman Is The Nigger
  Of The World"): *72* **10-15**
APPLE (1868; "Mind Games"): *73* **6-10**
GEFFEN (29855; "Happy Xmas"): *82* **2-3**
GEFFEN (49604; "Starting Over"): *80* **2-4**
GEFFEN (49644; "Woman"): *80* **2-4**
GEFFEN (49695; "Watching The
  Wheels"): *81* **2-4**
POLYDOR: *84* **2-4**

LPs: 10/12-Inch 33rpm

ADAM VIII LTD. (8018; "John Lennon
  Sings Great Rock & Roll
  Hits, Roots"): *75* **$150-250**
APPLE (3361; "Wedding
  Album"): *69* **75-90**
  (Price range is for complete boxed set with all in-
  serts.)
APPLE (3362; "Live Peace In
  Toronto"): *70* **30-40**
  (Includes 16-page calendar.)
APPLE (3362; "Live Peace In
  Toronto"): *70* **10-15**
  (Without 16-page calendar.)
APPLE (3372; "John Lennon, Plastic
  Ono Band"): *70* **12-15**
APPLE (3379; "Imagine"): *71* **15-20**
  (Includes bonus poster and photo card.)
APPLE (3414; "Mind Games"): *73* **8-12**
APPLE (3416; "Walls & Bridges"): *74* **8-12**
APPLE (3419; "Rock 'N' Roll"): *75* **8-12**
APPLE (3421; "Shaved Fish"): *75* **8-12**
APPLE/TETRAGRAMMATON (5001;
  "Two Virgins"): *68* **80-100**
  (With brown paper outer sleeve.)
APPLE/TETRAGRAMMATON (5001;
  "Two Virgins"): **5-8**
  (Reissue, with brown paper outer sleeve that does
  NOT cover entire jacket.)
APPLE/TETRAGRAMMATON (5001; "Two
  Virgins"): *68* **50-60**
  (Without brown paper outer sleeve.)
CAPITOL: *75-88* **5-10**
GEFFEN: *80-82* **8-10**
MFSL: *85* **15-25**
  (Half-speed mastered.)
NAUTILUS: *82* **20-25**
  (Half-speed mastered.)
POLYDOR: *84* **5-8**
SILHOUETTE: *84* **10-12**
ZAPPLE: *69* **20-30**

Promotional LPs

APPLE (3392; "Sometime In New
  York City"): *72* **125-150**
  (Issued on a white label.)
GEFFEN (2023; "John Lennon
  Collection"): *82* **20-25**
  (Quiex II "Limited Edition Pressing.")
POLYDOR (817 238-1; "Heart Play"): *83* **15-20**
  (Includes program notes and copy of a letter from
  Yoko on her stationery.)
SILHOUETTE (10014; "Reflections &
  Poetry"): *84* **35-50**
Also see BEATLES
Also see ELEPHANT'S MEMORY
Also see HAWKINS, Ronnie

Also see JOHN, Elton / John Lennon
Also see ONO, Yoko
Also see PEEL, David, & The Lower East Side

LENNON, Julian
Singles: 12-Inch 33/45rpm
ATLANTIC: 85 .... $5-8
Singles: 7-Inch
ATLANTIC: 84-86 1-3
Singles: 78rpm
BRUNSWICK: 57 2-4
CORAL: 56 2-4
Picture Sleeves
ATLANTIC: 84-85 1-3
LPs: 10/12-Inch 33rpm
ATLANTIC: 84-86 5-8

LENNON SISTERS
Singles: 7-Inch
BRUNSWICK: 57-59 3-6
CORAL: 56   3-6
DOT: 58-67 3-6
MERCURY: 68 3-5
LPs: 10/12-Inch 33rpm
BRUNSWICK: 57 5-15
DOT: 59-67 5-15
HAMILTON: 64 5-12
MERCURY: 68-69 8-12
RANWOOD: 68-81 4-8
VOCALION: 69-70 5-10
WING: 69 5-10
Members: Kathy Lennon; Peggy Lennon; Janet
Lennon; Dianne Lennon.
Also see WELK, Lawrence

LENNOX, Annie, & Al Green
Singles: 7-Inch
A&M: 88 1-3

LEON LEE: see LEE, Leon

LEONETTI, Tommy
Singles: 78rpm
CAPITOL: 54-56 3-5
Singles: 7-Inch
ATLANTIC: 60 3-6
CAPITOL: 54-56 5-10
COLUMBIA: 67-73 3-5
DECCA: 68-69 3-5
EPIC: 74 1-3
RCA VICTOR: 59-77 3-5
20TH CENTURY-FOX: 77 1-3
Picture Sleeves
COLUMBIA: 68 3-5
LPs: 10/12-Inch 33rpm
CAMDEN: 59 8-15
RCA VICTOR: 64-67 8-15

LEOPARDS
Singles: 7-Inch
LEOPARD: $10-15
VOXX: 85 2-3
LPs: 10/12-Inch 33rpm
MOON: 77 15-20
VOXX: 87 5-8

LE PAMPLEMOUSSE
Singles: 12-Inch 33/45rpm
A.V.I.: 78-85 4-6
Singles: 7-Inch
A.V.I.: 77-85 1-3
LPs: 10/12-Inch 33rpm
A.V.I.: 78-85 5-8

LEPPARD, Def: see DEF LEPPARD

LE ROUX
(Louisiana's LeRoux)
Singles: 7-Inch
CAPITOL: 78 2-3
RCA VICTOR: 82-83 1-3
LPs: 10/12-Inch 33rpm
CAPITOL: 78-81 5-8
RCA VICTOR: 82 5-8

LES COMPAGNONS DE LA CHANSON
Singles: 7-Inch
CAPITOL: 59-60 2-4

LESEAR, Anne
Singles: 7-Inch
H.C.R.C.: 84 1-3

LESTER, Bobby
Singles: 7-Inch
CHECKER: 59 5-10
COLUMBIA: 70 3-5
LPs: 10/12-Inch 33rpm
COLUMBIA: 70 10-15

LESTER, Bobby, & The Moonglows
Singles: 7-Inch
CHESS: 62 3-6
LPs: 10/12-Inch 33rpm
CHESS: 62 25-35
Also see LESTER, Bobby
Also see MOONGLOWS

LESTER, Bobby, & The Moonlighters
Singles: 78rpm
CHECKER: 54 5-10
Singles: 7-Inch
CHECKER: 54 10-12
Also see LESTER, Bobby

Ketty Lester

LESTER, Jerry
Singles: 78rpm
CORAL: 50 .... $2-4
Singles: 7-Inch
CORAL: 50 4-6

LESTER, Ketty
Singles: 7-Inch
COLLECTABLES: 1-3
ERA: 62-63 3-5
EVEREST: 62 3-5
PETE: 68-69 2-4
RCA VICTOR: 64 3-5
TOWER: 65-66 3-5

LPs: 10/12-Inch 33rpm
A.V.I.: 80 .... $5-8
ERA: 62 20-25
MEGA: 85 5-8
PETE: 69 10-12
RCA VICTOR: 64-65 10-15
SHEFFIELD: 77 8-10
TOWER: 66 10-15
  Also see EVERETT, Betty, & Ketty Lester

LET'S ACTIVE
LPs: 10/12-Inch 33rpm
I.R.S.: 84 5-8

LETTERMEN
Singles: 7-Inch
ALPHA-OMEGA: 78-88 2-4
APPLAUSE: 83 2-4
CAPITOL: 61-76 2-4
WARNER BROS: 60 3-6
Picture Sleeves
CAPITOL: 61-68 3-6
LPs: 10/12-Inch 33rpm
ALPHA-OMEGA: 77-88 5-15
APPLAUSE: 82 5-8
CANDELITE: 5-10
CAPITOL (147 through 836): 68-71 5-15
CAPITOL (1669 through 2934): 62-68 ... 10-20
  (With a "T" or "ST" prefix.)
CAPITOL (2500 & 2700 series): 4-8
  (With an "SM" prefix.)
CAPITOL (11000 series): 71-75 5-10
CAPITOL (16000 series): 80-83 4-8
LONGINES (220; "Time For
  Us"): 15-30
  (5-LP boxed set.)
LONGINES (220; "From The Lettermen,
  With Love"): 72 5-8
  (Bonus LP, issued with the above boxed set.)
PICKWICK: 77 5-8
  Members: Tony Butala; James Pike; Bob En-
  gemann; Gary Pike; Donny Pike; Chad Nichols;
  Don Campo.
  Also see PETER & GORDON / Lettermen
  Also see TONY, BOB & JIMMY

LEVEL 42
Singles: 7-Inch
A&M: 84 1-3
POLYDOR: 82-88 1-3
LPs: 10/12-Inch 33rpm
A&M: 84 5-8
POLYDOR: 82-87 5-8
  Members: Mark King; Mike Lindup; Phil Gould;
  Boon Gould; Krys Mach.

LEVERT
Singles: 7-Inch
ATLANTIC: *86-88* $1-3
TEMPRE: *85* 1-3
LPs: 10/12-Inch 33rpm
ATLANTIC: *86-88* 5-8
Members: Sean Levert; Gerald Levert; Marc Gordon.

LEVINE, Hank
(Hank Levine & The Minature Men)
Singles: 7-Inch
ABC-PARAMOUNT: *61* 2-4
DOLTON: *62-63* 2-4
TOPS: *60* 3-5
Also see MINIATURE MEN

LEVON & THE HAWKS
(Featuring Levon Helm)
Singles: 7-Inch
ATCO: *65-68* 5-8
Also see BAND
Also see HAWKINS, Ronnie
Also see HELM, Levon

LEVY, Marcy
Singles: 7-Inch
EPIC: *82* 1-3
LPs: 10/12 Inch 33rpm
EPIC: *82* 8-15
Also see CLAPTON, Eric

LEVY, Marcy, & Robin Gibb
Singles: 7-Inch
RSO: *80* 1-3
Picture Sleeves
RSO: *80* 1-3
Also see GIBB, Robin
Also see LEVY, Marcy

LEWIS, Barbara
Singles: 7-Inch
ATLANTIC: *62-67* 3-5
ENTERPRISE: *70-71* 2-3
REPRISE: *73* 2-3
LPs: 10/12-Inch 33rpm
ATLANTIC (Except 8286): *63-68* 20-35
ATLANTIC (8286; "Best Of Barbara
Lewis"): *71* 10-12
COLLECTABLES: *88* 6-8
ENTERPRISE: *70* 10-12
SOLID SMOKE: 8-10

LEWIS, Bobby
Singles: 78rpm
SPOTLIGHT: *57* 5-10
Singles: 7-Inch
ABC-PARAMOUNT: *64* 3-5
BELTONE: *61-62* 5-8

ERIC: $1-3
LANA: 1-3
ROULETTE: *59* 4-6
SPOTLIGHT: *57* 10-20
LPs: 10/12-Inch 33rpm
BELTONE: *61* 35-40

LEWIS, Gary, & The Playboys
Singles: 7-Inch
LIBERTY (Except 56144): *64-69* 3-5
LIBERTY (56144; "I Saw Elvis
Presley Last Night"): *69* 10-12
Picture Sleeves
LIBERTY: *65-67* 3-6
EPs: 7-Inch 33/45rpm
LIBERTY (227; "Doin' The Flake"): *65* . 10-20
(Liberty/Kellogg's Premium Record. Issued with paper sleeve.)
LPs: 10/12-Inch 33rpm
GUSTO: *72* 5-8
LIBERTY (Except 10000 series): *65-69* . 15-30
LIBERTY (10000 series): *81* 5-8
SUNSET: *69* 12-15
UNITED ARTISTS (Except 1000
series): *75* 8-10
UNITED ARTISTS (1000 series): *81* 5-8

LEWIS, Huey, & The News
Singles: 12-Inch 33/45rpm
CHRYSALIS: *84-86* 4-6
Singles: 7-Inch
CHRYSALIS: *80-88* 1-3
Promotional Singles
CHRYSALIS (43065; "Hip To
Be Square"): *85* 10-15
(Four-disc set, each of a different color vinyl.)
LPs: 10/12-Inch 33rpm
CHRYSALIS: *80-88* 5-8
MFSL: *85* 15-20
Members: Huey Lewis; Bill Gibson; Mario Cipollina; Sean Hopper; Chris Hayes; Johnny Colla.
Also see EDMUNDS, Dave
Also see U.S.A. FOR AFRICA

LEWIS, J.G.
Singles: 7-Inch
IX CHAINS: *76* 2-3

LEWIS, Jerry
Singles: 78rpm
CAPITOL: *50-53* 2-5
DECCA: *56-57* 2-4
Singles: 7-Inch
CAPITOL: *50-53* 3-5
DECCA: *56-62* 2-4
DOT: *60* 2-4
LIBERTY: *63* 2-4

Jerry Lee Lewis

EPs: 7-Inch 33/45rpm
CAPITOL: *56* $6-12
DECCA: *56* 5-10

LPs: 10/12-Inch 33rpm
CAPITOL: *64* 10-15
DECCA: *56* 15-25
DOT: *60* 10-15
VOCALION: *66* 8-12
Also see MARTIN, Dean, & Jerry Lewis

LEWIS, Jerry Lee
(Jerry Lee Lewis & His Pumping Piano)
Singles: 78rpm
SUN: *56-58* 8-12

Singles: 7-Inch
AMERICA SMASH: *86* 1-3
BUDDAH: *71* 2-3
ELEKTRA: *79-82* 2-3
MCA: *82-83* 1-3
MERCURY: *70-82* 2-3
SCR: *85* 2-3
SSS/SUN: *69-84* 1-3
(Includes numbers below 100 and over 1000.)
SMASH (1857 through 2122): *63-67* 4-8
SMASH (2146 through 2257): *68-70* 2-4
SUN (259; "Crazy Arms"): *56* 10-12
SUN (267 through 296): *56-58* 5-8
SUN (300 series): *58-65* 3-5

Picture Sleeves
SUN: *57-58* 10-20

EPs: 7-Inch 33/45rpm
MERCURY: *71-72* 15-20
(Promotional issues only.)
SCR: *86* 10-15
SSS/SUN: *69* 15-20
(Jukebox issues only.)
SMASH: *64-65* 20-25

SUN (107; "The Great Ball Of Fire"): *57* $25-50
(Issued with a paper sleeve.)
SUN (108; "Jerry Lee Lewis"): *57* 25-50
SUN (109; "Jerry Lee Lewis"): *58* 25-50
SUN (110; "High School
Confidential"): *58* 25-50

LPs: 10/12-Inch 33rpm
ACCORD: *81-82* 5-8
AURA: *82* 5-8
BUCKBOARD: *75* 8-10
ELEKTRA: *79-82* 5-8
EVEREST: *75* 8-10
HILLTOP: *72* 10-12
KOALA: *79* 5-8
MCA: *82-84* 5-8
MERCURY (SR series,
except 61318 & 61343): *70-72* 12-15
MERCURY (SR-61318; "In Loving
Memories"): *71* 15-20
MERCURY (SR-61343; "Touching
Home"): *71* 15-20
(Cover is mostly an artist's drawing with a small
photo of Lewis on the right side.)
MERCURY (SR-61343; "Touching
Home"): *71* 12-15
(Cover pictures Lewis standing in front of a brick
wall.)
MERCURY (SRM1 series): *72-78* 8-10
MERCURY (SRM2 series): *73* 15-20
OUT OF TOWN DIST: *82* 5-8
PICKWICK: *70-74* 10-12
POLYSTAR: 8-10
POWER PAK: *74* 8-10
RHINO: *83* 8-10
SCR: *85* 5-10
SSS/SUN: *69-84* 5-8
SEARS: 10-12
SMASH (040; "The Golden Hits Of
Jerry Lee Lewis"): *64* 20-25
SMASH (040; "The Golden Rock Hits
Of Jerry Lee Lewis"): 10-12
(Reissue, using a slightly different title.)
SMASH (056 through 086): *64-66* 20-25
SMASH (097; "Soul My Way"): *67* 25-30
(Smash numbers 040 through 097 were preceded
by a "27" for mono issues or a "67" for stereo
releases.)
SMASH (7000 series): *82* 5-8
SMASH (67104 through 67131): *68-70* .. 10-15
SUN (1230; "Jerry Lee Lewis"): *58* 45-55
SUN (1265; "Jerry Lee's
Greatest"): *62* 35-45
SUNNYVALE: *77* 8-10
TRIP: *74* 8-10

WING (Except PKW2 series): *66-67* . . . **$12-15**
WING (PKW2 series): *69* **20-25**
Promotional LPs
MERCURY (690; "Jerry Lee Lewis
Radio Special"): *73* **35-40**
Also see MEYERS, Augie
Also see NELSON, Willie / Jerry Lee Lewis /
Carl Perkins / David Allan Coe

LEWIS, Jerry Lee, & Friends
Singles: 7-Inch
SSS/SUN (1139; "Save The Last Dance
For Me"): *80* **2-3**
LPs: 10/12-Inch 33rpm
SSS/SUN (1011; "Duets"): *78* **8-10**
Members: Jerry Lee Lewis; Jimmy Ellis; Charlie
Rich.
Also see RICH, Charlie

LEWIS, Jerry Lee / Curly Bridges /
Frank Motley
LPs: 10/12-Inch 33rpm
DESIGN: *63* **10-15**

LEWIS, Jerry Lee / Johnny Cash
LPs: 10/12-Inch 33rpm
SSS/SUN: *71* **8-10**
Also see CASH, Johnny
Also see PERKINS, Carl, Jerry Lee Lewis,
Roy Orbison & Johnny Cash

LEWIS, Jerry Lee & Linda Gail
Singles: 7-Inch
SMASH: *69-70* **2-4**
SUN: *63* **3-5**
LPs: 10/12-Inch 33rpm
SMASH: *69* **15-20**

LEWIS, Jerry Lee / Roger Miller /
Roy Orbison
LPs: 10/12-Inch 33rpm
PICKWICK: **8-10**
Also see MILLER, Roger
Also see ORBISON, Roy

LEWIS, Jerry Lee, Carl Perkins &
Charlie Rich
LPs: 10/12-Inch 33rpm
SSS/SUN (1018; "Trio +"): *78* **8-10**
(With Jimmy Ellis.)
Also see ELLIS, Jimmy
Also see LEWIS, Jerry Lee, & Friends
Also see PERKINS, Carl

LEWIS, Jerry Lee / Charlie Rich /
Johnny Cash
LPs: 10/12-Inch 33rpm
POWER PAK: **8-10**

Also see CASH, Johnny, Carl Perkins & Jerry
Lee Lewis
Also see LEWIS, Jerry Lee
Also see RICH, Charlie

LEWIS, Jimmy
(Jimmy Lewis & The L.A. Street Band)
Singles: 7-Inch
HOTLANTA: *75* **$2-3**
MCA: *84* **1-3**
LPs: 10/12-Inch 33rpm
HOTLANTA: *74* **5-10**

LEWIS, Marcus
Singles: 7-Inch
AEGIS: *88* **1-3**

LEWIS, Ramsey
(Ramsey Lewis Trio; Ramsey Lewis & Co.)
Singles: 12-Inch 33/45rpm
COLUMBIA: *79-85* **4-6**
Singles: 7-Inch
ABC: *74* **1-3**
ARGO: *58-65* **2-4**
CADET: *65-72* **2-3**
CHESS: *73* **1-3**
COLUMBIA: *72-87* **1-3**
EMARCY: *59* **2-4**
EPs: 7-Inch 33/45rpm
ARGO: *61* **10-15**
LPs: 10/12-Inch 33rpm
ARGO (600 series): *58-62* **20-40**
ARGO (700 series): *62-65* **15-25**
CADET: *65-72* **8-15**
COLUMBIA: *72-85* **5-10**
EMARCY: *59* **20-40**
TRIP: *75* **5-8**
Members: Ramsey Lewis; Eldee Young; Red Holt.
Also see EARTH, WIND & FIRE & RAM-
SEY LEWIS
Also see WILSON, Nancy
Also see YOUNG-HOLT UNLIMITED

LEWIS, Smiley
Singles: 78rpm
COLONY: *52* **20-40**
DELUXE: *47* **20-40**
IMPERIAL: *50-57* **10-20**
Singles: 7-Inch
DOT: *64* **4-6**
IMPERIAL (5194; "The Bells Are
Ringing"): *52* **50-75**
IMPERIAL (5208 through 5279): *52-54* . **25-50**
(Black vinyl.)
IMPERIAL (5200 series): *53* **60-80**
(Colored vinyl.)
IMPERIAL (5296 through 5325): *54* **20-40**

IMPERIAL (5349 through 5418): *55-56* **$10-20**
IMPERIAL (5431 through 5820): *57-62* . . . **4-8**
KNIGHT: *59* **4-8**
LOMA: *65* **3-5**
OKEH: *62* **3-5**
LPs: 10/12-Inch 33rpm
IMPERIAL (9141; "I Hear You
Knocking"): *61* **125-200**

LEWIS, Webster
(Webster Lewis & The Post-Pop Space Rock Be-Bop Gospel Tabernacle Orchestra & Chorus; Webster Lewis & Love Unlimited Orchestra)
Singles: 12-Inch 33/45rpm
EPIC: *77* **4-6**
UNLIMITED GOLD: *81* **4-6**
Singles: 7-Inch
EPIC: *77-81* **1-3**
UNLIMITED GOLD: *81* **1-3**
LPs: 10/12-Inch 33rpm
EPIC: *78-80* **5-8**
UNLIMITED GOLD: *81* **5-8**

LEWIS & CLARKE
(Lewis & Clarke Expedition)
Singles: 7-Inch
CHARTMAKER: *66* **4-6**
COLGEMS: *67-68* **3-5**
Picture Sleeves
COLGEMS: *67* **5-10**
LPs: 10/12-Inch 33rpm
COLGEMS: *67* **12-15**
Members: Travis Lewis; Boomer Clarke.
Also see MURPHEY, Michael

LIA
Singles: 7-Inch
VIRGIN: *88* **1-3**

LIA, Orsa
Singles: 7-Inch
INFINITY: *79* **1-3**
RCA VICTOR: *68* **2-4**

LIBERACE
Singles: 78rpm
COLUMBIA: *52-57* **2-4**
DECCA: *52* **3-5**
Singles: 7-Inch
A.V.I.: *76-77* **1-3**
COLUMBIA (39000 through 41000
series): *52-58* **2-4**
CORAL: *59-61* **2-4**
DECCA (28000 series): *52* **3-5**
DOT: *64-67* **2-3**
MGM: *73* **1-3**
WARNER BROS: *71* **1-3**

EPs: 7-Inch 33/45rpm
COLUMBIA: *52-56* **$5-12**
DECCA (28000 series): *52* **8-12**
LPs: 10/12-Inch 33rpm
ABC: *74* **4-8**
A.V.I.: *73-79* **4-8**
COLUMBIA (500 through 1200
series): *53-58* **10-20**
COLUMBIA (6000 series): *52* **15-25**
COLUMBIA (9800 series): *69* **5-10**
CORAL: *59-64* **8-15**
DECCA: *72* **5-10**
DOT: *63-68* **5-15**
FORWARD: *69* **5-10**
HARMONY: *59-70* **5-10**
HAMILTON: *65* **5-10**
MISTLETOE: *74* **4-8**
PARAMOUNT: *73-74* **5-10**
TRIP: *76* **4-8**
VOCALION: *68* **5-10**
WARNER BROS: *71* **5-10**

LIEBERMAN, Lori
Singles: 7-Inch
CAPITOL: *72-75* **2-3**
MILLENIUM: *78* **2-3**
LPs: 10/12-Inch 33rpm
CAPITOL: *72-74* **8-10**

LIFESTYLE
Singles: 7-Inch
MCA: *77* **2-3**
LPs: 10/12-Inch 33rpm
MCA: *77* **8-10**

LIGGETT, Otis
Singles: 12-Inch 33/45rpm
EMERGENCY: *83* **4-6**
Singles: 7-Inch
EMERGENCY: *83* **1-3**

LIGGINS, Jimmy
(Jimmy Liggins & His 3-D Music)
Singles: 78rpm
ALADDIN: *54* **5-10**
SPECIALTY (500 series): *47-49* **5-10**
(The Specialty 500 series precedes the 300 & 400 series. Specialty's first 25 releases, all 78rpm only, were 500 series numbers. Then they began the 300 series and numbered consecutively until 499, at which time [August, 1954] they picked up at 526 and continued.)
Singles: 7-Inch
ALADDIN: *54* **15-25**
DUPLEX: **3-5**
SPECIALTY (300 & 400 series): *49-54* . . **15-25**
(Black vinyl.)
SPECIALTY (Colored vinyl): *53* **30-50**

WHISKEY, GIN & WINE
(Joe Liggins)
JOE LIGGINS
AND
HIS "HONEYDRIPPERS"
Vocal by Joe Liggins
SP 402 A

(Most Specialty singles are currently available, using original catalog numbers.)

LIGGINS, Joe
(Joe Liggins & His Honeydrippers)
Singles: 78rpm
DOT: $5-10
EXCLUSIVE: *45-48* 5-8
MERCURY: *54* 4-6
SPECIALTY: *49* 5-8
Singles: 7-Inch
ALADDIN. *56* 10-15
MERCURY: *54* 10-15
SPECIALTY: *51-54* 15-25
(Most Specialty singles are currently available, using original catalog numbers.)
Also see MILTON, Roy / Joe Liggins

LIGHT, Enoch, & His Orchestra
(Terry Snyder & The All-Stars; Command All-Stars; Enoch Light & The Light Brigade)
Singles: 7-Inch
COMMAND: *61* 2-4
LPs: 10/12-Inch 33rpm
COMMAND: *59-66* 5-15
GRAND AWARD: *59* 5-10
PROJECT: *67-71* 5-10

LIGHTFOOT, Gordon
(Gord Lightfoot)
Singles: 7-Inch
ABC-PARAMOUNT: *62* 8-15
REPRISE: *70-77* 2-5
UNITED ARTISTS: *65-69* 3-6
WARNER BROS (Except 5600
  series): *78-86* 1-3
WARNER BROS (5600 series): *65* 4-6
Picture Sleeves
UNITED ARTISTS (50152; "The Way
  I Feel"): *67* 5-10

LPs: 10/12-Inch 33rpm
LIBERTY: *80* $5-8
MFSL: *78* 25-50
PICKWICK: *79* 4-8
REPRISE (Except 2237): *70-76* 5-12
REPRISE (2237; "Gord's Gold"): *75* 10-15
UNITED ARTISTS (Except 400
  series): *70-74* 5-10
UNITED ARTISTS (400 series): *66-69* .10-15
  (U.A. 400 series numbers may be preceded by a
  "3," for monaural, or a "6," for stereo issues.)
WARNER BROS: *78-86* 5-8

LIGHTHOUSE
Singles: 7-Inch
EVOLUTION: *71-72* 2-4
POLYDOR: *73-74* 2-3
RCA VICTOR: *69-70* 2-4
LPs: 10/12-Inch 33rpm
EVOLUTION: *71-72* 10-12
JANUS: *76* 8-10
POLYDOR: *73-74* 8-10
RCA VICTOR: *69-70* 10-15

LIMAIIL
(Chris Hamill)
Singles: 12-Inch 33/45rpm
EMI AMERICA: *85-86* 4-6
Singles: 7-Inch
EMI AMERICA: *85-86* 1-3
LPs: 10/12-Inch 33rpm
EMI AMERICA: *85-86* 5-8
  Also see KAJAGOOGOO

LIME
Singles: 12-Inch 33/45rpm
PRISM: *83* 4-6
TSR: *85* 4-6
Singles: 7-Inch
PRISM: *83* 1-3
LPs: 10/12-Inch 33rpm
PRISM: *83* 5-8

LIMELITERS
Singles: 7-Inch
ELEKTRA: *60-61* 3-5
RCA VICTOR: *61-64* 3-5
WARNER BROS: *68* 2-4
Picture Sleeves
RCA VICTOR: *61-63* 5-10
LPs: 10/12-Inch 33rpm
CAMDEN: *74* 5-10
ELEKTRA: *60-61* 15-20
LEGACY: *70* 8-10
PICKWICK: *72* 5-8
RCA VICTOR (Except ANL1
  series): *61-68* 10-20

RCA VICTOR (ANL1 series): *77* **$5-8**
STAX: *74* **6-10**
WARNER BROS: *68* **8-15**
  Members: Glen Yarbrough; Lou Gottlieb; Alex
  Hassilev; Ernie Sheldon.
  Also see YARBROUGH, Glen

LIMIT
    Singles: 12-Inch 33/45rpm
PORTRAIT: *84* **4-6**
    Singles: 7-Inch
ARISTA: *82* **1-3**
PORTRAIT: *84* **1-3**

LIMITED WARRANTY
    Singles: 7-Inch
ATCO: *86* **1-3**

LIMMIE & FAMILY COOKIN'
    Singles: 7-Inch
AVCO: *72* **2-3**

LIND, Bob
    Singles: 7-Inch
CAPITOL: *71* **2-4**
VERVE/FOLKWAYS: *66* **3-5**
WORLD PACIFIC: *65-66* **3-5**
    LPs: 10/12-Inch 33rpm
CAPITOL: *71* **10-12**
VERVE/FOLKWAYS: *66* **10-15**
WORLD PACIFIC: *66* **10-15**
  Also see CASCADES

LINDEN, Kathy
    Singles: 7-Inch
CAPITOL: *62-63* **3-5**
FELSTED: *58-59* **4-6**
MONUMENT: *60-61* **3-5**
NATIONAL: **3-5**
RECORD PROD. CORP: *61* **3-5**
    Picture Sleeves
FELSTED: *58-59* **5-10**
MONUMENT: *60-61* **3-5**
    EPs: 7-Inch 33/45rpm
FELSTED: *58* **25-35**
    LPs: 10/12-Inch 33rpm
FELSTED: *59* **30-50**

LINDISFARNE
    Singles: 7-Inch
ATCO: *78* **1-3**
ELEKTRA: *72-73* **2-3**
    LPs: 10/12-Inch 33rpm
ATCO: *78* **8-10**
ELEKTRA: *71-74* **10-12**

LINDLEY, David
    Singles: 7-Inch
ASYLUM: *81* **1-3**

    LPs: 10/12-Inch 33rpm
ASYLUM: *81* **$5-8**
ELEKTRA: *88* **5-8**
  Also see BROWNE, Jackson

LINDSAY, Mark
    Singles: 7-Inch
COLUMBIA: *69-75* **2-4**
GREEDY: *76* **2-3**
WARNER BROS: *77* **2-3**
    LPs: 10/12-Inch 33rpm
COLUMBIA: *70-71* **10-12**
  Also see REVERE, Paul, & The Raiders

LINER
    Singles: 7-Inch
ATCO: *79* **1-3**
    LPs: 10/12-Inch 33rpm
ATCO: *79* **5-8**

LINK-EDDY COMBO
    Singles: 7-Inch
REPRISE: *61* **3-5**

LINKLETTER, Art
    Singles: 7-Inch
CAPITOL: *69* **2-3**
    EPs: 7-Inch 33/45rpm
COLUMBIA: *56* **5-10**
WORD: *69* **3-5**
    LPs: 10/12-Inch 33rpm
CAPITOL: *61* **8-15**
COLUMBIA: *56* **10-20**
HARMONY: *59* **8-15**
20TH CENTURY-FOX: *63-66* **8-15**
WORD: *68* **5-10**

LINX
    Singles: 7-Inch
CHRYSALIS: *81* **1-3**
    Picture Sleeves
CHRYSALIS: *81* **1-3**
    LPs: 10/12-Inch 33rpm
CHRYSALIS: *81* **5-8**
  Members: David Grant; Peter Martin.
  Also see GRANT, David

LIONS & GHOSTS
    LPs: 10/12-Inch 33rpm
EMI AMERICA: *87* **5-8**

LIPPS, INC.
    Singles: 7-Inch
CASABLANCA: *79-83* **1-3**
    LPs: 10/12-Inch 33rpm
CASABLANCA: *79-81* **5-8**

LIQUID GOLD
    Singles: 12-Inch 33/45rpm
CRITIQUE: *83* **4-6**

PARACHUTE: *79* $4-6
Singles: 7-Inch
CRITIQUE: *83* 1-3
PARACHUTE: *79* 1-3
LPs: 10/12-Inch 33rpm
PARACHUTE: *79* 5-8

LIQUID LIQUID
Singles: 12-Inch 33/45rpm
99 RECORDS: *83* 4-6

LIQUID SMOKE
Singles: 7-Inch
AVCO EMBASSY: *70* 2-3
LPs: 10/12-Inch 33rpm
AVCO EMBASSY: *70* 10-12

LISA
Singles: 12-Inch 33/45rpm
MOBY DICK: *83-84* 4-6

LISA LISA
(Lisa Lisa & Cult Jam With Full Force)
Singles: 12-Inch 33/45rpm
COLUMBIA: *85-86* 4-6
Singles: 7-Inch
COLUMBIA: *85-88* 1-3
LPs: 10/12-Inch 33rpm
COLUMBIA: *84-87* 5-8
Member: Lisa Velez.
Also see FULL FORCE
Also see KING DREAM CHORUS &
HOLIDAY CREW

LITES, Shirley
Singles: 12-Inch 33/45rpm
WEST END: *83* 4-6

LITTER
Singles: 7-Inch
PROBE: *69* 15-25
SCOTTY: 30-40
WARICK: *67* 30-40
LPs: 10/12-Inch 33rpm
HEXAGON (681; "$100 Fine"): *69* ...100-150
PROBE (4504; "Emerge"): *69* 50-100
WARICK (671; "Distortions"): *68* 150-200

LITTLE, Rich
Singles: 7-Inch
BOARDWALK: *82* 1-3
MERCURY: *71* 2-3
LPs: 10/12-Inch 33rpm
BOARDWALK: *82* 5-8
CAEDMON: *72* 5-10
KARR: *68* 8-15
MERCURY: *71* 8-10

LITTLE ANTHONY & THE
IMPERIALS
(Anthony & The Imperials; Imperials)
Singles: 7-Inch
APOLLO: *61* $5-10
AVCO: *74-75* 2-4
DCP: *64-66* 4-8
END (Except 1027): *58-62* 5-10
END (1027; "Tears On My Pillow"): *58* . 10-20
(Shown as by "The Imperials.")
END (1027; "Tears On My Pillow"): *58* .. 5-10
(Shown as by "Little Anthony & The Imperials.")
JANUS: *71-72* 2-4
MCA: *80* 1-3
OLD HIT: 1-3
PCM: *83* 1-3
PURE GOLD: *76* 1-3
ROULETTE: *61-63* 4-6
UNITED ARTISTS: *69-70* 3-5
VEEP: *66-68* 3-5
Picture Sleeves
DCP: *65* 6-12
VEEP: *66* 5-10
EPs: 7-Inch 33/45rpm
END: *58-59* 50-75
LPs: 10/12-Inch 33rpm
ACCORD: *83* 5-8
AVCO: *74* 8-10
DCP: *64-66* 15-20
END (303; "We Are The Imperials"): *59* 50-100
END (311; "Shades Of The '40s"): *60* ... 25-50
FORUM CIRCLE: 10-15
LIBERTY: *81* 5-8
ROULETTE: *65* 20-25
SUNSET: *70* 10-12
UNITED ARTISTS (Except 1000
series): *69-74* 10-15
UNITED ARTISTS (1000 series): *80* 5-8

VEEP: *66-68* $12-15
Members: Anthony Gourdine; Clarence Collins; Sam Strain; Tracy Lord; Ernie Wright; Gloucester Rogers.
Also see IMPERIALS
Also see O'JAYS

LITTLE ANTHONY & THE IMPERIALS / Platters
LPs: 10/12-Inch 33rpm
EXACT: *80* 5-8
Also see LITTLE ANTHONY & THE IMPERIALS
Also see PLATTERS

LITTLE BEAVER
Singles: 7-Inch
CAT: *72-76* 2-4

LITTLE BILL & THE BLUENOTES
Singles: 7-Inch
DOLTON: *59* 10-15
LPs: 10/12-Inch 33rpm
CAMELOT: *60* 50-75
Members: Bill Engelhart; Buck England; Tom Morgan.

LITTLE BO
(Eddie Bo)
Singles: 78rpm
ACE: *55* 10-20
Singles: 7-Inch
ACE: *55* 25-40

LITTLE BOOKER
(James Booker)
Singles: 78rpm
IMPERIAL: *54* 15-25
Singles: 7-Inch
ACE: *58* 5-10
IMPERIAL: *54* 30-50
Also see BOOKER, James

LITTLE CAESAR
Singles: 78rpm
BIG TOWN: *53* 5-10
RPM: *53* 5-10
RECORDED IN HOLLYWOOD: *53* 5-10
Singles: 7-Inch
BIG TOWN: *53* 10-20
RPM: *53* 10-20
RECORDED IN HOLLYWOOD: *53* ... 10-20

LITTLE CAESAR & THE CONSULS
Singles: 7-Inch
MALA: *65* 8-10

LITTLE CAESAR & THE ROMANS
Singles: 7-Inch
DEL-FI: *61* 10-15

LPs: 10/12-Inch 33rpm
DEL-FI (1218; "Memories Of Those Oldies But Goodies"): *61* $50-75
Members: Carl Burnett; David Johnson; Leroy Sanders; Johnny Simmons.
Also see BLUE JAYS / Little Caesar & The Romans

LITTLE DIPPERS
(Anita Kerr Singers)
Singles: 7-Inch
DOT: *64* 2-4
UNIVERSITY: *59-60* 3-5
Also see KERR, Anita

LITTLE ESTHER
(Little Esther Phillips)
Singles: 78rpm
DECCA: *54* 5-10
FEDERAL: *51-53* 10-20
SAVOY: *56* 3-6
Singles: 78rpm
MODERN: *49-50* 10-15
Singles: 7-Inch
ATLANTIC: *64-67* 3-5
DECCA: *54* 15-25
FEDERAL (12023; "I'm A Bad Girl"): *51* 35-40
FEDERAL (12042: "Crying & Sighing"): *51* 35-40
FEDERAL (12055 through 12142): *51-53* 20-30
Note: Federal 12100 is included in the LITTLE ESTHER & THE ROBINS section.
FEDERAL (12344; "Heart To Heart"): *58* 10-20
KUDU: *72-76* 2-3
LENOX: *62-63* 3-5
SAVOY (1100 series): *56* 5-8
SAVOY (1500 series): *58-59* 4-6
WARWICK: *60-61* 3-5
LPs: 10/12-Inch 33rpm
ATLANTIC (Except 8000 series): *70-76* ..8-10
ATLANTIC (8000 series): *65-66* 12-15
KING (622; "Memory Lane"): *59* 800-1000
KUDU: *72-76* 8-10
LENOX (227; "Release Me"): *62* 20-30
MERCURY: *78-81* 5-8
YORKSHIRE: 8-10
Also see PHILLIPS, Esther

LITTLE ESTHER & BIG AL DOWNING
Singles: 7-Inch
LENOX: *63* 3-5
Also see DOWNING, Al

LITTLE ESTHER & LITTLE WILLIE LITTLEFIELD
Singles: 78rpm
FEDERAL: 52 ....$5-10
Singles: 7-Inch
FEDERAL: 52 20-25
Also see LITTLEFIELD, Little Willie

LITTLE ESTHER & MEL WALKER
Singles: 78rpm
FEDERAL: 52 5-10
SAVOY: 50 8-15
Singles: 7-Inch
FEDERAL: 52 20-25
SAVOY: 50 25-35

LITTLE ESTHER & THE DOMINOES
Singles: 78rpm
FEDERAL: 51 40-80
Singles: 7-Inch
FEDERAL (12016; "The Deacon
Moves In"): 51 300-400
FEDERAL (12036; "Heart To
Heart"): 51 250-350
Also see DOMINOES

LITTLE ESTHER & THE ROBINS
Singles: 7-Inch
FEDERAL (12100, "Saturday Night
Daddy"): 52 100-175
SAVOY: 50 35-45
Also see LITTLE ESTHER
Also see OTIS, Johnny
Also see ROBINS

LITTLE EVA
Singles: 7-Inch
ABC: 74 1-3
AMY: 65-66 3-5
BELL: 72 2-3
DIMENSION: 62-65 4-6
MCA: 80 1-3
SPRING: 70 2-4
VERVE: 66 3-5
Picture Sleeves
DIMENSION: 64 20-30
LPs: 10/12-Inch 33rpm
DIMENSION: 62 35-45
Also see IRWIN, Big Dee
Also see KING, Carole / Little Eva / Cookies

LITTLE FEAT
Singles: 7-Inch
WARNER BROS: 70-78 2-3
LPs: 10/12-Inch 33rpm
MFSL (013; "Waiting For
Columbus"): 78 75-125
WARNER BROS: 70-88 ....$6-10
Promotional LPs
WARNER BROS (984; "Hoy Hoy"): 81 . 15-20
Members: Lowell George; Ken Gradney; Richard
Hayward; Kenny Gradney; Sam Clayton; Emilio
Castillo; Elliot Ingber; Steve Kupka; Fred Tackett;
Paul Barrere; Pete Kleinow; Bill Payne; Len Pick-
ett.
Also see BRAMLETT, Bonnie
Also see CARTER, Valerie
Also see COODER, Ry
Also see GEORGE, Lowell
Also see HARRIS, Emmylou
Also see ZEVON, Warren

LITTLE JO ANN
Singles: 7-Inch
KAPP: 62 8-10

LITTLE JOE & THE THRILLERS
(Little Joe; Little Joe The Thriller)
Singles: 7-Inch
ENJOY: 64 3-5
EPIC (9000 series): 58 4-6
MGM: 70-73 2-3
OKEH: 56-61 5-8
REPRISE: 63 3-5
ROSE: 63 3-5
20TH CENTURY-FOX: 61 3-5
EPs: 7-Inch 33/45rpm
EPIC (7198; "Little Joe &
The Thrillers"): 58 75-100
Member: Joe Cook.

LITTLE JOE BLUE
Singles: 7-Inch
CHECKER: 66 3-5
MOVIN': 66 3-5

LITTLE JOEY & THE FLIPS
(Joey Hall)
Singles: 7-Inch
JOY: 62 8-10

LITTLE JUNIOR'S BLUE FLAMES
(Junior Parker)
Singles: 78rpm
SUN: 53 15-25
Singles: 7-Inch
SUN: 53 35-50
Also see PARKER, Little Junior

LITTLE MAC & THE BOSS SOUNDS
Singles: 7-Inch
ATLANTIC: 65 3-5
Member: Ann Mason.

LITTLE MILTON
(Milton Campbell)
Singles: 78rpm
METEOR: 57 .... $15-25
Singles: 7-Inch
BOBBIN: *59-61* 6-12
CHECKER (1000 & 1100 series): *62-68* ... 3-6
CHECKER (1200 series): *68-71* 2-4
CHESS: *73-76* 2-3
GLADES: *76-78* 2-3
MCA: *83* 1-3
MALACO: *84-86* 1-3
METEOR: *57* 30-50
STAX: *72-82* 1-3
SUN (194; "Beggin' My
  Baby"): *53* 50-100
SUN (200; "If You Love
  Me"): *54* 50-100
SUN (220; "Homesick For
  My Baby"): *55* 100-200
LPs: 10/12-Inch 33rpm
CHECKER: *65-70* 10-15
CHESS: *72-76* 10-12
GLADES: *76-77* 8-10
MCA: *83* 5-8
MALACO: *84-86* 5-8
STAX: *73-81* 8-10

LITTLE MILTON & ALBERT KING
LPs: 10/12-Inch 33rpm
STAX: *79* 5-8
Also see KING, Albert
Also see LITTLE MILTON

LITTLE RICHARD
(Little Richard & His Band)
Singles: 78rpm
RCA VICTOR: *52* 20-40
SPECIALTY: *56-57* 5-10
Singles: 7-Inch
ABC: *73* 1-3
ATLANTIC: *63* 3-5
BELL: *73* 2-4
BRUNSWICK: *68* 3-5
CORAL: *63* 3-5
END: *59* 5-10
GREEN MOUNTAIN: *73* 2-4
KENT: *73* 2-4
MCA: *86* 1-3
MANTICORE: *75* 2-3
MERCURY: *61* 3-5
MODERN: *66-67* 3-5
OKEH: *66-69* 3-5
PEACOCK: *53-54* 15-20
RCA VICTOR (4392; "Taxi
  Blues"): *51* 75-100

RCA VICTOR (4582; "Get Rich
  Quick"): *52* $75-100
RCA VICTOR (4772; "Why Did
  You Leave Me?"): *52* 75-100
RCA VICTOR (5025; "Please Have
  Mercy On Me"): *52* 75-100
REPRISE: *70-72* 2-4
SPECIALTY (561 through 664): *56-59* ...5-10
SPECIALTY (670 through 699): *59-64* 4-8
SPECIALTY (SPBX series): *85* 12-15
(Boxed sets of six colored vinyl 45s. Most Special-
ty singles are currently available, using original
catalog numbers.)
TRIP: *71* 2-3
VEE JAY: *64* 3-5
WARNER BROS: *87* 1-3
Picture Sleeves
MODERN: *66* 10-20
OKEH: *66* 5-10
SPECIALTY: *57-58* 10-15
(Some Specialty singles with original catalog num-
bers are also currently available with picture
sleeves.)
EPs: 7-Inch 33/45rpm
CAMDEN: *56* 40-60
KAMA SUTRA: *70* 12-15
SPECIALTY: *56-57* 20-30
LPs: 10/12-Inch 33rpm
ACCORD: *81* 5-8
BUDDAH: *69* 10-12
CAMDEN (420; "Little
  Richard"): *56* 100-150
CAMDEN (2430; "Every Hour"): *70* 10-12
CORAL: *63* 15-20
CROWN: *63* 15-20
CUSTOM: 10-12
EPIC: *71* 10-12
EVEREST: *82* 5-8
EXACT: *80-81* 5-8
51 WEST: 5-8
GRT: *77* 5-8
GOLD DISC: 10-12
GUEST STAR: *64* 10-12
KAMA SUTRA: *70* 10-12
MERCURY: *61* 20-25
MODERN: *66* 10-15
OKEH: *67* 10-15
PICKWICK: *72* 10-12
REPRISE: *70-72* 10-12
ROULETTE: *68* 10-15
SCEPTER: 10-12
SPECIALTY (100; "Here's Little
  Richard"): *57* 200-250
(First pressings were numbered 100, later issues
were cataloged as 2100.)

FEDERAL (12100 series,
except 12148): *52-54* $30-60
FEDERAL (12148; "Miss K.C.'s
Fine"): *53* 50-75
FEDERAL (12200 series): *54* 25-50
FEDERAL (12300 series): *57-59* 8-15
RHYTHM: *56* 20-30
Also see LITTLE ESTHER & LITTLE WIL-
LIE LITTLEFIELD

LITTLEFIELD, Little Willie /
Goree Carter
Singles: 78rpm
FREEDOM: *49* 10-20
Also see LITTLEFIELD, Little Willie

LIVE
Singles: 7-Inch
T.S.O.B.: *81* 1-3

LIVERPOOL FIVE
Singles: 7-Inch
RCA VICTOR: *65-67* 5-10
LPs: 10/12-Inch 33rpm
RCA VICTOR: *66-67* 20-25

LIVIGNI, John
Singles: 7-Inch
RAINTREE: *75* 2-3

LIVIN' PROOF
Singles: 7-Inch
JU-PAR: *77* 2-4

LIVING COLOUR
LPs: 10/12-Inch 33rpm
EPIC: *88* 5-8

LIVING STRINGS
Singles: 7-Inch
COMMAND: *59* 1-3
GRAND AWARD: *59* 1-3
LPs: 10/12-Inch 33rpm
CAMDEN: *60-62* 4-8
COMMAND: *59* 4-8
GRAND AWARD: *59* 4-8

LIZARD, King:
see KING LIZARD

LIZZY BORDEN
LPs: 10/12-Inch 33rpm
ENIGMA/METAL BLADE: *86-87* 5-8

LLOYD, Charles, Quartet
LPs: 10/12-Inch 33rpm
ATLANTIC: *67* 8-12
COLUMBIA: *64-65* 8-15
Also see HAMILTON, Chico, & Charles
Lloyd

LLOYD, Ian
Singles: 7-Inch
POLYDOR: *76* $2-3
SCOTTI BROTHERS: *79* 2-3
LPs: 10/12-Inch 33rpm
POLYDOR: *76* 5-10
SCOTTI BROTHERS: *79* 5-8
Also see STORIES

LOAF, Meat: see MEAT LOAF

LOBO
(Kent Lavole)
Singles: 7-Inch
BIG TREE: *71-75* 3-5
ELEKTRA: *80* 2-3
EVERGREEN: 2-3
FLASHBACK: *73* 1-3
MCA: *79* 1-3
MARIANNE: *77* 2-3
WARNER BROS: *76-78* 2-4
LPs: 10/12-Inch 33rpm
BIG TREE: *71-75* 10-12
CALUMET: *73* 10-12
MCA: *79* 5-8

LOCKLIN, Hank
Singles: 78rpm
DECCA: *52* 3-5
FOUR STAR: *52-54* 3-5
Singles: 7-Inch
COUNTRY ARTISTS: *83* 1-3
DECCA (29000 series): *52* 4-6
FOUR STAR (1500 & 1600 series): *52-54* . . 4-6
KING (5000 series): *59* 3-5
MGM: *74* 2-3
PLANTATION: *76-77* 2-3
RCA VICTOR (0030 through 0900
series): *72-74* 2-3
RCA VICTOR (6100 through 7600
series): *55-59* 3-6
RCA VICTOR (7700 through 9900
series): *60-71* 2-5
EPs: 7-Inch 33/45rpm
RCA VICTOR: *58-61* 8-12
LPs: 10/12-Inch 33rpm
CAMDEN: *62-74* 8-15
DESIGN: *62* 10-15
INTERNATIONAL AWARD: 8-12
KING (600 & 700 series): *61* 12-18
MGM: *75* 5-10
METRO: *65* 10-15
PICKWICK/HILLTOP: *65-68* 8-15
PLANTATION: *77-81* 5-8
RCA VICTOR (Except 1600
series): *62-71* 8-15

RCA VICTOR (1600 series): *58* $20-25
SEARS: 8-12
WRANGLER: *62* 15-25
Also see SNOW, Hank / Hank Locklin / Porter
Wagoner

**LOCKLIN, Hank, With Danny Davis &
The Nashville Brass**
Singles: 7-Inch
RCA VICTOR: *69-70* 2-3
LPs: 10/12-Inch 33rpm
RCA VICTOR: *70* 6-10
Also see LOCKLIN, Hank

LOCKSMITH
Singles: 7-Inch
ARISTA: *80* 1-3
LPs: 10/12-Inch 33rpm
ARISTA: *80* 5-8

LODGE, John
Singles: 7-Inch
LONDON: *77* 2-3
LPs: 10/12-Inch 33rpm
LONDON: *76* 8-10
Also see HAYWARD, Justin, & John Lodge
Also see MOODY BLUES

LOFGREN, Nils
Singles: 7-Inch
A&M: *75-77* 2-3
LPs: 10/12-Inch 33rpm
A&M (Except 8362): *75-82* 8-10
A&M (8362; "Authorized Bootleg"): *76* . . 25-30
(Promotional issue only.)
BACKSTREET: *81* 5-8
EPIC: *76* 8-10
Also see GRIN

LOGG
Singles: 7-Inch
SALSOUL: *81* 1-3
LPs: 10/12-Inch 33rpm
SALSOUL: *81* 5-8

LOGGINS, Dave
Singles: 7-Inch
EPIC: *74-81* 1-3
VANGUARD: *72-74* 2-3
LPs: 10/12-Inch 33rpm
CAPITOL: *84* 5-8
EPIC: *74-81* 8-10
VANGUARD: *72* 8-10
Also see MURRAY, Anne, & Dave Loggins

LOGGINS, Kenny
Singles: 12-Inch 33/45rpm
COLUMBIA: *81-86* 4-6
Singles: 7-Inch

COLUMBIA: *77-88* $1-3
LPs: 10/12-Inch 33rpm
COLUMBIA (Except 45000 series): *72-88* 8-10
COLUMBIA (45000 series): *81* 10-15
(Half-speed mastered.)
Also see U.S.A. FOR AFRICA

LOGGINS, Kenny, & Stevie Nicks
Singles: 7-Inch
COLUMBIA: *78* 1-3
Also see NICKS, Stevie

LOGGINS, Kenny, & Steve Perry
Singles: 7-Inch
COLUMBIA: *82* 1-3
Also see LOGGINS, Kenny
Also see PERRY, Steve

LOGGINS & MESSINA
Singles: 7-Inch
COLUMBIA: *72-76* 2-3
LPs: 10/12-Inch 33rpm
COLUMBIA (30000 series): *72-82* 8-10
COLUMBIA (44000 series): *82* 10-15
(Half-speed mastered.)
Members: Kenny Loggins; Jim Messina.
Also see LOGGINS, Kenny
Also see MESSINA, Jim

**LOGGINS & MESSINA / David
Bromberg**
LPs: 10/12-Inch 33rpm
COLUMBIA: *72* 8-15
(Promotional issue only.)
Also see BROMBERG, David
Also see LOGGINS & MESSINA

LOLITA
Singles: 7-Inch
4 CORNERS: *65* 2-4
KAPP: *60-61* 3-5
Picture Sleeves
KAPP: *61* 8-12
LPs: 10/12-Inch 33rpm
KAPP: *61* 15-20

LOMAX, Jackie
Singles: 7-Inch
APPLE: *68-71* 3-5
CAPITOL: *77* 2-3
EPIC: *68* 3-5
WARNER BROS: *71-73* 2-4
LPs: 10/12-Inch 33rpm
APPLE: *69* 15-20
CAPITOL: *76-77* 5-10
WARNER BROS: *71-72* 8-12
Also see BADGER
Also see CLAPTON, Eric
Also see McCARTNEY, Paul

Also see STARR, Ringo

LOMBARDO, Guy
(Guy Lombardo & His Royal Canadians)
Singles: 7-Inch
CAPITOL: 59-67 .... $2-4
DECCA: 50-73 2-4
EPs: 7-Inch 33/45rpm
CAPITOL: 56-59 4-6
DECCA: 50-59 4-8
RCA VICTOR: 60 4-6
LPs: 10/12-Inch 33rpm
CAMDEN: 54-65 5-15
CAPITOL: 56-81 5-15
DECCA: 50-67 5-15
LONDON: 73 4-8
MCA: 75 4-8
RCA VICTOR: 72-77 4-8
VOCALION: 66-68 5-10
Also see ARMSTRONG, Louis, & Guy Lombardo

LONDON, Julie
Singles: 78rpm
LIBERTY: 55-57 3-5
Singles: 7-Inch
BETHLEHEM: 59 3-5
LIBERTY: 55-68 3-6
Picture Sleeves
LIBERTY: 61 5-10
EPs: 7-Inch 33/45rpm
BETHLEHEM: 59 10-20
LIBERTY: 55 10-20
LPs: 10/12-Inch 33rpm
GUEST STAR: 64 5-10
LIBERTY (Black vinyl,
green label): 55-57 20-40
LIBERTY (Colored vinyl): 58 20-40
LIBERTY (Black label): 58-68 10-20

SUNSET: 66-68 .... $8-12
UNITED ARTISTS: 75 5-8

**LONDON, Julie, & The Bud
Shank Quintet**
LPs: 10/12-Inch 33rpm
LIBERTY: 66 10-15
Also see LONDON, Julie
Also see SHANK, Bud

LONDON, Laurie
Singles: 7-Inch
CAPITOL: 58-59 4-6
ROULETTE: 59 3-5
EPs: 7-Inch 33/45rpm
CAPITOL: 58 20-30
LPs: 10/12-Inch 33rpm
CAPITOL: 58 30-45

LONDON SYMPHONY ORCHESTRA
(With Ian Anderson)
Singles: 7-Inch
RCA VICTOR (14262; "Elegy"): 86 1-3
LPs: 10/12-Inch 33rpm
RCA VICTOR (7067; "A Classic
Case"): 86 8-10

LONE JUSTICE
Singles: 7-Inch
GEFFEN: 85-87 1-3
LPs: 10/12-Inch 33rpm
GEFFEN: 85 5-8
Member: Tony Gilkyson.
Also see X

LONG, Shorty
Singles: 7-Inch
RCA VICTOR: 56 4-6
SOUL: 64-68 3-5
TRI-PHI: 62 4-6
VALLEY: 30-40
LPs: 10/12-Inch 33rpm
SOUL: 68-69 10-15

LONGET, Claudine
Singles: 7-Inch
A&M: 66-70 2-3
BARNABY: 70-73 1-3
LPs: 10/12-Inch 33rpm
A&M: 67-69 5-10
BARNABY: 70-72 5-8

LONGMIRE, Wilbert
Singles: 7-Inch
TAPPAN ZEE: 79-80 1-3
LPs: 10/12-Inch 33rpm
TAPPAN ZEE: 79-80 5-8

LOOKING GLASS
Singles: 7-Inch
EPIC: 72-74 .... $2-3
LPs: 10/12-Inch 33rpm
EPIC: 72-73 10-12

LOOSE CHANGE
Singles: 7-Inch
CASABLANCA: 79-80 1-3
LPs: 10/12-Inch 33rpm
CASABLANCA: 79 5-8

LOOSE ENDS
Singles: 12-Inch 33/45rpm
MCA: 85-86 4-6
Singles: 7-Inch
MCA: 85-88 1-3
LPs: 10/12-Inch 33rpm
MCA: 85-88 5-8

LOOSE JOINTS
Singles: 12-Inch 33/45rpm
4TH & BROADWAY: 84 4-6
Singles: 7-Inch
4TH & BROADWAY: 84 1-3

LOPEZ, Denise
Singles: 7-Inch
VENDETTA: 88 1-3
LPs: 10/12-Inch 33rpm
A&M: 88 5-8

LOPEZ, Trini
Singles: 7-Inch
CAPITOL: 71-72 2-3
D.R.A: 61 4-6
GRIFFIN: 73 2-3
KING (5100 series): 58-59 8-12
KING (5200 through 5400
series): 59-61 4-6
KING (5800 series): 63 3-5
MARIANNE: 77 1-3
PRIVATE STOCK: 75 2-3
REPRISE: 63-71 3-5
ROULETTE: 78 1-3
UNITED MODERN: 64 3-5
VOLK: 58 10-20
Picture Sleeves
REPRISE: 62-66 4-8
EPs: 7-Inch 33/45rpm
COLUMBIA/WARNER BROS (124178;
"Trini Lopez Sings His Greatest Hits"): 67 .. 4-8
(A Coca-Cola/Fresca special products issue.)
KING: 63 8-15
LPs: 10/12-Inch 33rpm
CAPITOL: 72 5-10
EXACT: 81 5-8
GRIFFIN: 72 8-10

HARMONY: 70 .... $8-10
KING: 63 10-15
REPRISE: 63-69 8-15
ROULETTE: 78 5-8
Also see LAWRENCE, Steve / Trini Lopez

LOR, Denise
Singles: 7-Inch
LIBERTY: 56 2-4
MAJAR: 54 3-5
MERCURY: 55 2-4
EPs: 7-Inch 33/45rpm
MERCURY: 55 5-8

LORBER, Jeff
(Jeff Lorber Fusion)
Singles: 12-Inch 33/45rpm
ARISTA: 85 4-6
Singles: 7-Inch
ARISTA: 79-85 1-3
INNER CITY: 78 2-3
WARNER BROS: 86 1-3
LPs: 10/12-Inch 33rpm
ARISTA: 79-85 5-8
INNER CITY: 78 5-10
Members: Kenny Gorelick; Karyn White; Michael
Jeffries.
Also see G., Kenny
Also see UNLIMITED TOUCH

LORD, C.M.
Singles: 12-Inch
MONTAGE: 82-84 4-6
WAVE: 83 4-6
Singles: 7-Inch
CAPITOL: 76 2-3
MONTAGE: 82-84 1-3
LPs: 10/12-Inch 33rpm
CAPITOL: 76 8-10
MONTAGE: 84 5-8

LORD ROCKINGHAM'S XI
Singles: 7-Inch
LONDON: 58 4-6

LORD SUTCH
(Lord Sutch & His Heavy Friends)
LPs: 10/12-Inch 33rpm
COTILLION: 70-72 15-20
Also see BECK, Jeff
Also see BLACKMORE, Ritchie
Also see HOPKINS, Nicky
Also see MOON, Keith
Also see PAGE, Jimmy

LORELEIS
Singles: 7-Inch
BRUNSWICK: 64 3-5
SPOTLIGHT: 55 5-8

LOREN, Bryan
Singles: 12-Inch 33/45rpm
PHILLY WORLD: 83-84 .... $4-6
Singles: 7-Inch
PHILLY WORLD: 83 1-3

LORETTA LYNN: see LYNN, Loretta

LORING, Gloria
Singles: 7-Inch
MGM: 72 2-3
LPs: 10/12-Inch 33rpm
ATLANTIC: 86 5-8

LORING, Gloria, & Carl Anderson
Singles: 7-Inch
CARRERE: 86 1-3
LPs: 10/12-Inch 33rpm
EPIC: 85 5-8
Also see ANDERSON, Carl
Also see LORING, Gloria

LOS ADMIRADORES
LPs: 10/12-Inch 33rpm
COMMAND: 60 8-15

LOS BRAVOS
Singles: 7-Inch
LONDON: 1-3
PARROT: 68 3-5
PRESS: 66-68 3-5
LPs: 10/12-Inch 33rpm
PARROT: 68 15-25
PRESS: 66 20-25
Member: Mike Kennedy.
Also see DRIFTERS / Lesley Gore / Roy Orbison / Los Bravos
Also see KENNEDY, Mike

LOS INDIOS TABAJARAS
Singles: 7-Inch
RCA VICTOR: 63-64 2-4
LPs: 10/12-Inch 33rpm
RCA VICTOR (1800 series): 58 15-20
RCA VICTOR (2800 & 2900
series): 63-64 8-15

LOS LOBOS
Singles: 12-Inch 33/45rpm
SLASH: 86 5-8
(Promotional issue only.)
Singles: 7-Inch
SLASH: 83-87 1-3
LPs: 10/12-Inch 33rpm
SLASH: 83-88 5-8
Member: David Hidalgo.

LOS POP-TOPS: see POP-TOPS

LOST GENERATION
Singles: 7-Inch
BRUNSWICK: 70-71 .... $2-4
INNOVATION: 74 2-4
LPs: 10/12-Inch 33rpm
BRUNSWICK: 70 10-12

LOU, Bonnie
Singles: 78rpm
KING: 55 3-5
Singles: 7-Inch
FRATERNITY: 58 4-8
KING: 55 4-8

LOUDERMILK, John D.
Singles: 7-Inch
COLUMBIA: 58-60 4-8
MUSIC IS MEDICINE: 78-79 2-3
RCA VICTOR: 61-69 3-5
WARNER BROS: 71 2-3
Picture Sleeves
COLUMBIA: 58 10-20
RCA VICTOR: 62 5-10
LPs: 10/12-Inch 33rpm
MUSIC IS MEDICINE: 78 5-8
RCA VICTOR: 61-69 15-20
WARNER BROS: 71 8-12
Also see DEE, Johnny

LOUDNESS
LPs: 10/12-Inch 33rpm
ATCO: 85-87 5-8

LOUISIANA'S LE ROUX:
see LE ROUX

LOVE
Singles: 7-Inch
BLUE THUMB: 69-70 3-5
ELEKTRA: 66-70 5-8
RSO: 74-75 3-5
LPs: 10/12-Inch 33rpm
BLUE THUMB: 69-70 12-15
ELEKTRA (4000 series): 66-67 30-50
(Monaural.)
ELEKTRA (74000 series,
except 74058): 66-70 20-30
ELEKTRA (74058; "Revisited"): 70 20-30
(With gatefold cover.)
ELEKTRA (74058; "Revisited"): 81 5-8
(With standard cover.)
MCA: 82 5-8
RSO: 74 8-10
RHINO (Except picture discs): 80 5-8
RHINO (Picture discs): 82 8-10
Members: Arthur Lee; John Echols; Ken Forssi;
Bryan Maclean; Alban Pfisterer.

LOVE, Candace
Singles: 7-Inch
AQUARIUS: *68* $3-6

LOVE, Darlene
Singles: 7-Inch
PHILLES (111; "The Boy I'm Gonna Marry"/
"My Heart Beat A Little Bit"): *63* 10-15
PHILLES (111; "The Boy I'm Gonna Marry"/
"Playing For Keeps"): *63* 8-10
PHILLES (114; "Wait Till My
Bobby Gets Home"): *63* 8-15
PHILLES (117; "A Fine, Fine Boy"): *63* ..8-15
PHILLES (119; "Christmas, Baby
Please Come Home"): *63* 15-25
PHILLES (123; "He's A Quiet Guy"): *64* 25-30
PHILLES (125; "Christmas, Baby
Please Come Home"): *64* 15-25
REPRISE: *66* 4-6
RHINO: *86*..........................5-8
WARNER/SPECTOR: *74-77* 2-4
LPs: 10/12-Inch 33rpm
CBS: *88* 5-10
Also see BOB B. SOXX & THE BLUE
JEANS
Also see BLOSSOMS
Also see CRYSTALS
Also see RONETTES / Crystals / Darlene
Love / Bob B. Soxx & The Blue Jeans

LOVE, Le Juan
Singles: 7-Inch
LUKE SKY: *88* 1-3
LPs: 10/12-Inch 33rpm
LUKE SKY: *88* 5-8

LOVE, Mary
Singles: 7-Inch
JOSIE: *68* 3-5
MODERN: *65-66* 3-5

LOVE, Ronnie
Singles: 7-Inch
D TOWN: 5-8
DOT: *60-61* 4-6

LOVE, Rudy, & The Love Family
Singles: 7-Inch
CALLA: *76* 2-3
LPs: 10/12-Inch 33rpm
CALLA: *76* 5-8

LOVE, Vikki, With Nuance
Singles: 12-Inch 33/45rpm
4TH & BROADWAY: *85* 4-6
Singles: 7-Inch
4TH & BROADWAY: *85* 1-3
Also see NUANCE

LOVE & KISSES
Singles: 7-Inch
CASABLANCA: *77-79* $1-3
LPs: 10/12-Inch 33rpm
CASABLANCA: *77-79* 8-10

LOVE & ROCKETS
Singles: 7 Inch
BIG TIME: *86* 1-3
LPs: 10/12-Inch 33rpm
BIG TIME: *86-87* 5-8
Members: David Jor; Kevin Haskins; Daniel Ash.

LOVE BUG STARSKI
Singles: 12-Inch 33/45rpm
ATLANTIC: *85* 1-3
FEVER: *83* 4-6

**LOVE CHILD'S AFRO CUBAN
BLUES BAND**
(Love Child's Latin Soul Afro Blues Band)
Singles: 7-Inch
A&M: *69*...........................2-4
ROULETTE: *75* 2-3

LOVE CLUB
Singles: 12-Inch 33/45rpm
WEST END: *83* 4-6

LOVE COMMITTEE
Singles: 7-Inch
ARIOLA AMERICA: *75-76* 2-3
GOLD MIND: *77-78* 2-3

LOVE GENERATION
Singles: 7-Inch
IMPERIAL: *67-68* 3-5
LPs: 10/12-Inch 33rpm
IMPERIAL: *68* 10-15
UNITED ARTISTS: *77* 8-10
Also see CLIMAX

LOVE, PEACE & HAPPINESS
Singles: 7-Inch
RCA VICTOR: *71-72* 2-3
LPs: 10/12-Inch 33rpm
RCA VICTOR: *71* 8-10

LOVE UNLIMITED
(Love Unlimited Orchestra)
Singles: 7-Inch
CASABLANCA: 1-3
MCA: 1-3
20TH CENTURY-FOX: *73-77* 2-3
UNI: *72* 2-4
UNLIMITED GOLD: *77-84* 1-3
LPs: 10/12-Inch 33rpm
20TH CENTURY-FOX: *74-76* 8-10
UNLIMITED GOLD: *77-84* 5-8
Also see WHITE, Barry

LOVELITES
Singles: 7-Inch
BANDERA: *67* $8-10
LOCK: *69* 3-5
LOVELITE: *70-71* 2-4
PHI-DAN: *66* 8-10
20TH CENTURY-FOX: *73* 2-4
UNI: *69-70* 2-4
LPs: 10/12-Inch 33rpm
UNI: *70* 10-15

LOVELY, Ike
Singles: 7-Inch
WAND: *73* 2-4

LOVERBOY
Singles: 7-Inch
COLUMBIA: *81-86* 1-3
Picture Sleeves
COLUMBIA: *81-85* 1-3
LPs: 10/12-Inch 33rpm
COLUMBIA (Except 169961): *80-86* 5-8
COLUMBIA (169961; "Loverboy"): *82* .. 8-12
Members: Mike Reno; Matthew Frenette; Paul
Dean; Doug Johnson; Scott Smith.
Also see RENO, Mike, & Ann Wilson

LOVERDE
Singles: 12-Inch 33/45rpm
MOBY DICK: *83* 4-6

LOVERS
Singles: 78rpm
DECCA: *56* 4-8
Singles: 7-Inch
ALADDIN: *58* 5-10
DECCA: *56* 8-15
IMPERIAL: *62-63* 4-6
KELLER: *61* 4-8
LAMP: *57-58* 15-20
POST: *63* 4-6
Member: Tarheel Slim.
Also see TARHEEL SLIM

LOVERS
Singles: 7-Inch
MARLIN: *77* 2-3

LOVESMITH
(Michael Lovesmith)
Singles: 7-Inch
MOTOWN: *81-85* 1-3
LPs: 10/12-Inch 33rpm
MOTOWN: *81* 5-8

LOVETT, Lyle
Singles: 7-Inch
MCA/CURB: *88-89* 1-3

LPs: 10/12-Inch 33rpm
MCA/CURB: *88-89* : $5-8

LOVETTE, Eddie
Singles: 7-Inch
STEADY: *69* 3-5
LPs: 10/12-Inch 33rpm
STEADY: *70* 8-10

LOVICH, Lene
Singles: 7-Inch
STIFF: *79-83* 1-3
LPs: 10/12-Inch 33rpm
STIFF: *79-83* 5-8

LOVIN' SPOONFUL
Singles: 7-Inch
ERIC: *78* 1-3
KAMA SUTRA: *65-72* 3-5
Picture Sleeves
KAMA SUTRA: *65-67* 5-10
LPs: 10/12-Inch 33rpm
BACK-TRAC: *85* 5-8
BUDDAH: *73* 8-10
51 WEST: 5-8
GRT: *76* 8-15
GUSTO: 5-8
KAMA SUTRA (Except 8000
series): *70-76* 10-15
KAMA SUTRA (8000 series): *65-69* 15-30
Members: John Sebastian; Zalman Yanovsky; Joe
Butler; Steve Boone; Jerry Yester.
Also see SEBASTIAN, John

LOW, Gary
Singles: 12-Inch 33/45rpm
QUALITY: *83* 4-6

LOWE, Bernie
(Bernie Lowe Orchestra)
Singles: 7-Inch
CAMEO: *58-63* 3-5
LPs: 10/12-Inch 33rpm
CAMEO: *62-63* 12-15

LOWE, Jim
Singles: 78rpm
DOT: *55-57* 3-5
MERCURY: *53-54* 3-5
Singles: 7-Inch
BUDDAH: *68* 2-4
DECCA: *60-61* 3-5
DOT (15300 through 16200
series): *55-60* 4-6
DOT (16600 series): *64* 3-5
MERCURY: *53-54* 4-6
20TH CENTURY-FOX: *63* 3-5
UNITED ARTISTS: *67* 2-4

EPs: 7-Inch 33/45rpm
DOT: *57* $10-20
MERCURY: *56* 10-20
LPs: 10/12-Inch 33rpm
DOT (3051; "The Green Door"): *57* 25-30
DOT (3681; "The Green Door"): *66* 10-15
(Monaural.)
DOT (25681; "The Green Door"): *66* 10-15
(Stereo.)
MERCURY: *56* 20-25

LOWE, Nick
(Nick Lowe & Rockpile; Nick Lowe & His Cowboy Outfit)
Singles: 7-Inch
COLUMBIA: *78-86* 1-3
LPs: 10/12-Inch 33rpm
COLUMBIA: *78-86* 5-10
Also see EDMUNDS, Dave, & Nick Lowe
Also see NICK & ELVIS
Also see ROCKPILE

LOWE, Nick, & Dave Edmunds
Singles: 7-Inch
COLUMBIA: *81* 2-3
EPs: 7-Inch 33/45rpm
COLUMBIA (1219; "Nick Lowe & Dave Edmunds Sing The Everly Brothers"): *80* .. 5-8
(Promotional issue only.)
Also see EDMUNDS, Dave
Also see LOWE, Nick

LOWRELL
Singles: 7-Inch
AVI: *78-80* 1-3
Also see SIMON, Lowrell

LOZ NETTO: see NETTO, Loz

L'TRIMM
Singles: 7-Inch
ATLANTIC: *88* 1-3
LPs: 10/12-Inch 33rpm
ATLANTIC: *88* 5-8

LUBOFF, Norman, Choir
Singles: 7-Inch
COLUMBIA: *54-59* 2-3
EPs: 7-Inch 33/45rpm
COLUMBIA: *54-59* 3-6
LPs: 10/12-Inch 33rpm
COLUMBIA: *54-60* 5-15
HARMONY: *61* 4-8
RCA VICTOR: *61-62* 4-8

LUCAS, Carrie
Singles: 12-Inch 33/45rpm
CONSTELLATION: *84-85* 4-6

Singles: 7-Inch
CONSTELLATION: *84-85* $1-3
SOLAR: *79-82* 1-3
SOUL TRAIN: *77* 2-3
LPs: 10/12-Inch 33rpm
CONSTELLATION: *85* 5-8
SOLAR: *79-82* 5-8
SOUL TRAIN: *77* 8-10

LUCAS, Carrie, & The Whispers
Singles: 7-Inch
CONSTELLATION: *85* 1-3
Also see LUCAS, Carrie
Also see WHISPERS

LUCAS, Frank
Singles: 7-Inch
ICA: *77-78* 2-3

LUCAS, Matt
Singles: 7-Inch
DOT: *63-64* 3-5
SMASH: *63* 3-5

LUGEE & THE LIONS
Singles: 7-Inch
ROBBEE: *61* 50-60
Members: Lou Christie; Kay Chick; Amy Sacco; Bill Faveck.
Also see CHRISTIE, Lou
Also see CLASSICS

LUGO, Danny, & The Destinations
Singles: 12-Inch 33/45rpm
C&M: *84* 4-6

LUKE, Robin
Singles: 7-Inch
BERTRAM INTERNATIONAL (Except 206): *58-59* 8-10
BERTRAM INTERNATIONAL (206; "Susie Darlin'"): *58* 15-20
DOT: *58-61* 4-6
Picture Sleeves
BERTRAM INTERNATIONAL (206; "Susie Darlin'"): *58* 25-35
DOT: *60* 8-10
EPs: 7-Inch 33/45rpm
DOT: *60* 20-30

LUKE, Robin, & Roberta Shore
Singles: 7-Inch
DOT: *62* 3-5
Also see LUKE, Robin

LULU
(Lulu & The Luvers)
Singles: 7-Inch
ALFA: *81-82* 1-3

ATCO: *69-72* $2-4
CHELSEA: *73-75* 2-4
EPIC: *67-68* 3-5
PARROT (9000 series): *64-65* 5-8
PARROT (40000 series): *67* 3-5
ROCKET: *78* 2-4

Picture Sleeves

ALFA (7006; "I Could Never
    Miss You More"): *81* 3-6
    (Pictures Lulu not wearing a headband.)
ALFA (7006; "I Could Never
    Miss You More"): *81* 1-3
    (Pictures Lulu wearing a headband.)
EPIC: *67-68* 3-6

LPs: 10/12-Inch 33rpm

ALFA: *81* 5-8
ATCO: *70-72* 10-12
CAPRICORN: *74* 8-10
CHELSEA: *73-77* 10-12
EPIC: *67-70* 10-15
HARMONY: *70* 10-12
PARROT (6/71016; "From Lulu
    With Love"): *67* 50-100
    (Monaural numbers begin with "6," stereo with
    "7.")
PICKWICK: *73* 8-10
ROCKET: *78* 5-8
Also see CLARK, Dave, Five / Lulu

LUMAN, Bob

Singles: 78rpm

IMPERIAL: *57* 10-20

Singles: 7-Inch

CAPITOL: *58* 10-20
EPIC: *68-77* 2-5
HICKORY (1200 series): *63-64* 4-8
HICKORY (1300 through 1500
    series): *65-70* 3-5
IMPERIAL (5705; "Red Cadillac &
    A Black Mustache"): *60* 10-20
    (Black label. Reissue of 8311.)
IMPERIAL (8311; "Red Cadillac &
    A Black Mustache"): *57* 25-50
    (Maroon label.)
IMPERIAL (8313; "Red Hot"): *57* 30-50
    (Maroon label.)
IMPERIAL (8313; "Red Hot"): *59* 20-25
    (Black label.)
IMPERIAL (8315; "Make Up
    Your Mind Baby"): *57* 15-25
    (Maroon label.)
IMPERIAL (8315; "Make Up
    Your Mind Baby"): *59* 5-8
    (Black label.)
POLYDOR: *77-78* 2-5
WARNER BROS: *59-62* 5-10

Bob Luman

Picture Sleeves

WARNER BROS: *60-62* $12-25

EPs: 7-Inch 33/45rpm

HICKORY (124-006: "Selections From
    Livin' Lovin' Sounds"): *65* 10-20
    (Promotional "Six-Pac" issue only.)
ROLLIN' ROCK: 4-6
WARNER BROS: *60* 15-25

LPs: 10/12-Inch 33rpm

EPIC: *68-77* 8-15
HARMONY: *72* 10-15
HICKORY (124; "Livin' Lovin'
    Sounds"): *65* 10-20
HICKORY (4000 series): *74* 8-10
POLYDOR: *78* 8-10
WARNER BROS: *60* 25-35

LUMAN, Bob, & Sue Thompson

Singles: 7-Inch

HICKORY: *63* 3-5
Also see LUMAN, Bob
Also see THOMPSON, Sue

LUNAR FUNK

Singles: 7-Inch

BELL: *72* 2-3

LUND, Art, & His Orchestra

Singles: 78rpm

CORAL: *52-57* 2-4
MGM: *47-55* 2-5

Singles: 7-Inch

CORAL: *52-58* 2-4
MGM: *50-55* 2-5
UNITED ARTISTS: *65* 2-3

EPs: 7-Inch 33/45rpm

MGM: *54-55* 4-8

LPs: 10/12-Inch 33rpm

MGM: *55* 5-15

LUNDBERG, Victor
Singles: 7-Inch
LIBERTY: *67* $2-4
LPs: 10/12-Inch 33rpm
LIBERTY: *68* 8-15

LUNDY, Pat
(Pat Lundi)
Singles: 7-Inch
COLUMBIA: *67-68* 2-4
DELUXE: *69* 2-4
HEIDI: *65* 3-5
LEOPARD: 2-5
PYRAMID: *76* 2-3
RCA VICTOR: *73* 2-3
TOTO: *62* 3-5
VIGOR: *75* 1-3
LPs: 10/12-Inch 33rpm
COLUMBIA: *68* 10-12
PYRAMID: *76* 5-8

LUNDY, Pat, & Bobby Harris
Singles: 7-Inch
HEIDI: *65* 3-5
Also see HARRIS, Bobby
Also see LUNDY, Pat

LUSHUS DAIM & THE PRETTY VAIN
Singles: 7-Inch
MOTOWN: *85* 1-3
LPs: 10/12-Inch 33rpm
MOTOWN: *85* 5-8

LUTHER
Singles: 7-Inch
COTILLION: *76-77* 2-3
LPs: 10/12-Inch 33rpm
COTILLION: *77* 8-10

LY-DELLS
Singles: 7-Inch
MASTER (111; "Genie Of
The Lamp"): *61* 30-35
MASTER (251; "Wizard Of Love"): *61* .. 15-20
ROULETTE: *63* 4-6
SCA: *62* 10-15
SOUTHERN SOUND: *65* 4-6
LPs: 10/12-Inch 33rpm
CLIFTON: 8-10

LYLE, Bobby
Singles: 7-Inch
CAPITOL: *78* 2-3

LYMAN, Arthur
(Arthur Lyman Group)
Singles: 7-Inch
GNP/CRESCENDO: *64-75* 1-3
HI FI: *59-69* 2-4

LPs: 10/12-Inch 33rpm
GNP/CRESCENDO: *63-75* $8-15
HI FI: *59-69* 8-18
OLYMPIC: *79* 5-8

LYME & CYBELLE
Singles: 7-Inch
WHITE WHALE: *66-67* 5-10

LYMON, Frankie
(Frankie Lymon & The Teenagers)
Singles: 78rpm
GEE: *55-57* 5-10
Singles: 7-Inch
ABC: *73* 1-3
COLUMBIA: *64* 3-5
GEE: *55-59* 6-10
ROULETTE: *58-61* 4-8
TCF: *64* 3-5
EPs: 7-Inch 33/45rpm
GEE: *56* 30-45
ROULETTE: *58* 25-35
LPs: 10/12-Inch 33rpm
GEE (701; "The Teenagers Featuring
Frankie Lymon"): *57* 100-175
(Red label.)
GEE (701; "The Teenagers Featuring
Frankie Lymon"): *61* 40-50
(Gray label.)
ROULETTE (25013; "Frankie Lymon
At The London Palladium"): *58* 50-65
ROULETTE (25036; "Rock & Roll"): *58* 50-65
ROULETTE (25250; "Frankie Lymon's
Greatest"): *64* 25-35
Members: Frankie Lymon; Herman Santiago; Sher-
man Garnes; Jim Merchant; Joe Negroni.
Also see TEENAGERS

LYMON, Lewis, & The Teenchords
Singles: 78rpm
END: *57* 10-15
FURY: *57* 6-12
Singles: 7-Inch
END (1000 series): *57* 20-30
END (1100 series): *62* 5-10
FURY: *57* 15-25
JUANITA: *58* 15-25
LPs: 10/12-Inch 33rpm
COLLECTABLES: *88* 6-8
LOST-NITE: *81* 5-8
Members: Lewis Lymon; Ralph Vaughan; David
Lyttle; Ross Rocco; Lyndon Harold; Jimmy Castor;
John Pruitt; Ed Pellegrino.

LYNCH, Ray
LPs: 10/12-Inch 33rpm
MUSIC WEST: *88* 5-8

LYNDELL, Linda
Singles: 7-Inch
VOLT: *68* $3-5

LYNN, Barbara
Singles: 7-Inch
ATLANTIC: *67-72* 2-4
COLLECTABLES: 1-3
JAMIE: *62-65* 3-5
TRIBE: *66-67* 3-5
LPs: 10/12-Inch 33rpm
ATLANTIC: *68* 10-15
JAMIE: *62-64* 20-25

LYNN, Barbara, & Lee Maye
Singles: 7-Inch
JAMIE: *65* 3-5
Also see LYNN, Barbara

LYNN, Cheryl
Singles: 12-Inch 33/45rpm
COLUMBIA: *78-85* 4-6
Singles: 7-Inch
COLUMBIA: *78-85* 1-3
MANHATTAN: *87* 1-3
PRIVATE I: *85* 1-3
LPs: 10/12-Inch 33rpm
COLUMBIA: *78-84* 5-8

LYNN, Cheryl, & Luther Vandross
Singles: 7-Inch
COLUMBIA: *82* 1-3
Also see LYNN, Cheryl
Also see VANDROSS, Luther

LYNN, Donna
Singles: 7-Inch
CAPITOL (Except 5127): *63-65* 3-5
CAPITOL (5127; "My Boyfriend Got
A Beatle Haircut"): *64* 15-20
EPIC: *63* 3-5
PALMER: *67* 3-5
LPs: 10/12-Inch 33rpm
CAPITOL: *64* 15-20

LYNN, Ginie
Singles: 7-Inch
ABC: *78* 2-3

LYNN, Loretta
(Loretta Lynn & The Coal Miners)
Singles: 7-Inch
DECCA (31000 series): *62-66* 3-5
DECCA (32000 series): *66-71* 2-4
MCA: *73-88* 1-3
ZERO (107; "I'm A Honky
Tonk Girl"): *60* 25-50
ZERO (110; "New Rainbow"): *61* 50-100

ZERO (112; "The Darkest
Day"): *61* $50-100
Picture Sleeves
DECCA (31000 series): *66* 5-10
DECCA (32000 series): *70* 3-5
MCA: *78* 1-3
EPs: 7-Inch 33/45rpm
DECCA: *64-65* 10-20
LPs: 10/12-Inch 33rpm
CORAL: *73* 4-8
COUNTRY MUSIC MAGAZINE: *76* ...12-18
(Special issue, available through *Country Music*
magazine's record catalog.)
DECCA (4457; "Loretta Lynn
Sings"): *63* 50-75
DECCA (4541 through 5000): *64-68* 15-25
(Decca numbers in the 4000 & 5000 series
preceded by a "DL7" are stereo issues.)
DECCA (75084; "Your Squaw Is
On The Warpath"): *69* 25-35
(Includes *Barney*, which was omitted from later
pressings.)
DECCA (75084; "Your Squaw Is
On The Warpath"): *69* 15-20
(Does not include *Barney*.)
DECCA (75115 through 75381): *69-72* ..10-20
L.L.: *76* 20-25
MCA: *73-88* 5-10
TEE VEE: *78* 8-12
TROLLEY CAR: *81* 8-10
VOCALION: *68-72* 8-15
Promotional LPs
MCA (1934; "Loretta Lynn's
Greatest Hits"): *74* 25-35
(Cover shows title as simply "Loretta Lynn.")
MCA (35013; "Allis-Chalmers Presents
Loretta Lynn"): *78* 20-25
MCA (35018; "Crisco Presents Loretta Lynn's
Country Classics"): *79* 20-30

Also see PIERCE, Webb / Loretta Lynn
Also see STARR, Kenny
Also see TWITTY, Conway

LYNN, Loretta / Tammy Wynette
LPs: 10/12-Inch 33rpm
RADIANT: *81* $5-8
Also see LYNN, Loretta
Also see WYNETTE, Tammy

LYNN, Vera
Singles: 78rpm
LONDON: *51-57* 2-4
Singles: 7-Inch
ARCO: *67* 1-3
DJM: *69* 1-3
LONDON: *51-64* 2-4
UNITED ARTISTS: *67* 1-3
EPs: 7-Inch 33/45rpm
LONDON: *52-56* 5-10
LPs: 10/12-Inch 33rpm
LONDON: *52-64* 8-15
MGM: *61* 6-12
UNITED ARTISTS: *67* 5-10

LYNNE, Gloria
Singles: 7-Inch
CANYON: *70* 1-3
EVEREST: *59-66* 2-4
FONTANA: *64-69* 2-4
HI FI: *66* 2-3
IMPULSE: *76* 1-3
MERCURY: *72* 1-3
SEECO: *61* 2-4
LPs: 10/12-Inch 33rpm
CANYON: *70* 5-10
DESIGN: *62* 10-15
EVEREST (300 series): *75* 5-8
EVEREST (5000 series): *59-60* 15-25
EVEREST (5100 & 5200 series): *60-65* . . 10-20
FONTANA: *64-69* 8-18
HI FI: *66* 8-15
IMPULSE: *76* 5-8
MERCURY: *69-72* 8-12
SUNSET: *66-67* 8-12
UPFRONT: *72* 5-10

LYNNE, Jeff
(Jeff Lynn)
Singles: 12-Inch 33/45rpm
JET: *77* 5-8
Singles: 7-Inch
JET: *77* 2-4
TWIN-SPIN: *65* 8-10
VIRGIN: *84* 1-3
Also see ELECTRIC LIGHT ORCHESTRA
Also see IDLE RACE

Also see MOVE

LYNYRD SKYNYRD
Singles: 7-Inch
ATNIA: *78* $2-3
MCA (Except 1966): *74-78* 2-3
MCA (1966; "Gimmie Back
  My Bullets"): *77* 8-10
(Promotional concert souvenir issue.)
EPs: 7-Inch 33/45rpm
MCA: *76* 10-15
(Promotional issue only.)
LPs: 10/12-Inch 33rpm
MCA (2000 & 3000 series,
  except 3029): *75-78* 8-10
MCA (3029; "Street Survivors"): *77* 30-35
(Front cover pictures the group in flames.)
MCA (3029; "Street Survivors"): *77* 8-10
(Front cover pictures the group without flames.)
MCA (5000 series): *79-82* 5-8
MCA (6000 series): *76-81* 10-15
MCA (10000 series): *79-81* 10-15
MCA (37000 series): *79-82* 5-8
MCA (42000 series): *87* 5-8
MCA/SOUNDS OF THE SOUTH
  (300 & 400 series): *73-74* 8-15
Promotional LPs
MCA (2170; "Gimmie Back
  My Bullets"): *76* 25-30
(White label. Concert souvenir copy.)
Members: Ronnie Van Zant; Gary Rossington;
Allen Collins; Steve Gaines; Cassie Gaines.
Also see ROSSINGTON-COLLINS BAND

LYTLE, Johnny
(Johnny Lytle Quintet; Johnny Lytle Trio)
Singles: 7-Inch
PACIFIC JAZZ: *68* 2-3
RIVERSIDE: *63* 2-4
SOLID STATE: *68* 2-3
TUBA: *65-66* 2-4
LPs: 10/12-Inch 33rpm
JAZZLAND: *60-62* 15-25
MILESTONE: *72* 5-10
MUSE: *78-81* 5-8
PACIFIC JAZZ: *67* 8-15
RIVERSIDE: *63-68* 10-20
SOLID STATE: *67-69* 8-15
TUBA: *66* 10-15

LYTLE, Johnny, & Ray Barretto
LPs: 10/12-Inch 33rpm
JAZZLAND: *62* 15-25
Also see BARRETTO, Ray
Also see LYTLE, Johnny

M

M
(Robin Scott)
Singles: 12-Inch 33/45rpm
SIRE: *79* $8-10
Singles: 7-Inch
SIRE: *79-81* 1-3
Picture Sleeves
SIRE: *79* 1-3
LPs: 10/12-Inch 33rpm
SIRE: *79-82* 6-10

M., Boney: see BONEY M

M/A/R/R/S
Singles: 7-Inch
4TH & B'WAY: *87-88* 1-3

M.C. CHILL
Singles: 12-Inch 33/45rpm
FEVER: *86* 4-6

M.C. HAMMER
Singles: 7-Inch
CAPITOL: *88* 1-3
LPs: 10/12-Inch 33rpm
CAPITOL: *88* 5-8

M.C. SHAN
(Featuring T.J. Swan)
Singles: 7-Inch
COLD CHILLIN': *87-88* 1-3

MC-5
(Motor City 5)
Singles: 7-Inch
A SQUARE: *67* 10-15
AMG: *66* 10-12
ATLANTIC: *69* 4-6
ELEKTRA: *69* 5-8
Picture Sleeves
A SQUARE: *67* 30-40
LPs: 10/12-Inch 33rpm
ATLANTIC: *70-71* 10-15
ELEKTRA (74042; "Kick Out
  The Jams"): *69* 30-35
(Title track has X-rated intro. Back cover has liner notes.)
ELEKTRA (74042; "Kick Out
  The Jams"): *69* 12-15
(Title track has censored intro. Back cover has no liner notes.)

MC SHY-D
LPs: 10/12-Inch 33rpm
LUKE SKYWALKER: *87-88* $5-8

MFSB
(Mothers, Fathers, Sisters, Brothers)
Singles: 7-Inch
PHILADELPHIA INT'L: *74-78* 2-3
TSOP: *81* 1-3
LPs: 10/12-Inch 33rpm
PHILADELPHIA INT'L: *73-78* 8-10
TSOP: *80* 5-8
Also see PEOPLE'S CHOICE
Also see THREE DEGREES

MGs
(Memphis Group)
Singles: 7-Inch
STAX: *73* 2-3
LPs: 10/12-Inch 33rpm
STAX: *73* 8-10
Also see BOOKER T. & THE MGs

M+M: see MARTHA & THE MUFFINS

M.O.D.
LPs: 10/12-Inch 33rpm
MEGAFORCE: *87-88* 5-8

MABLEY, Moms
Singles: 7-Inch
MERCURY: *69-71* 2-3
EPs: 7-Inch 33/45rpm
CHESS: *63* 5-8
LPs: 10/12-Inch 33rpm
CHESS: *61-64* 10-20
MERCURY: *64-70* 8-15

MABLEY, Moms, & Pigmeat Markham
LPs: 10/12-Inch 33rpm
CHESS: *64-71* 8-15
Also see MABLEY, Moms
Also see MARKHAM, Pigmeat

MABON, Willie
(Willie Mabon & His Combo)
Singles: 78rpm
CHESS (Except 1531): *52-56* 5-10
CHESS (1531; "I Don't Know"): *53* 25-50
Singles: 7-Inch
CHESS (Except 1531): *52-56* 10-20
CHESS (1531; "I Don't Know"): *53* 75-125
(Colored vinyl.)
CHESS (1531; "I Don't Know"): *53* 10-20
(Black vinyl.)
DELTA: 3-6
FEDERAL: *57* 10-15
FORMAL: *62* 4-6

MAD: *60* **$8-15**
PARROT (1050; "I Don't Know"): *53* . **100-150**
U.S.A.: *63-65* **3-5**

MAC, Fleetwood:
see FLEETWOOD MAC

MACARTHUR, James
Singles: 7-Inch
SCEPTER: *62-63* **3-6**
TRIODEX: *61* **3-6**

MAC BAND
(Featuring The Campbell Brothers)
Singles: 7-Inch
MCA: *88* **1-3**
LPs: 10/12-Inch 33rpm
MCA: *88* **5-8**

MACDONALD, Jeanette, &
Nelson Eddy
EPs: 7-Inch 33/45rpm
RCA VICTOR (Except 220): *61* **4-8**
RCA VICTOR (220; "Rose Marie"): *52* . . **10-20**
LPs: 10/12-Inch 33rpm
RCA VICTOR (16; "Rose Marie"): *52* . . **35-50**
(10-Inch LP.)
RCA VICTOR (526; "Rose Marie"): *66* . . **12-18**
(Soundtrack.)
RCA VICTOR (1000 series): *75* **4-8**
RCA VICTOR (1700 series): *59* **10-20**
RCA VICTOR (2400 series): *77* **5-8**
RCA VICTOR (3900 series): *81* **4-6**

MACDONALD, Ralph
Singles: 12-Inch 33-45rpm
POLYDOR: *84-85* **4-6**
Singles: 7-Inch
MARLIN: *76-79* **2-3**
POLYDOR: *84-85* **1-3**
LPs: 10/12-Inch 33rpm
MARLIN: *76-79* **6-10**
POLYDOR: *85* **5-8**

MACEO & ALL THE KINGS MEN
Singles: 7-Inch
EXCELLO: *72* **2-3**
HOUSE OF FOX: *70* **2-4**
LPs: 10/12-Inch 33rpm
EXCELLO: *72* **8-10**

MACEO & THE MACKS
Singles: 7-Inch
PEOPLE: *73-74* **2-3**
LPs: 10/12-Inch 33rpm
PEOPLE: *74* **8-10**

MACHINATIONS
Singles: 12-Inch 33/45rpm
A&M: *83* **4-6**

Singles: 7-Inch
A&M: *83* **$1-3**
LPs: 10/12-Inch 33rpm
A&M: *83* **5-8**

MACHINE
Singles: 7-Inch
RCA VICTOR: *79-80* **1-3**
LPs: 10/12-Inch 33rpm
RCA VICTOR: *80* **5-8**

MACGREGOR, Byron
Singles: 7-Inch
CAPITOL: *75* **1-3**
WESTBOUND: *74* **2-3**
LPs: 10/12-Inch 33rpm
WESTBOUND: *74* **5-10**

MACGREGOR, Mary
Singles: 7-Inch
ARIOLA: *78* **1-3**
ARIOLA AMERICA: *76-77* **2-3**
RSO: *79-80* **1-3**
LPs: 10/12-Inch 33rpm
ARIOLA AMERICA: *77* **8-10**

MACHO
Singles: 7-Inch
PRELUDE: *78* **1-3**
LPs: 10/12-Inch 33rpm
PRELUDE: *78* **5-8**

MACK, Lonnie
(Lonnie Mack & Pismo)
Singles: 7-Inch
ABC: *73* **1-3**
BARRY: **2-4**
CAPITOL: *77* **2-3**
COLLECTABLES: **1-3**
ELEKTRA: *71* **2-3**
FRATERNITY: *63-68* **5-8**
ROULETTE: *75* **1-3**
LPs: 10/12-Inch 33rpm
ALLIGATOR: *85-86* **5-8**
CAPITOL: *77* **8-10**
ELEKTRA: *69-71* **10-12**
FRATERNITY: *63* **20-25**
TRIP: *75* **8-10**
Members: Jim Keltner; Tim Drummond.

MACK, Lonnie, & Rusty York
LPs: 10/12-Inch 33rpm
QCA: *73* **10-12**
Also see MACK, Lonnie
Also see YORK, Rusty

MACK, Warner
Singles: 78rpm
DECCA: *57* **2-5**

Singles: 7-Inch
DECCA (Except 30000 series): *59-73* $2-4
DECCA (30000 series): *57-59* 3-6
KAPP: *61-62* 2-4
MCA: *73-76* 1-3
PAGEBOY: *77-81* 1-3
SCARLET: *60* 3-5
TOP RANK: *60* 2-4
EPs: 7-Inch 33/45rpm
DECCA: *65* 5-8
LPs: 10/12-Inch 33rpm
CORAL: *73* 4-6
DECCA: *65-70* 8-15
KAPP: *61-66* 10-18

MACKENZIE, Gisele
Singles: 78rpm
CAPITOL: *51-54* 2-5
VIK: *56* 2-4
X: *55* 2-4
Singles: 7-Inch
CAPITOL: *51-54* 3-5
EVEREST: *60* 2-3
MERCURY: *63* 2-3
VIK: *56* 2-4
X: *55* 2-4
Picture Sleeves
VIK: *56* 2-4
X: *55* 2-4
EPs: 7-Inch 33/45rpm
CAPITOL: *53-69* 5-10
VIK: *56* 5-10
LPs: 10/12-Inch 33rpm
CAMDEN: *59* 8-12
EVEREST: *60* 8-15
GLENDALE: *78* 4-8
MERCURY: *63* 8-12
RCA VICTOR: *59* 8-15
SUNSET: *67* 5-10
VIK: *56* 10-20

MACRAE, Gordon
Singles: 78rpm
CAPITOL: *53-57* 2-4
Singles: 7-Inch
CAPITOL: *53-68* 2-4
EPs: 7-Inch 33/45rpm
CAPITOL: *54-57* 5-8
ROYALE: 5-8
LPs: 10/12-Inch 33rpm
CAPITOL: *54-69* 8-18

MACRAE, Gordon, & Jo Stafford
Singles: 7-Inch
CAPITOL: *62* 2-3
LPs: 10/12-Inch 33rpm

CAPITOL (1600 & 1900 series): *62-63* .$10-15
CAPITOL (11000 series): *79* 4-8
Also see MAC RAE, Gordon
Also see STAFFORD, Jo

MAD LADS
Singles: 7-Inch
MARK-FI: *62* 8-10
CAPITOL: *64* 4-6
STAX: *64* 5-8
VOLT (100 series): *65-68* 4-8
VOLT (4000 series): *69-73* 3-5
LPs: 10/12-Inch 33rpm
COLLECTABLES: *86* 6-8
VOLT (400 series): *66* 15-20
VOLT (6000 series): *69-73* 10-15

MAD RIVER
Singles: 7-Inch
CAPITOL: *68-69* 5-8
EPs: 7-Inch 33/45rpm
WEE: *68* 15-20
LPs: 10/12-Inch 33rpm
CAPITOL: *68-69* 15-20

MADAGASCAR
Singles: 7-Inch
ARISTA: *81-82* 1-3

MADAME X
Singles: 7-Inch
LORIMAR: *88* 1-3

MADDOX, Johnny
(Johnny Maddox & The Rhythmasters)
Singles: 78rpm
DOT: *50-57* 2-4
Singles: 7-Inch
ABC: *74* 1-3
DOT: *50-63* 2-4
EPs: 7-Inch 33/45rpm
DOT: *52-56* 4-8
LPs: 10/12-Inch 33rpm
DOT: *55-67* 8-18
HAMILTON: *64* 5-10
PARAMOUNT: *74* 5-8

MADE IN U.S.A.
Singles: 7-Inch
DE-LITE: *77* 2-3

MADIGAN, Betty
Singles: 78rpm
CORAL: *57* 2-4
JAY DEE: *54* 2-5
MGM (11000 series): *53-56* 2-5
Singles: 7-Inch
CORAL: *57-59* 2-4
JAY DEE: *54* 3-5

MAGIC TOUCH
Singles: 7-Inch
BLACK FALCON: *71* $2-4

MAGIC TOUCH
(Vito & The Salutations)
Singles: 7-Inch
ROULETTE: *73* 4-6
Also see VITO & THE SALUTATIONS

MAGISTRATES
Singles: 7-Inch
MGM: *68-69* 3-5
Member: Jean Hillary.
Also see DOVELLS

MAGNIFICENT MEN
Singles: 7-Inch
CAPITOL: *66-68* 3-5
MERCURY: *69* 2-4
LPs: 10/12-Inch 33rpm
CAPITOL: *67-68* 10-15
MERCURY: *70* 8-10
Members: Bob Angelucci; Dave Buff; Buddy
King; Tom Pane.

MAGNIFICENTS
Singles: 7-Inch
CHECKER: *62* 3-5
COLLECTABLES: 1-3
KANSOMA: *62* 5-10
VEE JAY (183; "Up On
The Mountain"): *56* 30-60
VEE JAY (208; "Caddy Bo"): *56* 40-75
VEE JAY (235; "Off The Mountain"): *57* 30-60
VEE JAY (281; "Don't Leave
Me"): *58* 40-60
VEE JAY (367; "Up On The
Mountain"): *60* 5-10
Also see EL DORADOS

MAGNUM FORCE
Singles: 7-Inch
PAULA: *85* 1-3
LPs: 10/12-Inch 33rpm
WIZARD: *78* 5-8

MAHAL, TAJ: see TAJ MAHAL

MAHARIS, George
Singles: 7-Inch
EPIC: *62-66* 2-4
Picture Sleeves
EPIC: *62-64* 3-6
LPs: 10/12-Inch 33rpm
EPIC: *62-66* 8-15

MAHOGANY
Singles: 12-Inch 33/45rpm
WEST END: *83* 4-6

Singles: 7-Inch
WEST END: *83* $1-3

MAHOGANY RUSH
Singles: 7-Inch
COLUMBIA: *76* 2-3
20TH CENTURY-FOX: *74-75* 2-4
LPs: 10/12-Inch 33rpm
COLUMBIA: *76* 8-10
20TH CENTURY-FOX: *73-75* 10-12
Member: Frank Marino.
Also see MARINO, Frank, & Mahogany Rush

MAHONEY, Skip, & The Casuals
Singles: 7-Inch
ABET: *76-77* 2-3
D.C. INT'L: *74* 2-4

MAI TAI
Singles: 12-Inch 33/45rpm
MERCURY: *87* 4-6
Singles: 7-Inch
CRITIQUE: *86* 1-3
MERCURY: *87* 1-3
LPs: 10/12-Inch 33rpm
MERCURY: *87* 5-8
Members: Carol DeWindt; Jettie Well; Mildred
Douglas.

MAIN ATTRACTION
Singles: 7-Inch
RCA VICTOR: *86* 1-3
LPs: 10/12-Inch 33rpm
RCA VICTOR: *86* 5-8

MAIN INGREDIENT
Singles: 7-Inch
RCA VICTOR: *69-81* 2-4
ZAKIA: *86* 1-3
Picture Sleeves
RCA VICTOR: *70-81* 2-4
LPs: 10/12-Inch 33rpm
COLLECTABLES: *88* 6-8
RCA VICTOR: *70-81* 8-10
Member: Cuba Gooding.
Also see GOODING, Cuba
Also see POETS

MAINSTREETERS
Singles: 7-Inch
EVENT: *73* 2-3

MAJESTY
Singles: 7-Inch
GOLDEN BOY: *85* 1-3

MAJOR LANCE: see LANCE, Major

MAJORS
Singles: 7-Inch
IMPERIAL: *62-64* 4-6

LPs: 10/12-Inch 33rpm	
IMPERIAL: *63*	$25-30

Members: Ricky Cordo; Eugene Glass; Idella Morris; Frank Troutt; Ronald Gathers.

MAKEBA, Miriam
Singles: 7-Inch

KAPP: *62*	3-6
MERCURY: *66*	3-6
RCA VICTOR: *64*	3-6
REPRISE: *67-68*	3-6

LPs: 10/12-Inch 33rpm

KAPP: *62*	10-20
MERCURY: *66*	8-15
PETERS INT'L: *81*	5-8
RCA VICTOR: *60-68*	8-18
REPRISE: *67*	8-15

Also see BELAFONTE, Harry, & Miriam Makeba

Also see MANHATTAN BROTHERS & MIRIAM MAKEBA

MAKEM, Tommy:
see CLANCY BROTHERS & TOMMY MAKEM

MALCOLM X.
Singles: 7-Inch

TOMMY BOY: *83-84*	1-3

LPs: 10/12-Inch 33rpm

DOUGLAS: *68-71*	8-15

MALICE
LPs: 10/12-Inch 33rpm

ATLANTIC: *87*	5-8
ENIGMA:	5-8

MALMKVIST, Siw
(Siw Malmkvist & Umberto Marcato)
Singles: 7-Inch

JUBILEE: *64*	3-5
KAPP: *61*	3-5

MALO
Singles: 7-Inch

TRAQ: *81*	1-3
WARNER BROS: *72-73*	2-4

LPs: 10/12-Inch 33rpm

WARNER BROS: *72-74*	8-10

Also see AZTECA

Also see SANTANA, Jorge

MALMSTEEN, Yngwie J
(Yngwie J. Malmsteen's Rising Force)
LPs: 10/12-Inch 33rpm

POLYDOR: *88*	5-8

MALTBY, Richard, & His Orchestra
Singles: 78rpm

VIK: *56*	3-5
X: *54-55*	3-5

Singles: 7-Inch

COLUMBIA: *59*	$3-6
ROULETTE: *60-61*	3-6
VIK: *56*	3-6
X: *54-55*	3-6

Picture Sleeves

VIK: *56*	5-10

EPs: 7-Inch 33/45rpm

COLUMBIA: *59*	4-8
VIK: *56*	5-8
X: *54-55*	5-8

LPs: 10/12-Inch 33rpm

CAMDEN: *60-62*	8-12
COLUMBIA: *59*	10-15
HARMONY: *61*	8-12
ROULETTE: *60-62*	8-15
VIK: *56*	10-15
X: *54-55*	10-20

MAMA CASS: see ELLIOT, Cass

MAMA'S BOYS
LPs: 10/12-Inch 33rpm

JIVE: *84-87*	5-8

MAMAS & THE PAPAS
Singles: 7-Inch

ABC: *70*	1-3
DUNHILL: *65-72*	3-5
MCA: *80-82*	1-3

Picture Sleeves

DUNHILL (Except 4020 & 4083): *67*	4-8

DUNHILL (4020; "California
Dreamin'"): *65* ... 50-100
(Promotional issue only.)

DUNHILL (4083; "Creeque Alley"): *67* . 25-35
(Promotional issue only.)

EPs: 7-Inch 33/45rpm

ABC: *71*	8-15

(Promotional issues only.)

DUNHILL: *65*	10-15

LPs: 10/12-Inch 33rpm

ABC: *76*	6-10
DUNHILL: *66-73*	8-15
MCA: *80-82*	5-8
PICKWICK: *72*	6-10

Members: John Phillips; "Mama" Cass Elliot; Denny Doherty; Michelle Gilliam.

Also see BIG THREE

Also see ELLIOT, Cass

Also see PHILLIPS, John

MAMAS & THE PAPAS/ Association / Fifth Dimension
LPs: 10/12-Inch 33rpm

TEE VEE/WARNER SPECIAL
PROD: *79* ... 10-20

Also see ASSOCIATION
Also see FIFTH DIMENSION
Also see MAMAS & THE PAPAS

MAN PARRISH: see PARRISH, Man

MANCHA, Steve
Singles: 7-Inch
GROOVE CITY: $4-8
GROOVESVILLE: *65-67* 3-6
WHEELSVILLE: *65* 4-6
Also see BARNES, J.J., & Steve Mancha

MANCHESTER, Melissa
Singles: 12-Inch 33/45rpm
ARISTA: *82* 4-6
CASABLANCA: *84* 4-6
MCA: *85* 4-6
Singles: 7-Inch
ARISTA: *75-84* 1-3
BELL: *74* 2-3
CASABLANCA: *84* 1-3
MB: *67* 3-5
MCA: *85* 1-3
LPs: 10/12-Inch 33rpm
ARISTA: *75-83* 8-10
BELL: *73-74* 10-12
CASABLANCA: *84* 5-8
MCA: *79* 5-8
MFSL: *79* 25-50
Also see NATIONAL LAMPOON

MANCHESTER, Melissa, & Peabo Bryson
Singles: 7-Inch
ARISTA: *81* 1-3
Also see BRYSON, Peabo
Also see MANCHESTER, Melissa

MANCHILD
Singles: 7-Inch
CHI-SOUND: *77* 2-3
LPs: 10/12-Inch 33rpm
CHI-SOUND: *77* 8-10
Also see REDD HOTT

MANCINI, Henry
(Henry Mancini's Orchestra & Chorus)
Singles: 7-Inch
LIBERTY (1400 series): *82* 1-3
LIBERTY (55000 series): *58-59* 2-5
RCA VICTOR (Except 8184): *59-85* 2-5
RCA VICTOR (8184; "Banzai
Pipeline"): *63* 4-8
UNITED ARTISTS: *78* 1-3
WARNER BROS: *79-83* 1-3
Picture Sleeves
RCA VICTOR (Except 8184): *59-77* 5-12

RCA VICTOR (8184; "Banzai
Pipeline"): *63* $8-15
WARNER BROS: *79* 1-3
EPs: 7-Inch 33/45rpm
RCA VICTOR: *60-62* 5-15
LPs: 10/12-Inch 33rpm
AVCO EMBASSY: *70* 12-18
CAMDEN: *66-74* 5-10
LIBERTY (3000 series): *57-59* 10-20
LIBERTY (51000 series): *82* 4-8
MCA: *75-76* 6-12
PARAMOUNT: *70* 10-15
RCA VICTOR (0013 through
0098): *72-73* 5-10
RCA VICTOR (0231; "Visions Of
Eight"): *73* 20-25
(Soundtrack.)
RCA VICTOR (0270; "Country
Gentleman"): *74* 5-8
RCA VICTOR (0271; "Oklahoma
Crude"): *73* 10-15
(Soundtrack.)
RCA VICTOR (0672 through 1928): *74-76* 5-10
RCA VICTOR (1956; "The Music
From Peter Gunn"): *59* 15-20
(TV soundtrack.)
RCA VICTOR (2040; "More Music
From Peter Gunn"): *59* 15-25
(TV soundtrack.)
RCA VICTOR (2143; "The Music
From Peter Gunn"): *77* 4-8
(TV soundtrack.)
RCA VICTOR (2147; "The Blues &
The Beat"): *60* 10-20
RCA VICTOR (2198; "Music From
Mr. Lucky"): *60* 10-20
(TV soundtrack.)
RCA VICTOR (2314; "High Time"): *60* .. 20-30
(Soundtrack.)
RCA VICTOR (2360; "Mr. Lucky
Goes Latin"): *61* 10-20
RCA VICTOR (2362; "Just You & Me
Together Love"): *77* 4-8
RCA VICTOR (2362; "Breakfast At
Tiffany's"): *61* 25-35
(Soundtrack.)
RCA VICTOR (2258; "Combo"): *62* 10-20
RCA VICTOR (2442; "Experiment In
Terror"): *62* 35-50
(Cover pictures Lee Remick and her attacker.
Soundtrack.)
RCA VICTOR (2442; "Experiment In
Terror"): *62* 25-35
(Cover pictures mannequins. Soundtrack.)

RCA VICTOR (2484; "Love Story"): *77* . . **$4-8**
(Soundtrack.)
RCA VICTOR (2559; "Hatari"): *62* **25-35**
(Soundtrack.)
RCA VICTOR (2600 series): *63-64* **8-15**
RCA VICTOR (2755; "Charade"): *63* . . . **20-30**
(Soundtrack.)
RCA VICTOR (2795; "The Pink
Panther"): *64* **10-20**
(Soundtrack.)
RCA VICTOR (2800 & 2900
series): *64-65* **8-15**
RCA VICTOR (3000 series): *78* **4-8**
RCA VICTOR (3356; "The Latin Sound
Of Henry Mancini"): *65* **8-15**
RCA VICTOR (3347; "Best Of Henry
Mancini, Volume 3"): *79* **5-8**
RCA VICTOR (3402; "The Great
Race"): *65* **25-35**
(Soundtrack.)
RCA VICTOR (3500 series): *66* **6-12**
RCA VICTOR (3612; "Merry Mancini
Christmas"): *66* **6-12**
RCA VICTOR (3623; "Arabesque"): *66* . **30-40**
(Soundtrack.)
RCA VICTOR (3648; "What Did You Do
In The War Daddy"): *66* **20-30**
(Soundtrack.)
RCA VICTOR (3667; "Pure Gold"): *80* **4-8**
RCA VICTOR (3668; "Mancini
Country"): *80* **4-8**
RCA VICTOR (3694 through 3713): *66-67* **6-12**
RCA VICTOR (3756; "Warm Shade
Of Ivory"): *80* **4-8**
RCA VICTOR (3802; "Two For
The Road"): *67* **15-25**
(Soundtrack.)
RCA VICTOR (3822; "Best Of
Henry Mancini"): *80* **4-8**
RCA VICTOR (3877; "Music Of
Hawaii"): *81* **4-8**
RCA VICTOR (3887; "Encore"): *67* **8-15**
RCA VICTOR (3954; "Country
Gentleman"): *67* **4-8**
RCA VICTOR (3997 through
4689): *68-72* **5-10**
RCA VICTOR (5000 series): *85* **4-8**
RCA VICTOR (6000 series): *66-72* **8-15**
SUNSET: *66* **5-10**
UNITED ARTISTS: *70* **10-12**
WARNER BROS (Except 3339): *59-73* . . **10-20**
WARNER BROS (3339; "10"): *79* **5-10**
(Soundtrack.)
  Also see HIRT, Al / Henry Mancini / Perez
Prado

Also see MATHIS, Johnny, & Henry Mancini
MANCINI, Henry, & Charley Pride
  LPs: 10/12-Inch 33rpm
DECCA (79185; "Sometimes A
Great Notion"): *71* **$12-18**
(Soundtrack.)
  Also see PRIDE, Charley
MANCINI, Henry, & Doc Severinsen
  LPs: 10/12-Inch 33rpm
RCA VICTOR (3700 series): *80* **4-8**
  Also see MANCINI, Henry
  Also see SEVERINSEN, Doc
MANDEL, Harvey
  Singles: 7-Inch
PHILIPS: *68* **3-5**
  LPs: 10/12-Inch 33rpm
JANUS: *70-74* **8-10**
OVATION: *71* **8-10**
PHILIPS: *68-69* **10-12**
  Also see CANNED HEAT
MANDELL, Mike
  Singles: 7-Inch
VANGUARD: *81* **1-3**
MANDRE
  Singles: 7-Inch
MOTOWN: *77-79* **1-3**
  LPs: 10/12-Inch 33rpm
MOTOWN: *77-79* **5-8**
MANDRELL, Barbara
  Singles: 7-Inch
ABC: *78-79* **1-3**
ABC/DOT: *75-78* **2-3**
COLUMBIA: *69-75* **2-4**
EMI AMERICA: *87-88* **1-3**
MCA: *79-86* **1-3**
MOSRITE: *66* **5-8**
  Picture Sleeves
MCA: *79-85* **1-3**
  LPs: 10/12-Inch 33rpm
ABC: *78-79* **8-10**
ABC/DOT: *76-77* **8-12**
COLUMBIA: *71-81* **8-15**
COLUMBIA SPECIAL PRODUCTS: *82* . . **5-8**
MCA: *79-88* **5-10**
SONGBIRD: *82* **5-8**
TIME-LIFE: *81* **5-8**
  Also see HOUSTON, David, & Barbara
Mandrell
**MANDRELL, Barbara
& Lee Greenwood**
  Singles: 7-Inch
MCA: *84* **1-3**

LPs: 10/12-Inch 33rpm
MCA: *84* $5-8
Also see GREENWOOD, Lee

MANDRELL, Barbara, & The Oak Ridge Boys
Singles: 7-Inch
MCA: *86* 1-3
Also see MANDRELL, Barbara
Also see OAK RIDGE BOYS

MANDRILL
Singles: 7-Inch
ARISTA: *77-80* 1-3
LIBERTY: *83* 1-3
MONTAGE: *82* 1-3
POLYDOR: *71-74* 2-3
UNITED ARTISTS: *75-76* 2-3
LPs: 10/12-Inch 33rpm
ARISTA: *77-80* 8-10
LIBERTY: *83* 5-8
POLYDOR: *71-75* 10-12
UNITED ARTISTS: *75* 8-10
Also see MASSER, Michael, & Mandrill

MANFRED MANN:
see MANN, Manfred

MANGANO, Silvana
Singles: 7-Inch
MGM: *53* 3-5

MANGIONE, Chuck
(Chuck Mangione Quintet; Gap & Chuck Mangione)
Singles: 7-Inch
A&M: *75-80* 1-3
COLUMBIA: *82-84* 1-3
MERCURY: *71-77* 1-3
Picture Sleeves
A&M: *78-80* 1-3
LPs: 10/12-Inch 33rpm
A&M: *75-81* 5-10
COLUMBIA: *82-84* 5-8
JAZZLAND: *63* 30-50
MFSL: *82* 25-50
MERCURY: *71-78* 6-12
MILESTONE: *77* 5-8
RIVERSIDE: *61* 40-50

MANHATTAN BROTHERS & MIRIAM MAKEBA
Singles: 7-Inch
LONDON: *56* 3-5
Also see MAKEBA, Miriam

MANHATTAN TRANSFER
Singles: 7-Inch
ATLANTIC: *75-85* 1-3

LPs: 10/12-Inch 33rpm
ATLANTIC: *75-87* $8-10
COLLECTABLES: *88* 6-8
MFSL: *78* 25-50
Members: Tim Hauser; Alan Paul; Gary Chester; Garnett Brown; Ken Buttrey; Cheryl Bentyne; Janis Siegel; Don Roberts; Jay Graydon.

MANHATTANS
Singles: 12-Inch 33/45rpm
COLUMBIA: *84-85* 4-6
Singles: 7-Inch
AVANTI: *63* 4-6
CAPITOL: *61-62* 5-8
CARNIVAL: *64-69* 3-5
COLUMBIA: *73-87* 1-3
DELUXE: *69-73* 2-3
LPs: 10/12-Inch 33rpm
CARNIVAL: *66* 20-35
COLUMBIA: *73-83* 8-10
DELUXE: *70-72* 10-15
SOLID SMOKE: *81* 5-8
Members: George Smith; Ken Kelly; Sonny Bivens; Winfred Scott; Richard Taylor; Regina Bell.

MANILOW, Barry
Singles: 12-Inch 33/45rpm
ARISTA: *78-84* 4-6
Singles: 7-Inch
ARISTA: *74-85* 1-3
BELL: *73-74* 2-4
FLASHBACK: *76* 1-3
RCA VICTOR: *86* 1-3
Promotional Singles
ARISTA (11; "It's Just Another New Year's Eve"): *77* 3-5
Picture Sleeves
ARISTA (Except 11): *78-85* 1-3
ARISTA (11; "It's Just Another New Year's Eve"): *77* 4-8
(Promotional issue only.)
LPs: 10/12-Inch 33rpm
ARISTA: *74-87* 8-10
BELL: *74* 10-15
RCA VICTOR: *86* 5-8
Also see FEATHERBED
Also see LADY FLASH

MANILOW, Barry / Atlanta Rhythm Section
Singles: 7-Inch
WHAT'S IT ALL ABOUT: *79* 2-4
Also see ATLANTA RHYTHM SECTION

MANILOW, Barry / Firefall
Singles: 7-Inch
WHAT'S IT ALL ABOUT: 79 . . . . $2-4
Also see FIREFALL
Also see MANILOW, Barry

MANILOW, Barry / Kid Creole & The Coconuts
Singles: 7-Inch
ARISTA: 88 1-3

MANN, Barry
Singles: 7-Inch
ABC: 73 1-3
ABC-PARAMOUNT: 60-62 5-8
ARISTA: 76 2-4
CAPITOL: 66-68 3-5
CASABLANCA: 80 1-3
COLPIX: 63 4-6
JDS: 59 5-8
MCA: 1-3
NEW DESIGN: 71-72 2-4
RCA VICTOR: 74-76 2-4
RED BIRD: 64 4-6
ROULETTE: 1-3
SCEPTER: 70 2-4
UNITED ARTISTS: 77-78 1-3
WARNER BROS: 79 1-3
LPs: 10/12-Inch 33rpm
ABC-PARAMOUNT (399; "Who Put The
   Bomp"): 62 50-75
CASABLANCA: 80 5-8
NEW DESIGN: 71 10-12
RCA VICTOR: 75 8-10
UNITED ARTISTS: 77 8-10

MANN, Bobby
(Bobby Bloom)
Singles: 7-Inch
KAMA SUTRA: 66 3-5
Also see BLOOM, Bobby

MANN, Carl
Singles: 7-Inch
JAXON (502; "Gonna Rock & Roll
   Tonight"): 57 50-75
PHILLIPS INT'L: 59-61 5-8
SUN: 1-3
LPs: 10/12-Inch 33rpm
CHARLEY: 5-8
GRT/SUNNYVALE: 77 6-10
PHILLIPS INT'L (1960; "Like
   Mann"): 60 75-125

MANN, Charles
Singles: 7-Inch
ABC: 73 2-3

LANOR: $3-5

MANN, Gloria
(Gloria Mann & The Carter Rays)
Singles: 78rpm
DECCA: 56 3-6
DERBY: 56 4-8
JUBILEE: 54 4-8
SLS: 54 10-15
SOUND: 54-55 5-8
Singles: 7-Inch
DECCA: 56 4-6
DERBY: 56 5-8
JUBILEE: 54 8-10
SLS: 54 25-30
SOUND: 54-55 8-10

MANN, Herbie
Singles: 12-Inch 33/45rpm
ATLANTIC: 83 4-6
Singles: 7-Inch
A&M: 68 2-3
ATLANTIC: 60-83 1-3
BETHLEHEM: 59-62 2-4
COLUMBIA: 70 1-3
EMBRYO: 71 1-3
PRESTIGE: 66 2-3
LPs: 10/12-Inch 33rpm
A&M: 68 8-12
ATLANTIC (300 series): 72 8-12
ATLANTIC (1300 & 1400 series): 60-65 10-20
ATLANTIC (1500 & 1600 series): 69-76 . 8-12
ATLANTIC (8000 series): 67 8-15
ATLANTIC (18000 & 19000
   series): 77-83 5-10
BETHLEHEM (24 through 63): 55-56 . . 20-40
BETHLEHEM (1000 series): 54 40-60
   (10-Inch LPs.)
BETHLEHEM (6001; "The Bethlehem
   Years"): 76 5-8
BETHLEHEM (6067; "The Epitome
   Of Jazz"): 63 12-20
COLUMBIA: 65-81 8-15
EMBRYO: 70-71 8-12
EPIC: 57-58 20-35
FINNADAR: 76 5-10
INTERLUDE: 59 15-25
JAZZLAND: 60 15-25
MILESTONE: 73 8-12
MODE: 57 25-40
NEW JAZZ: 58 20-30
PREMIER: 63 10-20
PRESTIGE (7000 series): 57 30-50
   (Yellow label.)
PRESTIGE (7000 series): 65-69 10-20
   (Blue label.)

RIVERSIDE (03; "Blues For
  Tomorrow"): *82* $5-8
RIVERSIDE (200 & 300 series): *57* 20-35
RIVERSIDE (3000 series): *69* 8-12
ROULETTE: *67* 8-15
SAVOY (1100 series): *76* 5-8
SAVOY (12000 series): *57* 20-35
SOLID STATE: *68* 8-12
SURREY: *65* 10-15
UNITED ARTISTS (4000 & 5000
  series): *59* 20-40
UNITED ARTISTS (5300 series): *72* 8-10
UNITED ARTISTS (14000 & 15000
  series): *62-63* 20-35
VSP: *66* 8-15
VERVE: *57-61* 15-30
  (Reads "Verve Records, Inc." at bottom of label.)
VERVE: *63* 10-20
  (Reads "MGM Records - A Division Of Metro-
  Goldwyn-Mayer, Inc." at bottom of label.)
VERVE: *69-73* 5-10
  (Reads "Manufactured By MGM Record Corp.," or
  mentions either Polydor or Polygram at bottom of
  label.)
  Also see JONES, Tamiko, & Herbie Mann

MANN, Herbie, & Cissy Houston
  Singles: 7-Inch
ATLANTIC: *76* 2-3
  Also see HOUSTON, Cissy

**MANN, Herbie / Maynard
  Ferguson**
  LPs: 10/12-Inch 33rpm
ROULETTE: *71* 8-12
  Also see FERGUSON, Herbie
  Also see MANN, Herbie

MANN, Johnny, Singers
  Singles: 7-Inch
DECCA: *66* 1-3
EPIC: *72* 1-3
EUREKA: *60* 2-4
LIBERTY: *62-68* 2-3
  LPs: 10/12-Inch 33rpm
EPIC: *72* 4-8
LIBERTY: *59-69* 5-15
LIGHT: *76* 4-8
SUNSET: *66-70* 5-10
UNITED ARTISTS: *71* 5-10
  Also see Zentner, Si

MANN, Manfred
  (Manfred Mann's Earth Band)
  Singles: 7-Inch
ARISTA: *84-85* 1-3
ASCOT (Except 2157 & 2165): *64-68* 5-12

ASCOT (2157; "Do Wah Diddy
  Diddy"): *64* $3-5
ASCOT (2165; "Sha La La"): *64* 4-6
MERCURY: *66-69* 3-6
POLYDOR: *71-74* 2-4
PRESTIGE: *64* 8-10
UNITED ARTISTS: *66* 4-6
WARNER BROS: *76-81* 1-3
  EPs: 7-Inch 33/45rpm
UNITED ARTISTS (10030; "Manfred
  Mann"): *64* 10-20
  (Promotional issue only. Not issued with cover.)
  Picture Sleeves
ASCOT: *64* 10-20
MERCURY: *68* 8-15
  LPs: 10/12-Inch 33rpm
ARISTA: *83* 5-8
ASCOT: *64-66* 25-50
CAPITOL: *80* 5-8
EMI AMERICA: *77* 10-12
JANUS: *74* 12-15
MERCURY: *68* 15-20
POLYDOR: *70-74* 10-15
UNITED ARTISTS: *66-68* 20-25
WARNER BROS: *74-81* 5-8
  Members: Manfred Mann; Mike D'Abo; Paul
  Jones; Tom McGuinnes; Mick Rogers; Mick Vick-
  ers; Chris Slade; Colin Pattenden; Mike Hugg;
  Steve York.
  Also see FIRM
  Also see MC GUINNESS-FLINT
  Also see NIGHT

MANNA, Charlie
  Singles: 7-Inch
DECCA: *61* 2-4
JUBILEE: *65* 2-4
  Picture Sleeves
DECCA: *61* 3-6
  LPs: 10/12-Inch 33rpm
DECCA: *61-62* 10-20
VERVE: *66* 8-15

MANNHEIM STEAMROLLER
  LPs: 10/12-Inch 33rpm
AMERICAN GRAMAPHONE: *83-88* 5-8

MANONE, Wingy, & His Orchestra
  Singles: 78rpm
COLUMBIA: *54* 2-4
DECCA: *57* 2-4
  Singles: 7-Inch
COLUMBIA: *54* 2-4
DECCA: *57* 2-4
IMPERIAL: *62* 1-3
KEM: *61* 1-3
  EPs: 7-Inch 33/45rpm

COLUMBIA: *54* $4-8
VIK: *56* 4-6
LPs: 10/12-Inch 33rpm
IMPERIAL: *62* 8-15
MCA: *83* 4-8
PRESTIGE: *70* 5-10
RCA VICTOR: *69* 5-10
SAVOY: *73* 5-10
STORYVILLE: *83* 4-8
VIK: *56* 10-20

MANTOVANI
(Mantovani & His Orchestra)
Singles: 78rpm
LONDON (Except 1761): *51-65* 1-3
LONDON (1761; "Let Me Be
Loved"): *57* 2-4
Singles: 7-Inch
LONDON (Except 1761): *51-65* 1-3
LONDON (1761; "Let Me Be
Loved"): *57* 3-5
Picture Sleeves
LONDON (Except 1761): *57-65* 1-3
LONDON (1761; "Let Me Be
Loved"): *57* 10-20
(*Let Me Be Loved* was the main theme from the
film, *The James Dean Story*. Sleeve pictures Dean.)
EPs: 7-Inch 33/45rpm
LONDON: *51-59* 3-6
LPs: 10/12-Inch 33rpm
BAINBRIDGE: *82* 4-8
LONDON: *51-72* 5-15

MANTRA
Singles: 7-Inch
CASABLANCA: *81* 1-3
LPs: 10/12-Inch 33rpm
CASABLANCA: *81* 5-8

MANTRONIX
Singles: 12-Inch 33/45rpm
SLEEPING BAG: *85* 4-6
LPs: 10/12-Inch 33rpm
CAPITOL: *88* 5-8
SLEEPING BAG: *86* 5-8

MANU DIBANGO:
see DIBANGO, Manu

MANZANERA, Phil
**(Phil Manzanera Quiet Sun; Phil Manzanera &
801; Manzanera)**
Singles: 12-Inch 33/45rpm
EDITIONS E.G.: *82* 5-8
LPs: 10/12-Inch 33rpm
ANTILLES: 8-10
ATCO: 8-10
EDITIONS E.G.: *82* 5-8

POLYDOR: *78* $8-10
Also see 801
Also see ROXY MUSIC

MANZAREK, Ray
Singles: 7-Inch
MERCURY: *73-74* 3-5
LPs: 10/12-Inch 33rpm
A&M: *84* 5-8
MERCURY: *74-75* 8-10
Also see DOORS

MARA, Tommy
Singles: 7-Inch
B&F: *60* 4-8
FELSTED: *58-59* 4-8

MARATHONS
Singles: 7-Inch
ARGO: *61* 4-6
ARVEE (5027; "Peanut Butter"): *61* 10-12
(Other Arvee releases by the Marathons are actual-
ly by a different group. See the following section.)
CHESS: *61* 4-6
PLAZA: *62* 4-6
EPs: 7-Inch 33/45rpm
MARK '56 ("Laura Scudder's
Magic Record"): *69* 3-6
(A Laura Scudder's potato chip mail order coupon
giveaway item. Has three tunes, including *Peanut
Butter*, imbedded in a single band on each side.
When needle begins tracking, you don't know
which song will play. Price includes paper picture
sleeve.)
LPs: 10/12-Inch 33rpm
ARVEE: *61* 30-40
Members: James Johnson; Carl Fisher; Dick
Owens; Dave Govan; Don Bradley.
Also see JAYHAWKS
Also see VIBRATIONS

MARATHONS
Singles: 7-Inch
ARVEE (Except 5027): *61-62* 4-6
(Arvee 5027 is by a different group and is listed in
the preceding section.)

MARCELS
Singles: 7-Inch
COLPIX: *61-63* 10-25
ERIC: 1-3
QUEEN BEE: *73* 10-15
ST. CLAIR: 5-10
Picture Sleeves
COLPIX: *61-62* 30-50
LPs: 10/12-Inch 33rpm
COLPIX (416; "Blue Moon"): *61* 50-80
(Gold label.)

COLPIX (416; "Blue Moon"): *63* $25-45
(Blue label.)
MURRAY HILL: 8-10
Members: Cornelius Harp; Fred Johnson; Ron
Mundy; Gene Bricker; Richard Knauss; Walt Mad-
dox; Al Johnson.

MARCH, Little Peggy
(Peggy March)
Singles: 7-Inch
RCA VICTOR: *62-71* 4-6
Picture Sleeves
RCA VICTOR: *63* 10-15
EPs: 7-Inch 33/45rpm
RCA VICTOR: *63* 15-25
LPs: 10/12-Inch 33rpm
RCA VICTOR (Except 2732): *65-68* 15-20
RCA VICTOR (2732; "I Will
Follow Him"): *63* 50-70

MARCH, Little Peggy, & Bennie Thomas
LPs: 10/12-Inch 33rpm
RCA VICTOR: *65* 15-20
Also see MARCH, Little Peggy

MARCH, Peggy, & Gary Marshal
Singles: 7-Inch
RCA VICTOR: *66* 3-5
Also see MARCH, Little Peggy

MARCHAN, Bobby
(Bobby Marchon; Bobby Marchan & The Tick
Tocks; Bobby Marchan & The Clowns)
Singles: 78rpm
ACE: *56* 4-8
ALADDIN: *53* 5-10
DOT: *54* 5-10
GALE: *57* 4-8
Singles: 7-Inch
ABC: *73* 1-3
ACE: *56* 8-10
ALADDIN: *53* 20-25
CAMEO: *66-67* 3-5
DIAL: *64-74* 3-5
DOT: *54* 15-20
FIRE: *59-62* 5-10
FLASHBACK: *65* 1-3
GALE: *57* 5-8
GAMBLE: *68* 3-5
MERCURY: *77* 2-3
SPHERE SOUND: *65* 3-5
VOLT: *63* 3-5
LPs: 10/12-Inch 33rpm
COLLECTABLES: *88* 6-8
SPHERE SOUND: *64* 20-25

MARCHAN, Bobby, & The Clowns
Singles: 7-Inch
ACE: *59* $5-8
Also see MARCHAN, Bobby
Also see SMITH, Huey

MARCY JO & EDDIE RAMBEAU
Singles: 7-Inch
ROBBEE: *62* 4-6
SWAN: *63* 10-20
Also see MARCY JOE
Also see RAMBEAU, Eddie

MARCY JOE
(Marcy Jo)
Singles: 7-Inch
ROBBEE: *61* 4-6
SWAN: *62* 6-12
Also see CHRISTIE, Lou

MARDONES, Benny
Singles: 7-Inch
POLYDOR: *80* 1-3
PRIVATE STOCK: *78* 1-3
LPs: 10/12-Inch 33rpm
POLYDOR: *80* 5-8

MARESCA, Ernie
Singles: 7-Inch
LAURIE: *66* 4-6
RUST: *64* 5-10
SEVILLE: *60-65* 6-10
LPs: 10/12-Inch 33rpm
SEVILLE (87001; "Shout! Shout! Knock
Yourself Out"): *62* 40-80

MARGRET, Ann: see ANN-MARGRET

MARIACHI BRASS
LPs: 10/12-Inch 33rpm
WORLD PACIFIC: *66* 6-12
Member: Chet Baker.

MARIE, Diane
Singles: 12-Inch 33/45rpm
PRELUDE: *83* 4-6

MARIE, Teena
Singles: 12-Inch 33/45rpm
EPIC: *83-85* 4-6
Singles: 7-Inch
EPIC: *83-88* 1-3
GORDY: *79-81* 1-3
MOTOWN: 1-3
LPs: 10/12-Inch 33rpm
EPIC: *83-88* 5-8
GORDY: *79-81* 5-8
Also see KING DREAM CHORUS &
HOLIDAY CREW

MARIE & REX
Singles: 7-Inch
CARLTON: 59 .... $5-8
Members: Marie Knight; Rex Garvin.
Also see KNIGHT, Marie

MARIGOLDS
Singles: 78rpm
EXCELLO: 55 8-15
Singles: 7-Inch
EXCELLO: 55 20-30
Members: Johnny Bragg; Henry Jones; Hal Hebb;
Willie Wilson.

MARILLION
Singles: 7-Inch
CAPITOL: 83-87 1-3
LPs: 10/12-Inch 33rpm
CAPITOL: 83-86 5-8
Member: Jonathan Mover.
Also see GTR

MARIMBA CHIAPAS
Singles: 78rpm
CAPITOL: 56 2-4
Singles: 7-Inch
CAPITOL: 56 2-4

MARINERS
Singles: 78rpm
CADENCE: 55-56 2-5
COLUMBIA: 50-55 2-5
Singles: 7-Inch
CADENCE: 55-56 3-6
COLUMBIA: 50-55 3-6
TIARA: 58 3-5
EPs: 7-Inch 33/45rpm
COLUMBIA: 51-55 5-10
LPs: 10/12-Inch 33rpm
CADENCE: 56 15-25
COLUMBIA: 51-55 15-25
EPIC: 59 10-20
HARMONY: 59 10-20
Also see GODFREY, Arthur

MARINO, Frank
(Frank Marino & Mahogany Rush)
Singles: 7-Inch
COLUMBIA: 77-81 1-3
LPs: 10/12-Inch 33rpm
COLUMBIA: 77-81 5-8
Also see MAHAGONY RUSH

MARK II
Singles: 7-Inch
WYE: 60-61 3-6
Member: Winston Cogswell.

MARK IV
Singles: 7-Inch
COSMIC: 58 .... $8-10
MERCURY (71000 series): 59 4-6
MERCURY (73000 series): 72-73 2-3
LPs: 10/12-Inch 33rpm
MERCURY: 73 10-12

MARK-ALMOND BAND
Singles: 7-Inch
ABC: 75 2-3
BLUE THUMB: 72 2-4
COLUMBIA: 72-73 2-3
LPs: 10/12-Inch 33rpm
A&M: 78 8-10
BLUE THUMB: 70-71 10-12
COLUMBIA: 72-73 8-10
MCA: 5-8
PACIFIC ARTS: 81 8-10
Members: Jon Mark; Johnny Almond.

MARKETTS
(Mar-Kets)
Singles: 7-Inch
LIBERTY: 62 4-6
MERCURY: 73 2-4
UNI: 69 2-4
UNION: 61-62 8-10
WARNER BROS. (Except 5391): 63-66 ... 3-5
WARNER BROS (5391; "Outer
Limits"): 63 5-8
WARNER BROS (5391; "Out Of
Limits"): 63 3-5
WORLD PACIFIC: 67 3-5
LPs: 10/12-Inch 33rpm
DORE: 82 5-8
LIBERTY: 62-63 30-35
MERCURY: 73 10-15
PHONORAMA: 84 5-8
WARNER BROS: 63-66 25-35
WORLD PACIFIC: 67 15-20
Members: Ben Benay; Mike Henderson; Ray
Pohlman; Tommy Tedesco; Bill Pittman; Gene
Pello; Tom Hensley; Richard Hobaica.
Also see NEW MARKETTS

MAR-KEYS
Singles: 7-Inch
SATELITE: 61 8-10
STAX: 61-66 3-5
LPs: 10/12-Inch 33rpm
ATLANTIC: 61-62 20-25
STAX: 66-71 10-15
Members: Donald Dunn; Steve Cropper; Don Nix.

MAR-KEYS / Booker T. & The MGs
LPs: 10/12-Inch 33rpm
STAX: *67* $12-15
  Also see BOOKER T. & THE MGs
  Also see MAR-KEYS

MARKHAM, Pigmeat
Singles: 7-Inch
ABC: *74* 1-3
CHESS: *64-70* 2-3
WIG: 6-12
LPs: 10/12-Inch 33rpm
CHESS: *61-69* 8-18
JEWEL: *72-73* 5-10
  Also see MABLEY, Moms, & Pigmeat
  Markham

MARKS, Guy
Singles: 7-Inch
ABC: *68* 2-3
ARIOLA AMERICA: *76* 1-3
RADNOR: *70* 2-3
LPs: 10/12-Inch 33rpm
ABC: *66-68* 8-15

MARL, Marley
LPs: 10/12-Inch 33rpm
COLD CHILLIN': *88* 5-8

MARLEY, Bob, & The Wailers
(Wailers)
Singles: 7-Inch
COTILLION: *81* 1-3
ISLAND: *76-84* 1-3
SHELTER: *71* 2-4
LPs: 10/12-Inch 33rpm
CALLA (1200 series): *76* 10-15
CALLA (34000 series): *77* 8-10
COTILLION: *81* 5-8
ISLAND (Except 90000 series): *75-80* ... 8-10
ISLAND (90000 series): *83-86* 5-8
  Also see TOSH, Peter

MARLEY, Ziggy, & The Melody Makers
Singles: 7-Inch
VIRGIN: *88* 1-3
LPs: 10/12-Inch 33rpm
VIRGIN: *88* 5-8

MARLO, Micki
Singles: 78rpm
ABC-PARAMOUNT (Except 9841): *57* ... 3-6
ABC-PARAMOUNT (9841; "What
  You've Done To Me"): *57* 5-10
Singles: 7-Inch
ABC-PARAMOUNT (Except 9841): *57* ... 4-6

ABC-PARAMOUNT (9841; "What
  You've Done To Me"): *57* $8-12
(With "Vocal assist by Paul Anka.")
ABC-PARAMOUNT (9841; "What
  You've Done To Me"): *57* 4-6
(With singer humming the lines done by Paul Anka
on the above pressing.)
CAPITOL: *54-56* 5-8
LPs: 10/12-Inch 33rpm
ABC-PARAMOUNT: *60* 12-20
  Also see ANKA, Paul

MARLOWE, Marion
Singles: 78rpm
CADENCE: *55-56* 2-4
COLUMBIA: *53-54* 2-4
Singles: 7-Inch
CADENCE: *55-56* 2-4
COLUMBIA: *53-54* 2-4
EPs: 7-Inch 33/45rpm
COLUMBIA: *53-55* 4-8
LPs: 10/12-Inch 33rpm
BARNABY: *76* 5-8
COLUMBIA: *53-55* 10-20
HARMONY: *60* 8-12

MARMALADE
Singles: 7-Inch
ARIOLA AMERICA: *76* 2-3
EMI: *74* 2-3
EPIC: *67-69* 4-6
LONDON: *70-71* 3-5
LPs: 10/12-Inch 33rpm
EPIC: *70* 10-12
G&P: *81* 8-10
LONDON: *70* 10-15
  Member: Junior Campbell.
  Also see BLUE

MARSALIS, Branford
LPs: 10/12-Inch 33rpm
COLUMBIA: *84-86* 5-8

MARSALIS, Wynton
LPs: 10/12-Inch 33rpm
COLUMBIA: *82-87* 5-8
WHO'S WHO IN JAZZ: *83* 5-8

MARSH, Little Toni
Singles: 12-Inch 33/45rpm
PRISM: *83* 4-6

MARSHALL-HAIN
Singles: 7-Inch
HARVEST: *78* 1-3
LPs: 10/12-Inch 33rpm
HARVEST: *78* 5-8
  Members: Julian Marshall; Kit Hain.
  Also see EYE TO EYE

MARSHALL TUCKER BAND
Singles: 7-Inch
CAPRICORN: *73-78* $2-3
WARNER BROS: *79-80* 1-3
Picture Sleeves
WARNER BROS: *79* 1-3
LPs: 10/12-Inch 33rpm
CAPRICORN: *73-78* 10-12
WARNER BROS: *79-83* 8-10

MARTERIE, Ralph, & His Orchestra
Singles: 78rpm
MERCURY: *50-57* 2-4
Singles: 7-Inch
MERCURY: *50-60* 2-4
UNITED ARTISTS: *61-62* 2-3
EPs: 7-Inch 33/45rpm
MERCURY: *50-59* 3-6
LPs: 10/12-Inch 33rpm
MERCURY: *50-60* 5-15
UNITED ARTISTS: *61-62* 5-10
WING: *50-60* 4-8

MARTHA & THE MUFFINS
(M+M)
Singles: 12-Inch 33/45rpm
RCA VICTOR: *83-84* 4-6
Singles: 7-Inch
DINDISC/VIRGIN: *80* 1-3
RCA VICTOR: *83-84* 1-3
LPs: 10/12-Inch 33rpm
RCA VICTOR: *83* .5-8
VIRGIN: *80* 5-8

MARTHA & THE VANDELLAS
(Martha Reeves & The Vandellas)
Singles: 7-Inch
GORDY (7011; "I'll Have To
   Let Him Go"): *62* 8-12
GORDY (7014 through 7025): *62-63* 4-6
GORDY (7027 through 7110): *64-72* 3-5
MOTOWN: 1-3
MOTOWN/TOPPS ("Dancing In
   The Street"): *67* 50-75
(Topps Chewing Gum promotional item.
Cardboard flexi, picture disc. Issued with generic
paper sleeve.)
Picture Sleeves
GORDY: *64* 6-12
LPs: 10/12-Inch 33rpm
ERA: *79* 5-10
GORDY (902 & 907): *63* 35-50
GORDY (915 through 925): *65-67* 25-45
GORDY (926 through 958): *68-72* 15-20
MOTOWN (Except 100 & 200 series): *74* 12-15
MOTOWN (100 & 200 series): *81-82* 5-8
Also see GAYE, Marvin

Also see HONDELLS / Del Shannon / Martha
& The Vandellas
Also see REEVES, Martha
Also see VELVELETTES

MARTIKA
Singles: 7-Inch
COLUMBIA: *88* $1-3

MARTIN, Bobbi
Singles: 7-Inch
BUDDAH: *71-72* 1-3
CORAL: *61-67* 2-4
GREEN MENU: *75* 1-3
MGM: *73* 1-3
MAYPOLE: *60* 3-5
UNITED ARTISTS: *68 70* 2-3
Picture Sleeves
CORAL: *65* 3-6
EPs: 7-Inch 33/45rpm
CORAL: *65* 4-6
LPs: 10/12-Inch 33rpm
BUDDAH: *71* 5-10
CORAL: *65* 8-15
SUNSET: *71* 5-10
UNITED ARTISTS: *68-70* 5-10
VOCALION: *70* 5-10

MARTIN, Dean
Singles: 78rpm
APOLLO: *47-48* 25-50
CAPITOL : *48-58* 10-20
(Includes Capitol 2037/2038, *Hey, Brother, Pour
the Winell'd Cry Like a Baby*, a 7-inch 78 rpm.)
DIAMOND: *46* 40-60
EMBASSY (124; "One Foot
   In Heaven"): *49* 50-100
Singles: 7-Inch
CAPITOL (401; "Dean Martin
   Sings"): *53* 50-100
(Boxed set.)
CAPITOL (900 through 2000
   series): *50-54* 5-10
CAPITOL (3000 through 4500
   series): *55-61* 4-8
MCA: *85* 3-5
REPRISE (Except 40,000 series): *62-73* . . . 3-6
REPRISE (40,000 series): *62* 10-15
(Stereo 33 singles.)
WARNER BROS: *83* 1-3
Promotional Singles
CAPITOL (987/988; "Sleep Warm"): *59* . 15-25
(Issued with promo picture sleeve.)
REPRISE (200 "Sophia"): *65* 25-50

TEXAS DESERT CIRCUS WEEK (2160; "It's
1200 Miles From Texas To
Palm Springs"): *58* **$40-60**
(One-sided disc, with no actual label name.
Recorded especially for play in Palm Springs,
promoting a circus. Incorrect title is shown on
label. Should read "It's 1200 Miles From Palm
Springs To Texas.")

Picture Sleeves
CAPITOL: *58* **15-25**
REPRISE: *62* **15-20**

EPs: 7-Inch 33/45rpm
CAPITOL (401; "Dean Martin
Sings"): *53* **75-100**
(With an "EBF" prefix. Double EP boxed set.)
CAPITOL (400 through 700
series): *53-56* **25-75**
(With an "EAP" prefix.)
CAPITOL (800 through 1200
series): *57-59* **20-40**
CAPITOL (9000 series): *56* **25-50**
CAPITOL (Jukebox 33 Compacts): *62-66* **15-25**
18 TOP HITS: *54-55* **20-40**
(Includes both 45 and 78 rpm EPs.)
LLOYDS (705; "Dean Martin"): *54* **25-50**
(Mail-order bonus discs.)
REPRISE (Jukebox 33 Compacts): *63-70* **10-20**

LPs: 10/12-Inch 33rpm
CAPITOL (100 series): *69* **8-15**
CAPITOL (300 series): *69* **8-15**
CAPITOL (401; "Dean Martin
Sings"): *53* **50-100**
(With an "H" prefix. 10-Inch LP.)
CAPITOL (401; "Dean Martin
Sings"): *55* **25-50**
(With a "T" prefix. Red cover.)
CAPITOL (401; "Dean Martin
Sings"): *59* **10-20**
(With a "TT" prefix. Pink cover.)
CAPITOL (523; "Return To Me"/"You're
Nobody Til Somebody Loves You"): *70* . **8-12**
CAPITOL (576; "Swingin' Down
Yonder"): *55* **20-30**
CAPITOL (800 through 2600
series): *57-66* **10-20**
(With a "T" or "ST" prefix.)
CAPITOL (800 through 2600
series): *63-65* **8-15**
(With a "DT" prefix.)
CAPITOL (2815; "Dean Martin
Deluxe Set"): *67* **15-25**
(3-LP boxed set.)
CAPITOL (2900 series): *68* **8-12**
LONGINES (5234; "Memories Are
Made Of This"): *73* **25-50**
(5-LP boxed set. Includes booklet.)

LONGINES (5235; "That's Amore"): *73* . **$8-15**
PAIR: *83* **6-10**
PICKWICK: **6-12**
REPRISE: *63-78* **8-18**
S.M.I.: **10-20**
SEARS: **15-25**
TALKING BOOK (58007; "Look:
December 26, 1967"): *67* **50-75**
(Produced by the American Foundation for the
Blind. Plays at 16 2/3 rpm. Has an interview with
Dean on one side and an interview with Tom Stop-
pard on the reverse.)
TEE VEE: *78* **10-20**
TOWER: *65-66* **15-30**
WALDORF (27; "Dean Martin
Sings"): *53* **20-40**
(10-Inch LP.)
WARNER BROS.: *83* **5-8**

Promotional LPs
DEAN MARTIN TESTIMONIAL
DINNER: *59* **150-250**
(Presented by the Friars Club and sold as a "Collec-
tors Item" for $25 at the dinner. Three LPs in triple-
pocket jacket. No actual label name used. With
guest appearances by Jimmy Durante, Joey Bishop,
Tony Martin, George Burns, Dinah Shore, Mort
Sahl, Judy Garland, Sammy Cahn, Danny Thomas,
Sammy Davis Jr., Bob Hope, Frank Sinatra, and
others.)
REPRISE (246; "Dean Martin
Radio Sampler"): **25-50**
Also see BURNS, George
Also see DURANTE, Jimmy
Also see GARLAND, Judy
Also see GILKYSON, Terry
Also see GOLDDIGGERS
Also see LEE, Peggy, & Dean Martin
Also see MARTIN, Tony
Also see SAHL, Mort
Also see SHORE, Dinah
Also see SINATRA, Frank, & Sammy Davis,
Jr. / Dean Martin & Sammy Davis, Jr.
Also see SINATRA, Nancy

MARTIN, Dean / Glen Campbell
LPs: 10/12-Inch 33rpm
ZENITH/CAPITOL SPECIAL
PRODUCTS: *72* **10-20**
(Issued with a paper cover.)
Also see CAMPBELL, Glen

**MARTIN, Dean / Jeff Clark / Arlene
James**
EPs: 45/78rpm
POPULAR (1035; "Oh Marie"): *54* **8-15**
(78rpm. Not issued with special cover.)

VICTORY (1031; "Walking My Baby
Back Home"): *54* **$8-15**
(78rpm. Not issued with special cover.)
POPULAR (1035; "Oh Marie"): *54* **10-20**
(45rpm. Not issued with special cover.)
VICTORY (1031; "Walking My Baby
Back Home"): *54* **20-40**
(45rpm. Colored vinyl. Not issued with special
cover.)

MARTIN, Dean, & Nat "King" Cole
Singles: 78rpm
CAPITOL: *54* **3-6**
Singles: 7-Inch
CAPITOL: *54* **4-8**
Also see COLE, Nat "King"

MARTIN, Dean / Jane Froman
Singles: 78rpm
CAPITOL: *53* **3-6**
Singles: 7-Inch
CAPITOL (20030; "Who's Your Little
Who Zis"): *53* **8-15**
(Promotional issue only.)
Also see FROMAN, Jane

MARTIN, Dean / Jackie Gleason
LPs: 10/12-Inch 33rpm
CAPITOL SPECIAL MARKETS: **8-10**
Also see GLEASON, Jackie

MARTIN, Dean / Red Ingle &
The Natural Seven
Singles: 78rpm
CAPITOL (726; "Vieni Su"): *49* **8-15**
(Promotional issue only.)

MARTIN, Dean, & Jerry Lewis
Singles: 78rpm
CAPITOL (15000 series): *48* **5-8**
NATIONAL MASK & PUPPET CORP.
("Puppet Show"): **10-15**
(Promotional issue only.)
EPs: 7-Inch 33/45rpm
CAPITOL (533; "Living It Up"): *54* ... **100-150**
CAPITOL (752; "Pardners"): *56* **75-125**
Also see LEWIS, Jerry

MARTIN, Dean / Nicolini Lucchesi
LPs: 10/12-Inch 33rpm
AUDITION (5936; "Dean Martin Sings,
Niccolini Lucchesi Plays"): *56* **25-50**

MARTIN, Dean, & Ricky Nelson
WARNER BROS (2262; "My Rifle, My Pony
And Me"): *59* **50-100**
Also see NELSON, Rick

MARTIN, Dean, & The Nuggets
Singles: 78rpm
CAPITOL: *55* **$3-6**
Singles: 7-Inch
CAPITOL: *55* **5-8**

MARTIN, Dean, & Helen O'Connell
Singles: 78rpm
CAPITOL: *51* **3-6**
Singles: 7-Inch
CAPITOL: *51* **4-8**
Also see O'CONNELL, Helen

MARTIN, Dean / Patti Page
LPs: 10/12-Inch 33rpm
DECCA (79224; "Christmas Seals
For 1962"): *62* **20-40**
(Public service program for TB. Dean's show on
one side, Patti on flip.)
DECCA (79235; "Christmas Seals
For 1962"): *62* **20-30**
(Public service program for TB. Dean's and Patti's
shows on one side, flip has Si Zenter and Vaughn
Monroe.)
Also see MONROE, Vaughn
Also see PAGE, Patti
Also see ZENTER, Si

MARTIN, Dean, & Line Renaud
Singles: 78rpm
CAPITOL: *55* **3-6**
Singles: 7-Inch
CAPITOL: *55* **4-8**

MARTIN, Dean / Nelson Riddle
EPs: 7-Inch 33/45rpm
CAPITOL (1063; "Rio Bravo"): *59* **25-50**
(Promotional issue only. Issued with special paper
sleeve.)
Also see RIDDLE, Nelson

MARTIN, Dean, & Margaret Whiting
Singles: 78rpm
CAPITOL: 50 .... $3-6
Singles: 7-Inch
CAPITOL: 50 5-8
Also see MARTIN, Dean
Also see WHITING, Margaret

MARTIN, Derek
Singles: 7-Inch
BUTTERCUP: 3-5
CRACKERJACK: 63 4-6
ROULETTE: 65 3-5
SUE: 66 3-5
VOLT: 68 3-5

MARTIN, Eric
(Eric Martin Band)
Singles: 7-Inch
CAPTIOL: 85 1-3
ELEKTRA: 83 1-3
LPs: 10/12-Inch 33rpm
ELEKTRA: 83 5-8

MARTIN, Freddy, & His Orchestra
Singles: 78rpm
RCA VICTOR: 50-56 2-4
Singles: 7-Inch
CAPITOL: 63 2-3
DECCA: 67-68 1-3
KAPP: 61 2-3
RCA VICTOR: 50-56 2-4
EPs: 7-Inch 33/45rpm
CAMDEN: 54-56 4-8
RCA VICTOR: 50-54 5-10
LPs: 10/12-Inch 33rpm
CAMDEN: 54-56 5-15
CAPITOL: 59-79 5-15
DECCA: 67 5-10
KAPP: 61-66 5-15
MCA: 73-75 4-8
RCA VICTOR: 51-72 5-15
Also see GRIFFIN, Merv

MARTIN, George, & His Orchestra
Singles: 7-Inch
UNITED ARTISTS (745; "Ringo's
Theme"): 64 5-10
UNITED ARTISTS (750; "A Hard
Day's Night"): 64 5-10
UNITED ARTISTS (800 series): 65 2-3
UNITED ARTISTS (50148; "Love In
The Open Air"): 67 20-25
Picture Sleeves
UNITED ARTISTS (745; "Ringo's
Theme"): 64 35-40

UNITED ARTISTS (750; "A Hard
Day's Night"): 64 .... $175-200
Promotional Singles
UNITED ARTISTS (745; "Ringo's
Theme"): 64 10-15
(White label.)
LPs: 10/12-Inch 33rpm
UNITED ARTISTS (377; "Off The
Beatle Track"): 64 30-40
UNITED ARTISTS (383; "A Hard
Day's Night"): 64 20-30
UNITED ARTISTS (420; "George
Martin"): 65 15-25
UNITED ARTISTS (448; "Help"): 65 ...20-30
UNITED ARTISTS (539; "The Beatle
Girls"): 66 25-35
UNITED ARTISTS (647; "London
By George"): 68 10-15
Also see BEATLES
Also see GERRY & THE PACEMAKERS

MARTIN, Janis
Singles: 78rpm
RCA VICTOR: 56-57 4-8
Singles: 7-Inch
BIG DUTCH: 77 2-4
PALETTE: 61 5-8
RCA VICTOR (6400 & 6500
series): 56 10-12
RCA VICTOR (6652; "My Boy
Elvis"): 56 12-18
RCA VICTOR (6700 through
7300 series): 56-58 5-10
EPs: 7-Inch 33/45rpm
RCA VICTOR (4093; "Just Squeeze
Me"): 58 75-100

MARTIN, Kenny
Singles: 7-Inch
BIG TOP: 60 4-8
FEDERAL: 59-60 5-10
PJ: 66 3-5

MARTIN, Marilyn
Singles: 7-Inch
ATLANTIC: 86-87 1-3
LPs: 10/12-Inch 33rpm
ATLANTIC: 86-87 5-8
Also see COLLINS, Phil, & Marilyn Martin

MARTIN, Moon
(John Martin)
Singles: 7-Inch
CAPITOL: 78-79 1-3
LPs: 10/12-Inch 33rpm
CAPITOL: 78-82 5-8

MARTIN, Nancy
Singles: 7-Inch
ATLANTIC: 82 .... $1-3

MARTIN, Paul
Singles: 7-Inch
ASCOT: 65 3-5
IMPEX: 66 3-5

MARTIN, Ray, Orchestra
Singles: 7-Inch
RCA VICTOR: 61-62 2-3
UNITED ARTISTS: 58 2-3
Picture Sleeves
RCA VICTOR: 61 2-5
UNITED ARTISTS: 58 3-6
LPs: 10/12-Inch 33rpm
CAMDEN: 67-70 4-8
LONDON: 63 5-12
MONUMENT: 67 5-10
RCA VICTOR: 61 5-15

MARTIN, Steve
Singles: 7-Inch
WARNER BROS: 77-79 2-3
Picture Sleeves
WARNER BROS: 78 2-3
LPs: 10/12-Inch 33rpm
WARNER BROS: 77-81 5-8

MARTIN, Tony
Singles: 78rpm
RCA VICTOR: 50-57 2-4
Singles: 7-Inch
CHART: 70 1-3
DOT: 61-66 2-3
DUNHILL: 67 2-3
MOTOWN: 64-66 2-3
NAN: 64 2-3
PARK AVENUE: 63 2-3
RCA VICTOR: 50-60 2-4
EPs: 7-Inch 33/45rpm
DECCA: 51-56 5-10
MERCURY: 54-56 5-10
RCA VICTOR: 51-57 5-10
LPs: 10/12-Inch 33rpm
CAMDEN: 59-60 8-12
CHART: 70 5-8
CHARTER: 63 8-12
CORAL: 73 4-8
DECCA: 51-56 10-20
DOT: 61-62 8-15
MERCURY: 54-61 8-18
RCA VICTOR: 51-60 10-20
20TH CENTURY-FOX: 64 8-15
WING: 59-60 8-12
Also see MARTIN, Dean

MARTIN, Trade
Singles: 7-Inch
COED: 62-64 .... $5-10
GEE: 59 4-6
RCA VICTOR: 66-67 3-5
ROULETTE: 60 4-6
STALLION: 3-5
TOOT: 68 3-5
LPs: 10/12-Inch 33rpm
BUDDAH: 72 10-12

MARTIN, Vince
(Vince Martin & The Tarriers; Vince Martin & Fred Neil)
Singles: 78rpm
GLORY: 56 2-5
Singles: 7-Inch
ABC-PARAMOUNT: 59 3-5
GLORY: 56 3-5
ELEKTRA: 64 2-3
LPs: 10/12-Inch 33rpm
CAPITOL: 73 5-8
ELEKTRA: 64 8-15
Also see TARRIERS

MARTINDALE, Wink
Singles: 7-Inch
ABC/DOT: 76 1-3
DOT: 59-66 3-5
RANWOOD: 73 1-3
Picture Sleeves
DOT: 59-60 4-8
LPs: 10/12-Inch 33rpm
DOT: 59-66 15-20
HAMILTON: 64 10-15

MARTINDALE, Wink, & Robin Ward
Singles: 7-Inch
DOT: 63-64 3-5
LPs: 10/12-Inch 33rpm
DOT: 64 15-20
Also see MARTINDALE, Wink
Also see WARD, Robin

MARTINE, Layng, Jr.
Singles: 7-Inch
BARNABY: 71 2-4
DATE: 66 4-8
GENERAL INT'L: 66 3-5
PLAYBOY: 76 2-3

MARTINO, Al
Singles: 78rpm
BBS: 52 3-5
CAPITOL: 52-57 2-5
Singles: 7-Inch
BBS (Black vinyl): 52 3-5
BBS (Colored vinyl): 52 4-8

CAPITOL: *52-81* $2-5
20TH CENTURY-FOX: *59-64* 2-4
Picture Sleeves
CAPITOL: *63-66* 3-5
LPs: 10/12-Inch 33rpm
CAPITOL: *62-80* 5-15
GUEST STAR: *64* 5-10
MOVIETONE: *67* 5-10
SPRINGBOARD: *78* 4-8
20TH CENTURY-FOX: *59-65* 8-18

MARVELETTES
Singles: 7-Inch
MOTOWN: 1-3
TAMLA: *61-71* 4-8
Picture Sleeves
TAMLA: *61-64* 8-15
LPs: 10/12-Inch 33rpm
MOTOWN (Except 100 series): *75* 12-15
MOTOWN (100 series): *82* 5-8
TAMLA (228 through 243): *61-63* 30-50
TAMLA (253 through 288): *66-68* 20-30
TAMLA (300 series): *70* 12-15
Members: Gladys Horton; Kathy Anderson; Georgeanna Tillman; Wanda Young; Juanita Cowart.

MARVELOWS
(Mighty Marvelows)
Singles: 7-Inch
ABC: *66-69* 4-8
ABC-PARAMOUNT: *64-66* 8-10
LPs: 10/12-Inch 33rpm
ABC: *68* 12-20
Members: Melvin Mason; Frank Paden; Johnny Paden; Jesse Smith; Sonny Stevenson; Andrew Thomas.

MARVIN & JOHNNY
Singles: 78rpm
ALADDIN: *56* 5-10

Marvin and Johnny

MODERN: *54-56* $6-12
RAYS: *54* 5-10
SPECIALTY: *53-55* 5-10
Singles: 7-Inch
ALADDIN: *56* 10-20
ERIC: 1-3
FELSTED: *63* 3-5
FIREFLY: *60* 8-10
JAMIE: *61* 4-6
MODERN: *54-56* 15-25
RAYS: *54* 10-15
SPECIALTY (Black vinyl): *53-55* 10-20
SPECIALTY (Colored vinyl): *53* 20-35
(Most Specialty singles are currently available, using original catalog numbers.)
SWINGIN: *61* 5-10
LPs: 10/12-Inch 33rpm
CROWN (5381; "Marvin & Johnny"): *63* .25-50
Members: Marvin Phillips; Johnny Dean.
Also see ISLEY BROTHERS / Marvin & Johnny
Also see JESSE & MARVIN

MARX, Groucho
Singles: 7-Inch
A&M: *73* 1-3
LPs: 10/12-Inch 33rpm
A&M: *72* 5-10
DECCA: *69* 6-12
YOUNG PEOPLE'S RECORDS: *54* 4-8

MARX, Richard
Singles: 7-Inch
MANHATTAN: *87-88* 1-3
LPs: 10/12-Inch 33rpm
MANHATTAN: *87* 5-8

MARY JANE GIRLS
Singles: 12-Inch 33/45rpm
GORDY: *83-85* 4-6
MOTOWN: *85-87* 4-6
Singles: 7-Inch
GORDY: *83-87* 1-3
LPs: 10/12-Inch 33rpm
GORDY: *83-87* 5-8
Members: Joane "Jo Jo" McDuffie; Candice "Candy" Ghant; Kim "Maxi" Wuletich; Yvette "Corvette" Marine.

MAS, Carolyn
Singles: 7-Inch
MERCURY: *79* 1-3
LPs: 10/12-Inch 33rpm
MERCURY: *79* 5-8

MASCARA
Singles: 12-Inch 33/45rpm
OH MY: *84* 4-6

MASEKELA, Hugh
(Hugh Masekela & The Union Of South Africa)
Singles: 12-Inch 33/45rpm
JIVE AFRIKA: *84* $4-6
Singles: 7-Inch
BLUE THUMB: *74* 1-3
CASABLANCA: *75-77* 1-3
CHISA: *67-71* 2-3
JIVE AFRIKA: *84* 1-3
MGM: *66-68* 2-3
MERCURY: *63-68* 2-3
UNI: *67-69* 2-3
LPs: 10/12-Inch 33rpm
BLUE THUMB: *72-74* 5-10
CASABLANCA: *75-77* 5-10
CHISA: *67-71* 8-15
IMPULSE: *78* 5-10
MGM: *66-68* 8-15
MERCURY: *63-67* 8-18
UNI: *67-69* 8-12
UPFRONT: *77* 5-8
VERVE: *68* 8-15
WING: *68* 6-12
Also see ALPERT, Herb, & Hugh Masekela

MASHMAKHAN
Singles: 7-Inch
EPIC: *70* 2-4
JAMIE: *69* 3-5
LPs: 10/12-Inch 33rpm
EPIC: *70-71* 10-12

MASKED MARAUDERS
Singles: 7-Inch
DEITY: *69* 4-8
LPs: 10/12-Inch 33rpm
DEITY: *69* 15-20

MASKMAN & THE AGENTS
Singles: 7-Inch
DYNAMO: *68-69* 3-5
GAMA: *68* 3-5
LPs: 10/12-Inch 33rpm
DYNAMO: *69* 10-15

MASON, Barbara
(Barbara Mason & The Futures)
Singles: 12-Inch 33/45rpm
WEST END: *83-84* 4-6
Singles: 7-Inch
ARCTIC: *64-68* 3-5
BUDDAH: *71-75* 2-4
CHARGER: *65* 3-5
CRUSADER: *64* 4-6
NATIONAL GENERAL: *70* 2-3
PHONORAMA: *84* 1-3

PRELUDE: *78* $1-3
WMOT: *80-81* 1-3
WEST END: *83-84* 1-3
LPs: 10/12-Inch 33rpm
ARCTIC: *65-68* 15-20
BUDDAH: *72-75* 8-10
GNC: *70* 10-12
NATIONAL GENERAL: *70* 10-12
PHONORAMA: *84* 5-8
PRELUDE: *78* 8-10
WMOT: *81* 8-10
WARNER BROS: *77* 8-10
WIND: *81* 8-10
Also see FUTURES
Also see HIGGINS, Monk

MASON, Barbara, & Bunny Sigler
Singles: 7-Inch
WARNER BROS: *77* 2-3
Also see MASON, Barbara
Also see SIGLER, Bunny

MASON, Bonnie Jo
(Cher)
Singles: 7-Inch
ANNETTE: *64* 25-50
Also see CHER

MASON, Dave
Singles: 7-Inch
ABC: *74* 2-3
BLUE THUMB: *70-78* 2-4
COLUMBIA: *73-81* 1-3
MARBLE: *83* 1-3
LPs: 10/12-Inch 33rpm
ABC: *75* 8-10
BLUE THUMB (19; "Alone
   Together"): *70* 10-12
(Black vinyl.)
BLUE THUMB (19; "Alone
   Together"): *70* 20-25
(Colored vinyl.)
BLUE THUMB (34 through 54): *72-73* . 10-12
BLUE THUMB (800 series): *75* 8-10
BLUE THUMB (6000 series): *74-78* 8-10
COLUMBIA (Black vinyl): *73-81* 8-10
COLUMBIA (Colored vinyl): *73-81* 10-15
(Promotional issue only.)
ISLAND: *83* 5-8
Also see MERRYWEATHER, Neil
Also see TRAFFIC

MASON, Dave, & Cass Elliot
Singles: 7-Inch
DUNHILL: *70-71* 2-4
LPs: 10/12-Inch 33rpm
BLUE THUMB: *71* 12-15

Also see ELLIOT, Cass
Also see MASON, Dave

MASON, Harvey
Singles: 7-Inch
ARISTA: 76-81 .... $1-3
LPs: 10/12-Inch 33rpm
ARISTA: 78-81 5-8

MASON, Jackie
Singles: 7-Inch
VERVE: 62 2-4
LPs: 10/12-Inch 33rpm
VERVE: 62-64 8-18
WARNER BROS: 88 5-8

MASON, Nick
(Nick Mason's Fictitious Sports)
Singles: 12-Inch 33/45rpm
COLUMBIA: 85 4-6
Singles: 7-Inch
COLUMBIA: 81-85 1-3
LPs: 10/12-Inch 33rpm
COLUMBIA: 81-85 5-8
Also see PINK FLOYD

MASON, Nick, & Rick Fenn
Singles: 7-Inch
COLUMBIA: 85 1-3
LPs: 10/12-Inch 33rpm
COLUMBIA: 85 5-8
Also see MASON, Nick

MASON, Vaughan
(Vaughan Mason & Crew)
Singles: 12-Inch 33/45rpm
BRUNSWICK: 80 4-6
Singles: 7-Inch
BRUNSWICK: 80-81 1-3
LPs: 10/12-Inch 33rpm
BRUNSWICK: 80 5-8

MASON, Vaughan, & Butch Dayo
Singles: 12-Inch 33/45rpm
SALSOUL: 83 4-6
Singles: 7-Inch
SALSOUL: 82-83 1-3
LPs: 10/12-Inch 33rpm
SALSOUL: 83 5-8
Also see MASON, Vaughan

MASON DIXON DANCE BAND
Singles: 7-Inch
ALEXANDER STREET: 79 1-3

MASON PROFFIT
Singles: 7-Inch
AMPEX: 71 2-3
HAPPY TIGER: 70 2-4

LPs: 10/12-Inch 33rpm
AMPEX: 71 .... $6-10
HAPPY TIGER: 70-71 8-12
WARNER BROS: 72-73 6-10
Members: John Talbot; Terry Talbot.

MASQUERADERS
Singles: 7-Inch
ABC: 75 2-4
AMERICAN GROUP: 69 2-4
BANG: 80 1-3
BELL: 68 3-5
HI: 2-5
HOT BUTTERED SOUL: 75-76 2-3
TOWER: 66 3-5
WAND: 67 3-5
Members: Lee Hatim; Robert Wrightsil; David
Sanders; Harold Thomas; Sam Hutchins.

MASS PRODUCTION
Singles: 7-Inch
COTILLION: 76-83 1-3
LPs: 10/12-Inch 33rpm
COTILLION: 76-83 5-8

MASSER, Michael, & Mandrill
Singles: 7-Inch
ARISTA: 77 2-3
Also see MANDRILL

MASSEY, Wayne
Singles: 7-Inch
MCA: 83 1-3
POLYDOR: 80 1-3

MASSEY, Wayne, & Charly McClain
Singles: 7-Inch
EPIC: 85-86 1-3

MASSIAH, Maurice
Singles: 12-Inch 33/45rpm
RFC/QUALITY: 83 4-6

MASTER PLAN
Singles: 7-Inch
CRUSH: 88 1-3

MASTERDON COMMITTEE
Singles: 12-Inch 33/45rpm
PROFILE: 86-87 4-6
Singles: 7-Inch
PROFILE: 86-87 1-3
LPs: 10/12-Inch 33rpm
PROFILE: 86 5-8

MASTERPIECE
Singles: 7-Inch
WHITFIELD: 80 1-3
LPs: 10/12-Inch 33rpm
WHITFIELD: 80 5-8

MASTERS, Johnny
(Johnny Maestro)
Singles: 7-Inch
COED: 60 .... $15-20
Also see MAESTRO, Johnny

MASTERS, Sammy
Singles: 78rpm
DECCA: 57 3-5
4 STAR: 57 5-10
Singles: 7-Inch
DECCA: 57 4-8
DOT: 60-66 3-5
4 STAR: 57 20-30
GALAHAD: 62-72 3-5
KAPP: 64 3-5
LODE: 60-61 5-8
WARNER BROS: 60 3-5

MASTERS OF CEREMONY
LPs: 10/12-Inch 33rpm
4TH & B'WAY: 88 5-8

MATHEWS, Tobin
(Tobin Mathews & Co.; Tobin Matthews)
Singles: 7-Inch
CHIEF: 60-61 3-5
COLUMBIA: 63 3-5
U.S.A.: 61 3-5

MATHIS, Johnny
Singles: 78rpm
COLUMBIA: 57-58 2-5
Singles: 7-Inch
COLUMBIA (Except 40000
   series): 74-88 1-3
COLUMBIA (11000 & 12000
   series): 58-63 2-4
COLUMBIA (44000 through 46000
   series): 67-74 1-3
MERCURY: 63-66 2-3
Picture Sleeves
COLUMBIA (40000 series): 57 4-8
COLUMBIA (41000 & 42000
   series): 58-63 3-5
MERCURY: 63-66 2-5
EPs: 7-Inch 33/45rpm
COLUMBIA (Except 8800
   series): 57-59 5-10
COLUMBIA (8871 through
   8873): 56 10-20
LPs: 10/12-Inch 33rpm
COLUMBIA (Except 887): 57-87 5-15
COLUMBIA (887; "Johnny
   Mathis"): 56 25-50
CONCERT: 8-12
(TV mail-order offer.)

MFSL: 85 .... $15-20
MERCURY: 64-67 5-15
Also see KNIGHT, Gladys, & Johnny Mathis

MATHIS, Johnny, & Henry Mancini
LPs: 10/12-Inch 33rpm
COLUMBIA: 87 5-8
Also see MANCINI, Henry

MATHIS, Johnny, & Dionne Warwick
Singles: 7-Inch
ARISTA: 82 1-3
Also see WARWICK, Dionne

MATHIS, Johnny, & Deniece Williams
Singles: 7-Inch
COLUMBIA: 78-84 1-3
LPs: 10/12-Inch 33rpm
COLUMBIA: 78 5-8
Also see MATHIS, Johnny
Also see WILLIAMS, Deniece

MATHIS, Kathy
Singles: 7-Inch
TABU: 88 1-3

MATLOCK, Ronn
Singles: 7-Inch
COTILLION: 79 2-3

MATTHEWS, David
LPs: 10/12-Inch 33rpm
CTI: 77 5-8
Also see WASHINGTON, Grover, Jr.

MATTHEWS, Ian
Singles: 7-Inch
DECCA: 70 2-4
COLUMBIA: 76-77 2-3
ELEKTRA: 73 2-4
MUSHROOM: 78-79 1-3
VERTIGO: 71-72 2-4
LPs: 10/12-Inch 33rpm
COLUMBIA: 77 8-10
ELEKTRA: 73-74 8-10
MUSHROOM (Except "Stealin'
   Home" picture disc): 78 8-10
MUSHROOM ("Stealin' Home"
   picture disc): 78 35-40
VERTIGO: 71-72 10-12
Also see FAIRPORT CONVENTION
Also see MATTHEWS' SOUTHERN COMFORT

MATTHEWS, Milt
Singles: 7-Inch
H&L: 78 2-3

MATTHEWS' SOUTHERN COMFORT
(Featuring Ian Matthews)
Singles: 7-Inch
DECCA: 71 .... $2-4
LPs: 10/12-Inch 33rpm
DECCA: 70-71 10-12
MCA: 78 5-8
  Also see MATTHEWS, Ian
  Also see SOUTHERN COMFORT

MATYS BROS.
Singles: 7-Inch
ESSEX: 54 4-8
SELECT: 62 2-4
SOUND: 2-4

MAUDS
Singles: 7-Inch
DUNWICH: 67 4-6
MERCURY: 67-69 3-5
RCA VICTOR: 70 2-4
LPs: 10/12-Inch 33rpm
MERCURY: 67 15-20

MAURIAT, Paul, & His Orchestra
Singles: 7-Inch
PHILIPS: 67-71 1-3
Picture Sleeves
PHILIPS: 68 2-4
LPs: 10/12-Inch 33rpm
PHILIPS: 67-69 5-10

MAXAYN
Singles: 7-Inch
CAPRICORN: 72-74 2-4
LPs: 10/12-Inch 33rpm
CAPRICORN: 72-74 8-10

MAXWELL, Diane
Singles: 7-Inch
CAPITOL: 61 3-5
CHALLENGE: 59 4-6
LPs: 10/12-Inch 33rpm
CHALLENGE: 59 30-35
  Also see FULLER, Jerry, & Diane Maxwell

MAXWELL, Robert
(Bobby Maxwell)
Singles: 78rpm
MGM: 57 2-4
MERCURY: 52 2-4
TEMPO: 51-52 2-4
Singles: 7-Inch
DECCA: 64 2-3
MGM: 57 2-4
MERCURY: 52 2-4
TEMPO: 51-52 2-4

EPs: 7-Inch 33/45rpm
MGM: 57 .... $3-6
MERCURY: 52 4-8
TEMPO: 51-52 5-10
LPs: 10/12-Inch 33rpm
DECCA: 64 5-12
MGM: 57 10-15
TEMPO: 52 10-20

MAY, Billy, & His Orchestra
Singles: 78rpm
CAPITOL: 50-56 2-4
Singles: 7-Inch
CAPITOL: 50-56 2-4
EPs: 7-Inch 33/45rpm
CAPITOL: 50-56 4-8
LPs: 10/12-Inch 33rpm
CAPITOL: 50-56 5-15

MAY, Brian
(Brian May & Friends)
Singles: 7-Inch
CAPITOL: 83 1-3
LPs: 10/12-Inch 33rpm
CAPITOL: 83 5-8
  Also see QUEEN
  Also see REO SPEEDWAGON
  Also see VAN HALEN

MAYALL, John
(John Mayall & The Blues Breakers Featuring
Eric Clapton)
Singles: 7-Inch
IMMEDIATE: 67 4-6
LONDON: 66-68 5-8
POLYDOR: 69-74 2-4
LPs: 10/12-Inch 33rpm
ABC: 76-78 8-10
BLUE THUMB: 74 8-10
DJM: 79 8-10
LONDON: 67-78 10-15
MCA: 5-8
POLYDOR: 69-74 10-12
  Also see BRUCE, Jack
  Also see CLAPTON, Eric
  Also see FLEETWOOD MAC
  Also see HARTLEY, Keef, Band
  Also see TAYLOR, Mick

MAYANA
Singles: 12-Inch 33/45rpm
ATLANTIC: 83 4-6
Singles: 7-Inch
ATLANTIC: 83 1-3

MAYBE MENTAL
LPs: 10/12-Inch 33rpm
PLACEBO: 84-86 6-10

MAYER, Nathaniel
(Nathaniel Mayer & The Fabulous Twilights;
Nathaniel Mayer & The Fortune Braves)
Singles: 7-Inch
FORTUNE (400 series): *62* $10-15
FORTUNE (500 series): *62-69* 8-10
UNITED ARTISTS: *62* 4-6
LPs: 10/12-Inch 33rpm
FORTUNE: *64* 35-45

MAYFIELD, Curtis
Singles: 7-Inch
BOARDWALK: *81-82* 1-3
CRC: *85* 1-3
CURTOM: *70-80* 1-3
RSO: *80* 1-3
Picture Sleeves
CURTOM: *71-78* 1-3
LPs: 10/12-Inch 33rpm
ABC: *73* 12-15
BOARDWALK: *81-82* 5-8
CURTOM: *70-78* 10-12
RSO: *79-80* 5-8
Also scc IMPRESSIONS
Also see REED, Jimmy

MAYFIELD, Curtis, & Linda Clifford
Singles: 7-Inch
CURTOM: *79-80* 1-3
LPs: 10/12-Inch 33rpm
RSO: *80* 5-8
Also see CLIFFORD, Linda
Also see MAYFIELD, Curtis

MAYFIELD, Percy
Singles: 78rpm
SPECIALTY: *51-54* 5-10
Singles: 7-Inch
ATLANTIC: *74* 2-3
BRUNSWICK: *68* 2-4
CHESS: *55* 20-35
IMPERIAL: *59* 4-6
RCA VICTOR: *70* 2-3
SPECIALTY (300 series): *50-51* 15-25
SPECIALTY (400 series): *51-54* 10-20
(Black vinyl.)
SPECIALTY (400 series): *54* 25-40
(Colored vinyl.)
SPECIALTY (500 series): *55* 5-15
SPECIALTY (600 series): *60* 4-8
TANGERINE: *62-67* 3-5
LPs: 10/12-Inch 33rpm
BRUNSWICK: *69* 12-15
RCA VICTOR: *70-71* 10-12
SPECIALTY: *70* 8-10
TANGERINE: *66-67* $15-20

Maze featuring Frankie Beverly (Photo: Phil Bray)

Note: Most Specialty singles and LPs, reissued
using original catalog numbers, are currently
available.

MAZE
(Featuring Frankie Beverly)
Singles: 12-Inch 33/45rpm
CAPITOL: *84* $4-6
Singles: 7-Inch
CAPITOL: *77-86* 1-3
Picture Sleeves
CAPITOL: *81* 1-3
LPs: 10/12-Inch 33rpm
CAPITOL: *78-86* 6-10
MTA: 10-12

MBULU, Letta
Singles: 7-Inch
A&M: *77* 2-3
LPs: 10/12-Inch 33rpm
A&M: *77* 5-8

McANALLY, Mac
Singles: 7-Inch
ARIOLA: *78* 1-3
ARIOLA AMERICA: *77* 2-3
LPs: 10/12-Inch 33rpm
ARIOLA AMERICA: *78* 5-8

McCALL, Al
Singles: 7-Inch
PROFILE: *83* 1-3

McCALL, C.W.
Singles: 7-Inch
MGM: *74-75* 2-3
POLYDOR: *76* 1-3
LPs: 10/12-Inch 33rpm
MGM: *75* 5-10
POLYDOR: *76-79* 5-8

McCALL, Cash
Singles: 7-Inch
THOMAS: *66* 3-5

McCALL, Toussaint
Singles: 7-Inch
COLLECTABLES: $1-3
RONN: 67-68 3-5
LPs: 10/12-Inch 33rpm
RONN: 67 10-12
Also see NEVILLE, Aaron / Toussaint McCall

McCALLUM, David
Singles: 7-Inch
CAPITOL: 66 2-4
Picture Sleeves
CAPITOL: 66 4-8
LPs: 10/12-Inch 33rpm
CAPITOL: 66 5-15

McCANN, Les
Singles: 7-Inch
ATLANTIC: 69-75 1-3
LIMELIGHT: 65 2-4
PACIFIC JAZZ: 60-65 2-4
WORLD PACIFIC: 2-4
LPs: 10/12-Inch 33rpm
ATLANTIC: 69-75 5-10
LIMELIGHT: 65 10-20
PACIFIC JAZZ: 60-65 15-25
Also see FLACK, Roberta
Also see HOLMES, Richard "Groove," & Les McCann
Also see RAWLS, Lou, & Les McCann Ltd.

McCANN, Les, & Eddie Harris
Singles: 7-Inch
ATLANTIC: 69-70 2-3
LPs: 10/12-Inch 33rpm
ATLANTIC: 69-71 5-10
Also see HARRIS, Eddie
Also see McCANN, Les

McCANN, Peter
Singles: 7-Inch
COLUMBIA: 79 1-3
20TH CENTURY-FOX: 77 2-3
LPs: 10/12-Inch 33rpm
20TH CENTURY-FOX: 77 8-10

McCARTNEY, Paul
(Wings; Paul McCartney & Wings; Paul & Linda McCartney)
Singles: 12-Inch 33/45rpm
CAPITOL (15212; "Spies Like Us"): 85 ... 5-8
CAPITOL (15235; "Press"): 86 4-6
COLUMBIA (03019; "Take It Away"): 82 . 5-8
COLUMBIA (05077; "No More
Lonely Nights"): 84 5-8
("Playout version.")

COLUMBIA (05077; "No More
Lonely Nights"): 84 .... $10-15
("Special Dance Mix.")
COLUMBIA (10940; "Goodnight
Tonight"): 79 10-20
COLUMBIA (39927; "No More
Lonely Nights"): 84 8-12
(Picture disc.)
PROFILE (7147; "Let It Be"): 87 5-8
Promotional 12-Inch Singles
CAPITOL (8574; "Maybe I'm
Amazed"): 77 40-50
CAPITOL (9556; "Spies Like Us"): 85 ...20-25
CAPITOL (9763; "Press"): 86 10-15
CAPITOL (9797; "Angry"): 86 10-15
COLUMBIA (775 "Coming Up"): 80 50-60
(Red label.)
COLUMBIA (775 "Coming Up"): 80 45-55
(White label.)
COLUMBIA (1940; "No More
Lonely Nights"): 84 10-15
("Ballad" version.)
COLUMBIA (1990; "No More
Lonely Nights"): 84 10-15
("Special Dance Mix")
COLUMBIA (05077; "No More
Lonely Nights"): 84 10-15
("Ballad version")
COLUMBIA (10940; "Goodnight
Tonight"): 79 10-20
PROFILE (7147; "Let It Be"): 87 10-15
Singles: 7-Inch
APPLE (1829; "Another Day"): 71 3-5
APPLE (1837; "Uncle Albert-
Admiral Halsey"): 71 3-5
APPLE (1847; "Give Ireland Back
To The Irish"): 72 3-5
APPLE (1851; "Mary Had A
Little Lamb"): 72 3-5
APPLE (1857; "Hi Hi Hi"): 72 3-5
APPLE (1861; "My Love"): 73 3-5
APPLE (1863; "Live & Let
Die"): 73 3-5
APPLE (1869; "Helen Wheels"): 73 3-5
APPLE (1871; "Jet"/
"Mamunia"): 74 5-8
APPLE (1871; "Jet"/"Let Me
Roll It"): 74 3-5
APPLE (1873; "Band On The Run"): 74 ...3-5
APPLE (1875; "Junior's Farm"): 74 3-5
CAPITOL (1829; "Another Day"): 2-3
CAPITOL (1837; "Uncle Albert-Admiral
Halsey"): 2-3
CAPITOL (1847; "Give Ireland Back
To The Irish"): 2-3

CAPITOL (1851; "Mary Had A
Little Lamb"): $2-3
CAPITOL (1857; "Hi Hi Hi"): 2-3
CAPITOL (1861; "My Love"): 2-3
CAPITOL (1863; "Live & Let Die"): 2-3
CAPITOL (1869; "Helen Wheels"): 2-3
CAPITOL (1871; "Jet"): 2-3
CAPITOL (1873; "Band On The Run"): ... 2-3
CAPITOL (1875; "Junior's Farm"): 2-3
CAPITOL (4091; "Listen To What
The Man Said"): 75 2-3
CAPITOL (4145; "Letting Go"): 75 2-3
CAPITOL (4175; "Venus & Mars
Rock Show"): 75 2-3
CAPITOL (4256; "Silly Love Songs"): 76 .. 3-5
(Capitol custom label.)
CAPITOL (4256; "Silly Love Songs"): 2-3
(Black label.)
CAPITOL (4293; "Let 'Em In"): 76 3-5
(Capitol custom label.)
CAPITOL (4293; "Let 'Em In"): 2-3
(Black label.)
CAPITOL (4385; "Maybe I'm
Amazed"): 77 2-3
CAPITOL (4504; "Mull Of Kintyre"): 77 ... 2-3
CAPITOL (4559; "With A
Little Luck"): 78 2-3
CAPITOL (4594; "I've Had Enough"): 78 .. 2-3
CAPITOL (4625; "London Town"): 78 2-3
CAPITOL (5537; "Spies Like Us"): 85 2-3
CAPITOL (5597; "Press"): 86 2-3
CAPITOL (5636;
"Stranglehold"): 86 2-3
COLUMBIA (02171; "Silly Love
Songs"): 81 2-3
COLUMBIA (03018; "Take It Away"): 82 . 2-3
COLUMBIA (03235; "Tug Of War"): 82 .. 2-3
COLUMBIA (04296; "So Bad"): 83 2-3
COLUMBIA (04581; "No More
Lonely Nights"): 84 2-3
COLUMBIA (10939; "Goodnight
Tonight"): 79 2-3
COLUMBIA (11020; "Getting Closer"): 79 . 2-3
COLUMBIA (11070; "Arrow Through
Me"): 79 2-3
COLUMBIA (11162; "Wonderful
Christmastime"): 79 2-3
COLUMBIA (11263; "Coming Up"): 80 .. 2-3
COLUMBIA (11335; "Waterfalls"): 80 2-3
COLUMBIA (33405; "Goodnight
Tonight"): 80 2-3
COLUMBIA (33409; "My Love"): 80 2-3
COLUMBIA (33408; "Uncle Albert-
Admiral Halsey"): 80 2-3

COLUMBIA (33409; "Band On
The Run"): 80 .... $2-3
PROFILE (5147; "Let It Be"): 87 2-3
Picture Sleeves
APPLE (1847; "Give Ireland Back
To The Irish"): 72 10-15
APPLE (1851; "Mary Had A
Little Lamb"): 72 20-25
("Little Woman Love" printed under photo, on
reverse side of sleeve.)
APPLE (1851; "Mary Had A
Little Lamb"): 72 10-12
("Little Woman Love" not printed under photo, on
reverse side of sleeve.)
CAPITOL (4091; "Listen To What
The Man Said"): 75 4-6
CAPITOL (4504; "Mull Of Kintyre"): 77 . 8-10
CAPITOL (5537; "Spies Like Us"): 85 2-3
CAPITOL (5597; "Press"): 86 2-3
CAPITOL (5636; "Stranglehold"): 86 2-3
COLUMBIA (03018; "Take It Away"): 82 . 5-8
(Reads "Not For Sale" on back side. Promotional
issue only.)
COLUMBIA (03018; "Take It Away"): 82 . 2-4
COLUMBIA (04296; "So Bad"): 83 2-3
COLUMBIA (04296; "So Bad"): 83 5-8
(Reads "Not For Sale" on back side. Promotional
issue only.)
COLUMBIA (04581; "No More
Lonely Nights"): 84 5-8
COLUMBIA (11020; "Getting
Closer"): 79 20-25
COLUMBIA (11162; "Wonderful
Christmastime"): 79 3-5
COLUMBIA (11263 "Coming Up"): 80 ... 3-5
COLUMBIA (11335; "Waterfalls"): 80 .. 12-15
PROFILE (5147; "Let It Be"): 87 2-3
Promotional Singles
APPLE (1829; "Another Day"): 71 25-35
APPLE (1837; "Uncle Albert-
Admiral Halsey"): 71 15-20
APPLE (1851; "Mary Had A
Little Lamb"): 72 40-50
APPLE (1857; "Hi Hi Hi"): 72 10-15
APPLE (1861; "My Love"): 73 45-55
APPLE (1863; "Live & Let Die"): 73 ... 10-15
APPLE (1871; "Jet"): 74 20-30
APPLE (1873; "Band On The Run"): 74 . 20-30
APPLE (1875; "Junior's Farm"): 74 20-30
APPLE (1875; "Sally G"): 74 20-30
APPLE (6786; "Helen Wheels"): 73 25-35
APPLE (6787; "Country Dreamer"): 73 . 40-50
CAPITOL (4145; "Letting Go"): 75 12-15
CAPITOL (4175; "Venus & Mars
Rock Show"): 75 12-15

CAPITOL (4256; "Silly Love
Songs."): *76* $10-15
CAPITOL (4293; "Let 'Em In"): *76* 8-10
CAPITOL (4594; "I've Had
Enough"): *78* 10-15
(Add $3-$5 if accompanied by special promotional
flyer.)
CAPITOL (4625; "London Town"): *78* .. 10-15
CAPITOL (5537; "Spies Like Us"): *85* 5-8
CAPITOL (5597; "Press"): *86* 5-8
CAPITOL (5636; "Stranglehold"): *86* 5-8
CAPITOL (8138; "Listen To What
The Man Said"): *75* 10-15
CAPITOL (8570/1; "Maybe I'm
Amazed"): *77* 10-15
CAPITOL (8746/7; "Mull Of
Kintyre"): *77* 10-15
CAPITOL (8812; "With A
Little Luck"): *78* 10-15
COLUMBIA (1204 "Coming Up"): *80* 4-6
(One-sided disc.)
COLUMBIA (03018; "Take It Away"): *82* . 4-6
COLUMBIA (03235; "Tug Of War"): *82* . 8-10
COLUMBIA (04296; "So Bad"): *83* 5-8
COLUMBIA (04581; "No More
Lonely Nights"): *84* 5-8
COLUMBIA (10939; "Goodnight
Tonight"): *79* 5-8
COLUMBIA (11020; "Getting
Closer"): *79* 10-12
COLUMBIA (J1070; "Arrow
Through Me"): *79* 10-12
COLUMBIA (11162; "Wonderful
Christmastime"): *79* 10-12
COLUMBIA (11263; "Coming Up"): *80* .. 8-10
COLUMBIA (11335; "Waterfalls"): *80* ... 8-10
CREATIVE RADIO (PM-1; "Inside
Paul McCartney"): 10-20
(Radio show demo. Flip side is *The Beatle In-
vasion*.)
MIRAMAX (4202; "Rock Show"): *75* . 150-175
(Contains three radio spots. Issued to radio stations
only.)
PROFILE (5147; "Let It Be"): *87* 5-8
LPs: 10/12-Inch 33rpm
APPLE (3363; "McCartney"): *70* 12-15
(Label shows Paul's full name beneath LP title.)
APPLE (3363; "McCartney"): *70* 10-12
(Label doesn't show Paul's name beneath LP title.)
APPLE (3375; "Ram"): *71* 10-15
APPLE (3386; "Wild Life"): *71* 10-15
APPLE (3409; "Red Rose
Speedway"): *73* 10-15
APPLE (3415; "Band On The Run"): *73* . 10-15
(Price includes bonus poster.)

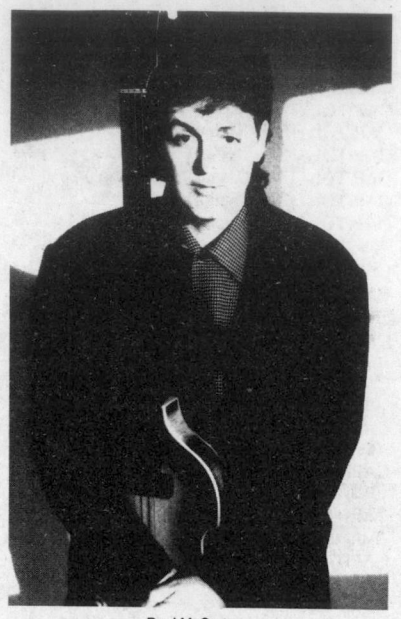

Paul McCartney

CAPITOL (3363; "McCartney"): $8-10
CAPITOL (3375; "Ram"): $8-10
CAPITOL (3386; "Wildlife"): $8-10
CAPITOL (3409; "Red Rose
Speedway"): $8-10
CAPITOL (3415; "Band On The Run"): . .8-10
(Price includes bonus poster.)
CAPITOL (11525; "Wings At The
Speed Of Sound"): *76* 8-10
CAPITOL (11593; "Wings Over
America"): *76* 12-15
CAPITOL (11905; "Greatest Hits"): *78* 5-8
(Price includes bonus poster.)
CAPITOL (11419; "Venus And
Mars"): *75* 10-12
(Price includes bonus posters & stickers.)
CAPITOL (11777; "London Town"): *78* .10-12
(Price includes bonus poster.)
CAPITOL (11901; "Band On The
Run," picture disc): *78* 18-20
CAPITOL (48287; "All The Best!"): *87* ..10-15
CAPITOL (91653; "Flowers In
The Dirt"): *89* 5-8
COLUMBIA (36057; "Back To
The Egg"): *79* 5-8
COLUMBIA (36478; "McCartney"): *80* 5-8
COLUMBIA (36479; "Ram"): *80* 5-8

COLUMBIA (36480; "Wild Life"): *80* **$5-8**
COLUMBIA (36481; "Red Rose
Speedway"): *80* **5-8**
COLUMBIA (36482; "Band On
The Run"): *80* **5-8**
COLUMBIA (36511;
"McCartney II"): *80* **12-15**
(Issued with bonus single, 1204, *Coming Up*,
which represents $4-$6 of the above price range.)
COLUMBIA (36801; "Venus And
Mars"): *80* **5-8**
(Price includes bonus posters.)
COLUMBIA (36987; "The McCartney
Interview"): *80* **8-10**
COLUMBIA (37409; "Wings At The
Speed Of Sound"): *81* **5-8**
COLUMBIA (37462; "Tug Of War"): *82* ... **5-8**
(With Stevie Wonder on *Ebony And Ivory*.)
COLUMBIA (39149; "Pipes
Of Peace"): *83* **5-8**
(With Michael Jackson on *Say Say Say*.)
COLUMBIA (39613; "Give My
Regards To Broad Street"): *84* **5-8**
COLUMBIA (46482; "Band On
The Run"): *80* **10-15**
(Half-speed mastered.)
LIBERTY (50100; "Live And
Let Die"): *84* **5-8**
(With McCartney on title track only.)
LONDON (76007; "The Family
Way"): *67* **50-60**
(Soundtrack. Monaural.)
LONDON (82007; "The Family
Way"): *67* **60-70**
(Soundtrack. Stereo.)
UNITED ARTISTS (100; "Live And
Let Die"): *73* **15-20**
(Copies of this LP with cut corners are valued at
about one-half of the above price range. With Mc-
Cartney on title track only.)
Promotional LPs
APPLE (3375; "Ram"): *71* **80-100**
(Monaural.)
APPLE (6210; "Brung To
Ewe By"): *71* **175-200**
COLUMBIA (821; "The McCartney
Interview"): *80* **40-50**
COLUMBIA (36057; "Back To
The Egg"): *79* **15-20**
COLUMBIA (36511;
"McCartney II"): *80* **15-20**
Also see BEATLES
Also see BRASS RING
Also see COUNTRY HAMS
Also see GREASE BAND

Also see LOMAX, Jackie
Also see NEWMAN, Thunderclap
Also see PERKINS, Carl
Also see SUZY & THE RED STRIPES

McCARTNEY, Paul, & Michael Jackson
Singles: 12-Inch 33/45rpm
COLUMBIA (1758; "Say Say Say"): *83* **$10-15**
COLUMBIA (04169; "Say Say Say"): *83* .. **5-8**
Promotional 12-Inch Singles
COLUMBIA (04169; "Say Say Say"): *83* **12-18**
Singles: 7-Inch
COLUMBIA (04168; "Say Say Say"): *83* .. **2-3**
EPIC (03288; "The Girl Is Mine"): *82* **2-3**
EPIC (03372; "The Girl Is Mine"): *82* **5-8**
(Special one-sided pressing with small, LP-size,
hole.)
Picture Sleeves
COLUMBIA (04168; "Say Say Say"): *83* .. **2-3**
Promotional Picture Sleeves
COLUMBIA (04168; "Say Say Say"): *83* .. **5-8**
EPIC (03288; "The Girl Is Mine"): *82* **5-8**
Promotional Singles
COLUMBIA (04168; "Say Say Say"): *83* .. **5-8**
EPIC (03288; "The Girl Is Mine"): *82* **5-8**
(Label shows matrix number as 169138.)
EPIC (03288; "The Girl Is Mine"): *82* ... **10-15**
(Label shows matrix number as 169202. Also reads
"New Edited Version.")
Also see JACKSON, Michael

**McCARTNEY, Paul / Rochestra /
Who / Rockpile**
Singles: 12-Inch 33/45rpm
ATLANTIC (388; "Every Night"): *81* ... **60-80**
(Promotional issue only.)
Also see ROCKPILE
Also see WHO

McCARTNEY, Paul, & Stevie Wonder
Singles: 12-Inch 33/45rpm
COLUMBIA (02878; "Ebony And
Ivory"): *82* **5-8**
Promotional 12-Inch Singles
COLUMBIA (1444; "McCartney"): *82* .. **25-30**
Singles: 7-Inch
COLUMBIA (02860; "Ebony And
Ivory"): *82* **2-3**
Promotional Singles
COLUMBIA (02860; "Ebony And
Ivory"): *82* **8-12**
Picture Sleeves
COLUMBIA (02860; "Ebony And
Ivory"): *82* **2-4**
Promotional Picture Sleeves
COLUMBIA (02860; "Ebony And
Ivory"): *82* **5-8**

Note: On all in this section, Stevie Wonder appears only on the track *Ebony And Ivory*.
Also see McCARTNEY, Paul
Also see WONDER, Stevie

McCLAIN, Alton, & Destiny
Singles: 7-Inch
POLYDOR: 79-81 .... $1-3
LPs: 10/12-Inch 33rpm
POLYDOR: 79-81 5-8
Also see BRISTOL, Johnny, & Alton McClain

McCLAIN, Janice
Singles: 12-Inch 33/45rpm
MCA: 86 4-6
Singles: 7-Inch
MCA: 86 1-3
RFC: 80 1-3
LPs: 10/12-Inch 33rpm
MCA: 86 5-8

McCLARY, Thomas
Singles: 7-Inch
MOTOWN: 84-85 1-3
LPs: 10/12-Inch 33rpm
MOTOWN: 85 5-8
Also see COMMODORES

McCLINTON, Delbert
Singles: 7-Inch
BOBILL: 67 3-5
BROWNFIELD: 65 3-5
CAPITOL: 80-81 1-3
CAPRICORN: 78 1-3
LPs: 10/12-Inch 33rpm
ACCORD: 81 5-8
CAPITOL: 81 5-8
INTERMEDIA: 84 5-8
MCA: 81 5-8
POLYDOR: 79 5-8
Also see DELBERT & GLEN

McCLINTON, O.B.
Singles: 7-Inch
MERCURY: 76 2-3
LPs: 10/12-Inch 33rpm
ENTERPRISE: 72-74 8-10

McCLURE, Bobby
Singles: 7-Inch
CHECKER: 66-67 3-5
Also see BASS, Fontella, & Bobby McClure

McCONNELL, C. Lynda
Singles: 12-Inch 33/45rpm
ATLANTIC: 84 4-6
Singles: 7-Inch
ATLANTIC: 84 1-3

McCOO, Marilyn
Singles: 7-Inch
RCA VICTOR: 83 .... $1-3
LPs: 10/12-Inch 33rpm
RCA VICTOR: 83 5-8

McCOO, Marilyn, & Billy Davis Jr.
Singles: 12-Inch 33/45rpm
COLUMBIA: 79 4-6
Singles: 7-Inch
ABC: 76-78 1-3
COLUMBIA: 78 1-3
LPs: 10/12-Inch 33rpm
ABC: 76 8-10
COLUMBIA: 78 5-8
Also see FIFTH DIMENSION
Also see McCOO, Marilyn

McCORMICK, Gayle
Singles: 7-Inch
DECCA: 72 2-4
DUNHILL: 71-72 2-4
MCA: 73 2-3
LPs: 10/12-Inch 33rpm
DECCA: 72 10-12
DUNHILL: 71 10-12
FANTASY: 74 8-10
Also see SMITH

McCOY, Charlie
Singles: 7-Inch
CADENCE: 61-62 2-4
MONUMENT: 68-81 1-3
LPs: 10/12-Inch 33rpm
EPIC: 82 5-8
MONUMENT: 69-78 5-10

McCOY, Freddie
Singles: 7-Inch
PRESTIGE: 67 2-4

McCOY, Van
(Van McCoy & The Soul City Symphony)
Singles: 12-Inch 33/45rpm
MCA: 79 4-6
Singles: 7-Inch
AMHERST: 1-3
AVCO: 74-75 2-3
CGC: 70 2-4
COLUMBIA: 65-66 3-5
EPIC: 69 2-4
H&L: 76 2-3
LIBERTY: 62 3-5
MCA: 78-79 1-3
ROCK 'N: 61 5-8
SILVER BLUE: 73 2-4
LPs: 10/12-Inch 33rpm
AVCO: 74-75 8-10

BUDDAH: *72-75* $8-10
COLUMBIA: *66* 12-15
H&L: *76* 8-10
MCA: *77-79* 8-10

McCOY BOYS
Singles: 7-Inch
VERVE: *60* 5-10
Members: Gil Garfield; Perry Botkin, Jr; Ray Campi.
Also see DE VORZON, Barry, & Perry Botkin, Jr.

McCOYS
Singles: 7-Inch
BANG: *65-67* 4-6
MERCURY: *68* 3-5
SOLID GOLD: *73* 1-3
LPs: 10/12-Inch 33rpm
BANG: *65-66* 20-25
MERCURY: *68-69* 15-20
Also see DERRINGER, Rick

McCRACKLIN, Jimmy
(Jimmy McCracklin & His Blues Blasters; Jimmie McCracklin)
Singles: 78rpm
ALADDIN: *51* 5-10
CAVATONE: *47* 8-12
COURTNEY: *45* 8-12
DOWN TOWN: *48* 10-15
EXCELSIOR: *45* 10-15
GLOBE: *45* 10-12
HOLLYWOOD: *55* 4-8
MODERN (700 series): *49* 5-10
PEACOCK: *52-54* 3-6
RPM: *50* 5-10
SWING TIME: *51-52* 5-10
TRILON: *49* 5-10
Singles: 7-Inch
ART-TONE: *61-62* 4-6
CHECKER: *58* 5-10
CHESS: *62* 3-5
GEDINSON'S: *61* 3-5
HI: *60* 4-6
HOLLYWOOD: *55* 10-15
IMPERIAL: *62-67* 3-5
IRMA: 8-12
KENT: *62* 3-5
LIBERTY: *70* 2-4
MERCURY: *59-61* 5-10
MINIT: *67-70* 3-5
MODERN (900 series): *54* 10-20
PEACOCK: *52-54* 10-20
LPs: 10/12-Inch 33rpm
CHESS: *62* 25-30
CROWN: *61* 15-20

IMPERIAL: *63-66* $15-20
MINIT: *67-69* 12-15
STAX: *72-81* 8-10
Also see BROWN, Charles, & Jimmy McCracklin

McCRAE, George
Singles: 7-Inch
GOLD MOUNTAIN: *84* 1-3
T.K.: *74-79* 2-3
LPs: 10/12-Inch 33rpm
CAT: *76* 8-10
GOLD MOUNTAIN: *84* 5-8
T.K.: *74-77* 8-10
Also see McCRAE, George & Gwen

McCRAE, George & Gwen
Singles: 7-Inch
CAT: *76* 2-3
Also see McCRAE, George
Also see McCRAE, Gwen

McCRAE, Gwen
Singles: 7-Inch
ATLANTIC: *81-83* 1-3
BLACK JACK: *84* 1-3
CAT: *74-75* 2-3
LPs: 10/12-Inch 33rpm
ATLANTIC: *81-83* 5-8
CAT: *74-76* 8-10
Also see McCRAE, George & Gwen

McCRARYS
Singles: 7-Inch
CAPITOL: *80-82* 1-3
PORTRAIT: *78-79* 1-3
LPs: 10/12-Inch 33rpm
CAPITOL: *80* 5-8
PORTRAIT: *78* 5-8
Members: Sam McCrary; Linda McCrary; Al McCrary; Charity McCrary.

McCULLOUGH, Ullanda
Singles: 7-Inch
ATLANTIC: *81* 1-3

McCURN, George
Singles: 7-Inch
A&M: *63-64* 3-5
LIBERTY: *62* 3-5
REPRISE: *66* 2-4
LPs: 10/12-Inch 33rpm
A&M: *63* 15-20

McDANIEL, Donna
Singles: 7-Inch
MIDLAND INT'L: *77* 2-3

McDANIELS, Gene
Singles: 7-Inch
COLUMBIA: *66-67* 2-4

LIBERTY: *60-65* $3-5
MGM: *73* 2-4
ODE '70: *75* 2-4
LPs: 10/12-Inch 33rpm
LIBERTY: *60-67* 15-20
ODE '70: *75* 8-10
SUNSET: *66* 10-15
UNITED ARTISTS: *75* 8-10

McDEVITT, Charles, Skiffle Group
(Featuring Nancy Wiskey)
Singles: 7-Inch
CHIC: *57* 3-6
ORIOLE: *57* 5-8

McDONALD, Country Joe
Singles: 7-Inch
FANTASY: *75-79* 2-4
VANGUARD: *71-74* 3-5
LPs: 10/12-Inch 33rpm
FANTASY: *75-79* 6-10
MFSL: *81* 25-50
PICCADILLY: *78* 10-15
VANGUARD: *69-76* 8-12
Also see COUNTRY JOE & THE FISH

McDONALD, Kathi
Singles: 7-Inch
CAPITOL: *74* 2-4
LPs: 10/12-Inch 33rpm
CAPITOL: *74* 12-15
Also see BALDRY, Long John, & Kathi Mc-
Donald

McDONALD, Michael
Singles: 7-Inch
MCA: *86* 1-3
WARNER BROS: *82-85* 1-3
Picture Sleeves
WARNER BROS: *82-85* 1-3
LPs: 10/12-Inch 33rpm
MCA: *86* 5-8
MFSL: *85* 15-25
WARNER BROS: *82* 5-8
Also see DOOBIE BROTHERS
Also see HOLLAND, Amy
Also see LABELLE, Patti, & Michael Mc-
Donald
Also see MEMPHIS HORNS
Also see PACK, David
Also see STEELY DAN
Also see WOOD, Lauren

McDONALD, Michael & James Ingram
Singles: 7-Inch
QWEST: *83* 1-3
Also see INGRAM, James
Also see McDONALD, Michael

McDOWELL, Carrie
Singles: 7-Inch
MOTOWN: *87* $1-3

McDOWELL, Ronnie
Singles: 7-Inch
CURB: *87-88* 1-3
EPIC: *79-85* 1-3
GRT: *77* 2-4
MCA: *87* 1-3
MCA/CURB: *86* 1-3
SCORPION (Except 0533): *77-79* 2-5
SCORPION (0533; "Only The Lonely"): *77* .4-6
LPs: 10/12-Inch 33rpm
DICK CLARK: *79* 8-10
EPIC: *79-85* 5-8
MCA/CURB: *86-88* 5-8
SCORPION: *77-79* 10-12
STRAWBERRY: 8-10

McDUFF, Brother Jack
Singles: 7-Inch
CADET: *68* 2-3
BLUE NOTE: *69* 2-3
LPs: 10/12-Inch 33rpm
BLUE NOTE: *69* 8-12
PRESTIGE (7000 series): *60-64* 25-50
(Yellow labels.)
PRESTIGE (7000 series): *64-65* 10-20
(Blue labels.)
Also see BENSON, George
Also see BURRELL, Kenny, & Brother Jack
McDuff

McDUFF, Brother Jack, & Gene Ammons
LPs: 10/12-Inch 33rpm
PRESTIGE: *61* 20-40
(Yellow label.)
Also see AMMONS, Gene

McDUFF, Brother Jack, & Willis Jackson
LPs: 10/12-Inch 33rpm
PRESTIGE: *66* 10-15
Also see JACKSON, Willis
Also see McDUFF, Brother Jack

McFADDEN, Bob
(Bob McFadden & Dor; Rod McKuen)
Singles: 7-Inch
BRUNSWICK: *59* 8-10
CORAL: *60* 8-10
Picture Sleeves
BRUNSWICK: *59* 12-25
LPs: 10/12-Inch 33rpm
BRUNSWICK: *59* 50-75
Also see McKUEN, Rod

McFADDEN & WHITEHEAD
Singles: 12-Inch 33/45rpm
PHILADELPHIA INT'L: 79 . . . . $4-6
SUTRA: 4-6
Singles: 7-Inch
CAPITOL: 82-83 1-3
PHILADELPHIA INT'L: 79 1-3
SUTRA: 1-3
TSOP: 80 1-3
LPs: 10/12-Inch 33rpm
CAPITOL: 83 5-8
PHILADELPHIA INT'L: 79 5-8
TSOP: 80 5-8
Members: Gene McFadden; John Whitehead.

McFARLAND, Gary
LPs: 10/12-Inch 33rpm
SKYE: 69 8-12

McFERRIN, Bobby
Singles: 7-Inch
EMI-MANHATTAN: 88 1-3
LPs: 10/12-Inch 33rpm
BLUE NOTE: 87 5-8
EMI-MANHATTAN: 88 5-8

McGEE, Parker
Singles: 7-Inch
BIG TREE: 77 2-3
LPs: 10/12-Inch 33rpm
BIG TREE: 76 5-8

McGHEE, Brownie
(Brownie McGhee & His Jook Block Dusters;
Brownie McGhee & His Sugar Men)
Singles: 78rpm
ALERT: 46-47 8-12
DERBY: 52 5-10
DISC: 47 5-10
DOT: 53 8-10
ENCORE: 53 5-10
HARLEM: 52 10-15
LONDON: 51 5-10
PAR: 52 5-10
RED ROBIN: 52-53 8-10
SAVOY: 44-57 5-15
SITTIN' IN WITH: 48 5-10
Singles: 7-Inch
DOT: 53 10-20
HARLEM: 52 25-35
JACKSON (2304; "Mean Old
Frisco"): 52 75-100
(Colored vinyl.)
JAX (Colored vinyl): 52 60-75
RED ROBIN (111; "Don't Dog
Your Woman"): 53 100-150
SAVOY (800 series): 51-52 10-20

SAVOY (1100 through 1500
series): 55-59 . . . . $5-15
LPs: 10/12-Inch 33rpm
FOLKWAYS (Except 20, 30, & 2000
series): 8-10
FOLKWAYS (20, 30, & 2000
series): 54-55 20-35
STORYVILLE: 5-8
VANGUARD: 8-10
Note: Though perhaps not credited, many of the
above feature Sonny Terry on harmonica.

McGHEE, Brownie, & Sonny Terry
Singles: 78rpm
SAVOY (5000 series): 44-48 8-12
Singles: 7-Inch
PRESTIGE BLUESVILLE: 60-62 1-5
LPs: 10/12-Inch 33rpm
A&M: 73 8-10
BLUESWAY: 69-73 10-12
EVEREST: 69 10-12
FANTASY (3000 series): 61-62 15-20
(Black vinyl.)
FANTASY (3000 series): 61-62 25-40
(Colored vinyl.)
FANTASY (8000 series): 62 15-20
(Black vinyl.)
FANTASY (8000 series): 62 25-40
(Colored vinyl.)
FANTASY (24000 series): 72-81 8-10
FOLKWAYS (2000 & 3000
series): 55-61 20-25
FOLKWAYS (31000 series): 8-10
FONTANA: 69 10-15
MAINSTREAM (6000 series): 65 15-20
MAINSTREAM (300 series): 71 8-10
MUSE: 81 5-8
OLYMPIC: 73 8-10
PRESTIGE (1000 series): 60 25-30
PRESTIGE (7000 series): 69-70 8-10
PRESTIGE BLUESVILLE: 60-62 20-25
PRESTIGE FOLKLORE: 12-15
ROULETTE: 59 25-30
SAVOY (1100 series): 84 5-8
SAVOY (12000 series): 73 8-10
SAVOY (14000 series): 58 25-30
SMASH: 65 15-20
VERVE: 61 20-25
VERVE/FOLKWAYS: 65 15-20
WORLD PACIFIC: 60 25-30
Also see McGHEE, Brownie
Also see TERRY, Sonny

McGHEE, Stick
(Stick McGhee & His Buddies; Sticks McGhee & The Ramblers)
Singles: 78rpm
ATLANTIC: 49-52 .... $10-15
DECCA: 47 10-20
ESSEX: 52 5-10
HARLEM: 47 15-20
KING: 53-55 6-12
LONDON: 51 25-50
SAVOY: 55 5-10
Singles: 7-Inch
ATLANTIC (955; "Wee Wee
    Hours"): 52 30-40
ATLANTIC (991; "New Found
    Love"): 52 30-40
GUSTO: 1-3
HERALD: 60 5-10
KING: 53-55 20-30
LONDON (978; "You Gotta Have Something
    On The Ball"): 51 75-150
SAVOY: 55 10-20

McGHEE, Sticks / John Lee Hooker
LPs: 10/12-Inch 33rpm
AUDIO LAB (1520; "Highway Of
    Blues"): 59 50-100
    Also see HOOKER, John Lee
    Also see McGHEE, Sticks

McGILPIN, Bob
Singles: 7-Inch
BUTTERFLY: 77-78 1-3
LPs: 10/12-Inch 33rpm
BUTTERFLY (Black vinyl): 78-79 5-8
BUTTERFLY (Colored vinyl): 78 12-15
CASABLANCA: 80 5-8

McGOVERN, Maureen
Singles: 7-Inch
CASABLANCA: 1-3
EPIC: 78 1-3
MAIDEN VOYAGE: 2-3
20TH CENTURY-FOX: 73-75 2-3
WARNER BROS: 79-80 1-3
WOODEN NICKEL: 73 2-4
LPs: 10/12-Inch 33rpm
20TH CENTURY-FOX: 73-75 8-10
WARNER BROS: 79 5-8

McGRIFF, Edna
Singles: 78rpm
JUBILEE: 51-53 6-12
Singles: 7-Inch
CAPITOL: 64-65 3-5
JUBILEE (Black vinyl): 51-53 15-20
JUBILEE (Colored vinyl): 53 25-40

WILLOW: 61 .... $4-8

McGRIFF, Edna, & Sonny Til
Singles: 78rpm
JUBILEE: 52 6-12
Singles: 7-Inch
JUBILEE: 52 15-25
    Also see McGRIFF, Edna
    Also see TIL, Sonny

McGRIFF, Jimmy
(Jimmy McGriff Trio)
Singles: 7-Inch
BLUE NOTE: 71 2-3
CAPITOL: 70-71 2-3
COLLECTABLES: 1-3
GROOVE MERCHANT : 75 2-3
JELL (100 series): 62 5-8
JELL (500 series): 65 3-5
MILESTONE: 83 1-3
SOLID STATE: 66-70 2-4
SUE: 62-64 3-5
UNITED ARTISTS: 71-78 1-3
LPs: 10/12-Inch 33rpm
BLUE NOTE: 70-71 8-12
COLLECTABLES: 88 6-8
51 WEST: 5-8
GROOVE MERCHANT: 71-76 8-10
LRC: 77-78 8-10
MILESTONE: 81-83 5-8
SOLID STATE: 66-70 10-15
SOUL SUGAR: 70 10-12
SUE: 62-65 15-30
UNITED ARTISTS: 71 8-12
VEEP: 68 10-12
    Also see HOLMES, Richard "Groove"
    Also see PARKER, Little Junior, & Jimmy McGriff

McGUFFEY LANE
Singles: 7-Inch
ATCO: 81-83 1-3
ATLANTIC AMERICA: 84 1-3
LPs: 10/12-Inch 33rpm
ATCO: 82 6-10

McGUINN, Roger
Singles: 7-Inch
COLUMBIA: 73-77 2-3
LPs: 10/12-Inch 33rpm
COLUMBIA: 77 8-10

McGUINN & HILLMAN
LPs: 10/12-Inch 33rpm
CAPITOL: 80 5-8
    Members: Roger McGuinn; Chris Hillman.
    Also see HILLMAN, Chris
    Also see McGUINN, Roger

McGUINN, CLARK & HILLMAN
Singles: 7-Inch
CAPITOL: 79 ....$1-3
LPs: 10/12-Inch 33rpm
CAPITOL: 79-82 5-8
Members: Roger McGuinn; Gene Clark; Chris
Hillman.
Also see BYRDS
Also see McGUINN & HILLMAN

McGUINESS, Wayne
Singles: 78rpm
METEOR: 56 15-25
Singles: 7-Inch
METEOR: 56 50-75

McGUINNESS-FLINT
Singles: 7-Inch
CAPITOL: 70-71 2-4
LPs: 10/12-Inch 33rpm
CAPITOL: 70-71 10-12
Members: Tom McGuinness; Hughie Flint.
Also see GALLAGHER & LYLE
Also see MANN, Manfred

McGUIRE, Barry
(Barry McGuire & The Horizon Singers)
Singles: 7-Inch
ABC: 70 1-3
DUNHILL: 65-66 3-5
HORIZON: 63 3-5
ODE '70: 70 2-3
MCA: 1-3
MOSAIC: 61-62 4-6
MYRRH: 73 1-3
ROULETTE: 1-3
Picture Sleeves
DUNHILL: 65 4-8
LPs: 10/12-Inch 33rpm
BIRDWING: 80 5-8
DUNHILL: 65 20-30
HORIZON: 63 15-20
MYRRH: 73-75 5-8
ODE '70: 70 8-10
SPARROW: 79 5-8
SURREY: 65 12-15
Also see NEW CHRISTY MINSTRELS

McGUIRE, Barry, & Barry Kane
Singles: 7-Inch
HORIZON: 62 3-5
LPs: 10/12-Inch 33rpm
HORIZON: 62 15-20
SURREY: 66 12-15

McGUIRE, Phyllis
Singles: 7-Inch
REPRISE: 64-65 2-4

ORPHEUM: 68 ....$2-3
LPs: 10/12-Inch 33rpm
ABC-PARAMOUNT: 66 10-15
Also see McGUIRE SISTERS

McGUIRE SISTERS
Singles: 78rpm
CORAL: 54-57 2-5
Singles: 7-Inch
ABC-PARAMOUNT: 66 2-4
CORAL (Except 61000 series): 58-65 3-5
CORAL (61000 series): 54-58 4-6
MCA: 1-3
REPRISE: 63-65 3-5
Picture Sleeves
CORAL: 56-61 5-10
EPs: 7-Inch 33/45rpm
CORAL: 55-60 8-12
LPs: 10/12-Inch 33rpm
ABC-PARAMOUNT: 66 10-15
CORAL (6; "Best Of The McGuire
Sisters"): 65 12-20
CORAL (56000 series): 55 25-30
CORAL (57000 series): 56-65 15-20
MCA: 78 5-8
VOCALION: 60-67 10-15
Members: Phyllis McGuire; Dorothy McGuire;
Christine McGuire.
Also see McGUIRE, Phyllis

McIAN, Peter
Singles: 7-Inch
COLUMBIA/ARC: 80 1-3
LPs: 10/12-Inch 33rpm
COLUMBIA/ARC: 80 5-8

McKEE, Lonett
Singles: 7-Inch
SUSSEX: 74 2-3

McKENDREE SPRING
Singles: 7-Inch
DECCA: 69-72 2-4
MCA: 73 2-3
PYE: 76 2-3
LPs: 10/12-Inch 33rpm
DECCA: 69-72 10-15
MCA: 73 8-10
PYE: 75 8-10

McKENZIE, Bob & Doug
Singles: 7-Inch
MERCURY: 82 1-3
LPs: 10/12-Inch 33rpm
MERCURY: 81 5-8

McKENZIE, Scott
(McKenzie's Musicians)
Singles: 7-Inch
CAPITOL: *65-67* $3-5
EPIC: *67-72* 3-5
ODE: *67-71* 3-5
LPs: 10/12-Inch 33rpm
ODE (44000 series): *67* 15-20
ODE (34000 series): *77* 8-10
ODE (77000 series): *70* 10-15

McKUEN, Rod
(Rod McKuen & The Keytones; Rod McKuen & The Horizon Singers)
Singles: 7-Inch
A&M: *63* 3-5
BUDDAH: *73-74* 2-3
DECCA: *59* 4-6
HORIZON: *63* 3-5
JUBILEE: *62* 4-6
KAPP: *61* 3-5
LIBERTY: *56* 5-8
RCA VICTOR: *66-67* 3-5
SPIRAL: *61-62* 4-6
VISTA: *71* 2-4
WARNER BROS: *68-72* 2-4
Picture Sleeves
VISTA: *71* 2-4
WARNER BROS: *71* 2-4
LPs: 10/12-Inch 33rpm
DECCA (4900 series): *68* 10-12
DECCA (8800 series): *59* 20-25
DECCA (75000 series): *69* 10-12
CAPITOL: *64* 15-20
HARMONY: *71* 8-10
HI FI: *58-59* 20-25
EPIC (600 & 3800 series): *62* 15-20
EPIC (26000 series): *68* 10-12
EVEREST: *68* 10-12
HORIZON: *63* 15-20
IN: *64* 15-20
JUBILEE: *62* 20-25
KAPP (1200 & 3200 series): *61* 15-20
KAPP (1500 & 3500 series): *67* 10-15
LIBERTY (Except 3011): *67* 10-15
LIBERTY (3011; "Songs For A
Lazy Afternoon"): *56* 25-35
RCA VICTOR: *65-68* 10-15
STANYAN: *66-72* 10-15
SUNSET: *70* 8-10
TRADITION: *68* 10-12
VISTA: *71* 8-10
WARNER BROS: *67-76* 8-12
Also see McFADDEN, Bob
Also see SAN SEBASTIAN STRINGS

McLAGAN, Ian
Singles: 7-Inch
MERCURY: *79* $1-3
LPs: 10/12-Inch 33rpm
MERCURY: *79* 5-8
Also see FACES
Also see SMALL FACES

McLAIN, Tommy
Singles: 7-Inch
COLLECTABLES: 1-3
JIN (Except 197): *66-69* 3-6
JIN (197; "Sweet Dreams"): *66* 5-10
MSL: *66* 3-5

McLANE, Jimmy
Singles: 7-Inch
SWAY: *61* 3-5

McLAREN, Malcom
(Malcom McLaren & The World's Famous Supreme Band)
Singles: 12-Inch 33/45rpm
ISLAND: *83-85* 4-6
Singles: 7-Inch
ISLAND: *83-85* 1-3
LPs: 10/12-Inch 33rpm
ISLAND: *83-85* 5-8
Also see WORLD'S FAMOUS SUPREME TEAM
Also see WORRELL, Bernie

McLAUGHLIN, John
LPs: 10/12-Inch 33rpm
COLUMBIA: *72-83* 5-10
DOUGLAS: *72* 8-12
POLYDOR: *69-72* 8-15

McLAUGHLIN, Pat
LPs: 10/12-Inch 33rpm
CAPITOL: *88* 5-8

McLAURIN, Bette
(Bette McLaurin & The Four Fellows; Bette McLaurin & The Striders; Betty McLaurin)
Singles: 7-Inch
CAPITOL: *59* 3-6
CENTRAL: *54* 5-10
CORAL: *53* 5-10
DERBY (700 series): *50-52* 8-12
DERBY (800 series): *52* 25-40
GLORY: *55* 10-20
JUBILEE: *55* 5-10
O GEE: *59* 4-8
PULSE: *65* 3-5
Also see FOUR FELLOWS

McLEAN, Don
Singles: 7-Inch
ARISTA: 78 ....$1-3
CAPITOL: 87-88 1-3
EMI AMERICA: 87 1-3
LIBERTY: 1-3
MILLENNIUM: 81-83 1-3
RCA VICTOR: 83 1-3
UNITED ARTISTS: 71-75 2-3
Picture Sleeves
UNITED ARTISTS: 71-73 2-4
LPs: 10/12-Inch 33rpm
CASABLANCA: 79 8-10
LIBERTY: 82-83 5-8
MILLENNIUM: 81 5-8
UNITED ARTISTS: 71-74 10-12
Promotional LPs
RCA VICTOR ("Special Radio
Series"): 81 10-15

McLEAN, Penny
Singles: 7-Inch
ATCO: 75-76 2-4
Also see SILVER CONVENTION

McLEAN, Phil
Singles: 7-Inch
VERSATILE: 61-62 4-6

McLOLLIE, Oscar
(Oscar McLollie & The Honey Jumpers; Oscar
Lollie)
Singles: 78rpm
CLASS: 57 3-6
MERCURY: 51-56 5-10
MODERN: 52-55 5-15
WING: 56 5-10
Singles: 7-Inch
CLASS: 57-59 4-8
MERCURY (70000 series): 56 5-10
MODERN (Except 902): 53-55 12-25
MODERN (902; "The Honey
Jump"): 52 20-30
WING: 56 8-12

McLOLLIE, Oscar, & Jeanette Baker
Singles: 7-Inch
CLASS: 58 4-6
Also see McLOLLIE, Oscar

McLOLLIE, Oscar, & Nancy Lamarr
Singles: 7-Inch
SAHARA: 63 3-5
Also see McLOLLIE, Oscar

McLYTE
LPs: 10/12-Inch 33rpm
FIRST PRIORITY: 88 5-8

McMAHON, Gerard
Singles: 7-Inch
FULL MOON: 83 ....$1-3
LPs: 10/12-Inch 33rpm
FULL MOON: 83 5-8

McNALLY, Larry John
Singles: 7-Inch
ARC: 81 1-3

McNAMARA, Robin
Singles: 7-Inch
STEED: 69-71 2-4
LPs: 10/12-Inch 33rpm
STEED: 70 10-15

McNEELY, Big Jay
(Big Jay McNeely & His Blue Jays; Big Jay Mc-
Neely With Little Sonny Warner)
Singles: 78rpm
ALADDIN: 49 5-10
BAYOU: 53 10-20
FEDERAL: 52-54 5-10
EXCLUSIVE: 46 5-10
IMPERIAL: 51-52 5-10
SAVOY: 48-49 5-10
VEE JAY: 55 5-10
Singles: 7-Inch
BAYOU: 53 25-40
FEDERAL: 52-54 10-20
IMPERIAL (5200 series): 53 15-25
SWINGIN': 59-61 4-8
VEE JAY: 55 15-30
WARNER BROS: 63 3-5
EPs: 7-Inch 33/45rpm
FEDERAL (246; "Go! Go! Go!
With Big Jay McNeely"): 100-200
LPs: 10/12-Inch 33rpm
COLLECTABLES: 88 6-8
FEDERAL (96; "Big Jay
McNeely"): 54 300-400
(10-Inch LP.)
FEDERAL (530; "Big Jay In
3-D"): 56 100-200
KING: 59 25-30
SAVOY (15045; "Rhythm & Blues
Concert"): 58 100-150
(10-Inch LP.)
WARNER BROS: 63 20-25
Also see OTIS, Johnny

McNEELY, Big Jay / Paul Williams
Singles: 78rpm
SAVOY: 49-55 5-10
Singles: 7-Inch
SAVOY (1100 series): 55 5-10
(Reissue of tracks originally on 78rpm only.)

Also see McNEELY, Big Jay
Also see WILLIAMS, Paul

McNEIR, Ronnie
Singles: 7-Inch
CAPITOL: *84* $1-3
PRODIGAL: *75* 2-3
LPs: 10/12-Inch 33rpm
CAPITOL: *84* 5-8

McNICHOL, Kristy & Jimmy
Singles: 7-Inch
RCA VICTOR: *78* 1-3
Picture Sleeves
RCA VICTOR: *78* 1-3

M'COOL, Shamus
Singles: 7-Inch
PERSPECTIVE: *81* 1-3

McPHATTER, Clyde
Singles: 78rpm
ATLANTIC: *56-57* 5-10
Singles: 7-Inch
AMY: *65-67* 3-5
ATLANTIC (1000 series): *56-58* 8-15
ATLANTIC (2000 series): *58-60* 5-10
DECCA: *70* 3-5
DERAM: *68-69* 3-5
MGM: *59-60* 4-6
MERCURY: *60-65* 4-6
Picture Sleeves
MGM: *60* 5-10
MERCURY: *60-65* 4-8
EPs: 7-Inch 33/45rpm
ATLANTIC: *58-59* 25-40

Clyde McPhatter

LPs: 10/12-Inch 33rpm
ALLEGIANCE: $5-8
ATLANTIC (8024; "Love
  Ballads"): *58* 50-100
  (Black label.)
ATLANTIC (8024; "Love
  Ballads"): *59* 20-25
  (Red label.)
ATLANTIC (8031; "Clyde"): *59* 35-50
ATLANTIC (8077; "Best Of Clyde
  McPhatter"): *63* 25-35
DECCA: *70* 15-20
MGM: *59-60* 25-30
MERCURY: *60-64* 20-30
WING: *62* 20-25
Also see DOMINOES
Also see DRIFTERS

McPHERSON, Wyatt "Earp"
Singles: 7-Inch
SAVOY: *61* 3-5

McPHERSON, Wyatt "Earp," & Paul Williams
Singles: 7-Inch
BATTLE: *63* $3-5
Also see McPHERSON, Wyatt "Earp"
Also see WILLIAMS, Paul

McRAE, Carmen
Singles: 78rpm
DECCA: *55-57* 2-4
VENUS: *54* 2-5
Singles: 7-Inch
COLUMBIA: *62* 2-4
DECCA: *55-57* 2-4
VENUS: *54* 3-5
Picture Sleeves
COLUMBIA: *62* 3-6
LPs: 10/12-Inch 33rpm
BETHLEHEM (1000 series): *54* 40-60
  (10-Inch LPs.)
COLUMBIA: *61-65* 15-25
DECCA (8100 through 8800
  series): *55-58* 25-50
  (Black & silver label.)
DECCA (8100 through 8800
  series): *64* 10-20
  (Black label with horizontal rainbow stripe.)
FOCUS: *65* 10-20
KAPP: *58-59* 20-35
MAINSTREAM: *65-67* 10-20
TIME: *63* 15-25
Also see DAVIS, Sammy, Jr., & Carmen
McRae
Also see SIMONE, Nina, Chris Connor & Carmen McRae

McSHANN, Jay
(Jay McShann & His Orchestra; Jay McShann
& His Combo; Jay McShann & His Trio; Jay
McShann Quartet; Jay McShann's Kansas City
Stompers; Jay McShann & His Jazz Men; Jay
McShann's Sextet)
Singles: 78rpm
ALADDIN: 50 ....$4-8
CAPITOL: 44-45 5-10
DECCA: 41-43 5-10
DOWN BEAT: 48-49 4-8
MERCURY: 45-46 4-8
MODERN: 50 4-8
PHILO/ALADDIN: 45 5-10
PREMIER: 45 5-10
SWING TIME: 48-50 4-8
VEE JAY: 55-56 3-6
Singles: 7-Inch
VEE JAY: 55-56 10-15
EPs: 7-Inch 33/45rpm
DECCA: 54 30-45
LPs: 10/12-Inch 33rpm
CAPITOL: 67 12-15
DECCA (5503; "Jay
McShann"): 54 125-175
(10-Inch LP.)
DECCA (9000 series): 68 10-12
Also see WITHERSPOON, Jimmy

McSHANN, Jay, With Johnny
Moore's Three Blazers
Singles: 78rpm
MODERN: 50 5-10
Also see MOORE, Johnny

McSHANN, Jay, & Priscilla Bowman
Singles: 78rpm
VEE JAY: 55 3-6
Singles: 7-Inch
VEE JAY: 55 10-15
Also see McSHANN, Jay

McSHY D
LPs: 10/12-Inch 33rpm
LUKE SKYWALKER: 88 5-8

McVIE, Christine
Singles: 7-Inch
WARNER BROS: 84 2-3
LPs: 10/12-Inch 33rpm
WARNER BROS: 84 5-8
Also see FLEETWOOD MAC
Also see PERFECT, Christine
Also see NEWMAN, Randy

McWILLIAMS, Paulette
Singles: 7-Inch
FANTASY: 77 2-3

MEAD, Sister Janet
Singles: 7-Inch
A&M: 74 ....$2-3

MEADER, Vaughn
LPs: 10/12-Inch 33rpm
CADENCE: 62-63 10-20
KAMA SUTRA: 8-15

MEADOWS BROTHERS
Singles: 7-Inch
KAYVETTE: 87 1-3

MEAGAN
Singles: 7-Inch
NEXT PLATINUM: 84 4-6

MEAN MACHINE
Singles: 7-Inch
SUGAR HILL: 81 2-3

MEAT LOAF
(Marvin Lee Aday)
Singles: 7-Inch
EPIC: 77-83 2-4
RSO: 74 2-4
LPs: 10/12-Inch 33rpm
CLEVELAND INT'L: 81-83 5-8
EPIC (30000 series, except
picture discs): 77-80 5-8
EPIC (34974; "Bat Out Of Hell"): 77 ... 15-20
(With bats on front cover.)
EPIC (34974; "Bat Out Of Hell"): 77 ... 25-30
(Without bats on front cover. Promotional issue
only.)
EPIC (40000 series): 80 12-15
(Half-speed mastered.)
Also see FOLEY, Ellen
Also see STONEY & MEATLOAF

MEAT PUPPETS
LPs: 10/12-Inch 33rpm
SST: 81-87 5-8
Members: Curt Kirkwood; Cris Kirkwood; Derrick
Bostrom.

MECO
(Meco Monardo)
Singles: 12-Inch 33/45rpm
ARISTA: 83 4-6
Singles: 7-Inch
ARISTA: 82-83 1-3
MILLENNIUM: 77-78 2-3
RSO: 80 1-3
LPs: 10/12-Inch 33rpm
ARISTA: 82-84 5-8
MILLENNIUM: 77-78 5-8
RSO: 80 5-8
Also see STAR WARS INTERGALACTIC
DROID CHOIR & CHORALE

MEDEIROS, Glenn
Singles: 7-Inch
AMHERST: 87-88 .... $1-3
LPs: 10/12-Inch 33rpm
AMHERST: 87 5-8

MEDLEY, Bill
Singles: 7-Inch
A&M: 71-73 2-4
LIBERTY: 81 1-3
MGM: 68 3-5
PARAMOUNT: 71 2-4
PLANET: 82-83 1-3
RCA VICTOR: 83-85 1-3
REPRISE: 65 4-6
SCOTTI BROS: 88 1-3
UNITED ARTISTS: 78-80 1-3
VERVE: 67 3-5
LPs: 10/12-Inch 33rpm
A&M: 71-73 8-10
LIBERTY: 81 5-8
MGM: 68-70 12-15
PLANET: 82 8-10
RCA VICTOR: 83-85 5-8
UNITED ARTISTS: 78-80 8-10
Also see RIGHTEOUS BROTHERS

MEDLEY, Bill, & Jennifer Warnes
Singles: 7-Inch
RCA VICTOR: 87 1-3
Also see MEDLEY, Bill
Also see WARNES, Jennifer

MEDLIN, Joe
Singles: 7-Inch
BRUNSWICK: 61 3-5
MERCURY: 59-60 4-6

MEGADETH
LPs: 10/12-Inch 33rpm
CAPITOL: 86-88 5-8
Members: Dave Mustaine; Dave Ellefson; Gar
Samuelson.

MEGATONS
Singles: 7-Inch
CHECKER: 62 3-5
DODGE: 62 8-10
FOREST: 63 3-5
JELL: 62 3-5

MEGATRONS
Singles: 7-Inch
ACOUSTICON: 59 4-8
AUDICON: 59-61 4-8

MEISNER, Randy
Singles: 7-Inch
ASYLUM: 78 2-3

EPIC: 80-82 .... $1-3
LPs: 10/12-Inch 33rpm
ASYLUM: 78 8-10
EPIC: 80-82 5-8
Also see EAGLES
Also see NELSON, Rick
Also see POCO

MEL & KIM
Singles: 7-Inch
ATLANTIC: 87 1-3

MEL & TIM
Singles: 7-Inch
BAMBOO: 69-70 2-4
COLLECTABLES: 1-3
ERIC: 1-3
STAX: 72-74 2-3
LPs: 10/12-Inch 33rpm
BAMBOO: 70 10-15
STAX: 72-74 8-10
Members: Mel Harden; Tim McPherson.

MELACHRINO, George, & His Orchestra
Singles: 78rpm
RCA VICTOR: 50-57 2-3
Singles: 7-Inch
RCA VICTOR: 50-59 2-3
EPs: 7-Inch 33/45rpm
RCA VICTOR: 50-59 3-6
LPs: 10/12-Inch 33rpm
RCA VICTOR: 50-61 5-15

MELANIE
(Melanie & The Edwin Hawkins Singers)
Singles: 7-Inch
ABC: 75 1-3
ATLANTIC: 77 2-3
BUDDAH: 69-73 2-4
CASABLANCA: 74 2-3
COLUMBIA: 67-68 3-5
ERIC: 78 1-3
MCA: 1-3
MIDSONG INT'L: 78 1-3
NEIGHBORHOOD: 71-75 2-3
PORTRAIT: 81 1-3
TOMATO: 78-79 1-3
Picture Sleeves
BUDDAH: 70-73 2-4
NEIGHBORHOOD: 72-73 2-3
LPs: 10/12-Inch 33rpm
ABC: 75 8-10
ACCORD: 81-82 5-8
ATLANTIC: 76 8-10
BLANCHE: 82 5-8
BUDDAH: 69-77 10-15

51 WEST: 79 .... $5-8
MCA/MIDSONG: 77-78 5-9
NEIGHBORHOOD: 71-75 8-10
PICKWICK: 71 8-10
TOMATO: 79 5-8
Also see HAWKINS, Edwin, Singers

MELLAA
Singles: 7-Inch
LARC: 83 1-3

MELLE MEL & DUKE BOOTEE
Singles: 12-Inch 33/45rpm
SUGAR HILL: 82 4-6
Also see GRANDMASTER FLASH & THE
FURIOUS FIVE

MELLENCAMP, John Cougar
(John Cougar; John Mellencamp)
Singles: 7-Inch
MERCURY: 87-88 1-3
RIVA: 79-85 1-3
Picture Sleeves
RIVA: 82 2-3
LPs: 10/12-Inch 33rpm
MAIN MAN: 83 5-8
MERCURY: 87 5-8
RIVA (Except picture discs): 79-85 5-8
RIVA (Picture discs): 30-40

MELLO-KINGS
(Mellokings; Mellotones)
Singles: 78rpm
HERALD (502; "Tonite Tonite"): 57 15-25
(With the group shown as "The Mellotones.")
HERALD (502; "Tonite Tonite"): 57 5-10
(With the group shown as "The Mello-Kings.")
Singles: 7-Inch
COLLECTABLES: 1-3
FLASHBACK: 65 1-3
HERALD (Except 502): 57-61 8-12
HERALD (502; "Tonite Tonite"): 57 30-60
(With the group shown as "The Mellotones.")
HERALD (502; "Tonite
Tonite"): 57 15-20
(With the group shown as "The Mello-Kings."
With logo in script print inside the flag.)
HERALD (502; "Tonite
Tonite"): 5-8
(With the group shown as "The Mello-Kings."
With logo in block print inside the flag.)
LESCAY: 62 4-6
EPs: 7-Inch 33/45rpm
HERALD (451; "The Fabulous
Mello-Kings"): 60 175-225
LPs: 10/12-Inch 33rpm
COLLECTABLES: 84 6-8

HERALD (1013; "Tonight
Tonight"): 60 .... $200-300
Members: Larry Esposita; Bob Scholl; Jerry
Scholl; Eddie Quinn; Neil Areana.

MELLO-MOODS
(Mellow Moods; Mellomoods; With The
Schubert Swanson Trio)
Singles: 78rpm
HAMILTON (143; "I'm Lost"): 53 50-100
PRESTIGE (799; "Call On Me"): 52 ... 75-150
PRESTIGE (856; "I'm Lost"): 52 75-150
ROBIN (104; "I Couldn't Sleep
A Wink Last Night"): 52 150-200
ROBIN (105; "Where Are You?"): 52 . 100-200
Singles: 7-Inch
HAMILTON (143; "I'm Lost"): 53 ... 200-300
PRESTIGE (799; "Call On Me"): 52 .. 400-500
PRESTIGE (856; "I'm Lost"): 52 400-500
ROBIN (105; "Where Are You?"): 52 . 500-700
Members: Ray "Buddy" Wooten; Bobby Williams;
Monte Owens; Bobby Baylor; Jimmy Bethea.

MELLO-TONES
Singles: 78rpm
FASCINATION ("Rosie Lee"): 57 20-30
GEE: 57 5-10
Singles: 7-Inch
FASCINATION ("Rosie Lee"): 57 50-75
GEE: 57 10-15

MELODIANS
Singles: 12-Inch 33/45rpm
REAL AUTHENTIC SOUND: 84 4-6
LPs: 10/12-Inch 33rpm
REAL AUTHENTIC SOUND: 84 5-8

MEL-O-DOTS
Singles: 7-Inch
APOLLO (1192; "One More
Time"): 52 400-600

MELVIN, Harold
(Harold Melvin & The Bluenotes)
Singles: 12-Inch 33/45rpm
PHILADELPHIA INT'L: 80 4-6
SOURCE: 79-80 4-6
Singles: 7-Inch
ABC: 77-78 1-3
ARCTIC: 67 3-5
LANDA: 64-65 4-6
MCA: 81 1-3
PHILADELPHIA INT'L: 72-79 2-3
PHILLY WORLD: 84-85 1-3
SOURCE: 79-80 1-3
Picture Sleeves
PHILADELPHIA INT'L: 72-75 2-3

LPs: 10/12-Inch 33rpm
ABC: 77 . . . . **$8-10**
MCA: 81 . . . . **5-8**
PHILADELPHIA INT'L: 72-76 . . . . **8-10**
PHILLY WORLD: 84-85 . . . . **5-8**
SOURCE: 80 . . . . **5-8**
  Also see BLUENOTES
  Also see PAIGE, Sharon
  Also see PENDERGRASS, Teddy

MEMPHIS HORNS
Singles: 7-Inch
RCA VICTOR: 76-78 . . . . **1-3**
LPs: 10/12-Inch 33rpm
RCA VICTOR: 77-78 . . . . **5-8**
  Also see McDONALD, Michael
  Also see POINTER SISTERS

MEN AT WORK
Singles: 12-Inch 33/45rpm
COLUMBIA: 82-83 . . . . **4-6**
Singles: 7-Inch
COLUMBIA: 82-83 . . . . **1-3**
LPs: 10/12-Inch 33rpm
COLUMBIA (1650; "Cargo - World
  Premier Weekend"): 83 . . . . **10-15**
  (Promotional issue only.)
COLUMBIA (30000 series): 82-83 . . . . **5-8**
COLUMBIA (40000 series): 83 . . . . **12-15**
  (Half-speed mastered.)

MEN WITHOUT HATS
Singles: 12-Inch 33/45rpm
BACKSTREET: 83 . . . . **4-6**
MCA: 83-84 . . . . **4-6**
Singles: 7-Inch
BACKSTREET: 83 . . . . **1-3**
MCA: 83-84 . . . . **1-3**
MERCURY: 87 . . . . **1-3**
LPs: 10/12-Inch 33rpm
BACKSTREET: 83 . . . . **5-8**
MCA: 84 . . . . **5-8**
MERCURY: 87 . . . . **5-8**

MENAGE
Singles: 12-Inch 33/45rpm
PROFILE: 83-85 . . . . **4-6**
Singles: 7-Inch
PROFILE: 83-85 . . . . **1-3**
LPs: 10/12-Inch 33rpm
PROFILE: 83 . . . . **5-8**

MENDES, Sergio
(Sergio Mendes & Brasil '66; Sergio Mendes & Brasil '77)
Singles: 12-Inch 33/45rpm
A&M: 82 . . . . **4-6**

Singles: 7-Inch
A&M (807 through 1257): 66-71 . . . . **$2-3**
A&M (1279 through 2700
  series): 71-85 . . . . **1-3**
ATLANTIC: 67-68 . . . . **2-3**
BELL: 73 . . . . **2-3**
ELEKTRA: 75-80 . . . . **1-3**
Picture Sleeves
A&M (807 through 1257): 66-71 . . . . **2-5**
LPs: 10/12-Inch 33rpm
A&M (Except 4100 series): 69-84 . . . . . . **6-10**
A&M (4100 series): 66-69 . . . . **10-15**
ATLANTIC: 65-67 . . . . **15-25**
BELL: 73-74 . . . . **8-10**
ELEKTRA: 75-79 . . . . **8-10**
EVEREST: 74 . . . . **8-10**
MFSL: 84 . . . . **15-25**
PHILIPS: 68 . . . . **10-12**
TOWER: 65 . . . . **40-60**
  Also see ADDERLEY, Julian "Cannonball,"
  & Sergio Mendes
  Also see HALL, Lani

MENUDO
Singles: 7-Inch
RCA VICTOR: 84-85 . . . . **1-3**
LPs: 10/12-Inch 33rpm
RCA VICTOR: 84 . . . . **5-8**
  Also see KING DREAM CHORUS &
  HOLIDAY CREW

MERC & MONK
Singles: 7-Inch
MANHATTAN: 85 . . . . **1-3**
  Members: Eric Mercury; Thelonious Monk.
  Also see MERCURY, Eric
  Also see MONK, Thelonious

MERCURY, Eric
LPs: 10/12-Inch 33rpm
AVCO EMBASSY: 69 . . . . **10-12**
CAPITOL: 81 . . . . **5-8**
ENTERPRISE: 72-73 . . . . **8-10**
  Also see FLACK, Roberta, & Eric Mercury
  Also see MERC & MONK

MERCURY, Freddie
Singles: 12-Inch 33/45rpm
COLUMBIA: 84 . . . . **4-6**
Singles: 7-Inch
COLUMBIA: 84-85 . . . . **1-3**
LPs: 10/12-Inch 33rpm
COLUMBIA: 85 . . . . **5-8**
  Also see QUEEN

MERCURY, Freddie / Giorgio Moroder
Singles: 12-Inch 33/45rpm
COLUMBIA: 84 . . . . **4-6**

Also see MERCURY, Freddie
Also see MORODER, Giorgio

MERCY
Singles: 7-Inch
SUNDI: *69* $3-5
WARNER BROS: *69* 3-5
LPs: 10/12-Inch 33rpm
SUNDI: *69* 15-20
WARNER BROS: *69* 10-15

MERMAIDS: see MURMAIDS

MERMAN, Ethel, & Dick Haymes
Singles: 7-Inch
DECCA: *51* 3-5
Also see HAYMES, Dick

MERRY-GO-ROUND
Singles: 7-Inch
A&M: *67-69* 3-6
LPs: 10/12-Inch 33rpm
A&M: *67* 12-20
RHINO: *85* 5-8
Members: Emitt Rhodes; Gary Kato; Joel Larson; Bill Rheinhart.
Also see RHODES, Emitt

MERRYWEATHER, Neil
(Merryweather)
Singles: 7-Inch
CAPITOL: *69* 2-4
LPs: 10/12-Inch 33rpm
CAPITOL: *69* 10-15
MERCURY: *74-75* 10-12
Also see MASON, Dave
Also see MERRYWEATHER & CAREY
Also see MILLER, Steve

MERRYWEATHER, Neil, & John Richardson
LPs: 10/12-Inch 33rpm
KENT: *72* 10-12
Also see MERRYWEATHER, Neil

MERRYWEATHER & CAREY
LPs: 10/12-Inch 33rpm
RCA VICTOR: *71* 8-10
Members: Neil Merryweather; Lynn Carey.
Also see MERRYWEATHER, Neil

MESA
Singles: 7-Inch
ARIOLA AMERICA: *77* 2-3

MESSENGERS
Singles: 7-Inch
BEAM: *64* 4-6
ERA: *65* 3-5
HOME MADE: 8-15
MGM: *64-65* 3-5

RARE EARTH: *71* $2-4
SOUL: *67* 3-5
LPs: 10/12-Inch 33rpm
RARE EARTH (509; "The
Messengers"): *69* 8-12
(With standard square cover.)
RARE EARTH (509; "The
Messengers"): *69* 15-25
(With rounded-top cover. Promotional issue.)

MESSINA, Jim
(Jim Messina & The Jesters)
Singles: 7-Inch
AUDIO FIDELITY: *64* 8-10
COLUMBIA: *79-80* 1-3
VIV: 8-10
WARNER BROS: *81-83* 1-3
LPs: 10/12-Inch 33rpm
AUDIO FIDELITY: *64* 25-30
COLUMBIA: *79* 5-8
THIMBLE: *73* 10-12
WARNER BROS: *81-83* 5-8
Also see BUFFALO SPRINGFIELD
Also see LOGGINS & MESSINA
Also see POCO
Also see YOUNG, Neil, & Jim Messina

MESSINA, Jim, & Pauline Wilson
Singles: 7-Inch
WARNER BROS: *81* 1-3
Also see MESSINA, Jim

METAL CHURCH
LPs: 10/12-Inch 33rpm
ELEKTRA: *86* 5-8

METALLICA
LPs: 10/12-Inch 33rpm
ELEKTRA: *84-88* 5-8
ENIGMA: *84* 5-8
MEGAFORCE: *84-86* 8-10
Members: James Hetfield; Jason Newsted; Kirk Hammett; Lars Ulrich.

METERS
Singles: 7-Inch
JOSIE: *69-71* 2-4
REPRISE: *74-76* 2-3
WARNER BROS: *77* 2-3
LPs: 10/12-Inch 33rpm
ISLAND: *75* 8-10
JOSIE: *69-70* 10-12
REPRISE: *72-74* 8-10
VIRGO: *75* 8-10
WARNER BROS: *77* 8-10
Also see NEVILLE BROTHERS

WILLOW: *61-62* $4-6
EPs: 7-Inch 33/45rpm
GROOVE: *57* 30-45
VIK: *58* 25-35
LPs: 10/12-Inch 33rpm
CAMDEN: *65* 25-40
RCA VICTOR: *73* 10-12
VIK (1102; "New Sounds"): *58* 75-125
Members: Mickey Baker; Sylvia Vanderpool.
Also see LITTLE SYLVIA
Also see SYLVIA

MICO WAVE
Singles: 7-Inch
COLUMBIA: *88* 1-3

MIDLER, Bette
Singles: 7-Inch
ATLANTIC: *72-85* 1-3
Picture Sleeves
ATLANTIC: *72-85* 1-3
LPs: 10/12-Inch 33rpm
ATLANTIC: *72-85* 5-8
Also see REDD, Sharon, Ula Hedwig & Char-
lotte Crossley
Also see U.S.A. FOR AFRICA

MIDNIGHT OIL
Singles: 12-Inch 33/45rpm
COLUMBIA: *84* 4-6
Singles: 7-Inch
COLUMBIA: *84-88* 1-3
LPs: 10/12-Inch 33rpm
COLUMBIA: *84-88* 5-8

MIDNIGHT STAR
Singles: 12-Inch 33/45rpm
SOLAR: *82-86* 4-6
Singles: 7-Inch
SOLAR: *80-88* 1-3
LPs: 10/12-Inch 33rpm
SOLAR: *82-88* 5-8

MIDNIGHT STRING QUARTET
LPs: 10/12-Inch 33rpm
VIVA: *66-68* 4-8

MIDNIGHTERS
Singles: 78rpm
FEDERAL: *54-57* 6-12
Singles: 7-Inch
FEDERAL (12169 through 12243): *54-55* **12-25**
FEDERAL (12251 through 12339): *56-58* **10-15**
EPs: 7-Inch 33/45rpm
FEDERAL: *54* 50-75
Members: Henry Booth; Hank Ballard; Sonny
Woods; Charles Sutton; Lawson Smith; Alonzo
Tucker. May be shown on some early releases as
"The Midnighters, Formerly The Royals."

Also see BALLARD, Hank, & The Midnighters
Also see ROYALS

MIDNIGHTERS:
see THEE MIDNIGHTERS

MIDWAY
Singles: 12-Inch 33/45rpm
PERSONAL: *84* $4-6
Singles: 7-Inch
PERSONAL: *84* 1-3

MIGHTY CLOUDS OF JOY
Singles: 12-Inch 33/45rpm
EPIC: *79* 4-6
Singles: 7-Inch
ABC: *76-77* 1-3
DUNHILL: *74-75* 1-3
EPIC: *79-80* 1-3
MYRRH: *82* 1-3
PEACOCK: *61-73* 1-3
LPs: 10/12-Inch 33rpm
ABC: *75-76* 4-6
DUNHILL: *74* 4-8
EPIC: *79* 5-8
MYRRH: *81-83* 4-6
PEACOCK: *65-73* 5-10
PRIORITY: *82* 4-8

MIGHTY FIRE
Singles: 7-Inch
ELEKTRA: *81-82* 1-3
ZEPHYR: *80* 2-3
LPs: 10/12-Inch 33rpm
ELEKTRA: *81-82* 5-8

MIGHTY FLEA
Singles: 7-Inch
ELDO: *67* 3-5

MIGHTY HANNIBAL
Singles: 7-Inch
DECCA: *65* 3-5
JOSIE: *66-67* 3-5
LOMA: *68* 3-5
SHURFINE: *66* 3-5

MIGHTY POPE
Singles: 7-Inch
PRIVATE STOCK: *77* 2-3

MIKE & BILL
Singles: 7-Inch
ARISTA: *75* 2-4

MIKE + THE MECHANICS
Singles: 7-Inch
ATLANTIC: *86-88* 1-3

LPs: 10/12-Inch 33rpm
ATLANTIC: 86-88 .... $5-8
Members: Mike Rutherford; Paul Carrack; Paul
Young; Peter Van Hooke; Adrian Lee.
Also see CARRACK, Paul
Also see RUTHERFORD, Mike
Also see SAD CAFE
Also see YOUNG, Paul

MIKKI
Singles: 7-Inch
EMERALD INT'L: 82-83 1-3
POP ART: 84 1-3

MILBURN, Amos
Singles: 78rpm
ALADDIN (100 & 200 series): 45-47 8-12
ALADDIN (3014 through 3300
  series): 48-57 5-10
Singles: 7-Inch
ALADDIN (3014; "Chicken Shack
  Boogie"): 50 40-60
ALADDIN (3018; "Bewildered"): 50 25-35
ALADDIN (3068 through 3197): 50-53 .. 20-25
ALADDIN (3200 & 3300 series): 53-57 . 10-20
IMPERIAL: 62 3-5
KING (5000 series): 60-61 4-8
KING (6000 series): 67 3-5
LE CAM: 62 3-5
MOTOWN: 63 15-20
LPs: 10/12-Inch 33rpm
ALADDIN (704; "Rockin' The
  Boogie"): 55 150-200
  (Black vinyl.)
ALADDIN (704; "Rockin' The
  Boogie"): 55 400-500
  (Colored vinyl.)
ALADDIN (810; "Rockin' The
  Boogie"): 56 75-125

IMPERIAL: 62 .... $25-35
MOTOWN (608; "The Blues Boss"): 63 .75-100
SCORE: 57 40-60
Also see BROWN, Charles, & Amos Milburn
Also see MILBURN, Amos / Wynonie Harris
/ Crown Prince Waterford
LPs: 10/12-Inch 33rpm
ALADDIN (703; "Party After
  Hours"): 56 150-250
  (Colored vinyl.)
Also see HARRIS, Wynonie
Also see MILBURN, Amos

MILES, Buddy
(Buddy Miles Express; Buddy Miles Band)
Singles: 7-Inch
CASABLANCA: 75-76 2-3
COLUMBIA: 73-74 2-4
MERCURY: 68-71 2-4
LPs: 10/12-Inch 33rpm
CASABLANCA: 75 8-10
COLUMBIA: 73-74 8-10
MERCURY: 68-72 12-15
Also see CALIFORNIA RAISINS
Also see ELECTRIC FLAG
Also see HENDRIX, Jimi, & Buddy Miles
Also see KARP, Charlie
Also see SANTANA, Carlos, & Buddy Miles

MILES, Garry
(Garry Miles & The Statues; Gary Miles)
Singles: 7-Inch
LIBERTY: 60-68 3-5
Picture Sleeves
LIBERTY: 60 10-20
EPs: 7-Inch 33/45rpm
LIBERTY: 60 35-45
Also see STATUES

MILES, John
Singles: 12-Inch 33/45rpm
LONDON: 77-80 5-8
Singles: 7-Inch
ARISTA: 78 2-3
LONDON: 76-77 2-3
LPs: 10/12-Inch 33rpm
ARISTA: 78 5-8
LONDON: 78-80 5-8

MILES, Lenny
Singles: 7-Inch
GROOVE: 62 3-5
SCEPTER: 61 3-5

MILITELLO, Bobby
Singles: 7-Inch
GORDY: 82-83 1-3

LPs: 10/12-Inch 33rpm
GORDY: 82-83 .... $5-8
Member: Jean Carn.
Also see CARN, Jean

MILLER, Chuck
Singles: 78rpm
MERCURY: 55-58 3-5
Singles: 7-Inch
MERCURY: 55-58 5-8
LPs: 10/12-Inch 33rpm
MERCURY: 56 25-30

MILLER, Clint
Singles: 7-Inch
ABC-PARAMOUNT: 58 5-8
BIG TOP: 59 4-6
HEADLINE: 60-61 4-8
LENOX: 62 3-5

MILLER, Frankie
Singles: 78rpm
COLUMBIA: 54-56 2-5
Singles: 7-Inch
COLUMBIA: 54-56 3-5
STARDAY: 59-67 2-5
UNITED ARTISTS: 62 2-4
EPs: 7-Inch 33/45rpm
STARDAY: 60 5-8
LPs: 10/12-Inch 33rpm
AUDIO LAB: 63 12-18
STARDAY: 61-65 10-20
UNITED ARTISTS: 62 12-18

MILLER, Frankie
(Frankie Miller Band)
Singles: 7-Inch
CAPITOL: 82 1-3
CHRYSALIS: 75-79 2-3
LPs: 10/12-Inch 33rpm
CAPITOL: 82 5-8
CHRYSALIS: 73-80 8-10

MILLER, Glenn, & His Orchestra
(New Glenn Miller Orchestra With Ray Mc-
Kinley; Buddy DeFranco & The Glenn Miller
Orchestra)
Singles: 7-Inch
EPIC: 65-69 1-3
RCA VICTOR: 50-67 2-4
EPs: 7-Inch 33/45rpm
EPIC: 54-56 5-15
RCA VICTOR (Except 6700
  series): 50-61 5-10
RCA VICTOR (6700 series): 53 20-40
LPs: 10/12-Inch 33rpm
BRIGHT ORANGE: 73 4-8
CAMDEN: 63-74 5-10

COLUMBIA: 82 .... $5-8
EPIC (1000 & 3000 series): 54-56 15-25
EPIC (16000 series): 60 10-20
EPIC (24000 & 26000 series): 65-66 5-10
EVEREST (Except 4004): 82 4-8
EVEREST (4004; "Glenn Miller"): 82 .. 15-25
  (5-LP set.)
GREAT AMERICAN
  GRAMOPHONE: 77 5-10
HARMONY: 70 4-8
KORY: 77 4-8
MOVIETONE: 67 8-12
RCA VICTOR (16 through 30): 51-52 .. 25-50
  (10-Inch LPs.)
RCA VICTOR (0600 through
  3800 series): 74-81 5-10
  (With an "ANL," "AYL," or "CPL" prefix.)
RCA VICTOR (3000 series): 52-54 20-40
  (10-Inch LPs.)
RCA VICTOR (1000 through
  1500 series): 54-57 10-20
  (Black labels.)
RCA VICTOR (1100 through
  1500 series): 68 4-8
  (Orange labels.)
RCA VICTOR (1600 through
  3900 series): 58-68 5-15
  (Black labels. With an "LPM" or "LSP" prefix.)
RCA VICTOR (1900 through
  4100 series): 68-69 4-8
  (Orange labels.)
RCA VICTOR (5000 series): 75-80 6-12
RCA VICTOR (6000 series): 69-73 8-15
RCA VICTOR (6100 series): 59-63 15-30
RCA VICTOR (6700 series): 53-62 60-80
  (5-LP set, with booklet and special gold or silver
  case.)
SPRINGBOARD: 77 4-6
20TH CENTURY-FOX (100
  series): 59 20-30
20TH CENTURY-FOX (900
  series): 73 5-10
20TH CENTURY-FOX (3000
  series): 59 15-20
20TH CENTURY-FOX (3100
  series): 65 10-15
20TH CENTURY-FOX (4100
  series): 65 10-15
20TH CENTURY-FOX (72000
  series): 73 6-10

MILLER, Jody
Singles: 7-Inch
CAPITOL: 63-70 2-5
EPIC: 70-79 1-3

Picture Sleeves
CAPITOL: 65 .... $3-6
LPs: 10/12-Inch 33rpm
CAPITOL (1900 series): 63 15-20
CAPITOL (2300 through 2900
  series): 65-69 12-15
CAPITOL (11000 series): 73 5-10
EPIC: 70-77 5-10
PICKWICK/HILLTOP: 66 10-15
Also see PAYCHECK, Johnny, & Jody Miller

MILLER, Marcus
Singles: 12-Inch 33/45rpm
WARNER BROS: 83-84 4-6
Singles: 7-Inch
WARNER BROS: 83-84 1-3

MILLER, Mrs. Elva
(Mrs. Miller)
Singles: 7-Inch
AMARET: 69-70 3-5
CAPITOL: 66 4-6
LPs: 10/12-Inch 33rpm
AMARET: 69 12-15
CAPITOL: 66-67 20-25

MILLER, Mitch
**(Mitch Miller's Orchestra & Chorus; Mitch
Miller & The Sing-Along Gang)**
Singles: 78rpm
COLUMBIA: 50-57 2-4
Singles: 7-Inch
COLUMBIA: 50-65 2-4
DECCA: 65-66 1-3
DIAMOND: 68 1-3
GOLD-MOR: 73 1-3
UNITED ARTISTS: 68 1-3
Picture Sleeves
COLUMBIA: 59-63 2-5
EPs: 7-Inch 33/45rpm
COLUMBIA: 55-61 4-8
LPs: 10/12-Inch 33rpm
ATLANTIC: 70 4-8
COLUMBIA (Except 2780/6380): 56-82 .. 5-15
COLUMBIA (2780; "Major
  Dundee"): 65 35-45
  (Soundtrack. Monaural.)
COLUMBIA (6380; "Major
  Dundee"): 65 45-55
  (Soundtrack. Stereo.)
DECCA: 66 5-10
HARMONY: 65-71 5-10

MILLER, Ned
Singles: 78rpm
DOT: 57 3-6

Singles: 7-Inch
CAPITOL (2000 series): 68 .... $2-3
CAPITOL (4600 series): 61 3-5
CAPITOL (5400 & 5800 series): 65-67 2-4
DOT (15000 series,
  except 15601): 57 3-5
DOT (15601; "From A Jack
  To A King"): 57 4-8
FABOR: 62-65 2-4
JACKPOT: 59 3-5
REPUBLIC: 69-70 1-3
LPs: 10/12-Inch 33rpm
CAPITOL: 65-67 10-15
FABOR (1001; "From A Jack
  To A King"): 63 15-20
  (Black vinyl.)
FABOR (1001; "From A Jack
  To A King"): 63 25-50
  (Colored vinyl.)
FABOR (Colored vinyl): 63 25-30
PLANTATION: 81 5-8
REPUBLIC: 70 8-10

MILLER, Roger
Singles: 7-Inch
BUENA VISTA: 70 2-4
COLUMBIA: 73-74 1-3
DECCA: 59 4-6
ELEKTRA: 81 1-3
MCA: 86 1-3
MERCURY: 70-72 2-3
MUSICOR: 65 2-4
RCA VICTOR (7000 series): 60-63 3-5
RCA VICTOR (8000 series): 65 2-4
SMASH: 64-76 2-4
STARDAY: 65 2-4
WINDSONG: 77 1-3
Picture Sleeves
BUENA VISTA: 70 3-5
SAMSH: 64-68 3-6
LPs: 10/12-Inch 33rpm
CAMDEN: 64-65 10-12
COLUMBIA: 73 6-10
EVEREST: 75 5-8
MCA: 86 5-8
MERCURY: 72 6-10
PICKWICK: 8-10
SMASH (Except 7000 series): 64-70 ... 10-12
SMASH (7000 series): 82 5-8
STARDAY: 65 10-15
20TH CENTURY-FOX: 79 5-8
WINDSONG: 77 5-8
WING: 69 8-12
Also see LEWIS, Jerry Lee / Roger Miller /
Roy Orbison

Also see NELSON, Willie, & Roger Miller

MILLER, Steve, Band
Singles: 12-Inch 33/45rpm
CAPITOL: *81-85* $4-6
Singles: 7-Inch
CAPITOL (2100 series): *68* 8-10
CAPITOL (2200 series): *68* 5-8
CAPITOL (2400 through 2600
series): *69* 4-6
CAPITOL (2800 through 3300
series): *70-72* 3-5
CAPITOL (3700 through 4400
series): *73-77* 2-4
CAPITOL (5000 series): *81-86* 1-3
Picture Sleeves
CAPITOL: *80-85* 1-3
LPs: 10/12-Inch 33rpm
CAPITOL (184 through 748): *69-71* 10-12
CAPITOL (2900 series): *68* 12-15
CAPITOL (11000 through
16000): *72-86* 5-10
CAPITOL (11872; "Greatest
Hits"): *78* 20-30
(Colored vinyl. Promotional issue only.)
CAPITOL (11903; "Book Of
Dreams"): *78* 15-20
(Picture disc.)
CAPITOL: *88* 5-8
MFSL: *78* 25-50
Also see MERRYWEATHER, Neil
Also see SCAGGS, Boz

MILLER, Steve, Band / Band /
Quicksilver Messenger Service
LPs: 10/12-Inch 33rpm
CAPITOL: *69* 35-45
(A 3-LP set, with one LP by each group.)
Also see BAND
Also see MILLER, Steve, Band
Also see QUICKSILVER

MILLINDER, Lucky, & His Orchestra
Singles: 78rpm
DECCA: *41-48* 5-10
KING: *51-57* 5-10
RCA VICTOR: *49-51* 4-8
Singles: 7-Inch
KING (4400 series): *51* 20-30
(Black vinyl.)
KING (4400 series): *51* 40-50
(Colored vinyl.)
KING (4500 series): *52* 10-15
KING (4700 & 4800 series): *55* 5-10
KING (5200 series): *59* 3-5
RCA VICTOR (50-0000 series): *51* 20-30
TODD: *59* 3-6

WARWICK: *60* $3-5
EPs: 7-Inch 33/45rpm
KING: *52* 20-35
Also see HARRIS, Wynonic

MILLS, Frank
Singles: 7-Inch
POLYDOR: *78 79* 1-3
SUNFLOWER: *72* 2-3
LPs: 10/12-Inch 33rpm
CAPITOL: *85* 5-8
POLYDOR: *79* 5-8
Also see BELLS

MILLS, Gary
Singles: 7-Inch
IMPERIAL: *60* 4-6
LONDON: *62* 3-5
TOP RANK: *60* 3-5

MILLS, Hayley
Singles: 7-Inch
BUENA VISTA: *61-62* 4-6
MAINSTREAM: *66* 3-5
Picture Sleeves
BUENA VISTA: *61-62* 6-12
EPs: 7-Inch 33/45rpm
DISNEYLAND: *60* 15-20
LPs: 10/12-Inch 33rpm
BUENA VISTA: *62* 20-25
MAINSTREAM (6090; "Gypsy
Girl"): *66* 15-25
(Soundtrack.)
Also see ANNETTE & HAYLEY MILLS

MILLS, Hayley, & Eddie Hodges
Singles: 7-Inch
BUENA VISTA: *63* 4-6
Picture Sleeves
BUENA VISTA: *64* 5-10
Also see HODGES, Eddie

MILLS, Hayley, & Burl Ives
(With Eddie Hodges & Deborah Walley)
Singles: 7-Inch
BUENA VISTA (4023; "Summer
Magic"): *63* 3-5
(Alcoa Wrap promotional issue.)
Picture Sleeves
BUENA VISTA (4023; "Summer
Magic"): *63* 8-15
(Alcoa Wrap promotional issue.)
Also see IVES, Burl

MILLS, Hayley, & Jimmie Bean
EPs: 7-Inch 33/45rpm
DISNEYLAND: *60* 15-20

MILLS, Hayley, & Maurice Chevalier
Singles: 7-Inch
BUENA VISTA: 62 .... $4-6
Also see MILLS, Hayley

MILLS, Stephanie
Singles: 12-Inch 33/45rpm
CASABLANCA: 82-85 4-6
MCA: 85-86 4-6
20TH CENTURY-FOX: 79-81 4-6
Singles: 7-Inch
ABC: 74 2-3
CASABLANCA: 82-86 1-3
MCA: 85-88 1-3
MOTOWN: 75 2-3
PARAMOUNT: 74 2-3
20TH CENTURY-FOX: 79-81 1-3
LPs: 10/12-Inch 33rpm
ABC: 75 8-10
CASABLANCA: 82-85 5-8
MCA: 87 5-8
MOTOWN (800 series): 75 8-10
MOTOWN (6000 series): 82 5-8
20TH CENTURY-FOX: 80-81 5-8
Also see KING DREAM CHORUS &
HOLIDAY CREW

MILLS, Stephanie, & Teddy Pendergrass
Singles: 7-Inch
20TH CENTURY-FOX: 81 1-3
Also see MILLS, Stephanie
Also see PENDERGRASS, Teddy

MILLS, Yvonne, & The Sensations
Singles: 78rpm
ATCO: 56-57 5-10
Singles: 7-Inch
ATCO: 56-58 10-15
Also see SENSATIONS

MILLS BROTHERS
Singles: 78rpm
BANNER: 34 5-10
BRUNSWICK: 31-47 4-8
CONQUEROR: 5-10
DECCA (100 through 4300
  series): 34-42 4-8
DECCA (11000 through 24000
  series): 42-57 3-6
Singles: 7-Inch
ABC: 64 1-3
DECCA: 50-61 2-4
DOT (15000 series): 58-59 2-4
DOT (17000 series): 68-69 1-3
MCA: 73-74 1-3
PARAMOUNT: 71-72 1-3
RANWOOD: 73-76 1-3

EPs: 7-Inch 33/45rpm
DECCA: 50-63 .... $5-15
DOT: 58-59 5-10
LPs: 10/12-Inch 33rpm
ABC: 74 4-8
DECCA (100 series): 66 8-15
DECCA (4000 series): 61-67 8-15
DECCA (5000 series): 51-55 15-25
  (10-Inch LPs.)
DECCA (7000 series): 55 15-20
DECCA (8000 series): 55-59 10-20
DECCA (75000 series): 70 5-10
DOT: 58-70 5-15
EVEREST: 75-77 4-8
GNP/CRESCENDO: 73 5-8
PARAMOUNT: 72-74 5-10
RANWOOD: 74-81 4-8
SONGBIRD: 74 4-6
VOCALION: 66-69 5-10
Members: Herb Mills; Harry Mills; Donald Mills;
John Mills.
Also see CROSBY, Bing, & The Mills
Brothers

MILLS BROTHERS, & Louis Armstrong
Singles: 7-Inch
DECCA: 61 2-4
Also see ARMSTRONG, Louis

MILLS BROTHERS, & Count Basie
LPs: 10/12-Inch 33rpm
ABC: 74 4-8
DOT: 68 5-10
Also see BASIE, Count
Also see MILLS BROTHERS

MILSAP, Ronnie
Singles: 7-Inch
BOBLO: 77 2-4
CHIPS: 70 3-5
FESTIVAL: 77 2-4
RCA VICTOR: 74-88 1-3
SCEPTER: 65-69 3-5
WARNER BROS (5000 series): 63 ... 5-8
WARNER BROS (8000 series): 76 ... 2-3
Picture Sleeves
RCA VICTOR: 79-85 1-3
LPs: 10/12-Inch 33rpm
BUCKBOARD: 76 8-10
CRAZY CAJUN: 75 8-10
51 WEST: 5-8
HSRD: 82 8-10
RCA VICTOR: 74-86 6-10
TRIP: 76 8-10
WARNER BROS: 71-75 8-10

Also see PRESLEY, Elvis

MILTON, Roy
(Roy Milton & His Band; Roy Milton & His Solid Senders; Roy Milton Sextet)
Singles: 78rpm

DOOTONE: *55-56* **$5-10**
DELUXE: **5-10**
HAMP-TONE: *45* **10-15**
JUKE BOX: *46* **15-25**
KING: *56-57* **3-6**
ROY MILTON: *46-47* **10-20**
SPECIALTY: *47-55* **5-10**

Singles: 7-Inch

CENCO: *61* **3-5**
DOOTONE: *55-56* **10-20**
KING (4900 & 5000 series): *56-58* **4-8**
KING (5600 series): *62* **3-5**
SPECIALTY (414 through 438): *50-52* .. **10-20**
SPECIALTY (446; "Believe Me,
Baby"): *52* **30-40**
SPECIALTY (458; "Some Day"): *53* **10-20**
(Black vinyl.)
SPECIALTY (458; "Some Day"): *53* **20-40**
(Colored vinyl.)
SPECIALTY (464; "Let Me Give
You All My Love"): *54* **10-20**
(Black vinyl.)
SPECIALTY (464; "Let Me Give
You All My Love"): *54* **20-40**
(Colored vinyl.)
SPECIALTY (480 through 545): *54-55* ... **5-10**
SPECIALTY (700 series): *69* **3-5**
(Most Specialty singles are currently available,
using original catalog numbers.)
WARWICK: *60* **4-8**

LPs: 10/12-Inch 33rpm

KENT: *63* **15-20**
Also see HOWARD, Camille, Trio

MILTON, Roy / Joe Liggins
Singles: 78rpm

SPECIALTY: *53* **4-8**
Singles: 7-Inch
SPECIALTY: *53* **10-12**
Also see LIGGINS, Joe
Also see MILTON, Roy

MIMMS, Garnet
(Garnet Mimms & The Enchanters; Garnet Mimms & The Trucking Co.)
Singles: 7-Inch

ARISTA: *77* **2-3**
GSF: *72* **2-4**
LIBERTY: *81* **1-3**
UNITED ARTISTS: *63-66* **3-5**
VEEP: *66* **3-5**

VERVE: *68-70* **$2-4**
Picture Sleeves
UNITED ARTISTS: *63* **4-8**
LPs: 10/12-Inch 33rpm
ARISTA: *78* **8-10**
GRAND PRIX: *63* **10-15**
GUEST STAR: *64* **12-15**
UNITED ARTISTS: *63-66* **20-25**

MIMMS, Garnet / Maurice Monk
LPs: 10/12-Inch 33rpm
GRAND PRIX: *63* **15-20**
Also see MIMMS, Garnet

MINA
Singles: 7-Inch
TIME: *61* **2-4**

MINDBENDERS
Singles: 7-Inch
FONTANA: *65-67* **4-6**
LPs: 10/12-Inch 33rpm
FONTANA: *66* **20-25**
Member: Eric Stewart.
Also see FONTANA, Wayne, & The
Mindbenders

MINEO, Sal
Singles: 78rpm
EPIC: *57* **4-6**
Singles: 7-Inch
DECCA: *64* **3-5**
EPIC: *57-59* **4-6**
FONTANA: *65* **3-5**

Sal Mineo

Picture Sleeves
EPIC: *57-59* $5-10
EPs: 7-Inch 33/45rpm
EPIC: *57-58* 20-30
LPs: 10/12-Inch 33rpm
EPIC: *58* 25-30

MINIATURE MEN
Singles: 7-Inch
DOLTON: *62* 3-5
Also see LEVINE, Hank

MINISTRY
Singles: 12-Inch 33/45rpm
ARISTA: *83* 4-6
SIRE: *86* 4-6
WAX TRAX: *85* 4-6
Singles: 7-Inch
ARISTA: *83* 1-3
SIRE: *86* 1-3
WAX TRAX: *85* 1-3
LPs: 10/12-Inch 33rpm
ARISTA: *83* 5-8
SIRE: *86-88* 5-8

MINK DE VILLE
Singles: 7-Inch
ATLANTIC: *81-84* 1-3
CAPITOL: *77-78* 2-3
LPs: 10/12-Inch 33rpm
ATLANTIC: *81-83* 5-8
CAPITOL: *77-82* 5-8

MINNEAPOLIS GENIUS 94 EAST
Singles: 7-Inch
HOT PINK: *86* 1-3

MINNELLI, Liza
Singles: 7-Inch
A&M: *68-71* 2-4
ABC: *73* 2-3
CADENCE: *63* 4-6
CAPITOL (4900 through 5700
series): *63-65* 2-5
COLUMBIA: *72-75* 2-3
UNITED ARTISTS: *77* 1-3
LPs: 10/12-Inch 33rpm
A&M: *68-73* 10-15
ABC (752; "Cabaret"): *72* 10-15
(Soundtrack. With Joel Grey.)
ARISTA (4069; "Lucky Lady"): *76* 8-10
(Soundtrack.)
CADENCE (4012; "Best Foot
Forward"): *63* 40-60
(Original cast.)
CAPITOL (2100 & 2400 series): *64-66* .. 10-20
(With a "T" or "ST" prefix.)
CAPITOL (2200 series): *78* 5-8

CAPITOL (11000 series): *72-78* $5-10
COLUMBIA: *72-77* 6-12
DRG (6101; "The Act"): *78* 8-10
MCA (752; "Cabaret"): 5-8
(Soundtrack. With Joel Grey.)
STET: 8-10
TELARC: *87* 10-12
Also see GARLAND, Judy, & Liza Minnelli

MINOGUE, Kylie
Singles: 7-Inch
GEFFEN: *88* 1-3
LPs: 10/12-Inch 33rpm
GEFFEN: *88* 5-8

MINOR DETAIL
Singles: 7-Inch
POLYDOR: *83-84* 1-3
LPs: 10/12-Inch 33rpm
POLYDOR: *83* 5-8
Members: John Hughes; Willie Hughes.

MIRABAI
LPs: 10/12-Inch 33rpm
ATLANTIC: *75* 5-10

MIRACLES
(Smokey Robinson & The Miracles; Miracles Featuring Bill Smokey Robinson)
Singles: 12-Inch 33/45rpm
COLUMBIA: *77* 4-6
Singles: 7-Inch
CHESS (119; "Bad Girl"): *84* 1-3
CHESS (1734; "Bad Girl"): *59* 10-15
CHESS (1768; "All I Want"): *60* 8-10
COLUMBIA: *77-78* 2-3
END: *58* 20-40
MOTOWN (G1; "Bad Girl"): *59* 275-300
MOTOWN (400 & 500 series): 1-3
MOTOWN (2207; "Bad Girl"): *59* 300-325
ROULETTE: 1-3
STANDARD GROOVE (13090; "I
Care About Detroit"): *68* 60-80
(Promotional issue only.)
TAMLA (009; "The Christmas
Song"): *63* 125-150
(Promotional issue only.)
TAMLA (54028; "Way Over There"/
"Depend On Me"): *60* 60-70
(With an alternate take of *Way Over There*, not
available elsewhere.)
TAMLA (54028; "Way Over There"/
"Depend On Me"): *60* 20-25
(With the hit version of *Way Over There*, the same
as is heard on their Tamla LPs.)

TAMLA (54028; "The Feeling Is So Fine"/
"You Can Depend On Me"): 60 .... $325-350
(Issued twice, first with the standard version of *You
Can Depend On Me*, then with an alternate take of
the tune. The alternate take can be identified by the
letter "A" following the matrix number in the
trailoff. There is no reportable difference in value.)

TAMLA (54034; "Shop Around"): 60 . .80-100
(With horizontal lines across top half of label. Contains an alternate version of *Shop Around*. Matrix
number is 45-I155518 A-2. Shows writer as
"Gordt" instead of Gordy.)

TAMLA (54034; "Shop Around"): 60 ...25-30
(Same as above, but with Tamla globe logo and no
lines on label.)

TAMLA (54034; "Shop Around"): 60 ...15-25
(Contains the hit version of *Shop Around*. Matrix
number is 45-L1 3. Shows writer as "Gordt." With
horizontal lines.)

TAMLA (54034; "Shop Around"): 60 4-6
(Contains the hit version of *Shop Around*. Matrix
number is 45-L1 3. Properly shows writer as
Gordy. With or without horizontal lines. Copies
exist of the record, as described here, but with the
H-55518-A2 matrix. We don't yet know which version of *Shop Around* is on this variation.)

TAMLA (54036; "Ain't It
Baby"): 61 8-10

TAMLA (54044; "Mighty Good
Lovin'"): 61 5-8

TAMLA (54048; "Everybody's Gotta
Pay Some Dues"): 61 5-8

TAMLA (54053 through 54069): 62 4-8

TAMLA (54073 through 54194): 62-70 3-6

TAMLA (54199 through 54268): 70-76 2-4

Picture Sleeves

TAMLA (54044; "Mighty Good
Lovin'"): 61 15-20

TAMLA (54059; "I'll Try Something
New"): 62 15-20

TAMLA (54073 through 54194): 62-70 4-6

LPs: 10/12-Inch 33rpm

COLUMBIA: 77-78 8-10

IMPERIAL HOUSE: 79 8-12

MOTOWN (Except 793): 82-84 5-8

MOTOWN (793; "Anthology"): 74 12-15

NATURAL RESOURCES: 78 5-8

TAMLA (220; "Hi! We're The
Miracles"): 61 100-200
(White label.)

TAMLA (220; "Hi! We're The
Miracles"): 61 100-150
(Yellow label with globes.)

TAMLA (223; "Cookin' With
The Miracles"): 62 100-150
(White label.)

TAMLA (223; "Cookin' With
The Miracles"): 62 ....$75-125
(Yellow label with globes.)

TAMLA (224; "Shop Around"): 62 40-60

TAMLA (230; "I'll Try Something
New"): 62 35-50

TAMLA (236; "Christmas With
The Miracles"): 63 100-125

TAMLA (238; "The Fabulous
Miracles"): 63 75-100

TAMLA (241 through 254): 63-65 25-35

TAMLA (267 through 297): 65-69 15-20

TAMLA (301 through 344): 70-76 10-15
Members: William "Smokey" Robinson; Pete
Moore; Bobby Rogers; Ron White; Claudette
Rogers.

Also see ROBINSON, Smokey

Also see RON & BILL

MIRAN, Wayne, & Rush Release
Singles: 7-Inch
ROULETTE: 75 2-4

MIRETTES
Singles: 7-Inch
REVUE: 67-69 3-5
UNI: 69 2-4
LPs: 10/12-Inch 33rpm
REVUE: 68 12-15
UNI: 69 10-12

MISS ABRAMS: see ABRAMS, Miss

MISS THANG
Singles: 12-Inch 33/45rpm
TOMMY BOY: 86 4-6

MISS TONI FISHER:
see FISHER, Miss Toni

MISSING PERSONS
Singles: 12-Inch 33/45rpm
CAPITOL: 82-86 4-6
Singles: 7-Inch
CAPITOL: 82-86 1-3
Picture Sleeves
CAPITOL: 82-84 1-3
EPs: 7-Inch 33/45rpm
KOMOS: 80 5-8
LPs: 10/12-Inch 33rpm
CAPITOL: 82-86 5-8
Members: Dale Bozzio; Terry Bozzio; Warren Cuc-
curullo.

Also see MOTHERS OF INVENTION

MISSION
Singles: 7-Inch
PARAMOUNT: 74 2-4

MISSION U.K.

LPs: 10/12-Inch 33rpm
MERCURY: 87-88 .... $5-8

MISSOURI
Singles: 7-Inch
PANAMA: 78 2-3
POLYDOR: 79 1-3
LPs: 10/12-Inch 33rpm
PANAMA: 77 8-10
POLYDOR: 79 5-8

MR. BIG
Singles: 7-Inch
ARISTA: 77 2-3
LPs: 10/12-Inch 33rpm
ARISTA: 76 8-10

MR. MISTER
Singles: 7-Inch
RCA VICTOR: 84-87 1-3
LPs: 10/12-Inch 33rpm
RCA VICTOR: 84-87 5-8
Members: Richard Page; Pat Mastelotto; Steve Farris; Steve George.
Also see PAGES

MR. T.
(Lawrence Tero)
Singles: 12-Inch 33/45rpm
COLUMBIA (Except picture
discs): 84 4-6
COLUMBIA (Picture discs): 84 5-8
Singles: 7-Inch
COLUMBIA: 84 1-3
MCA: 84 1-3
LPs: 10/12-Inch 33rpm
COLUMBIA: 84 5-8
MCA: 84 5-8

MISTRESS
Singles: 7-Inch
RSO: 79 1-3
LPs: 10/12-Inch 33rpm
RSO: 79 5-8

MITCHELL, Billy
(Billy Mitchell Group)
Singles: 7-Inch
CALLA: 69 2-4
JUBILEE: 61 3-5
RON: 61-62 3-5
UNITED ARTISTS: 60 3-5
WARWICK: 59 4-6
Also see CLOVERS
Also see MORRIS, Joe, & His Orchestra

MITCHELL, Bobby
(Bobby Mitchell & The Toppers)
Singles: 78rpm
IMPERIAL (5236; "I'm Cryin"): 53 .... $20-40
IMPERIAL (5250 through
5309): 53-54 15-30
IMPERIAL (5300 & 5400
series): 55-57 5-15
Singles: 7-Inch
IMPERIAL (5236; "I'm Cryin"): 53 75-100
IMPERIAL (5250; "One Friday
Morning"): 53 60-75
IMPERIAL (5270; "Baby's Gone"): 54 .. 35-50
IMPERIAL (5282; "Angel Child"): 54 ... 35-50
IMPERIAL (5295; "The Wedding
Bells Are Ringing"): 54 25-40
IMPERIAL (5309; "I'm A
Young Man"): 54 35-50
IMPERIAL (5326; "I Wish I
Knew"): 55 20-25
IMPERIAL (5346; "I Cried"): 55 15-25
IMPERIAL (5378 through 5558): 56-58 ... 8-15
IMPERIAL (5900 series): 63 4-8
RON: 61 4-6
SHOW-BIZ: 59 5-8

MITCHELL, Chad
Singles: 7-Inch
AMY: 68-69 3-5
WARNER BROS: 66-67 4-6
LPs: 10/12-Inch 33rpm
BELL: 69 10-12
WARNER BROS: 66-67 12-15
Also see MITCHELL, Chad, Trio

MITCHELL, Chad, Trio
(Mitchell Trio)
Singles: 7-Inch
COLPIX: 59-61 5-10
KAPP: 61-63 5-10
MAY: 62 5-10
MERCURY: 63-66 4-8
REPRISE: 67 4-6
Picture Sleeves
KAPP: 61 5-10
MERCURY: 63-66 5-10
LPs: 10/12-Inch 33rpm
COLPIX: 60 20-25
KAPP: 61-64 15-20
MERCURY: 63-66 15-20
REPRISE: 67 15-20
Members: Chad Mitchell; Joe Frazier; Mike
Kobluk; John Denver; Jim McGuinn.
Also see DENVER, John
Also see MITCHELL, Chad

MITCHELL, Chad, Trio, & The Gatemen
LPs: 10/12-Inch 33rpm
COLPIX: 64 .... $15-20
Also see MITCHELL, Chad, Trio

MITCHELL, Freddie, & Orchestra
Singles: 78rpm
ABC-PARAMOUNT: 57 2-4
BRUNSWICK: 53 2-5
CORAL: 53 2-5
DERBY: 49-52 3-6
MERCURY: 52 3-5
Singles: 7-Inch
ABC-PARAMOUNT: 57-61 3-5
BRUNSWICK: 53 4-6
CORAL: 53 4-6
DERBY: 49-52 4-6
MERCURY: 52 5-8
ROCK 'N ROLL: 5-8
LPs: 10/12-Inch 33rpm
TRIP: 10-15
VIK: 20-25
Also see KING CURTIS

MITCHELL, Guy
Singles: 78rpm
COLUMBIA: 50-57 2-5
Singles: 7-Inch
COLUMBIA: 50-62 4-8
ERIC: 83 1-3
JOY: 62-63 3-6
REPRISE: 66 3-5
STARDAY: 67-69 3-5
Picture Sleeves
COLUMBIA: 56-62 5-10
EPs: 7-Inch 33/45rpm
COLUMBIA: 54-57 5-12
LPs: 10/12-Inch 33rpm
COLUMBIA (6000 series): 53 15-25
(10-Inch LPs.)
KING: 59 25-50
NASHVILLE: 70 6-10
STARDAY: 68-69 8-12
Also see CLOONEY, Rosemary, & Guy Mitchell

MITCHELL, Guy, & Mindy Carson
Singles: 78rpm
COLUMBIA: 52-53 2-5
Singles: 7-Inch
COLUMBIA: 52-53 4-8
Also see CARSON, Mindy

MITCHELL, Guy / Eileen Rodgers
EPs: 7-Inch 33/45rpm
COLUMBIA: 56 5-8

Also see MITCHELL, Guy
Also see RODGERS, Eileen

MITCHELL, Joni
Singles: 7-Inch
ASYLUM: 72-80 .... $2-4
ELEKTRA: 75 2-4
GEFFEN: 82-86 1-3
REPRISE: 68-72 2-4
LPs: 10/12-Inch 33rpm
ASYLUM: 72-80 8-10
GEFFEN: 82-88 5-8
REPRISE: 68-71 10-20

MITCHELL, Joni, & The L.A. Express
LPs: 10/12-Inch 33rpm
ASYLUM: 74 8-10
Also see MITCHELL, Joni

MITCHELL, Kim
Singles: 7-Inch
BRONZE: 85 1-3

MITCHELL, McKinley
Singles: 7-Inch
BOXER: 59 8-10
CHIMNEYVILLE: 77-78 2-3
ONE-DERFUL: 62-65 4-8

MITCHELL, Philip
(Prince Philip Mitchell)
Singles: 7-Inch
ATLANTIC: 78-79 2-3
EVENT: 75 2-4
ICHIBAN: 86 1-3

MITCHELL, Rubin
Singles: 7-Inch
CAPITOL: 67-68 2-4
Picture Sleeves
CAPITOL: 67 3-5
LPs: 10/12-Inch 33rpm
CAPITOL: 67 8-15

MITCHELL, Willie
(Willie Mitchell & The Four Kings)
Singles: 7-Inch
HI: 62-69 4-8
HOME OF THE BLUES: 60-61 4-6
MOTOWN: 1-3
STOMPER TIME: 15-20
Picture Sleeves
HI: 68 3-5
LPs: 10/12-Inch 33rpm
BEARSVILLE: 81 5-8
HI (010 through 039): 63-67 15-20
HI (042 through 056): 68-71 10-15

(Hi 010 through 042 used a "12" prefix to indicate mono or a "32" prefix to indicate stereo releases.)
HI (8000 series): 77 . . . . $5-8
MOTOWN: 82 8-10

MITCHELL TRIO:
see MITCHELL, Chad, Trio

MITCHUM, Robert
Singles: 7-Inch
CAPITOL (Purple label): 57-58 5-10
CAPITOL (Orange/yellow label): 62 3-5
MONUMENT: 67 2-3
EPs: 7-Inch 33/45rpm
CAPITOL: 57-58 10-20
LPs: 10/12-Inch 33rpm
CAPITOL: 57-58 15-25
MONUMENT: 67 10-15

MIXTURES
Singles: 7-Inch
SIRE: 71 2-4

MOB
Singles: 7-Inch
COLOSSUS: 71-72 3-5
MERCURY: 68 4-8
PRIVATE STOCK: 76-77 2-5
Picture Sleeves
COLOSSUS: 71-72 2-4
LPs: 10/12-Inch 33rpm
COLOSSUS: 71 10-12
PRIVATE STOCK: 75 8-10

MOBY GRAPE
Singles: 7-Inch
COLUMBIA: 67-69 5-10
Picture Sleeves
COLUMBIA: 67 20-25
LPs: 10/12-Inch 33rpm
COLUMBIA (Except 2698 &
9498): 68-72 10-15
COLUMBIA (2698 & 9498; "Moby
Grape"): 67 35-50
(Cover pictures Don Stevenson's middle finger over washboard. Price includes bonus poster, which represents about $8-$10 of the value.)
COLUMBIA (2698/9498; "Moby
Grape"): 67 10-15
(Cover pictures Don Stevenson's hand closed. Price includes bonus poster, which represents about $4-$6 of the value. The "26" prefix indicates mono, the "94" stereo.)
ESCAPE: 78 8-10
HARMONY: 70-71 10-12
REPRISE: 71 10-12
SAN FRANCISCO SOUND: 83 10-15

Promotional LPs
COLUMBIA (MGS-1; "Grape
Jam"): 68 . . . .$10-15
(With Mike Bloomfield & Al Kooper.)
ESCAPE (95018; "Live Grape"): 78 15-20
(Colored vinyl.)
Members: Don Stevenson; Jerry Miller; Peter Lewis; Skip Spence; Jeff Blackburn.
Also see BLOOMFIELD, Mike, & Al Kooper

MOCEDADES
Singles: 7-Inch
TARA: 74 2-3
LPs: 10/12-Inch 33rpm
TARA: 74 5-10

MODEL 500
Singles: 12-Inch 33/45rpm
METROPLEX: 85 4-6

MODELS
Singles: 12-Inch 33/45rpm
GEFFEN: 86 4-6
Singles: 7-Inch
GEFFEN: 86 2-3
LPs: 10/12-Inch 33rpm
GEFFEN: 86 5-8
WINDSONG: 80 5-8

MODERN ENGLISH
Singles: 12-Inch 33/45rpm
SIRE: 82-86 4-6
Singles: 7-Inch
SIRE: 82-86 2-3
LPs: 10/12-Inch 33rpm
SIRE: 83-86 5-8

MODERN ROCKETRY
Singles: 12-Inch 33/45rpm
MEGATONE: 83 4-6

MODERNAIRES
(Modernaires With Paula Kelly)
Singles: 78rpm
COLUMBIA: 50 2-4
CORAL: 51-56 2-4
Singles: 7-Inch
CAPITOL: 69 .2-3
COLUMBIA (38000 series): 50 3-5
CORAL: 51-56 2-4
MERCURY: 59 2-3
UNITED ARTISTS: 62 2-3
EPs: 7-Inch 33/45rpm
CORAL: 51-55 3-5
LPs: 10/12-Inch 33rpm
COLUMBIA: 50-66 5-15
CORAL: 51-55 8-15
LIBERTY: 84 .4-8
MERCURY: 60 5-12

ROSS: 79 .... $4-8
UNITED ARTISTS: 61-62 5-10
WING: 62 5-10
  Members: Paula Kelly; John Drake; Allan
  Copeland; Francis Scott; Hal Dickenson.

MODUGNO, Domenico
Singles: 7-Inch
DECCA: 58-64 4-8
MCA: 78 1-3
MGM: 66 3-5
RCA VICTOR: 68-72 2-5
UNITED ARTISTS INT'L: 67 2-5
EPs: 7-Inch 33/45rpm
DECCA: 58 4-8
LPs: 10/12-Inch 33rpm
DECCA: 58-61 10-20
RCA VICTOR: 66 5-10
UNITED ARTISTS INT'L: 67 4-8

MODULATIONS
Singles: 7-Inch
BUDDAH: 74-75 2-4

MOJO MEN
(MoJo)
Singles: 7-Inch
AUTUMN: 65-66 8-10
GRT: 69 4-6
REPRISE: 66-68 4-8
LPs: 10/12-Inch 33rpm
GRT: 68 15-20

MOLLY HATCHET
Singles: 7-Inch
EPIC: 79-86 1-3
EPs: 7-Inch 33/45rpm
CSP: 81 3-6
  (Nestle's candy promotional issue.)
LPs: 10/12-Inch 33rpm
EPIC (1320; "Molly Hatchet"): 78 25-30
  (Picture disc. Promotional issue only.)
EPIC (1339; "Molly Hatchet"): 81 10-12
  (Promotional issue only.)
EPIC (30000 & 40000 series): 78-87 5-8
  Members: Danny Joe Brown; Jimmy Farrar.
  Also see BROWN, Danny Joe

MOM & DADS
Singles: 7-Inch
GNP/CRESCENDO: 71-80 1-3
LPs: 10/12-Inch 33rpm
GNP/CRESCENDO: 71-87 4-8

MOMENT OF TRUTH
Singles: 7-Inch
ROULETTE: 75 2-4

MOMENTS
Singles: 7-Inch
ERA: 63-64 .... $4-8
HIT: 63 3-6
WORLD ARTISTS: 64 3-5
Also see SHACKLEFORDS

MOMENTS
(Moments & Whatnauts)
Singles: 7-Inch
STANG: 68-78 2-5
SUGAR HILL: 80-81 1-3
LPs: 10/12-Inch 33rpm
STANG: 70-78 8-10
VICTORY: 82 5-8
Also see O'JAYS / Moments
Also see RAY, GOODMAN, & BROWN

MONAE, Tia
Singles: 12-Inch 33/45rpm
FIRST TAKE: 84 4-6

MONARCHS
Singles: 7-Inch
ERWIN: 64 4-8
MONUMENT: 1-3
SOUND STAGE 7: 64 5-10

MONDAY, Julie
Singles: 7-Inch
RAINBOW: 66 3-5
SSS INT'L: 68 2-4

MONDAY AFTER
Singles: 7-Inch
BUDDAH: 76 2-4

MONEY, Eddie
Singles: 12-Inch 33/45rpm
COLUMBIA: 84 4-6
Singles: 7-Inch
CBS ("Maybe I'm A Fool"): 79 20-25
  (Picture disc. Promotional issue only.)
COLUMBIA: 78-88 1-3
POLYDOR : 85 1-3
Picture Sleeves
COLUMBIA: 82-84 1-3
LPs: 10/12-Inch 33rpm
COLUMBIA: 77-88 6-9
POLYDOR : 85 5-8

MONEY, Eddie, & Zane Buzby
Singles: 7-Inch
COLUMBIA: 79 2-3
Also see MONEY, Eddie

MONEY, Eddie, & Valerie Carter
Singles: 7-Inch
COLUMBIA: 80 1-3
Also see CARTER, Valerie

MONEY, Eddie, & Ronnie Spector
Singles: 7-Inch
COLUMBIA: *86* $1-3
Also see MONEY, Eddie
Also see SPECTOR, Ronnie

MONGO SANTAMARIA:
see SANTAMARIA, Mongo

MONITORS
Singles: 7-Inch
BUDDAH: *72* 2-4
MOTOWN: 1-3
SOUL: *68* 2-4
V.I.P.: *65-68* 4-8
LPs: 10/12-Inch 33rpm
SOUL: *69* 12-15

MONK, T.S.
(Thelonious Monk, Jr.)
Singles: 7-Inch
MIRAGE: *80-82* 1-3
LPs: 10/12-Inch 33rpm
MIRAGE: *81-82* 5-8

MONK, Thelonious
Singles: 7-Inch
COLUMBIA: *63-69* 2-4
PRESTIGE: *60-69* 2-4
EPs: 7-Inch 33/45rpm
PRESTIGE: *52* 10-25
LPs: 10/12-Inch 33rpm
BLACK LION: *74* 6-10
BLUE NOTE (100 through
500 series): *73-76* 8-12
BLUE NOTE (1500 series): *56* 25-50
(Label reads "Blue Note Records Inc. - New York,
U.S.A.")
BLUE NOTE (1500 series): *58* 15-25
(Label reads "Blue Note Records Inc. - N.Y.,
U.S.A.")
BLUE NOTE: *63* 10-20
(Label reads "Blue Note Records - A Division Of
Liberty Records Inc.")
BLUE NOTE (5000 series): *52* 150-200
(10-Inch LPs.)
COLUMBIA (1900 through
2600 series): *63-67* 10-20
(Monaural.)
COLUMBIA (8700 through
9800 series): *63-69* 10-20
(Stereo.)
COLUMBIA (32000 through
38000 series): *74-83* 6-12
EVEREST: *78* 5-8
MILESTONE: *75-84* 6-12
PAUSA: *83* 5-8

PRESTIGE (100 series): *52-54* $50-80
(10-Inch LPs.)
PRESTIGE (7000 series): *56-62* 20-40
(Yellow labels.)
PRESTIGE (7000 through
7600 series): *65-69* 10-20
(Blue labels.)
PRESTIGE (7700 & 7800 series): *70-71* . .8-15
PRESTIGE (24000 series): *72* 8-15
RIVERSIDE (010 through
103): *82-84* 5-8
RIVERSIDE (200 & 300 series): *55-60* . .25-50
(Riverside 200 & 300 series numbers may be
preceded by a "12.")
RIVERSIDE (400 series): *62-67* 15-25
RIVERSIDE (1100 series): *58-60* 20-40
RIVERSIDE (3000 series): *68-69* 10-20
RIVERSIDE (9400 series): *62-63* 15-25
TOMATO: *78* 5-10
TRIP: *73* 5-10
Also see COLTRANE, John, & Thelonious
Monk
Also see DAVIS, Miles, & Thelonious Monk
Also see MERC & MONK
Also see MULLIGAN, Gerry, & Thelonious
Monk

MONK, Thelonious, & Sonny Rollins
EPs: 7-Inch 33/45rpm
PRESTIGE: *52* 25-50
LPs: 10/12-Inch 33rpm
PRESTIGE (100 series): *52* 100-150
(10-Inch LPs.)
PRESTIGE (7000 series): *57-59* 25-50
RIVERSIDE (200 series): *57-58* 25-50
RIVERSIDE (1100 series): *58* 20-40

MONKEES
Singles: 12-Inch 33/45rpm
ARISTA: *86* 5-10
(Promotional issue only.)
Singles: 7-Inch
ARISTA (0200 series): *76* 3-5
ARISTA (9000 series): *76-86* 1-3
COLGEMS: *66-70* 3-6
COLGEMS (Cardboard discs): *67* 6-10
(One-sided discs, each with four tracks, originally
attached to cereal boxes. Promotional special
products issues.)
FLASHBACK: *73* 2-3
RHINO: *87* 1-3
Picture Sleeves
COLGEMS (1000 series): *66-68* 5-15
COLGEMS (5000 series): *69-70* 20-25
EPs: 7-Inch 33/45rpm
COLGEMS (Cardboard discs): *67* 5-10

(One-sided discs, each with four tracks, originally attached to cereal boxes. Not issued with covers, although discs were illustrated.)

LPs: 10/12-Inch 33rpm

ARISTA (4000 series): *76* **$8-10**
ARISTA (8000 series): *86* **5-8**
BELL: *73* **12-15**
COLGEMS (101; "The
  Monkees"): *66* **10-15**
  (With the track "Papa Jean's Blues.")
COLGEMS (101; "The
  Monkees"): *66* **10-20**
  (With the track "Papa Gene's Blues.")
COLGEMS (102 through 109): *67-68* . . . **10-20**
COLGEMS (113; "Instant
  Replay"): *69* **25-35**
COLGEMS (115; "The Monkees
  Greatest Hits"): *69* **40-50**
COLGEMS (117; "The Monkees
  Present"): *69* **60-75**
COLGEMS (119; "Changes"): *70* **75-100**
COLGEMS (329; "Golden
  Hits"): *71* **100-125**
  (RCA Special Products issue.)
COLGEMS (1001; "A Barrel Full
  Of Monkees"): *71* **30-40**
COLGEMS (5008; "Head"): *68* **35-40**
LAURIE HOUSE: *73* **15-20**
  (Mail-order LP offer.)
RCA VICTOR (7000 series): **8-10**
RHINO: *82-87* **5-8**
Members: Michael Nesmith; Davy Jones; Mickey Dolenz; Peter Tork.
Also see DOLENZ, Mickey
Also see DOLENZ, JONES & TORK
Also see JONES, Davy
Also see NESMITH, Michael

MONOTONES

Singles: 7-Inch

ARGO (Except 5339): *58-59* **5-10**
ARGO (5339; "Tell It To
  The Judge"): *59* **15-20**
CHESS: *73* **1-3**
COLLECTABLES: **1-3**
ERIC: **1-3**
HICKORY: *64-65* **4-8**
HULL (735; "Reading The Book
  Of Love"): *60* **50-60**
HULL (743; "Daddy's Home But
  Momma's Gone"): *61* **15-20**
MASCOT (124; "Book Of
  Love"): *57* **75-100**
ROULETTE: *73* **3-5**

Members: Warren Davis; Frank Smith; John Raynes; George Malone; Charles Patrick; James Patrick.

MONRO, Matt

Singles: 7-Inch

CAPITOL: *66-72* **$2-3**
LIBERTY: *62-66* **2-4**
UNITED ARTISTS: *74* **1-3**
WARWICK: *61* **2-4**

LPs: 10/12-Inch 33rpm

CAPITOL: *67-70* **8-12**
LIBERTY: *62-66* **8-18**
WARWICK: *61* **10-20**
Also see BARRY, John
Also see LEGRAND, Michel, & Matt Monro

MONROE, Marilyn

Singles: 78rpm

RCA VICTOR: *54-55* **5-10**
UNITED ARTISTS: *59* **4-8**

Picture Sleeves

RCA VICTOR: *54-55* **12-25**

Singles: 7-Inch

RCA VICTOR: *54-55* **5-10**
20TH CENTURY-FOX: *62* **4-8**
UNITED ARTISTS: *59* **4-8**

Picture Sleeves

RCA VICTOR: *54-55* **12-25**
20TH CENTURY-FOX: *62* **25-50**

EPs: 7-Inch 33/45rpm

MGM (208; "Gentlemen Prefer
  Blondes"): *53* **15-25**
  (Soundtrack. With Jane Russell.)
RCA VICTOR (593; "There's No Business
  Like Show Business"): *55* **10-20**
UNITED ARTISTS: *59* **15-25**

LPs: 10/12-Inch 33rpm

ASCOT (13500; "Some Like
  It Hot"): *64* **15-20**
  (Monaural. Soundtrack.)
ASCOT (16500; "Some Like It Hot"): *64* **25-30**
  (Stereo. Soundtrack.)
COLUMBIA (1527; "Let's Make
  Love"): *60* **20-30**
  (Monaural. Soundtrack.)
COLUMBIA (8327; "Let's Make
  Love"): *60* **30-40**
  (Stereo. Soundtrack.)
COLUMBIA/CSP (8327; "Let's Make
  Love"): **8-10**
  (Soundtrack. With Yves Montand & Frankie Vaughan.)
MGM (208; "Gentlemen Prefer
  Blondes"): *53* **50-75**

MGM (3231; "Gentlemen Prefer
Blondes"): 55 . . . . $25-40
(Soundtrack. With Jane Russell.)
MOVIETONE: 67 10-20
STET: 5-10
20TH CENTURY-FOX: 62 15-30
UNITED ARTISTS (272; "Some Like
It Hot"): 74 8-10
(Soundtrack.)
UNITED ARTISTS (4030; "Some
Like It Hot"): 59 30-50
(Monaural. Soundtrack.)
UNITED ARTISTS (5030; "Some
Like It Hot"): 59 40-60
(Stereo. Soundtrack.)

MONROE, Vaughn
Singles: 78rpm
BLUEBIRD: 40-42 4-8
RCA VICTOR: 47-49 3-6
VICTOR: 42-47 3-6
Singles: 7-Inch
DOT: 62-63 2-5
JUBILEE: 61 2-4
MGM: 60 2-4
RCA VICTOR: 50-59 3-6
ROD: 68 1-3
UNITED ARTISTS: 60 2-4
Picture Sleeves
RCA VICTOR: 57 8-15
EPs: 7-Inch 33/45rpm
CAMDEN: 56 4-8
RCA VICTOR: 50-56 5-10
LPs: 10/12-Inch 33rpm
CAMDEN: 56 5-15
DOT: 62-64 10-20
HAMILTON: 65 5-10
KAPP: 65 5-10
RCA VICTOR (11 through 3066): 50-53 . 15-25
(10-Inch LPs.)
RCA VICTOR (1400 through 1700
series): 56-58 10-20
(12-Inch LPs.)
RCA VICTOR (1100 series): 75 4-8
RCA VICTOR (3800 series): 67 5-10
RCA VICTOR (6000 series): 72 5-10
Also see MARTIN, Dean / Patti Page

MONROES
Singles: 7-Inch
ALFA: 82 1-3
LPs: 10/12-Inch 33rpm
ALFA: 82 5-8

MONTANA ORCHESTRA
LPs: 10/12-Inch 33rpm
MJS: 81 5-8

MONTANA SEXTET
Singles: 12-Inch 33/45rpm
PHILLY SOUND: 83 . . . . $4-6

MONTANAS
Singles: 7-Inch
INDEPENDENCE: 67-69 4-6
WARNER BROS: 66-68 3-5

MONTCLAIRS
Singles: 7-Inch
PAULA: 71-74 2-4
LPs: 10/12-Inch 33rpm
PAULA: 72 8-12

MONTE, Lou
Singles: 78rpm
RCA VICTOR (Except 6704): 53-56 2-5
RCA VICTOR (6704; "Elvis Presley
For President"): 56 5-10
Singles: 7-Inch
GWP: 71-72 1-3
RCA VICTOR (5382 through 6600
series): 53-56 4-6
RCA VICTOR (6700 through 7600
series, except 6704): 56-60 3-5
RCA VICTOR (6704; "Elvis Presley
For President"): 56 10-15
RCA VICTOR (8700 through 9000
series): 65-67 2-4
RAGALIA: 69 2-3
REPRISE: 62-65 3-6
ROULETTE: 60-61 3-5
Picture Sleeves
REPRISE: 62-63 3-6
EPs: 7-Inch 33/45rpm
RCA VICTOR (Except 18): 57-59 8-10
RCA VICTOR (18; "Elvis Presley
For President"): 56 15-30
(Promotional issue only. Not issued with cover.)
LPs: 10/12-Inch 33rpm
CAMDEN: 58 15-20
HARMONY: 68 10-12
RCA VICTOR (1600 through 1900
series): 57-59 20-25
RCA VICTOR (3000 series): 66-67 12-15
ROULETTE: 60 15-20
REPRISE: 61-65 15-20
Also see PRESLEY, Elvis

MONTENEGRO, Hugo
(Hugo Montenegro's Orchestra & Chorus)
Singles: 7-Inch
RCA VICTOR: 64-75 1-3
TIME: 61-63 2-3
20TH CENTURY-FOX: 59 2-3

LPs: 10/12-Inch 33rpm

CAMDEN: 62 .... $5-10
GWP: 70 5-10
MAINSTREAM: 67-68 5-10
MOVIETONE: 67 5-10
PICKWICK: 4-8
RCA VICTOR (0025 through 2300
   series): 72-77 4-8
RCA VICTOR (1113; "Hurry
   Sundown"): 67 35-50
   (Soundtrack.)
RCA VICTOR (2900 series): 64 5-15
RCA VICTOR (3475; "The Man
   From Uncle"): 65 25-40
   (Soundtrack.)
RCA VICTOR (3574; "The Man
   From Uncle, Volume 2"): 66 35-45
   (Soundtrack.)
RCA VICTOR (3500 through 4600
   series): 66-71 5-15
RCA VICTOR (6000 series): 71 5-10
TIME: 60-64 8-15
20TH CENTURY-FOX: 59-68 5-15
   Also see HIRT, Al, & Hugo Montenegro

MONTEZ, Chris
Singles: 7-Inch

A&M: 65-68 3-5
COLLECTABLES: 1-3
ERA: 72 2-3
ERIC: 1-3
JAMIE: 73 2-3
MONOGRAM: 62-64 4-6
PARAMOUNT: 71-73 2-3
LPs: 10/12-Inch 33rpm
A&M: 66-67 12-15
MONOGRAM: 63 35-45
   Also see CHRIS & KATHY

MONTGOMERY, Melba
Singles: 7-Inch

CAPITOL: 69-76 1-3
COMPASS: 86 1-3
ELEKTRA: 73-75 1-3
MUSICOR: 66-69 2-4
UNITED ARTISTS (500 through
   900 series): 63-66 2-4
UNITED ARTISTS (1000 through
   1100 series): 77 1-3
Picture Sleeves
MUSICOR: 66 3-5
LPs: 10/12-Inch 33rpm
CAPITOL: 69-75 6-10
ELEKTRA: 73-75 5-10
MUSICOR: 66-68 10-15
UNART: 67 6-12

UNITED ARTISTS (Except 600
   series): 64 .... $10-20
UNITED ARTISTS (600 series): 78 5-8
   Also see JONES, George, Gene Pitney, &
Melba Montgomery
   Also see JONES, George, & Melba
Montgomery
   Also see PITNEY, Gene, & Melba
Montgomery
   Also see WEST, Dottie / Melba Montgomery

MONTGOMERY, Tammy
(Tammi Terrell)
Singles: 7-Inch

CHECKER: 64 4-8
SCEPTER: 61 4-8
TRY ME: 63 4-8
WAND: 62 4-8
   Also see TERRELL, Tammi

MONTGOMERY, Wes
(Wes Montgomery Quartet)
Singles: 7-Inch

A&M: 67-70 2-3
PACIFIC JAZZ: 60 2-4
RIVERSIDE: 61-64 2-4
VERVE: 65-68 2-3
LPs: 10/12-Inch 33rpm
A&M: 67-70 8-15
ACCORD: 82 5-8
BLUE NOTE: 75 6-12
MGM: 70 8-12
MILESTONE: 73-83 8-15
PACIFIC JAZZ (5;
   "Montgomeryland"): 60 15-25
PACIFIC JAZZ (10000 & 20000
   series): 66-68 10-15
RIVERSIDE (034 through 089): 82-83 5-8
RIVERSIDE (300 & 400 series): 59-67 . 15-25
RIVERSIDE (3000 series): 68-69 10-15
VERVE: 65-72 8-18
   (Reads "MGM Records - A Division Of Metro-
Goldwyn-Mayer, Inc." at bottom of label.)
VERVE: 73-84 5-10
   (Reads "Manufactured By MGM Record Corp.," or
mentions either Polydor or Polygram at bottom of
label.)
   Also see MONTGOMERY BROTHERS
   Also see SMITH, Jimmy, & Wes Montgomery

MONTGOMERY BROTHERS
Singles: 7-Inch

RIVERSIDE: 61 2-4
LPs: 10/12-Inch 33rpm
FANTASY: 60-62 15-25
PACIFIC JAZZ: 61 15-25
RIVERSIDE: 61 15-25

WORLD PACIFIC: *58* $20-40
Members: Wes Montgomery; Buddy Montgomery;
Monk Montgomery.
Also see MONTGOMERY, Wes
Also see SHEARING, George, & The
Montgomery Brothers

MONTRE-EL, Jackie
Singles: 7-Inch
ABC: *68* 3-5

MONTROSE
Singles: 7-Inch
WARNER BROS: *74-77* 2-3
LPs: 10/12-Inch 33rpm
WARNER BROS: *73-78* 6-10
Members: Ronnie Montrose; Sammy Hagar.
Also see HAGAR, Sammy

MONTROSE, Ronnie
Singles: 7-Inch
WARNER BROS: *78* 2-3
LPs: 10/12-Inch 33rpm
WARNER BROS: *78* 5-8
Also see GAMMA
Also see MONTROSE
Also see WINTER, Edgar

MONTY PYTHON
Singles: 7-Inch
ARISTA: *80* 2-3
LPs: 10/12-Inch 33rpm
ARISTA: *75-82* 5-8
MCA: *83* 5-8
PYE: *75* 5-10

MONYAKA
Singles: 12-Inch 33/45rpm
EASY STREET: *83* 4-6

MOODY BLUES
Singles: 7-Inch
DERAM: *68-72* 3-5
LONDON (Except 200, 9000, & 1000
series): 1-3
LONDON (200 series): *78* 2-4
LONDON (1000 series): *67* 5-10
LONDON (9000 series,
except 9726): *65-66* 10-15
LONDON (9726; "Go Now"): *65* . . . . : . 4-8
POLYDOR: *86-88* 1-3
THRESHOLD (600 series): *81-85* 1-3
THRESHOLD (67000 series): *70-72* 2-4
Picture Sleeves
POLYDOR: *86* 1-3
THRESHOLD (600 series): *81-85* 1-3
THRESHOLD (67000 series): *70-72* 2-4

LPs: 10/12-Inch 33rpm
DERAM (18012; "Days Of Future
Passed"): *68* $10-15
DERAM (18017; "In Search Of The
Lost Chord"): *68* 10-15
(With gatefold cover.)
DERAM (18017; "In Search Of The
Lost Chord"): 5-8
(With standard cover.)
DERAM (18025; "On The Threshold
Of A Dream"): *69* 10-15
(With gatefold cover.)
DERAM (18025; "On The Threshold
Of A Dream"): *69* 5-8
(With standard cover.)
DERAM (18051; "In The
Beginning"): *69* 12-15
DERAM (820006; "Days Of Future
Passed"): 5-8
LONDON (Except 428): *77-78* 8-10
LONDON (428; "Go Now"): *65* 20-25
(Reissues, using the same catalog number, are cur-
rently available.)
MFSL (042; "Days Of Future Past"): *80* . . 25-50
MFSL (151; "Seventh
Sojourn"): *85* 15-25
POLYDOR: *88* 5-8
THRESHOLD: *69-86* 6-12
Members: Michael Pinder; Ray Thomas; Graeme
Edge; Denny Laine; Brian Hines; Clint Warwick;
John Lodge; Justin Hayward; Patrick Moraz.
Also see EDGE, Graeme
Also see HAYWARD, Justin, & John Lodge
Also see LODGE, John
Also see MORAZ, Patrick
Also see PINDER, Michael
Also see THOMAS, Ray

MOON, Keith
Singles: 7-Inch
TRACK: *75* 2-4
LPs: 10/12-Inch 33rpm
MCA: *75* 8-10
Also see LORD SUTCH
Also see NELSON, Rick
Also see WHO

MOONEY, Art, & His Orchestra
Singles: 78rpm
MGM: *50-57* 2-5
VOGUE (Except 711 & 713): *46-48* 25-40
VOGUE (711; "I've Been Working
On The Railroad"): *46* 50-100
VOGUE (713; "I've Been Working
On The Railroad"): *46* 50-100

Singles: 7-Inch
DECCA: *61-62* $1-3
KAPP: *64-65* 1-3
MGM (Except 12312): *50-61* 2-4
MGM (12312; "Rebel Without A Cause")/
"East Of Eden"): *56* 4-6
RIVERSIDE: *62* 2-3

Picture Sleeves
MGM (12312; "Rebel Without A Cause")/
"East Of Eden"): *56* 10-20
(Billed as a "Tribute To James Dean.")

EPs: 7-Inch 33/45rpm
MGM: *55-56* 4-8

LPs: 10/12-Inch 33rpm
DECCA: *62* 5-10
KAPP: *64* 5-10
MGM: *55-61* 5-15
RCA VICTOR: *67* 5-8

MOONGLOWS
Singles: 78rpm
CHAMPAGNE (7500; "I Just Can't
Tell No Lie"): *52* 50-100
CHANCE (1147; "Whistle My
Love"): *53* 50-100
CHANCE (1150; "Just A Lonely
Christmas"): *53* 50-100
CHANCE (1152; "Secret Love"): *54* .. 50-100
CHANCE (1152; "I Was Wrong"): *54* .. 50-100
CHANCE (1161; "219 Train"): *54* 50-100
CHESS (1500 series): *54-55* 20-40
CHESS (1600 series): *55-57* 10-20

Singles: 7-Inch
BIG P: *71* 3-5
CHAMPAGNE (7500; "I Just Can't
Tell No Lie"): *52* 250-400
CHANCE (1147; "Whistle My
Love"): *53* 500-750
(Colored vinyl.)
CHANCE (1150; "Just A Lonely
Christmas"): *53* 300-500
CHANCE (1152; "Secret Love"): *54* .. 300-500
(Blue & silver label.)
CHANCE (1152; "Secret Love"): *54* .. 250-400
(Yellow & black label.)
CHANCE (1152; "I Was Wrong"): *54* . 250-400
(Yellow & black label.)
CHANCE (1152; "I Was Wrong"): *55* . 200-300
(White & black label.)
CHANCE (1161; "219 Train"): *54* 300-500
CHESS (1581; "Sincerely"): *54* 30-50
CHESS (1589; "Most Of All"): *54* 30-50
CHESS (1598; "Foolish Me"): *55* 20-25
CHESS (1605; "Starlite"): *55* 20-25
CHESS (1611; "In My Diary"): *55* 25-35

CHESS (1619 through 1689): *56-58* ... $10-20
CHESS (1700 series): *58* 5-10
CRIMSON: 3-5
LANA: *64* 3-5
RCA VICTOR: *72* 2-4
TIMES SQUARE: *64* 3-5
VEE JAY: *61* 3-5

EPs: 7-Inch 33/45rpm
CHESS: *59* 30-60

LPs: 10/12-Inch 33rpm
CHESS (701; "The Moonglows"): *76* 8-15
CHESS (1430; "Look, It's The
Moonglows"): *59* 50-75
CONSTELLATION: *64* 15-20
LOST-NITE: *81* 5-8
RCA VICTOR: *72* 10-15
Members: Harvey Fuqua; Bobby Lester; Alex
Graves; Prentiss Barnes; Marvin Gaye; Reese Pal-
mer; James Knowland; Chester Simmons; George
Thorpe; Dock Green; Berle Ashton.
Also see DIDDLEY, Bo
Also see DRIFTERS
Also see FLAMINGOS / Moonglows
Also see GAYE, Marvin
Also see HARVEY & THE MOONGLOWS
Also see LESTER, Bobby

MOONLION
Singles: 7-Inch
P.I.P.: *76* 1-3

MOORE, Bob
(Bob Moore & His Orchestra)
Singles: 7-Inch
HICKORY: *65-68* 2-3
MONUMENT: *59-64* 2-4

Picture Sleeves
MONUMENT: *62-63* 3-6

LPs: 10/12-Inch 33rpm
HICKORY: *66* 8-12
MONUMENT: *61-67* 10-20
Also see PRESLEY, Elvis

MOORE, Bobby
(Bobby Moore & The Rhythm Aces)
Singles: 12-Inch 33/45rpm
SCEPTER (12417; "Try To Hold On"): *75* . 5-8
(Promotional issue only.)
Singles: 7-Inch
CHECKER: *66-68* 3-5
SCEPTER: *75-76* 2-4
LPs: 10/12-Inch 33rpm
CHECKER: *66* 15-20

MOORE, Dorothy
(Dorothy Moore)
Singles: 12-Inch 33/45rpm
STREETKING: *84* 4-6

Singles: 7-Inch
GSF: *73* $2-4
HANDSHAKE: *82* 1-3
MALACO: *76-80* 1-3
STREETKING: *84* 1-3
LPs: 10/12-Inch 33rpm
MALACO: *76-78* 5-8
Also see POPPIES

MOORE, Dorothy, & Eddie Floyd
Singles: 7-Inch
MALACO: *77* 2-3
Also see FLOYD, Eddie
Also see MOORE, Dorothy

MOORE, Gary
(Gary Moore Band)
Singles: 7-Inch
JET: *79* 1-3
MIRAGE: *83-86* 1-3
LPs: 10/12-Inch 33rpm
JET: *78* 5-8
MIRAGE: *83-86* 5-8
PETERS INT'L (Red label): *73* 12-15
PETERS INT'L (Orange label): *73* 10-12
VIRGIN: *87* 5-8
Also see THIN LIZZY

MOORE, Jackie
Singles: 12-Inch 33/45rpm
COLUMBIA: *79-84* 4-6
Singles: 7-Inch
ATLANTIC: *70-73* 2-4
CATAWBA: *83* 1-3
COLUMBIA: *79-84* 1-3
KAYVETTE: *75-81* 1-3
SHOUT: *68* 3-5
LPs: 10/12-Inch 33rpm
COLUMBIA: *79* 5-8

MOORE, Johnny
**(Johnny Moore's Three Blazers; Johnny
Moore's Blazers; Johnny Moore's New Blazers;
Johnny Moore & The Twigs)**
Singles: 78rpm
ALADDIN: *45-48* 6-15
EXCLUSIVE: *46-48* 5-10
HOLLYWOOD: *55-56* 5-10
MODERN: *48-50* 5-10
MODERN MUSIC: *45-46* 5-10
PHILO: *46* 10-15
RCA VICTOR: *50-51* 6-12
SWING TIME: *51* 4-8
Singles: 7-Inch
ALADDIN (112; "Drifting Blues"): *51* .. 50-75
BLAZE: 10-20
HOLLYWOOD: *55-56* 10-20

MODERN (800 & 900 series): *53* $10-20
RCA VICTOR (50-0000 series): *50-51* ...15-25
RENDEZVOUS: *60* 4-8
Members: Johnny Moore; Charles Brown; Eddie
Williams.
Also see BROWN, Charles
Also see DIXON, Floyd, & Johnny Moore's
Three Blazers
Also see MC SHANN, Jay, & Johnny Moore's
Three Blazers

MOORE, Lee
Singles: 7-Inch
SOURCE: *79* 1-3

MOORE, Melba
Singles: 12-Inch 33/45rpm
CAPITOL: *83-86* 4-6
EPIC: *79-80* 4-6
Singles: 7-Inch
BUDDAH: *75-78* 2-3
CAPITOL: *82-88* 1-3
EMI AMERICA: *81-82* 1-3
EPIC: *78-80* 1-3
MERCURY: *69-72* 2-4
MUSICOR: *66* 3-5
LPs: 10/12-Inch 33rpm
ACCORD: *81* 5-8
BUDDAH: *75-79* 8-10
CAPITOL: *83-88* 5-8
EMI AMERICA: *81* 5-8
EPIC: *79-80* 5-8
MERCURY: *70-72* 10-12
Also see THOMAS, Lillo, & Melba Moore

MOORE, Melba, & Freddie Jackson
Singles: 7-Inch
CAPITOL: *86-88* 1-3
Also see JACKSON, Freddie

MOORE, Melba, & Kashif
Singles: 7-Inch
CAPITOL: *86* $1-3
  Also see KASHIF
  Also see MOORE, Melba

MOORE, Rene
Singles: 7-Inch
POLYDOR: *88* 1-3
LPs: 10/12-Inch 33rpm
POLYDOR: *88* 5-8

MOORE, Tim
Singles: 7-Inch
ASYLUM: *74-79* 1-3
DUNHILL: *73* 2-4

MOORE, Vinnie
LPs: 10/12-Inch 33rpm
SQUAWK: *88* 5-8

MORAZ, Patrick
LPs: 10/12-Inch 33rpm
ATLANTIC: *76* 8-10
CHRISIMA: *78* 5-8
IMPORT: *77* 8-10
PASSPORT: 5-8
  Also see MOODY BLUES
  Also see YES

MORGAN, Denroy
Singles: 12-Inch 33/45rpm
BECKET: *81-82* 4-6
Singles: 7-Inch
BECKET: *81* 1-3

MORGAN, Jane
Singles: 78rpm
KAPP: *54-57* 2-4
Singles: 7-Inch
ABC: *67-68* 1-3
EPIC: *65-68* 2-3
COLPIX: *63-65* 2-4
KAPP: *54-62* 2-4
RCA VICTOR: *69-70* 1-3
EPs: 7-Inch 33/45rpm
KAPP: *55-59* 4-8
Picture Sleeves
COLPIX: *63* 4-8
ELEKTRA: *82* 1-3
EPIC: *65* 3-6
KAPP: *57-59* 5-10
LPs: 10/12-Inch 33rpm
ABC: *68* 5-8
COLPIX: *63-66* 5-15
EPIC: *65-67* 5-10
KAPP: *56-63* 8-18
MCA: *73* 4-8

RCA VICTOR (Except 1160): *69-70* $5-8
RCA VICTOR (1160; "Marry Me,
  Marry Me"): *69* 10-15
  (Soundtrack.)
HARMONY: *70* 5-8
  Also see WILLIAMS, Roger, & Jane Morgan

MORGAN, Jaye P.
Singles: 78rpm
DECCA: *54-55* 2-5
DERBY: *53* 2-5
RCA VICTOR: *54-56* 2-5
Singles: 7-Inch
ABC-PARAMOUNT: *65* 2-5
BEVERLY HILLS: *69-72* 1-3
DECCA: *54-55* 4-8
DERBY: *53* 4-8
GIGOLO: 2-4
MGM: *59-63* 3-6
RCA VICTOR: *54-56* 4-8
EPs: 7-Inch 33/45rpm
DECCA: *55* 10-20
DERBY: *53* 10-20
LPs: 10/12-Inch 33rpm
BAINBRIDGE: *82* 4-8
BEVERLY HILLS: *70* 5-8
MGM: *59-61* 15-25
RCA VICTOR: *55* 15-25
  Also see COMO, Perry, & Jaye P. Morgan
  Also see PRESLEY, Elvis / Jaye P. Morgan

MORGAN, Lee
Singles: 7-Inch
BLUE NOTE: *64-69* 2-4
BUZZ: *79-80* 1-3
VEE JAY: *60* 2-4
LPs: 10/12-Inch 33rpm
BLUE NOTE (200 series): *74* 6-12
BLUE NOTE (900 & 1000
  series): *79-81* 5-8
BLUE NOTE (1500 series): *56-58* 25-50
  (Label gives New York street address for Blue
  Note Records.)
BLUE NOTE (1500 series): *58* 15-25
  (Label reads "Blue Note Records Inc. - New York,
  USA.")
BLUE NOTE (1500 series): *66* 10-20
  (Label shows Blue Note Records as a division of
  either Liberty or United Artists.)
BLUE NOTE (4000 series): *61* 20-40
  (Label gives New York street address for Blue
  Note Records.)
BLUE NOTE (4000 series): *62* 15-25
  (Label reads "Blue Note Records Inc. - New York,
  USA.")

BLUE NOTE (4000 series): *66* $10-20
(Label shows Blue Note Records as a division of
either Liberty or United Artists.)
BLUE NOTE (4100 through 4200
series): *63* 15-25
(Label reads "Blue Note Records Inc. - New York,
USA.")
BLUE NOTE (4100 through 4200
series): *66-67* 10-20
(Label shows Blue Note Records as a division of
either Liberty or United Artists.)
BLUE NOTE (84000 series): *61* 20-40
(Label gives New York street address for Blue
Note Records.)
BLUE NOTE (84000 series): *62* 15-25
(Label reads "Blue Note Records Inc. - New York,
USA.")
BLUE NOTE (84000 series): *66* 10-20
(Label shows Blue Note Records as a division of
either Liberty or United Artists.)
BLUE NOTE (84100 through 84200
series): *63-69* 15-25
(Label reads "Blue Note Records Inc. - New York,
USA.")
BLUE NOTE (84100 through 84300
series): *66-70* 10-20
(Label shows Blue Note Records as a division of
either Liberty or United Artists.)
BLUE NOTE (89000 series): *71* 10-15
GNP/CRESCENDO: *73* 6-12
JAZZLAND: *62* 15-25
MCA: *74* 5-8
PACIFIC JAZZ: *81* 5-8
PRESTIGE: *81* 5-8
SAVOY (12000 series): *56* 20-40
SUNSET: *69* 5-10
TRADITION: *68* 8-15
TRIP: *73* 6-10
VEE JAY: *60-65* 15-25

MORGAN, Meli'sa
Singles: 12-Inch 33/45rpm
CAPITOL: *86* 4-6
Singles: 7-Inch
CAPITOL: *86-88* 1-3
LPs: 10/12-Inch 33rpm
CAPITOL: *86-87* 5-8
Also see KASHIF & Meli'sa Morgan

MORGAN, Russ, & His Orchestra
Singles: 78rpm
DECCA: *50-56* 2-4
Singles: 7-Inch
DECCA: *50-56* 2-4
EVEREST: *61* 2-3
VEE JAY: *64-65* 1-3

EPs: 7-Inch 33/45rpm
DECCA: *51-56* $4-8
LPs: 10/12-Inch 33rpm
CAPITOL: *62* 5-10
CIRCLE: *81* 4-6
DECCA: *51-67* 5-15
EVEREST: *60-63* 5-12
GNP/CRESCENDO: *73* 4-8
MCA: *73* 4-8
PICKWICK: *65* 4-8
SUNSET: *66* 4-8
VEE JAY: *65* 5-10

MORGAN BROTHERS
Singles: 7-Inch
MGM: *58-60* 2-4
RCA VICTOR: *55* 2-4

MORISETTE, Johnnie
Singles: 7-Inch
SAR: *60-63* 4-6

MORLEY, Cozy
Singles: 7-Inch
ABC-PARAMOUNT: *57* 4-6

MORMON TABERNACLE CHOIR
Singles: 7-Inch
COLUMBIA: *59* 2-4
Picture Sleeves
COLUMBIA: *59* 3-6
LPs: 10/12-Inch 33rpm
COLUMBIA: *59-76* 5-10
RCA VICTOR: *60* 5-10

MORNING MIST
Singles: 7-Inch
EVENT: *71* 2-4
Members: Terry Cashman; Tommy West.
Also see CASHMAN & WEST

MORNING, NOON & NIGHT
Singles: 7-Inch
ROADSHOW: *77* 2-3
LPs: 10/12-Inch 33rpm
ROADSHOW: *77* 8-10

MORODER, Giorgio
(Giorgio)
Singles: 12-Inch 33/45rpm
COLUMBIA: *84* 4-6
MCA: *84* 4-6
Singles: 7-Inch
BACKSTREET: 1-3
CASABLANCA: *79-80* 1-3
COLUMBIA: *84* 1-3
DUNHILL: *72* 2-4
EMI AMERICA: *84* 1-3
MCA: *84* 1-3

POLYDOR: *80* $1-3
VIRGIN: 1-3
LPs: 10/12-Inch 33rpm
CASABLANCA: *77-79* 8-10
DUNHILL: *72* 10-12
POLYDOR: *80* 5-8
Also see MERCURY, Freddie / Giorgio
Moroder
Also see SUMMER, Donna

MORODER, Giorgio, & Phil Oakey
Singles: 12-Inch 33/45rpm
VIRGIN: *84* 4-6
Also see HUMAN LEAGUE
Also see MORODER, Giorgio

MORRILL, Kent
LPs: 10/12-Inch 33rpm
CREAM: 10-12
SUSPICIOUS: *88* 5-8
Also see WAILERS

MORRIS, David, Jr.
Singles: 7-Inch
BUDDAH: *76* 2-3
PHILIPS: *68* 3-5

MORRIS, Gary
Singles: 7-Inch
WARNER BROS: *80-87* 1-3
LPs: 10/12-Inch 33rpm
WARNER BROS: *82-86* 5-8
Also see ANDERSON, Lynn, & Gary Morris
Also see GAYLE, Crystal, & Gary Morris

MORRIS, Joe, & His Orchestra
(Joe Morris Orch. Featuring Mr. Stringbean)
Singles: 78rpm
ATLANTIC (Except 950, 954, &
974): *47-57* 4-8
ATLANTIC (950; "If I Had Known"): *51* **15-25**
(With vocals by Billy Mitchell & Teddy Smith.)
ATLANTIC (954; "Someday You'll
Be Sorry"): *52* 10-15
(With vocal by Billy Mitchell, though not credited.)
ATLANTIC (974; "Bald Headed
Woman"): *52* 10-15
(With vocal by Billy Mitchell, though not credited.)
DECCA: *49-50* 4-6
MANOR: *46-47* 4-6
Singles: 7-Inch
ATLANTIC (950; "If I Had Known"): *51* **50-65**
(With vocals by Billy Mitchell & Teddy Smith.)
ATLANTIC (954; "Someday You'll
Be Sorry"): *52* 25-35
(With vocal by Billy Mitchell, though not credited.)

ATLANTIC (974; "Bald Headed
Woman"): *52* $25-35
(With vocal by Billy Mitchell, though not credited.)
ATLANTIC (1100 series): *57* 5-10
HERALD (Black vinyl): *53-54* 8-15
HERALD (Colored vinyl): *54* 15-25
Also see ADAMS, Faye
Also see MITCHELL, Billy

MORRIS, Joe, & His Orchestra
(Featuring Billy Mitchell)
Singles: 78rpm
ATLANTIC: *51-52* 10-15
Singles: 7-Inch
ATLANTIC: *51-52* 20-30
Also see MITCHELL, Billy

MORRIS, Joe, & His Orchestra
(Featuring Laurie Tate)
Singles: 78rpm
ATLANTIC: *51-52* 4-8
Singles: 7-Inch
ATLANTIC (965; "Rock Me
Daddy"): *52* 20-30

MORRIS, Marlowe, Quintet
Singles: 7-Inch
COLUMBIA: *62* 2-4

MORRISON, Dorothy
Singles: 7-Inch
BUDDAH: *70* 2-4
ELEKTRA: *69* 2-4
LPs: 10/12-Inch 33rpm
BUDDAH: *70* 10-12
Also see HAWKINS, Edwin, Singers

MORRISON, Junie
Singles: 7-Inch
ISLAND: *84* 1-3
Also see JUNIE

MORRISON, Van
Singles: 7-Inch
BANG: *67-68* 3-6
MERCURY: *85* 1-3
SOLID GOLD: *73* 1-3
WARNER BROS: *70-83* 1-3
LPs: 10/12-Inch 33rpm
BANG (200 series): *67-70* 15-20
BANG (400 series): *74* 10-12
LONDON: *74* 10-12
MERCURY: *85-88* 5-8
WARNER BROS: *68-83* 8-12
Also see THEM

MORRISSEY
LPs: 10/12-Inch 33rpm
SIRE: *88* 5-8

MORROW, Buddy, & His Orchestra
Singles: 78rpm
MERCURY: *54-57* $2-4
RCA VICTOR: *50-57* 2-4
Singles: 7-Inch
EPIC: *64* 2-4
MERCURY: *54-62* 2-4
RCA VICTOR: *50-59* 2-4
UNITED ARTISTS: *68* 1-3
WING: *55-56* 2-4
EPs: 7-Inch 33/45rpm
MERCURY: *54-61* 5-10
RCA VICTOR: *52-61* 5-10
LPs: 10/12-Inch 33rpm
EPIC (Except 24095 & 26095): *64-65* 5-15
EPIC (24095 & 26095; "Big Band
  Beatlemania"): *64* 10-20
(The "24" indicates monaural, the "26" stereo.)
MERCURY: *54-62* 8-15
RCA VICTOR (2000 & 2100
  series): *59-60* 10-20
RCA VICTOR (2200 & series): *60* 5-15
RCA VICTOR (3100 & 3200
  series): *52-54* 15-25
(10-Inch LPs.)
UNITED ARTISTS: *68* 5-8
WING: *56* 10-20

MORSE, Ella Mae
(Ella Mae Morse & Freddie Slack)
Singles: 78rpm
CAPITOL: *50-56* 2-5
Singles: 7-Inch
CAPITOL (1600 through 3400
  series): *50-56* 3-6
EPs: 7-Inch 33/45rpm
CAPITOL: *54-55* 5-15
LPs: 10/12-Inch 33rpm
CAPITOL (H-500 series): *54* 25-40
(10-Inch LP.)
CAPITOL (T-500 series): *54* 20-30
CAPITOL (1800 series): *62* 8-15

MORSE, Steve, Band
LPs: 10/12-Inch 33rpm
MUSICIAN/ELEKTRA: *84* 5-8
  Also see DIXIE DREGS
  Also see KANSAS

MOSBY, Johnny & Jonie
Singles: 7-Inch
CAPITOL: *67-73* 2-3
CHALLENGE: *60* 3-5
COLUMBIA: *62-66* 2-4
STARDAY: *65* 2-4
TOPPA: *61* 3-5

Picture Sleeves
CAPITOL: *70* $2-3
LPs: 10/12-Inch 33rpm
CAPITOL: *68-71* 8-12
COLUMBIA: *65* 10-15
HARMONY: *70* 6-12

MOSS, Bill
Singles: 7-Inch
BELL: *69* 2-4

MOST, Donny
Singles: 7-Inch
UNITED ARTISTS: *76-77* 2-3
VENTURE: *78* 1-3
LPs: 10/12-Inch 33rpm
UNITED ARTISTS: *76* 8-10

MOST, Mickie
Singles: 7-Inch
LAWN: *64* 5-10

MOTELS
Singles: 7-Inch
CAPITOL: *79-84* 1-3
LPs: 10/12-Inch 33rpm
CAPITOL: *79-84* 5-8
  Member: Martha Davis.

MOTHER EARTH
Singles: 7-Inch
MERCURY: *68-69* 3-5
REPRISE: *70* 2-4
UNITED ARTISTS: *68* 4-6
LPs: 10/12-Inch 33rpm
MERCURY: *68-70* 10-15
REPRISE: *71* 10-12
UNITED ARTISTS: *68* 15-20
  Member: Tracy Nelson.
  Also see NELSON, Tracy

MOTHER'S FINEST
Singles: 12-Inch 33/45rpm
EPIC: *77-79* 4-6
Singles: 7-Inch
EPIC: *76-79* 2-3
LPs: 10/12-Inch 33rpm
ATLANTIC: *81* 5-8
EPIC: *77-79* 5-8
RCA VICTOR: *72* 8-10
  Also see KENNEDY, Joyce

MOTHERLODE
Singles: 7-Inch
BUDDAH: *69* 3-5
LPs: 10/12-Inch 33rpm
BUDDAH: *69-72* 10-15

MOTHERS OF INVENTION
(Mothers)
Singles: 7-Inch
BIZARRE/REPRISE: 70 . . . .$10-15
DISCREET: 73 .6-10
VERVE: 66-68 .10-20
Promotional Singles
BIZARRE/REPRISE: 70 12-15
DISCREET: 73 .8-10
VERVE: 66-68 .15-20
EPs: 7-Inch 33/45rpm
REPRISE (332; "Uncle Meat"): 69 35-40
(Promotional issue only.)
LPs: 10/12-Inch 33rpm
BIZARRE (2024; "Uncle Meat"): 69 20-25
(Blue label. With 12-page booklet.)
BIZARRE (2024; "Uncle Meat"): 69 10-15
(Blue label. Without booklet.)
BIZARRE (2028; "Weasles Ripped
  My Flesh"): 70 .10-15
(Blue label.)
BIZARRE (2042; "The Mothers Live/
  Fillmore East"): 71 15-20
(Blue label.)
BIZARRE (2075; "Just Another
  Band From L.A."): 72 10-12
(Blue label.)
BIZARRE (2093; "Grand Wazoo"): 72 . .10-12
(Blue label.)
BIZARRE (6370; "Burnt Weeny
  Sandwich"): 69 .25-30
(Blue label. With folder of bonus photos.)
BIZARRE (6370; "Burnt Weeny
  Sandwich"): 69 .10-15
(Blue label. Without folder of photos.)
DISCREET: 73 .10-12
MGM: 70-71 25-30
REPRISE: 73-74 8-10
(Reprise reissues of the Bizarre LPs.)
VERVE (5005; "Freak Out!"): 66 35-40
VERVE (5013; "Absolutely
  Free"): 67 40-45
(With mail-order bonus Freak map/poster, which
represents about $10 of the value.)
VERVE (5045; "We're Only In It
  For The Money"): 67 30-40
VERVE (5068; "Mothermania"): 69 15-20
VERVE (5074; "XXXX Of The
  Mothers"): 69 .20-25
Note: The price range of the Mothers' Verve LPs is
applicable for copies on the blue and the black
Verve labels as well as white MGM/Verve labels.
WARNER BROS: 77 8-10
Promotional LPs
BIZARRE: 69-72 20-30
(White labels.)

VERVE: 67-69 . . . . $50-75
(White or yellow labels.)
Members: Frank Zappa; Jimmy Carl Black; Roy
Estrada; Ray Collins; Elliot Ingber.
Also see CAPTAIN BEEFHEART
Also see DUKE, George
Also see MISSING PERSONS
Also see PRESTON, Billy
Also see RUBEN & THE JETS
Also see ZAPPA, Frank

MOTIVATION
Singles: 7-Inch
DE-LITE: 83 1-3

MOTLEY CRUE
Singles: 7-Inch
ELEKTRA: 83-87 1-3
LPs: 10/12-Inch 33rpm
ELEKTRA: 83-87 5-8
LEATHUR: 83 8-10
Member: Vince Neil; Nikki Sixx; Mick Mars;
Tommy Lee.

MOTORHEAD
Singles: 7-Inch
MERCURY: 80-83 1-3
LPs: 10/12-Inch 33rpm
EMI AMERICA: 85 5-8
GWR/PROFILE: 86-87 5-8
MERCURY: 80-83 5-8
Members: Ian "Lemmy" Kilmister; Phil Campbell;
Pete Gill; Mick "Wurzel" Burston.
Also see GLITTER BAND
Also see HAWKWIND
Also see SAXON

MOTORS
Singles: 7-Inch
VIRGIN: 77-80 1-3
LPs: 10/12-Inch 33rpm
VIRGIN: 77-80 8-10
Also see TCHAIKOVSKY, Bram

MOTT
Singles: 7-Inch
COLUMBIA: 75-76 2-3
LPs: 10/12-Inch 33rpm
COLUMBIA: 75-76 5-8
Also see MOTT THE HOOPLE

MOTT THE HOOPLE
Singles: 7-Inch
ATLANTIC: 70 3-5
COLUMBIA: 72-74 2-4
LPs: 10/12-Inch 33rpm
ATLANTIC: 70-74 12-15
COLUMBIA: 72-74 8-10
Member: Ian Hunter.

Also see BRITISH LIONS
Also see HUNTER, Ian
Also see MOTT

MOTTOLA, Tony
LPs: 10/12-Inch 33rpm
COMMAND: 62-65 .... $8-15
PROJECT 3: 67-70 5-10

MOUNTAIN
Singles: 7-Inch
WINDFALL: 69-71 2-4
LPs: 10/12-Inch 33rpm
COLUMBIA: 73-74 8-10
WINDFALL: 69-72 10-15
Members: Leslie West; Corky Laing.
Also see WEST, Leslie
Also see WEST, BRUCE, & LAING

MOUTH & MacNEAL
Singles: 7-Inch
PHILIPS: 72 2-4
Picture Sleeves
PHILIPS: 72 3-5
LPs: 10/12-Inch 33rpm
PHILIPS: 72-73 10-12
Members: Will Duyn; Maggie MacNeal.

MOUZON, Alphonse
(Alphonse Mouzon Featuring Carol Dennis; Alphonze Mouzon)
Singles: 12-Inch 33/45rpm
PRIVATE I: 84 4-6
Singles: 7-Inch
BLUE NOTE: 73-74 2-3
HIGHRISE: 82 1-3
PRIVATE I: 84 1-3
LPs: 10/12-Inch 33rpm
BLUE NOTE: 73-76 5-10
HIGHRISE: 82 5-8
OPTIMISM: 88 5-8
PAUSA: 81 5-8
PRIVATE I: 84 5-8

MOUZON, Alphonse, & Larry Coryell
LPs: 10/12-Inch 33rpm
ATLANTIC: 77 5-10
Also see CORYELL, Larry
Also see ELEVENTH HOUSE
Also see MOUZON, Alphonse

MOVE
Singles: 7-Inch
A&M: 67-69 4-6
CAPITOL: 70 8-10
DERAM: 67 4-6
MGM: 71 8-10
UNITED ARTISTS: 72-73 3-5

LPs: 10/12-Inch 33rpm
A&M (3181; "Shazam"): 82 .... $5-8
A&M (3625; "Best Of
    The Move"): 74 15-20
A&M (4259; "Shazam"): 69 20-25
CAPITOL: 71 20-25
PICKWICK: 10-15
UNITED ARTISTS: 73 10-15
Members: Jeff Lynne; Roy Wood.
Also see LYNNE, Jeff
Also see WOOD, Roy

MOVING PICTURES
Singles: 7-Inch
NETWORK: 82 1-3
LPs: 10/12-Inch 33rpm
NETWORK: 82 5-8

MOYET, Alison
Singles: 12-Inch 33/45rpm
COLUMBIA: 85 4-6
Singles: 7-Inch
COLUMBIA: 85 1-3
LPs: 10/12-Inch 33rpm
COLUMBIA: 85-87 5-8
Also see YAZ

MOZART, Mickey, Quintet
Singles: 7-Inch
ROULETTE: 59-61 2-4

MR.: see MISTER

MRS. MILLER: see MILLER, Mrs.

MTUME
(James Mtume)
Singles: 12-Inch 33/45rpm
EPIC: 79-86 4-6
Singles: 7-Inch
EPIC: 78-87 1-3
LPs: 10/12-Inch 33rpm
EPIC: 78-84 5-8

MUHAMMAD, Idris
Singles: 12-Inch 33/45rpm
FANTASY: 83 4-6
Singles: 7-Inch
FANTASY: 80-83 1-3
KUDU: 77-78 2-3
PRESTIGE: 72 2-3
LPs: 10/12-Inch 33rpm
FANTASY: 83 5-8
KUDU: 76 8-10
PRESTIGE: 72 8-10

MULDAUR, Maria
Singles: 7-Inch
REPRISE: 73-76 2-3
WARNER BROS: 78-79 1-3

LPs: 10/12-Inch 33rpm

MYRRH: 82 . . . .$5-8
REPRISE: 73-76 8-10
TAKOMA: 80 5-8
WARNER BROS: 78-79 5-8

MULL, Martin
(Martin Mull Orchestra)
Singles: 7-Inch

ABC: 77 2-3
CAPRICORN: 72-77 2-4
ELEKTRA: 79 1-3
LPs: 10/12-Inch 33rpm

ABC: 77-78 8-10
CAPRICORN: 73 .8-10
ELEKTRA: 79 5-8
MCA: 5-8

MULLIGAN, Gerry
(Gerry Mulligan Quartet)
Singles: 7-Inch

PACIFIC JAZZ: 61 .2-4
PHILIPS: 64 2-4
VERVE: 60 2-4
EPs: 7-Inch 33/45rpm

CAPITOL: 53 20-40
COLUMBIA: 59 .10-15
EMARCY (36000 series): 56 10-20
FANTASY: 53 20-40
PACIFIC JAZZ: 53-57 20-45
PRESTIGE: 52-53 25-50
UNITED ARTISTS: 58 10-20
LPs: 10/12-Inch 33rpm

A&M: 72 8-12
ABC-PARAMOUNT: 58 40-60
BLUE NOTE: 81 5-8
CTI: 75 6-12
CAPITOL (400 series): 53 50-75
(10-Inch LPs.)
CAPITOL (600 series): 56 30-50
CAPITOL (2000 series): 63 15-25
CAPITOL (11000 series): 72 5-10
CHIAROSCURO: 77 5-10
COLUMBIA (1300 through
    8700 series): 59-63 20-35
COLUMBIA (34000 series): 77 5-8
CROWN: 63-64 .10-20
DRG: 80 5-8
EMARCY (1000 series): 81 5-8
EMARCY (36000 series): 56-57 25-50
FANTASY (6; "Gerry Mulligan
    Quartet"): 53 .75-100
(10-Inch LP.)
FANTASY (200 series): 56 25-50
GRP: 83 5-8

GENE NORMAN PRESENTS: 52 . . . . $50-75
(10-Inch LPs.)
GENE NORMAN PRESENTS: 57-61 . . 20-40
(12-Inch LPs.)
INNER CITY: 80 5-8
KIMBERLY: 63 .15-25
LIMELIGHT (82000 & 86000
    series): 65-66 .10-20
(The 82000 series is mono, the 86000 series stereo.)
MERCURY (20000 series): 59 20-40
ODYSSEY: 68 8-15
PACIFIC JAZZ (1 through
    10): 53-54 60-80
(10-Inch LPs.)
PACIFIC JAZZ (7 through
    50): 60-62 20-40
(12-Inch LPs.)
PACIFIC JAZZ (1200 series): 55-57 25-50
PACIFIC JAZZ (10000 &
    20000 series): 66 10-15
PAUSA: 76 5-10
PHILIPS: 63-64 .10-20
PRESTIGE (003; "Mulligan
    Plays Mulligan"): 82 5-8
PRESTIGE (100 series): 52-53 150-200
(10-Inch LPs.)
PRESTIGE (7000 series): 55 25-50
(Yellow label.)
PRESTIGE (7200 series): 63 15-25
(Yellow label.)
RCA VICTOR (2600 series): 62 20-30
SUNSET: 66 8-15
TRIP: 75-76 5-12
UNITED ARTISTS (4000 &
    5000 series): 58-61 20-50
V.S.P: 66 10-20
VERVE: 58-60 20-40
(Reads "Verve Records, Inc." at bottom of label.)
VERVE: 61-72 10-20
(Reads "MGM Records - A Division Of Metro-
Goldwyn-Mayer, Inc." at bottom of label.)
VERVE: 73-84 5-10
(Reads "Manufactured By MGM Record Corp.," or
mentions either Polydor or Polygram at bottom of
label.)
WHO'S WHO IN JAZZ: 78 5-8
WING: 67 8-15
WORLD PACIFIC: 58-59 25-50
Also see BRUBECK, Dave, & Gerry Mulligan
Also see GETZ, Stan, & Gerry Mulligan

MULLIGAN, Gerry, & Paul Desmond
(Gerry Mulligan / Paul Desmond)
LPs: 10/12-Inch 33rpm

FANTASY: 56 25-50
(Colored vinyl.)

RCA VICTOR: *62* $20-30
VERVE: *58* 20-40
(Reads "Verve Records, Inc." at bottom of label.)
VERVE: *62* 15-20
(Reads "MGM Records - A Division Of Metro-
Goldwyn-Mayer, Inc." at bottom of label.)
Also see DESMOND, Paul, & Gerry Mulligan

MULLIGAN, Gerry, & Johnny Hodges
LPs: 10/12-Inch 33rpm
VERVE: *60* 20-40
(Reads "Verve Records, Inc." at bottom of label.)
VERVE: *64* 15-20
(Reads "MGM Records - A Division Of Metro-
Goldwyn-Mayer, Inc." at bottom of label.)
Also see HODGES, Johnny

MULLIGAN, Gerry, & Thelonious Monk
LPs: 10/12-Inch 33rpm
MILESTONE: *82* 8-12
RIVERSIDE: *57-58* 20-40
Also see MONK, Thelonious

MULLIGAN, Gerry, & Oscar Peterson
LPs: 10/12-Inch 33rpm
VERVE: *57* 20-40
(Reads "Verve Records, Inc." at bottom of label.)
VERVE: *63* 10-20
(Reads "MGM Records - A Division Of Metro-
Goldwyn-Mayer, Inc." at bottom of label.)
Also see MULLIGAN, Gerry
Also see PETERSON, Oscar

MUNDY, Nick
Singles: 7-Inch
COLUMBIA: *84* 1-3

MUNGO JERRY
Singles: 7-Inch
BELL: *71-73* 2-4
FLASHBACK: *73* 1-3
JANUS: *70-71* 2-4
PYE: *72-75* 2-3
LPs: 10/12-Inch 33rpm
JANUS: *70* 10-15

MUNICH MACHINE
Singles: 7-Inch
CASABLANCA: *78* 1-3
LPs: 10/12-Inch 33rpm
CASABLANCA: *78* 5-8

MUPPETS
(Sesame Street Muppets)
Singles: 7-Inch
ATLANTIC: *79-81* 1-3
SESAME STREET: *78* 1-3
Picture Sleeves
ATLANTIC: *79-81* 1-3
SESAME STREET: *78* 1-3

LPs: 10/12-Inch 33rpm
ARISTA: *77* $5-8
ATLANTIC: *79-81* 5-8
COLUMBIA: *70-72* 5-10
SESAME STREET: *78* 5-8
WARNER BROS: *71* 5-10
Also see DENVER, John, & The Muppets
Also see ERNIE
Also see HENSON, Jim
Also see KERMIT / Fozzie Bear

MURAD, Jerry: see HARMONICATS

MURDOCK, Lydia
Singles: 12-Inch 33/45rpm
TEEN: *83* 4-6
Singles: 7-Inch
TEEN: *83* 1-3

MURDOCK, Shirley
Singles: 12-Inch 33/45rpm
ELEKTRA: *86* 4-6
Singles: 7-Inch
ELEKTRA: *86-88* 1-3
LPs: 10/12-Inch 33rpm
ELEKTRA: *87-88* 5-8
Also see ZAPP

MURE, Billy
(Billy Mure & The Wild-Cats; Billy Mure & The
Trumpeteers; Billy Mure & The 7 Karats)
Singles: 7-Inch
DANCO: *65* 2-4
EVEREST: *60* 2-4
MGM: *60-66* 2-4
PARIS: *60* 2-5
RCA VICTOR: *57-58* 3-6
RIVERSIDE: *63* 2-4
SRG: *61* 2-4
SPLASH: *58* 2-5
STRAND: *61* 2-5
EPs: 7-Inch 33/45rpm
RCA VICTOR: *58* 8-15
LPs: 10/12-Inch 33rpm
EVEREST: *60-61* 15-20
KAPP: *61* 15-20
MGM: *59-66* 15-20
RCA VICTOR: *57-58* 25-30
STRAND: *61* 15-20
SUNSET: *67* 10-12
UNITED ARTISTS: *59* 20-25
Also see TRUMPETEERS
Also see WILD-CATS

MURE, Billy & Benny
Singles: 7-Inch
MGM: *64* 2-4
Also see MURE, Billy

MURMAIDS
(Mermaids)
Singles: 7-Inch
CHATTAHOOCHEE: 63-69 .... $4-6
LIBERTY: 68 3-5
LPs: 10/12-Inch 33rpm
CHATTAHOOCHEE: 81 8-10

MURPHEY, Michael
(Michael Martin Murphey)
Singles: 7-Inch
A&M: 72 2-4
CAPITOL: 74 2-3
EMI AMERICA: 84-85 1-3
EPIC: 74-79 1-3
LIBERTY: 82-84 1-3
WARNER BROS: 86-88 1-3
Picture Sleeves
EPIC: 74 1-3
LPs: 10/12-Inch 33rpm
A&M: 72-73 8-10
EMI AMERICA: 84-85 5-8
EPIC: 74-78 8-10
LIBERTY: 82 5-8
WARNER BROS. 86 5-8
Also see LEWIS & CLARKE

MURPHY, Eddie
Singles: 12-Inch 33/45rpm
COLUMBIA: 83-85 4-6
Singles: 7-Inch
COLUMBIA: 83-86 1-3
Picture Sleeves
COLUMBIA: 83-85 1-3
LPs: 10/12-Inch 33rpm
COLUMBIA (Except picture
discs): 82-86 5-8
COLUMBIA (Picture discs): 83 8-10

MURPHY, Peter
LPs: 10/12-Inch 33rpm
BEGGAR'S BANQUET: 88 5-8

MURPHY, Walter
(Walter Murphy & The Big Apple Band)
Singles: 12-Inch 33/45rpm
PRIVATE STOCK: 77 4-6
Singles: 7-Inch
MCA: 82 1-3
PRIVATE STOCK: 76-77 2-3
LPs: 10/12-Inch 33rpm
MCA: 82 5-8
PRIVATE STOCK: 76-77 5-8

MURPHYS
Singles: 7-Inch
VENTURE: 82 1-3

MURRAY, Anne
Singles: 7-Inch
CAPITOL: 70-88 .... $1-3
Picture Sleeves
CAPITOL: 80-86 ...., 1-3
LPs: 10/12-Inch 33rpm
CAPITOL: 70-88 5-10
Also see CAMPBELL, Glen, & Anne Murray
Also see WINCHESTER, Jesse

MURRAY, Anne, & Dave Loggins
Singles: 7-Inch
CAPITOL: 85 1-3
Also see LOGGINS, Dave
Also see MURRAY, Anne

MURRAY, Mickey
Singles: 7-Inch
SSS INT'L: 67-68 3-5
LPs: 10/12-Inch 33rpm
FEDERAL: 71 8-10
SSS INT'L: 67 10-15

MURRAY, Mickey & Clarence
Singles: 7-Inch
SSS INT'L: 68 3-5
Also see MURRAY, Mickey

MUSCLE SHOALS HORNS
Singles: 7-Inch
ARIOLA AMERICA: 77 2-3
BANG: 76 2-3
MONUMENT: 83 1-3
LPs: 10/12-Inch 33rpm
ARIOLA AMERICA: 77 5-8
BANG: 76 8-10
MONUMENT: 83 5-8

MUSIC EXPLOSION
Singles: 7-Inch
ATTACK: 66 8-10
LAURIE: 67-69 3-5
LPs: 10/12-Inch 33rpm
LAURIE: 67 25-30
Member: Jamie Lyons.
Also see BLOOM, Bobby
Also see KASENETZ-KATZ SINGING OR-
CHESTRAL CIRCUS

MUSIC MACHINE
Singles: 7-Inch
BELL: 69 5-10
ORIGINAL SOUND: 66-67 5-10
WARNER BROS: 68 5-10
Picture Sleeves
ORIGINAL SOUND (82; "Hey
Joe"): 67 15-25

LPs: 10/12-Inch 33rpm
ORIGINAL SOUND: *66* $25-30
Members: Sean Bonniwell; Mark Landon; Keith
Olsen; Doug Rhodes; Ron Edgar.

MUSIC MAKERS
Singles: 7-Inch
GAMBLE: *67-68* 3-5
LPs: 10/12-Inch 33rpm
GAMBLE: *68* 12-15

MUSICAL YOUTH
Singles: 12-Inch 33/45rpm
MCA: *82-84* 4-6
Singles: 7-Inch
MCA: *82-84* 1-3
LPs: 10/12-Inch 33rpm
MCA: *82-84* 5-8

MUSIQUE
Singles: 12-Inch 33/45rpm
PRELUDE: *78* 5-8
Singles: 7-Inch
PRELUDE: *78-79* 1-3
LPs: 10/12-Inch 33rpm
PRELUDE: *78* 5-8

MUSTANGS
Singles: 7-Inch
KEETCH: *64* 4-6
PROVIDENCE: *63-64* 5-8
SURE SHOT: *64* 4-6
VEST: 4-6
LPs: 10/12-Inch 33rpm
PROVIDENCE: *64* 30-40

MYERS, Alicia
Singles: 12-Inch 33/45rpm
MCA: *81-85* 4-6
Singles: 7-Inch
MCA: *81-85* 1-3
LPs: 10/12-Inch 33rpm
MCA: *84* 5-8

MYLES, Billy
Singles: 78rpm
EMBER: *57* 4-8
Singles: 7-Inch
COLLECTABLES: 1-3
EMBER: *57* 8-10
KING: *60* 4-6

MYRICK, Gary, & The Figures
Singles: 7-Inch
EPIC: *83-84* 1-3
LPs: 10/12-Inch 33rpm
EPIC: *83-84* 5-8

MYSTIC MERLIN
Singles: 7-Inch

CAPITOL: *80-82* $1-3
LPs: 10/12-Inch 33rpm
CAPITOL: *80-82* 5-8

MYSTIC MOODS ORCHESTRA
Singles: 7-Inch
PHILIPS: *66-70* 2-3
SOUNDBIRD: *75-78* 1-3
WARNER BROS: *72-73* 1-3
LPs: 10/12-Inch 33rpm
MFSL: *78* 20-40
PHILIPS: *66-70* .4-8
SOUNDBIRD: *75-78* 3-6
WARNER BROS: *72-73* 3-6

MYSTICS
Singles: 7-Inch
AMBIENT SOUND: *82* 3-5
COLLECTABLES: 1-3
LAURIE (3028; "Don't Take
The Stars"): *59* 10-15
LAURIE (3028; "Hushabye"): *59* 10-15
LAURIE (3028-S; "Hushabye"): *59* 20-30
(Stereo.)
LAURIE (3047 through 3086): *59* 10-15
LAURIE (3104; "Sunday Kind
Of Love"): *61* .15-20
LPs: 10/12-Inch 33rpm
AMBIENT SOUND: *82* 5-8
COLLECTABLES: *87* 6-8
Also see GARRETT, Scott

MYSTICS / Passions
LPs: 10/12-Inch 33rpm
LAURIE: *79* 5-8
Also see MYSTICS
Also see PASSIONS

MYSTIQUE
Singles: 7-Inch
CURTOM: *77* 2-3
LPs: 10/12-Inch 33rpm
CURTOM: *77* 5-8
Member: Ralph Johnson.
Also see IMPRESSIONS

N

N.C.C.U.
Singles: 12-Inch 33/45rpm
UNITED ARTISTS: *77* 4-6
Singles: 7-Inch
UNITED ARTISTS: *77* 2-3
LPs: 10/12-Inch 33rpm
UNITED ARTISTS: *77* 5-8

NRBQ
(New Rhythm & Blues Quintet)
Singles: 7-Inch
BEARSVILLE: 83 .... $1-3
BUDDAH: 74 2-4
COLUMBIA: 69 3-5
KAMA SUTRA: 73 2-4
MERCURY: 78 2-3
RED ROOSTER: 77 2-3
ROUNDER: 80 1-3
Picture Sleeves
RED ROOSTER: 77 2-3
LPs: 10/12-Inch 33rpm
ANNUIT COEPTIS: 76 10-15
BEARSVILLE: 83 5-8
KAMA SUTRA: 72-73 10-12
MERCURY: 78 8-10
COLUMBIA: 69 10-15
RED ROOSTER: 77 8-10
ROUNDER: 79-80 5-8
Members: Terry Adams; Don Adams; G. T. Stanley; Steve Ferguson; Al Anderson.
Also see ANDERSON, Al
Also see PERKINS, Carl, & NRBQ

NV
Singles: 12-Inch 33/45rpm
SIRE: 83-84 4-6
Singles: 7-Inch
SIRE: 83-84 1-3

N.W.A. AND THE POSSE
LPs: 10/12-Inch 33rpm
RUTHLESS: 88 5-8

NABORS, Jim
Singles: 7-Inch
COLUMBIA: 65-74 2-4
RANWOOD: 77 1-3
LPs: 10/12-Inch 33rpm
COLUMBIA: 65-75 5-15
HARMONY: 71 5-10
RANWOOD: 76-82 4-8

NAIROBI & THE AWESOME FOURSOME
Singles: 7-Inch
STREETWISE: 82 1-3

NAJEE
Singles: 7-Inch
EMI-MANHATTAN: 88 1-3
LPs: 10/12-Inch 33rpm
EMI-MANHATTAN: 88 5-8

NAKED EYES
Singles: 12-Inch 33/45rpm
EMI AMERICA: 83-84 4-6

Singles: 7-Inch
EMI AMERICA: 83-84 .... $1-3
LPs: 10/12-Inch 33rpm
EMI AMERICA: 83 5-8
Members: Pete Byrne; Rob Fisher.

NAPOLEON XIV
(Jerry Samuels)
Singles: 7-Inch
ERIC: 76 1-3
WARNER BROS (5800 series): 66 5-8
WARNER BROS (7700 series): 73 4-6
LPs: 10/12-Inch 33rpm
WARNER BROS (1661; "They're Coming
To Take Me Away"): 66 50-60
(With a "W" prefix. Monaural.)
WARNER BROS (1661; "They're Coming
To Take Me Away"): 66 75-100
(With a "WS" prefix. Stereo.)
WARNER BROS (1661; "They're Coming
To Take Me Away"): 66 75-100
(White label. Promotional issue only.)

NASH, Graham
Singles: 7-Inch
ATLANTIC (2000 series): 71-73 2-4
ATLANTIC (89000 series): 86 1-3
CAPITOL: 79-80 1-3
LPs: 10/12-Inch 33rpm
ATLANTIC (7000 series): 71-73 8-10
ATLANTIC (81000 series): 86 5-8
CAPITOL: 80 8-10
Also see CROSBY, David, & Graham Nash
Also see CROSBY, STILLS & NASH
Also see HOLLIES
Also see YOUNG, Neil, & Graham Nash

NASH, Johnny
Singles: 12-Inch 33/45rpm
EPIC: 79 4-6
Singles: 7-Inch
ABC-PARAMOUNT: 57-61 4-6
ARGO: 64-65 3-5
ATLANTIC: 66 3-5
BABYLON: 69 2-4
EPIC: 72-80 1-3
GROOVE: 63-64 3-5
JAD: 68-70 2-4
JANUS: 70 2-4
JODA: 65-66 3-5
MGM: 66-67 3-5
WARNER BROS: 62-63 3-5
Picture Sleeves
ABC-PARAMOUNT: 59-60 4-8
GROOVE: 63-64 4-6
EPs: 7-Inch 33/45rpm
ABC-PARAMOUNT: 58-61 10-15

LPs: 10/12-Inch 33rpm
ABC-PARAMOUNT: *58-61* $15-25
ARGO: *64* 12-20
CADET: *73* 10-12
EPIC: *72-74* 10-12
JAD: *68-69* 12-15
  Also see ANKA, Paul, George Hamilton IV,
  & Johnny Nash

NASH, Johnny, & Kim Weston
Singles: 7-Inch
BABYLON: *69* 2-4
  Also see NASH, Johnny
  Also see WESTON, Kim

NASHVILLE BRASS: see DAVIS, Danny

NASHVILLE TEENS
Singles: 7-Inch
LONDON: *64-65* 4-8
MGM: *65-67* 5-10
UNITED ARTISTS: *72* 3-5
LPs: 10/12-Inch 33rpm
LONDON: *64* 20-25

NATASHA
Singles: 12-Inch 33/45rpm
EMERGENCY: *83* 4-6

NATIONAL LAMPOON
Singles: 7-Inch
BLUE THUMB: *72-73* 3-5
EPIC (193; "Have A Kung-Fu
  Christmas"): *75* 2-4
  (Promotional issue only.)
LABEL 21: *78-80* 2-3
Picture Sleeves
EPIC (193; "Have A Kung-Fu
  Christmas"): *75* 4-6
  (Promotional issue only.)
LABEL 21: *78-80* 2-4
EPs: 7-Inch 33/45rpm
EPIC (1095; "A History Of
  The Beatles"): *75* 10-15
  (Promotional issue only.)
LPs: 10/12-Inch 33rpm
BANANA: *72* 10-15
BLUE THUMB: *72-74* 10-15
EPIC: *75-76* 8-12
IMPORT: *77* 8-10
LABEL 21 (Except picture discs): *78-80* ... 5-8
LABEL 21 (Picture discs): *80* 12-15
NATIONAL LAMPOON: *74* 15-20
PASSPORT: *82* 5-8
VISA: *78* 5-8

Members: John Belushi; Chevy Chase; Melissa
Manchester; Tony Hendra; Jim Payne; John
Lopresti.
  Also see BELUSHI, John
  Also see MANCHESTER, Melissa

NATIVE
Singles: 7-Inch
RCA VICTOR: *80* $1-3
LPs: 10/12-Inch 33rpm
RCA VICTOR: *80* 5-8

NATURAL FOUR
Singles: 7-Inch
ABC: *69* 2-4
CURTOM: *74-76* 2-3
LPs: 10/12-Inch 33rpm
CURTOM: *74-75* 8-10

NATURALS
Singles: 7-Inch
CALLA: *71* 2-4
MOTOWN: *72* 2-3

NATURE ZONE
Singles: 7-Inch
LONDON: *76* 2-3

NATURE'S DIVINE
Singles: 7-Inch
INFINITY: *79* 1-3
LPs: 10/12-Inch 33rpm
INFINITY: *79* 5-8

NATURE'S GIFT
Singles: 7-Inch
ABC: *74* 2-4

NAUGHTON, David
Singles: 7-Inch
RSO: *78-79* 1-3

NAYLOR, Jerry
Singles: 7-Inch
COLUMBIA: *68-71* 2-4
HITSVILLE: *76* 2-3
JEREMIAH: *79* 1-3
MC: *78* 1-3
MGM: *71-72* 2-3
MELODYLAND: *74-75* 2-3
OAK: *80* 1-3
PACIFIC CHALLENGER: *82* 1-3
SKLYA: *61-62* 5-8
SMASH: *65* 3-5
TOWER: *65-68* 2-4
WARNER BROS: *79* 1-3
WEST: *86* 1-3
  Also see ALLAN, Davie
  Also see CRICKETS

NAYOBE
Singles: 12-Inch 33/45rpm
FEVER: 85-86 . . . .$4-6
Singles: 7-Inch
FEVER: 85-86 1-3

NAZARETH
Singles: 7-Inch
A&M: 73-80 1-3
MCA: 83-84 1-3
WARNER BROS: 71 2-4
Picture Sleeves
A&M: 75-80 1-3
LPs: 10/12-Inch 33rpm
A&M: 73-82 5-8
MCA: 83-84 5-8
WARNER BROS: 72 10-12
Members: Dan McCafferty; Pete Agnew; Darrell
Sweet; Manny Charlton.

NAZTY
Singles: 7-Inch
MANKIND: 76 2-3
LPs: 10/12-Inch 33rpm
MANKIND: 76 5-10

NAZZ
Singles: 7-Inch
VERY RECORD (001; "Lay Down &
Die, Goodbye"): 67 225-300
Members: Vince "Alice Cooper" Furnier;
M. Bruce; G. Buxton; D. Dunaway; T. Speer.
Also see COOPER, Alice

NAZZ
Singles: 7-Inch
SGC: 68-69 4-6
Picture Sleeves
SGC: 68 6-12
LPs: 10/12-Inch 33rpm
SGC (5001; "Nazz"): 68 40-50
SGC (5002; "Nazz-Nazz"): 69 40-50
(Black vinyl.)
SGC (5002; "Nazz-Nazz"): 69 75-100
(Colored vinyl. Pink & orange label. SGC logo is
blue. Matrix number is 671531.)
SGC (5002; "Nazz-Nazz"): 69 75-125
(Colored vinyl. Mail-order edition. Red & orange
label. SGC logo is purple. Matrix number is
671531-MO.)
SGC (5004; "Nazz III"): 71 40-50
Member: Todd Rundgren.
Also see RUNDGREN, Todd

N'COLE
Singles: 7-Inch
MILLENNIUM: 78 .2-3

NDUGU & THE CHOCOLATE
JAM COMPANY
Singles: 7-Inch
EPIC: 80 . . . .$1-3

NECROPOLIS
LPs: 10/12-Inch 33rpm
BOMP: 88 5-8

NEELY, Sam
Singles: 7-Inch
A&M: 74-75 2-3
CAPITOL: 72-73 2-4
ELEKTRA: 77 2-3
MCA: 83 1-3
LPs: 10/12-Inch 33rpm
A&M: 74 8-10
CAPITOL: 72-73 .8-10

NEIGHBORHOOD
Singles: 7-Inch
BIG TREE: 70 3-5
BULLET: 69 5-10
LPs: 10/12-Inch 33rpm
BIG TREE: 70 10-12

NEIL & JACK
Singles: 7-Inch
DUEL (508; "You Are My
Love At Last"): 62 50-75
DUEL (517; "I'm Afraid"): 62 50-75
Members: Neil Diamond; Jack Parker.
Also see DIAMOND, Neil

NEIL & THE SHOCKING PINKS:
see YOUNG, Neil

NEKTAR
Singles: 7-Inch
PASSPORT: 74-75 .2-4
LPs: 10/12-Inch 33rpm
PASSPORT: 74-76 .8-10
POLYDOR: 77 8-10
VISA: 78 8-10

NELSON, Jimmy
Singles: 78rpm
CHESS: 53 8-15
Singles: 7-Inch
ALL BOY: 62 4-6
CHESS (1500 series): 53 15-25
CHESS (1800 series): 63 4-6
RPM: 53 15-25
Also see TURNER, Joe / Jimmy Nelson

NELSON, Karen, & Billy T.
Singles: 7-Inch
AMHERST: 77 8-10

NELSON, Phyllis
Singles: 12-Inch 33/45rpm
CARRERE: 85-86 . . . . $4-6
Singles: 7-Inch
CARRERE: 85-86 1-3
LPs: 10/12-Inch 33rpm
CARRERE: 86 5-8

NELSON, Rick
(Rick Nelson & The Stone Canyon Band; Ricky Nelson)
Singles: 12-Inch 33/45rpm
CAPITOL: 82 5-8
Singles: 78rpm
IMPERIAL: 57-58 10-20
VERVE: 57 10-20
Singles: 7-Inch
DECCA: 63-72 3-6
CAPITOL: 82 1-3
EPIC: 77-86 2-5
IMPERIAL (5400 series): 57 15-20
(Maroon labels.)
IMPERIAL (5463 through 5614): 57-59 . . 8-12
(Black labels. Black vinyl.)
IMPERIAL (5545; "Lonesome
Town"): 100-150
(Colored vinyl.)
IMPERIAL (5663 through 5985): 60-63 . . . 4-8
IMPERIAL (66000 series): 63-64 4-8
LIBERTY: 1-3
MCA: 73-75 2-5
VERVE (10047; "A Teenager's
Romance"): 57 10-15
VERVE (10070; "You're My One
& Only Love"): 57 10-15
(One side of this single is by Barney Kessell.)
Picture Sleeves
DECCA: 63-70 8-15
EPIC: 86 2-4

IMPERIAL (5463 through 5614): 57-59 . $10-20
IMPERIAL (5663 through 5935): 60-63 . . .8-12
MCA: 86 2-4
EPs: 7-Inch 33/45rpm
DECCA: 63-65 .15-25
IMPERIAL: 57-60 25-35
VERVE (5048; "Ricky"): 57 50-80
(Contains one track by Barney Kessell.)
LPs: 10/12-Inch 33rpm
CAPITOL: 81 5-8
DECCA (4419 through 4944): 63-67 20-25
(Decca numbers in this series preceeded by a "DL"
are mono. Stereo issues are indicated by a "DL7"
prefix.)
DECCA (75014 through 75391): 68-72 . .15-20
EPIC: 77-86 8-12
EPIC/NU-DISK: 81 10-15
IMPERIAL (9048 through 9082): 57-59 . .40-80
IMPERIAL (9122 through 9251): 60-63 . .25-30
(Imperial 9000 series issues were monaural LPs.)
IMPERIAL (12030; "Songs By
Ricky"): 59 30-35
IMPERIAL (12059; "More Songs
By Ricky"): 60 30-35
(Black vinyl.)
IMPERIAL (12059; "More Songs
By Ricky"): 60 200-400
(Colored vinyl. Thus far, colored vinyl copies of
this LP have always been stereo.)
IMPERIAL (12082 through
12244): 62-63 .25-30
(Imperial 12000 series issues were either stereo or
reprocessed stereo LPs.)
LIBERTY: 81-83 5-8
MCA (Except 1517): 73-74 10-12
MCA (1517; "The Decca Years"): 82 5-8
MCA/SILVER EAGLE: 86 5-10
MGM (4256; "Teen Time"): 65 10-20
(Reissue of Verve 2083, but with different Rivers
and Sparks tracks.)
RHINO: 85 5-8
SESSIONS (1003; "Ricky Nelson
Story"): 79 15-20
(3-LP mail-order offer.)
SUNSET: 66-68 12-15
UNITED ARTISTS (330; "Very Best
Of Rick Nelson"): 75 10-12
UNITED ARTISTS (1004; "Ricky"): 80 . .8-10
UNITED ARTISTS (9960;
"Legendary Masters"): 71 12-15
VERVE (2083; "Teen Time"): 57 100-200
(Also contains tracks by Randy Sparks, Jeff Allen,
Rock Murphy, Gary Williams, & Barney Kessell.)
Members: James Burton; Joe Osborn; Randy Meisner; Al Kemp; Steve Duncan.
Also see MEISNER, Randy

Also see MOON, Keith
Also see RIVERS, Johnny / Ricky Nelson /
Randy Sparks

NELSON, Rick, & Jack Lemmon
Singles: 7-Inch
THEATRE PROMOTION RECORD (760; "Do
You Know What It Means To Miss
New Orleans"): *60* $50-100
(Promotional issue, for theater play only.)

**NELSON, Rick / Joannie Sommers /
Dona Jean Young**
LPs: 10/12-Inch 33rpm
DECCA (4836; "On The Flip
Side"): *66* 20-25
Also see NELSON, Rick
Also see SOMMERS, Joannie

NELSON, Sandy
Singles: 7-Inch
COLLECTABLES: 1-3
ERA: *72* 1-3
IMPERIAL: *61-69* 4-6
LIBERTY: 1-3
ORIGINAL SOUND: *59* 5-8
UNITED ARTISTS: *74* 1-3
EPs: 7-Inch 33/45rpm
IMPERIAL: *65* 8-15
(Stereo jukebox "Little LPs.")
LPs: 10/12-Inch 33rpm
IMPERIAL (Except 9105/12044): *61-69* .10-20
IMPERIAL (9105 & 12044;
"Teen Beat"): *60* 20-25
(Imperial's 9000 series was for mono & 12000
series for stereo LPs.)
LIBERTY: *82-83* 5-8
SKYCLAD: *89* 5-8
SUNSET: *66-70* 12-15
UNITED ARTISTS: *75* 8-10
Also see TEDDY BEARS

NELSON, Tracy
Singles: 7-Inch
ATLANTIC: *75* 2-4
CAPITOL: *77* 2-3
MCA: *75* 2-4
LPs: 10/12-Inch 33rpm
ADELPHI: *83* 5-8
ATLANTIC: *74* 8-10
COLUMBIA: *73* 10-12
FLYING FISH: *78-80* 5-8
MCA: *75* 8-10
PRESTIGE (7303; "Deep Are
The Roots"): *65* 15-20
PRESTIGE (7726; "Deep Are
The Roots"): *69* 5-8

REPRISE: *72* $10-12
Also see MOTHER EARTH
Also see NELSON, Willie & Tracy

NELSON, Tyka
Singles: 7-Inch
COOLTEMPO: *88* 1-3

NELSON, Willie
Singles: 7-Inch
AMERICAN GOLD: *76* 2-3
ATLANTIC: *73-75* 1-3
BETTY: *64* 6-10
BELLAIRE (100 series): *63* 15-25
(Black vinyl.)
BELLAIRE (100 series): *63* 20-40
(Colored vinyl.)
BELLAIRE (5000 series): *76* 2-3
CAPITOL: *78* 1-3
COLUMBIA: *75-88* 1-3
D: *59-60* 8-15
LIBERTY (55000 series): *61-64* 4-6
LIBERTY (56000 series): *69* 2-4
LONE STAR: *78* 2-3
MONUMENT (800 series): *64* 3-5
RCA VICTOR (0100 through
0800 series): *69-72* 2-4
RCA VICTOR (8500 through
9900 series): *65-71* 3-5
RCA VICTOR (10000 through
12000 series): *75-81* 1-3
SONGBIRD: *80* 1-3
UNITED ARTISTS (600 series): *63* 4-6
UNITED ARTISTS (700 through
1200 series): *76-78* 1-3
Picture Sleeves
RCA VICTOR (12000 series): *81* 1-3
LPs: 10/12-Inch 33rpm
ACCORD: *83* 5-8
ALLEGIANCE: *83* 5-8
ATLANTIC: *73-74* 8-12
AURA: *83* 5-8
CAMDEN: *70-74* 8-12
CASINO: *84* 6-10
COLUMBIA (Except 38250): *75-88* 5-15
COLUMBIA (38250; "Willie
Nelson"): *83* 90-100
(10-LP set.)
DELTA: *82* 5-8
EXACT: *83* 5-8
H.S.R.D: *84* 8-10
HEARTLAND: *87* 10-15
HOT SCHATZ: *84* 5-8
LIBERTY (3200 series): *62* 25-35
LIBERTY (7200 series): *62* 30-40
LIBERTY (10000 series): 4-8

LONE STAR: 78 . . . . $8-12
MCA: 80 4-8
PICKWICK: 8-10
PLANTATION: 82 5-8
POTOMAC: 82 8-15
PREMORE: 5-10
RCA VICTOR (1100 through
    3200 series): 75-79 5-10
RCA VICTOR (3400 through
    4700 series): 65-72 10-20
    (With an "LPM" or "LSP" prefix.)
RCA VICTOR (3600 through
    4800 series): 80-83 4-8
    (With an "AYL1" prefix.)
RCA VICTOR/CANDELITE: 80 8-10
SHOTGUN: 77 12-18
SONGBIRD: 80 4-8
SUNSET: 66 10-18
TAKOMA: 83 5-8
TIME-LIFE (16000 series): 83 12-18
    (3-LP set.)
UNITED ARTISTS: 73-78 6-12
    Also see CHARLES, Ray, & Willie Nelson
    Also see COCHRAN, Hank, & Willie Nelson
    Also see COE, David Allan, & Willie Nelson
    Also see DARRELL, Johnny / George Jones /
    Willie Nelson
    Also see DAVIS, Danny, & The Nashville
    Brass, & Willie Nelson
    Also see HAGGARD, Merle, & Willie Nelson
    Also see IGLESIAS, Julio, & Willie Nelson
    Also see JENNINGS, Waylon, & Willie Nel-
    son
    Also see LEE, Brenda, & Willie Nelson
    Also see MEYERS, Augie
    Also see PRICE, Ray, & Willie Nelson

NELSON, Willie, & Johnny Lee
LPs: 10/12-Inch 33rpm
QUICKSILVER: 84 5-8
    Also see LEE, Johnny

NELSON, Willie / Johnny Lee /
Mickey Gilley
LPs: 10/12-Inch 33rpm
PLANTATION: 82 5-8
    Also see GILLEY, Mickey
    Also see LEE, Johnny

NELSON, Willie / Jerry Lee Lewis /
Carl Perkins / David Allan Coe
LPs: 10/12-Inch 33rpm
PLANTATION: 75 5-8
    Also see COE, David Allan
    Also see LEWIS, Jerry Lee
    Also see PERKINS, Carl

NELSON, Willie, & Roger Miller
LPs: 10/12-Inch 33rpm
COLUMBIA: 82 . . . . $5-8
    Also see MILLER, Roger

NELSON, Willie & Tracy
Singles: 7-Inch
ATLANTIC: 74 2-4
    Also see NELSON, Tracy

NELSON, Willie, & Dolly Parton
Singles: 7-Inch
MONUMENT: 82 1-3
    Also see PARTON, Dolly

NELSON, Willie, & Webb Pierce
Singles: 7-Inch
COLUMBIA: 82 1-3
LPs: 10/12-Inch 33rpm
COLUMBIA: 82 5-8
    Also see PIERCE, Webb

NELSON, Willie, & Leon Russell
Singles: 7-Inch
COLUMBIA: 79 1-3
LPs: 10/12-Inch 33rpm
COLUMBIA: 79 5-8
    Also see RUSSELL, Leon

NELSON, Willie / Faron Young
LPs: 10/12-Inch 33rpm
ROMULUS: 5-8
    Also see NELSON, Willie
    Also see YOUNG, Faron

NENA
Singles: 12-Inch 33/45rpm
EPIC: 83-84 4-6
Singles: 7-Inch
EPIC: 83-84 1-3
LPs: 10/12-Inch 33rpm
EPIC: 84 5-8

NEON PHILHARMONIC
Singles: 7-Inch
MCA: 76 2-3
TRX: 72 2-4
WARNER BROS: 69-71 3-5
LPs: 10/12-Inch 33rpm
WARNER BROS: 69 10-15

NERO, Peter
Singles: 7-Inch
ARIOLA AMERICA: 76 1-3
ARISTA: 75 1-3
COLUMBIA: 69-73 1-3
RCA VICTOR: 61-68 2-4
Picture Sleeves
RCA VICTOR: 62-63 2-5

LPs: 10/12-Inch 33rpm

ARISTA: 75 .... $4-8
CAMDEN: 67-73 5-10
COLUMBIA: 69-75 5-10
CONCORD JAZZ: 78 5-8
HARMONY: 71 4-8
PREMIER: 63 10-15
RCA VICTOR: 61-76 5-15

NERVOUS NORVUS
(Jimmy Drake; Nervous Norvus With Red
Blanchard)

Singles: 78rpm

DOT: 56-57 5-10

Singles: 7-Inch

BIG BEN: 10-12
DOT (15000 series): 56 10-12
(Maroon label.)
DOT (15000 series): 57 5-8
(Black label.)
DOT (16000 series): 65 2-4
EMBEE: 59 10-12

NESMITH, Michael
(Michael Nesmith & The First National Band;
Michael Nesmith & The Second National Band)

Singles: 7-Inch

EDAN (1001; "Just A Little
Love"): 65 10-15
ISLAND: 77 2-3
OMNIBUS: 63 10-15
PACIFIC ARTS: 75-79 5-8
RCA VICTOR: 70-75 5-15

LPs: 10/12-Inch 33rpm

PACIFIC ARTS (Except boxed 101,
"The Prison"): 77-79 5-15
PACIFIC ARTS (101; "The Prison,"
boxed edition): 78 10-15
(This LP was also issued in standard LP format.
Both issues were packaged with a special booklet.)
RCA VICTOR: 70-75 15-30

Promotional LPs

PACIFIC ARTS ("Conversation With
Music-Radio Special"): 78 12-15
Also see BLESSING, Michael
Also see MONKEES
Also see WICHITA TRAIN WHISTLE

NETTO, Loz

Singles: 7-Inch

21: 83 1-3

LPs: 10/12-Inch 33rpm

21: 82 5-8
Also see SNIFF 'N THE TEARS

NEVIL, Robbie

Singles: 12-Inch 33/45rpm

EMI-MANHATTAN: 86 4-6

Singles: 7-Inch

EMI-MANHATTAN: 86-88 .... $1-3

LPs: 10/12-Inch 33rpm

EMI-MANHATTAN: 86-88 5-8

NEVILLE, Aaron
(Arron Neville)

Singles: 7-Inch

AIRECORDS: 63 3-5
BELL: 68-69 2-4
HEAD: 2-4
MERCURY: 72-73 2-4
MINIT: 60-63 4-6
PAR-LO: 66-67 3-5
POLYDOR: 77 2-3
SAFARI: 67 3-5

LPs: 10/12-Inch 33rpm

COLLECTABLES: 88 6-8
MINIT: 67 15-20
PAR-LO: 67 15-20
Also see NEVILLE BROTHERS

NEVILLE, Aaron / Toussaint McCall

Singles: 7-Inch

TRIP: 1-3
Also see MC CALL, Toussaint
Also see NEVILLE, Aaron

NEVILLE, Ivan

Singles: 7-Inch

POLYDOR: 88 1-3

LPs: 10/12-Inch 33rpm

POLYDOR: 88 5-8

NEVILLE BROTHERS

Singles: 7-Inch

A&M: 81 1-3

LPs: 10/12-Inch 33rpm

A&M: 81 5-8
BLACK TOP: 86 5-8
CAPITOL: 78 15-30
EMI AMERICA: 87 5-8
RHINO: 87 5-8
SPINDLE TOP: 87 5-8
Members: Aaron Neville; Art Neville; Charles
Neville; Cyril Neville.
Also see METERS
Also see NEVILLE, Aaron

NEW BIRTH

Singles: 7-Inch

ARIOLA AMERICA: 79 2-3
BUDDAH: 75 2-4
RCA VICTOR: 71-75 2-4
WARNER BROS: 76-78 2-3

LPs: 10/12-Inch 33rpm

ARIOLA AMERICA: 79 5-8
BUDDAH: 75 8-10

COLLECTABLES: *88* $6-8
RCA VICTOR (Except LSP series): *73-82* **8-10**
RCA VICTOR (LSP series): *70-72* **10-12**
WARNER BROS: *77* **8-10**
Member: Harvey Fuqua.
Also see HARVEY

NEW CACTUS BAND
Singles: 7-Inch
ATCO: *73* **2-4**
LPs: 10/12-Inch 33rpm
ATCO: *73* **8-10**
Also see CACTUS

NEW CENSATION
Singles: 7-Inch
PRIDE: *74-75* **2-3**
LPs: 10/12-Inch 33rpm
PRIDE: *74* **8-10**

NEW CHOICE
Singles: 7-Inch
WARNER BROS: *88* **1-3**

NEW CHRISTY MINSTRELS
Singles: 7-Inch
COLUMBIA (42000 series): *62-63* **3-5**
COLUMBIA (43000 & 44000
series): *64-69* **2-4**
GREGAR: *70-72* **2-3**
WARNER BROS: *79* **1-3**
Promotional Singles
COLUMBIA (Colored vinyl): *63-65* **4-6**
LPs: 10/12-Inch 33rpm
COLUMBIA (1800 through 2500
series): *62-66* **10-20**
(Monaural.)
COLUMBIA (8600 through 9300
series): *62-66* **10-20**
(Stereo.)
COLUMBIA (9600 & 9700 series): *68* ... **8-15**
GREGAR: *70* **8-10**
HARMONY: *68-72* **8-10**
Members: Randy Sparks; Barry McGuire; Kenny
Rogers; Mike Settle; Thelma Lou Camacho; Terry
Williams; Mickey Jones.
Also see FIRST EDITION
Also see MC GUIRE, Barry

NEW COLONY SIX
Singles: 7-Inch
CENTAUR: *66* **4-6**
MCA: *74* **1-3**
MERCURY: *67-70* **3-5**
SENTAR: *66-67* **4-6**
SUNLIGHT: *71-72* **2-4**
TWILIGHT: *73* **2-4**

Picture Sleeves
MERCURY: *67-68* $4-8
LPs: 10/12-Inch 33rpm
MERCURY: *68-69* **20-25**
SENTAR (101;
"Breakthrough"): *66* **100-200**
SENTAR (3001;
"Colonization"): *67* **35-50**
Members: Ronnie Rice; Ray Graffia; Craig Kemp;
Jerry Kollenberg; Pat McBride.

NEW EDITION
Singles: 12-Inch 33/45rpm
MCA: *84-86* **4-6**
STREETWISE: *83* **4-6**
Singles: 7-Inch
MCA (Black vinyl): *84-88* **1-3**
MCA (Colored vinyl): *85* **3-5**
STREETWISE: *83* **5-8**
Picture Sleeves
MCA: *84-88* **2-5**
LPs: 10/12-Inch 33rpm
MCA: *84-88* **5-8**
STREETWISE: *83* **5-8**
Member: Johnny Gill.
Also see GILL, Johnny
Also see KING DREAM CHORUS &
HOLIDAY CREW

NEW ENGLAND
Singles: 7-Inch
ELEKTRA: *80-81* **1-3**
INFINITY: *79* **2-3**
LPs: 10/12-Inch 33rpm
ELEKTRA: *80-81* **5-8**
INFINITY: *79* **8-10**

NEW ENGLAND CONSERVATORY
RAGTIME ENSEMBLE
Singles: 7-Inch
ANGEL: *80* **1-3**
LPs: 10/12-Inch 33rpm
ANGEL: *73* **5-8**
GOLDEN CREST: *75* **4-8**

NEW ESTABLISHMENT
Singles: 7-Inch
COLGEMS: *69* **3-5**
MERCURY: *67* **3-5**

NEW GUYS ON THE BLOCK
Singles: 7-Inch
SUGAR HILL: *83* **1-3**

NEW HOLLYWOOD ARGYLES
Singles: 7-Inch
KAMMY: *66* **3-5**
Also see HOLLYWOOD ARGYLES

NEW HOPE
Singles: 7-Inch
JAMIE: *69-70* $3-5
LPs: 10/12-Inch 33rpm
JAMIE: *70* 20-25
LIGHT: *72* 8-10

NEW HORIZONS
Singles: 7-Inch
COLUMBIA: *83* 1-3
LPs: 10/12-Inch 33rpm
COLUMBIA: *83* 5-8

NEW JERSEY MASS CHOIR
Singles: 12-Inch 33/45rpm
SAVOY: *85* 4-6
Also see FOREIGNER

NEW KIDS ON THE BLOCK
Singles: 12-Inch 33/45rpm
COLUMBIA: *86* 4-6
Singles: 7-Inch
COLUMBIA: *86-88* 1-3
LPs: 10/12-Inch 33rpm
COLUMBIA: *88* 5-8

NEW KINGSTON TRIO
Singles: 7-Inch
CAPITOL: *71* 2-4
Also see KINGSTON TRIO

NEW MARKETTS
Singles: 7-Inch
FARR: *76* 2-4
SEMINOLE: *76* 2-4
LPs: 10/12-Inch 33rpm
CALLIOPE: *77* 8-12
Also see MARKETTS

NEW ORDER
Singles: 12-Inch 33/45rpm
FACTUS: *83* 4-6
QWEST: *85* 4-6
STREETWISE: *83* 4-6
Singles: 7-Inch
QWEST: *85-88* 1-3
STREETWISE: *83* 1-3
LPs: 10/12-Inch 33rpm
QWEST: *86* 5-8
QWEST (25621;
"Substance"): *87* 10-12

NEW RIDERS OF THE PURPLE SAGE
Singles: 7-Inch
COLUMBIA: *71-74* 2-5
MCA: *76-77* 2-3
LPs: 10/12-Inch 33rpm
A&M: *81* 5-8

BUDDAH: *75* $8-10
COLUMBIA: *71-75* 10-15
MCA: *77* 8-10
RELIX: *86-87* 5-8
Members: Skip Battin; David Turbert. Assorted
Grateful Dead members guested on Columbia and
Relix issues.
Also see GRATEFUL DEAD
Also see KINGFISH

NEW ROTARY CONNECTION
LPs: 10/12-Inch 33rpm
CHESS: *71* 8-10
Also see ROTARY CONNECTION

NEW SEEKERS
Singles: 7-Inch
ELEKTRA: *70-72* 2-4
MGM/VERVE: *73* 2-3
Picture Sleeves
MGM/VERVE: *73* 2-3
EPs: 7-Inch 33/45rpm
COCA-COLA: *69* 3-6
(Promotional issue only.)
LPs: 10/12-Inch 33rpm
ELEKTRA: *71-72* 10-12
MGM/VERVE: *73* 8-10
Member: Keith Potger.
Also see SEEKERS

NEW VAUDEVILLE BAND
Singles: 7-Inch
FONTANA: *66-68* 2-4
LPs: 10/12-Inch 33rpm
FONTANA: *67* 10-15

NEW VENTURES:
see VENTURES

NEW YORK CITI PEECH BOYS
Singles: 12-Inch 33/45rpm
GARAGE: *83-84* 4-6
ISLAND: *83-84* 4-6
Singles: 7-Inch
ISLAND: *83-84* 1-3
LPs: 10/12-Inch 33rpm
ISLAND: *84* 5-8

NEW YORK CITY
Singles: 7-Inch
CHELSEA: *73-75* 2-4
LPs: 10/12-Inch 33rpm
CHELSEA: *73-77* 10-12
Also see CADILLACS
Also see FIVE SATINS

NEW YORK COMMUNITY CHOIR
Singles: 7-Inch
RCA VICTOR: *77* 2-3

Mickey Newbury

NEW YORK DOLLS
Singles: 7-Inch
MERCURY: *73-76* $3-5
Picture Sleeves
MERCURY: *73* 4-8
LPs: 10/12-Inch 33rpm
MERCURY (675; "New York Dolls"): *73* **15-20**
MERCURY (1001; "Too Much
Too Soon"): *74* **10-15**
REACH OUT INT'L: *81* 5-8
Also see JOHANSEN, David
Also see SYLVAIN SYLVAIN
Also see W.A.S.P.

NEW YORKERS
Singles: 7-Inch
WALL: *61* **10-15**
Members: Fred Parris; Richard Freeman; Wesley
Forbes; Louis Peebles; Silvester Hopkins.
Also see FIVE SATINS

NEW YOUNG HEARTS
Singles: 7-Inch
ZEA: *70* 2-4

NEWBEATS
Singles: 7-Inch
ABC: *74* 1-3
HICKORY: *64-72* 3-5
PLAYBOY: *74* 2-3
LPs: 10/12-Inch 33rpm
HICKORY (Except 128): *64-65* **15-20**
HICKORY (128; "Run Baby Run"): *65* .. **20-25**
Members: Larry Henley; Dean Mathis; Mark
Mathis.
Also see DEAN & MARC

NEWBERRY, Booker, III
Singles: 12-Inch 33/45rpm
BOARDWALK: *83* $4-6
Singles: 7-Inch
BOARDWALK: *83* 1-3
OMNI: *86* 1-3

NEWBURY, Mickey
Singles: 7-Inch
AIRBORNE: *88* 1-3
ELEKTRA: *71-73* 2-3
HICKORY: *65-68* 2-4
MERCURY: *69-70* 2-4
RCA VICTOR: *68-70* 2-4
Picture Sleeves
RCA VICTOR: *68* 2-5
LPs: 10/12-Inch 33rpm
ABC/HICKORY: *77-79* 8-10
MCA: 5-8
ELEKTRA: *71-73* 8-10
MERCURY: *69* 10-12
RCA VICTOR: *68-72* 10-12

NEWCLEUS
Singles: 12-Inch 33/45rpm
SUNNYVIEW: *83-86* 4-6
Singles: 7-Inch
SUNNYVIEW: *83-86* 1-3
LPs: 10/12-Inch 33rpm
SUNNYVIEW: *85-86* 5-8

NEWCOMERS
Singles: 7-Inch
GIGOLO: *65* 3-5
STAX: *71* 2-4
TRUTH: *74-75* 2-3
VOLT: *69* 2-4

NEWHART, Bob
LPs: 10/12-Inch 33rpm
HARMONY: *69* 8-15
WARNER BROS (1300 through
1500 series): *60-65* 15-30
WARNER BROS (1600 through
1700 series): *66-67* 10-20

NEWLEY, Anthony
Singles: 7-Inch
KAPP: *69* 2-3
LONDON: *58-63* 2-5
MGM: *71-74* 1-3
RCA VICTOR: *66-67* 2-3
UNITED ARTISTS: *76-77* 1-3
WARNER BROS: *68* 2-3
LPs: 10/12-Inch 33rpm
BELL: *71* 8-10
LONDON: *62-66* 10-20

MGM: *71-73* $8-12
RCA VICTOR: *64-69* 8-15
UNITED ARTISTS: *77* 5-8

NEWMAN, Jimmy C.
(Jimmy Newman; Jimmy C. Newman & Cajun
Country)
Singles: 78rpm
DOT: *54-57* 3-5
Singles: 7-Inch
DECCA: *60-71* 2-4
DOT (Except 15766): *54-57* 3-6
DOT (15766; "Carry On"): *58* 25-30
MGM: *58-60* 3-5
MONUMENT: *72* 2-3
PLANTATION: *76-80* 1-3
SHANNON: *73* 2-3
EPs: 7-Inch 33/45rpm
DECCA: *64* 5-8
LPs: 10/12-Inch 33rpm
CROWN: 8-12
DECCA: *62-70* 10-20
DELTA: *82* 5-8
DOT: *66* 10-18
LA LOUISANNE: 5-8
MGM: *59-62* 15-25
PICKWICK/HILLTOP: 8-12
PLANTATION: *77-81* 5-8
SWALLOW: 5-8

NEWMAN, Jimmy C., Danny Davis &
The Nashville Brass
Singles: 7-Inch
RCA VICTOR: *80* 1-3
Also see DAVIS, Danny
Also see NEWMAN, Jimmy C.

NEWMAN, Randy
Singles: 78rpm
REPRISE: *78* 4-6
(Promotional issue only.)
Singles: 7-Inch
CHELSEA: *74* 2-3
DOT: *62* 3-5
REPRISE: *68-78* 2-4
REPRISE: *88* 1-3
WARNER BROS: *77-85* 1-3
LPs: 10/12-Inch 33rpm
EPIC (147; "Peyton Place"): *65* 20-25
(TV Soundtrack.)
REPRISE (Except 6286): *70-74* 6-10
REPRISE (6286; "Randy Newman"): *68* .10-12
(Cover pictures Randy in sweater & coat.)
REPRISE (6286; "Randy Newman"): *68* .12-15
(Cover picture is a close-up of Randy.)
REPRISE: *88* 5-8
WARNER BROS: *77-85* 5-8

Also see BISHOP, Stephen
Also see EAGLES
Also see MC VIE, Christine
Also see RONSTADT, Linda
Also see SEGER, Bob

NEWMAN, Randy, & Paul Simon
Singles: 7-Inch
WARNER BROS: *83* $1-3
Also see NEWMAN, Randy
Also see SIMON, Paul

NEWMAN, Ted
Singles: 78rpm
REV: *57* 3-5
Singles: 7-Inch
REV: *57* 4-6

NEWMAN, Thunderclap
Singles: 7-Inch
MCA: 1-3
TRACK (2000 series): *69-70* 4-6
TRACK (60000 series): *75* 2-4
LPs: 10/12-Inch 33rpm
ATLANTIC/TRACK: *70* 12-15
MCA/TRACK: *73* 6-10
Members: Andy Newman; Jimmy McCulloch;
Speedy Keen.
Also see McCARTNEY, Paul

NEWSOME, Bobby
Singles: 7-Inch
SPRING: *72* 2-4

NEWSOME, Frankie
Singles: 7-Inch
GWP: *69* 2-4

NEWTON, Juice
Singles: 7-Inch
CAPITOL: *78-84* 1-3
RCA VICTOR: *84-87* 1-3
Picture Sleeves
CAPITOL: *78-84* 1-3
RCA VICTOR: *84-85* 1-3
LPs: 10/12-Inch 33rpm
CAPITOL: *78-84* 5-8
RCA VICTOR: *84-86* 5-8
Also see RABBITT, Eddie, & Juice Newton

NEWTON, Juice, & Silver Spur
Singles: 7-Inch
CAPITOL: *77* 2-3
RCA VICTOR: *75-76* 2-4
LPs: 10/12-Inch 33rpm
CAPITOL (11000 series): *77* 8-10
CAPITOL (16000 series): *81* 4-8
RCA VICTOR (1000 series): *75* 8-12
RCA VICTOR (4000 series): *81* 4-8

Also see NEWTON, Juice

NEWTON, Wayne
Singles: 7-Inch
ARIES II: *79-80* **$1-3**
CAPITOL (Except 5338): *63-71* **2-5**
CAPITOL (5338; "Comin' On
Too Strong"): *64* **10-15**
(With Bruce Johnston & Terry Melcher.)
CHALLENGE: *64* **3-6**
CHELSEA: *72-76* **1-3**
GEORGE: *62* **4-8**
MGM: *68* **2-4**
20TH CENTURY-FOX: *78* **1-3**
WARNER BROS: *70-77* **1-3**
Picture Sleeves
CAPITOL: *65-66* **4-8**
LPs: 10/12-Inch 33rpm
AIRES II: *79-80* **5-8**
CAMDEN: *74* **5-10**
CAPITOL (573; "Wayne Newton"): *70* .. **12-25**
(A 3-LP set.)
CAPITOL (1973 through 2797): *63-67* .. **10-20**
(With a "T" or "ST" prefix.)
CAPITOL (2300 series): *75* **5-8**
(With an "SM" prefix.)
CAPITOL (11000 series): *79* **5-8**
CAPITOL (16000 series): *80* **5-8**
MGM: *68* **8-12**
MUSICOR: *79* **5-8**
20TH CENTURY-FOX: *78* **5-8**
Also see BRUCE & TERRY

NEWTON BROTHERS
(Newton Brothers Featuring Wayne)
Singles: 7-Inch
CAPITOL (4236; "The Real Thing"): *59* . **40-60**
GEORGE (Except 7778): *61* **5-10**
GEORGE (7778; "Little Jukebox"): *61* .. **10-20**
Members: Wayne Newton; Jerry Newton.
Also see NEWTON RASCALS

NEWTON RASCALS
Singles: 7-Inch
RANGER RECORDS (401; "If The Easter
Bunny Knew The Fun He'd
Have On Xmas"): *58* **10-15**
(Issued with a paper insert, picturing 12-year-old
Wayne & 14-year old Jerry as "The Rascals In
Rhythm." The value of the insert is about the same
as shown for the disc.)
Members: Wayne Newton; Jerry Newton.
Also see NEWTON, Wayne
Also see NEWTON BROTHERS

NEWTON-JOHN, Olivia
Singles: 12-Inch 33/45rpm
MCA (Except 1150): *81-84* **4-6**

MCA (1150; "Twist Of Fate"): *83* **$5-8**
(Promotional issue only.)
Singles: 7-Inch
KIRSHNER: *70* **5-8**
MCA: *73-88* **1-3**
RSO: *78* **1-3**
UNI (55281; "If Not For You"): *71* **3-5**
UNI (55304; "Banks Of The Ohio"): *71* ... **4-6**
UNI (55317; "What Is Life?"): *72* **4-6**
UNI (55348; "Just A Little
Too Much"): *72* **8-12**
Promotional Singles
MCA ("Deeper Than The Night"): *79* **25-30**
(Picture disc.)
WHAT'S IT ALL ABOUT: *74* **25-50**
Picture Sleeves
MCA (Except 40418): *73-84* **2-5**
MCA (40418; "Please Mr. Please"): *75* ... **6-10**
EPs: 7-Inch 33/45rpm
MCA: *73* **12-15**
(Promotional issues only.)
LPs: 10/12-Inch 33rpm
MCA (389; "Let Me Be There"): *73* **10-12**
MCA (411; "If You Love Me,
Let Me Know"): *74* **12-15**
(With *I Love You, I Honestly Love You.* Note
longer title.)
MCA (411; "If You Love Me,
Let Me Know"): *74* **8-10**
(With *I Honestly Love You.* Note shorter title.)
MCA (2000 & 3000 series): *75-78* **8-10**
MCA (5000 & 6000 series): *80-88* **5-8**
MCA (37000 series): *80-83* **5-8**
MFSL: *80* **25-50**
UNI (73117; "If Not For You"): *71* **50-75**
(Cover depicts a field scene.)
UNI (73117; "If Not For You"): *71* **20-30**
(Field scene removed from cover.)
Also see DENVER, John, & Olivia Newton-
John
Also see FOSTER, David, & Olivia Newton-
John
Also see WILSON, Carl

NEWTON-JOHN, Olivia, & The
Electric Light Orchestra
Singles: 7-Inch
MCA: *80* **1-3**
Picture Sleeves
MCA: *80* **1-3**
Also see ELECTRIC LIGHT ORCHESTRA

NEWTON-JOHN, Olivia, & Andy Gibb
Singles: 12-Inch 33/45rpm
POLYDOR (104; "Rest Your
Love On Me"): *79* **10-15**

Singles: 7-Inch
RSO: *80* **$1-3**
Also see GIBB, Andy

NEWTON-JOHN, Olivia, & Cliff Richard
Singles: 7-Inch
MCA: *80* **1-3**
Picture Sleeves
MCA: *80* **1-3**
Also see RICHARD, Cliff

NEWTON-JOHN, Olivia, & John Travolta
Singles: 7-Inch
RSO: *78* **1-3**
Picture Sleeves
RSO: *78* **1-3**
Also see NEWTON-JOHN, Olivia
Also see TRAVOLTA, John

NEXT MOVEMENT
Singles: 7-Inch
NUANCE: *84* **1-3**

NICE
Singles: 7-Inch
IMMEDIATE: *68* **3-5**
MERCURY: *70* **2-4**
LPs: 10/12-Inch 33rpm
CHARISMA: **8-10**
COLUMBIA: **8-10**
IMMEDIATE: *68-71* **10-15**
MERCURY: *71-72* **10-12**
SIRE: *75* **10-12**
Member: Keith Emerson.
Also see EMERSON, Keith, & The Nice

NICHOLAS, Paul
Singles: 7-Inch
COLUMBIA: *74* **2-4**
RSO: *76-78* **2-3**
LPs: 10/12-Inch 33rpm
RSO: *77* **5-10**

NICHOLS, Mike, & Elaine May
Singles: 7-Inch
MERCURY: **2-5**
LPs: 10/12-Inch 33rpm
MERCURY: *59-72* **10-20**

NICK & ELVIS
Singles: 12-Inch 33/45rpm
COLUMBIA: *84* **4-6**
Members: Nick Lowe; Elvis Costello.
Also see COSTELLO, Elvis
Also see LOWE, Nick

NICKIE LEE: see LEE, Nickie

NICKS, Stevie
Singles: 12-Inch 33/45rpm
MODERN: *81-86* **$4-6**
Singles: 7-Inch
MODERN: *81-86* **1-3**
Picture Sleeves
MODERN: *81-86* **1-3**
LPs: 10/12-Inch 33rpm
MFSL: *84* **20-30**
MODERN: *81-86* **5-8**
Also see BUCKINGHAM NICKS
Also see EGAN, Walter
Also see FLEETWOOD MAC
Also see LOGGINS, Kenny, & Stevie Nicks
Also see STEWART, John

NICKS, Stevie, & Don Henley
Singles: 7-Inch
MODERN: *81* **1-3**
Also see HENLEY, Don

NICKS, Stevie, & Tom Petty & The Heartbreakers
Singles: 7-Inch
MODERN: *81-86* **1-3**
Also see NICKS, Stevie
Also see PETTY, Tom, & The Heartbreakers

NICOLE
Singles: 12-Inch 33/45rpm
PORTRAIT: *85-86* **4-6**
Singles: 7-Inch
EPIC: *88* **1-3**
PORTRAIT: *85-86* **1-3**
LPs: 10/12-Inch 33rpm
PORTRAIT: *86* **5-8**

NIELSEN-PEARSON BAND
Singles: 7-Inch
CAPITOL: *80-83* **1-3**
EPIC: *78* **2-3**
LPs: 10/12-Inch 33rpm
CAPITOL: *80-81* **5-8**
EPIC: *78* **5-8**
Members: Reid Nielsen; Mark Pearson.

NIGHT
Singles: 7-Inch
PLANET: *79-81* **1-3**
Picture Sleeves
PLANET: *80-81* **1-3**
LPs: 10/12-Inch 33rpm
PLANET: *79-80* **8-10**
Member: Chris Thompson.
Also see MANN, Manfred
Also see THOMPSON, Chris, & Night

NIGHT RANGER
Singles: 7-Inch
BOARDWALK: 83 .... $1-3
MCA/CAMEL: 83-88 1-3
LPs: 10/12-Inch 33rpm
BOARDWALK: 82 8-10
MCA/CAMEL: 83-88 5-8

NIGHTCRAWLERS
Singles: 7-Inch
KAPP: 66-67 4-6
LEE: 66 10-12
LPs: 10/12-Inch 33rpm
KAPP: 67 25-30

NIGHTHAWK
Singles: 7-Inch
QUALITY: 82 1-3

NIGHTHAWKS
LPs: 10/12-Inch 33rpm
ADELPHI: 76-82 6-10
ALADDIN: 75 35-40
CHESAPEAKE (Black vinyl): 83 5-8
CHESAPEAKE (Colored vinyl): 83 10-15
VARRICK: 83 5-8
MERCURY: 80 5-8
Members: Mark Wenner; Jim Thackery.

NIGHTINGALE, Maxine
Singles: 7-Inch
A&M: 81 1-3
HIGHRISE: 82 1-3
RCA VICTOR: 80 1-3
UNITED ARTISTS: 76 2-3
WINDSONG: 79 1-3
LPs: 10/12-Inch 33rpm
UNITED ARTISTS: 77 8-10
WINDSONG: 80 5-8

NIGHTINGALE, Maxine, & Jimmy Ruffin
Singles: 7-Inch
HIGHRISE: 82 1-3
Also see NIGHTINGALE, Maxine
Also see RUFFIN, Jimmy

NIGHTINGALE, Ollie
Singles: 7-Inch
MEMPHIS: 71 2-4
PATHFINDER: 78 1-3
PRIDE: 72-73 2-4
LPs: 10/12-Inch 33rpm
PRIDE: 73 8-12

NIGHTNOISE
LPs: 10/12-Inch 33rpm
WINDHAM HILL: 88 5-8

NILE, Willie
Singles: 7-Inch
ARISTA: 80-81 .... $1-3
LPs: 10/12-Inch 33rpm
ARISTA: 80-81 5-8

NILSSON
(Harry Nilsson & The New Salvation Singers)
Singles: 7-Inch
POLYDOR: 85 1-3
RCA VICTOR: 67-77 2-4
TOWER (100 series): 64-65 3-5
TOWER (500 series): 69 2-4
Picture Sleeves
RCA VICTOR: 74-77 2-4
EPs: 7-Inch 33/45rpm
RCA VICTOR (248; "Excerpts From
   The Point"): 71 5-10
(Promotional issue only.)
LPs: 10/12-Inch 33rpm
51 WEST: 5-8
MUSICOR: 77 8-10
POLYDOR: 85 5-8
RCA VICTOR (0097 through
   0817): 73-75 8-10
RCA VICTOR (1003; "The Point"): 71 ..10-12
(With Davy Jones & Mickey Dolenz.)
RCA VICTOR (1031 through
   3811): 76-80 5-8
RCA VICTOR (3874; "Pandemonium
   Shadow Show"): 67 12-18
RCA VICTOR (3956; "Aerial Ballet"): 68 12-15
RCA VICTOR (4197 through
   4717): 69-72 8-12
SPRINGBOARD: 78 5-8
TOWER: 69 10-15
Promotional LPs
RCA VICTOR (567;
   "Scatalogue"): 25-30
Also see CHER & NILSSON
Also see DOLENZ, Mickey
Also see STARR, Ringo, & Harry Nilsson

NIMOY, Leonard
Singles: 7-Inch
DOT: 67-69 5-10
LPs: 10/12-Inch 33rpm
CAEDMON: 4-8
DOT: 67-69 25-50
JRT ("The Mysterious Golem"): 82 20-40
PARAMOUNT: 74 20-40
PICKWICK: 15-25

9TH CREATION
Singles: 7-Inch
HILLTAK: 79-80 1-3

PRELUDE: 77 ....$2-3
LPs: 10/12-Inch 33rpm
PRELUDE: 77 8-10
RITE TRACK: 10-12

9 9
Singles: 12-Inch 33/45rpm
RCA VICTOR: 85-86 4-6
Singles: 7-Inch
RCA VICTOR: 85-86 1-3
LPs: 10/12-Inch 33rpm
RCA VICTOR: 85 5-8

999
Singles: 7-Inch
POLYDOR: 81 1-3
LPs: 10/12-Inch 33rpm
PVC: 79 5-8
POLYDOR: 80-81 5-8

1910 FRUITGUM COMPANY
Singles: 7-Inch
ATTACK: 70 3-5
BUDDAH: 67-69 3-5
SUPER K: 70 3-5
LPs: 10/12-Inch 33rpm
BUDDAH: 68-70 12-15
Also see KASENETZ-KATZ SINGING OR-
CHESTRAL CIRCUS

1910 FRUITGUM COMPANY /
Lemon Pipers
LPs: 10/12-Inch 33rpm
BUDDAH: 68-70 12-15
Also see LEMON PIPERS
Also see 1910 FRUITGUM COMPANY

NINO & THE EBB TIDES
Singles: 7-Inch
MADISON: 61 10-15
MALA: 64 8-10
MARCO: 61 5-10
MR. PEACOCK: 61-62 15-20
MR. PEEKE: 63 10-15
RECORTE (Except 408): 58-59 25-30
RECORTE (408; "The Real Meaning
Of Christmas"): 58 40-45
Member: Nino Aiello.

NINO & THE EBB TIDES / Miss
Frankie Nolan
Singles: 7-Inch
MADISON: 61 10-15
Also see NINO & THE EBB TIDES

NITEFLYTE
Singles: 7-Inch
ARIOLA AMERICA: 79-81 1-3

LPs: 10/12-Inch 33rpm
ARIOLA AMERICA: 79-81 .... $5-8
NITE-LITERS
Singles: 7-Inch
RCA VICTOR: 71-72   2-4
LPs: 10/12-Inch 33rpm
RCA VICTOR: 71-72 8-10

NITTY GRITTY DIRT BAND
(Dirt Band)
Singles: 7-Inch
LIBERTY (1000 series): 81-84 1-3
LIBERTY (50000 series): 67-70 3-5
UNITED ARTISTS: 71-80 2-4
WARNER BROS: 84-88 1-3
Picture Sleeves
LIBERTY (1000 series): 81-84 1-3
LIBERTY (50000 series): 67 3-6
UNITED ARTISTS: 71-80 2-4
EPs: 7-Inch 33/45rpm
UNITED ARTISTS (69; "All The
Good Times"): 71 20-25
(Promotional issue only.)
LPs: 10/12-Inch 33rpm
LIBERTY (1100 series): 81 5-8
LIBERTY (3501; "Nitty Gritty
Dirt Band"): 67 15-20
(Monaural. The stereo of this issue was 7001.)
LIBERTY (7501 through 7611): 67-69 .. 12-18
LIBERTY (7642; "Uncle Charlie"): 70 .. 12-15
(With an "LST" prefix.)
LIBERTY (7642; "Uncle Charlie"): 5-8
(With an "LTAO" prefix.)
UNITED ARTISTS (117;
"Interview") : 75 15-20
(Promotional issue only.)
UNITED ARTISTS (184; "Stars &
Stripes Forever"): 74 12-15
(With a "UA-LA" prefix.)
UNITED ARTISTS (184; "Stars &
Stripes Forever"): 8-10
(With an "LWB" prefix.)
UNITED ARTISTS (469; "Dream"): 75 .. 8-10
UNITED ARTISTS (670; "Dirt,
Silver & Gold"): 76 15-20
(With a "UA-LA" prefix.)
UNITED ARTISTS (670; "Dirt,
Silver & Gold"): 10-12
(With an "LKCL" prefix.)
UNITED ARTISTS (854 through
1042) : 78-80 5-8
UNITED ARTISTS (5500 series): 71 8-10
UNITED ARTISTS (9800 series): 72 8-10
WARNER BROS: 84-88 5-8

NITTY GRITTY DIRT BAND, &
Roy Acuff
Singles: 7-Inch
UNITED ARTISTS: *71* $2-3
Also see NITTY GRITTY DIRT BAND

NITTY GRITTY DIRT BAND, &
Linda Ronstadt
Singles: 7-Inch
UNITED ARTISTS: *79* 2-3
Also see NITTY GRITTY DIRT BAND
Also see RONSTADT, Linda

NITZINGER
(John Nitzinger)
Singles: 7-Inch
CAPITOL: *72-73* 2-3
20TH CENTURY-FOX: *76* 2-3
LPs: 10/12-Inch 33rpm
CAPITOL: *72-73* 8-10
20TH CENTURY-FOX: *76* 8-10

NITZSCHE, Jack
Singles: 7-Inch
FANTASY: *76* 1-3
MCA: *78* 1-3
REPRISE: *63-65* 3-5
Picture Sleeves
REPRISE (20,202; "Lonely Surfer"): *63* . 10-20
LPs: 10/12-Inch 33rpm
MCA: *78* 8-10
REPRISE (2000 series): *73* 8-10
REPRISE (6100 series): *63-64* 15-25
REPRISE (6200 series): *66* 10-15

NIVENS, Pamela
Singles: 7-Inch
SUN VALLEY: *83* 1-3

NIX, Don
Singles: 7-Inch
CREAM: *76* 2-3
ELEKTRA: *71* 2-4
LPs: 10/12-Inch 33rpm
CREAM: *79* 5-8
ELEKTRA: *71* 8-10
ENTERPRISE: *73* 8-10

NIXON, Mojo, & Skid Roper
LPs: 10/12-Inch 33rpm
ENIGMA: *87* 5-8

NOBLE, Nick
Singles: 7-Inch
CAPITOL: *73* 1-3
CHESS: *63-64* 2-4
CHURCHILL: *77* 1-3
CORAL: *59-66* 2-4
DATE: *67-68* 2-3

EPIC: *77* $1-3
LIBERTY: *62-63* 2-4
MERCURY: *56-57* 2-4
TMS: *79* 1-3
20TH CENTURY-FOX: *65* 2-3
WING: *55-56* 3-5
LPs: 10/12-Inch 33rpm
COLUMBIA: *69* 8-12
LIBERTY: *63* 10-15
WING: *60* 10-20

NOBLES, Cliff
(Cliff Nobels & Co.)
Singles: 7-Inch
ATLANTIC: *66-67* 3-5
PHIL L.A. OF SOUL: *68-69* 3-5
JAMIE: *72* 2-3
ROULETTE: *73* 1-3
LPs: 10/12-Inch 33rpm
MOON SHOT: 8-10
PHIL L.A. OF SOUL: *68* 10-15

NOCERA
Singles: 7-Inch
SLEEPING BAG: *86-87* 1-3

NOEL
Singles: 7-Inch
4TH & BROADWAY: *88* 1-3
LPs: 10/12-Inch 33rpm
4TH & BROADWAY: *88* 5-8

NOGUEZ, Jacky, & His Orchestra
Singles: 7-Inch
JAMIE: *59-60* 2-4
Picture Sleeves
JAMIE: *60* 3-6
LPs: 10/12-Inch 33rpm
JAMIE: *60* 10-20

NOLAN: see PORTER, Nolan

NOLAN, Kenny
Singles: 7-Inch
CASABLANCA: *79-80* 1-3
DOT: *68* 3-5
FORWARD: *69* 3-5
HIGHLAND: *68* 3-5
LION: *72* 2-4
MGM: *71* 2-4
POLYDOR: *78* 2-3
20TH CENTURY-FOX: *76-77* 2-3
LPs: 10/12-Inch 33rpm
CASABLANCA: *79* 5-8
POLYDOR: *78* 8-10
20TH CENTURY-FOX: *77* 8-10

NORMA
Singles: 12-Inch 33/45rpm
ERC: *83* $4-6

NORMA JEAN
(Norma Jean Wright)
Singles: 12-Inch 33/45rpm
BEARSVILLE: *79-80* 4-6
Singles: 7-Inch
BEARSVILLE: *78-80* 1-3
LPs: 10/12-Inch 33rpm
BEARSVILLE: *78* 5-8
Also see CHIC

NORMAN, Jimmy
(Jimmy Norman & The Hollywood Teeners;
Jimmy Norman & The Viceroys)
Singles: 7-Inch
DOT: *59* 5-8
FUN: *60* 4-6
GOOD SOUND: *61* 4-6
JOSIE: *68* 3-5
LITTLE STAR: *62-63* 4-6
MERCURY: *67* 3-5
MUN RAB: *59* 5-8
POLO: *64* 3-6
RAY STAR: *61-62* 4-6
SAMAR: *66* 3-5
LPs: 10/12-Inch 33rpm
BADCAT: 6-8
Also see COASTERS
Also see DYNA-SORES
Also see HARLEM RIVER DRIVE

NORMAN, Jimmy, & Dorothy Berry
Singles: 7-Inch
LITTLE STAR: *62* 4-6

NORMAN, Jimmy / Willie
"The Moon Man" Echols
Singles: 7-Inch
GOOD SOUND: *61* 4-6

NORMAN, Jimmy, & The O'Jays
Singles: 7-Inch
LITTLE STAR: *63* 5-8
Also see NORMAN, Jimmy
Also see O'JAYS

NORTH, Freddie
Singles: 7-Inch
A-BET: *67-69* 3-5
CAPITOL: *62* 4-6
RIC: *64* 3-5
MANKIND: *71-76* 2-4
PHILLIPS INT'L: *61* 3-5
LPs: 10/12-Inch 33rpm
A-BET: 8-10

MANKIND: *71-75* $8-12
PHONORAMA: 5-8

NORTHCOTT, Tom
Singles: 7-Inch
UNI: *71* ....?-4
WARNER BROS: *67-69* 3-5
LPs: 10/12-Inch 33rpm
UNI: *71* 8-10

NORTHERN LIGHT
Singles: 7-Inch
COLUMBIA: *75* 2-3
GLACIER: *75-77* 2-4

NORVUS, Nervous:
see NERVOUS NORVUS

NORWOOD, Dorothy
(Dorothy Norwood & The Norwood Singers)
Singles: 7-Inch
GRC: *72-75* 2-3
JEWEL: *78* 1-3
SAVOY: *63-69* 1-3
LPs: 10/12-Inch 33rpm
JEWEL: *78* 4-8
SAVOY: *63-83* 5-15

NOTATIONS
Singles: 7-Inch
C.R.A.: *73* 2-4
GEMIGO: *75-76* 2-3
MERCURY: *77* 2-3
TWINIGHT: *70* 2-4
LPs: 10/12-Inch 33rpm
GEMIGO: *76* 8-10
Members: Clifford Curry; Bobby Thomas; Lasalle
Matthews; Jimmy Stroud; Walter Jones.

NOVA, Aldo
Singles: 12-Inch 33/45rpm
PORTRAIT: *82* 5-8
Singles: 7-Inch
PORTRAIT: *82* 1-3
LPs: 10/12-Inch 33rpm
PORTRAIT: *82-83* 5-8

NOVAS
Singles: 7-Inch
PARROT: *64* 40-50
TWIN TOWN: *65* 20-40

NOVELLE, Jay
Singles: 12-Inch 33/45rpm
EMERGENCY: *84* 4-6

NOVO COMBO
Singles: 7-Inch
POLYDOR: *82* 1-3
LPs: 10/12-Inch 33rpm

POLYDOR: *81-82* **$5-8**
Member: Mike Shrieve.
Also see SANTANA

NU SHOOZ
Singles: 7-Inch
ATLANTIC: *88* **1-3**
LPs: 10/12-Inch 33rpm
ATLANTIC: *88* **5-8**

NU TORNADOS
Singles: 7-Inch
CARLTON: *58-59* **3-5**
FELSTED: *59* **3-5**

NUANCE
(Featuring Vikki Love)
Singles: 12-Inch 33/45rpm
4TH & BROADWAY: *84-85* **4-6**
Singles: 7-Inch
4TH & BROADWAY: *84-85* **1-3**
Also see LOVE, Vikki, With Nuance

NUCLEAR ASSAULT
LPs: 10/12-Inch 33rpm
I.R.S.: *88* **5-8**

NUGENT, Ted
(Ted Nugent & The Amboy Dukes; Ted Nugent
& Brian Howe)
Singles: 7-Inch
ATLANTIC: *84-86* **1-3**
DISCREET: *74* **2-3**
EPIC: *76-80* **1-3**
LPs: 10/12-Inch 33rpm
ATLANTIC: *82-88* **5-8**
DISCREET: *74* **8-10**
EPIC (Except 607): *75-81* **6-10**
EPIC (607; "State Of Shock"): *79* **15-25**
(Picture disc.)
MAINSTREAM (10-01; "Ted Nugent
& The Amboy Dukes"): *82* **5-8**
MAINSTREAM (421; "Ted Nugent
& The Amboy Dukes"): **8-10**
POLYDOR: *71* **10-12**
Also see AMBOY DUKES
Also see BAD COMPANY

NUGGETS
Singles: 7-Inch
MERCURY: *79* **1-3**
LPs: 10/12-Inch 33rpm
MERCURY: *79* **5-8**

NUMAN, Gary
(Gary Numan & The Tubeway Army)
Singles: 7-Inch
ATCO: *79-81* **1-3**

LPs: 10/12-Inch 33rpm
ATCO: *79-81* **$5-8**

NUMONICS
Singles: 7-Inch
HODISK: *84* **1-3**

NUNN, Bobby
(Bobby Nunn & The Robbins)
Singles: 78rpm
MODERN: *51* **35-50**
Also see BYRD, Bobby
Also see COASTERS
Also see ROBINS

NURSERY SCHOOL
Singles: 12-Inch 33/45rpm
EPIC: *83* **4-6**

NUTMEGS
Singles: 78rpm
HERALD: *55-57* **5-10**
Singles: 7-Inch
COLLECTABLES: **1-3**
FLASHBACK: *65* **1-3**
HERALD (Except 574): *55-59* **10-20**
HERALD (574; "Rip Van Winkle"): *62* ...**8-10**
LANA: **2-3**
TEL: *60* **20-30**
TIMES SQUARE: *63* **4-6**
EPs: 7-Inch 33/45rpm
HERALD (452; "The
Nutmegs"): *60* **75-125**
LPs: 10/12-Inch 33rpm
COLLECTABLES: *84* **6-8**
RELIC: **8-10**
Members: Leroy Griffin; Jimmy Tyson; Leroy Mc-
Neil; James "Sonny" Griffin; Bill Emery; Ed Mar-
tin; Sonny Washburn; Harold Jones.

NUTMEGS / Volumes
Singles: 7-Inch
TIMES SQUARE: *63* **5-8**
Also see NUTMEGS
Also see VOLUMES

NUTTY SQUIRRELS
Singles: 7-Inch
COLUMBIA: *60* **3-5**
HANOVER: *59-60* **4-6**
RCA VICTOR: *64* **3-5**
Picture Sleeves
COLUMBIA: *60* **3-6**
HANOVER: *59* **4-8**
EPs: 7-Inch 33/45rpm
HANOVER: *60* **15-25**
LPs: 10/12-Inch 33rpm
COLUMBIA: *61* **20-25**
HANOVER: *60* **20-25**

MGM: *64* **$15-20**

NYRO, Laura
Singles: 7-Inch
COLUMBIA: *68-71* **2-4**
VERVE/FOLKWAYS: *66-67* **3-5**
VERVE/FORECAST: *68-69* **2-4**
Picture Sleeves
COLUMBIA: *68* **3-6**
LPs: 10/12-Inch 33rpm
COLUMBIA: *68-84* **6-10**
VERVE/FOLKWAYS: *67* **10-15**
VERVE/FORECAST: *69* **8-10**
Also see LABELLE, Patti

NYTRO
Singles: 12-Inch 33/45rpm
WHITFIELD: *79* **4-6**
Singles: 7-Inch
WHITFIELD: *76-79* **1-3**
LPs: 10/12-Inch 33rpm
WHITFIELD: *77-79* **5-8**

O

O., Jerry: see JERRY O

O ROMEO
Singles: 12-Inch 33/45rpm
BOB CAT: *83* **4-6**
OH MY: *84* **4-6**
Members: Lorilee Svedberg; Dora Suppes; Terry Weinberg.

O.M.D.
Singles: 12-Inch 33/45rpm
A&M: *84* **4-6**
Singles: 7-Inch
A&M: *84* **1-3**

O.R.S.
LPs: 10/12-Inch 33rpm
SALSOUL: *79* **5-8**

OAK
Singles: 7-Inch
MERCURY: *79-80* **1-3**
Also see PINETTE, Rick, & Oak

OAK RIDGE BOYS
(Oak Ridge Quartet; Oaks)
Singles: 7-Inch
ABC: *78-79* **2-3**
ABC/DOT: *77* **2-3**
CADENCE: *59* **2-4**
COLUMBIA: *73-76* **1-3**
HEARTWARMING: *71* **1-3**

IMPACT: *71* **$1-3**
MCA: *79-88* **1-3**
WARNER BROS: *63* **2-3**
LPs: 10/12-Inch 33rpm
ABC: *78-79* **5-10**
ABC/DOT: *77* **8-10**
ACCORD: *81-82* **4-8**
CADENCE: *58* **15-25**
CANAAN: *66* **8-15**
COLUMBIA: *74-83* **5-10**
EXACT: *83* **4-8**
51 WEST: **5-8**
HEARTWARMING: *71-74* **5-8**
INTERMEDIA: **5-8**
MCA: *80-88* **5-8**
NASHVILLE: *70* **8-10**
OUT OF TOWN DIST: *82* **4-8**
PHONORAMA: **5-8**
POWER PAK: **5-8**
PRIORITY: *82* **4-8**
SKYLITE: *64-66* **8-15**
STARDAY: *65* **8-15**
UNITED ARTISTS: *66* **8-15**
WARNER BROS: *63* **10-15**
Members: William Golden; Duane Allen; Rich Sterban; Joe Bonsall; Steve Sanders.
Also see LEE, Brenda, & The Oak Ridge Boys
Also see MANDRELL, Barbara, & The Oak Ridge Boys

OAKEY, Philip:
see MORODER, Giorgio, & Philip Oakey

OAS, Holly
Singles: 12-Inch 33/45rpm
DND: *84* **4-6**

O'BANION, John
Singles: 7-Inch
ELEKTRA: *81* **1-3**
LPs: 10/12-Inch 33rpm
ELEKTRA: *81* **5-8**

O'BRYAN
(O'Bryan Burnette)
Singles: 12-Inch 33/45rpm
CAPITOL: *82-86* **4-6**
Singles: 7-Inch
CAPITOL: *82-87* **1-3**
LPs: 10/12-Inch 33rpm
CAPITOL: *82-86* **5-8**

OCASEK, Ric
Singles: 12-Inch 33/45rpm
GEFFEN: *83* **4-6**
Singles: 7-Inch
GEFFEN: *83-86* **1-3**

LPs: 10/12-Inch 33rpm
GEFFEN: *83-86* $5-8
Also see CARS

OCEAN
Singles: 7-Inch
KAMA SUTRA: *71-72* 2-4
LPs: 10/12-Inch 33rpm
KAMA SUTRA: *71-72* 8-10

OCEAN, Billy
Singles: 12-Inch 33/45rpm
EPIC: *80-82* 4-6
JIVE: *84-86* 4-6
Singles: 7-Inch
ARIOLA AMERICA: *76* 2-3
EPIC: *77-82* 1-3
JIVE: *84-88* 1-3
LPs: 10/12-Inch 33rpm
EPIC: *82* 5-8
JIVE: *84-88* 5-8

OCHS, Phil
Singles: 7-Inch
A&M: *67-73* 3-5
LPs: 10/12-Inch 33rpm
A&M: *67-76* 10-15
ELEKTRA: *64-66* 15-20

O'CONNELL, Helen
Singles: 78rpm
CAPITOL: *51-54* 2-4
KAPP: *55* 2-4
VIK: *57* 2-4
Singles: 7-Inch
CAMEO: *63* 2-4
CAPITOL: *51-54* 2-4
KAPP: *55* 2-4
VIK: *57* 2-4
EPs: 7-Inch 33/45rpm
CAPITOL: *54* 5-8
VIK: *57* 5-8
LPs: 10/12-Inch 33rpm
CAMDEN: *59-62* 5-10
CAMEO: *63* 8-15
MARK '56: *77* 5-8
VIK: *57* 10-20
WARNER BROS: *61* 8-15
Also see MARTIN, Dean, & Helen O'Connell

O'CONNER, Carroll
LPs: 10/12-Inch 33rpm
A&M: *72* 5-10
AUDIO FIDELITY: *76* 5-10

O'CONNER, Carroll, & Jean Stapleton
Singles: 7-Inch
ATLANTIC: *71* 2-4

Also see O'CONNER, Carroll

O'CONNOR, Sinead
Singles: 7-Inch
CHRYSALIS: *86* $1-3
LPs: 10/12-Inch 33rpm
CHRYSALIS: *86-88* 5-8
Members: Sinead O'Connor; Andy Rourke; Mike Joyce.
Also see SMITHS

O'DAY, Alan
Singles: 7-Inch
PACIFIC: *77-85* 1-3
LPs: 10/12-Inch 33rpm
PACIFIC: *77* 5-8

O'DAY, Pat
Singles: 78rpm
MGM: *53-56* 2-4
Singles: 7-Inch
ARGO: *59* 2-4
MGM: *53-56* 2-4
SEVILLE: *59-60* 2-4
LPs: 10/12-Inch 33rpm
GOLDEN CREST: *56* 10-20

O'DAY, Anita
Singles: 7-Inch
CLEF: *53* 3-5
CLOVER: *66* 2-4
COLUMBIA: *76* 1-3
CORAL: *52* 3-5
EMILY: *79* 1-3
LONDON: *51* 3-5
MERCURY: *52-53* 3-5
VERVE: *56-62* 2-4
EPs: 7-Inch 33/45rpm
CLEF: *53* 25-50
COLUMBIA: *74* 8-10
NORGRAN: *54* 20-40
LPs: 10/12-Inch 33rpm
ADVANCE: *51* 100-175
(10-Inch LPs.)
AMERICAN RECORDING
    SOCIETY: *57* 30-60
ANITA O'DAY
    RECORDS: *72* 5-10
CLEF: *53* 75-100
CORAL: *53* 75-125
DOBRE: *78* 5-8
EMILY: *79-82* 5-8
FLYING DUTCHMAN: *74* 5-8
GNP/CRESCENDO: *79* 5-8
MPS: *73* 5-8
NORGRAN (30; "Anita O'Day"): *54* 50-80
(10-Inch LP.)

NORGRAN (1000 series): 55-56 ...... $30-60
PAUSA: 81 5-8
SIGNATURE: 75 5-8
VERVE (2000 series): 56 25-50
(Reads "Verve Records, Inc." at bottom of label.)
VERVE (2100 series): 56-61 20-40
(Reads "Verve Records, Inc." at bottom of label.)
VERVE (6000 series): 59-60 20-40
(Reads "Verve Records, Inc." at bottom of label.)
VERVE (8200 through 8500
series): 59-64 15-30
(Reads "Verve Records, Inc." at bottom of label.)
VERVE: 61-72 10-20
(Reads "MGM Records - A Division Of Metro-
Goldwyn-Mayer, Inc." at bottom of label.)
VERVE: 79-82 6-12
(Reads "Manufactured By MGM Record Corp." or
mentions either Polydor or Polygram at bottom of
label.)

O'DAY, Anita, & Cal Tjader
LPs: 10/12-Inch 33rpm
VERVE: 62 15-25
(Reads "MGM Records - A Division Of Metro-
Goldwyn-Mayer, Inc." at bottom of label.)
Also see O'DAY, Anita
Also see TJADER, Cal

ODDS & ENDS
Singles: 7-Inch
RED BIRD: 66 4-6
SOUTHBAY: 2-4
TODAY: 71-72 2-4

O'DELL, Brooks
Singles: 7-Inch
GOLD: 63 3-5

O'DELL, Kenny
Singles: 7-Inch
ABC: 73 2-3
CAPRICORN: 73-79 1-3
KAPP: 72 2-3
MAR-KAY: 65 4-6
VEGAS: 67-68 3-5
WHITE WHALE: 69 2-4
LPs: 10/12-Inch 33rpm
CAPRICORN: 74-78 5-10
VEGAS: 68 15-20

ODETTA
(Odetta Holmes)
Singles: 7-Inch
DUNHILL: 69 2-3
RCA VICTOR: 63 2-4
RIVERSIDE: 62 2-4
VANGUARD: 59 2-4
VERVE/FOLKWAYS: 66 2-4
VERVE/FORECAST: 68 2-3

LPs: 10/12-Inch 33rpm
EVEREST: 73 .... $5-8
FANTASY: 58 20-30
(Colored vinyl.)
POLYDOR: 70 5-10
RCA VICTOR: 62-66 8-15
RIVERSIDE (400 series): 62 15-25
RIVERSIDE (3000 series): 68 8-12
RIVERSIDE (9400 series): 62 15-25
TRADITION: 67 8-12
UNITED ARTISTS: 76 5-8
VANGUARD: 59-67 8-18
VERVE/FOLKWAYS: 67 8-12

ODYSSEY
Singles: 12-Inch 33/45rpm
RCA VICTOR: 77-82 4-8
Singles: 7-Inch
MOWEST: 72 2-4
RCA VICTOR: 77-82 1-3
LPs: 10/12-Inch 33rpm
MOWEST: 72 10-12
RCA VICTOR: 77-82 8-10
Members: Lillian Lopez; Louise Lopez.

OFARIM, Esther & Abraham
(Esther Ofarim; Esther & Abi Ofarim)
Singles: 7-Inch
PHILIPS: 64-68 2-3
LPs: 10/12-Inch 33rpm
CAPITOL: 68 5-10
PHILIPS: 63-70 5-15

OFF BROADWAY USA
Singles: 7-Inch
ATLANTIC: 80 1-3
LPs: 10/12-Inch 33rpm
ATLANTIC: 80 5-8

OFFITT, Lillian
Singles: 7-Inch
CHIEF: 60 5-8
EXCELLO: 57 4-6

OH ROMEO: see O ROMEO

O'HEARN, Patrick
LPs: 10/12-Inch 33rpm
PRIVATE: 88 5-8

O'HENRY, Lenny
(Lenny O'Henry & The Short Stories)
Singles: 7-Inch
ABC-PARAMOUNT: 61 8-10
ATCO: 64-67 5-8
SMASH: 63 5-8

OHIO EXPRESS
(Ohio Ltd.)

Singles: 7-Inch

ATTACK: 70	$2-3
BUDDAH: 68-73	2-4
CAMEO: 67	3-5
ERIC: 78	1-3
SUPER K: 69-70	2-4

LPs: 10/12-Inch 33rpm

BUDDAH: 68-70	10-15
CAMEO: 68	15-20

Also see IVY LEAGUE
Also see KASENETZ-KATZ SINGING OR-
CHESTRAL CIRCUS
Also see REUNION
Also see 10CC

OHIO LTD: see OHIO EXPRESS

OHIO PLAYERS

Singles: 7-Inch

AIR CITY: 84	1-3
ARISTA: 79	1-3
BOARDWALK: 81	1-3
CAPITOL: 69	2-4
COMPASS: 68	3-5
MERCURY: 74-78	1-3
TANGERINE: 67	3-5
TRACK: 88	1-3
WESTBOUND: 71-76	2-3

LPs: 10/12-Inch 33rpm

ACCORD: 81	5-8
ARISTA: 79	5-8
BOARDWALK: 81	5-8
CAPITOL (192; "Observations In Time"): 69	10-15
CAPITOL (11291; "The Ohio Players"): 74	8-10
MERCURY: 74-78	8-10
TRACK: 88	5-8
TRIP: 72	8-10
UNITED ARTISTS: 75	8-10
WESTBOUND: 72-75	8-10

Also see JUNIE

OINGO BOINGO

Singles: 12-Inch 33/45rpm

A&M: 81	4-6
MCA: 85-86	4-6

Singles: 7-Inch

A&M: 81-82	1-3
MCA: 85-86	1-3

LPs: 10/12-Inch 33rpm

A&M: 81-82	5-8
I.R.S.: 80	5-8
MCA: 85-88	5-8

Members: Danny Elfman; Steve Bartek; John Her-
nandez; Dale Turner; Kerry Hatch; Richard Gibbs.

O'JAYS

Singles: 12-Inch 33/45rpm

PHILADELPHIA INT'L: 83	$4-6

Singles: 7-Inch

ALL PLATINUM: 74	2-3
APOLLO: 63	5-8
ASTROSCOPE: 74	2-3
BELL: 67-73	2-4
IMPERIAL: 63-66	4-6
LIBERTY: 81	1-3
LITTLE STAR: 63	5-8
MINIT: 67	3-5
NEPTUNE: 69-70	2-4
PHILADELPHIA INT'L: 72-87	1-3
SARU: 71	2-3
TSOP: 80-81	1-3

LPs: 10/12-Inch 33rpm

BELL (6014; "Back On Top"): 68	10-15
BELL (6082; "The O'Jays"): 73	8-10
EMI MANHATTAN: 87	5-8
IMPERIAL: 65	30-40
KORY: 77	8-10
MINIT: 67	12-15
PHILADELPHIA INT'L: 72-86	5-10
SUNSET: 68	10-12
TSOP: 80	5-8
TRIP: 73	8-10
UNITED ARTISTS: 72	8-10

Members: Bob Massey; Eddie LeVert; Walt Williams; Bill Powell; Bill Isles; Sam Strain.

Also see LITTLE ANTHONY & THE IM-
PERIALS
Also see NORMAN, Jimmy, & The O'Jays
Also see PHILADELPHIA INTERNATION-
AL ALL STARS

O'JAYS / Moments

LPs: 10/12-Inch 33rpm

STANG: 74	8-10

Also see O'JAYS
Also see MOMENTS

O'KAYSIONS

Singles: 7-Inch

ABC: 68	3-5
COTILLION: 70	2-4
NORTH STATE (1001; "Girl Watcher"): 68	12-25
ROULETTE:	1-3

LPs: 10/12-Inch 33rpm

ABC: 68	15-20

O'KEEFE, Danny
Singles: 7-Inch
ATLANTIC: 75 .... $2-3
JERDEN: 66 3-5
SIGNPOST: 72 2-4
WARNER BROS. 77-78 1-3
Picture Sleeves
WARNER BROS: 77-78 1-3
LPs: 10/12-Inch 33rpm
ATLANTIC: 73-75 8-10
COTILLION: 70 10-12
FIRST AMERICAN: 8-10
SIGNPOST: 72 10-12
WARNER BROS: 77-79 5-8

OLA & THE JANGLERS
Singles: 7-Inch
GNP/CRESCENDO: 68-69 4-6
LONDON: 67 4-6
LPs: 10/12-Inch 33rpm
GNP/CRESCENDO: 69 12-15

OLD AND IN THE WAY
LPs: 10/12-Inch 33rpm
ROUND: 75 20-25
SUGAR HILL: 85 5-8
Members: Peter Rowan; Jerry Garcia; Vassar Clements; David Grisman.
Also see GARCIA, Jerry
Also see ROWANS

OLD AND IN THE WAY / Keith & Donna / Robert Hunter / Phil Lesh & Ned Lagin
Singles: 7-Inch
ROUND (02 & 03; "Sampler For Dead Heads"): 75 40-60
(Promotional fan club issue. A two-disc set. Price includes both discs and the following inserts: letter from Anton Round, letter about members of the Grateful Dead, miniature LP covers, and a mailer advertising posters available.)
ROUND (02 & 03; "Sampler For Dead Heads"): 75 20-30
(Price is for both discs, without inserts. Divide in half for either one of the two records.)
Also see OLD & IN THE WAY

OLDFIELD, Mike
(Mike & Sally Oldfield)
Singles: 7-Inch
EPIC: 81-82 1-3
VIRGIN: 73-82 2-3
LPs: 10/12-Inch 33rpm
EPIC: 81-82 5-8
VIRGIN (Except 2001): 73-82 6-12
VIRGIN (2001; "Tubular Bells"): 73 10-12
(Picture disc.)

VIRGIN: 88 .... $5-8

OLIVER
(Bill Oliver Swofford)
Singles: 7-Inch
CREWE: 69-70 3-6
JUBILEE: 69 2-4
LIBERTY: 1-3
PARAMOUNT: 73 2-3
PEOPLE SONG: 82 1-3
UNITED ARTISTS: 70-71 2-5
Picture Sleeves
CREWE: 69 2-4
LPs: 10/12-Inch 33rpm
CREWE: 69-70 10-12
UNITED ARTISTS: 71 8-10
Also see BILLY & SUE

OLIVER, David
Singles: 7-Inch
MERCURY: 78-80 1-3
LPs: 10/12-Inch 33rpm
MERCURY: 78-79 5-8

OLIVOR, Jane
Singles: 7-Inch
COLUMBIA: 77-85 2-3
LPs: 10/12-Inch 33rpm
COLUMBIA: 77-85 5-8

OLLIE & JERRY
Singles: 12-Inch 33/45rpm
POLYDOR: 84-85 4-6
Singles: 7-Inch
POLYDOR: 84-85 1-3
Members: Ollie Brown; Jerry Knight.
Also see KNIGHT, Jerry

OLLIE & THE NIGHTINGALES
Singles: 7-Inch
STAX: 68 4-6
LPs: 10/12-Inch 33rpm
STAX: 69 10-12

OLSON, Rocky
Singles: 7-Inch
CHESS: 59 8-10

OLSSON, Nigel
Singles: 7-Inch
BANG: 78-79 2-3
COLUMBIA: 78 2-3
ROCKET: 75 2-3
UNI: 71-72 2-4
LPs: 10/12-Inch 33rpm
BANG: 79-80 5-8
COLUMBIA: 78 5-8
ROCKET: 73-75 8-10
UNI: 71 8-10

Also see JOHN, Elton

OLYMPIC RUNNERS
Singles: 7-Inch
LONDON: *74-77* $2-4
POLYDOR: *79* 2-3
LPs: 10/12-Inch 33rpm
LONDON: *74-77* 8-10
POLYDOR: *79* 5-8

OLYMPICS
Singles: 7-Inch
ABC: *73* 1-3
ARVEE: *59-65* 5-10
COLLECTABLES: 1-3
DEMON: *58-60* 5-10
DUO DISC: *64* 4-8
ERIC: 1-3
JUBILEE: *69* 4-6
LIBERTY: *63* 2-4
LOMA: *65* 4-8
MGM: *73* 3-5
MIRWOOD: *66-67* 3-5
PARKWAY: *68* 3-5
TITAN: *61* 5-8
TRI DISC: *63* 5-8
WARNER BROS: *70* 2-4
EPs: 7-Inch 33/45rpm
ARVEE (423; "Doin' The
Hully Gully"): *60* 30-50
LPs: 10/12-Inch 33rpm
ARVEE (423; "Doin' The
Hully Gully"): *60* 40-80
ARVEE (424; "Dance By The Light
Of The Moon"): *61* 40-80
ARVEE (429; "Party Time"): *61* 40-80
EVEREST: *81* 5-8
MIRWOOD: *66* 12-20
POST: 8-10

YOKO ONO
LENNON
WHO HAS SEEN THE WIND?

PRODUCED BY
JOHN LENNON

RHINO: $5-8
TRI-DISC: *63* 20-30
Members: Walter Ward; Eddie Lewis; Melvin
King; Charles Figer; Julius McMichaels.
Also see PARAGONS
Also see REYNOLDS, Jody / Olympics

100 PROOF Aged In Soul
Singles: 7-Inch
HOT WAX: *69-72* 3-6
LPs: 10/12-Inch 33rpm
HOT WAX: *70-73* 10-12

101 NORTH
Singles: 7-Inch
CAPITOL: *88* 1-3
LPs: 10/12-Inch 33rpm
CAPITOL: *88* 5-8

101 STRINGS
Singles: 7-Inch
SOMERSET: *59* 2-3
LPs: 10/12-Inch 33rpm
SOMERSET: *59-61* 4-8
STEREO FIDELITY: *59-61* 4-8

ONE ON ONE
Singles: 7-Inch
KEE WEE: *84* 1-3

1 PLUS 1
Singles: 7-Inch
M.O.C.: *66* 3-5

ONE WAY
(Featuring Al Hudson)
Singles: 12-Inch 33/45rpm
MCA: *82-86* 4-6
Singles: 7-Inch
CAPITOL: *88* 1-3
MCA: *79-87* 2-3
LPs: 10/12-Inch 33rpm
MCA: *79-86* 5-8
Also see HUDSON, Al

O'NEAL, Alexander
Singles: 12-Inch 33/45rpm
TABU: *85-86* 4-6
Singles: 7-Inch
TABU: *85-88* 2-3
LPs: 10/12-Inch 33rpm
TABU: *85-88* 5-8
Also see CHERRELLE & Alexander O'Neal

ONO, Yoko
(Yoko Ono & The Plastic Ono Band)
Singles: 12-Inch 33/45rpm
POLYDOR: *85-86* 4-6
Singles: 7-Inch
APPLE: *71-73* 3-5

GEFFEN: *81*	$2-3
POLYDOR: *82-86*	1-3

Promotional Singles

GEFFEN: *81*	5-8
POLYDOR: *82-86*	4-6

Picture Sleeves

GEFFEN: *81*	2-4

LPs: 10/12-Inch 33rpm

APPLE: *71-73*	15-20
GEFFEN: *81*	5-8
POLYDOR: *82-86*	5-8

Promotional LPs

GEFFEN (934; "Walking On Thin Ice"): *81*	20-25
GEFFEN (975; "No No No"): *81*	25-30

Also see LENNON, John

OPUS SEVEN

Singles: 7-Inch

SOURCE: *79*	1-3

LPs: 10/12-Inch 33rpm

SOURCE: *79*	5-8

OPUS 10

Singles: 7-Inch

PANDISC: *85*	1-3

ORBISON, Roy
(Roy Orbison & The Teen Kings; Roy Orbison & The Candymen; Roy Orbison & The Roses)

Singles: 78rpm

SUN: *56-57*	8-15

Singles: 7-Inch

ASYLUM: *78 79*	2-4
COLLECTABLES: *85*	1-3
MGM: *65-73*	4-8
MGM CELEBRITY SCENE (CSN9 5; "Roy Orbison"): *66*	30-40

(Boxed set of five singles, bio insert & title strips. Jukebox issue only.)

MERCURY: *74*	2-3
MONUMENT (409; "Paper Boy"): *59*	10-20
MONUMENT (412; "Uptown"): *59*	10-15
MONUMENT (421 through 467): *60-62*	6-12
MONUMENT (800 & 900 series): *63-66*	4-8
MONUMENT (500 series): *63*	2-4
MONUMENT (8600 series): *76*	2-3
MONUMENT (8900 series): *72*	2-4
MONUMENT (45000 series): *76-77*	2-4
RCA VICTOR: *58-59*	10-20
SSS/SUN:	1-3
SUN (200 series): *56-58*	10-20
SUN (300 series): *61*	5-10
VIRGIN: *87*	1-3

Picture Sleeves

MGM: *65-67*	5-10
MONUMENT (400 series): *60-62*	10-20

MONUMENT (800 series): *63-64*	$10-15

EPs: 7-Inch 33/45rpm

MONUMENT (2; "Crying"): *62*	20-30

(Compact 33, "Special Promotional Six-Pac.")

STARS INC. (101; "Roy Orbison & The Teen Kings"): *59*	300-400

(Promotional issue, distributed to fan club members.)

LPs: 10/12-Inch 33rpm

ACCORD: *81*	5-8
ASYLUM: *78-79*	5-8
BUCKBOARD:	8-10
CANDLELITE MUSIC:	10-15
DESIGN:	10-15
HALLMARK:	10-12
MGM (4308 through 4514): *65-67*	15-20
MGM (4636 through 4934): *69-73*	10-15
MERCURY: *75*	8-10
MONUMENT (4002; "Lonely & Blue"): *61*	30-40

(Monaural.)

MONUMENT (14002; "Lonely & Blue"): *61*	45-60

(Stereo.)

MONUMENT (4007; "Crying"): *62*	30-35

(Monaural.)

MONUMENT (14007; "Crying"): *62*	45-50

(Stereo.)

MONUMENT (4009; "Greatest Hits"): *62*	25-30

(Monaural.)

MONUMENT (14009; "Greatest Hits"): *62*	35-40

(Stereo.)

MONUMENT (6600 series):	8-10
MONUMENT (7600; "Regeneration"): *76*	8-10
MONUMENT (8000; "Greatest Hits"): *63*	20-25

(Monaural.)

MONUMENT (18000; "Greatest Hits"): *63*	30-35

(Stereo. Apparently the number of this LP was changed when Monument switched from the 4000/14000 series to the 8000/18000 series. We're not positive that both a mono and a stereo exist for each series, but both are listed just in case.)

MONUMENT (8003; "In Dreams"): *63*	20-25

(Monaural.)

MONUMENT (18003; "In Dreams"): *63*	30-35

(Stereo.)

MONUMENT (8024; "More Greatest Hits"): *64*	20-25

(Monaural.)

MONUMENT (18024; "More Greatest Hits"): *64*	25-30

(Stereo.)

MONUMENT (8035; "Orbisongs"): *64* . **$15-20**
(Monaural.)
MONUMENT (18035; "Orbisongs"): *64* . **20-25**
(Stereo.)
Note: For the sake of continuity, the preceding
14000 & 18000 series stereo issues, requiring
separate pricing, are listed directly below their
4000 & 8000 series mono counterpart.
MONUMENT (8023/18023; "Early
Orbison"): *64* **20-25**
MONUMENT (8045/18045; "Very
Best"): *66* **15-20**
(Blue cover.)
MONUMENT (8045/18045; "Very
Best"): *66* **12-15**
(Purple cover.)
MONUMENT (38384; "All-Time
Greatest Hits"): *82* **8-10**
SPECTRUM: **15-20**
SSS/SUN: *69* **5-8**
SUN (1260; "Rock House"): *61* **75-150**
SUNNYVALE: *77* **8-10**
TRIP: *74* **8-10**
  Also see CANDYMEN
  Also see DRIFTERS / Lesley Gore / Roy Or-
bison / Los Bravos
  Also see GOLDSBORO, Bobby
  Also see JAN & DEAN / Roy Orbison / 4
Seasons / Shirelles
  Also see LEWIS, Jerry Lee / Roger Miller /
Roy Orbison
  Also see PERKINS, Carl, Jerry Lee Lewis,
Roy Orbison & Johnny Cash
  Also see TEEN KINGS

ORBISON, Roy / Bobby Bare /
Joey Powers
  LPs: 10/12-Inch 33rpm
CAMDEN: *64* **15-20**
  Also see BARE, Bobby
  Also see POWERS, Joey

ORBISON, Roy, & Emmylou
Harris / Craig Hundley
  Singles: 7-Inch
WARNER BROS: *80* **1-3**
  Also see HARRIS, Emmylou
  Also see ORBISON, Roy

ORBIT
  Singles: 12-Inch 33/45rpm
QUALITY/RFC: *82-84* **4-6**
  Singles: 7-Inch
QUALITY/RFC: *82-84* **1-3**
  Member: Carol Hall.

ORCHESTRAL MANOEUVRES IN
THE DARK
(OMD)
  Singles: 12-Inch 33/45rpm
A&M: *85-86* **$4-6**
  Singles: 7-Inch
A&M: *84-88* **1-3**
EPIC: *82-83* **1-3**
  LPs: 10/12-Inch 33rpm
A&M: *84-88* **5-8**
EPIC: *82-83* **5-8**

ORIGINAL ANIMALS: see ANIMALS

ORIGINAL CADILLACS
  Singles: 7-Inch
JOSIE: *57-58* **10-15**
  Members: Earl Carroll; Earl Wade; Charles
Brooks; Bobby Phillips; Junior Glanton; Roland
Martinez.
  Also see CADILLACS

ORIGINAL CAST
(Featuring Kacey Cisyk)
  Singles: 7-Inch
ARISTA: *77* **2-3**

ORIGINAL CASTE
(Featuring Dixie Lee Innes)
  Singles: 7-Inch
DOT: *68* **3-5**
T-A: *69-70* **2-4**
  LPs: 10/12-Inch 33rpm
T-A: *70* **10-12**

ORIGINAL CASUALS
(Featuring Gary Mears)
  Singles: 7-Inch
BACK BEAT: *58* **8-10**
  EPs: 7-Inch 33/45rpm
BACK BEAT: *58* **35-50**

ORIGINALS
  Singles: 7-Inch
MOTOWN: *75* **2-3**
PHASE II: *81* **1-3**
SOUL (35029 through 35061): *67-69* **3-5**
SOUL (35066 through 35119): *69-76* **2-3**
  LPs: 10/12-Inch 33rpm
FANTASY: *78-79* **5-8**
MOTOWN: *74-80* **5-8**
SOUL: *69-76* **8-12**
  Members: Ty Hunter; Henry Dixon; Joe Stubbs;
Walt Gaines; C.P. Spencer; Freddie Gorman.
  Also see HUNTER, Ty
  Also see VOICE MASTERS

ORIOLES
(Sonny Til & The Orioles)
Singles: 78rpm

IT'S A NATURAL: *48* $40-60
JUBILEE (5000; "It's Too Soon
  To Know"): *48* 15-25
JUBILEE (5001; "Dare To Dream"): *48* . . 15-20
JUBILEE (5001; "Lonely Christmas"): *48* 15-20
JUBILEE (5002; "Please Give My
  Heart A Break"): *49* 15-20
JUBILEE (5005; "Tell Me So"): *49* 15-20
JUBILEE (5008; "I Challenge
  Your Kiss"): *49* 15-20
JUBILEE (5009; "A Kiss & A Rose"): *49* 15-20
JUBILEE (5016; "So Much"): *49* 15-20
JUBILEE (5017; "What Are You
  Doing New Year's Eve?"): *49* 15-20
JUBILEE (5018; "Would You Still
  Be The One In My Heart?"): *50* 15-20
JUBILEE (5025; "At Night"): *50* 15-20
JUBILEE (5026; "Moonlight"): *50* 15-20
JUBILEE (5028; "You're Gone"): *50* 15-20
JUBILEE (5031; "I'd Rather Have You
  Under The Moon"): *50* 15-20
JUBILEE (5037; "I Need You So"): *50* . . 35-40
JUBILEE (5040; "I Cross My
  Fingers"): *50* 15-20
JUBILEE (5045; "Oh Holy Night"): *50* . . 15-20
JUBILEE (5057; "Would I
  Love You"): *51* 15-20
Note: At least ten of thes above 78rpm singles were
reissued around 1951 on 45s. It's likely that others
in the 5001-5061 series appeared on early fifties
Jubilee 45s, but those listed below are the only
ones we can verify.

JUBILEE (5061 through 5231): *51-56* 8-15
Singles: 7-Inch
ABNER: *58* 10-12
CHARLIE PARKER: *62-63* 3-5
COLLECTABLES: 1-3
JUBILEE (5000; "It's Too Soon
  To Know"): *51* 325-400
JUBILEE (5005; "Tell Me So"): *51* . . . 325-400
JUBILEE (5016; "So Much"): *51* 300-350
JUBILEE (5017; "What Are You
  Doing New Year's Eve?"): *51* 175-250
JUBILEE (5025; "At Night"): *51* 200-250
JUBILEE (5040; "I Cross My
  Fingers"): *51* 200-250
JUBILEE (5045; "Oh Holy Night"): *51* 150-200
JUBILEE (5051; "I Miss You So"): *51* . 175-200
  (Black vinyl.)
JUBILEE (5051; "I Miss You So"): *51* . 325-450
  (Colored vinyl.)
JUBILEE (5055; "Pal Of Mine"): *51* . . 200-250

JUBILEE (5061; "I'm Just A Fool
  In Love"): *51* $200-250
JUBILEE (5065; "Baby, Please
  Don't Go"): *51* 175-225
  (Black vinyl.)
JUBILEE (5065; "Baby, Please
  Don't Go"): *51* 275-350
  (Colored vinyl.)
JUBILEE (5071; "When You're
  Not Around"): *51* 150-200
JUBILEE (5074; "Trust In Me"): *52* . . 150-200
JUBILEE (5082; "It's Over Because
  We're Through"): *52* 150-200
JUBILEE (5084; "Barfly"): *52* 125-150
JUBILEE (5092; "Don't Cry
  Baby"): *52* 125-150
  (Black vinyl.)
JUBILEE (5092; "Don't Cry
  Baby"): *52* 275-350
  (Colored vinyl.)
JUBILEE (5102; "You Belong
  To Me"): *52* 125-150
JUBILEE (5107; "I Miss You So"): *53* 150-175
  (Reissued in 1963, using the same catalog number,
  and shown as by "Sonny Til & The Orioles." Black
  vinyl.)
JUBILEE (5107; "I Miss You So"): *53* 300-350
  (Colored vinyl.)
JUBILEE (5108; "Teardrops On
  My Pillow"): *53* 75-100
  (Black vinyl.)
JUBILEE (5108; "Teardrops On
  My Pillow"): *53* 200-250
  (Colored vinyl.)
JUBILEE (5115; "Bad Little Girl"): *53* . . 60-75
JUBILEE (5120; "I Cover The
  Waterfront"): *53* 75-100
  (Black vinyl.)
JUBILEE (5120; "I Cover The
  Waterfront"): *53* 175-225
  (Colored vinyl.)
JUBILEE (5122; "Crying In The
  Chapel"): *53* 20-25
JUBILEE (5127; "In The Mission Of
  St. Augustine"): *53* 15-20
JUBILEE (5134; "There's No
  One But You"): *54* 30-35
JUBILEE (5137; "Secret Love"): *54* 15-20
JUBILEE (5143; "Maybe You'll
  Be There"): *54* 20-25
JUBILEE (5154; "In The Chapel In
  The Moonlight"): *54* 20-25
JUBILEE (5161; "If You Believe"): *54* . . 20-25
JUBILEE (5172; "Runaround"): *54* 20-25

JUBILEE (5177; "I Love You
  Mostly"): 55 . . . . $20-25
JUBILEE (5189; "I Need You
  Baby"): 55 20-25
JUBILEE (5221; "Please Sing My
  Blues Tonight"): 55 20-25
JUBILEE (5231; "Angel"): 56 15-20
JUBILEE (5300 series): 59 4-6
  Note: There are probably other Jubilee colored
  vinyl issues, but those noted here are the only ones
  we've verified. Also, some Jubilee tracks were reis-
  sued, shown as by "Sonny Til & The Orioles," and
  are found in the "Til" section of this guide.
VEE JAY (Except 244): 56 15-25
VEE JAY (244; "Sugar Girl"): 57 30-35
  Picture Sleeves
JUBILEE (5017; "What Are You Doing
  New Year's Eve?"): 54 100-150
  (Sleeve for 78rpm single.)
JUBILEE (5017; "What Are You Doing
  New Year's Eve?"): 54 200-300
  (Sleeve for 45rpm single.)
JUBILEE (5045; "Oh Holy Night"): 54 200-300
  (Both Jubilee sleeves were issued in late 1954 and
  were sold with 1954 pressings of the discs, which
  would actually be second pressings of the two
  singles. These were blue script Jubilee labels with
  the line under the logo.)
LANA: 63 2-4
  EPs: 7-Inch 33/45rpm
JUBILEE (5000; "The Orioles
  Sing"): 400-600
  LPs: 10/12-Inch 33rpm
BIG A RECORDS: 69 15-25
CHARLIE PARKER: 62 25-35
COLLECTABLES: 84 6-8
MURRAY HILL: 30-35
  (5-LP set.)
ROULETTE: 5-8

Members: Sonny Til; Alex Sharp; George Nelson;
John Reed; Tom Gaither; Charles Harris; Greg Car-
roll; Billy Adams; Jerry Holman; Al Russell; Jerry
Rodriguez; Bill Taylor.
Also see CADILLACS / Orioles
Also see TIL, Sonny

ORION THE HUNTER
Singles: 7-Inch
PORTRAIT: 84-85 . . . . $1-3
LPs: 10/12-Inch 33rpm
PORTRAIT: 84 5-8
Member: Barry Goudreau.
Also see BOSTON

ORLANDO, Tony
Singles: 12-Inch 33/45rpm
CASABLANCA: 79 4-6
Singles: 7-Inch
ATCO: 65 3-6
CAMEO: 67 3-6
CASABLANCA: 79-80 2-3
EPIC (9000 series): 61-64 3-6
Promotional Singles
EPIC (55299; "Happy Times Are
  Here To Stay"): 61 8-10
LPs: 10/12-Inch 33rpm
EPIC (611; "Bless You"): 61 35-40
EPIC (33785; "Before Dawn"): 75 10-12
CASABLANCA: 79-80 5-8
Picture Sleeves
EPIC: 61-62 4-8
Also see SHIELDS, Billy
Also see SIMON, Paul
Also see WIND

ORLANDO, Tony, & Dawn
Singles: 7-Inch
ARISTA: 75 2-3
BELL: 71-74 2-4
ELEKTRA: 75-78 2-3
LPs: 10/12-Inch 33rpm
ARISTA: 75-76 6-10
ASYLUM: 75 6-10
BELL (6000 series): 70-71 10-12
BELL (1000 series): 73-75 8-10
ELEKTRA: 75-78 6-10
KORY: 74-77 8-10
Also see DAWN
Also see ORLANDO, Tony

ORLEANS
Singles: 7-Inch
ASYLUM: 75-77 2-3
INFINITY: 79 1-3
MCA: 86 1-3

LPs: 10/12-Inch 33rpm

ABC: *73-78* $10-12
ASYLUM: *75-76* 6-10
INFINITY: *79* 5-8
RADIO: *82* 5-8
Member: John Hall.
Also see HALL, John

ORLONS

Singles: 7-Inch

ABC: *67* 3-5
CALLA: *66* 3-5
CAMEO (198; "I'll Be True"): *61* 5-8
CAMEO (211; "Mr. 21"): *62* 5-8
CAMEO (218 through 384): *62-65* 3-5
Picture Sleeves
CAMEO: *62-64* 4-8
LPs: 10/12-Inch 33rpm
CAMEO: *62-63* 30-60
Members: Shirley Brickley; Rosetta Hightower;
Steve Caldwell; Marlena Davis.

ORLONS / Dovells

LPs: 10/12-Inch 33rpm

CAMEO: *63* 20-25
Also see DOVELLS
Also see ORLONS

ORPHEUS

Singles: 7-Inch

MGM: *68-69* 2-4
LPs: 10/12-Inch 33rpm
BELL: *71* 10-12
MGM: *68-69* 10-12

ORRALL, Robert Ellis
(Robert Ellis Orrall & Carlene Carter)
Singles: 7-Inch

RCA VICTOR: *81-83* 1-3
LPs: 10/12-Inch 33rpm
RCA VICTOR: *81-83* 5-8
Also see CARTER, Carlene

OSAMU

LPs: 10/12-Inch 33rpm

A&M: *88* 5-8

OSBORNE, Jeffrey
Singles: 12-Inch 33/45rpm

A&M: *82-86* 4-6
Singles: 7-Inch
A&M: *82-88* 1-3
LPs: 10/12-Inch 33rpm
A&M: *82-88* 5-8
Also see KENNEDY, Joyce, & Jeffrey Os-
borne
Also see L.T.D.

OSBORNE & GILES
LPs: 10/12-Inch 33rpm

RED LABEL: *85* $5-8
Members: Billy Osborne; A. Z. Giles.

OSBORNE BROTHERS
(Osborne Brothers & Red Allen)
Singles: 7-Inch

CMH: *80* 1-3
DECCA: *63-72* 2-4
MCA: *73-75* 1-3
MGM (100 series): *64* 2-3
MGM (12000 & 13000 series): *59-63* 3-5
EPs: 7-Inch 33/45rpm
MGM: *59* 8-15
LPs: 10/12-Inch 33rpm
CMH: *76-82* 5-10
CORAL: *73* 4-8
DECCA: *65-72* 8-18
MCA: *73-75* 5-8
MGM (100 series): *70* 5-10
MGM (3700 series): *59* 20-30
MGM (4000 series): *62-63* 10-20
ROUNDER: 5-8
SUGAR HILL: *84* 5-8
Members: Bobby Osborne; Sonny Osborne.

OSBOURNE, Ozzy
Singles: 7-Inch

CBS ASSOCIATED: *83-86* 1-3
JET: *82* 1-3
LPs: 10/12-Inch 33rpm
CBS ASSOCIATED: *83-88* 5-8
JET: *81-82* 5-8
Also see BLACK SABBATH
Also see MAGIC LANTERNS

OSBOURNE, Ozzy, & Randy Rhoads
LPs: 10/12-Inch 33rpm

CBS ASSOC: *87* 5-8
Also see OSBOURNE, Ozzy

OSIBISA
Singles: 7-Inch

DECCA: *72* 2-4
ISLAND: *76-77* 2-3
MCA: 1-3
WARNER BROS: *73-74* 2-4
LPs: 10/12-Inch 33rpm
BUDDAH: *73* 8-10
DECCA: *71-72* 10-12
ISLAND: *77* 8-10
MCA: 5-8
WARNER BROS: *73-74* 8-10

OSIRIS
Singles: 7-Inch

INFINITY: *79* 1-3

WARNER BROS: 79 .... $1-3
  LPs: 10/12-Inch 33rpm
INFINITY: 79 5-8
WARNER BROS: 79 5-8

OSKAR, Lee
  Singles: 7-Inch
ELEKTRA: 78-81 1-3
UNITED ARTISTS: 76 2-3
  LPs: 10/12-Inch 33rpm
ELEKTRA: 78-79 5-8
UNITED ARTISTS: 76 8-10
  Also see WAR

OSMOND, Donny
  Singles: 7-Inch
MGM: 71-75 2-3
POLYDOR: 76-78 1-3
  Picture Sleeves
MGM: 71-75 2-3
  LPs: 10/12-Inch 33rpm
MGM: 71-74 8-10
POLYDOR: 77 5-8
  Also see OSMONDS

OSMOND, Donny & Marie
  Singles: 7-Inch
MGM: 74-75 2-3
POLYDOR: 76-78 1-3
  LPs: 10/12-Inch 33rpm
MGM: 74-75 8-10
POLYDOR: 76-78 5-8
  Also see OSMOND, Donny
  Also see OSMOND, Marie

OSMOND, Jimmy
(Little Jimmy Osmond)
  Singles: 7-Inch
MGM: 70-75 2-3
MERCURY: 78 1-3
  LPs: 10/12-Inch 33rpm
MGM: 72 8-10
  Also see OSMONDS

OSMOND, Marie
  Singles: 7-Inch
CAPITOL: 85-88 1-3
ELEKTRA: 82-84 1-3
MGM: 73-75 2-3
POLYDOR: 76-78 1-3
RCA VICTOR: 84 1-3
  Picture Sleeves
MGM: 73-75 2-3
POLYDOR: 77 1-3
RCA VICTOR: 84 1-3
  LPs: 10/12-Inch 33rpm
CAPITOL: 85-88 5-8
MGM: 74-75 8-10

POLYDOR: 77 .... $5-8
  Also see OSMOND, Donny & Marie
  Also see OSMONDS
  Also see SEALS, Dan, & Marie Osmond

OSMOND, Marie, & Paul Davis
  Singles: 7-Inch
CAPITOL: 86-88 1-3
  Also see DAVIS, Paul
  Also see OSMOND, Marie

OSMONDS
(Osmond Brothers)
  Singles: 7-Inch
BARNABY: 68-69 3-5
EMI AMERICA: 85-86 1-3
ELEKTRA: 82-83 1-3
MGM (13126 through 14159): 63-70 3-5
MGM (14193 through 14831): 70-75 2-3
MERCURY: 79 1-3
POLYDOR: 76-77 1-3
UNI (55015; "I Can't Stop"): 67 4-6
UNI (55276; "I Can't Stop"): 71 2-4
WARNER BROS/CURB: 83-85 1-3
  Picture Sleeves
MGM: 73-74 2-3
  LPs: 10/12-Inch 33rpm
EMI AMERICA: 86 5-8
ELEKTRA: 82 5-8
MGM (7; "Preview: The Osmond
  Brothers"): 12-15
  (Promotional issue only.)
MGM (4100 & 4200 series): 63-65 10-20
MGM (4724 through 5012): 70-75 8-10
MERCURY: 79 5-8
METRO: 65 10-15
POLYDOR: 76-77 5-8
WARNER BROS/CURB: 83-85 5-8
  Members: Donny Osmond; Alan Osmond; Merrill
  Osmond; Wayne Osmond; Jimmy Osmond; Marie
  Osmond.
  Also see OSMOND, Donny
  Also see OSMOND, Jimmy
  Also see OSMOND, Marie

**OSMONDS, Steve Lawrence &
Eydie Gorme**
  Singles: 7-Inch
MGM: 72 2-3
  Also see LAWRENCE, Steve, & Eydie Gorme
  Also see OSMONDS

O'SULLIVAN, Gilbert
  Singles: 7-Inch
EPIC: 77-81 1-3
MAM: 71-76 2-3

Picture Sleeves
MAM: 72 .... $2-4
LPs: 10/12-Inch 33rpm
EPIC: 81 5-8
MAM: 72 10-12

OTIS, Johnny
(Johnny Otis Show; Johnny Otis & The
Peacocks; Johnny Otis Quintette)
Singles: 78rpm
CAPITOL: 57 5-10
DIG: 55-57 5-10
EXCELSIOR: 45-47 10-20
MERCURY: 51-53 6-12
PEACOCK (Except 1625): 52 5-10
PEACOCK (1625; "Young Girl"): 52 10-15
REGENT: 50-51 5-10
SAVOY: 50-54 5-10
Singles: 7-Inch
CAPITOL (3799-3802; "The Johnny
  Otis Show"): 57 250-350
  (Four discs with special four-pocket cover.)
CAPITOL (3799 through 3802): 57 5-8
  (Records without cover.)
CAPITOL (3852 through 4020): 58-60 4-6
  (Monaural.)
CAPITOL (4000 series): 59 10-15
  (Stereo.)
DIG: 55-59 10-20
ELDO (105; "The New Bo Diddley"): 60 ... 4-8
ELDO (153; "Long Distance"): 67 3-5
EPIC: 70 2-4
HAWK SOUND: 75 2-3
KENT: 69 2-4
KING: 61-63 3-5
MERCURY: 51-53 15-25
OKEH: 69 2-4
PEACOCK (Except 1625): 52 10-20
PEACOCK (1625; "Young Girl"): 52 25-35
SAVOY: 50-54 10-20
EPs: 7-Inch 33/45rpm
CAPITOL: 58-59 25-40
LPs: 10/12-Inch 33rpm
ALLIGATOR: 82 5-8
BLUES SPECTRUM: 10-12
CAPITOL: 58 50-75
DIG (104; "Rock & Roll
  Hit Parade"): 57 300-500
  (Yellow cover. Counterfeits exist, but can be easily
  identified by their gold cover.)
EPIC: 70-71 10-12
JAZZ WORLD: 78 5-10
KENT: 70 10-12
SAVOY: 78-80 5-8

Johnny Otis

Referenced below are some of the artists who per-
formed with the Johnny Otis Show, or with whom
he or his orchestra appeared.
Also see ADAMS, Marie
Also see FREEMAN, Ernie
Also see LITTLE ESTHER & THE ROBINS
Also see McNEELY, Big Jay
Also see WATSON, Johnny

OTIS, Johnny, & Preston Love
Singles: 7-Inch
KENT: 70 .... $2-4
Also see OTIS, Johnny
Also see OTIS, Shuggie, & Preston Love

OTIS, Shuggie
Singles: 7-Inch
EPIC: 70-74 2-4
LPs: 10/12-Inch 33rpm
EPIC: 70-74 10-12
Also see KOOPER, Al, & Shuggie Otis

OTIS, Shuggie, & Preston Love
Singles: 7-Inch
KENT: 70 2-4
Also see OTIS, Johnny, & Preston Love
Also see OTIS, Shuggie

OTIS & CARLA
Singles: 7-Inch
ATCO: 69 2-4
STAX: 67-68 3-5
LPs: 10/12-Inch 33rpm
STAX: 67 10-15
Members: Otis Redding; Carla Thomas.
Also see REDDING, Otis

Also see THOMAS, Carla

OUTLAWS
Singles: 7-Inch
ARISTA: *75-80* $1-3
LPs: 10/12-Inch 33rpm
ARISTA: *75-80* 5-8
Also see PAUL, Henry, Band

OUTLAWS
Singles: 7-Inch
PASHA: *86* 1-3
LPs: 10/12-Inch 33rpm
PASHA: *86* 5-8

OUTPUT
Singles: 12-Inch 33/45rpm
CBS ASSOCIATED: *83* 4-6
Singles: 7-Inch
CBS ASSOCIATED: *83* 1-3
TUFF CITY: *84* 1-3

OUTSIDERS
Singles: 7-Inch
BELL: *70* 3-5
CAPITOL: *66-68* 3-5
KAPP: *70* 3-5
Picture Sleeves
CAPITOL: *66-67* 4-8
LPs: 10/12-Inch 33rpm
CAPITOL: *66-67* 15-20
Members: Sonny Geraci; Bill Bruno; Tom King;
Rickey Baker; Merdin Madsen.
Also see CLIMAX

OVATIONS
(Ovation)
Singles: 7-Inch
CHESS: *75* 2-3
GOLDWAX: *64-69* 8-10
MGM: *73* 3-5
SOUNDS OF MEMPHIS: *72-73* 3-5
LPs: 10/12-Inch 33rpm
MGM: *73* 8-12
SOUNDS OF MEMPHIS: *72* 10-15
Member: Louis Williams.

OVERKILL
Singles: 7-Inch
SST: *86* 1-3
LPs: 10/12-Inch 33rpm
SST: *86* 5-8

OVERKILL
LPs: 10/12-Inch 33rpm
ATLANTIC: *86* 5-8

OVERLANDERS
Singles: 7-Inch
HICKORY: *64-66* 10-15

MERCURY: *63* $4-6

OVERTON, C.B.
Singles: 7-Inch
SHOCK: *78* 2-3

OVERTONES
LPs: 10/12-Inch 33rpm
TWIN/TONE: *88* 5-8

OWEN, B.
Singles: 7-Inch
JANUS: *70* 2-4

OWEN, Reg, & His Orchestra
Singles: 7-Inch
PALETTE: *58-62* 2-5
LPs: 10/12-Inch 33rpm
PALETTE: *59-60* 15-20

OWENS, Buck
(Buck Owens & The Buckaroos)
Singles: 78rpm
CAPITOL: *57* 5-10
Singles: 7-Inch
CAPITOL (2000 through 4000
series): *67-75* 2-3
(Orange label.)
CAPITOL (3824; "Come Back"): *57* 5-10
(Purple label.)
CAPITOL (3957; "Sweet Thing"): *58* 5-10
(Purple label.)
CAPITOL (4000 series): *59-63* 3-6
(Purple label.)
CAPITOL (5000 series): *63-67* 2-5
CAPITOL: *88* 1-3
HILLTOP: 20-30
NEW STAR: 50-75
PEP: *56-57* 10-20
STARDAY (500 series): *61* 3-5
STARDAY (5000 series): *64* 2-4
WARNER BROS (Except 8316): *76-80* 1-3
WARNER BROS (8316; "World
Famous Holiday Inn"): *77* 5-8
WARNER BROS (8316; "World
Famous Paradise Inn"): *77* 1-3
EPs: 7-Inch 33/45rpm
CAPITOL: *61-65* 10-20
LPs: 10/12-Inch 33rpm
CAPITOL (100 through 400 series): *68-70* .8-12
CAPITOL (500 series, except 574): *70* 8-10
CAPITOL (600 through 800 series): *70-72* .5-10
CAPITOL (574; "Buck Owens"): *70* 12-20
(3-LP set.)
CAPITOL (1400 through 1900
series): *61-63* 20-35
(With a "T" or "ST" prefix.)

LPs: 10/12-Inch 33rpm
CBS ASSOCIATED: *84* $5-8
UNCLE JAM: *84* 5-8

PG&E:
see PACIFIC GAS & ELECTRIC

PABLO CRUISE
Singles: 7-Inch
A&M: *75-84* 1-3
Picture Sleeves
A&M: *77-84* 1-3
LPs: 10/12-Inch 33rpm
A&M: *75-84* 6-10
MFSL: *79* 15-20
Members: Dave Jenkins; Steve Price; Cory Lerios; Bud Cockrell.
Also see IT'S A BEAUTIFUL DAY

PACIFIC GAS & ELECTRIC
(PG&E; Pacific Gas & Electric Blues Band)
Singles: 7-Inch
BRIGHT ORANGE: *68* 4-6
COLUMBIA: *69-72* 2-4
POWER: *69* 4-6
LPs: 10/12-Inch 33rpm
ABC: 8-10
BRIGHT ORANGE (701; "Get It
  On"): *68* 40-80
COLUMBIA: *69-73* 8-12
POWER: *69* 10-15
Also see SEEGER, Pete, & Pacific Gas & Electric

PACK, David
Singles: 7-Inch
WARNER BROS: *86* 1-3
Also see AMBROSIA
Also see MC DONALD, Michael

PACKERS
Singles: 7-Inch
HBR: *66* 3-5
IMPERIAL: *69* 2-4
PURE SOUL MUSIC: *65* 3-5
TANGERINE: *68* 2-4
LPs: 10/12-Inch 33rpm
IMPERIAL: *68* 10-12
PURE SOUL MUSIC: *66* 12-15

PAGAN, Bruni
Singles: 7-Inch
ELEKTRA: *79* 1-3

PAGAN, Ralfi
Singles: 7-Inch
FANIA: *71* 2-4

PAGE, Gene
Singles: 7-Inch
ARISTA: *78-80* $1-3
ATLANTIC: *74-75* 2-3
LPs: 10/12-Inch 33rpm
ARISTA: *78-80* 5-8
ATLANTIC: *74-75* 8-10

PAGE, Jimmy
LPs: 10/12-Inch 33rpm
SWAN SONG: *82* 5-8
Also see FIRM
Also see HERMAN'S HERMITS
Also see HONEYDRIPPERS
Also see LED ZEPPELIN
Also see LORD SUTCH
Also see STEWART, Al
Also see WILLIE & THE POOR BOYS
Also see YARDBIRDS

**PAGE, Jimmy, & Sonny Boy
Williamson**
LPs: 10/12-Inch 33rpm
SPRINGBOARD: *72* 8-10
Also see PAGE, Jimmy
Also see WILLIAMSON, Sonny Boy, & The
Yardbirds

PAGE, Patti
Singles: 78rpm
MERCURY: *48-58* 2-5
Singles: 7-Inch
AVCO: *74-75* 1-3
COLUMBIA: *63-70* 2-4

Patti Page

EPIC: 73 ....$1-3
MERCURY (5000 series): 50-52 4-8
MERCURY (70000 through 72000
  series): 52-63 3-5
MERCURY (73000 series): 71 2-4
PLANTATION: 81-82 1-3
      Picture Sleeves
MERCURY: 54-63 4-8
      EPs: 7-Inch 33/45rpm
MERCURY: 51-61 5-10
      LPs: 10/12-Inch 33rpm
ACCORD: 82........................4-8
CANDLELITE: 8-12
COLUMBIA: 63-70 5-15
EXACT: 80 5-8
HARMONY: 69-70 5-10
MERCURY (100 series): 69 6-12
MERCURY (20000 series): 55-64 10-25
MERCURY (25000 series): 50-54 15-30
  (10-Inch LPs.)
MERCURY (60000 series): 58-64 10-25
MERCURY (61000 series): 71 5-10
PLANTATION: 81 5-8
WING: 63-65 5-10
  Also see MARTIN, Dean / Patti Page

PAGE, Patti, & Tom T. Hall
      Singles: 7-Inch
MERCURY: 72 2-3
  Also see HALL, Tom T.
  Also see PAGE, Patti

PAGES
      Singles: 7-Inch
CAPITOL: 81 1-3
EPIC: 79-80 1-3
      LPs: 10/12-Inch 33rpm
CAPITOL: 81 5-8
EPIC: 78-79 5-8
  Members: Richard Page; Steve George; Russell
  Battelene; Jerry Manfredi; Peter Leinheiser.
  Also see MR. MISTER

PAIGE, Sharon
(Sharon Paige & Harold Melvin & The
Bluenotes)
      Singles: 7-Inch
PHILADELPHIA INT'L: 75 2-3
SOURCE: 80 1-3
  Also see MELVIN, Harold

PAINTER
      Singles: 7-Inch
ELEKTRA: 73 2-4
      LPs: 10/12-Inch 33rpm
ELEKTRA: 73 8-10

PALLAS, Laura
      Singles: 12-Inch 33/45rpm
TVI: 84 ....$4-6

PALM BEACH BAND BOYS
      Singles: 7-Inch
RCA VICTOR: 66-67 2-4
      LPs: 10/12-Inch 33rpm
RCA VICTOR: 66-67 5-10

PALMER, Robert
      Singles: 12-Inch 33/45rpm
ISLAND: 83-86 4-6
      Singles: 7-Inch
ISLAND: 75-86 1-3
      LPs: 10/12-Inch 33rpm
ISLAND (Except 819): 75-86 5-8
ISLAND (819; "Secrets"): 79 35-40
  (Picture disc. Promotional issue only.)
  Also see POWER STATION

PAMPLEMOUSSE, LE:
  see LE PAMPLEMOUSSE

PANIC BUTTON
      Singles: 7-Inch
CHALOM: 68 3-5
GAMBLE: 69 2-4

PAONE, Nicola
      Singles: 7-Inch
ABC-PARAMOUNT: 59 2-4
CADENCE: 59 2-4
      EPs: 7-Inch 33/45rpm
CADENCE: 59 4-8
      LPs: 10/12-Inch 33rpm
ABC-PARAMOUNT: 59-60 8-15
ROULETTE: 65 6-12

PAPER LACE
      Singles: 7-Inch
BANG: 72 2-4
MERCURY: 74-75 2-3
      LPs: 10/12-Inch 33rpm
MERCURY: 74 8-10

PARACHUTE CLUB
      Singles: 12-Inch 33/45rpm
RCA VICTOR: 83 4-6
      Singles: 7-Inch
RCA VICTOR: 83 1-3
      LPs: 10/12-Inch 33rpm
RCA VICTOR: 83 5-8

PARADE
      Singles: 7-Inch
A&M: 67-69 3-5
  Member: Jerry Riopelle.

PARADISE EXPRESS
Singles: 12-Inch 33/45rpm
FANTASY: *78-81* $4-6
Singles: 7-Inch
FANTASY: *78-81* 1-3
LPs: 10/12-Inch 33rpm
FANTASY: *78* 5-8

PARADONS
Singles: 7-Inch
COLLECTABLES: 1-3
ERA: *72* 1-3
MILESTONE: *60-61* 8-15
TUFFEST: 20-30
WARNER BROS: *60* 5-10
Members: Bill Myers; Chuck Weldon; Wes Tyler;
Bill Powers.

PARAGONS
Singles: 7-Inch
ABC: *73* 1-3
BUDDAH: *75* 2-4
COLLECTABLES: 1-3
MUSIC CLEF: *63* 4-6
MUSICRAFT: *60* 5-10
TAP: *62* 4-6
TIMES SQUARE: *63* 3-5
VIRGO: *72-73* 1-3
WINLEY (215; "Florence"): *57* 20-35
WINLEY (220; "Let's Start All
Over Again"): *57* 20-35
WINLEY (223 through 240): *57-60* 10-20
LPs: 10/12-Inch 33rpm
COLLECTABLES: *86* 6-8
LOST-NITE: *81* 5-8
RARE BIRD: 20-25
Members: Julius McMichaels; Mack Starr; Al
Brown; Don Travis; Ben Frazier; Bill Witt; Rick
Jackson.
Also see HARPTONES / Paragons
Also see OLYMPICS

PARAGONS / Jesters
LPs: 10/12-Inch 33rpm
JUBILEE : *59* 25-35
PAUL WINLEY PRODUCTIONS: *65* .. 20-25
WINLEY: *60* 50-75
Also see JESTERS
Also see PARAGONS

PARAMOR, Norrie, & His Orchestra
Singles: 78rpm
ESSEX: *53* 2-4
Singles: 7-Inch
ESSEX: *53* 2-4
EPs: 7-Inch 33/45rpm
CAPITOL: *56* 4-8

LPs: 10/12-Inch 33rpm
CAPITOL: *55-66* $5-15
ESSEX: *54* 8-15
HAYNES & SBARRA: *79* 4-8

PARAMOURS
Singles: 7-Inch
MOONGLOW (Black vinyl): *62* 10-15
MOONGLOW (Colored vinyl): *62* 20-30
SMASH: *61* 10-15
Members: Bill Medley; Bobby Hatfield.
Also see RIGHTEOUS BROTHERS

PARIS
Singles: 7-Inch
CAPITOL: *76* 2-3
LPs: 10/12-Inch 33rpm
CAPITOL: *76* 8-10
Members: Bob Welch; Glen Cornick; Bernie
Marsden; Thom Mooney.
Also see WELCH, Bob

PARIS SISTERS
Singles: 7-Inch
ABC: *73* 1-3
CAPITOL: *68* 3-5
COLLECTABLES: 1-3
DECCA: *54-58* 5-8
ERIC: 1-3
GNP/CRESCENDO: *68* 3-5
GREGMARK: *61-62* 4-6
IMPERIAL: *57-58* 5-8
MGM: *64* 3-5
MERCURY: *64-65* 3-5
REPRISE: *66-67* 3-5
Picture Sleeves
MGM: *64* 10-20
MERCURY: *64* 5-10
LPs: 10/12-Inch 33rpm
REPRISE: *67* 15-20
SIDEWALK: 12-15
UNIFILMS: 10-12
Members: Priscilla Paris; Sherrell Paris; Albeth
Paris.
Also see ALLAN, Davie

PARKAYS
Singles: 7-Inch
ABC-PARAMOUNT: *61* 3-5
FONTANA: *65* 3-5

PARKER, Bobby
Singles: 7-Inch
AMANDA: *60* 4-6
V-TONE: *61* 3-5

PARKER, Fess
(Fess Parker & Buddy Ebsen)
Singles: 78rpm
COLUMBIA: 55 .... $2-5
DISNEYLAND: 57 2-5
Singles: 7-Inch
BUENA VISTA: 63 2-4
CASCADE: 59 3-5
COLUMBIA: 55 4-6
DISNEYLAND: 57 3-5
GUSTO: 63 3-5
RCA VICTOR: 64-69 2-4
Picture Sleeves
BUENA VISTA: 63 4-6
DISNEYLAND: 57 5-10
RCA VICTOR: 64 3-5
EPs: 7-Inch 33/45rpm
COLUMBIA: 55 5-15
LPs: 10/12-Inch 33rpm
COLUMBIA (666; "Davy Crockett") : 55 15-30
DISNEYLAND (1200 series): 64-65 5-12
DISNEYLAND (1300 series): 70 5-10
DISNEYLAND (1900 series): 63 5-15
DISNEYLAND (3000 series): 55 10-20
DISNEYLAND (3900 series): 64 5-12
HARMONY: 60 5-15
RCA VICTOR: 64 8-15

PARKER, Graham
(Graham Parker & Rumour; Graham Parker & The Shot)
Singles: 7-Inch
ARISTA: 79-83 1-3
MERCURY (Black vinyl): 76-77 2-3
MERCURY (Colored vinyl): 77 2-4
Picture Sleeves
ARISTA: 80-83 1-3
LPs: 10/12-Inch 33rpm
ARISTA: 78-83 5-8
ELEKTRA: 85 5-8
MERCURY: 77-78 6-10
Promotional LPs
ARISTA (41; "Mercury Poisoning"): 78 .. 25-35
ARISTA (63; "Live Sparks"): 79 25-35
Also see RUMOUR
Also see SPRINGSTEEN, Bruce

PARKER, Little Junior
(Junior Parker; Little Junior & His Blue Flames; Little Junior Parker & The Blue Blowers)
Singles: 78rpm
DUKE: 54-58 4-8
MODERN: 52 5-10
Singles: 7-Inch
ABC: 73 2-3

BLUE ROCK: 68-69 .... $2-4
CAPITOL: 71 2-4
DUKE (100 series): 54-58 8-12
DUKE (300 series): 59-66 3-6
DUKE (400 series): 67 2-4
MCA. 1-3
MERCURY: 66-68 3-5
MINIT: 69 2-4
LPs: 10/12-Inch 33rpm
ABC: 76 8-10
BLUE ROCK: 69 10-12
BLUESWAY: 73 8-10
CAPITOL: 70 10-12
DUKE (76; "Driving Wheel"): 62 50-100
DUKE (83; "Best Of Junior Parker"): 74 .. 8-10
MCA: 5-8
MERCURY: 67 12-15
MINIT: 69 10-12
Also see BLAND, Bobby / Little Junior Parker
Also see LITTLE JUNIOR'S BLUE FLAMES

PARKER, Little Junior, With Bill Johnson's Blue Flames
Singles: 78rpm
DUKE: 54 5-10
Singles: 7-Inch
DUKE: 54 15-20

PARKER, Little Junior, & Jimmy McGriff
LPs: 10/12-Inch 33rpm
CAPITOL: 71 10-12
UNITED ARTISTS: 71 10-12
Also see MC GRIFF, Jimmy
Also see PARKER, Little Junior

PARKER, Little Willie, & Lorenzo Smith
Singles: 7-Inch
MAR-VEL: 64 3-5
Also see PARKER, Little Junior

PARKER, Paul
Singles: 12-Inch 33/45rpm
MEGATONE: 83 4-6

PARKER, Ray, Jr.
(Ray Parker Jr. & Raydio)
Singles: 12-Inch 33/45rpm
ARISTA: 84-85 4-6
Singles: 7-Inch
ARISTA (Except 1035): 80-85 1-3
ARISTA (1035; "Christmas Time Is Here"): 82 2-4
(Promotional issue only.)
FLASHBACK: 82 1-3
GEFFEN: 87 1-3

Picture Sleeves

ARISTA (Except 1035): *80-85* $1-3
ARISTA (1035; "Christmas Time
Is Here"): *82* 2-4
(Promotional issue only.)
LPs: 10/12-Inch 33rpm
ARISTA: *80-85* 5-8
GEFFEN: *87* 5-8
Members: J.D. Nicholas; Arnell Carmichael; Jack
Ashford; Ollie Brown.
Also see RAYDIO

PARKER, Robert
Singles: 7-Inch
HEAD: *72* 1-3
IMPERIAL: *62* 4-6
ISLAND: *75-76* 2-3
NOLA: *66-67* 3-5
RON: *59-60* 5-8
SILVER FOX: *69* 2-4
LPs: 10/12-Inch 33rpm
NOLA: *66* 15-20
Also see BO, Eddie

PARKER, Winfield
Singles: 7-Inch
ARCTIC: *69* 2-4
GSP: *72* 2-3
RU-JAC: *68* 3-5
SPRING: *71* 2-4

PARKING METER
Singles: 12-Inch 33/45rpm
ATLANTIC: *84* 4-6
Singles: 7-Inch
ATLANTIC: *84* 1-3

PARKS, Michael
Singles: 7-Inch
MGM: *70* 2-4
LPs: 10/12-Inch 33rpm
MGM: *69-70* 10-12
VERVE: *71* 8-10

PARLET
Singles: 7-Inch
CASABLANCA: *78-80* 1-3
LPs: 10/12-Inch 33rpm
CASABLANCA: *79* 5-8

PARLET & Jeanette Washington
Singles: 7-Inch
CASABLANCA: *80* 1-3
Also see WASHINGTON, Baby

PARLIAMENT
(Parliament Thang)
Singles: 12-Inch 33/45rpm
CASABLANCA: *78* 4-6

Singles: 7-Inch
CASABLANCA: *74-81* $1-3
INVICTUS: *70-71* 2-3
SOULTOWN: 2-4
LPs: 10/12-Inch 33rpm
CASABLANCA (Except picture
discs): *74-80* 5-8
CASABLANCA (Picture discs): *79* 10-15
INVICTUS: *70* 8-10
Also see BOOTSY'S RUBBER BAND
Also see BRIDES OF FUNKENSTEIN
Also see PARLIAMENTS

PARLIAMENTS
Singles: 7-Inch
ATCO: *69* 2-4
REVILOT: *67-68* 3-5
Also see CLINTON, George
Also see FUNKADELIC
Also see PARLIAMENT

PARR, John
Singles: 12-Inch 33/45rpm
ATLANTIC: *86* 4-6
Singles: 7-Inch
ATLANTIC: *84-86* 1-3
LPs: 10/12-Inch 33rpm
ATLANTIC: *86* 5-8

PARRIS, Fred
**(Fred Parris & The Satins; Fred Parris & The
Scarlets; Fred Parris & Black Satin; Fred Parris
& The Restless Hearts; Fred Paris)**
Singles: 7-Inch
ATCO: *66* 4-6
BIRTH: 3-5
BUDDAH: *75* 2-4
CANDLELITE: *63* 5-8
CHECKER: *65* 4-6
ELEKTRA: *82* 1-3
GREEN SEA: *66* 4-6
KLIK: *58* 30-35
MAMA SADIE: *67* 4-6
RCA VICTOR (9200 series): *67* 3-5
(In 1968, another Freddie Paris—note different
spelling— recorded for RCA. He had a 9300 series
single and an LP.)
LPs: 10/12-Inch 33rpm
BUDDAH: *75* 30-50
ELEKTRA: *82* 8-10
Also see FIVE SATINS

PARRISH, Dean
(Dean Parish)
Singles: 7-Inch
BOOM: *66* 3-5
LAURIE: *67* 3-5
MUSICOR: *65* 3-6

PARRISH, Man
Singles: 7-Inch
SUGAR SCOOP: 85 .... $1-3
LPs: 10/12-Inch 33rpm
IMPORTE: 83 5-8

PARSONS, Alan, Project
Singles: 7-Inch
ARISTA: 77-86 1-3
20TH CENTURY-FOX: 76 2-4
LPs: 10/12-Inch 33rpm
ARISTA: 77-87 5-8
20TH CENTURY-FOX: 76-77 8-10
MFSL (084; "I Robot"): 82 25-50
MFSL/UHQR (084; "I Robot"): 82 75-100
(Boxed set.)
MFSL (175; "Best Of The Alan
  Parsons Project): 85 15-25
Members: Alan Parsons; David Patton; Stuart
Tosh; Eric Woolfson; Lenny Zakatek; Ian
Bairnson; B.J. Cole; Stuart Elliott; Colin
Blunstone; Allan Clarke.
Also see PILOT

PARSONS, Bill
(Bobby Bare)
Singles: 7-Inch
ABC: 73 1-3
COLLECTABLES. 1-3
FRATERNITY (835; "The All
  American Boy"): 58 8-10
FRATERNITY (838; "Educated
  Rock & Roll"): 59 5-10
Also see BARE, Bobby

PARSONS, Bill
Singles: 7-Inch
STARDAY (Except 526): 61 3-6
STARDAY (526; "Hot Rod
  Volkswagen"): 60 10-15

PARSONS, Gram
(Gram Parsons & The Fallen Angels)
Singles: 7-Inch
REPRISE: 73 2-5
SIERRA: 79 2-3
EPs: 7-Inch 33/45rpm
SIERRA: 82 8-10
(Promotional issue only.)
LPs: 10/12-Inch 33rpm
REPRISE: 73 8-10
SHILOH: 73 8-12
SIERRA: 79-82 5-8
Also see BYRDS
Also see FLYING BURRITO BROTHERS
Also see HARRIS, Emmylou

PARTLAND BROTHERS
Singles: 7-Inch
MANHATTAN: 87 .... $1-3
LPs: 10/12-Inch 33rpm
MANHATTAN: 87 5-8

PARTON, Dolly
Singles: 12-Inch 33/45rpm
RCA VICTOR (Black vinyl): 78-83 4-6
RCA VICTOR (Colored vinyl): 78 8-10
Singles: 7-Inch
COLUMBIA: 87 1-3
GOLDBAND (1000 series): 59 10-20
MERCURY (71000 series): 62 5-10
MONUMENT (800 through 1000
  series): 65-68 3-5
RCA VICTOR (0100 & 0200
  series): 69-76 2-4
RCA VICTOR (5000 series): 86 1-3
RCA VICTOR (9500 through 9900
  series): 68-71 2-4
RCA VICTOR (10000 through
  14000 series): 74-87 1-3
Promotional Singles
RCA VICTOR (Colored vinyl): 77-85 3-5
Picture Sleeves
RCA VICTOR: 69-85 1-3
LPs: 10/12-Inch 33rpm
ALSHIRE: 69-71 8-10
CAMDEN: 72-78 5-10
COLUMBIA: 87 5-8
MONUMENT (7600 series): 78 5-8
MONUMENT (8085; "Hello, I'm
  Dolly"): 67 12-20
MONUMENT (18000 series): 67 10-20
MONUMENT (18100 series): 70 8-12
MONUMENT (31000 series): 72 8-15
MONUMENT (33000 series): 75 6-10
RCA VICTOR (0033 through 5000
  series): 73-87 5-12
(With an "AFL1," "AHL1," "APD1," "APL1," or
"AYL1" prefix.)
RCA VICTOR (3413; "Great Balls
  Of Fire"): 79 12-18
(Picture disc. With a "CPL1" prefix.)
RCA VICTOR (3900 through 4700
  series): 68-72 8-15
(With an "LPM" or "LSP" prefix.)
RCA VICTOR (4422; "Greatest
  Hits"): 82 25-50
(Without *Islands in the Stream*.)
RCA VICTOR (4422; "Greatest
  Hits"): 82 5-8
(With *Islands in the Stream*.)
RCA VICTOR (5000 series): 84 5-8

SOMERSET: *63-68* $10-20
STEREO-FIDELITY: *63-68* 10-20
TIME-LIFE: *81* 5-8
  Also see HARRIS, Emmylou
  Also see NELSON, Willie, & Dolly Parton
  Also see PHILLIPS, Bill, & Dolly Parton
  Also see ROGERS, Kenny, & Dolly Parton
  Also see WAGONER, Porter, & Dolly Parton

PARTON, Dolly / George Jones
LPs: 10/12-Inch 33rpm
STARDAY: *68* 25-35
  Also see JONES, George

PARTON, Dolly, Linda Ronstadt & Emmylou Harris
LPs: 10/12-Inch 33rpm
WARNER BROS: *87* 5-8
  Also see HARRIS, Emmylou
  Also see RONSTADT, Linda

PARTON, Dolly / Kitty Wells
LPs: 10/12-Inch 33rpm
EXACT: *80* 5-8
  Also see PARTON, Dolly
  Also see WELLS, Kitty

PARTRIDGE FAMILY
(Featuring David Cassidy)
Singles: 7-Inch
BELL: *70-73* 2-4
Picture Sleeves
BELL: *70-73* 2-5
LPs: 10/12-Inch 33rpm
BELL: *70-74* 8-10
  Also see CASSIDY, David

PASSIONS
Singles: 7-Inch
ABC-PARAMOUNT: *63* 8-10
AUDICON: *59-61* 12-20
COLLECTABLES: 1-3
DIAMOND: *63* 5-8
DORE: *58* 8-12
JUBILEE: *61* 8-12
LAURIE: 1-3
OCTAVIA: *62* 30-35
  Members: Jim Gallagher; Tony Armato; Al Galione; Vince Acerno; Louis Rotondo.
  Also see MYSTICS / Passions

PASSPORT
Singles: 7-Inch
ATCO: *76* 2-3
ATLANTIC: *78* 2-3
LPs: 10/12-Inch 33rpm
ATCO: *74-77* 8-10
ATLANTIC: *78-82* 5-8

REPRISE: *72* $8-10

PASTEL SIX
Singles: 7-Inch
CHATTAHOOCHEE: *65* 3-5
DOWNEY: *62-63* 5-10
ERA: *72* 1-3
ZEN: *62* 4-6
ZENITH: *63* 4-6
LPs: 10/12-Inch 33rpm
ZEN: *62* 50-100
  Member: Sonny Patterson.

PASTELS
Singles: 7-Inch
ARGO: *58* 10-15
CADET: 2-4
CHESS: *73* 1-3
MASCOT: *57* 50-75
  Members: Big Dee Irwin; Richard Travis; Tony Thomas; J.B. Wellington.
  Also see IRWIN, Big Dee

PASTORIUS, Jaco
LPs: 10/12-Inch 33rpm
WARNER BROS: *81* 5-8
  Also see WEATHER REPORT

PAT & THE SATELLITES
Singles: 7-Inch
ATCO: *59* 4-8
  Members: Pat Otts; King Curtis; Wayne Lips.
  Also see KING CURTIS

PAT & THE WILDCATS
Singles: 7-Inch
CRUSADER: *64* 3-5

PATE, Johnny
(Johnny Pate Trio)
Singles: 78rpm
FEDERAL: *57* 3-5
Singles: 7-Inch
ARGO: *64* 2-4
FEDERAL: *57-59* 3-5
GIG: *56* 3-5
LPs: 10/12-Inch 33rpm
GIG: *56* 20-40
KING (500 & 600 series): *58-59* 15-30
SALEM: *58* 15-30
STEPHENY: *57* 20-40

PATIENCE & PRUDENCE
Singles: 78rpm
LIBERTY: *56* 3-6
Singles: 7-Inch
CHATTAHOOCHEE: *64-65* 3-5
LIBERTY: *56* 5-8
UNITED ARTISTS: 1-3

Also see CLIFFORD, Mike, & Patience & Prudence

PATRIS
Singles: 12-Inch 33/45rpm
EMERGENCY: 85 .... $4-6

PATTERSON, Kellee
Singles: 7-Inch
SHADYBROOK: 75-77 2-3
LPs: 10/12-Inch 33rpm
SHADYBROOK: 76-79 5-8
Note: Shadybrook may also be shown as Shady Brook, two words.

PATTON, Robbie
Singles: 7-Inch
ATLANTIC: 83-85 1-3
BACKSTREET: 79 2-3
LIBERTY: 81 1-3
LPs: 10/12-Inch 33rpm
ATLANTIC: 85 5-8
LIBERTY: 81 5-8

PATTY & THE EMBLEMS
(Patti & The Emblems)
Singles: 7-Inch
COLLECTABLES: 1-3
CONGRESS: 66 5-8
HERALD: 64 10-12
KAPP: 66-68 5-8
SPHERE SOUND: 64 10-12

PAUL, Billy
Singles: 12-Inch 33/45rpm
PHILADELPHIA INT'L: 79 4-6
Singles: 7-Inch
FINCH: 60 8-10
PHILADELPHIA INT'L: 71-81 1-3
LPs: 10/12-Inch 33rpm
GAMBLE: 67 12-15
NEPTUNE: 70 10-12
PHILADELPHIA INT'L: 71-80 6-10
Also see PHILADELPHIA INTERNATIONAL ALL STARS

PAUL, Henry, Band
Singles: 7-Inch
ATLANTIC: 79-81 1-3
LPs: 10/12-Inch 33rpm
ATLANTIC: 79 5-8
Also see OUTLAWS

PAUL, Les
(Les Paul Trio)
Singles: 78rpm
CAPITOL: 50-53 2-5
DECCA: 54 2-5

Singles: 7-Inch
CAPITOL: 50-53 .... $3-5
DECCA: 54 3-5
EPs: 7-Inch 33/45rpm
DECCA: 50-53 5-15
LPs: 10/12-Inch 33rpm
CAPITOL (200 series): 77 5-8
CAPITOL (16000 series): 82 4-6
DECCA (5000 series): 50-53 30-50
(10-Inch LPs.)
GLENDALE: 78 5-8
LONDON: 68-79 6-12
VOCALION: 68 6-12
Also see ATKINS, Chet, & Les Paul

PAUL, Les, & Mary Ford
Singles: 78rpm
CAPITOL: 50-57 2-5
Singles: 7-Inch
CAPITOL: 50-57 3-5
COLUMBIA: 58-64 2-4
Picture Sleeves
COLUMBIA: 58-64 3-6
EPs: 7-Inch 33/45rpm
CAPITOL: 50-57 5-15
LPs: 10/12-Inch 33rpm
CAPITOL (200 series): 78 5-8
(With an "SM" prefix.)
CAPITOL (200 through 800 series): 50-56 15-30
(With an "H," "T," or "ST" prefix.)
CAPITOL (1400 & 1500 series): 60-61 10-20
CAPITOL (11000 series): 74 5-8
COLUMBIA: 61-63 8-15
HARMONY: 61-65 5-12
Also see PAUL, Les

PAUL, Pope: see POPE PAUL

PAUL & PAULA
Singles: 7-Inch
LE CAM (300 series): 74-82 2-3
LE CAM (900 series): 63 8-10
PHILIPS (40000 series): 62-66 3-5
PHILIPS (44000 series): 2-3
UNI: 68 3-5
UNITED ARTISTS: 70 2-4
Picture Sleeves
PHILIPS: 63 5-10
LPs: 10/12-Inch 33rpm
PHILIPS: 63 30-60
Members: Ray Hildebrand; Jill Jackson.
Also see CHANNEL, Bruce / Paul & Paula
Also see JILL & RAY

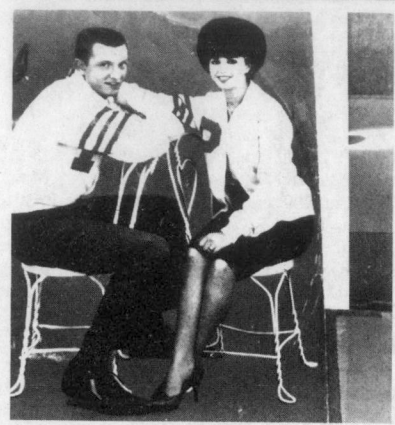

Paul and Paula

PAULETTE SISTERS
Singles: 78rpm
CAPITOL: 55 .... $2-5
Singles: 7-Inch
CAPITOL: 55 4-6
CONTEMPO: 63 3-5
DECCA: 58 3-6
RIBBON: 60 3-5
20TH CENTURY-FOX: 61 3-5

PAULSEN, Pat
LPs: 10/12-Inch 33rpm
MERCURY: 68-70 8-15

PAUPERS
Singles: 7-Inch
VERVE/FOLKWAYS: 66-67 4-8
VERVE/FORECAST: 67-68 4-8
Picture Sleeves
VERVE: 67 4-8
LPs: 10/12-Inch 33rpm
VERVE/FORECAST: 67-68 10-12

PAVLOV'S DOG
Singles: 7-Inch
COLUMBIA: 76 2-3
LPs: 10/12-Inch 33rpm
ABC: 75 10-12
COLUMBIA: 75-76 8-10
Members: David Surkamp; Mike Abebe; Murray Krugman; Sandy Pearlman; Mike Safron; Richard Stockton; David Hamilton; Doug Rayburn; Steve Scorfina.

PAVONE, Rita
Singles: 7-Inch
RCA VICTOR: 63-66 3-5

Picture Sleeves
RCA VICTOR: 64-65 .... $3-6
LPs: 10/12-Inch 33rpm
RCA VICTOR: 64-67 10-15

PAVAROTTI, Luciano
Singles: 7-Inch
LONDON: 79-84 1-3
LPs: 10/12-Inch 33rpm
LONDON: 76-84 5-8

PAXTON, Tom
Singles: 7-Inch
ASYLUM: 70 2-4
ELEKTRA: 69 4-8
REPRISE: 71 2-4
LPs: 10/12-Inch 33rpm
ANCHOR: 8-10
ELEKTRA: 64-71 10-15
FLYING FISH: 5-8
PRIVATE STOCK: 75 8-10
REPRISE: 71-73 10-15

PAYCHECK, Johnny
Singles: 7-Inch
ABC: 74 1-3
CUTLASS: 72 2-4
DESPERADO: 88 1-3
EPIC: 71-82 1-3
HILLTOP: 64-66 3-5
LITTLE DARLIN' (008 through
0072): 66-69 2-4
LITTLE DARLIN' (7000 series): 78-79 ...1-3
MERCURY: 86-87 1-3
LPs: 10/12-Inch 33rpm
ACCORD: 82 4-8
ALLEGIANCE: 83 4-8
CENTRON: 70 8-15
EPIC: 71-83 5-10
EXCELSIOR: 80 5-8
GUSTO: 83 4-8
IMPERIAL: 80 5-8
LITTLE DARLIN' (0500 through 0700
series): 79-80 5-8
LITTLE DARLIN' (8000 series): 66-69 ..10-18
LITTLE DARLIN' (10000 series): 79 8-12
MERCURY: 86 5-8
PICKWICK/HILLTOP: 72 6-10
  Also see HAGGARD, Merle, & Johnny Paycheck
  Also see JENNINGS, Waylon / Johnny Paycheck
  Also see JONES, George, & Johnny Paycheck

PAYCHECK, Johnny, & Jody Miller
Singles: 7-Inch
EPIC: 72 2-3

Also see MILLER, Jody
Also see PAYCHECK, Johnny

PAYNE, Freda
Singles: 12-Inch 33/45rpm
CAPITOL: 79 .... $4-6
Singles: 7-Inch
ABC: 75 1-3
ABC-PARAMOUNT: 62-63 3-5
CAPITOL: 77-78 2-3
DUNHILL: 74 2-4
IMPULSE: 63 3-5
INVICTUS: 69-73 2-4
MGM: 66 3-5
SUTRA: 82 1-3
Picture Sleeves
CAPITOL: 77-78 2-3
INVICTUS: 71-73 2-4
LPs: 10/12-Inch 33rpm
ABC: 75 8-10
CAPITOL: 78-79 5-8
DUNHILL: 74 8-10
IMPULSE: 64 12-18
INVICTUS: 70-72 10-12
MGM: 66-70 10-15
U.S.A: 71 10-12

PAYNE, Scherrie
Singles: 12-Inch 33/45rpm
MEGATONE: 84 4-6
Singles: 7-Inch
ALTAIR: 2-3
INVICTUS: 72 2-4
MOTOWN: 80 1-3
SUPERSTAR INT'L: 1-3
Also see GLASS HOUSE
Also see SUPREMES

PAYTON, Lawrence
Singles: 7-Inch
DUNHILL: 73-74 2-4
Also see FOUR TOPS

PEACHES & HERB
Singles: 7-Inch
COLUMBIA: 71-74 2-4
DATE: 66-70 3-5
MCA: 77 1-3
MERCURY: 73 2-3
Picture Sleeves
DATE: 67-68 3-5
LPs: 10/12-Inch 33rpm
DATE: 67-68 10-15
EPIC: 79 8-10
MCA: 77 8-10
Members: Francine Barker & Herb Fame.

PEACHES & HERB
Singles: 12-Inch 33/45rpm
POLYDOR: 78-79 .... $4-6
Singles: 7-Inch
COLUMBIA: 83 1-3
POLYDOR: 78-83 1-3
LPs: 10/12-Inch 33rpm
POLYDOR: 78-81 5-8
Members: Linda Green & Herb Fame.

PEANUT BUTTER CONSPIRACY
Singles: 7-Inch
CHALLENGE: 69 5-8
COLUMBIA: 67 8-10
VAULT: 66 10-15
LPs: 10/12-Inch 33rpm
CHALLENGE: 69 20-25
COLUMBIA (9000 series): 67-68 20-25
COLUMBIA (38000 series): 82 8-10
Member: Sandi Robison.

PEARL, Leslie
Singles: 7-Inch
RCA VICTOR: 82 1-3

PEARL HARBOR
(Pearl Harbor & The Explosions)
Singles: 7-Inch
WARNER BROS: 80-81 1-3
LPs: 10/12-Inch 33rpm
WARNER BROS: 80-81 5-8

PEARLETTES
Singles: 7-Inch
CRAIG: 61 8-10
VEE JAY: 61-62 6-10

PEARLS BEFORE SWINE
Singles: 7-Inch
ESP: 67 8-15
REPRISE: 69-70 5-10
LPs: 10/12-Inch 33rpm
ADELPHI: 80 5-8
ESP: 67-68 12-20
REPRISE: 69-71 10-15
Member: Tom Rapp.

PEARSON, Duke
Singles: 7-Inch
BLUE NOTE: 60-66 2-4
LPs: 10/12-Inch 33rpm
ATLANTIC: 66 8-15
BLUE NOTE: 59-61 20-35
(Label gives New York street address for Blue
Note Records.)
BLUE NOTE: 63-64 15-25
(Label reads "Blue Note Records Inc. - New York,
USA.")

BLUE NOTE: *66-74* $8-18
(Label shows Blue Note Records as a division of
either Liberty or United Artists.)
PRESTIGE: *70* **8-12**

PEARSON, Mr. Danny
Singles: 7-Inch
UNLIMITED GOLD: *78* **2-3**
LPs: 10/12-Inch 33rpm
UNLIMITED GOLD: *79* **5-8**

PEBBLES
Singles: 7-Inch
MCA: *87-88* **1-3**

PEDICIN, Mike
(Michael Pedicin Jr.; Mike Pedicin Quintet)
Singles: 12-Inch 33/45rpm
PHILADELPHIA INT'L: *79-82* **5-8**
Singles: 7-Inch
ABC-PARAMOUNT: *62* **3-5**
APOLLO: *59* **8-12**
CAMEO: *57* **4-8**
FEDERAL: *61* **3-5**
MALVERN: *57* **10-15**
PHILADELPHIA INT'L: *79-82* **1-3**
RCA VICTOR: *56* **4-6**
20TH CENTURY-FOX: **3-6**
EPs: 7-Inch 33/45rpm
RCA VICTOR: *56* **10-20**
(A "General Electric Flash Blub Limited Edition.")
LPs: 10/12-Inch 33rpm
APOLLO: *59* **25-30**
PHILADELPHIA INT'L: *79* **5-8**

PEDRICK, Bobby
(Bobby Pedrick, Jr.)
Singles: 7-Inch
BIG TOP: *58-60* **6-10**
DUEL: *62-63* **5-8**
MGM: *65* **4-6**
SHELL: *60* **10-12**
VERVE: *66* **10-15**
Also see JOHN, Robert

PEEBLES, Ann
Singles: 7-Inch
HI: *69-78* **2-4**
MOTOWN: *82* **1-3**
LPs: 10/12-Inch 33rpm
HI: *69-75* **8-10**
MOTOWN: *82* **5-8**

PEEK, Dan
Singles: 7-Inch
LAMB & LION: *79* **1-3**
SONGBIRD: *79* **1-3**
Also see AMERICA

PEEK, Paul
Singles: 7-Inch
COLUMBIA: *66* $3-5
FAIRLANE: *61* **6-10**
MERCURY: *62-63* **3-5**
NRC: *58-60* **8-12**
1-2-3: *69* **2-4**

PEEL, David, & The Lower East Side
Singles: 7-Inch
ORANGE: *77* **3-5**
LPs: 10/12-Inch 33rpm
APPLE: *72* **12-15**
ELEKTRA: *68-70* **12-15**
ORANGE: *77* **8-12**
Also see LENNON, John

PEELS
Singles: 7-Inch
KARATE: *66* **4-6**
LPs: 10/12-Inch 33rpm
KARATE: *66* **55-65**

PEEPLES
Singles: 7-Inch
MERCURY: *88* **1-3**

PEERCE, Jan
Singles: 7-Inch
BLUEBIRD: *60* **2-3**
RCA VICTOR: *51* **2-4**
UNITED ARTISTS: *63* **2-3**
EPs: 7-Inch 33/45rpm
RCA VICTOR: *51* **4-8**
LPs: 10/12-Inch 33rpm
RCA VICTOR (Except 2900 series): *51* ..**10-20**
RCA VICTOR (2900 series): *78* **4-8**
UNITED ARTISTS: *63-65* **5-15**
VANGUARD: *63-67* **5-15**

PEGGY LEE: see LEE, Peggy

PENDERGRASS, Teddy
Singles: 12-Inch 33/45rpm
PHILADELPHIA INT'L: *78-82* **4-6**
Singles: 7-Inch
ASYLUM: *84-88* **1-3**
PHILADELPHIA INT'L: *77-84* **1-3**
LPs: 10/12-Inch 33rpm
ASYLUM: *84-86* **5-8**
EPIC: *83* **5-8**
PHILADELPHIA INT'L (30000
series): *77-84* **6-10**
PHILADELPHIA INT'L (40000
series): *82* **10-15**
(Half-speed mastered.)

Promotional LPs
PHILADELPHIA INT'L ("Life Is
A Song"): *78* $20-30
(Picture disc. Promotional issue only.)
Also see HOUSTON, Whitney
Also see MELVIN, Harold
Also see MILLS, Stephanie, & Teddy
Pendergrass
Also see PHILADELPHIA INTERNATION-
AL ALL STARS

PENDULUM
Singles: 7-Inch
VENTURE: *80* 1-3
LPs: 10/12-Inch 33rpm
VENTURE: *81* 5-8

PENGUINS
(Penguins Featuring Cleve Duncan; Penquins)
Singles: 78rpm
ATLANTIC: *57* 5-10
DOOTO: *57* 8-15
DOOTONE: *54-55* 10-20
Singles: 7-Inch
ATLANTIC: *57* 10-15
DOOTO (348; "Earth Angel"): *62* 3-5
(Reissue of Dootone 348.)
DOOTO (400 series): *57-58* 15-25
DOOTONE (300 series): *54-55* 20-40
(Dootone 345 is found in the following section:
PENGUINS / Dootsie Williams Orchestra.)
GLENVILLE: 3-5
MERCURY: *55-57* 10-20
ORIGINAL SOUND: *63-65* 8-12
POWER: 3-5
SUN STATE: *62* .3-5
WING: *56* 8-10
Picture Sleeves
POWER: 4-8
EPs: 7-Inch 33/45rpm
DOOTO: *60* 10-15
DOOTONE: *55* 40-60
LPs: 10/12-Inch 33rpm
DOOTO (242; "Cool, Cool
Penguins"): *59* 100-200
(Yellow label with red lettering. Full-color cover.)
DOOTO: 8-10
(Multi-color label.)
Members: Cleve Duncan; Curtis Williams; Dexter
Tisby; Bruce Tate; Randy Jones; Ted Harper; Wal-
ter Saulsberry.
Also see JULIAN, Don, & The Meadowlarks

PENGUINS / Dootsie Williams Orchestra
Singles: 78rpm
DOOTONE (345; "Nore Ain't No
News Today"): *54* 75-100

Singles: 7-Inch
DOOTONE (345; "Nore Ain't No
News Today"): *54* $20-40

PENGUINS / Meadowlarks /
Medallions / Dootones
LPs: 10/12-Inch 33rpm
DOOTONE (204; "Best In
Rhythm & Blues"): *57* 50-80
(Black vinyl. Flat maroon label. Later pressings
have appeared on a glossy label stock and may, in
fact, be the currently available pressing. Current is-
sues may also be on the multi-color label. Accord-
ing to Dooto, this LP was black vinyl only. Colored
vinyl pressings are bootlegs.)
Also see PENGUINS

PENTAGONS
Singles: 7-Inch
DONNA: *61* 8-10
ERIC: 1-3
FLEET INT'L: *61* 12-20
JAMIE: *61-62* 5-10
SPECIALTY: *58* 5-10
(Most Specialty singles are currently available
using original catalog numbers.)

PENTAGONS / Earl Phillips
Singles: 7-Inch
OLDIES 45: *64* 2-3
Also see PENTAGONS

PENTANGLE
Singles: 7-Inch
REPRISE: *68-69* 3-5
TRANSATLANTIC: 3-5
LPs: 10/12-Inch 33rpm
REPRISE: *68-72* 10-15
Members: Jacqui McShee; Bert Jansch.

PEOPLE
Singles: 7-Inch
CAPITOL: *67-69* 5-8
PARAMOUNT: *69-70* 3-5
POLYDOR: *71* 2-4
ZEBRA (102; "Come Back
Beatles"): *78* 5-10
(Includes a note suggesting the Beatles reunite.)
LPs: 10/12-Inch 33rpm
CAPITOL: *68-69* 20-30
PARAMOUNT: *69-70* 10-15
Member: Larry Norman.

PEOPLE'S CHOICE
Singles: 7-Inch
CASABLANCA: *80* 1-3
PALMER: *67* 3-5
PHIL-L.A. OF SOUL: *71-73* 2-4
PHILADELPHIA INT'L: *71* 2-4

PHILIPS: 69 .... $2-4
TSOP: 74-77 2-3
LPs: 10/12-Inch 33rpm
CASABLANCA: 80 5-8
DECCA: 69 10-12
PHILADELPHIA INT'L: 78 5-8
TSOP: 75 8-10
Members: Roger Andrews; Guy Fiske; David
Thompson; Bob Eli; Frankie Brunson.
Also see MFSB

**PEPPERMINT, Danny, & The
Jumping Jacks**
Singles: 7-Inch
CARLTON: 61 5-8
LPs: 10/12-Inch 33rpm
CARLTON: 62 20-25
Member: Danny Lamego.

PEPPERMINT HARRIS
**(Peppermint Harris With Cross Town Blues
Band; Harrison Nelson)**
Singles: 78rpm
SITTIN' IN WITH: 50-51 5-10
Singles: 7-Inch
ALADDIN: 51-53 20-30
CASH: 54 15-20
DART: 60 5-8
DUKE: 60 5-8
JEWEL: 65-68 3-5
LUNAR: 2-4
MODERN: 51 15-25
MONEY: 54 15-20
SITTIN' IN WITH (543; "Rainin' In
My Heart"): 51 50-75
X: 55 40-60
LPs: 10/12-Inch 33rpm
TIME: 62 30-45

PEPPERMINT RAINBOW
Singles: 7-Inch
DECCA: 68-69 3-5
Picture Sleeves
DECCA: 69 3-5
LPs: 10/12-Inch 33rpm
DECCA: 69 10-15

PEPPERMINT TROLLEY COMPANY
Singles: 7-Inch
ACTA: 67-68 5-10
VALIANT: 66 8-12
LPs: 10/12-Inch 33rpm
ACTA: 68 15-20

PEPPERS
Singles: 7-Inch
BIG TREE: 75 2-3
EVENT: 74-75 2-3

LPs: 10/12-Inch 33rpm
EVENT: 74 .... $8-10

PEPSI & SHIRLIE
Singles: 7-Inch
POLYDOR: 87 1-3

PERCELLS
Singles: 7-Inch
ABC-PARAMOUNT: 63-64 5-8

PERCY & THEM
Singles: 7-Inch
PLAYBOY: 73 2-4

PERFECT, Christine
(Christine McVie)
Singles: 7-Inch
EPIC: 69 3-5
LPs: 10/12-Inch 33rpm
SIRE (6000 series): 77 5-8
SIRE (7000 series): 76 8-10
Also see MC VIE, Christine

PERICOLI, Emilio
Singles: 7-Inch
VESUVIUS: 62 2-4
WARNER BROS: 62-63 2-4
Picture Sleeves
WARNER BROS: 62 3-5
LPs: 10/12-Inch 33rpm
WARNER BROS: 63-66 5-15
VESUVIUS: 62 5-15

PERKINS, Al
Singles: 7-Inch
ATCO: 69-70 2-4
HI: 72 2-3
U.S.A: 64-65 3-5

PERKINS, Carl
(Carl Perkins & The C.P. Express)
Singles: 78rpm
FLIP (501; "Movie Magg"): 55 50-100
SUN (224; "Gone Gone Gone"): 56 10-20
SUN (234 through 287): 56-57 8-15
Singles: 7-Inch
AMERICA/SMASH: 86-87 1-3
COLUMBIA (41000 & 42000
series): 60-62 10-20
(With a "3" prefix. Compact 33 Singles.)
COLUMBIA (41000 through 43000
series): 58-64 4-6
COLUMBIA (44000 & 45000 series): 64-72 3-5
DECCA: 63-64 4-6
DOLLIE: 67 3-5
FLIP (501; "Movie Magg"): 55 300-350
JET: 79 2-3
MERCURY: 73-77 2-4

SSS/SUN: $1-3
SUN (224; "Gone Gone Gone"): *56* 35-45
SUN (234 through 287): *56-58* 10-15
Picture Sleeves
COLUMBIA: *58-62* 10-20
EPs: 7-Inch 33/45rpm
COLUMBIA (12341; "Whole Lotta
Shakin'"): *58* 100-200
SUN (115; "Blue Suede Shoes"): *58* 75-100
LPs: 10/12-Inch 33rpm
ACCORD: *82*.........................5-8
ALBUM GLOBE: 8-10
ALLEGIANCE: *84* 5-8
COLUMBIA (1234; "Whole Lotta
Shakin'"): *58* 60-75
COLUMBIA (9800 series): *69* 8-12
DESIGN: 10-15
DOLLIE: *67*........................10-15
GRT/SUNNYVALE: *77* 8-10
HARMONY: *72* 8-10
JET: *78*...........................8-10
KOALA: *80* 5-8
MERCURY: *73* 8-10
ROUNDER: *89* 5-8
SSS/SUN: *69-84* 5-8
SUEDE: *81* 8-10
SUN (1225; "Dance Album"): *57* 250-350
SUN (1225; "Teen Beat"): *61* 50-75
(Repackage of "Dance Album," using the same
catalog number.)
TRIP: *74*..........................8-10
UNIVERSAL: *89* 5-8
Also see McCARTNEY, Paul
Also see NELSON, Willie / Jerry Lee Lewis /
Carl Perkins / David Allan Coe
Also see YOUNG, Faron / Carl Perkins /
Claude King

PERKINS, Carl / Sonny Burgess
LPs: 10/12-Inch 33rpm
SSS/SUN: 5-8

**PERKINS, Carl, Jerry Lee Lewis,
Roy Orbison, & Johnny Cash**
LPs: 10/12-Inch 33rpm
AMERICA: *86*.....................20-25
(Mail-order only edition, includes souvenir booklet
and audio cassette with interviews of the singers.)
AMERICA/SMASH: *86* 5-8
Also see CASH, Johnny, Carl Perkins, & Jerry
Lee Lewis
Also see LEWIS, Jerry Lee, Carl Perkins, &
Charlie Rich
Also see ORBISON, Roy

PERKINS, Carl, & NRBQ
Singles: 7-Inch
COLUMBIA: *70* $2-4
LPs: 10/12-Inch 33rpm
COLUMBIA: *70*....................10-15
Also see NRBQ
Also see PERKINS, Carl

PERKINS, George
(George Perkins & The Silver Stars)
Singles: 7-Inch
SILVER FOX: *69* 2-4
SOUL POWER: *72*...................2-4
LPs: 10/12-Inch 33rpm
CRYIN' IN THE STREETS: *77* 8-10

PERKINS, Joe
Singles: 7-Inch
BERRY: 3-5
MUSICOR: *65* 3-5
SOUND STAGE 7: *63* 3-5

PERKINS, Tony
Singles: 78rpm
RCA VICTOR: *57* 3-6
Singles: 7-Inch
RCA VICTOR: *57* 3-6
Picture Sleeves
RCA VICTOR: *57* 8-12

PERRY, Greg
Singles: 7-Inch
ALFA: *82* 1-3
CASABLANCA: *74-75* 2-3
CHESS: *68* 3-5
RCA VICTOR: *77* 2-3
LPs: 10/12-Inch 33rpm
CASABLANCA: *75* 8-10

PERRY, Jeff
Singles: 7-Inch
ARISTA: *75-76* 2-3

EPIC: 77 .... $2-3

PERRY, Joe, Project
Singles: 7-Inch
COLUMBIA: 80-81 1-3
LPs: 10/12-Inch 33rpm
COLUMBIA: 80-81 5-8
MCA: 83 5-8
Also see AEROSMITH

PERRY, Linda
Singles: 7-Inch
MAINSTREAM: 73 2-3

PERRY, Roxy
Singles: 12-Inch 33/45rpm
PERSONAL: 83 4-6

PERRY, Steve
Singles: 7-Inch
COLUMBIA: 84-85 1-3
LPs: 10/12-Inch 33rpm
COLUMBIA: 84-85 5-8
Also see JOURNEY
Also see LOGGINS, Kenny, & Steve Perry
Also see U.S.A. FOR AFRICA

PERRY & SANLIN
Singles: 7-Inch
CAPITOL: 80 1-3
LPs: 10/12-Inch 33rpm
CAPITOL: 80 5-8

PERSIANS
Singles: 7-Inch
ABC: 68 3-5
CAPITOL: 71-72 2-4
GWP: 69-70 2-4

PERSON, Houston
Singles: 7-Inch
WESTBOUND: 75-76 2-3

PERSUADERS
Singles: 7-Inch
ATCO: 71-75 3-6
CALLA: 77 2-3
WIN OR LOSE: 71-72 3-5
LPs: 10/12-Inch 33rpm
ATCO: 73-74 8-10
CALLA: 77 8-10
WIN OR LOSE: 72 10-12

PERSUASIONS
Singles: 7-Inch
A&M: 74-75 2-4
CAPITOL: 71-72 2-4
CATAMOUNT: 2-4
MCA: 73 2-4
REPRISE: 70 2-4

TOWER: 65-66 ....$3-5
LPs: 10/12-Inch 33rpm
A&M: 74 8-10
CAPITOL: 71-72 6-10
ELEKTRA: 77 10-12
FLYING FISH: 79 5-8
MCA: 73 8-10
ROUNDER: 5-8
STRAIGHT: 70 15-20
Members: Jerry Lawson; Jimmy Hayes; Jayotis
Washington; Joe Russell; Herb Rhoad.

PET SHOP BOYS
Singles: 12-Inch 33/45rpm
EMI AMERICA: 86-87 4-6
Singles: 7-Inch
EMI AMERICA: 86-87 1-3
LPs: 10/12-Inch 33rpm
EMI AMERICA: 86-87 5-8
Members: Neil Tennant; Chris Lowe.
Also see SPRINGFIELD, Dusty

PETER & GORDON
Singles: 7-Inch
CAPITOL: 64-69 3-5
Picture Sleeves
CAPITOL: 64-67 4-8
LPs: 10/12-Inch 33rpm
CAPITOL (2500 series): 77 5-10
(With an "SM" prefix.)
CAPITOL (2100 through 2800
series): 64-68 10-20
(With a "T" or "ST" prefix.)
CAPITOL (16000 series): 80 5-8
Members: Peter Asher; Gordon Waller.

PETER & GORDON / Lettermen
Singles: 7-Inch
CAPITOL CREATIVE PRODUCTS: 66 ...4-6
(A Frito's company promotional issue.)
Also see LETTERMEN
Also see PETER & GORDON

PETER, PAUL & MARY
Singles: 7-Inch
EUGENE McCARTHY FOR
PRESIDENT: 68 10-20
(Promotional release, issued during McCarthy's
Democratic presidential nomination campaign. No
actual label name was shown.)
WARNER BROS (5000 series): 62-66 3-5
WARNER BROS (7000 series): 67-70 2-4
Picture Sleeves
WARNER BROS: 62-64 4-6
EPs: 7-Inch 33/45rpm
WARNER BROS: 63-64 4-8
(Jukebox issues only.)

LPs: 10/12-Inch 33rpm

GOLD C: *87* $5-8

WARNER BROS (1449 through
 1648): *62-66* 30-50
 (Quality of pressing is vital to grading with this
 series. Copies with poor fidelity, regardless of
 visual grade, cannot be considered near-mint.)

WARNER BROS (1700 through
 2552): *67-70* 8-12
 (At least four LPs from the 1400-1700 series are
 still in print; however, originals from that period
 are easily identified by their gray or gold labels.)

WARNER BROS (3000 series): *77-78* 5-8
 Members: Peter Yarrow; Paul Stookey; Mary
 Travers.
 Also see STOOKEY, Paul
 Also see TRAVERS, Mary
 Also see YARROW, Peter

PETERS, Bernadette
Singles: 7-Inch

ABC-PARAMOUNT: *65* 4-6
COLUMBIA: *67* 3-5
MCA: *78-81* 1-3
UNITED ARTISTS: *62* 5-8
Picture Sleeves
MCA: *80-81* 2-4
LPs: 10/12-Inch 33rpm
MCA: *80-81* 5-8

PETERSEN, Paul
Singles: 7-Inch

ABC: *74* 1-3
COLPIX (Except 720): *62-65* 3-5
COLPIX (720; "She Rides With Me"): *64* 15-20
 (With the Beach Boys.)
ERIC: 1-3
MCA: 1-3
MOTOWN: *67-68* 3-5
Picture Sleeves
COLPIX: *62* 5-8
LPs: 10/12-Inch 33rpm
COLPIX: *62-63* 15-20
 Also see BEACH BOYS
 Also see DARREN, James / Shelly Fabares /
 Paul Petersen

PETERSEN, Paul, & Shelly Fabares
Singles: 7-Inch

COLPIX: *62* 4-6
 Also see FABARES, Shelly
 Also see PETERSEN, Paul

PETERSON, Bobby
(Bobby Peterson Quintet)
Singles: 7-Inch

ATLANTIC: *62* 3-5
V-TONE: *59-60* 4-6

PETERSON, Lucky, Blues Band
Singles: 7-Inch

TODAY: *71* $2-4
LPs: 10/12-Inch 33rpm
TODAY: *71* 10-15

PETERSON, Oscar
(Oscar Peterson Trio)
Singles: 7-Inch

CLEF: *53-56* 3-5
LIMELIGHT: *65-66* 2-4
MERCURY (8900 series): *51-52* 4-6
MERCURY (72000 series): *64* 2-4
MERCURY (89000 series): *52-53* 3-5
NORGRAN: *55* 3-5
PRESTIGE: *69* 2-3
VERVE: *57-64* 2-4
EPs: 7-Inch 33/45rpm
CLEF: *52-53* 15-30
RCA VICTOR (3000 series): *51* 30-60
LPs: 10/12-Inch 33rpm
BASF: *74-76* 8-10
CLEF (100 series): *52-53* 50-75
 (10-Inch LPs.)
CLEF (600 series): *53-56* 30-60
EMARCY: *76* 8-12
LIMELIGHT (1000 series): *82* 5-8
LIMELIGHT (82000 & 86000
 series): *65-67* 8-18
MGM (100 series): *70* 8-10
MPS: *72-76* 8-12
MERCURY (20900 & 60900
 series): *64* 15-25
METRO: *65* 8-15
PABLO: *75-83* 6-12
PAUSA: *79-81* 5-8
PRESTIGE: *69-74* 8-12
RCA VICTOR (3006; "This Is
 Oscar Peterson"): *51* 75-150
 (10-Inch LP.)
TRIP: *75-76* 5-8
VSP: *66-67* 10-15
VERVE: *56-60* 20-45
 (Reads "Verve Records, Inc." at bottom of label.)
VERVE: *61-72* 10-25
 (Reads "MGM Records - A Division Of Metro-
 Goldwyn-Mayer, Inc." at bottom of label.)
VERVE: *73-83* 5-15
 (Reads "Manufactured By MGM Record Corp.," or
 mentions either Polydor or Polygram at bottom of
 label.)
WING: *67* 8-12
 Also see ARMSTRONG, Louis, & Oscar
 Peterson
 Also see BASIE, Count, & Oscar Peterson

Also see FITZGERALD, Ella, & Oscar Peterson

Also see GETZ, Stan, & Oscar Peterson

Also see HUBBARD, Freddie, & Oscar Peterson

Also see RIDDLE, Nelson

PETERSON, Oscar, & Buddy DeFranco
Singles: 7-Inch
NORGRAN: 55 .... $3-5
LPs: 10/12-Inch 33rpm
NORGRAN: 54 25-50
VERVE: 57 20-30
(Reads "Verve Records, Inc." at bottom of label.)

PETERSON, Oscar, & Sonny Stitt
LPs: 10/12-Inch 33rpm
VERVE: 60 15-25
(Reads "Verve Records, Inc." at bottom of label.)
Also see PETERSON, Oscar
Also see STITT, Sonny

PETERSON, Ray
Singles: 7-Inch
CLOUD 9 : 75 2-3
DECCA: 71 2-4
DUNES: 60-63 4-6
MGM: 64-66 3-5
POLYDOR: 1-3
RCA VICTOR (Stereo): 59-60 10-15
(With a "61" prefix.)
RCA VICTOR (Monaural): 59-64 4-8
(With a "47" prefix.)
REPRISE: 69 2-4
UNI: 70 2-4
Picture Sleeves
DUNES: 60 4-8
MGM: 64 3-6
RCA VICTOR: 59 6-10
EPs: 7-Inch 33/45rpm
RCA VICTOR: 60 20-35
LPs: 10/12-Inch 33rpm
CAMDEN: 66 10-15
DECCA: 71 8-10
MGM: 64-65 20-25
RCA VICTOR: 60 35-40
UNI: 70 8-15

PETITE
Singles: 7-Inch
YORK'S: 86 1-3

PETS
Singles: 7-Inch
ARWIN: 58 3-5
Member: Seph Acre.

PETTUS, Giorge
Singles: 7-Inch
MCA: 87-88 .... $1-3

PETTY, Frank, Trio
Singles: 78rpm
MGM: 50-57 2-4
Singles: 7-Inch
MGM: 50-57 2-4
EPs: 7-Inch 33/45rpm
MGM: 50-57 4-8
LPs: 10/12-Inch 33rpm
MGM: 50-57 8-15

PETTY, Norman, Trio
Singles: 78rpm
ABC-PARAMOUNT: 57 4-6
COLUMBIA (Except 41039): 57 4-6
COLUMBIA (41039; "Moondreams"): 57 10-20
(With Buddy Holly on guitar.)
NOR VA JAK: 57 5-10
X: 54-55 3-5
Singles: 7-Inch
ABC-PARAMOUNT: 57 4-6
COLUMBIA (Except 41039): 57 4-6
COLUMBIA (41039; "Moondreams"): 57 20-25
(With Buddy Holly on guitar.)
FELSTED: 62 3-5
JARO: 60 4-6
NOR VA JAK (Except 1325): 57-59 15-20
NOR VA JAK (1325; "True Love
  Ways"): 60 25-30
NORMAN: 60 4-6
X: 54-55 5-8
EPs: 7-Inch 33/45rpm
COLUMBIA: 58 20-25
X: 55 15-20
LPs: 10/12-Inch 33rpm
COLUMBIA: 58 30-40
TOP RANK: 60 25-30
VIK: 20-25
Members: Norman Petty; Vi Petty; Jack Petty.
Also see HOLLY, Buddy

PETTY, Tom, & The Heartbreakers
Singles: 7-Inch
BACKSTREET: 79-83 1-3
MCA: 85-87 1-3
SHELTER: 77-78 2-3
Picture Sleeves
BACKSTREET: 79-83 1-3
MCA: 85 1-3
SHELTER: 77-78 2-3
LPs: 10/12-Inch 33rpm
BACKSTREET: 79-82 5-8
MCA: 85-87 5-8

SHELTER: *76-78* $5-8
Promotional LPs
SHELTER (12677; "Official
Live 'Leg"): *76* 10-15
SHELTER (52029; "You're Gonna
Get It"). *76* 10-13
(Colored vinyl.)
Also see DYLAN, Bob, & The Heartbreakers /
Michael Rubini
Also see NICKS, Stevie, & Tom Petty & The
Heartbreakers

PHANTOM LIMBS
LPs: 10/12-Inch 33rpm
ROMANCE: *83-86* 5-8
Members: Jim Parks; Jeff Keenan; Peter"Splat"
Catalanotte.

PHANTOM, ROCKER & SLICK
Singles: 7-Inch
EMI AMERICA: *85-86* 1-3
LPs: 10/12-Inch 33rpm
EMI AMERICA: *85-86* 5-8
Members: Jim Phantom; Lee Rocker; Earl Slick.
Also see STRAY CATS

PHELPS, James
(Jimmy Phelps & The Du-Ettes)
Singles: 7-Inch
ARGO: *65* 3-5
CADET: *66* 3-5
FONTANA: *66-67* 3-5
MECCA: *60* 5-8
PARAMOUNT: *71-72* 2-4

PHILADELPHIA
INTERNATIONAL ALL STARS
Singles: 7-Inch
PHILADELPHIA INT'L: *77* 2-3
Members: Archie Bell; The O'Jays; Billy Paul;
Teddy Pendergrass; Lou Rawls; Dee Dee Sharpe.
Also see BELL, Archie
Also see O'JAYS
Also see PAUL, Billy
Also see PENDERGRASS, Teddy
Also see RAWLS, Lou
Also see SHARPE, Dee Dee

PHILADELPHIA STORY
Singles: 7-Inch
H&L: *77* 2-3

PHILHARMONICS
Singles: 7-Inch
CAPRICORN: *77* 2-3
LPs: 10/12-Inch 33rpm
CAPRICORN: *77* 5-8

PHILLINGANES, Greg
Singles: 12-Inch 33/45rpm
PLANET: *85* $1-3
Singles: 7-Inch
PLANET: *81-85* 1-3
LPs: 10/12-Inch 33rpm
PLANET: *81-85* 5-8

PHILLIPS, Anthony
Singles: 7-Inch
PASSPORT: *77-78* 1-3
LPs: 10/12-Inch 33rpm
PASSPORT: *77-78* 5-10
Also see GENESIS

PHILLIPS, Bill, & Dolly Parton
Singles: 7-Inch
DECCA (31901; "Put It
Off Until Tomorrow"): *66* 3-5
LPs: 10/12-Inch 33rpm
DECCA (4792; "Put It
Off Until Tomorrow"): *66* 15-20
(Monaural.)
DECCA (74792; "Put It
Off Until Tomorrow"): *66*   15-25
(Stereo.)
Also see PARTON, Dolly

PHILLIPS, Esther
(Little Esther Phillips)
Singles: 7-Inch
ATLANTIC: *64-70* 5-10
KUDU: *72-77* 2-4
LENOX: *62-63* 5-10
MERCURY: *77-79* 2-3
ROULETTE: *69* 2-4
WINNING: *83* 1-3
LPs: 10/12-Inch 33rpm
ATLANTIC: *65-76* 10-20
KUDO: *72-76* 8-10
LENOX: *62* 20-25
MERCURY: *77-81* 5-8
YORKSHIRE: 8-10
Also see LITTLE ESTHER

PHILLIPS, Esther, & Joe Beck
LPs: 10/12-Inch 33rpm
KUDU: *76* 8-10
Also see BECK, Joe

PHILLIPS, Esther, & Big Al Downing
Singles: 7-Inch
LENOX: *63* 3-5
Also see PHILLIPS, Esther

PHILLIPS, John
Singles: 7-Inch
ATCO: *74* 2-4

COLUMBIA: *73* $2-4
DUNHILL: *70* 2-4
LPs: 10/12-Inch 33rpm
DUNHILL: *70* 10-12
Also see MAMAS & THE PAPAS

PHILLIPS, Little Esther:
see PHILLIPS, Esther

PHILLIPS, Phil
(Phil Phillips With The Twilights)
Singles: 7-Inch
CLIQUE: *66* 3-5
KHOURY'S (711; "Sea Of Love"): *59* .. 50-75
MERCURY (10000 series): *59* 8-10
(Stereo.)
MERCURY (71000 series): *59-61* 4-6

PHILLIPS, Shawn
Singles: 7-Inch
A&M: *70-75* 2-4
ASCOT: *64* 3-5
LPs: 10/12-Inch 33rpm
A&M: *70-77* 8-10
RCA VICTOR: *78-81* 5-8

PHILLIPS, Stu
Singles: 7-Inch
CAPITOL: *73* 1-3
COLPIX: *62* 10-20
MCA: *78* 1-3
PARAGON: *76* 1-3
Also see HOLLYRIDGE STRINGS

PHILLIPS, Wes
Singles: 12-Inch 33/45rpm
QUALITY: *84* 4-6
Singles: 7-Inch
QUALITY: *84* 1-3

PHILLY CREAM
Singles: 12-Inch 33/45rpm
WMOT: *79* 4-6
Singles: 7-Inch
FANTASY: *79* 1-3
WMOT: *79* 1-3
LPs: 10/12-Inch 33rpm
WMOT: *79* 5-8

PHILLY DEVOTIONS
Singles: 7-Inch
COLUMBIA: *75-76* 2-3

PHOTOGLO, Jim
(Photoglo)
Singles: 7-Inch
CASABLANCA: *83* 1-3
20TH CENTURY-FOX: *80-81* 1-3

LPs: 10/12-Inch 33rpm
CASABLANCA: *83* $5-8
20TH CENTURY-FOX: *80-81* 5-8

PIAF, Edith
Singles: 7-Inch
CAPITOL: *56-61* 2-4
COLUMBIA: *50-52* 3-5
EPs: 7-Inch 33/45rpm
ANGEL: 5-15
COLUMBIA: *50-52* 5-15
DECCA (6000 series): 5-15
LPs: 10/12-Inch 33rpm
ANGEL: *55-56* 15-25
CAPITOL: *59-82* 5-15
COLUMBIA (Except 37000
series): *50-56* 15-30
COLUMBIA (37000 series): *81* 5-8
DECCA (6000 series): *54* 20-30
DISCOS: *56* 10-20
PHILIPS: *64-67* 8-15
RCA VICTOR: *64* 8-15
VOX: *53* 20-30

PIANO RED
(Willie Perryman)
Singles: 78rpm
CHECKER: *58* 3-6
GROOVE: *54-57* 5-8
RCA VICTOR: *50-57* 5-10
Singles: 7-Inch
CHECKER: *58* 8-10
GROOVE: *54-57* 10-15
JAX: *59* 4-6
RCA VICTOR (4000 series): *50-52* 15-20
RCA VICTOR (5000 series): *52-53* 10-20
RCA VICTOR (6000 & 7000
series): *57-58* 8-15
RCA VICTOR (50-0000 series): *50-51* ...15-20
(Black vinyl.)
RCA VICTOR (50-0000 series): *50-51* ...25-30
(Colored vinyl.)
EPs: 7-Inch 33/45rpm
GROOVE: *56* 30-50
RCA VICTOR (587; "Rockin'
With Red"): *54* 40-60
RCA VICTOR (5091; "Rockin'
With Red"): *59* 30-40
(Black label.)
RCA VICTOR (5091; "Rockin'
With Red"): *59* 40-60
(Maroon label.)
LPs: 10/12-Inch 33rpm
ARHOOLIE: 8-10
BLACK LION: *76* 8-10

GROOVE (1002; "Piano Red
 In Concert"): *56* $150-200
KING: *70* 10-12
RCA VICTOR: *74* 8-10
 Also see DOCTOR FEELGOOD

PICKETT, Bobby
(Bobby "Boris" Pickett & The Crypt-Kickers)
Singles: 12-Inch 33/45rpm
EASY STREET: *84* 4-6
        Singles: 7-Inch
ANTHEM: 3-5
ATMOSPHERE: *65* 4-6
CAPITOL: *63-64* 5-8
EASY STREET: *84* 1-3
GARPAX (1; "Monster Mash"): *62* 8-10
GARPAX (700 series): 4-6
GARPAX (44000 series): *62-64* 4-6
LONDON: 1-3
METROMEDIA (0089; "Me & My
 Mummy"): *68* 3-5
METROMEDIA (9989; "Me & My
 Mummy"): *73* 2-3
PARROT: *70-73* 2-3
RCA VICTOR: *64* 3-5
WHITE WHALE: *70* 2-4
        Picture Sleeves
GARPAX: *62-63* 8-15
        LPs: 10/12-Inch 33rpm
GARPAX: *62* 25-35
PARROT: *73* 8-10

PICKETT, Wilson
        Singles: 7-Inch
ATLANTIC (2200 through 2400
 series): *64-67* 3-5
ATLANTIC (2500 through 2900
 series): *68-72* 2-4
BIG TREE: *78* 2-3
CORREC-TONE: *62* 10-15
CUB: *62* 10-12
DOUBLE-L: *63* 4-6
EMI AMERICA: *79-81* 1-3
MOTOWN: *87* 1-3
RCA VICTOR: *73-74* 2-4
ROWE/AMI: *66* 4-8
 ("Play Me" Sales Stimulator promotional issue.)
VERVE: *65* 3-5
WICKED: *75-76* 2-3
        LPs: 10/12-Inch 33rpm
ATLANTIC (Except 8100 series): *69-73* ..8-12
ATLANTIC (8100 series): *65-68* 15-20
BIG TREE: *78* 5-8
BROOKVILLE: *77* 8-12
DOUBLE-L: *63* 25-35
EMI AMERICA: *79-81* 5-8

MONSTER MASH

44167
GARPAX
Records

RCA VICTOR: *73-77* $8-10
WAND: *68* 10-15
WICKED: *76* 8-10
 Also see FALCONS

PICKETTYWITCH
        Singles: 7-Inch
JANUS: *70* 2-4
PYE: *71* 2-4
        LPs: 10/12-Inch 33rpm
JANUS: *70* 8-10
 Members: Polly Brown.
 Also see BROWN, Polly

PICTURE PERFECT
        Singles: 7-Inch
ATLANTIC: *87* 1-3

PIECES OF A DREAM
        Singles: 12-Inch 33/45rpm
ELEKTRA: *84* 4-6
        Singles: 7-Inch
ELEKTRA: *81-84* 1-3
MANHATTAN: *88* 1-3
        LPs: 10/12-Inch 33rpm
ELEKTRA: *81-84* 5-8
MANHATTAN: *86* 5-8

PIECES OF EIGHT
        Singles: 7-Inch
A&M: *67-68* 5-10
ACTION: 4-8
MALA: *68* 4-8
 Also see SWINGIN' MEDALLIONS

PIERCE, Webb
        Singles: 78rpm
DECCA: *51-52* 3-6
FOUR STAR: *51-52* 4-8
        Singles: 7-Inch
DECCA (28000 through 30000
 series): *52-59* 5-10

DECCA (31000 through 33000
series): *59-73* **$2-5**
DECCA (46000 series): *51-52* **4-8**
FOUR STAR: *51-52* **5-10**
KING: *60* **3-5**
MCA: *73-74* **1-3**
PLANTATION: *75-77* **1-3**
SOUNDWAVES: *83* **1-3**
    EPs: 7-Inch 33/45rpm
DECCA: *53-65* **5-15**
    LPs: 10/12-Inch 33rpm
CORAL: *73* **4-6**
DECCA (100 series): *64* **15-20**
DECCA (4000 through 4800
series): *60-67* **10-20**
(Decca LP numbers in this series preceded by a "7"
or a "DL-7" are stereo issues.)
DECCA (5000 series): *53* **30-50**
(10-Inch LPs.)
DECCA (8000 series): *55-59* **20-40**
DECCA (74000 series): *68* **8-12**
ERA: *77* **8-10**
KING (600 series): *59* **25-35**
MCA: *73-78* **5-12**
PICKWICK/HILLTOP: *65* **10-15**
PLANTATION: *76-77* **5-8**
SEARS: **8-12**
SKYLITE: *77* **5-8**
VOCALION: *66-70* **5-15**
    Also see NELSON, Willie, & Webb Pierce

PIERCE, Webb / Loretta Lynn
    LPs: 10/12-Inch 33rpm
PHILCO/MCA: *59* **12-18**
    Also see LYNN, Loretta

PIERCE, Webb / Wynn Stewart
    LPs: 10/12-Inch 33rpm
DESIGN: *62* **10-15**
    Also see STEWART, Wynn

PIERCE, Webb, & Kitty Wells
    Singles: 7-Inch
DECCA: *64* **2-4**
    EPs: 7-Inch 33/45rpm
DECCA: *59* **5-10**
    Also see PIERCE, Webb
    Also see WELLS, Kitty

PILOT
    Singles: 7-Inch
ARISTA: *77* **2-3**
CAPITOL: *77* **2-3**
EMI: *75-76* **3-5**
    LPs: 10/12-Inch 33rpm
EMI: *75-76* **8-10**
    Also see PARSONS, Alan, Project

PILTDOWN MEN
    Singles: 7-Inch
CAPITOL: *60-62* **$5-10**
    Members: Lincoln Mayorga; Bob Bain; Earl
    Palmer; Jack Kel.

PINDER, Michael
    LPs: 10/12-Inch 33rpm
THRESHOLD: *76* **8-10**
    Also see MOODY BLUES

PINERA, Mike
    Singles: 7-Inch
CAPRICORN: *78* **2-3**
SPECTOR: *80* **2-3**
SRI: *79* **2-3**
    LPs: 10/12-Inch 33rpm
SRI: *79* **5-8**
    Also see BLUES IMAGE
    Also see CACTUS
    Also see IRON BUTTERFLY
    Also see RAMATAM

PINETOPPERS
    Singles: 78rpm
CORAL: *50-54* **2-4**
DECCA: *54-56* **2-4**
    Singles: 7-Inch
CORAL: *50-54* **3-6**
DECCA: *54-56* **3-6**
PEER SOUTHERN: *67* **2-4**
    EPs: 7-Inch 33/45rpm
CORAL: *50-56* **3-6**
    LPs: 10/12-Inch 33rpm
CORAL: *50-56* **5-15**

PINETTE, Rick, & Oak
    Singles: 7-Inch
MERCURY: *80* **2-3**
    LPs: 10/12-Inch 33rpm
MERCURY: *80* **5-8**
    Also see OAK

PINK FLOYD
    Singles: 7-Inch
CAPITOL: *71-78* **3-5**
COLUMBIA: *75-87* **1-3**
HARVEST: *73-74* **2-4**
TOWER: *67-68* **30-50**
    Picture Sleeves
COLUMBIA: *75-83* **1-3**
    EPs: 7-Inch 33/45rpm
HARVEST (6746/7; "Pink Floyd, From *Dark
Side Of The Moon*"): *73* **50-100**
(Promotional issue only.)
    LPs: 10/12-Inch 33rpm
CAPITOL (Except 11902): *78-83* **5-8**

CAPITOL (11902; "Dark Side
Of The Moon"): *78* $20-30
(Picture disc.)
COLUMBIA (Except 1636): *75-87* 6-10
COLUMBIA (1636; "Final Cut"): *83* 12-15
(Promotional issue only.)
HARVEST (300 series): *69-70* 18-20
HARVEST (700 & 800 series). *71* 10-15
HARVEST (11000 series): *72-73* 10-15
HARVEST (16000 series): *82* 5-8
MFSL (017; "Dark Side Of The
Moon"): *78* 40-80
MFSL/UHQR (017; "Dark Side
Of The Moon"): *78* 75-125
(Boxed set.)
TOWER (5093; "Piper At The Gates
Of Dawn"): *67* 50-100
(Orange label.)
TOWER (5093; "Piper At The Gates
Of Dawn"): *67* 30-50
(Striped label.)
TOWER (5131; "A Saucerful Of
Secrets"): *68* 50-100
(Orange label.)
TOWER (5131; "A Saucerful Of
Secrets"): *68* 50-100
(Striped label.)
TOWER (5169; "More"): *69* 20-40
Members: David Gilmour; Roger Waters; Rick
Wright; Nick Mason; Syd Barrett.
Also see BARRETT, Syd
Also see GILMOUR, David
Also see MASON, Nick
Also see WATERS, Roger

PINK LADY
Singles: 7-Inch
ELEKTRA: *79* 1-3
LPs: 10/12-Inch 33rpm
ELEKTRA: *79* 5-8
Members: Mie; Kei.

PIPEDREAM
Singles: 12-Inch 33/45rpm
ZOO YORK: *84* 4-6
LPs: 10/12-Inch 33rpm
ABC: *78* 5-8

PIPER, Wardell
Singles: 7-Inch
MIDSONG INT'L: *79-80* 1-3

PIPKINS
Singles: 7-Inch
CAPITOL: *70* 2-4
LPs: 10/12-Inch 33rpm
CAPITOL: *70* 10-15
Member: Chester Pipkin.

PIPS
Singles: 7-Inch
BRUNSWICK: *58* $30-40
CASABLANCA: *77-78* 2-3
EVERLAST: *63* 4-6
FURY: *62* 4-6
HUNTOM (2510; "Every Beat Of
My Heart"): *61* 75-100
VEE JAY: *61* 4-6
LPs: 10/12-Inch 33rpm
CASABLANCA: *77-78* 5-8
Members: Gladys Knight; Merald Knight; William
Guest; Edward Guest.
Also see KNIGHT, Gladys

PIRATES
(Temptations)
Singles: 7-Inch
MEL-O-DY (105; "Mind Over
Matter"): *62* 25-50
Also see TEMPTATIONS

PITNEY, Gene
Singles: 7-Inch
COLLECTABLES: 1-3
EPIC: *77* 2-3
ERIC: 1-3
FESTIVAL: *61* 8-10
MUSICOR (1000 series): *60-65* 4-6
MUSICOR (1100 through 1400
series): *65-72* 3-5
Picture Sleeves
MUSICOR (1000 series): *60-65* 5-10
MUSICOR (1100 through 1400
series): *66-69* 3-6
EPs: 7-Inch 33/45rpm
MUSICOR (500; "Looking Through
The Eyes Of Love"): *65* 15-20
(Issued without cover. Promotional issue only.)
LPs: 10/12-Inch 33rpm
COLUMBIA HOUSE: 10-15
(Columbia Record Club release.)
EVEREST: *81* 5-8
MUSIC DISC: *69* 10-12
MUSICOR (1 through 6): *62-63* 20-30
MUSICOR (8 through 134): *64-67* 12-15
(Gene's Musicor LPs 1 through 134 were num-
bered in the "2000" series for mono and the "3000"
series for stereo issues.)
MUSICOR (3148 through 3183): *67-70* . 10-12
MUSICOR (5026; "This Is Gene
Pitney"): *68* 12-15
(Columbia Record Club release.)
MUSICOR (5600 series): *78* 6-10
RHINO: *85* 5-8
SPRINGBOARD: *76* 6-10

TRIP: *76* $6-10
51 WEST: *79* 5-8
Also see BRYAN, Billy
Also see JAMIE & JANE
Also see JONES, George, & Gene Pitney

PITNEY, Gene, & Melba Montgomery
Singles: 7-Inch
MUSICOR: *65* 3-5
LPs: 10/12-Inch 33rpm
BUCKBOARD: *76* 8-10
MUSICOR: *66* 12-15
Also see MONTGOMERY, Melba

PITNEY, Gene / Newcastle Trio
LPs: 10/12-Inch 33rpm
DESIGN: 8-10
Also see PITNEY, Gene

PIXIES THREE
Singles: 7-Inch
MERCURY: *63-64* 6-8
Picture Sleeves
MERCURY: *63-64* 10-20
LPs: 10/12-Inch 33rpm
MERCURY: *64* 20-30

PIZANI, Frank
Singles: 78rpm
BALLY: *57* 3-5
Singles: 7-Inch
AFTON: *59* 3-5
BALLY: *57* 4-6
WARWICK: *59* 3-5
Also see HIGHLIGHTS

PLACE, Mary Kay
Singles: 7-Inch
COLUMBIA: *76-78* 1-3
LPs: 10/12-Inch 33rpm
COLUMBIA: *76-77* 5-10

PLANET P PROJECT
Singles: 7-Inch
GEFFEN: *83* 1-3
MCA: 1-3
LPs: 10/12-Inch 33rpm
GEFFEN: *83* 5-8
Member: Tony Carey.
Also see CAREY, Tony

PLANET PATROL
Singles: 12-Inch 33/45rpm
TOMMY BOY: *84* 4-6
Singles: 7-Inch
TOMMY BOY: *82-84* 1-3
LPs: 10/12-Inch 33rpm
TOMMY BOY: *84* 5-8

PLANT, Robert
Singles: 7-Inch
ATLANTIC: *83* $1-3
ESPARANZA: *83* 1-3
SWAN SONG: *82* 1-3
LPs: 10/12-Inch 33rpm
ATLANTIC/ESPARANZA: *83* 5-8
SWAN SONG: *82* 5-8
Also see HONEYDRIPPERS
Also see LED ZEPPELIN

PLASMATICS
(Featuring Wendy O. Williams)
LPs: 10/12-Inch 33rpm
CAPITOL: *82* 5-8
PVC: *84* 5-8
STIFF AMERICA: *80-81* 8-10
Also see BEAUVOIR, Jean

PLASTIC BERTRAND
Singles: 7-Inch
SIRE: *78* 2-3

PLASTIC COW
Singles: 7-Inch
DOT: *69* 2-4
LPs: 10/12-Inch 33rpm
DOT: *69* 10-12

PLASTIC ONO BAND:
see LENNON, John

PLATINUM BLONDE
Singles: 7-Inch
EPIC: *86-87* 1-3
LPs: 10/12-Inch 33rpm
EPIC: *86-87* 5-8

PLATT, Eddie, & His Orchestra
Singles: 7-Inch
ABC-PARAMOUNT: *58* 3-5
GONE: *58* 3-5

PLATTERS
Singles: 78rpm
FEDERAL (12153; "Give Thanks"): *53* ..25-50
FEDERAL (12164; "I Need You
All The Time"): *54* 25-50
FEDERAL (12181; "Roses Of
Picardy"): *54* 15-30
FEDERAL (12188 through 12204): *54-55* 10-20
FEDERAL (12244; "Only You"): *55* 15-25
FEDERAL (12250; "Tell The World"): *55* .6-12
FEDERAL (12271; "I Need You
All The Time"): *56* 5-10
MERCURY: *55-58* 5-10
Singles: 7-Inch
ANTLER: *82* 1-3
COLLECTABLES: 1-3

FEDERAL (12153; "Give
Thanks"): *53* $75-100
FEDERAL (12164; "I Need You
All The Time"): *54* 100-125
FEDERAL (12181; "Roses Of
Picardy"): *54* 60-80
FEDERAL (12188; "Tell The
World"): *54* 25-40
FEDERAL (12204; "Take Me
Back"): *54* 25-40
FEDERAL (12244; "Only You"): *55* 40-60
FEDERAL (12250; "Tell The
World"): *55* 20-25
FEDERAL (12271; "I Need You
All The Time"): *56* 15-20
GUSTO: 1-3
MERCURY (10000 series): *58-60* 10-20
(Stereo.)
MERCURY (70633; "Only You"): *55* ... 15-20
(Pink label.)
MERCURY (70633; "Only You"): *55* 5-10
(Black label.)
MERCURY (70753 through 71904): *55-61* 5-10
MERCURY (71921 through 72359): *62-64* .3-6
MUSICOR: *66-71* 3-5
OWL: *73* 2-4
POWER: 3-5

Picture Sleeves
MERCURY: *60-64* 4-8
EPs: 7-Inch 33/45rpm
FEDERAL (378; The Platters"): *56* ... 250-350
KING: *56* 25-40
MERCURY: *56-61* 15-25
LPs: 10/12-Inch 33rpm
CANDLELITE: 10-20
EVEREST: *81* 5-8
FEDERAL (549; "The Platters"): *56* ... 250-350
51 WEST: 5-8
KING (651; "The Platters"): *59* 50-75
MERCURY (4000 series): *82* 5-8
MERCURY (8000 series): 5-8
MERCURY (20146 through
20366): *56-58* 20-25
MERCURY (20410 through
20983): *59-65* 15-20
(Monaural.)
MERCURY (60043 through
60983): *59-65* 15-20
(Stereo.)
MUSIC DISC: *69* 10-12
MUSICO (1002; "Only You"): *70* 8-10
MUSICOR (2000 & 3000 series): *66-69* .10-15
MUSICOR (4600 series): *77* 10-12
PICKWICK: 8-10
SPRINGBOARD: *76* 8-10

THE PLATTERS

TRIP: *76* $8-10
WING: *62-67* 10-15
Members: Tony Williams; David Lynch; Herb
Reed; Linda Hayes: Sandra Dawn; Nate Nelson;
Sonny Turner; Zola Taylor; Paul Robi; Alex Hodge.
Also see FLAMINGOS
Also see HAYES, Linda, & The Platters
Also see LITTLE ANTHONY & THE IM-
PERIALS / Platters
Also see PLATTERS '65

**PLATTERS / Inez & Charlie Foxx /
Jive Five / Tommy Hunt**
LPs: 10/12-Inch 33rpm
MUSICOR: *67* 12-15
Also see FOXX, Inez
Also see HUNT, Tommy
Also see JIVE FIVE
Also see PLATTERS

PLATTERS '65
Singles: 7-Inch
ENTREE: *65* 3-5
Also see PLATTERS

PLAYBOYS
Singles: 7-Inch
ABC-PARAMOUNT: *59* 5-8
ACE: *64* 3-5
CAMEO: *58* 5-8
CATALINA: 4-6
CHANCELLOR: *61-62* 4-6
COTTON: *62* 5-8
DOLTON: *59* 4-6
HEARTBEAT: 3-5
IMPERIAL: *59* 5-8
JEWEL: *64* 3-5
LEGATO: *63* 4-6
MARTINIQUE (101; "Over The
Weekend"): *58* 10-15

MARTINIQUE (400; "Please
  Forgive Me"): *59* $8-10
MERCURY: *57* 5-10
RIK: *59* 4-6
SOUVENIR: *59* 4-6
TITAN: *65* 4-6
Note: This section is one of several in this edition
wherein listings by more than one group, using the
same name, are lumped together because we
haven't been able yet to accurately separate them.

PLAYER
Singles: 7-Inch
CASABLANCA: *80* 1-3
RCA VICTOR: *82* 1-3
RSO: *77-78* 2-3
LPs: 10/12-Inch 33rpm
CASABLANCA: *80* 5-8
RSO: *77-78* 5-8
RCA VICTOR: *81* 5-8
Also see BANDANA

PLAYERS ASSOCIATION
Singles: 12-Inch 33/45rpm
VANGUARD: *79-80* 4-6
Singles: 7-Inch
VANGUARD: *77-80* 1-3
LPs: 10/12-Inch 33rpm
VANGUARD: *77-80* 5-8

PLAYMATES
Singles: 78rpm
ROULETTE: *57* 4-6
Singles: 7-Inch
ABC-PARAMOUNT: *63-64* 3-5
BELL: *71* 2-4
COLPIX: *64-65* 3-5
CONGRESS: *65* 3-5
ROULETTE: *57-63* 4-8
LPs: 10/12-Inch 33rpm
FORUM: *60* 15-20
ROULETTE: *57-61* 20-25
Members: Donny Conn; Morey Carr; Chic Hetti.

PLEASURE
Singles: 12-Inch 33/45rpm
FANTASY: *76-80* 4-6
Singles: 7-Inch
FANTASY: *76-80* 1-3
RCA VICTOR: *82-83* 1-3
LPs: 10/12-Inch 33rpm
FANTASY: *76-80* 5-8
RCA VICTOR: *82* 5-8

PLEASURE, King
Singles: 78rpm
ALADDIN: *57* 3-6

JUBILEE: *55* $3-6
Singles: 7-Inch
ALADDIN: *57* 5-10
JUBILEE: *55* 5-10
PRESTIGE (800 & 900 series): *52-55* 5-8
UNITED ARTISTS: *62* 4-6
LPs: 10/12-Inch 33rpm
HI-FI: *60* 20-40
PRESTIGE (208; "King Pleasure
  Sings"): *55* 50-100
(10-Inch L.P.)
PRESTIGE (7000 series): *57* 30-60
UNITED ARTISTS: *62* 15-25

PLEASURE & THE BEAST
Singles: 12-Inch 33/45rpm
AIRWAVE: *84* 4-6

PLEIS, Jack, & His Orchestra
Singles: 7-Inch
ATCO: *65* 2-3
COLUMBIA: *61* 2-4
DECCA: *53-60* 2-4
LONDON: *50-51* 2-4
RANWOOD: *76* 1-3
EPs: 7-Inch 33/45rpm
DECCA: *55-57* 4-8
LPs: 10/12-Inch 33rpm
CAMEO: *63* 6-12
COLUMBIA: *61* 6-12
DECCA: *55-57* 6-15
RANWOOD: *76* 5-8

PLIMSOULS
Singles: 12-Inch 33/45rpm
BOMP: *80* 5-8
Singles: 7-Inch
BOMP: *80* 2-3
GEFFEN: *83* 1-3
Picture Sleeves
BOMP: *80* 2-3
LPs: 10/12-Inch 33rpm
GEFFEN: *83* 5-8
PLANET: *81* 5-8

PLUSH
Singles: 7-Inch
RCA VICTOR: *82* 1-3
LPs: 10/12-Inch 33rpm
RCA VICTOR: *82* 5-8

P-NUT GALLERY
Singles: 7-Inch
BUDDAH: *71* 2-4

POCKETS
Singles: 7-Inch
ARC: *79* 1-3

COLUMBIA: 77-78 .... $2-3
LPs: 10/12-Inch 33rpm
ARC: 79 5-8
COLUMBIA: 77-78 5-8

POCO
Singles: 7-Inch
ABC: 75-79 2-4
ATLANTIC: 82-84 1-3
EPIC: 69-75 3-5
MCA: 79-82 1-3
Picture Sleeves
EPIC: 70-72 3-5
MCA: 80 1-3
LPs: 10/12-Inch 33rpm
ABC: 75-78 8-10
ATLANTIC: 82-84 5-8
EPIC (26460 through 30753): 69-71 10-15
EPIC (31601 through 36210): 71-81 6-10
MCA: 80-82 5-8
MFSL: 78 25-50
   Members: Richie Furay; Jim Messina; Rusty
   Young; Timothy Schmit; Paul Cotton.
   Also see BUFFALO SPRINGFIELD
   Also see EAGLES
   Also see FURAY, Richie
   Also see ILLINOIS SPEED PRESS
   Also see MEISNER, Randy
   Also see MESSINA, Jim
   Also see SCHMIT, Timothy B.

POETS
Singles: 7-Inch
CHAIRMAN: 63 3-5
RED BIRD: 65 4-6
SYMBOL: 66 3-5
TRY ME: 63 3-5
VEEP: 68 3-5
   Also see MAIN INGREDIENT

POETS
Singles: 7-Inch
DYNO VOX: 64 3-6

POINT BLANK
Singles: 7-Inch
ARISTA: 76-77 2-3
MCA: 79-81 1-3
LPs: 10/12-Inch 33rpm
ARISTA: 77 5-8
MCA: 79-82 5-8

POINTER, Anita
Singles: 7-Inch
RCA VICTOR: 87-88 1-3

POINTER, Anita, & Earl Thomas Conley
Singles: 7-Inch
RCA VICTOR: 86 .... $1-3
   Also see POINTER SISTERS

POINTER, Bonnie
Singles: 12-Inch 33/45rpm
MOTOWN: 78-81 4-6
PRIVATE I: 84-85 4-6
Singles: 7-Inch
MOTOWN (Black vinyl): 78-81 1-3
MOTOWN (Colored vinyl): 78-81 3-6
PRIVATE I: 84-85 1-3
Promotional Singles
MOTOWN (Colored vinyl): 78 3-5
LPs: 10/12-Inch 33rpm
MOTOWN: 78-79 5-8
PRIVATE I: 84 5-8
   Also see POINTER SISTERS

POINTER, June
Singles: 12-Inch 33/45rpm
PLANET: 83-84 4-6
Singles: 7-Inch
PLANET: 83-84 1-3
LPs: 10/12-Inch 33rpm
PLANET: 83 5-8
   Also see POINTER SISTERS

POINTER, Noel
Singles: 12-Inch 33/45rpm
UNITED ARTISTS: 77 4-6
Singles: 7-Inch
BLUE NOTE: 77 1-3
LIBERTY: 81 1-3
UNITED ARTISTS: 78-80 1-3
LPs: 10/12-Inch 33rpm
BLUE NOTE: 77 5-10
LIBERTY: 81 5-8
UNITED ARTISTS: 78-80 5-8

POINTER SISTERS
Singles: 12-Inch 33/45rpm
PLANET: 78-85 4-6
RCA VICTOR: 85-86 4-6
Singles: 7-Inch
ABC: 75-78 2-3
ATLANTIC: 72 2-4
BLUE THUMB: 73-78 2-4
MCA: 87 1-3
PLANET: 78-85 1-3
RCA VICTOR: 85-88 1-3
Picture Sleeves
PLANET: 78-85 1-3
LPs: 10/12-Inch 33rpm
BLUE THUMB: 73-77 8-12
MCA: 81 5-8

PLANET: *78-84* $5-8
RCA VICTOR: *85-86* 5-8
Members: Bonnie Pointer; Anita Pointer; Ruth Pointer; June Pointer.
Also see MEMPHIS HORNS
Also see POINTER, Anita, & Earl Thomas Conley
Also see POINTER, Bonnie
Also see POINTER, June

POISON
Singles: 12-Inch 33/45rpm
ROULETTE: *76* 4-6
Singles: 7-Inch
ROULETTE: *75-76* 2-3
LPs: 10/12-Inch 33rpm
ROULETTE: *76* 5-8

POISON
Singles: 7-Inch
CAPITOL: *87* 1-3
ENIGMA: *86-87* 1-3
LPs: 10/12-Inch 33rpm
ENIGMA: *86* 5-8
Members: Bret Michaels; Rikki Rocket; C. C. De-Ville; Bobby Dall.

POISON DOLLYS
LPs: 10/12-Inch 33rpm
PVC: *86* 5-8

POLICE
Singles: 7-Inch
A&M (Except 25000 & picture discs): *79-84* 1-3
A&M (25000; "De Do Do Do, De Da Da Da"): *80* 2-4
(Spanish/Japanese language version.)
A&M (Picture disc singles): *79-80* 5-10
(Promotional issues only.)
SIRE: *86* 1-3
Picture Sleeves
A&M (Except 25000): *79-84* 1-3
A&M (25000; "De Do Do Do, De Da Da Da"): *80* 3-5
LPs: 10/12-Inch 33rpm
A&M (Except 3713): *79-86* 5-10
A&M (3713; "Reggatta de Blanc"): *79* .. 10-20
(Two 10-inch LPs. Includes poster. Promotional issue only.)
NAUTILUS: *81* 10-15
Members: Gordon "Sting" Sumner; Andy Summers; Stewart Copeland.
Also see COPELAND, Stewart
Also see FRIPP, Robert, & Andy Summers
Also see STING

POLITICIANS
Singles: 7-Inch
HOT WAX: *72* $2-4
LPs: 10/12-Inch 33rpm
HOT WAX: *72* 8-10
Members: McKinley Jackson.

POLNAREFF, Michel
Singles: 12-Inch 33/45rpm
ATLANTIC: *76* 4-6
Singles: 7-Inch
ATLANTIC: *76* 2-4
4 CORNERS: *67* 3-6
KAPP: *65-66* 3-6
LPs: 10/12-Inch 33rpm
ATLANTIC: *75* 8-10
4 CORNERS: *67* 10-15

PONDEROSA TWINS + ONE
Singles: 7-Inch
ASTROSCOPE: *72* 2-4
HOROSCOPE: *71* 2-4
LPs: 10/12-Inch 33rpm
HOROSCOPE: *71* 8-10

PONI-TAILS
Singles: 78rpm
ABC-PARAMOUNT: *57-60* 5-10
MARC: *57* 5-10
POINT: *57* 5-10
Singles: 7-Inch
ABC: *73* 1-3
ABC-PARAMOUNT: *57-60* 8-10
MCA: 1-3
MARC: *57* 10-15
POINT: *57* 10-15

PONSAR, Serge
Singles: 12-Inch 33/45rpm
WARNER BROS: *83* 4-6
Singles: 7-Inch
WARNER BROS: *83* 1-3

PONTY, Jean-Luc
Singles: 7-Inch
ATLANTIC: *76-85* 1-3
LPs: 10/12-Inch 33rpm
ATLANTIC: *75-85* 5-10
BLUE NOTE: *76-81* 5-10
MPS: *72-73* 5-10
PACIFIC JAZZ: *68-78* 8-18
PAUSA: *80* 5-8
PRESTIGE: *70* 8-15
WORLD PACIFIC: *69* 8-15

POOLE, Brian
(Brian Poole & The Tremeloes)
Singles: 7-Inch
DATE: *66* $4-6
LONDON: *63* 5-8
MONUMENT: *64-65* 4-6
LPs: 10/12-Inch 33rpm
AUDIO FIDELITY: *66-67* 15-20
Also see TREMELOES

POP, Iggy
(Iggy & The Stooges)
Singles: 12-Inch 33/45rpm
A&M: *86* 4-6
Singles: 7-Inch
A&M: *86* 1-3
RCA VICTOR: *77* 2-3
SIAMESE: *77* 2-3
EPs: 7-Inch 33/45rpm
BOMP: *78* 5-10
LPs: 10/12-Inch 33rpm
A&M: *86* 5-8
ANIMAL: *82* 5-8
ARISTA: *79-81* 8-10
BOMP (Black vinyl): *78* 10-15
BOMP (Colored vinyl): *78* 20-40
COLUMBIA: *73* 12-15
ENIGMA: *84* 5-8
IMPORT: *77* 8-10
INVASION: *83* 8-10
RCA VICTOR: *77-78* 5-8
Also see BOWIE, David / Iggy Pop
Also see STOOGES

POP, Iggy, & James Williamson
EPs: 7-Inch 33/45rpm
BOMP: *78* 5-10
LPs: 10/12-Inch 33rpm
BOMP: *78* 8-10
Also see POP, Iggy

POP TARTS
Singles: 7-Inch
FUNTONE USA: *88* 5-10
Members: Fenton Pop Tart; Randy Pop Tart; C.P.
Roth; Alan Bezoz; Gabriel Rotello; Simon Girl.

POP TOPS
Singles: 7-Inch
ABC: *71* 2-4
CALLA: *68* 3-5

POPE JOHN XXIII
LPs: 10/12-Inch 33rpm
MERCURY: *63* 5-10

POPE JOHN PAUL II
LPs: 10/12-Inch 33rpm
BETHLEHEM: *79* 4-8

INFINITY: *79* $4-8
VOX CHRISTIANA: *79* 4-8

POPE PAUL VI
LPs: 10/12-Inch 33rpm
A&M: *65* 5-10
AUDIO FIDELITY: *65* 5-10
MGM: *65* 5-10
20TH CENTURY-FOX: *64* 5-10

POPPIES
Singles: 7-Inch
EPIC: *66* 3-5
Picture Sleeves
EPIC: *66* 4-8
LPs: 10/12-Inch 33rpm
EPIC: *66* 20-25
Member: Dorothy Moore.
Also see MOORE, Dorothy

POPPY FAMILY
Singles: 7-Inch
LONDON: *70-72* 2-4
LPs: 10/12-Inch 33rpm
LONDON: *70-71* 10-12
Members: Susan Jacks; Terry Jacks.
Also see JACKS, Susan
Also see JACKS, Terry

PORTER, David
Singles: 7-Inch
ENTERPRISE: *70-72* 2-4
LPs: 10/12-Inch 33rpm
ENTERPRISE: *70-72* 8-10
Also see HAYES, Isaac & David Porter

PORTER, Nolan
(N.F. Porter; Nolan)
Singles: 7-Inch
ABC: *73* 2-3
LIZARD: *71* 2-4
LPs: 10/12-Inch 33rpm
LIZARD: *71* 8-10

PORTNOY, Gary
Singles: 7-Inch
APPLAUSE: *83* 1-3
EARTHTONE: *84* 1-3
Picture Sleeves
EARTHTONE: *84* 2-4

POSEY, Sandy
Singles: 7-Inch
AUDIOGRAPH: *83* 1-3
COLUMBIA: *71-72* 2-3
MGM: *66-67* 2-4
POLYDOR: *83* 1-3
WARNER BROS: *78-79* 1-3

Picture Sleeves
MGM: *66-67* $3-5
LPs: 10/12-Inch 33rpm
COLUMBIA: *72* 8-10
51 WEST: *83* 5-8
GUSTO: 5-8
MGM: *66-70* 10-12

POSEY, Sandy / Skeeter Davis
LPs: 10/12-Inch 33rpm
GUSTO: 5-8
Also see DAVIS, Skeeter
Also see POSEY, Sandy

POST, Mike
(Mike Post Coalition)
Singles: 7-Inch
BELL: *71* 2-3
ELEKTRA: *81-82* 1-3
EPIC: *77* 1-3
MGM: *75* 1-3
MUSIC FACTORY: *68* 2-3
POLYDOR: *87* 1-3
REPRISE: *65-66* 2-4
WARNER BROS: *69* 2-3
Picture Sleeves
ELEKTRA: *81-82* 1-3
LPs: 10/12-Inch 33rpm
ELEKTRA: *82* 5-8
RCA VICTOR: *83* 5-8
MGM: *75* 5-10
POLYDOR: *87* 5-8
WARNER BROS: *69* 8-12

POTLIQUOR
Singles: 7-Inch
CAPITOL: *79* 2-3
JANUS: *72* 2-4
LPs: 10/12-Inch 33rpm
CAPITOL: *79* 5-8
JANUS: *70-73* 10-15

POURCEL, Franck
(Franck Pourcel's French Fiddles)
Singles: 7-Inch
BLUE: *69* 1-3
CAPITOL: *59-64* 2-4
IMPERIAL: *66-68* 1-3
PARAMOUNT: *71-73* 1-3
EPs: 7-Inch 33/45rpm
CAPITOL: *59* 4-8
LPs: 10/12-Inch 33rpm
ATCO: *69* 5-10
CAPITOL: *56-79* 5-15
IMPERIAL: *66-68* 5-10
PARAMOUNT: *70-73* 5-8
WESTMINSTER: *54-55* 10-20

POUSETTE-DART BAND
Singles: 7-Inch
CAPITOL: *76-79* $2-3
LPs: 10/12-Inch 33rpm
CAPITOL: *76-80* 5-10
Member: Jon Pousette-Dart.

POWELL, Adam Clayton
LPs: 10/12-Inch 33rpm
JUBILEE: *67* 5-15

POWELL, Bobby
Singles: 7-Inch
JEWEL: *67* 3-5
WHIT: *65-71* 3-5
LPs: 10/12-Inch 33rpm
EXCELLO: *73* 8-10

POWELL, Cozy
Singles: 7-Inch
CHRYSALIS: *74* 2-3
Also see BECK, Jeff
Also see EMERSON, LAKE & POWELL

POWELL, Jane
Singles: 78rpm
VERVE: *56* 2-4
Singles: 7-Inch
RANWOOD: *68* 2-3
VERVE: *56* 2-4
LPs: 10/12-Inch 33rpm
COLUMBIA: *55-57* 10-25
LION: *59* 8-15
MGM: *55* 15-25
VERVE: *56* 15-25

POWER STATION
Singles: 12-Inch 33/45rpm
CAPITOL: *85* 4-6
Singles: 7-Inch
CAPITOL: *85* 1-3
LPs: 10/12-Inch 33rpm
CAPITOL: *85* 5-8
Members: Andy Taylor; John Taylor;
Robert Palmer.
Also see DURAN DURAN
Also see PALMER, Robert
Also see TAYLOR, Andy
Also see TAYLOR, John

POWERS, Joey
(Joey Powers' Flower)
Singles: 7-Inch
AMY: *63-67* 3-6
MGM: *65* 3-6
RCA VICTOR (8000 series): *62* 4-6
RCA VICTOR (9700 series): *69* 2-5
LPs: 10/12-Inch 33rpm
AMY: *64* 15-20

Also see ORBISON, Roy / Bobby Bare / Joey Powers

POWERS, Tom
Singles: 7-Inch
BIG TREE: 77 . . . . $2-3

POWERSOURCE
Singles: 7-Inch
POWERVISION: 87 1-3

POZO-SECO SINGERS
(Pozo Seco; Susan Taylor & The Pozo Seco Singers)
Singles: 7-Inch
CERTRON: 70 2-4
COLUMBIA: 65-70 3-5
EDMARK: 65 5-18
LPs: 10/12-Inch 33rpm
CERTRON: 70 8-12
COLUMBIA: 66-68 12-15
Members: Don Williams; Susan Taylor; Lofton Kline.
Also see WILLIAMS, Don

PRADO, Perez, & His Orchestra
Singles: 78rpm
RCA VICTOR: 50-58 2-4
Singles: 7-Inch
RCA VICTOR: 50-64 2-4
UNITED ARTISTS: 64 2-3
Picture Sleeves
RCA VICTOR: 59 3-5
EPs: 7-Inch 33/45rpm
RCA VICTOR: 54-61 4-8
LPs: 10/12-Inch 33rpm
CAMDEN: 60 5-10
RCA VICTOR: 76 5-8
(With an "ANL1" prefix.)
RCA VICTOR: 54-72 8-18
(With an "LPM," "LSP," or "VPS" prefix.)
SPRINGBOARD: 77 4-8
UNITED ARTISTS: 65-68 5-10
Also see CLOONEY, Rosemary, & Perez Prado
Also see HIRT, Al / Henry Mancini / Perez Prado

PRATT, Andy
Singles: 7-Inch
COLUMBIA: 73 2-4
NEMPEROR: 76-77 2-3
LPs: 10/12-Inch 33rpm
COLUMBIA: 73 8-10
NEMPEROR: 76-79 5-8
POLYDOR: 70 10-12
Also see SPRINGSTEEN, Bruce / Andy Pratt

PRATT-MC CLAIN
Singles: 7-Inch
REPRISE: 76-77 . . . . $2-3
LPs: 10/12-Inch 33rpm
DUNHILL: 73 8-10
REPRISE: 76 8-10
Members: Truett Pratt; Jerry McClain.

PRECISIONS
Singles: 7-Inch
ATCO: 69 2-4
D-TOWN: 65 4-6
DREW: 66-68 3-5
HEN-MAR: 73 2-4

PRELUDE
Singles: 7-Inch
ISLAND: 74 2-3
PYE: 75 2-3
LPs: 10/12-Inch 33rpm
ISLAND: 74 8-10
PYE: 76 8-10

PRELUDES FIVE
Singles: 7-Inch
PIK: 61 15-20

PREMIATA FORNERIA MARCONI:
see P.F.M.

PREMIERS
Singles: 7-Inch
FARO: 64-67 3-5
FINE: 4-6
LEO: 64 3-5
WARNER BROS: 64 3-5
LPs: 10/12-Inch 33rpm
WARNER BROS: 64 15-20

PRENTISS, Lee
Singles: 12-Inch 33/45rpm
MSB: 83 4-6

PREPARATIONS
Singles: 7-Inch
HEART & SOUL: 68 2-4

PRESIDENTS
Singles: 7-Inch
DELUXE: 69 2-5
HOLLYWOOD: 68 3-6
SUSSEX: 70-71 2-5
LPs: 10/12-Inch 33rpm
SUSSEX: 70 10-15

PRESLEY, Elvis
Singles: 78rpm
Includes Promotional 78s
RCA VICTOR (6357; "Mystery Train"): 55 75-100

RCA VICTOR (6380; "That's All
Right"): 55 .... $75-100
RCA VICTOR (6381; "Good Rockin'
Tonight"): 55 75-100
RCA VICTOR (6382; "Milkcow Blues
Boogie"): 55 75-100
RCA VICTOR (6383; "Baby, Let's
Play House"): 55 75-100
RCA VICTOR (6420; "Heartbreak
Hotel"): 56 60-75
(Black label.)
RCA VICTOR (6420; "Heartbreak
Hotel"): 56 175-200
(White label. Promotional issue only.)
RCA VICTOR (6540; "I Want You, I
Need You, I Love You"): 56 60-75
(Black label.)
RCA VICTOR (6540; "I Want You, I
Need You, I Love You"): 56 175-200
(White label. Promotional issue only.)
RCA VICTOR (6604; "Don't Be
Cruel"): 56 60-75
(Black label.)
RCA VICTOR (6604; "Don't Be
Cruel"): 56 175-200
(White label. Promotional issue only.)
RCA VICTOR (6636; "Blue Suede
Shoes"): 56 60-75
(Black label.)
RCA VICTOR (6637; "I Got
A Woman"): 56 60-75
(Black label.)
RCA VICTOR (6638; "I'm Gonna Sit
Right Down And Cry"): 56 60-75
(Black label.)
RCA VICTOR (6639; "Tryin' To
Get To You"): 56 60-75
(Black label.)
RCA VICTOR (6640; "Blue Moon"): 56 . 60-75
(Black label.)
RCA VICTOR (6641; "Money
Honey"): 56 60-75
(Black label.)
RCA VICTOR (6642; "Lawdy Miss
Clawdy"): 56 60-75
(Black label.)
RCA VICTOR (6643; "Love Me
Tender"): 56 50-75
(Black label.)
RCA VICTOR (6643; "Love Me
Tender"): 56 175-200
(White label. Promotional issue only.)
RCA VICTOR (6800; "Too Much"): 57 . 50-75
(Black label.)

RCA VICTOR (6800; "Too
Much"): 57 .... $175-200
(White label. Promotional issue only.)
RCA VICTOR (6870; "All Shook
Up"): 57 50-75
(Black label.)
RCA VICTOR (6870; "All Shook
Up"): 57 175-200
(White label. Promotional issue only.)
RCA VICTOR (7000; "Teddy
Bear"): 57 50-75
(Black label.)
RCA VICTOR (7000; "Teddy
Bear"): 57 175-200
(White label. Promotional issue only.)
RCA VICTOR (7035; "Jailhouse
Rock"): 57 50-75
(Black label.)
RCA VICTOR (7035; "Jailhouse
Rock"): 57 175-200
(White label. Promotional issue only.)
RCA VICTOR (7150; "Don't"): 58 60-75
RCA VICTOR (7240; "Wear My Ring
Around Your Neck"): 58 60-75
RCA VICTOR (7280; "Hard Headed
Woman"): 58 75-100
RCA VICTOR (7410; "One
Night"): 58 250-350
ROYAL ("Elvis Presley
Show"): 56 100-200
(One-sided disc, issued to radio stations to promote
Elvis in concert. Includes an excerpt of *Heartbreak
Hotel*.)
SUN (209; "That's All Right"): 54 175-250
SUN (210; "Good Rockin'
Tonight"): 54 175-250
SUN (215; "You're A
Heartbreaker"): 55 200-300
SUN (217; "Baby Let's
Play House"): 55 175-250
SUN (223; "Mystery Train"): 55 150-200
Note: All of the Elvis 78s were simultaneously is-
sued on 45rpm singles. All 78rpm plastic
soundsheets, or flexi-discs, are listed in a separate
section that follows. Sun and RCA 78s can be
found with label variations. Sun promotional
singles were so indicated with "Sample" rubber
stamped on the label.

Singles: 7-Inch
Commercial Issues
COLLECTABLES: 86-87 1-3
RCA VICTOR (0088; "Raised On
Rock"): 73 3-5
RCA VICTOR (0130; "How Great
Thou Art"): 69 15-20

RCA VICTOR (0196; "I've Got A Thing
About You Baby"): 74 . . . . $3-5
RCA VICTOR (0280; "If You Talk
In Your Sleep"): 74 3-5
RCA VICTOR (0572; "Merry Christmas
Baby"): 71 12-15
RCA VICTOR (0619; "Until It's Time
For You To Go"): 72 3-5
RCA VICTOR (0651; "He Touched
Me"); 72 3-5
RCA VICTOR (0651; "He Touched
Me"): 72 80-100
(With *He Touched Me* pressed at about 35rpm in-
stead of 45. These copies, the result of an error in
production, were commercial issues.)
RCA VICTOR (0672; "An American
Trilogy"): 72 10-12
RCA VICTOR (0769; "Burning Love"): 72 . 3-5
(Orange label.)
RCA VICTOR (0769; "Burning
Love"): 72 75-100
(Gray label.)
RCA VICTOR (0815; "Separate Ways"): 71 3-5
RCA VICTOR (0910; "Steamroller
Blues"): 73 3-5
RCA VICTOR (1017; "It's Only
Love"): 71 3-5
RCA VICTOR (2458; "My Boy"/
"Loving Arms"): 74 200-400
(Produced in the U.S. for European distribution.)
RCA VICTOR (6357; "Mystery
Train"): 55 40-60
(With horizontal silver line.)
RCA VICTOR (6357; "Mystery
Train"): 55 25-35
(Without horizontal silver line.)
RCA VICTOR (6380; "That's All
Right"): 55 40-60
(With horizontal silver line.)
RCA VICTOR (6380; "That's All
Right"): 55 25-35
(Without horizontal silver line.)
RCA VICTOR (6381; "Good Rockin'
Tonight"): 55 40-60
(With horizontal silver line.)
RCA VICTOR (6381; "Good Rockin'
Tonight"): 55 25-35
(Without horizontal silver line.)
RCA VICTOR (6382; "Milkcow Blues
Boogie"): 55 40-60
(With horizontal silver line.)
RCA VICTOR (6382; "Milkcow Blues
Boogie"): 55 25-35
(Without horizontal silver line.)

Elvis Presley

RCA VICTOR (6383; "Baby, Let's
Play House"): 55 . . . . $40-60
(With horizontal silver line.)
RCA VICTOR (6383; "Baby, Let's
Play House"): 55 25-35
(Without horizontal silver line.)
RCA VICTOR (6420; "Heartbreak
Hotel"): 56 25-50
(Turquoise label.)
RCA VICTOR (6420; "Heartbreak
Hotel"): 56 25-30
(Black label. With horizontal silver line.)
RCA VICTOR (6420; "Heartbreak
Hotel"): 56 15-20
(Black label. Without horizontal silver line.)
RCA VICTOR (6540; "I Want You, I
Need You, I Love You"): 56 25-30
(With horizontal silver line.)
RCA VICTOR (6540; "I Want You, I
Need You, I Love You"): 56 15-20
(Without horizontal silver line.)
RCA VICTOR (6604; "Don't Be
Cruel"): 56 25-30
(With horizontal silver line.)
RCA VICTOR (6604; "Don't Be
Cruel"): 56 15-20
(Without horizontal silver line.)
RCA VICTOR (6636; "Blue Suede
Shoes"): 56 40-50
(With horizontal silver line.)
RCA VICTOR (6636; "Blue Suede
Shoes"): 56 20-30
(Without horizontal silver line.)

RCA VICTOR (6637; "I Got
A Woman"): *56* $40-50
(With horizontal silver line.)
RCA VICTOR (6637; "I Got
A Woman"): *56* 20-30
(Without horizontal silver line.)
RCA VICTOR (6638; "I'm Gonna Sit
Right Down And Cry"): *56* 40-50
(With horizontal silver line.)
RCA VICTOR (6638; "I'm Gonna Sit
Right Down And Cry"): *56* 20-30
(Without horizontal silver line.)
RCA VICTOR (6639; "Tryin' To Get
To You"): *56* 40-50
(With horizontal silver line.)
RCA VICTOR (6639; "Tryin' To Get
To You"): *56* 20-30
(Without horizontal silver line.)
RCA VICTOR (6640; "Blue Moon"): *56* . 40-50
(With horizontal silver line.)
RCA VICTOR (6640; "Blue Moon"): *56* . 20-30
(Without horizontal silver line.)
RCA VICTOR (6641; "Money
Honey"): *56* 40-50
(With horizontal silver line.)
RCA VICTOR (6641; "Money
Honey"): *56* 20-30
(Without horizontal silver line.)
RCA VICTOR (6642; "Lawdy Miss
Clawdy"): *56* 125-150
(No dog on label.)
RCA VICTOR (6642; "Lawdy Miss
Clawdy"): *56* 40-50
(With horizontal silver line.)
RCA VICTOR (6642; "Lawdy Miss
Clawdy"): *56* 20-30
(Without horizontal silver line.)
RCA VICTOR (6643; "Love Me
Tender"): *56* 25-30
(With horizontal silver line.)
RCA VICTOR (6643; "Love Me
Tender"): *56* 15-20
(Without horizontal silver line.)
RCA VICTOR (6800; "Too
Much"): *57* 100-125
(No dog on label.)
RCA VICTOR (6800; "Too Much"): *57* . 25-30
(With horizontal silver line.)
RCA VICTOR (6800; "Too Much"): *57* . 15-20
(Without horizontal silver line.)
RCA VICTOR (6870; "All Shook
Up"): *57* 25-30
(With horizontal silver line.)
RCA VICTOR (6870; "All Shook
Up"): *57* 15-20
(Without horizontal silver line.)

RCA VICTOR (7000; "Teddy
Bear"): *57* $25-30
(With horizontal silver line.)
RCA VICTOR (7000; "Teddy
Bear"): *57* 15-20
(Without horizontal silver line.)
RCA VICTOR (7035; "Jailhouse
Rock"): *57* 35-40
(With horizontal silver line. This was the last silver
line single.)
RCA VICTOR (7035; "Jailhouse
Rock"): *57* 15-20
(Without horizontal silver line.)
RCA VICTOR (7150; "Don't"): *58* 10-15
RCA VICTOR (7240; "Wear My Ring
Around Your Neck"): *58* 10-15
RCA VICTOR (7280; "Hard Headed
Woman"): *58* 10-15
RCA VICTOR (7410; "One Night"): *58* .. 10-15
RCA VICTOR (7506; "A Fool
Such As I"): *59* 10-15
RCA VICTOR (7600; "A Big Hunk
O' Love"): *59* 10-15
RCA VICTOR (7740; "Stuck
On You"): *60* 8-10
RCA VICTOR (7740; "Stuck
On You"): *60* 175-200
(Living Stereo, numbered with a "61" prefix.)
RCA VICTOR (7777; "It's Now
Or Never"): *60* 8-10
RCA VICTOR (7777; "It's Now
Or Never"): *60* 250-300
(Living Stereo, numbered with a "61" prefix.)
RCA VICTOR (7810; "Are You
Lonesome To-night?"): *60* 8-10
RCA VICTOR (7810; "Are You
Lonesome To-night?"): *60* 250-300
(Living Stereo, numbered with a "61" prefix.)
RCA VICTOR (7850; "Surrender"): *61* ...8-10
RCA VICTOR (7850; "Surrender"): *61* 300-500
(Compact 33 Single, numbered with a "37" prefix.)
RCA VICTOR (7850; "Surrender"): *61* 225-275
(Living Stereo, numbered with a "61" prefix.)
RCA VICTOR (7850;
"Surrender"): *61* 1000-1200
(Stereo Compact 33 Single, numbered with a "68"
prefix.)
RCA VICTOR (7880; "I Feel
So Bad"): *61* 8-10
RCA VICTOR (7880; "I Feel
So Bad"): *61* 400-800
(Compact 33 Single, numbered with a "37" prefix.)
RCA VICTOR (7908; "His
Latest Flame"): *61* 8-10

RCA VICTOR (7908; "His
Latest Flame"): *61* **$500-1000**
(Compact 33 Single, numbered with a "37" prefix.)
RCA VICTOR (7968; "Can't Help
Falling In Love"): *61* **8-10**
RCA VICTOR (7968; "Can't Help
Falling In Love"): *61* **1000-1500**
(Compact 33 Single, numbered with a "37" prefix.)
RCA VICTOR (7992; "Good
Luck Charm"): *62* **8-10**
RCA VICTOR (7992; "Good
Luck Charm"): *62* **1500-2500**
(Compact 33 Single, numbered with a "37" prefix.)
RCA VICTOR (8041; "She's
Not You"): *62* **8-10**
RCA VICTOR (8100; "Return
To Sender"): *62* **8-10**
RCA VICTOR (8134; "One Broken
Heart For Sale"): *63* **8-10**
RCA VICTOR (8188; "Devil
In Disguise"): *63* **50-75**
(Flip side title incorrectly shown as *Please Don't
Drag That String ALONG.*)
RCA VICTOR (8188; "Devil
In Disguise"): *63* **5-8**
(Flip side title correctly shown as *Please Don't
Drag That String AROUND.*)
RCA VICTOR (8243; "Bossa Nova
Baby"): *63* **6-10**
RCA VICTOR (8307; "Kissin'
Cousins"): *64* **6-10**
RCA VICTOR (8360; "Viva
Las Vegas"): *64* **6-10**
RCA VICTOR (8400; "Such
A Night"): *64* **6-10**
RCA VICTOR (8440; "Ask Me"): *64* **6-10**
RCA VICTOR (8500; "Do The
Clam"): *65* **5-10**
RCA VICTOR (8585; "It Feels
So Right"): *65* **5-8**
RCA VICTOR (8657; "I'm Yours"): *65* **5-8**
RCA VICTOR (8740; "Tell Me Why"): *65* . **5-8**
RCA VICTOR (8780; "Frankie
& Johnny"): *66* **5-8**
RCA VICTOR (8870; "Love
Letters"): *66* **5-8**
RCA VICTOR (8941; "Spinout"): *66* **5-8**
RCA VICTOR (8950; "If Everyday
Was Like Christmas"): *66* **5-8**
RCA VICTOR (9056; "Indescribably
Blue"): *67* **5-8**
RCA VICTOR (9115; "Long
Legged Girl"): *67* **5-8**
RCA VICTOR (9287; "There's
Always Me"): *67* **5-8**

RCA VICTOR (9341; "Big
Boss Man"): *67* **$5-8**
RCA VICTOR (9425; "Guitar
Man"): *68* **5-8**
RCA VICTOR (9465; "U.S. Male"): *68* ... **5-8**
RCA VICTOR (9547; "Your Time
Hasn't Come Yet Baby"): *68* **5-8**
RCA VICTOR (9600; "You'll Never
Walk Alone"): *68* **5-10**
RCA VICTOR (9610; "Almost
In Love"): *68* **5-8**
RCA VICTOR (9670; "If I
Can Dream"): *68* **3-5**
RCA VICTOR (9731; "Memories"): *69* ... **3-5**
RCA VICTOR (9741; "In The
Ghetto"): *69* **3-5**
RCA VICTOR (9747; "Clean Up
Your Own Back Yard"): *69* **3-5**
RCA VICTOR (9764; "Suspicious
Minds"): *69* **3-5**
RCA VICTOR (9768; "Don't
Cry Daddy"): *69* **3-5**
RCA VICTOR (9791; "Kentucky
Rain"): *70* **3-5**
RCA VICTOR (9835; "The Wonder
Of You"): *70* **3-5**
RCA VICTOR (9873; "I've Lost You"): *70* **3-5**
RCA VICTOR (9916; "You Don't Have
To Say You Love Me"): *70* **3-5**
RCA VICTOR (9960; "I Really Don't
Want To Know"): *70* **3-5**
RCA VICTOR (9980; "Where Did
They Go Lord?"): *71* **3-5**
RCA VICTOR (9985; "Life"): *71* **3-5**
RCA VICTOR (9998; "I'm Leavin"): *71* ... **3-5**
Note: RCA numbers in the 10000-14000 series
with a "GB" prefix are Gold Standard Series issues
and are listed in a separate Gold Standard Singles
section. Those in the regular release series are
listed below.
RCA VICTOR (10074; "Promised
Land"): *74* **3-5**
(Orange label.)
RCA VICTOR (10074; "Promised
Land"): *74* **20-25**
(Gray label.)
RCA VICTOR (10191; "My Boy"): *75* **3-5**
(Orange label.)
RCA VICTOR (10191; "My Boy"): *75* ... **8-10**
(Tan or brown label.)
RCA VICTOR (10278; "T-r-o-u-b-l-e"): *75* **3-5**
(Orange label.)
RCA VICTOR (10278; "T-r-o-u-b-l-e"): *75* **8-10**
(Tan label.)

RCA VICTOR (10401; "Bringing
It Back"): 75 .... $45-55
(Orange label.)

RCA VICTOR (10401; "Bringing
It Back"): 75 3-5
(Tan label.)

RCA VICTOR (10601; "Hurt"): 76 3-5
(Tan label.)

RCA VICTOR (10601; "Hurt"): 76 90-100
(Black label.)

RCA VICTOR (10857; "Moody Blue"): 76 . 3-5
(Colored vinyl copies of *Moody Blue*, were experimental and are listed in the Promotional Singles
section that follows.)

RCA VICTOR (10998; "Way Down"): 77 . . 3-5

RCA VICTOR (11099 through 11113): 77 . 2-4
(Discs in this series were originally packaged in
either 11301 and/or 11340, both of which were
boxed sets of singles with sleeves.)

RCA VICTOR (11165; "My Way"): 77 3-5
(With flip side title shown as *America*.)

RCA VICTOR (11165; "My Way"): 77 . . 15-20
(With flip side shown as *America The Beautiful*.)

RCA VICTOR (11212; "Softly, As
I Leave You"): 78 3-5

RCA VICTOR (11301; "15 Golden
Records"): 77 40-50
(Boxed set of 15 Elvis singles, each with a picture
sleeve.)

RCA VICTOR (11320; "Teddy Bear"): 78 . 3-5

RCA VICTOR (11340; "20 Golden
Hits"): 77 65-75
(Boxed set of 10 Elvis singles, each with a picture
sleeve.)

RCA VICTOR (11533; "Are You
Sincere?"): 79 3-5

RCA VICTOR (11679; "There's A
Honky Tonk Angel"): 79 12-15
(With production and backing credits shown on
label.)

RCA VICTOR (11679; "There's A
Honky Tonk Angel"): 79 3-5
(With backing credits removed, leaving only
production credits.)

RCA VICTOR (12158; "Guitar Man"): 81 . . 3-5

RCA VICTOR (12205; "Lovin' Arms"): 81 3-5

RCA VICTOR (13058; "You'll Never
Walk Alone"): 82 3-5

RCA VICTOR (13351; "The Elvis
Medley"): 82 3-5

RCA VICTOR (13500; "I Was
The One"): 83 3-5

RCA VICTOR (13547; "Little Sister"): 83 . 3-5

RCA VICTOR (13875; "Baby, Let's
Play House"): 84 20-40
(Colored vinyl.)

RCA VICTOR (13885 through 13890): 84 .$1-3
(Discs in this series were originally packaged in
13897, *Golden Singles, Vol. I*. May include
jukebox title strips.)

RCA VICTOR (13891 through
13896): 84 1-3
(Discs in this series were originally packaged in
13898, *Golden Singles, Vol. II*. May include
jukebox title strips.)

RCA VICTOR (13897; "Golden
Singles, Vol. I"): 84 10-15
(Package of six colored vinyl singles with sleeves.)

RCA VICTOR (13898; "Golden
Singles, Vol. II"): 84 10-15
(Package of six colored vinyl singles with sleeves.)

RCA VICTOR (13929; "Blue Suede
Shoes"): 84 8-12
(Colored vinyl. With *Blue Suede Shoes* shown as
stereo; *Promised Land* as mono.)

RCA VICTOR (13929; "Blue Suede
Shoes"): 84 5-8
(Colored vinyl. With *Blue Suede Shoes* shown as
mono; *Promised Land* as stereo.)

RCA VICTOR (14090; "Always On
My Mind"): 85 5-8
(Colored vinyl.)

RCA VICTOR (14237; "Merry Christmas
Baby"): 85 5-8
(Black vinyl.)

RCA VICTOR (14237; "Merry Christmas
Baby"): 85 10-15
(Colored vinyl.)
Note: RCA numbers in the 10000-14000 series
with a "GB" prefix are Gold Standard Series issues
and are listed in a separate Gold Standard Singles
section. Regular series issues are in the preceding
section.

SUN (209; "That's All Right"): 54 400-450

SUN (210; "Good Rockin'
Tonight"): 54 400-450

SUN (215; "You're A
Heartbreaker"): 55 400-500

SUN (217; "Baby Let's
Play House"): 55 375-450

SUN (223; "Mystery Train"): 55 300-350
Note: Plastic soundsheets or flexi-discs are listed in
a separate section that follows.

Picture Sleeves
Includes Promotional Sleeves

LAUREL (41 623; "Treat Me
Nice"): 57 2000-3000
(Pictures Elvis but shows artist as Vince Everett.
This black and white "sleeve" was made as a prop
for the film, *Jailhouse Rock*. The printed sheet had
no reverse side, but was applied to a randomly
selected EP.)

RCA VICTOR (76; "Don't"/"Wear My Ring
Around Your Neck"): 60 .... **$1000-1500**
(Promotional issue only.)

RCA VICTOR (0088; "Raised On
Rock"): 73 .... **8-12**

RCA VICTOR (118; "King Of The
Whole Wide World"): 62 .... **150-175**
(Promotional issue only.)

RCA VICTOR (0130; "How Great
Thou Art"): 69 .... **75-100**

RCA VICTOR (162; "How Great
Thou Art"): 67 .... **125-150**
(Promotional issue only.)

RCA VICTOR (0196; "I've Got A Thing
About You Baby"): 74 .... **8-12**

RCA VICTOR (0280; "If You Talk
In Your Sleep"): 74 .... **8-12**

RCA VICTOR (0572; "Merry Christmas
Baby"): 71 .... **20-30**

RCA VICTOR (0619; "Until It's Time
For You To Go"): 71 .... **8-12**

RCA VICTOR (0651; "He Touched
Me"): 71 .... **40-50**

RCA VICTOR (0672; "An American
Trilogy"): 72 .... **15-25**

RCA VICTOR (0769; "Burning
Love"): 72 .... **8-12**

RCA VICTOR (0815; "Separate
Ways"): 71 .... **8-12**

RCA VICTOR (0910; "Steamroller
Blues"): 73 .... **8-12**

RCA VICTOR (1017; "It's Only
Love"): 71 .... **8-12**

RCA VICTOR (6540; "I Want You, I
Need You, I Love You"): 56 ...... **800-1200**
(Cartoon series "This Is His Life" sleeve. Promo-
tional issue only.)

RCA VICTOR (6604; "Don't Be
Cruel"): 56 .... **60-75**
(Showing *Don't Be Cruel* c/w *Hound Dog*.)

RCA VICTOR (6604; "Hound
Dog"): 56 .... **50-60**
(Showing *Hound Dog* c/w *Don't Be Cruel*.)

RCA VICTOR (6643; "Love Me
Tender"): 56 .... **100-150**
(Black and white sleeve.)

RCA VICTOR (6643; "Love Me
Tender"): 56 .... **60-75**
(Black and green sleeve.)

RCA VICTOR (6643; "Love Me
Tender"): 56 .... **35-45**
(Black and dark pink sleeve.)

RCA VICTOR (6643; "Love Me
Tender"): 56 .... **30-35**
(Black and light pink sleeve.)

RCA VICTOR (6800; "Too
Much"): 57 .... **$40-60**

RCA VICTOR (6870; "All Shook
Up"): 57 .... **40-60**

RCA VICTOR (7000; "Teddy
Bear"): 57 .... **40-60**

RCA VICTOR (7035; "Jailhouse
Rock"): 57 .... **40-60**

RCA VICTOR/MGM "Jailhouse
Rock" ticket/sleeve): 57 .... **400-600**
(MGM *Jailhouse Rock* film preview invitation ticket. Listed here because it was issued wrapped
around the standard 7035 disc & sleeve and distributed promotionally to the media.)

RCA VICTOR (7150; "Don't"): 58 ..... **40-50**

RCA VICTOR (7240; "Wear My Ring
Around Your Neck"): 58 .... **40-50**

RCA VICTOR (7280; "Hard Headed
Woman"): 58 .... **35-45**

RCA VICTOR (7410; "One Night"): 58 . **35-45**

RCA VICTOR (7506; "A Fool
Such As I"): 59 .... **150-200**
(With advertising for the *Elvis Sails* EP on reverse
side.)

RCA VICTOR (7506; "A Fool
Such As I"): 59 .... **25-35**
(With a listing of available Elvis EPs and 45s on
reverse side.)

RCA VICTOR (7600; "A Big Hunk
O' Love"): 59 .... **25-35**

RCA VICTOR (7740; "Stuck
On You"): 60 .... **15-25**

RCA VICTOR (7777; "It's Now
Or Never"): 60 .... **15-25**

RCA VICTOR (7810; "Are You
Lonesome To-night?"): 60 .... **15-25**

RCA VICTOR (7850; "Surrender"): 61 .. **15-20**

RCA VICTOR (7850; "Surrender"): 61 **300-500**
(Compact 33 Single sleeve, numbered with a "37"
prefix.)

RCA VICTOR (7880; "I Feel
So Bad"): 61 .... **15-25**

RCA VICTOR (7880; "I Feel
So Bad"): 61 .... **400-800**
(Compact 33 Single sleeve, numbered with a "37"
prefix.)

RCA VICTOR (7908; "His Latest
Flame"): 61 .... **15-25**

RCA VICTOR (7908; "His Latest
Flame"): 61 .... **500-1000**
(Compact 33 Single sleeve, numbered with a "37"
prefix.)

RCA VICTOR (7968; "Can't Help
Falling In Love"): 61 .... **15-20**

RCA VICTOR (7968; "Can't Help
Falling In Love"): *61* **$1000-1500**
(Compact 33 Single sleeve, numbered with a "37"
prefix.)

RCA VICTOR (7992; "Good Luck
Charm"): *62* **15-25**

RCA VICTOR (7992; "Good Luck
Charm"): *62* **1500-2500**
(Compact 33 Single sleeve, numbered with a "37"
prefix. This sleeve and its disc, priced separately in
the Singles section, is the rarest and most valuable
standard catalog Elvis release.)

RCA VICTOR (8041; "She's Not
You"): *62* **15-20**

RCA VICTOR (8100; "Return
To Sender"): *62* **15-20**

RCA VICTOR (8134; "One Broken
Heart For Sale"): *63* **15-20**

RCA VICTOR (8188; "Devil
In Disguise"): *63* **15-20**

RCA VICTOR (8243; "Bossa
Nova Baby"): *63* **15-20**

RCA VICTOR (8307; "Kissin'
Cousins"): *64* **15-20**

RCA VICTOR (8360; "Viva Las
Vegas"): *64* **15-20**

RCA VICTOR (8400; "Such A
Night"): *64* **15-20**

RCA VICTOR (8440; "Ask Me"): *64* . . . **15-20**

RCA VICTOR (8500; "Do The
Clam"): *65* **15-20**

RCA VICTOR (8585; "It Feels
So Right"): *65* **15-20**

RCA VICTOR (8657; "I'm Yours"): *65* . . **15-20**

RCA VICTOR (8740; "Tell Me
Why"): *65* **15-20**

RCA VICTOR (8780; "Frankie &
Johnny"): *66* **15-20**

RCA VICTOR (8870; "Love Letters"): *66* **15-20**

RCA VICTOR (8941; "Spinout"): *66* **15-20**

RCA VICTOR (8950; "If Everyday
Was Like Christmas"): *66* **15-20**

RCA VICTOR (9056; "Indescribably
Blue"): *67* **15-20**

RCA VICTOR (9115; "Long Legged
Girl"): *67* **15-20**

RCA VICTOR (9287; "There's
Always Me"): *67* **15-20**

RCA VICTOR (9341; "Big
Boss Man"): *67* **15-20**

RCA VICTOR (9425; "Guitar Man"): *68* . **10-20**

RCA VICTOR (9465; "U.S. Male"): *68* . . **10-20**

RCA VICTOR (9547; "Your Time
Hasn't Come Yet Baby"): *68* **10-20**

RCA VICTOR (9600; "You'll Never
Walk Alone"): *68* **$35-45**

RCA VICTOR (9610; "Almost In
Love"): *68* **10-15**

RCA VICTOR (9670; "If I
Can Dream"): *68* **10-15**

RCA VICTOR (9731; "Memories"): *69* . . **10-15**

RCA VICTOR (9741; "In The
Ghetto"): *69* **10-15**

RCA VICTOR (9747; "Clean Up
Your Own Back Yard"): *69* **10-15**

RCA VICTOR (9764; "Suspicious
Minds"): *69* **8-12**

RCA VICTOR (9768; "Don't Cry
Daddy"): *69* **8-12**

RCA VICTOR (9791; "Kentucky
Rain"): *70* **8-12**

RCA VICTOR (9835; "The Wonder
Of You"): *70* **8-12**

RCA VICTOR (9873; "I've Lost
You"): *70* **8-12**

RCA VICTOR (9916; "You Don't
Have To Say You Love Me"): *70* **8-12**

RCA VICTOR (9960; "I Really Don't
Want To Know"): *70* **8-12**

RCA VICTOR (9980; "Where Did
They Go Lord"): *71* **8-15**

RCA VICTOR (9985; "Life"): *71* **20-30**

RCA VICTOR (9998; "I'm Leavin'"): *71* . . **8-15**

RCA VICTOR (10074; "Promised
Land"): *74* **8-10**

RCA VICTOR (10191; "My Boy"): *75* **8-10**

RCA VICTOR (10278;
"T-r-o-u-b-l-e"): *75* **8-10**

RCA VICTOR (10401; "Bringing It
Back"): *75* **8-12**

RCA VICTOR (10601; "Hurt"): *76* **8-10**

RCA VICTOR (10857; "Moody
Blue"): *76* **6-10**

RCA VICTOR (10998; "Way Down"): *77* **.6-10**

RCA VICTOR (11099 through 11113): *77* . . **2-4**
(Sleeves in this series were originally packaged in
either RCA Victor 11301 and/or 11340, both boxed
sets of singles with sleeves.)

RCA VICTOR (11165; "My Way"): *77* . . . **6-10**
(With flip side title shown as *America*.)

RCA VICTOR (11165; "My Way"): *77* . . **15-25**
(With flip side title shown as *America The Beautiful*.)

RCA VICTOR (11212; "Softly, As I
Leave You"): *78* **5-10**

RCA VICTOR (11320; "Teddy
Bear"): *78* **5-10**

RCA VICTOR (11533; "Are You
Sincere?"): *79* **5-10**

RCA VICTOR (11679; "There's A
Honky Tonk Angel"): 79 . . . . $5-10
RCA VICTOR (12158; "Guitar
Man"): 81 5-10
RCA VICTOR (13058; "You'll Never
Walk Alone"): 82 5-10
RCA VICTOR (13302; "The
Impossible Dream"): 82 75-100
(Promotional issue only.)
RCA VICTOR (13351; "The Elvis
Medley"): 82 5-10
RCA VICTOR (13500; "I Was
The One"): 83 5-10
RCA VICTOR (13547; "Little Sister"): 83 . 5-10
RCA VICTOR (13875; "Baby, Let's
Play House"): 84 20-40
RCA VICTOR (13885 through 13896): 84 . 1-3
(Sleeves in this series were originally packaged in
RCA Victor 13897 and 13898, "Golden Singles.")
RCA VICTOR (13929; "Blue Suede
Shoes"): 84 5-10
RCA VICTOR (14090; "Always On
My Mind"): 85 5-10
RCA VICTOR (14237; "Merry Christmas
Baby"): 85 8-12
Note: There may be a slight price difference be-
tween "Coming Soon" and "Ask For" variations.
Likewise for variations in colors and paper stock
used. Often, the difference is simply which one is
needed to complete the set. Regardless, sleeve
variations within the price range given do not require separate listings. If the value varies beyond
the given range, a separate listing will be added.
Sleeves for the RCA "447" Gold Standard Series
are listed in a separate section that follows Gold
Standard Singles. Since there are but six promo
only sleeves, and considering they were rarely
marked as promo issues, they are combined in the
preceding section and identified as promotional issues only. A slight premium, perhaps $2-$5, may
be placed on RCA's "Living Stereo" paper sleeves.
These were used for many different RCA stereo
singles and were not exclusively an Elvis item.

Gold Standard Singles
With the "447" prefix
(Commercial Issues)

RCA VICTOR (0600 through
0639): 59-64 10-20
(Black label, dog on top.)
RCA VICTOR (0600 through 0639): 65-66 5-10
(Black label, dog on side.)
RCA VICTOR (0600 through
0639): 68-69 10-20
(Orange label.)
RCA VICTOR (0600 through 0639): 70-74 . 2-4
(Red label.)

RCA VICTOR (0600 through 0639): 77 . . $2-3
(Black label, dog near top.)
RCA VICTOR (0640 through
0642): 64 20-25
(Black label, dog on top.)
RCA VICTOR (0640 through 0642): 65-66 4-6
(Black label, dog on side.)
RCA VICTOR (0640 through 0642): 70-74 2-4
(Red label.)
RCA VICTOR (0643; "Crying In
The Chapel"): 65 5-8
(Black label, dog on side.)
RCA VICTOR (0643; "Crying In
The Chapel"): 70-74 2-4
(Red label.)
RCA VICTOR (0643; "Crying In
The Chapel"): 77 2-3
(Black label, dog near top.)
RCA VICTOR (0644 through
0646): 65 25-35
(Black label, dog on top.)
RCA VICTOR (0644 through 0646): 65 . . . 5-8
(Black label, dog on side.)
RCA VICTOR (0644 through
0646): 68-69 10-20
(Orange label.)
RCA VICTOR (0644 through 0646): 70-74 2-4
(Red label.)
RCA VICTOR (0644 through 0646): 77 . . . 2-3
(Black label, dog near top.)
RCA VICTOR (0647 through 0650): 65 . . . 5-8
(Black label, dog on side.)
RCA VICTOR (0647 through 0650): 70-74 2-4
(Red label.)
RCA VICTOR (0651 & 0652): 66 10-12
(Black label, dog on side.)
RCA VICTOR (0651 & 0652): 70-74 2-4
(Red label.)
RCA VICTOR (0653 through 0658): 66-68 4-6
(Black label, dog on side.)
RCA VICTOR (0653 through 0658): 70-74 2-4
(Red label.)
RCA VICTOR (0653 through 0658): 77 . . . 2-3
(Black label, dog near top.)
RCA VICTOR (0659; "Indescribably
Blue"): 70 10-15
(Red label.)
RCA VICTOR (0660; "Long Legged
Girl"): 70 25-35
(Red label.)
RCA VICTOR (0661; "Judy"): 70 10-15
(Red label.)
RCA VICTOR (0662; "Big Boss
Man"): 70 8-10
(Red label.)

RCA VICTOR (0663 through
0685): *70-73* **$2-4**
(Red label.)
RCA VICTOR (0663 through 0685): *77* ... **2-3**
(Black label, dog near top.)
RCA VICTOR (0720; "Blue
Christmas"): *64* **10-15**
(Black label, dog on top.)

*Gold Standard Singles
With the "GB" prefix
(Commercial Issues)*

RCA VICTOR (10156 through
10489): *75-76* **2-4**
(Red label.)
RCA VICTOR (10156 through
10489): *77* **2-3**
(Black label, dog near top.)
RCA VICTOR (11326 through
13275): *77* **2-3**
(Black label, dog near top.)
Note: Gold Standard promo singles are listed in
numerical sequence under Promotional Singles.

Gold Standard Picture Sleeves

RCA VICTOR (0601 through
0618): *64* **50-60**
RCA VICTOR (0639; "Kiss Me
Quick"): *64* **20-25**
RCA VICTOR (0643; "Crying In
The Chapel"): *65* **15-20**
RCA VICTOR (0647; "Blue
Christmas"): *65* **20-25**
(Pictures Elvis on a Christmas card amid wrapped
gifts.)
RCA VICTOR (0647; "Blue
Christmas"): *77* **8-10**
(Pictures Elvis in a circle amid colored ornaments.)
RCA VICTOR (0650; "Puppet On
A String"): *65* **20-25**
RCA VICTOR (0651; "Joshua Fit
The Battle"): *66* **50-75**
RCA VICTOR (0652; "Milky White
Way"): *66* **50-75**
RCA VICTOR (0651 & 0652; "Special
Programming Kit"): *66* **450-550**
(Picture sleeve-mailer. Contained both 1966 Easter
singles, *Joshua Fit The Battle* and *Milky White Way*
in their sleeves and an Easter greeting card from
Elvis. Price is for complete kit.)
RCA VICTOR (0651 & 0652; "Special Easter
Programming Kit"): *66* **300-400**
(Picture sleeve-mailer. Contained both Easter
singles, *Joshua Fit The Battle* and *Milky White Way*
in their sleeves and an Easter greeting card from
Elvis. Price is for sleeve-mailer only.)
RCA VICTOR (0720; "Blue
Christmas"): *64* **30-35**

Promotional Singles

CREATIVE RADIO ("Elvis 10th Anniversary"/
"The Elvis Hour"): *87* **$15-20**
(Demonstration disc, promoting the syndicated
10th anniversary radio special.)
CREATIVE RADIO ("Memories Of Elvis"/
"The Elvis Hour"): *87* **15-20**
(Demonstration disc, promoting the syndicated
10th anniversary radio special.)
Note: To find *Elvis-50th Birthday Special,* see
PRESLEY, Elvis / Buddy Holly. To find *The Elvis
Hour,* see PRESLEY, Elvis / Gary Owens.
CREATIVE RADIO ("Nearer My God
To Thee"): *89* **5-10**
(Promotional, souvenir issue only.)
PARAMOUNT PICTURES (2017; "Girls!
Girls! Girls!"): *64* **750-1000**
(Issued only to select theatres, designed for lobby
play.)
PARAMOUNT PICTURES (2413;
"Roustabout"): *64* **1000-1500**
(Issued only to select theatres, designed for lobby
play. Contains an otherwise unissued alternate take
of *Roustabout.*)
RCA VICTOR (15; "Old Shep"): *56* ... **600-650**
RCA VICTOR (76; "Don't"/"Wear My Ring
Around Your Neck"): *60* **500-550**
(Issued with a special sleeve, which is listed in the
Picture Sleeve section.)
RCA VICTOR (0088; "Raised On
Rock"): *73* **8-10**
(Yellow label.)
RCA VICTOR (118; "King Of The Whole
Wide World"): *62* **200-225**
(Issued with a special sleeve, which is listed in the
Picture Sleeve section.)
RCA VICTOR (0130; "How Great
Thou Art"): *69* **25-30**
(Yellow label.)
RCA VICTOR (139; "Roustabout"): *64* **175-200**
RCA VICTOR (162; "How Great
Thou Art"): *67* **100-125**
(Issued with a special sleeve, which is listed in the
Picture Sleeve section.)
RCA VICTOR (0196; "I've Got A
Thing About You Baby"): *74* **8-10**
(Yellow label.)
RCA VICTOR (0280; "If You Talk
In Your Sleep"): *74* **8-10**
(Yellow label.)
RCA VICTOR (0517; "Little
Sister"): *83* **100-125**
(12-Inch single.)
RCA VICTOR (0572; "Merry Christmas
Baby"): *71* **12-15**
(Yellow label.)

RCA VICTOR (0601 through
0618): *64* $40-50
(RCA "447" prefix Gold Standard Series. White
labels.)

RCA VICTOR (0619; "Until It's Time
For You To Go"): *72* 10-12
(Yellow label.)

RCA VICTOR (0639; "Kiss Me
Quick"): *64* 20-25
(RCA "447" prefix Gold Standard Series. White
label.)

RCA VICTOR (0643; "Crying In
The Chapel"): *65* 15-20
(RCA "447" prefix Gold Standard Series. White
label.)

RCA VICTOR (0647 & 0650): *65* 20-25
(RCA "447" prefix Gold Standard Series. White
labels.)

RCA VICTOR (0651 & 0652): *66* 30-40
(RCA "447" prefix Gold Standard Series. White
labels. See Gold Standard Picture Sleeve section
for special mailing sleeve used with these two
Easter singles.)

RCA VICTOR (0651; "He Touched
Me"): *72* 45-55
(Yellow label.)

RCA VICTOR (0672; "An American
Trilogy"): *72* 12-15
(Yellow label.)

RCA VICTOR (0720; "Blue
Christmas"). *64* 25-30
(RCA "447" prefix Gold Standard Series. White
label.)

RCA VICTOR (0769; "Burning
Love"): *72* 8-10
(Yellow label.)

RCA VICTOR (0808; "Blue
Christmas"): *57* 1000-1200

RCA VICTOR (0815; "Separate
Ways"): *72* 8-10
(Yellow label.)

RCA VICTOR (0910: "Steamroller
Blues"): *73* 8-10
(Yellow label.)

RCA VICTOR (6357; "Mystery
Train"): *55* 140-160
(White label.)

RCA VICTOR (8360; "Viva Las
Vegas"): *64* 20-25
(White label.)

RCA VICTOR (8400; "Such A
Night"): *64* 500-525
(White label.)

RCA VICTOR (8440; "Ask Me"): *64* 20-25
(White label.)

RCA VICTOR (8500; "Do The
Clam"): *65* $20-25
(White label.)

RCA VICTOR (8585; "It Feels
So Right"): *65* 20-25
(White label.)

RCA VICTOR (8657; "I'm Yours"): *65* . 20-25
(White label.)

RCA VICTOR (8740; "Tell Me
Why"): *65* 20-25
(White label.)

RCA VICTOR (8780; "Frankie &
Johnny"): *66* 20-25
(White label.)

RCA VICTOR (8870; "Love Letters"): *66* 20-25
(White label.)

RCA VICTOR (8941; "Spinout"): *66* ... 20-25
(White label.)

RCA VICTOR (8950; "If Everyday
Was Like Christmas"): *66* 20-35
(White label.)

RCA VICTOR (9056; "Indescribably
Blue"): *67* 20-25
(White label.)

RCA VICTOR (9115; "Long Legged
Girl"): *67* 20-25
(White label.)

RCA VICTOR (9287; "There's
Always Me"); *67* 20-25
(White label.)

RCA VICTOR (9341; "Big Boss
Man"): *67* 20-25
(White label.)

RCA VICTOR (9425; "Guitar Man"): *68* 15-20
(Yellow label.)

RCA VICTOR (9465; "U.S. Male"): *68* . 15-20
(Yellow label.)

RCA VICTOR (9547; "Your Time
Hasn't Come Yet Baby"): *68* 15-20
(Yellow label.)

RCA VICTOR (9600; "You'll Never
Walk Alone"): *68* 15-20
(Yellow label.)

RCA VICTOR (9610; "Almost In
Love"): *68* 10-15
(Yellow label.)

RCA VICTOR (9670; "If I
Can Dream"): *68* 10-15
(Yellow label.)

RCA VICTOR (9731; "Memories"): *69* . 10-15
(Yellow label.)

RCA VICTOR (9741; "In The
Ghetto"): *69* 10-15
(Yellow label.)

RCA VICTOR (9747; "Clean Up
Your Own Back Yard"): 69 .... $10-15
(Yellow label.)
RCA VICTOR (9764; "Suspicious
Minds"): 69 10-15
(Yellow label.)
RCA VICTOR (9768; "Don't Cry
Daddy"): 69 10-15
(Yellow label.)
RCA VICTOR (9791; "Kentucky
Rain"): 70 10-15
(Yellow label.)
RCA VICTOR (9835; "The Wonder
Of You"): 70 10-15
(Yellow label.)
RCA VICTOR (9873; "I've Lost
You"): 70 10-15
(Yellow label.)
RCA VICTOR (9916; "You Don't
Have To Say You Love Me"): 70 10-15
(Yellow label.)
RCA VICTOR (9960; "I Really Don't
Want To Know"): 70 10-15
(Yellow label.)
RCA VICTOR (9980; "Where Did
They Go Lord?"): 71 10-15
(Yellow label.)
RCA VICTOR (9985; "Life"): 71 10-15
(Yellow label.)
RCA VICTOR (9998; "I'm Leavin'"): 71   10-15
(Yellow label.)
RCA VICTOR (10074; "Promised
Land"): 74 8-10
(Yellow label.)
RCA VICTOR (10191; "My Boy"): 75 ... 8-10
(Yellow label.)
RCA VICTOR (10278;
"T-r-o-u-b-l-e"): 75 8-10
(Yellow label.)
RCA VICTOR (10401; "Bringing It
Back"): 75 8-10
(Yellow label.)
RCA VICTOR (10601; "Hurt"): 76 8-10
(Yellow label.)
RCA VICTOR (10857; "Moody Blue,"
black vinyl): 76 6-10
(Yellow label.)
RCA VICTOR (10857; "Moody Blue,"
colored vinyl): 76 900-1000
(Experimental pressings only. Never intended for
distribution.)
RCA VICTOR (10951; "Let Me
Be There"): 77 100-125
RCA VICTOR (10998; "Way
Down"): 77 125-150
(White label.)

RCA VICTOR (10998; "Way
Down"): 77 .... $6-10
(Yellow label.)
RCA VICTOR (11165; "My Way"): 77 ...6-10
(Yellow label.)
RCA VICTOR (11212; "Softly, As I
Leave You"): 78 6-10
(Yellow label.)
RCA VICTOR (11320; "Teddy
Bear"): 78 6-10
(Yellow label.)
RCA VICTOR (11533; "Are You
Sincere?"): 79 6-10
(Yellow label.)
RCA VICTOR (11679; "There's A
Honky Tonk Angel"): 79 6-10
(Yellow label.)
RCA VICTOR (12158; "Guitar Man,"
black vinyl): 81 6-10
(Yellow label.)
RCA VICTOR (12158; "Guitar Man,"
colored vinyl): 81 225-250
(Yellow label.)
RCA VICTOR (12205; "Lovin' Arms,"
black vinyl): 81 6-10
(Yellow label.)
RCA VICTOR (12205; "Lovin' Arms,"
colored vinyl): 81 250-275
(Bright yellow label.)
RCA VICTOR (13058; "You'll Never
Walk Alone"): 82 6-10
(Yellow label.)
RCA VICTOR (13302; "The Impossible
Dream"): 82 75-100
RCA VICTOR (13351; "The Elvis
Medley," black vinyl): 82 6-10
(Yellow label.)
RCA VICTOR (13351; "The Elvis
Medley," colored vinyl): 82 200-225
(Gold label.)
RCA VICTOR (13500; "I Was The
One," black vinyl): 83 6-10
(Yellow label.)
RCA VICTOR (13500; "I Was The
One," colored vinyl): 83 200-225
(Bright yellow label.)
RCA VICTOR (13547; "Little Sister,"
black vinyl): 83 6-10
(Yellow label.)
RCA VICTOR (13547; "Little Sister,"
colored vinyl): 83 175-200
(Blue label.)
RCA VICTOR (13875; "Baby, Let's Play
House," colored vinyl): 84 150-175
(Gold label.)

RCA VICTOR (13929; "Blue Suede
  Shoes," colored vinyl): *84* **$6-10**
  (Gold label.)
RCA VICTOR (14090; "Always On
  My Mind," colored vinyl): *85* **6-10**
  (Gold label.)
RCA VICTOR (14237; "Merry Christmas
  Baby"): *85* **6-10**
  50th Anniversary singles (RCA Victor 13875
  through 14237) used the same gold label for both
  commercial and promotional issues. Promo singles
  have "Not For Sale" printed on the label.
UNITED STATES AIR FORCE (125; "It's
  Now Or Never"): see PRESLEY, Elvis / Jaye
  P. Morgan.
UNITED STATES AIR FORCE (159;
  "Surrender"): see PRESLEY, Elvis / Lawrence
  Welk.
WHAT'S IT ALL ABOUT (78; "Life"): see
  PRESLEY, Elvis / Helen Reddy
WHAT'S IT ALL ABOUT (1840; "Elvis
  Presley"): *80* **70-75**
WHAT'S IT ALL ABOUT (3025; "Elvis
  Presley"): *82* **50-60**
  Note: Plastic soundsheets or flexi-discs are listed in
  a separate section that follows. Promotional 78s are
  listed with Singles: 78rpm, found at the beginning
  of the Presley section.

Plastic Soundsheets/Flexi-discs

EVA-TONE (38713; "Elvis Speaks! The
  Truth About Me"): **30-40**
  (Eva-Tone number is not on label but is etched in
  the trail-off.)
EVA-TONE (52578; "The King Is Dead,
  Long Live The King"): *78* **90-100**
EVA-TONE (831942; "50,000,000 Elvis
  Fans Weren't Wrong!"): *83* **5-10**
EVA-TONE (726771; "The Elvis Presley
  Story"): *77* **5-10**
EVA-TONE (1037710; "Elvis Live"): *78* . **30-40**
  (Price for magazine, titled *Collector's Issue*, with
  bound-in soundsheet.)
EVA-TONE (1037710; "Elvis Live"): *78* . **15-20**
  (Price for soundsheet only.)
EVA-TONE (1227785; "Thompson
  Vocal Eliminator"): *78* **15-20**
  (Contains segments of songs by three artists, includ-
  ing Elvis.)
EVA-TONE (10287733; "Elvis: Six
  Hour Special"): *77* **15-20**
EVA-TONE/RCA ("Love Me
  Tender"): *74* **15-25**
  (A Mick Ronson/*Teen Magazine* promotional
  issue.)

LYNCHBURG AUDIO ("The Truth
  About Me"): *56* **$125-150**
  (Lynchburg Audio number is not on label but is
  etched in the trail-off.)
RAINBO ("Elvis Speaks - In
  Person"): *56* **300-325**
  (Price for magazine, *Elvis Answers Back*, with
  78rpm flexi-disc still attached to front cover.)
RAINBO ("Elvis Speaks - In
  Person"): *56* **100-125**
  (Price for flexi-disc only.)
RAINBO ("The Truth About Me"): *56* **300-325**
  (Price for magazine, *Elvis Answers Back*, with
  78rpm paper flexi-disc still attached to front cover.)
RAINBO ("The Truth About Me"): *56* **100-125**
  (Price for flexi-disc only.)
  Note: All soundsheets & flexi-discs were used for
  some type of promotional purpose.

EPs: 7-Inch 33/45rpm
Commercial and Promotional Issues

RCA VICTOR (15; Extended Play
  Package): *56* **3500-4500**
  (Black labels. Only one of the ten EPs in this set is
  by Elvis. No box or package has yet been dis-
  covered for these discs. This value, however, is
  based on a complete set, which probably includes
  paper inserts, title strips, etc.)
RCA VICTOR (15; Extended Play
  Package): *56* **3000-4000**
  (Gray label edition. Otherwise, same as above.)
RCA VICTOR (15; Elvis disc 9089,
  black label): *56* **750-900**
RCA VICTOR (15; Elvis disc 9089,
  gray label): *56* **600-700**
  (The Elvis EP from the SPD-15 set. The gray press-
  ings were for jukebox operators and the black was
  probably a commercial release. The individual num-
  ber on this disc is 9089.)
RCA VICTOR (19; "The Sound Of
  Leadership"): *56* **1800-2000**
  (Eight-EP boxed set, with one EP containing one
  Elvis track. The number on the disc is 9113.
  Prepared as a souvenir for those attending a June,
  1956 convention. Price is for complete set includ-
  ing inserts.)
RCA VICTOR (19; "The Sound Of
  Leadership"): *56* **750-800**
  (Price for the EP from the SPD-19 set containing
  Elvis. This EP, numbered 9113, is actually untitled.)
RCA VICTOR (22; "Elvis
  Presley"): *56* **600-650**
  (Two-EP bonus promotional item. Discs are num-
  bered 9121 & 9122.)
RCA VICTOR (23; "Elvis
  Presley"): *56* **2000-2500**
  (Three-EP bonus promotional item. Discs are num-
  bered 9123, 9124, and 9125.)

RCA VICTOR (26; "Great Country /
Western Hits"): 56 .... **$900-1000**
(10-EP boxed set containing one Elvis EP with the
number 9141. Price is for the complete box set in-
cluding paper inserts.)
RCA VICTOR (26; "Great Country /
Western Hits"): 56 .... **200-250**
(Price for the EP from the SPD-26 set containing
Elvis. This EP, numbered 9141, is actually untitled.)
RCA VICTOR (27; "Save-On
Records"): 56 .... **600-650**
(Price for EP and paper sleeve. A sampler of music
by Elvis and others.)
RCA VICTOR (27; "Save-On
Records"): 56 .... **175-200**
(Price for EP only. A sampler of music by Elvis
and others.)
RCA VICTOR (37; "Perfect For
Parties"): 56 .... **75-90**
(Without horizontal silver line. Offered through
mail-order coupon ads. Contains six songs by dif-
ferent artists, including Elvis who is also the nar-
rator on the disc.)
RCA VICTOR (37; "Perfect For
Parties"): 56 .... **75-90**
(With horizontal silver line. Promotional issue,
reads "Not For Sale.")
RCA VICTOR (37; "Perfect For
Parties"): 56 .... **90-100**
(Paper sleeve for the *Perfect For Parties Highlight
Album.*)
RCA VICTOR (39; "Dealers'
Prevue"): 57 .... **600-650**
(Contains two songs each by six different artists, in-
cluding Elvis. Promotional issue only.)
RCA VICTOR (39; "Dealers'
Prevue" mailer): 57 .... **350-400**
(Paper mailing envelope used with the promotional
SDS-57-39 *Dealers' Prevue* EP.)
RCA VICTOR (61; Extended Play
Sampler): 57 .... **1000-1200**
(Sampler of 12 different RCA EPs, all by different
artists, including *Jailhouse Rock* by Elvis. No
sleeve or cover is known to exist for this disc.
Promotional issue only.)
RCA VICTOR (121; "RCA Family
Record Center"): 61 .... **1000-1200**
(Contains one song each by eight different artists in-
cluding Elvis. In-store Promotional issue only.)
RCA VICTOR (128; "Elvis By
Request"): 61 .... **50-60**
RCA VICTOR (747; "Elvis
Presley"): 56 .... **140-160**
(Black label, no dog.)

RCA VICTOR (747; "Elvis
Presley"): 56 .... **$70-90**
(Black label, dog on top. With horizontal silver
line. With song title strip across the top of front
cover.)
RCA VICTOR (747; "Elvis Presley"): 56 .**55-75**
(Black label, dog on top. Without horizontal silver
line. With song title strip across the top of front
cover.)
RCA VICTOR (747; "Elvis Presley"): 65 .**30-40**
(Black label, dog on side.)
RCA VICTOR (747; "Elvis Presley"): 69 .**30-40**
(Orange label.)
RCA VICTOR (747; "Blue Suede
Shoes"): 56 .... **500-525**
(Temporary paper sleeve for 1956 issue of EPA-
747. Price is for sleeve only.)
RCA VICTOR (821 through 994): 56 ..**140-160**
(Black label, no dog.)
RCA VICTOR (821 through 994): 56 ....**70-90**
(Black label, dog on top. With song title strip
across the top of front
cover.)
RCA VICTOR (821 through 994): 56 ....**55-75**
(Black label, dog on top. Without horizontal silver
line. With song title strip across the top of front
cover.)
RCA VICTOR (821 through 994): 65 ....**30-40**
(Black label, dog on side.)
RCA VICTOR (821 through 994): 69 ....**30-40**
(Orange label.)
Note: Not every EP in the 821-994 series was is-
sued with ALL of the possible label variations.
EPA-940 was the only EP from this period that was
reissued in the Gold Standard Series, as EPA-5120.
RCA VICTOR (1254; "Elvis
Presley"): 56 .... **350-400**
(Black label, no dog. A two EP set.)
RCA VICTOR (1254; "Elvis
Presley"): 56 .... **300-350**
(Black label, dog on top. With horizontal silver
line. A two EP set.)
RCA VICTOR (1254; "Elvis
Presley"): 56 .... **275-325**
(Black label, dog on top. Without horizontal silver
line. A two EP set.)
RCA VICTOR (1254; "Most Talked-About
New Personality"): 56 .... **1000-1200**
(Two EPs, also numbered 0793 and 0794, in a
single-pocket paper sleeve. Promotional issue only.)
RCA VICTOR (1254; "Most Talked-About
New Personality"): 56 .... **400-425**
(Price for the two EPs WITHOUT the sleeve.
Either disc would be worth about half the amount
shown for both. Discs, numbered 0793 and 0794,
are actually untitled. Promotional issue only.)

RCA VICTOR (1515; "Loving
You"): *57* $70-90
(Black label, dog on top. With horizontal silver
line. With song title strip across the top of front
cover.)

RCA VICTOR (1515; Loving You"). *57* 55-75
(Black label, dog on top. Without horizontal silver
line. With song title strip across the top of front
cover.)

RCA VICTOR (1515; "Loving You"): *65* 30-40
(Black label, dog on side.)

RCA VICTOR (1515; "Loving You"): *69* 30-40
(Orange label.)
(The above applies to both 1-1515 and 2-1515,
Loving You Volumes 1 and 2.)

RCA VICTOR (2006; "Aloha From
Hawaii"): *74* 60-75
(Price includes sheet of 10 title strips. Issued for
jukebox operators as one of four "Little LPs." The
other three in the campaign were by John Denver,
Harry Nilsson, and The Three Suns.)

RCA VICTOR (3736; "Pop Transcribed
30 Sec. Spot"): *58* 400-500
(No release number given, 3736 being the matrix
number on the Elvis side of this disc. Announcer
Vaughn Monroe presents sales pitch and excerpts
from four RCA LPs, including *Elvis' Golden
Records*.)

RCA VICTOR (4006; "Love Me
Tender"): *56* 150-200
(Black label, no dog. With song title strip across
the top of front cover.)

RCA VICTOR (4006; "Love Me
Tender"): *56* 75-80
(Black label, dog on top. With horizontal silver
line. With song title strip across the top of front
cover.)

RCA VICTOR (4006; "Love Me
Tender"): *56* 55-75
(Black label, dog on top. Without horizontal silver
line. With EP title strip across the top of front
cover.)

RCA VICTOR (4006; "Love Me
Tender"): *65* 30-40
(Black label, dog on side.)

RCA VICTOR (4006; "Love Me
Tender"): *69* 30-40
(Orange label.)

RCA VICTOR (4041; "Just For
You"): *57* 140-160
(Black label, no dog. With EP title strip across the
top of front cover.)

RCA VICTOR (4041; "Just For
You"): *57* 75-80
(Black label, dog on top. With horizontal silver
line. With EP title strip across the top of front
cover.)

RCA VICTOR (4041; "Just For
You"): *57* $55-65
(Black label, dog on top. Without horizontal silver
line. With EP title strip across the top of front
cover.)

RCA VICTOR (4041; "Just For
You"): *65* 30-40
(Black label, dog on side.)

RCA VICTOR (4041; "Just For
You"): *69* 30-40
(Orange label.)

RCA VICTOR (4054; "Peace In
The Valley"): *57* 75-80
(Black label, dog on top. With horizontal silver
line. With EP title strip across the top of front
cover.)

RCA VICTOR (4054; "Peace In
The Valley"): *57* 55-65
(Black label, dog on top. Without horizontal silver
line. With EP title strip across the top of front
cover.)
(Reissues of this EP were in the Gold Standard
Series, as EPA-5121.)

RCA VICTOR (4108; "Elvis Sings
Christmas Songs"): *57* 55-75
(Black label, dog on top. With EP title strip across
the top of front cover.)

RCA VICTOR (4108; "Elvis Sings
Christmas Songs"): *65* 30-40
(Black label, dog on side.)

RCA VICTOR (4108; "Elvis Sings
Christmas Songs"): *69* 30-40
(Orange label.)

RCA VICTOR (4114; "Jailhouse
Rock"): *57* 55-65
(Black label, dog on top.)

RCA VICTOR (4114; "Jailhouse
Rock"): *65* 30-40
(Black label, dog on side.)

RCA VICTOR (4114; "Jailhouse
Rock"): *69* 30-40
(Orange label.)

RCA VICTOR (4319; "King Creole"): *58* 55-70
(Reissues of this EP were in the Gold Standard
Series, numbered EPA-5122.)

RCA VICTOR (4321; "King Creole,"
Vol. 2): *58* 55-70
(Black label, dog on top.)

RCA VICTOR (4321; "King Creole,"
Vol. 2): *65* 30-40
(Black label, dog on side.)

RCA VICTOR (4321; "King Creole,"
Vol. 2): *69* 30-40
(Orange label.)

RCA VICTOR (4325; "Elvis Sails"): *58* . 70-80
(Reissues of this EP were in the Gold Standard
Series, numbered EPA-5157.)

RCA VICTOR (4340; "Christmas
With Elvis"): *58* $75-95
(Black label, dog on top.)
RCA VICTOR (4340; "Christmas
With Elvis"): *65* 30-40
(Black label, dog on side.)
RCA VICTOR (4340; "Christmas
With Elvis"): *69* 30-40
(Orange label.)
RCA VICTOR (4368; "Follow That
Dream"): *62* 45-60
(Black label, dog on top.)
RCA VICTOR (4368; "Follow That
Dream"): *62* 75-100
(Promotional issue only. Marked "Not For Sale.")
RCA VICTOR (4368; "Follow That
Dream"): *62* 100-150
(Special paper sleeve for this EP, issued to radio
stations and jukebox operators. Promotional issue
only. Price is for sleeve only.)
RCA VICTOR (4368; "Follow That
Dream"): *65* 30-40
(Black label, dog on side.)
RCA VICTOR (4368; "Follow That
Dream"): *69* 30-40
(Orange label.)
RCA VICTOR (4371; "Kid
Galahad"): *62* 45-60
(Black label, dog on top.)
RCA VICTOR (4371; "Kid
Galahad"): *65* 30-40
(Black label, dog on side.)
RCA VICTOR (4371; "Kid
Galahad"): *69* 30-40
(Orange label.)
RCA VICTOR (4382; "Viva Las
Vegas"): *64* 45-55
(Black label, dog on top.)
RCA VICTOR (4382; "Viva Las
Vegas"): *65* 30-40
(Black label, dog on side.)
RCA VICTOR (4382; "Viva Las
Vegas"): *69* 30-40
(Orange label.)
RCA VICTOR (4383; "Tickle Me"): *65* . . 40-50
(Black label, dog on side.)
RCA VICTOR (4383; "Tickle Me"): *69* . . 30-40
(Orange label.)
RCA VICTOR (4387; "Easy Come,
Easy Go"): *67* 40-50
(Black label, dog on side.)
RCA VICTOR (4387; "Easy Come,
Easy Go"): *67* 75-90
(White label. Promotional issue only.)

RCA VICTOR (4387; "Easy Come,
Easy Go"): *69* $30-40
(Orange label.)
RCA VICTOR (5088; "A Touch Of Gold,"
Vol. I): *59* 300-350
(Maroon label.)
RCA VICTOR (5088; "A Touch Of Gold,"
Vol. I): *59* 75-85
(Black label, dog on top.)
RCA VICTOR (5088; "A Touch Of Gold,"
Vol. I): *65* 30-40
(Black label, dog on side.)
RCA VICTOR (5088; "A Touch Of Gold,"
Vol. I): *69* 30-40
(Orange label.)
RCA VICTOR (5101; "A Touch Of Gold,"
Vol. II): *59* 300-350
(Maroon label.)
RCA VICTOR (5101; "A Touch Of Gold,"
Vol. II): *59* 75-85
(Black label, dog on top.)
RCA VICTOR (5101; "A Touch Of Gold,"
Vol. II): *65* 30-40
(Black label, dog on side.)
RCA VICTOR (5101; "A Touch Of Gold,"
Vol. II): *69* 30-40
(Orange label.)
RCA VICTOR (5120; "The Real
Elvis"): *59* 350-400
(Maroon label. Reissue of EPA-940.)
RCA VICTOR (5120; "The Real
Elvis"): *59* 50-60
(Black label, dog on top.)
RCA VICTOR (5120; "The Real
Elvis"): *65* 30-40
(Black label, dog on side.)
RCA VICTOR (5120; "The Real
Elvis"): *69* 30-40
(Orange label.)
RCA VICTOR (5121; "Peace In
The Valley"): *59* 350-400
(Maroon label. Reissue of EPA-4054.)
RCA VICTOR (5121; "Peace In
The Valley"): *59* 50-60
(Black label, dog on top.)
RCA VICTOR (5121; "Peace In
The Valley"): *65* 30-40
(Black label, dog on side.)
RCA VICTOR (5121; "Peace In
The Valley"): *69* 30-40
(Orange label.)
RCA VICTOR (5122; "King
Creole"): *59* 400-500
(Maroon label. Reissue of EPA-4319.)

RCA VICTOR (5122; "King
Creole"): 59 .... $50-60
(Black label, dog on top.)

RCA VICTOR (5122; "King
Creole"): 65 30-40
(Black label, dog on side.)

RCA VICTOR (5122; "King
Creole"): 69 30-40
(Orange label.)

RCA VICTOR (5141; "A Touch Of
Gold," Vol. 3): 60 250-300
(Maroon label.)

RCA VICTOR (5141; "A Touch Of
Gold," Vol. 3): 60 75-85
(Black label, dog on top.)

RCA VICTOR (5141; "A Touch Of
Gold," Vol. 3): 65 30-40
(Black label, dog on side.)

RCA VICTOR (5141; "A Touch Of
Gold," Vol. 3): 69 30-40
(Orange label.)

RCA VICTOR (5157; "Elvis Sails"): 65 . . 35-40
(Black label, dog on top. Reissue of EPA-4325.)

RCA VICTOR (5157; "Elvis Sails"): 65 . . 30-40
(Black label, dog on side.)

RCA VICTOR (5157; "Elvis Sails"): 69 . . 30-40
(Orange label.)

RCA VICTOR (8705; "TV Guide
Presents Elvis") 56 950-1000
(Price for disc without either insert sheet. No sleeve
or cover is known to exist for this disc. Promotional
issue only.)

RCA VICTOR (8705; "TV Guide
Presents Elvis"): 56 200-250
(Price for "Elvis Exclusively" gray insert.)

RCA VICTOR (8705; "TV Guide
Presents Elvis"): 56 125-150
(Price for "Elvis Exclusively" pink insert, with sug-
gested continuity.)

TUPPERWARE (11973; "Tupperware's
Hit Parade"): 73 50-60
(Contains excerpts of songs by numerous artists, in-
cluding Elvis. A promotional sales tool used by
Tupperware representatives.)

Notes: Unless listed and priced separately, all EP
values include both disc and cover with approximately half of the total attached to each.

Some of the rarer pieces that are often traded individually (disc or sleeve), as well as those sleeves
that have an exceptionally higher value than their
disc, are listed separately in this section.

All EPs in the 5000 series are Gold Standard
Series issues although not noted as such on the
labels, only on the covers.

EP label and cover variations that do not require
separate listing and pricing are not detailed in this
edition.

Remember, if you don't find the EP in this section
it may contain two, three, or four artists, and is
listed following the Presley section.

LPs: 10/12-Inch 33rpm
Commercial and Promotional Issues

ABC RADIO (1003; "Elvis
Memories"): 78 .... $425-500
(Three-LP boxed set. Price includes a 16-page
programmer's booklet and four pages of additional
information, which represents $40-$50 of the
value. Issued only to radio stations. A 7-inch reel
tape, with spots and promotional announcements,
accompanied this set and would be worth another
$45-$50. Highlights of this program were issued on
Michelob 810.)

ATV (1; "In The Beginning"): 80 50-75
(Contains 20 songs by 15 artists, including one by
Elvis. Promotional issue only.)

A&M (3930; "Heart Of Dixie"): 89 8-12
(Soundtrack. Contains 11 songs by 8 artists, including two by Elvis.)

ASSOCIATED BROADCASTERS (1001;
"Legend Of A King"): 80 125-150
(White label. Advance pressing.)

ASSOCIATED BROADCASTERS (1001;
"Legend Of A King"): 80 25-30
(Picture disc. First pressings were numbered from
3000 through 6000. Number appears under "Side
One" on the disc itself. Cover is standard, die-cut,
picture disc cover. Several spelling errors on back
cover, including "idle" for idol and "Jordinaires" instead of Jordanaires.)

ASSOCIATED BROADCASTERS (1001;
"Legend Of A King"): 80 20-25
(Picture disc. Second pressings were numbered
from 6001 through 9000. Most of the spelling errors were corrected on this cover.)

ASSOCIATED BROADCASTERS (1001;
"Legend Of A King"): 80 15-20
(Picture disc. Third pressings were numbered from
00001 through 02999 and 09001 through 15000.
Cover errors have all been corrected.)

ASSOCIATED BROADCASTERS (1001;
"Legend Of A King"): 84 10-12
(Picture disc. Fourth pressings were also numbered
from 3000 through 6000, but were packaged in a
clear plastic sleeve instead of a conventional cover.)

ASSOCIATED BROADCASTERS (1001;
"Legend Of A King"): 85 8-10
(Picture disc. Discs are not numbered. Packaged in
a plastic sleeve.)

ASSOCIATED BROADCASTERS ("Legend
Of A King"): 85 200-250
(Three-hour, three-LP set. Not boxed. Price includes 6 pages of cue sheets. Available to radio stations only.)

ASSOCIATED BROADCASTERS ("Legend
Of A King"): *85* $300-350
(Same as preceding set, but packaged in a specially
printed box.)

ASSOCIATED BROADCASTERS ("Legend
Of A King"): *86* 300-350
(Three-LP boxed set, same as above except time on
segment 1-B is increased from 14:25 to 15:15 in
order to include a Johnny Bernero interview.)

ASSOCIATED PRESS (1977; "The
World In Sound"): *78* 80-100
(Contains news highlights of 1977, including
coverage of Elvis' death.)

BEALE STREET ("Rebirth Of
Beale Street"): *84* 200-225
(Collection of songs by Memphis artists, including
one by Elvis. A promotionally distributed LP by
the city of Memphis. Price includes a photo booklet, which represents $20-$25 of the value.)

BILLBOARD ("Sound Of 77"): *77* ... 175-200
(Five-LP boxed set with various artists, including
eight songs by Elvis. Price includes a five-page
script, which represents about $5 of the value.
Promotional issue only.)

BILLBOARD ("1979 Yearbook"): *79* . 175-200
(Five-LP boxed set with various artists, including
one song by Elvis. Price includes a 10-page script,
which represents about $5 of the value. Promotion-
al issue only.)

BOXCAR ("Having Fun With
Elvis On Stage"): *74* 100-125
(Sold in conjunction with concert appearances.
Reissued as RCA Victor CPM1-0818.)

CBS SONGS (101; "Radio's Million
Performance Songs"): *84* 45-55
(Contains 15 songs by 15 artists, including Elvis.
Promotional issue only.)

CAEDMON (1572; "On The
Record"): *78* 50-75
(Contains news highlights of 1977, including
coverage of Elvis' death.)

CAMDEN (2304; "Flaming Star"): *69* ... 15-18
(First issued as RCA Victor 279, reissued in 1975
as Pickwick 2304.

CAMDEN (2408; "Let's Be Friends"): *70* 15-18
(Reissued in 1975 as Pickwick 2408.)

CAMDEN (2428; "Elvis' Christmas
Album"): *70* 15-18
(Eight songs on this LP were first issued on LOC-
1035. This package was reissued in 1975 as Pickwick 2428.)

CAMDEN (2440; "Almost In Love"): *70* . 25-30
(With *Stay Away Joe.*)

CAMDEN (2440; "Almost In Love"): *73* . 15-18
(With *Stay Away* replacing *Stay Away Joe*. Reissued in 1975 as Pickwick 2440.)

CAMDEN (2472; "You'll Never
Walk Alone"): *71* $15-18
(Reissued in 1975 as Pickwick 2472.)

CAMDEN (2518; "C'mon
Everybody"): *71* 15-18
(Reissued in 1975 as Pickwick 2518.)

CAMDEN (2533; "I Got Lucky"): *71* 15-18
(Reissued in 1975 as Pickwick 2533.)

CAMDEN (2567; "Elvis Sings Hits
From His Movies"): *72* 15-18
(Reissued in 1975 as Pickwick 2567.)

CAMDEN (2595; "Burning Love"): *72* . . 20-25
(Price includes 8x10 Elvis photo, which represents
$5-$7 of the value. Reissued in 1975 as Pickwick
2595.)

CAMDEN (2611; "Separate Ways"): *73* . . 15-18
(Reissued in 1975 as Pickwick 2611.)

CENTURY 21 PRODUCTIONS ("Epic
Of The '70s"): *76* 150-200
(Six-LP program of various '70s songs, including
one by Elvis. Promotional issue only. Not issued
with a special cover.)

COLLECTOR'S EDITION (505; "All-Time
Christmas Favorites"): *78* 250-275
(Five-LP boxed set, including one side of one disc
by Elvis.)

COUNTRY CROSSROADS (32-83; "Country
Crossroads"): *83* 75-100
(Southern Baptist Radio-TV issue. Contains one
track by Elvis.)

COUNTRY SESSIONS U.S.A. (122; "Best
Of Country Sessions U.S.A."): *83* 75-100
(Contains various country artists, including two
tracks by Elvis. Price includes cue sheets. Promotional issue only.)

COUNTRY SESSIONS U.S.A. (126; "A
Tribute To Elvis"): *83* 225-250
(Price includes cue sheets. Promotional issue only.)

CREATIVE RADIO ("Elvis
Remembered"): *78* 100-125
(Three-LP set. Price includes six insert pages,
which represent $25-$30 of the value. Advance
copies of this set, which was not issued with a special cover or package, had plain, white, handwrit-
ten, labels. These copies may be valued at
$150-$250. A promotional issue.)

CREATIVE RADIO ("Elvis, The
Country Side"): *84* 75-85
(Two-LP set. A promotional issue.)

CREATIVE RADIO ("Elvis-50th
Anniversary"): *85* 250-275
(Six-LP set. Price includes seven pages of programming instructions and cues. Packaged in a plain, un-
printed box. A promotional issue.)

CREATIVE RADIO ("Elvis-10th
Anniversary"): 87 .... $150-175
(Six-LP set. Price includes eight pages of program-
ming instructions and cues. Packaged in a custom
printed box. A promotional issue.)
~~CREATIVE RADIO ("Christmas With~~
Elvis"): 87 25-30
(Promotional issue. Not issued with special cover.)
CREATIVE RADIO ("Birthday Tribute
To Elvis"): 88 25-30
(Promotional issue. Not issued with special cover.)
CREATIVE RADIO ("The Elvis
Hour"): 86-88 10-12
(Price is for any of the weekly discs in this series.
The first 52 discs in the series have been selling as
a set for $450-$475. Promotional issues.)
CREATIVE RADIO ("Demo Of 10
Creative Radio Programs"): 25-30
(Includes segments of The Elvis Hour, 10th An-
niversary Special and Memories Of Elvis, plus por-
tions of other shows by other artists. A promotional
issue.)
CREATIVE RADIO (E1; "Elvis Exclusive
Interview"): 88 100-150
(Price for complete 1956 Little Rock concert
copies. The first 100 copies were pressed with the
full concert for promotional purposes. The only
way to visually identify these is to check the disc.
On the full concert pressings, the grooves take up
nearly the entire disc.)
CREATIVE RADIO (E1; "Elvis Exclusive
Interview"): 88 10-12
(Contains edited concert songs. On this pressing,
the grooves occupy only about two-thirds of the
disc.)
CREATIVE RADIO ("Between Takes
With Elvis"): 89 40-45
(Three-LP set. Promotional issue only.)
Note: Creative Radio issues may be shown as from
Creative Radio Shows or Creative Radio Network.
CURRENT AUDIO MAGAZINE (1; "Elvis
Press Conference"): 72 35-45
(Contains news and features on 13 topics, including
Elvis.)
DIAMOND P. PRODUCTIONS ("Reflections
Of Elvis"): 77 450-500
(Three-LP set. Price includes cue sheets. Promo-
tional issue only.)
DICK CLARK (402; "Rock, Roll &
Remember"): 77 225-250
(Six-LP set featuring various artists, including two
songs and a phone interview from Elvis. Price in-
cludes a six-page script. Not issued with a special
cover or package. For radio station use only.)

DICK CLARK ("Rock, Roll &
Remember, 1982"): 82 .... $250-300
(Four-LP boxed set, containing 48 songs by Elvis.
Price includes four programming sheets.)
DRAKE-CHENAULT ("Elvis: A
Three-Hour Special"): 77 300-350
(Three-LP boxed set. Price includes three pages of
cue sheets.)
DRAKE-CHENAULT ("Golden Years
Of Country"): 80 250-300
(25-LP set with one LP for each year, 1955-1979.
Includes eight songs by Elvis. Price includes 55-
page operations manual, which represents $25-$50
of the value. Issued to radio stations only.)
EMR ENTERPRISES (8; "The Age
Of Rock"): 69 100-125
(Promotional issue only.)
EARTH NEWS ("For August 29,
1977"): 77 300-350
(Contains 14 five minute programs, 12 of which are
about Elvis. For radio station use only. Not issued
with a special cover.)
ELEKTRA (60107; "Diner"): 82 8-12
(Contains 20 songs by 20 artists, including Elvis.)
GOLDEN EDITIONS LIMITED (1; "The
First Year"): 79 8-15
(Print in upper corners on front cover is in white.
Label is black. Includes 12-page booklet and one
page copy of a 1954 Elvis/Scotty Moore contract,
which represents $5-$8 of the value.)
GOLDEN EDITIONS LIMITED (101; "The
First Year"): 79 15-25
(Print in upper corners on front cover is in gold.
Label is white. Includes 12-page booklet and one
page copy of a 1954 Elvis/Scotty Moore contract,
which represents $5-$8 of the value. Most of the
material on this LP was previously issued on
HALW 00001.
GOODMAN GROUP (1; "Just Let Me Hear
Some Of That Rock'N'Roll
Music"): 79 75-150
(Two-LP set containing excerpts of 100 songs, in-
cluding three by Elvis. Promotional issue only.)
GREAT NORTHWEST (4005; "The Elvis
Tapes"): 77 10-15
(These interviews were repackaged on Starday
995.)
GREAT NORTHWEST (4006; "The King
Speaks"): 77 8-10
(First issued as Green Valley 2001.)
GREEN VALLEY (2001; "Elvis-1961
Press Conference"): 77 30-50
(Cover is thin, soft stock and does not have black
bar on spine. Label does not show the catalog num-
ber.)

GREEN VALLEY (2001; "Elvis-1961
Press Conference"): 77 . . . . $12-15
(Cover is standard stock and has black bar on
spine. Label has the catalog number on it. Repack-
aged as one-half of Green Valley 2001/2003. It was
later repackaged as Great Northwest 4006.)
GREEN VALLEY (2001/2003; "Elvis
Speaks To You"): 78 25-30
(GV-2001 was first issued as a single LP.)
HALW (00001; "The First Years"): 78 . . 25-30
(With embossed limited edition number on cover.)
HALW (00001; "The First Years"): 78 . . . 8-15
(No embossed number on cover. Repackaged in
1979 on Golden Editions 1.)
HEARTLAND/RCA VICTOR (1072/4;
"Unforgettable Fifties"): 88 18-22
(Four LPs. Contains 50 songs, including two by
Elvis. A TV mail-order offer.)
INTERNATIONAL HOTEL PRESENTS
ELVIS - 1969 (Boxed set): 69 1000-1500
(Custom gift box prepared by Col. Parker and RCA
for International Hotel guests. Contained: RCA Vic-
tor LPM-4088 and LSP-4155, three 8x10 Elvis
photos, RCA Elvis catalog, calendar, and a nine-
page letter. Price is for complete set, but box itself
represents 90-95% of value.)
INTERNATIONAL HOTEL PRESENTS
ELVIS - 1970 (Boxed set): 70 1000-1500
(Custom gift box prepared by Col. Parker and RCA
for International Hotel guests. Contained: RCA Victor LSP-6020 and 45-9791, one 8x10 Elvis photo,
photo album, RCA Elvis catalog, calendar, menu,
and letter. Price is for complete set, but box itself
represents 90-95% of value.)
K-TEL (9900; "Elvis Love
Songs"): 81 15-20
LOUISIANA HAYRIDE (3061; "The
Beginning Years"): 84 300-350
(White label advance pressing from RCA, In-
dianapolis, where this LP was manufactured.)
LOUISIANA HAYRIDE (3061; "The
Beginning Years"): 84 10-20
(Price includes 20-page *D.J. Fontana Remembers
Elvis* booklet, a four-sheet copy of Elvis' Hayride
contract, and a 10x10 *Presleyana, Second Edition*
flyer, all of which represent about $5-$8 of the
value. Selections from this LP were also issued on
The Music Works 3601 & 3602.)
LOUISIANA HAYRIDE (8454; "The
Louisiana Hayride"): 76 550-650
(Yellow label. A program of various artists, includ-
ing one song by Elvis. Issued to radio stations only.)
LOUISIANA HAYRIDE (8454; "The
Louisiana Hayride"): 81 300-325
(Gold label. A program of various artists, including
one song by Elvis.)

LOWERY GROUP (1; "25 Golden
Years"): 80 . . . . $40-60
(Two-LP set containing 25 songs by 21 artists, in-
cluding one by Elvis. Promotional issue only.)
MCA ("MCA Music"): 40-60
(No number shown on this four-LP set, containing
excerpts of 200 songs by various artists, including
five Elvis songs.)
MFSL (059; "From Elvis
In Memphis"): 82 25-40
(First issued as RCA Victor LSP-4155.)
MARCH OF DIMES (0653; "Discs
For Dimes"): 56 1400-1600
(Contains announcements by 20 artists, including
one by Elvis. Price includes a 16-page packet for
programmers, which represents $75-$100 of the
value. Promotional issue only. The other side of
this 16-inch LP is numbered 0654.)
MARCH OF DIMES (0657; "Disc Jockey
Interviews"): 56 1400-1600
(Contains songs and interviews with six artists, in-
cluding one by Elvis. Price includes an instruction
packet for programmers, which represents $75-
$100 of the value. Promotional issue only. The
other side of this 16-inch LP is numbered 0658.)
MARVENCO (101; "1954-1955, The
Beginning"): 88 10-15
(Contains material perviously issued on Golden
Editions 101.)
MEDIA ENTERTAINMENT ("The
King's Gold"): 85 50-75
(Three reel-to-reel tapes, issued only to radio sta-
tions. Price includes cue sheets, which represent $4-
$6 of the value. Not known to exist on disc.)
MICHELOB (810; "Highlights Of
Elvis Memories"): 78 175-200
(Michelob in-house promotional issue only. *Elvis
Memories* was first issued on ABC Radio 1003.)
MORE MUSIC (333-72; "A Chronology
Of American Music"): 72 500-600
(21 LPs of number one songs, including 16 Elvis
songs. For radio station use only. Not issued with
any special box or package.)
MUSIC WORKS (3601; "The First
Live Recordings"): 84 8-10
(First issued on Louisiana Hayride 3061.)
MUSIC WORKS (3602; "The
Hillbilly Cat"): 84 8-10
(First issued on Louisiana Hayride 3061.)
MUTUAL ("Super Songs"): 50-75
(Three-LP broadcast set. Contains one Elvis track.)
MUTUAL BROADCAST SYSTEM (4082;
"The Frantic Fifties"): 59 175-200
(Contains an excerpt of *Hound Dog*. Promotional
issue only.)

NEW WORLD (207; "Country Music
In The Modern Era"): 77 . . . . $40-60
(Contains 18 songs by 18 artists, including Elvis.
Produced for use by libraries.)

ORIGINAL SOUND RECORDINGS (11;
~~Rock Rock Rock~~): 72 45-55
(Contains 14 songs by 14 artists, including one by
Elvis. Title may also be shown as *All Star Rock,
Vol. 11*.)

PAIR (1010; "Double Dynamite"): 82 . . . 20-25
(First issued as Pickwick 5001.)

PAIR (1037; "Remembering Elvis"): 83 . . 20-25

PICKWICK (1; "We're Playing
Your Song"): 80 25-35
(Two-LP collection of various artists, including
three Elvis tracks. Promotional issue only.)

PICKWICK (2304; "Flaming Star"): 75 . . . 8-10
(First issued as RCA Victor 279.)

PICKWICK (2408; "Let's Be Friends,"
black vinyl): 75 8-10
(First issued as Camden 2408.)

PICKWICK (2408; "Let's Be Friends,"
colored vinyl): 500-600
(An experimental pressing. There was no colored
vinyl commercial or promotional edition of this
issue. Also, a series of standard catalog Elvis LPs
came out of RCA's Indianapolis plant, on colored
vinyl. These were experimental items, which sold
for approximately $1,000 each.)

PICKWICK (2428; "Elvis' Christmas
Album"): 75 8-10
(First issued as Camden 2428.)

PICKWICK (2440; "Almost In
Love"): 75 8-10
(First issued as Camden 2440.)

PICKWICK (2472; "You'll Never
Walk Alone"): 75 8-10
(First issued as Camden 2472.)

PICKWICK (2518; "C'mon
Everybody"): 75 8-10
(First issued as Camden 2518.)

PICKWICK (2533; "I Got Lucky"): 75 . . . 8-10
(First issued as Camden 2533.)

PICKWICK (2567; "Elvis Sings Hits
From His Movies"): 75 8-10
(First issued as Camden 2567.)

PICKWICK (2595; "Burning Love"): 75 . . 8-10
(First issued as Camden 2595.)

PICKWICK (2611; "Separate Ways"): 75 . 8-10
(First issued as Camden 2611.)

PICKWICK (5001; "Double
Dynamite"): 75 25-30
(Repackaged in 1982 as Pair 1010.)

PICKWICK (7007; "Frankie And
Johnny"): 76 10-12
(First issued as RCA Victor LPM/LSP-3553.)

PICKWICK (7064; "Mahalo From
Elvis"): 78 . . . . $15-20

PLAYBOY (7473; "The Playboy Music
Hall Of Fame Winners"): 78 100-150
(Contains 26 songs by 18 different artists, including Elvis. Includes the film version of *Long Lonely
Highway*, though titled "Moving Down the Line"
on this LP. A mail-order offer from *Playboy*
magazine.)

PROMO ("All Time Greats, Vol. 1"): . . . 20-30
(Collection of various artists, including one Elvis
track.)

PROMO ("All Time Greats,
Vol. 3"): 20-30
(Collection of various artists, including one Elvis
track.)

RCA VICTOR (EPC-1; "Special Christmas
Program" Reel Tape): 67 300-325
(Price includes programming insert, which repre-
sents $25-$35 of the value. This program was never
issued commercially on disc. All 10-inch red vinyl
LPs of this material are unauthorized.)

RCA VICTOR (TB-1; "A Collector's
Edition"): 76 75-100
(Five-disc boxed set. Price includes a 20-page booklet, which represents $10-$15 of the value. A TV
mail-order LP offer.)

RCA VICTOR (0001; "Robert W.
Sarnoff"): 73 600-800
(Contains a diverse assortment of RCA product, including four songs by Elvis. An RCA in-house
promotional item prepared as a tribute to Sarnoff's
25 years with the company.)

RCA VICTOR (4; Untitled RCA
Sampler): 56 1000-1500
(Contains 21 songs by 21 different artists, includ-
ing Elvis. Promotional issue only.)

RCA VICTOR (10; Untitled RCA
Sampler): 58 900-1000
(Contains 14 songs by 14 different artists, includ-
ing Elvis. Promotional issue only.)

RCA VICTOR (010; "Elvis! His
Greatest Hits"): 79 400-450
(WHITE box edition. An eight-LP boxed set, sold
mail-order by *Reader's Digest*.)

RCA VICTOR (010; "Elvis! His
Greatest Hits"): 83 40-60
(YELLOW box edition. A seven-LP boxed set,
sold mail-order by *Reader's Digest*. See RCA Victor 181 for the bonus LP offered with this edition.)

RCA VICTOR (016; "The Grammy
Award Winners"): *85* $75-100
(Four-LP boxed set, one in a series available
through the Franklin Mint by mail order. This set
features eight different artists, one of which is
Elvis—each heard on one full side of a disc. Includes six Elvis tracks. Issued on colored vinyl.)

RCA VICTOR (27; "August 1959
Sampler"): *59* 700-900
(Contains 13 songs by 13 different artists, includ-
ing Elvis. Promotional issue only.)

RCA VICTOR (0034; "QSP Presents A
Gift Of Music"): *84* 50-75
(Company promotional sampler, with 12 songs by
12 artists, including Elvis. QSP is a direct sales or-
ganization.)

RCA VICTOR RBA-040: see READER'S
DIGEST 040

RCA VICTOR (51; "February
Sampler"): *59* 700-900
(Contains 12 songs by 12 different artists, includ-
ing Elvis. Full number shown as SP-33-51.)

RCA VICTOR (54; "October Christmas
Sampler"): *59* 600-700
(Contains 13 songs by 13 different artists, includ-
ing Elvis. Promotional issue only.)

RCA VICTOR (0056; "Elvis"): *73* 40-50
(Mustard color label. Cover shows "Brookville
Records" in upper right. A mail-order offer.)

RCA VICTOR (0056; "Elvis"): *73* 20-25
(Blue label. Cover doesn't show "Brookville
Records." A mail-order offer.)
Repackaged in 1978 and titled *Elvis Commemora-
tive Album.*

RCA VICTOR (0056; "Elvis Commemorative
Album"): *78* 75-80
(Price includes a "Registered Certificate Of Owner-
ship," which represents $4-$6 of the value. A mail-
order offer. First titled *Elvis,* using the same catalog
number.)

RCA VICTOR (57; "November/December '59
Sampler"): *59* 700-900
(Contains 14 songs by 14 different artists, includ-
ing Elvis. Full number shown as SP-33-57.)

RCA VICTOR (59; "February
Sampler"): *59* 700-900
(Contains eight songs by eight different artists, in-
cluding Elvis. Full number shown as SP-33-59-7.
Has RCA Victor black label on one side and RCA
Camden label on side 2, thus sampling tunes from
LPs on both labels. Promotional issue only.)

RCA VICTOR (66; "Christmas Programming
From RCA"): *59* 500-600
(Contains 12 songs by 12 different artists, includ-
ing Elvis. Promotional issue only.)

RCA VICTOR (66; "Christmas Programming
From RCA"): *59* $500-600
(Special paper sleeve for SP-33-66. Promotional
issue only.)

RCA VICTOR (072; "Elvis Presley, Great
Hits Of 1956-57"): *87* 10-20
(Offered as a bonus LP by *Reader's Digest,* with
the purchase of one of their non-Elvis boxed sets.)

RCA VICTOR (0086; "Brightest Stars
Of Christmas"): *74* 35-45
(Contains 11 songs by 11 artists, including Elvis.
Custom made for J.C. Penney and sold only in their
stores.)

RCA VICTOR (96; "October 1960
Stereo Sampler"): *60* 500-600
(Contains 14 songs by 14 different artists, includ-
ing Elvis. Promotional issue only.)

RCA VICTOR (0108; "E-Z Country
No. 2"): *55* 250-275
(10-inch LP with 12 songs by 11 different artists,
including two by Elvis. Promotional issue only.
The other side of this LP is numbered 0109.)

RCA VICTOR (141; "October '61
Pop Sampler"): *61* 500-600
(Contains 11 songs by 11 different artists, includ-
ing Elvis. Promotional issue only.)

RCA VICTOR (0168; "Elvis In
Hollywood"): *76* 35-45
(Price includes a 20-page photo booklet, which rep-
resents $10-$15 of the value.)

RCA VICTOR (181; "Elvis Sings
Inspirational Favorites"): *83* 15-20
(Special Products *Reader's Digest* mail-order
bonus LP for buyers of the 1983 edition of RCA
Victor 010. Price includes 24-page *Reader's Digest
Music* catalog.)

RCA VICTOR (191; RCA
Sampler): *62* 500-600
(Promotional issue only. More information is
needed about this LP.)

RCA VICTOR (191; "Elvis, The Legend
Lives On"): *86* 40-45
(Seven-LP boxed set, sold mail-order by *Reader's
Digest.* Includes booklet.)

RCA VICTOR (0197; "E-Z Pop
No. 6"): *56* 250-275
(10-inch LP with 12 songs by 12 different artists,
including Elvis. Promotional issue only. The other
side of this LP is numbered 0198.)

RCA VICTOR (0199; "E-Z Country
No. 3"): *56* 250-275
(10-inch LP with 12 songs by nine different artists,
including two by Elvis. Promotional issue only.
The other side of this LP is numbered 0200.)

RCA VICTOR (215; "30 Years Of No. 1
Country Hits"): *86* $40-45
(Various artists, seven-LP boxed set, containing 84
songs, including three by Elvis. Includes booklet.)

RCA VICTOR (219; RCA
Sampler): *03* 500-600
(Promotional issue only. More information is
needed about this LP.)

RCA VICTOR (242; "Elvis Sings
Country Favorites"): *84* 20-30
(Offered as a bonus LP by *Reader's Digest* with the
purchase of their seven-disc boxed set, *The Great
Country Entertainers*.)

RCA VICTOR (247; "December '63
Pop Sampler"): *63* 500-600
(Contains 11 songs by 10 different artists, includ-
ing one by Elvis. Promotional issue only.)

RCA VICTOR (0263; "The Elvis
Presley Story"): *77* 30-40
(Special Products five-LP boxed set. A Candelite
Music mail-order offer.)

RCA VICTOR (0264; "Songs Of
Inspiration"): *77* 10-15
(Special Products issue. A Candelite Music mail-
order bonus LP for buyers of RCA Victor 0263.)

RCA VICTOR (272; "April '64
Pop Sampler"): *64* 500-600
(Contains 14 songs by 14 different artists, includ-
ing Elvis. Promotional issue only.)

RCA VICTOR (279; "Singer Presents
Elvis"): *68* 70-80
(Reissued in 1969 as Camden 2304 and in 1975 as
Pickwick 2304.)

RCA VICTOR (0283; "Elvis, Including
Fool"): *73* 50-60

RCA VICTOR (331; "April '65
Pop Sampler"): *65* 500-600
(Contains 14 songs by 14 different artists, includ-
ing Elvis. Promotional issue only.)

RCA VICTOR (0341; "Legendary
Performer," Vol. 1): *74* 20-25
(With die-cut cover. Price includes *The Early Years*
booklet, which represents $5-$8 of the value.)

RCA VICTOR (0341; "Legendary
Performer," Vol. 1): *83* 5-8
(With standard cover rather than die-cut.)

RCA VICTOR (0341; "Legendary
Performer," Vol. 1): *78* 800-1000
(Picture discs of the 0341 material but with pictures
from any of about six different LP covers pressed
on the disc. RCA experimental in-house item.)

RCA VICTOR (347; "August '65
Pop Sampler"): *65* 500-600
(Contains 12 songs by 12 different artists, includ-
ing Elvis. Promotional issue only.)

RCA VICTOR (0347; "Memories Of
Elvis"): *78* $35-45
(Special Products five-LP boxed set. A Candelite
Music mail-order offer. Price includes a 16-page
booklet and an Elvis print, which represent $8-$10
of the value. Apparently not all sets were issued
with the print and booklet.)

RCA VICTOR (0348; "Greatest Show
On Earth"): *78* 10-12
(Special Products issue. A Candelite Music mail-
order bonus LP for buyers of RCA Victor 0347.)

RCA VICTOR (0388; "Raised On
Rock"): *73* 15-20
(Orange label.)

RCA VICTOR (0388; "Raised On
Rock"): *77* 8-10
(Black label.)

RCA VICTOR (403; "April '66
Pop Sampler"): *66* 500-600
(Contains 14 songs by 14 different artists, includ-
ing Elvis. Promotional issue only.)

RCA VICTOR (0401; RCA Radio Victrola
Division Spots"): *56* 750-1000
(One-sided disc, containing four 50-second radio
commercials for RCA Victrolas, as well as for the
SPD-22 and SPD-23 EPs that were offered as a
bonus. Elvis is the announcer on all of the spots,
which include excerpts of some of his songs. Issued
only to radio stations scheduling the spots.)

RCA VICTOR (0412; "The Legendary
Recordings"): *79* 30-40
(Special Products six-LP boxed set. A Candelite
Music mail-order offer.)

RCA VICTOR (0413; "Greatest Moments
In Music"): *80* 10-15
(Special Products issue. A Candelite Music mail-
order bonus LP for buyers of RCA Victor 0412.)

RCA VICTOR (0437; "Rock 'N Roll
Forever"): *81* 10-15
(Candelite Music mail-order offer.)

RCA VICTOR (461; "Special Palm
Sunday Programming"): *67* 500-600
(Price includes programming packet, which represents $100-$125 of the value. Promotional issue
only.)

RCA VICTOR (0461; "The Legendary
Magic"): *80* 10-15
(Candelite Music mail-order LP offer.)

RCA VICTOR (CPL1-0475; "Good
Times"): *74* 15-20

RCA VICTOR (AFL1-0475; "Good
Times"): *77* 8-10

RCA VICTOR (0561; "Country
Gold"): *82* 20-25
(Contains 10 songs by 10 artists, including one by
Elvis. Special Products LP.)

RCA VICTOR (571; "Madison Square
Garden"): 72 .... **$250-300**
(Two-LP, double-pocket issue. Promotional issue
only. Commercially issued as RCA Victor LSP-
4776.)
RCA VICTOR (DJL1-0606; "On Stage
In Memphis"): 74 .... **250-275**
(Banded edition. Promotional issue only.)
RCA VICTOR (CPL1-0606; "On Stage
In Memphis"): 74 .... **15-18**
(Orange label.)
RCA VICTOR (CPL1-0606; "On Stage
In Memphis"): 76 .... **10-15**
(Tan label.)
RCA VICTOR (APD1-0606; "On Stage
In Memphis"): 74 .... **120-130**
(Quadradisc. Orange label.)
RCA VICTOR (AFL1-0606; "On Stage
In Memphis"): 77 .... **8-10**
RCA VICTOR (0608; "Happy
Holidays, Vol. 18"): 83 .... **8-10**
(Contains 10 songs by 10 artists, including Elvis.
Sold only at True Value Hardware Stores.)
RCA VICTOR (0632; "The Elvis Presley
Collection"): 84 .... **50-60**
(Special Products three-LP, mail-order boxed set,
produced for Candlelite Music. Includes booklet.)
RCA VICTOR (DPL1-0647; "Elvis
Country"): 84 .... **15-20**
(Special Products issue for ERA Records.)
RCA VICTOR (DPK1-0679; "Savage
Young Elvis"): 84 .... **5-8**
(Cassette tape of a package that was never avail-
able on LP. Price is for tape still attached to 12x12
photo card.)
RCA VICTOR (0704; "Elvis, HBO
Special"): 84 .... **25-35**
(Includes color poster. Special Products issue for
HBO cable TV subscribers. This material was first
issued as LPM-4088.
RCA VICTOR (0710; "Elvis: 50 Years,
50 Hits"): 85 .... **20-25**
(Three-LP set. Offered by TV mail-order and
through the RCA Record Club.)
RCA VICTOR (0713; "Happy Holidays,
Vol. 20"): 85 .... **8-10**
(Contains 14 songs by 14 artists, including Elvis.
Sold only at True Value Hardware Stores.)
RCA VICTOR (0716; "A Christmas Treasury
From Avon"): 85 .... **8-12**
(Contains 10 songs by 10 artists, including Elvis.
Available only from Avon as a Christmas bonus
item. Packaged in a specially printed cardboard
mailer which is included in the price.)
RCA VICTOR (0728; "Elvis, His Songs Of
Faith & Inspiration"): 86 .... **15-18**
(Two-LP, mail-order offer.)

RCA VICTOR (0739; "Happy Holidays,
Vol. 21"): 86 .... **$8-10**
(Contains 12 songs by 12 artists, including Elvis.
Sold only at True Value Hardware Stores.)
RCA VICTOR (0751; "Avon Valentine
Favorites"): 86 .... **10-15**
(Contains 10 songs by nine artists, including one by
Elvis. Available only from Avon as a bonus item.
Packaged in a specially printed cardboard mailer
which is included in the price.)
RCA VICTOR (DPL1-0803; "Celebrate
The Season With Tupperware"): 87 ... **20-30**
(Contains 10 songs by 10 artists, including one by
Elvis. Available only from Tupperware Home Par-
ties.)
RCA VICTOR (CPM1-0818; "Having Fun With
Elvis On Stage"): 74 .... **15-20**
(Orange label.)
RCA VICTOR (CPM1-0818; "Having Fun With
Elvis On Stage"): 76 .... **10-15**
(Tan label.)
RCA VICTOR (AFM1-0818; "Having Fun With
Elvis On Stage"): 77 .... **8-10**
(First issued on Boxcar, without a catalog number.)
RCA VICTOR (0835; "Elvis Presley
Interview Record"): 84 .... **75-100**
(Promotional issue only.)
RCA VICTOR (0842; "The Stars
Of Christmas"): 88 .... **8-12**
(Contains 12 songs by 12 artists, including Elvis.
Available only from Avon as a Christmas bonus
item. Includes 20-page lyrics/photo booklet.)
RCA VICTOR (0868; "Coming
Home"): 88 .... **15-20**
(Contains 24 songs by 23 artists, including one by
Elvis.)
RCA VICTOR (APL1-0873; "Promised
Land"): 75 .... **15-18**
(Orange label.)
RCA VICTOR (APL1-0873; "Promised
Land"): 76 .... **10-15**
(Tan label.)
RCA VICTOR (AFL1-0873; "Promised
Land"): 77 .... **8-10**
RCA VICTOR (APD1-0873; "Promised
Land"): 75 .... **100-125**
(Quadradisc. Orange label.)
RCA VICTOR (APD1-0873; "Promised
Land"): 77 .... **40-50**
(Quadradisc. Black label.)
RCA VICTOR (ANL1-0971; "Pure
Gold"): 75 .... **15-18**
(Orange label.)
RCA VICTOR (ANL1-0971; "Pure
Gold"): 76 .... **10-15**
(Yellow label.)

RCA VICTOR (ANL1-0971; "Pure
Gold"): 77 ....**$8-10**
(Black label. Reissued in 1980 as AYL1-3732.)

RCA VICTOR (1001; "The Sun
Collection"): 75 ....**20-25**
~~(Label does not have "Starcall" on it. Back cover~~
pictures other LPs.)

RCA VICTOR (1001; "The Sun
Collection"): 75 ....**15-20**
(Label has "Starcall" on it. Back cover with liner
notes. This U.K. import was distributed throughout
the U.S. It was repackaged in 1976 as RCA Victor
APM1-1675.)

RCA VICTOR (LOC-1035; "Elvis'
Christmas Album"): 57 ....**475-525**
(With gold foil gift-giving sticker.)

RCA VICTOR (LOC-1035; "Elvis'
Christmas Album"): 57 ....**350-400**
(Without gold foil gift-giving sticker. Repackaged
in 1958 as RCA Victor LPM-1951, in 1970 as Camden 2428, and in 1985 as RCA Victor AFM1-5486.
LOC-1035 may be found with both gold and silver
print on the spine.)

RCA VICTOR (APL1-1039;
"Today"): 75 ....**15-18**
(Orange label.)

RCA VICTOR (APL1-1039;
"Today"): 76 ....**10-15**
(Tan label.)

RCA VICTOR (AFL1-1039;
"Today"): 77 ....**8-10**

RCA VICTOR (APD1-1039;
"Today"): 75 ....**100-125**
(Quadradisc. Orange label.)

RCA VICTOR (APD1-1039;
"Today"): 77 ....**40-50**
(Quadradisc. Black label.)

RCA VICTOR (LPM-1254; "Elvis
Presley"): 56 ....**100-125**
(Black label with "Long Play" at bottom. Cover
with catalog number in upper right corner.)

RCA VICTOR (LPM-1254; "Elvis
Presley"): 63 ....**45-55**
(Black label with "Mono" at bottom. Cover with
catalog number on left.)

RCA VICTOR (LPM-1254; "Elvis
Presley"): 64 ....**25-30**
(Black label with "Monaural" at bottom. Cover
with catalog number on left.)

RCA VICTOR (LSP-1254e; "Elvis
Presley"): 62 ....**75-85**
(Black label, all print on label is silver.)

RCA VICTOR (LSP-1254e; "Elvis
Presley"): 64 ....**25-30**
(Black label, RCA logo is white, other label print is
silver.)

RCA VICTOR (LSP-1254e; "Elvis
Presley"): 68 ....**$10-20**
(Orange label.)

RCA VICTOR (LSP-1254e; "Elvis
Presley"): 76 ....**10-15**
~~(Tan label.)~~

RCA VICTOR (AFL1-1254e; "Elvis
Presley"): 77 ....**8-10**
(A digitally remastered edition of this LP was is-
sued in 1984 on RCA Victor 5198.)

RCA VICTOR (ANL1-1319; "His Hand
In Mine"): 76 ....**10-15**
(First issued as LPM/LSP-2328.)

RCA VICTOR (1349; "Legendary
Performer," Vol. 2): 76 ....**45-55**
(Pressed WITHOUT the studio out-takes. This was
a production error.)

RCA VICTOR (1349; "Legendary
Performer," Vol. 2): 76 ....**20-25**
(With die-cut cover. Price includes *The Early Years
Continued* booklet, which represents $5-$8 of the
value.)

RCA VICTOR (1349; "Legendary
Performer," Vol. 2): 83 ....**5-8**
(With standard cover rather than die-cut.)

RCA VICTOR (LPM-1382;
"Elvis"): 56 ....**750-1000**
(Black label with "Long Play" at bottom. Cover
with catalog number in upper right corner. Contains the otherwise unreleased alternate take of *Old
Shep*. This pressing has the designation "17S" following the matrix number stamped in the vinyl trailoff. We've yet to learn of any copies of this oddity
with a number OTHER than "17S.")

RCA VICTOR (LPM-1382;
"Elvis"): 56 ....**200-225**
(Black label, selections numbered as "Band 1"
through "Band 6.")

RCA VICTOR (LPM-1382;
"Elvis"): 56 ....**100-125**
(Black label with "Long Play" at bottom. Cover
with catalog number in upper right corner.)

RCA VICTOR (LPM-1382; "Elvis"): 63 . **45-55**
(Black label with "Mono" at bottom. Cover with
catalog number on left.)

RCA VICTOR (LPM-1382; "Elvis"): 64 . **25-30**
(Black label with "Monaural" at bottom. Cover
with catalog number on left.)

RCA VICTOR (LSP-1382e; "Elvis"): 62 **75-85**
(Black label, all print on label is silver.)

RCA VICTOR (LSP-1382e; "Elvis"): 64 **25-30**
(Black label, RCA logo is white, other print on
label is silver.)

RCA VICTOR (LSP-1382e; "Elvis"): 68 **10-20**
(Orange label.)

RCA VICTOR (LSP-1382e; "Elvis"): 76 **10-15**
(Tan label.)

RCA VICTOR (AFL1-1382e;
"Elvis"): 77 .... **$8-10**
(A digitally remastered edition of this LP was is-
sued in 1984 on RCA Victor 5199.)

RCA VICTOR (APL1-1506; "From Elvis
Presley Boulevard"): 76 .... **12-15**

RCA VICTOR (AFL1-1506; "From Elvis
Presley Boulevard"): 77 .... **8-10**

RCA VICTOR (LPM-1515; "Loving
You"): 57 .... **100-125**
(Black label with "Long Play" at bottom. Cover
with catalog number in upper right corner.)

RCA VICTOR (LPM-1515; "Loving
You"): 63 .... **45-55**
(Black label with "Mono" at bottom. Cover with
catalog number on left.)

RCA VICTOR (LPM-1515; "Loving
You"): 64 .... **25-30**
(Black label with "Monaural" at bottom. Cover
with catalog number on left.)

RCA VICTOR (LSP-1515e; "Loving
You"): 62 .... **75-85**
(Black label, all print on label is silver.)

RCA VICTOR (LSP-1515e; "Loving
You"): 64 .... **25-30**
(Black label, RCA logo is white, other label print is
silver.)

RCA VICTOR (LSP-1515e; "Loving
You"): 68 .... **10-20**
(Orange label.)

RCA VICTOR (LSP-1515e; "Loving
You"): 76 .... **10-15**
(Tan label.)

RCA VICTOR (AFL1-1515e; "Loving
You"): 77 .... **5-10**

RCA VICTOR (APM1-1675; "The Sun
Sessions"): 76 .... **12-15**

RCA VICTOR (AFM1-1675; "The Sun
Sessions"): 77 .... **8-10**
(First issued as RCA Victor HY-1001 and was reis-
sued in 1981 as RCA Victor AYM1-3893.)

RCA VICTOR (LPM-1707; "Elvis' Golden
Records"): 58 .... **100-125**
(Black label with "Long Play" at bottom. Cover
with catalog number in upper right corner and LP
title in light blue letters.)

RCA VICTOR (LPM-1707; "Elvis' Golden
Records"): 63 .... **45-55**
(Black label with "Mono" at bottom. Cover with
catalog number on left and LP title in white letters.)

RCA VICTOR (LPM-1707; "Elvis' Golden
Records"): 64 .... **25-30**
(Black label with "Monaural" at bottom. Cover
with catalog number on left.)

RCA VICTOR (LSP-1707e; "Elvis' Golden
Records"): 62 .... **$75-85**
(Black label, all print on label is silver.)

RCA VICTOR (LSP-1707e; "Elvis' Golden
Records"): 64 .... **25-30**
(Black label, RCA logo is white, other label print is
silver.)

RCA VICTOR (LSP-1707e; "Elvis' Golden
Records"): 68 .... **10-20**
(Orange label.)

RCA VICTOR (LSP-1707e; "Elvis' Golden
Records"): 76 .... **10-15**
(Tan label.)

RCA VICTOR (AFL1-1707e; "Elvis' Golden
Records"): 77 .... **8-10**

RCA VICTOR (AQL1-1707e; "Elvis' Golden
Records"): 79 .... **5-10**
(A digitally remastered edition of this LP was is-
sued in 1984 on RCA Victor 5196.

RCA VICTOR (1785; "WRCA Plays
The Hits"): 76 .... **300-350**
(Contains 16 songs by 16 artists, including Elvis.
Promotional issue only. Not issued with a special
cover.)

RCA VICTOR (LPM-1884; "King
Creole"): 58 .... **100-125**
(Black label with "Long Play" at bottom. Cover
with catalog number in upper right corner. Add
$75-$100 if accompanied by the 8x10 black and
white bonus photo of Elvis in uniform.)

RCA VICTOR (LPM-1884; "King
Creole"): 63 .... **45-55**
(Black label with "Mono" at bottom. Cover with
catalog number on left.)

RCA VICTOR (LPM-1884; "King
Creole"): 64 .... **25-30**
(Black label with "Monaural" at bottom. Cover
with catalog number on left.)

RCA VICTOR (LSP-1884e; "King
Creole"): 62 .... **75-85**
(Black label, all print on label is silver.)

RCA VICTOR (LSP-1884e; "King
Creole"): 62 .... **25-30**
(Black label, RCA logo is white, other label print is
silver.)

RCA VICTOR (LSP-1884e; "King
Creole"): 68 .... **10-20**
(Orange label.)

RCA VICTOR (LSP-1884e; "King
Creole"): 76 .... **10-15**
(Tan label.)

RCA VICTOR (AFL1-1884e; "King
Creole"): 77 .... **8-10**
(Reissued in 1980 as RCA Victor AYL1-3733.)

RCA VICTOR (ANL1-1936; "Wonderful
World Of Christmas"): 77 ....$5-10
(First issued as RCA Victor LSP-4579.)
RCA VICTOR (LPM-1951; "Elvis'
Christmas Album"): 58 90-100
(Black label with "Long Play" at bottom. Cover
with catalog number in upper right corner.)
RCA VICTOR (LPM-1951; "Elvis'
Christmas Album"): 63 45-55
(Black label with "Mono" at bottom. Cover with
catalog number on left.)
RCA VICTOR (LPM-1951; "Elvis'
Christmas Album"): 64 25-30
(Black label with "Monaural" at bottom. Cover
with catalog number on left.)
RCA VICTOR (LSP-1951e; "Elvis'
Christmas Album"): 64 25-30
(Black label, RCA logo is white, other label print is
silver.)
RCA VICTOR (LSP-1951e; "Elvis'
Christmas Album"): 68 20-25
(Orange label. Repackage of RCA Victor LOC-
1035, repackaged in 1970 as Camden 2428 and
again in 1985 as RCA Victor AFM1-5486.)
RCA VICTOR (1981; "Felton Jarvis
Talks About Elvis"): 81 150-200
(Price includes three script sheets, which represent
$5-$10 of the value. Price also includes Guitar
Man engraved Elvis belt buckle, which represents
$25-$50 of the value.)
RCA VICTOR (LPM-1990; "For LP
Fans Only"): 59 100-125
(Black label with "Long Play" at bottom. Cover
with catalog number in upper right corner.)
RCA VICTOR (LPM-1990; "For LP
Fans Only"): 63 45-55
(Black label with "Mono" at bottom. Cover with
catalog number on left.)
RCA VICTOR (LPM-1990; "For LP
Fans Only"): 65 25-30
(Black label with "Monaural" at bottom. Cover
with catalog number on left.)
RCA VICTOR (LSP-1990e; "For LP
Fans Only"): 65 25-30
(Black label, RCA logo is white, other label print is
silver.)
RCA VICTOR (LSP-1990e; "For LP
Fans Only"): 68 10-20
(Orange label.)
RCA VICTOR (LSP-1990e; "For LP
Fans Only"): 76 10-15
(Tan label.)
RCA VICTOR (AFL1-1990e; "For LP
Fans Only"): 77 8-10

RCA VICTOR (LPM-2011; "A Date
With Elvis"): 59 ....$300-500
(Black label with "Long Play" at bottom. With
gatefold cover and 1960 calendar. Has "New Gold-
en Age of Sound Album" wrap-around banner.)
RCA VICTOR (LPM-2011; "A Date
With Elvis"): 59 150-175
(Black label with "Long Play" at bottom. With
gatefold cover and 1960 calendar, but without
"New Golden Age of Sound Album" banner.)
RCA VICTOR (LPM-2011; "A Date
With Elvis"): 65 45-55
(Black label with "Mono" at bottom. Cover with
catalog number on left.)
RCA VICTOR (LPM-2011; "A Date
With Elvis"): 65 25-30
(Black label with "Monaural" at bottom. Cover
with catalog number on left.)
RCA VICTOR (LSP-2011e; "A Date
With Elvis"): 65 25-30
(Black label, RCA logo is white, other label print is
silver.)
RCA VICTOR (LSP-2011e; "A Date
With Elvis"): 68 10-20
(Orange label.)
RCA VICTOR (LSP-2011e; "A Date
With Elvis"): 76 10-15
(Tan label.)
RCA VICTOR (AFL1-2011e; "A Date
With Elvis"): 77 8-10
RCA VICTOR (LPM-2075; "Elvis' Golden
Records," Vol. 2): 59 100-125
(Black label with "Long Play" at bottom. Cover
with catalog number in upper right corner.)
RCA VICTOR (LPM-2075; "Elvis' Golden
Records, Vol. 2"): 63 45-55
(Black label with "Mono" at bottom. Cover with
catalog number on left.)
RCA VICTOR (LPM-2075; "Elvis' Golden
Records, Vol. 2"): 64 25-30
(Black label with "Monaural" at bottom. Cover
with catalog number on left.)
RCA VICTOR (LSP-2075e; "Elvis' Golden
Records, Vol. 2"): 62 75-85
(Black label, all print on label is silver.)
RCA VICTOR (LSP-2075e; "Elvis' Golden
Records, Vol. 2"): 64 25-30
(Black label, RCA logo is white, other label print is
silver.)
RCA VICTOR (LSP-2075e; "Elvis' Golden
Records, Vol. 2"): 68 10-20
(Orange label.)
RCA VICTOR (LSP-2075e; "Elvis' Golden
Records, Vol. 2"): 76 10-15
(Tan label.)

RCA VICTOR (AFL1-2075e; "Elvis' Golden
Records, Vol. 2"): 77 . . . . $8-10
(May also be shown as *50,000,000 Elvis Presley
Fans Can't Be Wrong.* A digitally remastered edi-
tion of this LP was issued in 1984 on RCA Victor
5197.)

RCA VICTOR (LPM-2231; "Elvis Is
Back"): 60 100-125
(Black label with "Long Play" at bottom. No song
titles printed on cover. May have a yellow sticker
on cover showing song titles.)

RCA VICTOR (LPM-2231; "Elvis Is
Back"): 63 45-55
(Black label with "Mono" at bottom. Cover with
catalog number on left.)

RCA VICTOR (LPM-2231; "Elvis Is
Back"): 64 25-30
(Black label with "Monaural" at bottom. Cover
with catalog number on left.)

RCA VICTOR (LSP-2231; "Elvis Is
Back"): 60 125-150
(Black label with "Living Stereo" at bottom. No
song titles printed on cover. May have a yellow
sticker on cover showing song titles.)

RCA VICTOR (LSP-2231; "Elvis Is
Back"): 64 25-30
(Black label, RCA logo is white, other label print is
silver.)

RCA VICTOR (LSP-2231; "Elvis Is
Back"): 68 10-20
(Orange label.)

RCA VICTOR (LSP-2231; "Elvis Is
Back"): 76 10-15
(Tan label.)

RCA VICTOR (AFL1-2231; "Elvis Is
Back"): 77 8-10

RCA VICTOR (LPM-2256; "G.I.
Blues"): 60 100-125
(Black label with "Long Play" at bottom. Price includes "Elvis Is Back" inner sleeve, which represents $15-$25 of the value.)

RCA VICTOR (LPM-2256; "G.I.
Blues"): 63 45-55
(Black label with "Mono" at bottom.)

RCA VICTOR (LPM-2256; "G.I.
Blues"): 64 25-30
(Black label with "Monaural" at bottom.)

RCA VICTOR (LSP-2256; "G.I.
Blues"): 60 100-125
(Black label with "Living Stereo" at bottom. Price
includes "Elvis Is Back" inner sleeve, which represents $15-$25 of the value.)

RCA VICTOR (LSP-2256; "G.I.
Blues"): 64 25-30
(Black label, RCA logo is white, other label print is
silver.)

RCA VICTOR (LSP-2256; "G.I.
Blues"): 68 . . . . $10-20
(Orange label.)

RCA VICTOR (LSP-2256; "G.I.
Blues"): 76 10-15
(Tan label.)

RCA VICTOR (AFL1-2256; "G.I.
Blues"): 77 8-10
(Reissued in 1980 as RCA Victor AYL1-3735.)

RCA VICTOR (APL1-2274; "Welcome To
My World"): 77 10-15

RCA VICTOR (AFL1-2274; "Welcome To
My World"): 77 8-10

RCA VICTOR (AQL1-2274; "Welcome To
My World"): 79 5-10

RCA VICTOR (LPM-2328; "His Hand
In Mine"): 60 75-90
(Black label with "Long Play" at bottom.)

RCA VICTOR (LPM-2328; "His Hand
In Mine"): 63 40-50
(Black label with "Mono" at bottom.)

RCA VICTOR (LPM-2328; "His Hand
In Mine"): 64 25-30
(Black label with "Monaural" at bottom.)

RCA VICTOR (LSP-2328; "His Hand
In Mine"): 60 90-100
(Black label with "Living Stereo" at bottom.)

RCA VICTOR (LSP-2328; "His Hand
In Mine"): 64 25-30
(Black label, RCA logo is white, other label print is
silver.)

RCA VICTOR (LSP-2328; "His Hand
In Mine"): 68 10-20
(Orange label.)

RCA VICTOR (LSP-2328; "His Hand
In Mine"): 76 10-15
(Tan label. Repackaged in 1976 as RCA Victor
ANL1-1319 and in 1981 as RCA Victor AYM1-
3935.)

RCA VICTOR (2347; "Elvis-Greatest Hits,
Vol. One"): 81 10-15
(With embossed letters on front cover.)

RCA VICTOR (2347; "Elvis-Greatest Hits,
Vol. One"): 83 5-8
(Standard printed cover. No embossed letters.)

RCA VICTOR (LPM-2370; "Something For
Everybody"): 61 75-90
(Black label with "Long Play" at bottom. Back
cover promotes Compact 33s.)

RCA VICTOR (LPM-2370; "Something For
Everybody"): 63 40-50
(Black label with "Mono" at bottom.)

RCA VICTOR (LPM-2370; "Something For
Everybody"): 64 25-30
(Black label with "Monaural" at bottom.)

RCA VICTOR (LSP-2370; "Something For
Everybody"): 61 .... $90-100
(Black label with "Living Stereo" at bottom. Back
cover promotes Compact 33s.)
RCA VICTOR (LSP-2370; "Something For
Everybody"): 64 23-30
(Black label, RCA logo is white, other label print is
silver.)
RCA VICTOR (LSP-2370; "Something For
Everybody"): 68 10-20
(Orange label.)
RCA VICTOR (LSP-2370; "Something For
Everybody"): 76 10-15
(Tan label.)
RCA VICTOR (AFL1-2370; "Something For
Everybody"): 77 8-10
(Reissued in 1981 as RCA Victor AYM1-4116.)
RCA VICTOR (LPM-2426; "Blue
Hawaii"): 61 75-90
(Black label with "Long Play" at bottom.)
RCA VICTOR (LPM-2426; "Blue
Hawaii"): 63 40-50
(Black label with "Mono" at bottom.)
RCA VICTOR (LPM-2426; "Blue
Hawaii"): 64 25-30
(Black label with "Monaural" at bottom.)
RCA VICTOR (LSP-2426; "Blue
Hawaii"): 61 90-100
(Black label with "Living Stereo" at bottom.)
RCA VICTOR (LSP-2426; "Blue
Hawaii"): 64 25-30
(Black label, RCA logo is white, other label print is
silver.)
RCA VICTOR (LSP-2426; "Blue
Hawaii"): 68 10-20
(Orange label.)
RCA VICTOR (LSP-2426; "Blue
Hawaii"): 76 10-15
(Tan label.)
RCA VICTOR (AFL1-2426; "Blue
Hawaii"): 77 8-10
Reissued in 1981 as RCA Victor AYL1-3683.
RCA VICTOR (AFL1-2428; "Moody
Blue"): 77 1000-1200
(Colored vinyl, other than blue. Experimental
production discs for RCA in-house use only.)
RCA VICTOR (AFL1-2428; "Moody
Blue"): 77 10-12
(Blue vinyl.)
RCA VICTOR (AFL1-2428; "Moody
Blue"): 77 125-150
(Black vinyl.)
RCA VICTOR (AQL1-2428; "Moody
Blue"): 79 8-10

RCA VICTOR (LPM-2523; "Pot
Luck"): 62 .... $75-90
(Black label with "Long Play" at bottom.)
RCA VICTOR (LPM-2523; "Pot
Luck"): 63 40-50
(Black label with "Mono" at bottom.)
RCA VICTOR (LPM-2523; "Pot
Luck"): 64 25-30
(Black label with "Monaural" at bottom.)
RCA VICTOR (LSP-2523; "Pot
Luck"): 62 90-100
(Black label with "Living Stereo" at bottom.)
RCA VICTOR (LSP-2523; "Pot
Luck"): 64 25-30
(Black label, RCA logo is white, other label print is
silver.)
RCA VICTOR (LSP-2523; "Pot
Luck"): 68 10-20
(Orange label.)
RCA VICTOR (LSP-2523; "Pot
Luck"): 76 10-15
(Tan label.)
RCA VICTOR (AFL1-2523; "Pot
Luck"): 77 8-10
RCA VICTOR (APL1-2558; "Harum
Scarum"): 77 8-10
(First issued as RCA Victor LPM/LSP-3468. It was
reissued in 1980 as RCA Victor AYL1-3734.)
RCA VICTOR (APL1-2560;
"Spinout"): 77 8-10
(First issued as RCA Victor LPM/LSP-3702. It was
reissued in 1980 as RCA Victor AYL1-3684.)
RCA VICTOR (APL1-2564; "Double
Trouble"): 77 8-10
(First issued as RCA Victor LPM/LSP-3787.)
RCA VICTOR (APL1-2565;
"Clambake"): 77 8-10
(First issued as RCA Victor LPM/LSP-3893.)
RCA VICTOR (APL1-2568; "It Happened At
The World's Fair"): 77 8-10
(First issued as RCA Victor LPM/LSP-2697.)
RCA VICTOR (APL2-2587; "Elvis
In Concert"): 77 15-20
(Price includes insert flyer listing other Elvis LPs,
which represents $2-$3 of the value.)
RCA VICTOR (CPL2-2587; "Elvis
In Concert"): 82 12-15
RCA VICTOR (LPM-2621; "Girls! Girls!
Girls!"): 62 75-90
(Black label with "Long Play" at bottom.)
RCA VICTOR (LPM-2621; "Girls! Girls!
Girls!"): 63 40-50
(Black label with "Mono" at bottom.)
RCA VICTOR (LPM-2621; "Girls! Girls!
Girls!"): 64 25-30
(Black label with "Monaural" at bottom.)

RCA VICTOR (LSP-2621; "Girls! Girls!
Girls!"): 62 . . . . $90-100
(Black label with "Living Stereo" at bottom.)
RCA VICTOR (LSP-2621; "Girls! Girls!
Girls!"): 64 25-30
(Black label, RCA logo is white, other label print is
silver.)
RCA VICTOR (LSP-2621; "Girls! Girls!
Girls!"): 68 10-20
(Orange label.)
RCA VICTOR (LSP-2621; "Girls! Girls!
Girls!"): 76 10-15
(Tan label.)
RCA VICTOR (AFL1-2621; "Girls! Girls!
Girls!"): 77 8-10
RCA VICTOR (CPD2-2642; "Aloha From
Hawaii"): 75 15-20
(Orange label.)
RCA VICTOR (CPD2-2642; "Aloha From
Hawaii"): 77 10-12
(Black label. First issued as RCA Victor VPSX-
6089.)
RCA VICTOR (LPM-2697; "It Happened At
The World's Fair"): 63 100-115
(Black label with "Long Play" at bottom. Price in-
cludes an 8x10 bonus color photo, which represents
$25-$35 of the value.)
RCA VICTOR (LPM-2697; "It Happened At
The World's Fair"): 63 40-50
(Black label with "Mono" at bottom.)
RCA VICTOR (LPM-2697; "It Happened At
The World's Fair"): 64 25-30
(Black label with "Monaural" at bottom.)
RCA VICTOR (LSP-2697; "It Happened At
The World's Fair"): 63 115-125
(Black label with "Living Stereo" at bottom. Price
includes an 8x10 bonus color photo, which repre-
sents $25-$35 of the value.)
RCA VICTOR (LSP-2697; "It Happened At
The World's Fair"): 64 25-30
(Black label, RCA logo is white, other label print is
silver. Reissued in 1977 as RCA Victor APL1-
2568.)
RCA VICTOR (LPM-2756; "Fun In
Acapulco"): 63 60-70
(Black label with "Mono" at bottom.)
RCA VICTOR (LPM-2756; "Fun In
Acapulco"): 64 25-30
(Black label with "Monaural" at bottom.)
RCA VICTOR (LSP-2756; "Fun In
Acapulco"): 63 60-70
(Black label, all print on label is silver.)
RCA VICTOR (LSP-2756; "Fun In
Acapulco"): 64 25-30
(Black label, RCA logo is white, other label print is
silver.)

RCA VICTOR (LSP-2756; "Fun In
Acapulco"): 68 . . . . $10-20
(Orange label.)
RCA VICTOR (LSP-2756; "Fun In
Acapulco"): 76 10-15
(Tan label.)
RCA VICTOR (AFL1-2756; "Fun In
Acapulco"): 77 8-10
RCA VICTOR (LPM-2765; "Elvis' Golden
Records, Vol. 3"): 63 90-100
(Black label with "Mono" at bottom. Price includes
bonus 8x10 photo booklet, which represents $30-
$40 of the value.)
RCA VICTOR (LPM-2765; "Elvis' Golden
Records, Vol. 3"): 64 25-30
(Black label with "Monaural" at bottom.)
RCA VICTOR (LSP-2765; "Elvis' Golden
Records, Vol. 3"): 63 90-100
(Black label, all print on label is silver. Price in-
cludes bonus 8x10 photo booklet, which represents
$30-40 of the value.)
RCA VICTOR (LSP-2765; "Elvis' Golden
Records, Vol. 3"): 64 25-30
(Black label, RCA logo is white, other label print is
silver.)
RCA VICTOR (LSP-2765; "Elvis' Golden
Records, Vol. 3"): 68 10-20
(Orange label.)
RCA VICTOR (LSP-2765; "Elvis' Golden
Records, Vol. 3"): 76 10-15
(Tan label.)
RCA VICTOR (AFL1-2765; "Elvis' Golden
Records, Vol. 3"): 77 8-10
RCA VICTOR (AFL1-2772; "He Walks
Beside Me"): 77 8-10
(Price includes a 20-page photo booklet, which rep-
resents $2-$3 of the value.)
RCA VICTOR (LPM-2894; "Kissin'
Cousins"): 64 100-150
(Black label with "Mono" at bottom. Does not pic-
ture film cast in lower right corner photo on cover.)
RCA VICTOR (LPM-2894; "Kissin'
Cousins"): 64 60-70
(Black label with "Mono" at bottom. Pictures film
cast in lower right corner photo on cover.)
RCA VICTOR (LPM-2894; "Kissin'
Cousins"): 64 25-30
(Black label with "Monaural" at bottom.)
RCA VICTOR (LSP-2894; "Kissin'
Cousins"): 64 100-150
(Black label, all print on label is silver. Does not
picture film cast in lower right corner photo on
cover.)

RCA VICTOR (LSP-2894; "Kissin'
Cousins"): *64* $60-70
(Black label, all print on label is silver. Pictures
film cast in lower right corner photo on cover.)

RCA VICTOR (LSP-2894; "Kissin'
Cousins"): *64* 25-30
(Black label, RCA logo is white, other label print is
silver.)

RCA VICTOR (LSP-2894; "Kissin'
Cousins"): *68* 10-20
(Orange label.)

RCA VICTOR (LSP-2894; "Kissin'
Cousins"): *76* 10-15
(Tan label.)

RCA VICTOR (AFL1-2894; "Kissin'
Cousins"): *77* 8-10
(Reissued in 1981 as RCA Victor AYM1-4115.)

RCA VICTOR (CPL1-2901; "Elvis Sings
For Children"): *78* 8-10
(Price includes "Special Memories" greeting card,
which represents $2-$4 of the value.)

RCA VICTOR (LPM-2999;
"Roustabout"): *64* 60-70
(Black label with "Mono" at bottom.)

RCA VICTOR (LPM-2999;
"Roustabout"): *65* 25-30
(Black label with "Monaural" at bottom.)

RCA VICTOR (LSP-2999;
"Roustabout"): *64* 500-700
(Black label. All print on label—including RCA
logo—is silver.)

RCA VICTOR (LSP-2999;
"Roustabout"): *64* 25-30
(Black label, RCA logo is white, other label print is
silver.)

RCA VICTOR (LSP-2999;
"Roustabout"): *68* 10-20
(Orange label.)

RCA VICTOR (LSP-2999;
"Roustabout"): *76* 10-15
(Tan label.)

RCA VICTOR (AFL1-2999;
"Roustabout"): *77* 8-10

RCA VICTOR (3078; "Legendary
Performer, Vol. 3"): *78* 15-20
(Picture disc. Price includes *Yesterdays* booklet,
which represents $5-$8 of the value. May be found
with the actual disc pressed on either blue or black
vinyl. Also issued on standard black vinyl as 3082.)

RCA VICTOR (3082; "Legendary
Performer, Vol. 3"): *78* 8-12
(Price includes *Yesterdays* booklet, which represents $5-8 of the value. Also issued on a picture
disc, as RCA Victor 3078.)

RCA VICTOR (3279; "Our Memories
Of Elvis"): *79* $8-10

RCA VICTOR (LPM-3338; "Girl
Happy"): *65* 35-45

RCA VICTOR (LSP-3338; "Girl
Happy"): *65* 35-45
(Black label.)

RCA VICTOR (LSP-3338; "Girl
Happy"): *68* 10-20
(Orange label.)

RCA VICTOR (LSP-3338; "Girl
Happy"): *76* 10-15
(Tan label.)

RCA VICTOR (AFL1-3338; "Girl
Happy"): *77* 8-10

RCA VICTOR (3448; "Our Memories
Of Elvis, Vol. 2"): *79* 8-10
(A sampling of tracks from this LP appeared on
RCA Victor 3455, *Pure Elvis*.)

RCA VICTOR (LPM-3450; "Elvis For
Everyone"): *65* 35-45

RCA VICTOR (LSP-3450; "Elvis For
Everyone"): *65* 35-45
(Black label.)

RCA VICTOR (LSP-3450; "Elvis For
Everyone"): *68* 10-20
(Orange label.)

RCA VICTOR (LSP-3450; "Elvis For
Everyone"): *76* 10-15
(Tan label.)

RCA VICTOR (AFL1-3450; "Elvis For
Everyone"): *77* 8-10
(Reissued in 1982 as RCA Victor AYL1-4232.)

RCA VICTOR (3455; "Pure
Elvis"): *79* 275-325
(Cover reads "Pure Elvis," but label says "Our
Memories Of Elvis - Vol. 2." Promotional issue
only.)

RCA VICTOR (LPM-3468; "Harum
Scarum"): *65* 65-75
(Price includes bonus 12x12 photo, which repre-
sents about $30 of the value.)

RCA VICTOR (LSP-3468; "Harum
Scarum"): *65* 65-75
(Price includes bonus 12x12 photo, which repre-
sents about $30 of the value. Reissued in 1977 as
RCA Victor APL1-2558 and in 1980 as RCA Vic-
tor AYL1-3734.)

RCA VICTOR (LPM-3553; "Frankie &
Johnny"): *66* 65-75
(Price includes bonus 12x12 photo, which repre-
sents about $30 of the value.)

RCA VICTOR (LSP-3553; "Frankie &
Johnny"): 66 .... $65-75
(Price includes bonus 12x12 photo, which repre-
sents about $30 of the value.)
Reissued in 1977 as RCA Victor APL1-2559. A
repackage appeared in 1976 on Pickwick 7007.
RCA VICTOR (LPM-3643; "Paradise
Hawaiian Style"): 66 35-45
RCA VICTOR (LSP-3643; "Paradise
Hawaiian Style"): 66 35-45
(Black label.)
RCA VICTOR (LSP-3643; "Paradise
Hawaiian Style"): 68 10-20
(Orange label.)
RCA VICTOR (LSP-3643; "Paradise
Hawaiian Style"): 76 10-15
(Tan label.)
RCA VICTOR (AFL1-3643; "Paradise
Hawaiian Style"): 77 8-10
RCA VICTOR (AYL1-3683; "Blue
Hawaii"): 80 5-10
(First issued as RCA Victor LPM/LSP-2426.)
RCA VICTOR (AYL1-3684;
"Spinout"): 80 5-10
(First issued as RCA Victor LPM/LSP-3702, but
was reissued in 1977 as RCA Victor APL1-2560.)
RCA VICTOR (CPL8-3699; "Elvis
Aron Presley"): 80 80-100
(An eight-LP boxed set. Price includes a 20-page
booklet, which represents $5-$8 of the value.)
RCA VICTOR (CPL8-3699; "Elvis
Aron Presley"): 80 450-500
(REVIEWER SERIES edition. Silver sticker on
back identifies the reviewer series edition as "NS-
3699." Price includes a 20-page booklet, which rep-
resents $5-$8 of the value.)
RCA VICTOR (CPK8-3699; "Elvis
Aron Presley"): 80 80-100
(Boxed set of four cassettes. Price includes a 20-
page booklet and eight 12x12 Elvis photos, which
represent $10-$15 of the value.)
RCA VICTOR (CPS8-3699; "Elvis
Aron Presley"): 80 100-125
(Boxed set of four 8-track tapes. Price includes a
20-page booklet and eight 12x12 Elvis photos,
which represent $10-$15 of the value. "Excerpts"
of songs in this set appeared on RCA Victor 3729.
"Selections" from this LP were issued on RCA Vic-
tor 3781. The tape sets contain some outtakes not
heard on the LP editions.)
RCA VICTOR (LSP-3702;
"Spinout"): 66 65-75
(Price includes bonus 12x12 photo, which repre-
sents about $30 of the value. Reissued in 1977 as
APL1-2560.)

RCA VICTOR (3729; "Elvis Aron
Presley, Excerpts"): 80 .... $100-125
(Contains 37 excerpts from RCA Victor 3699.
Promotional issue only.)
RCA VICTOR (AYL1-3732; "Pure
Gold"): 80 5-10
First issued as RCA Victor ANL1-0971.
RCA VICTOR (AYL1-3733; "King
Creole"): 80 5-10
(First issued as RCA Victor LSP-1884.)
RCA VICTOR (AYL1-3734; "Harum
Scarum"): 80 5-10
(First issued as RCA Victor LPM/LSP-3468.)
RCA VICTOR (AYL1-3735; "G.I.
Blues"): 80 5-10
(First issued as RCA Victor LPM/LSP-2256.)
RCA VICTOR (LPM-3758; "How Great
Thou Art"): 67 40-50
RCA VICTOR (LSP-3758; "How Great
Thou Art"): 67 35-45
(Black label.)
RCA VICTOR (LSP-3758; "How Great
Thou Art"): 68 10-20
(Orange label.)
RCA VICTOR (LSP-3758; "How Great
Thou Art"): 76 10-15
(Tan label.)
RCA VICTOR (AFL1-3758; "How Great
Thou Art"): 77 8-10
RCA VICTOR (3781; "Elvis Aron
Presley," Selections): 80 100-125
(Contains 12 selections from RCA Victor 3699.
Promotional issue only.)
RCA VICTOR (LPM-3787; "Double
Trouble"): 67 40-50
(Front cover notes "Special Bonus Full Color
Photo." Price includes 7x9 photo, which represents
about $5 of the value.)
RCA VICTOR (LPM-3787; "Double
Trouble"): 68 30-40
(Mention on cover of "Special Bonus Full Color
Photo" is replaced by "Trouble Double.")
RCA VICTOR (LSP-3787; "Double
Trouble"): 67 40-50
(Front cover notes "Special Bonus Full Color
Photo." Price includes 7x9 photo, which represents
about $5 of the value. Black label.)
RCA VICTOR (LSP-3787; "Double
Trouble"): 68 30-40
(Mention on cover of "Special Bonus Full Color
Photo" is replaced by "Trouble Double.")
RCA VICTOR (LSP-3787; "Double
Trouble"): 68 10-20
(Orange label.)

RCA VICTOR (LSP-3787; "Double
Trouble"): *76* **$10-15**
(Tan label. Reissued in 1977 as RCA Victor APL1-
2564.)

RCA VICTOR (AYL1-3892; "Elvis
In Person"): *81* **5-8**
First issued as RCA Victor LSP-4428.

RCA VICTOR (LPM-3893;
"Clambake"): *67* **150-200**
(Price includes bonus 12x12 photo, which repre-
sents about $30 of the value.)

RCA VICTOR (LSP-3893;
"Clambake"): *67* **60-70**
(Price includes bonus 12x12 photo, which repre-
sents about $30 of the value. Black label.)
Reissued in 1977 as RCA Victor APL1-2565.

RCA VICTOR (AYM1-3893; "The Sun
Sessions"): *81* **5-8**
(First issued as RCA Victor APM1-1675.)

RCA VICTOR (AYM1-3894; "Elvis
TV Special"): *81* **5-8**
(First issued RCA Victor LPM-4088.)

RCA VICTOR (3917; "Guitar Man"): *81* . .**8-12**
(Price includes a *This Is Elvis* flyer, which represents $3-$4 of the value. Producer Felton Jarvis
talks about Elvis and the making of this LP on
RCA Victor 1981.)

RCA VICTOR (LPM-3921; "Elvis' Gold
Records," Vol. 4): *68* **500-600**
(Price includes an 7x9 Elvis photo, which repre-
sents $25-$50 of the value.)

RCA VICTOR (LSP-3921; "Elvis' Gold
Records, Vol. 4"): *68* **60-90**
(Black label. Price includes an 7x9 Elvis photo,
which represents $25-$50 of the value.)

RCA VICTOR (LSP-3921; "Elvis' Gold
Records, Vol. 4"): *68* **10-20**
(Orange label.)

RCA VICTOR (LSP-3921; "Elvis' Gold
Records, Vol. 4"): *76* **10-15**
(Tan label.)

RCA VICTOR (AFL1-3921; "Elvis' Gold
Records, Vol. 4"): *77* **8-10**

RCA VICTOR (AYM1-3935; "His Hand
In Mine"): *81* **5-10**
(First issued as RCA Victor LPM/LSP-2328.)

RCA VICTOR (AYL1-3956; "That's The
Way It Is"): *81* **5-8**
(First issued as RCA Victor LSP-4460.)

RCA VICTOR (LPM-3989;
"Speedway"): *68* **800-900**
(Price includes an 8x10 Elvis photo, which repre-
sents $5-$10 of the value.)

RCA VICTOR (LSP-3989;
"Speedway"): *68* **35-45**
(Black label. Price includes an 8x10 Elvis photo,
which represents $5-10 of the value.)

RCA VICTOR (LSP-3989;
"Speedway"): *68* **$10-20**
(Orange label.)

RCA VICTOR (LSP-3989;
"Speedway"): *76* **10-15**
(Tan label.)

RCA VICTOR (AFL1-3989;
"Speedway"): *77* **8-10**

RCA VICTOR (4031; "This Is
Elvis"): *80* **10-15**

RCA VICTOR (LPM-4088; "Elvis
TV Special"): *68* **15-20**
(Orange label. Rigid disc.)

RCA VICTOR (LPM-4088; "Elvis
TV Special"): *72* **10-15**
(Orange label. Flexible disc.)

RCA VICTOR (LPM-4088; "Elvis
TV Special"): *76* **10-15**
(Tan label.)

RCA VICTOR (AFM1-4088; "Elvis
TV Special"): *77* **8-10**
(Reissued in 1981 as RCA Victor AYM1-3894. It
was repackaged for HBO as RCA Victor 0704.)

RCA VICTOR (AYL1-4114; "That's The
Way It Is"): *81* **5-10**
(First issued as RCA Victor LSP-4445.)

RCA VICTOR (AYM1-4115; "Kissin'
Cousins"): *81* **5-10**
(First issued as RCA Victor LPM/LSP 2894.)

RCA VICTOR (AYM1-4116; "Something For
Everybody"): *81* **5-10**
(First issued as RCA Victor LPM/LSP-2370.)

RCA VICTOR (LSP-4155; "From Elvis
In Memphis"): *69* **20-25**
(Orange label. Rigid disc. Price includes an 8x10
Elvis photo, which represents $5-$10 of the value.)

RCA VICTOR (LSP-4155; "From Elvis
In Memphis"): *72* **10-15**
(Orange label. Flexible disc.)

RCA VICTOR (LSP-4155; "From Elvis
In Memphis"): *69* **10-15**
(Tan label.)

RCA VICTOR (AFL1-4155; "From Elvis
In Memphis"): *77* **8-10**
(A half-speed mastered issue of this LP was
released in 1982 as MFSL 059.)

RCA VICTOR (AYL1-4232; "Elvis For
Everyone"): *82* **5-8**
First issued as RCA Victor LPM/LSP-3450.

RCA VICTOR (4351; "60 Years Of
Country Music"): *82* **8-10**
(Contains 24 songs by 24 artists, including Elvis.)

RCA VICTOR (LSP-4362; "On
Stage"): *70* **15-20**
(Orange label. Rigid disc.)

RCA VICTOR (LSP-4362; "On
Stage"): *72* $10-15
(Orange label. Flexible disc.)

RCA VICTOR (LSP-4362; "On
Stage"): *76* 10-15
(Tan label.)

RCA VICTOR (AFL1-4362; "On
Stage"): *77* 10-12

RCA VICTOR (AQL1-4362; "On
Stage"): *83* 5-10

RCA VICTOR (4395; "Memories Of
Christmas"): *82* 8-10
(Price includes a 7x9 calendar, which represents $2-
$4 of the value.)

RCA VICTOR (LSP-4428; "Elvis
In Person"): *70* 15-20
(Orange label.)

RCA VICTOR (LSP-4428; "Elvis
In Person"): *76* 10-15
(Tan label.)

RCA VICTOR (AFL1-4428; "Elvis
In Person"): *77* 8-10
(First released as half of RCA Victor LSP-6020,
was reissued in 1981 as RCA Victor AYL1-3892.)

RCA VICTOR (LSP-4429; "Elvis Back
In Memphis"): *70* 15-20
(Orange label.)

RCA VICTOR (LSP-4429; "Elvis Back
In Memphis"): *76* 10-15
(Tan label.)

RCA VICTOR (AFL1-4429; "Elvis Back
In Memphis"): *77* 8-10
(First issued as half of RCA Victor LSP-6020.)

RCA VICTOR (LSP-4445; "That's The
Way It Is"): *70* 15-20
(Orange label.)

RCA VICTOR (LSP-4445; "That's The
Way It Is"): *76* 10-15
(Tan label.)

RCA VICTOR (LSP-4445; "That's The
Way It Is"): *77* 8-10
(Black label.)

RCA VICTOR (AFL1-4445; "That's The
Way It Is"): *77* 8-10
(Reissued in 1981 as RCA Victor AYL1-4114.)

RCA VICTOR (LSP-4460; "Elvis
Country"): *71* 15-20
(Orange label. Price includes an 7x9 Elvis photo,
which represents $5-$10 of the value.)

RCA VICTOR (LSP-4460; "Elvis
Country"): *76* 10-15
(Tan label.)

RCA VICTOR (AFL1-4460; "Elvis
Country"): *77* 8-10
(Reissued in 1981 as RCA Victor AYL1-3956.)

RCA VICTOR (LSP-4530; "Love
Letters"): *71* $25-40
(Orange label. Full title, *Love Letters From Elvis,*
on TWO lines on front cover.)

RCA VICTOR (LSP-4530; "Love
Letters"): *71* 20-35
(Orange label. Full title, *Love Letters From Elvis,*
on THREE lines on front cover.)
Note: Conflicting opinions exist about which of the
Love Letters covers is the rarer. The first issue,
with "Love Letters From" on one line, theoretically
should be rarer. It was quickly replaced with the
three-line version, which has the letters "RE" (Reissue) in the lower left corner. However, quantities of
the first version have turned up to offset the difference in value. For now, we've put them in a
closer range than ultimately may exist. Additional
input is encouraged.

RCA VICTOR (LSP-4530; "Love
Letters"): *76* 10-15
(Tan label.)

RCA VICTOR (AFL1-4530; "Love
Letters"): *77* 8-10
Reissued in 1981 as RCA Victor AYL1-3956.

RCA VICTOR (AHL1-4530; "The Elvis
Medley"): *82* 8-10

RCA VICTOR (LSP-4579; "Wonderful
World Of Christmas"): *71* 20-25
(Price includes a 5x7 Elvis postcard, which repre-
sents $4-$6 of the value.)
Reissued in 1977 as RCA Victor ANL1-1936.

RCA VICTOR (LSP-4671; "Elvis
Now"): *72* 50-60
(With white titles/times sticker on front cover.
Promotional issue only.)

RCA VICTOR (LSP-4671; "Elvis
Now"): *72* 15-18
(Orange label.)

RCA VICTOR (LSP-4671; "Elvis
Now"): *76* 10-15
(Tan label.)

RCA VICTOR (AFL1-4671; "Elvis
Now"): *77* 8-10

RCA VICTOR (LSP-4690; "He Touched
Me"): *72* 50-60
(With white titles/times sticker on front cover.
Promotional issue only.)

RCA VICTOR (LSP-4690; "He Touched
Me"): *72* 15-18
(Orange label.)

RCA VICTOR (LSP-4690; "He Touched
Me"): *76* 10-15
(Tan label.)

RCA VICTOR (AFL1-4690; "He Touched
Me"): *77* 8-10

RCA VICTOR (4678; "I Was
The One"): *83* 8-10

RCA VICTOR (LSP-4776; "Madison
Square Garden"): 72 . . . . **$50-60**
(Orange label. With white programming stickers ap-
plied to front cover. Promotional issue only.)

RCA VICTOR (LSP-4776; "Madison
Square Garden"): 72 . . . . **15-20**
(Orange label.)

RCA VICTOR (LSP-4776; "Madison
Square Garden"): 76 . . . . **10-15**
(Tan label.)

RCA VICTOR (AQL1-4776; "Madison
Square Garden"): 77 . . . . **8-10**
(A two-LP promotional version of this LP was is-
sued as RCA Victor SPS-571.)

RCA VICTOR (4809; "A Country
Christmas, Vol. 2"): 83 . . . . **8-10**
(Contains eight songs by eight artists, including
Elvis.)

RCA VICTOR (4848; "Legendary
Performer, Vol. 4"): 83 . . . . **8-10**
(Price includes a 12-page *Memories Of The King*
booklet.)

RCA VICTOR (4941; "Elvis' Gold
Records, Vol. 5"): 84 . . . . **5-8**

RCA VICTOR (5172; "A Golden
Celebration"): 84 . . . . **40-50**
(Six-LP boxed set. Price includes custom inner
sleeves and an envelope containing an 8x10 Elvis
photo and a 50th Anniversary flyer, all of which
represents $5-$10 of the value.)

RCA VICTOR (5172; "A Golden
Celebration"): 84 . . . . **15-20**
(Special "Advance Cassette" sampler of the boxed
set.)

RCA VICTOR (5182; "Rocker"): 84 . . . . . . **5-8**

RCA VICTOR (5196; "Elvis' Golden
Records"): 84 . . . . **5-8**
(Digitally remastered quality mono pressing. Price
includes gold "The Definitive Rock Classic" banner. First issued as RCA Victor LPM-1707.)

RCA VICTOR (5197; "Elvis' Gold
Records," Vol. 2): 84 . . . . **5-8**
(Digitally remastered quality mono pressing. Price
includes gold "The Definitive Rock Classic" banner. First issued as RCA Victor LPM-2075.)

RCA VICTOR (5198; "Elvis
Presley"): 84 . . . . **5-8**
(Digitally remastered quality mono pressing. Price
includes gold "The Definitive Rock Classic" banner. First issued as RCA Victor LPM-1254.)

RCA VICTOR (5199; "Elvis"): 84 . . . . **5-8**
(Digitally remastered quality mono pressing. Price
includes gold "The Definitive Rock Classic" banner. First issued as RCA Victor LPM-1382.)

RCA VICTOR (5353; "A Valentine Gift
For You"): 85 . . . . **8-10**
(Colored vinyl.)

RCA VICTOR (5353; "A Valentine
Gift For You"): 85 . . . . **$5-8**
(Black vinyl.)

RCA VICTOR (5418; "Reconsider
Baby"): 85 . . . . **5-8**

RCA VICTOR (5430; "Always On
My Mind"): 85 . . . . **5-8**

RCA VICTOR (5463; "Rock And Roll,
The Early Days"): 85 . . . . **5-8**
(Contains 12 songs by 12 artists, including Elvis.)

RCA VICTOR (5486; "Elvis' Christmas
Album"): 85 . . . . **5-8**
(Colored vinyl.)

RCA VICTOR (5486; "Elvis' Christmas
Album"): 85 . . . . **20-40**
(Black vinyl. packaged with stickers reading
"pressed on green vinyl.")

RCA VICTOR (5600; "Elvis, Return Of
The Rocker"): 86 . . . . **5-8**

RCA VICTOR (5697; "Special Christmas
Programming"): 67 . . . . **800-1000**
(Promotional issue only.)

RCA VICTOR (5800; "Best Of
The '50s"): 86 . . . . **10-15**
(Contains 10 songs by 10 artists, including Elvis.)

RCA VICTOR (5802; "Best Of
The '60s"): 86 . . . . **10-15**
(Contains 10 songs by 10 artists, including Elvis.)

RCA VICTOR (5837; "Best Of
The '70s"): 86 . . . . **10-15**
(Contains 10 songs by 10 artists, including Elvis.)

RCA VICTOR (5838; "Best Of The
'50s, '60s, & '70s"): 86 . . . . **10-15**
(Contains 10 songs by 10 artists, including Elvis.)

RCA VICTOR (LSP-6020; "From Memphis
To Vegas"): 69 . . . . **30-40**
(Orange label. First pressing, incorrectly shows
writers of *Words* as Tommy Boyce and Bobby
Hart. Also shows writer of *Suspicious Minds* as
Frances Zambon. Price includes two 8x10 Elvis
photos, which represent $5-$10 of the value.)

RCA VICTOR (LSP-6020; "From Memphis
To Vegas"): 69 . . . . **20-30**
(Orange label. Correctly shows writers of *Words* as
Barry, Robin and Maurice Gibb, and writer of
Suspicious Minds as Mark James. Price includes
two 8x10 Elvis photos, which represent $5-$10 of
the value.)

RCA VICTOR (LSP-6020; "From Memphis
To Vegas"): 76 . . . . **15-20**
(Tan label.)

RCA VICTOR (LSP-6020; "From Memphis
To Vegas"): 77 .... **$10-15**
(Black label. Each of the two LPs in this set was
reissued individually, *Elvis In Person At The Inter-
national Hotel* as LSP-4428 and *Elvis Back In
Memphis* as LSP-4429, both in 1970.)

RCA VICTOR (VPSX-6089; "Aloha From
Hawaii"): 73 .... **1000-1500**
(With "Chicken Of The Sea," Quadradisc and contents stickers on cover. Promotional in-house issue
by the Van Camps Company.)

RCA VICTOR (VPSX-6089; "Aloha From
Hawaii"): 73 .... **200-250**
(With white titles/times sticker on front cover.
Promotional issue only.)

RCA VICTOR (VPSX-6089; "Aloha From
Hawaii"): 73 .... **75-90**
(With Quadradisc & contents stickers on cover.
Red/orange label.)

RCA VICTOR (VPSX-6089; "Aloha From
Hawaii"): 74 .... **25-30**
(With Quadradisc/RCA logo in lower right corner
of front cover. Titles are printed on back cover.
Orange label.)

RCA VICTOR (VPSX-6089; "Aloha From
Hawaii"): 76 .... **25-30**
(Tan label. Issued through the RCA Record Club as
RCA Victor 213736 and in 1977 as RCA Victor
CPD2-2642.)

RCA VICTOR (6221; "The Memphis
Record"): 87 .... **10-15**
(Includes a bonus color 15x22 poster and *Elvis
Talks* LP flyer.)

RCA VICTOR (6313; "Elvis Talks!"): 87 **10-15**
(Mail-order offer.)

RCA VICTOR (6382; "The Number
One Hits"): 87 .... **8-10**
(Includes a bonus color 15x22 poster and *Elvis
Talks* LP flyer.)

RCA VICTOR (6383; "The Top
Ten Hits"): 87 .... **10-12**
(Includes a bonus color 15x22 poster and *Elvis
Talks* LP flyer.)

RCA VICTOR (LPM-6401; "Worldwide 50
Gold Hits," Vol. 1): 70 .... **60-75**
(Orange label. Four-LP boxed set. Price includes
20-page Elvis photo booklet, which represents $10-
$20 of the value.)

RCA VICTOR (LPM-6401; "Worldwide 50
Gold Hits," Vol. 1): 76 .... **30-40**
(Tan label.)

RCA VICTOR (LPM-6401; "Worldwide 50
Gold Hits," Vol. 1): 77 .... **20-25**
(Black label. Two of the LPs in this set were
repackaged for the RCA Record Club in 1974 as
RCA Victor 213690 and the other two in 1978 as
RCA Victor 214657.)

RCA VICTOR (LPM-6402; "Worldwide 50
Gold Hits," Vol. 2): 71 .... **$60-75**
(Orange label. Price includes an
Elvis print and envelope with piece of material,
which represents $10-$20 of the value.)

RCA VICTOR (LPM-6402; "Worldwide 50
Gold Hits," Vol. 2): 76 .... **30-40**
(Tan label. With bonus items shown as included.)

RCA VICTOR (LPM-6402; "Worldwide 50
Gold Hits," Vol. 2): 76 .... **25-35**
(Tan label. No bonus items shown as being in-
cluded.)

RCA VICTOR (LPM-6402; "Worldwide 50
Gold Hits," Vol. 2): 77 .... **20-25**
(Black label.)
Two of the LPs in this set were repackaged for the
RCA Record Club in 1978 as RCA Victor 214567.

RCA VICTOR (6414; "The Complete
Sun Sessions"): 87 .... **10-15**
(Includes a bonus color 15x22 poster and *Elvis
Talks* LP flyer.)

RCA VICTOR (6738; "Essential
Elvis"): 88 .... **5-10**

RCA VICTOR (6985; "The Alternate
Aloha"): 88 .... **5-8**

RCA VICTOR (7004; "14 #1
Country Hits"): 85 .... **10-12**
(Contains 14 songs by 14 artists, including Elvis.)

RCA VICTOR (7013; "The Best
Of Christmas"): 85 .... **8-10**
(Contains eight songs by eight artists, including
Elvis.)

RCA VICTOR (7031; "Elvis
Forever"): 74 .... **25-35**
(TV mail-order offer.)

RCA VICTOR (8372; "Mistletoe And
Memories"): 88 .... **10-15**
(Contains nine songs by nine different artists, in-
cluding Elvis.)

RCA VICTOR (9681; "E-Z Pop
No. 5): 56 .... **250-275**
(Contains 16 songs by 12 different artists, including two by Elvis. Promotional issue only. The other
side of this LP is numbered 9682.)

RCA VICTOR (7065; "A Canadian
Tribute"): 78 .... **10-12**
(Price includes photo inner-sleeve, which represents $2-$3 of the value. Canadian issues of this LP
had the same number but are clearly marked on
back cover as Canadian.)

RCA VICTOR (8468; "Elvis In
Nashville"): 88 .... **5-8**

RCA VICTOR (8533; "Heartbreak
Hotel"): 88 .... **5-8**
(Four of the 10 songs are by Elvis.)

RCA VICTOR (9586; "Elvis Gospel,
1957-1971"): *89* **$5-8**
RCA VICTOR (9589; "Stereo '57,
Essential Elvis, Vol. 2"): *89* **5-8**
RCA VICTOR (213690; "Worldwide 50
Gold Hits, Parts 1&2"): *74* **75-100**
(Orange label. RCA Record Club issue only.)
RCA VICTOR (213690; "Worldwide 50
Gold Hits, Parts 1&2"): *76* **25-30**
(Tan label. RCA Record Club issue only.)
RCA VICTOR (213690; "Worldwide 50
Gold Hits, Parts 1&2"): *77* **12-15**
(Black label. RCA Record Club issue only. The
two discs in this set were first issued as half of
RCA Victor LPM-6401.)
RCA VICTOR (213736; "Aloha From
Hawaii"): *73* **45-55**
(Orange label.)
RCA VICTOR (213736; "Aloha From
Hawaii"): *76* **18-20**
(Tan label.)
RCA VICTOR (214657; "Worldwide 50
Gold Hits, Parts 3&4"): *78* **12-15**
(RCA Record Club issue only. The two discs in
this set were first issued as half of RCA Victor
LPM-6401.)
RCA VICTOR (233299; "Country
Classics"): *80* **20-25**
(RCA Record Club issue only.)
RCA VICTOR (234340; "From Elvis
With Love"): *78* **20-25**
(RCA Record Club issue only.)
RCA VICTOR (244047; "Legendary Concert
Performances"): *78* **20-25**
(RCA Record Club issue only.)
RCA VICTOR (244069; "Country
Memories"): *78* **20-25**
(RCA Record Club issue only.)
READER'S DIGEST (040; "Easy Listening
Hits of the '60s, & '70s"): *89* **20-30**
(Seven-LP boxed set with 81 songs, including three
by Elvis. Includes booklet.)
RHINO (71103; "The Sun Story"): *86* **8-12**
(Two-LP set, containing 27 songs by 15 artists, in-
cluding two by Elvis. Also includes booklet.)
RHINO (70618; "Billboard Top Rock 'N'
Roll Hits - 1957"): *88* **5-8**
(Two of the 10 songs are by Elvis.)
RHINO (70619; "Billboard Top Rock 'N'
Roll Hits - 1958"): *88* **5-8**
(One of the 10 songs is by Elvis.)
RHINO (70620; "Billboard Top Rock 'N'
Roll Hits - 1959"): *88* **5-8**
(One of the 10 songs is by Elvis.)

RHINO (70621; "Billboard Top Rock 'N'
Roll Hits - 1960"): *88* **$5-8**
(One of the 10 songs is by Elvis.)
SSS-SHELBY SINGLETON MUSIC
(1; "Songs For The Seventies"): *69* . .**300-325**
(Two-LP set with 48 songs by 34 artists, including
one by Elvis. Price includes a 66-page songbook,
which represents $50-$75 of the value. Promotional
issue only.)
SCANA (27022; "White Christmas,
Volume 1"): *86* **10-15**
(Has 10 songs by six artists, including one by Elvis.
A German import that was widely distributed in the
U.S.)
SCANA (27023; "White Christmas,
Volume 2"): *86* **10-15**
(Has 10 songs by six artists, including one by Elvis.
A German import that was widely distributed in the
U.S.)
SILHOUETTE (10001/10002;
"Personally Elvis"): *79* **20-25**
STARDAY (995; "Interviews With
Elvis"): *78* **30-50**
(These interviews were previously issued on Great
Northwest 4005.)
SUN (1001; "The Sun Years"): *77* **75-80**
(Light yellow label with "Memphis" at bottom.
Light yellow cover with light brown printing.)
SUN (1001; "The Sun Years"): *77* **15-20**
(Darker yellow label with four target circles. Dark
yellow cover with dark brown printing.)
SUN (1001; "The Sun Years"): *77* **20-25**
(White cover with brown printing.)
TM ("The Presley Years"): *81* **100-200**
(Boxed 12-LP syndicated radio show. Includes
script and cue sheets.)
TIME-LIFE (106; "Country Music"): *81* .**35-45**
TIME-LIFE (106; "Elvis Presley:
1954-1961"): *86* **15-18**
(Three-LP boxed set, part of the *Rock'N'Roll Era*
series of sets available from Time-Life by mail-
order. Other LPs in this series do not feature Elvis.
Includes fold-open brochure.)
TIME-LIFE (107; "The Time-Life Treasury
Of Christmas"): *85* **15-20**
(Three-LP boxed set with 45 songs by 33 artists, in-
cluding two by Elvis.)
TIME-LIFE (108; "The Time-Life Treasury
Of Christmas, Volume 2"): *87* **15-20**
(Three-LP boxed set with 48 songs by 31 artists, in-
cluding one by Elvis.)
TIME-LIFE (109; "Country
Christmas): *88* **15-20**
(Three-LP boxed set with 50 songs by 30 artists, in-
cluding four by Elvis.)

TIME-LIFE (127; "Songs Of Faith
And Inspiration"): *89* **$15-20**
(Three-LP boxed set with 40 songs by 32 artists, including two by Elvis.)
UNITED STATIONS (April 8-12, 1985;
"Solid Gold Country"): *85* **20-40**
(Five-LP boxed set, of which the LP for April 10th
is devoted to Elvis. Price includes six pages of
script and information and a "Proof Of Broadcasting" reply card. The Elvis disc is worth $15-$20 by
itself.)
WATERMARK ("The Elvis Presley
Story," 1975): *75* **800-900**
(13-LP set. White label with pink letters. Price includes a 48-page operations manual, which represents about $100 of the value. Promotional issue
only. Not issued with a special cover or package.)
WATERMARK ("The Elvis Presley
Story," 1977): *77* **700-800**
(13-LP set. White label with pink letters. Price includes a 48-page operations manual, which repre-
sents about $100 of the value. Promotional issue
only. Not issued with a special cover or package.)
WELK MUSIC GROUP (3002;
"Blue Christmas"): *84* **60-75**
(Has 15 versions of *Blue Christmas* by 15 artists, in-
cluding Elvis. Also includes five other Christmas
tunes, but none by Elvis. Promotional issue only.)
WELK MUSIC GROUP ("Sound
Ideas"): *86* **50-75**
(Six-LP set containing excerpts, including two of
Elvis songs. Promotional issue only.)
WESTWOOD ONE ("A Golden
Celebration"): *84* **200-250**
(Three-LP boxed set. Price includes instructions
and cue sheets, which represent $5-$10 of the
value. Issued to radio stations only.)
WORLD OF ELVIS PRESLEY: *83* **50-100**
(A one hour weekly radio show, on discs numbered
program 1 through program 30. The show ceased
operation after 30 programs. Each disc was accompanied by a single cue sheet. Price is for any one of
the discs.)
Notes:
• Prefix letters or numbers are used on some LP listings
in order to more quickly identify the variations available.
• A few items that have no label name are listed by title,
such as the International Hotel boxed sets.
• Beginning in 1961, many Elvis LPs had a separate
sticker, promoting such things as certain songs or
bonus photos. When not listed separately in this edition, a premium of 10-15% could be placed on LPs with
these original stickers.
• LPs with a sticker applied over the catalog number,
showing a new number, are valued approximately the
same as those without the sticker.
• Some albums were pressed with the "Dog Near Top"
label using the older LSP prefix, prior to being switched

to the AFL1 series. These are not listed separately
since there seems to be no consequential price dif-
ference between the two.
• Remember, if you don't find a record above, it may con-
tain two, three, or four artists, and is listed in a section
that follows.
Also see AUDREY
Also see BLACK, Bill
Also see BLOSSOMS
Also see CRAMER, Floyd
Also see CRICKETS
Also see DONNER, Ral
Also see HARRIS, Emmylou
Also see KERR, Anita
Also see MILSAP, Ronnie
Also see MOORE, Bob
Also see RANDOLPH, Boots
Also see REED, Jerry
Also see SINATRA, Nancy
Also see SWEET INSPIRATIONS

PRESLEY, Elvis / Beatles
Singles: 7-Inch
OSBORNE ENTERPRISES ("The 1967
Elvis Medley"): *88* **$3-5**
(Flip side is titled *The #1 Hits Medley, 1956-69*.)
OSBORNE ENTERPRISES ("The 1967
Elvis Medley"): *89* **4-8**
(Flip side is titled *The #1 Hits Medley, 1956-70*.)
Note change in year, from '69 to '70.)
LPs: 10/12-Inch 33rpm
UNITED DISTRIBUTORS (2382; "Lightning
Strikes Twice"): *81* **25-50**
(Promotional issue only. Has five songs by each art-
ist.)
Also see BEATLES

PRESLEY, Elvis / Martha Carson / Lou Monte / Herb Jeffries
EPs: 7-Inch 33/45rpm
RCA VICTOR (2; "Dealers'
Prevue"): *57* **700-750**
(Promotional only.)
RCA VICTOR (2; "Elvis Presley At
His Greatest"): *57* **350-400**
(Paper mailing envelope used with the preceding
Dealers' Prevue EP. Number on the envelope is
7000, the same as the *Teddy Bear/Loving You*
single, rather than SDS-7-2.)
Also see MONTE, Lou

PRESLEY, Elvis / Jean Chapel
EPs: 7-Inch 33/45rpm
RCA VICTOR (7; "Love Me
Tender"): *56* **125-140**
(Also shows the 45rpm number for *Love Me
Tender*, 6643. Not issued with a special sleeve or
cover. Promotional issue only.)

PRESLEY, Elvis / Buddy Holly
Singles: 7-Inch
CREATIVE RADIO ("Elvis-50th
Birthday Special"): *85* **$10-20**
(Demonstration disc. A promotional issue.)
Also see HOLLY, Buddy

PRESLEY, Elvis / Fear
LPs: 10/12-Inch 33rpm
DISCONET (309; "The Original Elvis
Presley Medley"/"Fear Medley"): *80* . . . **25-50**
(Promotional issue only.)

PRESLEY, Elvis / David Keith
Singles: 7-Inch
RCA VICTOR (8760; "Heartbreak
Hotel"): *88* **50-100**
(White label. Promotional issue only.)
RCA VICTOR (8760; "Heartbreak
Hotel"): *88* **3-5**
(Red label. Printing on both sides of label.)
RCA VICTOR (8760; "Heartbreak
Hotel"): *88* **4-8**
(Red label. Printing on Elvis side only.)
RCA VICTOR (8760; "Heartbreak
Hotel"): *88* **4-8**
(Red label. Printing on David Keith side only.)
Picture Sleeves
RCA VICTOR (8760; "Heartbreak
Hotel"): *88* **50-100**
(Pictures RCA's Butch Waugh. Promotional issue
only.)
RCA VICTOR (8760; "Heartbreak
Hotel"): *88* **4-8**
Also see KEITH, David

PRESLEY, Elvis / Jaye P. Morgan
Singles: 7-Inch
UNITED STATES AIR FORCE (125; "It's
Now Or Never"): *61* **300-325**
(Add approximately 10-15% if accompanied by
special mailing box. Issued only to radio stations.)
EPs: 7-Inch 33/45rpm
RCA VICTOR (992 & 689; "Elvis/Jaye
P. Morgan"): *56* **900-1000**
(Two-EP set, with 992 by Presley and 689 by Jaye
P. Morgan coupled together in a promotional
double-pocket package. Since the discs were stand-
ard pressings, at least 95% of the value here is rep-
resented by the custom EP cover.)
Also see MORGAN, Jaye P.

PRESLEY, Elvis / Gary Owens
Singles: 7-Inch
CREATIVE RADIO ("The Elvis
Hour"): *86* **20-30**
(Demonstration disc. Promotional issue only.)

PRESLEY, Elvis / Helen Reddy
Singles: 7-Inch
WHAT'S IT ALL ABOUT (78;
"Life"): *77* **$45-55**
(Issued only to radio stations.)
Also see REDDY, Helen

PRESLEY, Elvis / Dinah Shore
EPs: 7-Inch 33/45rpm
RCA VICTOR (56; "Too Much"): *57* . **125-140**
(Also shows the 45rpm number for *Too Much*,
6800. Not issued with a special sleeve or cover.
Promotional issue only.)
Also see SHORE, Dinah

**PRESLEY, Elvis / Frank Sinatra /
Nat King Cole**
EPs: 7-Inch 33/45rpm
CREATIVE RADIO ("Elvis
Remembered"): *79* **40-45**
(Demonstration disc. A promotional issue.)
Also see COLE, Nat "King"
Also see SINATRA, Frank

**PRESLEY, Elvis / Hank Snow /
Eddy Arnold / Jim Reeves**
EPs: 7-Inch 33/45rpm
RCA VICTOR (12; "Old Shep"): *56* . . **700-800**
(Promotional issue only.)
RCA VICTOR (12; "WOHO Featuring
RCA Victor"): *56* **800-1000**
(Special paper sleeve custom-made for WOHO
radio, Toledo, Ohio, and used with the PRO-12
disc for some promotional purpose.)
Also see ARNOLD, Eddy
Also see REEVES, Jim
Also see SNOW, Hank

PRESLEY, Elvis / Lawrence Welk
Singles: 7-Inch
UNITED STATES AIR FORCE (159;
"Surrender"): *61* **300-325**
(Add approximately 10-15% if accompanied by
special mailing box. Issued only to radio stations.)
Also see WELK, Lawrence

PRESLEY, Elvis / Hank Williams
LPs: 10/12-Inch 33rpm
SUNRISE MEDIA (3011; "History Of
Country Music"): *81* **10-15**
(With four songs by each artist.)
Also see PRESLEY, Elvis
Also see WILLIAMS, Hank

PRESLEY, Elvis
(Michael Conley)
Singles: 7-Inch
ELVIS CLASSIC (5478; "Tell Me
Pretty Baby"): 78 .... $3-5
(Despite being labeled a "1954 recording by Elvis
Presley," this track was simply a 1978 recording by
Michael Conley performing in an Elvis style. It is
listed separately to eliminate confusion.)
Picture Sleeves
ELVIS CLASSIC (5478; "Tell Me
Pretty Baby"): 78 5-10
(Sleeve pictures an artist's sketch of Elvis Presley.)

PRESSURE
Singles: 7-Inch
LAX: 79-80 1-3
LPs: 10/12-Inch 33rpm
LAX: 79 5-8

PRESSURE DROP
Singles: 12-Inch 33/45rpm
TOMMY BOY: 82 4-6
Singles: 7-Inch
TOMMY BOY: 82 1-3

PRESTON, Billy
Singles: 12-Inch 33/45rpm
MEGATONE: 84 4-6
MONTAGE: 84 4-6
Singles: 7-Inch
A&M: 72-78 2-4
APPLE: 69-72 3-5
CAPITOL: 66-69 3-5
CONTRACT: 61 8-10
MOTOWN: 79-82 1-3
VEE JAY: 65 5-8
Picture Sleeves
A&M: 73-75 2-4
APPLE: 69-70 4-8
LPs: 10/12-Inch 33rpm
A&M: 71-82 6-10
APPLE: 69-70 10-15
BUDDAH: 69 10-12
CAPITOL (ST series): 66 10-15
CAPITOL (SM series): 75 6-10
DERBY: 63 40-50
EXODUS: 65 12-15
GNP/CRESCENDO: 73 10-12
MOTOWN: 79-82 5-8
MYRRH: 78 5-8
PEACOCK: 73 8-10
SPRINGBOARD: 78 5-8
TRIP: 73 8-10
VEE JAY: 65 15-20
Also see BEATLES
Also see MOTHERS OF INVENTION

PRESTON, Billy, & Syreeta
Singles: 7-Inch
MOTOWN: 79-81 .... $1-3
TAMLA: 80 1-3
LPs: 10/12-Inch 33rpm
MOTOWN: 79-81 5-8
Also see PRESTON, Billy
Also see SYREETA

PRESTON, Johnny
Singles: 7-Inch
ABC: 68-73 2-4
HALL/HALL WAY: 64-66 3-5
IMPERIAL: 63 3-5
MERCURY: 59-62 4-6
TCF: 65 3-5
Picture Sleeves
MERCURY: 60-62 5-10
EPs: 7-Inch 33/45rpm
MERCURY: 60 20-30
LPs: 10/12-Inch 33rpm
MERCURY (Black label): 60-61 40-60
MERCURY (Chicago "Skyline"
label): 81 5-8
WING: 63 15-20

PRESTON, Mike
Singles: 7-Inch
LONDON: 58-63 3-5

PRESTON, Terry
(Ferlin Husky)
Singles: 78rpm
CAPITOL: 52-53 4-8
Singles: 7-Inch
CAPITOL: 52-53 8-12
Also see HUSKY, Ferlin

PRETENDERS
(Featuring Chrissie Hynde)
Singles: 7-Inch
SIRE: 79-87 1-3
Picture Sleeves
SIRE: 80-83 2-4
LPs: 10/12-Inch 33rpm
SIRE: 80-87 5-8
Also see UB40

PRETTY BOY
(Don Covay; With Johnny Fuller's Band)
Singles: 78rpm
RHYTHM: 54 20-30
Singles: 7-Inch
ATLANTIC: 57 30-40
BIG: 57 25-40
Also see COVAY, Don
Also see KING CURTIS

PRETTY MAIDS

LPs: 10/12-Inch 33rpm

EPIC: *87* $5-8

PRETTY POISON

Singles: 12-Inch 33/45rpm

MONTAGE: *84* 4-6
SVENGALI: *84* 4-6

Singles: 7-Inch

MONTAGE: *84* 1-3
SVENGALI: *84* 1-3
VIRGIN: *87-88* 1-3

PRETTY THINGS

Singles: 7-Inch

FONTANA: *64-66* 5-8
LAURIE: *68* 3-5
SWAN SONG: *75-76* 2-3

LPs: 10/12-Inch 33rpm

FONTANA: *66* 25-30
MOTOWN: *76* 10-12
RARE EARTH (506; "S.F. Sorrow"): *69* . 15-25
  (With standard square cover.)
RARE EARTH (506; "S.F. Sorrow"): *69* . 20-40
  (With rounded-top cover. Promotional issue.)
RARE EARTH (515; "Parachute"): *70* ... 15-20
RARE EARTH (549; "Rare Earth"): *76* ... 8-12
  (Reissue of material from 506 and 515.)
SIRE: *76* 8-10
SWAN SONG: *75-76* 8-10
WARNER BROS: *73-80* 8-10
  Also see GREEN, Jack

PRETTY TONY
(Tony Butler)

Singles: 7-Inch

MUSIC: *84* 1-3

PREVIN, Andre
(Andre Previn & David Rose's Orchestra)

Singles: 7-Inch

COLUMBIA: *60-64* 2-4
DECCA: *61* 2-4
MGM: *59* 2-4
RCA VICTOR: *67* 2-3

EPs: 7-Inch 33/45rpm

MGM: *59* 4-8

LPs: 10/12-Inch 33rpm

ALLEGIANCE: *84* 5-8
ANGEL: *80-81* 5-8
ASCOT (505; "Two For The Seesaw"): *64* 15-25
  (Soundtrack.)
CAMDEN: *64* 5-10
COLUMBIA: *60-65* 10-20
CONTEMPORARY: *57-60* 15-30
DECCA (4000 series): *61-63* 8-15
  (Decca LP numbers in this series preceded by a "7"
  or a "DL-7" are stereo issues.)

DECCA (8000 series): *55-56* $20-40
EVEREST: *70* 5-10
HARMONY: *67* 5-10
MFSL: *82* 20-40
MGM: *59-64* 10-15
METRO JAZZ: *59* 10-20
MONARCH: *54* 20-40
  (10-Inch LPs.)
ODYSSEY: *68* 8-12
RCA VICTOR (1000 series): *75* 5-10
  (With an "ARL1" prefix.)
RCA VICTOR (1000 series): *54* 20-45
  (With an "LPM" prefix.)
RCA VICTOR (1300 series): *56* 20-30
RCA VICTOR (2900 series): *67* 6-12
RCA VICTOR (3000 series): *52* 30-60
  (10-Inch LPs.)
RCA VICTOR (3400 through 3800
  series): *65-67* 6-12
20TH CENTURY-FOX (165; "Goodbye
  Charlie"): *65* 25-30
  (Soundtrack.)
UNITED ARTISTS (103; "Two For
  The Seesaw"): *62* 25-35
  (Soundtrack.)
UNITED ARTISTS (145; "The Fortune
  Cookie"): *66* 15-25
  (Soundtrack.)
UNITED ARTISTS (5200 series): *71* 5-10
VERVE: *63* 10-15
WARNER BROS. (1536; "Dead
  Ringer"): *64* 25-35
  (Soundtrack.)
  Also see ANDREWS, Julie & Andre Previn /
Vic Damone / Jack Jones / Marian Anderson
  Also see DAY, Doris, & Andre Previn
  Also see ROSE, David
  Also see SHORE, Dinah, & Andre Previn

PREVIN, Andre, & Diahann Carroll

Singles: 7-Inch

UNITED ARTISTS: *60* 3-5

LPs: 10/12-Inch 33rpm

UNITED ARTISTS: *60* 10-20
  Also see PREVIN, Andre

PREYER, Ron

Singles: 7-Inch

SHOCK: *78* 2-3

PRICE, Alan
(Alan Price Set)

Singles: 7-Inch

COTILLION: *69* 3-5
EPIC: *84* 1-3
JET: *77-79* 2-3
PARROT: *66-68* 4-6

WARNER BROS: *72* $2-4
LPs: 10/12-Inch 33rpm
ACCORD: *82* 5-8
JET: *77-80* 8-10
PARROT: *68* 15-20
TOWNHOUSE: *81* 5-8
WARNER BROS: *74* 8-10
Also see ANIMALS

PRICE, Lloyd
(Lloyd Price Orchestra; Lloyd Price & The
Dukes)
Singles: 78rpm
ABC-PARAMOUNT: *57* 5-10
SPECIALTY: *55-56* 5-10
Singles: 7-Inch
ABC: *67-73* 1-3
ABC-PARAMOUNT (Monaural): *57-60* .. 5-10
ABC-PARAMOUNT (Stereo): *59* 10-20
COLLECTABLES: 1-3
DOUBLE-L: *63-66* 4-8
GSF: *72-73* 2-4
JAD: *68* 2-4
KRC (Except 587): *57-59* 5-10
KRC (587; "Just Because"): *57* 35-45
LPG: *76* 2-3
LUDIX: 3-6
MCA: 1-3
MONUMENT: *64-65* 3-5
PARAMOUNT: *72* 2-4
REPRISE: *66* 3-5
ROULETTE: 1-3
SCEPTER: *71* 2-4
SPECIALTY (SPBX series): *86* 12-15
(Boxed sets of six colored vinyl 45s.)
SPECIALTY (400 series): *52-54* 15-25
(Black vinyl.)
SPECIALTY (400 series): *53-54* 30-40
(Colored vinyl.)
SPECIALTY (500 series): *55-56* 10-15
SPECIALTY (600 series): *59* 3-6
(Most Specialty singles are currently available,
using original catalog numbers.)
TURNTABLE: *69* 2-4
Picture Sleeves
DOUBLE-L: *64* 5-10
EPs: 7-Inch 33/45rpm
ABC-PARAMOUNT: *59-60* 20-35
LPs: 10/12-Inch 33rpm
ABC: *72-76* 8-10
ABC-PARAMOUNT: *59-61* 25-35
DOUBLE-L: *63* 20-25
GRAND PRIX: 10-12
GUEST STAR: *64* 10-12
JAD: *69* 10-12

MCA: *82* $5-8
MONUMENT: *65* 10-15
PICKWICK: *67* 8-12
SPECIALTY (2100 series): *59* 25-30
(Specialty LP reissues, using original catalog num-
bers, are currently available.)
TRIP: *76* 8-10
TURNTABLE: *69* 8-10
UPFRONT: 8-10
Also see COOKE, Sam / Lloyd Price / Larry
Williams
Also see DOMINO, Fats

PRICE, Priscilla
Singles: 7-Inch
BASF: *73* 2-4

PRICE, Ray
(Ray Price & The Cherokee Cowboys)
Singles: 78rpm
BULLET: *52* 25-50
COLUMBIA: *52-57* 4-8
Singles: 7-Inch
ABC: *75* 2-3
ABC/DOT: *75-77* 1-3
COLUMBIA (10000 series): *74-77* 1-3
COLUMBIA (20000 & 21000
series): *52-56* 4-8
COLUMBIA (40000 through
43000 series): *57-66* 3-5
COLUMBIA (44000 through
45000 series): *67-73* 2-4
DIMENSION: *81-82* 1-3
MONUMENT: *78-79* 1-3
MYRRH: *74-75* 1-3
STEP ONE: *85-88* 1-3
WARNER BROS: *82-83* 1-3
WORD: *78* 1-3
Picture Sleeves
COLUMBIA: *66* 3-5
EPs: 7-Inch 33/45rpm
COLUMBIA (1700 through
2800 series): *53-57* 10-20
COLUMBIA (8556; "Ray Price"): 10-20
COLUMBIA (10000 through
14000 series): *57-60* 8-15
(White label. Promotional issue only.)
LPs: 10/12-Inch 33rpm
ABC/DOT: *75-77* 6-10
COLUMBIA (28; "The World Of
Ray Price"): *70* 8-12
COLUMBIA (1015; "Ray Price Sings
Heart Songs"): *57* 30-40
COLUMBIA (1148; "Talk To Your
Heart"): *58* 25-35

COLUMBIA (1400 through
  2600 series): *60-67* $10-25
  (Monaural.)
COLUMBIA (8200 through
  9400 series): *60-67* 10-25
  (Stereo.)
COLUMBIA (9700 through
  9900 series): *68-70* 8-12
COLUMBIA (10000 series): *73* 5-10
COLUMBIA (30000 through
  37000 series): *70-81* 5-10
DIMENSION: *81* 5-8
51 WEST: *84* 5-8
HARMONY: *66-71* 8-15
MONUMENT: *79* 5-8
MYRRH: *74* 5-8
RADIANT: *81* 5-8
STEP ONE: *86* 5-10
WARNER BROS: *83* 5-8
WORD: *77* 5-8
  Also see ROBBINS, Marty / Johnny Cash /
  Ray Price

PRICE, Ray / Lefty Frizzell / Carl Smith
  LPs: 10/12-Inch 33rpm
COLUMBIA (1200 series): *59* 15-25
COLUMBIA (8700 series): *63* 12-18
  Also see FRIZZELL, Lefty
  Also see SMITH, Carl

PRICE, Ray, & Willie Nelson
  Singles: 7-Inch
COLUMBIA: *80* 1-3
  LPs: 10/12-Inch 33rpm
COLUMBIA: *80* 5-8
  Also see NELSON, Willie
  Also see PRICE, Ray

PRIDE, Charley
  (Country Charley Pride; Charley Pride & The
  Pridesmen)
  Singles: 7-Inch
RCA VICTOR (0100 through
  0500 series): *66-69* 2-5
RCA VICTOR (0600 through
  0900 series): *72-73* 1-3
RCA VICTOR (8700 & 8800
  series): *66* 3-5
RCA VICTOR (9000 through
  9900 series): *66-71* 2-4
RCA VICTOR (10000 through
  14000, except 11736): *74-86* 1-3
RCA VICTOR (11736; "Dallas
  Cowboys"): *79* 1-3
  (Black label.)

RCA VICTOR (11736; "Dallas
  Cowboys"): *79* $5-10
  (Gray and blue label. Special Dallas Cowboys edi-
  tion.)
16TH AVE: *87-88* 1-3
  Picture Sleeves
RCA VICTOR: *71-74* 2-4
  EPs: 7-Inch 33/45rpm
RCA VICTOR: 5-10
  (Jukebox issues.)
  LPs: 10/12-Inch 33rpm
RCA VICTOR (Except LPM/LSP 3700
  through 4800 series): *74-86* 5-10
RCA VICTOR (3700 through 4800
  series): *66-73* 8-18
  (With an "LPM" or "LSP" prefix.)
  Also see DAVE & SUGAR
  Also see MANCINI, Henry, & Charley Pride

PRIMA, Louis
  (Louis Prima & His Orchestra)
  Singles: 78rpm
COLUMBIA: *52-53* 3-5
DECCA: *54* 3-5
HIT: *44-45* 4-8
MERCURY: *50* 3-5
ROBIN HOOD: *50* 3-6
SAVOY: *53* 3-5
  Singles: 7-Inch
ABC: *68-74* 1-3
BUENA VISTA: *66-74* 1-3
CAPITOL: *62* 2-4
COLUMBIA: *52-53* 4-8
DECCA: *54* 3-6
DOT: *59-62* 2-4
HBR: *66* 2-3
KAMA SUTRA: *66* 2-3
MERCURY: *50* 4-8
PRIMA: *63-64* 4-8
ROBIN HOOD: *50* 4-8
SAVOY: *53* 4-8
UNITED ARTISTS: *67* 1-3
  EPs: 7-Inch 33/45rpm
CAPITOL: *56* 5-10
JUBILEE: *55* 5-10
VARSITY: *54* 6-12
  LPs: 10/12-Inch 33rpm
BUENA VISTA: *65-74* 8-18
CAPITOL: *56-62* 10-20
DE-LITE: *68* 5-10
DOT: *60* 10-15
HBR: *66* 5-12
HAMILTON: *65* 5-10
MERCURY (25000 series): *53* 15-30
  (10-Inch LPs.)

PRIMA: 72-76 .... $5-8
RONDO/RONDOLETTE: 59 10-20
UNITED ARTISTS: 67 5-10

PRIMA, Louis, & Keely Smith
Singles: 7-Inch
CAPITOL: 58-59 2-4
DOT: 59-61 2-4
Picture Sleeves
CAPITOL (4063; "That Old Black
  Magic"): 58 3-5
(Sleeve has a die-cut center hole)
DOT: 59 4-8
EPs: 7-Inch 33/45rpm
CAPITOL: 58 4-8
DOT: 60 3-6
LPs: 10/12-Inch 33rpm
CAPITOL: 75 5-8
(With an "SM" prefix.)
CAPITOL: 58-61 10-20
(With a "T" or "ST" prefix.)
DOT: 59-60 10-20
Also see SMITH, Keely

PRIMETTES
(Supremes)
Singles: 7-Inch
LUPINE (120; "Tears Of Sorrow"): 61 200-225
Also see SUPREMES

PRINCE
(Prince & The Revolution)
Singles: 12-Inch 33/45rpm
PAISLEY PARK: 85-89 4-6
WARNER BROS: 78-85 4-6
Promotional 12-Inch Singles
PAISLEY PARK: 85-89 5-8
WARNER BROS (Black vinyl): 78-85 5-8
WARNER BROS (Colored vinyl): 85 ... 10-15
Singles: 7-Inch
PAISLEY PARK: 85-89 1-3
WARNER BROS (Black vinyl): 78-85 1-3
WARNER BROS (Colored vinyl): 84 4-6
Picture Sleeves
PAISLEY PARK: 85-89 1-3
WARNER BROS: 80-85 1-3
LPs: 10/12-Inch 33rpm
PAISLEY PARK: 85-87 5-8
WARNER BROS (Black vinyl): 78-85 5-8
WARNER BROS (Colored vinyl): 84 ... 25-40
Also see E., Sheila

PRINCE BUSTER
(Prince Buster & The Sea Busters)
Singles: 7-Inch
AMY: 64 3-5
ATLANTIC: 64 3-5

PHILIPS: 67 .... $3-5
RCA VICTOR: 67 3-5
STELLAR: 64 3-5
LPs: 10/12-Inch 33rpm
RCA VICTOR: 67 10-15

PRINCE HAROLD
Singles: 7-Inch
MERCURY: 66 3-5
SPRING: 67 3-5
VERVE: 67 3-5

PRINCE LA LA
Singles: 7-Inch
AFO: 61-62 4-6

PRINCESS
Singles: 12-Inch 33/45rpm
NEXT PLATINUM: 85-86 4-6
POLYDOR: 86 4-6
Singles: 7-Inch
POLYDOR: 86-87 1-3

PRINCIPATO, Tom
LPs: 10/12-Inch 33rpm
POWERHOUSE: 88 5-8

PRINCIPLE, Jamie
Singles: 12-Inch 33/45rpm
PERSONA: 85 4-6

PRINE, John
Singles: 7-Inch
ASYLUM: 78 2-3
ATLANTIC: 71-75 2-4
OH BOY (Colored vinyl): 81-86 3-5
LPs: 10/12-Inch 33rpm
ASYLUM: 78-80 5-8
ATLANTIC: 71-76 8-10
OH BOY: 84-86 5-8

**PRINE, John / Daryl Hall & John
Oates / Barnaby Bye / Delbert & Glen**
EPs: 7-Inch 33/45rpm
ATLANTIC (195; "Something For
  Nothing"): 73 4-8
Also see DELBERT & GLEN
Also see HALL, Daryl, & John Oates
Also see PRINE, John

PRISCILLA:
see COOLIDGE-JONES, Priscilla

PRISM
Singles: 7-Inch
ARIOLA AMERICA: 77-79 2-3
CAPITOL: 82 1-3
LPs: 10/12-Inch 33rpm
ARIOLA AMERICA (Except
  50034): 77-79 10-12

ARIOLA AMERICA (50034; "Live
Tonite"): 78 . . . . $15-20
(Promotional issue only.)
CAPITOL: 80-82 5-8

PRISTER, Jerome "Secret Weapon"
TUFF CITY: 88 1-3

PROBY, P.J.
Singles: 7-Inch
IMPERIAL: 64 3-5
LIBERTY: 61-68 4-8
LONDON: 64 3-6
SURFSIDE: 65 5-8
Picture Sleeves
LIBERTY: 67 3-6
LPs: 10/12-Inch 33rpm
LIBERTY: 65-68 15-20
Also see FOCUS & P.J. PROBY

PROCESS & THE DOO RAGS
Singles: 7-Inch
COLUMBIA: 85-87 1-3

PROCOL HARUM
Singles: 7-Inch
A&M: 67-72 3-5
CHRYSALIS: 74-77 2-4
DERAM: 67 3-5
Picture Sleeves
A&M: 72 3-5
LPs: 10/12-Inch 33rpm
A&M (Except 4294 & 8053): 68-73 8-12
A&M (4294; "Broken
Barricades"): 71 12-15
(With die-cut gatefold cover.)
A&M (4294; "Broken
Barricades"): 72 10-12
(With standard cover.)
A&M (8053; "Procol Harum
Lives"): 15-25
CHRYSALIS: 73-77 8-10
DERAM (008; "Procol
Harum"): 67 40-60
(Issued with bonus poster.)
Members: Gary Brooker; Robin Trower.
Also see TROWER, Robin

PRODUCERS
Singles: 7-Inch
PORTRAIT: 81-82 1-3
LPs: 10/12-Inch 33rpm
PORTRAIT: 81-82 5-8

**PROFESSOR FUNK & HIS
EIGHTH STREET FUNK BAND**
Singles: 7-Inch
ROXBURY: 73 2-3

**PROFESSOR MORRISON'S
LOLLIPOP:**
see MORRISON, Professor

PROFILES
Singles: 7-Inch
BAMBOO: 69 . . . . $2-4
DUO: 68 3-5

PROJECT FUTURE
Singles: 12-Inch 33/45rpm
CAPITOL: 83 4-6
Singles: 7-Inch
CAPITOL: 83 1-3

PROPHECY
Singles: 7-Inch
AIRBORNE: 2-3
ALL PLATINUM: 74 2-3
MAINSTREAM: 75 2-3
Picture Sleeves
AIRBORNE: 2-4
Members: Mack Wolfman; Bernie Taylor.

PROPHETS: see THEE PROPHETS

PROTHEROE, Brian
Singles: 7-Inch
CHRYSALIS: 75 2-3
LPs: 10/12-Inch 33rpm
CHRYSALIS: 75-76 8-10

PROVINE, Dorothy
Singles: 7-Inch
WARNER BROS: 61 2-4
LPs: 10/12-Inch 33rpm
WARNER BROS: 60-61 10-20

**PROVINE, Dorothy, & Joe
"Fingers" Carr**
LPs: 10/12-Inch 33rpm
WARNER BROS: 60-62 10-20
Also see CARR, Joe "Fingers"
Also see PROVINE, Dorothy

PRUETT, Jeanne
(Jean Pruett)
Singles: 7-Inch
AUDIOGRAPH: 83 1-3
DECCA: 68-72 2-3
IBC: 79-80 1-3
MCA: 73-77 1-3
MERCURY: 78 1-3
MSR: 87 1-3
PAID: 81 1-3
RCA VICTOR: 63-64 2-4
LPs: 10/12-Inch 33rpm
ALLEGIANCE: 84 5-8
AUDIOGRAPH: 83 5-8
DECCA: 72 8-10

IBC: *79* $5-8
MCA: *73-75* 4-8
OUT OF TOWN DIST: *82* 5-8
Also see ROBBINS, Marty, & Jeanne Pruett

PRYOR, Richard
Singles: 7-Inch
LAFF: *80* 1-3
WARNER BROS: *76-79* 1-3
LPs: 10/12-Inch 33rpm
DOVE: *68* 8-15
LAFF: *71-81* 5-10
PARTEE: *74* 5-10
REPRISE: *68-77* 5-12
TIGER LILY: *77* 5-10
WARNER BROS: *76-85* 5-10

PRYSOCK, Arthur
Singles: 78rpm
DECCA: *52-54* 3-5
MERCURY: *54-55* 3-5
Singles: 7-Inch
MERCURY: *54-55* 3-5
BETHLEHEM: *72* 1-3
DECCA (25000 series): *65* 2-5
DECCA (27000 through 29000
series): *52-54* 4-8
DECCA (31000 series): *64-65* 2-5
GUSTO: *79* 1-3
KING: *69-71* 2-4
MCA: *78* 1-3
MERCURY: *54-55* 4-6
OLD TOWN (100 series): *73-76* 1-3
OLD TOWN (1000 series): *59-60* 3-5
(Light blue label.)
OLD TOWN (1000 series): *76-77* 1-3
(Dark blue or black label.)
OLD TOWN (1100 series): *61-66* 2-5
VERVE: *66-69* 2-4
LPs: 10/12-Inch 33rpm
DECCA: *64-65* 10-20
KING: *69-71* 8-12
MCA: *78* 5-8
MGM: *70* 2-3
OLD TOWN (100 series): *60-62* 20-30
OLD TOWN (2000 series): *62-65* 15-25
OLD TOWN (12000 series): *73-77* 6-10
POLYDOR: *77* 5-8
VERVE: *66-69* 10-20
Also see ECKSTINE, Billy / Arthur Prysock
Also see JOHNSON, Buddy

PRYSOCK, Arthur, & Count Basie
Singles: 7-Inch
VERVE: *66* 2-4

LPs: 10/12-Inch 33rpm
VERVE: *66* $10-20
Also see BASIE, Count

PRYSOCK, Arthur / Leroy Bivins
LPs: 10/12-Inch 33rpm
GUEST STAR: *64* 5-10
Also see PRYSOCK, Arthur

PSEUDO ECHO
Singles: 7-Inch
RCA VICTOR: *87* 1-3
LPs: 10/12-Inch 33rpm
RCA VICTOR: *87* 5-8

PSYCHEDELIC FURS
Singles: 12-Inch 33/45rpm
COLUMBIA: *84-86* 4-6
Singles: 7-Inch
COLUMBIA: *80-87* 1-3
LPs: 10/12-Inch 33rpm
COLUMBIA: *80-87* 5-8
Members: Tim Butler; Richard Butler; John Ashton; Mars Williams; Paul Garisto; Marty Williamson.

PUBLIC IMAGE LTD.
Singles: 12-Inch 33/45rpm
VIRGIN: *87* 4-6
LPs: 10/12-Inch 33rpm
ISLAND: *80* 8-10
VIRGIN: *87* 5-8
WARNER BROS: *81* 8-10
Also see SEX PISTOLS

PUCKETT, Gary
(Gary Puckett & The Union Gap; Union Gap
Featuring Gary Puckett)
Singles: 7-Inch
COLUMBIA: *67-72* 3-5
Picture Sleeves
COLUMBIA: *67-69* 4-6
LPs: 10/12-Inch 33rpm
BACK-TRAC: *85* 5-8
COLUMBIA: *68-71* 10-15
51 WEST: *82* 5-8
HARMONY: *72* 8-10

PULLINS, Leroy
Singles: 7-Inch
KAPP: *66* 2-4

PUMPKIN
(Pumpkin & The Profile All-Stars)
Singles: 12-Inch 33/45rpm
PROFILE: *84* 4-6
Singles: 7-Inch
PROFILE: *84* 1-3

PUPPETS
Singles: 12-Inch 33/45rpm
QUALITY/RFC: *84* $4-6
Singles: 7-Inch
QUALITY/RFC: *84* 1-3

PURDIE, Pretty
(Bernard Purdie)
Singles: 7-Inch
COLUMBIA: *69* 2-4
DATE: *67-68* 3-5
LPs: 10/12-Inch 33rpm
DATE: *67* 10-15
FLYING DUTCHMAN: *73* 8-10
PRESTIGE: *71* 8-10

PURE ENERGY
Singles: 12-Inch 33/45rpm
PRISM: *80-84* 4-6
Singles: 7-Inch
PRISM: *80-84* 1-3

PURE LOVE & PLEASURE
Singles: 7-Inch
DUNHILL: *70* 2-4
LPs: 10/12-Inch 33rpm
DUNHILL: *70* 10-12

PURE PRAIRIE LEAGUE
Singles: 7-Inch
RCA VICTOR: *72-79* 2-3
CASABLANCA: *80-81* 1-3
EPIC: *77* 2-3
LPs: 10/12-Inch 33rpm
CASABLANCA: *80-81* 5-8
RCA VICTOR: *72-80* 8-10
Also see AMERICAN FLYER

PURIFY, James & Bobby
Singles: 7-Inch
BELL: *66-69* 3-5
CASABLANCA: *74-75* 2-3
MERCURY: *76-77* 2-3
LPs: 10/12-Inch 33rpm
BELL: *66-67* 12-15
MERCURY: *77* 8-10
Members: James Purify; Bobby Dickey.

PURIM, Flora
LPs: 10/12-Inch 33rpm
MILESTONE: *74-77* 5-10
WARNER BROS: *78* 5-8
Also see HART, Mickey, Airto & Flora Purim

PURPLE REIGN
Singles: 7-Inch
GO-RILLA: *75* 3-5
PRIVATE STOCK: *75* 2-4

PURSELL, Bill
Singles: 7-Inch
COLUMBIA: *62-66* $2-3
DOT: *69* 1-3
EPIC: *67* 1-3
LPs: 10/12-Inch 33rpm
COLUMBIA: *63-65* 5-15

PUSHE
Singles: 12-Inch 33/45rpm
PARTYTYME: *84* 4-6

PYRAMIDS
Singles: 7-Inch
BEST: *63* 10-15
(Label makes no mention of "Distributed By London.")
BEST: *63-64* 4-6
(Label reads "Distributed By London.")
CEDWICKE: *64* 4-6
Picture Sleeves
BEST: *63* 15-25
LPs: 10/12-Inch 33rpm
BEST (36501; "Penetration"): *64* 50-100
WHAT: *83* 5-8

PYTHON LEE JACKSON
Singles: 7-Inch
GNP/CRESCENDO: *72* 3-5
LPs: 10/12-Inch 33rpm
GNP/CRESCENDO: *72* 10-15
Member: Rod Stewart.
Also see SMALL FACES
Also see STEWART, Rod

Q

Q
Singles: 7-Inch
EPIC: *77* 2-3
LPs: 10/12-Inch 33rpm
EPIC: *77* 8-10
Members: Robert Peckman; Don Garvin.
Also see JAGGERZ

QUADRANT SIX
Singles: 12-Inch 33/45rpm
ATLANTIC: *83* 4-6
Singles: 7-Inch
ATLANTIC: *83* 1-3

QUAITE, Christine
Singles: 7-Inch
WORLD ARTISTS: *64* 3-5

QUAKER CITY BOYS
Singles: 7-Inch
SWAN: *58-59* 4-6

QUANDO QUANDO
Singles: 12-Inch 33/45rpm
FACTORY: *83* $4-6

QUARTER NOTES
Singles: 78rpm
DOT: *57* 5-10
Singles: 7-Inch
DOT: *57* 10-15
GUYDEN: *63* 4-6
IMPERIAL: *60* 4-6
RCA VICTOR: *58* 4-8
WIZZ: *59* 10-15

QUARTERFLASH
Singles: 12-Inch 33/45rpm
GEFFEN: *81-82* 4-6
Singles: 7-Inch
GEFFEN: *81-85* 1-3
WARNER BROS: *82* 1-3
LPs: 10/12-Inch 33rpm
GEFFEN: *81-85* 5-8

QUARTERMAN, Joe, & Free Soul
Singles: 7-Inch
GSF: *72-74* 2-4
MERCURY: *74* 2-4

QUARTZ
Singles: 7-Inch
MARLIN: *78* 2-3
POLYDOR: *79* 1-3
LPs: 10/12-Inch 33rpm
POLYDOR: *79* 5-8

QUATEMAN, Bill
Singles: 7-Inch
COLUMBIA: *72-73* 2-4
RCA VICTOR: *77-78* 2-3
LPs: 10/12-Inch 33rpm
COLUMBIA: *73* 8-10
RCA VICTOR: *77-78* 5-8

QUATRO, Suzi
(Susie Quatro)
Singles: 7-Inch
ARISTA: *75* 2-3
BELL: *73-74* 2-4
BIG TREE: *76* 2-3
DREAMLAND: *80-81* 1-3
RAK: *72-74* 2-4
RSO: *79* 1-3
Picture Sleeves
DREAMLAND: *80* 1-3
LPs: 10/12-Inch 33rpm
ARISTA: *75* 8-10
BELL: *74* 10-12
DREAMLAND: *80* 5-8

RSO: *79* $5-8

QUATRO, Suzi, & Chris Norman
Singles: 7-Inch
RSO: *79* 1-3
Also see QUATRO, Suzi
Also see SMOKIE

QUAZAR
Singles: 7-Inch
ARISTA: *78* 2-3
LPs: 10/12-Inch 33rpm
ARISTA: *78* 5-8

QUEEN
Singles: 12-Inch 33/45rpm
CAPITOL: *84-86* 4-6
Singles: 7-Inch
CAPITOL: *84-86* 1-3
ELEKTRA: *74-82* 2-4
Picture Sleeves
CAPITOL: *84* 1-3
ELEKTRA: *77-82* 2-4
LPs: 10/12-Inch 33rpm
CAPITOL: *84-87* 5-8
ELEKTRA (Except 166): *73-82* 6-10
ELEKTRA (166; "Jazz"): *78* 40-50
(Picture disc. Promotional issue only.)
MFSL: *82* 25-50
Members: Freddie Mercury; John Deacon; Brian
May; Roger Taylor.
Also see MAY, Brian
Also see MERCURY, Freddie
Also see TAYLOR, Roger

QUEEN & DAVID BOWIE
Singles: 7-Inch
ELEKTRA: *81* 1-3
Picture Sleeves
ELEKTRA: *81* 1-3
Also see BOWIE, David
Also see QUEEN

QUEENSRYCHE
Singles: 7-Inch
EMI AMERICA: *83-86* 1-3
LPs: 10/12-Inch 33rpm
EMI AMERICA: *83-86* 5-8
EMI-MANHATTAN: *88* 5-8

? AND THE MYSTERIANS
(Question Mark & The Mysterians)
Singles: 7-Inch
ABKCO: 1-3
CAMEO: *66-67* 4-6
CAPITOL: *68* 5-8
CHICORY: *67* 12-15
LUV: *73* 4-6
PA-GO-GO: *66* 40-45

SUPER K: *69* **$3-5**
TANGERINE: **4-6**
LPs: 10/12-Inch 33rpm
CAMEO (2004; "96 Tears"): *66* **50-100**
CAMEO (2006; "Action"): *67* **50-100**
Members: Rudy Martinez; Robert Martinez; Frank
Rodriguez; Larry Borjas; Bob Balderamma; Frank
Lugo.

QUICK
Singles: 12-Inch 33/45rpm
EPIC: *82* **4-6**
PAVILLION: *81* **4-6**
Singles: 7-Inch
EPIC (37000 series): *82* **1-3**
PAVILLION: *81* **1-3**
LPs: 10/12-Inch 33rpm
EPIC: *82* **5-8**

QUICK
Singles: 7-Inch
EPIC (10516; "Ain't Nothin'
Gonna Stop Me"): *69* **10-15**
Member: Eric Carmen.
Also see CARMEN, Eric

QUICKEST WAY OUT
Singles: 7-Inch
WARNER BROS: *75-76* **2-4**

QUICKSILVER
(Quicksilver Messenger Service)
Singles: 7-Inch
CAPITOL: *68-76* **2-5**
LPs: 10/12-Inch 33rpm
CAPITOL (288; "Quicksilver
Messenger Service"): *69* **30-50**
CAPITOL (391 through 819): *69-71* **12-15**
CAPITOL (2904; "Quicksilver
Messenger Service"): *68* **15-20**
CAPITOL (11000 series): *72-75* **10-12**
CAPITOL (16000 series): *80* **5-8**
Also see HOPKINS, Nicky
Also see JEFFERSON AIRPLANE
Also see MILLER, Steve / Band / Quicksilver
Messinger Service
Also see VALENTI, Dino

QUIET RIOT
Singles: 12-Inch 33/45rpm
PASHA: *83-85* **4-6**
Singles: 7-Inch
CBS: *83* **2-4**
PASHA: *83-86* **1-3**
LPs: 10/12-Inch 33rpm
PASHA (Except picture discs): *83-88* **5-8**
PASHA (Picture discs): *83* **10-12**

QUINELLA
Singles: 7-Inch
BECKET: *81* **$1-3**

QUINN, Carmel
Singles: 78rpm
COLUMBIA: *55-56* **2-4**
Singles: 7-Inch
COLUMBIA: *55-56* **2-4**
DOT: *64* **2-3**
HEADLINE: *59-62* **2-4**
EPs: 7-Inch 33/45rpm
COLUMBIA: *55* **5-10**
LPs: 10/12-Inch 33rpm
CAMDEN: *65* **5-10**
COLUMBIA: *55-56* **10-20**
DOT: *65* **5-12**
HEADLINE: *59-62* **8-15**

QUIN-TONES
Singles: 7-Inch
COLLECTABLES: **1-3**
HUNT: *58* **10-15**
RED TOP: *58* **15-20**

R

RCR
Singles: 7-Inch
RADIO: *80* **1-3**
Members: Donna Rhodes; Charles Chalmers;
Sandy Rhodes.

R.E.M.
Singles: 7-Inch
HIBTONE: *81* **50-75**
I.R.S.: *82-88* **3-6**
Picture Sleeves
I.R.S.: *82-86* **4-8**
EPs: 7-Inch 33/45rpm
I.R.S.: *82* **5-10**
LPs: 10/12-Inch 33rpm
I.R.S: *82-88* **5-10**
Members: J. Michael Stipe; Bill Berry; Peter Buck;
Mike Mills.

REO SPEEDWAGON
Singles: 7-Inch
EPIC (Except 10000 & 11000 series): *75-88* **1-3**
EPIC (10000 & 11000 series): *72-74* **2-4**
Picture Sleeves
EPIC: *80-85* **1-3**
EPs: 7-Inch 33/45rpm
CSP: *81* **3-6**
(Nestle's candy promotional issue.)

LPs: 10/12-Inch 33rpm
EPIC (Except 40000 series): *71-87* **$6-10**
EPIC (40000 series): *81-82* **12-15**
(Half-speed mastered.)
        Promotional LPs
EPIC (643; "Nine Lives"): **12-15**
  Members: Kevin Cronin; Neal Doughty; Al Grat-
  zer; Bruce Hall; Terry Luttrell.
  Also see MAY, Brian

R.J.'S LATEST ARRIVAL
(Ralph James)
        Singles: 7-Inch
ARIOLA AMERICA: *79* **2-3**
ATLANTIC: *85* **1-3**
BUDDAH: *81* **1-3**
LARC: *83* **1-3**
EMI MANHATTAN: *88* **1-3**
MANHATTAN: *87* **1-3**
QUALITY/RFC: **1-3**
SUTRA: *81* **1-3**
ZOO YORK: *82* **1-3**
        LPs: 10/12-Inch 33rpm
ARIOLA AMERICA: *79* **5-8**
ATLANTIC: *85* **5-8**
EMI-MANHATTAN: *88* **5-8**

RABBITT, Eddie
        Singles: 7-Inch
DATE: *68* **2-4**
ELEKTRA: *74-83* **1-3**
RCA VICTOR: *86-88* **1-3**
20TH CENTURY-FOX: *64* **3-5**
WARNER BROS: *83-85* **1-3**
        Picture Sleeves
ELEKTRA: *81* **1-3**
        LPs: 10/12-Inch 33rpm
ELEKTRA: *75-82* **5-10**
RCA VICTOR: *86-88* **5-8**
WARNER BROS: *84-85* **5-8**

RABBITT, Eddie, & Crystal Gayle
        Singles: 7-Inch
ELEKTRA: *82* **1-3**
  Also see GAYLE, Crystal
  Also see RABBITT, Eddie

RABBITT, Eddie, & Juice Newton
        Singles: 7-Inch
RCA VICTOR: *86* **1-3**
  Also see NEWTON, Juice
  Also see RABBITT, Eddie

RABIN, Trevor
        Singles: 7-Inch
CHRYSALIS: *78-80* **1-3**
        LPs: 10/12-Inch 33rpm
CHRYSALIS: *78-80* **5-8**

RACE
        Singles: 7-Inch
OCEAN FRONT: *83* **$1-3**

RACING CARS
        Singles: 7-Inch
CHRYSALIS: *77-78* **2-3**
        LPs: 10/12-Inch 33rpm
CHRYSALIS: *77-78* **5-8**

RADIANCE
(Radiance With Andrea Stone)
        Singles: 12-Inch 33/45rpm
ARE 'N BE: *83* **4-6**
        Singles: 7-Inch
WARNER BROS: *85* **1-3**

RADIANTS
(Maurice McAlister & The Radiants; Maurice &
The Radiants)
        Singles: 7-Inch
CHESS: *62-69* **3-6**
ERIC: **1-3**
TWINIGHT: *71* **2-4**
  Members: Maurice McAlister; Wallace Sampson;
  Jerome Brooks; Elzie Butler; Green McLauren;
  Frank McCollum; Leonard Caston Jr.; James
  Jameson; Mitchell Bullock; Victor Caston.

RADIATORS
        Singles: 7-Inch
EPIC: *87* **1-3**
        LPs: 10/12-Inch 33rpm
EPIC: *87* **5-8**
  Members: Dave Malone; Frank Bua; Reggie Scan-
  lan; Ed Volker; Camile Baudoin; Glenn Sears.

RADICE, Mark
        Singles: 7-Inch
UNITED ARTISTS: *76* **2-4**
        LPs: 10/12-Inch 33rpm
ROADSHOW: *77* **8-10**

RADIO HEART
(Featuring Gary Numan)
        Singles: 7-Inch
CRITIQUE: *87* **1-3**
        LPs: 10/12-Inch 33rpm
CRITIQUE (Black vinyl): *87* **5-8**
CRITIQUE (Picture discs): *87* **8-12**

RADNER, Gilda
        Singles: 7-Inch
WARNER BROS: *79-80* **1-3**
        LPs: 10/12-Inch 33rpm
WARNER BROS: *79* **5-8**

RAE, Fonda
(Fonda Raye)
Singles: 12-Inch 33/45rpm
POSSE: *83* $4-6
VANGUARD: *82* 4-6
Singles: 7-Inch
VANGUARD: *82* 1-3
Also see WISH

RAE, Robbie
Singles: 7-Inch
QUALITY: *83* 1-3

RAELETTES
(Raeletts; Raelets)
Singles: 7-Inch
TRC: *70* 2-4
TANGERINE: *67-73* 2-4
LPs: 10/12-Inch 33rpm
TRC: *71-72* 8-10
TANGERINE: *72* 8-10
Also see CHARLES, Ray
Also see TURNER, Ike & Tina

RAES
Singles: 7-Inch
A&M: *78* 2-3
LPs: 10/12-Inch 33rpm
A&M: *79* 5-8

RAFFERTY, Gerry
Singles: 7-Inch
BLUE THUMB: *72* 2-4
LIBERTY: *82* 1-3
SIGNPOST: *72* 2-4
UNITED ARTISTS: *77-80* 1-3
Picture Sleeves
UNITED ARTISTS: *77-78* 1-3
LPs: 10/12-Inch 33rpm
BLUE THUMB: *73-78* 8-10
LIBERTY: *82* 5-8
MFSL: *81* 25-50
UNITED ARTISTS: *78-80* 8-10
VISA: *78* 5-8
Also see STEALERS WHEEL

RAG DOLLS
Singles: 7-Inch
MALA: *65* 8-10
Member: Jean Thomas.

RAG DOLLS / Caliente Combo
Singles: 7-Inch
PARKWAY: *64* 5-8
Also see RAG DOLLS

RAHEEM
LPs: 10/12-Inch 33rpm
A&M: *88* $5-8

RAIDERS, & Paul Revere:
see REVERE, Paul, & The Raiders

RAIK'S PROGRESS
Singles: 7-Inch
LIBERTY: *66* 5-10

RAIL
Singles: 7-Inch
EMI AMERICA: *84* 1-3
LPs: 10/12-Inch 33rpm
EMI AMERICA: *84* 5-8
PASSPORT: 5-8

RAILHEAD
Singles: 12-Inch 33/45rpm
WAX-TRAX: *87* 5-8
Singles: 7-Inch
WAX-TRAX: *87* 2-3

RAILWAY CHILDREN
LPs: 10/12-Inch 33rpm
VIRGIN: *87* 5-8

RAINBOW
Singles: 7-Inch
MERCURY: *82-83* 1-3
POLYDOR: *79* 2-3
LPs: 10/12-Inch 33rpm
MERCURY: *82-86* 5-10
OYSTER: *77* 8-10
POLYDOR: *78-81* 5-8
Member: Ritchie Blackmore.
Also see ALCATRAZZ
Also see BLACKMORE'S RAINBOW
Also see CAREY, Tony
Also see GLOVER, Roger

RAINDROPS
Singles: 7-Inch
JUBILEE: *63-65* 8-10
VIRGO: *73* 2-4
LPs: 10/12-Inch 33rpm
JUBILEE: *63* 30-35
MURRAY HILL: 5-8
Members: Jeff Barry; Ellie Greenwich.
Also see GREENWICH, Ellie

RAINES, Rita
Singles: 7-Inch
DEED: *56* 4-6

RAINMAKERS
Singles: 7-Inch
MERCURY: *86* 1-3

LPs: 10/12-Inch 33rpm
MERCURY: 86-87 .... $5-8

RAINWATER, Marvin
Singles: 78rpm
CORAL: 56 3-6
MGM: 55 3-6
Singles: 7-Inch
BRAVE: 63-67 2-4
CORAL: 56 5-10
HILLTOP: 5-10
MGM (12000 & 12100 series): 55 4-8
MGM (12200 series): 56 15-25
MGM (12300 series): 56 8-15
MGM (12400 through 12800
  series): 57-60 4-8
MGM (12900 series): 60 3-5
NU TRAYL: 76 2-3
UNITED ARTISTS: 65-66 2-4
WARNER BROS: 70 2-3
WARWICK: 61 5-8
EPs: 7-Inch 33/45rpm
MGM: 57 10-20
LPs: 10/12-Inch 33rpm
CROWN: 10-15
MGM (3500 & 3700 series): 57-58 50-75
MGM (4000 series): 62 40-50
MOUNT VERNON: 8-10
SPINORAMA: 8-10

RAINWATER, Marvin, & Connie Francis
Singles: 78rpm
MGM: 57 4-6
Singles: 7-Inch
MGM: 57 4-8
Also see FRANCIS, Connie
Also see RAINWATER, Marvin

RAINY DAZE
Singles: 7-Inch
CHICORY: 67 6-10
UNI: 67 3-5
WHITE WHALE: 68 3-5

Ram Jam

LPs: 10/12-Inch 33rpm
UNI: 67 .... $12-15

RAITT, Bonnie
Singles: 7-Inch
WARNER BROS: 72-86 1-3
LPs: 10/12-Inch 33rpm
WARNER BROS: 71-86 5-12

RAITT, Bonnie / Gilley's "Urban Cowboy" Band
Singles: 7-Inch
FULL MOON/ASYLUM: 80 1-3
Picture Sleeves
FULL MOON/ASYLUM: 80 1-3
Also see RAITT, Bonnie

RAKE
Singles: 7-Inch
PROFILE: 83 1-3

RALKE, Don
(Big Sound Of Don Ralke)
Singles: 78rpm
CROWN: 55 2-4
Singles: 7-Inch
CROWN: 55 2-4
DRUM BOY: 66 2-3
REAL: 56 2-4
WARNER BROS: 59-64 2-4
LPs: 10/12-Inch 33rpm
CROWN: 55 8-15
WARNER BROS: 59-60 8-15

RALPH, Sheryl Lee
Singles: 12-Inch 33/45rpm
NYM: 84-85 4-6
Singles: 7-Inch
NYM: 84-85 1-3

RAM JAM
Singles: 12-Inch 33/45rpm
EPIC: 77 6-10
Singles: 7-Inch
EPIC: 77-78 2-3
LPs: 10/12-Inch 33rpm
EPIC: 77-78 6-10
Also see LEMON PIPERS

RAMA
Singles: 12-Inch 33/45rpm
SUGARSCOOP: 84 4-6

RAMATAM
Singles: 7-Inch
ATLANTIC: 72-73 2-4
LPs: 10/12-Inch 33rpm
ATLANTIC: 72-73 10-12
Also see PINERA, Mike

RAMBEAU, Eddie
Singles: 7-Inch
BELL: 69 . . . .$2-4
DYNA VOICE: 65-66 3-5
SWAN: 61-62 3-5
20TH CENTURY-FOX: 64 3-5
VIRGO: 73 1-3
LPs: 10/12-Inch 33rpm
DYNO VOICE: 65 15-20
Also see MARCY JO & EDDIE RAMBEAU

RAMBLERS
Singles: 7-Inch
ADDIT: 60 5-8

RAMBLERS
Singles: 7-Inch
ALMONT: 64 4-8
SIDEWINDERS: 64 4-8

RAMIN, Sid, & Orchestra
LPs: 10/12-Inch 33rpm
RCA VICTOR: 63 5-10

RAMONES
Singles: 7-Inch
RSO: 81 2-4
SIRE: 76-80 4-6
Picture Sleeves
SIRE: 77 4-8
EPs: 7-Inch
SIRE: 79 5-8
(Promotional issues only.)
LPs: 10/12-Inch 33rpm
SIRE (Colored vinyl): 78 15-20
SIRE (Black vinyl, except 7528): 76-87 5-8
SIRE: 88 8-12
SIRE (7528; "Leave Home"): 77 15-25
(With the track "Carbona Not Glue.")

RAMRODS
Singles: 7-Inch
AMY: 60-62 4-6
PLYMOUTH: 66 3-5

RAMRODS
Singles: 7-Inch
QUEEN: 62 3-6
R&H: 63 4-8
Also see ROCKIN' RAMRODS

RAMRODS
Singles: 7-Inch
RAMPAGE: 72 2-4

RANDAZZO, Teddy
(Teddy Randazzo & All 6)
Singles: 7-Inch
ABC-PARAMOUNT: 59-62 3-6
COLPIX: 62-63 3-6

DCP: 64-66 . . . .$3-6
MGM: 66 3-5
VERVE/FOLKWAYS: 67 3-5
VIK: 58 4-8
LPs: 10/12-Inch 33rpm
ABC-PARAMOUNT: 61-62 15-25
MGM: 66 15-20
Also see CHUCKLES
Also see THREE CHUCKLES

RAN-DELLS
Singles: 7-Inch
R.S.V.P.: 64 5-8
CHAIRMAN: 63-64 4-8
Picture Sleeves
CHAIRMAN: 63 10-20

RANDOLPH, Boots
(Homer Randolph)
Singles: 7-Inch
MONUMENT: 61-83 2-4
PALO ALTO: 1-3
RCA VICTOR: 59-61 3-5
Picture Sleeves
MONUMENT: 64 3-5
LPs: 10/12-Inch 33rpm
CAMDEN: 64 12-15
GUEST STAR: 64 5-10
MONUMENT (Except 8000 & 18000
series): 71-82 5-12
MONUMENT (8000 & 18000
series): 63-71 8-18
PALO ALTO: 5-8
RCA VICTOR: 60 15-25
Also see HIRT, Al, & Boots Randolph
Also see KNIGHTSBRIDGE STRINGS
Also see PRESLEY, Elvis
Also see RANDOLPH, Randy

RANDOLPH, Cookie "Chainsaw"
Singles: 7-Inch
93-KDKB: 86 2-4

RANDOLPH, Randy
(Homer Randolph)
Singles: 7-Inch
RCA VICTOR: 58-59 4-6
Also see RANDOLPH, Boots

RANDY & THE RAINBOWS
Singles: 7-Inch
B.T. PUPPY: 67 5-8
LAURIE: 1-3
MIKE: 66 5-8
RUST (Blue label): 63 20-25
RUST (Rust & white label): 63 10-15
LPs: 10/12-Inch 33rpm
AMBIENT SOUND: 82 8-10

MAGIC CARPET: $8-10
Members: Dominick "Randy" Safuto; Frank
Safuto; Mike Zero; Sal Zero; Ken Arcipowski.

RANK & FILE
Singles: 7-Inch
SLASH: *83-84* 1-3
LPs: 10/12-Inch 33rpm
SLASH: *83-84* 5-8
Also see SEATRAIN

RANKIN, Billy
Singles: 7-Inch
A&M: *84* 1-3
LPs: 10/12-Inch 33rpm
A&M: *84* 5-8

RANKIN, Kenny
(Ken Rankin)
Singles: 7-Inch
ABC-PARAMOUNT: *61* 3-5
COLUMBIA: *63-65* 3-5
DECCA: *58-60* 4-6
LITTLE DAVID: *73-77* 2-3
MERCURY: *68-69* 2-4
Picture Sleeves
MERCURY: *68* 3-5
LPs: 10/12-Inch 33rpm
ATLANTIC: *80* 5-8
LITTLE DAVID: *72-75* 8-10
MERCURY: *67-69* 10-15

RANKING ROGER
LPs: 10/12-Inch 33rpm
I.R.S.: *88* 5-8

RAPPIN' DUKE
Singles: 12-Inch 33/45rpm
TOMMY BOY: *86* 4-6

RARE BIRD
Singles: 7-Inch
ABC: *72* 2-4
POLYDOR: *73-74* 2-4
PROBE: *70* 2-4
LPs: 10/12-Inch 33rpm
ABC: *72* 8-10
POLYDOR: *73-74* 8-10
PROBE: *70* 10-12

RARE EARTH
Singles: 7-Inch
MOTOWN: *81* 1-3
PRODIGAL: *78* 2-3
RARE EARTH: *70-76* 2-4
VERVE: *68* 3-5
Picture Sleeves
RARE EARTH: *71-73* 2-4

LPs: 10/12-Inch 33rpm
MOTOWN: *81* $5-8
PRODIGAL: *77-78* 5-8
RARE EARTH (Except 507): *70-76* 8-10
RARE EARTH (507; "Get Ready"): *69* ...8-12
(With standard square cover.)
RARE EARTH (507; "Get Ready"): *69* ..20-40
(With rounded-top cover. Promotional issue.)
VERVE: *68* 12-15

RARE ESSENCE
Singles: 12-Inch 33/45rpm
FANTASY: *82* 4-6

RASCALS
(Young Rascals)
Singles: 7-Inch
ATLANTIC: *65-70* 3-6
COLUMBIA: *71-72* 2-4
Picture Sleeves
ATLANTIC: *66-70* 4-8
LPs: 10/12-Inch 33rpm
ATLANTIC (137; "Freedom Suite"): *69* ..20-30
(Promotional issue only.)
ATLANTIC (901; "Freedom Suite"): *69* ..12-15
ATLANTIC (8123 through 8148): *66-67* .15-25
ATLANTIC (8169 through 8276): *68-71* .10-15
COLUMBIA: *71-72* 8-10
PAIR: *86* 6-10
RHINO: *87* 5-8
Members: Felix Cavaliere; Ed Brigati; Dino Danel-
li; Gene Cornish.
Also see BULLDOG
Also see CAVALIERE, Felix
Also see FOTOMAKER
Also see SWEET INSPIRATIONS

RASPBERRIES
Singles: 7-Inch
CAPITOL: *72-74* 3-5
Picture Sleeves
CAPITOL: *72-73* 5-10
LPs: 10/12-Inch 33rpm
CAPITOL (11036 through 11329): *72-74* .15-20
CAPITOL (11524; "Raspberries'
Best"): *76* 8-10
CAPITOL (16095; "Raspberries'
Best"): *80* 5-8
Members: Eric Carmen; Wally Bryson; Dave Smal-
ley; Jim Bonfanti.
Also see CARMEN, Eric
Also see FOTOMAKER

RATCHELL
Singles: 7-Inch
DECCA: *72* 2-4
LPs: 10/12-Inch 33rpm
DECCA: *71-72* 10-12

RATIONALS

Singles: 7-Inch

A SQUARE: *66* **$8-15**
CAMEO: *66-67* **5-10**
CAPITOL: *68* **5-10**
CREWE: *69* **4-8**
DANBY'S: **10-20**
GENESIS: **4-8**

LPs: 10/12-Inch 33rpm

CREWE: *69* **15-20**

RATT

Singles: 7-Inch

ATLANTIC: *84-87* **1-3**
TIME COAST: *83-84* **1-3**

LPs: 10/12-Inch 33rpm

ATLANTIC: *84-88* **5-8**
TIME COAST: *83-84* **5-8**

RATTLES

Singles: 7-Inch

LONDON: **3-5**
MERCURY: *66* **5-10**
PROBE: *70* **3-5**

LPs: 10/12 Inch 33rpm

MERCURY: *67* **15-25**
Also see SEARCHERS / Rattles

RAVAN, Genya

Singles: 7-Inch

COLUMBIA: *71-72* **2-4**
DE LITE: *75* **2-3**
DUNHILL: *73* **2-4**
20TH CENTURY-FOX: *78-79* **2-3**

LPs: 10/12-Inch 33rpm

COLUMBIA: *72* **8-10**
DUNHILL: *73* **8-10**
20TH CENTURY-FOX: *78-79* **5-8**
Also see TEN WHEEL DRIVE

RAVEN

Singles: 7-Inch

RAMPART: **1-3**

LPs: 10/12-Inch 33rpm

ATLANTIC: *85-86* **5-8**

RAVEN, Marcia

Singles: 12-Inch 33/45rpm

PROFILE: *83* **4-6**

Singles: 7-Inch

PROFILE: *83* **1-3**

RAVENS

Singles: 78rpm

ARGO: *56-57* **5-10**
CHECKER: *57* **5-10**
COLUMBIA: *50-51* **40-80**
HUB: *46* **20-40**

KING: *48* **$20-30**
JUBILEE: *55-56* **5-10**
MERCURY (5000 series,
except 5764): *52* **10-20**
MERCURY (5764; "There's No
Use Pretending"): *51* **30-60**
MERCURY (8000 series): *51-52* **15-25**
MERCURY (70060; "Don't Mention
My Name"): *52* **20-40**
MERCURY (70119 through
70554): *53-55* **15-25**
OKEH: *51-52* **40-80**
NATIONAL: *47-51* **20-40**
RENDITION: *51* **15-25**

Singles: 7-Inch

ARGO (5255; "Kneel & Pray"): *56* **20-25**
ARGO (5261; "A Simple Prayer"): *56* ... **25-35**
ARGO (5276; "That'll Be The Day"): *57* **10-20**
ARGO (5284; "Here Is My Heart"): *57* .. **10-20**
CHECKER: *57* **5-10**
COLUMBIA (1-903; "Time Takes
Care Of Everything"): *50* **250-350**
(Compact 33 Single.)
COLUMBIA (6-903; "Time Takes
Care Of Everything"): *50* **200-300**
COLUMBIA (1-925; "My Baby's
Gone"): *50* **250-350**
(Compact 33 Single.)
COLUMBIA (6-925; "My Baby's
Gone"): *50* **200-300**
COLUMBIA (39112; "You Don't Have To
Drop A Heart To Break It"): *51* **200-300**
COLUMBIA (39194; "You're Always
In My Dreams"): *51* **200-300**
COLUMBIA (39408; "You Foolish
Thing"): *51* **450-600**
JUBILEE: *55-56* **10-20**
MERCURY (5000 series,
except 5764): *52* **35-50**
MERCURY (5764; "There's No
Use Pretending"): *51* **100-200**
MERCURY (8000 series): *51-52* **25-40**
MERCURY (70060; "Don't Mention
My Name"): *52* **50-75**
MERCURY (70119 through
70240): *53-54* **35-50**
MERCURY (70307 through
70554): *54-55* **35-50**
NATIONAL: *50-51* **450-600**
OKEH (Except 6888): *51* **300-450**
OKEH (6888; "Mam'selle"): *52* **200-300**
SAVOY: *58* **5-10**
TOP RANK: *59* **4-8**
VIRGO: *72* **1-3**

EPs: 7-Inch 33/45rpm
KING (310; "Bye Bye Baby
 Blues"): *55* $250-350
RENDITION (104; "Ol' Man
 River"): *52* 300-450
LPs: 10/12-Inch 33rpm
HARLEM HITPARADE: *75* 10-12
REGENT (Green label): 25-35
REGENT (Red label): 15-25
SAVOY: *78* 10-12
 Members: Warren Suttles; Ollie Jones; Joe Van
 Loan; Jimmy Ricks; Leonard Puzey; Maithe Mar-
 shall; Joe Medlin; Louis Heyward; James Stewart;
 Louis Frazier; Tom Evans; James Van Loan; David
 Bowers; Paul Van Loan; Rich Cannon.
 Also see CUES

RAVENS & Dinah Washington
Singles: 78rpm
MERCURY (8257; "Out In The
 Cold Again"): *51* 15-25
Singles: 7-Inch
MERCURY (8257; "Out In The
 Cold Again"): *51* 40-60
 Also see WASHINGTON, Dinah

RAVENS / Three Clouds
Singles: 78rpm
KING: *48-49* 15-25
 Also see RAVENS

RAW SILK
Singles: 7-Inch
WEST END: *82* 1-3

RAWLS, Lou
Singles: 12-Inch 33/45rpm
PHILADELPHIA INT'L: *79* 4-6
Singles: 7-Inch
ARISTA: *75* 2-3
BELL: *74* 2-3
CANDIX: *60-61* 3-5
CAPITOL: *61-70* 2-5
EPIC: *82-85* 1-3
GAMBLE & H: *87* 1-3
MGM: *71-73* 2-3
PHILADELPHIA INT'L: *76-81* 1-3
SHAR-DEE: *60* 4-6
Picture Sleeves
CAPITOL: *67* 3-5
LPs: 10/12-Inch 33rpm
ALLEGIANCE: *84* 5-8
BELL: *74* 8-10
CAPITOL (Except 1700 through
 2900 series): *69-77* 5-12
CAPITOL (1700 through 2900
 series): *63-68* 10-25

EPIC: *82-83* $5-8
GAMBLE & HUFF: *88* 5-8
MGM: *71-73* 8-10
PHILADELPHIA INT'L: *76-80* 5-8
POLYDOR: *76* 8-10
 Also see COOKE, Sam
 Also see PHILADELPHIA INTERNATION-
 AL ALL STARS
 Also see VEGA, Tata

RAWLS, Lou, & Les McCann Ltd.
Singles: 7-Inch
CAPITOL: *62* 3-5
LPs: 10/12-Inch 33rpm
CAPITOL: *75* 5-8
(With an "SM" prefix.)
CAPITOL: *62* 20-30
(With a "T" or "ST" prefix.)
 Also see McCANN, Les
 Also see RAWLS, Lou

RAY, Baby: see BABY RAY

RAY, Diane
Singles: 7-Inch
MERCURY: *63-64* 3-5
Picture Sleeves
MERCURY: *63* 8-15
LPs: 10/12-Inch 33rpm
MERCURY: *64* 20-25

RAY, Don
Singles: 7-Inch
POLYDOR: *78* 2-3
LPs: 10/12-Inch 33rpm
POLYDOR: *78* 5-8

RAY, Harry
Singles: 7-Inch
SUGAR HILL: *82-83* 1-3
LPs: 10/12-Inch 33rpm
SUGAR HILL: *83* 5-8
 Also see RAY, GOODMAN & BROWN

RAY, James
Singles: 7-Inch
CAPRICE: *61-62* 3-6
CONGRESS: *63-64* 3-5
DYNAMIC: *62* 3-5
LPs: 10/12-Inch 33rpm
CAPRICE: *62* 35-50
 Also see GRANT, Janie

RAY, Johnnie
(Johnnie Ray & The Four Lads)
Singles: 78rpm
COLUMBIA: *57* 3-6
OKEH: *52* 3-6

XYZ (Except 100 & 102): *58-61* $4-8
XYZ (100; "My Steady Girl"): *57* 10-20
XYZ (102; "Silhouettes"): *57* 10-20
Singles: 7-Inch
ABKCO: 1-3
AMY: *64* 3-5
ARGO: 3-5
CAMEO: *57* 5-10
CHESS: *55-57* 8-12
PERRI (1004; "Are You
  Happy Now?"): *62* 15-20
(With Frankie Valli.)
XYZ (Except 100 & 102): *58-61* 8-12
XYZ (100; "My Steady Girl"): *57* 25-40
XYZ (102; "Silhouettes"): *57* 25-40
EPs: 7-Inch 33/45rpm
CHESS (5120; "The Rays"): *58* 100-150
Member: Hal Miller.

RAYS
Singles: 7-Inch
EMI-MANHATTAN: *88* 1-3

RAZE
Singles: 7-Inch
COLUMBIA: *88* 1-3

RAZOR'S EDGE
Singles: 7-Inch
POW: *66* 6-12

RAZZY: see BAILEY, Razzy

REA, Chris
Singles: 7-Inch
COLUMBIA: *82* 1-3
MOTOWN: *87* 1-3
RCA VICTOR: *84* 1-3
UNITED ARTISTS: *78-79* 2-3
Picture Sleeves
UNITED ARTISTS: *78* 2-3
LPs: 10/12-Inch 33rpm
COLUMBIA: *80-82* 5-8
RCA VICTOR: *84* 5-8
UNITED ARTISTS: *79* 5-8
  Also see WILLIE & THE POOR BOYS

READ, John Dawson
Singles: 7-Inch
CHRYSALIS: *75* 2-4
LPs: 10/12-Inch 33rpm
CHRYSALIS: *75-76* 5-10

READY FOR THE WORLD
Singles: 12-Inch 33/45rpm
MCA: *84-86* 4-6
Singles: 7-Inch
MCA: *84-88* 1-3

LPs: 10/12-Inch 33rpm
MCA: *86-88* $5-8

REAL LIFE
Singles: 12-Inch 33/45rpm
CURB/MCA: *83-86* 4-6
Singles: 7-Inch
CURB/MCA: *83-86* 1-3
LPs: 10/12-Inch 33rpm
CURB/MCA: *83-86* 5-8

REAL ROXANNE
(With Hitman Howie Tee)
Singles: 12-Inch 33/45rpm
SELECT: *85-86* 4-6
Singles: 7-Inch
SELECT: *88* 1-3
LPs: 10/12-Inch 33rpm
SELECT: *88* 5-8

REAL THING
Singles: 12-Inch 33/45rpm
BELIEVE IN A DREAM: *81* 4-6
EPIC: *79* 4-6
Singles: 7-Inch
BELIEVE IN A DREAM: *81* 1-3
EPIC: *79* 1-3
UNITED ARTISTS: *76-77* 2-3
WHIZ: *69* 2-4
LPs: 10/12-Inch 33rpm
UNITED ARTISTS: *76* 5-10

REAL TO REEL
Singles: 12-Inch 33/45rpm
ARISTA: *83-84* 4-6
Singles: 7-Inch
ARISTA: *83-84* 1-3
LPs: 10/12-Inch 33rpm
ARISTA: *83* 5-8

REAVES, Paulette
Singles: 7-Inch
BLUE CANDLE: *77-78* 2-3

REBELS
Singles: 7-Inch
MAR-LEE (0094; "Wild
  Weekend"): *60* 15-20
SWAN: *62-63* 8-10
  Also see BUFFALO REBELS
  Also see ROCKIN' REBELS

REBENNACK, Mac
Singles: 7-Inch
A.F.O.: *62* 5-10
ACE: *61* 10-15
REX: *59* 15-20
  Also see DR. JOHN

RECORD, Eugene
Singles: 12-Inch 33/45rpm
WARNER BROS: 79 ....$4-6
Singles: 7-Inch
WARNER BROS: 77-79 2-3
LPs: 10/12-Inch 33rpm
WARNER BROS: 77-79 5-8
Also see CHI-LITES

RECORDS
Singles: 7-Inch
VIRGIN: 79-81 2-3
Picture Sleeves
VIRGIN: 79-81 2-3
EPs: 7-Inch 33/45rpm
VIRGIN: 79 3-5
(Issued as a bonus with Virgin LP 13130, *The Records*.)
LPs: 10/12-Inch 33rpm
VIRGIN: 79-82 8-10

RED HOT CHILI PEPPERS
Singles: 12-Inch 33/45rpm
EMI AMERICA: 85 4-6
Singles: 7-Inch
EMI AMERICA: 84-85 1-3
LPs: 10/12-Inch 33rpm
EMI AMERICA: 84-85 5-8
EMI MANHATTAN: 87 5-8

RED RIDER
Singles: 7-Inch
CAPITOL: 80-84 1-3
Picture Sleeves
CAPITOL: 80-84 1-3
LPs: 10/12-Inch 33rpm
CAPITOL: 80-83 5-8
Member: Tom Cochrane.
Also see COCHRANE, Tom, & Red Rider

RED RIVER DAVE
(Dave McEnery)
Singles: 7-Inch
COPYRIGHT: 61 2-4
SAVOY: 60-65 2-4
EPs: 7-Inch 33/45rpm
VARSITY: 5-10
LPs: 10/12-Inch 33rpm
BLUEBONNET: 6-12
CONTINENTAL: 62 10-15
PLACE: 8-10
SUTTON: 5-8

RED ROCKERS
Singles: 12-Inch 33/45rpm
COLUMBIA: 84-85 4-6
Singles: 7-Inch
COLUMBIA: 84-85 1-3

LPs: 10/12-Inch 33rpm
COLUMBIA: 83 ....$5-8

RED 7
LPs: 10/12-Inch 33rpm
BCA: 87 5-8

REDBONE
Singles: 7-Inch
EPIC: 71-74 2-4
RCA VICTOR: 78 2-3
LPs: 10/12-Inch 33rpm
ACCORD: 82 5-8
EPIC: 70-75 8-12
RCA VICTOR: 77 8-10
Members: Pat Vegas; Lolly Vegas.

REDBONE, Leon
Singles: 78rpm
WARNER BROS: 78 5-10
(Promotional issue only.)
Singles: 7-Inch
EMERALD CITY: 81 2-4
WARNER BROS: 77-78 3-5
LPs: 10/12-Inch 33rpm
ACCORD: 82 8-12
EMERALD CITY: 81 8-12
WARNER BROS: 77-78 10-20

REDD, Sharon
Singles: 12-Inch 33/45rpm
PRELUDE: 81-83 4-6
Singles: 7-Inch
COLUMBIA: 78 2-3
PRELUDE: 81-83 1-3
VEEP: 67 3-5
LPs: 10/12-Inch 33rpm
COLUMBIA: 78 5-10
PRELUDE: 82 5-8

REDD, Sharon, Ula Hedwig, & Charlotte Crossley
Singles: 7-Inch
COLUMBIA: 77-78 2-3
Also see REDD, Sharon

REDD HOT
(Redd Hott)
Singles: 7-Inch
VENTURE: 81-82 1-3
Members: Kevin "Flash" Ferrell; Robert Parson; Daryl Simmons; Greg Russell; De Morris Smith.
Also see MANCHILD

REDD KROSS
LPs: 10/12-Inch 33rpm
BIT: 87 5-8
POSH BOY: 85-86 5-8

REDDING, Gene
Singles: 7-Inch
HAVEN: *74* $2-3

REDDING, Otis
(Otis Redding & The Pinetoppers; Otis Redding
& The Pinetones)
Singles: 7-Inch
ATCO: *68-71* 2-5
BETHLEHEM: *64* 5-10
CONFEDERATE: *62* 8-15
FINER ARTS: 4-8
KING: *68* 2-4
ORBIT: *61* 20-30
STAX: *68* 3-5
STONE: 3-6
VOLT: *62-68* 4-8
EPs: 7-Inch 33/45rpm
VOLT: *66* 12-15
LPs: 10/12-Inch 33rpm
ATCO (161; "Pain In
My Heart"): *64* 40-80
ATCO (200 series): *68-69* 8-15
ATCO (300 series): *70* 8-12
ATCO (801; "Best Of Otis Redding"): *72* 10-20
(Currently available, using the same catalog num-
ber.)
ATLANTIC: *82* 5-8
VOLT: *65-68* 20-45
  Also see BAR-KAYS
  Also see OTIS & CARLA

REDDING, Otis / Little Joe Curtis
LPs: 10/12-Inch 33rpm
ALSHIRE: *68* 6-10
SOMERSET: *68* 6-10
  Also see REDDING, Otis

REDDING, Otis / Jimi Hendrix
LPs: 10/12-Inch 33rpm
REPRISE: *70* 8-12
  Also see HENDRIX, Jimi
  Also see REDDING, Otis

REDDINGS
Singles: 12-Inch 33/45rpm
BELIEVE IN A DREAM: *83* 4-6
Singles: 7-Inch
BELIEVE IN A DREAM: *80-83* 1-3
POLYDOR: *85-88* 1-3
LPs: 10/12-Inch 33rpm
BELIEVE IN A DREAM: *80-83* 5-8
POLYDOR: *85-88* 5-8
Members: Otis Redding III; Dexter Redding; Mark
Locket.

REDDS & THE BOYS
Singles: 7-Inch
4TH & BROADWAY: *85* $1-3

REDDY, Helen
Singles: 12-Inch 33/45rpm
CAPITOL: *79* 4-6
Singles: 7-Inch
CAPITOL: *71-81* 1-3
FONTANA: *68* 3-5
MCA: *81-83* 1-3
LPs: 10/12-Inch 33rpm
CAPITOL: *71-81* 5-10
MCA: *81-83* 5-8
  Also see PRESLEY, Elvis

REDEYE
Singles: 7-Inch
PENTAGRAM: *70-71* 2-4
LPs: 10/12-Inch 33rpm
PENTAGRAM: *70-71* 10-12
Members: Doug "Red" Mark; David Hodkins;
Bobby Bereman; Bill Kman.
  Also see SUNSHINE COMPANY

REDJACKS
Singles: 7-Inch
APT: *58* 8-10
OKLAHOMA: *58* 10-15

REDNOW, Eivets
(Stevie Wonder)
Singles: 7-Inch
GORDY: *68* 4-6
LPs: 10/12-Inch 33rpm
GORDY: *68* 25-30
  Also see WONDER, Stevie

REDWAY, Michael
(Mike Redway)
Singles: 7-Inch
LONDON: *64* 3-5
PHILIPS: *73* 2-4

REED, Clarence: see REID, Clarence

REED, Dan, Network
Singles: 7-Inch
MERCURY: *88* 1-3
LPs: 10/12-Inch 33rpm
MERCURY: *88* 5-8

REED, Dean
Singles: 7-Inch
CAPITOL: *59-61* 5-8
IMPERIAL: *61* 3-5

REED, Denny
Singles: 7-Inch
ASPIRE: *77* 2-3
DOT: *62* 3-5

MCI: *60* $10-12
TREY: *60-61* 8-15
TOWER: *65* 3-5
UNITED ARTISTS: *61* 5-8

REED, Jerry
(Jerry Reed & The Hully Girlies)
Singles: 78rpm
CAPITOL: *55-56* 4-8
Singles: 7-Inch
CAPITOL: *55-56* 5-10
COLUMBIA: *61-63* 3-6
NRC: *59* 4-6
RCA VICTOR (Except 8500 through
9700): *69-85* 1-3
RCA VICTOR (8500 through
9700): *65-69* 3-5
Picture Sleeves
COLUMBIA: *61* 5-10
RCA VICTOR: *72-85* 1-3
LPs: 10/12-Inch 33rpm
CAMDEN: *72-74* 6-12
HARMONY: *71* 8-10
PICKWICK/HILLTOP: 6-10
RCA VICTOR (Except LPM & LSP
series): *73-83* 5-10
RCA VICTOR (LPM & LSP
series): *67-73* 8-15
Also see HART, Freddie / Sammi Smith /
Jerry Reed
Also see JENNINGS, Waylon, & Jerry Reed
Also see PRESLEY, Elvis

REED, Jerry, & Chet Atkins
LPs: 10/12-Inch 33rpm
RCA VICTOR: *72* 8-12
Also see ATKINS, Chet
Also see REED, Jerry

REED, Jimmy
Singles: 7-Inch
ABC: *73* 1-3
ABC-PARAMOUNT: *66* 2-4
BLUESWAY: *67* 2-4
CHANCE (1142; "High And
Lonesome"): *53* 250-350
(Reissue of Vee Jay 100.)
COLLECTABLES: 1-3
EXODUS: *66* 3-5
TRIP: 1-3
VEE JAY (100; "High And
Lonesome"): *53* 125-175
(Black vinyl.)
VEE JAY (100; "High And
Lonesome"): *53* 250-350
(Colored vinyl.)

VEE JAY (105; "I Found
My Baby"): *53* $100-150
(Black vinyl.)
VEE JAY (105; "I Found
My Baby"): *53* 200-300
(Colored vinyl.)
VEE JAY (119; "You Don't Have
To Go"): *54* 30-40
(Black vinyl.)
VEE JAY (119; "You Don't Have
To Go"): *54* 200-300
(Colored vinyl.)
VEE JAY (132; "Pretty Thing"): *55* 20-35
VEE JAY (153; "She Don't Want
Me No More"): *55* 20-30
VEE JAY (168 through 248): *56-57* 10-15
VEE JAY (253 through 298): *57-58* 5-10
VEE JAY (300 through 700 series): *59-65* . 3-6
LPs: 10/12-Inch 33rpm
BLUES ON BLUES: 8-10
BLUESWAY: *67-73* 8-12
BUDDAH: *69* 10-12
EVEREST: *69* 5-8
EXODUS: *66* 10-12
GNP/CRESCENDO: *74* 8-10
KENT: *69-71* 8-10
ROKER: 8-10
SUNSET: *68* 10-12
TRADITION: 5-8
TRIP: *71-78* 8-10
VEE JAY (Except 1004 through
1035): *62-65* 25-50
VEE JAY (1004 through
1035): *58-61* 30-60
VERSATILE: *78* 8-10
Also see MAYFIELD, Curtis
Also see UPCHURCH, Phil

REED, Lou
(Lou Reed & The Velvet Underground)
Singles: 12-Inch 33/45rpm
RCA VICTOR: *84* 4-6
Singles: 7-Inch
ARISTA: *76* 2-3
RCA VICTOR: *73-86* 2-4
LPs: 10/12-Inch 33rpm
ARISTA: *76-80* 5-8
PRIDE: *73* 8-10
RCA VICTOR (AFL1 series): *80-83* 5-8
RCA VICTOR (ANL1 series): *77* 5-8
RCA VICTOR (APL1 series): *73-77* 8-12
RCA VICTOR (AYL1 series): *80-83* 5-8
RCA VICTOR (CPL1 series): *74* 8-10
RCA VICTOR (LSP series): *72* 10-12
Also see VELVET UNDERGROUND

REED, Vivian
Singles: 7-Inch
ATCO: *73* $2-3
EPIC: *68-69* 2-4
UNITED ARTISTS: *78-79* 1-3
LPs: 10/12-Inch 33rpm
EPIC: *69* 10-12
UNITED ARTISTS: *78* 5-8

REESE, Della
(Della Reese & The Meditation Singers)
Singles: 78rpm
JUBILEE: *57* 3-5
Singles: 7-Inch
ABC: *67-73* 1-3
ABC-PARAMOUNT: *65-66* 2-4
AVCO EMBASSY: *69-72* 2-3
CHI-SOUND: *77* 1-3
JUBILEE: *57-59* 3-5
LMI: *73* 1-3
RCA VICTOR: *59-64* 2-5
VIRGO: *72* 1-3
Picture Sleeves
RCA VICTOR: *60-63* 3-6
EPs: 7-Inch 33/45rpm
RCA VICTOR: *61* 5-10
LPs: 10/12-Inch 33rpm
ABC: *76* 5-8
ABC-PARAMOUNT: *65-67* 10-12
JUBILEE (1000 & 5000 series): *57-63* .. 15-20
JUBILEE (6000 series): *69* 8-12
LMI: *73* 5-10
RCA VICTOR (2000 through 4600
  series): *60-72* 8-18
SUNSET: *71* 6-10
Also see ANN-MARGRET / Kitty Kallen /
Della Reese

REEVES, Del
(Del Reeves & The Goodtime Charlies)
Singles: 7-Inch
CHART: *70* 2-3
COLUMBIA: *64* 2-4
DECCA: *61-62* 3-5
KOALA: *80-82* 1-3
LAS VEGAS: *59* 3-6
PEACH: *60* 3-5
PLAYBACK: *86* 1-3
REPRISE: *63* 2-5
UNITED ARTISTS (Except 800 & 900
  series): *66-78* 1-3
UNITED ARTISTS (800 & 900
  series): *66-76* 2-4
Picture Sleeves
KOALA: *80* 1-3
UNITED ARTISTS: *67* 2-5

LPs: 10/12-Inch 33rpm
KOALA: *79-80* $5-8
STARDAY: 5-8
SUNSET: *69-70* 6-10
UNITED ARTISTS (200 through 600
  series): *73-76* 6-10
UNITED ARTISTS (3000 & 6000
  series): *65-71* 8-18

REEVES, Del, & Bobby Goldsboro
Singles: 7-Inch
UNITED ARTISTS: *65-71* 3-5
LPs: 10/12-Inch 33rpm
UNITED ARTISTS: *68* 10-15
Also see GOLDSBORO, Bobby

REEVES, Del / Red Sovine
LPs: 10/12-Inch 33rpm
EXACT: *80* 5-8
Also see SOVINE, Red

REEVES, Del, & Billie Jo Spears
Singles: 7-Inch
UNITED ARTISTS: *76* 2-3
LPs: 10/12-Inch 33rpm
LIBERTY: *82* 5-8
UNITED ARTISTS: *76* 6-10
Also see REEVES, Del
Also see SPEARS, Billie Jo

REEVES, Dianne
Singles: 7-Inch
BLUE NOTE: *87-88* 1-3
LPs: 10/12-Inch 33rpm
BLUE NOTE: *88* 5-8

REEVES, Jim
Singles: 78rpm
ABBOTT: *53-55* 5-10
FABOR: *54* 4-8
RCA VICTOR: *55-57* 4-8
Singles: 7-Inch
ABBOTT (100 series): *53-55* 5-15
  (Black vinyl.)
ABBOTT (116; "Mexican Joe"): *53* 25-50
  (Colored vinyl.)
ABBOTT (3000 series): *55* 5-10
ABBOTT (4000 series): 4-6
FABOR: *54* 5-8
RCA VICTOR (0100 through 0800
  series): *69-74* 2-3
RCA VICTOR (6200 through 7500
  series): *55-59* 3-6
RCA VICTOR (7600 through 9900
  series): *59-71* 2-4
RCA VICTOR (10000 through 13000
  series): *75-84* 1-3

Picture Sleeves
RCA VICTOR (Except 8252): *60-65* **$4-8**
RCA VICTOR (8252; "Señor Santa
  Claus"): *63* **10-15**
EPs: 7-Inch 33/45rpm
RCA VICTOR (Except 1200
  series): *56-61* **10-20**
RCA VICTOR (1200 series): *56* **20-30**
LPs: 10/12-Inch 33rpm
ABBOTT (5001; "Jim Reeves
  Sings"): *56* **500-600**
CAMDEN (Except 500 & 600
  series): *64-73* **5-15**
CAMDEN (500 & 600 series): *60-63* **10-20**
GUEST STAR: *64* **10-15**
HISTORY OF COUNTRY MUSIC: *72* ... **6-10**
PAIR: *82* **8-12**
PICKWICK: *72* **5-10**
PICKWICK/HILLTOP: *74* **5-10**
RCA VICTOR (0039 through 4800
  series): *73-83* **5-10**
  (With an "AHL1," "ANL1," "APL1," "AYL1," or
  "CPL1" prefix.)
RCA VICTOR (0587; "Golden
  Collection"): **25-35**
  (A Special Products 5-LP set.)
RCA VICTOR (1256; "Singing Down
  The Lane"): *56* **100-125**
  (With an "LPM" prefix.)
RCA VICTOR (1400 & 1500 series): *57* . **35-50**
  (With an "LPM" prefix.)
RCA VICTOR (1600 through 1900
  series): *58* **25-35**
  (With an "LPM" prefix.)
RCA VICTOR (2000 through 2300
  series): *59-61* **15-25**
  (With an "LPM" or "LSP" prefix.)
RCA VICTOR (2400 through
  3903): *62-67* **10-20**
  (With an "LPM" or "LSP" prefix.)
RCA VICTOR (3987; "A Touch Of
  Sadness"): *68* **40-50**
  (With an "LPM" prefix. Monaural.)
RCA VICTOR (3987; "A Touch Of
  Sadness"): *68* **10-12**
  (With an "LSP" prefix. Stereo.)
RCA VICTOR (4000 through 4700): *68-72* **8-12**
  (With an "LSP" prefix.)
READER'S DIGEST (210; "Unforgettable
  Jim Reeves"): *76* **40-50**
  (A 6-LP set.)
  Also see CRAMER, Floyd
  Also see KERR, Anita
  Also see PRESLEY, Elvis / Hank Snow /
Eddy Arnold / Hank Snow

Jim Reeves

REEVES, Jim, & Patsy Cline
Singles: 7-Inch
MCA: *82* **$1-3**
RCA VICTOR: *81* **1-3**
LPs: 10/12-Inch 33rpm
MCA: *82* **5-8**
RCA VICTOR: *81* **5-8**
  Also see CLINE, Patsy

REEVES, Jim, & Dottie West
Singles: 7-Inch
RCA VICTOR: *64* **2-4**
  Also see REEVES, Jim
  Also see WEST, Dottie

REEVES, Martha
Singles: 12-Inch 33/45rpm
FANTASY: *78-79* **4-6**
Singles: 7-Inch
ARISTA: *75-77* **2-3**
FANTASY: *78-80* **1-3**
MCA: *74* **2-3**
LPs: 10/12-Inch 33rpm
ARISTA: *76* **8-10**
FANTASY: *78-79* **5-8**
MCA: *74* **8-10**
PHONORAMA: **5-8**
  Also see MARTHA & THE VANDELLAS

REFLECTIONS
Singles: 7-Inch
ABC-PARAMOUNT: *66* **3-5**
ERIC: **1-3**
GOLDEN WORLD: *64-65* **3-5**
LPs: 10/12-Inch 33rpm
GOLDEN WORLD: *64* **30-35**
  Members: Tony Micale; John Dean; Phil
  Castrodale; Dan Bennie; Ray Steinberg.

REFLECTIONS
Singles: 7-Inch
CAPITOL: *75-76* $2-3
Members: Herman Edwards; Josh Pridgen; Ed-
mund "Butch" Simmons; John Simmons.

RE-FLEX
Singles: 12-Inch 33/45rpm
CAPITOL: *83-84* 4-6
Singles: 7-Inch
CAPITOL: *83-84* 1-3
LPs: 10/12-Inch 33rpm
CAPITOL: *83* 5-8

REGAL DEWY
Singles: 12-Inch 33/45rpm
MILLENNIUM: *77* 5-10
Singles: 7-Inch
MILLENNIUM: *77* 2-4

REGAN, Joan
Singles: 78rpm
LONDON: *55* 2-4
Singles: 7-Inch
COLUMBIA: *66* 2-3
LONDON: *55* 2-4
Picture Sleeves
COLUMBIA: *66* 2-5

REGENTS
Singles: 7-Inch
ABC: *73* 1-3
COUSINS (1002;
"Barbara-Ann"): *61* 75-100
GEE: *61-62* 10-15
ROULETTE: 1-3
LPs: 10/12-Inch 33rpm
CAPITOL: *64* 20-25
GEE (706; "Barbara-Ann"): *61* 75-100
MURRAY HILL: 5-8

Members: Guy Villari; Sal Cuomo; Chuck Fassert;
Don Jacobucci; Tony Gravagna.

REGINA
Singles: 7-Inch
ATLANTIC: *86* $1-3
LPs: 10/12-Inch 33rpm
ATLANTIC: *86* 5-8

REID, Clarence
(Clarence Reed)
Singles: 7-Inch
ALSTON: *68-74* 2-4
DIAL: *64* 3-5
PHIL-L.A. OF SOUL: *67* 3-5
SELMA: *63* 4-6
TAY-STER: *67* 3-5
WAND: *65* 3-5
LPs: 10/12-Inch 33rpm
ATCO: *69* 10-12

REID, Terry
Singles: 7-Inch
ATLANTIC: *73* 2-3
CAPITOL: *78* 2-3
EPIC: *69* 2-4
LPs: 10/12-Inch 33rpm
ATLANTIC: *73* 8-10
CAPITOL: *78* 5-10
EPIC: *68-69* 10-15

REILLY, Mike
Singles: 7-Inch
PARAMOUNT: *70-71* 2-4

REINER, Carl, & Mel Brooks
LPs: 10/12-Inch 33rpm
CAPITOL (1600 series): *61* 15-25
CAPITOL (2900 series): *68* 8-12
WARNER BROS (2741; "2000 &
Thirteen"): *73* 5-10
WARNER BROS (2744; "2000 Years With
Carl Reiner & Mel Brooks"): *73* 15-25
(3-LP set.)
WORLD PACIFIC: *60* 20-30

REIRRUC, Det: see DET REIRRUC

REISMAN, Joe, & His Orchestra
Singles: 78rpm
RCA VICTOR: *55-57* 2-4
Singles: 7-Inch
LANDA: *61* 2-4
RCA VICTOR: *55-59* 2-4
ROULETTE: *59-60* 2-3
EPs: 7-Inch 33/45rpm
RCA VICTOR: *56* 4-8
LPs: 10/12-Inch 33rpm
CAMDEN: *72* 5-10

RCA VICTOR: *56* **$8-18**
ROULETTE: *59-60* **5-15**

REJOICE
Singles: 7-Inch
DUNHILL: *68-69* **3-5**
LPs: 10/12-Inch 33rpm
DUNHILL: *69* **10-15**

RENAISSANCE
Singles: 7-Inch
CAPITOL: *72-73* **2-4**
SIRE: *76-78* **2-3**
LPs: 10/12-Inch 33rpm
CAPITOL: *72-78* **8-12**
I.R.S.: *81-83* **5-8**
MFSL: *82* **20-40**
SIRE: *74-79* **8-10**
SINGCORD: *76-77* **8-10**
SOVEREIGN: *73* **8-12**
Members: Annie Haslam; Keith Relf.
Also see ARMAGEDDON
Also see HASLAM, Annie

RENAISSANCE
Singles: 7-Inch
RANWOOD: *71* **1-3**
LPs: 10/12-Inch 33rpm
RANWOOD: *70* **4-8**
Also see HASLAM, Annie

RENAY, Diane
Singles: 7-Inch
ATCO: *62-63* **3-5**
DICE: *87* **1-3**
ERIC: **1-3**
FONTANA: *69* **2-4**
MGM: *64* **3-5**
NEW VOICE: *65* **3-5**
20TH CENTURY-FOX: *64* **3-5**
UNITED ARTISTS: *66* **3-5**
LPs: 10/12-Inch 33rpm
20TH CENTURY-FOX: *64* **20-25**

RENDER, Rudy
Singles: 78rpm
LONDON: *49-51* **3-6**
Singles: 7-Inch
DOT: *60-61* **3-5**
EDISON INT'L: *59* **4-6**
LONDON: *51* **6-10**

RENE, Delia
Singles: 7-Inch
AIRWAVE: *81* **1-3**

RENE, Googie
(Googie Rene & His Combo)
Singles: 7-Inch
CLASS: *57-66* **$4-8**
KAPP: *62* **3-5**
NEW BAG: *67* **2-5**
REED: *60* **3-6**
RENDEZVOUS: *60* **2-4**
Picture Sleeves
RENDEZVOUS: *60* **5-10**
LPs: 10/12-Inch 33rpm
CLASS: *59-63* **15-20**

RENE, Henri, & His Orchestra
Singles: 78rpm
RCA VICTOR: *51-56* **2-4**
STANDARD: *52-53* **2-4**
Singles: 7-Inch
DECCA: *62* **2-4**
IMPERIAL: *59* **2-3**
RCA VICTOR: *51-56* **2-4**
STANDARD: *52-53* **2-4**
Picture Sleeves
RCA VICTOR: *55* **5-10**
EPs: 7-Inch 33/45rpm
CAMDEN: *54-57* **4-8**
RCA VICTOR: *53-56* **4-8**
LPs: 10/12-Inch 33rpm
CAMDEN: *54-57* **5-15**
KAPP: *67* **5-10**
RCA VICTOR (Except 3000
series): *56-61* **5-15**
RCA VICTOR (3000 series): *53* **10-20**
(10-Inch LPs.)
Also see BELL SISTERS

RENE & ANGELA
Singles: 12-Inch 33/45rpm
MERCURY: *85-86* **4-6**
Singles: 7-Inch
CAPITOL: *80-83* **1-3**
MERCURY: *85-86* **1-3**
LPs: 10/12-Inch 33rpm
CAPITOL: *80-83* **5-8**
MERCURY: *85-86* **5-8**

RENE & RAY
Singles: 7-Inch
DONNA: *62* **4-6**

RENE & RENE
Singles: 7-Inch
ABC: *73* **1-3**
ABC-PARAMOUNT: *65* **3-5**
ARU: *64* **3-5**
CERTRON: *71* **2-3**
COBRA: *65* **3-5**

COLUMBIA: *64* $3-5
EPIC: *69* 2-4
FALCON: *68* 3-5
JOX: *64-66* 5-10
WHITE WHALE: *68-69* 2-4
Picture Sleeves
COLUMBIA: *64* 3-6
LPs: 10/12-Inch 33rpm
EPIC: *69* 10-12
WHITE WHALE: *68* 10-15
Members: Rene Ornelas; J. Ramirez.

RENEGADE
Singles: 7-Inch
ALLIED ARTISTS: *86* 1-3
LPs: 10/12-Inch 33rpm
ALLIED ARTISTS: *86* 5-8
Member: Luis Cardenas.

RENFRO, Anthony C., Orchestra
Singles: 7-Inch
RENFRO: *76* 2-3

RENO, Mike, & Ann Wilson
Singles: 7-Inch
COLUMBIA: *84* 1-3
Also see LOVERBOY
Also see WILSON, Ann, & The Daybreaks

RENTE, Damon
LPs: 10/12-Inch 33rpm
TBA: *86* 5-8

REO, Diamond: see DIAMOND REO

REPARATA & THE DELRONS
Singles: 7-Inch
BIG TREE: *71* 2-4
KAPP: *69-70* 3-5
MALA: *67-68* 4-6
NAMI: *74* 2-4
POLYDOR: *75* 2-4
RCA VICTOR: *65-67* 4-6
WORLD ARTISTS: *64-65* 4-8
LPs: 10/12-Inch 33rpm
AVCO EMBASSY: *70* 10-12
WORLD ARTISTS (3006; "Whenever A
Teenager Cries"): *65* 30-60
Members: Mary Aiese; Sheila Reillie; Carol Drob-
nicki; Nanette Licari; Lorraine Mazzola; Cookie
Sirico.

REPLACEMENTS
Singles: 7-Inch
SIRE: *85-86* 1-3
TWIN TONE: *82-84* 2-3
LPs: 10/12-Inch 33rpm
SIRE: *85-87* 5-8
TWIN/TONE: *84* 5-8

Promotional LPs
SIRE ("Interview With Paul
Westerberg"): *85* $20-25
Member: Paul Westerberg.

RESTIVO, Johnny
Singles: 7-Inch
EPIC: *62* 3-5
RCA VICTOR (7000 series): *59-60* 4-6
(With a "47" prefix. Monaural.)
RCA VICTOR (7000 series): *59-60* 10-15
(With a "61" prefix. Stereo.)
20TH CENTURY-FOX: *61* 8-12
Picture Sleeves
RCA VICTOR: *60* 8-15
20TH CENTURY-FOX: *61* 10-20
LPs: 10/12-Inch 33rpm
RCA VICTOR (LPM-2149; "Oh
Johnny"): *59* 25-30
(Monaural.)
RCA VICTOR (LSP-2149; "Oh
Johnny"): *59* 40-45
(Stereo.)
Also see KING CURTIS

RESTLESS HEART
Singles: 7-Inch
RCA VICTOR: *85-88* 1-3
LPs: 10/12-Inch 33rpm
RCA VICTOR: *87-88* 5-8

RETURN TO FOREVER
Singles: 7-Inch
COLUMBIA: *77-79* 2-3
POLYDOR: *75* 2-4
LPs: 10/12-Inch 33rpm
COLUMBIA: *76-79* 5-8
ECM: *75* 8-10
POLYDOR: *73-75* 8-10
Members: Chick Corea; Lenny White; Stanley
Clarke; Al DiMeola.
Also see CLARKE, Stanley
Also see DI MEOLA, Al
Also see WHITE, Lenny

REUNION
Singles: 7-Inch
MR. G: *68* 3-5
RCA VICTOR: *74-75* 2-4
Also see OHIO EXPRESS

REVELATION
Singles: 7-Inch
COMBINE: *67* 4-6
HANDSHAKE: *80-82* 1-3
MERCURY: *70* 2-4
MUSIC FACTORY: *68* 3-5
RCA VICTOR: *79* 1-3

RSO: *76* $2-3
LPs: 10/12-Inch 33rpm
HANDSHAKE: *82* 5-8
MERCURY: *70* 8-10
RCA VICTOR: *79* 5-8

REVELS
Singles: 7-Inch
NORGOLDE (103; "Dead Man's
Stroll"): *59* 20-25
NORGOLDE (103; "Midnight Stroll"): *59* . 8-10
NORGOLDE (104; "Foo Man Choo"): *59* . 8-15

REVERE, Paul, & The Raiders
(Paul Revere & The Raiders Featuring Mark Lindsay; Raiders)
Singles: 7-Inch
COLUMBIA (10000 series): *75* 3-5
COLUMBIA (42814 through
44970): *63-69* 4-8
(Black vinyl.)
COLUMBIA (43000 series): *66* 10-20
(Colored vinyl. Promotional issues only.)
COLUMBIA (45082 through
45898): *69-73* 3-5
COLUMBIA (105499; "SS 396"/
"Corvair Baby"): *66* 8-10
(Promotional issue only.)
DRIVE: *76* 3-5
GARDENA: *60-62* 10-20
JERDEN (807; "So Fine"): *66* 10-15
SANDE (101; "Louie Louie"): *63* 20-30
20TH CENTURY-FOX: *76* 3-5
Picture Sleeves
COLUMBIA: *65-66* 6-12
LPs: 10/12-Inch 33rpm
BACK-TRAC: *85* 5-8
COLUMBIA (12; "Two Great
Selling LPs"): *69* 15-20
COLUMBIA (462; "Greatest Hits"): *67* .. 20-25
COLUMBIA (2307 through 2721): *65-67* 20-25
(Monaural.)
COLUMBIA (2755/9555; "Christmas
Present & Past"): *67* 40-80
(Monaural/stereo numbers.)
COLUMBIA (2805/9605; "Goin'
To Memphis"): *68* 20-25
(Monaural/stereo numbers.)
COLUMBIA (9107 through 9521): *65-67* 25-40
(Stereo.)
COLUMBIA (9665 through 9964): *68-70* 15-20
COLUMBIA (30000 series): *71-76* 6-15
HARMONY: *70-72* 10-15
GARDENA (1000; "Like Long
Hair"): *61* 250-325

JERDEN (7004; "In The
Beginning"): *66* $75-125
PICKWICK: 10-12
SANDE (1001; "Paul Revere &
The Raiders"): *63* 200-300
SEARS: 40-50
(Special Products Sears promotional issue.)
Members: Mark Lindsay; Freddy Weller; Paul
Revere; Keith Allison; Joe Correro Jr.; Carl Driggs;
Omar Martinez; Doug Heath; Ron Foos; Danny
Krause.
Also see BROTHERHOOD
Also see LINDSAY, Mark
Also see WELLER, Freddy

REVERE, Paul, & The Raiders / Cyrkle
Singles: 7-Inch
COLUMBIA (466; "SS 396"/
"Camaro"): *66* 8-10
(Special Products Chevrolet promotional issue
only.)
Picture Sleeves
COLUMBIA (466; "SS 396"/
"Camaro"): *66* 10-20
Also see CYRKLE
Also see REVERE, Paul, & The Raiders

REX, T.: see T-REX

REYNOLDS, Burt
Singles: 7-Inch
MCA: *80* 1-3
MERCURY: *73-74* 2-4
Picture Sleeves
MCA: *80* 1-3
LPs: 10/12-Inch 33rpm
MERCURY: *73* 8-10

REYNOLDS, Debbie
Singles: 78rpm
CORAL: *57* 3-5
Singles: 7-Inch
ABC: *74* 1-3
ABC-PARAMOUNT: *65* 2-4
BEVERLY HILLS: *72* 2-3
CORAL: *57-58* 3-6
DOT: *59-63* 3-5
JANUS: *70* 2-3
MCA: 2-3
MGM (11000 & 12000 series): *55* 4-8
MGM (13000 series): *63* 5-10
PARAMOUNT: *73* 1-3
Picture Sleeves
MGM: *63-66* 8-15
EPs: 7-Inch 33/45rpm
CORAL: *58* 10-20
MGM: *55* 10-20

LPs: 10/12-Inch 33rpm
DOT (Black vinyl): *59-63* $15-20
DOT (Colored vinyl): *63* 20-35
MGM: *60-66* 10-25
METRO: *65* 10-15
Also see CARPENTER, Carleton, & Debbie Reynolds

REYNOLDS, Jeannie
Singles: 7-Inch
CASABLANCA: *75* 2-4

REYNOLDS, Jody
(Jody Reynolds & The Storms)
Singles: 78rpm
DEMON: *58* 5-10
Singles: 7-Inch
ABC: *73* 1-3
BRENT: *63* 3-6
COLLECTABLES: 1-3
DEMON: *58-59* 5-10
INDIGO: *61* 5-10
PULSAR: *69* 2-4
SMASH: *63* 4-6
TITAN: *66* 3-6
LPs: 10/12-Inch 33rpm
TRU-GEMS: *78* 8-10
Also see CASEY, Al

REYNOLDS, Jody, & Bobbie Gentry
Singles: 7-Inch
TITAN: *67* 3-5
Also see GENTRY, Bobbie
Also see REYNOLDS, Jody

REYNOLDS, Jody / Olympics
Singles: 7-Inch
LIBERTY: *63* 2-4
TITAN: *62* 3-5
Also see OLYMPICS
Also see REYNOLDS, Jody

REYNOLDS, L. J.
(L. J. Reynolds & The Chocolate Syrup)
Singles: 12-Inch 33/45rpm
CAPITOL: *82* 4-6
Singles: 7-Inch
CAPITOL: *81-82* 1-3
FANTASY: *85-87* 1-3
LAW-TON: *71-72* 2-4
MAINSTREAM: *69* 2-4
MERCURY: *84* 1-3
LPs: 10/12-Inch 33rpm
CAPITOL: *81-82* 5-8
MERCURY: *84* 5-8
Also see DRAMATICS

REYNOLDS, Lawrence
Singles: 7-Inch
COLUMBIA: *72* $2-3
WARNER BROS: *69-70* 2-4
LPs: 10/12-Inch 33rpm
WARNER BROS: *69* 8-10

RHEIMS, Robert
Singles: 7-Inch
RHEIMS: *59* 2-3
EPs: 7-Inch 33/45rpm
RHEIMS: *59* 3-6
LPs: 10/12-Inch 33rpm
MISTLETOE: *75* 4-6
RHEIMS: *58-63* 5-10
UNITED ARTISTS: *72-74* 4-8

RHINOCEROS
Singles: 7-Inch
ELEKTRA: *69-70* 2-5
LPs: 10/12-Inch 33rpm
ELEKTRA: *68-70* 10-12

RHODES, Emitt
Singles: 7-Inch
DUNHILL: *70-73* 2-4
LPs: 10/12-Inch 33rpm
A&M: *70* 10-12
DUNHILL: *70-73* 8-10
Also see MERRY-GO-ROUND

RHODES, Todd
Singles: 78rpm
KING: *48-54* 5-10
MODERN: *49* 5-10
SENSATION (Except 6): *47-49* 10-20
SENSATION (6; "Blues For The
Red Boy"): *47* 20-30
VITACOUSTIC: *47* 10-20
Singles: 7-Inch
KING (4469; "Gin Gin Gin"): *51* 30-40
KING (4486; "Good Man"): *51* 10-20
KING (4509; "Your Daddy's Doggin'
Around"): *51* 15-25
(Black vinyl.)
KING (4509; "Your Daddy's Doggin'
Around"): *51* 35-45
(Colored vinyl.)
KING (4528; "Rocket 69"): *52* 35-50
KING (4556 through 4601): *52-53* 10-15
(LaVern Baker is the vocalist on one side of each
of the four King issues in the 4556-4601 series.)
KING (4648 through 4775): *53-54* 5-8
EPs: 7-Inch 33/45rpm
KING: *53* 25-35

LPs: 10/12-Inch 33rpm
KING (88; "Todd Rhodes Plays
The Hits"): **$75-100**
KING (658; "Dance Music"): *60* **35-45**
Also see BAKER, LaVern

RHYTHM CORPS
LPs: 10/12-Inch 33rpm
PASHA: *88* **5-8**

RHYTHM HERITAGE
Singles: 12-Inch 33/45rpm
ABC: *78* **4-6**
Singles: 7-Inch
ABC: *75-78* **2-3**
LPs: 10/12-Inch 33rpm
ABC: *76-77* **5-10**

RHYTHM MAKERS
Singles: 7-Inch
VIGOR: *76* **2-3**
LPs: 10/12-Inch 33rpm
VIGOR: *76* **8-10**

RHYZE
Singles: 7-Inch
SAM: *80* **1-3**
20TH CENTURY-FOX: *81* **1-3**
LPs: 10/12-Inch 33rpm
20TH CENTURY-FOX: *81* **5-8**

RIBBONS
Singles: 7-Inch
ERA: *72* **1-3**
MARSH: *63* **4-6**
PARKWAY: *64* **3-5**

RICE, Mack
(Sir Mack Rice)
Singles: 7-Inch
ATCO: *69* **2-4**
BLUE ROCK: *65* **3-5**
LUPINE: *64* **3-5**
MERCURY: *66* **3-5**
STAX: *67-78* **2-4**

RICH, Buddy
(Buddy Rich Band)
Singles: 7-Inch
ARGO: *61* **2-4**
CLEF: *54* **3-5**
EVEREST: *71* **1-3**
GROOVE MERCHANT: *74* **1-3**
MCA: *81* **1-3**
NORGRAN: *55-56* **3-5**
PACIFIC JAZZ: *66-67* **2-3**
RCA VICTOR: *76* **1-3**
EPs: 7-Inch 33/45rpm
NORGRAN: *54-56* **10-25**

LPs: 10/12-Inch 33rpm
ARGO: *61* **$15-25**
CLEF: *56* **50-75**
EMARCY: *65-76* **10-20**
GREAT AMERICAN
GRAMOPHONE: *78* **5-8**
GROOVE MERCHANT: *74-75* **5-10**
GRYPHON: *79* **5-8**
LIBERTY: *70* **8-12**
MCA: *81* **5-8**
MERCURY: *59-60* **20-40**
(Black label.)
MERCURY: *69* **8-12**
(Red label.)
NORGRAN (26; "Buddy Rich
Swingin'"): *54* **50-75**
NORGRAN (1000 series): *55-56* **25-50**
PACIFIC JAZZ (Except 10000
series): *66-70* **8-15**
PACIFIC JAZZ (10000 series): *81* **5-8**
PAUSA: **5-8**
RCA VICTOR: *72-77* **5-10**
ROOST: *66* **10-20**
TRIP: *76* **5-8**
VSP: *67* **8-12**
VERVE: *57-58* **20-40**
(Reads "Verve Records, Inc." at bottom of label.)
VERVE: *61-69* **10-25**
(Reads "MGM Records - A Division Of Metro-
Goldwyn-Mayer, Inc." at bottom of label.)
VERVE: *73-84* **5-10**
(Reads "Manufactured By MGM Record Corp." or
mentions either Polydor or Polygram at bottom of
label.)
WHO'S WHO IN JAZZ: *78* **5-8**
WING: *69* **6-12**
WORLD PACIFIC: *68* **8-12**
Also see TORME, Mel

RICH, Buddy, & Max Roach
LPs: 10/12-Inch 33rpm
MERCURY: *81* **5-8**
Also see RICH, Buddy

RICH, Charlie
Singles: 7-Inch
ARISTA: *80* **1-3**
COLUMBIA: *82* **1-3**
EPIC: *70-81* **1-3**
ELEKTRA: *78-81* **1-3**
GROOVE: *63-64* **3-5**
HI: *66-67* **3-5**
MERCURY: *73-74* **2-3**
PHILLIPS INT'L: *59-63* **6-10**
RCA VICTOR (Except 8000 series): *74-77* **2-4**
RCA VICTOR (8000 series): *64-65* **3-5**

SSS/SUN: $1-3
SMASH: *65-66* 3-5
UNITED ARTISTS: *78-80* 1-3
Picture Sleeves
GROOVE: *63* 5-10
EPs: 7-Inch 33/45rpm
EPIC (1099; "Silver
Linings"): *76* 5-10
(Promotional issue only.)
LPs: 10/12-Inch 33rpm
BUCKBOARD: 8-10
CAMDEN: *70-74* 8-10
EPIC (Except 139): *68-78* 8-12
EPIC (139; "Everything You
Wanted To Hear"): *76* 12-15
(Promotional issue only.)
ELEKTRA: *80* 5-8
51 WEST: 5-8
GROOVE: *64* 20-25
HARMONY: *73* 8-10
HI (Except 32037): *74-77* 8-10
HI (32037; "Charlie Rich"): *67* 12-15
HILLTOP: 8-10
MERCURY: *74* 10-12
PHILLIPS INT'L (1970; "Lonely
Weekends"): *60* 200-300
PHONORAMA: 5-8
POWER PAK: *74* 8-10
RCA VICTOR (Except 3000
series): *73-77* 8-10
RCA VICTOR (3000 series): *65-66* 15-20
SSS/SUN: *69-79* 5-8
SMASH: *65-66* 15-20
TRIP: *74* 8-10
UNITED ARTISTS: *78-79* 8-10
WING: *69* 10-12
Also see CASH, Johnny
Also see LEWIS, Jerry Lee, Carl Perkins &
Charlie Rich
Also see SHERIDAN, Bobby

RICHARD, Cliff
(Cliff Richard & The Drifters; Cliff Richard &
The Shadows)
Singles: 12-Inch 33/45rpm
EMI AMERICA: *83* 4-6
Singles: 7-Inch
ABC-PARAMOUNT: *59-61* 6-12
BIG TOP: *62* 4-6
CAPITOL: *59* 10-15
DOT: *62* 3-5
EMI AMERICA: *79-84* 1-3
EPIC: *63-67* 3-5
MONUMENT: *70-72* 2-4
ROCKET: *76-79* 2-3

SIRE: *73* $2-3
UNI: *68-69* 3-5
WARNER BROS: *69* 2-4
Picture Sleeves
EMI AMERICA: *80-81* 1-3
EPIC: *63-66* 4-8
LPs: 10/12-Inch 33rpm
ABC-PARAMOUNT: *60-61* 25-40
EMI AMERICA: *79-83* 5-8
EPIC: *63-65* 15-25
ROCKET: *76-78* 8-10
VIRGIN: *88* 5-8
Also see NEWTON-JOHN, Olivia, & Cliff
Richard

RICHARD, Little:
see LITTLE RICHARD

RICHARDS, Diane
Singles: 7-Inch
ZOO YORK: *83* 1-3

RICHARDS, Turley
Singles: 7-Inch
ATLANTIC: *80* 1-3
COLUMBIA: *66-67* 3-5
EPIC: *76-78* 2-3
KAPP: *68* 2-4
MGM: *64* 3-5
20TH CENTURY-FOX: *65* 3-5
WARNER BROS: *70* 2-4
Picture Sleeves
COLUMBIA: *66* 3-5
LPs: 10/12-Inch 33rpm
ATLANTIC: *80* 5-8
EPIC: *76* 5-8
20TH CENTURY-FOX: *65* 12-15
WARNER BROS: *70-71* 10-12

RICHARDSON, Jape
(Jape Richardson & His Japettes)
Singles: 78rpm
MERCURY: *57* 10-15
Singles: 7-Inch
MERCURY: *57-58* 10-15
Also see BIG BOPPER

RICHIE, Lionel
Singles: 12-Inch 33/45rpm
MOTOWN: *83-86* 4-8
Singles: 7-Inch
MOTOWN: *82-87* 1-3
LPs: 10/12-Inch 33rpm
MOTOWN: *82-86* 5-8
Also see COMMODORES
Also see ROSS, Diana, & Lionel Ritchie
Also see U.S.A. FOR AFRICA

RICHIE, Lionel, & Alabama
Singles: 12-Inch 33/45rpm
MOTOWN (195; "Special Motown Service
To Country Radio"): *86* **$5-10**
(Promotional issue only.)
Singles: 7-Inch
MOTOWN: *86* **1-3**
Also see ALABAMA
Also see RICHIE, Lionel

RICHIE'S ROOM 222 GANG
Singles: 7-Inch
SCEPTER: *71* **2-4**

RICHMOND EXTENSION
Singles: 7-Inch
SILVER BLUE: *74* **2-4**

RICK & THE KEENS
Singles: 7-Inch
AUSTIN: *61* **15-20**
JAMIE: *62* **4-6**
LE CAM: *61-64* **8-12**
SMASH: *61* **3-5**
TOLLIE: *64* **10-15**
TROY: **20-25**

RIDDLE, Nelson, & His Orchestra
Singles: 78rpm
CAPITOL: *53-57* **2-5**
Singles: 7-Inch
CAPITOL: *53-62* **3-5**
EPIC: *67* **2-4**
LIBERTY: *67* **2-3**
REPRISE: *63-66* **2-3**
20TH CENTURY-FOX: *66* **2-3**
VERVE: *59* **2-5**
Picture Sleeves
CAPITOL: *60* **4-8**
EPIC: *67* **4-8**
EPs: 7-Inch 33/45rpm
CAPITOL: *55-59* **8-15**
VERVE: *59* **6-12**
LPs: 10/12-Inch 33rpm
ALSHIRE: *70-71* **4-8**
CAPITOL: *55-78* **5-15**
DAYBREAK: *73* **5-8**
EPIC (114; "El Dorado"): *67* **45-55**
(Soundtrack.)
HARMONY: *69* **5-8**
LIBERTY: *67* **5-10**
MPS: *73* **5-8**
PICKWICK: *65* **5-10**
RCA VICTOR (2976; "The Rogues"): *64* **15-25**
(Soundtrack.)
REPRISE: *63-65* **5-15**
SOLID STATE: *67* **5-10**

SUNSET: *68* **$5-10**
UNITED ARTISTS: *68* **5-10**
VERVE: *59* **5-15**
WARNER BROS. (1599; "Harlow"): *65* . **20-30**
(Soundtrack.)
Also see FITZGERALD, Ella
Also see MARTIN, Dean / Nelson Riddle
Also see PETERSON, Oscar

RIDGWAY, Stan
Singles: 7-Inch
I.R.S.: *86* **1-3**
LPs: 10/12-Inch 33rpm
I.R.S.: *86* **5-8**
Also see WALL OF VOODOO

RIGHT CHOICE
Singles: 7-Inch
MOTOWN: *88* **1-3**

RIGHT KIND
Singles: 7-Inch
GALAXY: *68* **3-5**

RIGHTEOUS BROTHERS
Singles: 7-Inch
HAVEN: *74-76* **2-4**
MGM: *78-79* **2-3**
MOONGLOW: *63-66* **4-6**
PHILLES: *64-66* **4-6**
POLYDOR: **1-3**
VERVE: *65-70* **3-5**
Picture Sleeves
PHILLES: *65-66* **5-10**
VERVE: *66-67* **4-8**

The Righteous Brothers: (L-R) Bill Medley; Bob Hatfield

FIRE-SIGN: 78 .... $10-15
MOTOWN: 74 8-10
QUALITY/RFC: 84 5-8

RIP CHORDS
Singles: 7-Inch
COLUMBIA (3-42000 series): 63 5-10
(Compact 33 singles.)
COLUMBIA (4-42000 & 4-43000
   series): 62-65 4-6
Promotional Singles
COLUMBIA (Colored vinyl): 63-64 10-15
Picture Sleeves
COLUMBIA: 63 12-20
(Promotional issue only.)
LPs: 10/12-Inch 33rpm
COLUMBIA: 64 20-30
Members: Bruce Johnston; Terry Melcher; Phil
Stewart; Ernie Bringas.
Also see BRUCE & TERRY

RIPERTON, Minnie
Singles: 12-Inch 33/45rpm
EPIC: 77 4-6
Singles: 7-Inch
CAPITOL: 79-81 2-3
EPIC: 74-77 2-4
GRT: 72 2-4
JANUS: 75-76 2-4
LPs: 10/12-Inch 33rpm
ACCORD: 82 5-8
CAPITOL: 79-81 5-8
EPIC: 74-77 10-12
51 WEST: 5-8
GRT: 70 12-15
JANUS: 74 8-10
Also see JONES, Quincy
Also see ROTARY CONNECTION

RIPPINGTONS FEATURING
RUSS FREEMAN
LPs: 10/12-Inch 33rpm
PASSPORT JAZZ: 88 5-8

RIPPLE
Singles: 7-Inch
GRC: 73-75 2-4
SALSOUL: 77-78 1-3
LPs: 10/12-Inch 33rpm
GRC: 74 8-10
SALSOUL: 77 5-8

RIPPLES & WAVES PLUS MICHAEL
(Jackson Five)
Singles: 7-Inch
STEELTOWN (688; "Let Me Carry
   Your School Books"): 69 .... $50-80
(Mono. "Steeltown" is in all upper-case letters on
label.)
STEELTOWN (688; "Let Me Carry
   Your School Books"): 69 75-100
(Stereo. "Steeltown" is in upper- and lower-case let-
ters.)
Also see JACKSONS

RITCHARD, Cyril
LPs: 10/12-Inch 33rpm
CAEDMON: 69 4-8
RIVERSIDE: 60-62 5-12

RITCHIE FAMILY
Singles: 12-Inch 33/45rpm
MARLIN: 76 4-6
RCA VICTOR: 82 4-6
Singles: 7-Inch
CASABLANCA: 79-80 1-3
MARLIN: 76-78 2-3
RCA VICTOR: 82-83 1-3
20TH CENTURY-FOX: 75 2-3
LPs: 10/12-Inch 33rpm
CASABLANCA: 79-80 5-8
MARLIN: 76-78 5-8
RCA VICTOR: 82 5-8
20TH CENTURY-FOX: 75 8-10

RITENOUR, Lee
Singles: 7-Inch
ELEKTRA: 81-82 1-3
EPIC: 76-80 1-3
Picture Sleeves
ELEKTRA: 81 1-3
LPs: 10/12-Inch 33rpm
ELEKTRA: 78-82 5-8
EPIC: 76-80 5-10
JVC: 78 5-8
MFSL: 85 15-25
Also see GRUSIN, Dave

RITTER, Tex
Singles: 78rpm
CAPITOL: 50-57 3-6
CHAMPION: 10-15
CONQUEROR: 10-15
Singles: 7-Inch
CAPITOL (1100 through 3900
   series): 50-58 3-5
(Purple labels.)

CAPITOL (2000 through 4000
series): *68-76* $1-3
(Orange labels.)
CAPITOL (4000 through 5900
series): *58-67* 2-4
Picture Sleeves
CAPITOL: *68* 3-5
EPs: 7-Inch 33/45rpm
CAPITOL: *53-60* 5-12
LPs: 10/12-Inch 33rpm
ALBUM GLOBE: 5-8
BUCKBOARD: 5-8
CAPITOL (200 through 400 series): *69-71* 8-12
CAPITOL (1100 through 2800
series): *59-68* 10-20
(With a "T" or "ST" prefix.)
CAPITOL (1200 series): *78* 4-6
(With an "SM" prefix.)
CAPITOL (1500 series): *61* 25-35
(With a "W" or "SW" prefix.)
CAPITOL (4000 series): *53* 25-40
(10-Inch LPs.)
CORONET: 8-12
HILLTOP: 10-15
LA BREA: *62* 15-25
PICKWICK/HILLTOP: *66-68* 6-12
SHASTA: 8-12
SPIN-O-RAMA: 8-12
Also see KENTON, Stan

RIVERA, Hector
Singles: 7-Inch
BARRY: *66* 3-5
LPs: 10/12-Inch 33rpm
EPIC: *61* 5-12
WING: *60* 5-15

RIVERS, Joan
LPs: 10/12-Inch 33rpm
BUDDAH: *69* 6-12
GEFFEN: *83* 5-8
WARNER BROS: *65* 8-15

RIVERS, Johnny
Singles: 7-Inch
ATLANTIC: *74* 2-5
BIG TREE: *77-78* 2-3
CAPITOL: *62-64* 4-6
CHANCELLOR: *61-62* 6-10
CORAL: *64* 5-8
CUB: *59-60* 8-10
DEE DEE: *59* 10-15
EPIC: *75-76* 2-4
ERA: *61* 5-8
GONE: *58* 20-25
GUYDEN (2003; "Hole In
The Ground"): *58* 10-12

GUYDEN (2110; "Hole In
The Ground"): *64* $4-6
IMPERIAL: *64-70* 3-5
MGM: *64* 4-6
RSO: *80* 1-3
RIVERAIRE: *59* 10-12
ROULETTE: *64* 8-12
ROWE/AMI: *66* 4-8
("Play Me" Sales Stimulator promotional issue.)
SOUL CITY (Except 008): *76-77* 2-3
SOUL CITY (008; "Slow
Dancing"): *77* 3-5
UNITED ARTISTS (Except 700
series): *71-73* 2-4
UNITED ARTISTS (700 series): *64* 4-6
Picture Sleeves
IMPERIAL: *64-69* 3-6
UNITED ARTISTS: *71* 2-4
LPs: 10/12-Inch 33rpm
ATLANTIC: *74* 8-10
CAPITOL (2161; "Sensational
Johnny Rivers"): *64* 50-75
CUSTOM: 10-12
EPIC: *75* 8-10
GUEST STAR: *64* 10-12
IMPERIAL: *64-70* 15-20
LIBERTY: *82* 5-8
PICKWICK: 8-10
PRIORITY: *83* 5-8
RSO: *80* 5-8
SEARS: 20-25
(Special Products issue for Sears stores.)
SOUL CITY: *77* 8-10
SUNSET: *67-69* 10-12
UNITED ARTISTS (Except UAL, UAS, &
UXS series): *73-75* 6-10
UNITED ARTISTS (UAL-3386; "Go
Johnny Go"): *64* 20-25
(Monaural.)
UNITED ARTISTS (UAS-6386; "Go
Johnny Go"): *64* 20-30
(Stereo.)
UNITED ARTISTS (UAS-5532;
"Homegrown"): *71* 10-12
UNITED ARTISTS (UAS-5650;
"L.A. Reggae"): *72* 10-12
UNITED ARTISTS (UXS-93;
"Johnny Rivers"): *72* 12-15
Also see JONES, Tom / Freddie & The
Dreamers / Johnny Rivers

RIVERS, Johnny / Ricky Nelson / Randy Sparks
LPs: 10/12-Inch 33rpm
MGM: *64* 20-25

Also see NELSON, Ricky
Also see RIVERS, Johnny
Also see SIMON, Paul

RIVIERAS
Singles: 7-Inch
COED (503 through 542): *58-60* **$10-20**
COED (592; "Moonlight
Cocktails"): *64* **5-8**
(Reissue of Coed 529.)
COLLECTABLES: **1-3**
ERIC: **1-3**
LOST-NITE: **1-3**
LPs: 10/12-Inch 33rpm
POST: **8-10**
Members: Ronald Cook; Homer Dunn; Andy
Jones; Charles Allen.

RIVIERAS
Singles: 7-Inch
LANA: **1-3**
RIVIERA: *63-65* **5-10**
LPs: 10/12-Inch 33rpm
RIVIERA (701; "Campus Party"): *64* ... **50-100**
USA (102; "Let's Have A Party"): *64* ... **50-100**
Members: Marty Fortson; Paul Dennert; Otto Nuss;
Doug Gean; Joe Pennell.

RIVINGTONS
Singles: 7-Inch
A.R.E. AMERICAN: *64* **10-15**
BATON MASTER: **4-6**
COLUMBIA: *66* **4-6**
J.D.: *76* **2-5**
LADERA: **2-4**
LIBERTY (Except 55610): *62-64* **4-8**
LIBERTY (55610; "Cherry"): *63* **20-25**
QUAN: *67* **3-5**
RCA VICTOR: *69* **3-5**
REPRISE: *64* **4-6**
VEE JAY: *64-65* **4-6**
WAND: *73* **2-4**
Picture Sleeves
LIBERTY: *63* **15-25**
LPs: 10/12-Inch 33rpm
LIBERTY (3282/7282; "Doin' The
Bird"): *63* **40-65**
LIBERTY (10184;
"Papa-Oom-Mow-Mow"): *82* **5-8**
Members: Carl White; Al Frazier; Sonny Harris;
Turner Wilson; Darryl White.

RIX, Jerry
Singles: 7-Inch
A.V.I.: *77* **2-3**

ROAD
Singles: 7-Inch
KAMA SUTRA: *68-71* **$2-4**
NATURAL RESOURCES: *72* **2-4**
LPs: 10/12-Inch 33rpm
KAMA SUTRA: *69-71* **10-12**
NATURAL RESOURCES: *72* **10-12**

ROAD APPLES
Singles: 7-Inch
POLYDOR: *75* **2-3**

ROB BASE & D. J. E-Z ROCK
Singles: 7-Inch
PROFILE: *88* **1-3**
LPs: 10/12-Inch 33rpm
PROFILE: *88* **5-8**

ROBBINS, Marty
Singles: 78rpm
COLUMBIA: *52-58* **5-10**
Singles: 7-Inch
COLUMBIA (02000 & 03000
series): *81-83* **1-3**
COLUMBIA (10305 through
11425): *76-81* **1-3**
COLUMBIA (20925 through
21324): *52-54* **15-30**
COLUMBIA (21351; "That's All
Right"): *54* **15-25**
COLUMBIA (21352 through
21414): *54-55* **5-10**
COLUMBIA (21446; "Maybellene"): *55* **15-25**
COLUMBIA (21461; "Pretty
Mama"): *55* **10-12**
COLUMBIA (21477; "Tennessee
Toddy"): *56* **15-25**
COLUMBIA (21508; "Singing The
Blues"): *56* **10-20**
COLUMBIA (21545; "Singing The
Blues"): *56* **5-10**
COLUMBIA (30000 series): *60* **10-15**
(Compact 33 stereo singles.)
COLUMBIA (40679; "Long Tall
Sally"): *56* **25-35**
COLUMBIA (40706; "Respectfully
Miss Brooks"): *56* **15-25**
COLUMBIA (40815 through
41408): *57-59* **5-10**
COLUMBIA (41511 through 43770): *59-66* **4-8**
COLUMBIA (43845 through 45775): *67-73* **2-4**
DECCA: *72-00* **2-4**
MCA: *73-75* **1-3**

Picture Sleeves

COLUMBIA (40815 through
41408): *57-59* **$8-15**
COLUMBIA (41511 through 43770): *59-66* **4-8**

EPs: 7-Inch 33/45rpm

COLUMBIA (1785; "Marty
Robbins"): *56* **15-25**
COLUMBIA (2116; "Singing The
Blues"): *56* **15-20**
COLUMBIA (2134; "A White
Sport Coat"): *57* **15-20**
COLUMBIA (2153; "Marty
Robbins"): *56* **15-20**
COLUMBIA (2808; "Marty
Robbins"): *57* **20-25**
COLUMBIA (2814; "Marty
Robbins"): *58* **8-12**
COLUMBIA (9700 series): *57* **15-20**
COLUMBIA (10000 through 14000
series): *57-60* **10-20**

LPs: 10/12-Inch 33rpm

ARTCO: *73* **30-40**
CANDLELITE: *77* **8-12**
COLUMBIA (15; "Marty's
Country"): *69* **8-12**
COLUMBIA (31; "Open-End Columbia
Artists Interviews"): **25-50**
(With a 3:00 Marty interview. Promotional issue
only.)
COLUMBIA (32; "Columbia Artists Interviews
With Frank Jones"): **50-75**
(With a 4:19 Marty interview. Includes 42-page
booklet. Promotional issue only.)
COLUMBIA (237; "Saddle
Tramp"): *66* **25-30**
(Columbia Record Club offer.)
COLUMBIA (445; "Bend In
The River"): *68* **35-45**
(Columbia Record Club offer.)
COLUMBIA (890; "Marty Robbins
Gold"): *75* **8-10**
COLUMBIA (976; "The Song
Of Robbins"): *57* **25-30**
COLUMBIA (1087; "Song Of
The Islands"): *57* **25-30**
COLUMBIA (1189; "Marty
Robbins"): *58* **25-30**
COLUMBIA (1256; "Return Of
The Gunfighter"): *69* **15-20**
(Columbia "Country Star" series issue.)
COLUMBIA (1325; "Marty's Greatest
Hits"): *59* **15-20**
COLUMBIA (1349; "Gunfighter Ballads
& Trail Songs"): *59* **15-20**

COLUMBIA (1481; "More Gunfighter Ballads
& Trail Songs"): *60* **$15-20**
COLUMBIA (1599; "Marty's Greatest
Hits"): *69* **$15-20**
(Columbia "Country Star" series issue.)
COLUMBIA (1635; "More Greatest
Hits"): *61* **15-20**
COLUMBIA (1666; "Just A Little
Sentimental"): *61* **15-20**
COLUMBIA (1801; "Marty After
Midnight"): *62* **40-50**
COLUMBIA (1855; "Portrait Of
Marty"): *62* **25-35**
(With bonus portrait of Marty.)
COLUMBIA (1855; "Portrait Of
Marty"): *62* **15-25**
(Without bonus portrait of Marty.)
COLUMBIA (1918; "Devil Woman"): *62* **15-20**
COLUMBIA (2016; "The Heart Of
Marty Robbins"): *69* **80-100**
(Columbia "Country Star" series issue.)
COLUMBIA (2040; "Hawaii's
Calling Me"): *62* **20-30**
COLUMBIA (2072; "Return Of
The Gunfighter"): *63* **15-20**
COLUMBIA (2167; "Island
Woman"): *64* **35-40**
COLUMBIA (2220; "R.F.D."): *64* **40-50**
COLUMBIA (2304; "Turn The Lights
Down Low"): *65* **15-25**
COLUMBIA (2448; "What God
Has Done"): *65* **15-20**
COLUMBIA (2527; "The Drifter"): *66* . . . **10-20**
COLUMBIA (2563; "What God
Has Done"): *69* **15-20**
(Columbia "Country Star" series issue.)
COLUMBIA (2601; "Rock'n Roll'n
Robbins"): *56* **500-550**
(10-Inch LP.)
COLUMBIA (2645; "My Kind
Of Country"): *67* **15-20**
COLUMBIA (2725; "Tonight
Carmen"): *67* **10-20**
COLUMBIA (2735; "Christmas With
Marty Robbins"): *67* **20-30**
COLUMBIA (2762; "More Gunfighter
Ballads & Trail Songs"): *69* **15-20**
(Columbia "Country Star" series issue.)
COLUMBIA (2817; "By The Time I
Get To Phoenix"): *68* **20-30**
COLUMBIA (3557; "The Drifter"): *69* . . . **15-20**
(Columbia "Country Star" series issue.)
COLUMBIA (3867; "My Kind
Of Country"): *69* **15-20**
(Columbia "Country Star" series issue.)

COLUMBIA (5489; "Tonight
   Carmen"): *69* **$15-20**
   (Columbia "Country Star" series issue.)
COLUMBIA (5498; "Christmas With
   Marty Robbins"): *69* **15-20**
   (Columbia "Country Star" series issue.)
COLUMBIA (5812; "Marty"): *72* **20-40**
   (5-LP set. Columbia Special Products issue.)
COLUMBIA (6994; "I Walk Alone"): *69* . **15-20**
   (Columbia "Country Star" series issue.)
COLUMBIA (8158; "Gunfighter Ballads
   & Trail Songs"): *59* **15-20**
   (With a "CS" prefix.)
COLUMBIA (8158; "Gunfighter Ballads
   & Trail Songs"): **5-8**
   (With a "PC" prefix.)
COLUMBIA (8272; "More Gunfighter
   Ballads & Trail Songs"): *60* **15-20**
   (With a "CS" prefix.)
COLUMBIA (8272; "More Gunfighter
   Ballads & Trail Songs"): **5-8**
   (With a "PC" prefix.)
COLUMBIA (8435; "More Greatest
   Hits"): *61* **15-20**
   (With a "CS" prefix.)
COLUMBIA (8435; "More Greatest
   Hits"): **5-8**
   (With a "PC" prefix.)
COLUMBIA (8466; "Just A Little
   Sentimental"): *61* **15-20**
COLUMBIA (8601; "Marty After
   Midnight"): *62* **40-50**
COLUMBIA (8655; "Portrait
   Of Marty"): *62* **25-35**
   (With bonus portrait of Marty.)
COLUMBIA (8655; "Portrait
   Of Marty"): *62* **15-25**
   (Without bonus portrait.)
COLUMBIA (8718; "Devil Woman"): *62* **15-20**
COLUMBIA (8840; "Hawaii's
   Calling Me"): *62* **20-30**
COLUMBIA (8872; "Return Of
   The Gunfighter"): *63* **15-20**
COLUMBIA (8976; "Island
   Woman"): *64* **35-40**
COLUMBIA (9020; "R.F.D."): *64* **40-50**
   (With a "CS" prefix.)
COLUMBIA (9020; "R.F.D."): **8-10**
   (With a "CSRP" prefix. Columbia Special Products
   issue.)
COLUMBIA (9104; "Turn The Lights
   Down Low"): *65* **20-30**
COLUMBIA (9248; "What God
   Has Done"): *65* **15-20**
   (With a "CS" prefix.)

COLUMBIA (9248; "What God
   Has Done"): **$5-8**
   (With an "ACS" prefix. Columbia Special Products
   issue.)
COLUMBIA (9327; "The Drifter"): *66* .. **10-20**
COLUMBIA (9421; "The Song
   Of Robbins"): *67* **30-40**
COLUMBIA (9445; "My Kind
   Of Country"): *67* **15-25**
COLUMBIA (9525; "Tonight
   Carmen"): *67* **10-20**
COLUMBIA (9535; "Christmas With
   Marty Robbins"): *67* **10-20**
COLUMBIA (9617; "By The Time I
   Get To Phoenix"): *68* **8-12**
COLUMBIA (9725; "I Walk Alone"): *68* . **8-15**
COLUMBIA (9811; "It's A Sin"): *69* ... **20-30**
COLUMBIA (9978; "My Woman, My Woman,
   My Wife"): *70* **8-12**
COLUMBIA (10022 through
   10579): *73-75* **8-10**
   (Columbia's Limited Edition series, identified with
   an "LE" prefix.)
COLUMBIA (10980; "Christmas With
   Marty Robbins"): *70* **15-20**
   (Columbia Special Products issue.)
COLUMBIA (11222; "Marty's Greatest
   Hits"): *75* **5-8**
COLUMBIA (11311; "By The Time I
   Get To Phoenix"): *70* **6-10**
   (Columbia Special Products issue.)
COLUMBIA (11513; "By The Time I
   Get To Phoenix"): *71* **15-20**
   (Columbia Special Products issue.)
COLUMBIA (12416; "Marty Robbins'
   Own Favorites"): *74* **12-15**
   (Special Products issue for Vaseline Hair Tonic.)
COLUMBIA (13358; "Christmas With
   Marty Robbins"): *72* **6-10**
   (Columbia Special Products issue.)
COLUMBIA (14035; "Legendary
   Music Man"): *77* **8-12**
   (Columbia Special Products issue.)
COLUMBIA (14613; "Best Of Marty
   Robbins"): *78* **5-8**
   (Columbia Special Products issue.)
COLUMBIA (15594; "Number One
   Cowboy"): *81* **5-8**
   (Columbia Special Products issue.)
COLUMBIA (15812; "Marty Robbins'
   Best"): *82* **5-8**
   (Columbia Special Products issue.)
COLUMBIA (16561;
   "Reflections"): *82* **5-8**
   (Columbia Special Products issue.)

COLUMBIA (16578; "Classics"): *83* ... **$15-20**
(3-LP set. Columbia Special Products issue.)
COLUMBIA (16914; "Country
Classics"): *83* **5-8**
(Columbia Special Products issue.)
COLUMBIA (17120;
"Sincerely"): *83* **5-8**
(Columbia Special Products issue.)
COLUMBIA (17136; "Forever Yours"): *83* . **5-8**
(Columbia Special Products issue.)
COLUMBIA (17137; "That Country
Feeling"): *83* **5-8**
(Columbia Special Products issue.)
COLUMBIA (17138; "Banquet
Of Songs"): *83* **5-8**
(Columbia Special Products issue.)
COLUMBIA (17159; "The Great
Marty Robbins"): *83* **5-8**
(Columbia Special Products issue.)
COLUMBIA (17206; "The Legendary
Marty Robbins"): *83* **5-8**
(Columbia Special Products issue.)
COLUMBIA (17209; "Country
Cowboy"): *83* **5-8**
(Columbia Special Products issue.)
COLUMBIA (17367; "Song Of
The Islands"): *83* **5-8**
(Columbia Special Products issue.)
COLUMBIA (30000 through 40000
series): *70-86* **5-12**
DECCA: *72* **8-12**
GUSTO/COLUMBIA: *81* **8-10**
HARMONY (Except 31258): *69-72* **8-15**
HARMONY (31258; "Song Of
The Islands"): *72* **20-25**
K-TEL: *77* **8-10**
MCA: *73-74* **5-12**
ORBIT: *84* **8-10**
PICKWICK: **5-10**
READER'S DIGEST (054; "Greatest
Hits"): *83* **20-30**
(5-LP set.)
SUNRISE MEDIA: *81* **5-8**
TIME-LIFE: *81* **5-8**
Note: When a Columbia LP title in the "1000" or
"2000" series is duplicated in the "8000" or "9000"
series, the lower number is a monaural issue, the
higher a stereo issue.
Also see SMITH, Carl / Lefty Frizzell / Marty
Robbins

ROBBINS, Marty / Johnny Cash / Ray Price
LPs: 10/12-Inch 33rpm
COLUMBIA: *70* **8-10**
Also see CASH, Johnny

Also see PRICE, Ray

ROBBINS, Marty, & Jeanne Pruett
Singles: 7-Inch
AUDIOGRAPH: *83* **$1-3**
Also see PRUETT, Jeanne
Also see ROBBINS, Marty

ROBBINS, Rockie
Singles: 7-Inch
A&M: *79-81* **1-3**
MCA: *85* **1-3**
Picture Sleeves
A&M: *80* **1-3**
LPs: 10/12-Inch 33rpm
A&M: *80-81* **5-8**
MCA: *85* **5-8**

ROBBS
Singles: 7-Inch
ATLANTIC: *68* **3-5**
DUNHILL: *69-70* **2-4**
MERCURY: *66-67* **3-5**
Picture Sleeves
MERCURY: *67* **4-8**
LPs: 10/12-Inch 33rpm
MERCURY: *67* **20-25**

ROBERT & JOHNNY
Singles: 78rpm
OLD TOWN: *57* **5-10**
Singles: 7-Inch
COLLECTABLES: **1-3**
OLD TOWN: *57-62* **8-10**
Members: Robert Carr; Johnny Mitchell.

ROBERT & JOHNNY / Fiestas
Singles: 7-Inch
ATCO: **1-3**
Also see FIESTAS
Also see ROBERT & JOHNNY

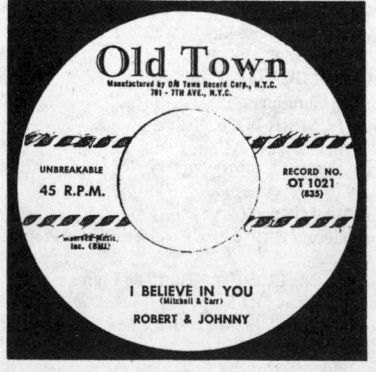

ROBERTA LEE: see LEE, Roberta

ROBERTINO
(Robertino Orchestra)
Singles: 7-Inch
4 CORNERS: *63* $2-4
KAPP: *61-62* 2-4
LPs: 10/12-Inch 33rpm
KAPP: *61-66* 5-15
UNITED ARTISTS INT'L: *67* 5-10

ROBERTS, Austin
Singles: 7-Inch
ARISTA: *78* 2-3
CHELSEA: *72-75* 2-4
COLLECTABLES: 1-3
GUSTO: 1-3
PHILIPS: *68-71* 2-4
PRIVATE STOCK: *75-76* 2-3
LPs: 10/12-Inch 33rpm
CHELSEA: *72-73* 8-10
PRIVATE STOCK: *75* 8-10

ROBERTS, John
Singles: 7-Inch
DUKE: *67-69* 3-5

ROBERTS, Lea
Singles: 7-Inch
MINIT: *69* 3-5
UNITED ARTISTS: *74-75* 2-3

ROBERTSON, Don
Singles: 78rpm
CAPITOL: *56-57* 2-4
Singles: 7-Inch
CAPITOL: *56-59* 2-4
MONUMENT: *66-76* 1-3
RCA VICTOR: *61-68* 2-4
LPs: 10/12-Inch 33rpm
RCA VICTOR: *65* 8-12

ROBERTSON, Robbie
Singles: 7-Inch
GEFFEN: *88* 1-3

ROBEY
Singles: 12-Inch 33/45rpm
SILVER BLUE: *84-85* 4-6
Singles: 7-Inch
SILVER BLUE: *84-85* 1-3

ROBIC, Ivo
Singles: 7-Inch
LAURIE: *59-60* 2-5
PHILIPS: *62* 2-4

ROBIN, Cock: see COCK ROBIN

ROBIN, Tina
Singles: 7-Inch
CORAL: *57-59* $5-8
MERCURY: *61-63* 3-5

ROBINS
(Robbins)
Singles: 78rpm
ALADDIN: *49* 40-50
ATCO: *55* 4-8
CROWN: *54* 25-50
RCA VICTOR: *53* 25-50
RECORDED IN HOLLYWOOD: *51* ...10-20
SAVOY: *50* 15-25
SCORE: *49* 20-30
SPARK: *54-55* 12-25
WHIPPET: *56-57* 5-10
Singles: 7-Inch
ARVEE: *60* 4-6
ATCO (6059; "Smokey Joe's Cafe"): *55* .. 5-10
CROWN (120; "Key To
My Heart"): *54* 100-150
GONE: *61* 4-6
KNIGHT: *58* 5-8
LAVENDER: *61* 10-15
PUSH: 3-5
RCA VICTOR (5175; "A Fool Such
As I"): *53* 100-150
RCA VICTOR (5271; "All Night
Baby"): *53* 100-150
RCA VICTOR (5434; "How Would
You Know"): *53* 75-100
RCA VICTOR (5486; "My Baby Done
Told Me"): *53* 75-100
RCA VICTOR (5489; "Ten Days
In Jail"): *53* 75-100
RCA VICTOR (5564; "Don't Stop
Now"): *53* 75-100
SPARK (103 through 110): *54-55* 30-50
SPARK (113 through 116): *55* 20-35
SPARK (122; "Smokey Joe's Cafe"): *55* . 40-60
WHIPPET: *56-58* 10-20
LPs: 10/12-Inch 33rpm
GNP/CRESCENDO: *75* 5-8
WHIPPET (703; "Rock 'N' Roll
With The Robins"): *58* 100-200
Members: Ty Terrell; Bobby Nunn; Carl Gardner;
Bill Richards; Grady Chapman; H.B. Barnum; Roy
Richards; Richard Berry.
Also see BARNUM, H.B.
Also see COASTERS
Also see LITTLE ESTHER & THE ROBINS
Also see NUNN, Bobby

ROBINS, Jimmy
Singles: 7-Inch
KENT: 68 .... $3-5

ROBINSON, Alvin
Singles: 7-Inch
ATCO: 68 2-4
BLUE CAT: 65 4-6
JOE JONES: 66 3-5
RED BIRD: 64 4-6
TIGER: 64 4-6

ROBINSON, Dutch
Singles: 7-Inch
CBS ASSOCIATED: 84-85 1-3

ROBINSON, Ed
Singles: 7-Inch
COTILLION: 70 2-4

ROBINSON, Floyd
Singles: 7-Inch
DOT: 61-62 3-5
GROOVE: 64 3-5
JAMIE: 61 3-5
RCA VICTOR: 59-60 4-6
UNITED ARTISTS: 63-66 4-8
EPs: 7-Inch 33/45rpm
RCA VICTOR: 59 15-25
LPs: 10/12-Inch 33rpm
RCA VICTOR: 60 20-30

ROBINSON, Freddy
Singles: 7-Inch
CHECKER: 66 3-5
LIBERTY: 70 2-4
LIMELIGHT: 58 5-8
MERCURY: 58 4-8
PACIFIC JAZZ: 69-70 2-4
QUEEN: 61 3-5
WORLD PACIFIC: 70 2-4
LPs: 10/12-Inch 33rpm
ENTERPRISE: 71 6-10
PACIFIC JAZZ: 69 8-12
Also see HOWLIN' WOLF
Also see LITTLE WALTER

ROBINSON, J. P.
Singles: 7-Inch
ALSTON: 68-69 2-4

ROBINSON, Jackie
Singles: 7-Inch
ARIOLA AMERICAN: 76 2-3

ROBINSON, Roscoe
(Rosco Robinson)
Singles: 7-Inch
ATLANTIC: 69 2-4
FAME: 70 2-4

PAULA: $2-4
SOUND STAGE 7: 67-69 3-5
WAND: 66-67 3-5

ROBINSON, Smokey
(William Robinson)
Singles: 7-Inch
TAMLA: 73-86 1-3
MOTOWN: 87-88 1-3
LPs: 10/12-Inch 33rpm
MOTOWN: 82-87 5-8
TAMLA: 73-86 6-10
Also see JAMES, Rick, & Friend
Also see MIRACLES
Also see PARTON, Dolly, & Smokey Robinson
Also see ROSS, Diana, Stevie Wonder, Marvin Gaye & Smokey Robinson
Also see TEMPTATIONS
Also see U.S.A. FOR AFRICA
Also see VANITY / Smokey Robinson

ROBINSON, Smokey, & Barbara Mitchell
Singles: 7-Inch
TAMLA: 83 1-3
Also see HIGH INERGY
Also see ROBINSON, Smokey

ROBINSON, Stan
Singles: 7-Inch
AMY: 60-61 3-5
MONUMENT: 59 3-5
TOTSY: 25-30

ROBINSON, Tom, Band
Singles: 7-Inch
HARVEST: 78-79 2-3
I.R.S.: 80 1-3
LPs: 10/12-Inch 33rpm
HARVEST: 78 8-10
I.R.S.: 80 5-8

ROBINSON, Vicki Sue
Singles: 12-Inch 33/45rpm
PROFILE: 83-84 4-6
Singles: 7-Inch
PROFILE: 83-84 1-3
RCA VICTOR: 76-77 2-3
LPs: 10/12-Inch 33rpm
PROFILE: 83 5-8
RCA VICTOR: 79-81 5-8

ROBINSON, Wanda
LPs: 10/12-Inch 33rpm
PERCEPTION: 71 5-10

ROBOTNICK, Alexander
Singles: 7-Inch
SIRE: 85 . . . . $1-3

ROCCA, John
Singles: 12-Inch 33/45rpm
STREETWISE: 84 4-6
Singles: 7-Inch
STREETWISE: 84 1-3
Also see FREEZ

ROCHELL
Singles: 12-Inch 33/45rpm
WARNER BROS: 85 4-6
Singles: 7-Inch
WARNER BROS: 85 1-3

ROCHELL & THE CANDLES
Singles: 7-Inch
CHALLENGE: 62-63 8-10
COLLECTABLES: 1-3
SWINGIN': 61 10-15
Members: Rochell Henderson; Johnny Wyatt.

ROCHES
LPs: 10/12-Inch 33rpm
WARNER BROS: 79-82 5-8
Members: Maggie Roche; Terre Roche; Suzzy Roche.

ROCK & ROLL DOUBLE BUBBLE TRADING CARD CO. OF PHILADELPHIA, 19141
Singles: 7-Inch
BUDDAH: 68 3-5

ROCK FLOWERS
Singles: 7-Inch
WHEEL: 71-73 2-4
LPs: 10/12-Inch 33rpm
WHEEL: 71-72 8-10

ROCK MASTER SCOTT & THE DYNAMIC THREE
Singles: 12-Inch 33/45rpm
REALITY: 84-85 4-6
Singles: 7-Inch
REALITY: 84-85 1-3

ROCK SQUAD
Singles: 12-Inch 33/45rpm
TOMMY BOY: 85 4-6

ROCK STEADY CREW
Singles: 12-Inch 33/45rpm
ATLANTIC: 83-84 4-6
Singles: 7-Inch
ATLANTIC: 83-84 1-3

ROCK-A-TEENS
Singles: 7-Inch
DORAN: 59 . . . . $25-35
ROULETTE: 59-60 10-15
LPs: 10/12-Inch 33rpm
MURRAY HILL: 5-8
ROULETTE (25109; "Woo-Hoo"): 60 . 80-100

ROCKER'S REVENGE
Singles: 12-Inch 33/45rpm
STREETWISE: 83-84 4-6
Singles: 7-Inch
STREETWISE: 82-84 1-3

ROCKET
Singles: 12-Inch 33/45
QUALITY/RFC: 83 4-6
LPs: 10/12-Inch 33rpm
QUALITY/RFC: 83 5-8

ROCKETS
Singles: 7-Inch
RSO: 79 1-3
TORTOISE INT'L: 77-78 2-3
LPs: 10/12-Inch 33rpm
RSO: 79-80 5-8
TORTOISE INT'L. 77 8-10
Also see DETROIT
Also see DETROIT WHEELS

ROCKIN' Rs
Singles: 7-Inch
STEPHENY: 60 4-6
TEMPUS: 59-60 15-20
VEE JAY: 60 4-6

ROCKIN' REBELS
Singles: 7-Inch
ABC: 73 1-3
ERIC: 1-3
ITZY: 5-8
STORK: 64 4-6
SWAN: 62-63 6-10
LPs: 10/12-Inch 33rpm
SWAN (509; "Wild Weekend"): 63 50-80
Members: Tom Gorman; Paul Balon; Mickey Kipler; Jim Kipler.
Also see BUFFALO REBELS
Also see HOT-TODDYS
Also see REBELS

ROCKINGHAM, David, Trio
Singles: 7-Inch
JOSIE: 63-64 3-5

ROCKPILE
Singles: 7-Inch
COLUMBIA: 80 1-3

EPs: 7-Inch 33/45rpm
COLUMBIA (1219; "Nick Lowe &
Dave Edmunds"): *80* $2-4
(Bonus EP, issued with the LP *Seconds Of
Pleasure*.)

LPs: 10/12-Inch 33rpm
COLUMBIA (36886; "Seconds Of
Pleasure"): *80* 5-8
(Includes the bonus EP, 1219, *Nick Lowe & Dave
Edmunds*.)
Members: Nick Lowe; Dave Edmunds.
Also see CARTER, Carlene
Also see LOWE, Nick
Also see McCARTNEY, Paul / Rochestra /
Who / Rockpile

ROCKWELL
Singles: 12-Inch 33/45rpm
MOTOWN: *84-86* 4-6
Singles: 7-Inch
MOTOWN: *84-86* 1-3
LPs: 10/12-Inch 33rpm
MOTOWN: *84-86* 5-8
Also see JACKSON, Michael

ROCKY FELLERS
Singles: 7-Inch
DONNA: *63* 4-6
PARKWAY: *62* 4-6
SCEPTER: *62-63* 4-8
WARNER BROS: *64-65* 4-6
LPs: 10/12-Inch 33rpm
SCEPTER: *63* 25-35
Members: Eddie; Albert; Tony; Junior; Pop.

ROD
Singles: 7-Inch
PRELUDE: *80* 1-3

RODGERS, Eileen
Singles: 78rpm
COLUMBIA: *56-57* 3-5
Singles: 7-Inch
COLUMBIA: *56-60* 3-5
KAPP: *61* 2-4
EPs: 7-Inch 33/45rpm
COLUMBIA: *58* 5-10
LPs: 10/12-Inch 33rpm
COLUMBIA: *58* 10-20
Also see MITCHELL, Guy / Eileen Rodgers

RODGERS, Jimmie
Singles: 78rpm
ROULETTE: *57* 3-6
Singles: 7-Inch
A&M: *67-70* 2-4
ABC: *73* 1-3
DOT: *62-67* 2-4

EPIC: *71-72* $2-3
RCA VICTOR: *73-75* 2-3
ROULETTE: *57-61* 3-6
SCRIMSHAW: *78* 1-3
Picture Sleeves
DOT: *62-64* 3-6
ROULETTE: *57-61* 5-10
EPs: 7-Inch 33/45rpm
ROULETTE: *57-60* 10-20
LPs: 10/12-Inch 33rpm
A&M: *67-70* 8-12
DOT: *62-67* 10-15
FORUM: *60* 12-15
HAMILTON: *64-65* 10-12
RCA VICTOR: *73-75* 8-10
ROULETTE (25000 series): *57-62* 15-20
ROULETTE (42000 series): 5-8
SCRIMSHAW: *78* 5-8

RODGERS, Michael
Singles: 7-Inch
WTG: *88* 1-3

RODGERS, Nile
Singles: 12-Inch 33/45rpm
WARNER BROS: *85* 4-6
Singles: 7-Inch
WARNER BROS: *85* 1-3
LPs: 10/12-Inch 33rpm
MIRAGE: *84* 5-8
WARNER BROS: *85* 5-8
Also see CHIC
Also see HONEYDRIPPERS

RODGERS, Paul
Singles: 7-Inch
ATLANTIC: *83* 1-3
LPs: 10/12-Inch 33rpm
ATLANTIC: *83* 5-8
Also see BAD COMPANY
Also see FIRM

RODNEY-O JOE COOLEY
LPs: 10/12-Inch 33rpm
EGYPTIAN EMPIRE: *88* 5-8

RODRIGUEZ, Johnny
Singles: 7-Inch
CAPITOL: *87-88* 1-3
COLUMBIA: *80* 1-3
EPIC: *79-85* 1-3
MERCURY: *72-79* 2-3
Picture Sleeves
MERCURY: *77* 2-3
LPs: 10/12-Inch 33rpm
EPIC: *80-84* 5-8
K-TEL: *77* 8-10
MERCURY: *74-79* 6-12

RODWAY
(Steve Rodway)
Singles: 7-Inch
MILLENNIUM: 82 .... $1-3
LPs: 10/12-Inch 33rpm
MILLENNIUM: 82 5-8

ROE, Tommy
(Tommy Roe & The Saints; Tommy Roe & The Flamingos)
Singles: 7-Inch
ABC: 66-71 3-5
ABC-PARAMOUNT: 62-66 3-5
JUDD (1018; "Caveman"): 60 15-20
JUDD (1022; "Sheila"): 62 20-25
MCA: 1-3
MCA/CURB: 86 1-3
MGM/SOUTH: 72-73 2-4
MARK IV: 60 10-15
MERCURY: 86-87 1-3
MONUMENT: 72-77 2-4
ROULETTE: 1-3
TRUMPET: 60 15-20
WARNER BROS: 78-80 1-3
Picture Sleeves
ABC-PARAMOUNT: 62-70 4-8
LPs: 10/12-Inch 33rpm
ABC (594 through 762): 67-72 10-15
ABC-PARAMOUNT (423 through 467): 62-64 25-50
ABC-PARAMOUNT (575; "Sweet Pea"): 66 15-20
ACCORD: 82 5-8
GUSTO: 5-8
MCA: 82 5-8
MONUMENT: 76-77 8-10

ROE, Tommy / Al Tornello
LPs: 10/12-Inch 33rpm
DIPLOMAT: 10-15
Also see ROE, Tommy

ROE, Tommy / Bobby Lee Trammell
LPs: 10/12-Inch 33rpm
CROWN: 63 12-15
Also see ROE, Tommy

ROGER
(Roger Featuring Shirley Murdock; Roger Troutman)
Singles: 7-Inch
REPRISE: 87-88 1-3
WARNER BROS: 81-85 1-3
LPs: 10/12-Inch 33rpm
REPRISE: 87 5-8
WARNER BROS: 81-84 5-8
Also see ZAPP

ROGERS, D. J.
Singles: 12-Inch 33/45rpm
COLUMBIA: 79 .... $4-6
Singles: 7-Inch
ARC: 79-80 1-3
COLUMBIA: 78-80 1-3
RCA VICTOR: 75-76 2-3
LPs: 10/12-Inch 33rpm
COLUMBIA: 78-80 5-8
RCA VICTOR: 76-77 6-10
SHELTER: 77 6-10
Also see RUSHEN, Patrice, & D. J. Rogers

ROGERS, Dann
Singles: 7-Inch
IA: 79 2-3
MCA: 87 1-3

ROGERS, Eric, & His Orchestra
LPs: 10/12-Inch 33rpm
LONDON/PHASE 4: 61-66 5-15

ROGERS, Jimmy
(Jimmy Rogers & His Trio; Jimmy Rogers & His Rocking Four)
Singles: 78rpm
CHESS: 50-57 10-20
Singles: 7-Inch
CHESS (1506; "I Used To Have A Woman"): 52 35-60
CHESS (1519; "The Last Time"): 52 35-60
CHESS (1543; "Left Me With A Broken Heart"): 53 30-50
CHESS (1574; "Chicago Bound"): 54 ... 25-45
CHESS (1600 series): 55-58 15-30
CHESS (1700 series): 59 5-10
LPs: 10/12-Inch 33rpm
CHESS: 8-12
Also see WATERS, Muddy

ROGERS, Jimmy, & Freddy King
LPs: 10/12-Inch 33rpm
SHELTER: 73 8-10
Also see KING, Freddy
Also see ROGERS, Jimmy

ROGERS, Julie
Singles: 7-Inch
MEGA: 72 2-3
MERCURY: 64-66 3-5
Picture Sleeves
MERCURY: 65 3-6
LPs: 10/12-Inch 33rpm
MEGA: 72 5-10
MERCURY: 65 10-20

Kenny Rogers

ROGERS, Kenny
(Kenneth Rogers)
Singles: 7-Inch

CARLTON: 58 .... $25-50
KEN-LEE: 8-10
LIBERTY: 80-86 1-3
MERCURY: 66 3-5
RCA VICTOR: 84-88 1-3
REPRISE: 88 1-3
UNITED ARTISTS: 76-80 1-3
Picture Sleeves
LIBERTY: 80-86 1-3
RCA VICTOR: 84-86 1-3
UNITED ARTISTS: 76-80 1-3
LPs: 10/12-Inch 33rpm
LIBERTY: 80-83 5-8
MFSL: 81 20-30
RCA VICTOR: 84-88 5-8
UNITED ARTISTS (Except "The Gambler,"
  picture disc): 76-80 5-8
UNITED ARTISTS ("The Gambler,"
  picture disc): 40-50
(Promotional issue only.)
Also see EASTON, Sheena, & Kenny Rogers
Also see U.S.A. FOR AFRICA

ROGERS, Kenny, & Kim Carnes
Singles: 7-Inch
UNITED ARTISTS: 80 .... $1-3
Picture Sleeves
UNITED ARTISTS: 80 1-3
Also see CARNES, Kim

ROGERS, Kenny, Kim Carnes & James Ingram
Singles: 7-Inch
RCA VICTOR: 84 1-3
Also see INGRAM, James

ROGERS, Kenny, & Ronnie Milsap
Singles: 7-Inch
RCA VICTOR: 87 1-3

ROGERS, Kenny, & Nickie Ryder
Singles: 7-Inch
RCA VICTOR: 86 1-3

ROGERS, Kenny, & The First Edition
Singles: 7-Inch
JOLLY ROGERS: 72-73 2-4
REPRISE: 68-72 3-5
LPs: 10/12-Inch 33rpm
JOLLY ROGERS: 72-73 8-12
REPRISE (Except 6276): 69-72 10-25
REPRISE (6276; "The First Edition"): 68 .15-30
Members: Kenny Rogers; Mike Settle; Terry Williams; Mickey Jones; Kin Vassey; Mary Arnold.
Also see FIRST EDITION

ROGERS, Kenny, & Dolly Parton
Singles: 7-Inch
RCA VICTOR: 83-85 1-3
LPs: 10/12-Inch 33rpm
RCA VICTOR: 88 5-8
Also see PARTON, Dolly

ROGERS, Kenny, & Dottie West
Singles: 7-Inch
UNITED ARTISTS: 78-79 1-3
LPs: 10/12-Inch 33rpm
UNITED ARTISTS: 78-79 5-8
LPs: 10/12-Inch 33rpm
Also see ROGERS, Kenny
Also see WEST, Dottie

ROGERS, Lee
Singles: 7-Inch
D-TOWN: 64-65 3-5
INSTANT: 72 2-4
LOADSTONE: 72 2-4
MAHS: 4-8
PLATINUM SOUND: 79 2-3
PREMIUM STUFF: 67 3-5
WHEELSVILLE: 66 3-5

ROGERS, Roy
(Roy Rogers & Dale Evans; Roy Rogers & The Sons Of The Pioneers)
Singles: 78rpm
DECCA: 40-44 .... $5-10
RCA VICTOR: 45-52 3-6
Singles: 7-Inch
CAPITOL: 70-71 2-4
MCA: 80 1-3
NEW DISC: 56 2-5
RCA VICTOR (Except 215): 51-52 3-6
RCA VICTOR (215; "Souvenir
Album"): 49 15-25
(Boxed set of three colored vinyl 45s.)
20TH CENTURY-FOX: 74-75 2-3
EPs: 7-Inch 33/45rpm
BLUEBIRD: 10-15
RCA VICTOR: 50-57 10-20
LPs: 10/12-Inch 33rpm
BLUEBIRD: 59 12-25
CAMDEN: 60-75 6-15
CAPITOL: 62-72 10-20
GOLDEN: 62 8-15
PICKWICK: 5-10
RCA VICTOR (1400 series): 57 20-25
RCA VICTOR (3000 series): 52-54 25-35
(10-Inch LPs.)
20TH CENTURY-FOX: 75 5-10
WORD: 73-77 4-8

ROGERS, Timmie
(Timmie "Oh Yeah" Rogers; Timmie Rogers & The Excelsior Hep Cats; Timmie Rogers & The Stomp Russell Trio; Timmy Rogers; Super Soul Brother Alias Clark Dark)
Singles: 78rpm
CAMEO: 57-58 3-6
CAPITOL: 53 3-6
EXCELSIOR: 45 10-15
MAJESTIC: 46 10-15
MERCURY: 54 10-15
REGIS: 45 10-15
VARSITY: 10-15
Singles: 7-Inch
CADET: 71 2-4
CAMEO: 57-58 4-8
CAPITOL: 53 5-8
EPIC: 65-66 3-5
MERCURY: 54 10-15
PARKWAY: 60 3-5
PARTEE: 73 2-4
PHILIPS: 62 3-5
SIGNATURE: 60 3-5
LPs: 10/12-Inch 33rpm
EPIC: 65 12-15

PARTEE: 73 .... $8-10
PHILIPS: 63 12-15

ROLLE, Ralph
Singles: 12-Inch 33/45rpm
STREETWISE: 85 4-6
Singles: 7-Inch
STREETWISE: 85 1-3

ROLLERS
Singles: 7-Inch
BELLE STAR: 62 4-8
LIBERTY: 61 4-8
Member: Al Wilson.
Also see WILSON, Al

ROLLERS
Singles: 7-Inch
ARISTA: 79 1-3
LPs: 10/12-Inch 33rpm
ARISTA: 79 5-8
Also see BAY CITY ROLLERS

ROLLIN, Dana
Singles: 7-Inch
TOWER: 67 3-5

ROLLING STONES
Singles: 12-Inch 33/45rpm
ATCO: 79 6-10
ROLLING STONES (70; "Hot
Stuff"): 76 35-45
(Promotional issue only.)
ROLLING STONES (119; "Miss
You"): 78 15-20
(Promotional issue only.)
ROLLING STONES (253; "If I Was
A Dancer"): 79 12-15
(Promotional issue only.)
ROLLING STONES (367; "Emotional
Rescue"): 80 15-20
(Promotional issue only.)
ROLLING STONES (397; "Start
Me Up"): 81 15-20
(Promotional issue only. Price includes special
cover.)
ROLLING STONES (574; "She Was
Hot"): 84 12-15
(Promotional issue only.)
ROLLING STONES (685; "Undercover
Of The Night"): 83 20-25
(White label. Promotional issue only.)
ROLLING STONES (685; "Undercover
Of The Night"): 83 12-15
(Yellow label. Promotional issue only.)
ROLLING STONES (692; "Too Much
Blood"): 85 15-20
(Promotional issue only. Price includes special
cover.)

ROLLING STONES (2275; "Harlem
Shuffle"): *86* $8-10
(Price includes special cover.)
ROLLING STONES (2275; "Harlem
Shuffle"): *86* 10-12
(Promotional issue only. Price includes special
cover.)
ROLLING STONES (2340; "One
Hit"): *86* 8-10
(Price includes color cover.)
ROLLING STONES (2340; "One
Hit"): *86* 20-25
(Price includes black and white cover. Promotional
issue only.)
ROLLING STONES (4609; "Miss
You"): *78* 8-10
(Price includes special cover.)
ROLLING STONES (4616; "Miss
You"/"Hot Stuff"): *78* 12-15
ROLLING STONES (96902; "Too
Much Blood"): *85* 8-10
(Price includes special cover.)
ROLLING STONES (96978: "Undercover Of
The Night"): *83* 8-10
(Price includes special cover.)
Singles: 7-Inch
ABKCO: *75* 2-4
LONDON (901 through 910): *66-69* 3-5
LONDON (9657 through 9725): *64-65* ... 8-12
(Purple & white labels.)
LONDON (9657 through 9725): *64-65* 3-5
(Blue swirl label.)
LONDON (9741 through 9823): *65-66* 3-5
ROLLING STONES (Except 99724): *71-86* 2-4
ROLLING STONES (99724; "Miss
You"/"Too Tough"): *78* 10-12
Picture Sleeves
LONDON (901 through 904): *66-67* 10-15
LONDON (905; "Dandelion"): *67* 80-100
LONDON (906; "She's A Rainbow"): *67* 10-15
LONDON (908; "Jumpin' Jack
Flash"): *68* 10-15
LONDON (909; "Street Fighting
Man"): *68* 1500-2000
LONDON (910; "Honky Tonk
Women"): *69* 8-10
LONDON (9657; "Not Fade Away"): *64* . 45-55
LONDON (9682; "Tell Me"): *64* 20-25
LONDON (9687; "It's All Over Now"): *64*15-20
LONDON (9708; "Time Is On
My Side"): *64* 15-20
LONDON (9725; "Heart Of
Stone"): *65* 125-150
LONDON (9741; "The Last Time"): *65* .. 20-25

LONDON (9766; "Satisfaction"): *65* ...$30-35
LONDON (9808; "As Tears Go By"): *65* .15-20
LONDON (9823; "19th Nervous
Breakdown"): *66* 15-20
ROLLING STONES (Except 228, 316,
& 19309): *78-86* 3-5
ROLLING STONES (228; "Time
Waits For No One"): *76* 15-20
(Promotional issue only.)
ROLLING STONES (316; "Before
They Make Me Run"): *78* 15-20
(Promotional issue only.)
ROLLING STONES (19309; "Beast Of
Burden"): *78* 250-300
Promotional Singles
ABKCO: *75* 5-8
LONDON (901 through 910): *66-69* 10-15
LONDON (9641; "Stoned"): *64* 275-375
LONDON (9657; "Not Fade
Away"): *64* 25-35
LONDON (9682 through 9823): *64-65* ...12-18
ROLLING STONES (228; "Time
Waits For No One"): *76* 12-15
ROLLING STONES (316; "Before
They Make Me Run"): *78* 10-12
ROLLING STONES (05000 series): *86* ...6-10
ROLLING STONES (19000 through
21301, except 19307): *71-82* 6-10
ROLLING STONES (19307; "Far
Away Eyes"): *78* 30-40
ROLLING STONES (90000 series,
except 99724): *82-85* 4-6
ROLLING STONES (99724; "Miss
You"/"Miss You"): *78* 12-15
EPs: 7-Inch 33/45rpm
ATLANTIC: *72-73* 25-35
(Jukebox issues only.)
LONDON: *64-67* 75-100
(Jukebox issues only.)
ROLLING STONES (287; "The
Rolling Stones"): *77* 15-25
(Promotional issue only.)
LPs: 10/12-Inch 33rpm
ABKCO (1; "Metamorphosis"): *75* 12-15
ABKCO (1; "Songs Of The
Rolling Stones"): *75* 100-150
(Promotional issue only.)
ABKCO (0268; "Greatest Hits"): 20-25
(A 2-LP TV mail-order offer.)
CRAWDADDY ("Rolling Stones
Tour Special"): *76* 150-175
(Promotional issue to college radio stations only.)
D.I.R. (312 & 325; "King Biscuit
Flower Hour"): *80* 150-200
(Promotional issue only.)

INS RADIO: *65* $50-75
LONDON (1; "Big Hits"): *66* 15-20
(Monaural.)
LONDON (2; "Their Satanic
Majesties Request"): *67* 40-50
(Monaural.)
LONDON (2; "Their Satanic
Majesties Request"): *67* 20-25
(Stereo.)
(With 3-D cover.)
LONDON (2; "Their Satanic
Majesties Request"): *70* 8-10
(Stereo.)
(With standard cover.)
LONDON (3; "Through The Past
Darkly"): *69* 8-10
LONDON (4; "Let It Bleed"): *69* 10-20
(With bonus poster.)
LONDON (4; "Let It Bleed"): *69* 8-10
(Without poster.)
LONDON (5; "Get Your Ya-Yas
Out"): *70* 8-10
LONDON (375; "The Rolling
Stones"): *64* 50-100
(Stereo.)
(Price includes a 12x12 bonus photo, which repre-
sents $25-$40 of the value. This issue also has a
printed promotional mention of the bonus photo on
the front cover.)
LONDON (375; "The Rolling
Stones"): *64* 8-10
(Stereo.)
(This issue has neither the 12x12 photo nor the
printed promotional mention of it on the front
cover.)
LONDON (402; "12 x 5"): *64* 8-10
(Stereo.)
LONDON (420; "Rolling Stones
Now"): *65* 8-10
(Stereo.)
LONDON (429; "Out Of Our Heads"): *65* . 8-10
(Stereo.)
LONDON (451; "December's
Children"): *65* 8-10
(Stereo.)
LONDON (476; "Aftermath"): *66* 8-10
(Stereo.)
LONDON (493; "Got Live If You
Want It"): *66* 8-10
(Stereo.)
LONDON (499; "Between The
Buttons"): *67* 8-10
(Stereo.)
LONDON (509; "Flowers"): *67* 8-10
(Stereo.)

LONDON (539; "Beggars Banquet"): *68* **$8-10**
(All songs are shown as written by Mick Jagger
and Keith Richard.)
LONDON (539; "Beggars Banquet"): ... 8-10
(*Prodigal Son* is shown as written by Rev. Wilkins.)
LONDON (600 series): *71* 10-12
LONDON (3375; "The Rolling
Stones" - mono): *64* 75-100
(Price includes a 12x12 bonus photo, which repre-
sents $10-$15 of the value. This issue also has a
printed promotional mention of the bonus photo on
the front cover.)
LONDON (3375; "The Rolling
Stones"): *64* 15-25
(Monaural. Has neither the 12x12 photo nor the
printed promotional mention of it on the front
cover.)
LONDON (3375; "The Rolling
Stones"): *64* 250-275
(White label. Promotional issue only.)
LONDON (3402; "12 x 5"): *64* 15-20
LONDON (3420; "Rolling Stones
Now"): *65* 20-30
(Monaural.)
LONDON (3429; "Out Of Our
Heads"): *65* 20-30
(Monaural.)
LONDON (3451; "December's
Children"): *65* 20-30
(Monaural.)
LONDON (3476; "Aftermath"): *66* 20-30
(Monaural.)
LONDON (3493; "Got Live If You
Want It"): *66* 20-30
(Monaural.)
LONDON (3499; "Between The
Buttons"): *67* 20-30
(Monaural.)
LONDON (3509; "Flowers"): *67* 20-30
(Monaural.)
MFSL (1; "Rolling Stones"): *85* 200-250
(11-LP boxed set, includes booklet, postcard and
alignment tool.)
MFSL (060; "Sticky Fingers"): *82* 25-50
MFSL (087; "Some Girls"): *82* 25-50
MUTUAL BROADCASTING SYSTEM ("The
Rolling Stones: Past & Present"): *84* **800-1000**
(12-LP boxed set, issued only to radio stations.
Price includes programming sheets.)
ROLLING STONES (2900; "Exile On
Main St."): *72* 12-15
(Price includes 12 bonus postcards, which represent
$2-$3 of the value.)
ROLLING STONES (9001; "Love You
Live"): *77* 10-15

ROLLING STONES (16015; "Emotional
Rescue"): *80* $5-8
ROLLING STONES (16028; "Sucking In
The Seventies"): *81* 5-8
ROLLING STONES (16052; "Tattoo
You"): *81* 5-8
ROLLING STONES (39108; "Some
Girls"): *78* 10-12
(With all girls' faces shown.)
ROLLING STONES (39108; "Some
Girls"): *78* 5-8
(Not all girls' faces shown. Cover is "Under Con-
struction.")
ROLLING STONES (39113; "Still
Life"): *82* 5-8
ROLLING STONES (40250; "Dirty
Work"): *86* 5-8
ROLLING STONES (59100; "Sticky
Fingers"): *71* 8-10
(Yellow label.)
ROLLING STONES (59100; "Sticky
Fingers"): *71* 125-150
(White label. Promotional issue only.)
ROLLING STONES (59101; "Goat's
Head Soup"): *73* 8-10
ROLLING STONES (79001; "It's
Only Rock & Roll"): *74* 8-10
ROLLING STONES (79002; "Made
In The Shade"): *75* 8-10
ROLLING STONES (90120;
"Undercover"): *83* 5-8
ROLLING STONES (90176;
"Rewind"): *84* 5-8
WESTWOOD ONE ("The Rolling
Stones Special"): *82* 175-200
(Promotional issue only.)
Members: Mick Jagger; Keith Richards; Bill
Wyman; Brian Jones; Charlie Watts; Mick Taylor;
Ron Wood.
Also see BEACH BOYS
Also see FAITHFUL, Marianne
Also see HOPKINS, Nicky
Also see JAGGER, Mick
Also see JONES, Brian
Also see SIMON, Carly
Also see TAYLOR, Mick
Also see WILLIE & THE POOR BOYS
Also see WOOD, Ron
Also see WYMAN, Bill

ROMAN HOLIDAY
Singles: 7-Inch
JIVE: *83-85* 1-3
LPs: 10/12-Inch 33rpm
JIVE: *83* 5-8

ROMANTICS
Singles: 12-Inch 33/45rpm
NEMPEROR: *83-85* $4-6
Singles: 7-Inch
BOMP: *78* 3-5
NEMPEROR: *80-85* 1-3
SPIDER: *77* 8-10
EPs: 7-Inch 33/45rpm
BOMP: *78* 5-8
LPs: 10/12-Inch 33rpm
NEMPEROR: *80-83* 5-8

ROMEO & JULIET
Singles: 7-Inch
CAPITOL: *69* 2-3

ROMEO VOID
Singles: 12-Inch 33/45rpm
COLUMBIA: *82-84* 4-6
Singles: 7-Inch
COLUMBIA: *82-84* 1-3
LPs: 10/12-Inch 33rpm
COLUMBIA: *82-84* 5-8
415: *82* 8-10

ROMEO'S DAUGHTER
Singles: 7-Inch
JIVE: *88* 1-3
LPs: 10/12-Inch 33rpm
JIVE: *88* 5-8

ROMEOS
Singles: 7-Inch
MARK II: *67* 3-5
LPs: 10/12-Inch 33rpm
MARK II: *67* 12-15

RON & BILL
Singles: 7-Inch
ARGO: *59* 15-25
TAMLA: *60* 25-35
Members: Ron White; Bill "Smokey" Robinson.
Also see MIRACLES

RONALD & RUBY
Singles: 7-Inch
RCA VICTOR: *58* 5-10
Member: Beverly Ross.

RONDELLS
(Ron-Dells; Rondels)
Singles: 7-Inch
ABC-PARAMOUNT: *65* 3-5
DOT (16000 series): *63-64* 4-8
DOT (17000 series): *70* 2-4
SHALIMAR: *63* 4-6
XPRESS: 3-5

RONDELS
Singles: 7-Inch
AMY: *61-62* $3-5
NOTE: *61* 3-5

RONDO, Don
Singles: 78rpm
DECCA: *55* 2-4
JUBILEE: *56-57* 2-5
Singles: 7-Inch
ATLANTIC: *63* 2-4
CARLTON: *60-61* 2-4
DECCA: *55* 2-4
JUBILEE: *56-66* 2-5
ROULETTE: *59-60* 2-4
TRIP: 1-3
TUBA: *65* 2-4
UNITED ARTISTS: *66-67* 2-4
VIRGO: *72* 1-3
LPs: 10/12-Inch 33rpm
JUBILEE: *57-58* 10-20
VOCALION: *70* 5-10

RONETTES
(Ronnettes)
Singles: 7-Inch
A&M: *69* 4-6
BUDDAH: *73-74* 5-10
COLPIX: *62* 25-30
MAY: *63* 15-20
PAVILLION: *82* 2-3
PHILLES: *63-66* 10-15
Promotional Singles
A&M: *69* 5-10
BUDDAH: *73-74* 10-15
COLPIX: *62* 25-35
MAY: *63* 15-25
PAVILLION: *82* 3-5
PHILLES: *63-66* 10-20
Picture Sleeves
PHILLES: *64-65* 15-30
LPs: 10/12-Inch 33rpm
COLPIX (486; "The Ronettes,
Featuring Veronica"): *65* 50-100
(Blue label. Monaural.)
COLPIX (486; "The Ronettes,
Featuring Veronica"): *65* 75-150
(Gold label. Monaural.)
COLPIX (486; "The Ronettes,
Featuring Veronica"): *65* 60-75
(Blue label. Stereo.)
COLPIX (486; "The Ronettes,
Featuring Veronica"): *65* 100-200
(Gold label. Stereo.)

COLPIX (486; "The Ronettes,
Featuring Veronica"): *65* $75-100
(White label. Promotional issue only.)
PHILLES (4006; "Presenting The
Fabulous Ronettes"): *64* 100-125
(Blue label. Monaural.)
PHILLES (4006; "Presenting The
Fabulous Ronettes"): *64* 75-150
(Yellow label. Monaural.)
PHILLES (4006; "Presenting The
Fabulous Ronettes"): *64* 200-300
(Yellow label with red print. Stereo.)
PHILLES (4006; "Presenting The
Fabulous Ronettes"): *64* 200-250
(Yellow label with black print. Stereo issue through
Capitol Record Club.)
MURRAY HILL: *86* 5-8
Members: Veronica Bennett-Spector; Estelle Bennett; Nedra Talley-Ross.
Also see RONNIE & THE RELATIVES
Also see SPECTOR, Ronnie

RONETTES / Crystals / Darlene Love
Singles: 7-Inch
PAVILLION (1354; "Phil Spector's
Christmas Medley"): *81* 3-5
(Promotional issue only.)

RONETTES / Crystals / Darlene Love / Bob B. Soxx & The Blue Jeans
EPs: 7-Inch 33/45rpm
PHILLES ("Christmas EP"): *63* 20-40
LPs: 10/12-Inch 33rpm
APPLE (3400; "Phil Spector's
Christmas Album"): *72* 10-12
PASSPORT (3604; "Phil Spector's
Christmas Album"): *85* 5-8
PAVILLION: *81* 5-10
PHILLES (4005; "A Christmas Gift
For You"): *63* 50-100
(Blue label.)
PHILLES (4005; "A Christmas Gift
For You"): *63* 40-60
(Yellow and red label.)
WARNER/SPECTOR: 8-12
Note: Phil Spector is heard speaking on this LP.
The Apple and Passport LPs are reissues of the Philles album.
Also see BOB. B. SOXX & THE BLUE
JEANS
Also see CRYSTALS
Also see LOVE, Darlene
Also see RONETTES

RONNIE & THE HI-LITES
Singles: 7-Inch
ABC-PARAMOUNT: *65* 3-5

Linda Ronstadt

COLLECTABLES: $1-3
ERIC: 1-3
JOY: 62 4-8
RAVEN: 63 5-8
WIN: 63 4-6

RONNIE & THE RELATIVES
(Ronettes)
Singles: 7-Inch
COLPIX: 61 30-35
MAY: 62 35-50
Promotional Singles
COLPIX: 61 30-40
MAY: 62 35-50
Also see RONETTES

RONNY & THE DAYTONAS
Singles: 7-Inch
MALA: 64-66 4-8
RCA VICTOR: 66-68 4-8
Picture Sleeves
RCA VICTOR: 66 15-25
LPs: 10/12-Inch 33rpm
MALA (4001; "G.T.O."): 64 50-100
MALA (4002; "Sandy"): 66 20-35
(Monaural.)
MALA (4002-S; "Sandy"): 66 75-100
(Stereo.)
Members: John "Bucky" Wilkin; Buzz Cason.

RONSON, Mick
LPs: 10/12-Inch 33rpm
RCA VICTOR: 74 8-10

RONSTADT, Linda
(Linda Ronstadt & The Stone Poneys)
Singles: 7-Inch
ASYLUM: 73-85 1-3

CAPITOL (2110 through 2438): 67-69 .... $4-6
CAPITOL (5000 series): 67 4-6
ELEKTRA: 75-78 1-3
SIDEWALK (937; "So Fine"): 66 50-100
(With Davie Allan.)
Picture Sleeves
ASYLUM: 73-85 1-3
CAPITOL: 68 5-10
LPs: 10/12-Inch 33rpm
ASYLUM (Except 401 & 60489): 73-85 ...5-8
ASYLUM (401; "Living In
The USA"): 78 10-15
(Picture disc.)
ASYLUM (60489; "Round
Midnight"): 86 10-15
CAPITOL (208 through 635): 69-72 10-15
CAPITOL (2000 series): 68 12-15
CAPITOL (11000 series): 74-75 8-10
CAPITOL (16000 series): 80 5-8
ELEKTRA: 80-87 5-8
MFSL: 85 15-20
Also see ALLAN, Davie
Also see CHRISTMAS SPIRIT
Also see EAGLES
Also see GLASS, Phillip
Also see NEWMAN, Randy
Also see NITTY GRITTY DIRT BAND, &
Linda Ronstadt
Also see PARTON, Dolly, Linda Ronstadt,
Emmylou Harris
Also see STONE PONEYS

RONSTADT, Linda, & Emmylou Harris
Singles: 7-Inch
ASYLUM: 75 2-3
Also see HARRIS, Emmylou

RONSTADT, Linda, & James Ingram
Singles: 7-Inch
MCA: 86 1-3
Also see INGRAM, James
Also see RONSTADT, Linda

ROOFTOP SINGERS
Singles: 7-Inch
ATCO: 67 2-4
VANGUARD: 62-65 3-5
Picture Sleeves
VANGUARD: 63 3-6
LPs: 10/12-Inch 33rpm
VANGUARD: 63-65 10-15
Members: Erik Darling; Lynne Taylor; Bill Svanoe.
Also see TARRIERS

ROOMATES
Singles: 7-Inch
ADDIT: *60* $10-15
CAMEO: *62* 10-15
CANADIAN AMERICAN: *64* 4-6
COLLECTABLES: 1-3
PHILIPS: *63-64* 25-30
PROMO: *60* 15-20
VALMOR: *61-62* 10-15
Also see CATHY JEAN & THE ROOMATES

ROQ-IN ZOO
Singles: 12-Inch 33/45rpm
MOTOWN: *86* 4-6
Singles: 7-Inch
MOTOWN: *86* 1-3

ROS, Edmundo, & His Orchestra
Singles: 78rpm
LONDON: *51-57* 1-3
Singles: 7-Inch
LONDON: *51-63* 1-3
EPs: 7-Inch 33/45rpm
CORAL: *54* 3-6
LONDON: *52-59* 3-6
LPs: 10/12-Inch 33rpm
CORAL: *54* 5-15
LONDON: *52-78* 5-15

ROSCOE & MABLE
Singles: 7-Inch
CHOCOLATE CITY: *77* 2-3

ROSE, Andy
(Andy Rose & The Thorns)
Singles: 7-Inch
AAMCO: *58* 4-6
CORAL: *59-62* 3-5
EMBER: *64* 3-5
GOLDEN CREST: *64* 3-5

ROSE, Biff
Singles: 7-Inch
BUDDAH: *71* 2-4
TETRAGRAMMATON: *68-70* 2-4
LPs: 10/12-Inch 33rpm
BUDDAH: *71* 8-10
TETRAGRAMMATON: *68-69* 10-12
UNITED ARTISTS: *73* 8-10

ROSE, David, & His Orchestra
Singles: 78rpm
MGM: *50-57* 2-4
Singles: 7-Inch
CAPITOL: *66-69* 1-3
MGM: *50-67* 2-4
Picture Sleeves
MGM: *56-62* 2-5

EPs: 7-Inch 33/45rpm
KAPP: *59* $3-6
MGM: *51-58* 5-10
ROYALE: 4-8
LPs: 10/12-Inch 33rpm
CAPITOL: *66-69* 5-12
DINO: *72* 5-10
KAPP: *59-61* 5-10
LION: *59* 5-10
MCA: *83* 5-8
MGM: *51-70* 5-15
METRO: *65-66* 5-10
Also see PREVIN, Andre

ROSE BROTHERS
Singles: 7-Inch
CAPITOL: *88* 1-3

ROSE COLORED GLASS
Singles: 7-Inch
BANG: *71* 2-4

ROSE GARDEN
Singles: 7-Inch
ATCO: *67-68* 4-6
LPs: 10/12-Inch 33rpm
ATCO: *68* 12-15

ROSE ROYCE
Singles: 12-Inch 33/45rpm
MONTAGE: *84* 4-6
Singles: 7-Inch
C&R: *84* 1-3
MCA: *76-77* 2-3
OMNI: *86-87* 1-3
WHITFIELD: *77-82* 1-3
LPs: 10/12-Inch 33rpm
EPIC: *82* 5-8
WHITFIELD: *77-81* 5-8

ROSE TATOO
Singles: 7-Inch
MIRAGE: *80-82* 1-3
LPs: 10/12-Inch 33rpm
MIRAGE: *80-82* 5-8

ROSELLI, Jimmy
Singles: 7-Inch
RIC: *65* 3-5
UNITED ARTISTS: *65-69* 1-3
LPs: 10/12-Inch 33rpm
RIC: *65* 10-15
UNITED ARTISTS: *65-72* 5-12

ROSIE
(Rosie & The Originals)
Singles: 7-Inch
ABC: *73* 1-3
HIGHLAND: *60-61* 10-20

BRUNSWICK: *61* $10-20
   LPs: 10/12-Inch 33rpm
BRUNSWICK: *61* 30-40
  Also see ROSIE & RON

ROSIE & RON
   Singles: 7-Inch
DONNA: *61* 4-8
  Members: Rosie Hamlin; Ron Holden.
  Also see HOLDEN, Ron
  Also see ROSIE

ROSS, Charlie
   Singles: 7-Inch
BIG TREE: *75-76* 2-3
TOWN HOUSE: *82-83* 1-3

ROSS, Diana
   Singles: 12-Inch 33/45rpm
MOTOWN: *78-80* 5-8
   Singles: 7-Inch
MCA: *88* 1-3
MOTOWN: *70-81* 1-3
RCA VICTOR: *81-87* 1-3
   Picture Sleeves
MOTOWN: *70-81* 1-3
   EPs: 7-Inch 33/45rpm
MOTOWN (7588; "Sneak Preview From
  Lady Sings The Blues"): *72* . . . . : 5-10
  (Promotional issue only.)
   LPs: 10/12-Inch 33rpm
DORAL: 150-200
  (Promotional mail-order issue, from Doral ciga-
  rettes.)
KORY: *77* 8-10
MOTOWN (100 series): *81-83* 5-8
MOTOWN (700 through 900
  series): *70-81* 8-12
  (Black vinyl.)
MOTOWN (Colored vinyl): *79* 10-20
  (Promotional issue only.)
MOTOWN (5000 series): *83* 5-8
MOTOWN (6000 series): *83* 8-12
RCA VICTOR: *81-87* 5-8
  Also see GAYE, Marvin, & Diana Ross
  Also see IGLESIAS, Julio, & Diana Ross
  Also see SUPREMES
  Also see TEMPTATIONS
  Also see U.S.A. FOR AFRICA

**ROSS, Diana, & Bill Cosby / Diana Ross
With The Jackson Five**
   EPs: 7-Inch 33/45rpm
MOTOWN: *70* 5-10
  Also see COSBY, Bill
  Also see JACKSONS

ROSS, Diana, & Michael Jackson
   Singles: 7-Inch
MCA: *78* $2-3
   Picture Sleeves
MCA: *78* 3-5
  Also see JACKSON, Michael

ROSS, Diana, & Lionel Richie
   Singles: 7-Inch
MOTOWN: *81* 1-3
POLYGRAM ("Dreaming Of You"): *81* . . . 8-15
  (Promotional issue only. No number given.)
  Also see RICHIE, Lionel

**ROSS, Diana, Stevie Wonder, Marvin
Gaye, & Smokey Robinson**
   Singles: 7-Inch
MOTOWN (Black vinyl): *79* 1-3
MOTOWN (Red vinyl): *79* 4-8
  (Heart-shaped disc.)
MOTOWN (Green vinyl): *79* 5-10
  (Promotional issue only.)
   LPs: 10/12-Inch 33rpm
MOTOWN: *79* 5-8
  Also see GAYE, Marvin
  Also see ROBINSON, Smokey
  Also see ROSS, Diana
  Also see WONDER, Stevie

ROSS, Jack
   Singles: 7-Inch
DOT: *61-63* 3-5
ROMAL: *61* 4-6
   LPs: 10/12-Inch 33rpm
DOT: *62* 15-20

ROSS, Jackie
   Singles: 7-Inch
BRUNSWICK: *67-68* 3-5
CAPITOL: *76* 2-3
CHESS: *64* 3-5
FOUNTAIN: *69* 2-4
GSF: *72-73* 2-4
MERCURY: *70-71* 2-4
SCEPTER: *72* 2-4
   LPs: 10/12-Inch 33rpm
CHESS: *64* 15-20

ROSS, Jimmy
   Singles: 7-Inch
RFC: *81* 1-3

ROSS, Spencer
   Singles: 7-Inch
COLUMBIA: *59-60* 2-4
   LPs: 10/12-Inch 33rpm
COLUMBIA: *60* 5-12

ROSSINGTON-COLLINS BAND
(Rossington Band)
Singles: 7-Inch
MCA: *80* $1-3
LPs: 10/12-Inch 33rpm
MCA: *80-88* 5-8
Members: Gary Rossington; Al Collins.
Also see LYNYRD SKYNYRD

ROTA, Nino
Singles: 7-Inch
PARAMOUNT: *72* 1-3
UNITED ARTISTS: *72* 1-3

ROTARY CONNECTION
Singles: 7-Inch
CADET CONCEPT: *68-70* 3-5
LPs: 10/12-Inch 33rpm
CADET CONCEPT: *68-70* 15-25
Member: Minnie Riperton.
Also see NEW ROTARY CONNECTION
Also see RIPPERTON, Minnie

ROTH, David Lee
Singles: 7-Inch
WARNER BROS: *85-88* 1-3
LPs: 10/12-Inch 33rpm
WARNER BROS: *85-88* 5-8
Also see BEACH BOYS
Also see VAN HALEN

ROUGH DIAMOND
Singles: 7-Inch
ISLAND: *77* 2-3
LPs: 10/12-Inch 33rpm
ISLAND: *77* 8-10
Members: Byron Britton; Geoff Britton.
Also see URIAH HEEP

ROUGH TRADE
Singles: 7-Inch
BOARDWALK: *82* 1-3
LPs: 10/12-Inch 33rpm
UMBRELLA: *77* 10-12

ROUND ROBIN
Singles: 7-Inch
CAPITOL: *67* 3-5
DOMAIN: *63-65* 3-5
LPs: 10/12-Inch 33rpm
CHALLENGE: *65* 15-20
DOMAIN: *64* 20-25

ROUNDTREE
Singles: 12-Inch 33/45rpm
ISLAND: *78* 4-6
Singles: 7-Inch
ISLAND: *78* 2-3

ROUNDTREE, Richard
Singles: 7-Inch
ARTISTS OF AMERICA: *76* $2-3
MGM: *73* 2-4
VERVE: *72-73* 2-4
LPs: 10/12-Inch 33rpm
MGM: *72* 8-12

ROUSSOS, Demis
Singles: 7-Inch
BIG TREE: *74-75* 2-4
MGM: *73* 2-4
MERCURY: *76-78* 2-3
LPs: 10/12-Inch 33rpm
BIG TREE: *74-75* 8-12
MGM: *72* 10-15
MERCURY: *76-78* 5-10

ROUTERS
Singles: 7-Inch
WARNER BROS: *62-64* 3-6
LPs: 10/12-Inch 33rpm
MERCURY: *73* 10-15
WARNER BROS: *63-65* 30-50
Members: Joe Saraceno; Rene Hall; Mike Gordon;
Ed Kay.

ROUX, Le: see LE ROUX

ROVER BOYS
Singles: 78rpm
ABC-PARAMOUNT: *56* 3-6
CORAL: *54* 3-6
Singles: 7-Inch
ABC: *73* 1-3
ABC-PARAMOUNT: *56* 4-6
CORAL: *54* 4-6
RCA VICTOR: *59* 3-5
UNITED ARTISTS: *61* 3-5
Member: Billy Albert.

ROVERS
Singles: 7-Inch
EPIC: *81* 1-3
LPs: 10/12-Inch 33rpm
CLEVELAND INT'L: *81-82* 5-8
Also see IRISH ROVERS

ROWANS
Singles: 7-Inch
ASYLUM: *75-76* 2-3
COLUMBIA: *72-73* 2-5
LPs: 10/12-Inch 33rpm
ASYLUM: *75-77* 8-10
COLUMBIA: *72* 10-15
Members: Peter Rowan; Chris Rowan; Lorin
Rowan.
Also see GARCIA, Jerry
Also see OLD & IN THE WAY

ROWLES, John
Singles: 7-Inch
KAPP: *68-71* $2-4
UNI: *68* 2-4
LPs: 10/12-Inch 33rpm
KAPP: *69* 10-12

ROXANNE
Singles: 7-Inch
SCOTTI BROS.: *88* 1-3

ROXANNE WITH UTFO
Singles: 12-Inch 33/45rpm
SELECT: *85* 4-6
Singles: 7-Inch
SELECT: *85* 1-3
Also see UTFO

ROXY MUSIC
Singles: 7-Inch
ATCO: *75-80* 2-5
WARNER BROS: *82-83* 2-3
Promotional Singles
ATCO: *75-80* 3-5
WARNER BROS: *82-83* 2-3
Picture Sleeves
WARNER BROS: *82-83* 1-3
LPs: 10/12-Inch 33rpm
ATCO (Except 106): *75-80* 8-10
ATCO (106; "Country Life"): *75* 20-35
(Cover pictures two women in their underwear.)
ATCO (106; "Country Life"): *75* 8-10
(Women are not pictured on cover.)
ATLANTIC: *74* 8-10
REPRISE: *72* 8-10
WARNER BROS (Except 2696): *82-83* ... 5-8
WARNER BROS (2696; "For Your
Pleasure"): *73* 15-25
Member: Bryan Ferry.
Also see ENO, Brian
Also see FERRY, Bryan
Also see MANZANERA, Phil

ROY, Barbara
Singles: 12-Inch 33/45rpm
ASCOT: *84* 4-6
Singles: 7-Inch
RCA VICTOR: *86* 1-3
Also see ECSTASY, PASSION & PAIN

ROY C.
(Roy Charles Hammond)
Singles: 7-Inch
ALAGA: *71* 2-4
BLACK HAWK: *65-66* 3-5
MERCURY: *73-77* 2-4
SHOUT: *66* 3-5
UPTOWN: *66* 3-5

LPs: 10/12-Inch 33rpm
MERCURY: *77* $8-10
Also see GENIES

ROYAL, Billy Joe
Singles: 7-Inch
ALL WOOD: *62* 5-10
ATLANTIC (2300 series): *66* 3-5
ATLANTIC (89000 series): *85-86* 1-3
ATLANTIC AMERICA: *86-88* 1-3
COLUMBIA: *65-73* 4-8
FAIRLANE: *61-62* 5-10
KAT FAMILY: *81* 2-3
MGM/SOUTH: *73* 3-5
MERCURY: *80-87* 2-3
PLAYER'S: *65* 4-8
PRIVATE STOCK: *78* 2-4
SCEPTER: *76* 2-4
TOLLIE: *64* 5-10
LPs: 10/12-Inch 33rpm
ATLANTIC AMERICA: *86* 5-8
BRYLEN: 5-8
COLUMBIA: *65-69* 15-25
51 WEST: *83* 5-8
KAT FAMILY: *81* 5-8
MERCURY: *80* 5-8

ROYAL GUARDSMEN
Singles: 7-Inch
LAURIE: *66-69* 4-6
LPs: 10/12-Inch 33rpm
LAURIE: *67-68* 12-15
Members: Chris Nunley; Barry Winslow.

ROYAL HOUSE
Singles: 7-Inch
IDLERS WAR: *88* 1-3

ROYAL JOKERS
Singles: 78rpm
ATCO: *55-56* 6-12
HI-Q: *57* 8-15
Singles: 7-Inch
ATCO: *55-56* 20-30
FORTUNE (500 series): *63* 8-12
FORTUNE (800 series): *58* 20-25
HI-Q: *57* 20-25

ROYAL PHILHARMONIC ORCHESTRA
Singles: 7-Inch
RCA VICTOR: *81-83* 1-3
LPs: 10/12-Inch 33rpm
RCA VICTOR: *81-83* 5-8
Conductor: Louis Clark.

ROYAL SCOTS DRAGOON GUARDS
Singles: 7-Inch
RCA VICTOR: 72 .... $1-3
LPs: 10/12-Inch 33rpm
RCA VICTOR: 72 5-8

ROYAL TEENS
Singles: 78rpm
ABC-PARAMOUNT: 57 4-8
Singles: 7-Inch
ABC: 73 1-3
ABC-PARAMOUNT: 57-58 5-8
ALLNEW: 62 3-5
ASTRA: 4-6
CAPITOL: 59-60 5-8
JUBILEE: 62 3-5
MCA: 1-3
MIGHTY (Except 112): 58-61 4-6
MIGHTY (112; "Cave Man"): 59 8-10
MUSICOR: 69-70 3-5
POWER: 57 25-30
SWAN: 65 5-8
TCF: 65 3-5
LPs: 10/12-Inch 33rpm
DEMAND: 10-15
MUSICOR: 70 10-15
TRU-GEMS: 75 8-10
Members: Bob Gaudio; Al Kooper; Buddy Randell; Joey Villa; Billy Crandall; Tom Austin; Tony Grochowski.
Also see KOOPER, Al

ROYALCASH
Singles: 12-Inch 33/45rpm
SUTRA: 83 4-6
Singles: 7-Inch
SUTRA: 83 1-3

ROYALETTES
Singles: 7-Inch
CHANCELLOR: 62-63 8-10
MGM: 64-66 5-8
ROULETTE: 67 5-8
WARNER BROS: 64 5-8
LPs: 10/12-Inch 33rpm
MGM: 65-66 15-25

ROYALS
Singles: 78rpm
FEDERAL (12064 through 12121): 52-53 **40-80**
FEDERAL (12133 through 12169): 53-54 **20-40**
Singles: 7-Inch
FEDERAL (12064; "Every Beat
Of My Heart"): 52 ....·..... 250-350
(Black vinyl.)

FEDERAL (12064; "Every Beat
Of My Heart"): 52 .... $500-700
(Colored vinyl.)
FEDERAL (12077; "Starting From
Tonight"): 52 400-500
FEDERAL (12088; "Moonrise"): 52 .. 350-400
FEDERAL (12098; "A Love In
My Heart"): 52 250-350
FEDERAL (12113; "Are You
Forgetting?"): 52 200-300
FEDERAL (12121; "The Shrine
Of St. Cecilia"): 53 200-300
FEDERAL (12133; "Get It"): 53 50-75
FEDERAL (12150; "Hey Miss
Fine"): 53 40-60
FEDERAL (12160; "That's It"): 54 40-60
FEDERAL (12169; "Work With
Me Annie"): 54 40-60
GUSTO: 1-3
Members: Henry Booth; Hank Ballard; Charles Sutton; Lawson Smith; Alonzo Tucker; Sonny Woods.
Also see BALLARD, Hank, & The Midnighters

ROYALTONES
Singles: 7-Inch
ABC: 73 1-3
GOLDISC: 60-61 8-10
JUBILEE (Blue label): 58-59 5-8
JUBILEE (Black label): 62 3-5
MALA: 63-64 4-6
PENTHOUSE: 59 20-25
ROULETTE: 71 1-3
VIRGO: 72 1-3

ROYALTY
Singles: 7-Inch
WARNER BROS: 88 1-3

RUBBER BAND
Singles: 7-Inch
ABC: 66 3-5
COLUMBIA: 66-67 3-5
REPRISE: 67 3-5

RUBBER RODEO
Singles: 7-Inch
MERCURY: 84-85 1-3
LPs: 10/12-Inch 33rpm
MERCURY: 85 5-8

RUBEN & THE JETS
(Mothers Of Invention)
Singles: 7-Inch
VERVE: 68 10-12

LPs: 10/12-Inch 33rpm
VERVE (5055; "Cruisin' With Ruben
& The Jets"): *68* $30-40
(Price includes paper inserts, which represent $10-
$15 of the value.)
Also see MOTHERS OF INVENTION

RUBEN & THE JETS
Singles: 7-Inch
MERCURY: *73* 2-4
LPs: 10/12-Inch 33rpm
MERCURY: *73* 10-12

RUBETTES
Singles: 7-Inch
MCA: *76* 2-3
POLYDOR: *74-75* 2-4
LPs: 10/12-Inch 33rpm
MCA: *76* 6-10

RUBICON
Singles: 7-Inch
20TH CENTURY-FOX: *78-79* 2-3
LPs: 10/12-Inch 33rpm
20TH CENTURY-FOX: *78-79* 5-8
Also see SLY & THE FAMILY STONE

RUBINOOS
Singles: 12-Inch 33/45rpm
WARNER BROS: *83* 4-6
Singles: 7-Inch
BESERKLEY: *77-79* 1-3
WARNER BROS: *84* 1-3
Picture Sleeves
BESERKLEY: *77-79* 1-3
LPs: 10/12-Inch 33rpm
BESERKLEY: *77-79* 5-8
Member: Jon Rubin.

RUBY & THE PARTY GANG
Singles: 7-Inch
GAMBLE: *72* 2-4
LAW-TON: *71* 2-4

RUBY & THE ROMANTICS
Singles: 7-Inch
A&M: *69* 2-4
ABC: *67-68* 3-5
KAPP: *62-67* 3-5
MCA: 1-3
Picture Sleeves
KAPP: *63-64* 3-6
LPs: 10/12-Inch 33rpm
ABC: *68* 10-15
KAPP: *63-67* 15-20
MCA: 5-8
Members: Ruby Nash; Edward Roberts; Ronald
Mosley; Leroy Fann; George Lee.

RUFFIN, David
Singles: 7-Inch
CHECK MATE: *61-62* $10-15
MOTOWN: *69-76* 2-4
WARNER BROS: *79-80* 1-3
LPs: 10/12-Inch 33rpm
MOTOWN (100 & 200 series): *82* 5-8
MOTOWN (600 series): *69* 10-15
MOTOWN (700 & 800 series): *73-76* 8-10
WARNER BROS: *77-80* 8-10
Also see HALL, Daryl, & John Oates
Also see NIGHTINGALE, Maxine, & Jimmy
Ruffin
Also see TEMPTATIONS
Also see VOICE MASTERS

RUFFIN, David, & Eddie Kendricks
Singles: 7-Inch
RCA VICTOR: *87-88* 1-3
Also see KENDRICKS, Eddie

RUFFIN, David & Jimmy
(Ruffin Brothers)
Singles: 7-Inch
SOUL: *70* 2-4
LPs: 10/12-Inch 33rpm
MOTOWN: *80* 5-8
SOUL: *70* 10-12
Also see RUFFIN, David
Also see RUFFIN, Jimmy

RUFFIN, Jimmy
Singles: 12-Inch 33/45rpm
EPIC: *77* 4-6
Singles: 7-Inch
EPIC: *77* 2-3
MIRACLE: *61* 20-25
MOTOWN: 1-3
RSO: *80* 1-3
SOUL: *64-71* 3-5
LPs: 10/12-Inch 33rpm
RSO: *80* 5-8
SOUL: *67-69* 10-15
Also see RUFFIN, David & Jimmy

RUFFNER, Mason
LPs: 10/12-Inch 33rpm
CBS ASSOC: *87* 5-8

RUFUS
(Rufus Featuring Chaka Khan)
Singles: 12-Inch 33/45rpm
WARNER BROS: *83-84* 4-6
Singles: 7-Inch
ABC: *74-78* 2-3
ATLANTIC: *74* 2-3
BEARSVILLE: *75* 2-3
EPIC: *70-71* 2-4

BEARSVILLE (6986; "Back To
The Bars"): *78* **$8-10**
BEARSVILLE (23732; "Ever Popular
Tortured Artist Effect"): *83* **5-8**
Also see NAZZ
Also see RUNT
Also see TYLER, Bonnie
Also see UTOPIA

RUNNER
Singles: 7-Inch
ISLAND: *79* **2-3**
LPs: 10/12-Inch 33rpm
ISLAND: *79* **5-8**

RUNT
(Featuring Todd Rundgren)
Singles: 7-Inch
AMPEX: *70* **4-8**
BEARSVILLE: *71* **4-8**
LPs: 10/12-Inch 33rpm
AMPEX (10105; "Runt"): *70* **50-100**
AMPEX (10116; "The Ballad Of
Todd Rundgren"): *71* **50-100**
Also see RUNDGREN, Todd

RUSH
Singles: 7-Inch
MERCURY: *75-87* **1-3**
Picture Sleeves
MERCURY: *81* **1-3**
EPs: 7-Inch 33/45rpm
MERCURY: *80* **5-10**
LPs: 10/12-Inch 33rpm
MERCURY (1000 through 4000 series,
except picture discs): *74-82* **5-8**
MERCURY (3743 "Hemispheres,"
picture disc): *78* **10-15**
MERCURY (7000 series): *76-81* **8-12**
MERCURY (9000 series): *76-81* **10-15**
MERCURY (800000 series): *84-87* **5-8**
Members: Geddy Lee; Neil Peart; Alex Lifeson.

RUSH, Bobby
Singles: 7-Inch
ABC: *68* **2-4**
CHECKER: *67* **3-5**
GALAXY: *71* **2-4**
JEWEL: **4-8**
PHILADELPHIA INT'L: *79* **1-3**
SALEM: *69* **2-4**
TOP: **3-5**
LPs: 10/12-Inch 33rpm
PHILADELPHIA INT'L: *79* **5-8**

RUSH, Jennifer
Singles: 7-Inch
EPIC: *86* **1-3**

LPs: 10/12-Inch 33rpm
EPIC: *86-87* **$5-8**

RUSH, Jennifer, & Elton John
Singles: 7-Inch
EPIC: *87* **1-3**
Also see JOHN, Elton
Also see RUSH, Jennifer

RUSH, Merrilee
(Merrilee Rush & The Turnabouts)
Singles: 7-Inch
AGP: *69-70* **2-4**
BELL: *68* **2-4**
GTP: *68* **2-4**
MERRILIN: **4-8**
RURO: **3-6**
SCEPTER: *71* **2-4**
UNITED ARTISTS: *77-78* **2-3**
LPs: 10/12-Inch 33rpm
BELL: *68* **12-15**
LIBERTY: *82* **5-8**
UNITED ARTISTS: *77* **8-10**

RUSH, Otis
Singles: 78rpm
COBRA: *56-57* **4-8**
Singles: 7-Inch
CHESS: *60* **4-8**
COBRA: *56-59* **6-12**
COTILLION: *69* **2-4**
DUKE: *62* **3-5**
LPs: 10/12-Inch 33rpm
BLUE HORIZON: *68-70* **10-12**
BULLFROG: *77* **8-10**
COTILLION: *69* **10-12**
DELMARK: *75-79* **5-8**
Also see KING, Albert, & Otis Rush

RUSH, Tom
Singles: 7-Inch
COLUMBIA: *72-74* **2-4**
ELEKTRA: *66-70* **3-5**
PRESTIGE: *64* **3-5**
LPs: 10/12-Inch 33rpm
COLUMBIA: *70-76* **6-10**
ELEKTRA: *65-70* **8-12**
FANTASY: *72* **5-8**
LY CORNU: *72* **15-20**
PRESTIGE: *64-68* **10-15**

RUSHEN, Patrice
Singles: 12-Inch 33/45rpm
ELEKTRA: *79-84* **4-6**
Singles: 7-Inch
ARISTA: *87* **1-3**
ELEKTRA: *80-84* **1-3**
PRESTIGE: *76* **2-3**

Picture Sleeves
ELEKTRA: *80* $1-3
LPs: 10/12-Inch 33rpm
ARISTA: *87* 5-8
ELEKTRA: *78-82* 5-8
PRESTIGE: *75-80* 5-10

RUSHEN, Patrice, & D. J. Rogers
Singles: 7-Inch
ELEKTRA: *80* 1-3
Also see ROGERS, D.J.
Also see RUSHEN, Patrice

RUSS, Lonnie
Singles: 7-Inch
4J: *62* 4-6

RUSSELL, Bobby
(Bobby Russell & The Beagles; Bobby & Sadie Russell)
Singles: 7-Inch
COLUMBIA: *73-74* 2-3
D: *60* 3-5
ELF: *68-69* 2-4
FELSTED: *59* 4-6
FILLY-COLT: *78* 1-3
IMAGE: *61* 4-6
MONUMENT: *65-66* 3-5
NATIONAL GENERAL: *70* 2-3
RISING SONS: *67* 2-4
SPAR: *64* 5-10
UNITED ARTISTS: *71-72* 2-3
VISTA: *69* 2-4
LPs: 10/12-Inch 33rpm
BELL: *69* 8-10
ELF: *68* 10-15
UNITED ARTISTS: *71* 8-10

RUSSELL, Brenda
Singles: 7-Inch
A&M: *79-88* 2-3
HORIZON: *79* 2-4
LPs: 10/12-Inch 33rpm
A&M: *79-88* 5-8
HORIZON: *79* 5-8

RUSSELL, Lee
(Leon Russell)
Singles: 7-Inch
BATON: *59* 8-12
ROULETTE: *58* 10-15
Also see RUSSELL, Leon

RUSSELL, Leon
(Leon Russell & The Shelter People; Leon Russell & The New Grass Revival)
Singles: 7-Inch
A&M (700 series): *64* 4-6
A&M (1200 series): *71* 2-4

ABC: *78* $2-3
COLUMBIA: 2-3
DOT: *65* 3-5
MCA: 1-3
PARADISE: *76-81* 1-3
SHELTER: *70-76* 2-4
Picture Sleeves
PARADISE: *78-84* 2-5
SHELTER: *74* 2-4
LPs: 10/12-Inch 33rpm
MCA: *79* 5-8
OLYMPIC: *73* 5-8
PARADISE: *78-81* 5-8
SHELTER (1000 & 2000 series): *70-75* . 10-20
SHELTER (8000 series, except 8917): *71-73* 10-15
SHELTER (8917; "Leon Live"): *73* 12-20
SHELTER (52000 series): *76* 8-10
Also see ASYLUM CHOIR
Also see CLAPTON, Eric
Also see COCKER, Joe
Also see DAVID & LEE
Also see HARRISON, George
Also see NELSON, Willie, & Leon Russell
Also see RUSSELL, Lee
Also see WILSON, Hank

RUSSELL, Leon & Mary
Singles: 7-Inch
PARADISE: *76-77* 2-4
LPs: 10/12-Inch 33rpm
PARADISE: *76-77* 8-10
Also see RUSSELL, Leon

RUSSELL, Sam
Singles: 7-Inch
PLAYBOY: *73* 2-4

RUSSO, Charlie
Singles: 7-Inch
DIAMOND: *63* 3-5
LAURIE: *67* 2-4
PART: *64* 3-5

RUTH, Babe: see BABE RUTH

RUTH & AL
Singles: 78rpm
IMPERIAL: *56* 3-5
Singles: 7-Inch
IMPERIAL: *56* 5-8

RUTH & SHERRY
Singles: 7-Inch
SWAN: *65* 3-5

RUTHERFORD, Don
Singles: 7-Inch
FINER ARTS: *65* 3-5

RECITAL: *64* $4-6

RUTHERFORD, Mike
Singles: 7-Inch
ATLANTIC: *83* 1-3
LPs: 10/12-Inch 33rpm
ATLANTIC: *83* 5-8
PASSPORT: 5-8
Also see GENESIS
Also see MIKE + THE MECHANICS

RUTLES
Singles: 12-Inch 33/45rpm
WARNER BROS (723; "The Rutles"): *78* **15-20**
(Colored vinyl. Promotional issue only.)
Singles: 7-Inch
PASSPORT: 1-3
WARNER BROS: *78* 2-4
LPs: 10/12-Inch 33rpm
WARNER BROS (3151; "The
Rutles"): *78* **10-12**
(Price includes bonus booklet, which represents $3-$5 of the value.)
Members: Neil Innes; Rikki Fataar; Erik Idle; John Hasley.
Also see BONZO DOG BAND

RYAN, Barry
Singles: 7-Inch
MGM: *68* 3-6
PRIDE: *71* 2-4

RYAN, Charlie
(Charlie Ryan & The Timberline Riders;
Charlie Ryan & The Livingston Brothers)
Singles: 7-Inch
FOUR STAR: *60-63* 2-5
SOUVENIR (101; "Hot
Rod Lincoln"): *55* 30-60
LPs: 10/12-Inch 33rpm
KING: *61* 20-30
PICKWICK/HILLTOP: *64* 10-15

RYDELL, Bobby
Singles: 7-Inch
ABKCO: 1-3
CAMEO ("Steel Pier"): 10-15
(Not numbered. A giveaway promotional item for
the Steel Pier in Atlantic City, NJ.)
CAMEO (160; "Please Don't
Be Mad"): *59* 10-15
CAMEO (164; "All I Want Is You"): *59* . 10-15
CAMEO (167 through 186): *59-61* 4-6
CAMEO (190 through 361): *61-65* 3-5
CAMEO (1070; "Forget Him"/"A Message
From Bobby"): *63* 5-10
(Packaged as a bonus single with the LP *Top Hits
Of 1963*.)

CAPITOL: *64-66* $3-5
P.I.P.: *76* 2-3
PERCEPTION: *74* 2-4
RCA VICTOR: *70* 2-4
REPRISE: *68* 3-5
TIME: *59* 5-8
VEKO: *58* 10-15
VENISE: *62* 5-8
Picture Sleeves
CAMEO: *59-64* 5-10
CAPITOL: *64* 5-10
EPs: 7-Inch
CAPITOL: *65* 10-15
LPs: 10/12-Inch 33rpm
CAMEO (1006; "We Got Love"): *59* 40-80
CAMEO (1007; "Bobby Sings,
Bobby Swings"): *60* 20-30
CAMEO (1009; "Bobby's Biggest
Hits"): *61* 40-50
(With gatefold cover and 12x12 photo insert.)
CAMEO (1009; "Bobby's Biggest
Hits"): *61* 30-35
(With gatefold cover, but without 12x12 photo insert.)
CAMEO (1009; "Bobby's Biggest
Hits"): *62* 15-20
(With standard cover; no gatefold, not die-cut.)
Copies with 1009 on the cover may have Cameo
1008 on the disc.)
CAMEO (1010 through 1055): *61-63* 15-25
CAMEO (1070; "Top Hits Of 1963
Sung By Robby Rydell"): *63* 20-30
(With bonus single *Forget Him/A Message From
Bobby*.)
CAMEO (1070; "Top Hits Of 1963
Sung By Robby Rydell"): *63* 15-20
(Without bonus single.)
CAMEO (1080; "Forget Him"): *64* 15-20
CAMEO (2000 series): 15-20
CAMEO (4017; "An Era Reborn"): *64* . . .15-25
CAPITOL: *65* 15-20
DESIGN: 10-15
P.I.P.: *76* 8-12
SPINORAMA: 10-15
STRAND: *60* 25-35
Also see CHECKER, Chubby, & Bobby
Rydell

RYDER, John & Anne
Singles: 7-Inch
DECCA: *69* 2-4
LPs: 10/12-Inch 33rpm
DECCA: *70* 10-12

RYDER, Mitch
(Mitch Ryder & The Detroit Wheels)
Singles: 7-Inch

ABC: 73	$1-3
AVCO EMBASSY: 70	3-5
DOT: 69	3-5
DYNO VOICE: 67-68	3-5
ERIC:	1-3
NEW VOICE (Except 820): 65-68	3-5
NEW VOICE (820; "Sock It To Me-Baby"): 67	4-6
(With "Feels like a punch" lyrics.)	
NEW VOICE (820; "Sock It To Me-Baby"): 67	3-5
(With "Hits me like a punch" lyrics.)	
RIVA: 83	1-3
VIRGO: 73	1-3

Picture Sleeves

NEW VOICE: 67	3-6

LPs: 10/12-Inch 33rpm

CREWE:	12-15
DOT: 69	12-15
DYNO VOICE: 67	12-15
NEW VOICE: 66 68	40-60
RIVA: 83	5-8
ROULETTE:	5-8
SEEDS & STEMS: 78-80	5-8
VIRGO: 73	8-10

Members: Mitch Ryder; Joe Kubert; Jim Mc-
Callister; Jim McCarty; Johnny Badanjek.
Also see DETROIT
Also see DETROIT WHEELS

RYLES, John Wesley
Singles: 7-Inch

ABC/DOT: 77	1-3
COLUMBIA: 68-70	2-3
GRT: 70	2-3
MCA: 79-83	1-3
MUSIC MILL: 75-76	1-3
PLANTATION: 72-73	2-3
PRIMERO: 82	1-3
RCA VICTOR: 74	2-3
16TH AVE: 84	1-3
WARNER BROS: 87-88	1-3

LPs: 10/12-Inch 33rpm

ABC: 78	6-10
ABC/DOT: 77	8-10
COLUMBIA: 69	8-12
MCA: 79-83	4-8
PLANTATION: 77	5-8

S

S.O.S. BAND
Singles: 12-Inch 33/45rpm

TABU: 80-85	$4-6

Singles: 7-Inch

TABU: 80-87	1-3

LPs: 10/12-Inch 33rpm

TABU: 80-85	5-8

S.O.U.L.
Singles: 7-Inch

MUSICOR: 71-74	2-4

LPs: 10/12-Inch 33rpm

MUSICOR: 72	8-10

SRC
(Scott Richard Case)
Singles: 7-Inch

A SQUARE: 67	5-10
BIG CASINO: 71	4-6
CAPITOL: 68-69	4-6

LPs: 10/12-Inch 33rpm

CAPITOL (134; "Milestones"): 69	25-40
CAPITOL (273; "Traveler's Tale"): 69	12-15
CAPITOL (2991; "SRC"): 68	40-65

SRC / Rationals
Singles: 7-Inch

A SQUARE: 67	5-10

Also see SRC

S.S.O.
Singles: 7-Inch

SHADY BROOK: 75-76	1-3

SSQ
Singles: 12-Inch 33/45rpm

ENIGMA: 84	4-6

Singles: 7-Inch

ENIGMA: 84	1-3

LPs: 10/12-Inch 33rpm

ENIGMA: 84	5-8

Also see ST. JAMES, Jon

SAAD, Sue, & The Next
Singles: 7-Inch

PLANET: 80	1-3

LPs: 10/12-Inch 33rpm

PLANET: 80	5-8

SACCO
(Lou Christie)
Singles: 12-Inch 33/45rpm

LIFESONG: 78	10-15

Singles: 7-Inch
LIFESONG: 78 .... $2-4
Also see CHRISTIE, Lou

SAD CAFE
Singles: 7-Inch
A&M: 78-79 2-3
SWAN SONG: 81 1-3
Picture Sleeves
SWAN SONG: 81 1-3
LPs: 10/12-Inch 33rpm
A&M: 78-79 6-10
SWAN SONG: 81 5-8
Members: Paul Young; Doreen Chanter; Irene
Chanter; John Stimpson; Vic Emerson; Ian Wilson;
Ashley Mulford; Lenni Zaksen.
Also see MIKE + THE MECHANICS
Also see YOUNG, Paul

SADANE, Marc
(Sadane)
Singles: 7-Inch
WARNER BROS: 81-82 1-3
Picture Sleeves
WARNER BROS: 81 1-3
LPs: 10/12-Inch 33rpm
WARNER BROS: 81 5-8

SADE
Singles: 12-Inch 33/45rpm
PORTRAIT: 84-86 4-6
Singles: 7-Inch
EPIC: 88 1-3
PORTRAIT: 84-86 1-3
LPs: 10/12-Inch 33rpm
EPIC: 88 5-8
PORTRAIT: 85-86 5-8

SADLER, Barry
(S/SGT. Barry Sadler)
Singles: 7-Inch
GAS: 78 1-3
RCA VICTOR: 66-67 2-5
Picture Sleeves
RCA VICTOR: 66-67 3-6
LPs: 10/12-Inch 33rpm
RCA VICTOR: 66-67 10-15
VETERAN: 74 10-20

SA-FIRE
Singles: 7-Inch
CUTTING: 88 1-3
LPs: 10/12-Inch 33rpm
CUTTING: 88 5-8

SAFARIS
(With The Phantom's Band)
Singles: 7-Inch
ELDO: 60-61 10-15

Members: Jimmy Stephens; Marv Rosenberg;
Richard Clasky; Shelly Briar.

SAGA
Singles: 7-Inch
POLYDOR: 79 .... $1-3
PORTRAIT: 82-85 1-3
LPs: 10/12-Inch 33rpm
ATLANTIC: 87 5-8
POLYDOR: 79 5-8
PORTRAIT: 82-85 5-8

SAGER, Carole Bayer
(Carole Bayer)
Singles: 7-Inch
BOARDWALK: 81 1-3
ELEKTRA: 77-78 1-3
METROMEDIA: 72 2-4
Picture Sleeves
BOARDWALK: 81 1-3
LPs: 10/12-Inch 33rpm
BOARDWALK: 81 5-8
ELEKTRA: 77-78 6-10

SAGITTARIUS
Singles: 7-Inch
COLUMBIA: 67-69 4-6
TOGETHER: 68-69 4-6
LPs: 10/12-Inch 33rpm
BACK-TRAC: 85 5-8
COLUMBIA: 68 15-20
TOGETHER: 69 20-25
Members: Gary Usher; Glen Campbell; Bruce
Johnston; Terry Melcher; Curt Boetcher.
Also see BRUCE & TERRY
Also see CAMPBELL, Glen

SAHL, Mort
LPs: 10/12-Inch 33rpm
GNP/CRESCENDO: 73 5-10
MERCURY: 67 5-12
REPRISE: 61 10-15
VERVE: 59-64 10-20
Also see MARTIN, Dean

SAHM, Doug
(Doug Sahm & The Mex Trip; Doug Sahm &
The Texas Tornados)
Singles: 7-Inch
ABC/DOT: 76 2-4
ATLANTIC: 73 8-10
CASABLANCA: 75 10-20
CHRYSALIS: 81 2-4
COBRA: 61 40-60
CRAZY CAJUN: 74 3-5
HARLEM: 60 20-35
PERSONALITY: 59 20-25
PLAYBOY: 76 2-4

RENNER (Colored vinyl): *61* $35-45
(Promotional issues only.)
RENNER (Black vinyl): *61-64* 15-30
SATIN: *59* 20-30
SOFT: *65* 10-15
SWINGIN': *60* 10-20
TEXAS RECORD: *76* 5-10
WARNER BROS: *74* 2-4
WARRIOR: *58* 30-35
Picture Sleeves
CHRYSALIS: *81* 2-4
LPs: 10/12-Inch 33rpm
ANTONE'S: *88* 5-8
ATLANTIC: *73* 8-10
HARLEM: *79* 8-10
MERCURY: *73* 8-10
TAKOMA: *80* 5-8
WARNER BROS: *74* 8-10
Also see BROMBERG, David
Also see DR. JOHN
Also see DYLAN, Bob
Also see SIR DOUGLAS QUINTET

SAHM, Doug, & Augie Meyers
Singles: 7-Inch
TEARDROP: *83* 1-3
Also see SAHM, Doug

SAILCAT
Singles: 7-Inch
ELEKTRA: *72-73* 2-4
LPs: 10/12-Inch 33rpm
ELEKTRA: *72* 10-12

SAIN, Oliver
Singles: 7-Inch
ABET: *71-77* 2-4
BOBBIN: *62* 3-5
HCRC: *82* 1-3
LPs: 10/12-Inch 33rpm
ABET (400 series): *71-73* 8-10
ABET (8700 series): *77* 5-8

ST. JAMES, Jon
Singles: 12-Inch 33/45rpm
EMI AMERICA: *84* 4-6
Singles: 7-Inch
EMI AMERICA: *84* 1-3
LPs: 10/12-Inch 33rpm
EMI AMERICA: *84* 5-8
Also see SSQ

ST. PETERS, Crispian
Singles: 7-Inch
JAMIE: *66-68* 3-5
LPs: 10/12-Inch 33rpm
JAMIE: *66* 20-25

Doug Sahm

ST. ROMAIN, Kirby
Singles: 7-Inch
INETTE: *63-64* $3-5
TEARDROP: *64* 3-5

SAINT TROPEZ
Singles: 12-Inch 33/45rpm
BUTTERFLY: *77-79* 4-6
DESTINY: *82* 4-6
Singles: 7-Inch
BUTTERFLY: *77-79* 2-3
DESTINY: *82* 1-3
LPs: 10/12-Inch 33rpm
BUTTERFLY (Black vinyl): *77-79* 6-10
BUTTERFLY (Colored vinyl): *77-79* ... 10-15
DESTINY: *82* 5-8

SAINTE-MARIE, Buffy
Singles: 7-Inch
ABC: *76* 1-3
MCA: *74-75* 1-3
VANGUARD: *65-72* 2-5
LPs: 10/12-Inch 33rpm
ABC: *76* 5-8
MCA: *74-75* 5-10
VANGUARD: *64-74* 8-15

SAKAMOTO, Kyu
Singles: 7-Inch
CAPITOL: *63-64* 3-5
EMI: *75* 2-3
LPs: 10/12-Inch 33rpm
CAPITOL: *63* 12-15

SALES, Soupy
Singles: 7-Inch
ABC-PARAMOUNT: *65* $3-6
CAPITOL: *66* 3-5
MOTOWN: *69* 3-5
REPRISE: *62* 3-6
Picture Sleeves
CAPITOL: *66* 3-6
LPs: 10/12-Inch 33rpm
ABC-PARAMOUNT: *64-65* 15-20
MOTOWN: *69* 10-15
REPRISE: *61-62* 15-20

SALSOUL ORCHESTRA
Singles: 12-Inch 33/45rpm
SALSOUL: *78-83* 4-6
Singles: 7-Inch
SALSOUL: *75-83* 1-3
LPs: 10/12-Inch 33rpm
SALSOUL: *75-83* 5-8
Also see CHARO
Also see HOLLOWAY, Loleatta

SALT-N-PEPA
Singles: 7-Inch
NEXT PLATEAU: *88* 1-3
LPs: 10/12-Inch 33rpm
NEXT PLATEAU: *88* 5-8

SALVAGE
Singles: 7-Inch
ODAX: *71* 2-4

SALVO, Sammy
Singles: 78rpm
RCA VICTOR: *57* 3-6
Singles: 7-Inch
DOT: *60* 3-5
HICKORY: *61-63* 5-10
IMPERIAL: *59-60* 3-5
MARK V: 5-8
RCA VICTOR: *57-59* 4-6

SAM, Butch, & The Station Band
Singles: 7-Inch
PRIVATE I: *85* 1-3

SAM & BILL
Singles: 7-Inch
DECCA: *67* 3-5
JODA: *65-66* 3-5
Members: Sam Gary; Bill Johnson.

SAM & DAVE
Singles: 7-Inch
ATLANTIC: *68-71* 2-4
ROULETTE: *62-66* 3-6
STAX: *65-68* 3-5
UNITED ARTISTS: *74-75* 2-4

LPs: 10/12-Inch 33rpm
ATLANTIC (8205; "I Thank
You"): *68* $12-15
ATLANTIC (8218; "Best Of Sam
& Dave"): *69* 8-10
GUSTO: 5-8
ROULETTE: *66* 12-15
STAX: *66-67* 15-30
UNITED ARTISTS: *74-75* 8-10
Members: Sam Moore; Dave Prater.
Also see STARS ON 45 (Featuring Sam &
Dave)

SAM THE SHAM & THE PHARAOHS
(Sam The Sham Revue; Sam; Sam Samudio)
Singles: 7-Inch
DINGO: *64* 5-8
MGM (13000 series): *64-69* 3-5
MGM (14000 series): *73* 2-4
POLYDOR: 1-3
TUPELO: *63* 5-8
WARRIOR: 20-30
XL: *64-65* 15-20
Picture Sleeves
MGM: *65-67* 5-10
LPs: 10/12-Inch 33rpm
MGM: *65-68* 12-15

SAMI JO
(Sami Jo Cole)
Singles: 7-Inch
FAME: *71-72* 2-4
MGM: *74-75* 2-3
POLYDOR: *76* 1-3
LPs: 10/12-Inch 33rpm
MGM: *74-75* 5-10

SAMPLE, Joe
Singles: 7-Inch
ABC: *78-79* 2-3
MCA: *80-83* 1-3
LPs: 10/12-Inch 33rpm
ABC: *78-79* 5-10
MCA: *81-83* 5-8
MFSL: *78* 25-50
Also see CRUSADERS

SAN REMO GOLDEN STRINGS
Singles: 7-Inch
GORDY: *67* 2-3
RIC-TIC: *65-66* 2-4
LPs: 10/12-Inch 33rpm
GORDY: *67-68* 8-12
RIC-TIC: *66* 10-15

SAN SEBASTIAN STRINGS
(Rod McKuen With The San Sebastian Strings)
Singles: 7-Inch
WARNER BROS: 67-73 .... $1-3
LPs: 10/12-Inch 33rpm
WARNER BROS (Except 2754): 67-75 ... 5-15
WARNER BROS (2754; "Spring, Summer,
Winter, Autumn"): 73 10-20
(4-LP set.)
Also see McKUEN, Rod

SANBORN, David
Singles: 12-Inch 33/45rpm
WARNER BROS: 81-85 4-6
Singles: 7-Inch
REPRISE: 88 1-3
WARNER BROS: 76-87 1-3
LPs: 10/12-Inch 33rpm
REPRISE: 88 5-8
WARNER BROS: 81-87 5-8
Also see JAMES, Bob, & David Sanborn

SANDALS
Singles: 7-Inch
WORLD PACIFIC (400 series): 64 4-6
WORLD PACIFIC (77000 series): 65-67 ... 3-5
Members: John Blakely; Danny Brawner; John Gibson; Gaston Georis; Walter Georis.

SANDERS, Felicia
Singles: 78rpm
COLUMBIA: 52-57 2-5
Singles: 7-Inch
COLUMBIA: 52-57 2-5
DECCA: 59-61 2-4
MGM: 65 2-3
TIME: 60 2-3
EPs: 7-Inch 33/45rpm
COLUMBIA: 55-56 5-10
LPs: 10/12-Inch 33rpm
COLUMBIA: 55-57 10-20
SPECIAL EDITIONS: 67 5-10
TIME: 60-64 5-15
Also see FAITH, Percy
Also see VALE, Jerry, Peggy King, & Felicia
Sanders

SANDERS, Pharoah
Singles: 7-Inch
ARISTA: 78 2-3
LPs: 10/12-Inch 33rpm
ARISTA: 78 5-8
IMPULSE: 69-74 8-12
INDIA NAVIGATION: 77 5-8
NOVUS: 81 5-8
THERESA: 80-81 5-12
TRIP: 71 5-10

SANDLER, Tony, & Ralph Young
(Sandler & Young)
Singles: 7-Inch
CAPITOL: 66-70 .... $2-4
LPs: 10/12-Inch 33rpm
A.V.I.: 79 4-8
CAPITOL: 66-78 5-15

SANDPEBBLES
Singles: 7-Inch
ABC: 73 1-3
CALLA: 67-69 3-5
Also see C & THE SHELLS

SANDPIPERS
Singles: 7-Inch
A&M: 66-72 2-5
KISMET: 66 3-5
TRU-GLOW-TOWN: 66 3-5
LPs: 10/12-Inch 33rpm
A&M: 66-73 8-12

SANDS, Evie
Singles: 7-Inch
ABC-PARAMOUNT: 63-64 3-5
A&M: 68-70 2-4
BLUE CAT: 65 4-6
CAMEO: 66-68 3-5
GOLD: 64 3-5
HAVEN: 75-76 2-3
RCA VICTOR: 79 1-3
LPs: 10/12-Inch 33rpm
A&M: 69 10-15
HAVEN: 74 8-10
RCA VICTOR: 79 5-8

SANDS, Jodie
Singles: 78rpm
BERNLO: 57 3-6
CHANCELLOR: 57 3-6
Singles: 7-Inch
ABC: 74 1-3
ABC-PARAMOUNT: 62-63 3-5
BERNLO: 57 4-6
CHANCELLOR: 57-59 4-6
PARIS: 60-61 3-5
SIGNATURE: 59 4-6
TEEN: 55 5-8
THOR: 59 4-6

SANDS, Tommy
(Tommy Sands & The Raiders)
Singles: 78rpm
CAPITOL: 57 4-8
RCA VICTOR: 54-56 5-8
Singles: 7-Inch
ABC-PARAMOUNT: 63-64 3-5
CAPITOL (3639 through 4082): 57-58 5-8

CAPITOL (4160 through 4580): *59-61* . . . **$4-6**
IMPERIAL: *66-67* **3-5**
LIBERTY: *65* **3-5**
RCA VICTOR: *54-56* **5-8**
SUPERSCOPE: *69* **2-4**
Picture Sleeves
CAPITOL: *58-59* **5-10**
EPs: 7-Inch 33/45rpm
CAPITOL: *57-59* **15-25**
LPs: 10/12-Inch 33rpm
BRUNSWICK: *78* **8-10**
CAPITOL (848 through 1239): *57-59* . . **25-30**
CAPITOL (1300 & 1400 series): *60* **20-25**
Also see ANNETTE & TOMMY SANDS

SANDS OF TIME
(Tokens)
Singles: 7-Inch
KIRSHNER: *76* **3-5**
Also see TOKENS

SANFORD-TOWNSEND BAND
Singles: 7-Inch
WARNER BROS: *77-79* **2-3**
LPs: 10/12-Inch 33rpm
WARNER BROS: *78-79* **5-8**
Members: Ed Sanford; John Townsend.

SANG, Samantha
Singles: 7-Inch
ATCO: *69* **3-5**
PRIVATE STOCK: *77-78* **2-3**
UNITED ARTISTS: *79* **1-3**
LPs: 10/12-Inch 33rpm
PRIVATE STOCK: *77-78* **5-8**
UNITED ARTISTS: *79* **5-8**
Also see BEE GEES

SANS, Billie
Singles: 7-Inch
INVICTUS: *71* **2-4**

SANTA ESMERALDA:
see ESMERALDA, Santa

SANTAMARIA, Mongo
(Mongo Santamaria & His Afro-Latin Group)
Singles: 12-Inch 33/45rpm
TAPPAN ZEE: *79* **4-6**
Singles: 7-Inch
ATLANTIC: *69-72* **2-4**
BATTLE: *63* **4-8**
COLLECTABLES: **1-3**
COLUMBIA: *64-69* **2-4**
FANTASY: *61-62* **2-4**
RIVERSIDE: *62-66* **2-4**
TAPPAN ZEE: *79* **1-3**
VAYA: *73* **2-3**

LPs: 10/12-Inch 33rpm
ATLANTIC: *70* **$8-10**
BATTLE: *63* **12-15**
COLUMBIA: *65-79* **5-12**
FANTASY: *59-62* **5-15**
(Many Fantasy LPs are still available, using
original catalog numbers in the 8000 series. Fan-
tasy 3000 series numbers were mono and are out of
print.)
MILESTONE: *73-76* **5-12**
PRESTIGE: *72* **6-12**
RIVERSIDE: *62-66* **8-15**
VAYA: *73-74* **5-10**

SANTANA
Singles: 12-Inch 33/45rpm
COLUMBIA: *85* **4-6**
Singles: 7-Inch
COLUMBIA: *69-82* **1-3**
Picture Sleeves
COLUMBIA: *70-82* **1-3**
LPs: 10/12-Inch 33rpm
COLUMBIA: *69-88* **8-15**
Members: Devadip Carlos Santana; Armando
Peraza; Graham Lear; David Margen; Richard
Baker; Alex Ligertwood; Orestes Vilato; Raul
Rekow.
Also see AZTECA
Also see BOOKER T. & THE MGs
Also see COLTRANE, Alice, & Carlos
Santana
Also see ESCOVEDO, Coke
Also see FABULOUS THUNDERBIRDS
Also see FRANKLIN, Aretha
Also see HAGAR, SCHON, AARONSON,
SHRIEVE
Also see HANCOCK, Herbie
Also see NOVO COMBO

SANTANA, Carlos, & Buddy Miles
Singles: 7-Inch
COLUMBIA: *72* **2-4**
LPs: 10/12-Inch 33rpm
COLUMBIA: *72* **6-10**
Also see MILES, Buddy
Also see SANTANA

SANTANA, Jorge
Singles: 7-Inch
TOMATO: *78-79* **2-3**
Also see MALO

SANTIAGO
Singles: 7-Inch
AMHERST: *76* **2-3**

SANTO & JOHNNY
Singles: 7-Inch
CANADIAN AMERICAN: 59-66 ...... $4-8
ERIC: 1-3
IMPERIAL: 67-68 3-6
ERIC: 1-3
UNITED ARTISTS: 66 3-6
Picture Sleeves
CANADIAN AMERICAN: 60-64 5-10
LPs: 10/12-Inch 33rpm
CANADIAN AMERICAN: 59-64 20-35
IMPERIAL: 67-69 10-15
Members: Santo Farina; Johnny Farina.

SANTOS, Larry
Singles: 7-Inch
ATLANTIC: 64 5-8
BATON: 8-10
CASABLANCA: 76-77 2-3
EVOLUTION: 69-71 2-4
LPs: 10/12-Inch 33rpm
CASABLANCA: 77 8-10
EVOLUTION: 69 10-12
Also see 4 SEASONS

SAPPHIRES
Singles: 7-Inch
ABC: 73 2-3
ABC-PARAMOUNT: 64-66 5-8
COLLECTABLES: 1-3
ERIC: 1-3
SWAN: 63-64 8-10
LPs: 10/12-Inch 33rpm
SWAN: 64 30-40

SARDUCCI, Father Guido
Singles: 7-Inch
A&M: 74 2-3
WARNER BROS: 80 1-3
LPs: 10/12-Inch 33rpm
WARNER BROS: 80 5-8

SARIDIS, Saverio
Singles: 7-Inch
UNITED ARTISTS: 66 1-3
WARNER BROS: 61-62 2-4
Picture Sleeves
WARNER BROS: 61 2-5
LPs: 10/12-Inch 33rpm
WARNER BROS: 62 5-10

SARSTEDT, Peter
Singles: 7-Inch
SIRE: 78 2-3
UNITED ARTISTS: 72 2-4
WORLD PACIFIC: 69 2-4
LPs: 10/12-Inch 33rpm
UNITED ARTISTS: 71 8-10

WORLD PACIFIC: 69 .... $10-12

SASS
Singles: 7-Inch
20TH CENTURY-FOX: 77 2-3

SATELLITE, Billy:
see BILLY SATELLITE

SATISFACTIONS
Singles: 7-Inch
CHESAPEAKE: 63 4-6
IMPERIAL: 66 3-5
LIONEL: 70-71 2-4
1-2-3: 69 2-4
SMASH: 66-67 3-5

SATTERFIELD, Esther
Singles: 7-Inch
A&M: 76 2-3
LPs: 10/12-Inch 33rpm
A&M: 76 5-10

SATURDAY NIGHT BAND
Singles: 7-Inch
PRELUDE: 78 2-3
LPs: 10/12-Inch 33rpm
PRELUDE: 78 5-8

SAULSBERRY, Rodney
Singles: 7-Inch
ALLEGIANCE: 84-85 1-3
RYAN: 88 1-3

SAUNDERS, Merl
(Merle Saunders & Heavy Turbulence)
Singles: 7-Inch
FANTASY: 64-69 3-6
GALAXY: 71 3-5
LPs: 10/12-Inch 33rpm
FANTASY: 68-73 10-20
Also see FOGERTY, Tom
Also see GARCIA, Jerry

SAUNDERS, Red
(Red Saunders Featuring Delores Hawkins)
Singles: 78rpm
BLUE LAKE: 54 3-6
OKEH: 51-53 4-8
SAVOY: 45 8-10
SULTAN: 46 10-15
SUPREME: 49 5-8
Singles: 7-Inch
BLUE LAKE (Colored vinyl): 54 5-8
OKEH (6000 series): 51-53 5-10
OKEH (7000 series): 63 3-5
Picture Sleeves
OKEH (7000 series): 63 4-8

SAVAGE GRACE
Singles: 7-Inch
REPRISE: 70-71 .... $2-4
LPs: 10/12-Inch 33rpm
REPRISE: 70-71 10-12

SAVALAS, Telly
Singles: 7-Inch
MCA: 74-75 2-3
LPs: 10/12-Inch 33rpm
AUDIO FIDELITY: 75 5-10
MCA: 74-76 5-10

SAVATAGE
Singles: 7-Inch
ATLANTIC: 86 1-3
LPs: 10/12-Inch 33rpm
ATLANTIC: 86-87 5-8

SAVOY, Ronnie
Singles: 7-Inch
CANDELO: 59 4-6
EPIC: 63-64 3-5
GONE: 59 4-6
MGM: 60-61 3-5
PHILIPS: 62-63 3-5
WINGATE: 65 3-5

SAVOY BROWN
(Savoy Brown Blues Band)
Singles: 7-Inch
LONDON: 74-75 2-4
PARROT: 69-73 3-5
TOWN HOUSE: 81 1-3
LPs: 10/12-Inch 33rpm
LONDON (600 & 700 series): 74-77 8-10
LONDON (50000; "Best Of
Savoy Brown"): 77 5-8
PARROT: 68-73 10-15
(Many Parrot LPs are currently available using
original catalog numbers.)
TOWN HOUSE (Except 7562): 81 8-12
TOWN HOUSE (7562; "Prime
Cuts"): 81 10-15
(Promotional issue only.)
Also see FOGHAT

SAWYER, Ray
Singles: 7-Inch
CAPITOL: 76-79 2-3
SANDY: 60-62 10-20
LPs: 10/12-Inch 33rpm
CAPITOL: 76 6-10
Also see DR. HOOK

SAWYER BROWN
Singles: 7-Inch
CAPITOL/CURB: 84-88 1-3

LPs: 10/12-Inch 33rpm
CAPITOL/CURB: 85-86 .... $5-8

SAWYER BROWN & "CAT" JOE BONSALL
Singles: 7-Inch
CAPITOL/CURB: 86 1-3
Also see SAWYER BROWN

SAXON
Singles: 7-Inch
CARRERE: 83-84 1-3
LPs: 10/12-Inch 33rpm
CAPITOL: 87 5-8
Also see MOTORHEAD

SAYER, Leo
Singles: 7-Inch
WARNER BROS: 73-84 1-3
LPs: 10/12-Inch 33rpm
WARNER BROS: 75-84 6-10

SCAFFOLD
Singles: 7-Inch
BELL: 68 4-6
WARNER BROS: 74 3-5
LPs: 10/12-Inch 33rpm
BELL: 68 25-30
Member: Mike McGear.

SCAGGS, Boz
Singles: 7-Inch
ATLANTIC: 69 3-5
COLUMBIA: 71-88 1-3
FULL MOON: 81 1-3
Picture Sleeves
COLUMBIA: 76-81 1-3
EPs: 7-Inch 33/45rpm
COLUMBIA: 76 5-8
LPs: 10/12-Inch 33rpm
ATLANTIC (8239; "Boz Scaggs"): 69 8-12
ATLANTIC (19166; "Boz Scaggs"): 78 5-8
COLUMBIA (Except 40000 series): 71-80 .6-10
COLUMBIA (40000 series): 80 12-15
(Half-speed mastered.)
Promotional LPs
COLUMBIA (203; "The Boz Scaggs
Sampler"): 76 10-15
Also see MILLER, Steve, Band

SCALES, Harvey
(Harvey Scales & The Seven Sounds)
Singles: 7-Inch
CASABLANCA: 2-4
CHESS: 70 2-4
MAGIC TOUCH: 67-68 3-5
MERCURY: 69 2-4
STAX: 2-4

LPs: 10/12-Inch 33rpm
CASABLANCA: 79 .... $5-8

SCANDAL
(Scandal Featuring Patty Smyth)
Singles: 12-Inch 33/45rpm
COLUMBIA (Except picture discs): 82-85 . 4-6
COLUMBIA (Picture discs): 82 10-12
Singles: 7-Inch
COLUMBIA: 82-85 1-3
LPs: 10/12-Inch 33rpm
COLUMBIA: 82-85 5-8

SCARBURY, Joey
Singles: 7-Inch
BELL: 71-73 2-4
BIG TREE: 73 2-4
COLUMBIA: 77-79 2-3
ELEKTRA: 81 1-3
LIONEL: 71 2-4
PLAYBOY: 74 .¦..................... 2-3
RCA VICTOR: 84 1-3
REENA: 68 3-5
Picture Sleeves
ELEKTRA: 81 1-3
LPs: 10/12-Inch 33rpm
ELEKTRA: 81 5-8

SCARLETT & BLACK
Singles: 7-Inch
VIRGIN: 88 1-3
LPs: 10/12-Inch 33rpm
VIRGIN: 88 5-8

SCHAFER, Kermit
Singles: 78rpm
JUBILEE: 56 5-10
Singles: 7-Inch
JUBILEE (5258; "Rock Around
The Blooper"): 56 10-15
LPs: 10/12-Inch 33rpm
AUDIO FIDELITY: 69 6-12
JUBILEE: 58-63 8-15
KAPP: 68-70 5-10
KING: 64 6-12
MCA: 74-77 5-8
Note: Kermit Schafer has released numerous com-
edy albums of "Bloopers," which we have not at-
tempted to list.

SCHENKER, Michael, Group
Singles: 7-Inch
CHRYSALIS: 80-83 1-3
LPs: 10/12-Inch 33rpm
CHRYSALIS: 80-83 5-8
Also see ALCATRAZZ
Also see UFO

SCHIFRIN, Lalo
Singles: 12-Inch 33/45rpm
TABU: 78-79 .... $4-6
Singles: 7-Inch
A&M: 75 1-3
CTI: 76-77 1-3
DOT: 67 2-4
MCA: 77-83 1-3
MGM: 63-70 2-3
PABLO: 77 1-3
PARAMOUNT: 69 2-3
TABU: 78-79 1-3
TETRAGRAMMATON: 69 2-3
20TH CENTURY-FOX: 74-75 1-3
UNITED ARTISTS: 70 1-3
VERVE: 63-71 2-3
WARNER BROS: 68-69 2-3
LPs: 10/12-Inch 33rpm
AUDIO FIDELITY: 62-68 5-15
CTI: 76-77 5-8
COLGEMS (5003; "Murderer's
Row"): 66 25-40
(Soundtrack.)
COLPIX: 64 10-20
DOT (831; "Mission Impossible"): 67 ... 12-20
(Soundtrack. Dot monaural issues are preceded by
a "3," stereo by a "25.")
DOT (833; "Cool Hand Luke"): 68 20-30
(Soundtrack. Dot monaural issues are preceded by
a "3," stereo by a "25.")
DOT (25852; "There's A Whole Lalo
Schifrin Goin' On"): 68 5-12
MCA (2284; "Rollercoaster"): 77 8-12
(Soundtrack.)
MCA (2374; "Nunzio"): 78 8-12
(Soundtrack.)
MCA (5000 series): 81 5-10
MGM: 63-70 5-15
PARAMOUNT (5002; "More Mission
Impossible"): 69 10-15
(Soundtrack.)
PARAMOUNT (5004; "Mannix"): 69 ... 15-20
(Soundtrack.)
ROULETTE: 62 8-15
TABU: 79 5-8
TETRAGRAMMATON (5006;
"Che"): 69 20-30
(Soundtrack.)
TICO: 60 8-15
VERVE (Except 8624): 63-69 8-15
VERVE (8624; "Music From Once A
Thief & Other Themes"): 65 20-35
(Soundtrack.)

WARNER BROS (1738; "The
Fox"): 68 .... $30-35
(Soundtrack.)
WARNER BROS (2727; "Enter The
Dragon"): 73 .... **10-15**
(Soundtrack.)

SCHILLING, Nina
Singles: 12-Inch 33/45rpm
MOBY DICK: 84 .... **4-6**

SCHILLING, Peter
Singles: 12-Inch 33/45rpm
ELEKTRA: 83 .... **4-6**
Singles: 7-Inch
ELEKTRA: 83 .... **1-3**
LPs: 10/12-Inch 33rpm
ELEKTRA: 83 .... **5-8**

SCHMIT, Timothy B.
Singles: 7-Inch
FULL MOON: 82 .... **1-3**
MCA: 87-88 .... **1-3**
LPs: 10/12-Inch 33rpm
ASYLUM: 84 .... **5-8**
MCA: 87 .... **5-8**
Also see EAGLES
Also see POCO

**SCHNEIDER, Fred, & The Shake
Society**
Singles: 12-Inch 33/45rpm
WARNER BROS: 84 .... **4-6**
Singles: 7-Inch
WARNER BROS: 84 .... **1-3**

SCHNEIDER, John
Singles: 7-Inch
MCA: 84-87 .... **1-3**
SCOTTI BROS: 81-83 .... **1-3**
Picture Sleeves
MCA: 84-86 .... **1-3**
SCOTTI BROS: 81-83 .... **1-3**
LPs: 10/12-Inch 33rpm
MCA: 84-86 .... **5-8**
SCOTTI BROS: 81-83 .... **5-8**

SCHNEIDER, John, & Jill Michaels
Singles: 7-Inch
SCOTTI BROS: 83 .... **1-3**
Also see SCHNEIDER, John

SCHON, Neal, & Jan Hammer
LPs: 10/12-Inch 33rpm
COLUMBIA: 81-83 .... **5-8**
Also see HAGAR, SCHON, AARONSON,
SHRIEVE
Also see HAMMER, Jan
Also see JOURNEY

SCHOOLBOYS
Singles: 78rpm
OKEH: 57 .... **$5-10**
Singles: 7-Inch
JUANITA: 58 .... **10-15**
OKEH: 57 .... **15-20**
EPs: 7-Inch 33/45rpm
MAGIC CARPET: **5-8**
Members: Les Martin; Jim Edwards; Roger Hayes;
Jim McKay; Renaldo Gamble.
Also see CADILLACS

SCHOOLLY D
LPs: 10/12-Inch 33rpm
JIVE: 88 .... **5-8**

SCHORY, Dick
(Dick Schory's Percussion Pops Orchestra)
LPs: 10/12-Inch 33rpm
RCA VICTOR: 59-63 .... **5-15**

SCHUMANN, Walter
(Voices Of Walter Schumann)
Singles: 78rpm
CAPITOL: 52 .... **2-4**
RCA VICTOR: 53-56 .... **2-4**
Singles: 7-Inch
CAPITOL: 52 .... **2-4**
RCA VICTOR: 53-56 .... **2-4**
EPs: 7-Inch 33/45rpm
CAPITOL: 52 .... **4-8**
RCA VICTOR: 53-56 .... **4-8**
LPs: 10/12-Inch 33rpm
CAPITOL: 52 .... **5-15**
RCA VICTOR: 53-56 .... **5-15**

SCHUUR, Diane
LPs: 10/12-Inch 33rpm
GRP: 88 .... **5-8**

SCHWARTZ, Eddie
Singles: 7-Inch
ATCO: 81-82 .... **1-3**
LPs: 10/12-Inch 33rpm
ATCO: 82 .... **5-8**

SCORPIONS
Singles: 7-Inch
MERCURY: 79-88 .... **1-3**
RCA VICTOR: 74-80 .... **2-4**
LPs: 10/12-Inch 33rpm
MERCURY: 79-88 .... **5-8**
RCA VICTOR: 74-84 .... **5-10**
Members: Klaus Meine; Francis Bucholz; Matt
Jabs; Herman Rarebell; Uli Roth; Rudolf Schenker.

SCOTT, Billy
Singles: 78rpm
CAMEO: 57 .... **3-6**

Singles: 7-Inch
CAMEO: *57-58* $4-6
EVEREST: *59* 5-8

SCOTT, Bobby
Singles: 78rpm
ABC-PARAMOUNT: *56* 4-8
Singles: 7-Inch
ABC: *73* 1-3
ABC-PARAMOUNT: *56* 8-10

SCOTT, Christopher
(Sir Christopher Scott)
LPs: 10/12-Inch 33rpm
DECCA: *69-70* 5-10
MCA: *73* 4-8

SCOTT, Freddie
(Freddy Scott)
Singles: 7-Inch
ABC: *74* 1-3
COLPIX: *63-64* 3-5
COLUMBIA: *64-65* 3-5
ERIC: *68* 1-3
JOY: *61-63* 3-5
P.I.P.: *72* 2-4
PROBE: *70* 2-4
SHOUT: *66-71* 3-5
SOLID GOLD: *73* 2-4
VANGUARD: *71* 2-3
LPs: 10/12-Inch 33rpm
COLPIX (Gold label): *64* 25-40
COLPIX (Blue label): *65* 15-20
COLUMBIA: *64-67* 10-15
PROBE: *70* 8-12
SHOUT: *67* 10-15

SCOTT, Gloria
Singles: 7-Inch
CASABLANCA: *75* 2-4

SCOTT, Jack
(Jack Scott & The Chantones)
Singles: 78rpm
ABC-PARAMOUNT: *57* 10-20
Singles: 7-Inch
ABC: *66* 4-6
ABC-PARAMOUNT: *57* 35-45
CAPITOL: *61-63* 6-10
CARLTON (Monaural): *58-59* 6-10
CARLTON (Stereo): *59* 12-15
COLLECTABLES: 1-3
DOT: *73* 2-4
ERIC: 1-3
GRT: *70* 2-4
GROOVE (0027; "There's Trouble
 Brewin'"): *63* 8-10

GROOVE (0031; "I Knew You
 First"): *64* $4-6
GROOVE (0037; "Wiggle On
 Out"): *64* 8-10
GROOVE (0042; "Thou Shalt
 Not Steal"): *64* 4-6
GROOVE (0049; "Flakey John"): *64* 8-10
GUARANTEED (209; "What Am I
 Living For"): *60* 4-6
GUARANTEED (211; "Go Wild Little
 Sadie"): *60* 10-12
JUBILEE: *67* 4-6
RCA VICTOR: *65* 4-6
TOP RANK: *60-61* 4-6
Picture Sleeves
CAPITOL: *61-62* 10-20
CARLTON: *58-59* 10-20
TOP RANK: *60-61* 10-20
EPs: 7-Inch 33/45rpm
CARLTON: *58-60* 40-55
TOP RANK: *60* 35-50
LPs: 10/12-Inch 33rpm
CAPITOL (2035; "Burning
 Bridges"): *61* 60-80
CARLTON (107; "Jack Scott"): *58* 75-100
CARLTON (122; "What Am I
 Living For"): *60* 75-100
JADE: 8-10
PONIE: *74-77* 8-12
TOP RANK (348; "The Spirit
 Moves Me"): *60* 75-100
TOP RANK (619; "I Remember
 Hank Williams"): *60* 75-100
TOP RANK (626; "What Am I
 Living For?"): *61* 75-100

SCOTT, Jay & Tommy
Singles: 7-Inch
FIDELITY: *63* 3-5

SCOTT, Judy
Singles: 78rpm
DECCA: *57* 3-6
Singles: 7-Inch
CAPITOL: *60* 3-5
DECCA: *57-59* 4-6
EMBER: *64* 3-5
TOP RANK: *59* 3-5

SCOTT, Linda
Singles: 7-Inch
CANADIAN AMERICAN: *61-62* 4-6
CONGRESS: *62-64* 3-5
ERIC: 1-3
KAPP: *64-66* 3-5
RCA VICTOR: *68* 3-5

EPs: 7-Inch 33/45rpm
CONGRESS (3001; "Linda Scott"): *62* . **$15-20**
(Promotional issue only. Issued with picture insert,
but not with cover.)
LPs: 10/12-Inch 33rpm
CANADIAN AMERICAN: *61-62* **35-40**
CONGRESS: *62* **25-35**
KAPP: *65* **20-25**

SCOTT, Marilyn
Singles: 7-Inch
BIG TREE: *77* **2-3**
MERCURY: *83-85* **1-3**
LPs: 10/12-Inch 33rpm
ATCO: *79* **5-8**
MERCURY: *83* **5-8**

SCOTT, Millie
Singles: 7-Inch
ISLAND: *88* **1-3**

SCOTT, Neal
**(Neal Scott & The Concords; Neil Scott; Neil
Bogart)**
Singles: 7-Inch
CAMEO: *67* **3-5**
CLOWN: *60* **4-6**
COMET: **5-8**
HERALD: *63* **8-10**
PORTRAIT: *61-62* **5-8**

SCOTT, Peggy, & Jo Jo Benson
Singles: 7-Inch
SSS INT'L: *68-69* **2-4**
SUN: **1-3**
LPs: 10/12-Inch 33rpm
AVI: *84* **5-8**
SSS INT'L: *69* **5-8**

SCOTT, Rena
Singles: 7-Inch
BUDDAH: *79* **2-3**
EPIC: *72-74* **2-4**
SEDONA: *88* **1-3**

SCOTT, Tom
**(Tom Scott & The L.A. Express; Tom Scott &
The California Dreamers)**
Singles: 12-Inch 33/45rpm
SIRE: *83* **4-6**
Singles: 7-Inch
A&M: *72* **2-4**
ATLANTIC: *83* **1-3**
COLUMBIA: *79* **1-3**
IMPULSE: *68* **3-5**
ODE: *74-79* **2-4**
SIRE: *83* **1-3**
LPs: 10/12-Inch 33rpm
COLUMBIA: *78-81* **5-8**

EPIC/ODE: *84* **$5-8**
IMPULSE: *68* **15-30**
ODE: *74-77* **8-10**
MUSICIAN: *82* **5-8**
RCA VICTOR: *81* **5-8**
Also see CLAYTON, Merry
Also see HARRISON, George

SCOTT-HERON, Gil
Singles: 7-Inch
ARISTA: *75-84* **1-3**
LPs: 10/12-Inch 33rpm
ARISTA: *75-84* **5-12**
FLYING DUTCHMAN (100 through
0600 series): *71-74* **8-15**
FLYING DUTCHMAN (3800 series): *80* ... **5-8**

SCOTT-HERON, Gil, & Brian Jackson
Singles: 7-Inch
ARISTA: *75-80* **1-3**
LPs: 10/12-Inch 33rpm
ARISTA: *75-80* **5-12**
STRATA-EAST: *74* **8-15**
Also see SCOTT-HERON, Gil

SCREAMING BLUE MESSIAHS
LPs: 10/12-Inch 33rpm
ELEKTRA: *88* **5-8**

SCRITTI POLITTI
Singles: 12-Inch 33/45rpm
WARNER BROS: *84-86* **4-6**
Singles: 7-Inch
WARNER BROS: *84-86* **1-3**
LPs: 10/12-Inch 33rpm
WARNER BROS: *84-88* **5-8**

SCRITTI POLITTI / Roger
Singles: 7-Inch
WARNER BROS: *88* **1-3**

SCRUFFY THE CAT
LPs: 10/12-Inch 33rpm
RELATIVITY: *88* **5-8**

SCRUGGS, Earl
(Earl Scruggs Revue)
Singles: 7-Inch
COLUMBIA: *70-83* **1-3**
LPs: 10/12-Inch 33rpm
COLUMBIA: *73-83* **5-10**
Also see FLATT, Lester, & Earl Scruggs
Also see HALL, Tom T., & Earl Scruggs
Also see SKAGGS, Ricky

SEA, Johnny
(Johnny Seay)
Singles: 7-Inch
CAPITOL: *61* **2-4**
COLUMBIA: *67-69* **2-4**

NRC: *59-60* $3-5
PHILIPS: *64-65* 3-5
VIKING: *70-71* 2-3
WARNER BROS: *66-67* 2-4
Picture Sleeves
COLUMBIA: *68* 2-4
LPs: 10/12-Inch 33rpm
GUEST STAR: *66* 5-10
PHILIPS: *64-65'* 10-15
PICKWICK/HILLTOP: *65* 6-12
WARNER BROS: *66* 10-15

SEA LEVEL
Singles: 7-Inch
ARISTA: *80* 1-3
CAPRICORN: *77-79* 2-3
LPs: 10/12-Inch 33rpm
ARISTA: *80* 5-8
CAPRICORN: *77-80* 8-10
Also see ALLMAN BROTHERS BAND

SEALS, Dan
(England Dan Seals)
Singles: 7-Inch
ATLANTIC: *80-82* 1-3
CAPITOL: *87-88* 1-3
EMI AMERICA: *84-87* 1-3
LIBERTY: *83-84* 1-3
LPs: 10/12-Inch 33rpm
ATLANTIC: *80-82* 8-1
CAPITOL: *88* 5-8
EMI AMERICA: *84-86* 5-8
LIBERTY: *83* 5-8
Also see ENGLAND DAN & JOHN FORD
COLEY

SEALS, Dan, & Marie Osmond
Singles: 7-Inch
CAPITOL: *85* 1-3
Also see OSMOND, Marie
Also see SEALS, Dan

SEALS & CROFTS
Singles: 7-Inch
T.A.: *69-71* 3-5
WARNER BROS: *71-80* 1-3
LPs: 10/12-Inch 33rpm
T.A.: *69-70* 20-25
WARNER BROS (Except 2809): *71-80* ... 6-10
WARNER BROS (2809; "Seals &
Crofts I & II"): *74* 10-12
Members: Jimmy Seals; Dash Crofts.
Also see CHAMPS

SEARCHERS
Singles: 7-Inch
ERIC: 1-3
KAPP: *64-67* 4-6

LIBERTY (55646; "Sugar & Spice"): *63* $5-10
LIBERTY (55689; "Sugar & Spice"): *63* .. 4-6
MERCURY: *63* 5-8
RCA VICTOR: *71-72* 3-5
SIRE: *80-81* 1-3
Picture Sleeves
KAPP: *64* 10-15
LPs: 10/12-Inch 33rpm
KAPP: *64-66* 20-30
MERCURY (Red label): *64* 25-30
MERCURY (White label): *64* 50-60
(Promotional issues only.)
PYE: *76* 10-12
SIRE: *80-81* 8-10

SEARCHERS / Rattles
LPs: 10/12-Inch 33rpm
MERCURY (Red label): *65* 35-45
MERCURY (White label): *64* 50-60
(Promotional issues only.)
Also see RATTLES
Also see SEARCHERS

SEASE, Marvin
LPs: 10/12-Inch 33rpm
LONDON: *88* 5-8

SEATRAIN
Singles: 7-Inch
A&M: *68* 4-6
CAPITOL: *71-72* 3-5
WARNER BROS: *73* 2-4
LPs: 10/12-Inch 33rpm
A&M: *69* 10-12
CAPITOL (600 series): *71* 8-10
CAPITOL (16000 series): *80* 5-8
WARNER BROS: *73* 8-10
Also see BLUES PROJECT
Also see RANK & FILE

SEAWIND
Singles: 7-Inch
A&M: 80-82 .... $1-3
CTI: 77-78 2-3
HORIZON: 79 2-3
LPs: 10/12-Inch 33rpm
A&M: 80-82 5-8
CTI: 77-78 8-10
HORIZON: 79 8-10

SEAY, Johnny: see SEA, Johnny

SEBASTIAN, John
Singles: 7-Inch
KAMA SUTRA: 68-70 3-5
MGM: 68-70 3-5
REPRISE: 70-77 2-4
Picture Sleeves
KAMA SUTRA: 69 3-5
LPs: 10/12-Inch 33rpm
KAMA SUTRA: 70 10-12
MGM: 69-70 12-15
REPRISE: 70-76 8-10
Also see LOVIN' SPOONFUL

SECO, Pozo, Singers:
see POZO SECO SINGERS

SECOND VERSE
Singles: 7-Inch
IX CHAINS: 74 2-4

SECRET TIES
Singles: 7-Inch
NIGHT WAVE: 86 1-3

SECRET WEAPON
Singles: 7-Inch
PRELUDE: 82-83 1-3

SECRETS
Singles: 7-Inch
DCP: 65 3-5
OMEN: 66 3-5
PHILIPS: 63-64 8-10
Picture Sleeves
PHILIPS: 64 4-8

SEDAKA, Neil
(Neil Sedaka & The Marvels)
Singles: 7-Inch
DECCA: 58 15-20
ELEKTRA: 77-80 1-3
GUYDEN: 58 15-20
KIRSHNER: 72-80 1-3
LEGION: 58 25-30
MCA: 75-84 1-3
MGM: 73 2-4
PYRAMID: 62 8-10

RCA VICTOR (7000 series): 58-61 ...... $4-6
(With a "47" prefix.)
RCA VICTOR (7000 series): 59-60 10-12
(With a "61" prefix. Stereo singles.)
RCA VICTOR (7000 & 8000
series): 60-62 12-15
(With a "37" prefix. Compact 33 Singles.)
RCA VICTOR (8000 & 9000 series): 62-67 . 3-5
(With a "47" prefix.)
ROCKET: 74-76 2-4
S.G.C.: 68-69 3-5
Promotional Singles
RCA VICTOR (7408; "The Diary"): 58 ... 8-10
(White label, with photo of Neil.)
Picture Sleeves
RCA VICTOR: 60-65 4-8
EPs: 7-Inch 33/45rpm
RCA VICTOR (EPA series): 59 20-30
RCA VICTOR (LPC series): 61 15-25
(Compact 33 Doubles.)
LPs: 10/12-Inch 33rpm
ACCORD: 81 5-8
CAMDEN: 8-10
ELEKTRA: 77-81 5-8
51 WEST: 5-8
INTERMEDIA: 85 5-8
KIRSHNER: 71-72 12-15
MCA: 84 5-8
RCA VICTOR (AFL1 & APL1
series): 75-78 8-10
RCA VICTOR (ANL1 series): 75-79 5-8
RCA VICTOR (VPL1 series): 76 10-12
RCA VICTOR (2035; "Neil Sedaka"): 59 . 25-40
(With an "LPM" prefix. Monaural.)
RCA VICTOR (2035; "Neil
Sedaka"): 59 50-100
(With an "LSP" prefix. Stereo.)
RCA VICTOR (2317 through
2627): 61-62 20-40
(With an "LPM" or "LSP" prefix.)
RCA VICTOR (10181;
"Smile"): 66 12-15
ROCKET: 74-77 8-10
Also see ANKA, Paul / Sam Cooke / Neil
Sedaka
Also see COOKE, Sam / Rod Lauren / Neil
Sedaka / Browns
Also see JOHN, Elton
Also see KING CURTIS
Also see 10CC
Also see SIMON, Paul
Also see WILLOWS

SEDAKA, Neil & Dara
Singles: 7-Inch
ELEKTRA: 80 1-3

MCA: *84* $1-3

SEDAKA, Neil, & The Tokens
LPs: 10/12-Inch 33rpm
GUEST STAR: 10-15
VERNON: 10-15
Also see TOKENS

SEDAKA, Neil, & The Tokens / Coins
LPs: 10/12-Inch 33rpm
CROWN: *63* 10-15
Also see SEDAKA, Neil
Also see TOKENS

SEEDS
(Featuring Sky Saxon)
Singles: 7-Inch
GNP/CRESCENDO (354; "Can't Seem To
Make You Mine"/"Daisy Mae"): *65* 5-8
GNP/CRESCENDO (354; "Can't Seem To
Make You Mine"/"I Tell Myself"): *67* 4-6
GNP/CRESCENDO (364; "Your Pushing
Too Hard"): *65* 8-10
(Reissued on 372, titled *Pushing Too Hard* and
with a different flip side, *Try To Understand*.)
GNP/CRESCENDO (370; "The Other
Place"): *65* 5-8
GNP/CRESCENDO (372 through
422): *66-69* 4-6
MGM: *69-70* 4-6
Picture Sleeves
GNP/CRESCENDO: *67* 10-15
LPs: 10/12-Inch 33rpm
GNP/CRESCENDO (2023 through
2043): *66-67* 25-45
(All Seeds LPs, except 2043, *Raw & Alive*, are
shown as currently available from GNP/Crescendo,
using the original catalog numbers. Original issue
1960s LPs have the GNP/Crescendo logo on a
horizontal line. Reissues have the label name in a
circular manner on the label.)
GNP/CRESCENDO (2100 series): *77* 5-8

SEEGER, Pete
Singles: 7-Inch
COLUMBIA: *63-67* 3-5
FOLKWAYS: *59* 3-5
PIONEER: *60* 3-5
LPs: 10/12-Inch 33rpm
ARAVEL: *63-64* 10-20
ARCHIVE OF FOLK MUSIC: *65* 8-15
BROADSIDE: *63* 10-20
CAPITOL: *64-67* 8-18
COLUMBIA: *63-72* 8-18
DISC: *64* 8-15
FOLKWAYS: *59-75* 8-18
(Black vinyl.)

FOLKWAYS (7610; "Animal Folk
Songs"): *59-75* $20-30
(Colored vinyl.)
HARMONY: *68-70* 5-10
ODYSSEY: *68* 5-12
OLYMPIC: *73* 5-10
PHILIPS: *63* 8-15
STINSON: *70* 5-10
TRADITION: *73* 5-10
VANGUARD: *78* 6-12
VERVE/FOLKWAYS: *65* 8-15
WARNER BROS: *79* 5-8
Also see SEEGERS
Also see WEAVERS

SEEGER, Pete, & Arlo Guthrie
LPs: 10/12-Inch 33rpm
REPRISE: *75* 8-12
WARNER BROS: *81* 6-10
Also see GUTHRIE, Arlo

SEEGER, Pete, & Pacific Gas & Electric
LPs: 10/12-Inch 33rpm
COLUMBIA (3540; "Tell Me That You
Love Me, Junie Moon"): *70* 8-15
(Soundtrack.)
Also see PACIFIC GAS & ELECTRIC
Also see SEEGER, Pete

SEEGERS
LPs: 10/12-Inch 33rpm
PRESTIGE: *65* 8-15
Members: Pete Seeger; Peggy Seeger; Mike
Seeger; Barbara Seeger; Penny Seeger.
Also see SEEGER, Pete

SEEKERS
Singles: 7-Inch
ATMOS: *65* 3-5
CAPITOL: *65-68* 3-5
MARVEL: *65* 3-5
Picture Sleeves
CAPITOL: *65* 4-6
LPs: 10/12-Inch 33rpm
CAPITOL (100 series): *69* 10-12
CAPITOL (2000 series): *65-67* 10-15
CAPITOL (16000 series): *80* 5-8
MARVEL: *65* 12-15
Members: Judy Durham; Keith Potger.
Also see JAMES, Sonny / Seekers
Also see NEW SEEKERS

SEELY, Jeannie
Singles: 7-Inch
CHALLENGE: *64-65* 3-5
COLUMBIA: *77-78* 1-3
DECCA: *69-73* 2-4
MCA: *73-75* 1-3

MONUMENT: *66-68* $2-4
LPs: 10/12-Inch 33rpm
DECCA: *69-70* 8-12
HARMONY: *72* 5-10
MCA: *73* 5-8
MONUMENT: *66-77* 6-12
Also see GREENE, Jack, & Jeannie Seely

SEGAL, George
(George Segal & The Imperial Jazzband)
Singles: 7-Inch
FLYING DUTCHMAN: *74* 1-3
PHILIPS: *67* 2-4
LPs: 10/12-Inch 33rpm
PHILIPS: *67* 8-15
SIGNATURE: *74* 5-10

SEGER, Bob
(Bob Seger & The Last Heard; Bob Seger
System; Bob Seger & The Silver Bullet Band)
Singles: 7-Inch
ABKCO: *72-75* 2-4
CAMEO: *66-67* 10-20
CAPITOL (Except 2000 series): *71-86* 1-3
CAPITOL (2000 series): *68-70* 3-6
HIDEOUT: *68* 10-15
MCA: *87* 1-3
PALLADIUM: *71-74* 2-4
REPRISE: *72* 2-4
Promotional Singles
CAPITOL (Colored vinyl): *78* 4-6
CAPITOL (9878; "Shame On
The Moon"): *82* 3-5
(This was an edited version, at 4:22, and not the
promo single of 5187, which ran 4:55.)
Picture Sleeves
CAPITOL: *78-84* 1-3

LPs: 10/12-Inch 33rpm
CAPITOL (172; "Ramblin' Gamblin'
Man"): *69* $12-15
(With an "ST" prefix.)
CAPITOL (172; "Ramblin' Gamblin'
Man"): *75* 8-10
(With an "SM" prefix.)
CAPITOL (236; "Noah"): *69* 40-70
(With an "ST" prefix.)
CAPITOL (499; "Mongrel"): *70* 12-15
(With an "SKAO" prefix.)
CAPITOL (499; "Mongrel"): *75* 8-10
(With an "SM" prefix.)
CAPITOL (731; "Brand New
Morning"): *71* 25-50
(With an "ST" prefix.)
CAPITOL (11000 series,
except 11904): *75-77* 6-12
CAPITOL (11904; "Stranger In Town,"
picture disc): *79* 15-20
CAPITOL (12000 series): *80-86* 6-10
CAPITOL (16000 series): *80* 5-8
MFSL (034; "Night Moves"): *79* 25-50
MFSL (127; "Against The Wind"): *85* ...15-25
PALLADIUM: *72-74* 10-15
Promotional LPs
CAPITOL ("Night Moves,"
picture disc): *78* 30-40
CAPITOL (8433; "Live Bullet,
Consensus Cuts"): *75* 15-20
Also see BEACH BUMS
Also see NEWMAN, Randy

SELECTOR
Singles: 7-Inch
CHRYSALIS: *79-81* 1-3
LPs: 10/12-Inch 33rpm
CHRYSALIS: *79-81* 5-8

SELF, Ronnie
Singles: 78rpm
ABC-PARAMOUNT: *56* 10-20
COLUMBIA: *57* 5-10
Singles: 7-Inch
ABC-PARAMOUNT: *56* 40-50
AMY: *68* 3-5
COLUMBIA (Except 41241): *57-58* 10-20
COLUMBIA (41241; "Petrified"): *58* 50-60
DECCA: *59-62* 4-6
KAPP: *63* 3-5
EPs: 7-Inch 33/45rpm
COLUMBIA (2149; "Ain't I'm
A Dog"): *57* 150-200

SELLARS, Marilyn
Singles: 7-Inch
MEGA: *74-77* 1-3

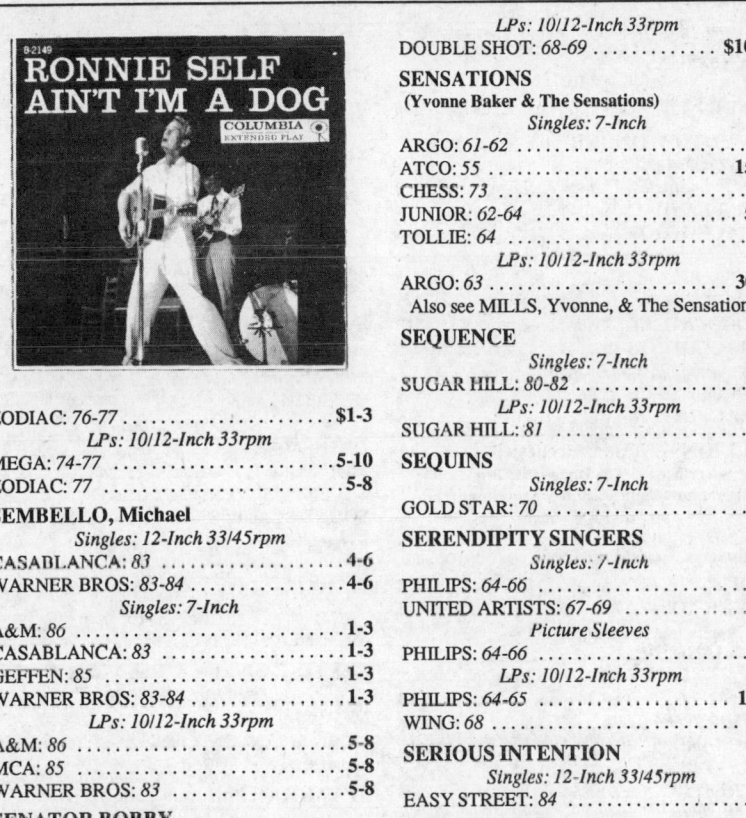

ZODIAC: 76-77 .... $1-3
    LPs: 10/12-Inch 33rpm
MEGA: 74-77 5-10
ZODIAC: 77 5-8

SEMBELLO, Michael
    Singles: 12-Inch 33/45rpm
CASABLANCA: 83 4-6
WARNER BROS: 83-84 4-6
    Singles: 7-Inch
A&M: 86 1-3
CASABLANCA: 83 1-3
GEFFEN: 85 1-3
WARNER BROS: 83-84 1-3
    LPs: 10/12-Inch 33rpm
A&M: 86 5-8
MCA: 85 5-8
WARNER BROS: 83 5-8

SENATOR BOBBY
    Singles: 7-Inch
RCA VICTOR: 67 3-5
  Also see HARDLY WORTHIT PLAYERS

SENATOR MC KINLEY:
  see HARDLY WORTHIT PLAYERS

SENAY, Eddy
    Singles: 7-Inch
SUSSEX: 72-73 2-4
    LPs: 10/12-Inch 33rpm
SUSSEX: 72 8-10

SENECA, Joe
    Singles: 7-Inch
EVEREST: 59-60 3-5

SEÑOR SOUL
    Singles: 7-Inch
DOUBLE SHOT: 67-68 3-5
WHIZ: 69-70 2-4

    LPs: 10/12-Inch 33rpm
DOUBLE SHOT: 68-69 .... $10-12

SENSATIONS
(Yvonne Baker & The Sensations)
    Singles: 7-Inch
ARGO: 61-62 3-5
ATCO: 55 15-20
CHESS: 73 1-3
JUNIOR: 62-64 5-10
TOLLIE: 64 3-5
    LPs: 10/12-Inch 33rpm
ARGO: 63 30-40
  Also see MILLS, Yvonne, & The Sensations

SEQUENCE
    Singles: 7-Inch
SUGAR HILL: 80-82 1-3
    LPs: 10/12-Inch 33rpm
SUGAR HILL: 81 5-8

SEQUINS
    Singles: 7-Inch
GOLD STAR: 70 2-4

SERENDIPITY SINGERS
    Singles: 7-Inch
PHILIPS: 64-66 3-5
UNITED ARTISTS: 67-69 2-4
    Picture Sleeves
PHILIPS: 64-66 3-6
    LPs: 10/12-Inch 33rpm
PHILIPS: 64-65 10-15
WING: 68 8-12

SERIOUS INTENTION
    Singles: 12-Inch 33/45rpm
EASY STREET: 84 4-6

SESAME STREET KIDS: see ERNIE

SETZER, Brian
    LPs: 10/12-Inch 33rpm
EMI-MANHATTAN: 88 5-8

SEVELLE, Taja
    Singles: 7-Inch
REPRISE: 88 1-3

7A3
    Singles: 7-Inch
GEFFEN: 88 1-3
    LPs: 10/12-Inch 33rpm
GEFFEN: 88 5-8

"707"
    Singles: 7-Inch
BOARDWALK: 82 1-3
CASABLANCA: 80 1-3
    LPs: 10/12-Inch 33rpm
BOARDWALK: 82 5-8

CASABLANCA: *80* $5-8

SEVEN SEAS
Singles: 7-Inch
GLADES: *75* **2-4**

SEVENTH WONDER
(7th Wonder)
Singles: 12-Inch 33/45rpm
CASABLANCA: *80* **4-6**
PARACHUTE: *79* **4-6**
Singles: 7-Inch
ABET: *73* **2-4**
CASABLANCA: *80* **1-3**
CHOCOLATE CITY: *80* **1-3**
PARACHUTE: *78-79* **2-3**
LPs: 10/12-Inch 33rpm
CHOCOLATE CITY: *80* **5-8**
PARACHUTE: *78-79* **5-8**

SEVERINSEN, Doc, Orchestra
(Doc Severinsen & The Dodge City Boys;
Tonight Show Band With Doc Severinsen)
Singles: 7-Inch
COMMAND: *65-70* **1-3**
EPIC: *59-76* **1-3**
FRONTLINE: *80* **1-3**
RCA VICTOR: *72-73* **1-3**
Picture Sleeves
COMMAND: *70* **1-3**
LPs: 10/12-Inch 33rpm
ABC: *71-73* **5-10**
AMHERST: *86* **5-8**
COMMAND: *61-73* **5-15**
EPIC: *76-81* **5-8**
EVEREST: *78* **5-8**
JUNO: *70-79* **5-8**
MCA: *82* **4-8**
RCA VICTOR: *71* **5-10**
Also see MANCINI, Henry, & Doc Severinsen

SEVILLE, David
(Ross Bagdasarian)
Singles: 78rpm
LIBERTY: *56-57* **3-6**
Singles: 7-Inch
LIBERTY: *56-61* **4-6**
Picture Sleeves
LIBERTY: *57* **6-10**
EPs: 7-Inch 33/45rpm
LIBERTY: *57* **20-25**
LPs: 10/12-Inch 33rpm
LIBERTY (3073; "The Music Of
David Seville"): *57* **25-35**
LIBERTY (3092; "The Witch
Doctor"): *58* **35-45**
Also see CHIPMUNKS

SEVILLES
Singles: 7-Inch
CAL-GOLD: *62* $3-5
GALAXY: *64* 3-5
J.C.: *61* 8-10

SEX PISTOLS
Singles: 7-Inch
WARNER BROS: *78* 2-3
LPs: 10/12-Inch 33rpm
WARNER BROS: *77* 5-8
Also see PUBLIC IMAGE LTD.
Also see SIOUXSIE & THE BANSHEES

S-EXPRESS
Singles: 7-Inch
CAPITOL: *88* 1-3

SEXTON, Ann
Singles: 7-Inch
DASH: *77* 2-5
MONUMENT: *77* .2-3
SEVENTY SEVEN: *72-74* 2-4
SOUND STAGE: *77* 2-3

SEXTON, Charlie
Singles: 7-Inch
MCA: *86* 1-3
LPs: 10/12-Inch 33rpm
MCA: *86* 5-8

SEXTON, Charlie, & Ron Wood
LPs: 10/12-Inch 33rpm
MCA: *84* 5-8
Also see SEXTON, Charlie
Also see WOOD, Ron

SEYMOUR, Phil
Singles: 7-Inch
BOARDWALK: *81* .1-3
LPs: 10/12-Inch 33rpm
BOARDWALK: *81* .5-8
Also see TEXTONES
Also see TWILLEY, Dwight, Band

SHA NA NA
Singles: 7-Inch
KAMA SUTRA: *70-75* 2-4
SUTRA: *74* 2-3
LPs: 10/12-Inch 33rpm
ACCORD: *81-83* 5-8
BUDDAH: *77* 5-8
CSP: *78* 8-10
EMUS: *78* 8-10
K-TEL: *81* 8-10
KAMA SUTRA: *69-76* 10-15
NASHVILLE: *80* .8-10
Members: Lennie Baker; Jon "Bowzer" Bauman;
Johnny Contardo; Denny Green; Henry Gross;

Sha Na Na

Jocko Marcellino; Danny McBride; Scott Powell; David-Allan "Chico" Ryan; "Screamin'" Scott Simon; Donny York.
Also see GROSS, Henry
Also see TRAVOLTA, John / Sha Na Na

SHACK
Singles: 7-Inch
VOLT: 71 .... $2-4

SHACKLEFORDS
Singles: 7-Inch
CAPITOL: 66 2-4
LHI: 67-68 2-4
MERCURY: 63 3-5
LPs: 10/12-Inch 33rpm
CAPITOL: 66 10-15
MERCURY: 63 15-20
Members: Lee Hazlewood; Marty Cooper; Al Stone; Garcia Nitzsche.
Also see HAZLEWOOD, Lee
Also see MOMENTS

SHADES OF BLUE
Singles: 7-Inch
COLLECTABLES: 1-3
IMPACT: 66-67 3-5
SHADES: 68 4-6
LPs: 10/12-Inch 33rpm
IMPACT: 66 20-25

SHADES OF LOVE
Singles: 7-Inch
VENTURE: 82 1-3

SHADOW
Singles: 7-Inch
ELEKTRA: 79-81 .... $1-3
LPs: 10/12-Inch 33rpm
ELEKTRA: 79-81 5-8

SHADOWFAX
Singles: 7-Inch
WINDHAM HILL: 82 1-3
LPs: 10/12-Inch 33rpm
CAPITOL: 88 5-8
PASSPORT: 76 8-10
WINDHAM HILL: 82-86 5-8

SHADOWS OF KNIGHT
Singles: 7-Inch
ATCO: 69 4-8
COLUMBIA/AURAVISION ("Potato Chip") 5-10
(5-inch, promotional flexi-disc.)
DUNWICH: 66-67 5-8
SUPER K: 69 4-8
TEAM: 68 4-8
Picture Sleeves
DUNWICH: 66 5-10
LPs: 10/12-Inch 33rpm
DUNWICH (666; "Gloria"): 66 50-100
DUNWICH (667; "Back Door Men"): 66 50-100
SUPER K: 69 10-15

SHAFTO, Bobby
Singles: 7-Inch
RUST: 64-65 4-8

SHAKATAK
Singles: 12-Inch 33/45rpm
POLYDOR: 82-84 4-6
Singles: 7-Inch
POLYDOR: 82-84 1-3
LPs: 10/12-Inch 33rpm
POLYDOR: 82 5-8

SHALAMAR
Singles: 12-Inch 33/45rpm
COLUMBIA: 84-85 4-6
SOLAR: 79-85 4-6
Singles: 7-Inch
COLUMBIA: 84-85 1-3
MCA: 84 1-3
SOLAR: 78-87 1-3
SOUL TRAIN: 77 2-3
LPs: 10/12-Inch 33rpm
SOLAR: 78-85 5-8
SOUL TRAIN: 77 8-10
Members: Howard Hewett; Jody Watley; Jeffrey Daniel.

SHANGO
Singles: 12-Inch 33/45rpm
CELLULOID: 83 .... $4-6
Singles: 7-Inch
A&M: 69 2-4
CELLULOID: 83 1-3
GNP/CRESCENDO: 69 2-4
LPs: 10/12-Inch 33rpm
A&M: 69 10-12
DUNHILL: 70 8-10
Also see BAMBAATAA, Afrika

SHANGRI-LAS
(Shangra-Las)
Singles: 7-Inch
COLLECTABLES: 1-3
ERIC: 1-3
MERCURY: 66-67 3-5
RED BIRD: 64-66 3-6
SSS INT'L: 1-3
SCEPTER: 65 3-6
SMASH: 63 4-8
SPOKANE: 64 5-8
TRIP: 1-3
LPs: 10/12-Inch 33rpm
BACK-TRAC: 85 5-8
COLLECTABLES: 83 6-8
MERCURY (21099; "Golden Hits Of
The Shangri-las"): 66 20-30
(Monaural.)
MERCURY (21099; "Golden Hits Of
The Shangri-las"): 66 50-75
(Shown as monaural but plays in true stereo.)
MERCURY (61099; "Golden Hits Of
The Shangri-las"): 66 25-35
(Stereo.)
POST: 10-12
RED BIRD (101; "Leader Of
The Pack"): 65 30-50
RED BIRD (104; "Shangri-Las
'65"): 65 30-50
RED BIRD (104; "I Can Never Go
Home Anymore"): 65 30-50
Members: Mary Weiss; Marge Ganser; Mary Ann
Ganser.

SHANK, Bud
Singles: 78rpm
GOOD TIME JAZZ: 54 3-5
Singles: 7-Inch
GOOD TIME JAZZ: 54 3-5
PACIFIC JAZZ: 61-70 2-4
WORLD PACIFIC: 64-68 2-4
EPs: 7-Inch 33/45rpm
NOCTURNE: 53 20-40
PACIFIC JAZZ: 54-58 15-30

LPs: 10/12-Inch 33rpm
CONCORD JAZZ: 76 .... $5-8
CROWN: 63 10-20
KIMBERLY: 63 10-20
LIBERTY: 56 20-40
NOCTURNE (2; "The Bud Shank
Quintet"): 53 75-125
(10-Inch LPs.)
PACIFIC JAZZ (14 through 20): 54-55 ..40-60
(10-Inch LPs.)
PACIFIC JAZZ (4 through 89): 60-65 ...10-20
(12-Inch LPs.)
PACIFIC JAZZ (400 series): 57 15-30
PACIFIC JAZZ (1200 series): 55-57 20-40
PACIFIC JAZZ (10000 & 20000
series): 66-81 5-15
SUNSET: 66 5-12
WORLD PACIFIC (1000 through
1200 series): 58-60 15-30
WORLD PACIFIC (1400 series): 61-63 ..10-20
WORLD PACIFIC (1800 series): 64-67 ...5-15
WORLD PACIFIC (21000 series): 68 5-12
Also see FOLKSWINGERS
Also see LONDON, Julie, & The Bud Shank
Quintet

SHANKAR, Ravi
Singles: 7-Inch
APPLE: 71 3-6
DARK HORSE: 75 2-3
WORLD PACIFIC: 59-68 2-4
Picture Sleeves
APPLE (1838; "Joi Bangla"): 71 20-25
LPs: 10/12-Inch 33rpm
ANGEL: 67 8-15
APPLE: 71-73 8-15
CAPITOL: 67-72 5-12
COLUMBIA: 66-68 5-15
DARK HORSE: 74-76 5-10
FANTASY: 73 8-12
PRESTIGE: 68 5-12
SPARK: 73 5-10
WORLD PACIFIC: 59-69 5-15
Also see BEATLES
Also see HARRISON, George

SHANNON
(Marty Wilde)
Singles: 7-Inch
EPIC/MAGNET: 75 2-3
HERITAGE: 69 2-4
Also see WILDE, Marty

SHANNON
(Shannon Greene)
Singles: 12-Inch 33/45rpm
EMERGENCY: 83-84 4-6

MIRAGE: *84-85* $4-6
Singles: 7-Inch
ATLANTIC: *86* 1-3
EMERGENCY: *83-84* 1-3
MIRAGE: *84-85* 1-3
LPs: 10/12-Inch 33rpm
MIRAGE: *84-85* 5-8

SHANNON, Del
Singles: 7-Inch
AMY: *64-65* 4-6
BERLEE: *63-64* 5-8
BIG TOP: *61-63* 6-10
COLLECTABLES: 1-3
DUNHILL: *69* 3-6
ERIC: 1-3
ISLAND: *75* 2-4
LANA: 1-3
LIBERTY: *66-68* 4-6
NETWORK: *81-82* 1-3
TERRIFIC: 2-4
WARNER BROS: *85* 1-3
Picture Sleeves
LIBERTY: *68* 4-8
LPs: 10/12-Inch 33rpm
AMY: *64-65* 25-30
BIG TOP (1303; "Runaway"): *61* 50-75
(Monaural.)
BIG TOP (1303; "Runaway"): *61* 400-500
(Stereo.)
BIG TOP (1308; "Little Town Flirt"): *63* .35-45
BUG: *85* 5-8
DOT: *67* 15-20
LIBERTY: *66-68* 15-20
NETWORK/ELEKTRA: *81* 5-8
PHOENIX 20: *80* 5-10
PICKWICK: 8-10
POST: 10-12
SIRE: *75* 10-12
SUNSET: *70* 10-12
UNITED ARTISTS: *73* 10-12
Also see HONDELLS / Del Shannon / Martha
& The Vandellas

SHANNON, Jackie
(Jackie Shannon & The Cajuns; Jackie De-
Shannon)
Singles: 7-Inch
DOT: *59* 10-12
FRATERNITY: *59* 10-15
P.J.: *59* 25-35
SAGE: *59* 20-25
SAND: *59* 15-20
Also see DE SHANNON, Jackie

SHANTE, Roxanne
Singles: 12-Inch 33/45rpm
POP ART: *85* $4-6
Singles: 7-Inch
POP ART: *85* 1-3
LPs: 10/12-Inch 33rpm
POP ART: *85* 5-8
Also see JAMES, Rick, & Roxanne Shante

SHANTELLE
Singles: 7-Inch
PANDISC: *85* 4-6

SHAPIRO, Helen
Singles: 7-Inch
CAPITOL: *61-62* 2-5
EPIC: *62-63* 2-4
JANUS: *70* 1-3
MUSICOR: *65* 2-3
TOWER: *67* 2-3
Picture Sleeves
EPIC: *62* 2-5
LPs: 10/12-Inch 33rpm
EPIC: *63* 5-15

SHA-RAE, Billy
(Sha-Rae)
Singles: 7-Inch
BAY-UKE: *61-62* 4-6
HOUR GLASS: 2-5
LAURIE: 2-3
SPECTRUM: *71* 2-4

SHARKEY, Feargal
Singles: 12-Inch 33/45rpm
A&M: *86* 4-6
Singles: 7-Inch
A&M: *86* 1-3
LPs: 10/12-Inch 33rpm
A&M: *86* 5-8
Also see UNDERTONES

SHARKS
Singles: 7-Inch
MCA: *73-74* 2-4
LPs: 10/12-Inch 33rpm
MCA: *73-74* 8-12

SHARP, Dee Dee
(Dee Dee Sharp Gamble)
Singles: 7-Inch
ABKCO: *83-84* 1-3
ATCO: *66-68* 3-5
CAMEO: *62-66* 3-5
FAIRMOUNT: *66* 3-5
GAMBLE: *68* 2-4
PHILADELPHIA INT'L: *77-81* 1-3
TSOP: *76* 2-3

Picture Sleeves
CAMEO: *62-65* $4-8
LPs: 10/12-Inch 33rpm
CAMEO: *62-63* 20-25
PHILADELPHIA INT'L: *75-81* 8-10
Also see CHECKER, Chubby, & Dee Dee
Sharp
Also see KING, Ben E., & Dee Dee Sharp
Also see PHILADELPHIA
INTERNATIONAL ALL STARS

SHARPE, Mike
Singles: 7-Inch
LIBERTY: *66-69* 3-5
LPs: 10/12-Inch 33rpm
LIBERTY: *67-69* 10-15

SHARPE, Ray
(Ray Sharpe & The Blues Whalers; Ray Sharpe
& The Soul Set)
Singles: 7-Inch
A&M: *71* 2-4
ATCO: *66* 3-5
DOT: *59* 4-6
FLYING HIGH: 2-4
GAREX: *63* 4-8
GREGMARK: *62* 3-6
HAMILTON: *59* 8-10
JAMIE (Except 1128): *58-60* 4-6
JAMIE (1128; "Linda Lu"/
"Monkey's Uncle"): *59* 8-10
JAMIE (1128; "Linda Lu"/
"Red Sails In The Sunset"): *59* 5-8
(Note different flip side.)
LHI: 3-5
MONUMENT: *65* 3-5
PARK AVE: 3-5
SOCK & SOUL: 3-5
TREY: *61* 4-6
LPs: 10/12-Inch 33rpm
AWARD: 15-20
Also see KING CURTIS

SHARPEES
Singles: 7-Inch
ONE-DERFUL: *65-66* 5-8
Members: Herbert Reeves; Vernon Guy; Stacy
Johnson.

SHARPLES, Bob
(Bob Sharples' Living Strings)
Singles: 78rpm
LONDON: *56-57* 2-4
Singles: 7-Inch
LONDON: *56-61* 2-4
LPs: 10/12-Inch 33rpm
CAMDEN: *60* 5-10

LONDON: *61-64* $5-15
METRO: *65* 5-10

SHAW, Georgie
Singles: 78rpm
DECCA: *53-56* 2-4
Singles: 7-Inch
DECCA: *53-56* 2-4
EPs: 7-Inch 33/45rpm
DECCA: *56* 4-8
LPs: 10/12-Inch 33rpm
DECCA: *53-56* 8-15
Also see KALLEN, Kitty, & Georgie Shaw

SHAW, Marlena
Singles: 12-Inch 33/45rpm
COLUMBIA: *79* 4-6
SOUTH BAY: *83* 4-6
Singles: 7-Inch
BLUE NOTE: *72-76* 2-3
CADET: *66-69* 2-5
COLUMBIA: *77-79* 2-3
SOUTH BAY: *83* 1-3
Picture Sleeves
CADET: *67* 3-5
LPs: 10/12-Inch 33rpm
BLUE NOTE: *72-75* 6-12
CADET: *68-69* 8-15
COLUMBIA: *77-79* 5-8

SHAW, Robert, Chorale
Singles: 7-Inch
RCA VICTOR: *50-62* 2-4
EPs: 7-Inch 33/45rpm
RCA VICTOR: *54-56* 4-8
LPs: 10/12-Inch 33rpm
ALMANAC: *66* 4-8
CAMDEN: *64* 4-8
RCA VICTOR: *50-70* 5-15
VICTROLA: *70* 4-8

SHAW, Roland, Orchestra
Singles: 7-Inch
LONDON: *56-67* 2-4
LPs: 10/12-Inch 33rpm
LONDON: *64-78* 5-15

SHAW, Sandie
Singles: 7-Inch
MERCURY: *64* 3-5
RCA VICTOR: *68-70* 2-4
REPRISE: *64-67* 3-5
LPs: 10/12-Inch 33rpm
REPRISE: *65-66* 15-20

SHAW, Timmy
Singles: 7-Inch
JAMIE: *61-62* 3-5

SCEPTER: *73* $1-3
WAND: *63-64* 3-5

SHAW, Tommy
Singles: 7-Inch
A&M: *84-85* 1-3
ATLANTIC: *88* 1-3
LPs: 10/12-Inch 33rpm
A&M: *84* 5-8
  Also see STYX

SHAWN, Damon
Singles: 7-Inch
WESTBOUND: *73* 2-4

SH-BOOMS
(Chords)
Singles: 78rpm
CAT: *55* 5-10
VIK: *57* 5-10
Singles: 7-Inch
ATCO: *61* 5-10
ATLANTIC: *60* 15-20
CAT: *55* 10-15
VIK: *57* 8-12
  Also see CHORDS

SHEAR, Jules
Singles: 12-Inch 33/45rpm
EMI AMERICA: *84-85* 4-6
Singles: 7-Inch
EMI AMERICA: *84-85* 1-3

SHEARING, George, Quintet
Singles: 7-Inch
CAPITOL: *55-67* 2-4
LONDON: *63* 2-3
MGM: *50-56* 2-5
SHEBA: *71* 1-3
EPs: 7-Inch 33/45rpm
CAPITOL: *55-60* 4-8
MGM: *51-55* 5-15
LPs: 10/12-Inch 33rpm
ARCHIVE OF FOLK
  MUSIC: *68* 5-10
BASF: *73* 5-8
CAPITOL: *55-77* 5-15
CONCORD JAZZ: *80-82* 4-8
DISCOVERY: *50* 15-30
(10-Inch LPs.)
EVEREST: *69* 4-8
LION: *59* 5-10
MGM (90 through 252): *51-53* 15-30
(10-Inch LPs.)
MGM (100 series): *70* 5-8
(12-Inch LPs.)
MGM (3000 series): *55-60* 8-18
MGM (4000 series): *62-63* 6-12

MPS: *74-75* $5-8
METRO: *65* 5-10
PAUSA: *79-82* 5-8
SAVOY (15000 series): *50* 15-30
SHEBA: *71-76* 5-10
VSP: *66-67* 5-10
  Also see COLE, Nat "King," & George Shearing
  Also see LEE, Peggy, & George Shearing

SHEARING, George
& The Montgomery Brothers
Singles: 7-Inch
JAZZLAND: *62* 2-4
LPs: 10/12-Inch 33rpm
JAZZLAND (55; "George Shearing
  And The Montgomery Brothers): *61* ... 20-35
(Cover pictures Shearing with the three brothers.)
JAZZLAND (55; "George Shearing
  And The Montgomery Brothers): *62* ... 10-20
(Cover pictures a woman.)
RIVERSIDE: *82* 5-8
  Also see MONTGOMERY BROTHERS
  Also see SHEARING, George, Quintet
  Also see WILSON, Nancy, & George Shearing

SHEEN, Bobby
Singles: 7-Inch
CAPITOL: *66-69* 3-5
CHELSEA: *75* 2-4
DIMENSION: *65* 4-6
LIBERTY: *62* 5-8
WARNER BROS: *72* 2-4
  Also see BOB B. SOXX & THE BLUE
JEANS

SHEEP
Singles: 7-Inch
BOOM: *66* 10-20
  Also see STRANGELOVES

SHEILA
(Sheila & B. Devotion)
Singles: 7-Inch
CARRERE: *80-81* 1-3
CASABLANCA: *78* 2-3
Picture Sleeves
CARRERE: *80-81* 1-3
Promotional Singles
CARRERE (37675; "Little
  Darlin'"): *81* 3-5
(Price includes special sleeve.)
LPs: 10/12-Inch 33rpm
CARRERE: *80* 5-8
CASABLANCA: *78* 5-8

SHEILA E: see E., Sheila

SHELLEY, Pete
(Peter Shelley)
Singles: 12-Inch 33/45rpm
ARISTA: 82-83 .... $4-6
Singles: 7-Inch
ARISTA: 82-83 1-3
BELL: 74 2-4
LPs: 10/12-Inch 33rpm
ARISTA: 82 5-8
Also see BUZZCOCKS

SHELLS
Singles: 78rpm
CANDLELITE (436; "Baby Oh Baby"): 72 5-8
(Colored vinyl.)
Singles: 7-Inch
ABC: 75 1-3
BOARDWALK: 75 3-5
COLLECTABLES: 1-3
END: 58 40-50
GONE: 61 10-15
JOHNSON (099; "My Cherie"): 72 3-5
JOHNSON (104; "Baby Oh Baby"/
"Angel Eyes"): 57 15-20
JOHNSON (104; "Baby Oh Baby"/
"What's In An Angel Eyes?"): 60 5-8
(The 1960 issue label has two parallel lines with
one thinner than the other. These lines are both the
same thickness on the '57 issue. MOST 1957 issues
have the shorter flip side title, but ALL 1960 issues
have the longer title.)
JOHNSON (106; "Pleading No
More"): 58 45-55
JOHNSON (107 through 127): 61-63 8-12
JOHNSON (300 series): 61 5-8
JOSIE: 63 4-6
ROULETTE: 59 8-10
SELSOM: 65 3-5

JOHNSON RECORDS

45 R.P.M.
(J-351)
JOLI MUSIC
INC. (BMI)
TIME 2:10

A
JOEY DUKE
PRODUCTION
And Wayne Stierle

DEEP IN MY HEART
(BOB STAUNTON)
THE SHELLS
119

SNOWFLAKE (1959; "If You Were
Gone From Me"/"Misty"): 64 .... $10-20
(Blank, orange labels.)
SOUNDS FROM THE SUBWAY: 77 3-5
(Colored vinyl.)
LPs: 10/12-Inch 33rpm
CANDLELITE: 10-12
JUBILEE: 10-15
Members: Nat Burknight; Shade Alston; Bobby
Nurse; Danny Small; Gus Geter; Roy Jones.
Also see DUBS / Shells

SHELTO, Steve
Singles: 12-Inch 33/45rpm
SAM: 83 4-6

SHELTON, Anne
Singles: 7-Inch
COLUMBIA: 56 3-5
EPIC: 59 2-4

SHELTON, Ricky Van
LPs: 10/12-Inch 33rpm
COLUMBIA: 87-88 5-8

SHELTON, Roscoe
Singles: 7-Inch
BATTLE: 62-63 3-5
EXCELLO: 59-61 4-6
SIMS: 64-65 3-5
SOUND STAGE 7: 65-68 3-5
LPs: 10/12-Inch 33rpm
EXCELLO: 61 20-30
SOUND STAGE 7: 66 12-15

SHEP & THE LIMELITES
(Featuring James Sheppard)
Singles: 7-Inch
ABC: 73 1-3
HULL (Except 770): 61-65 6-12
HULL (770; "A Party For Two"): 65 20-40
ROULETTE: 73 2-3
LPs: 10/12-Inch 33rpm
HULL (1001; "Our Anniversary"): 62 ..200-400
ROULETTE: 67 35-40
Also see HEARTBEATS
Also see HEARTBEATS / Shep & The
Limelites

SHEPARD, Jean
Singles: 78rpm
CAPITOL: 53-57 2-5
Singles: 7-Inch
CAPITOL: 53-61 3-6
(Purple labels.)
CAPITOL: 61-72 2-4
(Orange or orange/yellow labels.)
MERCURY: 72 2-3
SCORPION: 78 1-3

UNITED ARTISTS: *73-77* **$1-3**
EPs: 7-Inch 33/45rpm
CAPITOL: *56-61* **5-10**
LPs: 10/12-Inch 33rpm
CAPITOL (100 through 800 series): *69-71* **5-10**
CAPITOL (700 through 1200
series): *56-59* **15-20**
(With a "T" prefix.)
CAPITOL (1500 through 2900
series): *61-68* **8-15**
CAPITOL (11000 series): *72-79* **5-8**
MERCURY: *71* **5-10**
PICKWICK/HILLTOP: *67-68* **6-12**
POWER PAK: **5-8**
UNITED ARTISTS: *73-76* **5-10**

SHEPARD, Jean, & Ferlin Huskey
Singles: 78rpm
CAPITOL: *53* **3-5**
Singles: 7-Inch
CAPITOL: *53* **4-6**
Also see HUSKY, Ferlin
Also see SHEPARD, Jean

SHEPHERD SISTERS
(Sheppard Sisters; Shepard Sisters; Shephard Sisters)
Singles: 78rpm
LANCE: *57* **3-5**
MELBA: *56* **4-6**
MERCURY: *57* **3-5**
Singles: 7-Inch
ABC: *73* **1-3**
ATLANTIC: *63* **6-10**
COLLECTABLES: **1-3**
LANCE: *57* **4-6**
MGM: *59* **3-5**
MELBA: *56* **4-6**
MERCURY: *57* **4-6**
20TH CENTURY-FOX: *64* **3-5**
UNITED ARTISTS: *61* **3-5**
WARWICK: *59-60* **3-5**
YORK: *65* **3-5**

SHEPPARD, T.G.
Singles: 7-Inch
COLUMBIA: *85-88* **1-3**
HITSVILLE: *76* **2-3**
MELODYLAND: *74-75* **2-3**
WARNER BROS: *77-85* **1-3**
LPs: 10/12-Inch 33rpm
COLUMBIA: *85* **5-8**
CURB: *84* **5-8**
HITSVILLE: *76* **5-10**
MELODYLAND: *75-76* **8-10**
WARNER BROS: *78-83* **1-3**

Also see COLLINS, Judy, & T.G. Sheppard
Also see EASTWOOD, Clint, & T.G. Sheppard

SHERBET
(Sherbs)
Singles: 7-Inch
ATCO: *81* **$1-3**
MCA: *76-77* **2-3**
LPs: 10/12-Inch 33rpm
ATCO: *80-82* **5-8**
MCA: *76-77* **8-10**

SHERIDAN, Bobby
(Charlie Rich)
Singles: 7-Inch
SUN: *61* **5-8**
Also see RICH, Charlie

SHERIDAN, Tony & The Beat Brothers: see BEATLES

SHERIFF
Singles: 7-Inch
CAPITOL: *83-88* **1-3**
LPs: 10/12-Inch 33rpm
CAPITOL: *83* **5-8**
OBSERVATORY: *79* **8-10**

SHERMAN, Allan
(Allan Sherman & Friends)
Singles: 7 Inch
RCA VICTOR: *68* **2-3**
WARNER BROS: *63-66* **3-5**
Picture Sleeves
WARNER BROS: *63-64* **3-6**
LPs: 10/12-Inch 33rpm
JUBILEE: *62* **8-15**
RCA VICTOR: *64* **10-15**
RHINO: *85-86* **5-8**
WARNER BROS: *62-65* **10-15**

SHERMAN, Bobby
Singles: 7-Inch
CAMEO: *66* **3-5**
CONDOR: *69* **3-5**
DECCA: *64-65* **4-6**
DOT: *63* **4-6**
EPIC: *67* **3-5**
GRT: *76* **1-3**
JANUS: *75* **2-3**
METROMEDIA: *69-73* **2-5**
PARKWAY: *65* **4-6**
STARCREST: *62* **5-8**
Picture Sleeves
DECCA: *65* **5-10**
METROMEDIA: *69-72* **2-5**

EPs: 7-Inch 33/45rpm
METROMEDIA ("Bobby Sherman"): 70 . **$3-5**
(Flexi-disc.)
LPs: 10/12-Inch 33rpm
METROMEDIA: 69-73 .... **8-12**

SHERMAN, Joe, & His Orchestra
(Joe Sherman & The Arena Brass)
Singles: 78rpm
KAPP: 56-57 .... **2-4**
Singles: 7-Inch
EPIC: 65-66 .... **2-3**
KAPP: 56-61 .... **2-4**
WORLD ARTISTS: 63-65 .... **2-4**
LPs: 10/12-Inch 33rpm
COLUMBIA: 68 .... **5-10**
EPIC: 66 .... **5-10**
RCA VICTOR: 67.................... **5-10**
WORLD ARTISTS: 63-64 .... **5-12**

SHERRYS
Singles: 7-Inch
GUYDEN: 62-63 .... **8-10**
MERCURY: 64 .... **3-6**
ROBERTS: **5-10**
LPs: 10/12-Inch 33rpm
GUYDEN (503; "At The Hop"): 62 ..... **60-80**

SHERWOOD, Roberta
Singles: 78rpm
DECCA: 56-57 .... **2-4**
Singles: 7-Inch
DECCA: 56-64 .... **2-4**
DUNHILL: 68 .... **2-3**
HAPPY TIGER: 69 .... **1-3**
HARMON: 62-63 .... **2-3**
KING: 71-72 .... **1-3**
MCA: 73 .... **1-3**
OLEN: 65 .... **2-3**
EPs: 7-Inch 33/45rpm
DECCA: 56-59 .... **5-10**
LPs: 10/12-Inch 33rpm
ABC-PARAMOUNT: 63-64 .... **5-10**
DECCA: 56-65 .... **5-15**
HARMON: 63 .... **5-10**
KING: 70 .... **5-8**
VOCALION: 66-68 .... **5-8**

SHIELDS
Singles: 7-Inch
DOT (136; "You Cheated"): 66 .... **20-25**
(Colored vinyl. Promotional issue only.)
DOT (15805; "You Cheated"): 58 ..... **10-15**
DOT (15856; "I'm Sorry Now"): 58 .... **15-20**
DOT (15940; "Play The Game Fair"): 59 . **15-20**
TENDER: 58-59 .... **30-40**
(Label reads "Dist. By Dot.")

TENDER: 58 .... **$15-20**
(Label does NOT read "Dist. By Dot.")
TRANSCONTINENTAL: **15-20**
LPs: 10/12-Inch 33rpm
BRYLEN: **5-8**
Members: Frankie Ervin; Charles Wright;
Nathaniel Wilson.
Also see WRIGHT, Charles

SHIELDS, Billy
(Tony Orlando)
Singles: 7-Inch
HARBOUR: 69 .... **5-8**
Also see ORLANDO, Tony

SHINDOGS
Singles: 7-Inch
VIVA: 66 .... **4-6**
WARNER BROS: 65 .... **4-6**
Members: Delaney Bramlet; Bonnie Bramlett.
Also see DELANEY & BONNIE

SHINEHEAD
LPs: 10/12-Inch 33rpm
ELEKTRA: 88 .... **5-8**

SHIRELLES
Singles: 7-Inch
COLLECTABLES: **1-3**
BLUE ROCK: 68 .... **3-5**
DECCA: 58-61 .... **10-15**
ERIC: **1-3**
GUSTO: **1-3**
RCA VICTOR: 71-73 .... **5-10**
SCEPTER (White label): 59-60 .... **10-15**
SCEPTER (Red label): 60-68 .... **8-10**
TIARA (6112; "I Met Him
On A Sunday"): 57 .... **100-125**
UNITED ARTISTS: 70-71 .... **2-4**
Picture Sleeves
SCEPTER: 63 .... **8-15**
LPs: 10/12-Inch 33rpm
BACK-TRAC: 85 .... **5-8**
EVEREST: 81 .... **5-8**
GUSTO: **5-8**
PHOENIX: 81 .... **5-10**
PRICEWISE: **15-20**
RCA VICTOR: 71-72 .... **10-15**
RHINO: 85 .... **5-8**
SCEPTER (501; "Tonight's The
Night"): 61 .... **75-100**
SCEPTER (502 through 562): 61-67 .... **25-35**
SCEPTER (599; "Remember
When"): 72 .... **15-20**
SPRINGBOARD: 72 .... **8-10**
UNITED ARTISTS: 71-75 .... **10-12**

Members: Shirley Jackson-Alston; Beverly Lee;
Doris Coley-Jackson; Addie "Micki" Harris-
McFadden.
Also see JAN & DEAN / Roy Orbison / 4
Seasons / Shirelles
Also see KING, Carole
Also see SHIRLEY & THE SHIRELLES

SHIRELLES, & King Curtis
LPs: 10/12-Inch 33rpm
SCEPTER: 62 .... $25-30
Also see KING CURTIS
Also see SHIRELLES

SHIRLEY, Donald
(Don Shirley Trio)
Singles: 7-Inch
BARNABY: 76 1-3
CADENCE: 60-64 2-4
COLUMBIA: 68-69 1-3
LPs: 10/12-Inch 33rpm
ATLANTIC: 72 5-12
AUDIO FIDELITY: 59 10-25
CADENCE: 55-63 10-20
COLUMBIA: 65-69 8-12

SHIRLEY & COMPANY
(Shirley Goodman)
Singles: 7-Inch
VIBRATION: 75-76 2-4
LPs: 10/12-Inch 33rpm
VIBRATION: 75 8-10
Also see SHIRLEY & LEE

SHIRLEY & LEE
Singles: 78rpm
ALADDIN (3152 through 3205): 52-53 .. 10-20
ALADDIN (3222 through 3258): 54 8-15
ALADDIN (3289 through 3455): 55-57 4-8
Singles: 7-Inch
ABC: 73 1-3
ALADDIN (3152 through 3205): 52-53 .. 40-60
ALADDIN (3222 through 3258): 54 20-30
ALADDIN (3289 through 3455): 55-59 .. 8-12
IMPERIAL: 62-63 3-6
LIBERTY: 1-3
UNITED ARTISTS: 73 2-4
WARWICK: 60-61 4-6
LPs: 10/12-Inch 33rpm
ALADDIN (807; "Let The Good
Times Roll"): 56 200-400
IMPERIAL (9179; "Let The Good
Times Roll"): 62 25-50
SCORE (4023; "Let The Good
Times Roll"): 57 75-100
UNITED ARTISTS: 73-74 20-25

WARWICK (2028; "Let The Good
Times Roll"): 61 .... $50-75
Members: Shirley Goodman; Leonard Lee.
Also see SHIRLEY & COMPANY

SHIRLEY & SQUIRRELY
Singles: 7-Inch
GRT: 76 2-4
LPs: 10/12-Inch 33rpm
GRT: 76 5-8
Also see SHIRLEY, SQUIRRELY & MEL-
VIN

SHIRLEY & THE SHIRELLES
(Featuring Shirley Alston)
Singles: 7-Inch
BELL: 69 5-8
Also see SHIRELLES

SHIRLEY, SQUIRRELY & MELVIN
Singles: 7-Inch
EXCELSIOR: 81 1-3
Picture Sleeves
EXCELSIOR: 81 1-3
LPs: 10/12-Inch 33rpm
EXCELSIOR: 81 5-8
Also see SHIRLEY & SQUIRRELY

SHOCK
Singles: 7-Inch
DOWNTOWN: 78 2-4
(Colored vinyl.)
Picture Sleeves
DOWNTOWN: 78 2-4
EPs: 7-Inch 33/45rpm
IMPACT: 78 6-10
(Colored vinyl. Issued with a paper sleeve.)
Members: Paul Lesperance; Steve Reiner; Kip
Brown; Gaylord.

SHOCK
Singles: 12-Inch 33/45rpm
FANTASY: *81-83* $4-6
Singles: 7-Inch
FANTASY: *81-83* 1-3
LPs: 10/12-Inch 33rpm
FANTASY: *81-82* 5-8

SHOCK-A-RA
Singles: 7-Inch
FUTURE: *88* 1-3

SHOCKED, Michelle
Singles: 7-Inch
MERCURY: *88* 1-3
LPs: 10/12-Inch 33rpm
MERCURY: *88* 5-8

SHOCKING BLUE
Singles: 7-Inch
BUDDAH: *71* 2-4
COLOSSUS: *69-71* 3-5
MGM: *72-73* 2-4
Picture Sleeves
COLOSSUS: *69-70* 3-5
LPs: 10/12-Inch 33rpm
COLOSSUS: *70* 12-15

SHOES
Singles: 7-Inch
BOMP: *78* 2-3
ELEKTRA: *79* 1-3
Picture Sleeves
ELEKTRA: *79* 1-3
EPs: 7-Inch 33/45rpm
BOMP: *78* 5-8
LPs: 10/12-Inch 33rpm
BLACK VINYL: 10-12
ELEKTRA: *77-82* 5-8
PVC: *78* 5-8

SHONDELL, Troy
(Troy Shondel; Troy Shundell; Gary Shelton)
Singles: 7-Inch
AVM: *88* 1-3
BRITE STAR: *73-74* 2-4
COLLECTABLES: 1-3
COMMERCIAL: *78* 2-3
DECCA: *64* 3-5
EVEREST: *62-64* 3-5
GAYE: *61* 15-20
GOLDCREAST: *61* 10-15
GOLDCREST: *61* 8-10
LIBERTY: *61-62* 4-6
LUCKY: *75* 2-4
MASTER: 10-15
RIC: *65* 3-5
SUNSHINE: *76* 2-4

TRX: *67-69* $2-4
TELESONIC: *80-81* 1-3
3 RIVERS: 4-6
WRITERS & ARTISTS: *61* 15-25
LPs: 10/12-Inch 33rpm
EVEREST: *63* 20-25
STAR-FOX: 10-12
SUNSET: *67* 12-15

SHONDELLS / Rod Bernard / Warren Storm / Skip Stewart
LPs: 10/12-Inch 33rpm
LA LOUISIANNE: *64* 35-40
Also see BERNARD, Rod
Also see STORM, Warren

SHONDELLS
(Featuring Tommy James)
Singles: 7-Inch
RED FOX: *66* 10-15
SELSOM: *65* 8-10
SNAP: *65* 15-20
Also see JAMES, Tommy

SHO-NUFF
Singles: 12-Inch 33/45rpm
MALACO: *81-84* 4-6
Singles: 7-Inch
MALACO: *81-84* 1-3
STAX: *78-79* 2-3
LPs: 10/12-Inch 33rpm
STAX: *78* 5-8

SHOOTING STAR
Singles: 7-Inch
EPIC: *82* 1-3
VIRGIN: *80* 1-3
Picture Sleeves
VIRGIN: *80* 1-3
LPs: 10/12-Inch 33rpm
EPIC: *82* 5-8
VIRGIN: *80-82* 5-8

SHORE, Dinah
Singles: 78rpm
BLUEBIRD: *40-42* 5-10
RCA VICTOR: *50-57* 3-6
VICTOR: *42-46* 4-8
Singles: 7-Inch
CAPITOL: *60-62* 3-5
DECCA: *69* 2-3
MERCURY: *74* 1-3
PROJECT 3: *67-68* 2-5
RCA VICTOR: *50-57* 4-8
Picture Sleeves
RCA VICTOR: *53* 5-10
EPs: 7-Inch 33/45rpm
CAMDEN: *56* 5-10

Singles: 7-Inch
WARNER BROS: *83* $1-3
LPs: 10/12-Inch 33rpm
ISLAND: *87-88* 5-8
WARNER BROS: *83* 5-8
Members: Barry Andrews; David Allen.
Also see GANG OF FOUR
Also see XTC

SIBERRY, Jane
Singles: 7-Inch
OPEN AIR: *86* 1-3
LPs: 10/12-Inch 33rpm
OPEN AIR: *86* 5-8

SIDE EFFECT
Singles: 12-Inch 33/45rpm
FANTASY: *78-81* 4-6
Singles: 7-Inch
ELEKTRA: *80-82* 1-3
FANTASY: *75-81* 1-3
LPs: 10/12-Inch 33rpm
ELEKTRA: *80-82* 5-8
FANTASY: *75-81* 5-8
Member: Miki Howard.
Also see HOWARD, Miki

SIDEKICKS
Singles: 7-Inch
RCA VICTOR: *66-67* 3-6
LPs: 10/12-Inch 33rpm
RCA VICTOR: *66* 12-15

SIEGEL, Dan
Singles: 7-Inch
CBS ASSOC: *88* 1-3

SIEGEL-SCHWALL BAND
Singles: 7-Inch
DEUTSCHE GRAMMOPHON: *73* 2-4
WOODEN NICKEL: *72-74* 2-4
LPs: 10/12-Inch 33rpm
VANGUARD: *66-70* 20-25
WOODEN NICKEL: *72-74* 20-35
Members: Corky Siegel; Jim Schwall.

SIFFRE, Labi
Singles: 7-Inch
CHINA: *87* 1-3

SIGLER, Bunny
(Mr. Emotions)
Singles: 12-Inch 33/45rpm
SALSOUL: *80* 4-6
Singles: 7-Inch
BEE: *59* 4-6
CRAIG: *61* 3-5
DECCA: *65-67* 2-4
GOLD MINE: *78-79* 2-3

NEPTUNE: $3-6
PARKWAY: *67-69* 2-4
PHILADELPHIA INT'L: *71-76* 2-3
SALSOUL: *80* 1-3
LPs: 10/12-Inch 33rpm
PARKWAY: *67* 10-12
SALSOUL: *80* 5-8
Also see HOLLOWAY, Loleatta, & Bunny
Sigler
Also see MASON, Barbara, & Bunny Sigler

SIGUE SIGUE SPUTNIK
Singles: 12-Inch 33/45rpm
MANHATTAN: *86* 4-6
Singles: 7-Inch
MANHATTAN: *86* 1-3
LPs: 10/12-Inch 33rpm
MANHATTAN: *86* 5-8
Member: Tony James.

SILAS, Alfie
(Alfie)
Singles: 7-Inch
MOTOWN: *84-86* 1-3
RCA VICTOR: *82-84* 1-3
LPs: 10/12-Inch 33rpm
MOTOWN: *85* 5-8
RCA VICTOR: *82-84* 4-8
Also see KING, Bobby

SILENCERS
Singles: 7-Inch
PRECISION: *80* 1-3
LPs: 10/12-Inch 33rpm
PRECISION: *80-81* 5-8

SILENCERS
Singles: 7-Inch
RCA VICTOR: *87* 1-3
LPs: 10/12-Inch 33rpm
RCA VICTOR: *87* 5-8

SILENT UNDERDOG
Singles: 12-Inch 33/45rpm
PROFILE: *85* 4-6

SILHOUETTES
Singles: 78rpm
EMBER: *57* 5-10
JUNIOR: *57* 15-25
Singles: 7-Inch
ABC: *73* 1-3
ACE: *58* 10-15
COLLECTABLES: 1-3
EMBER (Except 1037): *57-58* 10-15
EMBER (1037; "Bing Bong"): *58* 35-50
FLASHBACK: *65* 1-3
IMPERIAL: *62* 4-6

JUNIOR (391; "Get A Job"): *57* $50-75
JUNIOR (396; "I Sold My Heart
  To The Junkman"): *58* 15-20
JUNIOR (400; "Evelyn"): *59* 10-20
JUNIOR (993; "Your Love"): *63* 5-10
      LPs: 10/12-Inch 33rpm
GOODWAY (100; "Get A Job"): 75-125

SILK
      Singles: 7-Inch
ABC: *69* 2-4
DECCA: *71* 2-4
      LPs: 10/12-Inch 33rpm
ABC: *69* 10-15
  Member: Michael Stanley.
  Also see STANLEY, Michael, Band

SILK
      Singles: 12-Inch 33/45rpm
PHILADELPHIA INT'L: *79-80* 4-6
      Singles: 7-Inch
PHILADELPHIA INT'L: *79-80* 1-3
PRELUDE: *77* 2-3
PYE: *76* 2-3
      LPs: 10/12-Inch 33rpm
ARISTA: *77* 5-8
PHILADELPHIA INT'L: *79* 5-8
  Members: Debra Henry.
  Also see BUTLER, Jerry, & Debra Henry

SILK, J.M.
      Singles: 12-Inch 33/45rpm
D.J. INT'L: *85* 4-6

SILKIE
      Singles: 7-Inch
FONTANA: *65-66* 3-6
      LPs: 10/12-Inch 33rpm
FONTANA: *65* 20-30

SILVA-TONES
      Singles: 7-Inch
ARGO: *57* 10-15
MONARCH (Yellow label): *57* 25-30
MONARCH (Black label): *57* 10-15

SILVER
      Singles: 7-Inch
ARISTA: *76-77* 2-4
      LPs: 10/12-Inch 33rpm
ARISTA: *76* 6-10
  Members: John Batdorf; Brent Mydland.
  Also see BATDORF, John
  Also see BATDORF & RODNEY
  Also see GRATEFUL DEAD

SILVER, Horace, Quintet
      Singles: 7-Inch
BLUE NOTE (300 through
  1000 series): *73-77* $1-3
BLUE NOTE (1600 & 1700
  series): *54-61* 3-5
BLUE NOTE (1800 & 1900
  series): *61-69* 2-4
      LPs: 10/12-Inch 33rpm
BLUE NOTE: *56-59* 20-50
  (Label gives New York street address for Blue
  Note Records.)
BLUE NOTE: *59-65* 15-25
  (Label reads "Blue Note Records Inc. - New York,
  U.S.A.")
BLUE NOTE: *66-80* 8-18
  (Label shows Blue Note Records as a division of
  either Liberty or United Artists.)
BLUE NOTE (5000 series): *53-55* 50-80
  (10-Inch LPs.)
EPIC (3300 series): *56* 25-50
EPIC (16000 series): *56* 20-40

**SILVER, Horace, Quintet, &
Stanley Turrentine**
      LPs: 10/12-Inch 33rpm
BLUE NOTE: *68* 8-12
  Also see SILVER, Horace, Quintet
  Also see TURRENTINE, Stanley

SILVER APPLES
      Singles: 7-Inch
KAPP: *68-69* 2-4
      LPs: 10/12-Inch 33rpm
KAPP: *68-69* 10-15

SILVER CONDOR
      Singles: 7-Inch
COLUMBIA: *81* 1-3
      Picture Sleeves
COLUMBIA: *81* 1-3
      LPs: 10/12-Inch 33rpm
COLUMBIA: *81* 5-8
  Members: Joe Cerisano; Earl Slick; John Corey;
  Claude Pepper; Jay Davis.

SILVER CONVENTION
      Singles: 7-Inch
MIDLAND INT'L: *75-78* 1-3
MIDSONG INT'L: *78* 1-3
      Picture Sleeves
MIDLAND INT'L: *76* 1-3
      LPs: 10/12-Inch 33rpm
MIDSONG INT'L: *75-78* 8-10
  Member: Penny McLean.
  Also see McCLEAN, Penny

SILVER PLATINUM
Singles: 7-Inch
SRI: *81* $1-3
SPECTOR: *81* 1-3
LPs: 10/12-Inch 33rpm
SPECTOR: *81* 5-8

SILVER, PLATINUM & GOLD
Singles: 7-Inch
FARR: *76-77* 2-3
WARNER BROS: *74-75* 2-4
LPs: 10/12-Inch 33rpm
NEPTUNE: *82* 5-8

SILVERADO
Singles: 7-Inch
PAVILLION: *81* 1-3
RCA VICTOR: *77* 2-3
LPs: 10/12-Inch 33rpm
PAVILLION: *81* 5-8
RCA VICTOR: *77* 6-10

SILVERSPOON, Dooley
Singles: 7-Inch
COTTON: *74-75* 2-4

SILVERSTEIN, Shel
Singles: 7-Inch
COLUMBIA: *71-75* 2-4
ELEKTRA: *60* 3-6
RCA VICTOR: *69-70* 2-4
LPs: 10/12-Inch 33rpm
ATLANTIC (8000 series): *63* 15-20
ATLANTIC (8200 series): *70* 8-15
CADET: *65-66* 12-20
COLUMBIA: *72-84* 5-12
CRESTVIEW: *63* 12-20
ELEKTRA: *59* 20-30
FLYING FISH: *80* 5-8
JANUS: *73* 8-10
PARACHUTE (Except 20512): *78* 5-8
PARACHUTE (20512; "Selected Cuts
  From Songs & Stories"): *78* 12-15
  (Promotional issue only.)
RCA VICTOR: *69* 10-15

SILVETTI
Singles: 7-Inch
SALSOUL: *77* 2-3
LPs: 10/12-Inch 33rpm
SALSOUL: *77* 5-8

SIMEONE, Harry, Chorale
Singles: 7-Inch
COLUMBIA: *66-67* 1-3
KAPP: *64-68* 1-3
MERCURY: *62-64* 1-3
MISTLETOE: *74* 1-3

20TH CENTURY-FOX: *58-79* $1-3
Picture Sleeves
MERCURY: *62* 3-5
20TH CENTURY-FOX: *58-63* 3-6
Promotional Picture Sleeve
20TH CENTURY-FOX (121; "The
  Little Drummer Boy"): *58* 4-8
  (Labeled "Prepare To Be Enchanted," this sleeve
  was sent only to radio stations.)
LPs: 10/12-Inch 33rpm
DECCA: *62-64* 5-10
KAPP: *65* 5-10
MERCURY: *63-64* 5-10
MISTLETOE: *73* 4-8
MOVIETONE: *67* 4-8
20TH CENTURY-FOX: *58-79* 5-15
WING: *69* 4-8

SIMMONS, Aleese
. Singles: 7-Inch
ORPHEUS: *88* 1-3

SIMMONS, Gene
(Jumpin' Gene Simmons; Morris Gene Simmons)
Singles: 7-Inch
AGP: 3-5
CHECKER: *60* 5-8
EPIC: *70* 2-4
DELTUNE: *78* 2-3
HI: *61-67* 4-6
HURSHEY: *73* 2-4
MALA: *68* 3-5
SANDY: 4-6
SUN: *58* 10-15
TUPELO: 3-5
LPs: 10/12-Inch 33rpm
HI: *64* 20-25

SIMMONS, Gene
Singles: 7-Inch
CASABLANCA: *78-79* 2-3
LPs: 10/12-Inch 33rpm
CASABLANCA (Except picture
  discs): *78-80* 20-30
CASABLANCA (Picture discs): *79* 40-50
Also see KISS

SIMMONS, Patrick
Singles: 12-Inch 33/45rpm
ELEKTRA: *83* 4-6
Singles: 7-Inch
ELEKTRA: *83* 1-3
LPs: 10/12-Inch 33rpm
ELEKTRA: *83* 5-8
Also see DOOBIE BROTHERS
Also see EAGLES

SIMMONS, Simtec
Singles: 7-Inch
INNOCATION: 75 .... $2-4

SIMMS, John & Arthur
Singles: 7-Inch
CASABLANCA: 80 1-3
LPs: 10/12-Inch 33rpm
CASABLANCA: 80 5-8

SIMMS TWINS: see SIMS TWINS

SIMON, Carly
Singles: 7-Inch
ARISTA: 86-88 1-3
COLUMBIA: 73 2-4
ELEKTRA: 71-79 2-3
EPIC: 85-86 1-3
MIRAGE: 82 1-3
WARNER BROS: 80-83 1-3
Picture Sleeves
ARISTA (9525; "Coming Around
   Again"): 86 3-6
(Pictures Meryl Streep and Jack Nicholson.)
ARISTA (9525; "Coming Around
   Again"): 86 2-4
(Pictures Carly Simon.)
ELEKTRA: 75-79 2-3
WARNER BROS: 80-83 1-3
LPs: 10/12-Inch 33rpm
ARISTA: 86-88 5-8
ELEKTRA: 71-79 6-10
EPIC: 85-86 5-8
WARNER BROS: 80-83 5-8
   Also see ROLLING STONES
   Also see SIMON SISTERS

SIMON, Carly, & James Taylor
Singles: 7-Inch
ELEKTRA: 74-78 2-3
   Also see SIMON, Carly
   Also see TAYLOR, James

SIMON, Joe
(Joe Simon & The Checkmates; Joe Simon &
The Mainstreeters)
Singles: 7-Inch
COMPLEAT: 2-3
DOT: 64 3-5
HUSH: 60-62 5-8
IRRAL: 63 4-6
MONUMENT: 70-72 2-3
POSSE: 81-82 1-3
SOUND STAGE 7: 66-72 3-5
SPRING: 69-75 2-4
VEE JAY: 64-65 3-5
Picture Sleeves
SPRING: 71-73 2-4

LPs: 10/12-Inch 33rpm
BUDDAH: 69 .... $10-15
POSSE: 81-82 5-8
SOUND STAGE 7: 67-75 10-15
SPRING: 71-78 8-10

SIMON, Lowrell
Singles: 12-Inch 33/45rpm
ZOO YORK: 81 4-6
Singles: 7-Inch
ZOO YORK: 81 1-3
   Also see LOWRELL

SIMON, Paul
(Paul Simon & Urubamba; Paul Simon & Los
Incas)
Singles: 7-Inch
COLUMBIA: 72-77 2-4
WARNER BROS: 80-87 1-3
Picture Sleeves
COLUMBIA: 73-77 3-8
WARNER BROS: 80 1-3
LPs: 10/12-Inch 33rpm
COLUMBIA (Except C5X & 43000
   series): 72-77 6-12
COLUMBIA (C5X series): 81 25-35
(5-LP set.)
COLUMBIA (43000 series): 81 12-15
(Half-speed mastered.)
DMG (1; "The Songs Of Paul Simon,
   Collection Of Hits"): 75 15-20
(Contains Paul Simon compositions performed by:
Paul Simon; Simon & Garfunkel; Aretha Franklin;
Yes; Crykle; Booker T. & The MGs. Promotional
issues only.)
DMG (2; "The Songs Of Paul Simon,
   Easy Listening Collection"): 75 10-15
(Contains Paul Simon compositions performed by
easy listening artists. Promotional issue only.)
MCP (8027; "Paul Simon Plus"): 15-20
(Contains three true stereo tracks issued as by Jerry
Landis. Also has tracks by Tony Orlando, Neil
Sedaka, Johnny Rivers, and The 4 Seasons.)
WARNER BROS: 80-86 5-8
   Also see BOOKER T. & THE MGs
   Also see CYRKLE
   Also see 4 SEASONS
   Also see FRANKLIN, Aretha
   Also see KANE, Paul
   Also see LANDIS, Jerry
   Also see NEWMAN, Randy, & Paul Simon
   Also see ORLANDO, Tony
   Also see RIVERS, Johnny
   Also see SEDAKA, Neil
   Also see SIMON & GARFUNKEL
   Also see TAYLOR, True
   Also see TICO & THE TRIUMPHS

Also see U.S.A. FOR AFRICA
Also see VALERY, Dana
Also see YES

SIMON, Paul, & Phoebe Snow
(With The Jessy Dixon Singers)
Singles: 7-Inch
COLUMBIA: 75 . . . . $2-3
Also see SIMON, Paul
Also see SNOW, Phoebe

SIMON & GARFUNKEL
Singles: 7-Inch
ABC-PARAMOUNT: 66 8-12
COLUMBIA (10000 series): 75 2-4
COLUMBIA (11000 series): 66 5-8
COLUMBIA (43000 through 45000
series): 65-72 3-5
WARNER BROS: 82 1-3
Promotional Singles
COLUMBIA (43396; "The Sounds
Of Silence"): 65 25-30
(Colored vinyl.)
COLUMBIA (43617; "I Am A
Rock"): 66 15-20
(Colored vinyl.)
TEEN SCOOP (789; "Visits With
Simon & Garfunkel"): 66 5-10
(*Teen Scoop* magazine bonus soundsheet.)
Picture Sleeves
COLUMBIA: 66-75 4-8
EPs: 7-Inch 33/45rpm
COLUMBIA: 68-69 10-15
(Jukebox issues only.)
LPs: 10/12-Inch 33rpm
COLUMBIA (C5X series): 81 25-30
COLUMBIA (CL-2000 series): 64-68 . . . 10-20
COLUMBIA (CS-9000 series): 64-70 . . . 10-20
COLUMBIA (CQ series): 71 10-15
COLUMBIA (JS series): 68 10-12
COLUMBIA (OS series): 68 12-15
COLUMBIA (PC series): 72 5-8
COLUMBIA (40000 series): 80-81 12-15
(Half-speed mastered.)
MFSL: 85 15-20
OFFSHORE: 10-15
PICKWICK (3059; "Hit Sound Of Simon
& Garfunkel"): 66 50-75
SEARS: 20-25
WARNER BROS: 82 5-8
Members: Paul Simon; Art Garfunkel.
Also see GARFUNKEL, Art
Also see SIMON, Paul
Also see TOM & JERRY

SIMON SAID
Singles: 7-Inch
ATCO: 75-76 . . . . $2-4
ROULETTE: 75 2-4

SIMON SISTERS
Singles: 7-Inch
COLUMBIA (02600 series): 82 1-3
COLUMBIA (45000 series): 73 2-4
KAPP: 64-65 3-5
LPs: 10/12-Inch 33rpm
COLUMBIA (21525; "Lobster
Quadrille"): 69 12-15
COLUMBIA (21539; "Simon Sisters
Sing For Children"): 73 10-12
COLUMBIA (24506; "Lobster
Quadrille"): 69 15-20
(Special childrens' book edition.)
COLUMBIA (37000 series): 82 5-8
KAPP: 64 15-20
WARNER BROS: 80 5-8
Members: Carly Simon; Lucy Simon.
Also see DOOBIE BROTHERS / Kate Taylor
& The Simon-Taylor Family
Also see SIMON, Carly

SIMONE, Nina
Singles: 7-Inch
BETHLEHEM: 59-70 2-4
CTI: 78 1-3
COLPIX: 59-63 2-4
PHILIPS: 64-66 2-4
RCA VICTOR: 67-71 2-4
TRIP: 72 1-3
EPs: 7-Inch 33/45rpm
BETHLEHEM: 59 .4-8
LPs: 10/12-Inch 33rpm
ACCORD: 80 4-8
BETHLEHEM: 59 15-25
CTI: 78-79 5-8
COLPIX: 59-66 10-20
PHILIPS: 64-69 10-20
QUINTESSENCE: 80 4-8
RCA VICTOR: 67-76 6-12
STROUD: 73 5-10
TRIP: 72-77 5-10
UPFRONT: 72 5-10
VERSATILE: 78 .6-10

SIMONE, Nina, Chris Connor & Carmen McRae
LPs: 10/12-Inch 33rpm
BETHLEHEM: 60 15-25
Also see CONNOR, Chris
Also see MC RAE, Carmen
Also see SIMONE, Nina

SIMPLE MINDS
Singles: 12-Inch 33/45rpm
A&M: *82-86* $4-6
Singles: 7-Inch
A&M: *82-86* 1-3
Picture Sleeves
A&M: *84* 1-3
LPs: 10/12-Inch 33rpm
A&M: *82-86* 5-8
A&M (6850;"Simple Minds Live:
In The City Of Light"): *87* 10-12
PVC: *79* 8-10
Members: John Giblin; Charles Burchill; Jim Kerr;
Michael MacNeil; Mel Gaynor.

SIMPLY RED
Singles: 12-Inch 33/45rpm
ELEKTRA: *85-86* 4-6
Singles: 7-Inch
ELEKTRA: *85-87* 1-3
LPs: 10/12-Inch 33rpm
ELEKTRA: *85-87* 5-8

SIMPSON, Paul
(Paul Simpson Connection)
Singles: 12-Inch 33/45rpm
EASY STREET: *85* 4-6
STREETWISE: *83* 4-6
Singles: 7-Inch
STREETWISE: *83* 1-3

SIMPSON, Valerie
Singles: 7-Inch
TAMLA: *71-72* 2-4
LPs: 10/12-Inch 33rpm
TAMLA: *71-77* 8-10
Also see ASHFORD & SIMPSON

SIMS, Joyce
Singles: 7-Inch
SLEEPING BAG: *86-88* 1-3

SIMS, Marvin L.
Singles: 7-Inch
KAREN: *69* 2-4
MELLOW: *66-67* 3-5
MERCURY: *72* 2-4
REVUE: *68-69* 3-5

SIMS TWINS
(Simms Twins)
Singles: 7-Inch
ABKCO: 1-3
CROSSOVER: *74* 2-3
KENT: *71* 2-4
PARKWAY: *68* 3-5
SAR: *61-62* 4-6
SPECIALTY: 2-3

SIMTEC & WYLIE
Singles: 7-Inch
MISTER CHAND: *70-72* $2-4
SHAMA: *69-70* 2-4
LPs: 10/12-Inch 33rpm
MISTER CHAND: *71-72* 8-10
Also see SOUTHSIDE MOVEMENT

SINATRA, Frank
Singles: 78rpm
BLUEBIRD: *42-43* 25-50
BRUNSWICK (8443; "From The Bottom Of
My Heart"): *39* 100-150
(With Harry James & His Orchestra.)
CAPITOL: *53-58* 4-8
COLUMBIA: *39-52* 5-15
(With Harry James & His Orchestra.)
RCA VICTOR ("Oh Look At
Me Now"). 50-100
(Promotional issue only. Numbered edition of
1,000 issued.)
Singles: 7-Inch
CAPITOL (2450; "Lean Baby"): *53* 12-25
CAPITOL (2500 through 4800
series): *53-62* 5-15
COLUMBIA (100 through 900
series): *50-52* 15-30
(Microgroove 33 single series.)
COLUMBIA (38000 & 39000
series): *50-51* 5-10
"HIGH HOPES WITH JACK KENNEDY"/
"Jack Kennedy All The Way": *60* ... 150-250
(Presidential campaign promotional issue only. No
label name or artist shown, only titles.)
REPRISE (45; "Gunga Din"): *66* 25-50
(Promotional issue only.)
REPRISE (0249 through 1335): *64-75* 3-6
REPRISE (20001 through 20151): *61-63* .. 4-8

REPRISE (20157; "California"): *63* . . . **$50-100**
(White label. Promotional issue only.)
REPRISE (20157; "California"): *77* . . . **100-200**
(Brown label. Promotional issue only.)
REPRISE (29000 series): *82* **1-3**
REPRISE (49000 series): *80-83* **1-3**
REPRISE/CAL NEVADA LODGE
(101; "Ring-A-Ding-Ding"): *61* **20-40**
Picture Sleeves
REPRISE (0249 through 1300
series): *64-76* **5-15**
REPRISE (20001 through 20151): *61-63* . **10-20**
REPRISE/CAL NEVADA LODGE
(101; "Ring-A-Ding-Ding"): *61* **40-60**
(Promotional souvenir, available from the lodge.)
SINATRA: *75* **2-3**
EPs: 7-Inch 33/45rpm
CAPITOL: *54-61* **15-30**
COLUMBIA: *50-59* **20-40**
RCA VICTOR (3000 series): *52* **40-60**
RCA VICTOR (5000 series): *60* **15-25**
LPs: 10/12-Inch 33rpm
CAMDEN: *72-73* **5-10**
CAPITOL ("Radio/TV Sampler"): *58* . **200-250**
(Number unknown. Yellow label. Promotional
issue only.)
CAPITOL (200 & 300 series): *69* **8-15**
CAPITOL (400 through 1100
series): *54-59* **15-30**
(With a "T" prefix.)
CAPITOL (500 through 1600
series): *61-78* **5-15**
(With a "DT," "DW," "SM," "STBB," "SW," or
"W" prefix.)
CAPITOL (1200 through 1600
series): *59-62* **10-20**
(With a "T" or "ST" prefix.)
CAPITOL (1729; "Love & Things"): *62* . **10-20**
CAPITOL (1762; "Great Years"): *62* **20-30**
(3-LP set.)
CAPITOL (1800 through 2700
series): *62-67* **10-20**
CAPITOL (2814; "Frank Sinatra
Deluxe Set"): *67* **35-50**
(6-LP set.)
CAPITOL (11000 & 12000
series): *74-80* **5-10**
CAPITOL (16000 series): *80-82* **5-8**
COLUMBIA (6; "The Frank
Sinatra Story"): *58* **10-20**
COLUMBIA (42; "Essential
Frank Sinatra"): *67* **15-30**
COLUMBIA (606 through 803): *55-57* . . **15-25**
COLUMBIA (842; "Essential Frank
Sinatra"): *67* **15-30**

COLUMBIA (855 through 1400
series): *57-59* **$12-25**
COLUMBIA (2400 & 2500 series): *66* **8-15**
(12-Inch LPs.)
COLUMBIA (2500 series): *55* **15-30**
(10-Inch LPs.)
COLUMBIA (2900 series): *69* **5-10**
COLUMBIA (6000 series): *50-54* **30-60**
(10-Inch LPs. Some LPs in this series have paper
sleeves.)
COLUMBIA (9200 & 9300 series): *66* **8-15**
COLUMBIA (10000 series): *73* **5-10**
COLUMBIA (31000 series): *72* **5-10**
HARMONY: *66-71* **5-12**
MFSL (1; "Frank Sinatra"): *85* **300-400**
(16-LP boxed set. Includes booklet and alignment
tool.)
MFSL (100 series): *84-86* **15-30**
ODYSSEY: *68* **8-15**
QWEST: *84* **5-8**
RCA VICTOR (400 through 1500
series): *72-76* **5-10**
RCA VICTOR (3000 series): *52* **20-40**
(10-Inch LP.)
RCA VICTOR (4300 series): *82* **8-12**
RCA VICTOR (4700 series): *83* **4-8**
REPRISE (1001 through 1024): *61-68* . . . **10-20**
REPRISE (1025 through 1034): *68-72* **8-12**
REPRISE (2020 through 2275): *64-77* **5-15**
REPRISE (2300; "Trilogy"): *80* **15-25**
(3-LP set.)
REPRISE (2305; "She Shot Me Down"): *81* . **5-8**
REPRISE (6000 series): *65* **10-15**
SINATRA: *75* **5-10**
Also see ANTHONY, Ray
Also see CROSBY, Bing, & Frank Sinatra
Also see DAY, Doris & Frank Sinatra
Also see DORSEY, Tommy, Orchestra
Also see JAMES, Harry
Also see PRESLEY, Elvis / Frank Sinatra /
Nat "King" Cole
Also see ZENTER, Si

SINATRA, Frank, & The Charioteers
Singles: 78rpm
COLUMBIA: *45* **5-10**

SINATRA, Frank, & Count Basie
LPs: 10/12-Inch 33rpm
REPRISE: *63-66* **10-20**
Also see BASIE, Count

SINATRA, Frank, & Doris Day
Singles: 78rpm
COLUMBIA: *49* **5-10**
Also see DAY, Doris / Frank Sinatra

SINATRA, Frank, & Duke Ellington
Singles: 7-Inch
REPRISE: 68 . . . . $2-3
LPs: 10/12-Inch 33rpm
REPRISE: 68 8-15
Also see ELLINGTON, Duke

SINATRA, Frank & Antonio
Carlos Jobim
LPs: 10/12-Inch 33rpm
REPRISE: 69-71 8-12
Also see JOBIM, Antonio Carlos

SINATRA, Frank, & Keely Smith
Singles: 7-Inch
CAPITOL: 58 3-5
Also see SMITH, Keely

SINATRA, Frank, Sammy Davis Jr., &
Dean Martin
Singles: 7-Inch
REPRISE (20,128; "Me And My Shadow"/
"Sam's Song"): 62 3-5
Picture Sleeves
REPRISE (20,128; "Me And My Shadow"/
"Sam's Song"): 62 5-10
LPs: 10/12-Inch 33rpm
LATIMER (247-17; "Summit Meeting At
The 500 Club"): 64 50-100
(Promotional issue only.)
Also see DAVIS, Sammy, Jr.
Also see MARTIN, Dean

SINATRA, Frank & Nancy
(Sinatra Family)
Singles: 7-Inch
REPRISE: 66-71 2-4
LPs: 10/12-Inch 33rpm
REPRISE: 69 8-15
Members: Sinatra Family included Frank Sinatra;
Frank Jr.; Nancy; & Tina.
Also see SINATRA, Nancy

SINATRA, Nancy
Singles: 7-Inch
ELEKTRA: 80 1-3
PRIVATE STOCK: 75-77 2-3
RCA VICTOR: 72-73 2-4
REPRISE: 61-71 3-5
Picture Sleeves
REPRISE: 62-67 3-6
EPs: 7-Inch 33/45rpm
REPRISE: 66 10-12
(Jukebox issue only.)
LPs: 10/12-Inch 33rpm
RCA VICTOR: 72 8-10
REPRISE: 66-72 15-30
Also see BARRY, John

Also see MARTIN, Dean
Also see PRESLEY, Elvis
Also see SINATRA, Frank & Nancy

SINATRA, Nancy, & Lee Hazlewood
Singles: 7-Inch
PRIVATE STOCK: 76 . . . . $2-3
RCA VICTOR: 72 2-3
REPRISE: 67-68 3-5
LPs: 10/12-Inch 33rpm
RCA VICTOR: 72 8-10
REPRISE: 68 10-15
Also see HAZLEWOOD, Lee
Also see SINATRA, Nancy

SINCLAIR, Gordon
Singles: 7-Inch
AVCO: 74 2-4

SINFIELD, Pete
Singles: 7-Inch
MANTICORE: 73 2-4
LPs: 10/12-Inch 33rpm
MANTICORE: 73 8-10

SINGING BELLS
Singles: 7-Inch
MADISON: 60 5-8

SINGING DOGS
(Don Charles Presents The Singing Dogs)
Singles: 78rpm
RCA VICTOR: 55 2-5
Singles: 7-Inch
RCA VICTOR: 55-72 3-5
Picture Sleeves
RCA VICTOR: 55-56 5-10

SINGING NUN
(Soeur Sourire)
Singles: 7-Inch
PHILIPS: 63-64 2-4
Picture Sleeves
PHILIPS: 63-64 3-5
LPs: 10/12-Inch 33rpm
PHILIPS: 63-69 6-15

SINGLE BULLET THEORY
Singles: 7-Inch
NEMPEROR: 83 1-3
LPs: 10/12-Inch 33rpm
NEMPEROR: 83 5-8

SINGLETON, Charlie
Singles: 7-Inch
ARISTA: 85 1-3
LPs: 10/12-Inch 33rpm
ARISTA: 85 5-8
Also see CAMEO
Also see COBHAM, Billy

SINGLETON, Charlie, & Modern Man
Singles: 7-Inch
EPIC: *87-88* $1-3

SINNAMON
Singles: 12-Inch 33/45rpm
BECKET: *82-83* 4-6
JIVE: *84* 4-6
Singles: 7-Inch
BECKET: *82-83* 1-3

SIOUXSIE & THE BANSHEES
Singles: 12-Inch 33/45rpm
GEFFEN: *84-86* 4-6
PVC: *80-82* 4-6
Singles: 7-Inch
GEFFEN: *84-88* 1-3
PVC: *80-82* 1-3
POLYDOR: *79* 1-3
LPs: 10/12-Inch 33rpm
GEFFEN: *84-88* 5-8
PVC: *80-82* 6-10
POLYDOR: *79* 8-10
Also see SEX PISTOLS

SIR CHAUNCEY
(Ernie Freeman)
Singles: 7-Inch
PATTERN: *60* 3-6
WARNER BROS: *60* 2-4
Also see FREEMAN, Ernie

SIR DOUGLAS QUINTET
(Sir Douglas Band)
Singles: 7-Inch
ATLANTIC: *73* 4-8
CASABLANCA (0828; "Roll With
The Punches"): *75* 5-15
MERCURY: *71* 2-4
PACEMAKER: *64* 10-20
PHILIPS: *70-71* 2-4
SMASH: *68-70* 3-5
TRIBE: *65* 5-8
(Plain label, no Indian pictured.)
TRIBE: *65-67* 3-6
(Label pictures Indian.)
Picture Sleeves
PHILIPS: *70-71* 2-4
LPs: 10/12-Inch 33rpm
ACCORD: *82* 5-8
ATLANTIC: *73* 10-15
MERCURY: *72* 10-12
PHILIPS: *70-71* 10-15
SMASH: *68-70* 15-30
TAKOMA: *80-83* 5-8
TRIBE (47001; "Best Of Sir
Douglas Quintet"): *66* 40-80

Members: Doug Sahm; Augie Meyers; Jack Barber; Leon Baetty; John Perez; Frank Morin; Jim Stallings.
Also see CASCADES / Sir Douglas Quintet
Also see SAHM, Doug

SIR LORD BALTIMORE
Singles: 7-Inch
MERCURY: *70-71* $2-4
LPs: 10/12-Inch 33rpm
MERCURY: *70-71* 8-10

SIR MIX-A-LOT
Singles: 7-Inch
NASTYMIX: *88* 1-3
LPs: 10/12-Inch 33rpm
NASTYMIX: *88* 5-8

SIREN
Singles: 7-Inch
MIDSONG INT'L: *79* 2-3
LPs: 10/12-Inch 33rpm
ELEKTRA: *71* 8-10
DANDELION: *70* 10-12

SIRENNE, Gianni
Singles: 12-Inch 33/45rpm
ATLANTIC: *84* 4-6
Singles: 7-Inch
ATLANTIC: *84* 1-3

SISTER & BROTHERS
Singles: 7-Inch
CALLA: *71* 2-4
UNI: *70* 2-4

SISTER SLEDGE
Singles: 12-Inch 33/45rpm
ATLANTIC: *85* 4-6
COTILLION: *79-83* 4-6
Singles: 7-Inch
ATCO: *73-75* 2-4
ATLANTIC: *85* 1-3
COTILLION: *76-83* 1-3
LPs: 10/12-Inch 33rpm
ATCO: *75* 8-10
ATLANTIC: *85* 5-8
COTILLION: *76-83* 5-8

SISTERS LOVE
Singles: 7-Inch
A&M: *69-71* 2-4
MOWEST: *73* 2-4

SISTERS OF MERCY
LPs: 10/12-Inch 33rpm
ELEKTRA: *88* 5-8

SIX TEENS
Singles: 7-Inch
FLIP (Except 338): *56-60* 10-15

Ricky Skaggs (Photo: Beverly Parker)

FLIP (338; "Baby-O"): 58 .... $20-25
  Members: Trudy Williams; Louise Williams; Ed
  Wells; Bev Pecot; Ken Sinclair; Darrell Lewis.

SKA KINGS
Singles: 7-Inch
ATLANTIC: 64 3-5

SKAGGS, Ricky
Singles: 7-Inch
EPIC: 81 88 1-3
ROUNDER: 80 1-3
SUGAR HILL: 80 2-3
LPs: 10/12-Inch 33rpm
EPIC: 81-88 5-8
ROUNDER: 82 5-8
SUGAR HILL: 79-80 5-8
WEL DUN: 78 8-10
  Also see SCRUGGS, Earl

SKELLERN, Peter
Singles: 7-Inch
LONDON: 72 2-4
PRIVATE STOCK: 75 2-3
LPs: 10/12-Inch 33rpm
LONDON: 76 6-10

SKELTON, Red
Singles: 7-Inch
CBS/BURGER KING ("Pledge Of
  Allegiance"): 69 8-12
  (Promotional paper soundsheet.)
COLUMBIA: 69 2-4
LPs: 10/12-Inch 33rpm
LIBERTY: 65-66 5-15

SKHY, A.B: see A.B. SKHY

SKIP & FLIP
Singles: 7-Inch
BRENT: 59-62 .... $4-6
CALIFORNIA: 63 3-5
COLLECTABLES: 1-3
ERIC: 1-3
TIME: 61 8-10
  Members: Clyde Batton; Gary Paxton.

SKIP & THE CASUALS
Singles: 7-Inch
D.C. INT'L: 74 2-4

SKIPWORTH & TURNER
Singles: 12-Inch 33/45rpm
4TH & BROADWAY: 85 4-6
WARNER BROS: 86 4-6
Singles: 7-Inch
4TH & BROADWAY: 85 1-3
WARNER BROS: 86 1-3
LPs: 10/12-Inch 33rpm
WARNER BROS: 86 5-8
  Members: Rodney Skipworth; Philip Turner.

SKOOL BOYZ
Singles: 12-Inch 33/45rpm
COLUMBIA: 84-85 4-6
Singles: 7-Inch
COLUMBIA: 84-85 1-3
DESTINY: 81-82 1-3
LPs: 10/12-Inch 33rpm
DESTINY: 81 5-8
  Also see TRIPLE "S" CONNECTION

SKRATCH
Singles: 12-Inch 33/45rpm
PASSION: 85 4-6

SKWARES
Singles: 7-Inch
MERCURY: 88 1-3

SKY
Singles: 7-Inch
RCA VICTOR: 71-72 2-4
LPs: 10/12-Inch 33rpm
RCA VICTOR: 70-71 10-12

SKY
Singles: 7-Inch
ARISTA: 81 1-3
LPs: 10/12-Inch 33rpm
ARISTA: 81 8-10
  Member: Doug Fieger.
  Also see KNACK

SKYLARK
Singles: 7-Inch
CAPITOL: 72-73 2-4

LPs: 10/12-Inch 33rpm
CAPITOL: 72-74 .... $8-10
Members: Donny Gerrard; Carl Graves.
Also see GERRARD, Donny

SKYLINERS
Singles: 7-Inch
ATCO: 63 4-6
CALICO: 59-60 10-15
CAMEO: 62 4-6
CAPITOL: 75 2-4
COLPIX: 61 20-30
JUBILEE: 65-66 4-6
ORIGINAL SOUND: 1-3
TORTOISE INT'L: 78 2-3
VIRGO: 73 1-3
VISCOUNT: 62 4-6
LPs: 10/12-Inch 33rpm
CALICO (3000; "The Skyliners"): 59 . 100-200
KAMA SUTRA: 71 10-20
ORIGINAL SOUND: 63 15-25
TORTOISE INT'L: 78 8-10
Members: Jimmy Beaumont; Janet Vogel; Wally
Lester; Jack Taylor; Joe Verscharen.
Also see BEAUMONT, Jimmy

SKYNYRD, Lynyrd:
see LYNYRD SKYNYRD

SKYY
Singles: 12-Inch 33/45rpm
CAPITOL: 86 4-6
SALSOUL: 79-85 4-6
Singles: 7-Inch
CAPITOL: 86 1-3
SALSOUL: 79-85 1-3
LPs: 10/12-Inch 33rpm
CAPITOL: 86 5-8
SALSOUL: 79-82 5-8

SLADE
Singles: 7-Inch
CBS ASSOCIATED: 84-85 1-3
COTILLION: 71-72 2-4
POLYDOR: 72-73 2-4
REPRISE: 73 2-4
WARNER BROS: 73-76 2-3
LPs: 10/12-Inch 33rpm
CBS ASSOCIATED: 84 5-8
COTILLION: 70 10-15
POLYDOR: 72-73 8-10
REPRISE: 73 10-12
WARNER BROS: 74-76 8-10

SLADES
Singles: 7-Inch
DOMINO: 58-61 15-20
LIBERTY: 58 8-10

Also see SPADES

SLATKIN, Felix, Orchestra
Singles: 7-Inch
LIBERTY: 60-62 .... $2-4
LPs: 10/12-Inch 33rpm
ANGEL: 72 5-8
CAPITOL: 59 5-15
LIBERTY: 60-64 5-15
SUNSET: 66-68 5-10
UNITED ARTISTS: 71 5-10

SLAVE
(Slave-Arrington)
Singles: 12-Inch 33/45rpm
COTILLION: 83 4-6
Singles: 7-Inch
COTILLION: 77-84 1-3
ICHIBAN: 86-87 1-3
LPs: 10/12-Inch 33rpm
COTILLION: 77-84 5-8
ICHIBAN: 86 5-8
Member: Steve Arrington.
Also see ARRINGTON, Steve

SLAY, Emitt
(Emitt Slay Trio; Emitt Slay's Slayriders With
Sweetie Dolores)
Singles: 78rpm
SAVOY: 52-53 5-10
Singles: 7-Inch
CHECKER: 58 5-10
J.V.B.: 59 5-8
SAVOY: 52-53 10-20

SLAY, Frank, & His Orchestra
Singles: 7-Inch
SCA: 63 2-4
SWAN: 61 2-4
Also see CANNON, Freddy

SLAYER
Singles: 7-Inch
METAL BLADE: 85 1-3
LPs: 10/12-Inch 33rpm
DEF JAM: 86-88 5-8
ENIGMA/METAL BLADE: 85 5-8

SLEDGE, Percy
Singles: 7-Inch
ATLANTIC: 66-72 3-5
CAPRICORN: 74-76 2-4
MONUMENT: 83 1-3
LPs: 10/12-Inch 33rpm
ATLANTIC: 66-69 10-15
CAPRICORN: 74-75 8-10
MONUMENT: 83 5-8
Also see JACKSON, Chuck / Percy Sledge

SLEDGE, Sister: see SISTER SLEDGE

SLEEPY KING
Singles: 7-Inch
AWAKE: $10-15
JOY: *61* 3-5

SLICK
Singles: 12-Inch 33/45rpm
FANTASY: *80* 4-6
Singles: 7-Inch
FANTASY: *80* 1-3
LPs: 10/12-Inch 33rpm
FANTASY: *80* 5-8
WMOT: *79* 5-8

SLICK, Grace
(Grace Slick & The Great Society)
Singles: 7-Inch
GRUNT: *72-74* 2-4
RCA VICTOR: *80-81* 1-3
Picture Sleeves
RCA VICTOR: *80* 1-3
LPs: 10/12-Inch 33rpm
COLUMBIA (9624; "Conspicuous
Only"): *68* 20-30
(With a "CS" prefix.)
COLUMBIA (9624; "Conspicuous
Only"): 5-8
(With a "PC" prefix.)
COLUMBIA (9702; "How It Was"): *68* ..12-15
(With a "CS" prefix.)
COLUMBIA (30459; "Collector's
Item"): *71* 10-12
GRUNT: *74* 8-10
HARMONY: *71* 10-12
RCA VICTOR: *80-83* 5-8
Promotional LPs
RCA VICTOR ("Dreams"
Interview LP): *80* 25-30
RCA VICTOR (3922; "Wrecking
Ball" Interview LP): *81* 25-30
RCA VICTOR (3923; "Special
Radio Series"): *81* 10-15
RCA VICTOR (13708; "Interview LP"): ..5-10
Also see CROSBY, David
Also see GREAT!! SOCIETY!!
Also see JEFFERSON AIRPLANE
Also see KANTNER, Paul, & Grace Slick

SLIM, Guitar: see GUITAR SLIM

SLIM, Tarheel: see TARHEEL SLIM

SLIM & ANN:
see TARHEEL SLIM & LITTLE ANN

SLIM HARPO: see HARPO, Slim

SLINGSHOT
Singles: 12-Inch 33/45rpm
QUALITY/RFC: *83* $4-6
Singles: 7-Inch
QUALITY/RFC: *83* 1-3

SLOAN, P.F.
(Phil Sloan)
Singles: 7-Inch
ATCO: *69* 2-4
DUNHILL: *65-67* 3-5
MART: *60* 8-10
MUMS: *72* 2-4
LPs: 10/12-Inch 33rpm
ATCO: *68* 10-12
DUNHILL: *65-66* 12-15
MUMS: *72* 8-10

SLONIKER, Mark
LPs: 10/12-Inch 33rpm
SANDSTONE: *88* 5-8

SLY
(Sly Stone; Sly Stewart)
Singles: 7-Inch
AUTUMN: *65* 4-6
Also see SLY & THE FAMILY STONE

SLY & ROBBIE
Singles: 7-Inch
ISLAND: *86-87* 1-3
LPs: 10/12-Inch 33rpm
ISLAND: *86-87* 5-8
Members: Sly Dunbar; Robbie Shakespeare.

SLY & THE FAMILY STONE
Singles: 12-Inch 33/45rpm
EPIC: *79* 4-6
Singles: 7-Inch
EPIC: *67-75* 2-5
WARNER BROS: *79-85* 1-3
Picture Sleeves
EPIC: *68-70* 2-5
LPs: 10/12-Inch 33rpm
EPIC (264; "Everything You Always
Wanted To Hear"): *76* 10-15
(Promotional issue only.)
EPIC (26000 series): *67-69* 10-12
EPIC (30325; "Greatest Hits"): *70* 8-10
(With a "KE" prefix.)
EPIC (30325; "Greatest Hits"): 5-8
(With a "PE" prefix.)
EPIC (30325; "Greatest Hits"): *73* 25-50
(With an "EQ" prefix. Quad issue. Contains some
true stereo tracks that were only available in rechan-
neled stereo on the "KE" & "PE" 30325 issues.)
EPIC (30335 through 37071): *70-81* 6-10
WARNER BROS: *79-83* 5-8

Members: Sylvester "Sly Stone" Stewart; Rose
Stone; Larry Graham; Fred Stone; Gregg Errico;
Jerry Martini.
Also see BANKS, Rose
Also see GRAHAM, Larry
Also see RUBICON
Also see SLY
Also see STONE, Sly

SLY FOX
Singles: 12-Inch 33/45rpm
CAPITOL: 85-86 . . . . $4-6
Singles: 7-Inch
CAPITOL: 85-86 1-3
LPs: 10/12-Inch 33rpm
CAPITOL: 86 5-8
Members: Mike Camacho; Gary Cooper.

SMALL, Karen
Singles: 7-Inch
VENUS: 66 3-5

SMALL, Millie
(Blue Beat Girl)
Singles: 7-Inch
ATCO: 65 5-8
ATLANTIC: 64 5-8
BRIT: 65 4-6
SMASH: 64 4-8
LPs: 10/12-Inch 33rpm
SMASH: 64 15-20

SMALL FACES
Singles: 7-Inch
IMMEDIATE: 67-68 4-6
PRESS: 65-68 8-15
RCA VICTOR: 66 8-10
WARNER BROS: 70 3-5
LPs: 10/12-Inch 33rpm
ACCORD: 82 5-8
ATLANTIC: 77-78 8-10
COMPLEAT: 86 5-8

IMMEDIATE (002; "There Are But
Four Small Faces"): 68 . . . . $20-25
IMMEDIATE (008; "Ogden's Nut
Gone Flake"): 68 20-25
IMMEDIATE (4225; "Ogden's Nut
Gone Flake"): 73 10-12
MGM: 74 10-15
PRIDE: 72-73 10-15
SIRE: 10-15
WARNER BROS: 70 12-15
Members: Steve Marriott; Ronnie Lane.
Also see FACES
Also see HUMBLE PIE
Also see McLAGAN, Ian
Also see PYTHON LEE JACKSON

SMASH PALACE
Singles: 7-Inch
EPIC: 86 1-3
LPs: 10/12-Inch 33rpm
CBS: 85 5-8

SMITH
Singles: 7-Inch
DUNHILL: 69-70 2-4
ROULETTE: 1-3
Picture Sleeves
DUNHILL: 69 3-5
LPs: 10/12-Inch 33rpm
DUNHILL: 69-70 10-15
Member: Gayle McCormack.
Also see MC CORMACK, Gayle

SMITH, Betty
(Betty Smith Group)
Singles: 7-Inch
ECHO: 10-15
LONDON: 58 4-6

SMITH, Bro
Singles: 7-Inch
BIG TREE: 76 2-4
Picture Sleeves
BIG TREE: 76 2-5

SMITH, Bobby
LPs: 10/12-Inch 33rpm
RIPSAW: 87 5-8
Members: Danny Gatton; Johnny Castle; Mitch
Collins.

SMITH, Cal
Singles: 7-Inch
DECCA: 70-73 2-3
KAPP: 66-70 2-4
PLAID: 60 3-5
MCA: 73-79 1-3
SOUNDWAVES: 82 1-3
STEP ONE: 86 1-3

LPs: 10/12-Inch 33rpm

CORAL: 73	$4-8
DECCA: 72	8-10
KAPP: 66-70	8-12
MCA: 73-77	4-8

SMITH, Carl
(Carl Smith & The Tunesmiths)
Singles: 78rpm

COLUMBIA: 51-57	2-5

Singles: 7-Inch

ABC/HICKORY: 76-78	1-3
COLUMBIA (20000 & 21000 series): 51-56	3-6
COLUMBIA (40000 through 45000 series): 56-72	2-4
HICKORY: 74-76	1-3

Picture Sleeves

COLUMBIA: 59	4-8

EPs: 7-Inch 33/45rpm

COLUMBIA: 57-58	6-12

LPs: 10/12-Inch 33rpm

ABC/HICKORY: 77-78	5-8
COLUMBIA (31; "Anniversary Album"): 70	8-12
COLUMBIA (900 through 1100 series): 57-58	15-25
COLUMBIA (1500 through 2600 series): 60-67	10-20
COLUMBIA (2500 series): 56 (10-Inch LPs.)	20-35
COLUMBIA (8300 through 9800 series): 60-72 (12-Inch LPs.)	10-20
COLUMBIA (9000 series): 54 (10-Inch LPs.)	20-35
COLUMBIA (10000 series): 73	5-10
COLUMBIA (30000 series): 70-84	5-10
GUSTO: 80	5-8
HICKORY: 75	5-10
HARMONY: 64-72	5-15
LAKE SHORE:	5-8

Also see PRICE, Ray / Lefty Frizzell / Carl Smith

SMITH, Carl / Lefty Frizzell / Marty Robbins
LPs: 10/12-Inch 33rpm

COLUMBIA (2544; "Carl, Lefty, And Marty"): 56 (10-Inch LP.)	200-300

Also see FRIZZELL, Lefty
Also see ROBBINS, Marty
Also see SMITH, Carl

SMITH, Connie
Singles: 7-Inch

COLUMBIA: 73-77	$1-3
EPIC: 85	2-3
MONUMENT: 77-83	1-3
RCA VICTOR: 64-74	2-4

Picture Sleeves

RCA VICTOR: 67	3-5

LPs: 10/12-Inch 33rpm

CAMDEN: 67-72	5-10
COLUMBIA: 73-77	5-10
MONUMENT: 77-78	5-8
RCA VICTOR (0100 series through 1200 series): 73-75	5-10
RCA VICTOR (3300 series through 4800 series): 65-73	8-15

SMITH, Dawson
Singles: 7-Inch

ROADSHOW/SCEPTER: 75	2-4

SMITH, Effie
Singles: 78rpm

ALADDIN: 46-53	5-10
G&G: 45	8-12
GEM: 45	8-12
MILTONE: 47	5-10
VITA: 56	5-10

Singles: 7-Inch

ALADDIN (3200 series): 53	15-20
DUO DISC: 64-65	3-5
EEE CEE: 68	2-4
SPOT: 59	4-8
VITA: 56	10-15

LPs: 10/12-Inch 33rpm

JUBILEE: 66	15-20

SMITH, Frankie
Singles: 12-Inch 33/45rpm

WMOT: 81	4-6

Singles: 7-Inch

WMOT: 81	1-3

LPs: 10/12-Inch 33rpm

WMOT: 81	5-8

SMITH, Helene
Singles: 7-Inch

DEEP CITY: 68	4-8
PHIL-L.A. OF SOUL: 67-69	3-5

SMITH, Huey
(Huey Smith & His Band; Huey "Piano" Smith & His Clowns; Huey Smith & The Pitter Pats)
Singles: 7-Inch

ABC: 73	1-3
ACE (521 through 571): 56-59	8-15
ACE (584 through 672): 60-65	4-8
COLLECTABLES:	1-3

CONSTELLATION: *63* $3-5
COTILLION: *72* 2-4
IMPERIAL: *61* 4-6
INSTANT: *68-69* 3-5
SAVOY: *54* 30-35
VIN: *60* 4-6

EPs: 7-Inch 33/45rpm
ACE: *59* 25-35

LPs: 10/12-Inch 33rpm
ACE (1000 series): *59-62* 40-50
ACE (2000 series): *74* 25-35
GRAND PRIX: 10-15
Also see FORD, Frankie
Also see MARCHAN, Bobby, & The Clowns

SMITH, Hurricane
Singles: 7-Inch
CAPITOL: *72-73* 2-4
EMI: *74* 2-4
LPs: 10/12-Inch 33rpm
CAPITOL: *72* 8-10

SMITH, Jerry
(Jerry Smith & His Pianos)
Singles: 7-Inch
ABC: *69* 2-3
AD: *59-61* 2-5
CHART: *67* 2-3
DECCA: *70-72* 1-3
RANWOOD: *73-78* 1-3
RICE: *67* 2-3
SOUND STAGE 7: *65* 2-4
LPs: 10/12-Inch 33rpm
ABC: *69* 5-10
DECCA: *70-72* 5-10
RANWOOD: *73-75* 5-8
Also see DIXIEBELLES
Also see MAGIC ORGAN

SMITH, Jimmy
Singles: 7-Inch
BLUE NOTE: *56-63* 2-5
MGM: *78* 1-3
MERCURY: *77* 1-3
PRIDE: *74* 1-3
VERVE: *62-73* 2-4
LPs: 10/12-Inch 33rpm
BLUE NOTE: *56-60* 25-50
(Label gives New York street address for Blue
Note Records.)
BLUE NOTE: *61-63* 15-25
(Label reads "Blue Note Records Inc. - New York,
USA.")
BLUE NOTE: *66-73* 10-20
(Label shows Blue Note Records as a division of
either Liberty or United Artists.)
COBBLESTONE: *72* 6-12

ELEKTRA: *82-83* $5-8
GUEST STAR: *64* 8-12
INNER CITY: *81* 5-8
MGM: *70* 8-12
MERCURY: *77-78* 5-10
METRO: *67* 8-15
MOJO: *75* 5-10
PRIDE: *74* 5-10
SUNSET: *70* 5-10
VERVE: *63-72* 10-25
(Reads "MGM Records - A Division Of Metro-
Goldwyn-Mayer, Inc." at bottom of label.)
VERVE: *73-84* 5-10
(Reads "Manufactured By MGM Record Corp.," or
mentions either Polydor or Polygram at bottom of
label.)

SMITH, Jimmy, & Wes Montgomery
LPs: 10/12-Inch 33rpm
VERVE: *66-69* 10-20
Also see MONTGOMERY, Wes
Also see SMITH, Jimmy

SMITH, Kate
Singles: 78rpm
COLUMBIA: *27-46* 3-6
VICTOR: *38-42* 3-5
MGM: *48* 3-5
Singles: 7-Inch
ATLANTIC: *74* 1-3
MGM: *78* 1-3
RCA VICTOR: *63-68* 1-3
TOPS: *60* 2-3
Picture Sleeves
RCA VICTOR: *63-64* 2-5
EPs: 7-Inch 33/45rpm
MGM: *52-57* 4-8
RCA VICTOR: *59* 4-8
LPs: 10/12-Inch 33rpm
CAMDEN: *70-73* 4-8
CAPITOL: *54-57* 5-15
COLUMBIA (6000 series): *50* 10-20
(10-Inch LPs.)
HARMONY: *57* 5-12
KAPP: *58* 5-15
LION: *57-60* 5-12
MGM: *52-66* 5-15
METRO: *67* 5-10
RCA VICTOR: *63-80* 5-12

SMITH, Keely
Singles: 78rpm
CAPITOL: *56-58* 2-4
Singles: 7-Inch
ATLANTIC: *67* 1-3
CAPITOL: *56-58* 2-4
DOLTON: *64* 2-3

DOT: *59-62* $2-3
RCA VICTOR: *66-71* 1-3
REPRISE: *63-66* 1-3
Picture Sleeves
DOT: *60* 3-5
EPs: 7-Inch 33/45rpm
CAPITOL: *58-59* 4-8
DOT: *60* 4-8
LPs: 10/12-Inch 33rpm
CAPITOL: *58-75* 5-15
DOT: *59-62* 5-15
HARMONY: *69* 5-10
REPRISE: *63-65* 5-10
Also see PRIMA, Louis, & Keely Smith
Also see SINATRA, Frank, & Keely Smith

SMITH, Leslie, & Merry Clayton
Singles: 7-Inch
ELEKTRA: *82* 1-3
Also see CLAYTON, Merry

SMITH, Lonnie
Singles: 7-Inch
BLUE NOTE: *69-70* 1-3
GROOVE MERCHANT: *75* 2-3
LRC: *78-79* 1-3
LPs: 10/12-Inch 33rpm
BLUE NOTE: *68-70* 8-15
COLUMBIA: *67* 10-15
GROOVE MERCHANT: *75-76* 5-10
KUDU: *71* 5-10
LRC: *78* 5-8

SMITH, Lonnie Liston
(Lonnie Liston Smith & The Cosmic Echoes)
Singles: 12-Inch 33/45rpm
COLUMBIA: *79* 4-6
Singles: 7-Inch
COLUMBIA: *78-80* 1-3
DOCTOR JAZZ: *83* 1-3
FLYING DUTCHMAN: *75-76* 2-3
RCA VICTOR: *77* 1-3
LPs: 10/12-Inch 33rpm
COLUMBIA: *78-79* 5-8
DOCTOR JAZZ: *83* 5-8
FLYING DUTCHMAN: *73-76* 8-12
RCA VICTOR: *76-77* 5-10

SMITH, O.C.
(Ocie Smith)
Singles: 78rpm
CADENCE: *56-57* 3-6
Singles: 7-Inch
BIG TOP: *60* 3-5
CADENCE: *56-57* 5-8
CARIBOU: *76-77* 2-3
CITATION: *59* 3-5

COLUMBIA: *66-74* $2-4
FAMILY: *80* 1-3
GORDY: *82* 1-3
MGM: *56* 4-6
MOTOWN: *82* 1-3
RENDEZVOUS: *86-87* 1-3
SHADYBROOK: *78* 2-3
SOUL WEST: *72* 2-4
SOUTH BAY: *82* 1-3
Picture Sleeves
COLUMBIA: *69* 2-5
LPs: 10/12-Inch 33rpm
CARIBOU: *79* 5-8
COLUMBIA: *67-74* 8-12
HARMONY: *71* 8-10
MGM: *72* 8-10
MOTOWN: *82* 5-8
SOUTH BAY: *82* 5-8

SMITH, Patti
(Patti Smith Group)
Singles: 7-Inch
ARISTA: *76-79* 2-3
MER (601; "Hey Joe"): *74* 30-35
SIRE: *77* 2-3
Picture Sleeves
ARISTA: *78* 2-3
LPs: 10/12-Inch 33rpm
ARISTA (Except "Easter" picture
disc): *75-79* 8-10
ARISTA ("Easter" picture disc): *79* 15-20
ARISTA: *88* 5-8
(Promotional issue only.)

SMITH, Ray
Singles: 7-Inch
ABC: *73* 1-3
CELEBRITY CIRCLE: *64* 3-5
CINNAMON: *73-74* 2-4
COLLECTABLES: 1-3
CORONA: *75-77* 2-3
DIAMOND: *65* 3-5
HEART (250; "Gone Baby,
Gone"): 100-150
INFINITY: *61* 3-5
JUDD: *59-61* 5-10
NU-TONE: *64* 3-5
SMASH: *62* 3-5
SSS INT'L: 1-3
SSS/SUN: 1-3
SUN (298; "Right Behind You Baby"): *58* 10-20
SUN (308; "Why Why Why"): *59* 8-12
SUN (319 through 375): *59-62* 6-10
TOLLIE: *64* 8-10
TOPPA: *62* 3-5
VEE JAY: *64* 3-5

WARNER BROS: *63* $3-5
WIX: *78* 2-3
    LPs: 10/12-Inch 33rpm
BOOT: *78* 5-8
COLUMBIA: *63* 20-25
JUDD (701; "Travelin' With Ray"): *60* **100-150**
T: 10-12
WIX: 10-12
    Also see DONNER, Ral / Ray Smith / Bobby
Dale

SMITH, Rex
    Singles: 7-Inch
COLUMBIA: *76-81* 1-3
    Picture Sleeves
COLUMBIA: *79-80* 1-3
    LPs: 10/12-Inch 33rpm
COLUMBIA: *76-81* 5-8

SMITH, Rex, & Rachel Sweet
    Singles: 7-Inch
COLUMBIA: *81* 1-3
    Picture Sleeves
COLUMBIA: *81* 1-3
    Also see SMITH, Rex
    Also see SWEET, Rachel

SMITH, Richard Jon
    Singles: 12-Inch 33/45rpm
JIVE: *83* 4-6
    Singles: 7-Inch
JIVE: *83* 1-3
    LPs: 10/12-Inch 33rpm
JIVE: *83* 5-8

SMITH, Roger
    Singles: 7-Inch
JEROME: *61* 3-5
WARNER BROS: *59* 3-6
    Picture Sleeves
WARNER BROS: *59* 4-8
    LPs: 10/12-Inch 33rpm
WARNER BROS: *59* 20-25

SMITH, Sammi
    Singles: 7-Inch
COLUMBIA: *67-69* 2-4
CYCLONE: *79* 1-3
ELEKTRA: *75-78* 1-3
MEGA: *70-76* 1-3
SOUND FACTORY: *80-82* 1-3
STEP ONE: *86* 1-3
TRIP: *74* 1-3
ZODIAC: *76* 1-3
    Picture Sleeves
MEGA: *70* 2-3
    LPs: 10/12-Inch 33rpm
CYCLONE: *79* 5-8

ELEKTRA: *76-78* $5-8
HARMONY: *71* 5-10
MEGA: *70-75* 5-10
TRIP: *74* 5-8
UNITED ARTISTS: *75* 5-8
ZODIAC: *76* 5-8
    Also see HART, Freddie / Sammi Smith /
Jerry Reed

SMITH, Somethin', & The Redheads
    Singles: 78rpm
EPIC: *54-57* 2-4
    Singles: 7-Inch
EPIC: *54-59* 3-5
MGM: *61* 2-4
    Picture Sleeves
EPIC: *58* 4-8
    EPs: 7-Inch 33/45rpm
EPIC: *59* 10-20
    LPs: 10/12-Inch 33rpm
EPIC: *59* 10-20
MGM: *61* 5-15

SMITH, Tab
(Tab Smith & His Band)
    Singles: 78rpm
ARCO: *48* 4-6
ATLANTIC: *52* 4-8
CHESS: *52* 4-8
DECCA: *44* 5-8
EBONY: *46* 4-6
HARLEM: *46* 5-8
HUB: *45-46* 4-6
KING: *46* 4-8
MANOR: *44-48* 4-6
QUEEN: *46* 4-6
REGIS: *44* 5-8
SOUTHERN: *46* 4-6
20TH CENTURY: *45* 4-6
UNITED: *51-57* 4-8
    Singles: 7-Inch
ARGO: *58-59* 4-6
ATLANTIC: *52* 10-12
B&F: *61* 3-5
CHECKER: *59* 4-6
CHESS: *52* 8-10
KING (4000 series): *52* 5-8
KING (5000 series): *60-61* 3-5
UNITED (Black vinyl): *51-57* 8-15
UNITED (Colored vinyl): *51* 15-20
    EPs: 7-Inch 33/45rpm
KING: 10-15
    LPs: 10/12-Inch 33rpm
CHECKER: *59* 15-20
UNITED (001; "Music Styled
    By Tab Smith"): 30-35

UNITED (003; "Red Hot & Cool
   Blue Moods"): $20-25

SMITH, Verdelle
Singles: 7-Inch
CAPITOL: 66-67 3-5
COLUMBIA: 65 3-5
JANUS: 75 2-4
Picture Sleeves
COLUMBIA: 65 3-6
LPs: 10/12-Inch 33rpm
CAPITOL: 66 15-20
JANUS: 75 8-10

SMITH, Vince
Singles: 7-Inch
FOUR WINDS: 86-88 2-4
LPs: 10/12-Inch 33rpm
FOUR WINDS: 87-88 5-8

SMITH, Warren
Singles: 78rpm
SUN: 57 5-10
Singles: 7-Inch
LIBERTY: 60-64 3-5
MERCURY: 68 2-4
SUN (239; "Rock 'N' Roll Ruby"): 56 ... 20-30
SUN (250; "Ubangi Stomp"): 56 10-20
SUN (268 through 314): 57-59 5-10
SSS/SUN: 80 1-3
WARNER BROS: 59 4-6
LPs: 10/12-Inch 33rpm
LIBERTY: 61 30-40

SMITH, Whistling Jack
Singles: 7-Inch
DERAM: 67-69 2-4
LPs: 10/12-Inch 33rpm
DERAM: 67 10-12

SMITH CONNECTION
Singles: 7-Inch
MUSIC MERCHANT: 73 2-4

SMITHEREENS
Singles: 7-Inch
CAPITOL/ENIGMA: 88 1-4
ENIGMA: 85-86 1-3
LPs: 10/12-Inch 33rpm
CAPITOL/ENIGMA: 88-89 5-8
ENIGMA: 85-86 5-8
   Members: Pat Dinizio; Jim Babjak; Dennis Diken;
   Mike Mesaros.

SMITHS
Singles: 12-Inch 33/45rpm
SIRE: 84-86 4-6
Singles: 7-Inch
SIRE: 84-86 1-3

LPs: 10/12-Inch 33rpm
SIRE: 84-88 .... $5-8
   Members: Andy Rourke; Mike Joyce.
   Also see O'CONNOR, Sinead

SMOKE CITY
Singles: 7-Inch
EPIC: 84-85 1-3

SMOKE RING
Singles: 7-Inch
BUDDAH: 69 3-5

SMOKE RINGS
Singles: 7-Inch
DOT: 66 4-8

SMOKESTACK LIGHTNIN'
Singles: 7-Inch
BELL: 68-70 3-5
WHITE WHALE: 67 4-6
LPs: 10/12-Inch 33rpm
BELL: 69 10-15

SMOKIE
(Smokey)
Singles: 7-Inch
MCA: 75 2-4
RSO: 76-79 2-3
LPs: 10/12 Inch 33rpm
MCA: 75 8-10
RSO: 76-79 5-8
   Member: Chris Norman.
   Also see QUATRO, Suzi, & Chris Norman

SMOTHERS BROTHERS
Singles: 7-Inch
MERCURY: 62-66 3-5
Picture Sleeves
MERCURY: 64-65 4-8
LPs: 10/12-Inch 33rpm
MERCURY (20000 & 60000
   series): 61-68 10-20
   Members: Dick Smothers; Tom Smothers.

SNAIL
Singles: 7-Inch
CREAM: 78-79 2-3
LPs: 10/12-Inch 33rpm
CREAM: 78-79 5-8

SNEAKER
Singles: 7-Inch
HANDSHAKE: 81-82 1-3
LPs: 10/12-Inch 33rpm
HANDSHAKE: 81 5-8

SNEED, Lois
Singles: 7-Inch
CAPITOL: 73 2-4

SNELL, Annette
Singles: 7-Inch
DIAL: 73-74 .... $2-4
EPIC: 77 2-3

SNIFF 'N' THE TEARS
Singles: 7-Inch
ATLANTIC: 79-80 1-3
MCA: 81 1-3
LPs: 10/12-Inch 33rpm
ATCO: 79 5-8
ATLANTIC: 80 5-8
MCA: 81 5-8
Also see NETTO, Loz

SNOW, Hank
Singles: 78rpm
BLUEBIRD: 15-30
RCA VICTOR: 49-57 5-10
Singles: 7-Inch
RCA VICTOR (0100 & 0900 series): 69-74 2-4
(Orange labels.)
RCA VICTOR (0300 & 0400
series): 50-51 5-10
(Gray labels.)
RCA VICTOR (4300 through 7700
series): 52-60 4-8
RCA VICTOR (7800 through 9900
series): 61-70 2-5
RCA VICTOR (10000 & 11000
series): 74-80 1-3
Picture Sleeves
RCA VICTOR: 63 3-6
EPs: 7-Inch 33/45rpm
RCA VICTOR (295 through
1113): 54-56 10-25
RCA VICTOR (1156; "Old Doc
Brown"): 55 30-40
RCA VICTOR (1200 series): 55 15-20
RCA VICTOR (1400 series): 57 8-12
RCA VICTOR (4000 series): 58 8-12
RCA VICTOR (5000 series): 58-60 8-12
RCA VICTOR (3000 & 3100
series): 52-53 35-45
LPs: 10/12-Inch 33rpm
CAMDEN: 59-74 8-15
HANK SNOW SCHOOL OF MUSIC
(1149/50; "The Guitar"): 58 175-225
(Special issue from the Hank Snow School Of
Music. Includes guitar instruction booklet.)
PICKWICK: 75-76 5-10
RCA VICTOR (0134; "The Living
Legend"): 78 100-125
(RCA Special Products issue.)
RCA VICTOR (0162 through 0900
series): 73-75 5-10

RCA VICTOR (1004; "I'm
Movin' On"): 82 .... $15-20
(RCA Special Products issue.)
RCA VICTOR (1052 through 3500
series): 75-79 5-10
(With an ""AHL1," "ANL1," or APL1" prefix.)
RCA VICTOR (1113; "Just Keep
A-Movin"): 55 25-35
(With an "LPM" prefix.)
RCA VICTOR (1156; "Old Doc
Brown"): 55 125-175
RCA VICTOR (1200 through 1800
series): 55-58 25-40
RCA VICTOR (2000 through 4700
series): 60-72 10-25
RCA VICTOR (3000 & 3100
series): 52-54 40-60
(10-Inch LPs.)
RCA VICTOR (6014; "This Is
My Story"): 66 20-30
READER'S DIGEST (216; "I'm
Movin' On"): 125-150
(6-LP set.)
Also see PRESLEY, Elvis / Hank Snow /
Eddy Arnold / Hank Snow

SNOW, Hank, & Chet Atkins
Singles: 78rpm
RCA VICTOR: 55 4-8
Singles: 7-Inch
RCA VICTOR (5900 series): 55 3-5
LPs: 10/12-Inch 33rpm
RCA VICTOR (2900 through 4200
series): 64-70 20-25
Also see ATKINS, Chet

SNOW, Hank / Hank Locklin /
Porter Wagoner
LPs: 10/12-Inch 33rpm
RCA VICTOR: 63 10-20
Also see LOCKLIN, Hank
Also see SNOW, Hank
Also see WAGONER, Porter

SNOW, Phoebe
Singles: 7-Inch
COLUMBIA: 76-78 2-3
MIRAGE: 81 1-3
SHELTER: 74-75 2-4
LPs: 10/12-Inch 33rpm
COLUMBIA: 76-81 5-8
MCA: 79 5-8
MIRAGE: 81 5-8
SHELTER: 74 8-10
Also see GOODMAN, Steve, & Phoebe Snow
Also see SIMON, Paul, & Phoebe Snow

SNUFF
Singles: 7-Inch
WARNER BROS/CURB : *83* $1-3

SO
Singles: 7-Inch
EMI-MANHATTAN: *88* 1-3
LPs: 10/12-Inch 33rpm
EMI-MANHATTAN: *88* 5-8

SOBER, Errol
Singles: 7-Inch
ABC: *74* 2-3
ABNAK: *70* 2-4
BELL: *72* 2-4
CAPITOL: *76* 2-3
NUMBER ONE: *79* 1-3

SOCCIO, Gino
Singles: 12-Inch 33/45rpm
ATLANTIC: *80-84* 4-6
WARNER BROS/RFC: *79-80* 4-6
Singles: 7-Inch
ATLANTIC: *80-84* 1-3
WARNER BROS/RFC: *79-82* 1-3
LPs: 10/12-Inch 33rpm
ATLANTIC: *80-84* 5-8
WARNER BROS/RFC: *79-80* 5-8

SOFFICI, Piero
Singles: 7-Inch
JUBILEE: *61* 3-5
KIP: *61* 3-5

SOFT CELL
Singles: 12-Inch 33/45rpm
SIRE: *82* 4-6
Singles: 7-Inch
SIRE: *82* 1-3
Picture Sleeves
SIRE: *82* 1-3
LPs: 10/12-Inch 33rpm
ACCORD: *82* 5-8
SIRE: *82-83* 5-10
Members: Marc Almond; David Ball.
Also see ALMOND, Marc

SOFT MACHINE
Singles: 7-Inch
PROBE: *69* 3-5
LPs: 10/12-Inch 33rpm
ACCORD: *82* 5-8
COLUMBIA: *70-73* 8-10
COMMAND: *73* 12-15
PROBE (4500; "The Soft Machine"): *68* . 20-25
(With movable parts cover.)
PROBE (4500; "The Soft Machine"): *69* . 15-20
(With standard cover.)

PROBE (4505; "The Soft
Machine, Vol. 2"): *69* $15-20
RECKLESS: *88* 6-8

SOFTONES
(Soft Tones)
Singles: 7-Inch
AVCO: *73-75* 2-4
H&L: *77* 2-3
Picture Sleeves
H&L: *77* 2-3

SOLARIS
Singles: 7-Inch
DANA: *80* 1-3
LPs: 10/12-Inch 33rpm
DANA: *80* 5-8

SOLO
Singles: 12-Inch 33/45rpm
NEXT PLATINUM: *84* 4-6

SOME, Belouis: see BELOUIS SOME

SOMMER, Bert
Singles: 7-Inch
BUDDAH: *71* 2-4
CAPITOL: *77-78* 2-3
ELEUTHERA: *70* 2-4
LPs: 10/12-Inch 33rpm
BUDDAH: *71* 8-12
CAPITOL: *77* 8-10
ELEUTHERA: *70* 8-12

SOMMERS, Joanie
Singles: 7-Inch
ABC: *78* 1-3
CAPITOL: *67* 2-4
COLUMBIA: *66* 2-4
HAPPY TIGER: *70* 2-3
WARNER BROS (107; "Sommers'
Hot, Sommers' Here"): *60* 5-10
(Promotional issue only.)
WARNER BROS (5000 series): *60-65* 3-5
WARNER BROS (7000 series): *68* 2-4
LPs: 10/12-Inch 33rpm
COLUMBIA: *66* 10-15
DISCOVERY: *83* 5-8
WARNER BROS: *59-62* 15-20
Also see BYRNES, Edd "Kookie," With
Joanie Sommers & The Mary Kaye Trio
Also see NELSON, Rick / Joanie Sommers /
Dona Jean Young

SOMMERS, Joanie & Laurindo Almeida
LPs: 10/12-Inch 33rpm
WARNER BROS: *64* 10-20
Also see ALMEIDA, Laurindo
Also see SOMMERS, Joanie

SOMMERS, Ronny
(Sonny Bono)
Singles: 7-Inch
SWAMI: 61 .... $8-12
Also see SONNY

SONNY
(Sonny Bono)
Singles: 7-Inch
ATCO: 65-67 3-5
HIGHLAND: 63 5-8
MCA: 72-74 2-4
SPECIALTY: 65-72 2-5
LPs: 10/12-Inch 33rpm
ATCO: 67 12-15
Also see CHRISTY, Don
Also see SOMMERS, Ronny
Also see SONNY & CHER

SONNY & CHER
Singles: 7-Inch
ATCO: 65-70 4-8
KAPP: 71-72 3-5
MCA: 73-74 3-5
REPRISE: 64-65 5-10
VAULT (916; "The Letter"): 65 8-12
WARNER BROS: 77 2-4
Picture Sleeves
VAULT: 65 10-15
EPs: 7-Inch 33/45rpm
ATCO: 65 5-10
(Jukebox issues only.)
REPRISE: 65 15-20
LPs: 10/12-Inch 33rpm
ATCO: 65-72 12-15
KAPP: 71-72 10-12
MCA: 73-74 8-12
REPRISE (6177; "Baby Don't Go"): 65 .. 20-30
(Shown as by "Sonny & Cher & Friends." Includes
tunes by the Righteous Brothers, and the Letter-
men.)
TVP: 77 8-10
Members: Salvatore Bono; Cher LaPiere.
Also see CAESAR & CLEO
Also see CHER
Also see RIGHTEOUS BROTHERS
Also see SONNY

SONS OF CHAMPLIN
(Sons)
Singles: 7-Inch
ARIOLA AMERICA: 75-77 2-3
CAPITOL: 69-70 4-6
COLUMBIA: 73 2-4
GOLDMINE: 8-12
VERVE : 67 5-8

LPs: 10/12-Inch 33rpm
ARIOLA AMERICA: 75-76 .... $8-10
CAPITOL: 69 10-15
COLUMBIA: 73 10-12

SOPHISTICATED LADIES
Singles: 7-Inch
MAYHEW: 77 2-3

SOPWITH CAMEL
Singles: 7-Inch
KAMA SUTRA: 66-67 3-5
REPRISE: 73 2-4
Picture Sleeves
KAMA SUTRA: 67 4-8
LPs: 10/12-Inch 33rpm
KAMA SUTRA: 67-73 15-20
REPRISE: 73 15-20

SOUL: see S.O.U.L.

SOUL, David
Singles: 7-Inch
MGM: 66-67 3-5
PARAMOUNT: 70 2-4
PRIVATE STOCK: 77 2-3
LPs: 10/12-Inch 33rpm
PRIVATE STOCK: 77 8-10

SOUL, Jimmy
(Jimmy Soul & The Chants)
Singles: 7-Inch
S.P.Q.R.: 62-65 4-6
20TH CENTURY-FOX: 63 3-5
Picture Sleeves
S.P.Q.R.: 62-63 10-15
LPs: 10/12-Inch 33rpm
S.P.Q.R.: 63 30-40

SOUL, Jimmy / Belmonts
LPs: 10/12-Inch 33rpm
SPINORAMA: 63 20-25
Also see BELMONTS
Also see SOUL, Jimmy

SOUL ASYLUM
LPs: 10/12-Inch 33rpm
TWIN/TONE: 88 5-8
Members: Dan Murphy; Grant Young; Dave
Pirner; Karl Mueller.

SOUL BROTHERS SIX
Singles: 7-Inch
ATLANTIC: 67-69 4-6
PHIL-L.A. OF SOUL: 72-74 2-5

SOUL CHILDREN
Singles: 12-Inch 33/45rpm
STAX: 78-79 4-6
Singles: 7-Inch
EPIC: 75-76 2-4

STAX: 69-74 ....$2-5
LPs: 10/12-Inch 33rpm
EPIC: 76 8-10
STAX: 69-79 8-10

SOUL CLAN
Singles: 7-Inch
ATLANTIC: 68 3-6
Picture Sleeves
ATLANTIC: 68 3-5
Members: Solomon Burke; Arthur Conley; Don
Covay; Ben E. King; Joe Tex.
Also see BURKE, Solomon
Also see CONLEY, Arthur
Also see COVAY, Don
Also see KING, Ben E.
Also see TEX, Joe

SOUL DOG
Singles: 7-Inch
AMHERST: 76 2-5
LPs: 10/12-Inch 33rpm
AMHERST: 77 8-12

SOUL GENTS
(Soul Generation)
Singles: 7-Inch
EBONY SOUNDS: 72-74 2-5
FROS RAY: 68-71 3-5
LPs: 10/12-Inch 33rpm
EBONY SOUNDS: 72 8-12

SOUL RUNNERS
Singles: 7-Inch
MO SOUL: 66-67 4-6

SOUL SEARCHERS
Singles: 7-Inch
POLYDOR: 75 2-4
SUSSEX: 72-74 2-4
LPs: 10/12-Inch 33rpm
SUSSEX: 73-74 8-10

SOUL SISTERS
Singles: 7-Inch
GUYDEN: 62 3-6
KAYO: 63 3-6
SUE: 64-65 3-6
VEEP: 68 3-5
LPs: 10/12-Inch 33rpm
SUE: 64 20-25

SOUL SURVIVORS
Singles: 7-Inch
ATCO: 68-69 3-5
CRIMSON: 67-68 3-5
DECCA: 67 4-6
PHILADELPHIA INT'L: 76............2-3
TSOP: 74-75 2-4

LPs: 10/12-Inch 33rpm
ATCO: 69 ....$12-15
CRIMSON: 67 15-20
TSOP: 75 8-10
Members: Richard Ingui; Charles Ingui; Kenny
Jeremiah.

SOUL TORNADOS
Singles: 7-Inch
BURT: 69 3-5

SOUL TRAIN GANG
Singles: 7-Inch
SOUL TRAIN: 75-77 2-3
LPs: 10/12-Inch 33rpm
SOUL TRAIN: 76 8-10

SOULE, George
Singles: 7-Inch
LA LOUISIANNE: 65 3-5
FAME: 73 2-4
TETRAGRAMMTON: 69 2-4

SOULE, George, & Ava Aldridge
Singles: 7-Inch
MCA: 78 2-3
Also see SOULE, George

SOULFUL STRINGS
Singles: 7-Inch
CADET: 66-73 2-4
LPs: 10/12-Inch 33rpm
CADET: 67-73 8-10

SOUND EXPERIENCE
Singles: 7-Inch
SOULVILLE: 74 2-4

SOUNDGARDEN
EPs: 7-Inch 33/45rpm
"SCREAMING LIFE": 87 5-8
(Colored vinyl)
Members: Chris Cornell; Hiro Yamamoto; Mat-
thew Cameron; Kim Thayil.

SOUNDS OF SUNSHINE
Singles: 7-Inch
P.I.P.: 76 1-3
RANWOOD: 71-73 1-3
LPs: 10/12-Inch 33rpm
P.I.P.: 76 4-8
RANWOOD: 71-72 4-8

SOUNDS ORCHESTRAL
Singles: 7-Inch
PARKWAY: 62-66 2-4
LPs: 10/12-Inch 33rpm
PARKWAY: 62-67 5-15

SOUPY SALES: see SALES, Soupy

SOURIRE, Soeur: see SINGING NUN

SOUTH, Joe
(Joe South & The Believers)
Singles: 7-Inch
A&M: *68* $2-4
ALL WOOD: *62* 4-6
APT: *65* 4-6
CAPITOL: *67-75* 3-5
COLUMBIA: *67* 3-5
FAIRLANE: *61-62* 4-6
ISLAND: *75* 2-3
MGM: *63-64* 4-6
NRC (Except 002): *58-60* 6-10
NRC (002; "I'm Snowed"): *58* 20-30
LPs: 10/12-Inch 33rpm
ACCORD: *81* 5-8
CAPITOL: *68-72* 8-12
ISLAND: *70* 10-12
MINE: *70* 10-12

SOUTH, Joe / Dells
LPs: 10/12-Inch 33rpm
APPLE: *71* 15-20
   Also see DELLS
   Also see SOUTH, Joe

SOUTH SHORE COMMISSION
Singles: 7-Inch
WAND: *75-76* 2-4

SOUTHCOTE
Singles: 7-Inch
BUDDAH: *74* 3-5

SOUTHER, J.D.
(John David Souther)
Singles: 7-Inch
ASYLUM: *74-76* 2-4
COLUMBIA: *79* 2-3
WARNER BROS: *85* 1-3
LPs: 10/12-Inch 33rpm
ASYLUM: *72-76* 8-10
COLUMBIA: *79* 5-8
WARNER BROS: *85* 5-8
   Also see TAYLOR, James, & J.D. Souther
   Also see TILLOTSON, Johnny, & J.S. Souther

SOUTHER-HILLMAN-FURAY BAND
Singles: 7-Inch
ASYLUM: *74-75* 2-4
LPs: 10/12-Inch 33rpm
ASYLUM: *74-75* 8-10
   Members: J. D. Souther; Chris Hillman; Richie Furay.
   Also see FURAY, Richie
   Also see HILLMAN, Chris
   Also see SOUTHER, J.D.

SOUTHERN, Jeri
Singles: 7-Inch
CAPITOL: *59* $2-4
DECCA: *51-58* 2-4
EPs: 7-Inch 33/45rpm
DECCA: *55-56* 4-8
LPs: 10/12-Inch 33rpm
CAPITOL: *59* 8-15
DECCA: *55-58* 10-20
ROULETTE: *57-59* 8-15

SOUTHERN BELL SINGERS
Singles: 7-Inch
VEE JAY: *63* 3-5

SOUTHERN COMFORT
Singles: 7-Inch
CAPITOL: *71-72* 2-4
COTILLION: *69* 3-5
LPs: 10/12-Inch 33rpm
BRYLEN: 5-8
CAPITOL: *71* 10-12
COLUMBIA: *70* 10-12
SIRE: *69* 12-15
   Also see MATTHEWS' SOUTHERN COMFORT

SOUTHERN COOKIN'
Singles: 7-Inch
POLYDOR: *79* 1-3
LPs: 10/12-Inch 33rpm
POLYDOR: *79* 5-8

SOUTHROAD CONNECTION
Singles: 12-Inch 33/45rpm
UNITED ARTISTS: *79-80* 4-6
Singles: 7-Inch
LIBERTY: *80* 1-3
MAHOGANY: *78* 2-3
UNITED ARTISTS: *79-80* 1-3
LPs: 10/12-Inch 33rpm
UNITED ARTISTS: *80* 5-8

SOUTHSIDE JOHNNY
LPs: 10/12-Inch 33rpm
CYPRESS: *88* 5-8

SOUTHSIDE JOHNNY
& THE ASBURY JUKES
(Jukes; Southside Johnny & The Jukes)
Singles: 7-Inch
ATLANTIC: *86* 1-3
EPIC: *77-78* 2-4
MERCURY: *79* 2-3
MIRAGE: *83-84* 1-3
LPs: 10/12-Inch 33rpm
ATLANTIC: *86* 5-8
EPIC: *76-79* 8-10

MERCURY: *79-81* $5-8
MIRAGE: *83-84* 5-8
   Also see FIVE SATINS

SOUTHSIDE MOVEMENT
Singles: 7-Inch
20TH CENTURY-FOX: *74-75* 2-3
WAND: *73* 2-4
    LPs: 10/12-Inch 33rpm
20TH CENTURY-FOX: *75* 6-10
WAND: *73* 8-10
   Also see SIMTEC & WYLIE

SOUTHWEST F.O.B.
Singles: 7-Inch
GPC: *68* 3-5
HIP: *68-69* 5-10
    LPs: 10/12-Inch 33rpm
HIP: *69* 20-30
Members: Dan Seals; John Ford Coley.
   Also see ENGLAND DAN & JOHN FORD
COLEY

SOVINE, Red
Singles: 78rpm
DECCA (Except 30239): *54-66* 2-5
DECCA (30239; "Juke Joint
  Johnny"): *57* 5-10
MGM: *50-53* 3-5
    Singles: 7-Inch
CHART: *71-75* 1-3
DECCA (Except 30239): *54-66* 2-5
DECCA (30239; "Juke Joint Johnny"): *57* . 8-12
GUSTO: *79-80* 1-3
MGM: *50-53* 3-6
RCA VICTOR: *62* 2-4
RIC: *64-65* 2-4
STARDAY (Except 500 through 800
  series): *70-78* 1-3
STARDAY (500 through 800
  series): *60-70* 2-4
    EPs: 7-Inch 33/45rpm
MGM: *57* 8-15
    LPs: 10/12-Inch 33rpm
CMI: *77* 5-8
CHART: *72-74* 6-10
DECCA (4400 series): *64* 15-25
DECCA (4700 series): *66* 10-15
GUSTO: 4-8
LAKE SHORE: 8-12
MGM (3465; "Red Sovine"): *57* 30-40
METRO: *67* 8-15
NASHVILLE: *70* 6-12
POWER PAK: 4-8
RIC: *65* 10-15
SOMERSET: *63* 8-12

STARDAY (Except 100 series): *65-70* .. $5-15
STARDAY (100 series): *61-62* 15-25
STEREO FIDELITY: *63* 8-12
VOCALION: *68* 8-12
   Also see FELTS, Narvel / Red Sovine / Mel
Tillis
   Also see REEVES, Del / Red Sovine

SOX, Bob B.:
  see BOB B. SOXX & THE BLUE JEANS

SPACE
Singles: 12-Inch 33/45rpm
CASABLANCA: *79-80* 4-6
    Singles: 7-Inch
CASABLANCA: *79-80* 1-3
UNITED ARTISTS: *77* 2-3
    LPs: 10/12-Inch 33rpm
CASABLANCA: *78-79* 5-8
UNITED ARTISTS: *77* 8-10

SPACEMEN
(Space Men)
Singles: 7-Inch
ALTON: *59-60* 4-6
FELSTED: *59* 4-6
JAMECO: *65* 4-6
JUBILEE: *59* 4-6
MARKEY: *62* 3-5
    LPs: 10/12-Inch 33rpm
ROULETTE: *64-66* 15-20

SPADES
(Slades)
Singles: 7-Inch
LIBERTY: *58* 10-20
   Also see SLADES

SPADES
(13th Floor Elevators)
Singles: 7-Inch
ZERO (10002; "You're Gonna
  Miss Me"): *66* 100-150
   Also see 13TH FLOOR ELEVATORS

SPAIN, Joanne
Singles: 7-Inch
CASINO: *77* 2-3

SPANDAU BALLET
Singles: 12-Inch
CHRYSALIS: *84-85* 4-6
    Singles: 7-Inch
CHRYSALIS: *84-85* 1-3
    LPs: 10/12-Inch 33rpm
CHRYSALIS: *84-85* 5-8
MFSL: *85* 15-25
   Also see BAND AID

SPANIELS

Singles: 78rpm

CHANCE (1141; "Baby, It's You"): *53* . **$50-75**
VEE JAY (101; "Baby, It's You"): *53* .. **60-100**
VEE JAY (103; "The Bells
Ring Out"): *53* **30-60**
VEE JAY (107; "Goodnite Sweetheart,
Goodnite"): *53* **25-50**
VEE JAY (116; "Play It Cool"): *54* **15-25**
VEE JAY (131; "Do-Wah"): *55* **15-25**
VEE JAY (154; "You Painted
Pictures"): *55* **10-20**
VEE JAY (154; "Painted Picture"): *55* ... **15-25**
(Shown on this pressing as by The Spanials.)
VEE JAY (178 through 200 series): *56-57* . **5-15**

Singles: 7-Inch

BUDDAH: *69* **3-5**
CALLA: *70* **2-4**
CANTERBURY: *74* **2-4**
CHANCE (1141; "Baby,
It's You"): *53* **200-300**
(Black vinyl.)
CHANCE (1141; "Baby,
It's You"): *53* **300-500**
(Colored vinyl.)
COLLECTABLES: **1-3**
ERIC: **1-3**
NORTH AMERICAN: *70* **2-4**
OWL: *73* **2-4**
VEE JAY (101; "Baby,
It's You"): *53* **300-500**
(Black vinyl.)
VEE JAY (101; "Baby,
It's You"): *53* **500-750**
(Colored vinyl.)
VEE JAY (103; "The Bells
Ring Out"): *53* **100-250**
(Black vinyl.)
VEE JAY (103; "The Bells
Ring Out"): *53* **250-400**
(Colored vinyl.)
VEE JAY (107; "Goodnite Sweetheart,
Goodnite"): *53* **75-100**
(Black vinyl.)
VEE JAY (107; "Goodnite Sweetheart,
Goodnite"): *53* **200-300**
(Colored vinyl.)
VEE JAY (116; "Play It Cool"): *54* **50-75**
(Black vinyl.)
VEE JAY (116; "Play It Cool"): *54* ... **250-300**
(Colored vinyl.)
VEE JAY (131; "Do-Wah"): *55* **40-60**
(Black vinyl.)
VEE JAY (131; "Do-Wah"): *55* **250-350**
(Colored vinyl.)

VEE JAY (154; "You Painted
Pictures"): *55* **$20-40**
VEE JAY (154; "Painted
Picture"): *55* **20-30**
(Shown on this pressing as by The Spanials.)
VEE JAY (178; "False Love"): *56* **25-50**
VEE JAY (189; "Dear Heart"): *56* **25-50**
VEE JAY (202; "Since I Fell
For You"): *56* **25-40**
VEE JAY (229 through 301): *56-58* **15-25**
VEE JAY (310 through 350): *59-60* **10-20**

LPs: 10/12-Inch 33rpm

LOST-NITE (19; "The Spaniels"): *81* **5-8**
LOST-NITE (137; "The Spaniels"): **10-15**
VEE JAY (1002; "Goodnite, It's
Time To Go"): *59* **175-250**
(Maroon label.)
VEE JAY (1002; "Goodnite, It's
Time To Go"): *61* **50-75**
(Black label.)
VEE JAY (1024; "The Spaniels"): *60* .. **150-250**
UPFRONT: **10-15**
Members: Pookie Hudson; Jerry Gregory; Ernest
Warren; Willie Jackson; Opal Courtney; James
Cochran; Carl Rainge; Don Porter; Andy
Magruder; Bill Carey.
Also see HUDSON, Pookie

SPANKY & OUR GANG

Singles: 7-Inch

EPIC: *75-76* **2-4**
MERCURY: *67-69* **3-5**

Picture Sleeves

MERCURY: *67-68* **3-6**

LPs: 10/12-Inch 33rpm

EPIC: *75* **8-10**
MERCURY: *67-71* **10-15**
Member: Spanky McFarlane.

SPARKLETONES, With Joe Bennett:
see BENNETT, Joe, & The Sparkletones

SPARKS

Singles: 12-Inch 33/45rpm

ATLANTIC: *84* **4-6**

Singles: 7-Inch

ATLANTIC: *82-84* **1-3**
BEARSVILLE: *72* **3-5**
COLUMBIA: *78* **2-3**
ELEKTRA: *79* **2-3**
FINE ARTS: *88* **1-3**
ISLAND: *73-76* **2-4**
RCA VICTOR: *81* **1-3**

LPs: 10/12-Inch 33rpm

ATLANTIC: *82-84* **5-8**
BEARSVILLE: *72-73* **12-15**
COLUMBIA (Black vinyl): *77* **8-10**

COLUMBIA (Colored vinyl): 77 ..... $12-15
ELEKTRA: 79 8-10
ISLAND: 74-76 8-10
RCA VICTOR: 81 5-8
Members: Ron Mael; Russell Mael.

SPARKS & JANE WIEDLIN
Singles: 12-Inch 33/45rpm
ATLANTIC: 83 4-6
Singles: 7-Inch
ATLANTIC: 83 1-3
Also see SPARKS
Also see WIEDLIN, Jane

SPARKY D
Singles: 12-Inch 33/45rpm
NIA: 85 4-6

SPARQUE
Singles: 12-Inch 33/45rpm
WEST END: 84 4-6

SPATS
Singles: 7-Inch
ABC-PARAMOUNT: 64-66 4-6
ENITH: 64 8-10
JANO: 67 3-6
LPs: 10/12-Inch 33rpm
ABC-PARAMOUNT: 65 20-25
Member: Dick Johnson.

SPEARS, Billie Jo
Singles: 7-Inch
CAPITOL: 68-71 2-4
LIBERTY: 81 1-3
PARLIAMENT: 84 1-3
UNITED ARTISTS (Except 50000
series): 74-80 1-3
UNITED ARTISTS (50000 series): 66-67 ..2-5
LPs: 10/12-Inch 33rpm
CAPITOL: 68-79 5-15
LIBERTY: 81 4-8
PICKWICK/HILLTOP: 5-8
UNITED ARTISTS: 75-80 5-10
Also see REEVES, Del, & Billie Jo Spears

SPECIAL AKA
Singles: 12-Inch 33/45rpm
CHRYSALIS: 84 4-6
Singles: 7-Inch
CHRYSALIS: 84 1-3
LPs: 10/12-Inch 33rpm
CHRYSALIS: 84 5-8
Also see SPECIALS

SPECIAL DELIVERY
Singles: 7-Inch
MAINSTREAM: 75-76 2-4
SHIELD: 77-78 2-3

Member: Terry Huff.

SPECIALS
Singles: 7-Inch
CHRYSALIS: 79-80 .... $1-3
Picture Sleeves
CHRYSALIS: 79 1-3
LPs: 10/12-Inch 33rpm
CHRYSALIS: 80 5-8
Also see FUN BOY THREE
Also see SPECIALS AKA

SPECTOR, Ronnie
(Ronnie Spector & The Ronettes; Ronnie Spector & The E Street Band)
Singles: 7-Inch
ALSTON: 78 5-8
APPLE: 70-71 5-8
BUDDAH: 74 3-5
EPIC/CLEVELAND INT'L: 77 5-10
COLUMBIA: 87 1-3
POLISH: 80 3-5
TOM CAT (Black vinyl): 75-76 2-4
TOM CAT (Colored vinyl): 75 4-6
(Promotional issues only.)
WARNER BROS/SPECTOR: 76 2-4
Picture Sleeves
APPLE: 71 5-10
COLUMBIA: 87 1-3
EPIC/CLEVELAND INT'L. 77 5-10
LPs: 10/12-Inch 33rpm
POLISH: 80 8-12
Also see MONEY, Eddie, & Ronnie Spector
Also see RONETTES
Also see SPRINGSTEEN, Bruce
Also see VERONICA

SPEEDO & THE CADILLACS
(Cadillacs)
Singles: 7-Inch
JOSIE: 60 10-15
Also see CADILLACS

SPELLBINDERS
Singles: 7-Inch
COLUMBIA: 65-66 3-5
DATE: 67 3-5
MIRAMAR: 3-5
LPs: 10/12-Inch 33rpm
COLUMBIA: 66 12-15

SPELLBOUND
Singles: 7-Inch
EMI AMERICA: 78 2-3
LPs: 10/12-Inch 33rpm
EMI AMERICA: 78 5-8

SPELLMAN, Benny
Singles: 7-Inch
ACE: *61* $4-8
ALON: *66* 3-5
ATLANTIC: *65* 3-5
MINIT: *62* 4-6
SANSU: *67* 3-5
WATCH: *64* 3-5
Also see K-DOE, Ernie

SPENCE, Judson
Singles: 7-Inch
ATLANTIC: 88 1-3
LPs: 10/12-Inch 33rpm
ATLANTIC: *88* 5-8

SPENCER, Sonny
Singles: 7-Inch
MEMO: *59* 5-10
MUSIC HALL: 4-6
ONDA: 10-15

SPENCER, Tracie
Singles: 7-Inch
CAPITOL: *88* 1-3
LPs: 10/12-Inch 33rpm
CAPITOL: *88* 5-8

SPENCER & SPENCER
Singles: 7-Inch
ARGO: *59* 5-8
GONE: *59* 8-10

SPERRY, Steve
Singles: 7-Inch
MERCURY: *77* 2-3

SPHEERIS, Chris
LPs: 10/12-Inch 33rpm
COLUMBIA: *88* 5-8

SPHEERIS, Jimmie
Singles: 7-Inch
COLUMBIA: *72* 2-4
EPIC: *75* 2-3
LPs: 10/12-Inch 33rpm
EPIC: *75* 8-10

SPIDER
Singles: 7-Inch
CAPITOL: *72* 2-4
LPs: 10/12-Inch 33rpm
CAPITOL: *72* 8-10

SPIDER
Singles: 7-Inch
DREAMLAND: *80-81* 1-3
Picture Sleeves
DREAMLAND: *80* 1-3
LPs: 10/12-Inch 33rpm

DREAMLAND: *80* $5-8

SPIDERS
Singles: 78rpm
IMPERIAL: *54-57* 10-20
Singles: 7-Inch
IMPERIAL (5265 through 5344): *54-55* . . 25-50
IMPERIAL (5354; "Bells In
My Heart"): *55* 40-65
IMPERIAL (5366 through 5423): *55-56* . . 15-25
IMPERIAL (5618 through 5739): *59-61* . . . 5-10
OWL: *73* 2-4
LPs: 10/12-Inch 33rpm
IMPERIAL (9142; "I Didn't Want
To Do It"): *61* 100-125
Member: Chuck Carbo.

SPIDERS
Singles: 7-Inch
NASCOT (112; "Why Don't
You Love Me"): *65* 100-125
SANTA CRUZ (003; "Don't Blow
Your Mind"): *66* 80-100
Member: Alice Cooper.
Also see COOPER, Alice

SPIDERS FROM MARS
Singles: 7-Inch
PYE: *76* 2-4
LPs: 10/12-Inch 33rpm
PYE: *76* 8-10
Also see BOWIE, David

SPIN
Singles: 7-Inch
ARIOLA AMERICA: *76* 2-3
LPs: 10/12-Inch 33rpm
ARIOLA AMERICA: *76* 8-10

SPINAL TAP
Singles: 7-Inch
POLYDOR: *84* 1-3
LPs: 10/12-Inch 33rpm
POLYDOR: *84* 5-8

SPINNERS
Singles: 7-Inch
ATLANTIC: *72-85* 2-4
MOTOWN (1000 & 1100 series): *64-68* . . . 3-5
MOTOWN (1200 series): *73* 2-4
TRI-PHI: *61-62* 5-8
V.I.P.: *70* 3-5
LPs: 10/12-Inch 33rpm
ATLANTIC: *73-84* 6-10
MOTOWN (Except 639): *73-82* 6-10
MOTOWN (639; "The Original
Spinners"): *67* 12-15
PICKWICK: *76* 8-10

V.I.P.: *70* **$10-15**
  Members: Bobby Smith; Henry Fambrough; Pervis
  Jackson; Bill Henderson; G.C. Cameron; Philippe
  Wynne; Reese Palmer; Jim Knowland; Ed
  Edwards; Chester Simmons.
  Also see ABBA / Spinners / Firefall / England
  Dan & John Ford Coley
  Also see CAMERON, G.C.
  Also see WARWICK, Dionne, & The Spinners

SPIRAL STARECASE
         Singles: 7-Inch
COLUMBIA: *69-70* **3-5**
         LPs: 10/12-Inch 33rpm
COLUMBIA: *69* **15-20**
  Member: Pat Upton.

SPIRIT
         Singles: 12-Inch 33/45rpm
MERCURY: *84* **4-6**
         Singles: 7-Inch
EPIC: *70-74* **3-5**
MERCURY: *75-76* **2-4**
ODE: *68-70* **4-6**
POTATO: *78* **2-3**
RHINO: *81* **1-3**
         Picture Sleeves
EPIC: *74* **4-8**
POTATO: *78* **2-4**
         LPs: 10/12-Inch 33rpm
EPIC: *70-73* **8-12**
MERCURY (Except 818514): *75-77* **10-15**
MERCURY (818514; "Spirit Of '84"): *84* ..**5-8**
ODE (44003; "Spirit"): *68* **15-20**
  (Monaural.)
ODE (44004; "Spirit"): *68* **12-15**
  (Stereo.)
**ODE (44014; "The Family That
  Plays Together"):** *68* **10-15**
ODE (44016; "Clear"): *69* **10-12**
POTATO: **10-12**
RHINO: *81* **5-8**
  Members: Jay Ferguson; Randy California; Mark
  Andes; Ed Cassidy; John Locke; John Arliss.
  Also see FERGUSON, Jay
  Also see HEART
  Also see YELLOW BALLOON

SPLINTER
         Singles: 7-Inch
DARK HORSE: *74-77* **3-5**
         LPs: 10/12-Inch 33rpm
DARK HORSE: *74-77* **8-10**
  Members: Bill Elliott; Bob Purvis.

SPLIT ENZ
         Singles: 7-Inch
A&M: *80-81* **1-3**

         Picture Sleeves
A&M: *81* **$1-3**
         LPs: 10/12-Inch 33rpm
A&M (Except picture discs): *80-82* **5-8**
A&M (Picture discs): *81* **20-25**
  (Promotional issues only.)
CHRYSALIS: *77* **8-10**
  Members: Tim Finn; Neil Finn.
  Also see CROWDED HOUSE
  Also see FINN, Tim

SPLIT IMAGE
         Singles: 7-Inch
BENTLEY: *88* **1-3**
         LPs: 10/12-Inch 33rpm
BENTLEY: *88* **5-8**

SPOKESMEN
         Singles: 7-Inch
DECCA: *65-66* **4-6**
WINCHESTER: *67* **3-5**
         LPs: 10/12-Inch 33rpm
DECCA: *65* **25-30**
  Members: Johnny Madara; David White.

SPOOKY TOOTH
         Singles: 7-Inch
A&M: *69* **3-5**
MALA: *68* **5-10**
ISLAND: *72* **2-4**
         LPs: 10/12-Inch 33rpm
A&M: *69-73* **10-12**
ACCORD: *82* **5-8**
BELL: *68* **15-20**
ISLAND: *73-74* **8-10**
  Members: Gary Wright; Mike Harrison; Luther
  Grosvenor.
  Also see WRIGHT, Gary

SPOONBREAD
         Singles: 7-Inch
STANG: *72* **2-4**

SPOONIE GEE
         Singles: 12-Inch 33/45
CBS ASSOCIATED: *83* **4-6**
         Singles: 7-Inch
CBS ASSOCIATED: *83* **1-3**
TUFF CITY: *83* **1-3**

SPORTS
         Singles: 7-Inch
ARISTA: *79* **1-3**
         LPs: 10/12-Inch 33rpm
ARISTA: *79-80* **5-8**

SPRING
         Singles: 7-Inch
IX CHAINS: *73* **2-4**

SPRING, McKendree:
see McKENDREE SPRING

SPRINGERS
Singles: 7-Inch
WAY OUT: *65* $5-8

SPRINGFIELD, Dusty
Singles: 7-Inch
ATLANTIC: *68-71* 2-4
CASABLANCA: *82* 1-3
DUNHILL: *73* 2-4
PHILIPS: *63-68* 3-5
20TH CENTURY-FOX: *80* 1-3
UNITED ARTISTS: *77-79* 2-3
Picture Sleeves
PHILIPS: *64-67* 3-6
ATLANTIC: *68* 2-5
LPs: 10/12-Inch 33rpm
ATLANTIC: *69-70* 10-15
CASABLANCA: *82* 5-8
DUNHILL: *73* 8-10
PHILIPS: *64-67* 12-15
UNITED ARTISTS: *78-79* 5-8
WING: *68* 10-12
Also see PET SHOP BOYS
Also see SPRINGFIELDS

SPRINGFIELD, Rick
Singles: 12-Inch 33/45rpm
RCA VICTOR: *83-84* 4-6
Singles: 7-Inch
CAPITOL: *72-73* 3-5
CHELSEA: *76-77* 2-4
COLUMBIA: *74* 3-5
MERCURY: *84-85* 1-3
RCA VICTOR: *81-88* 1-3
Picture Sleeves
CAPITOL: *72* 3-5
RCA VICTOR: *81-85* 1-3
LPs: 10/12-Inch 33rpm
CAPITOL (11000 series): *72-73* 15-20
CAPITOL (16000 series): *81* 5-8
CHELSEA: *76* 8-12
COLUMBIA (32000 series): *73* 8-12
(With a "KC" prefix.)
COLUMBIA (32000 series): 5-8
(With a "PC" prefix.)
MERCURY: *84* 5-8
RCA VICTOR: *80-88* 5-8

SPRINGFIELD, Rick, & Randy Crawford
Singles: 7-Inch
RCA VICTOR: *84* 1-3
Also see CRAWFORD, Randy
Also see SPRINGFIELD, Rick

SPRINGFIELDS
Singles: 7-Inch
PHILIPS: *62-63* $3-5
LPs: 10/12-Inch 33rpm
PHILIPS: *62-63* 15-20
Members: Dusty Springfield; Tom Springfield; Tim Field.
Also see SPRINGFIELD, Dusty

SPRINGSTEEN, Bruce
(Bruce Springsteen & The E Street Band)
Singles: 12-Inch 33/45rpm
COLUMBIA (1332; "Santa Claus
Is Comin' To Town"): *81* 30-40
(White label. Promotional issue only.)
COLUMBIA (2007; "I'm On
Fire"): *85* 20-25
(Red label. Black and white cover. Promotional issue only.)
COLUMBIA (2082; "Glory Days"): *85* .. 20-25
(Red label. Black and white cover. Promotional issue only.)
COLUMBIA (2174; "I'm Goin'
Down"): *85* 20-25
(Red label. Black and white cover. Promotional issue only.)
COLUMBIA (2233; "My
Hometown"): *85* 20-25
(Red label. Black and white cover. Promotional issue only.)
COLUMBIA (05028; "Dancing In
The Dark"): *84* 5-8
COLUMBIA (05028; "Dancing In
The Dark"): *84* 20-30
(With black and white cover. Promotional issue only.)
COLUMBIA (05028; "Dancing In
The Dark"): *84* 15-20
(Promotional issue with color cover and gold promo stamp.)
COLUMBIA (05087; "Cover Me"): *84* 5-8
COLUMBIA (05147; "Born In
The U.S.A."): *84* 4-6
COLUMBIA (05147; "Born In
The U.S.A."): *84* 15-20
(White label. Promotional issue only.)
Singles: 7-Inch
COLUMBIA (03243; "Hungry Heart"): *84* .. 1-3
COLUMBIA (04463; "Dancing In
The Dark"): *84* 1-3
COLUMBIA (04561; "Cover Me"): *84* 1-3
COLUMBIA (04680; "Born In
The U.S.A."): *84* 1-3
COLUMBIA (04772; "I'm On Fire"): *85* ... 1-3
COLUMBIA (04924; "Glory Days"): *85* ... 1-3

COLUMBIA (05606; "I'm Goin'
Down"): 85 ....$1-3
COLUMBIA (05728; "My
Hometown"): 85 1-3
COLUMBIA (06432; "War"): 86 1-3
COLUMBIA (06657; "Fire"): 87 1-3
COLUMBIA (07595; "Brilliant
Disguise"): 87 1-3
COLUMBIA (07663; "Tunnel of
Love"): 87 1-3
COLUMBIA (07726; "One Step Up"): 88 . .1-3
COLUMBIA (08400 series): 88 1-3
(Columbia Hall of Fame series.)
COLUMBIA (10209; "Born To Run"): 75 . .4-6
COLUMBIA (10274; "Tenth Avenue
Freeze-Out"), 75 4-6
COLUMBIA (10763; "Prove It
All Night"): 78 5-8
COLUMBIA (10801; "Badlands"): 78 2-4
COLUMBIA (11391; "HungryHeart"): 80 . .2-4
COLUMBIA (11431; "Fade Away"/
"To Be True"): 81 30-40
COLUMBIA (11431; "Fade Away"/
"Be True"): 81 2-4
COLUMBIA (33323; "Born To Run"): 76 . .3-6
(Red label. Columbia Hall of Fame series.)
COLUMBIA (33323; "Born To Run"): 84 . .1-3
(Gray label. Columbia Hall of Fame series.)
COLUMBIA (45805; "Blinded By
The Light"): 73 75-90
COLUMBIA (45864; "Spirit In
The Night"): 73 100-125

Promotional Singles: 7-Inch

COLUMBIA (1332; "Santa Claus Is
Comin' To Town"): 81 10-15
COLUMBIA (04463; "Dancing In
The Dark"): 84 6-10
COLUMBIA (04561; "Cover Me"): 84 . . .6-10
COLUMBIA (04680; "Born In
The U.S.A."): 84 6-10
COLUMBIA (04772; "I'm On Fire"): 85 . .6-10
COLUMBIA (04924; "Glory Days"): 85 . .6-10
COLUMBIA (05606; "I'm Goin'
Down"): 85 6-10
COLUMBIA (05728; "My
Hometown"): 85 6-10
COLUMBIA (06432; "War"): 86 5-8
COLUMBIA (07595; "Brilliant
Disguise"): 87 5-8
COLUMBIA (10209; "Born To
Run"): 75 25-35
(With large letters on label.)
COLUMBIA (10209; "Born To
Run"): 75 15-20
(With small letters on label.)

Santa Claus Is Comin' To Town
BRUCE SPRINGSTEEN
DEMONSTRATION—NOT FOR SALE

COLUMBIA (10274; "Tenth Avenue
Freeze-Out"): 75 ....$15-20
COLUMBIA (10763; "Prove It
All Night"): 78 15-20
COLUMBIA (10801; "Badlands"): 78 . . 15-20
COLUMBIA (11391; "Hungry
Heart"): 80 15-20
COLUMBIA (11431; "Fade Away"): 81 . 10-15
COLUMBIA (45805; "Blinded By
The Light"): 73 45-55
COLUMBIA (45864; "Spirit In
The Night"): 73 35-45

Picture Sleeves

COLUMBIA (1332; "Santa Claus
Is Comin' To Town"): 81 15-20
(Promotional issue only.)
COLUMBIA (03000 through 07000
series): 84-87 1-3
COLUMBIA (11391; "Hungry Heart"): 80 . 4-6
COLUMBIA (11431; "Fade Away"): 81 . . . 3-5
COLUMBIA (45805; "Blinded By
The Light"): 73 100-125

LPs: 10/12-Inch 33rpm

COLUMBIA (31903; "Greetings
From Asbury Park"): 73 15-20
(With a "KC" prefix.)
COLUMBIA (31903; "Greetings
From Asbury Park"): 75 8-12
(With a "PC" prefix.)
COLUMBIA (31903; "Greetings
From Asbury Park"): 78 5-8
(With a "JC" prefix.)
COLUMBIA (32432; "The Wild Innocent
& The E Street Shuffle"): 73 15-18
(With a "KC" prefix.)
COLUMBIA (32432; "The Wild Innocent
& The E Street Shuffle"): 73 10-15
(With a "PC" prefix.)

COLUMBIA (32432; "The Wild Innocent & The E Street Shuffle"): 78 . . . . $5-8
(With a "JC" prefix.)
COLUMBIA (33795; "Born To Run"): 75 25-30
(With a "PC" prefix and credits showing Jon as "John.")
COLUMBIA (33795; "Born To Run"): 75 15-20
(With a "PC" prefix and "Jon" correction strip applied to cover.)
COLUMBIA (33795; "Born To Run"): 75 . 8-12
(With a "PC" prefix and correction to "Jon" printed on cover.)
COLUMBIA (33795; "Born To Run"): 78 . . 5-8
(With a "JC" prefix.)
COLUMBIA (35318; "Darkness On The Edge Of Town"): 78 5-8
(With a "JC" prefix.)
COLUMBIA (36854; "The River"): 80 . . 10-15
COLUMBIA (38358; "Nebraska"): 82 5-8
COLUMBIA (38653; "Born In The U.S.A."): 84 5-8
COLUMBIA (40558; "Bruce Springsteen & The E Street Band Live,1975-85"): 86 30-40
(Includes 36-page booklet.)
COLUMBIA (40999; "Tunnel Of Love"): 87 5-8
COLUMBIA (43795; "Born To Run"): 80 12-15
(With an "HC" prefix. Half-speed mastered.)
COLUMBIA (45318; "Darkness On The Edge Of Town"): 81 12-15
(With an "HC" prefix. Half-speed mastered.)
Promotional LPs
COLUMBIA (978; "Bruce Springsteen As Requested Around The World"): 81 30-40
COLUMBIA (1957; "Born In The U.S.A."): 84 15-20
COLUMBIA (31903; "Greetings From Asbury Park"): 73 25-30
(White label.)
COLUMBIA (32432; "The Wild Innocent & The E Street Shuffle"): 73 30-35
(White label.)
COLUMBIA (33795; "Born To Run"): 75 225-250
(With special "script" cover.)
COLUMBIA (33795; "Born To Run"): 75 40-50
(White label.)
COLUMBIA (35318; "Darkness On The Edge Of Town"): 78 30-40
(White label.)

COLUMBIA (35318; "Darkness On The Edge Of Town"): 78 . . . . $75-100
(Picture disc.)
COLUMBIA (36854; "The River"): 80 . . 25-35
(White label.)
COLUMBIA (38358; "Nebraska"): 82 . . . 15-20
(White label.)
COLUMBIA (38653; "Born In The U.S.A."): 84 12-15
(White label.)
Also see BONDS, Gary "U.S."
Also see CLEMONS, Clarence, & The Red Bank Rockers
Also see LITTLE STEVEN & THE DISCIPLES OF SOUL
Also see PARKER, Graham
Also see SPECTOR, Ronnie
Also see THOMPSON, Robbin, Band
Also see U.S.A. FOR AFRICA

SPRINGSTEEN, Bruce / Andy Pratt
Singles: 7-Inch
COLUMBIA/PLAYBACK (AS-45; "Blinded By The Light"): 73 35-45
Picture Sleeves
COLUMBIA/PLAYBACK (AS-45; "Blinded By The Light"): 73 10-15
Also see PRATT, Andy

SPRINGSTEEN, Bruce / Albert Hammond / Loudon Wainwright III / Taj Mahal
Singles: 7-Inch
COLUMBIA/PLAYBACK (AS-52; "The Circus Song"): 73 50-75
Picture Sleeves
COLUMBIA/PLAYBACK (AS-52; "The Circus Song"): 73 40-60
Also see HAMMOND, Albert
Also see TAJ MAHAL
Also see WAINWRIGHT, Loudon, III

SPRINGSTEEN, Bruce / Johnny Winter / Hollies
Singles: 7-Inch
COLUMBIA/PLAYBACK (AS-66; "Rosalita"): 73 .30-50
Picture Sleeves
COLUMBIA/PLAYBACK (AS-66; "Rosalita"): 73 .15-25
Also see HOLLIES
Also see SPRINGSTEEN, Bruce
Also see WINTER, Johnny

SPRINGWELL
Singles: 7-Inch
PARROT: 71 2-4

SPUNK
Singles: 7-Inch
GOLD COAST: *81* $1-3
LPs: 10/12-Inch 33rpm
GOLD COAST: *81* 5-8

SPYDER-D
(Spyder-D & D.J. Divine
Singles: 12-Inch 33/45rpm
PROFILE: *84-86* 4-6

SPYRO GYRA
Singles: 7-Inch
AMHERST: *78* 2-3
INFINITY: *79* 2-3
MCA: *80-85* 1-3
Picture Sleeves
INFINITY: *79* 2-3
LPs: 10/12-Inch 33rpm
AMHERST: *78* 5-8
INFINITY: *79* 5-8
MCA (5000 series): *80-86* 5-8
MCA (6000 series): *84* 8-10
MCA (42000 series): *87* 5-8
Members: Chet Catallo; Jay Beckenstein; Eli
Konikoff; Jeremy Wall; Tom Schuaman; Rick
Strauss; Will Lee; Tom Walsh; Greg Millar.

SPYS
Singles: 7-Inch
EMI AMERICA: *82* 1-3
LPs: 10/12-Inch 33rpm
EMI AMERICA: *82* 5-8
Also see FOREIGNER

SQUEEZE
(U.K. Squeeze)
Singles: 7-Inch
A&M: *79-87* 1-3
Picture Sleeves
A&M: *80* 1-3
LPs: 10/12-Inch 33rpm
A&M (Black vinyl): *72-87* 5-10
A&M (Colored vinyl): *78* 10-20
Members: Chris Difford; Glenn Tilbrook; Jools
Holland; Gilson Lavis; Keith Wilkinson; Andy
Metcalfe.
Also see CARRACK, Paul
Also see DIFFORD & TILBROOK

SQUIER, Billy
Singles: 7-Inch
CAPITOL: *80-86* 1-3
Picture Sleeves
CAPITOL: *80-86* 1-3
LPs: 10/12-Inch 33rpm
CAPITOL: *80-85* 5-8

SQUIRE, Chris

Billy Squier (Photo: Richard Noble)

Singles: 7-Inch
ATLANTIC: *76* $2-3
LPs: 10/12-Inch 33rpm
ATLANTIC: *76* 8-10
Also see YES

STACEY Q
Singles: 7-Inch
ATLANTIC: *88* 1-3
LPs: 10/12-Inch 33rpm
ATLANTIC: *88* 5-8

STACKRIDGE
Singles: 7-Inch
DECCA: *71-72* 2-4
MCA: *73* 2-4
ROCKET: *76* 2-3
SIRE: *74-75* 2-4
LPs: 10/12-Inch 33rpm
DECCA: *71* 10-12
MCA: *73* 8-10
ROCKET: *76* 5-8
SIRE: *74-75* 8-10
Member: Mutter Slater.

STACY, Clyde
(Clyde Stacy & The Nitecaps)
Singles: 7-Inch
ARGYLE: *59* 5-10
BULLSEYE (Except 1008): *58* 5-10
BULLSEYE (1008; "Sure Do Love
You Baby"): *58* 25-35
CANDLELIGHT: *57* 25-35
G&H: *58* 10-20
LEN: *61* 8-12

STACKHOUSE, Ruby
(Ruby Andrews)
Singles: 7-Inch
KELLMAC: 65 . . . . $3-5
 Also see ANDREWS, Ruby

STAFFORD, Jim
Singles: 7-Inch
COLUMBIA: 84 1-3
ELEKTRA: 80-81 1-3
ISLAND: 74 2-4
MGM: 73-75 2-4
POLYDOR: 75-78 1-3
TOWNHOUSE: 82 1-3
WARNER BROS: 76-80 1-3
LPs: 10/12-Inch 33rpm
MGM: 74-75 8-10
POLYDOR: 76 5-8

STAFFORD, Jo
Singles: 78rpm
CAPITOL: 43-50 3-6
COLUMBIA: 50-57 2-5
Singles: 7-Inch
COLPIX: 62 2-4
COLUMBIA: 50-60 2-5
DECCA: 68 2-3
DOT: 65 2-3
REPRISE: 63 2-4
EPs: 7-Inch 33/45rpm
CAPITOL: 50-57 5-15
COLUMBIA: 50-59 5-15
LPs: 10/12-Inch 33rpm
BAINBRIDGE: 82 5-8
CAPITOL (75 through 435): 50-53 20-35
 (10-Inch LPs.)
CAPITOL (400 through 1600
 series): 55-62 10-20
 (12-Inch LPs.)

CAPITOL (1900 through 2100
 series): 63-64 . . . . $8-15
CAPITOL (9000 series): 54 15-25
 (10-Inch LPs.)
CAPITOL (11000 series): 79 5-8
COLUMBIA (600 through 1300
 series): 55-59 10-25
COLUMBIA (1561; "Jo Plus Jazz"): 60 . . 25-50
 (Monaural.)
COLUMBIA (2500 series): 55 15-30
 (10-Inch LPs.)
COLUMBIA (6000 series): 50-54 20-35
 (10-Inch LPs.)
COLUMBIA (8361; "Jo Plus Jazz"): 60 . . 30-60
 (Stereo.)
DECCA: 68 5-15
DOT: 66 5-15
TRIBUTE: 71 5-10
VOCALION: 68-69 5-10
 Also see LAINE, Frankie, & Jo Stafford
 Also see MacRAE, Gordon, & Jo Stafford
 Also see WESTON, Paul

STAFFORD, Terry
Singles: 7-Inch
ATLANTIC: 73-74 2-4
COLLECTABLES: 1-3
CRUSADER: 64 4-6
ERIC: 1-3
FIRSTLINE: 81 1-3
MGM: 71 2-4
MELODYLAND: 75 2-4
MERCURY: 66 3-5
SIDEWALK: 66-67 3-5
WARNER BROS: 69 2-4
LPs: 10/12-Inch 33rpm
ATLANTIC: 73 8-10
CRUSADER (1001; "Suspicion!"): 64 . . . 25-35
 (Stereo.)
CRUSADER (1001; "Suspicion!"): 64 . . . 20-25
 (Monaural.)
 Also see ALLAN, Davie

STAIRSTEPS
Singles: 7-Inch
BUDDAH: 71-72 2-4
DARK HORSE: 75-76 2-4
 Also see FIVE STAIRSTEPS

STALLION
Singles: 7-Inch
CASABLANCA: 77-78 2-3
LPs: 10/12-Inch 33rpm
CASABLANCA: 77-78 5-8

STALLONE, Frank
Singles: 12-Inch 33/45rpm
RSO: 83 4-6

Singles: 7-Inch
POLYDOR: 84-85 . . . . $1-3
SCOTTI BROS: 80 1-3
LPs: 10/12-Inch 33rpm
POLYDOR: 84 5-8

STAMPEDERS
Singles: 7-Inch
BELL: 71 2-4
CAPITOL: 73 2-4
FLASHBACK: 74 .1-3
MGM: 68 3-5
QUALITY: 76 2-4
LPs: 10/12-Inch 33rpm
BELL: 71 10-12
CAPITOL: 73-74 8-10
PRIVATE STOCK/QUALITY: 76 8-10
Also see WOLFMAN JACK

STAMPLEY, Joe
Singles: 7-Inch
ABC: 77 1-3
ABC/DOT: 75-76 2-3
CHESS: 63 4-6
COLUMBIA: 81-84 1-3
DOT: 70-74 2-4
EPIC: 75-86 1-3
EVERGREEN: 88 1-3
IMPERIAL: 59 5-8
PARAMOUNT. 70 2-4
PAULA: 74 2-3
LPs: 10/12-Inch 33rpm
ABC: 77 10-12
ABC/DOT: 74-76 8-10
ACCORD: 82 5-8
COLUMBIA: 82-84 5-8
EPIC: 75-83 6-10
PHONORAMA: 5-8
Also see UNIQUES

STANDELLS
Singles: 7-Inch
COLLECTABLES: 1-3
LIBERTY: 64 10-15
MGM: 65 10-15
SUNSET: 66 10-15
TOWER: 66-68 .5-10
VEE JAY: 65 8-10
Picture Sleeves
TOWER: 67 10-15
VEE JAY: 65 15-25
LPs: 10/12-Inch 33rpm
LIBERTY: 64 40-50
RHINO: 5-8
SUNSET: 66 15-20
TOWER: 66-67 .40-65

Joe Stampley

Members: Dick Dodd; Larry Tamblyn; Gary Lane;
Tony Valentino; Dave Burke.

STANDLEY, Johnny
Singles: 78rpm
CAPITOL: 52-56 . . . . $2-5
Singles: 7-Inch
CAPITOL: 52-56 2-5
MAGNOLIA: 60 20-25

STANKY-BROWN GROUP
Singles: 7-Inch
SIRE: 76-78 2-3
LPs: 10/12-Inch 33rpm
SIRE: 76-78 8-10

STANLEY, Michael, Band
Singles: 7-Inch
ARISTA: 78-79 2-3
EMI AMERICA: 80-82 1-3
EPIC: 77 2-3
TUMBLEWEED: 72-73 2-4
LPs: 10/12-Inch 33rpm
ARISTA: 78-79 5-8
EMI AMERICA: 80-82 5-8
EPIC: 75-76 8-10
MCA: 73 10-12
TUMBLEWEED: 73 8-12
Also see SILK

STANLEY, Pamala
Singles: 12-Inch 33/45rpm
KOMANDER: 83 4-6
MIRAGE: 84-85 4-6

TSR: *84* $4-6
Singles: 7-Inch
EMI AMERICA: *79* 2-3
MIRAGE: *84-85* 1-3
LPs: 10/12-Inch 33rpm
EMI AMERICA: *79* 5-8

STANLEY, Paul
Singles: 7-Inch
CASABLANCA: *78* 2-3
LPs: 10/12-Inch 33rpm
CASABLANCA (Except picture
discs): *78-80* 20-30
CASABLANCA (Picture discs): *79* 40-50
Also see KISS

STAPLE SINGERS
(Staples)
Singles: 7-Inch
ABC: *73* 2-3
CURTOM: *75-77* 2-3
EPIC: *64-71* 2-4
PRIVATE I: *84-86* 1-3
RIVERSIDE: *62-63* 2-4
SHARP: *60* 3-5
STAX: *68-74* 2-4
20TH CENTURY-FOX: *81* 1-3
VEE JAY: *59-62* 4-8
WARNER BROS: *76-80* 1-3
LPs: 10/12-Inch 33rpm
BUDDAH: *69* 6-10
CREED: *73* 5-10
CURTOM: *76* 5-10
EPIC: *65-71* 10-12
EVEREST: *68-69* 8-12
FANTASY: *73* 5-10
51 WEST: 5-8
GOSPEL: *59* 5-15
HARMONY: *72* 5-10
MILESTONE: *75* 5-10
PRIVATE I: *84-86* 5-8
RIVERSIDE: *62-65* 10-15
STAX: *68-81* 5-10
20TH CENTURY-FOX: *81* 5-8
TRIP: *71-77* 5-10
VEE JAY (5000 through 5030): *59-63* ... 10-15
WARNER BROS: *77-78* 5-8
Members: Mavis Staples; Roebuck Staples; Cleo
Staples; Yvonne Staples.
Also see STAPLES, Mavis

STAPLES, Mavis
Singles: 7-Inch
CURTOM: *77* 2-3
PHONO: *84* 1-3
VOLT: *70-72* 2-4

WARNER BROS: *79-86* $1-3
LPs: 10/12-Inch 33rpm
VOLT: *69-70* 8-12
WARNER BROS: *79-86* 5-8
Also see BELL, William, & Mavis Staples
Also see FLOYD, Eddie, & Mavis Staples
Also see STAPLE SINGERS

STAPLETON, Cyril, & His Orchestra
Singles: 78rpm
LONDON: *51-63* 2-4
MGM: *55-56* 2-4
Singles: 7-Inch
DECCA: *67* 1-3
LONDON: *51-63* 2-4
MGM: *55-56* 2-4
STAGE: *62* 1-3
EPs: 7-Inch 33/45rpm
LONDON: *55-57* 4-8
MGM: *55-56* 4-8
LPs: 10/12-Inch 33rpm
IMPERIAL: *61* 5-10
LONDON: *55-59* 5-15
MGM: *55-56* 5-15
RICHMOND: *59-61* 5-15

**STAR WARS INTERGALACTIC
DROID CHOIR & CHORALE**
Singles: 7-Inch
RSO: *80* 1-3
Also see MECO

STARBUCK
Singles: 7-Inch
A.V.I.: *84* 1-3
ATCO: *73* 2-4
ELEKTRA: *71* 2-4
PRIVATE STOCK: *76-77* 2-4
UNITED ARTISTS: *78-79* 2-3
LPs: 10/12-Inch 33rpm
PHONORAMA: 5-8
PRIVATE STOCK: *77* 8-10
UNITED ARTISTS: *78* 8-10
Member: Bruce Blackman.

STARCASTLE
Singles: 7-Inch
EPIC: *76-78* 2-4
LPs: 10/12-Inch 33rpm
EPIC (Except "Citadel," picture
disc): *76-79* 8-10
EPIC ("Citadel," picture disc): *79* 50-60
(Promotional issue only.)

STARCHER, Buddy
Singles: 7-Inch
BOONE: *66* 2-4
DECCA: *66* 2-4

RCA VICTOR (0100 series): *73* $1-3
RCA VICTOR (6000 & 7000 series): *55-59* 2-5
Picture Sleeves
CAPITOL: *62* 3-6
EPs: 7-Inch 33/45rpm
CAPITOL: *50-61* 5-15
RCA VICTOR: *55-58* 5-10
LPs: 10/12-Inch 33rpm
ABC: *68* 5-15
CAMDEN: *60-61* 5-15
CAPITOL (211; "Songs By
Kay Starr"): *50* 40-60
(10-Inch LP. With an "H" prefix.)
CAPITOL (211; "Songs By
Kay Starr"): *55* 20-40
(With a "T" prefix.)
CAPITOL (415; "The Hits Of
Kay Starr"): *53* 20-35
(10-Inch LP. With an "H" prefix.)
CAPITOL (400 through 1200
series): *53-59* 15-30
(With a "T" or "ST" prefix.)
CAPITOL (400 through 900 series): *63-75* 5-15
(With a "DT" or "SM" prefix.)
CAPITOL (1300 series): *60* 10-20
CAPITOL (1438; "Kay Starr,
Jazz Singer"): *60* 20-35
CAPITOL (1468 through 2100
series): *61-64* 8-15
CAPITOL (11000 series): *74-79* 5-8
CORONET: *63* 10-20
GNP/CRESCENDO: *74-75* 5-10
LIBERTY (3200 series): *63* 10-20
LIBERTY (9000 series): *56* 20-40
RCA VICTOR (1100 through 1700
series): *55-57* 15-25
RONDO-LETTE: *58* 15-35

STARR, Kay, & Count Basie
LPs: 10/12-Inch 33rpm
MCA: *83* 5-8
PARAMOUNT: *69* 8-15
Also see BASIE, Count

STARR, Kay, & Tennessee Ernie Ford
Singles: 78rpm
CAPITOL: *50-56* 2-5
Singles: 7-Inch
CAPITOL: *50-56* 3-6
EPs: 7-Inch 33/45rpm
CAPITOL: *56* 5-15
Also see FORD, Tennessee Ernie

STARR, Kay / Erroll Garner
LPs: 10/12-Inch 33rpm
CROWN: *57* 15-30
MODERN: *56* 20-45

Also see GARNER, Erroll
Also see STARR, Kay

STARR, Kenny
Singles: 7-Inch
MCA: *73-78* $2-3
S.S. TITANIC: *81* 1-3
LPs: 10/12-Inch 33rpm
MCA: *75* 5-8
Also see LYNN, Loretta

STARR, Lucille
Singles: 7-Inch
A&M: *66* 2-4
ALMO: *64-65* 3-5
EPIC: *67-69* 2-4
LPs: 10/12-Inch 33rpm
EPIC: *69* 8-10

STARR, Randy
Singles: 78rpm
DALE: *57* 3-5
Singles: 7-Inch
DALE: *57-59* 6-10
MAYFLOWER: *59* 3-5
Also see ISLANDERS

STARR, Randy, & Frank Metis
LPs: 10/12-Inch 33rpm
MAYFLOWER: *59* 15-20
Also see STARR, Randy

STARR, Ringo
Singles: 12-Inch 33/45rpm
ATLANTIC (93; "Drowning In The
Sea Of Love"): *77* 15-20
(Promotional issue only.)
Singles: 7-Inch
APPLE (1831; "It Don't Come Easy"): *71* ..4-6
APPLE (1849; "Back Off Boogaloo"): *72* .10-15
(With a blue apple on the label.)
APPLE (1849; "Back Off Boogaloo"): *73* ...3-5
(With a green apple on the label.)
APPLE (1865; "Photograph"): *73* 3-5
APPLE (1870; "You're Sixteen"): *73* 5-8
(With standard apple label.)
APPLE (1870; "You're Sixteen"): *73* 3-5
(With 5-point star label.)
APPLE (1872; "Oh My My"): *74* 3-5
APPLE (1876; "Only You"): *74* 3-5
APPLE (1880; "No No Song"): *75* 3-5
APPLE (1882; "It's All Down To
Goodnight Vienna"): *75* 3-5
APPLE (2969; "Beaucoups Of Blues"): *70* ..4-6
ATLANTIC (3361; "Dose Of
Rock 'N' Roll"): *76* 5-8
ATLANTIC (3371; "Hey Baby"): *76* 8-12

ATLANTIC (3412; "Drowning In
The Sea Of Love"): 77 .... $10-20
ATLANTIC (3429; "Wings"): 77 8-12
BOARDWALK (130; "Wrack My
Brain"): 81 2-3
BOARDWALK (134; "Private
Property"): 82 2-3
CAPITOL (Orange label): 75 3-6
CAPITOL (Purple label): 78 2-3
CAPITOL (Black label): 83 1-3
PORTRAIT (70015; "Lipstick
Traces"): 78 6-10
PORTRAIT (70018; "Heart On
My Sleeve"): 78 4-8

Picture Sleeves

APPLE (1826; "Beaucoups Of
Blues"): 70 20-25
(With the 2969 catalog number mistakenly shown
as Apple 1826.)
APPLE (1831; "It Don't Come Easy"): 71 10-12
APPLE (1849; "Back Off
Boogaloo"): 72 10-12
APPLE (1865; "Photograph"): 73 8-10
APPLE (1870; "You're Sixteen"): 73 8-10
APPLE (1876; "Only You"): 74 5-8
APPLE (1882; "It's All Down To
Goodnight Vienna"): 75 6-10
APPLE (2969; "Beaucoups Of
Blues"): 70 12-15
(With the catalog number correctly shown.)
BOARDWALK (130; "Wrack My
Brain"): 81 2-4

Promotional Singles

APPLE (1831; "It Don't Come Easy"): 71 12-15
APPLE (1849; "Back Off Boogaloo"): 72 35-45
(White label.)
APPLE (1865; "Photograph"): 73 20-25
APPLE (1870; "You're
Sixteen"): 73 20-25
APPLE (1872; "Oh My My"): 74 20-25
APPLE (1876; "Only You"): 74 20-25
APPLE (1880; "No No Song"): 75 20-25
APPLE (1882; "It's All Down To
Goodnight Vienna"): 75 20-25
APPLE (1882; "Oo-Wee"): 75 25-30
ATLANTIC (3361; "Dose Of
Rock 'N' Roll"): 76 20-25
(White label.)
ATLANTIC (3361; "Dose Of
Rock 'N' Roll"): 76 10-12
(Blue label.)
ATLANTIC (3371; "Hey Baby"): 76 20-25
(White label.)
ATLANTIC (3371; "Hey Baby"): 76 10-12
(Red-white and blue labels.)

ATLANTIC (3371; "Hey Baby"): 76 .. $25-30
(One-sided disc.)
ATLANTIC (3412; "Drowning In The
Sea Of Love"): 77 10-20
ATLANTIC (3429; "Wings"): 77 20-25
(White label.)
ATLANTIC (3429; "Wings"): 77 10-12
(Red-white and blue labels.)
BOARDWALK (130; "Wrack My
Brain"): 81 8-10
BOARDWALK (134; "Private
Property"): 82 8-10
PORTRAIT (70015; "Lipstick
Traces"): 78 8-12
PORTRAIT (70018; "Heart On
My Sleeve"): 78 8-12

LPs: 10/12-Inch 33rpm

APPLE (3365; "Sentimental
Journey"): 70 10-15
APPLE (3417; "Goodnight Vienna"): 75 . 10-15
APPLE (3422; "Blast From
Your Past"): 75 10-15
APPLE (3413; "Ringo"): 73 12-15
(Issued with 20-page booklet.)
APPLE (3413; "Ringo"): 73 10-15
(With the 4:05 version of *Six O'Clock*.)
ATLANTIC (18193; "Ringo's
Rotogravure"): 76 8-12
ATLANTIC (19108; "Ringo
The 4th"): 77 8-12
BOARDWALK (33246; "Stop And
Smell The Roses"): 81 8-10
CAPITOL: 80-81 5-12
PORTRAIT (35378; "Bad Boy"): 78 8-10

Promotional LPs

APPLE (3413; "Ringo"): 73 75-100
(With the 5:26 version of *Six O'Clock*. Some
copies list the track at 5:26, when it actually runs
only 4:05.)

ATLANTIC (18193; "Ringo's
Rotogravure"): 76 .... $10-20
(With programming sticker on front cover.)
ATLANTIC (19108; "Ringo
The 4th"): 77 10-20
(With programming sticker on front cover.)
PORTRAIT (35378; "Bad Boy"): 78 25-30
(Labels reads "Advance Promotion.")
PORTRAIT (35378; "Bad Boy"): 78 15-20
(Labels reads "Demonstration, Not For Sale.")
Also see BEATLES
Also see CLAPTON, Eric
Also see FRAMPTON, Peter
Also see JOHN, Elton
Also see LOMAX, Jackie
Also see NILSSON

STARS ON
(Stars On 45; Stars On Long Play)
Singles: 12-Inch 33/45rpm
RADIO: 81-82 5-8
Singles: 7-Inch
RADIO: 81-82 1-3
TWENTY-ONE: 83 1-3
LPs: 10/12-Inch 33rpm
RADIO: 81-82 8-10
TWENTY-ONE: 83 5-8

STARS ON 45
(Featuring Sam & Dave)
Singles: 7-Inch
TWENTY-ONE: 85 1-3
Also see SAM & DAVE

STARSHINE
Singles: 12-Inch 33/45rpm
PRELUDE: 83 4-6
Singles: 7-Inch
PRELUDE: 83 1-3

STARSHIP
(Jefferson Starship)
Singles: 7-Inch
GRUNT: 85-88 1-3
LPs: 10/12-Inch 33rpm
GRUNT: 85-87 5-8
Also see JEFFERSON STARSHIP

STARSKI, Love Bug
Singles: 7-Inch
ATLANTIC: 85 1-3

STARZ
Singles: 7-Inch
CAPITOL: 76-79 2-3
Picture Sleeves
CAPITOL: 76-79 2-3
LPs: 10/12-Inch 33rpm
CAPITOL (Black vinyl): 76-78 8-10

CAPITOL (Colored vinyl): 77 .... $12-15
VIOLATION: 83 5-8
Member: Richie Ranno; Joe Dube; Brenda Harkin.

STATE OF GRACE
Singles: 12-Inch 33/45rpm
PROFILE: 83 4-6
Singles: 7-Inch
PROFILE: 83 1-3

STATLER BROTHERS
Singles: 7-Inch
COLUMBIA: 64-69 2-5
MERCURY: 70-88 1-3
LPs: 10/12-Inch 33rpm
COLUMBIA (2000 series): 66-67 15-25
COLUMBIA (9000 series): 66-69 12-25
(With a "CS" prefix.)
COLUMBIA (9000 series): 5-8
(With a "PC" prefix.)
COLUMBIA (31000 series): 5-10
51 WEST: 5-8
HARMONY: 71-73 6-12
MERCURY: 71-88 5-12
PRIORITY: 82 5-8
TIME-LIFE: 81 5-8
Members: Harold Reid; Don Reid; Lew DeWitt;
Phil Balsley; Jimmy Fortune.
Also see CASH, Johnny

STATON, Candi
Singles: 7-Inch
FAME: 69-73 2-4
L.A.: 81 1-3
SUGAR HILL: 82 1-3
WARNER BROS: 74-80 2-5
LPs: 10/12-Inch 33rpm
FAME: 70-72 10-12
SUGAR HILL: 82 5-8
WARNER BROS: 74-80 8-10

STATON, Dakota
Singles: 7-Inch
CAPITOL: 55-63 2-5
GROOVE MERCHANT: 72 1-3
EPs: 7-Inch 33/45rpm
CAPITOL: 58-60 5-15
LPs: 10/12-Inch 33rpm
CAPITOL (800 through
1600 series): 58-63 15-35
HALF MOON: 83 5-8
LONDON: 67 10-15
UNITED ARTISTS: 63-64 10-20
VERVE: 71 8-12

STATUES
Singles: 7-Inch
LIBERTY: 60 10-15

Member: Garry Miles.
Also see MILES, Garry

STATUS QUO
Singles: 7-Inch
A&M: 73-74 .... $2-4
CADET/CONCEPT: 68-69 3-5
CAPITOL: 75-77 2-3
JANUS: 72 2-4
PYE: 75 2-4
RIVA: 80 1-3
LPs: 10/12-Inch 33rpm
A&M: 73-74 8-10
CADET CONCEPT: 68 10-15
CAPITOL: 74-79 8-10
JANUS: 71 10-12
PYE: 72 10-12
Also see BAND AID

STATUS VI
Singles: 12-Inch 33/45rpm
RADAR: 83 4-6

STEADY B
LPs: 10/12-Inch 33rpm
JIVE: 88 5-8

STEALERS WHEEL
Singles: 7-Inch
A&M: 73-78 2-4
Picture Sleeves
A&M: 73 2-4
LPs: 10/12-Inch 33rpm
A&M: 73-78 6-10
PICKWICK: 80 5-8
Members: Gerry Rafferty; Joe Egan.
Also see RAFFERTY, Gerry

STEALIN' HORSES
LPs: 10/12-Inch 33rpm
ARISTA: 88 5-8

STEAM
Singles: 7-Inch
FONTANA: 69 2-4
MERCURY: 70-76 2-4
Picture Sleeves
MERCURY (30160; "Na Na Hey Hey
  Kiss Him Goodbye"): 76 8-10
(Promotional Chicago White Sox sleeve.)
LPs: 10/12-Inch 33rpm
MERCURY: 69 12-15

STEEL, Jake & Jeff
Singles: 7-Inch
PEACH/MINT: 74 2-4

STEEL BREEZE
Singles: 7-Inch
RCA VICTOR: 82-83 1-3

LPs: 10/12-Inch 33rpm
RCA VICTOR: 82 .... $5-8

STEEL PULSE
Singles: 7-Inch
ELEKTRA: 82 1-3
LPs: 10/12-Inch 33rpm
ELEKTRA: 82 5-8
MCA: 88 5-8
MANGO: 80 5-8

STEELE, Ben, & His Bare Hands
Singles: 12-Inch 33/45rpm
VANITY: 83 4-6

STEELERS
Singles: 7-Inch
DATE: 69 2-4
EPIC: 71 2-4

STEELEYE SPAN
Singles: 7-Inch
CHRYSALIS: 72-78 2-4
LPs: 10/12-Inch 33rpm
BIG TREE: 71 12-15
CHRYSALIS: 72-78 8-12
MFSL: 79 25-50
TAKOMA: 81 8-10

STEELY DAN
Singles: 7-Inch
ABC: 72-78 2-4
MCA: 78-81 1-3
EPs: 7-Inch 33/45rpm
ABC: 73-77 5-10
(Jukebox issues only.)
LPs: 10/12-Inch 33rpm
ABC: 72-78 6-10
COMMAND: 74 8-10
MCA: 79-82 5-8
MFSL: 79 25-50
Members: Donald Fagen; Walter Beckers.
Also see FAGEN, Donald
Also see McDONALD, Michael

STEIN, Lou
Singles: 78rpm
BRUNSWICK: 52-53 2-4
EPIC: 55-56 2-4
JUBILEE: 54 2-4
MERCURY: 55-58 2-4
RKO UNIQUE: 57 2-4
Singles: 7-Inch
BRUNSWICK: 52-53 2-4
EPIC: 55-56 2-4
JUBILEE: 54 2-4
MERCURY: 55-58 3-6
MURBO: 69 1-3

RKO UNIQUE: 57 .... $2-4
EPs: 7-Inch 33/45rpm
EPIC: 55-56 4-8
JUBILEE: 54 4-8
LPs: 10/12-Inch 33rpm
CHIAROSCURO: 76-81 4-8
CORAL: 53 5-15
EPIC: 55-56 5-15
EVEREST: 60 5-12
JUBILEE: 54 5-15
MERCURY: 55-60 5-15
MUSICOR: 67-68 5-10
OLD TOWN: 61 5-15
WING: 62 5-10
WORLD JAZZ: 81 4-8

STEINBERG, David
Singles: 7-Inch
COLUMBIA: 74 2-3
LPs: 10/12-Inch 33rpm
COLUMBIA: 74-75 5-10
ELEKTRA: 70 5-10
UNI: 68 8-15

STEINMAN, Jim
Singles: 7-Inch
EPIC/CLEVELAND INT'L: 81 1-3
LPs: 10/12-Inch 33rpm
EPIC/CLEVELAND INT'L: 81 5-8

STEPHENS, Tennyson
(Tenison Stephens)
Singles: 7-Inch
ARIES: 69 2-4
CHESS: 69 2-4
BACK BEAT: 61 3-5
  Also see HUGHES, Rhetta, & Tennyson
Stephens
  Also see UPCHURCH, Phil, & Tennyson
Stephens

STEPHENSON, Van
Singles: 7-Inch
HANDSHAKE: 81 1-3
MCA: 84 1-3
LPs: 10/12-Inch 33rpm
HANDSHAKE: 81 5-8
MCA: 84 5-8

STEPPENWOLF
Singles: 7-Inch
ABC: 70 2-4
DUNHILL: 67-71 3-5
IMMEDIATE: 67 4-6
MCA: 1-3
MUMS: 74-75 2-4
ROULETTE: 1-3

Steppenwolf: (L-R) Michael Wilk; Ron Hurst; Rocket Ritchotte; John Kay (Photo: Amy Etra)

Picture Sleeves
DUNHILL: 71 .... $3-5
MUMS: 74 2-4
EPs: 7-Inch 33/45rpm
DUNHILL: 68 5-10
(Jukebox issues only.)
LPs: 10/12-Inch 33rpm
ABC: 75-76 8-10
ALLEGIANCE: 5-8
DUNHILL: 68-73 15-30
EPIC: 75-76 6-10
MCA: 79 5-8
MUMS: 74 8-10
Members: John Kay; Goldy McJohn; Michael
Monarch; Jerry Edmonton; Nick St. Nicholas.
  Also see HARD TIMES
  Also see KAY, John

STEPTOE
Singles: 12-Inch 33/45rpm
FANTASY: 82 4-6
Singles: 7-Inch
FANTASY: 82 1-3

STEREO FUN INC.
Singles: 12-Inch 33/45rpm
MOBY DICK: 83 4-6

STEREOS
Singles: 7-Inch
MINK (22; "Memory Lane"): 59 10-20
(*Memory Lane* was reissued later in 1959, showing
the group as the Tams. The same track was again is-
sued in 1963, shown as by the Tams and then by
the Hippies.)
  Also see HIPPIES / Reggie Harrison
  Also see TAMS

STEREOS
Singles: 7-Inch
CADET: *67-68* $3-5
COLLECTABLES: *86* 1-3
CUB: *61-62* 10-15
GIBRALTAR: *59* 8-12
WORLD ARTISTS: *63* 4-8

STERLING, Michael
Singles: 7-Inch
SUCCESS: *83* 1-3

STETSASONIC
Singles: 7-Inch
TOMMY B: *88* 1-3
LPs: 10/12-Inch 33rpm
TOMMY B: *88* 5-8

STEVE & EYDIE:
see LAWRENCE, Steve, & Eydie Gorme

STEVENS, April
Singles: 7-Inch
A&M: *72* 3-5
ATCO: *65* 4-8
CONTRACT: *61* 4-8
IMPERIAL: *59-65* 4-8
KING: *64* 4-6
MGM: *67* 3-6
RCA VICTOR: *51-52* 5-10
VERVE: *71* 2-4
LPs: 10/12-Inch 33rpm
IMPERIAL: *61-64* 15-20
LIBERTY: *83* 5-8
Also see TEMPO, Nino, & April Stevens

STEVENS, April / Marg Phelan
LPs: 10/12-Inch 33rpm
AUDIO LAB: *59* 15-20
Also see STEVENS, April

STEVENS, Cat
Singles: 12-Inch 33/45rpm
A&M: *77* 5-8
Singles: 7-Inch
A&M: *70-79* 2-5
DERAM: *66-72* 4-8
Picture Sleeves
A&M: *71-78* 2-3
EPs: 7-Inch 33/45rpm
A&M: *70* 8-10
(Jukebox issue only.)
LPs: 10/12-Inch 33rpm
A&M: *69-84* 6-10
DERAM: *67-72* 10-15
LONDON: *78* 5-8
MFSL (035; "Tea For The
Tillerman"): *79* 15-20

MFSL/UHQR (035; "Tea For The
Tillerman"): *79* $25-40
(Boxed set.)

STEVENS, Connie
Singles: 7-Inch
BELL: *70-72* 4-8
MGM: *68* 10-15
PARAMOUNT ("Why Can't He
Care For Me?"): *58* 25-50
(Promotional issue only. No label name or number
shown. Distributed by Paramount to promote *Rock-
A-Bye Baby*, a film starring Connie Stevens.)
WARNER BROS: *59-66* 5-10
Picture Sleeves
WARNER BROS: *60* 15-25
LPs: 10/12-Inch 33rpm
HARMONY: *69* 10-20
WARNER BROS: *58-62* 25-50
Also see BYRNES, Edward

STEVENS, Dodie
Singles: 7-Inch
CRYSTALETTE: *59* 10-15
DOLTON: *63* 4-8
DOT: *59-62* 5-10
IMPERIAL: *63* 4-8
Picture Sleeves
CRYSTALETTE: *59* 10-20
LPs: 10/12-Inch 33rpm
DOT: *60-61* 20-25

STEVENS, Ray
(Ray Stevens & The Merry Melody Singers)
Singles: 7-Inch
BARNABY: *70-76* 3-5
CAPITOL: *58-59* 10-15
MCA: *85-89* 2-4
MERCURY (71000 & 72000
series): *61-68* 5-10
MERCURY (810000 series): *83* 2-3
MONUMENT: *65-69* 4-8
NRC: *59-60* 8-10
PREP: *57* 10-20
PRIORITY: 2-3
RCA VICTOR: *81-82* 2-4
WARNER/AHAB: *76-79* 3-5
Picture Sleeves
BARNABY: *70* 3-6
MCA: *86* 2-3
MERCURY: *61-64* 8-15
WARNER/AHAB: *79* 2-4
Promotional Singles
MERCURY (66; "Butch Barbarian"): *64* . 8-12
EPs: 7-Inch 33/45rpm
MERCURY (85; "Ray Stevens"): *62* 10-20
(Promotional issue only. Not issued with cover.)

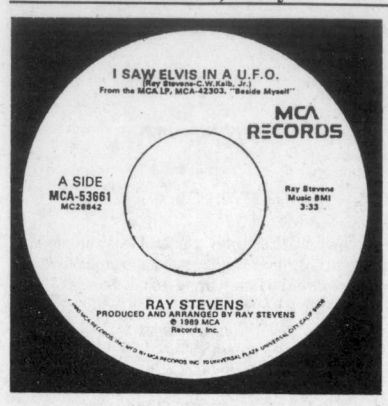

STEWART, Baron
Singles: 7-Inch
UNITED ARTISTS: 75 . . . . $2-3
LPs: 10/12-Inch 33rpm
UNITED ARTISTS: 75 8-10

STEWART, Billy
Singles: 78rpm
ARGO: 56 8-12
Singles: 7-Inch
ARGO: 56 8-12
CHESS: 62-73 3-5
ERIC: 1-3
UNITED ARTISTS: 61 4-6
LPs: 10/12-Inch 33rpm
CADET: 74 8-10
CHESS: 65-67 15-20

STEWART, Billy, & The Marquees
Singles: 7-Inch
OKEH: 57 50-75
Also see STEWART, Billy

STEWART, Bobby
Singles: 12-Inch 33/45rpm
WARNER BROS: 83 4-6
Singles: 7-Inch
WARNER BROS: 83 1-3

STEWART, Dave, & Barbara Gaskin
Singles: 7-Inch
PLATINUM: 81 1-3

STEWART, Gary
(Gary Stewart & Dean Dillon)
Singles: 7-Inch
CORY: 8-12
DECCA: 71 2-3
HIGHTONE: 88 1-3
KAPP: 68-70 2-4
MCA: 75 2-3
RED ASH: 84 1-3
RCA VICTOR: 73-83 1-3
Picture Sleeves
RCA VICTOR: 82 1-3
LPs: 10/12-Inch 33rpm
MCA: 75 4-8
RCA VICTOR: 75-83 5-10

STEWART, Jermaine
Singles: 12-Inch 33/45rpm
ARISTA: 84-86 4-6
Singles: 7-Inch
ARISTA: 84-88 1-3
LPs: 10/12-Inch 33rpm
ARISTA: 85-88 5-8

STEWART, John
Singles: 7-Inch
ALLEGIANCE: $1-3
CAPITOL: 69 2-4
RCA VICTOR: 73 2-4
RSO: 79 1-3
WARNER BROS: 71 2-4
LPs: 10/12-Inch 33rpm
ALLEGIANCE: 5-8
CAPITOL: 69-70 10-12
RCA VICTOR: 73 8-10
RSO: 79 5-8
SHIP: 87 5-8
WARNER BROS: 71 8-10
Also see BUCKINGHAM, Lindsey
Also see KINGSTON TRIO
Also see NICKS, Stevie

STEWART, John, & Buffy Ford
LPs: 10/12-Inch 33rpm
CAPITOL: 68 10-12

STEWART, John, & Nick Reynolds
LPs: 10/12-Inch 33rpm
TAKOMA: 5-8
Also see KINGSTON TRIO
Also see STEWART, John

STEWART, John, & Scott Engel:
see ENGEL, Scott, & John Stewart

STEWART, Mel
Singles: 12-Inch 33/45rpm
MERCURY: 83 4-6
Singles: 7-Inch
MERCURY: 83 1-3

STEWART, Rod
(Rod Stewart & The Faces)
Singles: 12-Inch 33/45rpm
WARNER BROS: 78-82 5-8
Singles: 7-Inch
GEFFEN: 87 1-3
GNP/CRESCENDO: 73 3-5
MERCURY: 70-76 3-5
PRESS: 65 10-20
PRIVATE STOCK: 76 2-4
WARNER BROS: 75-88 1-3
Picture Sleeves
MERCURY: 72-73 4-8
WARNER BROS: 75-88 1-3
LPs: 10/12-Inch 33rpm
ACCORD: 81 5-8
MERCURY (Except 61000 series): 71-76 . 8-12
MERCURY (61000 series): 69-70 10-20
MFSL: 81 25-50
PRIVATE STOCK: 77 8-10
SPRINGBOARD: 72 8-12

TRIP: 77 .... $8-10
WARNER BROS (Except "Blondes Have
More Fun" picture discs): 75-86 6-10
WARNER BROS ("Blondes Have More
Fun" picture disc): 79 10-15
   Also see BECK, Jeff, & Rod Stewart
   Also see FACES
   Also see PYTHON LEE JACKSON

STEWART, Sandy
Singles: 78rpm
EPIC: 54 3-5
OKEH: 53 3-5
20TH CENTURY: 54 3-5
X: 55 3-5
Singles: 7-Inch
ATCO: 59 3-5
COLPIX: 62-63 2-5
DCP: 64 2-5
EAST WEST: 58 4-6
EPIC: 54 3-6
OKEH: 53 3-6
20TH CENTURY: 54 3-6
UNITED ARTISTS: 60-61 3-5
X: 55 3-6
Picture Sleeves
COLPIX: 62 4-8
LPs: 10/12-Inch 33rpm
COLPIX: 63 10-20

STEWART, Wynn
(Wynn Stewart & The Tourists)
Singles: 78rpm
CAPITOL: 56-57 3-5
Singles: 7-Inch
ATLANTIC: 74 2-3
CAPITOL (2000 series): 67-71 2-4
CAPITOL (3000 series): 56-57 3-6
CAPITOL (5000 series): 62-67 2-4
CHALLENGE: 59-64 2-5
4 STAR: 80 1-3
JACKPOT: 59 10-15
PLAYBOY: 75-76 2-3
PRETTY WORLD: 85 1-3
RCA VICTOR: 72-73 2-3
WINS: 79 1-3
Picture Sleeves
CAPITOL: 67-69 2-5
LPs: 10/12-Inch 33rpm
CAPITOL: 67-75 5-12
PICKWICK/HILLTOP: 67 6-12
PLAYBOY: 76 6-10
STARDAY: 68 8-12
WRANGLER: 62 15-25
   Also see PIERCE, Webb / Wynn Stewart

STILLS, Stephen
(Stephen Stills & Manassas)
Singles: 7-Inch
ATLANTIC: 70-73 .... $2-4
COLUMBIA: 75-78 1-3
Picture Sleeves
ATLANTIC: 71 2-4
LPs: 10/12-Inch 33rpm
ATLANTIC: 70-84 6-10
COLUMBIA (Except PCQ series): 75-78 . . 5-10
COLUMBIA (PCQ series): 75 10-15
(Quadrophonic issues.)
   Also see BLOOMFIELD, Mike, Al Kooper, &
Steve Stills
   Also see BUFFALO SPRINGFIELD
   Also see CROSBY, STILLS & NASH
   Also see CROSBY, STILLS, NASH &
YOUNG
   Also see STILLS-YOUNG BAND

STILLS-YOUNG BAND
Singles: 7-Inch
REPRISE: 77 2-3
LPs: 10/12-Inch 33rpm
REPRISE: 76 5-8
Members: Stephen Stills; Neil Young.
   Also see STILLS, Stephen
   Also see YOUNG, Neil

STILLWATER
Singles: 7-Inch
CAPRICORN: 77-78 2-3
LPs: 10/12-Inch 33rpm
CAPRICORN: 78-79 5-8

STING
(Gordon Sumner)
Singles: 12-Inch 33/45rpm
A&M: 85-87 4-6
Singles: 7-Inch
A&M: 85-88 1-3
ABC: 78 2-3
LPs: 10/12-Inch 33rpm
A&M: 85-87 5-8
ABC: 78 6-10
   Also see BAND AID
   Also see POLICE

STIRLING SILVER
Singles: 7-Inch
COLUMBIA: 76 2-3
Member: Gery Sterling.

STITES, Gary
Singles: 7-Inch
CARLTON: 59-60 10-15
EPIC: 66 3-5
MADISON: 60-61 10-15

MR. PEEKE: *62* $4-6
    LPs: 10/12-Inch 33rpm
CARLTON: *60* 40-50

STITT, Sonny
Singles: 7-Inch
ARGO: *58-65* 2-4
ATLANTIC: *63* 2-4
CADET: *74* 1-3
CATALYST: *77* 1-3
ENTERPRISE: *69* 2-3
IMPULSE: *64* 2-4
PRESTIGE: *63-69* 2-4
ROULETTE: *65-67* .2-3
WINGATE: *65* 2-4
WORLD PACIFIC: *63* 2-4
    EPs: 7-Inch 33/45rpm
PRESTIGE: *53* 10-25
    LPs: 10/12-Inch 33rpm
ARGO: *58-65* 15-30
ATLANTIC: *62-64* 15-25
CADET: *65-74* 8-18
CATALYST: *76-77* 5-10
CHESS: *76* 8-12
COLPIX: *66* 10-20
EVEREST: *82* 5-8
FLYING DUTCHMAN: *75-76* 5-10
IMPULSE: *63-64* .15-25
JAMAL: *71* 8-12
JAZZLAND: *62* 20-35
JAZZTONE: *56* 20-40
MUSE: *73-82* 5-12
PACIFIC JAZZ: *63* 15-25
PAULA: *74* 5-10
PRESTIGE (060; "Kaleidoscope"): *83* 5-8
PRESTIGE (100 series): *51-53* 50-75
  (10-Inch LPs.)
PRESTIGE (7000 series): *56-64* 20-45
  (Yellow labels.)
PRESTIGE (7000 series): *65-70* 10-20
  (Blue labels.)
PRESTIGE (10000 series): *71-74* 8-12
PRESTIGE (20000 series): *74* 8-15
ROOST (400 series): *52* 75-150
  (10-Inch LPs.)
ROOST (1200 series): *56* 20-40
ROOST (2200 series): *57-66* 10-30
ROULETTE: *65-70* 10-25
SAVOY (9000 series): *53* 40-60
  (10-Inch LPs.)
SOLID STATE: *69* 8-15
TRIP: *73* 6-12
UPFRONT: *77* 5-8
VERVE: *57-59* 20-40
  (Reads "Verve Records, Inc." at bottom of label.)

VERVE: *62-72* $10-20
  (Reads "MGM Records - A Division Of Metro-
  Goldwyn-Mayer, Inc." at bottom of label.)
VERVE: *73-84* 5-10
  (Reads "Manufactured By MGM Record Corp." or
  mentions either Polydor or Polygram at bottom of
  label.)
  Also see AMMONS, Gene, & Sonny Stitt
  Also see PETERSON, Oscar, & Sonny Stitt

STOKES, Simon T.
(Simon Stokes & The Nighthawks)
Singles: 7-Inch
CASABLANCA: *74* 2-4
ELEKTRA: *69-70* 2-4
IN SOUND: *68* 3-5
UNITED ARTISTS: *77* 2-4
    LPs: 10/12-Inch 33rpm
MGM: *70* 10-12
SPINDIZZY: *73* 8-10
UNITED ARTISTS: *77* 8-10

STOLOFF, Morris
**(Morris Stoloff Conducts The Columbia Studio
Orchestra)**
Singles: 78rpm
DECCA: *56* 2-4
MERCURY: *54* 2-4
Singles: 7-Inch
COLPIX: *59* 2-4
DECCA: *56* 2-4
MERCURY: *54* 2-4
REPRISE: *65* 2-3
    LPs: 10/12-Inch 33rpm
DECCA: *56* 5-15
WARNER BROS. (1416; "Fanny"): *61* . . 25-35
  (Soundtrack.)

STOMPERS
Singles: 7-Inch
GONE: *61* 10-12
LANDA: *61-62* 8-10
MERCURY (72000 series): *63* 4-6

STOMPERS
Singles: 7-Inch
BOARDWALK: *83* 1-3
MERCURY (880000 series): *84* 1-3
    LPs: 10/12-Inch 33rpm
MERCURY: *84* 5-8

STONE
Singles: 7-Inch
WEST END: *82* 1-3

STONE, Cliffie
(Cliffie Stone Singers)
Singles: 78rpm
CAPITOL (Except 2910): *50-69* 2-5

CAPITOL (2910; "Blue Moon Of
Kentucky"): *54* $4-8
Singles: 7-Inch
CAPITOL (Except 2910): *50-69* 3-5
CAPITOL (2910; "Blue Moon Of
Kentucky"): *54* 8-10
TOWER: *67* 2-3
LPs: 10/12-Inch 33rpm
CAPITOL (100 through 300 series): *68-69* 5-10
CAPITOL (1000 through
1600 series): *58-62* 15-30
CAPITOL (2100 series): *64* 5-15
TOWER: *67* 8-12

STONE, Kirby, Four
(Kirby Stone Quartet)
Singles: 78rpm
COLUMBIA: *57* 2-4
Singles: 7-Inch
COLUMBIA: *57-65* 2-4
MGM: *67* 2-3
WARNER BROS: *63-64* 2-4
LPs: 10/12-Inch 33rpm
COLUMBIA: *58-62* 8-15
WARNER BROS: *63-64* 5-12
Members: Kirby Stone; Edward Hall; Michael
Gardner; Larry Foster.

STONE, Sly
(Sylvester "Sly Stone" Stewart)
Singles: 12-Inch 33/45rpm
EPIC: *80* 4-6
Singles: 7-Inch
EPIC: *75-79* 2-4
LPs: 10/12-Inch 33rpm
EPIC: *79* 5-8
Also see JOHNSON, Jesse
Also see SLY & THE FAMILY STONE

STONE CITY BAND
Singles: 7-Inch
GORDY: *80-83* 1-3
LPs: 10/12-Inch 33rpm
GORDY: *80-83* 5-8
Also see JAMES, Rick

STONE FURY
Singles: 7-Inch
MCA: *84* 1-3
LPs: 10/12-Inch 33rpm
MCA: *84* 5-8

STONE PONEYS
(Featuring Linda Ronstadt)
Singles: 7-Inch
CAPITOL: *67* 5-10
LPs: 10/12-Inch 33rpm
CAPITOL (2600 & 2700 series): *67* 15-20

Members: Linda Ronstadt; Bob Kimmel; Ken
Edwards.
Also see RONSTADT, Linda

STONEBOLT
Singles: 7-Inch
PARACHUTE: *78-79* $2-3
RCA VICTOR: *80* 1-3
LPs: 10/12-Inch 33rpm
PARACHUTE: *78* 8-10
RCA VICTOR: *80* 5-8

STONEY & MEAT LOAF
Singles: 7-Inch
RARE EARTH: *71* 2-4
LPs: 10/12-Inch 33rpm
PRODIGAL: *78* 5-8
RARE EARTH: *71* 10-15
Also see MEAT LOAF

STOOGES
(Featuring Iggy Pop)
Singles: 7-Inch
ELEKTRA: *69-70* 3-5
LPs: 10/12-Inch 33rpm
ELEKTRA: *69-70* 12-15
Also see POP, Iggy

STOOKEY, Paul
Singles: 7-Inch
ERIC: 1-3
WARNER BROS: *71-72* 2-4
LPs: 10/12-Inch 33rpm
NEWPAX: 5-8
WARNER BROS: *71* 8-10
Also see PETER, PAUL & MARY

STOREY SISTERS
Singles: 7-Inch
BATON: *58* 8-10
CAMEO: *58* 8-10
MERCURY: *59* 4-6

STORIES
Singles: 7-Inch
ERIC: 1-3
KAMA SUTRA: *72-74* 2-4
RADIOACTIVE GOLD: *74* 2-4
LPs: 10/12-Inch 33rpm
KAMA SUTRA: *72-73* 8-10
Members: Ian Lloyd; Michael Brown.
Also see LLOYD, Ian

STORM
Singles: 7-Inch
PHI KAPPA: *74* 2-3
LPs: 10/12-Inch 33rpm
CAPITOL: *83* 5-8
MCA: *77* 5-8

STORM, Billy
(Billy Storm & The Valiants)
Singles: 7-Inch

ATLANTIC: *60-61* $3-5
BUENA VISTA: *63* 3-5
COLUMBIA: *59* 4-6
ENSIGN: *59* 4-6
GREGMARK: *61* 3-5
HBR: *66* 3-5
INFINITY: *62-63* 3-5
LOMA: *64-65* 3-5
ODE: *69* 2-4
Picture Sleeves
HBR: *66* 3-5
LPs: 10/12-Inch 33rpm
BUENA VISTA: *63* 15-20
FAMOUS: *69* 15-20
Also see VALIANTS

STORM, Gale
Singles: 78rpm
DOT: *55-56* 3-6
Singles: 7-Inch
DOT (Maroon label): *55-56* 5-10
DOT (Black label): *57-60* 3-6
DOT (Orange label): *57-60* 2-4
Picture Sleeves
DOT: *58* 10-15
EPs: 7-Inch 33/45rpm
DOT: *55-56* 15-25
LPs: 10/12-Inch 33rpm
DOT: *56-59* 20-25
HAMILTON: *66* 8-10
MCA: *82* 5-8

STORM, Warren
Singles: 7-Inch
ATCO: *68* 2-4
DOT: *61* 4-6
KINGFISH: 4-6
NASCO: *58-60* 4-6
ROCKO: 5-10
SOUTH STAR: *83* 1-3
STARFLITE: *79* 2-3
ZYNN: 5-10
Also see SHONDELLS / Rod Bernard / Warren Storm / Skip Stewart

STOTT, Lally
Singles: 7-Inch
PHILIPS: *71* 2-4

STRAIT, George
Singles: 7-Inch
MCA: *81-88* $1-3
LPs: 10/12-Inch 33rpm
MCA: *81-88* 5-8

STRAKER, Nick, Band
Singles: 7-Inch
PRELUDE: *82* $1-3
LPs: 10/12-Inch 33rpm
PRELUDE: *82* 5-8

STRANGE, Billy
(Billy Strange & The Telstars; Billy Strange & The Transients)
Singles: 78rpm
CAPITOL: *54-55* 2-5
DECCA: *55* 2-5
Singles: 7-Inch
BUENA VISTA: *62-63* 2-5
CAPITOL: *54-55* 3-6
COLISEUM: *63* 2-5
DECCA: *55* 4-6
GNP/CRESCENDO: *64-65* 3-5
LIBERTY: *61-62* 2-5
TOWER: *69* 2-4
LPs: 10/12-Inch 33rpm
COLISEUM: *62* 10-15
GNP/CRESCENDO: *63-75* 6-10
HORIZON: *63* 10-15
SUNSET: *68* 8-10
SURREY: *65* 10-15
TRADITION: *68* 6-10
Also see CAMPBELL, Glen, & Billy Strange

STRANGELOVES
Singles: 7-Inch
BANG: *65-67* 4-6
SIRE: *68* 3-5
SWAN: *64* 5-8
LPs: 10/12-Inch 33rpm
BANG: *65* 30-35
Members: Bob Feldman; Jerry Goldstein; Richie Gottehrer.
Also see SHEEP

STRANGERS
Singles: 7-Inch
TITAN: *59-60* 10-15
Member: Joel Hill.

STRAWBERRY ALARM CLOCK
Singles: 7-Inch
ALL AMERICAN: *67* 5-8
MCA: 1-3
UNI: *67-70* 3-5
LPs: 10/12-Inch 33rpm
BACK-TRAC: *85* 5-8
UNI: *67-70* 20-35
VOCALION: *71* 12-15
Member: Randy Seol.
Also see THEE SIXPENCE
Also see WHO / Strawberry Alarm Clock

STRAWBS
Singles: 7-Inch
A&M: *68-75* $4-8
ARISTA: *78* 1-3
OYSTER: *76-77* 2-4
LPs: 10/12-Inch 33rpm
A&M: *71-78* 8-15
ARISTA: *78* 5-8
OYSTER: *76-77* 8-10
Also see WAKEMAN, Rick

STRAY CATS
Singles: 7-Inch
EMI AMERCIA: *82-84* 1-3
Picture Sleeves
EMI AMERCIA: *82-84* 1-3
LPs: 10/12-Inch 33rpm
EMI AMERICA: *82-86* 5-8
Members: Brian Setzer; Lee Rocker; Slim Jim
Phantom.
Also see PHANTOM, ROCKER & SLICK

STREEK
Singles: 7-Inch
COLUMBIA: *81* 1-3
LPs: 10/12-Inch 33rpm
COLUMBIA: *81* 5-8

STREET, Janey
Singles: 7-Inch
ARISTA: *84* 1-3
LPs: 10/12-Inch 33rpm
ARISTA: *84-85* 5-8

STREET CHRISTIANS
Singles: 7-Inch
P.I.P.: *73* 2-3

STREET PEOPLE
Singles: 7-Inch
MUSICOR: *69-70* 2-4
VIGOR: *75-77* 2-3
LPs: 10/12-Inch 33rpm
MUSICOR: *70* 12-15
PICKWICK: *72* 8-10
Also see HOLMES, Rupert

STREET PLAYERS
Singles: 7-Inch
ARIOLA AMERICA: *79* 1-3
LPs: 10/12-Inch 33rpm
ARIOLA AMERICA: *79* 5-8

STREETS
Singles: 7-Inch
ATLANTIC: *83-84* 1-3
EPIC: *79* 1-3
LPs: 10/12-Inch 33rpm
ATLANTIC: *83-84* 5-8

EPIC: *79* $5-8
Member: Steve Walsh.
Also see KANSAS

STREISAND, Barbra
Singles: 12-Inch 33/45rpm
COLUMBIA (White labels): *79-85* 12-25
(Promotional issues only.)
Singles: 7-Inch
COLUMBIA (04000 & 05000 series): *83-86* 1-3
COLUMBIA (08000 series): *88* 1-3
COLUMBIA (10000 & 11000
series): *76-80* 1-3
COLUMBIA (3-42648; "My Coloring
Book"): *62* 20-25
(Compact 33 Single.)
COLUMBIA (4-42648; "My Coloring
Book"): *62* 8-10
COLUMBIA (42631; "Happy Days
Are Here Again"): *63* 5-8
COLUMBIA (42965 through 43469): *64-65* 3-5
COLUMBIA (43518 through 46024): *66-74* 2-4
Promotional Singles
COLUMBIA (04000 & 05000 series): *83-86* 2-3
COLUMBIA (10000 & 11000
series): *76-80* 2-4
COLUMBIA (4-42648; "My Coloring
Book"): *62* 10-20
COLUMBIA (42631; "Happy Days Are
Here Again"): *63* 10-15
COLUMBIA (42965 through
43469): *64-65* 5-10
COLUMBIA (43518 through
46024): *66-74* 3-8
Picture Sleeves
COLUMBIA (Except 43000 series): *73-84* .. 1-3
COLUMBIA (43000 series): *66* 3-6
LPs: 10/12-Inch 33rpm
COLUMBIA (1779; "The Legend Of
Barbra Streisand"): *83* 20-40
(Promotional issue only. A one hour interview pro-
gram.)
COLUMBIA (2007 through
2682): *63-67* 15-25
(With a "CL" prefix. Black vinyl.)
COLUMBIA (2478; "Color Me
Barbra"): *66* 25-50
(Colored vinyl. Promotional issue only.)
COLUMBIA (8807 through
9482): *63-67* 15-25
(With a "CS" prefix. Black vinyl.)
COLUMBIA (8854; "The Second Barbra
Streisand Album"): *63* 30-60
(Colored vinyl. Promotional issue only.)
COLUMBIA (9710 through 9968): *68-70* 10-15

COLUMBIA (8000 & 9000 series): $5-8
(With a "PC" prefix.)
COLUMBIA (9000 series): 5-8
(With a "JC" prefix.)
COLUMBIA (30086 through 40000
series): *70-88* 6-15
Also see ARLEN, Harold, With "Friend"

STREISAND, Barbra, & Kim Carnes
Singles: 7-Inch
COLUMBIA: *84* 1-3
Also see CARNES, Kim

STREISAND, Barbra, & Neil Diamond
Singles: 7-Inch
COLUMBIA: *78* 2-3
Also see DIAMOND, Neil

STREISAND, Barbra, & Barry Gibb
Singles: 7-Inch
COLUMBIA: *80-81* 1-3
Also see GIBB, Barry

STREISAND, Barbra, & Donna Summer
Singles: 12-Inch 33/45rpm
COLUMBIA/CASABLANCA: *79* 8-10
(Promotional issue only. Issued with special cover.)
Singles: 7-Inch
COLUMBIA: *79* 1-3
Picture Sleeves
COLUMBIA: *79* 2-3
Also see STREISAND, Barbra
Also see SUMMER, Donna

STRIKERS
Singles: 7-Inch
PRELUDE: *81* 1-3
LPs: 10/12-Inch 33rpm
PRELUDE: *81* 5-8

STRING-A-LONGS
Singles: 7-Inch
ATCO (6694; "Popi"): *69* 3-5
(Reportedly recorded by the Fireballs but credited
to the String-A-Longs.)
DOT: *62-65* 3-5
WARWICK (Except 603 & 606): *61-62* ...4-6
WARWICK (603; "Wheels"/"Tell
The World"): *60* 10-15
WARWICK (603; "Wheels"/"Am I
Asking Too Much?"): *61* 4-6
WARWICK (606; "Tell The World"): *61* ..8-10
LPs: 10/12-Inch 33rpm
ATCO (241; "World Wide
Hits"): *68* 10-20
(Reportedly recorded by the Fireballs but credited
to the String-A-Longs.)
DOT: *62-66* 15-20
WARWICK: *61* 30-40

Members: Keith McCormick; Jimmy Tores.
Also see FIREBALLS

STROKE
Singles: 12-Inch 33/45rpm
OMNI: *85* $4-6

STROLLERS
Singles: 7-Inch
CARLTON: *61* 10-15

STRONG, Barrett
Singles: 7-Inch
ANNA: *60* 15-20
ATCO: *62* 3-5
CAPITOL: *75* 2-4
EPIC: *73* 2-4
MOTOWN: 1-3
TAMLA (54027; "Money"): *60* 25-30
(With horizontal lines on label.)
TAMLA (54027; "Money"): *60* 10-12
(With Tamla globe logo on label.)
TAMLA (54029; "Money"): *60* 50-60
(With horizontal lines on label.)
TAMLA (54033; "Whirlwind"): *60* 4-6
TAMLA (54035; "Money And Me"): *61* ...5-8
TAMLA (54043; "Misery"): *61* 20-25
TOLLIE: *64* 5-8
Picture Sleeves
EPIC: *73* 2-4
LPs: 10/12-Inch 33rpm
CAPITOL: *74* 8-10

STRUNK, Jud
(Jud Strunk & The Coplin Kitchen Band)
Singles: 7-Inch
CAPITOL: *74* 2-4
COBURT: *71* 2-4
COLUMBIA: *70* 2-4
MCA: *77* 2-3
MGM: *72-73* 2-4
MELODYLAND: *75-76* 2-4
LPs: 10/12-Inch 33rpm
COLUMBIA: *70* 8-12
HARMONY: *73* 5-10
MCA: *77* 5-8
MGM: *71-73* 6-10

STRYPER
Singles: 7-Inch
ENIGMA: *88* 1-3
LPs: 10/12-Inch 33rpm
ENIGMA: *88* 5-8

STUDENTS
Singles: 7-Inch
ARGO: *61* 5-8
CHECKER: *58-62* 8-12
CHESS: *73* 1-3

COLLECTABLES: $1-3
NOTE (10012; "I'm So Young"): *58* .. **100-200**
NOTE (10019; "My Vow
 To You"): *58* **100-200**
RED TOP (100; "My Heart Is
 An Open Door"): *58* **40-60**
Member: Leroy King.

STUFF
Singles: 7-Inch
WARNER BROS: *76-80* **1-3**
LPs: 10/12-Inch 33rpm
WARNER BROS: *76-80* **5-8**

STUFF 'N' RAMJETT
Singles: 7-Inch
CHELSEA: *76* **2-3**

STYLE COUNCIL
Singles: 7-Inch
GEFFEN: *84* **1-3**
POLYDOR: *83* **1-3**
LPs: 10/12-Inch 33rpm
GEFFEN: *84* **5-8**
POLYDOR: *83-88* **5-8**
 Also see BAND AID
 Also see JAM

STYLERS
Singles: 78rpm
GOLDEN CREST: *57* **4-8**
JUBILEE: *55-57* **4-8**
KICKS: *54* **25-50**
Singles: 7-Inch
GOLDEN CREST: *57-58* **5-10**
JUBILEE: *55-57* **5-10**
KICKS (2; "Gentle As
 A Teardrop"): *54* **100-200**

STYLISTICS
Singles: 7-Inch
AMHERST: *85* **1-3**
AVCO: *70-76* **2-4**
H&L: *76-79* **2-3**
MERCURY: *79* **2-3**
PHILADELPHIA INT'L: *82* **1-3**
STREETWISE: *84-86* **1-3**
TSOP: *80-84* **1-3**
Picture Sleeves
AVCO: *76* **2-4**
LPs: 10/12-Inch 33rpm
AVCO: *71-75* **8-10**
H&L: *78-79* **5-8**
MERCURY: *78-79* **5-8**
PHILADELPHIA INT'L: *82* **5-8**
STREETWISE: *84-86* **5-8**
TSOP: *80-81* **5-8**

Members: Russell Tompkins, Jr.; Airrion Love;
Herb Murrell; James Dunn; James Smith.

STYX
Singles: 7-Inch
A&M: *76-84* $1-3
PARAMOUNT: *71-72* **2-4**
RCA VICTOR: *76* **2-3**
WOODEN NICKEL: *72-78* **2-4**
Picture Sleeves
A&M: *77-84* **2-5**
LPs: 10/12-Inch 33rpm
A&M (Except picture
 discs): *75-84* **5-8**
A&M (Picture discs): *79* **10-15**
MFSL: *79* **25-50**
NAUTILUS: *81* **10-15**
RCA VICTOR: *72-82* **5-8**
WOODEN NICKEL: *72-77* **8-10**
Promotional LPs
A&M (8431; "Styx Radio Special"): *77* ..**15-20**
A&M (17053; "Styx Radio Special"): *78* .**35-40**
 Members: Dennis DeYoung; James Young;
 Tommy Shaw; John Panozzo; Chuck Panozzo.
 Also see DE YOUNG, Dennis
 Also see SHAW, Tommy

SUAVÉ
Singles: 7-Inch
CAPITOL: *88* **1-3**
LPs: 10/12-Inch 33rpm
CAPITOL: *88* **5-8**

SUE ANN
Singles: 7-Inch
MCA: *88* **1-3**
WARNER BROS: *81* **1-3**
LPs: 10/12-Inch 33rpm
WARNER BROS: *81* **5-8**

SUGAR BEARS
Singles: 7-Inch
BIG TREE: *72* **2-4**
LPs: 10/12-Inch 33rpm
BIG TREE: *71* **10-12**

SUGAR BILLY
Singles: 7-Inch
FAST TRACK: *75* **2-3**
LPs: 10/12-Inch 33rpm
FAST TRACK: *75* **6-10**

SUGAR DADDY
Singles: 12-Inch 33/45rpm
BC: *81* **4-6**
Singles: 7-Inch
BC: *81* **1-3**

SUGARCUBES
LPs: 10/12-Inch 33rpm
ELEKTRA: *88* $5-8

SUGARHILL GANG
Singles: 12-Inch 33/45rpm
SUGAR HILL (Except 542): *80-85* 5-10
SUGAR HILL (542; "Rapper's
Delight"): *79* 20-30
Singles: 7-Inch
SUGAR HILL: *79-85* 1-3
LPs: 10/12-Inch 33rpm
SUGAR HILL: *80-85* 5-8
Members: Michael "Wonder Mike" Wright; Guy "Master Gee" O'Brien; Henry "Big Hank" Jackson. Also see FURIOUS FIVE & THE SUGAR-HILL GANG

SUGARLOAF
(Sugarloaf With Jerry Corbetta)
Singles: 7-Inch
BRUT: *73-74* 2-4
CLARIDGE: *74-76* 2-3
LIBERTY: *70-71* 2-4
UNITED ARTISTS: *71* 2-4
Picture Sleeves
BRUT: *73-74* 3-6
LIBERTY: *71* 2-4
LPs: 10/12-Inch 33rpm
BRUT: *73* 8-10
CLARIDGE: *75* 8-10
LIBERTY: *70-71* 12-15
Members: Jerry Corbetta; Bob Webber.

SUICIDAL TENDENCIES
Singles: 7-Inch
FRONTIER: *84* 2-4
LPs: 10/12-Inch 33rpm
CAROL: *87* 5-8
EPIC: *88* 5-8
JANA: *86* 8-10

SULTON, Kasim
Singles: 7-Inch
EMI AMERICA: *82* 1-3
LPs: 10/12-Inch 33rpm
EMI AMERICA: *82* 5-8

SUMMER, Donna
Singles: 12-Inch 33/45rpm
CASABLANCA: *78-80* 5-8
GEFFEN: *80-86* 4-6
MERCURY: *83* 4-6
OASIS: *75-76* 5-8
Singles: 7-Inch
CASABLANCA: *75-80* 1-3
GEFFEN: *80-87* 1-3
OASIS: *75-76* 2-4

Picture Sleeves
GEFFEN: *80-84* $1-3
OASIS: *76* 1-3
LPs: 10/12-Inch 33rpm
CASABLANCA (Except 20110): *75-80* ... 5-8
CASABLANCA (20110; "Once
Upon A Time"): *77* 12-15
(Promotional issue only.)
GEFFEN: *80-87* 5-8
MERCURY: *83* 5-8
OASIS: *75-76* 8-10
Also see BROOKLYN DREAMS
Also see MORODER, Giorgio
Also see STREISAND, Barbra, & Donna Summer

SUMMER, Henry Lee
Singles: 7-Inch
CBS ASSOC: *88* 1-3
LPs: 10/12-Inch 33rpm
CBS ASSOC: *88* 5-8

SUMMERS, Andy, & Robert Fripp:
see FRIPP, Robert, & Andy Summers

SUMMERS, Bill
(Bill Summers & Summers Heat)
Singles: 12-Inch 33/45rpm
MCA: *81-84* 4-6
Singles: 7-Inch
MCA: *81-84* 1-3
PRESTIGE: *77-80* 1-3
LPs: 10/12-Inch 33rpm
MCA: *81* 5-8
Also see HANCOCK, Herbie

SUN
Singles: 7-Inch
AIR CITY: *84* 1-3
CAPITOL: *76-82* 1-3
Picture Sleeves
CAPITOL: *76-82* 1-3
LPs: 10/12-Inch 33rpm
CAPITOL: *77-82* 5-8

SUN, Joe
Singles: 7-Inch
A.M.I.: *85* 1-3
ELEKTRA: *82-83* 1-3
OVATION: *78-80* 1-3
LPs: 10/12-Inch 33rpm
ELEKTRA: *82-83* 5-8
OVATION: *78-80* 5-8

SUNBEAR
Singles: 7-Inch
SOUL TRAIN: *77* 1-3
LPs: 10/12-Inch 33rpm
SOUL TRAIN: *77* 5-8

SUNDANCE / Kevin Stevenson
Singles: 7-Inch
FATIMA: *88* $1-3

SUNDOWN COMPANY
Singles: 7-Inch
POLYDOR: *76* 2-3

SUNFIRE
Singles: 12-Inch 33/45rpm
WARNER BROS: *82* 4-6
Singles: 7-Inch
WARNER BROS: *82* 1-3
LPs: 10/12-Inch 33rpm
WARNER BROS: *82* 5-8

SUNGLOWS
(Sunny & The Sunglows; Sunny & The Sun-
liners; Sunny Ozuna & The Sunliners)
Singles: 7-Inch
DISCO GRANDE: *65* 4-6
KEY LOC: *66* 3-5
OKEH: *61* 4-6
RPR: *69* 2-4
SUNGLOW: *62-66* 3-5
TEAR DROP: *63-64* 3-5
LPs: 10/12-Inch 33rpm
KEY LOC: *66* 10-15
SUNGLOW: *65* 15-20
TEAR DROP: *63* 20-25

SUNNY & THE SUNGLOWS/
SUNLINERS: see SUNGLOWS

SUNNYSIDERS
Singles: 78rpm
KAPP: *55-57* 2-4
MARQUEE: *55-56* 2-4
Singles: 7-Inch
KAPP: *55-60* 2-4
MARQUEE: *55-56* 2-4
NRC: *60* 2-4
ZENITH: *60* 2-4
EPs: 7-Inch 33/45rpm
KAPP: *56* 4-8
LPs: 10/12-Inch 33rpm
KAPP: *56* 5-15

SUNRAYS
Singles: 7-Inch
TOWER: *64-67* 5-8
WARNER BROS: *62* 5-8
Picture Sleeves
TOWER: *67* 10-15
LPs: 10/12-Inch 33rpm
TOWER (5017; "Andrea"): *66* 50-100
Members: Rick Henn; Bryon Case; Vince Hozier;
Ed Medora; Marty DiGiovanni.

SUNRIZE
Singles: 7-Inch
BOARDWALK: *82* $1-3

SUNSHINE BAND:
see KC & THE SUNSHINE BAND

SUNSHINE COMPANY
Singles: 7-Inch
IMPERIAL: *67-68* 3-5
LPs: 10/12-Inch 33rpm
IMPERIAL: *67-68* 10-15
Members: Doug "Red" Mark; Maury Manseau;
Larry Sims; Merle Bregante; Mary Nance.
Also see REDEYE

SUPER LOVER CEE &
CASANOVA RUD
LPs: 10/12-Inch 33rpm
ELEKTRA: *88* 5-8

SUPER MAX
Singles: 7-Inch
VOYAGE: *79* 1-3

SUPER NATURE
Singles: 12-Inch 33/45rpm
POP ART: *85* 4-6

SUPERBS
Singles: 7-Inch
COLLECTABLES: 1-3
DORE: *64-67* 3-5
HERITAGE: *61* 4-6

SUPERIOR MOVEMENT
Singles: 7-Inch
CHYCAGO INT'L: *81-82* 1-3
LPs: 10/12-Inch 33rpm
CHYCAGO INT'L: *82* 5-8

SUPERLATIVES
Singles: 7-Inch
UPTITE: *66* 3-5
WESTBOUND: *69* 2-4

SUPERSAX
LPs: 10/12-Inch 33rpm
CAPITOL: *73-74* 5-10

SUPERTRAMP
Singles: 12-Inch 33/45rpm
A&M: *82-85* 4-6
Singles: 7-Inch
A&M: *71-85* 1-3
Picture Sleeves
A&M: *77-85* 1-3
LPs: 10/12-Inch 33rpm
A&M: *70-87* 8-12
MFSL (005; "Crime Of The
Century"): *78* 30-60

SUPERTRAMP — TAKE THE LONG WAY HOME

MFSL/UHQR (005; "Crime Of
The Century"): *78* $50-100
(Boxed set.)
MFSL (045; "Breakfast In America"): *80* . 25-50
Members: Rick Davies; Roger Hodgson; Doug
Thomson; Bob Benberg; John Helliwell.
Also see HODGSON, Roger

SUPREMES
Singles: 12-Inch 33/45rpm
MOTOWN: *79-81* 6-10
Singles: 7-Inch
GEORGE ALEXANDER INC. (1079;
"The Only Time
I'm Happy"): *65* 20-30
(Special premium record, with a Supremes inter-
view on the flip.)
MOTOWN (400 series): 1-3
MOTOWN (1027; "Your Heart
Belongs To Me"): *62* 10-15
MOTOWN (1034; "Let Me Go The
Right Way"): *62* 10-15
MOTOWN (1040; "My Heart Can't Take
It No More"): *63* 20-30
MOTOWN (1044; "A Breath Taking, First
Sight Soul Shaking, One Night Love Making,
Next Day Heart Breaking Guy"): *63* ...20-30
MOTOWN (1044; "A Breath Taking
Guy"): *63* 4-8
(Reissue, using a much shorter title.)
MOTOWN (1051; "When The Lovelight Starts
Shining Through His Eyes"): *63* 4-8
MOTOWN (1054; "Run, Run,
Run): *64* 15-25
MOTOWN (1060 through 1156): *64-69* 3-6
MOTOWN/TOPPS ("Where Did Our
Love Go"): *67* 50-75
MOTOWN/TOPPS ("Baby Love"): *67* ...50-75

MOTOWN/TOPPS ("Stop In The
Name Of Love"): *67* $50-75
(Topps Chewing Gum promotional items.
Cardboard flexi, picture discs. Issued with generic
paper sleeves.)
TAMLA (54038; "I Want A Guy"): *61* .. 60-75
TAMLA (54045; "Buttered
Popcorn"): *61* 35-45
Picture Sleeves
MOTOWN (1027; "Your Heart
Belongs To Me"): *62* 25-40
MOTOWN (1074 through 1156): *64-69* .. 5-12
(Not ALL of the numbers in this series were issued
with picture sleeves.)
Promotional Singles
AMERICAN INTERNATIONAL PICTURES
("Dr. Goldfoot And The
Bikini Machine"): *66* 20-40
(One-sided disc, used to promote the film of the
same name.)
EEOC ("Things Are Changing"): *65* 15-30
MOTOWN (1027 through 1054): *62-64* . 10-15
MOTOWN (1060 through 1156): *64-69* ... 5-8
(Black vinyl.)
MOTOWN (Colored vinyl): *65* 10-20
TOPPS: *67* 5-15
(Cardboard flexi-discs from the makers of Topps
chewing gum.)
EPs: 7-Inch 33/45rpm
MOTOWN: *64* 20-25
LPs: 10/12-Inch 33rpm
MOTOWN (100 & 200 series): *80-82* 5-8
MOTOWN (606; "Meet The
Supremes"): *63* 100-125
(Front cover pictures each member sitting on a
chair.)
MOTOWN (606; "Meet The
Supremes"): *63* 30-35
(Front cover pictures the head of each group mem-
ber.)
MOTOWN (621 through 638): *64-65* ... 20-25
MOTOWN (643 through 708): *66-70* ... 15-20
MOTOWN (794; "Anthology"): *74* 15-20
(3-LP set. Includes 12-page booklet.)
MOTOWN (900 series): *75* 6-10
MOTOWN (5000 series, except
5381): *83-84* 5-10
MOTOWN (5381; "25th
Anniversary"): *86* 15-20
(3-LP set. Includes 12-page booklet.)
NATURAL RESOURCES: *78* 6-10
Members: Diana Ross; Mary Wilson; Florence Bal-
lard; Cindy Birdsong.
Also see DIAMOND, Neil / Diana Ross &
The Supremes
Also see PRIMETTES

MOTOWN 1044
2648 W. Grand Boulevard
Detroit 8, Mich. 48 (3549)
Jobete, BMI
Produced by Smokey
TIME 2:20
DM 8-03930*
33 RPM

PROMOTIONAL   NOT FOR SALE

A BREATH TAKING, FIRST SIGHT SOUL
SHAKING, ONE NIGHT LOVE MAKING,
NEXT DAY HEART BREAKING GUY
(Wm. Robinson)

THE SUPREMES

Also see ROSS, Diana
Also see WILSON, Mary

SUPREMES
Singles: 7-Inch
MOTOWN (400 series): **$1-3**
MOTOWN (1162 through 1415): 70-77 ... **2-4**
LPs: 10/12-Inch 33rpm
MOTOWN (102; "Touch"): 71 .... **15-20**
(Open-end interview LP. Price includes script.
Promotional issue only.)
MOTOWN (700 through 900
series): 70-78 .... **8-12**
Members: Jean Terrell; Mary Wilson; Cindy
Birdsong.
Also see PAYNE, Scherrie
Also see TERRELL, Jean

SUPREMES, & The Four Tops
Singles: 7-Inch
MOTOWN (400 series): **1-3**
MOTOWN (1100 series): 70-71 .... **2-4**
EPs: 7-Inch 33/45rpm
MOTOWN (717; "Magnificant
Seven"): 70 .... **5-15**
(Jukebox issue.)
LPs: 10/12-Inch 33rpm
MOTOWN (100 series): 82 .... **5-8**
MOTOWN (700 series): 70-71 .... **10-12**
Also see FOUR TOPS

SUPREMES, & The Temptations
Singles: 7-Inch
MOTOWN (400 series): **1-3**
MOTOWN (1100 series): 68-69 .... **3-5**
Picture Sleeves
MOTOWN: 68 .... **3-5**
LPs: 10/12-Inch 33rpm
MOTOWN (100 series): 82 .... **5-8**
MOTOWN (600 series): 68-69 .... **10-12**

Also see SUPREMES
Also see TEMPTATIONS

SURF TRIO
LPs: 10/12-Inch 33rpm
VOXX: 87-88 .... **$5-8**

SURFACE
Singles: 12-Inch 33/45rpm
COLUMBIA: 86 .... **4-6**
SALSOUL: 83 .... **4-6**
Singles: 7-Inch
COLUMBIA: 86-88 .... **1-3**
SALSOUL: 83 .... **1-3**
LPs: 10/12-Inch 33rpm
COLUMBIA: 86-88 .... **5-8**

SURFARIS
Singles: 7-Inch
ABC: 74 .... **1-3**
CHANCELLOR: 63 .... **5-8**
DFS (11; "Wipe Out"): 63 .... **50-75**
DECCA: 63-66 .... **5-8**
DEL-FI: 63 .... **5-8**
DOT (Except 144 & 16479): 65-67 .... **5-8**
DOT (144; "Wipe Out"): 66 .... **3-5**
DOT (16479; "Wipe Out"): 63 .... **4-6**
FELSTED: 64 .... **5-8**
MCA: **1-3**
PRINCESS (50; "Wipe Out"): 63 .... **25-50**
(Longer version. Does not have "RE-1" etched in
the vinyl trailoff.)
PRINCESS (50; "Wipe Out"): 63 ...... **20-35**
(Short version, same as Dot issue. With "RE-1"
etched in the vinyl trailoff.)
REGANO: 63 .... **5-8**
Promotional Singles
DOT (144; "Wipe Out"): 66 .... **25-30**
(Colored vinyl.)
EPs: 7-Inch 33/45rpm
DECCA (2765; "Wipe Out"): 63 .... **20-30**
LPs: 10/12-Inch 33rpm
DECCA: 63-65 .... **25-30**
DOT (535; "Wipe Out"): 63 .... **30-35**
(Front cover reads "The Original Hit Version, Wipe
Out.")
DOT (535; "Wipe Out"): 63 .... **25-30**
(Front cover reads "Wipe Out & Surfer Joe and
Other Popular Selections By Other Instrumental
Groups." The Surfaris are heard only on *Wipe Out*
and *Surfer Joe*. Other tracks on this LP are by the
Challengers.)
DIPLOMAT: **12-15**
PICKWICK: 78 .... **8-10**
Members: Ron Wilson; Jim Fuller; Jim Pash; Pat
Connolly; Bob Berryhill; Ken Forssi. Though not
actual members, Richie Podolor, Chuck Girard, and
Gary Usher made appearances on Surfaris releases.

Also see BEACH BOYS / Dick Dale / Surfaris / Surf Kings

SURFARIS / Biscaynes
Singles: 7-Inch
NORTHRIDGE: *63* **$8-12**
REPRISE: *63* **4-8**
Also see SURFARIS (Original Surfaris)

SURRETT, Alfonzo
Singles: 7-Inch
MCA: *80* **1-3**

SURVIVOR
Singles: 12-Inch 33/45rpm
SCOTTI BROS: *79-86* **4-6**
Singles: 7-Inch
CASABLANCA: *84* **1-3**
SCOTTI BROS: *80-88* **1-3**
LPs: 10/12-Inch 33rpm
SCOTTI BROS (Except 362): *79-88* **5-8**
SCOTTI BROS (362; "Rebel
Girl"): *80* **10-12**
(Promotional issue only.)
Members: Jim Peterik; Jim Jameson.

SURVIVORS
Singles: 7-Inch
CAPITOL (5102; "Pamela
Jean"): *64* **100-125**
Members: Brian Wilson; Dave Nowlen; Bob Norberg; Rich Peterson.
Also see BEACH BOYS

SUSAN
Singles: 7-Inch
RCA VICTOR: *79* **1-3**
SCEPTER: *70* **2-4**
LPs: 10/12-Inch 33rpm
RCA VICTOR: *79* **5-8**

SUTCH, Screaming Lord:
see LORD SUTCH

SUTHERLAND BROTHERS
(Sutherland Brothers & Quiver)
Singles: 7-Inch
COLUMBIA: *75-79* **2-3**
ISLAND: *72-73* **2-4**
LPs: 10/12-Inch 33rpm
COLUMBIA: *75-76* **8-10**
ISLAND: *72-74* **8-10**

SUTTON, Glenn
Singles: 7-Inch
ABC: *73* **1-3**
EPIC: *67* **2-4**
MGM: *64-65* **3-5**
MERCURY: *78-86* **1-3**

LPs: 10/12-Inch 33rpm
MERCURY: *79* **$5-8**
Also see KELLUM, Murray / Glenn Sutton

SUTTON, Mike & Brenda
Singles: 7-Inch
SAM: *81-82* **1-3**

SUTTONS
Singles: 7-Inch
ROCSHIRE: *84* **1-3**
LPs: 10/12-Inch 33rpm
ROCSHIRE: *84* **5-8**

SUZY & THE RED STRIPES
(Linda McCartney & Wings)
Singles: 12-Inch 33/45rpm
CAPITOL: **4-8**
EPIC (361; "Seaside Woman"): *77* **20-30**
(Promotional issue only.)
Singles: 7-Inch
CAPITOL: **1-3**
EPIC (50403; "Seaside Woman"): *77* **4-6**
Promotional Singles
EPIC (50403; "Seaside Woman"): *77* ... **30-40**
(Colored vinyl.)
EPIC (50403; "Seaside Woman"): *77* ... **10-20**
(Black vinyl.)
Also see MC CARTNEY, Paul

SUZY Q
Singles: 7-Inch
ATLANTIC: *81* **1-3**

SVENSSON, Bo
LPs: 10/12-Inch 33rpm
GOLDEN BOY: *88* **5-8**

SWALLOWS
Singles: 78rpm
AFTER HOURS (104; "My Baby"): *54* . **50-75**
KING (4466; "Since You've
Been Away"): *51* **50-100**
KING (4458; "Will You Be Mine?"): *51* **50-100**
KING (4466; "Since You've
Been Away"): *51* **50-100**
KING (4501; "Eternally"): *51* **40-60**
KING (4515; "Tell Me Why"): *51* **40-60**
KING (4525; "Beside You"): *52* **25-50**
KING (4533; "I Only Have
Eyes For You"): *52* **40-60**
KING (4579; "Where Do I
Go From Here?"): *52* **40-60**
KING (4612; "Laugh"): *53* **25-50**
KING (4632; "Nobody's Lovin' Me"): *53* **25-50**
KING (4656; "Trust Me"): *53* **25-50**
KING (4676; "I'll Be Waiting"): *53* **25-50**

Singles: 7-Inch

AFTER HOURS (104; "My
Baby"): *54* $300-400
GUSTO: 1-3
KING (4458; "Will You
Be Mine?"): *51* 400-600
KING (4466; "Since You've
Been Away"): *51* 400-600
KING (4501; "Eternally"): *51* 350-500
(Black vinyl.)
KING (4501; "Eternally"): *51* 400-600
(Colored vinyl.)
KING (4515; "Tell Me Why"): *51* 350-500
(Based on other King numbers on colored plastic,
this issue could also have been. However, none are
yet confirmed.)
KING (4525; "Beside You"): *52* 100-200
KING (4533; "I Only Have
Eyes For You"): *52* 300-400
KING (4579; "Where Do I
Go From Here?"): *52* 300-400
KING (4612; "Laugh"): *53* 150-250
KING (4632; "Nobody's
Lovin' Me"): *53* 150-250
KING (4656; "Trust Me"): *53* 100-200
KING (4676; "I'll Be Waiting"): *53* ... 150-200
Members: Junior Denby; Ed Rich; Earl Hurley;
Fred Johnson; Norris Mack; Dee Bailey; Buddy
Bailey; Irving Turner; Al France; Cal Kollette.

SWALLOWS

Singles: 7-Inch

FEDERAL: *58* 8-10

SWAMP DOGG

(Jerry Williams; Swamp Dogg With The Riders
Of The New Funk)

Singles: 7-Inch

ALA: *82* 1-3
ATOMIC ARTS: *79* 2-3
BRUT: *73* 2-4
CANYON: *70* 2-5
CREAM: *73* 2-4
ELEKTRA: *72* 2-4
ISLAND: *73* 2-4
MUSICOR: *77* 2-3
RARE BULLET: *83-85* 1-3
ROKER: *71* 2-4
STONEDOGG: *73* 2-4
SWAMP DOGG PRESENTS: *72* 2-4
WIZARD: *77* 2-4

LPs: 10/12-Inch 33rpm

ALA: *82* 5-8
CANYON: *70* 10-15
CREAM: *72* 8-10
ELEKTRA: *71* 8-10

ISLAND: *73* $8-10
MUSICOR: *77* 5-8
TAKOMA: *81* 5-8
WAR BRIDE: *82* 5-8
WIZARD: *78* 5-8

SWAN, Billy

Singles: 7-Inch

A&M: *78-79* 2-3
COLUMBIA: *76-77* 2-3
EPIC: *81-83* 1-3
MGM: *68* 5-10
MERCURY: *86-87* 1-3
MONUMENT: *66-76* 2-4
RISING SONS: *67* 2-4

LPs: 10/12-Inch 33rpm

A&M: *78* 5-8
COLUMBIA/MONUMENT: *77* 5-8
EPIC: *81* 5-8
MONUMENT: *74-78* 6-10

SWANN, Bettye

Singles: 7-Inch

A-BET: *72-74* 2-4
ATLANTIC: *72-76* 2-4
BIG TREE: 2-3
CAPITOL: *68-70* 2-4
FAME: *71* 2-4
MONEY: *65-67* 3-5

Picture Sleeves

CAPITOL: *69* 2-4

LPs: 10/12-Inch 33rpm

A-BET: *72* 8-10
ATLANTIC: *72-75* 8-10
CAPITOL: *69* 10-12
MONEY: *67* 10-15
Also see DEES, Sam, & Bettye Swann

SWANS

Singles: 7-Inch

CAMEO: *64* 20-25
SWAN: *63* 8-10

SWANSON, Brad, & His Whispering Organ

LPs: 10/12-Inch 33rpm

THUNDERBIRD: *69* 5-10

SWAYZE, Patrick, & Wendy Fraser

Singles: 7-Inch

RCA VICTOR: *88* 1-3

SWEAT, Keith

Singles: 7-Inch

ELEKTRA: *87* 1-3
VINTERTAINMENT: *88* 1-3

LPs: 10/12-Inch 33rpm

VINTERTAINMENT: *88* 5-8

SWEAT BAND
Singles: 7-Inch
UNCLE JAM: *80* $1-3
LPs: 10/12-Inch 33rpm
UNCLE JAM: *80* 5-8
Also see BOOTSY'S RUBBER BAND

SWEATHOG
Singles: 7-Inch
COLUMBIA: *71* 2-4
LPs: 10/12-Inch 33rpm
COLUMBIA: *71-72* 8-10

SWEENEY, Jimmy
(Jimmy Sweeney & The Varieteers)
Singles: 78rpm
HICKORY: *53* 20-40
TENNESSEE: *50* 5-10
Singles: 7-Inch
BUCKLEY: *62* 4-6
COLUMBIA: *59* 5-8
DATE: 3-6
HICKORY (1004; "Deep Blues"): *53* ... 75-100

SWEENY TODD
Singles: 7-Inch
LONDON: *76* 2-4
Member: Bryan Guy Adams.
Also see GILDER, Nick

SWEET
Singles: 7-Inch
BELL: *71-74* 2-4
CAPITOL: *75-79* 2-3
LPs: 10/12-Inch 33rpm
BELL: *73* 10-20
CAPITOL (Except 16000
series): *75-79* 8-10
CAPITOL (16000 series): *80-82* 5-8
KORY: *77* 8-10
Promotional LPs
CAPITOL (8849; "Short &
Sweet"): *78* 20-25
CAPITOL (11129; "Cut Above
The Rest"): *79* 45-55
(Boxed set, containing the LP, 8-track and cassette
issues of *Cut Above The Rest*, plus a group photo &
biography.)

SWEET, Rachel
Singles: 12-Inch 33/45rpm
STIFF/COLUMBIA: *79* 10-15
(Promotional issue only.)
Singles: 7-Inch
COLUMBIA: *81-83* 1-3
DERRICK: *76-78* 2-4
STIFF/COLUMBIA: *79-80* 1-3

LPs: 10/12-Inch 33rpm
COLUMBIA: *81-82* $5-8
STIFF/COLUMBIA: *79-80* 5-8
Also see SMITH, Rex, & Rachel Sweet

SWEET CREAM
Singles: 12-Inch 33/45rpm
SHADYBROOK: *78* 4-6
Singles: 7-Inch
SHADYBROOK: *78* 2-3

SWEET DREAMS
Singles: 7-Inch
ABC: *74* 2-4

SWEET G.
Singles: 12-Inch 33/45rpm
FEVER: *83* 4-6

SWEET INSPIRATIONS
Singles: 12-Inch 33/45rpm
RSO: *79* 4-6
Singles: 7-Inch
ATLANTIC: *67-71* 2-4
CARIBOU: *77* 2-3
RSO: *79* 2-3
STAX: *73-74* 2-4
LPs: 10/12-Inch 33rpm
ATLANTIC: *68-70* 10-12
RSO: *79* 5-8
STAX: *73* 8-10
Members: Cissy Houston; Sylvia Shemwell; Myrna
Smith; Estelle Brown.
Also see FRANKLIN, Aretha
Also see HOUSTON, Cissy
Also see PRESLEY, Elvis
Also see RASCALS

SWEET MUSIC
Singles: 7-Inch
WAND: *76* 2-3

SWEET OBSESSION
Singles: 7-Inch
EPIC: *88* 1-3
LPs: 10/12-Inch 33rpm
EPIC: *88* 5-8

SWEET SENSATION
Singles: 7-Inch
ATCO: *88* 1-3
PYE: *74-75* 2-3
LPs: 10/12-Inch 33rpm
ATCO: *88* 5-8
PYE: *75* 6-10

SWEET TEE
Singles: 7-Inch
PROFILE: *88* 1-3

LPs: 10/12-Inch 33rpm
PROFILE: 88 .... $5-8

SWEET THUNDER
Singles: 7-Inch
FANTASY: 79 1-3
WMOT: 79 1-3
LPs: 10/12-Inch 33rpm
WMOT: 79 5-8

SWEETWATER
Singles: 7-Inch
REPRISE: 68-71 3-5
LPs: 10/12-Inch 33rpm
REPRISE: 68-71 10-15

SWING OUT SISTER
Singles: 7-Inch
MERCURY: 87-88 1-3
LPs: 10/12-Inch 33rpm
MERCURY: 87 5-8

SWINGIN' MEDALLIONS
Singles: 7-Inch
CAPITOL: 68 3-5
COLLECTABLES: 1-3
DOT: 65 5-8
4 SALE: 66 12-15
1-2-3: 70 2-4
SMASH: 66-67 4-6
LPs: 10/12-Inch 33rpm
SMASH: 66 25-30
Also see PIECES OF EIGHT

SWINGING BLUE JEANS
Singles: 7-Inch
IMPERIAL: 64-67 5-8
LPs: 10/12-Inch 33rpm
IMPERIAL: 64 25-35
LIBERTY: 82 5-8

SWINGLE SINGERS
LPs: 10/12-Inch 33rpm
COLUMBIA: 76 4-6
PHILIPS: 63-72 4-10

SWISS MOVEMENT
Singles: 7-Inch
CASABLANCA: 74 3-5
PERKY: 68 15-25
RCA VICTOR: 73 2-4
LPs: 10/12-Inch 33rpm
RCA VICTOR: 73 8-12

SWITCH
Singles: 7-Inch
GORDY (Black vinyl): 78-82 1-3
GORDY (Colored vinyl): 78-82 4-6
(Promotional issues only.)
TOTAL EXPERIENCE: 82-84 1-3

LPs: 10/12-Inch 33rpm
GORDY: 78-81 .... $5-8
TOTAL EXPERIENCE: 82-84 5-8

SYBIL
Singles: 7-Inch
NEXT PLATEAU: 87-88 1-3

SYKES, Keith
Singles: 7-Inch
BACKSTREET: 80 1-3
LPs: 10/12-Inch 33rpm
BACKSTREET: 80 5-8
MIDLAND INT'L: 77 8-10
VANGUARD: 70-71 10-12

SYLVAIN SYLVAIN
Singles: 7-Inch
RCA VICTOR: 79 2-3
LPs: 10/12-Inch 33rpm
RCA VICTOR: 79 5-8
Also see NEW YORK DOLLS

SYLVERS
Singles: 12-Inch 33/45rpm
CASABLANCA: 79 4-6
GEFFEN: 84-85 4-6
SOLAR: 81-82 4-6
Singles: 7-Inch
CAPITOL: 75-78 2-3
CASABLANCA: 78-79 1-3
GEFFEN: 84-85 1-3
MGM: 72-74 2-3
PRIDE: 72-73 2-4
SOLAR: 81-82 1-3
VERVE: 71 2-4
Picture Sleeves
GEFFEN: 84-85 1-3
LPs: 10/12-Inch 33rpm
CAPITOL: 75-78 5-8
CASABLANCA: 78-79 5-8
CONCEPT: 81 5-8
GEFFEN: 84 5-8
MGM: 72-74 8-10
PRIDE: 72-73 8-10
SOLAR: 81 5-8
Members: Foster Sylvers; Edmund Sylvers; Pay
Sylvers; Angie Sylvers.
Also see SYLVERS, Edmund
Also see SYLVERS, Foster

SYLVERS, Edmund
Singles: 7-Inch
CASABLANCA: 80 1-3
LPs: 10/12-Inch 33rpm
CASABLANCA: 80 5-8
Also see SYLVERS

SYLVERS, Foster
Singles: 7-Inch
MGM: *73* $2-3
PRIDE: *73* 2-4
LPs: 10/12-Inch 33rpm
MGM: *74* 6-10
PRIDE: *73* 8-10
Also see SYLVERS

SYLVESTER
(Sylvester James)
Singles: 12-Inch 33/45rpm
FANTASY: *78-79* 4-6
MEGATONE: *83-86* 4-6
Singles: 7-Inch
FANTASY (Black vinyl): *78-79* 1-3
FANTASY (Colored vinyl): *78-79* 4-8
(Promotional issues only.)
HONEY: *80-81* 1-3
MEGATONE: *83-86* 1-3
WARNER BROS: *87* 1-3
LPs: 10/12-Inch 33rpm
FANTASY: *78-81* 5-8
HONEY: *80-81* 5-8
MEGATONE: *83-86* 5-8
WARNER BROS: *87* 5-8

SYLVESTER, Tony, & The New Ingredient
Singles: 7-Inch
MERCURY: *76* 2-3

SYLVIA
(Sylvia Vanderpool; Sylvia Robinson)
Singles: 12-Inch 33/45rpm
SUGARHILL: *82* 4-6
VIBRATION: *77* 4-6
Singles: 7-Inch
ALL PLATINUM: *74* 2-4
STANG: *70* 2-4
SUGARHILL: *81* 1-3
VIBRATION: *73-78* 2-4
LPs: 10/12-Inch 33rpm
SUGARHILL: *81* 5-8
VIBRATION: *73-78* 6-10
Also see LITTLE SYLVIA
Also see MICKEY & SYLVIA
Also see SYLVIA & RALFI PAGAN
Also see TURNER, Ike & Tina

SYLVIA
(Sylvia Kirby Allen)
Singles: 7-Inch
RCA VICTOR: *81-87* 1-3
Picture Sleeves
RCA VICTOR: *81-86* 1-3

LPs: 10/12-Inch 33rpm
RCA VICTOR: *81-86* $5-8

SYLVIA & RALFI PAGAN
Singles: 7-Inch
VIBRATION: *73* 2-4
Also see SYLVIA

SYMBA
Singles: 7-Inch
VENTURE: *80* 1-3

SYMBOL 8
Singles: 7-Inch
SHOCK: *77-78* 2-3

SYMS, Sylvia
Singles: 78rpm
ATLANTIC: *52-53* 2-5
DECCA: *56-57* 2-5
Singles: 7-Inch
ATLANTIC: *52-53* 3-6
COLUMBIA: *59-65* 2-5
DECCA: *56-64* 2-5
PRESTIGE: *67* 2-3
RORI: *62* 2-4
EPs: 7-Inch 33/45rpm
ATLANTIC: *56* 5-15
DECCA: *55* 5-15
LPs: 10/12-Inch 33rpm
A&M: *78* 5-8
ATLANTIC (137; "Songs By
Sylvia Syms"): *53* 50-75
(10-Inch LPs.)
ATLANTIC (1243; "Songs By
Sylvia Syms"): *56* 20-40
(With Atlantic logo at top of label.)
ATLANTIC (1243; "Songs By
Sylvia Syms"): *60* 15-25
(With Atlantic logo on side of label.)
ATLANTIC (18000 series): *76* 5-8
COLUMBIA: *60* 15-25
DECCA: *55* 20-40
KAPP: *61* 10-20
MOVIETONE: *67* 10-15
PRESTIGE: *65-67* 10-25
REPRISE: *82* 5-8
20TH CENTURY-FOX: *64* 10-20
VERSION: *54* 20-40
(10-Inch LPs.)

SYNDICATE OF SOUND
Singles: 7-Inch
BELL: *66-67* 3-5
BUDDAH: *70* 2-4
CAPITOL: *69* 2-4
DEL-FI: *66* 4-6
HUSH: *66* 8-10

Syndicate of Sound

SCARLET: *66* **$8-10**
LPs: 10/12-Inch 33rpm
BELL: *66* **25-30**
PERFORMANCE: *88* **5-8**
Members: Jim Sawyers; Bob Gonzalez; John
Sharkey; Don Baskin; John Duckworth; Larry Roy;
Carl Scott; Barrie Thompson; Dennis Tracy.

SYNERGY
Singles: 7-Inch
PASSPORT: *76* **2-3**
LPs: 10/12-Inch 33rpm
PASSPORT (Black vinyl): *75-84* **5-8**
PASSPORT (Clear vinyl): *78* **8-10**

SYREETA
(Syreeta Wright)
Singles: 7-Inch
MOTOWN: *74-80* **1-3**
MOWEST: *72* **2-4**
TAMLA: *80-83* **1-3**
LPs: 10/12-Inch 33rpm
MOTOWN: *74-77* **6-10**
MOWEST: *72* **8-12**
TAMLA: *77-81* **5-8**
Also see PRESTON, Billy, & Syreeta

SYSTEM
Singles: 12-Inch 33/45rpm
MIRAGE: *83-86* **4-6**
Singles: 7-Inch
ATCO: *88* **1-3**
ATLANTIC: *87* **1-3**
MIRAGE: *83-86* **1-3**
LPs: 10/12-Inch 33rpm
ATLANTIC: *87* **5-8**

MIRAGE: *83-86* **$5-8**

SZABO, Gabor
Singles: 7-Inch
BLUE THUMB: *70* **2-3**
BUDDAH: *70* **2-3**
CTI: *73* **1-3**
IMPULSE: *66-68* **2-4**
MERCURY: *76-77* **1-3**
REPRISE: *73* **1-3**
SKYE: *68-70* **2-3**
LPs: 10/12-Inch 33rpm
BLUE THUMB: *70* **8-12**
BUDDAH: *70* **8-12**
CTI: *73-74* **8-12**
IMPULSE: *66-70* **10-20**
MCA: *82* **5-8**
MERCURY: *76* **5-10**
SALVATION: *75* **5-10**
SKYE: *68-70* **8-12**
Also see HORNE, Lena, & Gabor Szabo
Also see WOMACK, Bobby

T

TFO
Singles: 7-Inch
VENTURE: *80-81* **1-3**

T.H.P. ORCHESTRA
Singles: 7-Inch
ATLANTIC: *79* **1-3**
BUTTERFLY (Black vinyl): *77-78* **2-3**
BUTTERFLY (Colored vinyl): *77-78* **3-5**
LPs: 10/12-Inch 33rpm
ATLANTIC: *79* **5-8**
BUTTERFLY: *77* **8-10**

TKA
(Total Knowledge in Action)
Singles: 12-Inch 33/45rpm
TOMMY BOY: *86* **4-6**
Singles: 7-Inch
TOMMY BOY: *86-88* **1-3**
LPs: 10/12-Inch 33rpm
TOMMY BOY: *88* **5-8**

TKO
Singles: 7-Inch
INFINITY: *79* **2-3**
LPs: 10/12-Inch 33rpm
INFINITY: *79* **5-8**

T.M.G.
Singles: 7-Inch
ATCO: *79* **2-3**

LPs: 10/12-Inch 33rpm
ATCO: 79 .... $5-8

TMP BAND
Singles: 7-Inch
CRITIQUE: 86 1-3

TNT BAND
Singles: 7-Inch
COTIQUE: 69 2-5

T.S.U. TORONADOS
Singles: 7-Inch
ATLANTIC: 68-69 2-4
VOLT: 69-70 2-4

TTF
(Today, Tomorrow, Forever)
Singles: 7-Inch
CURTOM: 80 1-3
GOLD COAST: 81 1-3
RSO: 80 1-3
LPs: 10/12-Inch 33rpm
GOLD COAST: 81 5-8

T.Z.
Singles: 12-Inch 33/45rpm
STREET SOUND: 83 4-6

TA MARA & THE SEEN
Singles: 12-Inch 33/45rpm
A&M: 85-86 4-6
Singles: 7-Inch
A&M: 85-88 1-3
LPs: 10/12-Inch 33rpm
A&M: 85 5-8

TA'BOO
Singles: 12-Inch 33/45rpm
ACME: 84 4-6

TACO
(Taco Ockerse)
Singles: 12-Inch 33/45rpm
RCA VICTOR: 83-84 4-6
Singles: 7-Inch
RCA VICTOR: 83-84 1-3
LPs: 10/12-Inch 33rpm
RCA VICTOR: 83-84 5-8

TAFF, Russ
Singles: 7-Inch
HORIZON: 85-86 1-3
LPs: 10/12-Inch 33rpm
MYRRH: 5-8

TAIL GATORS
LPs: 10/12-Inch 33rpm
RESTLESS: 88 5-8
WRESTLER: 87 5-8

TAJ MAHAL
Singles: 7-Inch
COLUMBIA (10000 series): 75 .... $2-3
COLUMBIA (44000 series): 67-69 3-5
COLUMBIA (45000 series): 69-74 2-4
Picture Sleeves
COLUMBIA: 67 3-5
LPs: 10/12-Inch 33rpm
COLUMBIA: 68-81 6-12
WARNER BROS: 77 5-10
Also see SPRINGSTEEN, Bruce / Albert
Hammond / Loudon Wainwright III / Taj Mahal

TAKA BOOM: see BOOM, Taka

TALK TALK
Singles: 12-Inch 33/45rpm
EMI AMERICA: 82-86 4-6
Singles: 7-Inch
EMI AMERICA: 82-86 1-3
LPs: 10/12-Inch 33rpm
EMI AMERICA: 82-86 5-8

TALKING HEADS
Singles: 12-Inch 33/45rpm
SIRE: 79-86 4-6
Singles: 7-Inch
SIRE: 77-86 1-3
Picture Sleeves
SIRE: 78-85 1-3
LPs: 10/12-Inch 33rpm
SIRE: 77-86 5-8
WARNER BROS (104; "Live On
Tour"): 79 10-15
(Promotional issue only.)
Member: David Byrne.
Also see BYRNE, David

TAMI SHOW
Singles: 7-Inch
CHRYSALIS: 88 1-3

TAMPA RED
(Hudson Whittaker)
Singles: 78rpm
BLUEBIRD: 44-45 10-20
RCA VICTOR: 45-54 5-10
Singles: 7-Inch
RCA VICTOR (47-4000 & 47-5000
series): 51-54 25-35
RCA VICTOR (50-0000 series): 49-51 .. 30-50
LPs: 10/12-Inch 33rpm
BLUEBIRD: 75 10-15
BLUES CLASSICS: 5-8
PRESTIGE BLUESVILLE: 61-62 20-25
YAZOO: 10-12

TAMS

Singles: 7-Inch

MINK (22; "Memory Lane"): *59* $10-20
(*Memory Lane* was first issued in 1959 showing
the group as the Stereos. The same track was reis-
sued in 1963, shown as by the Tams and then by
the Hippies.)
PARKWAY (863; "Memory
Lane"): *63* 10-15
Also see HIPPIES / Reggie Harrison
Also see STEREOS

TAMS

Singles: 7-Inch

ABC: *68-73* 2-4
ABC-PARAMOUNT: *63-64* 3-5
APT/ABC: *72* 2-4
ARLEN: *62-63* 4-6
CAPITOL: *71* 3-5
COLLECTABLES: 1-3
COMPLEAT: *83* 1-3
DAISY: 5-10
DUNHILL: *71* 2-4
GENERAL AMERICAN: *62* 5-8
GUSTO: *80* 1-3
1-2-3: *70* 2-4
KING: *65* 3-5
MCA: 1-3
RIPETE: *82* 2-3
ROULETTE: 1-3
SOUTH: *73* 2-4
SWAN: *60* 5-8
WONDER: *82* 2-3

LPs: 10/12-Inch 33rpm

ABC: *67-69* 10-12
ABC-PARAMOUNT: *64* 15-20
BRYLEN: *84* 5-8
CAPITOL: *79* 5-8
COMPLEAT: *83* 5-8
1-2-3: *70* 8-10
SOUNDS SOUTH: *77* 8-10
Members: Joe Pope; Charles Pope; Robert Lee
Smith; Horace Key; Albert Cottle.

TANEGA, Norma

Singles: 7-Inch

ABC: *73* 2-4
ERIC: 1-3
NEW VOICE: *66-67* 3-5
VIRGO: *73* 1-3

LPs: 10/12-Inch 33rpm

NEW VOICE: *66* 15-20

TANGERINE DREAM

Singles: 7-Inch

EMI AMERICA: *84* 1-3
VIRGIN: *75-77* 2-3

LPs: 10/12-Inch 33rpm

EMI AMERICA: *84* $5-8
ELEKTRA: *81* 5-8
MCA: *77* 5-8
PRIVATE: *88* 5-8
VIRGIN: *74-77* 8-12
Members: Peter Baumann; Chris Franks; Ed Froese.
Also see BAUMANN, Peter

TANGERINE DREAM / Jon Anderson / Bryan Ferry

LPs: 10/12-Inch 33rpm

MCA (6165; "Legend"): *86* 6-10
(Soundtrack.)
Also see ANDERSON, Jon
Also see FERRY, Bryan
Also see TANGERINE DREAM

TANNER, Gary

Singles: 7-Inch

20TH CENTURY-FOX: *78* 2-3

TANNER, Marc, Band

Singles: 7-Inch

ELEKTRA: *79* 1-3
PRIVATE I: 1-3

LPs: 10/12-Inch 33rpm

ELEKTRA: *78-80* 5-8
PRIVATE I: 5-8

TANTRUM

Singles: 7-Inch

OVATION: *79* 1-3

LPs: 10/12-Inch 33rpm

OVATION: *79* 5-8

TARHEEL SLIM
(Alden Bunn)

Singles: 78rpm

FIRE: *59-60* 15-25

Singles: 7-Inch

FIRE: *59-60* 10-20
FURY: *59* 10-20
Also see BUNN, Allen
Also see LOVERS

TARHEEL SLIM & LITTLE ANN
(Slim & Ann; Slim & Little Ann; Tarheel Slim &
Lil' Annie)

Singles: 78rpm

FIRE: *59-60* 15-25

Singles: 7-Inch

ATCO: *63* 4-6
FIRE: *59-62* 10-20
PORT: *65* 3-5
Also see TARHEEL SLIM

TARNEY-SPENCER BAND
Singles: 7-Inch
A&M: 78-81 ....$1-3
PRIVATE STOCK: 76 2-3
LPs: 10/12-Inch 33rpm
A&M: 79 5-8
Members: Alan Tarney; Trevor Spencer.

TARRIERS
Singles: 78rpm
GLORY: 56 4-8
Singles: 7-Inch
DECCA: 63-64 2-4
GLORY: 56 4-8
UNITED ARTISTS: 59 2-5
LPs: 10/12-Inch 33rpm
ATLANTIC: 60 15-20
DECCA: 62-64 10-15
GLORY: 57 40-50
KAPP: 63 10-15
UNITED ARTISTS: 59 15-20
Members: Erik Darling; Alan Arkin; Bob Carey.
Also see MARTIN, Vince
Also see ROOFTOP SINGERS
Also see WEISSBERG, Eric

TASSELS
Singles: 7-Inch
AMY: 66 3-5
MADISON: 59 10-15

TASTE
Singles: 7-Inch
ATCO: 69-70 2-4
LPs: 10/12-Inch 33rpm
ATCO: 69-70 10-15
Member: Rory Gallagher.
Also see GALLAGHER, Rory

TASTE OF HONEY
Singles: 12-Inch 33/45rpm
CAPITOL (Except 9572): 78-79 4-6
CAPITOL (9572; "Sukiyaki): 80 8-10
(Fan-shaped disc. Promotional issue only.)
MCA: 84 4-6
Singles: 7-Inch
CAPITOL: 78-82 1-3
MCA: 84 1-3
Picture Sleeves
CAPITOL: 78-82 1-3
LPs: 10/12-Inch 33rpm
CAPITOL: 78-82 5-8
Members: Janice Johnson; Hazel Payne.
Also see FELDER, Wilton

TATE, Howard
Singles: 7-Inch
TURNTABLE: 69-70 3-5

VERVE: 66-68 ....$3-6
LPs: 10/12-Inch 33rpm
ATLANTIC: 69 10-15
TURNTABLE: 8-10
VERVE: 67-68 12-20

TATE, Tommy
Singles: 7-Inch
JACKSON SOUND: 70 2-4
KOKO: 72-76 2-3
OKEH: 66 3-5

TAVARES
Singles: 12-Inch 33/45rpm
CAPITOL: 77-79 4-6
RCA VICTOR: 82-84 4-6
Singles: 7-Inch
CAPITOL: 73-80 1-3
RCA VICTOR: 82-84 1-3
LPs: 10/12-Inch 33rpm
CAPITOL: 73-81 8-10
RCA VICTOR: 82-83 5-8

TAWATHA
Singles: 7-Inch
EPIC: 87 1-3

TAXXI
Singles: 7-Inch
FANTASY: 82 1-3
LPs: 10/12-Inch 33rpm
FANTASY: 82 5-8
MCA: 85 5-8

TAYLOR, Alex
Singles: 7-Inch
BANG: 78-79 1-3
CAPRICORN: 71 2-4
DUNHILL: 74 2-4
LPs: 10/12-Inch 33rpm
CAPRICORN: 71 8-10
DUNHILL: 74 8-10

TAYLOR, Andy
Singles: 12-Inch 33/45rpm
ATLANTIC: 86 4-6
Singles: 7-Inch
ATLANTIC: 86 1-3
MCA: 86-87 1-3
Also see DURAN DURAN
Also see POWER STATION

TAYLOR, Austin
Singles: 7-Inch
LAURIE: 60-61 4-6
Also see TAYLOR, Ted

TAYLOR, B. E., Group
Singles: 12-Inch 33/45rpm
EPIC: 84 4-6

Singles: 7-Inch
EPIC: *84-86* $1-3
MCA: *83-84* 1-3
LPs: 10/12-Inch 33rpm
MCA: *82* 5-8

TAYLOR, Bobby
(Bobby Taylor & The Vancouvers)
Singles: 7-Inch
BUDDAH: *72* 2-4
GORDY: *68-69* 3-5
INTEGRA: *68* 8-12
PLAYBOY: *75* 2-4
SUNFLOWER: *72* 2-4
TOMMY: *73* 2-4
LPs: 10/12-Inch 33rpm
GORDY: *68-69* 10-15
Members: Bobby Taylor; Wes Henderson; Eddie
Patterson; Robbie King; Ted Lewis; Tommy
Chong.
Also see CHEECH & CHONG

TAYLOR, Debbie
Singles: 7-Inch
ARISTA: *75-76* 2-3
DECCA: *68* 2-4
GWP: *69* 2-4
POLYDOR: *74* 2-4
TODAY: *72* 2-4
LPs: 10/12-Inch 33rpm
TODAY: *72* 6-10

TAYLOR, Felice
Singles: 7-Inch
KENT: *68* 3-5
MUSTANG: *67* 4-6

TAYLOR, Gary
Singles: 7-Inch
VIRGIN: *88* 1-3
LPs: 10/12-Inch 33rpm
VIRGIN: *88* 5-8

TAYLOR, Gloria
Singles: 7-Inch
COLUMBIA: *74* 2-4
GLO-WHIZ: *69* 3-5
SILVER FOX: *69* 2-4

TAYLOR, James
(James Taylor & The Original Flying Machine)
Singles: 7-Inch
APPLE: *69-70* 2-4
CAPITOL: *76* 2-3
COLUMBIA: *77-88* 1-3
EUPHORIA: *71* 2-4
WARNER BROS: *70-76* 2-4
LPs: 10/12-Inch 33rpm
APPLE: *69* 10-15

COLUMBIA: *77-88* $5-10
EUPHORIA: *71* 12-15
TRI: *73* 8-10
WARNER BROS: *70-77* 8-10
Also see DOOBIE BROTHERS, James Hall,
& James Taylor
Also see DOOBIE BROTHERS / Kate Taylor
& The Simon-Taylor Family
Also see FLYING MACHINE
Also see GARFUNKEL, Art
Also see KING DREAM CHORUS &
HOLIDAY CREW
Also see SIMON, Carly, & James Taylor

TAYLOR, James, & J. D. Souther
Singles: 7-Inch
COLUMBIA: *81* 1-3
Also see SOUTHER, J. D.
Also see TAYLOR, James

TAYLOR, John
Singles: 12-Inch 33/45rpm
CAPITOL: *86* 4-6
Singles: 7-Inch
CAPITOL: *86* 1-3
LPs: 10/12-Inch 33rpm
CAPITOL: *86* 5-8
Also see DURAN DURAN
Also see POWER STATION

TAYLOR, Johnnie
(Johnny Taylor)
Singles: 7-Inch
BEVERLY GLEN: *82* 1-3
COLUMBIA: *76-80* 1-3
DERBY: *63-64* 3-5
MALACO: *83-87* 1-3
RCA VICTOR: *77* 2-3
SAR: *61-65* 3-5
STAX: *66-77* 2-4
LPs: 10/12-Inch 33rpm
BEVERLY GLEN: *82* 5-8
COLUMBIA: *76-81* 6-10
MALACO: *83-88* 5-8
RCA VICTOR: *77* 8-10
STAX: *67-83* 6-10

TAYLOR, Johnnie, & Carla Thomas
Singles: 7-Inch
STAX: *69* 2-4
Also see TAYLOR, Johnnie
Also see THOMAS, Carla

TAYLOR, Kate
Singles: 7-Inch
COLUMBIA: *77-79* 2-3
COTILLION: *71* 2-4

LPs: 10/12-Inch 33rpm
COLUMBIA: 78-79 .... $5-8
COTILLION: 71 8-10
  Also see DOOBIE BROTHERS / Kate Taylor
& The Simon-Taylor Family

TAYLOR, Koko
(Cocoa Taylor)
Singles: 7-Inch
CHECKER: 66-68 3-5
U.S.A.: 63 5-8
LPs: 10/12-Inch 33rpm
ALLIGATOR: 76-81 5-8
CHESS: 69-72 10-12

TAYLOR, Little Johnny
Singles: 7-Inch
GALAXY: 63-64 3-5
RONN: 71-79 2-4
LPs: 10/12-Inch 33rpm
BEVERLY GLEN: 87 5-8
GALAXY: 63 15-20
ICHIBAN: 88 5-8
RONN: 72-79 6-10

TAYLOR, Little Johnny, & Ted Taylor
LPs: 10/12-Inch 33rpm
RONN: 73 8-10
  Also see TAYLOR, Little Johnny
  Also see TAYLOR, Ted

TAYLOR, Livingston
Singles: 7-Inch
CAPRICORN: 70-73 2-4
CRITIQUE: 88 1-3
EPIC: 78-80 1-3
LPs: 10/12-Inch 33rpm
CAPRICORN: 79 5-8
EPIC: 78 5-8
  Also see DOOBIE BROTHERS / Kate Taylor
& The Simon-Taylor Family

TAYLOR, Mick
Singles: 7-Inch
COLUMBIA: 79 2-3
LPs: 10/12-Inch 33rpm
COLUMBIA: 79 5-8
  Also see MAYALL, John
  Also see ROLLING STONES

TAYLOR, R. Dean
Singles: 7-Inch
AUDIO MASTER (1; "At The High
  School Dance"): 60 75-150
BARRY (3023; "At The High
  School Dance"): 60 50-100
  (Canadian.)
FARR: 76 2-4

JANE: 77 .... $2-3
MALA: 62 5-8
MOTOWN: 1-3
RAGAMUFFIN: 79 1-3
RARE EARTH: 70-72 2-4
20TH CENTURY-FOX: 81 1-3
V.I.P.: 65-68 3-5
Picture Sleeves
RARE EARTH: 71 2-4
LPs: 10/12-Inch 33rpm
RARE EARTH: 70 10-12

TAYLOR, Roger
Singles: 7-Inch
CAPITOL: 84 1-3
ELEKTRA: 81 1-3
LPs: 10/12-Inch 33rpm
CAPITOL: 84 5-8
ELEKTRA: 81 5-8
  Also see ARCADIA
  Also see QUEEN

TAYLOR, Ted
Singles: 7-Inch
ALARM: 76 2-4
APT: 62 3-5
ATCO: 65-66 3-5
DADE: 63 3-5
DUKE: 59 4-6
EPIC: 66 3-5
GOLD EAGLE: 61 4-6
JEWEL: 66-67 3-5
OKEH: 62-65 3-5
RONN: 67-72 2-4
SONCRAFT: 61 3-5
TOP RANK: 60-61 4-6
WARWICK: 61 3-5
LPs: 10/12-Inch 33rpm
OKEH: 63-66 15-20
MCA: 78 5-8
RONN: 69-72 8-10
  Also see CADETS
  Also see TAYLOR, Austin
  Also see TAYLOR, Little Johnny & Ted
Taylor

TAYLOR, True
(Paul Simon)
Singles: 7-Inch
BIG: 58 15-20
  Also see SIMON, Paul

T-BONES
Singles: 7-Inch
LIBERTY: 64-66 3-6

EPs: 7-Inch 33/45rpm
LIBERTY: *65* $4-8
(Jukebox issues only.)
LPs: 10/12-Inch 33rpm
LIBERTY: *64-66* **15-20**
SUNSET: *66* **10-12**
Members: Dan Hamilton; Joe Frank Carollo; Tom
Reynolds.
Also see HAMILTON, JOE FRANK &
REYNOLDS

TCHAIKOVSKY, Bram
Singles: 7-Inch
ARISTA: *81* **1-3**
POLYDOR: *79* **1-3**
LPs: 10/12-Inch 33rpm
ARISTA: *81* **5-8**
POLYDOR: *79-80* **5-8**
Also see MOTORS

T-CONNECTION
Singles: 12-Inch 33/45rpm
CAPITOL: *81-84* **4-6**
Singles: 7-Inch
CAPITOL: *81-84* **1-3**
DASH: *77-79* **2-3**
LPs: 10/12-Inch 33rpm
CAPITOL: *81-84* **5-8**
DASH: *77-79* **5-8**

TEARDROP EXPLODES
Singles: 7-Inch
MERCURY: *81-82* **1-3**
LPs: 10/12-Inch 33rpm
MERCURY: *81-81* **5-8**

TEARS FOR FEARS
Singles: 12-Inch 33/45rpm
MERCURY: *83-86* **4-6**
Singles: 7-Inch
MERCURY: *83-86* **1-3**
LPs: 10/12-Inch 33rpm
MERCURY: *83-86* **5-8**
SELECT ONE: **12-18**

TEASE
Singles: 12-Inch 33/45rpm
EPIC: *86* **4-6**
RCA VICTOR: *83* **4-6**
Singles: 7-Inch
EPIC: *86-88* **1-3**
RCA VICTOR: *83* **1-3**
LPs: 10/12-Inch 33rpm
EPIC: *86* **5-8**
RCA VICTOR: *83* **5-8**

TECHNIQUE
Singles: 12-Inch 33/45rpm
ARIAL: *83* **4-6**

TECHNIQUES
Singles: 78rpm
ROULETTE: *57* $3-5
Singles: 7-Inch
ROULETTE: *57-58* **4-6**
STARS: *57* **8-10**

TEDDY & THE TWILIGHTS
Singles: 7-Inch
SWAN: *62* **10-15**

TEDDY BEARS
Singles: 7-Inch
COLLECTABLES: **1-3**
DORE: *58-59* **5-8**
IMPERIAL: *58-59* **8-10**
LPs: 10/12-Inch 33rpm
IMPERIAL (12010; "The Teddy
Bears Sing"): *59* **100-150**
(Monaural.)
IMPERIAL (9067; "The Teddy
Bears Sing"): *59* **300-400**
(Stereo.)
Members: Phil Spector; Annette Kleinbard; Mar-
shall Leib.
Also see NELSON, Sandy

TEE, Willie
Singles: 7-Inch
A.F.O: *62* **4-8**
ATLANTIC: *65* **3-6**
CAPITOL: *68-70* **2-4**
GATOR: *71* **2-4**
NOLA: *65* **5-10**
UNITED ARTISTS: *76* **2-3**
LPs: 10/12-Inch 33rpm
CAPITOL: *69* **10-12**
UNITED ARTISTS: *76* **5-10**

TEE SET
Singles: 7-Inch
COLLECTABLES: **1-3**
COLOSSUS: *70-71* **2-4**
Picture Sleeves
COLOSSUS: *70* **2-4**
LPs: 10/12-Inch 33rpm
COLOSSUS: *70* **10-12**

TEEGARDEN & VAN WINKLE
Singles: 7-Inch
ATCO: *68* **3-5**
PLUMM: *70* **3-6**
WESTBOUND: *69-72* **2-4**
Picture Sleeves
WESTBOUND: *70* **2-4**
LPs: 10/12-Inch 33rpm
ATCO: *68* **10-15**
WESTBOUND: *69-72* **10-12**

Members: David Teegarden; Skip Knape.

TEEN DREAM
(Teen Dream With Valentino)
Singles: 7-Inch
WARNER BROS: *87-88* $1-3

TEEN KINGS
Singles: 78rpm
JE-WEL (101; "Ooby Dooby"): *56* 50-100
Singles: 7-Inch
JE-WEL (101; "Ooby Dooby"): *56* 250-350
(May read "Vocal Roy Oribson," instead of "Roy
Orbison," on some labels.)
Members: Roy Orbison; Johnny "Peanuts" Wilson;
Billy Par Ellis; James Monroe; Jack Kennelly.
Also see ORBISON, Roy

TEEN QUEENS
Singles: 78rpm
RPM: *56-57* 4-8
Singles: 7-Inch
ANTLER: *60-61* 5-8
COLLECTABLES: 1-3
KENT: *61* 3-5
RCA VICTOR: *58* 5-10
RPM: *56-57* 8-12
Picture Sleeves
ANTLER: *60* 10-15
LPs: 10/12-Inch 33rpm
CROWN (5022, "Eddie My
Love"): *56* 35-40
CROWN (5373; "The Teen
Queens"): *63* 15-20
UNITED: 6-10
Members: Rose Collins; Betty Collins.

TEENA MARIE:
see MARIE, Teena

TEENAGERS
Singles: 78rpm
GEE (1046; "Flip-Flop"): *57* 4-8
Singles: 7-Inch
END: *60* 20-25
GEE (1046; "Flip-Flop"): *57* 5-10
Billy Lobrano; Herman Santiago; Sherman Garnes;
Jim Merchant; Joe Negroni.
Also see LYMON, Frankie

TEMPER
Singles: 12-Inch 33/45rpm
MCA: *84* 4-6
Singles: 7-Inch
MCA: *84* 1-3

TEMPO, Nino
(Nino Tempo & 5th Ave. Sax)
Singles: 7-Inch
A&M: *73-74* 2-4

RCA VICTOR: *59-60* $3-5
TOWER: *67* 2-4
UNITED ARTISTS: *60* 3-5
LPs: 10/12-Inch 33rpm
A&M: *74* 8-10
ATCO: *66* 10-12
Also see ARCHIES

TEMPO, Nino, & April Stevens
Singles: 7-Inch
A&M: *72-75* 2-4
ABC: *73* 1-3
ATCO: *62-66* 2-5
BELL: *69* 2-4
CHELSEA: *76* 2-3
MARINA: *72* 2-4
WHITE WHALE: *66-68* 2-5
LPs: 10/12-Inch 33rpm
ATCO: *63-66* 10-15
CAMDEN: *64* 10-15
WHITE WHALE: *69* 10-15
Also see STEVENS, April
Also see TEMPO, Nino

TEMPOS
Singles: 78rpm
KAPP: *57* 5-8
Singles: 7-Inch
CLIMAX: *59* 5-8
KAPP: *57-58* 5-8
PARIS: *59* 4-6
ROULETTE: 1-3

TEMPREES
Singles: 7-Inch
EPIC : *76* 2-4
STAX: *84* 1-3
WE PRODUCE: *72-74* 2-4
LPs: 10/12-Inch 33rpm
STAX: *84* 5-8
WE PRODUCE: *72-74* 8-10

TEMPTATIONS
Singles: 7-Inch
GOLDISC (Multi-color label): *60* 10-15
GOLDISC (Black label): *60* 5-10
ROULETTE: *71* 1-3

TEMPTATIONS
Singles: 7-Inch
ATLANTIC: *77-78* 1-3
GORDY (1600 through 1800
series): *82-86* 1-3
GORDY (7001; "Dream Come
True"): *62* 15-25
GORDY (7010; "Paradise"): *62* 10-20
GORDY (7015; "I Want A Love
I Can See"): *63* 8-15

GORDY (7020; "May I Have This
Dance?"): *63* **$6-12**
GORDY (7028 through 7074): *64-68* **4-8**
GORDY (7081 through 7213): *68-81* **2-5**
MIRACLE (5; "Oh Mother Of
Mine"): *61* **60-75**
MIRACLE (12; "Check Yourself"): *62* .. **15-20**
MOTOWN: *84-88* **1-3**
MOTOWN/TOPPS ("My Girl"): *67* **50-75**
(Topps Chewing Gum promotional item.
Cardboard flexi, picture disc. Issued with generic
paper sleeve.)
Picture Sleeves
GORDY (Except 7038): *66-70* **4-8**
GORDY (7038; "My Girl"): *65* **10-20**
LPs: 10/12-Inch 33rpm
ATLANTIC: *77-78* **8-10**
GORDY (911 through 927): *64-68* **15-20**
GORDY (938 through 1006): *68-80* **10-15**
GORDY (6000 series): *82-86* **5-8**
KORY: *77* **8-10**
MOTOWN (100 & 200 series): *81-82* **5-8**
MOTOWN (782; "Anthology"): *73* **12-20**
(Includes 12-page color booklet.)
MOTOWN (998; "Give Love At
Christmas"): *80* **12-15**
(Promotional issue only.)
MOTOWN (5389; "25th
Anniversary"): *86* **10-15**
(Includes 8-page color booklet.)
MOTOWN (6246; "Together Again"): *87* .. **5-8**
NATURAL RESOURCES: *78* **5-8**
Members: David Ruffin; Eddie Kendricks; Melvin
Franklin; Otis Williams; Paul Williams; Damon
Harris; Dennis Edwards.
Also see EDWARDS, Dennis
Also see FOUR TOPS / Temptations
Also see KENDRICKS, Eddie
Also see LANDS, Liz, & The Temptations
Also see PIRATES
Also see ROBINSON, Smokey
Also see ROSS, Diana
Also see RUFFIN, David
Also see SUPREMES & TEMPTATIONS

TEMPTATIONS & RICK JAMES
Singles: 12-Inch 33/45rpm
GORDY: *82* **4-6**
Singles: 7-Inch
GORDY: *82* **1-3**
Also see JAMES, Rick

TEMPTATIONS / Stevie Wonder
LPs: 10/12-Inch 33rpm
TAMLA (101; "The Sky's The
Limit"): *71* **$18-20**
(Promotional issue only.)
Also see TEMPTATIONS
Also see WONDER, Stevie

10CC
Singles: 7-Inch
MERCURY: *75-77* **2-4**
POLYDOR: *78* **2-4**
UK: *72-74* **3-5**
Picture Sleeves
MERCURY: *75-77* **5-8**
LPs: 10/12-Inch 33rpm
MERCURY: *75-77* **10-15**
POLYDOR: *78-79* **5-8**
UK: *73-75* **10-15**
WARNER BROS: *80* **8-10**
Members: Kevin Godley; Lol Creme; Graham
Gouldman; Eric Stewart; Paul Burgess;
Rick Fenn; Tony O'Malley; Stuart Tosh.
Also see GODLEY, Kevin, & Lol Creme
Also see HOTLEGS
Also see KASENETZ-KATZ SINGING OR-
CHESTRAL CIRCUS
Also see KOKOMO
Also see OHIO EXPRESS
Also see SEDAKA, Neil
Also see WAX

10DB
Singles: 7-Inch
CRUSH: *88* **1-3**

10-SPEED
Singles: 12-Inch 33/45rpm
QUALITY/RFC: *83* **4-6**
Singles: 7-Inch
QUALITY/RFC: *83* **1-3**

10,000 MANIACS
Singles: 7-Inch
ELEKTRA: *88* **1-3**

TEN WHEEL DRIVE
Singles: 7-Inch
CAPITOL: *73* **2-4**
POLYDOR: *69-71* **2-4**
LPs: 10/12-Inch 33rpm
CAPITOL: *73* **8-10**
POLYDOR: *69-71* **10-12**
Member: Genya Ravan.
Also see RAVAN, Genya
Also see ZAGER, Michael, Band

TEN YEARS AFTER
Singles: 7-Inch
COLUMBIA: 71-73 .... $2-4
DERAM: 68-70 3-5
LPs: 10/12-Inch 33rpm
CHRYSALIS: 83 5-8
COLUMBIA: 71-76 8-12
DERAM: 68-75 8-12
LONDON: 77 5-8
Member: Alvin Lee.
Also see LEE, Alvin

TENANT, Jimmy:
see TENNANT, Jimmy

TENDER SLIM
Singles: 7-Inch
GREY CLIFF: 59 4-6
HERALD: 62 4-6

TENNANT, Jimmy
(Jimmy Velvet; Jimmy Tenant)
Singles: 7-Inch
AMP: 59 4-6
WARWICK: 60 8-10
Also see VELVET, Jimmy

TENNESSEE ERNIE:
see FORD, "Tennessee" Ernie

TENNILLE, Toni
Singles: 7-Inch
MIRAGE: 84 1-3
LPs: 10/12-Inch 33rpm
GAIA: 87 5-8
MIRAGE: 84 5-8
Also see CAPTAIN & TENNILLE

TEPPER, Robert
Singles: 7-Inch
SCOTTI BROTHERS: 85-86 1-3
LPs: 10/12-Inch 33rpm
SCOTTI BROTHERS: 85-86 5-8

TERMINATORS OF
ENDEARMENT
Singles: 7-Inch
"STRANGER IN THE MANGER": 88 3-5
Picture Sleeves
"STRANGER IN THE MANGER": 88 4-8
(Listed by title since label is not yet known.)
Members: Michael Monahan; Steven Strauss.

TERRELL, Jean
Singles: 7-Inch
A&M: 78 2-3
LPs: 10/12-Inch 33rpm
A&M: 78 8-10
Also see SUPREMES

Ten Years After: (L-R) Rick Lee; Leo Lyons; Alvin Lee;
Chick Churchill (Photo: Alen Macweeney)

TERRELL, Tammi
Singles: 7-Inch
MOTOWN: 65-69 .... $3-5
LPs: 10/12-Inch 33rpm
MOTOWN (200 series): 82 5-8
MOTOWN (600 series): 67 12-15
Also see GAYE, Marvin, & Tammi Terrell
Also see JACKSON, Chuck, & Tammi Terrell
Also see MONTGOMERY, Tammy

TERRY, Sonny
(Sonny "Hootin'" Terry & His Night Owls;
Sonny Terry & His Buckshot Five)
Singles: 78rpm
ASCH: 45 10-15
CAPITOL: 47-50 5-10
GOTHAM: 51 5-10
GRAMERCY: 52 5-10
GROOVE: 54-55 4-8
HARLEM: 52 8-15
JACKSON: 52 10-15
JAX: 10-15
JOSIE: 56 10-15
OLD TOWN: 56 10-15
RCA VICTOR: 53 5-10
RED ROBIN: 53 15-25
SAVOY: 48 5-10
SOLO: 49 8-12
Singles: 7-Inch
CAPITOL (900 series): 50 25-40
CHOICE: 61 3-5
GOTHAM: 51 15-20
GRAMERCY (Black vinyl): 52 15-25
GRAMERCY (Colored vinyl): 52 25-50
GROOVE: 54-55 10-20
HARLEM: 52 25-35
JACKSON (Colored vinyl): 52 35-50
JAX (Colored vinyl): 30-50
JOSIE: 56 10-15
OLD TOWN: 56 10-15
RCA VICTOR: 53 15-20
RED ROBIN: 53 50-75

LPs: 10/12-Inch 33rpm
ARCHIVE OF FOLK MUSIC: *65* **$12-15**
EVEREST: **5-8**
PRESTIGE BLUESVILLE: *61-63* **20-30**
WASHINGTON: *61* **20-30**
Note: Most of the Sonny Terry sessions included
Brownie McGhee on guitar.
Also see BAGBY, Doc
Also see HOPKINS, Lightnin', & Sonny Terry
Also see McGHEE, Brownie, & Sonny Terry

TERRY, Todd, Project
LPs: 10/12-Inch 33rpm
FRESH: *88* **5-8**

TERRY, Tony
Singles: 7-Inch
EPIC: *87-88* **1-3**

TESLA
Singles: 7-Inch
GEFFEN: *87* **1-3**
LPs: 10/12-Inch 33rpm
GEFFEN: *87* **5-8**

TESTAMENT
LPs: 10/12-Inch 33rpm
MEGAFORCE: *88* **5-8**

TETES NOIRES
EPs: 7-Inch 33/45rpm
RAPUNZEL: *85* **4-6**
LPs: 10/12-Inch 33rpm
RAPUNZEL: *85* **5-10**
ROUNDER: *87* **5-8**
Members: Jennifer Holt; Cindy Bartell; Renee
Kayon; Camille Gage; Polly Alexander; Angela
Frucci.

TEX, Joe
(Joe Tex & The Class Mates)
Singles: 12-Inch 33/45rpm
EPIC: *77* **4-6**
Singles: 7-Inch
ACE: *58-60* **6-10**
ANNA: *60-61* **5-8**
ATLANTIC: *72* **2-4**
CHECKER: *63* **3-5**
DIAL (1000 series): *71-76* **2-4**
DIAL (2800 series): *78* **2-3**
DIAL (3000 series): *61-64* **4-6**
DIAL (4000 series): *64-69* **3-5**
EPIC: *77-79* **2-3**
HANDSHAKE: *81* **1-3**
JALYNNE: *61* **4-6**
KING: *55-57* **6-10**
LPs: 10/12-Inch 33rpm
ACCORD: *82* **5-8**
ATLANTIC: *65-72* **10-15**

Matt Johnson of The The

CHECKER: *64* **$12-15**
DIAL: *72-79* **8-10**
EPIC: *77-78* **8-10**
KING: *65* **12-15**
LONDON: *79* **5-8**
PARROT: *65* **12-15**
PRIDE: *73* **8-10**
Members: Mike Appell; Rod Bristow.
Also see KELLY, Paul
Also see SOUL CLAN

TEXANS
Singles: 7-Inch
GOTHIC: *61* **10-15**
INFINITY: *61* **10-15**
JOX: *64* **5-8**
VEE JAY: *65* **3-5**
Members: Dorsey Burnette; Johnny Burnette.
Also see BURNETTE, Johnny & Dorsey

TEXAS GUITAR SLIM
(Johnny Winter)
Singles: 7-Inch
MOON-LITE: *60* **40-50**
Also see WINTER, Johnny

TEXTONES
Singles: 7-Inch
GOLD MOUNTAIN: *84* **1-3**
I.R.S./FAULTY PRODUCTS: *80* **1-3**
LPs: 10/12-Inch 33rpm
GOLD MOUNTAIN: *84* **5-8**
Members: Carla Olson; Mark Cuff; Kathy Valen-
tine; David Provost; George Callins; Phil Seymour;
Tom Morgan; Joe Read.
Also see DREAM SYNDICATE
Also see GO-GOs

Also see SEYMOUR, Phil

THE
(The The; Matt Johnson)
Singles: 12-Inch 33/45rpm
EPIC: *84-85* $4-6
SIRE: *84* 4-6
Singles: 7-Inch
EPIC: *84-85* 1-3
LPs: 10/12-Inch 33rpm
EPIC: *84-87* 5-8

THEE MIDNITERS
Singles: 7-Inch
CHATTAHOOCHEE: *65-66* 5-8
UNI: *69* 3-5
WHITTIER: *66-68* 4-8
LPs: 10/12-Inch 33rpm
CHATTAHOOCHEE: *65* 20-25
RHINO: *83* 5-8
WHITTIER: *66-67* 15-20

THEE PROPHETS
Singles: 7-Inch
KAPP: *69* 3-5
LPs: 10/12-Inch 33rpm
KAPP: *69* 15-20

THEE SIXPENCE
(Strawberry Alarm Clock)
Singles: 7-Inch
DOT: *66* 10-15
Also see STRAWBERRY ALARM CLOCK

THELONIOUS MONK
see: MONK, Thelonious

THEM
(Featuring Van Morrison)
Singles: 7-Inch
HAPPY TIGER: *69-70* 3-6
KING: *65* 8-10
LOMA: *66* 5-8
LONDON: 1-3
PARROT (Except 365): *64-66* 6-10
PARROT (365; "Gloria"): *65* 10-15
(Copies with later copyright dates are reissues.)
RUFF: *67* 8-10
SULLY: 15-20
TOWER: *67-69* 4-6
LPs: 10/12-Inch 33rpm
HAPPY TIGER: *69-71* 10-15
LONDON: *77* 5-8
PARROT (71005; "Them"): *65* 50-100
(Cover does NOT emphasize *Gloria*.)
PARROT (71005; "Them"): *65* 30-35
(Cover emphasizes *Gloria*.)
PARROT (71008; "Them
Again"): *66* 25-30

PARROT (71053; "Them Featuring
Van Morrison"): *72* $12-15
TOWER: *68* 20-25
Also see MORRISON, Van

THEO VANESS
Singles: 7-Inch
PRELUDE: *79* 1-3
LPs: 10/12-Inch 33rpm
PRELUDE: *79* 5-8

THEODORE, Mike, Orchestra
Singles: 7-Inch
WESTBOUND: *77-79* 2-3
LPs: 10/12-Inch 33rpm
WESTBOUND: *77-79* 5-8

THERESA
Singles: 7-Inch
RCA VICTOR: *87-88* 1-3

THEY MIGHT BE GIANTS
LPs: 10/12-Inch 33rpm
BAR/NONE: *88* 5-8

THIN LIZZY
Singles: 12-Inch 33/45rpm
WARNER BROS: *78* 4-8
(Promotional issues only.)
Singles: 7-Inch
LONDON: *73* 2-4
MERCURY: *76-77* 2-3
VERTIGO: *75* 2-4
WARNER BROS: *78-79* 2-3
Picture Sleeves
VERTIGO: *75* 1-3
LPs: 10/12-Inch 33rpm
LONDON (500 & 600 series): *71* ... 10-15
LONDON (50000 series): *77* 5-8
MERCURY: *76-77* 8-12
VERTIGO: *74-75* 10-12
WARNER BROS: *78-82* 5-8
Members: Philip Lynott; Gary Moore; Brian Robertson.
Also see MOORE, Gary

THINK
Singles: 7-Inch
BIG TREE: *74* 2-4
COLUMBIA: *68-69* 3-5
LAURIE: *71* 2-4
LPs: 10/12-Inch 33rpm
LAURIE: *72* 8-10
Member: Lou Stallman.

THIRD POWER
Singles: 7-Inch
BARON: 5-10
VANGUARD: *70* 3-6

LPs: 10/12-Inch 33rpm
VANGUARD: *70* **$10-15**

THIRD RAIL
Singles: 7-Inch
CAMEO: *66* **4-6**
EPIC: *67-69* **3-5**
LPs: 10/12-Inch 33rpm
EPIC: *67* **20-25**

THIRD WORLD
Singles: 12-Inch 33/45rpm
COLUMBIA: *81-82* **4-6**
ISLAND: *78-80* **4-6**
Singles: 7-Inch
ABRAXAS: *76* **2-4**
COLUMBIA: *81-85* **1-3**
ISLAND: *79* **2-3**
LPs: 10/12-Inch 33rpm
COLUMBIA: *81-82* **5-8**
ISLAND: *76-80* **6-9**
Also see WONDER, Stevie

13TH FLOOR ELEVATORS
Singles: 7-Inch
CONTACT: *66* **25-35**
HBR: *66* **40-50**
INTERNATIONAL ARTISTS: *66-68* ... **10-20**
LPs; 10/12-Inch 33rpm
INTERNATIONAL ARTISTS (1;
"Psychedelic Sounds"): *67* **75-100**
(Does NOT have "Masterfonics" stamped in the vinyl trailoff.)
INTERNATIONAL ARTISTS (5; "Easter
Everywhere"): *67* **40-60**
(Does NOT have "Masterfonics" stamped in the vinyl trailoff.)
INTERNATIONAL ARTISTS (8;
"Live"): *68* **40-60**
(Does NOT have "Masterfonics" stamped in the vinyl trailoff.)
INTERNATIONAL ARTISTS (9; "Bull
Of The Woods"): *68* **40-60**
(Does NOT have "Masterfonics" stamped in the vinyl trailoff.)
INTERNATIONAL ARTISTS
(Reissues): **10-15**
(With "Masterfonics" stamped in the vinyl trailoff.)
INTERNATIONAL ARTISTS (White
Label): *67-68* **150-225**
(Promotional issues only.)
TEXAS ARCHIVE: *85* **8-10**
Members: Roky Erickson; Tommy Hall; Stacy
Sutherland; John Ike Walton; Benny Thurman.
Also see SPADES

.38 SPECIAL
Singles: 7-Inch
A&M: *77-88* **$1-3**
CAPITOL: *84* **1-3**
Picture Sleeves
A&M: *80-83* **1-3**
LPs: 10/12-Inch 33rpm
A&M: *77-88* **5-8**
CAPITOL: *84* **5-8**
Member: Dave Van Zandt.

THOMAS, B. J.
(B. J. Thomas & The Triumphs)
Singles: 7-Inch
ABC: *75* **2-4**
CLEVELAND INT'L: *83* **1-3**
COLLECTABLES: **1-3**
COLUMBIA: *83-86* **1-3**
HICKORY: *66* **3-5**
MCA: *77-82* **1-3**
MYRRH: *77-81* **1-3**
PACEMAKER: *66* **10-15**
PARAMOUNT: *73-74* **2-4**
SCEPTER (12100 series): *66-67* **3-5**
SCEPTER (12200 & 12300
series): *68-72* **2-4**
SCEPTER (21000 series): *73-74* **2-3**
VALERIE: **3-5**
Picture Sleeves
MCA: *79* **1-3**
LPs: 10/12-Inch 33rpm
ABC: *74-77* **8-10**
ACCORD: *81-82* **5-8**
BUCKBOARD: **5-8**
CLEVELAND INT'L: *83* **5-8**
COLUMBIA: *86* **5-8**

VALERIE
Distributed by LONDON RECORDS, INC.

Pub: Ka-Boo Music
Pub. Co.-BMI
Time: 2:15
VL - 12

45-226V

Produced by
Charlie Booth

PROMOTIONAL COPY

HEY, JUDY!
(M. Charron)
**B. J. THOMAS and
THE TRIUMPHS**
Made in U.S.A.

DORAL: $15-25
(Promotional mail-order issue from Doral
cigarettes.)
EXACT: *80* 5-8
EXCELSIOR: *80* 5-8
EVEREST: *81* 5-8
51 WEST: *79* 5-8
IIICKORY: *66* 35-45
MCA: *77-82* 5-8
MCA/SONGBIRD: *80* 5-8
MYRRII: *78-83* 5-8
PACEMAKER: *66* 40-50
PARAMOUNT: *73-74* 8-10
PHOENIX 20: *81* 8-10
PICKWICK: *78* 5-8
PRIORITY: *83* 5-8
SCEPTER: *69-73* 8-12
SPRINGBOARD: *73-79* 6-10
STARDAY: *77* 5-8
TRIP: *76* 8-10
UNITED ARTISTS: *74* 8-10
  Also see EDDY, Duane

THOMAS, B. J., & Ray Charles
Singles: 7-Inch
COLUMBIA: *85* 1-3
  Also see CHARLES, Ray
  Also see THOMAS, B.J.

THOMAS, Carla
Singles: 7-Inch
ATLANTIC: *60-65* 4-8
STAX: *65-72* 3-6
Picture Sleeves
STAX: *67* 4-8
EPs: 7-Inch 33/45rpm
STAX: *66* 10-15
(Jukebox issues only.)
LPs: 10/12-Inch 33rpm
ATLANTIC (8057; "Gee Whiz"): *61* 20-30
ATLANTIC (8232; "Best Of Carla
  Thomas"): *69* 10-15
STAX: *66-71* 10-15
  Also see BELL, William, & Carla Thomas
  Also see OTIS & CARLA
  Also see RUFUS & CARLA
  Also scc TAYLOR, Johnnie

THOMAS, Evelyn
Singles: 12-Inch 33/45rpm
TSR: *84* 4-6
Singles: 7-Inch
CASABLANCA: *78* 2-3
TSR: *84* 1-3
VANGUARD: *85* 1-3

LPs: 10/12-Inch 33rpm
A.V.I.: *79* $5-8
CASABLANCA: *78* 5-8

THOMAS, Gene
Singles: 7-Inch
HICKORY: *71* 2-4
TRX: *69* 2-4
UNITED ARTISTS: *61-65* 3-5
VENUS: *61-62* 8-12
  Also see GENE & DEBBE

THOMAS, Ian
Singles: 7-Inch
ATLANTIC: *78* 2-3
CHRYSALIS: *75* 2-3
JANUS: *73-74* 2-4
MERCURY: *84* 1-3
LPs: 10/12-Inch 33rpm
ATLANTIC: *78* 5-8
JANUS: *73* 8-10
MERCURY: *84* 5-8

THOMAS, Irma
Singles: 7-Inch
BANDY: 3-5
CANYON: *70* 2-4
CHESS: *68* 2-4
COTILLION: *71-72* 2-4
FUNGUS: *73* 2-4
IMPERIAL: *64-66* 3-5
MINIT: *61-63* 3-5
RCS: *79-81* 1-3
ROKER: *71* 2-4
RONK: *59-60* 4-6
LPs: 10/12-Inch 33rpm
FUNGUS: *73* 8-10
IMPERIAL (266; "Wish Someone
  Would Care"): *64* 15-25
IMPERIAL (302; "Take A Look"): *66* .. 12-15
RCS: *80* 5-8
  Also scc BROWN, Maxine / Irma Thomas

THOMAS, Jamo, & The Party Brothers
Singles: 7-Inch
CHESS: *66* 3-5
DECCA: *68* 2-4
SOUND STAGE 7: *67* 3-5
THOMAS: *66* 4-6

THOMAS, Joe
Singles: 78rpm
KING: *49-51* 4-8
Singles: 7-Inch
KING (Black vinyl): *51* 10-20
KING (Colored vinyl): *51* 30-40

THOMAS, Joe
Singles: 7-Inch
GROOVE MERCHANT: 76 .... $2-4
LRC: 77-79 2-3
SUE: 64 3-5
LPs: 10/12-Inch 33rpm
LRC: 77-78 5-8
TODAY: 72 8-10

THOMAS, Joe, & Bill Elliott
LPs: 10/12-Inch 33rpm
SUE: 64 10-20
Also see THOMAS, Joe

THOMAS, Jon
(John Thomas)
Singles: 78rpm
CHECKER: 55 4-8
Singles: 7-Inch
ABC-PARAMOUNT: 60-61 4-6
CHECKER: 55 5-8
JUNIOR: 64 3-5
VEEP: 67-68 3-5
LPs: 10/12-Inch 33rpm
ABC-PARAMOUNT: 60 20-30
MERCURY: 63 15-20

THOMAS, Leone
Singles: 7-Inch
DON: 76 2-4

THOMAS, Lillo
Singles: 12-Inch 33/45rpm
CAPITOL: 83-85 4-6
Singles: 7-Inch
CAPITOL: 83-87 1-3
LPs: 10/12-Inch 33rpm
CAPITOL: 83-85 5-8

THOMAS, Lillo, & Melba Moore
Singles: 7-Inch
CAPITOL: 84 1-3
Also see MOORE, Melba
Also see THOMAS, Lillo

THOMAS, Nolan
Singles: 12-Inch 33/45rpm
EMERGENCY: 84-85 4-6
Singles: 7-Inch
MIRAGE: 84-85 1-3

THOMAS, Pat
Singles: 7-Inch
MGM: 62-63 2-4
VERVE: 62-64 2-4
Picture Sleeves
MGM: 62 3-5
LPs: 10/12-Inch 33rpm
MGM: 62-64 10-20

STRAND: 61 .... $10-20

THOMAS, Philip-Michael
Singles: 7-Inch
ATLANTIC: 88 1-3
LPs: 10/12-Inch 33rpm
ATLANTIC: 88 5-8

THOMAS, Ray
Singles: 7-Inch
THRESHOLD: 75-76 2-4
LPs: 10/12-Inch 33rpm
THRESHOLD (Except 102): 75-76 8-10
THRESHOLD (102; "Ray Thomas Discusses
From Mighty Oaks"): 75 12-20
(Promotional issue only.)
Also see MOODY BLUES

THOMAS, Rufus
(Rufus "Bearcat" Thomas)
Singles: 12-Inch 33/45rpm
A.V.I.: 78 4-6
Singles: 78rpm
CHESS: 52 15-25
STAR TALENT: 50 20-30
SUN: 53 25-50
Singles: 7-Inch
A.V.I.: 77-78 2-3
ARTISTS OF AMERICA: 76 2-3
HI: 78 2-3
METEOR (5039; "I'm Steady
Holdin' On"): 56 75-150
STAX (100 & 200 series): 62-68 3-5
STAX (0010 through 0236): 68-75 2-4
SUN (181; "Bearcat"): 53 100-150
SUN (188; "Tiger Man"): 53 100-150
LPs: 10/12-Inch 33rpm
A.V.I.: 77-78 5-8
ARTISTS OF AMERICA: 76 8-10
GUSTO: 80 5-8
STAX (Except 704): 70-79 6-10
STAX (704; "Walking The Dog"): 63 15-20
Also see RUFUS & CARLA

THOMAS, Tasha
Singles: 7-Inch
ATLANTIC: 78-79 2-3

THOMAS, Timmy
Singles: 12-Inch 33/45rpm
GOLD MOUNTAIN: 84 4-6
SPECTOR: 83 4-6
Singles: 7-Inch
GLADES: 72-77 2-4
GOLD MOUNTAIN: 84-85 1-3
GOLDWAX: 67 3-5
MARLIN: 80-81 1-3
SPECTOR: 83 1-3

TM: 78 .... $2-3
LPs: 10/12-Inch 33rpm
GLADES: 72-76 8-10
GOLD MOUNTAIN: 84 5-8

THOMAS, Vaneese
Singles: 7-Inch
GEFFEN: 88 1-3

THOMPSON, Chris, & Night
Singles: 7-Inch
PLANET: 79 2-3
Also see NIGHT

THOMPSON, Hank
(Hank Thompson & The Brazos Valley Boys)
Singles: 78rpm
CAPITOL: 47-57 3-6
GLOBE: 46 25-50
Singles: 7-Inch
ABC: 75-79 1-3
ABC/DOT: 74-77 2-3
CAPITOL (1000 through 3000
  series): 50-58 5-10
CAPITOL (4000 & 5000 series): 58-66 3-6
CHURCHILL: 83 1-3
DOT: 68-74 2-3
MCA: 79-80 1-3
WARNER BROS: 66-67 2-4
Picture Sleeves
CAPITOL: 61 3-6
EPs: 7-Inch 33/45rpm
CAPITOL: 53-59 10-20
LPs: 10/12-Inch 33rpm
ABC: 78 5-8
ABC/DOT: 74-77 5-10
CAPITOL (400 series): 53 40-60
  (With an "H" prefix. 10-Inch LPs.)
CAPITOL (400 series): 55 25-40
  (With a "T" prefix.)
CAPITOL (600 series): 55 35-50
  (With an "H" prefix. 10-Inch LPs.)
CAPITOL (600 series): 55 25-40
  (With a "T" prefix.)
CAPITOL (700 series): 56 30-45
CAPITOL (800 & 900 series): 57-58 20-30
CAPITOL (1100 through 2100
  series): 59-64 15-25
CAPITOL (2000 series): 75 5-8
  (With an "SM" prefix.)
CAPITOL (2200 through 2800
  series): 65-67 10-20
  (With a "T" or "ST" prefix.)
CAPITOL (9000 series): 53 40-60
  (10-Inch LPs.)
CAPITOL (11000 series): 79 5-8
CHURCHILL: 84 5-8

DOT: 68-74 .... $6-15
GUSTO: 80 5-8
PICKWICK/HILLTOP: 67-68 6-15
TOWER: 68 8-15
WACO: 8-10
Also see BRAZOS VALLEY BOYS

THOMPSON, Kay
Singles: 78rpm
CADENCE: 56 2-4
MGM: 54-55 2-4
Singles: 7-Inch
CADENCE: 56 2-4
MGM: 54-55 2-4

THOMPSON, Richard
Singles: 7-Inch
HANNIBAL: 83 1-3
POLYDOR: 85-86 1-3
REPRISE: 72 2-4
LPs: 10/12-Inch 33rpm
CAPITOL: 88 5-8
HANNIBAL: 83 5-8
POLYDOR: 85-86 5-8
REPRISE: 72 8-10
Also see FAIRPORT CONVENTION

THOMPSON, Richard & Linda
Singles: 7-Inch
CHRYSALIS: 78 2-3
ISLAND: 74-75 2-4
LPs: 10/12-Inch 33rpm
CHRYSALIS: 78 5-8
ISLAND: 74-75 8-10
Also see THOMPSON, Richard

THOMPSON, Robbin, Band
Singles: 7-Inch
NEMPEROR: 76-77 2-3
OVATION: 80 1-3
LPs: 10/12-Inch 33rpm
NEMPEROR: 76 8-10
OVATION: 80 5-8

THOMPSON, Roy
Singles: 7-Inch
OKEH: 66-67 3-5

THOMPSON, Sonny
Singles: 78rpm
CHART: 56 5-10
KING: 50-57 5-10
Singles: 7-Inch
CHART: 56 10-20
KING (4500 through 5300
  series): 52-60 5-10
KNIGHT: 61 3-5

Sue Thompson displays her Gold Record award for *Norman*

EPs: 7-Inch 33/45rpm
KING: $20-30
LPs: 10/12-Inch 33rpm
KING (500 series): *56* 30-40
KING (600 series): *59* 20-25
  Also see KING, Freddie / Lulu / Sonny
Thompson

THOMPSON, Sue
Singles: 78rpm
DECCA: *55* 5-8
MERCURY: *51-54* 5-10
Singles: 7-Inch
DECCA: *55* 8-10
GUSTO: 1-3
HICKORY (Except 1100 & 1200
series): *66-76* 2-5
HICKORY (1100 & 1200 series): *61-65* ... 4-8
MERCURY: *51-54* 10-20
Picture Sleeves
HICKORY: *64* 4-6
LPs: 10/12-Inch 33rpm
HICKORY (Except 104 through
121): *69-74* 8-12
HICKORY (104 through 121): *62-65* 15-20
WING: *66* 8-15
  Also see GIBSON, Don, & Sue Thompson
  Also see LUMAN, Bob, & Sue Thompson

THOMPSON TWINS
Singles: 12-Inch 33/45rpm
ARISTA: *83-86* 4-6
Singles: 7-Inch
ARISTA: *82-87* 1-3

LPs: 10/12-Inch 33rpm
ARISTA: *82-88* $5-8
  Members: Tom Bailey; Alannah Currie; Joe
Leeway; Chris Bell.
  Also see GENE LOVES JEZEBEL

THOMSON, Ali
Singles: 7-Inch
A&M: *80-81* 1-3
LPs: 10/12-Inch 33rpm
A&M: *80* 5-8

THORNE, David
(David Throne)
Singles: 7-Inch
ADMIRAL: *64-65* 3-5
CHOICE: *60* 4-6
RIVERSIDE: *62* 3-5
SAVOY: *59* 3-5

THORNTON, Fonzi
Singles: 12-Inch 33/45rpm
RCA VICTOR: *83* 4-6
Singles: 7-Inch
RCA VICTOR: *83* 1-3
LPs: 10/12-Inch 33rpm
RCA VICTOR: *83* 5-8

THORNTON, Willie Mae
(Big Mama Thornton)
Singles: 78rpm
PEACOCK: *52-57* 5-10
Singles: 7-Inch
ABC: *73* 1-3
ARHOOLIE: *68* 2-4
BAY TONE: *61* 8-10
GALAXY: *66* 3-5
KENT: *65* 4-6
MERCURY: *69* 2-4
PEACOCK (Maroon label): *52* 15-30
PEACOCK (Red label): *53-55* 15-25
PEACOCK (White label): *56-57* 8-15
  (White label numbers below 1676 are reissues,
which Peacock continued carrying in their catalog
through the seventies.)
SOTOPLAY: *65* 6-10
LPs: 10/12-Inch 33rpm
ARHOOLIE: *66-67* 10-15
BACK BEAT: *70* 20-25
MERCURY: *69-70* 10-15
PENTAGRAM: *71* 10-12
ROULETTE: *70* 10-12
VANGUARD: *74-75* 8-10

THOROGOOD, George, & The Destroyers
Singles: 12-Inch 33/45rpm
EMI AMERICA: 83-85 . . . . $4-6
Singles: 7-Inch
EMI AMERICA: 82-86 1-3
MCA: 79 1-3
ROUNDER: 78-80 1-3
LPs: 10/12-Inch 33rpm
EMI AMERICA: 82-86 5-8
EMI/MANHATTAN: 88 5-8
MCA: 79 5-8
ROUNDER: 77-80 5-8

THORPE, Billy
Singles: 7-Inch
CAPRICORN: 79 3-5
POLYDOR: 79 2-3
PASHA (Except "Retail
Teaser"): 85 2-3
PASHA ("Retail Teaser"): 85 4-8
LPs: 10/12-Inch 33rpm
CAPRICORN: 79 15-20
ELEKTRA: 80 5-8
PASHA: 82-85 8-12

3
Singles: 7 Inch
GEFFEN: 88 1-3
LPs: 10/12-Inch 33rpm
GEFFEN: 88 5-8
Members: Keith Emerson; Carl Palmer.
Also see EMERSON, LAKE & PALMER

THREE CHUCKLES
(Featuring Teddy Randazzo)
Singles: 78rpm
BOULEVARD: 53 5-10
VIK: 56 3-6
X: 54-56 3-6
Singles: 7-Inch
BOULEVARD: 53 25-35
CLOUD: 66 3-5
VIK: 56 5-8
X: 54-56 10-15
EPs: 7-Inch 33/45rpm
RCA VICTOR: 55 10-20
VIK (4; "The Three Chuckles"): 57 10-20
(Promotional issue only. Not issued with cover.)
LPs: 10/12-Inch 33rpm
VIK: 55 35-45
Members: Teddy Randazzo; Phil Benti; Tom
Romano; Russ Gilberto.
Also see CHUCKLES
Also see RANDAZZO, Teddy

THREE DEGREES
Singles: 7-Inch
ARIOLA AMERICA: 78-80 . . . . $1-3
EPIC: 76 2-3
METROMEDIA: 69 2-4
NEPTUNE: 70 2-4
PHILADELPHIA INT'L: 73-76 2-4
ROULETTE: 70-73 2-4
SWAN: 64-66 6-10
WARNER BROS: 68 2-4
LPs: 10/12-Inch 33rpm
ARIOLA AMERICA: 78-81 5-8
EPIC: 77 8-10
PHILADELPHIA INT'L: 74-76 8-10
ROULETTE: 70-75 10-15
Also see MFSB

THREE DOG NIGHT
(3 Dog Night)
Singles: 7-Inch
ABC: 70-76 2-4
DUNHILL (Except 4168): 69-75 2-4
DUNHILL (4168; "Nobody"): 68 5-8
PASSPORT: 83 1-3
Promotional Singles
DUNHILL (4168; "Nobody"): 68 5-8
(White label.)
Picture Sleeves
DUNHILL (Except 4168): 70 2-5
DUNHILL (4168; "Nobody"): 68 20-30
(Promotional issue only.)
LPs: 10/12-Inch 33rpm
ABC: 75-76 8-12
COMMAND: 74-75 10-15
DUNHILL (50048 through
50068): 68-69 10-15
DUNHILL (50078; "It Ain't
Easy"): 70 15-20
(Cover pictures nude people.)

DUNHILL (50078; "It Ain't
Easy"): *70* $10-12
(Cover doesn't show nudes.)
DUNHILL (50088 through
50158): *70-73* **10-15**
DUNHILL (50168; "Hard Labor"): *74* ... **15-18**
(With baby delivery cover.)
DUNHILL (50168; "Hard Labor"): *74* ... **10-12**
(With Band-Aid cover.)
DUNHILL (50178; "Joy To The
World"): *74* **8-10**
MCA: *82* **5-8**
PASSPORT: *83* **5-8**
Members: Danny Hutton; Cory Wells; Chuck
Negron.
Also see HUTTON, Danny

3 FRIENDS
Singles: 7-Inch
CAL-GOLD: *61* **4-8**
IMPERIAL: *61* **4-8**

THREE Gs
Singles: 7-Inch
COLUMBIA: *58-61* **5-8**

3 MAN ISLAND
Singles: 7-Inch
CHRYSALIS: *88* **1-3**

THREE MILLION
Singles: 12-Inch 33/45rpm
COTILLION: *84-84* **4-6**
Singles: 7-Inch
COTILLION: *83-84* **1-3**

3 OUNCES OF LOVE
Singles: 7-Inch
MOTOWN: *78* **2-3**
LPs: 10/12-Inch 33rpm
MOTOWN: *78* **5-8**

THREE PLAYMATES
Singles: 7-Inch
SAVOY: *58* **4-6**

THREE SUNS
Singles: 78rpm
RCA VICTOR: *50-57* **2-4**
Singles: 7-Inch
RCA VICTOR: *50-64* **2-4**
EPs: 7-Inch 33/45rpm
RCA VICTOR: *50-61* **4-8**
ROYALE: **4-8**
LPs: 10/12-Inch 33rpm
CAMDEN: *60-64* **5-10**
MUSICOR: *66* **5-10**
RCA VICTOR: *50-76* **5-15**
RONDO: *59* **5-12**

Members: Al Nevins; Marty Nevins; Art Dunn.

THRILLS
Singles: 7-Inch
G&P: *80* $1-3
LPs: 10/12-Inch 33rpm
G&P: *80* **5-8**

THUNDER, Johnny
Singles: 7-Inch
ABC: *74* **1-3**
CALLA: *69* **2-4**
DIAMOND: *62-68* **3-6**
EPIC: *59* **5-8**
UNITED ARTISTS: *70* **2-4**
Picture Sleeves
DIAMOND: *63* **5-10**
LPs: 10/12-Inch 33rpm
DIAMOND: *63* **20-30**
REAL RECORDS: **10-12**

THUNDER, Johnny, & Ruby Winters
Singles: 7-Inch
DIAMOND: *67-68* **3-5**
Also see THUNDER, Johnny
Also see WINTERS, Ruby

THUNDER, Margo
Singles: 7-Inch
HAVEN: *74* **2-4**

THUNDERCLAP NEWMAN:
see NEWMAN, Thunderclap

THUNDERFLASH
Singles: 7-Inch
JAMPOWER: *83* **1-3**

THUNDERKLOUD, Billy, & The Chieftones
Singles: 7-Inch
POLYDOR: *76-77* **2-3**
20TH CENTURY-FOX: *74-75* **2-4**
LPs: 10/12-Inch 33rpm
SUPERIOR: *74* **8-12**
20TH CENTURY-FOX: *74-75* **6-10**

THURSTON, Bobby
Singles: 7-Inch
PRELUDE: *80* **1-3**

TIA
Singles: 7-Inch
RCA VICTOR: *87* **1-3**

TIC TOC
Singles: 12-Inch 33/45rpm
RCA VICTOR: *84* **4-6**
Singles: 7-Inch
RCA VICTOR: *84* **1-3**

LPs: 10/12-Inch 33rpm
RCA VICTOR: *84* $5-8

TICO & THE TRIUMPHS
(Featuring Paul Simon)
Singles: 7-Inch
AMY (Except 876): *61-62* **10-15**
AMY (876; "Cards Of Love"): *62* **25-30**
MADISON: *62* **25-30**
 Also see SIMON, Paul

TIERRA
Singles: 7-Inch
ASI: *80* **1-3**
BOARDWALK: *80-82* **1-3**
SALSOUL: *81* **1-3**
MCA: *79* **1-3**
TODY: **2-4**
LPs: 10/12-Inch 33rpm
ASI: *80* **5-8**
BOARDWALK: *80* **5-8**
SALSOUL: *81* **5-8**
 Members: Salas Brothers.
 Also see EL CHICANO

TIFFANY
Singles: 7-Inch
MCA: *88* **1-3**
LPs: 10/12-Inch 33rpm
MCA: *88* **5-8**

TIGGI CLAY
Singles: 7-Inch
MOROCCO: *84* **1-3**
LPs: 10/12-Inch 33rpm
MOROCCO: *84* **5-8**

TIGHT FIT
Singles: 12-Inch 33/45rpm
ARISTA: *81* **4-6**
JIVE: *81* **4-6**
Singles: 7-Inch
ARISTA: *81* **1-3**
JIVE: *81* **1-3**

TIJUANA BRASS: see ALPERT, Herb

TIL, Sonny
(Sonny Til & The Orioles)
Singles: 78rpm
JUBILEE: *53* **10-15**
Singles: 7-Inch
JUBILEE (Blue label): *53* **25-40**
JUBILEE (Black label): *59-60* **4-8**
RCA VICTOR: *69-72* **2-4**
ROULETTE: *58* **4-6**
LPs: 10/12-Inch 33rpm
DOBRE: *78* **5-8**
RCA VICTOR: *70-71* **10-15**

Also see McGRIFF, Edna, & Sonny Til
Also see ORIOLES

'TIL TUESDAY
Singles: 7-Inch
EPIC: *85-88* $1-3
LPs: 10/12-Inch 33rpm
EPIC: *85-88* **5-8**
 Members: Aimee Mann; Michael Hausman; Robert
 Holmes; Joey Pesce.

TILLMAN, Bertha
Singles: 7-Inch
BRENT: *62* **15-20**

TILLOTSON, Johnny
Singles: 7-Inch
AMOS: *69-70* **2-4**
BARNABY: *76* **2-3**
BUDDAH: *71-73* **2-4**
CADENCE (1300 series): *58-61* **4-6**
CADENCE (1400 series): *61-63* **3-5**
COLUMBIA: *73-75* **2-4**
ERIC: **1-3**
MGM: *63-68* **3-5**
REWARD: *82-84* **1-3**
UNITED ARTISTS: *76-77* **2-3**
Picture Sleeves
CADENCE: *60* **8-12**
MGM: *63-66* **4-6**
EPs: 7-Inch 33/45rpm
CADENCE: *60-61* **20-30**
LPs: 10/12-Inch 33rpm
ACCORD: *82* **5-8**
AMOS: *69* **10-15**
BARNABY: *77* **8-10**
BUDDAH: *72* **10-12**
CADENCE: *61-63* **30-40**
EVEREST: *82* **5-8**
METRO: *66* **10-15**
MGM: *66-71* **12-15**
ROWE/AMI: *66* **4-8**
("Play Me" Sales Stimulator promotional issue.)
UNITED ARTISTS: *77* **8-10**
 Also see IVAN / Johnny Tillotson

TILLOTSON, Johnny / J.D. Souther
Singles: 7-Inch
BUDDAH: *71* **2-4**
 Also see SOUTHER, J.D.
 Also see TILLOTSON, Johnny

TIM TAM & THE TURN-ONS
Singles: 7-Inch
PALMER (5002; "Wait A Minute"): *66* .. **5-10**
PALMER (5003; "Cheryl Ann"): *66* **15-20**
PALMER (5006; "Kimberly"): *66* **20-25**
PALMER (5014; "Don't Say Hi"): *67* **5-8**

TIMBUK 3
Singles: 7-Inch
I.R.S.: *86* $1-3
LPs: 10/12-Inch 33rpm
I.R.S.: *88* 5-8

TIME
Singles: 12-Inch 33/45rpm
WARNER BROS: *82-84* 4-6
Singles: 7-Inch
WARNER BROS: *81-84* 1-3
LPs: 10/12-Inch 33rpm
WARNER BROS: *81-84* 5-8
Members: Morris Day; Jesse Johnson; Jimmy Jam;
Monte Moir; Jellybean Johnson; Stacy Adams;
Terry Lewis.
Also see DAY, Morris
Also see JOHNSON, Jesse
Also see VANITY 6

TIME BANDITS
Singles: 12-Inch 33/45rpm
COLUMBIA: *85* 4-6

TIME ZONE
Singles: 12-Inch 33/45rpm
CELLULOID: *84* 4-6

TIMES TWO
Singles: 7-Inch
REPRISE: *88* 1-3
LPs: 10/12-Inch 33rpm
REPRISE: *88* 5-8

TIMELORDS
Singles: 7-Inch
TVT: *88* 1-3

TIMETONES
Singles: 7-Inch
ATCO: *61* 10-15
TIMES SQUARE (Except 421): *64* 5-8
TIMES SQUARE (421; "Here In
My Heart"): *61* 15-20
TIMES SQUARE (421; "In My
Heart"): *61* 8-10
Member: Slim Rose.

TIMEX SOCIAL CLUB
Singles: 12-Inch 33/45rpm
DANYA: *86* 4-6
JAY: *86* 4-6
Singles: 7-Inch
DANYA: *86-87* 1-3
JAY: *86* 1-3

TIN TIN
Singles: 12-Inch 33/45rpm
SIRE: *81-83* 4-6

Singles: 7-Inch
ATCO: *71* $2-4
LPs: 10/12-Inch 33rpm
ATCO: *70-71* 12-15
Members: Steve Kipner; Steve Groves.

TINA B.
Singles: 12-Inch 33/45rpm
ATLANTIC: *82* 4-6
ELEKTRA: *83* 4-6
Singles: 7-Inch
ATLANTIC: *82* 1-3
ELEKTRA: *83* 1-3
LPs: 10/12-Inch 33rpm
ATLANTIC: *82* 5-8
ELEKTRA: *83* 5-8

TINDLEY, George
**(George Tindley & The Modern Red Caps;
George Tinley)**
Singles: 7-Inch
EMBER: *60* 4-6
HERALD: *61* 4-6
ROWAX: 4-6
PARKWAY: *62* 3-5
SMASH: *62* 3-5
WAND: *69-70* 2-4

TINGSTAD, Eric, & Nancy Rumbel
LPs: 10/12-Inch 33rpm
SONA GAIA: *88* 5-8

TINY TIM
(Herbert Khaury)
Singles: 7-Inch
BLUE CAT: *65* 5-10
NLT: *88* 1-3
REPRISE: *68-71* 3-5
ROULETTE: 1-3
VIC TIM: *71* 2-4
LPs: 10/12-Inch 33rpm
REPRISE: *68* 12-15

TINY TIM & MISS VICKI
Singles: 7-Inch
REPRISE: *71* 2-4

TINY TIM / Michelle Ramos /
Bruce Haack
LPs: 10/12-Inch 33rpm
RA-JO INT'L: *86* 5-8
Also see TINY TIM

TJADER, Cal
Singles: 78rpm
FANTASY: *54-57* 2-5
SAVOY: *53-54* 3-5
Singles: 7-Inch
FANTASY: *54-71* 2-5

SAVOY: *53-54* $3-5
SKYE: *68* 2-3
VERVE: *61-66* 2-4
EPs: 7-Inch 33/45rpm
FANTASY: *54-55* 10-20
SAVOY: *54* 10-20
LPs: 10/12-Inch 33rpm
BUDDAH: *70* 8-12
CLASSIC JAZZ: *80* 5-8
CONCORD JAZZ: *80-82* 5-8
FANTASY (3-9 through 3-17
series): *54* 30-60
(10-Inch LPs.)
FANTASY (200 series): *54-56* 10-25
FANTASY (3200 series): *55-60* 20-45
FANTASY (3300 series): *60-65* 15-30
FANTASY (8000 & 8100
series): *58-61* 20-45
FANTASY (8300 series): *65* 15-30
FANTASY (8400 series): *71-72* 8-12
FANTASY (9000 series): *72-77* 6-12
GALAXY: *78-79* 5-8
METRO: *67* 8-15
PRESTIGE: *73* 6-10
SAVOY (9000 series): *54* 25-50
(10-Inch LPs.)
SAVOY (12000 series): *56* 20-40
SKYE: *68-69* 8-12
VERVE. *61-69* 10-20
(Reads "MGM Records - A Division Of Metro-
Goldwyn-Mayer, Inc." at bottom of label.)
VERVE: *73-84* 5-12
(Reads "Manufactured By MGM Record Corp.," or
mentions either Polydor or Polygram at bottom of
label.)
Also see BRUBECK, Dave, Quartet
Also see O'DAY, Anita, & Cal Tjader

TJADER, Cal, & Stan Getz
LPs: 10/12-Inch 33rpm
FANTASY (3200 series): *58* 20-40
FANTASY (3300 series): *65* 10-20
FANTASY (8000 series): *58* 20-40
FANTASY (8300 series): *65* 10-20
Also see GETZ, Stan
Also see TJADER, Cal

TOBY BEAU
Singles: 7-Inch
RCA VICTOR: *78-80* 1-3
LPs: 10/12-Inch 33rpm
RCA VICTOR (Except 2994): *78-81* 5-8
RCA VICTOR (2994; "Three You
Missed, One You Didn't"): *78* 10-15
(Promotional issue only.)

TODAY
Singles: 7-Inch
MOTOWN: *88* $1-3
LPs: 10/12-Inch 33rpm
MOTOWN: *88* 5-8
Members: Lee Drakeford; Larry McCain; Wesley
Adams; Larry Singletary.

TODAY'S PEOPLE
Singles: 7-Inch
20TH CENTURY-FOX: *73* 2-4

TODD, Art & Dotty
Singles: 7-Inch
CAPITOL: *62* 3-5
COLLECTABLES: 1-3
DAKAR: *63* 3-5
DART: *59-67* 3-5
DECCA: *61* 3-5
DOT: *66* 2-4
ERA: *58-59* 4-6
M.O.L.: *68* 2-4
SIGNET: *65* 2-4
LPs: 10/12-Inch 33rpm
BEVERLY HILLS: *73* 8-10
DART: *60* 15-20
DOT: *66* 10-15
REPRISE: *65* 10-15

TODD, Nick
Singles: 78rpm
DOT: *57* 4-8
Singles: 7-Inch
DOT: *57-60* 4-8

TOKENS
Singles: 78rpm
MELBA: *56* 5-10
Singles: 7-Inch
ABC: *73* 1-3
ATCO: *74* 2-4
B.T. PUPPY: *64-69* 4-6
BELL: *72* 2-4
BUDDAH: *69-70* 3-5
LAURIE: *63* 5-8
MELBA: *56* 20-25
RCA VICTOR (7000 & 8000
series): *61-65* 6-10
(With a "47" prefix.)
RCA VICTOR (7000 & 8000
series): *61-62* 15-20
(With a "37" prefix. Compact 33 Singles.)
WARNER BROS: *67-69* 3-5
WARWICK: *61* 8-10
Picture Sleeves
B.T. PUPPY: *66* 5-10
RCA VICTOR: *61-63* 5-12

BIG
RECORDS

VOCAL WITH
ORCHESTRA

613
(3420)
Village Music Co.
Time 2:15 (BMI)

HEY, SCHOOLGIRL
(A. Garfunkel & P. Simon)
TOM & JERRY
With Orchestra Accomp.

BIG RECORDS, INC., NEW YORK, N. Y.

LPs: 10/12-Inch 33rpm

ABC: 77	$8-10
DECCA: 60	30-45
ELEKTRA: 81	5-8
MGM: 67-75	8-15
UNITED ARTISTS: 66	25-30
VOCALION: 67	8-12

TOMS, Gary
(Gary Toms' Empire)
Singles: 12-Inch 33/45rpm

MCA: 77	4-6

Singles: 7-Inch

MCA: 77	2-3
MERCURY: 78	2-3
P.I.P.: 75-76	2-4

LPs: 10/12-Inch 33rpm

MCA: 77	5-10
MERCURY: 78	5-8
P.I.P.: 75	8-10

TONE LOC
Singles: 7-Inch

DELICIOUS: 88	1-3

TONES
Singles: 7-Inch

CRIMINAL: 83	1-3

TONEY, Oscar, Jr.
Singles: 7-Inch

BELL: 67-69	3-5
CAPRICORN:	2-4
KING: 64	3-5

LPs: 10/12-Inch 33rpm

BELL: 67	12-15

TONEY LEE: see LEE, Toney

TONY & CAROL
Singles: 7-Inch

ROULETTE: 72	2-4

TONY & JOE
Singles: 7-Inch

DORE: 61-62	3-6
ERA: 58	4-8
FLYTE: 59	4-6
GARDENA: 60	4-6

Members: Tony Savonne; Joe Saraceno.
Also see BEACH BOYS / Tony & Joe

TONY, BOB & JIMMY
Singles: 7-Inch

CAPITOL: 62	3-5

Members: Tony Butala; Bob Engemann; Jim Pike.
Also see LETTERMEN

TONY! TONI! TONE!
Singles: 7-Inch

WING: 88	1-3

LPs: 10/12-Inch 33rpm

WING: 88	$5-8

TOO SHORT
LPs: 10/12-Inch 33rpm

JIVE: 88	5-8

TOOTS & THE MAYTALS
Singles: 12-Inch 33/45rpm

MANGO: 82	4-6

Singles: 7-Inch

MANGO: 76-82	1-3

LPs: 10/12-Inch 33rpm

MANGO: 76-82	5-8

Members: Toots Hibbert; Nathaniel Mathias;
Releigh Gordon; Paul Douglas; Jackie Jackson;
Winston Wright.
Also see WINWOOD, Steve

TOP SHELF
Singles: 7-Inch

LO LO: 69-70	2-4
SOUND TOWN: 80	1-3

TORCH
Singles: 12-Inch 33/45rpm

PACIFIC: 83	4-6

TORCHSONG
Singles: 12-Inch 33/45rpm

I.R.S.: 83-84	4-6

Singles: 7-Inch

I.R.S.: 83-84	1-3

LPs: 10/12-Inch 33rpm

I.R.S.: 83	5-8

TORME, Mel
(Mel Torme & The Meltones)
Singles: 78rpm

BETHLEHEM: 56-57	2-5
CAPITOL (1000 & 2000 series): 50-53	3-6

Singles: 7-Inch

ATLANTIC: 62-64	2-4
BETHLEHEM: 56-58	2-5
CAPITOL (1000 & 2000 series): 50-53	3-6
(Purple labels.)	
CAPITOL (2000 series): 69-70	2-3
(Orange labels.)	
COLUMBIA: 64-67	2-4
CORAL: 53-56	2-5
LIBERTY: 68	2-4
VERVE: 59-61	2-4

EPs: 7-Inch 33/45rpm

CAPITOL: 50	5-15

LPs: 10/12-Inch 33rpm

ATLANTIC (8000 series): 62-64	10-25
ATLANTIC (18000 series): 75	5-8
ATLANTIC (80000 series): 83	5-8
BETHLEHEM (34 through 52): 55-56	20-35

BETHLEHEM (4000 series): *65* $10-20
BETHLEHEM (6000 series): *58-60* 15-35
  (Maroon labels.)
BETHLEHEM (6000 series): *77-78* 5-10
  (Gray labels.)
CAPITOL (200 series): *50* 15-30
  (10-Inch LPs.)
CAPITOL (300 & 400 series): *69-70* 8-12
COLUMBIA (2000 series): *64-66* 10-20
  (Monaural.)
COLUMBIA (9000 series): *64-66* 10-20
  (Stereo.)
CONCORD JAZZ: *82* 5-8
CORAL (57000 series): *54-55* 25-50
EVEREST: *76* 5-8
GLENDALE: *78-79* 5-8
GRYPHON: *79* 5-8
LIBERTY: *68* 8-15
MGM (500 series): *52* 30-60
  (10-Inch LPs.)
MAYFAIR: *58* 20-30
METRO: *65* 10-20
MUSICRAFT: *83* 5-8
STRAND: *60* 12-25
VERVE: *58-60* 15-30
  (Reads "Verve Records, Inc." at bottom of label.)
VERVE: *61-72* 10-20
  (Reads "MGM Records - A Division Of Metro-
  Goldwyn-Mayer, Inc." at bottom of label.)
VERVE: *73-84* 5-10
  (Reads "Manufactured By MGM Record Corp.," or
  mentions either Polydor or Polygram at bottom of
  label.)
VOCALION: *70* 5-10
  Also see CROSBY, Bing, & Mel Torme
  Also see LEE, Peggy, & Mel Torme
  Also see RICH, Buddy
  Also see WHITING, Margaret

TORNADER
Singles: 7-Inch
POLYDOR: *77* 2-3

TORNADOES
Singles: 7-Inch
LONDON: *62-63* 3-5
TOWER: *65* 3-5
LPs: 10/12-Inch 33rpm
LONDON: *62-63* 20-30
  Members: Alan Caddy; Clem Cattini; Heinz Burt;
  George Bellamy.

TOROK, Mitchell
(Mitchell Torok & The Louisiana Hayride Band;
Mitchell Torok & The Matches)
Singles: 7-Inch
ABBOTT: *53-54* 5-10
CAPITOL: *62-63* 3-5

DECCA: *57-59* $4-6
GUYDEN: *59-60* 4-6
INETTE: *63* 3-5
MERCURY: *61* 3-5
RCA VICTOR: *65* 3-5
REPRISE: *66-67* 2-4
Picture Sleeves
GUYDEN: *59-60* 8-12
LPs: 10/12-Inch 33rpm
GUYDEN: *60* 25-35
REPRISE: *66* 10-15

TORONTO
Singles: 7-Inch
NETWORK: *82* 1-3
SOLID GOLD: 1-3
LPs: 10/12-Inch 33rpm
A&M: *80-81* 5-8
NETWORK: *82* 5-8
SOLID GOLD: 5-8

TORRANCE, George
(George Torrance & The Naturals; Georgie Tor-
rance & The Dippers)
Singles: 7-Inch
DUO DISC: *66* 3-5
EPIC: *61* 5-8
KING: *60* 4-8
SHOUT: *68* 3-5

TORRANCE, Richard
(Richard Torrance & Eureka)
Singles: 7-Inch
CAPITOL: *77-79* 2-3
SHELTER: *75* 2-4
LPs: 10/12-Inch 33rpm
CAPITOL: *77* 5-8
SHELTER: *74-75* 8-10

TOSH, Peter
Singles: 12-Inch 33/45rpm
EMI AMERICA: *83* 4-6
Singles: 7-Inch
COLUMBIA: *77* 2-3
EMI AMERICA: *81-84* 1-3
ROLLING STONES: *78-79* 2-3
Picture Sleeves
ROLLINS STONES: *78* 3-5
EPs: 7-Inch 33/45rpm
COLUMBIA: *76* 4-8
  (Promotional issue only.)
LPs: 10/12-Inch 33rpm
COLUMBIA: *77* 5-8
EMI AMERICA: *81-84* 5-8
ROLLING STONES: *79* 5-8

TOSH, Peter, & Mick Jagger
Singles: 7-Inch
ROLLING STONES (19308; "Don't
Look Back"): 78 .... $3-5
(With "Rolling Stones" at top of label.)
ROLLING STONES (19308; "Don't
Look Back"): 78 2-3
(Without "Rolling Stones" at top of label.)
Promotional Singles
ROLLING STONES (130; "Don't
Look Back"): 78 12-15
ROLLING STONES (7500; "Don't
Look Back"): 78 5-8
LPs: 10/12-Inch 33rpm
ROLLING STONES: 78 5-8
Also see JAGGER, Mick
Also see MARLEY, Bob, & The Wailers

TOTAL COELO
Singles: 12-Inch 33/45rpm
CHRYSALIS: 83 4-6
Singles: 7-Inch
CHRYSALIS: 83 1-3
Picture Sleeves
CHRYSALIS: 83 2-4

TOTAL CONTRAST
Singles: 12-Inch 33/45rpm
LONDON: 85-86 4-6
Singles: 7-Inch
LONDON: 85-88 1-3
LPs: 10/12-Inch 33rpm
LONDON: 86 5-8

TOTO
Singles: 12-Inch 33/45rpm
COLUMBIA: 79-85 4-6
Singles: 7-Inch
COLUMBIA: 78-88 1-3
Promotional Singles
COLUMBIA ("Hold The Line"): 78 20-25
(Licorice Pizza picture disc. Issued with special in-
sert.)
LPs: 10/12-Inch 33rpm
COLUMBIA ("Isolation"): 84 8-12
(Picture disc.)
COLUMBIA ("Toto"): 79 30-40
(Picture disc. Promotional issue only.)
COLUMBIA (30000 series): 78-86 5-10
COLUMBIA (47000 series): 83 10-15
(Half-speed mastered.)
COLUMBIA: 88 5-8
POLYDOR: 84 5-8
Members: Steve Porcaro; David Paich; Steve
Lukather; David Hungate; Jeffrey Porcaro; Bobby
Kimball.

Also see VOICES OF AMERICA / U.S.A.
For Africa

TOUCH
Singles: 7-Inch
ATCO: 80-81 .... $1-3
BRUNSWICK: 77 2-3
COLISEUM: 69 4-6
LECASVER: 69 5-8
LPs: 10/12-Inch 33rpm
ATCO: 80 5-8
COLISEUM: 68 15-20
Member: Don Gallucci.
Also see DON & THE GOODTIMES

TOUCH
Singles: 7-Inch
SUPERTRONICS: 87 1-3

TOUCH OF CLASS
Singles: 12-Inch 33/45rpm
NEXT PLATINUM: 84 4-6
Singles: 7-Inch
ATLANTIC: 82 1-3
MIDLAND INT'L: 75-77 2-4
ROADSHOW: 79-81 1-3
LPs: 10/12-Inch 33rpm
MIDLAND INT'L: 76 5-10
ROADSHOW: 79 5-8

TOURISTS
Singles: 7-Inch
EPIC: 80 2-3
LPs: 10/12-Inch 33rpm
EPIC: 81 6-10
Members: Annie Lennox; David Stewart; Ed Chin;
Pete Coombes; Jim Toomey.
Also see EURYTHMICS

TOWER OF POWER
Singles: 7-Inch
COLUMBIA: 76-78 2-3
SAN FRANCISCO: 64-73 4-6
WARNER BROS: 72-75 2-4
LPs: 10/12-Inch 33rpm
COLUMBIA: 78-79 5-8
SAN FRANCISCO: 71 10-15
WARNER BROS: 72-76 8-10
Also see WILLIAMS, Lenny

TOWNES, Carol Lynn
Singles: 12-Inch 33/45rpm
POLYDOR: 84-85 4-6
Singles: 7-Inch
POLYDOR: 84-85 1-3
LPs: 10/12-Inch 33rpm
POLYDOR: 84 5-8

TOWNS, Eddie
(ET)
Singles: 12-Inch 33/45rpm
TOTAL EXPERIENCE: *86* $4-6
Singles: 7-Inch
TOTAL EXPERIENCE: *86* 1-3
LPs: 10/12-Inch 33rpm
TOTAL EXPERIENCE: *86* 5-8

TOWNSEND, Ed
Singles: 7-Inch
CAPITOL: *58-59* 4-6
CHALLENGE: *61-62* 3-5
DYNASTY: *60* 3-5
GLO-TOWN: *66* 2-4
LIBERTY: *62-63* 3-5
MGM: *67* 2-4
MAXX: *64* 3-5
POLYDOR: *70* 2-4
WARNER BROS: *60-61* 3-5
EPs: 7-Inch 33/45rpm
CAPITOL: *58* 10-20
LPs: 10/12-Inch 33rpm
CAPITOL: *59* 15-25
CURTOM: *76* 8-12

TOWNSHEND, Pete
Singles: 7-Inch
ATCO: *80-85* 1-3
LPs: 10/12-Inch 33rpm
ATCO: *80-87* 5-10
DECCA: *72* 10-12
Also see WHO

TOWNSHEND, Pete, & Ronnie Lane
Singles: 7-Inch
MCA: *77-78* 2-3
LPs: 10/12-Inch 33rpm
MCA: *77* 8-10
Also see CLAPTON, Eric
Also see ENTWISTLE, John
Also see TOWNSHEND, Pete
Also see WOOD, Ron, & Ronnie Lane

TOWNSHEND, Simon
Singles: 7-Inch
21: *83* 1-3
LPs: 10/12-Inch 33rpm
21: *83* 5-8

TOY DOLLS
Singles: 7-Inch
ERA: *62* 5-8

TOYS
Singles: 7-Inch
ABC: *73* 1-3
DYNO VOICE: *65-66* 3-5

ERIC: $1-3
GUSTO: 1-3
MUSICOR: *68* 3-5
PHILIPS: *67* 3-5
VIRGO: *72* 1-3
LPs: 10/12-Inch 33rpm
DYNO VOICE: *66* 25-30
SECTET: *81* 5-8

TRACY, Jeanie
(Jeanne Tracy)
Singles: 12-Inch 33/45rpm
MEGATONE: *84-85* 4-6
Singles: 7-Inch
FANTASY: *83* 1-3
SMOGSVILLE: *67* 3-5

TRADE WINDS
Singles: 7-Inch
ERIC: 1-3
KAMA SUTRA: *66-67* 3-5
RED BIRD: *65* 10-15
LPs: 10/12-Inch 33rpm
KAMA SUTRA: *67* 20-30
Members: Pete Anders; Vinnie Poncia.

TRADEWINDS
Singles: 7-Inch
RCA VICTOR: *59* 4-6

TRAFFIC
Singles: 7-Inch
ASYLUM: *74* 2-4
ISLAND: *72-73* 2-4
UNITED ARTISTS: *67-72* 3-5
Picture Sleeves
UNITED ARTISTS: *67* 3-6
LPs: 10/12-Inch 33rpm
ASYLUM: *74* 8-10
ISLAND (Except 9000 series): *83* 5-8
ISLAND (9000 series): *71-75* 8-10
UNITED ARTISTS: *68-75* 10-20
Members: Jim Capaldi; Dave Mason; Steve Winwood; Chris Wood.
Also see CAPALDI, Jim
Also see MASON, Dave
Also see WINWOOD, Steve

TRAITS
Singles: 7-Inch
ASCOT: *62* 8-10
PACEMAKER: *67* 5-10
RENNER: *62* 10-15
SCEPTER: *66* 3-5
TNT: *59-60* 10-15
LPs: 10/12-Inch 33rpm
TNT (101; "Roy Head &
The Traits"): *65* 100-150

Member: Roy Head.
Also see HEAD, Roy

TRAITS
Singles: 7-Inch
UNIVERSAL: *66* $20-30
Member: Johnny Winter.
Also see WINTER, Johnny

TRAMAINE
(Tramaine Hawkins)
Singles: 12-Inch 33/45rpm
A&M: *85-86* 4-6
Singles: 7-Inch
A&M: *85-87* 1-3
LPs: 10/12-Inch 33rpm
A&M: *86* 5-8

TRAMMPS
Singles: 7-Inch
ATLANTIC: *75-80* 1-3
BUDDAH: *72-76* 2-4
ERIC: *78* 1-3
GOLDEN FLEECE: *73-75* 2-4
VENTURE: *83* 1-3
Picture Sleeves
ATLANTIC: *77* 1-3
LPs: 10/12-Inch 33rpm
ATLANTIC: *76-80* 6-10
BUDDAH: *75* 8-10
GOLDEN FLEECE: *75* 8-10
PHILADELPHIA INT'L: *77* 8-10

TRANSVISION VAMP
Singles: 7-Inch
UNI: *88* 1-3
LPs: 10/12-Inch 33rpm
UNI: *88* 5-8

TRANS-X
Singles: 12-Inch 33/45rpm
ATCO: *86* 4-6
MIRAGE: *86* 4-6
Singles: 7-Inch
ATCO: *86* 1-3

TRAPEZE
Singles: 7-Inch
PAID: *81* 1-3
THRESHOLD: *72* 2-4
WARNER BROS: *74-75* 2-4
LPs: 10/12-Inch 33rpm
MEDUSA: 40-60
PAID: *81* 5-8
SHARK: 8-10
THRESHOLD: *70-74* 20-30
WARNER BROS: *74-75* 8-10
Also see DEEP PURPLE

TRASHMEN
Singles: 7-Inch
ARGO: *66* $5-10
BEAR: *66* 5-10
ERA: *72* 2-3
ERIC: 1-3
GARRETT: *63-64* 5-10
LANA: 2-4
METROBEAT: *68* 4-6
TRIBE: *66* 5-8
Picture Sleeves
GARRETT: *64* 10-20
LPs: 10/12-Inch 33rpm
GARRETT: *64* 35-45
Members: Tony Andreason; Bob Reed; Dal
Winslow; Steve Wahrer.

TRAVELING WILBURYS
Singles: 7-Inch
WILBURY: *88* 1-3
LPs: 10/12-Inch 33rpm
WILBURY: *88* 5-8

TRAVERS, Mary
Singles: 7-Inch
CHRYSALIS: *78-79* 1-3
WARNER BROS: *71-73* 2-3
LPs: 10/12-Inch 33rpm
CHRYSALIS: *78* 5-8
WARNER BROS: *71-74* 8-10
Also see PETER, PAUL & MARY

TRAVERS, Pat
(Pat Travers Band; Pat Travers' Black Pearl)
Singles: 7-Inch
POLYDOR: *77-80* 1-3
LPs: 10/12-Inch 33rpm
POLYDOR: *76-84* 5-8

TRAVIS, McKinley
Singles: 7-Inch
PRIDE: *70* 2-4

TRAVIS, Randy
Singles: 7-Inch
WARNER BROS: *85-88* 1-3
LPs: 10/12-Inch 33rpm
WARNER BROS: *87-88* 5-8

TRAVIS & BOB
Singles: 7-Inch
BIG TOP: *60* 3-5
MERCURY: *61* 3-5
SANDY: *59* 4-6
(Reads "Distributed By Dot" on label.)
SANDY: *59* 5-10
(Does not read "Distributed By Dot" on label.)
Members: Travis Pritchett; Bob Weaver.

TRAVOLTA, Joey
Singles: 7-Inch
CASABLANCA: 78-79 .... $2-3
MILLENIUM: 78 2-3
Picture Sleeves
MILLENNIUM: 78 2-3
LPs: 10/12-Inch 33rpm
CASABLANCA: 78-79 5-8
MILLENNIUM: 78 5-8

TRAVOLTA, John
Singles: 7-Inch
MIDLAND INT'L: 76-80 1-3
RCA VICTOR: 77 2-3
RSO: 78-79 1-3
Picture Sleeves
MIDLAND INT'L (Except 10623): 76-80 .. 2-4
MIDLAND INT'L (10623; "Let
 Her In"): 76 4-8
RCA VICTOR: 77 2-3
RSO: 78-79 1-3
LPs: 10/12-Inch 33rpm
MIDLAND INT'L: 76-77 8-10
MIDSONG INT'L: 78 8-10
 Also see NEWTON-JOHN, Olivia, & John
Travolta

TRAVOLTA, John / Sha Na Na
Singles: 7-Inch
RSO: 78 2-3
 Also see SHA NA NA
 Also see TRAVOLTA, John

TREASURES
Singles: 7-Inch
EPIC: 77 2-3
MERCURY: 76 2-4
LPs: 10/12-Inch 33rpm
EPIC: 77 5-8

TREAT HER RIGHT
LPs: 10/12-Inch 33rpm
RCA VICTOR: 88 5-8

TREE SWINGERS
Singles: 7-Inch
GUYDEN: 60 8-10

TREMELOES
Singles: 7-Inch
DJM: 74-75 2-4
EPIC (Except 10075): 67-70 3-5
EPIC (10075; "Good Day
 Sunshine"): 66 4-6
Picture Sleeves
EPIC: 67 3-5
LPs: 10/12-Inch 33rpm
DJM: 74 8-10

EPIC: 67-68 .... $15-20
 Also see POOLE, Brian

T-REX
(Tyrannosaurus Rex)
Singles: 7-Inch
A&M: 68 5-8
BLUE THUMB: 71-72 4-6
CASABLANCA: 75 2-4
REPRISE: 71-74 3-5
LPs: 10/12-Inch 33rpm
A&M (3000 series): 72 10-15
A&M (4000 series): 68 15-20
BLUE THUMB: 71-72 10-15
CASABLANCA: 74 8-10
REPRISE: 71-73 8-12
 Members: Marc Bolan; Jack Green.
 Also see GREEN, Jack

TRIBE
Singles: 7-Inch
ABC: 73-74 2-4
C & CT: 71 2-4
LPs: 10/12-Inch 33rpm
ABC: 73-74 8-10
FARR: 77 8-10
PICKWICK: 75 10-15

TRINERE
Singles: 7-Inch
JAMPACKED: 85-87 1-3
LPs: 10/12-Inch 33rpm
JAMPACKED: 86 5-8

TRIO+ :
 see LEWIS, Jerry Lee, Carl Perkins, & Charlie
 Rich

TRIPLE "S" CONNECTION
Singles: 12-Inch 33/45rpm
20TH CENTURY-FOX: 79-80 4-6
Singles: 7-Inch
20TH CENTURY-FOX: 79-80 1-3
LPs: 10/12-Inch 33rpm
20TH CENTURY-FOX: 79 5-8
 Also see SKOOL BOYZ

TRIUMPH
Singles: 7-Inch
MCA (Black vinyl): 85-86 1-3
MCA (Colored vinyl): 85-86 3-5
RCA VICTOR: 78-84 1-3
LPs: 10/12-Inch 33rpm
MCA: 85-87 5-8
RCA VICTOR: 78-84 5-8
 Members: Mike Levine; Gil Moore; Rik Emmett.

TRIUMVIRAT
Singles: 7-Inch
CAPITOL: 79 ....$1-3
LPs: 10/12-Inch 33rpm
CAPITOL: 74-80 6-10
HARVEST: 74 10-12

TRIXXX
Singles: 12-Inch 33/45rpm
COTILLION: 86 4-6
Singles: 7-Inch
COTILLION: 86 1-3

TROGGS
Singles: 7-Inch
ATCO: 66-67 5-8
BELL: 73 ....3.5
FONTANA: 66-69 4-6
PAGE ONE: 69-70 3-5
PRIVATE STOCK: 77 2-4
PYE: 75-76 2-4
LPs: 10/12-Inch 33rpm
ATCO: 66 35-45
FONTANA: 66-68 20-30
LIBERTY: 66 20-30
MKC: 80 8-10
PRIVATE STOCK: 76 10-15
PYE: 75 10-15
SIRE: 76 12-15

TROLLS
Singles: 7-Inch
ABC: 66-67 3-5
RUFF: 66 5-8
WARRIOR: 4-6
LPs: 10/12-Inch 33rpm
SMASH: 69 10-15

TROLLS
Singles: 7-Inch
U.S.A.: 68 4-8

TROOP
Singles: 7-Inch
ATLANTIC: 88 1-3
LPs: 10/12-Inch 33rpm
ATLANTIC: 88 5-8

TROOPER
Singles: 7-Inch
LEGEND: 75-77 2-4
MCA: 77-78 2-3
LPs: 10/12-Inch 33rpm
LEGEND: 75-76 8-10
MCA: 78-80 5-8
RCA VICTOR: 82 5-8

TROPEA
Singles: 7-Inch
MARLIN: 76-77 ....$2-3
LPs: 10/12-Inch 33rpm
MARLIN: 76-77 8-10

TROUBADOURS DU ROI BAUDOUIN
LPs: 10/12-Inch 33rpm
PHILIPS: 63-69 4-10

TROUBLE
Singles: 7-Inch
AL & THE KIDD: 80 1-3
UNITED ARTISTS: 77 2-3
LPs: 10/12-Inch 33rpm
UNITED ARTISTS: 77 8-10

TROUBLE FUNK
Singles: 12-Inch 33/45rpm
ISLAND: 85-86 4-6
SUGAR HILL: 82 4-6
Singles: 7-Inch
D.E.T.T.: 83 1-3
ISLAND: 85-86 1-3
LPs: 10/12-Inch 33rpm
ISLAND: 86 5-8
SUGAR HILL: 82 5-8

TROUTMAN, Tony
Singles: 7-Inch
GRAM-O-PHONE: 75 2-4
T. MAIN: 82-83 1-3

TROWER, Robin
Singles: 7-Inch
CHRYSALIS: 72-78 2-3
LPs: 10/12-Inch 33rpm
ATLANTIC: 88 5-8
CHRYSALIS: 73-82 5-12
GNP/CRESCENDO: 86 5-8
Also see BRUCE, Jack, & Robin Trower
Also see PROCOL HARUM

TROY, Benny
(Benny Troy & Maze)
Singles: 7-Inch
DE-LITE: 75 2-4
20TH CENTURY-FOX: 1-3

TROY, Doris
Singles: 7-Inch
APPLE: 70 2-4
ATLANTIC: 63-65 3-5
CALLA: 66 3-5
CAPITOL: 67 2-4
MIDLAND INT'L: 76 2-3
LPs: 10/12-Inch 33rpm
APPLE: 70 15-20

ATLANTIC: *64* $20-25

TROYER, Eric
Singles: 7-Inch
CHRYSALIS: *80* 1-3
LPs: 10/12-Inch 33rpm
CHRYSALIS: *80* 5-8

TRUE, Andrea
(Andrea True Connection)
Singles: 7-Inch
BUDDAH: *76-78* 2-4
ERIC: *78* 1-3
LPs: 10/12-Inch 33rpm
BUDDAH: *76-78* 5-8

TRUE LOVE
Singles: 7-Inch
CRITIQUE: *87* 1-3
LPs: 10/12-Inch 33rpm
CRITIQUE: *88* 5-8

TRUMPETEERS
Singles: 7-Inch
SPLASH: *59* 2-4
Member: Billy Mure.
Also see MURE, Billy

Tanya Tucker

TRUSSELL
Singles: 7-Inch
ELEKTRA: *80* $1-3
LPs: 10/12-Inch 33rpm
ELEKTRA: *80* 5-8

TRUTH
Singles: 7-Inch
DEVAKI: *80-81* 1-3
ROULETTE: *74-75* 2-3
LPs: 10/12-Inch 33rpm
PARAGON: *78* 5-8
ROULETTE: *75* 8-10

TRYTHALL, Gil
Singles: 7-Inch
ATHENA: *69-70* 1-3
LPs: 10/12-Inch 33rpm
ATHENA: *69-70* 5-8
PANDORA: *81* 5-8

TUBES
Singles: 12-Inch 33/45rpm
CAPITOL: *83* 4-6
Singles: 7-Inch
A&M: *75-79* 2-4
CAPITOL: *81-85* 1-3
Picture Sleeves
CAPITOL: *81* 1-3
LPs: 10/12-Inch 33rpm
A&M: *75-81* 6-10
CAPITOL: *81-85* 5-8
Members: Fee Waybill; Roger Steen.
Also see WAYBILL, Fee

TUCKER, Junior
Singles: 7-Inch
GEFFEN: *83* 1-3
LPs: 10/12-Inch 33rpm
GEFFEN: *83* 5-8

TUCKER, Louis
Singles: 7-Inch
ARISTA: *83* 1-3
LPs: 10/12-Inch 33rpm
ARISTA: *83* 4-8

TUCKER, Marshall:
see MARSHALL TUCKER BAND

TUCKER, Tanya
Singles: 7-Inch
ARISTA: *82-84* 1-3
CAPITOL: *85-88* 1-3
COLUMBIA: *72-77* 2-4
MCA: *75-81* 1-3
Picture Sleeves
COLUMBIA: *72-75* 3-5
MCA: *75-81* 1-3

LPs: 10/12-Inch 33rpm

ARISTA: 82-84	$5-8
CAPITOL: 86-88	5-8
COLUMBIA ("KC" series): 72-75	8-10
COLUMBIA ("PC" series): 77	5-8
MCA: 75-81	5-8

Also see CAMPBELL, Glen, & Tanya Tucker
Also see HARRIS, Emmylou

TUCKER, Tommy
Singles: 7-Inch

CHECKER: 64-67	3-5
FESTIVAL: 66	3-5
HI: 59-60	4-6
RCA VICTOR (37-7800 series): 61	5-8
(Compact 33 Single.)	
RCA VICTOR (47-7800 series): 61	3-5
RCA VICTOR (68-7800 series): 61	10-15
(Stereo Compact 33 Single.)	
SUNBEAM: 59	4-6
XL: 66	3-5

LPs: 10/12-Inch 33rpm

CHECKER: 64	15-20

TUFANO & GIAMMERSE
Singles: 7-Inch

ODE: 73-76	2-4

LPs: 10/12-Inch 33rpm

EPIC/ODE: 76-77	8-10
ODE. 73-74	10-12

Members: Dennis Tufano; Carl Giammerese.
Also see BUCKINGHAMS

TUFF DARTS
Singles: 7-Inch

SIRE: 78	2-4

LPs: 10/12-Inch 33rpm

SIRE: 78	5-8

TULL, Jethro:
see JETHRO TULL

TUNE ROCKERS
Singles: 7-Inch

PET: 58	5-8
UNITED ARTISTS: 58	4-6

TUNE WEAVERS
(Margo Sylvia & The Tune Weavers)
Singles: 78rpm

CASA GRANDE: 57	10-15
CHECKER: 57	5-10

Singles: 7-Inch

CASA GRANDE (Except 4037): 57-60	15-30
CASA GRANDE (4037; "Happy,	
Happy Birthday Baby"): 57	25-50
CHECKER: 57-62	10-15
CHESS: 73	1-3
CLASSIC ARTISTS: 88-89	2-3

COLLECTABLES:	$1-3
ERIC:	1-3

LPs: 10/12-Inch 33rpm

CASA GRANDE:	10-15

Members: Margo Sylvia; Charlotte Davis; Gil
Lopez; John Sylvia.

TUNETOPPERS:
see BROWN, Al, & His Tunetoppers

TUNNELL, Jimi
Singles: 12-Inch 33/45rpm

MCA: 84	4-6

Singles: 7-Inch

MCA: 84	1-3

TURBANS
Singles: 7-Inch

ABC: 73	1-3
COLLECTABLES:	1-3
FLASHBACK: 65	1-3
HERALD: 55-57	15-20
HI-OLDIES:	1-3
IMPERIAL: 61-62	4-6
MONEY: 55	15-25
PARKWAY: 61	5-8
RED TOP: 60	10-15
ROULETTE: 60-61	5-8

LPs: 10/12-Inch 33rpm

COLLECTABLES: 84	6-8
LOST-NITE: 81	5-8
RELIC:	1-3

Members: Al Banks; Matt Platt; Andrew Jones;
Charles Williams.

TURBANS / Turks
Singles: 7-Inch

MONEY: 55	30-35

Also see TURBANS

TURNER, Ike
(Ike Turner & The Kings Of Rhythm)
Singles: 78rpm

CHESS: 51	8-15
FEDERAL: 57	3-6
FLAIR: 52	5-10
RPM: 52	6-12

Singles: 7-Inch

ARTISTIC: 59	5-8
COBRA: 59	5-8
FEDERAL: 57	5-8
FLAIR: 52	15-20
KING: 61	3-5
LIBERTY: 70	2-4
RPM: 52	20-30
SUE (100 series): 66	3-5
SUE (700 series): 59	4-6
UNITED ARTISTS: 71-74	2-4

LPs: 10/12-Inch 33rpm

CROWN: *63* $20-25
POMPEII: *69* 10-12
UNITED ARTISTS: *72-73* 8-10
Also see BLAND, Bobby, & Ike Turner

TURNER, Ike & Tina
(Ike & Tina Turner & The Ikettes; Ike & Tina Turner & Home Grown Funk)
Singles: 7-Inch

A&M: *69* 2-4
BLUE THUMB: *69-71* 2-4
COLLECTABLES: 1-3
FANTASY: *80* 2-3
INNIS: *68-71* 3-5
KENT (400 series): *64* 3-5
KENT (4500 series): *70* 2-4
LIBERTY: *70-71* 2-4
LOMA: *65* 3-5
MINIT: *69-70* 2-4
MODERN: *65* 3-5
PHILLES (Yellow label): *66* 5-10
PHILLES (White label): *66* 10-15
(Promotional issues only.)
POMPEII: *68-70* 3-5
SONJA: *63-64* 3-5
SUE (100 series): *65-66* 3-5
SUE (700 series): *60-63* 4-6
TRC: *71* 2-4
TANGERINE: *66* 3-6
UNITED ARTISTS: *71-75* 2-4
WARNER BROS: *64* 3-5
Picture Sleeves
POMPEII: *69* 3-5
WARNER BROS: *64* 5-8
LPs: 10/12-Inch 33rpm
A&M (3000 series): *82* 5-8
A&M (4000 series): *69* 10-15
ABC: 8-10
ACCORD: *81* 5-8
BLUE THUMB: *69-73* 8-12
CAPITOL (500 series): *75* 5-8
(With an "SM" prefix.)
CAPITOL (500 series): *69* 10-12
(With an "ST" prefix.)
CENCO: 15-20
COLLECTABLES: *88* 6-8
FANTASY: *80* 5-8
HARMONY (11000 series): *69* 10-12
HARMONY (30000 series): *71* 8-10
KENT: *61-64* 15-20
LIBERTY (7000 series): *70* 10-12
LIBERTY (51000 series): *85* 5-8
LOMA: *66* 10-15
MINIT: *70* 10-12

PHILLES (4011; "River Deep,
Mountain High"): *66* $750-1000
PICKWICK: 6-10
POMPEII: *68-69* 10-12
SUE: *61-65* 40-75
SUNSET: *69-70* 8-10
UNART: 5-10
UNITED ARTISTS: *71-78* 8-12
UNITED SUPERIOR: 8-10
WARNER BROS: *65-69* 12-15
Also see IKETTES
Also see RAELETTES
Also see SYLVIA
Also see TURNER, Tina

TURNER, Jesse Lee
Singles: 7-Inch

CARLTON: *59* 4-6
FRATERNITY: *59* 4-6
GENE NORMAN PRESENTS (184;
"All You Gotta Do"): *62* 4-6
GENE NORMAN PRESENTS (188;
"Shotgun Boogie"): *62* 20-25
IMPERIAL: *60* 5-8
SUDDEN: 3-5
TOP RANK: *60* 3-5
Picture Sleeves
CARLTON: *59* 5-15
FRATERNITY: *59* 25-50

TURNER, Joe
(Big Joe Turner; Joe Turner & His Blues Kings; Joe Turner With Pete Johnson & His Orchestra)
Singles: 78rpm

ALADDIN: *49-50* 5-10
ATLANTIC: *51-57* 4-8
BAYOU: *53* 10-20
COLONY: *52* 4-8
CORAL (65000 series): *48* 5-10
DECCA: *41-56* 5-10
DOWN BEAT: *48* 8-10
EXCELSIOR: *49* 5-10
FIDELITY: *51-52* 5-8
FREEDOM: *50* 5-10
IMPERIAL: *50* 5-10
MGM: *48-50* 5-10
NATIONAL: *46-51* 6-10
RPM: *51* 15-25
SWING BEAT: *49* 5-18
VOCALION: *39* 10-15
Singles: 7-Inch
ATLANTIC (939; "Chains Of
Love"): *51* 35-40
ATLANTIC (949; "Bump Miss
Susie"): *51* 30-35
ATLANTIC (960; "Sweet Sixteen"): *52* .. 30-35

ATLANTIC (970; "Don't You
  Cry"): *52* **$25-30**
ATLANTIC (982; "Don't You
  Cry"): *52* **20-25**
ATLANTIC (1001; "Honey Hush"): *53* .. **12-15**
ATLANTIC (1016; "TV Mama"): *53* **20-25**
ATLANTIC (1026 through 1184): *54-58* .. **6-10**
ATLANTIC (2000 series): *59-60* **4-6**
BAYOU: *53* **40-50**
BLUESWAY: *67* **3-5**
CORAL (62000 series): *64* **3-5**
DECCA (29000 series): *55-56* **10-15**
KENT: *69-71* **2-4**
RPM: *51* **50-75**
RONN: *69* **2-4**
          EPs: 7 Inch 33/45rpm
ATLANTIC: *55-57* **20-35**
EMARCY: *56* **25-35**
          LPs: 10/12-Inch 33rpm
ARHOOLIE: *62* **15-20**
ATCO: *71* **8-10**
ATLANTIC (1234; "Boss Of
  The Blues"): *58* **30-40**
ATLANTIC (1332; "Big Joe
  Rides Again"): *60* **25-30**
ATLANTIC (8005; "Joe Turner"): *57* ... **35-45**
  (Black label.)
ATLANTIC (8005; "Joe Turner"): *59* ... **20-25**
  (Red label.)
ATLANTIC (8023; "Rockin'
  The Blues"): *58* **50-80**
  (Black label.)
ATLANTIC (8023; "Rockin'
  The Blues"): *59* **20-25**
  (Red label.)
ATLANTIC (8033; "Big Joe
  Is Here"): *59* **50-80**
  (Black label.)
ATLANTIC (8033; "Big Joe
  Is Here"): *59* **20-25**
  (Red label.)
ATLANTIC (8081; "Best Of
  Joe Turner"): *63* **15-20**
ATLANTIC (8812; "Boss Of
  The Blues"): *81* **5-8**
BIG TOWN: *78* **5-8**
BLUES SPECTRUM: **10-12**
BLUESWAY: *67-73* **8-12**
CHIARASCURO: *76* **8-10**
CLASSIC JAZZ: *79* **5-8**
EMARCY (36014; "Joe Turner With
  Pete Johnson"): *56* **50-100**
INTERMEDIA: *83-84* **5-8**
LMI: *74* **8-10**
MCA: *80* **5-8**

PABLO: *76-83* **$5-8**
SAVOY: *77* **5-8**
UNITED: **8-10**
  Also see KING CURTIS

TURNER, Joe / Jimmy Nelson
          LPs: 10/12-Inch 33rpm
CROWN: *62* **10-20**
  Also see NELSON, Jimmy
  Also see TURNER, Joe

TURNER, Ruby
(Ruby Turner Featuring Jonathan Butler)
          Singles: 7-Inch
JIVE: *86* **1-3**
          LPs: 10/12-Inch 33rpm
JIVE: *86* **5-8**
  Also see BUTLER, Jonathan

TURNER, Sammy
(Sammy Turner & The Twisters)
          Singles: 7-Inch
BIG TOP (3007 & 3016): *59* **4-6**
BIG TOP (3029; "Always"): *59* **4-6**
BIG TOP (3029; "Always"): *59* **8-10**
  (Stereo.)
BIG TOP (3032 through 3070): *60-61* **3-5**
BIG TOP (3089; "Falling"): *61* **8-10**
ERIC: **1-3**
MILLENNIUM: *78* **2-3**
MOTOWN: *64* **10-15**
PACIFIC: *59* **15-20**
20TH CENTURY-FOX: *65* **3-5**
VERVE: *66* **3-5**
          LPs: 10/12-Inch 33rpm
BIG TOP: *60* **20-30**
  Also see KING CURTIS

TURNER, Spyder
          Singles: 7-Inch
KWANZA: *73* **2-5**
MGM: *66-71* **3-5**
POLYDOR: *84* **1-3**
WHITFIELD: *78-79* **2-3**
          LPs: 10/12-Inch 33rpm
MGM: *67* **15-20**
WHITFIELD: *78-79* **5-8**
  Also see BRISTOL, Johnny, & Spyder Turner

TURNER, Tina
          Singles: 12-Inch 33/45rpm
CAPITOL: *84-87* **4-6**
          Singles: 7-Inch
CAPITOL: *84-87* **1-3**
POMPEII: *68* **3-5**
UNITED ARTISTS: *75-78* **2-4**
WAGNER: *79* **2-3**

Tina Turner

Picture Sleeves
CAPITOL: *84-87* $1-3
LPs: 10/12-Inch 33rpm
CAPITOL: *84-88* 5-8
FANTASY: 5-8
SPRINGBOARD: *72* 8-10
UNITED ARTISTS (Except 200): *75-78* . . 8-10
UNITED ARTISTS (200; "Tina Turner
    Turns The Country On"): *67* 8-15
WAGNER: *79* 5-8
    Also see ADAMS, Bryan, & Tina Turner
    Also see BOWIE, David
    Also see JOHN, Elton / Tina Turner
    Also see TURNER, Ike & Tina
    Also see U.S.A. FOR AFRICA

TURNER, Titus
Singles: 78rpm
ATLANTIC: *57* 3-6
Singles: 7-Inch
ATCO: *64* 3-5
ATLANTIC: *57* 5-10
COLUMBIA: *63* 3-5
ENJOY: *62-63* 3-5
GLOVER (Except 302): *59-60* 4-6
GLOVER (302; "When The Sergeant
    Comes Marching Home"): *60* 10-15
GUARANTEED: *61-62* 3-5
JAMIE: *61* 3-5
JOSIE: *68-69* 2-4
KING (Monaural singles): *57-61* 4-6
KING (Stereo singles): *59* 5-8
MURBO: *65* 3-5
OKEH (6844 through 7038): *52-54* 10-15
OKEH (7200 series): *66* 3-5
PHILIPS: *67* 3-5
WING: *55* 8-10

LPs: 10/12-Inch 33rpm
JAMIE: *61* $20-25
TURRENTINE, Stanley
Singles: 7-Inch
BLUE NOTE: *61-69* 2-4
CTI: *72* 1-3
ELEKTRA: *79-81* 1-3
FANTASY: *74-78* 1-3
IMPULSE: *67* 2-4
LPs: 10/12-Inch 33rpm
BAINBRIDGE: *81* 5-8
BLUE NOTE: *60-61* 25-50
    (Label gives New York street address for Blue
    Note Records.)
BLUE NOTE: *62-65* 15-25
    (Label reads "Blue Note Records Inc. - New York,
    U.S.A.")
BLUE NOTE: *66-85* 8-18
    (Label shows Blue Note Records as a division of
    either Liberty or United Artists.)
CTI: *71-75* 8-12
ELEKTRA: *79-81* 5-8
FPM: *75* 5-8
FANTASY: *74-78* 6-12
IMPULSE: *67-78* 8-15
MAINSTREAM: *65* 12-25
PRESTIGE: *70-71* 5-10
SUNSET: *69* 5-10
TIME: *62-63* 25-50
UPFRONT: *72* 6-10
    Also see BYRD, Donald, & Stanley Turrentine
    Also see GILBERTO, Astrud, & Stanley Tur-
rentine
    Also see HUBBARD, Freddie, & Stanley Tur-
rentine
    Also see SILVER, Horace, Quintet, & Stanley
Turrentine

TURTLES
Singles: 7-Inch
COLLECTABLES: 1-3
WHITE WHALE: *65-70* 3-5
Picture Sleeves
WHITE WHALE: *66-69* 3-6
LPs: 10/12-Inch 33rpm
RHINO (Except picture discs): *82-86* 5-8
RHINO (Picture discs): *83* 8-10
SIRE: *74* 10-15
TRIP: 5-8
WHITE WHALE: *65-71* 20-25
Members: Howard Kaylan; Mark Volman; Don
Murray; Chuck Portz; Al Nichol; Jim Tucker; John
Barbata; John Seiter; Jim Pons.
Also see CHRISTMAS SPIRIT

TURZY, Jane
Singles: 78rpm
DECCA: *51-54* $2-4
Singles: 7-Inch
DECCA: *51-54* 2-4

TUTONE, Tommy: see Tommy Tutone

TUXEDO JUNCTION
Singles: 12-Inch 33/45rpm
BUTTERFLY: *78-80* 4-6
Singles: 7-Inch
BUTTERFLY (Black vinyl): *78-80* 1-3
LPs: 10/12-Inch 33rpm
BUTTERFLY (Black vinyl): *77-79* 5-8
BUTTERFLY (Colored vinyl): *77* 10-12
(Promotional issues only.)

TWENNYNINE
Singles: 7-Inch
ELEKTRA: *79-81* 1-3
LPs: 10/12-Inch 33rpm
ELEKTRA: *79-81* 5-8
Member: Lenny White.
Also see WHITE, Lenny

20-20
Singles: 7-Inch
PORTRAIT: *79* 1-3
EPs: 7-Inch 33/45rpm
BOMP: 5-10
LPs: 10/12-Inch 33rpm
ENIGMA: *83* 5-8
PORTRAIT: *79-81* 5-8

21ST CENTURY
Singles: 7-Inch
RCA VICTOR: *75* 2-4

TWILIGHT 22
Singles: 12-Inch 33/45rpm
VANGUARD: *83-84* 4-6
Singles: 7-Inch
VANGUARD: *83-84* 1-3
LPs: 10/12-Inch 33rpm
VANGUARD: *84* 5-8

TWILLEY, Dwight, Band
Singles: 7-Inch
ARISTA: *77-79* 2-3
EMI AMERICA: *82-84* 1-3
SHELTER: *75-76* 2-4
Picture Sleeves
SHELTER: *75-76* 2-4
LPs: 10/12-Inch 33rpm
ARISTA: *77-79* 5-8
EMI AMERICA: *82-84* 5-8
SHELTER: *75-76* 8-10
Also see SEYMOUR, Phil

TWIN IMAGE
Singles: 12-Inch 33/45rpm
CAPITOL: *84-85* $4-6
Singles: 7-Inch
CAPITOL: *84-85* 1-3
LPs: 10/12-Inch 33rpm
CAPITOL: *84* 5-8

TWINS
Singles: 12-Inch 33/45rpm
QUALITY/RFC: *83* 4-6

TWISTED SISTER
Singles: 7-Inch
ATLANTIC: *83-86* 1-3
LPs: 10/12-Inch 33rpm
ATLANTIC: *83-87* 5-8
Member: Dee Snider.

TWITTY, Conway
Singles: 78rpm
MERCURY: *57* 5-10
Singles: 7-Inch
ABC-PARAMOUNT (10507; "Go On
And Cry"): *63* 5-8
ABC-PARAMOUNT (10550; "My
Baby Left Me"): *64* 8-12
DECCA: *65-72* 2-4
ELEKTRA: *82-83* 1-3
MCA: *73-88* 1-3
MGM (500 series): *78* 1-3
MGM (12000 & 13000 series): *58-62* 4-6
MGM (14000 series): *71-72* 2-4
MGM (50000 series): *58-59* 15-25
(Stereo.)
MERCURY: *57-58* 15-25
MUSIGRAM: 2-4
(Flexi-disc.)
POLYDOR: 1-3
WARNER BROS: *83-86* 1-3
Picture Sleeves
ELEKTRA: *82* 1-3
MGM: *58-62* 10-15
EPs: 7-Inch 33/45rpm
MGM: *58-59* 15-20
LPs: 10/12-Inch 33rpm
ACCORD: *82* 5-8
ALLEGIANCE: *84* 5-8
CANDLELITE: 10-12
CORAL: *73* 4-8
DECCA: *66-72* 8-15
DEMAND: *72* 8-12
ELEKTRA: *82-83* 5-8
MCA: *73-85* 5-12
MCA: *88* 5-8
MGM (110; "Conway Twitty"): *70* 10-15

MGM (3744; "Conway Twitty
Sings"): *59* $30-40
MGM (3786; "Saturday Night With
Conway Twitty"): *59* 30-40
MGM (3818; "Lonely Blue Boy"): *60* . . . 20-30
MGM (3849; "Conway Twitty's
Greatest Hits"): *60* 30-40
(Black label. With gatefold cover and poster.)
MGM (3849; "Conway Twitty's
Greatest Hits"): *68* 10-12
(Blue and yellow label. With standard cover.)
MGM (3907; "The Rock &
Roll Story"): *61* 30-40
MGM (3943; "The Conway Twitty
Touch"): *61* 20-30
MGM (4019 through 4217): *62-64* 20-30
MGM (4650 through 4884): *69-73* 10-15
METRO: *65* 15-20
OPRYLAND (12636; "Conway
Twitty, Then And Now"): 60-80
(6-LP set. Promotional issue only.)
PICKWICK: *72* 10-12
TEE VEE: *78* 5-10
TROLLY CAR: 5-8
WARNER BROS: *83-86* 5-8

TWITTY, Conway, & Loretta Lynn
Singles: 7-Inch
DECCA: *71-72* 2-4
MCA: *73-81* 1-3
LPs: 10/12-Inch 33rpm
DECCA: *71-72* 8-15
MCA: *73-84* 5-10
MCA: *88* 5-8
TVP: *76* 8-12
Also see LYNN, Loretta
Also see TWITTY, Conway

2 LIVE CREW
Singles: 7-Inch
LUKE SKYW: *88* 1-3
LPs: 10/12-Inch 33rpm
LUKE SKYW: *87-88* 5-8

2 OF CLUBS
Singles: 7-Inch
FRATERNITY: *66-67* 3-5

TWO SISTERS
Singles: 12-Inch 33/45rpm
SUGARSCOOP: *83* 4-6

TWO TONS O' FUN
(Two Tons)
Singles: 12-Inch 33/45rpm
FANTASY: *80* 4-6
Singles: 7-Inch
FANTASY: *80* 1-3

HONEY: *80-81* $1-3
LPs: 10/12-Inch 33rpm
FANTASY: *80* 5-8
HONEY: *80* 5-8
Members: Martha Wash; Izora Armstead.
Also see WEATHER GIRLS

TYCOON
Singles: 7-Inch
ARISTA: *79* 1-3
LPs: 10/12-Inch 33rpm
ARISTA: *78-81* 5-8

TYLER, Bonnie
Singles: 7-Inch
CHRYSALIS: *77* 2-4
COLUMBIA: *83-86* 1-3
RCA VICTOR: *78-79* 2-3
LPs: 10/12-Inch 33rpm
CHRYSALIS: *77* 10-12
COLUMBIA: *83-86* 5-8
RCA VICTOR: *78-81* 5-8
Also see RUNDGREN, Todd

TYLER, Frankie
(Frankie Valli)
Singles: 7-Inch
OKEH (7103; "I Go Ape"): *58* 45-55
Promotional Singles
OKEH (7103; "I Go Ape"): *58* 25-35
Also see VALLI, Frankie

TYMES
Singles: 7-Inch
ABKCO: 1-3
COLUMBIA: *68-70* 2-4
MGM: *66* 3-5
PARKWAY (Except 871): *63-64* 4-8
PARKWAY (871; "So In Love"): *63* 8-10
PARKWAY (871; "So Much In Love"): *63* .4-8
RCA VICTOR: *74-77* 2-4
WINCHESTER: *67* 3-5
Picture Sleeves
PARKWAY: *63-64* 4-8
LPs: 10/12-Inch 33rpm
KABKCO: *74* 5-8
COLUMBIA: *69* 10-15
PARKWAY: *63-64* 15-25
RCA VICTOR: *74-77* 8-10
Members: George Williams Jr.; Donald Banks; Al
Berry; Norman Burnett; George Hilliard.

TYNER, McCoy
(McCoy Tyner Trio)
Singles: 7-Inch
COLUMBIA: *82* 1-3
IMPULSE: *65* 2-4

LPs: 10/12-Inch 33rpm
BLUE NOTE: *66-76* $8-15
COLUMBIA: *82* 5-8
FPM: *75* 5-8
IMPULSE: *62-78* 10-20
MCA: *81* 5-8
MILESTONE: *72-82* 6-12
PAUSA: *82* 5-8

TYRANNOSAURUS REX:
see T-REX

TYZIK
(Jeff Tyzik)
Singles: 12-Inch 33/45rpm
POLYDOR: *84* 4-6
Singles: 7-Inch
CAPITOL: *82* 1-3
POLYDOR: *84* 1-3
LPs: 10/12-Inch 33rpm
CAPITOL: *82* 5-8
POLYDOR: *84* 5-8

U

UB40
(UB40 With Chrissie Hynde)
Singles: 12-Inch 33/45rpm
A&M: *83-86* 4-6
Singles: 7-Inch
A&M: *83-88* 1-3
LPs: 10/12-Inch 33rpm
A&M: *83-88* 5-8
Also see PRETENDERS

UFO
Singles: 7-Inch
CHRYSALIS: *73-86* 1-3
LPs: 10/12-Inch 33rpm
CHRYSALIS: *74-86* 5-12
RARE EARTH: *71* 10-15
Also see SCHENKER, Michael, Group

U.K.
Singles: 7-Inch
POLYDOR: *78-79* 2-3
LPs: 10/12-Inch 33rpm
POLYDOR: *78-79* 5-8
Members: John Wetton; Eddie Jobson; Terry Bozzio; Bill Bruford; Allan Holdsworth.

U.K. SQUEEZE: see SQUEEZE

U.S.A.- EUROPEAN CONNECTION
Singles: 7-Inch
MARLIN: *78-79* 2-3

LPs: 10/12-Inch 33rpm
MARLIN: *78-79* $5-8

U.S.A. FOR AFRICA
Singles: 12-Inch 33/45rpm
COLUMBIA: *85* 4-6
Singles: 7-Inch
COLUMBIA: *85* 1-3
LPs: 10/12-Inch 33rpm
COLUMBIA: *85* 5-8
Members: Dan Aykroyd; Kim Carnes; Ray Charles; Bob Dylan; Daryl Hall; James Ingram; Michael Jackson; Jean-Michael Jarre; Al Jarreau; Waylon Jennings; Billy Joel; Quincy Jones; Cyndi Lauper; Huey Lewis; Kenny Loggins; Bette Midler; Steve Perry; Lionel Richie; Smokey Robinson; Kenny Rogers; Diana Ross; Paul Simon; Bruce Springsteen; Tina Turner; Dionne Warwick; Stevie Wonder.
Also see CARNES, Kim
Also see CHARLES, Ray
Also see DYLAN, Bob
Also see HALL, Daryl
Also see INGRAM, James
Also see JACKSON, Michael
Also see JARRE, Jean-Michael
Also see JARREAU, Al
Also see JENNINGS, Waylon
Also see JOEL, Billy
Also see JONES, Quincy
Also see LAUPER, Cyndi
Also see LEWIS, Huey, & The News
Also see LOGGINS, Kenny
Also see MIDLER, Bette
Also see PERRY, Steve
Also see RICHIE, Lionel
Also see ROBINSON, Smokey
Also see ROGERS, Kenny
Also see ROSS, Diana
Also see SIMON, Paul
Also see SPRINGSTEEN, Bruce
Also see TURNER, Tina
Also see VOICES OF AMERICA / U.S.A. FOR AFRICA
Also see WARWICK, Dionne
Also see WONDER, Stevie

U.S. BONDS:
see BONDS, Gary U.S.

U.S. 1
Singles: 7-Inch
PRIVATE STOCK: *75* 2-4

UTFO
Singles: 12-Inch 33/45rpm
SELECT: *85-86* 4-6

Singles: 7-Inch
SELECT: *85-87* $1-3
LPs: 10/12-Inch 33rpm
SELECT: *85-86* 5-8
Also see ROXANNE WITH UTFO

U2
Singles: 12-Inch 33/45rpm
ISLAND: *83* 4-6
Singles: 7-Inch
ISLAND: *81-89* 1-3
Picture Sleeves
ISLAND: *81-89* 1-3
LPs: 10/12-Inch 33rpm
ISLAND: *81-89* 5-10
Members: Paul "Bono Vox" Hewson; David "The Edge" Evan; Adam Clayton; Larry Mullen.
Also see BAND AID

UBIQUITY
Singles: 7-Inch
ELEKTRA: *78* 2-3
LPs: 10/12-Inch 33rpm
ELEKTRA: *78* 5-8
Also see AYERS, Roy

UGGAMS, Leslie
Singles: 7-Inch
ATLANTIC: *65-70* 2-3
COLUMBIA: *59-64* 2-4
GORDY: *76* 1-3
MGM: *54-55* 2-5
SONDAY: *71* 1-3
EPs: 7-Inch 33/45rpm
MGM: *54* 5-10
LPs: 10/12-Inch 33rpm
ATLANTIC: *66-69* 5-10
COLUMBIA: *59-63* 5-15
MOTOWN: *75* 5-10
SONDAY: *72* 5-10

ULLANDA
Singles: 7-Inch
OCEAN: *79* 2-3

ULLMAN, Tracey
Singles: 7-Inch
MCA: *84-85* 1-3
LPs: 10/12-Inch 33rpm
MCA: *84* 5-8

ULTIMATE
Singles: 7-Inch
CASABLANCA: *78-80* 1-3
LPs: 10/12-Inch 33rpm
CASABLANCA: *78-80* 5-8

ULTIMATE SPINACH
Singles: 7-Inch
MGM: *68-69* $3-6
LPs: 10/12-Inch 33rpm
MGM: *68-69* 20-30

ULTRAMAGNETIC MC'S
LPs: 10/12-Inch 33rpm
NEXT PLATEAU: *88* 5-8

ULTRAVOX
Singles: 12-Inch 33/45rpm
CHRYSALIS: *83* 4-6
Singles: 7-Inch
ANTILLES: *78-80* 1-3
CHRYSALIS: *80-83* 1-3
ISLAND: *77* 8-10
LPs: 10/12-Inch 33rpm
ANTILLES: *78-80* 5-8
CHRYSALIS: *80-83* 5-8
ISLAND: *77* 8-10
Also see BAND AID

UMILANI, Piero
Singles: 7-Inch
ARIEL: *69* 2-3
LPs: 10/12-Inch 33rpm
ARIEL: *69* 8-12

UNCLE DOG
Singles: 7-Inch
MCA: *73* 2-3
LPs: 10/12-Inch 33rpm
MCA: *73* 8-10

UNCLE LOUIE
Singles: 7-Inch
MARLIN: *79* 2-3
LPs: 10/12-Inch 33rpm
MARLIN: *78* 5-8

UNDERGROUND SUNSHINE
Singles: 7-Inch
INTREPID: *69* 3-6
LPs: 10/12-Inch 33rpm
INTERPID: *69* 10-15

UNDERTONES
Singles: 7-Inch
CAPITOL: *84* 1-3
HARVEST: *81* 1-3
SIRE: *80* 1-3
LPs: 10/12-Inch 33rpm
CAPITOL: *84* 5-8
HARVEST: *81* 8-10
SIRE: *80* 5-8
Member: Feargal Sharkey.
Also see SHARKEY, Feargal

UNDERWOOD, Veronica
Singles: 7-Inch
PHILLY WORLD: 85 .... $1-3

UNDERWORLD
Singles: 7-Inch
SIRE: 88 1-3
LPs: 10/12-Inch 33rpm
SIRE: 88 5-8

UNDISPUTED TRUTH
Singles: 12-Inch 33/45rpm
WHITFIELD: 77-79 4-6
Singles: 7-Inch
GORDY: 71-75 2-4
MOTOWN: 1-3
WHITFIELD: 76-79 2-3
LPs: 10/12-Inch 33rpm
GORDY: 71-75 8-10
WHITFIELD: 77-79 5-8
Members: Joe Harris; Brenda Evans; Billie Calvin;
Carl Smalls.
Also see DRAMATICS

UNICORN
Singles: 7-Inch
CAPITOL: 74-77 2-3
LPs: 10/12-Inch 33rpm
CAPITOL: 74-77 8-10

UNIFICS
Singles: 7-Inch
FOUNTAIN: 71 2-4
KAPP: 68-69 3-5
MCA: 1-3
Picture Sleeves
KAPP: 68-69 3-6
LPs: 10/12-Inch 33rpm
KAPP: 68 10-15

UNION GAP: see PUCKET, Gary

UNIPOP
Singles: 7-Inch
KAT FAMILY: 82 1-3
LPs: 10/12-Inch 33rpm
KAT FAMILY: 82 5-8

UNIQUE
Singles: 12-Inch 33/45rpm
PRELUDE: 83 4-6
Singles: 7-Inch
PRELUDE: 83 1-3

UNIQUES
Singles: 7-Inch
PARAMOUNT: 70-72 2-4
PAULA: 65-70 3-5
LPs: 10/12-Inch 33rpm
PAULA: 66-70 12-20

Members: Joe Stampley; Bobby Stampley; Jim
Woodfield; Mike Love; Ray Mills; Bobby Sims;
Ronnie Weiss.
Also see STAMPLEY, Joe

UNIT 4+2
Singles: 7-Inch
LONDON: 65-66 .... $3-5
LPs: 10/12-Inch 33rpm
LONDON: 65 25-35
Member: Russ Ballard.
Also see BALLARD, Russ

UNITED STATES AIR FORCE BAND
LPs: 10/12-Inch 33rpm
RCA VICTOR: 63 5-10

UNITED STATES MARINE BAND
LPs: 10/12-Inch 33rpm
RCA VICTOR: 63 5-10

UNITED STATES NAVY BAND
LPs: 10/12-Inch 33rpm
RCA VICTOR: 63 5-10

UNITED STATES OF AMERICA
LPs: 10/12-Inch 33rpm
COLUMBIA: 68 5-20
Members: Dorothy Moskowitz; Joseph Byrd;
Gordon Marron; Rand Forbes; Craig Woodson.

UNITS
Singles: 12-Inch 33/45rpm
EPIC: 83-84 4-6
UPROAR: 83 4-6
Singles: 7-Inch
EPIC: 84 1-3
LPs: 10/12-Inch 33rpm
EPIC: 84 5-8

UNIVERSAL ROBOT BAND
Singles: 7-Inch
GREG RED: 77 2-3
LPs: 10/12-Inch 33rpm
GREG RED: 77 5-8

UNKNOWNS
Singles: 7-Inch
MARLIN: 67 3-5
PARROT: 66 4-6
SHIELD: 4-6
LPs: 10/12-Inch 33rpm
SIRE: 81 8-10
INVASION: 83 8-10
Member: Keith Allison.

UNLIMITED TOUCH
Singles: 12-Inch 33/45rpm
PRELUDE: 81-84 4-6
Singles: 7-Inch
PRELUDE: 81-84 1-3

LPs: 10/12-Inch 33rpm
PRELUDE: *81-84* $5-8
Also see LORBER, Jeff

UP WITH PEOPLE
LPs: 10/12-Inch 33rpm
PACE : *66-70* 4-8

UPBEATS
Singles: 7-Inch
JOY: *58-59* 4-6
PREP: *57-58* 4-6
SWAN: *58* 4-6

UPCHURCH, Phil
(Phil Upchurch Combo)
Singles: 7-Inch
BOYD: *61* 4-6
GOLDEN FLEECE: *74* 2-3
MARLIN: *79* 1-3
UNITED ARTISTS: *61-62* 3-5
LPs: 10/12-Inch 33rpm
BLUE THUMB : *73* 8-10
BOYD: *61* 20-25
CADET: *69* 8-10
MILESTINE: 5-8
UNITED ARTISTS: *61-62* 15-20
Also see REED, Jimmy

UPCHURCH, Phil, & Tennyson
Stephens
LPs: 10/12-Inch 33rpm
KUDU: *75* 8-10
Also see STEPHENS, Tennyson
Also see UPCHURCH, Phil

UPFRONT
Singles: 12-Inch 33/45rpm
SILVER CLOUD: *83* 4-6

URGENT
Singles: 7-Inch
MANHATTAN: *85* 1-3

URIAH HEEP
Singles: 7-Inch
CHRYSALIS: *78* 2-3
MERCURY: *70-82* 2-4
WARNER BROS: *73-78* 2-4
Picture Sleeves
MERCURY: *70-82* 2-4
LPs: 10/12-Inch 33rpm
CHRYSALIS: *78-79* 5-8
MERCURY: *70-82* 6-10
WARNER BROS: *73-81* 8-10
Also see HENSLEY, Ken
Also see ROUGH DIAMOND

UTOPIA
Singles: 7-Inch
BEARSVILLE: *76-80* $2-4
NETWORK: *82* 1-3
PASSPORT: *84-85* 1-3
LPs: 10/12-Inch 33rpm
BEARSVILLE: *80-82* 5-8
KENT: *73* 10-15
NETWORK: *82* 8-10
PASSPORT: *84-85* 5-8
Members: Todd Rundgren; Willie Wilcox; Roger
Powell; Kasim Sulton.
Also see CASSIDY, Shaun, & Todd
Rundgren's Utopia
Also see RUNDGREN, Todd

V

V.S.O.P.
LPs: 10/12-Inch 33rpm
COLUMBIA: *77* 5-8
Members: Herbie Hancock; Wayne Shorter; Fred-
die Hubbard; Tony Williams.

VACELS
Singles: 7-Inch
KAMA SUTRA: *65* 4-6

VALADIERS
Singles: 7-Inch
GORDY: *62-63* 25-30
MIRACLE: *61* 30-35

VALE, Jerry
Singles: 78rpm
COLUMBIA: *51-57* 2-4
Singles: 7-Inch
BUDDAH: *78* 1-3
COLUMBIA: *51-74* 2-5
Picture Sleeves
COLUMBIA: *64-65* 2-4
EPs: 7-Inch 33/45rpm
COLUMBIA: *56-59* 5-10
LPs: 10/12-Inch 33rpm
COLUMBIA: *58-75* 5-15
HARMONY: *69-74* 5-10

VALE, Jerry, Peggy King, &
Felicia Sanders
LPs: 10/12-Inch 33rpm
COLUMBIA: *56* 10-15
Also see KING, Peggy
Also see SANDERS, Felicia
Also see VALE, Jerry

VALENS, Ritchie
Singles: 12-Inch 33/45rpm
DEL-FI: $10-15
Singles: 7-Inch
ABC: *74* 1-3
DEL-FI: *58* 15-20
(Solid green label with black print.)
DEL-FI: *58-60* 8-15
(With rows of circles on label.)
ERIC: 1-3
GOODIES: 1-3
KASEY: 5-8
LANA: 1-3
Picture Sleeves
DEL-FI (4114: "That's My
Little Suzie"): *59* 15-25
DEL-FI (4117: "Little Girl"): *59* 20-35
(With explanatory "Concerning This Record" insert.)
DEL-FI (4117: "Little Girl"): *59* 15-25
(Without insert.)
DEL-FI (4128: "Stay Beside Me"): *60* ... 15-25
EPs: 7-Inch 33/45rpm
DEL-FI (111; "Ritchie Valens"): *60* 50-75
LPs: 10/12-Inch 33rpm
DEL-FI (Except 1214): *59-65* 50-75
DEL-FI (1214; "Ritchie Valens
In Concert"): *61* 60-80
GUEST STAR: *64* 15-20
MGM: *70* 10-15
RHINO (Except 2798): *81-87* 5-8
RHINO (2798; "History Of
Ritchie Valens"): *81* 20-25

VALENS, Ritchie / Jerry Kole
LPs: 10/12-Inch 33rpm
CROWN: *63* 20-30
Also see VALENS, Ritchie

VALENTE, Caterina
Singles: 78rpm
DECCA: *54-57* 2-4
Singles: 7-Inch
DECCA: *54-59* 2-5
LONDON: *60-68* 2-4
RCA VICTOR: *59* 2-4
TELEFUNKEN: *59* 2-4
EPs: 7-Inch 33/45rpm
DECCA: *55* 5-10
LPs: 10/12-Inch 33rpm
DECCA: *55-64* 5-15
LONDON: *59-72* 5-15
RCA VICTOR: *61* 5-15

VALENTE, Dino
Singles: 7-Inch
ELEKTRA: *64* 5-8

LPs: 10/12-Inch 33rpm
EPIC: *68* $15-20
Also see QUICKSILVER MESSENGER SERVICE

VALENTI, John
Singles: 7-Inch
ARIOLA AMERICA: *76-77* 2-3

VALENTIN, Dave
Singles: 7-Inch
GRP: *80-81* 1-3
LPs: 10/12-Inch 33rpm
GRP: *80-81* 5-8

VALENTINE, Lezli
Singles: 7-Inch
ALL PLATINUM: *68* 2-4

VALENTINE BROTHERS
Singles: 12-Inch 33/45rpm
SOURCE: *78* 4-6
Singles: 7-Inch
A&M: *84* 1-3
BRIDGE: *82* 1-3
SOURCE: *79* 1-3
LPs: 10/12-Inch 33rpm
A&M: *84* 5-8
BRIDGE: *82* 5-8
SOURCE: *79* 5-8

VALENTINO, Danny
Singles: 7-Inch
CONTRAST: *67* 3-5
MGM: *59-60* 4-6

VALENTINO, Mark
Singles: 7-Inch
SWAN: *62-63* 5-8
(May be erroneously shown as Mark
Valentinon on some Swan pressings.)

LPs: 10/12-Inch 33rpm
SWAN: *63* $30-40

VALENTINOS
Singles: 7-Inch
ABKCO: 1-3
ASTRA: 4-6
CHESS: *66* 3-5
CLEAN: *73* 2-4
JUBILEE: *68-69* 2-4
SAR: *62-64* 4-6
Members: Bobby Womack; Curtis Womack.
Also see WOMACK, Bobby
Also see WOMACK BROTHERS

VALERIE & NICK
Singles: 7-Inch
GLOVER: *64* 5-8
Members: Valerie Simpson; Nick Ashford.
Also see ASHFORD & SIMPSON

VALERY, Dana
Singles: 7-Inch
ABC: *68-69* 3-5
COLUMBIA: *67* 8-10
LIBERTY: *70* 2-4
PHANTOM: *75* 2-4
SCOTTI BROS: *79* 2-3
Picture Sleeves
PHANTOM: *75* 2-4
Also see SIMON, Paul

VALIANTS
(Featuring Billy Storm)
Singles: 78rpm
KEEN: *57* 5-8
Singles: 7-Inch
KEEN: *57-58* 15-20
SHAR-DEE: *59* 10-15
Also see STORM, Billy

VALINO, Joe
Singles: 78rpm
UNITED ARTISTS: *57* 3-5
VIK: *56* 3-5
Singles: 7-Inch
BANDBOX: *61* 3-5
CROSLEY: *59-60* 3-6
DEBUT: *67-68* 2-4
RCA VICTOR: *59* 3-6
UNITED ARTISTS: *57-58* 6-12
VIK: *56* 4-8
Picture Sleeves
UNITED ARTISTS (101; "Legend
Of The Lost"): *57* 20-30
LPs: 10/12-Inch 33rpm
DEBUT: *67* 8-12

VALJEAN
(Valjean Johns)
Singles: 7-Inch
CARLTON: *62-63* $2-4
Picture Sleeves
CARLTON: *62* 3-5
LPs: 10/12-Inch 33rpm
CARLTON: *62-63* 10-20

VALLI, Frankie
**(Frankie Valley & The Travelers; Frankie Valle;
Frankie Vally; Frankie Vallie & The Romans)**
Singles: 10/12-Inch 33/45rpm
MOTOWN: *73* 15-20
PRIVATE STOCK: *77* 10-15
Singles: 7-Inch
CINDY: *59* 75-100
COLLECTABLES: 1-3
CORONA (1234; "My Mother's
Eyes"): *53* 200-300
DECCA (30994; "Please Take
A Chance"): *59* 75-100
MERCURY (70381; "Forgive &
Forget"): *54* 75-125
(Maroon label.)
MERCURY (70381; "Forgive &
Forget"): *54* 40-60
(Black label.)
MOTOWN: *73* 8-10
MOWEST: *72* 5-8
PHILIPS (40407 through 45098): *66-70* 4-6
PHILIPS (40661 & 40680): *69-70* 10-12
PRIVATE STOCK: *74-78* 2-4
RSO: *78* 2-4
SMASH: *65-66* 5-10
WARNER/CURB: *78-80* 2-4
Promotional Singles
BOB CREWE PRESENTS (1; "The
Girl I'll Never Know"): *69* 25-30
DECCA (30994; "Please Take
A Chance"): *59* 30-40
MERCURY (70381; "Forgive &
Forget"): *54* 50-75
MOWEST (5025; "The Night"): *71* 12-15
PHILIPS: *66-70* 8-12
PRIVATE STOCK: *74-78* 8-10
SMASH: *65-66* 8-12
Picture Sleeves
PHILIPS: *66-69* 8-15
LPs: 10/12-Inch 33rpm
MOTOWN (100 series): *81* 5-8
MOTOWN (800 series): *75* 8-12
MCA: *79-80* 5-8
PHILIPS (200000 series): *67* 35-40
PHILIPS (600000 series): *67-68* 20-25

PRIVATE STOCK: 75-78 . . . . $8-10
WARNER BROS: 78 8-10
  Also see FOUR LOVERS
  Also see 4 SEASONS
  Also see LEE, Larry
  Also see TYLER, Frankie

VALLI, Frankie, & Chris Forde
Singles: 7-Inch
MCA: *80* 3-5

VALLI, Frankie, & Cheryl Ladd
Singles: 7-Inch
CAPITOL: *82* 2-3
  Also see LADD, Cheryl
  Also see VALLI, Frankie

VALLI, June
Singles: 78rpm
RCA VICTOR: *52-56* 2-4
Singles: 7-Inch
ABC-PARAMOUNT: *63* 2-4
DCP: *64* 2-4
MERCURY: *58-61* 2-4
RCA VICTOR: *52-56* 2-5
UNITED ARTISTS: *62* 2-4
Picture Sleeves
MERCURY: *61* 2-5
EPs: 7-Inch 33/45rpm
RCA VICTOR: *55-56* 5-10
LPs: 10/12-Inch 33rpm
AUDIO FIDELITY: *69* 5-10
MERCURY: *60* 8-15
RCA VICTOR: *55-56* 10-20
  Also see ZABACH, Florian

VALLIE, Frankie: see VALLI, Frankie

VALLY, Frankie: see VALLI, Frankie

VAN & TITUS
Singles: 7-Inch
ELF: *68* 3-5

VANCE, Paul
Singles: 7-Inch
ROULETTE: *62* 3-5
SCEPTER: *66* 3-5
LPs: 10/12-Inch 33rpm
SCEPTER: *66* 10-15
  Also see LEE & PAUL

VANDENBERG
(Adrian Vandenberg)
Singles: 7-Inch
ATCO: *83-84* 1-3
LPs: 10/12-Inch 33rpm
ATCO: *83-84* 5-8

VANDROSS, Luther
Singles: 12-Inch 33/45rpm
EPIC: *82-85* $4-6
Singles: 7-Inch
COTILLION: *76* 2-4
EPIC: *81-88* 1-3
LPs: 10/12-Inch 33rpm
EPIC: *81-88* 5-8
  Also see BOWIE, David
  Also see CHANGE
  Also see LYNN, Cheryl, & Luther Vandross
  Also see WARWICK, Dionne, & Luther
Vandross

VANDROSS, Luther, & Gregory Hines
Singles: 7-Inch
EPIC: *87* 1-3

VAN DYKE, Leroy
Singles: 78rpm
DOT (Except 15698): *56-57* 3-6
DOT (15698; "Leather Jacket"): *57* 5-10
Singles: 7-Inch
ABC: *74-75* 1-3
ABC/DOT: *75-77* 1-3
DECCA: *70-72* 2-3
DOT (except 15698): *56-57* 4-8
DOT (15698; "Leather Jacket"): *57* 20-30
KAPP: *68-70* 2-3
MCA: *73* 2-3
MERCURY: *61-64* 3-5
PLANTATION: *78* 1-3
SUN: *79* 1-3

Leroy Van Dyke

WARNER BROS: 65-67 .... $2-4
Picture Sleeves
MERCURY: 64 3-5
LPs: 10/12-Inch 33rpm
DECCA: 72 8-10
HARMONY: 69 8-12
KAPP: 68-69 8-12
MCA: 73 5-10
MERCURY: 62-64 10-20
PLANTATION: 77-79 5-8
SUN: 74 5-8
WARNER BROS: 65-66 10-15
WING: 65-66 8-12

VAN DYKES
Singles: 7-Inch
DELUXE: 61 5-10
KING: 58 25-40

VAN DYKES
Singles: 7-Inch
DONNA: 60 5-10
FELSTED: 59 5-10
SPRING: 60 10-12

VAN DYKES
Singles: 7-Inch
MALA: 65-67 3-5
LPs: 10/12-Inch 33rpm
BELL: 67 12-15

VANGELIS
Singles: 7-Inch
POLYDOR: 81 1-3
RCA VICTOR: 78 1-3
Picture Sleeves
POLYDOR: 81 1-3
LPs: 10/12-Inch 33rpm
ARISTA: 88 5-8
POLYDOR: 81-86 5-10
RCA VICTOR: 78-82 5-8
Also see JON & VANGELIS

VANGUARDS
Singles: 7-Inch
LAMP: 70 2-4
WHIZ: 69 2-4

VAN HALEN
Singles: 12-Inch 33/45rpm
WARNER BROS: 83-84 4-6
Singles: 7-Inch
WARNER BROS: 78-88 1-3
Picture Sleeves
WARNER BROS: 78-84 1-3
LPs: 10/12-Inch 33rpm
WARNER BROS: 78-88 5-8

WARNER BROS/LOONEY
TUNES (705; "Van Halen"): 78 ...... $10-20
(Colored vinyl. Promotional issue only.)
Members: David Lee Roth; Edward Van Halen;
Alex Van Halen; Michael Anthony; Sammy Hagar.
Also see HAGAR, Sammy
Also see MAY, Brian
Also see ROTH, David Lee
Also see VAN HALEN, Edward

VAN HALEN, Edward
LPs: 10/12-Inch 33rpm
MCA: 86 5-8
Also see VAN HALEN

VANILLA FUDGE
Singles: 7-Inch
ATCO: 67-70 3-5
LPs: 10/12-Inch 33rpm
ATCO (200 & 300 series): 67-69 15-20
ATCO (90000 series): 82 5-8
Also see BECK, BOGERT & APPICE

VANITY
(Denise Matthews)
Singles: 12-Inch 33/45rpm
MOTOWN: 84-86 4-6
Singles: 7-Inch
MOTOWN: 84-86 1-3
LPs: 10/12-Inch 33rpm
MOTOWN: 84-86 5-8
Also see VANITY 6

VANITY / Smokey Robinson
LPs: 10/12-Inch 33rpm
MOTOWN (179; "Superstar
Interviews"): 84 10-15
(Promotional issue only.)
Also see ROBINSON, Smokey
Also see VANITY

VANITY FARE
Singles: 7-Inch
BRENT: 67 3-5
DJM: 75 2-4
PAGE ONE: 68-70 2-4
SOMA: 68 8-12
20TH CENTURY-FOX: 73 2-4
LPs: 10/12-Inch 33rpm
PAGE ONE: 70 10-15

VANITY 6
Singles: 12-Inch 33/45rpm
WARNER BROS: 82-83 4-6
Singles: 7-Inch
WARNER BROS: 82-83 1-3
LPs: 10/12-Inch 33rpm
WARNER BROS: 82 5-8
Member: Denise Matthews.

Also see APOLLONIA 6
Also see TIME
Also see VANITY

VANN, Teddy
Singles: 7-Inch
CAPITOL: 67 .... $2-4
COLUMBIA: 61 4-6
END: 59 5-8
JUBILEE: 62 3-5
ROULETTE: 60 4-6
TRIPLE-X: 60 5-8

VANNELLI, Gino
Singles: 12-Inch 33/45rpm
HME: 85 4-6
Singles: 7-Inch
A&M: 74-79 2-3
ARISTA: 81-82 1-3
CBS ASSOCIATES: 85-87 1-3
HME: 85 1-3
Picture Sleeves
A&M: 76-79 2-3
ARISTA: 81-82 1-3
LPs: 10/12-Inch 33rpm
A&M (3000 series): 81 5-8
A&M (4000 series): 74-78 8-10
ARISTA: 81-82 5-8
CBS ASSOCIATES: 87 5-8
HME: 85 5-8
MFSL: 80 20-35
NAUTILUS: 81 15-20
(Half-speed mastered.)

VAN TIEGHEM, David
Singles: 12-Inch 33/45rpm
WARNER BROS: 84 4-6
Singles: 7-Inch
WARNER BROS: 84 1-3
LPs: 10/12-Inch 33rpm
WARNER BROS: 84 5-8

VANWARMER, Randy
Singles: 7-Inch
BEARSVILLE: 79 2-3
16TH AVE: 88 1-3
LPs: 10/12-Inch 33rpm
BEARSVILLE: 79-83 5-8

VAN ZANDT, Johnny, Band
Singles: 7-Inch
POLYDOR: 80-82 1-3
LPs: 10/12-Inch 33rpm
POLYDOR: 80-82 5-8

VAPORS
Singles: 7-Inch
LIBERTY: 81 1-3

UNITED ARTISTS: 80 .... $1-3
LPs: 10/12-Inch 33rpm
LIBERTY: 81 5-8
UNITED ARTISTS: 80 5-8

VASEL, Marianne, & Erich Storz
Singles: 7-Inch
MERCURY: 58 2-4
LPs: 10/12-Inch 33rpm
DANA: 59 8-15

VAUGHAN, Frankie
Singles: 7-Inch
COLUMBIA: 59-60 2-4
EPIC: 58 3-5
PHILIPS: 62-66 2-4
LPs: 10/12-Inch 33rpm
COLUMBIA: 60 8-15
PHILIPS: 62 5-15

VAUGHAN, Sarah
Singles: 78rpm
COLUMBIA: 51-53 3-5
MGM: 50-51 3-5
MERCURY: 53-57 2-5
Singles: 7-Inch
ATLANTIC: 81 1-3
COLUMBIA (38000 & 39000
series): 51-53 3-6
MGM (10000 & 30000 series): 50-51 4-8
MAINSTREAM: 71-74 2-3
MERCURY (70000 series): 53-66 2-5
ROULETTE: 60-64 2-4
WARNER BROS: 81 1-3
Picture Sleeves
MERCURY: 65 3-5
EPs: 7-Inch 33/45rpm
ATLANTIC: 55 8-15
COLUMBIA: 50-56 8-18
EMARCY: 54-56 8-18
MGM: 52-55 5-15
MERCURY: 53-59 5-15
LPs: 10/12-Inch 33rpm
ALLEGRO: 5-10
ATLANTIC: 81 5-8
COLUMBIA (600 & 700 series): 55-56 . 20-40
COLUMBIA (900 series): 57 15-25
COLUMBIA (6000 series): 50 50-80
(10-Inch LPs.)
COLUMBIA (37000 series): 82 5-8
CONCORD: 56 15-25
EMARCY (400 series): 77 8-12
EMARCY (1000 series): 81 5-8
EMARCY (26000 series): 54 30-60
(10-Inch LPs.)
EMARCY (36000 series): 54-57 20-40

EVEREST: 70-76 .... **$5-10**
HARMONY: 59-69 .... **5-12**
MGM (070 through 500 series): 51-54 ... **40-60**
(10-Inch LPs.)
MGM (3200 series): 55 .... **25-50**
MAINSTREAM: 71-75 .... **6-12**
MERCURY (100 series): 57 .... **15-25**
MERCURY (1000 series): 82 .... **5-8**
MERCURY (20000 series): 58-64 ...... **15-25**
MERCURY (21000 series): 65-67 ...... **10-20**
(Monaural.)
MERCURY (25000 series): 53 .... **30-60**
(10-Inch LPs.)
MERCURY (60000 series): 59-64 ...... **15-25**
MERCURY (61000 series): 65-67 ...... **10-20**
(Stereo.)
METRO: 65 .... **8-15**
MUSICRAFT: 83-84 .... **5-8**
PABLO: 78-82 .... **5-8**
REMINGTON (1024; "Hot Jazz"): 53 ... **50-75**
(10-Inch LPs.)
RIVERSIDE: 55 .... **20-40**
RONDO: 59 .... **20-40**
RONDOLETTE: 59 .... **20-40**
ROULETTE (100 series): 71 .... **8-15**
ROULETTE (52000 series): 60-67 ..... **10-25**
(Black vinyl.)
ROULETTE (52082; "You're Mine"): 62 **20-40**
(Colored vinyl.)
SCEPTER: 74 .... **5-10**
SUTTON: **5-10**
TRIP: 74-76 .... **5-10**
WING: 63-68 .... **5-15**
Also see BASIE, Count, & Sarah Vaughan
Also see BASIE, Count, Sarah Vaughan, &
Joe Williams
Also see ECKSTINE, Billy, & Sarah Vaughan
Also see LEGRAND, Michel

Also see WASHINGTON, Dinah, & Sarah
Vaughan

VAUGHAN, Sarah, & Quincy Jones
LPs: 10/12-Inch 33rpm
MERCURY: 59 .... **$15-25**
Also see JONES, Quincy
Also see VAUGHAN, Sarah

VAUGHAN, Stevie Ray
(Stevie Ray Vaughan & Double Trouble)
Singles: 7-Inch
COLUMBIA: 87 .... **1-3**
EPIC: 85 .... **1-3**
LPs: 10/12-Inch 33rpm
COLUMBIA: 87 .... **5-6**
EPIC (Except picture discs): 84-86 ...... **5-10**
EPIC (Picture discs): 84 .... **8-12**

VAUGHN, Billy, Orchestra
Singles: 78rpm
DOT: 54-57 .... **2-5**
Singles: 7-Inch
ABC: 74 .... **1-3**
DOT: 54-70 .... **2-5**
PARAMOUNT: 70-72 .... **1-3**
Picture Sleeves
DOT: 58-67 .... **2-5**
EPs: 7-Inch 33/45rpm
DOT: 55-59 .... **4-8**
LPs: 10/12-Inch 33rpm
ABC: 74 .... **4-8**
DOT: 55-70 .... **5-15**
HAMILTON: 65-66 .... **5-10**
MCA: 83 .... **4-8**
MISTLETOE: 76 .... **4-8**
MUSICOR: 77 .... **4-8**
PARAMOUNT: 70-74 .... **4-8**
PICKWICK: 68 .... **4-8**
RANWOOD: 83 .... **4-8**
Also see HILLTOPPERS

VAUGHN, Denny
Singles: 78rpm
KAPP: 56 .... **2-4**
Singles: 7-Inch
KAPP: 56 .... **2-5**

VEE, Bobby
**(Bobby Vee & The Shadows; Bobby Vee & The
Eligibles; Bobby Vee & The Strangers; Bobby
Vee & The Johnny Mann Singers; Robert
Thomas Velline)**
Singles: 7-Inch
LIBERTY (3300 series): 61 .... **10-12**
(Stereo Compact 33 Single.)
LIBERTY (55208; "Suzie Baby"): 59 .... **10-12**

LIBERTY (55234 through 55325): *60-61* . $4-6
LIBERTY (55234 through 56208): *61-70* . .3-5
SHADYBROOK: *75-77* 2-4
SOMA: *59* 25-30
UNITED ARTISTS: *71-78* 2-3
Picture Sleeves
LIBERTY: *60-68* 5-10
EPs: 7-Inch 33/45rpm
LIBERTY: *60-62* 25-35
UNITED ARTISTS: *72* 10-12
LPs: 10/12-Inch 33rpm
LIBERTY (181 through 385): *61-64* 20-25
LIBERTY (448 through 612): *66-69* 15-20
(Liberty 181 through 534 numbers were preceded
by a "3" for mono issues. Numbers 181 through
612 were preceded by a "7" for stereo LPs.)
LIBERTY (10000 series): *84* 5-8
SUNSET: *66-67* 12-15
UNITED ARTISTS (300 series): *73* 8-10
UNITED ARTISTS (1000 series): *80* 5-8

VEE, Bobby / Johnny Burnette /
Ventures / Fleetwoods
LPs: 10/12-Inch 33rpm
LIBERTY (5503 "Teensville"): *61* 15-20
Also see BURNETTE, Johnny
Also see FLEETWOODS
Also see VENTURES

VEE, Bobby, & The Crickets
Singles: 7-Inch
LIBERTY: *62* 4-6
Picture Sleeves
LIBERTY: *60-63* 10-15
LPs: 10/12-Inch 33rpm
LIBERTY: *62* 20-25
Also see CRICKETS

VEE, Bobby, & The Ventures
LPs: 10/12-Inch 33rpm
LIBERTY: *63* 20-25
Also see VEE, Bobby
Also see VENTURES

VEGA, Suzanne
Singles: 7-Inch
A&M: *85-87* 1-3
LPs: 10/12-Inch 33rpm
A&M: *85-87* 5-8

VEGA, Tata
Singles: 12-Inch 33/45rpm
TAMLA: *79* 4-6
Singles: 7-Inch
TAMLA: *76-80* 1-3
LPs: 10/12-Inch 33rpm
TAMLA: *76-80* 5-8
Also see RAWLS, Lou

VEJTABLES
Singles: 7-Inch
AUTUMN: *65-66* $5-8
UPTOWN: *67* 4-6

VELAIRES
Singles: 7-Inch
HI MAR: *65* 4-6
JAMIE: *61-62* 8-10

VELEZ, Martha
Singles: 7-Inch
MCA: *80* 1-3
POLYDOR: *73* 2-4
SIRE: *69-76* 2-4
LPs: 10/12-Inch 33rpm
SIRE (7000 series): *74-76* 8-10
SIRE (97000 series): *69* 10-12

VELLINE, Robert Thomas:
see VEE, Bobby

VELOURS
Singles: 78rpm
ONYX (Except 508): *56-57* 15-25
ONYX (508; "Romeo"): *57* 25-50
Singles: 7-Inch
CUB: *58-59* 10-20
END: *61* 8-12
GOLDISC: *60* 10-15
GONE: *60* 10-15
ONYX (501; "My Love Come
   Back"): *56* 50-75
ONYX (508; "Romeo"): *57* 125-150
ONYX (512; "Can I Come
   Over Tonight?"): *57* 50-75
ONYX (515; "This Could Be
   The Night"): *57* 40-60
ONYX (520; "Remember"): *58* 25-40
ORBIT: *58* 10-20
ROULETTE: 1-3
STUDIO: *59* 8-12
Members: Jerry Ramos; Pete Winston; John Pear-
son; Don Heywood; John Cheetom; Charles Mof-
fett; Keith Williams; Troyce Key.

VELS
Singles: 12-Inch 33/45rpm
MERCURY: *84-85* 4-6
Singles: 7-Inch
MERCURY: *84-85* 1-3
LPs: 10/12-Inch 33rpm
MERCURY: *84* 5-8

VELVELETTES
Singles: 7-Inch
I.P.G.: *63* 4-6
SOUL: *66* 3-5

Jimmy Velvet

V.I.P.: *64-65* **$3-5**
Members: Carolyn Gill, Sandra Tilley; Betty Kelly.
Also see MARTHA & THE VANDELLAS

VELVET, Jimmy
(Jimmy Velvet Five; James Velvet; Jimmy
Velvit)
Singles: 7-Inch
ABC-PARAMOUNT: *63-64* **3-5**
BELL: *67* **3-5**
CAMEO: *67* **3-5**
CORREC-TONE: *62* **4-8**
CUB: *61-62* **4-6**
DIVISION: *61* **5-8**
PHILIPS: *65* **3-5**
ROYAL AMERICAN: *69* **3-5**
TOLLIE: *64* **3-5**
UNITED ARTISTS: *68* **3-5**
VELVET: *61* **5-8**
VELVET TONE (Except 102): *67* **3-5**
VELVET TONE (102; "It's Almost
Tomorrow"): *65* **4-6**
LPs: 10/12-Inch 33rpm
VELVET TONE: *67* **12-15**
Also see TENNANT, Jimmy

VELVET UNDERGROUND
Singles: 7-Inch
COTILLION: *71* **3-5**
MGM: *69* **4-6**
VERVE: *67* **4-6**
LPs: 10/12-Inch 33rpm
COTILLION: *70-72* **10-15**
MGM (100 series): *71* **8-10**
MGM (4000 series): *69-74* **10-15**
MERCURY: *72* **12-15**

PRIDE: *73* **$10-15**
VERVE (5046; "White Light/White
Heat"): *67* **20-30**
VERVE (800000 series): *84* **5-8**
Members: Lou Reed; John Cale; Sterling Morrison;
Maureen Tucker; Doug Yule.
Also see AMERICAN FLYER
Also see CALE, John
Also see REED, Lou

VELVET UNDERGROUND, & Nico
Singles: 7-Inch
VERVE: *66-67* **5-8**
LPs: 10/12-Inch 33rpm
VERVE (5008; "Velvet Underground
& Nico"): *67* **30-35**
(With banana sticker on front cover.)
VERVE (5008; "Velvet Underground
& Nico"): *67* **20-25**
(Without banana sticker on front cover.)
VERVE (800000 series): *84* **5-8**
Also see VELVET UNDERGROUND

VELVETS
Singles: 7-Inch
MONUMENT (400 series): *61-62* **8-10**
MONUMENT (800 & 900
series): *63-66* **3-5**
PLAID: *59* **5-8**
20TH CENTURY-FOX: *59* **5-8**
Member: Virgil Johnson.

VENETIANS
Singles: 7-Inch
CHRYSALIS: *87* **1-3**

VENTURES
Singles: 12-Inch 33/45rpm
TRIDEX (1245; "Surfin' & Spyin'"): *81* ...**5-8**
(With vocals by Charlotte Caffey and Jane
Weidlin.)
Singles: 7-Inch
BLUE HORIZON: *59-60* **8-10**
DOLTON: *61-66* **4-8**
LIBERTY: *66-70* **3-6**
TRIDEX: *81* **1-3**
UNITED ARTISTS: *70-78* **2-4**
Picture Sleeves
DOLTON: *60-66* **5-10**
EPs: 7-Inch 33/45rpm
DOLTON: *60* **20-25**
LPs: 10/12-Inch 33rpm
AWARD: *84* **8-12**
DOLTON (003; "Walk Don't Run"): *60* ..**25-35**
(With light blue label.)
DOLTON (003; "Walk Don't Run"): *61* ..**20-25**
(With dark blue label.)
DOLTON (004 through 035): *61-65* **20-25**

DOLTON (037 through 050): *65-67* **$15-20**
DOLTON (17000 series): *65-66* **15-20**
LIBERTY (052 through 060): *67-70* **10-15**
 (Liberty and Dolton numbers, under 100, that are
 preceded by a "2" are mono. Stereo LPs in this
 series were preceded by an "8.")
LIBERTY (10000 series): *81-84* **5-8**
LIBERTY (35000 series): *70* **12-15**
SUNSET: *66-71* **10-15**
TRIDEX: *81-83* **5-8**
UNITED ARTISTS: *71-77* **10-15**
 Members: Don Wilson; Bob Bogle; Mel Taylor;
 Nokie Edwards; Jerry McGee.
 Also see GO-GOs
 Also see VEE, Bobby, & The Ventures

VENUS, Vic
Singles: 7-Inch
BUDDAH: *69* **3-5**

VERA, Billy
(Billy Vera & The Contrasts; Billy Vera & The
Beaters; Billy Vera & Blue Eyed Soul)
Singles: 7-Inch
ATLANTIC: *68-69* **3-5**
CAPITOL: *88* **1-3**
MACOLA: *87* **1-3**
RHINO: *86-87* **1-3**
RUST: *62* **4-6**
LPs: 10/12-Inch 33rpm
ALFA: *82* **5-8**
ATLANTIC: *68* **10-15**
MIDSONG INT'L: *77* **8-10**
RHINO: *86* **5-8**
 Also see BILLY & THE BEATERS

VERA, Billy & Judy Clay
Singles: 7-Inch
ATLANTIC: *67-68* **3-5**
LPs: 10/12-Inch 33rpm
ATLANTIC: *68* **10-15**
 Also see CLAY, Judy
 Also see VERA, Billy

VERA LYNN: see LYNN, Vera

VERLAINE, Tom
Singles: 7-Inch
ELEKTRA: *80* **1-3**
WARNER BROS: *83-84* **1-3**
LPs: 10/12-Inch 33rpm
ELEKTRA: *80* **5-8**
WARNER BROS: *83-84* **5-8**

VERNE, Larry
Singles: 7-Inch
COLLECTABLES: **1-3**
ERA: *60-64* **5-8**

Picture Sleeves
ERA: *60* **$8-12**
LPs: 10/12-Inch 33rpm
ERA: *60* **25-30**

VERONICA
(Veronica "Ronnie" Spector)
Singles: 7-Inch
PHIL SPECTOR: *64* **20-25**
 Also see SPECTOR, Ronnie

VERTICAL HOLD
Singles: 7-Inch
CRIMINAL: *88* **1-3**

VIA AFRIKA
Singles: 12-Inch 33/45rpm
EMI AMERICA: *84* **4-6**
Singles: 7-Inch
EMI AMERICA: *84* **1-3**
LPs: 10/12-Inch 33rpm
EMI AMERICA: *84* **5-8**

VIBRATIONS
Singles: 7-Inch
ABC: *74* **1-3**
ATLANTIC: *63-64* **3-5**
BET: *60* **8-10**
CHECKER: *60-63* **10-15**
CHESS: *74* **2-4**
EPIC: *68* **2-4**
MANDALA: *72* **2-4**
NEPTUNE: *69-70* **2-4**
OKEH: *64-68* **3-5**
LPs: 10/12-Inch 33rpm
CHECKER: *61* **20-30**
MANDALA: *72* **12-15**
OKEH: *65-69* **20-30**
 Also see JAYHAWKS
 Also see MARATHONS

VICKY D
Singles: 7-Inch
SAM: *82* $1-3

VICTIMS FAMILY
LPs: 10/12-Inch 33rpm
MORDAM: *88* 5-8

VIDAL, Maria
Singles: 12-Inch 33/45rpm
EMI AMERICA: *84* 4-6
Singles: 7-Inch
EMI AMERICA: *84* 1-3
Also see CHILD, Desmond, & Rouge

VIDEEO
Singles: 7-Inch
H.C.R.C.: *82* 1-3

VIDELS
(Vi-Dels)
Singles: 7-Inch
COLLECTABLES: 1-3
DUSTY DISC: 5-8
JDS: *60* 15-25
KAPP: *61* 30-35
MEDIEVAL: *59* 4-6
MUSICNOTE: *63* 8-10
RHODY: *59* 35-40
Members: Pete Anders; Vinnie Poncia.

VIEW FROM THE HILL
Singles: 7-Inch
CAPITOL: *88* 1-3

VIGRASS & OSBORNE
Singles: 7-Inch
EPIC: *74* 2-3
UNI: *72* 2-4
LPs: 10/12-Inch 33rpm
EPIC: *74* 8-10
UNI: *71* 10-15
Members: Paul Vigrass; Gary Osborne.

VILLAGE PEOPLE
Singles: 12-Inch 33/45rpm
CASABLANCA: *78-79* 4-6
Singles: 7-Inch
CASABLANCA: *78-79* 1-3
RCA VICTOR: *81* 1-3
Picture Sleeves
CASABLANCA: *78-79* 1-3
RCA VICTOR: *81* 1-3
LPs: 10/12-Inch 33rpm
CASABLANCA (Except picture
 discs): *77-79* 5-8
CASABLANCA (Picture discs): *78* 10-15
RCA VICTOR: *81* 5-8

Members: Victor Willis; Alexander Briley; Felipe
Rose; Randy Jones; David Hodo; Glenn Hughes.

VILLAGE SOUL CHOIR
Singles: 7-Inch
ABBOTT: *69-70* $2-4

VILLAGE STOMPERS
Singles: 7-Inch
EPIC: *63-67* 2-4
Picture Sleeves
EPIC: *63-65* 2-5
LPs: 10/12-Inch 33rpm
EPIC: *63-67* 10-15
Also see VINTON, Bobby, & The Village
Stompers

VINCENT, Gene
(Gene Vincent & His Blue Caps)
Singles: 78rpm
CAPITOL: *56-57* 8-15
Singles: 7-Inch
CAPITOL (3450 through 3617): *56-57* ... 8-10
CAPITOL (3678;
 "B-I-Bickey-Bi-Bo-Bo-Go"): *57* 10-15
CAPITOL (3763 through 4665): *57-61* ... 6-10
CHALLENGE: *6-67* 4-6
FOREVER: *69-70* 3-5
KAMA SUTRA: *70-73* 2-4
PLAYGROUND: *68* 60-75
Picture Sleeves
CAPITOL (4237; "Right Now"): *60* ... 200-300
Promotional Singles
CAPITOL (White label): *56-61* 15-20
EPs: 7-Inch 33/45rpm
CAPITOL (Except 985): *57-59* 50-75
CAPITOL (985; "Hot Rod Gang"): *58* . 150-250
CAPITOL (985; "Hot Rod Gang"): *58* . 250-350
(White label. Promotional issue.)
LPs: 10/12-Inch 33rpm
CAPITOL (380; "Gene Vincent's
 Greatest"): *69* 10-15
(With a "DKAO" prefix.)
CAPITOL (380; "Gene Vincent's
 Greatest"): *78* 5-8
(With an "SM" prefix.)
CAPITOL (764; "Bluejean Bop"): *57* .. 100-150
CAPITOL (811; "Gene Vincent &
 His Blue Caps"): *57* 100-150
CAPITOL (970; "Gene Vincent
 Rocks"): *58* 100-150
CAPITOL (1059; "Gene Vincent
 Record Date"): *58* 100-150
CAPITOL (1207; "Sounds Like
 Gene Vincent"): *59* 100-150
CAPITOL (1342; "Crazy Times"): *60* ... 85-100
CAPITOL (11000 series): *74* 8-10

CAPITOL (16000 series): *81* **$5-8**
DANDELION: *70* **10-15**
KAMA SUTRA: *70-71* **10-15**
ROLLIN' ROCK: *80-81* **5-8**
  Also see MEYERS, Augie

VINCENT, Vinnie, Invasion
  LPs: 10/12-Inch 33rpm
CHRYSALIS: *86-88* **5-8**
  Also see KISS

VINTON, Bobby
(Bobby Vinton Orchestra)
  Singles: 7 Inch
ABC: *74-77* **1-3**
ALPINE: *59* **5-10**
DIAMOND: *62* **3-5**
CURB: *88* **1-3**
ELEKTRA: *78* **1-3**
EPIC (9000 series): *60-66* **3-5**
  (Black vinyl.)
EPIC (9000 series): *64* **5-10**
  (Colored vinyl.)
EPIC (10000 series): *66-75* **2-4**
LARC: *83* **1-3**
TAPESTRY: *79-84* **1-3**
  Picture Sleeves
EPIC: *62-72* **2-5**
TAPESTRY: *80* **1-3**
  EPs: 7-Inch 33/45rpm
EPIC: *63-64* **6-12**
  LPs: 10/12-Inch 33rpm
ABC: *74-77* **8-10**
COLUMBIA: *73* **8-10**
EPIC (500 series): *60* **20-25**
EPIC (3000 series): *60* **15-20**
EPIC (20000 series): *62-70* **8-15**
  (Black vinyl.)

EPIC (20468; "Blue On Blue"): *63* **$20-40**
  (Colored vinyl. Promotional issue only.)
EPIC (30000 series): *72-79* **5-10**
HARMONY: *70* **6-10**
TAPESTRY: *80* **5-8**

**VINTON, Bobby, & The Village
Stompers**
  LPs: 10/12-Inch 33rpm
EPIC: *66* **10-15**
  Also see VILLAGE STOMPERS
  Also see VINTON, Bobby

VIOLENCE
  LPs: 10/12-Inch 33rpm
MECHANIC: *88* **5-8**

VIPERS
  Singles: 12-Inch 33/45rpm
MIDNIGHT: *88* **4-6**
  Singles: 7-Inch
MIDNIGHT: *84-88* **2-3**
  LPs: 10/12-Inch 33rpm
MIDNIGHT: *84-88* **5-8**
PVC: *85* **5-8**
  Members: David Andrew Mann; Graham May;
  Paul Martin; Pat Brown; Jonithan Weiss; John
  England; Bill McGarvey; Anders Thomsen.
  Also see FLESHTONES

VIRTUES
(Frank Virtue & The Virtues; Frank Virtuoso &
The Virtues)
  Singles: 7-Inch
ABC: *73* **1-3**
ABC-PARAMOUNT: *59* **3-5**
FAYETTE: *64* **3-5**
HIGHLAND: *60* **3-5**
HUNT (Monaural): *59* **5-8**
HUNT (Stereo): *59* **15-20**
SURE (500 series): *59* **8-10**
SURE (1700 series): *62* **3-5**
VIRNON: *60* **4-6**
VIRTUE: *66-69* **3-5**
WYNNE: *60* **3-5**
  LPs: 10/12-Inch 33rpm
STRAND: *60* **20-25**
WYNNE: *60* **25-30**

VISAGE
  Singles: 12-Inch 33/45rpm
POLYDOR: *80-82* **4-6**
  Singles: 7-Inch
POLYDOR: *81* **1-3**
  LPs: 10/12-Inch 33rpm
POLYDOR: *80-82* **5-8**

VISCOUNTS
(Vicounts)

Singles: 7-Inch
AMY: *65-66* $3-5
CORAL: *66-67* 3-5
MADISON: *59-61* 4-6
MR. PEACOCK: *61* 3-5
MR. PEEKE: *63* 3-5
LPs: 10/12-Inch 33rpm
AMY: *65* ....'................... 20-25
MADISON: *60* 30-40
Members: Bobby Spievak; Joe Spievak; Harry Haller; Larry Vecchio; Clark Smith.

VISUAL
Singles: 12-Inch 33/45rpm
PRELUDE: *83-84* 4-6
Singles: 7-Inch
PRELUDE: *83-84* 1-3

VITALE, Joe
Singles: 7-Inch
ASYLUM: *82* 1-3
ATLANTIC: *74* 2-4
LPs: 10/12-Inch 33rpm
ASYLUM: *82* 5-8
ATLANTIC: *74* 8-10
Also see EAGLES
Also see WALSH, Joe

VITAMIN E
Singles: 7-Inch
BUDDAH: *77* 2-3

VITAMIN Z
Singles: 12-Inch 33/45rpm
GEFFEN: *85* 4-6
Singles: 7-Inch
GEFFEN: *85* 1-3
LPs: 10/12-Inch 33rpm
GEFFEN: *85* 5-8

VITO & THE SALUTATIONS
Singles: 7-Inch
APT: *65* 8-10
BOOM: *66* ..../.... 10-15
CRYSTAL BALL: *78* 3-5
HAROLD: *62* 4-8
HERALD: *63-64* 15-20
KRAM: *62* 30-35
RAYNA: *62* 20-25
RED BOY: *66* 3-5
REGINA: *64* 5-8
RUST: *66* 4-6
SANDBAG: *68* 3-5
WELLS (Black vinyl): *64* 10-15
WELLS (Colored vinyl): *64* 20-25

LPs: 10/12-Inch 33rpm
RED BOY: *81* $20-30
Members: Vito Balsamo; Shelly Buchansky; Randy Silverman; Len Citrin; Frank Fox.
Also see MAGIC TOUCH

VIXEN
Singles: 7-Inch
EMI/MANHATTAN: *88* 1-3
Picture Sleeves
EMI/MANHATTAN: *88* 1-3
LPs: 10/12-Inch 33rpm
EMI/MANHATTAN: *88* 5-8

VOCALEERS
Singles: 7-Inch
OLD TOWN: *60* 8-12
OLDIES 45: *65* 2-4
PARADISE: *59* 20-25
RED ROBIN (113; "Be True"): *52* 75-100
RED ROBIN (114; "Is It
A Dream?"): *52* 75-100
RED ROBIN (119; "I Walk
Alone"): *53* ./.................. 75-100
RED ROBIN (125; "Will You
Be True?"): *54* 75-100
RED ROBIN (132; "Angel Face"): *54* ..75-100
TWISTIME: *62* 10-20
VEST: *60* 8-10
Members: Joe Duncan; Curtis Dunham; Ted Williams; Mel Walton; Bill Walker; Lamarr Cooper; Joe Powell; Richard Blandon; Leo Fuller; Curtis Blandon; Caesar Williams.

VOGUES
Singles: 7-Inch
ABC: *73* 1-3
ABC-PARAMOUNT: *65* 3-5
ASTRA: *73* 2-4
BELL: *71* 2-4
BLUE STAR: *65* 8-10
CASCADE: *59* 4-6
CO & CE: *65-67* 3-5
DOT: *58-59* 5-8
GUSTO: 1-3
MGM: *67* 3-5
MAINSTREAM: *72* 2-4
REPRISE: *68-71* 2-4
REVUE: *68* 3-6
SUN: *79* 1-3
20TH CENTURY-FOX: *73* 2-4
LPs: 10/12-Inch 33rpm
CO & CE: *65-66* 25-30
51 WEST: 5-8
PICKWICK: *71* 8-10
REPRISE: *68-70* 10-15
SSS INT'L: *77* 5-8

Member: Bob Bush.

VOICE MASTERS
Singles: 7-Inch
ANNA (100 series): *59* $15-20
ANNA (1100 series): *60* 8-10
BAMBOO: *68* 3-5
  Members: Ty Hunter; C.P. Spencer; Lamont
  Dozier; David Ruffin; Freddie Gorman.
  Also see DOZIER, Lamont
  Also see HUNTER, Ty
  Also see ORIGINALS
  Also see RUFFIN, David

VOICES OF AMERICA / U.S.A.
 For Africa
Singles: 7-Inch
EMI AMERICA: *86* 1-3
  Also see TOTO
  Also see U.S.A. FOR AFRICA

VOICES OF EAST HARLEM
Singles: 7-Inch
ELEKTRA: *70-72* 2-4
JUST SUNSHINE: *73-74* 2-4
LPs: 10/12-Inch 33rpm
ELEKTRA: *70* 8-10
JUST SUNSHINE: *73-74* 5-10

VOLCANOS
Singles: 7-Inch
ARCTIC: *65-67* 3-5
VIRTUE: *70* 2-4

VOLLENWEIDER, Andreas
Singles: 12-Inch 33/45rpm
COLUMBIA: *86* 4-6
Singles: 7-Inch
COLUMBIA: *86* 1-3
LPs: 10/12-Inch 33rpm
COLUMBIA: *86* 5-8

VOLTAGE BROTHERS
Singles: 12-Inch 33/45rpm
MTM: *86* 4-6
Singles: 7-Inch
LIFESONG: *78* 2-3
MTM: *86* 1-3
LPs: 10/12-Inch 33rpm
LIFESONG: *78* 5-8
MTM: *86* 5-8

VOLUMES
Singles: 7-Inch
ABC: *73* 1-3
AMERICAN ARTS: *64-65* 4-6
CHEX: *62* 5-10
IMPACT: *66* 3-5
INFERNO: *67-68* 3-5

OLD TOWN: *64* $3-5
JUBILEE: *63* 5-8
VIRGO: *73* 1-3
LPs: 10/12-Inch 33rpm
RELIC: *85* 5-8
  Also see NUTMEGS / Volumes

VOLUMES
Singles: 7-Inch
JAGUAR (3004; "I Won't Tell
  A Soul"): *54* 60-75

VONTASTICS
Singles: 7-Inch
CHESS: *67* 3-5
ST. LAWRENCE: *65-66* 3-5
SATELLITE: *65* 4-6

VOUDOURIS, Roger
Singles: 7-Inch
WARNER BROS: *78-79* 2-3
LPs: 10/12-Inch 33rpm
WARNER BROS: *79* 5-8

VOXPOPPERS
Singles: 7-Inch
AMP 3: *58* 10-15
MERCURY: *58* 5-8
POPLAR: *58* 8-10
VERSAILLES: *59* 10-20
EPs: 7-Inch 33/45rpm
MERCURY (3391; "The
  Voxpoppers"): *58* 50-75

VOYAGE
Singles: 7-Inch
ATLANTIC: *82* 1-3
MARLIN: *78-79* 2-3
LPs: 10/12-Inch 33rpm
ATLANTIC: *82* 5-8
MARLIN: *78* 5-8

VOYEUR
Singles: 7-Inch
MCA: *85* 1-3

W

W.A.G.B.
Singles: 7-Inch
STREET SOUNDS: *82* 1-3

W.A.S.P.
Singles: 7-Inch
CAPITOL: *84-87* 1-3
Picture Sleeves
CAPITOL: *84-87* 2-4

LPs: 10/12-Inch 33rpm

CAPITOL: *84-87* $5-8
  Members: Blackie Lawless; Randy Piper; Chris
  Holmes; Steve Riley.
  Also see NEW YORK DOLLS

WA WA NEE
Singles: 7-Inch

EPIC: *87-88* 1-3
LPs: 10/12-Inch 33rpm

EPIC: *87* 5-8

WACKERS
Singles: 7-Inch

BOMP: *75* 3-5
ELEKTRA: *71-73* 2-4
LPs: 10/12-Inch 33rpm

ELEKTRA: *71-72* 8-10

WADE, Adam
Singles: 7-Inch

COED: *59-61* 4-8
EPIC: *62-66* 3-5
KIRSHNER: *77* 2-3
REMEMBER: *69* 2-4
WARNER BROS: *67-68* 2-4
Picture Sleeves

COED: *60-61* 4-8
EPIC: *62-63* 2-5
LPs: 10/12-Inch 33rpm

COED: *60* 20-25
EPIC: *62* 15-20
KIRSHNER: *77* 5-10

WADSWORTH MANSION
Singles: 7-Inch

SUSSEX: *70* 2-4
LPs: 10/12-Inch 33rpm

SUSSEX: *71* 12-15
  Note: Some Sussex issues showed the group as
  "Wadsworth Manison."

WAGNER, Jack
Singles: 7-Inch

QWEST: *84-87* 1-3
LPs: 10/12-Inch 33rpm

QWEST: *84-87* 5-8

WAGONER, Porter
Singles: 78rpm

RCA VICTOR: *56-57* 2-5
Singles: 7-Inch

ACCORD: *82* 5-8
RCA VICTOR (0013 through 1000
  series): *69-73* 1-3
RCA VICTOR (5600 through 6500
  series): *56-56* 4-8
RCA VICTOR (6600 through 9900
  series): *56-71* 2-5

RCA VICTOR (10000 through 11000
  series): *74-79* $1-3
WARNER BROS: *82-83* 1-3
EPs: 7-Inch 33/45rpm

RCA VICTOR: *56* 8-12
LPs: 10/12-Inch 33rpm

CAMDEN: *63-73* 5-15
H.S.R.D.: *81* 6-10
PICKWICK: *75-77* 5-10
RCA VICTOR (Except 1300 through
  2900 series): *66-79* 5-15
RCA VICTOR (1300 series): *56* 30-40
RCA VICTOR (2700 through 2900
  series): *63-65* 15-25
  (With an "LPM" or "LSP" prefix.)
TUDOR: *84* 5-8
WARNER BROS: *83* 5-8
  Also see SNOW, Hank / Hank Locklin / Porter
  Wagoner

WAGONER, Porter, & Skeeter Davis
LPs: 10/12-Inch 33rpm

RCA VICTOR: *62* 10-15
  Also see DAVIS, Skeeter

WAGONER, Porter, & Dolly Parton
Singles: 7-Inch

RCA VICTOR: *67-71* 2-5
LPs: 10/12-Inch 33rpm

RCA VICTOR: *68-80* 10-15
  (With an "LPM" or "LSP" prefix.)
RCA VICTOR: *74-80* 5-10
  (With an "APL1" or "AHL1" prefix.)
  Also see PARTON, Dolly
  Also see WAGONER, Porter

WAIKIKIS
Singles: 7-Inch

KAPP: *64-68* 2-4
PALETTE: *62-63* 2-5
LPs: 10/12-Inch 33rpm

BOOT: *78* 4-8
KAPP: *64-69* 8-12
MCA: 5-8

WAILERS
Singles: 7-Inch

BELL: *67* 3-5
ETIQUETTE: *63-66* 4-6
GOLDEN CREST: *59* 10-15
  (Label pictures the group.)
GOLDEN CREST: *60-64* 8-10
  (No picture on label.)
IMPERIAL: *64* 3-5
VIVA: *67* 2-5
LPs: 10/12-Inch 33rpm

BELL: *68* 10-15

ETIQUETTE (1; "The Fabulous
Wailers At The Castle"): *66* $75-100
ETIQUETTE (022; "The Wailers &
Company"): *66* 40-60
ETIQUETTE (023; "Wailers Wailers
Everywhere"): *66* 75-100
ETIQUETTE (026; "Out Of
Our Tree"): 40-60
Note: Recent reissues of Etiquette LPs have a
1980s date on back cover.
ETIQUETTE (1100 series); *86* 5-8
GOLDEN CREST (3075; "The
Fabulous Wailers"): *60* 20-30
GOLDEN CREST (3075; "The
Wailers Wail"): 15-20
IMPERIAL: *64* 15-20
Members: Kent Morrill; Robin Roberts; Gail Har-
ris; Mark Marush; Rich Dangel; Buck Ormsby;
Mike Burk.
Also see MORRILL, Kent

WAINWRIGHT, Loudon, III
Singles: 7-Inch
ARISTA: *76-78* 2-3
COLUMBIA: *73* 2-4
LPs: 10/12-Inch 33rpm
ARISTA: *76-78* 5-8
ATLANTIC: *70-71* 12-15
COLUMBIA (KC series): *72-73* 10-15
COLUMBIA (PC series): *75* 5-10
ROUNDER: *80-83* 5-8
Also see SPRINGSTEEN, Bruce / Albert
Hammond / Loudon Wainwright III / Taj Mahal

WAITE, John
Singles: 12-Inch 33/45rpm
EMI AMERICA: *84* 4-6
Singles: 7-Inch
CHRYSALIS: *82-85* 1-3
EMI AMERICA: *84-87* 1-3
LPs: 10/12-Inch 33rpm
CHRYSALIS: *82* 5-8
EMI AMERICA: *84-87* 5-8
Also see BABYS

WAITRESSES
Singles: 7-Inch
ANTILLES: *80* 2-5
POLYDOR: *82* 1-3
LPs: 10/12-Inch 33rpm
POLYDOR: *82-83* 5-8

WAITS, Tom
Singles: 7-Inch
ASYLUM: *74* 2-3
ELEKTRA: *83* 1-3
ISLAND: *83* 1-3

LPs: 10/12-Inch 33rpm
ASYLUM: *73-80* $6-10
ELEKTRA: *83* 5-8
ISLAND: *83-88* 5-8
Also see GAYLE, Crystal, & Tom Waits

WAKELY, Jimmy
Singles: 78rpm
CAPITOL: *50-52* 3-5
CORAL: *53-55* 2-5
DECCA: *55-70* 2-4
Singles: 7-Inch
ARTCO: *74* 1-3
CAPITOL (1300 through 2100
series): *50-52* 4-6
CORAL: *53-55* 3-6
DECCA: *55-70* 2-5
DOT: *66* 2-4
SHASTA (100 series): *58-67* 2-5
SHASTA (200 series): *71* 2-3
Picture Sleeves
SHASTA: *58* 4-8
EPs: 7-Inch 33/45rpm
CAPITOL: *50-53* 8-15
CORAL: *54* 8-15
DECCA: *58* 6-12
LPs: 10/12-Inch 33rpm
ALBUM GLOBE: *81* 5-8
CAPITOL: *50-53* 20-30
CORAL: *73* 4-6
DANNY: 8-10
DECCA (8400 through 8600): *56-57* 20-30
DECCA (75000 through 78000
series): *67-70* 8-15
DOT: *66* 8-12
MCA: 4-6
MCR: *74* 6-10
SHASTA: *58-75* 5-15
TOPS: 8-15
VOCALION: *68-70* 5-10
Also see CHANDLER, Karen, & Jimmy
Wakely
Also see WHITING, Margaret, & Jimmy
Wakely

**WAKELIN, Johnny, & The
Kinshasa Band**
Singles: 7-Inch
PYE: *75* 2-4

WAKEMAN, Rick
(Rick Wakeman With The London Symphony
Orchestra & English Chamber Choir; Rick
Wakeman & The English Rock Ensemble)
Singles: 7-Inch
A&M: *73* 2-4

LPs: 10/12-Inch 33rpm
A&M (3000 series): *74* $5-8
A&M (4000 series): *73-77* 8-10
A&M (6000 series): *79* 10-12
Also see DALTREY, Roger, & Rick Wakeman
Also see STRAWBS
Also see YES

WALDEN, Narada Michael
(Narada)
Singles: 12-Inch 33/45rpm
ATLANTIC: *82-83* 4-6
WARNER BROS: *85* 4-6
Singles: 7-Inch
ATLANTIC: *77-83* 1-3
REPRISE: *88* 1-3
WARNER BROS: *85* 1-3
LPs: 10/12-Inch 33rpm
ATLANTIC: *79-83* 5-8
REPRISE: *88* 5-8

**WALDEN, Narada Michael, &
Patti Austin**
Singles: 7-Inch
WARNER BROS: *85* 1-3
Also see AUSTIN, Patti
Also see WALDEN, Narada Michael

WALDMAN, Wendy
Singles: 7-Inch
EPIC: *82-83* 1-3
WARNER BROS: *77-78* 2-3
LPs: 10/12-Inch 33rpm
EPIC: *82-83* 5-8
WARNER BROS: *78* 5-8

WALDO
Singles: 7-Inch
COLUMBIA: *82* 1-3
LPs: 10/12-Inch 33rpm
COLUMBIA: *82* 5-8

WALKER, Billy
Singles: 78rpm
COLUMBIA: *54-56* 2-5
Singles: 7-Inch
CAPRICE: *79* 1-3
COLUMBIA (21000 series): *54-56* 4-6
COLUMBIA (40000 series): *56-60* 3-5
COLUMBIA (42000 & 43000
series): *61-65* 2-4
DIMENSION: *83* 1-3
MCA: *77* 1-3
MGM: *70-74* 2-3
MRC: *78* 1-3
MONUMENT: *66-70* 2-4
RCA VICTOR: *75-76* 2-3
SCORPION: *78* 1-3

TALL TEXAN: *83-88* $1-3
Picture Sleeves
COLUMBIA: *63-67* 2-5
LPs: 10/12-Inch 33rpm
COLUMBIA: *63-69* 8-18
GUSTO: 5-8
H.S.R.D.: *84* 5-8
HARMONY: *64-70* 8-15
MGM: *70-74* 8-12
MONUMENT: *66-72* 8-15
RCA VICTOR: *75-76* 5-8

WALKER, Billy, & Barbara Fairchild
Singles: 7-Inch
PAID: *81* 1-3
LPs: 10/12-Inch 33rpm
PAID: *81* 5-8
Also see FAIRCHILD, Barbara
Also see WALKER, Billy

WALKER, Bobbi
Singles: 7-Inch
CASABLANCA: *80* 1-3

WALKER, Boots
Singles: 7-Inch
PROVIDENCE: *66* 3-6
RUST: *67-68* 3-5

WALKER, David T.
Singles: 7-Inch
ODE: *73-76* 2-4
REVUE: *69-69* 2-5
ZEA: *70* 2-4
LPs: 10/12-Inch 33rpm
ODE: *74-76* 8-10
REVUE: *68-69* 10-15

WALKER, Gloria
(Gloria Walker & The Chevelles)
Singles: 7-Inch
FLAMING ARROW: *68-69* 3-5
PEOPLE: 2-4

WALKER, Jay
(Jay Walker & The Pedestrians)
Singles: 7-Inch
AMY: *62* 3-5
VEE JAY: *61* 3-5

WALKER, Jerry Jeff
Singles: 7-Inch
ATCO: *68-70* 2-5
MCA: *73-80* 1-3
LPs: 10/12-Inch 33rpm
ATCO (Except 297): *68-70* 15-20
ATCO (297; "Five Years
Gone"): *69* 40-50
DECCA: *72* 10-12

ELEKTRA: **$8-10**
MCA: *73-80* **6-10**
SOUTH COAST: *81* **5-8**
VANGUARD: *69* **10-12**

WALKER, Jimmy
Singles: 7-Inch
BUDDAH: *75* **2-4**
LPs: 10/12-Inch 33rpm
BUDDAH: *75* **8-10**

WALKER, Junior
(Junior Walker & The All Stars; Junior Walker & All The Stars)
Singles: 12-Inch 33/45rpm
WHITFIELD: *79* **4-6**
Singles: 7-Inch
HARVEY: *62-64* **5-8**
MOTOWN: *83* **1-3**
SOUL: *65* **4-8**
(With black band on label, printed over the words: "Distributed By Bell Records.")
SOUL (Except 35003): *65-76* **2-5**
(Without black band.)
SOUL (35003; "Monkey Jump"): *64* **4-6**
WHITFIELD: *79* **2-3**
Picture Sleeves
SOUL: *65-66* **3-6**
LPs: 10/12-Inch 33rpm
MOTOWN (Except 700 series): *80-83* **5-8**
MOTOWN (700 series): *74* **8-12**
SOUL (701 through 721): *65-70* **10-15**
SOUL (725 through 750): *70-78* **8-10**
WHITFIELD: *79* **5-8**

WALKER BROTHERS
Singles: 7-Inch
SMASH: *64-66* **4-6**
Picture Sleeves
SMASH: *65-66* **5-10**
LPs: 10/12-Inch 33rpm
SMASH: *66-67* **20-25**
Members: Scott Engel; John Maus; Gary Leeds.

WALL OF VOODO
Singles: 12-Inch 33/45rpm
I.R.S.: *83* **4-6**
Singles: 7-Inch
I.R.S.: *81-83* **1-3**
LPs: 10/12-Inch 33rpm
I.R.S: *81-83* **5-8**
Member: Stan Ridgway.
Also see COPELAND, Stewart, & Stan Ridgway
Also see RIDGWAY, Stan

WALLACE, Jerry
(Jerry Wallace & The Jewels)
Singles: 78rpm
ALLIED: *54* **$4-8**
CHALLENGE: *57* **4-8**
Singles: 7-Inch
ALLIED: *54* **5-8**
BMA: *77-78* **2-3**
CHALLENGE (1000 series): *57* **8-12**
CHALLENGE (9100 series): *61-63* **3-5**
CHALLENGE (59013 through 59098): *58-60* **5-10**
CHALLENGE (59200 series): *63-65* **3-5**
CLASS: *53* **5-8**
DECCA: *71-72* **2-4**
DOOR KNOB: *80* **1-3**
ERIC: **1-3**
4-STAR: *78-79* **1-3**
GLENOLDEN: *68* **2-4**
GUSTO: **1-3**
LIBERTY: *67-70* **2-4**
MCA: *73-74* **2-3**
MGM: *75* **2-3**
MERCURY (Except 72000 series): *55-56* .. **3-6**
MERCURY (72000 series): *64-66* **2-5**
TOPS: *53* **4-6**
UNITED ARTISTS: *72-75* **2-4**
VOGUE: *52* **8-10**
WING: *56* **4-6**
Picture Sleeves
CHALLENGE (59013 through 59098): *58-60* **5-10**
CHALLENGE (59200 series): *63-65* **3-6**
EPs: 7-Inch 33/45rpm
CHALLENGE: *60* **15-25**
LPs: 10/12-Inch 33rpm
BMA: *77* **8-10**
CHALLENGE (606; "Just Jerry"): *59* ... **30-35**
CHALLENGE (612; "There She Goes"): *61* **20-25**
CHALLENGE (616; "Shutters & Boards"): *63* **15-20**
CHALLENGE (619; "In The Misty Moonlight"): *64* **15-20**
CHALLENGE (2002; "Greatest Hits"): *69* **10-15**
DECCA: *71* **8-12**
4-STAR: *83* **5-8**
LIBERTY: *68* **10-12**
MCA: *73-74* **8-10**
MGM: *75* **8-10**
MERCURY: *66* **10-15**
UNITED ARTISTS: *72-75* **8-12**
WING: *68* **10-12**

Also see BARE, Bobby / Donna Fargo / Jerry
Wallace

WALLACE, Jerry / Soul Surfers
Singles: 7-Inch
CHALLENGE: *64* $3-5
Also see WALLACE, Jerry

WALLACE BROTHERS
Singles: 7-Inch
JEWEL: *68-69* 2-4
SIMS: *63-67* 3-5
LPs: 10/12-Inch 33rpm
SIMS: *65* 15-20

WALSH, James, Gypsy Band
Singles: 7-Inch
RCA VICTOR: *78-79* 2-3
LPs: 10/12-Inch 33rpm
RCA VICTOR: *79* 5-8
Also see GYPSY

WALSH, Joe
Singles: 7-Inch
ABC: *75-78* 2-3
ASYLUM: *78-81* 1-3
DUNHILL: *73-75* 2-4
FULL MOON: *80* 1-3
MCA: *79* 1-3
LPs: 10/12-Inch 33rpm
ABC: *76-78* 8-10
ASYLUM: *78-81* 5-8
COMMAND: *74-75* 8-12
DUNHILL: *72-74* 8-10
MCA: *79* 5-8
WARNER BROS: *83-87* 5-8
Also see EAGLES
Also see JAMES GANG
Also see VITALE, Joe

WALSH, Steve
Singles: 7-Inch
KIRSHNER: *80* 1-3
LPs: 10/12-Inch 33rpm
KIRSHNER: *80* 5-8

WAMMACK, Travis
Singles: 7-Inch
ARA: *64-65* 3-5
ATLANTIC: *66* 3-5
CAPRICORN: *75* 2-3
FAME: *72-73* 2-4
FRATERNITY: *58* 45-55
LPs: 10/12-Inch 33rpm
CAPRICORN: *75* 8-10
FAME: *72* 8-12
PHONORAMA: 5-8

WANDERERS
Singles: 78rpm
ONYX: *57* $10-15
ORBIT: *58* 5-10
SAVOY (1109; "We Could Find
Happiness"): *53* 20-40
Singles: 7-Inch
CUB: *58-62* 10-20
MGM: *62* 4-6
ONYX: *57* 20-30
ORBIT: *58* 10-15
SAVOY (1109; "We Could Find
Happiness"): *53* 75-100
UNITED ARTISTS: *62* 3-5
Members: Ray Pollard; Bob Yarborough; Sheppard
Grant; Frank Joyner.

WANDERLEY, Walter
Singles: 7-Inch
A&M: *69* 1-3
GNP/CRESCENDO: *81* 1-3
TOWER: *66-67* .2-4
VERVE: *66-68* 2-4
WORLD PACIFIC: *66* 2-4
LPs: 10/12-Inch 33rpm
A&M: *69* 6-10
CAPITOL: *63* 8-15
GNP/CRESCENDO: *81* 5-8
PHILIPS: *67* 8-12
TOWER: *66-67* .8-15
VERVE: *66-68* .8-15
WORLD PACIFIC: *66-67* 8-15
Also see GILBERTO, Astrud

WANG CHUNG
(Huang Chung)
Singles: 12-Inch 33/45rpm
GEFFEN: *84* 4-6
Singles: 7-Inch
GEFFEN: *84-87* .1-3
LPs: 10/12-Inch 33rpm
ARISTA: *83* 5-8
GEFFEN: *85* 5-8

WANSEL, Dexter
Singles: 12-Inch 33/45rpm
PHILADELPHIA INT'L: *79* 4-6
Singles: 7-Inch
PHILADELPHIA INT'L: *76-79* 1-3
LPs: 10/12-Inch 33rpm
PHILADELPHIA INT'L: *76-79* 5-8

WAR
Singles: 12-Inch 33/45rpm
MCA: *78-79* 4-6
Singles: 7-Inch
BLUE NOTE: *77* .2-3

COCO PLUM: *85*	$1-3
LAX: *81*	1-3
MCA: *77-82*	1-3
PRIORITY: *87*	1-3
RCA VICTOR: *82-83*	1-3
UNITED ARTISTS: *71-78*	3-6
WAR: *77*	2-3

Picture Sleeves

MCA: *77*	1-3
UNITED ARTISTS: *71-75*	2-4

LPs: 10/12-Inch 33rpm

BLUE NOTE: *76*	8-10
MCA: *77-82*	5-8
PRIORITY: *87*	5-8
RCA VICTOR: *82-83*	5-8
UNITED ARTISTS (Except 103): *71-76*	8-10
UNITED ARTISTS (103; "Radio Free War"): *74*	12-15

(Promotional issue only.)
Members: Howard Scott; Lonnie Jordan; Dee Allen; B.B. Dickerson; Lee Oskar; Charles Miller; Harold Brown.
Also see BURDON, Eric, & War
Also see JORDAN, Lonnie
Also see OSKAR, Lee

WARD, Anita

Singles: 7-Inch

JUANA: *79*	2-3

LPs: 10/12-Inch 33rpm

JUANA: *79*	5-8

WARD, Billy, & The Dominoes

Singles: 78rpm

DECCA: *56-57*	5-10
FEDERAL (12105; "I'd Be Satisfied"): *52*	10-20
FEDERAL (12106; "Yours Forever"): *52*	10-20
FEDERAL (12114; "Pedal Pushin' Papa"): *52*	20-40
FEDERAL (12129; "These Foolish Things"): *53*	15-25
FEDERAL (12139 through 12380): *53-57*	5-15

Singles: 7-Inch

ABC-PARAMOUNT: *60*	4-6
DECCA: *56-57*	10-20
FEDERAL (12105; "I'd Be Satisfied"): *52*	35-50
FEDERAL (12106; "Yours Forever"): *52*	30-50
FEDERAL (12114; "Pedal Pushin' Papa"): *52*	75-100
FEDERAL (12129; "These Foolish Things"): *53*	60-80

FEDERAL (12139 through 12218): *53-55*	$20-40
FEDERAL (12163 through 12380): *56-57*	10-20
GUSTO:	1-3
JUBILEE: *54-55*	10-20
KING (1000 series, except 1281): *53-55*	20-30
KING (1281; "Christmas In Heaven"): *53*	35-50
KING (5000 series): *60-61*	4-6
KING (6000 series): *65*	3-5
LIBERTY (54000 series): *57-59*	5-10
LIBERTY (55000 series): *62*	3-5
RO-ZAN: *62*	3-5

Picture Sleeves

LIBERTY: *57*	10-20

EPs: 7-Inch 33/45rpm

DECCA: *58*	40-60
FEDERAL (Silver Top label): *54-56*	50-75
FEDERAL (Green label): *57*	25-40
LIBERTY: *59*	20-30

LPs: 10/12-Inch 33rpm

DECCA (8621; "Billy Ward & His Dominoes"): *58*	75-100
FEDERAL (94; "Billy Ward & His Dominoes"): *54*	800-1000

(10-Inch LP.)

FEDERAL (548; "Billy Ward & His Dominoes"): *56*	400-800
FEDERAL (559; "Clyde McPhatter With Billy Ward & His Dominoes"): *57*	300-500
KING (548; "Billy Ward & His Dominoes"): *58*	60-80
KING (559; "Clyde McPhatter With Billy Ward & His Dominoes"): *61*	50-60
KING (733; "Billy Ward & His Dominoes, Featuring Clyde McPhatter & Jackie Wilson"): *61*	50-60
KING (952; "24 Songs"): *66*	20-30
KING/GUSTO:	5-8
LIBERTY: *59*	25-35

Members: Clyde McPhatter; Jackie Wilson; Billy Ward; Gene Mumford; Milton Merle; Milton Grayson; William Lamont; Cliff Givens.
Also see DOMINOES
Also see MUMFORD, Gene
Also see WILSON, Jackie

WARD, Dale

Singles: 7-Inch

BIG WAY:	3-5
BOYD: *62-65*	3-6
DOT (16000 series): *63-65*	3-5
DOT (17000 series): *71-72*	2-4
MONUMENT: *66-69*	3-5
PARAMOUNT: *69-70*	2-4

Picture Sleeves
BOYD: *62* $10-20
  Also see CRESCENDOS
  Also see WARD, Robin

WARD, Joe
  Singles: 78rpm
KING: *55-56* 3-6
  Singles: 7-Inch
KING: *55-56* 6-10

WARD, Robin
  Singles: 7-Inch
DOT: *63-64* 3-5
SONGS UNLIMITED: *63* 3-5
  Picture Sleeves
SONGS UNLIMITED: *63* 4-8
  LPs: 10/12-Inch 33rpm
DOT: *63* 25-35
  Also see MARTINDALE, Wink, & Robin
  Ward
  Also see WARD, Dale

WARD, Singin' Sammy
  Singles: 7-Inch
SOUL: *64* 3-5
TAMLA (54030; "What Makes You
  Love Him?"): *61* 25-30
  (With horizontal lines.)
TAMLA (54030; "What Makes You
  Love Him?"): *61* 15-20
  (With Tamla globe logo.)
TAMLA (54049; "What Makes You
  Love Him?"): *62* 15-20
TAMLA (54057; "Everybody
  Knows It"): *62* 30-35
TAMLA (54071; "Part Time Love"): *62* ... 5-8

WARE, Leon
  Singles: 7-Inch
ELEKTRA: *81* 1-3
FABULOUS: *79* 1-3
UNITED ARTISTS: *72* 2-4
  LPs: 10/12-Inch 33rpm
FABULOUS: *79* 5-8
GORDY: *76* 6-10
UNITED ARTISTS: *72* 8-12

WARINER, Steve
  Singles: 7-Inch
MCA: *88* 1-3

WARING, Fred
  (Fred Waring & The Pennsylvanians)
  Singles: 7-Inch
CAPITOL: *57-59* 2-4
DECCA: *50-68* 2-4
REPRISE: *64* 1-3

EPs: 7-Inch 33/45rpm
CAPITOL: *57-58* $3-6
DECCA: *50-59* 3-8
  LPs: 10/12-Inch 33rpm
CAPITOL: *57-69* 5-12
DECCA: *50-68* 5-15
HARMONY: *69* 4-8
MCA: *77* 4-8
MEGA: *71* 4-8
REPRISE: *64-65* 4-8
RCA VICTOR: *68* 4-8

WARNES, Jennifer
  (Jennifer Warren)
  Singles: 12-Inch 33/45rpm
20TH CENTURY-FOX ("It Goes Like
  It Goes"): *79* 4-6
  (Shown as by Jennifer Warnes. No catalog number
  used.)
20TH CENTURY-FOX (379; "It Goes
  Like It Goes"): *79* 5-8
  (Shown as by Jennifer Warren.)
  Singles: 7-Inch
ARISTA: *77-82* 1-3
PARROT: *68* 3-5
WARNER BROS: *83* 1-3
  LPs: 10/12-Inch 33rpm
ARISTA: *76-82* 5-8
CYPRESS: *87* 5-8
REPRISE: *72* 8-10
  Also see COCKER, Joe, & Jennifer Warnes
  Also see JENNIFER
  Also see MEDLEY, Bill, & Jennifer Warnes

WARP 9
  Singles: 12-Inch 33/45rpm
PRISM: *83-84* 4-6
  Singles: 7-Inch
PRISM: *83-84* 1-3

WARREN, Rusty
  Singles: 7-Inch
JUBILEE: *60* 5-10
  EPs: 7-Inch 33/45rpm
JUBILEE: *62* 10-15
  LPs: 10/12-Inch 33rpm
GNP/CRESCENDO: *74-77* 5-12
JUBILEE: *60-68* 10-20

WARRIOR, Jade:
  see JADE WARRIOR

WARWICK, Dee Dee
  (Dee Dee Warwick & The Dixie Flyers)
  Singles: 7-Inch
ATCO: *70-71* 2-4
BLUE ROCK: *65* 3-5
HURT: *66* 3-5

JUBILEE: *63* $3-5
MERCURY: *66-69* 3-5
PRIVATE STOCK: *75* 2-3
SUTRA: 2-3
TIGER: *64* 3-5
LPs: 10/12-Inch 33rpm
ATCO: *70* 8-10
HERITAGE SOUND: *83* 5-8
MERCURY: *67-69* 10-15

WARWICK, Dionne
(Dionne Warwicke)
Singles: 12-Inch 33/45rpm
ARISTA: *84* 4-6
Singles: 7-Inch
ARISTA: *79-88* 2-4
COLLECTABLES: 1-3
ERIC: 1-3
MUSICOR: *77* 2-4
SCEPTER (1200 series): *62-65* 4-8
SCEPTER (12000 series): *65-71* 3-6
WARNER BROS: *72-78* 3-5
Picture Sleeves
SCEPTER: *63-71* 2-5
LPs: 10/12-Inch 33rpm
ARISTA: *79-87* 5-8
CIRCA: 5-8
EVEREST: *81* 5-8
51 WEST: 5-8
MFSL: *82* 25-50
MUSICOR: *77* 5-8
PHOENIX: *81* 5-8
RHINO: 5-8
SCEPTER (Except 200): *64-72* 10-15
SCEPTER (200; "March Is Dionne
   Warwick Month"): *67* 20-25
   (Promotional issue only.)
UNITED ARTISTS: *74* 8-10
TRIP: *76* 8-10
WARNER BROS: *72-77* 8-10
   Also see DIONNE & FRIENDS
   Also see GIBB, Barry
   Also see HAYES, Isaac, & Dionne Warwick
   Also see MATHIS, Johnny, & Dionne War-
wick
   Also see U.S.A. FOR AFRICA
   Also see WONDER, Stevie / Dionne Warwick

WARWICK, Dionne, & Howard Hewett
ARISTA: *88* 1-3
   Also see HEWETT, Howard

WARWICK, Dionne, & Glenn Jones
Singles: 7-Inch
ARISTA: *85* 2-3
   Also see JONES, Glenn

WARWICK, Dionne, & Kashif
Singles: 7-Inch
ARISTA: *87* $1-3
   Also see KASHIF

WARWICK, Dionne, & The Spinners
Singles: 7-Inch
ATLANTIC: *74* 3-5
   Also see SPINNERS

WARWICK, Dionne, & Luther Vandross
Singles: 7-Inch
ARISTA: *83* 2-3
   Also see VANDROSS, Luther
   Also see WARWICK, Dionne

WAS
(NOT WAS)
Singles: 12-Inch 33/45rpm
ISLAND: *82* 4-6
Singles: 7-Inch
CHRYSALIS: *88* 1-3
GEFFEN: *83* 2-3
ISLAND: *81-82* 2-3
ZE: *82* 1-3
LPs: 10/12-Inch 33rpm
CHRYSALIS: *88* 5-8
GEFFEN: *83* 5-8
ISLAND: *81* 5-8
Members: Don Fagenson; David Weiss.

WASHINGTON, Baby
(Jeanette Washington; Justine Washington)
Singles: 7-Inch
ABC-PARAMOUNT: *61* 5-10
A.V.I.: *78* 2-4
CHECKER: *59* 5-10
CHESS: *70* 3-5
COLLECTABLES: 1-3
COTILLION: *69-70* 3-5
J&S: *59* 5-10
MASTER FIVE: *73-75* 2-5
NEPTUNE: *60-61* 10-15
SIXTH AVENUE: *76* 2-4
SUE: *62-67* 5-10
LPs: 10/12-Inch 33rpm
A.V.I.: *78* 5-8
COLLECTABLES: *87-88* 6-8
SUE: *63-65* 15-20
TRIP: *71* 8-10
VEEP: *68* 10-15
   Also see HEARTS
   Also see PARLET & Jeanette Washington

WASHINGTON, Baby, & Don Gardner
Singles: 7-Inch
MASTER FIVE: *73-74* 3-5

LPs: 10/12-Inch 33rpm
MASTER FIVE: *74* **$8-10**
  Also see WASHINGTON, Baby

WASHINGTON, Deborah
Singles: 7-Inch
ARIOLA: *78* **2-3**
. *LPs: 10/12-Inch 33rpm*
ARIOLA: *78* **5-8**

WASHINGTON, Dinah
Singles: 78rpm
APOLLO: *45-47* **5-10**
KEYNOTE: *44* **8-15**
MERCURY: *46-57* **4-8**
Singles: 7-Inch
MERCURY (5000 series): *50-52* **10-15**
MERCURY (8200 series): *52* **8-12**
MERCURY (70046 through 70968): *52-56* **5-10**
MERCURY (71000 & 72000 series): *57-63* **3-8**
ROULETTE: *62-63* **3-5**
Picture Sleeves
MERCURY: *61-62* **5-10**
EPs: 7-Inch 33/45rpm
EMARCY: *54-56* **10-25**
MERCURY (3000 through 3200
series): *51-57* **15-20**
MERCURY (3300 series): *60* **10-15**
MERCURY (4000 series): *61* **8-12**
LPs: 10/12-Inch 33rpm
EMARCY (400 series): *76* **8-12**
EMARCY (26000 series): *54* **40-50**
  (10-Inch LPs.)
EMARCY (36000 series): *54-58* **25-35**
EVEREST: *75* **8-10**
MERCURY (103; "This Is
My Story"): *63* **20-25**
MERCURY (121; "Original Queen
Of Soul"): *69* **12-15**
MERCURY (603; "This Is
My Story"): *63* **20-25**
MERCURY (20100 & 20200
series): *55-58* **30-40**
MERCURY (20400 through 20900
series): *59-63* **15-20**
MERCURY (21100 series): *67* **10-12**
MERCURY (25000 series): *50-51* **50-60**
  (10-Inch LPs.)
MERCURY (60100 through 60900
series): *59-63* **15-25**
MERCURY (61100 series): *67* **10-12**
ROSETTA: *84* **5-8**
ROULETTE (100 series): *71-72* **10-12**
ROULETTE (25000 series): *62-65* **12-15**
TRIP: *73-78* **8-10**
WING: *59-64* **15-20**

Also see BENTON, Brook, & Dinah
Washington
Also see HAMPTON, Lionel, & Dinah
Washington
Also see JONES, Quincy
Also see RAVENS & Dinah Washington

**WASHINGTON, Dinah / Joe Williams /
Sarah Vaughan**
LPs: 10/12-Inch 33rpm
ROULETTE: *64* **$15-20**
  Also see VAUGHAN, Sarah
  Also see WASHINGTON, Dinah

WASHINGTON, Donna
* *Singles: 7-Inch*
CAPITOL: *81* **1-3**
LPs: 10/12-Inch 33rpm
CAPITOL: *81* **5-8**

WASHINGTON, Ella
Singles: 7-Inch
ATLANTIC: *67* **3-5**
SOUND STAGE: *67-69* **2-4**
LPs: 10/12-Inch 33rpm
SOUND STAGE: *69* **10-12**

WASHINGTON, Grover, Jr.
Singles: 7-Inch
COLUMBIA: *87* **1-3**
ELEKTRA: *79-84* **1-3**
KUDU: *71-78* **2-3**
MOTOWN: *78-83* **1-3**
Picture Sleeves
ELEKTRA: *80* **1-3**
LPs: 10/12-Inch 33rpm
COLUMBIA: *87* **5-8**
ELEKTRA: *79-84* **5-8**
KUDO: *71-77* **8-12**
MOTOWN: *78-83* **6-10**
  Also see COSBY, Bill
  Also see LABELLE, Patti, & Grover
Washington Jr.
  Also see WITHERS, Bill

**WASHINGTON, Jeanette:
see WASHINGTON, Baby**

WASHINGTON, Jerry
Singles: 7-Inch
EXCELLO: *73* **2-4**

WATANABE, Kazumi
LPs: 10/12-Inch 33rpm
GRAMAVISION: *88* **5-8**

WATERBOYS
LPs: 10/12-Inch 33rpm
CHRYSALIS: *88* **5-8**

WATERS, Freddie
Singles: 7-Inch
KARI: *81* $1-3
OCTOBER: *77* 2-3

WATERS, Muddy
Singles: 78rpm
ARISTOCRAT: *48-49* 20-30
CHESS: *50-55* 5-12
Singles: 7-Inch
CHESS (1509 through 1542): *52-53* 30-50
CHESS (1550 through 1571): *53-54* 20-35
CHESS (1579 through 1596): *54-55* 10-20
CHESS (1600 series): *55-59* 5-8
CHESS (1700 series): *59-61* 4-6
CHESS (1800 & 1900 series): *62-66* 3-5
CHESS (2000 series): *67-73* 2-4
LPs: 10/12-Inch 33rpm
BLUE SKY: *77-81* 5-8
CADET CONCEPT: *68-69* 10-12
CHESS (1427; "The Best Of
  Muddy Waters"): *57* 35-45
CHESS (1444; "Muddy Waters
  Sings Big Bill"): *60* 25-35
CHESS (1449; "Muddy Waters
  At Newport"): *64* 20-25
CHESS (1483; "Folk Singer"): *64* 15-20
CHESS (1500 series): *66-71* 10-15
CHESS (50012 through 50023): *72-73* 6-10
CHESS (50033; "Fathers & Sons"): *75* ... 15-20
CHESS (60006; "McKinley
  Morganfield"): *71* 10-12
CHESS (60013 through 60035): *72-75* 6-10
DOUGLAS: *68* 10-12
MUSE: *73* 5-8
TESTAMENT: 10-12
  Also see COTTON, James
  Also see ROGERS, Jimmy
  Also see WELLS, Junior
  Also see WINTER, Johnny

WATERS, Muddy, & Howlin' Wolf
LPs: 10/12-Inch 33rpm
CHESS: *74* 8-10
  Also see DIDDLEY, Bo, Howlin' Wolf, &
  Muddy Waters
  Also see HOWLIN' WOLF
  Also see WATERS, Muddy

WATERS, Patty
LPs: 10/12-Inch 33rpm
ESP: *66* 12-15

WATERS, Roger
(With Madeline Bell, Katie Kissoon, Eric Clapton ,& Doreen Chanter; Roger Waters & The Bleeding Heart Band)
Singles: 12-inch
COLUMBIA: *84* $4-6
Singles: 7-Inch
COLUMBIA: *84* 1-3
LPs: 10/12-Inch 33rpm
COLUMBIA: *84-87* 5-8
  Also see BELL, Madeline
  Also see CLAPTON, Eric
  Also see KISSOON, Mac & Katie
  Also see PINK FLOYD

WATKINS, Tip
Singles: 7-Inch
H&L: *77* 2-4

WATLEY, Jody
Singles: 7-Inch
MCA: *88* 1-3

WATSON, Doc
Singles: 7-Inch
POPPY: *72-74* 2-3
UNITED ARTISTS: *75-79* 1-3
LPs: 10/12-Inch 33rpm
FLYING FISH: *81* 5-8
FOLKWAYS: *63-69* 8-18
LIBERTY: *83* 5-8
POPPY: *72* 6-12
UNITED ARTISTS: *75-76* 8-15
VANGUARD: *64-77* 8-18
VERVE/FOLKWAYS: *66* 10-15
  Also see FLATT, Lester, Earl Scruggs & Doc Watson

WATSON, Johnny
(Johnny Guitar Watson; Young John Watson; Johnny Watson Trio)
Singles: 78rpm
FEDERAL: *53-54* 10-15
KEEN: *57* 4-8
RPM: *55-56* 5-10
Singles: 7-Inch
ALL STAR: *58* 5-8
ARVEE: *60* 4-6
CLASS: *59* 4-6
DJM: *77* 2-3
ESCORT: 4-6
FANTASY: *73-75* 2-3
FEDERAL: *53-54* 30-40
GOTH: *60* 4-6
KEEN: *57* 8-10
KENT: *60* 3-5
KING: *61-64* 3-5

OKEH: *66-67* $3-5
RPM: *55-56* 10-15
VALLEY VUE: *84* 1-3
LPs: 10/12-Inch 33rpm
A&M: *81* 5-8
BIG TOWN: *77* 8-10
CADET: *67* 10-15
CHESS: *64* 15-20
DJM: *76-81* 5-8
FANTASY: *73-81* 5-8
KING: *63* 40-50
OKEH: *67* 10-15
MCA: *81* 5-8
Also see BLAND, Bobby / Johnny Guitar
Watson
Also see OTIS, Johnny
Also see WATSONIAN INSTITUTE
Also see WILLIAMS, Larry, & Johnny
Watson

WATSONIAN INSTITUTE
Singles: 7-Inch
DJM: *78* 2-3
LPs: 10/12-Inch 33rpm
DJM: *78* 5-8
Also see WATSON, Johnny

WATTS, Ernie
Singles: 7-Inch
QWEST: *82* 1-2
LPs: 10/12-Inch 33rpm
QWEST: *82* 5-8

WATTS, Noble
(Noble "Thin Man" Watts & His Rhythm
Sparks; Noble Watts Quintet; Nobel Watts With
Paul "Hucklebuck" Williams)
Singles: 78rpm
BATON: *57* 4-6
DELUXE: *54* 4-8
Singles: 7-Inch
BATON: *57* 4-6
BRUNSWICK: *68* 3-5
CLAMIKE: *63-64* 3-5
CUB: *60* 3-5
DELUXE: *54* 5-8
Also see WILLIAMS, Paul

WATTS, Noble, & June Bateman
Singles: 7-Inch
ENJOY: *63* 3-5
Also see WATTS, Noble

WATTS 103RD ST. RHYTHM BAND
(Featuring Charles Wright)
Singles: 7-Inch
KEYMEN: *67* 3-5
WARNER BROS: *68-69* 3-5

LPs: 10/12-Inch 33rpm
WARNER BROS: *68-69* $10-15
Also see WRIGHT, Charles

WAX
Singles: 12-Inch 33/45rpm
RCA VICTOR: *86* 4-6
Singles: 7-Inch
RCA VICTOR: *81-86* 1-3
LPs: 10/12-Inch 33rpm
COTILLION: *80* 5-8
RCA VICTOR: *81-86* 5-8
Members: Graham Gouldman; Andrew Gold.
Also see GOLD, Andrew
Also see 10CC

WAYBILL, Fee
Singles: 7-Inch
CAPITOL: *84* 1-3
LPs: 10/12-Inch 33rpm
CAPITOL: *84* 5-8
Also see TUBES

WAYLON & WILLIE:
see JENNINGS, Waylon, & Willie Nelson

WAYNE, Bobby
Singles: 78rpm
MERCURY: *51-54* 3-6
Singles: 7-Inch
MERCURY: *51-54* 3-6
EPs: 7-Inch 33/45rpm
MERCURY: *53* 5-10

WAYNE, James
(James Waynes; Wee Willie Wayne)
Singles: 78rpm
ALADDIN: *54* 4-8
IMPERIAL: *51-57* 4-8
MILLION: *54* 5-10
PEACOCK: *57* 4-8
SITTIN' IN WITH: *51-52* 5-10
Singles: 7-Inch
ANGELTONE: *60* 5-8
ALADDIN: *54* 15-20
IMPERIAL (5200 series): *53* 20-30
IMPERIAL (5300 series): *55* 10-20
IMPERIAL (5600 & 5700
series): *60-61* 3-5
MILLION: *54* 15-20
PEACOCK: *57* 5-10
LPs: 10/12-Inch 33rpm
IMPERIAL: *61* 40-50

WAYNE, John
Singles: 7-Inch
CASABLANCA: *79* 1-3
RCA VICTOR: *73* 2-3

LPs: 10/12-Inch 33rpm
RCA VICTOR (3000 series): *79-81* **$4-8**
RCA VICTOR (4800 series): *73* **8-15**

WAYNE, Thomas
(Thomas Wayne & The DeLons)
Singles: 7-Inch
CAPEHART: *61* **3-5**
CHALET: *69* **2-4**
COLLECTABLES: **1-3**
ERIC: **1-3**
FERNWOOD (Except 106): *59-60* **4-6**
FERNWOOD (106; "You're The
One That Done It"): *58* **35-40**
MERCURY (71287; "You're The
One That Done It"): *58* **25-35**
MERCURY (71454; "You're The
One That Done It"): *59* **20-25**
OLDIES 45: *64* **1-3**
PHILLIPS INT'L: *62* **3-5**
RACER: *65* **3-5**
SANTO: *62* **3-5**

WE FIVE
Singles: 7-Inch
A&M: *65-69* **3-5**
MGM: *73* **2-4**
VAULT: *67* **3-5**
VERVE: *68-73* **2-4**
LPs: 10/12-Inch 33rpm
A&M: *65-69* **10-15**
A.V.I: *77* **5-8**
VAULT: *70* **10-12**
Members: Mike Stewart; Pete Fullerton; Beverly
Bivens; Bob Jones; Jerry Burgan.

WE THE PEOPLE
Singles: 7-Inch
CHALLENGE: *66-67* **8-12**
DAVEL: *75* **2-3**
IMPERIAL: *69* **2-4**
LION: *72-74* **2-4**
MAP CITY: *69* **2-4**
RCA VICTOR: *67* **4-8**
REENA: *68* **2-4**
VERVE: *71* **2-4**

WEAPONS OF PEACE
Singles: 7-Inch
PLAYBOY: *76-77* **2-3**
LPs: 10/12-Inch 33rpm
PLAYBOY: *77* **5-8**

WEATHER GIRLS
Singles: 12-Inch 33/45rpm
COLUMBIA: *83-85* **4-6**
Singles: 7-Inch
COLUMBIA: *83-85* **1-3**

LPs: 10/12-Inch 33rpm
COLUMBIA: *84* **$5-8**
Also see TWO TONS O' FUN

WEATHER REPORT
Singles: 7-Inch
COLUMBIA: *73-84* **1-3**
LPs: 10/12 Inch 33rpm
ARC/COLUMBIA: *78-82* **5-10**
COLUMBIA: *71-86* **5-10**
Also see PASTORIUS, Jaco
Also see SHORTER, Wayne

WEATHERLY, Jim
Singles: 7-Inch
ABC: *76-77* **2-3**
BUDDAH: *74-75* **2-4**
ELEKTRA: *79-80* **1-3**
ERIC: *78* **1-3**
RCA VICTOR: *72-74* **2-4**
20TH CENTURY-FOX: *65* **3-5**
Picture Sleeves
BUDDAH: *74* **2-4**
LPs: 10/12-Inch 33rpm
ABC: *77* **5-8**
BUDDAH: *74-75* **8-10**
RCA VICTOR: *72* **8-10**

WEATHERS, Carl
Singles: 7-Inch
MIRAGE: *81* **1-3**

WEATHERS, Oscar
Singles: 7-Inch
BLUE CANDLE: *73* **2-4**
TOP & BOTTOM: *69-72* **2-4**

WEAVER, Dennis
(Dennis Weaver & The Good Time People)
Singles: 7-Inch
CASCADE: *59* **5-8**
CENTURY CITY: *69* **2-4**
EVA: *63* **4-6**
IM'PRESS: *72* **2-4**
OVATION: *75* **2-3**
WARNER BROS: *63* **3-5**
LPs: 10/12-Inch 33rpm
IM'PRESS: *72* **8-10**
OVATION: *75* **5-10**

WEAVERS
(Weavers With Gordon Jenkins' Orchestra)
Singles: 78rpm
DECCA: *50-57* **2-4**
Singles: 7-Inch
DECCA (27000 through 29000
series): *50-55* **4-8**
DECCA (31000 series): *62* **2-4**

NSD: 82 .... $1-3
VANGUARD: 60-62 3-5
    EPs: 7-Inch 33/45rpm
DECCA: 51-52 5-15
    LPs: 10/12-Inch 33rpm
DECCA (Except 5000 series): 58-70 8-18
DECCA (5000 series): 51-52 15-30
  (10-Inch LPs.)
VANGUARD (15-16; "Greatest
  Hits"): 71 8-12
VANGUARD (2000 series): 59-63 10-20
VANGUARD (3000 through 6000
  series): 67-70 8-15
VANGUARD (9000 series): 56-63 12-25
VANGUARD (9100 series): 65 10-20
  Members: Pete Seeger; Lee Hays; Fred Hellerman;
  Ronnie Gilbert.
  Also see JENKINS, Gordon, & His Orchestra
  Also see SEEGER, Pete

WEB, Ebony: see EBONEE WEBB

WEBB, Jack
(Jack Webb & Jazz Combo)
    EPs: 7-Inch 33/45rpm
RCA VICTOR (0342/3; "The
  Christmas Story"): 15-25
RCA VICTOR (1126; "Pete Kelly's
  Blues"): 55 20-35
    LPs: 10/12-Inch 33rpm
RCA VICTOR (1126; "Pete Kelly's
  Blues"): 55 25-40
RCA VICTOR (2040; "Pete Kelly's
  Blues"): 59 15-25
WARNER BROS: 58 10-20
  Members: Jack Webb; Matty Matlock; Dick Cath-
  cart; Nick Fatool; Elmer "Moe" Schneider; George
  Van Eps; Ray Sherman; Jud DeNaut.

WEBB, Paula
    Singles: 7-Inch
WESTBOUND: 75 2-3

WEBER, Joan
    Singles: 78rpm
COLUMBIA: 54-56 2-5
    Singles: 7-Inch
COLUMBIA: 54-56 3-5
CROSLEY: 63 2-4
MAPLE: 61 2-4
    EPs: 7-Inch 33/45rpm
COLUMBIA: 55 5-10

WEBS
    Singles: 7-Inch
GUYDEN: 63 4-6
HEART: 61-62 3-5
MGM: 66 3-5

POPSIDE: 67-68 ....$3-5
VERVE: 68 3-5

WEDNESDAY
    Singles: 7-Inch
CELEBRATION: 76 2-3
SKY: 76 2-3
SUSSEX: 73-74 2-4
    LPs: 10/12-Inch 33rpm
SUSSEX: 74 8-10

WEE GEE
    Singles: 7-Inch
COTILLION: 80 1-3
JUNEY: 78 2-3

WEEKS & CO.
    Singles: 12-Inch 33/45rpm
SALSOUL: 83 4-6
    Singles: 7-Inch
CHEZ RO: 81 1-3
SALSOUL: 83 1-3
    LPs: 10/12-Inch 33rpm
SALSOUL: 83 5-8

WEIDER, John
    LPs: 10/12-Inch 33rpm
ANCHOR: 76 8-10
GOLD CASTLE: 88 5-8
  Also see ANIMALS
  Also see FAMILY

WEIR, Bob
    Singles: 7-Inch
ARISTA (315; "Bombs Away"): 77 2-4
ARISTA (336; "I'll Be
  Doggone"): 77 5-10
  (Promotional issue only.)
WARNER BROS: 72 3-5
    LPs: 10/12-Inch 33rpm
ARISTA: 78 5-8
WARNER BROS: 72 10-15
  Also see BOBBY & THE MIDNITES
  Also see GRATEFUL DEAD
  Also see KINGFISH

WEIR, Frank, Orchestra
    Singles: 78rpm
CAPITOL: 56 2-4
COLUMBIA: 57 2-4
LONDON: 54-57 2-4
    Singles: 7-Inch
CAPITOL: 56 2-4
COLUMBIA: 57 2-4
LONDON: 54-63 2-4
    EPs: 7-Inch 33/45rpm
LONDON: 54-55 4-8

LPs: 10/12-Inch 33rpm

COLUMBIA: *57*	$8-15
LONDON: *54*	8-15

WEISBERG, Tim
Singles: 7-Inch

A&M: *71-79*	2-3
MCA: *79*	1-3
UNITED ARTISTS: *77-80*	1-3

LPs: 10/12-Inch 33rpm

A&M: *73-79*	5-10
MCA: *79-80*	5-8
NAUTILUS: *80*	12-15
UNITED ARTISTS: *77-78*	5-10

Also see FOGELBERG, Dan, & Tim Weisberg

WEISSBERG, Eric
(Eric Weissberg & Steve Mandell; Eric
Weissberg & Marshall Brickman)
Singles: 7-Inch

WARNER BROS: *72-73*	2-3

LPs: 10/12-Inch 33rpm

ELEKTRA: *63*	15-25
WARNER BROS: *73*	5-10

Also see TARRIERS

WELCH, Bob
Singles: 7-Inch

CAPITOL: *77-81*	1-3
RCA VICTOR: *81-83*	1-3

Picture Sleeves

CAPITOL: *81*	1-3

LPs: 10/12-Inch 33rpm

CAPITOL (Except 16000 series): *77-80*	8-10
CAPITOL (16000 series): *80-82*	5-8
RCA VICTOR: *81-83*	5-8

Promotional LPs

CAPITOL ("French Kiss," picture
disc): *79* 25-30
Also see FLEETWOOD MAC
Also see PARIS

WELCH, Honey
Singles: 7-Inch

CHEVELL: *65*	3-5

WELCH, Lenny
Singles: 7-Inch

ATCO: *72*	2-4
BARNABY: *76*	1-3
BIG TREE: *78-83*	1-3
CADENCE (Except 1422): *59-64*	4-8
CADENCE (1422; "Congratulations Baby"): *62*	10-20
COLUMBIA: *67*	3-5
COMMONWEALTH UNITED: *69*	2-4
DECCA: *59*	4-6
KAPP: *65-67*	3-5

MAINSTREAM: *73-74*	$2-4
MERCURY: *68*	3-5
ROULETTE: *71*	2-3

LPs: 10/12-Inch 33rpm

CADENCE: *64*	15-20
COLUMBIA: *65*	10-15
KAPP: *66-67*	10-15

WELK, Lawrence, & His Orchestra
Singles: 78rpm

CORAL: *50-57*	2-4
MERCURY: *50-55*	2-4

Singles: 7-Inch

CORAL: *50-66*	2-4
DOT: *59-67*	1-3
MERCURY: *50-55*	2-4
RANWOOD: *68-77*	1-3

EPs: 7-Inch 33/45rpm

CORAL: *50-58*	3-8
DOT: *59-60*	3-6
MERCURY: *50-55*	4-8

LPs: 10/12-Inch 33rpm

CORAL: *50-65*	5-15
DECCA: *72*	5-10
DOT: *59-67*	4-12
HAMILTON: *64-66*	4-8
HARMONY: *68-70*	4-8
MCA: *74-76*	4-8
RANWOOD: *68 85*	4-8
SUNNYVALE: *79*	4-6
TRADITION: *75*	4-8
VOCALION: *59-70*	4-8
WING: *60-62*	4-8

Also see HODGES, Johnny, & Lawrence Welk
Also see HUDSON, Emperor Bob, &
Lawrence Welk
Also see LENNON SISTERS
Also see PRESLEY, Elvis / Lawrence Welk

WELLER, Freddy
Singles: 7-Inch

ABC/DOT: *75*	2-3
APT: *65*	4-6
COLUMBIA: *69-80*	1-3
DORE: *61*	5-8

LPs: 10/12-Inch 33rpm

COLUMBIA: *69-80*	5-10
EPIC: *74*	8-10
51 WEST:	5-8

Also see REVERE, Paul, & The Raiders

WELLES, Orson
LPs: 10/12-Inch 33rpm

MEDIARTS: *70*	8-12

Also see CROSBY, Bing, & Orson Welles

WELLS, Brandi
Singles: 7-Inch
WMOT: *81-82* $1-3

WELLS, Jean
Singles: 7-Inch
ABC-PARAMOUNT: *65* 3-5
CALLA: *67-68* 3-5
VOLARE: *69* 2-4

WELLS, Junior
(Junior Wells & His Eagle Rockers; Junior
Wells' Chicago Blues Band)
Singles: 7-Inch
BLUE ROCK: *68-69* 3-5
BRIGHT STAR: *66-67* 3-5
CHIEF: *57-62* 8-10
PROFILE: *59-60* 4-6
SHAD: *59* 5-8
STATES (122; "Cut That Out"): *52* 50-75
(Colored vinyl.)
STATES (134; "Hodo Man"): *53* 50-75
(Colored vinyl.)
STATES (139; "Lawdy Lawdy"): *53* 50-75
(Colored vinyl.)
STATES (143; "So All Alone"): *53* 50-75
(Colored vinyl.)
U.S.A.: *63-64* 4-6
VANGUARD: *67* 3-5
LPs: 10/12-Inch 33rpm
BLUE ROCK: *68* 10-12
DELMARK: *66-69* 10-15
VANGUARD: *66-68* 10-15
Also see WATERS, Muddy

WELLS, Junior, & Buddy Guy
LPs: 10/12-Inch 33rpm
BLIND PIG: *82* 5-8
INTERMEDIA: 5-8
Also see GUY, Buddy
Also see WELLS, Junior

WELLS, Kitty
Singles: 78rpm
DECCA: *52-57* 2-5
Singles: 7-Inch
CAPRICORN: *74-76* 2-3
DECCA (28000 & 29000
series): *52-56* 4-8
DECCA (30000 through 32000
series): *56-71* 2-5
MCA: *73* 1-3
RUBOCA: *79-80* 1-3
Picture Sleeves
DECCA: *69* 2-4
EPs: 7-Inch 33/45rpm
DECCA: *55-65* 6-15

LPs: 10/12-Inch 33rpm
CAPRICORN: *74* $6-10
DECCA (Except 8800 series): *61-72* 12-25
DECCA (8800 series): *56-59* 30-40
EXACT: *80* 5-8
IMPERIAL HOUSE: *80* 5-10
KOALA: *79* 5-8
MCA: *73-83* 4-8
MISTLETOE: 5-8
PICKWICK/HILLTOP: 6-12
ROUNDER: *82* 5-8
RUBOCA: *79* 8-12
SUFFOLK MARKETING: *80* 5-10
VOCALION: *66-69* 8-15
Also see PARTON, Dolly / Kitty Wells
Also see PIERCE, Webb, & Kitty Wells

WELLS, Kitty, & Roy Drusky
Singles: 7-Inch
DECCA: *60* 2-4
Also see DRUSKY, Roy

WELLS, Kitty, & Red Foley
Singles: 78rpm
DECCA: *54* 2-5
Singles: 7-Inch
DECCA: *54-69* 2-5
EPs: 7-Inch 33/45rpm
DECCA: *59* 8-12
LPs: 10/12-Inch 33rpm
DECCA: *61-67* 15-20
Also see FOLEY, Red
Also see WELLS, Kitty

WELLS, Mary
Singles: 12-Inch 33/45rpm
EPIC: *82* 4-6
Singles: 7-Inch
ATCO: *66-67* 3-5
EPIC: *82* 1-3
JUBILEE: *68-71* 2-4
MOTOWN (1003; "Bye Bye
Baby"): *60* 15-20
(Pink label.)
MOTOWN (1011; "I Don't Want To
Take A Chance"): *61* 10-15
(Pink label.)
MOTOWN (1011; "I Don't Want To
Take A Chance"): *61* 8-10
(Blue label.)
MOTOWN (1024 through 1056): *62-64* 4-6
REPRISE: *71-74* 2-4
20TH CENTURY-FOX: *64-66* 3-5
Picture Sleeves
MOTOWN: *61-62* 20-25
20TH CENTURY-FOX: *65* 3-6

LPs: 10/12-Inch 33rpm

WELLS, Terri
Singles: 12-Inch 33/45rpm
Singles: 7-Inch

WERNER, David
Singles: 7-Inch
LPs: 10/12-Inch 33rpm

WERNER, Max
Singles: 7-Inch

WESLEY, Fred
(Fred Wesley & The Horny Horns; Fred Wesley
& The J.B.s)
Singles: 7-Inch
LPs: 10/12-Inch 33rpm

WEST, Belinda
Singles: 7-Inch

WEST, Dr.:
see DR. WEST'S MEDICINE SHOW & JUNK
BAND

WEST, Dottie
Singles: 7-Inch
Picture Sleeves
LPs: 10/12-Inch 33rpm

WEST, Dottie / Melba Montgomery
LPs: 10/12-Inch 33rpm

WEST, Leslie
(Leslie West Band)
Singles: 7-Inch
LPs: 10/12-Inch 33rpm

Leslie West and friend (Photo: Hugh Brown)

WEST, Mae
Singles: 78rpm
BRUNSWICK: *33* **$10-15**
Singles: 7-Inch
MGM: *73* **2-4**
PLAZA: *62* **3-6**
TOWER: *66* **3-5**
20TH CENTURY-FOX (6718; "Hard To
Handle"): *70* **15-30**
EPs: 7-Inch 33/45rpm
DECCA (838; "The Fabulous
Mae West"): *55* **50-75**
(Triple EP set.)
LPs: 10/12-Inch 33rpm
DAGONET: *66* **10-15**
DECCA (9016; "The Fabulous
Mae West"): *55* **30-50**
DECCA (79016; "The Fabulous
Mae West"): *70* **10-15**
MGM: *72* **10-15**
TOWER: *66* **10-20**
Also see FIELDS, W.C.

WEST, BRUCE & LAING
Singles: 7-Inch
COLUMBIA: *73* **2-4**
LPs: 10/12-Inch 33rpm
COLUMBIA: *74* **8-10**
COLUMBIA/WINDFALL: *72-73* **8-12**
Members: Leslie West; Jack Bruce; Corky Laing.
Also see BRUCE, Jack
Also see MOUNTAIN
Also see WEST, Leslie

WEST STREET MOB
Singles: 12-Inch 33/45rpm
SUGAR HILL: *81-83* **4-6**
Singles: 7-Inch
SUGAR HILL: *81-83* **1-3**
LPs: 10/12-Inch 33rpm
SUGAR HILL: *82* **5-8**

WESTON, Kim
Singles: 7-Inch
ENTERPRISE: *74* **2-4**
GORDY: *65-66* **3-5**
MGM: *67-68* **2-5**
MIKIM: *71-72* **2-4**
PEOPLE: *69-70* **2-4**
PRIDE: *70* **2-4**
TAMLA: *63-65* **4-6**
Picture Sleeves
MGM: *67* **3-5**
LPs: 10/12-Inch 33rpm
ENTERPRISE: *74* **8-10**
MGM: *67-68* **15-20**

VOLT: *71* **$10-12**
Also see GAYE, Marvin, & Kim Weston
Also see NASH, Johnny, & Kim Weston

WESTON, Paul, Orchestra
Singles: 78rpm
CAPITOL: *45-57* **2-4**
COLUMBIA: *50-56* **2-4**
Singles: 7-Inch
CAPITOL: *57-60* **1-3**
COLUMBIA: *50-56* **2-4**
EPs: 7-Inch 33/45rpm
COLUMBIA: *50-56* **3-8**
LPs: 10/12-Inch 33rpm
CAPITOL: *57-61* **5-15**
COLUMBIA: *50-56* **5-15**
CORINTHIAN: *78* **4-8**
HARMONY: *72* **4-8**
Also see STAFFORD, Jo

WET WET WET
Singles: 7-Inch
UNI: *88* **1-3**
LPs: 10/12-Inch 33rpm
UNI: *88* **5-8**

WET WILLIE
Singles: 7-Inch
CAPRICORN: *74-76* **2-4**
EPIC: *77-79* **2-3**
LPs: 10/12-Inch 33rpm
CAPRICORN: *71-77* **6-10**
EPIC: *78-79* **5-8**
Member: Jimmy Hall.
Also see HALL, Jimmy

WHALUM, Kirk
LPs: 10/12-Inch 33rpm
COLUMBIA: *88* **5-8**

WHAM!
(Wham! U.K.)
Singles: 12-Inch 33/45rpm
COLUMBIA: *82-86* **4-6**
Singles: 7-Inch
COLUMBIA: *83-86* **1-3**
Picture Sleeves
COLUMBIA: *82-86* **1-3**
LPs: 10/12-Inch 33rpm
COLUMBIA (Except 40062): *83-86* **5-8**
COLUMBIA (40062; "Make It
Big"): *84* **8-10**
(Picture disc.)
Members: George Michael; Andrew Ridgely.
Also see BAND AID
Also see MICHAEL, George

WHATNAUTS
(Whatnauts & The Whatnaut Band)
Singles: 7-Inch
A&I: 70 .... $2-4
GSF: 73 2-4
HARLEM INT'L: 82 1-3
STANG: 71 2-4
LPs: 10/12-Inch 33rpm
STANG: 70-71 10-20

WHEELER, Billy Edd
Singles: 7-Inch
CAPITOL: 75-76 2-3
KAPP: 63-68 2-5
NSD: 80-81 1-3
RCA VICTOR: 70-73 2-3
RADIO CINEMA: 79 1-3
UNITED ARTISTS: 69 2-4
Picture Sleeves
KAPP: 67 2-5
LPs: 10/12-Inch 33rpm
AVALANCHE: 73 8-10
FLYING FISH: 79 5-8
KAPP: 64-68 10-18
MONITOR: 61-62 15-25
RCA VICTOR: 71 8-10
UNITED ARTISTS: 69 8-12

WHEN IN ROME
Singles: 7-Inch
VIRGIN: 88 1-3
LPs: 10/12-Inch 33rpm
VIRGIN: 88 5-8

WHIRLWIND
Singles: 12-Inch 33/45rpm
ROULETTE: 77 4-6
Singles: 7-Inch
ROULETTE: 76 2-3

WHISPERS
Singles: 12-Inch 33/45rpm
SOLAR: 80-84 4-6
Singles: 7-Inch
COLLECTABLES: 1-3
DORE: 65-66 3-6
FONTANA: 66 4-8
JANUS: 70-75 2-4
SOLAR: 79-88 1-3
SOUL CLOCK: 69-70 2-4
SOUL TRAIN: 75-77 2-3
LPs: 10/12-Inch 33rpm
ACCORD: 81 5-8
ALLEGIANCE: 84 5-8
DORE: 80 5-8
JANUS: 72-75 8-10
SOLAR: 78-87 5-8

SOUL TRAIN: 76-77 .... $8-10
Members: Walter Scott; Wallace Scott; Nicholas
Caldwell; Marcus Hudson; Leaveil DeGree.
Also see LUCAS, Carrie, & The Whispers

WHISTLE
Singles: 7-Inch
SELECT: 88 1-3
LPs: 10/12-Inch 33rpm
SELECT: 88 5-8

WHITCOMB, Ian
(Ian Whitcomb & Bluesville; Ian Whitcomb & Somebody's Chyldren)
Singles: 7-Inch
JERDEN: 64-65 8-15
TOWER: 65-68 3-5
UNITED ARTISTS: 73 2-4
Picture Sleeves
TOWER: 66 4-8
LPs: 10/12-Inch 33rpm
FIRST AMERICAN: 78-82 5-8
SIERRA: 80 5-8
TOWER: 65-68 15-20
UNITED ARTISTS : 72 8-10

WHITE, Artie "Blues Boy"
Singles: 7-Inch
ALTEE: 77 2-3
RONN: 2-3

WHITE, Barry
(Barry White With Love Unlimited & The Love Unlimited Orchestra; Barry White & Glodean)
Singles: 12-Inch 33/45rpm
20TH CENTURY-FOX: 73-78 4-6
UNLIMITED GOLD: 83 4-6
Singles: 7-Inch
A&M: 87 1-3
BRONCO: 67 3-5
CASABLANCA: 1-3
20TH CENTURY-FOX: 73-78 1-3
UNLIMITED GOLD: 79-83 1-3
LPs: 10/12-Inch 33rpm
A&M: 87 5-8
20TH CENTURY-FOX (Except 1): 73-81 6-10
20TH CENTURY-FOX (1; "Barry
White Radio Special"): 10-15
(Promotional issue only.)
UNLIMITED GOLD: 79-81 6-10
Also see BOB & EARL
Also see LOVE UNLIMITED

WHITE, Barry, & The Atlantics / Atlantics
Singles: 7-Inch
FARO: 63 5-8
Also see WHITE, Barry

WHITE, Danny
Singles: 7-Inch
ABC-PARAMOUNT: *64* $3-5
ATLAS: *66* 3-5
DECCA: *66-67* 2-5
DOT: *61* 3-5
FRISCO: *62* 3-5
KING: *58* 10-15
ROCKY COAST: *77* 2-3
SSS INT'L: *69* 2-4

WHITE, Karyn
Singles: 7-Inch
WARNER BROS.: *88* 1-3
LPs: 10/12-Inch 33rpm
WARNER BROS.: *88* 5-8

WHITE, Kitty
Singles: 78rpm
DECCA: *51* 3-5
MERCURY: *55-56* 2-4
Singles: 7-Inch
CLOVER: *66* 2-4
DECCA: *51* 3-6
DOT: *60* 2-4
GNP/CRESCENDO: *59* 2-4
MERCURY: *55-56* 3-6
EPs: 7-Inch 33/45rpm
EMARCY: *54* 5-15
PACIFIC JAZZ: *54* 5-15
LPs: 10/12-Inch 33rpm
EMARCY: *54* 20-40
CLOVER: *66* 6-12
MERCURY: *55* 15-30
PACIFIC JAZZ: *54-55* 20-40

WHITE, Lenny
Singles: 7-Inch
ELEKTRA: *78-83* 1-3
NEMPEROR: *76* 2-4
LPs: 10/12-Inch 33rpm
ELEKTRA: *78-83* 5-8
NEMPEROR: *75-77* 8-10
Also see RETURN TO FOREVER
Also see TWENNYNINE

WHITE, Maurice
Singles: 12-Inch 33/45rpm
COLUMBIA: *86* 4-6
Singles: 7-Inch
COLUMBIA: *85-86* 1-3
GOLD: *59* 8-10
PRIDE: *60* 5-8
LPs: 10/12-Inch 33rpm
COLUMBIA: *85-86* 5-8

WHITE, Tony Joe
(Tony Joe White & The Mojos)
Singles: 7-Inch
ARISTA: *79* $1-3
CASABLANCA: *80* 1-3
COLUMBIA: *83-85* 1-3
J-BECK: 5-8
MONUMENT: *67-70* 3-6
20TH CENTURY-FOX: *76* 2-3
LPs: 10/12-Inch 33rpm
CASABLANCA: *80* 5-8
COLUMBIA: *83* 5-8
MONUMENT: *69-70* 8-12
20TH CENTURY-FOX: *77* 5-8
WARNER BROS: *71-73* 8-10

WHITE LION
LPs: 10/12-Inch 33rpm
ATLANTIC: *87* 5-8
GRAND SLAM: *88* 5-8

WHITE PLAINS
Singles: 7-Inch
DERAM: *70-71* 2-4
LONDON: 1-3
LPs: 10/12-Inch 33rpm
DERAM: *70* 10-15
Members: Roger Greenaway; Roger Cook.
Also see DAVID & JONATHAN

WHITE WOLF
Singles: 7-Inch
RCA VICTOR: *85-86* 1-3
LPs: 10/12-Inch 33rpm
RCA VICTOR: *85-86* 5-8

WHITEHEAD, Charles
(Charlie Whitehead & The Swamp Dogg Band)
Singles: 7-Inch
ISLAND: *75* 2-4
LPs: 10/12-Inch 33rpm
FUNGUS: 10-15
WIZARD: *78* 5-10

WHITEHEAD, John
Singles: 7-Inch
MERCURY: *88* 1-3

WHITEHEAD, Kenny & Johnny
Singles: 12-Inch 33/45rpm
PHILADELPHIA INT'L: *86* 4-6
Singles: 7-Inch
PHILADELPHIA INT'L: *86* 1-3
LPs: 10/12-Inch 33rpm
PHILADELPHIA INT'L: *86* 5-8
Also see KENNY & JOHNNY

WHITEMAN, Paul, Orchestra
Singles: 78rpm
CAPITOL: 42-43 .... $2-4
COLUMBIA: 28-32 2-5
CORAL: 50-56 2-4
DECCA: 38-39 2-5
VICTOR: 20-36 3-5
Singles: 7-Inch
CORAL: 50-56 2-4
EPs: 7-Inch 33/45rpm
CORAL: 50-56 3-8
LPs: 10/12-Inch 33rpm
CAPITOL: 62 5-10
CORAL: 50-56 5-15
GRAND AWARD: 56-59 5-15
RCA VICTOR: 68-69 4-8
WESTMINSTER: 74 4-8

WHITESNAKE
Singles: 12-Inch 33/45rpm
GEFFEN: 86 4-6
Singles: 7-Inch
GEFFEN: 82-88 1-3
MIRAGE: 80 1-3
UNITED ARTISTS: 79 2-3
Picture Sleeves
MIRAGE: 80 1-3
LPs: 10/12-Inch 33rpm
GEFFEN: 82-87 5-8
MIRAGE: 80-81 5-8
UNITED ARTISTS: 79 6-10
Members: David Coverdale; Jon Lord; Aynsley
Dunbar; John Sykes; Neil Murray; Tommy
Aldridge; Rudy Sarzo; Vivian Campbell; Adrian
Vandenberg.
Also see DEEP PURPLE

WHITFIELD, David
Singles: 78rpm
LONDON: 53-57 2-4
Singles: 7-Inch
LONDON: 53-63 2-4
EPs: 7-Inch 33/45rpm
LONDON: 54 4-8
LPs: 10/12-Inch 33rpm
LONDON: 54-66 5-15

WHITING, Margaret
Singles: 78rpm
CAPITOL: 46-56 2-5
DOT: 57 2-4
Singles: 7-Inch
CAPITOL: 50-56 2-5
DOT: 57-59 2-4
LONDON: 66-70 2-4
VERVE: 60 2-4

EPs: 7-Inch 33/45rpm
CAPITOL: 50-56 .... $4-8
LPs: 10/12-Inch 33rpm
CAPITOL: 50-56 8-18
DOT: 57-67 5-15
HAMILTON: 59-65 5-12
LONDON: 67-68 6-12
VERVE: 60 5-15
Also see MARTIN, Dean, & Margaret Whiting
Also see TORME, Mel

WHITING, Margaret, & Jimmy Wakely
Singles: 78rpm
CAPITOL: 50 2-4
Singles: 7-Inch
CAPITOL: 50 3-5
EPs: 7-Inch 33/45rpm
CAPITOL: 53 8-12
LPs: 10/12-Inch 33rpm
PICKWICK: 67 8-12
Also see WAKELY, Jimmy
Also see WHITING, Margaret

WHITLOCK, Bobby
Singles: 7-Inch
DUNHILL: 72 2-4
LPs: 10/12-Inch 33rpm
CAPRICORN: 76 8-10
DUNHILL: 72 10-12
Also see BELL, Maggie, & Bobby Whitlock
Also see DELANEY & BONNIE
Also see DEREK & THE DOMINOES

WHITMAN, Slim
Singles: 78rpm
IMPERIAL: 52-57 2-5
Singles: 7-Inch
CLEVELAND INT'L: 80-82 1-3
EPIC: 84 1-3
IMPERIAL (5000 series): 61-63 3-5
IMPERIAL (8000 through 8200
series): 52-58 5-10
IMPERIAL (8300 series): 59-60 3-6
IMPERIAL (50000 series): 70-71 2-3
IMPERIAL (65000 & 66000
series): 61-69 2-5
UNITED ARTISTS: 70-77 2-3
EPs: 7-Inch 33/45rpm
IMPERIAL: 54-65 30-50
RCA VICTOR (3217; "Slim Whitman
Sings & Yodels"): 54 100-150
LPs: 10/12-Inch 33rpm
CAMDEN: 66 8-12
CLEVELAND INT'L: 80-81 5-8
EPIC: 84 5-8

IMPERIAL (3004; "America's Favorite
Folk Artist"): *54* **$400-500**
(10-Inch LP.)
IMPERIAL (9000 series): *56-60* **25-40**
(Maroon labels, or black with "Imperial" at top.)
IMPERIAL (9000 series): *66* **8-12**
(Black labels with "Imperial" on left side.)
IMPERIAL (9100 series): *60-62* **15-30**
(Black labels with "Imperial" at top.)
IMPERIAL (9100 series); *66* **8-12**
(Black labels with "Imperial" on left side.)
IMPERIAL (9200 & 9300 series): *63-67* . **10-25**
IMPERIAL (12100 series): *62* **15-25**
(Black labels with "Imperial" at top.)
IMPERIAL (12100 series): *66* **8-12**
(Black labels with "Imperial" on left side.)
IMPERIAL (12200 & 12300
series): *65-68* **10-25**
IMPERIAL (12400 series): *68-69* **8-12**
LIBERTY: *80-82* **5-8**
PICKWICK: **5-10**
RCA VICTOR (3217; "Slim Whitman
Sings & Yodels"): *54* **250-350**
RCA VICTOR (3700 series): *80* **5-8**
SUFFOLK MARKETING: *79-82* **8-12**
SUNSET: *66-70* **8-12**
UNITED ARTISTS: *70-80* **6-12**
Also see WILLIAMS, Hank / Slim Whitman

WHITNEY, Marva
Singles: 7-Inch
KING: *67-69* **2-4**
T-NECK: *70* **2-4**
LPs: 10/12-Inch 33rpm
KING: *69* **8-12**
Also see BROWN, James, & Marva Whitney

WHITNEY, Marva, & Ellie Taylor
Singles: 7-Inch
EXCELLO: *72* **2-4**
Also see WHITNEY, Marva

WHITTAKER, Roger
Singles: 7-Inch
MAIN STREET: *84* **1-3**
RCA VICTOR: *70-86* **1-3**
Picture Sleeves
RCA VICTOR: *80* **1-3**
LPs: 10/12-Inch 33rpm
MAIN STREET: *84* **5-8**
RCA VICTOR: *70-86* **5-12**

WHO
Singles: 7-Inch
ATCO (6409; "Substitute"): *67* **15-20**
ATCO (6509; "Substitute"): *67* **12-20**
DECCA (31725; "I Can't Explain"): *64* . . **12-15**

DECCA (31801; "Anyway Anyhow
Anywhere"): *65* **$15-20**
DECCA (31877; "My Generation"): *65* . **10-15**
DECCA (31988; "The Kids Are
Alright"): *66* **15-20**
DECCA (32058; "I'm A Boy"): *66* **12-15**
DECCA (32114; "Happy Jack"): *67* **8-10**
DECCA (32156; "Pictures Of Lily"): *67* . . **8-10**
DECCA (32206; "I Can See For Miles"): *67* **4-6**
DECCA (32288; "Call Me Lightning"): *68* . **8-10**
DECCA (32362; "Magic Bus"): *68* **4-6**
DECCA (32465; "Pinball Wizard"): *69* **4-6**
DECCA (32519; "I'm Free"): *69* **4-6**
DECCA (32670; "The Seeker"): *70* **5-8**
DECCA (32708; "Summertime Blues"): *70* . **4-6**
DECCA (32729; "See Me, Feel Me"): *70* . . **4-6**
DECCA (32737; "Young Man
Blues"): *70* **10-15**
DECCA (32846; "Won't Get Fooled
Again"): *71* **4-6**
DECCA (32888; "Behind Blue Eyes"): *71* . . **5-8**
DECCA (32983; "Join Together"): *72* **4-6**
DECCA (33041; "The Relay"): *72* **4-6**
Note: Some Decca numbers in the 30000 series
may be preceded by a "7."
MCA: *74-79* **2-4**
POLYDOR: *75-79* **2-4**
TRACK: *72-74* **3-5**
WARNER BROS: *81-83* **1-3**
Picture Sleeves
DECCA: *67-70* **5-15**
WARNER BROS: *81-83* **1-3**
LPs: 10/12-Inch 33rpm
DECCA (4664; "My Generation"): *66* . **50-100**
(With a "DL" prefix. Monaural.)
DECCA (4664; "My Generation"): *66* . . **30-40**
(With a "DL7" prefix. Stereo.)
DECCA (4892; "Happy Jack"): *67* **30-40**
(With a "DL" prefix. Monaural.)
DECCA (4892; "Happy Jack"): *67* **20-30**
(With a "DL7" prefix. Stereo.)
DECCA (4950; "The Who Sell Out"): *67* . **30-40**
(With a "DL" prefix. Monaural.)
DECCA (4950; "The Who Sell Out"): *67* . **20-30**
(With a "DL7" prefix. Stereo.)
DECCA (7205; "Tommy"): *69* **20-30**
(Includes 12-page booklet.)
DECCA (75064; "Magic Bus"): *68* **25-30**
DECCA (79175; "Live At Leeds"): *70* . . . **15-20**
DECCA (79182; "Who's Next"): *71* **15-20**
DECCA (79184; "Meaty Beaty Big
& Bouncy"): *71* **15-20**
MCA (2023; "Who's Next?"): **8-15**
MCA (2126; "Odds & Sods"): *74* **10-20**
(Includes insert.)

MCA (2161; "The Who By
   Numbers"): *75* $8-10
MCA (3050; "Who Are You?"): *78* 8-10
   (Black vinyl.)
MCA (3050; "Who Are You?"): *78* 15-20
   (Colored vinyl.)
MCA (4000 series): *74* 10-12
MCA (5000 series): *83-85* 5-8
MCA (6000 series): *74* 10-12
MCA (8000 series): *84* 10-12
MCA (10004; "Quadrophenia"): *81* 10-12
MCA (10005; "Tommy"): *77* 10-12
MCA (11005; "The Kids Are
   Alright"): *79* 10-12
MCA (12001; "Hooligans"): *81* 10-12
MCA (14950; "Who Are You?"): *79* 12-15
   (Picture disc.)
MCA (37000 series): *79* 5-8
MFSL: *84* 15-25
TRACK (10004; "Quadrophenia"): *73* ... 15-20
   (Includes 44-page booklet.)
WARNER BROS: *81-82* 5-8
   Promotional LPs
DWJ: *78* 30-40
DECCA (7205; "Excerpts
   from *Tommy*): *69* 50-75
MCA (1987; "Who Are You?"): *78* 15-20
   Members: Roger Daltrey; Pete Townshend; John
   Entwistle; Keith Moon; Kenny Jones.
   Also see DALTREY, Roger
   Also see ENTWISTLE, John
   Also see McCARTNEY, Paul / Rochestra /
   Who / Rockpile
   Also see MOON, Keith
   Also see TOWNSHEND, Pete

WHO / Strawberry Alarm Clock
   LPs: 10/12-Inch 33rpm
DECCA: *69* 45-55
   (Philco-Ford Special Products promotional issue.)
   Also see STRAWBERRY ALARM CLOCK
   Also see WHO

WHODINI
   Singles: 12-Inch 33/45rpm
JIVE: *84-86* 4-6
   Singles: 7-Inch
JIVE: *82-87* 1-3
   LPs: 10/12-Inch 33rpm
JIVE: *84-87* 5-8
   Members: Jalil Hutchins; John Fletcher; Drew
   Carter.
   Also see JACKSON, Millie
   Also see KING DREAM CHORUS &
   HOLIDAY CREW

WHOLE DARN FAMILY
   Singles: 7-Inch
SOUL INT'L: *76-77* $2-4
   LPs: 10/12-Inch 33rpm
SOUL INT'L: *76* 8-10

WHOLE OATS
   Singles: 7-Inch
ATLANTIC: *72* 4-6
   Members: Daryl Hall; John Oates.
   Also see HALL, Daryl, & John Oates

WICHITA TRAIN WHISTLE
   Singles: 7-Inch
DOT: *68* 5-8
   LPs: 10/12-Inch 33rpm
DOT: *68* 15-20
PACIFIC ARTS: *78* 8-10
   Member: Michael Nesmith.
   Also see NESMITH, Michael

WIDE BOY AWAKE
   Singles: 12-Inch 33/45rpm
RCA VICTOR: *83* 4-6
   Singles: 7-Inch
RCA VICTOR: *83* 1-3
   LPs: 10/12-Inch 33rpm
RCA VICTOR: *83* 5-8

WIDOWMAKER
   Singles: 7-Inch
JET: *76-77* 2-3
   LPs: 10/12-Inch 33rpm
UNITED ARTISTS: *76-77* 8-10
   Members: John Butler; Aerial Bender.

WIEDLIN, Jane
   Singles: 7-Inch
EMI/MANHATTAN: *88* 1-3
I.R.S.: *85* 1-3
   LPs: 10/12-Inch 33rpm
EMI/MANHATTAN: *88* 5-8
I.R.S.: *85* 5-8
   Also see GO-GOs
   Also see SPARKS, & Jane Wiedlin

Jane Wiedlin

WIER, Rusty
Singles: 7-Inch
ABC: *74* $2-4
COLUMBIA: *76* 2-3
COMPLEAT: *83-84* 1-3
20TH CENTURY-FOX: *75-76* 2-4
LPs: 10/12-Inch 33rpm
ABC: *74* 8-12
COLUMBIA: *76* 8-10
20TH CENTURY-FOX: *75* 8-10

WIGGINS, Spencer
Singles: 7-Inch
FAME: *69-70* 2-4
GOLDWAX: *66-69* 3-5

WILCOX, Eddie, Orchestra
(Featuring Sunny Gale)
Singles: 78rpm
DERBY: *52* 3-6
Singles: 7-Inch
DERBY (Colored vinyl): *52* 10-15
Also see GALE, Sunny

WILCOX, Harlow
(Harlow Wilcox & The Oakies)
Singles: 7-Inch
PLANTATION: *69* 2-4
SSS INT'L: 1-3
LPs: 10/12-Inch 33rpm
PLANTATION: *70-71* 5-8

WILD, Jack
Singles: 7-Inch
BUDDAH: *71* 2-4
CAPITOL: *70* 2-4
Picture Sleeves
CAPITOL: *70* 2-4

WILD CHERRY
Singles: 12-Inch 33/45rpm
EPIC: *76-79* 4-6
Singles: 7-Inch
A&M: *75* 2-3
BROWN BAG: *72-73* 2-4
EPIC: *76-79* 1-3
LPs: 10/12-Inch 33rpm
EPIC: *76-79* 6-10
Members: Robert Parissi; Allen Wentz; Ronald
Beitle; Bryan Bassett.

WILD MAGNOLIAS
Singles: 7-Inch
POLYDOR: *74* 2-4
LPs: 10/12-Inch 33rpm
POLYDOR: *74* 8-10

WILD MAN STEVE
(Steve Gallon)
LPs: 10/12-Inch 33rpm
RAW: *69-70* $6-12

WILD ONES
Singles: 7-Inch
MAINLINE: *65* 4-6
MALA: *67* 4-6
UNITED ARTISTS: *65-66* 4-6
LPs: 10/12-Inch 33rpm
UNITED ARTISTS: *65* 15-20
Also see ANTELL, Peter

WILD TURKEY
Singles: 7-Inch
CHRYSALIS: *72-73* 2-4
REPRISE: *72* 2-4
LPs: 10/12-Inch 33rpm
CHRYSALIS: *72-73* 8-10
REPRISE: *72* 10-12
Also see JETHRO TULL

WILD-CATS
Singles: 7-Inch
UNITED ARTISTS (154;
"Gazachstahagen"): *58* 5-8
UNITED ARTISTS (169; "King Size
Guitar"): *59* 5-8
UNITED ARTISTS (1154;
"Gazachstahagen"): *58* 10-12
Also see MURE, Billy

WILDE, Danny
LPs: 10/12-Inch 33rpm
GEFFEN: *88* 5-8

WILDE, Eugene
Singles: 12-Inch 33/45rpm
PHILLY WORLD: *84-86* 4-6
Singles: 7-Inch
MCA: *86* 1-3
PHILLY WORLD: *84-86* 1-3
LPs: 10/12-Inch 33rpm
PHILLY WORLD: *84-86* 5-8

WILDE, Kim
Singles: 12-Inch 33/45rpm
MCA: *85* 4-6
Singles: 7-Inch
EMI AMERICA: *82* 1-3
MCA: *85-88* 1-3
LPs: 10/12-Inch 33rpm
EMI AMERICA: *82* 5-8
MCA: *85-88* 5-8

WILDE, Marty
Singles: 7-Inch
BELL: *74* 2-4

EPIC: *58-60* $6-10
    LPs: 10/12-Inch 33rpm
EPIC: *60* 25-30
  Also see SHANNON

WILDER, Matthew
    Singles: 12-Inch 33/45rpm
PRIVATE I: *83-85* 4-6
    Singles: 7-Inch
PRIVATE I: *83-85* 1-3
    LPs: 10/12-Inch 33rpm
PRIVATE I: *83-85* 5-8

WILDFIRE
    Singles: 7-Inch
CASABLANCA: *77* 2-3

WILDWEEDS
    Singles: 7-Inch
CADET: *67-68* 4-6
CADET CONCEPT: *68* 4-6
VANGUARD: *71* .2-4
    LPs: 10/12-Inch 33rpm
VANGUARD: *70* 10-15

WILEY, Ed
  (With Teddy Reynolds & King Tut)
    Singles: 78rpm
SITTIN' IN WITH (Except 545): *50* 10-15
    Singles: 7-Inch
ATLANTIC: *51* .50-75
SITTIN' IN WITH (545; "Cry, Cry
  Baby"): *50* 50-75
  Members: Teddy Reynolds; King Tut.

WILEY, Michelle
    Singles: 7-Inch
20TH CENTURY-FOX: *77* 2-3

WILL & THE KILL
    LPs: 10/12-Inch 33rpm
MCA: *88* 5-8

WILL TO POWER
    Singles: 7-Inch
EPIC: *88* 1-3
    LPs: 10/12-Inch 33rpm
EPIC: *88* 5-8

WILLESDEN-DODGERS
    Singles: 12-Inch 33/45rpm
JIVE: *83* 4-6
    Singles: 7-Inch
JIVE: *83* 1-3

WILLIAMS, Andre
  (Andre Williams & The Don Juans; Andre Wil-
  liams & The Five Dollars; Andre Wiliams &
  Diablos; Andre "Bacon Fat" Williams With The
  Inspirations; Andre "Mr. Rhythm" Williams)
    Singles: 78rpm
EPIC: *57* $3-5
FORTUNE: *55 57* 4-8
    Singles: 7-Inch
AVIN: *66* 3-5
CHECKER: *68-69* 2-4
EPIC: *57* 5-10
FORTUNE: *55-58* 10-15
SPORT: *67* 3-5
WINGATE: *66* 3-5
    LPs: 10/12-Inch 33rpm
FORTUNE: *86* 5-8

WILLIAMS, Andre, & Gino Parks
    Singles: 7-Inch
FORTUNE: *60* 5-8
  Also see WILLIAMS, Andre

WILLIAMS, Andy
    Singles: 12-Inch 33/45rpm
COLUMBIA: *79* 4-6
    Singles: 78rpm
CADENCE: *56-57* 2-5
    Singles: 7-Inch
CADENCE: *56-64* 3-5
COLUMBIA: *61-79* 1-3
    Picture Sleeves
CADENCE: *59* 3-6
COLUMBIA: *61-76* 2-5
    EPs: 7-Inch
CADENCE: *57-59* 8-15
COLUMBIA: *62-66* 5-10
(Jukebox issues only.)

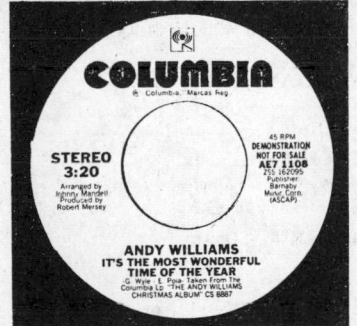

LPs: 10/12-Inch 33rpm
CADENCE: *58-62* $15-25
COLUMBIA: *62-77* 5-15

WILLIAMS, Andy & David
Singles: 7-Inch
BARNABY: *74-75* 1-3
KAPP: *72-73* 2-3
LPs: 10/12-Inch 33rpm
KAPP: *72* 5-10

WILLIAMS, Anson
Singles: 7-Inch
CHELSEA: *77* 2-4
Picture Sleeves
CHELSEA: *77* 2-4

WILLIAMS, Billy
(Billy Williams Quartet)
Singles: 78rpm
CORAL: *54-57* 3-5
Singles: 7-Inch
CORAL (61200 through 61800
series): *54-57* 5-10
CORAL (61900 through 65500
series): *58-64* 4-8
MCA: 1-3
MGM (10000 & 11000 series): *50-52* 5-10
MGM (12000 series): *57* 5-10
MERCURY: *52-54* 5-10
EPs: 7-Inch 33/45rpm
CORAL: *57* 10-20
MGM: *57* 10-20
MERCURY: *53-55* 15-20
LPs: 10/12-Inch 33rpm
CORAL: *57-60* 25-35
MGM: *57* 25-35
MERCURY: *58* 25-35
WING: *59* 15-20
Members: Billy Williams; Claude Riddick; John
Ball; Eugene Dixon.

WILLIAMS, Bobby Earl
Singles: 7-Inch
IV CHAINS: *74* 3-5

WILLIAMS, Carol
Singles: 7-Inch
SALSOUL: *76* 2-4

WILLIAMS, Danny
Singles: 7-Inch
PILOT: *62* 3-5
UNITED ARTISTS: *61-66* 3-5
LPs: 10/12-Inch 33rpm
UNITED ARTISTS: *63-66* 15-20

WILLIAMS, Deniece
Singles: 12-Inch 33/45rpm
COLUMBIA: *77-86* $4-6
Singles: 7-Inch
ARC: *79-82* 1-3
COLUMBIA: *76-88* 2-3
LPs: 10/12-Inch 33rpm
COLUMBIA: *76-88* 5-8
Also see MATHIS, Johnny, & Deniece Williams
Also see WONDER, Stevie

WILLIAMS, Diana
Singles: 7-Inch
CAPITOL: *76* 2-3
LITTLE GEM: *77* 2-4

WILLIAMS, Don
Singles: 7-Inch
ABC: *75-78* 2-4
ABC/DOT: *74-77* 2-4
CAPITOL: *86-88* 1-3
DOT: *74* 2-4
JMI: *72-74* 3-5
MCA: *79-85* 2-3
LPs: 10/12-Inch 33rpm
ABC (Except 28): *77-78* 5-10
ABC (28; "Don Williams"): *77* 10-15
(Promotional issue only.)
ABC/DOT: *74-77* 8-10
CAPITOL: *86* 5-8
JMI: *73-74* 15-20
MCA (Except 44): *75-85* 4-8
MCA (44; "Expressions"): *78* 12-18
(Picture disc.)
Also see POZO SECO SINGERS

WILLIAMS, Esther
Singles: 7-Inch
FRIENDS & CO: *76-78* 2-4

WILLIAMS, Geoffrey
Singles: 7-Inch
ATLANTIC: *88* $1-3

WILLIAMS, Hank
(Hank Williams & The Drifting Cowboys; Hank
Williams as "Luke The Drifter"; Hank &
Audrey Williams)
Singles: 78rpm
MGM: *47-55* 5-10
STERLING (201; "Calling You"): *47* . 200-400
STERLING (204; "Wealth Won't
Save Your Soul"): *47* 150-300
STERLING (208; "I Don't Care"): *47* . 100-200
STERLING (210; "Pan
American"): *47* 100-200
Singles: 7-Inch
MGM (10000 & 11000 series): *50-55* 10-20
MGM (12000 series): *55-59* 5-15
MGM (13000 series): *64-67* 3-6
EPs: 7-Inch 33/45rpm
ARHOOLIE: *83* 4-6
(Not issued with cover.)
MGM (100 & 200 series): *52-54* 25-50
MGM (1000 through 1600 series): *55-60* . 15-30
LPs: 10/12-Inch 33rpm
BLAINE HOUSE: *72* 15-20
BOLL WEEVIL: *76* 8-12
COLUMBIA (5616; "Hank Williams
Treasury"): 35-45
(4-LP set offered through the Columbia House
record club.)
GOLDEN COUNTRY: 5-8
MGM (2; "36 Of Hank Williams'
Greatest Hits"): *57* 80-100
(A 3 LP set.)
MGM (4; "36 More Of Hank
Williams' Greatest Hits"): *58* 80-100
(3-LP set.)
MGM (100 & 200 series): *52-54* 50-100
(10-Inch LPs.)
MGM (240-2; "24 Karat Hits,
Hank Williams"): *68* 15-20
MGM (1000 series): *76* 8-10
(Special Products issue.)
MGM (3200 through 3900 series): *55-61* . 25-50
(With an "E" prefix.)
MGM (3200 through 3900 series): *63-70* . 10-20
(With an "SE" prefix.)
MGM (4000 through 4700 series,
except 4267): *63-71* 10-20
MGM (4267; "The Hank Williams
Story"): *66* 50-75
(4-LP set.)
MGM (4900 through 5400 series): *75-77* . . 5-10
METRO: *65-67* 10-15

POLYDOR: *83-84* $6-12
SUNRISE MEDIA: *81* 8-10
TIME-LIFE: *82* 5-8
Also see PRESLEY, Elvis / Hank Williams

WILLIAMS, Hank / Slim Whitman
LPs: 10/12-Inch 33rpm
SUNRISE MEDIA: *81* 8-10
Also see WHITMAN, Slim

**WILLIAMS, Hank, & Hank
Williams, Jr.**
LPs: 10/12-Inch 33rpm
MGM (4200 series): *65* 15-25
MGM (4300 through 4900 series): *66-74* 10-15
Also see WILLIAMS, Hank, Jr.

WILLIAMS, Hank, Jr.
(Hank Williams Jr. & The Cheatin' Hearts;
Hank Williams Jr. With The Mike Curb Con-
gregation; Hank Williams Jr. & Lois Johnson)
Singles: 7-Inch
CONSOL: 10-20
(Promotional issue from Consolidation Coal.)
ELEKTRA/CURB: *79-82* 1-3
MGM (13000 series): *64-68* 4-8
MGM (14000 series): *68-76* 2-5
WARNER BROS/CURB (Except
8000 series): *82-88* 1-3
WARNER BROS/CURB (8000
series): *77-78* 2-4
Picture Sleeves
MGM (13000 series): *64-68* 5-10
LPs: 10/12-Inch 33rpm
CURB: *83-84* 1-3
ELEKTRA: *79-82* 5-8
MGM (Except 5009): *64-76* 10-20
MGM (5009; "Hank Williams Jr.
& Friends"): *76* 40-60
WARNER BROS: *77-88* 5-10
Also see CHARLES, Ray, & Hank Williams,
Jr.
Also see FRANCIS, Connie, & Hank Wil-
liams, Jr.
Also see WILLIAMS, Hank, & Hank Wil-
liams, Jr.

WILLIAMS, James "D-Train"
Singles: 12-Inch 33/45rpm
COLUMBIA: *86* 4-6
Singles: 7-Inch
COLUMBIA: *86-88* 1-3
LPs: 10/12-Inch 33rpm
COLUMBIA: *86-88* 5-8

WILLIAMS, Jeanette
Singles: 7-Inch
BACK BEAT: *66-69* 3-5

WILLIAMS, John, Orchestra
Singles: 7-Inch
ARISTA: 77-80 .... $1-3
COLUMBIA: 83 1-3
MCA: 74-76 1-3
RCA VICTOR: 79 1-3
20TH CENTURY-FOX: 77-78 1-3
WARNER BROS: 79 1-3
Picture Sleeves
ARISTA: 77 1-3
20TH CENTURY-FOX: 78 1-3
WARNER BROS: 79 1-3
EPs: 7-Inch 33/45rpm
ARISTA (AS-9500; "Close Encounters
Of The Third Kind"): 78 3-5
(LP bonus, one-sided disc.)
LPs: 10/12-Inch 33rpm
ARISTA (9500; "Close Encounters
Of The Third Kind"): 78 8-12
(Soundtrack.)
CAPITOL: 71 5-10
COLUMBIA (3510; "The Reivers"): 70 . 15-20
(Soundtrack.)
COLUMBIA (31091; "Changes"): 71 5-10
COLUMBIA (37000 series): 81 5-8
DISCOVERY: 84 4-8
MCA (2087; "Jaws"): 75 8-10
(Soundtrack.)
MCA (2088; "The Eiger Sanction"): 75 ... 8-10
(Soundtrack.)
MCA (3045; "Jaws 2"): 78 8-10
(Soundtrack.)
RCA VICTOR: 77 5-8
UNITED ARTISTS (623; "Missouri
Breaks"): 76 8-10
(Soundtrack.)
Also see BOSTON POPS ORCHESTRA

WILLIAMS, Johnny
Singles: 7-Inch
BASHIE: 70 2-4
CUB: 68 2-4
PHILADELPHIA INT'L: 73 2-4

WILLIAMS, L. C.
(L. C. Williams Orchestra; L. C. Williams With
Conney's Combo)
Singles: 78rpm
BAYOU: 53 10-15
FREEDOM: 49-50 8-12
GOLD STAR: 48 10-15
IMPERIAL: 52 5-8
JAX: 52 8-10
MERCURY: 52 5-8
SITTIN' IN WITH: 52 8-10

Singles: 7-Inch
BAYOU: 53 .... $30-40

WILLIAMS, Larry
Singles: 7-Inch
CHESS: 59-60 4-6
MERCURY: 63 3-5
OKEH: 66-67 3-5
SMASH: 66 3-5
SPECIALTY (SPBX series): 85 12-15
(Boxed set of six colored vinyl 45s.)
SPECIALTY (608 through 658): 57-59 ... 5-10
SPECIALTY (665 through 682): 59-60 4-6
(Most Specialty singles are currently available,
using original catalog numbers.)
VENTURE: 68 3-5
Picture Sleeves
SPECIALTY: 58 10-20
LPs: 10/12-Inch 33rpm
OKEH: 67 10-15
SPECIALTY (2109; "Here's Larry
Williams"): 59 40-50
(Specialty LP reissues, using original catalog num-
bers, are currently available.)
SPECIALTY (2158; "Unreleased Larry
Williams"): 88 6-10
(With Art Neville.)
Also see COOKE, Sam / Lloyd Price / Larry
Williams

WILLIAMS, Larry, & Johnny Watson
Singles: 7-Inch
OKEH (7300; "Nobody"): 67 15-25
(With Kaleidoscope.)
LPs: 10/12-Inch 33rpm
OKEH: 67 10-15
Also see KALEIDOSCOPE
Also see WATSON, Johnny
Also see WILLIAMS, Larry

WILLIAMS, Lee
(Lee Williams & The Moonrays; Lee Williams &
The Cymbals; Lee "Shot" Williams)
Singles: 7-Inch
CARNIVAL: 66-69 3-5
FEDERAL: 63-64 3-5
KING: 60 8-10
SHAMA: 69 2-4

WILLIAMS, Lenny
Singles: 12-Inch 33/45rpm
ABC: 78 4-6
ROCSHIRE: 83-84 4-6
Singles: 7-Inch
ABC: 77-78 2-3
CRUSH: 88 1-3
KNOBHILL: 86 1-3
MCA: 79-81 1-3

MOTOWN: 75 .... $2-3
ROCSHIRE: 83-84 1-3
    LPs: 10/12-Inch 33rpm
ABC: 77-78 8-10
MOTOWN: 75 8-10
ROCSHIRE: 83-84 5-8
WARNER BROS: 74 8-12
  Also see G., Kenny, & Lenny Williams
  Also see TOWER OF POWER

WILLIAMS, Linda
Singles: 7-Inch
ARISTA: 79 1-3

WILLIAMS, Little Jerry
Singles: 7-Inch
ACADEMY: 64 4-6
CALLA: 65-66 3-5
COTILLION: 69 3-5
LOMA: 64 3-5
SOUTHERN SOUND: 64-65 4-6

WILLIAMS, Mason
Singles: 7-Inch
WARNER BROS: 68-71 2-4
    LPs: 10/12-Inch 33rpm
EVEREST: 69 6-12
FLYING FISH: 78 5-8
VEE JAY: 64 10-20
WARNER BROS: 68-71 6-12

WILLIAMS, Mason, &
Mannheim Steamroller
    LPs: 10/12-Inch 33rpm
AMERICAN G: 87 5-8

WILLIAMS, Maurice
(Maurice Williams & The Zodiacs)
Singles: 7-Inch
ATLANTIC: 70 2-4
COLLECTABLES: 1-3
DEESU: 67 3-5
ERIC: 1-3
FLASHBACK: 65 1-3
HERALD: 60-62 4-6
OWL: 73 2-4
SEA HORN: 64 3-5
SPHERE SOUND: 65 3-5
VEE JAY: 65 3-6
VEEP: 69 2-4
    LPs: 10/12-Inch 33rpm
COLLECTABLES: 84 6-8
HERALD (1014; "Stay"): 61 50-100
RELIC: 10-12
SNYDER: 25-30
SPHERE SOUND: 66 15-20
  Also see GLADIOLAS

"LOLLIPOP"
(Beverly Ross-Julius Dixon)
MAURICE WILLIAMS
VJ-678

WILLIAMS, Mike
Singles: 7-Inch
ATLANTIC: 65-66 .... $3-6
KING: 66 3-6

WILLIAMS, Otis
(Otis Williams & The Midnight Cowboys)
Singles: 7-Inch
DELUXE (6100 series): 59 4-6
KING: 60-64 3-5
OKEH: 66 3-5
STOP: 71 2-3
    LPs: 10/12-Inch 33rpm
POWER PAK: 74 8-10
STOP: 71 8-12
  Also see CHARMS

WILLIAMS, Paul
(Paul Williams & His Orchestra)
Singles: 78rpm
CAPITOL: 55 3-5
CLEF: 52 4-6
GROOVE: 54 4-8
JAX: 54 4-8
JOSIE: 56 3-6
RAMA: 55 15-30
SAVOY: 49-57 4-6
Singles: 7-Inch
ASCOT: 62 3-5
CAPITOL: 55 5-10
GROOVE: 54 10-15
JAX (Colored vinyl): 54 25-30
JOSIE: 56 6-10
RAMA (167; "Ring-A-Ling"): 55 50-75
  (Vocalist is not credited, but is believed to be Little
  Willie John.)
SAVOY (1100 series): 54-59 4-6
VEE JAY: 57 4-6
  Also see JOHN, Little Willie

Also see MC NEELY, Big Jay / Paul Williams
Also see MC PHERSON, Wyatt "Earp," &
Paul Williams
Also see WATTS, Noble

WILLIAMS, Paul
Singles: 7-Inch
A&M: 72-77 .... $2-3
PAID: 81 1-3
PORTRAIT: 79 1-3
REPRISE: 70 2-4
LPs: 10/12-Inch 33rpm
A&M: 71-77 6-10
PAID: 81 5-8
PORTRAIT: 79 5-8
REPRISE: 70 8-12

WILLIAMS, Robin
Singles: 12-Inch 33/45rpm
CASABLANCA: 79 4-6
Singles: 7-Inch
BOARDWALK: 80 1-3
Picture Sleeves
BOARDWALK: 80 1-3
LPs: 10/12-Inch 33rpm
CASABLANCA: 79-83 5-8

WILLIAMS, Roger
Singles: 78rpm
KAPP: 55-57 2-4
Singles: 7-Inch
KAPP: 55-72 2-4
MCA: 73-78 1-3
WARNER BROS: 80 1-3
Picture Sleeves
KAPP: 55-66 2-5
EPs: 7-Inch 33/45rpm
KAPP: 55-58 3-6
LPs: 10/12-Inch 33rpm
KAPP: 55-72 5-15
MCA: 73-83 4-8
VOCALION: 71 4-8

WILLIAMS, Roger, & Jane Morgan
Singles: 78rpm
KAPP: 56 2-4
Singles: 7-Inch
KAPP: 56 2-4
Also see MORGAN, Jane
Also see WILLIAMS, Roger

WILLIAMS, Vanessa
Singles: 7-Inch
WING: 88 1-3
LPs: 10/12-Inch 33rpm
WING: 88 5-8

WILLIAMS, Vesta
Singles: 12-Inch 33/45rpm
A&M: 86 .... $4-6
Singles: 7-Inch
A&M: 86-88 1-3
LPs: 10/12-Inch 33rpm
A&M: 86-88 5-8

WILLIAMSON, Sonny Boy
(John Lee Williamson)
Singles: 78rpm
BLUEBIRD: 45 6-10
RCA VICTOR (20-0000 & 22-0000
series): 46-49 5-8
Singles: 7-Inch
RCA VICTOR (50-0000 series): 49 30-40

WILLIAMSON, Sonny Boy
(Aleck "Rice" Miller)
Singles: 78rpm
ACE: 54 10-15
CHECKER: 55-57 5-10
TRUMPET: 51-54 6-12
Singles: 7-Inch
ACE: 54 25-30
CHECKER (800 series): 55-58 10-15
CHECKER (900 series): 58-62 5-8
CHECKER (1000 & 1100 series): 62-66 ... 3-5
TRUMPET (100 series): 51-52 20-30
TRUMPET (200 series): 53-54 15-20
LPs: 10/12-Inch 33rpm
ARHOOLIE: 8-12
BLUES CLASSICS: 64 15-20
CHESS (200 series): 76 10-12
CHESS (1400 series): 60 30-40
CHESS (1500 series): 66-69 10-15
CHESS (50000 series): 72 10-12
STORYVILLE: 80 5-8

WILLIAMSON, Sonny Boy, & Big
Joe Williams
LPs: 10/12-Inch 33rpm
BLUES CLASSICS: 5-8
Also see WILLIAMSON, Sonny Boy (Aleck
"Rice" Miller)

WILLIAMSON, Sonny Boy, & The
Yardbirds
LPs: 10/12-Inch 33rpm
MERCURY: 66 15-20
Also see PAGE, Jimmy, & Sonny Boy Wil-
liamson
Also see WILLIAMSON, Sonny Boy (Aleck
"Rice" Miller)
Also see YARDBIRDS

WILLIAMSON, Sonny Boy
Singles: 7-Inch
RAM: *61* $10-15

WILLIE, Wet: see WET WILLIE

WILLIE & THE POOR BOYS
LPs: 10/12-Inch 33rpm
PASSPORT: *85* 5-8
Members: Andy Fairweather-Low; Mickey Gee;
Kenny Jones; Jimmy Page; Chris Rea; Paul
Rodgers; Geraint Watkins; Charlie Watts; Bill
Wyman.
Also see FAIRWEATHER-LOW, Andy
Also see PAGE, Jimmy
Also see REA, Chris
Also see ROLLING STONES

WILLIS, Chuck
(Chuck Willis & The Royals; Chuck Willis &
The Sandmen)
Singles: 78rpm
ATLANTIC: *56-57* 4-8
COLUMBIA: *51* 10-15
OKEH: *53-56* 5-10
Singles: 7-Inch
ATLANTIC (1000 & 1100 series): *56-59* .8-15
COLUMBIA (30238; "Can't You
See?"): *51* 25-40
OKEH (6000 series, except 6985): *51-53* .10-20
OKEH (6985; "Don't Deceive Me"): *53* ..15-20
OKEH (7000 series): *53-56* 8-12
EPs: 7-Inch 33/45rpm
ATLANTIC: *57-58* 30-40
EPIC: *56* 35-50
LPs: 10/12-Inch 33rpm
ATCO: *71* 10-12
ATLANTIC (8018; "King Of
The Stroll"): *58* 50-100
(Black label.)
ATLANTIC (8018; "King Of
The Stroll"): *59* 20-30
(Red label.)
ATLANTIC (8079; "I Remember
Chuck Willis"): *63* 30-35
COLUMBIA: *80* 5-8
EPIC (3425; "Chuck Willis Wails
The Blues"): *58* 100-175
EPIC (3728; "A Tribute To
Chuck Willis"): *58* 100-175

WILLIS, M-D-L-T
Singles: 7-Inch
IVORY TOWER: *74* 2-4

WILLIS, Timmy
Singles: 7-Inch
JUBILEE: *69* 2-4

VEEP: *68* $3-5

WILLIS "THE GUARD" & VIGORISH
Singles: 7-Inch
HANDSHAKE: *80* 2-4
Members: Jerry Buckner; Gary Garcia.
Also see BUCKNER & GARCIA

WILL-O-BEES
Singles: 7-Inch
DATE: *67* 3-5
SGC: *68-69* 3-5

WILLOWS
Singles: 78rpm
MELBA (Except 102): *56-57* 5-10
MELBA (102; "Church Bells
Are Ringing"): *56* 15-25
MELBA (102; "Church Bells
May Ring): *56* 5-10
(Note slightly different title.)
Singles: 7-Inch
ABC: *73* 1-3
COLLECTABLES: 1-3
MELBA (Except 102): *56-57* 15-20
MELBA (102; "Church Bells
Are Ringing"): *56* 50-60
MELBA (102; "Church Bells
May Ring): *56* 10-15
Members: Tony Middleton; Richard Davis; Ralph
Martin; Joe Martin; John Steele; Richard Simon;
Dotty Martin.
Also see SEDAKA, Neil

WILMER & THE DUKES
Singles: 7-Inch
APHRODISIAC: *69* 2-4
LPs: 10/12-Inch 33rpm
APHRODISIAC: *69* 10-15

WILSON, Al
Singles: 7-Inch
BELL: *70* 2-4
BELL GOLD: 1-3
CAROUSEL: *71* 2-4
PLAYBOY: *76* 2-4
ROADSHOW: *79* 2-3
ROCKY ROAD: *72-75* 2-4
SOUL CITY: *67-69* 3-5
LPs: 10/12-Inch 33rpm
PLAYBOY: *76* 8-10
ROADSHOW: *79* 5-8
ROCKY ROAD: *73-74* 8-10
SOUL CITY: *69* 10-15
Also see ROLLERS

WILSON, Ann
(Ann Wilson & The Daybreaks)
Singles: 7-Inch
CAPITOL: *86* $1-3
TOPAZ: *67* 10-15
  Also see HEART
  Also see RENO, Mike, & Ann Wilson

WILSON, Ann, & Robin Zander
Singles: 7-Inch
CAPITOL: *88* 1-3

WILSON, Bobby
Singles: 7-Inch
BUDDAH: *75* 2-4
CHAIN: *73* 2-4

WILSON, Brian
(Brian Wilson & Mike Love)
Singles: 7-Inch
BROTHER: *67* 12-18
CAPITOL: *66* 12-18
SIRE: *87-88* 2-5
Picture Sleeves
SIRE: *87-88* 2-5
LPs: 10/12-Inch 33rpm
SIRE: *88* 5-10
  Also see BEACH BOYS
  Also see BERRY, Jan
  Also see HONDELLS
  Also see CAMPBELL, Glen

WILSON, Carl
Singles: 7-Inch
CARIBOU: *81-83* 2-3
LPs: 10/12-Inch 33rpm
CARIBOU: *81-82* 5-8
  Also see ANGEL
  Also see BEACH BOYS
  Also see NEWTON-JOHN, Olivia

WILSON, Dennis
Singles: 7-Inch
CARIBOU: *77* 4-6
LPs: 10/12-Inch 33rpm
CARIBOU: *77* 10-15
  Also see BEACH BOYS

WILSON, Flip
Singles: 7-Inch
FLIP WILSON (SK-1; "Flip Wilson"): . . . 5-10
(Promotional issue only. No title or label shown.)
LITTLE DAVID: *72-75* 2-3
LPs: 10/12-Inch 33rpm
ATLANTIC: *67-68* 8-15
IMPERIAL: *61* 10-20
LITTLE DAVID: *70-72* 5-10
MINIT: *68* 8-15

SUNSET: *70* $8-10

WILSON, Hank
(Leon Russell)
Singles: 7-Inch
SHELTER: *73-74* 2-4
LPs: 10/12-Inch 33rpm
SHELTER: *73* 8-10
  Also see RUSSELL, Leon

WILSON, J. Frank
(J. Frank Wilson & The Cavaliers)
Singles: 7-Inch
ABC: *73* 1-3
APRIL: 3-5
CHARAY: *69* 3-5
COLLECTABLES: 1-3
ERIC: 1-3
JOSIE: *64-65* 3-5
LE CAM (500 series): *81* 1-3
LE CAM (722; "Last Kiss"): *64* 10-20
LE CAM (1000 series): *65* 3-5
LE CAM (12000 series): 2-3
SOLLY: *66* 3-5
TAMARA: *64* 8-15
VIRGO: *72* 1-3
LPs: 10/12-Inch 33rpm
DILL PICKEL: *71* 8-10
JOSIE (4006; "Last Kiss"): *64* 40-50

WILSON, Jackie
Singles: 78rpm
BRUNSWICK: *57* 5-10
Singles: 7-Inch
BRUNSWICK (7-38000 series): *60* 10-20
(Stereo compact 33 singles.)
BRUNSWICK (55024 through
  55086): *57-58* 8-12
BRUNSWICK (55105 through
  55165): *58-59* 5-8
BRUNSWICK (55166 through
  55236): *60-62* 4-6
BRUNSWICK (55238 through
  55504): *63-73* 2-5
COLUMBIA: *87* 1-3
ERIC: *83* 1-3
GUSTO: 1-3
Picture Sleeves
BRUNSWICK (55166 through
  55236): *60-62* 8-12
BRUNSWICK (55238 through
  55467): *63-72* 4-8
COLUMBIA: *87* 2-3
EPs: 7-Inch 33/45rpm
BRUNSWICK: *59-63* 20-35

LPs: 10/12-Inch 33rpm
BRUNSWICK (111; "Solid Gold"): . . . **$10-15**
(Brunswick Special Products, mail-order offer.)
BRUNSWICK (54045; "Lonely
Teardrops"): *59* **50-100**
BRUNSWICK (54042; "He's So
Fine"): *59* **50-100**
BRUNSWICK (54050; "So Much"): *60* . .**40-80**
BRUNSWICK (54055; "Jackie Sings
The Blues"): *60* **30-50**
BRUNSWICK (54058; "My Golden
Favorites"): *60* **30-40**
BRUNSWICK (54059; "A Woman, A
Lover, A Friend"): *60* **30-40**
BRUNSWICK (54100; "You Ain't
Heard Nothin' Yet"): *61* **25-30**
BRUNSWICK (54101; "By Request"): *61* **25-30**
BRUNSWICK (54105; "Body
& Soul"): *62* **25-30**
BRUNSWICK (54108; "At The
Copa"): *62* **25-30**
BRUNSWICK (54110 through
54130): *63-67* **20-25**
(Beginning with 54050, Brunswick indicated stereo
LPs with a "7" preceding the catalog number. Num-
bers after 54130 were available as stereo issues
only, and are shown here as the 75000 series.)
BRUNSWICK (754138 through
754167): *68-71* **15-20**
BRUNSWICK (754185 through
754212): *72-77* **10-15**
COLUMBIA: *87* **5-8**
DISCOVERY: *78* **8-10**
EPIC: *83* **10-12**
Also see WARD, Billy, & The Dominoes

WILSON, Jackie, & Lavern Baker
Singles: 7-Inch
BRUNSWICK: *65* **3-5**
Also see BAKER, Lavern

WILSON, Jackie, & Count Basie
Singles: 7-Inch
BRUNSWICK: *68* **3-5**
LPs: 10/12-Inch 33rpm
BRUNSWICK: *68* **15-20**
Also see BASIE, Count

WILSON, Jackie, & The Chi-Lites
Singles: 7-Inch
BRUNSWICK: *75* **2-4**
Also see CHI-LITES

WILSON, Jackie, & Linda Hopkins
Singles: 7-Inch
BRUNSWICK: *62-65* **3-5**

EPs: 7-Inch 33/45rpm
BRUNSWICK: *63* **$15-20**
LPs: 10/12-Inch 33rpm
BRUNSWICK: *68* **25-35**
Also see WILSON, Jackie

WILSON, Mary
Singles: 7-Inch
MOTOWN: *79* **2-3**
LPs: 10/12-Inch 33rpm
MOTOWN: *79* **5-8**
Also see SUPREMES

WILSON, Meri
Singles: 7-Inch
GRT: *77* **2-3**
LPs: 10/12-Inch 33rpm
GRT: *77* **5-10**

WILSON, Murray
Singles: 7-Inch
CAPITOL: *67* **5-10**
LPs: 10/12-Inch 33rpm
CAPITOL: *67* **15-25**

WILSON, Nancy
Singles: 12-Inch 33/45rpm
CAPITOL: *79* **4-6**
Singles: 7-Inch
CAPITOL (Except 4000 & 5000
series): *68-79* **1-3**
CAPITOL (4000 & 5000 series): *59-67* **2-5**
(Includes both purple and orange/yellow labels. See
"Label Identification" chapter to differentiate be-
tween Capitol's purple labels.)
Picture Sleeves
CAPITOL: *65* **2-5**
LPs: 10/12-Inch 33rpm
ASI: *81* **5-8**
CAPITOL (100 through 800
series): *69-71* **5-12**
CAPITOL (1300 through 1700
series): *59-62* **15-30**
CAPITOL (1800 through 2900
series): *63-68* **8-18**
(With a "T," "ST," or "SKAO" prefix.)
CAPITOL (1800 through 2900 series): *78* . **5-8**
(With an "SM" prefix.)
CAPITOL (11000 & 12000 series): *74-80* **5-10**
CAPITOL (16000 series): *80* **5-8**
COLUMBIA: *84* **5-8**
Also see LEWIS, Ramsey

WILSON, Nancy, & Julian
"Cannonball" Adderley
Singles: 7-Inch
CAPITOL: *62* **2-5**

LPs: 10/12-Inch 33rpm
CAPITOL (1657; "Nancy Wilson &
Cannonball Adderley"): 62 . . . . $15-25
(With a "T" or "ST" prefix.)
CAPITOL (1657; "Nancy Wilson &
Cannonball Adderley"): 75 5-8
(With an "SM" prefix.)
CAPITOL (16000 series): 81 4-8
Also see ADDERLEY, Cannonball

WILSON, Nancy, & George Shearing
Singles: 7-Inch
CAPITOL: 61 2-5
LPs: 10/12-Inch 33rpm
CAPITOL (1524; "Swingin's
Mutual"): 61 15-25
(With a "T" or "ST" prefix.)
CAPITOL (1524; "Swingin's
Mutual"): 75 5-8
(With an "SM" prefix.)
Also see SHEARING, George
Also see WILSON, Nancy

WILSON, Phill
Singles: 7-Inch
HURON: 61 3-5

WILSON, Precious
Singles: 7-Inch
JIVE: 86 1-3
LPs: 10/12-Inch 33rpm
JIVE: 86 5-8

WILSON, Shanice
Singles: 7-Inch
A&M: 88 1-3

WILSON, Timothy
Singles: 7-Inch
BLUE ROCK: 69 2-4
BUDDAH: 67-68 3-5
VEEP: 65 3-5

WILSON BROTHERS
Singles: 7-Inch
ATCO: 79 2-3
LPs: 10/12-Inch 33rpm
ATCO: 79 5-8

WILTON PLACE STREET BAND
Singles: 7-Inch
ISLAND: 77 2-3

WINANS, Bebe & Cece
Singles: 7-Inch
CAPITOL: 88 1-3

WINBUSH, Angela
Singles: 7-Inch
MERCURY: 88 1-3

WINCHESTER, Jesse
Singles: 7-Inch
AMPEX: 70 . . . . $2-4
BEARSVILLE: 76-81 1-3
LPs: 10/12-Inch 33rpm
BEARSVILLE/AMPEX: 70 15-20
BEARSVILLE: 71-81 6-10
Promotional LPs
BEARSVILLE (692; "Live At
The Bijou"): 75 20-25
BEARSVILLE (693; "Live At The
Bijou/Live Interview"): 75 30-40
Also see HARRIS, Emmylou
Also see LARSON, Nicolette
Also see MURRAY, Anne

WIND
Singles: 7-Inch
LIFE: 69 4-6
LPs: 10/12-Inch 33rpm
LIFE: 69 15-20
Member: Tony Orlando.
Also see COOL HEAT
Also see ORLANDO, Tony

WIND IN THE WILLOWS
Singles: 7-Inch
CAPITOL: 68 4-6
LPs: 10/12-Inch 33rpm
CAPITOL (2956; "The Wind In
The Willows"): 68 40-75
Members: Deborah Harry; Paul Klein; Peter Brit-
tain; Anton Carysforth; Steve DePhillips.
Also see HARRY, Debbie

WINDING, Kai, & His Orchestra
(Kai Winding & J.J. Johnson)
Singles: 7-Inch
BETHLEHEM: 60 2-4
COLUMBIA: 56-59 2-5
IMPULSE: 61 2-4
MGM: 78 1-3
VERVE: 62-67 2-4
EPs: 7-Inch 33/45rpm
COLUMBIA: 58-59 5-15
SAVOY: 53 10-20
LPs: 10/12-Inch 33rpm
A&M: 68 8-12
COLUMBIA (900 through 1300
series): 56-59 15-30
COLUMBIA (8100 series): 59 15-25
GLENDALE: 76-77 5-8
IMPULSE: 61 15-25
JAZZTONE: 56 20-35
PICKWICK: 65-70 5-10
ROOST (400 series): 52 60-80
(10-Inch LPs.)

SAVOY (9000 series): *53* $50-75
(10-Inch LPs.)
VERVE: *61-67* 10-25
  (Reads "MGM Records - A Division Of Metro-
  Goldwyn-Mayer, Inc." at bottom of label.)
VERVE: *73-84* 5-10
  (Reads "Manufactured By MGM Record Corp.," or
  mentions either Polydor or Polygram at bottom of
  label.)
WHO'S WHO IN JAZZ: *78* 5-8

WINDJAMMER
Singles: 7-Inch
MCA: *83-85* 1-3
LPs: 10/12-Inch 33rpm
MCA: *83* 5-8

WINDSTORM
Singles: 7-Inch
POLYDOR: *80* 1-3

WINDY CITY
Singles: 7-Inch
CHI-SOUND: *77* 2-3
KELLI-ARTS: *80* 1-3

WINE, April: see APRIL WINE

WING & A PRAYER FIFE & DRUM CORPS
Singles: 7-Inch
WING & A PRAYER: *75-77* 2-3
LPs: 10/12-Inch 33rpm
WING & A PRAYER: *76-77* 5-8

WINGER
LPs: 10/12-Inch 33rpm
ATLANTIC: *88* 5-8

WINGFIELD, Pete
Singles: 7-Inch
ISLAND: *75-77* 2-3
LPs: 10/12-Inch 33rpm
ISLAND: *75* 5-8

WINGS (With Paul McCartney): see McCARTNEY, Paul

WINNERS
Singles: 7-Inch
ARIOLA-AMERICA: *78* 2-3
LPs: 10/12-Inch 33rpm
ARIOLA-AMERICA: *78* 5-8
ROADSHOW: *78* 5-10

WINSTON, George
Singles: 7-Inch
WINDHAM HILL: 1-3
LPs: 10/12-Inch 33rpm
WINDHAM HILL: *83-88* 5-8

WINSTONS
Singles: 7-Inch
METROMEDIA: *69* $2-4
LPs: 10/12-Inch 33rpm
METROMEDIA: *69* 8-12

WINTER, Edgar
(Edgar Winter Group; Edgar Winter's White Trash)
Singles: 12-Inch 33/45rpm
BLUE SKY: *80* 4-6
BODY ROCK: *83* 4-6
Singles: 7-Inch
BLUE SKY: *75-81* 1-3
EPIC: *70-75* 2-4
LPs: 10/12-Inch 33rpm
BACK-TRAC: *85* 5-8
BLUE SKY: *75-81* 6-10
EPIC: *70-75* 10-15
  Also see DERRINGER, Rick
  Also see HARTMAN, Dan
  Also see MONTROSE, Ronnie
  Also see WINTER, Johnny & Edgar

WINTER, Jimmy: see WINTER, Johnny

WINTER, Johnny
(Johnny Winter & The Crystaliers; Jimmy Winter)
Singles: 7-Inch
ATLANTIC: *64* 5-10
BLUE SKY: *75* 2-4
COLUMBIA: *69-74* 2-4
FROLIC: 20-30
GRT: *69* 3-5
IMPERIAL: *69* 3-5
KRCO: *61* 50-75
MGM: *65* 4-6
PACEMAKER: *66* 5-8
SONOBEAT: *68* 5-8
TODD: *63* 8-10
Picture Sleeves
SONOBEAT: *68* 40-60
  (Some sleeves picture the Vulcan Gas Co., an Aus-
  tin nightclub, and those are at the high end of the
  price range given. Sleeves that do not picture the
  club are priced at the lower end.)
LPs: 10/12-Inch 33rpm
ACCORD: *81* 5-8
ALLIGATOR: *85* 5-8
BLUE SKY: *74-80* 6-10
BUDDAH: *69* 10-15
CBS ASSOCIATED: 5-8
COLUMBIA (9800 & 9900 series): *69* .. 15-20
COLUMBIA (30000 through
  33000 series): *70-75* 10-15
CRAZY CAJUN: 8-10

GRT: *69* $10-15
IMPERIAL: *69* 15-20
JANUS: *69-70* 10-12
SONOBEAT ("Progressive
  Blues Experiment"): *68* 100-150
  (Limited edition autographed issue.)
SONOBEAT ("Progressive
  Blues Experiment"): *68* 75-125
  (Limited edition, NOT autographed.)
UNITED ARTISTS: *73-74* 8-10
  Also see JOHNNY & THE JAMMERS
  Also see GREAT BELIEVERS
  Also see GUITAR SLIM
  Also see SPRINGSTEEN, Bruce / Johnny
  Winter / Hollies
  Also see TEXAS GUITAR SLIM
  Also see TRAITS
  Also see WATERS, Muddy

WINTER, Johnny & Edgar
Singles: 7-Inch
BLUE SKY: *76* 2-4
CASCADE: *64* 35-45
LPs: 10/12-Inch 33rpm
BLUE SKY (Except 242): *76* 5-8
BLUE SKY (242; "Johnny & Edgar Winter
  Discuss *Together*"): *76* 10-20
  (Promotional issue only.)
  Also see WINTER, Edgar
  Also see WINTER, Johnny

WINTER, Paul
**(Paul Winter & Winter Consort; Paul Winter
Sextet)**
Singles: 7-Inch
A&M: *69-77* 2-4
COLUMBIA: *62* 2-5
EPIC: *72-73* 2-4
LPs: 10/12-Inch 33rpm
A&M: *69-78* 8-12
COLUMBIA: *62-65* 10-20
EPIC: *72* 8-10
LIVING MUSIC: *83-86* 5-8
  Also see WINTER CONSORT

WINTER, Ruby: see WINTERS, Ruby

WINTER CONSORT
Singles: 7-Inch
A&M: *69* 3-5
  Also see WINTER, Paul

WINTERHALTER, Hugo, & His Orchestra
Singles: 78rpm
RCA VICTOR: *50-57* 2-4
Singles: 7-Inch
ABC-PARAMOUNT: *63* 1-3

COLUMBIA: *50* $2-4
KAPP: *64-65* 1-3
MUSICOR: *68-70* .1-3
RCA VICTOR: *50-63* 2-4
EPs: 7-Inch 33/45rpm
RCA VICTOR: *50-59* 3-6
LPs: 10/12-Inch 33rpm
ABC-PARAMOUNT: *63* 4-8
CAMDEN: *69-72* .4-8
KAPP: *65* 4-8
MUSIC DISC: *69* .4-8
MUSICOR: *68-71* 5-10
RCA VICTOR: *50-77* 5-15
TRIP: *76* 4-8
  Also see HEYWOOD, Eddie

WINTERS, Jonathan
LPs: 10/12-Inch 33rpm
COLUMBIA: *68-73* 8-15
VERVE: *59-60* 15-30
  (Reads "Verve Records, Inc." at bottom of label.)
VERVE: *61-67* 10-20
  (Reads "MGM Records - A Division Of Metro-
  Goldwyn-Mayer, Inc." at bottom of label.)
VERVE: *73-84* 5-10
  (Reads "Manufactured By MGM Record Corp.," or
  mentions either Poly dor or Polygram at bottom of
  label.)

WINTERS, Robert, & Fall
Singles: 7-Inch
BUDDAH: *80-81* .1-3
CASABLANCA: *82-84* 1-3
LPs: 10/12-Inch 33rpm
CASABLANCA: *82-83* 5-8

WINTERS, Ruby
(Ruby Winter)
Singles: 7-Inch
CERTRON: *71* 2-4
DIAMOND: *66-69* 3-5
MILLENNIUM: *78* 2-3
POLYDOR: *73-75* 2-4
LPs: 10/12-Inch 33rpm
MILLENNIUM: *78* 5-8
  Also see THUNDER, Johnny, & Ruby Winters

WINWOOD, Steve
Singles: 7-Inch
ISLAND: *77-88* 1-3
UNITED ARTISTS: *71* 3-5
VIRGIN: *88* 1-3
Picture Sleeves
ISLAND: *80-84* 1-3
LPs: 10/12-Inch 33rpm
ISLAND: *77-87* 5-8

UNITED ARTISTS (9950;
"Winwood"): 71 ....$20-30
(With liner notes by Bobby Abrahms.)
UNITED ARTISTS (9964;
"Winwood"): 71 10-15
(Without liner notes.)
VIRGIN: 88 5-8
Also see BAKER, Ginger
Also see BLIND FAITH
Also see DAVIS, Spencer
Also see TOOTS & THE MAYTALS
Also see TRAFFIC
Also see YAMASHTA, Stomu

WIRE TRAIN
Singles: 12-Inch 33/45rpm
COLUMBIA: 84 4-6
Singles: 7-Inch
COLUMBIA: 84 .....'................1-3
LPs: 10/12-Inch 33rpm
COLUMBIA: 84-87 5-8

WISH
'(Featuring Fonda Rae)
Singles: 12-Inch 33/45rpm
KN: 84 4-6
Singles: 7-Inch
PERSONAL: 84-85 1-3
Also see RAE, Fonda

WISHBONE ASH
Singles: 7-Inch
ATLANTIC: 77 2-3
DECCA: 71-72 2-4
MCA: 73-77 2-3
LPs: 10/12-Inch 33rpm
ATLANTIC: 76 6-10
DECCA (Except 1922): 71-72 10-15
DECCA (1922; "Live From
Memphis"): 72 15-20
(Promotional issue only.)
MCA: 73-82 5-8
Also see FOGHAT

WITCH QUEEN
Singles: 7-Inch
ROADSHOW: 79 2-3
LPs: 10/12-Inch 33rpm
ROADSHOW: 79 5-8

WITHERS, Bill
Singles: 12-Inch 33/45rpm
COLUMBIA: 79 4-6
Singles: 7-Inch
COLUMBIA: 75-85 1-3
SUSSEX: 71-75 2-4
Picture Sleeves
SUSSEX: 72 2-4

LPs: 10/12-Inch 33rpm
COLUMBIA: 75-81 ....$5-8
SUSSEX: 71-75 8-12
Also see WASHINGTON, Grover, Jr.
Also see WOMACK, Bobby, & Bill Withers

WITHERSPOON, Jimmy
(Jimmy Witherspoon & Groove Holmes; Jimmy
Witherspoon With Jay McShann & His Band;
Jimmy Witherspoon & Ben Webster; Jimmy
Witherspoon With Panama Francis & The
Savoy Sultans)
Singles: 78rpm
CHECKER: 54-55 5-10
FEDERAL: 52-53 5-10
DOWN BEAT: 48-49 5-8
MODERN (665 through 845): 49-51 4-6
RCA VICTOR: 57 4-8
SUPREME: 48-49 5-8
SWING BEAT: 49 4-8
SWING TIME: 51 4-6
Singles: 7-Inch
ABC: 71 2-4
BLUE NOTE: 75 2-3
BLUESWAY: 69 2-4
CAPITOL: 74 2-3
CHECKER (Black vinyl): 54-55 15-20
CHECKER (Colored vinyl): 54 50-75
FEDERAL: 52-53 15-20
GNP/CRESCENDO: 59 4-6
HI FI: 60 4-6
KENT: 71 2-4
KING: 65 3-5
MODERN (857 through 903): 52-53 15-20
PACIFIC JAZZ: 62 3-5
PRESTIGE: 63-65 3-5
RCA VICTOR: 57 5-8
REPRISE: 61-64 3-5
RIP: 58 5-8
VEE JAY: 59 4-6
VERVE: 66-67 3-5
WORLD PACIFIC: 59 4-6
LPs: 10/12-Inch 33rpm
ABC: 70 8-10
BLUE NOTE: 75 8-10
BLUESWAY: 69-73 8-10
CAPITOL: 74 8-10
CONSTELLATION: 64 15-20
CROWN (215; "Jimmy Witherspoon
Sings The Blues"): 61 15-20
(Black Vinyl.)
CROWN (215; "Jimmy Witherspoon
Sings The Blues"): 61 20-40
(Colored Vinyl.)
FANTASY: 72 10-12

HI FI: *59* $20-30
INNER CITY: *81* 5-8
MCA: *83* 5-8
MUSE: *83* 5-8
OLYMPIC: *73* 8-10
PRESTIGE: *64-69* 10-15
(Many Prestige LPs remain currently available, using original catalog numbers.)
RCA VICTOR (1048; "Goin' To
Kansas City Blues"): *75* 6-10
RCA VICTOR (1639; "Goin' To
Kansas City Blues"): *58* 30-40
REPRISE: *61-62* 20-30
SURREY: *65* 12-15
UNITED: 8-10
VERVE (5000 series): *66-68* 12-15
VERVE (8000 series): *74* 8-10
VERVE/FOLKWAYS (3011; "Blues
Box"): *66* 25-30
WORLD PACIFIC: *59-61* 20-30
Also see BURDON, Eric, & Jimmy
Witherspoon
Also see FREEMAN, Ernie
Also see HOLMES, Richard "Groove"
Also see McSHANN, Jay

WITHERSPOON, Jimmy, & The Lamplighters
Singles: 78rpm
FEDERAL: *52* 10-20
Singles: 7-Inch
FEDERAL: *52* 25-50

WITHERSPOON, Jimmy, & The Quintones
Singles: 78rpm
ATCO: *57* 5-10
Singles: 7-Inch
ATCO: *57* 10-20

WITHERSPOON, Jimmy / Eddie Vinson
LPs: 10/12-Inch 33rpm
KING (634; "Battle Of The
Blues, Vol. 3"): *59* 200-300
Also see WITHERSPOON, Jimmy

WITT, Joachim
Singles: 12-Inch 33/45rpm
W.E.A. INTERNATIONAL: *84* 4-6

WITTER, Jimmy
Singles: 7-Inch
ELVIS (900; "If You Love
My Woman"): 150-175
NEPTUNE: *61* 20-35
UNITED ARTISTS: *61* 8-10

WOLCOTT, Charles, Orchestra
Singles: 7-Inch
MGM: *60* $2-4

WOLF
(Bill Wolfer)
Singles: 7-Inch
CONSTELLATION: *81-83* 1-3
LPs: 10/12-Inch 33rpm
CONSTELLATION: *83* 5-8

WOLF, Peter
Singles: 12-Inch 33/45rpm
EMI AMERICA: *84-85* 4-6
Singles: 7-Inch
EMI AMERICA: *84-87* 1-3
LPs: 10/12-Inch 33rpm
EMI AMERICA: *84-87* 5-8
Also see FRANKLIN, Aretha
Also see GEILS, J., Band

WOLFMAN JACK
(Wolfman Jack & The Wolf Pack; Bob Smith)
Singles: 7-Inch
BREAD: 4-6
WOODEN NICKEL: *72-73* 2-4
LPs: 10/12-Inch 33rpm
BREAD: 15-20
COLUMBIA: *75* 8-10
WOODEN NICKEL: *72-73* 8-10
Also see FLASH CADILLAC & THE CON-
TINENTAL KIDS
Also see GUESS WHO
Also see STAMPEDERS

WOMACK, Bobby
(Bobby Womack & Brotherhood; Bobby
Womack & Peace)
Singles: 12-Inch 33/45rpm
ELEKTRA/WOMACK: *83* 4-6
Singles: 7-Inch
ARISTA: *79* 2-3
ATLANTIC: *67* 3-5
BEVERLY GLEN: *81-84* 1-3
CHECKER: *65* 3-5
COLUMBIA: *76-78* 2-3
COLUMBIA/BROTHERHOOD: *76-77* 2-3
ELEKTRA/WOMACK: *83* 1-3
LIBERTY: *70* 2-4
MCA: *86* 1-3
MINIT: *67-70* 2-4
UNITED ARTISTS: *71-76* 2-4
EPs: 7-Inch 33/45rpm
UNITED ARTISTS: *72* 10-15
(Promotional issue only.)
LPs: 10/12-Inch 33rpm
ARISTA: *79* 5-8

BEVERLY GLEN: *81-84* $5-8
COLUMBIA: *75-78* 8-10
COLUMBIA/BROTHERHOOD: *76* 8-10
ELEKTRA/WOMACK: *83* 5-8
LIBERTY (7600 series): *70* 8-10
LIBERTY (10000 series): 5-8
MCA: *86* 5-8
MINIT: *68-70* 10-12
UNITED ARTISTS: *71-76* 8-10
    Also see BROTHERHOOD
    Also see FELDER, Wilton, & Bobby Womack
    Also see VALENTINOS
    Also see SZABO, Gabor
    Also see WOMACK BROTHERS

WOMACK, Bobby, & Patti Labelle
Singles: 7-Inch
BEVERLY GLEN: *84* 1-3
    Also see LABELLE, Patti
    Also see WOMACK, Bobby

WOMACK, Bobby, & Bill Withers
Singles: 7-Inch
UNITED ARTISTS: *75* 2-4
    Also see WITHERS, Bill

WOMACK & WOMACK
Singles: 7-Inch
ELEKTRA: *84-85* 1-3
    LPs: 10/12-Inch 33rpm
ELEKTRA: *84-85* 5-8
ISLAND. *88* 5-8
    Members: Linda Womack; Cecil Womack.

WOMACK BROTHERS
Singles: 7-Inch
SAR: *61* 4-6
    Also see VALENTINOS
    Also see WOMACK, Bobby

WOMBLES
Singles: 7-Inch
COLUMBIA: *74-75* 2-4
    LPs: 10/12-Inch 33rpm
COLUMBIA: *74* 8-10
    Member: Mike Batt.

WOMENFOLK
Singles: 7-Inch
RCA VICTOR: *64-66* 2-4
    LPs: 10/12-Inch 33rpm
RCA VICTOR: *63-66* 10-15

WONDER, Stevie
(Little Stevie Wonder)
Singles: 12-Inch 33/45rpm
MOTOWN: 4-6
TAMLA: 4-6

FINGERTIPS - PT 2
(Paul, Cosby)
LITTLE STEVIE WONDER

Singles: 7-Inch
MOTOWN: *84-88* $1-3
MOTOWN/TOPPS ("Fingertips
    Part 2"): *67* 50-75
    (Topps Chewing Gum promotional item.
    Cardboard flexi, picture disc. Issued with generic
    paper sleeve.)
TAMLA (1600 through 1800 series): *82-86* 1-3
TAMLA (54061; "I Call It Pretty
    Music"): *62* 8-12
TAMLA (54074; "Contract
    On Love"): *63* 5-8
TAMLA (54080; "Fingertips"): *63* 3-5
TAMLA (54086; "Workout Stevie,
    Workout"): *63* 3-5
TAMLA (54090; "Castles In The Sand"): *64* 4-6
TAMLA (54096; "Hey Harmonica
    Man"): *64* 3-5
TAMLA (54103; "Happy Street"): *64* 8-12
TAMLA (54119 through 54139): *65-66* ... 3-5
TAMLA (54142; "Someday At
    Christmas"): *66* 6-10
TAMLA (54147 through 54323): *67-81* ... 2-4
    (Black vinyl.)
TAMLA (54147 through 54323): *69-78* ... 4-8
    (Colored vinyl. Promotional issues only.)
MOTOWN: *82* 1-3
    Picture Sleeves
TAMLA (54061; "I Call It
    Pretty Music"): *62* 12-25
TAMLA (54080 through 54096): *63-64* ... 4-8
TAMLA (54136 through 54317): *66-80* ... 2-5
    EPs: 7-Inch 33/45rpm
TAMLA (340; "Something Extra For
    Songs In The Key Of Life"): *76* 10-15
    LPs: 10/12-Inch 33rpm
MOTOWN (100 & 200 series): *82* 5-8
MOTOWN (800 series): *77* 12-15

MOTOWN (6000 series): *87* $5-8
TAMLA (232; "Tribute To
Uncle Ray"): *63* 50-65
TAMLA (233; "The Jazz Soul Of
Stevie Wonder"): *63* 50-65
TAMLA (240; "Little Stevie
Wonder"): *63* 40-50
TAMLA (232 through 255): *63-64* 30-40
TAMLA (268 through 279): *66-67* 15-20
TAMLA (281; "Someday At
Christmas"): *67* 30-40
TAMLA (282 through 371): *68-79* 10-15
TAMLA (373; "Hotter Than July"): *80* 5-8
TAMLA (6000 series): *82* 10-12
Promotional LPs
MOTOWN (PR-77; "Hotter Than
July"): *80* 10-15
TAMLA (PR-61; "Stevie Wonder's Journey
Through The Secret
Life Of Plants"): *79* 10-15
TAMLA (PR 98/99; "Radio Programmer's
Special"): 15-20
  Also see CHARLENE & STEVIE WONDER
  Also see DIONNE & FRIENDS
  Also see JACKSONS
  Also see MC CARTNEY, Paul, & Stevie
Wonder
  Also see REDNOW, Eivets
  Also see ROSS, Diana, Stevie Wonder, Mar-
vin Gaye, & Somkey Robinson
  Also see TEMPTATIONS / Stevie Wonder
  Also see THIRD WORLD
  Also see U.S.A. FOR AFRICA
  Also see WILLIAMS, Deniece

WONDER, Stevie, & Michael Jackson
Singles: 7-Inch
MOTOWN: *88* 1-3
  Also see JACKSON, Michael

WONDER, Stevie, & Clarence Paul
(Little Stevie Wonder & Clarence Paul)
Singles: 7-Inch
TAMLA: *62* 25-35

WONDER, Stevie / Dionne Warwick
LPs: 10/12-Inch 33rpm
MOTOWN: *84* 5-8
  Also see WARWICK, Dionne
  Also see WONDER, Stevie

WONDER BAND
Singles: 7-Inch
ATCO: *79* 2-3
LPs: 10/12-Inch 33rpm
ATCO: *79* 5-8

WONDER-LAND, Alice
see: ALICE WONDER-LAND

WONDER WHO?
(4 Seasons)
Singles: 7-Inch
COLLECTABLES: $1-3
PHILIPS: *65-67* 3-5
VEE JAY: *64* 12-15
Picture Sleeves
PHILIPS: *65-67* 15-20
  Also see 4 SEASONS

WOO, Gerry
Singles: 7-Inch
POLYDOR: *87-88* 1-3

WOOD, Bobby
Singles: 7-Inch
CHALLENGE: *62* 3-5
CINNAMON: *74* 2-3
JOY: *63-65* 3-5
LUCKY ELEVEN: *73* 2-3
MALA: *66* 3-5
MGM: *67-69* 2-4
SUN: *63* 3-5
LPs: 10/12-Inch 33rpm
JOY: *64* 10-15

WOOD, Brenton
Singles: 7-Inch
BRENT: *66* 3-5
CREAM: *76-78* 2-3
DOUBLE SHOT: *67-71* 2-4
MR. WOOD: *72-73* 2-4
PRESIDENT: *60* 4-6
PROPHESY: *73* 2-4
WAND: *64* 8-12
WARNER BROS: *75* 2-3
LPs: 10/12-Inch 33rpm
CREAM: *77* 5-8
DOUBLE SHOT: *67* 12-15

WOOD, Del
Singles: 78rpm
DECCA: *53-54* 2-4
MERCURY: *62-64* 2-4
RCA VICTOR: *55-59* 2-4
REPUBLIC: *51-54* 2-4
TENNESSEE: *51* 3-6
Singles: 7-Inch
CHART: *71-72* 1-3
DECCA: *53-54* 3-5
MERCURY: *62-64* 2-4
RCA VICTOR: *55-59* 2-5
REPUBLIC: *51-54* 3-8
TENNESSEE: *51* 5-10

Also see COLDER, Ben

WOOLIES
Singles: 7-Inch
DUNHILL: *66-67* $4-8
SPIRIT: *66* 5-8
LPs: 10/12-Inch 33rpm
SPIRIT: *66* 20-30

WOOLLEY, Bruce, & The Camera Club
Singles: 7-Inch
COLUMBIA: *80* 2-3
Picture Sleeves
COLUMBIA: *80* 2-3
LPs: 10/12-Inch 33rpm
COLUMBIA: *80* 5-8

WORD OF MOUTH
(Featuring D. J. Cheese)
Singles: 12-Inch 33/45rpm
BEAUTY & THE BEAST: *85* 4-6
PROFILE: *86* 4-6

WORLD CLASS WRECKIN CRU
(Lonzo & The World Class Wreckin Cru)
Singles: 7-Inch
KRU'-CUT: *88* 1-3
LPs: 10/12-Inch 33rpm
TECHNO KUT: *88* 5-8

WORLD PARTY
Singles: 7-Inch
CHRYSALIS: *86-87* 1-3
LPs: 10/12-Inch 33rpm
CHRYSALIS: *86* 5-8

WORLD PREMIER
Singles: 12-Inch 33/45rpm
CAPITOL: *84* 4-6
Singles: 7-Inch
CAPITOL: *84* 2-3

WORLD'S FAMOUS SUPREME TEAM
Singles: 12-Inch 33/45rpm
ISLAND: *84* 4-6
Singles: 7-Inch
ISLAND: *84* 1-3
Also see McLAREN, Malcom

WORRELL, Bernie
Singles: 7-Inch
ARISTA: *79* 2-3
LPs: 10/12-Inch 33rpm
ARISTA: *79* 5-8
Also see PARLIAMENT

WORTH, Marion
Singles: 7-Inch
CHEROKEE: *59* $4-8
COLUMBIA: *60-67* 3-6
DECCA: *67-70* 2-5
GUYDEN: *59-60* 4-8
Picture Sleeves
COLUMBIA: *61-62* 3-5
LPs: 10/12-Inch 33rpm
COLUMBIA: *63-64* 10-20
DECCA: *67* 8-12

WRABIT
Singles: 7-Inch
MCA: *82* 2-3
LPs: 10/12-Inch 33rpm
MCA: *82* 5-8

WRAY, Bill
Singles: 7-Inch
ABC: *79* 2-3

WRAY, Link
(Link Wray & His Ray Men; Link Wray & His Wray Men; Link Ray)
Singles: 78rpm
CADENCE: *58* 5-10
Singles: 7-Inch
ATLAS: *62* 5-10
BARNABY: *76* 2-4
CADENCE: *58* 8-15
EPIC: *59-61* 5-10
HEAVY: *68* 3-5
KAY: *58* 50-65
MR. G: *69* 4-6
OKEH: *67* 4-6
POLYDOR: *70-74* 3-5
RUMBLE: *61* 15-20
SWAN (4137; "Jack The Ripper"): *63* ... 8-10
SWAN (4154; "Week End"): *63* 6-10
SWAN (4163 through 4187): *63-64* 5-8
SWAN (4201; "Good Rockin'
     Tonight"): *65* 10-15
SWAN (4211 through 4232): *65* 5-8
SWAN (4239; "Ace Of Spades"): *65* 10-12
SWAN (4244; "The Batman Theme"): *66* ... 5-8
SWAN (4261; "Ace Of Spades"): *66* 8-10
SWAN (4273 through 4282): *66-67* 4-8
Picture Sleeves
EPIC: *59* 20-35
LPs: 10/12-Inch 33rpm
EPIC (3661; "Link Wray & The
     Wraymen"): *60* 40-50
POLYDOR: *71-74* 8-10
RECORD FACTORY: *74* 20-25
SWAN: *63* 50-60

VERMILLION: 75 .... $20-25
VISA: 79-80 5-8
Also see DUDLEY, Dave / Link Wray
Also see GORDON, Robert
Also see WRAY BROTHERS

WRAY, Link / Red Saunders
Singles: 7-Inch
OKEH (7100 series): 63 4-6
OKEH (7200 series): 67 3-5

WRAY, Lucky
(Link Wray)
Singles: 78rpm
STARDAY: 56 6-12
Singles: 7-Inch
STARDAY (500 series): 56 20-25
STARDAY (600 series): 57 50-75

WRAY, Vernon
(With Link Wray)
LPs: 10/12-Inch 33rpm
VERMILLION: 20-25
Also see WRAY BROTHERS

WRAY BROTHERS
(Wray Family)
Singles: 7-Inch
INFINITY: 62 6-10
LAWN: 63 6-10
Members: Link Wray; Doug Wray; Vernon Wray.
Also see WRAY, link
Also see WRAY, Vernon

WRECKING CREW
Singles: 12-Inch 33/45rpm
ERECT: 83 4-6
Singles: 7-Inch
ERECT: 83 1-3
SOUND OF FLORIDA: 83 1-3

WRIGHT, Bernard
Singles: 12-Inch 33/45rpm
ARISTA: 83 4-6
Singles: 7-Inch
ARISTA: 83-84 1-3
GRP: 81-82 1-3
MANHATTAN: 86 1-3
LPs: 10/12-Inch 33rpm
ARISTA: 83 5-8
GRP: 81 5-8
MANHATTAN: 86 5-8

WRIGHT, Betty
Singles: 12-Inch 33/45rpm
EPIC: 81 4-6
JAMAICA: 84-85 4-6
Singles: 7-Inch
ALSTON: 68-79 2-4

ATCO: 83 .... $1-3
EPIC: 81-83 1-3
FIRST STRING: 86 1-3
JAMAICA: 84-85 1-3
M.S.B.: 88 1-3
LPs: 10/12-Inch 33rpm
ALSTON: 72-79 6-10
ATCO: 68 10-15
COLLECTABLES: 88 6-8
EPIC: 81-83 5-8
MS.B: 88 5-8
Also see ALAIMO, Steve, & Betty Wright
Also see BROWN, Peter, & Betty Wright
Also see KC & THE SUNSHINE BAND

WRIGHT, Billy
Singles: 78rpm
SAVOY: 49-52 4-6
Singles: 7-Inch
CARROLLTON: 59 4-6
SAVOY (776; "Mean Old Wine"): 51 ... 15-20
SAVOY (827; "Drinkin' &
Thinkin'"): 52 8-12

**WRIGHT, Charles, & The Watts
103rd Street Rhythm Band**
Singles: 7-Inch
ABC: 75 2-4
DUNHILL: 73-74 2-4
WARNER BROS: 70-71 2-4
LPs: 10/12-Inch 33rpm
ABC: 75 6-10
DUNHILL: 73-74 6-10
WARNER BROS: 70-72 8-12
Also see SHIELDS
Also see WATTS 103RD STREET RHYTHM
BAND

WRIGHT, Dale
(Dale Wright & The Rock-Its; Dale Wright With
The Wright Guys & The Dons)
Singles: 7-Inch
ALCAR: 60 8-10
FRATERNITY: 58-59 10-15

WRIGHT, Duke
Singles: 7-Inch
MOOLA: 60 4-6

WRIGHT, Gary
(Gary Wright & Spooky Tooth)
Singles: 7-Inch
A&M: 70-72 2-4
WARNER BROS: 75-81 1-3
LPs: 10/12-Inch 33rpm
A&M: 70-76 8-12
WARNER BROS: 75-79 5-8
Also see SPOOKY TOOTH

WRIGHT, O.V.
Singles: 7-Inch
ABC: 75-76 .... $2-4
BACK BEAT: 65-74 3-5
GOLDWAX: 64 4-6
HI: 76-79 2-3
LPs: 10/12-Inch 33rpm
BACK BEAT: 65-72 10-15
HI: 78-79 5-8

WRIGHT, Priscilla
Singles: 78rpm
UNIQUE: 55 3-6
Singles: 7-Inch
20TH CENTURY-FOX: 59 4-6
UNIQUE: 55 5-8

WRIGHT, Ruben
Singles: 7-Inch
CAPITOL: 64-67 3-5
WYNNE: 60 3-5

WRIGHT, Ruby
Singles: 78rpm
FRATERNITY: 57 3-6
Singles: 7-Inch
FRATERNITY: 57 4-6
KING (Monaural): 59 3-5
KING (Stereo): 59 4-8

WRIGHT, Ruby, & Dick Pike
Singles: 7-Inch
KING (5192; "Three Stars"): 59 8-10
Also see WRIGHT, Ruby

WRITERS
Singles: 12-Inch 33/45rpm
COLUMBIA: 79 4-6
Singles: 7-Inch
COLUMBIA: 78-79 2-3
LPs: 10/12-Inch 33rpm
COLUMBIA: 79 5-8

WUF TICKET
Singles: 12-Inch 33/45rpm
PRELUDE: 81 4-6
Singles: 7-Inch
PRELUDE: 81 1-3

WYCOFF, Michael
Singles: 12-Inch 33/45rpm
RCA VICTOR: 83 4-6
Singles: 7-Inch
RCA VICTOR: 80-84 1-3
LPs: 10/12-Inch 33rpm
RCA VICTOR: 83 5-8
Also see CLAYTON, Merry

WYLIE, Richard
(Richard "Popcorn" Wylie)
Singles: 7-Inch
ABC: 75 .... $2-4
EPIC: 62-63 3-5
KAREN: 68 2-4
MOTOWN: 61 30-40
SOUL: 71 2-4
Picture Sleeves
EPIC: 62 4-8
LPs: 10/12-Inch 33rpm
ABC: 74 8-10

WYMAN, Bill
Singles: 12-Inch 33/45rpm
A&M (12041; "Je Suis Un Rock Star"): 81 .6-10
Singles: 7-Inch
A&M (2367; "Je Suis Un Rock Star"): 81 ...2-4
ROLLING STONES: 74-75 4-6
Promotional Singles
A&M (2367; "Je Suis Un Rock Star"): 81 ...4-6
A&M (12041; "Je Suis Un
Rock Star"): 81 15-20
(12-Inch single.)
Picture Sleeves
A&M (2367; "Je Suis Un Rock Star"): 81 ...3-5
LPs: 10/12-Inch 33rpm
ROLLING STONES: 74-76 8-10

WYMAN, Bill / Rolling Stones
Singles: 7-Inch
LONDON (907; "In Another Land"): 67 4-6
Promotional Singles
LONDON (907; "In Another Land"): 67 ...8-10
Picture Sleeves
LONDON (907; "In Another Land"): 67 ..10-15
Also see ROLLING STONES
Also see WYMAN, Bill

WYND CHYMES
Singles: 7-Inch
RCA VICTOR: 82-83 1-3
LPs: 10/12-Inch 33rpm
RCA VICTOR: 82 5-8

WYNETTE, Tammy
Singles: 7-Inch
EPIC (Except 1): 66-88 1-3
EPIC (1; "The Wonders You Perform"): 70 .3-5
(Colored vinyl. Promotional issue only.)
Picture Sleeves
EPIC: 69-76 2-4
LPs: 10/12-Inch 33rpm
COLUMBIA: 73 5-10
EPIC: 68-86 5-15
HARMONY: 70-71 5-10
TIME-LIFE: 81 5-8

Tammy Wynette (Photo: Randee St. Nicholas)

Also see CASH, Johnny / Tammy Wynette
Also see HOUSTON, David, & Tammy
Wynette
Also see JONES, George, & Tammy Wynette
Also see LYNN, Loretta / Tammy Wynette

WYNNE, Philippe
Singles: 12-Inch 33/45rpm
FANTASY: *83* $4-6
Singles: 7-Inch
COTILLION: *77* 1-3
FANTASY: *83* 1-3
SUGAR HILL: *83* 1-3
UNCLE JAM: *80* 1-3
LPs: 10/12-Inch 33rpm
COTILLION: *77* 5-8
Also see DUNLAP, Gene

X
Singles: 7-Inch
ELEKTRA: *82* 1-3
LPs: 10/12-Inch 33rpm
ELEKTRA: *82-88* 5-8
ROCSHIRE: *83* 5-8
SLASH: *80-81* 10-20
Members: Dave Alvin; Exene Cervenka; John Doe;
D.J. Bonebrake; Tony Gilkyson.
Also see ALVIN, Dave
Also see BLASTERS
Also see LONE JUSTICE

X, Malcolm: see MALCOLM X

XTC
Singles: 7-Inch
EPIC: *82* $1-3
GEFFEN (Except PRO series): *83-89* 1-3
GEFFEN (PRO series): *83-84* 3-5
(Promotional issues only.)
RSO: *81* 2-3
VIRGIN: *79-81* 2-3
LPs: 10/12-Inch 33rpm
EPIC: *82* 5-10
GEFFEN: *84-89* 5-8
RSO: 5-10
VIRGIN: *78-82* 5-10
Members: Andy Partridge; Barry Andrews; Colin
Moulding; Terry Chambers; Dave Gregory.
Also see DUKES OF STRATOSPHERE
Also see SHRIEKBACK

XAVIER
(Xavier Smith)
Singles: 12-Inch 33/45rpm
LIBERTY: *82* 4-6
Singles: 7-Inch
LIBERTY: *82* 1-3
LPs: 10/12-Inch 33rpm
LIBERTY: *82* 5-8

XAVION
Singles: 7-Inch
ASYLUM: *84-85* 1-3
LPs: 10/12-Inch 33rpm
ASYLUM: *84* 5-8

XENA
Singles: 12-Inch 33/45rpm
EMERGENCY: *83* 4-6

X-25 BAND
Singles: 7-Inch
H.C.R.C.: *82* 1-3

Y&T
(Yesterday & Today)
Singles: 7-Inch
A&M: *81-85* 1-3
LPs: 10/12-Inch 33rpm
A&M: *81-85* 5-8
GEFFEN: *87* 5-8
LONDON: *78* 8-10

YACHTS
Singles: 7-Inch
POLYDOR: *79* 2-3

LPs: 10/12-Inch 33rpm
POLYDOR: *79-80* **$5-8**
RADAR: **6-10**

YAMASHTA, Stomu
LPs: 10/12-Inch 33rpm
ARISTA: *77* **5-8**
ISLAND: *76-78* **5-8**
VANGUARD: *71-74* **8-10**
Also see WINWOOD, Steve

YAMBU
Singles: 7-Inch
MONTUNO GRINGO: *75* **2-4**

YANKOVIC, "Weird Al"
Singles: 12-Inch 33/4rpm
ROCK 'N' ROLL: *84* **4-6**
Singles: 7-Inch
CAPITOL: *79* **2-4**
ROCK 'N' ROLL: *83-88* **1-3**
TK: *81* **1-3**
LPs: 10/12-Inch 33rpm
ROCK 'N' ROLL: *83-88* **5-8**

YANNI
LPs: 10/12-Inch 33rpm
PRIVATE: *88* **5-8**

YARBROUGH, Glenn
Singles: 7-Inch
PRIDE: *72* **2-3**
RCA VICTOR: *64-68* **2-4**
STAX: *73-74* **2-3**
WARNER BROS: *68-71* **2-3**
Picture Sleeves
RCA VICTOR: *65* **3-6**
LPs: 10/12-Inch 33rpm
FIRST AMERICAN: *81* **5-8**
IM'PRESS: *71* **8-10**
RCA VICTOR: *64-69* **8-18**
STAX: *74* **8-10**
TRADITION: *67-70* **8-15**
WARNER BROS: *68-71* **8-12**
Also see LIMELITERS

YARBROUGH & PEOPLES
Singles: 12-Inch 33/45rpm
TOTAL EXPERIENCE: *82-86* **4-6**
Singles: 7-Inch
MERCURY: *80-81* **1-3**
TOTAL EXPERIENCE: *82-86* **1-3**
LPs: 10/12-Inch 33rpm
MERCURY: *80* **5-8**
TOTAL EXPERIENCE: *82-86* **5-8**
Members: Calvin Yarbrough; Alisa Peoples.

YARDBIRDS
Singles: 7-Inch
EPIC (9709; "I Wish You Could"): *64* . .**$15-20**
EPIC (9790 through 10204): *65-67* **5-8**
EPIC (10248; "Ten Little Indians"): *67* ...**10-15**
EPIC (10303; "Goodnight Sweet
Josephine"): *68* **15-20**
Picture Sleeves
EPIC (Except 9709): *65-66* **10-15**
EPIC (9709; "I Wish You Could"): *64* ..**75-125**
(Promotional issue only.)
LPs: 10/12-Inch 33rpm
ACCORD: *81-83* **5-8**
COLUMBIA (11311; "Live
Yardbirds"): *72* **25-35**
(Columbia Special Products issue.)
COMPLEAT: *86* **8-12**
EPIC (24167; "For Your Love"): *65* **50-100**
(Monaural.)
EPIC (24177; "Having A Rave Up"): *65* ..**40-60**
(Monaural.)
EPIC (24210; "Over Under
Sideways Down"): *66* **40-60**
(Monaural.)
EPIC (24246; "Yardbirds' Greatest
Hits"): *66* **30-40**
(Monaural.)
EPIC (24313; "Little Games"): *67* **40-60**
(Monaural.)
EPIC (26167; "For Your Love"): *65* **30-40**
(Stereo.)
EPIC (26177; "Having A Rave Up"): *65* ..**30-40**
(Stereo.)
EPIC (26210; "Over Under
Sideways Down"): *66* **30-45**
(Stereo.)
EPIC (26246; "Yardbirds'
Greatest Hits"): *66* **30-40**
(Stereo.)
EPIC (26313; "Little Games"): *67* **35-50**
(Stereo.)
EPIC (30135; "The Yardbirds Featuring
Performances By Jeff Beck, Eric
Clapton, Jimmy Page"): *70* **75-100**
EPIC (30615; "Live Yardbirds"): *71* **50-75**
EPIC (34490; "Yardbirds' Favorites"): *77* .**8-10**
EPIC (34491; "Yardbirds' Great Hits"): *77* .**8-10**
EPIC (38455; "The Yardbirds"): *83* **5-8**
EPIC (48455; "The Yardbirds"): *83* **12-15**
(Half-speed mastered.)
RHINO: *82-86* **6-10**
SPRINGBOARD: *72* **8-10**
Members: Eric Clapton; Jeff Beck; Keith Relf;
Jimmy Page; Jim McCarty; Chris Dreja.
Also see ARMAGEDDON

Also see BECK, Jeff
Also see BOX OF FROGS
Also see CACTUS
Also see CLAPTON, Eric
Also see PAGE, Jimmy
Also see WILLIAMSON, Sonny Boy, & The
Yardbirds

YARROW, Peter
Singles: 7-Inch
WARNER BROS: 68-75 . . . . $2-4
LPs: 10/12-Inch 33rpm
WARNER BROS: 72-75 8-10
Also see PETER, PAUL & MARY

YAZ
(Yazoo)
Singles: 12-Inch 33/45rpm
SIRE: 82-84 4-6
Singles: 7-Inch
SIRE: 82-84 1-3
LPs: 10/12-Inch 33rpm
SIRE: 82-83 5-8
Members: Alison Moyet; Vince Clarke.
Also see MOYET, Alison

YAZZ & THE PLASTIC POPULATION
Singles: 7-Inch
ELEKTRA: 88 1-3

YELLO
Singles: 12-Inch 33/45rpm
ELEKTRA: 83-85 4-6
RALPH: 81 5-8
STIFF: 4-8
Singles: 7-Inch
ELEKTRA: 83-85 1-3
MERCURY: 87 1-3
RALPH: 81 2-4
STIFF (Picture discs): 4-8
LPs: 10/12-Inch 33rpm
ELEKTRA: 83-85 5-8
MERCURY: 87 5-8
RALPH: 81 8-10

YELLOW BALLOON
Singles: 7-Inch
CANTERBURY: 67-68 4-6
LPs: 10/12-Inch 33rpm
CANTERBURY: 67 15-20
Members: Alex Valdez; Don Grady; Don Braucht;
Forrest Green; Paul Cannella; Darryl Dragon.
Also see CAPTAIN & TENNILLE
Also see SPIRIT

YELLOW JACKETS
Singles: 7-Inch
SMASH: 68 3-5

YELLOW MAGIC ORCHESTRA
Singles: 12-Inch 33/45rpm
A&M: 80 . . . . $4-6
Singles: 7-Inch
A&M: 80 1-3
HORIZON: 80 1-3
LPs: 10/12-Inch 33rpm
A&M: 80-81 5-8

YELLOWMAN
Singles: 12-Inch 33/45rpm
COLUMBIA: 84 4-6
Singles: 7-Inch
COLUMBIA: 84 1-3
LPs: 10/12-Inch 33rpm
COLUMBIA: 84 5-8

YES
Singles: 12-Inch 33/45rpm
ATCO: 83-86 4-6
Singles: 7-Inch
ATCO: 83-88 1-3
ATLANTIC (Black vinyl): 70-78 2-4
ATLANTIC (Colored vinyl): 70-78 4-8
Promotional Singles
ATLANTIC: 70-78 3-6
LPs: 10/12-Inch 33rpm
ATCO: 83-87 5-8
ATLANTIC (100 series): 73 12-15
ATLANTIC (500 series): 80 8-12
ATLANTIC (900 series): 74 12-15
ATLANTIC (7000 series): 71 10-12
ATLANTIC (8000 series): 69-71 10-15
ATLANTIC (16000 series): 80 5-8
ATLANTIC (19000 series): 77-82 5-8
MFSL: 82 25-50
Promotional LPs
ATLANTIC ("Solos"): 76 10-15
Members: Jon Anderson; Rick Wakeman; Steve
Howe; Chris Squire; Tony Kaye; Alan White; Bill
Bruford; Patrick Moraz; Geoff Downes; Trevor
Horn.
Also see ANDERSON, Jon
Also see BANKS, Peter
Also see BUGGLES
Also see HOWE, Steve, Band
Also see MORAZ, Patrick
Also see SIMON, Paul
Also see SQUIRE, Chris
Also see WAKEMAN, Rick

YIPES
Singles: 7-Inch
MILLENNIUM: 79-80 1-3
LPs: 10/12-Inch 33rpm
MILLENNIUM: 79-80 5-8

YOAKAM, Dwight
Singles: 7-Inch
REPRISE: *86-89* $1-3
LPs: 10/12-Inch 33rpm
REPRISE: *86-89* 5-8
Also see OWENS, Buck

YORK, Dave, & The Beachcombers
Singles: 7-Inch
LANCELOT: *62* 8-12
P.K.M.: *62* 4-6

YORK, Rusty
Singles: 7-Inch
CAPITOL: *61* 3-5
CHESS: *59* 5-8
GAYLORD: *63* 3-5
KING (5100 series): *58* 5-8
KING (5500 series): *61-62* 4-6
NOTE: *59* 20-30
P.J.: *59* 10-15
SAGE: *60* 10-15
Also see MACK, Lonnie, & Rusty York

YOST, Dennis
Singles: 7-Inch
MGM: *75* 2-4
ROBOX: *81* 1-3
LPs: 10/12-Inch 33rpm
ACCORD: *81* 5-8
ROBOX: *82* 5-8
Also see CLASSICS IV

YOU KNOW WHO GROUP
Singles: 7-Inch
CASUAL: *65* 4-6
4 CORNERS: *64* 4-6
LPs: 10/12-Inch 33rpm
INTERNATIONAL ALLIED: *65* 15-20

YOUNG, Barry
Singles: 7-Inch
COLUMBIA: *66* 2-4
DOT: *65-66* 3-5
EVA: *63* 3-6
HOOKS BROTHERS: *66* 2-4
Picture Sleeves
COLUMBIA: *66* 3-6
LPs: 10/12-Inch 33rpm
DOT: *65* 10-20

YOUNG, Faron
(Faron Young & Margie Singleton)
Singles: 78rpm
CAPITOL: *53-57* 3-6
Singles: 7-Inch
CAPITOL (2200 through 3900
series): *53-58* 4-8

CAPITOL (4000 through 4800
series): *58-62* $3-5
MCA: *79-81* 1-3
MERCURY: *63-78* 2-4
STEP ONE: *88* 1-3
Picture Sleeves
CAPITOL: *61* 3-6
MERCURY: *62-68* 2-5
EPs: 7-Inch 33/45rpm
CAPITOL: *54-61* 8-15
LPs: 10/12-Inch 33rpm
ALBUM GLOBE: *81* 5-8
ALLEGIANCE: *84* 5-8
CAPITOL (700 series): *57* 30-40
CAPITOL (1000 series): *58-59* 20-25
CAPITOL (1100 series): *59* 30-40
CAPITOL (1400 through 2500
series): *60-66* 12-25
(With a "T," "DT," or "ST" prefix.)
CAPITOL (1500 series): *75* 5-8
(With an "SM" prefix.)
CASTLE: 5-8
EXACT: *80* 5-8
FARON YOUNG: 15-20
MCA: *79-83* 4-8
MARY CARTER PAINTS (1000; "Faron
Young Sings On Stage"): 35-45
(Promotional issue only.)
MERCURY: *63-77* 5-15
PICKWICK/HILLTOP: *66-68* 8-12
SEARS: 8-12
TOWER: *66-68* 12-15
WING: *68* 8-12
Also see ATKINS, Chet / Faron Young
Also see NELSON, Willie / Faron Young
Also see OWENS, Buck / Faron Young / Ferlin Husky

YOUNG, Faron / Carl Perkins / Claude King
LPs: 10/12-Inch 33rpm
PICKWICK/HILLTOP: *65* 8-15
Also see KING, Claude
Also see PERKINS, Carl

YOUNG, Georgie
(Georgie Young & The Rockin' Bocs; George Young)
Singles: 7-Inch
CAMEO: *58-59* 4-6
CHANCELLOR: *61* 3-5
FORTUNE: *57* 5-8
MERCURY (71259; "Can't
Stop Me"): *58* 30-40
PACE SETTER: 5-8
SWAN: *60* 4-6

YOUNG, Jesse Colin
(Jesse Colin Young With The Youngbloods)
Singles: 7-Inch
ELEKTRA: 78 .... $2-3
REPRISE: 73 2-4
WARNER BROS: 70-77 2-4

LPs: 10/12-Inch 33rpm
CAPITOL (2000 series): 64 20-25
CAPITOL (11000 series): 74 8-10
CAPITOL (16000 series): 80 5-8
ELEKTRA: 78 5-8
MERCURY (61005; "Young
  Blood"): 65 20-25
MERCURY (61273; "Two
  Trips"): 70 10-15
WARNER BROS: 72-75 8-10
Also see YOUNGBLOODS

YOUNG, John Paul
Singles: 7-Inch
ARIOLA AMERICA: 75-76 2-3
SCOTTI BROTHERS: 78 2-3
LPs: 10/12-Inch 33rpm
SCOTTI BROTHERS: 78 5-8

YOUNG, Karen
Singles: 7-Inch
WEST END: 78 2-3

YOUNG, Kathy
(Kathy Young & The Innocents)
Singles: 7-Inch
COLLECTABLES: 1-3
ERA: 72 1-3
ERIC: 1-3
INDIGO: 60-62 10-15
MONOGRAM: 62 8-10
STARFIRE: 79 3-6
VIRGO: 72 1-3
Picture Sleeves
INDIGO: 60-61 6-12
LPs: 10/12-Inch 33rpm
INDIGO (504; "The Sound Of
  Kathy Young"): 61 50-100
Also see CHRIS & KATHY
Also see INNOCENTS

YOUNG, Neil
(Neil Young & Crazy Horse; Neil & The Shock-
ing Pinks; Neil Young & The Bluenotes)
Singles: 12-Inch 33/45rpm
GEFFEN: 86 4-6
Singles: 7-Inch
GEFFEN: 83-86 1-3
REPRISE (0785 through 0898): 68-70 3-5
REPRISE (0911 through 1396): 70-79 2-3

Neil Young (Photo: Ebet Roberts)

REPRISE (49000 series): 79-81 .... $1-3
Picture Sleeves
REPRISE: 78-81 1-3
EPs: 7-Inch 33/45rpm
REPRISE: 72 10-15
(Jukebox issue only.)
LPs: 10/12-Inch 33rpm
GEFFEN: 83-87 5-8
REPRISE (2000 series,
  except 2257 & 2296): 72-81 5-8
REPRISE (2257; "Decade"): 77 12-15
REPRISE (2296; "Live Rust"): 79 10-12
REPRISE (6317; "Neil Young"): 68 40-50
(Front cover does NOT have Neil Young's name
on it.)
REPRISE (6317; "Neil Young"): 68 8-12
(Front cover has Neil Young's name on it.)
REPRISE (6349; "Everybody Knows
  This Is Nowhere"): 69 10-12
REPRISE (6383; "After The
  Gold Rush"): 70 10-12
REPRISE (6480; "Journey Through
  The Past"): 72 12-15
REPRISE: 88 5-8
WARNER BROS (Except 358): 79 5-8
WARNER BROS (358; "The Big
  Ball"): 79 12-15
(Promotional issue only.)
Also see BUFFALO SPRINGFIELD
Also see CASCADES
Also see CRAZY HORSE

Also see CROSBY, STILLS, NASH, &
YOUNG
Also see HARRIS, Emmylou
Also see LARSON, Nicolette

YOUNG, Neil, & Jim Messina
Singles: 7-Inch
REPRISE: 70 . . . . $3-5
Also see MESSINA, Jim

YOUNG, Neil, & Graham Nash
Singles: 7-Inch
REPRISE: 72 2-4
Also see NASH, Graham
Also see STILLS-YOUNG BAND
Also see YOUNG, Neil

YOUNG, Nelson
Singles: 7-Inch
LUCKY: 59 60-75
MADISON: 25-30
RUBY: 57 25-35

YOUNG, Paul
Singles: 12-Inch 33/45rpm
COLUMBIA: 83-86 4-6
Singles: 7-Inch
COLUMBIA: 83-86 1-3
EPIC: 74 2-4
LPs: 10/12-Inch 33rpm
COLUMBIA: 84-86 5-8
Also see BAND AID
Also see MIKE + THE MECHANICS
Also see SAD CAFE

YOUNG, Retta
Singles: 7-Inch
ALL PLATINUM: 75 2-4

YOUNG, Tommie
Singles: 7-Inch
MCA: 78 2-3
SOUL POWER: 73-75 2-4
LPs: 10/12-Inch 33rpm
MCA: 78 5-8

YOUNG, Val
Singles: 12-Inch 33/45rpm
GORDY: 85-86 4-6
Singles: 7-Inch
AMHERST: 87 1-3
GORDY: 85-86 1-3
LPs: 10/12-Inch 33rpm
GORDY: 85-86 5-8

YOUNG, Victor
Singles: 78rpm
DECCA: 50-57 2-4
Singles: 7-Inch
DECCA: 50-57 2-4

EPs: 7-Inch 33/45rpm
DECCA: 50-57 . . . . $3-6
LPs: 10/12-Inch 33rpm
DECCA: 50-59 5-15
Also see CROSBY, Bing
Also see GARLAND, Judy

YOUNG AMERICANS
LPs: 10/12-Inch 33rpm
ABC: 69 5-10

YOUNG & COMPANY
Singles: 7-Inch
BRUNSWICK: 81 1-3
RCA VICTOR: 69 2-4
LPs: 10/12-Inch 33rpm
BRUNSWICK: 81 5-8

YOUNG FRESH FELLOWS
Singles: 7-Inch
POPLLAMA: 85-86 1-3
EPs: 7-Inch 33/45rpm
POPLLAMA: 87 3-5
LPs: 10/12-Inch 33rpm
POPLLAMA: 84-86 5-8
POPLLAMA/FRONTIER: 87 5-8
Members: Scott McCaughey; Tad Hutchison; Jim
Sangster; Chuck Carroll.

YOUNG HEARTS
Singles: 7-Inch
AVCO EMBASSY: 70 2-4
MINIT: 68-69 3-5
20TH CENTURY-FOX: 74-75 2-3
LPs: 10/12-Inch 33rpm
MINIT: 69 10-12

YOUNG HOLT UNLIMITED
(Young-Holt Trio)
Singles: 7-Inch
BRUNSWICK: 66-69 2-4
COTILLION: 70-71 2-3
ERIC: 83 1-3
PAULA: 73 2-3
LPs: 10/12-Inch 33rpm
ATLANTIC: 73 8-10
BRUNSWICK: 67-69 10-15
COTILLION: 70-71 8-10
PAULA: 73 5-8
Members: Eldee Young; Isaac Holt.
Also see LEWIS, Ramsey

YOUNG RASCALS: see RASCALS

YOUNG VANDALS
Singles: 7-Inch
T-NECK: 70 2-4

YOUNGBLOOD, Lonnie
Singles: 7-Inch
FAIRMOUNT: *67* $3-5
LOMA: *67-68* 3-5
RADIO: *81* 1-3
SHAKAT: *74* 2-4
TURBO: *71-73* 2-4
LPs: 10/12-Inch 33rpm
RADIO: *81* 5-8
TURBO: *71* 8-10
Also see HENDRIX, Jimi, & Lonnie
Youngblood

YOUNGBLOODS
(Featuring Jesse Colin Young)
Singles: 7-Inch
MERCURY: *66-69* 5-8
RCA VICTOR: *66-71* 4-6
WARNER/RACCOON: *70-72* 2-4
Picture Sleeves
RCA VICTOR: *66* 4-6
LPs: 10/12-Inch 33rpm
RCA VICTOR (3000 series): *80* 5-8
(With an "ALY1" prefix.)
RCA VICTOR (3000 series): *67* 12-15
(With an "LPM" or "LSP" prefix.)
RCA VICTOR (4000 series): *70-71* 10-15
(With an "LPM" or "LSP" prefix.)
RCA VICTOR (6000 series): *72* 12-15
WARNER BROS/RACOON: *70-72* 10-12
Members: Jesse Colin Young; Jerry Corbit; Joe
Cauer; Lowell "Banana" Levinger.
Also see BOWIE, David / Joe Cocker /
Youngbloods
Also see YOUNG, Jesse Colin

YOUNGHEARTS
Singles: 7-Inch
ABC: *77* 2-3
CANTERBURY: *67* 3-5
20TH CENTURY-FOX: *73-76* 2-4
LPs: 10/12-Inch 33rpm
ABC: *77* 5-8
20TH CENTURY-FOX: *73-74* 8-10

YURO, Timi
Singles: 7-Inch
LIBERTY (55000 series): *61-64* 3-5
LIBERTY (56000 series): *68* 2-4
MERCURY: *64-67* 2-4
PLAYBOY: *75* 2-4
EPs: 7-Inch 33/45rpm
LIBERTY: *61* 8-12
(Jukebox issues only.)
LPs: 10/12-Inch 33rpm
COLGEMS: *68* 8-10
LIBERTY (Except 7500 series): *61-63* ... 15-20

LIBERTY (7500 series): *68* $8-10
MERCURY: *65* 10-15
SUNSET: *66-70* 6-12
UNITED ARTISTS: *75-76* 5-8
WING: *68* 8-10
Also see RAY, Johnnie, & Timi Yuro

YUTAKA
Singles: 7-Inch
ALFA: *81* 1-3
Picture Sleeves
ALFA: *81* 1-3
LPs: 10/12-Inch 33rpm
ALFA: *81* 5-8
Also see AUSTIN, Patti

Z

ZZ TOP
Singles: 12-Inch 33/45rpm
WARNER BROS: *84-86* 4-6
Singles: 7-Inch
LONDON: *70-77* 2-4
SCAT: 5-8
WARNER BROS: *80-86* 1-3
Picture Sleeves
LONDON: *75* 2-4
LPs: 10/12-Inch 33rpm
LONDON (Except 1001): *71-77* 8-12
LONDON (1001; "World Wide
Texas Tour"): *76* 12-15
(Promotional issue only.)
WARNER BROS: *79-86* 5-8
Members: Bill Gibbons; Frank Beard; Dusty Hill.

ZABACH, Florian
Singles: 78rpm
DECCA: *51-54* 2-4
MERCURY: *56-57* 2-4
Singles: 7-Inch
CADENCE: *61* 2-3
DECCA: *51-54* 2-4
MERCURY: *56-58* 2-4
EPs: 7-Inch 33/45rpm
DECCA: *51-54* 4-8
MERCURY: *56-58* 3-6
LPs: 10/12-Inch 33rpm
DECCA: *51-65* 5-15
MERCURY: *56-60* 5-15
VOCALION: *63-66* 4-8
WING: *63* 4-8
Also see VALLI, June

ZACHARIAS, Helmut
(Helmut Zacharias' Magic Violins)
Singles: 78rpm
DECCA: 56-57 .... $2-3
Singles: 7-Inch
CAPITOL: 69 1-3
DECCA: 56-64 2-3
EPs: 7-Inch 33/45rpm
DECCA: 56-58 3-6
LPs: 10/12-Inch 33rpm
CAPITOL: 69 4-8
DECCA: 56-61 5-15
PHILIPS: 62 4-8
RCA VICTOR: 66 4-8

ZACHERLEY, John
(Zacherle; Zacherley; John Zacherlie; "Cool Ghoul")
Singles: 7-Inch
ABKCO: 1-3
CAMEO: 58 5-8
COLPIX: 64 4-6
ELEKTRA: 60 4-6
PARKWAY: 62 3-5
LPs: 10/12-Inch 33rpm
CRESTVIEW: 63 25-35
ELEKTRA: 60 25-35
PARKWAY: 62-63 25-35

ZADORA, Pia
(Pia Zadora & The London Symphony Orchestra)
Singles: 12-Inch 33/45rpm
MCA: 83 4-6
Singles: 7-Inch
CURB: 83 1-3
ELEKTRA: 82-83 1-3
MCA: 83-84 1-3
WARNER BROS: 78 2-3
LPs: 10/12-Inch 33rpm
CBS ASSOCIATED: 86 5-8
ELEKTRA: 82 5-8
Also see JACKSON, Jermaine, & Pia Zadora

ZAGER, Michael, Band
Singles: 12-Inch 33/45rpm
CBS ASSOCIATED: 84 4-6
COLUMBIA: 79 4-6
Singles: 7-Inch
BANG: 78 2-3
CBS ASSOCIATED: 84 1-3
PRIVATE STOCK: 78 2-3
LPs: 10/12-Inch 33rpm
COLUMBIA: 79 5-8
PRIVATE STOCK: 78 5-8
Also see TEN WHEEL DRIVE

ZAGER, Michael, Moon Band, & Peabo Bryson
Singles: 7-Inch
BANG: 76 .... $2-3
Also see BRYSON, Peabo
Also see ZAGER, Michael, Band

ZAGER & EVANS
Singles: 7-Inch
RCA VICTOR: 69-70 3-5
TRUTH: 69 8-12
VANGUARD: 71 2-4
LPs: 10/12-Inch 33rpm
RCA VICTOR (1000 series): 75 8-10
RCA VICTOR (4000 series): 69-70 ... 12-15
VANGUARD: 71 10-12
WHITE WHALE: 69 12-15
Members: Denny Zager; Rick Evans.

ZAHND, Ricky, & The Blue Jeaners
Singles: 7-Inch
COLUMBIA: 55-56 3-5

ZAPP
Singles: 7-Inch
WARNER BROS: 80-86 1-3
LPs: 10/12-Inch 33rpm
WARNER BROS: 80-86 5-8
Members: Roger Troutman; Shirley Murdock.
Also see BOOTSY'S RUBBER BAND
Also see MURDOCK, Shirley
Also see ROGER

ZAPPA, Frank
(Frank Zappa & The Mothers; Francis Vincent Zappa)
Singles: 12-Inch 33/45rpm
BARKING PUMPKIN (1114; "Goblin Girl"): 79 15-20
(Picture disc.)
ZAPPA (1001; "I Don't Want To Get Drafted"): 80 8-10
Singles: 7-Inch
BARKING PUMPKIN: 82 2-3
BIZARRE/REPRISE (0800 series): 69-70 10-15
BIZARRE/REPRISE (0900 series): 70 6-10
DISCREET: 73-74 3-5
UNITED ARTISTS: 71 5-8
VERVE: 66-68 8-12
WARNER BROS: 76-77 4-6
ZAPPA: 79-80 2-4
Promotional Singles
DISCREET (586; "Cosmik Debris"): 74 .. 10-12
EPs: 7-Inch 33/45rpm
REPRISE (336; "Hot Rats"): 72 35-40
(Promotional issue only.)

UNITED ARTISTS ("200 Motels"): *71* . **$35-40**
(Promotional issue only.)
Picture Sleeves
ZAPPA: *80* **1-3**
LPs: 10/12-Inch 33rpm
BARKING PUMPKIN (37000
series): *81* **10-15**
BARKING PUMPKIN (38000
series): *82-83* **5-8**
BARKING PUMPKIN (74000
series): *84-86* **5-8**
BIZARRE: *69-72* **10-15**
DISCREET (2100 series): *74* **10-15**
DISCREET (2200 series): *74-79* **10-12**
VERVE (8741; "Lumpy Gravy"): *68* **25-30**
UNITED ARTISTS: *71* **15-20**
ZAPPA (1500 series): *79* **12-15**
ZAPPA (1600 series): *79* **8-12**
Promotional LPs
BARKING PUMPKIN (1111; "Shut
Up 'N' Play Yer Guitar"): *81* **12-15**
(Mail-order offer.)
BARKING PUMPKIN (1112; "Shut Up
'N' Play Yer Guitar Some More"): *81* .. **12-15**
(Mail-order offer.)
BARKING PUMPKIN (1113; "Return
Of Shut Up 'N' Play Yer
Guitar"): *81* **12-15**
(Mail-order offer.)
BIZARRE (368; "Zapped"): *69* **20-25**
(With cartoon cover.)
WARNER BROS. (368;
"Zapped"): *69* **12-15**
(Cover pictures Frank Zappa.)
ZAPPA (78; "Sheik Yerbouti,
Clean Cuts"): *79* **15-20**
ZAPPA (129; "Joe's Garage,
Acts I, II, & III"): *79* **15-20**
Also see BABY RAY & THE FERNS
Also see GUY, Bob
Also see MOTHERS OF INVENTION

ZAPPA, Frank & Moon
Singles: 12-Inch 33/45rpm
BARKING PUMPKIN (03069; "Valley
Girl"): *82* **5-8**
Singles: 7-Inch
BARKING PUMPKIN (02972; "Valley
Girl"): *82* **2-3**
Promotional Singles
BARKING PUMPKIN (1490; "Valley
Girl"): *82* **4-6**
Also see ZAPPA, Frank

ZAVARONI, Lena
Singles: 7-Inch
STAX: *74* **$2-4**
ZEBRA
Singles: 7-Inch
ATLANTIC: *83-84* **1-3**
LPs: 10/12-Inch 33rpm
ATLANTIC: *83-84* **5-8**
ZELLA, Danny, & His Zell Rocks
Singles: 7-Inch
FOX: *59* **5-10**
RED ROCKET: **10-20**
SHO-BIZ: **4-6**
ZENTER, Si, & His Orchestra
(Si Zentner's Orchestra & The Johnny Mann
Singers)
Singles: 7-Inch
BEL CANTO: *59* **2-4**
LIBERTY: *59-67* **2-4**
RCA VICTOR: *64-66* **1-3**
Picture Sleeves
LIBERTY: *62* **2-5**
EPs: 7-Inch 33/45rpm
LIBERTY: *59-67* **5-8**
LPs: 10/12-Inch 33rpm
BEL CANTO: *59* **8-15**
LIBERTY: *59-67* **5-15**
RCA VICTOR: *65-66* **5-10**
SUNSET: *66* **5-10**
Also see DENNY, Martin
Also see MANN, Johnny, Singers
Also see MARTIN, Dean / Patti Page
Also see SINATRA, Frank
ZEPHYR
Singles: 7-Inch
PROBE: *70* **5-8**
WARNER BROS: *70* **2-4**
Promotional Singles
PROBE: *70* **10-12**
LPs: 10/12-Inch 33rpm
PROBE: *69* **30-40**
RED SNEAKERS: *82* **5-10**
WARNER BROS: *71-72* **25-30**
Members: Candy Givens; Tommy Bolin.
Also see BOLIN, Tommy
ZEPPELIN, Led: see LED ZEPPELIN
ZEVON, Warren
(Zevon)
Singles: 7-Inch
ASYLUM: *77-80* **1-3**
LPs: 10/12-Inch 33rpm
ASYLUM: *78-82* **5-8**
IMPERIAL: *70* **10-12**

Warren Zevon (Photo: Herb Ritts)

VIRGIN: 87 . . . . $5-8
  Members: Richard Hayward; Kenny Gradney;
  Greg Beck; Karen Childs.
  Also see LITTLE FEAT

ZILL, Pat
Singles: 7-Inch
BIG C: 62 3-5
ERA: 63 3-5
INDIGO: 61 3-5
SAND: 61 5-8

ZINGARA
Singles: 7-Inch
WHEEL: 80-81 1-3
LPs: 10/12-Inch 33rpm
WHEEL: 81 5-8

ZINO
Singles: 12-Inch 33/45rpm
PACIFIC 6: 84 4-6

ZION BAPTIST CHURCH CHOIR
Singles: 7-Inch
MYRRH: 73 1-3

Z'LOOKE
Singles: 7-Inch
ORPHEUS: 88 1-3

**ZODIAC MINDWARP & THE
  LOVE REACTION**
LPs: 10/12-Inch 33rpm
VERTIGO: 88 5-8

ZOMBIES
Singles: 7-Inch
DATE: 68-69 . . . . $3-5
EPIC: 74 2-4
ERIC: 83 1-3
LONDON: 1-3
PARROT: 64-66 4-6
Picture Sleeves
PARROT: 65 10-20
LPs: 10/12-Inch 33rpm
BACK-TRAC: 85 5-8
DATE (4013; "Odessey &
  Oracle"): 68 20-25
  (No promotional mention of *Time Of The Season*
  on front cover.)
DATE (4013; "Odessey &
  Oracle"): 68 15-20
  (With promo for *Time Of The Season* on front
  cover.)
EPIC: 74 10-12
LONDON: 69 10-15
PARROT: 65 30-35
RHINO: 5-8
  Members: Colin Blunstone; Rod Argent.
  Also see ARGENT

ZOOM
Singles: 7-Inch
MCA: 83 1-3
POLYDOR: 81-82 1-3
LPs: 10/12-Inch 33rpm
A&M: 74 8-10
MCA: 83 5-8
POLYDOR: 81 5-8

ZULEMA
(Zulema Cusseaux)
Singles: 7-Inch
LE JOINT: 78-79 2-3
RCA VICTOR: 74-76 2-4
SUSSEX: 72-73 2-4
LPs: 10/12-Inch 33rpm
LE JOINT: 78 5-8
RCA VICTOR: 75-76 5-8
SUSSEX: 72-74 8-10

ZWOL
(Walter Zwol)
Singles: 7-Inch
EMI AMERICA (Except 8905): 78-79 2-3
EMI AMERICA (8905; "New
  York City"): 78 4-8
  (Alternate version, white vinyl. Promotional issue
  only.)
LPs: 10/12-Inch 33rpm
EMI AMERICA: 78-79 5-8

DIRECTORY OF BUYERS AND SELLERS

After you have learned the current value of your records, you may wish to offer them for sale. Just as likely, you may decide you would like to purchase out-of-print records for your collection.

Either way, the author recommends you do two things:

First, request a sample issue of *DISCoveries* magazine, the record collector's publication where buyers and sellers get together each month. From the pages of *DISCoveries* you'll get an idea of what's being traded and the prices being asked for music collectibles of all types, especially records and compact discs (*DISCoveries*, P.O. Box 255, Port Townsend, WA 98368. Call toll-free: 1-800-666-DISC).

Second, contact other collectors and dealers. To assist in this regard, here is a random sampling of well-known buyers and sellers of collectible music and memorabilia, any of whom may be the right one to assist you.

ACE-HIGH RECORDS
5708 Winona Ave.
Des Moines, IA 50312

ALPHA RECORDS
6918 Madison Ave.
Indianapolis, IN 46227
(317) 784-7582

ANTONE'S RECORD SHOP
2928 Guadalupe
Austin, TX 78705

ARC PROMOTIONS
P.O. Box 215
Chesterfield, IN 46017
(317) 646-5305
Information about upcoming conventions.

BAGATELLE RECORDS
140 E. Third St.
Long Beach, CA 90802
(213) 432-7534

STANLEY BAUMRUK
15840 Ventura Blvd., Ste. 384
Encino, CA 91436
(818) 990-1847

BLUESLAND OLDIES RECORD SHOP
P.O. Box 1247
Daphne, AL 36526
(205) 626-0272

CALIFORNIA ALBUMS
P.O. Box 3426-D
Hollywood, CA 90078

COLLECTOR'S RECORDS
2631 E. Platte Ave.
Colorado Springs, CO 80909
(303) 577-4653

COLLECTOR'S RECORDS
10616 Garland
Dallas, TX 75218
(214) 327-0262

COLLECTOR'S CLEARINGHOUSE
P.O. Box 135
North Syracuse, NY 13212

CONNOISSEUR'S GROOVY ORIGINALS
1815 B East Park Row
Arlington, TX 76010
(817) 265-8023

CONTINENTAL RECORDS CO. LTD.
P.O. Box 2103
Bramalea, Ontario, Canada L6T 3S3

VERNON EDWARDS
103 Yellowhammer Circle
Montevallo, AL 35115
(205) 663-5185

ELLIS AUDIOTICS
247 Garfield-3A
Brooklyn, NY 11215
(718) 662-0923

FINEST RECORD STORE
2400 8th Ave.
Greeley, CO 80631
(303) 352-5390

GOLDEN OLDIES
201 NE 45th St.
Seattle, WA 98105

P.D. HAMLIN
P.O. Box 1981
Susanville, CA 96130
(916) 257-0596

INFINITE RECORDS
528 Westheimer
Houston, TX 77006
(713) 521-0187

LES HARRIS RECORDS
7243 Split Creek
San Antonio, TX 78238

HOT PLATTERS
P.O. Box 2793
Los Angeles, CA 90078

JELLYROLL PRODUCTIONS
P.O. Box 255
Port Townsend, WA 98368
(206) 385-3029
Distributor of assorted music publications.

JLO WEST
P.O. Box 8892
Universal City, CA 91608

LP LARRY
P.O. Box 349
Bay Ridge Station
Brooklyn, NY 11220

LYNN'S RECORDS
P.O. Box 5321
Walnut Creek, CA 94521

MEMORY LANE RECORDS
1940 E. University Dr.
Tempe, AZ 85281
(602) 968-1512

METRO MUSIC
P.O. Box 1000
Silver Spring, MD 20904
(301) 622-2473

√ MIDNIGHT RECORDS
P.O. Box 390
new York, NY 10011
(212) 675-2768

CRAIG MOERER
P.O. Box 19231
Portland, OR 97219
(503) 244-5527

√ SCOTT NEUMAN'S RECORD SHOP
P.O. Box 1048
Hightstown, NJ 08520
(609) 426-4730

RICHARD OCHOA
1206 N. 15th St.
Coeur d'Alene, ID 83814
(208) 664-4549

√ VICTOR PEARLIN
P.O. Box 199
Greendale Station
Worcester, MA 01606

BOB PEGG
8420 S. 16th St.
Tacoma, WA 98465
(206) 564-2846

POSITIVELY 4TH STREET
208 W. 4th Ave.
Olympia, WA 98501
(206) SUN-TAPE

√ PRINCETON RECORD EXCHANGE
20 S. Tulane St.
Princeton, NJ 08542
(609) 921-0881

RANDY'S RECORD SHOP
157 E. 900 South
Salt Lake City, UT 84111
(801) 532-4413

RICK RANN BEATLELIST
P.O. Box 877
Oak Park, IL 60303
(312) 442-7907

RECORD EXCHANGE
5840 Hampton
St. Louis, MO 63109
(314) 832-2249

RECORD SHOWCASE
228 Redbank Rd.
Goose Creek, SC 29445
(803) 553-1991

CLIFF ROBNETT
7804 NW 27th
Bethany, OK 73008
(405) 787-6703

ROCK ISLAND
3331 Foxridge Dr.
Tampa, FL 33618
(813) 969-2299

ROCKIN' ROBIN
1657 S. Wooster St.
Los Angeles, CA 90035
(213) 275-0808

ROWE'S RARE RECORDS
54 W. Santa Clara St.
San Jose, CA 95113
(408) 294-7200

LYNN RUSSWURM
Box 63,
Elmira, Ontario, Canada N3B 2Z5
(519) 669-2386

SALTY'S RECORD ATTIC
1326 9th St.
Modesto, CA 95354
(209) 527-4010

TOM SCANDARIATO
2310 Spring Wagon Lane
Austin, TX 70720

JOEL SCHERZER RARE RECORDS
P.O. Box 222
Pueblo, CO 81002

JOE SCOTT RECORDS
P.O. Box 464
Crystal River, FL 32629

DAVE SLOBODIAN
4533 Napier St.
Burnaby, B.C., Canada V5C 3H4
(604) 299-7902

SOCIAL INSECT RECORDS
923 Baldwin
Danville, IL 61832
(217) 443-3321

JOHN TEFTELLER
P.O. Box 1727
Grants Pass, OR 97526

TIMES SQUARE RECORDS
P.O. Box 391, Knightsbridge Sta.
Bronx, NY 10463
(212) 549-7497

TRACKS IN WAX RECORDS
4741 N. Central Ave.
Phoenix, AZ 85012
(602) 274-2660

USED (BUT NOT ABUSED) RECORDS
P.O. Box 2456
Russellville, AR 72801

VERY ENGLISH & ROLLING STONE
P.O. Box 7061
Lancaster, PA 17604
(717) 627-2081

VINTAGE MUSIC
316 Boro Rd.
Primos, PA 19108

VINYL VENDORS
1800 S. Robertson Blvd. #279
Los Angeles, CA 90035
(213) 935-6553

♪ ROCK WITH THE LEGENDS! ♪

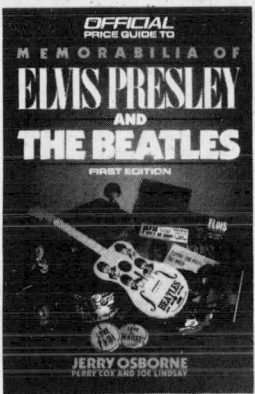

Experts JERRY OSBORNE ("Mr. Music"; author of *The Official® Price Guide to Records*), PERRY COX, and JOE LINDSAY don't miss a beat in *The Official® Price Guide to Memorabilia of Elvis Presley and The Beatles*. This is the first book ever to bring two of the greatest names in rock 'n' roll history together — a nostalgic compilation of the astounding array of memorabilia that make Elvis and The Beatles the cultural idols they remain today.

☆ Over 200 photos... eight-page color insert... fully indexed!

TAKE A MAGICAL MYSTERY TOUR THROUGH THIS BOOK!